Maloney's

ANTIQUES &

COLLECTIBLES

RESOURCE

DIRECTORY — 5th Edition

Maloney's

ANTIQUES & COLLECTIBLES RESOURCE DIRECTORY — 5th Edition

David J. Maloney, Jr., ISA CAPP

ANTIQUE TRADER BOOKS
A Division of Krause Publications
Iola, WI

To my grandson,
Cedric Shane Maloney,
and to the memory of the Grandmother he will not be fortunate enough to know,
Bonnie Sue Schroyer
1943 — 1999

ISBN: 1-58221-016-0

ISSN: 1083-8449

Published by Antique Trader Books, a Division of Krause Publications, Iola, WI 54990

Manufactured in the United States of America

TABLE OF CONTENTS

General Listings:

Continued on page vi

Continued from page v

Continued on page vii

Continued from page vi

Continued on page viii

Continued from page vii

Continued on page ix

Continued from page viii

Continued on page x

Continued from page ix

Continued on page xi

Continued from page x

Continued on page xii

Continued from page xi

Continued on page xiii

Continued from page xii

Continued on page xiv

Continued from page xiii

ABOUT THE AUTHOR

David J. Maloney, Jr., ISA CAPP is a nationally known appraiser, author, radio talk-show guest, and lecturer. His reputation is based on over 30 years of practical experience, extensive academic and personal study, teaching and lecturing. As a graduate of the U.S. Coast Guard Academy, he earned his BS in Engineering and, later, his Masters in Management. Following his career in the Coast Guard, Maloney operated an antiques business for several years prior to founding Frederick Appraisal, Claims & Estate Services.

He is now a full-time professional personal property appraiser specializing in the valuation of antiques, collectibles, residential contents, vehicles, and business equipment for several functions including insurance, probate, business valuation, divorce, and charitable contribution. Maloney also provides appraisal consulting services to bank trust departments, personal representatives, accountants, lawyers, estate planners, insurance agents, and the moving industry. In addition, he advises his clients on the best options available for disposing of antiques and collectibles.

Maloney is a Certified Member of the International Society of Appraisers (ISA) and is currently a member of the ISA Board of Directors. He writes and teaches ISA courses in appraisal principles and practice across the country, is ISA's representative to The Appraisal Foundation's Advisory Council, and has been awarded ISA's coveted Member of the Year Award and President's Award for his efforts in developing the new and highly-acclaimed ISA educational programs.

In addition to appraisals, Maloney provides damage claims and inspection services for major van lines operating in the Maryland, Washington DC, Virginia, and West Virginia area. He has served as a member of the Board of Directors of the moving industry's Claims Prevention and Procedure Council. Maloney has written and spoken extensively on the role of an appraiser in the claims process, and he is a contributing author of the *California Household Goods Carriers Claims Training & Reference Manual*.

Maloney resides with his family in Frederick, Maryland.

FOREWORD

I was honored when David Maloney asked me to write the foreword to the fifth edition of *Maloney's Antiques & Collectibles Resource Directory.* I use this book every day, and it is one of the most important resources in the antiques and collectibles field.

No reference book in my library gets as much use as does my copy of *Maloney's*. The copy I have of the 4th edition is tattered and torn, the cover is taped together, and the interior pages are dog-eared and coffee-stained. This copy has traveled with me from Las Vegas, NV, to Atlantic City, NJ. I absolutely never leave home without it. Whenever it is time for a new edition of this book, we order four or five copies so that everyone on our staff can have one. I also keep a copy by my desk in my office at home. Other books may stay neatly stacked on shelving units, but *Maloney's* is always within easy reaching distance from my computer or my telephone.

For the last 10 years *Maloney's* has made me look like a Whiz Kid by providing me with the answers to thousands of antiquers' questions. As an editor of *AntiqueWeek* newspaper and the leader of several on-line antiquing forums, I spend many hours each week trying to help people find the information they need to learn more about their treasured items. People ask me if there is a club for Roseville collectors, or how they can learn more about their Dracula figure. I thumb through *Maloney's* and always find someone I can refer them to.

Things have changed a lot since the first *Maloney's* came out 10 years ago. At that time the Internet was but a distant rumor for most people, and sending a letter or making a phone call were about the only ways a person could reach anyone. The fifth edition of *Maloney's* will have over 18,100 listings and over half of those listings will contain an e-mail address, while almost 7,500 of the listings will contain web sites.

No longer will people have to wait weeks for their mail to be sent, read, answered and then returned. With the Internet many people will be able to find the help they need within days or even hours by using e-mail addresses and visiting web sites.

Many people look at *Maloney's Antiques & Collectibles Resource Directory* as just a place to find a contact in order to buy or sell an item, but the book is much, much more than that. It is a place where you can meet lifelong collecting friends who share your passion for oil drilling memorabilia or Judaic needlework. The book also provides valuable information on the legalities of buying and selling certain types of items as well as resources on how to learn more about fakes and reproductions. Readers will be able to find appraisers, repair services, matching services, suppliers of parts and even auction services within the pages of this book. With more than 2,200 clubs listed in the fifth edition of *Maloney's*, collectors will be able to find the educational resources they need. Reference book sellers, museums, periodicals and libraries of interest are also listed. The best part of all this is that everything in *Maloney's* is also on-line in an easily searchable format.

If you are surfing the Internet and suddenly decide you want to learn more about souvenir buildings, you can pop over to **http://www.maloneysonline.com**, type in "souvenir buildings" and instantly find seven contacts.

In short, if you need to find out about something, the first place you should look is *Maloney's Antiques & Collectibles Resource Directory.*

Connie Swaim, Editor
AntiqueWeek
June 1999

INTRODUCTION

Welcome to the 5th edition of *Maloney's Antiques & Collectibles Resource Directory.* This massive compilation contains over 18,000 resources to assist you in the location, study and authentication, replacement, repair, valuation, or buying and selling of over 3,100 categories of art, antiques, collectibles and other types of personal property including gems & jewelry, race cars and boats — even tree and shrub appraisers!

Maloney's Antiques & Collectibles Resource Directory is a pioneer in gathering and disseminating information about antiques-related resources to the public. Since its debut eight years ago, this book has been hailed as the "...best one-volume research tool in print" by the *Gannett News Service* and has been listed as a Best Reference Book by the *Library Journal. Kipplinger's Personal Finance Magazine* refers to *Maloney's* as "...the industry bible..." This book is a unique and comprehensive, all-in-one resource for hard-to-find information about the personal property you own. And now with more than 3,100 new listings (several thousand of which now have e-mail and Internet addresses) in scores of new categories, the 5th edition of *Maloney's* is better than ever!

Please note that a listing should not be considered an endorsement, and no guarantee of satisfactory service is made. Comments I receive regarding service will be weighed in considering those to be included in future editions.

Specialized resources contained within *Maloney's* include buyers, collectors, dealers, experts, appraisers, periodicals, suppliers of parts, reproduction sources, reference book sellers, manufacturers/distributors/producers, clubs, societies and associations, museums and libraries, centers for specialized research, matching services, repair/restoration/conservation specialists, vendors to the trade, Internet resources, and mail-bid, Internet and gallery auctions. Many other miscellaneous services ranging from free-lance writers and antique buying trips to collector computer software and bottle cleaning kits are also included.

In addition to thousands of new and updated listings and scores of new categories, the 5th edition of *Maloney's* includes the following important features:

— A greatly expanded **cross-referencing system**. Readers are directed to other relevant categories which might contain information of interest. No other publication has ever cross-referenced antiques and collectibles to this degree.

— Four important **appendices**:
1. Educated and Tested ISA Appraisers
2. Auction Services
3. General Interest Periodicals
4. Repair Firms

— A redesigned and highly-detailed **index**.

— Nearly 7,500 listings with Internet **web sites** and over 9,500 with **e-mail** addresses.

The goal of this book is to place as much information as possible at the user's fingertips to allow him or her to make decisions based on knowledge and fact. Veteran dealers and collectors are well aware that knowledge and information are the keys to success in the world of antiques and collectibles. Unfortunately, such informational resources are minimal is scope, widely scattered and often short-lived or frequently changing. Prior to *Maloney's* there was no organized method to capture, preserve, collate, and distribute collector resource information to efficiently keep the public accurately informed on a continuing basis. *Maloney's* is designed to overcome this shortfall through frequent updating and regular publication.

My personal experience as an appraiser demonstrates quite dramatically that most non-collectors are unaware of the value and historical/cultural significance of many of their own possessions. Even when people do realize that their collectible items are valuable and/or of interest to others, they are often at a loss as to how to set a price, find a buyer (should they choose to sell), or locate information to learn more about their collectible.

This directory is an ideal source for locating potential buyers. Individual buyers are listed as are associated clubs (*Maloney's* lists over 2,200) and periodicals (over 1,200) which are themselves excellent sources of information about potential buyers. New research, repair techniques, theft and fraud alerts, reproductions, and an ever-changing value structure makes specialized serial publications and collectors' clubs more important than ever as the primary source of current and topical news in all fields of antiques and collectibles. The periodicals, trade publications and collector clubs/associations listed in *Maloney's* disseminate a wealth of timely information that is of great importance to the collector and researcher. In addition, the listed auction services (often specializing in a narrow area of collector interest) provide alternatives to selling to an individual.

For professionals such as appraisers, dealers, estate liquidators, repairers, attorneys, claims adjusters, *Maloney's Antiques & Collectibles Resource Directory* is the unrivaled source of information to find those who can aid in the authentication and valuation of antiques and collectibles, help settle a legal dispute, or who can help with the successful resolution of a loss or damage claim. Experts found among dealers, collectors, clubs and specialized periodicals offer an unparalleled source of specialized knowledge to help in confirming bona fide claims or in disproving fraudulent ones.

Of special interest to the moving, claims, and repair industries, *Maloney's* lists suppliers of such items as replacement crystals for chandeliers, furniture hardware, curved glass, tools, lamp parts, upholstery and caning supplies, clock parts, refinishing supplies and other obscure and hard-to-find items such as bed rail extenders and icebox hardware. The directory lists matching services for silver, crystal, dinnerware ("china"), conservation and repair supply sources, specialized repair services and, through the dealer listings, replacement sources for just about anything antique or collectible. Also listed are computer programs for collectors and sources of supplies for the collector and dealer such as bubble wrap, Mylar sleeves, acid-free storage containers, and display cases.

Maloney's also provides public awareness resources which disseminate information about recognizing fakes & reproductions, and reporting and recovering stolen art. In addition, there are listings for federal and state offices which provide information regarding the laws which govern the gathering, owning, transporting, or selling of items made from endangered species or of items classified as heritage resources such as certain Native American Indian relics or buried historical artifacts.

We are always interested in correcting, updating and adding sources of information and in improving category nomenclature and structure. Please e-mail, write or call with your suggestions for changes. At the end of this Directory you will find a "Listing Registration & Change Form" which you can submit at any time to either change your present listing or to add a new one. There is also an on-line form at or web site, **http://www.maloneysonline.com**. By the way, listings in *Maloney's Antiques & Collectibles Resource Directory* are free.

A special thanks to all those who are listed, and to our users for their feedback, suggestions, and overwhelming encouragement. I continue to strive for excellence in providing a thorough, accurate and all-encompassing antiques and collectibles resource directory. To that end, I encourage and welcome your comments and suggestions.

David J. Maloney, Jr., ISA CAPP
P.O. Box 2049
Frederick, MD 21702-1049
phone 301-695-8544
fax 301-695-6491
dave@maloney.com

USER'S GUIDE

Description of the General Listings

The main section of this book, the General Listings, contains more than 18,000 specific entries in over 3,100 subject categories arranged alphabetically by primary classification in CAPITAL LETTERS. Subclassifications appear where there are recognized subcategories in Upper and Lower case letters. Of particular importance is the extensive and comprehensive cross-referencing system which directs the user to related subject matter and which is unique to this publication. The following is a sample of headings and subheadings found in the General Listings:

ADVERTISING COLLECTIBLES
(see also BREWERIANA; BUTTONS, Pin-Back; COFFEE; GAS STATION COLLECTIBLES; GLASSES; LABELS; MAGAZINES, Covers & Tear Sheets; PAPER COLLECTIBLES; POCKET MIRRORS; TIN COLLECTIBLES)

Alka Seltzer
Beer & Soda

AIR LABELS

AIRLINE MEMORABILIA
(see, also AIRPLANES; AVIATION; AVIATION MEMORABILIA; LUGGAGE LABELS; STAMP COLLECTING, Air Mail Related; TOYS, Airplane Related; TRANSPORTATION COLLECTIBLES)

Baggage I.D. Labels
Models, desk
Pan-American Airways
Pilot Wings

Each entry contains as much of the following information as is applicable and available:

1) **PRIMARY CLASSIFICATION**
2) **Subclassification**
3) Entry Type (i.e. Dealer, Collector, Club, etc.; entries are in ZIP Code order)
4) Contact person's name
5) Business, organization, club, or museum name
6) Periodical type and name
7) Address
8) Phone and fax numbers
9) E-mail address
10) Internet web site
10) Descriptive comment

Primary Classifications and Subclassifications

Of critical importance was the establishment of a classification system which employs a well-defined system that is sensitive to nomenclature currently in vogue within the collecting community. A bi-level system of nomenclature which includes primary classifications and, where necessary, subclassifications, was adopted. Additional flexibility is afforded within either level by employing parenthetical terms such as **CERAMICS (AMERICAN), Stoneware**, or **GLASS, Carnival (Post-1960)**.

Entry Type

The entry type heading identifies the listing as an appraiser, auction service, book seller, collector, collector club, dealer, expert, manufacturer/distributor/producer, matching service, miscellaneous service of special interest, museum or library, on-line (Internet) service, periodical, repair/restoration/conservation service, reproduction source, or supplier. Entries are listed *alphabetically by entry type* and then in *ZIP Code order* for ease in locating services or specialists in your area. Entry types are self explanatory, hut the following warrant additional comment:

- "Collectors" buy or trade primarily for their own enjoyment, and with any profit motive being secondary.
- "Dealers" buy, sell, or trade. They may also be "Collectors", but dealers anticipate making a profit.
- "Experts" (while they may also be a "Collector" and/or "Dealer") are considered to be expert because they have lectured or written extensively on the subject, have authored books or articles, have curated exhibits or managed collections, have dealt extensively in the subject, appraise within a specialized field, have conducted lengthy studies on the subject, or otherwise have such a degree of experience that they are recognized within the trade as having an uncommonly high degree of knowledge about the subject.
- "Man./Dist./Prod." are businesses which either manufacturer, distribute or produce items such as modem collectibles or reproductions.
- "Suppliers" are sources of replacement parts or supplies. Included in this category are vendors who cater to the needs of collectors, dealers, repairers and restorers, conservators, etc.
- As a general rule, only "periodicals" (newsletters, magazines, newspapers, journals, etc.) issued more than once a year are included in this directory. Price guides and books about antiques and collectibles are not listed. Such reference sources are available through your local library or from the book sellers listed in this Directory under **BOOKS, Reference**. General interest periodicals appear in Appendix C. They also appear within the General Listings if they also focus on a particular specialty area. Periodicals, such as newsletters or magazines, issued by a club or society are listed with that club within its specialty area and are not also listed separately as a "Periodical." By the way, many fine club periodicals are available to members only, so you may wish to join in order to receive them.

NOTE: Always check the comment lines in each listing for additional information. For instance, often *collectors* or *experts* might also buy and sell, supply parts, do repairs or provide other services relevant to the classification.

Names, Addresses and Phone Numbers

As appropriate, listings include a contact person's name, a business and periodical name, address, phone and fax numbers. Requests not to list a street address but rather only phone numbers or e-mail addresses have been honored. A requirement for being listed in *Maloney's* is that there be either a bona fide mailing address or e-mail address listed (preferably both).

E-Mail Address

Nearly ten thousand of those listed in this edition of *Maloney's* are also accessible by means of electronic mail (e-mail) via computer. With the growing popularity of electronic on-line communications and the abundance of resources now on the Internet, savvy antiques and collectibles enthusiasts are speeding down the information super-highway to take advantage of information often found nowhere else.

Internet Web Site

Almost 7,500 listings in *Maloney's* also feature an Internet web site. With over 50 million users, the Internet offers an unparalleled opportunity for you to learn more about what you own and who shares your particular areas of interest worldwide! The Internet can also increase the world's awareness of you and improve your efforts to gain publicity for your group, business, or area of interest.

Comment Line

Most entries include a comment line of amplifying information which users will find extremely valuable. Comment space was limited, so at times editorial license was taken to shorten or otherwise modify comments submitted by those listed.

Tips for Searching *Maloney's*

- Sellers of new books focusing on antiques & collectibles are listed under **BOOKS, Reference.**
- Repair, restoration and conservation services will be found 1) under the heading **REPAIR/RESTORATION/CONSERVATION**, 2) in the *Repair Firm* appendix, or 3) within their specialty classification listed in the General Listings under the entry type, *Repair Services.*
- Objects made of fired clay (pottery, earthenware, stoneware, and porcelain) will be found under the primary classification of **CERAMICS**, which is further subdivided according to place of origin and type, e.g., **CERAMICS (AMERICAN ART POTTERY), Roseville Pottery Co.** By cross-reference, users are directed to such related areas as **COOKIE JARS**, **FAIRINGS** and **DINNERWARE** (a generic classification which contains most "china").
- Matching services locate replacement pieces for dinnerware, glassware and flatware tableware services. Matching services will be found primarily under the categories **DINNERWARE**; **FLATWARE**; **GLASS, Elegant** and **GLASS, Crystal**.
- Sports-related collectibles are listed alphabetically by sport subclassification under the primary classification of **SPORTS COLLECTIBLES**. By the way, **SPORTS COLLECTIBLES** should not be confused with **SPORTING COLLECTIBLES.** (The latter includes items relating to the hunting sports such as decoys, hunting prints and paintings, sporting art, target shooting, duck game calls, etc.)
- Contemporary collectibles, including limited editions, can be found under **COLLECTIBLES (MODERN)**.
- Many supplies for the dealer and collector can be found under **ANTIQUES DEALERS & COLLECTORS, Supplies for**. Certain specific categories such as **STAMP COLLECTING, Supplies for** and **COINS & CURRENCY, Supplies for** also list sources of supplies for those specialties.

- Listings with the subcategory *Computer Programs For* contain vendors of computer programs for cataloging and maintaining collections. As an example, see **STAMP COLLECTING, Computer Programs For**.

- While many listings now include an Internet web site, those listees who operate primarily on the Internet can be found listed within their specialty area under the entry type *Internet Resources*.

- The category **REPRODUCTION SOURCES** (sometimes catering only to the wholesale trade) lists businesses offering copies of antiques and collectibles — everything from R.S. Prussia porcelain and oak furniture to Diamond Dye lithographed tins and jukeboxes.

- See the categories **HERITAGE RESOURCES** and **ENDANGERED SPECIES** for federal and state resources which disseminate information regarding the regulations governing the gathering, owning and selling of certain types of artifacts and items made from parts of endangered species.

- While appraisers, auction services, periodicals, and repair services that specialize are listed within the General Listings under their areas of expertise, the Appendices list other appraisers, auction services, periodicals, and repair services which have more general coverage

The Appendices

There are four appendices that you will find very useful:

- Appendix A: Appraisers - Several hundred educated and tested members of the International Society of Appraisers listed in ZIP Code order.

- Appendix B: Auction Services - General line auction services listed in ZIP Code order.

- Appendix C: General Interest Periodicals - Periodicals of general interest to the antiques and collectibles trade listed in alphabetical order.

- Appendix D: Repair Firms - Hundreds of repair firms that specialize in the repair and restoration of household goods listed in ZIP Code order. All firms are members of the moving industry's Claims Prevention & Procedure Council.

The Index

The Directory offers a detailed index to help you readily find both major and minor subject categories of interest. It features an exhaustive cross-reference system that will efficiently guide you to other categories of related interest.

Skim through the index - you'll be amazed at the diversity of items people collect. The index will also help you think of things you might own that may be valuable.

Can't locate information about an item? Try looking under related subjects. Our extensive cross-reference will usually guide you, but use your imagination. Many collectibles are crossovers, i.e. they have collector appeal in more than one field. For instance, an early 20th century calendar depicting bicyclists has appeal not only to paper collectors but also to bicycle enthusiasts.

Useful and Important Suggestions

- When writing and requesting a reply from those listed, always send a long self-addressed and stamped envelope (LSASE) to help ensure and expedite a reply. Many collector clubs operate on a shoestring budget and require that a request for information be accompanied with an LSASE. Everyone will appreciate your courtesy. Include your phone number as well so the party can call you if they need additional information concerning your query. If you are selling, many would-be buyers are anxious to speak to you personally as soon as possible. They will often have specific questions to ask that can be best answered over the phone.

- When calling, DON'T CALL COLLECT unless otherwise directed (and very few do!); respect time zone differences; don't leave telephone or answering service messages unless you want the call returned collect. Suggest a time that the party should call back collect to ensure that you will be there. When calling about an item you own, be prepared. Have the item in hand (or good photographs of the item), along with notes on its dimensions, maker's mark, condition, signature, and any other identifying marks such as a patent number or date, model/serial number, etc.

- Don't send items without first notifying the receiving party and getting their permission. Items sent without permission can be considered "gifts" and do not need to be returned. When sending photographs, be sure that they are clear, close-up and in focus. Polaroids are seldom useful. Often, relatively flat objects such as small textiles, medals, ribbons, or paper items can be photocopied.

- When asking for help in identifying or authenticating an item, in addition to photos send complete descriptions including dimensions, maker's marks, materials, how long you've had it, how you acquired it, and its provenance (who owned it before you and for how long.)

- If selling, always state the price you would be willing to sell the item for. Most authorities agree that it's up to the seller to set the asking price although some dealers or buyers will help you. Unable to determine a fair price to ask? Your options are to seek comparable items in one of many price guide available today (booksellers are listed under **BOOKS, Reference**), or to retain the services of an expert, dealer or appraiser to assist you (look for appraisers within the general listings or in Appendix A, or call the International Society of Appraisers (see below) for a free referral.) By the way, the person you retain to do the appraisal should have no interest in purchasing the items you are selling.

- When you receive a reply from someone you've offered to sell an item to, make sure you respond promptly. If the party wants to buy the items you are offering, make sure you let him know of your final intentions to sell to him or otherwise. Don't keep him wondering whether or not you even received his reply. Often listees spend their valuable time and money in researching and/or corresponding with you. Make sure you are courteous and thoughtful in return.

- Buying through an Internet auction? Here are some tips to avoid getting burned:
  —**Use an escrow account**. Escrow accounts protect both the buyer and seller by releasing payment only after notification from the buyer that the item has bee received, inspected and accepted. Either party can arrange for an escrow account which are offered by such companies as i-Escrow (www.iescrow.com) and TradeSafe (www.tradesafe.com).
  —**Use an on-line auction web site with a guarantee**. Amazon.com (www.amazon.com) and eBay (www.ebay.com) offer fraud insurance up to about $200 to $250 to protect the buyer if the item purchased is not as represented on-line by the seller.

—**Pay be credit card**. Using a credit card to make a purchase enables the buyer to withhold payment if the merchandise is not as promised. Using a credit card is not a problem when the auction house is the seller of the property such as Onsale (www.onsale.com), but using a credit card with an individual is normally not possible. However, Auction Universe (www.auctionuniverse.com) will process the credit card transaction on behalf of the seller for a nominal fee.

—**Know who you are dealing with**. Many on-line auction sites maintain a database buyers' comments about sellers (and vice versa). While this is a good way to get a feel for the past performance of the person you are dealing with, it is not a guarantee that you will be treated in the same manner. As a further check, get the seller's address and phone number and use an on-line phone directory such as Switchboard (www.switchboard.com) to verify the information.

- Be sensitive to the possible need for paying a few dollars when requesting catalogs, lists, samples or brochures. Always ask if there are charges for the service or product you are requesting, such as an appraisal or authentication.

- If an expert is not listed for your particular area of interest, try contacting a related collector's club or periodical. Often the club's contact or the periodical's editor or publisher are themselves experts. In any case, they are always excellent sources of information.

- Another excellent source when trying to locate an expert in your area is to call the International Society of Appraisers, a nonprofit organization and the largest association of educated and tested personal property appraisers in North America. For a free, no-obligation referral to an appraiser in your area, call the ISA at 888-472-4732, e-mail at ISAHQ@cs.com, or write the ISA at 16040 Christensen Rd., Ste. 120, Seattle, WA 98188. You can also check for an appraiser by going to the ISA's web site at http://www.isa-appraisers.org.

- Finally, when looking for an expert, advice or service, don't forget to contact your own neighborhood resources. Museums, libraries, historical societies, and moving company claims departments (a great source for talented repairers) are just a few of the local sources to turn to when seeking advice. If you locate an unusual source, let us know about it, too. We'd love to include it in the next edition of this book. Don't forget to consult your local telephone Yellow Pages, too. Look under "Antique - Dealers," "Antiques - Repairing & Restoring," "Appraisers," "Furniture Repairing & Refinishing," "Jewelers," "Lamps," and "Moving & Storage" for local businesses which may also be able to help.

If you wish to be listed in a future edition of the *Resource Directory*, complete and return the form located at the end of this book. Remember, there is no charge for being listed in *Maloney's Antiques & Collectibles Resource Directory*.

007

(see CHARACTER COLLECTIBLES, Spy Memorabilia [James Bond]; TELEVISION SHOWS & MEMORABILIA, Private Eye)

1930s to 1960s

(see MODERNISM; POPULAR CULTURE; SOCIAL CAUSES)

20TH CENTURY

(see ART, Outsider; ART DECO; ELECTRICITY RELATED ITEMS, Appliances; MODERNISM; POPULAR CULTURE; SOCIAL CAUSES)

3-D PHOTOGRAPHICA

(see also CAMERAS & CAMERA EQUIPMENT; OPTICAL ITEMS; STEREO VIEWERS & STEREOVIEWS)

Clubs/Associations

John W. Bordner
National Collectors Association of Die Doubling
Newsletter: Hub, The
P.O. Box 119
White Plains, NY 10604-0119
ph: 717-453-9530
e-mail: jwb209@epix.net
web: http://www.geocities.com/ResearchTriangle/Facility/4968/NCADD.html
Club is devoted to the study of die varieties; bi-monthly newsletter with information covering die varieties; attributions, micro and macro photography available.

Collectors

Harry Poster
P.O. Box 1883
South Hackensack, NJ 07606-0483
ph: 201-794-9606
fax: 201-794-9553
e-mail: hposter@att.net
web: http://www.harryposter.com
Buying Tru-Vue rolls and viewers, View Master singles and three packs; wants Military, Cactus, Wildflowers, gold centers, Movie Pre-views ($50 ea.!); VM and Tru-Vue dealer displays, advertising, Novel View, and similar stereo slides.

Sheldon Aronowitz
487 Palmer Ave.
Teaneck, NJ 07666-3251
ph: 201-837-9508 or 800-982-7401
fax: 201-861-8648
Specializes in View-Master, Tru-Vue, Stori-Vue, Anaglyph, Lenticular, holograms, stereo cards, 3-D literature, 3-D cameras, 3-D views.

Kyle Spain
423 Knight Way
La Canada, CA 91011
ph: 818-449-9179
e-mail: kyle_spain@warnerbros.com
Collector wants to buy 3D/stereo slides (4"x1 5/6") made by amateur photographers from 1950s stereo cameras; also wants viewers.

Chris Perry
Doctor 3D
7470 Church St., Ste. A
Yucca Valley, CA 92284-3248
ph: 760-365-0475
fax: 760-365-0495
Buys anything that is 3D: 3D cameras, projectors, viewers, Viewmaster, TRU-VUE, Realist slides, lenticular 3D pictures, holograms, novelviews, 3D filmstrips; 3D magazines that you view with 3D glasses or viewer; and any other 3D items.

Dealers

Dalia Miller
3Dstereo.com, Inc.
1930 Village Center Circle, PMB 3-333
Las Vegas, NV 89134
ph: 702-838-7015 or 702-838-7021
fax: 702-838-7016
e-mail: ddd@3dstereo.com
web: http://www.3dstereo.com
Buys and sells 3-D supplies, equipment, stereo cameras, projectors, viewers, lenticulars, books, stereorama, View-Master reels and packets, Tru-Vue strips; great catalog.

David Starkman
Reel 3-D Enterprises, Inc.
P.O. Box 2368
Culver City, CA 90231-2368
ph: 310-837-2368
fax: 310-558-1653
e-mail: reel3d@aol.com
web: http://www.stereoscopy.com/reel3d
A catalog about 3-D photography and 3-D equipment collecting.

John Saddy
Jefferson Stereoptics
50 Foxborough Grove
London, Ontario N6K 4A8
Canada
ph: 519-641-4431
fax: 519-641-2899
e-mail: john.saddy.3d@sympatico.ca
web: http://www3.sympatico.ca/john.saddy.3d/home.htm
Specializes in consignments for international phone and mail auctions; also buys and sells stereo photography and equipment.

Experts

Roger T. Nazeley
4921 Castor Ave.
Philadelphia, PA 19124-2411
ph: 215-535-9021 or 215-743-8999
fax: 215-288-8030
Buy, sell, trade View-Master reels and packets, Tru-Vue cards & film strips, look-a-like View-Masters, etc.; author of book on subject.

John Waldsmith
Antique Graphics
302 Granger Rd.
Medina, OH 44256-8434
ph: 330-239-1944 or 330-239-2212
fax: 330-239-1944
e-mail: vansywalsy@aol.com
Wants stereoscopic views, View-Master reels, photographica; conducts mail/phone auctions on regular basis; also direct sales; author of "Stereo Views: An Illustrated History and Price Guide."

Internet Resources

MaryAnn & Wolfgang Sell
View-Master Homepage, The
3752 Broadview Dr.
Cincinnati, OH 45208
ph: 513-871-1026 or 513-871-1657
fax: 513-321-5398
e-mail: vmmasell@cinti.net
web: http://www.cinti.net/~vmmasell/
View-Master expert and general interest 3-D information source; curators of Holmes Stereo Research Library in Cincinnati.

Periodicals

Dalia Miller
3Dstereo.com, Inc.
Magazine: Inside 3-D
1930 Village Center Circle, PMB 3-333
Las Vegas, NV 89134
ph: 702-838-7015 or 702-838-7021
fax: 702-838-7016
e-mail: ddd@3dstereo.com
web: http://www.3dstereo.com
Quarterly publication for 3D enthusiasts; information on stereo cameras, projectors, viewers, View-Master, Tru-Vue and other 20th century 3D.

Tru-View

Experts

Tom Martin
2510 Douglas Dr. N
Golden Valley, MN 55422
ph: 612-591-9453
e-mail: tlmartin@bitstream.net
web: http://www2.bitstream.net/~tlmartin/index.html
Has been collecting Tru-Vue, Novelview, View-Master and other 3-D transparencies for several years; has written articles on the subject; currently writing a book on Tru-Vue; helps edit on-line Tru-Vue newsletter.

View-Masters

Clubs/Associations

National Stereoscopic Association
Magazine: Stereo World
P.O. Box 14801
Columbus, OH 43214
ph: 614-263-4296
e-mail: nsa@nsa-3d.org
web: http://nsa-3d.org/
Members collect stereo views, stereoscopes, stereo cameras; View-Master reels, viewers, packets; all other 3-D collectibles; the glossy colorful magazine is published six timer per year.

Tom Martin
View-Master & Tru-Vue Collectors Association
Newsletter: ReView
2510 Douglas Dr. N
Golden Valley, MN 55422
ph: 612-591-9453
e-mail: tlmartin@bitstream.net
web: http://www2.bitstream.net/~tlmartin/index.html

Collectors

Jim Rohacs
9721 Lomond Dr.
Manassas, VA 22110-3104
ph: 703-369-5578
Wants to buy View-Masters and similar 3D items.

Howard & Jane Hazelcorn
6731 Ashley Ct.
Sarasota, FL 34241-9696
ph: 941-921-1815
Wants to buy early viewers and rare reels.

Bob Zeuschel
1638 Highland Valley Ctr.
Chesterfield, MO 63005-4919
ph: 314-537-3145
Wants to buy View-Masters, Tru-Vue 3-D slide formats.

Kyle Spain
423 Knight Way
La Canada, CA 91011
ph: 818-449-9179
e-mail: kyle_spain@warnerbros.com
Collector wants to buy View-Master reels and packets; all types especially scenic, "Made in Belgium" reels (scenic).

Dealers

Steve Schuler
ph: 419-738-7551
e-mail: sschuler@bright.net
web: http://www.bright.net/~sschuler/vmfs.html
Site has lots of reels for sale.

Diane Davison
A Different View of the World
1517 Reisterstown Rd., Ste. 101
Baltimore, MD 21208
ph: 410-486-0900
fax: 410-486-0901
e-mail: lawgal@usa.net
web: http://mail.bcpl.lib.md.us/~ddavison/home.html
Collects, buys and sells View-Master, 3-D, stereoscopy.

John & Dana Achziger
10016 E 10th
Spokane, WA 99206
ph: 509-924-9199
Have a large variety of View-Master reels for sale.

Experts

Sheldon Aronowitz
487 Palmer Ave.
Teaneck, NJ 07666-3251
ph: 201-837-9508 or 800-982-7401
fax: 201-861-8648
Specializes in View-Master, Tru-Vue, Stori-Vue, Anaglyph, Lenticular, holograms, stereo cards, 3-D literature, 3-D cameras, 3-D views.

Walter Sigg
3-D Entertainment
P.O. Box 208
Swartswood, NJ 07877-0208
Buys and sells View-Master, Tru-Vue, 3-D cameras, projectors, reels, and most 3-D items; also early non-cartoon single View-Master reels and the three reel packets, and reels and 3-D cameras by Sawyers and G.A.F.

John Waldsmith
Antique Graphics
302 Granger Rd.
Medina, OH 44256-8434
ph: 330-239-1944 or 330-239-2212
fax: 330-239-1944
e-mail: vansywalsy@aol.com
Wants stereoscopic views, View-Master reels, photographica; conducts mail/phone auctions on regular basis; also direct sales; author of "Stereo Views: An Illustrated History and Price Guide."

MaryAnn & Wolfgang Sell
View-Master Homepage, The
3752 Broadview Dr.
Cincinnati, OH 45208
ph: 513-871-1026 or 513-871-1657
fax: 513-321-5398
e-mail: vmmasell@cinti.net
web: http://www.cinti.net/~vmmasell/
View-Master expert and general interest 3-D information source; curators of Holmes Stereo Research Library in Cincinnati.

Internet Resources

Keith Baird
View-Master Ultimate Reel List
701 Winflo
Austin, TX 78703
ph: 512-474-6759
e-mail: kbaird@mail.utexas.edu
web: http://ccwf.cc.utexas.edu/~number6/vm/
Lists of reels, history of View-Master, numbering system.

A.C. GILBERT

(see TOYS, Construction Sets [Erector]; TRAINS, Toy [American Flyer])

ABRAHAM LINCOLN

(see CIVIL WAR ARTIFACTS; PERSONALITIES [HISTORICAL], Abraham Lincoln)

ACCOUNT BOOKS

(see also PAPER COLLECTIBLES)

Collectors

Roy C. Kulp
P.O. Box 264
Hatfield, PA 19440-0264
ph: 215-362-0732
Wants to buy account books and day books by farmers, carpenters, blacksmiths, coffin & carriage makers, and weavers; also wants pre-1890 hand written travel diaries.

ACTING

(see PERFORMING ARTS)

ADDING MACHINES

(see also CALCULATORS; OFFICE EQUIPMENT; TYPEWRITERS)

Clubs/Associations

Darryl Rehr, Ed.
Early Typewriter Collectors Association
Magazine: ETCetera
P.O. Box 641824
Los Angeles, CA 90064
ph: 310-477-5229
fax: 310-268-8420
e-mail: dcrehr@earthlink.net
web: http://home.earthlink.net/~dcrehr/
An international club for collectors of old office equipment; provides contact with worldwide network of over 500 members; free ads.

Collectors

Peter Frei
P.O. Box 500
Brimfield, MA 01010-0500
ph: 800-942-8968 or 413-245-4660
web: http://www.peterfrei.com/
Wants to buy hand powered vacuum cleaners, pre-1875 sewing machines, typewriters, calculators, and adding machines.

Anthony Casillo
Antique Typewriter Collecting
325 Nassau Blvd.
Garden City, NY 11530-5313
ph: 516-489-8300 or 516-742-4919
fax: 516-489-6501
e-mail: typebar@aol.com
web: http://members.aol.com/typesite
Wants to buy old and unusual pre-1920 adding machines.

Arthur Cheslock
514 Paul St.
Baltimore, MD 21202
ph: 410-962-8580
fax: 410-752-8112
Wants pre-1945 calculators, adding machines and scientific instruments; also wants related literature.

Darryl Rehr
P.O. Box 641824
Los Angeles, CA 90064
ph: 310-477-5229
fax: 310-268-8420
e-mail: dcrehr@earthlink.net
web: http://home.earthlink.net/~dcrehr/
Wants adding machines (machines that only add) of unusual and early designs; send SASE for free information packet.

ADIRONDACK

(see FURNITURE [ANTIQUE], Rustic)

ADS

Magazine

(see ADVERTISING COLLECTIBLES; MAGAZINES, Covers & Tear Sheets; PAPER COLLECTIBLES)

ADVERTISING COLLECTIBLES

(see also BREWERIANA; BUTTONS, Pin-Back; COFFEE; DINNERWARE, Advertising; GAS STATION COLLECTIBLES; GLASSES; LABELS; MAGAZINES, Covers & Tear Sheets; PAPER COLLECTIBLES; POCKET MIRRORS; POPULAR CULTURE; THERMOMETERS; WATCH FOBS)

Auction Services

Randy Inman
James D. Julia Auctioneers Inc.
Rt. 201, Skowhegan Rd.
P.O. Box 830
Fairfield, ME 04937
ph: 207-453-7125
fax: 207-453-2502
e-mail: jjulia@juliaauctions.com
web: http://www.juliaauctions.com
Conducts specialized auctions of advertising and country store items; one of the leaders in the field; trade signs coin-operated items, gambling devices, syrup dispensers; uses nationally recognized experts to catalog specialty sales.

Howard Parzow
Howard B. Parzow, Auctioneers
P.O. Box 3464
Gaithersburg, MD 20885-3464
ph: 301-977-6741
fax: 301-208-8947
e-mail: hparzow@aol.com
Conducts specialized auctions of country store, advertising, drug store, apothecary and medical related items, and Americana; advertises nationally; auction house located at 10 South Main St., Mt. Airy, MD.

Richard W. Opfer, Jr.
Richard Opfer Auctioneering, Inc.
1919 Greenspring Dr.
Lutherville Timonium, MD 21093-4113
ph: 410-252-5035
fax: 410-252-5863
e-mail: info@opferauction.com
web: http://www.opferauction.com/
Specializes in auctioning toys, dolls, games, black memorabilia, and advertising items; weekly estate auctions including antiques, fine art; monthly eclectic collector sales feature a wide variety of collectibles.

Dave Beck
Beck Auctions
P.O. Box 435
Mediapolis, IA 52637-0435
ph: 319-394-3943
fax: 319-394-3943
Conducts mail auctions of advertising watch fobs, mirrors, pin-back buttons, etc.; send stamp for illustrated auction catalog.

Buffalo Bay Antiques
11 E. Division St.
Buffalo, MN 55313
ph: 612-682-1825
Holds regular absentee advertising auctions.

Clubs/Associations

Ephemera Society of America Inc., The
Newsletter: Ephemera News
P.O. Box 95
Cazenovia, NY 13035-0095
ph: 315-655-9139
fax: 315-655-9139
e-mail: info@ephemerasociety.org
web: http://www.ephemerasociety.org/
The major organization for collectors and dealers of paper collectibles; focuses on the preservation and study of ephemera (short-lived printed matter); also publishes "The Ephemera Journal."

David Schnakenberg
Farm Machinery Advertising Collectors
10108 Tamarack Drive
Vienna, VA 22182-1843
e-mail: schnakenbergdd@erols.com

David Hirsch
Antique Advertising Association of America
Newsletter: Past Times
P.O. Box 1121
Morton Grove, IL 60053
ph: 708-446-0904
e-mail: quadanews@aol.com
web: http://www.pastimes.org
Dedicated to collecting ALL forms of quality advertising: tobacco, coffee, whiskey, beer, candy, gum, clocks, country store, cabinets, etc.

Collectors

April Rhodes
RR 1 Box 284-E
Sunbury, PA 17801-9618
Wants to buy sample advertising tins; prefers cosmetic and toiletry sample tins.

Barry Hunsberger
2300 Meadowlane Dr.
Easton, PA 18042
ph: 610-253-2477
e-mail: barryMGC@aol.com
Beer, soda, whiskey, other advertising lithos: calendars, signs, trays, match holders.

Jerry A. Phelps
1500 Van Buren Boat Deck Rd.
Mount Eden, KY 40046
ph: 502-859-4063
Wants pre-1900 country store and advertising items: signs, broadsides, clocks, tins, bins, display cases, etc.

Mark S. McNee
1009 Vassar Dr.
Kalamazoo, MI 49001-4483
ph: 616-343-8393
Wants to buy all forms of early advertising including signs, posters, tin containers, and store displays.

Tom Rutledge
3015 Bever Ave., SE
Cedar Rapids, IA 52403-3028
ph: 319-399-1427
Wants country store advertising items, calendars, signs, broadsides, tins, posters for all types of products, especially ammunition, beer, whiskey, tobacco, and soft drink companies; also old mail order catalogs and flyers.

Mike Kranz
463 Stage Line Rd.
Hudson, WI 54016-7849
ph: 715-386-7333 or 715-386-9212
e-mail: juliekr@pressenter.com
Wants to buy old store stock and store advertisements.

Steve Ketcham
P.O. Box 24114
Minneapolis, MN 55424-0114
ph: 612-920-4205
e-mail: s.ketcham@unique-software.com
Seeking pre-1940 advertising signs, trays, mirrors, calendars, posters, etc. for all types of products, especially beer, whiskey, patent medicine, tobacco; send SASE with all inquiries.

Dale B. Peterson
Past Times Treasures
22762 Woodridge Drive
Claremore, OK 74017
ph: 918-341-5475
e-mail: cpeters2@webzone.net
web: http://www.webzone.net/cpeters2/
Actively seeking drug store and country store show globes, pedestal candy jars, old shelf stock, advertising, and especially counter top containers used for serving or displaying candy, gum, nuts, etc.; appraisals given.

Roger V. Baker
P.O. Box 620417
Redwood City, CA 94062-0417
ph: 369-851-7188
Wants signs, calendars, trays, etc. advertising firearms, ammunition, beer, whiskey, tobacco, and general store companies.

Neal Austinson
P.O. Box 1691
Windsor, CA 95492-1691
ph: 707-837-9685
Wants to buy old advertising collectibles including signs, trays, etc.

Ludovic Kintgen
6 Rue De Longpont
Neuilly
Seine, 92200
France
Buys, trades and collects advertising items.

Dealers

Leila Dunbar
Dunbar's Gallery
76 Haven St.
Milford, MA 01757-3821
ph: 508-634-8697 or 508-634-8097
fax: 508-634-8698
Mail order Americana - no reproductions; buys, sells and specializes in vintage character and comic toys, banks, advertising, automobilia, and Halloween related items.

Rudy Franchi
Nostalgia Factory, The
51 North Margin St.
Boston, MA 02113
ph: 617-720-2211 or 800-479-8754
e-mail: posters@nostalgia.com
web: http://www.nostalgia.com
Buys and sells all forms of old advertising, from Victorian trade cards to contemporary billboards; 25 years in business.

Robb Sequin
P.O. Box 1126
Dennis Port, MA 02639
ph: 508-760-2599
e-mail: rsequin@capecod.net
Wants advertising signs with interesting subject matter either by company or graphically: signs, displays, products and calendars; no tear sheets, please.

Phelps Fullerton
Great Bay Trading Co.
281 Atlantic Ave.
North Hampton, NH 03862-2103
ph: 603-964-7093 or 603-964-9928
e-mail: pfullerton@aol.com
Buys and sells paper, tin, porcelain, and wood advertising signs, trays, tins, calendars, die-cuts, mirrors, display cases, country store items, etc. for all types of products.

Mary Ann Hahn
Second Hand Mary Ann's
103 Ocean Point Road
Boothbay Harbor, ME 04538
ph: 207-633-2426
fax: 207-633-2586
e-mail: maryann@gwi.net
Wants to buy old advertising die-cuts (cardboard signs with easels on back).

Louise Pennisi
Around the Kitchen
P.O. Box 840
Georgetown, CT 06829
ph: 203-438-2338
e-mail: louise@aroundthekitchen.com
web: http://www.aroundthekitchen.com
Buys and sells food and kitchen advertising, including kitchen appliance, recipe pamphlets, cookery booklets (Pillsbury, Baker's Chocolate, Jell-O, etc.), and collectible cookbooks (19th & 20th cent.); catalogs, searches, co. histories.

Marc Zydiak
Star Archives
P.O. Box 285
Westfield, NJ 07091-0285
ph: 908-654-6505

Alice Kasten
Alice's Advertising Antiques
131 Allenwood Rd.
Great Neck, NY 11023
ph: 516-466-8954
e-mail: alicek13@aol.com
web: http://members.aol.com/AliceK13/
Buys and sells advertising collectibles; thousands of trade cards, advertising blotters, pamphlets, etc. on database; can send list tailored to your wants.

Harvey Leventhal
Harvey's Antique Advertising
412 Circle Drive
Ellwood City, PA 16117
ph: 724-752-1068
e-mail: harvey@antiqueadvertising.com
web: http://www.antiqueadvertising.com
Website filled with photos, facts, fun and links to other antique advertising sites; lots of old tins, antique advertising and country store items.

George Goehring
Dennis & George Collectibles
3407 Lake Montebello Dr.
Baltimore, MD 21218
ph: 410-889-3964
e-mail: dandgtins@aol.com
With Dennis O'Brien runs collectibles mail order firm; collectors and dealers of upright pocket tobacco tins, advertising, etc.

Steve Colby
Off The Deep End
712 East St.
Frederick, MD 21701-5239
ph: 301-698-9006
e-mail: chilimon@offthedeepend.com
web: http://www.offthedeepend.com/
Antique to contemporary; also ephemera, 1950s home accessories, Playboy magazines, diner collectibles, pin-ups, nudes and Hula Girls (all types), used books.

J. Glen & Violet Moore
Main Street Antiques
47 W. Main St.
P.O. Box 627
New Market, MD 21774
ph: 301-865-3710
Buys and sells antique advertising items; signs (including neon), catalogs, trade cards and more; large selection specializing in earlier items; appointments preferred.

Willisia Holbrook
Armbrook Antiques
531 Doub Rd.
Lewisville, NC 27023
ph: 888-393-8025 or 336-945-9477
fax: 336-945-9914
e-mail: olestuff@armbrookantiques.com
web: http://www.armbrookantiques.com
Buys and sells early country store advertising items; web site has full online catalog including descriptions and photos.

Vic Kroll
Kroll's Kollectibles
3451 Nighthawk Ct.
Punta Gorda, FL 33950-6675
ph: 941-575-0303
e-mail: beer@sunline.net
Buys, sells, trades beer, whiskey, soda and tobacco advertising items.

Coshocton Art Works
P.O. Box 1146
Coshocton, OH 43812
Wants tin and celluloid advertising items.

Mike Schwimmer
Collectors Center
325 East Blodgett
Lake Bluff, IL 60044-2112
ph: 847-295-1901
Collector of cigar memorabilia; dealer in all forms of vintage advertising; buys and sells.

Robert M. Levine
#2 Troll Court
Ballwin, MO 63011
ph: 314-394-4370
fax: 314-391-6618
Buys, sells, trades and collects advertising items with company logo; must be at least 25 years old.

Jim & Rita Hinton
Collector's Choice
P.O. Box 104284
Jefferson City, MO 65110-4284
ph: 573-636-7567

Kim & Mary Kokles
P.O. Box 495092
Garland, TX 75049
Buys and sells advertising; promotes national all-advertising show.

Stephen Hansrote
Griffin Trading Company
159 Howell St.
Dallas, TX 75207
ph: 214-747-9234
fax: 214-747-0660
e-mail: griffintc@aol.com
web: http://members.aol.com/griffintc/website.htm
Buying and selling all types of American and European advertising such as displays, props, figures, paper goods, wood and metal signs.

John D. McKenna
McKenna Bros. Wholesale
801-803 W Cucharras St.
Colorado Springs, CO 80905
ph: 719-630-8732
Always buying, selling, trading antique signs, tins, trays, posters, and country store items; best prices paid for mint condition items.

Ruth A. Miller Knott
Paperpeneur, The
2601 Kittias Highway
Ellensburg, WA 98926
ph: 509-962-8840
fax: 509-962-3609
e-mail: ruthie@ellensburg.com
Offers a unique selection of paper ephemera, historical documents, and collectibles: advertising, Americana, agriculture, Colonial, maritime, transportation, fraternal; does research and will answer questions.

Alma
MPA Collections
20, rue des Poissonniers
Neuilly sur Sein
Paris, 92200
France
ph: 01 40 8 01 52
e-mail: alma@mpacollections.com
web: http://www.mpacollections.com
Specializes in antique advertising, tins, toys, vintage Disney.

Experts

Dawn E. Reno
3280 Shingler Terrace
Deltona, FL 32738-5351
ph: 904-532-1960
fax: 904-532-1960
e-mail: DawnReno@juno.com
Author of "Advertising Collectibles" (1993, Avon).

Craig & Donna Stifter
P.O. Box 6514
Naperville, IL 60540-6514
ph: 630-789-5780 or 630-939-7479
e-mail: cocacola@enteract.com
Wants to buy older Coca-Cola, Pepsi-Cola, Dr. Pepper, Orange-Crush, Hire Root Beer and other brand soda memorabilia; writes columns for several antiques periodicals; also interested in items pertaining to country (general) stores.

Museums/Libraries

Warsaw Collection of Business Americana
Smithsonian Institution
Washington, DC 20560
ph: 202-357-2414
e-mail: webmaster@si.edu
web: http://www.si.edu/organiza/museums/nmah/nmah.htm

National Museum of American History, Archives Center, Smithsonian Institution
14th & Constitution Ave. NW
Room C340, MRC 601
Washington, DC 20560
ph: 202-357-3270 or 202-357-1789
fax: 202-786-2453
e-mail: webmaster@si.edu
web: http://www.si.edu/organiza/museums/nmah/nmah.htm
Dedicated to advertising and American business ephemera from the late 1700s to 1980; also ethnic ephemera from 1890s to present.

Periodicals

Denise M. Sater, Ed.
Newspaper: Paper & Advertising Collector (P.A.C.)
P.O. Box 500
Mount Joy, PA 17552-0500
ph: 717-492-2540 or 800-800-2833
fax: 717-653-6165

Annie Morrel
Magazine: Collectors' Mart
Pargate House
27 High Street
Hampton Hill, Middlesex TW12 1BN
U.K.
ph: (0) 181 941 4512
fax: (0) 181 941 8630
e-mail: cmart@easynet.co.uk
web: http://www.worldcollectorsnet.com/cmart/
A quarterly magazine of advertising collectibles and other collecting lines; THE leading international collectibles magazine in print; available by subscription.

A & P Items

Dealers

Syd E. Pitzer
Cherished Antiques & Collectibles
425 Old Bethel Church Rd.
Winchester, VA 22603-4050
ph: 540-667-4255

Absinthe

Dealers

Mike Lavarone
Absinthe Collectibles
611 Marengo Ave.
Forest Park, IL 60130-1916
ph: 312-407-5639
e-mail: mikei@mcs.com
web: http://www.mcs.net/~mikei/absinthe/
Offering the finest in French bistro, absinthe and pastis items: spoons, glassware, books, posters.

Absolut Vodka

Clubs/Associations

Absolut Collectors Society
P.O. Box 4038
Philadelphia, PA 19118
e-mail: membership@absolutsociety.com
web: http://www.absolutsociety.com/
Collectors interested in Absolut Vodka advertisements and associated paraphernalia.

Alka Seltzer

Collectors

Darlene Shidler
58999 Lower Dr.
Goshen, IN 46528-6731
ph: 219-533-6102
e-mail: precmom48@aol.com
Wants Alka Seltzer and Miles Laboratories, Inc. (Elkhart, IN) items: bottles, boxes, toys, "Speedy" figures, advertising, etc.

Ammunition

Collectors

Bill Bramlett
P.O. Box 1105
Florence, SC 29503-1105
ph: 803-393-7390 or 843-665-3165
e-mail: bbramlett@webtv.net
Wants to buy 1890-1931 calendars, posters and signs advertising shotgun shells and cartridges from companies such as Peters, Austin, Remington, U.S. Cartridge Co., The Black Shells, Western.

Aunt Jemima

Collectors

Lynn Burkett
P.O. Box 671
Hillsdale, MI 49242-0671
ph: 517-437-2149
e-mail: slburkett@dmci.net
Wants Aunt Jemima pancake advertising: recipe booklets, flyers, maps, paper masks, signs, posters, product containers, premium items, china, etc.

Beech-Nut

Collectors

Bruce A. Van Evera
94 Montgomery St.
Canajoharie, NY 13317-1213
ph: 518-673-3522
Wants to buy Beech-Nut Brand glass, tin or cardboard containers with excellent paper label intact: catsup, mustard, chili sauce, slice beef, ginger ale, sarsparilla, peanut butter, jams, K-rations, gum, biscuit tins, olive oil, etc.

Biblical

Collectors

Burke O. Long
16 McLellan St.
Brunswick, ME 04011
ph: 207-725-8920
fax: 207-725-3495
e-mail: blong@polar.bowdoin.edu
Does not buy bibles; wants old advertising using Bible scenes, quotes, or themes: paper, postcards, trade cards, signs, celluloids, tin, etc.

Billboard Signs

Dealers

Randy Littlefield
Billboards of the Past
5654 S.E. King Rd.
Portland, OR 97222
ph: 503-659-0266
e-mail: randy@worldstar.com
web: http://www.worldstar.com/~randy/
Offers original full size billboard signs dating from 1945 to 1967; subjects include auto, beer, Coca-Cola, gas, oil, Levis, food, politics, tires, tractors, household, and many others.

Black & White Scotch

Collectors

Paul Stookey
Olde Towne Collectables
3436 Pointe Creek Ct. #202
Cape Coral, FL 34134-2005
ph: 941-498-4502
Wants to buy any "Black and White" Scotch advertising: signs, trays, bottles, back bar pieces, all black and white dogs, etc.

Counter Jars

(see also BOTTLES; BISCUIT BARRELS/JARS/TINS; CANDY CONTAINERS, Jars; FRUIT JARS; JELLY CONTAINERS; TOBACCO COLLECTIBLES, Jars)

Experts

Craig Ehlenberger
Abalone Cove Antiques
7 Fruit Tree Rd.
Rancho Palos Verdes, CA 90275
ph: 310-377-4609
fax: 310-377-8049
e-mail: cehlenberger@worldnet.att.net
Collector, dealer, expert; collects, trades, deals in pre-1950 counter display jars, glass trays, etc.; primarily those with names embossed in the glass, but also all others.

Figures

(see also DOLLS, Advertising; PHONOGRAPHS, Nipper)

Collectors

Roland Coover
1537 E. Strasburg Rd.
West Chester, PA 19380-6380
ph: 610-692-3112
e-mail: rlcoover@aol.com
Wants to buy figures of trademark characters such as Speedy Alka-Seltzer, Mr. Clean, Reddy Kilowatt, Quisp, Otto the Orkin Man, Raid Bug, etc.

Dealers

Marty Blank
P.O. Box 405
Flushing, NY 11365-0405
ph: 516-485-8071
e-mail: martyadver@aol.com
Wants to buy Elsie, Campbell Kids, Reddy Kilowatt, Coke, figural vinyl advertising and Country Store items.

Museums/Libraries

Creatability Toys Museum of Advertising Icons
1550 Maruga Ave., Ste. 504
Miami, FL 33146
ph: 305-663-7374
fax: 305-669-0092
web: http://toymuseum.com/main.html
Museum has over 650 nostalgic advertising icons; website allows you to search and obtain detailed descriptions and identification of all items in the collection.

Figures (Charlie Tuna)

Clubs/Associations

Cathy C. Runyan, Pres.
Charlie Tuna Collectors Club
7812 N.W. Hampton Rd.
Kansas City, MO 64152-4940
ph: 816-587-8687
fax: 816-587-8687
e-mail: marbleldy@aol.com

Experts

Cathy C. Runyan
Right Brain Publishing
7812 N.W. Hampton Rd.
Kansas City, MO 64152-4940
ph: 816-587-8687
fax: 816-587-8687
e-mail: marbleldy@aol.com
Collector, appraiser and specialist in Charlie Tuna memorabilia and promotional items.

Figures (Reddy Kilowatt)

Collectors

Carolyn T. Little
725 Esla Dr.
Chula Vista, CA 91910
Collects and specializes in light bulbs; wants light bulbs with tips or unusual light bulbs, Glow Lamps (neon) with figurals inside, meters, sockets, bulbs with figural or decorative filaments, Edison, Westinghouse, Reddy Kilowatt, etc.

Experts

Warren Dotz
2999 Regent St., Ste. 300
Berkeley, CA 94705-2118
ph: 510-652-1159
fax: 510-540-0325
e-mail: wellipsis@aol.com
Buys & specializes in advertising character figural store displays, banks, statuettes, and dolls; cartoonish trademark characters (Speedy Alka Seltzer, Reddy Kilowatt, Elsie the Cow, etc.); author of "Advertising Character Collectibles."

Firearms Related

Collectors

Bill Bramlett
P.O. Box 1105
Florence, SC 29503-1105
ph: 803-393-7390 or 843-665-3165
e-mail: bbramlett@webtv.net
Wants 1890-1931 firearms-related advertising items such as calendars, signs and posters that advertise firearms, shotgun shells, gunpowders from Remington, Marlin, Peters, U.M.C., DuPont, Winchester, U.S. Cartridge Co., Savage, etc.

Gerber Baby

Experts

Joan Stryker Grubaugh
2342 Hoaglin Rd.
Van Wert, OH 45891
ph: 419-622-4411
fax: 419-622-3026
Author of "Gerber Baby Dolls & Advertising Collectibles."

Hormel

Museums/Libraries

SPAM Museum
P.O. Box 800
Austin, MN 55912
ph: 507-437-5345
Museum of the Hormel Company; history, artifacts, advertisements, SPAM history and exhibit.

Johnson & Johnson

Collectors

Vi Leibecki
34 Westlawn Place
Palm Coast, FL 32164
ph: 904-446-9499
Interested in all pre-1940 Johnson & Johnson items.

Loose-Wiles

Collectors

Liz & Dick Wilmes
38W567 Brindlewood Ave.
Elgin, IL 60123-7976
ph: 847-697-9679
fax: 847-742-1054
e-mail: Bblocks@cris.com
Wants to buy items produced by or for the Sunshine Biscuit Co. (or formally Loose-Wiles Company): display racks, containers, photos, trade cards, artwork, signs, toys, stationary, brochures, invoices, pins, calendars, etc.; SASE for reply.

Lucky Strike

Collectors

John Van Alstyne
85 Brooks Ave.
Rochester, NY 14619-2453
Wants to buy Lucky Strike items: tobacco (including R.A. Patterson brand) and cigarettes; any kind of advertising or product item; American Tobacco Co.; pre-1912 advertising or products.

Harvey Leventhal
Harvey's Antique Advertising
412 Circle Drive
Ellwood City, PA 16117
ph: 724-752-1068
e-mail: harvey@antiqueadvertising.com
web: http://www.antiqueadvertising.com

Barnaby Conrad III
2101 Pacific Ave.
San Francisco, CA 94115
ph: 415-563-7418
Wants Lucky Strike vintage displays, ads, and related memorabilia.

Monarch Food Products

Collectors

Bruce & Nada Ferris
Ev'ry Nook & Cranny
3094 Oakes Dr.
Hayward, CA 94542-1234
ph: 510-581-5285
fax: 510-581-4469
e-mail: Nada.Ferris@ncal.kaiperm.org
Wants Monarch food products items from the 1920s: glass items with paper labels, tins, Monarch cookbook, teenie weenie popcorn, etc.; also Toledo, OH advertising, Atlas, Woolson Spice & Coffee, Toledo Biscuit, Buckey Beer.

Nabisco Food Group

Clubs/Associations

Charlie & Prissy Brown
Inner Seal Club
Newsletter: Colophon, The
6609 Billtown Rd.
Louisville, KY 40299
ph: 502-231-9379
A club dedicated to the collection and discussion of antique and nostalgic items carrying or relating to the

INNER SEAL trademark of the Nabisco Foods Group; National Biscuit Company (NABISCO), Americana, country store.

Phillip Morris

Collectors

Stuart Morrell
8925 Laureate Lane
Richmond, VA 23236-4406
Wants old Phillip Morris items.

Piano Related

Collectors

Philip Jamison
17 Sharon Alley
West Chester, PA 19382
ph: 610-696-8449
fax: 610-696-8449
Wants piano related material such as advertising signs and posters, catalogs, photographs of factory interiors, piano trade publications, etc.

Janice E. Kelsh
633 Pennsylvania Ave.
Hagerstown, MD 21740-3769
ph: 301-797-7675
fax: 301-496-7383
e-mail: jkelsh@niaid.nih.gov
Wants to buy piano advertising items; also piano related trade cards and postcards.

Pillsbury

Collectors

David & Brenda Wendel
F.E.I.
P.O. Box 1187
Poplar Bluff, MO 63902-1187
ph: 573-785-2075
fax: 573-686-8990
e-mail: bwendel@ldd.net
Wants advertising and other memorabilia related to Pillsbury Doughboy, Green Giant, Sprout.

Potteries Related

Collectors

Harvey Duke
577 Avenue Y
Brooklyn, NY 11235
Wants catalogs, brochures, flyers and other paper material from U.S. potteries; also wants advertising signs, dealer signs, ceramic Christmas cards and calling cards, sample plates, plant visit souvenirs, etc. from U.S. potteries only.

Signs

Clubs/Associations

Robert C. English
Porcelain Advertising Collectors Club
P.O. Box 381
Marshfield Hills, MA 02051-0381
ph: 781-837-0111
Informal membership that acts as a clearinghouse for collectors & dealers interested in porcelain signs in all categories. e.g. country store & automobile products as well as directional and street signs; 1900-1950; call for more info.

Collectors

Paul G. Engelke
23399 Rio Del Mar Dr.
Boca Raton, FL 33486-8504
ph: 561-338-3332
e-mail: keytelco@bellsouth.net
Wants to buy porcelain signs that advertise any type of merchandise: food, gas, oil, services, etc.

Michael Bruner
2615 Echo Lane
Ortonville, MI 48462
ph: 248-627-6351
Wants pre-1950 American or Canadian porcelain signs with good colors or graphics.

Richard Trautwein
Toys N Such
437 Dawson St.
Sault Sainte Marie, MI 49783-2119
ph: 906-635-0356
e-mail: rtraut@portup.com
Especially interested in porcelain advertising signs, neon clocks, and Coca Cola items.

Dealers

Robert C. English
P.O. Box 381
Marshfield Hills, MA 02051-0381
ph: 781-837-0111
Buys and sells porcelain signs including country store and automobile products as well as directional and street signs; 1900-1950.

Darrow's Fun Antiques
1101 1st Ave.
New York, NY 10021-8737
ph: 212-838-0730
fax: 212-838-3617
e-mail: george@fun-antiques.com
web: http://www.fun-antiques.com/
Buys & sells antique games, toys, ad signs, animated art, jukeboxes, slot machines, comic watches, bicycles & memorabilia of all types.

Walt Feiger
Walt's Antiques
2513 Nelson Rd.
Traverse City, MI 49686-8557
ph: 231-223-7386 or 231-223-4123
Wants to buy old porcelain or tin advertising signs.

Dave Beck
P.O. Box 435
Mediapolis, IA 52637-0435
ph: 319-394-3943
fax: 319-394-3943
Buys all kinds of signs in any quantity; may be fairly new (but not reproductions) or 100 years old; tin, porcelain, cardboard, or paper; advertising soda, beer, tobacco, farm related items, or anything else.

Doug Clemence
Treasure Chest
436 North Chicago
Salina, KS 67401-2020
ph: 785-827-9371 or 785-825-4111
e-mail: clemence@midusa.net
Buys, sells, trades old advertising signs.

Robert Newman
10809 Charnock Rd.
Los Angeles, CA 90034-6606
ph: 310-559-0539
Wants to buy neon and lighted clocks; also tin, cardboard and porcelain 1920s-1950s oil, auto, soft drink, bus and motorcycle advertising signs: Coca-Cola, Harley-Davidson, etc.; condition important; with graphics or pictures.

Museums/Libraries

Museum of Transportation at Larz Anderson Park
15 Newton St.
Brookline, MA 02146
ph: 617-522-6547
web: http://www.mot.org/

Repro. Sources

Terri McCoy
AAA Sign Co.
354 S. State Line Rd.
Lowellville, OH 44436-9508
ph: 330-964-8394
fax: 330-964-1013
Manufactures and carries over 800 different reproduction (nostalgic) embossed tin sign designs; full color catalog $5; wholesale only, so send your business card and tax number.

4x1 Imports Inc.
5873 Day Rd.
Cincinnati, OH 45251
ph: 513-385-8185
fax: 513-385-8182
Over 250 signs in stock; painted on heavy die-cut metal stock; send $4 for catalog.

Seay Marketing
1325 Tarman Circle
Norman, OK 73071
ph: 405-321-8797
e-mail: seaymktg@telepath.com
web: http://www.seaymarketing.com
Offers high quality reproduction advertising signs for the shop of gameroom: automotive dealership, beverage, petroliana.

Spintops

Collectors

Glenn A. Scott
29 Upton Lane
Morrisville, PA 19067-2710
Wants to buy metal or celluloid spintops (half dollar size disk with wooden shaft) with advertising.

Sunshine Biscuit

Collectors

Liz & Dick Wilmes
38W567 Brindlewood Ave.
Elgin, IL 60123-7976
ph: 847-697-9679
fax: 847-742-1054
e-mail: Bblocks@cris.com
Wants to buy items produced by or for the Sunshine Biscuit Co. (or formally Loose-Wiles Company): display racks, containers, photos, trade cards, artwork, signs, toys, stationary, brochures, invoices, pins, calendars, etc.; SASE for reply.

Talcum Powder

Collectors

Millie Vaccarella
1955 Hythe St.
Roseville, MN 55113
ph: 651-631-2201
Wants to buy talcum powder tins, especially with babies or beautiful ladies.

Telephone & Telegraph

Experts

Michael Bruner
2615 Echo Lane
Ortonville, MI 48462
ph: 248-627-6351
Co-author with Bob Alexander of "A Collectors Guide to Telephone, Telegraph and Express Co. Advertising."

Tin Vienna Art Plates

Dealers

Tom Lavely
Neat Olde Stuff
16935 N. Main St.
P.O. Box 9
Galesville, WI 54630-0009
ph: 608-582-2082
fax: 608-582-2180
e-mail: tglavely@aol.com
Collector, expert and dealer in tin Vienna Art Plates; collecting since 1965.

Experts

Howard & Jane Hazelcorn
6731 Ashley Ct.
Sarasota, FL 34241-9696
ph: 941-921-1815
Authors of "Hazelcorn's Price Guide to Tin Vienna Art Plates"; tin advertising plates made from the 1890s to the 1950s. (Vienna Art is a

trademark used by the H.D. Beach Co., OH.)

Tins

Collectors

Ed Natale, Jr.
P.O. Box 222
Wyckoff, NJ 07481
ph: 201-848-8485
fax: 201-848-8485
Wants to buy automotive related tin container: oil, grease, bulb, fuse, spark plug, tube patch, etc.; motorcycle, household oil, handy oil, gun oil, coffee, condom; also related signage: tin, porcelain, paper; photos helpful.

Michael R. Reilly
W259 N9116 City Rd. J
Hartland, WI 53029-9010
ph: 414-246-3017 or 888-246-4017
e-mail: ChipTin@aol.com
web: http://www.usadvertising.com
Collector of antique and collectibles tins.

Ken Kennedy, Sr.
7824 South 113th St.
Seattle, WA 98178-3238
ph: 206-772-4358
e-mail: spiceking@isomedia.com
Wants to buy colorful old spice tins with interesting graphics.

Dealers

Pat Dowis
Tin Lizzie's
6448 Dearborn Dr.
Acworth, GA 30102-1228
ph: 770-924-9637
e-mail: gals@mindspring.com
web: http://members.tripod.com/~TIN_LIZZIES/
Wants to buy mostly modern advertising tins and collectibles; also some of the older ones.

Charles & Joan Rhoden
Rhoden's Antiques
8693 N 1950 East Road
Georgetown, IL 61846-6264
ph: 217-662-8046 or 217-662-8440
fax: 217-662-8223
Wants to buy pre-1960 lard tins and spice tins; send brand name and describe, include photo if possible.

Experts

David Zimmerman
6834 Newtonsville Rd.
Pleasant Plain, OH 45162
ph: 513-625-5188
Wants to buy advertising tin cans (smalls and samples): aspirins, condoms, needles, typewriter ribbons, medicines, etc. to publish "Encyclopedia of Advertising Tins, Vol. II"; send SASE plus 3 stamps for 20-page wants list with prices.

Internet Resources

Tin Talk
e-mail: collect@telepath.com
web: http://www.telepath.com/collect/

Michael R. Reilly
Antique & Collectible Advertising Tins & Cans
W259 N9116 City Rd. J
Hartland, WI 53029-9010
ph: 414-246-3017 or 888-246-4017
e-mail: ChipTin@aol.com
web: http://www.usadvertising.com
Web site is in the form of a "book" on collecting antique and collectible tins; a guide and source of information; FREE e-mail newsletter, "Tin Gathering", every two weeks.

Trade Cards

(see also TRADING CARDS, Non-Sport)

Auction Services

Russell Mascieri
Victorian Images
P.O. Box 284
Marlton, NJ 08053
ph: 609-985-7711
fax: 609-985-8513
e-mail: RMascieri@aol.com
web: http://www.tradecards.com/vi
Conducts specialized trade card mail and telephone auctions.

Murray Cards (International) Ltd.
51 Watford Way
Hendon Central, London NW4 3JH
U.K.
ph: 0181-2025688
fax: 0181-2037878
e-mail: murraycards@ukbusiness.com
web: http://www.murraycards.com
Stocks and auctions trade cards; also publishes "Cigarette Card Values" - a catalog of cigarette and other trade cards.

Clubs/Associations

Trade Card Collector's Association
Journal: Advertising Trade Card Quarterly
3706 S. Acoma St.
Englewood, CO 80110
ph: 303-761-7906
e-mail: tccadc@aol.com
web: http://members.aol.com/tccahomepg/index.html
Helps unify advertising trade card collectors through informative publications and an annual national convention.

John W. Townsend
Cartophilic Society of Great Britain
63 Ferndale Road
Church Crookham
Fleet, Hants. GU13 OLN
U.K.
e-mail: librarian@cardclubs.ndirect.co.uk
web: http://www.cardclubs.ndirect.co.uk/
Non-profit club founded in 1935 devoted to the research and collecting of all trade advertisement cards, especially tobacco/cigarette/gum.

Dealers

Dave & Nancy Dawson
P.O. Box 750
Marstons Mills, MA 02648-0750
ph: 508-420-3872
e-mail: dawson95@aol.com
Has an inventory of thousands of trade cards in addition to a variety of other 19th century ephemera such as rewards of merit, valentines, business cards, broadsides, billheads.

Kit Barry
Kit Barry Ephemera
88 High Street Box S-I
Brattleboro, VT 05301
ph: 802-254-3634
web: http://www.tradecards.com/kb/
Specializes in fine ephemera, scarce and rare, including trade cards, billheads, labels, and posters; also sells a complete line of ephemera supplies: plastic pages, matchbook pages, rigid print holders, soft plastic sleeves, et.

Jean & Howard Berg
P.O. Box 343
Granby, CT 06035
ph: 860-653-7982
e-mail: JandHBERG@aol.com
Buys and sells quality trade cards, seed and garden trade catalogs, and related ephemera.

Marcy & Mindi Brahin
100 Sargent Rd.
Freehold, NJ 07728
ph: 732-462-7923
e-mail: Atprints@aol.com
Buys and sells trade cards and business cards; also specializes in matted Harpers and Leslie prints.

Bill Mobley
P.O. Box 10
Schoharie, NY 12157

Stephen C. Jones
P.O. Box 267
Homer, NY 13077-0267
ph: 607-753-8822
e-mail: stevejones@a-znet.com
Wants pre-1910 advertising trade cards illustrating products or services, mechanical bank trade cards, Currier & Ives trade cards, Victorian scrapbooks, illustrated business cards, cigar box sample labels and sample books of labels.

Ron Schieber
Mad Money
P.O. Box 72057
Akron, OH 44372
ph: 330-836-9442
e-mail: dschiebe@neo.rr.com
web: http://www.tradecards.com/pages/rsListsForm.html
Author of a series of 30 checklists of Trade Cards and other ephemera.

Jimmy & Amanda Greene
A & J Trade Cards
9453 Carlton Hills Blvd.
Santee, CA 92071-2504
ph: 619-562-0320 or 619-562-0320
e-mail: jgreene@inetworld.net
Buys and sells trade cards; wants Victorian trade card categories such as food-related items and odds and ends as long as they're attractive and/or bizarre.

Albert Van den Bosch
Collectomania
Stenenbrug 14
Antwerp, Flanders 2140
Netherlands
ph: 003 343 365952 or 003 232 711588
fax: 003 232 711583
e-mail: Albert.vandenBosch@ping.be
web: http://www.ping.be/card/index.html
Buys and sells European trade cards; also calendars, menus and all other European ephemera.

Bob Coalbran
Card Mine, The
21 Pine View, Muxton
Telford, Shropshire TF2 8QX
U.K.
ph: 01952 410774
fax: 01952 411083
e-mail: bob.coalbran@cableinet.co.uk
web: http://wkweb4.cableinet.co.uk/card.mine/
Dedicated to the collection and study of Trade Cards from around the world, particularly Europe; website includes illustrated catalogs produced by Verkade plus details of Chocolat d"aiguebelle Natural History series; regular auctions.

Experts

Ben Crane
Trade Card Place, The
P.O. Box 4885
Wheaton, IL 60189
ph: 630-665-5662
fax: 630-665-2826
e-mail: bcrane@tradecards.com
web: http://www.tradecards.com/
Author of "The Before and After Trade Card"; website is about Victorian trade cards that advertise American goods and services during the late 1800s; website has for sale

ads, articles, collectors and dealers, organizations,

Internet Resources

Bob Coalbran
Card Mine, The
21 Pine View, Muxton
Telford, Shropshire TF2 8QX
U.K.
ph: 01952 410774
fax: 01952 411083
e-mail: bob.coalbran@cableinet.co.uk
web: http://wkweb4.cableinet.co.uk/card.mine/
Dedicated to the collection and study of Trade Cards from around the world, particularly Europe; website includes illustrated catalogs produced by Verkade plus details of Chocolat d"aiguebelle Natural History series; regular auctions.

Trade Cards (Tobacco)

(see also CIGARETTE COLLECTIBLES; SMOKING COLLECTIBLES)

Auction Services

Murray Cards (International) Ltd.
Newsletter: Cigarette Cards
51 Watford Way
Hendon Central, London NW4 3JH
U.K.
ph: 0181-2025688
fax: 0181-2037878
e-mail: murraycards@ukbusiness.com
web: http://www.murraycards.com
Stocks in excess of 20M cigarette & trade cards; monthly specialist auctions; publisher of card values & books on card collecting.

Bob Coalbran
Card Mine, The
21 Pine View, Muxton
Telford, Shropshire TF2 8QX
U.K.
ph: 01952 410774
fax: 01952 411083
e-mail: bob.coalbran@cableinet.co.uk
web: http://wkweb4.cableinet.co.uk/card.mine/
A variety of unusual ephemera items are included within each of the regular Card Mine Auctions.

Collectors

William Nielsen
1379 Main St.
Brewster, MA 02631-1723
ph: 508-896-7389
Wants U.S. tobacco related trade cards.

Paul Davis
308 Landsende Rd.
Devon, PA 19333
ph: 610-644-1216
Wants insert and trade cards of tobacco companies; also wants Liebig and Au Bon Marche trade cards.

Ron Stevenson
4920 Armoury St.
Niagara Falls, Ontario L2E 1T1
Canada
ph: 905-358-5497
Interested in American cigarette cards and albums; Brooke-Bond/Red Rose Tea cards and related ephemera; Liebig trade cards, English language; also other ephemera.

Dealers

David Grimes
P.O. Box 354
Hopewell, NJ 08525
ph: 609-446-0303
fax: 609-466-8790
e-mail: noblegb@aol.com
web: http://members.aol.com/noblegb/Page/Text.html
Buys and sells 19th and 20th century American cigarette and tobacco cards, silks, leathers, etc.

Franklyn Roberts
Franklyn Cards
26 The Parade
Walton on the Naze
Essex, CO14 8EA
U.K.
e-mail: 106325.464@compuserve.com
web: http://ourworld.compuserve.com/homepages/Franklyn_Roberts/
One of the best resources on the Internet for 1880 to 1940 cigarette cards.

Periodicals

David Stuckey
Magpie Publications
Magazine: Card Times
70 Winifred Lane
Aughton
Ormskirk, Lancashire L39 5DL
U.K.
ph: 0169 542 3470
fax: 0151 430 7836
A monthly magazine focusing on trade cards, cigarette silks and cards, also trade cards of celebrities, politicians, athletes, etc.; club activities, sales/show calendars, ads.

Typewriter Related

Collectors

Darryl Rehr
P.O. Box 641824
Los Angeles, CA 90064
ph: 310-477-5229
fax: 310-268-8420
e-mail: dcrehr@earthlink.net
web: http://home.earthlink.net/~dcrehr/
Wants pre-1920 ads for typewriters and office equipment; also trade catalogs and business magazines, e.g. "Business Man's Monthly."

Woolson Spice Co.

Collectors

Bruce & Nada Ferris
Ev'ry Nook & Cranny
3094 Oakes Dr.
Hayward, CA 94542-1234
ph: 510-581-5285
fax: 510-581-4469
e-mail: Nada.Ferris@ncal.kaiperm.org
Wants Monarch food products items from the 1920s: glass items with paper labels, tins, Monarch cookbook, teenie weenie popcorn, etc.; also Toledo, OH advertising, Atlas, Woolson Spice & Coffee, Toledo Biscuit, Buckey Beer.

Experts

Randy Webb
42217 Cochran Mill Rd.
Leesburg, VA 20175
ph: 703-777-3600 or 540-668-6071
fax: 703-478-1160
e-mail: thewebbs3@aol.com
Wants Wooson Spice Co. (Lion Coffee) items: bags, cans, cards, diecuts, premiums, store posters, games, etc.; these materials needed for entry into database and book on everything Woolson Spice Co.

AFRICAN AMERICANS

(see BLACK MEMORABILIA)

AGRICULTURE RELATED ITEMS

(see FARM COLLECTIBLES; FARM MACHINERY; TOYS, Farm; TRACTORS)

AIR LABELS

(see AIRLINE MEMORABILIA; LABELS, Luggage)

AIRGUNS

(see also TOY GUNS, BB Guns)

Clubs/Associations

John Quiter, Sec./Treas.
American Airgun Field Target Association
Newsletter: AAFTA Newsletter
180 Mill Creek Rd.
Bayville, NJ 08721
ph: 732-269-3303
web: http://www.airguns.net/aafta/aafta.html

Mike Ahuna
Carolina Airgun Club
Newsletter: Carolina Airgun Club Newsletter
689 Highland Ridge Rd.
Mooresville, NC 28115
ph: 704-660-3400
fax: 704-660-3401
The Club holds Target Matches, Field Target Matches, and Silhouette Matches the year round; Matches are open to the public and Club members.

Dealers

Mike Ahuna
Mike's Crosman Service
689 Highland Ridge Rd.
Mooresville, NC 28115
ph: 704-660-3400
fax: 704-660-3401
Buys and sells old and new airguns; authorized Crosman airgun service station, and is an authorized Beeman 5 Star Dealer.

Periodicals

Edith Gaylord
Newsletter: Airgun Letter, The
4614 Woodland Rd.
Ellicott City, MD 21042-6329
ph: 410-730-5496
fax: 410-730-9544
e-mail: staff@airgunletter.net
web: http://www.airgunletter.net
A monthly newsletter for airgun users and collectors.

Barry Abel, Ed.
Newsletter: Airgun Ads
P.O. Box 33
Hamilton, MT 59840-0033
ph: 406-363-3805
fax: 406-363-4117
e-mail: airgunads@bitterroot.net
Published monthly to enable subscribers to buy and sell airguns of all types, from Olympic match grade to smooth bore, including parts, accessories and literature.

AIRLINE MEMORABILIA

(see also AIRPLANES; AIR SICKNESS BAGS; AVIATION; AVIATION MEMORABILIA; LABELS, Luggage; MODELS, Aircraft; STAMP COLLECTING, Air Mail Related; TOYS, Airplane Related; TRANSPORTATION COLLECTIBLES)

Clubs/Associations

Paul F. Collins
World Airline Historical Society
Magazine: Captain's Log
13739 Picarsa Dr.
Jacksonville, FL 32225-3265
ph: 904-221-1446
web: http://www.aircruise.com/wahs/
Members are interested in the collecting of airline memorabilia and

in the study of airlines, airliners, kits, models and related items.

Louis Wendruck
Gay Airline & Travel Club, The
Magazine: Gay Airline & Travel Club Newsletter, The
P.O. Box 69A04 - Dept. Mal
West Hollywood, CA 90069-0066
ph: 323-650-5112
e-mail: gayboylaca@writeme.com
web: http://members.tripod.com/~gatc/
A club for gay men interested in meeting others who collect airline memorabilia, travel or work in the airline and travel industry; quarterly magazine has ads for airline collectibles wanted and for sale.

Collectors

Jay T. Schulz
Advanced Air Cargo Logistics
134 Rossevelt Blvd.
Hauppauge, NY 11788
ph: 516-234-0103
e-mail: anjcrane@aol.com
Wants airline memorabilia from the 1970s: public relations materials, photos, wings, safety cards, aircraft models, etc.

Steve & Larry Charter
8249 Cavalry Run
Mechanicsville, VA 23111
ph: 804-779-3142
Wants to buy airline memorabilia: playing cards, wings, matchbooks, metal travel agency display model airplanes, etc.

Charles C. Quarles
204 Reservation Dr.
Spindale, NC 28160-1534
ph: 828-286-2962 or 828-245-7803
fax: 828-286-3224
Wants pilot and steward/ess wings, hat badges, metal travel agency display model airliners, etc. from 1930s to 1960s U.S. airlines.

Randy Ridgely
447 Oglethorpe Ave.
Athens, GA 30606-2236
ph: 706-549-9264
e-mail: erie@negia.net
Wants railroad, steamship and airline items.

Bill Rosenbloom
1893 Worcester
Saint Paul, MN 55116-2614
ph: 651-699-2784
Wants all older logoed airline items: playing cards, schedules, posters, kiddie wings, and all other logo-marked items.

Dick Wallin
P.O. Box 1784
Springfield, IL 62705-1784
ph: 217-498-9279
e-mail: rrwallin@aol.com
Wants airline logo items: dishes, glassware, playing cards, crew wings and badges, silverplate pitchers, creamers; also large travel agency size plane models, chrome ashtrays with plane models.

Craig Morris
105 Silver Willow Ct.
Galt, CA 95632-2442
ph: 209-745-4539
Wants to buy airline memorabilia: 1920-1960 airline postcards, time tables, posters, paper ephemera, etc.; will pay postage.

Peter van Meerten
Peavy's Aviation Memorabilia
Heerenbeekplantsoen 6
Almere, 1333XG
The Netherlands
ph: 0031-(0)36-5370913
e-mail: peavey@tref.nl
web: http://leden.tref.nl/peavey/
Wants to trade or buy passenger safety instruction cards.

Dealers

Bizarre Bazarre
130 1/4 East 65th St.
New York, NY 10021-7007
ph: 212-517-2100
fax: 212-517-2283
Wants museum quality aviation models, metal models of propellered aircraft, airline and travel agent display airplane models, factory and industrial design models.

William Gawchick
88 Clarendon Ave.
Yonkers, NY 10701
ph: 914-965-3010
fax: 914-966-1055
e-mail: panam314@aol.com
web: http://www.freeyellow.com/members2/mrpanam
Expert, dealer, collector, appraiser wants to buy pilot and steward(ess) wings, hat badges, kiddie wings, and all other logo-marked items from the 1930 to 1970s for Pan Am and other domestic airlines.

Jeffrey D. Boutin
JB Airline Collectibles
705 White Bluff Ave.
Savannah, GA 31419-3140
ph: 912-920-9907
fax: 912-920-9906
Wants to buy memorabilia from U.S. airlines, past or present; postcards, flight schedules/time tables, glassware, dinnerware, flatware/silverware, baggage tags, etc., especially Northeast, National, Braniff.

Mike Fleming
Mike Fleming Antiques & Aviation Collectibles
432 S. Main St.
Princeton, IL 61356
ph: 773-267-8595
fax: 773-267-8596
e-mail: FAAsale@aol.com
Wants aviation items that display airline and manufacturing logos: playing cards, travel agency models, manufacturer's models, ashtrays, lighters, timetables, company annual reports, flight manuals, crew items, hat badges, service pins.

Experts

Larry McLaughlin
17 Seventh Ave.
Smithtown, NY 11787-4508
ph: 516-265-9224
e-mail: larrymak@erols.com
Buys, collects and specializes in airline items: travel agency models, ashtrays, lighters, timetables, crew hat badges, pins, wings, commercial or military models, helmets, manuals; also wants tin airplane toys.

John R. Joiner
173 Green Tree Dr.
Newnan, GA 30265-2066
ph: 770-502-9565
e-mail: propjoiner@mindspring.com
Wants pilot and flight attendant wings, hat badges; also wants display models, early signs, anniversary pins, postcards, time tables, playing cards from commercial airlines, pre-1970s; no military items, please.

Dick Wallin
P.O. Box 1784
Springfield, IL 62705-1784
ph: 217-498-9279
e-mail: rrwallin@aol.com
Author of "Airline Collectibles General Information"; he will try to answer questions and provide information on buying and selling of specific items, or he will direct you to someone who can.

Museums/Libraries

Art Thomas
Don Thomas Foundation
5134 Sugar Camp Rd.
Milford, OH 45150-9674
ph: 513-248-0485 or 513-248-4650
fax: 513-248-0485
Buys, sells and specializes in airline memorabilia; Don Thomas is author of "Nostalgia Panamerican", "Poster Art of the Airlines", "Lindbergh & Commercial Aviation", "Nostalgia North Americana", "Airline Artistry," "Nostalgia Artistica."

Periodicals

R.D. Roland
R.S. & T. Ry. Co.
Ad Paper: Main Line Journal, The
P.O. Box 121
Streamwood, IL 60107-0121
A bi-monthly "ad" paper exclusively for buying and selling railroad collectibles as well as airline and steamship memorabilia; subscribers receive FREE ads.

Airways International, Inc.
Magazine: Airways
P.O. Box 1109
Sandpoint, ID 83864-0872
ph: 208-263-2098 or 800-440-5166
fax: 208-263-5906
e-mail: airways@nidlink.com
web: http://www.airwaysmag.com/
International bi-monthly magazine devoted to airlines and commercial aircraft; a global review of commercial flight; periodically contains articles of interest to the collector of airline memorabilia.

Air Sickness Bags

Collectors

Steve Silberberg
Air Sickness Bag Virtual Museum
P.O. Box 821384
Dallas, TX 75206
ph: 214-696-0543
e-mail: stevebo@onramp.net
web: http://www.airsicknessbags.com/
Curator of the On-Line Air Sickness Bag Museum; collects all kinds of air sickness bags but specializes in one-of-a-kind bags usually not found on commercial flights; seeking a Space Shuttle bag.

Dr. Walter Brinker
Niedernfeld 2
Radevormwald, 42477
Germany
ph: 49-219540928
fax: 49-21956517
A collector with about 1100 air sickness bags from 500 air lines.

Rune Tapper
Sweden
ph: +46 70 5750232
e-mail: rune@tapper.com
web: http://home1.swipnet.se/~w-14429/puke.htm
Collector of barf bags from airlines all over the world; bags to swap listed on website.

Graham Curran
Vomitorium, The
Greenacres, Old Hall
Hanmer, SY13 3BX
U.K.
ph: +44 (0) 1948 830461
e-mail: grcurran@csi.com
web: http://ourworld.compuserve.com/homepages/grcurran/vomitum.htm
Bags of fun from the colorful world of

international air sickness; see what nauseous air travelers have in their laps.

Baggage I.D. Labels

(see also LABELS, Luggage)

Experts

H. Van Dyk
7 Birchwood Ave.
Peabody, MA 01960
ph: 978-535-0353
Author of "Catalog of Baggage I.D. Labels, Vol. 1, U.S.A. & Canada" & "..Vol. 2, Europe & Middle East"; buys airline baggage I.D. labels (for travelers' name/address); 1st Class, cabin baggage, crew, fragile, etc.; no destination labels.

Models

Collectors

Michael Walters
P.O. Box 31
Scottsdale, AZ 85252-0031
ph: 602-946-7454
fax: 602-946-8729
e-mail: michwalt@aol.com
Collector wants good condition chrome desk display pieces and ashtrays that have plane models attached.

Experts

Bob Keller
Starline Hobbies
P.O. Box 38
Stanton, CA 90680-0038
ph: 714-826-5216
e-mail: prsdog@aol.com
web: http://members.aol.com/PRSdog/kitshow.html
Especially wants to buy plastic model kits; can provide professional appraisals of collections.

Models (Desk)

(see also TOYS, Airplane)

Collectors

Ira S. Kuperstein
22 Brush Hill Terrace
Butler, NJ 07405-2439
ph: 973-283-2420 or 800-526-5177
fax: 973-283-2426
e-mail: kuperstein@nac.net
Wants to buy airplane display models.

David Ostrowski
5411 Masser Lane
Fairfax, VA 22032-3817
ph: 703-323-6674

Experts

Larry McLaughlin
17 Seventh Ave.
Smithtown, NY 11787-4508
ph: 516-265-9224
e-mail: larrymak@erols.com
Wants to buy airplane, rocket, missile desk models: manufacturers' display models, travel agency models, commercial or military, etc.; has written articles for aviation toy magazines; staff editor for "Miniature Aircraft Quarterly."

Pilots Wings

(see also AVIATION MEMORABILIA, Military Insignia)

Collectors

Michael Dusek
1058 Lupin Dr. #5
Salinas, CA 93906
ph: 831-757-2526
Wants to buy military wings, civilian wings, sterling silver wings; also wants China, Burma, or India bracelets related to aviation.

Playing Cards

Collectors

Fred Chan
Top Flite Information
P.O. Box 2744
Sequim, WA 98382-2744
ph: 360-681-4671
fax: 360-681-4671
e-mail: topflite@olympus.net
Author of "Airline Playing Cards" with supplements; buys, trades, and sells airline playing cards (decks and singles); appraises airline playing card collections.

Timetables

Collectors

Jerry Hughes
Jerry's Airline Timetable Collection
843 W 146th St.
Gardena, CA 90247-2711
ph: 310-769-6208
e-mail: fromfay@aol.com
web: http://members.aol.com/fromfay/
A private collector of airline timetables from very old to present from all around the world.

AIRPLANES

(see also AIRLINE MEMORABILIA; AVIATION; AVIATION MEMORABILIA; MODELS, Aircraft; TOYS, Airplane Related)

Appraisers

Michael Bonventre
MJB Aviation
P.O. Box 1136
Seaford, NY 11783
ph: 516-328-0847
fax: 516-783-2536
e-mail: airdrv@aol.com
Airplane appraisal and consulting service: valuations, estates, bankruptcy, tax appeals, repossessions, matrimonial, insurance, corporate, condemnations, condition surveys.

National Aircraft Appraisers Association
P.O. Box 528
Hillsboro, MO 63050
ph: 314-285-4768

Auction Services

Jon Baddeley
Sotheby's
34-35 New Bond St.
London, W1A 2AA
U.K.
ph: 44 171 293 5000
fax: 44 171 293 5989
web: http://www.sothebys.com/
Conducts regular specialized auctions of vintage aircraft.

Clubs/Associations

Great War Aeroplanes Association, The
Newsletter: Great Times, The
18 Journey's End
Mendon, VT 05701
e-mail: mlewis@cfanet.com
web: http://www.cfanet.com/mlewis/gwaa.htm
This organization is for anyone that has an interest in WWI, especially aviation.

L.E. Opdycke
World War I Aeroplanes, Inc.
15 Crescent Rd.
Poughkeepsie, NY 12601-4405
ph: 914-473-3679
A service organization devoted to those magnificent flying machines of 1900-1919 and 1920-1940; for builders, museums, restorers, historians, modelers and collectors; publishes the journals "WWI Aero" and "Skyways."

Robert Taylor, Pres.
Antique Airplane Association, Inc.
Magazine: Antique Airplane News & Digest
22001 Bluegrass Rd.
Ottumwa, IA 52501-8569
ph: 515-938-2773
fax: 515-938-2773
e-mail: aaaapmhq@pcsia.com
web: http://www.aaa-apm.org/aaa/
The organization for antique and classic airplane owners, pilots and enthusiasts.

Antique Aeroplane Association of Australia, Inc.
Magazine: Rag & Tube
P.O. Box 1036
South Melbourne, Victoria 3205
Australia
e-mail: rclark@aardvark.apana.org.au
web: http://members.ocean.com.au/aaaa/
Australia's only dedicated old aeroplane magazine; published four times per year.

Popular Flying Association
Terminal Building, Shoreham Airport
Shoreham-by-Sea, West Sussex BN43 5FF
U.K.
ph: +44 (0)1273 461616
fax: +44 (0)1273 463390
e-mail: office@pfa.org.uk
web: http://www.pfa.org.uk/
The United Kingdom's association for the construction of amateur-built aircraft and vintage aircraft restoration.

Dealers

Bob Von Willer
Exotic Aircraft Company
1719 North Marshall Ave.
El Cajon, CA 92020
ph: 619-562-7467
fax: 619-448-2110
e-mail: baron@skyguy.com
web: http://www.barnstormers.com/
Specializes in the restoration and marketing of antique aircraft, including warbirds; appraiser, dealer, expert, collector, and repair services offered.

Experts

Bob Von Willer
Exotic Aircraft Company
1719 North Marshall Ave.
El Cajon, CA 92020
ph: 619-562-7467
fax: 619-448-2110
e-mail: baron@skyguy.com
web: http://www.barnstormers.com/
Specializes in the restoration and marketing of antique aircraft, including warbirds; appraiser, dealer, expert, collector, and repair services offered.

Periodicals

L.E. Opdycke
World War I Aeroplanes, Inc.
Journal: WWI Aero
15 Crescent Rd.
Poughkeepsie, NY 12601-4405
ph: 914-473-3679
A quarterly magazine for collectors, restorers, replica builders, historians, and modelers focusing on 1900-1919 aircraft.

L.E. Opdycke
World War I Aeroplanes, Inc.
Journal: Skyways
15 Crescent Rd.
Poughkeepsie, NY 12601-4405
ph: 914-473-3679
A quarterly magazine for collectors, restorers, replica builders, historians, and modelers focusing on 1920-1940 aircraft.

Trader Publishing Company
Magazine: Aero Trader & Chopper Shopper
P.O. Box 9059
Clearwater, FL 34618-9059
ph: 727-712-0035 or 800-548-8889
fax: 727-712-0034
e-mail: webmaster@traderonline.com
web: http://www.traderonline.com

TAP Publishing Co.
Newspaper: Trade-A-Plane
174 Fourth St.
P.O. Box 509
Crossville, TN 38557
ph: 800-337-5263 or 931-484-5137
fax: 931-484-2532
e-mail: webmaster@trade-a-plane.com
web: http://trade-a-plane.com/
Published three times each month; huge advertising newspaper containing everything to keep you flying: from antique airplanes to parts, electronics and related services.

Christina Gargano
Heartland Communications Group, Inc.
Magazine: Aviators Hot Line
1003 Central Ave.
P.O. Box 1052
Fort Dodge, IA 50501
ph: 800-247-2000 or 515-955-1600
fax: 515-574-2233
e-mail: libbie@hlipublishing.com
web: http://www.hlipublishing.com
The national and international marketplace for active buyers and sellers of corporate and general aircraft, parts and service.

H.G. Frautschy
Experimental Aircraft Association
Magazine: Vintage Airplane
P.O. Box 3086
Oshkosh, WI 54903-3086
ph: 800-843-3612 or 920-426-4800
fax: 920-426-4873
e-mail: communication@eaa.org
web: http://www.eaa.org/

H.G. Frautschy
Experimental Aircraft Association
Magazine: Sport Aviation
P.O. Box 3086
Oshkosh, WI 54903-3086
ph: 800-843-3612 or 920-426-4800
fax: 920-426-4873
e-mail: communication@eaa.org
web: http://www.eaa.org/

H.G. Frautschy
Experimental Aircraft Association
Magazine: Sport Aerobatics
P.O. Box 3086
Oshkosh, WI 54903-3086
ph: 800-843-3612 or 920-426-4800
fax: 920-426-4873
e-mail: communication@eaa.org
web: http://www.eaa.org/

Kathy Kingston
Intertec Publishing Corp.
Price Guide: Aircraft Bluebook - Price Digest
P.O. Box 12901
Overland Park, KS 66282
ph: 800-654-6776 or 913-341-1300
web: http://www.intertec.com/books/ablubok.htm
Comprehensive quarterly index of the value of used fixed wing aircraft and helicopters; controlled availability; no vintage, antique, military, kit or experimental planes.

Steven D. Werner
Werner Publishing Corp.
Magazine: Plane & Pilot
12121 Wilshire Blvd., Ste. 1220
Los Angeles, CA 90025-1175
ph: 310-820-1500
fax: 310-826-5008
e-mail: editors@planeandpilotmag.com
web: http://www.planeandpilotmag.com/
Articles on general aviation from light single-engine planes to medium-weight twins and related products.

Fancy Publications, Inc.
Magazine: Private Pilot
3 Burroughs
Irvine, CA 92718
ph: 714-855-8822
fax: 714-855-3045

Sclair Ben
Newspaper: Flyer
P.O. Box 39099
Tacoma, WA 98439
ph: 800-426-8538
fax: 253-471-9911
e-mail: comments@flyer-online.com
web: http://www.flyer-online.com/
Bi-weekly newspaper serving the aviation industry nationwide; containing thousands of ads for aircraft, avionics, equipment, instruction, aviation businesses, etc.

Cessna

Clubs/Associations

Richard Heckenlaible
Cessna Owners Organization
Magazine: Cessna Owners
P.O. Box 5000
Iola, WI 54945
ph: 715-445-5000 or 800-331-0038
fax: 715-445-4053
e-mail: aircraft@aircraftownergroup.com
web: http://aircraftownergroup.com
Magazines cover trouble-shooting, maintenance tips, product reviews, airworthiness alerts, etc.

Ford Tri-Motors

Dealers

Tim O'Callaghan
305 St. Lawrence Rd.
P.O. Box 512
Northville, MI 48167
ph: 248-449-2652
e-mail: timothyo@ameritech.net
Author of "Henry Ford's Airport & Other Aviation Interests 1909-1954" and producer of a video on Ford's aviation ventures; always willing to answer questions; buys items relating to Ford Tri-Motor airplanes; also other Ford memorabilia.

Model

(see also KITS; MODELS)

Clubs/Associations

Larry Clark
Society of Antique Modelers
Newsletter: Sam Speaks
P.O. Box 528
Lucerne Valley, CA 92356
ph: 714-542-8294
e-mail: CWReich@aol.com
web: http://www.antiquemodeler.org/
Focuses on the collecting, restoring and operating of free flight and R/C model model airplanes of vintage design; chapters worldwide.

Periodicals

Erika Daileda
Wise Owl Worldwide Publications
Magazine: Scale Aircraft Modeling
4314 West 238th St. - Dept. MACR
Torrance, CA 90505-4509
ph: 310-375-6258
fax: 310-375-0548
e-mail: wiseowl@sprintmail.com
A monthly English publication; gives details, historical facts, and photos on specific aircraft each month.

Model (Remote Control)

(see also MODELS, Aircraft [Flying])

Periodicals

Magazine: FlightSmith Radio Control Magazine
P.O. Box 59905
Chicago, IL 60659-0905
Bi-monthly publication for radio control flying; includes construction articles, beginner sections, product reviews.

Magazine: R/C Modeler Magazine
144 West Sierra Madre Blvd.
Sierra Madre, CA 91024
ph: 626-355-1476
e-mail: rcmcorp@aol.com
web: http://www.mag-web.com/rc-modeler/
Complete R/C publication for the remote control enthusiast; construction, how-to's; equipment, contests, etc.

Piper

Clubs/Associations

Richard Heckenlaible
Piper Owner Society
Magazine: Pipers
P.O. Box 5000
Iola, WI 54945
ph: 715-445-5000 or 800-331-0038
fax: 715-445-4053
e-mail: aircraft@aircraftownergroup.com
web: http://aircraftownergroup.com
Magazines cover trouble-shooting, maintenance tips, product reviews, airworthiness alerts, etc.

Sailplanes

Clubs/Associations

Raul Blacksten, Archivist
Vintage Sailplane Association
Magazine: Bungee Cord
13312 Scotsmore Way
Norcross, GA 20171
ph: 770-446-5533
e-mail: raulb@earthlink.net
web: http://www.iac.net/~feguy/VSA/
Soaring enthusiasts who are keeping our gliding history and heritage alive by building, restoring, flying gliders from the past; interested in vintage sailplanes (pre-1958) and classic sailplanes (25 years or older but post-1958).

Austen Wood
Vintage Gliding Club
Magazine: VGC News
6 Buckwood Close
Hazel Grove
Stockport, SK7 4NG
U.K.
ph: 0161 487 4522
e-mail: vgc@datron.co.uk
web: http://www.tally.co.uk/guests/vgc/
Members focus mainly on gliders designed during the 1930s, but includes some earlier and later; vintage gliders throughout the world, rallies, history.

Collectors

J. Scott
4310 River Bottom Dr.
Norcross, GA 30092
ph: 540-882-5504
Private collector of rare and restorable gliders.

AIRSHIPS

(see also KITES; STAMP COLLECTING, Covers [Balloon Related])

Balloons

Clubs/Associations

Dr. A.D. Topping
Lighter-Than-Air Society
1436 Triplett Blvd.
Akron, OH 44306
e-mail: aa208@freenet.akron.oh.us
web: http://spot.colorado.edu/~dziadeck/lta.html

Collectors

Mark Walberg
P.O. Box 130
Sunbury, PA 17801
ph: 570-286-1617
fax: 570-286-9686
Wants anything with balloon subjects: letters, medals, drawings, fans, books, posters, prints, coins, etc.; 18th century to 19th century.

Alan Zimkus
1290 Creek Point Dr.
Rochester, MI 48307-1727
ph: 800-886-3766
fax: 248-650-3361
e-mail: azimkus@aol.com
Wants to buy items relating to early gas balloons: postcards, posters, memorabilia, books, medals, etc.

Dirigibles, Zeppelins, Blimps

Collectors

Hank Loescher
90 Scofield Rd.
Bridgeport, CT 06605-2953
ph: 203-368-4983
Wants zeppelin or dirigible related items: books, charts, photos, relics, souvenirs, fabric, personal items, info., etc.

Henry Heiman, III
P.O. Box 316
South Salem, NY 10590-0316
Specializes in Zeppelins, German flying boats.

Frederick Lingenfelser
814 Byram St.
Reading, PA 19606-1446
Wants to buy pre-1945 Zeppelin items, must be passenger lines: post cards, letters, deck plans, books, tickets, brochures, dinnerware, souvenirs, models, menus, etc.

Charles M. Jacobs
P.O. Box 785
Kenton, OH 43326-0785
ph: 419-675-2435
e-mail: zeppo@kenton.com
Especially interested in popular culture and historical artifacts related to lighter-than-air aeronautics.

Alan Zimkus
1290 Creek Point Dr.
Rochester, MI 48307-1727
ph: 800-886-3766
fax: 248-650-3361
e-mail: azimkus@aol.com
Wants to buy items relating to dirigibles, zeppelins, and blimps: postcards, posters, memorabilia, books, medals, etc.

Dealers

Jody Stamp Studio Inc.
6001 Riverdale Ave.
Bronx, NY 10471-1615

Experts

Art Bink
Zeppelin
609 Hamilton Dr.
Riverton, NJ 08077-4250
ph: 856-829-3959
Historian not dealer wants airship items: zeppelin, blimp, dirigible memorabilia; pieces, toys, photos, books, medals, china, etc.; no balloons.

Charles Ira Sachs
TransAtlantic Research
P.O. Box 8005
Universal City, CA 91618-8005
ph: 818-985-1345
fax: 818-985-1345
e-mail: onrs@earthlink.net
web: http://www.titanic.org/
Buys/sells/specializes/lectures on ocean liner and zeppelin history & memorabilia from the high seas (i.e. none from coastal or river steamers) dating from 1840 to 1960s; posters, postcards and related material for collectors/museums.

Museums/Libraries

Art Bink
Navy Lakehurst Historical Society
609 Hamilton Dr.
Riverton, NJ 08077-4250
ph: 856-829-3959

ALARM BOXES

Collectors

Tom Mills
30 Bay Path Rd.
Spencer, MA 01562-1602
ph: 508-885-9550
Wants fire alarm and police boxes especially ones with dates cast into them; seeks cast iron signs and street letter pickup boxes marked "U.S. MAIL"; best to write and send photos.

ALBUMS

(see also AUTOGRAPHS; CELLULOID ITEMS; PAPER COLLECTIBLES; RECORDS)

Dealers

Barbara & Richard DePalma
Deer Park Books
609 Kent Rd., Route 7
Gaylordsville, CT 06755
ph: 860-350-4140
fax: 860-350-4140
e-mail: DeerParkBk@aol.com
web: http://www.abebooks.com/home/BARBDE/
Fine books bought and sold; antiquarian books, modern first editions, children's and illustrated; also maps, autographs, etc.; all subjects; also wants handwritten diaries, travel journals, scrapbooks, albums.

Autograph

Dealers

M. McGovern
Home Grown
1012 Manoa Rd.
Wynnewood, PA 19096
ph: 610-649-6316
fax: 610-649-2369
Wants to buy 19th century "Friendship" Autograph Albums, female Americans only with multiple entries.

ALCOHOLICS ANONYMOUS ITEMS

Collectors

PREP
12 Crest Rd. E.
Rolling Hills, CA 90274
ph: 323-541-5256
fax: 323-541-0332
Wants Alcoholics Anonymous 1st edition books, with or without dust jackets and 2nd editions wit dust jackets; also wants literature from 1939 through 1975.

Dealers

Clark Phelps
Amusement Sales Co.
7610 South Main St.
Midvale, UT 84047
ph: 801-255-4731
Historian and book seller wants AA books, pamphlets, etc. before 1974.

Experts

Charles Bishop, Jr.
Bishop of Books, The
46 Eureka Ave.
Wheeling, WV 26003-1424
ph: 304-242-2937
e-mail: bishopbks@aol.com
Buy, sell, appraise books, magazines, posters, postcards, etc. relating to alcoholism or Alcoholics Anonymous.

ALMANACS

(see BOOKS)

ALUMINUM

Hammered

Clubs/Associations

Dannie Woodard
Hammered Aluminum Collectors Association
Newsletter: Aluminist, The
P.O. Box 1346
Weatherford, TX 76086
ph: 817-594-4680
e-mail: al1310@aol.com
Newsletter provides updated information on prices, patterns, ads and companies; group organized in 1990; 200 members.

Collectors

Danielle Lanier
Wendell August Collectors Guild
P.O. Box 107
Grove City, PA 16127-0107
ph: 800-386-6155

Mike Landis
P.O. Box 814
Adamstown, PA 19501
ph: 888-248-2291
e-mail: landis2@desupernet.net
Wants to buy hammered aluminum with the following marks: Arthur Armour, Palmer Smith, Cellini; also wants old Wendell August; call toll free or send picture and information.

James Londe
10374 Chimnet Rock Dr., #5
Saint Louis, MO 63146-5751
fax: 314-692-7071
e-mail: jamlon@usa.net
Wants to buy most hammered aluminum with special interest in works of Palmer Smith and Clayton Sheasley.

Bonita Campbell, Ph.D.
P.O. Box 3151
Granada Hills, CA 91394
e-mail: hcspc003@csun.edu
Collector and researcher actively engaged in academic research of artisans, companies, marks, times of production, and other information pertinent to hammered aluminum; also preparing research monographs as appropriate.

Dealers

John M. Rowley
Eye-Openers
HC 63, Box 356
South Acworth, NH 03607
ph: 603-835-2281 or 8888-OPENER
e-mail: eyeopeners@webtv.net
Buys and sells kitchen collectibles,

gadgets, openers, and especially hammered aluminum.

Chuck Haley
Sherlock's
13926 Double Girth Ct.
Matthews, NC 28105-4068
ph: 704-847-5480
Dealing primarily in totally handwrought pieces, especially Wendell August and Arthur Armour, as well as Kensington.

Experts

Ed Gangawere
American Dream Collectibles
5128 Schultz Bridge Rd.
Zionsville, PA 18092-2542
ph: 215-679-2254
Buys, sells, collects hammered aluminum; National Hammered Aluminum Show held the last full weekend in October; call for location and time.

Dannie Woodard
P.O. Box 1346
Weatherford, TX 76086
ph: 817-594-4680
e-mail: al1310@aol.com
Author of "Hammered Aluminum - Hand Wrought Collectibles Book II."

Periodicals

Ed Gangawere
American Dream Collectibles
Newsletter: Continental Report, The
5128 Schultz Bridge Rd.
Zionsville, PA 18092-2542
ph: 215-679-2254
Published quarterly; focuses on all aspects of the Hammered Aluminum trade done by the Continental Company.

AMERICAN BANDSTAND

(see also MUSIC, Rock 'N' Roll)

Clubs/Associations

Dave Frees
American Bandstand 1950's Fan Club
Magazine: Bandstand Boogie
P.O. Box 131
Adamstown, PA 19501-0131
ph: 717-738-2513
Focuses on "American Bandstand" from the 1950s and 1980s; magazine published twice a year; sells "Dave's Collectables Catalog" (50s through 80s photos, magazines, etc.) for $1 - free to members.

Collectors

Lana Director
1 Gwizdak Court
Sayreville, NJ 08872
ph: 732-727-8647
Wants to buy pre-1964 American Bandstand, Teen-related magazines; also Ponytail, Dateline, and similar vinyl items.

AMERICAN INDIAN

(see also ARCHAEOLOGY; BASKETS; BEADS, Trade; BOOKS, Reference [American Indian]; CIGAR STORE COLLECTIBLES; EDGED WEAPONS; HERITAGE RESOURCES; INDIAN WARS; PREHISTORIC ARTIFACTS; TEXTILES, Blankets; WESTERN AMERICANA)

Appraisers

Gary L. Fogelman
RD 1 Box 240
Turbotville, PA 17772-9599
ph: 570-437-3698
fax: 570-437-3411
e-mail: iam@csrling.net
web: http://www.iampub.com/
Author of "A Projectile Point Typology for PA and the Northeast" and "An Identification and Price Guide for Indian Artifacts of the Northeast."

Maryann L'Heureux
Native American Arts Appraisals
P.O. Box 267
Hockessin, DE 19707-0267
ph: 302-234-3190 or 302-234-1358
fax: 302-234-3190
e-mail: maryann_lheureux@msn.com
Senior member of the American Society of Appraisers, tested in North American Indian art and artifacts.

John C. Hill
Gallery of American Indian Art
6962 East First Ave., Ste. 104
Scottsdale, AZ 85251-4302
ph: 602-946-2910
fax: 602-946-7410
e-mail: antqindart@aol.com
Expert dealer and appraiser of old Southwestern Indian, and Indian beadwork.

Gene Quintana
P.O. Box 533
Carmichael, CA 95609
ph: 916-485-8232
Collector and appraiser of American Indian basketry and blankets.

Brill Lee
P.O. Box 244
Bellevue, WA 98009-0244
ph: 425-885-4518
fax: 425-885-2473
e-mail: BrillLee@hotmail.com
Buys, sells and appraises pre-1960 American Indian artifacts.

Auction Services

Linda Dyer
Skinner, Inc.
357 Main St.
Bolton, MA 01740-1104
ph: 978-779-6241
fax: 978-779-5144
e-mail: info@skinnerinc.com
web: http://www.skinnerinc.com
Established in 1964, Skinner Inc. is the fifth largest auction house in the US; has offices in Bolton and Boston, MA.

Willis Henry
Willis Henry Auctions, Inc.
22 Main St.
Marshfield, MA 02050
ph: 781-834-7774 or 800-244-8466
fax: 781-826-3520
e-mail: wha@willishenry.com
web: http://www.willishenry.com/
Specializes in the sale of American antiques of all kinds, particularly Shaker, American Indian and early American.

Sotheby's
1334 York Ave.
New York, NY 10021
ph: 212-606-7000
fax: 212-606-7107
web: http://www.sothebys.com
Over 70 collecting areas are featured at Sotheby's auctions including toys, dolls, porcelain, furniture, silver, art, books; exhibitions are free and everyone is welcome; for a free copy of "Sotheby's Newsletter", call 212-606-7245.

Garth's Auction, Inc.
2690 Stratford Rd.
P.O. Box 369
Delaware, OH 43015
ph: 614-362-4771 or 614-369-5085
fax: 614-363-0164
e-mail: info@garths.com
web: http://www.garths.com
Specializing in Early American, English, Continental, Oriental antiques and accessories; paintings, fine art, folk art, American Indian, military, jewelry, toys, dolls, advertising, collectibles.

Jan Sorgenfrei
Old Barn Auction
10040 S.R. 224 West
Findlay, OH 45840
ph: 419-422-8531
fax: 419-522-5321
web: http://www.oldbarn.com/
Conducts specialized auctions of American Indian items.

Doug Allard
Allard Indian Auctions
P.O. Box 460
Saint Ignatius, MT 59865
ph: 406-745-2951 or 800-821-3318
fax: 406-745-2961
e-mail: stephan@allardauctions.com
web: http://www.allardauctions.com
Conducts auctions specializing in Indian items.

Preston E. Miller
Four Winds Indian Auction
P.O. Box 580
Saint Ignatius, MT 59865-0580
ph: 406-745-4336
fax: 406-745-3595
e-mail: 4winds@bigsky.net
web: http://www.4winds.com/
Conducts mail/phone bid auctions of contemporary Indian artifacts and collectibles: beadwork, old photos, stone relics, parfleches, weapons, pottery, trade beads, baskets, replicas, Navajo rugs, etc.; photo illustrated catalog $20.

Butterfield & Dunning
755 Church Rd.
Elgin, IL 60123
ph: 847-741-3483
fax: 847-741-3589
e-mail: info@butterfields.com
web: http://www.butterfields.com
Conducts semiannual Native American auctions.

Joy Luke
Joy Luke Auction Gallery
300 E. Grove St.
Bloomington, IL 61701-5232
ph: 309-828-5533
fax: 309-829-2266
e-mail: robert@joyluke.com
web: http://www.joyluke.com/
Conducts periodic auctions specializing Indian items.

Butterfield & Butterfield
220 San Bruno Ave.
San Francisco, CA 94103-5018
ph: 415-861-7500
fax: 415-861-8951
e-mail: info@butterfields.com
web: http://www.butterfields.com/
Specialties include posters, toys, decorative arts, furniture, photography, etc.; the largest full service auction in the west.

Clubs/Associations

John Berner
Genuine Indian Relic Society
195 Barringon Dr. E
Roswell, GA 30076
ph: 770-998-5682

Collectors

Dr. Fred Cesana
49 E. Main St.
Plainville, CT 06062
ph: 860-747-2759
Wants pre-1880 Plains Indian weapons: tomahawks, knives, lances, clubs, rifles; also wants important beadwork.

Brian L. Ebosh
17738 Indian Hollow rd.
Grafton, OH 44044
ph: 440-355-8118
Wants Indian and pioneer metal axes: pipe tomahawks, spike, spontoon, Missouri, and related items.

Jan Sorgenfrei
10040 S.R. 224 West
Findlay, OH 45840
ph: 419-422-8531
fax: 419-522-5321
web: http://www.oldbarn.com/

Larry Jarvinen
313 Condon Rd.
Manistee, MI 49660
ph: 616-723-5063
Wants to buy American Indian trade beads, silver, axes, beadwork, brass kettles, etc.

Mike Kramer
P.O. Box 3257
Vallejo, CA 94590-0676
ph: 800-568-8883 or 800-446-6581
fax: 707-642-2456
Wants early American Indian items: model totems, trade totems, quality baskets.

Daniel Brown
P.O. Box 149
Davenport, CA 95017-0149
ph: 831-426-0134 or 800-492-6786
Wants to buy museum quality Indian relics: pre-1900 Plains Indian material including shirts, shields, weapons, beadwork, quillwork; large Pueblo pots, early Navajo blankets, saltillos, old Navajo jewelry, fine baskets, NW coast, etc.

Dealers

Norman Hurst, ISA
Hurst Gallery
53 Mount Auburn St.
Cambridge, MA 02138
ph: 617-491-6888
fax: 617-661-0439
e-mail: NHurst@compuserve.com
web: http://www.hurstgallery.com
Buys, sells, appraises, restores African, Oceanic, Native American, pre-Columbian and Asian art; has been appraising, dealing and publishing American Indian & Eskimo art for over 20 years: baskets, pottery, beadwork, masks, ivory.

Carol Halberstadt
Migrations
P.O. Box 543
Newton, MA 02258
e-mail: carol@migrations.com
web: http://www.migrations.com
Specializes in older and contemporary Native American and Inuit/Eskimo art: weavings, pottery, baskets, jewelry, sculpture; online gallery with links to a wide variety of Native American resources.

David Summers
Native American Artifacts
45 West Parkway
Victor, NY 14564-1243
ph: 716-924-5167
e-mail: naasummers@aol.com
One of the world's largest dealers in American Indian art and antiquities; buys and sells; specializing in Northeastern Indian specimens.

Von Hilliard
Indian Shop, The
P.O. Box 246
Independence, KY 41051-0246
ph: 606-441-0773
For $5 you receive the current relic catalog consisting of 50 to 80 pages filled with arrowheads, spearheads, axes, pre-Columbian, Plains Indian and Eskimo items, and more - all photographed.

Randy Sandler
Cincinnati Art Galleries
225 E 6th St.
Cincinnati, OH 45202
ph: 513-381-2128
fax: 513-381-7527
e-mail: mail@cincinnatiartgalleries.com
web: http://www.cincinnatiartgalleries.com/

Bradley S. Vite
Bradley Vite Fine Arts
1600 West Beardsley Ave.
Elkhart, IN 46514-1800
ph: 219-293-1616
fax: 219-293-1616
e-mail: bradley@finearts.com
web: http://vitefinearts.com/
Interested in Native American weavings and basketry.

World City, Inc.
6935 James Ave. South
Minneapolis, MN 55423-2147
Buys and sells Indian items such as beaded items, pottery, Navajo rugs, quilled items, Kachinas, Northwest Coast items; both pre-historic and historic; send price wanted (unless unsure), description, photos, and SASE.

John Buxton
Shango Galleries
6717 Spring Valley
Dallas, TX 75240
ph: 972-239-4620 or 972-239-9943
fax: 972-239-9766
e-mail: jbuxton@arttrak.com
web: http://www.arttrak.com
Buys, sells, and appraises African, Precolumbian, Oceanic, and American Indian art.

Pat Dunnegan
Pat's Authentic Indian Artifacts
201 Harrison Ave.
Gustine, TX 76455
ph: 888-841-9386 or 915-667-7210
e-mail: teddun@itexas.net
web: http://www2.itexas.net/~teddun/
Online close-up photos of quality authentic American Indian artifacts offered for sale; also a selected list of related books; over 40 years in business.

Donna McMenamin
5001 Woodway #1002
Houston, TX 77056-1718
ph: 713-622-7252
fax: 281-780-9723
e-mail: DMcMenamin@msn.com
web: http://www.donnamcmenamin.com
Buys and sells historical Native American baskets, pre-1900 beadwork, and Navajo rugs.

Christopher A. Jones
Squash Blossom, The
2531 W. Colorado Ave.
Colorado Springs, CO 80904
ph: 719-632-1899
Dealer/appraiser specializing in Southwestern Native American jewelry and art including pottery, weaving, Kachinas (both prehistoric and historic.)

John Hartman
Globalarts
17897 Hwy. 160
Durango, CO 81301
ph: 970-247-5589
fax: 970-259-6020
e-mail: hartman@rmi.net
web: http://www.globalarts.com
Buys and sells antique Frontier memorabilia, Native American Indian items, Cowboy items; also Ethnic Rarities from around the world.

John C. Hill
Gallery of American Indian Art
6962 East First Ave., Ste. 104
Scottsdale, AZ 85251-4302
ph: 602-946-2910
fax: 602-946-7410
e-mail: antqindart@aol.com
Wants to buy early Southwest Indian items including classic Navajo & Pueblo silver & turquoise, Indian blankets and other textiles, Kachina dolls, early pottery; also wants Plains and Northeast Indian beadwork, and fine Indian basketry.

Richard B. Troyanowski
Rich Relics
P.O. Box 432
Sandia Park, NM 87047-0432
ph: 505-281-2611 or 505-281-2329
Buys/sells prehistoric/historic Indian artifacts, cowboy, militaria, old world antiquities & coins, fossils & ethnographic collectibles.

Thomas Baker
Tanner Chaney Gallery
410 Romero NW
Albuquerque, NM 87104
ph: 505-247-2242
fax: 505-298-3434
e-mail: tbaker@tannerchaneygallery.com
web: http://www.tannerchaneygallery.com
Sells and appraises contemporary and antique Native American jewelry, weavings and pottery.

Morningstar Gallery
513 Canyon Rd.
Santa Fe, NM 87501
ph: 505-982-8187
fax: 505-984-2368
e-mail: indian@morningstargallery.com
web: http://www.morningstargallery.com
Pottery, baskets, bags, textiles, rugs, parfleche, moccasins, clothing, jewelry, weapons, musical instruments, dolls.

Jeff Mark
P.O. Box 5178
Santa Monica, CA 90409-5178
ph: 800-666-9553 or 310-396-9767
fax: 310-396-2666
Wants to buy American Indian rugs, blankets, baskets, dolls, clothing, beadwork weapons, pots, historical memorabilia.

Barry Friedman
P.O. Box 55492
Valencia, CA 91385-0492
ph: 805-255-2365

Jimmy Vitanza
Peregrine Galleries
508 Brinkerhoff Ave.
Santa Barbara, CA 93101-3441
ph: 805-963-3134
fax: 805-963-3134

John W. Barry
Indian Rock Arts
P.O. Box 583
Davis, CA 95617-0583
ph: 530-758-2561
e-mail: jackbarr@pacbell.net
Wants California Indian baskets, Pueblo Indian pottery, beadwork, Navajo rugs, old Navajo jewelry.

Syd Bottomley, ISA
P.O. Box 1842
Nevada City, CA 95959
ph: 530-272-5400
fax: 530-272-2820
Buys, collects, appraises and specializes in American Indian art: baskets, rugs, pottery, early California paintings.

Randeen Cummings, ISA CAPP
Cummings & Associates
P.O. Box 5484
Eugene, OR 97405-0484
ph: 541-345-5856 or 541-485-3068
fax: 541-345-8192
e-mail: rmcummings@ibm.net
web: http://www.antiquesinn.com
Specializes in selling & appraising residential contents, fine art, estate jewelry, 18th & 19th century antiques, American Brilliant period cut glass; also specialized marketing for clients: consultations, estate, and Internet sales.

Kevin C. McIntosh
Kevin's Fine American Indian Art
270 Southridge Way
Grants Pass, OR 97527
ph: 541-476-1028
e-mail: formacs@terragon.com
web: http://www.kevinsindianart.com
Collector and dealer of southern OR and northern CA native American Indian basketry and related ethnographic material; specializes in Hupa, Yurok, and Karuk areas; seeking sinew-backed painted bows, wood stemmed pipes, elk horn items.

Douglas Vincent
Far West Antiques
P.O. Box 371
Redmond, OR 97756-0070
ph: 541-923-1847 or 541-923-2140
fax: 541-923-3874
e-mail: farwest@empnet.com
web: http://www.farwestantiques.com
Buys, sells, trades in older Native American items and Western Americana inducing gambling collectibles; also collects native American beadwork, baskets, jewelry and Kachina dolls.

Brill Lee
P.O. Box 244
Bellevue, WA 98009-0244
ph: 425-885-4518
fax: 425-885-2473
e-mail: BrillLee@hotmail.com

Experts

Gary L. Fogelman
RD 1 Box 240
Turbotville, PA 17772-9599
ph: 570-437-3698
fax: 570-437-3411
e-mail: iam@csrling.net
web: http://www.iampub.com/
Specializes in and buys Indian artifacts: single pieces or entire collections; appraisals; author of "A Projectile Point Typology for PA and the Northeast" and "An Identification and Price Guide for Indian Artifacts of the Northeast."

Roy Harrell
46 Davis Rd.
Street, MD 21154
ph: 410-399-0448
e-mail: aiashow@aol.com
Expert in Native American Indian items.

Dawn E. Reno
3280 Shingler Terrace
Deltona, FL 32738-5351
ph: 904-532-1960
fax: 904-532-1960
e-mail: DawnReno@juno.com
Author of "Native American Collectibles" (1994, Avon), and "Today's Native American Artists" (1995, Alliance).

Terry L. Schafer
American Indian Art & Antiques
Rte. 2 Box 298
Marietta, OH 45750-9358
ph: 740-374-2807
e-mail: amindart@marietta.edu
web: http://www.marietta.edu/~amindart/
Wants old Indian items: baskets, blankets, beadwork, Navajo rugs and old pawn jewelry.

Peter Eller, ISA
Peter Eller Gallery & Appraisers
206 Dartmouth
Albuquerque, NM 87106
ph: 505-268-7437
fax: 505-268-6442
e-mail: pelgal@nmia.com
web: http://www.peterellergallery.com/
Specializes in and appraises American, Southwest, and "Western" art; also Pueblo pottery, Navajo rugs and other weavings, Spanish colonial artifacts.

Mary Elizabeth McDonald
620 Sierra Dr. SE
Albuquerque, NM 87108-3377
ph: 505-265-2842

Don Bennett
Don Bennett & Associates
P.O. Box 283
Agoura Hills, CA 91376-0283
ph: 818-991-5596
fax: 818-991-6866
e-mail: artofwest@aol.com
Collects, buys and sells high quality antique American Indian items and paintings by deceased Western artists; since 1968.

Internet Resources

Longhouse Marketplace
1425 NE Irving, Ste. 225
Portland, OR 97232
e-mail: longhouse@indianbaskets.com
web: http://www.indianbaskets.com/
A web site bringing together buyers and sellers of authentic American Indian baskets and clothing.

Museums/Libraries

Joe Liberkowski
Museum of Classical Antiquities & Primitive Arts
P.O. Box 2161
Medford, NJ 08055-7161
Wants American Indian items; also pre-1940 Mexican and South American Santos, Retablos, Ex Votos, crucifixes, religious, historical autographs/documents.

U.S. Department of the Interior Museum, The
1849 C. St. NW
Mail Stop 1024
Washington, DC 20240
ph: 202-208-4743
web: http://www.doi.gov/museum/

National Museum of Natural History
10th St. & Constitution Ave.
Washington, DC 20560
ph: 202-357-2700
web: http://www.mnh.si.edu/

National Museum of the American Indian
470 L'Enfant Plaza, SW, Ste. 7102
Washington, DC 20560
web: http://www.si.edu/nmai/
The museum will open on the Mall in Washington, DC, in the year 2002, on a site between the National Air & Space Museum and the U.S. Capitol; will be a center for exhibitions, ceremonies, performances, and educational activities

Museum of the Cherokee Indian
P.O. Box 1599
Cherokee, NC 28719-1599
ph: 828-497-3481
fax: 828-497-4985
e-mail: brenda_germano@ibm.net
web: http://www.hightopmedia.com/musofthecherin/
Located on the Cherokee Indian Reservation, the museum tells the story of the Cherokee Indians through dramatic exhibits.

Erik Alexander
Grand Rapids Public Museum
272 Pearl St. NW
Grand Rapids, MI 49504-5371
ph: 616-456-3977
fax: 616-456-3873
e-mail: staff@grmuseum.org
web: http://www.grmuseum.org/
Exhibits, publications and research information relating to West Michigan's Ottawa, Potawatomi, and Chippewa people; also Great Lakes Indian beadwork.

Field Museum of Natural History
Roosevelt Rd. at Lake Shore Dr.
Chicago, IL 60605
ph: 312-642-4600
web: http://www.fmnh.org/

Jerry P. Martin, Dir.
Indian Center Museum
650 North Seneca
Wichita, KS 67203
ph: 316-262-5221
fax: 316-262-4216
e-mail: icm@southwind.net
web: http://www2.southwind.net/~icm/museum/
Dedicated to the preservation of Native American Heritage; features a wide range of exhibitions displaying contemporary art as well as traditional artifacts.

Diana Pardue
Heard Museum, The
2301 N. Central Ave.
Phoenix, AZ 85004
ph: 602-252-8848 or 602-252-8840
fax: 602-252-9757
e-mail: webmaster@heard.org
web: http://www.heard.org
Has over 32,000 works of art and ethnographic objects including more than 4,000 objects from the Fred Harvey Company Fine Art Collection.

Betty L. Cornelius
Colorado River Indian Tribes Museum
Rte. 1 Box 23-B
Parker, AZ 85344-9704
ph: 520-669-9211
fax: 520-669-8262
Displays Mohave, Chemehuevi, Navajo, and Hopi artifacts and prehistoric Mogollon, Anasazi, Hohokam, and Patayan collections.

Dr. Anne I. Woosley, Dir.
Amerind Foundation, Inc.
P.O. Box 400
Dragoon, AZ 85609
ph: 520-586-3666
fax: 520-586-4679
e-mail: amerind@amerind.org
web: http://www.amerind.org/
Archaeology and ethnology museum, art gallery, and research library; archaeological collections from the Americas; ethnological material from the SW, Mexico, Great Plains, Eastern Woodlands, CA, Arctic.

Jonathan Batkin, Dir.
Wheelwright Museum of the American Indian, The
Newsletter: Messenger, The
P.O. Box 5153
Santa Fe, NM 87502
ph: 505-982-4636 or 800-607-4636
fax: 505-988-7386
e-mail: ybond@nmhu.campus.mci.net
web: http://www.nmculture.org/cgi-bin/showlnst.pl?InstlD-WHEE

Southwest Museum
234 Museum Drive
Los Angeles, CA 90065
ph: 323-221-2164
e-mail: info@southwestmuseum.org
web: http://www.southwestmuseum.org
Holds one of the nation's most important collections related to the American Indian; also extensive holdings of prehistoric, Spanish Colonial, Latino, and Western American art and artifacts.

Favell Museum of Western Art & Indian Artifacts
125 W. Main St.
Klamath Falls, OR 97601
ph: 541-882-9996
fax: 541-882-9996
web: http://www.ohwy.com/or/f/favemwaa.htm

Josie De Falla, Dir.
Maryhill Museum of Art
35 Maryhill Museum Drive
Goldendale, WA 98620-4601
ph: 509-773-3733
fax: 509-773-6138
e-mail: MaryHill@gorge.net
web: http://www.maryhillmuseum.org/
The extensive 5000 piece Native American collection comprises rare prehistoric rock carvings, baskets, beadwork, and other objects which are seen as both art and artifact.

Periodicals

Gary L. Fogelman
Magazine: Indian-Artifact Magazine
RD 1 Box 240
Turbotville, PA 17772-9599
ph: 570-437-3698
fax: 570-437-3411
e-mail: iam@csrling.net
web: http://www.iampub.com/
An easy reading quarterly focusing on American Indian prehistory: artifacts, tools, lifestyles, customs, archaeology, book reviews; everything about collecting, buying, finding and enjoying Indian artifacts.

Written Heritage, Inc.
Magazine: Whispering Wind Magazine
P.O. Box 1390
Folsom, LA 70437
ph: 504-796-5433 or 800-301-8009
fax: 504-796-9236
e-mail: whiswind@i-55.com
web: http://www.whisperingwind.com/
Crafts, pow-wows, books, history, tradition; subscribers are crafts people, book buyers and Indian art and antique collectors.

American Indian Art, Inc.
Magazine: American Indian Art Magazine
7314 E. Osborn Dr.
Scottsdale, AZ 85251-6418
ph: 480-994-5445
fax: 480-945-9533
Quarterly art journal devoted to native American art from prehistoric to modern; gorgeous photographs, auction reports, reports on ethnographic and fine arts items, "Legal Briefs" column.

Martin Link, Pub.
Newspaper: Indian Trader, The
P.O. Box 1421
Gallup, NM 87305-1421
ph: 505-722-6694 or 800-748-1624
fax: 505-722-6696
e-mail: trader@cia-g.com
web: http://www.cia-g.com/~trader/index.htm
Focuses on old and new Indian art and artifacts.

John M. Gogol
Magazine: American Indian Basketry
P.O. Box 66124
Portland, OR 97266
ph: 503-233-8131
A magazine dedicated to Native American Indian arts: basketry, beadwork, pottery, baskets and weaving, textiles, masks, jewelry, etc.

Basketry

Experts

Chris L. Moser
Riverside Municipal Museum
3580 Mission Inn Ave.
Riverside, CA 92501
ph: 909-782-5273
fax: 909-369-4970
e-mail: cmoser@ci.riverside.ca.us
web: http://www.ci.riverside.ca.us/museum/
Can identify Native American basketry; Riverside Museum Press published 3 catalogs written by Chris Moser: 1986 "Basketry of Central California," 1989 "Basketry of Northern California," 1993 "Basketry of Southern California."

Baskets

Dealers

Syd Bottomley, ISA
P.O. Box 1842
Nevada City, CA 95959
ph: 530-272-5400
fax: 530-272-2820
Buys, collects, appraises and specializes in American Indian art: baskets, rugs, pottery, early California paintings.

Experts

Barry Friedman
P.O. Box 55492
Valencia, CA 91385-0492
ph: 805-255-2365
Wants to buy pre-1940 undamaged Indian baskets; please send good photo, dimensions and price; all letters answered!

Museums/Libraries

Diana Pardue
Heard Museum, The
2301 N. Central Ave.
Phoenix, AZ 85004
ph: 602-252-8848 or 602-252-8840
fax: 602-252-9757
e-mail: webmaster@heard.org
web: http://www.heard.org
Has over 32,000 works of art and ethnographic objects including more than 4,000 objects from the Fred Harvey Company Fine Art Collection; has an extensive collection of Native American baskets.

Eskimo & Northwest Coast

Auction Services

Seahawk Auctions
P.O. Box 231
Aldergrove, British Columbia V2X 7G1
Canada
ph: 604-657-1147 or 604-657-2072
fax: 604-462-7228
e-mail: info@seahawkauctions.com
web: http://www.seahawkauctions.com/
Specializes in the sale of Northwest Indian items.

Waddington's
11 Bathurst Street
Toronto, Ontario M5V 2R1
Canada
ph: 416-504-9100
fax: 416-504-0033
e-mail: info@waddingtonsauctions.com
web: http://www.waddingtonsauctions.com
Canada's oldest and largest auction house specializing in decorative arts, jewelry, antique furniture, Inuit and native Canadian arts, European and Canadian arts, books, militaria, Orientalia, toys, ceramics, etc.

Dealers

Norman Hurst, ISA
Hurst Gallery
53 Mount Auburn St.
Cambridge, MA 02138
ph: 617-491-6888
fax: 617-661-0439
e-mail: NHurst@compuserve.com
web: http://www.hurstgallery.com
Buys, sells, appraises, restores African, Oceanic, Native American, pre-Columbian and Asian art; has been appraising, dealing and publishing American Indian & Eskimo art for over 20 years: baskets, pottery, beadwork, masks, ivory.

Carol Halberstadt
Migrations
P.O. Box 543
Newton, MA 02258
e-mail: carol@migrations.com
web: http://www.migrations.com
Specializes in older and contemporary Native American and Inuit/Eskimo art: weavings, pottery, baskets, jewelry, sculpture; online gallery with links to a wide variety of Native American resources.

Hedy Mann
Alaska on Madison - Gallery of Eskimo Art
937 Madison Ave.
New York, NY 10021
ph: 212-879-1782
fax: 212-327-4877

Jeffrey R. Myers
Jeffrey R. Myers, Primitive Arts
12 East 86th St.
New York, NY 10028-0506
ph: 212-472-0115
fax: 212-472-1665
Buys, sells, specializes and appraises pre-1915 NW masks, rattles, frontlets, bowls, textiles, boxes; pre-1915 Eskimo masks, carved boxes, bow drills, figural pieces, etc.

Arthur W. Erickson
Arthur E. Erickson, Inc.
1030 SW Taylor
Portland, OR 97205-2504
ph: 503-227-4710
fax: 503-279-9146
e-mail: erickson@inetarena.com
Buys and sells antique Native American and Eskimo arts with an emphasis on Columbian River items such as Wasco Sally bags, cork husk bags, Klicitat baskets and plateau figural and contour beadwork.

Lee
Northwest Tribal Art
1417 1st Ave.
Seattle, WA 98101
ph: 206-467-9330
fax: 206-624-6154
Carries a wide assortment of contemporary Native Eskimo and Pacific Northwest Coast Indian art, carvings, petrified walrus tusk, stone carvings, textiles, etc.

Curtright & Son Tribal Art
759 St. Helens Ave.
Tacoma, WA 98402
ph: 253-383-2969 or 360-705-4567
e-mail: JCurtri286@aol.com
web: http://www.web-pac.com/mall/Indian/
Specialty is Northwest Coat materials, plains beadwork, and Eskimo art: Baskets, beadwork, carvings, jewelry, pottery, rugs.

Richard A. Wood
Alaskan Heritage Bookshop
P.O. Box 22165
Juneau, AK 99802-2165
ph: 907-789-8450
fax: 907-789-8450
e-mail: akrare@alaska.net
web: http://www.alaska.net/~akrare/
Buys and sells Northwest Coast antique Indian art objects including model boats, canoes, and kayaks, masks, baskets, handmade silver spoons, totem poles, Athabaskan beadwork, photographs.

Geoff Ryan
Uqqurmiut Centre for Arts & Crafts
P.O. Box 453
Pangnirtung, Northwest Territory X0A 0R0
Canada
ph: 867-473-8870 or 867-473-8669
fax: 867-473-8634
e-mail: inuitart@nunanet.com
web: http://www.uqqurmiut.com
Producers of the Annual Pangnirtung limited edition Community Print Collection, Pangnirtung limited edition Tapestries, and hand made crafts.

Victor Topper
Topper Gallery
2900 John Street, Ste. 402
Markham, Ontario L3R 5G3
Canada
ph: 905-513-8070 or 416-633-4518
fax: 905-513-6628
e-mail: toppart@pathcom.com
web: http://www.topperart.com/
Chinese art, Japanese art, Buddhistic art, pre-Columbian, Judaica, Inuit art, Northwest Coast Indians.

Museums/Libraries

Samuel K. Fox Museum
P.O. Box 237
Dillingham, AK 99576
ph: 907-842-2322
fax: 907-842-2322

Carolyn Young
Sheldon Jackson Museum
104 College Dr.
Sitka, AK 99835-7657
ph: 907-747-8981
fax: 907-747-3004
e-mail: bruce_kato@educ.state.ak.us
web: http://www.educ.state.ak.us/lam/museum/sjhome.html
Focuses on Aleut, Athabaskan, and Northwest Coast Indians: Haida argillite carvings, Eskimo implements, ivory carvings, masks, skin clothing, baskets, kayaks, umiaks, totem poles, garments, ceremonial equipment, etc.

Totem Heritage Center
629 Dock St.
Ketchikan, AK 99901
ph: 907-225-5900
fax: 907-225-5602

Grenfell Labrador Industries

Experts

Barry Friedman
P.O. Box 55492
Valencia, CA 91385-0492
ph: 805-255-2365
Wants to buy any textile or purses labeled "Grenfell Labrador Industries." These always picture Northern scenes (polar bears, Eskimos, etc.); undamaged pieces only; send photo, dimensions, and price; all letters answered!

Repro. Sources

Grenfell Handicrafts
P.O. Box 290
St. Anthony, Newfoundland AOK 4S0
Canada
ph: 709-454-3576
Send for free catalog of new Grenfell mats currently for sale.

Kachina Dolls

Dealers

World City, Inc.
6935 James Ave. South
Minneapolis, MN 55423-2147
Buys and sells Indian items such as beaded items, pottery, Navajo rugs, quilled items, Kachinas, Northwest Coast items; both pre-historic and historic; send price wanted (unless unsure), description, photos, and SASE.

Christopher A. Jones
Squash Blossom, The
2531 W. Colorado Ave.
Colorado Springs, CO 80904
ph: 719-632-1899
Dealer/appraiser specializing in Southwestern Native American jewelry and art including pottery, weaving, Kachinas (both prehistoric and historic.)

John C. Hill
Gallery of American Indian Art
6962 East First Ave., Ste. 104
Scottsdale, AZ 85251-4302
ph: 602-946-2910
fax: 602-946-7410
e-mail: antqindart@aol.com
Wants to buy early Southwest Indian items including classic Navajo & Pueblo silver & turquoise, Indian blankets and other textiles, Kachina dolls, early pottery; also wants Plains and Northeast Indian beadwork, and fine Indian basketry.

Alexander Anthony, Jr.
Adobe Gallery
413 Romero NW
Albuquerque, NM 87104-1421
ph: 505-243-8485 or 800-821-5221
fax: 505-243-8403
Specializing in art of the Southwest Indian: historic Pueblo pottery, Navajo blankets and rugs, Hopi Kachina dolls and Navajo and Pueblo pawn jewelry.

Museums/Libraries

Diana Pardue
Heard Museum, The
2301 N. Central Ave.
Phoenix, AZ 85004
ph: 602-252-8848 or 602-252-8840
fax: 602-252-9757
e-mail: webmaster@heard.org
web: http://www.heard.org
Has over 32,000 works of art and ethnographic objects and one of the largest collections of Hopi Kachina dolls including 437 historic Kachina dolls from the Barry Goldwater Collection.

Navajo

Collectors

Andrew Nagen
P.O. Box 1306
Corrales, NM 87408
ph: 505-898-5058
Wants Navajo rugs and blankets; also Rio Grande, Pueblo, and Mexican textiles.

Dealers

Tyrone & Una Campbell
Una
7103 E. Main St.
Scottsdale, AZ 85251-4315
ph: 602-423-9160
Buys and sells antique American Indian weavings: Navajo, Pueblo and Hispanic weavings and folk art; specializes in appraising collections, consultations, and research of 19th & 20th C. Navajo weavings.

Experts

Gregg Leighton
Notah Dineh
345 West Main
Cortez, CO 81321
ph: 800-444-2024 or 970-565-9607
e-mail: notah@subee.com
web: http://subee.com/nd/home.html
Buys and sells wide range of Navajo rugs, antique and contemporary; also carries large assortment of contemporary American Indian crafts and jewelry.

Steve Getzwiller
Classic & Contemporary Amerind Art
P.O. Box 36
Spear G Ranch
Benson, AZ 85602
ph: 520-586-2579
fax: 520-586-2960
e-mail: getzwiller@theriver.com
web: http://navajorug.com
Recognized authority, dealer and collector of American Indian art; specializing in Navajo weavings, historic and contemporary; author of "The Fine Art of Navajo Weaving;" buys and sells Indian art collections.

Barry Friedman
P.O. Box 55492
Valencia, CA 91385-0492
ph: 805-255-2365
Wants to purchase pre-1940 Navajo rugs; send photo, condition, and price; undamaged items only; all letters answered!

Museums/Libraries

Navajo National Monument Museum
HC 71 Box 3
Tonalea, AZ 86044-9704
ph: 520-672-2366 or 520-672-2367
fax: 520-672-2345
web: http://www.nps.gov/nava/
A national monument featuring the best preserved cliff dwellings in the SW; small museum and library (no checkout) for research (copier not available); prehistoric Pueblo and Navajo exhibits.

Pottery

Appraisers

Casey Reed
Material Culture
1727 Dietz Plaza, NW
Albuquerque, NM 87107
ph: 505-344-8492
fax: 505-344-8492
e-mail: Casey@material-culture.com
web: http://material-culture.com/PuebloPotteryRestoration.htm
Conservation and restoration of Pueblo pottery; application of traditional and unique methodologies to preserve the past; also collects and appraises Pueblo pottery.

Experts

John W. Barry
Indian Rock Arts
P.O. Box 583
Davis, CA 95617-0583
ph: 530-758-2561
e-mail: jackbarr@pacbell.net
Appraises Pueblo Indian pottery; author of "American Indian Pottery" (Books Americana), 1981; contributor to "Encyclopedia Native American in the 20th Century" (Garland Publishing) and "North American Artifacts" by Lar Hothem.

Museums/Libraries

Cherokee National Museum
P.O. Box 515
Tahlequah, OK 74465-0515
ph: 918-456-6007
fax: 918-456-6165
web: http://www.powersource.com/heritage/museum.html
The only facility devoted to the preservation of the heritage of the Cherokee Nation, the second largest American tribe.

Diana Pardue
Heard Museum, The
2301 N. Central Ave.
Phoenix, AZ 85004
ph: 602-252-8848 or 602-252-8840
fax: 602-252-9757
e-mail: webmaster@heard.org
web: http://www.heard.org
Has over 32,000 works of art and ethnographic objects including an extensive collection of pottery, especially pieces made by Native American cultures in the Southwestern United States.

Institute of American Indian Arts Museum
108 Cathedral Place
Santa Fe, NM 87501
ph: 509-988-6281
web: http://hanksville.phast.umass.edu/misc/IAIA.html

Repair Services

Andy Goldschmidt
Ceramicare
P.O. Box 1812
Corrales, NM 87048
ph: 505-898-2728
e-mail: agoldschmidt@earthlink.net
web: http://home.earthlink.net/~agoldschmidt/wizzg.html
Repairs and restores ceramic art; specializing in Native American Indian pottery - prehistoric, historic and contemporary.

Casey Reed
Material Culture
1727 Dietz Plaza, NW
Albuquerque, NM 87107
ph: 505-344-8492
fax: 505-344-8492
e-mail: Casey@material-culture.com
web: http://material-culture.com/PuebloPotteryRestoration.htm
Conservation and restoration of Pueblo pottery; application of traditional and unique methodologies to preserve the past; also collects and appraises Pueblo pottery.

Skookum Dolls

Dealers

William W. Wynn
2117 Hillcrest St.
Fort Worth, TX 76107-4329
ph: 817-763-8424
Wants to buy Skookum Indian dolls, beaded Zuni dolls, pre-1950 Plains Indian and Navajo rag dolls.

Experts

Linda Larouche
Linda Larouche Antiques & Collectibles
18 Polhemus Place
Brooklyn, NY 11215-2231
ph: 718-230-3830
e-mail: skookumgal@aol.com
web: http://www.skookumgal.com
Wants to buy Skookum Indian dolls in good condition; wants all sizes from 3" to 36".

Barry Friedman
P.O. Box 55492
Valencia, CA 91385-0492
ph: 805-255-2365
Wants to buy undamaged Skookum Indian dolls over 12"; these dolls wear colorful Indian design blankets; send photo, size, and price; all letters answered!

Souvenirs

Experts

Abby Irons
Dave Irons Antiques
223 Covered Bridge Rd.
Northampton, PA 18067
ph: 610-262-9335
fax: 610-262-2853

Souvenirs (Beadwork)

Experts

Marty & Mike Irons
Dave Irons Antiques
223 Covered Bridge Rd.
Northampton, PA 18067
ph: 610-262-9335
fax: 610-262-2853

Totems

Dealers

John Cavanagh
Linda Larouche Antiques & Collectibles
18 Polhemus Place
Brooklyn, NY 11215-2231
ph: 718-230-3830 or 212-594-1009
e-mail: jcav@stray-light.com
web: http://www.skookumgal.com/
Buys and sells well carved pre-1945 Pacific NW and Eskimo model totems in wood, bone or ivory; also wants ivory carved animals, fish, salt & peppers, etc.

AMERICAN INDIAN (MODERN)

Clubs/Associations

Susan McGuire
Indian Arts & Crafts Association
Newsletter: IACA Newsletter
122 Laveta NE, Ste. B
Albuquerque, NM 87108-1613
ph: 505-265-9149 or 505-255-6032
e-mail: iaca@ix.netcom.com
web: http://www.iaca.com/
Purpose is to collect, promote, preserve, protect and enhance the understanding of authentic American Indian crafts and arts.

Dealers

Carol Halberstadt
Migrations
P.O. Box 543
Newton, MA 02258
e-mail: carol@migrations.com
web: http://www.migrations.com
Specializes in older and contemporary Native American and Inuit/Eskimo art: weavings, pottery, baskets, jewelry, sculpture; online gallery with links to a wide variety of Native American resources.

Ian M. Schwartz
Adobe East
4454 Springfield Avenue
Summit, NJ 07901
ph: 908-273-8282 or 800-242-3623
e-mail: ian@adobe-east.com
web: http://www.adobe-east.com/
Hopi, Kachina dolls, Native American Pueblo pottery and jewelry, sculpture, paintings, Zuni fetishes.

Richard Sutton
Kiva Trading Company
117 Main St.
Cold Spring Harbor, NY 11724
ph: 516-367-2875 or 800-947-8461
fax: 516-367-2834
e-mail: kiva1@ibm.net
web: http://www.kivatrading.com
NY metro's most complete selection of authentic American Indian handcrafted arts: jewelry, pottery, Kachina dolls, fetish carvings, weavings, fine hanging arts, sculpture; no imports or knock-offs; website has lots of images.

Peyton M. Alexander
Native American Traders
3463 Evans Ridge Dr.
Atlanta, GA 30341-5848
ph: 404-371-8108 or 770-491-8100
fax: 770-496-9797
e-mail: pma@nativeamericantraders.com
web: http://www.nativeamericantraders.com
Carries Native arts including Kachina dolls, weavings, prehistoric pots, paintings.

Red Crow Snapp
Native American Connection
3215 Brainerd Rd
Chattanooga, TN 37411
ph: 423-624-5061
e-mail: redcrow@warlance.com
web: http://www.warlance.com/redcrow/
Specializes in antique repair and replating, and design and creation of custom jewelry; carries a variety of Native American crafts.

WhiteBark Design
P.O. Box 6739
Kokomo, IN 46904-6739
ph: 765-459-8741
e-mail: barri@iquest.net
web: http://www.nativecreations.com
Native American made and related art, artifacts, books, apparel, supplies and more.

Harry Bradshaw
Reflections of Culture
145 W. Main Street
Cambridge, WI 53523
ph: 800-655-0553 or 608-423-3223
fax: 608-423-9744
e-mail: culture@idcnet.com
web: http://www.reflectionsofculture.com
Specializing in the sale of Native art from all North America; member of the Indian Arts & Crafts Association; galleries located in Cambridge, WI and Monona, WI.

Colleen Miller
Prairie Edge, Inc.
P.O. Box 8303
Rapid City, SD 57709
ph: 605-342-3086
fax: 605-341-6415
e-mail: prairie@rapidnet.com
web: http://www.prairieedge.com
Deals in contemporary reproductions of Plains Indians arts, crafts and jewelry.

Jill Giller
Native American Collections, Inc.
338 Eudora St.
Denver, CO 80220
ph: 303-321-1071
fax: 303-321-1071
e-mail: Jillspots@aol.com
web: http://www.nativepots.com
A unique contemporary gallery showcasing the finest in handmade Pueblo pottery, Zuni Fetishes, Hopi Kachinas, sculpture, and Indian jewelry; welcomes special orders.

Anne Goldstein
Elk Ridge Art Company
P.O. Box 1917
Evergreen, CO 80439-1917
ph: 303-526-1561 or 800-713-0763
fax: 303-526-5271
e-mail: GoldAnne@aol.com
web: http://www.elkridgeart.com
Carries fine Native American art, paintings, pottery, Navajo rugs and jewelry.

Georgiana Kennedy Simpson
Kennedy Indian Arts
P.O. Box 39
Bluff, UT 84512
ph: 435-672-2405
fax: 435-672-2406
e-mail: georgiana@kennedyindianarts.com
web: http://www.kennedyindianarts.com
Since 1908 specializing in pottery, jewelry, fetishes, rugs, baskets, Kachinas, novelties, folk art.

John & Sharon Bryant
Dancing Horses
P.O. Box 30357
Mesa, AZ 85275-0357
ph: 602-924-3226
fax: 602-981-6281
e-mail: jsbryant@amug.org
web: http://www.galaxymall.com/shops/dancing_horses.html/
Authentic Native American collectibles handcrafted by artists: dream catchers,to tomahawks.

Stephen Osborne
Desert Son American Indian Art
4759 E Sunrise Dr.
Tucson, AZ 85718
ph: 520-299-0818
e-mail: elrey@azstarnet.com
web: http://www.desertson.com/desertson/
Dealing in quality Indian goods for over 30 years; handmade traditional Southwestern moccasins, gold and silver jewelry, Kachinas, rugs, pottery, buckles, belts; excellent buckle collection including Ranger sets; Hopi Kachina repair.

Jay Tallant
Canyon Country Originals
6030 E. Fangio Place
Tucson, AZ 85750
ph: 520-529-5545
fax: 520-529-1456
e-mail: cainfo@canyonart.com
web: http://canyonart.com
Web site has large collection of Southwestern Indian arts & crafts; specializing in pottery from Hopi, Acoma, Zuni, Jemez, Cochiti, San Ildefonso, Santa Clara, San Juan pueblos; authentic Navajo rugs, jewelry.

Ron McGee
McGee's Indian Art
P.O. Box 607, Hwy. 264
Keams Canyon, AZ 86034
ph: 520-738-2295
fax: 520-738-5250
e-mail: rmcgee@hopiart.com
web: http://www.hopiart.com
Located on the Hopi Reservation for over 50 years; specializing in Hopi jewelry, Kachinas and pottery.

Ledge House Indian Craft Store
HC 71 Box 3
Tonalea, AZ 86044-9704
ph: 520-672-2366 or 520-672-2367
fax: 520-672-2345
web: http://www.nps.gov/nava/
Sells contemporary Indian crafts.

Lucky Mokhesi
Van's Trading Company
P.O. Box 7
Tuba City, AZ 86045
ph: 520-283-5343 or 800-798-9849
fax: 520-283-4333
e-mail: lm1@tubacity.net
web: http://vanstrading.com
Navajo owned and operated trading post on the Navajo Reservation; dating back to 1940s; authentic Navajo arts & crafts, rugs, Hopi Kachina carvings; pawn jewelry; monthly auctions.

Pueblo Pottery Gallery
P.O. Box 366
San Fidel, NM 87049
ph: 505-552-6748 or 800-933-5771
fax: 505-552-6748
web: http://www.collectorsguide.com/ab/g313.html
Featuring quality pottery, Kachinas, jewelry, fetishes, rugs, Acoma photographs and prints; numerous artists represented.

Thomas Baker
Tanner Chaney Gallery
410 Romero NW
Albuquerque, NM 87104
ph: 505-247-2242
fax: 505-298-3434
e-mail: tbaker@tannerchaneygallery.com
web: http://www.tannerchaneygallery.com
Sells and appraises contemporary and antique Native American jewelry, weavings and pottery.

Alexander Anthony, Jr.
Adobe Gallery
413 Romero NW
Albuquerque, NM 87104-1421
ph: 505-243-8485 or 800-821-5221
fax: 505-243-8403
Specializing in art of the Southwest Indian: historic Pueblo pottery, Navajo blankets and rugs, Hopi Kachina dolls and Navajo and Pueblo pawn jewelry.

Georgiana Kennedy Simpson
Kennedy Gallery
P.O. Box 6526
Albuquerque, NM 87197
ph: 505-344-7538
fax: 505-343-1382
e-mail: georgiana@kennedygallery.com
web: http://www.kennedygallery.com
Showcases top examples of contemporary Native American art: weavings, basketry, Navajo folk art, contemporary Indian jewelry, pottery.

Bien Mur Indian Market Center
I-25 N & Tramway Rd.
P.O. Box 91148
Albuquerque, NM 87199
ph: 505-821-5400 or 800-365-5400
e-mail: info@bienmur.com
web: http://www.bienmur.com
Sells original Native American Indian art & crafts: fetishes, turquoise, Kachinas, Navajo rugs, sand paintings, jewelry, pottery, etc.

Bill Foutz
Foutz Trading Co.
P.O. Box 1894
Shiprock, NM 87420
ph: 505-368-5790 or 800-383-0615
fax: 505-368-4441
Specializing in Navajo rugs, sand paintings, Kachinas, sculptures, Navajo pottery, beadwork.

Arch Thiessen
Sunshine Studio
3180 Vista Sandia
Santa Fe, NM 87501
ph: 800-348-9273 or 505-985-3216
fax: 505-986-0765
e-mail: sunshine@sunshinestudio.com
web: http://www.sunshinestudio.com/
Specializes in Southwest American Indian art, but antique and contemporary: Zuni fetishes, American Indian silver and turquoise jewelry, Pueblo pottery, Navajo rugs, Hopi Kachinas, Native American paintings, baskets, etc.

Peter Kahn
Keshi the Zuni Connection
227 Don Gaspar
Santa Fe, NM 87501
ph: 509-989-8728
e-mail: zuniart@keshi.com
web: http://www.keshi.com
Your connection to authentic arts & crafts from the Zuni Pueblo: traditional Zuni jewelry, fetish carvings and medicine bags.

Buzz Trevathan
Cristof's
106 West San Francisco St.
Santa Fe, NM 87501
ph: 505-988-9881 or 505-988-9882
fax: 505-986-8652
e-mail: buzzart@cristofs.com
web: http://www.cristofs.com
An internationally recognized primary source for contemporary museum quality Navajo weavings such as rugs, tapestries, wall hangings; also carries Hopi Kachinas, Navajo sand paintings, Navajo Yeibichai carvings, and other works of art.

Julie Anne Overton
Native Hands Gallery
460 St. Michaels Drive, Ste. 1000
Santa Fe, NM 87505
ph: 505-820-6600
fax: 505-820-6900
e-mail: info@nativehands.com
web: http://www.nativehands.com
Brings the finest in traditional and contemporary Native American jewelry to the Internet; website contains the work of award-winning Navajo, Hopi and Zuni artists who continue the rich history of Indian silver jewelry.

Janet Aper
159 E. 5th Ave.
Sun Valley, NV 89433
ph: 702-674-6366
Native American art, bronzes, carvings, clothing, jewelry, Kachinas, pottery, weapons.

Rainmaker-Art
P.O. Box 3801
Hollywood Station
Los Angeles, CA 90078-3801
ph: 818-951-3663
fax: 818-951-3663
e-mail: Rainmaker@Rainmaker-art.com
web: http://www.Rainmaker-Art.com
Dealer, expert, appraiser of modern Native American arts & crafts for over 20 years: Hopi Kachina dolls, Navajo rugs, Zuni fetishes, old pawn jewelry, beadwork, weapons, clothing, basketry, pottery.

Paul Larson
Eagle Wing Indian Art
P.O. Box 1741
San Juan Capistrano, CA 92693-1741
ph: 714-493-5760
fax: 714-493-3967
e-mail: plarson@eaglewingart.com
web: http://www.eaglewingart.com
Deals in Southwestern U.S. Native American art: Kachina dolls, pottery, jewelry; website had in-depth information and research; free newsletter.

Gallery of the American West
121 K Street
Sacramento, CA 95814
ph: 916-446-6662
fax: 916-446-1432
e-mail: gallerywest@webtv.net
web: http://www.gallerywest.com
Buys and sells highest quality Native American handmade pieces.

Joseph Ramos II
RedRoad
401 1/2 Newton St.
Medford, OR 97501
ph: 541-779-0863 or 541-779-0780
e-mail: beyond@cdsnet.net
web: http://home.cdsnet.net/~beyond/
Collector, dealer, expert; dedicated to bringing cultural education of the

Native American to the world through both art and artifact.

Patricia Hudson
Potcarrier American Indian Arts
P.O. Box 727
Vashon, WA 98070
ph: 206-463-5998
fax: 206-463-3435
e-mail: paia@potcarrier.com
web: http://www.potcarrier.com
Specializing in the traditional Native American arts of the Southwest including Pueblo pottery, Zuni fetish carvings, Navajo rugs, Hopi Kachina dolls, baskets, jewelry and other arts.

Raheema Vasudevan
Chakra
8249 Shaughnessy St.
Vancouver, British Columbia V6P 3X9
Canada
ph: 604-325-5092
e-mail: chakra@smarttnet.com
web: http://www.grantbc.com/chakra/
Provides authentic, Southwestern native art and craft to collectors, interior designers, and retailers; collection consists of contemporary Navajo and Pueblo art and craft of exceptional quality.

Misc. Services

Indian Arts & Crafts Board
U.S. Dept. Of The Interior
Room 4004 - MIB
Washington, DC 20240-0001
ph: 202-208-3773
Write for information on how to order a "Source Directory" which lists Indian-owned and operated arts & crafts businesses throughout the country.

Periodicals

American Indian Art, Inc.
Magazine: American Indian Art Magazine
7314 E. Osborn Dr.
Scottsdale, AZ 85251-6418
ph: 480-994-5445
fax: 480-945-9533
Quarterly art journal devoted to native American art from prehistoric to modern; gorgeous photographs, auction reports, reports on ethno-graphic and fine arts items, "Legal Briefs" column.

Martin Link, Pub.
Newspaper: Indian Trader, The
P.O. Box 1421
Gallup, NM 87305-1421
ph: 505-722-6694 or 800-748-1624
fax: 505-722-6696
e-mail: trader@cia-g.com
web: http://www.cia-g.com/~trader/index.htm
Focuses on old and new Indian art and artifacts.

John M. Gogol
Magazine: American Indian Basketry
P.O. Box 66124
Portland, OR 97266
ph: 503-233-8131
A magazine dedicated to Native American Indian arts: basketry, beadwork, pottery, baskets and weaving, textiles, masks, jewelry, etc.

AMMUNITION & EXPLOSIVE ORDNANCE

(see also ADVERTISING COLLECTIBLES, Ammunition; ARMS & ARMOR; CANNONS; CIVIL WAR ARTIFACTS; FIREARMS; MILITARIA; TOYS, Cannons; TRENCH ART)

Auction Services

Dr. J.R. Crittenden Schmitt
Crittenden Schmitt Archives
Court House Station
P.O. Box 4253
Rockville, MD 20849-4253
ph: 301-946-2643
Only video auctions in the world of ordnance material: collector ammunition, bombs, grenades, mines; inert only, from all countries; includes reference material in all formats and languages.

Clubs/Associations

Dr. J.R. Crittenden Schmitt
International Ammunition Association, Inc.
Journal: International Ammunition Journal
Court House Station
P.O. Box 4253
Rockville, MD 20849-4253
ph: 301-946-2643
Association has over 1000 members; membership open to all; Journal published bimonthly for members only.

International Cartridge Collectors Association
Journal: International Ammunition Journal
5032 Grave Run Rd.
Manchester, MD 21102

Madeline Bruemmer
Shotshell Historical & Collectors Society
3886 Dawley Rd.
Ravenna, OH 44266
Focuses exclusively on shotshells.

Bob Cameron
Sioux Empire Cartridge Collectors Association
14597 Glendale Ave. SE
Prior Lake, MN 55372

Don MacChesney
Greater St. Louis Cartridge Collectors Association
145 East Maple
Kirkwood, MO 63122

Gary Muckel
Nebraska Cartridge Collectors Club
Newsletter: NCCC Newsletter
P.O. Box 84442
Lincoln, NE 68501
ph: 402-483-2484
Appraisals and buyers located; items identified; assistance offered to locate antique wants in small arms ammunition; bimonthly newsletter.

George Blakslee
Rocky Mountain Cartridge Collectors Association
15072 E. Mississippi Ave.
Aurora, CO 80012

Rick Montgomery
California Cartridge Collectors Association
1728 Christina
Stockton, CA 95204

Robert T. Jardin
Association of Cartridge Collectors of the Pacific North-West
14214 Meadowlark Drive KPN
Gig Harbor, WA 98329

Graham Irving
European Cartridge Research Associa-tion
Newsletter: Cartridge Researcher, The
P.O. Box 55
Spa, girving@skynet.be 4900
Belgium
ph: +32 (0)87-77-43-40
fax: +32 (0)87-77-27-51
Publishes its monthly bulletin in English, French, German and Dutch; holds cartridge meetings in Belgium, Holland, Germany, Switzerland, and France; has members world wide.

Collectors

Ron Willoughby
1072 Rte. 171
Woodstock, CT 06281-2134
ph: 860-974-1226
fax: 860-974-3190
e-mail: swillo@neca.com
web: http://www.neca.com/swillo
Wants to buy shotshell boxes, gun company posters and calendars, glass target balls and traps, gunpowder cans, animal traps, and related items; a very serious buyer; free appraisals; estate purchases.

Guy Hildebrand
6748 Johnstown Loop
Tallahassee, FL 32308
ph: 850-893-9503
e-mail: mg64guy@aol.com
web: http://members.aol.com/~mg64guy/index.htm
Interested in collecting old cartridges and related boxes.

Dealers

Ray T. Giles
RTG Sporting Collectibles, LLC
P.O. Box 670894
Dallas, TX 75367
ph: 214-361-6577
e-mail: ray@rtgammo.com
web: http://rtgammo.com/
Buys and sells antique and obsolete ammunition in original boxes; specializing in U.S. sporting calibers; no military or reloaded ammo; very few shotshells, mostly metallics wanted; no lists; see web site or call.

John Spangler
John Spangler Professional Services, LC
P.O. Box 711282
Salt Lake City, UT 84171
ph: 801-947-9442
e-mail: hq@oldguns.net
web: http://oldguns.net
Buys and sells ammunition for the collector.

Experts

Dr. J.R. Crittenden Schmitt
Crittenden Schmitt Archives
Court House Station
P.O. Box 4253
Rockville, MD 20849-4253
ph: 301-946-2643
Family in business since 1849; full line of consulting expertise in all areas of munitions: grenades, land mines, bombs, etc.; ordnance consulting support for government, industry, entertainment and private collectors.

Periodicals

Magazine: Artilleryman, The
RR 1 Box 36
Tunbridge, VT 05077-9707
ph: 802-889-3500 or 800-777-1862
fax: 802-889-5627
e-mail: mail@civilwarnews.com
web: http://www.civilwarnews.com/
Published quarterly, the only magazine exclusively for the 1750-1898 artillery enthusiast: artillery history, unit profiles, shell collecting, etc.

Badges

Collectors

Dr. J.R. Crittenden Schmitt
Crittenden Schmitt Archives
Court House Station
P.O. Box 4253
Rockville, MD 20849-4253
ph: 301-946-2643
Wants only metal badges & pins relating to bomb squads, explosive ordnance disposal units, ammunition & weapons companies of the world.

Shell Casings

Collectors

Charles Eberhart
Lead Cannon, The
3616 Seward
Topeka, KS 66616-1652
ph: 785-235-1016
Wants to buy large brass military casings - the longer the better; also wants to buy decorated "Trench Art" shells.

AMUSEMENT PARK ITEMS

(see also CAROUSELS & CAROUSEL FIGURES; CARNIVAL ITEMS; COIN-OPERATED MACHINES, Arcade Games; ROLLER COASTERS; TARGETS, Shooting Gallery)

Auction Services

David A. Norton
Norton Auctioneers of Michigan, Inc.
50 W. Pearl St.
Coldwater, MI 49036-1967
ph: 517-279-9063
fax: 517-279-9191
e-mail: nortonsold@cbpu.com
Specializing in the auctioning of amusement rides, carousels, amusement parks, arcades, museums, etc.

Clubs/Associations

International Association of Amusement Parks & Attractions
1448 Duke St.
Alexandria, VA 22314
ph: 703-836-4800
fax: 703-836-4801
e-mail: lhunnewe@iaapa.org
web: http://www.iaapa.org

Historic Amusement Foundation
Newsletter: HAF Times
4410 North Keystone Ave.
Indianapolis, IN 46205
ph: 317-841-7677

Ty Fluharty
National Amusement Park Historical Association
Newsletter: NAPHA News
P.O. Box 83
Mount Prospect, IL 60056
ph: 412-831-6315
fax: 412-343-0971
e-mail: info@napha.org
web: http://www.napha.org/
The world's only educational and enthusiast's organization dedicated to all aspects of the amusement park.

Collectors

Ty Fluharty
P.O. Box 83
Mount Prospect, IL 60056
ph: 412-831-6315
fax: 412-343-0971
e-mail: info@napha.org
web: http://www.napha.org/
Collector of amusement park memorabilia.

Jim Abbate
7936 Park Ave.
Skokie, IL 60077
ph: 847-675-4511
Wants roller coaster, carousel, amusement park ephemera; photos, brochures, stationery, ride manufacturers' catalogs, tickets, sheet music, letterheads, matchbooks, signs, advertisements, pamphlets, trade cards, postcards, etc.

Tom Keefe
P.O. Box 464
Tinley Park, IL 60477-0464
Wants signs, tickets, carousel horses, tokens, photos, movies, letterheads, ride manufacturer's catalogs, posters, advertising items.

Peter Dusza
305 Mathew St.
Santa Clara, CA 95050
ph: 408-988-8161 or 408-723-0722
fax: 408-988-2206
e-mail: pdusza@ix.netcom.com
Wants to buy roller coaster souvenirs and memorabilia: coffee cups, drinking and shot glasses, pins, patches, post cards, posters, and buttons.

Experts

Thomas G. Morris
Prize Publishers
P.O. Box 8307
Medford, OR 97504-0307
ph: 541-779-3164
e-mail: chalkman@cdsnet.net
Specializing in carnival chalkware figures; author of "The Carnival Chalk Prize Vol. I and II"; will assist with information or appraisals on the subject.

Museums/Libraries

Knoebels Amusement Park & Carousel Museum
P.O. Box 317, Rte. 487
Elysburg, PA 17824-0317
ph: 570-672-2572 or 800-ITS-4FUN
e-mail: magicusa@microserve.net
web: http://www.microserve.net/~magicusa/knoebels.html

Periodicals

Mark Wyatt, Ed.
Newspaper: Inside Track
P.O. Box 7956
Newark, DE 19714-7956
ph: 302-737-3667
fax: 302-368-8329
web: http://www.insidetrackonline.com/
Monthly international amusement and theme park newspaper.

Don Schockow
Rainbow Ridge Productions
VHS: Disney TV
P.O. Box 1064
Ojai, CA 93024-1064
ph: 805-640-8101
fax: 805-640-8101
e-mail: disnyanatv@aol.com
web: http://www.disneyanatv.com/
"Disneyana TV" is a quarterly VHS television show covering everything Disney; from behind the scenes to future projects...it's all on Disneyana TV.

Chalkware

Museums/Libraries

Val Seath
Chalkware Museum On-Line
R.R. #6
Eganville, Ontario K0J 1TO
Canada
ph: 613-628-9489
e-mail: val@canadianantiques.com
web: http://www.canadianantiques.com/1chalk.htm
An on-line virtual museum of carnival chalkware prizes: animals, ashtrays, banks, birds, cats, cartoon characters, character figures, cowboys, dogs, history, hula girls, Kewpies, Jenkins pieces, lamps, monkeys, pigs, vases, etc.

Coney Island

Collectors

Stanley Fried
195 Froehlich Farm Blvd.
Woodbury, NY 11797-2931
ph: 516-364-1112
fax: 516-625-4220
Wants Coney Island related items such as old postcards, souvenirs.

ANCIENT COINS

(see COINS & CURRENCY, Coins [Ancient])

ANGELS

Clubs/Associations

Barbara Lopatin
National Angel Collector's Club
Newsletter: On the Wings of Angels
P.O. Box 1847
Annapolis, MD 21404
ph: 410-349-1158
fax: 410-349-1158
e-mail: Balopatin@aol.com
web: http://members.delphi.com/angelcollect/index.html
A club for collectors of all categories of angel collectors.

Jeanne Kehe
Angel Collector Club
Newsletter: Angels of the World
14 Parkview Ct.
Crystal Lake, IL 60012-3540
ph: 815-459-9259
Members are collectors of any type of angels; membership is limited to 225; newsletter published 6 timer per year.

Alberta Hedstrom
Angels Collectors' Club of America
Newsletter: Halo Everybody!
12225 South Patomac
Phoenix, AZ 85044-2231
ph: 602-598-0458
e-mail: eahedstrom@aol.com
Over 1,000 members who collect angels in any form.

ANIMAL COLLECTIBLES

(see also ANIMAL CONTROL COLLECTIBLES; ANIMAL TROPHIES; AQUARIUMS; BOOKS, Poultry; DINOSAURS; ENDANGERED SPECIES; FARM COLLECTIBLES; FIGURINES, Mortens; HORSES; INSECTS; LICENSES, Animal; VETERINARY MEDICINE ITEMS; WHALES & DOLPHINS)

Dealers

Barbara Framke
"Just Animals"
15525 Fitzgerald
Livonia, MI 48154-1805
ph: 734-464-8493
Buys and sells animal collectibles, especially dog, cat and horse figurines.

Bears

(see SMOKEY BEAR ITEMS; TEDDY BEARS)

Cats

(see also CERAMICS [AMERICAN], Black Cats; HALLOWEEN COLLECTIBLES)

Clubs/Associations

Peggy Way
Northeast Regional Cat Collector's Club
5091 Beatty St.
Piscataway, NJ 08854
ph: 732-699-9297
e-mail: rjway@worldnet.att.net
web: http://www.hairballs.com

Marilyn Dipboye
Cat Collectors
Newsletter: Cat Talk
33161 Wendy Dr.
Sterling Heights, MI 48310-6473
ph: 810-264-0285
web: http://www.hairballs.com/collectors/
For ailurophiles (cat lovers), this club focuses on all types of cat collectibles; offers catalog of extensive line of antique/older cat collectibles for sale.

Collectors

Peggy Way
5091 Beatty St.
Piscataway, NJ 08854
ph: 732-699-9297
e-mail: rjway@worldnet.att.net
web: http://www.hairballs.com
Cat collector specializing in Shafford and Wales Black Cats, antique toy cats, games featuring cats, cookie jars and teapots in a cat motif, jewelry, etc.

Renae Giles
P.O. Box 6
Carver, MN 55315-0006
ph: 612-448-7046
e-mail: zelda0555@aol.com
Advanced collector seeks all types of cat collectibles, especially Goebel, Hagen-Renaker, Josef Originals, Lowell Davis, Border FIne Arts and novelty salt and pepper shakers; also trades.

Mercedes DiRenzo
Jazz'e Junque
3831 N. Lincoln
Chicago, IL 60613
ph: 773-463-7411
fax: 773-463-3687
e-mail: JazzyJunk@aol.com
web: http://www.jazzejunque.com

Dealers

Billie J. Parsons
431 Thomas Dr.
Webster, NY 14580
ph: 716-671-9388
Specializes in canine, equine, and feline collectibles: large dog figurines, Western Hartlands, Kay Finch, Hagen-Renaker, Breyer Horses.

Barbara Framke
"Just Animals"
15525 Fitzgerald
Livonia, MI 48154-1805
ph: 734-464-8493
Buys and sells all cat related items, especially figurines and collector plates, both current and secondary market; current sale lists available for SASE; if selling, please price and describe items.

Experts

Marbena "Jean" Fyke
132 North Montgomery, Ste. D-12
Walden, NY 12586-1165
ph: 914-778-7327
fax: 914-564-1421
Author of "Collectible Cats," books I and II (Collector's Books).

Joyce & Judy
Krazy Cat Collectibles
P.O. Box 21727
Emmitsburg, MD 21727
ph: 301-309-2513
e-mail: KrazyCatCo@aol.com
Specializing in unique and interesting old cat items: toys, postcards, advertising, jewelry, pictures, cookie jars, sale & peppers, plates, vintage clothing, figurines, etc.; will buy one piece or entire collection.

Marilyn Dipboye
33161 Wendy Dr.
Sterling Heights, MI 48310-6473
ph: 810-264-0285
web: http://www.catwriters.org/articles/m-dipboye.html
Wants antique cat memorabilia in all collecting categories.

Cats (Goebel Figurines)

Experts

Linda Nothnagel
Rte. 3 Box 30
Shelbina, MO 63468-9406
ph: 573-588-4958 or 816-781-5291
e-mail: katzen630@hotmail.com
Wants out-of-production Goebel cat figurines and Goebel cat related items.

Cats (Kliban)

Collectors

Sue Lucente
115 Marbeth Ave.
Carlisle, PA 17013-1626
ph: 717-249-9343
e-mail: Sooloo@webtv.net
Wants B. Kliban cat items: teapots, candy dishes, pillows and sheets, Christmas items, figurines, banks, salt & pepper shakers, mugs, cookie jars, cat feeders, framed pictures, book ends, T-shirts, stuffed animals, kitchen towels, etc.

Dogs

(see also LICENSES, Dog; TELEVISION SHOWS & MEMORABILIA, Lassie)

Clubs/Associations

Jane Swanson
Canine Collectors Club
Magazine: Canine Collectibles Quarterly
10290 Hill Road
Erie, IL 61250
ph: 309-659-2166
A publication devoted to the promotion, enjoyment and collecting of dog memorabilia. Information on a wide range of dog items, as well as a classified ad section to buy and sell.

Collectors

Jeffrey Jacobson
860 Graegin Place
Dyer, IN 46311-2215

Dealers

Annie Alpert
Maiasaura Books & Canine Collectibles
405 Lexington Ave.
Cranford, NJ 07016-2729
ph: 908-276-2847
fax: 908-276-2954
e-mail: maiasaura@home.com
web: http://www.maiasaura.com
Carries interesting dog art for the collector including the full line of Ron Hevener dog figurines.

Billie J. Parsons
431 Thomas Dr.
Webster, NY 14580
ph: 716-671-9388
Specializes in canine, equine, and feline collectibles: large dog figurines, Western Hartlands, Kay Finch, Hagen-Renaker, Breyer Horses.

Denise Hamilton
899 Latta Brook Rd.
Elmira, NY 14901-9226
ph: 607-732-2550
Buys dogs collectibles: figurines, old dog postcards, jewelry with dogs in it, etc.; Borzoi (Russian Wolfhound), greyhound, all Morten Studio and Erphila dogs and animals.

Meg Weitz
Tigger's Dog Stuff
601 Rockwood Rd.
Wilmington, DE 19802
ph: 302-762-8939
Buys and sells fine dog collectibles and prints.

Jo Ellen Arnold
Dog Lady, The
P.O. Box 2641
Springfield, VA 22152-0641
ph: 703-644-5201
fax: 703-644-5401
Specializes in fine canine collectibles.

Jane & John Carroll
2894 John Tyler Highway
Williamsburg, VA 23185-1335
ph: 757-258-9322
fax: 757-258-9552
Buys and sells canine collectibles; a poodle authority.

Mary Blacker
610 W. Siebenthaler Ave.
Dayton, OH 45405
ph: 937-278-6153
Antique & collectible dog figurines and art; Royal Doulton, Mortens Studio, Rosenthal, Boehm, Kirmse, Dennis, Thorne, Eberhardt.

Barbara Framke
"Just Animals"
15525 Fitzgerald
Livonia, MI 48154-1805
ph: 734-464-8493
Buys and sells all dog related items, especially figurines and collector plates, both current and secondary market; current sale lists available for SASE; if selling, please price and describe items.

Sharlene Beckwith
Exclusively Dogs!
P.O. Box 1858
Upland, CA 91785-1858
ph: 909-946-1544
fax: 909-949-4796
Specializing in fine canine collectibles, especially fine porcelains (Rosenthal, Boehm, etc.), Kay Finch dog figurines and any large or unusual Kay Finch animals, including cookie jars; also wants Kay Finch bronzes and dog jewelry.

Museums/Libraries

Barbara Kolk, Lib.
American Kennel Club, Inc. Library
260 Madison Ave., 4th Floor
New York, NY 10016
ph: 212-696-8254 or 212-696-8348
fax: 212-696-8299
e-mail: library@akc.org
web: http://www.akc.org/library.htm
Research library open to the public; 17,000 volumes on dogs and related areas.

Dog Museum, The
1721 S. Mason Rd.
Saint Louis, MO 63131
ph: 314-821-3647
Commemorates every aspect of a dog's life; collection includes dog art and artifacts.

Dogs (Collies)

Collectors

Joan L. Neidhardt
331 Regal Drive
Abingdon, MD 21009
e-mail: JLNCollies@aol.com
Wants to buy anything relating to

Collies or to Lassie; old, new, unique; toys, figurines, character collectibles.

Debby Stratman
10851 Rosalie Dr.
Northglenn, CO 80233-3553
ph: 303-457-8665
Wants anything pertaining to Collie dogs, including paper, any condition considered; please write first.

Periodicals

Joan L. Neidhardt
Newsletter: COLLIEctively Speaking!
331 Regal Drive
Abingdon, MD 21009
e-mail: JLNCollies@aol.com

Dogs (German Shepherds)

Collectors

Henry Heiman, III
P.O. Box 316
South Salem, NY 10590-0316
Wants to buy German Shepherd dog items.

Dogs (Poodles)

Collectors

Mickey Kern
NewMont Toy Poodles
124 North Crawford Ave.
Hardin, MT 59034
ph: 406-665-1097 or 406-679-1170
fax: 406-665-6127
e-mail: mmkern@mcn.net
web: http://www.mcn.net/~mmkern/
Collects, dealer, expert in poodle items; prefers high quality items, spaghetti, slaw, and similar varieties; please no stuffed, mechanical, or plastic poodles; also does not want poodle hats, musical instruments, or glasses.

Dealers

Betty Hannigan
12509 Biscayne Dr.
Philadelphia, PA 19154
ph: 215-632-7247
e-mail: wayback@webtv.net
Carries a selection of spaghetti poodles.

Jane & John Carroll
2894 John Tyler Highway
Williamsburg, VA 23185-1335
ph: 757-258-9322
fax: 757-258-9552
Buys and sells canine collectibles; a poodle authority.

Dogs (Scotties)

Clubs/Associations

David Bohnlein
Wee Scots
Magazine: Scottie Sampler
P.O. Box 450
Danielson, CT 06239-0450
ph: 850-564-6660
e-mail: dbohnlein@snet.net
web: http://campbellscotties.com/
A quarterly publication with historical data, current market prices, photos, ads, etc. for Scottie collectors and dealers.

Dogs (War Dogs)

Collectors

James Flurchick
395 Paramus Rd.
Paramus, NJ 07652
ph: 201-444-3403
Collects war dog militaria: equipment, postcards, insignia, back packs, awards, books, toys.

Elephants

Clubs/Associations

Richard W. Massiglia
National Elephant Collectors Society, The
380 Medford St.
Somerville, MA 02145-3810
ph: 617-625-4067
For information send LSASE plus $1.

Collectors

Rosita Williams
14357 Georgia Ave., Apt. T-2
Silver Spring, MD 20906
ph: 301-871-3135

Experts

Richard W. Massiglia
380 Medford St.
Somerville, MA 02145-3810
ph: 617-625-4067

Periodicals

Joan L. Huegel
Newsletter: Jumbo Jargon
1002 West 25th St.
Erie, PA 16502-2427
Quarterly publication; free ad for subcribers; articles, meet other collectors, "from the expert" column, classified ads, etc.; available only by subscription.

Flamingos

Collectors

Suzy Holleron
624 Morningside Dr.
San Antonio, TX 78209-2808
ph: 210-826-6663
Known as the "Flamingo Lady;" collects everything with a flamingo motif.

Lynn Fry
P.O. Box 5495
Coos Bay, OR 97420
ph: 541-888-4177
Wants flamingo figurines, lamps, pictures, mirrors, etc.

Lynn Rogers
P.O. Box 5495
Coos Bay, OR 97420
ph: 541-888-4177
Wants flamingo items.

Dealers

Steve Colby
Off The Deep End
712 East St.
Frederick, MD 21701-5239
ph: 301-698-9006
e-mail: chilimon@offthedeepend.com
web: http://www.offthedeepend.com/
Wide assortment of flamingo collectibles.

Frogs

(see also FLOWER "FROGS")

Clubs/Associations

Ms. Merelaine Haskett, Ed.
Frog Pond, The
Newsletter: Ribbit Ribbit
P.O. Box 193
Beech Grove, IN 46107-0193
Newsletter has articles and buy/sell/ trade ads; open to all who are interested in collecting frog related items.

Chicago Herpetological Society
Journal: Bulletin of the Chicago Herpetological Society
2060 N. Clark St.
Chicago, IL 60614
ph: 773-281-1800
e-mail: chsinfo@chicagoherp.org
web: http://www.chicagoherp.org/
Affiliated with the Chicago Academy of Sciences; focuses on the study of reptiles and amphibians; offers books about frogs and reptiles; 8 1/2" x 11" journal published monthly.

Dealers

Louise Mesa
"Frog Fantasies" Museum & Frogs Only Gift Shop
151 Spring St.
Eureka Springs, AR 72632
ph: 501-253-7227

Museums/Libraries

Louise Mesa
Frog Fantasies Museum, The
151 Spring St.
Eureka Springs, AR 72632
ph: 501-253-7227
Has over 6,000 frogs.

Horse Related

(see also FARM COLLECTIBLES; HORSE-DRAWN VEHICLES; HORSES; LEATHER; RIDING TOYS, Rocking Horses; SADDLES; SPORTS COLLECTIBLES, Polo; SPORTS COLLECTIBLES, Thoroughbred Racing; WESTERN AMERICANA)

Collectors

Bill Mackin
1137 Washington St.
Craig, CO 81625-1613
ph: 970-824-6717 or 970-824-6360
fax: 970-824-7175
Author of "Cowboy and Gunfighter Collectibles" with 1993-94 updated price guide; sells books for Old West collectors by mail and at shows; over 45 years collecting; wants nice gun leather and cowboy gear; appraises, consults, lectures.

Linda Paich
Bookends
P.O. Box 445
Los Olivos, CA 93441
ph: 805-688-3484
fax: 805-688-0307
e-mail: bookends@utech.net
Wants items relating to horses: postcards, books, statues, antique Western tack, etc.; antique and out-of-print on all types of horses and horse sport; buys and sells.

Dealers

Billie J. Parsons
431 Thomas Dr.
Webster, NY 14580
ph: 716-671-9388
Specializes in canine, equine, and feline collectibles: large dog figurines, Western Hartlands, Kay Finch, Hagen-Renaker, Breyer Horses.

Barbara Cole
October Farm
2609 Branch Rd.
Raleigh, NC 27610-9213
ph: 919-772-0482
fax: 919-779-6265
e-mail: octoberfarm@bellsouth.net
web: http://www.octoberfarm.com/
Buys and sells horse books and paper ephemera, especially relating to polo, carriages & driving, Morgan horses, American Saddlebred horses, and veterinary medicine; also old farm horse equipment and catalogs; mail order only.

Barbara Framke
"Just Animals"
15525 Fitzgerald
Livonia, MI 48154-1805
ph: 734-464-8493
Buys porcelain and ceramic horse figurines, especially by Hagen-Renaker, Beswick and Goebel; also wants horse related books; all items considered.

Museums/Libraries

Keith D. Bartz, Dir.
American Saddle Horse Museum
4093 Iron Works Pike
Lexington, KY 40511
ph: 606-259-2746
fax: 606-259-1628
web: http://www.american-saddlebred.com/museum/
To learn about the American saddlebred horse, and to preserve and maintain artifacts pertinent to the history of the breed.

Bill Cooke, Dir.
International Museum of the Horse, Kentucky Horse Park
4089 Iron Works Pike
Lexington, KY 40511
ph: 606-233-4304
fax: 606-259-4212
e-mail: khp@mis.net
web: http://www.imh.org/

Horse Related (Draft)

Collectors

Jim Richendollar
508 W. Columbia Ave.
Belleville, MI 48111
ph: 734-699-3805
Wants draft (work horse like Clydesdales) horse memorabilia: books, magazines, photos, prints, paintings, sale catalogs, statues, figurines, etc.

Horse Related (Models)

Stephanie Macejko
Stallions USA
14 Industrial Rd.
Pequannock, NJ 07440
ph: 973-694-5006
e-mail: breyerhrs@aol.com
web: http://www.horsecollector.com/
(see also Offers fine porcelain horse sculptures, also Breyers.)

Clubs/Associations

North American Model Horse Shows Association
e-mail: troyb@cts.com
web: http://www.namhsa.org/

Daralyn Wallace
Equine Miniaturists & Collectors Association of Texas
Newsletter: EMCAT News
1311 Garden Lane
Bryan, TX 77802
e-mail: RaunFalcon@aol.com
web: http://hometown.aol.com/emcattx/
Formed for the purpose of promoting interest and involvement in model horse collecting and showing; all are welcome.

Collectors

Chelle Fulk
1793 Ivy Oak Sq.
Reston, VA 20190-4723
ph: 703-471-1968 or 202-626-9773
e-mail: anthem2@juno.com
Wants plastic horses, dogs, etc.: Breyer, Hartland, others; any size, condition, color.

Jessica Prior-Jennings
621 Pierson St.
Flint, MI 48503
ph: 810-239-6326
Wants Breyer and Hartland plastic model horses, rider and animal models; will buy collections; also wants Hagen-Renaker, Designer's Workshop, or Beswick china horse figurines.

Dealers

Terri Mardis-Ivers
Terri's Toys & Nostalgia
419 S. First St.
Ponca City, OK 74601
ph: 580-762-8697
Specializes in Breyer and Hartland figures.

Black Horse Ranch
1024 Nobles Court
Minden, NV 89423
ph: 800-360-5BHR

Internet Resources

Model Horse Web
e-mail: kira@metronet.com
web: http://www.lightsphere.com/model-horse/
Web site packed with resources for model horse hobbyists; dealers, classified ads, clubs, publications, artists, art supplies, shows, etc.

Janet Piercy
Model Horse Gallery
e-mail: jpiercy@linex.com
web: http://www.astroarch.com/modelhorse/
The largest and only model horse gallery in the world; over 10,000 photos, 100 galleries and over 600 pages.

Model Horse Enthusiasts' Site
e-mail: emilynchris@geocities.com
web: http://www.geocities.com/Heartland/Plains/6871
For collectors of plastic, porcelain, pottery, or resin model horses.

Periodicals

Paula Hecker
Magazine: Hobby Horse News, The
2053 Dryehaven Dr.
Tallahassee, FL 32311-8656
ph: 850-216-2983
e-mail: thhn@aol.com
web: http://www.vistech.net/users.thhn/
Bi-monthly magazine with hobby horse articles, shows, ads, etc.

Sheryl Leisure
Newsletter: Model Horse Trader, The
34428 Yucaipa Blvd., #E119
Yucaipa, CA 92399
ph: 909-446-0233
fax: 909-795-2474
Ads-only newsletter consisting of dealers' lists from across the country; not a reference or price guides; models identified only be model number; send $15, photos and LSASE for appraisals; checks payable to Sheryl Leisure.

Repair Services

Sue Thiessen
25115 Cemetery Rd.
Middleton, ID 83644-5103
ph: 208-585-3243
Specializing in restoring model horses, Roseville, and other pottery; also collector of Hagen Renaker horse and animal figurines.

Horse Related (Models/Breyer)

Clubs/Associations

Stephanie Macejko
Breyer Collectors Club
Magazine: Just About Horses
14 Industrial Rd.
Pequannock, NJ 07440
ph: 973-694-5006
e-mail: breyerhrs@aol.com
Offers information on model horse collecting and hobbying including customization, vintage models & horse model showing; no paid ads.

Dealers

Sue Coffee
Laysville Hardware
10 Saunders Hollow Rd.
Old Lyme, CT 06371-1126
ph: 860-434-5641
fax: 860-434-2653
e-mail: SueCoffee@aol.com
web: http://www.suecoffee.com/
Buys and sells: present to discontinued; send SASE with .78 cent postage for list or visit web site; wants Breyer from the 1950s and 1960s, especially woodgrains and decorators (gold, blue and dapple).

Arlene Bentley
Bentley Sales Company
642 Sandy Lane
Des Plaines, IL 60016
ph: 847-439-2049
fax: 847-439-2071
e-mail: bentleysales@mw.sisna.com
web: http://www.modelhorses.com/bentley/pl.html
Carries entire Breyer Model Horse line plus limited editions, discontinued and special run models.

Terry & Antina Richards
5838 Darlene Dr.
Rockford, IL 61109
Specialize in vintage Breyer horse models; please include SASE when writing.

Experts

Kimberly Grackowski
23046 Bagpipe Ct.
Long Grove, IL 60047
e-mail: springfvr@aol.com
Publishes a value guide of ALL Breyer models ever created; buys collections.

Kimberly Gackowski
23046 Bagpipe Ct.
Long Grove, IL 60047-7524
ph: 847-203-5809 or 847-827-1657
e-mail: SpringFvr@aol.com
Author of "Breyer Model Collector's Value Guide"; detailed descriptions and production years of regular models, special runs, lamps, night lights, music boxes; contains current market values, photos, etc.

Nancy Atkinson Young
Nancy Young's Books
268 Ross Court
Claremont, CA 91711-3139
ph: 909-621-7872
e-mail: Nancy_Young@earthlink.net
web: http://home.earthlink.net/~nancy_young/
Author of "Breyer Molds and Models," (available from author) the most comprehensive book available on Breyer model horses and other animals; does not do appraisals; please include SASE when writing.

Man./Prod./Dist.

Bentley Sales Co.
642 Sandy Lane
Des Plaines, IL 60016
ph: 847-439-2049
Contact for information on the new Breyer line.

Mules

Collectors

Gene Hammerlun
1350 Cal Ct.
Gardnerville, NV 89410-6123
ph: 775-782-5945
Wants to buy anything related to

mules: pictures, advertising, stories, etc.

Periodicals

Magazine: Western Mule Magazine
P.O. Box 46
Marshfield, MO 65706
ph: 417-859-6853
fax: 417-859-2814
e-mail: ben@westernmulemagazine.com
web: http://www.westernmulemagazine.com/
Pleasure, cutting, show and pack mules' training, health, trail riding, mule rodeos and more.

Owls

Clubs/Associations

Elise Mann
International Owl Collectors Club
Newsletter: Life's a Hoot
54 Triverton Rd.
Edgware, Middlesex HA8 6BE
U.K.
ph: +44 181 952 2888
e-mail: CraftyUK@aol.com
Hundreds of members worldwide who collect owl items.

Experts

Donna Russell
RR 1 Box 990
Coquille, OR 97423-9752
ph: 541-396-2688

Internet Resources

Donna Howard
Owl's Nest, The
P.O. Box 990
Depoe Bay, OR 97341-0990
ph: 541-765-2473 or 888-345-OWLS
fax: 800-352-6024
e-mail: owlsnest@owlsnestcatalog.com
web: http://www.owlsnestcatalog.com
The catalog for owl collectors of the world; owl merchandise, events, clubs, newsletters, magazines for the owl collector.

Pigs

Clubs/Associations

Gene Holt
Happy Pig Collectors Club, The
Newsletter: Happy Pig, The
P.O. Box 17
Oneida, IL 61467-0017
ph: 309-483-6192
e-mail: pigclub@netins.net
For collectors of pigs items, so that they may gain more enjoyment from their hobby and mingle with others cursed with the same strange affliction; it's respectful to say "When I see a Pig, I think of you."

Collectors

Arlene McNaught
136 Edwards St.
Kewanee, IL 61443-3538
ph: 309-853-4960
e-mail: happypig@cin.net

Gene Holt
P.O. Box 17
Oneida, IL 61467-0017
ph: 309-483-6192
e-mail: pigclub@netins.net

Experts

Mary Hamburg
Tootsie's Antiques
20 Cedar Ave.
Danville, IL 61832-1525
ph: 217-446-2323 or 217-442-2725
Buys, sells, collects, and specializes in German china pig figurines; advisor to "Warman's Americana & Collectibles Price Guide."

Plastic Models

Collectors

Chelle Fulk
1793 Ivy Oak Sq.
Reston, VA 20190-4723
ph: 703-471-1968 or 202-626-9773
e-mail: anthem2@juno.com
Wants plastic horses, dogs, cattle, wildlife, etc.; especially Breyer; any size, condition or color.

Possums

Collectors

Van Matre
15 S. Blaine
Hinsdale, IL 60521-4208
e-mail: lvanmatre@tribune.com
Wants possum-related items: vintage postcards, tins, games, children's books, anything featuring happy and healthy possums; all replies answered.

Reptiles

Experts

Mark F. Miller
Herpetology.com
P.O. Box 52261
Philadelphia, PA 19115-7261
ph: 215-464-3561
fax: 215-464-3561
e-mail: reptiles@earthling.net
web: http://www.herpetology.com
Author of numerous articles regarding reptile care, reptile books, and collecting reptile literature, sculptures, prints, and postcards; past Editor or the "Bulletin of the Philadelphia Herpetology Society."

ANIMAL CONTROL COLLECTIBLES

Collectors

Wayne M. Besenty
9060 Hegel St.
Bellflower, CA 90706-4216
ph: 562-925-8574 or 562-570-3057
e-mail: CaSrACO@wentv.net
Collector of historical animal control and Humane Society items: patches, badges, pins, banners, animal humane magazines, posters, photographs of dog catchers, animal control or humane officers, ASPCA, trucks; anything animal control.

ANIMAL TROPHIES

(see also ENDANGERED SPECIES; SKELETONS; SPORTING COLLECTIBLES)

Auction Services

Gerard Giguere
Giguere Auction Co.
P.O. Box 1272
Windham, ME 04062
ph: 207-892-3800
fax: 207-892-3800
Conducts sporting auctions: fishing, hunting, decoys, sporting art, taxidermy.

Dealers

Bob Hoffman
Moose River Lake & Lodge Store
69 Railroad St.
Barnet, VT 05821
ph: 802-748-2423 or 802-633-4031
Old taxidermy; deer, moose, elk, caribou antlers; skulls, folk art, prints, paintings and photos; snowshoes, pack baskets, creels, rustic & camp furnishings; open daily.

Gene Harris
Art By God
50 Upper Alabama, Store No. 248
Underground Atlanta
Atlanta, GA 30303
ph: 404-577-7311 or 800-940-4449
fax: 305-573-9343
e-mail: artbygod@netside.net
Mineral specimens, fossils, gems, sea shells, animal mounts, animal pelts, insects/butterflies, snail shells, skulls.

Gene Harris
Art By God
3705 Biscayne
Miami, FL 33137
ph: 305-573-3011 or 305-573-3691
fax: 305-573-9343
e-mail: artbygod@netside.net
Mineral specimens, fossils, gems, sea shells, animal mounts, animal pelts, insects/butterflies, snail shells, skulls.

Edward Leep
American Natural Resources
128 N. Broad St.
Griffith, IN 46319-2219
ph: 219-922-6444
Sells mounts from around the world: full mounts, shoulder mounts, bear rugs, birds, etc.

David Boone
Boone's Trading Company
P.O. Box BB
Brinnon, WA 98320
ph: 360-796-4330 or 800-423-1945
fax: 360-796-4551
Buys and sells legal ivory, scrimshaw, furs and skulls: scrimshaw, netsuke, Eskimo artifacts, carvings, walrus, hippo, warthog, mammoth, jewelry, pistol grips, ivory beads, old trade beads, scrimshaw supplies and reproductions.

Experts

Gerard Giguere
Giguere Auction Co.
P.O. Box 1272
Windham, ME 04062
ph: 207-892-3800
fax: 207-892-3800
Conducts sporting auctions: fishing, hunting, decoys, sporting art, taxidermy; very knowledgeable about the regulations related to the sale of animal parts.

Museums/Libraries

Call of the Wild, The
850 S. Wisconsin Ave.
Gaylord, MI 49735
ph: 517-732-4336 or 517-732-4087

Suppliers

Van Dykes Supply Company
P.O. Box 278
Woonsocket, SD 57385-0278
ph: 800-558-1234 or 605-796-4425
fax: 605-796-4085
web: http://www.vandykes.com/
Issues large catalog of taxidermy supplies.

ANIMATION FILM ART

(see also AUDIO-VISUAL; CARTOON ART; CHARACTER COLLECTIBLES; SCIENCE FICTION)

Appraisers

Pam Martin
CEL-EBRATION!
P.O. Box 123
Little Silver, NJ 07739
ph: 732-842-8489 or 842-842-0494
fax: 732-842-8489
e-mail: cel-ebration@monmouth.com
web: http://www.cel-ebration.com
Appraises, buys and sells vintage and contemporary animation art from all studios; storefront in Red Bank, NJ;

also mail order; offers hard-to-find rare cels.

Pamela Scoville, AAA
330 W. 45th St., Ste. 9D
New York, NY 10036-3864
ph: 212-765-3030
fax: 212-765-2727
e-mail: TheAAGLtd@aol.com
Offers appraisal services for animation film art; certified member, Appraiser Association of America.

Melanie Smith, ISA
Seaside Art Gallery
P.O. Box 1
2716 Virginia Dare Trail S
Nags Head, NC 27959
ph: 252-441-5418 or 800-828-2444
fax: 252-441-8563
e-mail: seaside@interpath.com
web: http://www.seasideart.com
Accredited member of the International Society of Appraisers; specializes in fine art (paintings, graphics, sculpture) and animation art.

Michael Austin
Great American Ink
11633 San Vicente Blvd.
Los Angeles, CA 90049
ph: 310-447-6490 or 800-552-BUGS
fax: 310-447-1831
e-mail: GreatAmeri@compuserve.com
web: http://www.cartoongallery.com
Appraiser, collector, dealer and expert in animation artworks from the early 1900s through the 1960s; strong collector of Disney, Lantz, Warner Brothers Studios original production artworks including cels, story paintings, backgrounds.

Clubs/Associations

Pamela Scoville
Animation Art Guild, Ltd.
Newsletter: Update, The
330 W. 45th St., Ste. 9D
New York, NY 10036-3864
ph: 212-765-3030
fax: 212-765-2727
e-mail: TheAAGLtd@aol.com
Established in 1990; offers reliable, unbiased information; member services include book finders, auction hotline, appraisal services, flash advisories, art theft advisories, world's most comprehensive database on animation art values.

Nancy McClellan
Animation Art Collectors Club of Washington
2972 Yarling Ct.
Falls Church, VA 22042-4475
ph: 703-876-0891 or 202-364-0842
fax: 202-364-0002
e-mail: antiques@erols.com
web: http://www.antiquesdc.com/
Regional club interested in promotion and education of animation as an art form.

Steven Worth
Association Internationale Du Film D'Animation (ASIFA)
725 South Victory Blvd.
Burbank, CA 91502
ph: 818-842-8330
fax: 818-842-5645
e-mail: sworth@vintageip.com
web: http://home.earthlink.net/~asifa/
A worldwide organization dedicated to the art of animation.

Dealers

Steve Grossfeld
Newsletter: Celmail
P.O. Box 1787
Manchester Center, VT 05255
ph: 802-362-4766
fax: 802-362-4745
e-mail: CELMAIL@thegremlin.com
web: http://www.thegremlin.com/CELMAILhome.html
An online animation film newsletter; join to be connected to thousands of other enthusiasts who share the hobby; member participation and monitored by industry professionals, industry publications and galleries alike.

Herb Barker
Barker Animation Art Galleries
1188 Highland Ave.
Cheshire, CT 06410-1624
ph: 800-227-5372 or 800-995-2357
fax: 203-699-1188
e-mail: fun@barkeranimation.com
web: http://www.BarkerAnimation.com

William Gunn
All American Collectibles, Inc.
24-04 Broadway
Fair Lawn, NJ 07410
ph: 201-797-2555 or 800-778-2847
fax: 201-797-8668
e-mail: all-american-collectibles@worldnet.att.net
web: http://www.allamericancollectible.com/

Pam Martin
CEL-EBRATION!
P.O. Box 123
Little Silver, NJ 07739
ph: 732-842-8489 or 842-842-0494
fax: 732-842-8489
e-mail: cel-ebration@monmouth.com
web: http://www.cel-ebration.com
Appraises, buys and sells vintage and contemporary animation art from all studios; storefront in Red Bank, NJ; also mail order; offers hard-to-find rare cels.

Animazing Gallery
415 West Broadway
New York, NY 10012
ph: 800-303-4848 or 212-226-7374
fax: 212-226-7428
e-mail: animazing@worldnet.att.net
web: http://animazing.com
New York City's largest authorized animation gallery featuring vintage and contemporary cels and drawings from all studios; a Disney exclusive gallery; hosts industry events; publishers of Underdog artwork.

Debbie Weiss
Wonderful World of Animation Art
51 E. 74th St., Ste. 1R
New York, NY 10022
ph: 212-472-1720
e-mail: debbiew@animationartgallery.com
web: http://www.animationartgallery.com
Buys, sells, appraises animation art; specializes in original art from Disney, Simpsons, Warner, Hanna, and others; over 2000 original production pieces in stock.

Ari S. Goldman
355 E. 88th St.
New York, NY 10128-4904
Collector and dealer of fine animation art.

Cartoon Gallery
69-40 108th St.
Forest Hills, NY 11375
ph: 718-793-4714 or 800-715-4776
fax: 718-793-0698
e-mail: info@cartoon-gallery.com
web: http://www.cartoon-gallery.com
Buys and sells animation cels of your favorite cartoon characters from all of the major studios; limited edition and production cels.

Stu & Miriam Reisbord
Cartoon Carnival Gallery, The
2 Rabbit Run
Wallingford, PA 19086-6218
ph: 610-566-4343 or 610-566-1292
fax: 610-566-2727
e-mail: stureis@erols.com
Specializing in Disney vintage drawings, cels and backgrounds for over 20 years; also original pen & ink classic syndicated art.

Bryan Guarnieri
Animation & Fine Art Galleries
200 N. Greensboro Street
Car Mill Mall
Carrboro, NC 27510
ph: 919-968-8008 or 888-968-8008
fax: 919-968-8064
e-mail: fineart@mindspring.com
web: http://animationandfineart.com/
Specializes in original production animation art cels and drawings as well as original paintings, drawings and sculpture by world-renowned museum-exhibited 20th century artists.

Melanie Smith, ISA
Seaside Art Gallery
P.O. Box 1
2716 Virginia Dare Trail S
Nags Head, NC 27959
ph: 252-441-5418 or 800-828-2444
fax: 252-441-8563
e-mail: seaside@interpath.com
web: http://www.seasideart.com
Wants original oils, graphics, sculpture, and animation film art; also buys and sells old and new animation art; Accredited Member of the International Society of Appraisers.

Elvena Green
One-of-a-Kind Cartoon Art, Inc.
775 Livingstone Place
Decatur, GA 30030-3950
ph: 404-377-3333
fax: 404-377-6011

Taylor R. Robinson
3844 Oakbridge Lane
Dublin, OH 43017
ph: 614-799-0547 or 614-799-0541
fax: 614-799-0542
Buys, sells and trades fine animation art.

Dan & Mary Anne Ergezi
Art-Toons
P.O. Box 670600
Northfield, OH 44067-0600
ph: 330-468-2655
fax: 330-468-2644
e-mail: ergezi@ct.picker.com
A family-owned business dedicated to give the public the enjoyment of owning animation art at affordable prices: Warner Bros., Walt Disney, commercials, MGM, super heroes, cult classics such as Heavy Metal, Wizards, Hanna Barbera.

Cartoon Factory Animation Art Gallery
1400 South Foothill Drive
Salt Lake City, UT 84108-2300
ph: 801-583-3700
fax: 801-583-3713
e-mail: gallery@cartoon-factory.com
web: http://www.cartoon-factory.com/
Large selection of animation art on the web; original and limited edition art cels from Disney, Warner Bros., Hanna-Barbera, The Simpsons, Peanuts, and many other studios.

Michael Austin
Great American Ink
11633 San Vicente Blvd.
Los Angeles, CA 90049
ph: 310-447-6490 or 800-552-BUGS
fax: 310-447-1831
e-mail: GreatAmeri@compuserve.com
web: http://www.cartoongallery.com
Appraiser, collector, dealer and expert in animation artworks from the early 1900s through the 1960s; strong collector of Disney, Lantz, Warner Brothers Studios original production artworks including cels, story paintings, backgrounds.

Ron Silverstein
Silver Stone Gallery
2005 Palo Verde Ave., Ste. 205
Long Beach, CA 90815-3399
ph: 562-598-7600
fax: 562-598-7700
e-mail: silverston@aol.com
A private gallery for the discerning collector, specializing in buying & selling Disney Studio vintage animation art.

Joseph Cesaro
Sunday Funnies LLC
10010 Canoda Ave., Ste. B1
Chatsworth, CA 91311
ph: 818-341-9040 or 800-693-2369
fax: 818-341-4850
e-mail: joecesaro@sundayfunniesllc.com
web: http://www.sundayfunniesllc.com/
Sells animated art: production cells, limited edition cels, and seri-cels; includes Archie, Fat Albert, Heckle & Jeckle, Blondie, Beetle Bailey, Star Trek, Star Wars, Lone Ranger, Lassie, etc.; represents Filmation, Lucas Films, etc.

Stephen Worth
Vintage Ink & Paint
5701 Klump Ave. #7
North Hollywood, CA 91601
ph: 818-980-7637
e-mail: sworth@vintageip.com
web: http://www.vintageip.com/
Buys, sells, repairs, appraises; the leading authority on animation art authentication & restoration; all paints manufactured in-house using same formulas and techniques used at Disney Studios; has worked with several major studios.

Steve Oakley
Acme Animation Art Cel Galleries
10938 Magnolia Blvd.
North Hollywood, CA 91601
ph: 909-899-5400 or 888-988-6667
fax: 818-768-4841
e-mail: wag@westworld.com
web: http://www.acmeanimation.com/
A premier animation art gallery specializing in fine animation cels and cartoon character art as well as figurines and other collectibles.

Richard L. Trethewey
Rainbo Animation Art
8 Duran Court
Pacifica, CA 94044-4231
ph: 800-647-5085 or 950-359-0221
fax: 413-643-0711
e-mail: rainbo@hooked.net
web: http://www.hooked.net/~rainbo
Carries a wide range of animation art from production cells to posters; also carries animation collectibles featuring Toy Story toys and collectibles.

Vincent Sean Monico
Animation Artshop, The
P.O. Box 10014
Anchorage, AK 99510-0114
ph: 907-274-1894 or 800-646-5967
e-mail: animate@alaska.net
web: http://www.alaska.net/~animate/
Collects, buys and sells all types of original Disney production artwork.

Experts

Debbi Grossfeld
Gremlin Animation
Newsletter: Celmail
646 Richville Rd.
P.O. Box 1787
Manchester Center, VT 05255
ph: 877-GREMLIN or 802-362-4766
fax: 802-362-4745
e-mail: gallery@thegremlin.com
web: http://www.thegremlin.com
Animation film art dealer, expert and appraiser; one of the largest resources in the world for animation art from all studios; currently maintains an inventory of over 25,000 original cels, drawings and limited editions.

Ron Stark, ISA
S/R Laboratories, Animation Art Conservation Center
Newsletter: Today
31200 Via Colinas, Ste. 210
Thousand Oaks, CA 91362-3939
ph: 818-991-9955
fax: 818-991-5418
e-mail: srlabs@earthlink.net
web: http://www.srlabs.com/srindex.html
Appraiser, dealer, restorer, expert in animation art; also Disneyana.

Stephen Worth
Vintage Ink & Paint
5701 Klump Ave. #7
North Hollywood, CA 91601
ph: 818-980-7637
e-mail: sworth@vintageip.com
web: http://www.vintageip.com/
Buys, sells, repairs, appraises; the leading authority on animation art authentication & restoration; all paints manufactured in-house using same formulas and techniques used at Disney Studios; has worked with several major studios.

Museums/Libraries

Herb Barker
Barker Character, Comic & Cartoon Museum
1188 Highland Ave.
Cheshire, CT 06410-1624
ph: 800-227-5372 or 800-995-2357
fax: 203-699-1188
e-mail: fun@barkeranimation.com
web: http://www.BarkerAnimation.com
Features comic character collectibles, television collectibles, cartoon character collectibles, toys, and comic memorabilia.

Museum of Modern Art, The
11 W. 53rd. St.
New York, NY 10019
ph: 212-708-9400 or 800-447-6662
e-mail: comments@moma.org
web: http://www.moma.org/

Baltimore Museum of Art, The
10 Art Museum Dr.
Baltimore, MD 21218-3898
ph: 410-396-7100
fax: 410-396-7153
web: http://www.artbma.org/

Dave Smith
Walt Disney Archives
500 South Buena Vista St.
Burbank, CA 91521-3040
ph: 818-560-5424
Comprehensive Disney collection including complete U.S. and most foreign Disney comics; comics not available to researchers for preservation reasons; usage limited to approved projects.

Periodicals

Source Publications, Inc.
Magazine: Collectors' Showcase
7134 S. Yale, Ste. 720
Tulsa, OK 74136
ph: 918-491-9088
fax: 918-491-9946
e-mail: bwilkerson@sourcepub.com
web: http://www.cslive.com/
Bi-monthly full-color magazine focusing on contemporary and vintage character collectibles from animation film art, comics and entertainment studios like Disney Warner Bros., and many more.

Magazine: Animation World
6525 Sunset Blvd., Garden Ste. 10
Los Angeles, CA 90028
ph: 323-468-2554
fax: 323-464-5914
e-mail: info@awn.com
web: http://www.awn.com/mag/

Magazine: Animation Magazine
30101 Agoura Court, Ste. 110
Agoura Hills, CA 91301
ph: 818-991-2884 or 800-996-TOON
fax: 818-991-3773
e-mail: animag@aol.com
web: http://www.animag.com/
A monthly magazine about the animation industry: animators, special effects, commercials, festivals, contests, fans, international animation, collecting animation art, ads for dealers selling animation art and related services.

Directory: Animation Industry Directory
30101 Agoura Court, Ste. 110
Agoura Hills, CA 91301
ph: 818-991-2884 or 800-996-TOON
fax: 818-991-3773
e-mail: animag@aol.com
web: http://www.animag.com/
The most comprehensive reference guide to the people and companies active in the animation industry today.

Repair Services

Ron Stark, ISA
S/R Laboratories, Animation Art Conservation Center
Newsletter: Today
31200 Via Colinas, Ste. 210
Thousand Oaks, CA 91362-3939
ph: 818-991-9955
fax: 818-991-5418
e-mail: srlabs@earthlink.net
web: http://www.srlabs.com/srindex.html
First and only animation art conservation center in the world featuring restoration, ink & paint lab, frame shop, accredited appraisals, expert witness and trial consultation, and much more.

Stephen Worth
Vintage Ink & Paint
5701 Klump Ave. #7
North Hollywood, CA 91601
ph: 818-980-7637
e-mail: sworth@vintageip.com
web: http://www.vintageip.com/
Buys, sells, repairs, appraises; the leading authority on animation art authentication & restoration; all paints manufactured in-house using same formulas and techniques used at Disney Studios; has worked with several major studios.

ANTIQUES & COLLECTIBLES

(see also ANTIQUES DEALERS & COLLECTORS, Supplies For; ANTIQUES SHOP DIRECTORIES; ANTIQUES SHOW PROMOTERS; ART; ART THEFT & FRAUD; BOOKS, Reference [Antiques]; FLEA MARKET GUIDES; INTERNET CLASSIFIEDS FOR COLLECTORS; POPULAR CULTURE; PAWNBROKERS; TOURS/BUYING TRIPS)

Appraisers

(see also "APPRAISERS" Appendix in the back of this book for hundreds of educated, tested, and trained professional personal property appraisers - all credentialed members of the International Society of Appraisers.)

Dewey W. Smith, ASA
Dewey W. Smith, ASA Antique Appraisals
7346 S. Alton Way #10-G
Littleton, CO 80120-2327
ph: 303-930-9899
fax: 303-930-9919
e-mail: dwsmithasa@aol.com

Barbara Pickett, GCA, MCA, GGAC
Antique Rose, The
P.O. Box 771
Lakewood, CA 90714-0771
ph: 562-425-4149
fax: 562-425-4149
Personal property appraisals of antiques, collectibles, estates, insurance, probate, divorce, IRS.

Christian Coleman, Ex. Dir.
International Society of Appraisers
Newsletter: Professional Appraisers Information Exchange
16040 Christensen Rd., Ste. 102
Seattle, WA 98188
ph: 206-241-0359 or 888-472-4732
fax: 206-241-0436
e-mail: ISA_HQ@compuserve.com
web: http://www.isa-appraisers.org
Largest association of professional personal property appraisers; over 1,300 members specializing in all areas of antiques & residential contents, gems & jewelry, fine art, machinery & equipment; free referrals; directory available.

Clubs/Associations

Donna Carlson, Dir.
Art Dealers Association of America
575 Madison Ave.
New York, NY 10022-2511
ph: 212-940-8590
fax: 212-940-7013
e-mail: artdeal@rosenman.com
web: http://www.artdealers.org/
Non-profit organization of nation's leading dealers in fine art.

Dora Lerch
World of Collectibles - Collector Club International
P.O. Box 245
Garnerville, NY 10923-0245
ph: 914-362-4657
fax: 914-362-3258
e-mail: WorldofCollectibles@juno.com
Over 200 members.

Betty McKenna, Pres.
American Antique Arts Association
Newsletter: A.A.A.A. Journal
1240 Colonial Rd.
Mc Lean, VA 22101-2965
ph: 703-827-0867
The AAAA is devoted to the appreciation, study and preservation of American antiques, architecture, art, crafts and local history; the 14 chapters with 1000 members in MD, N. VA, and DC invite membership of any interested individual.

Lois R. Newton
Questers, The
8420 E. San Candido
Scottsdale, AZ 85258-2402
Offers members a unique opportunity to study and appreciate antiques; new chapters are organized whenever eight or more interested people apply for a charter from the International Organization.

Victorian Homeowner's Association
Newsletter: Victorian Homeowner's Association Newsletter
P.O. Box 846
Sutter Creek, CA 95685-0846
ph: 209-267-0774
For owners of Victorian homes; home renovation, antiques and collecting info.

Tom Fritz, Pres.
Wild Rose Antique Collectors Club
P.O. Box 1471
Main Post Office
Edmonton, Alberta T5J 2N5
Canada
ph: 780-454-7480
Large club of antiques and collectibles enthusiasts; meets monthly with speaker program.

Experts

George E. Michael
P.O. Box 2087
Merrimack, NH 03054-2087
ph: 603-424-7400
fax: 603-424-7400
e-mail: gitius@aol.com
Specialist in fine arts and antiques: appraiser, expert witness, auctioneer, writer, editor, consultant, lecturer and instructor.

Harry L. Rinker
Rinker Enterprises, Inc.
5093 Vera Cruz Rd.
Emmaus, PA 18049-9554
ph: 610-965-1122
fax: 610-965-1124
e-mail: rinker@fast.net
web: http://www.rinker.com
Maintains research files, library (books, periodicals, etc.), photos and slides covering over 1500 antiques & collectibles categories.

Internet Resources

Dave Cunningham
CompuServe, Dave Cunningham's Collectibles Forum
56 Hubbard Ave.
Stamford, CT 06905
ph: 203-323-4872
e-mail: 76702.453@compuserve.com
web: http://go.compuserve.com/collectibles
Join the Collectibles Forum or Antiques Forum via computer modem or via the Internet: philatelists, numismatics and other collectors (books, sports, dolls, figurines, cards, pins, and more; an online club atmosphere founded in 1989.

David J. Maloney, Jr., ISA CAPP
MaloneysOnline Antiques & Collectibles Resource Directory
P.O. Box 2049
Frederick, MD 21702-1049
ph: 301-695-8544
fax: 301-695-6491
e-mail: dave@maloney.com
web: http://www.maloneysonline.com/
Online resource information source for collectors, sellers, claims adjusters, etc.: includes experts, buyers, clubs, periodicals, repairers, museums/libraries, appraisers, auctioneers, matching services, dealers, etc.

Nidus Group, The
292 South County Rd.
Palm Beach, FL 33480
ph: 888-GO-NIDUS or 561-793-3493
fax: 561-793-1779
An international collaborative effort in the Art & Antique community offering FREE membership and the following services: Directory Listing, Brokerage, Locator, Internet Resource Guide.

Mitchell Koester
ClickAbout.com
4611 Sandy Park Dr.
Memphis, TN 38141
ph: 901-368-4362 or 901-362-9986
e-mail: admin@clickabout.com
web: http://www.clickabout.com
This web site contains 70 categories of categorized links for collectors.

Lee Bernstein
Lee Bernstein Antiques & Collectibles
Newsletter: Attic Muse, The
1631 Novo Drive
Schererville, IN 46375
ph: 219-322-4272
e-mail: info@elee.com
web: http://www.eLee.com
Free electronic newsletter with HOT collectible news; specializes in helping serious collectors buy and sell collectibles; author of eBay's Collectibles "Inside Scoop."

Ron McCoy
Collectorsweb.com
P.O. Box 703095
Tulsa, OK 741703095
ph: 918-747-1344
e-mail: ron@collectorsweb.com
web: http://www.collectorsweb.com
Free antiques & collectibles online twice-monthly newsletter available to anyone with an email address; keeps subscribers informed and up-to-date on general news/tidbits regarding the antiques and collecting hobby.

John Blatt
Planet Earth Antiques & Collectables E-Mail
876 Curtis St., Ste. 2709
Honolulu, HI 96813
ph: 808-596-8708
fax: 808-596-8708
e-mail: admin@peacelist.com
web: http://www.peacelist.com
A FREE listserve which allows subscribers to reach a targeted audience of subscribers worldwide to buy, sell, or publicize.

Jose Nunez
Kaleden.com
6600 Trans-canada Hwy.
Pointe-Claire, Quebec H9R 4S2
Canada
ph: 514-426-2557 or 877-525-3336
fax: 514-426-1642
e-mail: Jjones@kaleden.com
web: http://www.kaleden.com
An umbrella site for magazines and newspapers, both national and international, publishing on the topic of art, antiques and collectibles.

Misc. Services

Leon Castner, ISA CAPP
National Appraisal Consultants
P.O. Box 482
Hope, NJ 07844
ph: 800-323-5996 or 908-459-5996
fax: 908-459-4899
e-mail: castner@garden.net
web: http://www.nacvalue.com
Popular and knowledgeable speaker, teacher, seminar leader in most areas of antiques & collectibles; offers both lighthearted and serious presentations to civic groups or national organizations.

Periodicals

David J. Maloney, Jr., ISA CAPP
Collector's Information Clearinghouse (CIC)
Directory: Maloney's Antiques & Collectibles Resource Dir.
P.O. Box 2049
Frederick, MD 21702-1049
ph: 301-695-8544
fax: 301-695-6491
e-mail: dave@maloney.com
web: http://www.maloney.com/
Publishes major resource information source for collectors, sellers, claims adjusters, etc.: includes experts, buyers, clubs, periodicals, repairers, museums/libraries, appraisers, auctioneers, matching services, dealers, etc.

Appraisers

(see APPRAISAL ASSOCIATIONS as well as the "APPRAISERS" Appendix and Appraisers listed under specific categories throughout this Directory.)

Auction Services

(see "AUCTION SERVICES" Appendix as well as Auction Services listed under specific categories throughout this Directory.)

Canadian

Appraisers

Lorraine Pierce-Hull
Pierce-Hull & Associates & Advisors
23 Seaforth Road
Carelton Place, Ontario K7M 1E1
Canada
ph: 613-542-2228 or 888-205-5866
fax: 613-542-1474
e-mail: lphull@magi.com
Appraiser of Canadian and European paintings, textiles, sculpture, photographs and prints.

Kathryn Minard, ISA
Contemporary Fine Art Services, Inc.
413 Dundas St. East
Toronto, Ontario M5A 2A9
Canada
ph: 416-366-9770
fax: 416-366-8541
e-mail: kathryn_minard@compuserve.com
Expert and appraiser specializing in Canadian contemporary and historical art; also Canadian Indian and Inuit.

Auction Services

Erik J. Peters, ISA
Maynards Auctioneers
415 West 2nd Ave.
Vancouver, British Columbia V5Y 1E3
Canada
ph: 604-876-6787 or 604-531-0166
fax: 604-876-2678
e-mail: Erik@Maynards.com
web: http://www.maynards.com
Quarterly auctions of Canadian, American & Western European fine art, antiques, silver, jewellery, china, glass, carpets and specialty collectables; Accredited Member of International Society of Appraisers.

Collectors

Colin R. Voorneveld, MD
27 Roncesvalles Ave., #408
Toronto, Ontario M6R 3B2
Canada
ph: 416-516-4751
e-mail: 72774.257@compuserve.com
Avid collector specializing in pre-1900 medical and pharmaceutical antiques; actively seeks medical instruments, spectacles, historic medicine, etc.

Dealers

Angey Sabourin
Do You Remember When
311 Elm St.
Sudbury, Ontario P3C 1V6
Canada
ph: 705-673-4430
e-mail: jim.hendry@sympatico.ca

Internet Resources

Val Seath
R.R. #6
Eganville, Ontario K0J 1TO
Canada
ph: 613-628-9489
e-mail: val@canadianantiques.com
web: http://www.canadianantiques.com/
Web site is dedicated to bringing you up-to-date information on where to find quality Canadian information regarding the online Canadian antiques scene.

Periodicals

Paul Fiocca
Trajan Publishing Corp.
Magazine: Antique Showcase
103 Lakeshore Rd., Ste. 202
St. Catharines, Ontario L2N 2T6
Canada
ph: 905-646-7744
fax: 905-646-0995
e-mail: bret@trajan.com
web: http://www.vaxxine.com/trajan/
National magazine with diverse articles, show and auction reports, museum exhibits, book reviews, upcoming trends, etc.; also contains lots of display and classified ads for buyers of Canadian, US and European antiques; 9 times per year.

German

Auction Services

Jane Herz, US Rep.
Auction Team Koln
6731 Ashley Ct.
Sarasota, FL 34241-9696
ph: 941-925-0385
fax: 941-925-0487
e-mail: auction@breker.com
web: http://www.breker.com/
Specializes in the sale of old office equipment, scientific instruments and devices, photographica, and old technology including toasters, typewriters, sewing machines, posters and lobby cards, tools telecommunications, etc.

Mexican

Dealers

El Paso Saddle Blanket Co.
601 N. Oregon
El Paso, TX 79901
Wants to buy old Mexican rugs, blankets, Sarahs; also old Navajo rugs and weavings, Tarahumara Indian art, Mexican ranch collectibles.

Museums/Libraries

Joe Liberkowski
Museum of Classical Antiquities & Primitive Arts
P.O. Box 2161
Medford, NJ 08055-7161
Wants American Indian items; also pre-1940 Mexican and South American Santos, Retablos, Ex Votos, crucifixes, religious, historical autographs/documents.

Periodicals

(see "GENERAL INTEREST PERIODICALS" Appendix as well as Periodicals listed under specific categories throughout this Directory.)

Repair Services

(see "REPAIR SERVICES" Appendix as well as Repair Services listed under REPAIR/RESTORATION/ CONSERVATION and other specific categories throughout this Directory)

Reproductions

Clubs/Associations

Bill Mergenthal
American Antique Association
702 W. 76th St.
Davenport, IA 52806
ph: 800-473-7816 or 319-386-7866
A non-profit organization with the goal to stop the sale of unmarked reproductions; a consumer-oriented organization designed to help people who feel they may have purchased a reproduction.

Experts

Norman S. Young
Fake Publications
P.O. Box 766
Nassau, NY 12123-0766
e-mail: nsyoung@aol.com
Author of "Fabulous But Fake" (H/C book), the professional's guide to fake antiques; available from the author for $44.95.

Periodicals

Mark Chervenka
Newsletter: Antique & Collectors Reproduction News
P.O. Box 12130
Des Moines, IA 50312-9403
ph: 515-274-5886 or 800-227-5531 (orders)
fax: 515-255-4530
e-mail: acrn@repronews.com
web: http://www.repronews.com/
Monthly newsletter showing differences between old originals & new reproductions and fakes; 30-60 close-up photos of new and old side-by-side in each issue; all subjects; printed on glossy paper; annual index.; orders 800-227-5531.

Repro. Sources

Museum of Fine Arts, Boston - Catalogue Sales Department
465 Huntington Ave.
P.O. Box 1044
Boston, MA 02120
ph: 800-225-5592
e-mail: webmaster@mfa.org
web: http://www.mfa.org
Not needed

Upper Deck, Ltd.
P.O. Box 1705
New Bedford, MA 02741
ph: 508-992-5424 or 508-992-3827
fax: 508-997-2123
Sells reproduction tin toys, weathervanes, decoys, glassware, etc. to the trade only.

G.R.'s Trading
108 Chester Rd.
Derry, NH 03038
ph: 603-434-0220
fax: 603-425-2199
Sells repro. roll top desks, ice boxes, lamps, dolls, baskets, wicker, iron banks & toys, clocks, prints, pie safes, iron & brass beds, china cabinets, etc.

Renovator's Supply
P.O. Box 2515
Conway, NH 03818
ph: 800-659-2211 or 603-447-8500
fax: 603-447-1717
Offers catalog of Victorian reproduction accessories, lighting, hardware, bath fixtures, and door, window and cabinet hardware.

Sturbridge Yankee Workshop
90 Blueberry Rd.
Portland, ME 04102-1989
ph: 800-343-1144
fax: 207-774-2561
web: http://www.st3.yahoo.net/sturbridgeyankee/
Furniture, floor coverings, lamps & lighting, framed prints, household textiles, garden & hearth, mirrors & wall art; Shaker, Country, Mission styles.

Artique Inc.
259 Godwin Ave.
Midland Park, NJ 07432-1808
ph: 201-444-8989
Repro. clay pipes, fraktur, advertising memorabilia, Christmas tree ornaments, pottery, flags, 19th century engravings, old maps, bells, sleigh bells, etc.

A.A. Importing Company, Inc.
30 Northfield Ave.
Raritan Center
Edison, NJ 08837
ph: 732-225-0770
Repro. Orientalia, porcelains, stoneware, cast iron banks and toys, simulated ivory, weathervanes, oak furniture; to the trade only.

World Collectible Center
18 Vesey St.
New York, NY 10007
ph: 212-267-7100
Wholesale prices for reproduction collectibles: mammy cookie jar, Coca-Cola tip tray, KISS poster, gumball machines, Howdy Doody Western Set, etc.

Museum of Modern Art, The
11 W. 53rd. St.
New York, NY 10019
ph: 212-708-9400 or 800-447-6662
e-mail: comments@moma.org
web: http://www.moma.org/

Castle Antiques & Reproductions
515 Welwood Ave. & Rte. #6
Hawley, PA 18428
ph: 800-345-1667 or 570-226-8550
fax: 570-226-0454
web: http://www.castleantiques.com/castleantiques/
They publish a full catalog of a large line of antique reproductions.

Fred & Dottie's Inc.
6711 Perkiomen Ave.
Birdsboro, PA 19508
ph: 610-582-1506
Reproduction ceramics, glass, cast iron; wholesale only.

Merritt's Antiques, Inc.
P.O. Box 277
Douglassville, PA 19518
ph: 610-689-9541
fax: 610-689-4538
e-mail: info@merritts.com
web: http://www.merritts.com
Carries a large line or reproduction clocks, ceramics, brass, dolls, furniture, glass, etc.

Winterthur Museum
Direct Mail Marketing Office
Winterthur, DE 19735-0001
ph: 800-448-3883
e-mail: Winterthur@udel.edu
web: http://www.udel.edu/winterthur/
Sells museum reproductions.

Avalon Forge
409 Gun Rd.
Baltimore, MD 21227
ph: 410-242-8431
e-mail: avlonfrg@bcpl.net
Offers documented 18th century replicas for living history such as military goods, farm and home items.

Kristina Neiman
Victorian Rapture Company
198 Garibaldi Rd.
Winnsboro, SC 29180-6788
Custom makes high Victorian shades; 16" beaded fringe patterns & 85 frame choices to order; also covers old frames and supplier of reproduction Victorian lighting, jewelry (14K plated), bronzes, perfume bottles.

IAC International
4001 Hiawatha Ave.
Minneapolis, MN 55406
ph: 612-724-7244
fax: 612-724-1238
Repro. Peanut jar and salt shakers, hen-on-a-nest, blue baby bottles, cast iron horse beer wagon and 5-car train, cast iron tractors, porcelain tea sets, and much more.

A.A. Importing Company, Inc.
7700 Hall St.
Saint Louis, MO 63147
ph: 314-383-8800
fax: 314-383-2608
Repro. Orientalia, porcelains, stoneware, cast iron banks and toys, simulated ivory, weathervanes, oak furniture; to the trade only.

ReproCrafters, Inc.
11578 Industrial Park
Forney, TX 75126
ph: 800-654-8830 or 972-564-4441
fax: 214-552-9867
An import-direct warehouse carrying reproduction carousel horses, wicker doll carriages, bird cages, ship paintings, tricycles, sleds, etc.

Jim "Bud" Burton
Burton's Antiques & Antique Reproductions
9333 Harwin Dr.
Houston, TX 77036
ph: 713-789-9333 or 281-977-5885
fax: 713-789-8181
Carries furniture and aluminum reproductions such as light poles, carousel horses, patio tables & chairs, etc.

A.A. Importing Company, Inc.
352 Shaw Rd.
South San Francisco, CA 94080
ph: 650-589-4422
Repro. Orientalia, porcelains, stoneware, cast iron banks and toys, simulated ivory, weathervanes, oak furniture; to the trade only.

ANTIQUES DEALERS & COLLECTORS

Clubs/Associations

National Antique & Art Dealers Association of America
220 East 57th St.
New York, NY 10022
ph: 212-826-9707
fax: 212-832-9493
e-mail: naadaa@dir-dd.com
web: http://www.dir-dd.com/naadaa.html
Trade group represents art and antique dealers; sponsors antique and art exhibitions; promotes ethical trade practices among its members; free membership directory available.

Jim Tucker
Antiques & Collectibles Dealer Association (ACDA)
Newsletter: ACDA News
P.O. Box 2782
Huntersville, NC 28070-2782
ph: 800-287-7127 or 704-895-9088
fax: 704-895-0230
e-mail: acda@ix.netcom.com
web: http://www.acda.org
Provides a variety of services to dealers, such as insurance, merchant services, newsletter, seminars, travel and product discounts and more.

Jim Tucker
National Association of Collectors
Newsletter: NAC News
P.O. Box 2782
Huntersville, NC 28070-2782
ph: 800-287-7127 or 704-895-9088
fax: 704-895-0230
e-mail: info@collectors.org
web: http://www.collectors.org/
Provides a variety of services to collectors, such as insurance programs, newsletter, biennial meeting, travel and product discounts and more.

Jim Tucker
National Association of Antique Malls
P.O. Box 2782
Huntersville, NC 28070-2782
ph: 800-287-7127 or 704-895-9088
fax: 704-895-0230
e-mail: info@naam.org
web: http://www.naam.org/
Association for owners and managers of antiques malls; membership benefits include a newsletter directed at specific problems and needs of the antique mall, insurance benefits, merchant services, supply discounts, annual meetings.

Lester E. Sender
National Association of Dealers in Antiques
23500 Mercantile Rd.
Cleveland, OH 44122-5914
ph: 216-595-1111
fax: 216-595-1111
e-mail: antiques@nadaweb.org
web: http://www.nadaweb.org
Representing ethical antiques dealers nationally; also representing antique collectors in their "Collector Membership" category; write for details; pin, professional courtesies, Hdq. as a source of information, roster, current pricing.

Internet Resources

Martin Marcus
Antique Advertiser, The
P.O. Box 608
Marblehead, MA 01945
e-mail: martinnm@ix.netcom.com
web: http://antiqueadvertiser.com
An on-line only advertisement source and antique shop directory for Eastern Massachusetts antiques buyers and sellers: articles, free advertising, complete directory of dealers.

Kovels Online Price Guide
P.O. Box 22200
Beachwood, OH 44122-0200
ph: 800-571-1555 or 800-829-9158
fax: 216-752-3115
e-mail: kovels@usbrands.com
web: http://www.kovel.com

Antique Trader OnLine Price Guide
P.O. Box 1050
Dubuque, IA 52004-1050
ph: 800-482-3158 or 800-480-6169
fax: 800-531-0880
e-mail: randylte@mwci.net
web: http://www.collect.com/priceguide/
Antique Trader's annual price guide database with a huge number of items priced in thousands of categories.

Periodicals

Antoinette Knopp Powers, Pub.
AMQ Group Ltd.
Magazine: Professional Antique Mall
P.O. Box 219
Western Springs, IL 60558
ph: 708-246-4990
fax: 708-246-1559
A quarterly periodical with antique mall related ads, articles, computer software.

Computer Programs For *Man./Prod./Dist.*

Tom Bilotta
Carlisle Development Corp.
Software: Collector's Assistant
P.O. Box 291
Carlisle, MA 01741-0291
ph: 800-219-0257
e-mail: carlisleDC@aol.com
web: http://www.csmonline.com/carlisledc/
Software for collectors and dealers; standard versions are available for over 40 collectibles categories: coins, currency, figurines, toys, autographs, sports cards, knives, military, etc.; custom versions available.

Stephen J. Abt, III
ArtFact, Inc.
Price Guide: ArtFact
1130 Ten Rod Rd., Ste. E104
North Kingstown, RI 02852-4158
ph: 401-295-2656 or 800-278-3228
fax: 401-295-2629
e-mail: sales@artfact.com
web: http://www.artfact.com
A computerized library recording auction sales of art and antiques; complete descriptions, prices realized, on-screen images.

Russ Wood
Collector's Marketplace
Software: Intelligent Collector Software
RD 1 Box 213B
Montrose, PA 18801-9779
ph: 570-278-2099
e-mail: cmonline@epix.net

Michael Belofsky
MSdataBase Solutions
Software: Collectibles Database for Collectors
614 Warrenton Terrace NE
Leesburg, VA 22076-2465
ph: 800-407-4147 or 703-777-5660
fax: 703-777-5440
e-mail: techsupport@collectorsoft.com
web: http://www.collectorsoft.com
Windows: How many items to you own? How much have you spent? How much insured for? What items do you want? Includes on-line price guides for Prec. Mom., Hallmark Orns., Swarovski, D56, Tender Touches, Cher. Teddies, Disney Classics, others.

Michael Belofsky
MSdataBase Solutions
Software: Collectibles Database for Dealers
614 Warrenton Terrace NE
Leesburg, VA 22076-2465
ph: 800-407-4147 or 703-777-5660
fax: 703-777-5440
e-mail: techsupport@collectorsoft.com
web: http://www.collectorsoft.com
DOS: Keep track of inventory in stock, sold, sales tax, customers; print receipts, targeted mailings, price lists, inventory sheets, etc.; great for secondary market dealers! Refer to collector version for list of included price guides.

John Silling
Niche Software, Inc.
4342 N.W. 51st Court
Coconut Creek, FL 33073
ph: 954-418-0730
e-mail: sales@collectiblessoftware.com
web: http://www.collectiblessoftware.com/
Different programs designed for collectors of: Beanie Babies; bottles and glass; books, magazines and paper; Civil War relics; coins; dolls & figurines; comic books; toys & diecast cars; guns; knives; sports; stamps; sports collectibles.

GEW
Software: Collector Series, The
1224 S. Federal Highway
Lake Worth, FL 33460
web: http://gardian.com/collectr.htm
Sells several different software programs for collectors of coins, stamps, baseball cards, autographs, silverware; also orchids and videos.

Charles E. Crume
Charles Crume Software
Software: Charles Crume Software
P.O. Box 5054
Cincinnati, OH 45205
ph: 513-471-0479
fax: 513-471-2590
e-mail: ccsmain@concentric.net
web: http://www.concentric.net/~Ccsmain/
IBM compatible program versions for malls, single dealers, collectors, consignment shops; optional modules for auction houses; bar coding, credit card verification, extended inventory information, remote inventory entry, phone bids.

Lee Mellinger
Anteq Software Corporation
Software: Anteq Collection Manager
4201 N.Main, Ste. 403
Findlay, OH 45840
ph: 888-223-6359 or 419-353-1004
fax: 216-274-6385
e-mail: admin@anteq.com
web: http://www.anteq.com
Software for antique dealers, shops, malls and collectors.

Linda Hiatt
Dimark Group
Software: Collectorpro 97
211 Surrey Trail Drive
Saint Peters, MO 63376
ph: 314-272-2113 or 800-336-7692
e-mail: info@collectorpro.com
web: http://www.collectorpro.com
Software to catalog collections; keep track of item information, financial information, customer information and expense tracking; record sales and track sales tax; many reports and labels; stores and prints photos; WIN or WIN95 only.

James S. Nixon
Whirlwind Technologies
Software: Collect!
P.O. Box 450907
Garland, TX 75045-0907
e-mail: jnixon@wwtech.com
web: http://www.wwtech.com/coll.htm
A system that allows you to work with collections of any type; program your own collection information in minutes; pre-defined templates for 15 types of collections including coins, stamps, comics, antiques, books, videos and more.

Fusion Software
Software: Value Vision
9337-B Katy Freeway, Ste. 444
Houston, TX 77024
ph: 713-465-6363
fax: 713-465-9749
A personal inventory manager; Windows program to capture the contents of your home or office; quick, fun and easy; over 600 colorful icons to help you identify rooms and items; produces insurance claims form.

Bette Laswell
BDL Homeware
Software: BDL
P.O. Box 18385
Tucson, AZ 85731-8385
ph: 520-298-4212 or 800-487-5206
fax: 520-885-1606
e-mail: bdlhomeware@juno.com
Sells software for collectors and dealers; no computer skills required; inventories collections for insurance, keeps track of sales, does mailings, etc.; free catalog; also general bookkeeping software.

Third Rail
Software: Collector, The
3377 Cimarron Dr.
Santa Ynez, CA 93460
ph: 805-688-7370
e-mail: webmaster@thirdrail.com
web: http://www.thirdrail.com/
Sells computer inventory program for collectors; organize your collectibles; store up to 225,000 items.

ArtStacks
Software: ArtStacks
57 Marguerite Ave.
Mill Valley, CA 94941
ph: 415-388-6917
fax: 415-389-6172
e-mail: bruce@artstacks.com
web: http://www.artstacks.com/
A collection management software program for Macintosh computers: purchase and appraisal information, images, framing information, edition information, provenance, exhibitions, bibliography, maintenance and restoration records, etc.

Roger Graham
Every Era Antiques
855 57th St.
Sacramento, CA 95819-3300
ph: 916-456-1767
e-mail: roger@every-era.com
web: http://www.every-era.com
Sells eBay software for auto search, auto submit, and auto respond; aids buyers and sellers by making eBay auction process quicker and easier.

Steven Hudgik
PSG - HomeCraft Software
Software: HomeCraft
P.O. Box 974
Tualatin, OR 97062-0974
ph: 503-692-3732
fax: 503-692-0382
e-mail: info@homecraft.com
web: http://www.homecraft.com
A leading publisher of software for cataloging collections of music, books, videos, coins, stamps, Beanie Babies, license plates, and baseball cards.

Innovative Logic Corp.
Software: Collector Pro
330 Jasper Highway
Smith Falls, Ontario K7A 4S5
Canada
ph: 613-284-0647 or 800-242-4775
e-mail: dalest@innovativelogic.com
web: http://www.innovativelogic.com/collector/
Computerized collections database program.

PrimaSoft PC, Inc.
Software: Collectibles Catalog
P.O. Box 456
Surrey, British Columbia V3T 5B7
Canada
ph: 800-371-7520 or 604-951-1085
fax: 604-951-7797
e-mail: support@primasoft.com
web: http://www.primasoft.com/co.htm
For beginners and advanced users; designed to help to store information about different types of collectibles such as bears, dolls, miniatures, house plants, jewelry, Precious Moments figurines, Coca-Cola memorabilia, etc.

Insurance

Misc. Services

Tony Bucci
International Collectors Insurance Agency
P.O. Box 6991
Warwick, RI 02886-6991
ph: 800-691-1114
fax: 401-823-0240
Insurer of collections; specializing in china, porcelain, glass, crystal, ceramics, figurines, pottery; comprehensive coverage including accidental breakage, flood and earthquake.

Patty Rickey
RL & G Agency, Inc.
P.O. Box 426
Norwich, CT 06360
ph: 800-962-0431
Offers special protection policies for collectors.

American Collectors Insurance, Inc.
P.O. Box 8343
Cherry Hill, NJ 08002-0343
ph: 800-360-2277 or 609-779-7212
fax: 609-779-7289
Provides "agreed value" insurance protection to collectors of dolls, model trains, vintage toys, limited edition figurines, plates/steins, ornaments; "paper" collectibles (e.g. stamps) and coins ineligible; call for free quote.

W. Danforth Walker
Collectibles Insurance Agency, Inc.
P.O. Box 1200
Westminster, MD 21158-0299
ph: 410-876-8833 or 888-837-9537
fax: 410-876-9233
e-mail: collectinsure@pipeline.com
web: http://www.collectinsure.com
Insurance for collectibles, collectors, dealers and collector/dealers; all risk coverage; no listing required unless an item is over $5,000 in value; no appraisal required; specialized collectibles coverage for over 30 years.

Jim Tucker
Association Insurance Administrators
P.O. Box 2963
Huntersville, NC 28070
ph: 800-618-1787 or 704-895-9209
fax: 704-895-0230
Provides property and liability insurance to all dealers, mall owners, collectors, show promoters; programs sponsored by the Antiques & Collectibles Dealer Association.

Mercy A. Komar, CIC
Insurance Center, The
P.O. Box 271
Warren, OH 44482-0271
ph: 330-394-6444 or 800-546-6444
fax: 330-393-8118
e-mail: insurancecenter@neonet.net
web: http://www.inscntrs.com/
Specializing in insurance for dealers and collectors; member of Antiques & Collectibles Dealers Association and of the Society of Certified Insurance Counselors.

Unirisc, Inc.
450 East 22nd St.
Lombard, IL 60148-6113
ph: 630-620-6562
fax: 630-932-8688
Provides fine arts insurance coverage for shops, galleries and collections; also coverage for shipping and storing.

Services For

Misc. Services

Dave Clark
National Collector Library
1331 Pleasant St.
Barre, MA 01005
ph: 978-355-6362
A nationwide clearinghouse and lifetime search service for collectors and collecting.

Bill Firla
Antique Researchers
P.O. Box 79
Waban, MA 02168-0001
ph: 617-449-1122
Research detectives specializing in all types of questions, problems, or issues relating to collectibles, art, antiques; identify artists, careers, craft persons, hallmarks, initials, logos, trademarks, provenance; does not buy or sell.

David & Becky Beane
Beane's Antiques & Photography
92 River Rd.
Benton, ME 04901
ph: 207-453-6790
fax: 207-453-6790
e-mail: dbeane@mint.net
web: http://www.metigues.com/catgalog/beane.html
A photography business specializing in illustrations of antiques for antiques publications, auctions, dealer advertisements and all relating photography; travels and covers the northern New England area.

Andrew Katz
Windham Antiques Research Service
P.O. Box 1212
Norwich, VT 05055-1212
ph: 802-649-5712
e-mail: windham@bmark.com
web: http://bmark.com/windham.antiques/
Specialty is research providing identification, documentation, historical and biographical background information pertaining to antiques, silver, ceramics and fine art for dealers, appraisers, and collectors.

Edward J. Pfeiffer
361 Lovely St.
Avon, CT 06001-4071
ph: 860-673-4120
fax: 860-676-9481
Publicity & public relations services for auctions, shows, dealers, museums; writing speeches, scripts, presentations.

Stanley & Bob Block
Block's Box
P.O. Box 51
Trumbull, CT 06611-0051
ph: 203-261-0057 or 203-926-8448
fax: 203-261-7033
e-mail: blockschip@aol.com
web: http://www.blocksite.com/
Produce video tapes & catalogs for auctioneers and appraisers; full state-of-the-art video tape production facility.

Flora Hanst
Thesaurus Group Ltd.
111 5th Ave.
New York, NY 10003
ph: 800-491-FIND
fax: 516-944-5278
e-mail: Jason@thesaurus.co.uk
web: http://www.thesaurus.co.uk/
A pre-sale auction search service; a fee based service for subscribers to get advanced notice of upcoming items for sale at auctions around the world.

Richard Michael Gramly, PhD
Great Lakes Artifact Repository
79 Perry St.
Buffalo, NY 14203-3037
ph: 716-849-0149
fax: 716-852-0093
Stores, sells, and conserves artifacts from all parts of the world in a secure, fireproof, climate-controlled working room and vault; examining room with drafting and photographic facilities; cataloguing of incoming collections, etc.

Harry L. Rinker
Institute for the Study of Antiques & Collectibles
5093 Vera Cruz Rd.
Emmaus, PA 18049-9554
ph: 610-965-1122
fax: 610-965-1124
e-mail: rinker@fast.net
web: http://www.rinker.com
Educational organization that offers seminars and workshops designed to improve business and object skills in the field of antiques and collectibles.

Donald L. Raleigh
Period Antiques Delivery Service, Inc.
P.O. Box 205
Millington, MD 21651
ph: 410-778-4357 or 800-962-1424
e-mail: pads@dmv.com
web: http://www.padsinc.com/index.html
Specializes in the professional transportation of antiques and works of art.

Joan C. Browning
Papilion Lane Press
P.O. Box 436
Ronceverte, WV 24970-0436
ph: 304-645-6799
fax: 304-645-6799
e-mail: oma00013@mail.wvnet.edu
Syndicate distributing antiques/history features to subscribing newspapers and periodicals; publicist for history/antiques entities on contract basis; research in material culture; lectures to historical organizations & college classes.

Asheford Institute of Antiques
775 Gulf Shore Dr.
Destin, FL 32541
e-mail: antqcourse@aol.com
web: http://members.aol.com/antqcourse
Offers a home study course for those wishing to start an antiques business.

Timothy Haines
Auction Consultants
1077 Celestial St.
Rookwood Bldg. 3, Ste. 400
Cincinnati, OH 45202
ph: 513-961-5794
fax: 513-651-0860
e-mail: advigroup@aol.com
web: http://members.aol.com/advigroup
Consulting individuals on auction consignments; finding the best auction for their art and antiques.

Robert Reed, Ed.
Antique & Collectible News Service
P.O. Box 204
Knightstown, IN 46148-0204
ph: 765-345-7479
fax: 765-345-7479
e-mail: ACNS@aol.com
Provides articles and book reviews to publications around the US and worldwide; more than 500 topics; lists available.

Judy L. Campbell
Attic Antiques
P.O. Box 27
Midland, MI 48640-0027
ph: 517-631-9263 or 517-631-4874
Syndicated antiques columnist specializing in answering readers' questions regarding the history and status of their antiques and collectibles in today's market; also refers readers to specialists, clubs and other related resources.

Mary Antoine deJulio
Antoine & Associates
317 S. Wacouta Ave.
Prairie Du Chien, WI 53821
ph: 608-326-8225 or 608-326-6626
fax: 608-326-8225
Assistance in the care, management, protection, conservation, research, and documentation of American 18th and 19th century antiques.

Jim Crawford
Crawford Direct Marketing
7944 Curtis Ave.
Omaha, NE 68134-2162
ph: 402-571-0736
e-mail: fair@tias.com
web: http://www.CrawfordDirect.com
A direct marketing company specializing in the antiques and collectibles industry; offers imaginative ideas in mail and internet advertising; also provides information on how to create and design successful web sites.

David Lisot
Advision, Inc.
3100 Arrowwood Lane
Boulder, CO 80303
ph: 303-444-2320 or 800-876-2320
Advision specializes in producing and distributing videotapes about coins and collectibles; currently over 100 video titles available.

Supplies For

(see also ANTIQUES & COLLECTIBLES; ANTIQUES DEALERS & COLLECTORS, Computer Programs For; AUCTION CATALOGS; BLACKLIGHTS [UV LAMPS]; GEMS & JEWELRY Suppliers; REPAIR/RESTORATION/ CONSERVATION, Archival Supplies For; REPAIR/RESTORATION/ CONSERVATION, Woodworking)

Suppliers

Arlington Industries
2617 Vermont Route 7A
Arlington, VT 05250-8882
ph: 802-375-6139 or 888-308-4333
fax: 802-375-9549
e-mail: info@plateholders.com
web: http://www.plateholders.com
Sells sturdy, safe and crystal clear plateholders for museums, galleries and collectors.

Kit Barry
Kit Barry Ephemera Supplies
88 High Street Box S-I
Brattleboro, VT 05301
ph: 802-254-3634
web: http://www.tradecards.com/kb/
Sells ephemera supplies: plastic pages, matchbook pages, rigid print holders, soft plastic sleeves, et.

Russell Norton
Photographic Antiques
P.O. Box 1070
New Haven, CT 06504-1070
ph: 203-562-7800
Carries 14 sizes of clear 2.5 mil polypropylene archival sleeves for photos and postcards up to 16" x 20".

Collector's House
1739 Hwy. 9 North
Howell, NJ 07731
ph: 800-448-9298 or 732-845-3260
fax: 732-845-3236
e-mail: collectorshouse@iop.com
web: http://www.cardmall.com/collectors-house/
Showcases, tabletop display cases, jewelry displays, display mounts, butterfly boxes, fitted table covers, wrapping pads, Beanie Baby cases.

Dealers Supply, Inc.
P.O. Box 717
Matawan, NJ 07747
ph: 732-591-2883 or 800-524-0576
fax: 732-591-8571
e-mail: dlrsply@worldnet.att.net
web: http://www.dlrsupply.com
Carries table covers, aluminum show cases, canopies, lights, alarms, etc.

Robbins Container Corp.
222 Conover St.
Brooklyn, NY 11231-1033
ph: 718-875-3204
fax: 718-797-3529
Carries corrugated mailers, cartons, boxes, stretch film, stackable cardboard bins, tote boxes, storage chests, strapping and sealing tape, foam, polystyrene chips, mailing envelopes, twine, bubble wrap, etc.

Mega-National Industries Inc.
P.O. Box 538
Round Lake, NY 12151-0538
ph: 518-899-6190 or 518-827-4443
Supplier of canopy tent units, and dealer display equipment; also archival quality protection polysleeves, archival rigids, semi-rigid sleeves for postcards, currency, stereoviews; archival pocket pages, backing boards, etc.

Bags Unlimited
7 Canal St.
Rochester, NY 14608-1910
ph: 800-767-2247 or 716-436-9006
fax: 716-328-8526
e-mail: bags@frontiernet.net
web: http://www.frontiernet.net/~bags/
Sells collector supplies: poly and paper sleeves, mailers, filler pads, album jackets, storage boxes, divider cards, etc.

Brodart Company
P.O. Box 300
Mc Elhattan, PA 17748
ph: 800-820-4377 or 570-769-3265
fax: 800-283-6087
e-mail: supplies@brodart.com
web: http://www.brodart.com
Carries clear protective covers for books; protect book dust jackets - they may represent half or more of the value of a book.

SAFE Publications, Inc.
P.O. Box 263
Southampton, PA 18966-0263
ph: 215-357-9049
fax: 215-357-5202
Sells collecting systems for postcards, covers, documents, pins, medals, badges, stamps, coins, banknotes, telephone cards, etc.; crystal clear sleeves are PVC free.

W.C. Golden, Sr.
GOlden's Antique Supply
311 Independence Way
Woodstock, GA 30188
ph: 888-202-1029 or 770-924-8528
fax: 770-924-5991
e-mail: wcgolden@antiquesupply.com
web: http://www.antiquesupply.com
An extensive on-line site for antique related supplies and equipment for the beginner to the professional.

Terri Harlan
Mylan Enterprises
P.O. Box 971002
Boca Raton, FL 33497-1002
ph: 800-852-8119 or 561-852-0861
fax: 561-852-0862
e-mail: sales@mylanusa.com
web: http://www.mylanusa.com/
Carries a wide assortment of Wrapping Pads, Bubble Packs and Bubble Bags.

Allan Koskela
Allan Koskela Restorations
P.O. Box 186
Webster City, IA 50595
ph: 515-832-1131
Sells extremely durable high impact polyethylene containers; never wear out; light weight; airtight lockable; safer and more cost effective than cardboard boxes or wooden crates.

Demco
P.O. Box 7488
Madison, WI 53707
Carries clear protective covers for books; protect book dust jackets - they may represent half or more of the value of a book.

Kurt Keifer
Kiefer Supply
417 Stanton Ave.
Fergus Falls, MN 56537
ph: 218-736-7000 or 888-543-3377
fax: 218-736-7474
e-mail: service@kiefers.com
web: http://www.kiefers.com/
Acrylic stands, wrapping pads, banners, blacklights, bubble wrap, cartons, cash boxes, dollies, easels, fasteners, forms holders, inventory items, jewelry tags, knobs & finials, labels, laminated signs, magnifiers, pennants, etc.

Ronald Nootbaar
Roberts Colonial House, Inc.
570 W. 167th St.
South Holland, IL 60473
ph: 708-331-6233
fax: 708-331-0538
Sells plate hangers, plate stands, Plexiglass display cubes, quilted vinyl china cases, and over 1600 other items; send for catalog.

Maas International
1500 West 55th St.
La Grange, IL 60525
ph: 708-246-8581
fax: 708-246-8690
Sells Maas Polishing Creme, an amazing product that cleans, polishes and protects all metals: gold, pewter, dirigold, silver, aluminum, chrome, brass, dirilyte, Plexiglas, copper, stainless steel, enamel, and more.

Sandler Products, Inc.
2229 S. Halsted St.
Chicago, IL 60608
ph: 312-226-1414
Sells blue underpads - very useful for wrapping fragile items.

Boss Mfg. Co.
221 West First St.
Kewanne, IL 61443
ph: 800-447-4581 or 309-852-2131
fax: 309-852-0848
Carries a line of nylon tricot inspectors gloves for the safe handling of silver, glass, jewelry, etc.

Collector's Care
4455 Torrance Blvd., #297
Torrance, CA 90503-4398
ph: 800-595-ACID or 805-497-7445
Supplies acid-free paper, boxes and related products for storing dolls, doll clothing, teddy bears, pressed flowers, wedding and christening gowns, quilts, needlepoint, heirlooms and linens.

Jones West Packaging Co.
P.O. Box 1084 - Dept. DL
Rohnert Park, CA 94927-1084
ph: 707-795-8552
Supplier of all sizes of ZIP CLOSE plastic bags and flat bags in small or large quantities; since 1981; credit cards accepted; catalog available.

Collector Items
P.O. Box 55511
Seattle, WA 98155
ph: 206-365-1188
fax: 206-367-1188
Sells nylon bubble bags.

Supplies For (Lighting)

Suppliers

Jon Wokuluk
Westgate Enterprises
2118 Wilshire Blvd., Ste. 612
Santa Monica, CA 90403-5784
ph: 310-477-5891
fax: 310-478-1954
e-mail: daylight@ix.netcom.com
Carries over 100 different full spectrum light bulbs and tubes; improved, glare-free, color corrected light bulbs that improve display lighting.

Supplies For (Safes)

Suppliers

Kingsberry Mfg. Corp.
715 W. Zavale
Crystal City, TX 78839
ph: 800-445-0763
Sells new safes for collectors.

Supplies For (Showcases)

Dealers

GEMO Display Cases
6952 Ponteberry Street
Canton, OH 44718
ph: 330-499-2023
fax: 330-499-3382
e-mail: info@gemodisplays.com
web: http://www.gemodisplays.com/
Glass and mirror contemporary design display cases; anti-static, dust

proof, scratch proof, non tarnishing; large sizes available.

Man./Prod./Dist.

Roger Kleinschmidt
Golf Ball Art & Custom Displays
21218 St. Andrews Blvd., Ste. 620
Boca Raton, FL 33486
ph: 888-296-4133 or 561-417-5010
fax: 561-417-5010
e-mail: golfart@icanect.net
web: http://golfballart.com/
Builds golf ball display cases for collectors or to be given as awards of gifts; unique because of a new concept of attaching balls to a surface; made of oak or acrylic and of any size; takes up less wall or desk space.

Charles Wood
McAvoy/Wood-Working Co.
P.O. Box 27
Bethel, OH 45106
ph: 513-734-7374 or 513-752-2559
fax: 513-752-8156
e-mail: mac2wood@one.net
web: http://w3.one.net/~mac2wood/
Makes antique type chests, gun and knife cases; Civil War period camp chests, antique style gun and knife cases, logo golf ball display cases, custom jewelry boxes.

Suppliers

Megaworks
P.O. Box 341
East Hampton, CT 06424
ph: 860-267-7640
fax: 860-267-7641
Carries displays and aluminum show cases.

Dave Cohen
Dave Cohen & Associates
P.O. Box 868
Westwood, NJ 07675-0868
ph: 201-666-2222
fax: 201-666-2282
Supplier of glass display show cases for antiques shops, malls, co-ops, and private collectors.

Showcases by Lin Terry
1000 Airport Rd., #103
Lakewood, NJ 08701-5960
ph: 732-370-5252
fax: 732-370-4114
e-mail: linterry@aol.com
Sells handcrafted acrylic collectible display cases for trains, dolls, ships, sports memorabilia, comic books, magazines, wax boxes, figurines, etc.; many sizes; call or write for free catalog.

Monique Caron-Krug, CEO
Showcase Sales Gallery, Inc.
43 Main Street
P.O. Box 312
Otego, NY 13825
ph: 607-988-9173 or 800-246-2940
fax: 607-988-9173
e-mail: showcase@telenet.net
web: http://www.showcasesales.com
Showcases, display cases and cabinets for a beautiful presentation of collectibles or shop merchandise; various styles and sizes.

National Showcase Company
49 West Aylesbury
Timonium, MD 21093
ph: 800-628-2352 or 410-252-7700
Distributes Allstate aluminum showcases.

Chris R. Jensen
Streamwood, Inc.
121 Gulf St.
P.O. Box 1841
Easley, SC 29641-1841
ph: 864-859-2915 or 800-453-0398
fax: 864-855-5010
e-mail: cjensen@streamwood.net
web: http://www.streamwood.net
Sells BoxWare display cases made from tough injection molded plastic, not cardboard; latched lids so no more straight pins; replaceable glass or acrylic lenses.

Antique Mall Showcases
3039 W. Antioch Rd.
Springville, TN 38256
ph: 800-839-4928
Large capacity showcases, 40 watt fluorescent bulbs.

Bluegrass Case Company
272 Airport Rd.
P.O. Box 386
Stanton, KY 40380
ph: 606-663-9871 or 800-668-9871
fax: 606-663-6369
Sells black collector frames; also walnut, cherry or oak frames with locks.

Janie Jinks-Weidner
13706 Robins Rd.
Westerville, OH 43082
ph: 614-965-2868 or 800-444-1280
fax: 614-965-5913
e-mail: janiew48@aol.com
web: http://members.aol.com/JanieW48/
Sells hand-held display frames good for displaying scouting, arrowheads, knives, jewelry, fossils, minerals, militaria, Indian artifacts, spoons, Civil War relics, poker chips; 186 different sizes.

Coneaut Glass
200 East Main Rd.
Conneaut, OH 44030
ph: 440-593-6622
fax: 440-593-6015
Makes glass enclosures with oak bases for Barbie dolls, Ginny dolls, and Madam Alexander dolls.

Sales Dept.
Jamar Company
5015 State Rd.
Dept. MACR
Medina, OH 44256-8427
ph: 330-239-2889
fax: 330-239-2889
Manufactures and sells a wide selection of acrylic display cases and cabinets.

Specialty Plastic Fabrications
972 Kahn Ave.
Hamilton, OH 45011-4458
ph: 800-582-9038 or 513-856-9475
fax: 513-856-9133
e-mail: cases@zoomtown.com
web: http://www.specialtyplasticfab.com
Sells crystal clear acrylic display cases for dolls, antiques, toys, and other fine collectibles.

Collectible Displays, Inc.
9846 Crescent Park Dr.
West Chester, OH 45069
ph: 513-777-7784
fax: 513-777-7761
Solid wood lit display cabinets of the highest quality: hidden compartment under each shelf for wire storage, adjustable shelves, beveled glass, etc.

Douglas Hammetter
Creative Store Design, Inc.
3728 N Fratney St.
Milwaukee, WI 53212-1749
ph: 800-865-9595 or 414-963-1900
fax: 414-963-4445
Sells upright display cases or trophy cases; full vision, glass cube displays, countertop showcases; delivery and setup available.

Crystal Showcase Design
315 Atwater St.
Saint Paul, MN 55117
ph: 651-489-5328
Makes specialized showcases.

D. Roberts
139 W. Montana Ave.
Glendale Heights, IL 60139
ph: 630-690-0848
fax: 630-690-2756
e-mail: deroberts@super-highway.net
web: http://www.geocities.com/RodeoDrive/2504/glassdomes.html
Leading supplier of show cases and shadow boxes for collectibles; also carries a wide selection of glass domes.

Michael Cosentino
Marble Show-Case
6936 N. Overhill Ave.
Chicago, IL 60631
fax: 773-594-9479
e-mail: mikecoz@aol.com
web: http://marbleshowcase.com/
Sells display cases for marbles and other small collectibles; also sells and appraises marbles.

Militaire Promotions
6427 W. Irving Park Rd., Ste. 160
Chicago, IL 60634-2437
ph: 312-777-0499
Sell J-mount display boxes; glass-top display boxes for small collectibles: jewelry, watches, buttons, badges, etc.; all sizes.

Steve Lundin
Action Figure Display Case Co.
P.O. Box 7954
Chicago, IL 60680
ph: 773-395-3395
fax: 773-395-3495
e-mail: actioncc@enteract.com
web: http://www.enteract.com/~actioncc
Manufactures high quality display cases for all 12" action figures; full color combat backgrounds or cityscapes for Barbie; perfect for gifts, home or office.

Garrett's
1264 East 2073 Rd.
Eudora, KS 66025
ph: 785-542-2339 or 800-447-7508
Sells black collector frames and aluminum or cherry sales/display/ show cases.

Paul F. Gabel
Clear-View Display Cases
9251 Minnesota Ave.
Kansas City, KS 66112
ph: 913-299-8366
Manufacturers clear plastic display cases with solid oak, cherry, or walnut bases; ideal for model tractors, cars, trucks, etc.

Michael A. Pratt, Sr.
Collector's Display Case Co.
687 Co. Rd. “”U””
Rt. 2 Box 73
Fremont, NE 68025-9635
ph: 402-721-4765
fax: 402-721-4765
e-mail: mp@mb3.net
web: http://www.mb3.net/display/
Manufactures unique inexpensive cases to display, organize, and protect small collectibles of all types including marbles; send SASE for more information.

ANTIQUES SHOP DIRECTORIES

(see also FLEA MARKETS, Directories)

Periodicals

Lisa Freeman
AntiqueSource, Inc.
Guide: Sloan's Green Guide to Antiquing in New England
P.O. Box 270
Belmont, VT 05730
ph: 802-259-3614
fax: 802-259-3615
e-mail: info@antiquesource.com
web: http://www.antiquesource.com
The definitive guide to antiques dealers and related services in the New England region (ME, NH, VT, RI, CT, MA, Eastern NY, Long Island); dealer inventory, hours of operation, detailed directions, services offered.

Lisa Freeman
AntiqueSource, Inc.
Guide: Green Guide to Antiquing in the Midwest
P.O. Box 270
Belmont, VT 05730
ph: 802-259-3614
fax: 802-259-3615
e-mail: info@antiquesource.com
web: http://www.antiquesource.com
The definitive guide to antiques dealers and related services in the Midwest (IL, IN, MI, MN, OH, WI); dealer inventory, hours of operation, detailed directions, services offered.

Southern Antiques
Guide: Southern Antiques Shop Guide
P.O. Drawer 1107
Decatur, GA 30031-1107
ph: 404-289-0054 or 888-800-4997
fax: 404-286-9727
Lists the South's best antiques shops, hundreds of antiques shows, top auction houses, and special products and services.

Joan Bryant, Ed.
Antiques & Art Around Publishing, Inc.
Guide: Antiques & Art Around Florida
P.O. Box 2481
Fort Lauderdale, FL 33303-2481
ph: 954-768-9430 or 800-248-9430
fax: 954-768-0621
e-mail: aarf@shadow.com
web: http://www.aarf.com
Full color guide to Florida's antique shops; maps, shows, museums; feature articles on antiques and FL heritage.

David & Kim Leggett
Rainy Day Publishing
Directory: Antique Atlas, The
1740 N. Germantown Pkwy, Ste. 18
Cordova, TN 38018
ph: 800-456-9326 or 901-755-5233
fax: 901-755-2529
web: http://www.antiqnet.com/atlas/
A comprehensive guide to antiquing in America: over 15,000 shops and malls.

Judy Lloyd
FDS, Inc.
Directory: No Nonsense Antique Mall Directory
4 Brown Street
P.O. Box 188
Higginsport, OH 45131
ph: 937-375-3009
Directory of over 5,200 antique malls/multi-dealer antique shops in the US; alphabetically arranged by state/city; contains standardized listings of name, address, size, phone, hours and directions (when available); SASE for info.

Judy Lloyd
NoNonsense Antique Mall Directory
P.O. Box 188
101 Brown St.
Higginsport, OH 45131
ph: 937-375-4395
fax: 937-375-4394
e-mail: fdsinc@bright.net
web: http://www.AntiqueMallsUSA.com
Nationwide antique mall directory with over 5,000 multi-dealer listings; all states, easy to use; alphabetical format by state and city; name, size, address, phone, hours, directions.

Connie Swaim, Ed.
Mayhill Publications, Inc.
Guide: AntiqueWeek Antique Shop Directory
P.O. Box 90
Knightstown, IN 46148
ph: 765-345-5133 or 800-876-5133
fax: 800-695-8153
e-mail: antiquewk@aol.com
web: http://www.antiqueweek.com
AntiqueWeek Shop Guide is an annual directory that lists antique shops and malls; two editions are published: Eastern and Central.

Janice Reittinger
DJ's Publishing
Guide: Iowa's Complete Guide to Antique Shops & Malls
424 1st Ave. East
Dyersville, IA 52040-1301
ph: 319-875-8640 or 877-226-5351
web: http://www.collectoronline.com/guides/Iowa.html
Published every March; over 800 shops, shows, maps, want ad section.

Terri Vopelak
CarPac Publishing Co.
Guide: Antiques Shops Directory
1800 W. D St.
P.O. Box 601
Vinton, IA 52349-0601
ph: 319-472-4763 or 319-472-4764
fax: 319-472-3117
web: http://www.collectorsjournal.com/
Lists antiques shops in Illinois, Nebraska, Wisconsin, Kansas, Minnesota, Missouri, South Dakota, Texas and Iowa.

Shepart Swift
Moonlight Press
Guide: Taylor's Guide to Antique Shops in IL & So. WI
P.O. Box 5095
Buffalo Grove, IL 60089
ph: 847-465-3314
fax: 847-465-3307
e-mail: stiver@ix.com
web: http://www.collectoronline.com/guides/taylors.html
Address and phone numbers of all known antique shops in northern Illinois and southern Wisconsin; includes antiques show dates; repair people; maps; published every April.

Jan Lindenberger
Guide: Antique Buyer's Guide
P.O. Box 7224
Colorado Springs, CO 80933
ph: 719-591-9558
fax: 719-591-9558
Covering the states of KS, OK, NM, CO, MO, NE and TX; addresses, ads, maps.

Patricia F. Doering
Guide: Second Hand News
3120 41st St.
San Diego, CA 92105-4133
ph: 619-283-5245
fax: 800-243-8892
e-mail: secondhand@earthlink.net
web: http://www.bargainlink.com
A comprehensive 52 page 5"x8" guide to San Diego's thrift stores, rummage sales, swap meets, calendar of events, feature articles.

Bliss Cochran
Guide: Cochran's Collector's Guide for the West Coast
P.O. Box 750895
Petaluma, CA 94975-0895
ph: 707-769-9916 or 800-648-0526
fax: 707-769-0669
e-mail: cochran@sonic.net
web: http://www.cochrans.com
This directory is a map book covering the entire state of California with an annual listing of antique shows; free at stores and shows; $5 by mail.

British

Periodicals

Carol Fisher
Carol Fisher Publishing
Guide: Touring British Antique Shops
P.O. Box 531
Melksham, Wiltshire SN12 8SL
U.K.
ph: 01225-700085
fax: 01225-790939
Annual paperback containing 60 illustrated guided tours of 3,500 antique shops in over 1400 towns and villages throughout Britain; compact and portable with 65 maps and full historic/tourist info enroute; $33.95 US airmail.

ANTIQUES SHOW PROMOTERS

Clubs/Associations

Mitchell Sorenson, Ex. Dir.
Professional Show Manager's Association
P.O. Box 30
Bloomfield, CT 06002
ph: 860-243-3977
fax: 860-286-0787
e-mail: msorensen@ssmgt.com
Promotes a Code of Ethics for the benefit of the consumer show industry and to facilitate the exchange of information among show managers of consumer shows.

Diana Bittel, Pres.
Antiques Council, The
P.O. Box 574
Southport, CT 06490
ph: 203-396-0192
fax: 203-396-0193
e-mail: info@antiquescouncil.com
web: http://www.antiquescouncil.com/home.htm
An association of approximately 80 members across the nation who manage antiques shows for charity sponsors; members abide by code of ethics; show schedule now includes seven annual shows; founded in 1990.

Jim Tucker
Antiques & Collectibles Show Promoters Association
P.O. Box 2782
Huntersville, NC 28070-2782
ph: 800-287-7127 or 704-895-9088
fax: 704-895-0230
e-mail: info@showpromoters.org
web: http://www.showpromoters.org
Provides benefits directed solely to the show promoter and manager; 5 regions nationwide with annual meetings in each region and nationally; benefits include a newsletter with contributions from show managers, networking, insurance.

Misc. Services

Vivien Cord
Cord Shows, Ltd.
4 Whippoorwill Lane
Armonk, NY 10504
ph: 914-273-4667
fax: 914-273-4656
e-mail: shows@cordshows.com
web: http://www.cordshows.com/
Has been running antiques shows and fine art and crafts fairs for over thirty years.

ANTIQUITIES

(see also ARCHAEOLOGY; COINS & CURRENCY, Coins [Ancient]; PRECOLUMBIAN; PREHISTORIC ARTIFACTS)

Appraisers

Frederick P. Dose, Jr.
Frederick Dose Appraisals Ltd.
778 Pleasant Ave.
Highland Park, IL 60035-4613
ph: 847-433-7870 or 847-433-1090
Appraises Egyptian, Greek, Roman, etc. art for insurance, corporate, private, and attorneys; references on request; 6 year full-time as University art historian.

Auction Services

Greg Manning
Greg Manning Auctions, Inc.
775 Passaic Ave.
West Caldwell, NJ 07006
ph: 973-882-0004 or 800-221-0243
fax: 973-882-3499
e-mail: gmauction@aol.com
web: http://www.gregmanning.com/
Since 1905, a leading auctioneer of Americana, glass, stoneware, and antiquities.

Howard Rose
Arte Primitivo
3 East 65th St., Ste. 2
New York, NY 10021
ph: 212-570-6999
fax: 212-570-1899
e-mail: arteprim@idt.net
web: http://www.arteprimitivo.com/
Specializes in Classical and Egyptian antiquities, pre-Columbian art, ethnographic art, Asian antiquities, and books; conducts absentee/callback auctions biannually and publishes lavish color catalog with each auction.

Christie's
502 Park Ave.
New York, NY 10022
ph: 212-546-1000
fax: 212-980-8163
web: http://www.christies.com

Alex G. Malloy
Alex G. Malloy, Inc.
P.O. Box 38
South Salem, NY 10590-0038
ph: 203-438-0396 or 203-438-9652
fax: 203-438-6744
e-mail: alexmalloy@aol.com
web: http://members.aol.com/AlexMalloy/agmalloy.htm
Issues fixed price lists and mail bid sales of ancient and medieval coinage, and of ancient art and antiquities for sale; author of "Official Price Guide to Artifacts of Ancient Civilizations."

Dealers

John Ambrose
Fragments of Time
P.O. Box 376
Marshfield Hills, MA 02051
ph: 508-359-0090
fax: 508-390-0090
e-mail: fragments@aol.com
web: http://www.antiquities.net
Collector, dealer, expert, and appraiser of ancient Greek, Roman, Egyptian, Etruscan and Near Eastern art; known worldwide for museum-quality art at competitive prices; authenticity guaranteed.

Norman Hurst, ISA
Hurst Gallery
53 Mount Auburn St.
Cambridge, MA 02138
ph: 617-491-6888
fax: 617-661-0439
e-mail: NHurst@compuserve.com
web: http://www.hurstgallery.com
Has been consulting, appraising and dealing in Ancient art for over 25 years: Greek, Roman, Egyptian, ancient glass, Osiris, Isis, bronze, faience.

Allen G. Berman
Allen G. Berman Professional Numismatist
P.O. Box 605
Fairfield, CT 06430-0605
ph: 914-434-6090 or 914-434-6079
fax: 914-434-6079
e-mail: agberman@aol.com
Medieval, Byzantine and European seals including sealed documents, lead seals to modern times, medieval pilgrim badges; consultant to auction houses on attribution of seals, oil lamps and pottery; no New World or Far Eastern handled.

Sadigh Gallery
303 Fifth Ave., Ste. 1603
New York, NY 10016
ph: 800-426-2007 or 212-725-7537
fax: 212-545-7612
e-mail: sales@ipgroup.com
web: http://www.ipgroup.com/sadigh/
Framed antiquities, arrowheads and stone tools, ancient coins and jewelry, fossils, biblical artifacts, Persian ceramics.

Alex G. Malloy
Alex G. Malloy, Inc.
P.O. Box 38
South Salem, NY 10590-0038
ph: 203-438-0396 or 203-438-9652
fax: 203-438-6744
e-mail: alexmalloy@aol.com
web: http://members.aol.com/AlexMalloy/agmalloy.htm
Issues fixed price lists and mail bid sales of ancient and medieval coinage, and of ancient art and antiquities for sale; author of "Official Price Guide to Artifacts of Ancient Civilizations."

Frank J. Wagner
Classica Antiquities
P.O. Box 509
Syracuse, NY 13201-0509
ph: 315-687-0036 or 315-457-7249
e-mail: clasant@servtech.com
web: http://www.servtech.com/~clasant/
For over 30 years buying/selling ancient and medieval Greek, Roman, Egyptian, Near Eastern coins and antiquities.

Allan Anawati
Medusa Antiquities
10 Notre Dame East, Ste. 310
Montreal, Quebec H2Y 1B7
Canada
ph: 514-874-0337 or 514-876-1373
fax: 514-876-7998
e-mail: anawti@bam.net
web: http://www.anawati.com
Dealing in Egyptian, Greek, Roman, and Near Eastern antiquities for over 30 years.

Museums/Libraries

Abbe Museum
P.O. Box 286
Bar Harbor, ME 04609
ph: 207-288-3519
web: http://www.abbemuseum.org/
Discover 10,000 years of Indian culture, history and art through changing exhibits, hands-on programs and workshops taught by Native artists.

British Museum, The
Great Russell Street
London, WC1B 3DG
U.K.
ph: 0171 636 1555 or 0171 580 1788
fax: 0171 323 8614
e-mail: info@british-museum.ac.uk
web: http://www.british-museum.ac.uk/
World famous collections housed in beautiful neoclassical building; covering humankind's artistic achievements from Ancient Egypt, Greece and Rome to Anglo-Saxon England and Renaissance Europe.

Periodicals

Magazine: Celator, The
P.O. Box 911
Gainesville, MO 65655
ph: 417-679-2142
fax: 417-679-2524
e-mail: wayne@celator.com
web: http://www.celator.com/
A monthly magazine focusing on antiquities and ancient coins; ads, articles, auction reports, etc.

Emma Beatty
Aurora Publications Ltd.
Magazine: Minerva
14 Old Bond St.
London, W1X 3BD
U.K.
ph: 44 171 495 2590
fax: 44 171 491 1595
The international review of ancient art and archaeology; a bi-monthly illustrated magazine focusing on ancient art, antiquities, archaeology and numismatic discoveries worldwide.

Egyptian

Dealers

David Markarian
Markarian Ancient Artifacts
P.O. Box 2476
Rancho Mirage, CA 92270-1087
ph: 760-202-5000
e-mail: orion@inland.net
web: http://www.ancientart.org/
Buys and sells Egyptian artifacts.

Allan Anawati
Medusa
10 Notre Dame East, Ste. 310
Montreal, Quebec H2Y 1B7
Canada
ph: 514-874-0337 or 514-876-1373
fax: 514-876-7998
e-mail: anawti@bam.net
web: http://www.anawati.com
Dealing in Egyptian, Greek, Roman, and Near Eastern antiquities for over 30 years.

Henk F. Dijkstra
Anubis Ancient Art
P.O. Box 24340
Rotterdam, 3007 DJ
Netherlands
ph: +31 (10) 4332236
fax: +31 (10) 4332236
e-mail: anubis@worldonline.nl
web: http://www.antiquities-on-line.com/dealers/anubis/
Buys and sells high quality ancient Egyptian, Roman and Greek art; specializes in Egyptian art.

Greek & Roman

Dealers

Allan Anawati
Medusa Ancient Art
10 Notre Dame East, Ste. 310
Montreal, Quebec H2Y 1B7
Canada
ph: 514-874-0337 or 514-876-1373
fax: 514-876-7998
e-mail: anawti@bam.net
web: http://www.anawati.com
Dealing in Egyptian, Greek, Roman, and Near Eastern antiquities for over 30 years.

Museums/Libraries

Ellen Reeder
Walters Art Gallery
600 N. Charles St.
Baltimore, MD 21201
ph: 410-547-9000
e-mail: lwolfe@thewalters.org
web: http://www.thewalters.org/
One of only a few museums worldwide to present a comprehensive history of art from the third millennium B.C. to the early 20th century.

Toledo Museum of Art, The
2445 Monroe St.
P.O. Box 1013
Toledo, OH 43697
ph: 419-255-8000 or 800-644-6862
web: http://www.toledomuseum.org/
Internationally-recognized collection of Greek vases, as well as glass, paintings, and decorative arts.

Medieval

Museums/Libraries

Dr. Gary Vikan
Walters Art Gallery
600 N. Charles St.
Baltimore, MD 21201
ph: 410-547-9000
e-mail: lwolfe@thewalters.org
web: http://www.thewalters.org/
One of only a few museums worldwide to present a comprehensive history of art from the third millennium B.C. to the early 20th century.

Repro. Sources

Medieval Replicas
1925 Marber ave.
Long Beach, CA 90815-3111
ph: 562-431-0402
Excellent quality weapons and armor; write for free catalog.

ANTLERS

(see ANIMAL TROPHIES; FURNITURE [ANTIQUE], Antler & Horn)

APOTHECARY ANTIQUES

(see MEDICAL, DENTAL & PHARMACEUTICAL)

APPLE PARERS

(see also KITCHEN COLLECTIBLES)

Clubs/Associations

Gerald W. Laverty
International Society of Apple Parer Enthusiasts
Newsletter: ISAPE Newsletter
735 Cedarwood Terrace
Rochester, NY 14609
ph: 716-654-6998
web: http://www.collectoronline.com/clubs/ISAPE/
Holds conventions; 12-page newsletter contains articles, old ads, patents and a buy/sell section; to date over 100 photos of different models have been presented.

Collectors

Johnny Appleseed
8060 Sierra St.
Fair Oaks, CA 95628-7549
ph: 916-961-7174
Apple peelers wanted; give patent dates, model and description.

APPLIANCES

(see ELECTRICITY RELATED ITEMS, Appliances; FANS, Mechanical; KITCHEN COLLECTIBLES; STOVES; RANGES; TOASTERS, Electric)

APPRAISAL ASSOCIATIONS

(see also "APPRAISERS" Appendix in the back of this book for hundreds of educated, trained and tested ISA appraisers; additional Appraisers are also listed under specific categories throughout this Directory.)

Clubs/Associations

Victor Wiener, Ex. Dir.
Appraisers Association of America
Newsletter: Appraiser, The
386 Park Ave. S #2000
New York, NY 10016-8804
ph: 212-889-5404
fax: 212-889-5503
e-mail: AppraisersAssn@compuserve.com
web: http://www.appraisersassoc.org/
Oldest nonprofit association of personal property appraisers with approximately 1,000 members in more than 600 subspecialties in all areas of fine art, antiques, and collectibles; membership directory available.

Deborah A. Sharpe
Appraisal Foundation, The
Newsletter: Foundation News
1029 Vermont Ave. NW, Ste. 900
Washington, DC 20005-3517
ph: 202-347-7722
fax: 202-347-7727
e-mail: staff@appraisalfoundation.org
web: http://www.appraisalfoundation.org
Authorized by Congress as the source of appraisal standards and appraiser qualifications.

Rebecca L. Maxey
American Society of Appraisers
P.O. Box 17265
Washington, DC 20071
ph: 703-478-2228 or 800-ASA-VALU
fax: 703-742-8471
e-mail: asainfo@appraisers.org
web: http://www.appraisers.org
Publishes "Business Valuation Review," "Personal Property Journal," and "MTS Journal"; contact ASA for subscription information.

Christian Coleman, Ex. Dir.
International Society of Appraisers
Newsletter: Professional Appraisers Information Exchange
16040 Christensen Rd., Ste. 102
Seattle, WA 98188
ph: 206-241-0359 or 888-472-4732
fax: 206-241-0436
e-mail: ISA_HQ@compuserve.com
web: http://www.isa-appraisers.org
Largest association of professional personal property appraisers; over 1,300 members specializing in all areas of antiques & residential contents, gems & jewelry, fine art, machinery & equipment; free referrals; directory available.

Canadian Association of Personal Property Appraisers
Newsletter: CAPPA News
2 Briar Place
Halifax, Nova Scotia B3M 2X2
Canada
ph: 902-443-5698
fax: 902-443-5698
Membership consists of individuals covering all areas of personal property appraising, excluding vehicles of all types and heavy industrial equipment.

Internet Resources

David J. Maloney, Jr., ISA CAPP
MaloneysOnline Antiques & Collectibles Resource Directory
P.O. Box 2049
Frederick, MD 21702-1049
ph: 301-695-8544
fax: 301-695-6491
e-mail: dave@maloney.com
web: http://www.maloneysonline.com/
Online resource information source for collectors, sellers, claims adjusters, etc.: includes experts, buyers, clubs, periodicals, repairers, museums/libraries, appraisers, auctioneers, matching services, dealers, etc.

Misc. Services

Stephen J. Abt, III
ArtFact, Inc.
Price Guide: ArtFact
1130 Ten Rod Rd., Ste. E104
North Kingstown, RI 02852-4158
ph: 401-295-2656 or 800-278-3228
fax: 401-295-2629
e-mail: sales@artfact.com
web: http://www.artfact.com
A computerized library recording auction sales of art and antiques; complete descriptions, prices realized, on-screen images.

William D. Hoefer, FGA, GG
Hoefers' Gemological Services
5016 Alan Ave., Ste. B4
San Jose, CA 95124-5741
ph: 408-264-0670
fax: 408-264-0725
e-mail: editor@appraiserunderoath.com
web: http://www.appraiserunderoath.com/
Offers experts consultation and expert testimony to attorneys on personal property appraisal methodology, legal research, etc.

AQUARIUMS

Collectors

Tim LaGanke
14054 Sweetbriar Lane
Novelty, OH 44072
ph: 440-338-8745
Wants to buy antique and old aquariums; also wants old toy and model divers.

Gary Bagnall
3090 McMillan Rd.
San Luis Obispo, CA 93401-6730
ph: 805-542-9988 or 805-782-0238
fax: 805-542-9295
e-mail: zoomed@zoomed.com
Buys and sells antique aquariums and related pet products.

Magazines

Dealers

Steve Stewart
Steve Stewart "Aquarium Literature"
P.O. Box 610118
Flushing, NY 11361-0118
ph: 718-352-2242
Wants freshwater aquarium literature: books, magazines, ephemera on tropical, gold, native fish; thousands of issues in stock, including various full sets; claims to have the largest assortment available.

Ornaments

Collectors

Darryl Rehr
P.O. Box 641824
Los Angeles, CA 90064-6824
ph: 310-477-5229
fax: 310-268-8420
e-mail: dcrehr@earthlink.net
web: http://www.earthlink.net/~dcrehr/trans1.html
Wants attractive aquarium ornaments used in home aquariums: castles, sea creatures, divers, etc.

ARCHAEOLOGY

(see also AMERICAN INDIAN; ANTIQUITIES; HERITAGE RESOURCES; NATURAL HISTORY; FOSSILS; MINERAL SPECIMENS; PREHISTORIC ARTIFACTS; TREASURE HUNTING)

Clubs/Associations

Archaeological Institute of America
Magazine: Archaeology
656 Beacon St.
Boston, MA 02215-2006
ph: 617-353-9361
fax: 617-353-6550
e-mail: aia@BU.EDU
web: http://www.he.net/~archaeol/
Has phone numbers and addresses for all state archaeological departments; "Archaeology" is published bi-monthly; also publishes the "American Journal of Archaeology" quarterly; write for details.

Society for American Archaeology
900 2nd St. NE, #12
Washington, DC 20002
ph: 202-789-8200
fax: 202-789-0284
e-mail: headquarters@saa.org
web: http://www.saa.org/
Promotes interest in American archaeology; stimulates research, fosters professional associations, advocates the conservation of artifacts; works to eliminate the commercialization of antiquities.

Nancy Geasey, Mem. Sec.
Archeological Society of Maryland, Inc.
4302 Crow Rock Rd.
Myersville, MD 21773
ph: 301-293-2708
e-mail: ngeasey@kis.net
web: http://www.smcm.edu/Academics/soan/asm/home.htm

Joe Andrews, Sec./Treas.
Piedmont Archaeological Society of North & South Carolina
159 Marshdale Ave. SW
Concord, NC 28025

Robert K. Beasley, Sec.
Peach State Archaeological Society of Georgia
360 Copeland Lane
Marietta, GA 30063-7302

Troy Futral
Rebel State Archaeological Society of Alabama
85 Lee Road
Auburn, AL 36830

Jim Butler
Volunteer State Archaeological Society of Tennessee
510 N. Russell St.
Portland, TN 37148-2009

Barbara Tully
Green River Archaeological Society of Kentucky
P.O. Box 923
Benton, KY 42025-0903

Pete Schwinn, Sec.
Indiana Archaeological Society
14378 N. 400 W. Elwood
Elwood, IN 46036-9230

Mary Ann Freudenberg
Wolverine State Archaeological Society of Michigan
611 Niles Road
Saint Joseph, MI 49085

Belinda Filbrandt, Sec./Treas.
Hawkeye State Archaeological Society of Iowa
3967 Highway 22
Blue Grass, IA 52726-9400

Cathy Norton
Badger State Archaeological Society of Wisconsin
Journal: Central States Archaeological Journal
W7103 Cty C.
Monticello, WI 53570-9790
e-mail: cnorton@utelco.tds.net
web: http://www.csas-archaeology.org/

Carl Becker
Illinois State Archaeological Society
Newsletter: Field Notes
7941 St. James.
Springfield, IL 62707
Collectors of prehistoric Native American and Pre Columbian artifacts: arrowheads, axes, pottery, inc.

John Crowley, Ed.
Central States Archaeological Societies, Inc.
Journal: Central States Archaeological Journal
11552 Patty Ann
Saint Louis, MO 63146-5471
e-mail: C21stlouis@aol.com
web: http://www.csas-archaeology.org/
Endeavors to develop a better understanding among students and collectors of archaeological material, professional and nonprofessional, as well as museums and institutions of learning.

David Meiser, Sec.
Greater St. Louis Archaeological Society
3248 Brightwood
St. Charles, MO 63305-6510

Larry Swaim, Sec.
Arkansas Archaeological Society
20 Evesham Ln.
Bella Vista, AR 72714-4307

Brad Sather
Lone Star State Archaeological Society of Texas
812 Wagon Trail
Austin, TX 78758-1805

Michael J. Rodeffer
Society for Historical Archaeology
Newsletter: Historical Archaeology
P.O. Box 30446
Tucson, AZ 85751
ph: 520-886-8006
e-mail: sha@azstarnet.com
web: http://www.sha.org
The largest scholarly group concerned with the archaeology of the modern world (A.D. 1400 to present); promotes scholarly research and the dissemination of knowledge concerning historical archaeology.

Collectors

Tommy W. Bryden
7941 St. James.
Springfield, IL 62707
Collector of prehistoric Native American artifacts such s arrowheads, axes, pottery.

Internet Resources

Hugh Jarvis
Lithics Site, The
e-mail: hjarvis@acsu.buffalo.edu
web: http://wings.buffalo.edu/go?lithics
Great page with lots of links to all kinds of archaeological resources: lithics research projects, literary resources, related institutional sites, archaeological courses on lithics, artifact information, commercial concerns.

Museums/Libraries

Kelsey Museum of Archaeology, University of Michigan
434 S. State St.
Ann Arbor, MI 48109
ph: 734-764-9304
fax: 734-763-8976
web: http://www.umich.edu/~kelseydb/

Periodicals

Boston University Scholarly Publications
Journal: Journal of Field Archaeology
985 Commonwealth Ave.
Boston, MA 02215
ph: 617-353-4106c
e-mail: abw@crsa.bu.edu
web: http://jfa-www.bu.edu
This quarterly journal publishes articles that deal with reports of field excavations and surveys the world over; provides coverage of studies of methodological and technical matters as well as scientific advances in archaeology.

Athena Publications
Journal: Athena Review
P.O. Box 10904
Naples, FL 34101
fax: 941-594-2163
e-mail: athenarev1@aol.com
web: http://www.athenapub.com/
Quarterly journal of archaeology, history and exploration.

Magazine: Ancient
82 Hythe Road
Brighton, East Sussex BN1 6JS
U.K.
Bi-monthly review of antiquity.

Emma Beatty
Aurora Publications Ltd.
Magazine: Minerva
14 Old Bond St.
London, W1X 3BD
U.K.
ph: 44 171 495 2590
fax: 44 171 491 1595
The international review of ancient art and archaeology; a bi-monthly illustrated magazine focusing on ancient art, antiquities, archaeology and numismatic discoveries worldwide.

Oxford University Press
: Antiquity
Antiquity Office
New Hall
Cambridge, CB3 0DF
U.K.
ph: (01223) 426164
fax: (01223) 423353
e-mail: catm20@cam.ac.uk
web: http://intarch.ac.uk/antiquity/
Reports on specialist work in archaeology; an academic and scholarly publication; contains reviews, bibliographies, and provides a cumulative index for very 50 issues; published quarterly.

ARCHITECTURAL ELEMENTS

(see also DOORKNOBS; FIREPLACE ITEMS, Mantels; GARDEN FURNITURE, Furniture & Ornaments; PLUMBING; STAINED GLASS)

Auction Services

Julie Lewis
Great Gatsby's, The
5070 Peachtree Industrial Blvd
Atlanta, GA 30341
ph: 770-457-1903 or 800-GATSBYS
fax: 770-457-7250
e-mail: greatgatsbys@mindspring.com
web: http://www.gatsbys.com
Specializes in the sale of architectural antiques.

Dealers

Aardvark Antiques
475 Thames St.
Newport, RI 02840
ph: 800-446-1052 or 401-849-7233
fax: 401-849-1591
e-mail: ardvarkan@aol.com
web: http://www.aardvarkantiques.com/
Lighting, stained glass, statuary, planters, sconces, pedestals, fountains, fireplaces, gates, fences, marble, iron, cast iron.

H. Weber Wilson
Oltz-Wilson Antiques
P.O. Box 506
Portsmouth, RI 02871
ph: 800-508-0022
fax: 401-683-1644
e-mail: hww@edgenet.net
web: http://www.antiqnet.com/webwilson/
Sells architectural antiques; garden ornaments, vintage plumbing, quality furniture, antique door hardware.

Chris McMahon
Architectural Salvage, Inc.
#1 Mill Street
Exeter, NH 03833
ph: 603-642-4348
fax: 603-642-4348
e-mail: arch@ttlc.net
web: http://www.oldhousesalvage.com/
Deals in all types of old house parts from the smallest hardware to grand entrance ways and everything in between.

Allan Soll
Soll's Antiques
P.O. Box 307
Route 2
Canaan, ME 04924-0307
ph: 207-474-5396
e-mail: solantiq@somtel.com
web: http://www.somtel.com/solantiq/
Carries over 150 architectural c. 1900 stained and beveled glass windows; also antique doors, mantles, lighting fixtures, and other architectural items; also wholesales antique furniture.

United House Wrecking
535 Hope St.
Stamford, CT 06906-1316
ph: 203-348-5371
fax: 203-961-9472
web: http://www.united-antiques.com
Sells architectural elements; stained and beveled glass, fireplace mantels and accessories, brass & copper, plumbing & lighting fixtures, Victorian gingerbread, etc.

Matthew White
Recycling the Past
381 N. Main
Barnegat, NJ 08005
ph: 609-660-9790
e-mail: whitey99@cybercomm.net
web: http://www.recyclingthepast.com
Specializing in iron gates and fencing, garden urns, doors, windows, mantels, statuary, terra-cotta building parts, fireplace mantels, building parts of wood and metal, lighting, hardware.

Jeffery Venturella
Architectural Emporium
207 Adams Ave.
Canonsburg, PA 15317
ph: 724-222-8586 or 724-746-3861
e-mail: salesml@architectural-emporium.com
web: http://architectural-emporium.com
Carries a full line of architectural antiques; specializes in restoring antique lighting, chandeliers, and sconces.

Stephen G. Del Sordo
Heritage Resource Group
305 Oakley St.
Cambridge, MD 21613
ph: 410-228-8934
fax: 410-221-8061
e-mail: delsordo@shore.intercom.net
web: http://www.heritageresource.com/
A cultural resource management/historic preservation firm that has contracts to locate, provide, authenticate artifacts for museums and collectors; areas of expertise include architecture, industry, domestic, agriculture, and maritime.

Salvage One
1524 South Sangamon St.
Chicago, IL 60608
ph: 312-733-0098
fax: 312-733-6829
Maintains large inventory of American and European architectural elements from the 18th through 20th centuries.

Architectural Antiques
403 Dawson St.
San Antonio, TX 78202
ph: 210-226-6863
Buys and sells architectural elements including antique hardware, old pine doors, mantles, porch spindles and posts and brackets, old iron fencing, etc.

Perry Prince
Perry S. Prince, Asian Antiques
P.O. Box 1364
Ashland, OR 97520
ph: 541-488-1989
fax: 541-488-1989
e-mail: perry@asianarts.com
web: http://www.asianarts.com
Carries architectural antiques, Southeast Asian, Asian art, Asian antiques, interior decorating, interior design, Asian folk art, salvage, Chinese antiques, Chinese architecture.

Cathy Black
Traders of the Lost Art
1303 17th Avenue SW
Calgary, Alberta T2T 0C4
Canada
ph: 403-229-0234
fax: 403-229-0565
e-mail: traders@telusplanet.net
web: http://www.traders.ab.ca
Specializing in Western Canadian architectural salvage: decorative iron, country doors, fireplace mantels, fixtures and fittings, etc.

John Rawlinson
Original Reclamation Trading Co. Ltd.
22 Elliott Rd.
Love Lane Estate
Cirencester, Gloucestershire GL7 1YS
U.K.
ph: +44 1 285 653 532
fax: +44 1 285 644 383
e-mail: john@ortc.co.uk
web: http://www.ortc.co.uk
Offers period stone, wood and cast iron fireplaces, oak flooring and doors, quality stone items for the garden, statuary, panelling, period garden seats.

Thornton Kay
Salvo
18 Ford Village
Berwick-upon-Tweed, Northumberland TD15 2QG
U.K.
ph: 01890 820333
fax: +44 1890 820499
e-mail: salvo@salvo.co.uk
web: http://www.salvo.co.uk
Great source for information about antique and reclaimed materials for buildings and gardens, worldwide.

Alexander Puddy
Architectural Heritage, Ltd.
Taddington Manor, Taddington
Nr. Cutsdean
Cheltenham, Gloucestershire GL54 5RY
U.K.
ph: 01386-584414
fax: 01386-584236
e-mail: puddy@architectural-heritage.co.uk
web: http://www.architectural-heritage.co.uk
In business since 1976; carries one of the largest stocks of fine quality architectural antiques and garden ornaments.

Museums/Libraries

Octagon, The; The Museum of the American Architectural Foundation
1735 New York Ave., NW
Washington, DC 20006
ph: 202-638-3105
fax: 202-626-7420
web: http://www.amerarchfoundation.com/

Periodicals

Hanley-Wood, Inc.
Magazine: Old-House Journal, The
Two Main Street
Gloucester, MA 01930
ph: 800-234-3797
e-mail: jbutterf@hanley-wood.com
web: http://www.oldhousejournal.com/
Monthly magazine focusing on the repair of old houses; publishes "The Old-House Journal Catalog"-hundreds of sources for products & services.

Hanley-Wood, Inc.
Directory: Old-House Journal Restoration Directory
Two Main Street
Gloucester, MA 01930
ph: 800-234-3797
e-mail: jbutterf@hanley-wood.com
web: http://www.oldhousejournal.com/
Sourcebook listing companies large and small which manufacture and sell traditional hard-to-find items for the old house owner: sinks, siding, lumber, plumbing, stoves, etc.; also call 800-931-2931.

Ray Shepherd
Magazine: Traditional Building
69A 7th Ave.
Brooklyn, NY 11217-3618
ph: 718-636-0788
fax: 718-636-0750
e-mail: htcstaff@traditional-building.com
web: http://www.traditional-building.com
Great source for products for historical buildings.

Victorian Homes, Inc.
Directory: Victorian Homes Sourcebook
265 South Anita Dr., Ste. 120
Orange, CA 92868
ph: 800-999-9718
April issue has articles and ads on restoration philosophy, moldings, wallpapers, restoring old windows, kitchen renovations; a complete directory of products and services for the Victorian Revival home market.

Victorian Gingerbread

Suppliers

Vintage Woodworks
Highway 34 South
P.O. 39, MSC 2534
Quinlan, TX 75474
ph: 903-356-2158
fax: 903-356-3023
e-mail: mail@vintagewoodworks.com
web: http://www.vintagewoodworks.com
Sells solid wood gingerbread suitable for Victorian homes: brackets, stair parts, gazebo, newel posts, balusters, moldings, gables, shelves, spandrels, window cornices, etc.; send $2 for a copy of their catalog of architectural details.

ARCHITECTURAL TOYS

(see TOYS, Construction Sets)

ARCHITECTURE & RELATED ITEMS

(see also CATALOGS, Trade [Homebuilding]; FRANK LLOYD WRIGHT; HARDWARE; PLANNING ITEMS)

ARCTIC EXPLORERS

Museums/Libraries

Bowdoin College, Peary-MacMillan Arctic Museum
Hubbard Hall
Brunswick, ME 04011
ph: 207-725-3416
e-mail: cpayson@bowdoin.edu
web: http://www.bowdoin.edu/dept/arctic/

ARMS & ARMOR

(see also AMERICAN INDIAN, Tomahawks; BAYONETS; EDGED WEAPONS; FIREARMS; KNIVES; MILITARIA; ORIENTALIA; POWDER HORNS; SWORDS)

Auction Services

Sotheby's
1334 York Ave.
New York, NY 10021
ph: 212-606-7000
fax: 212-606-7107
web: http://www.sothebys.com
Over 70 collecting areas are featured at Sotheby's auctions including toys, dolls, porcelain, furniture, silver, art, books; exhibitions are free and everyone is welcome; for a free copy of "Sotheby's Newsletter", call 212-606-7245.

Christie's
502 Park Ave.
New York, NY 10022
ph: 212-546-1000
fax: 212-980-8163
web: http://www.christies.com

Butterfield & Butterfield
220 San Bruno Ave.
San Francisco, CA 94103-5018
ph: 415-861-7500
fax: 415-861-8951
e-mail: info@butterfields.com
web: http://www.butterfields.com/

Roy Butler
Wallis & Wallis
West Street Auction Galleries
Lewes, East Sussex BN7 2NJ
U.K.
ph: 01273-480208
fax: 01273-476562
e-mail: wallisandwallis@mcmail.com
web: http://www.wallisandwallis.co.uk/
Britain's specialist auctioneers of arms, armor, militaria and military orders.

Clubs/Associations

Arms & Armour Society, The
P.O. Box 10232
London, SW19 2ZD
U.K.
ph: 01323 844278
fax: 01232 449430
e-mail: edmund@jbgreenwood.force9.co.uk
web: http://www.armourer.u-net.com/arms.htm
To further the study of arms & armour; two journals and four newsletters per year.

Collectors

Jim Manteris
P.O. Box 40
Manvel, TX 77578
ph: 281-489-8074
fax: 281-489-4784
e-mail: manteris1@webtv.net
Wants clubs, saps, billy clubs, blackjacks, brass knuckles, and old knives; also wants African and Asian weapons.

David J. DeLaurant
1505 N. Lafayette
Fresno, CA 93728-1123
ph: 559-488-3229 or 559-233-1492
e-mail: dlaurant@sjvls.lib.ca.us
Serious student of post-1914 military helmets & other body armor items from all nations; communicates with other body armor collectors via the "Body Armor Reporter", a quarterly newsletter; will identify armor free - send SASE.

Dealers

Terry Porter
Fine Antique Arms
P.O. Box 59028
Mesquite, TX 75150
ph: 214-679-7410
fax: 972-681-8992
e-mail: Terry.Porter@FineAntiqueArms.com
web: http://www.fineantiquearms.com
Dealing in fine antique arms, rapiers, swords, pistols, guns, muskets.

Brian R. Price
Arms & Armour
4226 Cambridge Way
Union City, CA 94587
ph: 650-961-2187
e-mail: brian@chronique.com
web: http://www.chronique.com/
Arms & armor dealer, expert, repair and reproduction source; website focuses on medieval times and has a complete online glossary for arms and armor.

Experts

Charles H. Clements, III
1741 Dallas St.
Aurora, CO 80010-2018
ph: 303-364-0403
fax: 303-739-9824
e-mail: gryphons@worldnet.att.net
Appraises and specializes in arms & armor, hunting, gaming, military and leisure material for men, frontier, fur trade and Indian artifacts, etc.

Internet Resources

Brian R. Price
Arms & Armour Glossary of Terms
4226 Cambridge Way
Union City, CA 94587
ph: 650-961-2187
e-mail: brian@chronique.com
web: http://www.chronique.com/
Arms & armor dealer, expert, repair and reproduction source; website focuses on medieval times and has a complete online glossary for arms and armor.

Museums/Libraries

Higgins Armory Museum
100 Barber Ave.
Worcester, MA 01606-2444
ph: 508-853-6015
fax: 508-852-7697
e-mail: higgins@higgins.org
web: http://www.higgins.org/
Step in the Higgins Armory Museum and step back in time to medieval and Renaissance Europe, feudal Japan, and even to the Mediterranean cradles of civilization; has 70 suits of armor - the heroic legacies of another world and time.

Periodicals

David J. DeLaurant
Newsletter: Body Armor Reporter
1505 N. Lafayette
Fresno, CA 93728-1123
ph: 559-488-3229 or 559-233-1492
e-mail: dlaurant@sjvls.lib.ca.us
For the collector of post-1914 military helmets & other body armor items from all nations.

Brian R. Price
Journal: Journal of Chivalry, The
4226 Cambridge Way
Union City, CA 94587
ph: 650-961-2187
e-mail: brian@chronique.com
web: http://www.chronique.com/
A quarterly print journal.

Repro. Sources

Pamela Lemieux
Swords n Stuff
123 Wolf Neck Road
Freeport, ME 04032
ph: 800-286-4143 or 207-865-3542
fax: 207-865-0385
e-mail: swords@swords-n-stuff.com
web: http://www.swords-n-stuff.com
Offers a large selection of replica swords, daggers, shields and armor from medieval, Renaissance, Celtic and Roman times.

Iron Guard
155 North May St.
Southern Pines, NC 28387
e-mail: 72774.2240@compuserve.com
web: http://www.skirmisher.com/SWORDS.htm
Sells high quality swords from all periods of history.

Museum Replicas Limited
P.O. Box 840
Gees Mill Road
Conyers, GA 30012
ph: 800-883-8838
fax: 770-388-0246
e-mail: musrep@mindspring.com
web: http://www.museumreplicas.com/
Sells authentic replica edged weapons, battle gear, period clothing; swords, daggers, axes, shields, helmets, tunics, etc.

Japanese

Collectors

Raymond Macy
P.O. Box 11
West Alexandria, OH 45381-0011
ph: 937-839-5721 or 937-839-5203
Wants Japanese swords, daggers, sword parts, matchlock guns, anything samurai.

Don Beck
P.O. Box 15305
Fort Wayne, IN 46885-5305
ph: 219-486-3010
Wants Japanese swords and sword items, guns, medals, daggers, head gear, from any war 1860 to 1945.

Japanese (Swords)

Clubs/Associations

Dr. T.C. Ford, Ed.
Japanese Sword Society of the United States, Inc.
Newsletter: Japanese Sword Society of U. S. Newsletter
P.O. Box 712
Breckenridge, TX 76024-0712
e-mail: barry_hennick@nynet.nybe.on.ca
web: http://www.jssus.org/
Focuses on the study and preservation of Japanese swords.

Jim Kurrasch
Japanese Sword Society of Southern California
7612 Newport Drive
Goleta, CA 93117-2418
ph: 805-968-8278
e-mail: kurrasch@west.net
web: http://www.west.net/~kurrasch/jsssc.htm
Formed in the late 1950s to study and appreciate the Arts of the Japanese Sword; meets once a month and publishes a monthly newsletter on various aspects of the Japanese Sword.

Society for the Preservation of Japanese Art Swords, The
Journal: SPJAS Journal
NBTHK, 4-25-10, Yoyogi
Shibuya-Ku
Tokyo, 151
Japan
web: http://anime.jyu.fi/~saren/Docs/Sword.html
Yearly dues are 19,500 yen; members receive a Japanese language journal four times per year.

Collectors

S.J. Moore
5 E. Genesee St.
Skaneateles, NY 13152-1317
ph: 315-685-8758
fax: 315-685-1564
e-mail: moore90w@aol.com
Buys and sells Japanese samurai swords and fittings: tsuba, menuki, fushi, kashira, kogai, kazuka, scabbards.

Robert Navrotski
1024 4th St.
Canonsburg, PA 15317-1910
ph: 724-745-4840
Wants to buy Samurai swords; free information and appraisal.

Greg Souchik
P.O. Box 161
Custer City, PA 16725-0161
ph: 814-362-2642
fax: 814-362-7356
e-mail: AlleghenyArsenal@compuserve.com
Wants to buy all WWII German and Japanese swords and daggers.

Mark Walberg
P.O. Box 130
Sunbury, PA 17801
ph: 570-286-1617
fax: 570-286-9686
Wants to buy Japanese swords, sword fittings, matchlock rifles, Samurai armor.

Ed Hicks
819 Hope Mills Rd.
Fayetteville, NC 28304-2224
ph: 910-425-7000
Wants Japanese swords and armor: daggers, bronzes, iron teapots, helmets, masks, lacquer, matchlock guns, Samurai relics, sword guards, sword fittings, metal work, tea ceremony artifacts and ceramics; free research on Samurai.

R.W. Lightner
P.O. Box 320042
Cocoa Beach, FL 32932-0042
ph: 407-783-0314 or 800-752-6135
Japanese swords and sword items; also guns, medals, daggers, head gear; member NBTHK, Tokyo.

Bill Simmons
8955 NW 19th St.
Coral Springs, FL 33071-6109
ph: 954-340-0734
e-mail: wsim1206@aol.com
Wants any and all Japanese and Chinese swords and daggers: military, ivory, Katanasa, short, long.

K. Wiley
719 Baldwin SE
Grand Rapids, MI 49503-4470
ph: 616-451-8410
e-mail: quillion1@aol.com
Wants Japanese swords, daggers, sword parts. Also German 3rd Reich daggers, swords, bayonets. References available.

Ron Hartmann
5907 Deerwood Dr.
Saint Louis, MO 63123-2707
ph: 314-577-2873 or 314-832-3477
e-mail: swords@usroute66.net
Wants to buy Japanese swords, daggers, sword guards, and other parts; over 20 years experience; life member of Japanese Sword Society; always willing to help others realize fair price for their items; send photos and SASE with inquiries.

Dealers

Fred Coluzzi
Frederick's Swords
6919 Westview Dr.
Oak Forest, IL 60452-1566
ph: 708-687-3647
Buys and sells antique swords and daggers from all countries and all periods; issues 3 to 4 major catalogs per year: Japanese, US, German, Turkish, Moro, Indonesian, Philippine, Chinese.

Experts

Dale Garbutt
7 St. Paul St., Ste. 1400
Baltimore, MD 21202-1626
ph: 410-347-8710 or 410-358-1228
fax: 410-347-9475
e-mail: dgarbutt@wtplaw.com
Collects Japanese swords, sword fittings, matchlocks, and armor; member of the Japanese Sword Society of the U.S. and of The Society of Japanese Art Swords, Tokyo, Japan; will provide no-obligation evaluation by mail or in person.

Richard Fleming
P.O. Box 8394
Virginia Beach, VA 23450-8394
ph: 757-622-1343
fax: 757-463-3052
e-mail: rfleming@milcom-systems.com
Buys and specializes in Japanese swords; free translation of signed pieces; research, identification, evaluation performed and restoration services arranged; Gendaito Oshigata needed for future publication; literature bought.

David McDonald
P.O. Box 265
Sidney, MT 59270
ph: 406-482-3243
e-mail: jswords@mcn.net
web: http://www.mcn.net/~jswords/
Collector, dealer, expert in Japanese swords; swords and fittings bought, sold appraised and repaired; specializes in Japanese sword Tsuka-maki (hilt wrapping) services.

Jim Kurrasch
7612 Newport Drive
Goleta, CA 93117-2418
ph: 805-968-8278
e-mail: kurrasch@west.net
web: http://www.west.net/~kurrasch/jsssc.htm
Specializes in Japanese swords and some Japanese armor and fittings; does not sell or charge for services.

Jim Kurrasch
7612 Newport Dr.
Goleta, CA 93117-2418
ph: 805-968-8278
e-mail: kurrasch@west.net
Collector and expert in Japanese swords; active in the Japanese Sword Society of Southern California.

Fred Lohman
Fred Lohman Co.
3405 N.E. Broadway
Portland, OR 97232
ph: 503-282-4567
fax: 503-287-2678
e-mail: lohman@katana4u.com
web: http://www.Japanese-Swords.com/
The ultimate source for parts and supplies relating to the restoration and maintenance of the Japanese sword; restoration service backed up with 30 years of Nihon-to experience (references available.)

Internet Resources

Richard Stein
Japanese Sword, The
P.O. Box 339
Locust Grove, VA 22508
e-mail: rstein@ns.gemlink.com
web: http://www.gemlink.com/rstein/nihonto.htm
Japanese sword history, care, illustrated glossary, articles, clubs, sword sites, Japanese military swords, sword care, martial arts, etc.; links to related sites that contain great research information about swords.

SamuraiSword.com
P.O. Box 718
Grant Park, IL 60940
ph: 800-534-5119
e-mail: dpepin@ibm.net
web: http://www.samuraisword.com/
Buys, sells, appraises Samurai swords; web site contains many good sword related links.

Bob McCoy
Oshigata Project Web Site, The
ph: 970-491-8638
e-mail: mccoy@atmos.colostate.edu
web: http://optical.atmos.colostate.edu/sword/sword.html
The Oshigata Project is a free online resource for Japanese sword characters; over 500 examples provided.

Bob McCoy
Nihonto Classified Ad Web Page, The
ph: 970-491-8638
e-mail: mccoy@atmos.colostate.edu
web: http://mccoyresearch.com/sword/sword.html
A free service for posting for sale ads and wanted ads for all Japanese swords and related items.

Alan Quinn
Nihonto - Japanese Sword
U.K.
e-mail: alan@meiboku.demon.co.uk
web: http://www.meiboku.demon.co.uk/
Provides a wealth of information about Japanese swords.

Museums/Libraries

Museum of Fine Arts, Boston
465 Huntington Ave.
Boston, MA 02115-5523
ph: 617-267-9300
e-mail: webmaster@mfa.org
web: http://www.mfa.org/home.html
Home to more than 500 swords and thousands of sword fittings.

Repair Services

David McDonald
P.O. Box 265
Sidney, MT 59270
ph: 406-482-3243
e-mail: jswords@mcn.net
web: http://www.mcn.net/~jswords/
Collector, dealer, expert in Japanese swords; swords and fittings bought, sold appraised and repaired; specializes in Japanese sword Tsuka-maki (hilt wrapping) services.

Bushido Japanese Sword Polishing & Restoration
P.O. Box 61783
Honolulu, HI 96839
ph: 808-988-9908
fax: 808-988-9908
e-mail: bushidoswd@aol.com
web: http://togishi.com/
Specializes in Japanese sword polishing and restoration.

Fred Lohman
Fred Lohman Co.
3405 N.E. Broadway
Portland, OR 97232
ph: 503-282-4567
fax: 503-287-2678
e-mail: lohman@katana4u.com
web: http://www.Japanese-Swords.com/
The ultimate source for parts and supplies relating to the restoration and maintenance of the Japanese sword; restoration service backed up with 30 years of Nihon-to experience (references available.)

Miniature

Clubs/Associations

Miniature Arms Collectors/Makers Society
Newsletter: MAC/MS Newsletter
4910 Kilburn Ave.
Rockford, IL 61101-1746
e-mail: gin40@msn.com

ARROWHEADS & POINTS

(see AMERICAN INDIAN; ARCHAEOLOGY; PREHISTORIC ARTIFACTS, Arrowheads & Points)

ART

(see also BRONZES; CARTOON ART; CRAFTS; FOLK ART; FRAMES; ILLUSTRATORS; LAPIDARY; MEDALLIC SCULPTURES; ORIENTALIA; PERSONALITIES [ARTISTS]; PRINTS; PRINTS [MODERN]; REPAIR/RESTORATION/ CONSERVATION, Art; SCULPTURE; TATTOO; WESTERN ART & CRAFTS)

Appraisers

Peter C. Sorlien, ASA
Accredited Appraisers
17 1/2 State St.
Marblehead, MA 01945-3536
ph: 781-631-5956
fax: 781-631-6550
e-mail: appraisr@shore.net
Professional art appraisals; experience with divorce, donation, estate, insurance, litigation, and tax matters; does not buy or sell.

Stephen van Cline, CAPP
van Cline & Davenport, Ltd.
792 Franklin Ave.
Franklin Lakes, NJ 07417-1343
Specializes in paintings, watercolors, drawings, bronze & marble sculpture; appraisals, authentication, lectures, expert testimony; minimum $25 charge; letter request only, SASE.

Judith S. Jordan
Perrinart Associates
140 Scarborough Rd.
Briarcliff Manor, NY 10510-2006
ph: 914-762-1438 or 802-869-2784

Dr. Charles J. Semowich
242 Broadway
Rensselaer, NY 12144-2705
ph: 518-449-4756
e-mail: semowich@webtv.net
Appraiser of art, antiques and decorative arts.

Pamela E. Mayo, ISA
710 Washington St.
Sewickley, PA 15143-1845
ph: 412-749-0760 or 412-201-1760
fax: 412-201-1747
e-mail: pandjr@usaor.net
Fine art appraiser (paintings, drawings, prints, sculpture), specializing in 19th and early 20th century American art with a general background in 18th-20th century American and European art; specializes in Southern art.

Rochelle Eisenberg, ASA
Art Directives, Inc.
P.O. Box 173
Ambler, PA 19002
ph: 215-646-0233
fax: 215-542-7015
e-mail: artappr@aol.com
Appraiser, consultant, writer, lecturer, author, advisor for Montgomery County newspapers, appeared on "Chubb Antiques Roadshow", instructor at Temple University.

Randall C. Hunt
3503 Fulton St., NW
Washington, DC 20007-1438
ph: 202-333-4035
fax: 202-333-1354
e-mail: randall@appraiser.net
Specializes in fine art.

Elen W. Shea, ISA
Antiques Critiques, Inc.
P.O. Box 34586
Bethesda, MD 20827-0586
ph: 301-299-7314

Melanie Smith, ISA
Seaside Art Gallery
P.O. Box 1
2716 Virginia Dare Trail S
Nags Head, NC 27959
ph: 252-441-5418 or 800-828-2444
fax: 252-441-8563
e-mail: seaside@interpath.com
web: http://www.seasideart.com
Accredited member of the International Society of Appraisers; specializes in fine art (paintings, graphics, sculpture) and animation art.

James Corcoran, ISA
Corcoran Fine Arts Limited, Inc.
2915 Fairfax Rd.
Cleveland, OH 44118-4015
ph: 216-397-0777
fax: 330-379-0222
e-mail: corcoran@aol.com
Appraisals, consulting, private dealer.

Caroline Ashleigh
Caroline Ashleigh Associates, Inc.
P.O. Box 2022
Birmingham, MI 48012
ph: 248-646-3045
fax: 248-647-2861
e-mail: carolineashleigh@msn.com
Specializes in professional appraisals of fine art, antiques and residential contents for insurance, divorce, and donation purposes; participating appraiser in the "Antiques Roadshow," member of the Appraisers Association of America.

Patricia M. Knight
Finetooth Comb Antiques Research & Appraisal Service
P.O. Box 1177
Ames, IA 50010-1177
ph: 515-292-9028
e-mail: ftcres@aol.com
Consultant and qualified appraiser of 19th century and early 20th century oil paintings; also Oriental images on paper; please send SASE for reply.

Frederick P. Dose, Jr.
Frederick Dose Appraisals Ltd.
778 Pleasant Ave.
Highland Park, IL 60035-4613
ph: 847-433-7870 or 847-433-1090
Appraises US, British, Continental paintings and furniture, prints, porcelain, silver, decorative arts, coins, antiquities; for corporate, private, and attorneys; references on request; 6 year full-time as University art historian.

Sybil Tillman, ISA
Artco Inc.
Box 3148 RFD Cuba Rd.
Long Grove, IL 60047-9606
ph: 847-438-8420
fax: 847-438-6464
e-mail: smbm04b@prodigy.com
Specializing in fine art appraisals and research; also buying and selling 19th and 20th century, important and contemporary American artists and American Indian Art.

Bob & Maloree Banks
Banks Fine Art
3316 Royal Lane
Dallas, TX 75229-5061
ph: 214-352-1811
fax: 214-352-6360
e-mail: artman2@ix.netcom.com
web: http://www.banksfineart.com
Buys, sells, auctions, appraises oil paintings and other 19th and 20th century fine art.

Jane Cowan, ISA
Cowan & Company
2100 Tanglewild #735
Houston, TX 77063
ph: 713-532-7203
fax: 713-532-7214
e-mail: janecowan@cowanco.com
web: http://www.cowanco.com
Specializes in Wildlife and Sporting art; 19th and 20th century fine art appraisals, consultations and sales.

Richard Casagrande, ISA CAPP
Casagrande Appraisals
8546 Broadway, Ste. 203
San Antonio, TX 78217
ph: 210-820-3097
fax: 210-820-3097
e-mail: 104411.545@compuserve.com
Appraiser specializing in 19th century American art; also the art of Texas and the San Antonio region.

Jan Wilson, ISA
Jan Wilson Gallery
P.O. Box 6649
Ketchum, ID 83340
ph: 208-622-7799
fax: 208-726-5975
e-mail: jan@janwilsongallery.com
web: http://www.janwilsongallery.com/
Specializes in appraising fine art, prints & sculpture.

Corinne Cain
Corinne Cain Ltd.
326 West Harmont Dr.
Phoenix, AZ 85021
ph: 602-906-1633
fax: 602-906-0677
e-mail: kogyo@primenet.com
Appraises Fine Arts and Native American arts.

Jnanideva Shanmuga
Appraisal & Connoisseur Associates
620 Sierra Dr. SE
Albuquerque, NM 87108-3377
ph: 505-265-2842
e-mail: jshan@highfiber.com
Appraisers, artists and brokers serving the Southwest in painting, prints and sculpture; also appraise residential contents nationwide.

James Haddad, ISA
Poulsen Galleries, Inc.
910 San Pasqual St.
Pasadena, CA 91106
ph: 626-792-7410
fax: 626-792-7247
e-mail:
poulsengalleries@compuserve.com

Marcia Osterkamp, ISA
Poulsen Galleries, Inc.
327 Terrace Dr.
Brawley, CA 92227-3040
ph: 760-344-4810
fax: 760-344-4778
e-mail:
poulsengalleries@compuserve.com
web: http://www.artnet.com/poulsen.html
Fine art appraiser; buys and sells 19th and 20th century American and European paintings; also California paintings.

Richard C. Frey, ISA
R.T.L.H. Enterprises
1275 East Ave.
Chico, CA 95926-1020
ph: 530-343-4528 or 800-567-7854
fax: 530-343-9380
e-mail: RFREYRTLH@aol.com
Qualified appraiser of American and European art, paintings, watercolors, drawings, prints, sculpture, bronzes, etc.; appraises for estates, arbitration, and has testified as expert witness.

Candy Moffett
Alder Gallery
55 W. Broadway
Eugene, OR 97401
ph: 541-342-6411
fax: 541-683-9797
e-mail: candy@alderart.com
web: http://www.alderart.com
Buys, sells, repairs and restores art; specializes in the appraisal of fine art and antiques; Accredited Member of the International Society of Appraisers (ISA).

Christian Coleman, Ex. Dir.
International Society of Appraisers
Newsletter: Professional Appraisers Information Exchange
16040 Christensen Rd., Ste. 102
Seattle, WA 98188
ph: 206-241-0359 or 888-472-4732
fax: 206-241-0436
e-mail: ISA_HQ@compuserve.com
web: http://www.isa-appraisers.org
Largest association of professional personal property appraisers; members specialize in antiques & residential contents, gems & jewelry, fine art, and machinery & equipment; call for appraiser nearest you.

Andrew Steven White, ISA
Andrew White Fine Art
#31396 W. 71 Ave.
Vancouver, British Columbia V6P 3B5
Canada
ph: 604-261-4801
e-mail: anwhite@direct.ca
Accredited Member of the International Society of Appraisers; provides appraisal services for corporate and private art collectors in Vancouver and surrounding area.

Edith Yeomans, ISA
Appraisal Associates
80 Richmond Street West, Ste. 1101
Toronto, Ontario M5H 2A4
Canada
ph: 416-368-4334
fax: 416-368-6679
e-mail: aaci@pathcom.com
web: http://www.appraise.org/
Specialist in the valuation of fine art, antiques, decorative art, including Canadian, American and European art.

Stephen P. Sweeting, ISA
Appraisal Associates
80 Richmond Street West, Ste. 1101
Toronto, Ontario M5H 2A4
Canada
ph: 416-368-4334
fax: 416-368-6679
e-mail: aaci@pathcom.com
web: http://www.appraise.org/
Specialist in the valuation of fine art, antiques, decorative art, including Canadian, American and European art.

Andrew Steven White, ISA
1396 W 71 Ave., #3
Vancouver, British Columbia V6P 3B5
Canada
ph: 604-261-4801
e-mail: anwhite@direct.ca
An independent personal property appraiser specializing in the valuation of fine art in private, corporate, estate and community art collections; Accredited Member of the International Society of Appraisers.

Nicholas Fairrie
Appraisal Information Exchange
1106 Montgomery St., Ste. 300
San Francisco, CA 94133-4107
U.K.
ph: 415-986-6066
fax: 415-989-7285
e-mail: info@aix.net
web: http://www.aix.net/
Identification, authentication and appraisal services; also functions in advisory capacity to new collectors and acts on their behalf to make new acquisitions.

Auction Services

Colleen Fesko
Skinner, Inc.
357 Main St.
Bolton, MA 01740-1104
ph: 978-779-6241
fax: 978-779-5144
e-mail: info@skinnerinc.com
web: http://www.skinnerinc.com
Established in 1964, Skinner Inc. is the fifth largest auction house in the US; has offices in Bolton and Boston, MA.

Philip C. Shute
Shute Auction Gallery
850 W. Chestnut St.
Brockton, MA 02401
ph: 508-588-0022 or 508-588-7833
fax: 508-559-6687
Antique and custom furniture, art, silver, glass and china, collectibles, etc.

George M. Young
Young Fine Arts Auctions, Inc.
P.O. Box 313
Providence, RI 02906
ph: 207-676-3104
fax: 207-676-3105
e-mail: gyoung@gwi.net
web: http://www.maine.com/yfa
Complete no-frills online art auction catalogs; every lot illustrated with jpeg image; prices listed after each auction; four to five auctions per year; specializes in pre-1950 American & European paintings.

Young Fine Arts Auctions, Inc.
P.O. Box 313
North Berwick, ME 03906
ph: 207-676-3104
fax: 207-676-3105
e-mail: gyoung@maine.com
web: http://www.maine.com/yfa/
Lots of good information on their website about works they have sold in the past including thousands of images and prices realized.

Annette & Rob Elowitch
Barridoff Galleries
P.O. Box 9715
Portland, ME 04104
ph: 207-772-5011
fax: 207-772-5049
e-mail: fineart@barridoff.com
web: http://www.barridoff.com/
Specializing in the auction sale of fine art.

Caroline Birenbaum
Swann Galleries, Inc.
104 E. 25th St.
New York, NY 10010-2977
ph: 212-254-4710
fax: 212-979-1017
e-mail: swann@swanngalleries.com
web: http://www.swanngalleries.com/
Oldest/largest U.S. auctioneer specializing in rare books, autographs & manuscripts, maps, atlases, photographs, and works of art on paper including vintage posters.

Christie's East
219 E. 67th St.
New York, NY 10021
ph: 212-606-0400
web: http://www.christies.com

Sotheby's
1334 York Ave.
New York, NY 10021
ph: 212-606-7000
fax: 212-606-7107
web: http://www.sothebys.com

Christie's
502 Park Ave.
New York, NY 10022
ph: 212-546-1000
fax: 212-980-8163
web: http://www.christies.com

Amory Spizzirri, Client Svc.
William Doyle Galleries
175 E. 87th St.
New York, NY 10128-2205
ph: 212-427-2730
fax: 212-369-0892
e-mail: info@doylegalleries.com
web: http://www.doylegalleries.com
Holds over 50 auctions annually of furniture and decorations, paintings and sculpture, jewelry, books and prints, couture and textiles, 20th century art & design, majolica, Lalique, Asian works of art and other specialty categories.

Margot Chuatal
Weschler's
909 E St. NW
Washington, DC 20004-2006
ph: 202-628-1281 or 800-331-1430
fax: 202-628-2366
web: http://www.weschlers.com/
Conducts specialized auction sales of art, paintings, prints and graphics.

Frank Boos
Boos Gallery, Inc.
420 Enterprise Court
Bloomfield Hills, MI 48013
ph: 248-332-1500

Clubs/Associations

Archaeological Institute of America
Magazine: Archaeology
656 Beacon St.
Boston, MA 02215-2006
ph: 617-353-9361
fax: 617-353-6550
e-mail: aia@BU.EDU
web: http://www.he.net/~archaeol/
Has phone numbers and addresses for all state archaeological departments; "Archaeology" is published bi-monthly; also publishes the "American Journal of Archaeology" quarterly; write for details.

National Antique & Art Dealers Association of America
220 East 57th St.
New York, NY 10022
ph: 212-826-9707
fax: 212-832-9493
e-mail: naadaa@dir-dd.com
web: http://www.dir-dd.com/naadaa.html
Trade group represents art and antique dealers; sponsors antique and art exhibitions; promotes ethical trade practices among its members; free membership directory available.

Donna Carlson, Dir.
Art Dealers Association of America
575 Madison Ave.
New York, NY 10022-2511
ph: 212-940-8590
fax: 212-940-7013
e-mail: artdeal@rosenman.com
web: http://www.artdealers.org/
Non-profit organization of nation's lading dealers in fine art.

American Association of Museums
1575 Eye Street, Ste. 400
Washington, DC 20005
ph: 202-289-1818
fax: 202-289-6578
e-mail: info@aam-us.org
web: http://www.aam-us.org/
A professional society of museums which has established an accrediting system for museums.

N. J. Fregin
American Society of Artists, Inc.
Newsletter: Art Lovers & Craft Fair Bulletin
P.O. Box 1326
Palatine, IL 60078
ph: 312-751-2500 or 847-991-4748
e-mail: amersocofartist@webtv.com
National professional membership organization; membership is juried, with a crafts division - American Artisans; presents shows, has lecture and demonstration service; "ASA Artisan" published quarterly for members.

Ruth Redmond-Cooper, Dir.
Institute of Art & Law
: Art Antiquity & Law
Bank Chambers
121 London Road
London, LE2 0QT
U.K.
ph: +44 (0)116 255 5146
fax: +44 (0)116 255 1782
e-mail: ruth.redmond-cooper@inst-of-art-and-law.co.uk
web: http://www.pipemedia.net/ial/
A small independent institution, founded in 1995, that aims to bridge the divide between the worlds of art and law by organizing seminars and publishing books and periodicals; membership is open to the public; many related links.

Collectors

John Clement
36 Oakwood Ave.
Fitchburg, MA 01420-7421
ph: 978-345-5863
Collector and expert, special interests include worldwide master works of art, particularly works on paper, including Japanese woodblock prints; also fine paintings.

Dealers

Henry B. Holt
125 Golden Hill
P.O. Box 699
Lee, MA 01238-0699
ph: 413-243-3184
fax: 413-243-9918
e-mail: hbholt@vgernet.net
Buys and sells American art, oils or watercolors; conservation, framing and appraisals available; wants to buy marines, still life, impressionist, Hudson River, and folk art; member Appraisers Association of America, Inc.

Paul Lantagne
Paul Lantagne Fine Art
P.O. Box 3117
Westford, MA 01886
ph: 978-692-4961
Appraiser and dealer of antiques and American/European paintings.

Tony Fusco
Fusco & Four, Associates
One Murdock Terrace
Brighton, MA 02135-2817
ph: 617-787-2637
fax: 617-782-4430
e-mail: fuscofour@aol.com
Specializes in European and American paintings from 1900-1950, with an emphasis on Art Deco, WPA, Modernist, Regionalists and American Scene; will assist individuals and organizations buying and selling paintings and fine art.

Sonnie Cucinotti
Spirits in the Attic
201 Msgr. O'Brien Hwy.
Cambridge, MA 02141
ph: 617-738-6054
Buys and sells watercolors by listed artists.

Jane Allinson
Allinson Gallery, Inc.
P.O. Box 646
Storrs, CT 06268-2022
ph: 860-429-2322
fax: 860-429-2825
e-mail: allinson@neca.com
web: http://www.allinsongallery.com
Buys and sells American & European fine prints, drawings, paintings, watercolors; also offers fine art appraisals; member of Appraisers Association of America, International Fine Print Dealers Association.

Peter Falk
P. Hastings Falk, Inc.
859 Boston Post Rd.
P.O. Box 833
Madison, CT 06443
ph: 203-245-2246
fax: 203-245-5116
e-mail: info@folkart.com
Researches, writes and sells books about artists listed in "Who Was Who in American Art"; also publishes/sells art reference dictionaries and the ADEC/API CD-ROM of art prices.

Don Barese
Don Barese Fine Art & Antiques
47 Wakefield St.
Hamden, CT 06517-1328
ph: 203-281-7438
fax: 203-281-7438
Buys and sells American & European fine art, 19th and 20th century paintings and prints.

Ellen Sragow
Sragow Gallery
73 Spring St.
New York, NY 10012-5800
ph: 212-219-1793
Specializes in American art from the 1920s to the 1950s: paintings, prints, sculpture; WPA era, abstract expressionist prints, Mexican prints, works by African American artists.

Alex Acevedo
Alexander Gallery
942 Madison Ave.
New York, NY 10021
ph: 212-472-1636
fax: 212-734-6937
e-mail: hudson3@worldnet.att.net
Specializes in 18th, 19th, and 20th century art.

Graham Gallery
1014 Madison Ave.
New York, NY 10021-0103
ph: 212-535-5767
e-mail: JGSgal@aol.com
Specializes in 19th and early 20th century American paintings, American and European sculpture, contemporary art.

Arthur S. Liss
Marineart Gallery
151 East 83rd St.
Penthouse D
New York, NY 10028-1958
ph: 212-772-2737
fax: 212-861-4754
e-mail: info@marineart.com
web: http://www.marineart.com
An art gallery specializing in fine 18th and 19th century British and American marine art; the gallery's watercolor and painting exhibition catalog is available on-line.

Margaret McAuliffe
ARDAGH
P.O. Box 810
Carmel, NY 10512
ph: 914-225-1746 or 800-217-1746
Buys and sells fine art: oils, watercolors, prints, sculpture, photographs.

Sydney L. Germansky
Europa Master Gallery
16 A Lafayette Ave.
Suffern, NY 10901-5406
ph: 914-368-2707

P. Bruce Marine
Marine-Hardy Collection
2918 M. St. NW
Washington, DC 20007-3713
ph: 202-337-2224
fax: 202-337-2224
Specializes in 19th century through 1940s African-American art; buys, sells, collects; oils, drawings, watercolors; by Bannister, Lawrence, Lewis, Douglas, Lee-Smith, etc.

Robert B. Mayo
Gallery Mayo, Inc.
11758 River Crest Dr.
Gloucester, VA 23061-2516
ph: 804-693-2516
e-mail: hightide@visi.net
Buys and sells 19th through early 20th century American art, with a specialty in Southern and sporting art.

Paul G. Hughes, ISA
Tudor House Galleries
4126 Park Rd., Ste. E.
Charlotte, NC 28209
ph: 704-676-4871 or 704-676-4872
e-mail: tudorhouse@aol.com
web: http://www.tudorhouse.com
Buys, sells and appraises 19th century oil paintings and watercolors;

Accredited Member, International Society of Appraisers.

Stephen Dillon
S & S Dillon, Ltd.
P.O. Box 830
Depot Center
Clayton, GA 30525
Fine art expert.

Peter Thurber
Ritzi & Thurber, Inc.
160 S. Beach St.
Daytona Beach, FL 32114
ph: 904-252-2552 or 904-226-8489
fax: 904-226-8490
e-mail: ritzi1881@earthlink.net
web: http://www.ritzi-thurber.com/
Founded in 1881, gallery buys and sells 18th to early 20th century works of art; up-to-date, comprehensive art reference library is maintained; all subjects sought, especially still lifes, animals, and marine subjects.

James & Timothy Keny
Keny Galleries, Inc.
300 East Beck St.
Columbus, OH 43206
ph: 614-464-1228
fax: 614-464-1992
Buys, sells, specializes in, and appraises 19th, and 20th century art; historic Ohio artists.

Ivan Gilbert, MD
Miran Art & Books
2824 Elm Ave.
Columbus, OH 43209
ph: 614-231-3707 or 614-818-3222
fax: 614-818-3223
e-mail: IGilbert@ahhinc.com
Interested especially in prints and paintings by 20th century artists, but only if of quality and with adequate provenance.

Randy Sandler
Cincinnati Art Galleries
225 E 6th St.
Cincinnati, OH 45202
ph: 513-381-2128
fax: 513-381-7527
e-mail: mail@cincinnatiartgalleries.com
web: http://
www.cincinnatiartgalleries.com/
Buying paintings.

Timothy Haines
1077 Celestial St.
Rookwood Bldg. #3, Ste. 400
Cincinnati, OH 45202-1629
ph: 513-559-1405
fax: 513-651-0860
e-mail: relostrat1@aol.com
web: http://members.aol.com/ReyneH
Wants to buy 19th-20th century American and European paintings, watercolors and drawings by listed artists.

Bradley S. Vite
Bradley Vite Fine Arts
1600 West Beardsley Ave.
Elkhart, IN 46514-1800
ph: 219-293-1616
fax: 219-293-1616
e-mail: bradley@finearts.com
web: http://vitefinearts.com/
Buys, sells and appraises 19th and 20th century American and European prints, paintings, watercolors, and sculpture; especially interested in Audubon prints and McKenney & Hall prints.

Sybil Tillman, ISA
Artco Inc.
Box 3148 RFD Cuba Rd.
Long Grove, IL 60047-9606
ph: 847-438-8420
fax: 847-438-6464
e-mail: smbm04b@prodigy.com
Specializing in fine art appraisals and research; also buying and selling 19th and 20th century, important and contemporary American artists and American Indian Art.

Susan Larson, ISA
Susan Larson Fine Art
1150 Old Mill Dr.
Palatine, IL 60067
ph: 847-359-7799
fax: 847-359-6796
Specialist in buying, selling and appraising fine art including paintings and prints; also consults and advises on the development of private and corporate fine art collections.

Farhad Radfar, ISA
MIR International Gallery, Inc.
332 n. Michigan Ave., 2nd Floor
Chicago, IL 60611
ph: 312-814-8510
fax: 312-814-8511
e-mail: mirgallery@aol.com
web: http://www.mirgallery.com/

Taylor Clark
Taylor Clark Gallery
2623 Government St.
Baton Rouge, LA 70806-5408
ph: 225-383-4929
fax: 225-383-3043
Specializes in 18th, 19th, and 20th century oil paintings, watercolors, and prints, especially all editions of Audubon prints.

Bob Banks
Banks Fine Art
3316 Royal Lane
Dallas, TX 75229-5061
ph: 214-352-1811
fax: 214-352-6360
e-mail: artman2@ix.netcom.com
web: http://www.banksfineart.com
Buys, sells, auctions, appraises oil paintings and other 19th and 20th century fine art.

Stephen Hansrote
Griffin Trading Company
13663 Jupiter Rd., Ste. 406
Dallas, TX 75238
ph: 214-342-9234
fax: 214-341-0660
e-mail: griffintc@aol.com

Jan Wilson, ISA
Jan Wilson Gallery
P.O. Box 6649
Ketchum, ID 83340
ph: 208-622-7799
fax: 208-726-5975
e-mail: jan@janwilsongallery.com
web: http://www.janwilsongallery.com/
Buys and sells print, fine art, sculpture.

De Ville Galleries
8751 Melrose Ave.
Los Angeles, CA 90069
ph: 310-652-0525
Specializes in 19th, and 20th century art.

Goldfield Galleries
8380 Melrose Ave.
West Hollywood, CA 90069-5422
ph: 323-651-1122
fax: 323-651-1168
Specializes in 19th and 20th century American Impressionist art, and California and Western art.

James Haddad, ISA
Poulsen Galleries, Inc.
910 San Pasqual St.
Pasadena, CA 91106
ph: 626-792-7410
fax: 626-792-7247
e-mail:
poulsengalleries@compuserve.com

Christine Daniels
Christine Daniels Antiques
135 E. Shiloh Rd.
Santa Rosa, CA 95403-1254
ph: 707-838-6083
fax: 707-838-6083
e-mail: ctiques@aol.com
Buys and sells art: Maxfield Parrish, R. Atkinson Fix prints; also R. Atkinson oils, Louis Icart etchings, and early California oil paintings.

Richard C. Frey, ISA
R.T.L.H. Enterprises
1275 East Ave.
Chico, CA 95926-1020
ph: 530-343-4528 or 800-567-7854
fax: 530-343-9380
e-mail: RFREYRTLH@aol.com
Buys, sells and appraises fine art: paintings, watercolors, prints, drawings, sculpture, bronzes, etc.; American or European; Accredited Member of the International Society of Appraisers.

Elizabeth Wenner-Madison
ARTLister
12162 SW Scholls Ferry Rd., Ste 117
Portland, OR 97223
ph: 503-579-9295
e-mail: art@artlister.com
web: http://www.artlister.com
Assisting dealers and private collectors in pricing, marketing, and shipping of limited edition prints, sculpture, and original fine art.

Candy Moffett
Alder Gallery
55 W. Broadway
Eugene, OR 97401
ph: 541-342-6411
fax: 541-683-9797
e-mail: candy@alderart.com
web: http://www.alderart.com
Buys, sells, repairs and restores art; specializes in the appraisal of fine art and antiques; Accredited Member of the International Society of Appraisers (ISA).

Randeen Cummings, ISA CAPP
Cummings & Associates
P.O. Box 5484
Eugene, OR 97405-0484
ph: 541-345-5856 or 541-485-3068
fax: 541-345-8192
e-mail: rmcummings@ibm.net
web: http://www.antiquesinn.com
Specializes in selling & appraising residential contents, fine art, estate jewelry, 18th & 19th century antiques, American Brilliant period cut glass; also specialized marketing for clients: consultations, estate, and Internet sales.

Lewis & Bond Fine Art
209 W. Houghton St.
Medford, OR 97501
ph: 541-988-5484 or 800-667-0562
e-mail: sales@lewisbond.com
web: http://www.lewisbond.com
Brokers, buys and sells most well-known artist works; originals, limited edition prints and posters; Red Skelton, Bob Byerley, Norman Rockwell.

Experts

Rosemary & Mike McKittrick
McKittrick Fine Arts
Price Guide: McKittrick's Art Price Guide
237 Kennedy Dr.
Sewickley, PA 15143-8716
ph: 412-741-0743
fax: 412-741-7802
Publishes an annual comprehensive listing of art auction sales results including over 50,000 works of art.

Myreen Moore
1404 Gates Ave.
Norfolk, VA 23507
ph: 757-623-7827
fax: 757-855-4312
Appraises, repairs, restores art,

paintings, prints; twenty-five years experience as researcher/artist/writer; staff writer for "Mid-Atlantic Antiques Magazine"; listed in "Who's Who in American Art."

Bob Banks
Banks Fine Art
3316 Royal Lane
Dallas, TX 75229-5061
ph: 214-352-1811
fax: 214-352-6360
e-mail: artman2@ix.netcom.com
web: http://www.banksfineart.com
Buys, sells, auctions, appraises oil paintings and other 19th and 20th century fine art.

Alan Bamberger
Art Talk
2510 Bush St.
San Francisco, CA 94115-3002
ph: 415-931-7875
fax: 415-922-3580
e-mail: alanb@artbusiness.com
web: http://www.artbusiness.com
Author of "Buy Art Smart" and "Art For All"; syndicated columnist who answers questions about art.

Naomi Welch
Images of the Past
309 Playa Blvd., Ste. 110
La Selva Beach, CA 95076-1737
fax: 831-689-0318
e-mail: naomi@harrisonfisher.com
web: http://www.harrisonfisher.com/
Collector, dealer, expert specializes in Harrison Fisher; author of two books, published in 1999, entitled "The Complete Works of Harrison Fisher Illustrator," and "American & European Postcards of Harrison Fisher Illustrator."

Internet Resources

Artists Online
ph: 214-255-6861
e-mail: onlineart@onlineart.com
web: http://www.onlineart.com
A resource for contemporary artists in sculpture, painting, photography, monotype print, drawings, tapestry; buy art or list your own art; silent auctions, search database of artists; upcoming events.

Artnet.com
61 Broadway, 23rd Floor
New York, NY 10006-2701
ph: 800-427-8638 or 212-497-9700
fax: 212-497-9707
e-mail: sites@artnet.com
web: http://www.artnet.com
The portal to the world of art for dealers, collectors, artists and enthusiasts; online auctions of blue-chip art; inventory from over 700 galleries; auction results and previews, fine art auction database.

David J. Maloney, Jr., ISA CAPP
MaloneysOnline Antiques & Collectibles Resource Directory
P.O. Box 2049
Frederick, MD 21702-1049
ph: 301-695-8544
fax: 301-695-6491
e-mail: dave@maloney.com
web: http://www.maloneysonline.com/
Online resource information source for collectors, sellers, claims adjusters, etc.: includes experts, buyers, clubs, periodicals, repairers, museums/libraries, appraisers, auctioneers, matching services, dealers, etc.

Scott Kublin
Art Directory
P.O. Box 1616
Rincon, GA 31326
ph: 912-826-6840
e-mail: admin@artframing.com
web: http://www.artframing.com
Centralized resource for businesses in the art and framing industry.

World Wide Arts Resource
761 Franklin Ave.
Columbus, OH 43205
e-mail: info@wwar.com
web: http://wwar.com/
The biggest gateway for the arts on the Internet: events, exhibitions, museums, cyber galleries, art schools, galleries, museums, art for sale, arts publications, arts agencies, literary and theatre resources, crafts, antiques.

Art Brokerage, Inc.
P.O. Box 3730
Ketchum, ID 83340
ph: 208-788-1484 or 208-788-1491
fax: 208-788-1492
e-mail: drose@earthlink.net
web: http://www.artbrokerage.com/
Online service for buying and selling art.

Art Buys
369 Montezuma Ave., Ste 422
Santa Fe, NM 87501
ph: 505-988-5484 or 800-667-0562
e-mail: sales@artbuys.com
web: http://www.artbuys.com
Online classified ads for art; Red Skelton, Chagall, Peter Max, Steve Kaufman, Thomas Kinkade, Joan Miro, Leroy Neiman, Norman Rockwell, Salvador Dali, and many others.

Art Library Online
Avenue Louise 65, Box 11
Brussels, 1050
Belgium
ph: +32 (0)2 535 7893
fax: +32 (0)2 535 7700
e-mail: adminb@artlibrary.com
web: http://www.artlibrary.com/
A subscription service: American art directory, international directory of arts, Who's Who in American Art, museums of the world, the Official Museum Directory, auction sales database, art auctioneers online, galleries, and more.

Davie Cirese
Net-ArT Virtual Space for Art & Photography
via Palermn 6/a
Rome, 00184
Italy
ph: +39 06 4883253
fax: +39 06 48916583
e-mail: netart@netart.it
web: http://www.netart.it
Internet art resource from Italy; presenting international art and artists; offers useful free search services for art-workers; go to the website to subscribe to Net-ArT Newsletter, a free online newsletter.

Ashleigh Ogier, G.M.
Arthema Limited
338 Old York Road
London, London SW18 1SS
U.K.
ph: 0181 870 9389
fax: 0181 870 4673
e-mail: email@arthema.com
web: http://www.arthema.com/
Items for sale and wanted listings plus valuation service, international events listings, directories of 30 categories of arts related businesses, internet site design tailored to the art and antiques industry.

Misc. Services

Stephen J. Abt, III
ArtFact, Inc.
Price Guide: ArtFact
1130 Ten Rod Rd., Ste. E104
North Kingstown, RI 02852-4158
ph: 401-295-2656 or 800-278-3228
fax: 401-295-2629
e-mail: sales@artfact.com
web: http://www.artfact.com
A computerized library recording auction sales of art and antiques; complete descriptions, prices realized, on-screen images.

Peter Falk
Institute for Art Research & Documentation
170 Boston Post Rd., Box 150
Madison, CT 06443-2164
ph: 203-245-2246 or 203-849-1655
fax: 203-245-5116
Service bureau for museums, archives, and scholarly art reference publishers; compiles and transcribes original historical documents into database format; also provides extensive appraisal services for the public.

Flora Hanft
Thesaurus Group Ltd.
111 5th Ave.
New York, NY 10003
ph: 800-491-FIND
fax: 516-944-5278
e-mail: Jason@thesaurus.co.uk
web: http://www.thesaurus.co.uk/
A pre-sale auction search service; a fee based service for subscribers to get advanced notice of upcoming items for sale at auctions around the world.

M. Barden Prisant
Telepraisal
P.O. Box 20686
New York, NY 10009-8973
ph: 212-614-9090 or 800-645-6002
fax: 212-780-9539
e-mail: bprisant@telepraisal.com
web: http://www.telepraisal.com
Computerized works of art data base search for art auctions and prices realized; verbal or written reports on paintings, sculptures and prints.

OmniGuard Corporation
730 Fifth Ave.
New York, NY 10019-4105
ph: 800-808-2882 or 212-577-9000
fax: 212-577-9220
e-mail: info@omniguard.com
web: http://www.omniguard.com/
Guarantees the authenticity of fine art; also registers art.

Anna J. Kisluk
International Foundation for Art Research (IFAR)
Magazine: IFAR Reports
500 Fifth Ave., Ste 1234
New York, NY 10110
ph: 212-391-6234
fax: 212-391-8794
e-mail: kferg@ifar.org
web: http://www.ifar.org
Clearinghouse for information on art theft, fraud, forgery; promotes recovery of stolen art & prevention of circulation of forged works; publishes Stolen Art Alert notices of art thefts and recoveries.

National Gallery of Art
Dept. of Education Resources
6th & Constitution Ave. NW
Washington, DC 20565-0001
ph: 202-737-4215
e-mail: webfeedback@nga.gov
web: http://www.nga.gov/
FREE loan program of VHS, 16mm film, and slide/tape programs covering many facets of art and antiques. Send for free Extension Programs Catalogue.

Elly Friedman
Award Video & Film Distributors, Inc.
3520 Bayou Louise Ln.
Sarasota, FL 34242-1102
ph: 941-955-1818
fax: 941-346-2583
A distribution company handling

quality art and collector videos including a Contemporary Art Series and a Collector Series.

Gordon's Art Reference, Inc.
Price Guide: Davenport's Art Reference & Price Guide
306 West Coronado Rd.
Phoenix, AZ 85003
ph: 602-253-6948 or 800-892-4622
fax: 602-253-2104
e-mail: info@gordonart.com
web: http://www.gordonart.com
Comprehensive bi-annual directory of over 175,000 artists, their work, auction dates and prices.

ISIS Secure Registry System
257 Grant Ave.
San Francisco, CA 94108
ph: 415-788-8411 or 415-788-6008
Uses advanced digital and forensic technologies to identify and register fine art to facilitate later identification and recovery should it be stolen.

Elizabeth Wenner-Madison
ARTLister
12162 SW Scholls Ferry Rd., Ste 117
Portland, OR 97223
ph: 503-579-9295
e-mail: art@artlister.com
web: http://www.artlister.com
Assisting dealers and private collectors in pricing, marketing, and shipping of limited edition prints, sculpture, and original fine art.

Art Library Online
Avenue Louise 65, Box 11
Brussels, 1050
Belgium
ph: +32 (0)2 535 7893
fax: +32 (0)2 535 7700
e-mail: adminb@artlibrary.com
web: http://www.artlibrary.com/
A subscription service: American art directory, international directory of arts, Who Was Who in American Art, museums of the world, the Official Museum Directory, auction sales database, art auctioneers online, galleries, and more.

ADEC Art Price Annual & Falk's Art Price Index
B.P. 69
St. Romain au Mont d'Or, 69270
France
ph: 33 478 220 000
fax: 33 478 220 606
e-mail: info@adec.com
web: http://www.artmarket.com/
An annual art price index having over 1,300,000 prices for catalogued works of art; 142,000 listed artists; updated daily; paintings, photography, prints, drawings; online or CD-ROM searchable.

Duncan Hislop
Art Sales Index, Ltd.
Price Guide: Artquest Computer Service
1 Thames St.
Weybridge, Surrey KT13 8JG
U.K.
ph: 01932-856426
fax: 01932-842482
e-mail: asi@art-sales-index.com
ARTQUEST on-line computer art database (also on CD-ROM) of art auction prices since 1970 (over 1.7 million records); also publishes the Annual Art Sales Index, Auction Prices of American Artists.

Museums/Libraries

Rhode Island School of Design Museum
224 Benefit St.
Providence, RI 02903-2723
ph: 401-454-6500
fax: 401-454-6556
e-mail: rbenefie@risd.edu
web: http://www.risd.edu/museum.html
Apparel, architecture, furniture, graphic design, industrial design, interior architecture, landscape architecture.

Archives of American Art, New York Research Center
1285 Avenue of the Americas
New York, NY 10019
ph: 212-399-5015
fax: 212-399-6890
e-mail: aaaemref@aaa.si.edu
web: http://www.si.edu/artarchives
Important source of biographical material on American artists; maintains records of paintings by subject & artist; regional offices in Boston, Detroit, New York, and San Marino, CA.

Whitney Museum of American Art
945 Madison Ave. at 75th St.
New York, NY 10021
ph: 212-570-3676
web: http://www.echonyc.com/~whitney/

Heidi Rosenau, Comm. Off.
Frick Collection, The
1 East 70th St.
New York, NY 10021-4967
ph: 212-288-0700
fax: 212-628-4417
e-mail: info@frick.org
web: http://www.frick.org/
Housed in the Gilded Age mansion of Henry Clay Frick (1849-1919), the museum is one of the most important private collections of Western fine art and decorative arts in the world: Bellini, El Greco, Rembrandt, Titian, Whistler.

Metropolitan Museum of Art
1000 Fifth Ave.
New York, NY 10028
ph: 212-570-3838
fax: 212-794-9316
web: http://www.metmuseum.org/
One of the largest and finest art museums on the world; over 2 million works of art spanning more than 5,000 years of world culture.

Philadelphia Museum of Art
P.O. Box 7646
Philadelphia, PA 19101-7646
ph: 215-684-7860 or 215-763-8100
fax: 215-235-0050
e-mail: pr@philamuseum.org
web: http://www.philamuseum.org
More than 400,000 works in the permanent collection; 3rd largest museum in the country; more than 200 galleries containing a myriad of artistic treasures from many continents and cultures.

Museum of American Art of the Pennsylvania Academy of Fine Arts
118 N Broad St.
Philadelphia, PA 19102
ph: 215-972-7600
e-mail: pafa@pafa.org
web: http://www.pafa.org/museum/museum.html
America's first art museum.

Corcoran Museum of Art
1701 E Street
Washington, DC 20002
ph: 202-639-1700 or 202-639-1725
e-mail: webmaster@corcoran.org
web: http://www.corcoran.org/

Holly Crider
National Museum of Women in the Arts
Magazine: Women in the Arts
1250 New York Ave. NW
Washington, DC 20005-3920
ph: 202-783-5000
fax: 202-393-3235
e-mail: NMWAmem@aol.com
web: http://www.nmwa.org/
Brings recognition to the achievements of women artists of all periods and nationalities by exhibiting, preserving, acquiring, and researching art by women and by educating the public concerning their accomplishments.

National Museum of American Art
Catalog: Smithsonian Art Index
8th & G Sts. N.W.
Washington, DC 20560
ph: 202-357-2504
e-mail: nmaainfo@nmaa.si.edu
web: http://www.nmaa.si.edu/
Identifies drawings, prints, paintings and sculpture in Smithsonian divisions but not part of the museum collection.

National Museum of American Art
Catalog: Peter A. Juley & Son Collection
8th & G Sts. N.W.
Washington, DC 20560
ph: 202-357-2504
e-mail: nmaainfo@nmaa.si.edu
web: http://www.nmaa.si.edu/
Over 127,000 photographic negatives of art now lost, destroyed or altered.

National Museum of American Art
Catalog: Slide & Photograph Archives
8th & G Sts. N.W.
Washington, DC 20560
ph: 202-357-2504
e-mail: nmaainfo@nmaa.si.edu
web: http://www.nmaa.si.edu/
Over 60,000 35mm color slides and over 200,000 photographs and negatives for visual documentation of American art.

National Museum of American Art
Catalog: Pre-1877 Art Exhibition Catalogue Index
8th & G Sts. N.W.
Washington, DC 20560
ph: 202-357-2504
e-mail: nmaainfo@nmaa.si.edu
web: http://www.nmaa.si.edu/
A computerized index from over 700 rare catalogs of exhibitions held between 1790 and 1876; art unions, fairs, museums, etc.

National Museum of American Art
Catalog: Permanent Collection Data Base
8th & G Sts. N.W.
Washington, DC 20560
ph: 202-357-2504
e-mail: nmaainfo@nmaa.si.edu
web: http://www.nmaa.si.edu/
A computerized listing providing information on the over 300,000 objects in the museum's permanent collection.

Archives of American Art, Washington D.C. Center
Journal: Archives of American Art Journal
901 D St. SW
Washington, DC 20560-0937
ph: 202-314-3900
e-mail: aaaemref@aaa.si.edu
web: http://www.si.edu/artarchives
Important source of biographical material on American artists; maintains records of paintings by subject & artist; regional offices in Boston, Detroit, New York, and San Marino, CA.

Joaneath Spicer
Walters Art Gallery
600 N. Charles St.
Baltimore, MD 21201
ph: 410-547-9000
e-mail: lwolfe@thewalters.org
web: http://www.thewalters.org/
One of only a few museums worldwide

to present a comprehensive history of art from the third millennium B.C. to the early 20th century.

Chrysler Museum, Art Reference Library, The
245 West Olney Road
Norfolk, VA 23510-1587
ph: 757-664-6200
fax: 757-664-6201
e-mail: museum@chrysler.org
web: http://www.chrysler.org

High Museum of Art, The
1280 Peachtree St.
Atlanta, GA 30309
ph: 404-733-4400
fax: 404-733-4502
web: http://www.high.org/

Toledo Museum of Art, The
2445 Monroe St.
P.O. Box 1013
Toledo, OH 43697
ph: 419-255-8000 or 800-644-6862
web: http://www.toledomuseum.org/
One of America's finest art collections American and European paintings in a building of exceptional beauty

Cleveland Museum of Art
11150 East Boulevard
Cleveland, OH 44106-1797
ph: 216-421-7340
e-mail: info@cma-oh.org
web: http://www.clemusart.com/
One of the world's great art museums with a collection of more than 30,000 works of art ranging over 5,000 years, from ancient Egypt to present; masterpieces from Europe, Asia, Africa and the Americas.

Detroit Institute of Arts
5200 Woodward Ave.
Detroit, MI 48202
ph: 313-833-7900
e-mail: Erickson@dia.ci.detroit.mi.us
web: http://www.dia.org/
The fifth largest fine arts museum in the U.S. with holdings of over 60,000 works: paintings, sculpture, and graphic and decorative arts.

Art Institute of Chicago
111 S. Michigan Ave.
Chicago, IL 60603
ph: 312-443-0849
e-mail: webmaster@artic.edu
web: http://www.artic.edu/aic/firstpage.html

Milan R. Hugston, Librarian
Amon Carter Museum
3501 Camp Bowie Blvd.
Fort Worth, TX 76107-2695
ph: 817-738-1933
fax: 817-377-8523
e-mail: milan.hughston@cartermuseum.org
web: http://www.cartermuseum.org
Has large and distinguished collection of paintings and sculpture by Frederic Remington and Charles M. Russell.

Los Angeles County Museum of Art
5905 Wilshire Blvd.
Los Angeles, CA 90036
ph: 323-857-6000
e-mail: publicinfo@lacma.org
web: http://www.lacma.org

Getty Center, The
1200 Getty Center Drive
Los Angeles, CA 90049
ph: 310-440-7300
web: http://www.getty.edu/
J.Paul Getty Museum of European and American art and sculpture; The Getty Research Institute for the History of Art and the Humanities; The Getty Conservation Institute; The Getty Information Institute.

Archives of American Art, West Coast Research Center
Huntington Library
1151 Oxford Rd.
San Marino, CA 91108
ph: 626-583-7847
fax: 626-583-7207
e-mail: aaaemref@aaa.si.edu
web: http://www.si.edu/artarchives
Important source of biographical material on American artists; maintains records of paintings by subject & artist; regional offices in Boston, Detroit, New York, and San Marino, CA.

Musee du Louvre
75058 Cedex 01
France
ph: (33) 01 40 20 51 51
fax: (33) 01 40 20 54 42
e-mail: info@louvre.fr
web: http://www.louvre.fr/

Periodicals

Fine Arts Trader, The
P.O. Box 1273
Randolph, MA 02368
ph: 800-332-5055 or 781-961-9045
fax: 781-961-9044
e-mail: info@fineartstrader.com
web: http://www.fineartstrader.com/
Published monthly to bring buyers and sellers of fine art together; ads, articles, happenings, upcoming antique shows.

Zachary P. Morfogen
Newsletter: Morgogen Associates NEWS
P.O. Box 324
Mountain Lakes, NJ 07046
ph: 973-334-0675
fax: 973-334-7458
e-mail: mmmzpm@aol.com
Published quarterly for museums and galleries, performing art institutions, corporate and foundation sponsors, art media; devote to previewing and promoting major museum and gallery exhibitions.

Newspaper: Art Newspaper, The
P.O. Box 3000
Denville, NJ 07834-9776
ph: 800-875-2997
U.S. subscription office for "the international journal of art"; prints, paintings, antiques, sculpture; articles, reviews, schedule of events, museum and gallery exhibits, fairs; published ten times per year in England.

Reed Reference Publishing
Directory: Official Museum Directory
121 Chanlon Rd.
New Providence, NJ 07974-1541
ph: 800-521-8110
Profiles more than 7,600 American institutions in 85 categories; aquariums, historic homes, museums, zoos; handy for those looking for information about specific types of antiques, fine art & collectibles; annual.

Magazine: Art & Auction
440 Park Ave. South
14th Floor
New York, NY 10016
ph: 800-777-8718 or 212-447-9555
fax: 212-447-5221
e-mail: editorial@artandauction.com
web: http://www.artandauction.com/
Covers the international art markets, from antiquities to contemporary art; articles include pieces on artists or schools of art/furniture, analyses of trends in the market, auction reviews and previews, calendar of events, etc.

Art & Auction Magazine
Directory: International Directory for Collectors
440 Park Ave. South
14th Floor
New York, NY 10016
ph: 800-777-8718 or 212-447-9555
fax: 212-447-5221
e-mail: editorial@artandauction.com
web: http://www.artandauction.com/
One issue per year of "Art & Auction Magazine" includes the Annual Directory of Galleries and Auction Houses International (including shows, art associations, fairs, art services, appraisers, conservators, etc.)

Newsletter: ARTnewsletter
48 West 38th St.
New York, NY 10018-6211
ph: 212-398-1690
fax: 212-819-0394
e-mail: goARTnews@aol.com
web: http://www.artnewsonline.com/
A biweekly international business report of the art market; has the latest news on auctions and trends in the art market.

Journal: Art On Paper
39 E 78th St., #501
New York, NY 10021-0213
ph: 212-988-5959
fax: 212-988-6107
e-mail: info@artonpaper.com
web: http://www.artonpaper.com
Published bi-monthly, this journal reports on the entire print and photograph market and is considered a must by print collectors and dealers; also contains scholarly articles and reviews, and auction results.

Walter de Gruyter, Inc.
Magazine: International Journal of Cultural Property
200 Saw Mill River Rd.
Hawthorne, NY 10532-1525
ph: 914-747-0110
fax: 914-747-1326
e-mail: degruyter.ny@worldnet.att.net
web: http://www.degruyter.de
Addresses such issues as contested attributions, ethics of art historians and museum personnel, looting, national retention and protection, legal issues and evolving law regarding art.

Haworth Press
Journal: Art Reference Services Quarterly
10 Alice St.
Binghamton, NY 13904-9981
ph: 800-895-0582 or 607-722-5857
fax: 607-722-6362
e-mail: getinfo@haworthpressinc.com
web: http://www.haworthpressinc.com/
Publication geared to art librarians focusing on reference services for art history, architecture, and the studio arts; legal resources for art, index to reviews of art reference titles, book reviews, etc.

Barbara Dougherty
Magazine: Art Calendar
27528 Fairmount Rd.
P.O. Box 199
Upper Fairmount, MD 21867
ph: 800-597-5988 or 410-651-9150
fax: 410-651-5313
e-mail: barbdoug@dmv.com
web: http://www.artcalendar.com/
A monthly magazine with artist and dealer interviews plus articles on art fraud, art scams, artist block, internships, shows, artist opportunities.

Barbara Dougherty
Directory: Annual Artists' Resource Directory
27528 Fairmount Rd.
P.O. Box 199
Upper Fairmount, MD 21867
ph: 800-597-5988 or 410-651-9150
fax: 410-651-5313
e-mail: barbdoug@dmv.com
web: http://www.artcalendar.com/
Annual containing art consultants, arts agencies and councils, college

galleries, corporate collections, artwork insurers, etc.

Magazine: Art & Antiques
2100 Powers Ferry Rd.
Atlanta, GA 30339
ph: 770-955-5656 or 800-274-7594
e-mail: art&antiques@billian.com
web: http://www.billian.com/artantiques/
Glossy magazine focusing on the fine and decorative arts and in antiques: colorful ads, articles, auction reports, etc.

Chicago New Art Association
Magazine: New Art Examiner
314 W. Institute Place
Chicago, IL 60610
ph: 312-649-9900
fax: 312-649-9935
e-mail: examiner@newartexaminer.org
web: http://www.newartexaminer.org/

Magazine: American Art Review
1200 East 104th St.
Kansas City, MO 64131
ph: 913-451-8801
Bi-monthly magazine devoted to America's artistic heritage.

Fred B. Rothman & Co.
Newsletter: Critical Issues
10368 W. Centennial Rd.
Littleton, CO 80127
ph: 800-457-1986
fax: 303-978-1457
e-mail: orders@rothman.com
A bi-monthly newsletter presenting legal and business information about art and antiques.

Anthony Westbridge
Westbridge Publications Ltd.
Newsletter: Westbridge Art Market Report
2339 Granville St.
Vancouver, British Columbia V6H 3G4
Canada
ph: 604-736-1014
fax: 604-734-4944
A bi-monthly newsletter for fine art collectors and investors; extensive auction coverage, including results and analysis, as well as market movements and trends, interviews, advice and opinion pertinent to art as an investment.

Magazine: Apollo Magazine
1 Castle Lane
London, SW1E 6DR
U.K.
ph: 0171-233 6640
fax: 0171-233-6307
e-mail: editorial@apollomag.com
web: http://www.apollomagazine.com/
The international magazine of art and antiques; an English monthly publication with detailed articles and glossy color photos; for U.S. postal subscriptions write P.O. Box 47, North Hollywood, CA 91603-0047.

African & Tribal

(see also BLACK MEMORABILIA; SAFARI)

Appraisers

Norman Hurst, ISA
Hurst Gallery
53 Mount Auburn St.
Cambridge, MA 02138
ph: 617-491-6888
fax: 617-661-0439
e-mail: NHurst@compuserve.com
web: http://www.hurstgallery.com
Buys, sells, appraises, restores African, Oceanic, Native American, PreColumbian and Asian art; dealing in, authenticating and appraising African art and artifacts for over 25 years; sculptures, masks.

Auction Services

Norman Hurst, ISA
Hurst Gallery
53 Mount Auburn St.
Cambridge, MA 02138
ph: 617-491-6888
fax: 617-661-0439
e-mail: NHurst@compuserve.com
web: http://www.hurstgallery.com
Buys, sells, appraises, restores African, Oceanic, Native American, PreColumbian and Asian art; dealing in, authenticating and appraising African art and artifacts for over 25 years; sculptures, masks.

Clubs/Associations

Deborah Begner, Mem.
Antique Tribal Art Dealers Association, The
215 Sierra SE
Albuquerque, NM 87108
ph: 602-423-8777
fax: 602-423-8778
e-mail: acek33@aol.com
web: http://www.atada.org/
Offers buyers a guarantee that objects members sell are as represented regarding age, authenticity and extent of restoration (if any); members also guarantee refunds if objects prove to be other than represented.

Collectors

Marcia Hersey
P.O. Box 976
Ansonia Station
New York, NY 10023-0976
ph: 212-877-5328 or 212-874-3946
Specializes in primitive art: African, Indonesian, Himalayan, Pre-Columbian; wants to buy authentic old objects.

Richard McCoy
2719 Lakeview Ave.
St. Joseph, MI 49085
Wants African and South American artifacts: spears, masks, shields, arrows, weapons, skins, mounts, ivory, art, tools, body adornments.

Dealers

Norman Hurst, ISA
Hurst Gallery
53 Mount Auburn St.
Cambridge, MA 02138
ph: 617-491-6888
fax: 617-661-0439
e-mail: NHurst@compuserve.com
web: http://www.hurstgallery.com
Buys, sells, appraises, restores African, Oceanic, Native American, PreColumbian and Asian art.

Phillip A. Alotta
Images Africaines
P.O. Box 8604
Saddle Brook, NJ 07663
ph: 201-797-3823 or 800-609-7565
Buys and sells African art.

Dominick Cardella
Artifactory
641 Indiana Ave. NW
Washington, DC 20004
ph: 202-393-2727
Sells new and old African, Asian and other foreign souvenir, arts and craft items including carvings and textiles.

Charles Jones
Charles Jones African Art
6716 Barren Inlet Rd.
Wilmington, NC 28405
ph: 910-686-0717
fax: 910-686-1313

John Buxton
Shango Galleries
6717 Spring Valley
Dallas, TX 75240
ph: 972-239-4620 or 972-239-9943
fax: 972-239-9766
e-mail: jbuxton@arttrak.com
web: http://www.arttrak.com
Buys, sells, and appraises African, Precolumbian, Oceanic, and American Indian art.

Joel & Michael Malter
Malter Galleries, Inc.
17005 Ventura Blvd.
Encino, CA 91316-4128
ph: 818-784-7772 or 818-784-2181
fax: 818-784-4726
e-mail: rarearts@earthlink.net
web: http://www.maltergalleries.com/

Experts

Scott Nelson
P.O. Box 6081
Santa Fe, NM 87502-6081
ph: 505-986-1176
Wants authentic African, Oceanic, and American Indian art and artifacts; consultant to "Schroeder's Antiques Price Guide."

Internet Resources

Conrad Schuler
masks.org
P.O. Box 11441
Olympia, WA 98508
web: http://www.masks.org
An online resource for masks, mask makers, and masquerade.

Museums/Libraries

SMA African Art Museum
23 Bliss Ave.
Tenafly, NJ 07042
ph: 201-894-8611
fax: 201-541-1280
e-mail: smausa-E@ix.netcom.com
web: http://www.smafathers.org/society/tenafly.htm

National Museum of African Art Smithsonian Institution
950 Independence Ave.
Washington, DC 20560-0001
ph: 202-357-4600 or 202-357-2700
fax: 202-357-4879
e-mail: webmaster@si.edu
web: http://www.si.edu/organiza/museums/africart/nmafa.htm
Museum's primary focus is collecting & exhibiting the traditional arts of Africa south of the Sahara; also collects & exhibits the arts of other African areas, including the arts of northern Africa; also ancient and contemporary arts.

Periodicals

Jonathan Fogel, Ed.
Tribarts, Inc.
Magazine: Tribal Arts
2261 Market St., #644
San Francisco, CA 94114
ph: 415-677-7917
fax: 415-431-8321
e-mail: fogel@mediacity.com
web: http://www.tribalarts.com/
The only magazine about the art, ethnography, and culture of tribal and ancient cultures around the world.

Alabama

Dealers

Marcia Weber - Art Objects
1050 Woodley Rd.
Montgomery, AL 36106
ph: 334-262-5349
fax: 334-567-0060
e-mail: weberart@mindspring.com
web: http://weberart.home.mindspring.com
Specializes in locating and selling antique art by important Alabama artists: Anne Goldthwaite, J. Kelly Fitzpatrick, Zelda Fitzgerald, Bill Taylor and the artists of the New South group; gallery opened by appointment.

Andy Warhol

Museums/Libraries

Andy Warhol Museum
117 Sandusky St.
Pittsburgh, PA 15212-5890
ph: 724-237-8300
fax: 724-237-8340
e-mail: warhol@alphaclp.clpgh.org
web: http://www.warhol.org/
Focuses on the American artist, Andy Warhol; also is a primary resource for anyone who wishes to gain insights into contemporary art and popular culture.

Asian

(see also ART, Oriental; INDONESIA; ORIENTALIA)

Appraisers

Norman Hurst, ISA
Hurst Gallery
53 Mount Auburn St.
Cambridge, MA 02138
ph: 617-491-6888
fax: 617-661-0439
e-mail: NHurst@compuserve.com
web: http://www.hurstgallery.com
Buys, sells, appraises, restores African, Oceanic, Native American, PreColumbian and Asian art.

Elisabeth Weikert Douglas
China Coast Oriental Art Appraisal Services
11266 Taylor Draper Lane, Apt. 2024
Austin, TX 78759-3972
ph: 512-288-3043
fax: 512-345-8420
e-mail: wien@texas.net
Active in the field of Asian art and antiques for over 20 years; owned and operated antiques export service in Bangkok, Thailand; owned and operated Oriental art and antiques shop in Washington DC.

Book Sellers

Paragon Book Gallery, Inc.
1507 S Michigan Ave.
Chicago, IL 60605-2812
ph: 312-663-5155
fax: 312-663-5177
e-mail: paragon@paragonbook.com
web: http://www.paragonbook.com/
Carries rare, out-of-print, and scholarly books on Asia; specializes in books on Asian arts and Asian studies; new and out of print.

Clubs/Associations

John van Breeman
Asia Society of Central Florida
Newsletter: ASCF Bulletin
2599 Via Tuscany
Winter Park, FL 32789
ph: 407-644-5190
A non-profit cultural organization; members interested in Asian art and culture; monthly meetings held Sept. to May with lectures and demonstrations on art of all Asian countries.

Collectors

John Rudak
32 Princess Lane
North Stonington, CT 06359-1117
ph: 860-599-8489
Wants Buddhist & Hindu art of SE Asia; all representations desired; interested in all Asian artistic mediums including metalwork, wood carvings, porcelain, pottery, works on paper, etc.; special interest in Buddhist art & artifacts.

Dealers

Norman Hurst, ISA
Hurst Gallery
53 Mount Auburn St.
Cambridge, MA 02138
ph: 617-491-6888
fax: 617-661-0439
e-mail: NHurst@compuserve.com
web: http://www.hurstgallery.com
Buys, sells, appraises, restores African, Oceanic, Native American, PreColumbian and Asian art.

Art of the Past
1242 Madison Ave.
New York, NY 10128-0515
ph: 212-860-7070
fax: 212-876-5373
Specializing in paintings, sculptures, textiles, Islamic and other works of art from India, Tibet, Nepal, and Southeast Asia.

Peaceful Wind
129 West San Francisco St.
Santa Fe, NM 87501
e-mail: asianart@nets.com
web: http://www.asianart.com/pw/
Expert and dealer specializes in high quality Asian art and antiquities, with a special emphasis on Himalayan art from Tibet and Nepal, and the art of Southeast Asia.

Perry Prince
Perry S. Prince, Asian Antiques
P.O. Box 1364
Ashland, OR 97520
ph: 541-488-1989
fax: 541-488-1989
e-mail: perry@asianarts.com
web: http://www.asianarts.com
Carries architectural antiques, Southeast Asian, Asian art, Asian antiques, interior decorating, interior design, Asian folk art, salvage, Chinese antiques, Chinese architecture.

Experts

Pratapaditya Pal, Cur.
Los Angeles County Museum of Art
5905 Wilshire Blvd.
Los Angeles, CA 90036
ph: 323-857-6000
e-mail: publicinfo@lacma.org
web: http://www.lacma.org
Senior curator of Indian and Southeast Asian Art; author of "Tibetan Paintings"; specializes in Indian and Himalayan arts; Tibetan thankas, Hinduism and Buddhism.

Internet Resources

Ian Alsop
Asian Arts
129 "B" West San Francisco
Santa Fe, NM 87501
ph: 505-983-7658
fax: 505-983-7613
e-mail: asianart@webart.com
web: http://www.asianart.com/
The on-line journal for the study and exhibition of the arts of Asia; offers buy and sell service.

Museums/Libraries

Hiram Woodward
Walters Art Gallery
600 N. Charles St.
Baltimore, MD 21201
ph: 410-547-9000
e-mail: lwolfe@thewalters.org
web: http://www.thewalters.org/
One of only a few museums worldwide to present a comprehensive history of art from the third millennium B.C. to the early 20th century.

Los Angeles County Museum of Art
5905 Wilshire Blvd.
Los Angeles, CA 90036
ph: 323-857-6000
e-mail: publicinfo@lacma.org
web: http://www.lacma.org

Pacific Asia Museum
Newsletter: Pacific Asia Museum Member Newsletter
46 N. Los Robles Ave.
Pasadena, CA 91101
ph: 626-449-2742
fax: 626-449-2754
web: http://www.sppsr.ucla.edu/dup/courses/s97/comdev/pamuseum/
Preserves, presents, and interprets to the public the arts and culture of the Pacific Islands and Asia.

Periodicals

Wendy Holden, Co-Ed.
Journal: Newsletter, East Asian Art & Archaeology
Dept. of the History of Art, 50 Tappan Hall
Univ. of Michigan
Ann Arbor, MI 48109-1357
ph: 734-936-2539
fax: 734-647-4121
e-mail: wholden@umich.edu
web: http://www.umich.edu/~hartspc/NEAAA.html
Published three times per year, NEAAA focuses on current exhibitions, symposia, newly published books, scholarly news, etc.

Elizabeth Knight, Pub.
Orientations Magazine Limited
Magazine: Orientations
200 Lockhart Road, 17th Floor
Hong Kong
ph: 2511 1368
fax: 2507 4620
e-mail: info@orientations.com.hk
web: http://www.orientations.com.hk/
Brings readers informed articles on all aspects of the arts of East Asia, the Indian Subcontinent and Southeast Asia; beautifully illustrated articles on the ancient arts of painting, calligraphy, bronzes, ceramics.

HALI Publications, Ltd.
Magazine: HALI
Kingsgate House
Kingsgate Place, London NW6 4TA
U.K.
ph: 44 171 328 9341 or 44 171 328 1998
fax: 44 171 372 5924
e-mail: hali@centaur.co.uk
"HALI" is the leading bi-monthly international publication in the field of carpet and textile art; an invaluable encyclopedic source of information with original research articles, reviews of museum collections, etc.; high color.

Australia

Dealers

Ian Johnson
Harden, Johnson & Assoc.
1616 Whisper Way
Goose Creek, SC 29445
ph: 843-572-7968
fax: 843-572-7968
24 years experience in Australian, New Zealand, South African paintings, drawings, and watercolors from 1797 to present; also specializing in British, Scottish, and Irish paintings from 1880-1950; daily contact with these countries.

Bad

Internet Resources

Vito Salvatore
Vito Salvatore Virtual Collection
e-mail: vito@badart.com
web: http://www.badart.com/
Scours the US for the most appallingly bad art; much is on this online virtual gallery.

Lauren Wood
Laruen Wood's Wacky World of Bad Art!
11684 Ventura Blvd., Ste 515
Studio City, CA 91604
e-mail: bighairdo@laurenwood.com
web: http://laurenwood.com/badart.htm

Museums/Libraries

Museum of Bad Art
10 Vogel St.
Boston, MA 02123
ph: 781-325-8224 or 781-444-6757
e-mail: moba@wworld.std.com
web: http://glyphs.com/moba/
Museum is located at 580 High Street, Dedham MA 02026; a community-based, private institution dedicated to the collection, preservation, exhibition and celebration of bad art in all its glory.

Botanical

Museums/Libraries

James J. White
Hunt Institute for Botanical Documentation
Journal: Huntia
Carnegie Mellon University
Pittsburgh, PA 15213-3890
ph: 412-268-2434 or 412-268-2440
fax: 412-268-5677
e-mail: jw3u@andrew.cmu.edu
web: http://huntbot.andrew.cmu.edu/HIBD/HuntInstitute.html
Collection documents botanical imagery from Renaissance onward; center for research/documentation into botanical science, history, art, biography, bibliography; conducts exhibitions of botanical art and illustration; no appraisals.

British

Auction Services

Ian Johnson
Harden, Johnson & Assoc.
1616 Whisper Way
Goose Creek, SC 29445
ph: 843-572-7968
fax: 843-572-7968
24 years experience in Australian, New Zealand, South African paintings, drawings, and watercolors from 1797 to present; also specializing in British, Scottish, and Irish paintings from 1880-1950; daily contact with these countries.

Dealers

Ian Johnson
Harden, Johnson & Assoc.
1616 Whisper Way
Goose Creek, SC 29445
ph: 843-572-7968
fax: 843-572-7968
24 years experience in Australian, New Zealand, South African paintings, drawings, and watercolors from 1797 to present; also specializing in British, Scottish, and Irish paintings from 1880-1950; daily contact with these countries.

Jeffery Measamer
Art Connections
8315 E. Copper Village Dr.
Houston, TX 77095
ph: 281-861-0244
fax: 281-861-0266
e-mail: ArtConnections@worldnet.att.net
web: http://www.erols.com/villej/alldlr/artconn/artconn.htm
Specialists in fine prints and drawings from 1750-1950; deals primarily in British prints and drawings; always has a wide selection of American and European works in stock.

Museums/Libraries

Duncan Robinson, Dir.
Yale Center for British Art
P.O. Box 208280
New Haven, CT 06520-8280
ph: 203-432-2800 or 203-432-2850
fax: 203-432-9695
e-mail: bacinfo@minerva.cis.yale.edu
web: http://pantheon.cis.yale.edu/~yups/bac/
Largest museum and research center for British paintings, sculpture, prints, drawings, and rare books outside England; no decorative arts.

Byzantine

Museums/Libraries

Dumbarton Oaks Research Library & Collection
1703 32nd St. NW
Washington, DC 20007
ph: 202-339-6400
e-mail: DumbartonOaks@doaks.org
web: http://www.doaks.org/

California

Appraisers

Richard C. Frey, ISA
R.T.L.H. Enterprises
1275 East Ave.
Chico, CA 95926-1020
ph: 530-343-4528 or 800-567-7854
fax: 530-343-9380
e-mail: RFREYRTLH@aol.com
Qualified appraiser of American and European art, paintings, watercolors, drawings, prints, sculpture, bronzes, etc.; appraises for estates, arbitration, and has testified as expert witness.

Auction Services

Butterfield & Butterfield
7601 Sunset Blvd.
Los Angeles, CA 90046-2714
ph: 323-850-7500
fax: 323-850-5843
e-mail: info@butterfields.com
web: http://www.butterfields.com/

John Moran
John Moran Auctioneers, Inc.
735 W. Woodbury Rd.
Altadena, CA 91001-5310

Dealers

Goldfield Galleries
8380 Melrose Ave.
West Hollywood, CA 90069-5422
ph: 323-651-1122
fax: 323-651-1168
Specializes in 19th and 20th century American Impressionist art, and California and Western art.

Marcia Osterkamp, ISA
Poulsen Galleries, Inc.
327 Terrace Dr.
Brawley, CA 92227-3040
ph: 760-344-4810
fax: 760-344-4778
e-mail: poulsengalleries@compuserve.com
web: http://www.artnet.com/poulsen.html
Fine art appraiser; buys and sells 19th and 20th century American and European paintings; also California paintings.

Ray Redfern
Redfern Galleries
1540 South Coast Hwy.
Laguna Beach, CA 92651
ph: 949-497-3356

Jimmy Vitanza
Peregrine Galleries
508 Brinkerhoff Ave.
Santa Barbara, CA 93101-3441
ph: 805-963-3134
fax: 805-963-3134

Paul Galli
ph: 408-730-4010
e-mail: paul.galli@lmco.com
Buys and sells San Francisco abstract expressionist art by John Saccard, James Budd Dixon, Edward Corbett, and other artists.

Alfred C. Harrison, Jr.
Northpoint Gallery, The
250 Sutter St., 4th Floor
San Francisco, CA 94108
ph: 415-781-7550

Garzoli Gallery
930 B. St.
San Rafael, CA 94901
ph: 415-459-4321

Christine Daniels
135 E. Shiloh Rd.
Santa Rosa, CA 95403-1254
ph: 707-838-6083
fax: 707-838-6083
e-mail: ctiques@aol.com
Buys and sells art: Maxfield Parrish, R. Atkinson Fix prints; also R. Atkinson oils, Louis Icart etchings, and early California oil paintings.

Syd Bottomley, ISA
P.O. Box 1842
Nevada City, CA 95959
ph: 530-272-5400
fax: 530-272-2820
Buys, collects, appraises and specializes in American Indian art: baskets, rugs, pottery, early California paintings.

Museums/Libraries

Irvine Museum, The
18881 Von Karman Ave., 12th Floor
Irvine, CA 92612
ph: 949-476-0294 or 949-476-2565
web: http://www.irvinemuseum.org/
Dedicated to the preservation and display of California art of the Impressionist Period (1890-1930).

Canadian

Appraisers

Kathryn Minard, ISA
Contemporary Fine Art Services, Inc.
413 Dundas St. East
Toronto, Ontario M5A 2A9
Canada
ph: 416-366-9770
fax: 416-366-8541
e-mail: kathryn_minard@compuserve.com
Expert and appraiser specializing in Canadian contemporary and historical art; also Canadian Indian and Inuit.

Auction Services

Waddington's
11 Bathurst Street
Toronto, Ontario M5V 2R1
Canada
ph: 416-504-9100
fax: 416-504-0033
e-mail: info@waddingtonsauctions.com
web: http://www.waddingtonsauctions.com
Canada's oldest and largest auction house specializing in decorative arts, jewelry, antique furniture, Inuit and native Canadian arts, European and Canadian arts, books, militaria, Orientalia, toys, ceramics, etc.

Periodicals

Wendy Ingram, Pub.
Magazine: Canadian Art
70 The Esplanade, 2nd Floor
Toronto, Ontario M5E 1R2
Canada
ph: 416-368-8854
fax: 416-368-6135
e-mail: canart@istar.ca

Magazine: C Magazine
P.O. Box 5, Station B
Toronto, Ontatio M5T 2T2
Canada
ph: 416-539-9495
fax: 416-539-9903

Magazine: Arts Atlantic
Confederation Center
145 Richmond St.
Charlottetown, Prince Edward C1A 1J1
Canada
ph: 902-628-6138
fax: 902-566-4648
e-mail: artsatlantic@isn.net
web: http://www.isn.net/artsatlantic
Atlantic Canada's only arts periodical; features and reviews work of practicing painters, print makers, sculptors, photographers and craftspeople; also performances staged by theatre and dance companies.

Magazine: Border Crossings
500-70 Arthur St.
Winnipeg, Manitoba R3B 1G7
Canada
ph: 204-942-5778
fax: 204-949-0793
e-mail: bordercr@escape.ca

Magazine: Innuit Art Quarterly
2081 Merivale Road
Nepean, Ontario K2G 1G9
Canada
ph: 613-224-8189
fax: 613-224-2907
e-mail: iaf@inuitart.org
web: http://www.inuitart.org

Canvas Marks

Collectors

Alexander Katlan
Alexander Katlan Conservation Inc.
5638 Main St.
Flushing, NY 11355-5046
ph: 718-445-7458
Interested in collecting American canvas marks or maker's labels found on the backs of paintings.

Commercial Advertising

Man./Prod./Dist.

Craig Wolfe
Name That Toon Icons of Happiness
28 Mountain View Ave.
San Rafael, CA 94901
ph: 415-456-3452 or 800-550-5202
fax: 415-456-9045
e-mail: response@namethattoon.com
web: http://www.namethattoon.com
World's largest publisher of commercial advertising/animation art; framed and matted prints: Coca-Cola, Anheuser-Busch, M&M/Mars, Pillsbury, Hershey's, Campbell Soup, Nabisco, Planter's, Life Savers, Oreo, Ritz, etc.

Contemporary

Auction Services

Christie's
502 Park Ave.
New York, NY 10022
ph: 212-546-1000
fax: 212-980-8163
web: http://www.christies.com

Dealers

Knoedler & Company
19 East 70th St.
New York, NY 10021
ph: 212-794-0550
fax: 212-772-6932

Andre Emmerich Gallery
41 East 57th St.
New York, NY 10022
ph: 212-752-0124
fax: 212-371-7345

Museums/Libraries

Museum of Modern Art, The
11 W. 53rd. St.
New York, NY 10019
ph: 212-708-9400 or 800-447-6662
e-mail: comments@moma.org
web: http://www.moma.org/

William Johnston
Walters Art Gallery
600 N. Charles St.
Baltimore, MD 21201
ph: 410-547-9000
e-mail: lwolfe@thewalters.org
web: http://www.thewalters.org/
One of only a few museums worldwide to present a comprehensive history of art from the third millennium B.C. to the early 20th century.

Contemporary Arts Center
115 E. Fifth St.
Cincinnati, OH 45202
ph: 513-345-8400
fax: 513-721-7418
e-mail: admin@spiral.org
web: http://www.spiral.org/

Cranbrook Art Museum
1221 N. Woodward Ave.
Bloomfield Hills, MI 48013
ph: 248-645-3323 or 248-645-3361
fax: 248-645-3324
e-mail: caa_info@cc.cranbrook.edu
web: http://www.cranbrookart.edu/museum/

Museum of Contemporary Art
220 East Chicago Ave.
Chicago, IL 60611-2604
ph: 312-280-2660
fax: 312-397-4095
web: http://www.mcachicago.org/

Periodicals

Mercury Subscription Service
Magazine: Modern Painters
2323 Randolf Ave.
Avenel, NJ 07001
ph: 44 171 626 6305 or 44 171 636 6058
fax: 44 171 580 5615
web: http://www.bowieart.com/mp.html
An English quarterly journal of the fine arts.

Magazine: Artforum International
350 7th Ave., 19th Floor
New York, NY 10001
fax: 212-529-1257
e-mail: generalinfo@artforum.com
web: http://www.artforum.com/

Brant Art Publications
Magazine: Art in America
575 Broadway
New York, NY 10012
ph: 212-941-2800 or 800-925-8059
fax: 212-941-2897
e-mail: brantpubs@aol.com
A full-color monthly magazine focusing on contemporary art.

Art in America Magazine
Directory: Annual Art Directory
575 Broadway
New York, NY 10012
ph: 212-941-2800 or 800-925-8059
fax: 212-941-2897
e-mail: brantpubs@aol.com
The August issue of "Art in America" includes an annual directory of art galleries, museums art associations, fairs, art services, appraisers, conservators, etc.

Magazine: ARTnews
48 West 38th St.
New York, NY 10018-6211
ph: 212-398-1690
fax: 212-819-0394
e-mail: goARTnews@aol.com
web: http://www.artnewsonline.com/
A monthly magazine that reports on the contemporary art forms, personalities, issues, exhibitions, trends, and events that shape the international art world; subscriptions call 800-284-4625

Newspaper: West Art
P.O. Box 6868
Auburn, CA 95604-6868
ph: 530-885-0969
West Coast biweekly art publication; information and photographs of current West Coast fine art and craft exhibitions.

German

Collectors

Tony Vehr
4118 East Vernon Ave.
Phoenix, AZ 85008-2333
ph: 602-957-0653
fax: 602-957-1631
Wants to buy pen and ink sketches and prints by German artist Heinrich Kley.

Museums/Libraries

Busch-Reisinger Museum, Harvard University Art Museums
32 Quincy St.
Cambridge, MA 02138
ph: 617-495-2317 or 617-495-9400
fax: 617-495-9936
web: http://www.artmuseums.harvard.edu/Busch_Pages/BuschMain.html
Harvard University Art Museum's collection of Germanic art: masterpieces of Vienna Secession art, German Expressionism, 1920s abstraction, decorative arts and architectural drawings; also late Medieval, Renaissance, Baroque sculpture.

Grandma Moses

Museums/Libraries

Bennington Museum, The
W. Main St.
Bennington, VT 05201
ph: 802-447-1571
fax: 802-442-8305
web: http://www.bennington.com/museum/
One of the finest regional art history museums in the country; works by Grandma Moses, American glass, VT furniture, Bennington pottery, the oldest Stars & Stripes in existence, the 1925 luxury touring car "The Wasp", and much more.

Haitian

Dealers

Le Jardin Cultured Art Gallery
225-09 Linden Blvd.
Jamaica, NY 11411
ph: 718-712-9377
fax: 718-528-1799

Art of Haiti, The - MedaliaArt
6 Fox Rd.
East Setauket, NY 11733
ph: 516-246-5527 or 800-984-2065
e-mail: webmaster@medalia.net
web: http://www.medalia.net/

Bill Bollendorf
Galerie Macondo
406 S. Craig St.
Pittsburgh, PA 15213-3720
ph: 412-683-6486 or 412-661-1498
Devoted to informing collectors on trends in Haitian art, price trends, news of the Haitian art community and interviews with established and emerging artists.

Ireland

Dealers

Ian Johnson
Harden, Johnson & Assoc.
1616 Whisper Way
Goose Creek, SC 29445
ph: 843-572-7968
fax: 843-572-7968
24 years experience in Australian, New Zealand, South African paintings, drawings, and watercolors from 1797 to present; also specializing in British, Scottish, and Irish paintings from 1880-1950; daily contact with these countries.

Islamic

Dealers

Mehmet Nabi Israfil
Fil Caravan Inc.
240 Eat 56th St., Ste. 2E
New York, NY 10022
ph: 212-421-5972
fax: 212-421-5976
e-mail: filcaravan@worldnet.att.net
web: http://www.citysearch.com/nyc/filcaravan
Established in 1976, Serves an international clientele in all aspects of Islamic Art including antiques, jewelry, textiles and fine Oriental rugs; has large selection of authentic Russian samovars.

Italian Renaissance

Museums/Libraries

Joan Norris
Isabella Stewart Gardner Museum
280 The Fenway
Boston, MA 02115-5809
ph: 617-566-1401
fax: 617-232-8039
web: http://www.boston.com/gardner/
Museum is the remarkable achievement of Isabella Stewart Gardner, who formed the collection, designed the building; opened in 1903; built in the style of the 15th century Venetian palazzo; houses 2,500 works of art spanning 30 centuries.

Jasper F. Cropsey

Museums/Libraries

Newington-Cropsey Foundation
25 Cropsey Lane
Hastings On Hudson, NY 10706
ph: 914-478-7990
web: http://www.newingtoncropsey.com/
Concentrates on figurative and classical works, with good color illustrations, and comments on art, architecture, and culture in general.

Jewish

(see also JUDAICA)

Museums/Libraries

Center for Jewish Art, Hebrew University of Jerusalem
Journal: Jewish Art
P.O. Box 4262
Jerusalem, 91042
Israel
ph: 972 02 6586605 or 972 02 658664
fax: 972 02 6586672
e-mail: cja@vms.huji.ac.il
web: http://www.hum.huji.ac.il/cja/
Dedicated to research, documentation, publication and education in the field of Jewish art.

Jo Mora

Collectors

Terry Ahlberg
1000 Irvine Blvd.
Tustin, CA 92680-3527
ph: 714-730-1000 or 949-654-1331
fax: 714-730-1752
e-mail: emailit@earthlink.net
Collecting all art of Jo Mora (a.k.a. J.J. Mora, Joseph J. Mora, J.M.M.) (1876-1947) including posters, pictorial maps, sculpture, illustrated and/or authored books, photos of Mora or his art.

Marine

(see also NAUTICAL ANTIQUES)

Collectors

Kerry James McCaffrey
6 Senate Pl.
P.O. Box 6686
Jersey City, NJ 07306
Collector, expert.

Dealers

James & Ann Marenakos
Quester Gallery
77 Main St.
P.O. Box 446
Stonington, CT 06378
ph: 860-535-3860
fax: 860-535-3533
e-mail: questergal@snet.net
web: http://www.artnet.com/quester.html
Buys, sells, consults on 19th & 20th century marine paintings, ships models, bronzes, campaign furniture, etc.

Rod & Becky Cardoza
West Sea Company
2495 Congress St.
San Diego, CA 92110-2820
ph: 619-296-5356
fax: 619-296-1097
Buys, sells all types of marine paintings, scrimshaw, ships' carvings, ship models, navigational and scientific instruments, sailor handcrafts, campaign furniture, hard hat diving, antique marine photography, nautical books, ceramics.

Experts

Sara Conklin
Nautical Appraisals
239 Sierra Pt. Rd.
Brisbane, CA 94005-1664
ph: 415-467-6249
fax: 415-467-6249
e-mail: sconklin2@earthlink.com
Managed the collections of the National Maritime Museum in San Francisco for ten years and is an expert in appraising marine fine art.

Internet Resources

Arthur S. Liss
Marine Art Information Center
151 East 83rd St.
Penthouse D
New York, NY 10028-1958
ph: 212-772-2737
fax: 212-861-4754
e-mail: info@marineart.com
web: http://www.marineart.com
An on-line resource center for all manner of topics relating to marine art, including a link to The American Society of Marine Artists.

Periodicals

Robert R. McKenna, Ed.
Magazine: Nautical Collector
One Whale Oil Row
New London, CT 06320
ph: 860-444-0127
fax: 860-444-0129
e-mail: nautworld@aol.com
An authoritative bi-monthly magazine on the antiques, collectibles, art, artifacts, literature and memorabilia associated with the seas, lakes and waterways.

New Mexico

Dealers

Eller, ISA
Peter Eller Gallery & Appraisers
206 Dartmouth
Albuquerque, NM 87106
ph: 505-268-7437
fax: 505-268-6442
e-mail: pelgal@nmia.com
web: http://www.peterellergallery.com/
Specializes in works by Albuquerque artists and minor New Mexico artists, traditional and modernist, 1925-1965, for beginning and intermediate collectors; appraising art, antiques, Spanish Colonial, religious and SW Indian artifacts.

New Zealand

Dealers

Ian Johnson
Harden, Johnson & Assoc.
1616 Whisper Way
Goose Creek, SC 29445
ph: 843-572-7968
fax: 843-572-7968
24 years experience in Australian, New Zealand, South African paintings, drawings, and watercolors from 1797 to present; also specializing in British, Scottish, and Irish paintings from 1880-1950; daily contact with these countries.

Oceanic

Appraisers

Norman Hurst, ISA
Hurst Gallery
53 Mount Auburn St.
Cambridge, MA 02138
ph: 617-491-6888
fax: 617-661-0439
e-mail: NHurst@compuserve.com
web: http://www.hurstgallery.com
Buys, sells, appraises, restores African, Oceanic, Native American, PreColumbian and Asian art; one of the leading appraisers of the Pacific including Melanesian, Polynesian, Micronesian, and Southeast Asian art.

Dealers

Norman Hurst, ISA
Hurst Gallery
53 Mount Auburn St.
Cambridge, MA 02138
ph: 617-491-6888
fax: 617-661-0439
e-mail: NHurst@compuserve.com
web: http://www.hurstgallery.com
Buys, sells, appraises, restores African, Oceanic, Native American, PreColumbian and Asian art; one of the leading appraisers of the Pacific including Melanesian, Polynesian, Micronesian, and Southeast Asian art.

John Buxton
Shango Galleries
6717 Spring Valley
Dallas, TX 75240
ph: 972-239-4620 or 972-239-9943
fax: 972-239-9766
e-mail: jbuxton@arttrak.com
web: http://www.arttrak.com
Buys, sells, and appraises African, Precolumbian, Oceanic, and American Indian art.

Oriental

(see also ART, Asian; BRONZES, Oriental; CERAMICS [ORIENTAL]; COLLECTIBLES [MODERN], Sculptures [Japanese Themes]; ORIENTALIA; PRINTS, Woodblock [Japanese])

Auction Services

William P. Weschler
Weschler's
909 E St. NW
Washington, DC 20004-2006
ph: 202-628-1281 or 800-331-1430
fax: 202-628-2366
web: http://www.weschlers.com/
Conducts specialized auction sales of antique Oriental Art.

Dealers

Floating World Gallery
P.O. Box 148200
Chicago, IL 60614
ph: 312-587-7800
fax: 312-587-7888
e-mail: artwork@floatingworld.com
web: http://www.floatingworld.com
Seeking paintings and prints from the Far East; antique to the present; Japan, Philippines, Indonesia, Singapore, Bali, China.

Experts

Dr. Daphne L. Rosenzweig
Rosenzweig Associates
P.O. Box 16187
Tampa, FL 33687-6187
ph: 813-988-0880
fax: 813-989-8091
e-mail: rosetwig@aol.com
Consultant and appraiser dealing with Oriental Art; author of the books "Selected Works from the Fine Arts Group of Later Chinese Painting" and "The Appraisal of Oriental Art", and of Chinese jade and other Orientalia catalogues.

Misc. Services

Arthur M. Sackler Gallery
Smithsonian Institution
1050 Independence Ave. SW
Washington, DC 20560
ph: 202-357-3200
e-mail: edsonmi@asia.si.edu
web: http://www.si.edu/organiza/museums/freer/start.htm
Will authenticate your Japanese, Chinese, Near East and South & Southeast works of art; call for an appt.; limit 5 items/visit, 10 items/year; may be able to work from good photographs.

Museums/Libraries

Arthur M. Sackler Museum, Harvard University of Art Museums
32 Quincy Street
Cambridge, MA 02138
ph: 617-495-9400
web: http://www.artmuseums.harvard.edu/Sackler_Pages/SacklerMain.html
Houses collections of Ancient, Asian, Islamic, and Later Indian art: the world's finest collection of Chinese jades, Korean ceramics, and Chinese cave temple paintings and sculpture, Japanese woodblock prints, Chinese bronzes, etc.

Freer Gallery of Art
Smithsonian Institution
12th & Jefferson Dr. SW
Washington, DC 20560
ph: 202-357-3200
e-mail: edsonmi@asia.si.edu
web: http://www.si.edu/organiza/museums/freer/start.htm
The Freer Gallery of Art and the Arthur M. Sackler Gallery are the two national museums of Asian art at the Smithsonian Institution.

Arthur M. Sackler Gallery
Smithsonian Institution
1050 Independence Ave. SW
Washington, DC 20560
ph: 202-357-3200
e-mail: edsonmi@asia.si.edu
web: http://www.si.edu/organiza/museums/freer/start.htm
The Freer Gallery of Art and the Arthur M. Sackler Gallery are the two national museums of Asian art at the Smithsonian Institution.

Periodicals

Wendy Holden, Co-Ed.
Newsletter: Newsletter, East Asian Art & Archaeology
Dept. of the History of Art, 50 Tappan Hall
Univ. of Michigan
Ann Arbor, MI 48109-1357
ph: 734-936-2539
fax: 734-647-4121
e-mail: wholden@umich.edu
web: http://www.umich.edu/~hartspc/NEAAA.html
Published three times per year, NEAAA focuses on current exhibitions, symposia, newly published books, scholarly news, etc.

Jenny Marsh, Ex. Dir.
Magazine: Arts of Asia
1309 Kowloon Centre
29-39 Ashley Rd.
Hong Kong
ph: (852) 23762228
fax: (852) 23763713
e-mail: artasia@hk.linkage.net
web: http://user.hk.linkage.net/~artasia/
A bi-monthly fully illustrated, scholarly magazine about the Oriental arts.

Repair Services

Janice & Dennis Dobson
Dobson Studios
810 N. Daniel St.
Arlington, VA 22201-1944
ph: 703-243-7363
fax: 703-243-2382
e-mail: ddobson@erols.com
Conservator of Oriental screens, scrolls and wood block prints; repairs and conservation to other paper items as well.

Outsider

(see also FOLK ART)

Auction Services

Steve Slotin
Slotin Folk Art Auction House
Newspaper: 20th Century Folk Art News
5967 Blackberry Lane
Buford, GA 30518
ph: 770-932-1000
fax: 770-932-0506
Leading venue for self-taught, Outsider, Folk Art and Southern folk pottery; published newspaper twice each year chronicling important happenings in the field of 20th century folk art as the most popular feature, New, True & Blue Artists.

Clubs/Associations

Jeff Cory
Intuit: The Center for Intuitive & Outsider Art
Newsletter: Outsider, The
756 N. Milwaukee Ave.
Chicago, IL 60622
ph: 312-243-9088
fax: 312-243-9089
e-mail: intuit@art.org
web: http://outsider.art.org
Committed to fostering and expanding the awareness of outsider, intuitive, and visionary art.

Bill Rose, Sec.
Deep South Society, Art & Pleasure Club
3500 St. Charles Ave., #204
New Orleans, LA 70115
To study and promote the understanding of self-taught artists and their art, and to disseminate relevant information.

Dealers

Frank Maresca
Ricco/Maresca Gallery
529 W. 20th Street, 3rd Floor
New York, NY 10011
ph: 212-627-4819
fax: 212-627-5117
e-mail: rmgal@aol.com
web: http://www.riccomaresca.com/
Deals in American self-taught, folk and outsider art.

William K. Jones
Folk Art Net
4026 Melrose Ave.
Roanoke, VA 24017
ph: 800-476-4215 or 540-362-3751
fax: 540-563-0545
e-mail: asnake65@aol.com
Collects, buys and sells self-taught, folk, outsider art.

America - Oh, Yes
17 Pope Ave. Executive Park, Bldg. 4
P.O. Box 3075
Hilton Head Island, SC 29928
ph: 843-785-2649
e-mail: folkart@hargray.com
web: http://www.americaohyes.com

Matt Lippa
Artisans
P.O. Box 256
Mentone, AL 35984-0256
ph: 256-634-4037
fax: 256-634-4037
e-mail: artisans@folkartisans.com
web: http://www.folkartisans.com
Buy and sell folk art, outsider art, fine art; Internet WWW site offers links to additional dealers; also offers non-profit clubs and museums with an outlet to post notices, press releases, calendar items, etc. at no charge.

Marcia Weber - Art Objects
1050 Woodley Rd.
Montgomery, AL 36106
ph: 334-262-5349
fax: 334-567-0060
e-mail: weberart@mindspring.com
web: http://weberart.home.mindspring.com
Has specialized in collecting and art created by self-taught artists for many years; has an inventory of over 400 works available through photographs sent to prospective purchasers; gallery opened by appointment only.

Anton Haardt Gallery
2714 Coliseum St.
New Orleans, LA 70130
ph: 504-897-1172
Specializes in contemporary folk art from the Deep South.

Lois Zetter
Zetter Collection, The
5570 Old Highway 395 N.
Carson City, NV 89704
ph: 702-885-2827
fax: 702-885-6850
e-mail: lzmgmt@pyramid.net
Specializing in the self-taught artist.

Ames Gallery, The
2661 Cedar St.
Berkeley, CA 94708
ph: 510-845-4949
fax: 510-845-6219
Specializes in self-taught, visionary, outsider, intuitive, art brut, folk art.

Internet Resources

William Swislow
Outsider Pages, The
e-mail: billsw@mcs.com
web: http://www.interestingideas.com/

David A. Crotty
e-mail: dacrotty@cco.caltech.edu
web: http://www.cco.caltech.edu/~dacrotty/folkart.html
Website has lots of information about self-taught artists of the United States.

Steve Slotin
Self-Taught Art Online
5967 Blackberry Lane
Buford, GA 30518
ph: 770-932-1000
fax: 770-932-0506
The website for collectors and galleries of the self-taught artist; promotes the folk art field, helps sell inventory.

Periodicals

Journal: Raw Vision
163 Amsterdam Ave., #203
New York, NY 10023-5001
ph: 212-714-8381
e-mail: rawvision@btinternet.com
web: http://www.rawvision.com/
A semiannual journal devoted outsider art (works ignored by the conventional art press).

Paint-By-Numbers

Internet Resources

Le Salon de PAINT-BY-NUMBERS
e-mail: eddertoo@paintbynumberz.com
web: http://www.paintbynumberz.com/directory.html
History of paint-by-numbers, articles, conservation tips, photos, related links.

Periodicals

Larry Rubin
Newsletter: By The Numbers
725 N.E. 17th Road
Fort Lauderdale, FL 33304
e-mail: rub@icanect.net
web: http://www.paintbynumberz.com/larry.html
A quarterly paint-by-numbers publication containing history, auction reports, preservation, pricing tips.

Paintings

Appraisers

Charles B. Goldstein, ISA CAPP
Charles Barry International
8 Hardwicke Place
Rockville, MD 20850-3010
ph: 301-340-6775
fax: 301-340-1726
Buys, sells, and appraises 19th and 20th century, modern and contemporary American and European paintings; Certified Member, International Society of Appraisers; expert witness and trial consultant.

William Lavendusky, M.S., ISA
William Lavendusky, Fine Art
3345 So. Harvard, Bldg. 100
Tulsa, OK 74135
ph: 918-747-5336
fax: 918-742-3425
Dealer and appraiser of paintings and sculpture; specialist in 19th century French animal bronzes.

Dealers

Hirschl & Adler Galleries, Inc.
21 East 70th St.
New York, NY 10021
ph: 212-535-8810
fax: 212-772-7237
Specializing in fine paintings, prints and furniture.

Don Treadway
2029 Madison Rd.
Cincinnati, OH 45208
ph: 513-321-6742 or 800-526-0491
fax: 513-871-7722
e-mail: info@treadwaygallery.com
web: http://www.treadwaygallery.com

Marcia Osterkamp, ISA
Poulsen Galleries, Inc.
327 Terrace Dr.
Brawley, CA 92227-3040
ph: 760-344-4810
fax: 760-344-4778
e-mail: poulsengalleries@compuserve.com
web: http://www.artnet.com/poulsen.html
Fine art appraiser; buys and sells 19th and 20th century American and European paintings; also California paintings.

Jimmy Vitanza
Peregrine Galleries
508 Brinkerhoff Ave.
Santa Barbara, CA 93101-3441
ph: 805-963-3134
fax: 805-963-3134

Experts

Terry L. Schafer
American Indian Art & Antiques
Rte. 2 Box 298
Marietta, OH 45750-9358
ph: 740-374-2807
e-mail: amindart@marietta.edu
web: http://www.marietta.edu/~amindart/
Expert in old oil paintings and period frames.

Museums/Libraries

Jan Ramierz
Museum of the City of New York
1220 5th Ave.
New York, NY 10029-5221
ph: 212-534-1672
fax: 212-534-5974
e-mail: mcny@mcny.org
web: http://www.mcny.org/mcny/
Special paintings and sculpture collections; access by appointment; research fee charged.

National Museum of American Art
Catalog: Inventory of Amer. Paintings Executed Before 1914
8th & G Sts. N.W.
Washington, DC 20560
ph: 202-357-2504
e-mail: nmaainfo@nmaa.si.edu
web: http://www.nmaa.si.edu/
A computerized index of over 230,000 records of pre-1914 paintings in public and private collections; artist, location, subject, photo.

Repro. Sources

Isabel Art Gallery
241, route de Longwy
Luxembourg, L-1941
Luxembourg
web: http://www.isabel.com/
Reproduces thousands of works by Old Masters; high quality oil reproductions, entirely hand crafted by specialized and talented artists: Carraaci, Cezanne, David, Degas, Goya, Klimt, Renoir, Van Gogh, Vermeer, Manet, and others.

Vincent Art Gallery
Hoge Slagen 343
SM's - Hertogenbosch, 5233
The Netherlands
ph: +31 73 6417807
fax: +31 73 6400576
e-mail: theo@vincent.nl
web: http://www.vincent.nl/
Oil painting on canvas reproductions: Van Gogh, Aersten, Botticelli, Boudin, Cabanel, Constable, Degas, Fragonard, Goya, Klimt, Lastman, Leyden, Mauve, Orley, Patinir, Parmigianino, and others.

Paintings (Reverse on Glass)

Experts

Shirley R. Mace
Shadow Enterprises
P.O. Box 1602
Mesilla Park, NM 88047-1602
ph: 505-524-6717
fax: 505-523-0940
e-mail: shadow-ent@zianet.com
Author of "Silhouette Collectibles on Glass" (1992) and price guide to silhouette collectibles; painted black on reverse of glass; sold in dimestores from the 1920s to 1950s; often with advertising and attached thermometers or calendars.

Peale Papers

Museums/Libraries

National Portrait Gallery
Catalog: Charles Wilson Peale Papers
8th & F Streets N.W.
Washington, DC 20560-0001
ph: 202-357-2866
fax: 202-786-2565
web: http://www.npg.si.edu
Specializing in documenting and cataloging all Peale family paintings and manuscripts.

Polynesia

Collectors

M.A. Blackburn
Antique Hawaiiana
2448 Lincoln Highway East
Lancaster, PA 17602
ph: 800-346-7847 or 717-295-9078
fax: 717-295-3494
e-mail: MBlackburn@aol.com
web: http://www.csmonline.com/blackburn/
Wants to buy over 50 year old art and artifacts from Polynesia; coral pounders, wood bowls, god figures, jewelry, personal adornment items, wood headrests, tapa cloth; from Tahiti, Cook Islands, New Zealand, Samoa, Fiji, Hawaii, etc.

Portraits

Misc. Services

Robert Stewart, Sr. Curator
4104 46th St. NW
Washington, DC 20016-5608
ph: 202-357-2866
Will authenticate paintings and sculpture brought in for inspection; make an appointment first; may be able to work from good photographs.

Museums/Libraries

Linda Thrift, Keeper
National Portrait Gallery
Catalog: Catalog of American Portraits
8th & F Streets N.W.
Washington, DC 20560-0001
ph: 202-357-2578
fax: 202-786-2565
e-mail: npgweb@npg.si.edu
web: http://www.npg.si.edu
Research database documenting more than 100,000 American portraits in public and private collections; offers on-line catalog on the INTERNET.

Portraits (Miniature)

Collectors

Sheldon Lerman
7505 Osler Dr.
Baltimore, MD 21204-7736
ph: 410-321-1514 or 410-828-1928
fax: 410-825-5710
Wants to buy American portrait miniatures on ivory.

Experts

Lester E. Sender
Galerie Nouvelle
23500 Mercantile Rd.
Cleveland, OH 44122-5914
ph: 216-595-0000
fax: 216-595-1111
Buys and sells portrait miniatures on paper, ivory, canvas, porcelain or metal from the 17th century through 1930, American and Continental.

Prison Related

Dealers

Matt Lippa
Artisans
P.O. Box 256
Mentone, AL 35984-0256
ph: 256-634-4037
fax: 256-634-4037
e-mail: artisans@folkartisans.com
web: http://www.folkartisans.com
Buy and sell folk art, outsider art, fine art; Internet WWW site offers links to additional dealers; also offers non-profit clubs and museums with an outlet to post notices, press releases, calendar items, etc. at no charge.

Public

Experts

Joyce Pomeroy Schwartz
Works of Art for Public Spaces, Inc.
17 West 54th St.
New York, NY 10019
ph: 212-245-6468
fax: 212-333-3250
Specializes in large scale, outside or inside, public art: sculpture, fountains, landscape environment, murals, terra-cotta and stone reliefs, frescoes, etc.

Pulp

Collectors

Tim Isaacson
1002 Clinton
Oak Park, IL 60304-1824
ph: 708-383-5646
e-mail: TFIsaacson@aol.com
Wants to buy original pulp art (paintings used for pulp magazines); covers and interior black and white drawings; all types - detective, science fiction, horror, mystery, The Shadow; also wants men's magazines and paperback book cover art.

Remington

Museums/Libraries

Frederic Remington Art Museum
303 Washington St.
Ogdensburg, NY 13669
ph: 315-393-2425
fax: 315-393-4464
e-mail: broncho@northnet.org
web: http://thames.northnet.org/broncho
The only museum dedicated to the life and works of the renown artist of the Old West, Frederic Remington.

Rodin

Museums/Libraries

Josie De Falla, Dir.
Maryhill Museum of Art
35 Maryhill Museum Drive
Goldendale, WA 98620-4601
ph: 509-773-3733
fax: 509-773-6138
e-mail: MaryHill@gorge.net
web: http://www.maryhillmuseum.org/
The museum contains an internationally recognized collection of sculpture and drawings by the great French master Auguste Rodin.

Musee Rodin
77 Rue de Varenne
Paris, 75007
France
ph: 00 33 (0) 1 44 18 61 10
fax: 00 33 (0) 1 45 51 17 52
e-mail: penseur@musee-rodin.fr
web: http://www.musee-rodin.fr/

Scottish

Dealers

Ian Johnson
Harden, Johnson & Assoc.
1616 Whisper Way
Goose Creek, SC 29445
ph: 843-572-7968
fax: 843-572-7968
24 years experience in Australian, New Zealand, South African paintings, drawings, and watercolors from 1797 to present; also specializing in British, Scottish, and Irish paintings from 1880-1950; daily contact with these countries.

South Africa

Dealers

Ian Johnson
Harden, Johnson & Assoc.
1616 Whisper Way
Goose Creek, SC 29445
ph: 843-572-7968
fax: 843-572-7968
24 years experience in Australian, New Zealand, South African paintings, drawings, and watercolors from 1797 to present; also specializing in British, Scottish, and Irish paintings from 1880-1950; daily contact with these countries.

Southern

Dealers

Robert B. Mayo
Gallery Mayo, Inc.
11758 River Crest Dr.
Gloucester, VA 23061-2516
ph: 804-693-2516
e-mail: hightide@visi.net
Buys and sells 19th through early 20th century American art, with a specialty in Southern and sporting art.

Henry Barnet
516 Maverick Circle
Spartanburg, SC 29307-3707
ph: 864-579-2112
e-mail: yourtowninc@compuserve.com
Buys, sells and appraises 18th through 20th C. American art, specializing in Southern art, genre, sporting art; originals and prints.

Spanish

Museums/Libraries

Hispanic Society of America, The
613 W. 155th St.
New York, NY 10032
ph: 212-926-2234
e-mail: info@hispanicsociety.org
web: http://www.hispanicsociety.org/

Sporting

(see also ART, Wildlife; SPORTING COLLECTIBLES)

Appraisers

Jane Cowan, ISA
Cowan & Company
2100 Tanglewild #735
Houston, TX 77063
ph: 713-532-7203
fax: 713-532-7214
e-mail: janecowan@cowanco.com
web: http://www.cowanco.com
Specializes in Wildlife and Sporting art; 19th and 20th century fine art appraisals, consultations and sales.

Collectors

Robert B. Mayo
Gallery Mayo, Inc.
11758 River Crest Dr.
Gloucester, VA 23061-2516
ph: 804-693-2516
e-mail: hightide@visi.net
Wants American sporting art through the mid-20th century; author of "America, The Sporting View."

Dealers

James & Ann Marenakos
Quester Gallery
77 Main St.
P.O. Box 446
Stonington, CT 06378
ph: 860-535-3860
fax: 860-535-3533
e-mail: questergal@snet.net
web: http://www.artnet.com/quester.html
Buys, sells, consults on 19th & 20th century sporting art and marine paintings.

J.N. Bartfield
J.N. Bartfield Galleries, Inc.
30 West 57th St.
Third Floor
New York, NY 10019
ph: 212-245-8890
fax: 212-541-4860
Buys and sells sporting, Western, and 19th century American art.

Tony Laws
Woods & Water, Inc.
1019 McFarland Blvd.
Northport, AL 35476
ph: 205-333-1214
fax: 205-339-9573
Buys and sells sporting art: paintings, prints, drawings, classic firearms, rods & reels, sporting bronzes, wood carvings, advertising art, catalogs, brochures, books.

Robert Krause
Ravenwood Gallery
38745 Butternut Ridge Rd.
Elyria, OH 44035
ph: 440-458-4929
Wants to buy paintings, prints, etchings, calendars, and posters relating to hunting and fishing, birds, dogs, guns, ammunition and power companies; also duck and crow calls, decoys, sporting books, bamboo fly rods, rods, reels, etc.

Collectors Choice
10725 Equestrian Dr.
Santa Ana, CA 92705
ph: 714-730-2082
Buys and sells fine paintings, etchings and prints by artists such as Hagerbaumer, Maass, Reneson, Hardie, Schaldach, Bishop, Osthaus, Kouba, and others.

Frank J. Mikesh
1356 Walden Rd.
Walnut Creek, CA 94596-3158
ph: 510-934-9243
fax: 510-947-6113
e-mail: natscibooks@netvista.net
web: http://www.netvista.net/~natscibooks/
Interested in out-of-print natural history, hunting, fishing, sporting, and wildlife books, and related art.

Sports

(see also SPORTS COLLECTIBLES)

Museums/Libraries

National Art Museum of Sport, Inc.
Newsletter: Museum of Sport Newsletter
850 W. Michigan St.
Indianapolis, IN 46202-5198
ph: 317-274-3627
fax: 317-274-3878
e-mail: arein@iupui.edu
web: http://namos.iupui.edu
Promotes sports art, e.g. paintings, sculptures, prints depicting fishing, track, boxing, racquet games, auto racing, baseball, etc.

Western

(see also WESTERN AMERICANA)

Dealers

J.N. Bartfield
J.N. Bartfield Galleries, Inc.
30 West 57th St.
Third Floor
New York, NY 10019
ph: 212-245-8890
fax: 212-541-4860
Wants anything of American Historical interest, especially having to do with the West: paintings, bronzes, drawings, water colors; Cowboy and Indian, Western landscapes, Remington, Farny, Hansen, Krieghoff, Bierstadt, Homer, etc.

William L. King
Bozeman Trail Gallery
214 N. Main
Sheridan, WY 82801
ph: 307-672-3928 or 307-672-8318
fax: 307-672-2616
e-mail: btg@bozemantrailgallery.com
web: http://www.bozemantrailgallery.com/
Wants 19th and early 20th cent. Western art, especially by Joe DeYong, E.W. Gollings, Hans Kleiber; also wants No. Plains Indian beadwork and related items, cowboy equipment, Colt Bisley's, mod. 1885 Remington pistols.

Peter Eller, ISA
Peter Eller Gallery & Appraisers
206 Dartmouth
Albuquerque, NM 87106
ph: 505-268-7437
fax: 505-268-6442
e-mail: pelgal@nmia.com
web: http://www.peterellergallery.com/
Specializes in and appraises American, Southwest, and "Western" art; also Pueblo pottery, Navajo rugs and other weavings, Spanish colonial artifacts.

Museums/Libraries

M.J. VanDeventer
National Cowboy Hall of Fame & Western Heritage Center
Magazine: Persimon Hill
1700 N.E. 63rd St.
Oklahoma City, OK 73111-7906
ph: 405-478-2250
fax: 405-478-4714
e-mail: nchf@aol.com
web: http://www.cowboyhalloffame.org/
NCHA represents 17 western states; preserves the rich heritage of the Old West and the memory of those who contributed to it.

Periodicals

Duerr & Tierney, Inc.
Magazine: Art of the West
15612 Hwy. 7, Ste. 235
Hopkins, MN 55345-3559
ph: 612-935-5850
fax: 612-935-6546
e-mail: aotw@aotw.com
Magazine featuring art of the West: cowboys, American landscapes, western wildlife, etc.

Wildlife

Dealers

Bob Dumaine
Sam Houston Philatelics
13310 Westheimer, Ste. 150
Houston, TX 77077-3506
ph: 281-493-6386 or 800-231-5926
fax: 281-496-1445
e-mail: rwhouduck@aol.com
Specializing in Wildlife Art, including originals, prints, sculptures, and gifts.

Periodicals

Pothole Publishing, Inc.
Magazine: Wildlife Art Magazine
5230 W. 73rd
Edina, MN 55439
ph: 612-835-5353 or 800-626-0934
fax: 612-835-5554
e-mail: publisher@mail.winternet.com
web: http://www.wildlifeartmag.com/
Largest magazine focusing on art relating to animals, birds, and art of the natural world; international in scope; full-color award-winning magazine; artists from around the world; painters, sculptors, wood carvers, etc.; bi-monthly.

William Aiken Walker

Experts

John Fowler
P.O. Box 15529
New Orleans, LA 70175
ph: 504-888-2380
fax: 504-899-0843
e-mail: fowl@gateway.net
Currently researching the works of William Aiken Walker (1838-1921) in the preparation of a catalogue raisonne.

ART DECO

(see also ARCHITECTURAL ELEMENTS; CERAMICS; CLOCKS; ELECTRICITY RELATED ITEMS, Appliances; FRANKART; FURNITURE [ANTIQUE]; GEMS & JEWELRY; GLASS; MODERNISM; RADIOS; SALOON & BAR COLLECTIBLES, Cocktail Shakers)

Auction Services

Christie's East
219 E. 67th St.
New York, NY 10021
ph: 212-606-0400
web: http://www.christies.com
Christie's East is well known in the collecting field for its Art Deco auctions.

Amory Spizzirri, Client Svc.
William Doyle Galleries
175 E. 87th St.
New York, NY 10128-2205
ph: 212-427-2730
fax: 212-369-0892
e-mail: info@doylegalleries.com
web: http://www.doylegalleries.com
Holds over 50 auctions annually of furniture and decorations, paintings and sculpture, jewelry, books and prints, couture and textiles, 20th century art & design, majolica, Lalique, Asian works of art and other specialty categories.

Savoia's Auction Inc.
Rte. 23
South Cairo, NY 12482
ph: 518-622-8000
fax: 518-622-9453

Ronald Baker
Art Deco Auction House
1600 Whitman, Ste. 100
Wheaton, IL 60187
ph: 630-665-5279
fax: 630-462-1750
e-mail: service@virtualauctions.com
web: http://www.virtualauctions.com/
If you are the type of person who fully appreciates all types of distinctive Art Deco, this is the place for you; from sparkling chrome cocktail shakers to elegant telephones, you will find them at this live, interactive auction.

Butterfield & Butterfield
7601 Sunset Blvd.
Los Angeles, CA 90046-2714
ph: 323-850-7500
fax: 323-850-5843
e-mail: info@butterfields.com
web: http://www.butterfields.com/
Two specialty auction each year.

Clubs/Associations

Tony Fusco, Pres.
Art Deco Society of Boston
Newsletter: Motif
One Murdock Terrace
Brighton, MA 02135-2817
ph: 617-787-2637
fax: 617-782-4430
e-mail: fuscofour@aol.com
Purpose is to educate, and to preserve items and architecture relating to the Art Deco period.

Art Deco Society of New York
Newsletter: Modernist
P.O. Box 160
Planetarium Station
New York, NY 10024
ph: 212-679-3326
web: http://www.artdeco.org/

Art Deco Society of Washington
Newsletter: Translux
P.O. Box 11090
Washington, DC 20008-0290
ph: 202-298-1100
e-mail: info@adsw.org
web: http://www.adsw.org/
Non-profit organization to foster public awareness and appreciation of the Art Deco period (1925-1950) through volunteer actions to preserve the decorative, industrial, architectural, and cultural arts of that era.

George Neary
Miami Design Preservation League
Newsletter: Impressions
P.O. Box 190180
Miami Beach, FL 33119-0180
ph: 305-672-2014 or 305-672-1836
fax: 305-672-4319
Non-profit Art Deco preservation society devoted to preserving, protecting and promoting the cultural, social, economic, environmental, and architectural integrity of the Miami Beach architectural district.

Sharon Koskoff, Pres.
Art Deco Society of the Palm Beaches
Newsletter: Streamline
325 SW 29th Ave.
Delray Beach, FL 33444
ph: 561-276-9925
e-mail: sharon@flinet.com
web: http://www.gopbi.com/community/groups/artdeco
A non-profit organization dedicated to the preservation, education and awareness of Art Deco Architecture and design; custom Art Deco design

services also available; newsletter published quarterly.

Art Deco Society of Cleveland
Newsletter: Newsreel
3439 West Brainard Rd., #260
Woodmere, OH 44122
ph: 330-382-3283 or 330-721-2274

Art Deco Society of Northern Ohio
3439 West Brainard Rd., Ste. 260
Cleveland, OH 44122-4273
ph: 216-831-9110
fax: 216-292-7529

Detroit Area Art Deco Society
Newsletter: Modern, The
P.O. Box 1393
Royal Oak, MI 48068-1393
ph: 248-582-3326
e-mail: membership@daads.org
web: http://www.daads.org/

Chicago Art Deco Society
Magazine: Chicago Art Deco Society Magazine
400 Skokie #270
Northbrook, IL 60062-7902
ph: 847-291-4440
fax: 847-291-6677
Promotes the appreciation of the Art Deco era through publications and meetings.

Bill McDevitt, Dir.
Kansas Art Deco Society
201 Wyandotte
Kansas City, MO 64105
ph: 816-471-3391
web: http://www.smartkc.com/sections/albumkcartdecocon.html

Art Deco Society of Louisiana
P.O. Box 1326
Baton Rouge, LA 70821-6367
ph: 225-275-6367

Friends of Fair Park
P.O. Box 150248
Dallas, TX 75315
ph: 214-426-3400

Art Deco Society of Los Angeles
Newsletter: Exposition, The
P.O. Box 972
Los Angeles, CA 90078-0972
ph: 213-659-3326
web: http://www.adsla.org/

Art Deco Society of California
Magazine: Sophisticate, The
100 Bush St., Ste. 511
San Francisco, CA 94104-3908
ph: 415-982-DECO
web: http://www.art-deco.org/deco/
Dedicated to the preservation of California's Art Deco (1920s-1940s) artistic expression heritage; also publishes the newsletter "Streamlined Times."

Richard Unger
Sacramento Art Deco Society
Newsletter: Moderne Times Newsletter, The
P.O. Box 162836
Sacramento, CA 95816-2836
ph: 916-736-1929
Non-profit organization dedicated to preserving all aspects of the Art Deco period (1925-1945); monthly lectures on architecture, design, jewelry, music, art, etc.; offers walking tours; educational and fun events.

Canadian Art Deco Society
626 Pender St., #800
Vancouver, British Columbia V6B 1V9
Canada
ph: 604-688-1216
e-mail: luxton@portal.ca

Twentieth Century Society, The
Journal: Journal, The
70 Cowcross St.
London, EC1M 6DR
U.K.
ph: 0171-2503857
fax: 0171-2503022
e-mail: knewton@c20society.freeserve.co.uk
web: http://www.c20society.freeserve.co.uk/
Conservation and preservation group for post-1914 buildings; also concerned with visits, lectures and publications.

Collectors

Carl Ratner
550 Lamoka Ave.
Staten Island, NY 10312
ph: 718-317-1838
e-mail: artdeco@nyct.net
Buy, sell, trade a wide range of Art Deco items: Chase, Manning Bowman and Revere chrome; clocks, cameras, lighters, radios, telephones; Frankart; lamps and lighting fixtures; kitchen appliances; Roseville Futura pottery, etc.

Richard Trautwein
Toys N Such
437 Dawson St.
Sault Sainte Marie, MI 49783-2119
ph: 906-635-0356
e-mail: rtraut@portup.com
Collector, dealer wants to buy quality Art Deco items in glass, ceramics, sculpture, metalwork, silver, jewelry, and rugs.

John M. England, Jr.
P.O. Box 393
Lincolnshire, IL 60069
ph: 847-823-5287
fax: 847-823-5287
e-mail: triodes@sprintmail.com
Buys, sells, collects Art Deco items, industrial design, Moderne furnishings, radios, streamline.

Clint Miller
1604 N. Harrison St.
Little Rock, AR 72207-5322
ph: 501-664-8424 or 501-682-7466
Wants to buy Art Deco bookends, radios, paperweights, book jackets, posters, etc.

Dealers

William Sakas
20th Century Antiques
P.O. Box 586
Wayne, NJ 07474
ph: 973-783-7174
e-mail: decobill@aol.com
web: http://www.machineage.com/decobill/
Buys and sells 20th Century antiques, furniture, and collectibles; specializes in radios, cameras and paper items.

Deco Deluxe
993 Lexington Ave.
New York, NY 10021
ph: 212-472-7222

Ron Savino
Times & Moments Antiques & Collectibles
378 Atlantic Ave.
Brooklyn, NY 11217-1703
ph: 718-625-3145 or 718-497-4529
e-mail: moments@webtv.net
With John Thomas Lee specializes in Art Deco furniture, enamel-top kitchen tables, waterfall furniture, especially cedar chests.

Joseph D. Cantara
Cantara/Galletti
ph: 718-352-7273
fax: 718-352-6661
e-mail: Deco11358@aol.com
web: http://www.antiqnet.com/da/tiffany.html
Buys, sells and specializes in art glass and in Tiffany items such as lamps, desk sets, glass and accessories; also buys and sells Art Deco - especially French & Austrian.

Norman Karp
Time & Again Antiques
855 E. Broadway, Box 47 Apollo Plaza
Monticello, NY 12701
ph: 914-791-5247
e-mail: deco4u@aol.com
Buys and sells art deco bronzes, bronze dogs, deco lamps; small items only.

Bob Aibel
Moderne Gallery
111 N. 3rd St.
Philadelphia, PA 19106-1903
ph: 215-923-8536
fax: 215-619-0068
e-mail: raibel@aol.com
Wants to buy Art Deco items - glass, ceramics, furniture, sculpture, paintings, catalogs, etc.; specialty areas include Ruba Rombic art glass and Nakashima furniture.

Bruce Marine
Cherub Antiques Gallery
2918 M. St. NW
Washington, DC 20007-3713
ph: 202-337-2224
fax: 202-337-2224
Buys and sells Art Deco glass, artwork, and metal wares.

Ken Forster
5501 Seminary Rd., Ste. 1311 South
Falls Church, VA 22041
ph: 703-379-1142
Dealer in American art pottery and tiles, specializing in American tiles from 1860 to 1940; also Art Nouveau, Art Deco, Georg Jensen silver, and American Modernism.

Ric Emmett
Modernism Gallery
1622 Ponce de Leon Blvd.
Miami, FL 33134-4012
ph: 305-442-8743
fax: 305-443-3074
e-mail: artdeco@modernism.com
web: http://www.modernism.com
Wants to buy Deco and 1950s furniture by Deskey, Rhode, Nelson, Frankl, Nakashima, Mont, and other designers; also wants lamps, pottery, glass, bronzes, chrome and Mexican silver.

Connie Zeigler
Durwyn Smedley Antiques
431 Massachusetts Ave.
Indianapolis, IN 46204
ph: 317-822-0102
e-mail: smedley@iquest.net
web: http://www.smedley.com/smedley/
Buys and sells 20th Century design: Arts & Crafts era, Art Deco, Mid-Century Modern, upscale 50's; art pottery from all eras and designer dinnerware; the first Indiana antique shop in the World Wide Web.

Steve Savitt
Josie's
545 Ridge Rd.
Wilmette, IL 60091-2439
ph: 847-256-7646
fax: 847-256-7004
Specializes in Art Deco, 20th Century Modern, art pottery, art glass and jewelry; no reproductions.

Ronald Baker
Art Deco Auction House
1600 Whitman, Ste. 100
Wheaton, IL 60187
ph: 630-665-5279
fax: 630-462-1750
e-mail: service@virtualauctions.com
web: http://www.virtualauctions.com/
Buys, sells, collects and has an online auction of Art Deco items.

Anita Cochran
Anita's Antiques
2730 Virginia Pl.
Homewood, IL 60430-1135
ph: 708-957-2241
e-mail: lcoch37469@aol.com
Buys and sells Art Deco; also Depression glass and china; collects Art Deco figurines.

Frank Piccolo
Piccolo Pete's
13814 Ventura Blvd.
Sherman Oaks, CA 91423
ph: 818-990-5421
fax: 818-990-5421
e-mail: artdeco@piccolopetes.com
web: http://www.piccolopetes.com/
First Art Deco establishment in Los Angeles' San Fernando Valley; Art Deco furniture, glassware, pottery, jewelry, period lighting, etc.

Experts

Tony Fusco
Fusco & Four, Associates
One Murdock Terrace
Brighton, MA 02135-2817
ph: 617-787-2637
fax: 617-782-4430
e-mail: fuscofour@aol.com
Author of "The Confident Collector Identification and Price Guide to Art Deco"; offers appraisal and brokerage services for 1909-1939 Art Deco collectors; appraise and broker fine Art Deco European and American decorative arts.

Ira & Miriam Raskin
Try To Remember
5120 Wilson Ln.
Bethesda, MD 20814-2436
ph: 301-652-1695
fax: 301-986-4528
e-mail: iraskin@aol.com
Buys and sells functional nostalgia from the 1920s to 1950s: radios, clocks, watches, jewelry, books, etc.

Internet Resources

Adam Schoolsky
ArtDeco.com
P.O. Box 23182
Portland, OR 97281-3162
ph: 503-579-3162
fax: 503-579-5046
e-mail: Adam@ArtDeco.com
web: http://www.ArtDeco.com
If it's from the 1920s-1940s, you'll find it here: music, fashion, designers, lifestyles,a nd much more; secure on-line multi-dealer Art Deco store.

Museums/Libraries

Newark Museum, The
49 Washington St.
P.O. Box 540
Newark, NJ 07101-0540
ph: 973-596-6550 or 800-7-MUSEUM
fax: 973-642-0459

Barbara Livenstein
Cooper-Hewitt Museum National Museum of Design, Smithsonian Institution
2 East 91st St.
New York, NY 10128
ph: 212-860-8400 or 212-849-8349
e-mail: liven@ch.si.edu
web: http://www.si.edu/organiza/museums/design/ndm.htm

Frederick R. Brandt
Virginia Museum of Fine Arts
2800 Grove Ave.
Richmond, VA 23221-2466
ph: 804-367-0844
fax: 804-367-9393
e-mail: webmaster@vmfa.state.va.us
web: http://dit1.state.va.us/vmfa/index.html
Fine arts museum covering the entire range of history of art.

Repro. Sources

Kenneth F. Kalbleish, Sr.
Sun Foundry
299 S. Lake St.
Burbank, CA 91502
ph: 818-841-7979 or 800-367-3479
fax: 818-955-9690
e-mail: sunfoundry@earthlink.net
web: http://home.earthlink.net/~sunfoundry/
Manufactures bronze statues; send for catalog of reproduction Art Deco items.

Chase Brass & Copper Co.

Book Sellers

Jo-D Books
81 Willard Terrace
Stamford, CT 06903-4927
ph: 203-322-0568
Books on Art Deco chrome, especially by Chase.

Clubs/Associations

Barry L. Van Hook
Chase Collectors Society
2149 West Jibsail Loop
Mesa, AZ 85202-5524
ph: 480-838-6971 or 480-965-1217
fax: 480-965-8314
e-mail: vanhook@asu.edu
web: http://www.public.asu.edu/~icblv/chase.htm

Collectors

Barry L. Van Hook
2149 West Jibsail Loop
Mesa, AZ 85202-5524
ph: 480-838-6971 or 480-965-1217
fax: 480-965-8314
e-mail: vanhook@asu.edu
web: http://www.public.asu.edu/~icblv/chase.htm
Avid collector of items made by the Chase Brass & Copper Company of Waterbury, CT.

Lamps & Lighting

Dealers

Jack Beeler
Decorum
1400 Vallejo St.
San Francisco, CA 94109-2608
Specializes in buying and selling French and American Art Deco lighting.

Neon

Dealers

Dennis Clark
Off the Wall Antiques, Inc.
7325 Melrose Ave.
Los Angeles, CA 90046
ph: 323-930-1185
fax: 323-930-1595

ART MODERNE

(see MODERNISM)

ART NOUVEAU

(see also CERAMICS; FURNITURE [ANTIQUE]; GEMS & JEWELRY; GLASS)

Auction Services

Butterfield & Butterfield
7601 Sunset Blvd.
Los Angeles, CA 90046-2714
ph: 323-850-7500
fax: 323-850-5843
e-mail: info@butterfields.com
web: http://www.butterfields.com/
Two specialty auction each year.

Dealers

Joseph D. Cantara
Cantara/Galletti
ph: 718-352-7273
fax: 718-352-6661
e-mail: Deco11358@aol.com
web: http://www.antiqnet.com/da/tiffany.html
Buys, sells and specializes in art glass and in Tiffany items such as lamps, desk sets, glass and accessories; also buys and sells Art Deco - especially French & Austrian.

Bruce Marine
Cherub Antiques Gallery
2918 M. St. NW
Washington, DC 20007-3713
ph: 202-337-2224
fax: 202-337-2224
Buys and sells Art Nouveau glass, artwork, and metal wares.

Museums/Libraries

Frederick R. Brandt
Virginia Museum of Fine Arts
2800 Grove Ave.
Richmond, VA 23221-2466
ph: 804-367-0844
fax: 804-367-9393
e-mail: webmaster@vmfa.state.va.us
web: http://dit1.state.va.us/vmfa/index.html
Fine arts museum covering the entire range of history of art.

ART POTTERY

(see CERAMICS [AMERICAN ART POTTERY]; CERAMICS [ENGLISH], Art Pottery; CERAMICS [CONTINENTAL], Art Pottery)

ART THEFT & FRAUD

Clubs/Associations

Society to Prevent Trade in Stolen Art
1920 N Street NW, Ste. 620
Washington, DC 20036
ph: 202-872-7869
fax: 202-457-0662
e-mail: director@stop.org
web: http://www.stop.org/
Services include a lecture series, research library, referral program that will link victims of art crimes with detectives, appraisers, and insurance companies; on-line database of pre-1987 auction house records.

Ruth Redmond-Cooper, Dir.
Institute of Art & Law
: Art Antiquity & Law
Bank Chambers
121 London Road
London, LE2 0QT
U.K.
ph: +44 (0)116 255 5146
fax: +44 (0)116 255 1782
e-mail: ruth.redmond-cooper@inst-of-art-and-law.co.uk
web: http://www.pipemedia.net/ial/
A small independent institution, founded in 1995, that aims to bridge the divide between the worlds of art and law by organizing seminars and publishing books and periodicals; membership is open to the public; many related links.

Internet Resources

Art Theft/Most Wanted Art/Recovery Project
e-mail: art-theft@webtv.net
web: http://www.saztv.com/

FBI, National Stolen Art File
IT/GRCU, Room 5096
935 Pennsylvania Ave., NW
Washington, DC 20535
ph: 202-324-4192
fax: 202-324-1504
web: http://www.fbi.gov/art.htm

Alert All - The Stolen Property Guide
Box 24109
Stockholm, 104 51
Sweden
ph: +46 8 663 86 60 or +46 70 471 35 81
fax: +46 70 511 07 08
e-mail: info@alert-all.se
web: http://www.alert-all.se/
Enables insurance companies, police authorities, auction houses, antique dealers, collectors, burglarized individuals to give and receive information about stolen valuables: clocks, paintings, vehicles, jewelry, yachts, prints, etc.

Ton Cremers
Museum Security Network
P.O. Box 74888
Amsterdam, 3032 XD
The Netherlands
ph: _31 10 4653837 or +31 20 6747000
fax: +31 10 4653837
e-mail: TonCremers@museum-security.org
web: http://www.museum-security.org/
Website collects and disseminates information about incidents and the trade involving stolen cultural property; offers related information such as publications, security products, safety and salvage plans, and related links.

Misc. Services

OmniGuard Corporation
730 Fifth Ave.
New York, NY 10019-4105
ph: 800-808-2882 or 212-577-9000
fax: 212-577-9220
e-mail: info@omniguard.com
web: http://www.omniguard.com/
Guarantees the authenticity of fine art; also registers art.

Art Loss Register, New York Office
666 Fifth Ave.
New York, NY 10103
ph: 212-262-4831
fax: 212-262-4838
e-mail: artloss@artloss.com
web: http://www.artloss.com/
A service to register lost art to assist in recovery; a permanent computerized database of stolen and missing works of art, antiques and valuables, operating on an international basis to assist law enforcement agencies.

Anna J. Kisluk
International Foundation for Art Research (IFAR)
Magazine: IFAR Reports
500 Fifth Ave., Ste 1234
New York, NY 10110
ph: 212-391-6234
fax: 212-391-8794
e-mail: kferg@ifar.org
web: http://www.ifar.org
Clearinghouse for information on art theft, fraud, forgery; promotes recovery of stolen art & prevention of circulation of forged works; publishes Stolen Art Alert notices of art thefts and recoveries.

Nancy J. Little
International Foundation for Art Research (IFAR) Authentication Serv.
500 Fifth Ave., Ste 1234
New York, NY 10110
ph: 212-391-6234
fax: 212-391-8794
e-mail: kferg@ifar.org
web: http://www.ifar.org
Offers a unique authentication service which examines works of art to assist in the resolution of questions of authenticity and attribution; for individuals, art dealers, museums, etc.

Federal Trade Commission
6th St. & Pennsylvania Ave., Room 130
Washington, DC 20580
ph: 202-326-2222
web: http://www.cotu.com/infopage/consumers/artfrd1.htm
Has jurisdiction over art dealers; send for free copy of a "Art Fraud" brochure.

Robert E. Spiel
Robert E. Spiel Associates
Newsletter: Art Intelligence Newsletter
549 West Randolph St., Ste. 425
Chicago, IL 60661-2208
ph: 312-258-0646
fax: 312-258-0815
e-mail: spiel@arttheft.com
web: http://www.arttheft.com/
Offers global stolen art investigations & security services for appraisers, conservators, private & corporate collectors, dealers, insurance professionals, interior designers, museums, private & public investigators, moving companies.

Art Loss Register, London Office
12 Grosvenor Place
London, London SW1 X7HH
U.K.
ph: 0171 235 3393
e-mail: artloss@artloss.com
web: http://www.artloss.com/
A service to register lost art to assist in recovery; a permanent computerized database of stolen and missing works of art, antiques and valuables, operating on an international basis to assist law enforcement agencies.

Periodicals

Robert E. Spiel
Robert E. Spiel Associates
Newsletter: Art Intelligence Newsletter
549 West Randolph St., Ste. 425
Chicago, IL 60661-2208
ph: 312-258-0646
fax: 312-258-0815
e-mail: spiel@arttheft.com
web: http://www.arttheft.com/
Articles and commentary on art crimes; typical art fraud and their discovery; criminal techniques; former FBI Special Agent, Mr. Spiel dedicated most of his 20-year career to the recovery of stolen fine art and rare collectibles.

Magazine: Trace
U.K.
e-mail: trace@thesaurus.co.uk
web: http://www.trace.co.uk/
A monthly, glossy published monthly; focuses on locating and retrieving stolen art, antiques and collectibles.

ARTIFACTS

(see AMERICAN INDIAN; ANTIQUITIES; HERITAGE RESOURCES; NATURAL HISTORY; FOSSILS; MINERAL SPECIMENS; PREHISTORIC ARTIFACTS; TREASURE HUNTING)

ARTILLERY

(see CANNONS; MILITARIA; AMMUNITION & EXPLOSIVE ORDNANCE)

ARTS & CRAFTS

(see also ARCHITECTURAL ELEMENTS, Arts & Crafts; CERAMICS [AMERICAN]; FRANK LLOYD WRIGHT; FURNITURE [ANTIQUE], Stickley; COPPER ITEMS, Stickley)

Auction Services

Jerry Cohen
Craftsman Auctions
1485 Weset Housatonic
Pittsfield, MA 01201
ph: 800-448-7828 or 413-448-8922
fax: 413-442-1550
e-mail: aurora@neca.com
web: http://www.artsncrafts.com/
Conducts periodic Arts & Crafts auction sales of period furniture, metalwork, lighting, and pottery; full-color catalogs, national delivery, absentee bids welcome.

Garrett Sheahan
Skinner, Inc.
357 Main St.
Bolton, MA 01740-1104
ph: 978-779-6241
fax: 978-779-5144
e-mail: info@skinnerinc.com
web: http://www.skinnerinc.com
Established in 1964, Skinner Inc. is the fifth largest auction house in the US; has offices in Bolton and Boston, MA.

David Rago
David Rago Auctions Inc.
333 North Main St.
Lambertville, NJ 08530
ph: 609-397-9374 or 609-397-1802
fax: 609-397-9377
e-mail: info@ragoarts.com
web: http://www.ragoarts.com
Specializing in the sale of American art pottery and Arts and Crafts items.

Don Treadway
Treadway Auctions
2029 Madison Rd.
Cincinnati, OH 45208
ph: 513-321-6742 or 800-526-0491
fax: 513-871-7722
e-mail: info@treadwaygallery.com
web: http://www.treadwaygallery.com
Specializes in the sale of Arts and Crafts pottery.

Butterfield & Butterfield
7601 Sunset Blvd.
Los Angeles, CA 90046-2714
ph: 323-850-7500
fax: 323-850-5843
e-mail: info@butterfields.com
web: http://www.butterfields.com/
Two specialty auction each year.

Clubs/Associations

Kitty Turgeon, Ex. Dir.
Foundation for the Study of the Arts & Crafts Movement
Roycroft Campus
31 South Grove St.
East Aurora, NY 14052
ph: 716-652-3333 or 716-655-0562
e-mail: rycrft@aol.com
The foundation's mission is to study, teach & preserve the philosophical and artistic legacy of the International Arts & Crafts Movement; meetings, seminars, appraisals, consultations.

Roycrofters-At-Large Association
Newsletter: RALA Newsletter
P.O. Box 417
East Aurora, NY 14052
ph: 716-652-0213
e-mail: tomboj@buffnet.net
web: http://www.roycrofter.com/rala/rala.html
Studies the Arts & Crafts Movement and fosters new crafts people at the Roycroft Campus in East Aurora, NY; lecture series, tours, sponsors a winter and a summer crafts show.

Collectors

Richard L. Sasicki
P.O. Box 3113
Glen Ellyn, IL 60138-3113
ph: 630-682-8706
e-mail: artware@sprynet.com
Wants to buy books, catalogs, pamphlets, or any ephemera related to American Art Pottery and Ceramics or to the Arts & Crafts period.

Bruce Richards
508 N. Belmont Ave.
Los Angeles, CA 90026-4124
ph: 213-413-4517
Wants Roycroft, Karl Kipp, and The Too Kay Shop handwrought copper items in good condition with original patina: letter openers, bookends, candlesticks, desk sets, vasettes, vases, trays, bowls.

Dealers

Jim Messineo
JMW Gallery
144 Lincoln St.
Boston, MA 02111-2523
ph: 617-338-9097
fax: 617-338-7636
e-mail: jmwgallery@tiac.net
web: http://www.jmwgallery.com/
Buys, sells and specializes along with co-owner Mike Witt in the Arts & Crafts movement. Mission furniture: Lifetime, Limbert, Stickley; American Art Pottery 1875 to 1950s: Grueby, Newcomb, Marblehead, etc.; metalwork, Roycroft.

John S. Zuk
106 Orchard St.
Belmont, MA 02478
ph: 617-489-7540
fax: 617-484-4800
e-mail: jzuk@integral-inc.com
Buys and sells metal work (Roycroft), furniture (Stickley, Limbert), pottery (Newcomb, Marblehead, SEG, Grueby, Rookwood) in the Mission period.

Rosalie & Aram Berberian
ARK Antiques
P.O. Box 3133
New Haven, CT 06515
ph: 203-498-8572
fax: 203-776-4397
e-mail: crshburn@ct1.nai.net
Wants American craftsman silver, jewelry and metal of the first half of the 20th century.

David Rago
Perrault Rago Gallery
333 North Main St.
Lambertville, NJ 08530
ph: 609-397-9374 or 609-397-1802
fax: 609-397-9377
e-mail: info@ragoarts.com
web: http://www.ragoarts.com
Wants American art pottery, and Arts and Crafts items such as furniture and metal items by Stickley, Rohlfs, Wright, Roycroft, etc.

Bruce A. Austin
c/o RIT/College Liberal Arts
92 Lomb Memorial Dr.
Rochester, NY 14623-5604
ph: 716-475-2879 or 716-387-9820
fax: 716-475-7732
e-mail: baagll@rit.edu
Wants to buy L & JG Stickley, Stickley Bros., Gustav Stickley, Limbert, Roycroft, Rohlfs, Mission Oak furniture, clocks, art pottery; also hammered copper and lighting by Roycroft, Dirk Van Erp, Jarvie, Tiffany, Heintz, Albert Berry.

Steve Traband
P.O. Box 7064
Saint Petersburg, FL 33734-7064
ph: 813-896-2308
Buys and sells Mission style furniture: Stickley, Roycroft, Limbert, Lifetime, Rohlfs, F.L. Wright, etc.

Tony McCormak
McCormack & Company
P.O. Box 49093
Sarasota, FL 34320
ph: 941-952-1244 or 941-350-2785
e-mail: birdkey@aol.com
web: http://www.antiqnet.com/McCormack
Dealer, expert, appraiser specializing in Arts & Crafts furniture, metals, pottery, and lighting; always buying Stickley, Limbert, Roycroft, and other examples of Mission style furniture.

Don Treadway
2029 Madison Rd.
Cincinnati, OH 45208
ph: 513-321-6742 or 800-526-0491
fax: 513-871-7722
e-mail: info@treadwaygallery.com
web: http://www.treadwaygallery.com

Reyne Haines
405 Lafayette Ave.
Cincinnati, OH 45220
ph: 513-559-1405
e-mail: themvmt@aol.com
web: http://members.aol.com/TheMvmt

Connie Zeigler
Durwyn Smedley 20th Century
431 Massachusetts Ave.
Indianapolis, IN 46204
ph: 317-822-0102
e-mail: smedley@iquest.net
web: http://www.smedley.com/smedley/
Buys and sells 20th Century design: Arts & Crafts era, Art Deco, Mid-Century Modern, upscale 50's; art pottery from all eras and designer dinnerware; the first Indiana antique shop in the World Wide Web.

Ned & Ann Duke
Duke Gallery
312 W. Fourth
Royal Oak, MI 48067-2502
ph: 248-547-5511

John Toomey
John Toomey Gallery
818 North Blvd.
Oak Park, IL 60302
ph: 708-383-5234
fax: 708-383-4828
e-mail: toomey@interaccess.com
Conducts Arts and Crafts auctions in association with Don Treadway.

Experts

Rosalie & Aram Berberian
ARK Antiques
P.O. Box 3133
New Haven, CT 06515
ph: 203-498-8572
fax: 203-776-4397
e-mail: crshburn@ct1.nai.net
Specializing in American Arts & Crafts Movement silver, jewelry and metal items.

Carole Hibel
Art & Antiques
131-B Broadview Road
Woodstock, NY 12498
ph: 914-679-2966 or 800-426-3357
fax: 914-679-9101
Author of "The Fulper Book," wants to buy Fulper, Grueby, Marblehead, Teco, etc. pottery, Gustav Stickley, L & JG Stickley, Limberts, Roycroft, Van Erp furniture and lamps, etc.

Fritz Gram
357 North Shore Rd.
Cuba, NY 14727-9227

Jim Graham
1407 S Street NW
Washington, DC 20009

Bruce Johnson
P.O. Box 8773
Asheville, NC 28814-8773
ph: 828-628-1915
fax: 828-628-4070
e-mail: bj1912@aol.com
Writes furniture repair/refinishing column. Wrote "Price Guide to Arts and Crafts Movement" items.

Internet Resources

Reyne Haines
Movement, The
405 Lafayette Ave.
Cincinnati, OH 45220
ph: 513-559-1405
e-mail: themvmt@aol.com
web: http://members.aol.com/TheMvmt
A website dedicated to the Arts & Crafts Movement; items for sale and wanted to buy, discussion group information, links to other great Arts & Crafts areas on the internet.

Carol Kamm, Dir. of Oper.
Arts & Crafts Society
1194 Bandera
Ann Arbor, MI 48103
ph: 734-665-4729
fax: 734-213-0045
e-mail: info@arts-crafts.com
web: http://www.arts-crafts.com/
Interactive electronic community dedicated to the philosophy and spirit of the original Arts & Crafts Movement of the late 19th and early 20th centuries.

On-Line Arts & Crafts Movement Resource Directory
2612 Clermont St.
Denver, CO 80207
ph: 303-388-2560
e-mail: stermitz@ragtime.org
web: http://www.sni.net/ragtime
On-line Arts & Crafts movement resource directory dedicated to the Craftsman period (1890-1920).

Periodicals

David Rago
Journal: Style: 1900
333 North Main St.
Lambertville, NJ 08530
ph: 609-397-9374 or 609-397-1802
fax: 609-397-9377
e-mail: info@ragoarts.com
web: http://www.ragoarts.com
The only periodical devoted entirely to the Arts & Crafts movement.

John Brinkmann
Magazine: American Bungalow
P.O. Box 756
Glendale, CA 91205-0756
ph: 626-355-3363 or 800-350-3363
fax: 626-355-1220
e-mail: john@ambungalow.com
web: http://www.ambungalow.com/
Focusing on Bungalow and Arts & Crafts architecture, design, how-to's, sources, interior and exterior decor, furniture, craftsmen, etc.

Furniture

Dealers

Douglass White
Classic Interiors & Antiques
2042 N Rio Grande Ave., Ste. E
Orlando, FL 32804-5644
ph: 407-839-0004
Wants to buy American Arts & Crafts period furniture.

Experts

Bruce Johnson
P.O. Box 8773
Asheville, NC 28814-8773
ph: 828-628-1915
fax: 828-628-4070
e-mail: bj1912@aol.com
Writes furniture repair/refinishing column. Wrote price guide to arts and crafts movement items. Hosts annual Grove Park Inn Arts & Crafts Conference & Antiques Show, Asheville, NC.

Roycroft

(see also BOOKS, Roycroft)

Collectors

Richard Blacher
209 Plymouth Colony Rd.
Branford, CT 06405-4753
ph: 203-481-3321
e-mail: dblacher@javanet.com
Wants all types of Roycroft items,

especially books; also wants other American Private Presses of the period, especially limited editions, illuminations, illustrations, and fine bindings; please describe and price; all quotes answered.

Gary Wood
733 Myrtle Rd.
North Brunswick, NJ 08902-2549
ph: 732-821-7633
e-mail: woodrasp@aol.com
Collector seeks single issues or bound volumes of all Roycroft magazines including "The Philistine," "Roycrofter," "The Fra," as well as books published by The Roycroft Press and craft items bearing the Roycroft cross-and-orb mark.

Francesca Gern
P.O. Box 2161
Hudson, OH 44236-0161
ph: 330-655-9325 or 888-RUM-RILL
fax: 330-655-9347
e-mail: rumrill2@aol.com
Wants to buy Roycroft desk sets, vases, sconces, candleholders, lamps, etc.

Experts

Fritz Gram
357 North Shore Rd.
Cuba, NY 14727-9227
Appraises and specializes in Roycroft items.

Charles F. Hamilton
P.O. Box 769
Tavares, FL 32778
Author of "Roycroft Collectibles."

Museums/Libraries

Elbert Hubbard Roycroft Museum
363 Oakwood Ave.
East Aurora, NY 14052-2319
ph: 716-652-4735 or 716-634-1231
e-mail: ebert@earthlink.net
web: http://www.roycrofter.com/museum.htm

Van Erp-Style Lamps

Repro. Sources

Jerry Cohen
Aurora Studios
109 Main St.
Putnam, CT 06260
ph: 860-928-1965 or 800-448-7828
fax: 860-928-1966
e-mail: Aurora@neca.com
web: http://www.artsncrafts.com
Makes handcrafted, hand-hammered copper lighting fixtures of the highest quality; in the style of Dick Van Erp and Gustav Stickley, plus own custom designs and custom work.

William Morris

Clubs/Associations

William Morris Society of Canada, The
Journal: Journal, The
52 Berkeley Court
Unionville, Ontario L3R 6LP
Canada
e-mail: hedgerow@wwonline.com
web: http://www.yorku.ca/faculty/academic/mckenna/society.html
Exists to foster knowledge about the life, works and philosophy of the gifted and multi-faceted 19th century artist, author and craftsman William Morris (1834-1896.)

ASHTRAYS

Periodicals

Chuck Thompson
Directory: Ashtray Collectors Directory and Source Book
10802 Greencreek Dr., Ste. 703
Houston, TX 77070-5367
For collectors of smokers' ashtrays; porcelain, glass, metal, brass, china, Bakelite, etc.

Casino

Experts

Art Anderson
P.O. Box 4103
Flint, MI 48504-0103
ph: 810-234-3400 or 810-659-4446
fax: 810-234-8656
e-mail: cashtrays@aol.com
web: http://members.aol.com/cashtrays
Author of "Casinos and Their Ashtrays."

Smokers

Collectors

Betty Franks
1831 Penthley Ave.
Akron, OH 44312-1915
ph: 330-784-2869
Wants china or ceramic figural ashtrays with a big mouth or holes in nose, ears, or head for escaping smoke.

Tire

Collectors

Jim Olean
115 MacBeth Drive
Lower Burrell, PA 15068-2628
e-mail: candy@microconnect.net
Avid collector of tire ashtrays, toy candy containers and American glass target balls.

Bill Akers
1969 Whitnet Way
Clearwater, FL 33760
ph: 813-535-7797 or 813-531-7340
fax: 813-532-9087
e-mail: billcat@gte.net
web: http://home1.gte.net/billcat/
Avid tire ashtray collector welcomes any news or comments about tire ashtrays or tire company related items; always buying and have tire ashtrays for sale or trade; interested in starting a tire ashtray collectors club.

ASPHALT

Museums/Libraries

Scott Gordon, Cur.
World Famous Asphalt Museum
ph: 707-664-2344
e-mail: sgordon@cs.sonoma.edu
web: http://www.cs.sonoma.edu/~sgordon/asphalt.html
A breathtaking <g> exhibit of famous asphalt from such notable byways as ROute 66 and Hwy 1 (Pacific Coast Highway).

ASTRONAUT MEMORABILIA

(see SPACE COLLECTIBLES)

ASTRONOMICAL ITEMS

(see also BOOKS, Astronomy; INSTRUMENTS & DEVICES, Scientific; SPACE COLLECTIBLES)

Comets

Experts

Stuart Schneider
P.O. Box 64
Teaneck, NJ 07666-0064
ph: 201-261-1983
fax: 201-599-1950
e-mail: stuarts1031@erols.com
web: http://www.geocities.com/Yosemite/Geyser/7949/
Collector, writer wants items relating to Haley's comets; author of "Haley's Comet - Memories of 1910."

Meteorites

Collectors

Q. David Bowers
Bowers & Merena, Inc.
P.O. Box 1224
Wolfeboro, NH 03894-1224
ph: 800-458-4646 or 603-569-5095
fax: 603-569-5319
e-mail: bowersmerena@conknet.com
web: http://web.coin-universe.com/bowers/index.html
Wants pre-1950 books, catalogs, and monographs describing meteorites, cataloging collections, offering specimens for sale.

Blaine Reed
P.O. Box 1183
Durango, CO 81302-1183
ph: 970-259-5326
fax: 970-254-5326
Buy, sell, trade all types of meteorites; free list; free identification on suspected meteorites for people who believe they may have found one.

Robert Haag
P.O. Box 27527
Tucson, AZ 85726
ph: 520-882-8804
fax: 520-743-7225

Dealers

Michael Casper
Michael I. Casper Meteorites, Inc.
P.O. Drawer J
Ithaca, NY 14851
ph: 607-257-5349
fax: 607-266-7904
e-mail: casper@meteorites.com
web: http://www.meteorites.com/
Meteorite dealer, collector, expert and appraiser; buys, sells, trades meteorites; has an extensive inventory; guarantees authenticity; world's largest volume meteorite dealer.

Marvin Killgore
P.O. Box 95
Payson, AZ 85547
ph: 520-474-9515
fax: 520-474-2474

Eric Twelker
Meteorite Market, The
P.O. Box 33873
Juneau, AK 99803
ph: 907-789-6800
fax: 907-789-3742
e-mail: twelker@alaska.net
web: http://www.alaska.net/~meteor/
A place to buy or learn about meteorites; a full-color on-line catalog of hundreds of affordable meteorite specimens.

Experts

Michael Casper
Michael I. Casper Meteorites, Inc.
P.O. Drawer J
Ithaca, NY 14851
ph: 607-257-5349
fax: 607-266-7904
e-mail: casper@meteorites.com
web: http://www.meteorites.com/
Meteorite dealer, collector, expert and appraiser; buys, sells, trades meteorites; has an extensive inventory; guarantees authenticity; world's largest volume meteorite dealer.

Randy D. Watson, M.D.
545 SE Oak, Ste. D
Hillsboro, OR 97123-4147
ph: 503-297-7424 or 503-640-1614
fax: 503-681-0925
e-mail: gate@teleport.com
Advanced collector pays top dollar; will buy any and all meteorites; also wants to buy meteorite books and pictures; says "I never met a meteorite I didn't like!"; has private museum of

over 2500 microscopes and 200 meteorites.

Periodicals

Joel Schiff
Pallasite Press
Magazine: Meteorite!
P.O. Box 33-1218
New Zealand
ph: +69-9-486-6750
fax: +64-9-489-6750
e-mail: j.schiff@auckland.ac.nz
web: http://crash.ihug.co.nz/~afs/
Meteorite collecting and collections, scientific research, new falls and finds, craters, asteroids, Tektites, historical events, new discoveries, and more.

Telescopes

Clubs/Associations

Walter H. Breyer, Sec.
Antique Telescope Society
Journal: Journal of the Antique Telescope Society
1275 Poplar Grove Lane
Cumming, GA 30041
ph: 770-887-6359
e-mail: whbreyer@mindspring.com
web: http://www1.tecs.com/oldscope/
Members collect, study, restore, preserve and use antique telescopes & other early astronomical instruments, books, atlases, & related items; glossy stock journal published quarterly: technical, historical, restoration articles.

Experts

Bart Fried
P.O. Box 444
Conshohocken, PA 19428
ph: 610-825-6600
e-mail: 71223.3430@compuserve.com
web: http://www1.tecs.com/oldscope/
Specializes in the history of telescopes, astronomical instruments, atlases, astronomical books; special area of interest is in 19th & 20th century telescope makers; will assist with appraisals, restorations problems, authentication.

John W. Briggs
Yerkes Observatory
373 W. Geneva St.
Williams Bay, WI 53191-0258
ph: 414-245-5555 or 505-437-6822
fax: 505-434-5555
e-mail: jwb@hale.yerkes.uchicago.edu
web: http://www1.tecs.com/oldscope/
Specializes in early American telescopes; familiar with details relating to value, original construction, and restoration; historian of the various makers.

Repair Services

Bart Fried
P.O. Box 444
Conshohocken, PA 19428
ph: 610-825-6600
e-mail: 71223.3430@compuserve.com
web: http://www1.tecs.com/oldscope/
Specializes in the history of telescopes, astronomical instruments, atlases, astronomical books; special area of interest is in 19th & 20th century telescope makers; will assist with appraisals, restorations problems, authentication.

ATLANTIC CITY COLLECTIBLES

Dealers

M. McGovern
Home Grown
1012 Manoa Rd.
Wynnewood, PA 19096
ph: 610-649-6316
fax: 610-649-2369
Wants to buy dated ruby flash glass from Atlantic City.

ATLASES

(see also BOOKS; GAS STATION COLLECTIBLES, Road Maps; GLOBES; MAPS & CHARTS)

Dealers

Murray Hudson
Murray Hudson - Antiquarian Books, Maps, Prints & Globes
109 S. Church St.
P.O. Box 163
Halls, TN 38040-0163
ph: 901-836-9057 or 800-748-9946
fax: 901-836-9017
e-mail: mapman@usit.net
web: http://www.murrayhudson.com
Buys/sells pre-1900 antique maps (especially pocket, wall, Civil War and railroad maps) & books with maps (e.g. atlases, travel guides, geographies, land surveys, etc.); esp. of S.E. & S.W. US; also wants pre-1950 world globes.

Paul Mahoney
Old Map Gallery, The
1746 Blake St.
Denver, CO 80202
ph: 303-296-7725
fax: 303-296-7725
e-mail: oldmapgallery@denver.net
web: http://www.oldmapgallery.com
Wants atlases and folding pocket maps.

Lahaina Printsellers, Ltd.
636 Luakini St.
Lahaina, HI 96761
ph: 808-667-7843 or 800-669-7843
e-mail: info@printsellers.com
web: http://ww.printsellers.com/
Wants to buy pre-1900 atlases.

AUCTION CATALOGS

Auction Services

Don Hockman
Hockman Auction Center
Rt. 2 Box 290
Kearneysville, WV 25430
ph: 304-264-0311 or 800-404-8515
fax: 304-264-8261
e-mail: hockman@intrepid.net
web: http://www.hockmanauction.com
Specializes in antiques and collectibles auctions; monthly auctions on the first Sunday of each month with additional estate auctions held throughout the month; consignments accepted.

Doug Davies
Davies Auctions
P.O. Box 5542
Lafayette, IN 47903-5542
ph: 765-449-4515
e-mail: sales@daviesauctions.com
web: http://www.dcwi.com/~davies/Welcome.html
Specializes in antiques auctions.

Book Sellers

Andrew Rose
Catalog Kid
3 Seward Dr.
Ocean, NJ 07712-3724
ph: 800-258-2056 or 732-918-2546
fax: 732-918-8121
e-mail: catalogs@injersey.com
web: http://www.catalogkid.com/
Distributes post sale auction catalogs from Christie's, Sotheby's, Phillips, Lelends, Treadway, Craftsman, Butterfield, Bourne at remaindered prices; domestic and foreign sales.

Kathe Quinn
Auction Catalog, Co., The
503 Live Oak St.
Miami, AZ 85539-1226
ph: 520-473-4088 or 800-487-0428
fax: 520-473-4110
e-mail: auctioncatalog@theriver.com
Sells most definitive, up-to-date reference in art, antiques & collectible market: Sotheby, Christie, Skinner post auction catalogs.

Dealers

Wendy Kenney
EphemeraArts
229 E. 31st St., #4
New York, NY 10016
ph: 212-481-0138
e-mail: wendy@ephemerarts.com
web: http://ephemerarts.com
Carries auction catalogs, exhibition catalogs, reference books and out-of-print books on antiques & collectibles; online catalog includes Asian arts, Americana, decorative arts, dolls, pottery, porcelain, glass jewelry, toys, etc.

Misc. Services

Stanley & Bob Block
Block's Box
P.O. Box 51
Trumbull, CT 06611-0051
ph: 203-261-0057 or 203-926-8448
fax: 203-261-7033
e-mail: blockschip@aol.com
web: http://www.blocksite.com/
Produce video tapes & catalogs for auctioneers and appraisers; full state-of-the-art video tape production facility.

AUCTION SERVICES

(see also "AUCTION SERVICES" Appendix in the back of this book as well as Auction Services listed under specific categories throughout this Directory.)

Clubs/Associations

Joe Keefhaver, Ex. Dir.
National Auctioneers Associations
Magazine: Auctioneer, The
8880 Ballentine
Shawnee Mission, KS 66214
ph: 913-541-8084
fax: 913-894-5281
e-mail: joe@auctioneers.org
web: http://www.auctioneers.org/

Internet Resources

David J. Maloney, Jr., ISA CAPP
MaloneysOnline Antiques & Collectibles Resource Directory
P.O. Box 2049
Frederick, MD 21702-1049
ph: 301-695-8544
fax: 301-695-6491
e-mail: dave@maloney.com
web: http://www.maloneysonline.com/
Online resource information source for collectors, sellers, claims adjusters, etc.: includes experts, buyers, clubs, periodicals, repairers, museums/libraries, appraisers, auctioneers, matching services, dealers, etc.

Misc. Services

Timothy Haines
Auction Consultants
1077 Celestial St.
Rookwood Bldg. 3, Ste. 400
Cincinnati, OH 45202
ph: 513-961-5794
fax: 513-651-0860
e-mail: advigroup@aol.com
web: http://members.aol.com/advigroup
Consulting individuals on auction consignments; finding the best auction for their art and antiques.

Ronald P. Hume
Ottawa Valley Auctions
121 Woodbury Cr.
Ottawa, Ontario K1G 5C6
Canada
ph: 613-733-0900
fax: 613-733-2728
e-mail: spider1@capitalnet.com
web: http://www.capitalnet.com/~spider1/homepage.html
Provides day/date listings of auctions in the Ottawa Valley Region.

Periodicals

Newsmagazine: Auction World
417 W. Stanton
P.O. Box 745
Fergus Falls, MN 56537
ph: 218-739-4408
fax: 218-736-7474
The monthly newsmagazine for professional auctioneers featuring news, feature stories and columns on auctions all over the U.S.; also auctioneer supplies and services.

Government Contract

Auction Services

Government Asset Sales
e-mail: support@financenet.gov
web: http://www.financenet.gov/sales.htm
A one-stop portal website for information on the sale or auction of all manner of public assets and surplus from real property and loans to planes, cars, jewelry.

GSA, Property Management Division, Federal Supply Service
web: http://tsd.r3.gsa.gov/fss/auction.htm
Sells various types of property including cars, vans, trucks, plumbing equipment, heating equipment, paper products, typewriters, computers, other office machines, medical equipment, tools, etc.; expect to pay a fair price.

Government Auction Listings
e-mail: webmaster@govauctions.org
web: http://www.govauctions.org/
Complete, up-to-date information about Government Federal auctions all over the US: Department of Defense, U.S. Customs Service, U.S. Marshals, General Services Administration, Housing & Urban Development, etc.; small fee for services.

United States Treasury Auctions Page
c/o Office of Public Correspondence
1500 Pennsylvania Ave., NW
Washington, DC 20220
ph: 202-622-2000
fax: 202-622-6415
web: http://www.ustreas.gov/auctions/
Customs, IRS, USSS and ATF seized property.

Manheim Auctions Government Services
1400 Lake Hearn Dr., NE
Atlanta, GA 30319
ph: 800-222-9885
Has a government contract to conduct government auctions of personal property including antiques, rare books, jewelry, collectibles, etc; call to be placed on their mailing list.

United States Postal Service Auctions, Atlanta Mail Recovery Center
P.O. Box 4416
Atlanta, GA 30336-9590
web: http://www.usps.gov/consumer/auctions.htm
Auctions of damaged and unclaimed goods are held periodically at each Mail Recovery Center in Atlanta, Saint Paul, San Francisco.

Internet

(see INTERNET CLASSIFIEDS FOR COLLECTORS as well as the "Auction Services" appendix in the back of this Directory)

AUDIO EQUIPMENT

(see AUDIO-VISUAL; HI-FI EQUIPMENT)

AUDIO-VISUAL

(see also BROADCASTING; CAMERAS & CAMERA EQUIPMENT; FILMS; GAMES, Video Games; HI-FI EQUIPMENT; MOVIE MEMORABILIA; PHOTOGRAPHS; RADIO SHOWS, Old Time; RECORDS; TELEVISION SHOWS & MEMORABILIA)

Appraisers

Steven Smolian
Smolian Sound Preservation Studios
1 Worman's Mill Court #4
Frederick, MD 21701
ph: 301-694-5134
fax: 301-694-5179
Record collections appraised for tax donation, estate & insurance loss purposes; all formats - 78s, 45s, LPs, cylinders, radio disks, etc.; rock, classical, country, old news broadcasts; over 20 years appraising major archives.

Paul Willigan, Pres.
NICE Network, Inc.
2126 Alpine Place
Cincinnati, OH 45206-2603
ph: 513-961-1052 or 800-837-NICE
fax: 513-961-0538
e-mail: paul@nicenetwork.com
web: http://www.nicenetwork.com/
Appraisers of high tech and high value electronic equipment including computers, PBX telephone systems, medical equipment, copiers, software, film printers, optical jukeboxes, mainframe computers, audio-visual systems, etc.

Experts

Dr. Steve Johnson
Behavioral Images, Inc.
Newsletter: Ten Thousands Words
302 Leland St., Ste. 101
Bloomington, IL 61701-5646
ph: 309-829-3931 or 800-988-6427
fax: 309-829-9677
e-mail: sjohnson@mediavalue.com
web: http://www.mediavalue.com
Film, video, recordings, photographs, negatives; author of "Appraising Audio-Visual Media; A Guide for Attorneys, Trust Officers, Insurance Professionals, & Archivists" (1993); $34.95 & $3 S&H; publishes newsletter ten times per year.

Misc. Services

Steven Smolian
Smolian Sound Preservation Studios
1 Worman's Mill Court #4
Frederick, MD 21701
ph: 301-694-5134
fax: 301-694-5179
Old recordings transferred from your squealing tapes, home discs, radio transcriptions, shellac records, etc. to tape and CD; uses a full range of professional equipment; over 30 years experience restoring audio for companies.

Repair Services

S.P.E.C.S. Bros. Video Services
P.O. Box 5
Ridgefield Park, NJ 07660
ph: 201-440-6589
Offers a videotape rejuvenation and reclamation service; reclaim deteriorating or contaminated video material; optimize tapes for signal retrieval; special fire damage and environmental damage reclamation services.

Analogique Systems Labs
17 West 17th St.
New York, NY 10011
ph: 212-989-4240
fax: 212-633-9389
e-mail: analogique@earthlink.net
web: http://www.analogique.com/
Factory authorized repair of stereos, hi-fi and audio equipment, video and speaker repair, tube equipment repair, turntables, tape recorders, DAT and VCR repair.

AUTO RACING MEMORABILIA

(see also AUTOMOBILES; AUTOMOBILES, Racing; TOYS, Cars [Racing])

Collectors

George Spruce
33 Washington St.
Sayville, NY 11782-2003
ph: 516-563-4211
e-mail: gspruce@earthlink.net
Wants Vanderbilt Cup Auto Race Long Island Motor Parkway items and other pre-1917 auto racing memorabilia.

George Koyt
8 Lenora Ave.
Morrisville, PA 19067-1206
ph: 215-295-4908
Wants all types of auto racing items: programs, postcards, books, toys, games, anything auto racing, A to Z, old/new, large or small; will buy one piece or entire collections.

Museums/Libraries

International Motorsports Hall of Fame
3198 Speedway Blvd.
Talladega, AL 35160
ph: 256-362-5002 or 256-362-5003
fax: 256-362-3717
web: http://www.olcg.com/al/atc/central/imhf.html
Preserves the worldwide history of motor sports; over $7M in racing vehicles and memorabilia on display; Hall of Fame.

Indianapolis Motor Speedway Hall of Fame Museum
P.O. Box 24152
Speedway, IN 46224
e-mail: leisure@infinet.com
web: http://www.automuseum.com/INDYmuse.html

Drag

Collectors

Mike & Cheryl Goyda
P.O. Box 192
East Petersburg, PA 17520-0192
ph: 717-569-7149
fax: 717-569-0909
e-mail: Goydagang@aol.com
Wants to purchase drag racing newspapers and magazines, handouts, trophies, jackets, posters, programs, etc.

Museums/Libraries

Don Garlits
Don Garlits Museum of Drag Racing
13700 SW 16th Ave.
Ocala, FL 34473-3970
ph: 352-245-8661
fax: 352-245-6895
web: http://www.garlits.com
Classic car and antique museum encompasses 20,000 square feet of displays, mostly auto related though plenty of old "Americana" as well; adjacent to the Auto Racing Hall of Fame & Museum.

Periodicals

Geoff Stunkard
Newsletter: Quarter Milestones
53 Milligan Ln.
Abbeville, MS 38601
ph: 423-928-7741

Indy 500

Clubs/Associations

John E. Blazier
National Indy 500 Collectors Club
Newsletter: Short Chute, The
10505 N. Delaware St.
Indianapolis, IN 46280-1353
ph: 317-848-4750
Goal is to preserve the history of the Indy 500 Mile Race; newsletter has club notes, member spotlight, articles, want, sell, trade, etc.

Collectors

John E. Blazier
10505 N. Delaware St.
Indianapolis, IN 46280-1353
ph: 317-848-4750
Founder of the National Indy 500 Collectors Club.

Eric Jungnickel
P.O. Box 4674
Naperville, IL 60567-4674
ph: 630-983-8339
Wants Indy 500 items: auto racing items including felt pennants, programs, posters, tickets, passes, toys, board games, bobbin' head dolls, trophies, any race track; prefers pre-WWII items.

Experts

Jack Mackenzie
6940 Wildridge Rd.
Indianapolis, IN 46256
Author of "Indy 500 Buyers Guide."

Museums/Libraries

Indianapolis Motor Speedway Hall of Fame Museum
P.O. Box 24152
Speedway, IN 46224
e-mail: leisure@infinet.com
web: http://www.automuseum.com/INDYmuse.html

NASCAR

Clubs/Associations

National Racing Club, The
Newsletter: Inside Track
615 Hwy. A1A North, Ste. 105
Ponte Vedra Beach, FL 32082
ph: 904-285-9409
fax: 904-285-5408
For NASCAR enthusiasts: club members get exclusive racing collectibles, product discounts, special member-only events.

Collectors

John Adipotti
2728 Fifth St.
Monroeville, PA 15146
ph: 412-823-5095
fax: 412-856-3377

Dealers

Tom & Joanne Schwarz
3125 E. Main St.
Endicott, NY 13760
ph: 607-785-0707
fax: 607-785-0707
e-mail: nascartoys@aol.com

Brickel's Racing Collectibles
P.O. Box 205
Leesport, PA 19533
ph: 610-926-6719
fax: 610-926-6977
Stock cars, sprints, late model dirt cars, funny cars, top fuel dragsters, Dually's, 1/18 racer toys, RCCA club pieces, fan fueler items.

Randy Kerschner
Randy Kershner's Racing Collectibles
871 Scenic Drive
Mohnton, PA 19540
ph: 610-777-5736
Glassware, ceramics, mail order.

Keith Moore
Last Lap Replicas
15 Park Ave.
Hagerstown, MD 21740
ph: 301-733-5019
Specializes in NASCAR custom-built models, banks and diecasts.

A & L Racing Collectibles
13945 Statesville Blvd., #73
Cleveland, NC 27013
ph: 704-278-2122
fax: 704-278-2124

Luke Krisher
A & L Racing Collectibles
13945 Statesville Blvd., #73
Cleveland, NC 27013
ph: 704-278-2122
fax: 704-278-2124
e-mail: krishers@salisbury.net
Specializes in NASCAR trading cards.

John Williams
John's Wholesale Sports Collectibles
801 N. Salisbury St.
Lexington, NC 27292
ph: 336-476-9153 or 336-249-1622

Cathy's Racing Collectibles
1829 Old Watkins Rd.
Henderson, NC 27536
ph: 252-438-8614
fax: 252-438-9563
e-mail: CRCRacing@aol.com

Greg Toney
JSI Motorsports Collectibles
P.O. Box 478
Sandy Springs, SC 29677-0478
ph: 864-231-9491
e-mail: jsi@carol.net
web: http://members.carol.net/jsi/
Specializes in motorsports collectibles: autographs and rare memorabilia, postcards, trading cards, uniforms, programs.

White Rhino Racing Collectibles
7592 W. Farmington Blvd., Ste. 206
Memphis, TN 38138
ph: 901-753-4027
e-mail: wrracing@aol.com
NASCAR diecast model cars and trucks, funny cars, Ertl.

Dean Knight
Kathy's Kards
7700 E. 42nd Place
Tulsa, OK 74145
ph: 800-435-3570 or 918-664-3232
fax: 918-664-7018
e-mail: kathy@nascarshop.com
web: http://www.nascarshop.com
One of the largest racing collectibles companies in the U.S.; specializes in diecast of all makes; also carries cards and many racing related souvenirs.

Cross Roads Racing
1260 Brentwood St.
Lakewood, CO 80215
ph: 877-880-6500
e-mail: racing@racingstuff.com
web: http://www.racingstuff.com/
NASCAR die cast racing collectibles and merchandise; over 1400 different race collector toys in stock.

Experts

Whit King
Racing Collector's Price Guide
5620 Highway 29 N., Ste. 202
Harrisburg, NC 28075
ph: 704-455-1702
fax: 704-455-1707
e-mail: rcpg@bellsouth.net
web: http://www.racingcollectors.com/
Editor-at-large of "Racing Collector's Price Guide."

Museums/Libraries

Hendrick Motorsports Museum & Gift Shop
4400 Papa Joe Hendrick Blvd.
Harrisburg, NC 28075
ph: 704-455-0342
fax: 704-455-0341
25 acre, 200,000 square foot racing complex; display exhibits, souvenir sales, race shop viewing.

Jerry Cashman, Ex. Dir.
North Carolina Auto Racing Hall of Fame
119 Knob Hill Rd.
Mooresville, NC 28115
ph: 704-663-5331
fax: 704-663-6949
e-mail: webmaster@ncarhof.com
web: http://www.ncarhof.com/
Features over 30 race cars dedicated to al types of auto racing; racing history films, Indy Simulator, showcases of uniforms, helmets, and photographs.

Gloria Durant
NMPA Stock Car Hall of Fame - Joe Weatherly Museum
P.O. Box 500
Darlington, SC 29532
ph: 843-395-8821
web: http://www.autospeak.com/museum03.htm
Has the largest collection of stock cars in the world; fans can see the pioneers who made the sport of NASCAR what it is today; housed at Darlington Raceway, NASCAR's original Superspeedway.

Periodicals

Magazine: RACE Magazine
P.O. Box 716
Kannapolis, NC 28082-0716
ph: 704-788-4660
fax: 704-786-3781
e-mail: racecollexch@prodigy.com
The racing collector's exchange; race fan guides, race schedules, collectibles ads.

NASCAR
Magazine: Inside NASCAR
888 W. Big Beaver, Ste. 600
Troy, MI 48084
ph: 800-996-4300
web: http://www.nascar.com/pubs/inside/
Official publication of the National Association for Stock Car Auto Racing.

AUTOGRAPHS

(see also ALBUMS, Autograph; BOOKS, Reference [Autographs]; HISTORICAL AMERICANA; MANUSCRIPTS; PAPER COLLECTIBLES; PERSONALITIES; PHOTOGRAPHS, Celebrity; PLAYBOY ITEMS; SPORTS COLLECTIBLES; PERFORMING ARTS)

Appraisers

Brian Kathenes
Brian Kathenes Autographs & Collectibles
P.O. Box 482
Hope, NJ 07844-0482
ph: 908-459-5225 or 800-323-5996
fax: 908-459-4899
e-mail: Brian@nacvalue.com
web: http://www.nacvalue.com
Specialist-Certified Appraiser of autographs, manuscripts and historical documents, with a specialty in sports and celebrity memorabilia, collectibles, stamps, coins, and rare books.

Stephen Koschal
P.O. Box 1581
Boynton Beach, FL 33425-1581
ph: 407-736-8409
fax: 407-736-5902
Buys, sells, and appraises autographs, signatures, letters, documents, books, signed photographs or anyone famous; former director UACC; catalogs issued; live auctions twice a year.

Auction Services

Stanley J. Richmond
Daniel F. Kelleher Company, Inc.
24 Farnsworth St., Ste. 605
Boston, MA 02210-1264
ph: 617-443-0033
fax: 617-443-0789
e-mail: kelleher@tiac.net
web: http://www.tiac.net/users/kelleher/
U.S. and BNA stamps at auction; also autographs and documents.

Tom Beaber Jolie
Recollections Autographs
2-40 Bridge Ave.
Red Bank, NJ 07701
ph: 800-315-1776 or 732-747-3858
fax: 732-758-9730
Full-time autograph dealers; holds bi-monthly auctions and issues free catalogs; publishers of "The Robot That Helped to Make a President", the definitive study of the John F. Kennedy autograph.

Caroline Birenbaum
Swann Galleries, Inc.
104 E. 25th St.
New York, NY 10010-2977
ph: 212-254-4710
fax: 212-979-1017
e-mail: swann@swanngalleries.com
web: http://www.swanngalleries.com/
Oldest/largest U.S. auctioneer specializing in rare books, autographs & manuscripts, maps, atlases, photographs, and works of art on paper including vintage posters.

Chris Coover
Christie's
502 Park Ave.
New York, NY 10022
ph: 212-546-1000
fax: 212-980-8163
web: http://www.christies.com

Robert H. Snyder
Cohasco, Inc.
P.O. Box 821
Yonkers, NY 10702-0821
ph: 914-476-8500
fax: 914-476-8573
e-mail: cohascodpc@earthlink.net
web: http://home.earthlink.net/~cohascodpc/index.html
In business over 50 years, specializing in paper collectibles, autographs, documents, Americana, ephemera, etc.; mail auction catalogs issued.

Herman Darvick
Herman Darvick Autograph Auctions
P.O. Box 467
Rockville Centre, NY 11571
ph: 516-766-0289
fax: 516-766-7459
Conducts six specialty auction auctions per year; faxed and mail bids accepted.

Kurt R. Krueger
Krueger Auctions
P.O. Box 275
Iola, WI 54945-0275
ph: 715-445-3845
fax: 715-445-4100
Conducts periodic specialized auction sales of autographs and documents.

George Baker
Baker's Eclectibles
P.O. Box 580466
Modesto, CA 95358
ph: 290-537-5221
fax: 209-531-0233
e-mail: georgeb1@thevision.net
web: http://www.collectorsmart.com/
Buys, sells, appraises, auctions authentic autographs and movie memorabilia, music collectibles, art, trading cards, etc.; monthly autograph, coin/currency/token, and general auctions; 25 years in service; member UACC, TAMS.

Trevor Vennett-Smith
T. Vennett-Smith Chartered Auctioneer
11 Nottingham Rd.
Gotham, Nottingham NG11 OHE
U.K.
ph: 0115-9830541
fax: 0115-9830114
web: http://www.thesaurus.co.uk/vennett-smith/
Great Britain's leading professional autograph auction house, specializing in bi-monthly auctions of fine and varied autographs.

Clubs/Associations

Douglas Wertman, Sec.
Universal Autograph Collectors Club
Magazine: Pen & Quill, The
P.O. Box 6181
Washington, DC 20044-6181
e-mail: bardwell@nh.ultranet.com
web: http://www.uacc.org/
The UACC has over 2000 members worldwide; offers a bi-monthly magazine with reports on facsimiles, forgeries, authentication, auctions, shows, celebrity addresses, etc.

George Teas
Washington Historical Autograph & Certificate Organization (WHACO)
Newsletter: WHACO! News
P.O. Box 2428
Springfield, VA 22152-2428
ph: 703-866-0175
fax: 703-866-0175
e-mail: gteas@erols.com
web: http://www.whaco.com
Formed to bring collectors together to promote the hobby of antique stock and bond certificates and historical autographs; database of prices, featured articles, listings of dealers.

International Autograph Collectors Club & Dealers Alliance
4575 Sheridan St., Ste. 111
Hollywood, FL 33021-3515
ph: 561-736-8409
fax: 561-736-5902
web: http://www.iacc-da.com/
Largest autograph collectors club in the world devoted exclusively to autograph collecting.

David R. Smith, Ex. Dir.
Manuscript Society, The
Magazine: Manuscripts
350 N. Niagara St.
Burbank, CA 91505-3648
e-mail: manuscrip@aol.com
web: http://www.manuscript.org
An organization of collectors, dealers, librarians, archivists, scholars and others interested in autographs and manuscripts.

Urs Thoma
Swiss Autograph Collectors Association
Magazine: Swiss Autograph Magazine
Oberdorf 3
Schaenis, CH-8778
Switzerland

Collectors

Stan Block
128 Cynthia Rd.
Newton, MA 02159
Wants autographs, banners, leathers, political pins, baseball cards, silks, sports memorabilia.

Kenneth Schwartz
World Jeep
79 Rte. 35
Eatontown, NJ 07724-3425
ph: 732-542-1111
fax: 932-935-7467
e-mail: kenneth@monmouth.com
Autograph collector, authenticator, expert wants to buy autographs, documents, or letters from famous people; coauthored author of "The Robot That Helped Make a President" with Charles Hamilton, a recognized authority on autographs.

Steven Spalten
P.O. Box 3726
Albany, NY 12203
e-mail: spalten@wizvax.net
web: http://www.wizvax.net/spalten/autograph
Website about autograph collecting; addresses, tips, success stories; great for both new and old collectors.

Edward Bomsey
Edward N. Bomsey Autographs, Inc.
7317 Farr St.
Annandale, VA 22003
ph: 703-642-2040
fax: 703-642-2040
e-mail: enbainc@compuserve.com
web: http://www.abaa-booknet.com/usa/bomsey/
Wants letters, photographs, signatures of personalities in politics, military, science, history, music, arts, etc.

Ralf Mulhern
3722 Alabama #130
San Diego, CA 92104
Wants to buy autographs; send photocopy of items for sale and asking price; send lists and auction catalogs of items for sale.

Michael Reese II
P.O. Box 5704
South San Francisco, CA 94083-5704
ph: 415-641-5920
e-mail: creole@shutmymouth.com
web: http://www.shutmymouth.com
Wants autographs: early aviation (1910-1939), letters, Presidents letters, any Civil War (Union or Confederate); also signed photos, California Gold Rush period (1848-1851).

Dealers

Jerry Rubackin
Jerry's Cards & Collectibles
P.O. Box 1271
Framingham, MA 01701-0207
ph: 508-788-5197
fax: 508-788-5197
Buys and sells WWII fighter aces autographs and other WWII military signatures; also want autographed material by the crew of the Enola Gay which dropped the first atomic bomb on Hiroshima.

Paul Longo
Paul Longo Americana
P.O. Box 5510
Gloucester, MA 01930-0007
ph: 978-525-2290
Wants autographs of Presidents, famous athletes, world famous inventors, statesmen, actors and actresses, etc.

Mark Vardakis
P.O. Box 1430
Coventry, RI 02816
ph: 401-823-8440 or 800-342-0301
fax: 401-823-8861
e-mail: 75253.3166@compuserve.com
web: http://ourworld.compuserve.com/homepages/markvautographs
Buying and selling autographs: presidents, authors, musicians, celebrities, scientists, etc.; also conducts autograph auctions.

George & Julie Perron
Old Paperphiles, The
P.O. Box 135
Tiverton, RI 02878-0135
ph: 401-624-9420
fax: 401-624-4204
Buys and sells paper collectibles: books, autographs, sheet music, postcards, photos, stereoviews, documents, old letters; issues periodic catalog of items for sale.

George H. La Barre
La Barre Galleries
P.O. Box 746
Hollis, NH 03049
ph: 603-882-2411
fax: 603-882-4979
e-mail: collect@glabarre.com
web: http://www.glabarre.com/
Specializes in collectible stocks and bonds, autographs, paper money; also deals with other areas of Americana; retail and wholesale to other dealers including large marketing companies; inventory includes over 5.7 million pieces in stock.

Bob Eaton
R & R Enterprises
3 Chestnut Dr.
Bedford, NH 03110
ph: 603-471-0808
fax: 603-471-2844
Buys and sells photographs, signatures, letters and documents signed by famous personalities in all fields: presidential, historical, sports, music, film.

Alexander Autographs, Inc.
100 Melrose Ave.
Greenwich, CT 06830
ph: 203-622-8444 or 203-622-8765
e-mail: info@alexautographs.com
web: http://www.alexautographs.com/
Conducts mail, phone, fax and Internet auctions approximately every four months featuring thousands of autographs in all fields.

University Archives
600 Summer St.
Stamford, CT 06901-1403
ph: 800-237-5692 or 203-975-9291
fax: 203-348-3560
Buying and selling fine historical autographs, manuscripts, documents, autographed books and autographed photographs of notable people including U.S. presidents, Revolutionary and Civil War, literary, aviation, science, art, and music.

Marc Zydiak
Star Archives
P.O. Box 285
Westfield, NJ 07091-0285
ph: 908-654-6505

Tom Beaber Jolie
Recollections Autographs
2-40 Bridge Ave.
Red Bank, NJ 07701
ph: 800-315-1776 or 732-747-3858
fax: 732-758-9730
Full-time autograph dealers; holds bi-monthly auctions and issues free catalogs; publishers of "The Robot That Helped to Make a President", the definitive study of the John F. Kennedy autograph.

Seth Kaller
M. Kaller & Assoc., Inc.
P.O. Box 173
Allenhurst, NJ 07711
ph: 732-774-0222
fax: 732-774-9401
Buys and sells historical autographs & documents: Civil War, Lincoln items, U.S. Presidents, etc.

Mara Urciuoli
Lion Heart Autographs
470 Park Avenue South - Penthouse
New York, NY 10016
ph: 212-779-7050 or 800-969-1310
fax: 212-779-7066
e-mail: lhaautog@aol.com
web: http://www.lionheartinc.com/
Offers the finest in historical autographs and manuscripts in the fields of American and world history, science, art, literature, and music.

Susan Levin Hoffman
North Shore Manuscript Company, Inc.
P.O. Box 458
Roslyn Heights, NY 11577
ph: 516-484-6828
fax: 516-625-3327
e-mail: nsmc@earthlink.net
Buys and sells historical manuscripts, documents, letters, signatures, and photos in the fields of politics, science, business, art, literature; specializing in Presidents and signers of the Declaration of Independence.

Jerry Docteur
Pages of History
P.O. Box 2840
Binghamton, NY 13902-2840
ph: 607-724-4943
fax: 607-724-0120
e-mail: 71064.3342@compuserve.com
Wants presidential and other historical autographs and material; buys autographs in all fields; also wants Civil War letters and documents.

Robert Batchelder
1 West Butler Ave.
Ambler, PA 19002-5701
ph: 215-643-1430
fax: 215-643-6613
Wants autograph letters, manuscripts & documents (American & European in all fields): Presidents, historical, literary, musical, etc.; issues periodic catalogs of items for sale.

Steven S. Raab
Steven S. Raab Autographs
P.O. Box 471
Ardmore, PA 19003
ph: 610-446-6193 or 800-977-8333
fax: 610-446-4514
e-mail: raab@raabautographs.com
web: http://www.raabautographs.com/
Buying and selling autographs, manuscripts documents and signed photographs in all fields of interest; American history and vintage entertainment are specialties; issues illustrated catalogs.

Catherine Barnes
Catherine Barnes Autographs
P.O. Box 27782
Philadelphia, PA 19118
ph: 215-247-9240
Wants autographs, letters, documents, etc. signed by historic individuals, e.g. Presidents, government, science, medicine, the arts, law, etc.

Mr. Carmen D. Valentino
Rare Books & Manuscripts
2956 Richmond St., Drawer 19
Philadelphia, PA 19134-5720
ph: 215-739-6056
Antiquarian bookseller specializing in rare books, manuscripts, documents, early newspapers, handwritten diaries, account books and ledgers, ephemera, broadsides; pre-WWI.

Nate Dresler
Nate's Autograph Hound
10020 Raynor Road
Silver Spring, MD 20901
e-mail: autohnd@access.digex.net
web: http://www.access.digex.net/~autohnd/
Carries only authentic autographs form celebrities in rock/pop, movie/TV, political/presidential, space, to name a few; over 300 signed photos, books, cards; some presidential memorabilia, too; member UACC.

Barbara Pengelly
Barb Pengelly, Autographs
13917 No. Meadow Road
Hagerstown, MD 21742
ph: 301-733-9070
fax: 301-416-7891
e-mail: BarbPengly@aol.com
web: http://www.civilwarmall.com/pengly.htm
Authenticate, appraise, buy and sell quality autographs, documents, signed photos, letters and diaries; member of UACC and of The Manuscript Society; premium paid for Civil War-related material; references available.

Peter Thurber
Ritzi & Thurber, Inc.
160 S. Beach St.
Daytona Beach, FL 32114
ph: 904-252-2552 or 904-226-8489
fax: 904-226-8490
e-mail: ritzi1881@earthlink.net
web: http://www.ritzi-thurber.com/
Firm has one of central Florida's largest biographical and historical reference libraries, with over 400 volumes containing 4 million names on the Civil War alone.

Al Wittnebert
Al Wittenbert Autographs, Inc.
P.O. Box 821297
South Florida, FL 33082-1297
ph: 954-437-5562
fax: 954-450-6585
e-mail: signhere@msn.com
Author of "Signature of the Stars" (1989) and "The Study of Star Trek Autographs" (1994); dealer in all fields of autographs with over 30 years experience.

Cordelia & Tom Platt
Platt Autographs
1040 Bayview Dr., #428
Fort Lauderdale, FL 33306
ph: 954-564-2002
fax: 954-564-2002
e-mail: ctplatt@ctplatt.com
web: http://www.ctplatt.com/
Members of IADA, Manuscript Society, UACC.

Ed London
Autographs Incorporated
9408 NW 70 St.
Fort Lauderdale, FL 33321-3002
ph: 954-724-4274 or 954-726-4107
Buys and sells autographs; free giant super sale autograph catalog available upon request.

Joseph Rubinfine
American Historical Autographs
505 S. Flagler Dr., Ste. 1301
West Palm Beach, FL 33401-5923
ph: 561-659-7077
Advanced, experienced dealer; catalog of autograph and document offerings available for $5; focuses on 18th century autographs and documents.

Pieces of the Past
4521 PGA Blvd., #258
West Palm Beach, FL 33418

Stephen Koschal
P.O. Box 1581
Boynton Beach, FL 33425-1581
ph: 407-736-8409
fax: 407-736-5902
Buys, sells, and appraises autographs, signatures, letters, documents, books, signed photographs or anyone famous; former director UACC; catalogs issued; live auctions twice a year.

Richard Kohl
1840 N. Federal Highway
Boynton Beach, FL 33435
ph: 800-344-9103
fax: 561-364-8765
Wants to buy autographs and historical documents: artists, authors, poets, entertainers, musicians/ composers, astronauts, explorers, inventors, aviators, presidents, political/foreign/military/religious leaders; also Americana.

R. Greg Albach
Sign Here...Autographs
P.O. Box 3777
Plant City, FL 33564
ph: 813-757-0076
e-mail: autographs@combase.com
web: http://www.autographweb.com/signhere/
Collector, dealer, expert with online resource for authentic autographs on the Internet; huge selection, secure ordering, monthly auctions.

W. Noble
1705 W Broad St.
Tampa, FL 33604-4637
ph: 813-930-6202
fax: 813-930-6202
Buys, sells and trades autographs in all fields; holds bi-monthly mail bid autograph auction; also sells celebrity address list.

J.D. Bardwell
J.D. Bardwell Autographs
9131 College Parkway, Ste. 13B, Box 101
Fort Myers, FL 33919-4827
ph: 941-481-5629
fax: 941-481-1487
Offers quality autographs at wholesale prices; issuing catalogs since 1986; specializes in autographs from those in the entertainment field; author of "In-Person Facsimile Guide of Celebrity Autographs."

Ivan Gilbert, MD
Miran Art & Books
2824 Elm Ave.
Columbus, OH 43209
ph: 614-231-3707 or 614-818-3222
fax: 614-818-3223
e-mail: IGilbert@ahhinc.com
Wants autographs, manuscript materials, letters, note books, documents, etc.

Ramparts, Inc.
P.O. Box 9429
Dayton, OH 45409
ph: 800-463-1932
fax: 937-299-2151

Steve H. Nowlin
History Makers, Inc.
4040 E. 82nd St.
Indianapolis, IN 46250
ph: 800-424-9259 or 317-842-5828
fax: 317-842-5845
e-mail: steven@indy.net
web: http://www.a1.com/history/
Wants autographs of heroes, legends, superstars; any famous autographs from 1600 to present.

Linda Payne
Linda Payne Autographs
P.O. Box 081336
Racine, WI 53408-1336
ph: 414-663-7478
fax: 414-663-7525
e-mail: Pinda@aol.com
Wants all items signed by famous people; from 1 item to entire collections, especially good vintage items; catalog available.

William Butts
Main Street Fine Books & Manuscripts
206 N. Main St.
Galena, IL 61035-2244
ph: 815-777-3749
fax: 815-777-8950
e-mail: msfb@galenalink.com
web: http://www.wcinet.com/msfbooks
Open shop dealing in autographs and out-of-print books in most fields; specializing in all aspects of American history; books and autograph catalogs issued regularly; member of A.B.A.A.; author of column, "Sign Here."

Robert A. LeGresley
P.O. Box 1199
Lawrence, KS 66044-8199
ph: 785-331-0782 or 785-749-5458
fax: 785-331-0782
e-mail: rlegres@aol.com
Buys and sells autographs, specializing in historical, scientific, literary, musicians, composers, aviation, Civil War, entertainers, Papal and Saints, William Randolph Hearst.

PM Antiques & Collectibles
P.O. Box 224
Coffeyville, KS 67337
ph: 316-251-5308
e-mail: pagrundy@webtv.net
Specializes in autographs and sports memorabilia.

Classic Rarities & Co.
P.O. Drawer 29109
Lincoln, NE 68529
ph: 402-467-2948
fax: 402-467-3780

Larry F. Vrzalik
Lone Star Autographs
P.O. Drawer 500
Kaufman, TX 75142
ph: 972-932-6050
fax: 972-932-7742

Tim Anderson
Autographs of America
P.O. Box 461
Provo, UT 84603-0461
e-mail: tanders3@autographsofamerica.com
web: http://www.autographsofamerica.com/
Buy, sell, trade autographs: historical, Mormons, sports figures, etc.; specializing in movie stars of the 1930s, '40s and '50s.

Rocky Whitehead
P.O. Box 36561
Tucson, AZ 85740-6561
ph: 520-297-7811
fax: 520-297-7811
e-mail: aautograph@aol.com
web: http://members.aol.com/aautograph/index.html
Sells autographs and other memorabilia; also promotes shows.

Joseph Maddalena
Profiles in History
345 North Maple Dr., Ste. 202
Beverly Hills, CA 90210-3859
ph: 800-942-8856 or 310-859-7701
fax: 310-859-3842
web: http://www.profilesinhistory.com/
Wants original letters, manuscripts, rare books of famous people. Cash paid. Serious inquiries only.

Myron Ross
Heroes & Legends
P.O. Box 9088
Calabasas, CA 91372
ph: 818-346-9220
e-mail: heroesross@aol.com
Wants character memorabilia, books, comic books, Fanzines, movie memorabilia, etc.; science fiction or fantasy, rock 'n roll, autographs.

Darrell Talbert
Odyssey Group, Inc.
510-A S. Corona Mall
Corona, CA 91720-1420
ph: 909-371-7137 or 800-99-ODYSSEY
fax: 909-371-7139
e-mail: DBTOGI@aol.com
web: http://www.odysseygroup.com/odyssey.htm
One of the world's leading companies in rare autographs and popular culture memorabilia.

George Baker
Baker's Eclectibles
P.O. Box 580466
Modesto, CA 95358
ph: 290-537-5221
fax: 209-531-0233
e-mail: georgeb1@thevision.net
web: http://www.collectorsmart.com/
Buys, sells, appraises, auctions authentic autographs and movie memorabilia, music collectibles, art, trading cards, etc.; monthly autograph, coin/currency/token, and general auctions; 25 years in service; member UACC, TAMS.

Daniel Cohen
Daniel Cohen Autographs & Memorabilia
869 Nashville Rd., Box #55
Kleinburg, Ontario L0J 1C0
Canada
ph: 905-893-2328
e-mail: dcohen@danielcohen.com
web: http://www.danielcohen.com/
Specializes in vintage to contemporary celebrity autographs in all fields.

Experts

Kenneth Schwartz
World Jeep
79 Rte. 35
Eatontown, NJ 07724-3425
ph: 732-542-1111
fax: 932-935-7467
e-mail: kenneth@monmouth.com
Autograph collector, authenticator, expert wants to buy autographs, documents, or letters from famous people; coauthored author of "The Robot That Helped Make a President" with Charles Hamilton, a recognized authority on autographs.

Helen & George Sanders
Autograph House
2 Lake Dr.
P.O. Box 658
Enka, NC 28728-0658
ph: 828-667-9835
Co-authors with Ralph Roberts of "Collector's Guide to Autographs" (Wallace-Homestead, 1991); also other books; own one of the largest and extensive autograph collections; buys, sells, authenticates and appraises autographs.

Al Wittnebert
Al Wittenbert Autographs, Inc.
P.O. Box 821297
South Florida, FL 33082-1297
ph: 954-437-5562
fax: 954-450-6585
e-mail: signhere@msn.com
Author of "Signature of the Stars" (1989) and "The Study of Star Trek Autographs" (1994); dealer in all fields of autographs with over 30 years experience.

Internet Resources

Steven Spalten
Autograph Collectors Database
P.O. Box 3726
Albany, NY 12203
e-mail: spalten@wizvax.net
web: http://www.wizvax.net/spalten/autograph
Website about autograph collecting; addresses, tips, success stories; great for both new and old collectors.

Misc. Services

Jim Romeo
Directory: Resource for Autograph Collectors
1008 Weeping Willow Dr.
Chesapeake, VA 23322-7701
Publishes a directory of resources for autograph collectors: dealers, clubs, associations, auction houses.

Museums/Libraries

New York Public Library, The
455 5th Ave.
New York, NY 10016-0118
ph: 212-340-0833
web: http://www.nypl.org/branch/central_units/mm/midman.html

Periodicals

Christopher C. Jaeckel
Walter R. Benjamin Autographs, Inc.
Magazine: Collector, The
P.O. Box 255
Hunter, NY 12442-0255
ph: 518-263-4133
fax: 518-263-4134

Jeffrey Morey
Newsletter: Autograph Review, The
305 Carlton Rd.
Syracuse, NY 13207-1530
ph: 315-474-3516
A bi-monthly 21-year publication for the serious collector; collector growth oriented: sports, military, actors' addresses, ads, mail-bid auctions, information and news. Courtesy sample $1 + LSASE.

Marty Marsh
Marlan Group
Newspaper: Autograph Times
1125 W. Baseline Rd., #2-153-M
Mesa, AZ 85210-9501
ph: 480-777-8552 or 480-777-0842
fax: 480-777-0844
e-mail: MarlanPub@aol.com
web: http://celebrityconnection.com/at.htm
News and information on all aspects of autograph collecting including historical, space, sports, entertainment and through the mail.

Magazine: V.I.P. Autogramm-Magazin
3000 W. Olympic Blvd., Bld.3, Ste. 2415
Santa Monica, CA 90404
ph: 310-264-4274
e-mail: vip@cube.net
web: http://www.vip-entertainment.com/
The European autograph collector's magazines.

Ev Phillips
Oddesy Publications
Magazine: Autograph Collector
510-A S. Corona Mall
Corona, CA 91720-1420
ph: 909-371-7137 or 800-99-ODYSSEY
fax: 909-371-7139
e-mail: DBTOGI@aol.com
web: http://www.autographcollector.com/acm.htm
A bi-monthly magazine covering all aspects of autograph and historical document collecting: entertainment, sports, historical, etc.; for all ages; sample autographs, free celebrity addresses, detailed how-to articles, auctions, ads, etc.

Ev Phillips
Oddesy Publications
Magazine: Pop Culture Collecting
510-A S. Corona Mall
Corona, CA 91720-1420
ph: 909-371-7137 or 800-99-ODYSSEY
fax: 909-371-7139
e-mail: DBTOGI@aol.com
web: http://www.odysseygroup.com/collect.htm
A monthly magazine focusing on collecting autographs, movie memorabilia, movie posters, television, rock & roll, props, costumes, sports, space collectibles, animation art and more.

Astronaut

Dealers

Adam Harwood
Astronaut Autographs
1414 West Aries
Edmond, OK 73003-5826
ph: 405-359-7678
fax: 405-341-8405
e-mail: 75717.1061@compuserve.com
Over eight years experience buying and selling astronaut autographs; has worked with former astronauts and NASA employees to bring their collections to the space collectibles market; writes space memorabilia column for collectibles mag.

Celebrity

(see also PHOTOGRAPHS, Celebrity)

Auction Services

Alan Sherred
Non Stop Auction of Autographs
P.O. Box 255
Deland, FL 32721-255
ph: 904-943-9500
fax: 904-943-4115
e-mail: auction@n-jcenter.com
web: http://www.auctionautograph.com/
Online internet auction including autographed photos, autographed 3x5 cards of movie and TV stars of the past and present, super models, Star Trek, Sci-Fi, horror and much more.

Dealers

Robert Jones
Autograph World
12 Benajah Drive
Barrington, NH 03825
ph: 603-644-5767
fax: 207-363-5303
e-mail: jones@autographworld.com
web: http://www.autographworld.com
Specializes in the sale of celebrity autographs; on-line catalog features hundreds of stars from vintage Hollywood through today; every item in catalog is pictured.

Jon Allan
Elmer's Nostalgia, Inc.
3 Putnam St.
Sanford, ME 04073-2024
ph: 207-324-2166

Doug Wirth
Hummerdude's
P.O. Box 4348
Dunellen, NJ 08812
ph: 732-424-9367
Buys and sells celebrity photos and autographs.

Safka & Bareis Autographs
P.O. Box 886
Flushing, NY 11375
ph: 718-263-2276
Collections bought and sold; specializing in cinema, music, opera and ballet.

Searle's Autographs
P.O. Box 9369
Asheville, NC 28815
Monthly catalog of celebrity autographs with emphasis on TV, movies, and theatre.

Alan Sherred
Walk of Fame Autographs
P.O. Box 255
Deland, FL 32721-255
ph: 904-943-9500
fax: 904-943-4115
e-mail: autogrph@n-jcenter.com
web: http://www.alansherred.com/
Buys and sells celebrity autographs: Hollywood, TV, models, political, sports, music, celebrities.

J.D. Bardwell
J.D. Bardwell Autographs
9131 College Parkway, Ste. 13B, Box 101
Fort Myers, FL 33919-4827
ph: 941-481-5629
fax: 941-481-1487
Offers quality autographs at wholesale prices; issuing catalogs since 1986; specializes in autographs from those in the entertainment field; author of "In-Person Facsimile Guide of Celebrity Autographs."

Barbara Meyrowitz
Star-Shots
5389 Bearcup St.
Port Charlotte, FL 33981
ph: 941-697-6935
fax: 941-698-0811
e-mail: autos@star-shots.com
web: http://www.star-shots.com
Celebrity autographs and photographs of all kinds; signed photos, 3x5 signature cards, books, Y-shirts.

Steve Nowlin
Rare Find Gallery, A
4040 E. 82nd St.
Indianapolis, IN 46250
ph: 800-424-9259
fax: 317-842-5845
Buys and sells autographs of Hollywood movie stars.

Merit Adventures
P.O. Box 66262
Houston, TX 77266-6262
ph: 281-680-0325
fax: 281-680-2233

Gary Price
Autograph Central
P.O. Box 441615
Aurora, CO 80044
e-mail: webmaster@autographcentral.com
web: http://www.autographcentral.com

Golden State Autographs
P.O. Box 14776
Albuquerque, NM 87191
ph: 505-293-7407

Mike Gould
Hollywood Legends
6621A Hollywood Blvd.
Los Angeles, CA 90028
ph: 323-962-7411
fax: 323-962-6742
Specializes in signed photographs of

contemporary movie stars; also autographs of television stars.

Phil Sears
24592 Via Carissa
Laguna Niguel, CA 92677-7034
ph: 949-643-1477
fax: 949-643-8376
e-mail: Sears@pacbell.net
web: http://www.phil-sears.com
Buys and sells 1930-1950 movie star autographs.

Trudy Prescott
Star Struck International
2791 F. North Texas St., Ste. 112
Fairfield, CA 94533
ph: 707-426-4056
e-mail: starcollectibles@juno.com
web: http://www.star-collectibles.com
Publishes an illustrated catalog of celebrity autographs, costumes and memorabilia.

Thomas Burford
Celebrity Access
20 Sunnyside Ave., Ste. A241
Mill Valley, CA 94941-1928
ph: 415-389-8133
e-mail: AccessStar@aol.com
web: http://members.aol.com/AccessStar/
Autograph dealers for over 2 decades, specializing mostly in Hollywood; publishes a celebrity address book with over 7000 (mostly Hollywood) celebrity addresses; members of several organizations and are active on TV and radio.

cindy Starr
Starr Autographs, Inc.
P.O. Box 68618
Portland, OR 97268
ph: 503-659-3333
e-mail: starr@teleport.com
web: http://www.4collecting.com
Website has thousands of items for sale with all items pictured; on-line auctions; certificates of authenticity with every purchase.

Internet Resources

Scott Johnson
Celebrity Locators
P.O. Box 12
North Whitefield, ME 04353
ph: 207-832-6687
fax: 207-832-0546
e-mail: Scott@CelebrityLocators.com
web: http://www.CelebrityLocators.com
Specialist in putting fans in contact with celebrities; carries a variety of celebrity-related products; publisher of "The Big Book of Celebrity Addresses," and "The Autograph Collecting News" (a free email newsletter).

Misc. Services

Cardiff Publishing Company
Directory: Christensens Celebrity Addresses
6065 Mission Gorge Rd.
San Diego, CA 92120
Publishes annual directory of over 40,000 celebrity addresses.

Periodicals

Hollywood Movie Archives
Directory: Celebrity Address Book
P.O. Box 1566
Apple Valley, CA 92307-0030
ph: 760-247-6819 or 800-771-6746
e-mail: sales@accidental.com
web: http://24.0.45.221/archives/index.htm
Addresses for thousands of stars - screen, stage, television, musicians, singers, teenager, actors, industry executives, ice skaters.

Thomas Burford
Celebrity Access
Directory: Celebrity Access - The Directory
20 Sunnyside Ave., Ste. A241
Mill Valley, CA 94941-1928
ph: 415-389-8133
e-mail: AccessStar@aol.com
web: http://members.aol.com/AccessStar/
Autograph dealers for over 2 decades, specializing mostly in Hollywood; publishes a celebrity address book with over 7000 (mostly Hollywood) celebrity addresses; members of several organizations and are active on TV and radio.

Music Related

Dealers

John & Jude Lubrano
J & J Lubrano, Music Antiquarians
8 George Street
Great Barrington, MA 01230
ph: 413-528-5799
fax: 413-528-4164
e-mail: lubrano@bcn.net
web: http://www.abaa-booknet.com/usa/lubrano/
Buys and sells autograph manuscripts from famous musicals and dance; rare printed music and books about music, musical autographs and manuscripts, rare dance books 16th to 20th centuries; established in 1977; member ABAA, ILAB.

Roger Gross
Roger Gross, Ltd.
225 East 57th St.
New York, NY 10022-2822
ph: 212-759-2892
fax: 212-838-5425
e-mail: rogergross@earthlink.net
web: http://www.rgrossmusicautograph.com/
Buys and sells signed photos of singers, instrumentalists, conductors and composers; letters, musical quotes; classical music and operatic books, memorabilia, ephemera, unsigned photos, etc.

J.B. Muns
Fine Arts Books & Musical Autographs
1162 Shattuck Ave.
Berkeley, CA 94707-2635
ph: 510-525-2420
fax: 510-525-1126
Buys and sells musical autographs (classical musicians, composers and singers) as well as books on music.

AUTOMATA

(see CLOCKS; DOLLS, Automatons; MUSIC BOXES; MUSIC BOXES, Birds & Bird Boxes [Singing])

AUTOMATONS

(see DOLLS, Automatons; CLOCKS; COIN-OPERATED MACHINES; MUSIC BOXES; MUSIC BOXES, Birds & Bird Boxes [Singing]; MUSICAL INSTRUMENTS, Mechanical; TOYS)

AUTOMOBILES

(see also AUTOMOBILIA; BOOKS, Reference [Automobiles]; BUSES; KITS; MILITARIA, Vehicles; MODELS, Cars; AUTO RACING MEMORABILIA; TAXI RELATED COLLECTIBLES; TOYS, Diecast; TRACTORS & RELATED ITEMS; TRAILERS & RV'S; TRUCKS; VOLKSWAGEN RELATED ITEMS)

Appraisers

James Wetzel
Automobile Appraisal Source
40 Plank Rd.
Newburgh, NY 12550
ph: 800-820-0333
fax: 914-561-1745
e-mail: jimwetzel@hvaa.com
web: http://www.hvaa.com
The source for vehicle appraising; in business for over 30 years and performed over 200,000 appraisals; the internet source for appraising.

Terry Shaw
Automotive Legal Service
P.O. Box 626
Dresher, PA 19025-0626
ph: 800-487-4947 or 215-659-4947
fax: 215-659-4947
Government licensed appraisers for all appreciable, collectible quality vehicles; specialists in insurance claims, restoration disputes, IRS donations, estate & equity matters, Lemon Law; qualified expert witness; free information.

Dorothy Balzer, ISA
Accurate Auto Appraisal
P.O. Box 459
Bear, DE 19701
ph: 302-836-5167 or 888-836-7340
e-mail: balzer_g@msn.com
web: http://www.autoappraising.com/
Determines value of vehicles for insurance, estate settlements, etc.; requires inspection of vehicle; serves MD, DE, PA, and NJ.

Larry Batton
Auto Appraisal Group
RR 3 Box 184E
Charlottesville, VA 22903-9322
ph: 800-848-2886 or 804-295-1722
fax: 804-295-7918
e-mail: AAG@autoappraisal.com
web: http://www.autoappraisal.com/
Nationwide appraisal service for all classic and collectible type automobiles: prepurchase inspections, insurance documentation, property and divorce settlements, expert witness testimony; also originality and historical research.

Wayne Merritt
Merritt Appraisal Service
P.O. Box 664
Taylors, SC 29687-0664
ph: 864-297-3999 or 864-420-8844
fax: 804-297-3999
Over 30 years experience in appraising automobiles for insurance claims and coverage.

Dean Kruse
Kruse International
P.O. Box 190
Auburn, IN 46706
ph: 800-968-4444 or 219-925-5600
fax: 219-925-5467
e-mail: skruse@kruseinternational.com
web: http://www.kruseinternational.com
Appraises all collector cars.

Carl T. Roedel, Jr., ISA
Automobile Appraisal Service
10097 Manchester
Saint Louis, MO 63122
ph: 314-821-4015
fax: 314-821-4015
Appraiser of antique, classic and special interest cars & trucks, both foreign and late models, sports cars, muscle cars, street rods, replicas, RVs, SUVs, motorcycles, boats; also consignments of collector cars for sale.

R.W. "Bob" Ryan
Auto Evaluators
5062 S. 108th St., Ste. 225
Omaha, NE 68137
ph: 402-681-2968
fax: 402-331-1638
Custom and classic auto appraiser; automotive legal consultant; court-tested expert witness; mail appraisals nationwide since 1983.

Chris M. Zora
P.O. Box 9939
The Woodlands, TX 77386
ph: 281-362-8258
Specializes in appraising special interest automobiles; classics, street rods, muscle cars.

Mike Grippo, ISA
M & M Automobile Appraisers, Inc.
584 Broomspun St.
Hendersonville, NV 89015
ph: 702-568-5120
fax: 702-568-5158
Special interest, collectible and antique cars, machinery & equipment; expert witness, marriage or business dissolution, loan valuation and insurance coverage; Accredited Member, International Society of Appraisers.

C. Erik Baltzar
Consulting Distributors
P.O. Box 1331
Palm Desert, CA 92261
ph: 760-346-1984
fax: 760-568-6354
Vehicle appraiser.

Dennis Mitosinka
Dennis Mitosinka's Classic Cars
619 E. Fourth St.
Santa Ana, CA 92701-4705
ph: 714-953-5303
fax: 714-953-1810
Appraises all types of autos from 1900 to present; appraisals accepted by FBI, IRS, FSLIC and insurance companies; member of the Inter. Soc. of Appraisers & the Antique Appraisers of Amer.

Randy Hilberg
Collector's Nectar
Box 431
Morro Bay, CA 93443
ph: 805-772-2968
fax: 805-772-2968
e-mail: nectar@thegrid.net
Always buying antique cars; offers complete restoration services; appraisals; master technician; all makes and models; no collection too big or too small to purchase or restore; the only lifetime guarantee in the business.

Auction Services

Kruse International
P.O. Box 190
Auburn, IN 46706
ph: 800-968-4444 or 219-925-5600
fax: 219-925-5467
e-mail: skruse@kruseinternational.com
web: http://www.kruseinternational.com
Specializes in auctioning antique, classic and other special interest automobiles, planes, motorcycles, trucks, etc.

Bruce Knox
Kruse International Southwest
P.O. Box 792427
San Antonio, TX 78279-2427
ph: 210-495-4777
fax: 210-697-4217
e-mail: info@dkccp.com
web: http://www.dankruseclassic.com/
Specializes in auction sales of classic collector cars.

Specialty Sales
4321 First St.
Pleasanton, CA 94566
ph: 510-484-2262 or 800-600-2262
fax: 510-426-8535
e-mail: jdnye@sfnet.com
web: http://www.specialty-sales.com/
Auctions antiques, classics, exotics; largest indoor showroom; ships overseas.

Clubs/Associations

Society of Automotive Historians, Inc.
Magazine: Automotive History Review
1102 Long Cove Rd.
Gales Ferry, CT 06335-1812
e-mail: foster@netbox.com
web: http://www.classicar.com/bombsight/sah.html
Interested in the preservation of historically valuable materials.

COVA/CVGA Inc.
P.O. Box 2136
Little Falls, NJ 07424-3311
ph: 973-881-8831 or 800-227-7166
fax: 973-297-3779
e-mail: info@covacvag.org
web: http://www.covacvag.org/
Not-for-profit special interest group representing all automotive enthusiasts regarding regulation and legislation potentially contrary to collector interest.

William Schmoll
Fifties Automobile Club of America
1114 Furman Dr.
Linwood, NJ 08234
ph: 609-927-4967
Purpose of the club is to encourage the restoration, preservation and use of historic, sports and racing cars.

Antony S. Carroll, Mem.
Vintage Sports Car Club of America
170 Wetherill Road
Garden City, NY 11530
ph: 516-248-6237
e-mail: edwardh@ct1.nai.net
web: http://w3.nai.net/~edwardh/ed8.htm
Emphasis is on pre-1960 cars rare and unusual racing cars.

Ray Hernandez
Wanderers Car Club, The
2620 Old Elizabeth Road
West Mifflin, PA 15122
ph: 412-466-8626

William H. Smith, Ex. Dir.
Antique Automobile Club of America
Magazine: Antique Automobile
501 West Governor Rd.
P.O. Box 417
Hershey, PA 17033
ph: 717-534-1910
fax: 717-534-9101
e-mail: peterg@aaca.org
web: http://www.aaca.org/
Dedicated to the history of the automobile; focuses on "antique" cars - (or by state registration a vehicle at least 25 years old); sponsors AACA tours, meets and discussions; regions and chapters across the U.S.

National Muscle Car Association
Magazine: Muscle Monthly Magazine
3404 Democrat Rd.
Memphis, TN 38118
ph: 901-365-3779
fax: 901-366-1807
e-mail: nmca@netten.net
web: http://www.goracing.com/nmca/

William E. Donze, ExSec
Veteran Motor Car Club of America
Magazine: Bulb Horn
P.O. Box 360788
Strongsville, OH 44136-0014
ph: 440-238-2771
e-mail: vmcca@aol.com
A hobby club organized in 1938 to serve the needs of those interested in the preservation of collector vehicles and related memorabilia.

Milestone Car Society
Magazine: Mile Post
P.O. Box 24612
Indianapolis, IN 46224
ph: 317-259-0959
Focuses on "milestone" cars; certain club-approved 1946-1974 cars which are gaining popularity with the passage of time.

James Garman
Historical Automobile Association
P.O. Box 10313
Fort Wayne, IN 46851-0313

Vintage Sports Car Drivers Association
3160 Thornapple River Dr.
Grand Rapids, MI 49546
ph: 616-949-8281
fax: 616-949-0191
e-mail: vscda@iserv.net
web: http://www.vscda.org/

George Koehler
'48 'n Under, Inc.
708 Water St.
Sauk City, WI 53583
ph: 608-643-8146
For owners and enthusiasts of pre-1949 automobiles.

James J. Baxter
National Motorists Association
Newsletter: NMA News
402 W 2nd St.
Waunakee, WI 53597
ph: 608-849-6000
fax: 608-849-8697
e-mail: nma@motorists.org
web: http://www.motorists.org
For the protection of the rights of motorists, enhancing personal mobility, encouraging rational traffic laws.

Mike Giel
Perfect "10" Motor Vehicle Club
P.O. Box 1890
Saint Paul, MN 55101
ph: 651-639-1928
e-mail: tdgiel@aol.com
Vintage and collector automobiles, motorcycles and scooters; runs a small museum/display area; puts on annual car show.

Classic Car Club of America
1645 Des Plaines River Road, Ste. 7
Des Plaines, IL 60018
ph: 847-390-0443
fax: 847-390-7118
web: http://www.classiccarclub.org/
For owners of select cars from 1925 through 1948.

Mary Jean Flory
Contemporary Historical Vehicle Association
Magazine: Action Era Vehicle
P.O. Box 98
Tecumseh, KS 66542-0098
ph: 785-233-6715
web: http://www.classicar.com/clubs/chva/chva.htm
For cars from 1928 through cars at least 25 years old.

Buddy Hoelzeman
Mid-America Old Time Automobile Association, The
Magazine: Antique Car Times
8 Jones Lane
Petit Jean Mountain
Morrilton, AR 72110
ph: 501-727-5427
fax: 501-727-5427
web: http://www.classicar.com/clubs/motaa/motaa.htm
M.O.T.A.A. represents approximately 26 affiliated antique car clubs; "Antique Car Times" filled with articles featuring antique cars; recognizes cars manufactured through 1972.

Sports Car Club of America, Inc.
Magazine: SportsCar Magazine
9033 East Easter Pl.
Englewood, CO 80112
ph: 303-694-7222
fax: 303-694-7391
e mail: admin@scca.com
web: http://www.scca.com/
Sanctions amateur and professional

auto sports events throughout the U.S., and has done so for over 50 years.

World Organization of Automotive Hobbyists
P.O. Box 1331
Palm Desert, CA 92261-1331
ph: 760-568-6354
Representing automotive hobbyist interests vis-a-vis regulation and/or legislation.

Todd Miller, Ex. Sec.
Horseless Carriage Club of America
Newsletter: Horseless Carriage Gazette
49239 Golden Oak Loop
Oakhurst, CA 93644
ph: 559-658-8800
e-mail: office@horseless.com
web: http://www.horseless.com/
Interested in brass-era touring cars.

Ralph Linnell
Inliners International
Newsletter: 12 Port News, The
14408 SE 169th
Renton, WA 98058
ph: 425-228-2028
e-mail: ChevySix@seatac.net
web: http://www.inliners.org/
For enthusiasts of all makes, models, years of stock, mild, or racing engines that are 4, 6, or 8 cylinders in-lines.

Harry Snoeyer, Sec.
Southern Alberta Antique & Classic Automobile Club
P.O. Box 1723
Lethbridge, Alberta T1J 4K4
Canada
ph: 403-345-4796
web: http://www.classicar.com/clubs/saacac/saacac.htm

Dealers

Duffy Schamberger
Duffy's Collectible Cars
250 Classic Car Court S.W.
Cedar Rapids, IA 52404-4665
ph: 319-364-7000
fax: 319-364-4036
e-mail: duffys@aol.com
web: http://www.duffys.com/

Carl T. Roedel, Jr., ISA
Automobile Appraisal Service
10097 Manchester
Saint Louis, MO 63122
ph: 314-821-4015
fax: 314-821-4015
Appraiser of antique, classic and special interest cars & trucks, both foreign and late models, sports cars, muscle cars, street rods, replicas, RVs, SUVs, motorcycles, boats; also consignments of collector cars for sale.

Dennis Mitosinka
Dennis Mitosinka's Classic Cars
619 E. Fourth St.
Santa Ana, CA 92701-4705
ph: 714-953-5303
fax: 714-953-1810
Auto dealer in antique, classic and special interest cars.

Randy Hilberg
Collector's Nectar
Box 431
Morro Bay, CA 93443
ph: 805-772-2968
fax: 805-772-2968
e-mail: nectar@thegrid.net
Always buying antique cars; offers complete restoration services; appraisals; master technician; all makes and models; no collection too big or too small to purchase or restore; the only lifetime guarantee in the business.

Experts

Tad Burness
Auto Album
P.O. Box 247
Pacific Grove, CA 93950-0247
ph: 831-649-4864
Classic and antique car historian; writes and illustrates syndicated "Auto Album" column for newspapers including "AntiqueWeek"; author of 24 books, most on transportation subjects.

Internet Resources

Auto Restorer Online
e-mail: autobuff@autorestorer.com
web: http://www.autorestorer.com/
A collection of auto restoration information to help with auto restoration projects and car repair needs.

Edmund's
e-mail: editor@edmunds.com
web: http://www.edmunds.com/edweb/used/usedcars.html
On-line values (trade in and resale) for used cars; also comprehensive guide to buying and selling used cars; new cars and trucks, consumer advice, vehicle reviews, financial loan calculator.

Stefan Conrady
Special Car Journal
1730 Christopher Dr.
Deerfield, IL 60015
ph: 847-945-7135
fax: 847-945-9636
e-mail: editor@specialcar.com
web: http://www.specialcar.com
The premier on-line magazine for enthusiasts of classic, exotic, luxury and sports cars; automotive articles, news, featured marques, directories, auction catalogs, classifieds, advertisements, and other related links.

Kelley Blue Book
Price Guide: Kelley Blue Book
5 Oldfield
Irvine, CA 92618
ph: 949-770-7704
fax: 949-837-1904
e-mail: kelley@kbb.com
web: http://www.kbb.com/indexv.html
Website offers current trade-in values for all makes and model cars for the past 21 years; also publishes printed value guides for cars, RV's, motorcycles, snowmobiles, motor homes, travel trailers, personal watercraft, etc.

Steve Ferguson, Ed.
National Automobile Dealers Association
Price Guide: N.A.D.A. Official Used Car Guide
P.O. Box 7800
Costa Mesa, CA 92628
ph: 800-544-6232
fax: 714-556-8715
e-mail: nada@nada.org
web: http://www.nada.org/
A series of value guides for domestic and foreign cars, trucks, vans, RV's, mobile homes, motorcycles, snowmobiles, and boats, small and large; also Heavy Duty Trucks and Aircraft Book, car clubs & organizations, museums.

Lou Ann Hammond
Car-List
P.O. Box 460070
San Francisco, CA 94146-0070
ph: 530-823-6865
e-mail: lou@car-list.com
web: http://www.car-list.com
An on-line Internet service; Car-List is a used car locating service; you can also get a new car price quote; locate a car club from around the world, or list your car club for free.

ClassicCar.com
1200 Harris Ave., #104
Bellingham, WA 98225
ph: 360-738-7018
fax: 360-738-4815
e-mail: editor@classicar.com
web: http://www.classicar.com/
Premier on-line source for classic vehicles, automobilia and rare parts, technical information; great website for all sorts of classic car information: clubs, chat, swap meet, museums, suppliers, articles, etc.

Nicholas Froome
Classic Car Club
The Tomato Building
London, W1R 3HQ
U.K.
ph: 0171 439 0481
fax: 0171 439 0485
e-mail: cars@classic-car-club.co.uk
web: http://www.classic-car-club.co.uk
Web site with news, features, events from the world of classic cars.

Misc. Services

Bob Amott
Horizon Productions Inc.
2321 Kemper Lane
Cincinnati, OH 45206
ph: 513-559-0550 or 800-899-1020
e-mail: hotizon_productions@msn.com
web: http://www.carestoration.com
Produces a series of videos on car restorations; also internet resource for all things concerning automotive restoration: tips, links, parts, clubs, and more.

Museums/Libraries

James A. Harwick, Cur.
J. K. Lilly III Automobile Museum at Heritage Plantation
P.O. Box 566
Sandwich, MA 02563
ph: 508-888-3300 or 508-888-1222
fax: 508-833-2916
e-mail: heritage@heritageplantation.org
web: http://www.heritageplantation.org/autos.htm

Kenneth E. Creed
Auto Museum at Wells, The
1181 Post Rd.
P.O. Box 496
Wells, ME 04090
ph: 207-646-5051 or 207-646-9064
web: http://www.classicar.com/MUSEUMS/WELLS/WELLS.HTM
Over 70 vehicles from 1894 to 1963; fine collection of nickelodeons and antique games (all working!).

Jeffrey A. Gast
Gast Classic Motorcars Exhibit
Route 896
421 Hartman Bridge Rd.
Strasburg, PA 17579-9601
ph: 717-687-9500
web: http://www.classicar.com/MUSEUMS/GAST/GAST.HTM
Over 50 outstanding antique, classic, sports, and hi-performance cars immaculately displayed in "state of the art" lighting; cameras and camcorders are welcome.

Bellm Cars & Music of Yesterday
5500 North Tamiami Trail
Sarasota, FL 34243
ph: 941-355-6228
web: http://www.classicar.com/MUSEUMS/BELLMCAR/BELLMCAR.HTM

Don Garlits
Don Garlits Auto Racing Hall of Fame & Museum
13700 SW 16th Ave.
Ocala, FL 34473-3970
ph: 352-245-8661
fax: 352-245-6895
web: http://www.garlits.com
Classic car and antique museum encompasses 20,000 square feet of displays, mostly auto related though plenty of old "Americana" as well.

Dixie Gun Work's Old Car & Steam Engine Museum
1412 Reelfoot Ave.
Union City, TN 38261
ph: 901-885-0561
fax: 901-885-0440
e-mail: dixiegun@iswt.com
web: http://www.dixiegun.com

Charlie Sens Antique Auto Museum
2074 Marion-Mt. Gilead Rd.
Marion, OH 43302
ph: 740-389-4686 or 740-386-2521
web: http://www.classicar.com/MUSEUMS/SENS/SENS.HTM

Jim Johnson
Alfred P. Sloan Museum
Newsletter: Sloan News
1221 E. Kearsley St.
Flint, MI 48503
ph: 810-760-1169
web: http://www.classicar.com/MUSEUMS/SLOAN/SLOAN.HTM
Features vintage automobiles built in Flint, MI; especially Buick and Chevrolet, but also early marques such as Whitney, Mason, Little, Samson, Durant, Dart and others.

Thomas A. Kayser, Ex. Dir.
Gilmore Classic Car Club Museum
6865 Hickory Rd.
Hickory Corners, MI 49060
ph: 616-671-5089
fax: 616-671-5843
e-mail: gcm@telecity.org
web: http://www.gilmorecarmuseum.org/
Over 140 antique, classic and collector cars are displayed in six large historic Michigan barns; exhibits range from a 1899 Locomobile to a Cadillac styling concept car destined for the year 2002.

Duffy Schamberger
Duffy's Collectible Cars
250 Classic Car Court S.W.
Cedar Rapids, IA 52404-4665
ph: 319-364-7000
fax: 319-364-4036
e-mail: duffys@aol.com
web: http://www.duffys.com/
A car museum with 100 fully restored cars from the 1940s through 1960s; along with other memorabilia from the eras such as gas pumps, barber poles, phone booths, wall murals, and a 1950s diner with neon signs.

Hartford Heritage Auto Museum
147 North Rural St.
Hartford, WI 53027
ph: 414-673-7999
web: http://www.classicar.com/MUSEUMS/HARTFORD/HARTFORD.HTM
Home of the Kissel.

Greg Grams
Volo Auto Museum
27582 Volo Village Rd.
Round Lake, IL 60073-9613
ph: 815-385-3644
fax: 815-344-0703
web: http://www.voloautomuseum.com
Over 200 collector cars on display; featuring muscle cars from the 50s to 70s; one entire building dedicated to pre-1948 autos; inventory changing constantly; admission charged; opened daily 10 to 5.

Keith R. Gill
Museum of Science & Industry
57th St. & Lake Shore Dr.
Chicago, IL 60637
ph: 773-684-1414
fax: 773-684-5580

Buddy Hoelzeman
Museum of Automobiles, The
Route 3, Box 306
Petit Jean Mountain
Morrilton, AR 72110
ph: 501-727-5427
fax: 501-727-5427
web: http://www.classicar.com/MUSEUMS/MUSEAUTO/MUSEAUTO.HTM
Founded in 1964 by the late Winthrop Rockefeller; over 50 cars on display from 1904 to 1967 models; open year round 10 a.m. to 5 p.m.; gift shop.

Hagan Stewart, Dir.
Imperial Palace Auto Collection
3535 Las Vegas Blvd., So.
Las Vegas, NV 89109
ph: 702-794-3174 or 702-731-3311
fax: 702-369-7430
e-mail: ip@imperialpalace.com
web: http://www.autocollection.com/auto/
Incredible collection of hundreds of classic cars: Dusenbergs, Cords, Auburns, etc.; also celebrity cars: Elvis, Marilyn Monroe, Steve McQueen, Al Capone, and presidential cars from Wilson to Nixon.

National Automobile Museum (The Harrah Collection)
Newsletter: Precious Metal
10 Lake Street South
Reno, NV 89501-1558
ph: 775-333-9300
fax: 775-333-9309
e-mail: leisure@infinet.com
web: http://www.automuseum.com/
Museum depicts the history of the automobile; exhibiting over 220 classic, vintage, and special interest vehicles; automobile library offering research by mail; multimedia theater; educational programs; museum store.

Petersen Automotive Museum
6060 Wilshire Blvd.
Los Angeles, CA 90036
ph: 323-930-CARS
web: http://www.petersen.org/
300,000 square feet showcases over 200 vehicles, from rare to classics.

Kristin Hartley
Towe Auto Museum
2200 Front St.
Sacramento, CA 95818
ph: 916-442-6802
fax: 916-442-2646
e-mail: towe_auto_museum@email.msn.com
web: http://www.classicar.com/MUSEUMS/TOWEFORD/TOWEFORD.HTM
A museum of automobile history, explaining the impact of the development of the automobile on our lives; exhibits are constantly changing; monthly activities; annual collector car auction.

Periodicals

Hemmings Motor News
Newsmagazine: Hemmings Motor News
P.O. Box 76
Bennington, VT 05201-0076
ph: 802-442-3101 or 800-227-4373
fax: 802-447-1561
e-mail: terry@hmn.com
web: http://www.hmn.com
Newsmagazine for antique and special interest auto enthusiasts; auctions, ads, services, insurance, restorations, etc.

David Brownell
Hemmings Motor News
Magazine: Special Interest Autos
P.O. Box 196
Bennington, VT 05201-0196
ph: 802-442-3101 or 800-227-4373
fax: 802-447-1561
e-mail: davehmn@sover.net
web: http://www.hmn.com
A bi-monthly magazine focusing on special interest vehicles.

Jonathan A. Stein
Automobile Quarterly, Inc
Magazine: Automobile Quarterly
P.O. Box 348
Kutztown, PA 19530
ph: 610-683-3169
fax: 610-683-3287
e-mail: aqspec@fast.net
web: http://www.autoquarterly.com
Hardbound magazine totally without advertising features in-depth articles on automotive history, nostalgia, art and much more for the serious auto collector and historian; packed with fine color and rare b&w photographs.

Eric Lawrence, Pres.
Price Guide: CPI Value Guide
P.O. Box 3190
Laurel, MD 20709-3190
ph: 301-317-4228 or 800-972-5312
e-mail: Eric.Lawrence@jhu.edu
web: http://www.cpivalueguide.com/
Published quarterly; covers more than 4,000 collectible and exotic cars and light trucks made since 1945; current market values of imported and domestic collectible, exotic and high-line cars.

National Auto Research
Magazine: Black Book Official Auction Report
2620 Barrett Rd.
P.O. Box 758
Gainesville, GA 30503
ph: 770-532-4111 or 800-554-1026
fax: 770-532-4792
web: http://hearstcorp.com/bpub14.html
Publishes weekly, monthly, bimonthly, annual guides (Black Books) containing new and used car and truck values for the automotive and finance industries including used and new car dealers, bankers, wholesale buyers, credit unions.

Magazine: Car Collector & Car Classics
5211 S. WAshington Ave.
Titusville, FL 32780
ph: 407-268-5010
fax: 407-269-2025
e-mail: sales@carcollector.com
web: http://www.carcollector.com/
A monthly glossy magazine with articles about classic, antique and special interest cars; also ads, parts sources and restoration services.

Jeff Broadus
Magazine: Car Collector Magazine
5211 S. Washington Ave.
Titusville, FL 32780
ph: 407-268-5010 or 800-376-2237
fax: 407-269-2025
e-mail: editorial@carcollector.com
web: http://www.carcollector.com
Monthly glossy magazine for the car collector; restoration tips, museums, show previews.

Tim Abbey
Trader Publishing Company
Magazine: Old Car Trader
P.O. Box 9059
Clearwater, FL 34618-9059
ph: 727-712-0035 or 800-548-8889
fax: 727-712-0034
e-mail: webmaster@traderonline.com
web: http://www.traderonline.com

Kelly McKnight
DuPont Registry
Magazine: DuPont Registry
2325 Ulmerton Rd., Ste. 16
Clearwater, FL 34622
ph: 727-573-9339 or 800-233-1731
fax: 727-572-5523
e-mail: mobordo@earthlink.net
web: http://www.dupontregistry.com/
A buyer's gallery of fine automobiles - classics, luxury, exotic, and muscle cars - plus worldwide auction coverage, drive tests, recommendations, profiles, book reviews.

Pat DuChene, PR
Krause Publications
Newsmagazine: Old Cars
700 E. State St.
Iola, WI 54990-0001
ph: 715-445-2214
fax: 715-445-4087
e-mail: info@krause.com
web: http://www.krause.com/
Weekly coverage of antique automobiles of all ages; auction reports, hobby events, car shows, swap meets, ads, club activities, etc.

Pat DuChene, PR
Krause Publications
Magazine: Old Cars Price Guide
700 E. State St.
Iola, WI 54990-0001
ph: 715-445-2214
fax: 715-445-4087
e-mail: info@krause.com
web: http://www.krause.com/
Bi-monthly lists current values in five grading categories for all American cars made from 1901-1989.

Don Nelson, Ed.
Deals on Wheels Publications
Magazine: Deals on Wheels
P.O. Box 205
Sioux Falls, SD 57101
ph: 605-338-7666 or 800-334-1886
fax: 605-338-5337
e-mail: donnelson@dealsonwheels.com
web: http://www.dealsonwheels.com
A comprehensive monthly listing with photo ads of cars for sale nationwide; also classified and display ads for the car enthusiast.

Deals on Wheels Publications
Magazine: Specialty Car Marketplace
P.O. Box 205
Sioux Falls, SD 57101
ph: 605-338-7666 or 800-334-1886
fax: 605-338-5337
e-mail: donnelson@dealsonwheels.com
web: http://www.dealsonwheels.com
Photo-ad magazine listing cars and trucks for sale.

Magazine: Special Car Journal
1730 Christopher Dr.
Deerfield, IL 60015
ph: 847-808-7620
fax: 847-808-7640
e-mail: editor@SpecialCar.com
web: http://www.specialcar.com

Magazine: Skinned Knuckles
175 May Ave.
Monrovia, CA 91016-2227
ph: 626-358-6255
fax: 626-358-6255
e-mail: skpubs@earthlink.net
The hobby's premier monthly auto restoration magazine.

Kelley Blue Book
Price Guide: Kelley Blue Book
5 Oldfield
Irvine, CA 92618
ph: 949-770-7704
fax: 949-837-1904
e-mail: kelley@kbb.com
web: http://www.kbb.com/indexv.html
Website offers current trade-in values for all makes and model cars for the past 21 years; also publishes printed value guides for cars, RV's, motorcycles, snowmobiles, motor homes, travel trailers, personal watercraft, etc.

Steve Ferguson, Ed.
National Automobile Dealers Association
Price Guide: N.A.D.A. Official Used Car Guide
P.O. Box 7800
Costa Mesa, CA 92628
ph: 800-544-6232
fax: 714-556-8715
e-mail: nada@nada.org
web: http://www.nada.org/
A series of value guides for domestic and foreign cars, trucks, vans, RV's, mobile homes, motorcycles, snowmobiles, and boats, small and large; also Heavy Duty Trucks and Aircraft Book, car clubs & organizations, museums.

John Hudson
CMM Publications
Magazine: Classic Motor Monthly
P.O. Box 129
Bolton, Lancashire BL3 4YQ
U.K.
ph: +44 1204 657212
fax: +44 1204 62479
e-mail: editor@classicmotor.demon.co.uk
web: http://www.classicmotor.demon.co.uk/
One of the UK's leading publications for classic, vintage and veteran auto owners; each issue is packed with ads, events, news and much more; the online version reflects the character of the magazines.

Repair Services

Antique Vehicle Maintenance
57 Cannonball Rd.
Pompton Lakes, NJ 07442
ph: 973-616-6300

Martin Lum
Older Car Restoration
304 S. Main St.
P.O. Box 428
Mont Alto, PA 17237-0428
ph: 717-749-3383 or 717-352-7701
fax: 717-749-3383
e-mail: jlum@epix.net
Manufactures and sells reproduction parts for antique cars; also chrome plating.

Realistic Auto Restorations, Inc.
2519 6th Ave. S.
Saint Petersburg, FL 33712-1640
ph: 727-327-5162 or 727-327-1877
e-mail: jsamu58686@aol.com
Offers restoration services for antiques, classics, street rods, Corvettes and all sports cars; paint & body, upholstery, mechanics, woodwork, welding, wiring, stainless steel repair; since 1978; many Concours winners.

David Ten Brink
Beckley Auto Restoration Inc.
4405 S.W. Capital Ave.
Battle Creek, MI 49015
ph: 616-979-3013
fax: 616-979-1261
Offers complete classic and antique car restoration.

Dave Lewis
Dave Lewis Restorations
3825 South Second St.
Springfield, IL 62703
ph: 217-529-5290
fax: 217-529-8452
Partial or complete show quality restorations; over 20 years experience.

Randy Hilberg
Collector's Nectar
Box 431
Morro Bay, CA 93443
ph: 805-772-2968
fax: 805-772-2968
e-mail: nectar@thegrid.net
Always buying antique cars; offers complete restoration services; appraisals; master technician; all makes and models; no collection too big or too small to purchase or restore; the only lifetime guarantee in the business.

Suppliers

John Kutarna
Wheels of Wood
3235 Hill Ave.
Regina, Saskatchewan S4S 0W5
Canada
ph: 306-586-8658
fax: 306-586-2617
e-mail: jkutarna@cableregina.com
web: http://www.saskmaple.net/geodetic/wow/
Makes replacement wood spoked wheels for classic automobiles; also rebuilds and restores wood wheels.

Alfa Romeo

Clubs/Associations

Alfa Romeo Owners Club
3105 E. Skelly Dr., Stge. 607
Tulsa, OK 74105-6358

AMC

Clubs/Associations

Darryl A. Salisbury, Pres.
American Motors Owners Association
Newsletter: American Motoring
6756 Cornell St.
Portage, MI 49024-3412
ph: 616-323-0369
fax: 616-387-4806
e-mail: salisbury@wmich.edu
Founded in 1974 for AMC enthusiasts to distribute information pertaining to AMC cars and hobby; international convention and several regional meets around the world; for all AMC-built products from 1958 through 1988.

Larry Mitchell
AMC World Clubs
7963 Depew St.
Arvada, CO 80003-2527
ph: 303-428-8760
fax: 303-428-1070
web: http://www.amcwc.com/
For owners of 1955 - 1999 American Motors Corp. automobiles: AMX, Spirit, Eagle, Rebel, Pacer, Marlin, Hornet, Javelin, Classic, Gremlin, Rambler, Matador, AMC/Jeep, Concord, American, Ambassador, Metropolitan.

AMC Pacer

Clubs/Associations

AMC Pacer Club
2628 Queenstown Road
Cleveland, OH 44118
ph: 216-371-0226
web: http://www.classicar.com/clubs/pacer/pacer.htm

AMC Rambler

Clubs/Associations

AMC Rambler Club
2645 Ashton Rd.
Cleveland, OH 44118
ph: 216-371-5946
web: http://www.classicar.com/clubs/rambler/rambler.htm

Aston Martin

Clubs/Associations

Jim Whyman, Sec.
Aston Martin Owners Club
1A Hight Street
Sutton
Nr Ely, Cambridgeshire CB6 2RB
U.K.
ph: +44 1353 777353
fax: +44 1353 777648
e-mail: hgstaff@amoc.org
web: http://www.amoc.org/contacts.html

Auburn-Cord-Duesenberg

Clubs/Associations

Matt Bogart, Mem.
Auburn-Cord-Duesenberg Club
P.O. Box 403
Chardon, OH 44024-0403

Museums/Libraries

Auburn-Cord-Duesenberg Museum
1600 South Wayne St.
P.O. Box 271
Auburn, IN 46706
ph: 219-925-1444
web: http://www.classicar.com/MUSEUMS/AUBURN/AUBURN.HTM

Austin-Healey

Clubs/Associations

Edie Anderson, Mem.
Austin-Healey Club of America, Inc., The
Magazine: Healey Marque
P.O. Box 3220
Monroe, NC 28111-3220
ph: 877-5-HEALEY
fax: 704-288-7765
e-mail: secyahca@aol.com
web: http://www.healeyclub.org/
For owners or those interested in Austin-Healey, Austin-Healey Sprite and other Healey marques; mission is to preserve the Austin-Healey and to maintain the highest standards by sharing technical and mechanical information.

Carroll Goldsworth
Austin-Healey Association
Newsletter: Healey Motor News
20702 Linear Lane
Lake Forest, CA 92630
ph: 979-770-3279
e-mail: whocares56@aol.com
Dedicated to the enjoyment of a fine automobile.

Austin-Healey Club USA
Magazine: Austin-Healey Magazine
P.O. Box 6197
San Jose, CA 95150
ph: 888-4AHCUSA
fax: 925-484-2764
e-mail: info@healey.org
web: http://www.healey.org/
Established in 1970; members interested in the history, maintenance, restoration and enjoyment of all Austin-Healeys; ownership of an Austin-Healey not required for membership.

Avanti

Clubs/Associations

Total Performance Avanti Club
P.O. Box 49614
Sarasota, FL 34230-6614

Avanti Owners Association International
Magazine: Avanti Magazine
P.O. Box 28788
Dallas, TX 75228-0788
ph: 972-709-6185 or 800-527-3452
fax: 972-296-7920
e-mail: t442163@Rutadmin.rutgers.edu
web: http://www.classicar.com/clubs/aoai/aoaihome.htm

Bentley

Clubs/Associations

Bentley Drivers Club
223 West Malvern
Fullerton, CA 92832
ph: 714-992-2757

Bentley Drivers Club Ltd.
16 Chearsley Rd.
Long Crendon
Aylesbury, Bucks HP18 9AW
U.K.
ph: 01844-208233
fax: 01844-208923

BMW

Clubs/Associations

Membership
BMW Car Club of America
2130 Mass. Ave.
Cambridge, MA 02140-9850
ph: 617-492-2500 or 800-878-9292
fax: 617-876-3424
e-mail: 102514.2477@compuserve.com
web: http://www.bmwcca.org/

BMW Vintage Club of America
P.O. Box S
San Rafael, CA 94913-4358
ph: 415-897-0220
fax: 415-898-0831
For owners of 1929 through 1965 BMW automobiles.

British

Misc. Services

Karen Miller, Archivist
Jaguar Cars Inc.
555 MacArthur Blvd.
Mahwah, NJ 07430-2326
ph: 201-818-8144 or 914-221-0293
fax: 201-818-0281
A corporate archives offering individual vehicle research from original Jaguar Cars Ltd. build records; verify authenticity of Jaguar and Daimler (from 1960) automobiles.

Repair Services

Ed Miller
Reward Service, Inc.
172 Overhill Rd.
Stormville, NY 12582-5415
ph: 914-227-7647
fax: 914-221-0293
Appraisals, repair & restoration of classic British automobiles by an expert with more than 30 years experience in the field; own research library; family owned and operated.

Bugatti

Clubs/Associations

American Bugatti Club
142 Berkeley St.
Boston, MA 02116-5166
ph: 617-266-1271
fax: 617-266-8572

Bugatti Owners Club
Prescott Hill, Gotherington
Nr. Cheltenham, Glos. GL52 4RD
U.K.
ph: 1242 67 3136
fax: 1241 67 7001

Collectors

Stanley King
260 Fifth Ave.
New York, NY 10001-6408
ph: 212-447-1880
fax: 212-447-0728
Wants to buy anything relating to the Bugatti automobile: car models, posters, auto parts, literature and sales brochures, etc.

Museums/Libraries

Bugatti Trust, The
Prescott Hill, Gotherington
Nr. Cheltenham, Glos. GL52 4RD
U.K.
fax: 44 1242 674191
e-mail: trust@bugatti.co.uk
A museum with Bugatti related material.

Buick

Clubs/Associations

Val Ingram
Buick Club of America
Magazine: Bugle
P.O. Box 401927
Hesperia, CA 92340-1927
ph: 760-947-2485
fax: 760-947-2485
e-mail: peterg@buickclub.org
web: http://www.buickclub.org/
Over 10,000 members; "Bugle" published monthly; members share an interest in the cars made by the Buick Motor Division, their restoration, and preservation.

Cadillac

Clubs/Associations

Jay Ann Edmunds, Mem. Sec.
Cadillac-LaSalle Club, Inc.
Magazine: Self-Starter, The
P.O. Box 1916
Lenoir, NC 28645-1916
ph: 828-757-9919
fax: 828-757-0367
e-mail: CadLaSal@twave.net
web: http://www.cadillaclasalleclub.com
Worldwide organization with 6000+ members; technical service, monthly magazine, annual issue, directory, and annual meet held in various parts of the U.S.

Wray Tibbs
Cadillac Drivers Club
Newsletter: Leland Letters, The
5825 Vista Ave.
Sacramento, CA 95824-1428
ph: 916-421-3193 or 916-421-3105
fax: 702-972-1726
e-mail: jbraun6668@aol.com
Keep your Cadillac on the road forever!

Checker

Clubs/Associations

Roy Dickinson, Ed.
Checker Car Club of America
Newsletter: CCCA Newsletter
10530 W. Alabama Ave.
Sun City, AZ 85351-3544
ph: 623-974-4987
fax: 623-974-4987
e-mail: carclub@gte.net
web: http://www.classicar.com/clubs/checker/checker.htm
For the preservation and enjoyment of Checker automobiles from 1922-1982.

Chevrolet

Clubs/Associations

Bow Tie Chevrolet Association
P.O. Box 607458
Orlando, FL 32860
ph: 407-889-5387
fax: 407-886-7571
e-mail: CHEVY55-72@ao.net
web: http://www.ao.net/CHEVY55-72/
For 1955 to 1957 Chevys only.

Late Great Chevrolet Association
P.O. Box 607458
Orlando, FL 32860
ph: 407-889-5387
fax: 407-886-7571
e-mail: CHEVY55-72@ao.net
web: http://www.ao.net/CHEVY55-72/
For 1958 to 1972 Chevys.

Classic Chevy International
P.O. Box 607188
Orlando, FL 32860-7188
ph: 407-880-1505 or 800-456-1957
fax: 407-299-3341
e-mail: cciworld@aol.com
web: http://www.classicchevy.com/
108 chapters; and '55 to '57 Chevrolet, including Corvette and pickup.

National Chevy Association
Newsletter: Partsline
947 Arcade
Saint Paul, MN 55106-3850
ph: 651-778-9522
fax: 651-778-9686
'54-'54 Chevrolet specialists.

Dennis Fink
Vintage Chevrolet Club of America
P.O. Box 5387
Orange, CA 92863-5387
ph: 818-963-CHEV
e-mail: wtb@swbell.net
web: http://www.classicar.com/clubs/vccaclub/vccaclub.htm

Periodicals

Magazine: Corvette & Chevy Trader
P.O. Box 9059
Clearwater, FL 34618-9059
ph: 727-712-0035 or 800-548-8889
fax: 727-712-0034
e-mail: webmaster@traderonline.com
web: http://www.traderonline.com

Chevrolet Camaro

Clubs/Associations

International Camaro Club, Inc.
Magazine: In The Fast Lane
2001 Pittson Ave.
Scranton, PA 18505-3233
ph: 570-585-4082
Club for all Camaro owners, from the 1967 Classic Collectibles to the present; bi-monthly magazine has technical tips, trim tag ID, classifieds; newsletter is an award winning publication for all Camaro fans!

Worldwide Camaro Association
Magazine: Camaro World
522 Hunt Club Blvd., #415
Apopka, FL 32703
ph: 407-774-4922
fax: 407-774-0329
e-mail: wca@camaroclub.com
web: http://www.camaroclub.com/

Repair Services

Camaro Specialties
112 Elm St.
East Aurora, NY 14052-2536
ph: 716-652-7086
fax: 716-652-2279
e-mail: camarospecial@wzrd.com
web: http://www.camaros.com/
Parts and restorations for '66-'72 GM muscle cars; Camaro and Firebird specialists.

Chevrolet Chevelle

Clubs/Associations

Mark Meekins
National Chevelle Owners Association
Newsletter: Chevelle Report, The
7343-J West Friendly Ave.
Greensboro, NC 27410-6209
ph: 336-854-8935
Focus on interest is on 1964-1987 Chevelle and El Camino; monthly color magazine featuring members' cars, tech tips, factory photos, production information, parts sources, classified ads, chapter club news; over 6,000 members.

American Chevelle Enthusiasts Society
4636 Lebanon Pike, Ste. 195
Hermitage, TN 37076-1316
ph: 615-773-2237
web: http://www.chevelles.com/aces/

Chevrolet Corvair

Clubs/Associations

Harry Jensen
Corvair Society of America
Magazine: CORSA Communique
P.O. Box 607
Lemont, IL 60439-0607
ph: 630-257-6530
fax: 630-257-5540
e-mail: corvair@corvair.org
web: http://www.corvair.org/

Chevrolet Corvette

Clubs/Associations

D. Sandoval
National Corvette Owners Association
Newsletter: For Vettes Only
900 So. Washington St., Ste. G-13
Falls Church, VA 22046-4009
ph: 703-533-7222
fax: 703-533-1153
e-mail: ncoassoc@aol.com
web: http://www.ncoa-vettes.com/
Dedicated to the concept of uniting all Corvette enthusiasts with a common goal, i.e. that of encouraging and increasing the Corvette enjoyment among all members.

Garnett Rogers
Corvette Club of America
Newsletter: Corvette Capers
P.O. Box 9879
Bowling Green, KY 42102
ph: 502-737-6022 or 800-801-7329
fax: 502-737-6022
e-mail: ccabg@ekx.infi.net
web: http://www.corvetteclubofamerica.com

Gary Mortimer
National Corvette Restorers Society
6291 Day Road
Cincinnati, OH 45252-1334
ph: 513-395-8526
fax: 513-385-8554
e-mail: info@ncrs.org
web: http://www.ncrs.org
For people interested in 1953 through 1982 Corvettes; 32 chapters.

Nancy Sable
National Council of Corvette Clubs, Inc.
P.O. Box 5032
Lafayette, IN 47903-5032
ph: 800-245-VETT or 765-447-7412
web: http://www.classicar.com/clubs/NCCCBLUE/NCCCBLUE.HTM
Founded in 1960; non-profit, all volunteer national organization of more that 280 member clubs that sponsor more than 1000 competitive events each year; Concours, wheel-to-wheel drags, autocrosses, rallies, economy runs.

Rob Weaver
Western States Corvette Council
2321 Falling Water Court
Santa Clara, CA 95054
ph: 800-409-9722 or 408-778-5164
web: http://www.geocities.com/MotorCity/3289/

Museums/Libraries

National Corvette Museum
350 Corvette Dr.
Bowling Green, KY 42102
ph: 800-53V-ETTE or 502-781-7973
fax: 502-781-5286
e-mail: ncm@ky.net
web: http://www.corvettemuseum.com
A 68,000 sq. ft. building housing more than 50 Corvette models and one-of-a-kind concept cars spanning the history of Corvette; also thousands of Corvette-related photos, movies, videos, advertisements, models and rare memorabilia.

Periodicals

Petersen Companies, Inc.
Magazine: Corvette Fever
3816 Industry Blvd.
Lakeland, FL 33811
ph: 941-644-0449 or 800-999-3269
e-mail: leeke@petersenpub.com
web: http://www.d-p-g.com/
For enthusiasts who take the love of their automobile seriously; do-it-yourself technical articles, beautiful color features, advice from top Corvette industry experts, interesting news and events listings.

Magazine: Corvette & Chevy Trader
P.O. Box 9059
Clearwater, FL 34618-9059
ph: 727-712-0035 or 800-548-8889
fax: 727-712-0034
e-mail: webmaster@traderonline.com
web: http://www.traderonline.com

Chevrolet Impala

Clubs/Associations

Dennis Naasz
National Impala Association
Magazine: National Impala Association Magazine
P.O. Box 968
Spearfish, SD 57783-0968
ph: 605-642-5864
fax: 605-642-5868
e-mail: impala@blackhills.com
web: http://www.impala.blackhills.com/
Dedicated to the preservation of all full-size Chevrolets from 1958 through 1969; bi-monthly magazine.

Chevrolet Monte Carlo

Clubs/Associations

National Monte Carlo Owners Association
P.O. Box 187
Independence, KY 41051
ph: 606-491-2378
e-mail: nmcoa@juno.com
web: http://www.montecarloclub.com/

Chevrolet Nova

Clubs/Associations

National Nostalgic Nova
Magazine: Nova Times
P.O. Box 2344
York, PA 17405
ph: 717-252-4192 or 717-252-2383
fax: 717-252-1666
web: http://nnova.com/

Chrysler

Clubs/Associations

Ray Montgomery
Chrysler Product Owners Club, Inc.
Newsletter: Torsion Bar
806 Winhall Way
Silver Spring, MD 20904-2072
ph: 301-622-2962
Club is dedicated to the preservation, restoration, and enjoyment of all vehicles built by The Chrysler Corporation and its antecedent companies: Plymouth, DeSoto, Imperial, Dodge.

Wendy McKenney
National Hemi Owners Association
1693 S. Reese Rd.
P.O. Box 171
Reese, MI 48757
ph: 517-868-4921
For enthusiasts of hemi-engined Chrysler products.

Richard Bowman
Walter P. Chrysler Club, Inc.
Newsmagazine: W.P.C. News
P.O. Box 3504
Kalamazoo, MI 49003-3504
ph: 616-375-5535
fax: 616-375-5535
e-mail: wpc@pacificcoast.net
web: http://www.pacificcoast.net/~wpc/
Dedicated to the preservation, restoration, enjoyment of Chrysler products: Plymouth, Dodge, DeSoto, Chrysler, Imperial, Jeep, Eagle, and related vehicles including antecedents Maxwell and Chalmers Motor Cars.

Eleanor Riehl
Chrysler 300 Club International, Inc.
Magazine: Club News
4900 Jonesville Rd.
Jonesville, MI 49250-9439
ph: 517-849-2783
fax: 517-849-7445
e-mail: mayerd@hartwick.edu
web: http://www.classicar.com/clubs/chrysler/300club.htm
Of particular interest to owners of Chrysler 300 letter series automobiles.

Periodicals

Petersen Companies, Inc.
Magazine: Mopar Muscle
3816 Industry Blvd.
Lakeland, FL 33811
ph: 941-644-0449 or 800-999-3269
e-mail: leeke@petersenpub.com
web: http://www.d-p-g.com/
Covers all aspects of interest to Chrysler-oriented performance car enthusiasts; articles ranging from concours-restored cars to all-out Pro Street modifieds to street rods, drag cars, even Chrysler-powered race boats!

Citroen

Clubs/Associations

Citroen Car Club
Magazine: Citronenian
P.O. Box 348
Bromely, Kent BR2 8QT
U.K.
ph: +44 1689 853999
fax: +44 1689 853999
e-mail: webmaster@CitroenCarClub.org.uk
web: http://www.ccc-uk.demon.co.uk/welcome.htm
Founded in 1949; now with over 3000 members worldwide.

Periodicals

Michael Cox, Ed.
Citroen Club
Magazine: Citroen Quarterly
P.O. Box 130030
Boston, MA 02113-0001
ph: 617-742-6606
e-mail: citq@aol.com
web: http://members.aol.com/citq/CitroenClub.html
The "Citroen Quarterly" contains technical information, Citroen history and events; also publishes "Citroen Quarterly Archives"; sponsors and organizes the "Citroen Quarterly" Rendezvous on Fathers Day weekend in Northfield, MA.

Convertible

Clubs/Associations

Joyce Barrow
National Convertible Association & Registry
1314 Rollins Rd.
Burlingame, CA 94010
ph: 650-348-8269

Crosley

Clubs/Associations

Crosley Automobile Club, Inc.
217 North Gilbert St.
Iowa City, IA 52245
e-mail: Jim@Bollman.com
web: http://www.ggw.org/freenet/c/cac/

Custom

Clubs/Associations

National Street Rod Association
4030 Park Ave.
Memphis, TN 38111
ph: 901-452-4030
e-mail: clandsr@avana.net
web: http://www.hotrodsworldwide.com/nsra/nsra.htm

Darryl Starbird
National Rod & Custom Car Hall of Fame
Magazine: Fun on Wheels
Rte. 3, No. 2 Star Kustom Ave.
Afton, OK 74331
ph: 918-257-4234
fax: 918-257-8224
Aims to establish rules for indoor specialty vehicle car shows; national events.

Periodicals

Buzz Kanter, Pub.
TAM Communications, Inc.
Magazine: Rodder's Digest
6 Prowitt St.
Norwalk, CT 06855-1204
ph: 203-855-0008
fax: 203-852-9980
e-mail: buzz@americaniron.com
web: http://www.americaniron.com
Designed for the traditional street-rod enthusiast with a heavy emphasis on do-it-yourself building articles.

Paisano Publications
Magazine: American Rodder
28210 Dorothy Dr.
Agoura Hills, CA 91301-2605
ph: 818-889-8740
fax: 818-889-5214
e-mail: jtinnion@easyrider.net
Focuses on latest trends and techniques in the field of street rodding.

Kelsey Publishing Ltd.
Magazine: Custom Car
Cudham Tithe Barn
Berrys Hill
Cudham, Kent TN16 3AG
U.K.
ph: 01959 541444
fax: 01959 541400
e-mail: info@kelsey.co.uk
web: http://www.kelsey.co.uk
A 68-page monthly British magazine dealing with customization, hot-rodding and cruising, low-riders, lead sleds, drag racing, practical how-to's.

Datsun Roadster

Clubs/Associations

Datsun Roadster Association
Magazine: Datsun Roadster Review
11520 Seahurst Road
Pasadena, CA V7A 3P2
Canada
ph: 604-271-1902

Datsun/Nissan Z Cars

Clubs/Associations

Mike Willemsen, Pres.
Capital Z of Texas
P.O. Box 80844
Austin, TX 78708-0844
ph: 512-458-9924
e-mail: mikew@mip.com
web: http://www.capitalzoftexas.com/

DeLorean

Clubs/Associations

John Truscott, Mem.
DeLorean Owners Association
Magazine: DeLorean World
879 Randolph Rd.
Santa Barbara, CA 93111-1030
ph: 805-964-5296
e-mail: delorean@impulse.net
web: http://www.delorean-owners.org

DeSoto

Clubs/Associations

Ray Montgomery
Chrysler Product Owners Club, Inc.
Newsletter: Torsion Bar
806 Winhall Way
Silver Spring, MD 20904-2072
ph: 301-622-2962
Club is dedicated to the preservation, restoration, and enjoyment of all vehicles built by The Chrysler Corporation and its antecedent companies: Plymouth, DeSoto, Imperial, Dodge.

Walter O'Kelly, Ed.
DeSoto Club of America
Newsletter: DeSoto Days
403 S. Thornton
Richmond, MO 64085
ph: 816-470-3048
Get information about DeSotos, restoration and locating parts.

Leslie Howard, Mem.Sec.
National DeSoto Club, Inc.
Magazine: DeSoto Adventures
3567 Daniel Paul Court
Reno, NV 89506
e-mail: desoto@one.net
web: http://www.desoto.org/
Purpose of the club is to promote the restoration, preservation and enjoyment of the DeSoto automobile; non-profit corporation with international membership.

Dodge

Clubs/Associations

Mike Wenis
Dodge Brothers Club, Inc.
P.O. Box 151
North Salem, NY 10560
ph: 914-669-5509
1914 to 1938 dodge Bros. motor vehicles and Graham Bros. commercial vehicles.

Ray Montgomery
Chrysler Product Owners Club, Inc.
Newsletter: Torsion Bar
806 Winhall Way
Silver Spring, MD 20904-2072
ph: 301-622-2962
Club is dedicated to the preservation, restoration, and enjoyment of all vehicles built by The Chrysler Corporation and its antecedent companies: Plymouth, DeSoto, Imperial, Dodge.

Shelby Dodge Automobile Club
P.O. Box 4631
Lutherville Timonium, MD 21094-4631
ph: 410-821-7322
e-mail: sdac@sdac.org
web: http://www.sdac.org/
Committed to preserving the history of Shelby-built and inspired Dodge-powered automobiles.

Edsel

Clubs/Associations

International Edsel Club
P.O. Box 371
Sully, IA 50251-0371
e-mail: intledselclub@yahoo.com
web: http://www.classicar.com/clubs/intledselclub/index.htm

Mike Read, Treas.
Edsel Owners Club, Inc.
1234 Bayview Heights Rd.
Los Osos, CA 93402-4406

Electric

Clubs/Associations

Frank Didik
Electric Car Owners Club
167 Concord St.
Brooklyn, NY 11201
ph: 718-797-4311
fax: 718-596-4852

Electric Automobile Association
Newsletter: Current Events
2710 St. Giles Lane
Mountain View, CA 94040
ph: 800-537-2882 or 925-685-7580
e-mail: eaanews@juno.com
web: http://www.eaaev.org

Emergency

Clubs/Associations

Emergency Vehicle Owners & Operators Association
14311 W. Lincoln Rd.
Spokane, WA 99224-9398
ph: 509-244-4062
e-mail: evooa@spokane.net
web: http://www.intrlink.net/evooa/
Formed to unite individuals who are interested in the collection, restoration and preservation of "Emergency" vehicles.

Ferrari

Clubs/Associations

Ferrari Club of America, Inc.
P.O. Box 720597
Atlanta, GA 30358
ph: 800-328-0444
fax: 800-328-0444
e-mail: info@ferrariclubofamerica.org
web: http://www.ferrariclubofamerica.org/

Ferrari Owners Club
2012 La Cuesta Drive
Santa Ana, CA 92705
ph: 714-832-2657
fax: 714-832-0004
e-mail: info@ferrariownersclub.org
web: http://www.ferrariownersclub.org/

Fiat

Clubs/Associations

Fiat America
P.O. Box 391068
Mountain View, CA 94039-1068
e-mail: fiatamer@cris.com
web: http://www.concentric.net/~fiatamer/

Ford

Clubs/Associations

Barbara Lemaster
Performance Ford Club of America, Inc.
Magazine: Ford Enthusiast Magazine, The
13155 U.S. Route 23
Ashville, OH 43103
ph: 740-983-2273
fax: 740-983-9691
For all Ford-powered vehicle enthusiasts; hosts car shows, swap meets, and cruise-ins; magazine published bi-monthly.

Toby & Sandy Gorny
Crown Victoria Association
Newsletter: FoMoCo Times
P.O. Box 6
Bryan, OH 43506
ph: 419-636-2475
fax: 419-636-8449
e-mail: fordpart@bright.net
web: http://www.classicar.com/clubs/crownvictoria/index.htm
For owners of all 1954 through 1956 Fords.

Dan Wittern
Early Ford V-8 Club of America
Newsletter: V-8 Times
P.O. Box 2122
San Leandro, CA 94577-2122
ph: 619-283-8117
e-mail: fordv8club@aol.com
web: http://www.earlyfordv8.org/
For 1932 through 1953 V-8 Ford, Mercury, Lincoln owners.

Periodicals

Petersen Companies, Inc.
Magazine: Ford Marketplace
3816 Industry Blvd.
Lakeland, FL 33811
ph: 941-644-0449 or 800-999-3269
e-mail: leeke@petersenpub.com
web: http://www.d-p-g.com/
Buy and sell Ford cars, parts, and services.

Petersen Companies, Inc.
Magazine: Super Ford Magazine
3816 Industry Blvd.
Lakeland, FL 33811
ph: 941-644-0449 or 800-999-3269
e-mail: leeke@petersenpub.com
web: http://www.d-p-g.com/
The only monthly all-Ford magazine.

Magazine: Ford & Mustang Trader
P.O. Box 9059
Clearwater, FL 34618-9059
ph: 727-712-0035 or 800-548-8889
fax: 727-712-0034
e-mail: webmaster@traderonline.com
web: http://www.traderonline.com

Ford Econoline

Clubs/Associations

Jay Long
Econo Club
15039 Costela St.
San Leandro, CA 94579-1524
For owners of 1961-1967 Econoline and Falcon vans and pickups.

Ford Escort

Clubs/Associations

Ford Escort Owners Association
e-mail: dustin@feoa.net
web: http://www.feoa.net/

Ford Fairlane

Clubs/Associations

Mike Mieth
Fairlane Club of America
Magazine: Fairlaner, The
2116 Manville Rd.
Muncie, IN 47302-4854
ph: 765-282-4308
e-mail: fairlaners@aol.com
web: http://www.classicar.com/clubs/fairlane/fairlane.htm
For owners of '62 through '75 Fairlanes and Torinos; impressive colorful "Fairlaner" published six times per year: restoration tips, how-to's, ads, color photos.

Ford Falcon

Clubs/Associations

Falcon Club of America
Newsletter: Falcon News, The
P.O. Box 113
Jacksonville, AR 72078-0113
ph: 501-982-9721
e-mail: fca@falconclub.com
web: http://www.falconclub.com/
For owners of 1960 through 1970 1/2 Falcons.

Ford Galaxie

Clubs/Associations

Mark Reynolds
Ford Galaxie Club of America
Newsletter: Ford Galaxies
P.O. Box 178
Hollister, MO 65672-0178
e-mail: galaxieclub@collector.org
web: http://www.galaxieclub.com/
For owners of 1959 through 1974 Ford Galaxies.

Ford Model A

Clubs/Associations

Model "A" Restorers Club
Magazine: Model "A" News, The
24800 Michigan Ave.
Dearborn, MI 48124-1713
ph: 313-278-1455
fax: 313-278-2624
web: http://www.classicar.com/clubs/marc/marc.htm
To encourage members to acquire, preserve, restore, exhibit and make use of Model A Fords (1928-1931); many regional chapters; articles, event reviews, lots of ads for parts, supplies, and services.

Jerry Wilhelm
Model A Ford Club of America
Magazine: Restorer, The
250 S. Cypress
La Habra, CA 90631-5515
ph: 562-697-2712 or 888-2-MODELA
fax: 562-690-7452
e-mail: webmaster@mafca.com
web: http://www.mafca.com
Over 15,000 members; dedicated to the restoration and preservation of the 1928-1931 Model A Ford.

Ford Model T

Clubs/Associations

Model T Ford Club International
Magazine: Model-T Times
P.O. Box 276236
Boca Raton, FL 33427-6236
e-mail: karens@xnet.com
web: http://www.modelt.org/theclub.html
Dedicated to the preservation and enjoyment of the 1909 to 1927 Model T Ford automobile.

Jay Klehfoth
Model T Ford Club of America
Magazine: Vintage Ford
P.O. Box 743936
Dallas, TX 75374-3936
ph: 972-783-7531
fax: 972-783-0575
e-mail: jay@mtfca.com
web: http://www.MTFCA.com

Ford Mustang

Clubs/Associations

Mustang Club of America, Inc.
Magazine: Mustang Times
3588 Highway 138, Ste. 365
Stockbridge, GA 30281
ph: 770-477-1965
fax: 770-477-1965
e-mail: mustang@mustang.org
web: http://www.mustang.org/
An association for the Ford Mustang and Shelby collector, restorer and enthusiast.

Paul McLaughlin, Pres.
Mustang Owners Club International
Newsletter: Pony Express
2720 Tennessee N.E.
Albuquerque, NM 87110
ph: 505-296-2554
web: http://www.classicar.com/clubs/mustang/mustang.htm
For all Mustang enthusiasts.

Vintage Mustang Owners Association
P.O. Box 5772
San Jose, CA 95150-5772
e-mail: webmaster@vmoa.org
web: http://www.vmoa.org/
Members interested in 1964 1/2 to present Ford Mustangs.

Museums/Libraries

Mustang Museum
432 Lakeshore St.
Jasper, GA 30143
ph: 888-687-8397
e-mail: jburgy@ford.com
web: http://www.mustangmuseum.org/

Periodicals

Petersen Companies, Inc.
Magazine: Mustang Monthly
3816 Industry Blvd.
Lakeland, FL 33811
ph: 941-644-0449 or 800-999-3269
e-mail: leeke@petersenpub.com
web: http://www.d-p-g.com/
Dedicated to the entire scope of Mustang production: repair, restoration, how-to's, performance modifications, etc.

Magazine: Ford & Mustang Trader
P.O. Box 9059
Clearwater, FL 34618-9059
ph: 727-712-0035 or 800-548-8889
fax: 727-712-0034
e-mail: webmaster@traderonline.com
web: http://www.traderonline.com

Repair Services

Joe Palmere
Garden State Mustang
160 Horseneck Rd.
Fairfield, NJ 07004-2328
ph: 973-227-0364
fax: 973-227-0282
Specializes in restoration and general service/repairs of Ford Mustangs and Mustang II's; also supply parts: new, used, repro, and NOS for same.

Ford Ranchero

Clubs/Associations

Gene Makrancy
Ranchero Club
Newsletter: Ranchero Courier
1339 Beverly Rd.
Port Vue, PA 15133
ph: 412-678-2670
For all Ranchero and Courier enthusiasts.

Ford Thunderbird

Clubs/Associations

Kenneth Leaman
International Thunderbird Club
Magazine: Script
8 Stag Trail
Fairfield, NJ 07004
e-mail: 60tbird@intergrafix.net
web: http://intl-tbirdclub.com
For those interested in all Thunderbirds from 1955 to present.

Alan Tast Pres.
Vintage Thunderbird Club International
Magazine: Thunderbird Scoop
P.O. Box 2250
Dearborn, MI 48123-2250
ph: 316-674-7251
fax: 316-794-8132
e-mail: tast@feist.com
web: http://www.classicar.com/clubs/vintbird/vintbird.htm
Focuses on vintage Thunderbirds, 1958 to present.

John Draxler
Thunderbirds of America
P.O. Box 2766
Cedar Rapids, IA 52406
ph: 712-884-6546

Don Kimrey
Heartland Vintage Thunderbird Club of America
Newsletter: Heartland Newsletter
P.O. Box 18113
Kansas City, MO 64133
For owners of 1958 to 1969 Thunderbirds.

Classic Thunderbird Club International
Newsletter: Early Bird
1308 E. 29th St.
Long Beach, CA 90806-1842
ph: 562-426-2709
e-mail: office@ctci.org
web: http://www.ctci.org/
For owners and enthusiasts of 1955 through 1957 T-Birds; 110 local chapters.

Hupmobile

Clubs/Associations

Steve Christie
Hupmobile Club
Magazine: Hupp Herald
158 Pond Rd.
North Franklin, CT 06254-1217
ph: 860-642-6997
Dedicated to the restoration, preservation and enjoyment of Hupmobiles, RCH and Hupp-Yeats automobiles; worldwide membership in excess of 600; also publishes a bi-monthly parts locator newsletter.

Collectors

L. Robert Hurwitz
P.O. Box 243
Syracuse, NY 13215-0243
ph: 315-468-4281
Wants to buy 1909-1941 Hupmobile related items, literature, dealer giveaways and related collectibles such as factory badges, stickpins, fobs, lapel pins, signs, postcards, trohpies, toys, banners, signs, clocks, etc.

Italian

Clubs/Associations

John DeBoer
Italian Car Registry
3305 Valley Vista Rd.
Walnut Creek, CA 94598-3943
ph: 925-458-1163
fax: 925-458-1163
e-mail: icar@deboer.net
Research association devoted to the study of the Italian automobile industry; directory includes information on more than 15,000 limited production automobiles; SASE for details.

Jaguar

Clubs/Associations

Mason Roe
Classic Jaguar Association
1324 East LeParc Dr.
Fresno, CA 93720
ph: 209-434-7626

Jerry Parkhill, Membr.
Jaguar Clubs of North America
9685 McLeod Rd., RR #2
Chilliwack, British Columbia V2P 6H4
Canada
ph: 604-794-3652
fax: 604-794-3654
e-mail: parkhill@uniserve.com
International organization of Jaguar enthusiasts; over 5000 members; sponsors car shows, Concours D'Elegance, rallies and slaloms.

Experts

Karen Miller, Archivist
Jaguar Cars Inc.
555 MacArthur Blvd.
Mahwah, NJ 07430-2326
ph: 201-818-8144 or 914-221-0293
fax: 201-818-0281
Research service; maintains facility housing an extensive photographic collection, technical library, service & parts bulletins, technical bulletins, owner, parts and service manuals, advertising, and paint & upholstery information.

Periodicals

Kelsey Publishing Ltd.
Magazine: Jaguar World
Cudham Tithe Barn
Berrys Hill
Cudham, Kent TN16 3AG
U.K.
ph: 01959 541444
fax: 01959 541400
e-mail: info@kelsey.co.uk
web: http://www.kelsey.co.uk
A 130-page monthly British magazine for the Jaguar enthusiast covering all aspects of Jaguar ownership from buying to restoration: rallies, projects.

Jeep

Clubs/Associations

Jeep Registry
172 Long Hill Rd.
Oakland, NJ 07436-1331
ph: 201-405-0480
For 1946 through 1987 Jeeps.

Periodicals

Petersen Companies, Inc.
Magazine: JP Magazine
3816 Industry Blvd.
Lakeland, FL 33811
ph: 941-644-0449 or 800-999-3269
e-mail: leeke@petersenpub.com
web: http://www.d-p-g.com/
The only all-Jeep periodical about Jeeps and the Jeep lifestyle (no Broncos, Samurais, Explorers, Hummers, Blazers, Scouts, just Jeeps); bi-monthly covering from the first military models to the current TJ Wranglers, Cherokees, etc.

Kit Built

Clubs/Associations

Vintage Kit & Custom Club
RR 1, Box 185
Jacksonville, IL 62650

Lamborghini

Clubs/Associations

Jim Kaminski
Lamborghini Owners Club
Newsletter: LOC Newsletter
P.O. Box 7214
Saint Petersburg, FL 33734
ph: 727-392-3474
fax: 727-392-3474
Organized in 1978; members in 15 countries; tech tips, services sources, parts information, collectibles, and meeting information.

Lamborghini Club of America
170 Monte Vista Rd.
Orinda, CA 94563
ph: 415-254-2107

Land Rover

Clubs/Associations

New York Land Rover Club
Newsletter: Roverfile
P.O. Box 2235
Halesite, NY 11743
ph: 516-271-4808
e-mail: roversny@aol.com
web: http://www.nyroverclub.com/

Rover Owners Club of North America
P.O. Box 43005
Tucson, AZ 85719

Ottawa Valley Land Rovers
P.O. Box 36055
1318 Wellington St.
Ottawa, Ontario K1Y 4V3
Canada
e-mail: david.meadows@sympatico.ca
web: http://www.ovlr.org/

Lincoln

Clubs/Associations

Jim Griffin
Lincoln Owners Club
P.O. Box 660
Lake Orion, MI 48361
ph: 715-356-3039
fax: 810-274-1010
Primarily for those interested in Lincolns built between 1921 and 1939.

Lincoln & Continental Owners Club
Magazine: Continental Comments
P.O. Box 28788
Dallas, TX 75228-0788
ph: 972-709-6185 or 800-527-3452
fax: 972-296-7920
e-mail: webmaster@lcoc.org
web: http://www.lcoc.org/
International club dedicated to the preservation and restoration of all Lincolns, Lincoln Continentals, and Continentals; three national meets every year; magazine published 7 times per year.

Locomobile

Clubs/Associations

Norm Buckhart
Locomobile Society of America
3165 California St.
San Francisco, CA 94115-2412
ph: 415-563-1771

Lotus

Clubs/Associations

Mark Winston
Lotus, Ltd.
P.O. Box L
College Park, MD 20741-3010
ph: 301-982-4054
fax: 301-982-4054

Maserati

Clubs/Associations

Maserati Club, The
Newsletter: Il Tridente
P.o. Box 5300
Somerset, NJ 08875-5300
ph: 732-249-2177
e-mail: email@themaseraticlub.com
web: http://www.themaseraticlub.com/
A nationwide, non-profit member-run club for Maserati enthusiasts; holds major events from Maine to Florida.

Maserati Owners Club of North America
14220 Saddlebow Ct.
Reno, NV 89511
fax: 775-853-7212
e-mail: Rileysboss@aol.com

Maserati Club International
P.O. Box 772
Mercer Island, WA 98040
ph: 206-455-4707 or 206-455-4449
fax: 425-646-5458
e-mail: spdracer@america.com
web: http://maserati.worldwide.net

Mazda

Clubs/Associations

Mazda Club
P.O. Box 11238
Chicago, IL 60611
ph: 773-769-6262
fax: 773-769-3240
e-mail: tnwb52A@prodigy.com
web: http://pages.prodigy.com/IL/franko/mazdaclub.html
For all Mazdas including the RX-7, Miata, MX-6, 626, MX-3, 424, Millenia, Protege/323, and trucks.

Mercedez-Benz

Clubs/Associations

Ron Farrar
Mercedez-Benz Club of America, Inc.
Magazine: Star, The
1907 Leleray St.
Colorado Springs, CO 80909
ph: 800-637-2360 or 716-633-6427
fax: 716-633-9283
e-mail: info@mbca.org
web: http://www.mbca.org/

Internet Resources

Stefan Conrady
Mercedez-Benz Classic On-Line E-Zine
R 051
Stuttgart, D-70322
Germany
ph: +49 711/17-83453
fax: +49 711/17-83455
e-mail: classic-center@str.daimler-benz.com
web: http://www.mercedes-benz.com/e/hist/index_cl.htm
The official Mercedez-Benz Classic website offer: a center for sales, rentals, restorations, parts and accessories; the famous museum collection; clubs around the world; archive of 110 years of automotive tradition; news and reports.

Mercury

Clubs/Associations

Jerry Robbin
International Mercury Owners Association
Newsletter: Quicksilver
6445 West Grand Ave.
Chicago, IL 60635-3410
ph: 773-622-6445
fax: 773-622-3602
web: http://www.classicar.com/clubs/INTMERC/INTMERC.HTM
Open to all Mercury owners (regardless of year or make) and Mercury enthusiasts alike; over 900 members.

Mercury Comet

Clubs/Associations

John Howell
Comet Cyclone Registry
6609 Grey Fox Dr.
Springfield, VA 22152
ph: 703-569-0174

Mercury Cougar

Clubs/Associations

Ron & Sally Crouch, Mem.
Cougar Club of America
Magazine: At the Sign of the Cat
1637 Skyline Dr.
Norfolk, VA 23518-4327
e-mail: cougr351c@aol.com
web: http://members.aol.com/Cougr351c/CCOA.html
Dedicated to the preservation of 1967 through 1973 Mercury Cougars.

MG

Clubs/Associations

Eliot Ganek
MG Car Club
P.O. Box 435
Morristown, NJ 07961
ph: 973-762-8116
fax: 973-376-0687

MG Car Club Ltd., The
P.O. Box 251
Abingdon, Oxfordshire OX14 1FF
U.K.
ph: 01235-555552
fax: 01235-533755
e-mail: carclub@mgcars.org.uk
web: http://www.mgcars.org.uk/mgcc/
U.S. chapters and clubs.

Richard Mong
MG Owners Club, The
Magazine: Enjoying MG
Octagon House
Swavesey, Cambridge CB4 5Qz
U.K.
ph: 01954 231125
fax: 01954 232106
e-mail: RichardM@mgownersclub.co.uk
web: http://www.mgownersclub.co.uk
Largest single marque car club in the world offering advice, spares, events, camaraderie, accessories, insurance, rallies: everything for the MG owner.

MG A Series

Clubs/Associations

Jonathan A. Stein
A Coupe Group
7450 Valley View Lane
Reading, PA 19606
ph: 610-779-9710
fax: 610-779-9710
An informal registry for MGA coupes, offering free information and assistance.

Don Holle
North American MGA Register
P.O. Box 11746
Albuquerque, NM 87192-0746
ph: 505-29309085
fax: 505-332-3116
e-mail: jzorn@ameritech.net
web: http://www.mgcars.org.uk/namgar/
Register for the English MGA series sports car.

MG B Series

Clubs/Associations

Frank Ochal
American MGB Association
P.O. Box 11401
Chicago, IL 60611-0401
ph: 800-723-MGMG or 773-878-5055
fax: 773-769-3240
e-mail: amgba@aol.com
web: http://www.british-cars.org.uk/

Miniature

Clubs/Associations

Kaz Wysocki
Microcar & Minicar Club
Magazine: Minutia
P.O. Box 43137
Montclair, NJ 07043
ph: 201-342-3685
e-mail: minutiamag@aol.como
web: http://www.montclair.edu/pages/FineArts/Faculty/Luttropp/MMwww/MM.html
For the preservation and restoration of small cars usually under 1,000 cc; foreign and domestic; national and regional meets.

Marc Delmont
MicroCar Club
6675 South Sherman St.
Littleton, CO 80121
ph: 303-798-8589

Muscle Cars

Periodicals

Petersen Companies, Inc.
Magazine: Muscle Car Review
3816 Industry Blvd.
Lakeland, FL 33811
ph: 941-644-0449 or 800-999-3269
e-mail: leeke@petersenpub.com
web: http://www.d-p-g.com/
Bi-monthly magazine dedicated to the American muscle car.

Nash

Clubs/Associations

Jim & Dorothy Bracewell
Nash Car Club of America
Newsletter: Nash Times
1N274 Prarie
Glen Ellyn, IL 60137
e-mail: bracewell@nashcarclub.org
web: http://www.nashcarclub.org
A worldwide club over 1900 strong.

Oldsmobile

Clubs/Associations

Charles Degges
National Antique Oldsmobile Club
Magazine: Runabouts to Rockets
11730 Moffitt Lane
Manassas, VA 20112-3122
ph: 703-791-3065
e-mail: NAOC@HotMail.com
1897 through 1964 Oldsmobiles only.

Penny Casteele
Oldsmobile Club of America, Inc.
Magazine: Journey With Olds
P.O. Box 80318
Lansing, MI 48908-0318
ph: 517-321-8825
fax: 517-321-8770
e-mail: krwright@flash.net
For owners and enthusiasts of all Oldsmobile products.

Opel

Clubs/Associations

Opel Association of North America
394 Mystic Lane
Wirtz, VA 24184
ph: 804-379-9737
e-mail: OpelPrez@opel-na.com
web: http://www.opel-na.com/

Opel Motorsport Club
5161 Gelding Circle
Huntington Beach, CA 92649
ph: 714-525-1443
e-mail: president@opelclub.com
web: http://www.opelclub.com/

Opel Drivers Club of America
P.O. Box 385
Pebble Beach, CA 93953

Packard

Clubs/Associations

Packard Automobile Classics, Inc.
Magazine: Cormorant News Bulletin
P.O. Box 28788
Dallas, TX 75228-0788
ph: 972-709-6185 or 800-527-3452
fax: 972-296-7920
e-mail: PACwebmaster@packardclub.org
web: http://www.packardclub.org
Worldwide club for fans of the Packard automobile; monthly newsletter and quarterly magazine; national meet for all members.

Richard Hack, Pres.
Packards International Motor Car Club
Magazine: Packards International Magazine
302 French St.
Santa Ana, CA 92701-4845
ph: 714-541-8431
e-mail: rlh@ucicl.eng.uci.edu
web: http://www.classicar.com/clubs/PACKINTL/PACKINTL.HTM
Dedicated to the preservation and driving of the Packard auto; technical information, source of parts, free classified ads for members.

Periodicals

Dr. Robert B. Marvin
R-Mac Publications
Magazine: Packard Motor Car Magazine
Rt. 3, Box 425
Jasper, FL 32052
ph: 904-792-2480
e-mail: rbm@isgroup.net
web: http://www.vintagevehicle.com/MASTOF97.htm
Bi-monthly magazine dedicated to the Packard company and to the Packard brothers who established the Packard Motor Company.

Dr. Robert B. Marvin
R-Mac Publications
Newsletter: Packard Shop, The
Rt. 3, Box 425
Jasper, FL 32052
ph: 904-792-2480
e-mail: rbm@isgroup.net
web: http://www.vintagevehicle.com/MASTOF97.htm
Monthly newsletter of Packard classifieds.

Pantera

Clubs/Associations

Pantera Owners Club of America
P.O. Box 91773
San Dimas, CA 91773
e-mail: poca1@aol.com
web: http://www.panteraclub.com/

Linda & David Adler
Pantera International Car Club
18586 Main St., Ste. 100
Huntington Beach, CA 92648-1720
ph: 714-848-6674
fax: 714-843-5851
e-mail: pantera@home.com
web: http://www.panteracars.com/

Pierce-Arrow

Clubs/Associations

Pierce-Arrow Society, Inc.
Magazine: Arrow, The
P.O. Box 637
La Grange, TX 78945-0637
e-mail: webmaster@pierce-arrow.org
web: http://www.pierce-arrow.org/
Provides technical and historical information on all Pierce vehicles through "The Arrow" magazine, the "Service Bulletin" (technical bulletin) and "The Emporium" (current events and advertising newsletter.)

Plymouth

Clubs/Associations

Ray Montgomery
Chrysler Product Owners Club, Inc.
Newsletter: Torsion Bar
806 Winhall Way
Silver Spring, MD 20904-2072
ph: 301-622-2962
Club is dedicated to the preservation, restoration, and enjoyment of all vehicles built by The Chrysler Corporation and its antecedent companies: Plymouth, DeSoto, Imperial, Dodge.

Larry Nuesch, Corr. Sec.
Plymouth Owners Club, Inc.
Magazine: Plymouth Bulletin
P.O. Box 416
Cavalier, ND 58220-0416
ph: 701-549-3746
fax: 701-549-3744
e-mail: LNuesch@aol.com
web: http://www.classicar.com/clubs/plymouth/home.htm
Recognizes all 4, 6 & V8 powered Plymouth cars, Plymouth trucks and Fargo commercial vehicles built from 1928 through cars over 25 years of age.

Plymouth Barracuda

Clubs/Associations

Plymouth Barracuda/Cuda Owners Club
64898 Lutz Rd.
Constantine, MI 49042

Police & Sheriff

Clubs/Associations

Sgt. James Post
Police Car Owners of America
15677 Highway 62 West
Eureka Springs, AR 72632
ph: 501-253-4948
fax: 501-253-4949
e-mail: jcasey@policeguide.com
web: http://www.policeguide.com/police-car-club.htm
A club for owners of restored police vehicles - any year and any make; also for collectors of police car models and photographs.

Pontiac Fiero

Clubs/Associations

Fiero Owners Association
Magazine: Pontiac Fiero Connection
9507 Jones Road, #234
Houston, TX 77065
ph: 281-897-0813
e-mail: newboy@flash.net
web: http://www.flash.net/~newboy/foa.html

Fiero Owners Club of America
Magazine: Fiero Owner
7200 Hazard
Westminster, CA 92683
ph: 714-903-6186
fax: 714-903-6196
web: http://www.fieroowners.com/
The only Fiero network resource; informational data, historical info, restorative facts and modification upgrades; magazine has articles, car parts for sale.

Pontiac Firebird

Clubs/Associations

Tom Scherer
National Firebird Club
P.O. Box 11238
Chicago, IL 60611-0238
ph: 773-769-6262
fax: 773-769-3240
e-mail: FirebirdClub@prodigy.com
web: http://www.classicar.com/clubs/nfc/nfc.htm
For all Firebirds including the Trans AM Formula and Firehawk.

Pontiac GTO

Clubs/Associations

GTO Association of America
Magazine: Legend, The
5829 Stroebel Road
Saginaw, MI 48609
ph: 800-486-1964

Porsche

Clubs/Associations

Judy Hendrickson, Mem.
Porsche Club of America
Magazine: Porsche Panorama
P.O. Box 30100
Alexandria, VA 22310-8100
ph: 703-922-9300
e-mail: DH993@aol.com
web: http://www.pca.org/
Members must own a Porsche to join; over 46,000 members and 139 Chapters across US and Canada.

Laurie Taylor, Mem.
Porsche Owners Club, Inc.
: P.O. Box 9000-277
ph: 760-244-1996 or 760-240-6114
e-mail: hirev321@aol.com
web: http://www.porscheclub.com

Preservation

Clubs/Associations

Gary Derner
Auto Restorers Club
308 11th St. SE
Waseca, MN 56093
ph: 507-625-9226

Elaine Jordan
International Society for Vehicle Preservation
Magazine: Restoration Magazine
P.O. Box 50046
Tucson, AZ 85703
ph: 520-622-2201
fax: 520-792-8501
e-mail: isvp@aztexcorp.com
web: http://www.aztexcorp.com/root/isvp.html
For appreciation, preservation, restoration of self-propelled vehicles; how-to help in restoring, sourcing of materials.

Professional

Clubs/Associations

Beverly Ruff, Mem.
Professional Car Society
Magazine: Professional Car, The
P.O. Box 9636
Columbus, OH 43209
ph: 614-237-2350
e-mail: blruff@freenet.columbus.oh.us
web: http://www.professionalcar.org/
For all interested in the preservation of hearses, flower cars, ambulances, limousines, and service cars.

Periodicals

Kelsey Publishing Ltd.
Magazine: Commercial Vehicles
Cudham Tithe Barn
Berrys Hill
Cudham, Kent TN16 3AG
U.K.
ph: 01959 541444
fax: 01959 541400
e-mail: info@kelsey.co.uk
web: http://www.kelsey.co.uk
A 48-page monthly British magazine dealing with only classic and vintage commercial vehicles: rallies, auctions, restorations.

Racing

Clubs/Associations

Sportscar Vintage Racing Association
Newsletter: Line, The
1 Maple St.
Hanover, NH 03755-2007
ph: 603-640-6161
web: http://www.chicago-soft.com/svra/

Charles Gilmore
Eastern States Timing Association
Newsletter: ESTA Nostalgia News
P.O. Box 176
Lahaska, PA 18931
ph: 215-794-8611
Promotes nostalgia drag racing shows throughout the northeast; over 200 members interested in drag racing restored or relics of pre-1972 drag racing cars.

Antique Auto Racing Association
P.O. Box 486
Fairview, NC 28730
Opened to vintage race car owners and enthusiasts.

Thomas Seal
National Auto Racing Historical Society
121 Mt. Vernon St.
Lakewood, OH 44107-3309
ph: 617-723-2661
Shares resources among members, assists publishing and advertising efforts; provides documentation.

International Hot Rod Association
9 1/2 E. Main St.
Norwalk, OH 44857
ph: 419-663-6666
fax: 419-663-4472
e-mail: ihra@goracing.com
web: http://www.ihra.com/
A sanctioning organization for drag strips and racing events throughout N.A. and Europe; 70 member tracks; produces Snap-on Tools Drag Racing Series of professional and sportsman drag racing.

Historic Stock Car Racing Group
5418 Reeve Rd.
Mazomanie, WI 53560
ph: 800-677-6171

Vintage Auto Racing Association
Magazine: Vintage Voice
207 W. Los Angeles Ave., Ste 304
Los Angeles, CA 90068
ph: 800-280-8272
fax: 805-533-0672
e-mail: vara@msn.com
web: http://www.vararacing.com/

Nostalgia Drag Racing Association
10922 Chestnut Ave
Stanton, CA 90680
ph: 714-229-9422

American Nostalgia Racing Association
Magazine: Drag Racing Monthly
7342 East Saddlehorn Way
Orange, CA 92869
ph: 714-744-0844
fax: 714-744-8306
e-mail: anra@anra.com
web: http://www.anra.com/

Steve Earle
Historic Motor Sports Association
P.O. Box 489
Buellton, CA 93427-0489
ph: 805-686-9292

Collectors

Megan Collins
2925 Denison Ave.
San Pedro, CA 90731
ph: 310-833-6757

Renault

Clubs/Associations

Kurt Triffet, Mem.
Renault Owners Club of North America
Newsletter: Renault Report, The
7418 Collet Ave.
Van Nuys, CA 91406
ph: 619-561-6687
e-mail: cdavid@Dreamsoft.com
web: http://web.dreamsoft.com/renaul~1/home.htm

REO

Clubs/Associations

REO Club of America
P.O. Box 336
Rumson, NJ 07760

Periodicals

Ray Wood
Newsletter: Reo Echo
20 Arbor Rd.
South Burlington, VT 05403-5743

Rolls-Royce

Clubs/Associations

Rolls-Royce Owners' Club
Magazine: Flying Lady, The
191 Hempt Rd.
Mechanicsburg, PA 17055
ph: 717-697-4671
fax: 717-697-7820
e-mail: rroc@rroc.org
web: http://www.rroc.org/

Silver Ghost Association
1700 East Iron
P.O. Box 737
Salina, KS 67401
ph: 785-827-9331
e-mail: rroc@rroc.org
web: http://www.rroc.org/regions/sga/sga.htm

Collectors

Glyn Morris
1730 Christopher Dr.
Deerfield, IL 60015-3912
ph: 847-945-9603
fax: 847-945-9636
e-mail: belmont@wwa.com
web: http://www.SpecialCar.com
Wants any paper items relating to Rolls-Royce and Bentley: books, manuals, photos, etc.

SAAB

Clubs/Associations

Stephen Goldberger, Pub.
SAAB Club of North America
Magazine: Nines
2389 Chestnut Hill St.
Canton, OH 44720
ph: 330-497-0346
fax: 330-497-0346
e-mail: publisher@saabclub.com
web: http://www.saabclub.com
Magazine contains valuable information for owners of all SAAB cars; from 2-stroke through Turbomobiles - tech tips, SAAB news, history, service bulletins, classified ads, and business ads.

Shelby

Clubs/Associations

Rick Kopec
Shelby American Automobile Club
Magazine: Shelby American, The
P.O. Box 788
Sharon, CT 06069-0788
ph: 860-364-0449
fax: 860-364-0769
e-mail: saac@discovernet.net
web: http://www.saac.com
SAAC is dedicated to the preservation, care, history and enjoyment of the World Championship cars created by Carroll Shelby from 1962 to present; club in operation since 1975; approx. 5000 members world wide.

Shelby Owners of America, Inc.
P.O. Box 54
Arnold, KS 67515-0054
ph: 913-731-2873
Annual convention; bi-monthly newsletter.

Station Wagons

Clubs/Associations

Ken McDaniel
American Station Wagon Owners Association
Magazine: Wagon Roundup
6110 Bethesda Way
Indianapolis, IN 46254-5060
ph: 317-291-0321
e-mail: aswoa@aol.com
web: http://www.stationwagon.com/
Dedicated to the preservation of American-built station wagons.

Jim Fisher
Station Wagons U.S.A.
5433 Whitsett Ave.
Valley Village, CA 91607
ph: 818-509-9640
G.M. station wagons up to 1972.

Steam

Clubs/Associations

G.T. Elliott, Treas.
Steam Automobile Club of America
Newsletter: Steam Automobile Bulletin
1680 Dartmouth Ln.
Deerfield, IL 60015-3945
ph: 847-945-1975
e-mail: JReynol@aol.com
web: http://www.classicar.com/clubs/STEAM/STEAM.HTM
Encourages the preservation of steam cars and the design of modern ones.

Studebaker

Clubs/Associations

Studebaker Drivers Club
Magazine: Turning Wheels
P.O. Box 28788
Dallas, TX 75228-0788
ph: 214-709-6185 or 800-527-3452
fax: 214-296-7920
e-mail: brady@interaccess.com
web: http://www.studebakerclubs.com/sdc/index.htm

Sheldon Harrison
Antique Studebaker Club
Magazine: Antique Studebaker Review
P.O. Box 28845
Dallas, TX 75228-0845
ph: 972-709-6185 or 800-527-3452
fax: 972-296-7920
e-mail: dochemp@c-zone.net
web: http://www.dochemp/9stude.html
For pre-1946 Studebakers.

Museums/Libraries

Studebaker National Museum
525 South Main St.
South Bend, IN 46601-2225
ph: 219-235-9108 or 219-235-9479
web: http://www.classicar.com/MUSEUMS/STUDE/STUDE.HTM

Stutz

Clubs/Associations

William Greer
Stutz Club
Magazine: Stutz News
7400 Lantern Rd.
Indianapolis, IN 46256-2120
ph: 317-849-3443

Subaru

Clubs/Associations

Ed Parsil
Subaru 360 Drivers' Club
Newsletter: Quarterly Newsletter
1421 North Grady Ave.
Tucson, AZ 85715-5013
ph: 520-290-6492
All-volunteer association of owners/drivers of 2-cylinder Subarus.

Sunbeam

Clubs/Associations

Doug Ferrell
Midwest Sunbeam Club
3701 NW Eric Dr.
Topeka, KS 66618-3631
ph: 785-286-2987
e-mail: rootesclub@cjnetworks.com

Sunbeam Owners Group of San Diego
2250 Rosecrans
San Diego, CA 92106
ph: 619-223-0496
e-mail: oldealp@aol.com

Triumph

Clubs/Associations

Andrew Mace
Vintage Triumph Register, The
Magazine: Vintage Triumph, The
15218 W Warren Ave.
Dearborn, MI 48126-1356
ph: 404-475-1088
e-mail: vtr-www@www.vtr.org
web: http://www.vtr.org/
Focuses on all Triumphs; magazine published quarterly; also publishes "The English Channel" newsletter; annual convention; nearly 70 local affiliate clubs in the US and Canada.

Tucker

Clubs/Associations

William E. Pommering
Tucker Automobile Club of America, Inc.
Newsletter: Tucker Topics
9509 Hinton Dr.
Santee, CA 92071-2760
ph: 619-596-3028
fax: 815-346-6398
e-mail: TuckerClub@aol.com
web: http://www.TuckerClub.org/

Volkswagen

Clubs/Associations

Vintage Volkswagen Club of America
5705 Gordon Dr.
Harrisburg, PA 17112
ph: 717-540-9972
e-mail: eppy@cysource.com
web: http://www.cris.com/~Vvwca/

Volkswagen Club of America
P.O. Box 154
North Aurora, IL 60542-0154
ph: 630-896-2803
e-mail: vwclub@aol.com
web: http://www.vwclub.org

Collectors

Volksgallery
P.O. Box 517
Crompond, NY 10517
Wants Volkswagen-related memorabilia: advertising, brochures, accessories, pictures, toys, etc.

Frank Koinsky
290 Third Ave. Extension
Rensselaer, NY 12144
ph: 518-465-0477
Wants anything to do with Volkswagens: toys, models, literature, memorabilia.

Volvo

Clubs/Associations

Gretchen Adams
Volvo Club of America
Magazine: Rolling
P.O. Box 16
Afton, NY 13730-0016
ph: 607-639-2279
fax: 607-639-2279
e-mail: rollingmag@aol.com
web: http://www.vcoa.org

Willys

Clubs/Associations

Willys Club
Magazine: Willys World
P.O. Box 5466
Plainfield, NJ 07060
ph: 908-757-8807
For help in the restoration of Willys cars, trucks, and Jeeps from 1933 through 1963.

Woodies

Clubs/Associations

John Lee
National Woodie Club
Newsletter: Woodie Times
P.O. Box 6134
Lincoln, NE 68506-0134
ph: 402-488-0990
e-mail: woodcar@tiac.net
web: http://www.classicar.com/clubs/woodie/woodhome.htm
For restorers and owners of wood-bodied cars; advice, ads, information.

AUTOMOBILIA

(see also FARM MACHINERY; FORD MOTOR COMPANY ITEMS; GAS STATION COLLECTIBLES; KEY CHAINS; LICENSE PLATES; LICENSES, Driver; MODELS; MOTORCYCLES; MOTOR SCOOTERS; TOYS, Cars; TRANSPORTATION COLLECTIBLES)

Auction Services

Kruse International
P.O. Box 190
Auburn, IN 46706
ph: 800-968-4444 or 219-925-5600
fax: 219-925-5467
e-mail: skruse@kruseinternational.com
web: http://www.kruseinternational.com

Clubs/Associations

David K. Bausch
Automobile Objects D'Art Club
Newsletter: Automobile Objects D'Art Newsletter
252 N. 7th St.
Allentown, PA 18102-4024
ph: 610-432-3355
fax: 610-820-9368
e-mail: oldtoy@aol.com
A club for collectors interested in early automobile history as shown through art and objects of art.

Collectors

Dave Ogden
P.O. Box 223
Northbrook, IL 60062-0223
ph: 847-564-2893
fax: 847-564-2893
e-mail: musical@flash.net
Wants to buy early automobile lights, horns, radiator caps, and accessories.

Mike Diafera
605 Samoset Lane
Schaumburg, IL 60193
ph: 630-980-6869
Wants to buy automobile memorabilia: oil cans, grease tins, dealership signs, etc.

Dealers

Leila Dunbar
Dunbar's Gallery
76 Haven St.
Milford, MA 01757-3821
ph: 508-634-8697 or 508-634-8097
fax: 508-634-8698
Mail order Americana - no reproductions; buys, sells and specializes in vintage character and comic toys, banks, advertising, automobilia, and Halloween related items.

Robert H. Snyder
P.O. Box 821
Yonkers, NY 10702-0821
ph: 914-476-8500
fax: 914-476-8573
e-mail: cohascodpc@earthlink.net
web: http://home.earthlink.net/~cohascodpc/index.html
Wants automobile literature, materials, periodicals, artifacts & collectibles of all kinds relating to autos, trucks, motorcycles, etc.; collections assembled for institutions & specialists; also Duryea, Napier/Edge, pre-war Japanese.

Ron & Deb Ladley
1850 Valley Forge Rd.
Lansdale, PA 19446
ph: 610-584-1665
fax: 610-584-8537
Wants pre-1970 auto, truck and motorcycle literature, ephemera, catalogs, brochures, manuals, signs, dealership items, etc.; any age.

Experts

Jim & Nancy Schaut
Aquarius Antiques
7147 W. Angela Dr.
Glendale, AZ 85308-8507
ph: 623-878-4293
fax: 623-878-2458
e-mail: jnschaut@aol.com
web: http://members.aol.com/jr1955/web.html
Buys, sells; publishes a quarterly automobilia catalog: gas station maps, dealer signs, automobile literature, oil company items, service station giveaways, etc.; authors of "American Automobilia", illustrated history & price guide.

Internet Resources

Mobilia.com
P.O. Box 575
Middlebury, VT 05753-0575
ph: 800-967-8068 or 802-388-3071
fax: 802-388-2215
e-mail: subs@mobilia.com
web: http://www.mobilia.com/
Online auction of automobilia and related toys, accessories, models, parts, toys, vehicles; also scale model dealers, price guide, car books, events, and more.

Museums/Libraries

Museum of Transportation at Larz Anderson Park
15 Newton St.
Brookline, MA 02146
ph: 617-522-6547
web: http://www.mot.org/

William E. Swigart, Jr.
Swigart Museum
Rte. 22 E
P.O. Box 214
Huntingdon, PA 16652
ph: 814-643-0885 or 814-643-2024
fax: 814-643-2857
e-mail: tours@swigartmuseum.com
web: http://www.swigartmuseum.com/
Cars, toys, lights, license plates, emblems, bicycles, clothing, and much more.

Periodicals

Eric Killorin
Hyatt Research Corp.
Magazine: Mobilia Magazine
P.O. Box 575
Middlebury, VT 05753-0575
ph: 800-967-8068 or 802-388-3071
fax: 802-388-2215
e-mail: subs@mobilia.com
web: http://www.mobilia.com/hotspots/articles.asp
Monthly magazine focusing on automobile collectibles: petroliana, toys, books, car art, models, pedal cars, sculpture; market outlook, price guides, news, auction reports, restoration hints, buy/sell ads.

Sue Elliott, Pub.
Full Throttle Enterprises
Magazine: Car Toys
7950 Deering Ave.
Canoga Park, CA 91304-5063
ph: 818-887-0550
fax: 818-884-1343
e-mail: mail@challengeweb.com
web: http://www.challengeweb.com/
Bi-monthly magazine covers model cars of all types, sizes, materials, and vintage; also covers automobilia from automotive art and racing collectibles to pedal cars, porcelain signs, neon clocks, apparel, literature, gas pumps, etc.

Buick Related

Collectors

Alvin Heckard
RD 1 Box 88
Lewistown, PA 17044-9801
ph: 717-248-7071 or 717-248-2816
Wants pre-1965 Buick promotional items: paperweights, desk sets, ash trays, key chains, promotional models, matchbooks, awards, literature, etc.

Car Club Badges (Grille)

Clubs/Associations

Kayes Chu
Car Badge Collectors' Club of the WWW
P.O. Box 105
Taiping, Perak 34000
Malaysia
e-mail: kayes@pc.jaring.my
web: http://www.geocities.com/MotorCity/Downs/2163
An international on-line club for collectors of car grille badges.

Collectors

Dan Morris
1225 Ramblewood Dr.
Annapolis, MD 21401
ph: 410-757-6430
e-mail: epstein73@aol.com
Collects European car club badges and vintage Volkswagon accessories.

Kayes Chu
P.O. Box 105
Taiping, Perak 34000
Malaysia
e-mail: kayes@pc.jaring.my
web: http://www.geocities.com/MotorCity/Downs/2163
Has the only on-line collection of car grille badges on the Internet.

Dealers

John A. Boggs, Jr.
2665 Quail Hill Dr.
Pittsburgh, PA 15241
ph: 412-833-6565
e-mail: john_boggs@hotmail.com
Collector, dealer, expert specializing in automobile badges: AAA, NMA, AA, RAC, breakdown organizations, clubs, racing, sports car clubs and organizations; specialty is early badges - radiator cap mount, brass, enamel.

Experts

Raymond A.R.J. Gelder
Duinwetering 29
Noordwijk, 2203 HL
The Netherlands
ph: 0031 713618 678
fax: 0031 713618 678
e-mail: gelder.r.a.r.j@kivi.nl
Collector of metal car club badges; national, regional, local, veteran/vintage car, company, marque clubs; trades, buys and sells.

Tony Phillips
"Lelystad" 2 Chalfont Square
Oakwood Park, Oakwood
Derby, Derbyshire DE21 2LQ
U.K.
ph: 01332 666702
e-mail: TonyFanum@msn.com
Collector, dealer, expert, appraiser of AA and associated car club badges from the UK and overseas; always interested in exchange or purchase of interesting badges; can date all UK AA badges from the badge number.

Flower Vases

Collectors

Dulce Holt
504 Broadway
Chesterton, IN 46304-2320
ph: 219-926-2838 or 219-926-4170
fax: 219-929-4580
e-mail: rick@carvase.com
web: http://www.carvase.com/
Wants to buy 1900-1930 flower vases (with or without metal attaching brackets) from old cars; also wants related information.

Roger Olszewski
1509 Lamplighter Lane
Fort Worth, TX 76134
ph: 817-293-3013
Wants to buy all types, sizes and colors of automobile flower vases that were used in vintage cars.

Internet Resources

Dulce Holt
504 Broadway
Chesterton, IN 46304-2320
ph: 219-926-2838 or 219-926-4170
fax: 219-929-4580
e-mail: rick@carvase.com
web: http://www.carvase.com/
The internet site for collectors of car vases: what they are, photos, information, movies with vases, how to fine vases, etc.

Hood Ornaments

Collectors

Sy & Ronnie Margolis
17853 Santiago Blvd., #170-210
Villa Park, CA 92861-4113
ph: 714-974-5938
fax: 714-921-0731
e-mail: smargol@ibm.net
Wants pre-WWII hood ornaments/mascots; also wants related signs, brochures, catalogs.

Dealers

Mike Z. Kleba
P.O. Box 70
Mallorytown, Ontario K0E 1R0
Canada
ph: 613-923-5934
Wants to buy hood ornaments from old cars; good or broken; metal or glass; one piece or many; roosters, eagles, aeroplanes, flying man and lady, Superman, Uncle Sam, devil, Indian head, etc.

Hubcaps

Clubs/Associations

Dennis Kuhn
Hubcap Collectors Club
Newsletter: Hubcapper
P.O. Box 54
Buckley, MI 49620
ph: 616-269-3555
Focus on the older threaded hubcaps.

Dealers

Hubcaps
2825 Selzer
Evansville, IN 47712-3884
Buys and sells; thousands available from 1949 through 1982.

Instruments

Repair Services

John Wolf & Co., Inc.
36420 Biltomre Place
Willoughby, OH 44094
ph: 440-942-0083
e-mail: johnwolfco@aol.com
web: http://www.tempman.qpg.com/
Provides functional and cosmetic restoration of gauges and instrumentation; also restores antique auto and aircraft instruments.

Literature

Collectors

Peter Tilp
B & T Publications
P.O. Box 580
Summit, NJ 07901-0580
Wants to buy automobile showroom catalogues for 1925-1048 classic cars.

Walter Miller
6710 Brooklawn Pkwy.
Syracuse, NY 13211-2104
ph: 315-432-8282
fax: 315-432-8256
e-mail: info@autolit.com
Buys 1900-1975 automobile sales brochures, repair manuals, parts catalogs, showroom items or any other related literature.

Bob Olds
364 Vinewood Ave.
Tallmadge, OH 44278
ph: 330-633-5938
Wants to buy auto, truck, motorcycle, bicycle sales and dealer literature, owner's manuals, shop manuals, and any related memorabilia or scale model cars.

Jay Ketelle
Jay Ketelle Collectibles, Inc.
3721 Farwell
Amarillo, TX 79109
ph: 806-355-3456
Wants to buy automobile literature.

Ralph Dunwoodie
5935 Calico
Sun Valley, NV 89433-6910
ph: 702-673-3811
Wants truck, car and motorcycle magazines, literature and catalogs from 1895 to 1942; seeking select magazines to complete collection.

Dealers

Bob Johnson
Bob Johnson's Auto Literature
92 Blandin Ave.
Framingham, MA 01702
ph: 508-872-9173 or 800-334-0688
fax: 508-626-0991
e-mail: bjohnson@autopaper.com
web: http://www.autopaper.com
Buying & selling 1900-present auto, truck, motorcycle, farm, construction, factory sales brochures, owner & repair manuals, parts books, showroom albums, data books, color & upholstery books, paint chips, auto dealer promotional items.

J.B. Hoffert
P.O. Box 801
Reading, PA 19607-0801
ph: 610-777-0105
e-mail: jhofflit@aol.com
Wants automotive sales brochures and manuals for any kind of vehicle; also buys antique toys, trains, banks, dolls, antique & classic cars, slot machines, beer items, sports cards, early baseball, and old photographs.

Rob & Sharon McLellan
McLellan's Automotive History
9111 Longstaff Dr.
Houston, TX 77031-2711
ph: 713-772-3285
fax: 713-772-3287
e-mail: mclellans@worldnet.att.net
web: http://www.mclellansautomotive.com/
Buys and sells books, sales literature, art, programs, magazines and memorabilia on sport, luxury, classic, antique and racing cars; quarterly catalogs of items for sale; publishes catalog 4 timer per year.

W.R. Sewell
Model Auto
P.O. Box 79253
Houston, TX 77279-9253
ph: 713-468-4461
fax: 713-468-4461
e-mail: modelaut@ix.netcom.com
Buys and trades all makes of auto sales literature: dealer albums, promotional model cars and old model car kits, shop manuals.

Museums/Libraries

Walter Miller
Museum of Automobile History, The
321 Clinton St.
Syracuse, NY 13203
ph: 315-478-CARS
fax: 315-432-8256
e-mail: info@autolit.com
web: http://www.autolit.com/autolit/museum.htm
More than 10,000 items pertaining to more than 1,000 makes of automobiles, motorcycles and trucks; the first institution to trace the social effect of the century's favorite machine; no cars displayed.

Model A Advertising

Dealers

Jim Thomas
8165 Glenmill Ct.
Cincinnati, OH 45249
ph: 513-774-0350
e-mail: jthoms@aol.com
Wants 1928-1931 Ford Model "A" car and truck advertising, sales literature, posters, dealer items, memorabilia; buy/sell/trade.

Plaques (Car Club)

Collectors

Malcolm Andrus
420 Jackson Dr.
Vidor, TX 77662
ph: 409-769-4607 or 717-248-2816
Wants old car club plaques.

Spark Plugs

Clubs/Associations

Jeff Bartheld
Spark Plug Collectors of America
Magazine: Ignitor, The
14018 NE 85th St.
Elk River, MN 55330-6818
ph: 612-441-7059
Dedicated to the promotion of spark plug collecting and research, and the preservation of spark plug history; the magazine is published quarterly; also publishes the "Hot Sheet" newsletter.

Collectors

Robert J. Harrington
6 Village Rd.
Milford, CT 06460
ph: 203-878-8013
fax: 203-878-8013
e-mail: rharrington03@snet.net
Wants to buy old and unusual spark plugs.

Charles Langley
825 N. Meridian St.
Greentown, IN 46936
ph: 317-628-7579
Wants to buy antique brand name spark plugs; also wants related catalogs and charts, and auto magazines from 1900 to 1925.

Bill Bond
P.O. Box 2229
Ann Arbor, MI 48106
Has a collection of over 2,000 spark plugs.

Don McKinsey
P.O. Box 94
Wilkinson, IN 48186-0094
ph: 765-785-6284
Buying spark plugs: wants obsolete spark plugs from 1900 to 1950, all offers given consideration; will buy a few later ones; also wants spark plug advertising items and pre-1931 spark plug application guides; send #10 SASE for buying list.

Jeff Bartheld
14018 NE 85th St.
Elk River, MN 55330-6818
ph: 612-441-7059

Experts

Cornelius Bergbower
P.O. Box 144
Bluford, IL 62814-0144
ph: 618-732-6195
Author of "Spark Collector's Guide", available from the author - Vol I $11 ppd., Vol. II $14 ppd.; also wants to buy spark plugs with odd names and shapes, especially plugs with priming cups, gadgets, etc.

Studebaker Related

Collectors

Paul Straughn
4111 Carnation Dr.
Arlington, TX 76016
ph: 817-572-2817
Wants Studebaker related memorabilia, 1852-1966: car/truck/horse-drawn items: literature, photographs, catalogs, signs, sheet music, stock certificates, pins, badges, promotional and dealership items, models, china, banners, etc.

Barry Mann
10602 Denell Circle
Austin, TX 78753
Wants anything related to the Studebaker.

AVIATION

(see also AIRLINE MEMORABILIA; AIRPLANES; AIRSHIPS; AVIATION MEMORABILIA; BOOKS, Reference [Aviation]; MILITARIA; MODELS, Aircraft; PERSONALITIES [FAMOUS], Charles A. Lindbergh; STAMP COLLECTING, Air Mail Related; TOYS, Airplane Related)

Clubs/Associations

Maine Aviation Historical Society/ Maine Air Museum
Newsletter: MAHS Newsletter
P.O. Box 2641
Bangor, ME 04402-2641
ph: 207-941-6757 or 877-280-MAHS
e-mail: townsend@acadia.net
web: http://www.acadia.net/mahs/
A Historical Society dealing with aviation in Maine; currently starting Maine Air Museum in Bangor at airport.

American Aviation Historical Society
Magazine: AAHS Journal
2333 Otis St.
Santa Ana, CA 92704-3846
ph: 714-549-4818
fax: 714-549-3657
e-mail: aahs2333@aol.com
web: http://www.aahs-online.org
Provides source of factual historical data compiled by leading historians; quarterly newsletter and journal contain articles on personalities, unit histories, machines, aviation history, buy and sell ads, etc.

Canadian Aviation Historical Society
P.O. Box 224, Station A
Willowdale, Ontario M2N 5S8
Canada
ph: 416-410-9774
e-mail: cahsnatsec@idirect.com
web: http://www.cahs.com/
Members are writers, photographers, artists, model builders and others with an interest in the history of aviation.

Popular Flying Association
Magazine: Popular Flying
Term. Bldg., Shoreham Airport
Shoreman-by-Sea, Sussex BN43 5FF
U.K.
ph: (+44) 0 1273 461616
fax: (+44) 0 1273 463390
e-mail: office@pfa.org.uk
web: http://www.pfa.org.uk/
The United Kingdom Association of amateur-built and vintage aircraft restoration.

Collectors

Alan C. King
P.O. Box 86
Radnor, OH 43066-0086
ph: 614-595-3332
Wants aviation related repair manuals, magazines, handbooks, etc.

Experts

Frank Strnad
Aero Collectables
P.O. Box 240
Northport, NY 11768-0240
ph: 516-261-0140
Wants to buy aviation books and magazines (Aero Digest, Popular Aviation, MAN), erection and maintenance manuals, engine manuals, factory brochures and drawings, instruments, models, name plates, photos, memorabilia, etc.

Jon Aldrich
Pine Mountain Lake Airport
Airport Box 9
Big Oak Flat, CA 95305
ph: 209-962-6121
Long time dealer in vintage aeronautical memorabilia, both civil and military; wants to buy aviation autographs, books, war relics, pilot memorabilia, airplane parts, aero nostalgia; please send price and description; appraisal.

Internet Resources

Thomas Van Hare
Historic Wings
200 W. Palmetto Park Rd., Ste. 201
Boca Raton, FL 33432
ph: 561-347-0181 or 561-483-7450
fax: 561-347-2240
e-mail: hw@historicwings.com
web: http://www.historicwings.com/
An online aviation magazine featuring stories from the past and present, a full range of articles and aviation poetry; download aviation back-grounds for your compute desktop.

Aviation Home Page, The
2520 Kempton St. SE
Olympia, WA 98501
e-mail: garret@avhome.com
web: http://www.avhome.com
Airlines and airports, art, photogra-phy, poetry, weather, meteorology, academies, universities, flight schools, classifieds, flight simulation, aviation news, forums.

Museums/Libraries

New England Air Museum of the Connecticut Aeronautical Historical Assoc.
Bradley International Airport
Windsor Locks, CT 06096
ph: 860-623-3305
fax: 860-627-2820
e-mail: staff@neam.org
web: http://www.neam.org/

Piper Aviation Museum
One Piper Way
Lock Haven, PA 17745
ph: 717-748-8283
fax: 717-893-8357
e-mail: piper@cub.kcnet.org
web: http://www.kcnet.org/~piper

Mid Atlantic Air Museum
11 Museum Drive
Reading, PA 19605
ph: 610-372-7333
e-mail: fpierce@avialantic.com
web: http://www.maam.org/

National Air & Space Museum
6th St. & Independence Ave. SW
Washington, DC 20560
ph: 202-357-2700
e-mail: web@nasm.edu
web: http://www.nasm.edu/

Experimental Aircraft Association Air Adventure Museum
P.O. Box 3065
Oshkosh, WI 54093-3065
ph: 920-426-4818
fax: 920-426-6174
e-mail: communication@eaa.org
web: http://www.eaa.org/education/museum/
Collection of over 90 vintage airplanes.

Keith R. Gill
Museum of Science & Industry
57th St. & Lake Shore Dr.
Chicago, IL 60637
ph: 773-684-1414
fax: 773-684-5580

Air Museum Planes of Fame - AZ
HCR 34, Box B
Vale-Williams, AZ 86046
ph: 520-635-1000
e-mail: fly1katana@aol.com
web: http://www.planesoffame.org/
One of the first air museums in the US; the collection spans from the Chanute Hang Glider of 1896 to jet fighters of the 1960s.

Air Museum Planes of Fame - CA
7000 Merrill Ave.
Box 17
Chino, CA 91710
ph: 909-597-3722
fax: 909-597-4755
e-mail: fly1katana@aol.com
web: http://www.planesoffame.org/

Byron Reynolds
Reynolds Aviation Museum
P.O. Box 6360
Wetaskiwin, Alberta T9A 2G1
Canada
ph: 800-661-4726
fax: 780-361-1239
e-mail: ram@mcd.gov.ab.ca
web: http://www.gov.ab.ca/mcd/mhs/ram/aviation.htm

Fiona Hale, Lib.
National Aviation Museum
11 Aviation Parkway, Bldg. 194
P.O. Box 9724, Station T
Ottawa, Ontario K1G 5A3
Canada
ph: 613-993-2010 or 800-463-2038
e-mail: aviation@nmstc.ca
web: http://www.aviation.nmstc.ca/e-home.htm
One of the world's great aeronautical collections.

Periodicals

Hachette Filipacchi Magazines, Inc.
Magazine: Flying Magazine
500 West Putnam Ave.
Greenwich, CT 06830
ph: 203-622-2700
fax: 203-622-2725

Cowles Magazines, Inc.
Magazine: Aviation History
741 Miller Dr. SE, Ste. D2
Harrisburg, PA 20175
ph: 717-540-6617 or 800-829-3340
fax: 717-540-6706
e-mail: brentd@cowles.com
web: http://www.cowles.com/maglist.html
Offers readers in-depth articles on the history of world aviation from its earliest beginnings to the present day.

Rozonna Kinlen
Magazine: Flying Review
4801 Charlotte Ct. NE
Albuquerque, NM 87109-3009
ph: 505-836-4646 or 505-842-4184
fax: 505-842-4405

Small Air Forces Clearing House
Magazine: Small Air Forces Observer
27965 Berwick Dr.
Carmel, CA 93923
e-mail: webmaster@bartoli.com
web: http://bartoli.com/safo/
Promotes interest in the history and modeling of aircraft of the smaller countries.

Nick Veronico
Magazine: In Flight Aviation News
P.O. Box 620447
Woodside, CA 94062
ph: 650-364-8110
fax: 650-364-1359
e-mail: editor@inflightusa.com
web: http://www.inflightusa.com/
A 120 page newspaper devoted to aviation & aviation history; editors will answer questions about memorabilia and refer sellers to buyers.

Magazine: FlyPast
P.O. Box 100
Stamford, Lincs PE9 1XQ
U.K.
ph: 01780 755131
fax: 01780 757261
e-mail: flypast@keymags.demon.co.uk
web: http://www.keymags.co.uk/flypast/
Britain's top selling aviation monthly.returned

Art

Dealers

Jerry Beach
Aeronautical Classics & Fine Arts
1305 King Street
Alexandria, VA 22314
ph: 703-548-7122
fax: 703-548-6414
Fine aviation prints, paintings,

memorabilia, books, desk models, propellers, gifts, etc.

Steve Ornelas
Aviation Arts
533 South Coast Hwy.
Laguna Beach, CA 92651
ph: 949-494-4303
fax: 760-744-7204
web: http://www.aircruise.com/aviationart/
Offers new aviation related art of interest to collectors.

Stephen Remington
AviationArt
2555 Robert Fowler Way, #A
Reid-Hillview Airport
San Jose, CA 95148-1011
ph: 408-259-3366
fax: 408-259-4223
e-mail: 72245.747@compuserve.com
web: http://www.bayarea.net/~hanger/Collectair/collectair.htm
Original aviation art, limited edition prints, bronze sculptures, display models, display models, aeronautical collectibles, aviation books, model airplane exhibits, museum.

Military

Dealers

Bob Von Willer
Exotic Aircraft Company
1719 North Marshall Ave.
El Cajon, CA 92020
ph: 619-562-7467
fax: 619-448-2110
e-mail: baron@skyguy.com
web: http://www.barnstormers.com/
Specializes in the restoration and marketing of antique aircraft, including warbirds; appraiser, dealer, expert, collector, and repair services offered.

Museums/Libraries

National Warplane Museum, Elmira-Corning Regional Airport
17 Aviation Dr.
Horseheads, NY 14845
ph: 607-739-8200
e-mail: nwm@warplane.org
web: http://www.warplane.org/

U.S. Army Aviation Museum
P.O. Box 620610
Fort Rucker, AL 36362-5134
ph: 334-255-4507 or 888-ARMYAVN
e-mail: manager@aviationmuseum.org
web: http://aviationmuseum.org/

Richard L. Uppstrom, Dir.
U.S. Air Force Museum
1100 Spaatz Street
Dayton, OH 45433-7102
ph: 937-255-3286
fax: 937-255-3910
e-mail: champpa.rr@usafa.af.mil
web: http://129.48.104.231/museum/
World's largest aviation museum with 10 1/2 acres of aircraft and other exhibits under roof.

Yankee Air Force Museum
P.O. Box 590
Belleville, MI 48112
ph: 734-483-4030
e-mail: yankeeairmuseum@provide.net
web: http://www.yankeeairmuseum.org/

Combat Air Museum
Hangars 602-604 ""J"" Street
P.O. Box 19142
Topeka, KS 66619
ph: 785-862-3303
fax: 785-862-3304
web: http://combatairmuseum.org/

Cavanaugh Flight Museum
Addison Airport
4572 Claire Chennault
Addison, TX 75001
ph: 972-380-8800 or 800-206-3953
e-mail: jef@cavanaughflightmuseum.com
web: http://www.cavanaughflightmuseum.com/
Historic warbirds, trainers, fighters, jets and other aircraft chronicle heroes, battles and technological advances from WWI to present.

Col. J. Ward Boyce, USAF (Ret.)
Museum of the American Fighter Aces Association
Magazine: American Fighter Aces Bulletin
P.O. Box 2020
San Antonio, TX 78297-2020
ph: 210-354-2322
fax: 210-354-0575
e-mail: aftrac@goodnet.com
web: http://www.fighteraces.org/
Friends of the American Fighter Aces formed to provide funding support to American Fighter Ace Museum; open to all interested in American Fighter Aces and fighter aircraft.

War Eagles Air Museum
8012 Airport Rd.
Santa Teresa, NM 88008
ph: 505-589-2000
e-mail: information@war-eagles-air-museum.com
web: http://www.war-eagles-air-museum.com/
A non-profit organization dedicated to the restoration of vintage WWII and Korean War planes.

Periodicals

H.G. Frautschy
Experimental Aircraft Association
Magazine: Warbirds Magazine
P.O. Box 3086
Oshkosh, WI 54903-3086
ph: 800-843-3612 or 920-426-4800
fax: 920-426-4873
e-mail: communication@eaa.org
web: http://www.eaa.org/

Magazine: Air Wars
8931 Kittyhawk Ave.
Los Angeles, CA 90045-4128
Focuses on the restoration of classic (1919-1939) fighter planes; how-to articles and photos, museum articles, plans for models, etc.

Erika Daileda
Wise Owl Worldwide Publications
Magazine: Windsock
4314 West 238th St. - Dept. MACR
Torrance, CA 90505-4509
ph: 310-375-6258
fax: 310-375-0548
e-mail: wiseowl@sprintmail.com
A bi-monthly English publication; the journal for WWI aeroplane enthusiasts and modelers.

Challenge Publications, Inc.
Magazine: Air Classics
7950 Deering Ave.
Canoga Park, CA 91304
ph: 818-887-0550
fax: 818-884-1343

Magazine: Airpower
P.O. Box 881526
San Diego, CA 92168
e-mail: aenyedy@millennianet.com
web: http://www.airpoweronline.com/

Magazine: Classic Wings Magazine
P.O. Box 534
New Zealand
e-mail: admin@classicwings.com
web: http://classicwings.com/
The only journal dedicated exclusively to vintage and warbird aeroplanes in Australia and New Zealand; high quality publication packed with in-depth articles, news and superb photographs.

Warbirds Worldwide International, Inc.
Magazine: Warbirds Worldwide
The Studio, Brunts Business Centre
Samuel Brunts Way
Mansfield, Notts NG18 2AH
U.K.
ph: +44 1623 624288
fax: +44 1623 622659
e-mail: web@warbirdsww.com
web: http://www.warbirdsww.com/
A quarterly journal for serious vintage airplane enthusiasts: worldwide news reports on fighters, bombers and vintage jets, pilot reports, features on museums and high quality photo-graphic coverage of aircraft being rebuilt.

Races & Meets

Clubs/Associations

Herman Schaub, Sec.
Society of Air Racing Historians
168 Marian Lane
Berea, OH 44017-1566
ph: 440-234-2301
e-mail: bill@airrace.com
web: http://www.airrace.com
Dedicated to preserving air racing history from 1909 to the present.

Collectors

Pete Kramer
P.O. Box 52
Glen Ellyn, IL 60138-0052
ph: 630-627-4051
Wants to buy 1909-1939 aviation meet and air race programs, posters, tickets, autographed photos, and souvenirs.

AVIATION MEMORABILIA

(see also AIRLINE MEMORABILIA; AIRPLANES; AVIATION; BADGES; MILITARIA; MODELS, Aircraft; POSTCARDS, Aviation Related; STAMP COLLECTING, Air Mail Related; TOYS, Airplane Related)

Collectors

Talbert Kanigher
Tal's Nostalgia
P.O. Box 6294
Burbank, CA 91505-6294
ph: 818-848-6469
fax: 818-848-6469
Collecting aviation memorabilia for over 30 years: photographs, programs, autographs, etc.

Dealers

Dixie Aviation Collectibles
P.O. Box 382
Holmdel, NJ 077332
ph: 732-946-8528
fax: 732-332-1068
e-mail: GenDixie@aol.com
Buys and sells die-cast, wood, resin & plastic limited edition aircraft models.

Frank Cea
Barnstormer Enterprises & Auctions
P.O. Box 260331
Jamaica, NY 11426-0331
ph: 516-741-3694 or 516-727-6191
fax: 516-877-0646
Buys and sells aviation and model aircraft items; memorabilia, photos, magazines, brochures, artifacts, books, model kits, model motors, race cars, catalogs, built planes, airline models and ephemera.

Tom Heitzman
Stuffinder
P.O. Box 222
Deansboro, NY 13328
ph: 315-841-4444
fax: 315-841-3488
e-mail: gyro@stuffinder.com
web: http://www.stuffinder.com
Buys and sells aviation memorabilia: original art, scratch-built models, aircraft/engine sales literature and photos, post card, books, magazines and manuals, airline time tables, crew insignia, etc., especially pre-1960.

Peter DeNevai
20th C. Aviation Collectibles
HC63 Box 5
Duchesne, UT 84021-9701
e-mail: Pinyon99@yahoo.com
Buys, sells, trades all manner of aviation artifacts and publications; military and civilian; parts, equipment, uniform items, manuals, periodicals, books, airline timetables and handouts, postcards, toys, model kits, etc.

Experts

Tom Heitzman
Stuffinder
P.O. Box 222
Deansboro, NY 13328
ph: 315-841-4444
fax: 315-841-3488
e-mail: gyro@stuffinder.com
web: http://www.stuffinder.com
Buys and sells aviation memorabilia: original art, scratch-built models, aircraft/engine sales literature and photos, post card, books, magazines and manuals, airline time tables, crew insignia, etc., especially pre-1960.

Herb Jacobs
P.O. Box 5390
Pompano Beach, FL 33074-5390
ph: 954-943-4213
Buys, sells, appraises and specializes in aviation memorabilia.

Russ Huff
P.O. Box 17276
Sarasota, FL 34276-0276
ph: 941-923-3600
e-mail: russhuff@aol.com
Buys, sells and specializes in military aviation qualification badges of the world; also other aviation memorabilia.

Museums/Libraries

Stephen Remington
CollectAir/Museum of Aircraft Recognition
Newsletter: News & Views
2555 Robert Fowler Way, #A
Reid-Hillview Airport
San Jose, CA 95148-1011
ph: 408-259-3366
fax: 408-259-4223
e-mail: 72245.747@compuserve.com
web: http://www.bayarea.net/~hanger/Collectair/collectair.htm
Associated with aviation for over 40 years; has his own art gallery and museum of aircraft recognition items; art gallery with originals and prints, aviation memorabilia; always buying pre-1950 aviation memorabilia.

Boeing 747

Collectors

Francis Smith
Francis Smith's Boeing 747 Page
213 S. Harrison
Garrett, IN 46738
e-mail: smitfj01@holmes.ipfw.edu
web: http://www.geocities.com/CapeCanaveral/Hangar/4653/index.htm
A Boeing 747 enthusiast wants to buy Boeing 747s memorabilia (especially the older 747s): 747-related airline postcards, models, and other memorabilia (especially from Aer Lingus, Braniff, Pam Am, and other old 747 airlines.)

Civil Air Patrol

Collectors

Ace Browning
e-mail: alamrcn@sparc.isl.net
web: http://www.isl.net/~alamrcn/
Collects, trades, buys and sometimes sells Civil Air Patrol patches and insignia.

Helicopters

Collectors

Skip Robinson
18653 Ventura Blvd., #419B
Tarzana, CA 91367
ph: 818-883-9494
Wants anything related to helicopters: books, photos, models, manuals, sales and technical brochures, paper items.

Military

Clubs/Associations

Jan Jaobs
F-4 Phantom II Society
Magazine: Smoke Trails
P.O. Box 900174
San Diego, CA 92190-0174
ph: 619-689-9227
fax: 619-578-8839
e-mail: f14ro@aol.com
web: http://www.f4phantom.org
Focuses on the F-4 Phantom II; "Smoke Trails" is published quarterly.

Collectors

Charles Donald
P.O. Box 822
Union City, NJ 07087-0822
ph: 201-330-9619
Wants WWI squadron memorial volumes and squadron histories 1914 to 1918, aviation-related photos from 1920s to 1940s, photo albums, log books, groups of negatives; only wants to buy negative collections, not individual negatives.

David Ostrowski
5411 Masser Lane
Fairfax, VA 22032-3817
ph: 703-323-6674
Wants to buy military and civilian aircraft models, ID/recognition aircraft models, photos/negatives/slides of military and civilian aircraft.

Dennis Gordon
1246 N Ave.
Missoula, MT 59801-6602
ph: 406-549-6280
Wants World War I (c. 1914-1918) aviation items and American Volunteer items: U.S. and foreign; pilot log books, I.D. cards, books, photos, aircraft instruments, souvenir items, insignia, helmets, uniforms, medals, documents.

Dealers

Bob McKowen
215 S. Ace. C
Washington, IA 52353
ph: 319-653-5776
Specializes in WWII aircraft cockpit instruments.

Robert Chad LeBeau
Aviation Artifacts, Inc.
1213 Sandstone Dr.
Saint Charles, MO 63304-6830
ph: 636-441-2706
fax: 636-447-4071
web: http://www.aviationartifactsinc.com/
Buys flight gear: flight helmets, oxygen masks, parachutes, ejection seats, aircraft parts, instruments.

James E. Garcia
9 Atumnwood Ct.
Edgewood, NM 87015
Buys and sells vintage helmets, goggles, maps, pilot wrist watches, clocks, flight manuals, and other aviation items.

Aviators World
P.O. Box 2441
Big Bear City, CA 92314-2441
ph: 909-584-2527
fax: 909-584-4721
e-mail: nasmith@compuserve.com
web: http://www.aviatorsworld.com.default.htm
Buys and sells plane and pilot collectibles from all eras: air combat, military, civil, space; issues detailed illustrated catalog of items for sale four times each year.

Experts

Jeff Mark
P.O. Box 5178
Santa Monica, CA 90409-5178
ph: 800-666-9553 or 310-396-9767
fax: 310-396-2666
Wants to buy Air Force and 1900-1970 aviation related items including flying jackets, airplane parts, silver wings, medals, memorabilia, patches, helmets, goggles, etc.; wants U.S., German, Japanese, or British.

Military Insignia

(see also AIRLINE MEMORABILIA, Pilots Wings; MILITARIA; BADGES)

Collectors

Robert Missero
4 Kakiat Lane
Spring Valley, NY 10977-2009
ph: 914-425-0013
Wants all types of WWII sterling silver U.S. Army Air Force wings; 1", 2", 3"; also wing bracelets.

Experts

Russ Huff
P.O. Box 17276
Sarasota, FL 34276-0276
ph: 941-923-3600
e-mail: russhuff@aol.com
Buys, sells and specializes in military aviation qualification badges of the world; also other aviation memorabilia.

Propellers

Dealers

Philip Wallick
Vintage Aeroplane Propellers
P.O. Box 3699
Chico, CA 95927-3699
ph: 530-877-0352
Buys and sells wooden airplane propellers; original or reconditioned; also offers for sale high quality vintage reproduction propellers for wall decoration and display; write or call for color brochure.

Safety Briefing Cards

Collectors

Keith L. Mock
41214 North Woodbury Green Dr.
Belleville, MI 48111
ph: 734-699-9217
fax: 734-699-9163
e-mail: DuckBoyFL@aol.com
Buys, sells, trades and provides information on aviation passenger safety briefing cards.

AVON COLLECTIBLES

(see also BOTTLES, Perfume & Scent; CALIFORNIA PERFUME COMPANY)

Clubs/Associations

Connie Clark, Pres.
National Association of Avon Collectors, Inc.
Newsletter: Avon Times
P.O. Box 7006
Kansas City, MO 64113-0006
ph: 816-822-2347
A national association of Avon collectors; promotes the hobby of Avon collecting; many members clubs throughout the U.S. and Canada; newslettter has buy/sell ads, upcoming shows schedules.

Dealers

Rhonda Schriver
Avon Collector's Lost & Found
7646 Nancy Drive
Elkridge, MD 21075
ph: 410-799-2881
e-mail: alkmon@msn.com
web: http://www.icollectavon.com/
Website where hundreds of collectors gather to buy and sell Avon collectibles.

Dwight & Vera Young
P.O. Box 9868
Kansas City, MO 64134-0868
ph: 816-537-8223
fax: 816-737-8223
e-mail: avontimes@aol.com
Buys and sell Avon collectibles.

Experts

Bud Hastin
Hastin Books
P.O. Box 11530
Fort Lauderdale, FL 33339
ph: 954-566-0691
e-mail: avonman@pstcomputers.com
Author of "Avon Collectors Encyclopedia - 15th Edition", 640 pages, 6000 pictures; 1886 to present; lists all Avon products and California Perfume Products (early Avon); all priced with current market value.

Internet Resources

Rhonda Schriver
Avon Collector's Lost & Found
7646 Nancy Drive
Elkridge, MD 21075
ph: 410-799-2881
e-mail: alkmon@msn.com
web: http://www.icollectavon.com/
Hundreds of ads from buyers and sellers of all Avon collectibles; browse the ads, contact buyers and sellers online, place your own ad; site updated daily.

Periodicals

Gere Reed
RR 1, box 99B
Montrose, PA 18801
e-mail: bookworm@epix.net
web: http://www.angelfire.com/sc/beachlady/
Expert capable of aiding in the description of year of production of Avon items; also sells.

Dwight & Vera Young
Avon Times
Newsletter: Avon Times
P.O. Box 9868
Kansas City, MO 64134-0868
ph: 816-537-8223
fax: 816-737-8223
e-mail: avontimes@aol.com
A monthly newsletter with international circulation that contains articles, ads, photos, history, convention and show news; buy and sell ads from around the world; devoted strictly to the hobby of Avon collecting.

AWARDS

(see MEDALS, ORDERS & DECORATIONS; PINS, Award)

Here are some tips when contacting someone listed in this book:

■ When requesting information about a particular item, include a description (material, dimensions, maker's mark, model number, etc.) and a photo, sketch, or photocopy of the item in question.

■ Always ask if there are charges for samples or for the services requested.

■ When writing, please be sure to include a Large (#10 business size) Self-Addressed and Stamped Envelope (LSASE) if requesting a reply or the return of photographs.

■ Never call collect unless otherwise directed. When calling, be considerate of time zone differences and always ask if the party you are calling has time to talk. When leaving an answering machine message, always instruct the party to call you back collect.

BABY CARRIAGES

(see CHILDREN'S THINGS; PERAMBULATORS)

BADGES

(see also AUTOMOBILIA; AVIATION MEMORABILIA; FRATERNAL ORGANIZATION ITEMS; MEDALS, ORDERS & DECORATIONS; LAW ENFORCEMENT MEMORABILIA; MILITARIA; AMMUNITION & EXPLOSIVE ORDNANCE, Badges; PATCHES; PINS; SOCIAL CAUSES; TAXI; VETERAN ITEMS)

Collectors

Ken Mitzel
5225 N. George
Manchester, PA 17345-9400
ph: 717-266-2783
Wants to buy Game Warden badges, Fish Warden badges, Forestry badges, Guide badges, Fire Warden badges.

R. MacVicar
P.O. Box 337
Houghton Lake, MI 48629
Wants to buy country club and taxi badges.

Steve Mizroch
99 Monticello Rd.
San Rafael, CA 94903
Badge collector specializing in California badges: police, fire, taxi, post office, humane society.

Chauffeurs

Collectors

Albert Velocci
62 Cherrywood Dr.
Hillside Manor, NY 11040
Wants to buy chauffeur badges, especially early and undated badges.

George A. Coupe
1243 1st St. S.E.
Washington, DC 20003
ph: 202-554-1000 or 800-368-5466
fax: 202-863-0775
Wants to buy chauffeur badges; one or whole collections.

Howard Share
4349 LaVale Ct.
Clemmons, NC 27012-9009
ph: 336-766-6579
fax: 336-766-5445
e-mail: HowSha43@aol.com
Wants to buy chauffeur or driver license badges, especially from Southern states and Hawaii; will also trade.

Trent Culp
P.O. Box 550
Misenheimer, NC 28109-0550
ph: 704-279-6242
Collects chauffeurs' badges from all states and all years, especially badges from the Southern states.

Jerome Schaeper, Jr.
705 Philadelphia St.
Covington, KY 41011-1252
ph: 606-581-3729
Collects and appraises city or state issued driving badges, early Southern badges especially wanted.

Mike O'Brien
215 Meadowlark
Sandwich, IL 60548
Wants to buy chauffeur's badges from all states and cities: licensed, registered, conditional, professional, taxi driver, chauffeur, etc.

Dealers

Walt Feiger
Walt's Antiques
2513 Nelson Rd.
Traverse City, MI 49686-8557
ph: 231-223-7386 or 231-223-4123
Wants to buy Michigan chauffeur badges.

Experts

Dr. Edward H. Miles
888 Eighth Ave.
New York, NY 10019-5704
ph: 212-765-2660
Editor/publisher "Chauffeurs Badges & Transportation Related Badges of the World" Vol. I N.Y. State & City Badges, Vol. II New England City & State Badges. There is a price guide.

John Connors
3811 Grantley Rd.
Toledo, OH 43613-4218
Author of "Price Guide to American & Canadian Chauffeur Badges."

Employee

Collectors

Gary Wood
733 Myrtle Rd.
North Brunswick, NJ 08902-2549
ph: 732-821-7633
e-mail: woodrasp@aol.com
Collector seeking "plant badges" with photos; these are pinback buttons worn by employees; often included a photo of the employee for identification; used primarily 1930s through 1960s; pays $5 to $50 each depending on type.

Douglas W. Tietze
4909 Harter Rd.
Slatington, PA 18080
Collects 1920s to 1950s employee badges: oval, round, square; brass, copper, plated steel, plastic; many contain a photograph of the employee.

Federal

Experts

Ken W. Lucas, Sr.
3052 Bel Pre Rd., Apt. 101
Silver Spring, MD 20906-2415
ph: 301-871-0877
Author of "Federal Law Enforcement Badges"; Agriculture, Commerce, Defense, Energy, Health & Human Services, Interior, Park Police, Fish & Wildlife, Indian, Justice, U.S. Marshals, FBI, DEA, Labor, CIA, Postal, Customs, etc.

BAGS

(see AIRLINE MEMORABILIA, Airline Sickness Bags; FEED SACKS; PURSES)

BAKELITE

(see GEMS & JEWELRY, Vintage & Costume; PLASTIC COLLECTIBLES)

BALLS

Agitator

Collectors

Fred Meadows
Crew Chief, Auto Fac., American Airlines
3707 North Harbor Dr.
San Diego, CA 92101
ph: 619-231-5483
Collects the little agitator balls found inside aerosol cans.

BANANA COLLECTIBLES

Clubs/Associations

L. Ken Bannister, T.B.
International Banana Club
Newsletter: Woddis Newsletter
2524 N. El Molino Ave.
Altadena, CA 91001-2318
ph: 626-798-2272
e-mail: bananasTB@aol.com
web: http://www.banana-club.com
A "fun" humorous club founded in 1972; purpose is to keep people smiling and exercising their sense of humor each day.

Museums/Libraries

Ann Lovell, Cur.
Banana Museum
ph: 253-833-8043
e-mail: abanana@mail.gr.cc.wa.us
web: http://www.geocities.com/NapaValley/1799/

L. Ken Bannister, T.B.
International Banana Club Museum
2524 N. El Molino Ave.
Altadena, CA 91001-2318
ph: 626-798-2272
e-mail: bananasTB@aol.com
web: http://www.banana-club.com
More than 17,000 items on display; opened by prearranged appointment only; featured on national TV and magazines.

Stickers

Periodicals

George Griffin
Newsletter: Banana Label Times
P.O. Box 159
Old Town, FL 32680-0159
ph: 352-542-3447
fax: 352-542-3447
Published quarterly: for collectors of banana stickers by Chiquita, DelMonte, Dole, Turbana, Fielder, Banacol, Sunisa, and all other banana stickers.

BAND ORGANS

(see MUSICAL INSTRUMENTS, Mechanical [Band Organs])

BANKING

(see also COINS & CURRENCY; CREDIT CARDS & CHARGE ITEMS; MONEYCARDS; PAPER COLLECTIBLES; SCRIP; STAMP COLLECTING, Revenue & Tax Stamps; TELEPHONE CARDS; TOKENS; WOODEN MONEY)

Collectors

Frederick Lingenfelser
814 Byram St.
Reading, PA 19606-1446
Grandson of an engraver, wants to buy anything related to Western, Republic, or Security bank note companies: books, advertising, histories; will also share information.

Museums/Libraries

Wells Fargo Bank History Museum
420 Montgomery St.
San Francisco, CA 94163
ph: 415-396-2619
web: http://www.wellsfargo.com/about/museum/info/

Bank Checks

Clubs/Associations

Coleman Leifer, Sec.
American Society of Check Collectors
Journal: Check Collector, The
P.O. Box 577
Garrett Park, MD 20896-0577
ph: 301-493-5755
e-mail: cal493@aol.com
web: http://www.members.aol.com/asccinfo
Founded in 1969, ASCC is open to collectors of all types of fiscal paper: engravings, revenue stamps on checks; over 400 members; journal published quarterly.

Collectors

Gary Ronk
6247 Cove Rd.
Roanoke, VA 24019-1715
ph: 540-562-2368
Wants to buy pre-1900 bank checks, especially those that are illustrated with vignettes or have imprinted revenue stamps.

Lee Poleske
P.O. Box 871
Seward, AK 99664-0871
Wants pre-1900 bank checks, drafts, and bills of exchange; please send photocopy or sample with price.

Dealers

Douglas McDonald
Gypsyfoot Enterprises, Inc.
P.O. Box 5833
Helena, MT 59604-5833
ph: 406-449-8076
fax: 406-443-8514
Buys, sells and collects old pre-1902 bank checks, drafts, exchanges, money orders, warrants, etc.; please send photocopies for offer.

Warren Anderson
America West Archives
P.O. Box 100
Cedar City, UT 84721-0100
ph: 435-586-9497 or 435-586-7323
e-mail: awa@netutah.com
web: http://www.americawestarchives.com/
Buys and sells pre-1910 issued bank checks and other financial papers from the Western U.S.; catalogs issued; author of "Owning Western History."

Periodicals

Pat DuChene, PR
Krause Publications
Newspaper: Bank Note Reporter
700 E. State St.
Iola, WI 54990-0001
ph: 715-445-2214
fax: 715-445-4087
e-mail: info@krause.com
web: http://www.krause.com/
Monthly news source and marketplace for collectors of U.S. and world paper money, notes, checks and related fiscal paper.

BANKS

(see also BANKING; LOCKS; SOUVENIR & COMMEMORATIVE ITEMS, Buildings; STOCKS & BONDS; TOYS)

Auction Services

Bill Bertoia
Bill Bertoia Auctions
1881 Spring Rd.
Vineland, NJ 08631
ph: 609-692-1881
fax: 609-692-8697
e-mail: webmaster@billbertoiaauctions.com
web: http://www.billbertoiaauctions.com/
Specializing in the auctioning of antique toys, banks, trains, and doorstops.

Sam Haney
Haney Auction Co.
2686 Green St.
Eden, NY 14057
ph: 716-992-3300
Specializes in the auctioning of toys and banks.

Henry/Pierce Auctioneers
1525 S. Arcadian Dr.
New Berlin, WI 53151
ph: 414-797-7933

Mike Henry
Henry/Pierce Auctioneers
1456 Carson Court
Homewood, IL 60430-4013
ph: 708-799-1732 or 414-797-7933
Appraises and auctions still and mechanical banks.

Collectors

Bob Brady
2341 Woodwick Rd.
Lancaster, PA 17601
ph: 717-569-7408
Wants to buy mechanical and still banks.

George A. Coupe
1243 1st St. S.E.
Washington, DC 20003
ph: 202-554-1000 or 800-368-5466
fax: 202-863-0775
Collector looking for old cast iron or tin mechanical banks or toys; will buy one or whole collection; call toll free 24 hours.

Jim Conley
2758 Coventry Lane
Canton, OH 44708-1320
ph: 330-477-7725 or 330-499-9283
fax: 330-879-2950
Very interested in buying mechanical and still banks; OK for sellers to call collect.

Mike Henry
1456 Carson Court
Homewood, IL 60430-4013
ph: 708-799-1732 or 414-797-7933
Mechanical and still banks wanted.

Dealers

David A. Hull
Small Town Coins & Collectibles
7498 E. Davison Rd.
Davison, MI 48423-2014
ph: 810-658-1992
fax: 810-658-2977
Buys and sells still and mechanical cast iron banks.

Norman Bowers
1916 Cleveland St.
Evanston, IL 60202-1910
ph: 847-866-7165 or 708-333-7880
fax: 708-333-9561
Buys, sells, trades, and appraises old still and mechanical banks.

Clive Devenish
Whitney Antiques
P.O. Box 907
Orinda, CA 94563
ph: 925-254-8383
Wants to buy old penny banks; still and mechanical.

Experts

Robert L. McCumber
201 Carriage Dr.
Glastonbury, CT 06033-3231
ph: 860-633-4984
Author of several books about toy banks covering repros and fakes, mechanical and still banks, Chein banks, registering banks, building banks, iron safe banks, penny banks, and more.

Charles Reynolds
Reynolds Toys
2836 Monroe St.
Falls Church, VA 22042-2007
ph: 703-533-1322
e-mail: reynoldstoys@erols.com
web: http://www.reynoldstoys.com
Specializes in mechanical and still banks.

Ross Hermann
c/o AntiqueWeek
P.O. Box 90
Knightstown, IN 46148
Writes column about mechanical and still banks for "AntiqueWeek", will answer questions, but a SASE must be enclosed if photos are to be returned.

Earnest & Ida Long
Long's Americana
P.O. Box 90
Mokelumne Hill, CA 95245
ph: 209-286-1348
Specializes in toys, banks, games and other children's items; publishes "Dictionary of Toys, Vol I & II" and "Penny Lane."

Ceramic

Collectors

Brian Cleary
P.O. Box 155
Poland, NY 13431-0155
ph: 315-826-3610
Wants pottery or ceramic banks that DO NOT have a place to remove coins (need to break bank to remove coins), especially those marked Germany, Austria, Japan, or Occupied Japan.

Dealers

Carol Silagyi
C.S. Antiques & Jewelry
P.O. Box 151
Wyckoff, NJ 07430
ph: 201-934-6528
Has collection of over 400 figural ceramic banks; wants to buy cartoon, Disney, ABC, Leeds, McCoy, Japanese, etc.

Glass

Collectors

Brian Cleary
P.O. Box 155
Poland, NY 13431-0155
ph: 315-826-3610
Wants to buy glass bottle banks with labels, ANY amber glass bottle bank, Guttuso rabbit, Snow Crest seal, BUBBLE banks, fish bowl banks, glass block banks, war related glass banks, glass candy container banks, etc.

John Honl
P.O. Box 1201
Kailua Kona, HI 96745-1201
ph: 808-325-9905
e-mail: jonhonl@konacoast.net
Wants to buy glass bottle banks including Galaxy Spaceman, Snowcrest seal clown and penguin, administration building, Jumbo peanut butter elephant, Guttuso rabbit, Jocko monkey (prepared mustard), etc.

Periodicals

Brian Cleary, Ed.
Newsletter: Glass Bank Collector
P.O. Box 155
Poland, NY 13431-0155
ph: 315-826-3610
Issued three times per year: articles about glass banks and glass container banks; subscribers entitled to "Free" ad in the For Sale/For Trade/Wanted section of each newsletter; please send SASE for more information.

Mechanical

Clubs/Associations

Rick Mihlhiem, Sec.
Mechanical Bank Collectors of America
Newsletter: Mechanical Banker
P.O. Box 13323
Pittsburgh, PA 15234
e-mail: info@mechanicalbanks.org
web: http://www.mechanicalbanks.org/

Dealers

Bill Bertoia
1881 Spring Rd.
Vineland, NJ 08631
ph: 609-692-1881
fax: 609-692-8697
e-mail: bill@billbertoiaauctions.com

Paris Pierce
Mechanical Bank Zone
118 Montgomery Ave.
Bala Cynwyd, PA 19004
ph: 215-557-0400
fax: 215-665-1976
e-mail: paris@pond.com
web: http://www.pond.com/~paris/bankzone.htm
Collector, dealer, expert in mechanical banks (1930 to modern); first on-line Mechanical Bank Museum and collectors' web site.

Stephen Steckbeck
200 W. Superior St.
Fort Wayne, IN 46802
ph: 219-625-3537
Buys, sells and appraises old mechanical banks.

David Markarian
P.O. Box 2476
Rancho Mirage, CA 92270-1087
ph: 760-202-5000
e-mail: orion@inland.net
Wants to buy old cast iron mechanical banks; member of the Mechanical bank Collectors of America.

David Markarian
Markarian Ancient Artifacts
P.O. Box 2476
Rancho Mirage, CA 92270-1087
ph: 760-202-5000
e-mail: orion@inland.net
Wants to buy cast iron mechanical banks and old toys; Member of the Mechanical Bank Collectors of America.

Experts

Mark Suozzi
P.O. Box 102
Ashfield, MA 01330
ph: 413-628-3241
fax: 413-628-3241
e-mail: marklyn@valinet.com
web: http://www.marklynantiques.com/
Antique penny banks, 1 cent arcade machines, advertising signs, folk art, and wind-up clockwork toys.

Leon M. Weiss
Gemini Antiques Ltd.
P.O. Box 1752
2418 Montauk Highway
Water Mill, NY 11976
ph: 516-537-4565 or 212-316-6380
fax: 516-726-9366
e-mail: julgert@geminiantiques.com
web: http://www.geminiantiques.com/
Buys and sells mechanical still banks, cast iron toys, door stops, folk art and more.

James S. Maxwell, Jr.
P.O. Box 367
Lampeter, PA 17537
ph: 717-464-5573 or 717-464-5572
Advisor to "Warman's Antiques & Collectibles Price Guide."

Paris Pierce
Mechanical Bank Zone
118 Montgomery Ave.
Bala Cynwyd, PA 19004
ph: 215-557-0400
fax: 215-665-1976
e-mail: paris@pond.com
web: http://www.pond.com/~paris/bankzone.htm
Collector, dealer, expert in mechanical banks (1930 to modern); first on-line Mechanical Bank Museum and collectors' web site.

Dr. Greg Zemenick
Dr. "Z"
1350 Kirts, Ste. 160
Troy, MI 48084-4852
ph: 248-642-8129 or 248-244-9430
fax: 248-244-9495
e-mail: drzzeezzi@aol.com
web: http://www.drzzeezzi.com/
Buys, sells, brokers and specializes in mechanical banks, any condition or completeness; wooden or cardboard packing boxes; trade cards, catalogs; also bell toys; member ATCA, MBCA, SBCA and others.

Repro. Sources

Charles Reynolds
Reynolds Toys
2836 Monroe St.
Falls Church, VA 22042-2007
ph: 703-533-1322
e-mail: reynoldstoys@erols.com
web: http://www.reynoldstoys.com
Offers limited editions of new original penny banks, of sand-cast aluminum; political, holiday and event themes; over 100 editions produced from 1970-1990.

Oil Can (Miniature)

Collectors

Peter Capell
1838 West Grace St.
Chicago, IL 60613-2724
ph: 773-871-8735
e-mail: pcapell@netware.net
Wants tin or tin with paper label miniature oil can banks produced as promotional giveaways for gasoline and motor oil dealers.

Penny

Experts

Sy Schreckinger
P.O. Box 104
East Rockaway, NY 11518-0104
ph: 516-536-4154
Buy/sell mechanical and still banks: cast iron, tin, wood or lead; also wooden bank shipping boxes, bank trade cards, catalogs, etc.; also wants old photos of children with banks and toys.

Repair Services

Sy Schreckinger
P.O. Box 104
East Rockaway, NY 11518-0104
ph: 516-536-4154
Offers professional, museum quality repair, restoration and cleaning of iron and tin mechanical and still banks.

Registering

Collectors

Goerge P. Juergens
35 Farrah Dr.
Elkton, MD 21921
ph: 410-398-5041
Wants to buy Uncle Sam, Add-o-Bank and other registering banks.

Stanley D. Watson
2959 Hundred Oaks Ave.
Baton Rouge, LA 70808-1536
ph: 504-383-1594
e-mail: sdwatson@earthlink.net
Collector of antique registering banks (US mfg. only) by Durable Toy, Hoge, Kingsbury, Shonk, and other early manufacturers.

Experts

Robert L. McCumber
201 Carriage Dr.
Glastonbury, CT 06033-3231
ph: 860-633-4984
Author of "Registering Banks"; registering banks (e.g. pocket tube banks) show amount as coins are deposit.

Rocket/Space

Collectors

Anthony Glab
6708 Duluth Ave.
Baltimore, MD 21222
e-mail: glab@aol.com
Wants to buy rocket/space banks in mint condition by Astro Mfg.

Safe Shaped

Collectors

Larry Egelhoff
4175 Millersville Rd.
Indianapolis, IN 46205-2966
ph: 317-846-7228
e-mail: egelhoffl@juno.com
Collector and appraiser.

Still

Clubs/Associations

Larry Egelhoff, Mem.
Still Bank Collectors Club of America
Newsletter: Penny Bank Post
4175 Millersville Rd.
Indianapolis, IN 46205-2966
ph: 317-846-7228
e-mail: egelhoffl@juno.com
web: http://www.stillbankclub.com/
To stimulate knowledge of, interest in, and the collection of antique and contemporary still banks and, further, within the limits of friendly rivalry, to assist members in adding to and enhancing the value of their collections.

Collectors

Harry Ward
153 Scott Ave.
Bloomsburg, PA 17815-1020
ph: 570-784-3946

Tom Kellogg
6125 Rockdale Lane
Sylvania, OH 43560-3644
ph: 419-885-5562
fax: 419-261-1988
e-mail: ironbanks@aol.com
Wants to buy still banks in the form of buildings; also wants other forms of still and mechanical banks.

Dealers

Mike Henry
1456 Carson Court
Homewood, IL 60430-4013
ph: 708-799-1732 or 414-797-7933
Buys and sells still banks.

Experts

Leon M. Weiss
Gemini Antiques Ltd.
P.O. Box 1752
2418 Montauk Highway
Water Mill, NY 11976
ph: 516-537-4565 or 212-316-6380
fax: 516-726-9366
e-mail: julgert@geminiantiques.com
web: http://www.geminiantiques.com/
Buys and sells mechanical still banks, cast iron toys, door stops, folk art and more.

Repro. Sources

Charles Reynolds
Reynolds Toys
2836 Monroe St.
Falls Church, VA 22042-2007
ph: 703-533-1322
e-mail: reynoldstoys@erols.com
web: http://www.reynoldstoys.com
Offers limited editions of new original still banks of sand-cast aluminum; political, holiday, and event themes; flyer on request.

BANKS (MODERN)

(see also TOYS, Diecast)

Dealers

Donald Amnott
Small Wheels of America
34 Huckleberry Lane
Southington, CT 06489
ph: 800-258-7776
fax: 860-621-8885
Diecast cars, trucks, planes and blimps by Ertl, First Gear, Spec-Cast, PEM; oil company tankers by Hess, Texaco, Servco and many others.

Kathy & Walter Easterbrook
Eastco Banks & Collectibles
P.O. Box 412
Hancock, NY 13783-0412
ph: 607-467-3040
Diecast banks and toys: Ertl, Spec-Cast, First Gear, plastic gas station promotions.

Art & Judy Turner
Homestead Collectibles
P.O. Box 173
Mill Hall, PA 17751
ph: 570-726-3597
Specializing in diecast metal banks and airplane banks; over 3,200 different banks in stock; send $1 for price list.

Toy Collector Club of America
P.O. Box 368
Dyersville, IA 52040-0368
ph: 800-452-3303 or 319-875-9223
fax: 319-875-8056
For collectors of contemporary diecast banks and vehicles; gives collectors the opportunity to purchase diecast metal banks; newsletter lists what is available for purchase and discounts on products.

Darryl & Georgia Schulz
Georgia's Replica of Yesterday
6945 S 155th W Ave.
Sapulpa, OK 74066
ph: 918-224-2259
Specializes in die cast collectibles and banks; Ertl, JLE, Spec-Cast, First Gear.

Experts

Richard L. Heuser
Heuser Publishing Div. of Heuser Enterprises
508 Clapson Rd.
P.O. Box 300
West Winfield, NY 13491-0300
ph: 315-822-4804
fax: 315-822-4804
e-mail: toybanks@concentric.net
web: http://www.concentric.net/~Toybanks/
Buys, collects, appraises and specializes in modern collectible toy banks and diecast toys.

Periodicals

Richard L. Heuser
Heuser Publishing Div. of Heuser Enterprises
Price Guide: Heuser's Price Guide to Official Collectible Banks
508 Clapson Rd.
P.O. Box 300
West Winfield, NY 13491-0300
ph: 315-822-4804
fax: 315-822-4804
e-mail: toybanks@concentric.net
web: http://www.concentric.net/~Toybanks/
Quarterly price guide features Ertl, First Gear, Liberty Classics, Spec Cast, Action Racing Collectibles, Gearbox, Crown Premium/Vees Collectibles, DG Productions and others; listed by name, no., quantity, color, year made and value.

Richard L. Heuser
Heuser Publishing Div. of Heuser Enterprises
Newsletter: Heuser's Quarterly Collectible Diecast Newsletter
508 Clapson Rd.
P.O. Box 300
West Winfield, NY 13491-0300
ph: 315-822-4804
fax: 315-822-4804
e-mail: toybanks@concentric.net
web: http://www.concentric.net/~Toybanks/
Focuses on modern diecast collectible banks and custom imprinted replicas; new issues; articles of interest to collectors; listing of dealers and manufacturers; listing of upcoming toy shows.

BAR COLLECTIBLES

(see SALOON & BAR COLLECTIBLES)

BARBED WIRE

(see also FENCE COLLECTIBLES)

Clubs/Associations

Dan & Nancy Sowle
New Mexico Barbed Wire Collectors Association
Newsletter: Wire Barb & Nail
P.O. Box 102
Stanley, NM 87056-0102
ph: 505-832-4339 or 505-832-2552
fax: 505-832-2552

John Mantz
American Barbed Wire Collectors Society
Newsletter: Wire Collector News
1023 Baldwin Rd.
Bakersfield, CA 93304-4203
ph: 805-397-9572
fax: 805-831-3491
The only national association for collectors of barbed wire and associated fencing tools.

Collectors

Bill Prain
129 West Homewood Ct.
Genoa, IL 60135-1134
ph: 815-784-2663
Collects, trades barbed wire and barbed wire related items.

Experts

Charles & Rosie Dalton
1322 Lark
Lewisville, TX 75067-7606
ph: 972-317-7999
Buys, sells, collects and auctions barbed wire; authors of "Pocket Book of Wires", publishers of "The Barbed Wire Collector" newsletter.

John Mantz
1023 Baldwin Rd.
Bakersfield, CA 93304-4203
ph: 805-397-9572
fax: 805-831-3491

Museums/Libraries

Director
Barbed Wire Museum
P.O. Box 716
La Crosse, KS 67548-0716
ph: 785-222-9900
e-mail: broax@southwind.net
web: http://www2.southwind.net/~broax/bwire.html
Exhibit includes thousands examples of barbed wire plus related tools.

M.J. VanDeventer
National Cowboy Hall of Fame & Western Heritage Center
Magazine: Persimon Hill
1700 N.E. 63rd St.
Oklahoma City, OK 73111-7906
ph: 405-478-2250
fax: 405-478-4714
e-mail: nchf@aol.com
web: http://www.cowboyhalloffame.org/
NCHA represents 17 western states; preserves the rich heritage of the Old West and the memory of those who contributed to it.

Delbert Trew, Dir.
Devil's Rope Museum
Magazine: Barbed Wire Collector
100 Kingsley St.
P.O. Box 290
Mclean, TX 79057-0290
ph: 806-779-2225 or 806-779-3164
e-mail: barbwiremueum@centramedia.com
Largest barbed wire collection in the world; over 14,000 sq. ft. with over 6,000 artifacts on display; stocks and publishes books on barbed wire; hosts 2-day Barbed Wire Collectors Show annually in April.

Barbed Wire Museum
116 S. Cuyler
Pampa, TX 79065
ph: 806-665-5521

BARBERSHOP COLLECTIBLES

(see also BEAUTY SHOP COLLECTIBLES; BOTTLES, Barber; HAIRWORK; SHAVING COLLECTIBLES)

Auction Services

James Hagenbuch
Glass Works Auctions
P.O. Box 180
102 Jefferfson St.
East Greenville, PA 18041
ph: 215-679-5849
fax: 215-679-3068
e-mail: glswrk@enter.net
web: http://www.glswrk-auction.com/
Specializes in the auction of historical flasks, fruit jars, food & milk bottles, sodas, poisons, whiskeys, medicines, inks, barber bottles, bitters bottles, scent bottles, shaving mugs, target & range balls, etc.

Tony Nard
Nard Auctions
U.S. Rte. 220
Milan, PA 18831
ph: 570-888-9404
fax: 570-888-7723
Conducts specialized auctions of occupational shaving mugs, barber bottles, razors, country store and advertising items, etc.

Clubs/Associations

Penny Nader
National Shaving Mug Collectors Association
Newsletter: Barbershop Collectibles Newsletter
320 S. Glenwood St.
Allentown, PA 18104-6529
ph: 610-437-2534
fax: 610-770-1818
Mission is to stimulate the study of

shaving mugs, razors, barber bottles, and all related barbering items.

Collectors

Burton Handelsman
18 Hotel Dr.
White Plains, NY 10605-3531
ph: 914-428-4480
fax: 914-428-2145
Wants to buy shaving mugs, personalized barber bottles decorated with glass labels, barbershop photos and related catalogs.

Mike Griffin
11 Walton Ave.
White Plains, NY 10606-3212
ph: 914-949-7041
Buys early shaving mugs, occupational shaving mugs, barber bottles, signs, old barber photos; editor of the "National Shaving Mug Collectors Association Newsletter."

Bill Campesi
P.O. Box 140
Merrick, NY 11566-0140
ph: 516-546-9630
Collector of straight razors, especially fancy handles; also wants related trade catalogs, advertising, show cases, postcards, etc.

D. Perkins
6335 W. 62nd St.
Indianapolis, IN 46278-1906
ph: 317-293-9962
Wants fancy backbars, mugs, cabinets, shaving mugs with names and scenes, handpainted barber bottles, shave paper, vases, signs, shop photos, wooden chairs, salesman sample chairs, and child chairs, etc.

Dealers

Chris Jones
Barbershop Museum, The
1959 Rte. 33, Ste. A
Trenton, NJ 08690-1713
ph: 609-261-4258
fax: 609-261-4258
e-mail: barbrpole@aol.com
Buys and sells anything barbershop related; wants signs, tools, backbar items, bleeding/cupping and leeching utensils, furniture.

Sigmund Wohl
Razor's Edge, The
P.O. Box 429
Bronxville, NY 10708-0429
ph: 914-476-5939
fax: 914-376-4160
e-mail: swohl@compuserve.com
Buys and sells barber and shaving collectibles, fancy and unusual razors, and related advertising.

Mike & Mary Sparks
Antiquities, Ltd.
305 Carriage Crossing
Lansing, KS 66043
ph: 913-250-0697
web: http://www.unlimited-ltd.com/dealers/Antiquities.html
Buys and sells barber and shaving related items, especially shaving mugs, barber bottles, fancy straight and early safety razors, and barbershop furnishings.

Jo Havens-Wright
Wright Enterprises
610 N. Delaware Ave.
Roswell, NM 88201-2135
ph: 505-623-8053
e-mail: johavens@dfn.com
web: http://www.dfn.com/~johavens
Collector of barbershop items.

Experts

Chris Jones
Barbershop Museum, The
1959 Rte. 33, Ste. A
Trenton, NJ 08690-1713
ph: 609-261-4258
fax: 609-261-4258
e-mail: barbrpole@aol.com
Educational lectures, slide presentations, stage and movie prop rentals; also does appraisals of barbershop and shaving antiques.

Museums/Libraries

Lester DeQuaine, Dir.
National Shaving & Barbershop Museum
39 West Main St.
Meriden, CT 06451-4110
ph: 203-639-9778
Displays barbershop and shaving furnishings and artifacts with on-site theater, sidewalk cafe, and museum store which buys and sells related collectibles and books including razor blade price guide.

Chris Jones
Barbershop Museum, The
1959 Rte. 33, Ste. A
Trenton, NJ 08690-1713
ph: 609-261-4258
fax: 609-261-4258
e-mail: barbrpole@aol.com
Over 3000 items of barbering/shaving history documenting the subject from the stone age to present; highlights include complete, working 1896 barbershop; tours available by appointment only.

Edwin Jeffers
Barber Museum, The
2 1/2 S. High St.
Canal Winchester, OH 43110
ph: 614-833-9931
Collection includes straight razors, shaving mugs, barber poles, wooden chairs, bloodletting tools, etc.

Barber Poles

Book Sellers

Robert Marvy
William Marvy Company
1540 St. Clair Ave.
Saint Paul, MN 55105-2344
ph: 651-698-0726 or 800-874-2651
fax: 651-698-4048
e-mail: marvys@aol.com
Manufactures barber poles and replacement parts: domes, motors, glass and paper cylinders, etc.; also sells barbershop books.

Collectors

John & Joanna Kille
1319 Farley Court South
Arnold, MD 21012
ph: 410-757-8118
Buys early wooden and porcelain barber poles and chairs; also wants unusual barber signs and advertising.

Suppliers

Robert Marvy
William Marvy Company
1540 St. Clair Ave.
Saint Paul, MN 55105-2344
ph: 651-698-0726 or 800-874-2651
fax: 651-698-4048
e-mail: marvys@aol.com
Manufactures barber poles and replacement parts: domes, motors, glass and paper cylinders, etc.; also sells barbershop books.

Furnishings

Collectors

Joel Scheckner
15 Glendale Dr.
Englishtown, NJ 07726
ph: 732-462-3827
Wants to buy barbershop contents: wooden barber chairs, child's chairs, salesman samples, barber poles, mug racks, shoeshine stands, backbars, etc.

Shaving Mugs

Clubs/Associations

Penny Nader
National Shaving Mug Collectors Association
Newsletter: Barbershop Collectibles Newsletter
320 S. Glenwood St.
Allentown, PA 18104-6529
ph: 610-437-2534
fax: 610-770-1818
Mission is to stimulate the study of shaving mugs, razors, barber bottles, and all related barbering items.

Collectors

Lester Dequaine
155 Brewester St.
Bridgeport, CT 06605-3149
ph: 203-335-6833
Wants to buy shaving mugs in figural shapes of animals, humans, birds; also shaving brushes with handles in figural shapes; also early safety razors, mechanical blade sharpeners, razor blade banks, and related advertisements.

Joseph Albanese
70 Loretta Dr.
Torrington, CT 06790-5914
ph: 860-482-1854
e-mail: JCL.Albanese@juna.com
Buys, collects shaving mugs: occupational, fraternal, and photographical; also wants to buy interior and exterior photographs of barbershops.

Edward J. Meschi
129 Pinyard Rd.
Monroeville, NJ 08343-1870
ph: 609-358-7293
fax: 609-358-7789
e-mail: emfinearts@yahoo.com
Wants to buy occupational shaving mugs.

Mike Griffin
11 Walton Ave.
White Plains, NY 10606-3212
ph: 914-949-7041
Buys early shaving mugs, occupational shaving mugs, barber bottles, signs, old barber photos; editor of the "National Shaving Mug Collectors Association Newsletter."

Robert Fortin
5334 Strawflower Dr.
Syracuse, NY 13212-1243
Buys and sells barbershop collectibles: occupational shaving mugs, wooden barber poles, child's barber chair, salesman barber chair, good barber signs.

Ralph Nix
P.O. Box 655
Red Bay, AL 35582-0655
ph: 256-356-2997
e-mail: ralphn@getaway.net
web: http://www.shavingmug.com
Wants old, personalized shaving mugs including Occupational and Fraternal mugs.

Morris Pickerell, Jr.
103 South Crawford St.
Tompkinsville, KY 42167
ph: 800-826-4499 or 502-678-5848
fax: 502-678-7888
Wants to buy occupational, fraternal, and decorative shaving mugs.

Richard Hebel
233 Dietrich Crescent Dr.
Lawrenceburg, IN 47025
ph: 812-537-0150
e-mail: bhebel@seidata.com
Interested in occupational shaving mugs, especially those that are railroad related.

Experts

Burton Handelsman
18 Hotel Dr.
White Plains, NY 10605-3531
ph: 914-428-4480
fax: 914-428-2145
Buys and sells occupational shaving mugs and personalized barber bottles; author of the "Shaving Mugs" section in the Time-Life "Encyclopedia of Collectibles" series.

Museums/Libraries

Atwater Kent Museum - the History Museum of Philadelphia
15 S. 7th St.
Philadelphia, PA 19143
ph: 610-922-3031
web: http://www.fieldtrip.com/pa/59223031.htm

Lightner Museum
P.O. Box 334
75 King St.
Saint Augustine, FL 32085
ph: 904-824-2874

BAROMETERS

(see also INSTRUMENTS & DEVICES, Scientific)

Collectors

Paul H. Hayashi, PE
18 Tarabrook Dr.
Orinda, CA 94563-3121
ph: 925-254-5074 or 925-253-1038
fax: 925-253-0592
Wants to buy old stick barometers.

Dealers

Jill & Chuck Probst
Charles Edwin Antiques
P.O. Box 1340
Louisa, VA 23093-1340
ph: 540-967-0416
fax: 540-967-0416
e-mail: cei@charles-edwin.com
web: http://www.charles-edwin.com
Buys, sells, repairs mercury barometers only.

Bob Elsner
Heights Antiques
29 Clubhouse Ln.
Boynton Beach, FL 33436-6056
ph: 561-736-1362
fax: 561-736-1914
e-mail: rjelsner@aol.com
Barometer expert who buys, sells, appraises and repairs all types of barometers: gimbaled, mercury, aneroid, altimeters, barographs; antique and reproduction.

Don Levison
Don Levison Antiques
P.O. Box 22262
San Francisco, CA 94122
ph: 415-753-0455
fax: 415-753-5206
e-mail: dlevison@juno.com
web: http://www.antiquehorology.com
Buys and sells antique and better quality pocket and wrist watches, clocks, music boxes, singing birds, and other small automata; also mercury barometers from the 17th century to present.

Experts

Jill & Chuck Probst
Charles Edwin Antiques
P.O. Box 1340
Louisa, VA 23093-1340
ph: 540-967-0416
fax: 540-967-0416
e-mail: cei@charles-edwin.com
web: http://www.charles-edwin.com
Buys, sells, repairs mercury barometers only.

John Forster
Barometer Fair
P.O. Box 25502
Sarasota, FL 34277
ph: 941-923-6136
fax: 941-923-6136
e-mail: barometer@glimmer.com
Buys, sells, restores all antique barometers; also deals in antique maps, globes, compasses, telescopes and other scientific instruments.

Repair Services

Jim Mulhern
Medford Clock Shop
3 Union Street
Medford, NJ 08055
ph: 609-953-0014
fax: 609-953-0411
e-mail: medclock@aol.com
web: http://www.medfordclock.com
Specializes in the repair of all types of antique clocks; also antique mercury and aneroid barometers repaired and restored; mercury barometer tubes made to fit old barometers.

Jill & Chuck Probst
Charles Edwin Antiques
P.O. Box 1340
Louisa, VA 23093-1340
ph: 540-967-0416
fax: 540-967-0416
e-mail: cei@charles-edwin.com
web: http://www.charles-edwin.com
Buys, sells, repairs mercury barometers only.

Bob Elsner
Heights Antiques
29 Clubhouse Ln.
Boynton Beach, FL 33436-6056
ph: 561-736-1362
fax: 561-736-1914
e-mail: rjelsner@aol.com
Barometer expert who buys, sells, appraises and repairs all types of barometers: gimbaled, mercury, aneroid, altimeters, barographs; antique and reproduction.

BARS

(see BREWERIANA)

BARWARE

(see SALOON & BAR COLLECTIBLES)

BASEBALL CAPS

(see CAPS)

BASKETS

(see also AMERICAN INDIAN; CRAFTS, Basketry; KITCHEN COLLECTIBLES; REPAIR/RESTORATION/CONSERVATION, Cane & Basketry)

Internet Resources

WeaveNet
25 Florida St.
Long Beach, NY 11561
web: http://www.weavenet.com/
This web site provides a complete source of basketry, weaving and caning information; restoration supplies, ash strips, chair cane, dyes, patterns, raffia, seagrass, weaving guilds and associations, etc.

Museums/Libraries

Old Salem, Inc.
Salem Station
Drawer F
Winston Salem, NC 27108-0346
ph: 336-721-7350 or 888-348-5422
fax: 336-721-7335
e-mail: webmaster@oldsalem.org
web: http://oldsalem.org/
Old Salem, a living history town, is a repository of era baskets and other collection items from the late 1700s and early 1800s.

Repro. Sources

Stephen Zeh
Stephen Zeh, Basketmaker
Newsletter: News From the Basket Shop
P.O. Box 381
Temple, ME 04984-0381
ph: 207-778-2351
fax: 207-778-6439
Handcrafted brown ash splint baskets in the tradition of Maine woodsmen, Shakers, and the Native American basket makers; catalog $2.

Darryl & Karen Arawjo
P.O. Box 477
Bushkill, PA 18324-0477
ph: 570-588-6957
Reproduction of Nantucket, Shaker and Appalachian baskets in hand-split white oak; brochure available.

Longaberger

Auction Services

Greg Michael
Craft & Michael Auctioneers
P.O. Box 7
Camden, IN 46917-0007
ph: 219-686-2615 or 219-967-4442
fax: 219-686-9100
Conducts periodical basket auctions.

Internet Resources

Brett Rabideau
Basket Collector's Emporium, The
P.O. Box 16722
West Haven, CT 06516
e-mail: baskets@basketcollector.com
web: http://www.basketcollector.com
Secondary market for Longaberger baskets, accessories and pottery; buys, sells, auctions.

Man./Prod./Dist.

Longaberger
e-mail: webmaster@longaberger.com
web: http://www.longaberger.com

Periodicals

Suzy Metzler
Newsletter: Basket Collector's Gazette, The
P.O. Box 100
Pitkin, CO 81241-0100
ph: 970-641-5838
fax: 970-641-2624
e-mail: BasColGaz@aol.com
web: http://www.basketlover.com/
A monthly newsletter designed for avid collectors of Longaberger baskets, ideas, recipes; free Longaberger buy/sell/swap ads for subscribers.

BATHING BEAUTIES

Nudies & Naughties

(see also EROTICA)

Collectors

Lori Landgrebe
2331 E. Main St.
Decatur, IL 62521-2263
ph: 217-423-2254
Wants German bathing beauties.

BATHROOM FIXTURES

(see PLUMBING)

BATTERSEA ENAMEL BOXES

(see BOXES, Enamel [Battersea]; ENAMELS)

BAUHAUS

(see MODERNISM)

BAYONETS

(see also ARMS & ARMOR; FIREARMS; MILITARIA; SWORDS; KNIVES; MILITARIA)

Clubs/Associations

Roy P. Anderson, Sec.
Society of American Bayonet Collectors, The
P.O. Box 234
East Islip, NY 11730-0234
e-mail: Bayonets4u@usa.net
web: http://www.whidbey.com/sabc/
An organization for collectors of bayonets made or used in the U.S.

Mery Christian
Association of French Bayonet Collectors
Newsletter: Baionette
France
ph: 03 80 29 82 30
fax: 03 80 29 82 30
e-mail: christian.mery@wanadoo.fr
web: http://perso.wanadoo.fr/christian.mery/
Web site is in English and French.

Collectors

Derek Complin
ph: 613-547-9595
fax: 613-549-2528
e-mail: unilink@istar.ca
web: http://www.cybertap.com/brothers/Derek-2.htm
Over 30 years collecting bayonets; interests focus on all British and British Commonwealth bayonets, and plug bayonets from any country; buys, sells and trades.

Ron Riede
e-mail: driver@inil.com
web: http://www.inil.com/users/driver/
Collector of Imperial German bayonets; always interested in unusual or rare world bayonets; also has many bayonet duplicates for sale or trade.

Eric Fuchslocher
8050 Ventura Cyn Ave.
Panorama City, CA 91402
ph: 818-994-1492
Wants German bayonets; Imperial through WWII in unaltered condition.

Shawn K. Gibson
Bayonet Connection, The
P.O. Box 1533
Travis AFB, CA 94535
fax: 707-429-9406
e-mail: shawn@bayonets.com
web: http://bayonets.com

R.J. Reeves
2623 Bruce Rd., R.R. 7
Duncan, British Columbia V9L 4W4
Canada
ph: 250-746-9521
e-mail: rreeves@duncan.island.net
Interested in all types of bayonets; specializing in British and Commonwealth countries (Australia, Canada, India, etc.); duplicates occasionally available for sale or trade.

Jerrey Hayes
12 Crawford Rd.
Hatfield, Hertfordshire AL10 OPG
U.K.
ph: 0410 095027
e-mail: jeff@hayestech.demon.co.uk
Collector of world bayonets of all types, from plug bayonets to current issue.

Dealers

Bayonet Trader
e-mail: driver@inil.com
web: http://www.inil.com/users/driver/
Web site has many bayonets for sale; also examples of bayonet styles from various periods.

Experts

Jim Maddox
Maddox Collection, The
34 east 50th Street
Savannah, GA 31405
e-mail: bayonets@geocities.com
web: http://www.geocities.com/Pentagon/6591/
Bayonet collector for over 38 years; website features "The Maddox Collection" and posts six featured bayonets at all times with frequent updates; also Wants List and For Sale List and links; will identify and appraise unknown items.

Internet Resources

Bayonet Collector's Network
e-mail: jlsmjacobi@worldnet.att.net
web: http://www.geocities.com/Athens/Oracle/2691/bcn.htm
Comprehensive web site for the bayonet collector.

BEADS

(see also AMERICAN INDIAN; GEMS & JEWELRY; PURSES)

Clubs/Associations

Beadesigner International, The New England Area Bead Society
135 Aspinwall Ave.
Brookline, MA 02146
ph: 617-499-9432
e-mail: beadesigner@geocities.com
web: http://www.geocities.com/SoHo/3542/

Peter Francis, Jr.
Center for Bead Research
Newsletter: Margaretologist, The
4 Essex St.
Lake Placid, NY 12946-1236
ph: 518-523-1794
e-mail: pfjr@northnet.org
web: http://www.thebeadsite.com
The New York Times calls Mr. Francis "the world's leading authority on beads." The Center is internationally known for its work: research; publications, workshops, lectures, tours, website; devoted to all kinds of beads.

Bead Society of Greater Washington
P.O. Box 70036
Bethesda, MD 20813-0036
ph: 202-462-8933 or 301-656-9255
e-mail: bsgw@erols.com
web: http://www.bsgw.org/
Monthly meetings featuring slide-illustrated lectures, how-to workshops about beads and related topics; newsletter five times a year with articles on bead research, travel, collecting, bead bazaars, bead books for sale, etc.

Baltimore Bead Society, The
P.O. Box 311
Riderwood, MD 21139-0311
e-mail: wheat@craftwolf.com
web: http://www.craftwolf.com/baltbd01.htm

Lynn Smythe
Palm Beach Bead Society
Newsletter: Bead Gazette
5416 Cleveland Road
Delray Beach, FL 33484
ph: 561-496-7673
e-mail: dlphcrft@aol.com
web: http://www.gopbi.com/community/groups/pbbeadsociety/
Holds monthly meetings; membership includes monthly newsletter, discount at local bead stores; free listing including photos of beadwork and society websites.

Lara Gambony
Treasure Coast Bead Society
Newsletter: Bead Gazette
634 S. Degan Drive
Port Saint Lucie, FL 34983
ph: 561-871-6144
e-mail: snooch101@aol.com
Holds monthly meetings; membership includes monthly newsletter, discount at local bead stores; free listing including photos of beadwork and society websites.

Judith Schwab
Bead Society of Greater Chicago
Newsletter: BSGC Newsletter
P.O. Box 8103
Wilmette, IL 60091-8103
ph: 312-458-0519 or 847-699-7959
fax: 847-699-7959
Offers members monthly slide lectures and workshops.

Chicago Midwest Bead Society
Newsletter: Chicago Midwest Bead Society
1511 Sherman Ave.
Evanston, IL 60201-4416
ph: 847-328-4040
e-mail: info@aylasoriginals.com
web: http://www.aylasoriginals.com/CMBS.html
Focuses on glass, organic and metal beads and beadwork from ancient to contemporary; workshops, speakers, bazaar.

Courtney Emken
Austin Bead Society
P.O. Box 656
Austin, TX 78767-0656
e-mail: info@austin.beads.org
web: http://austin.beads.org

Kohler Dena
Bead Society of Orange County, The
Bowers Museum of Cultural Art, The
2002 North Main St.
Santa Ana, CA 92706
ph: 714-828-8468
e-mail: udok@wdc.net
Main goal is to provide an educational resource in the artistic, historical, and intercultural significance of beads; supports The Bowers Museum of Cultural Art, including fund raising and volunteer support of Museum programs.

Paula Althoff, Mem.
Northern California Bead Society
Newsletter: Northern California Bead Society Bulletin
1650 Lower Grand Ave.
Piedmont, CA 94611
ph: 510-655-5332
web: http://www.norcalbead.org/
Dedicated to the study of beads; meetings have lecture slide presentations; members wear beads pertaining to the announced meeting topic; major annual sale open to the public.

Alice Scherer, Dir.
Center for the Study of Beadwork
Newsletter: Notes From a Beadworker's Journal
P.O. Box 13719
Portland, OR 97213-0719
ph: 503-657-0583
fax: 503-657-0583
web: http://www.europa.com/~alice/
Purpose is to gather and disseminate information on beadwork; maintains a study collection, library, articles file, and slide bank; quarterly newsletter.

Lester A. Ross
Society of Bead Researchers
Journal: Bead Forum, The
P.O. Box 7304
Eugene, OR 97401
e-mail: lross@bigfoot.com
web: http://www.spiretech.com/~lester/sbr/index/index.htm
Formed in 1981 to foster research on beads of all materials and periods; membership is open to all.

Dealers

Barbara VanDusen
Bishop's Gambit
3210 Dover Road
Pompano Beach, FL 33062
e-mail: vandusen@gate.net
web: http://www.gate.net/~vandusen
Makes, collects and sells glass beads and jewelry; collects glass beads and Victorian jewelry; recycles broken necklaces for the glass beads and components; sells beads (vintage and new lampwork), costume jewelry, and buttons.

Lynn Smythe
Dolphin Crafts
5416 Cleveland Road
Delray Beach, FL 33484
ph: 561-496-7673
e-mail: dlphcrft@aol.com
web: http://members.aol.com/dlphcrft/
Mail order catalog of beads, books, buttons and related supplies; also beaded jewelry kits and finished jewelry.

Ayla's Originals
1511 Sherman Ave.
Evanston, IL 60201-4416
ph: 847-328-4040
e-mail: info@aylasoriginals.com
web: http://www.aylasoriginals.com/CMBS.html
Buys and sells a wide selection of beads and components for designing and collecting; also design and repair of beaded jewelry.

Ari Imports, Inc.
8 South Michigan Ave., Ste. 2008
Chicago, IL 60603
ph: 312-263-3313
fax: 312-263-3314
e-mail: ari@mcs.net
web: http://www.czechmate.com/
Direct importer and distributor of glass beads from the Czech Republic.

Christina Blessing
Lost Cities
2802 Juan Street, #14
San Diego, CA 92110
ph: 800-525-3053 or 619-692-1114
fax: 619-692-0841
Sells old unusual beads: coral, Tibetan, turquoise, amber.

Simma Chester
Chester Bead
205 Camino Alto, Ste. 130
Mill Valley, CA 94941
ph: 415-381-3934
fax: 415-381-3934
e-mail: simma@altavista.net
web: http://www.geocities.com/Paris/7137/
Beads, supplies, jewelry.

Experts

Peter Francis, Jr.
Center for Bead Research
4 Essex St.
Lake Placid, NY 12946-1236
ph: 518-523-1794
e-mail: pfjr@northnet.org
web: http://www.thebeadsite.com
The New York Times calls Mr. Francis "the world's leading authority on beads."

Judy Kovl
JuDeSigns
P.O. Box 99006
Troy, MI 48099-9066
ph: 248-680-8860
e-mail: jude@elbbs.com
web: http://www.elbbs.com/elbbs/jude/amulet.html
Beadwork expert; website has pictures and descriptions of handmade beaded jewelry and wearable art.

Internet Resources

BeadNet
e-mail: simone@mcs.net
web: http://www.mcs.net/~simone/beadnet.html
Bead newsgroups, on-line resources, commercial sites, bead artists, bead societies, African inspired beadwork, Native American beadwork, and more.

Man./Prod./Dist.

Lucinda Brown
Cindybeads
6240 Everett Ct. #C
Arvada, CO 80004
ph: 303-423-1616
e-mail: beads@ecentral.com
web: http://www.cindybeads.com/
Makes glass beads lovingly by hand.

Museums/Libraries

Corning Museum of Glass, The
One Museum Way
Corning, NY 14830-2253
ph: 607-937-5371
fax: 607-937-3352
e-mail: cmg@cmog.org
web: http://www.pennynet.org/glmuseum/
Over 24,000 glass objects, innovative exhibits, videos, models; glass history, archaeology, and early manufacturing; great website with lots of information about glass.

National Museum of the American Indian
470 L'Enfant Plaza, SW, Ste. 7102
Washington, DC 20560
web: http://www.si.edu/nmai/
The museum will open on the Mall in Washington, DC, in the year 2002, on a site between the National Air & Space Museum and the U.S. Capitol; will be a center for exhibitions, ceremonies, performances, and educational activities

Bead Museum, The
5754 W. Glenn Dr.
Glendale, AZ 85301
ph: 623-931-2737
fax: 623-930-8561
e-mail: cheryl@thebeadmuseum.com
web: http://www.thebeadmuseum.com/
Collects, preserves, identifies, documents and displays beads and ornaments used in personal adornment from ancient, ethnic and contemporary cultures, covering all periods of history.

Periodicals

Kalmbach Publishing Co.
Magazine: Bead & Button
P.O. Box 1612
21027 Crossroads Circle
Waukesha, WI 53187
ph: 414-796-8776 or 800-533-6644
fax: 414-796-1615
e-mail: customerservice@kalmbach.com
web: http://www.beadandbutton.com
Dedicated to helping all bead and button enthusiasts with creative projects and providing collectible information; how-to projects, beading tips and techniques, historical articles.

Magazine: Jewelry Crafts
5000 Eagle Rock Blvd., #105
Los Angeles, CA 90041
ph: 800-528-1024
e-mail: jwlrymag@flex.net
web: http://www.jewelrycrafts.com
A bi-monthly magazine for those with a passion for beads: how-to-make-it projects from beading to lampworking; also silversmithing and cane making.

Suppliers

Gampel Supply Corp.
11 West 37th St.
New York, NY 10018-6235
ph: 212-398-9222
fax: 212-575-0931
Bead work and jewelry making supplies.

John & Jaqueline Foutz
550 Silver & Supply
4187 US Highway 64
Kirtland, NM 87417
ph: 505-598-5322
fax: 505-598-0974
e-mail: sales@beadsource.com
web: http://www.beadsource.com/
Supplies metal and bead crafters with the finest possible jewelry supplies, tools, materials and services: sterling silver, .999 fine silver, silver filled, 14k gold, gold filled, nickel, copper, red and yellow brass, bead supplies, etc.

Barry
Berger Specialty Company
413 E 8th St.
Los Angeles, CA 90014-2301
ph: 213-627-8785
fax: 213-680-9743
e-mail: Bergers@earthlink.net
Mail order OK.

BEAM BOTTLES

(see DECANTERS, Figural Whiskey [Beam])

BEAUTY SHOP COLLECTIBLES

(see also HAIRWORK)

Collectors

Michael Warner
Beauty Shoppe Archives
e-mail: mwarner@net-link.net
web: http://www.net-link.net/~mwarner/BSA.html
Wants barbershop or hair dressers collectibles: trade magazines or texts, old barber or beauty shop tools or furniture; also any photos or material on bobbed hair fad of the 1920s.

BEEKEEPING MEMORABILIA

Collectors

John O. Burgess
10738 Harley Rd.
Lorton, VA 22079-3908
Wants to buy beekeeping memorabilia especially glass honey containers.

BEER CAN OPENERS

(see CAN OPENERS)

BEER CANS

(see also BREWERIANA)

Clubs/Associations

Doug Blegen
Gambrinus Chapter of the Beer Can Collectors of America
985 Maebelle Way
Westerville, OH 43081-1273
ph: 614-890-0835
fax: 614-890-0812
e-mail: drblegen@aol.com
Sponsors annual breweriana show.

Beer Can Collectors of America
Newsletter: Beer Can Collectors News
747 Merus Court
Fenton, MO 63026-2092
ph: 314-343-6486
fax: 314-343-6486
e-mail: bcca@bcca.com
web: http://www.bcca.com/index.html
A not-for-profit organization founded in 1974; over 4,000 members worldwide who share an interest in brewery history and/or collect beer cans and other breweriana; also publishes the "BCCA Want Ad Bulletin" newsletter.

Collectors

John Gruskin
P.O. Box 53
Northport, NY 11768
ph: 516-262-0338
e-mail: jlgruskin@aol.com
web: http://www.angelfire.com/ny/beerstuff/
Beer can collector and expert; has over 10,000 beer cans in his collection.

Frank Munshower
355 W. 8th Ave.
Tarentum, PA 15084
e-mail: ftmmlm@usaor.net
Wants to buy straight steel tab tops, flat tops, and cone tops; member of The Olde Frothingslosh Chapter of the BCCA.

Steve Gordon
P.O. Box 632
Olney, MD 20830-0632
ph: 301-774-7651 or 301-439-4116
fax: 301-439-7296
e-mail: gono@clark.net
web: http://www.geocities.com/Heartland/pointe/8848/beer.html
Wants to buy pre-1970s U.S. cans, especially 12 ounce conetops and flat tops; will answer any letter or call promptly; also will consider other beer-related items; singles of entire collections.

Dick Caughey
1410 Brookside Dr.
Memphis, TN 38138
ph: 901-754-4609
Wants to buy cone top soda and beer cans.

Jon Williams
Busch Brothers
2712 Jefferson Ave., Apt. #2
Cincinnati, OH 45219
ph: 513-861-3813 or 305-932-1205
e-mail: buschbros@geocities.com
web: http://www.travel.to/buschmountains/
Collection consists of over 25,000 Busch beer cans from different eras.

John Conrad
3245 N. 650 East
Churubusco, IN 46723-9510
ph: 219-693-3507 or 219-693-2464
Old beer cans & advertisements; also 1 qt. old metal oil cans.

Jerry Glader
1017 Villa Gran Way
Fenton, MO 63026
ph: 314-343-9433
e-mail: jerry@primary.net
web: http://www.angelfire.com/mo/JerryBeerCans/
Collects beer cans; specializes in one can from every country in the world, also in cans from Africa.

Dealers

AAACRC
P.O. Box 8061
Saddle Brook, NJ 07662-8061
Buys, trades and sells beer cans, complete sets; bottom opened; will sell or trade for silver coins. 12 oz size only, US.

Paul Ash
Ash's Beer Cans & Breweriana
1295 Caudle St.
Orlando, FL 32828
ph: 407-568-4220
e-mail: pash@gdi.net
web: http://www.angelfire.com/biz2/beercans/
Appraiser, dealer, collector and specialist in American 12 oz. beer cans; free appraisals; buys and sells better beer can collections; specializes in opening instruction flat top and cone top cans.

Jeff Grissop
2530 W. Main St.
Rapid City, SD 57702
ph: 605-343-2006
fax: 605-341-6945
e-mail: grissop@enetis.net
web: http://www.enetis.net/~grissop/beercans.html
Collector and dealer of beer cans; buys, sells and trades; has 1500 cans to trade (over 450 different cans); specializes in beer cans relating to motorcycles, and has many Harley beer cans to trade, especially from the Sturgis Rally.

Jim Wicker
Jim's Breweriana
426 Old Country Way
Chicago, IL 60684
ph: 847-487-4697 or 847-895-3640
fax: 847-497-4698
e-mail: wicker@interaccess.com
web: http://homepage.interaccess.com/~wicker/
Buys, sells, appraises beer cans and cone top cans which were made from 1935 to 1956 and have spouts on them.

Art LaComb
Art's Beer Cans
3208 Parkwood Dr.
Flower Mound, TX 75022
ph: 972-539-9820
e-mail: jazbo@concentric.net
web: http://www.concentric.net/~jazbo/beercans.htm
Offers an extensive list of top grade cone top, flat top, and pull tab beer cans; always looking to purchase cone top and flat top beer cans in excellent condition.

Experts

Allan Aprea
24 Chestnut Road
Chatham, NJ 07928-1120
ph: 973-635-6099
e-mail: ajaprea@pica.army.mil
Collector, appraiser, expert specializing in U.S. and Canadian 12 oz. beer cans as well as other forms of breweriana (signs, lights, etc.) from the G. Krueger Brewery of Newark, NJ and the Trommer's Brewery of Brooklyn, NY & Orange, NJ.

Museums/Libraries

Museum of Beverage Containers & Advertising, The
1055 Ridgecrest Dr.
Goodlettsville, TN 37072
ph: 615-859-5236 or 877-859-4929
fax: 615-859-5238
e-mail: mbca@gono.com
web: http://gono.com/vir-mus/museum.htm
The largest collection of soda and beer cans in the world; buy, sell, trade beer & soda advertising items; also cleans rust from old beer cans.

Suppliers

Soda Mart - Can World
1055 Ridgecrest Dr.
Goodlettsville, TN 37072
ph: 615-859-5236 or 877-859-4929
fax: 615-859-5238
e-mail: mbca@gono.com
web: http://gono.com/vir-mus/museum.htm
Sells breweriana books; also cleans and de-rusts on cans, and sells supplies for the beer can collector.

BEER RELATED COLLECTIBLES

(see BEER CANS; BREWERIANA; STEINS)

BEER STEINS

(see STEINS)

BELIEVE IT OR NOT! COLLECTIBLES

(see RIPLEY'S BELIEVE IT OR NOT!)

BELLS

Clubs/Associations

American Bell Association
Magazine: Bell Tower, The
P.O. Box 19443
Indianapolis, IN 46219-0443
ph: 210-674-1814
e-mail: jfforman@loop.com
web: http://www.collectoronline.com/club-ABA.html
Over 1,700 members with 48 chapters worldwide; purpose is primarily education in the field of bells; the bi-monthly publication is filled with bell related articles.

Collectors

George A. Coupe
1243 1st St. S.E.
Washington, DC 20003
ph: 202-554-1000 or 800-368-5466
fax: 202-863-0775
Wants unusual bells, tap bells, figural, but no bells with handles.

Bells
207 Irwin St.
Brooklyn, MI 49230
ph: 517-592-9030
fax: 517-592-4511
Wants bronze or brass bells from 9" to huge.

Don Mathews
3215 Garner Ave.
Ames, IA 50010-4225
ph: 515-232-0938
Wants to buy metal, figural and figurine bells; needs descriptions, photos and asking price.

Don Hicks
747 Merus Court
Fenton, MO 63026-2092
ph: 314-343-6486
fax: 314-343-6486
e-mail: bcca@bcca.com
web: http://www.bcca.com/index.html

Kay Weaver
7210 Bellbrook Dr.
San Antonio, TX 78227-1002
ph: 210-674-1814
e-mail: aba-ron@juno.com

Dealers

R.C. Brosamer
Brosamer's Bells
207 Irwin Street
Brooklyn, MI 49230-9282
ph: 517-592-9030 or 888-592-3557
fax: 517-592-4511
e-mail: sales@brosamersbells.com
web: http://www.brosamersbells.com/
Advertises as the largest dealer of pre-owned bronze and cast iron bells, mostly from churches, railroads and ships.

Experts

Dorothy Malone Anthony
World of Bells
2401 S. Horton
Fort Scott, KS 66701
ph: 316-223-3404
e-mail: worldofbells@terraworld.net
Over 200 bells in color in each of the 12 books published to date in the "World of Bells" book series; flyer on request.

Suppliers

Smucker's Harness Shop
2014 Main St.
Narvon, PA 17555
ph: 717-445-5956
fax: 717-445-7752
Carries complete line of leather working supplies including solid brass and plated brass bells for harnesses and decorative purposes.

Tap

Collectors

T.C. Scott
8511 Cathedral Forest Dr.
Fairfax Station, VA 22039
ph: 703-548-5454 or 800-368-5466
fax: 703-549-3439
Collector wants to buy ornate "tap" bells that were used on counters in hotels, etc.; brass, silver, unusual; will buy single piece or whole collection.

BELT BUCKLES

(see also CLOTHING & ACCESSORIES, Vintage; CUFF LINKS)

John Deere

Clubs/Associations

John Cooklin
International Association of John Deere Buckle Collectors
14 Forest Rd.
Rock Island, IL 61201-6140
ph: 309-786-9747
fax: 309-786-0392
e-mail: www.jmcooklin@aol.com

Collectors

John Cooklin
14 Forest Rd.
Rock Island, IL 61201-6140
ph: 309-786-9747
fax: 309-786-0392
e-mail: www.jmcooklin@aol.com

BERMUDA COLLECTIBLES

Collectors

Ernest M. Roberts
5 Corsa St.
Huntington Station, NY 11746-6607
ph: 516-586-1462
e-mail: roberer@mail.northgrum.com
Wants pre-1950 postcards, covers, hotel stationery, maps, prints, old books, photographs, and other paper ephemera relating to Bermuda; old plates, mugs, cups, silver spoons and all tourist trinkets from Bermuda.

BIBLES

(see also BOOKS; RELIGIOUS COLLECTIBLES, Holy Cards)

Dealers

Phil Barber
Historic Newspapers & Early Imprints
P.O. Box 8694
Boston, MA 02114-0036
ph: 617-492-4653
fax: 617-868-1534
e-mail: barber10@channel1.com
web: http://www.channel1.com/barbernews/
Buying and selling fine paper collectibles since 1979; specializes in historic newspapers from the period 1775 to 1865; also early Bible leaves, and ephemera dating 1440 to 1940.

Museums/Libraries

American Bible Society Library
Magazine: Record
1865 Broadway
New York, NY 10023-7503
ph: 212-408-1204
fax: 212-408-1546
e-mail: pwaller@americanbible.org
web: http://www.americanbible.org/LOCALNAGIM.nsf/Pages/Library
Collection of nearly 50,000 bibles, testaments, and scripture portions in approximately 2,000 languages, dating from the 15th cent.

BICYCLES & RELATED MEMORABILIA

(see also RIDING TOYS)

Auction Services

Michael Fallon
Copake Country Auction
P.O. Box H, 266 Rt. 7A
Copake, NY 12516
ph: 518-329-1142
fax: 518-329-3369
e-mail: info@copakeauction.com
web: http://www.copakeauction.com/
Conducts auctions specializing in the sale of classic bicycles.

Clubs/Associations

Wheelmen, The
Magazine: Wheelmen Magazine, The
63 Stonebridge Road
Allen Park, NJ 07042-1631
ph: 609-587-6487
e-mail: hoehne@aol.com
web: http://www.thewheelmen.org
A club with about 800 members dedicated to the enjoyment and preservation of our bicycle heritage.

Jody Newman, Ex. Dir.
League of American Bicyclists
Magazine: Bicycle USA
1612 K Street, NW
Washington, DC 20006
ph: 202-822-1333
fax: 202-822-1334
e-mail: bikexec@aol.com
web: http://www.bikeleague.org
Bicycle advocacy, bicycle safety promotion, schedules bike events; many antique bike collectors as well as replica builders; newsletter has frequent articles about antique bikes.

Richard Truett
Vintage Bicycle Club of America
325 West Hornbeam Dr.
Longwood, FL 32779-2532
ph: 407-862-0031
e-mail: thecabe@aol.com
web: http://www.tiac.net/users/cabe/
Formed to promote the preservation and restoration of classic and antique American bicycles made from 1917 to present.

Robert B. Balcomb, Past-Pres.
International Veteran Cycle Association
Newsletter: Veteran Cyclist, The
248 Highland Dr.
Findlay, OH 45840-1207
ph: 419-423-2760
e-mail: bobalcomb@aol.com
International umbrella organization for national clubs of bicycle collectors, historians, enthusiasts; promotes the heritage of the bicycle; focuses on pre-1918 bicycles.

Scott Allison
North Park Cycle
826 Orange Ave., #180
Coronado, CA 92118
ph: 619-448-2543 or 619-338-6493
fax: 619-448-2543
Bicycles are an important factor in world history; this club focuses on bicycles from the 1860s through the 1960s.

Collectors

Don Peoples
63 Stonebridge Road
Allen Park, NJ 07042-1631
ph: 609-587-6487
e-mail: hoehne@aol.com
web: http://www.thewheelmen.org
Wants antique pre-1900 highwheel bicycles and related items such as bells, cyclometers, lamps, etc.

Ron Klaus
35769 Simon Dr.
Clinton Township, MI 48035
ph: 810-791-5594

Dealers

Donald Paquette
BikeIcons
3 Grove Circle
Saco, ME 04072
ph: 207-282-7336 or 207-282-4910
fax: 207-770-4455
e-mail: ride@bikeicons.com
web: http://www.bikeicons.com/
Buys, sells, trades, appraises and restores antique & classic bicycles; want to buy old bicycles, parts & collections.

Village Schwinn Shop
606 New Road
Somers Point, NJ 08244
ph: 609-927-3775

Keith Murdock
Keith's Bikes
e-mail: keithm@boulder.earthnet.net
web: http://www.keithsbikes.com/
Buys and sells antique bicycles including Schwinn, Roadmaster, Shelby, Huffman, Dayton, Elgin, Sting-Ray and others.

Experts

Lorne Shields
Vintage Cycling
P.O. Box 211
Chagrin Falls, OH 44022
ph: 416-733-3777 or 416-744-0747
fax: 416-744-8042
e-mail: vintage@globalserve.net
Buys, sells, appraises, consults on cycling and related historical objects; generally 1817 through 1950s; collections or singles purchased; all bicycles, ephemera, memorabilia such as clocks, trophies, bells, lamps, parts, books, etc.

Jerry Peters
Chestnut Hollow, Ltd.
6060 Bordman Rd.
P.O. Box 6
Almont, MI 48003-0006
ph: 810-798-3158
Largest collector of classic bicycles in the US with over 1000; free museum/ showroom with 300 of rarest and finest bicycles; issues catalog of parts and accessories for sale ($6); offers free bicycle identification service.

Leon Dixon
P.O. Box 28242
Santa Ana, CA 92799-8242
ph: 714-647-1949
e-mail: Oldbicycle@aol.com
web: http://members.aol.com/oldbicycle/
Wants old deluxe, streamlined (1920-1965) bicycles, bicycle literature, memorabilia, catalogs, parts, etc.; curator of the National Bicycle History Archive; makes personal appearances with slide shows, old movies etc. on bicycles.

Internet Resources

Menotomy Vintage Bicycles
P.O. Box 2864
Acton, MA 01720
e-mail: Menotomy@aol.com
web: http://uses.aol.com/menotomy/index.htm
Lots on on-line information: collector reference books, discussion areas, old maps and pictures, bicycles for sale, parts, literature, etc.

Museums/Libraries

Carl & Clarice Burgwardt
Pedaling History Bicycle Museum
3943 N. Buffalo Rd.
Orchard Park, NY 14127-1841
ph: 716-662-3853 or 716-662-7882
fax: 716-662-4594
e-mail: BicycleMus@aol.com
web: http://www.pedalinghistory.com
Contains a sizable collection of bicycles and related items such as carbide & kerosene lamps, photographs, advertising & nearly 100 antique steins; will help with research or appraisals.

Jerry Peters
Chestnut Hollow, Ltd.
6060 Bordman Rd.
P.O. Box 6
Almont, MI 48003-0006
ph: 810-798-3158
Largest collector of classic bicycles in the US with over 1000; free museum/ showroom with 300 of rarest and finest bicycles; issues catalog of parts and accessories for sale ($6); offers free bicycle identification service.

Leon Dixon, Curator
National Bicycle History Archive
P.O. Box 28242
Santa Ana, CA 92799-8242
ph: 714-647-1949
e-mail: Oldbicycle@aol.com
web: http://members.aol.com/oldbicycle/
NBHA performs research on old bicycles and bicycle history; archive includes in excess of 30,000 original catalogs, movies, photos, advertisements, books, etc.; each research based on fee which varies according to services needed.

Periodicals

Richard Truett
Arjay Communications, Inc.
Directory: North Amer. Dir. of Vintage Bicycle Collectors
325 West Hornbeam Dr.
Longwood, FL 32779-2532
ph: 407-862-0031
e-mail: thecabe@aol.com
web: http://www.tiac.net/users/cabe/
Listing phone numbers and addresses of people in the hobby.

Richard Truett
Arjay Communications, Inc.
Newsletter: Classic & Antique Bicycle Exchange
325 West Hornbeam Dr.
Longwood, FL 32779-2532
ph: 407-862-0031
e-mail: thecabe@aol.com
web: http://www.tiac.net/users/cabe/

Steve Culver
Newsletter: Classic Bike News
5046 East Wilson Rd.
Clio, MI 48420-9712
ph: 810-687-3528
fax: 810-687-3528
News, history, restoration tips, photo classifieds and much more.

Newsletter: Bicycle Trader, The
510 Frederick
San Francisco, CA 94117
ph: 415-876-1999 or 415-564-2304
fax: 415-876-4507
e-mail: info@bicycletrader.com
web: http://www.bicycletrader.com/

Repair Services

Donald Paquette
BikeIcons
3 Grove Circle
Saco, ME 04072
ph: 207-282-7336 or 207-282-4910
fax: 207-770-4455
e-mail: ride@bikeicons.com
web: http://www.bikeicons.com/
Buys, sells, trades, appraises and restores antique & classic bicycles; want to buy old bicycles, parts & collections.

Suppliers

Larry Busch
Memory Lane Classics
12551 Jefferson St.
Perrysburg, OH 43551
ph: 419-874-4501
e-mail: info@memorylane-classics.com
web: http://www.memorylane-classics.com
Publishes a catalog of old and reproduction parts for sale; also published the "Bicycle Blue Book" which lists current prices for vintage bikes.

Golden Era Bikes
26448 Rialto
Madison Heights, MI 48071
ph: 248-546-0842
Carries a wide variety of reproduction parts for vintage bicycles.

Maple Island Sales
59 W.S. 5th Lane
Lamar, MO 64759
ph: 417-682-6655
Carries a wide variety of reproduction parts for vintage bicycles.

Bikes-R-Us
P.O. Box 5065
Bossier City, LA 71171-5065
Supplier of parts for vintage bicycles; fully illustrated 60 page catalog for $7.50.

License Plates

Collectors

James C. Case
10189 Crane Rd.
Lindley, NY 14858-9719
ph: 607-524-6606
e-mail: hftlicense@aol.com
Wants pre-1920 sidepath tags (early bike licenses) from all states but especially New York.

Schwinn

Internet Resources

Schwinn Bicycle Company
1690 38th Street
Boulder, CO 80301
ph: 800-SCHWINN or 303-473-9609
fax: 303-473-9754
e-mail: schwinn@schwinn.com
web: http://www.schwinn.com/forums/collectornet.html
Website has Schwinn bicycle CollectorNet Online Forum, restoration forum, buy/sell/trade forum, collector forum archive, collector links, dating old bikes.

BILLIARD RELATED ITEMS

Collectors

Tim Lawrence
2489 Bexford Place
Columbus, OH 43209-1710
ph: 614-235-9472
Wants to buy billiard and pool tables, magazines, books, ivory balls, catalogs, art, old prints, billiard cigarette cards and postcards, antique cues and cue racks, and all other billiard related collectibles; pool table expert.

Maccoun
77 Beale #2313
San Francisco, CA 94106
ph: 415-973-2954
Wants to buy billiard memorabilia from Brunswick, Balke, Collender: catalogs, etc.

Dealers

Ed Lanza
Ed Lanza Billiard Co.
209 W. Evesham Ave.
Magnolia, NJ 08049
ph: 609-346-0384
Antique billiard and pool table accessories.

Paul Giammatteo
Yesteryear Billiards
509 Woodlawn Ave.
Newark, DE 19711-5537
ph: 302-453-8788 or 302-453-8823
fax: 302-454-1550
e-mail: pgiammatte@aol.com
Dealer and appraiser of antique pool and billiard tables, pool room accessories: cues, chairs, lights, catalogs, trade catalogs, books, ephemera, and related memorabilia; also does restoration of old pool tables.

Dilworth Billiards
300 East Tremont
Charlotte, NC 28203
ph: 704-333-3021
Wants pool tables, cues and accessories.

Mark Stellinga
416 Sierra Trail
Coralville, IA 52241-1124
ph: 319-354-7287
fax: 319-466-1989
e-mail: billiard@avalon.net
web: http://www.avalon.net/~billiard
Buys, sells, trades Victorian tables, cue and ball racks, lights, ivory balls, and related collectibles and accessories.

Steven Sawyer
Billiard Warehouse
103 Hardaman Ave.
South Saint Paul, MN 55075
ph: 800-422-7665 or 651-455-1150
fax: 651-455-1150
Wants pool and billiard items: old catalogs, books, posters, letterhead, racks, balls, cues, or anything billiard related.

Al Schwinghammer
Antique Billiard Tables & Accessories
3735 18th St. South
Saint Cloud, MN 56301
ph: 320-259-0294
e-mail: schwing@gte.net
web: http://home1.gte.net/schwing/index.htm
Featuring the finest in antique billiards restorations; 19th century Brunswick tables and rare accessories; buy, sell, trade; website has great billiards related links.

Simpson Ltd.
140 S Seminary St.
Galesburg, IL 61401-4805
ph: 309-342-5800
fax: 309-342-5730
e-mail: simpsonltd@misslink.net
web: http://www.simpsonltd.com/
Author of "Blue Book on Pool Cues"; want to buy old cues, cue racks, pool tables, old sets of ivory balls in boxes, old pool hall photos or prints, billiard trophies and medals - anything old that relates to pool or billiards.

Walt Baxley
Be-Bop Jukeboxes & Gameroom Goodies
11441 Stemmons Frwy., Ste. 133
Dallas, TX 75229
ph: 972-243-5725
fax: 972-243-2179
e-mail: bebops@aol.com
web: http://www.2nd-sight.com/bebop
Southwest's largest retailer of antique and collectible jukeboxes, pool tables, and other gameroom items; sales, service, restoration, and party rentals.

Alan Conway
1696 W. Morton Ave.
Porterville, CA 93257
ph: 559-782-0505
Wants to buy pre-1970 custom pool, billiard, and snooker cues with decoration or inlay; also wants pre-1930 pool tables with decoration or carving, and decorated cue and ball racks.

Dan M. Jacobson
P.O. Box 277101
Sacramento, CA 95827-7101
Wants to buy pool hall, billiard, snooker, and related advertising material.

Experts

Ken Hash
Classic Billiards
4302 Chapel Rd.
Perry Hall, MD 21128-9714
ph: 410-391-3333
e-mail: CBilliards@aol.com
Buys, sells, appraises and specializes in antique pool tables or related items; also offers repair/restoration/conservation services.

Periodicals

Sports Publications Ltd.
Magazine: Pool & Billiard Magazine
810 Travelers Blvd., #D
Summerville, SC 29485
ph: 843-875-5115 or 888-766-5624
fax: 843-875-5171
e-mail: shari@poolmag.com
web: http://www.poolmag.com/
Monthly magazine serving the sports industry and its participants; some articles feature antique and collectible tables and other equipment and related memorabilia.

Repair Services

Edward O'Connell
Time After Time
5 Padanaran Rd.
Danbury, CT 06811-4835
ph: 203-743-2801
e-mail: tatpool@snet.net
web: http://www.bca-pool.com/tat/
Wants pool tables, cues and accessories; sells museum quality antique pocket billiard tables; complete restoration service.

Brunswick

Collectors

Dave Wicker
Antique Billiard Center
400 S. Church St.
Monroe, NC 28112
ph: 704-289-4302
Wants Brunswick billiard items from 1845 to 1930: billiard table catalogs, posters, trade cards, lion's head pool tables (Monarchs), and any old paper memorabilia.

BILLIKENS

Collectors

Ronnie Kaplan
209 Harvard St.
Brookline, MA 02146
ph: 617-964-0619
Wants billikens or any information about them.

Judy A. Knauer
1224 Spring Valley Lane
West Chester, PA 19380-5112
ph: 610-431-3477
Wants items that feature a Billiken on them; anything from postcards to dolls and flatware; not interested in carved ivory, gemstones, or novelties from Alaska. Billiken - The God of Good Luck or The God of Things As They Ought To Be.

Belva Green
90 Highland Ave., #1204
Tarpon Springs, FL 34689
ph: 727-942-7354
e-mail: comber@iserv.net
Collecting anything Billikens, Royal Order of Jesters (ROJ): jewelry, figurines (ivory or other material), toys; old or new; query with SASE.

BINOCULARS

(see also OPTICAL ITEMS)

Experts

William M. Beacom
Quality Binoculars
2423 Jackson St.
Sioux City, IA 51104-3548
ph: 712-255-3412
fax: 712-255-0844
Wants binoculars of all types, foreign and domestic; can identify and appraise; also does repairs on some models or will buy any and all for parts.

BIRD DECOYS

(see DECOYS, Waterfowl)

BIRD'S-EYE-MAPLE

Collectors

Norwood H. Keeney, III
P.O. Box 1026
Georges Mills, NH 03751-1026
ph: 603-763-9157
e-mail: keeney@kear.tds.net
Wants items made from bird's-eye-maple, any period; also wants information about this wood and its use; photos encouraged.

BIRTH RELATED ITEMS

(see also PERSONALITIES [Famous], Dionne Quintuplets)

Museums/Libraries

"Miss Helen" Kirk
Multiple Birth Museum
P.O. Box 254
Galveston, TX 77553-0254
ph: 409-762-4792
Interested in anything related to any multiple births (triplets and above).

BISCUIT BARRELS/JARS/TINS

Collectors

Trudie & Les Anderson
Anderson Antiques & Gifts
5224 Sue Marie Lane
Houston, TX 77091
ph: 713-697-1858
Compiling complete history of the biscuit barrel/jar and cracker jars; seeking research material and ephemera; buys and collects Victorian and early 20th century biscuit and cracker barrels/jars.

BISQUE

(see CERAMICS, Bisque; CERAMICS [AMERICAN PRODUCTION ARTWARE], American Bisque Company)

BLACK MEMORABILIA

(see also ART, African & Tribal; CHARACTER COLLECTIBLES, Uncle Remus; CIVIL WAR ARTIFACTS; COLLECTIBLES [MODERN], Black Related; DOLLS, Black; MOVIE MEMORABILIA, Movie Posters [Black]; SLAVERY ITEMS)

Appraisers

Virgil J. Mayberry
V.J.M. Unlimited, Inc.
559 22nd Ave.
Rock Island, IL 61201-4129
ph: 309-786-6595
fax: 309-786-2114
Appraises one item or complete collections for insurance companies, individuals, and museums; over 30 years experience with black memorabilia; deals only in black memorabilia.

Clubs/Associations

Black Memorabilia Collector's Association
Newsletter: Collecting Our Culture
2482 Devoe Terrace
Bronx, NY 10468
ph: 212-946-1281
Provides information and promotes activities that encourage the

collecting, preservation and documentation of black memorabilia.

Collectors

Jan Thalberg
23 Mountain View Dr.
Weston, CT 06883-1317
ph: 203-227-8175
Wants early rag dolls, greeting cards, sewing items, children's books, kitchen items, Aunt Jemima items, playing cards, games & puzzles, canes, perfume bottles, mini bronzes, candy containers; photocopy helpful; please send SASE.

Constance Brendel
P.O. Box 8226
Jersey City, NJ 07308
ph: 201-451-7653
Wants to buy African American early quality photos, historical, military, occupations, Western, children.

Ed Natale, Jr.
P.O. Box 222
Wyckoff, NJ 07481
ph: 201-848-8485
fax: 201-848-8485
Wants to buy black memorabilia: insulting, exaggerated features; figurines, paper, signs; photos helpful.

Dr. E. Maynard
224 Mine Road
Monroe, NY 10950
ph: 914-783-1552
fax: 914-783-2480
e-mail: emayn37868@aol.com
Wants black American books and memorabilia: history, biography, fiction, non-fiction.

Richard Newman
83 Chauncey St.
Brooklyn, NY 11233
ph: 718-778-6614
Wants to buy/trade smoking items, toys, figurines, jewelry.

Gene Peters
'Tiques
P.O. Box 3267
Farmingdale, NY 11735-0679
ph: 516-842-9549
Wants documents, pictures, articles and artifacts relating to African-American life from the 18th century through the Civil Rights movement.

Judy Posner
4195 South Tamiami Trail, Ste. 183
Venice, FL 34293-5112
ph: 941-497-7149
fax: 941-493-8085
e-mail: jpc@tias.com
web: http://www.tias.com/stores/jpc/
Wants black Mammy and Chef cookie jars, salt & pepper shakers and kitchen items.

David L. Hartline
P.O. Box 775
Columbus, OH 43085-0775
Wants 1860-1950 medals, badges and awards given to Black soldiers; also wants military uniforms from Black regiments; prefers if inscribed; all letters answered; 30 years experience.

Mike Kranz
463 Stage Line Rd.
Hudson, WI 54016-7849
ph: 715-386-7333 or 715-386-9212
e-mail: juliekr@pressenter.com
Wants Black memorabilia: cookie jars, string holders, toys, salt & peppers, linens, advertising, etc.

John Hamilton
100 Military Rd.
Newport, MN 55055-1572
ph: 651-458-3939
e-mail: hammer3b@webtv.net
Wants to buy black collectibles: quality cookie jars, salt and peppers, humidors, toys, string holders, figures, advertising; wants one piece or entire collection.

Esther Roman
6087 Glen Harbor Drive
San Jose, CA 95123-4321
ph: 408-227-1162
Wants to buy Black memorabilia.

Dealers

Leslie Fleuranges
Mahogany Curio Collection
85 Maple St.
Teaneck, NJ 07666
ph: 201-836-7234
Specializing in black porcelain collectibles.

Rose Rontanella
324 Avenue F
Brooklyn, NY 11218
ph: 718-436-2099
Specializes in black memorabilia: books, dolls, toys, jewelry, magazines, prints, paintings, slave papers, ads, photos, posters, postcards, ceramics, linens, kitchen items.

Mark E. Mitchell
African-American History
3002 Winter Pine Ct.
Fairfax, VA 22031-1125
ph: 703-591-3150
fax: 703-385-3152
e-mail: info@mitchellarchives.com
web: http://www.mitchellarchives.com/
Buying and selling African-American letters, documents, prints, etc.

Arnold F. Winfield
Winfield Associates
P.O. Box 181
North Chicago, IL 60064-0181
ph: 847-475-8049
Buys and sells black exonumia including tokens, medals and other unusual collectibles.

Bindy Bitterman
Eureka! Antiques
705 W. Washington
Evanston, IL 60202-2214
ph: 847-869-9090
Wants to buy black memorabilia; everything from kitsch to historical; a small shop - they send no lists but write detailed individual letters; SASEs get first attention.

Experts

Dawn E. Reno
3280 Shingler Terrace
Deltona, FL 32738-5351
ph: 904-532-1960
fax: 904-532-1960
e-mail: DawnReno@juno.com
Author of "Encyclopedia of Black Collectibles" (1995, Chilton).

Jan Lindenberger
P.O. Box 7224
Colorado Springs, CO 80933
ph: 719-591-9558
fax: 719-591-9558
Buys and sells black memorabilia; author of "Black Memorabilia for the Kitchen - Information and Price Guide" and "Black Memorabilia Around the House - Information & Price Guide" (Schiffer Pub., 1993).

Misc. Services

UNICA Shows Unlimited
5406 9th St. NW
Washington, DC 20011
ph: 202-726-8931 or 301-445-2495

Esther Roman
6087 Glen Harbor Drive
San Jose, CA 95123-4321
ph: 408-227-1162
Exhibitions and lectures relating to Black memorabilia; workshops on how to start and build a Black collection.

Museums/Libraries

Anacostia Museum & Center for African American History & Culture
web: http://www.si.edu/organiza/museums/anacost/start.htm

African American Museum
1765 Crawford Rd.
Cleveland, OH 44106
ph: 216-791-1700
fax: 216-791-1774
e-mail: AfricanAmericanMuseum@clarence-webpage.com
web: http://www.ben.net/aamuseum/

Dr. John E. Fleming, Dir.
National Afro-American Museum & Culture Center
P.O. Box 578
Wilberforce, OH 45384-0578
ph: 937-376-4944
fax: 937-376-2007
e-mail: naamcc@erinet.com
web: http://winslo.ohio.gov/ohsww/places/afroam/index.html
Mission is to educate the public about African American heritage and culture from the African origins to the present by collecting, preserving, and interpreting material evidence of the Black experience.

Museum of African American History
315 E. Warren St.
Detroit, MI 48201
ph: 313-494-5800
fax: 313-494-5855
web: http://www.detnews.com/maah/
Dedicated to the preservation and presentation of African and African American history and culture.

Great Plains Black Museum
2213 Lake St.
Omaha, NE 68110
ph: 402-345-2212
web: http://www.omaga.org/oma/black.htm
One of 120 American museums belonging to the African American Museum Association; rare photographs, relics and historical displays.

Periodicals

Virgil J. Mayberry
V.J.M. Unlimited, Inc.
Newsletter: Blackin'
559 22nd Ave.
Rock Island, IL 61201-4129
ph: 309-786-6595
fax: 309-786-2114
Designed to inform subscribers of the different black memorabilia items being bought and sold; send $3 for sample issue.

Postcards (Dance Related)

Collectors

William G. Sommer, MD
9 W. 10th St.
New York, NY 10011-8748
ph: 212-260-0999
Wants post cards depicting African-American dancing, e.g. Cake Walk, Jitterbug; also Waltz, Tango, etc. & dance items in other media.

Sheet Music (Dance Related)

Collectors

William G. Sommer, MD
9 W. 10th St.
New York, NY 10011-8748
ph: 212-260-0999
Wants sheet music depicting African-American dancing, e.g. Cake Walk,

Jitterbug; also Waltz, Tango, etc. & dance items in other media.

BLACK POWDER RIFLES

(see FIREARMS, Rifles [Single Shot])

BLACKLIGHTS (UV LAMPS)

Dealers

Rick Morris
Rick's Black Lights & Art Glass
194 Stonefield Circle
Macon, GA 31206
ph: 912-781-5119
e-mail: southern@mindspring.com
web: http://www.mindspring.com/~southern1/blacklig.htm
Detect fakes and reproductions in cut glass, cast iron, paper products, pattern glass, vaseline glass, art glass and more.

Man./Prod./Dist.

A & B Jewels & Tools
350 West Grand River
Williamston, MI 48895
ph: 800-628-6657 or 517-655-4664
fax: 517-655-4665
e-mail: tooline@voyager.net
web: http://abtool.com/
Distributor for all Raytech products including ultraviolet lights, lapidary products, magnetic pin polishers, and glass restoration centers; also sells tools, supplies, equipment to make jewelry items; diamond testers.

UVP Inc.
2066 W 11th St.
Upland, CA 91786-3509
ph: 909-946-3197 or 800-452-6788
fax: 909-946-3597
e-mail: uvp@uvp.com
web: http://www.uvp.com
Manufacturers a wide range of ultraviolet lamps in long wave, shortwave, and midrange UV for brilliant fluorescence of rocks and minerals, and for use in detecting damages or repairs; battery-operated and standard voltage models available.

Don Newsome
UV Systems
16605 127th Ave. SE
Renton, WA 98058
ph: 425-228-9988 or 888-228-9988
fax: 425-228-9988
e-mail: uvsystems@aol.com
Sells the Superbright 2000SW and 2010LW short wave and long wave ultraviolet lights that are used primarily for mineralogical and geology applications, such as fluorescent minerals; also sells parts and supplies for other UV lights.

Misc. Services

Mark Chervenka
Antique & Collectors Reproduction News
P.O. Box 12130
Des Moines, IA 50312-9403
ph: 515-274-5886 or 800-227-5531 (orders)
fax: 515-255-4530
e-mail: acrn@repronews.com
web: http://www.repronews.com/
Sells pocket size to professional size models of readmission lights, invisible marking pens, etc.; publishes "Black Light for Antiques & Collectibles" 84 pg. book of tests for damages/repairs, fakes, reproductions on glass, china, paper.

BLACKSMITHING ITEMS

(see also KNIVES; TOOLS)

Collectors

Richard L. Weiss
1885 Klines Mill Rd.
Breinigsville, PA 18031
ph: 610-285-4122
e-mail: mrsdlw@prodigy.net
Wants rare and unusual blacksmithing tools, literature, advertising signs and related items.

Museums/Libraries

Eugene I. Morris, Dir.
New England Fire & History Museum
Newsletter: Siren Soundings
1439 Main St. (Rte. 6A)
Brewster, MA 02631
ph: 508-896-5711 or 508-432-2450
Mr. Morris appraises and has written many articles relating to fire fighting, apothecary and blacksmithing material.

BLIMPS

(see AIRSHIPS)

BLOTTERS

(see also INKWELLS & INKSTANDS; PAPER COLLECTIBLES; PENS)

Collectors

Homer Neel
4213 Westridge Dr.
North Little Rock, AR 72116
Wants old advertising ink blotters: all subjects, must be in mint condition.

Elaine Hinkle Crittenden
Calligraphy Heaven
14902 Preston Rd., Ste. 216
Dallas, TX 75240-9103
ph: 972-934-1055
fax: 972-934-1055
Buys inkwells and related items such as blotters, desk sets, dip pen points, etc.

John E. Kochenburger
1304 Robertson St.
Fort Collins, CO 80524-4258
ph: 304-484-0274
Collects a variety of inkstands, inkwells, ink bottles and "go-withs"; also buys and sells.

Dealers

Sam Fiorella
Pendemonium
15231 Larkspur Lane
Dumfries, VA 22026-1075
ph: 703-670-8549
fax: 703-670-3785
e-mail: sam@pendemonium.com
web: http://www.pendemonium.com
Buys and sells fountain pens, inkwells, ink bottles, pen stands, blotters, pen catalogs, magazine covers and advertisements; write for current "Writing Collectibles" catalog, it's FREE!

Bill Thompson
502 Woodhaven Rd.
Centerville, GA 31028-1327
Buys and sells anything related to writing; inkwells, rocker blotters, letter openers, lap desks, etc.

BLUE JEANS

(see CLOTHING & ACCESSORIES, Denim)

BLUE RIDGE

(see CERAMICS [AMERICAN DINNERWARE], Southern Potteries/ Blue Ridge)

BOATS

(see also OUTBOARD MOTORS; MODELS; NAUTICAL ANTIQUES; STEAMBOAT COLLECTIBLES; TOYS, Boats & Outboards)

Auction Services

David A. Norton
Norton Auctioneers of Michigan, Inc.
50 W. Pearl St.
Coldwater, MI 49036-1967
ph: 517-279-9063
fax: 517-279-9191
e-mail: nortonsold@cbpu.com
Conducts specialized auctions for antique, classic and collectible boats.

Clubs/Associations

Antique & Classic Boat Society
Magazine: Rusty Rudder
442 James St.
Clayton, NY 13624
ph: 315-686-2680
e-mail: hqs@acbs.org
web: http://www.acbs.org/
Has over 40 U.S. and Canadian chapters; not necessary to own a boat in order to be a member.

Collectors

C.E. Berry
13375 Havelock Trail
Apple Valley, MN 55124
Wants to buy boat catalogs and related literature; also factory items for any wooden boat from the 1890s to 1960s: Hacker, Garwood, Chris-Craft, Century, and others.

James King
1178 Chillem Dr.
Batavia, IL 60510-3309
ph: 630-879-2263
Wants to buy mahogany boats; inboard launches, runabouts, racers. Chris-Craft, Garwood, Greavette, Century, Streblow, etc.

Dealers

Antique Boat Connection
5521 Vine Street
Cincinnati, OH 45217
ph: 513-242-0808
fax: 513-242-0555
e-mail: lou@antiqueboat.com
web: http://www.antiqueboat.com
Specializes in the sale of classic boats: utilities, cruisers, runabouts, speedboats, launches, mahogany,inboard and outboard.

Lou Rauh
Antique Boat Connection
5521 Vine St.
Cincinnati, OH 45217
ph: 513-242-0808
fax: 513-242-0555
e-mail: lou@antiqueboat.com
web: http://www.antiqueboat.com
Collector, expert, appraiser, buyer, seller, and broker of antique and classic boats; also seller of reproduction wooden boats.

Experts

Wilson W. Wright
217 South Adams St.
Tallahassee, FL 32301-1708
ph: 850-224-2628
fax: 850-224-1033
e-mail: WWright@nettally.com
web: http://www.Chris-Craft.org
Specializes in antique boats.

Museums/Libraries

carlton J. Pinhiero
Herreshoff Marine Museum
One Burnside Street
P.O. Box 450
Bristol, RI 02809
ph: 401-253-5000
fax: 401-253-6222
e-mail: herreshoff@ids.net
web: http://www.naut-res-guild.org/museums/herreshf.html
Collection covers yachting, sail and power, Herreshoff and America's Cup memorabilia from 1840 to 1945; 2000 volume library, 500 photos, 100 other documents.

Maine Maritime Museum
Journal: Rumb Line, The
243 Washington St.
Bath, ME 04530
ph: 207-443-1316
fax: 207-443-1665
web: http://www.bathmaine.com
The repository and exhibition space for the premier collection of objects illustrating Maine's maritime heritage.

Adirondack Museum, The
Rte. 30
P.O. Box 99
Blue Mountain Lake, NY 12812-0099
ph: 518-352-7311
fax: 518-352-7653
web: http://www.adkmuseum.org/
Sponsors wooden boat regatta to learn about the rich heritage of boats in the region; has an extensive boat collection.

Antique Boat Museum
750 Mary St.
Clayton, NY 13624
ph: 315-686-4104
fax: 315-686-2775
e-mail: abm@gisco.net
web: http://it.stlawu.edu/~slcha/slip/abm.htm
General focus in on freshwater boats and engines: 150 antique and classic boats, 300 engines and related objects; conducts annual boat auction.

Pete Lesher, Cur.
Chesapeake Bay Maritime Museum
Magazine: Weather Gauge, The
P.O. Box 636
Saint Michaels, MD 21663-0636
ph: 410-745-2916
fax: 410-745-6088
e-mail: letters@cbmm.org
web: http://www.cbmm.org
A major regional maritime museum with a 10,00 volume research library; collections include 7,500 objects, 12,000 photos, 1,200 ships' plans, 100 linear feet of manuscripts; decoys, oystering, lighthouses, charts, nautical, tools.

Center for Wooden Boats, The
1010 Valley Street
Seattle, WA 98109-4332
ph: 206-382-2628
fax: 206-382-2699
e-mail: cwb@cwb.org
web: http://www.cwb.org/
Collection of over 100 historically significant boats; rental fleet; community outreach program.

Periodicals

Bob Hicks
Magazine: Messing About In Boats
29 Burley St.
Wenham, MA 01984
ph: 978-774-0906
Great biweekly magazine about interesting boats & people who design, build, restore and/or use them - sail, oar, antique, steam, etc.

Matt Murphy, Ed.
Magazine: WoodenBoat
P.O. Box 78
Brooklin, ME 04616
ph: 207-359-4651 or 800-877-5284
fax: 207-359-8920
e-mail: woodenboat@woodenboat.com
web: http://www.woodenboat.com
A glossy bi-monthly magazine for wooden boat owners, builders, and designers; construction plans and techniques, calendar of events, ads, navigation, wood and other boat building supplies, etc.

Trader Publishing Company
Magazine: Boat Trader
P.O. Box 9059
Clearwater, FL 34618-9059
ph: 727-712-0035 or 800-548-8889
fax: 727-712-0034
e-mail: webmaster@traderonline.com
web: http://www.traderonline.com
Offers hundreds of boats for sale by both private individuals, brokers and dealers.

Kelley Blue Book
Price Guide: Kelley Blue Book
5 Oldfield
Irvine, CA 92618
ph: 949-770-7704
fax: 949-837-1904
e-mail: kelley@kbb.com
web: http://www.kbb.com/indexv.html
Website offers current trade-in values for all makes and model cars for the past 21 years; also publishes printed value guides for cars, RV's, motorcycles, snowmobiles, motor homes, travel trailers, personal watercraft, etc.

Steve Ferguson, Ed.
National Automobile Dealers Association
Price Guide: N.A.D.A. Official Used Car Guide
P.O. Box 7800
Costa Mesa, CA 92628
ph: 800-544-6232
fax: 714-556-8715
e-mail: nada@nada.org
web: http://www.nada.org/
A series of value guides for domestic and foreign cars, trucks, vans, RV's, mobile homes, motorcycles, snowmobiles, and boats, small and large; also Heavy Duty Trucks and Aircraft Book, car clubs & organizations, museums.

Nic Compton, Ed.
Link House Magazines
Magazine: Classic Boat
Link House, Dingwall Ave.
Croydon, Surrey CR9 2TA
U.K.
ph: +44 (0) 181 686 2599
fax: +44 (0) 181 781 6535
e-mail: cb@lhm.co.uk
web: http://www.classicboat.co.uk/
Britain's best selling traditional boat magazine; monthly articles on yachting and work boat histories by leading writers' lively news and opinion pages debating all the current issues in the traditional boat world; restoration tips.

Repair Services

Clawson Classic Instruments
2402 30th Street
Anacortes, WA 98221
ph: 360-299-8636
fax: 360-299-2836
Specializes in the professional restoration of boat instruments.

Repro. Sources

Lou Rauh
Antique Boat Connection
5521 Vine St.
Cincinnati, OH 45217
ph: 513-242-0808
fax: 513-242-0555
e-mail: lou@antiqueboat.com
web: http://www.antiqueboat.com
Collector, expert, appraiser, buyer, seller, and broker of antique and classic boats; also seller of reproduction wooden boats.

Suppliers

Wooden Boat Shop, The
1007 Northeast Boat Street
Seattle, WA 98105
ph: 206-634-3600 or 800-933-3600
fax: 206-632-9101
e-mail: wbs@halcyon.com
web: http://www.halcyon.com/wbs/wbs1.htm
A retail and mail order store supplying kits, plans, materials, tools, books, technical assistance, and classes to hundreds of backyard boat builders and boat owners.

Canoes

Clubs/Associations

P. Christopher Merigold, Pres.
Wooden Canoe Heritage Association, Ltd.
Magazine: Wooden Canoe
P.O. Box 226
Blue Mountain Lake, NY 12812
ph: 803-643-3800
e-mail: webmaster@wcha.org
web: http://www.wcha.org/
Non-profit association dedicated to preserving, studying, building, restoring and using wooden and birch bark canoes; articles and ads for supplies, restorers, parts, gatherings, etc.; chapters across the U.S. and Canada.

Canadian Recreational Canoeing Association
Magazine: Kanawa
P.O. Box 398
446 Main St. West
Merrickville, Ontario K0G 1N0
Canada
ph: 888-252-6292 or 613-269-2910
fax: 613-269-2908
e-mail: staff@crca.ca
web: http://www.crca.ca/kanawa.html
The "Voice of Paddling in Canada", 72-page full color magazine covering everything you need to know about canoeing and kayaking.

Misc. Services

David Gidmark
Box 26
Maniwaki, Quebec J9E 3B3
Canada
Offers course on birch bark canoe building.

Periodicals

Magazine: Canoe Magazine
P.O. Box 420235
Palm Coast, FL 32142-0235
ph: 800-829-3340
e-mail: wembaster@canoekayak.com
web: http://www.canoekayak.com/
Glossy magazine for the canoe and kayak enthusiast; occasional articles on collectible boats and kayaks.

Repair Services

Northwoods Canoe Co.
RFD 3 Box 118-A2
Dover Foxcroft, ME 04426
Restores classic boats and builds custom boats.

McGreivey's Canoe Shop
1379 Old State Rd.
Cato, NY 13033
ph: 315-626-6635
Restorers of classic canoes and guide boats.

Gilbert Cramer
Wooden Canoe Shop, Inc.
03583 RD 13
Bryan, OH 43506-9804
ph: 419-636-1689
e-mail: gcramer@williams-net.com
Repairs and restorations of wood/ canvas canoes and boats; buys and sells unrestored canoes and sells restored canoes.

West Coast Canoe Company
P.O. Box 143
Campbell River, British Columbia V9W 5A7
Canada
ph: 250-287-7348
Wooden canoe restoration and repairs.

Chris Crafts

Clubs/Associations

Wilson W. Wright, Ex.Dir.
Chris Craft Antique Boat Club, Inc.
Newsletter: Brass Bell
217 South Adams St.
Tallahassee, FL 32301-1708
ph: 850-224-2628
fax: 850-224-1033
e-mail: WWright@nettally.com
web: http://www.Chris-Craft.org
Assists members with collecting, restoring, maintaining vintage Chris Crafts; quarterly newsletter has antique boat show calendar, articles, how-to hints, ads, restorers/boat works, model builders, marine instrument repairs, etc.

Engines

Collectors

James King
1178 Chillem Dr.
Batavia, IL 60510-3309
ph: 630-879-2263
Wants to buy old inboard marine engines, one to twelve cylinders. Marinized aero engines, racing engines. Scripps, Kermath, Hisso, Packard, etc.

Model

Clubs/Associations

John Snow
U.S. Vintage Model Yacht Group
Newsletter: Vintage Model Yacht Newsletter
78 East Orchard St.
Marblehead, MA 01945
ph: 781-631-4203 or 781-639-0779
e-mail: boebert@swcp.com
web: http://www.swcp.com/usvmyg
Devoted to the preservation and sailing of older wooden model sailboats (pond boats) and to the study of the history of model yachting in North America; library of old model yachting, periodicals, articles and design plans available.

Collectors

Susan P. Meisel
135 Prince St.
New York, NY 10012
ph: 212-254-0137
fax: 212-533-7340
e-mail: susan@meisels.com
web: http://www.spyonthis.com/spmda
Wants to buy pond sailboats, big and small, whole or parts.

Dealers

J. Tobin
Antique & Classic Boats
12 Carstead Dr.
Slingerlands, NY 12159
ph: 518-439-0477
fax: 518-439-0477
Buys and sells pond boats - late 19th and early 20th century sail boats designed to be sailed on ponds.

Steam

Clubs/Associations

Bill Mueller
International Steamboat Society
Journal: Steamboating
Rte. 1 Box 262
Middlebourne, WV 26149-9748
ph: 304-386-4434
fax: 304-386-4868
e-mail: steam@steamboating.com
web: http://www.steamboating.com/
"Steamboating" magazine provides contemporary information on how to acquire, build, operate, maintain, and enjoy a steam-powered vessel.

Collectors

Robin Corsiglia
Toy Steam Engines
5200 NE 9th Lane
Ocala, FL 34470
ph: 352-236-2635 or 352-680-3022
e-mail: marklinc@atlantic.net
web: http://members.atlantic.net/~marklinc/
Buys, sells and collects toy steam engines (stationary with real boilers and flywheels) and tin pop-pop boats, tin wind up boats, and tin battery boats; mainly collects buy also buys, sells, trades and gives out information.

Internet Resources

Al Dunlop
Steamboating
e-mail: djd@openix.com
web: http://www.openix.com/steamboating/
Publications, societies, museums, lots of steam boat links.

Periodicals

David Thompson
Newsletter: Stem to Stern
P.O. Box 175
Moultonborough, NH 03254

Tug

Clubs/Associations

Tugboat Enthusiasts Society of the Americas
Magazine: Tug Bitts
308 Quince St.
Mount Pleasant, SC 29464-3420
ph: 843-881-1173
Published quarterly; covers steamboat & inland river history; packed with news, photos, articles on all types of tow boats, tugboats (harbor, ocean, military) and work boat salvage, restoration and history; a must for tugboat enthusiasts.

Yachts

Appraisers

John E. Bakken, ASA
Business Appraisal Associates, Inc.
2777 South Colorado Blvd., Ste. 200
Denver, CO 80222
ph: 303-758-8818
fax: 303-758-6164
e-mail: jbakken@juno.com
Specializes in yacht appraisals; also has ASA designations in business valuation and in oil and gas valuation.

Clubs/Associations

Scottie Dobson
Classic Yacht Association
149-b West Ave. Marquita
San Clemente, CA 92672
fax: 714-366-2987
e-mail: georgeh@classicyacht.org
web: http://www.classicyacht.org
A non-profit organization of collectors, restorers and skippers of classic (pre-1942) yachts and boats; a major influence in growing awareness and appreciation for the classic.

Periodicals

Trader Publishing Company
Magazine: Yacht Trader
P.O. Box 9059
Clearwater, FL 34618-9059
ph: 727-712-0035 or 800-548-8889
fax: 727-712-0034
e-mail: webmaster@traderonline.com
web: http://www.traderonline.com
Offers hundreds of luxury motor and sailing yachts for sale by both private individuals, brokers and dealers.

BONES

(see ANIMAL TROPHIES; FURNITURE [ANTIQUE], Antler & Horn; ODDITIES & THE MORBID; SKELETONS)

BOOK ARTS

(see also BOOKS, Repair Services for; PRINTING EQUIPMENT)

Museums/Libraries

University of California, Special Collections Department
P.O. Box 5900
Riverside, CA 92517
ph: 909-787-3233 or 909-784-7324
fax: 909-787-3285
e-mail: sidney.berger@ucr.edu
web: http://library.ucr.edu/about/services/spec_coll/spec_main.html
Collection of material on the Book Arts, especially book binding, papermaking, fine presses, forgeries, etc.

BOOKENDS

Clubs/Associations

Louis Kuritzky
Bookend Collectors Club
Newsletter: Bookend Collectors Club Newsletter
4510 N.W. 17th Place
Gainesville, FL 32605-3479
ph: 352-376-3884 or 352-377-3193
fax: 352-377-3193
e-mail: lkuritsky@aol.com
Color newsletter published quarterly.

Experts

Gerald P. (Jerry) McBride
4005 Dellbrook Drive
Tampa, FL 33624
ph: 813-264-4005
e-mail: charlotteweb@earthlink.net
Specialist in metal bookends; author of "A Collector's Guide to Cast Metal Bookends."

BOOKLETS

(see PAPER COLLECTIBLES)

BOOKMARKS

(see also PAPER CLIPS; STEVENGRAPHS)

Collectors

Joan L. Huegel
1002 West 25th St.
Erie, PA 16502-2427

Experts

Dr. Judith Ackerman
P.O. Box 354
West Long Branch, NJ 07764-0354
ph: 732-531-3624
fax: 732-222-9214
e-mail: ackerman1@home.com
Researching and writing about all aspects of bookmarks, including all materials, periods and styles.

Periodicals

Joan L. Huegel
Newsletter: Bookmark Collector
1002 West 25th St.
Erie, PA 16502-2427
A friendly, informative newsletter for all collectors; for those wanting only antique as well as those who collect new and modern bookmarks, too; published quarterly.

Notched

Collectors

John T. Ogle
P.O. Box 252
Ocean Springs, MS 39566-0252
Wants to buy paper clips and notched bookmarks: antique, foreign, plastic, novelty, advertising; also wants early paper clip advertising.

BOOKPLATES

Clubs/Associations

Audrey Spencer Arellanes, Ed.
American Society of Bookplate Collectors & Designers
Newsletter: Bookplates in the News
605 N. Stoneman Ave., No. F
Alhambra, CA 91801-1406
ph: 626-570-9404
Quarterly newsletter features articles on contemporary bookplate artists & collectors, news of exhibitions, competitions, literature.

Bryan Welch, Sec.
Bookplate Society
Journal: Bookplate Society Newsletter
11 Nella Road
London, W6 9PB
U.K.
Write for details; membership includes journal and newsletter, free book and bookplates.

Collectors

Lewis Jaffe
1919 Chestnut St., Apt. 1117
Philadelphia, PA 19103-3418
fax: 610-568-6768
e-mail: exlibris@webtv.net
Active buyer of bookplate (exlibris) collections and accumulations.

Dealers

Thomas G. Boss
Thomas G. Boss Fine Books
355 Boylston St.
Boston, MA 02116-3313
ph: 617-427-1880
fax: 617-536-7072
e-mail: boss@tiac.net
web: http://www.tiac.net/users/boss/
Carries the largest stock of bookplates in the U.S.; Art Deco, Art Nouveau, Arts & Crafts; also fine bindings.

James Wilson
22 Castle St.
Berkhamsted, Hertfordshire HP4 2DW
U.K.
ph: 01442-873396
Largest dealer in England for bookplates and books about bookplates.

BOOKS

(see also ACCOUNT BOOKS; AUTOGRAPH BOOKS; ATLASES; AUCTION CATALOGS; BIBLES; BOOK ARTS; COMIC BOOKS; COOKBOOKS; DIARIES; HYMNALS; ILLUSTRATORS; MAPS & CHARTS; MYSTERY/DETECTIVE ITEMS; PAPER COLLECTIBLES; PERSONALITIES [LITERARY]; SCIENCE FICTION)

Appraisers

Lee Temares
50 Heights Rd.
Plandome, NY 11030-1413
ph: 516-627-8688 or 516-627-2647
fax: 516-627-7822
e-mail: tembooks@aol.com
Buys children's series books; must have dust jackets if they originally had them; also wants Limited Editions Club and Heritage Press books, but must be in very good condition and in fine boxes; appraises all books except law & medicine.

Kevin T. Ransom
Kevin T. Ransom Bookseller
P.O. Box 176
Amherst, NY 14226
ph: 716-839-1510
First editions and rare books.

David Szewczyk
Philadelphia Rare Books & Manuscripts Company
P.O. Box 9536
Philadelphia, PA 19124
ph: 215-744-6734
fax: 215-755-6137
e-mail: rarebks@prbm.com
web: http://www.prbm.com
Buying and selling books printed in England from before 1801, on the European continent before 1750, and in the Americas before 1830; all languages, most topics; manuscripts of a substantive nature, not autographs; member ABAA, ILAB.

Auction Services

Richard & Mary Sykes
New Hampshire Book Auctions
P.O. Box 460
Weare, NH 03281
ph: 603-529-7432
Specializes in the auction of books, maps, prints and ephemera.

Caroline Birenbaum
Swann Galleries, Inc.
104 E. 25th St.
New York, NY 10010-2977
ph: 212-254-4710
fax: 212-979-1017
e-mail: swann@swanngalleries.com
web: http://www.swanngalleries.com/
Oldest/largest U.S. auctioneer specializing in rare books, autographs & manuscripts, maps, atlases, photographs, and works of art on paper including vintage posters.

Lynn Martin
Freeman/Fine Arts of Philadelphia
1808 Chestnut St.
Philadelphia, PA 19103
ph: 610-563-9275 or 610-563-9453
fax: 610-563-8236
web: http://www.artlibrary.com/freeman/
America's oldest auction house: Continental, English and American furniture, paintings, silver and decorative arts; Oriental rugs, rare books, fine jewelry, Orientalia.

Dale Sorenson
Waverly Auctions, Inc.
4931 Cordell Ave.
Bethesda, MD 20814-2508
ph: 301-951-8883
fax: 301-718-8375
e-mail: wavauc@clark.net
web: http://www.waverlyauctions.com
Specializes in the auction of graphic art, books, paper, atlases, prints, postcards, autographs, and other paper ephemera.

Chris Bready
Baltimore Book Co., Inc.
2114 N. Charles St.
Baltimore, MD 21218
ph: 410-659-0550
Buys and auctions books, prints, paintings, autographs, photographs, and ephemera.

Stephen Neil Greengard
California Book Auction Galleries
220 San Bruno Ave.
San Francisco, CA 94103-5018
ph: 415-861-7500
fax: 415-861-8951
e-mail: info@butterfields.com
web: http://www.butterfields.com/

George K. Fox
Pacific Book Auction Galleries
133 Kearny St., 4th Floor
San Francisco, CA 94108-4805
ph: 415-989-2665
fax: 415-989-1664
e-mail: pba@slip.net
web: http://www.pacificbook.com
Conducts numerous auctions each year of rare books, manuscripts, maps, autographs, historical material, early photography, prints, and fine literary property; all auction catalogs are on the web, so bid by e-mail directly from the site.

Book Sellers

Beverly Joy-Karno
Howard Karno Books, Inc.
P.O. Box 2100
Valley Center, CA 92082
ph: 760-749-2304 or 800-345-2766
fax: 760-749-4390
e-mail: info@karnobooks.com
web: http://www.karnobooks.com
Book dealer, appraiser, expert; specialists in Latin American subjects, including the Caribbean.

Clubs/Associations

Antiquarian Booksellers' Association of America (ABAA)
Newsletter: ABAA Newsletter
20 West 44th St., 4th Floor
New York, NY 10036
ph: 212-944-8291
fax: 212-944-8293
e-mail: abaa@panix.com
web: http://www.abaa-booknet.com/booknet1.html
A non-profit association; publishes a membership directory and a newsletter.

Lee Temares
Long Island Antiquarian Book Dealers Association
Newsletter: LIABDA Newsletter
P.O. Box 622
Plandome, NY 11030
ph: 516-627-8688 or 516-627-2647
fax: 516-627-7822
e-mail: Tembooks@aol.com

Lee Harrer
Florida Bibliophile Society
Newsletter: FBL Newsletter
P.O. Box 3887
Saint Petersburg, FL 33731-3887
ph: 727-536-4029
Newsletter is published monthly.

Antiquarian Booksellers' Association
Sackville House
40 Piccadilly, London W1V 9PA
U.K.
ph: 44-171-439-3118
fax: 44-171-439-3119
e-mail: info@aba.org.uk
web: http://www.aba.org.uk
The senior trade body for dealers in rare and fine books, manuscripts and allied material in the British Isles and elsewhere; founded in 1906.

Collectors

Tom Rutledge
3015 Bever Ave., SE
Cedar Rapids, IA 52403-3028
ph: 319-399-1427
Wants rare & antiquarian books, manuscripts, autographs, first editions, children's books, fore-edge painted books, illustrated books, Modern Library books, pop-ups, Asian art, and collectible paperbacks.

Dealers

Robert Lucas
Robert F. Lucas Antiquarian Books
P.O. Box 63
Blandford, MA 01008
ph: 413-848-2061
e-mail: books@lucasbooks.com
web: http://www.lucasbooks.com
Mail order, on-line sales of antiquarian books, ephemera; specializing in books, ephemera by & about Emily Dickinson and Henry D. Thoreau, 19th century Americana, and manuscript Americana; member ABAA; online essay on book collecting.

Steve Finer
Steve Finer Rare Books
38 Grinnell St.
Greenfield, MA 01302-3621
ph: 413-773-5811
e-mail: finerbks@crocker.com

Thomas G. Boss Fine Books
355 Boylston St.
Boston, MA 02116-3313
ph: 617-427-1880
fax: 617-536-7072
e-mail: boss@tiac.net
web: http://www.tiac.net/users/boss/
Fine printing, fine binding and illustration, especially in the 1890-1946 period; also bookplates, drawings, posters, and prints.

Clare Murphy
Payson Hall Books
321 Trapelo Road
Belmont, MA 02178
ph: 617-484-2020
fax: 617-484-0580
e-mail: payson@oldbooks.com
web: http://www.tiac.net/users/payson/

Jeff Gubitosi
Booktiques
165 Palmer St.
Arlington, MA 02474-3328
ph: 781-648-3328
e-mail: booktiques@aol.com

Karen & Jim Weyant
Scribe's Perch, The
P.O. Box 3295
Newport, RI 02840-0324
ph: 401-682-1743
fax: 401-682-1752
e-mail: karen@scribesperch.com
web: http://www.scribesperch.com/
Dealers in out-of-print and collectible books; specializing in childrens, Americana, military history, nautical, literature; has searchable database on web site.

George & Julie Perron
Old Paperphiles, The
P.O. Box 135
Tiverton, RI 02878-0135
ph: 401-624-9420
fax: 401-624-4204
Buys and sells paper collectibles: books, autographs, sheet music, postcards, photos, stereoviews, documents, old letters; issues periodic catalog of items for sale.

Jon Mayo
Tuttle Antiquarian Books Inc.
28 South Main St.
Rutland, VT 05701
ph: 802-773-8229
fax: 802-773-1493
e-mail: tuttbook@together.net
web: http://www.tuttlebooks.com
Three floors of used books specializing in Americana, Orientalia, genealogy; welcomes quotations and inquiries concerning miniature books, genealogies, and family histories.

Barbara & Richard DePalma
Deer Park Books
609 Kent Rd., Route 7
Gaylordsville, CT 06755
ph: 860-350-4140
fax: 860-350-4140
e-mail: DeerParkBk@aol.com
web: http://www.abebooks.com/home/BARBDE/
Fine books bought and sold; antiquarian books, modern first editions, children's and illustrated; also maps, autographs, etc.; all subjects; also wants handwritten diaries, travel journals, scrapbooks, albums.

Bel Canto Books
P.O. Box 55
Metuchen, NJ 08840-0055
ph: 732-548-7371
Wants books about music and dance.

J.N. Bartfield
J.N. Bartfield Books, Inc.
30 West 57th St.
Third Floor
New York, NY 10019
ph: 212-245-8890
fax: 212-541-4860
Wants to buy fine books: Americana, atlases, Canadiana, color plate books, fore-edge painting, fine leather bindings, rare books, first editions, sporting books, autographs, manuscripts, original diaries and journals.

Bibi Mohamed
Imperial Fine Books, Inc.
790 Madison Ave. Ste. 200
New York, NY 10021
ph: 212-861-6620
fax: 212-249-0333
e-mail: Imperial@dir-dd.com
web: http://dir-dd.com/imperial-fine-books.html
Fine books bought and sold; sets, fine and decorative bindings, first editions, fore-edge paintings, children's & illustrated books, etc.; issues catalogs; bookbinding.

Argosy Book Store
116 East 59th St.
New York, NY 10022
ph: 212-753-4455
Carries rare books in all subject areas.

Antipodean Books, Maps & Prints
P.O. Box 189
Cold Spring, NY 10516
ph: 914-424-3867
fax: 914-424-3617
e-mail: Antipbooks@highlands.com
web: http://www.highlands.com/Business/Antipodean.html
Books, maps, prints.

Joanmarie Dale
Stray Books
192 Pinewood Road, #87
Hartsdale, NY 10530-1414
ph: 914-761-1198 or 914-761-1198
e-mail: StrayBks@compuserve.com
web: http://ourworld.compuserve.com/homepages/StrayBks/
Specializes in mail order Modern First Editions; offers free book searches.

Helen & Marc Younger
Aleph-Bet Books, Inc.
218 Waters Edge
Valley Cottage, NY 10989
ph: 914-268-7410
fax: 914-268-5942
e-mail: helen@alephbet.com
web: http://www.alephbet.com/
Specializing in fine first editions of collectible and rare children's and illustrated books; always interested in buying books in fine condition; business established in 1978.

Diana Rudy
Book Look
P.O. Box 450
Warwick, NY 10990
ph: 800-223-0540
fax: 914-651-1233
e-mail: sales@booklook.com
web: http://www.booklook.com
Largest out-of-print book search service in the U.S.; any book located.

Dan Weaver
Daniel T. Weaver, Bookseller
21 Bunn St.
Amsterdam, NY 12010-3505
ph: 518-842-3498
Buys and sells used and out-of-print books in almost all subject areas, but especially Protestant religion, children's books and books for home schoolers; also offers search service.

Darrel Dillon
Stone House Books
2635 Valley Dr.
Nedrow, NY 13120
ph: 315-469-6432
e-mail: shbooks@mail.concentric.net
web: http://www.concentric.net/~shbooks/
Dealer in fine used and rare books; specialty is Sci/Fi, Mystery, Horror, and Juvenile; house authors include Edgar Rice Burroughs, Michael Crichton, Stephen King, Douglas Adams, Issac Asimov, Ian Fleming; has over 10,000 books.

Michael Tokman
A-ha! Books, Inc.
3 Cedar Lane
Ithaca, NY 14850
ph: 607-257-9200
fax: 607-257-1540
e-mail: ahabooks@lightlink.com
web: http://www.lightlink.com/tokman/
Buys and sells rare, antiquarian and out-of-print books, autographs, and maps; online catalog, book search service.

George S. MacManus Co.
1317 Irving St.
Philadelphia, PA 19107
ph: 215-735-4456
fax: 215-735-3635
e-mail: macmanus9@aol.com

David Szewczyk
Philadelphia Rare Books & Manuscripts Company
P.O. Box 9536
Philadelphia, PA 19124
ph: 215-744-6734
fax: 215-755-6137
e-mail: rarebks@prbm.com
web: http://www.prbm.com
Buying and selling books printed in England from before 1801, on the European continent before 1750, and in the Americas before 1830; all languages, most topics; manuscripts of a substantive nature, not autographs; member ABAA, ILAB.

Carmen D. Valentino
Rare Books & Manuscripts
2956 Richmond St., Drawer 19
Philadelphia, PA 19134-5720
ph: 215-739-6056
Antiquarian bookseller specializing in rare books, manuscripts, documents, early newspapers, handwritten diaries, account books and ledgers, ephemera, broadsides; pre-WWI.

Howard Weetall
Antiquarian Bookworm, The
7315 Wisconsin Ave.
Bethesda, MD 20814-3202
ph: 301-656-3779
Buying and selling out-of-print books since 1968; Americana, Civil War, non-fiction, natural History; interested in purchasing good quality books, maps, and prints.

Stan Modjesky
Book Miser, Inc.
2133 Gwynn Oak Ave., Ste. 200
Baltimore, MD 21207
ph: 410-281-2121
fax: 410-281-2121
e-mail: Books@bookmiser.com
web: http://www.bookmiser.com/
Dealer in used, rare and new books; specializes in music, opera, ballet, theatre, motion pictures, history and Americana books; ABE participants; Bibliofind participants; open by appointment.

Jack Hamilton
Hamilton's Book Store
1784 Jamestown Rd.
Williamsburg, VA 23185
ph: 757-220-3000
fax: 757-220-1820
e-mail: goodbook@goodbooks.com
web: http://www.goodbooks.com/
Books, autographs, black history, documents, ephemera, illustrated, maps, genealogy.

Bookpress, Ltd., The
P.O. Box KP
Williamsburg, VA 23187
ph: 757-229-1260
fax: 757-229-0498
e-mail: bookpress@widowmaker.com
web: http://www.bookpress.com
A rare book service buying and selling fine books, old maps and prints.

Jim Reed
Reed Books
P.O. Box 55893
Birmingham, AL 35255-5893
ph: 205-326-4460
fax: 205-326-4468
e-mail:
JimReedBooks@compuserve.com
Reed Books is a specialized, international book search company that finds old out-of-print books and magazines.

Ivan Gilbert, MD
Miran Art & Books
2824 Elm Ave.
Columbus, OH 43209
ph: 614-231-3707 or 614-818-3222
fax: 614-818-3223
e-mail: IGilbert@ahhinc.com
Specializing in illustrated books, in particular color plates, childrens, medical, photography, erotica, 16th/17th/18th century.

Joe Davidson
Aaron's Archives
5185 Windfall Rd.
Medina, OH 44256-8703
ph: 330-723-7172
Wants to buy pre-1895 books containing color plates, etchings, engravings plus pre-1600 Medieval books and manuscripts.

Richard D. Hendrickson
ArchBooks, Inc.
P.O. Box 24642
Minneapolis, MN 55424
ph: 612-927-0298
fax: 612-927-0550
e-mail: info@archbooks.com
web: http://www.archbooks.com/
One of the largest inventories of out-of-print or hard-to-find children's titles in the U.S.; over 55,000 titles in stock; in business for over 20 years.

William Butts
Main Street Fine Books & Manuscripts
206 N. Main St.
Galena, IL 61035-2244
ph: 815-777-3749
fax: 815-777-8950
e-mail: msfb@galenalink.com
web: http://www.wcinet.com/msfbooks
Open shop dealing in autographs and out-of-print books in most fields; specializing in all aspects of American history; books and autograph catalogs issued regularly; member of A.B.A.A.

Bob & Beverlee Reimers
Peddler's Wagon
P.O. Box 109
Lamar, MO 64759-0109
ph: 417-682-3734
Buys and sells books on quilting, needlework, children's illustrated books, Little Golden books, and series books; mail order only.

Coyote Shadow
A Sentimental Journey
Figger-Dude Rance
4501 Pyeatt
Gladewater, TX 75647-9232
ph: 903-845-6693
fax: 903-845-5621
e-mail: asjourney@texramp.net
web: http://www.texramp.net/~asjourney/
Specializes in fine books and books about religion.

Nita Anderson
2812 Country Road 920
Crowley, TX 76036-5732
ph: 817-297-7287

Barbara Ruppert
Alcott Books
5909 Darnell
Houston, TX 77074-7719
ph: 713-774-2202
Wants to buy books: Dick and Jane Readers, first edition mysteries with dust jackets, signed editions, early first editions of Stephen King, books illustrated by Maxfield Parrish, OZ books.

Barrie D. Watson
Barrie D. Watson Bookseller
8760 Grand Ave.
P.O. Box 38
Beulah, CO 81023
ph: 719-485-3136 or 800-785-3136
fax: 719-485-3838
e-mail: watsonbk@usa.net
web: http://members.iex.net/~watsonbk/

Len Unger
Len Unger Rare Books
P.O. Box 5858
Sherman Oaks, CA 91413
ph: 818-990-7569
fax: 818-905-7909
e-mail: lenunger@ix.netcom.com
web: http://www.abaa-booknet.com/usa/len.unger/
Specializes in modern first editions, mystery, Western fiction, Zane Grey, signed books, autographs, and books made into movies.

Howard L. Karon
Howard Karno Books, Inc.
P.O. Box 2100
Valley Center, CA 92082
ph: 760-749-2304
fax: 760-749-4390
e-mail: howard@karnobooks.com
web: http://www.cts.com/~karnobks/
Particular specialty area is in Latin American arts: graphic, architecture, archaeology, dance, music.

Barbara Gelink
OTENTO Book Search
4756 Terrace Dr.
San Diego, CA 92116-2514
ph: 619-281-8962
e-mail: cookwithbabs@home.com
web: http://www.sandiegoinsider.com/community/groups/cookbook/
Book finder for out-of-print books; places ads in national book magazines and has realized a 50% success rate; charges $2 per title to locate book which usually takes 2-3 months; specializes in cookbooks, children's books, and bibles.

Jean Parmer
Parmer Books
7644 Forrestal Rd.
San Diego, CA 92120-2203
ph: 619-287-0693
fax: 619-287-6135
e-mail: parmerbook@aol.com
Polar, Arctic, Antarctic, voyages, sail, Pacific, exploration.

Richard Gilbo
Richard Gilbo - Bookseller
P.O. Box 12
Carpinteria, CA 93014-0012
ph: 805-684-2892
Specializes in books about food and drink, cats; also specializes in literature.

Thorn Books
P.O. Box 1244
Moorpark, CA 93020
ph: 805-529-3647
fax: 805-529-0022
e-mail: info@thornbooks.com
web: http://www.thornboks.com/
Offers antiquarian, rare and out-of-print books.

David B. Ogle
Antiquarian Archive, The
379 State St.
Los Altos, CA 94022-2816
ph: 650-949-1593
e-mail: archive@batnet.com
web: http://www.ippi.com/antiquarian-archive.html
Specialist in Western Americana, railroadiana, nautical & maritime, military history & memoirs, books of the Roycroft printing shop.

Tom Haydon
Wessex Books
558 Santa Cruz Ave.
Menlo Park, CA 94025
ph: 650-321-1333
fax: 650-856-1984
e-mail: info@wessexbooks.com
web: http://www.wessexbooks.com
Over 12,000 modern literary first editions, related criticism, and biography for sale: fiction, poetry, University Press titles, Literature in Translation, British and American first editions.

Brick Row Book Shop
49 Geary St. #235
San Francisco, CA 94108-5705
ph: 415-398-0414
fax: 415-398-0435
e-mail: crichton@brickrow.com
web: http://www.brickrow.com
Specializes in first editions of English and American literature, especially of the 18th and 19th centuries; over 8,000 titles in stock; want lists accepted; buys fine and rare books.

Alan Bamberger
2510 Bush St.
San Francisco, CA 94115-3002
ph: 415-931-7875
fax: 415-922-3580
e-mail: alanb@artbusiness.com
web: http://www.artbusiness.com
Buys and sells rare, out-of-print and collectible reference books on the fine and decorative arts; member Antiquarian Booksellers Association of America, Intentional League of Antiquarian Booksellers.

J.B. Muns
Fine Arts Books & Musical Autographs
1162 Shattuck Ave.
Berkeley, CA 94707-2635
ph: 510-525-2420
fax: 510-525-1126
Buys and sells books: art, architecture, dance, photography; member

ABAA, Manuscript Society, UACC, PADA; serving libraries, the public and other dealers since 1964; by appointment only.

Sandi Pitcher
18610 Castle Hill Drive
Morgan Hill, CA 95037
ph: 408-782-1987
fax: 408-782-1488
e-mail: sewinsandi@aol.com
Liquidating estates; has extensive old book collection; many first editions, autographed, leather bound, uncut pages; contact for complete listing.

Steve Mauer
BookMine.com
1015 2nd St.
Sacramento, CA 95814
e-mail: books@bookmine.com
web: http://www.bookmine.com/
Specializes in rare books: Western Americana, railroading, science & medicine, children's literature, travel & exploration.

Great Northwest Book Store
1234 SW Stark
Portland, OR 97205-2310
ph: 503-223-8098

David Morrison
David Morrison Books
530 NW 12th
Portland, OR 97209
ph: 503-295-6882
fax: 503-295-6947
e-mail: morrison@teleport.com
web: http://www.teleport.com/~morrison/
One of the largest collection of out-of-print and rare books on the arts in the Northwest; always interested in buying material in these subjects; offers worldwide book search and appraisal service.

Robert Gavora
Robert Gavora, Fine & Rare Books
P.O. Box 448
Talent, OR 97541
ph: 541-512-9000
e-mail: rgavora@teleport.com
web: http://www.teleport.com/~rgavora/
ABAA member specializing in first and limited editions of science fiction, horror, mystery, Western Americana, railroading; current inventory on the web site; wants to buy single items or entire collections.

Wessel & Lieberman
121 First Ave. S.
Seattle, WA 98104
ph: 206-682-3545
fax: 206-682-2391
e-mail: wlbooks@wlbooks.com
web: http://www.wlbooks.com/

Louis Collins
Louis Collins Books
1211 East Denny Way
Seattle, WA 98122
e-mail: collinsbooks@collinsbooks.com
web: http://www.collinsbooks.com/hannah/
Specializes in all fields of old books with an emphasis on anthropology/archaeology and American Indian studies; books in all fields are searched rather successfully; no fee or obligation for searches.

Randolph M. Moss
Eclectic Books
2740 Hannah Place
Friday Harbor, WA 98250
ph: 360-378-5732
e-mail: eclecticbk@aol.com
Buys and sells National Geographic: pre-1915 magazines, bound sets, reprint, books; all publications by The National Geographic Society; also non-fiction books such as art, archaeology, anthropology.

William Mathews
William Matthews Books
16 Jarvis St.
Fort Erie, Ontario L2A 2S1
Canada
ph: 905-871-8484
fax: 905-871-9857
e-mail: matthews@vaxxine.com
web: http://www.vaxxine.com/matthews/
Carries a very large stock of used and rare books in all fields; specializes in sensational fiction and early fantasy.

Otto Graser
Arlington Books
21 Arlington Ave.
Ottawa, Ontario K2P 1C1
Canada
ph: 613-232-6975
e-mail: ograser@arlingtonbooks.on.ca
web: http://www.arlingtonbooks.on.ca
Buys and sells modern first editions, nautical, naval, sailing, true crime, biography, occult.

W.D.J. Bennett
Postaprint
Taidswood House
Iver Heath, Bucks SL0 0PQ
U.K.
ph: +44 1 895 833 720
fax: +44 1 895 834 890
e-mail: Postaprint@btinternet.com
web: http://www.postaprint.co.uk/
Antique maps, prints, historic engravings, antiquarian atlases and books; has an online database of over 200,000 antique maps, steel, copper or wood engravings available for searching; items date from 1550 to 1899.

Nigel P. Burwood
Any Amount of Books
56 Charing Cross Road
London, WC2 HOBB
U.K.
ph: 00441718363697
fax: 00441712401769
e-mail: charingx@anyamountofbooks.com
web: http://www.anyamountofbooks.com
Specializes in selling second hand and rare books.

Experts

Pat & Allen Ahearn
Quill & Brush
P.O. Box 5365
Rockville, MD 20853-5365
ph: 301-870-3200
fax: 301-874-0424
e-mail: firsts@qb.com
web: http://www.qb.com/
Author of "Book Collecting, A Comprehensive Guide", "Collected Books, The Guide to Values" and "Author Price Guides."

Douglas O'Dell
Chapel Hill Rare Books
P.O. Box 456
Carrboro, NC 27510
ph: 919-929-8351
fax: 919-967-2532
e-mail: rarebooks@mindspring.com
Fine rare books in all fields, first editions in literature and Americana; inscribe copies, bindings, travels, etc.; author on books.

Ray Walsh
Curious Book Shop
307 E. Grand River
East Lansing, MI 48823-4324
ph: 517-332-0112
Dealer/expert; owner of three book shops in Michigan; hosts radio call-in show about books and paper collectibles; writes columns; send a SASE for reply when writing.

Internet Resources

Online Booksellers Union
e-mail: union@olbu.com
web: http://www.olbu.com
An online book search service.

BookSearch, Inc.
ph: 651-292-1842
fax: 651-292-1742
e-mail: bksearch@bitstream.net
web: http://www.booksearch.com
An online book search service.

Bibliocity
e-mail: bibliocity@bibliocity.com
web: http://www.bibliocity.com
An online book search service.

Barnes & Noble
ph: 800-843-2665 or 201-750-4426
e-mail: service@barnesandnoble.com
web: http://bn.bfast.com/booklink/click?sourceid=38698&categoryid=oop
Web site has millions of out-of-print, rare and used books for sale with a searchable database; book sizes & condition, glossary of out-of-print books.

Fiona Smythe
Bibliofind, Inc.
875 Massachussets Ave.
Cambridge, MA 02139
e-mail: admin@bibliofind.com
web: http://www.bibliofind.com/
Over a thousand booksellers listing millions of books for sale from around the world.

Shoshana Edwards
Auldbooks Resources Page/Books from Bree
7795 SW Hall Boulevard
Beaverton, OR 97008-6925
ph: 503-644-7218
e-mail: bree@auldbooks.com
web: http://www.auldbooks.com/biblio/other/op_services.html
Offers a listing of online book search services; also buys and sells scientific and technical books.

Richard M. Weatherford
Alibris
P.O. Box 5
Southworth, WA 98386-0005
ph: 360-871-3617
fax: 360-871-5626
e-mail: adamw@alibris.com
web: http://www.alibris.com
The electronic marketplace for books; reach more buyers and sellers; select from 2+ million titles offered by booksellers worldwide; book searching; appraisal offerings.

Cathy Waters
Advanced Book Exchange (ABE)
#4-415 Dunedin Street
Victoria, British Columbia V8T 5GB
Canada
ph: 250-475-6013
fax: 250-475-6014
e-mail: buyertech@abebooks.com
web: http://www.abebooks.com
A premier internet marketplace for out-of-print, used, rare, and antiquarian books; over 10 million of books listed in a searchable database.

Ton Cremers
Book Information Website
Rechter Rottekade 171
Rotterdam, 3032 XD
The Netherlands
ph: 31 10 4653837
fax: 21 10 4653837
Website devoted to all aspects of books, bookarts, book history, letterpress printing, fine printing, book schools, paper and paper

making, book artists, bookbinding and book binders, antiquarian books, search services, auctions, etc.

Museums/Libraries

Library of Congress
101 Independence Ave. SE
Washington, DC 20540
ph: 202-707-5000 or 202-707-8000
e-mail: lcinfo@loc.gov
web: http://www.loc.gov

Consortium of Popular Culture Collections
Popular Culture Library
Bowling Green State University
Bowling Green, OH 43403-0001
ph: 419-372-2450
fax: 419-372-7996
e-mail: ascott@bgnet.bgsu.edu
web: http://www.bgsu.edu/colleges/library/pcl/cpccm.html
Consortium composed of Bowling Green State U., Kent State U., Michigan State U., and Ohio State U.; the largest academic library collections of primary research material in comic art, popular fiction, popular music, performing arts.

Toledo Museum of Art, The
2445 Monroe St.
P.O. Box 1013
Toledo, OH 43697
ph: 419-255-8000 or 800-644-6862
web: http://www.toledomuseum.org/
Internationally-recognized collection of artist-illustrated books, as well as paintings, decorative arts, graphic arts, and glass.

Periodicals

Price Guide: American Book Prices Current
P.O. Box 1236
Washington Depot, CT 06793
ph: 860-868-7408
fax: 860-868-0080
e-mail: abpc@snet.net
web: http://etext.lib.virginia.edu/rbs/rbs-abpc.html
ABPC is an annual volume listing over 35,000 prices of books, serials, autographs & manuscripts, broadsides, and maps from actual auction sales in U.S. and abroad; the standard reference work in the field.

Magazine: AB Bookman's Weekly
P.O. Box AB
Clifton, NJ 07015
ph: 973-772-0020
fax: 973-772-9281
e-mail: abbookman@aol.com
web: http://www.abbookman.com/
Weekly magazine for the book collecting world; excellent guide to out-of-print and rare books.

John C. Huckans, Ed.
Magazine: Book Source Monthly
2007 Syossett Dr.
P.O. Box 567
Cazenovia, NY 13035-0567
ph: 315-655-8499
fax: 315-655-8499
Book Source Monthly serves both members of the antiquarian book trade and private collectors; books, paper ephemera; contains book fair calendar, book auction calendar, specialists' directories, catalogs received, open shop guide.

Ruth E. Robinson
Ruth E. Robinson Books
Directory: Buy Books Where - Sell Books Where
Rte. 7 Box 162A
Morgantown, WV 26505
An annual directory listing people who sell and buy specialties.

Newsletter: Bookseller
P.O. Box 8183
Ann Arbor, MI 48107-8183
ph: 734-930-0450
fax: 734-930-0450
Covers out-of-print, rare and used books; published 24 times per year; oversized newsletter filled with names of book searchers, dealers, and collectors in search of specific books; books wanted and book for sale ads; free sample copy.

Doug Watson
Magazine: Paper Collectors' Marketplace
470 Main St.
P.O. Box 128
Scandinavia, WI 54977-0128
ph: 715-467-2379
fax: 715-467-2243
e-mail: pcmpaper@gglbbs.com
web: http://www.pcmpaper.com/
Monthly magazine for collectors of autographs, paperbacks, postcards, advertising, photographica, magazines; all types of paper ephemera.

Charles Amery
Newsletter: Rare Book Bulletin
P.O. Box 201
Peoria, IL 61650-0201
A bi-monthly newsletter focusing on books: paperback, hardback, book reviews, coming events, antique & collectible books, buy/sell/trade ads, etc.

First Magazine Inc.
Magazine: Firsts: The Book Collector's Magazine
P.O. Box 65166
Tucson, AZ 85728-5166
ph: 520-529-1355
fax: 520-529-5847
web: http://www.fists.com/
The monthly magazine for book collectors: surveys of various collecting areas, checklists of authors' published works, retail prices for collectible books, keys to identification.

Colleen Sell, Ed.
Aster Publishing Corporation
Magazine: Biblio Magazine
845 Williamette St.
Eugene, OR 97401-2918
ph: 800-840-3810 or 541-345-3800
fax: 541-302-9872
e-mail: csell@bibliomag.com
web: http://www.bibliomag.com
Explores the art, history, science/technology, and culture of books and other "archives of civilization"—from illuminated manuscripts, to journals, gov. documents, autographs, cuneiform tablets; for book lovers and collectors.

Repair Services

Don E. Sanders
Don E. Sanders Bookbinder
1116 Pinion Dr.
Austin, TX 78748
ph: 512-282-4774
30 years experience; custom binding & cases, restoration and repair.

Peregrine Arts Bookbindery
P.O. Box 1691
Santa Fe, NM 87504
ph: 505-982-0490
Book repair, marbling.

Gary D. Muir
Muir's Book Repair
2115 Garden Ave.
Redding, CA 96001
ph: 530-243-3920
Repair/restore any and all types of books, bibles, cookbooks, newspapers and magazines; also other historical documents; chewed-up by dog, moisture or water damage, fire damage, lost spine, lost front or back, loose or torn pages.

Astronomy

Book Sellers

Lee & Peggy Price
Knollwood Books
P.O. Box 197
Oregon, WI 53575-0197
ph: 608-835-8861
fax: 608-835-8421
e-mail: books@tdsnet.com
Issues quarterly catalogs; buys and sells out-of-print books on astronomy, meteorology, and space exploration; also books about microscopes, old scientific instruments, optics, and related areas.

Aviation Related

Collectors

Paul Davis
308 Landsende Rd.
Devon, PA 19333
ph: 610-644-1216
Wants books on general aviation and military aviation history, airplanes, etc.

Big Little

Clubs/Associations

Larry Lowery
Big Little Book Collectors Club of America
Newsletter: Big Little Times
P.O. Box 1242
Danville, CA 94526-8242
ph: 510-837-2086
e-mail: larry@biglittlebooks.com
web: http://www.biglittlebooks.com/
Club provides a conduit among collectors and dealers interested in Big Little Books and similar books; publishes research and other information pertaining to Big Little Books; bi-monthly newsletter.

Experts

Larry Lowery
P.O. Box 1242
Danville, CA 94526-8242
ph: 510-837-2086
e-mail: larry@biglittlebooks.com
web: http://www.biglittlebooks.com/
Author of "The Collector's Guide to Big Little and Similar Books," "Guide to the Tarzan Big Little Books," "Guide to the Dick Tracy Big Little Books."

Ken Mitchell
710 Conacher Dr.
Willowdale, Ontario M2M 3N6
Canada
ph: 416-222-5808
Buys and sells comic character collectibles (comic books, Sunday funnies, "Big Little Books", etc.) and other nostalgic paper including music (Pop) magazines and books from 1890 through 1960s.

Boys'

Collectors

Joseph A. Ruttar
3116 Teesdale
Philadelphia, PA 19152-4514
Wants boys' series books: Andy Blake, Trigger Berg, Hal Keen, Conquest of U.S., Sam Steele, Boy Fortune Hunters, Jack Race, Jack Straw, Dave Porter (no Special Edition), Square Dollar Boys, Boys of Liberty.

British

Clubs/Associations

Ellie Luchinsky, Sec.
Lewis Carroll Society of North America
Newsletter: Knights Letter, The
18 Fitzharding Place
Owings Mills, MD 21117
ph: 410-356-5110
e-mail: eluchin@erols.com
web: http://www.lewiscarroll.org
Many members also collect books and other Lewis Carroll related materials.

Children's

(see also BOOKS, Pop-up & Movable)

Collectors

Alan Levine
P.O. Box 1577
Bloomfield, NJ 07003
ph: 973-743-5288

Mary Young
P.O. Box 9244
Dayton, OH 45409-9244
Wants to buy children's school readers (primarily first and second grade readers) from the 1920s to 1960s, 1930-1960s coloring and punch-out books, and girls' series books, storybooks by Platt and Munk, Whitman, Beckley Cardy Co.

Margery Wilder
1409 1st St.
Port Townsend, WA 98368-3078
Wants Tasha, Tudor, Maurice Sendak and various other charming illustrated books.

Dealers

Marion F. Adler
P.O. Box 627
Stockbridge, MA 01262
ph: 413-298-3559
Specializing in out-of-print children's books.

Ten Eyck Books
P.O. Box 84
Southborough, MA 01772
ph: 508-481-3517
Specializing in out-of-print children's books.

Greg Gillert
Justin G. Shiller Ltd.
1270 Avenue of the Americas
Rockefeller Center, Ste. 302
New York, NY 10020
ph: 212-332-7070 or 914-331-3309
fax: 212-332-7028
e-mail: early@childlit.com
web: http://www.abaa-booknet.com/usa/schiller/
Established in 1959, claims to be the oldest antiquarian book firm in the US continuously specializing in rare and collectible children's books in all languages and covering all time periods especially 17th to mid-19th century.

Helen & Marc Younger
Aleph-Bet Books, Inc.
218 Waters Edge
Valley Cottage, NY 10989
ph: 914-268-7410
fax: 914-268-5942
e-mail: helen@alephbet.com
web: http://www.alephbet.com/
Specializing in fine first editions of collectible and rare children's and illustrated books; always interested in buying books in fine condition; business established in 1978.

Lee Temares
50 Heights Rd.
Plandome, NY 11030-1413
ph: 516-627-8688 or 516-627-2647
fax: 516-627-7822
e-mail: tembooks@aol.com
Buys children's series books; must have dust jackets if they came originally had them; also wants Limited Editions Club and Heritage Press, but must be very good condition and in fine boxes; appraises all books except law & medicine.

Michael Kelly
Paper Pandemonium
1321 Jack's Mountain Road
Fairfield, PA 17320
ph: 717-642-8019
e-mail: kellym@mail.cvn.net
web: http://www.tias.com/stores/pp
Collector and dealer carries a large selection of early children's books including Little Golden Books and other favorites.

Debbi Manley
306 Willowbrook Dr.
Norristown, PA 19403-3425
Wants to buy vintage children's books: juvenile series, pop-ups, mechanicals, color illustrated, cookbooks, black children's, anything Dick & Jane; authors/illustrators Maud Hart Lovelace, Tasha Tudor, Maud Humphrey, etc.

Jo Ann Reisler
360 Glyndon St., NE
Vienna, VA 22180-3537
ph: 703-938-2967
fax: 703-938-9057
e-mail: Reisler@clark.net
web: http://www.clark.net/pub/reisler
Wants to buy fine and unusual children's and illustrated books.

Daniel Hirsch
Daniel Hirsch Rare Books
P.O. Box 5096
Chapel Hill, NC 27514
ph: 919-542-1816
fax: 919-542-1817
e-mail: rhirsch@interserv.com
Wants Dr. Seuss posters, books, dolls, etc.; also wants fairy tale books, pop-ups, movable books.

Cattermole
9880 Fairmont Rd.
Newbury, OH 44065
ph: 216-338-3253
Specializes in buying and selling 20th century children's books.

David B. Mischke
ARMS
120 Cedar Street
Ringsted, IA 50578
ph: 712-866-0191
e-mail: mischke@netins.net
Buys, sells, collects late 19th and early 20th century children's books as well as nonfiction books of the same period.

Helmar & Dorothy Kern
Marvelous Books
P.O. Box 1510
Ballwin, MO 63022-1510
ph: 314-256-0425
fax: 314-256-0894
e-mail: marvbooks@aol.com
Buy/sell quality children's books and illustrated books; search service available; catalogs issued $5; want list available; friendly service for 20 years.

Ruppert Books
5909 Darnell
Houston, TX 77074-7719
ph: 713-774-2202
fax: 713-774-2202
Wants books: Nancy Drew, Hardy Boys, Dana Girls, Judy Bolton, Tom Swift, Rick Brant, Little Black Sambo, Raggedy Ann, Dick and Jane Readers, OZ, all children's series books in fine conditions, with dust jackets, illustrated.

James Keeline
Prince & the Pauper Collectible Children's Books
3201 Adams St.
San Diego, CA 92116-1654
ph: 619-283-4380
fax: 619-283-4666
Largest book store specializing exclusively in children's books; 50,000 out-of-print and collectibles children's books; maintains active, long-term search service and research library related to children's books.

Experts

E. Lee Baumgarten
718 1/2 W. John St.
Martinsburg, WV 25401-2204
ph: 304-267-2711
Compiler of "Price Guide & Bibliographic Checklist for Children's Illustrated Books - 1880-1960"; write or call anytime for free information; separate, related printing available featuring Library of Congress call numbers.

James Keeline
Prince & the Pauper Collectible Children's Books
3201 Adams St.
San Diego, CA 92116-1654
ph: 619-283-4380
fax: 619-283-4666
Specializes in children's books: Dick & Jane textbooks, Little Golden Books, L.M. Montgomery, Jules Verne, Hardy Boys series, Nancy Drew Series, Tom Swift series, Clive Cussler (modern author), and others.

Museums/Libraries

American Antiquarian Society
185 Salisbury St.
Worcester, MA 01609
ph: 508-755-5221
fax: 508-753-3311
e-mail: library@mwa.org
web: gopher://mark.mwa.org/
A learned society founded in 1812; maintains a research library of American history and culture in order to collect, preserve, and make available for study the printed record of the U.S.; 3 million books, maps, pamphlets, etc.

Free Library of Philadelphia
1901 Vine St.
Philadelphia, PA 19103
ph: 215-686-5322 or 215-686-5416
e-mail: webteam@library.phila.gov
web: http://www.library.phila.gov/

Lucile Clarke Memorial Children's Library
Central Michigan University
Mount Pleasant, MI 48859
ph: 517-774-3197
e-mail: clarke@cmich.edu
web: http://www.lib.cmich.edu/clarke/

Periodicals

Rebecca Grayson
Newspaper: Gold Mine Review, The
P.O. Box 209
Hershey, PA 17033-0209
ph: 717-533-3039
For collectors of all children's illustrated books from 1900-1970, e.g. those published by the Golden Book Company.

Martha Rasmussen
Newsletter: Martha's KidLit Newsletter
P.O. Box 1488
Ames, IA 50010-1488
e-mail: mart515@aol.com
web: http://www.kidlitonline.com/
Published bi-monthly; your guide to out-of-print antiquarian children's books; ads, reviews, articles about favorite books and authors or illustrators, want lists.

Clothing & Accessories

Book Sellers

Fred Struthers
Fred Struthers Books
P.O. Box 2706
Fort Bragg, CA 95437-2706
ph: 707-964-8662
e-mail: fsbks@mcn.org
An important source to collectors and researchers for hard-to-find and out-of-print books on costume, textiles, tailoring; caries period sewing and etiquette books and periodicals; publishes two catalogs per year for $2.50.

Computer Programs For

Man./Prod./Dist.

PrimaSoft PC, Inc.
Software: Book Organizer
P.O. Box 456
Surrey, British Columbia V3T 5B7
Canada
ph: 800-371-7520 or 604-951-1085
fax: 604-951-7797
e-mail: support@primasoft.com
web: http://www.primasoft.com/bko.htm
A complete program that allows book collectors, hobbyists, book clubs, small private or public libraries to organize, catalog, and manage their collections on their computers; organize all your information in one place; free downloads.

Dictionaries

Collectors

Edwin A. Miles
2645 Alta Glen Dr.
Birmingham, AL 35243-4509
ph: 205-967-2504
e-mail: samnoah@aol.com
Wants pre-1865 English-language dictionaries (including medical, scientific, technological, legal, musical, fine arts, agricultural, commercial, etc.); also works of slang, Americanisms, and lexicography.

Etiquette

Collectors

Maret Webb
4118 East Vernon Ave.
Phoenix, AZ 85008-2333
ph: 602-957-0653
fax: 602-957-1631
Wants vintage etiquette books, pre-1875, pretty bindings, gilded edges, "deportment", "decorum", manners.

First Editions

Collectors

Maria E. Raymond
Plow & Pen, Inc.
P.O. Box 251
Robbins, CA 95676-0251
ph: 530-735-6596
fax: 530-735-6112
e-mail: M_Raymond@compuserve.com
Wants first editions only: Atwood, Sarton, Plath, Sexton, Duras, Walker, Hurston.

Dealers

Joanmarie Dale
StrayBooks
192 Pinewood Road, #87
Hartsdale, NY 10530-1414
ph: 914-761-1198
fax: 914-761-1198
e-mail: JDale@StrayBooks.com
web: http://www.StrayBooks.com
Online mail order book shop specializing in First Editions, many signed; free book searches.

Ron Lieberman
Family Album, The
RD 1 Box 42
Glen Rock, PA 17327-9707
ph: 717-235-2134
fax: 717-235-8765
e-mail: ronbiblio@delphi.com
web: http://www.auldbooks.com/biblio/clients/lieberman.html
Buys and sells fine books in all fields, specializing in American and European first editions; advisor to "Warman's Antiques & Collectibles Price Guide."

Pat & Allen Ahearn
Quill & Brush
P.O. Box 5365
Rockville, MD 20853-5365
ph: 301-870-3200
fax: 301-874-0424
e-mail: firsts@qb.com
web: http://www.qb.com/
Book dealer specializing in 19th & 20th century first editions.

Fishing

Dealers

Steve & Susan Starrantino
Armchair Angler
35 Rockland Ave.
Hillburn, NY 10931
ph: 914-357-8746
Sells out-of-print fishing books and related material.

Flip

(see BOOKS, Pop-Ups & Movable [Flip])

Fore-Edge Painted

Experts

Ron Lieberman
Family Album, The
RD 1 Box 42
Glen Rock, PA 17327-9707
ph: 717-235-2134
fax: 717-235-8765
e-mail: ronbiblio@delphi.com
web: http://www.auldbooks.com/biblio/clients/lieberman.html
Buys and sells fine books in all fields, specializing in American and European first editions; advisor to "Warman's Antiques & Collectibles Price Guide."

German

Collectors

R.L. Rice
612 E. Front St.
Bloomington, IL 61701-5314
Wants oversized illustrated language books and handwritten diaries in German including Bibles, children's, fashion, art; also wants art books and magazines 1830s -1920s.

Ghosts

Book Sellers

Chris Woodyard
Invisible Ink: Books on Ghosts & Hauntings
1811 Stonewood Dr.
Beavercreek, OH 45432-4002
ph: 937-426-5110
fax: 937-320-1832
e-mail: invisiblei@aol.com
web: http://www.invink.com
Collector of nonfiction books on ghosts & hauntings; also dealer in new and paranormal books; founder of Invisible Ink Collection at BGSU Popular Collection Library.

Horatio Alger, Jr.

(see also PERSONALITIES [LITERARY], Horatio Alger, Jr.)

Collectors

George Owens
23 Kiowa Lane
Palmyra, VA 22963
ph: 804-589-3373
e-mail: caddowens@juno.com
Wants Horatio Alger, Jr. books; state title, publisher, condition and price.

Illustrated

(see also ILLUSTRATORS)

Dealers

Helen & Marc Younger
Aleph-Bet Books, Inc.
218 Waters Edge
Valley Cottage, NY 10989
ph: 914-268-7410
fax: 914-268-5942
e-mail: helen@alephbet.com
web: http://www.alephbet.com/
Specializing in fine first editions of collectible and rare children's and illustrated books; always interested in buying books in fine condition; business established in 1978.

Jo Ann Reisler
360 Glyndon St., NE
Vienna, VA 22180-3537
ph: 703-938-2967
fax: 703-938-9057
e-mail: Reisler@clark.net
web: http://www.clark.net/pub/reisler
Wants to buy fine and unusual children's and illustrated books.

Joseph L. Mashburn
Colonial House
P.O. Box 609 - M
Enka, NC 28728-0609
ph: 828-667-1427
fax: 828-667-1111
e-mail: jmashb0135@aol.com
web: http://www.postcard-books.com
Wants large gift books with illustrations by Harrison Fisher, Coles Phillips, Clarence Underwood, Henry Hutt, Howard C. Christy, Charles Gibson, Pogany, Dulac, Erte.

Periodicals

Denis C. Jackson, Ed.
Newsletter: Illustrator Collector's News, The
P.O. Box 1958
Sequim, WA 98382-1958
ph: 360-452-3810
e-mail: ticn@olypen.com
web: http://www.olypen.com/ticn/
A monthly publication for collectors of magazines, books and other paper illustrations; free classifieds for subscribers; send LSASE for free information guide offer.

Jules Verne

Collectors

Dana V. Eales
2447 Delta Dr.
Uniontown, OH 44685-8117
ph: 303-699-5341
e-mail: deals@sssnet.com
Collects French, English and American translations of Jules Verne novels; primarily early editions but also little known or unusual titles.

Dealers

James Keeline
Prince & the Pauper Collectible Children's Books
3201 Adams St.
San Diego, CA 92116-1654
ph: 619-283-4380
fax: 619-283-4666
Largest book store specializing exclusively in children's books; 50,000 out-of-print and collectibles children's books; maintains active, long-term search service and research library related to children's books.

Juvenile Series

Clubs/Associations

Horatio Alger Society
Newsletter: Newsboy, The
P.O. Box 70361
Richmond, VA 23255
e-mail: alger-l@listserv.wuacc.edu
web: http://www.wuacc.edu/sobu/broach/algerres.html
To further the philosophy of Horatio Alger, Jr. and to encourage the spirit of Strive & Succeed.

Collectors

Mike DeBaptiste
4402 Prasse Rd.
Cleveland, OH 44121
ph: 216-381-8092
Wants Nancy Drew books in dust jackets; also similar series books such as Hardy Boys, Tom Swift, Judy Bolton, Rick Brant, etc.

Jeff Escue
164 Larchmont Ln.
Bloomingdale, IL 60108-1412
ph: 630-307-6415
e-mail: jsq2@yahoo.com
Buying kids series books: Hardy Boys, Nancy Drew, Rick Brant, Judy Bolton, Tom Swift, Three Investigators, Big Little Books, Ken Holt, Leo Edwards, Hal Keen, Sue Barton, Chip Hilton, etc.

Van Matre
15 S. Blaine
Hinsdale, IL 60521-4208
e-mail: lvanmatre@tribune.com
Wants hardcover books by Emma Bugbee, the author who wrote girls' series books about a girl reporter; all replies answered.

Victoria Broadhurst
5009 Queen Victoria Rd.
Woodland Hills, CA 91364-4757
ph: 818-883-3127
fax: 818-887-3739
e-mail: mrscdrew@aol.com
Wants to buy Nancy Drew and Hardy Boys books in dust jackets.

Dealers

Terri Pointon
RR 6, Box 6523
Moscow, PA 18444
e-mail: tmp95@mindspring.com
web: http://tmp95.home.mindspring.com/
Buys and sells old juvenile series books.

James Keeline
Prince & the Pauper Collectible Children's Books
3201 Adams St.
San Diego, CA 92116-1654
ph: 619-283-4380
fax: 619-283-4666
Largest book store specializing exclusively in children's books; 50,000 out-of-print and collectibles children's books; maintains active, long-term search service and research library related to children's books.

Gary Nerman
Nerman's Books & Collectibles
721 Osborne St. South
Winnipeg, Manitoba R3L 2C1
Canada
ph: 204-475-1050 or 204-255-2196
fax: 204-947-0753
e-mail: nerman@escape.ca
Publishes a highly informative catalog; always interested in buying children and juvenile books.

Experts

Virginia & David Brown
RR 1, Box 73
Machias, ME 04654-9711
ph: 207-255-4223
e-mail: cybertiques@nemaine.com
web: http://www.cybertiques.com/
Buys and sells; newsletter covers all aspects of collecting, caring for and enjoying the Whitman Publishing Company's juvenile books.

Periodicals

Gil O'Gara
Yellowback Press
Magazine: Yellowback Library
P.O. Box 36172
Des Moines, IA 50315-0310
ph: 515-287-0404
Focuses on juvenile series books and dime novels; largest circulation in the hobby.

Fred Woodworth, Pub.
Magazine: Mystery & Adventure Series Review
P.O. Box 3488
Tucson, AZ 85722-3488
Quarterly magazine devoted to collecting and preserving c. 1925-1965 series-books, e.g. Hardy Boys, Ken Holt & Rick Brant.

Kate Emburg
Society of Phantom Friends, The
Newsletter: Whispered Watchword, The
P.O. Box 1437
North Highlands, CA 95660-1437
ph: 916-331-7435 or 916-331-7352
e-mail: dolladopt@aol.com
A club for readers and collectors of girls' juvenile fiction from 1900 to present, including but not limited to Nancy Drew, Judy Bolton, Trixie Belden, and Beany Malone; books bought and sold; please send SASE with inquiries.

Law Reference

Collectors

Clint Miller
1604 N. Harrison St.
Little Rock, AR 72207-5322
ph: 501-664-8424 or 501-682-7466
Wants to buy books on legal reasoning, legal writing, jurisprudence, criminal law, American constitutional law and legal questions.

Dealers

Luke Pavone, VP
National Law Resource, Inc.
328 S. Jefferson
Chicago, IL 60661-5605
ph: 800-279-7799 or 800-886-1800
fax: 773-382-0323
e-mail: lawstuff@aol.com
Book dealer of up-to-date, excellent quality, pre-owned law books; carries inventories of all Federal, National, Regional and state sets; also tax libraries, labor law libraries, GPO titles, bound legal periodicals, ultra-fiche.

Little Golden Books

Collectors

Ilene Kayne
1308 S. Charles St.
Baltimore, MD 21230-4219
ph: 410-685-3923
Wants Little Golden Books; especially those with dust jackets or in a foreign language.

Dealers

James Keeline
Prince & the Pauper Collectible Children's Books
3201 Adams St.
San Diego, CA 92116-1654
ph: 619-283-4380
fax: 619-283-4666
Largest book store specializing exclusively in children's books; 50,000 out-of-print and collectibles children's books; maintains active, long-term search service and research library related to children's books.

Experts

Steve Santi
19626 Ricardo Ave.
Hayward, CA 94541
ph: 510-481-2586
e-mail: lgbsteve@aol.com
web: http://www.jps.net/lgbsteve
Buys and sells Little Golden Books by Books Americana; author of "Collecting Little Golden Books."

Periodicals

Rebecca Grayson
Newspaper: Gold Mine Review, The
P.O. Box 209
Hershey, PA 17033-0209
ph: 717-533-3039
For collectors of all children's illustrated books from 1900-1970, e.g. those published by the Golden Book Company.

Metaphysics

Dealers

Dennis E. Whelan
Samadhi Metaphysical Literature
781 Eagle Lane
Lakeview, AR 72642
ph: 870-431-8830
Collector and seller of metaphysical books/magazines: esoterica, mysticism, yoga, astrology, Tibet, Egypt, Atlantis, herbalism, UFO, tarot, crystal balls, the unexplained, etc.; SASE plus $1 for annual catalog; free search service.

Meteorology

Book Sellers

Lee & Peggy Price
Knollwood Books
P.O. Box 197
Oregon, WI 53575-0197
ph: 608-835-8861
fax: 608-835-8421
e-mail: books@tdsnet.com
Issues quarterly catalogs; buys and sells out-of-print books on astronomy, meteorology, and space exploration; also books about microscopes, old scientific instruments, optics, and related areas.

Military History

(see also MILITARY HISTORY)

Dealers

Paul Hunt
Book Castle, Inc.
P.O. Box 10907
Burbank, CA 91510-0907
ph: 818-409-9761 or 818-845-6467
fax: 818-845-0460
e-mail: paulhunt@netroplex.com
Buys and sells books, specialty: back issue magazines, and military and history.

Miniature

Experts

Ron Lieberman
Family Album, The
RD 1 Box 42
Glen Rock, PA 17327-9707
ph: 717-235-2134
fax: 717-235-8765
e-mail: ronbiblio@delphi.com
web: http://www.auldbooks.com/biblio/clients/lieberman.html

Modern Library

Periodicals

A. Oestreich
Newsletter: Modern Library Collector, The
340 Warren Ave.
Cincinnati, OH 45220-1135
For collectors of "Modern Library" and "Viking Portable" books; published twice a year.

Mountaineering

Book Sellers

Chessler Books
P.O. Box 399
Kittredge, CO 80457
ph: 800-654-8502 or 303-670-0093
fax: 303-670-9727
Extensive selection of books on mountaineering, rock climbing, exploration, guidebooks.

Movable

(see BOOKS, Children's; BOOKS, Pop-Up & Movable)

Movie & TV Related

Dealers

Paul Hunt
Book Castle, Inc.
P.O. Box 10907
Burbank, CA 91510-0907
ph: 818-409-9761 or 818-845-6467
fax: 818-845-0460
e-mail: paulhunt@netroplex.com
Buys and sells books, specialty: back issue magazines, and military and history.

Mystery

Collectors

Beverley Furlow-Cleary
1555 N. Arcadia Ave.
Tucson, AZ 85712-4010
ph: 520-323-1709
e-mail: beverleyf@aol.com
Buys, sells, and appraises collectible mystery/detective items: books, vintage clothing and hats.

Dealers

Peggy Ell
Peggy's Paper
218 Gratton
Burlington, IA 52601
ph: 319-752-7670
Buys and sells mystery magazines such as Alfred Hitchcock and Ellery Queen mystery magazines; also wants hardback mystery books.

Michael S. Greenbaum
Janus Books, Ltd.
P.O. Box 40787
Tucson, AZ 85717
ph: 520-881-8192
fax: 520-323-3351
e-mail: janus@azstarnet.com
web: http://janusbooks.com
Buys and sells first edition of detective, mystery, and suspense fiction; related bibliography and criticism; Sherlock Holmes; catalog available by snail mail or online.

New York

Collectors

James L. Sedore, Jr. CPA
431 McGrath Blvd.
Fishkill, NY 12524-2831
ph: 914-831-8535 or 831-297-1111
fax: 914-297-1432
Wants to buy books on New York State; Dutchess City, NY; Hudson Valley, NY; also of Indians of the Hudson River Valley; also wants American history books and books about the American Revolution.

Paperback

(see also MAGAZINES, Pulp)

Clubs/Associations

Paul Duncan
British Association of Paperback Collectors
17 Tregullan Rd.
Coventry, CV7 9NG
U.K.
International club interested in vintage paperback books.

Dealers

R.C. & Elwanda Holland
Books Are Everything!
302 Martin Drive
Richmond, KY 404753505
ph: 606-624-9176
fax: 606-623-9354
e-mail: holland@zeus.chapel1.com
web: http://www.booksareeverything.com/
Mail-order paperback book company with over 500,000 vintage paperbacks in stock.

Nancy Mancing
Buck Creek Books, Ltd.
838 Main St.
Lafayette, IN 47901
ph: 765-742-6618
Publishes a free catalog of vintage paperbacks; also sells hardback books.

Experts

Ray Walsh
Curious Book Shop
307 E. Grand River
East Lansing, MI 48823-4324
ph: 517-332-0112
Dealer/expert; owner of three book shops in Michigan; hosts radio call-in show about books and paper collectibles; writes columns; send a SASE for reply when writing.

Periodicals

Gary Lovisi
Gryphon Publications
Magazine: Paperback Parade
P.O. Box 209
Brooklyn, NY 11228-0209
ph: 718-646-6126
web: http://www.gryphonbooks.com/
A magazine for paperback readers and collectors; news, articles, lists, interviews; a hobby publication full of news and info about paperbacks; issues are 100+ pages with color covers; $7 each, subscriptions $35/year.

Randy Cox
Journal: Dime Novel Round-Up
P.O. Box 226
Dundas, MN 55019-0226
A magazine devoted to the collecting, preservation and literature of the old-time dime and nickel novels and popular story papers.

Pocket

Collectors

Bruce Axler
Ansonia Station
P.O. Box 1288
New York, NY 10023-1288
ph: 212-362-4429
fax: 212-579-1274
Wants to buy pocket books from the 19th century (1800s) that people carried which were loaded with information, e.g. dictionaries, almanacs, encyclopedias, reckoners; no fiction, religious, poetry, foreign, speeches, or bio.

Pop-Up & Movable

(see also BOOKS, Children's)

Clubs/Associations

Ann Montanaro
Movable Book Society
Newsletter: Movable Stationery
P.O. Box 11645
New Brunswick, NJ 08906-1645
ph: 732-247-6071 or 732-445-5896
fax: 732-846-7928
e-mail: montanar@rci.rutgers.edu
web: http://www.rci.rutgers.edu/~montanar/mbs.html
Forum for collectors of pop-up and movable books to share collecting resources, research, and questions about individual titles.

Collectors

Ann Montanaro
P.O. Box 11645
New Brunswick, NJ 08906-1645
ph: 732-247-6071 or 732-445-5896
fax: 732-846-7928
e-mail: montanar@rci.rutgers.edu
web: http://www.rci.rutgers.edu/~montanar/
Wants to buy pop-up and movable books.

Margery Wilder
1409 1st St.
Port Townsend, WA 98368-3078
Collecting pop-up, mechanical, fold-out, unusual children's books.

Dealers

Helen & Marc Younger
Aleph-Bet Books, Inc.
218 Waters Edge
Valley Cottage, NY 10989
ph: 914-268-7410
fax: 914-268-5942
e-mail: helen@alephbet.com
web: http://www.alephbet.com/
Specializing in fine first editions of collectible and rare children's and illustrated books; always interested in buying books in fine condition; business established in 1978.

A. Dalrymple
1791 Graefield
Birmingham, MI 48009
Always wants to buy pop-ups and movable books.

Mr. Books
2814 W Bell Rd., Ste. 1495
Phoenix, AZ 85023-7532
Issues catalog of pop-up books for sale.

Ampersand Books
Ludford Mill
Ludlow, Shropshire SY8 1PP
U.K.
ph: +44 1584 877813
fax: +44 1584 877519
e-mail: ampersand.books@mcmail.com
web: http://www.ampersand.books.mcmail.com/
Specializes exclusively in dimensional and interactive books: antiquarian,

rare, second-hand; pop-ups, movables, children's novelty books, peep show and tunnel books, panoramas, flicks, carousels, tab-operated animations, revolving, etc.

Pop-Up & Movable (Flip)

Collectors

Robin Klein
801 Welington St.
Baltimore, MD 21211-2513
Interested in contacting other collectors of flip books.

Poultry

Collectors

Carl Kidder
3219 E. County Rd. "N"
Milton, WI 53563
ph: 608-868-4185
fax: 608-868-6808
e-mail: ckidder@jvlnet.com
web: http://www.jvlnet.com/bus/marilynhelp.htm
Expert, collector of pre-1926 books on fancy show-type poultry that feature color plates of chickens, ducks, geese, or turkeys.

Railroad

Experts

Jim Younger
4628 Old Dragon Path
Ellicott City, MD 21042-5970
ph: 410-964-1949
e-mail: jmyr@erols.com
Buys, sells, trades out-of-print railroad-themed fiction (novels, short stories, juveniles, poetry, dime novels, paperbacks, etc.) and true stories (autobiographies, biographies, reminiscences of or by railroaders, c. 1830-1990.

Reference (American Indian)

Book Sellers

Lar Hothem
Hothem House
P.O. Box 458
Lancaster, OH 43130-0458
ph: 740-653-9030
Buys and sells Indian related books covering archaeology, artifacts, earthworks, U.S. prehistory.

Reference (Antiques)

Book Sellers

Grace Miller Dickinson
Miller's Daughter, The
21 Poplar Hill Rd.
Haydenville, MA 01039-9602
ph: 877-829-9114
Essential reference books on furniture, the decorative arts, tools, antiques, glass and collectibles; appearing at select shows; also by mail order and from the shop.

A-Book & Company
54 Redstone Hill
Lancaster, MA 01523-1858
ph: 800-47A-BOOK or 978-365-6456
Send for free catalog; over 1,700 titles in stock.

Joslin Hall Rare Books
P.O. Box 516
Concord, MA 01742
ph: 978-371-3101
fax: 978-371-6445
e-mail: jhall@tiac.net
web: http://www.joslinhall.com
Specialists in rare books on the decorative arts and American fine art.

John Hart
John Hart - Wellesley Antiques & Books
P.O. Box 620268
Newton, MA 02162-0268
ph: 800-867-7019 or 617-964-6979
fax: 617-243-0202
e-mail: welbooks@tiac.net
web: http://www.antiqnet.com/wellesley/
New reference books on antiques and collectibles; over 1200 titles, mail order and shows, catalog available; Arts & Crafts Movement and 20th Century Design a specialty.

F. Russack Antiques & Books
20 Beach Plain Rd.
Danville, NH 03819
ph: 603-642-7718
fax: 603-642-7718
Specializes in out-of-print books about decorative arts, folk art, Americana.

Greg Johnson
Books About Antiques
168 New Milford Tpke.
P.O. Box 2358
New Preston, CT 06777
ph: 860-868-1611
fax: 860-868-1620

John-Peter J. Hayden, Jr.
Hayden & Fandetta
Radio City Station
P.O. Box 1549
New York, NY 10101-1549
ph: 212-582-2505 or 917-972-6161
Foremost source for rare, obscure, and old books on antiques and gardens.

Timothy Trace Booksellers
144 Red Mill Rd.
Cortdandt Manor, NY 10566
ph: 914-528-4074
Sells out-of-print books about furniture and the decorative arts: ceramics, silver, jewelry, metalwork, textiles, rugs and carpets, wallpaper, clocks and watches, China Trade, glass, folk art, and art reference.

Christie's Publications
21-44 44th Ave.
Long Island City, NY 11101
ph: 718-784-1480

Richard & Eileen Dubrow
Richard & Eileen Dubrow Antiques & Books
P.O. Box 128
Flushing, NY 11361-0128
ph: 718-767-9758
fax: 718-767-8172
Sells books (out of print and current) about 19th C. furniture and about furniture and decorative arts.

Antique Collectors' Club, Ltd.
91 Market Street Industrial Park
Wappingers Falls, NY 12590
ph: 800-247-9955 or 914-297-1312
fax: 914-297-0068
e-mail: webmaster@antiquecc.com
web: http://www.antiquecc.com/
Carries the best books and price guides on the fine and decorative arts; also on architecture and garden design; retail sales; Mayer's on CD, Gordon's, art books, price guides, furniture, glass, textiles, metalwork, ceramics

Doris Motta
ArtBooks
P.O. Box 745
Cooperstown, NY 13326-0745
e-mail: artbooksdm@aol.com
web: http://www.oldbooks.com/
Books and catalogs on fine and decorative arts.

Whitehouse-Books.com
32 E. Market St.
Corning, NY 14830
ph: 607-936-8536 or 800-935-8536
fax: 607-936-2465
e-mail: elizabeth@whitehouse.com
web: http://www.whitehouse-books.com
One of the world's largest selections of new and out-of-print books about glass; also books about ceramics, silver, furniture, jewelry, textiles, and other antiques & collectibles.

William Blystone
Blystone Books
2132 Delaware Ave.
Pittsburgh, PA 15218-1811
ph: 724-371-3511
Sells in print & out of print collectibles books by mail; specialty areas are dolls, toys and train books; looking for new book sources.

Betty Johnston
Reference Rack, Inc., The
P.O. Box 445
Orefield, PA 18069-0445
ph: 800-722-7279 or 610-395-0004
fax: 610-706-0229
e-mail: laviniaj@aol.com
web: http://www.referencerack.com
New reference books on antiques, art and collectibles; issues one free catalog per year.

Geraud Schultz
Antique Gallery, The
8523 Germantown Ave.
Philadelphia, PA 19118
ph: 215-248-1700
fax: 215-247-8411
Sells reference books on decorative arts.

Schiffer Publishing, Ltd.
4880 Lower Valley Rd.
Atglen, PA 19310-9717
ph: 610-593-1777
fax: 610-593-2002
e-mail: schifferbk@aol.com
web: http://www.schifferbooks.com
Carries a line of high quality books focusing on antiques and collectibles.

Winterthur Museum Bookstore
ph: 800-448-3883 or 302-888-4600
e-mail: winterthur@udel.edu
web: http://www.udel.edu/winterthur/

Edward Johnson
Nancy Antiques & Books
P.O. Box 4894
Lutherville Timonium, MD 21094
ph: 410-683-1519
fax: 410-683-4894
e-mail: nancyant@erols.com
web: http://www.bookmallventura.com/nancyantiques.html
Reference books on 20th century design and the decorative arts: antiquarian, in-print, European, Art Deco, Art Nouveau, industrial design, furniture, glass, ceramics, silver, jewelry, fashion, textiles, posters.

Random House Inc./House of Collectibles
400 Hahn Rd.
Westminster, MD 21157
ph: 800-733-3000 or 410-848-1900
fax: 800-659-2436
e-mail: customerservice@randomhouse.com
web: http://www.randomhouse.com

Crown Publishers, Inc.
c/o Random House
400 Hahn Rd.
Westminster, MD 21157
ph: 410-848-1900 or 800-733-3000
e-mail: crownpublicity@randomhouse.com
web: http://www.randomhouse.com/
Offers books about antiques and collectibles.

David & Kathleen Way
Antique Books
P.O. Box 6395
Annapolis, MD 21401-0395
ph: 410-268-0845
fax: 410-268-0845
Sells quality new and out-of-print books about antiques and collectibles.

Carl Mikalauskas
Country Lane Books
P.O. Box 656
Braddock Heights, MD 21714-0656
ph: 800-769-5961 or 301-371-5846
fax: 603-754-3964
e-mail: sales@countrylane.com
web: http://www.countrylane.com
Specializing in antiques and collectibles price guides and reference books from both major publishers and private publishers; discounts; most books are in stock and are shipped within 24 hours; free catalog.

Perry Franks
Collector's Companion
P.O. Box 935
Mechanicsville, VA 23111-0935
ph: 804-321-9212
e-mail: bookscc@aol.com
Offering over 6,500 different new and out-of-print reference/price guides dealing with antiques and collectibles; exhibits at many Virginia shows; limited book displays at selected Virginia antique malls; mail order available.

B.J. Hicks
Homebiz Books & More
2919 Mistwood Forest Dr.
Chester, VA 23831-7043
ph: 804-748-3645
Offers antique and collectible reference books; also buys bottle books.

Merrill Thompson
Books on Antiques & Collectibles
2103 North Decatur Road, #149
Decatur, GA 30033
ph: 404-248-1725 or 404-248-8905
fax: 404-235-0278
e-mail: agoodbook@aol.com
web: http://www.booksoncollectibles.com
Carries hundreds of reference books and price guides on antiques and collectibles; all at 25% off cover.

Harold Haskins
Southeastern Library Service
P.O. Box 44
Gainesville, FL 32602-0044
ph: 352-466-4789
Sells wholesale to booksellers and libraries; bi-monthly catalogs.

Gerry Haskins
Haskins House
P.O. Box 44
Gainesville, FL 32602-0044
ph: 352-466-4789

Bill Schroeder
Collector Books
P.O. Box 3009
Paducah, KY 42002-3009
ph: 800-626-5420 or 502-898-6211
fax: 502-898-8890
e-mail: antiques@apex.net
Publishers of books on antique and collectibles; specializes in full color value guides; since 1970.

Karen Nester
Green Gate Books
P.O. Box 989
Lima, OH 45802-0989
ph: 419-222-3816 or 800-228-3816 orders
fax: 419-227-3816
e-mail: ggb@wcoil.com
web: http://www.greengatebooks.com/
Offers almost 2,000 titles at retail and wholesale on books about antiques, collectibles and related crafts; also carries dealer's stickers, book display racks and plate racks.

L-W Book Sales
P.O. Box 69, Dept. 105
Gas City, IN 46933-0069
ph: 800-777-6450 or 765-674-6450
fax: 765-674-3503
e-mail: catalogs@lwbooks.com
web: http://www.lwbooks.com
Distributor of over 1000 titles of reference books on antiques & collectibles; wholesale and retail; call 1-800-777-6450, Dept. 105 for a FREE catalog.

Nancy Johnson
Library, The
P.O. Box 37
Des Moines, IA 50301-0037
ph: 515-262-6714
fax: 515-263-8116
e-mail: njohnson@collectorsextravaganza.com
Reference books on antiques, collectibles and the decorative arts; including foreign and private presses; over 7500 titles in stock; sells at antiques shows in Midwest and West and by mail order.

Mark Chervenka
P.O. Box 12130
Des Moines, IA 50312-9403
ph: 515-274-5886 or 800-227-5531 (orders)
fax: 515-255-4530
e-mail: acrn@repronews.com
web: http://www.repronews.com/
Buys and sells used reference books on antiques.

Antique Trader Books
P.O. Box 1050
Dubuque, IA 52004-1050
ph: 800-334-7165
fax: 800-531-0880
web: http://www.collect.com
Offers best selling price guides and reference books on nearly every antique and collectible category imaginable; quality purchase discounts available; send or call for free catalog.

Pat DuChene, PR
Krause Publications
700 E. State St.
Iola, WI 54990-0001
ph: 715-445-2214
fax: 715-445-4087
e-mail: info@krause.com
web: http://www.krause.com/

Charles & Joan Rhoden
"MEMORIES" Book Sales
8693 N 1950 East Road
Georgetown, IL 61846-6264
ph: 217-662-8046 or 217-662-8440
fax: 217-662-8223
Carries over 1300 new books on antiques and collectibles; send for free catalog; wholesale and retail; mail order and open shop.

Enid & Len Waska
Bookworm, The
P.O. Box 90063
Houston, TX 77290-0063
ph: 281-583-7448
e-mail: bookworm@blkbox.com
web: http://www.houstonet.com/bookworm/
Specializing in price guides and reference books on antiques and collectibles; over 1900 titles available.

Herzinger & Co.
144 Horizon Dr.
Sagle, ID 83860
ph: 800-428-2670
fax: 800-285-1502
Sells reference books on antiques, collectibles, dolls, and art.

Mickey Kaz
BooksR4U
P.O. Box 606
Woodland Hills, CA 91365-0606
ph: 818-703-6173
fax: 818-703-6173
e-mail: booksr4u@aol.com
web: http://www.collect.com/booksr4u/
Specializing in price guides on antiques, collectibles, dolls, toys, jewelry, etc.; online secure shopping cart service, searchable index by keyword; in business since 1977.

Mary M. Claret
Ms. Information
P.O. Box 262
El Granada, CA 94018-0262
ph: 650-726-1367
fax: 650-726-1367
e-mail: msinfo@mail.coastside.net
web: http://www.coastside.net/msinfobooks/
Sells out-of-print, used & new books about antiques & collectibles; website has extensive on-line catalog of books for sale; also provides new (in-print) books and used titles, bibliographical database and free search service.

Paul Brannan
Brannan Books
P.O. Box 475
Garberville, CA 95542
ph: 707-923-3552
fax: 707-923-2560
e-mail: brannan@humboldt.net
web: http://www.humboldt.net/~brannan/
Stocks out-of-print and rare books and exhibition catalogs on European, American, and Oriental art, artists, and antiques.

Sam's Books
7875 SE 13th Ave.
Portland, OR 97202-6307
ph: 503-232-3755
Large selection of collectors' reference books - new, used and out-of-print; buys and sells.

Richard J. Perry
Collectors Press, Inc.
P.O. Box 230986
Portland, OR 97281-0986
ph: 503-684-3030 or 888-680-3030
fax: 503-684-3777
e-mail: rperry@collectorspress.com
web: http://www.collectorspress.com/
Publishes books on nostalgia, art, and collecting; always looking for new book submissions and/or ideas.

J.R.'s Collector Reference Books
934 SW 8th St.
Newport, OR 97365-5135
ph: 800-726-5086
Wholesale mail order source for newly published antiques and collectibles reference books.

Estella Gelder
Estella G. Gelder Books
2728 Iron Street
Bellingham, WA 98225
ph: 360-733-7809
e-mail: egelder@nas.com
web: http://www.abebooks.com/home/estellasbooks
Internet online source for books about antiques & collectibles.

Dave McGee
Diversity Antiques & Collectibles Incorporated
P.O. Box 31275
Halifax, Nova Scotia B3K 5Y5
Canada
ph: 902-425-5331
e-mail: BooksAboutAntiques@canada.com
web: http://www.angelfire.com/ns/books
Carries selected American, English and Canadian titles; also Canadian stockist for publications of the Torquay Pottery Collectors' Society,

W. K. Cross, Pres.
Charlton Press, The
2040 Yonge St., Ste. 208
Toronto, Ontario M4S 1Z9
Canada
ph: 800-442-6042 or 416-488-1418
fax: 416-488-4656
e-mail: chpress@charltonpress.com
web: http://www.charltonpress.com
Specializes in books on Royal Doulton, Beswick, Chintz, Wade, Coalport, Royal Worcester, coins, paper money, country store collectibles.

John Ives
John Ives Antiquarian Books
5 Normanhurst Dr.
Twickenham, Middlesex TW1 1NA
U.K.
ph: 0181-8926265
fax: 0181-7443944
e-mail: jives@btconnect.com
Supplies specialist reference books on antiques and collecting to customers all over the world; send for free catalog.

Collectors

Karen S. Rabe, ISA CAPP
Appraisal Specialists
P.O. Box 21
Lake Forest, IL 60045
ph: 847-356-2094
fax: 847-356-2139
e-mail: ksrabe@ameritech.net
Wants to buy out-of-print books about the fine arts and decorative arts, furniture, glass, ceramics, and silver.

Dealers

Wendy Kenney
EphemeraArts
229 E. 31st St., #4
New York, NY 10016
ph: 212-481-0138
e-mail: wendy@ephemerarts.com
web: http://ephemerarts.com
Carries auction catalogs, exhibition catalogs, reference books and out-of-print books on antiques & collectibles; online catalog includes Asian arts, Americana, decorative arts, dolls, pottery, porcelain, glass jewelry, toys, etc.

Richard Olsen
Antiques & Collectibles Book Club
333 E. 38th St.
New York, NY 10016
ph: 800-257-8345 or 212-455-5000
fax: 609-786-3439
e-mail:
Richard_Olsen@mail.booksonline.com
web: http://www.booksonline.com/acbc
Only book club of its kind; offers hundreds of titles that have been reviewed and recommended by experts; members receive a monthly catalog featuring a wide range of topics; every book is offered at a discount.

J. M. Cohen
J.M. Cohen, Rare Books
2 Karin Court
New Paltz, NY 12561
ph: 914-883-9720
fax: 914-883-9142

Reference (Architecture)

Dealers

Arcade Books
P.O.Box 5176
FDR Station
New York, NY 10150-5176
ph: 212-724-5371

Reference (Art)

Book Sellers

Currier Fine Art, Inc.
Price Guide: Currier Price Guides
35 Centre St.
Brockton, MA 02401-4014
ph: 508-588-4509
Publisher of four art and print price guides including guides to American artists at auction, European artists at auction, American & European prints at auction, and Currier & Ives prints.

Arthur Fraumeni
New England Gallery
367 Gov. Wentworth Hwy.
Wolfeboro, NH 03894-4616
ph: 603-569-3501 or 954-7289
fax: 603-569-3501
e-mail: scollysq@aol.com
Distributor of "Benezit", the dictionary of painters; ADEC International Art Price Annual, and other reference books; also dealer in American and European art & antiques.

Peter Falk
Sound View Press
859 Boston Post Rd.
P.O. Box 833
Madison, CT 06443
ph: 203-245-2246
fax: 203-245-5116
e-mail: info@folkart.com
Researches, writes and sells books about artists listed in "Who's Who in American Art"; also publishes/sells art reference dictionaries and the ADEC/API CD-ROM of art prices.

Dealer's Choice Books
P.O. Box 710
Land O Lakes, FL 34639-0710
ph: 813-996-6599 or 800-238-8288
fax: 813-996-5226
e-mail: booksales@art-amer.com
web: http://www.Art-Amer.com
Sells art reference books (new only), e.g. Hislop's "Art Sales Index", "Who Was Who in American Art", "Signatures of American Artists", "Davenport's Art Price Guide", "Benezit", "Meyer's", Falk's "Print Price Index", etc.

Paul Brannan
Brannan Books
P.O. Box 475
Garberville, CA 95542
ph: 707-923-3552
fax: 707-923-2560
e-mail: brannan@humboldt.net
web: http://www.humboldt.net/~brannan/
Stocks out-of-print and rare books and exhibition catalogs on European, American, and Oriental art, artists, and antiques.

Collectors

Karen S. Rabe, ISA CAPP
Appraisal Specialists
P.O. Box 21
Lake Forest, IL 60045
ph: 847-356-2094
fax: 847-356-2139
e-mail: ksrabe@ameritech.net
Wants to buy out-of-print books about the fine arts and decorative arts, furniture, glass, ceramics, and silver.

Reference (Art, Asian)

Book Sellers

Jerrold G. Stanoff
Rare Oriental Book Co.
P.O. Box 1599
Aptos, CA 95001-1599
ph: 831-689-0203
fax: 831-689-0204
e-mail: jgs@rareorientbooks.com
web: http://www.rareorientbooks.com
Sells old, rare choice books on Japan, Korea, China, Tibet, S.E. Asia, Philippines, Hong Kong, Macau, Indonesia, Siam, Malaya, Singapore, Cambodia, Laos, Burma, Vietnam, Mongolia, New Guinea, Central Asia, Indonesia, Bali, etc.

Reference (Autographs)

Book Sellers

Brian Kathenes
Brian Kathenes Autographs & Collectibles
P.O. Box 482
Hope, NJ 07844-0482
ph: 908-459-5225 or 800-323-5996
fax: 908-459-4899
e-mail: Brian@nacvalue.com
web: http://www.nacvalue.com

Reference (Automobiles)

Book Sellers

Eric Waiter Associates
205 US Hwy. 22
Dunellen, NJ 08812
ph: 732-424-0200 or 732-424-7811
fax: 732-424-7814
e-mail: ewa@ewacars.com
web: http://www.ewacars.com
Carries large selection of automobile related books, magazines and videos; over 1500 titles on a wide variety of subjects; catalog sent free on request.

Dennis Mitosinka
Dennis Mitosinka's Classic Cars
619 E. Fourth St.
Santa Ana, CA 92701-4705
ph: 714-953-5303
fax: 714-953-1810
Over 400 titles of car-related out-of-print books including large selection of Clymer books, Indy 500 Year Books, Salt Flat Racing.

Reference (Aviation)

Book Sellers

Historic Aviation
211 Alpha Lane
South Saint Paul, MN 55075
ph: 800-225-5575 or 651-453-1875
fax: 651-453-1895
Sells aviation related books, videos and prints.

Reference (Breweriana)

Book Sellers

Soda Mart - Can World
1055 Ridgecrest Dr.
Goodlettsville, TN 37072
ph: 615-859-5236 or 877-859-4929
fax: 615-859-5238
e-mail: mbca@gono.com
web: http://gono.com/vir-mus/museum.htm
Sells breweriana books; also cleans and de-rusts on cans, and sells supplies for the beer can collector.

Reference (Cameras)

Book Sellers

Jim McKeown
Centennial Photo Service
11595 State Route 70
Grantsburg, WI 54840
ph: 715-689-2153
fax: 715-689-2277
e-mail: mckeown@camera-net.com
web: http://www.camera-net.com/
Publisher of "McKeown's Price Guide to Antique & Classic Cameras", the world's leading camera reference work; over 9,000 different models with values; heavily illustrated; send for details on latest edition; dealer inquiries invited.

William P. Carroll
ACR Books
P.O. Box 4294
Whittier, CA 90607-4294
ph: 562-693-8421
fax: 562-945-6011
Antique and classic cameras for sale; offers new and used books on kaleidoscopes, cameras and the history of photography.

Reference (Ceramics)

Book Sellers

Bradshaw & Whelan Ceramic Books
P.O. Box 18521
Asheville, NC 28814
ph: 828-253-1829
fax: 828-281-4798
e-mail: anhua@att.net
web: http://www.att.net/~anhua/
Specializes in out-of-print, used and new ceramic reference books including British, Continental, Oriental, and American pottery and porcelain books; offers a free book search service for ceramics and other decorative arts titles.

David Richardson
Antique Publications
217 Union St.
P.O. Box 553
Marietta, OH 45750-0553
ph: 800-533-3433 or 740-373-6146
fax: 740-373-6917
e-mail: info@antiquepublications.com
web: http://www.antiquepublications.com/
Offers a wide selection of books about pottery and glass.

Reference (Civil War)

Book Sellers

Nancy Dearing Rossbacher
North South Trader
P.O. Drawer 631
Orange, VA 22960-0370
ph: 540-67C-IVIL
fax: 540-672-7283
e-mail: nstcw@msn.com
web: http://www.nstcivilwar.com
Carries extensive inventory of hardbound and softbound books for Civil War historians, enthusiasts and collectors.

First Corps Books
42 Eastgrove Ct.
Columbia, SC 29212-2404
ph: 803-781-2709
Carries hundreds of Civil War books, both new and out-of-print.

Theodore P. Savas
SAVAS Publishing Company
1475 S. Bascom Ave., Ste. 204
Campbell, CA 95008-0629
ph: 408-879-9039 or 800-848-6585
fax: 408-879-9327
e-mail: mhbooks@aol.com
Publisher of Civil War books.

Reference (Clocks)

Book Sellers

Heart of America Press
55 N. Central
Umatilla, FL 32784
ph: 352-669-4791
fax: 352-669-6969
e-mail: sales@hoapress.com
web: http://www.hoapress.com/
Issues catalog of horological books and literature.

Loren Scalon
Scalon American Reprints Co.
P.O. Box 379
Modesto, CA 95353-0379
ph: 209-667-2906 or 800-854-8639
fax: 209-521-2777
e-mail: dlscanlon@aol.com
Large selection of watch and clock books and price guides - over 800 titles.

Reference (Coin-Operated)

Book Sellers

Ken Durham
909 26th St. NW
Washington, DC 20037-2029
e-mail: durham@gameroomantiques.com
web: http://www.GameRoomAntiques.com
Sells large selection of books and service manuals on same; send SASE for information.

Russell's Antiques
2404 W. 111th St.
Chicago, IL 60655
ph: 773-233-3205
Sells books and literature related to coin-operated machines.

Rosanna Harris
5815 W. 52nd Ave.
Denver, CO 80212-7503
ph: 303-431-9266
fax: 303-431-6978
e-mail: info@royalbell.com
Carries selection of books and service manuals relating to slot machines.

Peter Movsesian
Coin-Op Classics
17844 Toiyabe St.
Fountain Valley, CA 92708
ph: 714-968-3020
fax: 714-963-1716
e-mail: pmovsesian@aol.com
web: http://www.coin-opclassics.com
Publishes books on vintage coin-operated machines; books include photos, history, original service manuals, schematics, etc.; all books include price guides.

Reference (Coins)

Book Sellers

Q. David Bowers
Bowers & Merena, Inc.
P.O. Box 1224
Wolfeboro, NH 03894-1224
ph: 800-458-4646 or 603-569-5095
fax: 603-569-5319
e-mail: bowersmerena@conknet.com
web: http://web.coin-universe.com/bowers/index.html
Sells books relating to all areas of the US coin business and hobby; gold, silver, tokens, and all other areas of numismatics including exonumia; member International Association of Professional Numismatists.

George F. Kolbe
Fine Numismatic Books
P.O. Drawer 3100
Crestline, CA 92325-3100
ph: 909-338-6527
fax: 909-338-6980
e-mail: numislit@compuserve.com
web: http://www.numislit.com
Sells numismatic literature.

Reference (Dolls)

Book Sellers

F. Russack Antiques & Books
20 Beach Plain Rd.
Danville, NH 03819
ph: 603-642-7718
fax: 603-642-7718

Hobby House Press, Inc.
One Corporate Drive
Grantsville, MD 21536
ph: 301-895-3792 or 800-554-1447
fax: 301-895-5029
e-mail: hobbyhouse@aol.com
Specializes on books dealing with Dolls, Teddy Bears, Paper Dolls, Vintage Clothing.

Reference (Exonumia)

Book Sellers

Rich Hartzog
World Exonumia
P.O. Box 4143
Rockford, IL 61110-0643
ph: 815-226-0771
fax: 815-397-7662
e-mail: hartzog@exonumia.com
web: http://www.exonumia.com/
Carries a large selection of titles relating to tokens, medals, and exonumia.

Reference (Farm Toys)

Book Sellers

Shawn Van Meeuwen
Diamond Enterprises & Book Publishers
P.O. Box 537
Alexandria Bay, NY 13607-0537
ph: 613-475-1771 or 800-481-1353
fax: 613-475-3748
e-mail: info@yesteryeartoys.com
web: http://www.yesteryeartoys.com
Offers a complete line of hobby and toy publications; specialty in hobby steam and farm toys including antique tractor books.

Reference (Firearms)

Book Sellers

Ray Riling Arms Books Co.
6844 Gorsten St.
Philadelphia, PA 19119
ph: 215-438-2456
Carries every gun book in print.

Bill Williams
Guncraft Sports Inc.
10737 Dutchtown Rd.
Knoxville, TN 37932-3208
ph: 423-966-4545
fax: 423-966-4500
e-mail: findit@guncraft.com
web: http://www.usit.net/hp/guncraft/
Serving the shooting public since 1947; a multi-faceted supplier of guns, accessories, appraisal services, training, gunsmithing, gun related books.

Reference (Gems/Jewelry)

Book Sellers

Stuart M. Matlins
Gemstone Press
P.O. Box 237
Woodstock, VT 05091-0237
ph: 802-457-4000 or 800-962-4544
fax: 802-457-4004
e-mail: everyone@longhillpartners.com
web: http://www.gemstonepress.com/
International source for books and other items designed to help people in the gem trade and consumers learn more about gems & jewelry.

Gemological Institute of America Bookstore
5345 Armada Dr.
Carlsbad, CA 92008
ph: 760-603-4200
fax: 760-603-4266
web: http://www.gia.org

Reference (Glass)

Book Sellers

Robert Eaton
Eaton's Glass Books on the Web
18 Folson Road
P.O. Box 1081
Derry, NH 03038-1081
fax: 603-434-3588
e-mail: reaton@glassbooks.com
web: http://www.glassbooks.com/
Sells glass books via the Internet.

David Richardson
Antique Publications
217 Union St.
P.O. Box 553
Marietta, OH 45750-0553
ph: 800-533-3433 or 740-373-6146
fax: 740-373-6917
e-mail: info@antiquepublications.com
web: http://www.antiquepublications.com/
Offers a wide selection of books about pottery and glass.

Reference (Japanese Items)

Book Sellers

Yoneyama
Ginza, "Things Japanese"
1721 Connecticut Ave., NW
Washington, DC 20009-1108
ph: 202-331-7991
Carries a wide assortment of Japan related books in English: art, crafts, history, fiction, tea ceremony, Zen, cooking, martial arts, poetry, some graphic novels, origami, architecture, interior design, fengshui/geomancy, tapes, etc.

Reference (Japanese Prints)

Book Sellers

G. C. Uhlenbeck
Ukiyo-E Books B.V./Anthro Books
Breestraat 113a
CL Leiden, 23211
The Netherlands
ph: (071) 514 35 52/512 44 59
fax: (071) 514 14 88/512 38 55
e-mail: ukiyoe@xs4all.nl
web: http://www.nvva.nl/hotei/

Reference (Jukeboxes)

Book Sellers

Michael F. Baute
Always Jukin'
1952 1st Avenue S. #6
Seattle, WA 98134-1406
ph: 206-652-4005
fax: 972-783-0705
e-mail: alwaysjuke@aol.com
web: http://www.alwaysjukin.com/
Sells books about jukeboxes, jukebox service manuals and records.

Reference (Knives)

Book Sellers

Knife World Books
P.O. Box 3395
Knoxville, TN 37927-3395
ph: 423-397-1955 or 800-828-7751
fax: 423-397-1969
e-mail: knifepub@knifeworld.com
web: http://www.knifeworld.com
Specializes in books about knives.

Louise Weyer
Weyer International - Book Division
2740 Nebraska Ave.
Toledo, OH 43607-3245
ph: 419-534-2020
e-mail: law-weyerinternational@msn.com
Specializes in books about knives.

Reference (Law Enforcement)

Book Sellers

Matthew G. Forte
Turn of the Century Publishers
P.O. Box 3114
Memorial Station
Montclair, NJ 07043-3114
ph: 973-746-8686
fax: 973-746-8686
Publisher of "American Police Collectibles": billy clubs, nightsticks, handcuffs, mechanical and chain nippers, rattles, bullseye lanterns.

Reference (Maps & Charts)

Book Sellers

Kimmel Publications
P.O. Box 12
Amherst, MA 01004-0012
ph: 413-256-8900
fax: 413-256-6291
e-mail: navigateur@aol.com
Publisher of the "Antique Map Price Record & Handbook"; news, comments, recommended references, book reviews, collectors' considerations, glossary of terms, directory of dealers, price listing, title and geographical index, etc.

Map Collector Publications, Ltd.
48 High Street
Tring, Hertfordshire HP23 5AH
U.K.
ph: 011 44 1442 824977
fax: 011 44 1442 827712
e-mail: gp86@dial.pipex.com
web: http://www.mapcolelctor.com/
Publishers and distributors of books about collecting maps and the history of early maps.

Reference (Militaria)

Book Sellers

Military Bookman, The
29 East 93rd St.
New York, NY 10128
ph: 212-348-1280
fax: 212-427-5588
e-mail: history@militarybookman.com
web: http://www.militarybookman.com
Deals exclusively in military, naval and aviation history o/p books, with related pictorial items; by mail or on site; catalogs available.

Nate Rind
Antheil Booksellers
2177 Isabelle Court
Bellmore, NY 11710-1599
ph: 516-826-2094
fax: 516-826-3101
e-mail: antheil231@aol.com
web: http://www.antheilbooksellers.com/
Specializes in naval, maritime, military and aviation books, both new and used; many books from Germany, Great Britain, Japan, and Australia; business done exclusively by mail; 48-page catalog subscription $6 for four catalogs.

Terry Hannon
Phoenix Militaria, Inc. Military Bookstore
116 Lyons Rd.
Mertztown, PA 19539-9801
ph: 610-682-1010 or 800-446-0909
fax: 610-682-1066
e-mail: TerryHannon@msn.com
web: http://www.phoenixmilitaria.com
Sells a wide variety of military-related books and publications.

LTC(Ret) Thomas Johnson
Johnson Reference Books & Militaria
312 Butler Road, Bldg. 403
Fredericksburg, VA 22405-2514
ph: 540-373-9150 or 540-371-2665
fax: 540-373-0087
e-mail: ww2daggers@aol.com
web: http://www.ww2daggers.com
Wants to buy German War booty; specific interest is in edged weapons (dress swords, daggers, bayonets); author of seventeen books about Imperial and 3rd Reich German edged weapons, and militaria.

Nautical & Aviation Publishing Co. of American Inc.
1250 Fairmont Ave.
Mount Pleasant, SC 29464
ph: 843-856-0561
fax: 843-856-3164
e-mail: milesadler@aol.com
web: http://www.sonic.net/~bstone/nautical/
Carries naval, aviation and Civil War military books; many titles are primary sources, i.e. memoirs, biographies, etc.

C. Clayton Thompson
P.O. Box 5033
Pleasanton, CA 94566
ph: 510-462-5211
fax: 510-462-5211
e-mail: Greatbooks@aol.com
web: http://members.aol.com/Greatbooks
Specialist in Civil War military books and has one of the largest selections on the internet; also Regimental histories, first editions and reprints.

Collectors' Library
P.O. Box 263
Eugene, OR 97440
Publisher and book dealer for key reference books and reprints on equipment of the US military; extensive offering in free catalog.

Service Publications
55 Abingdon Drive
Nepean, Ontario K2H 7M5
Canada
ph: 613-820-7350
fax: 613-820-1288
e-mail: service@magi.com
web: http://infoweb.magi.com/~service/home/se09000.htm
Specializes in publishing books about firearms and collectible military artifacts.

Dealers

Last Square, The
5944 Odana Rd.
Madison, WI 53719
ph: 800-750-4401 or 608-278-4401
fax: 608-278-4402
e-mail: orders@lastsquare.com
web: http://www.lastsquare.com
A military/militaria art & books/historical miniatures dealer catering to all aspects of the military history hobby; from collectible art to large-scale hand-painted figures to wargaming miniatures.

Reference (Music)

Book Sellers

Linda Osborne
Jellyroll Productions
P.O. Box 255
Port Townsend, WA 98368
ph: 360-385-1200
fax: 360-385-6572
e-mail: jpo@olympus.net
web: http://www.jerryosborne.com
Specializes in books relating to the hobby of music & music memorabilia collecting; artists, titles, price guides, etc.

Reference (Natural History)

Book Sellers

Donald E. Hahn
Natural History Books
P.O. Box 1004
Cottonwood, AZ 86326-1004
ph: 520-634-5016 or 520-634-1217
fax: 520-634-1217
Offers technical publications about earth, biological sciences, and meteorites.

Reference (Nautical)

Book Sellers

Bob Glick
Columbia Trading Company
1 Barnstable Rd.
Hyannis, MA 02601
ph: 508-778-2929
fax: 508-778-2922
e-mail: nautical@capecod.net
web: http://www.columbiatrading.com/
Issues 6 catalogs a year each offering 600 nautical, boating, and naval books, magazines and ephemera for sale.

Reference (Orientalia)

Book Sellers

Paragon Book Gallery, Inc.
1507 S Michigan Ave.
Chicago, IL 60605-2812
ph: 312-663-5155
fax: 312-663-5177
e-mail: paragon@paragonbook.com
web: http://www.paragonbook.com/
Carries rare, out-of-print, and scholarly books on Asia; specializes in books on Asian arts and Asian studies; new and out of print.

Jerrold G. Stanoff
Rare Oriental Book Co.
P.O. Box 1599
Aptos, CA 95001-1599
ph: 831-689-0203
fax: 831-689-0204
e-mail: jgs@rareorientbooks.com
web: http://www.rareorientbooks.com
Sells old, rare choice books on Japan, Korea, China, Tibet, S.E. Asia, Philippines, Indonesia, Siam, Malaya, Singapore, Cambodia, Laos, Burma, Vietnam, Mongolia, New Guinea, Bali, etc.

Reference (Paperweights)

Book Sellers

Paul H. Dunlop
Dunlop Collection, The
P.O. Box 6269
Statesville, NC 28687-6269
ph: 800-227-1996 or 704-871-2626
fax: 704-871-2329
"Paperweights of the 19th & 20th Centuries," (Paul Jokelson & Gerald Ingold); "Old Glass Paperweights of Southern New Jersey," (Clarence Newell), "The Jokelson Collection of Antique Cameo Incrustation," (Paul H. Dunlop).

Lawrence H. Selman
L.H. Selman, Ltd.
761 Chestnut St.
Santa Cruz, CA 95060-3751
ph: 800-538-0766 or 831-427-1177
fax: 831-427-0111
e-mail: lselman@got.net
web: http://www.paperweight.com/
Carries over 50 books about paperweights.

Reference (Phonographs)

Book Sellers

Allen Koenigsberg
502 E. 17th St.
Brooklyn, NY 11226-6606
ph: 718-941-6835
fax: 718-941-1408
e-mail: AllenAmet@aol.com
web: http://members.aol.com/allenamet/PhonoBooks.html
Carries the most complete list of phonograph related books, catalogs, manuals, discographies, posters and magazines; "The Antique Phonograph Monthly" available for $15 per volume, or sample for $3 in stamps.

Reference (Postcards)

Book Sellers

Dr. James Lewis Lowe, Dir.
Deltiologists of America
Magazine: Postcard Classics
P.O. Box 8
Norwood, PA 19074
ph: 610-485-8572
International postcard society for collectors, dealers, librarians, and archivist; offers several postcard related books for sale.

Reference (Quilts)

Book Sellers

Kris Driessen
Hickory Hill Antique Quilts
P.O. Box 273
Esperance, NY 12066
ph: 518-875-6133
fax: 518-875-9141
e-mail: oldquilt@albany.net
web: http://www.HickoryHillQuilts.com
Offers antique quilt tops, blocks by catalog; also offers vintage and reproduction fabrics, as well as restoration supplies and Quilt Heritage reference books.

Reference (Railroads)

Book Sellers

Harold H. Carstens
Carstens Publications
108 Phil Hardin Road
P.O. Box 700
Newton, NJ 07860-0700
ph: 973-383-3355 or 800-474-6995
fax: 973-383-4064
e-mail: carstens@carstens-publications.com
web: http://www.carstens-publications.com/mainindex.html
Carries large line of books about railroads.

Richard C. Barrett
Railroad Research Publications
3400 Ridge Rd. West, Ste. 5-266
Rochester, NY 14626-3458
ph: 716-227-6903
Publishes and sells books on railroad collectibles and railroad history; send SASE for catalog.

Reference (Records)

Book Sellers

Linda Osborne
Jellyroll Productions
P.O. Box 255
Port Townsend, WA 98368
ph: 360-385-1200
fax: 360-385-6572
e-mail: jpo@olympus.net
web: http://www.jerryosborne.com
Offers an assortment of publications for the record collector.

Reference (Reptile/Amphibians)

Book Sellers

Mark F. Miller
Herpetology.com
P.O. Box 52261
Philadelphia, PA 19115-7261
ph: 215-464-3561
fax: 215-464-3561
e-mail: reptiles@earthling.net
web: http://www.herpetology.com
Buys reptile or amphibian books, serials, monographs, PH.D. thesis, etc.; please quote anytime; do not send books or other items unless instructed.

Reference (Space Collectibles)

Book Sellers

Richard H. Jackson
Missile, Space or Rocket Used Books
P.O. Box 93
Mount Vernon, VA 22121-0093
ph: 703-360-7677
fax: 703-360-2886
e-mail: spacebooks@csgi.com
web: http://www.ari.net/nss/msrb/
Buys and sells used books about missile, space or rockets; mail order; quarterly price lists.

Reference (Stamps)

Book Sellers

Leonard H. Hartmann
Philatelic Bibliophile
P.O. Box 36006
Louisville, KY 40233-6006
fax: 502-459-8538
e-mail: pbbooks@ibm.net
web: http://www.pbbooks.com
Sells new books (no annual catalogs such as Scott's, S.G., Minkus, Yvert) stocked from over 100 publishers plus used stamp books; does not drop ship; check out website.

Newspaper: Linn's Stamp News
P.O. Box 29
Sidney, OH 45365-0029
ph: 937-498-0801 or 800-448-7293
fax: 800-340-9501
e-mail: linns@linns.com
web: http://www.linns.com
World's largest stamp marketplace with up-to-the-minute hobby news, reports on topics from trends in values, special interest collections to under-collected stamps; well-respected in the hobby; indispensable for the stamp collector.

Reference (Teddy Bears)

Book Sellers

Hobby House Press, Inc.
One Corporate Drive
Grantsville, MD 21536
ph: 301-895-3792 or 800-554-1447
fax: 301-895-5029
e-mail: hobbyhouse@aol.com
Specializes on books dealing with Dolls, Teddy Bears, Paper Dolls, Vintage Clothing.

Reference (Telegraph Items)

Book Sellers

Tom French
Artifax Books
P.O. Box 88
Maynard, MA 01754-0088
ph: 978-562-5573
fax: 978-562-3043
e-mail: artifaxbooks@yahoo.com
web: http://home.fiam.net/tfrench/artifax.htm
Sells books for telegraph instrument collectors, including Vibroplex and McElroy keys; reprints of early books on telegraphy; send for free list.

Reference (Textiles)

Book Sellers

Mary Chapman
Mary Chapman, Booksellers
P.O. Box 304
College Park, MD 20741
Specialists in out-of-print books on all textile and needle arts; mail order only; catalogs issues; want lists solicited.

Reference (Tiles)

Book Sellers

Joseph Taylor
Tile Heritage Foundation
P.O. Box 1850
Healdsburg, CA 95448
ph: 707-431-8453
fax: 707-431-8455
web: http://www.aimnet.com/~tcolson/pages/tileorgs/thfinfo.htm
Offers a large line of books about tile: terra cotta, foreign, decorated tiles, Delftware, English medieval, Victorian tiles, etc.

Chris Blanchett
Buckland Books
Holly Tree House
18 Woodlands Rd.
Littlehampton, West Sussex BN17 5PP
U.K.
ph: +44 1903 717648
fax: +44 1903 717648
e-mail: clbanchett@lineone.net
A mail-order service selling new and secondhand books about tiles and associated subjects such as architecture, bricks, terra-cotta & mosaics; publishes six monthly book lists.

Reference (Tools)

Book Sellers

Lisa J. Pollak
Astragal Press, The
P.O. Box 239
Mendham, NJ 07945-0239
ph: 973-543-3045
fax: 973-543-3044
e-mail: astragalpress@ibm.net
web: http://www.astragalpress.com/
Publishes and distributes books on early tools, trades, and technology including books on woodworking tools, metalworking, scientific instruments, architecture, wood turning, machinists' tools, and reprints of early trade catalogs.

Martin J. Donnelly
Martin J. Donnelly Antique Tools
P.O. Box 281
Bath, NY 14810-0281
ph: 800-869-0695 or 607-776-9322
fax: 607-776-6064
e-mail: mjd@mjdtools.com
web: http://www.mjdtools.com
Website offers a long list of books about tools for sale.

Bob & Maxine Finch
Glen Moor Press
1864 Glen Moore Dr.
Lakewood, CO 80215-3038
ph: 303-232-1932
fax: 303-232-8826
e-mail: rffinch@aol.com
Published reprint "Woodworking Machinery - Its Rise, Progress, and Construction - 1800 - 1880," illustrated; 400 pp.; $12.

Reference (Toys)

Book Sellers

F. Russack Antiques & Books
20 Beach Plain Rd.
Danville, NH 03819
ph: 603-642-7718
fax: 603-642-7718

Joseph E. Freed
Freedom Publishing Co., Inc.
6209 Sandy Forks Rd.
Raleigh, NC 27624-9534
ph: 919-847-7365
fax: 919-847-3822

Patricia Mullins
P.E.I. International
6001 Johns Rd., Ste. 148
Tampa, FL 33634
ph: 813-855-4213
Publishers and distributors of reference books about rocking horses, toy soldiers, penny toys, dolls, teddy bears, war toys, and all types of other toys.

Reference (Vintage Clothing)

Book Sellers

Hobby House Press, Inc.
One Corporate Drive
Grantsville, MD 21536
ph: 301-895-3792 or 800-554-1447
fax: 301-895-5029
e-mail: hobbyhouse@aol.com
Specializes on books dealing with Dolls, Teddy Bears, Paper Dolls, Vintage Clothing.

Wooden Porch Books
Rte. 1 Box 262
Middlebourne, WV 26149-9748
ph: 304-386-4434
fax: 304-386-4868
e-mail: books@woodenporch.com
web: http://www.woodenporch.com/
6 catalogs per year listing approximately 2400 out-of-print books and magazines on the fiber arts and kindred subjects.

Fred Struthers
R.L. Shep Publications
P.O. Box 2706
Fort Bragg, CA 95437
ph: 707-964-8662
fax: 707-964-8662
e-mail: fsbks@mcn.org
web: http://www.mcn.org/e/fsbks/
Reprints of Victorian and Edwardian costume books stressing patterns, instructions, embroidery, etc.; women and men; practical manuals; also Civil War books about women's activities.

Reference (Watches)

Book Sellers

Heart of America Press
55 N. Central
Umatilla, FL 32784
ph: 352-669-4791
fax: 352-669-6969
e-mail: sales@hoapress.com
web: http://www.hoapress.com/
Issues catalog of horological books and literature.

Reference (Western Americana)

Book Sellers

Early West, The
P.O. Box 9292
College Station, TX 77842
ph: 800-245-5841
fax: 409-764-7758
Sells, buys and trades non-fiction books on the old west: outlaws, lawmen, towns, areas.

Bill Mackin
1137 Washington St.
Craig, CO 81625-1613
ph: 970-824-6717 or 970-824-6360
fax: 970-824-7175
Sells books and reprinted catalogs for Old West and cowboy collectors; over 50 titles including his own "Cowboy and Gunfighter Collectibles" with updated prices; $25 plus $3 postage.

Kenneth Asher
Maverick Distributors
P.O. Drawer 7289
Bend, OR 97708
ph: 541-382-2728
fax: 541-382-8444
e-mail: kenasher@teleport.com
Sells Western Americana books: Indian art & artifacts, bottles, cowboy & horse collectibles, fruit jars, railroad, logging, fur trade, history. etc.

Dealers

David B. Ogle
Antiquarian Archive, The
379 State St.
Los Altos, CA 94022-2816
ph: 650-949-1593
e-mail: archive@batnet.com
web: http://www.ippi.com/antiquarian-archive.html
Specialist in Western Americana, railroadiana, nautical & maritime, military history & memoirs, books of the Roycroft printing shop.

Roycroft

Collectors

Gary Wood
733 Myrtle Rd.
North Brunswick, NJ 08902-2549
ph: 732-821-7633
e-mail: woodrasp@aol.com
Collector seeks single issues or bound volumes of all Roycroft magazines including "The Philistine," "Roycrofter," "The Fra," as well as books published by The Roycroft Press and craft items bearing the Roycroft cross-and-orb mark.

Scientific

Book Sellers

Lee & Peggy Price
Knollwood Books
P.O. Box 197
Oregon, WI 53575-0197
ph: 608-835-8861
fax: 608-835-8421
e-mail: books@tdsnet.com
Issues quarterly catalogs; buys and sells out-of-print books on astronomy, meteorology, and space exploration; also books about microscopes, old scientific instruments, optics, and related areas.

Scottish

Periodicals

Jennie Renton
Magazine: Scottish Book Collector
36 Lauriston Place
Edinburgh, EH3 9EZ
U.K.
e-mail: jennie@scotbooksmag.demon.co.uk
web: http://www.scotbooksmag.demon.co.uk/
A quarterly magazine that specializes in in-depth features about collectible, old and rare Scottish books alongside profiles of contemporary Scottish writers and publishers.

Sports

Collectors

John Buonaguidi
540 Reeside Ave.
Monterey, CA 93940-1828
ph: 831-375-7345
Wants 19th century non-fiction books about baseball, football, or boxing.

Yearbooks

Collectors

Seth & Danine Poppel
Yearbook Archives
38 Range Dr.
Merrick, NY 11566
ph: 516-867-6280
fax: 516-546-4128
e-mail: Sethpoppel@aol.com
web: http://www.highschool.com
Always eager to buy high school yearbooks that feature the senior pictures of famous and infamous people; if you don;t know whether

there is a famous person in the yearbook just e-mail, mail or fax year, school, city and state.

Experts

Mitchell Moore
Bygone Era
5203 16th St.
Lubbock, TX 79416
ph: 806-785-1823
e-mail: mlmoore@llano.net
Specializing in all sections of both high school and college yearbooks spanning over 120 years; call for specifics or general yearbook trends over the years; also searching for additional copies.

BORGHESE

Collectors

David Elder
306 South Chapman St.
Greensboro, NC 27403
Wants Borghese decorative boxes, lamps, pictures, plaques, figurines, bookends, etc.; usually made from plaster and painted gold, green, maroon, etc., sometimes with pictures of flowers pasted on; black felt bottom with paper label.

BOSSONS

Clubs/Associations

Dr. Robert E. Davis, ExDir
International Bossons Collectors Society, Inc.
Newsletter: Bossons Briefs
1787 Morgan Valley Road
Rockmart, GA 30153
ph: 770-684-1922
fax: 770-684-0300
e-mail: bossonboss@aol.com
web: http://hometown.aol.com/bossonboss/collect/
Bossons character heads or figurines.

Collectors

Bruce Bleier
73 Riverdale Rd.
Valley Stream, NY 11581
ph: 516-791-4353
fax: 516-792-0519
e-mail: emeralite@aol.com
Buys and sells BOSSONS artware including faces, animals and plaques.

Andy Jackson
501 Falcon Lane
West Chester, PA 19382-5716
ph: 610-692-0269 or 610-272-7900
Wants all Bossons artware: face masks, dogs, animals and plaques; will buy, sell or trade.

Dealers

Donald M. Hardisty
Don's Collectibles
3020 E. Majestic Ridge
Las Cruces, NM 88011
ph: 505-522-3721
fax: 505-522-7909
e-mail: donsbossons@zianet.com
web: http://www.zianet.com/donsbossons/
Internationally recognized expert, collector, supplier, appraiser, and restoration artist recommended by Bossons; also specializes in Hummels and rare coins; member Inter. Bossons Collectors Society, MI Hummel Club, Amer. Numismatic Assoc.

Lynda Meek
Bossons Australia Pty Ltd.
P.O. Box 92
Five Dock
Sydney, New South Wales 2046
Australia
ph: 612 97132122
fax: 612 97131784
e-mail: bosngals@redback.com.au
web: http://www.asiapacific.com.au/~owent/
Large assortment of Bossons pieces for sale; wants to purchase any items made by Bossons Co., Congleton, England.

Experts

Dr. Robert E. Davis
International Bossons
1787 Morgan Valley Road
Rockmart, GA 30153
ph: 770-684-1922
fax: 770-684-0300
e-mail: bossonboss@aol.com
web: http://hometown.aol.com/bossonboss/collect/
Author of "The Imagical World of Bossons" and "The Imagical World of Bossons - Book II."

Donald M. Hardisty
Don's Collectibles
3020 E. Majestic Ridge
Las Cruces, NM 88011
ph: 505-522-3721
fax: 505-522-7909
e-mail: donsbossons@zianet.com
web: http://www.zianet.com/donsbossons/
Internationally recognized expert, collector, supplier, appraiser, and restoration artist recommended by Bossons; also specializes in Hummels and rare coins; member Inter. Bossons Collectors Society, MI Hummel Club, Amer. Numismatic Assoc.

John & Joanna Cassidy
Ultimate Bosson Website, The
1317 N. San Fernanto Blvd., Ste. #3
Burbank, CA 91504
ph: 818-238-3575 or 818-734-7007
e-mail: bossonsman@aol.com
web: http://www.bossons.com
Online resource for Bossons artware; information and photos of the character wall masks, figurines, and many other items produced by the W.H. Bossons, Co., of Congleton, England.

Internet Resources

John & Barb Spinner
Bossons
e-mail: johnspinner@fuse.net
web: http://home.fuse.net/johnspinner/

BOTTLE CAPS

(see also BOTTLES, Milk; BREWERIANA; DAIRY COLLECTIBLES; SOFT DRINK COLLECTIBLES)

Crown

Clubs/Associations

John Vetter
Crown Collectors Society International
Newsletter: Crown Cappers Exchange
4300 San Juan Dr.
Fairfax, VA 22030-5351
ph: 703-591-3060
fax: 703-591-3197
e-mail: crownking@erols.com
A collector's organization dedicated to helping those interested in collecting and working to preserve the rich colorful history of the bottle crown closure as used for beer, soda, mineral water, etc. bottles.

Collectors

Barry Oremland
1260 Washington St.
Walpole, MA 02081-3116
ph: 508-688-9086 or 617-864-0161
fax: 617-864-4422
e-mail: crownclctr@aol.com
web: http://members.aol.com/crownclctr
Collects, trades, buys, sells crown caps of all types; all origins, and all reasonable conditions; also wants crown industry material, reseal caps, signs, pictures, articles, letters, etc. depicting or mentioning crown caps.

Christopher Leppek
1016 S. Washington St.
Denver, CO 80209-4318
ph: 303-744-8385
e-mail: redraven75@aol.com
Buys, sells and trades crowns (bottle caps); vintages, nationalities of all types - beers, sodas, waters, oddball. Will buy loners, groups or entire collections.

David Friedman
11129 Barman Ave.
Culver City, CA 90230
ph: 310-837-3089
Runs the ABA Crown Cap Exchange.

Konstantin Levochkin
Kievskaya ul 16-7
Moscow, 121151
Russia
e-mail: kostya@invsbank.glasnet.ru
web: http://www.geocities.com/NapaValley/2544/
A beer cap collector from Moscow; wants to trade with other collectors.

Edward Veld
Verschoorstraat 25 B
Rotterdam, 3081 JT
The Netherlands
e-mail: seine@dds.nl
web: http://www.crowncap.demon.nl
Collector of crown bottle caps; website is for collectors of Williams Painters crown bottle caps.

Experts

Robert Walters
RTW Services
63 Mount Batten Street
Rochester, NY 14623
ph: 716-359-4917
fax: 716-359-4917
e-mail: beercap@lsweb.com
web: http://www.lsweb.com/crowns/
Historian, collector, dealer of beer crowns from U.S. breweries; knowledgeable in grading and valuation of all U.S. beer crowns; web site has member listings, crowns for sale, convention information, buy-sell-trade ads, links.

Internet Resources

Beer Cap Page, The
web: http://www.cam.org/~kibi/TBCP/

Eric Budesheim
Bottle Caps Via the Internet
e-mail: buda@global2000.net
web: http://www.members.global2000.net/~buda/

Wietze Veld
Crown Cap Page, The
The Netherlands
e-mail: seine@dds.nl
web: http://www.crowncap.demon.nl/
Online resources for crown cap collecting on the Internet.

Milk

(see also POGS)

Dealers

Carole Schauer
Carole's Collectibles
W10642 Elm St.
Elcho, WI 54428-9572
ph: 715-275-5200
Buys and sells milk bottle caps and small dairy items.

Experts

Dan Ryan
45 Sunnyside Ave.
Putnam, CT 06260-1830
ph: 860-928-5014
e-mail: milkcaps@worldnet.att.net
web: http://home.att.net/~milkcaps/
Writes "Covering Caps" column for "The Milk Route", newsletter of The National Association of Milk Bottle Collectors.

BOTTLE OPENERS

Figural

(see also BREWERIANA; CAN OPENERS; CORKSCREWS)

Clubs/Associations

John T. Fitzsimmons
Figural Bottle Opener Collectors Club
Newsletter: Opener, The
9697 Gwynn Park Dr.
Ellicott City, MD 21042
e-mail: johnf129@aol.com
web: http://www.dol.net/~c-llesser/
Formed to promote interest in and knowledge about figural bottle openers.

John Stanley
Just for Openers
Newsletter: Just for Openers Newsletter
P.O. Box 64
Chapel Hill, NC 27514
ph: 919-419-1546 or 919-966-5794
e-mail: jfo@mindspring.com
web: http://www.mindspring.com/~jfo
Just for Openers is a club for bottle and corkscrew collectors; quarterly newsletter.

Collectors

John Stanley
P.O. Box 64
Chapel Hill, NC 27514
ph: 919-419-1546 or 919-966-5794
e-mail: jfo@mindspring.com
web: http://www.mindspring.com/~jfo
Wants any bottle opener or corkscrew from the Southeast U.S.; also wants to buy any beer advertising items.

Marc Benjamin
167 Nixon Beach Rd.
Edenton, NC 27932
ph: 252-482-2099
Wants flat figural bottle openers; beer and non-beer.

Kurt Bachmann
57883 Hanover Rd.
Washington, MI 48094
ph: 810-677-3284
fax: 248-745-1221
e-mail: kbach@clearr.com
Dealing with all types of breweriana advertising including, but not limited to, beer advertising bottle openers.

Kelly C. Devlin
Rte. 1 Box 93
Wahoo, NE 68066-9730
ph: 402-443-4305
fax: 402-443-4849
e-mail: kd31202@navix.net
Wants to buy figural bottle openers.

Experts

Charles Reynolds
Reynolds Toys
2836 Monroe St.
Falls Church, VA 22042-2007
ph: 703-533-1322
e-mail: reynoldstoys@erols.com
web: http://www.reynoldstoys.com
An advanced collector paying top dollar for openers, e.g. wall mount boy winking, Amish Man, Skull, Coyote, Bear, Eagle, Standing College Figures, etc.

Phyllis Eisenach
3759 SW Whispering Sound Dr.
Palm City, FL 34990-7735
ph: 561-223-8275
e-mail: eisenach@webtv.net
Interested in figural (three-dimensional) bottle openers; 16 years collecting; member of the Figural Bottle Opener Collectors Club; prefers iron or other metal openers.

Repro. Sources

Charles Reynolds
Reynolds Toys
2836 Monroe St.
Falls Church, VA 22042-2007
ph: 703-533-1322
e-mail: reynoldstoys@erols.com
web: http://www.reynoldstoys.com
Offers limited editions of new original figural bottle openers of sand-cast aluminum; flyer on request.

BOTTLES

(see also BOTTLE CAPS; BREWERIANA; DAIRY COLLECTIBLES; DECANTERS, Figural Whiskey; FRUIT JARS; INFANT FEEDERS; INKWELLS & INKSTANDS; INSULATORS; SALOON & BAR COLLECTIBLES; SODA FOUNTAIN COLLECTIBLES; SOFT DRINK COLLECTIBLES; TREASURE HUNTING)

Appraisers

David Robinson
Antique Bottle Collectors
W142 N4896 Fieldcrest Court
Menomonee Falls, WI 53051
ph: 414-790-18781
e-mail: dave@antiquebotl.com
web: http://www.antiquebotl.com
Source for antique bottle collectors; website has information on shows, books, magazines, for sale, want to buy, questions, appraisals, identification.

Auction Services

James A. Megura
Skinner, Inc.
357 Main St.
Bolton, MA 01740-1104
ph: 978-779-6241
fax: 978-779-5144
e-mail: info@skinnerinc.com
web: http://www.skinnerinc.com
Established in 1964, Skinner Inc. is the fifth largest auction house in the US; has offices in Bolton and Boston, MA.

Norman C. Heckler
Norman C. Heckler & Company
79 Bradford Corner Rd.
Woodstock Valley, CT 06282-2002
ph: 860-974-1634
fax: 860-974-2003
e-mail: heckler@neca.com
web: http://www.hecklerauction.com/
Specializes in the sale of early glass and bottles; Heckler & Co. sold a single bottle for $66,000 at auction in 1993.

James Hagenbuch
Glass Works Auctions
P.O. Box 180
102 Jefferfson St.
East Greenville, PA 18041
ph: 215-679-5849
fax: 215-679-3068
e-mail: glswrk@enter.net
web: http://www.glswrk-auction.com/
Specializes in the auction of historical flasks, fruit jars, food & milk bottles, sodas, poisons, whiskeys, medicines, inks, barber bottles, bitters bottles, scent bottles, shaving mugs, target & range balls, etc.

Pacific Glass Auctions
1507 21st St., Ste. 203
Sacramento, CA 95814
ph: 916-443-3296 or 916-443-3210
fax: 916-443-3199
e-mail: info@pacglass.com
web: http://www.pacglass.com/
The largest antique bottle auction house currently on the internet.

A.R. Blakeman
B.B.R. Auctions
Elsecar Heritage Centre
Nr Barnsley, S. Yorks S74 8HJ
U.K.
e-mail: sales@bbrauctions.co.uk
web: http://www.bbracutions.co.uk/
England's leading specialists and auction house for antique bottles, pot lids and related advertising material.

Clubs/Associations

Creighton Hall
Yankee Bottle Club
382 Court St.
Keene, NH 03431
ph: 603-352-2959
fax: 603-352-7919

William Yellenik
New England Antique Bottle Club
Newsletter: NEABC News
18 Linden Dr.
Brentwood, NH 03833
Membership throughout New England; meets 2nd Sunday of each month (except July & August) in Kennebunk, ME; newsletter published 10 times per year; for club information pack or bottle related questions please send SASE.

Joe Maggi
North Jersey Antique Bottle Collectors Association
117 Lincoln Pl.
Waldwick, NJ 07463-2114
ph: 201-445-9079

Jersey Shore Bottle Club
P.O. Box 995
Toms River, NJ 08754-0649
e-mail: jsbc@stufforsale.com
web: http://www.cybercomm.net/~shadowin/jsbc/jsbc.html

Kim Bloomer
Hudson Valley Antique Bottle Club
6 Columbus Ave.
Cornwall On Hudson, NY 12520
web: http://members.aol.com/JBishop701/Harps.html

Bruce Babcock, Show Ch.
Empire State Bottle Collectors Association
Newsletter: ESBCA Newsletter
115 Marshia Ave.
North Syracuse, NY 13212
ph: 315-458-3627

Genessee Valley Bottle Collectors Association
P.O. Box 7528
Rochester, NY 14615

Engvard Johnson
Pittsburgh Antique Bottle Club
RD 3 Box 280
Indiana, PA 15701
ph: 724-465-8287

Pennsylvania Bottle Collector's Association
Newsletter: Dirty Bottle, The
251 Eastland Ave.
York, PA 17402-1105
ph: 717-854-4965
Members collect or are interested in antique bottles and are from various states with the majority of members from the York-Lancaster-Harrisburg area.

Richard Tucker
Forks of the Delaware Bottle Collectors Association
3105 Hecktown Rd.
Easton, PA 18045
ph: 610-258-5776

Kevin A. Sives, Mem.
Federation of Historical Bottle Collectors, Inc.
Magazine: Bottles & Extras
P.O. Box 1558
Southampton, PA 18966
ph: 215-953-1686
fax: 215-953-1104
e-mail: sives@antiquez.com
web: http://www.fohbc.com/
"Bottles & Extras" contains articles, pictures, letters, show dates, and show and auction reports in the field of antique bottles, insulators, fruit jars and associated items; check website for list of scores of clubs by region.

Bill Baumgardner
Delmarva Antique Bottle Club
57 Lakewood Dr.
Lewes, DE 19958
ph: 302-945-2025

Jim Choplick
Baltimore Antique Bottle Club
Newsletter: Baltimore Bottle Digger
P.O. Box 36061
Townson, MD 21286-6061
ph: 301-997-1999
e-mail: jimchoplick@hotmail.com
web: http://www.antiquebottles.com/baltimore/
Monthly meetings include displays, selling/trading and speaker programs about bottles & related items: jugs, fruit jars, etc.

Ken Anderson
Potomac Bottle Collectors
4028 Williamsburg Court
Fairfax, VA 22032-1139
ph: 703-273-7415 or 703-360-8181
fax: 703-385-7330
e-mail: pehraug@aol.com
web: http://members.aol.com/potomacbtl/bottle2.htm

Mike Jordan
Potomac Bottle Club
Newsletter: Potomac Pontil, The
8411 Porter Ln.
Alexandria, VA 22308-2140
ph: 703-360-8181
e-mail: bjordan@aol.com
web: http://members.aol.com/Potomacbtl/bottle2.htm
Club serves the metropolitan Washington, D.C. area; provides a monthly meeting with educational programs, library, public speakers, annual bottle show, and other services of interest to collectors of antique bottles and jars.

Frank Kowalski
Apple Valley Bottle Collectors Club
Newsletter: Bottle Worm, The
3015 Northwestern Pike
Winchester, VA 22603-3825
ph: 540-877-1093
e-mail: polishbn@shentel.net
web: http://www.antiquebottles.com/apple/
Members are interested antique bottles: bitters, whiskeys, beers, mineral waters, White House vinegars, milks, medicines, cures, Depression glassware, local pottery, postcards and milk glass; annual show in Winchester.

Historical Bottle Diggers of Virginia, The
Newsletter: HBDV Newsletter
242 E. Grattan St.
Harrisonburg, VA 22801
Member of National Federation of Historical Bottle Collectors; newsletter published bi-monthly.

Ed Faulkner
Richmond Area Bottle Collectors Association
4718 Kyloe Lane
Moseley, VA 23120
e-mail: efaulk@erols.com
web: http://www.antiquebottles.com/rabca/

Fred Taylor, Ed.
Southeastern Antique Bottle Club
Newsletter: Whittle Mark, The
143 Scatterfoot Dr.
Peachtree City, GA 30269-1853
ph: 770-487-2468
e-mail: Fred-Taylor@worldnet.att.net
web: http://home.att.net/~fred-taylor/
Holds monthly meetings and an annual "Bottle Show & Auction" each year in April; all are welcome to join.

M-T Bottle Collectors Association, Inc.
Newsletter: Diggers Dispatch
P.O. Box 1581
De Land, FL 32721
Sponsors an annual bottle show usually in March.

Ed Herrold
Sarasota-Manatee Antique Bottle Collectors Association
P.O. Box 3105
Sarasota, FL 34230-3105
ph: 941-923-6550
Networking for education and pleasure of antique bottle, insulator, and fruit jar collectors; only interested in 19th century and earlier; no Jim Beam bottles or Avon bottles.

Nancy Pennington
Middle Tennessee Bottle & Collector's Club
Newsletter: MTBCC Newsletter
1750 Keyes Rd.
Greenbrier, TN 37073
ph: 615-643-0290
fax: 615-643-0290

Larry W. Acuff
East Tennessee Antique Bottle & Collectibles Society
Newsletter: ETABCS Newsletter
220 N. carter School Road
Strawberry Plains, TN 37871
ph: 423-933-2333
Newsletter published bi-monthly; club sponsors annual antique bottle, advertising and collectibles show on 2nd Saturday in June at Knoxville Convention Center, Knoxville, TN; largest show of its kind in the country.

Dave Merker
Ohio Bottle Club
7126 12th St.
Minerva, OH 44657
web: http://www.antiquebottles.com/ohio/
One of the largest bottle clubs in the country.

Norman & Junne Barnett
Midwest Antique Fruit Jar & Bottle Club
Newsletter: Midwest Glass Chatter, The
P.O. Box 38
Flat Rock, IN 47234
ph: 812-587-5560
Sponsors two fruit and bottle shows each year in Indianapolis.

Shaun Kotlarsky
Huron Valley Antique Bottle & Insulator Club
2475 West Walton Blvd.
Waterford, MI 48329-4435
ph: 248-673-1650
e-mail: hvbic@insulators.com
web: http://www.insulators.com/clubs/hvbic.htm

Glenn Poch
Antique Bottle Club of Northern Illinois
1537 Silver Strand
Palatine, IL 60074
ph: 847-705-6572 or 847-259-3500
e-mail: pochg@phl.alibrary.com
web: http://www.antiquebottles.com/poch/

John E. Panek
First Chicago Bottle Club
Newsletter: Midwest Bottle News, The
P.O. Box A3382
Chicago, IL 60690
ph: 847-945-5493
Organization of antique bottle and stoneware collectors who research, educate, buy and sell at monthly meetings, annual shows, and annual auctions.

Tino Romero
New Mexico Historical Bottle Society
3256 c/s
Socorro, NM 87801
ph: 505-838-1636
e-mail: tromero@nmt.edu
web: http://www.nmt.edu/~tromero/nmhbs.html
Focus in on the education preservation, and history of historical bottles.

Dottie Daugherty
Las Vegas Antique Bottle & Collectibles Club
Newsletter: Punkin Seed, The
3901 E. Stewart #19
Las Vegas, NV 89110-3152
ph: 702-452-1263
Members promote the hobby of collecting, researching, displaying and trading of antique bottles and collectibles; sponsors an annual collectibles show and sale in February of each year.

Willy Young
Antique Bottle & Collectibles Club
P.O. Box 1061
Verdi, NV 89439
ph: 775-746-0922
e-mail: wilyoung@ix.netcom.com

San Bernardino County Historical Bottle & Collectible Club
P.O. Box 6759
San Bernardino, CA 92412

San Jose Antique Bottle Collectors Association
P.O. Box 5432
San Jose, CA 95150-5432

Collectors

Leo A. Bedard
39 Chestnut St., Apt. 102
Ludlow, MA 01056-3462
ph: 413-583-5746
Collects antique bottles, specializing in embossed, strapsided, and coffin flasks.

Philip R. Donovan, Jr.
18 Linden Dr.
Brentwood, NH 03833
Collect/buy/trade 1870s to 1920s bottles: medicine, soda, milk; will buy collections of dug bottles of all types; purchases labeled embossed 1800s-1910s medicines, sodas, beers, foods, etc. for personal collection; also digs.

Douglas Anderson
112 S. Commerce St.
Centreville, MD 21617-1116
ph: 410-758-3278

Dan Argentati
61342 Creekview Dr.
South Lyon, MI 48178
ph: 248-437-6104
Collector of antique bottles,

specializing in bitters bottles and any bottles from Michigan cities.

Mark S. McNee
1009 Vassar Dr.
Kalamazoo, MI 49001-4483
ph: 616-343-8393
Wants to buy early American bottles of all types including bitters, poisons, historical flasks, and medicines.

Steve Ketcham
P.O. Box 24114
Minneapolis, MN 55424-0114
ph: 612-920-4205
e-mail: s.ketcham@unique-software.com
Buying pre-1900 American bottles with embossed or paper labels: especially flasks, bitters, cures, figurals, barber bottles, etc.; please send SASE with inquiries; $1 plus SASE for illustrated bottle dating pamphlet.

John E. Panek
P.O. Box A3382
Chicago, IL 60690
ph: 847-945-5493
Specialists in historical flasks, bitters, sodas and Chicago bottles and stoneware.

Tino Romero
3256 c/s
Socorro, NM 87801
ph: 505-838-1636
e-mail: tromero@nmt.edu
web: http://www.nmt.edu/~tromero/nmhbs.html
Specializes in New Mexico bottles, Dr. Kilmer, embalming fluids, poisons and narcotic bottles.

Kitty & Russell Umbraco
P.O. Box 5331
Richmond, CA 94805-0331
ph: 510-235-1656
Wants to buy Western bottles, especially Nevada, San Francisco and related advertising.

John Goetz
P.O. Box 1570
Cedar Ridge, CA 95924
ph: 530-272-4644
Buying pre-1920 embossed glass bottles: bitters, fifths, flasks, mineral water, beer, California bottles.

Scott Grandstaff
63742 Applegate Dr.
Happy Camp, CA 96039
ph: 530-493-2032

Dealers

Jack Pelletier
211 Main St.
Gorham, ME 04038
ph: 207-839-4389
Buying and selling antique bottles for over 30 years; expert on Bininger bottles.

John Brandt
Historic Glasshouse
200 Mile Common Road
Easton, CT 06612
ph: 718-855-3776 or 203-254-2183
e-mail: info@antiquebottles-glass.com
web: http://www.antiquebottles-glass.com
One of the largest dealers in 17th - 19th century antique bottles and glass; website lists a wide variety of fine quality items for sale; professionally cleans staining on glass items; will search for specific items; also appraises.

Kevin A. Sives
Kevin A. Sives, Antiques
P.O. Box 1558
Southampton, PA 18966
ph: 215-953-1686
fax: 215-953-1104
e-mail: sives@antiquez.com
web: http://www.antiquez.com
Collects, buys and sells antique blown glass, bottles, and flasks.

Frank Kowalski
Polish Barn Antiques, The
3015 Northwestern Pike
Winchester, VA 22603-3825
ph: 540-877-1881 or 540-877-1093
e-mail: polishbn@shentel.net
Bottle collector, dealer, appraiser; interested in Winchester VA antique bottles: bitters, whiskeys, beers, mineral waters, White House vinegars, milks, medicines, cures, Depression glassware, local pottery, postcards and milk glass.

Duane Combs
Mountain State Bottle Exchange
P.O. Box 181
Burlington, WV 26710
ph: 304-788-5517
fax: 304-788-5517
Buys, sells, trades old bottles: bitters, medicines, poisons, flasks, White House vinegars, early sodas, Warner Safe Cures, etc.

William E. Bowen
Auction Price Report for Antique Bottles
8251 NW 49th Court
Pompano Beach, FL 33067
ph: 954-344-0023
fax: 954-757-7625
e-mail: auctionp@bellsouth.net
Publisher of a current price guide based on prices realized at major bottle auctions over the past ten years; included are bitters, historical flasks, whiskeys, sodas and mineral waters, medicines, and poisons.

Earl's Bottles
108 Crystal Lane
Aurora, OH 44202

Don Dzuro
Antique of Copley
1442 St. Michaels Ave.
Akron, OH 44320-3236
ph: 330-867-8024
Buys, sells and trades bottles, jars and pottery; author of "Ohio Bottles."

David Robinson
Antique Bottle Collectors
W142 N4896 Fieldcrest Court
Menomonee Falls, WI 53051
ph: 414-790-18781
e-mail: dave@antiquebotl.com
web: http://www.antiquebotl.com
Source for antique bottle collectors; website has information on shows, books, magazines, for sale, want to buy, questions, appraisals, identification.

Glenn Poch
1537 Silver Strand
Palatine, IL 60074
ph: 847-705-6572 or 847-259-3500
e-mail: pochg@phl.alibrary.com
web: http://www.antiquebottles.com/poch/
Appraises, buys, sells, collects, repairs antique bottles; specializes in pre-1900 bottles, flasks, bitters, medicines, inks, scents, etc.

Freds Bottles
P.O. Box 1423
Cheyenne, WY 82003

Keith Lunt
Antique Bottle Trader
2668 Montara Dr.
Medford, OR 97504
ph: 541-773-2404
fax: 541-772-1515
e-mail: vlunt@ccountry.net
web: http://www.ccountry.net/~vlunt/bottle.htm
Avid antique bottle collector, dealer, trader, and appraiser for over 25 years; member of The Oregon Bottle Collectors Association and The Antique Poison Bottle Collectors Association; also a bottle show promoter.

Rob Sturrock
Old Bottles from British Columbia
Canada
ph: 604-980-3679
e-mail: primex@portal.ca
web: http://www.geocities.com/Eureka/Promenade/4600/
Buys, sells, trades bottles: sodas, ginger beers, milks, poisons, fruit jars, etc.

Mike Sheridan
30 Brabant Rd.
Cheadle Hulme
Cheadle, Cheshire SK8 7AU
U.K.
ph: 0961 172 197
fax: 0961 172 197
e-mail: mike@bygones.demon.co.uk
web: http://www.bygones.demon.co.uk/bottle.htm
English dealer/collector seeks old English bottles now resident in the US: stenciled Scots/Irish whiskeys, pontiled medicine, including Turlingtons, old stoneware bottles, highly pictorial and colorful old labels of all types.

Experts

Mike Jordan
Jordan Antiques & Research Co.
8411 Porter Ln.
Alexandria, VA 22308-2140
ph: 703-360-8181
e-mail: bjordan@aol.com
web: http://members.aol.com/Potomacbtl/bottle2.htm
Buy, sells, appraises and specializes in rare, early American bottles.

Reggie Lynch
P.O. Box 13736
Durham, NC 27709
ph: 919-661-8167
e-mail: rlynch@antiquebottles.com
web: http://www.antiquebottles.com/
Buys, sells, collects and specializes in antique bottles such as inks, medicine and Coke.

Jamie Houdeshell
16255 Normandy South
Perrysburg, OH 43551
ph: 419-872-1966
Buys, sells, appraises and specializes in antique bottles and early American glass.

Keith Lunt
Antique Bottle Trader
2668 Montara Dr.
Medford, OR 97504
ph: 541-773-2404
fax: 541-772-1515
e-mail: vlunt@ccountry.net
web: http://www.ccountry.net/~vlunt/bottle.htm
Avid antique bottle collector, dealer, trader, and appraiser for over 25 years; member of The Oregon Bottle Collectors Association and The Antique Poison Bottle Collectors Association; also a bottle show promoter.

Internet Resources

Reggie Lynch
Antique Bottle Collectors Haven
P.O. Box 13736
Durham, NC 27709
ph: 919-661-8167
e-mail: rlynch@antiquebottles.com
web: http://www.antiquebottles.com/
Website is a haven for antique bottle collectors: information on clubs, shows, books, magazines, newsletters, newsgroups, for sale, auctions, want to buy, questions, etc.

Bottles & Bygones
30 Brabant Rd.
Cheadle Hulme
Cheadle, Cheshire SK8 7AU
U.K.
ph: 0961 172 197
fax: 0961 172 197
e-mail: mike@bygones.demon.co.uk
web: http://www.bygones.demon.co.uk/bottle.htm
Britain's biggest and busiest internet site relating to old bottles, pot lids and old advertising.

Misc. Services

Jerry Stokes
11 Wilson Ave.
Cheswick, PA 15024
ph: 724-274-6438
Offers professional bottle cleaning and stain removal.

Paul Mendik
Precision Bottle Cleaning
929 State Route 305
Cortland, OH 44410
ph: 330-847-8375
Professional cleaning of dug bottles to upgrade most to mint condition.

Wayne Lowry
Jar Doctor
20812 S. State Route J
Peculiar, MO 64078
ph: 816-779-4982
e-mail: jalowry53@aol.com
Manufacturers a bottle and jar cleaning system.

Museums/Libraries

Jan Rutland, Dir.
National Bottle Museum
Newsletter: Bottle Muse, The
76 Milton Ave.
Ballston Spa, NY 12020-1405
ph: 518-885-7589
fax: 518-885-0317
e-mail: nbm@crisny.org
web: http://www.crisny.org/not-for-profit/nbm/
Open year round; exhibits, videos and library deal with the history and beauty of 18th and 19th century bottles manufactured with hand tools and lung power; artifacts represent an industry and way of life that has vanished.

Hawaii Bottle Museum
Newsletter: Hawaii Bottle Museum News
27 Kalopa Mauka Road
P.O. Box 1635
Honokaa, HI 96727-1635
ph: 808-775-0411
Collection contains bottles from 1776 to 1900.

A.R. Blakeman
National Bottle Museum
Elsecar Heritage Centre
Nr Barnsley, S. Yorks S74 8HJ
U.K.
e-mail: sales@bbrauctions.co.uk
web: http://www.bbracutions.co.uk/
Specialist museum covering all areas of bottles: wines, medicines, inks, brewery, etc.

Periodicals

James Hagenbuch
Magazine: Antique Bottle & Glass Collector
P.O. Box 180
102 Jefferfson St.
East Greenville, PA 18041
ph: 215-679-5849
fax: 215-679-3068
e-mail: glswrk@enter.net
web: http://www.glswrk-auction.com/
A monthly magazine for the glass and bottle collector.

Glenn Poch
Newsletter: Glenn Poch's Bottle Collecting Newsletter
1537 Silver Strand
Palatine, IL 60074
ph: 847-705-6572 or 847-259-3500
e-mail: pochg@phl.alibrary.com
web: http://www.antiquebottles.com/poch/

A.R. Blakeman
B.B.R. Publishing
Magazine: British Bottle Review
Elsecar Heritage Centre
Nr Barnsley, S. Yorks S74 8HJ
U.K.
e-mail: sales@bbrauctions.co.uk
web: http://www.bbracutions.co.uk/
The world's longest continuous running publication covering the multitudinous areas of antique bottles; including world news; published quarterly.

Magazine: Antique Bottle Collecting Magazine
4 Lower Clifton Hill
Clifton, Bristol B5
U.K.

Mike Sheridan
Magazine: Bottles & Bygones
30 Brabant Rd.
Cheadle Hulme
Cheadle, Cheshire SK8 7AU
U.K.
ph: 0961 172 197
fax: 0961 172 197
e-mail: mike@bygones.demon.co.uk
web: http://www.bygones.demon.co.uk/bottle.htm
Magazine loaded with articles and photos about glass and stoneware bottles and related items; published quarterly; Britain's most informative bottle magazine; company histories, new discoveries, digging articles; great source for info!

Suppliers

Dexter's Stain Remover
15140 Washington St.
Riverside, CA 92506
Sells a stain remover advertised as a cure for sick glass; for all stained antique glass; mineral, rust, and calcium deposits removed.

Barber

(see also BARBERSHOP COLLECTIBLES)

Collectors

George A. Coupe
1243 1st St. S.E.
Washington, DC 20003
ph: 202-554-1000 or 800-368-5466
fax: 202-863-0775
Wants barber bottles; must be in good condition.

Bitters

Experts

Robert Daly
10341 Jewell Lake Ct.
Fenton, MI 48430-2418
ph: 810-629-4934
fax: 810-714-1009
e-mail: ldaly1@aol.com
Serious collector wants old colored bottles, hand blown in shapes; must have a "pontil" mark (a rough break-off) on the bottom of the bottle.

Periodicals

Greg Price
Newsletter: Bitters Report, The
P.O. Box 1253
Bunnell, FL 32110-1253
ph: 904-437-2807
e-mail: GregTBR@aol.com
A newsletter for bitters bottle enthusiasts.

Bubble Bath

Collectors

Pete Nowicki
1531 39th Ave.
San Francisco, CA 94122-3015
ph: 415-566-7506
e-mail: portfire86@aol.com
Collects plastic Soaky and Purex containers which came in the shape of figures such as Donald Duck, Batman, Mr. Magoo; were filled with soap to get kids clean; when empty they became a new toy.

Ginger Beer

Collectors

Keith Roloson
6220 Carriage Ct.
Cumming, GA 30040-9111
ph: 770-781-5021 or 770-750-6429
e-mail: kroloson@mindspring.com
web: http://www.insulators.com/clubs/djic.htm
Wants to buy American, Canadian, South African, Australian, and other stone ginger beer bottles with pictorials.

Historical Flasks

Experts

John Crary
P.O. Box 417
Canton, NY 13617
ph: 315-386-8715
Author of "Guide to the Value of Historical Flasks."

Robert Daly
10341 Jewell Lake Ct.
Fenton, MI 48430-2418
ph: 810-629-4934
fax: 810-714-1009
e-mail: ldaly1@aol.com
Serious collector wants old colored bottles, hand blown in shapes; must have a "pontil" mark (a rough break-off) on the bottom of the bottle.

Japanese

Collectors

Al Sparacino
743 La Huerta Way
San Diego, CA 92154-2656
ph: 619-690-3632
Wants Japanese figural sake, wine, liquor bottles: House of Koshu, Kikukawa, Kamotsuru, Kikkoman, Sasaiti Shuzo, Okura Shuzu, etc.

Japanese/German Giveaway

Collectors

Paul Stookey
3436 Pointe Creek Ct. #202
Cape Coral, FL 34134-2005
ph: 941-498-4502
Wants Japanese and German giveaway bottles - "nippers."

Milk

(see also BOTTLE CAPS, Milk; DAIRY COLLECTIBLES)

Clubs/Associations

Thomas Gallagher
National Association of Milk Bottle Collectors, Inc.
Newsletter: Milk Route, The
4 Ox Bow Rd.
Westport, CT 06880-2602
ph: 203-227-5244
fax: 203-227-2206
e-mail: milkroute@yahoo.com
web: http://www.collectoronline.com/club-NAMBC-wp.html
Focuses on milk and dairy history and related memorabilia; membership includes the newsletter and directory of members; newsletter has articles, ads, show dates, information exchange, patents, events, etc.

Collectors

Gus Dueben
10215 117th Dr.
Largo, FL 33773-2336

Dealers

O. B. Lund
13009 So. 42nd St.
Phoenix, AZ 85044-3917
ph: 602-893-3567
Buy, sell, trade milk bottles; round, long neck bottles only, in good condition; bottles must have name of dairy, city and state; they may be embossed or painted (pyro-glazed).

Experts

Thomas Gallagher
4 Ox Bow Rd.
Westport, CT 06880-2602
ph: 203-227-5244
fax: 203-227-2206
e-mail: milkroute@yahoo.com
web: http://www.collectoronline.com/club-NAMBC-wp.html

Tony Knipp
P.O. Box 105
Blooming Grove, NY 10914-0105
ph: 914-496-6841 or 914-938-4580

Robert Bickel
7545 US Highway 522 S
Mc Veytown, PA 17051-7450
Wants milk bottles from Mifflin Co., PA (McVeytown, Lewistown, Milroy, Reedsville, Burnham, McClure, Belleville, Allensville, Granville, Matawana, Newton); also wants beer cans from PA breweries and stoneware marked "Lewistown".

Ralph Riovo
686 Franklin St.
Alburtis, PA 18011-9578
ph: 610-966-2536
Buying and selling milk and dairy items for 18 years; wants milk bottles with Hopalong Cassidy, Annie Oakley, Disney characters, etc.

John Tutton
Early American Workshop
1967 Ridgeway Rd.
Front Royal, VA 22630-8652
ph: 540-635-7058 or 540-635-6141
e-mail: jtutton@rma.edu
web: http://www.erols.com/stutton/eaw/
Involved in milk bottles for 23 years; covering collecting, buying and selling; lecturer and author of three books on milk bottles; author of "Udderly Beautiful", updated in 1997.

Periodicals

Mike & Naomi Hull
Newsletter: Milk Bottle News
Stonemasons
Burleigh
Stroud, Gloucester GL5 2PJ
U.K.
ph: 01453 884922
e-mail: mbnews@artisan.abel.co.uk
web: http://www.artisan.uk.com/mbnews/
A British newsletter for collectors of milk bottles and dairy related memorabilia.

Miniature

Clubs/Associations

Butch Jones
Midwest Miniature Bottle Collector
Newsletter: MMBC
7866 Millerton Dr.
Centerville, OH 45459
ph: 937-428-9364
e-mail: fmjmini@aol.com
20 year old club with over 400 members in 10 countries; quarterly newsletter.

Collectors

Butch Jones
7866 Millerton Dr.
Centerville, OH 45459
ph: 937-428-9364
e-mail: fmjmini@aol.com

Lee Weiss
5626 Corning Ave.
Los Angeles, CA 90056-1305
ph: 310-546-5117
Buys, trades miniature bottles such as whiskey, beer, liquor and pop containers.

Harry Ford
54 Village Circle
Manhattan Beach, CA 90266-7222

Dealers

Flask Wine & Spirits, The
12194 Ventura Blvd.
Studio City, CA 91604
ph: 818-761-5373
Carries large selection of minis.

Periodicals

David Spaid
Briscoe Publications
Magazine: Miniature Bottle Collector, The
P.O. Box 2161
Palos Verdes Peninsula, CA 90274-8161
ph: 310-534-4943
fax: 310-534-8437
e-mail: editor@bottlecollecting.com
web: http://www.bottlecollecting.com/
For collectors of modern or old miniature bottles; published six times per year.

Miniature Beer & Soda

Dealers

Alexander Mullin
Miscellanea
331 North Lehigh Circle
Swarthmore, PA 19081
ph: 610-328-7381
Wants American and foreign MINIATURE beer bottles (3"-6" high), 1880-1960; bottles may be embossed; most will have paper, decal, or foil labels; labels must be in good condition; small breweries bring premium; describe, especially label.

Miniature Liquor

Auction Services

Albert Rieland
Mini-Bottle Auction Club
Nording 16A
Babenhausen, 064832
Germany
Bi-monthly auctions; 1600 to 2500 bottles in each issue.

Clubs/Associations

Wayne L. Full
Western New York Miniature Liquor Bottle Club
Newsletter: How Little We Know About Bottler
P.O. Box 182
Cheektowaga, NY 14225-0182
ph: 716-683-8939

Norm Luber
Del-Val Miniature Bottle Club
Newsletter: It's A Small World
57104 Del Aire Landing Rd.
Philadelphia, PA 19114
Members show and exchange information on miniature liquor bottles; club meets every other month; two shows every year.

Paul M. Murray
Great Lakes Miniature Bottle Club
Newsletter: GLMBC Newsletter
19745 Woodmont
Harper Woods, MI 48225-1873
ph: 313-882-8917
Club is devoted to collecting miniature liquor bottles and related items such as giveaways and mini beers; all are welcome.

Harry Ford, Treas.
Lilliputian Bottle Club, The
Newsletter: Gulliver's Gazette
54 Village Circle
Manhattan Beach, CA 90266-7222
215 member club is 20 years old and very active; meets monthly, sponsors a mini-bottle show and sale each October.

Errol Brassett
Port Nicholson Miniature Bottle Club
P.O. Box 384
Wellington, Wellington 6006
New Zealand
ph: 64-4-232-8051 or 64-4-239-9536
e-mail: errolb2@voyager.co.nz
web: http://www.voyager.co.nz/~errolb2/index.htm
New Zealand's only miniature bottle collectors club; members throughout the world.

U.K. Mini Bottle Club, The
Newsletter: Mini Bottle Club Newsletter
47 Burradon Rd.
Burradon
Cramlington, Northumberland NE23 7NF
U.K.
ph: 0191 2686561
fax: 0191 2160787
e-mail: mini_bottle_club@compuserve.com
web: http://www.toddalyth.freeserve.co.uk/mbc.html
Large bi-monthly newsletter with latest information on old & new miniatures as well as members' buy/sell ads, feature articles, and bottle outlets; primarily scotch whisky but also gins, cognacs, rums, vodkas, liquors, and ceramics.

Collectors

Dr. Dana Cable
8605 Pinecliff Dr.
Frederick, MD 21701
ph: 301-694-9297
fax: 301-694-3539
e-mail: danacable@msn.com
Buys and sells miniature liquor bottles; interested in purchase of individual bottles; send description and price.

Paul Stookey
3436 Pointe Creek Ct. #202
Cape Coral, FL 34134-2005
ph: 941-498-4502
Buys, sells, trades miniature whiskey jugs and older miniature whiskey bottles.

M.L. Trangmoe
Roscoes Restaurant
22746 Roscoe Blvd.
Canoga Park, CA 91304-3350
ph: 818-883-5597
fax: 818-883-5541
1000s of mini's on display.

Thomas F. Nagelin, Sr.
13271 Clinton St.
Garden Grove, CA 92643
ph: 714-638-3041 or 714-554-8000
fax: 714-554-1798
Wants miniature liquor bottles; 1930s and 1940s; has collection of over 11,000 minis.

Fred Hawley
1311 Montero Ave.
Burlingame, CA 94010
ph: 650-342-7085
Collector of miniature liquor bottles wants minis with labels from pre-prohibition through the 1950s; especially interested in 1930s minis from California.

John Goetz
P.O. Box 1570
Cedar Ridge, CA 95924
ph: 530-272-4644
Buy/sell ceramic & glass figural mini bottles: dancers, pigs, drunks, Santas, octopus and other whimsical figures; sorry, no Beam types.

Perfume & Scent

(see also AVON COLLECTIBLES; PERFUME LAMPS)

Auction Services

Randy Monsen
Monsen & Baer Inc.
P.O. Box 529
Vienna, VA 22183-0529
ph: 703-938-2129
fax: 703-242-1357
e-mail: monsenbaer@erols.com
Cataloged auctions of perfume bottles: commercial, Czechoslovakian, Lalique, Baccarat, Victorian, Crown Top, Factices, miniatures.

Clubs/Associations

Lenore Hiers, Mem.
International Perfume Bottle Association
Newsletter: Perfume Bottle Quarterly
3314 Shamrock Rd.
Tampa, FL 33629
ph: 813-837-5845
fax: 813-837-8567
e-mail: Lhiers@compuserve.com
web: http://www.perfumebottles.org
Informative quarterly newsletter, annual meeting, membership directory, special programs for members.

Sandy Katz-Leegood
Lone Star Chapter of the International Perfume Bottle Association
Newsletter: Lone Star Scents
P.O. Box 596553
Dallas, TX 75359-6653
ph: 214-824-7917
fax: 214-824-7917
e-mail: decolectibles@cyberramp.net
Members receive two newsletters, regional meetings and opportunities to participate in Annual Vintage Vanity Convention featuring all ladies vanity items: perfumes, compacts, vintage purses, powders, hat pins, combs, etc.

Collectors

Vallerie Roberts Shutterly
Victorian Touch
P.O. Box 4
Micanopy, FL 32667
ph: 352-466-4022
fax: 351-591-2872
Wants to buy ornate jeweled perfume bottles and powder jars: colored glass bottles covered with fancy brass filigree and jewels; especially cut-to-clear in pinks and roses with jeweled ornamentation; marked Czechoslovakia.

Donna G. Sims
P.O. Box 187
Galena, OH 43021-0187
ph: 614-965-5693
Editor of the "Perfume Bottle Quarterly," the quarterly publication of the International Perfume Bottle Association.

Janice Holton
Passion for Perfume
5106 Meadowlark Lane
Nampa, ID 83687
ph: 208-467-7604
e-mail: janice@micron.net
web: http://www.webpak.net/~janice/
Website has everything you can think of that is perfume related plus places to list wants or advertise for missing parts; list of good perfume bottle shopping places, and perfume bottle books for sale.

Jeane Parris
Sugarplums, etc.
2022 E. Charleston Blvd.
Las Vegas, NV 89104-2018
ph: 702-385-6059
fax: 702-388-1202

Arielle Hart
1123 North Flores St., #21
West Hollywood, CA 90069-2978
ph: 323-654-0277
fax: 323-656-7477
e-mail: aaahart@earthlink.net
Collector of commercial perfume bottles; would enjoy hearing from anyone who would like to sell or trade; or anyone who would just like to chat about perfumes.

Beverly Nelson
1010 Lorna St.
Corona, CA 91720
ph: 909-737-0977
e-mail: nelac@earthlink.net
Specializes in perfume bottles, sets, compacts, lipsticks, and counter displays from the Bourjois Co. (makers of Evening in Paris, Mais Oui, Kobako) and Woodworth Co. (makers of Karess, Viegay, Fiancee); price guide available for $15.

Dealers

Ken Leach
Gallery #47
1050 2nd Ave.
New York, NY 10022
ph: 800-942-0550 or 212-888-0165
fax: 212-355-4403
Buys and sells commercial and Czechoslovakian perfume bottles.

Oldies But Goodies
P.O. Box 217
Hankins, NY 12741-0217
ph: 914-887-5272
fax: 914-887-5272
e-mail: oldgood@catskill.net
web: http://www.catskill.net/oldgood/
Buys, sells perfume bottles (Czech, DeVilbiss, R. Lalique, crown tops, etc.)

Randy Monsen
Monsen & Baer Inc.
P.O. Box 529
Vienna, VA 22183-0529
ph: 703-938-2129
fax: 703-242-1357
e-mail: monsenbaer@erols.com
Wants commercial perfume bottles, especially with original boxes: by Guerlain, Coty, Nina Ricci, Dior, Corday, Lalique, etc.

Tina Schaare
2331 D2 E Ave. S, #275
Palmdale, CA 93550
fax: 661-538-9240
e-mail: crowns97@aol.com
web: http://home.earthlink.net/~schaare4/
Buy, sell, trade high quality commercial perfume bottles; specializing in minis, samplers and testers, solid perfume compacts.

Experts

Christie Mayer Lefkowith
FDR Station
P.O. Box 5200
New York, NY 10150-5200
ph: 212-838-2932 or 212-758-8550
fax: 212-688-9313
e-mail: mayerlef@panix.com
web: http://www.panix.com/~mayerlef/
Buys all sizes of commercial perfume bottles, preferably with boxes: Lalique, Baccarat, and others from 1850 to 1960; author of "The Art of Perfume, Discovering and Collecting Perfume Bottles."

Madeleine France
Madeleine France Antiques
P.O. Box 15555
Fort Lauderdale, FL 33318-5555
ph: 305-584-0009 or 305-921-0022
fax: 305-584-0014
e-mail: mady@MadeleineFrance.com
web: http://www.MadeleineFrance.com/
Wants perfume bottles and boudoir items: Lalique, Baccarat, Viard, St. Louis, Moser, Sterling Scents, Steuben, DeVilbiss, Victorian laydowns, etc.

Emily Hart Killian
1211 E. Front St., Ste. 131
Traverse City, MI 49684-2928
ph: 616-946-7144
Author of "Perfume Bottles Remembered"; available from the author for $16 plus $2 S&H.

Internet Resources

Montage
e-mail: montage@cicat.com
web: http://www.cicat.com/montage/

Periodicals

Christie Mayer Lefkowith
Newsletter: Phillips Perfume Presentations
FDR Station
P.O. Box 5200
New York, NY 10150-5200
ph: 212-838-2932 or 212-758-8550
fax: 212-688-9313
e-mail: mayerlef@panix.com
web: http://www.panix.com/~mayerlef/
A bi-annual review of specialty perfume bottle auctions at Phillips International Auctions.

Repair Services

Oldies But Goodies
P.O. Box 217
Hankins, NY 12741-0217
ph: 914-887-5272
fax: 914-887-5272
e-mail: oldgood@catskill.net
web: http://www.catskill.net/oldgood/
Will custom fit their atomizer perfume parts onto your bottle or top; send SASE for information.

Shari Hopper
Paradise & Co.
2902 Neal Rd.
Paradise, CA 95969-6169
ph: 530-872-5020
fax: 530-872-5022
e-mail: paradise@sunset.net
web: http://www.paradise-co.com/
Replacement parts for atomizers: cords, balls, tassels; metal sprayer tops and collars; glass siphon tubing and daubers; also repairs, restoration

and conservation available for perfume bottles.

Suppliers

Shari Hopper
Paradise & Co.
2902 Neal Rd.
Paradise, CA 95969-6169
ph: 530-872-5020
fax: 530-872-5022
e-mail: paradise@sunset.net
web: http://www.paradise-co.com/
Replacement parts for atomizers: cords, balls, tassels; metal sprayer tops and collars; glass siphon tubing and daubers; also repairs, restoration and conservation available for perfume bottles.

Perfume & Scent (Miniature)

Clubs/Associations

Melinda Churchfield
Miniature Perfume Bottle Collectors
Newsletter: Mini-Scents
28227 Paseo El Siena
Laguna Niguel, CA 92677-4500
ph: 949-364-9510
e-mail: perfumeme1@aol.com
For collectors of miniature perfume bottles; newsletter includes what's new, history of perfume houses, different versions and a color center page.

Collectors

Arielle Hart
1123 North Flores St., #21
West Hollywood, CA 90069-2978
ph: 323-654-0277
fax: 323-656-7477
e-mail: aaahart@earthlink.net
Collector of commercial perfume bottles; would enjoy hearing from anyone who would like to sell or trade; or anyone who would just like to chat about perfumes.

Dealers

Eric Lipson
1700 University Drive, Ste. 205
Pompano Beach, FL 33071
ph: 800-735-2805 or 954-340-9400
fax: 954-755-3061
e-mail: perfumedad@aol.com
Appraiser, dealer, collector specializes in vintage miniature perfume samples and commercial perfume bottles; reseller of fine perfume display bottles (FACTICES).

Melinda Churchfield
My Mom & Me
28227 Paseo El Siena
Laguna Niguel, CA 92677-4500
ph: 949-364-9510
e-mail: perfumeme1@aol.com
Collector, dealer of commercial miniature/sample perfume bottles; in business for over 12 years.

Poison

Clubs/Associations

Joan Cabaniss
Antique Poison Bottle Collectors Association
312 Summer Lane
Huddleston, VA 24104
e-mail: Jjcab@aol.com
web: http://www.antiquebottles.com/apbca/

Collectors

Mary Riggin
Rt. 617
Marionville, VA 23408
ph: 757-442-5321
fax: 757-442-5321
Collector wants to buy old poison bottles.

Gren Mckenzie
Old Bottles & Collectibles
48 Maxton Road
Dover, Kent CT17 9JL
U.K.
ph: 01304 215023
e-mail: oldbottles@oldbottles.co.uk
web: http://www.oldbottles.co.uk
Buys and sells old and antique poison bottles; also other bottles.

Experts

Noel Cook
Mr. Poison
6601 Woodbine Rd.
Woodbine, MD 21797-9403
ph: 410-781-7013
Buys trades, and sells embossed poison bottles from anywhere in the world; willing to help any new poison bottle collector.

Puzzle

Collectors

Alvin Schenk
5728 Pimlico Rd.
Baltimore, MD 21209
ph: 410-367-4371
Collects puzzle bottles - small, handcarved curiosities placed in bottles with small openings.

Soda

(see also SODA FOUNTAIN COLLECTIBLES; SOFT DRINK COLLECTIBLES)

Experts

Paul & Karen Bates
Interactive Publishers
1055 Ridgecrest Dr.
Goodlettsville, TN 37072
ph: 615-859-5236 or 877-859-4929
fax: 615-859-5238
e-mail: mbca@gono.com
web: http://gono.com/vir-mus/museum.htm
Publishes always-current price updates to earlier soda bottle books.

Ron Fowler
Seattle History Company
P.O. Box 45251
Seattle, WA 98145-0251
ph: 206-525-1050
e-mail: SodaBottles@yahoo.com
web: http://www.members.tripod.com/~SodaBottles/
Author of "Ice-Cold Soda Pop 5 Cents", "Washington Sodas:, "The Bottler's Helper", and "An Introduction to Collecting Soda Pop Bottles."

Western Whiskey

Clubs/Associations

John Goetz
49'er Historical Bottle Club
P.O. Box 1570
Cedar Ridge, CA 95924
ph: 530-272-4644
Always glad to provide information on West coast bottles or on club membership.

Experts

Bob Barnett
P.O. Box 109
Lakeview, OR 97630
ph: 541-947-2415
fax: 541-947-2642
Author of "Western Whiskey Bottles."

BOW HUNTING

(see SPORTING COLLECTIBLES, Archery)

BOXES

(see also ADVERTISING COLLECTIBLES; BATTERSEA ENAMEL BOXES; CEREAL BOXES; CIGAR BOXES, LABELS & BANDS; ENAMELS; ORIENTALIA; PLASTIC COLLECTIBLES, Celluloid; RUSSIAN ITEMS; SMOKING COLLECTIBLES, Snuff Boxes; STAMP BOXES)

Collectors

Betty Bird
107 Ida St.
Mount Shasta, CA 96067-2629
ph: 530-926-4331 or 530-926-2231
Wants any type of figural or unusual boxes and containers: enamels, glass, porcelain, metal; also small scent containers.

Dealers

Sally Kaltman
Sallea Antiques
66 Elm St.
New Canaan, CT 06840
ph: 203-972-1050
fax: 203-972-1567
Buys, sells and specializes in distinctive antique boxes; all shapes, styles, materials and sizes.

Experts

Janice & Richard Vogel
4720 SE Fort King St.
Ocala, FL 34470-1501
ph: 352-694-5776
fax: 352-694-7330
e-mail: vogels@atlantic.net
Authors of "Victorian Trinket Boxes," a handbook with price guide for the porcelain trinket box collector.

Candy

Collectors

Lynn Goldfinger
P.O. Box 4962
Burlingame, CA 94011-4962
ph: 650-342-7829
fax: 650-343-3269
e-mail: goldie1943@aol.com
Wants to buy Victorian cardboard candy boxes; all styles and sizes with artwork on the box.

Enamel

Dealers

Bob Smith
Cameron & Smith Ltd.
P.O. Box 637
Vero Beach, FL 32961-0637
ph: 800-472-9862 or 561-778-7862
fax: 561-794-0544
e-mail: enamels@cameronsmith.com
web: http://www.cameronsmith.com/
Buys and sells enamel boxes: Halcyon Days, Staffordshire, Crummles, Bilston, Battersea, etc.; limited editions wanted; specializing in retired limited editions Beatrix Potter enamels and any Royalty enamels; also Holiday boxes.

Enamel (Battersea)

Dealers

John Harrigan
1900 Hennepin
Minneapolis, MN 55403-3160
ph: 612-872-0226
fax: 612-872-0224
Prefers to buy motto boxes, but will consider others.

Experts

Mel & Barbara Alpren
14 Carter Rd.
West Orange, NJ 07052-4612
ph: 201-731-9427
Advisor to "Warman's Antiques & Collectibles Price Guide."

Enamel (Halcyon)

Man./Prod./Dist.

Halcyon Days Enamels
14-16 Barton Park Mount Pleasant
Bilston, West Midlands WV14 7LH
U.K.
ph: 011 44 1902 408440
fax: 011 44 1902 498008

BOY SCOUT MEMORABILIA

(see also CAMPING EQUIPMENT; GIRL SCOUT MEMORABILIA; LONE SCOUT MEMORABILIA; STAMP COLLECTING, Boy Scouting)

Book Sellers

Doug Bearce
Scouting Collectables
P.O. Box 4742
Salem, OR 97302-8742
ph: 503-399-9872
fax: 503-399-0559
e-mail: bearce@prodigy.net
Publishes and sells books on collecting Boy Scout items.

Clubs/Associations

Glen T. Wright
International Badgers Club
Magazine: SETT
2903 W Woodbine Dr.
Maryville, TN 37803
ph: 423-984-8856
fax: 423-984-8856
e-mail: IBCBadger@aol.com
Members interested in collecting Scout and Guide badges of the entire world; an international organization with representatives all around the world.

Billie Lee
National Scouting Collectors Society
Newsletter: Scouting Collectors Quarterly
806 E. Scott St.
Tuscola, IL 61953-1726
ph: 217-253-3243

American Scouting Traders Association, Inc.
Newsletter: American STAR, The
P.O. Box 210013
San Francisco, CA 94121-0013
ph: 714-641-4845
e-mail: asta@scouter.org
web: http://asta.scouter.org/
ASTA members share an interest in the collecting and trading of Scouting memorabilia; primary purpose is to educate the membership and others regarding Scouting memorabilia; for Scouts and Scouters only.

Collectors

Norm Sapolnick
P.O. Box 5
Hillside, NJ 07205-0005
ph: 908-687-3920 or 908-964-5800
fax: 908-687-6300

Bruce White
3 Woodfern Ave.
Trenton, NJ 08628
ph: 609-882-5584
Wants Boy Scouts of America patches, pins, literature, WWW items, jamboree, etc.

John Burch
173 Hutton Dr.
Williamsburg, KY 40769
ph: 606-539-4160
e-mail: jburch@cc.cumber.edu
web: http://hagan.cumber.edu/trade.html

Michael Bungo
Scout Place
229 S. Chillicothe Rd.
Aurora, OH 44202
ph: 330-562-4880
e-mail: bungo@bigfoot.com
web: http://www.geocities.com/Yosemite/Trails/8210/
Collector of Boy Scout patches: council shoulder patches, anniversary patches, Jamboree patches, Council/Camp patches.

Mike Wroblewski
5526 E. County Rd. 100 N.
Greensburg, IN 47240-8805
ph: 812-663-9403
e-mail: bwrob00@mail.hsonline.net
Wants all Boy Scout related memorabilia: books, pictures, OA items, uniforms, patches, equipment, unusual items, etc.; special interest in all Indiana related Scouting items.

Dr. Larry Ruehlen, Sr.
21124 Hoffman St.
Saint Clair Shores, MI 48082-1517
Wants Scout rings, square merit badges and ranks, Air Scout items, Eagle items, OA vigil items.

Robert N. Hightower
Rt. 11 Box 469
Palestine, TX 75801
ph: 903-723-0418
Buys Boy Scout items: patches, pins, books, uniforms, medals, equipment, etc.

John C. Williams
Heart O' Texas Trader
P.O. Box 23374
Waco, TX 76702-3374
ph: 254-772-1106
fax: 254-741-9715
e-mail: jconleywilliams@prodigy.net
web: http://www.hottrader.com
Dealer, collector, appraiser, on-line resource specializing in Boy Scouting; wants to buy Boy Scout patches: Order of the Arrow (WWW), Philmont, High Adventure, Jamboree; also wants other Boy Scout related memorabilia.

Doug Bearce
P.O. Box 4742
Salem, OR 97302-8742
ph: 503-399-9872
fax: 503-399-0559
e-mail: bearce@prodigy.net
Wants Boy Scout items: books, uniforms, patches, pins, OA items, Jamboree, etc.

Dealers

James W. Clough
Scout Collectors Shop
9 Elmwood Dr.
South Glens Falls, NY 12803-5454
ph: 518-793-4037
Wants Boy Scout items; sashes, medals, pins, patches, uniforms, etc.

Richard Shields
Carolina Trader, The
P.O. Box 769
Monroe, NC 28111-0769
ph: 704-282-1339 or 704-289-1604
e-mail: carotrader@trellis.net
web: http://www.trellis.net/carotrader
Buys anything associated with the Boy Scouts of America; author of "Patrol Yell - History of the Patrol Medallions of the BSA"; publishes large catalog of BSA items for sale.

Roland Sayers
Southeastern Antiques & Collectibles
305 N. Main St.
Hendersonville, NC 28792
ph: 826-697-6064
fax: 826-883-9562
Wants to buy pre-1960 Boy and Girl Scout collectibles.

Darrell Wessinger
Wessingers, The
17 Sandy Bank Dr.
Lexington, SC 29072-9185
ph: 803-356-0161 or 800-572-2427
fax: 803-957-4147
e-mail: Darrwess@aol.com
web: http://www.scsn.net/users/darrwess/
Specializing in Boy Scout and Girl Scout memorabilia; publishes several sales/auction lists each year.

Chris R. Jensen
Streamwood, Inc.
Newsletter: Scout Stuff
121 Gulf St.
P.O. Box 1841
Easley, SC 29641-1841
ph: 864-859-2915 or 800-453-0398
fax: 864-855-5010
e-mail: cjensen@streamwood.net
web: http://www.streamwood.net
Wants Boy Scout memorabilia: pre-1936 handbooks, Order of the Arrow (WWW), merit badges, jamboree, medals, patches, insignia, uniforms; publishes extensive catalog four/five times a year; 40-page tabloid paper; send for free sample.

Randall M. MacDonald
Suncoast Patch Supply
4310 Creekglen Lane
Lakeland, FL 33811
ph: 941-644-4177
e-mail: macdonr@tfn.net
web: http://www.angelfire.com/fl/thetrader/index.html
Avid collector and dealer of Boy Scout patches since 1973; also wants patches and memorabilia from Philmont Scout Ranch in Cimarron, NM.

Nancy & Glenn Darst
Boston Store, The
P.O. Box 190394
Mobile, AL 36619
ph: 334-666-9265 or 334-666-2079
e-mail: gdarst@zebra.net
Buys and sells fishing collectibles from 1800s to 1950s: landing & trout nets, backpacks, lures, bobbers, knives, creels, pack baskets, fishing catalogs, old hunting and fishing signs; also Scout knives, hatchets, axes; pre-1950 LLBean.

Mark Browning
Ploughshare Trades
12300 E 5th St.
Kansas City, MO 64133
ph: 816-353-2876
e-mail: mbrownin@qni.com
web: http://www.jccc.net/~mbrownin/scouts/mark.html
Buys and sells all sorts of Boy Scout collectibles; specializes in Order of the Arrow and Council Shoulder patches.

Experts

Chris R. Jensen
Streamwood, Inc.
121 Gulf St.
P.O. Box 1841
Easley, SC 29641-1841
ph: 864-859-2915 or 800-453-0398
fax: 864-855-5010
e-mail: cjensen@streamwood.net
web: http://www.streamwood.net
30 years experience as dealer/collector/appraiser; largest sale list of exclusive Scouting items in the world; largest inventory of Scout collecting guide books available anywhere; author of 7 Scout collecting books and price guides.

Fran & Cal Holden
P.O. Box 264 - M264
Doylestown, OH 44230-0264
ph: 800-663-2793
Wants old or unusual pins, badges, medals; from O/A, Jamboree, Senior Scouts; also uniforms, games, official literature, postcards, etc.; offers subscription sales lists to collectors of Boy Scout literature.

Roy More
Scout Patch Auction
2484 Dundee
Ann Arbor, MI 48103
ph: 734-663-6203
fax: 734-663-7227
e-mail: spa@msen.com
web: http://www.tspa.com
Collector, dealer, appraiser expert in Boy Scout memorabilia.

Jack O'Brian
Memory Tree
P.O. Box 9462
Madison, WI 53715
ph: 414-261-6641
fax: 414-261-9461
Buys and sells Eagle Scout and Air Scout medals and ribbons, enamel pins, Lone Scout, posters, banks, tins, toys, watch fobs; will help identify and date items if inquiries are accompanied by a SASE.

Jim & Bea Stevenson
Stevensons, The
316 Sage Lane
Euless, TX 76039-7906
ph: 817-354-8903
fax: 817-354-9382
e-mail: the_stevensons@msn.com
Wants Boy Scout handbooks, paper items, Jamboree items, uniforms, insignia, Sea Scouts, Skippers, Order of the Arrow, etc.; issues 10 catalogs per year for $10/yr.

John C. Williams
Heart O' Texas Trader
P.O. Box 23374
Waco, TX 76702-3374
ph: 254-772-1106
fax: 254-741-9715
e-mail: jconleywilliams@prodigy.net
web: http://www.hottrader.com
Dealer, collector, appraiser, on-line resource specializing in Boy Scouting; wants to buy Boy Scout patches: Order of the Arrow (WWW), Philmont, High Adventure, Jamboree; also wants other Boy Scout related memorabilia.

Museums/Libraries

Dr. Edward Rowan, Ed.
Lawrence L. Lee Scout Museum & Max I. Silber Scouting Library
Magazine: Scout Memorabilia
P.O. Box 1121
Manchester, NH 03105-1121
ph: 603-627-1492 or 603-669-8919
fax: 603-641-6436
web: http://www.scoutingmuseum.org
Home to one of the finest collections of Boy Scout memorabilia; "Scout Memorabilia" has insert listing sales, auctions, ads, etc.

Susan K. Crawford
Murray State University National Museum of the Boy Scouts of America
16th & Calloway
Murray, KY 42071
ph: 502-762-3383 or 800-303-3047
e-mail: webmaster@murraystate.edu
web: http://www.mursuky.edu/cam/Nat-sct.htm
Displays 54 original Rockwell Scouting paintings.

Ottawa Scouting Museum
1100 Canal Street
P.O. Box 2241
Ottawa, IL 61350
ph: 815-431-9353
e-mail: scouter@theramp.net
web: http://sever8.hypermart.net/osm/osm.htm
Houses the Zitelman Collection of Rockford, the Sullivan Collection of Friendship Village, and memorabilia from local donors: covers Boy Scouting, Girl Scouting, and Camp Fire.

Ed W. Hillenberg, Curator
Hillenberg Scout Museum
123 Beard St.
Danville, IL 61832-6009
ph: 217-442-6678

Periodicals

Dr. Edward Rowan, Ed.
Lawrence L. Lee Scout Museum & Max I. Silber Scouting Library
Magazine: Scout Memorabilia
P.O. Box 1121
Manchester, NH 03105-1121
ph: 603-627-1492 or 603-669-8919
fax: 603-641-6436
web: http://www.scoutingmuseum.org
Home to one of the finest collections of Boy Scout memorabilia; "Scout Memorabilia" has insert listing sales, auctions, ads, etc.

Ken Wiltz
Magazine: Fleur-de-Lis
5 Dawes Ct. - Dept. CIC
Novato, CA 94947-4406
ph: 415-892-5977
fax: 415-892-5977
An international scouting memorabilia magazine now read in 30 countries.

Camps

Periodicals

David Minnihan
Newsletter: Camp Patch Collector, The
P.O. Box 210013
San Francisco, CA 94121-0013
ph: 714-641-4845
e-mail: asta@scouter.org
web: http://asta.scouter.org/
Newsletter dealing with history and memorabilia of Boy Scout Camps.

Neckerchief Slides

Collectors

John Koppen
12705 N.W. Puddy Gulch Rd.
Yamhill, OR 97148-8020
ph: 503-662-3953

Order Of The Arrow

Collectors

Paul Judge
4 Winthhrop Place
Maplewood, NJ 07040
e-mail: PaulBJudge@aol.com
web: http://members.aol.com/PaulBJudge/pjudge.html
Collector and expert who specializes in collecting and trading Order of the Arrow Boy Scout patches, especially OA flap patches from past and present New Jersey Lodges.

Greg Souchik
P.O. Box 161
Custer City, PA 16725-0161
ph: 814-362-2642
fax: 814-362-7356
e-mail: AlleghenyArsenal@compuserve.com
Wants to buy "Order of the Arrow" embroidered patches; may have "W.W.W.", "Lodge", or "O.A." on them; will pay up to $1000 for some patches; send photos or photocopies.

John E. Pannell
600-C Tracy Dr.
Burlington, NC 27215
e-mail: pannellj@netpath.net
web: http://www.netpath.net/~pannellj/oaguide/

Internet Resources

John E. Pannell
Internet Guide to Order of the Arrow Insignia
600-C Tracy Dr.
Burlington, NC 27215
e-mail: pannellj@netpath.net
web: http://www.netpath.net/~pannellj/oaguide/
The internet's largest collection of Order of the Arrow insignia; more than 590 lodges are represented with over 3600 images.

Seals

Clubs/Associations

Murray Fried
World Scout Sealers
Newsletter: World Scout Sealers
509-11 Margaret Ave.
Kitchener, Ontario N2H 6M4
Canada
ph: 519-745-7947
e-mail: murryfried@golden.net
Members buy, sell and trade Scout seals, decals and other Boy Scout memorabilia; publishes an 8-page newsletter twice a year.

BRASS ITEMS

(see also BELLS; CANDLEHOLDERS; FIREPLACE ITEMS; GARDEN HOSE NOZZLES; INSTRUMENTS & DEVICES; LAMPS & LIGHTING; MEDICAL, DENTAL & PHARMACEUTICAL; REPAIR/RESTORATION/CONSERVATION, Metal Items; TRENCH ART)

Repair Services

Don L. Reedy
Brass & Copper Polishing Shop
13 South Carroll St.
Frederick, MD 21701-5606
ph: 301-663-4240 or 301-662-5503
fax: 301-694-9190
e-mail: shineit4u@aol.com
Repairs and polishes or lacquers brass and copper items.

Repro. Sources

Becky Ballew
Virginia Metalcrafters
1010 East Main St.
Waynesboro, VA 22980-5855
ph: 540-949-9400 or 800-368-1002
fax: 540-949-9446
e-mail: vametal@rica.net
web: http://www.vametal.com/
Makes and sells andirons, fireplace tools and fenders, chandeliers, candlesticks, sconces, garden sculpture.

BREWERIANA

(see also ADVERTISING COLLECTIBLES; BEER CANS; BOTTLES; BOTTLE CAPS; BOTTLE OPENERS; COLLECTIBLES [MODERN], Steins; CORKSCREWS; GLASSES, Drinking; NEON; PAPER COLLECTIBLES; PROHIBITION ITEMS; SALOON & BAR COLLECTIBLES; STEINS)

Appraisers

Judy Owen, ISA
Antique Appraisers - Grand Traverse
10332 Stoneybeach Pointe
Traverse City, MI 49686-8584
ph: 231-946-2534
fax: 231-946-2573
e-mail: judy@antiqueappraisers.com
web: http://www.antiqueappraisers.com/
Collects, specializes in, and appraises breweriana: Strohs, Goebels, all Michigan breweries, pre-prohibition trays and signs, etched glasses, bottle-shaped openers, etc.

Lynn Geyer
300 Trail Ridge
Silver City, NM 88061-6071
ph: 505-538-2341
fax: 505-388-9000
Appraiser, expert specializes in all aspects of breweriana and soda-pop; also contemporary steins, mugs & drinking glasses; advertising trays, advertising signs, tap knobs; member

of Certified Appraiser Guild of America.

Auction Services

Don Fink
Fink's Off the Wall Auctions
108 E. Seventh St.
Lansdale, PA 19446-2622
ph: 215-855-9732
fax: 215-855-6325
e-mail: lansbeer@finksauctions.com
web: http://www.finksauctions.com/
Deals in a wide range of brewery collectibles.

Pete Kroll
Glasses, Mugs & Steins Auction
P.O. Box 207
Sun Prairie, WI 53590-0207
ph: 608-837-4818
fax: 608-825-4205
e-mail: pkroll@chorus.net
web: http://www.gmskroll.com/
Produces a semi-annual mail auction featuring collectible advertising glasses, mugs & steins: beer, soda, horse racing, cartoon, Disney, root beer, Budweiser, whiskey shot glasses, whiskey pitchers, etc.

Lynn Geyer
Lynn Geyer Advertising Auctions
300 Trail Ridge
Silver City, NM 88061-6071
ph: 505-538-2341
fax: 505-388-9000
Conducts semi-annual mail/phone bid specialized auctions on all aspects of breweriana and soda-pop; also contemporary steins, mugs & drinking glasses; advertising trays, advertising signs, tap knobs.

Clubs/Associations

Chris & Roger Levesque
Microbes
Newsletter: Micro Connection, The
P.O. Box 826
South Windsor, CT 06074
ph: 860-644-9582
e-mail: chris.roger@snet.net
Focuses on collecting breweriana relating to micro breweries.

John Stanley
East Coast Breweriana Association
Newsletter: Keg, The
P.O. Box 64
Chapel Hill, NC 27514
ph: 919-419-1546 or 919-966-5794
e-mail: jfo@mindspring.com
web: http://www.mindspring.com/~jfo
The oldest breweriana collectors organization; serving collectors of all types of brewery advertising; emphasis on Eastern US; write and request a membership application.

Kurt Bachmann
Dog Gone Good
Newsletter: Dog Gone Good Dispatch
57883 Hanover Rd.
Washington, MI 48094
ph: 810-677-3284
fax: 248-745-1221
e-mail: kbach@clearr.com
Dealing with all types of breweriana advertising including, but not limited to, beer advertising bottle openers; official chapter of the National Association of Breweriana Advertising dedicated to breweriana history and collecting.

Keith Ajayan
Beer Can & Breweriana Collectors of America, Mile High Chapter
414 Wright St. #107
Lakewood, CO 80228
ph: 303-763-5811
e-mail: beerstuff@aol.com

Stan Galloway, Ex. Dir.
American Breweriana Association, Inc.
Journal: American Breweriana Journal
P.O. Box 11157
Pueblo, CO 81001-0157
ph: 719-544-9267
e-mail: breweriana@aol.com
web: http://www.a-b-a.com
Association of brewery historians and collectors of beer advertising and collectibles; offers seven free exchange services for collectors, Lending Library, and annual meeting for members to buy/sell/trade breweriana; 3,300 members.

Andy Reiner
Canadian Brewerianist, The
19 Lambert Road
Thornhill, Ontario L3T 7E6
Canada

Martin Apeler, Treas.
German Breweriana Collector Society
Brinkstr. 52
Hess. Oldendorf, D-31840
Germany

John Mann
Association of Bottled Beer Collectors
Newsletter: What's Bottling
4 Willow Road
Basingstoke, Hampshire RG26 4LU
U.K.
ph: (44) 118 981 6092
e-mail: John_Mann@compuserve.com
web: http://ourworld.compuserve.com/homepages/John_Mann/abbchome.htm
Collectors of (mainly) British commemorative bottled beers, beer labels and other breweriana.

Collectors

Ed Natale, Jr.
P.O. Box 222
Wyckoff, NJ 07481
ph: 201-848-8485
fax: 201-848-8485
Wants to buy beer trays with brewery scenes, women, dogs, children; foam scrapers, NJ & NYC brewery items, painted label bottles, punch-top and spout-top cans, signs; photos helpful.

Ron Gavin
1721 Depot Rd.
Duanesburg, NY 12056
ph: 518-895-8165
Wants breweriana items; specializes in trays, signs, bottles, and coasters; wants items from upstate New York cities such as Albany, Troy, Schenectady, Amsterdam, Utica, Rome, Cohoes, Hudson, and Binghamton.

Kurt Bachmann
57883 Hanover Rd.
Washington, MI 48094
ph: 810-677-3284
fax: 248-745-1221
e-mail: kbach@clearr.com
Dealing with all types of breweriana advertising including, but not limited to, beer advertising bottle openers.

Mike England
718 NW Scott St.
Ankeny, IA 50021-2267
ph: 515-965-2448
e-mail: menglan@bcca.com
Want old cone top & flat top beer & soda cans; also breweriana (beer advertising) items; especially interested in pre-prohibition era, anything from Iowa breweries, Dr. Pepper, etc.; look in crawl spaces, attics, walls, under stoop.

Steve Ketcham
P.O. Box 24114
Minneapolis, MN 55424-0114
ph: 612-920-4205
e-mail: s.ketcham@unique-software.com
Wants pre-prohibition brewery memorabilia: calendars, publications, brewery signs, trays, glasses, posters, pocket mirrors, steins, etc.; please send SASE with inquiries.

Dale Schmidt
610 Howell Prairie Rd. SE
Salem, OR 97301-9097
ph: 503-364-0499
fax: 503-585-3071
e-mail: jschm62655@aol.com
Wants anything pre-Prohibition that is related to beer and/or breweries.

Jeroen Dubois
Belgium
e-mail: jeroendubois@hotmail.com
web: http://www.angelfire.com/ne/jeroendubois/
Trades beer mats or coasters, labels and crowncaps from different countries.

Dealers

Dan Morean
www.breweriana.com
13 Greenleaf St.
Malden, MA 02148
ph: 781-324-3330 or 781-322-3725
fax: 781-324-3320
e-mail: dan@breweriana.com
web: http://www.breweriana.com
Collects MA breweriana, buys and sells all other breweriana items; specializes in pre-prohibition brewery advertising, beer cans, bottles, trays, lithographs, trade cards, openers, matchbooks, labels; also soda collectibles.

Bob Miller
P.O. Box 640245
Flushing, NY 11364-0245
ph: 718-776-7409
Wants old (pre-Prohibition up to 1940s) American beer advertising items such as match safes, trays, signs, corkscrews, unusual bottle openers, paperweights, signs, etched glassware, etc.

Bob Lucian
33 Merritts Road
Farmingdale, NY 11735-1820
ph: 516-293-3927
e-mail: bbluc@erols.net
Buys and sells old pre-prohibition American beer items: mugs, steins, advertising signs, bottle openers, match safes, glasses, "giveaways", etc.; prefers items from the NYC and L.I. area; also wants prohibition items; call collect.

John Gruskin
P.O. Box 53
Northport, NY 11768
ph: 516-262-0338
e-mail: jlgruskin@aol.com
web: http://www.angelfire.com/ny/beerstuff/
Buys and sells beer cans, trays, steins, advertising.

Louis DiDona
Lou's Breweriana Unlimited
623 Center Street
Bethlehem, PA 18018-4035
ph: 610-866-2373
fax: 610-866-2373
e-mail: lou@lousbreweriana.com
web: http://www.lousbreweriana.com/
Specializes in fine collectible beer advertising and beer cans; also in soda advertising items; website has large database of items for sale.

Paul Jarmusz
Vintage Original Fruit Crate Labels
2845 D St. N.E.
Salem, OR 97301-1600
ph: 503-371-0868
fax: 503-371-0868
e-mail: mail@labelcollector.com
web: http://www.labelcollector.com
Buys and sells old can labels, beer labels, soda labels; unused stock found from breweries, old packing houses, canneries, produce businesses.

Bill Mugrage
Pacific Coast Breweriana
3819 190th Pl. S.W.
Lynnwood, WA 98036
ph: 425-774-9849
e-mail: premium@pc-breweriana.com
web: http://www.pc-breweriana.com/
Dealing in all aspects of U.S. breweriana; buys, sells, trades all forms of beer advertising; free appraisals; inquiries promptly answered.

Experts

Tom Terwilliger, CAGA
Pro Auction Company
707 230th Street
Algona, IA 50511
ph: 515-295-7819
fax: 515-295-7742
e-mail: proauct@ncn.net
web: http://www.proauctionusa.com
Collects and specializes in breweriana.

Bill Mugrage
Pacific Coast Breweriana
3819 190th Pl. S.W.
Lynnwood, WA 98036
ph: 425-774-9849
e-mail: premium@pc-breweriana.com
web: http://www.pc-breweriana.com/
Dealing in all aspects of U.S. breweriana; buys, sells, trades all forms of beer advertising; free appraisals; inquiries promptly answered.

Museums/Libraries

American Museum of Brewing History & Arts, Oldenberg Brewing Company
400 Buttermilk Pike Exit
Ft. Mitchell, KY 41017
ph: 606-341-7223
web: http://realbeer.com/oldenberg/Museum.html
World's largest collection of breweriana: tens of thousands of labels, coasters, bottles, cans, match boxes, signs, foam scrapers, etc.

Periodicals

Michael Allison
Magazine: All About Beer
1627 Marion Ave.
Durham, NC 27705-5808
ph: 800-977-2337
fax: 919-490-0865
e-mail: allabtbeer@aol.com
web: http://www.allaboutbeer.com
For fifteen years the voice of beer lovers; brew pub finder, homebrewing, beer links, some discussion of beer collectibles, calendar of events, beer & food, beer travelers, beer talk.

Sandra L. Powers
Bosak Publishing Co.
Magazine: Suds 'N Stuff
4764 Galicia Way
Oceanside, CA 92056
ph: 760-724-4447 or 800-457-6543
Bi-monthly beer publication; articles, history, memorabilia, ads, etc.

Advertising

Clubs/Associations

Robert E. Jaeger
National Association of Breweriana Advertising
Newsletter: Breweriana Collector, The
2343 Met-To-Wee Lane
Milwaukee, WI 53226-1612
ph: 414-257-0158
Focuses on anything with the word "Beer" or "Brewery" on it; encourage the collection, preservation and study of American brewery advertising on a national level; membership directory and annual convention; 4 newsletters per year.

Collectors

David Donovan, Sr.
129 S. Linwood Ave.
Baltimore, MD 21224-2246
ph: 410-276-7577 or 410-732-2778
e-mail: bowery@erols.com
Interested in all types of advertising from any Baltimore or Maryland brewery, especially pre-prohibition.

Robert E. Jaeger
2343 Met-To-Wee Lane
Milwaukee, WI 53226-1612
ph: 414-257-0158
Wants any advertising item with the word "Beer" or "Brewery" on it.

Back Bar Statues

Experts

George Baley
310 Grandview Ave.
Kalamazoo, MI 49001-3609
ph: 616-382-4833
Author of "Back Bar Breweriana."

Canadian

Dealers

Phil Greenwood
6 Wildrose Place
Sherwood Park, Alberta T8H 1H1
Canada
ph: 780-449-7048
e-mail: pgreenwood@home.com
web: http://members.ebay.com/aboutme/chmee
Collects, buys and sells Canadian breweriana: cans, trays, signs, calendars, labels, crowns, etc.; welcomes contact with others who might have questions about Canadian breweriana.

Coasters

Clubs/Associations

Terry Lavell
British Beermat Collectors' Society
6 Salcombe Road
London, E17 8JH
U.K.

Collectors

George Barone
94 Ridgeview Place
Cheshire, CT 06410
e-mail: geobaron@ix.netcom.com
web: http://members.aol.com/gbarone/
Author of "Coasters of New England."

George Barone
Beer Coaster Mania
94 Ridgeview Place
Cheshire, CT 06410
ph: 203-272-2656
e-mail: geobaron@ix.netcom.com
web: http://members.aol.com/gbarone/
Website has all the information you need on collecting beer coasters: mystery coasters, rare new finds, trade lists, coaster guides, recent news, and more.

Steve Barile
Stogie Steve
1905 Hunter Lane
Brandon, FL 33510
e-mail: SEBDGB@aol.com
web: http://members.aol.com/sebdgb/collect/
WAnts to buy beer mats (beer coasters); trade or purchase.

Ken Kositzke
1623 N. Linwood Ave.
Appleton, WI 54914
Runs the ABA Coaster Exchange.

Scott deMasi
5610 Kiowa Timbers Dr.
Humble, TX 77346-1929
ph: 281-852-0077
e-mail: demasi@flash.net

Dealers

George Barone
94 Ridgeview Place
Cheshire, CT 06410
ph: 203-272-2656
e-mail: geobaron@ix.netcom.com
Coaster collector, dealer, and expert.

Vic Kroll
Kroll's Kollectibles
3451 Nighthawk Ct.
Punta Gorda, FL 33950-6675
ph: 941-575-0303
e-mail: beer@sunline.net
Buys, sells, trades U.S. brewery coasters, postcards, letterheads, tokens, stock certificates and other advertising items.

Experts

George Barone
94 Ridgeview Place
Cheshire, CT 06410
ph: 203-272-2656
e-mail: geobaron@ix.netcom.com
Coaster collector, dealer, and expert.

Internet Resources

George Klann
George's Tegestology Page
2316 Telemark Ln., N.W.
Rochester, MN 55901
e-mail: klann.george@mayo.edu
web: http://stoopidsoftware.com/brad/beer/
Beer coaster collecting is known as tegestology.

Hamm's Beer

Collectors

Jim Welytok
W241 N8938 Penny Lane
Sussex, WI 53089
ph: 414-246-7171
Wants 1954-1968 Hamm's Beer items: animated moving store displays, statues, artwork, advertising, signs, etc.

Craig Ventzke
1837 Park Blvd.
Fargo, ND 58103-4735
ph: 701-293-1547
e-mail: kicrvi@aol.com
Looking for Hamm's Beer signs, point of sale displays, neon signs, old grain belt signs; pre-prohibition items.

Pete Nowicki
1531 39th Ave.
San Francisco, CA 94122-3015
ph: 415-566-7506
e-mail: portfire86@aol.com
Collector desires to obtain older Hamm's Beer advertising: glasses, signs, neons, etc.; the older the better.

Heineken

Collectors

Jan Stabij
Suideinde 382
Amsterdam, NH 1035 PP
Holland
ph: +31206332257
e-mail: stabij@excite.com
web: http://angelfire.com/ns/stabij/
Collects anything from the Heineken beer company, especially advertising items.

Peter van Otterloo
Libanonstraat 12
Delft HS, 2622
The Netherlande
ph: 015-2564580
e-mail: 106254.3013@compuserve.com
Collects all kind of items of Heineken beer, especially pre-1950 glasses and mugs from all countries of the world.

Labels

Collectors

Pat Wheeler
4330 W 152nd St.
Cleveland, OH 44135-1367
e-mail: abalabex@aol.com
web: http://members.aol.com/abalabex/labex.htm
Coordinates the ABA Label Exchange program.

Petr Vaverka
Labolog Club
Palackeho 13
Litomerice, 4120
Czech Republic
e-mail: petr.vaverka@zero.cz
web: http://labolog.zero.cz
Largest beer label collection on the internet.

Dealers

Nelson V. Rich, III
12479 Windcliff
Davisburg, MI 48350

Adrian Angleton
1303 Main
South Roxana, IL 62087
ph: 618-254-0401

Napkins

Collectors

Jeff Coolaw
5132 Round Rock Drive
El Paso, TX 79924
Runs the ABA Napkin Exchange.

Openers

(see also BOTTLE OPENERS)

Collectors

Lawrence Biehl
448 Crandon
Calumet City, IL 60449
Wants to buy beer can, bottle or cork openers that have name of brewery on them.

Trays

Collectors

Floyd Buck
P.O. Box 9
Wolcott, VT 05680
Wants to buy beer trays.

BREYER HORSE MODELS

(see ANIMAL COLLECTIBLES, Horses [Models/Breyer])

BRICKS

Clubs/Associations

Bill & Barb Brownlee
International Brick Collectors Association
Journal: International Brick Collectors Association Journal
80 E. 106th Terrace
Kansas City, MO 64114-5080
e-mail: somer-set@msn.com
Organization trades bricks at swap meets.

Collectors

Bill & Barb Brownlee
80 E. 106th Terrace
Kansas City, MO 64114-5080
e-mail: somer-set@msn.com

Ken Jones
100 Manor Dr.
Columbia, MO 65203
ph: 573-445-7171

Museums/Libraries

Museum of Ancient Brick, The
General Shale Corp.
3211 North Roan St.
Johnson City, TN 37601
ph: 423-282-4661
fax: 423-828-0491

BRIDAL COLLECTIBLES

Experts

Ann C. Bergin
P.O. Box 105
Amherst, NH 03031-0105
fax: 508-649-6807
e-mail: acbergin@aol.com

Periodicals

Ann C. Bergin
Newsletter: Bridal Collector's Roster
P.O. Box 105
Amherst, NH 03031-0105
fax: 508-649-6807
e-mail: acbergin@aol.com
Wants wedding and bride related pictorial books, dolls, music boxes, etc.; also first communions, Christenings, "rites" of passage.

Cake Toppers

Collectors

Jeff Dykes
6 Wildwood Terrace
Glen Ridge, NJ 07028
ph: 973-748-4990
e-mail: lja@viconet.com
Wants to buy German bisque and spun sugar wedding cake tops from 1890s to 1940s; especially wants military groom pieces; all must be in excellent condition; also look for bride/groom photo mirrors from 1910-1930s.

Jeannie Greenfield
310 Parker Rd.
Stoneboro, PA 16153-2810
ph: 724-376-2584
Wants pre-1950 cake toppers, any condition.

Experts

Cathy Cook
10 E. 13th St., #2D
New York, NY 10003-4467
ph: 212-691-2406
fax: 212-691-2406
e-mail: ccook710@aol.com
Collector always looking for historical information on bride-and-groom cake toppers; also wants to buy vintage toppers.

Wedding Gowns

Dealers

Lauren Lavonne Pritchett
Gulden & Brown Antique Wedding Gowns
1144 Koko Head Ave., Ste. 244
Honolulu, HI 96816
ph: 808-737-4696
e-mail: design-house@worldnet.att.net
web: http://home.att.net/~design-house/
Carries a large assortment of antique vintage wedding gowns and dresses, wax blossom headpieces, veils, and vintage bridal handbags from the 30s; specializes in evening gowns from the 30s and 40s; also carries Japanese kimonos.

BRIDGE

(see also PLAYING CARDS)

Dealers

Bill Sachen
Wankegan Bridge Center
927 Grand Ave.
Waukegan, IL 60085-3709
ph: 847-662-7204
e-mail: futilewill@aol.com
web: http://members.aol.com/FutileWill/
Buys and sells items relating to bridge and other indoor games as well as playing cards; many books in foreign languages.

Periodicals

Magazine: Bridge Buff's Bulletin
927 Grand Ave.
Waukegan, IL 60085-3709
ph: 847-662-7204
e-mail: futilewill@aol.com
web: http://members.aol.com/FutileWill/
A quarterly publication for collectors of bridge books and periodicals.

BROADCASTING

(see also AUDIO-VISUAL; FILMS; MOVIE MEMORABILIA; RADIO SHOWS, Old Time; RADIOS; TELEVISION SHOWS & MEMORABILIA; TELEVISIONS; TELEGRAPH ITEMS)

Experts

Mike Adams
112 Crescent Ct.
Scotts Valley, CA 95066-2815
ph: 408-924-4545
fax: 408-924-4543
Specialty area is radio and broadcast history; produced "Radio Collector" series for PBS TV; writes for "Antique Radio Classified."

Museums/Libraries

Pavek Museum of Broadcasting
3515 Raleigh Ave.
Minneapolis, MN 55416
ph: 612-926-8198
fax: 612-926-9761
e-mail: sraymer@pavekmuseum.org
web: http://www.pavekmuseum.org/
Houses one of the world's finest collections of antique radio, television, and broadcast equipment.

Military

Collectors

Bob Putnam
9140 Conversation Way
Springfield, VA 22153
ph: 703-644-9711
Serious collector wants all items, transcripts, pictures, etc. concerning military broadcasters who served in WWII, Korea and Vietnam as well as in all other military campaigns.

BROADSIDES

(see PAPER COLLECTIBLES; POSTERS)

BRONZES

(see also ART; COLLECTIBLES [MODERN], Sculptures; ORIENTALIA; SCULPTURE)

Appraisers

Stephen van Cline, CAPP
van Cline & Davenport, Ltd.
792 Franklin Ave.
Franklin Lakes, NJ 07417-1343
Specializes in paintings, watercolors, drawings, bronze & marble sculpture; appraisals, authentication, lectures, expert testimony; minimum charge $25; letter request only, SASE.

Faber Donoughe
201 W. 89th St.
New York, NY 10024
ph: 212-873-5882
A recognized appraiser of bronze sculptures.

Jerry Bengis, ISA
9860 SW 122nd St.
Miami, FL 33176-4928
ph: 305-232-1143
fax: 305-251-1450
e-mail: yascha7@netrox.net
Fine art appraiser specializing in prints (especially Salvador Dali), graphics (Miro, Chagall, Picasso, Warhol), etchings, engravings, prints, bronzes.

William Lavendusky, M.S., ISA
William Lavendusky, Fine Art
3345 So. Harvard, Bldg. 100
Tulsa, OK 74135
ph: 918-747-5336
fax: 918-742-3425
Dealer and appraiser of paintings and sculpture; specialist in 19th century French animal bronzes.

Dealers

Cameron Shay
James Graham & Sons
1014 Madison Ave. at 78th St.
New York, NY 10021
ph: 212-535-5767
fax: 212-794-2454
e-mail: jgsgal@aol.com
Specializes in fine bronze sculptures: Akeley, Baryre, Bonheur, Bugatti, Carpeaux, Remington, Russell, St. Gaudens, etc.

Experts

Henry Swiggum, ISA
4246 Glencove Trl
Saint Paul, MN 55214-5517
ph: 612-891-1514
fax: 612-891-1514
Specialist in bronzes and marble sculptures, prints, paintings, and Oriental art.

Repro. Sources

Jim Solk
Jim Solk Co., Inc.
4073 Glencoe Ave.
Marina Del Rey, CA 90292
ph: 310-448-4433 or 800-835-3600
fax: 310-448-4435
e-mail: solk@ix.netcom.com
web: http://www.solk.com
Extensive selection of reproduction bronzes after famous artists.

Deborah Lopez
Everything Metal Imaginable, Inc.
401 E. Cypress
Visalia, CA 93277-2834
ph: 559-732-8126 or 800-777-8126
fax: 559-732-5961
e-mail: webmaster@emiartbronze.com
web: http://www.emiartbronze.com
Buy foundry direct bronze sculptures by Remington, Russell, Mene, Bonhuer; over 300 quality "lost wax" bronze reproductions; send $10 for 56 page full-color catalog.

Foundry

Man./Prod./Dist.

Fine Arts Sculpture Centre, Inc.
4975 Waldon Road
Clarkston, MI 48348
ph: 248-391-3010
web: http://www.igfa.com/sculpture/index.html
A foundry offering mold-making, lost-wax shell casting, sand casting, repair & restoration, patina application, installation.

Ed Pogue
Pogue Sculpture
400 Monterey Blvd., #13
San Francisco, CA 94127
ph: 415-585-7462
fax: 415-585-7462
e-mail: ed34sculpt@aol.com
Specializing in all types of metal casting with specific expertise in the lost wax, ceramic shell, and resin bonded sand mold casting processes for non-ferrous metals.

Vince Maggiore
Bronze Works, The
W. 50 Fredson Road
Shelton, WA 98584
ph: 360-427-3857 or 360-427-9435
fax: 360-427-9464
e-mail: Bronzeworks@olywa.net
web: http://www.olywa.net/bronzeworks/
A full service sculpture foundry specializing in fine art; can also repair, recondition, or reproduce metal sculpture or artifacts; also offers sculpting classes.

Remington

Repro. Sources

Manny Shaool
Manny's Oriental Rugs
72 W. Washington St.
Hagerstown, MD 21740
ph: 301-797-7434
Importer of Oriental ivory, porcelain, reverse paintings, rugs; also Remington recast bronzes, clocks, lacquered furniture.

Vienna

Dealers

Joe Zobel
P & S Antiques
P.O. Box 741
Crompond, NY 10517
ph: 914-528-7209
Deals in fine quality 19th and early 20th century cold painted Austrian bronze figures.

BROTHER JUNIPER

Collectors

John Ferry
36 West Nyack Rd.
Nanuet, NY 10954
ph: 914-627-2163
Wants Brother Juniper figurines, bookends, ashtrays, etc.

BROWNIES

(see ELVES; ILLUSTRATORS, Palmer Cox)

BUBBLE GUM & CANDY WRAPPERS

Collectors

David Welch
P.O. Box 714
Murphysboro, IL 62966-0714
ph: 618-687-2282
fax: 618-684-2243
e-mail: PezDude1@aol.com
Wants pre 1970 chewing gum items: Wrigleys, Beechnut, Adams, Clarks, etc.; wrappers, packages, advertising (no magazine ads), displays, boxes, etc.; especially wants gum/candy items with cartoon, TV, movie character tie-ins.

Carl Lepiane
104 Karina Ct.
San Jose, CA 95131
ph: 408-436-1727 or 408-356-8474
Wants old chewing gum: pre-1950s tins, full boxes, packs, sticks, or wrappers; also gum cases, store displays and advertising.

Periodicals

Craig Willardson
Newsletter: Chewing Gum Times
P.O. Box 8296
Spokane, WA 99203-0296
ph: 509-624-0772
e-mail: cwillardsn@aol.com
Semi-annual newsletter for collectors of early chewing gum packs, sticks, wrappers, displays and related advertising; classified and display ad space available; published in April and November.

BUBBLE GUM CARDS

(see also TRADING CARDS, Non-Sport)

BUCKLES

(see BELT BUCKLES; CLOTHING & ACCESSORIES, Vintage)

BUGGIES

(see HORSE-DRAWN VEHICLES, Carriages)

BUILDERS ITEMS

(see ARCHITECTURE & RELATED ITEMS)

BUILDING BLOCKS

(see TOYS, Construction Sets)

BUILDING REPLICAS

(see SOUVENIR & COMMEMORATIVE ITEMS, Buildings)

BULLION

(see GOLD; PLATINUM; SILVER)

BUMPER STICKERS

Radio Station

Collectors

Doreen Lynn Hansen
2311 Morris Thomas Rd.
Duluth, MN 55811
ph: 218-628-3462
e-mail: dhansen@d.umn.edu
Collector/trader of bumper stickers from AM/FM radio stations in the USA, Canada and Mexico; will trade other promo items for stickers.

BURLESQUE

(see STRIPTEASE)

BURMA SHAVE COLLECTIBLES

Collectors

Steve Soelberg
29126 Laro Dr.
Agoura Hills, CA 91301-1635
ph: 818-889-9909
Burma Shave collectibles bought and sold, especially road signs; write with complete description and price; sorry, no list available; world's largest Burma Shave collector.

Internet Resources

Burma Shave Slogans
web: http://www.iea.com/~dgookin/burma.htm
Burma Shave signs from 1927 to 1963.

BURNT WOOD COLLECTIBLES

(see PYROGRAPHY ITEMS)

BUS LINE COLLECTIBLES

(see also TRANSPORTATION COLLECTIBLES)

Collectors

Charles Wotring
Royal Coach
911 Conley Dr.
Mechanicsburg, PA 17055
Wants to buy bus-related memorabilia from models to paper ephemera; also sells promotional bus banks.

Bernard F. Lopez
Bernie's Model & Classic Bus Depot
2 East Eighth St., #2412
Chicago, IL 60605
e-mail: bflop@idt.net
web: http://idt.net/~bflop/

Internet Resources

Bernard F. Lopez
Bernie's Model & Classic Bus Depot
2 East Eighth St., #2412
Chicago, IL 60605
e-mail: bflop@idt.net
web: http://idt.net/~bflop/
Internet resource for model, toy and classic bus collectors and enthusiasts; lots of photos.

BUSES

Clubs/Associations

Motor Bus Society
Magazine: Motor Coach Age
P.O. Box 251
Paramus, NJ 07653
e-mail: mct@shore.net
web: http://motorbussociety.org/
Publishes "Motor Coach Age" which emphasizes history and "Motor Coach Today" which provides fresh coverage of ever-changing bus fleets from charter operators to transit to over-the-road companies.

Robert B. Redden, Sr.
International Bus Collectors Club
Newsletter: IBCC Newsletter
1518 ""C"" Trailee Dr.
Charleston, SC 29407-4144
ph: 843-571-2489
The definitive bus club in the U.S.; work as consultants to the movie industry and media; produces the only American line of bus models; 20+ original video productions available; send for catalog.

Bernard Drovillard
Bus History Association
Magazine: Bus Industry Magazine
965 McEwan
Windsor, Ontario N9B 2G1
Canada
ph: 519-977-0664
Founded to preserve and record data, information and other materials related to the bus industry in North America and worldwide.

Collectors

Eugene R. Farha
P.O. Box 633
Cedar Grove, WV 25039-0633
ph: 304-340-3229 or 304-595-2296
fax: 304-340-3315
e-mail: farha@mail.wvnet.edu
Wants Greyhound and Trailways memorabilia: 10-yr. and 20-yr. service watch, years-of-service pins, match covers, Greyhound Bus Depot sign with dog; also wants Trailways items and Greyhound data, Greyhound Bus Lines rings.

Steve Wessing
P.O. Box 3050
Madison, WI 53704
e-mail: pstevew@madison.tds.net
Wants to buy bus items: tokens, passes, tickets, maps, schedules, advertising, promo items, bus driver hats, uniforms, badges, bus toys, signs, photos, postcards with bus station or buses, bus company items, etc.

Museums/Libraries

Pacific Bus Museum
P.O. Box 91
San Anselmo, CA 94979-0091
ph: 415-661-4408
e-mail: pbmbuses@sanfrantours.com
web: http://www.sanfrantours.com/PBM.HTML

Periodicals

Kelsey Publishing Ltd.
Magazine: Bus & Coach Preservation
Cudham Tithe Barn
Berrys Hill
Cudham, Kent TN16 3AG
U.K.
ph: 01959 541444
fax: 01959 541400
e-mail: info@kelsey.co.uk
web: http://www.kelsey.co.uk
A 56-page monthly British magazine dealing with British bus and coach preservation and restoration.

BUSINESS CARD HOLDERS

Collectors

Stephen Seltzer
7912 Georgia Ave.
Silver Spring, MD 20910-4837
ph: 301-565-2444 or 301-565-3339
fax: 301-565-2228
e-mail: eseltzer@aol.com
Wants to buy business cards and wallets - any material.

BUSINESS CARDS

(see also PAPER COLLECTIBLES)

Clubs/Associations

American Business Card Club
Newsletter: Card Talk
P.O. Box 460297-BC
Dept. #838
Aurora, CO 80046-0297
e-mail: bettycrow@worldnet.att.net
web: http://www.geocities.com/Wellesley/Garden/4757/club.html
The American Business Card Club is a unique resource for business people and collectors alike; please provide SASE with inquiries.

Collectors

Stephen Seltzer
7912 Georgia Ave.
Silver Spring, MD 20910-4837
ph: 301-565-2444 or 301-565-3339
fax: 301-565-2228
e-mail: eseltzer@aol.com
Wants to buy unusual business cards.

Jack Gurner
116 Dupuy St.
Water Valley, MS 38965-2901
ph: 601-473-1154
e-mail: jgurner@watervalley.net
web: http://www.watervalley.net/users/jgurner/bizcard.htm
Wants to buy OLD business cards; also wants some trade cards related to photographers and newspapers; main interest is in illustrated, odd or unusual.

Experts

Avery N. Pitzak
P.O. Box 460297-BC
Dept. #838
Aurora, CO 80046-0297
e-mail: bettycrow@worldnet.att.net
web: http://www.geocities.com/Wellesley/Garden/4757/club.html
Author of "Make Your Business Cards INCREDIBLE EFFECTIVE!"

Internet Resources

Terry Stewart
Collector Link
71 John St. East
Waterloo, Ontario N2J 1G2
Canada
ph: 519-745-1745
e-mail: stewart@collector-link.com
web: http://www.collector-link.com/
Catalogs over 2,000 trading card related web sites for: baseball, hockey, basketball, football, other sports, non-sports, phone cards, credit-debit cards, business cards, postcards.

BUTTER PATS

Clubs/Associations

Alice Black
Butter Pats International Collectors Club
Newsletter: BPICC Newsletter
38 Acton St.
Maynard, MA 01754
ph: 978-897-2434
For collectors of porcelain and other 3 inch butter pats; newsletter, buy, sell, trade, research, appraisals.

Mary Dessoie
Butter Pat Patter Association
Newsletter: Butter Pat Patter
280 Bronxville Road, Apt. 5-0
Bronxville, NY 10708-2849
ph: 914-337-1557
Association is for the serious collector of Victorian-era 3 inch butter pats and 19th century to modern day hotel and transportation pats; monthly newsletter with research, buy and sell ads, and butter pat values.

Collectors

Fred & Lila Schrader
2025 Highway 199
Crescent City, CA 95531
ph: 707-458-3525

Experts

Alice Black
38 Acton St.
Maynard, MA 01754
ph: 978-897-2434
Author of "The Joy of Collecting: Butter Pats and Miniature Plates."

Mary Dessoie
280 Bronxville Road, Apt. 5-0
Bronxville, NY 10708-2849
ph: 914-337-1557
Buys, sells, collects, appraises and specializes in butter pats.

Periodicals

Newsletter: Butter Pat Collectors' Notebook
5955 S.W. 179th Ave.
Beaverton, OR 97007

BUTTON COVERS

(see CLOTHING & ACCESSORIES, Vintage; CUFF LINKS)

BUTTONHOOKS

Clubs/Associations

Buttonhook Society, The
Newsletter: Boutonneur, The
2 Romney Place
Maidstone, Kent ME15 6LE
U.K.
ph: 01622 752949
To promote interest and research in the history, origins, uses and the collecting of buttonhooks; newsletters, exhibitions; new American point of contact: Priscilla Stoffel, Box 287, White Marsh, MD 21162-0287.

Collectors

Richard Mathes
P.O. Box 1408
Springfield, OH 45501-1408
Wants all types of buttonhooks to add to substantial collection; boot/shoe hooks, glove hooks, loop buttoners, or collar buttoners.

Paul Moorehead
2 Romney Place
Maidstone, Kent ME15 6LE
U.K.
ph: 01622 752949
Seeks unusual buttonhooks singles or in sets.

Dealers

Priscilla Washed
Victorian Lady, The
102 South Main St.
P.O. Box 424
Waxhaw, NC 28173-0424
ph: 704-843-4467 or 800-786-1886
A Victorian specialty store featuring 19th century ladies decorative & fashion accessories; buys and sells purses; also sewing and needlework tools, vintage fashion, Victoriana, and combs; mail order; catalog $5.

BUTTONS

(see also CUFF LINKS; SEWING ITEMS & GO-WITHS)

Appraisers

Lisa Schulz
1317 Lynndale Rd.
Madison, WI 53711-3316
ph: 608-271-4566
fax: 608-271-4566
e-mail: buttonldy@aol.com
web: http://www.buttonimages.com/
Collectible clothing buttons appraised, bought and sold; also sells button collecting products (mounting cards and wire, storage envelopes); catalog on request; e-mail on CompuServe at 70137,3556 or on America On Line at ButtonLdy.

Clubs/Associations

Lois Pool, Sec.
National Button Society
Newsletter: National Button Bulletin
2733 Juno Place, Apt. 4
Akron, OH 44313-4137
ph: 330-864-3296
Over 4000 members worldwide; focuses on preserving buttons and learning button history; one national show each year.

Joyce McGrath
Michigan Button Society
8215 Amelia Rd.
Jenison, MI 49428

California State Button Society
Newsletter: California Button Brief
P.O. Box 3084
Grass Valley, CA 95945-3084
e-mail: csbsweb@aol.com
web: http://members.aol.com/csbsweb/csbsweb/Default.htm

Pioneer Button Club
102 Frederick St.
Oshawa, Ontario L1G 2B3
Canada

Collectors

Warren K. Tice
W. Tice & Company
8 Orchard Terrace
Essex Junction, VT 05452-3501
ph: 802-878-3835
e-mail: wtice@vbimail.champlain.edu
Wants to purchase decorative ladies buttons.

A. Barth
1120 Laurelwood Dr.
Mc Lean, VA 22102-1519
ph: 703-734-0306
Wants fine quality 19th century buttons of all materials and sizes.

Michelle Revoir
2121 North Bayshore Dr. #716
Miami, FL 33137
ph: 305-573-6855
e-mail: OhRevoir@iname.com
Collector of antique and vintage clothing buttons and sewing items of all kinds.

Dealers

Debbie Woolley
Favorite Past-Times
6 Main Hill
Bridgton, ME 04009
ph: 207-647-5286
e-mail: woolley@maine-antiques.com
web: http://www.maine-antiques.com/fpt/Index/
Buys and sells antique buttons and button collections.

Gail Busche
Archangel Antiques
334 East Ninth St.
New York, NY 10003-7924
ph: 212-260-9313
Buying antique buttons, cuff links, eye glasses, and vintage lighters; always seeking fine examples such as enamel Deco and Art Nouveau.

Linda Kent
Antique Buttons & Collectibles
1 Campbell Rd. Ct.
Binghamton, NY 13905-4301
ph: 607-723-0644
e-mail: AntqBttn@ix.netcom.com
Buying and selling antique and collectible clothing buttons; member of National Button Society and past secretary of New York State Button Society.

Gale VerHague
Gale's Gallery
2646 Mezzio Rd.
Forestville, NY 14062
e-mail: galesgallery@netscape.net
web: http://www.antiquebuttons.com/

Kevin & Marilyn Kinne
Grist Books & Stuff
P.O. Box 91375
East Ridge, TN 37412-6375

Lisa Schulz
Button Images
1317 Lynndale Rd.
Madison, WI 53711-3316
ph: 608-271-4566
fax: 608-271-4566
e-mail: buttonldy@aol.com
web: http://www.buttonimages.com
Buys, sells, collects collectible clothing buttons and button display products; buttons can be shipped on approval; $15 minimum purchase.

Gwen Daniel
18 Belleau Lake Ct.
O Fallon, MO 63366-3144
ph: 314-978-3190
e-mail: gdaniel@mail.win.org
Buys and sells old interesting sewing buttons (picture buttons, Oriental buttons, carved Bakelite buttons) and related items.

Buttons, Etc.
P.O. Box 7572
Dallas, TX 75209
e-mail: buttons@ont.com
web: http://www.onlinetoday.com/users/buttons

Jude Allen
Vintage Collection
356 Main St.
Half Moon Bay, CA 94019
ph: 650-712-0366
fax: 650-654-0842
Buys and sells linen and lace; also old yardage, buttons, quilts, sewing implements, sewing machines and miniature sewing machines.

Eureka, I Found It! Antiques & Collectibles
P.O. Box 2192
Petaluma, CA 94953-2192
e-mail: eureka@erueka-i-found-it.com
web: http://www.eureka-i-found-it.com
An online dealer specializing in vintage textiles and clothing, toy and model steam engines, buttons, fans, Art Deco, costume jewelry, toy sewing machines.

Veronica Wexler
Button Bytes
840 Blossom Dr.
Santa Clara, CA 95050-5115
ph: 408-261-9742 or 408-984-2423
e-mail: rwexler@tias.com
web: http://www.tias.com/lists/buttons.shtml
Collector, dealer specializing in collectible clothing buttons; moderates a button chat list.

Georgia Fox
Foxes' Den Antiques
P.O. Box 846
Sutter Creek, CA 95685-0846
ph: 209-267-0774
Wants antique clothing buttons: porcelain, metal, gilt and Satsuma buttons with pictures, fables,

buildings, and heads of famous people.

Experts

Tender Buttons
143 East 62nd St.
New York, NY 10021
ph: 212-758-7004 or 212-980-3540
fax: 212-319-8474
Has the largest collection of antique buttons in America for both the collector and the wholesale dealers; author of "A Collector's Guide to Buttons" and co-author with Millicent Safro of "Buttons."

Lois Pool
2733 Juno Place, Apt. 4
Akron, OH 44313-4137
ph: 330-864-3296

Debra J. Wisniewski
410 Bond St.
Hastings, MI 49058
Author of "Antique & Collectible Buttons."

Internet Resources

Cecile T. Kohrs
Button Bytes
7303 Mallory Lane
Alexandria, VA 22315
e-mail: wyeknott@pop.dn.net
web: http://www.tias.com/articles/buttons
Internet site devoted to the hobby of button collecting; has an online 'zine, Button Bytes Light.

Linda Stark
Our Button Box
1113 Wheelis Road
Wylie, TX 75098
ph: 972-442-1410
e-mail: LL2Starks@aol.com
web: http://www.buttonworld.com/LL2Starks/
Not-for-profit informational web site for button collectors.

Linda Stark
Our Button Box
1113 Wheelis Rd.
Wylie, TX 75098
ph: 972-442-1410
e-mail: LL2Starks@aol.com
web: http://members.aol.com/LL2Starks/index.htm
A website for button lovers; links to dozens of button dealers, informative sites, a pictorial glossary of button terms, club listings, and more.

Man./Prod./Dist.

Donald B. Petersen
Waterbury Companies, Inc.
P.O. Box 1812
Waterbury, CT 06722
ph: 203-596-0800
fax: 203-574-1040
web: http://www.watco.com/buttons/buttons.htm
Manufacturer of metal buttons for uniforms and fashion garments since 1812; oldest continuous producer of metal buttons in the US.

Museums/Libraries

Gay Nineties Button & Doll Museum
Rte. 4 Box 420
Berryville, AR 72616
ph: 870-253-8588 or 800-645-8588
fax: 870-253-5444
Vintage doll and button collection; tours, lectures, exhibits.

Suppliers

Lisa Schulz
1317 Lynndale Rd.
Madison, WI 53711-3316
ph: 608-271-4566
fax: 608-271-4566
e-mail: buttonldy@aol.com
web: http://www.buttonimages.com/
Collectible clothing buttons appraised, bought and sold; also sells button collecting products (mounting cards and wire, storage envelopes); catalog on request; e-mail on CompuServe at 70137,3556 or on America On Line at ButtonLdy.

Military (American)

Collectors

Warren K. Tice
W. Tice & Company
8 Orchard Terrace
Essex Junction, VT 05452-3501
ph: 802-878-3835
e-mail: wtice@vbimail.champlain.edu
Wants to purchase U.S. Military, Confederate, and high quality decorative buttons; also wants to buy military antiques.

Experts

Bob French
Military Buttons
P.O. Box 79
Fairfax, VA 22030-0079
ph: 703-369-0031
fax: 703-369-0031
Noted expert in American Military Buttons 1776-1865; buys and sells all types of American uniform and historical buttons; written appraisals available.

Daniel J. Binder
927 20th St.
Rockford, IL 61104-3508
ph: 815-226-9056 or 815-654-2501
Wants 1812-1865 U.S. military buttons, especially Confederate States, Southern State seals, and Southern military school buttons.

Pin-Back

(see also PINS; POLITICAL COLLECTIBLES)

Collectors

Bob Cereghino
6400 Baltimore National Pike, Ste. 170A-319
Baltimore, MD 21228-3914
ph: 410-766-7593
e-mail: jwbc@juno.com
Wants advertising, entertainment and political pin-back buttons.

Millie Vaccarella
1955 Hythe St.
Roseville, MN 55113
ph: 651-631-2201
Wants to buy pin-back buttons: advertising, sports, movie stars, etc.; interested in single items or large collections.

Scott Weiss
1158 26th St., #489
Santa Monica, CA 90403
ph: 310-442-0040
fax: 310-442-5530
e-mail: sweiss5905@aol.com
Wants to buy TV and movie pinback buttons, pins, badges, and ribbons; promotional, licensed, product tie-ins, prop or cast and crew; wants from all years.

Experts

Ted Hake
Hake's Americana & Collectibles Auction
P.O. Box 1444
York, PA 17405-1444
ph: 717-848-1333
e-mail: Ted@hakes.com
web: http://www.hakes.com/
Always purchasing items for mail-bid auctions of Disneyana, historical Americana, toys, premiums, political items, character and other collectibles; author of "Price Guide to Collectible Pin-Back Buttons."

Pin-Back (Advertising)

Dealers

Dave Beck
P.O. Box 435
Mediapolis, IA 52637-0435
ph: 319-394-3943
fax: 319-394-3943
Buys and sells advertising watch fobs, mirrors and pin-backs; send stamp for illustrated mail auction catalog.

Pin-Back (Character/Comic)

Collectors

Walter Koenig
P.O. Box 4395
North Hollywood, CA 91617-0395
e-mail: gineokw@aol.com
Wants to buy comic (strip kind) pin-back buttons 1890s-1960s; no pep cereal buttons.

Transportation Employees'

Experts

Donald P. Van Court
41 Hillcrest Rd.
Madison, NJ 07940-2559
ph: 973-377-2676
Author of books illustrating the monograms, sets of initials, trade marks and designs on uniform buttons; historical notes on companies (land, sea and air) for which uniform button designs were created; also sells own book.

BUYING TRIPS

(see TOURS/BUYING TRIPS)

Here are some tips when contacting someone listed in this book:

- **When requesting information about a particular item, include a description (material, dimensions, maker's mark, model number, etc.) and a photo, sketch, or photocopy of the item in question.**
- **Always ask if there are charges for samples or for the services requested.**
- **When writing, please be sure to include a Large (#10 business size) Self-Addressed and Stamped Envelope (LSASE) if requesting a reply or the return of photographs.**
- **Never call collect unless otherwise directed. When calling, be considerate of time zone differences and always ask if the party you are calling has time to talk. When leaving an answering machine message, always instruct the party to call you back <u>collect</u>.**

CABINET CARDS

(see PHOTOGRAPHS)

CALCULATORS

(see also ADDING MACHINES; COMPUTERS; OFFICE EQUIPMENT; SLIDE RULES; TYPEWRITERS)

Clubs/Associations

Guy Ball
International Association of Calculator Collectors
Newsletter: International Calculator Collector, The
P.O. Box 345
Tustin, CA 92781-0345
ph: 714-730-6140 or 949-380-5748
fax: 714-730-6140
e-mail: mrcalc@usa.net
web: http://www.oldcalcs.com
Informative quarterly newsletter about collecting calculators from the "golden years" (1971-1978); send SASE for more information.

Collectors

Peter Frei
P.O. Box 500
Brimfield, MA 01010-0500
ph: 800-942-8968 or 413-245-4660
web: http://www.peterfrei.com/
Wants to buy hand powered vacuum cleaners, pre-1875 sewing machines, typewriters, calculators, and adding machines.

Arthur Cheslock
514 Paul St.
Baltimore, MD 21202
ph: 410-962-8580
fax: 410-752-8112
Wants pre-1945 calculators, adding machines and scientific instruments; also wants related literature.

Dale R. Beeks
Perceptions Scientifica
P.O. Box 117
Mount Vernon, IA 52314-0117
ph: 800-880-5178 or 319-895-0506
e-mail: dbeeksci@aol.com
Wants to buy pre-1960 pocket-sized adders and slide rules; also any in unusual forms.

Bruce Flamm
P.O. Box 70513
Riverside, CA 92513-0513
fax: 909-353-5625
e-mail: bflamm@ix.netcom.com
Wants pocket or hand-held calculators.

Robert Otnes
2160 Middlefield Rd.
Palo Alto, CA 94301-4022
ph: 650-324-1821
e-mail: bobotnes@mediacity.com
A leading collector of calculating machines and slide rules.

Robert De Cesaris
7429 Bree Ann Ct.
Citrus Heights, CA 95610-2455
ph: 916-356-5769
e-mail: rdecesar@pcocd2.intel.com
Very serious collector of mechanical calculators, early adders, and slide rules; seeking lever-set (Marchant, Brunsviga, Odhner, etc.), Arithometers, small adders (Calcumeter, Webb, Stephenson, etc.), Curta calculators, and others.

Erez Kaplan
Calculating Machines Website
20A Harkafot St.
Kefar Shemaryahu, 46910
Israel
ph: 972-9-584552
e-mail: calcmach@shani.net
web: http://www.webcom.com/calc/main.html
Interested in collecting mechanical calculating machines (non-electrical) dating from 1642 through 1965.

Dealers

Calculator World, Inc.
1086 S. Delaware Dr.
Mount Bethel, PA 18343
ph: 610-588-2600
fax: 610-588-1727
Buy, sell, trade, and repairs all Hewlett Packard calculators and palmtops.

Joe Pfeiffer
Zapper Technologies
P.O. Box 253
Sandy, UT 84091-0253
ph: 801-571-5453
e-mail: joep@antiquesecrets.com
web: http://www.antiquesecrets.com/
Buy, sell, trade early portable and pocket L.E.D. calculators: Summit, NCE, PRA, Hewlett Packard and other "lighted" display electronic calculators.

Experts

Darryl Rehr
P.O. Box 641824
Los Angeles, CA 90064
ph: 310-477-5229
fax: 310-268-8420
e-mail: dcrehr@earthlink.net
web: http://home.earthlink.net/~dcrehr/
Wants early calculators (they subtract, multiply, divide and add) such as the "Comptometer", "Curta", and "Millionaire."

Guy Ball
P.O. Box 345
Tustin, CA 92781-0345
ph: 714-730-6140 or 949-380-5748
fax: 714-730-6140
e-mail: mrcalc@usa.net
web: http://www.oldcalcs.com
Recognized authority on early, electronic, pocket calculators; co-author of "Collector's Guide to Pocket Calculators" (1997); producer of "Collecting Calculators" video; send SASE with requests for rarity and/or pricing information.

Internet Resources

Guy Ball
Collecting Calculators Website
P.O. Box 345
Tustin, CA 92781-0345
ph: 714-730-6140 or 949-380-5748
fax: 714-730-6140
e-mail: mrcalc@usa.net
web: http://www.oldcalcs.com
This site contains historical and collectible information for calculator collectors; focus is on early electronic calculators of the 1960s and 1970s, but also covers the older and larger electro-mechanical "monsters".

Erez Kaplan
20A Harkafot St.
Kefar Shemaryahu, 46910
Israel
ph: 972-9-584552
e-mail: calcmach@shani.net
web: http://www.webcom.com/calc/main.html
Pictorial views of calculators, old ads, related links, magazines, organizations, other sites of interest; covers all aspects of mechanical calculating machines.

Hewlett-Packard

Museums/Libraries

Dave Hicks
Museum of HP Calculators
e-mail: dgh@hpmuseum.org
web: http://www.hpmuseum.org
Displays and describes Hewlett-Packard calculators introduced from 1968 to 1986 plus a few interesting later models; also sections on calculating machines and slide rules; plus sections for buying and selling HP calculators.

Novelty

Collectors

Janice Goings-Flamm
P.O. Box 70513
Riverside, CA 92513-0513
fax: 909-353-5625
e-mail: bflamm@ix.netcom.com
Wants to buy novelty calculators, i.e. those with odd shapes.

CALENDAR PLATES

Collectors

Carole Melfi
Carole Melfi's Calendar Plates
407 Holly Drive
Levittown, PA 19055
e-mail: cmelfi@jersey.net
web: http://www.jersey.net/~wmelfi/cmelfi/
Has a web site devoted to her calendar plate collection; site features the history of calendar plates, images, and links to related sites.

Jane M. Cummings
37943 Wright St.
Willoughby, OH 44094-5851
ph: 440-946-2174
Wants any '20s, '30s & '40s or earlier calendar plates, especially the unusual or pre-1906.

Dealers

Alan Gumtow
Odd Things
710 N. Lake Shore Drive
Tower Lakes, IL 60010-1277
ph: 847-526-5319
e-mail: agumtow@aol.com
Buys and sells 1880-1933 calendar plates with or without store, town or person on it, old giveaways.

Periodicals

Alan Gumtow
Newsletter: Calendar, The
710 N. Lake Shore Drive
Tower Lakes, IL 60010-1277
ph: 847-526-5319
e-mail: agumtow@aol.com
A quarterly newsletter for collectors and dealers of old calendar plates from 1880-1949.

CALENDARS

(see also ADVERTISING COLLECTIBLES; ILLUSTRATORS; PAPER COLLECTIBLES)

Clubs/Associations

Larry L. Krug
Calendar Collector Society
18222 Flower Hill Way, #299
Gaithersburg, MD 20879-5300
ph: 301-926-8663
fax: 301-926-7648
e-mail: ccs-info@collectors.org
web: http://www.collectors.org/ccs/

Collectors

Larry L. Krug
Americana Resources, Inc.
18222 Flower Hill Way, #299
Gaithersburg, MD 20879-5300
ph: 301-926-8663
fax: 301-926-7648
e-mail: info@amres.com
web: http://www.amres.com

Dealers

Robb Sequin
P.O. Box 1126
Dennis Port, MA 02639
ph: 508-760-2599
e-mail: rsequin@capecod.net
Strong buyer of calendars dating from 1900 to 1970 relating to advertising, pin-ups, celebrities, commercial artists; condition and interesting subject matter are important; quantities wanted too.

Mary Ann Hahn
Second Hand Mary Ann's
103 Ocean Point Road
Boothbay Harbor, ME 04538
ph: 207-633-2426
fax: 207-633-2586
e-mail: maryann@gwi.net
Wants to buy calendars of all kinds and categories: pin-up, scenics, hunting & fishing, children's illustrators, advertising, auto, Coca-Cola.

Firearms Related

Collectors

Bill Bramlett
P.O. Box 1105
Florence, SC 29503-1105
ph: 803-393-7390 or 843-665-3165
e-mail: bbramlett@webtv.net
Wants to buy 1897-1927 calendars, posters and signs advertising shotgun shells and cartridges from companies such as Peters, Austin Cartridge Co., Remington-UMC, Selby shells, Union Metallic Cartridge Co., Western, Winchester.

CALIFORNIA PERFUME COMPANY

(see also AVON COLLECTIBLES; BOTTLES, Perfume & Scent)

Collectors

Patrick Brady
210 Fulton St.
Elmira, NY 14904-1215
ph: 607-732-2894
Wants CPC paper, tins, bottles, anything.

Experts

Dick Pardini
3107 N. El Dorado St., Dept. MACRD
Stockton, CA 95204-3412
ph: 209-466-5550
Wants certain boxed CPC items (1886 to 1929); no AVON please; will help with CPC prices and identification; enclose LSASE for information; LSASE NOT necessary when offering items for sale.

CALLING CARDS

(see BUSINESS CARDS)

CALLIOPES

(see CAROUSELS & CAROUSEL FIGURES; MUSICAL INSTRUMENTS, Mechanical [Band Organs])

CALLS

(see SPORTING COLLECTIBLES, Game Calls)

CAMERAS & CAMERA EQUIPMENT

(see also BOOKS, Reference [Cameras]; 3-D PHOTOGRAPHICA; MAGIC LANTERNS; PHOTOGRAPHS; PHOTOGRAPHY; SPY EQUIPMENT; STEREO VIEWERS & STEREOVIEWS; TOYS, Optical)

Appraisers

David L. Studebaker
300 Pease Road
Cle Elum, WA 98922
ph: 509-647-1916
e-mail: pspcs@geocities.com
web: http://www.geocities.com/Eureka/Park/3740/
Specializes in classic old cameras, colored cameras, subminiatures, stanhopes, old images, and photographs and daguerreotypes.

Auction Services

Bryan W. Ginns
2109 Cty. Rte. 21
Valatie, NY 12184-6001
ph: 518-392-5805
fax: 518-392-7925
e-mail: the3dman@aol.com
Conducts mail sales specializing in optical items such as cameras, magic lantern slide projectors, stereographica, polyorama pantoptiques, praxinoscopes, zeotropes, kinoras, coin-operated mutoscopes, etc.

Michael Pritchard
Christie's South Kensington, Ltd.
85 Old Brompton Rd.
London, SW7 3LD
U.K.
ph: 0171 581 7611 or 0171 321 3279
fax: 0171 321 3321
e-mail: mpritchard@christies.com
web: http://www.cskart.com/
An international auction house specializing in the sale of rare and collectible cameras, photographic equipment and optical toys.

Clubs/Associations

Gerald Fine
American Photographic Historical Society, Inc.
Magazine: Photographica
1150 Avenue of the Americas
New York, NY 10036
ph: 212-575-0483 or 732-617-3142
fax: 732-617-1360
e-mail: gfine@monmouth.com
web: http://www.superexpo.com/aphs/
International organization with educational meetings six times each year in NYC; conducts two fairs for the selling of antique cameras, equipment & photos; publishes "Photographica" quarterly and a monthly newsletter, "In Focus".

Paul K. Kirchner
Camera & Memorabilia Enthusiasts Regional Association (C.A.M.E.R.A.)
103 Greenwich Dr.
Albany, NY 12203

Pennsylvania Photographic Historical Society, Inc.
P.O. Box 862
Beaver Falls, PA 15010-0862
ph: 724-843-5688

John Durand
Ohio Camera Collectors Society, The
Newsletter: Developments, The Members Memo
P.O. Box 282
Columbus, OH 43216-0282
ph: 614-885-3224
Focuses on cameras, camera equipment, images and photographic history; holds annual show, sale, auction, guest speakers on Memorial Day weekend; various members have considerable camera expertise about cameras and makers; annual auction.

William S. Nehez, Mem. Ch.
Photographic Historical Society of the Western Reserve
Newsletter: Collector, The
P.O. Box 25663
Cleveland, OH 44125
ph: 216-662-9008
To further advance the collection and preservation of historical photographic material; for those with an interest in photography and photographic equipment; bi-monthly newsletter; holds annual Photographic Flea Market.

Bill Bond, Pres.
Tri-State Photographic Collectors Society
8910 Cherry St.
Blue Ash, OH 45242
ph: 513-891-5266
Collectors of cameras and various photographic equipment, prints, books and anything related to photography.

Michigan Photographic Historical Society
Newsletter: Photogram, The
P.O. Box 2278
Birmingham, MI 48012-2278
ph: 313-882-1113 or 245-549-6026
e-mail: pmotz@worldnet.att.net

Marv B. Chait, Pres.
Chicago Photographic Collectors Society
Newsletter: CPCS Bulletin
P.O. Box 303
Grayslake, IL 60030
ph: 773-262-5979 or 847-223-4348
e-mail: info@chicagophotographic.org
web: http://www.chicagophotographic.org/
A non-profit organization since 1971; over 200 U.S. and foreign members; sponsors two trade shows a year in the Chicago area; "CPCS Bulletin" is published monthly; also publishes the journal "By Daylight" periodically.

Photographic Collectors of Houston
1201 McDuffie #104
Houston, TX 77019
e-mail: jdunn@pop3.wt.net
web: http://web.wt.net/~jdunn/

American Society of Camera Collectors
7952 Genesta Ave.
Van Nuys, CA 91406-1624
ph: 818-776-9991
fax: 818-776-9993
e-mail: cameraderi@aol.com
An educational society dedicated to the restoration and preservation of all types of photographica.

David Silver
Bay Area Photographica Association
Newsletter: BAPA News
2538 34th Ave.
San Francisco, CA 94116-2801
ph: 415-664-6498 or 415-681-4356
e-mail: silver@well.com
A collectors' group specializing in cameras, photographs and related materials; members buy, sell and trade collectibles as well as share information on the field of photo-history.

Shirley Sparrow
Puget Sound Photographic Collectors Society
Newsletter: Bellows
300 Pease Road
Cle Elum, WA 98922
ph: 509-647-1916
e-mail: pspcs@geocities.com
web: http://www.geocities.com/Eureka/Park/3740/
Dedicated to the collection and preservation of historical photographica; holds monthly meetings, sponsors annual camera show, publishes monthly newsletter.

Rolf Eipper, Pres.
Western Canada Photographic Historical Association
P.O. Box 78082
2606 Commercial Drive
Vancouver, British Columbia V5N 5W1
Canada
ph: 604-254-6778
fax: 604-254-6778

Michael Pritchard, Editor
Photographic Collectors Club of Great Britain
Magazine: Photographica World
1B Church Street Industrial Estate
Haydon Bridge
Hexham, Northumberland NE47 6JG
U.K.
ph: (0044) (0)1434 688129
e-mail: pccgb@lightwave.demon.co.uk
web: http://www.lightwave.demon.co.uk/pccgb/pccgb.htm
Club aims to promote the study and collection of photographic equipment and images by publications, meetings, auctions and shows; covers cameras, lenses, photographers, optical toys, stereoscopes, magic lanterns, and related areas.

Collectors

J. Hemenway
ph: 781-729-8956
fax: 781-729-2959
e-mail: Cameras@SouthPawCorp.com
web: http://www1.shore.net/~hemenway/selcam/welcome.htm
Buys cameras for own collection and sells surplus items.

Dan Colucci
82 Brick Kiln Rd.
Chelmsford, MA 01824
ph: 617-790-4915
e-mail: DColucci@aol.com
web: http://members.aol.com/dcolucci/index.html

Norman D. Leckert
P.O. Box 363
Bethel, VT 05032-0363
ph: 802-234-5657 or 800-717-2021
fax: 802-234-6104
Wants to buy old cameras, lenses and accessories; any age, type or condition.

Harry Poster
P.O. Box 1883
South Hackensack, NJ 07606-0483
ph: 201-794-9606
fax: 201-794-9553
e-mail: hposter@att.net
web: http://www.harryposter.com
Wants early wooden cameras and lenses; stereo 3D cameras, viewers, projectors; Pathe and 16mm movie cameras and projectors; Polaroid models 180, 185, 190, 195 only; old film, accessories, flash units; press cameras; buys camera shops.

Fred Spira
158-17 Riverside Dr.
Flushing, NY 11357-1341
ph: 718-767-6761 or 718-767-5297
Private collector buys early (Daguerreian, wet-plate), color, detective and other rare and unusual cameras and camera accessories; single items or entire collections; also pre-1900 photographic images and photo albums.

George Elmore
408 - 8B West University Ave.
Gainesville, FL 32601
ph: 352-377-3602
fax: 352-377-3601
e-mail: kj4ig@aol.com
Wants to buy large format cameras.

Bob Coyle
1006 Lincoln
Dubuque, IA 52001-3457
ph: 319-588-9464
fax: 319-583-9083
Private collector (not a dealer) wants to buy collectible cameras, lenses and accessories; please send price and description; does not do appraisals.

Dave Gorski
244 Cutler St.
Waukesha, WI 53186-4943
ph: 414-542-3069
fax: 414-542-9730
e-mail: camera19@idt.net
web: http://www.davegorski.com/
Wants to buy stereo cameras, wood cameras with two or more lenses, folding or box cameras, any multi-lens camera, 1920s movie cameras or projectors; also cameras by Canon, Nikon, Leica, Zeiss, Voightlander, Alpa, Ernemann.

Marv B. Chait
P.O. Box 1979
Evanston, IL 60204-1979
ph: 312-262-5979
e-mail: Marv5555@aol.com

Richard Ogden
P.O. Box 210
Chapman, NE 68827
ph: 308-986-2247
fax: 308-986-2247
e-mail: exoticam@kdsi.net
Wants exotic cameras: such as cameras that look like machine guns, aerials, military, medical, concealed, special purpose, swinging lens, Cirkuts, subminiature cameras, beverage can shaped cameras and others that are odd or unusual.

Charles R. Scribner
555 Sherwood Lane
Muskogee, OK 74403-8300
ph: 918-687-9639
e-mail: scrib@ok.azalea.net
web: http://www.azalea.net/~scrib/
Private collector who enjoys sharing information about cameras.

Jim Kopke
P.O. Box 4310
Dillon, CO 80435-4310
Wants to buy old, odd and unique cameras and related equipment.

Mike Kramer
P.O. Box 3257
Vallejo, CA 94590-0676
ph: 800-568-8883 or 800-446-6581
fax: 707-642-2456
Collector wants to buy pre-1960 range-finder cameras such as Nikon, Canon, Leica, Zeiss plus all stereo, subminiature and colored cameras.

Henk van Roy
235 Kelvin Grove Rd.
Kelvin Grove
Brisbane, Queensland 4059
Australia
ph: +61 7 3856 4757
fax: +61 7 3856 4790
e-mail: freemana@powerup.com.au
web: http://www.freeman.powerup.com.au
Collector and appraiser of cameras of yesteryear; buys, sell, swap.

Dealers

Gary Dicker
Photon Enterprises
173 Park Street
Putnam, CT 06260
ph: 860-963-7611
e-mail: garyd@neca.com
web: http://users.neca.com/kaycee/
Buys, sells trades cameras and related equipment - one item of a whole collection; provides accurate and honest evaluations of your vintage or modern camera equipment; years of experience.

John S. Craig
Craig Camera
P.O. Box 1637
Torrington, CT 06790
ph: 860-496-9791
fax: 860-496-0664
e-mail: john@craigcamera.com
web: http://www.craigcamera.com/
Buys and sells antique and collectible photographica: cameras, daguerreotypes, stereos, literature.

Allen & Hilary Weiner
80 Central Park West
New York, NY 10023-5204
ph: 212-787-8357
fax: 212-496-6502
e-mail: amwcameras@msn.com
Well-established and respected dealers who are always interested in buying entire collections or fine individual items.

Konny Lang, Pres.
Atlantic Camera Repair
276 Higbie Lane
West Islip, NY 11795-2822
ph: 516-587-7959
fax: 516-587-7750
Buys and sells cameras and photographic equipment.

Bryan W. Ginns
2109 Cty. Rte. 21
Valatie, NY 12184-6001
ph: 518-392-5805
fax: 518-392-7925
e-mail: the3dman@aol.com
Wants large collections of stereo views, old cameras, daguerreotypes, magic lanterns, optical toys; anything relating to photographics.

Jim O'Neil
Fredonia Camera
60 West Main St.
Fredonia, NY 14063
ph: 716-679-4582 or 800-786-6861
Buying Leica, Nikon, Minox, Super Ikonta, Unhof, Stereo Realist, Rolleiflex, Contarex, Hasselblad, Retina, Voigtlander, Plaubel, and many others.

Herb Halsman
Camera Man, The
1614 Bethlehem Pike
Flourtown, PA 19031-2026
ph: 215-233-4025 or 800-396-0506
fax: 215-233-4025
Wants to buy Leica, Zeiss, Nikon, Minox, wood cameras, toy cameras, miniatures, stereo, German cameras: Hasselblad, Rolleiflex, Alpa, etc.

Bruce Walker
Camera Web
2347 E Lincoln Highway
Coatesville, PA 19320
ph: 610-383-7094
fax: 610-383-7240
e-mail: webmaster@cameraweb.com
web: http://www.cameraweb.com/
A great place to buy, sell, trade cameras and camera equipment; free online ads; free photographic tips.

Bill Green
Classic & Used Cameras
3735 Franklin Rd., #191
Roanoke, VA 24014
ph: 540-985-0682
fax: 540-343-1149
e-mail: cameras@ibm.net
web: http://www.classic-cameras.com
Buys, sells, trades, repairs classic and used cameras.

John Starace
Camera Exchange International, The
P.O. Box 982
Swansboro, NC 28584
ph: 910-326-1563
fax: 910-326-1563
e-mail: johntcei@coastalnet.com
web: http://www.cardmall.com/camera-exchange/
Selling pre-owned cameras.

Robert L. Johnson
North Georgia Graphics
P.O. Box 309
Chickamauga, GA 30707-0309
ph: 706-375-4326
e-mail: oldgoat@voy.net
Specializing in large-format (view and studio) cameras, panoramic and banquet cameras and enlargers, lenses, accessories, books on photography history, collectible cameras.

Eric Mehl
Columbus Camera Group, Inc.
55 East Blake Ave.
Columbus, OH 43202-2905
ph: 614-267-0686
fax: 614-267-5526
e-mail: colscamr@infinet.com
web: http://www.columbuscamera.com/
Buys and sells all photographic equipment new and old; Nikon, Stereo, Rollei, Linhof, Canon, Leica, Pentax, Zeiss; appraises estates; also buy current equipment as well as photos and darkrooms.

T.K. Treadwell
4201 Nagle Rd.
Bryan, TX 77801-3938
ph: 409-846-0209
e-mail: 71222.1571@compuserve.com

Brian P. Wolfe
BPW Limited Photographic
4351 S. Sepulveda Blvd.
Culver City, CA 90230-4715
ph: 310-397-5576
fax: 310-391-6478
e-mail: caameras@bpwltd.com
web: http://www.bpwltd.com
Used and collectible cameras, lenses and accessories; buy, sell, trade, repair and restore all types of photographic equipment; also rents photo equipment to film makers: Hasselblad, Rolleiflex, Nikon, Japanese, German, Russian, etc.

William P. Carroll
ACR Books
P.O. Box 4294
Whittier, CA 90607-4294
ph: 562-693-8421
fax: 562-945-6011
Antique and classic cameras for sale; offers new and used books on kaleidoscopes, cameras and the history of photography.

Alex Beringer
Online Camera Exchange
P.O. Box 1711
Imperial Beach, CA 91933
ph: 760-739-7601
fax: 760-739-7601
e-mail: aderr@tfb.com
web: http://www.tfb.com/oce/oce.htm
Buys and sells fine used and collectible cameras; specialty is wooden cameras, spy cameras, 1950s-1960s rangefinder cameras, military cameras and other unusual equipment.

Dale Lampson
Pacific Rim Camera
P.O. Box 4475
Salem, OR 97302
ph: 503-370-7461 or 503-585-3230
fax: 503-370-8301
e-mail: pacrim@teleport.com
web: http://www.pacificrimcamera.com
Collector, appraiser, expert, dealer in collectible cameras since 1986; handles a wide variety of photographica; specializes in cameras from the 1930s through the 1960s; over 10,000 items in stock.

Experts

Fred Waterman
1704 Valencia Dr.
Rockford, IL 61108
Buys and specializes in novel cameras with unusual devices or appearances; also in camera accessories such as meters, exposure guides, darkroom equipment, etc.

William P. Carroll
ACR Books
P.O. Box 4294
Whittier, CA 90607-4294
ph: 562-693-8421
fax: 562-945-6011
Buys, specializes in early shutters, small format roll-film cameras, mechanically complex cameras (built-in motor drives or other unusual features); also wants camera look-alikes (flasks, compacts, etc.)

Mike & Gladys Kessler
25749 Anchor Circle
San Juan Capistrano, CA 92675-4002
ph: 949-661-3320
Buys and specializes in unusual 1880-1890s disguised or detective cameras; also Simon Wing cameras.

Internet Resources

Dan Colucci
Internet Directory of Camera Collectors
82 Brick Kiln Rd.
Chelmsford, MA 01824
ph: 617-790-4915
e-mail: DColucci@aol.com
web: http://members.aol.com/dcolucci/index.html
An Internet directory of camera collectors; this is a free on-line subscription e-mail list of serious camera collectors; 110 members from around the world; lots of good camera links.

Museums/Libraries

Jack Naylor
Naylor Museum of Photographic History
P.O. Box 23
Waltham Station
Waltham, MA 02254-0023
ph: 617-731-6603
fax: 617-277-7878
e-mail: jacknaylor@aol.com
A private museum with photographic exhibitions for collectors and historians; pre-photography, the first photograph, wet and dry plate, roll film, research library.

Fleetwood Museum of Art & Photographica
614 Greenbrook Rd.
North Plainfield, NJ 07063
ph: 908-757-5507
Exhibits a collection of vintage cameras and images; maintains a photo-techniques and photo-history library.

Periodicals

Magazine: Shutterbug
5211 S. Washington Ave.
Titusville, FL 32780
ph: 407-269-3212
fax: 407-269-2025
web: http://www.shutterbug.net/
Geared to the advanced to professional photographer; articles about new/old equip. & access., collectibles and new products; many ads.

Neil Smith
Magazine: Photographic Trader
P.O. Box 95
Carina, QLD 4152
Australia
ph: 0167 3843 2319 or 0167 398 3801
fax: 0167 3842 0135
e-mail: neil@phototrader.com.au
Australia's marketplace for photographic equipment and collectors news.

Fred & Stephanie Marriott
Magazine: Classic Camera Magazine
28 The Colonnade
Piece Hall
Halifax, HX1 1RE
U.K.
e-mail: photo@marriott.u-net.com
web: http://www.marriott.u-net/ccm.htm
Quarterly magazine devoted to classic still and cine equipment.

Repair Services

Konny Lang, Pres.
Atlantic Camera Repair
276 Higbie Lane
West Islip, NY 11795-2822
ph: 516-587-7959
fax: 516-587-7750
Repairs cameras, studio equipment, 35mm SLRs, video and movie cameras, VCRs, meters, graphic art lenses, projectors, electronic strobes, surveillance equipment, underwater cameras; also modifies or restores cameras including antique.

Cliff Ratcliff
Cameratek
1780 N. Market St.
Frederick, MD 21701
ph: 301-695-9733
Professional repair service; also buy, sell, trade, used cameras.

Ed Romney
Romney Publishing
P.O. Box 487
Drayton, SC 29333
ph: 864-597-1882
e-mail: Romney@edromney.com
web: http://www.edromney.com
Fix your own cameras! Romney offers camera repair manuals, courses, tools and restoration supplies for most cameras, old or new: Leica Graflex, Rolleiflex, Nikon, Canon and many more; also books on repairing old radios.

Ken Ruth
Photography on Bald Mountain
113 Bald Mountain
Davenport, CA 95017-0113
ph: 831-423-4465
Repairs only older and classic mechanical cameras; parts fabrication, modifications, adaptations.

Suppliers

Ed Romney
Romney Publishing
P.O. Box 487
Drayton, SC 29333
ph: 864-597-1882
e-mail: Romney@edromney.com
web: http://www.edromney.com
Fix your own cameras! Romney offers camera repair manuals, courses, tools and restoration supplies for most cameras, old or new: Leica Graflex, Rolleiflex, Nikon, Canon and many more; also books on repairing old radios.

Exakta

Clubs/Associations

Maruizio Frizziero
Exakta Circle
via De Gaspari 1
Genova, 16146
Italy
ph: +3910365999 or +3910365996
fax: +3919364316
e-mail: mfrizzi@tin.it
web: http://www.exakta.org/
The Exakta camera was the first 35mm SLR in the world; the website offers lots of information about this camera.

Film

Suppliers

Dick Haviland
Film for Classics
P.O. Box 486
Jamaica, NY 11472-0486
ph: 716-624-4945
e-mail: joankay@frontiernet.net
web: http://www.simplyrochester.com/directory/photography/equipment.html
Provides film for collectors/users of classic and antique cameras all over the world.

Kodak

Clubs/Associations

Dr. George Layne
International Kodak Historical Society
P.O. Box 21
Paoli, PA 19301-0021
e-mail: glayne@msn.com

Dr. David L. Jentz
Historical Society for Retina Cameras
51312 Mayflower Road
South Bend, IN 46628
ph: 219-272-0599
fax: 219-232-2162
e-mail: retinacam@msn.com
web: http://www.netins.net/showcase/crye/retina.htm
The Kodak Retina was first introduced in 1934; it featured the new development of a daylight loading 35 mm format film cartridge that made quality cameras and pictures available to the ordinary person.

Collectors

Greg Milneck
9146 Jefferson Hwy.
Baton Rouge, LA 70809
ph: 504-928-4814
e-mail: camcollect@aol.com
web: http://www.digitalfxinc.com/kodak/
Wants to buy Kodak cameras in mint condition; from 1928-1933 Kodak made several colored and deco-style cameras designed for women: Beau Brownie, Bantam, Special, Coquette, Ensemble, Vanity Ensemble, Petites, and Vanity.

Walker Mangum
Kodak Collector's Page
15910 Laurelfield Dr.
Houston, TX 77059-6432
e-mail: mangum@ghg.net
web: http://www.ghg.net/mangum/Kodak/
Private collector with comprehensive online collection of Eastman Kodak cameras and collectibles with information about each.

Joe Fix
10315 Timberloch
Houston, TX 77070
e-mail: jdfix@thompson-grp.com
web: http://www.thompson-grp.com/fix/images/instamatic.htm
Specializes in Kodak Instamatic cameras.

Chris Eve
Flat 2 The Elms
Rue Des Cosnets
St. Ouen, Jersey JE3 2BJ
U.K.
e-mail: kypfer@itl.net
web: http://user.itl.net/~kypfer/intro.htm
Website contains a private collection in virtual museum format of about 300 Kodak cameras, including Box cameras, Brownie cameras, Instamatic cameras, Instant Picture cameras, Retina and Retinette cameras.

Kodak Brownie

Collectors

Donald Bridge
194 Kempton Drive
Berea, OH 44017
A collector who pays book value of $20 minimum; pays in advance with a money order for Brownies in very good or better condition; see want list with prices on web site.

Dealers

Jeff Jost
West Valley Webs
23705 Vanowen Street, Ste. 288
West Hills, CA 91307
ph: 818-888-5050
fax: 818-888-9923
e-mail: brownielover@westval.com
web: http://westval.com/brownie/
Avid collector/dealer buys, sells, and trades Eastman Kodak Brownie cameras; when dead wants his ashes placed inside an original Brownie Box camera and buried somewhere between Henry Ford's, Thomas Edison's & George Eastman's graves.

Internet Resources

Brownie Page, The
e-mail: Chuck9toe@aol.com
web: http://users.aol.com/Chuck02178/brownie.htm

Jeff Jost
Brownie Camera Discussion Group
23705 Vanowen Street, Ste. 288
West Hills, CA 91307
ph: 818-888-5050
fax: 818-888-9923
e-mail: brownielover@westval.com
web: http://westval.com/brownie/
Discussion group and mailing list of hundreds of Kodak Brownie camera collectors; join now for free and have access to these experts for your Brownie camera questions.

Leica

Clubs/Associations

Tom Snyder
Leica Historical Society of America
Journal: Viewfinder, The
7611 Dornoch Lane
Dallas, TX 75248-2327
ph: 972-386-4005
e-mail: tom_snyder@ed.gov
web: http://www.lhsa.org/
An international group of photographers, collectors, enthusiasts and historians dedicated to the use of the Leica system and the preservation of its heritage.

Military

Collectors

Richard J. Kimmel
P.O. Box 19
Bayville, NJ 08721-1412
ph: 732-269-8581
e-mail: cmbtcamera@aol.com
Wants WWII combat cameras: military versions with subdued olive drab and black finish only.

Movie

(see also MOVIE PROJECTORS)

Clubs/Associations

Robert Sieberg, Pres.
Movie Machine Society, The
Newsletter: Sixteen Frames
903 Maryland Dr.
Austin, TX 78758
ph: 512-836-2244
fax: 512-836-2146
e-mail: movmacso@satx.net
web: http://www.moviemachinesociety.org/
Devoted to the exchange of information among those interested in the technical history of all kinds of apparatus designed to create a moving image, from Arriflexes to Zoopraxiscopes.

Collectors

David Hale
17 West Broad St.
Hazleton, PA 18201
ph: 570-459-7049
Wants hand crank movie cameras and hand crank movie projectors from the 1940s through 1960s; any condition.

Gregory J. Vonderheide
29032 Rivergate Run
Zephyrhills, FL 33543-6544
ph: 813-907-9291
fax: 813-949-9252
e-mail: gvondo1@aol.com
Wants to buy wind-up movie cameras; all mm, prefer pre-1940; must be working.

Michael Zaiontz
1946 Gentilly Blvd.
New Orleans, LA 70119
ph: 504-566-6090
Wants to buy 3-strip film, lens, projection equipment, manuals, theatre blueprints, etc.

Alan Heim
8007 West 4th St.
Los Angeles, CA 90048
ph: 213-935-0865
fax: 213-931-9549
e-mail: klippar@primenet.com
Collector and sometimes trader of all forms of early film equipment with a focus on editing equipment.

Wes Lambert
1568 Dapple Ave.
Camarillo, CA 93010
ph: 805-482-5331
Early cine collector wants to buy pre-1923, hand-crank, 35, 28 & 17 1/2 mm, motion picture cameras; will correspond with other cine collectors.

Michael Rogge
The Netherlands
e-mail: wichm@xs4all.nl
web: http://www.xs4all.nl/~wichm/cinemat.html
Wants to buy vintage movie equipment; website contains information on collecting vintage movie equipment; an article is provided on "100 Years of Film Sizes"; buy and sell ads; links and other information is provided.

Dealers

International Cinema Equipment Company, Inc.
100 NE 39th St.
Miami, FL 33137
ph: 305-573-7339
fax: 305-573-8101
Sells pre-owned, rebuilt, refurbished,

and secondhand professional cinema equipment.

Randy Donley
Donley's Wild West Town & Museum
8512 S. Union Rd.
Union, IL 60180-9661
ph: 815-923-9000
fax: 815-923-2253
web: http://www.wildwesttown.com/
Wants pre-1930 34mm hand-crank movie projectors and cameras.

Experts

Alan Kattelle
50 Old Country Rd.
Hudson, MA 01749-3026
ph: 978-562-9184
e-mail: alankatt@aol.com
Wants unusual amateur movie cameras & projectors: Devry 16 Deluxe, Pathe KOK Projector, "Wedding Brownie" movie camera, Duplex 11mm camera and projector, and Victor Cine cameras & projectors.

Periodicals

Antique Trader Publications, Inc.
Newspaper: Big Reel
P.O. Box 1050
Dubuque, IA 52004-1050
ph: 800-334-7165 or 800-482-4155
fax: 800-531-0880
e-mail: atpzines@aol.com
web: http://www.collect.com/bigreel
A monthly tabloid for movie and television memorabilia collectors and fans: ads, news, current & nostalgic feature articles, obits, etc.

Nikon

Clubs/Associations

Robert J. Rotoloni
Nikon Historical Society
Magazine: Nikon Journal, The
P.O. Box 3213
Hammond, IN 46321-0213
e-mail: rotoloni@msn.com
web: http://www.nikonhs.org/
Focuses on the history of Nikon cameras; magazine contains articles and ads for the Nikon collector.

Collectors

Harry Poster
P.O. Box 1883
South Hackensack, NJ 07606-0483
ph: 201-794-9606
fax: 201-794-9553
e-mail: hposter@att.net
web: http://www.harryposter.com
Wants early Nikons and Nikon accessories.

Experts

Robert J. Rotoloni
P.O. Box 3213
Hammond, IN 46321-0213
e-mail: rotoloni@msn.com
web: http://www.nikonhs.org/
Author of "The Nikon..An Illustrated History of the Nikon Camera", founder of the Nikon Historical Society.

Stereo Cameras

(see also STEREOVIEWERS & STEREOGRAPHS)

Clubs/Associations

Betty Graham
Vintage Camera Club
2562 Victoria St.
Wichita, KS 67216
ph: 316-265-0393
For collectors of vintage stereo cameras and stereo images.

Dealers

Harry Poster
P.O. Box 1883
South Hackensack, NJ 07606-0483
ph: 201-794-9606
fax: 201-794-9553
e-mail: hposter@att.net
web: http://www.harryposter.com
Since 1979; wants 3D stereo cameras and accessories including Macro Realist and Donaldson, Belplasca, Verascope f40, Realist, Wollensak, TDC, Realist, Kodak, Delta, Sputnik, plus other stereoscope cameras, viewers, projectors, etc.

Subminiature

(see also SPY EQUIPMENT)

Collectors

Don Carter
P.O. Box 142164
Gainesville, FL 32614-2164
ph: 352-376-6668
fax: 352-376-6668
Wants to buy spy cameras and equipment.

Dave Gorski
244 Cutler St.
Waukesha, WI 53186-4943
ph: 414-542-3069
fax: 414-542-9730
e-mail: camera19@idt.net
web: http://www.davegorski.com/
Wants to buy cameras disguised in hats, binoculars, canes, guns, lighters, purses, pens or watches; or just very tiny cameras.

Internet Resources

Joe McGloin
Sub Club, The
3271 S. Clay St.
Sheridan, CO 80110
e-mail: xkaes@aol.com
web: http://members.aol.com/xkaes/index.htm
A web site that covers all aspects of subminiature photography; various resources such as descriptions of all subminiature cameras (half-frame and smaller), lists of books and articles, how to use, processing film, photo gallery, etc.

Zeiss

Clubs/Associations

Zeiss Historica Society
Journal: Zeiss Historica Society Journal
300 Waxwing Drive
Cranbury, NJ 08512
ph: 540-981-1036
e-mail: msmall@roanoke.infi.net
web: http://www.netins.net/showcase/crye/zi-hist.htm
Dedicated to the study & exchange of information on the history of Carl Zeiss Optical Co. and Zeiss-Ikon, its people and products (cameras, accessories, and optical equipment of all types) from 1846 to present; semi-annual journal.

CAMPBELL SOUP COLLECTIBLES

Clubs/Associations

David R. Young
Campbell Soup Collectors Club
Newsletter: Soup Collector, The
414 Country Lane Ct.
Wauconda, IL 60084
ph: 847-487-4917
e-mail: soupclub@yahoo.com
web: http://www.soupcollector.com/
Networking; quarterly newsletter features articles and classified ads; write for more information.

Experts

Mary Jane Lamphier
Quilted Keepsakes & Unique Dolls Exhibit
577 Main St.
Arlington, IA 50606-9712
ph: 319-633-5885
Specializes in Campbell's Soup Kids; please include a SASE if requesting a reply or the return of photos.

Man./Prod./Dist.

Campbell Shop
e-mail: campbells@harrisondirect.com
web: http://www.campbellshop.com/
For collectors of contemporary Campbell Soup memorabilia: dolls vehicles, kitchen, porcelains, etc.; a Campbell Company sponsored web site.

CAMPING EQUIPMENT

(see also BOY SCOUT MEMORABILIA; SPORTING COLLECTIBLES; TRAILERS & RV'S)

Coleman

Clubs/Associations

Ron Bowers
Coleman Collector's Network, The
Newsletter: Coleman Collector, The
2282 W. Caley Ave.
Littleton, CO 80120
ph: 303-794-2415
e-mail: ron@colemancollectors.com
web: http://www.colemancollectors.com/
For collectors of any Coleman products such as lamps, lanterns, irons, camp stoves and other pressurized liquid fuel appliances; also literature, old repair manuals, sales samples.

Collectors

Levi Esh
Rt. 2, Kesslet Rd.
Millersburg, PA 17061

Bud Michael
P.O. Box 1236
Lincolnton, NC 28093-1236
ph: 704-735-8643
e-mail: bud@vnet.net

Jim Adkins
808 Turner Rd.
Independence, MO 64056
ph: 816-796-9205

Jay Poirier
5964 S. Lee Way
Littleton, CO 80127
ph: 303-973-4255
fax: 303-288-1790
Wants Coleman items: lamps, lanterns, stoves, parts, irons, sales catalogs, advertising, military.

Experts

Carl R. Tucker
3715 Riveria N.W.
Massillon, OH 44546
Author of "Coleman Collector's Guide."

Man./Prod./Dist.

Coleman Company, The
P.O. Box 2931
Wichita, KS 67201
ph: 316-261-3211
e-mail: consumerservice@coleman.com
web: http://www.coleman.com/
Manufacturer of quality sporting and camping equipment.

CAN OPENERS

Collectors

Stan Dickinson
307 1/2 E. Lake St., Apt. B
Petoskey, MI 49770
ph: 616-347-1022
Have about 225 different can openers; all for sale.

Joe Young
P.O. Box 587
Elgin, IL 60121-0587
ph: 847-695-0108 or 847-254-8208
fax: 847-695-1679
e-mail: sagphu@aol.com
Wants to buy unusual can openers; also interested in combination tools with can openers; all correspondence answered.

CAN-CAN

Collectors

Taylor Warren
P.O. Box 1802
Williamsburg, VA 23187-1802
Wants stills and clippings of can-can dancers; wants girls wearing skirts, especially Las Vegas can-can programs and can-can items from the movies.

CANAL COLLECTIBLES

Clubs/Associations

American Canal Society, Inc.
Newsletter: American Canals
P.O. Box 842
Shepherdstown, WV 25443
web: http://www.blacksheep.org/canals/ACS/acs.html
Focuses on the preservation, restoration, interpretation and use of the historic navigational canals of the Americas.

Collectors

Harry L. Rinker
5093 Vera Cruz Rd.
Emmaus, PA 18049-9554
ph: 610-965-1122
fax: 610-965-1124
e-mail: rinker@fast.net
web: http://www.rinker.com
Seeks artifacts, books, paper ephemera and commemorative objects associated with America's mule-drawn canal era.

Museums/Libraries

Canal Society of New York State, Inc.
7308 Jamesville Rd.
Manlius, NY 13104

Erie Canal Museum
Newsletter: Canal Packet, The
318 Erie Blvd.
Syracuse, NY 13202
ph: 315-471-0593

National Canal Museum & Hugh Moore historical Park & Museums, Inc.
30 Centre Square
Easton, PA 18042-7743
ph: 610-559-6613
e-mail: ncm@canals.org
web: http://canals.org

Cape Cod Canal

Collectors

N.H. Webber
126 Westfield St.
Dedham, MA 02026
ph: 781-326-5329
Wants to buy items related to the Cape Cod Canal: postcards, photos, souvenirs, china, pamphlets, log books, schedules, maps.

Erie Canal

Collectors

Robert Preston
8 Newman St.
Gloversville, NY 12078
ph: 518-725-8214
e-mail: rpreston@superior.net

Panama Canal

Collectors

Frederick Lingenfelser
814 Byram St.
Reading, PA 19606-1446
Collecting anything related to the construction of the Panama Canal, 1870-1914, the French or American effort: maps, letters, photographs, books, autographs, diaries, etc.

CANCELLATIONS

Postal

(see STAMP COLLECTING, Cancels)

CANDY

(see also BOXES, Candy; BUBBLE GUM & CANDY WRAPPERS; MOLDS, Candy; PEZ)

Museums/Libraries

Michelle Havrilla
Wilbur Chocolate's Candy Americana Museum
48 N. Broad St.
Lititz, PA 17543-1026
ph: 717-626-3249 or 888-294-5287
web: http://www.800padutch.com/wilbur.html
Collection of the making of candy: antique novelty candy containers, cocoa tins, chocolate molds.

CANDY BARS

(see BUBBLE GUM & CANDY WRAPPERS; CANDY)

CANDY CONTAINERS

(see also BUBBLE GUM & CANDY WRAPPERS; CANDY; PEZ)

Collectors

Douglas Dezso
864 Paterson Ave.
Maywood, NJ 07607
ph: 201-845-7707

Terry Whitmeyer
88 Woodbine Dr.
Hershey, PA 17033-2668
ph: 717-533-3716

Kit Carter Weilage
506 Briar Hill Rd.
Louisville, KY 40206
ph: 502-561-5030
Buys and sells Christmas collectibles, specializing in German-made Santa candy containers.

Dealers

Paul W. Schofield
Lion's Den Antiques
7988 Bethel Burley Rd. SE
Port Orchard, WA 98366
ph: 360-876-3364
fax: 360-876-5421
Buys, sells, appraises, and specializes in old Santas, candy containers, Halloween, Easter, Christmas, Easter, Dresden, figural lights.

Museums/Libraries

Cambridge Glass Museum, The
812 Jefferson Ave.
Cambridge, OH 43725
ph: 740-432-3045
Over 5000 pieces of Cambridge glass on display; also 100 pieces of Cambridge Art Pottery; private museum.

Jars

Collectors

Tom "The Jar Man"
421 De La Vina
Santa Barbara, CA 93101
ph: 805-966-3076
Wants pedestal candy jars, any size or condition.

CANES & WALKING STICKS

(see also PIPES)

Auction Services

Nancy & Henry Taron
Tradewinds Auctions
63 Main St.
Essex, MA 01929
ph: 978-526-4085 or 978-768-3327
fax: 978-526-4085
Conducts all-cane auctions twice a year.

Henry Taron
Tradewinds Antiques & Auctions
24 Magnolia Ave.
P.O. Box 249
Manchester, MA 01944
ph: 978-768-3327 or 978-526-4085
fax: 978-526-4085
e-mail: taron@tiac.net
web: http://www.tradewindsantiques.com/
Conducts at least two all antique cane auctions each year; operates the only exclusively canes retail shop in America at 63 Main St., Essex, MA 01929.

Joel & Michael Malter
Malter Galleries, Inc.
17005 Ventura Blvd.
Encino, CA 91316-4128
ph: 818-784-7772 or 818-784-2181
fax: 818-784-4726
e-mail: rarearts@earthlink.net
web: http://www.maltergalleries.com/
Conducts periodic auction sales of canes and walking sticks.

Collectors

Sherlock S. Holmes, D.D.
P.O. Box 3
Worcester, MA 01613-0003
ph: 508-754-9907
e-mail: mail@SherlockHolmes.com
web: http://www.SherlockHolmes.com
Wants to buy pre-1940 walking stocks (or rare canes); especially interested in walking sticks with guns, swords or other items hidden inside.

Bruce Thalberg
23 Mountain View Dr.
Weston, CT 06883-1317
ph: 203-227-8175
Wants to buy canes: carved wood, ivory and bone figural handles and knobs, container and gadget canes; handles without shafts are acceptable; photocopy helpful; please send SASE.

Barry Koffman
1 Vincent St.
Binghamton, NY 13905
ph: 607-723-5167
fax: 607-797-6959
e-mail: caneman94@aol.com
Specializes in carved folk art canes.

R.W. Carlson
7718 Georgetown Pike
Mc Lean, VA 22102
Wants to buy unusual walking sticks,

especially "gadget" canes or heavily carved or personalized sticks.

F. Monek
P.O. Box 528
Richmond, IL 60071
ph: 815-678-2000 ext. 117
Wants canes or walking sticks of the gadget, weapon, folk art, or ivory type.

Arnold Scher
Beaver Bros. Antiques
1637 Market St.
San Francisco, CA 94103-1217
ph: 415-863-4344
fax: 415-863-4399
e-mail: www.beaverprop@aol.com
Wants dual purpose, container, weapon, gadget, fancy carved ivory, gold or silver canes; also wants carved folk art canes.

Dealers

Nancy & Henry Taron
Tradewinds Antiques
63 Main St.
Essex, MA 01929
ph: 978-526-4085 or 978-768-3327
fax: 978-526-4085

Henry Taron
Tradewinds Antiques & Auctions
24 Magnolia Ave.
P.O. Box 249
Manchester, MA 01944
ph: 978-768-3327 or 978-526-4085
fax: 978-526-4085
e-mail: taron@tiac.net
web: http://www.tradewindsantiques.com/
Buys, sells, appraises and specializes in walking sticks: carved ivory, folk art, nautical, gadget, etc., also Victorian style cane stands; the only exclusively canes retail shop in America, located at 63 Main St., Essex, MA 01929.

Brian J. Kiracofe
Newport Scrimshander, The
14 Bowen's Wharf
Newport, RI 02840
ph: 401-849-5680 or 800-635-5234
fax: 401-849-9306
e-mail: newportscrimshaw@juno.com
web: http://www.scrimshanders.com
Carries an extensive collection of canes and walking sticks; mostly ivory handles.

Kim Robertson
Robertsons
6365 Greenhill Rd.
New Hope, PA 18938
ph: 215-297-5068
fax: 215-297-5669
Buys and sells walking sticks, especially quality decorative, ivory, system and defense walking sticks.

C.B. Grissom
Cane Man, The
2180 Stephens Lane
Lexington, KY 40504-3020
ph: 606-277-7665
Wants to buy antique canes, walking sticks, umbrella handles; karat gold, sterling, ivory, V.I.P., container, watch.

Keeil's Antiques
325 Royal St.
New Orleans, LA 70130
ph: 504-522-4552
fax: 504-522-8754
Specializes in walking and "system" sticks: shaving knife & brush, sewing kits, animal sticks, flask sticks, sword and dagger sticks, camera and opium pipe sticks, gaming and writing canes, etc.

M.S. Rau Antiques
630 Royal Street
New Orleans, LA 70130
ph: 504-523-5660 or 800-544-9440
fax: 504-566-0057
e-mail: info@rauantiques.com
web: http://www.rauantiques.com
Specializes in fine canes and walking sticks.

Experts

George H. Meyer
100 West Long Lake Rd., Ste. 100
Bloomfield Hills, MI 48304
ph: 248-646-2907
fax: 248-647-6079
e-mail: mkss@michbar.org
Author of "American Folk Art Canes - Personal Sculpture."

Museums/Libraries

Peabody Essex Museum
Essex & Libert Streets
Salem, MA 01970
ph: 978-745-9500 or 800-745-4054
e-mail: pem@pem.org
web: http://www.pem.org

Curator
Fairfield Historical Society
636 Old Post Rd.
Fairfield, CT 06430-6647
ph: 203-259-1598
fax: 203-255-2716

Remington Firearms Museum
P.O. Box 179
Ilion, NY 13357-0179
ph: 315-895-3200
fax: 315-895-3237
e-mail: webmaster@remington.com
Affiliated with the Remington Arms Company, Inc.

Periodicals

Patrick Arthur
Newsletter: Cane Collector's Chronicle, The
P.O. Box 271668
Houston, TX 77277
ph: 713-669-9810
fax: 206-441-4459
e-mail: p-arthur@juno.com
A quarterly newsletter for the collector of antique walking sticks: articles, ads, photographs, auction results, book reviews, Q&A, etc.

Political

Collectors

Jim Gifford
P.O. Box 51
Bath, OH 44210-0051
ph: 330-666-3692
Specializes in collecting canes that have a political theme or motif.

CANNING JARS

(see BOTTLES; FRUIT JARS; JELLY CONTAINERS)

CANNONS

(see also ARMS & ARMOR; CIVIL WAR ARTIFACTS; FIREWORKS MEMORABILIA; MILITARIA: AMMUNITION & EXPLOSIVE ORDNANCE; TOYS, Cannons; TOY GUNS)

Collectors

Charles G. Kratz, Jr.
17821 Golfview
Homewood, IL 60430-1210
ph: 708-799-8478 or 312-951-0336
Wants old muzzle loading military cannons (only full-size, authentic type) in any condition; also want U.S. artillery clothing and equipment such wooden artillery carriages and ammunition chests.

Man./Prod./Dist.

Marshall Steen
Steen Cannons
520 13th Street
Ashland, KY 41102
ph: 606-329-2477
e-mail: steencannons@wwd.net
web: http://www.wwd.net/steen/
Manufacturer of Civil War period artillery, carriages, and limbers.

South Bend Replicas, Inc.
61650 Oak Road
South Bend, IN 46614

Starter

Man./Prod./Dist.

Robert B. George
R. B. G. Cannons
20 Amber Trail
Madison, CT 06443-2037
ph: 203-245-1216 or 800-327-2193
fax: 860-669-6982
e-mail: rbgeorge@snet.net
Cannon manufacturers for over 35 years; most cannons are scale reproductions, meticulously finished with special attention to details; used as starting cannons and trophies; units fire black powder or 10 ga. black powder shells.

CANS

(see ADVERTISING COLLECTIBLES; BEER CANS; BREWERIANA; OYSTER RELATED COLLECTIBLES; SOFT DRINK COLLECTIBLES, Soft Drink Cans)

CANTON

(see CERAMICS [ORIENTAL], Chinese Export Porcelain)

CAP PISTOLS

(see TOY GUNS)

CAPODIMONTE

(see also COLLECTIBLES [MODERN], Flowers [Capodimonte])

Dealers

James R. Highfield
Diamonds & Gold
6301 D University Commons
South Bend, IN 46635
ph: 219-272-4200
e-mail: diamondjrh@aol.com
Wants old blue crown N relief style capodimonte to purchase; please send picture and price; also need pictures and information for upcoming book.

CAPS

(see also BOTTLE CAPS; POGS)

Clubs/Associations

Gene Dittman
National Cap Association
Newsletter: NCPA Newsletter
2503 Cty. Rd. G
Emerald, WI 54012-8127
ph: 715-265-7407
Members collect baseball-style caps with logos on them; quarterly newsletter, members receive annual

cap printed with the year and different logo.

CARDS

(see also ADVERTISING COLLECTIBLES, Trade Cards; BUBBLE GUM CARDS; CREDIT CARDS & CHARGE ITEMS; HOLIDAY COLLECTIBLES; GAMES, Cards; PLAYING CARDS; RELIGIOUS COLLECTIBLES, Holy Cards; SPORTS COLLECTIBLES; TRADING CARDS, Non-Sport)

Clubs/Associations

John W. Townsend
Mice Information Collectors Exchange Free Card Guild
4 Stiles Avenue
Marple
Stockport, Cheshire SK6 6LR
U.K.
e-mail: anonymouse@cardclubs.co.uk
web: http://www.cardclubs.ndirect.co.uk/mice.html
For collectors of pictorial non-insert advertising/publicity cards which are given away free: postcards, bookmarks, tourist information cards, radio/TV presenter cards, recipe cards, telephone publicity cards, pocket calendars, etc.

Tarot

Collectors

Joan Iris Eisenberg
176 East 77th Street, Apt. #2F
New York, NY 10021-1909
ph: 212-879-9013
fax: 212-879-9525
e-mail: Joaniris@aol.com
Wants to buy unusual and quality fortune telling cards and tarot cards.

CARNEGIE HALL ITEMS

Collectors

Gino Francesconi
Carnegie Hall Corporation
881 Seventh Ave.
New York, NY 10019-3210
ph: 212-903-9629
fax: 212-424-2026
web: http://www.carnegiehall.org/
Wants house programs, stagebills, photographs of building, posters of events, other early memorabilia.

CARNIVAL ITEMS

(see also AMUSEMENT PARK ITEMS; CAROUSELS & CAROUSEL FIGURES)

Collectors

David Gaylin
P.O. Box 9686
Rosedale, MD 21237
ph: 410-665-6295
Always seeking carnival-related advertising, posters, promotional items, literature, ride manufacturers' literature, games, etc.

Allen Franklin
Rt. 3, Box 470
Farmville, VA 23901
ph: 804-392-6578
e-mail: afrankli@longwood.lwc.edu
Wants to buy Carnival & Fair prizes from the 1940s through the 1960s: chalkware, dolly canes, fur monkeys, china cane tops, dolls with feathers; games of skill pieces such as knock-down cats & clowns, bottles, and rings from toss games.

Chalkware

Experts

Cathy Cook
10 E. 13th St., #2D
New York, NY 10003-4467
ph: 212-691-2406
fax: 212-691-2406
e-mail: ccook710@aol.com
Interested in historical information about carnival chalkware and carnivals in general.

Thomas G. Morris
Prize Publishers
P.O. Box 8307
Medford, OR 97504-0307
ph: 541-779-3164
e-mail: chalkman@cdsnet.net
Buys, sells and specializes in carnival chalkware figures; author of "The Carnival Chalk Prize" Vol. I and Vol. II; will assist with information or appraisals on the subject; SASE for info.

Periodicals

John & Cathy Daniel
Newsletter: Chalk Talk
ph: 323-682-3557
e-mail: jadsden1@aol.com

Repro. Sources

Peg McCormack
Folkwerks
1760 Elbow Lane
Allentown, PA 18103-9639
ph: 610-398-3328
fax: 610-398-3328
e-mail: folkwerks@aol.com
web: http://www.members.aol.com/folkwerks
Sculpts original pieces in earth clay; a mold is made, each piece is cast, handpainted, signed, dated, and numbered.

CAROUSELS & CAROUSEL FIGURES

(see also AMUSEMENT PARK ITEMS; CARNIVAL ITEMS; COLLECTIBLES [MODERN], Figurines [Carousels]; FOLK ART; MUSICAL BOXES; MUSICAL INSTRUMENTS, Mechanical [Band Organs])

Appraisers

Ken Weaver
Weavers Antiques
7 Cooks Glen Road
Spring City, PA 19475-3303
ph: 610-469-6331
fax: 610-469-6845
e-mail: BarbMGR@aol.com
Auctions, buys, sells, restores and appraises carousel figures.

Mary Jenkins
3845 Telegraph Rd.
Elkton, MD 21921-2442
ph: 410-392-4289
fax: 410-392-6129
e-mail: carousel@dol.net
web: http://www.carousel.org/acs/
Collects, appraises and specializes in carousels and carousel art; Executive Secretary of the American Carousel Society.

Auction Services

Arlan Ettinger
Guernsey's Auction
108 East 73rd St.
New York, NY 10021
ph: 212-794-2280
fax: 212-744-3638
e-mail: catalogues@guernseys.com
web: http://www.guernseys.com/
Specializes in the sale of carousel figures.

Gordon Riewe
2287 Millville Rd.
Lapeer, MI 48446
ph: 810-664-5648
fax: 810-664-7141
Dealer of carousel horses; carousel auctions.

David A. Norton
Norton Auctioneers of Michigan, Inc.
50 W. Pearl St.
Coldwater, MI 49036-1967
ph: 517-279-9063
fax: 517-279-9191
e-mail: nortonsold@cbpu.com
Specializing in the auctioning of amusement rides, carousels, amusement parks, arcades, museums, etc.

Clubs/Associations

Mary Jenkins, Ex. Sec.
American Carousel Society
Newsletter: Rounding Board, The
3845 Telegraph Rd.
Elkton, MD 21921-2442
ph: 410-392-4289
fax: 410-392-6129
e-mail: carousel@dol.net
web: http://www.carousel.org/acs/
The goal of the ACS is to preserve operating carousels and carousel art; please send SASE for information.

National Carnival Association
Magazine: Carousel Magazine
P.O. Box 4165
Salisbury, NC 28145-4165
ph: 704-636-0841
fax: 704-636-1051
e-mail: support@carouselmagazine.com
web: http://www.carouselmagazine.com/
A quality monthly publication for the amusement industry: articles about current carnival activities, midway talk and personalities, manufacturers' showcase, rides of the past, carnival modeling of miniature creations.

Edward F. Gallenstein
National Wood Carvers Association
Magazine: Chip Chats
P.O. Box 43218
Cincinnati, OH 45243
ph: 513-561-0627 or 513-561-9051
fax: 513-561-0627
e-mail: nwca@chipchats.org
web: http://www.chipchats.org/
NWCA's aims are to promote woodcarving and fellowship among members; encourage exhibitions; list tool and wood suppliers, and find markets for those who sell their work - in short, anything that aids the carver and/or whittler.

Terry Blake, ExSec.
National Carousel Association
Magazine: Merry-Go-Roundup
P.O. Box 4333
Evansville, IN 47724-0333
ph: 812-428-3675
e-mail: terrybnca@juno.com
web: http://www.carousel.org/nca/
Primary goal is to protect existing wooden operating carousels; please send SASE for information.

Jean Martell
Colorado Carousel Society
6651 Metropolitan
Colorado Springs, CO 80911
ph: 719-392-9826

Collectors

Tommy Sciortino
3723 Nebraska Ave.
Tampa, FL 33603
ph: 813-248-9911
Restores antique carousels; buys and sells whole carousels, horses, chariots, parts, etc.

Dealers

Bruce Zubee
Carousel Classifieds
15 Jerome Ave.
Burlington, CT 06013-2407
ph: 860-675-7653
e-mail: webmaster@carousels.com
web: http://www.carousels.com/
Wants to buy any old wooden carousel horses or menagerie figures in any condition; also buying band organs, carousel scenery panels and rounding boards, etc.; sales, purchases, museum quality restorations, worldwide service.

Ken Weaver
Weavers Antiques
7 Cooks Glen Road
Spring City, PA 19475-3303
ph: 610-469-6331
fax: 610-469-6845
e-mail: BarbMGR@aol.com
Auctions, buys, sells, restores and appraises carousel figures.

Steve Crescenze
Restorations by Wolf
8480 Gunston Rd.
Welcome, MD 20693
ph: 301-932-2734
web: http://www.carousel.net/wolf
Buys, sells, trades carousel figures (one to a whole carousel); professional restoration services with photo documentation of each figure.

Craig Swanson
Midwest Carousel Organization
1952 Lake Drive
Independence, MO 64055-1863
ph: 816-685-6602 or 800-896-9661
e-mail: extra@finest1.com
web: http://www.finest1.com/hand/
World famous woodcarver, professional animal restorations; also buys, sells, and trades.

Don Snider
Merry-Go-Art
2606 Jefferson
Joplin, MO 64804
ph: 417-624-7281
e-mail: hsnider@clandjop.com
web: http://www.janics.com/~hsnider
Buys and sells carousel figures, and video tapes of antique carousels.

John & June Reely
Flying Tails
1209 Indiana Ave.
South Pasadena, CA 91030-3611
ph: 223-256-8657
Send 2 stamp SASE for catalog of carousel figures hair tails.

Danie Horenberger
Brass Ring Entertainment
11001 Peoria St.
Sun Valley, CA 91352
ph: 818-394-0028
fax: 818-394-0062
e-mail: sales@carousell.com
web: http://www.carousell.com
20 years experience, sales, restoration, parts, service.

Experts

William Manns
P.O. Box 6459
Santa Fe, NM 87502-6459
ph: 505-995-0102
fax: 505-995-0103
e-mail: zon@nets.com
Author of "Painted Ponies, American Carousel Art." Send photo and request for information about your carving and its authenticity.

Marianne Stevens
Wooden Horse, The
920 W. Mescalero Rd.
Roswell, NM 88201
ph: 505-622-7397
fax: 505-622-7397
Buys, sells, trades, brokers, and appraises carousel figures.

Internet Resources

Bruce Zubee
Carousel Classifieds
15 Jerome Ave.
Burlington, CT 06013-2407
ph: 860-675-7653
e-mail: webmaster@carousels.com
web: http://www.carousels.com/
The "World's Source" for the collector of antique carousel figures and related collectibles.

Man./Prod./Dist.

Bill Dentzel
Dentzel Carousel Company
843 53rd St.
Port Townsend, WA 98368
ph: 360-385-0304
fax: 360-385-1067
e-mail: bill@dentzel.com
web: http://www.dentzel.com

Misc. Services

Tommy Sciortino
American Carousel & Novelty
3723 Nebraska Ave.
Tampa, FL 33603
ph: 813-248-9911
Experienced in relocation, setup and dismantling of carousels.

Museums/Libraries

Heritage Plantation of Sandwich
P.O. Box 566
Sandwich, MA 02563
ph: 508-888-3300 or 508-888-1222
fax: 508-833-2916
e-mail: heritage@heritageplantation.org
web: http://www.heritageplantation.org/autos.htm

Louise L. DeMars, Ex. Dir.
New England Carousel Museum, Inc.
Newsletter: Carousel, The
95 Riverside Ave.
Bristol, CT 06010
ph: 860-585-5411
web: http://www.carousel.org/newengl.html
One of the nation's largest collections of historic carousel art, figurines and memorabilia.

Elizabeth Brick, Dir.
Herschell Carousel Factory Museum
Newsletter: Carousel Newsletter
180 Thompson St.
P.O. Box 672
North Tonawanda, NY 14120-0672
ph: 716-693-1885 or 716-693-7972
fax: 716-693-1885
web: http://www.carousel.org/hersch.html
Allen Herschell wooden carousel c. 1916 (wood), a metal children's carousel c. 1946, and original Allan Herschell factory site; exhibit on history of Herschell Co., carousels, amusement rides, and band organs.

Tamara Humphrey, Dir.
Merry-Go-Round Museum
W. Washington & Jackson Sts.
P.O. Box 718
Sandusky, OH 44870-0718
ph: 419-626-6111 or 419-627-5412
fax: 419-626-1297
e-mail: MerryGoR@aol.com
web: http://www.carousel.org/sandusky/
Features a working carousel, and master carver Gustav Dentzel's 19th century carving shop; carving & restoration demonstrations of carousel animals & band organs.

Children's Museum of Indianapolis, The
P.O. Box 3000
Indianapolis, IN 46206
ph: 800-208-KIDS or 317-924-KIDS
e-mail: tcmi@childrensmuseum.org
web: http://www.childrensmuseum.org/
The museum's carousel was originally installed at White City Park (now called Broad Ripple Park) in 1917.

Carol Perron
International Museum of Carousel Art
500 North Second St.
Hood River, OR 97031
ph: 541-387-2979
Historical museum dedicated to preserving the carousel.

Periodicals

Walter Loucks
Magazine: Carousel News & Trader, The
87 Park Ave. West, Ste. 206
Mansfield, OH 44902
ph: 419-529-4999
fax: 419-529-2321
e-mail: cnsam@aol.com
web: http://www.carousel.net/trader/
Monthly magazine serving the carousel enthusiast since 1985; color photos, ads, stories, auctions, restoring, events, etc.

William Manns
Zon International Publishing
Directory: Carousel Shopper
P.O. Box 6459
Santa Fe, NM 87502-6459
ph: 505-995-0102
fax: 505-995-0103
e-mail: zon@nets.com
A carousel resource directory: suppliers, museums, carousel events, shows, restorers, auctions, reproductions, cards, posters, etc.

Repair Services

Steve Crescenze
Restorations by Wolf
8480 Gunston Rd.
Welcome, MD 20693
ph: 301-932-2734
web: http://www.carousel.net/wolf
Buys, sells, trades carousel figures (one to a whole carousel); professional restoration services with photo documentation of each figure.

Marsha A. Schloesser
Carousel Workshop, The
218 High St.
De Land, FL 32720
ph: 904-738-4229
web: http://www.carousel.net/workshop/
Dealer and lecturer; buys, sells, restores carousel figures; also gliding & rocking horses.

Sherrell Anderson
Carousel Magic!
P.O. Box 1466
Mansfield, OH 44901-1466
ph: 419-526-4009
fax: 419-526-4561
e-mail: carmagic@richnet.net
web: http://carouselmagic.com/
Highest quality custom made full size carousels, individual animals, restorations, carving classes and carving kits.

Craig Swanson
Midwest Carousel Organization
1952 Lake Drive
Independence, MO 64055-1863
ph: 816-685-6602 or 800-896-9661
e-mail: extra@finest1.com
web: http://www.finest1.com/hand/
World famous woodcarver, professional animal restorations; also buys, sells, and trades.

Pegi Sanders
Sanders Carousel Company
1203 Greenstone Lane
Santa Maria, CA 93454
ph: 805-948-3268
fax: 805-928-3908
e-mail: horse@carouselvend.com
web: http://www.carouoselvend.com/
Complete, basket cases to final paint.

Bill Hughes
Hughes Carousel Restoration
10325 Dougherty Ave.
Morgan Hill, CA 95037-9241
ph: 408-778-5077
Museum quality restorations.

Repro. Sources

Bob Morris
Wooden Horse Studio, The
11152 Kootenay Path
Lakeview, OH 43331
ph: 937-843-3346
e-mail: bmorris@mail.bright.net
web: http://www.bright.net/~bmorris/
Contemporary carvings; does not do reproductions.

Joe & Susan Leonard
Custom Woodcarving
12107 St. Rt. 88
Garrettsville, OH 44231
ph: 330-527-2307
Specializing in restoring and carving carousel figures.

Sherrell Anderson
Carousel Magic!
P.O. Box 1466
Mansfield, OH 44901-1466
ph: 419-526-4009
fax: 419-526-4561
e-mail: carmagic@richnet.net
web: http://carouselmagic.com/
Highest quality custom made full size carousels, individual animals, restorations, carving classes and carving kits.

Suppliers

Sally Craig
Nostalgia
336 W. High St.
Elizabethtown, PA 17022-2140
ph: 717-295-9188
Reins, stirrups, jewels, tails, twisted brass; send SASE for list; also sells antique carousel horses and other figures.

Peter Millar
Quill, Hair & Ferrule, Ltd.
P.O. Box 23927
Columbia, SC 29224-3927
ph: 800-421-7961 or 803-788-4499
fax: 803-736-4731
e-mail: pmillar@paint-info.com
Professional restoration supplies: Japan & oil colors, brushes, abalone & mother-of-pearl, aluminum, copper, composition, gold leaf, burnishing tools, imported gold sizes, non-tarnish iridescent & metallic pigments, etc.

George Faircloth
Faircloth Carousel Restoration Studios
4633 Coolidge St.
Concord, CA 94521-1347
ph: 415-682-7669
Eyes, tails, stands, restoration guide, materials.

Miniature

Clubs/Associations

Jerry Defenderfer
Miniature Carousel Builders, Inc.
2746 Warmspring Rd.
Chambersburg, PA 17201
ph: 717-375-4256

Patrick Wentzel
Carousel Modelers & Miniatures Association
Magazine: Horse Tales
2310 Highland Ave.
Parkersburg, WV 26101-2920
ph: 304-428-3544
Formed in 1986 for those interested in the building miniature carousels and related items.

Collectors

Patrick Wentzel
2310 Highland Ave.
Parkersburg, WV 26101-2920
ph: 304-428-3544
Wants to buy carousel, carnival, amusement park, and circus items including photographs, miniature carvings, books, and related articles.

Suppliers

Patrick Wentzel
2310 Highland Ave.
Parkersburg, WV 26101-2920
ph: 304-428-3544
Sells scale wood carving kits in 1", 1 1/2", and 2" scales; over 50 different kits available.

Albert Krueger
Merry-Go-Rounds
19771 Lexington Lane
Huntington Beach, CA 92646
ph: 714-963-2676
Miniature kits, five sizes, scale, operating.

CARPENTER ITEMS

(see ARCHITECTURE & RELATED ITEMS)

CARPET SWEEPERS

(see VACUUM CLEANERS)

CARRIAGES

(see HORSE-DRAWN VEHICLES, Carriages)

CARS

(see AUTOMOBILES; AUTOMOBILIA; AUTO RACING MEMORABILIA; KITS; MILITARIA, Vehicles; MODELS, Cars; TOYS, Diecast; TRAILERS & RV'S)

CARTE-DE-VISITES

(see CIVIL WAR ARTIFACTS, Photographs; PHOTOGRAPHS)

CARTOON ART

(see also ANIMATION FILM ART; CHARACTER COLLECTIBLES; COMIC BOOKS; COMIC STRIPS, Sunday Newspaper; POLITICAL COLLECTIBLES, Nast Cartoons; POPULAR CULTURE; POSTERS, Cartoon; SCIENCE FICTION)

Clubs/Associations

National Cartoonists Society
Magazine: Cartoonist, The
Columbus Circle Station
P.O. Box 20267
New York, NY 10023
web: http://www.reuben.org/main.asp
National club interested in professional cartooning.

Metropolitan Cartoon Art & Collectibles Club
P.O. Box 414
Manhasset, NY 11030
ph: 516-627-2123
e-mail: toonclb@ibm.net
For collectors of cartoon art and character collectibles.

Collectors

Tim Isaacson
1002 Clinton
Oak Park, IL 60304-1824
ph: 708-383-5646
e-mail: TFIsaacson@aol.com
Wants to buy original comic art: comic book covers and pages, Sunday and daily comic strip art; Dick Tracy, Prince Valiant, The Phantom, Little Orphan Annie, etc.

Bill Bush
P.O. Box 61868
Houston, TX 77208-1868
Wants to buy original cartoons and comic art by Caniff, Baker, Eisner, Interlandi, Kaufman, Kremos, Lichty, Machamer, Priscilla, Rayon, Ross, Ben Roth, Shermund, Simms Campbell, Troop, Wenzel, Wood, and Wolfe.

Lee Aronsohn
16430 Westfall Place
Encino, CA 91436
ph: 818-905-0225
fax: 818-905-6334
e-mail: overpaid@metawire.com
Collects material relating to cartoonist Gary Trudeau and the "Doonesbury" comic strip; also wants humorous 3-D postcards marked "Eden Plastics," "Postplax," or "Cardell."

Dealers

Bill & Joanne Bruegman
Toy Scouts, Inc.
137 Casterton Ave.
Akron, OH 44303-1543
ph: 330-836-0668
fax: 330-869-8668
e-mail: toyscout@akron.infi.net
Wants to buy original artwork from comic books, especially super hero; artists such as Jack Kirby, Steve Ditko, Will Eisner, John Comita.

Robert A. LeGresley
P.O. Box 1199
Lawrence, KS 66044-8199
ph: 785-331-0782 or 785-749-5458
fax: 785-331-0782
e-mail: rlegres@aol.com
Buys and sells original comic art.

Cartoon Museum, The
814 Mission St.
San Francisco, CA 94103
ph: 415-227-8666
Buys and sells original cartoon art of all types; also "spin offs": books, collectibles, comic books, magazines, etc.; a private museum with original art for more than 2,500 cartoons of all kinds, especially comic art.

Experts

Frederick P. Dose, Jr.
Frederick Dose Appraisals Ltd.
778 Pleasant Ave.
Highland Park, IL 60035-4613
ph: 847-433-7870 or 847-433-1090
Has verified and valued over 60,000 original gag and political cartoons for the Cartoon Museum of Ohio State University, plus 5,000 Chester Gould Dick Tracy and Gravies strips.

Museums/Libraries

International Museum of Cartoon Art
201 Plaza Real
Boca Raton, FL 33429
ph: 561-391-2200

Curator
Cartoon Research Library, University of Ohio
023L Wexner
27 West 17 Avenue Mall
Columbus, OH 43210-1393
ph: 614-292-0538
fax: 614-292-9101
e-mail: cartoons@osu.edu
web: http://www.lib.ohio-state.edu
Houses more than 200,000 original cartoons including editorial cartoons, comic strips, sports cartoons, magazine cartoons, and comic book art; several hundred cartoonists are represented including Milton Caniff and Walt Kelly.

Consortium of Popular Culture Collections
Popular Culture Library
Bowling Green State University
Bowling Green, OH 43403-0001
ph: 419-372-2450
fax: 419-372-7996
e-mail: ascott@bgnet.bgsu.edu
web: http://www.bgsu.edu/colleges/library/pcl/cpccm.html
Consortium composed of Bowling Green State U., Kent State U., Michigan State U., and Ohio State U.; the largest academic library collections of primary research material in comic art, popular fiction, popular music, performing arts.

Molly Kiely
Cartoon Art Museum
Newsletter: Cartoon Times
814 Mission St., 2nd Floor
San Francisco, CA 94103
ph: 415-546-3922 or 415-CAR-TOON
fax: 415-243-8666
Broad collection of original daily and Sunday comic strip art, editorial and political cartoons, animation cels, magazine panels, comic book pages and covers, and toy-related items.

San Francisco Academy of Comic Art
170 W. Cliff Dr., #15
Santa Cruz, CA 95060-5440
ph: 831-427-1737
fax: 831-427-1737
Millions of newspaper strips, bound files, major dailies from 1890-1960, pulps, all science fiction, crime fiction, film history, children's books, comic books; excellent copies made of all graphic material; dup material for trade.

Comics

Collectors

John S. Fawcett
P.O. Box 1156
Waldoboro, ME 04572-1156
ph: 207-832-7398
Wants to buy original comic art: wants original Krazy Kat by George Herriman, original Lone Ranger art and pulp cover paintings of Lone Ranger; also Pogo originals by Walt Kelly.

Milton Caniff

Collectors

Bill Bush
P.O. Box 61868
Houston, TX 77208-1868
Wants to buy Milton Caniff sketches, color guides and proofs, letters, photos, audios, VHS videos and other ephemera.

Periodicals

Carl Horak
Journal: Caniffites Journal
1319 108 Avenue SW
Calgary, Alberta T2W 0C6
Canada
ph: 403-252-0878
Members focus on the works of Milton Caniff - original art or Sunday comic strips: Terry and the Pirates, Steve Canyon, etc.; newsletter published 4 times a year.

Walt Kelly

Experts

Steve Thompson
6908 Wentworth Ave. South
Minneapolis, MN 55423-2363
ph: 612-869-6320
e-mail: thompson_2@epi.umn.edu
Internationally-known bibliographer and biographer of Walt Kelly and "Pogo"; active collector of unusual and esoteric Kellyana.

CARTRIDGES

(see AMMUNITION & EXPLOSIVE ORDNANCE)

CARTS

(see RIDING TOYS)

CASH REGISTERS

Clubs/Associations

Mike Hennessey
Cash Register Collectors Club of America
Newsletter: Bronze Idol
P.O. Box 20534
Dayton, OH 45420
ph: 937-433-3529
e-mail: jmarkner@aol.com

Collectors

Lt. Col. B.A. Gill (Ret.)
P.O. Box 381
Clifton Park, NY 12065
ph: 513-371-6035
Brass or wood in any condition; also literature, ads, sales brochures.

Hayne Dominick
562 Gammon Rd.
Kingsport, TN 37663-4119
ph: 423-323-9579
fax: 423-323-9579
e-mail: domndom@jun.com
Buying early and unusual cash registers; specializing in National Cash Register, related memorabilia & advertising; sales, repairs and restorations.

Lewis
18915 Los Palominos Dr.
Yorba Linda, CA 92886-2649
ph: 714-970-8390
e-mail: BookEmDano@webtv.net
Wants to buy cash registers and related items, especially small wooden, figural, ornate, unusual machines.

Dealers

Bill Heuring
Hickory Bend Antiques & Collectibles
2995 Drake Hill Rd.
Jasper, NY 14855-9715
ph: 607-792-3343
fax: 607-792-3309
Cash registers bought and sold; professional restoration and repair; also sells parts.

Experts

Sam Robins
Play It Again Sam's, Inc.
8218 Lowell Ave.
Skokie, IL 60076-2624
Buys, sells, trades machines; has extensive register parts inventory; also offers a full restoration service for cash registers.

John Gillman
2125 Seneca Street
Kingman, AZ 86401
ph: 520-753-1192
Buys, sells, repairs and completely restores NCR cash registers for customers throughout the U.S.

Henry Bartsch
Antique Registers
P.O. Box 444
Rockaway Beach, OR 97136-0444
ph: 503-355-2932
Author of "Antique Cash Registers 1880-1920"; offers antique cash register sales and service.

CASINO COLLECTIBLES

(see ASHTRAYS, Casino; GAMBLING COLLECTIBLES; MATCHCOVERS, Casino)

CAST IRON ITEMS

(see also BANKS; FARM COLLECTIBLES, Cast Iron Seats; FIREPLACE ITEMS; GARDEN FURNITURE; KITCHEN COLLECTIBLES; METAL ITEMS; PAPERWEIGHTS, Cast Iron; STOVES; TARGETS; TOYS; WATER SPRINKLERS; WINDMILL COLLECTIBLES, Weights)

Collectors

Dave Johnson
113 Hix Ave.
Rye, NY 10580
ph: 914-967-4809
Wants cast iron match safes, string holders, muffin pans, etc.

Craig Dinner
P.O. Box 4399
Long Island City, NY 11104-0399
ph: 718-729-3850 or 802-365-7181

Dealers

Sonnie Cucinotti
Spirits in the Attic
201 Msgr. O'Brien Hwy.
Cambridge, MA 02141
ph: 617-738-6054
Wants to buy cast and and wrought iron decorative and utilitarian items.

John & Nancy Smith
American Sampler
P.O. Box 371
Barnesville, MD 20838-0371
ph: 301-972-6250
Wants cast iron doorstops, figural bottle openers, doorknockers, paperweights, banks, bookends, etc.

Louis Picek
Main Street Antiques & Art
110 West Main
P.O. Box 340
West Branch, IA 52358-0340
ph: 319-643-2065
Buys and sells figural iron of all types; offers a monthly list of items for sale.

J.M. Ellwood
Irontiques
7050 E. Main
Scottsdale, AZ 85251
ph: 602-947-6220 or 602-947-9679
fax: 602-947-2501
e-mail: irontiques@aol.com
Wants trivets, match holders, irons, banks, children's stoves and irons, advertising items, cigar cutters, cap exploders, figural bottle openers, miners candlesticks.

Experts

Craig Dinner
P.O. Box 4399
Long Island City, NY 11104-0399
ph: 718-729-3850 or 802-365-7181
Wants cast iron doorstops, figural

bottle openers, doorknockers, paperweights, lawn sprinklers, shooting gallery targets, architectural items, etc.

Richard Tucker
Argyle Antiques
P.O. Box 262
Argyle, TX 76226-0262
ph: 940-464-3752
fax: 940-464-7293
e-mail: lead1234@gte.net

Museums/Libraries

Birmingham Museum of Art
2000 8th Ave. N.
Birmingham, AL 35203
ph: 205-254-2565
fax: 205-254-2714
web: http://www.artsbma.org/
Holds the Lamprecht Collection of decorative cast iron, the largest in the world.

Repair Services

Rocco V. DeAngelo
Antique Cast Iron
425 Hoose Rd.
Cherry Valley, NY 13320
ph: 607-264-3607
fax: 607-264-3607
Quality restoration of antique cast iron; sandblasting, painting, repair, fabrication of parts; garden furniture, urns, fences installed, handwrought iron, brass & iron beds, etc.

Cookware

Collectors

Jim Bell
P.O. Box 355
Swainsboro, GA 30401
ph: 912-237-7815
Wants to buy old cast iron cookware.

Patrick Bedwell
4200 Bohannon Drive
Menlo Park, CA 94025
ph: 650-473-2456
e-mail: mrpotatohead@earthlink.net
web: http://www.mrpotatohead.net
Collector of cast iron cookware from manufacturers such as Griswold, Wagner, Wapak, Favorite, and Filley; website has historical information about these companies and lots of images of skillets, muffin pans, waffle irons, etc.

Steve Stephens
28 Angela Ave.
San Anselmo, CA 94960
ph: 415-453-7790
A 6-issue-per-volume (about 40 pages) newsletter (one volume every 1-2 years); illustrated and packed with detailed information focusing on cast iron kitchen cookware (including Griswold.)

Dealers

David G. Smith
Pan Man, The
P.O. Box 247
Perrysburg, NY 14129
ph: 716-532-5154
e-mail: panman@utec.net
web: http://www.panman.com
Cast iron collector specializing in cast iron muffin pans; has over 250 different patterns and/or variations; buys, sells and trades cast iron cookware; author of "The Book of Griswold & Wagner."

LaVon Deatsman
609 1st Street
Lake Odessa, MI 48849
ph: 616-374-5482
Buys and sells Griswold and Wagner cast iron cookware items.

Bernie Ver Hey
623 Watkins Glen
Saint Charles, MO 63304
ph: 314-441-9936
e-mail: bverhey@mail.win.org
Buys and sells Griswold, Wagner, Erie, Wapak, G.F. Filley, Favorite cast iron cookware.

Darvin King
Cast Iron Cowboy
248 PR 4839
Baird, TX 79504
ph: 915-854-1046
Specializes in Griswold and Wagner cast iron collectibles.

Experts

David G. Smith
Pan Man, The
P.O. Box 247
Perrysburg, NY 14129
ph: 716-532-5154
e-mail: panman@utec.net
web: http://www.panman.com
Cast iron collector specializing in cast iron muffin pans; has over 250 different patterns and/or variations; buys, sells and trades cast iron cookware; author of "The Book of Griswold & Wagner."

Periodicals

David G. Smith, Ed.
Newsletter: Kettles 'n Cookware
P.O. Box 247
Perrysburg, NY 14129
ph: 716-532-5154
e-mail: panman@utec.net
web: http://www.panman.com
Focuses on cast iron, aluminum, tin and other items made by the Griswold and other manufacturers.

Cookware (Erie)

Collectors

Joan Baldini
3007 Plum St.
Erie, PA 16508
ph: 814-868-1316
e-mail: duner1@aol.com
Collects Erie related cast iron items.

Cookware (Griswold)

Clubs/Associations

Joanie Baldini, Sec.
Griswold & Cast Iron Cookware Association
3007 Plum St.
Erie, PA 16508
ph: 814-868-1316
e-mail: duner1@aol.com
web: http://www.panman.com/association.html
Dedicated to the promotion and education of its members in cast iron kitchen collectibles; 650+ members nationwide; annual swap meet and meeting.

Collectors

Sally Swanson
3302 West 11th St.
Erie, PA 16505-3710
ph: 814-838-1866
Wants to buy cast iron items made by the Griswold Manufacturing Co.

Dealers

Scott Lamb
1550 Kennelworth Court
State College, PA 16801
ph: 814-237-3303
Buys, sells, trades Griswold cast iron cookware.

Larry & Sue Foxx
400 Creek Rd.
Carlisle, PA 17013-9645
ph: 717-243-9231
Interested in collecting cast iron, aluminum, tin and other items made by the Griswold Manufacturing Co., Erie, PA; also wants items marked Selden & Griswold and Erie.

Cookware (Wagner)

Man./Prod./Dist.

WagnerWare Corporation
440 Fair Road
Sidney, OH 45365
ph: 888-457-COOK
fax: 888-457-BAKE
e-mail: wagnerware@worldnet.att.net
web: http://www.wagnerware.com/
Manufacturer of Wagner cast iron products.

CATALOGS

(see also ADVERTISING COLLECTIBLES; AUCTION CATALOGS; HARDWARE; MACHINERY & EQUIPMENT, Catalogs; MAGAZINES; PAPER COLLECTIBLES; PLUMBING; SEEDS)

Christmas

Dealers

Christmas Catalog Collector, The
175 East Delaware, #7403
Chicago, IL 60611-1731
ph: 800-879-6948 or 312-337-3123
fax: 312-266-7982
Seeks toy and Christmas catalogs and flyers from Sears, Wards, all retailers, wholesalers and manufacturers; also buying toy magazines and general merchandise catalogs if containing many toys.

Mail Order

Dealers

Judy Hesson
Hesson Collectables
1261 S. Lloyd
Lombard, IL 60148-4234
ph: 630-627-3298
fax: 630-627-3298
e-mail: jhesson@mediaone.net
Buys & sells mail order catalogs: Sears, Montgomery Ward, Penny, Aldens, Spiegel: 1900-1990; also other catalogs; send $4 for list of 2000 for sale.

Trade

(see also ADVERTISING COLLECTIBLES; MACHINERY & EQUIPMENT, Catalogs; MAGAZINES)

Collectors

Tom Rutledge
3015 Bever Ave., SE
Cedar Rapids, IA 52403-3028
ph: 319-399-1427
Wants to buy old trade catalogs and flyers; all companies desired; all retailers, wholesalers, manufacturers, distributors, etc.

Don Hooper
9645 Sylvia Ave.
Northridge, CA 91324-1756
ph: 818-772-1721
fax: 818-772-4647
e-mail: vntgplbg@aol.com
Wants early pre-1910 plumbing trade catalogs showing ornamental bath fixtures.

Dealers

Steve Finer
38 Grinnell St.
Greenfield, MA 01302-3621
ph: 413-773-5811
e-mail: finerbks@crocker.com

Joseph F. Loccisano
Historic Photographs & Paper Americana
2264 Nicholson Square Dr.
Lancaster, PA 17601-3966
ph: 717-560-5182
Wants to buy pre-1915 catalogs (hardcover or softcover) illustrating hardware specialties, tinware, occupational supplies, photographic apparatus, architectural supplies, toys, etc.; send asking price with photos.

Kenneth Schneringer
Old-Paper.Com
271 Sabrina Ct.
Woodstock, GA 30188-4228
ph: 770-926-9383
e-mail: trademan68@aol.com
web: http://www.old-paper.com
Buys and sells trade catalogs, old paper and other ephemera.

Judy Hesson
Hesson Collectables
1261 S. Lloyd
Lombard, IL 60148-4234
ph: 630-627-3298
fax: 630-627-3298
e-mail: jhesson@mediaone.net
Buys and sells trade catalogs: sports, fashion, hardware, architectural, wholesale, retail; send $4 for list of 900 for sale.

Robert D. Verhines
1705 Longwood Dr., Apt. 202
Sycamore, IL 60178-2743
ph: 815-899-3121
Buys and sells trade catalogs, e.g. Sears, Wards, Penny's, Alden, Spiegel, etc.; especially wants Christmas issues.

Trade (Furniture)

Museums/Libraries

Christian G. Carron
Grand Rapids Public Museum
272 Pearl St. NW
Grand Rapids, MI 49504-5371
ph: 616-456-3977
fax: 616-456-3873
e-mail: staff@grmuseum.org
web: http://www.grmuseum.org/
Large collection of 20th century furniture and furniture manufacturing trade catalogs.

Trade (Homebuilding)

Collectors

Charles W. Wardell
P.O. Box 195
Trinity, NC 27370-0195
ph: 336-434-1145
Wants early (1870-1910) manufacturers' catalogs of ornate builders' hardware such as doorknobs, escutcheon plates, doorknobs, store door handles, etc.

Jerry L. Wilson
1002 E. Main St.
P.O. Box 220
Cherryvale, KS 67335-0220
ph: 316-336-2495 or 316-336-2176
fax: 316-336-2177
Wants to buy millwork or sash & door company catalogs from the 1800s to 1920; also wants any other building related catalogs such as stained glass, paint, general hardware, metal ceilings, etc. from the same era.

Trade (Kitchen Collectibles)

Collectors

Reid Cooper
32942 Josheroo Ct.
Temecula, CA 92592
ph: 909-302-3348
e-mail: rcoop4129@aol.com
Advanced collector/researcher wants to buy pre-1920 trade catalogs of kitchen implements, gadgets, eggbeaters, etc.; also interested in old advertising, billheads, and trade cards that relate to same; send price, sample photocopy.

Trade (Medical)

Museums/Libraries

Michael Rhode, Archivist
Otis Historical Archives, National Museum of Health & Medicine
Bldg. 54
Walter Reed Medical Center
Washington, DC 20306
ph: 202-782-2200
fax: 202-782-3573
e-mail: rhode@afip.osd.org/
web: http://bubba.afip.org/
Federal government museum archives that collects catalog material related to the history of medicine, especially military medicine.

Trade (Woodworking)

Collectors

John Treggiari
ph: 978-744-2897
fax: 978-744-5572
e-mail: micrometer@juno.com
Serious collector wants to buy tool catalogs: woodworking, machinist, drafting, and hardware store catalogs showing tools are all needed, but should have been published prior to 1920.

CAVE RELATED ITEMS

Collectors

Jack Speece
711 East Atlantic Ave.
Altoona, PA 16602-5405
ph: 814-946-3155 or 814-342-0470
fax: 814-342-5660
Wants items pertaining to caves, caverns, speleo history and folklore.

Bert Ashbrook
Cave Investigation & Exploration
1257 Lehigh Parkway South
Allentown, PA 18103-3875
ph: 610-797-3981
Collects books, ephemera, antiques, and memorabilia related to caves, commercial caverns, wild caves, cave history, and cave science.

Anthony Glab
6708 Duluth Ave.
Baltimore, MD 21222
e-mail: glab@aol.com
Wants to buy cave memorabilia such as paperweights, signs, souvenirs, etc.

Gordon Smith
P.O. Box 217
Marengo, IN 47140-0217
ph: 812-945-5721
e-mail: glstis@aol.com
Wants items pertaining to caves and caverns: books, pamphlets, brochures, photos, souvenir plates and spoons, stereo views, sheet music, etc.

CELEBRITIES

(see AUTOGRAPHS; MOVIE MEMORABILIA; PERSONALITIES; PHOTOGRAPHS, Celebrity; TELEVISION SHOWS & MEMORABILIA)

CELLULOID ITEMS

(see also ALBUMS)

Auction Services

Kurt R. Krueger
Krueger Auctions
P.O. Box 275
Iola, WI 54945-0275
ph: 715-445-3845
fax: 715-445-4100

Clubs/Associations

Victorian Era Celluloid Collectors Association
P.O. Box 470
Alpharetta, GA 30239-0470
Club for collectors of Victorian celluloid covered boxes, photo albums, tri-fold mirrors and other Victorian celluloid covered items; send SASE for info.

Collectors

John Andreae
P.O. Box 156
Granger, IN 46530-0156
ph: 219-272-2337
fax: 219-271-1146
e-mail: jkandreae@aol.com
Wants celluloid pieces with advertising on them: pocket mirrors, pinback buttons, bookmarks and blotters; anything that is made of celluloid and that has advertising on it.

Andra Behrendt
P.O. Box 217
Western Springs, IL 60558
ph: 708-246-26767
e-mail: andra@lady-a.com
web: http://www.lady-a.com/
Collects decorative Celluloid glove, collar, trinket, dresser set boxes and celluloid autograph albums; must be in mint condition; also wants 1895-1910 catalogs that advertise these items.

Sherry & Mike Miller
303 Holiday Dr. #130
Tuscola, IL 61953-2118
ph: 217-253-4991
e-mail: miller@tuscola.net
web: http://www.tuscola.net/~miller/
Wants to buy Victorian era boxes which held collars/cuffs, gloves, neckties, shaving sets, etc.; also photograph albums and autograph albums; must have lithograph prints of scenes or people; all covered in thin layer of clear Celluloid.

Dealers

Judith Rubin
This Time Around Antiques
9226 Cynthia Street
Centreville, VA 20111
ph: 703-303-8167
e-mail: judy.harveyr@erols.com
Buys and sells Victorian (1895-1910) celluloid boxes (collar/cuff, vanity, etc.), photo albums, autograph albums, 3-way shaving mirrors; excellent condition only; contents not necessary in boxes or albums; no ivorine, or French ivory.

Andra Behrendt
Lady A Antiques
P.O. Box 217
Western Springs, IL 60558
ph: 708-246-26767
e-mail: andra@lady-a.com
web: http://www.lady-a.com/
Buys, sells and collects decorative Celluloid glove, collar, trinket, dresser set boxes and celluloid autograph and photograph albums; must be in mint condition; also wants 1893-1910 catalogs that advertise these items.

Experts

Julie Robinson
P.O. Box 744
Davidsville, PA 15928
ph: 814-479-2212
Identification of natural and synthetic moldable materials: Gutta Percha, Vulcanite, Horn, Tortoise shell, Ivory imitations, Celluloid, Casine, bakelite, Beetleware, Acrylic, Acetate, and early poly plastics; written extensively.

CELS

(see ANIMATION FILM ART; AUDIO-VISUAL)

CERAMICS

(see also ADVERTISING COLLECTIBLES, Potteries Related; CALENDAR PLATES; COOKIE JARS; DINNERWARE; FAIRINGS; FIGURINES; POT LIDS; PRECOLUMBIAN; REPAIR/ RESTORATION/CONSERVATION; RAILROAD COLLECTIBLES, China; RESTAURANT COLLECTIBLES; STEINS; TILES)

Appraisers

Karen J. Russo, G.G., ISA
Karen Jocelyn, Inc.
792 Partridge Dr.
P.O. Box 6795
Bridgewater, NJ 08807
ph: 908-526-8440
fax: 908-526-8348
Specializing in 19th and 20th century ceramics; has constant contact with metropolitan area galleries that specialize in this area; appraisal, photography, market research.

Patricia M. Knight
Finetooth Comb Antiques Research & Appraisal Service
P.O. Box 1177
Ames, IA 50010-1177
ph: 515-292-9028
e-mail: ftcres@aol.com
Consultant and qualified appraiser of ceramics of Oriental, European, English and American origin or style, including "American Satsuma"; please send SASE for reply.

Linda H. Richard, ISA
Cajun Collection
3308 White Oak
Temple, TX 76502
ph: 254-774-8608
e-mail: cajun@vvm.com
web: http://www.vvm.com/~cajun/
Specializing in pottery, porcelain, with emphasis on American & European pottery.

Kathleen M. Bailey, ISA CAPP
Antique Appraisal & Estate Sale Services
9416 1st Ave., NE, #311
Seattle, WA 98115
ph: 425-746-2777
fax: 425-746-3793

Robert G. Jason-Ickes
3600 Elizabeth Ave., SE #19-203
Olympia, WA 98501-7458
ph: 360-455-9914
Specializes in American ceramics and American art pottery; also lectures.

Auction Services

Butterfield & Butterfield
7601 Sunset Blvd.
Los Angeles, CA 90046-2714
ph: 323-850-7500
fax: 323-850-5843
e-mail: info@butterfields.com
web: http://www.butterfields.com/

Clubs/Associations

Nancy K. Lester, Ex. Dir.
American Ceramic Circle
Journal: American Ceramic Circle Journal
520 16th St.
Brooklyn, NY 11215
fax: 718-832-5446
e-mail: nlester@earthlink.net
Founded in 1970, a nonprofit organization that promotes scholarship and research in the history, use, and preservation of ceramics of all kinds, periods, and origins; membership restricted; Journal available for purchase by public.

San Francisco Ceramic Circle
P.O. Box 15163
San Francisco, CA 94115
ph: 510-752-3830
web: http://www.patriciananantiques.com/sfcc.html
Monthly lectures and meetings; affiliated with the Fine Arts Museum of San Francisco; a valuable resource for anyone with an interest in antique ceramics or ceramic art.

Ontario Clay & Glass Association, The
Magazine: Fusion Magazine
80 Spadina Ave., Ste. 204
Toronto, Ontario MV5 2J3
Canada
ph: 416-504-9899
Focuses on contemporary potters and techniques.

Dealers

Pat Dillon
Antique Legacy - Online Catalog
P.O. Box 12
Portville, NY 14770
ph: 716-928-2334
e-mail: alegacy@worldnet.att.net
Buys and sells hand painted china, Limoges, Bavaria, Staffordshire, Majolica, etc.

Paul G. Hughes, ISA
Tudor House Galleries
4126 Park Rd., Ste. E.
Charlotte, NC 28209
ph: 704-676-4871 or 704-676-4872
e-mail: tudorhouse@aol.com
web: http://www.tudorhouse.com
Buys, sells and appraises 18th and 19th century ceramics; Accredited Member, International Society of Appraisers.

Ron McCoy
P.O. Box 703095
Tulsa, OK 741703095
ph: 918-747-1344
e-mail: ron@collectorsweb.com
web: http://www.collectorsweb.com

Kathleen M. Bailey, ISA CAPP
Antique Appraisal & Estate Sale Service - K. Bailey
9416 1st Ave., NE, #311
Seattle, WA 98115
ph: 425-746-2777
fax: 425-746-3793
Specializes in 18th and 19th century porcelain, plaques, enamels.

Experts

Susan & Jim Harran
World of Ceramics, The
208 Hemlock Dr.
Neptune, NJ 07753
e-mail: antique208@msn.com
Authors of "World of Ceramics" column.

Susan & Al Bagdade
Country Peasants, The
1325 North State Parkway, Apt. 15A
Chicago, IL 60610
ph: 312-397-1321
fax: 312-543-2544
e-mail: ADBSDB@aol.com

Dr. Dorothy I. Godfrey-Smith
TOSL Research Laboratory
Department of Earth Sciences
Dalhousie University
Halifax, Novia Scotia B3H 3J5
Canada
ph: 902-494-1451 or 902-494-2358
fax: 902-494-6889
e-mail: digs@is.dal.ca
Offers an analytical service using thermoluminescence to analyze ceramic artifacts and art objects; used by museums, art galleries, private collectors and estate appraisers wishing to ensure authenticity of ceramic objects.

Elinor Racine, ISA
175 Bessborough Drive
Toronto, Ontario M4G 3J8
Canada
ph: 416-483-8675
fax: 416-440-2809
e-mail: 75317.2337@compuserve.com
Specialist in contemporary ceramics: appraiser, collector, author.

Man./Prod./Dist.

Dona Danziger
Clay Works, The
4058 S. Main St.
P.O. Box 352
Exmore, VA 23350
ph: 757-414-0567
fax: 757-414-0571
e-mail: clayworks@esva.net
web: http://www.esva.net/~clayworks
Hand painted pottery and art tiles in current studio productions; brochures and shipping available.

Misc. Services

Shirley Vickers
Shirley Vickers School of China Repair
P.O. Box 688
Pine, AZ 85544-0688
ph: 520-476-3703
fax: 520-476-3703
e-mail: shirley@shirleyvickers.com
web: http://www.shirleyvickers.com
Will buy damaged pottery of any kind; call or fax or write with descriptions of damage and price.

Museums/Libraries

Miss Dorothy Lee Jones, Founder/Cur.
Jones Museum of Glass & Ceramics, The
35Douglas Mountain Rd.
East Sebago, ME 04029
ph: 207-787-3370 or 207-787-2800
fax: 207-787-2800
Unique museum: over 7500 examples of glass & ceramics ranging from ancient to modern; holdings include Chinese export, Wedgwood, Spode, and other 18th & 19th c. English potters; 19th c. European ceramics; American ceramics; library.

National Museum of American History
14th & Constitution Ave. NW
Washington, DC 20560
ph: 202-357-2700
e-mail: webmaster@si.edu
web: http://www.si.edu/organiza/museums/nmah/nmah.htm

George Gardiner Museum of Ceramic Art
0111 Queen's Park
Toronto, Ontario M5S 2C7
Canada
ph: 416-586-8080
fax: 416-586-8085
The only specialized museum of its kind in North America; internationally-renowned collection of ceramics ranging from pre-Columbian artifacts

of 3,000 BC to 20th-century wares from around the world including Europe and South America.

Periodicals

Lladro USA
Newsletter: Lladro Antique News
1 Lladro Dr.
Moonachie, NJ 07074
ph: 201-807-1177 or 800-634-9088
fax: 201-807-1168
e-mail: lladrosociety@worldnet.att.net
web: http://www.lladro.com
Focuses on the current secondary market values of Lladro's 3,000 hard-paste porcelain figurines produced since 1941; also covers history of hard-paste porcelain (1000 AD to present) such as Meissen, Sevres, Nymphenburg, etc.

Magazine: Ceramics Monthly
P.O. Box 6102
Westerville, OH 43086-6102
ph: 614-488-4561
fax: 614-891-8960
e-mail: editorial@ceramicsmonthly.org
web: http://www.ceramicsmonthly.org/
A trade publication for ceramic artists and art education institutions; a glossy, quality magazine!

Scott Publications
Magazine: Ceramic Arts & Crafts
30595 Eight Mile
Livonia, MI 48152-1798
ph: 800-458-8237 or 248-477-6650
fax: 248-477-6795
e-mail: 104137.1254@compuserve.com
The "Bible" for the ceramic hobbyist since 1955; each monthly issue filled with projects and patterns, celebrity clips, new products, show listings, industry news, shoppers guides, book reviews, ads and classifieds.

Paradise Publications
Newsletter: Pottery Collectors Express, The
P.O. Box 221
Mayview, MO 64071-0221
ph: 660-584-6309

Belleek

Clubs/Associations

Belleek Collectors' Society, The
Newsletter: Belleek Collector, The
9893 Georgetown Pike, Ste. 525
Great Falls, VA 22066
ph: 800-235-5335 or 703-847-6207
fax: 703-847-6201
e-mail: info@belleek.com
web: http://www.belleek.com/
Membership of over 10,000; biennial conferences; for collectors of new or antique Belleek.

Experts

Miriam & Aaron Levine
881 Whalley Ave.
New Haven, CT 06515
ph: 203-389-5440

Jack Mulhern
3212 Winterset Dr.
Dayton, OH 45440-3630
ph: 937-426-2592
Collector specializes in Irish Belleek.

Kathleen Mitchell
Old Pump Antiques
P.O. Box 774
San Bruno, CA 94066-0774
ph: 650-588-9514 or 650-588-4894
fax: 650-875-7556
Buys, sells, appraises and specializes in 18th and 19th century porcelain including black mark Irish Belleek, Dresden, and Meissen; also specializes in Irish Belleek stoneware.

Museums/Libraries

Mark Twyford
Museum of Ceramics
400 E. 5th St.
East Liverpool, OH 43920-3134
ph: 330-386-6001
Detailed exhibit of the local ceramic industry; "The East Liverpool, Ohio Pottery District: Identification of Manufacturers & Marks" by Wm. Gates, Jr. and Dana Ormerod can be obtained by contacting the museum.

Belleek (American)

Appraisers

Peggy Sebek, ISA, AAA
Century Antiques & Appraisals, Inc.
3255 Glencairn Rd.
Shaker Heights, OH 44122-3407
ph: 216-991-2356
fax: 216-991-2935
e-mail: peggylane@worldnet.att.net
Specializes in and appraises American Belleek; also residential contents, Victorian furniture, and silver; Accredited Member of the International Society of Appraisers, Member of the Appraisers Association of America.

Bisque

Collectors

Dave Harris
1206- 1101 Bay St.
Toronto, Ontario M5S 2W8
Canada
ph: 416-972-6331 or 416-928-8579
Wants quality continental European bisque; marked or unmarked; send photo; will travel.

Blue & White Pottery

Clubs/Associations

Howard Gardner
Blue & White Pottery Club
Newsletter: Blue & White Pottery Club Newsletter
224 12th St. NW
Cedar Rapids, IA 52405-3913
ph: 319-362-8116
For collectors of blue and white stoneware, blue and white spongeware, and related blue stoneware; annual convention for members only; 650 members.

Alan Myers Riley
Friends of Blue Society
18 St. George's Place
Northamton, NN2 6EP
U.K.

Dealers

Susan Lengyel
Blue & White Dinnerware
4800 Crestview Dr.
Carmichael, CA 95608
ph: 916-961-7406
e-mail: TheFourLs@aol.com
web: http://members.aol.com/TheFourLs/NEWSLETR.HTM
Appraiser, dealer, collector, expert in blue and white pottery; replacements for discontinued Staffordshire patterns such as Liberty Blue, Blue Danube.

Experts

Gregg Ellington
Upper Loft Antiques
47 Columbus St.
Wilmington, OH 45177
ph: 937-382-4311
Buys, sells, trades and collects graniteware and American ceramics including mochaware, yellowware, spongeware, etc.

Blue Willow

(see CERAMICS, Willow Pattern)

Chintz

(see also CERAMICS [ENGLISH], Royal Winton)

Clubs/Associations

Chintz Connection
Newsletter: Chintz Connection Newsletter
P.O. Box 222
Riverdale, MD 20738-0222
ph: 301-937-8270
e-mail: welshjo@webtv.net
web: http://www.chintzconnection.com/welcome.html

Jane Fehrenbacher
Chintz China Collector, The
Newsletter: Chintz Collector, The
P.O. Box 50888
Pasadena, CA 91115
ph: 626-441-4708
fax: 626-441-4122
e-mail: chintz4u@aol.com
web: http://www.chintznet.com
An international club for collectors of chintz china; colorful quarterly newsletter has news, convention information, auction results, educational articles, buy/sell ads.

Ken Glibbery, Sec.
ChintzWorld International
Newsletter: RWICC NewsLetter
Dancer's End
Northall, Bedfordshire LU6 2EU
U.K.
ph: +44 (0) 1525 220272
fax: +44 (0) 1525 222442
e-mail: royalwinton@dial.pipex.com
web: http://www.chintzworld-intl.com/

Collectors

Bruce E. Thulin
P.O. Box 121
Ellsworth, ME 04605
ph: 207-667-5225
e-mail: thulin@acadia.net
Wants chintz ceramics with all over decoration: Royal Winton, Shelley, Lord Nelson, James Kent, Crown Ducal, Midwinter; teapots, plates, stacking teapots, cups, etc.

Jane Fehrenbacher
California Associates
600 Columbia St.
Pasadena, CA 91105
ph: 626-441-2490
fax: 616-441-4122
e-mail: chintz4u@aol.com
web: http://chintznet.com
Buying and selling chintz; specializing in English Chintz china, primarily Royal Winton, James Kent, Lord Nelson, and Crown Ducal.

Dealers

Joyce Settel
Joyce Settel Ltd.
P.O. Box 94
Quogue, NY 11959
ph: 516-653-5670 or 516-288-0431
Specializes in English porcelain, Chintz, Royal Winton, James Kent, Lord Nelson, Crown Ducal.

Dianne Howerton
Royal Pair Antiques, The
12707 Hillcrest Dr.
Longmont, CO 80501-1162
ph: 303-772-2760 or 303-772-2309
Buys and sells English semi-porcelain chintzware in Royal Winton, Lord Nelson, James Kent, Midwinter, Myott, Crown Ducal, Ridgeway, Shelley, Wood & Sons and Empire Porcelain Co. patterns.

Experts

Linda Eberle
P.O. Box 50888
Pasadena, CA 91115
ph: 626-441-4708
fax: 626-441-4122
e-mail: chintz4u@aol.com
web: http://www.chintznet.com
Co-author with Susan Scott of "Charlton Standard Catalogue of Chintz, 2nd Edition."

Susan Scott
882 Queen Street West
Toronto, Ontario M6J 1G3
Canada
ph: 416-538-8536
fax: 416-534-4814
e-mail: scottca@ibm.net
web: http://www.collecting20thcentury.com/
Specializing in chintz ceramics, especially by Royal Winton, Crown Ducal, James, Kent, Elijah Cotton; author of "Charlton Standard Catalogue of Chintz, 3nd Edition" (1999).

Internet Resources

Jane Fehrenbacher
ChintzNet
600 Columbia St.
Pasadena, CA 91105
ph: 626-441-2490
fax: 616-441-4122
e-mail: chintz4u@aol.com
web: http://chintznet.com
Chintz sellers ads, Chintz conventions.

Clay Art

Man./Prod./Dist.

Thomas Biela
Clay Art, Inc.
239 Utah Ave.
South San Francisco, CA 94080-6802
ph: 415-244-4970 or 800-252-9555
fax: 415-244-4979
e-mail: clayartinc@aol.com
Specializes in collectible giftware and tabletop accessories; handcrafted ceramic masks, salt & peppers, cookie jars, creamers & sugars, mugs, plates, and more designed with a unique and whimsical nature.

Cups & Saucers

Experts

Susan & Jim Harran
World of Ceramics, The
208 Hemlock Dr.
Neptune, NJ 07753
e-mail: antique208@msn.com
Authors of "Collectible Cups & Saucers," the only book of its kind with over 400 full color photos, history, dates, sizes, makers and facts; 184 pages; $21.95 ppd.

Flow Blue

Appraisers

Robert G. Jason-Ickes
3600 Elizabeth Ave., SE #19-203
Olympia, WA 98501-7458
ph: 360-455-9914

Clubs/Associations

James McClain, Mem.
Flow Blue International Collectors Club
Newsletter: Blue Berry Notes
P.O. Box 1021
South Houston, TX 77587
ph: 281-944-2004
e-mail: debj@megahaus.com
web: http://www.flowblue.org

Norman Wolfe
Transferware Collector's Club
Morris Street Antiques, Space #60
503 E. Morris St.
La Conner, WA 98257
e-mail: floboo@pacificrim.net
web: http://www.pacificrim.net/~floboo/
An organization of collectors, dealers and museum personnel interested in English transferware, c. 1760-1880.

Dealers

John Bove
Pedigree Antiques
61 West Shore Road
Bristol, NH 03222
ph: 603-744-5346
e-mail: pedigree1@usa.net
web: http://angelfire.com/nh/pedigreeantiques/
Large selection of Flow Blue; also Roseville, Lundberg Art Glass, Majolica.

Anne & Dave Middleton
Pot O Gold Antiques
P.O. Box 124
Allenwood, NJ 08720-0124
ph: 732-528-6648
fax: 732-528-6648
e-mail: pot-o-goldantiques@worldnet.att.net
Interested in flow blue china, epergnes, and Historical Staffordshire.

Carl McCann
Troy & Black, Inc.
P.O. Box 228
Red Creek, NY 13143-0228
ph: 315-754-8115
e-mail: tbrc@banet.net
Buys and sells high quality flow blue, Staffordshire figurines, American painted furniture, stoneware, redware, coverlets, samplers, and other American textiles, folk art, etc.

Louise M. Loehr
Louise's Old Things
163 W. Main St.
P.O. Box 208
Kutztown, PA 19530-0208
ph: 610-683-8370
fax: 610-683-6865
e-mail: louises@bellatlantic.net
Co-author of "Willow Pattern China." Specializing in willow, flow blue, and early children's china. Wants one piece or collections.

Pam & Ralph Krainik
Seven Gables Antiques
P.O. Box 204
Baraboo, WI 53913

Experts

Sunny Lenzer
1345 Sierra Linda Dr.
Escondido, CA 92025
Buys and sells flow blue; also offers seminars on flow blue.

Gaudy

Experts

John D. Querry
RD 2 Box 137B
Martinsburg, PA 16662-9655
ph: 814-793-3185 or 814-693-7985
fax: 814-793-3802
e-mail: JDQuerry@aol.com
Specializes in Gaudy Dutch; advisor to "Warman's Antiques & Collectibles Price Guide."

Handpainted

Clubs/Associations

World Organization of China Painters, The
Magazine: China Painter, The
2641 N.W. 10th St.
Oklahoma City, OK 73107-5407
ph: 405-521-1234
fax: 405-521-1265
e-mail: wocporg@theshop.net
web: http://www.theshop.net/wocporg/
Organization with 7000 members; online museum dedicated to handpainted china; seminars, courses, library.

Museums/Libraries

World Organization of China Painters, The
Magazine: China Painter, The
2641 N.W. 10th St.
Oklahoma City, OK 73107-5407
ph: 405-521-1234
fax: 405-521-1265
e-mail: wocporg@theshop.net
web: http://www.theshop.net/wocporg/
Museum houses examples of handpainted porcelain from all over the U.S. and from several foreign countries.

Head Vase Planters

Clubs/Associations

Maddy Gordon
Head Vase Convention
Newsletter: Head Hunters Newsletter
P.O. Box 83H
Scarsdale, NY 10583-8583
ph: 914-472-0200

Collectors

Dan Morphy
121 Moorland Ct.
Lititz, PA 17543-8016
Top dollar paid for Disney, Marilyn Monroe, unusual lady head vases.

Sharon Stogner
Sharon's Head Vase Collection
P.O. Box 373
Imperial, CA 92251
e-mail: dstog@c2i2.com
web: http://www.c2i2.com/~dstog/
Great resource web site with information and photos.

Dealers

Diane Leach
201 Filors La.
Stony Point, NY 10980-2641
ph: 914-942-2074
fax: 914-942-2320
e-mail: cupplate@aol.com
Wants to buy Betty Lou Nichols head vases, figurines and planters; also any head vases 7" or larger; call collect.

Millie Miller
1027 Emory Lane
Indianapolis, IN 46241
ph: 317-241-4123
Buys, sells, or trades head vases.

Lois & Ralph Behm
Lois' Collectibles of Antique Market III
413 W. Main St.
Saint Charles, IL 60174-1815
ph: 630-377-5599 or 847-831-5997
Buys and sells lady head vases; will buy entire collections.

Christina Stelzer
Chrissy's Lady Head Vases
10300 Grand Oak Drive
Austin, TX 78750
ph: 512-918-2576
e-mail: chrissy@chrissy.com
web: http://www.chrissy.com/heads.html
Offers a huge selection of Limoges and porcelain hinged boxes, Halcyon Days enamels, and Lady Head Vases.

Jennifer Sykes
Jennifer Sykes Antiques
9018 Balboa Blvd. #595
Northridge, CA 91325-2610
ph: 818-993-1916
fax: 818-993-7612
e-mail: Veeda10@aol.com
Buys, sells Lady Head vases, especially those over 7" tall; also

buying Head Vases by Betty Lou Nichols.

Peggy Cole
134 E. Laveta
Orange, CA 92666-1908
ph: 714-997-7379
Wants to buy ladies head vases, especially Jackie Kennedy, Carmen Miranda, and any Ceramic Arts Studio ladies head vases.

Experts

Maddy Gordon
P.O. Box 83H
Scarsdale, NY 10583-8583
ph: 914-472-0200
Head vase collector, dealer and expert.

D.L. Barron
Head Vase Collectors Corner
P.O. Box 7901
Columbus, MS 39705-7901
e-mail: dlb@ebicom.net
web: http://www.ebicom.net/~dlb/heads.htm
Author of "Head Vases by numbers 1999 Price Guide."

Mike Posgay
P.O. Box 93022
Brampton, Ontario LGY 4V8
Canada
ph: 905-453-9074
Specializes in head-vase planters; co-author with Ian Warner of "Head Vases Identification and Values."

Ironstone (Mason's)

Clubs/Associations

Susan Hirshman
Mason's Ironstone Collectors' Club
Newsletter: MICC Newsletter
2011 E. Main St.
Medford, OR 97504
ph: 541-608-9594

Gerard Larkin Haverstock Esq.
Mason's Ironstone China Society
Glendermont House
109 Noble Ave.
Winnipeg, Manitoba R2L 0J5
Canada
ph: 204-667-3248 or 204-663-1151
fax: 204-667-3248
e-mail: larkinh@escape.ca
web: http://www.webhaven.com/gerard/
Non-profit society open to all; Purpose is to propagate the study and appreciation of the pottery and porcelain manufactured by Mason's Ironstone China Company of England; info as to patterns and marks; late 18th century to present.

Ironstone (Tea Leaf)

Clubs/Associations

Dale Abrams
Tea Leaf Club International
Newsletter: Tea Leaf Readings
960 Bryden Rd.
Columbus, OH 43205-1809
ph: 614-258-5258
fax: 614-258-6663
e-mail: TLAntiques@aol.com
web: http://ourworld.compuserve.com/homepages/da/
Purpose is to inform membership about Tea Leaf Ironstone and its copper lustre variants.

Collectors

Dick Brackin
15565 Willow Creek Rd.
Athens, OH 45701
Purpose is to inform membership about Tea Leaf Ironstone and its copper lustre variants.

Chris Weinbrenner
2216 B Avenue NE
Cedar Rapids, IA 52402

Experts

Julie Rich
411 Kinross Dr.
Newark, DE 19711-1535
ph: 302-456-5769
fax: 302-454-8538
e-mail: RRich411@aol.com
Buys, sells, collects and specializes in Tea Leaf & White Ironstone; writes and lectures on American ironstone, especially Tea Leaf.

Dale Abrams
Tea Leaf Ironstone China Home Page
960 Bryden Rd.
Columbus, OH 43205-1809
ph: 614-258-5258
fax: 614-258-6663
e-mail: TLAntiques@aol.com
web: http://ourworld.compuserve.com/homepages/da
Buys and sells quality Tea Leaf and Teaberry ironstone china and other white ironstone decorated with copper lustre motifs.

William Durham
Hospice House Antiques
9633 Beaver Valley Rd.
Belvidere, IL 61008-8057
ph: 815-547-5128

Ironstone (White)

Clubs/Associations

White Ironstone China Association, Inc.
Newsletter: White Ironstone Notes
P.O. Box 536
Redding Ridge, CT 06876
fax: 203-936-8378
e-mail: Dieringer1@aol.com
web: http://www.ironstonechina.org/

Collectors

Ernie & Bev Dieringer
Dieringer's Antiques
P.O. Box 536
Redding Ridge, CT 06876
fax: 203-938-8378
e-mail: Dieringer1@aol.com
Editors of "White Ironstone Notes," newsletter for The White Ironstone China Association, Inc.; send e-mail for membership information; ask about the web site under construction.

Experts

Jean Wetherbee
P.O. Box 856
Hillsborough, NH 03244
ph: 603-464-5462 or 603-464-6747
Author of "A Look at White Ironstone."

Julie Rich
411 Kinross Dr.
Newark, DE 19711-1535
ph: 302-456-5769
fax: 302-454-8538
e-mail: RRich411@aol.com
Buys, sells, collects and specializes in Tea Leaf & White Ironstone; writes and lectures on American ironstone, especially Tea Leaf.

Dale Abrams
960 Bryden Rd.
Columbus, OH 43205-1809
ph: 614-258-5258
fax: 614-258-6663
e-mail: TLAntiques@aol.com
web: http://ourworld.compuserve.com/homepages/da
Buys and sells quality Tea Leaf and white ironstone china.

William Durham
Hospice House Antiques
9633 Beaver Valley Rd.
Belvidere, IL 61008-8057
ph: 815-547-5128

Jugs (Molded)

Experts

Kathy Hughes
Tudor House Galleries
4126 Park Rd., Ste. E.
Charlotte, NC 28209
ph: 704-676-4871 or 704-676-4872
e-mail: tudorhouse@aol.com
web: http://www.tudorhouse.com
Specializes in 19th century relief-molded jugs (pitchers); author of "A Collector's Guide to 19th Century Jugs" Vol. I and Vol. II.

Jugs (Puzzle)

Collectors

Don Berey
151 Prospect Ave., Ste. 7A
Hackensack, NJ 07601
ph: 201-498-0944
fax: 201-498-0988
Wants to buy puzzle jugs.

Lefton

Clubs/Associations

Loretta DeLozier
National Society of Lefton Collectors
Newsletter: Lefton Collector
1101 Polk Street
Bedford, IA 50833
ph: 712-523-2289
fax: 712-523-2624
e-mail: LeftonLady@aol.com
web: http://members.aol.com/leftonlady
Members are interested in dinnerware and figurines made by Lefton.

Collectors

Loretta DeLozier
1101 Polk Street
Bedford, IA 50833
ph: 712-523-2289
fax: 712-523-2624
e-mail: LeftonLady@aol.com
web: http://members.aol.com/leftonlady
Wants to buy Lefton porcelain dinnerware and figurines.

Man./Prod./Dist.

Mark Holmen
George Zoltan Lefton Co., Imports
3622 South Morgan St.
Chicago, IL 60609
ph: 773-254-4344 or 800-938-1800
fax: 773-254-4545

Majolica

Auction Services

Amory Spizzirri, Client Svc.
William Doyle Galleries
175 E. 87th St.
New York, NY 10128-2205
ph: 212-427-2730
fax: 212-369-0892
e-mail: info@doylegalleries.com
web: http://www.doylegalleries.com
Holds over 50 auctions annually of furniture and decorations, paintings and sculpture, jewelry, books and prints, couture and textiles, 20th century art & design, majolica, Lalique, Asian works of art and other specialty categories.

Michael G. Strawser
Strawers Auctions
P.O. Box 332
Wolcottville, IN 46795-0332
ph: 219-854-2859 or 219-854-2235
fax: 219-854-3979
web: http://www.majolicaauctions.com/
Specializing in Majolica auctions in the U.S.

Clubs/Associations

Majolica International Society
Newsletter: Majolica Matters
1275 First Ave., Ste. 103
New York, NY 10021-5601
fax: 212-744-1124
Conventions held in April/May each year with international speakers and show/sale; members are collectors, dealers, experts.

Debora Lamm
Pacific Northwest Majolica Club
Newsletter: Majolica Madness
16302 - 34th St. NE
Snohomish, WA 98290
ph: 425-334-6585
e-mail: danes90@aol.com
web: http://hometown.aol.com/danes90/homepage3.html

Collectors

Michael G. Strawser
P.O. Box 332
Wolcottville, IN 46795-0332
ph: 219-854-2859 or 219-854-2235
fax: 219-854-3979
web: http://www.majolicaauctions.com/

Dealers

Nancy Kramer
Sparrows
4115 Howard Ave.
Kensington, MD 20895-2417
ph: 301-530-0175
fax: 301-530-0189
e-mail: NSKramer@aol.com
web: http://www.sparrows.com
Specializes in mid-19th through mid 20th century French majolica.

Hardy Hudson
Our Antiques Market
5453 Lake Howell Rd.
Winter Park, FL 32792-1033
ph: 407-657-2100 or 407-647-3454
e-mail: todiefor@mindspring.com
Buys and sells and specializes in majolica by Minton, George Jones, Hold Croft, Wedgwood, Fielding, Copeland, Etruscan, James Carr; majolica oyster plates.

Majolica Wares, Inc.
2314 Guthrie Ave., N.W.
Cleveland, TN 37311
ph: 423-339-3975
Collects originals in order to make reproductions; buys and sells antique Victorian majolica upon availability and request.

Experts

Nicholas Dawes
67 East 11th St.
New York, NY 10003-4613
ph: 212-473-5111
fax: 212-353-3845
e-mail: nmdawes@aol.com
web: http://www.pbs.org/wgbh/pages/roadshow/appraisers/dawes.html
Buys, sells and specializes in Victorian majolica; author of "Majolica" (Crown Publishers, 1989).

Linda Kettering
3202 E. Lincolnshire Blvd.
Toledo, OH 43606-1207
ph: 419-536-5531
Buys and sells English, American and French majolica; good condition only; unusual pieces particularly desired.

Brenda Wilson
2720 N. 45th Road
Manton, MI 49663
ph: 616-824-3043
fax: 616-824-9357
Will answer collectors questions to help identify majolica; please include SASE for reply.

Repro. Sources

Majolica Wares, Inc.
2314 Guthrie Ave., N.W.
Cleveland, TN 37311
ph: 423-339-3975
Produces high-quality American-made majolica reproductions.

Majolica (Palissy Ware)

Experts

Marshall P. Katz
Gateway Towers, Suite 24A
Pittsburgh, PA 15222
ph: 412-471-1600
fax: 412-471-0250
e-mail: palissy@usaor.net
web: http://www.palissy.com
Co-author with Robert Lehr of "Palissy Ware: Nineteenth Century French Ceramists From Avisseau to Renoleau." Write for list of dealers specializing in 19th century French Palissy ware in the U.S. and Europe.

Mexican

Collectors

Kier Linn
P.O. Box 641824
Los Angeles, CA 90064
ph: 310-477-5229
fax: 310-268-8420
e-mail: dcrehr@earthlink.net
Seeking Mexican pottery sold to tourists from the 1930s to 1960s; of particular interest are large pieces, and those with black backgrounds in design.

Military Related

Collectors

Rex Stark
P.O. Box 1029
Gardner, MA 01440-6029
ph: 978-630-3237
fax: 978-630-2388
Wants to buy china with American political and military portraits or scenes; Liverpool, lustreware, parian ware, Staffordshire, etc.

Mochaware

Experts

Gregg Ellington
Upper Loft Antiques
47 Columbus St.
Wilmington, OH 45177
ph: 937-382-4311
Buys, sells, trades and collects graniteware and American ceramics including mochaware, yellowware, spongeware, etc.

Picasso Editions

Appraisers

Stephen van Cline, CAPP
van Cline & Davenport, Ltd.
792 Franklin Lakes Ave.
Franklin Lakes, NJ 07417-1343
Minimum charge $25; letter request only, SASE.

Collectors

Albert Merola
Universal Fine Objects, Inc.
424 Commercial Street
Provincetown, MA 02657
ph: 508-487-4424
fax: 508-487-4743
e-mail: ufoarts@capecod.net
web: http://www.universalfineobjects.com/
Fine art dealer in contemporary prints, paintings, and ceramic; primary interest is Picasso ceramic editions and other Madoura ceramics.

Pixieware

Dealers

Joe Iozzia
P.O. Box 1005
Pomona, NJ 08240-1005
ph: 609-652-8504
fax: 609-652-8888
e-mail: pinflyers@aol.com
web: http://members.aol.com/NUTS4SALE/HOLT.html
Appraisers, collector, dealer, expert buys and sells Hold Howard Pixieware ceramics; buys entire collections.

Political Related

Collectors

Rex Stark
P.O. Box 1029
Gardner, MA 01440-6029
ph: 978-630-3237
fax: 978-630-2388
Wants to buy china with American political and military portraits or scenes; Liverpool, lustreware, parian ware, Staffordshire, etc.

Redware

Dealers

Richard Hume
American Stoneware Collectors
P.O. Box 281
Point Pleasant Beach, NJ 08742-0281
ph: 732-899-8707 or 732-295-9285
Collects, appraises, buys, sells, auctions American decorated stoneware: jugs, crocks, etc.; also Southern pottery, American redware, folk pots, etc.; conducts auctions twice a year.

Carl McCann
Troy & Black, Inc.
P.O. Box 228
Red Creek, NY 13143-0228
ph: 315-754-8115
e-mail: tbrc@banet.net
Buys and sells high quality flow blue, Staffordshire figurines, American painted furniture, stoneware, redware, coverlets, samplers, and other American textiles, folk art, etc.

Repro. Sources

Stephen Nutt
Steve Nutt, Potter
25 Ellicott Place
Staten Island, NY 10301
ph: 718-273-6815
e-mail: yankeered@aol.com
Reproductions of 19th century Mid-Atlantic and New England redware plates; also designs and make seasonal, holiday and thematic plates; send $2 for catalog and sample newsletter.

James Nyeste
RD #3
Seven Valleys, PA 17360
ph: 717-428-3314
Makes figural redware sculptures: animals and figures in the Pennsylvania and Shenandoah Valley traditions.

Lester Breininger
Breininger Pottery
476 S. Church St.
Robesonia, PA 19551
ph: 610-693-5344

Rockingham

Experts

George Eck
1987 Limewood Dr.
San Jose, CA 95132
Collector and expert who has been specializing in Rockingham for 10 years; has researched every U.S. and English museum that has a ceramics collection.

Souvenir & Commemorative

(see also SOUVENIR & COMMEMORATIVE ITEMS)

Dealers

Tom & Barbara Tripp
P.O. Box 366
Peterborough, NH 03458
ph: 603-924-6106
e-mail: tripptom@aol.com
Wants to buy antique souvenir china from New England towns.

Spongeware

Experts

Gregg Ellington
Upper Loft Antiques
47 Columbus St.
Wilmington, OH 45177
ph: 937-382-4311
Buys, sells, trades and collects graniteware and American ceramics including mochaware, yellowware, spongeware, etc.

Studio Pottery

Experts

Jim Messineo
JMW Gallery
144 Lincoln St.
Boston, MA 02111-2523
ph: 617-338-9097
fax: 617-338-7636
e-mail: jmwgallery@tiac.net
web: http://www.jmwgallery.com/
Buys, sells and specializes along with co-owner Mike Witt in the Arts & Crafts movement. Mission furniture: Lifetime, Limbert, Stickley; American Art Pottery 1875 to 1950s: Grueby, Newcomb, Marblehead, etc.; metalwork, Roycroft.

Terra Cotta

Clubs/Associations

Susan Tunick
Friends of Terra Cotta
771 West End Avemue, #10E
New York, NY 10025-5539
ph: 212-932-1750
fax: 212-662-0768
web: http://www.preserve.org/fotc/
Formed to promote and educate and research architectural terra cotta and related ceramic materials.

Texas

Collectors

James E. Kattner
P.O. Box 11132
Spring, TX 77391
ph: 281-986-6916 or 281-376-4826
Wants to buy Texas whiskey jugs which display the merchant's name and town; some may display saloon name and town; especially want Texas jugs, but will pay equally well for same from other Southern and Western states.

Willow Pattern

Clubs/Associations

Jeff Siptak
Willow Society of Tennessee
P.O. Box 41312
Nashville, TN 37204
ph: 615-383-7855
fax: 615-269-7123
e-mail: WillowWare@aol.com
For collectors interested in Willow pattern china and collectibles; open to all; meetings throughout the year in Tennessee.

Marge LaLonde
Ohio Willow Society
4820 Center Rd., Rte 83
Avon, OH 44011

International Willow Collectors
1232 Anthony Trace
Waynesville, OH 45068
web: http://www.willowcollectors.org/
Members interested in collecting and studying of ceramics and other materials decorated with the willow pattern.

Collectors

Joyce LaFont
331 Edenwood
Jackson, TN 38301
ph: 901-668-5974

Al Little
151 Highway 173
Antioch, IL 60002
ph: 847-395-7752
fax: 847-395-7703
Buy, sells and trades Blue Willow china.

Dealers

Louise M. Loehr
Louise's Old Things
163 W. Main St.
P.O. Box 208
Kutztown, PA 19530-0208
ph: 610-683-8370
fax: 610-683-6865
e-mail: louises@bellatlantic.net
Co-author of "Willow Pattern China." Specializing in willow, flow blue, and early children's china. Wants one piece or collections.

Experts

Connie Rogers
1733 Chase St.
Cincinnati, OH 45223-2057
ph: 513-541-2013
Editor of "American Willow Report" 7/87 through 5/90; consultant to "The Official Price Guide to Pottery and Porcelain"; author of "Willow Ware Made in the USA," (1996), available from author.

Periodicals

Jeff Siptak
Newsletter: Willow Review, The
P.O. Box 41312
Nashville, TN 37204
ph: 615-383-7855
fax: 615-269-7123
e-mail: WillowWare@aol.com
The only international newsletter devoted to collecting and enjoying willow pattern china and collectibles; quarterly issues featuring photos, prices, trends in collecting, articles on a wide variety of subjects, and more.

Mary Lina Berndt, Pub.
Newsletter: Willow Word, The
1232 Anthony Trace
Waynesville, OH 45068
web: http://www.willowcollectors.org/
A newsletter addressing all aspects of "Blue Willow", the world's most popular china pattern; its 200 year history, the "Willow Legend", current sources for both old and new willowware; a forum for questions, gossip, convention news.

Yellowware

Collectors

Bill Carroll
RR 1, Box 62
Hope, ND 58046-9760
ph: 701-945-2416
fax: 701-945-2772
e-mail: BillND29@ictc.com
web: http://www.collectoronline.com/booths/booth-74/
Wants to buy yellowware!

Experts

Gregg Ellington
Upper Loft Antiques
47 Columbus St.
Wilmington, OH 45177
ph: 937-382-4311
Buys, sells, trades and collects graniteware and American ceramics including mochaware, yellowware, spongeware, etc.

CERAMICS (AMERICAN)

Clubs/Associations

Jim Riordan, Pres.
Wisconsin Pottery Association
P.O. Box 46
Madison, WI 53701-0046
ph: 608-249-6898 or 608-241-9138
fax: 608-241-8770
e-mail: ceramics@execpc.com
web: http://www.wisconsinpottery.com/
Club meets monthly; meetings include guest speakers on featured pottery or various lines of vintage pottery; affiliated with the State Historical Society of Wisconsin.

Dealers

Naomi's Antiques To Go
1817 Polk St.
San Francisco, CA 94109
ph: 415-775-1207
Buys/sells American dinnerware: Hall, Bauer, Tepco, Wallace, Coors, Autumn Leaf, Russel Wright, American Modern, Iroquois, etc.

Experts

Harvey Duke
577 Avenue Y
Brooklyn, NY 11235
Author of "Price Guide to Pottery and Porcelain"; covering 90 collectible American potteries with 22,000 items priced; $15 + P&H, call 800-726-0600; specializes in Ohio and West Virginia dinnerware made from the 1890s to 1950s.

Lorrie Kitchen
3905 Torrance Dr.
Toledo, OH 43612
ph: 419-475-1759 or 419-478-3815
web: http://www.dealersdirect.com/Dealer/Tucker/
With Dan Tucker specializes in American dinnerware such as Hall China, Fiesta, Blue Ridge and Shawnee; sells labels for Anchor Hocking or Owens Illinois glass kitchen canisters.

Susan & Al Bagdade
Country Peasants, The
1325 North State Parkway, Apt. 15A
Chicago, IL 60610
ph: 312-397-1321
fax: 312-543-2544
e-mail: ADBSDB@aol.com
Author of "Warman's American Pottery & Porcelain" (Krause).

Museums/Libraries

Everson Museum of Art of Syracuse & Onondaga County
401 Harrison St.
Syracuse, NY 13202
ph: 315-474-6064
Contains one of the most important collections of American ceramics.

Mark Twyford
Museum of Ceramics at East Liverpool
400 E. 5th St.
East Liverpool, OH 43920-3134
ph: 330-386-6001
Detailed exhibit of the local ceramic industry; "The East Liverpool, Ohio Pottery District: Identification of Manufacturers & Marks" by Wm. Gates, Jr. and Dana Ormerod can be obtained by contacting the museum.

Periodicals

Teri Steele, Ed.
Depression Glass Daze, Inc.
Newspaper: Daze, The
P.O. Box 57
Otisville, MI 48463-0057
ph: 810-631-4593 or 800-336-9927
fax: 810-631-4567
web: http://www.thedaze.com
A monthly newspaper catering to the dealers and collectors of glass, china and pottery from the 1920s and 1930s.

Art Deco

Museums/Libraries

Megan Allen
Cowan Pottery Museum at the Rocky River Public Library
1600 Hampton Rd.
Rocky River, OH 44116-2699
ph: 440-333-7610
e-mail: allenme@oplin.lib.oh.us
web: http://www.rrpl.org/rrpl_cowan.stm
Features a collection of over 700 pieces by the artists of the Cowan Pottery Studio of Lakewood and Rocky River, Ohio, 1912-1932.

Cranbrook Art Museum
1221 N. Woodward Ave.
Bloomfield Hills, MI 48013
ph: 248-645-3323 or 248-645-3361
fax: 248-645-3324
e-mail: caa_info@cc.cranbrook.edu
web: http://www.cranbrookart.edu/museum/

Bennington

(see also CERAMICS [AMERICAN], Stoneware)

Experts

Gregg Ellington
Upper Loft Antiques
47 Columbus St.
Wilmington, OH 45177
ph: 937-382-4311
Buys, sells, trades and collects graniteware and American ceramics including mochaware, yellowware, spongeware, etc.

Museums/Libraries

Bennington Museum, The
W. Main St.
Bennington, VT 05201
ph: 802-447-1571
fax: 802-442-8305
web: http://www.bennington.com/museum/
One of the finest regional art history museums in the country; works by Grandma Moses, American glass, VT furniture, Bennington pottery, the oldest Stars & Stripes in existence, the 1925 luxury touring car "The Wasp", and much more.

George Ohr

Experts

Dr. Eugene Hecht
Adelphi University Physics Department
Adelphi University
Garden City, NY 11530
e-mail: genehecht@aol.com
Is available by mail to help authenticate George Ohr pottery; send SASE with inquiry; this is not an appraisal service.

Marty Shack
P.O. Box 25
Bellmore, NY 11710-0025
Is available by mail to help authenticate George Ohr pottery; send SASE with inquiry; this is not an appraisal service.

Museums/Libraries

George E. Ohr Arts & Cultural Center
136 G. E. Ohr St.
Biloxi, MS 39530
ph: 228-374-5547
e-mail: info@georgeohr.org
web: http://www.georgeohr.org/
Exhibits over 250 works by the potter George Ohr.

Illinois

Clubs/Associations

Norma Sams
Collectors of Illinois Pottery & Stoneware
Newsletter: Collectors of Ill. Pottery & Stoneware Newsletter
308 N. Jackson St.
Clinton, IL 61727-1320
ph: 217-935-6825
An organization for persons interested in collecting Illinois pottery; quarterly newsletter features photos and information.

Lewistown Pottery

Collectors

Scott Armstrong
RD 4 Box 115
Lewistown, PA 17044-9364
ph: 717-248-5285
Wants pieces marked Lewistown Pottery.

Limoges

Experts

Mrs. Raymonde Limoges
Raymonde Limoges
P.O. Box 73263
Puyallup, WA 98373-0263
ph: 253-845-3889
fax: 253-845-3889
e-mail: r.limoges@worldnet.att.net
Specializes in American Limoges china made in Sebring Ohio (1900-1955); mostly dinnerware; author of "American Limoges - A Collector's Guide."

Russel Wright Designs

(see also RUSSEL WRIGHT)

Collectors

Chad Sutton
1344 N. Westeview
Derby, KS 67037
e-mail: thesuttons@feist.com
web: http://www.feist.com/~thesuttons/rw/wright.html

Dealers

Robert & Nancy Perzel
Popkorn Antiques
3 Mine St.
P.O. Box 1057
Flemington, NJ 08822-1057
ph: 908-782-9631
Buys and sells American ceramics including Franciscan Apple, Dessert Rose, Metlox, Vernon plaids, Currier & Ives, Pennsbury, Puritan, Russel Wright designs, Stangl, Fulper, Homer Laughlin Fiesta.

Kathryn Wiese
Retrospective Modern Designs
3225 Yellowstone Dr.
Lawrence, KS 66047
ph: 785-832-0972
e-mail: modern@hialoha.net
web: http://www.retrospective.net/
Russel Wright dinnerware, metals and home designs sold exclusively on the internet and by phone; featuring American Modern, Casual by Iroquois, Harkerware, Knowles, Chase and more; no storefront sales.

Experts

Ann M. Kerr
P.O. Box 437
Sidney, OH 45365-0437
ph: 937-492-6369
fax: 937-492-6369
e-mail: raintree@bright.net
Wants Russel Wright dinnerware, stainless, chrome; Bauer art ware, etc.; author of "Collector's Encyclopedia of Russell Wright Designs", updated with 1993 prices; $21.95 ppd. from author.

Internet Resources

Chad Sutton
Russel Wright Web Page
1344 N. Westeview
Derby, KS 67037
e-mail: thesuttons@feist.com
web: http://www.feist.com/~thesuttons/rw/wright.html
Online resource for Russel Wright collectors; contains new and historical photos, sale/trade pages, and contacts with other collectors.

Southern Folk Pottery

Auction Services

Billy Ray & Susan Hussey
Southern Folk Pottery Collectors Society
Newsletter: SFPCS Newsletter
1828 N. Howard Mill Rd.
Robbins, NC 27325-7477
ph: 910-464-3961
fax: 910-464-2530
Formed for the purpose of educating and continuing the role of the self-taught Southern folk potter of the 18th and 19th centuries and today; holds two absentee auctions per year.

Steve Slotin
Slotin Folk Art Auction House
Newspaper: 20th Century Folk Art News
5967 Blackberry Lane
Buford, GA 30518
ph: 770-932-1000
fax: 770-932-0506
Leading venue for self-taught, Outsider, Folk Art and Southern folk pottery; published newspaper twice each year chronicling important happenings in the field of 20th century folk art as the most popular feature, New, True & Blue Artists.

Clubs/Associations

Billy Ray & Susan Hussey
Southern Folk Pottery Collectors Society
Newsletter: SFPCS Newsletter
1828 N. Howard Mill Rd.
Robbins, NC 27325-7477
ph: 910-464-3961
fax: 910-464-2530
Formed for the purpose of educating and continuing the role of the self-taught Southern folk potter of the 18th and 19th centuries and today; holds two absentee auctions per year.

Experts

Roy Thompson
19 Hubbard Run
Glastonbury, CT 06033-2323
ph: 860-633-3121
Author of "Face Jugs, Chickens and Other Whimseys."

Museums/Libraries

Billy Ray & Susan Hussey
Southern Folk Pottery Collectors Society Shop/Museum
Newsletter: SFPCS Newsletter
1828 N. Howard Mill Rd.
Robbins, NC 27325-7477
ph: 910-464-3961
fax: 910-464-2530
Formed for the purpose of educating and continuing the role of the self-taught Southern folk potter of the 18th and 19th centuries and today; holds two absentee auctions per year.

Stoneware

Auction Services

Richard Hume
American Stoneware Collectors
P.O. Box 281
Point Pleasant Beach, NJ 08742-0281
ph: 732-899-8707 or 732-295-9285
Collects, appraises, buys, sells, auctions American decorated stoneware: jugs, crocks, etc.; also Southern pottery, American redware, folk pots, etc.; conducts auctions twice a year in April and October.

Vicki & Bruce Waasdorp
Antiques & Americana
Newsletter: Stoneware
10931 Main St.
P.O. Box 434
Clarence, NY 14031
ph: 716-759-2361
fax: 716-759-2397
e-mail: waasdrop@antiques-stoneware.com
web: http://www.antiques-stoneware.com
Provides a mail and phone bid auction service for both collectors and dealers of Decorated American Stoneware; also appraisals, category history, and pertinent information on request; newsletter has post-sale auction prices.

Wayne Arthur
Arthur Auctioneering
563 Reed Road
Hughesville, PA 17737
ph: 570-584-3697 or 800-278-4873
Conducts specialized sales of decorated stoneware.

Clubs/Associations

American Stoneware Collectors Society
Newsletter: ASCC Newsletter
P.O. Box 281
Point Pleasant Beach, NJ 08742-0281
ph: 732-899-8707 or 732-295-9285
A growing society of stoneware collectors; call or write for more information.

Collectors

Ivy & Geoff Bean
8200 Mountain Laurel Ln.
Gaithersburg, MD 20879-1558
ph: 301-963-7469
e-mail: gibpbean@email.msn.com
Wants blue decorated American stoneware: crocks, jugs, jars, etc.; specific interest is in Western Pennsylvania region; buys, sells, trades all regions and areas.

Ed McDermott
1415 McKendree
Kevil, KY 42053
ph: 502-488-3420
e-mail: emcdermott@brtc.net
Wants stencil or scratch advertising stoneware from pre-1920 grocery and whiskey firms; especially wants whiskey jugs from small towns located in Southern and Western states; pays premium for saloon whiskey jugs.

Don Johnson
5110 S. Greensboro Pike
Knightstown, IN 46148-9596
ph: 765-345-5758
e-mail: djohnson@comsys.net
Buys, sells and collects all types of Indiana stoneware and pottery.

Steve Ketcham
P.O. Box 24114
Minneapolis, MN 55424-0114
ph: 612-920-4205
e-mail: s.ketcham@unique-software.com
Primarily interested in crocks, jugs, etc. which carry name of product or advertising such as liquor dealers, medicines, etc.; especially wants Red Wing stoneware; please send SASE with all inquiries.

James E. Kattner
P.O. Box 11132
Spring, TX 77391
ph: 281-986-6916 or 281-376-4826
Wants to buy Texas whiskey jugs which display the merchant's name and town; some may display saloon name and town; especially want Texas jugs, but will pay equally well for same from other Southern and Western states.

Bruce & Nada Ferris
Ev'ry Nook & Cranny
3094 Oakes Dr.
Hayward, CA 94542-1234
ph: 510-581-5285
fax: 510-581-4469
e-mail: Nada.Ferris@ncal.kaiperm.org
Wants mini advertising jugs, advertising 7" spongeband pitcher, advertising spongeware bowls, dometop stoneware jars; Ferris jugs from NY; any dated or holiday mini advertising jugs.

Scott Grandstaff
63742 Applegate Dr.
Happy Camp, CA 96039
ph: 530-493-2032

Dealers

Richard Hume
American Stoneware Collectors
P.O. Box 281
Point Pleasant Beach, NJ 08742-0281
ph: 732-899-8707 or 732-295-9285
Collects, appraises, buys, sells, auctions American decorated stoneware: jugs, crocks, etc.; also Southern pottery, American redware, folk pots, etc.; conducts auctions twice a year.

Greg Walsh
32 River View Lane
P.O. Box 747
Potsdam, NY 13676-0747
ph: 315-265-9111 or 800-371-9286
fax: 315-265-9222
e-mail: gwalsh@northnet.org
web: http://www.walshauction.com/
Stoneware dealer since 1979 wants to buy blue decorated stoneware of exceptional quality; also appraises.

Anthony & Barb Zipp
Anthony & Barbara Zipp Antiques
P.O. Box 725
Riderwood, MD 21139-0725
ph: 410-337-5090
Buys and sells quality, 19th century, blue decorated stoneware.

Barry Friedman
P.O. Box 55492
Valencia, CA 91385-0492
ph: 805-255-2365
Seeking stoneware bottles with maker's names; no unmarked bottles; also American only, please.

Experts

Vicki & Bruce Waasdorp
Antiques & Americana
10931 Main St.
P.O. Box 434
Clarence, NY 14031
ph: 716-759-2361
fax: 716-759-2397
e-mail: waasdrop@antiques-stoneware.com
web: http://www.antiques-stoneware.com
Provides a mail and phone bid auction service for both collectors and dealers of Decorated American Stoneware; also buys, sells, appraisals, category history, and pertinent information on request.

Museums/Libraries

Mark Twyford
Museum of Ceramics at East Liverpool
400 E. 5th St.
East Liverpool, OH 43920-3134
ph: 330-386-6001
Detailed exhibit of the local ceramic industry; "The East Liverpool, Ohio Pottery District: Identification of Manufacturers & Marks" by Wm. Gates, Jr. and Dana Ormerod can be obtained by contacting the museum.

Repro. Sources

Rowe Pottery Works
404 England St.
Cambridge, WI 53523
ph: 608-764-5435 or 800-356-5003
fax: 608-423-9826
e-mail: sales@rowepottery.com
web: http://www.rowepottery.com/
Produces authentic reproductions of 19th century salt-glaze stoneware plates, figurines, miniatures and steins; also wrought iron.

Stoneware (Red Wing Pottery)

Clubs/Associations

John & Kim Key
Red Wing Collectors Society, Inc.
Newsletter: Red Wing Collectors Newsletter
P.O. Box 50
Red Wing, MN 55066
ph: 800-977-7927 or 651-388-4004
e-mail: rwcs1@win.bright.net
web: http://www.redwingcollectors.org
Dedicated to the preservation of Red Wing and American pottery.

Collectors

Peter M. Naysmith
Mounted Rte. Box 444
Two Harbors, MN 55616
ph: 218-834-4770
Collector of Red Wing stoneware always looking for advertising pieces including moonshine jugs; will pay up to $50 for stoneware (jugs preferred) with advertising on the side and the name of the pottery on the bottom.

Ken & Dee Dee Gorgan
P.O. Box 184
Galesburg, IL 61402-0184

Charles W. Casad
801 Tyler Ct.
Monticello, IL 61856-2246
ph: 217-762-2303
Wants Red Wing crocks, beehive jugs, shoulder jugs, water coolers, commemorative pieces, Red Wing advertising pieces and any other unusual Red Wing pieces; mint or near-mint only, please.

Dealers

Byron Bush
3314 E. Overdale Dr.
Pearland, TX 77584
ph: 281-489-3003
e-mail: ByronBush@RedWingNet.com
web: http://www.RedWingNet.com
Experts specializing, buying and selling Red Wing ceramics.

Pat Puckett
Teacherage, The
1583 Ranch Road
San Bernardino, CA 92407
ph: 909-887-8383
fax: 909-887-8383
e-mail: tcherage@aol.com
web: http://members.aol.com/tcherage/index.html
Specializes in Red Wing and RumRill art pottery, stoneware and ephemera; visitors may post want ads or items for sale at no charge; also trades.

Internet Resources

Byron Bush
Wing Tips
3314 E. Overdale Dr.
Pearland, TX 77584
ph: 281-489-3003
e-mail: ByronBush@RedWingNet.com
web: http://www.RedWingNet.com
This site is committed to antique Red Wing artware; pottery, dinnerware, stoneware, crocks/crockery and anything else associated with Red Wing.

CERAMICS (AMERICAN ART POTTERY)

Appraisers

Tony McCormak
McCormack & Company
P.O. Box 49093
Sarasota, FL 34320
ph: 941-952-1244 or 941-350-2785
e-mail: birdkey@aol.com
web: http://www.antiqnet.com/McCormack
Collector, dealer, expert, appraiser specializing in American art pottery; always buying Rookwood, Grueby, Newcomb College, Teco, Marblehead, Overbeck; dated Van Briggle, George Ohr, Weller & Roseville pottery; member ISA.

Auction Services

Louise Luther
Skinner, Inc.
357 Main St.
Bolton, MA 01740-1104
ph: 978-779-6241
fax: 978-779-5144
e-mail: info@skinnerinc.com
web: http://www.skinnerinc.com
Established in 1964, Skinner Inc. is the fifth largest auction house in the US; has offices in Bolton and Boston, MA.

Barry Brooks
Pottery Auction
P.O. Box 224
Winter Park, FL 32789
ph: 407-740-8260
e-mail: admin@potteryauction.com
web: http://www.potteryauction.com
An online auction featuring American art pottery.

Mike Clum
Mike Clum, Inc.
7795 Cincinnati Zanesvile Rd.
Rushville, OH 43150
ph: 740-536-7421
Conducts periodic auctions specializing in American art pottery.

Riley Humler
Cincinnati Art Galleries
225 E 6th St.
Cincinnati, OH 45202
ph: 513-381-2128
fax: 513-381-7527
e-mail: mail@cincinnatiartgalleries.com
web: http://www.cincinnatiartgalleries.com/
Conducts specialty auctions of American art pottery including Rookwood, Van Briggle, Newcomb, Grueby, etc.

Don Treadway
Treadway Auctions
2029 Madison Rd.
Cincinnati, OH 45208
ph: 513-321-6742 or 800-526-0491
fax: 513-871-7722
e-mail: info@treadwaygallery.com
web: http://www.treadwaygallery.com
Specializes in the sale of Arts and Crafts pottery: Grueby, Teco, Newcomb, Van Briggle, Marblehead.

Jon Crisman, ISA
Jackson's Auctioneers & Appraisers
2229 Lincoln St.
Cedar Falls, IA 50613
ph: 319-277-2256
fax: 319-277-1252
e-mail: jacksons@jacksonsauction.com
web: http://www.jacksonsauction.com
Conducts specialty auctions of art pottery including Rookwood, Van Briggle, Roseville, Weller, Grueby, Teco, etc.

Clubs/Associations

Patti Bourgeois
American Art Pottery Association
Magazine: Journal of the AAPA
P.O. Box 834
Westport, MA 02790-0697
e-mail: PotsEtAl@aol.com
web: http://www.amartpot.org/
Content heavy information site for lovers of American art pottery including Mystery pot ID, "fakes" information, pottery events calendar, hundreds of selected hot links, and more.

Pat Sallaz
Pottery Lovers Reunion
Newsletter: Pottery Lovers Newsletter
4969 Hudson Dr.
Stow, OH 44224
e-mail: potlvrs@neo.lrun.com
Publishes a quarterly newsletter describing activities and plans for the upcoming Pottery Lovers Reunion and show.

Gordon Hoppe
Minnesota Art Pottery Association
10120 32nd Ave.
Minneapolis, MN 55441

Collectors

Bruce E. Thulin
P.O. Box 121
Ellsworth, ME 04605
ph: 207-667-5225
e-mail: thulin@acadia.net
Wants to buy pottery signed Grand Feu Pottery, Flame, Losanti, Pauleo, etc.

Bob Hut
P.O. Box 1495
Grand Central Station
New York, NY 10163-1495
ph: 800-321-7687
Wants to buy dated Van Briggle, artist-signed Rookwood, decorated Marblehead and Grueby; also any and all unusual pre-1930 high quality American and French Art Nouveau and Art Deco pottery (no Roseville, Fulper, Hull, McCoy).

Richard L. Sasicki
P.O. Box 3113
Glen Ellyn, IL 60138-3113
ph: 630-682-8706
e-mail: artware@sprynet.com
Wants to buy Van Briggle, Pine Ridge, Broadmoor, Coors Pottery, Teco, Grueby, Fulper, Newcomb, Arts & Crafts style and other American Art pottery; author of "The Collector's Encyclopedia of Van Briggle Art Pottery."

Dealers

John Keaveny
222 Fitchburg Rd.
Ashburnham, MA 01430
ph: 978-827-6809
Wants to buy Roseville, Weller, Rookwood, and other art potteries.

Jim Messineo
JMW Gallery
144 Lincoln St.
Boston, MA 02111-2523
ph: 617-338-9097
fax: 617-338-7636
e-mail: jmwgallery@tiac.net
web: http://www.jmwgallery.com/
Buys, sells and specializes along with co-owner Mike Witt in the Arts & Crafts movement. Mission furniture: Lifetime, Limbert, Stickley; American Art Pottery 1875 to 1950s: Grueby, Newcomb, Marblehead, etc.; metalwork, Roycroft.

Patti's Past Perfect Pottery
P.O. Box 1226
Westport, MA 02790
ph: 508-679-5910

Marvin McKee
65 Chase Rd.
Bangor, ME 04401-2633
ph: 207-945-3450
e-mail: mmckee@mint.net
Buys and sells American art pottery, especially Roseville.

William Banks
Classical Glass
P.o. Box 364
Wiscasset, ME 04578
ph: 207-882-9393
e-mail: inventor@lincoln.midcoast.com
web: http://lincoln.midcoast.com/~inventor
Specializing in antique and collectible glassware and art pottery; author of a price guide on Victorian opalescent glass.

Edward E. Stump
6 High St.
Mullica Hill, NJ 08062-9540
ph: 609-478-4488
e-mail: ractrale@fast.net
Wants Roseville and Weller art pottery.

David Rago
Perrault Rago Gallery
333 North Main St.
Lambertville, NJ 08530
ph: 609-397-9374 or 609-397-1802
fax: 609-397-9377
e-mail: info@ragoarts.com
web: http://www.ragoarts.com
Wants American art pottery, and Arts and Crafts items such as furniture and metal items by Stickley, Rohlfs, Wright, Roycroft, etc.

Bob Berman
441 S. Jackson St.
Media, PA 19063-3715
ph: 610-566-1516
Wants to buy American art pottery by Teco, Rookwood, George Ohr, Van Briggle, Cowan, Newcomb College, Fulper, Grueby, etc.

Martin Kramer
313 Arch St., Ste. 203
Philadelphia, PA 19106-1810
ph: 610-592-0103
fax: 610-592-0103
Wants to buy American art pottery: Rookwood, Fulper, Roseville, Weller, Cowan, UND, Van Briggle, SEG, Pewabic, Niloak, Marblehead, Hampshire, Grueby, Newcomb Art Pottery; also anything by The Cleveland School ceramic artists.

Caren Fine
11603 Gowrie Ct.
Potomac, MD 20854-3623
ph: 301-299-6886 or 301-299-2116
Wants art pottery: Overbeck, Newcomb College, Van Briggle, Grueby, Teco, Roseville, Marblehead, SEG, Ohr, Paul Revere, North Dakota School of Mines, Walrath, Tiffany, Robineau, Redlands, Arequipa, Cowan, sculptures.

Ken Forster
5501 Seminary Rd., Ste. 1311 South
Falls Church, VA 22041
ph: 703-379-1142
Dealer in American art pottery and

tiles, specializing in American tiles from 1860 to 1940; also Art Nouveau, Art Deco, Georg Jensen silver, and American Modernism.

Stephanie Hull Winters
Classic Treasures
3232 Morgan Rd.
Temple, GA 30179
ph: 770-562-1332
e-mail: swinters@bellsouth.net
Buys, sells, collects American art pottery including Hull, McCoy, Shawnee, Stangl, Royal Copley, Red Wing, Frankoma, Haeger, Niloak, Weller, etc.

Hardy Hudson
Our Antiques Market
5453 Lake Howell Rd.
Winter Park, FL 32792-1033
ph: 407-657-2100 or 407-647-3454
e-mail: todiefor@mindspring.com
Buys and sells Grueby, Newcomb, Ohr, Weller animals/birds/garden ornaments, Roseville, Teco, Cowan figurals, Overbeck, S.E.G., Marblehead, Fulper, Arequipa, Owens, Clifton, Avon, Niloak Swirl, Kay Finch, Dedham, Rookwood, Pewabic.

Steve Traband
P.O. Box 7064
Saint Petersburg, FL 33734-7064
ph: 813-896-2308
Buys and sells American Art Pottery: Rookwood, Grueby, Newcomb, Teco, Marblehead, Fulper, Dedham, Hampshire, S.E.G.-O.B.K., early Van Briggle, etc.

Tony McCormak
McCormack & Company
P.O. Box 49093
Sarasota, FL 34320
ph: 941-952-1244 or 941-350-2785
e-mail: birdkey@aol.com
web: http://www.antiqnet.com/McCormack
Collector, dealer, expert, appraiser specializing in American art pottery; always buying Rookwood, Grueby, Newcomb College, Teco, Marblehead, Overbeck; dated Van Briggle, George Ohr, Weller & Roseville pottery; member ISA.

Tina & Mark Richey
Spotted Horse Collectibles
12141 Couch Mill Rd.
Knoxville, TN 37932-1102
e-mail: shcollect@aol.com
web: http://members.aol.com/shcollect/homepage.html
Collectors and dealers of American Art Pottery including Rookwood, Fulper, Niloak, Missionware, Cowan, Van Briggle, Weller.

Betty Powell
Pottery Place, The
P.O. Box 571
Columbus, OH 43085-0571
fax: 614-885-1962
e-mail: potteryplace@worldnet.att.net
Buys and sells American art pottery, specializing in Rookwood, Roseville, Arts & Crafts style.

Joan Wurmbrand
Good Buy Girls
176 S. Merkle Rd.
Columbus, OH 43209
ph: 614-231-9636
fax: 614-231-9656
e-mail: wurmbrand@aol.com
Buys and sells art pottery including Rookwood, Roseville, Van Briggle, Weller, Hull; also Desert Rose, Apple, Coronado, Franciscan.

Don Treadway
2029 Madison Rd.
Cincinnati, OH 45208
ph: 513-321-6742 or 800-526-0491
fax: 513-871-7722
e-mail: info@treadwaygallery.com
web: http://www.treadwaygallery.com

Connie Zeigler
Durwyn Smedley Antiques
431 Massachusetts Ave.
Indianapolis, IN 46204
ph: 317-822-0102
e-mail: smedley@iquest.net
web: http://www.smedley.com/smedley/
Buys and sells 20th Century design: Arts & Crafts era, Art Deco, Mid-Century Modern, upscale 50's; art pottery from all eras and designer dinnerware; the first Indiana antique shop in the World Wide Web.

Gary Moore
e-mail: gemoore@flash.net
web: http://www.flash.net/~gemoore/arkpotx.htm
Collector of Camark pottery, dealer in American art pottery, publisher of the National Association of Arkansas Pottery Collector's newsletter.

Kathy Flynn
Art Pottery Exchange
200 A Avenue
Coronado, CA 92118
ph: 619-435-4350
e-mail: akalmans@nassco.com

Sue Morse
Emma's Trunk
1701 Orange Tree Lane
Redlands, CA 92374-2857
ph: 909-798-7865 or 909-864-8445
fax: 909-798-7386
Wants to buy Clemison, Roseville, Weller, Hull, Bauer; marked pieces only; please call, write or fax for specifics on pricing.

Barry & Donna Williams
300 San Antonio Rd.
Santa Barbara, CA 93110-1316
ph: 805-964-4820
Special interest in Walrath, Newcomb, and Rhead pottery.

Bill Warmboe
1003 California Dr.
Burlingame, CA 94010
ph: 650-579-7908
Buys and sells art pottery: Catalina Island, Bauer, Roseville, Batchelder, Rookwood, Arequipa, Van Briggle, Fiesta, Weller, Teco, Rhead, Robertson, McCoy, Newcomb College, California Faience, Peters & Reed, Vernon Kilns.

Patricia Huerta
Another Man's Treasure
45 Palm Drive
Union City, CA 94587
ph: 510-487-5330
e-mail: patih@webtv.net

Michael Lindsey
Vintage American Pottery
116 S. Washington St.
Seattle, WA 98104-2522
ph: 206-682-6162
fax: 206-405-3561
e-mail: oiljars@aol.com
Wants collectible and discontinued American dinnerware and art pottery by Franciscan, Metlox, Heath, Fiesta, Russel Wright, Vernon, Roseville, Rookwood, Grueby, Teco, Weller, Catalina, Newcomb, Owens, Voulkos and many others.

Experts

Geraud Schultz
Antique Gallery, The
8523 Germantown Ave.
Philadelphia, PA 19118
ph: 215-248-1700
fax: 215-247-8411
Buys, sells, and specializes in Weller, Sicard, Roseville, Fulper, Cowan, Matt Morgan, Rookwood, Grueby, Pillin, California - all American art pottery.

Riley Humler
Cincinnati Art Galleries
225 E 6th St.
Cincinnati, OH 45202
ph: 513-381-2128
fax: 513-381-7527
e-mail: mail@cincinnatiartgalleries.com
web: http://www.cincinnatiartgalleries.com/
Rookwood is their specialty; also want Van Briggle, Newcomb, Grueby, etc.

Norman Haas
264 Clizbe Rd.
Quincy, MI 49082-9586
ph: 517-639-8537
Owns and manages the APEC (American Pottery, Earthenware & China) Show and Sale held annually in Springfield, IL in late summer.

Internet Resources

Barry Brooks
Pottery Auction
P.O. Box 224
Winter Park, FL 32789
ph: 407-740-8260
e-mail: admin@potteryauction.com
web: http://www.potteryauction.com
Online person-to-person auction specializing in American art pottery.

Museums/Libraries

Everson Museum of Art of Syracuse & Onondaga County
401 Harrison St.
Syracuse, NY 13202
ph: 315-474-6064

Zanesville Art Center
620 Military Rd.
Zanesville, OH 43701
ph: 740-452-0741
fax: 740-452-0797
e-mail: zac@zanesvilleoh.com
web: http://www.zanesvilleoh.com/art/zac/

Cincinnati Art Museum
Eden Park
Cincinnati, OH 45202
ph: 513-721-5204
e-mail: cincyart@fuse.net
web: http://www.cincinnatiartmuseum.com/

Newcomb Art Gallery
1229 Broadway
New Orleans, LA 70118
ph: 504-865-5327
e-mail: webmaster@tulane.edu
web: http://www.newcomb.tulane.edu/

American Art Clay Co.

Experts

Virginia Heiss
7777 N. Alton Ave.
Indianapolis, IN 46268-7901
ph: 317-875-6797
Specializes in pottery made by the American Art Clay Co., Indianapolis, IN.

Clewell Pottery

Museums/Libraries

Jan McLean, Ex. Dir
Jesse Besser Museum
491 Johnson St.
Alpena, MI 49707
ph: 517-356-2202
fax: 517-356-3133
e-mail: jbmuseum@northland.lib.mi.us
web: http://www.ogdennews.com/upnorth/museum/home.html
Owns a large and important collection of Clewell Pottery.

Cowan Pottery Co.

Collectors

Ann M. Kerr
P.O. Box 437
Sidney, OH 45365-0437
ph: 937-492-6369
fax: 937-492-6369
e-mail: raintree@bright.net
Wants Cowan figural items done by Guy Cowan, Gregory, Schrekengast, Winter, etc.

Experts

Timothy & Jamie Saloff
P.O. Box 339
Edinboro, PA 16412
ph: 814-734-5189
fax: 814-734-7162
e-mail: jlsaloff@erie.net
web: http://www.erie.net/~jlsaloff
Authors of "The Collectors Encyclopedia of Cowan Pottery."

Museums/Libraries

Victoria F. Peltz
Cowan Pottery Museum at the Rocky River Public Library
Journal: Cowan Pottery Journal
1600 Hampton Rd.
Rocky River, OH 44116-2699
ph: 440-333-7610
e-mail: allenme@oplin.lib.oh.us
web: http://www.rrpl.org/rrpl_cowan.stm
Features a collection of over 700 pieces by the artists of the Cowan Pottery Studio of Lakewood and Rocky River, Ohio, 1912-1932.

Cowan Pottery Museum, Rocky River Public Library
1600 Hampton Rd.
Rocky River, OH 44116-2699
ph: 440-333-7610
e-mail: allenme@oplin.lib.oh.us
web: http://www.rrpl.org/cowan_associates.stm

Dedham Pottery Co.

Clubs/Associations

Jim Kaufman
Dedham Pottery Collectors Society
Newsletter: Dedham Pottery Collectors Society Newsletter
248 Highland St.
Dedham, MA 02026-5833
ph: 800-283-8070 or 781-329-8070
fax: 781-329-9538
e-mail: dpcurator@aol.com
web: http://www.dedhampottery.com/
Devoted to the history and study of Dedham and Chelsea Keramic Art Works pottery; published by Jim Kaufman, curator for Dedham pottery at the Dedham Historical Society, Dedham, MA; quarterly newsletter.

Collectors

Jane Lee
P.O. Box 134
Monmouth Junction, NJ 08852-0134
ph: 201-429-1531
Wants to buy Dedham dinnerware and service pieces produced in the late 1800s and early 1900s in Massachusetts; "Bunny" items preferred.

Dealers

Jim Kaufman
248 Highland St.
Dedham, MA 02026-5833
ph: 800-283-8070
e-mail: dpcurator@aol.com
web: http://www.dedhampottery.com/
Wants to buy Dedham pottery and Chelsea Keramic Art Works pottery and related papers or other historical information; all calls are welcome.

Experts

Jim Kaufman
248 Highland St.
Dedham, MA 02026-5833
ph: 800-283-8070 or 781-329-8070
fax: 781-329-9538
e-mail: dpcurator@aol.com
web: http://www.dedhampottery.com/
Wants to buy Dedham pottery and Chelsea Keramic Art Works pottery and related papers or other historical information; all calls are welcome.

Museums/Libraries

Dedham Historical Society
612 High Street
P.O. Box 215
Dedham, MA 02027-0215
ph: 781-326-1385
fax: 781-326-5762
e-mail: dhs@dedham.com
web: http://www.dedham.com/dhs/pottery.htm
The Society's museum displays the largest public collection of Dedham pottery as well as Chelsea Keramic Art Works pottery.

Repro. Sources

Potting Shed Inc., The
P.O. Box 1287
Concord, MA 10742
ph: 978-369-1382 or 800-722-2487
fax: 978-369-1416
Hand made Dedham reproduction pottery; each piece signed by the artist.

Fulper Pottery Co.

Collectors

Terry Seger
880 Foxcreek Ln.
Cincinnati, OH 45233-1462
ph: 513-941-9689
Wants to buy Stickley Brothers copper; also large examples of Fulper pottery.

Dealers

David Rago
Perrault Rago Gallery
333 North Main St.
Lambertville, NJ 08530
ph: 609-397-9374 or 609-397-1802
fax: 609-397-9377
e-mail: info@ragoarts.com
web: http://www.ragoarts.com

Robert & Nancy Perzel
Popkorn Antiques
3 Mine St.
P.O. Box 1057
Flemington, NJ 08822-1057
ph: 908-782-9631
Buys and sells American ceramics including Franciscan Apple, Dessert Rose, Metlox, Vernon plaids, Currier & Ives, Pennsbury, Puritan, Russel Wright designs, Stangl, Fulper, Homer Laughlin Fiesta.

Experts

Douglass White
Classic Interiors & Antiques
2042 N Rio Grande Ave., Ste. E
Orlando, FL 32804-5644
ph: 407-839-0004

Man./Prod./Dist.

Fulper Tile
P.O. Box 373
Morrisville, PA 19067
ph: 215-736-8512
For information on current production.

Gonder Pottery

Clubs/Associations

Jim & Carol Boshears
Gonder Collectors Club
Newsletter: Gonder Collector
917 Hurl Drive
Pittsburgh, PA 15236-3636
ph: 412-655-1380
e-mail: gondernut@aol.com

Collectors

Jim & Carol Boshears
917 Hurl Drive
Pittsburgh, PA 15236-3636
ph: 412-655-1380
e-mail: gondernut@aol.com

James Persinger
Happy's Antiques & Auctions
115 West Third St.
Ayden, NC 28513
ph: 252-746-2188
e-mail: persinger@starfishnet.com
web: http://www.happysemporium/gonderMuseum.htm
Collector and webmaster of the Gonder Pottery Museum on the Internet.

Dealers

Mike Landis
P.O. Box 814
Adamstown, PA 19501
ph: 888-248-2291
e-mail: landis2@desupernet.net
Buys and sells Gonder pottery; especially interested in larger pieces, pieces in gold crackle glaze, other crackle glazes, or red flambe.

Experts

Ron Hoppes
P.O. Box 21
Crooksville, OH 43731

John & Marilyn McCormick
6400 Payne St.
Shawnee Mission, KS 66226
Buys and sells; consultant to "The Official Price Guide to Pottery and Porcelain."

Internet Resources

James Persinger
Gonder Museum, The
115 West Third St.
Ayden, NC 28513
ph: 252-746-2188
e-mail: persinger@starfishnet.com
web: http://www.happysemporium/gonderMuseum.htm

Houghton/Dalton

Experts

Jim & Mira Houdeshell
JMJ Antiques
1801 N. Main St.
Findlay, OH 45840-3815
ph: 419-423-2895 or 419-424-4551
fax: 419-424-6974
Author of "Houghton and Dalton Pottery."

Muncie Pottery Co.

Experts

Brent & Donna Holloway
2006 S. Spruce St.
Muncie, IN 47302-1929
ph: 765-282-3772
e-mail: Gillclay@aol.com
web: http://members.aol.com/gillclay/
An advanced collector of Muncie pottery for over ten years; always buying including entire collections; can advise on current market prices and trends.

Newcomb College

Dealers

David Rago
Perrault Rago Gallery
333 North Main St.
Lambertville, NJ 08530
ph: 609-397-9374 or 609-397-1802
fax: 609-397-9377
e-mail: info@ragoarts.com
web: http://www.ragoarts.com
Wants American art pottery, and Arts

and Crafts items such as furniture and metal items by Stickley, Rohlfs, Wright, Roycroft, etc.

Clifford P. Catania
David Chase Gallery
518 Kimberton Road
Phoenixville, PA 19460
ph: 610-917-1167
web: http://www.davidchase.net/
Buy and sell Newcomb pottery; special interest in early, high-glaze pieces.

Caren Fine
11603 Gowrie Ct.
Potomac, MD 20854-3623
ph: 301-299-6886 or 301-299-2116
Wants to buy all decorated pieces, vases, plaques, lamps, jardiniers; special interest in large pieces, even if not perfect; all Newcomb College arts and crafts objects.

North Dakota

Clubs/Associations

Sandy Short, Mem. Ch.
North Dakota Pottery Collectors Society
Newsletter: North Dakota Pottery Collectors Society Newsletter
P.O. Box 14
Beach, ND 58621-0014
ph: 701-872-3236
fax: 701-872-3236
e-mail: csshortnd@mcn.net
Focuses on North Dakota potteries, e.g. Rosemeade (Wahpeton Pottery Co.), WPA, Dakota, UND School of Mines.

Collectors

Bill Carroll
RR 1, Box 62
Hope, ND 58046-9760
ph: 701-945-2416
fax: 701-945-2772
e-mail: BillND29@ictc.com
web: http://www.collectoronline.com/booths/booth-74/
Wants to buy North Dakota art pottery: Rosemeade, ND School of Mines, Dickota, 3 Tribes; please send info and asking price.

Owens Pottery Co.

Experts

Frank L. Hahn
P.O. Box 934
Lima, OH 45802-0934
ph: 419-225-3816 or 419-222-3816
fax: 419-227-3816
e-mail: ggb@wcoil.com
Expert and avid collector of J.B. Owens Pottery of Zanesville, OH; also buys, sells and appraises; has published a book on Owens Pottery.

Jeanette Stofft
45 12th St.
Tell City, IN 47586
ph: 812-547-5707
Co-managers along with Kristy & Rick McKibben of the Pottery Lovers American Art Pottery Show and Sale and co-authors of "Owens Pottery Unearthed."

Kristy & Rick McKibben
45 12th St.
Tell City, IN 47586
ph: 812-547-5707
Co-managers along with Jeanette & Marvin Stofft of the Pottery Lovers AMerican Art Pottery Show and Sale and co-authors of "Owens Pottery Unearthed."

Pisgah Forest

Collectors

Roland Sayers
305 N. Main St.
Hendersonville, NC 28792
ph: 826-697-6064
fax: 826-883-9562
Wants to buy Pisgah Forest and Nonconnah Pottery, most are dated; also wants Pisgah Forest cameo pieces with designs.

Red Wing

Experts

Ron Linde
500 South Water Street
Northfield, MN 55057-2060
ph: 507-645-6946
Collects and consultant to "The Official Price Guide to Pottery and Porcelain."

Ray Reiss
2144 North Leavitt
Chicago, IL 60647
ph: 773-384-3245 or 800-355-2324
fax: 773-384-3252
e-mail: rayreiss@earthlink.net
web: http://www.rayreiss.com/
Author of "Red Wing Art Pottery" (including pottery made for RumRill), classic American pottery from the 1930s through 1960s; interested in buying Red Wing art pottery; published Red Wing dinnerware price & identification guide.

Rookwood Pottery Co.

Auction Services

Don Treadway
Treadway Auctions
2029 Madison Rd.
Cincinnati, OH 45208
ph: 513-321-6742 or 800-526-0491
fax: 513-871-7722
e-mail: info@treadwaygallery.com
web: http://www.treadwaygallery.com
Specializes in the sale of Arts and Crafts pottery.

Collectors

Bob Hut
P.O. Box 1495
Grand Central Station
New York, NY 10163-1495
ph: 800-321-7687
Wants to buy Rookwood pottery, artist signed by Schmidt, Valentine, Daly, Toohey, Horsfall, McDonald, Laurence, Nichols, Wilcox, Storer, Wareham, Hurley, Shirayamadani, Artus Van Briggle, Conant, Robineau, Losanti, Natzler.

Man./Prod./Dist.

Art Townley
Rookwood Pottery Co.
10696 Hewitt Rd.
Brooklyn, MI 49230-9760
ph: 517-592-2169
Company makes new pottery.

Roseville Pottery Co.

Clubs/Associations

Jack & Nancy Bomm
Rosevilles of the Past Pottery Club
Newsletter: Roseville Connection
P.O. Box 656
Clarcona, FL 32710-0656
ph: 407-294-3980
fax: 407-294-7836
e-mail: rosepast@bellsouth.net
web: http://members.tripod.com/~rosepast/
For Roseville pottery collectors, dealers, and enthusiasts; bi-monthly newsletter contains articles, buy/sell/trade ads, commentary, collector profiles, etc.; complete information on all aspects of Roseville Pottery.

Roseville Historical Society
91 Main St.
Roseville, OH 43777
ph: 740-697-7127
e-mail: pchs@netpluscom.com
web: http://www.netpluscom.com/~pchs/rosevill.htm

Andrew E. Thomas, Pres.
Valley of the Sun Roseville Collectors Club
Newsletter: Chasing the Clay
4681 North 84th Way
Scottsdale, AZ 85251-1864
ph: 888-255-0664 or 480-947-5693
fax: 480-994-4382
Meets quarterly in collectors' homes or local restaurants; purpose is to increase level of knowledge regarding Roseville; welcomes collectors, dealers and all Roseville enthusiasts.

Collectors

Todd P. Violette
P.O. Box 2594
Waterville, ME 04901-2594
ph: 207-873-8898
Wants Roseville Pottery pieces: vases, umbrella stands, pedestals.

John Overton
3601 Connecticut Ave. NW, Ste. 609
Washington, DC 20008
ph: 202-244-2609

Jack & Nancy Bomm
P.O. Box 656
Clarcona, FL 32710-0656
ph: 407-294-3980
fax: 407-294-7836
e-mail: rosepast@bellsouth.net
web: http://members.tripod.com/~rosepast/

Andrew E. Thomas
Chasing the Clay
4681 North 84th Way
Scottsdale, AZ 85251-1864
ph: 888-255-0664 or 480-947-5693
fax: 480-994-4382
Buys, sells, trades all patterns of Roseville pottery from Apple Blossom to Zephyr Lily; any condition from mint to severely damaged; the larger and older the better.

Dealers

Debbie Woolley
Favorite Past-Times
6 Main Hill
Bridgton, ME 04009
ph: 207-647-5286
e-mail: woolley@maine-antiques.com
web: http://www.maine-antiques.com/fpt/Index/
Buys and sells authentic Roseville pottery.

Marvin McKee
65 Chase Rd.
Bangor, ME 04401-2633
ph: 207-945-3450
e-mail: mmckee@mint.net
Buys and sells American art pottery, especially Roseville.

Randy Monsen
Monsen & Baer Inc.
P.O. Box 529
Vienna, VA 22183-0529
ph: 703-938-2129
fax: 703-242-1357
e-mail: monsenbaer@erols.com

Experts

Tom Rago
716 Silver Court
Hamilton Square, NJ 08690
Buys and sells; consultant to "The Official Price Guide to Pottery and Porcelain."

Gordon Hoppe
10120 32nd Ave.
Minneapolis, MN 55441
Buys and sells; consultant to "The Official Price Guide to Pottery and Porcelain."

John W. Humphries
P.O. Box 965
Los Molinos, CA 96055-0965
Author of "A Price Guide to Roseville Pottery by the Numbers"; does radio talk shows.

San Jose Pottery

Experts

Susan Frost
806 Rosedale Terrace
Austin, TX 78704-3159
ph: 512-447-2575 or 512-447-0407
e-mail: Reuter@io.com
web: http://www.io.com/~reuter/
Researches and collects San Jose Pottery, San Jose Mission Crafts, Mexican Arts & Crafts, Inc., and other related San Antonio pottery and tiles.

Van Briggle Pottery Co.

Clubs/Associations

Van Briggle Collectors Society
600 S. 21st St.
Colorado Springs, CO 80901
ph: 719-633-7729 or 800-847-6341
fax: 719-633-7720
e-mail: VANpottery@aol.com
web: http://electricstores.com/pottery/default.htm
A company sponsored club; members receive quarterly newsletter, logo tile, product catalog.

Dealers

Gary Lickver
P.O. Box 1778
San Marcos, CA 92079-1778
ph: 760-744-5686
Buys, sells, collects 1901-1940 Van Briggle art pottery; at most quality indoor antique shows in California.

Experts

Richard L. Sasicki
P.O. Box 3113
Glen Ellyn, IL 60138-3113
ph: 630-682-8706
e-mail: artware@sprynet.com
Author of "The Collector's Encyclopedia of Van Briggle Art Pottery."

Scott Nelson
P.O. Box 6081
Santa Fe, NM 87502-6081
ph: 505-986-1176
Wants early and dated Van Briggle, decorated North Dakota, Hylong, and any fine pottery, damage OK if priced accordingly; consultant to "The Official Price Guide to Pottery and Porcelain," author of book on Van Briggle.

Man./Prod./Dist.

Van Briggle Pottery Co.
600 S. 21st St.
Colorado Springs, CO 80901
ph: 719-633-7729 or 800-847-6341
fax: 719-633-7720
e-mail: VANpottery@aol.com
web: http://electricstores.com/pottery/default.htm
In continuous operation since 1899. Free tour through production facility. Showroom for retail sales of beautiful pottery figurines and tiles.

Weller Pottery Co.

Internet Resources

WellerPottery.com
e-mail: webmaster@wellerpottery.com
web: http://www.wellerpottery.com
An online Weller museum.

CERAMICS (AMERICAN DINNERWARE)

(see also DINNERWARE; MODERNISM)

Collectors

Dave Folckemer
RD2 Box 394
Hollidaysburg, PA 16648-9200
ph: 814-696-0301
e-mail: mcfol@nb.net
Advisor to "Warman's" for Royal China.

Dealers

Karin Stafford
Great American Dinnerware
P.O. Box 4202
Burlington, VT 05406
ph: 802-660-9570
e-mail: karins@together.net
web: http://homepages.together.net/~karins/gad.htm
Collector, dealer specializing in American dinnerware and pottery produced from the 1930s to the 1960s.

Carolyn Brooks
Neat Stuff
7808 Scotia Dr.
Dallas, TX 75248-3115
ph: 972-404-1951
fax: 972-404-1870
e-mail: carolyn@neatstuff2.com
web: http://www.neatstuff2.com/
Specializes in Franciscan handpainted dinnerware, Fiestaware, Coors Rosebud.

Joanne Jasper
28005 Balkins Dr.
Agoura Hills, CA 91301-1801
ph: 818-597-0234
fax: 818-597-9503
Author of "The Collectors Encyclopedia of Homer Laughlin China" (Collector Books); autographed copies available; buys and sells Home Laughlin Decorated china and turn of the century American china.

Experts

Harvey Duke
577 Avenue Y
Brooklyn, NY 11235
Author of "Price Guide to Pottery and Porcelain"; covering 90 collectible American potteries with 22,000 items priced; $15 + P&H, call 800-726-0600; specializes in Ohio and West Virginia dinnerware made from the 1890s to 1950s.

Blair Ceramics

Collectors

Lori Hinterleiter
P.O. Box 9394
Arlington, VA 22219
ph: 703-729-1310
e-mail: lhinterl@aol.com
Wants to buy Blair Ceramics in all patterns.

Buffalo Pottery Co.

Collectors

Fred & Lila Schrader
2025 Highway 199
Crescent City, CA 95531
ph: 707-458-3525
Wants to buy Buffalo pottery: Deldare, Blue Willow, jugs and pitchers, game and fish sets.

Experts

Phillip M. Sullivan
P.O. Box 69
South Orleans, MA 02662
Collector and consultant to "The Official Price Guide to Pottery and Porcelain."

Vi & Si Altman
Vi & Si's Antiques
39 Spice Bush
Williamsville, NY 14221
ph: 716-688-6925
Buys, sells, appraises and specializes in all ceramic items marked Buffalo Pottery Co. and Buffalo China; authors of "The Book of Buffalo Pottery" $30.50 ppd.

Man./Prod./Dist.

Buffalo China, Inc./Oneida Food Service
658 Bailey Ave.
Buffalo, NY 14206
ph: 716-824-8515 or 800-828-7033

Buffalo Pottery Co. (Deldare)

Collectors

John & Joanna Kille
1319 Farley Court South
Arnold, MD 21012
ph: 410-757-8118
Wants to buy Emerald Deldare; also wants Dr. Syntax items, especially wants "Dr. Syntax Returns Home" humidor.

Coors Porcelain Co.

Collectors

Ed Bour
6110 W Pleasant Ridge Rd., #4771
Arlington, TX 76016
Wants Coors Pottery items: vases, Rosebud, Rockmount, Thermoporcelain, etc.

Jo Ellen Winther
8449 W. 75th Way
Arvada, CO 80005-4533
ph: 800-872-2345 or 303-421-2371
fax: 303-431-5350
e-mail: repofam@aol.com

Experts

Robert Schneider
3808 Carr Pl. N.
Seattle, WA 98103-8126
ph: 206-632-1144
Author of "Coors Rosebud Pottery"; general knowledge of all Coors Pottery and thermo-porcelain including Rosebud, Rockmount, Mello-Tone, Coorado and Art Vases.

Periodicals

Robert Schneider
Newsletter: Coors Pottery Newsletter
3808 Carr Pl. N.
Seattle, WA 98103-8126
ph: 206-632-1144

Gladding-McBean/Franciscan

Clubs/Associations

James Elliot
Franciscan Pottery Collectors Society
Newsletter: Franciscan Newsletter
8412 5th Ave. NE
Seattle, WA 98115
ph: 206-525-8818
fax: 206-362-5520
e-mail: gmcb@ix.netcom.com
web: http://www.gmcb.com/franciscan/
Club is devoted to the preservation of the history of Gladding McBean and Franciscan Ware.

Dealers

Alan Phair
Alan's Antiques
P.O. Box 30373
Long Beach, CA 90853-0373
ph: 562-983-7020
e-mail: AlanPhair@aol.com
Buys pieces marked "Catalina Pottery" made by Gladding-McBean; shells and some pieces marked with blue ink stamp "MADE IN U.S.A."; G.M.B., Franciscan and Catalina Pottery advertising items and price lists; also Franciscan dinnerware.

Experts

Marv Fogleman
1914 West Carriage Dr.
Santa Ana, CA 92704
Buys and sells; consultant to "The Official Price Guide to Pottery and Porcelain."

James Elliot
8412 5th Ave. NE
Seattle, WA 98115
ph: 206-525-8818
fax: 206-362-5520
e-mail: gmcb@ix.netcom.com
web: http://www.gmcb.com/franciscan/
Buys and sells; consultant to "The Official Price Guide to Pottery and Porcelain."

Matching Services

Delleen Enge
Franciscan Dinnerware Matching
323 E. Matilija, Ste. 112
Ojai, CA 93023-2775
fax: 805-646-0927
Specializing in mail order sales of Franciscan (trade name used by Gladding McBean and Co.) china, earthenware, and stoneware; large inventory in stock; author of "Franciscan Ware" and "Embossed and Handpainted Franciscan."

Gorham

Man./Prod./Dist.

Gorham, Inc.
100 Lenox Dr.
Lawrenceville, NJ 08648
ph: 609-896-2800 or 800-635-3669
web: http://www.lenox.com
Sterling and stainless steel flatware, sterling and silverplated hollowware; fine china, crystal stemware, giftware and dolls; a division of Lenox Brands.

Hall China Co.

Clubs/Associations

Virginia Lee
Hall China Collector's Club
Newsletter: Hall China Collector's Club Newsletter
P.O. Box 360488
Cleveland, OH 44136
ph: 330-220-7456
web: http://www.chinaspecialties.com/hallnews.html
Association commissions Hall China to produce unique, limited edition items in the Autumn Leaf, Silhouette, Red Poppy, crocus and other patterns; newsletter published yearly; 2000+ members; send SASE for free information.

Experts

Fred Squicciarini
3360 Culver Rd.
Rochester, NY 14622
ph: 716-336-9294
Expert, collector of Hall China Co. Refrigerator Ware and china.

Elizabeth Boyce
38 Carlotia Dr.
Jeffersonville, IN 47130-5278
ph: 812-282-8697
Buys and sells; collecting Hall China for over 24 years; consultant to "The Official Price Guide to Pottery and Porcelain."

Jane & Don Warner-Smith
RR1, Box 94B
Farmersville, IL 62533
Buys and sells; consultant to "The Official Price Guide to Pottery and Porcelain."

Internet Resources

Marty Kennedy
Hall China Collectors Home Page
4711 SW Brentwood Road
Topeka, KS 66606
ph: 785-273-4981
e-mail: mkennedy@cjnetworks.com
web: http://www.inter-services.com/HallChina/
Comprehensive services for Hall China collectors and dealers; site includes items for sale, bulletin board, classified ads, item identification services, historical information.

Hall China Co./Autumn Leaf

Clubs/Associations

Frances Downing
National Autumn Leaf Collectors Club
P.O. Box 162961
Fort Worth, TX 76161-0961

Dealers

Virginia Lee
China Specialties, Inc.
P.O. Box 361280
Strongsville, OH 44136
ph: 330-220-7456
web: http://www.chinaspecialties.com/
Specializes in the Autumn Leaf pattern.

Experts

Harvey Duke
577 Avenue Y
Brooklyn, NY 11235
Author of "Superior Quality Hall China" and "Hall 2", the authoritative books on the Hall China Company; each is $16.95 ppd.; Price Update is $8.50 ppd.

Margaret & Kenn Whitmyer
P.O. Box 30806
Columbus, OH 43230
e-mail: junquer9@idt.net
web: http://www.kandmantiques.com
Author of "The Collector's Guide to Hall China."

Ben Moulton
300 West York Dr.
Terre Haute, IN 47802-4492
ph: 812-234-3870
Specializes in Hall China: refrigerator ware, kitchenware, dinnerware, novelties, tea pots, etc.

Jo Cunningham
535 E. Normal
Springfield, MO 65807-1659
ph: 417-831-1320
Author of "The Autumn Leaf Story," "The Collectors' Encyclopedia of American Dinnerware," and "The Best of Collectible Dinnerware."

Man./Prod./Dist.

Hall China Company, The
1 Anna Street
East Liverpool, OH 43920
ph: 330-385-2900 or 800-445-4255
fax: 330-385-6185
e-mail: custserv@hallchina.com
web: http://www.hallchina.com/
Maker of Hall China since 1903.

Homer Laughlin China Co.

Clubs/Associations

Matthew Whalen
Homer Laughlin China Collectors Association
Magazine: Dish, The
P.O. Box 26021
Arlington, VA 22215-6201
ph: 500-674-5222
e-mail: hlcaa-info@mediumgreen.com
web: http://www.mediumgreen.com/hlcca/
For collectors of Homer Laughlin China Company dinnerware including Fiestaware; provides educational material and resources to collectors, dealers, museums, and other interested parties; quarterly magazine.

Dealers

Edward E. Stump
6 High St.
Mullica Hill, NJ 08062-9540
ph: 609-478-4488
e-mail: ractrale@fast.net
Specializes in Homer Laughlin China Company's Fiesta, Harlequin and Riviera patterns; buying and selling.

Experts

Michael Haas
Rte. 46E Box 106
Buttzville, NJ 07829
ph: 908-453-2918
Buys and sells; consultant to "The Official Price Guide to Pottery and Porcelain."

Matthew Whalen
P.O. Box 26021
Arlington, VA 22215-6201
ph: 500-674-5222
e-mail: hlcaa-info@mediumgreen.com
web: http://www.mediumgreen.com/hlcca/
Specialist in dinnerware made by the Homer Laughlin China Company.

Jo Cunningham
535 E. Normal
Springfield, MO 65807-1659
ph: 417-831-1320
Author of "Homer Laughlin China - A Giant Among Dishes 1873-1939)."

Joanne Jasper
28005 Balkins Dr.
Agoura Hills, CA 91301-1801
ph: 818-597-0234
fax: 818-597-9503
Author of "The Collectors Encyclopedia of Homer Laughlin China" (Collector Books); autographed copies available; buys and sells Home Laughlin Decorated china and turn of the century American china.

Man./Prod./Dist.

Homer Laughlin Co., The
6th & Harrison Sts.
Newell, WV 26050
ph: 304-387-1300 or 800-452-4462
fax: 304-387-0593
e-mail: hlc@hlchina.com
web: http://www.hlchina.com/
Vitrified china and ironstone dinnerware; web site has a page for collectors.

Periodicals

Richard Racheter, Ed.
Newsletter: Laughlin Eagle, The
1270 63rd Terrace So.
Saint Petersburg, FL 33705-5842
ph: 727-867-3982
fax: 727-867-3982
Published quarterly.

Homer Laughlin/Fiesta

Auction Services

Ronald E. Kay
P.O. Box 15383
Machesney Park, IL 61115-5383
ph: 815-282-3104 or 815-282-2585
fax: 815-282-3179
Conducts annual Fiesta auction.

Clubs/Associations

Virginia Lee
Fiesta Collectors Club
Newsletter: Fiesta Collectors Quarterly
P.O. Box 471
Valley City, OH 44280
ph: 330-220-7456
web: http://www.chinaspecialties.com/fiesta.html
The original association for Fiesta Collectors, now in its fourth year; newsletter dedicated to Fiesta, Harlequin Riviera and other 1930s to 1970s solid-glazed dinnerware from the Newell/East Liverpool region; buy and sell ads.

Ronald E. Kay, Pres.
Fiesta Club of America, Inc.
Newsletter: Fiesta Club of America Newsletter
P.O. Box 15383
Machesney Park, IL 61115-5383
ph: 815-282-3104 or 815-282-2585
fax: 815-282-3179
Club objective is to promote Fiesta while having fun; club meetings, newsletter; annual convention; send LSASE for sample newsletter.

Collectors

Michael Fellenzer
P.O. Box 551081
Indianapolis, IN 46205-1081
e-mail: felenzer@in.net
web: http://www.in.net/~felenzer/
Fiestaware collector and specialist; website has general information regarding Fiesta dinnerware produced by the Homer Laughlin China factory; photos, links, etc.

Dealers

Jay McKinsey
ph: 405-946-5385
e-mail: mckinsey@flash.net
web: http://www.flash.net/~mckinsey/
Buys and sells Fiestaware and Franciscan.

Fred & Linda Suzman
Suzman's Antiques
P.O. Box 301
Rehoboth, MA 02769
ph: 508-252-5729
e-mail: suzmanf@ride.ri.net
Buys and sells Depression glass and Fiestaware.

Larry Sherman
Fiesta Dish
12 Skip Lane
Burlington, CT 06013
ph: 860-675-3159
e-mail: fiestadish@aol.com
web: http://members.aol.com/FiestaDish/index.html
Buys and sells original 1950s colors of Fiesta; website has a listing and prices of pieces for sale; mail order only.

Helene Guarnaccia
52 Coach Lane
Fairfield, CT 06430
ph: 203-374-6034

Gus Gustafson
Buttzville Center
Rte. 46E Box 106
Buttzville, NJ 07829-9999
ph: 908-453-2918
Buys and sells, specializes in Homer Laughlin China Company's Fiesta pattern; consultant to "The Official Price Guide to Pottery and Porcelain."

Robert & Nancy Perzel
Popkorn Antiques
3 Mine St.
P.O. Box 1057
Flemington, NJ 08822-1057
ph: 908-782-9631
Buys and sells American ceramics including Franciscan Apple, Dessert Rose, Metlox, Vernon plaids, Currier & Ives, Pennsbury, Puritan, Russel Wright designs, Stangl, Fulper, Homer Laughlin Fiesta.

Liz Kramar
Kramar's Kollectible Korner
P.O. Box 30
Elk Mills, MD 21920-0030
ph: 410-398-0105
e-mail: lizk@iximd.com

Chester Sturm
Fiesta Antiques
P.O. Box 1325
Harpers Ferry, WV 25425
ph: 304-535-2456
Specializing in American art pottery.

Mick & Lorna Chase
Fiesta Plus
380 Hawkins Crawford Rd.
Cookeville, TN 38501-6658
ph: 931-372-8333
Buys and sells Fiesta, Franciscan USA, Metlox, Lu Ray, Vernon Kilns, Harlequin, Riviera, Kitchen Kraft; ships anywhere; ironclad money back guarantee; credit cards welcome.

Virginia Lee
China Specialties, Inc.
P.O. Box 361280
Strongsville, OH 44136
ph: 330-220-7456
web: http://www.chinaspecialties.com/
Buys and sells Fiesta, all colors and all pieces; carries full line of new Fiesta as well.

Experts

Ronald E. Kay
P.O. Box 15383
Machesney Park, IL 61115-5383
ph: 815-282-3104 or 815-282-2585
fax: 815-282-3179
Has written price guide for the club and has traveled throughout the US giving appraisals of vintage Fiesta.

Internet Resources

R. L. Steeves
Fiesta Pages for Collectors
e-mail: rlsteeves@cyberzone.net
web: http://www3.edgenet.net/rlsteeves/index.htm
Collector with a great website: the story of Fiesta, Fiesta color chart, web pages to other collectors of Fiesta, sources of Fiesta, Fiesta for sale or trade, images of vintage and new Fiesta.

Matthew Whalen
mediumgreen.com
734 S. 26th St.
Arlington, VA 22202
e-mail: fiesta@mediumgreen.com
web: http://www.mediumgreen.com
Online resource for the Fiesta collector; descriptions and pictures of items, suggested pricing, bulletin board, database to keep track of your current collection and its value.

Joe & Michele Boeckholt
FiestaWire
5348A Russell
Shawnee Mission, KS 66202
ph: 913-722-3672
e-mail: fiestawire@bigplanet.com
web: http://www.myplanet.net/fiestawire/
An Internet resource with links to Fiestaware and related collectibles.

Candy Fagerlin
Fiesta Fanatic @ Work
c/o QL Capital
5161 "C" CLayton Road
Concord, CA 94521
e-mail: fiestafanatic@fiestafanatic.com
web: http://www.fiestafanatic.com/
A website devoted to vintage and reissue Fiesta dinnerware produced by Homer Laughlin China Co; up-to-the-minute news of soon-to-be released additions to the Fiesta line, photos, updated daily with answers on "How to Find Fiesta."

Repair Services

Fiestoration
4011 Butterfield Trail
Fayetteville, AR 72701
Specializing in the invisible restoration of all sizes of chips in FiestaWare.

Iroquois China Co.

Experts

Paul Beedenbender
1203 East Paris St.
Tampa, FL 33604
Collects and consultant to "The Official Price Guide to Pottery and Porcelain."

Metlox Potteries

Experts

Carl Gibbs, Jr.
P.O. Box 131584
Houston, TX 77219-1584
ph: 713-521-9661
Author of "Collector's Encyclopedia of Metlox Potteries"; autographed copies for $24.95 plus $3 postage.

Marv Fogleman
1914 West Carriage Dr.
Santa Ana, CA 92704
Buys and sells; consultant to "The Official Price Guide to Pottery and Porcelain."

Pennsbury Pottery Co.

Collectors

Mark Supnick
2771 Oakbrook Manor
Fort Lauderdale, FL 33332
ph: 954-578-8787
Author of "Shawnee Pottery", and "Collecting Hull's Little Red Riding Hood."

Dealers

Bret Foreman
West Coast Stangl & Pennsbury Connection
13720 Valley View Ave.
La Mirada, CA 90638
ph: 562-903-2396
Buys, sells and specializes in Stangl and Pennsbury pottery.

Experts

Joe Simone
6 Duchess Lane
Dayton, NJ 08810
Buys and sells; consultant to "The Official Price Guide to Pottery and Porcelain."

Pfaltzgraff Pottery Co.

Clubs/Associations

Vicki Quint
Pfaltzgraff America Collectors Club
Newsletter: America Messenger, The
2536 Quint Lane
Columbia, IL 62236
ph: 618-281-7963 or 314-791-8162
e-mail: quint@wholenet.net
web: http://clubs.yahoo.com/clubs/pfaltzgraffamericacollectors
Members interested in the "America" or "Americana" pattern of Pfaltzgraff dinnerware (made from 1983 to 1989.)

Collectors

Vicki Quint
2536 Quint Lane
Columbia, IL 62236
ph: 618-281-7963 or 314-791-8162
e-mail: quint@wholenet.net

Melody Schoeppel
401 South Walnut Street
P.O. Box 50
Pinckneyville, IL 62274
ph: 618-357-5123
fax: 618-357-6089
e-mail: ppd1@midwest.net

Experts

David Zeiger
P.O. Box 105
Spring Grove, PA 17362
ph: 717-632-5912
Buys and sells anything "Pfaltzgraff": Salt, Albany, and Bristle glazed stoneware Art Pottery, dinner ware patterns, old brochures and catalogs, etc.; consultant to "The Official Price Guide to Pottery and Porcelain."

Man./Prod./Dist.

Dave Walsh
Pfaltzgraff Co., The
140 East Market
York, PA 17401
ph: 717-848-5500 or 800-999-2811
fax: 717-846-1133
web: http://www.pfaltzgraff.com/
Begun in 1811 in York, PA, Pfaltzgraff manufactured cobalt-decorated salt-glazed stoneware, Bristol-glazed ware, blue sponge, yellowware, Art Pottery, kitchen and ovenware, etc.; today a leading manufacturer of ceramic dinnerware.

Matching Services

David Zeiger
P.O. Box 105
Spring Grove, PA 17362
ph: 717-632-5912
Matching and/or replacements for old and new Pfaltzgraff dinner ware patterns; also others upon request.

Pickard

Auction Services

Joy Luke
Joy Luke Auction Gallery
300 E. Grove St.
Bloomington, IL 61701-5232
ph: 309-828-5533
fax: 309-829-2266
e-mail: robert@joyluke.com
web: http://www.joyluke.com/
Conducts periodic auctions specializing in the sale of toys, banks, trains and dolls.

Clubs/Associations

Jackie Pope
Pickard Collectors Club
Newsletter: Pickard Collectors Club Newsletter
300 E. Grove St.
Bloomington, IL 61701-5232
ph: 309-828-5533
fax: 309-829-2266
e-mail: joyluke@aol.com
Organized to advance the knowledge of collectors and dealers about this fine porcelain hand decorated in America.

Dealers

Glenda Ridgway
P.O. Box 231
Anna, IL 62906
ph: 618-833-7971
Charter member, Pickard Collectors Club.

Experts

Alan Reed
Firstlight, Inc.
723 N. Linden Ave.
Oak Park, IL 60302
ph: 708-383-1817
fax: 708-383-9256
Author of the "Collector's Encyclopedia of Pickard China"; lists Pickard and all major Chicago china decorators.

Man./Prod./Dist.

Pickard China Co.
782 Pickard Ave.
Antioch, IL 60002
ph: 847-395-3800
fax: 847-395-3827
e-mail: Finest@pickardchina.com
web: http://www.pickardchina.com/
Fine china dinnerware and giftware; limited edition plates.

Porcelier

Clubs/Associations

Shirley Hall
Porcelier Collectors Club
Newsletter: Porcelier Paper, The
21 Tamarac Swamp Rd.
Wallingford, CT 06492-5529
ph: 203-265-5791
e-mail: ThePPLady@aol.com
For collectors of Porcelier dinnerware, service pieces and all-ceramic small electrical kitchen appliances; bi-monthly newsletter features information and pictures of patterns, new finds, and research; free ads for members.

Collectors

Shirley Hall
21 Tamarac Swamp Rd.
Wallingford, CT 06492-5529
ph: 203-265-5791
e-mail: ThePPLady@aol.com
Collectors of Porcelier china, coffee pots, teapots, service pieces and all-ceramic small electrical kitchen appliances.

Experts

Susan Grindberg
1412 Pathfinder Road
Henderson, NV 89014
ph: 702-898-7535
e-mail: porcelier@anv.net
Author of "Collector's Guide to Porcelier China;" buys and sells Porcelier china; especially interested in toasters, waffle irons, sandwich grills and percolators.

Periodicals

Eileen Holt
Antique Cupboard
e-mail: fdholt@aol.com
web: http://www.in1era.com/AntiqueCupboard/pottery.html

Red Wing

Collectors

Doug Way
1215 Packard
Ann Arbor, MI 48104
ph: 734-741-1349
e-mail: dway@mat.net
web: http://www.mindspring.com/~dway/town.html
Specializes in the Town & Country pattern dinnerware designed by Eva Zeisel for Red Wing Pottery.

Experts

Monna Erickson
1712 Harrison Court
Northfield, MN 55057
Collects and consultant to "The Official Price Guide to Pottery and Porcelain"; specializing in Red Wing hand-painted dinnerware.

Reed & Barton

Man./Prod./Dist.

Reed & Barton
144 W. Britannia St.
Taunton, MA 02780
ph: 508-824-6611 or 800-822-1824
fax: 508-822-7269
Produces china, crystal, silver, silverplate, and stainless flatware, collectible plates, bells, dolls, ornaments and accessories.

Royal China Co./Currier & Ives

Clubs/Associations

Dave Folckemer, Pres.
Currier & Ives Dinnerware Collectors Club
Newsletter: Currier & Ives Collectors' Newsletter
RD2 Box 394
Hollidaysburg, PA 16648-9200
ph: 814-696-0301
e-mail: mcfol@nb.net
For collectors all items made by the Royal China Co. of Sebring, OH, including Currier & Ives dinnerware.

Collectors

Dave Folckemer
RD2 Box 394
Hollidaysburg, PA 16648-9200
ph: 814-696-0301
e-mail: mcfol@nb.net
Advisor to "Warman's" for Royal China.

Eldon R. "Bud" Aupperle
29470 Saxon Rd.
Toulon, IL 61483-9206
ph: 309-896-3331
fax: 309-856-6005
Author of "A Collector's Guide for Currier & Ives Dinnerware by Royal China Co."

Experts

Jack & Treva Hamlin
RR 4 Box 150, Kaiser St.
Proctorville, OH 45669

Eldon R. "Bud" Aupperle
29470 Saxon Rd.
Toulon, IL 61483-9206
ph: 309-896-3331
fax: 309-856-6005
Author of "A Collector's Guide for Currier & Ives Dinnerware by Royal China Co."

Betsey Edmondson
Betsey's Collectibles
1404 Sylan Dr.
Plano, TX 75074
Buys and sells; consultant to "The Official Price Guide to Pottery and Porcelain."

Periodicals

Patti Street
Newsletter: Currier & Ives Newsletter
P.O. Box 504
Riverton, KS 66770-0504
ph: 316-848-3529
A newsletter especially for enthusiasts of Currier & Ives china by the Royal China Co. of Sebring, OH; also covers other china patterns by Royal China Co. as well as other Currier & Ives collectibles.

Scio Pottery

Man./Prod./Dist.

Scio Pottery Museum
38500 Crimm Rd.
P.O. Box 565
Scio, OH 43988
ph: 740-945-3111 or 740-945-3121
fax: 740-945-1575
e-mail: sciopackage@eohio.net
Antique dinnerware made by the Scio Pottery Company.

Southern Potteries/Blue Ridge

Clubs/Associations

Wanda Hashe
Blue Ridge Collectors Club
208 Harris St.
Erwin, TN 37650
ph: 423-743-9337
fax: 423-743-4629
e-mail: jwbh@prefered.com

Collectors

Linda Weeks
22 Stevens Ave.
Meredith, NH 03253-5855
ph: 603-279-3357
Wants to buy Blue Ridge - Homer Laughlin dishes.

Don & Susan Burkett
233 East Wesley Rd.
Atlanta, GA 30305
Your Southern Potteries and Blue Ridge ideas, questions and pictures are always welcome; please include a SASE if requesting a reply; consultant to "The Official Price Guide to Pottery and Porcelain."

Dealers

Diana E. Bullock
Bullock Antiques
P.O. Box 5427
Somerset, NJ 08875
ph: 732-846-1368
Buys and sells Blue Ridge/Southern Pottery dinnerware and Stangl dinnerware.

Mary & Ray Farley
B R Barn, The
1379 West Commerce
Lewisburg, TN 37091-3158
ph: 931-359-2906
fax: 931-359-2906
e-mail: rfarley@vallnet.com

Wanda Hashe
Main St. Antiques Mall
105 S. Main St.
Erwin, TN 37650
ph: 423-743-9337
fax: 423-743-4629
e-mail: jwbh@prefered.com

Experts

Norma Lilly
144 Highland Dr.
Blountville, TN 37617-5404
ph: 423-323-5247
Wants Blue Ridge china made by Southern Potteries, Inc.; any unusual form or pattern.

Susan Moore
51803 Windyridge Dr.
South Bend, IN 46628-9290
Collects and consultant to "The Official Price Guide to Pottery and Porcelain."

Periodicals

Bryan & Kim Snyder
Magazine: Blue Ridge Beacon Magazine
P.O. Box 629
Mountain City, GA 30562-0629
ph: 800-851-6481
e-mail: bksnyder@acme-brain.com
16 pages in full color; includes articles on collecting Blue Ridge, rare and unusual Blue Ridge, interesting Erwin history, interviews with Southern Potteries employees, old photographs and advertisements, new patterns, classifieds, etc.

Norma Lilly
Newsletter: National Blue Ridge Newsletter
144 Highland Dr.
Blountville, TN 37617-5404
ph: 423-323-5247
10 pre-punched pages; Q&A up-date, articles, new patterns, readers comment section; published bi-monthly.

Stangl Pottery Co.

(see also CERAMICS [AMERICAN FIGURES], Stangl Pottery Co.)

Dealers

Diana E. Bullock
Bullock Antiques
P.O. Box 5427
Somerset, NJ 08875
ph: 732-846-1368
Buys and sells Blue Ridge/Southern Pottery dinnerware and Stangl dinnerware.

Bret Foreman
West Coast Stangl & Pennsbury Connection
13720 Valley View Ave.
La Mirada, CA 90638
ph: 562-903-2396
Buys, sells and specializes in Stangl and Pennsbury pottery.

Experts

Robert & Nancy Perzel
Popkorn Antiques
3 Mine St.
P.O. Box 1057
Flemington, NJ 08822-1057
ph: 908-782-9631
Offers a Stangl Pottery dinner matching service; also Stangl birds and Artware; consultant to "The Official Price Guide to Pottery and Porcelain," "Schroeder's," and "Warman's."

Taylor, Smith & Taylor/LuRay

Collectors

Joe Zacharias
P.O. Box 99516
Raleigh, NC 27624-9516
ph: 919-848-6966
e-mail: IBUYLURAY2@aol.com
Wants LuRay PASTELS: chocolate/ straight-sided A/D pots, sugars, creamers; blue/green, 7" mini-platters; grey 36's bowls, chop plate; 8", 9", 10" LuRay Calendar plaques; LuRay backstamped items of ANY color; also ed ads, brochures.

Dealers

Edward E. Stump
6 High St.
Mullica Hill, NJ 08062-9540
ph: 609-478-4488
e-mail: ractrale@fast.net
Specializes in Taylor, Smith and Taylor Company's LuRay Pastels line.

Experts

Ray & Virginia Cramble
Antiques From Memory Lane
7340 Memory Lane Lane NE
Minneapolis, MN 55432-3217
Buys, sells, collects and appraises almost all Abingdon and rare LuRay.

Periodicals

Moira Forbes
Newsletter: LuRay Relay
P.O. Box 3512
Arlington, VA 22203
e-mail: mforbes@lewin.com
Quarterly newsletter for collectors of LuRay.

Vernon Kilns Co.

Collectors

Kevin H. Souza
Vernon Kilns Plaid Dinnerware Web Site
e-mail: vernonplaid@geocities.com
web: http://www.geocities.com/~vernonplaid/
Looking for Vernon Kiln Plaid collection.

Bill Stern
361 North Orange Dr.
Los Angeles, CA 90036

Dealers

Judi & Dave Thompson
1668 Melissa Way
Anaheim, CA 92802

Experts

Harold Mathews
24 Church St.
Honeoye, NY 14471
Consultant to "The Official Price Guide to Pottery and Porcelain."

Maxine Nelson
7657 E. Hazelwood St.
Scottsdale, AZ 85251-1510
Author of "Collectible Vernon Kilns" (out-of-print).

Bess Christensen
1313 East Locust Ave.
Lompoc, CA 93436-7442
Consultant to "The Official Price Guide to Pottery and Porcelain."

Periodicals

Newsletter: Vernon Views
P.O. Box 945
Scottsdale, AZ 85252
The newsletter for collectors of Vernon Kilns pottery; recent finds, free ads, interesting articles.

Wallace China Co.

Collectors

Terry Ahlberg
1000 Irvine Blvd.
Tustin, CA 92680-3527
ph: 714-730-1000 or 949-654-1331
fax: 714-730-1752
e-mail: emailit@earthlink.net
Wants the Westward Ho series in the following pattern: Rodeo, Pioneer Trails, Boots & Saddle, Longhorn, Little Buckaroo.

Experts

Marv Fogleman
1914 West Carriage Dr.
Santa Ana, CA 92704
Buys and sells; consultant to "The Official Price Guide to Pottery and Porcelain."

Warwick China Co.

Experts

Donald C. Hoffmann, Sr.
1291 N. Elmwood Dr.
Aurora, IL 60506
ph: 630-859-3435
Author of "Why Not Warwick," "Warwick A to W"; also advisor to Schroeder's Price Guide.

Watt Pottery Co.

Clubs/Associations

Dennis Thompson, Dir.
Watt Pottery Collectors USA
Newsletter: Spoutings
P.O. Box 26067
Cleveland, OH 44126-0067
ph: 216-235-8548
e-mail: dthomp@stratos.net
web: http://www.execpc.com/~wmhill/wpcusa2.html
Publishes original research on the Watt Pottery, its history and wares; provides identification of wares produced under trade names used by Watt and other potteries; national conventions in Cooksville, OH, home of Watt pottery.

Wendy Stinocher
Watt Collectors Association
Newsletter: Watt's News
P.O. Box 1995
Iowa City, IA 52244-1995
ph: 319-338-9181
web: http://www.execpc.com/~wmhill/wcapg1.html
A non-profit educational organization dedicated to the study and preserva-

tion of this unique segment of the pottery world.

Experts

Dennis Thompson
P.O. Box 26067
Cleveland, OH 44126-0067
ph: 216-235-8548
e-mail: dthomp@stratos.net
web: http://www.execpc.com/~wmhill/wpcusa2.html
Author of "Watt Pottery, a Collectors Reference with Price Guide" (Schiffer, 1994); 240 pages; 800 color photos; $43ppd from author; consultant to "The Official Price Guide to Pottery and Porcelain."

Dave & Sue Morris
3388 Merlin Rd., Ste. 351
Grants Pass, OR 97526
ph: 541-955-8411
e-mail: sue@wattpottery.com
web: http://www.wattpottery.com
Buys and sells Watt pottery; authors of "Watt Pottery - An Identification and Value Guide"; available from authors for $22 ppd.

CERAMICS (AMERICAN FIGURES)

Ceramic Arts Studio

Clubs/Associations

Jim Petzold
Ceramic Arts Studio Collectors Association
Newsletter: CAS Collector
P.O. Box 46
Madison, WI 53701-0046
ph: 608-241-9138
fax: 608-241-8770
e-mail: ceramics@execpc.com
Provides accurate information on authentic Ceramic Arts Studio (Madison, WI) works; quarterly newsletter with stories and memories of the Studio and the collecting experience; "Inventory Record & Price Guide" lists 800+ works; conventions.

Collectors

Tim Holthaus
P.O. Box 46
Madison, WI 53701-0046
ph: 608-241-9138
fax: 608-241-8770
e-mail: ceramics@execpc.com
Co-editor with of "CAS Collector"; wants to buy all Ceramic Arts Studio & Royal Copley creations including shakers, figurines, dolls, lamps, and metal art.

Dealers

Lana Walker
House of Storybook Antiques & Collectibles
ph: 408-866-5404
fax: 603-853-4508
e-mail: lanawalker@houseofstorybook.com
web: http://www.houseofstorybook.com/
Wants to buy Ceramic Arts Studio items.

Experts

Jim Petzold
P.O. Box 46
Madison, WI 53701-0046
ph: 608-241-9138
fax: 608-241-8770
e-mail: ceramics@execpc.com
Co-editor with of "CAS Collector"; wants to buy all Ceramic Arts Studio & Royal Copley creations including shakers, figurines, dolls, lamps, and metal art.

Florence

Clubs/Associations

Beth Dunigan
Florence Collectors Club
Newsletter: Florence Collectors Club Newsletter
P.O. Box 122
Richland, WA 99352-0122
ph: 909-683-1485 or 509-943-0971
e-mail: dunigan@3-cities.com
web: http://www.florenceceramics.simplenet.com/

Dealers

Mike & Bev
637 E. Main St.
Cottage Grove, OR 97424
ph: 541-942-3664

Experts

Sue & Jerry Kline
2070 Sugarwood Dr.
Kodak, TN 37764
ph: 423-933-4011
fax: 423-433-4492
e-mail: chintzlady@earthlink.net
web: http://www.sweetpea.net/
Buys and sells; author and consultant to "The Official Price Guide to Pottery and Porcelain" and "Schroeder's."

Jeanne Fredericks
12364 Downey Ave.
Downey, CA 90242-3556
ph: 562-861-4781
e-mail: jeenrob@aol.com
Collector and consultant to "The Official Price Guide to Pottery and Porcelain" and "The Florence Collectibles - An Era of Elegance" by Doug Foland.

Rita Bee
6960 Abel Stearns Ave.
Riverside, CA 92509
ph: 909-683-1485
e-mail: AR2Bee@aol.com
Editor of the "Florence Collector's Club Newsletter."

Kay Finch

Dealers

Sharlene Beckwith
Exclusively Dogs!
P.O. Box 1858
Upland, CA 91785-1858
ph: 909-946-1544
fax: 909-949-4796
Specializing in fine canine collectibles, especially Kay Finch dog figurines and any large or unusual Kay Finch animals, including cookie jars; also wants Kay Finch bronzes and dog jewelry.

Experts

Frances Finch Webb
1589 Gretel Lane
Mountain View, CA 94040-3704
ph: 650-968-0739
Author of "The New Kay Finch Field Identification Guide," available from author; keeper of FINCH archival and historic records; research consultant for other authors on Kay Finch.

Stangl Pottery Co.

(see also CERAMICS [AMERICAN DINNERWARE], Stangl Pottery Co.)

Clubs/Associations

Robert Runge, Pres.
Stangl/Fulper Club
Newsletter: Stangl/Fulper Club Newsletter
P.O. Box 538
Flemington, NJ 08822
ph: 908-995-2696 or 908-782-9631
e-mail: kenlove508@aol.com
web: http://www.stanglpottery.org/
Promotes Stangl/Fulper pottery, dinnerware, birds, animals.

Dealers

Liz Kramar
Kramar's Kollectible Korner
P.O. Box 30
Elk Mills, MD 21920-0030
ph: 410-398-0105
e-mail: lizk@iximd.com
Wants to buy Stangl birds.

Experts

Harvey Duke
577 Avenue Y
Brooklyn, NY 11235
Author of "Stangl Pottery", the most comprehensive and authoritative price and identification guide on Stangl; $22.45 ppd.

CERAMICS (AMERICAN PRODUCTION ARTWARE)

(see also COOKIE JARS; MODERNISM)

Auction Services

Michael Verlangieri
Verlangieri Gallery
P.O. Box 844
Cambria, CA 93428-0844
ph: 805-927-4428
fax: 805-924-0110
e-mail: michael@calpots.com
web: http://www.calpots.com
Periodic auctions of Bauer, Russel Wright, Gladding McBean, Catalina Island, Pacific, Sascha Brastoff, Matthew Addame, Metlox, Vernon Kilns, Franciscan, Modglins, Halderman, Camark, Brayton Laguna, Batchelder, and more.

Dealers

Dave DeWitt
Mad Dog Pottery
8712 N. Eastern Ave.
Oklahoma City, OK 73131
ph: 405-478-1725
e-mail: maddogpot@aol.com
Buys and sells Frankoma pottery; website updated weekly with new products.

Susan & Mark Wiskow
5214 F Diamond Heights #302
San Francisco, CA 94131
ph: 415-587-9133
fax: 415-239-5148
Buys and sells American-made pottery and glass figurines from the period 1920 to 1950.

Internet Resources

Sierra Bufe
American Pottery Exchange
e-mail: bufe@earthlink.net
web: http://home.earthlink.net/~bufe/APX/
A Place on the web for people to buy, sell, trade 20th century American pottery: Russel Wright, Fiesta, Franciscan, Lu-Ray, Ben Seibel, Harlequin, McCoy, Bauer, Stangl, Hall, Blue Ridge, Metlox, Vernon Kilns, Red Wing, etc.

Abingdon

Clubs/Associations

Elaine Westover
Abingdon Pottery Club
Newsletter: Abingdon Pottery Collectors Newsletter
210 Knox Hwy. 5
Abingdon, IL 61410-9332
ph: 309-462-3267
Sponsors annual show and flea market on the 3rd Saturday in August of every year.

Collectors

Don King
7474 Jason Ave. NE
Monticello, MN 55362-3000
ph: 612-295-8405
Wants Abingdon Pottery decorated pieces, tableware, salesman samples, cookie jars.

Dealers

Barbara Stevens
Some Where in Time Antiques
4490 Cricket Ridge Dr., #204
Holt, MI 48842
ph: 517-699-8372 or 517-337-4988
fax: 517-337-4560
e-mail: stevensg44@aol.com
Buys and sells Abingdon pottery.

Vicki Quint
Quintiques
2536 Quint Lane
Columbia, IL 62236
ph: 618-281-7963 or 314-791-8162
e-mail: quint@wholenet.net
Buys and sells Abingdon pottery.

Experts

Ray & Virginia Cramble
Antiques From Memory Lane
7340 Memory Lane Lane NE
Minneapolis, MN 55432-3217
Buys, sells, collects and appraises almost all Abingdon and rare LuRay.

Robert Rush
210 North Main St.
Abingdon, IL 61410
Collects and consultant to "The Official Price Guide to Pottery and Porcelain."

Elaine Westover
210 Knox Hwy. 5
Abingdon, IL 61410-9332
ph: 309-462-3267
Collects and consultant to "The Official Price Guide to Pottery and Porcelain."

American Bisque Company

Experts

Joyce Roerig
1501 Maple Ridge Rd.
Walterboro, SC 29488-9278
ph: 843-538-2487
fax: 843-538-4263
e-mail: ckejrn@lowcountry.com
Buys and sells; consultant to "Official Price Guide to Pottery & Porcelain"; founded in 1919, American Bisque Company produced florist ware, kitchenware, and cookie jars.

Arkansas Potteries

Clubs/Associations

Gary Moore, Pub.
National Association of Arkansas Pottery Collectors
Newsletter: Arkansas Pottery Exchange
e-mail: gemoore@flash.net
web: http://www.flash.net/~gemoore/arkpotx.htm
Will answer questions about Arkansas pottery such as Camark, Niloak and Ouchita pottery; please include LSASE with questions.

Bauer

Collectors

James L. Harmon
P.O. Box 25
Banks, OR 97106
ph: 503-324-7041
Wants to buy Bauer; Bauer ringware wanted in all colors; top dollar paid for black; bowls especially wanted.

Experts

Jack Chipman
P.O. Box 1079
Venice, CA 90294-1079
ph: 310-396-5320
e-mail: jchipman@amerimail.net
web: http://members.tripod.com/~ChipmanJ/chipman1.htm
Buys and sells; consultant to "The Official Price Guide to Pottery and Porcelain" (1992) and "Schroeder's Antiques Price Guide", author of "Collector's Guide to Bauer Pottery" (1997).

Internet Resources

Bauer Pottery Page, The
e-mail: DMagnon@aol.com
web: http://users.aol.com/Stadelbach/BauerPottery.htm

Periodicals

Magazine: Bauer Quarterly
P.O. Box 2524
Berkeley, CA 94702-0524
ph: 510-540-8960
e-mail: bauerpot@ix.netcom.com
A quarterly color magazine devoted to Bauer pottery; features articles and photos for Bauer enthusiasts, collectors and dealers; one subscriber describes the BQ as "historical, aesthetic, intelligent and a little irreverent."

Brush-McCoy Pottery

Experts

Martha & Steve Sanford
230 Harrison Ave.
Campbell, CA 95008
ph: 408-978-8408
Authors of "The Guide to Brush-McCoy Pottery."

California Potteries

(see also CERAMICS [AMER. PROD. ARTWARE], Bauer; CERAMICS [AMER. PROD. ARTWARE], Catalina Island Pottery; CERAMICS [AMER. PROD. ARTWARE], deLee; CERAMICS [AMER. PROD. ARTWARE], Hedi Schoop; CERAMICS [AMER. PROD. ARTWARE], Sascha Brastoff)

Dealers

Rick & Sharon Blumenthal
California Dreamin'
5436 Matilija Ave.
Van Nuys, CA 91401
ph: 818-781-7589
Buys, collects and sells Catalina, Howard Pierce, Roselane, Kay Finch, Hedi Schoop.

Experts

Jack Chipman
P.O. Box 1079
Venice, CA 90294-1079
ph: 310-396-5320
e-mail: jchipman@amerimail.net
web: http://members.tripod.com/~ChipmanJ/chipman1.htm
Buys and sells; consultant to "The Official Price Guide to Pottery and Porcelain" (1992), author of "Collector's Encyclopedia of California Pottery, 2nd Edition" (1999)

Steve Soukup
California Crazed
P.O. Box 7662
Van Nuys, CA 91406-7662
ph: 818-787-5990 or 818-781-9262
Buys and sells California pottery and tiles: Bauer, Catalina, Batchelder, Pacific Pottery, Romanelli, Vernon Kilns, Metlox, Meyers, Poxon, Padre, California Rainbow, Tropico Pottery, GMB, Brayton, etc.

Susan Cox
800 Murray Dr.
El Cajon, CA 92020
ph: 619-697-5922
e-mail: antiqfever@aol.com

Periodicals

Michael Verlangieri
Verlangieri Gallery
Newsletter: California Pottery Trader, The
P.O. Box 844
Cambria, CA 93428-0844
ph: 805-927-4428
fax: 805-924-0110
e-mail: michael@calpots.com
web: http://www.calpots.com
Features dealer ads, pottery news, pottery show coverage, and books on California pottery.

Camark Pottery Co.

Experts

Letitia Landers
Colony Publishing
P.O. Box 203
Camden, AR 71711
ph: 870-231-6861 or 870-836-3022
fax: 870-836-0127
e-mail: camark@cei.net
web: http://www.cei.net/~camark/
Expert, collector, author on Camark pottery which was made in Camden, AR from 1920s through 1960s; "Camark Pottery, An Identification and Value Reference," Vol. 1 & 2, price guide, photographs, catalog pages; $24.90 ea.

David Gifford
e-mail: gemoore@flash.net
web: http://www.flash.net/~gemoore/arkpotx.htm
Buys and sells; consultant to "The Official Price Guide to Pottery and Porcelain."

Cardinal China Co.

Collectors

Trish Claar
2621 Manor Court
Owings, MD 20736-9145
ph: 301-855-6531
Collector and consultant to "The Official Price Guide to Pottery and Porcelain."

Catalina Island Pottery

Collectors

Steven Hoefs
P.O. Box 1024
Avalon, CA 90704
ph: 310-510-2623
Wants to buy Catalina Island Pottery.

Walter Sanford
321 Redondo Ave.
Long Beach, CA 90814-2652
ph: 562-434-7253
fax: 562-434-6353
Buy, sells and specializes in ceramics produced by the Catalina Island Pottery from 1927 through 1937.

Dealers

Alan Phair
Alan's Antiques
P.O. Box 30373
Long Beach, CA 90853-0373
ph: 562-983-7020
e-mail: AlanPhair@aol.com
Buys pieces marked "Catalina Pottery" made by Gladding-McBean; shells and some pieces marked with blue ink stamp "MADE IN U.S.A."; G.M.B., Franciscan and Catalina Pottery advertising items and price lists; also Franciscan dinnerware.

Cliftwood

Experts

Doris & Burdell Hall
B & B Antiques
210 West Sassafras Dr.
Morton, IL 61550-1254
ph: 309-263-2988
e-mail: bnbhall@mtco.com
Buys and sells; specializing in Morton potteries including Cliftwood Art Potteries Inc (Midwest Potteries Inc.), and American dinnerware.

deLee

Experts

Joanne Schaefer
S & S Publishing
3184 Williams Rd.
Butte Valley, CA 95965-8300
ph: 800-897-6263
fax: 530-894-5302
e-mail: JSchaef@sprintmail.com
Author and publisher of "deLee Art - The Pictorial History - 1937-1958" including price guide.

Eva Zeisel

Clubs/Associations

Eva Zeisel Collectors Club
22781 Flamingo St.
Woodland Hills, CA 91364

Frankoma Pottery Co.

Clubs/Associations

Nancy Littrell
Frankoma Family Collectors Association
Journal: Pot & Puma Journal
P.O. Box 32571
Oklahoma City, OK 73123-0771
ph: 405-722-2941 or 918-224-6610
fax: 405-728-3332
e-mail: slittrell@frankoma.org
web: http://www.frankoma.org/
A national non-profit organization dedicated to the appreciation, preservation and promotion of Frankoma Pottery as a collectible; quarterly journal and Trader; annual show and auction; complete resource for the dedicated collector.

Collectors

Steve & Nancy Littrell
P.O. Box 32571
Oklahoma City, OK 73123-0771
ph: 405-722-2941
fax: 405-728-3332
e-mail: selittrell@aol.com
Major collectors of Frankoma.

Donna Frank
1300 Luker Lane
Sapulpa, OK 74066-6024
ph: 918-224-6610
e-mail: ffc4donna@aol.com
Author of "Clay in the Master's Hands," a history of Frankoma founder and artist John Frank, his family and Frankoma Pottery; a must for all Frankoma collectors; details evolution of ceramics in American Southwest.

Dealers

Aaron's
P.O. Box 1303
Bethany, OK 73008
Wants to buy Frankoma pottery: early vases, statues of ladies, horses, dogs, buffalo, dealer signs.

Homespun Treasures Antiquity
209 E. Dewey Ave.
Sapulpa, OK 74066
ph: 918-227-4508
e-mail: antique@galstar.com
web: http://www.homespun.tulsa.net/images/frnk.html

Experts

Ray Stoll
4618 NW 34th St.
Oklahoma City, OK 73122-1330
ph: 405-947-8505
fax: 405-947-8505
e-mail: ffca4ray@aol.com
Specializes in Frankoma and Gracetone pottery, most other Oklahoma potteries; also elephants of all kinds, particularly Disney Dumbos.

Tom & Phyllis Bess
14535 East 13th St.
Tulsa, OK 74108-4527
ph: 918-437-7776
Buys and sells; authors of "Frankoma Treasurers" with price guide; $24 postpaid; consultant to "The Official Price Guide to Pottery and Porcelain."

Susan Cox
800 Murray Dr.
El Cajon, CA 92020
ph: 619-697-5922
e-mail: antiqfever@aol.com
Author of "The Collectors Guide to Frankoma, Book 2," "How to Successfully Own a Booth in a Mart," Antique Trader's "20th Century American Ceramics"; columnist for "The Antique Trader Weekly" and "The Collector."

Man./Prod./Dist.

Frankoma Pottery, Inc.
2400 Frankoma Rd.
P.O. Box 789
Sapulpa, OK 74067
ph: 918-224-5511 or 800-331-3650
fax: 918-227-3117
e-mail: frankoma@frankoma.com
web: http://www.frankoma.com/
Earthenware dinnerware, serving accessories, floral containers.

Haeger/Royal Haeger

Clubs/Associations

Dennis & Lanette Clarke
Haeger Pottery Collectors of America
Newsletter: HPCA Newsletter
5021 Toyon Way
Antioch, CA 94509-8426
ph: 925-776-7784
fax: 925-942-0706
e-mail: lanettec@colorspot.com

Dealers

Mike Landis
P.O. Box 814
Adamstown, PA 19501
ph: 888-248-2291
e-mail: landis2@desupernet.net
Buys and sells Royal Haeger, Haeger, Royal Hickman pottery; especially interested in pieces marked "Royal Haeger by Royal Hickman."

Dennis & Lanette Clarke
Haeger Pottery Collectors of America
5021 Toyon Way
Antioch, CA 94509-8426
ph: 925-776-7784
fax: 925-942-0706
e-mail: lanettec@colorspot.com
Collectors, dealers, appraisers specializing in Haeger pottery.

Experts

David D. Dilley
312 W. Weber Dr.
Muncie, IN 47303
ph: 765-284-7443
e-mail: advertising@lwbooks.com
Author of "Haeger Potteries - Through the Years;" collects Haeger in these glazes: anything purple, Mandarin Orange, Pearl Shell, Ebony, Lilac, Turquoise-Blue, Black Mystique and others; planters, bowls, figurals, wall pockets, lamps, etc.

Man./Prod./Dist.

Haeger Potteries
7 Maiden Lane
Dundee, IL 60118-2307
ph: 847-426-3441
fax: 847-426-0017
e-mail: haegerpotteries@msn.com
web: http://haegerpotteries.com/

Museums/Libraries

Gene D'Amico
Haeger Potteries
7 Maiden Lane
Dundee, IL 60118-2307
ph: 847-426-3441
fax: 847-426-0017
e-mail: haegerpotteries@msn.com
web: http://haegerpotteries.com/

Harker

Experts

Neva Colbert
69565 Crescent Rd.
Saint Clairsville, OH 43950-9350
ph: 740-695-2355
e-mail: colbert@1st.net
web: http://users.1st.net/colbert/harker/harker.htm
Author of "The Collector's Guide to Harker Pottery"; writes and distributes "The Harker Arrow", a newsletter about cameoware and other Harker pottery; also is a contributor to "American Country Collectibles" magazine.

Periodicals

Neva Colbert
Newsletter: Harker Arrow, The
69565 Crescent Rd.
Saint Clairsville, OH 43950-9350
ph: 740-695-2355
e-mail: colbert@1st.net
web: http://users.1st.net/colbert/harker/harker.htm

Harlequin

Collectors

Jim Stewart
807 Twin Pine
St. Louis, MO 63122
ph: 314-821-9913
Wants to buy Harlequin ceramic animal figurines; also any unusual Harlequin items.

Hedi Schoop

Collectors

Steve Hughes
1701 East Kati Ave., #36
Las Vegas, NV 89119
e-mail: tudorhouse@aol.com
Hedi Schoop Art Creations 1942-1958 North Hollywood, CA.

Hull Pottery

Clubs/Associations

Lowell Thomsen
Hull Pottery Association
15475 Hilltop Rd.
Council Bluffs, IA 51503

Collectors

Joe & Betty Yonis
11023 Tunnell Hill NE
New Lexington, OH 43764
ph: 740-982-6763
e-mail: jyonis@crsville.net

Marilyn Felkins
P.O. Box 221
Atlanta, TX 75551
ph: 903-796-6055
e-mail: Mfelkins@aol.com
Wants to buy Hull pottery pieces in the white gloss water lily pattern.

Experts

Joan Gray Hull
1376 Nevada S.W.
Huron, SD 57350-3135
ph: 605-352-1685
Author of "Hull - The Heavenly Pottery", an alphabetized, numerical, pictorial, pocket size price guide; all newly revised 6th edition with updated prices; advisor to "Warman's Antiques & Collectibles Price Guide", $24 ppd.

Brenda Roberts
Country Side Antiques
RR 2, Box 14-B
Marshall, MO 65340-9802
ph: 660-886-8888
Author of "The Collector's Encyclopedia of Hull Pottery", "Roberts' Ultimate Encyclopedia of Hull Pottery" and "The Companion Guide to Roberts' Ultimate Encyclopedia of Hull Pottery."

Periodicals

Kimberly Edmonds-Smith
Newsletter: Hull Pottery Newsletter
7768 Meadow Dr.
Hillsboro, MO 63050
ph: 314-274-2749
e-mail: kimcopubl@aol.com
Monthly newsletter directed to Hull Pottery collectors; designed to bring collectors the most up-to-date information on the subject and an outlet to meet other collectors and share collecting interests and experiences.

Hull Pottery/Red Riding Hood

Experts

Mark Supnick
2771 Oakbrook Manor
Fort Lauderdale, FL 33332
ph: 954-578-8787
Author of "Shawnee Pottery", and "Collecting Hull's Little Red Riding Hood."

Twins Antiques & Collectibles, The
Highway 242
Wayne City, IL 62895
Buys and sells; consultant to "The Official Price Guide to Pottery and Porcelain."

Kreiss

Collectors

Michells & Mike King
P.O. Box 3519
Alliance, OH 44601

Barb & Russ Vandervate
1430 Oak Court
Lafayette, IN 47905-2115

Pat & Larry Aikins
P & L Collectibles
Rt. 5, Box 5174
Athens, TX 75751
ph: 903-675-3765
fax: 903-677-3643
e-mail: Texasboxer@aol.com
web: http://www.mrlunchbox.com/
Authors of "The World of Kreiss Ceramics" price guide covering the Kreiss Psuchoss, Elegant Heirs, Naplin Ladies, and salt & pepper shakers.

James Casey
8004 Gault Street #A
Austin, TX 78757-8413

Carol & Mike Shong
2500 S. 370th #265
Federal Way, WA 98003

McCoy Pottery Co.

Collectors

Geri Strebel
P.O. Box 277
East Moriches, NY 11940
Wants McCoy Pottery items: vases, planters, baskets, etc.

Laura Simecek
McCoy Pottery Collectors Home Page
9296 Liberty Road
Twinsburg, OH 44087
ph: 330-963-1096
e-mail: Nuts4McCoy@aol.com
web: http://members.aol.com/nuts4mccoy
Collecting McCoy since 1993; always looking for maroon and cobalt colored pieces; website is an internet resource for all McCoy collectors; links to anything and everything McCoy.

Carol Seman
8934 Brecksville Road
Brecksville, OH 44141-2318
ph: 440-526-2094
fax: 440-526-2094
e-mail: McCjs@aol.com
web: http://members.aol.com/nmxpress/nmxpress.htm
Editor of "The NM Express" McCoy newsletter.

Dealers

Ruth Weeks
Borrowed Time
Uniontown Rd.
Phillipsburg, NJ 08865
ph: 908-859-0097
Wants to buy McCoy pottery from the 1930s and 1940s; prefers decorative vases in matte glazes and animal figures and planters, especially animal-form pitchers.

John Marshall
For Love or Money
16693 NW Meadowgrass Ct.
Beaverton, OR 97006
e-mail: john@europa.com
web: http://www.europa.com/~john/
Buys and sells all types of McCoy pottery.

Experts

Joanne Lindberg
79 Lexington Dr.
Metuchen, NJ 08840
Buys and sells; consultant to "The Official Price Guide to Pottery and Porcelain."

Chiquita Prestwood
1559 Echo Dr.
Lenoir, NC 28645
Buys and sells; consultant to "The Official Price Guide to Pottery and Porcelain."

Craig Nissen
P.O. Box 223
Grafton, WI 53024-0223
ph: 414-377-7932
e-mail: McCoyCN@aol.com
Co-author with Bob & Margaret Hanson of "McCoy Pottery Collectors' Reference & Value Guide," Vols. I & II.

Periodicals

Carol Seman
Newsletter: NM Xpress, The
8934 Brecksville Road
Brecksville, OH 44141-2318
ph: 440-526-2094
fax: 440-526-2094
e-mail: McCjs@aol.com
web: http://members.aol.com/nmxpress/nmxpress.htm
Monthly newsletter "for, by and about McCoy lovers everywhere"; read about rare finds, meet fellow collectors, stay abreast of McCoy pottery and cookie jar sales, shows and auctions; free classifieds for all subscribers.

Morton Potteries

Experts

Doris & Burdell Hall
B & B Antiques
210 West Sassafras Dr.
Morton, IL 61550-1254
ph: 309-263-2988
e-mail: bnbhall@mtco.com
Buys and sells; specializing in Morton pottery and American dinnerware; author of "Morton's Potteries: 99 Years."

Muncie Pottery Co.

Collectors

Barbara Norman
P.O. Box 251382
West Bloomfield, MI 48325-1382
ph: 248-855-7766
fax: 248-855-5224
Wants to buy Ruba Rombic, red or cased pieces of PHOENIX or Consolidated Art Glass, Catalonian, and Muncie Ruba Rombic pottery.

Paul Galli
ph: 408-730-4010
e-mail: paul.galli@lmco.com
Wants to buy or trade Muncie Pottery, Ruba Rombic line.

Experts

Virginia Heiss
7777 N. Alton Ave.
Indianapolis, IN 46268-7901
ph: 317-875-6797
Specializes in pottery made by the Muncie Clay Products Co., of Muncie, IN.

Jack D. Wilson
3926 N. Keeler Ave.
Chicago, IL 60641-2915
ph: 773-282-9553
e-mail: jdwilson1@earthlink.net
web: http://home.earthlink.net/~jdwilson1/
See website for information on this company.

Nemadji Tile & Pottery Co.

Clubs/Associations

Michelle Lee
Nemadji Collectors
Newsletter: Left Hand Gazette
P.O. Box 95
Moose Lake, MN 55767
ph: 218-485-8173
e-mail: nemadji@computerpro.com
web: http://www.computerpro.com/~nemadji/
Members share information about this swirl pottery made in Moose Lake, MN; while not made by Native Americans, Nemadji pottery is often referred to as "Indian" pottery; newsletter published quarterly; free sample newsletter with SASE.

Collectors

Michelle Lee
P.O. Box 95
Moose Lake, MN 55767
ph: 218-485-8173
e-mail: nemadji@computerpro.com
web: http://www.computerpro.com/~nemadji/
Specializes in Nemadjy pottery, "Indian" pottery, and tiles; Nemadji is a hand painted, swirl pottery made in Moose Lake, MN from 1923 to 1972; since 1972 it has been produced in Kettle River, MN.

V. Chermishnok
726 Beech St.
Redwood City, CA 94063
ph: 650-368-3070

Niloak Pottery

Experts

David Gifford
e-mail: gemoore@flash.net
web: http://www.flash.net/~gemoore/arkpotx.htm
Author of "Collector's Encyclopedia of Niloak Pottery."

Pewabic Pottery

Man./Prod./Dist.

Pewabic Pottery
10125 East Jeferson
Detroit, MI 48214
ph: 313-823-0954

Purinton

Experts

Jamie Johnson
228 Egbert Hall
Clarion, PA 16214
ph: 800-820-5087

Lori Hinterleiter
P.O. Box 9394
Arlington, VA 22219
ph: 703-729-1310
e-mail: lhinterl@aol.com
Specializes and always seeking rare and unusual pieces of Purinton Pottery, especially signed pieces, souvenir items, kiddie ware, and the following patterns: Pennsylvania Dutch, Chartreuse, Peasant Garden, Petals, Cactus, Ribb.

Dave & Sue Morris
3388 Merlin Rd., Ste. 351
Grants Pass, OR 97526
ph: 541-955-8411
e-mail: sue@wattpottery.com
web: http://www.wattpottery.com
Buys and sells Purinton pottery; author of "Purinton Pottery - An Identification and Value Guide" available from author for $27.95.

Periodicals

Lori Hinterleiter
Newsletter: Purinton Pastimes
P.O. Box 9394
Arlington, VA 22219
ph: 703-729-1310
e-mail: lhinterl@aol.com
Published quarterly, devoted solely to Purinton Pottery; research, historical articles, photos, recent finds, auction updates and prices, and free classified ads; annual convention.

Ransburg

Experts

Jo Lauderdale
2014 Richmond Rd.
Decatur, IL 62521
Collects and consultant to "The Official Price Guide to Pottery and Porcelain."

Regal China Corp.

Experts

Judy Posner
4195 South Tamiami Trail, Ste. 183
Venice, FL 34293-5112
ph: 941-497-7149
fax: 941-493-8085
e-mail: jpc@tias.com
web: http://www.tias.com/stores/jpc/
Collects and consultant to "The Official Price Guide to Pottery and Porcelain."

Rumrill Pottery Co.

Clubs/Associations

Francesca Malone-Gern
Rumrill Society, The
Newsletter: Rumrill Society Newsletter, The
P.O. Box 2161
Hudson, OH 44236-0161
ph: 330-655-9325 or 888-RUM-RILL
fax: 330-655-9347
e-mail: rumrill2@aol.com
Quarterly newsletter discusses RumRill art pottery and post Redwing RumRill art pottery.

Dealers

Pat Puckett
Teacherage, The
1583 Ranch Road
San Bernardino, CA 92407
ph: 909-887-8383
fax: 909-887-8383
e-mail: tcherage@aol.com
web: http://members.aol.com/tcherage/index.html
Specializes in Red Wing and RumRill art pottery, stoneware and ephemera; visitors may post want ads or items for sale at no charge; also trades.

Experts

Francesca Gern
P.O. Box 2161
Hudson, OH 44236-0161
ph: 330-655-9325 or 888-RUM-RILL
fax: 330-655-9347
e-mail: rumrill2@aol.com
Expert and avid collector of Rumrill pottery; also buys and sells and appraises; publisher of The Rumrill Society Newsletter.

Mike Zaeske
1796 North 9th St.
Kalamazoo, MI 49099
Collects and consultant to "The Official Price Guide to Pottery and Porcelain."

Ron Linde
500 South Water Street
Northfield, MN 55057-2060
ph: 507-645-6946
Collects and consultant to "The Official Price Guide to Pottery and Porcelain."

Sascha Brastoff

Experts

De Wayne Bethany
256 S. Robertson Blvd., Ste. 109
Beverly Hills, CA 90211
Co-author with Bill Seay (assisted by Steve Conti) of the "Collector's Encyclopedia of Sascha Brastoff."

Shawnee Pottery Co.

Clubs/Associations

Pamela D. Curran
Shawnee Pottery Collectors Club
Newsletter: Exclusively Shawnee
P.O. Box 713
New Smyrna Beach, FL 32170-0713
ph: 904-760-6600
fax: 904-760-5004
A club for Shawnee Pottery (made in Zanesville until 1961) collectors and enthusiasts; send LSASE for information. Monthly newsletter with plenty of pictures, letters, buy/sell classifieds, and new discoveries; chartered 1990.

Collectors

Pamela D. Curran
P.O. Box 713
New Smyrna Beach, FL 32170-0713
ph: 904-760-6600
fax: 904-760-5004
Buys, collects, and specializes in Shawnee Pottery; interested in purchasing all Shawnee Pottery including cookie jars, Valencia, salt & pepper shakers, miniatures, lamps, and most gold-trimmed planters.

Experts

Pamela D. Curran
P.O. Box 713
New Smyrna Beach, FL 32170-0713
ph: 904-760-6600
fax: 904-760-5004
Author of "Shawnee Pottery, The Full Encyclopedia"; publishes the Shawnee newsletter, "Exclusively Shawnee."

Mark Supnick
2771 Oakbrook Manor
Fort Lauderdale, FL 33332
ph: 954-578-8787
Author of "Shawnee Pottery", and "Collecting Hull's Little Red Riding Hood."

Bev & Jim Mangus
5147 Broadway NE
Louisville, OH 44641
Collects and consultant to "The Official Price Guide to Pottery and Porcelain."

Duane & Janice Vanderbilt
6038 E. Country Road 800 N
Brownsburg, IN 46112-8820
Collects and consultant to "The Official Price Guide to Pottery and Porcelain."

Spaulding China/Royal Copley

Collectors

Barbara Burke
4028 Palo Alto Ct.
Orlando, FL 32817-3803

Experts

Joe Devine
1411 3rd St.
Council Bluffs, IA 51503
Collects and consultant to "The Official Price Guide to Pottery and Porcelain."

Jim Petzold
P.O. Box 46
Madison, WI 53701-0046
ph: 608-241-9138
fax: 608-241-8770
e-mail: ceramics@execpc.com
Co-editor with of "CAS Collector"; wants to buy all Ceramic Arts Studio & Royal Copley creations including shakers, figurines, dolls, lamps, and metal art.

Periodicals

Dan Benton
Newsletter: Copley Courier, The
1639 N. Catalina St.
Burbank, CA 91505-1605
ph: 818-848-6541
For collectors of Royal Copley china which was made by the Spaulding China of Sebring, OH (1942-1957); Spaulding also made the Royal Windsor and the Spaulding patterns; published bi-monthly.

Stanford Pottery

Experts

Kathy Kimball
140 Linnell Rd.
Grand Marais, MN 55604
Collects and consultant to "The Official Price Guide to Pottery and Porcelain."

Tamac Pottery

Experts

Kelly Alworth
Tamac Web Page
415 NW 8th
Oklahoma City, OK 73102
ph: 405-272-0773
e-mail: gecko@ionet.net
web: http://www.ionet.net/~gecko/tamac/tamac1.html
Appraiser, collector, dealer, expert in Tamac pottery.

Tom & Phyllis Bess
14535 East 13th St.
Tulsa, OK 74108-4527
ph: 918-437-7776
Buys and sells; consultant to "The Official Price Guide to Pottery and Porcelain."

Treasure Craft Pottery

Experts

Joyce Roerig
1501 Maple Ridge Rd.
Walterboro, SC 29488-9278
ph: 843-538-2487
fax: 843-538-4263
e-mail: ckejrn@lowcountry.com
Buys and sells; consultant to "Official Price Guide to Pottery & Porcelain."

Twin Winton

Experts

Joyce Roerig
1501 Maple Ridge Rd.
Walterboro, SC 29488-9278
ph: 843-538-2487
fax: 843-538-4263
e-mail: ckejrn@lowcountry.com
Buys and sells; consultant to "Official Price Guide to Pottery & Porcelain."

Uhl Pottery Co.

Clubs/Associations

Don Schwartz
Uhl Collectors Society, Inc.
Newsletter: Uhl Collectors Society Newsletter
P.O. Box 1081
Michigan City, MI 46361-8281
ph: 219-872-2308
Purpose is the preservation and sharing of information relating to the production of Uhl pottery; production dates back to 1849 and ran through the mid-1940s when the company ceased operation.

Collectors

Tom & Donna Uebelhor
233 E. Timberlin Lane
Jasper, IN 47546-7303
ph: 812-482-9575
Lives in the area where Uhl pottery was made.

Joseph Erbacher
P.O. Box 98
St. Anthony, IN 47565-0098
ph: 812-326-2777
President of Uhl Collectors Society; membership info sent on request; annual convention.

Dave & Donna Swick
506 Martin St.
Newton, IL 62448-1340
ph: 618-783-3455
e-mail: ddswick@psbnewton.com
Publish the Uhl Pottery Newsletter for the Uhl Collectors Society.

Dealers

Don Schwartz
P.O. Box 1081
Michigan City, MI 46361-8281
ph: 219-872-2308

Experts

Tim Hodges
1378 West Andrew Lane
Jasper, IN 47546
Consultant to "The Official Price Guide to Pottery and Porcelain."

CERAMICS (CONTINENTAL)

(see also DINNERWARE)

Auction Services

Christie's
502 Park Ave.
New York, NY 10022
ph: 212-546-1000
fax: 212-980-8163
web: http://www.christies.com

Collectors

John Coates
324 Woodland Dr.
Stevens Point, WI 54481-9285
ph: 715-341-6113
e-mail: jcoaates@coredcs.com
Especially interested in Boch Feres/ Keramis Belgium art pottery depicting animals or birds, and those pieces with strong Art Deco design.

Dealers

Gerald Shultz
Antique Gallery, The
8523 Germantown Ave.
Philadelphia, PA 19118-3316
ph: 215-248-1700
fax: 215-247-8411
18th century Sevres, Coalport, Worcester, Meissen, Bow, Chelsea.

Farhad Radfar, ISA
MIR International Gallery, Inc.
332 n. Michigan Ave., 2nd Floor
Chicago, IL 60611
ph: 312-814-8510
fax: 312-814-8511
e-mail: mirgallery@aol.com
web: http://www.mirgallery.com/
Specializing in Meissen, KPM and Vienna porcelain.

Experts

Geraud Schultz
Antique Gallery, The
8523 Germantown Ave.
Philadelphia, PA 19118
ph: 215-248-1700
fax: 215-247-8411
Buys, sells and specializes in 18th century Delft, Sevres, Meissen, Longwy, Galle, Massier, Quimper, Doat, Boch, etc.

Susan & Al Bagdade
Country Peasants, The
1325 North State Parkway, Apt. 15A
Chicago, IL 60610
ph: 312-397-1321
fax: 312-543-2544
e-mail: ADBSDB@aol.com
Author of "Warman's English & Continental Pottery & Porcelain" (Krause); advisor to "Warman's Antiques & Collectibles Price Guide."

Museums/Libraries

Wadsworth Atheneum
600 Main St.
Hartford, CT 06103
ph: 860-278-2670
fax: 860-527-0803
e-mail: info@wadsworthatheneum.org
web: http://www.wadsworthatheneum.org/
Featured displays include the Harold & Wendy Newman Collection of Veilleuses, the J. Pierpont Morgan Collection of Meissen Porcelain, and other diverse examples of fine European ceramics.

Amphora

Clubs/Associations

Wilf Pegg
Amphora Collectors Club
Newsletter: Amphora Files
129 Bathurst St.
Toronto, Ontaria M5V 2R2
Canada
ph: 416-703-0338
fax: 416-703-1330
e-mail: amphora@idirect.com
Newsletter is published quarterly; articles about Amphora and related wares (particularly Austrian); articles, photos, reader exchanges.

Collectors

John Cobabe
800 South Pacific Hwy., Ste. 8-301
Redondo Beach, CA 90277
ph: 310-316-2982
e-mail: johncobabe@aol.com
Wants to buy Amphora; send photo, size and price.

Experts

Les & Irene Cohen
P.O. Box 17001
Pittsburgh, PA 15235-0001
ph: 412-793-0222 or 412-795-3030
fax: 412-793-0222
e-mail: www.am4ah@hotbot.com
Buys, collects and specializes in Austrian Amphora art pottery; prefers vases.

Jack Gunsaulus
Gray's Gallery
583 W. Ann Arbor Trail
Plymouth, MI 48170-1627
ph: 734-455-2373
Buys and sells Teplitz-Turn art pottery, e.g. items made by the Amphora Porcelain Works and Alexandra Works.

Art Pottery

Dealers

Gerald Shultz
Antique Gallery, The
8523 Germantown Ave.
Philadelphia, PA 19118-3316
ph: 215-248-1700
fax: 215-247-8411
Boch, Pilkington, B. Moore, Martin Bros., Moorecroft, DeMorgan, Amphora, Wedgwood, Crimson, B. Leach, Doulton, Rambervillers, T. Deck, T. Doat, Clarice Cliff, S. Cooper, Carltonware.

Alain Fournier
La Verrerie D'Art
P.O. Box 757
Bowie, MD 20718-0757
ph: 301-464-3251
e-mail: grafour@aol.com
Buys, sells, specializes in European art pottery from the Art Nouveau and Art Deco eras; C. Catteau, Dage, Amphora, early Sarraguemine, Czech, Austrian, French, Belgian.

Conta & Boehme

Experts

Janice & Richard Vogel
4720 SE Fort King St.
Ocala, FL 34470-1501
ph: 352-694-5776
fax: 352-694-7330
e-mail: vogels@atlantic.net

Ray Begley
2 Lydiate Ash Road
Bromsgrove, Worcestershire B61 OHU
U.K.
ph: (44) 121 457 9181
fax: (44) 121 457 9212
e-mail: fairings@globalnet.co.uk
web: http://www.users.global.net.co.uk/~fairings/
Collector and expert in Conta & Boehme fairings and match holders/strikers.

Czechoslovakian

Clubs/Associations

Kathy Foster
Czechoslovakian Collectors Guild International
Newsletter: CCGI Newsletter
P.O. Box 901395
Kansas City, MO 64190-1395
ph: 816-891-9115 or 888-910-2424
fax: 816-891-0988
e-mail: ccgi@kc.net
For collectors of anything Czechoslovakian and Bohemian: glass, pottery, art.

Collectors

Burt Smith
2000 Commonwealth Ave.
Brighton, MA 02135
ph: 617-787-6336
e-mail: burtczecho@aol.com
Wants large unusual pieces of Czech porcelain with dime-size round label marked "Made in Czechoslovakia"; figurals of birds, animals, people; also wants pitchers, urns, vases.

Mike & Cheryl Goyda
P.O. Box 192
East Petersburg, PA 17520-0192
ph: 717-569-7149
fax: 717-569-0909
e-mail: Goydagang@aol.com
Wants to buy Czech pottery.

Dealers

R. Snaith
8446 W. 3rd St.
Los Angeles, CA 90048
ph: 323-930-2930
Buys, sells, trades Czech pottery.

Danish

Dealers

Phil Anderson
Anderson & Associates
2147 W. Farwell
Chicago, IL 60645-4900
ph: 773-338-1758
fax: 773-338-1758
e-mail: philtanderson@msw.com
Buys and sells porcelain figurines and vases from the Denmark, especially Royal Copenhagen, Bing & Grondahl, and Dahl Jensen; also collects Scandinavian wood carvings especially those signed Trygg and/or Gunnarsson.

Dutch

Experts

Marty Wittenbols
Martin Wittenbols' Dutch Pottery
e-mail: wittenbols@spanit.com
web: http://www.spanit.com/~wittenbols/
Expert in Dutch Art Nouveau, Art Deco pottery and ceramics including Rozenburg, Purmerend, Amstelhoek, Gouda, Amphora, De Distel, Velsen, Arnhem, Ram, Ultrecht, etc.

French

Experts

Martin Spickler, PhD
Tova's Treasures
11410 Strand Dr., #207
Rockville, MD 20852-2938
ph: 301-984-5954
Specializes in English, French, Meissen, Wedgwood, and Oriental ceramics.

Haviland

(see also CERAMICS [CONTINENTAL], Limoges; DINNERWARE, Haviland)

Clubs/Associations

Susan Carter, Mem.
Haviland Collectors International Foundation
Newsletter: HCIF Newsletter
P.O. Box 802462
Santa Clarita, CA 91380-2462
ph: 805-297-0132
e-mail: HCIF@mwci.net
web: http://www.havilandcollectors.com/
An organization dedicated to the study and promotion of porcelain and pottery made by the Haviland companies of France and America; newsletter published quarterly.

Dealers

Grace Graves
Haviland Matching Service, Ltd.
219 N. Milwaukee St.
Milwaukee, WI 53202-5818
ph: 414-291-9111
fax: 414-291-9018
e-mail: hmsgraves@aol.com
Collector, dealer in porcelains and pottery by the Haviland families of Limoges, France; specialists in identifying and locating French & American Haviland patterns; use Schleiger number or send photocopy for pattern identification.

Experts

Dee Hooks
Dee's China Shop
13050 Blackstump Rd.
Percy, IL 62272
ph: 618-965-3832

Dick & Dona Schleiger
1626 Crestview Rd.
Redlands, CA 92374
Son and daughter-in-law of Arlene & Dick Haviland, original authors of Haviland pattern books and developers of the "Schleiger" numbers for Haviland identification; currently authors of more recent Haviland pattern books.

Matching Services

Jan Cruikshank
Coleman's Antiques
3313 N. Sepulveda Blvd.
Manhattan Beach, CA 90266-3626
ph: 888-458-4988 or 310-545-6699
fax: 310-545-6699
e-mail: jcruikshank@earthlink.net
web: http://www.colemansantiques.com/
Has been in business for 50 years; specializes in pre-1930 French Haviland; also sells English, German, Bohemian and Delft porcelain, silver and glassware; send Schleiger number or photocopy for Haviland matching.

Herend

Dealers

Rumson China & Glass Shop
125 East River Road
Rumson, NJ 07760
ph: 732-842-2322 or 888-800-0020
web: http://rumsongiftgallery.com/
Sells Herend porcelain, Waterford crystal, Lynn Chase Designs, Mottahedeh, Vietri, Yeoward Crystal, Agresti, Orrefors, Casafina, Buccellati, Lalique, Laura Slatkin, Christian Tortu, Chelsea clocks, and more.

Scully & Scully
504 Park Ave.
New York, NY 10022
ph: 212-755-2590 or 800-223-3717
e-mail: info@scullyscully.com
web: http://www.scullyscully.com/
Offering distinctive gifts since 1934: Herend porcelain, Limoges & Halcyon Days, Murano glass.

Museums/Libraries

Herend Porcelain Museum
Herend
Kossuth ut 140, 8440
Hungary
ph: +36 88 261-159 or +36 88 261-144
fax: +36 88 261-801
e-mail: simon_magdolna@galamb.net
web: http://www.c3.hu/~porcelan/angolf.htm
Specializes in Herend and Zsolnay porcelain; carries the largest inventory of Herend in the U.S.; buys, sells and appraises Herend and Zsolnay.

Hutschenreuther

Experts

Jack Gunsaulus
Gray's Gallery
583 W. Ann Arbor Trail
Plymouth, MI 48170-1627
ph: 734-455-2373

Italian

Dealers

Kenneth P. Lesko
Kenneth Paul Lesko 20th Century Decorative Arts
P.O. Box 16099
Rocky River, OH 44116-0099
ph: 216-356-0275
fax: 216-331-1280
e-mail: kplesko@aol.com
web: http://members.aol.com/kplesko/kplesko.html
Specialist in Italian ceramics 1900-1970; wants to buy ADCF/Firenze, Albisola, G. Andloviz, Baldelli, Bassanelli, Roberto Bertagnin, Bertetti, R. Bevilacqua, Biancini, B. Brunetti, A Bucci/Faenza, C.A.S., CD or DC, and all others.

Shaw
P.O. Box 5096
Southfield, MI 48086
Wants to buy Italian ceramics: Gamboni, Fantoni, Melotti, Gratti, Melandri, Campi, Ginori, Garaboldi, Mazzotti, Albisola, Fabbari, Tasca, Fontana, Patrinini, Arte Della Ceramica, etc.

KPM

Man./Prod./Dist.

KPM (Royal Porcelain Manufacturer)
Wegley Str. #1
Berlin 12, W-1000
Germany

Limoges

Dealers

Susan Leite
44 Glenwood Rd.
Brewster, MA 02631-2202
ph: 508-385-4905
Wants to buy undamaged Limoges items.

Massier

Collectors

John Cobabe
800 South Pacific Hwy., Ste. 8-301
Redondo Beach, CA 90277
ph: 310-316-2982
e-mail: johncobabe@aol.com

Meissen

Dealers

Martin & Helene Schwalberg
Meissen Shop, The
329 Worth Ave.
Palm Beach, FL 33480-6012
ph: 561-832-2504
fax: 561-833-4171
Devoted exclusively to antique Meissen porcelain.

Experts

Martin Spickler, PhD
Tova's Treasures
11410 Strand Dr., #207
Rockville, MD 20852-2938
ph: 301-984-5954
Specializes in English, French, Meissen, Wedgwood, and Oriental ceramics.

Mimi Levine
Mimi & Steve Levine Antiques, Inc.
6205 Marilyn Drive
Alexandria, VA 22310
ph: 703-971-3941
e-mail: mimilev@erols.com
Buys and sells pre-1900 English, American, and German porcelains and English pottery: Meissen, Wedgwood, Worcester, Minton, and other excellent companies; also appraises and lectures.

Mottahedeh

Man./Prod./Dist.

Mottahedeh & Co.
225 Fifth Ave.
New York, NY 10010
ph: 212-685-3050
fax: 212-889-9483
Porcelain, pottery, glassware, brassware; antique reproductions, metal and wood and ceramics; china dinnerware.

Old Ivory

Clubs/Associations

Darlene Warembourg, Sec.
Old Ivory Porcelain Society
5946 West Morraine Ave.
Littleton, CO 80128
ph: 303-972-2799

Collectors

John Harms
P.O. Box 326
Osage, IA 50461
ph: 515-732-3872

Periodicals

Pat Fitzwater
Newsletter: Elegance of Old Ivory, The
28101 St. Petes Mtn. Rd.
West Linn, OR 97068-9537
ph: 503-655-1420
fax: 503-655-1420
Focuses on the Old Ivory (Silesia) patterns of porcelain dinnerware produced in Germany during the late 1800s by the Ohme factory; send a LSASE for a sample copy.

Portuguese

Dealers

Tucha Gift Shop, Inc.
110 Ferry St.
Newark, NJ 07105
ph: 973-589-3681 or 973-589-6672
fax: 973-589-8284
Carries a large line of contemporary items made in Portugal, especially handpainted ceramics.

Quimper

Auction Services

Sandra Bondhus
New England Absentee Auctions, Inc.
16 Sixth St.
Stamford, CT 060905
ph: 203-975-9055
fax: 203-323-6407
e-mail: neaauction@aol.com
web: http://www.members.tripod.com/~bondhus/
Specializing in the auctions of Quimper Pottery; accepts Quimper and related accessories for consignment; two or three sales per year.

Clubs/Associations

Lucy Williams
USA Quimper Club
2519 Kansas Ave., Ste. 108
Santa Monica, CA 90404
ph: 310-286-6762
fax: 310-969-8883
e-mail: usaquimper@aol.com
web: http://members.aol.com/usaquimper/pubpage.htm

Dealers

Gerald Shultz
Antique Gallery, The
8523 Germantown Ave.
Philadelphia, PA 19118-3316
ph: 215-248-1700
fax: 215-247-8411

Charles & Marianne Wilson
Thistle Hill Bed & Breakfast Inn
5541 Sperryvile Pike
Boston, VA 22713
ph: 540-987-9142

Experts

Sandra Bondhus
P.O. Box 100
Unionville, CT 06085-0100
ph: 860-678-1808
e-mail: nbondhus@polnet.com
Author of "Quimper Pottery"; specializes in 19th & 20th century Quimper of fine artistic merit; always buying and selling Quimper.

Noelle B. Beatty
Old Quimper Pottery
3438 34th Place, NW
Washington, DC 20016-3136
ph: 202-537-0855
fax: 202-537-1609
e-mail: gw-nb-beatty@email.msn.com
web: http://www.nsws.com/quimper/
Buys, sells, specializes in Quimper; wide variety of 19th and 20th century Quimper for sale; will answer collectors' questions about old Quimper.

Joan Datesman
105 Market St.
Annapolis, MD 21401
ph: 410-268-6233
fax: 410-268-3061
Author of "Collecting Quimper; Quimper Collections"; trips to France maintains large 1860-1930 inventory; rustic to elaborate designs.

Susan & Al Bagdade
Country Peasants, The
1325 North State Parkway, Apt. 15A
Chicago, IL 60610
ph: 312-397-1321
fax: 312-543-2544
e-mail: ADBSDB@aol.com
Buys and sells Quimper pottery, especially unusual pieces: figures and early decorative examples; authors, lecturers, staff writers.

Man./Prod./Dist.

Quimper Faience
Newsletter: Le Monde de Quimper
141 Water St.
Stonington, CT 06378-1323
ph: 860-535-1712
fax: 860-535-3509
e-mail: mail@quimperfaience.com
web: http://www.quimperfaience.com/
The American branch of the French Quimper factory; retail mail order available; publishes newsletter twice a year; newsletter includes topics on interest to the Quimper collector including articles about Brittany.

Periodicals

Millicent S. Mali
Newsletter: Old Quimper Review
P.O. Box 377
East Greenwich, RI 02818-0377
Twelve-page periodical with color photos featuring articles on the history and production of different factories in Quimper, France; contains advertisements by leading Quimper dealers.

R.S. Prussia

Clubs/Associations

Frances Coy
International Association of R. S. Prussia Collectors Inc.
Newsletter: IARSPC Newsletter
212 Wooded Falls Rd.
Louisville, KY 40243
ph: 502-244-5391
e-mail: jaynes@in.on.ca
web: http://www.rsprussia.com/

Dealers

Mary McCaslin
6887 Black Oak Ct. East
Avon, IN 46123
ph: 317-272-7776
fax: 317-272-7776
e-mail: maryjack@iquest.net
Author of "Royal Bayreuth: A Collector's Guide", past-president of International Assoc. of RS Prussia Collectors and the Royal Bayreuth Collectors Club.

Ward Stewart
Stewart's Antiques
1000 Coolidge
Lafayette, LA 70503-2336
ph: 318-232-2957

Experts

Mary McCaslin
6887 Black Oak Ct. East
Avon, IN 46123
ph: 317-272-7776
fax: 317-272-7776
e-mail: maryjack@iquest.net
Author of "Royal Bayreuth: A Collector's Guide", past-president of International Assoc. of RS Prussia Collectors and the Royal Bayreuth Collectors Club.

Dee Hooks
Dee's China Shop
13050 Blackstump Rd.
Percy, IL 62272
ph: 618-965-3832
Has been buying and selling R.S. Prussia for 20 years.

Rosenthal

Experts

Ann M. Kerr
P.O. Box 437
Sidney, OH 45365-0437
ph: 937-492-6369
fax: 937-492-6369
e-mail: raintree@bright.net
Author of a book on Rosenthal.

Man./Prod./Dist.

Rosenthal USA Limited
355 Michele Pl.
Carlstadt, NJ 07072-2304
ph: 201-804-8000
e-mail: chris@rosusa.com
web: http://www.rosenthalchina.com/index.html
Glassware, giftware, flatware, dinnerware, china and stoneware, stemware, silverplate, stainless steel, figurines, ceramic, glass, wood serving accessories.

Royal Bayreuth

Clubs/Associations

Howard & Sarah Wade
Royal Bayreuth International Collectors' Society
Newsletter: RBICS Newsletter
P.O. Box 325
Orrville, OH 44667-0325
ph: 330-682-8551
fax: 330-682-3655
e-mail: ukdolls@aol.com
Bi-monthly newsletter with information on members' collections, new finds, price trends across the country and classified ads.

Judith White
Royal Bayreuth Collectors' Club
926 Essex Circle
Kalamazoo, MI 49008
ph: 616-343-6066
e-mail: judykazoo@aol.com

Collectors

Eric Sidman
Eric's Antiques
381 Elliot St.
Newton, MA 02164
ph: 617-332-3744
Wants old blue mark Royal Bayreuth items; all figurals but especially Santa Claus, Tiger, Squirrel, Rabbit, etc.; Rose Tapestry items, Sunbonnets, Snow Babies, Beach Babies; any unusual or rare items; will pay for photos; prompt reply.

Howard & Sarah Wade
P.O. Box 325
Orrville, OH 44667-0325
ph: 330-682-8551
fax: 330-682-3655
e-mail: ukdolls@aol.com

Dealers

Mary McCaslin
6887 Black Oak Ct. East
Avon, IN 46123
ph: 317-272-7776
fax: 317-272-7776
e-mail: maryjack@iquest.net
Author of "Royal Bayreuth: A Collector's Guide", past-president of International Assoc. of RS Prussia Collectors and the Royal Bayreuth Collectors Club.

Experts

Mary McCaslin
6887 Black Oak Ct. East
Avon, IN 46123
ph: 317-272-7776
fax: 317-272-7776
e-mail: maryjack@iquest.net
Author of "Royal Bayreuth: A Collector's Guide", past-president of International Assoc. of RS Prussia Collectors and the Royal Bayreuth Collectors Club.

Dee Hooks
Dee's China Shop
13050 Blackstump Rd.
Percy, IL 62272
ph: 618-965-3832

Royal Copenhagen

Dealers

Pat Owen
Viking Import House, Inc.
690 NE 13th St.
Ft. Lauderdale, FL 33304-1110
ph: 954-763-3388 or 800-327-2297
fax: 954-462-2317
e-mail: vikingimp@aol.com
Operates the VIDEX, a buy/sell service for any and all Royal Copenhagen and Bing & Grondahl collectibles.

Man./Prod./Dist.

Josephine Dillon
Royal Scandinavian
140 Bradford Dr.
West Berlin, NJ 08091
ph: 609-768-5400 or 800-431-1992
fax: 800-448-7553
Royal Copenhagen, Bing & Grondahl, Holmegaard, and Georg Jensen are the best of Scandinavian collectibles; manufactures dinnerware, cobalt blue underglaze collector plates, figurines, bells, dolls, ornaments and gift accessories.

Royal Copenhagen/Flora Danica

Dealers

Jeff E. Purtell
P.O. Box 28
Amherst, NH 03031-0028
ph: 603-673-4331 or 800-973-4331
fax: 603-673-1525
Specializes in Royal Copenhagen Flora Danica.

Scandinavian

Dealers

Anita L. Grashof
Gallerie Ani'tiques
Stage House Village
Park & Front Streets
Scotch Plains, NJ 07076
ph: 908-322-4600 or 201-377-3032
fax: 973-765-9565
Buys, sells, appraises Swedish art pottery such as Argenta by Kage, Gustavsberg, Rorstrand; also Finnish Arabia pottery.

Schlegelmilch

(see CERAMICS [CONTINENTAL], R.S. Prussia)

Sevres

Experts

Ann Friedman
Meadow Brook Hall
Oakland University
Rochester, MI 48309
e-mail: friedman@oakland.edu

Sitzendorf

Man./Prod./Dist.

Sitzendorfer Porzellanmanufaktur
Hautstr. 26
Sitzendorfe, 07429
Germany

Teplitz-Turn

Experts

Les & Irene Cohen
P.O. Box 17001
Pittsburgh, PA 15235-0001
ph: 412-793-0222 or 412-795-3030
fax: 412-793-0222
e-mail: www.am4ah@hotbot.com
Buys, collects and specializes in Teplitz-Turn art pottery such as Amphora Porcelain Works, Alexandra Works, Heliosine Ware, "PD" marked Teplitz; prefers vases.

Jack Gunsaulus
Gray's Gallery
583 W. Ann Arbor Trail
Plymouth, MI 48170-1627
ph: 734-455-2373
Buys and sells Teplitz-Turn art pottery, e.g. items made by the Amphora Porcelain Works and Alexandra Works.

Villeroy & Boch

Collectors

Steve Elliott
1600 Tennessee St.
Vallejo, CA 94590
ph: 707-552-8400 or 707-642-1949
fax: 707-552-0881
Wants antique Villeroy & Boch Mettlach items.

Man./Prod./Dist.

Villeroy & Boch Co.
5 Vaugh Drive, Ste. 303
Princeton, NJ 08540
ph: 212-683-1747 or 800-515-7444
fax: 212-481-0283
Imported dinnerware, glassware.

Museums/Libraries

Keramikmuseum
Schloss Ziegelberg
Mettlach/Saar, 66693
Germany
web: http://www.sr-online.de/fahr-mal-hin/keramikmuseum-mettlach/

Zsolnay

Collectors

Les & Irene Cohen
P.O. Box 17001
Pittsburgh, PA 15235-0001
ph: 412-793-0222 or 412-795-3030
fax: 412-793-0222
e-mail: www.am4ah@hotbot.com
Buys and collects Zsolnay art pottery vases with ocean glaze made during the period 1895 to 1910.

John Cobabe
800 South Pacific Hwy., Ste. 8-301
Redondo Beach, CA 90277
ph: 310-316-2982
e-mail: johncobabe@aol.com

Dealers

Federico Santi
Zsolnay Store, The
152 Spring St.
Newport, RI 02840-6806
ph: 401-841-5060
fax: 401-848-0953
e-mail: zsolnay@drawrm.com
web: http://www.drawrm.com
Buys and sells Hungarian Zsolnay and Eastern European pottery; interested in Zsolnay, Amphora, Turin-Tepliz art pottery; send photos and price; can buy from photo; website has virtual museum of Zsolnay ceramics.

Agnes Kalmar
Transdanubian Treasures
P.O. Box 840009
New Orleans, LA 70184-0009
ph: 504-283-1712
fax: 504-288-2564
e-mail: Angyali@aol.com
web: http://www.zsolnay.com/
Unique, iridescent porcelain from the Zsolnay factory (Hungary) is available online; artistic vases, figurines, animal figures.

Frank Juhasz
Diamond & Gem Trading USA, Co.
Herend
Kossuth ut 140, 8440
Hungary
ph: +36 88 261-159 or +36 88 261-144
fax: +36 88 261-801
e-mail: simon_magdolna@galamb.net
web: http://www.c3.hu/~porcelan/angolf.htm
Specializes in Herend and Zsolnay porcelain; carries the largest inventory of Herend in the U.S.; buys, sells and appraises Herend and Zsolnay.

Experts

John Gacher
Zsolnay Store, The
152 Spring St.
Newport, RI 02840-6806
ph: 401-841-5060
fax: 401-848-0953
e-mail: zsolnay@drawrm.com
web: http://www.drawrm.com
Author of "Zsolnay: Collecting a Culture"; wants to buy fine examples of Zsolnay pottery; will purchase from photo.

Laszlo Gyugyi
P.O. Box 17329
Pittsburgh, PA 15235
ph: 412-256-2300 or 412-731-1753
fax: 412-256-2223
Collector wants to buy quality Zsolnay pieces from the Art Nouveau period and from the preceding classical periods; quality more important than price; send photo and/or description; all letters answered; information seekers welcome.

Misc. Services

American Hungarian Foundation, The
300 Somerset St.
P.O. Box 1084
New Brunswick, NJ 08903
ph: 732-846-5777
fax: 732-249-7033
e-mail: info@ahfoundation.org
web: http://www.ahfoundation.org/
Devoted to furthering the understanding and appreciation of the Hungarian cultural and historical heritage in U.S.; held exhibit of art pottery from the factory of Vilmos Zsolnay in Pecs, Hungary.

CERAMICS (ENGLISH)

(see also DINNERWARE)

Auction Services

Stuart Slavid
Skinner, Inc.
357 Main St.
Bolton, MA 01740-1104
ph: 978-779-6241
fax: 978-779-5144
e-mail: info@skinnerinc.com
web: http://www.skinnerinc.com
Established in 1964, Skinner Inc. is the fifth largest auction house in the US; has offices in Bolton and Boston, MA.

W. Buckley
Potteries Antique Centre Auctions
271 Waterloo Road
Cobridge
Stoke on Trent, Staffordshire ST6 3HR
U.K.
ph: 01782-201455
fax: 01782-201518
e-mail: potteriesantiquecentre@compuserve.com
web: http://www.potteriesantiquecentre.com/
Conducts three specialized British pottery auctions each year.

Clubs/Associations

Dr. Keith McLeod
Wedgwood International Seminar
Newsletter: WIS Proceedings
22 DeSavry Crescent
Toronto, Ontario M4S 2L2
Canada
ph: 416-978-7011
fax: 416-489-4089
e-mail: k.mcleod@utoronto.ca
An educational association sharing the latest information in the field of English ceramics; also publishes the "Annual Proceedings"; also lectures and annual seminars; annual conference.

Dealers

Wynn A. Sayman
Wynn A. Sayman, Inc.
Old Fields
Richmond, MA 01254-9585
ph: 413-698-2272
fax: 413-698-3282
e-mail: wynnasayman@taconic.net
web: http://www.wynnasayman.com
Specializes in English pottery and porcelain of the 18th and early 19th century: salt-glaze, redware, tortoise shell wares, creamware, pearlware and Staffordshire bocage figures; some Chelsea, Bow, Worcester, and Derby; by appointment.

Leo Kaplan
Leo Kaplan, Ltd.
967 Madison Ave.
New York, NY 10021
ph: 212-249-6766 or 212-249-7574
Specializes in early English pottery and porcelain.

Mimi Levine
Mimi & Steve Levine Antiques, Inc.
6205 Marilyn Drive
Alexandria, VA 22310
ph: 703-971-3941
e-mail: mimilev@erols.com
Buys and sells pre-1900 English, American, and German porcelains and English pottery: Meissen, Wedgwood, Worcester, Minton, and other excellent companies; also appraises and lectures.

Dennis Lockard
2 Hats Collectibles
P.O. Box 1192
Clarksville, VA 23927
Specializes in 20th century English dinnerware.

W. Buckley
Potteries Antique Center Auctions
271 Waterloo Road
Cobridge
Stoke on Trent, Staffordshire ST6 3HR
U.K.
ph: 01782-201455
fax: 01782-201518
e-mail: potteriesantiquecentre@compuserve.com
web: http://www.potteriesantiquecentre.com/
Antique store with large stocks of British pottery from the 19th and 20th centuries.

Experts

Stuart Slavid
9 Gryzboska Circle
Farmingham, MA 01702
ph: 508-620-2531
e-mail: wedghead@pop.ma.ultranet.com
Specializes in Wedgwood, Staffordshire, and Royal Worcester.

David & Linda Arman
P.O. Box 39
Portsmouth, RI 02871-0039
ph: 401-841-8403
fax: 401-841-8403
e-mail: info@oaklandpublications.com
web: http://oaklandpublications.com/new%20pubs.html
Experts, dealers, auction sales; monthly sales of Historical Staffordshire, Liverpool, and War of 1812 ceramics; also sales of American glass and references dealing with English ceramics and American glass.

Geraud Schultz
Antique Gallery, The
8523 Germantown Ave.
Philadelphia, PA 19118
ph: 215-248-1700
fax: 215-247-8411
Buys, sells and specializes in English ceramics: Coalport, Worcester, Bow, Chelsea, Davenport, Doulton.

Martin Spickler, PhD
Tova's Treasures
11410 Strand Dr., #207
Rockville, MD 20852-2938
ph: 301-984-5954
Specializes in English, French, Meissen, Wedgwood, and Oriental ceramics.

E. Jefferson Hynds
1317 Cranbrook Dr.
Saginaw, MI 48603-5470
Interested in English transferware of the 18th and 19th centuries. Most interested in acquiring the wares of Spode and Copeland, particularly the 18th century blue and white Spode. Also collect antique Adams jasperware.

Susan & Al Bagdade
Country Peasants, The
1325 North State Parkway, Apt. 15A
Chicago, IL 60610
ph: 312-397-1321
fax: 312-543-2544
e-mail: ADBSDB@aol.com
Author of "Warman's English & Continental Pottery & Porcelain" (Krause); advisor to "Warman's Antiques & Collectibles Price Guide."

Susan Scott
882 Queen Street West
Toronto, Ontario M6J 1G3
Canada
ph: 416-538-8536
fax: 416-534-4814
e-mail: scottca@ibm.net
web: http://www.collecting20thcentury.com/
Specializes in 20th century English ceramics.

Periodicals

David & Linda Arman
Magazine: China & Glass Quarterly
P.O. Box 39
Portsmouth, RI 02871-0039
ph: 401-841-8403
fax: 401-841-8403
e-mail: info@oaklandpublications.com
web: http://oaklandpublications.com/new%20pubs.html
Deals with the fields of English ceramics 1750-1865 (Historical Staffordshire, Pratt Ware, Lustre, Figures, transferware) and Early American glass 1750-1880 (blown three mold, freeblown, pattern molded, pressed, paperweights.)

ABC Plates

Clubs/Associations

Dr. Joan M. George
ABC Collectors' Circle
Newsletter: ABC Collectors' Circle Newsletter
67 Stevens Ave.
Old Bridge, NJ 08857-2244
ph: 732-679-8924
fax: 732-679-6102
e-mail: drjgeorge@nac.net
Collectors of educational plates and mugs in china, tin and glass; many collect only those with alphabet displayed; most prefer 19th century items; buy, sell, trade through quarterly newsletter.

Applied Sprig Wares

Experts

Stephanie M. Schnatz
17 Tallow Ct.
Baltimore, MD 21244-2516
ph: 410-944-0819
e-mail: chelsealady@hotmail.com
Buying applied sprig ware (called

Chelsea or Grandmother's Ware); willing to buy any motif in lavender on white china, or white motifs/ decorations on lavender china: jugs, foot bath, soup tureen, miniatures, toast rack, creamers, etc.

Art Pottery

Experts

Geraud Schultz
Antique Gallery, The
8523 Germantown Ave.
Philadelphia, PA 19118
ph: 215-248-1700
fax: 215-247-8411
Buys, sells and specializes in Bernard Moore, Doulton, Pilkington, Clarice Cliff, Susie Cooper, Moorcroft, Roole, Minton, Carlton Ware.

Beswick

Periodicals

Laura J. Rock-Smith
Newsletter: Beswick Quarterly
10 Holmes Court
Sayville, NY 11782-2408
ph: 516-589-9027
fax: 516-589-9027
e-mail: beswickquarterly@yahoo.com
web: http://members.tripod.com/~BeswickQuarterly/
A quarterly newsletter for Beswick collectors: photographs, columns, articles, up-to-date information on Beswick, for sale and wanted ads.

Bunnykins

Dealers

Wendy Link
Pascoe & Company
101 Alameria Ave.
Coral Gables, FL 33134
ph: 800-872-0195 or 305-445-3229
fax: 305-445-3305
e-mail: webmaster@pascoeandcompany.com
web: http://www.pascoeandcompany.com
Buying Royal Doulton figurines, character jugs, and coaching ware; carries large inventory for sale.

Periodicals

Leah Selig
Newsletter: Rabbiting On
2 Harper Street
Merrylands, New South Wales 2160
New Zealand
ph: 612 9637 2410
fax: 612 9637 2410

Carlton Ware

Clubs/Associations

Helen & Keith Martin
Carlton Ware Collectors International
Newsletter: Carlton Times
P.O. Box 161
Sevenoaks, Kent TN15 6GA
U.K.
ph: 01474 853630 or 01374-147197
fax: 01474 854480
e-mail: cwciclub@aol.com
Leading Carlton Ware club.

Dealers

Helen & Keith Martin
P.O. Box 161
Sevenoaks, Kent TN15 6GA
U.K.
ph: 01474 853630 or 01374-147197
fax: 01474 854480
e-mail: cwciclub@aol.com
World's leading Carlton Ware specialists.

Clarice Cliff

Clubs/Associations

Andrew Hutton
Clarice Cliff Collector's Club
1 Foxdell Way
Chellaston
Derby, Derbyshire DE73 1PU
U.K.
ph: +44(0) 133 2691931
fax: +44(0) 870 0522364
e-mail: webmaster@claricecliff.com
web: http://www.claricecliff.com/
The "Official" web site for collectors of Clarice Cliff pottery - Art Deco "masterpieces" from the 1920s and 1930s.

Collectors

Darryl Rehr
P.O. Box 641824
Los Angeles, CA 90064
ph: 310-477-5229
fax: 310-268-8420
e-mail: dcrehr@earthlink.net
web: http://home.earthlink.net/~dcrehr/
Wants handpainted "Bizarre-Ware" only; many patterns including "Fantasque", "Cruise Ware" and others; please send photos.

Experts

Carole A. Berk
Carole A. Berk, Ltd.
4918 Fairmont Ave.
Bethesda, MD 20814
ph: 800-382-2413 or 301-656-0355
fax: 301-652-5859
e-mail: cab@caroleberk.com
web: http://www.caroleberk.com/
Specializes in 20th century decorative art: Clarice Cliff, Keith Murray, Charlotte Rhead, Mexican silver, Bakelite, and costume jewelry; co-author of "Mexican Silver."

Susan Scott
882 Queen Street West
Toronto, Ontario M6J 1G3
Canada
ph: 416-538-8536
fax: 416-534-4814
e-mail: scottca@ibm.net
web: http://www.collecting20thcentury.com/

Doulton

(see also CERAMICS [ENGLISH], Royal Doulton; COLLECTIBLES [MODERN], Royal Doulton)

Dealers

Yesterdays, Inc.
P.O. Box 296
New City, NY 10956
ph: 800-Toby-Jug or 914-634-8456
Send LSASE for brochure; buys single pieces or entire collections; will arrange to come to your house to inspect/pack collections; after 7:00 pm call 800-Toby Mug or 914-634-8456.

Arnie Berger
Yesterdays South, Inc.
P.O. Box 565097
Miami, FL 33256
ph: 800-368-5866 or 305-251-1988
fax: 305-254-5977
e-mail: aberger@yesterdayssouth.com
web: http://www.yesterdayssouth.com/
Send SASE for list of almost 1000 Doultons, Hummels, and Lladros for sale.

Tom & Annette Power
Collector, The
4 Queens Parade Close
London, N11 3FY
U.K.
ph: +44 181 361 7787
e-mail: collector@globalnet.co.uk
Specializing in discontinued Doulton: character jugs, figurines, seriesware, Kingsware, Bunnykins, Flambe, stoneware, etc.

Goss China/Crested Ware

Clubs/Associations

Alisa Schofield, Sec.
Goss Collectors Club
Magazine: Gosshawk, The
31a The Crescent
Stanley Common, Derbyshire DE7 6GL
U.K.
ph: +44 0181 491 4035
fax: +44 0181 262 9713
e-mail: frank@gosscrestedchina.demon.co.uk
web: http://www.gosscrestedchina.demon.co.uk/Club.html
Worldwide membership with regional meetings held in England; W.H. Goss (1833-1906) of Stoke-on-Trent produced a variety of china, parian and terra-cotta ware including decorative busts.

Lynda & Nicholas Pine
Goss & Crested China Club
62 Murray Road
Waterlooville, Hants P08 9JL
U.K.
ph: (011 44 23) 92597440
fax: (011 44 23) 92591975
e-mail: lynda@gosschinaclub.demon.co.uk
web: http://www.gosscrestedchina.demon.co.uk/Club.html

Collectors

Jeanne Goss Spaulding
1325 West Ave.
Hilton, NY 14468
ph: 716-392-2706
Only wants pieces marked "W.H. Goss"; pictorials, parian busts, cottages, monuments, and animals preferred.

Dealers

Lynda & Nicholas Pine
62 Murray Road
Waterlooville, Hants P08 9JL
U.K.
ph: (011 44 23) 92597440
fax: (011 44 23) 92591975
e-mail: lynda@gosschinaclub.demon.co.uk
web: http://www.gosscrestedchina.demon.co.uk/Club.html
Dealers for over 25 years in Goss and all crested china made from 1857 to 1939; has a showroom and a free museum; offers mail order catalog; writes the definitive price guide and other books on Goss & crested ware.

Man./Prod./Dist.

Mike Wallington
Sixpenny Pig, The
75 Cannon Grove
Fetcham
Leatherhead, Surrey KT22 9LP
U.K.
ph: 01372-376612
A Goss and Crested China Company.

Periodicals

Robert Southall
Newsletter: Crested Circle
42 Douglas Road, Tolworth
Surbiton, Surrey KT6 7SA
U.K.
ph: 0181 3990898

Honiton

Clubs/Associations

Robin Tinkler, Pub.
Honiton Pottery Collectors' Society
e-mail: rjohnd@cix.co.uk
web: http://www.cix.co.uk/~moshpit/Hpcshome.html
A society for collectors interested in

Honiton and Crown Dorset pottery and in particular the work of Charles Collard.

Maling

Clubs/Associations

Maling Collectors' Society
P.O. Box 1762
North Shields, NE30 4YJ
U.K.
e-mail: david@cello.easynet.co.uk
web: http://www.geocities.com/RodeoDrive/6544/
For those interested in ceramics manufactured by the C.T. Maling company, England.

Minton

Museums/Libraries

Joan Jones, Cur.
Minton Museum
Minton House
London Road
Stoke-on-Trent, Staffordshire ST4 5DH
U.K.
ph: (01782) 292292
fax: (01782) 292099
e-mail: jmjones@royal-doulton.com
web: http://www.royal-doulton.com/
The Minton Museum is currently available to visit by prior appointment with the Curator, Mrs. Joan Jones; please call in advance to arrange for a visit; the museum contains an unrivaled variety of Minton ceramics dating back to 1793.

Moorcroft

Clubs/Associations

Moorcroft Collectors Club
c/o W. Moorcroft PLC
Sandbach Road
Burslem, Stoke on Trent ST6 2DG
U.K.
ph: 01782 820500
fax: 01782 820501
e-mail: oberon@globalnet.co.uk
web: http://www.moorcroft.com/

Collectors

Leo & Susan Poole
P.O. Box 692
Mill City, OR 97360
ph: 503-897-2625
e-mail: susita@wvi.com

Dealers

John Harrigan
1900 Hennepin
Minneapolis, MN 55403-3160
ph: 612-872-0226
fax: 612-872-0224
Please write with pictures of items.

Man./Prod./Dist.

W. Moorcroft PLC
Sandbach Road
Burslem, Stoke-on-Trent ST6 2DQ
U.K.
ph: 01782 820500
fax: 01782 820501
e-mail: oberon@globalnet.co.uk
web: http://www.moorcroft.com/

Museums/Libraries

Moorcroft Museum
c/o W. Moorcroft PLC
Sandbach Road
Burslem, Stoke-on-Trent ST6 2DQ
U.K.
ph: 01782 820500
fax: 01782 820501
e-mail: oberon@globalnet.co.uk
web: http://www.moorcroft.com/

Rabbitware

Collectors

William F. Oliver, Jr.
P.O. Box 886
Fernandina Beach, FL 32035-0886
ph: 904-261-5328
Wants to buy rabbitware - a colorful Staffordshire ceramic; comes in four patterns: Virginia Rose, Single Rose, Adams Rose and Bullseye, with rabbits around the rim or in the center; usually in form of plates, platters, mugs, chargers.

Royal Crown Derby

Clubs/Associations

Royal Crown Derby Collectors' Guild
Minton House, London Road
Stoke-on-Trent, Staffordshire ST4 7QD
U.K.
ph: 00 44 1782 292292
fax: 00 44 1782 292099
e-mail: icc@royal-doulton.com
web: http://www.royal-doulton.com/rcd/gd_index.html
A company-sponsored collectors club.

Man./Prod./Dist.

Royal Crown Derby
U.K.
e-mail: SecretaryRCD@royal-doulton.com
web: http://www.royal-doulton.com/rcd/
Royal Crown Derby museum, Collectors Guild, Discussion forum.

Royal Doulton

(see also CERAMICS [ENGLISH], Doulton; COLLECTIBLES [MODERN], Royal Doulton)

Dealers

Peggy Guy
Happy Pastime
P.O. Box 1225
Ellicott City, MD 21041-1225
ph: 410-203-1101
e-mail: hpastime@bellatlantic.net
web: http://www.happypastime.com/
Buys and sells; specializes in Royal Doulton, M.I. Hummel, Royal Copenhagen, Bing & Grondahl, Lladro, Goebel, Beswick, Royal Worcester.

Jean-Paul Iannantuoni
455 Concord Parkway N., #5500
Dept. CIC
Concord, NC 28027-6736
ph: 704-786-7758
fax: 704-795-7975
e-mail: AnteekBear@aol.com
web: http://www.freeyellow.com/members/royaldoulton/index.html
Buys and sells Doulton and Royal Doulton character jugs, figurines and series ware; dinnerware search service for all manufacturers; send; send $2 for current price list; appraisals by fee only.

Wendy Link
Pascoe & Company
101 Alameria Ave.
Coral Gables, FL 33134
ph: 800-872-0195 or 305-445-3229
fax: 305-445-3305
e-mail: webmaster@pascoeandcompany.com
web: http://www.pascoeandcompany.com
Buying Royal Doulton figurines, character jugs, and coaching ware; carries large inventory for sale.

Stan Worrey
Colonial House Antiques
182 Front St.
Berea, OH 44017-1920
ph: 440-826-4169 or 800-344-9299
fax: 440-826-0839
e-mail: ywhorrey@aol.com
web: http://www.colonial-house-clltbs.com/
Specializes in old and new Royal Doulton figurines and character jugs; mail lists on request.

Seaway China
135 Broadway
Marine City, MI 48039-1607
ph: 800-968-2424
fax: 800-968-9005
e-mail: sales@seawaychina.com
web: http://www.collectoronline.com/booth-5.html
Specialists in both new and discontinued Royal Doulton including character jugs; also offers a full line of new Bunnykins and Beatrix Potter figurines as well as hundreds of discontinued figurines.

John Harrigan
1900 Hennepin
Minneapolis, MN 55403-3160
ph: 612-872-0226
fax: 612-872-0224
Interested in Toby jugs; please write with pictures of items.

Wellington & Co.
2394 Leeward Circle
Westlake Village, CA 91361
ph: 805-379-3066
Wants old Royal Doulton mugs.

Carol Payne
Carol's Antique Gallery
14455 Big Basin Way
Saratoga, CA 95070-6008
ph: 408-867-7055
Wants to buy animal figurines; will also consider lady figurines, series ware (teapots, or plates with scenes, etc.), stoneware, Toby jugs, teapots and cups.

David Harcourt
Thorndon Antiques & Collectibles
Newsletter: Dounton News
P.O. Box 12076
Thorndon
Wellington, Wgtn 6000
New Zealand
ph: 64-4-4730173 or 64-4-4733560
e-mail: thorndon@paradise.net.nz
web: http://www.thorndon.co.nz
Dealer, expert, appraiser specializes in Shelley, Lilliput Lane, and Royal Doulton.

Experts

Fred Dearden
ph: 561-736-4598
fax: 561-736-9095
e-mail: Fredolt@icanect.net
web: http://www.collectoronline.com/booths/booth-1/
Royal Doulton collector for over 45 years, former consultant to the Royal Doulton International Collectors Club; promoter of Royal Doulton conventions; well networked throughout the US and England.

Man./Prod./Dist.

Customer Service
Royal Doulton USA Inc.
701 Cottontail Lane
Somerset, NJ 08873
ph: 732-356-7880 or 800-682-4462
fax: 732-764-4974
e-mail: usa@royal-doulton.com
China, dinnerware; cups and saucers, figurines, crystal giftware and stemware; US offices.

Museums/Libraries

Ian Howe
Royal Doulton Museum, Royal Doulton Visitor Centre
Nile Street
Burslem
Stoke-on-Trent, Staffordshire ST4 2AJ
U.K.
ph: (01782) 292434 or (01782) 291770
fax: (01782) 292424
e-mail: visitor@royal-doulton.com
web: http://www.royal-doulton.com/rd/visitors/
Home of the Royal Doulton Figure; located within the original factory building; contains the world's largest public display of figures past and present; also the Sir Henry Doulton Gallery, displaying pieces dating from 1815.

Periodicals

Doug Pinchin
B.B.R. Publishing
Magazine: Collecting Doulton
Elsecar Heritage Centre
Nr Barnsley, S. Yorks S74 8HJ
U.K.
e-mail: sales@bbrauctions.co.uk
web: http://www.bbracutions.co.uk/
Leading magazine for the coverage of all aspects of Royal Doulton pottery: character jugs, figurines, advertising items, etc.; published bi-monthly.

Royal Winton

Clubs/Associations

Ken Glibbery, Sec.
Royal Winton International Collectors' Club
Newsletter: RWICC NewsLetter
Dancer's End
Northall, Bedfordshire LU6 2EU
U.K.
ph: +44 (0) 1525 220272
fax: +44 (0) 1525 222442
e-mail: royalwinton@dial.pipex.com
web: http://www.chintzworld-intl.com/
Based in England, this club focuses on chintz, cottage, luster and other wares made by Grimwade Brothers and Royal WInton from 1886 until the 1960s; club newsletter four times per year.

Man./Prod./Dist.

Royal Winton, Unit 1, Lompark Estate
Chadwick Street, Longton
Stoke on Trent, Staffordshire ST3 1PJ
U.K.
ph: 01782 598811
fax: 01782 342737

Royal Worcester

Dealers

Peg Zurkowski
Becker Brooks Antiques
8027 Ellingson Dr.
Chevy Chase, MD 20815
ph: 301-588-8558
fax: 301-608-2167
e-mail: pzrkwski@ix.netcom.com

Gwendolyn R. Reasoner, Ph.D.
Re Vann Galleries
125 Arthur Lane
Hackberry, LA 70645-3001
ph: 609-345-7474 or 800-821-4278
e-mail: revanngal@aol.com
Largest Boehm dealer in the U.S.; specializes in the Boehm secondary market; also Cybis, Royal Worcester, Erte; also appraises.

Man./Prod./Dist.

Royal Worcester Limited
Severn St.
Worcester, Worcestshire WR1 2NE
U.K.
ph: (01905) 23221
fax: (01905) 23601
Plates, figurines.

Museums/Libraries

Museum of Worcester Porcelain, The
Severn St.
Worcester, Worcestshire WR1 2NE
U.K.
ph: (01905) 23221
fax: (01905) 23601
The largest and most comprehensive collection of Worcester porcelain in the world, 1751-2000; situated on the factory site; tours available seven days a week.

Seacombe

Collectors

Peter Blundell
P.O. Box 6
Vernon, British Columbia V1T 6M1
Canada
ph: 250-542-4540
e-mail: peterblundell@bc.sympatico.ca
English-born collector, born where this pottery existed in the 1850s near Liverpool; has researched extensively this poor quality pottery that was made wharfside for export to the US, Canada, West Indies, Australia.

Shelley Potteries

Clubs/Associations

Curt Leiser
National Shelley China Club
Newsletter: NSCC Newsletter
12010 38th Ave. NE
Seattle, WA 98125
ph: 206-362-7136
fax: 206-362-7136
e-mail: cleiser@compuserve.com
Over 550 members world-wide; provides information and services to member and regional units; holds national conferences; quarterly color newsletter with listed Shelley pubs and ads.

Shelley Group
Newsletter: Shelley Group Newsletter
12 Lilleshall Rd.
Clayton
Newcastle-Under-Lyme, Staffordshire ST5 3BX
U.K.

Experts

Phyllis Osjecki
Phyllis'
P.O. Box 792
Canyonville, OR 97417
ph: 541-839-4135 or 541-839-6151
Buys, sells, and appraises Shelley china.

Spode

Clubs/Associations

Rosalind Pulver, Mem.
Spode Society, The
Newsletter: Review
P.O. Box 1812
London, NW4 4NW
U.K.
ph: 0181 203 1769
e-mail: spode@spode.co.uk
web: http://www.spode.co.uk/spode7.htm
Brings together collectors and lovers of Spode; founded in 1986.

Dealers

Carol Payne
Carol's Antique Gallery
14455 Big Basin Way
Saratoga, CA 95070-6008
ph: 408-867-7055
Wants to purchase any pre-1950 Spode; one item or sets; must be in perfect condition; especially likes the "Mayfair" pattern.

Don Hasse
Mr. Spode - D & D Antiques
P.O. Box 818
Mukilteo, WA 98275-0818
ph: 425-348-7443
e-mail: mrspode@aol.com
web: http://www.mrspode.com/
Pattern matching service for Spode/Copeland china from 1770 to present.

Man./Prod./Dist.

Spode
Church St.
Stoke, Stoke-on-Trent ST4 1BX
U.K.
ph: 01782 744011
fax: 01782 747612
e-mail: spode@spode.co.uk
web: http://www.spode.co.uk
Will answer questions about Spode and Copeland factory wares.

Museums/Libraries

Curator
Spode Museum
Church St.
Stoke, Stoke-on-Trent ST4 1BX
U.K.
ph: 01782 744011
fax: 01782 747612
e-mail: spode@spode.co.uk
web: http://www.spode.co.uk

Staffordshire

Appraisers

Stephen van Cline, CAPP
van Cline & Davenport, Ltd.
792 Franklin Ave.
Franklin Lakes, NJ 07417-1343
Specializes in English Staffordshire & Wedgwood ceramics; appraisals, authentication, lectures, expert testimony; minimum charge $25; letter request only, SASE.

Auction Services

Joseph Arman
Collector's Sales & Services
P.O. Box 4073
Middletown, RI 02842
ph: 401-849-5012
e-mail: collectors@antiquechina.com
web: http://www.antiquechina.com
Specialize in mail-bid auctions for historical Staffordshire, Quimper, American glass, paperweights, bottles, etc.

Dealers

Anita L. Grashof
Gallerie Ani'tiques
Stage House Village
Park & Front Streets
Scotch Plains, NJ 07076
ph: 908-322-4600 or 201-377-3032
fax: 973-765-9565
Buys, sells and appraises 19th century English figurines and dogs; royalty, theater, naval and army, sports and miscellaneous groups; also all animals and breeds of dogs in pairs.

Carl McCann
Troy & Black, Inc.
P.O. Box 228
Red Creek, NY 13143-0228
ph: 315-754-8115
e-mail: tbrc@banet.net
Buys and sells high quality flow blue, Staffordshire figurines, American painted furniture, stoneware, redware, coverlets, samplers, and other American textiles, folk art, etc.

Dennis Lockard
2 Hats Collectibles
P.O. Box 1192
Clarksville, VA 23927

J. Wagner
Bygones
P.O. Box 1558
North Bend, OR 97459-0090
ph: 541-756-7111
Buyers of English Staffordshire transferware, old blue and colors; specializes in the Adams potteries.

Experts

Adele Kenny
c/o Schiffer Publishing, Ltd.
77 Lower Valley Road
Atglen, PA 19310
ph: 908-889-7223
Author of "Staffordshire Spaniels: A Collector's Guide to History and Values" (Schiffer); wants to buy and trade all types of Staffordshire figures 1740-1900.

Staffordshire (Historical)

Dealers

William & Teresa Kurau
1617 Lampeter Rd.
Lancaster, PA 17602
ph: 717-464-0731
Wants dark blue and lighter colors; Arms of the States by Mayer; Erie Canal and Liverpool pitchers; list of items for sale available.

Norman Wolfe
Flo Boo - Staffordshire Plus Antiques
Morris Street Antiques, Space #60
503 E. Morris St.
La Conner, WA 98257
e-mail: floboo@pacificrim.net
web: http://www.pacificrim.net/~floboo/
Specializes in flow blue, Mulberry ironstone, all colors of transferware, Historical Staffordshire, cup plates and child's dishes.

Staffordshire (Romantic)

Experts

Mark Brown
Seekers Antiques
P.O. Box 10083
Columbus, OH 43201
ph: 614-291-2203
Advisor to "Warman's Antiques & Collectibles Price Guide."

Tim Sublette
Seekers Antiques
P.O. Box 10083
Columbus, OH 43201
ph: 614-291-2203
Advisor to "Warman's Antiques & Collectibles Price Guide."

Susie Cooper China Ltd.

Clubs/Associations

Alison Dodds
Susie Cooper Collectors Group
Newsletter: Susie Cooper Collectors Group Newsletter
P.O. Box 7436
London, N12 7QF
U.K.
web: http://www.lattimore.co.uk/deco/susie.htm
An international organization for collectors of Susie Cooper ceramics; quarterly newsletter with news, buy/sell ads, auctions, etc.; please send SASE with inquiries.

Collectors

Darryl Rehr
P.O. Box 641824
Los Angeles, CA 90064
ph: 310-477-5229
fax: 310-268-8420
e-mail: dcrehr@earthlink.net
web: http://home.earthlink.net/~dcrehr/
Wants Art Deco style patterns and shapes; please send photo and SASE for guaranteed reply.

Experts

Susan Scott
882 Queen Street West
Toronto, Ontario M6J 1G3
Canada
ph: 416-538-8536
fax: 416-534-4814
e-mail: scottca@ibm.net
web: http://www.collecting20thcentury.com/

Torquay

Clubs/Associations

Marlene Graham
North American Torquay Society
Magazine: Torquay Collector, The
214 N. Ronda Rd.
Mc Henry, IL 60050
For the enhancement of knowledge and enjoyment of Torquay pottery; magazine offers articles, ads, convention news; magazine published quarterly; send LSASE for membership form.

Joy Griffiths
Torquay Pottery Collectors Society
5 Claverdon Dr.
Little Aston
Sutton Coldfield, West Midlands B74 3AH
U.K.
ph: 0121 353 9156
e-mail: tpcs@macatala.demon.co.uk
web: http://www.macatala.demon.co.uk

Collectors

Joseph Brewer
P.O. Box 397
Dalton, GA 30722

Gerry & Jerry Kline
604 Orchard View Dr.
Maumee, OH 43537
ph: 419-893-1226

Experts

Cynthia Holt
c/o Rumbo
8738 1/2 Hunting Drive
San Gabriel, CA 91775-1265
ph: 818-286-6223
Collector and expert in Torquay pottery from all the major firms (Aller Vale, Longpark, Watcombe, etc.); especially wants pottery with scrolls, scenes, figurals; also exceptional motto-ware, especially "Kerswell Daisy."

Transferware

(see also CERAMICS, Ironstone; CERAMICS [ENGLISH], Staffordshire)

Clubs/Associations

Norman Wolfe
Transferware Collector's Club
Morris Street Antiques, Space #60
503 E. Morris St.
La Conner, WA 98257
e-mail: floboo@pacificrim.net
web: http://www.pacificrim.net/~floboo/
An organization of collectors, dealers and museum personnel interested in English transferware, c. 1760-1880.

Internet Resources

Jeff
Antique English Transferware
U.K.
web: http://www.concentric.net/~Jspode/
Great English transferware website with essays, discussion groups, and other information about English transferware.

Wade

Clubs/Associations

Wade Watch
Newsletter: Wade Watch Newsletter
8199 Pierson Ct.
Arvada, CO 80005
ph: 303-421-9655 or 303-424-4401
fax: 303-721-0317
e-mail: webmaster@wadewatch.com
web: http://www.wadewatch.com/

Official International Wade Collectors Club
Royal Works
Westport Road
Burslem, Stoke-on-Trent ST6 4AP
U.K.
ph: 01782 255 255
fax: 01782 575 195
e-mail: info@wade.co.uk
web: http://www.wade.co.uk/
A company-sponsored collectors' club.

Dealers

Patty Keenan
Keenan Antiques
P.O. Box 111
Dover, PA 17315
ph: 717-292-4820
fax: 717-292-4664
Dealer in commissioned Christmas ornaments from Wade; major dealer in English/Irish Wade.

Liz Kramar
Kramar's Kollectible Korner
P.O. Box 30
Elk Mills, MD 21920-0030
ph: 410-398-0105
e-mail: lizk@iximd.com
Wants to buy English/Irish Wade.

Experts

Ian Warner
POS-NER Associates
P.O. Box 93022
Brampton, Ontario LGY 4V8
Canada
ph: 905-453-9074
Co-author with Mike Posgay of "The World of Wade," "The World of Wade Book 2," and "Wade Price Trends First Edition."

Man./Prod./Dist.

Jenny Wright
Wade Ceramics Limited
Royal Works
Westport Road
Burslem, Stoke-on-Trent ST6 4AP
U.K.
ph: 01782 255 255
fax: 01782 575 195
e-mail: info@wade.co.uk
web: http://www.wade.co.uk/

Wedgwood

Appraisers

Stephen van Cline, CAPP
van Cline & Davenport, Ltd.
792 Franklin Ave.
Franklin Lakes, NJ 07417-1343
Specializes in English Staffordshire & Wedgwood ceramics; appraisals, authentication, lectures, expert testimony; minimum charge $25; letter request only, SASE.

Auction Services

Carolyn Remmey
Lincoln Galleries
225 Scotland Rd.
Orange, NJ 07050
ph: 973-677-2000
fax: 973-677-1176
e-mail: warehouses@aol.com
web: http://cybergsi.com/lincoln/

Clubs/Associations

Ronald F. Frazier
Wedgwood Society of Boston, Inc.
Newsletter: WSB Newsletter
Frazier at D.H.S./Wedgwood
P.O. Box 215
Dedham, MA 02027-0215
ph: 781-843-5091
e-mail: wedgwood@hotmail.com
web: http://www.angelfire.com/ma/wsb
Publishes regular newsletter with in-depth articles on Wedgwood; holds regular meetings with speakers on Wedgwood.

Wedgwood Society of New York
Magazine: ARS Ceramica
5 Dogwood Ct.
Glen Head, NY 11545-2740
ph: 516-626-3427
fax: 516-626-3430
e-mail: www@wsny.org
web: http://www.wsny.org/
An annual publication with in-depth articles about Wedgwood and other English ceramics, ads and auctions; also publishes a bi-monthly newsletter.

Wedgwood Society of Great Britain
89 Andrewes House
Barbican
Longon, ECY 8AY
U.K.
web: http://www.geocities.com/Heartland/3203/WSGB.html

Collectors

Stuart Slavid
9 Gryzboska Circle
Farmingham, MA 01702
ph: 508-620-2531
e-mail: wedghead@pop.ma.ultranet.com
Wants to buy old Wedgwood; one piece or entire collections.

B. Stern
56 Center St.
Clinton, NJ 08809
Wants to buy yellow, pink, lilac or other unusual colors of Wedgwood.

Bernard Starr
5 Dogwood Ct.
Glen Head, NY 11545-2740
ph: 516-626-3427
fax: 516-626-3430
e-mail: bstarr12b4@aol.com
Specializes in Wedgwood and other English ceramics.

K. Paterson
2772 Windmill View Rd.
El Cajon, CA 92020
ph: 619-562-4136
Collecting Wedgwood Jasperware boxes and jars; send email with information on ones for sale; also wants out-of-print books on Wedgwood.

Karen Patterson
2772 Windmill View Rd.
El Cajon, CA 92020
ph: 619-581-9844
e-mail: kcp@home.com
Wants to buy Wedgwood Jasperware boxes; also Queensware dishes, cream-on-cream of cream-on-lavender.

Dealers

Benton & Beverly Rosen
Mansion House, Inc.
9 Kenilworth Way
Pawtucket, RI 02860-5607
ph: 401-722-2927 or 508-759-4303
Dealers and collectors; want to buy Wedgwood transfer print decorated commemorative items.

Eric H. Granberg
Deja Vue Antiques
428 Branch Ave.
Providence, RI 02904
ph: 401-521-0872 or 508-226-1816
fax: 401-272-8446
e-mail: dejavue@aol.com
Specialist in Wedgwood; also buys complete or partial dinnerware sets.

Howard Lewis
Howard Lewis Antiques
P.O. Box 5911
Wilmington, DE 19808-0911
ph: 302-731-5597
Buying and selling 18th, 19th and collectible 20th century Wedgwood: Jasper, Basalt, Caneware, Rosso Antico, Drabware, etc.; also wants non-Wedgwood porcelain and china of all types.

Collector's Wedgwood
P.O. Box 462
Newbury Park, CA 91319-0462
Specializes in antique and collectors' Jasper, Fairyland, Creamware, Basalts, Dry Bodies, Majolica; all shapes; no dinnerware, please; send SASE for list.

Experts

Ronald F. Frazier
Frazier at D.H.S./Wedgwood
P.O. Box 215
Dedham, MA 02027-0215
ph: 781-843-5091
e-mail: wedgwood@hotmail.com
web: http://www.angelfire.com/ma/wsb
Collects and lectures on Wedgwood; freelance writer/contributor for periodicals' member of most major Wedgwood collector organizations.

Miriam & Aaron Levin
881 Whalley Ave.
New Haven, CT 06515
ph: 203-389-5440

Martin Spickler, PhD
Tova's Treasures
11410 Strand Dr., #207
Rockville, MD 20852-2938
ph: 301-984-5954
Specializes in English, French, Meissen, Wedgwood, and Oriental ceramics.

Leslie V. Canavan
Alexis Antiques
6348 S. Rosebury Ave.
Saint Louis, MO 63105-2207
ph: 314-863-7897 or 877-WEDGWOOD
fax: 314-863-1176
e-mail: wedgwood@alexisantiques.com
web: http://www.alexisantiques.com
Appraiser, dealer, collector specializing in Wedgwood products of all types and eras; china matching, giftware; college, commemorative & historical plates; appraisals.

Man./Prod./Dist.

Waterford/Wedgwood USA Inc.
P.O. Box 1276
Wall, NJ 07719
ph: 732-938-5800 or 800-444-1997
fax: 732-938-6915
web: http://www.wedgwood-usa.com/
Bone china and earthenware.

Museums/Libraries

Birmingham Museum of Art
2000 8th Ave. N.
Birmingham, AL 35203
ph: 205-254-2565
fax: 205-254-2714
web: http://www.artsbma.org/
Holds the Beeson Collection of Wedgwood, the largest and finest outside England.

Wedgwood Visitor Center & Museum
Barlaston
Stoke-on-Trent, ST12 9ES
U.K.
ph: 01782-204218
fax: 01782-204141
web: http://www.wedgwood.co.uk/visitors_centre.htm/

CERAMICS (ORIENTAL)

(see also DINNERWARE; ORIENTALIA)

Appraisers

Stephen van Cline, CAPP
van Cline & Davenport, Ltd.
792 Franklin Ave.
Franklin Lakes, NJ 07417-1343
Specializes in Japanese and Chinese porcelains; minimum charge $25; letter request only, SASE.

Experts

Martin Spickler, PhD
Tova's Treasures
11410 Strand Dr., #207
Rockville, MD 20852-2938
ph: 301-984-5954
Specializes in English, French, Meissen, Wedgwood, and Oriental ceramics.

Chinese Export Porcelain

Appraisers

Patricia M. Knight
Finetooth Comb Antiques Research & Appraisal Service
P.O. Box 1177
Ames, IA 50010-1177
ph: 515-292-9028
e-mail: ftcres@aol.com
Consultant and qualified appraiser and lecturer on Chinese export porcelains; please send SASE for reply.

Experts

Stuart Slavid
9 Gryzboska Circle
Farmingham, MA 01702
ph: 508-620-2531
e-mail: wedghead@pop.ma.ultranet.com

Hobart D. Van Deusen
28 The Green
Watertown, CT 06795-2118
ph: 860-945-3456
e-mail: rtn.hoby@worldnet.att.net
Wants to buy rare & unusual forms of blue & white Canton; willing to assist others in identifying and pricing their Canton.

Elinor Gordon
P.O. Box 211
Villanova, PA 19085
ph: 610-525-0981

Museums/Libraries

Peabody Essex Museum
Essex & Libert Streets
Salem, MA 01970
ph: 978-745-9500 or 800-745-4054
e-mail: pem@pem.org
web: http://www.pem.org

Dr. Dana D. Ricciardi
Captain Robert Bennet Forbes House
215 Adams St.
Milton, MA 02186-4215
ph: 617-696-1815
web: http://key-biz.com/ssn/Milton/forbes.html
A Boston China trade merchant family's country mansion; 19th century furnishings, American and Chinese export porcelain, prints, paintings, furniture; also Abraham Lincoln and Civil War memorabilia.

Dragonware

Clubs/Associations

Suzi Hibbard
Dragonware Club
2570 Walnut Blvd. #10
Walnut Creek, CA 94596
ph: 925-947-1076
Please include SASE with inquiries.

Collectors

Joyce Lynn
3201 Miami
Wichita Falls, TX 76309
ph: 940-696-1930
e-mail: drgnlady@wf.quik.com
Dragonware expert has been collecting dragonware ceramics for 30 years.

Geisha Girl Porcelain

Experts

E. Litts
P.O. Box 394
Morris Plains, NJ 07950-0394
ph: 973-361-4087
e-mail: happy-memories@worldnet.att.net
web: http://home.att.net/~happy-memories
Author of "The Collector's Encyclopedia of Geisha Girl Porcelain."

Nippon

Auction Services

James W. Breadmore, Sr.
J. Breadmore & Co.
P.O. Box 1679
Andover, MA 01810
ph: 978-975-8926 or 978-682-0705
e-mail: breadmor@aol.com

Jon Crisman, ISA
Jackson's Auctioneers & Appraisers
2229 Lincoln St.
Cedar Falls, IA 50613
ph: 319-277-2256
fax: 319-277-1252
e-mail: jacksons@jacksonsauction.com
web: http://www.jacksonsauction.com
Specializes in Nippon.

Clubs/Associations

Janice C. Eldridge
New England Nippon Collectors Club
64 Burt Rd.
Springfield, MA 01118-1848
ph: 413-783-4629
e-mail: eldride@ix.netcom.cm
Regional chapter of the International Nippon Collectors' Club.

Tim Trapani
Long Island Nippon Collectors Club
145 Andover Pl.
West Hempstead, NY 11552-1603
ph: 516-292-8355 or 718-464-9009
fax: 718-464-8448
e-mail: ttrapani@aol.com
Members study, trade, and discuss Nippon and Noritake; regional chapter of the international Nippon Collectors' Club.

Yvonne Matlosz, Mem.
International Nippon Collectors' Club
Magazine: INCC Journal
9101 Sulkirk Dr.
Raleigh, NC 27613
ph: 941-278-4239
web: http://www.nipponcollectorsclub.com
Fun club specializing in Nippon porcelain; annual convention with seminars, in-room selling, auction, etc.; focusing now on education regarding danger of reproduction items; INCC Journal 3 times a year; INCC Newsletter 3 times a year.

Anne Dickinson
Sunshine State Nippon Collectors' Club
P.O. Box 425
Frostproof, FL 33843-0425
ph: 941-635-4866 or 941-635-4121
fax: 941-635-4866
Regional chapter of the International Nippon Collectors' Club.

Kathy Wojciechowski
Lakes & Plains Nippon Collectors Club
4305 W. Beecher Rd.
P.O. Box 230
Peotone, IL 60468-0230
ph: 708-258-6105
fax: 708-258-6105
Please include a LSASE when requesting a reply; regional chapter of the International Nippon Collectors' Club.

Collectors

Tim Trapani
145 Andover Pl.
West Hempstead, NY 11552-1603
ph: 516-292-8355 or 718-464-9009
fax: 718-464-8448
e-mail: ttrapani@aol.com
Wants to buy Art Deco Noritake, especially women and men figurals; no dinnerware, please.

Mark Griffin
1417 Steele St.
Fort Myers, FL 33901-8431
ph: 800-726-1489
e-mail: nippon준only@aol.com
Buys quality Nippon: chocolate & tea sets, molded, portraits, wall plaques, coralene, urns, jugs, moriage, figural, Deco Noritake.

Debra Tuttle
112 Ascot Dr.
Southlake, TX 76092-5117
ph: 817-481-4129 or 972-242-2160
fax: 972-466-0532

Dealers

Janice C. Eldridge
64 Burt Rd.
Springfield, MA 01118-1848
ph: 413-783-4629
e-mail: eldride@ix.netcom.cm
Wants to buy Nippon - moriage, coralene, high quality vases, urns, etc..

Susan Leite
44 Glenwood Rd.
Brewster, MA 02631-2202
ph: 508-385-4905
Wants to buy undamaged Nippon items.

Deborah Smallwood
Seller of Dreams
P.O. Box 428
Powell, OH 43065
ph: 614-436-8393
Buys and sells all types of quality Nippon.

Alison Libby
Nippon Collection, The
ph: 616-895-6445
e-mail: auntieal@aol.com
web: http://members.aol.com/AuntieAl/index.html
Collector and dealer of authentic, quality Nippon antique porcelain items; Internet website has photos and descriptions of items for sale.

Ward Stewart
Stewart's Antiques
1000 Coolidge
Lafayette, LA 70503-2336
ph: 318-232-2957

Experts

Kathy Wojciechowski
Quality Nippon
4305 W. Beecher Rd.
P.O. Box 230
Peotone, IL 60468-0230
ph: 708-258-6105
fax: 708-258-6105
Pays top dollar for high quality undamaged Nippon: large vases, urns, portraits, moriage, coralene, tapestry, dresser sets, dolls, etc.; author of "The Wonderful World of Nippon Porcelain (1891-1921)", appraiser, lecturer on Nippon.

Wilf Pegg
129 Bathurst St.
Toronto, Ontaria M5V 2R2
Canada
ph: 416-703-0338
fax: 416-703-1330
e-mail: amphora@idirect.com
Advanced collector specializing in early "blown-out" or relief-molded Nippon (1891-1921); features animals, birds and humans in relief.

Noritake

Clubs/Associations

Tim Trapani
Noritake Collectors' Society
Newsletter: Noritake News
145 Andover Pl.
West Hempstead, NY 11552-1603
ph: 516-292-8355 or 718-464-9009
fax: 718-464-8448
e-mail: ttrapani@aol.com
Art Deco, 1920s through 1940s Noritake Lustreware, excluding dinnerware; quarterly newsletter, holds annual convention.

Collectors

Adrienne Leff
1550 S Dixie Hwy. #210
Coral Gables, FL 33146-3034
ph: 305-667-4214
fax: 305-668-2592
Buys, sells, collects Art Deco Noritake, hand painted ladies, clowns, figural ladies and clowns, and strong geometric designs.

Mark Griffin
1417 Steele St.
Fort Myers, FL 33901-8431
ph: 800-726-1489
e-mail: nipponʼonly@aol.com
Wants to buy Noritake Art Deco men and women, also figural and Deco floral decors.

Dealers

Gloria Munsell
Allenwood Americana Antiques
P.O. Box 116
Allenwood, PA 17810-0116
ph: 570-538-1440
Wants the Azalea pattern & scenic Noritake (Tree-in-The Meadow) china only; largest dealer of these patterns in the country; over 20 years experience; always buying & selling.

Experts

David H. Spain
1237 Federal Ave. E
Seattle, WA 98102-4329
ph: 206-323-8102
fax: 206-328-8264
e-mail: Spain3@gateway.net
Publishes books and lectures on Art Deco, 1920s through 1940s Noritake Lustreware, excluding dinnerware; editor of "Noritake News," the official publication of the Noritake Collectors Society; interested ONLY in Noritake non-dinnerware.

Phoenix Bird Pattern

Clubs/Associations

Joan Oates
Phoenix Bird Collectors of America
Newsletter: Phoenix Bird Discoveries
685 S. Washington
Constantine, MI 49042-1407
ph: 616-435-8353
e-mail: koates@remc12.k12.mi.us
Members interested in ceramics decorated in the blue-and-white Phoenix Bird pattern and variants; advisor to "Warman's Antiques & Collectibles Price Guide," "Schroeder's Price Guide," and to "Garage Sale & Flea Market Annual."

Collectors

Dalen Whitt
Rte. 6 - Unus Road
Lewisburg, WV 24901-9834
ph: 304-497-2425
Wants to buy rare items in Phoenix Bird China (spots on breast of bird); also Jadite kitchenware by McKee, Noritake HOWO China, and Delphite kitchenware.

Dealers

Seth Price
Antiques Nook, The
402 Benfield Road
Severna Park, MD 21146
ph: 410-544-5607
e-mail: sprice@clark.net
web: http://www.clark.net/pub/aaccspri/home.html
Buys and sells Phoenix Bird china; mail order or internet sales; no shop.

Carleton L. Cotting
1441 Crowell Rd.
Vienna, VA 22182-1512
ph: 703-759-5646
Collects, buys and sells Phoenix Bird pattern china.

Experts

Joan Oates
685 S. Washington
Constantine, MI 49042-1407
ph: 616-435-8353
e-mail: koates@remc12.k12.mi.us
Collector, historian, consultant; also author of "Phoenix Bird Chinaware" Books I, II, III and IV; available from the author; also specializes in the Flying Turkey pattern variant.

Satsuma

Dealers

Joseph Belperio
1303 Hawthorne Ct.
Sewell, NJ 08080
ph: 609-256-0791
Specializes in fine quality Japanese Satsuma and cloisonne.

Bill Eberhardt
Harry A. Eberhardt & Son
2010 Walnut St.
Philadelphia, PA 19103-5608
ph: 610-568-4144
Specializes in Japanese cloisonne and fine Satsuma.

CEREAL BOXES

(see also PAPER COLLECTIBLES; PREMIUMS, Cereal Boxes)

Auction Services

Jack O'Brian
Memory Tree
P.O. Box 9462
Madison, WI 53715
ph: 414-261-6641
fax: 414-261-9461
Conducts specialty mail auctions of cereal boxes and backs, and character premium rings.

Clubs/Associations

Kevin Meisner
Sugar-Charged Cereal Collectors
Magazine: Freakie Magnet, The
5400 Cheshire Meadows Way
Fairfax, VA 22032-3216
ph: 703-527-3485
e-mail: slid-erkev@aol.com
High-quality magazine for cereal box and cereal box prize collectors; articles, photos, artwork featuring cereals from 1960s to present; buy/sell cereal boxes, prizes, cereal art.

Collectors

John S. Fawcett
P.O. Box 1156
Waldoboro, ME 04572-1156
ph: 207-832-7398
Wants all boxes showing Disney, cowboys, radio premiums, Bugs Bunny; top dollar for a Kix Atomic Bomb Ring Cereal Box.

Steve Roden
P.O. Box 36B16
Los Angeles, CA 90036-1154
ph: 323-933-3158
fax: 323-933-3158
Wants to buy cereal boxes, back panels and premiums; also trading cards, bubble gum items, and radio premiums.

Dan Goodsell
P.O. Box 342
Culver City, CA 90232
ph: 310-815-0465
Interested in all 1950s to 1970s kid's food packaging and premiums such as cereal boxes.

Experts

Scott Bruce
P.O. Box 481
Cambridge, MA 02140-0004
ph: 617-492-5004
e-mail: scottbruce@flake.com
web: http://www.flake.com
Buy, sell, trade cereal prizes, displays and boxes from 1950s to 1970s; especially interested in character material such as Quisp, Quake, monsters and personalities.

David Welch
P.O. Box 714
Murphysboro, IL 62966-0714
ph: 618-687-2282
fax: 618-684-2243
e-mail: PezDude1@aol.com
Wants pre-1975 food or household product boxes showing TV, movie, cartoon, sports, or comic characters or premium offers, especially super heroes; up to $1500 for 1940s-1950s Batman or Superman.

Oats

Collectors

Mike Boggs
2075 Beaver Valley Rd.
Beaver Creek, OH 45385-9521
ph: 937-426-2171
Wants pre-1965 oat boxes; either round or rectangular; Rolled Oats or Quick Oats; such brands as Kamo, Friends, Purity, etc.; any oat boxes with pictures or early artwork.

Sports Related

Experts

Steve Wronker
39 Boswell Rd.
West Hartford, CT 06107
ph: 860-561-8910
fax: 860-561-8910
e-mail: FunnyBusiness2@msn.com
web: http://pages.prodigy.com/funnybusiness/cbox.htm
This web site is the ultimate source about collectors of sport Wheaties cereal boxes; a collector for over 10 years; writes a column about sports related cereal boxes in Beckett Publications and is considered an expert in the field.

CHARACTER COLLECTIBLES

(see also COMIC BOOKS; COMIC COLL.; COMIC STRIPS; COWBOY HEROES; DISNEY COLLECTIBLES; FAN CLUBS; MOVIE MEMORABILIA; POPULAR CULTURE; PREMIUMS; TELEVISION SHOWS & MEMORABILIA; TOYS, Character; WATCHES, Character/Comic)

Clubs/Associations

Metropolitan Cartoon Art & Collectibles Club
P.O. Box 414
Manhasset, NY 11030
ph: 516-627-2123
e-mail: tooncIb@ibm.net
For collectors of cartoon art and character collectibles.

Collectors

Warren Dotz
2999 Regent St., Ste. 300
Berkeley, CA 94705-2118
ph: 510-652-1159
fax: 510-540-0325
e-mail: wellipsis@aol.com
Wants to buy advertising trademark character figures in the form of store displays, banks, statuettes, premiums and dolls; characters include Speedy Alka-Seltzer, PEP Boys, Reddy Kilowatt, Mido Watch Robot, Elsie the Cow, etc.

Dealers

Dave Haveles
Extensive Search Service
51 Squaw Rock
Danielson, CT 06239
ph: 860-774-1203
fax: 860-774-7137
Catalogs of special mailings available for $3 per category; bona-fide dealers are eligible to receive special wholesale character and toy collectibles catalog; obtains large quantities and pass savings on to dealers.

Greg Quire
Cool Toy Shop, The
1008 Fairview Street
Stroudsburg, PA 18360
ph: 717-424-0354
e-mail: cooltoys@epix.net
web: http://www.cooltoys.com
Featuring over 3,000 collectible toys from the 1970s to present; action figures, Barbie, Hot Wheels, Cabbage Patch, California Raisins, character glasses, Disney, Looney Tunes, PEZ, Snoopy, Smurfs, McDonald's, 101 Dalmatians, etc.

Gary Lundquist
Oasis of Quality
336 Shamrock Rd.
Saint Augustine, FL 32086-6560
ph: 904-797-9745
Beatles pinback buttons, Hopalong Cassidy badge, Marilyn Monroe ring; also reproduction Batman, KISS, Lone Ranger, Popeye, Casper, Tom Mix, Shirley Temple related collectibles.

Rod W. Carnahan
Classic Antiques-Toys
541 El Paso St.
Jacksonville, TX 75766
ph: 903-586-1355
e-mail: rodcarnahan_toys@tyler.net

Experts

John Marshall
P.O. Box 340
Rancocas, NJ 08073-0340
ph: 609-267-6903
Buys, sells, collects and specializes in character collectibles, e.g. Mickey Mouse watches.

Doug & Pat Wengel
P.O. Box 305
Skillman, NJ 08558-0305
ph: 609-466-2461
fax: 609-466-8911
e-mail: wengel@njcc.com
web: http://pluto.njcc.com/~wengel
Buys, sells and specializes in vintage character collectibles, especially those with early images of Disney characters Mickey, Minnie, Horace and Clarabelle.

Judith Katz-Schwartz
Twin Brooks Antiques & Collectibles
P.O. Box 6572
New York, NY 10128-0006
ph: 212-876-3512
fax: 212-876-3512
e-mail: twinb@msjudith.net
web: http://www.msjudith.net
Buys, sells, appraises vintage character items, especially early Disneyana, Popeye, Betty Boop, Felix, G.I Joe, Charlie McCarthy, Howdy Dowdy, etc.

Mary Jane Lamphier
Quilted Keepsakes & Unique Dolls Exhibit
577 Main St.
Arlington, IA 50606-9712
ph: 319-633-5885
Buys, sells and trades advertising dolls and characters such as Jolly Green Giant, the Ronald McDonald collection, Campbell Soup Kids, etc.; author of "Zany Characters of the Ad World" (Collector Books, 1995).

Warren Dotz
2999 Regent St., Ste. 300
Berkeley, CA 94705-2118
ph: 510-652-1159
fax: 510-540-0325
e-mail: wellipsis@aol.com
Buys & specializes in advertising character figures including statuettes, banks, store displays, vinyl dolls, cartoonish trademark figurals (Speedy, Alka-Seltzer, Reddy Kilowatt, Mr. Clean, etc.); author of books on the subject.

Museums/Libraries

Herb Barker
Barker Character, Comic & Cartoon Museum
1188 Highland Ave.
Cheshire, CT 06410-1624
ph: 800-227-5372 or 800-995-2357
fax: 203-699-1188
e-mail: fun@barkeranimation.com
web: http://www.BarkerAnimation.com
Features comic character collectibles, television collectibles, cartoon character collectibles, toys, and comic memorabilia.

Periodicals

Antique Trader Publications, Inc.
Newspaper: Toy Trader
P.O. Box 1050
Dubuque, IA 52004-1050
ph: 800-334-7165 or 800-482-4155
fax: 800-531-0880
e-mail: jmkoenig@execpc.com
web: http://www.collect.com/toytrader
Monthly newspaper with information on how to buy, sell and trade all types of toys; market trends, the latest prices, "how-to" columns, listings of toy clubs and upcoming toy shows and auctions; also full of buy and sell ads.

Source Publications, Inc.
Magazine: Collectors' Showcase
7134 S. Yale, Ste. 720
Tulsa, OK 74136
ph: 918-491-9088
fax: 918-491-9946
e-mail: bwilkerson@sourcepub.com
web: http://www.cslive.com/
Bi-monthly full-color magazine focusing on contemporary and vintage character collectibles from animation film art, comics and entertainment studios like Disney Warner Bros., and many more.

101 Dalmatians

Collectors

Kyla Covington
14 Elm St.
Saraland, AL 36571
ph: 334-679-0049
Collects anything to do with the movie "101 Dalmatians."

Alf

Clubs/Associations

Thomas Cannavo
ALFmeisters - ALF Collector Fan Club
25 Arizona Ave.
Jackson, NJ 08527-2134
ph: 732-364-0104
e-mail: tntvg@aol.com

Collectors

Thomas Cannavo
25 Arizona Ave.
Jackson, NJ 08527-2134
ph: 732-364-0104
e-mail: tntvg@aol.com
Buys, sells, trades anything ALF.

Scott Brodnax
225 Church
Clover, SC 29710
ph: 803-222-1066
Wants to buy Alf related toys, books, paper items, fan club items, and NBC material, etc. Fellow ALF collectors please write.

Val Bendel
4072 Tumbleweed Trail
Loves Park, IL 61111

Alice In Wonderland

Clubs/Associations

Ellie Luchinsky, Sec.
Lewis Carroll Society of North America
Newsletter: Knights Letter, The
18 Fitzharding Place
Owings Mills, MD 21117
ph: 410-356-5110
e-mail: eluchin@erols.com
web: http://www.lewiscarroll.org
Many members also collect books and other Lewis Carroll related materials.

Joel Birenbaum
Alice in Wonderland Collectors Network
Newsletter: Alice in Wonderland Collectors Network Newsletter
2765 Shellingham Dr.
Lisle, IL 60532-4245
ph: 630-637-8530
e-mail: birenbau@netwave.net
An organization of collectors, buyers and sellers of Alice In Wonderland and Lewis Carroll items.

Collectors

Alice Berkey
127 Alleyne Dr.
Pittsburgh, PA 15215-1401
ph: 412-782-2686
Wants old Alice in Wonderland items: Alice dolls, toys, figurines, books (especially translations into foreign languages), etc.; anything Alice! Complete and original only, please.

Joel Birenbaum
2765 Shellingham Dr.
Lisle, IL 60532-4245
ph: 630-637-8530
e-mail: birenbau@netwave.net

Betty Boop

Clubs/Associations

Kim Gordon
Betty Boop Fan Club
P.O. Box 42
Moorhead, MN 56561
e-mail: klovesboop@aol.com

Barbara West
Official Betty Boop Fan Club, The
Newsletter: Betty Boop Fan Club Newsletter
6025 Fullerton Ave., Apt. 2
Buena Park, CA 90621-2345
ph: 714-994-1948
Publishes places to find Betty Boop items, special stories about members, pictures for members to use, stories about Betty's past and old "Boopabelia"; newsletter published quarterly.

Collectors

Susan Gahan, ISA
13225 Davisburg Rd.
Davisburg, MI 48350
ph: 248-634-5252
e-mail: trgmich@tir.com

Dealers

Gina Forlano
390 Ridgeview Rd.
Orange, CT 06477
ph: 203-795-0070
Buying, collecting and selling Betty Boop for over 12 years.

Barbara West
6025 Fullerton Ave., Apt. 2
Buena Park, CA 90621-2345
ph: 714-994-1948
Buys and sells "Betty Boop"-a-bilia, both new and old; will buy collections or will sell collections on consignment; send LSASE for latest catalog.

Internet Resources

Gene King
Friends of Betty Boop, The
2307 W. Dearfield Rd.
Mount Pleasant, MI 48858
ph: 517-772-4625
e-mail: gking@edcen.ehhs.cmich.edu
web: http://members.xoom.com/Mr_Boop
An online resource for facts and information on Betty Boop, with a free fan club; sounds, images, links.

Man./Prod./Dist.

Connie Bingaman
P.O. Box 370
Brownstown, IL 62418
ph: 618-427-2761
fax: 314-230-9559
e-mail: mr356@aol.com
Sells many new different Betty Boop collectible items; send SASE for list.

California Raisins

Collectors

Ken Alexander
415 Morgan St.
Elgin, IL 60123-7537
ph: 847-931-0174
Wants to buy items relating to the California Raisins.

Experts

Larry DeAngelo
516 King Arthur Dr.
Virginia Beach, VA 23464-2236
ph: 757-424-1691
Wants to buy or trade California Raisin figurines: surfboards, tambourines, Mom, AC, Graduates, Leonard and Cecil; buys old store stock and closeouts; has appeared on the TV shoe "Collecting Across America" his with extensive collection.

George & Pam Curran
P.O. Box 713
New Smyrna Beach, FL 32170-0713
ph: 904-760-6600
fax: 904-760-5004
Advanced collector looking for PVC characters and any of the related California Raisins products; prefers mint in box, but will consider rarity of item; author of "Collectible California Raisins."

Cartoon & Comic

(see also ANIMATION FILM ART; COMIC BOOKS; COMIC STRIPS, Sunday Newspaper; POLITICAL COLLECTIBLES, Nast Cartoons; POSTERS, Cartoon; SCIENCE FICTION)

Dealers

Cartoon Museum, The
Newsletter: Cartoon Times
814 Mission St.
San Francisco, CA 94103
ph: 415-227-8666
Buys and sells original cartoon art of all types; also "spin offs": books, collectibles, comic books, magazines, etc.; a private museum with original art for more than 2,500 cartoons of all kinds, especially comic art.

Experts

Norm Vigue
62 Bailey St.
Stoughton, MA 02072
ph: 781-344-5441
Wants to buy character collectibles: ceramic figures, banks, movie sheets, tin toys, dolls - Rocky & Bullwinkle, Tom & Jerry, Dick Tracy, Flintstones, Roy Rogers, Howdy Doody, Buck Rogers, Superman, Warner Bros., Terry Toons, etc.

Dagwood-Blondie

Collectors

Rod W. Carnahan
541 El Paso St.
Jacksonville, TX 75766
ph: 903-586-1355
e-mail: rodcarnahan_toys@tyler.net
Wants to buy Dagwood and Blondie collectibles.

Davy Crockett

Collectors

Gary Pimenta
64 Lakeside Dr.
Tiverton, RI 02878-3111
Wants to buy Davy Crockett, The Alamo, and Zorro character collectibles including toys, banks, magazines, comic books, trading cards, records, etc.

Experts

Howard Bender
Crocket Craze
515 Buxton Rd.
Toms River, NJ 08755
e-mail: croktcraze@aol.com
web: http://www.geocities.com/TelevisionCity/Set/1486/
Appraises, buys, sells, collects and specializes in memorabilia related to Davy Crockett.

Dick Tracy

Clubs/Associations

Dick Tracy Fan Club
Magazine: Dick Tracy Fan Club Magazine
P.O. Box 632
Manitou Springs, CO 80829-0632
ph: 719-685-9086
Newsletter published quarterly.

Experts

Larry Doucet
2351 Sultana Dr.
Yorktown Heights, NY 10598-3706
ph: 914-245-1320
fax: 914-739-9094
e-mail: ldoucet@aol.com
Buys, sells, appraises, Dick Tracy; co-author of "The Authorized Guide to Dick Tracy Collectibles"; will appraise Dick Tracy collectibles and memorabilia free of charge; wants to buy anything from premiums and toys to ephemera and art.

Felix The Cat

Collectors

Jason Schmidt
3567 Benton St., #500
Santa Clara, CA 95051
ph: 408-248-5741
fax: 408-248-5551
Wants to buy Felix the Cat items from the 1920s through the 1960s: furniture, toys, games, cells, postcards.

Dealers

Jan Wachtel
Felix Old & New
316 Midvalley Center #115
Carmel, CA 93923
ph: 408-626-8125 or 408-624-4906
fax: 408-622-0225
e-mail: felixtc@redshift.com
web: http://www.redshift.com/~felixtc/
Specializes in Felix the Cat collectibles of all vintages; antique Felix as well as newer collectibles including figures, plushes, jewelry, watches, toys, clothing, etc.

Garfield

Clubs/Associations

Denise Karl
Garfield Connection, The
Newsletter: Garfield Connection Newsletter
2 Lyons Rd.
Armonk, NY 10504-2224
ph: 914-273-3575
e-mail: garfconect@aol.com

Collectors

Adrienne Warren
1032 Feather Bed Lane
Edison, NJ 08820
ph: 732-381-7083
Wants Garfield items: ceramics, figurines, banks, water domes, musicals, plush, promotional items, displays, European items.

Dealers

Denise Karl
2 Lyons Rd.
Armonk, NY 10504-2224
ph: 914-273-3575
e-mail: garfconect@aol.com
Buys, sells, trades Garfield collectibles; entire collections wanted.

Carolyn Berens
Collection Connection, The
P.O. Box 18552
Hamilton, OH 45018
ph: 513-851-9217
Has hundreds of Garfield items in stock.

Hanna-Barbera

Collectors

John Krupienski
5200 Hilltop Dr.
P.O. Box AA6
Brookhaven, PA 19015-1200
ph: 610-874-3003
Collector specializing in Hanna-Barbera character collectibles: Flintstones, Jetsons, Huckleberry Hound, Pixie and Dixie, Quick Draw McGraw, Yogi Bear and Top Cat.

Howdy Doody

Clubs/Associations

Jeff Judson
Howdy Doody Memorabilia Collectors Club
Newsletter: Howdy Doody Times
8 Hunt Court
Flemington, NJ 08822-3349
ph: 908-782-1159
fax: 908-782-0188
e-mail: jjudson@ptd.net
Members are interested in anything related to Howdy Doody - old or new; also known as the Doodyville Historical Society.

Collectors

Chris Swain
P.O. Box 513
Williamsburg, MA 01096
ph: 413-628-3213
e-mail: Bluejettoy@aol.com
Wants Howdy Doody memorabilia.

Jeff Judson
8 Hunt Court
Flemington, NJ 08822-3349
ph: 908-782-1159
fax: 908-782-0188
e-mail: jjudson@ptd.net
World's foremost Howdy Doody collector.

Christmas Catalog Collector, The
175 East Delaware, #7403
Chicago, IL 60611-1731
ph: 800-879-6948 or 312-337-3123
fax: 312-266-7982
Major and enthusiastic collector wants more Howdy Doody toys and other Howdy items; also wants all pre-1985 toy/Christmas catalogs.

Experts

Jack Koch
P.O. Box 428
Morrisville, PA 19067
Author of "Howdy Doody Collector's Reference and Trivia Guide."

Humpty Dumpty

Clubs/Associations

Dee Sharp
Humpty Dumpty Club, The
P.O. Box 328
Fairview, NC 28730
ph: 828-628-0520
e-mail: humptyclub@aol.com
web: http://members.aol.com/humptyclub/
Club for Humpty Dumpty collectors and enthusiasts; free membership.

Collectors

Dee Sharp
P.O. Box 328
Fairview, NC 28730
ph: 828-628-0520
e-mail: humptyclub@aol.com
web: http://members.aol.com/humptyclub/
Wants old Humpty Dumpty related items: paper, wooden, metal, figurines, etc.

Jigglers

Collectors

Debra Sellitti
23 Miller Rd.
Farmingdale, NY 11735
ph: 516-249-1332
Wants jigglers, thick rubbery critters marked "RDF"; some sat, some hung; with ribbon marked "Untouchables" Russberry.

Greg Whitaker
2535 Marsh Lane, #506
Carrollton, TX 75006
ph: 972-418-9442
Wants to buy "jigglers", rubbery creatures from the 1960s.

Li'l Abner

Collectors

Wilma Schiebel
No Place Like Home Collectibles
HCR 63 Box 116C
Yellville, AR 72687-9512
ph: 870-436-5874
e-mail: grantiques@alltel.net
Wants any souvenir related to Dogpatch USA Theme Park; also wants anything related to Li'l Abner such as books, snowdomes, Schmoo, Mammy & Pappy Yokum, etc.

Mystery Science Theater 3000

Clubs/Associations

MST3K Information Club
P.O. Box 5325
Hopkins, MN 55343
e-mail: juliewa@aol.com
Interested in the low-budget cable show featuring Tom Servo, Mike Nelson, and Crow T. Robot.

Peanuts Characters

Clubs/Associations

Andrea C. Podley
Peanuts Collector Club, Inc.
Newsletter: Peanuts Collector Club Newsletter
539 Sudden Valley
Bellingham, WA 98226-4811
ph: 360-733-5209
fax: 360-733-5239
e-mail: acpodley@nas.com
web: http://www.dcn.davis.ca.us/~bang/peanuts/
A privately-owned club dedicated to the art & memorabilia associated with "Peanuts" and with its creator, Charles M. Schulz; also interested in memorabilia associated with the related characters in the "Peanuts" strip.

Experts

Freddi Karin Margolin
12 Lawrence Lane
Bay Shore, NY 11706
ph: 516-666-6861
fax: 516-665-7986
e-mail: snupius@li.net
Wants to buy Snoopy/Peanuts character items; especially wants older wooden music musicals, ephemera, old catalogs from 1967 through the 70s showing Peanuts items; author of "Peanuts ... The Home Collection."

Andrea C. Podley
539 Sudden Valley
Bellingham, WA 98226-4811
ph: 360-733-5209
fax: 360-733-5239
e-mail: acpodley@nas.com
web: http://www.dcn.davis.ca.us/~bang/peanuts/
Co-author with Freddi Margolin of "The Official Price Guide to Peanuts Collectibles."

Pee-Wee Herman

Collectors

Barry Mann-Pee-Wee-Man
10602 Denell Circle
Austin, TX 78753
Wants anything to do with Pee-Wee Herman.

Pink Panther

Collectors

Cheryl Dickinson
P.O. Box 36
Montague, MA 01351
ph: 413-367-9389
Wants all Pink Panther collectibles: toys, ceramics, books, and ephemera; U.S. or foreign.

Pogo

Clubs/Associations

Steve Thompson
Pogo Fan Club
Magazine: Fort Mudge Most, The
6908 Wentworth Ave. South
Minneapolis, MN 55423-2363
ph: 612-869-6320
e-mail: thompson_2@epi.umn.edu
International club explores all aspects of Walt Kelly's career; magazine reprints scarce and unpublished Kellyana, ads, letters, strip; magazine published bi-monthly.

Dealers

Dave Haveles
Extensive Search Service
51 Squaw Rock
Danielson, CT 06239
ph: 860-774-1203
fax: 860-774-7137
Catalogs of special mailings available for $3 per category; bona-fide dealers are eligible to receive special wholesale character and toy collectibles catalog; obtains large quantities and pass savings on to dealers.

Marilyn White
14099 Lakeshore Drive
Nampa, ID 83686
ph: 208-466-1746
e-mail: igopogo@micron.net
web: http://www.webpak.net/~igopogo/
Long time collector and active buyer of rarer Pogo and Walt Kelly items; offers list of Pogo items for sale by mail or on internet.

Experts

Steve Thompson
6908 Wentworth Ave. South
Minneapolis, MN 55423-2363
ph: 612-869-6320
e-mail: thompson_2@epi.umn.edu
Author of "The Walt Kelly Collector's Guide: A Bibliography and Price Guide."

Marilyn White
14099 Lakeshore Drive
Nampa, ID 83686
ph: 208-466-1746
e-mail: igopogo@micron.net
web: http://www.webpak.net/~igopogo/
Long time collector and active buyer of rarer Pogo and Walt Kelly items; offers list of Pogo items for sale by mail or on internet.

Popeye

Clubs/Associations

Official Popeye Fan Club
Newsletter: Popeye Fan Club Newsletter
1001 State St.
Chester, IL 62233
ph: 618-826-4567
fax: 618-826-3322
e-mail: ace1@midwest.net
web: http://www.midwest.net/orgs/ace1/
Specializes in Popeye related collectibles; quarterly newsletter.

Collectors

Patricia L. Norberg
1135 W. 18th Ave.
Eugene, OR 97402-3951
ph: 541-345-9409
Collects Popeye the Sailor Man toys, art and other related collectibles.

Dealers

Spinach Can Collectibles
1001 State St.
Chester, IL 62233
ph: 618-826-4567
fax: 618-826-3322
e-mail: ace1@midwest.net
web: http://www.midwest.net/orgs/ace1/

Punch & Judy

Dealers

Jonathan & Lisa Reynolds
Dramatis Personae - Booksellers
P.O. Box 1070
Sheffield, MA 01257-1070
ph: 413-229-7735
fax: 413-229-7735
Wants to buy pre-1890 Punch and Judy books, prints, ephemera, puppets, pottery, memorabilia, etc.

Red Riding Hood

Clubs/Associations

Ann C. Bergin
Red Riding Hood!
Newsletter: Red Riding Hood Network
P.O. Box 105
Amherst, NH 03031-0105
fax: 508-649-6807
e-mail: acbergin@aol.com
For collectors of (Little) Red Riding Hood.

Road Runner

Collectors

Rik
P.O. Box 681045
Indianapolis, IN 46268
ph: 317-290-9274
Wants Road Runner related toys, books, puzzles, games, lunch boxes and drinking glasses.

Rocky & Bullwinkle

Dealers

Dudley Do-Right Emporium
8218 Sunset Blvd.
Los Angeles, CA 90046
Filled with T-shirts, keychains, charms, pictures, Wossammatta U sweatshirts, and many other types of merchandise, all related to the Jay Ward characters; mail order also.

Periodicals

Gary David
Newsletter: Frostbite Falls Far-Flung Flier
P.O. Box 39
Macedonia, OH 44056-0039
ph: 330-467-1074
fax: 330-468-6936
e-mail: gdcomputer@aol.com
Focuses on Rocky & Bullwinkle and Jay Ward cartoons.

Sherlock Holmes

(see also BOOKS, Mystery; MAGAZINES, Mystery; MYSTERY/ DETECTIVE ITEMS; PIPES; SMOKING COLLECTIBLES)

Collectors

Sherlock S. Holmes, D.D.
P.O. Box 3
Worcester, MA 01613-0003
ph: 508-754-9907
e-mail: mail@SherlockHolmes.com
web: http://www.SherlockHolmes.com
Collects Sherlockiana; wants items relating to, covering, showing, the great detective Sherlock Holmes and/ or Dr. John H. Watson: books, memorabilia, cups, magazines, videos, etc.; contact if you are unsure.

Robert C. Hess
559 Potter Blvd.
Brightwaters, NY 11718-1615
ph: 516-665-8365
e-mail: two21@aol.com
Wants Sherlock Holmes/Sir Arthur Conan Doyle items: figurines, sculpture, statuary, dolls, original artwork, illustrations, etc.

Jerry Margolin
10007 SW Quail Post Rd.
Portland, OR 97219-6368
ph: 503-293-7274
Wants to buy and and all things relating to Sherlock Holmes.

Dealers

Chuck Haley
Sherlock's
13926 Double Girth Ct.
Matthews, NC 28105-4068
ph: 704-847-5480
Interested on all things Sherlockian.

Michael S. Greenbaum
Janus Books, Ltd.
P.O. Box 40787
Tucson, AZ 85717
ph: 520-881-8192
fax: 520-323-3351
e-mail: janus@azstarnet.com
web: http://janusbooks.com
Buys and sells first edition of detective, mystery, and suspense fiction; related bibliography and criticism; Sherlock Holmes; catalog available by snail mail or online.

Simpsons

Collectors

William LaRue
P.O. Box 292
Liverpool, NY 13088
ph: 315-451-2397
e-mail: BartFan@aol.com
web: http://members.aol.com/bartfan
Web site contains an online price guide for Simpson collectibles.

Jay Shearer
2325 Middleton Dr.
North Little Rock, AR 72116
ph: 501-758-2617
e-mail: shearer100@aol.com
Wants Bart Simpson memorabilia.

Dealers

Scott Carruthers
Scott's Simpsons Merchandise Page
10507 NE 269th St.
Battle Ground, WA 98604
e-mail: carrwash@prodigy.net
web: http://www.geocities.com/TelevisionCity/Studio/2930/merchandise.html
Sells rare and new Simpsons merchandise.

Internet Resources

William LaRue
Collecting Simpsons!
P.O. Box 292
Liverpool, NY 13088
ph: 315-451-2397
e-mail: BartFan@aol.com
web: http://members.aol.com/bartfan
A comprehensive online resource to collecting licensed merchandise from Fox's "The Simpsons."

Smurf

Clubs/Associations

Suzanne Lipschitz
Smurf Collectors Club International
Newsletter: Smurf Collectors Newsletter
24 Cabot Road W.
Massapequa, NY 11758
ph: 516-799-3221
e-mail: NYSmurfette@juno.com
Focuses on Smurf memorabilia from 56 countries including fast food, cartoon art, porcelain, puzzles, Pez, plushes, etc.; quarterly newsletter; send SASE for more information.

Collectors

Kerry Culhane
129 58th St.
West New York, NJ 07093-2713
Wants to buy and Smurf or related items.

Suzanne Lipschitz
24CH Cabot Road W.
Massapequa, NY 11758
ph: 516-799-3221
e-mail: nysmurf@aol.com
Wants European items only; post cards, metal cars, books, figurines; must have "Peyo" (creator's name) license mark.

Isabel Haecker
160 Mail St. S., PO Box 92508
Brampton, Ontario L6W 2G0
Canada
e-mail: astro@websmurfclub.org
web: http://www.websmurfclub.org
Collector and expert who wants to buy Smurf collectibles.

Dealers

Colleen Lewis
Buffalo Road Hobby
10120 Main St.
Clarence, NY 14031-2049
ph: 716-759-7541
fax: 716-759-7462
web: http://www.toyline.com/clubs/pcc
Carries complete line of Smurfs, including figures, supers, playsets, super playsets, cottages, castle, displays, key chains, mugs, jewelry, toys, etc.; $3 for catalog; collections sought to buy.

Experts

Greg Quire
Cool Toy Shop, The
1008 Fairview Street
Stroudsburg, PA 18360
ph: 717-424-0354
e-mail: cooltoys@epix.net
web: http://www.cooltoys.com

Internet Resources

Isabel Haecker
Ultimate Web Smurf Club
160 Mail St. S., PO Box 92508
Brampton, Ontario L6W 2G0
Canada
e-mail: astro@websmurfclub.org
web: http://www.websmurfclub.org
Free online collectors club with worldwide connections; the latest information on Smurf figurines and other collectibles; the place to buy, sell and trade Smurf items; free membership entitles you to free ads.

Periodicals

Alan G. Rennard
Newsletter: Smurfing Times
3 Indian Lane
Burlington, NJ 08016-5123
ph: 609-386-8186
fax: 609-386-8186
e-mail: arennard@juno.com
A bi-monthly newsletter dedicated to creating a worldwide Smurf collectors network.

Snoopy

(see CHARACTER COLLECTIBLES, Peanuts Characters)

Soupy Sales

Collectors

Bob Averill
1942 W. Market St.
Pottsville, PA 17901-2043
ph: 800-637-6484 or 570-628-3084
Wants Soupy Sales collectibles: board games, dolls, pencil cases, cards, pencils, pens, cereal boxes, books, clothing, anything Soupy.

Spy Memorabilia

Clubs/Associations

Charles Helfenstein
Secret Agent Fan Club
Newsletter: Spies
P.O. Box 476
Frederick, MD 21705-0476
ph: 301-695-4367
e-mail: ohmss@erols.com
Spies, 007, Avengers, Mission Impossible, Man from U.N.C.L.E.

Dealers

Spy Guise, Inc.
261 Central Ave.
P.O. Box 205
Jersey City, NJ 07307
ph: 201-653-7395
e-mail: spyguise@msn.com
web: http://www.spyguise.com/
Buys, sells, trades; world's largest dealer of spy memorabilia: James Bond 007, Our Man Flint, Man From U.N.C.L.E., I Spy, Avengers; toys, games, novelties, records, lobby cards, posters from around the world.

Spy Memorabilia (James Bond)

Clubs/Associations

Graham Rye
James Bond 007 Fan Club & Archive, The
Magazine: 007 Magazine
P.O. Box 007
Addlestone, Surrey KT15 1DY
U.K.
ph: 01483-756007
fax: 01483-756007
e-mail: jbifc@globalnet.co.uk
web: http://www.thejamesbondfanclub.com/
Focuses on James Bond; publishes "007 Magazine" (glossy, professionally produced, many never-before-seen photographs) and "007 Extra" newsletter (James Bond news worldwide) three times each year.

Collectors

Gary Pimenta
64 Lakeside Dr.
Tiverton, RI 02878-3111
Wants to buy James Bond 007 related toys, clothes, posters, records, magazines, books, etc.; also wants first edition books by Ian Fleming (with dust jackets.)

Tarzan

(see also PERSONALITIES [LITERARY], Edgar Rice Burroughs)

Collectors

Jim Gerlach
2206 Greenbrier Dr.
Irving, TX 75060
ph: 972-790-0922

The Shadow

(see also MAGAZINES, Pulp; PREMIUMS, Radio Show; RADIO SHOWS, Old Time)

Collectors

Karl Schadow
221-A Kirkland Dr.
Richmond, VA 23227
ph: 804-228-8159
Wants any item, collectible or memorabilia related to "The Shadow": radio episodes on discs or reels, LPs, ads, comics, pulp magazines, movies, ephemera, prints, toys, books, premiums, etc.

Three Stooges

Clubs/Associations

Gary Lassin
Three Stooges Fan Club
Newsletter: Three Stooges Journal
P.O. Box 747
Gwynedd Valley, PA 19437-0747
ph: 215-654-9466
fax: 215-368-3595
e-mail: garystooge@aol.com

Collectors

Frank R. Levine
393 Charles St.
Malden, MA 02148-6318
ph: 781-321-0639
Wants 3 Stooges memorabilia.

John Krupienski
5200 Hilltop Dr.
P.O. Box AA6
Brookhaven, PA 19015-1200
ph: 610-874-3003

Gary Lassin
P.O. Box 747
Gwynedd Valley, PA 19437-0747
ph: 215-654-9466
fax: 215-368-3595
e-mail: garystooge@aol.com
Wants 3 Stooges memorabilia; toys, games, posters, stills, anything.

Harry S. Ross
P.O. Box 72
Skokie, IL 60076-0072
ph: 847-432-4820
fax: 847-432-4820
Wants to buy Three Stooges toys, games, original movie posters, props, autographs, autographs, and more!

Mark Lyons
544 Crest Dr.
Encinitas, CA 92024-4145
ph: 760-431-5397
fax: 760-431-1515
Wants pre-1970 Three Stooges toys, games, puppets, promotional items, autographs; also wants newer advertising tie-ins.

Neil J. Teizeira
P.O. Box 20812
Piedmont, CA 94620
ph: 510-658-9938
Wants anything related to The Three Stooges: posters, lobby cards, toys, memorabilia, promotional items.

Neal Austinson
P.O. Box 1691
Windsor, CA 95492-1691
ph: 707-837-9685
Wants to buy Three Stooges 1930s composition head hand puppets, toys, etc.

Man./Prod./Dist.

David Blaise
Soitenly Stooges, Inc.
P.O. Box 72
Skokie, IL 60076-0072
ph: 800-378-6643
fax: 800-329-8735
web: http://www.opendoor.com/stooges/
Catalog of new Three Stooges gifts - dolls, books, videos, posters, T-shirts, watches, ties, magnets, comics, photos, clocks, etc.; send for quarterly "Soitenly Stooges" catalog.

Uncle Remus

Museums/Libraries

Uncle Remus Museum
P.O. Box 3184
Highway 441 S.
Eatonton, GA 31024
ph: 706-485-6856
web: http://www.oconee.com/epchamber/remus.html
Collection of items related to Joel Chandler Harris, author of the fables of Br'er Rabbit and Br'er Fox.

Uncle Wiggily

Collectors

Martin McCaw
P.O. Box 9
Prescott, WA 99348
ph: 800-451-9755
e-mail: mcca2@bmi.net
Wants to buy Uncle Wiggly items including puzzles, books, Sunday comics, candy tins, cloth dolls (Nurse Jane, too), animal cracker box, all dishes, advertising items, etc.; call toll free about anything Uncle Wiggily; finder's fees paid.

Yellow Kid

Clubs/Associations

Richard Olson
R. F. Outcault Society
Newsletter: R. F. Outcault Reader, The
103 Doubloon Dr.
Slidell, LA 70461-2715
ph: 504-641-5173 or 504-280-6778
fax: 504-280-6049
e-mail: olson32@ibm.net
Members collect the art and history of Richard F. Outcault, creator of The Yellow Kid, Buster Brown, and Poor Li'l Mose.

Collectors

William Nielsen
1379 Main St.
Brewster, MA 02631-1723
ph: 508-896-7389
Wants Yellow Kid items.

Craig Koste
2187 State Route 22B
Morrisonville, NY 12962-3423
ph: 518-643-8173
Serious collector buying or trading for all Yellow Kid items.

Richard Olson
103 Doubloon Dr.
Slidell, LA 70461-2715
ph: 504-641-5173 or 504-280-6778
fax: 504-280-6049
e-mail: olson32@ibm.net
Wants all Yellow Kid items including pin-backs, gum cards, toys, ads, magazines, comic supplements, etc.

CHARACTER JUGS

(see CERAMICS [ENGLISH], Royal Doulton; COLLECTIBLES [MODERN], Toby Jugs)

CHARGE CARDS

(see CREDIT CARDS & CHARGE ITEMS)

CHARLIE TUNA

(see ADVERTISING COLLECTIBLES, Figures [Charlie Tuna])

CHARMS

(see also PLASTIC COLLECTIBLES)

Clubs/Associations

Maureen McCaffrey
Bubble-Gum Charm Collector's Club
Newsletter: Charmed I'm Sure!
24 Seafoam St.
Staten Island, NY 10306-5770
ph: 718-979-8496
fax: 718-351-8832
e-mail: McCaf@worldnet.att.net

Plastic

Collectors

Jeffrey Maxwell
Alphabet26 Web Site
213 East Wells Blvd.
Sapulpa, OK 74066-6439
ph: 918-227-0657 or 918-594-8280
fax: 918-594-8281
e-mail: alphabet26@aol.com
web: http://members.aol.com/Alphabet26
A website dedicated to the study of 1940 to 1960s plastic prizes from gum machines and Cracker Jacks with an alphabet theme.

Leo & Susan Poole
P.O. Box 692
Mill City, OR 97360
ph: 503-897-2625
e-mail: susita@wvi.com
Wants older plastic charms.

CHARTS

(see MAPS & CHARTS)

CHECKS

(see BANKING, Bank Checks; COINS & CURRENCY)

CHESS SETS

(see also GAMES)

Appraisers

Jeffrey Litwin, ISA
Litwin Antiques
P.O. Box 5865
Trenton, NJ 08638-0865
ph: 609-275-1427 or 609-275-0996
fax: 609-275-1427
Buys, sells and appraises chess sets, chess books, chess art and chess ephemera. Please send description and/or photo of items for sale; Accredited Member of the international Society of Appraisers.

Clubs/Associations

Dr. Thomas Thomsen
Chess Collectors International
Newsletter: Chess Collector, The
P.O. Box 166
Commack, NY 11725-0166
ph: 516-543-1330
fax: 516-543-7901
e-mail: lichess@aol.com
International membership interested in collecting chess sets, chess stamps, chess books, chess art, and other chess related items; meetings held biennially in the even numbered years.

Collectors

Jim Stephens
10906 Watermill Ct.
Oakton, VA 22124-1024
ph: 703-620-2031
Wants chess sets and related books, pictures, catalogs, etc.; fabricates decorated chess sets from molds; member of Chess Collectors International.

David Warther II
David Warther Carving Museum
2561 Crestview Dr. NW
Dover, OH 44622-7405
ph: 330-852-3455 or 330-343-1868
Collects quality antique chess sets; greatest interest is in wood or ivory sets of European on Indian origin.

Dennis Horwitz
P.O. Box 301
Topanga, CA 90290-0301
e-mail: hellcats99@hotmail.com
Collects antique or unusual chess sets, especially figural sets based on themes; describe condition and composition of set; height of pawn and king; date, location and price of purchase; board or box; include SASE and photo for reply.

Ned Munger, Ph.D.
1201 East California
Pasadena, CA 91125-0001
ph: 626-395-3634
fax: 626-795-1547
e-mail: munger@hss.caltech.edu
Wants ethnic, historic, or geographic theme chess sets; no boards.

Experts

Floyd Sarisohn
P.O. Box 166
Commack, NY 11725-0166
ph: 516-543-1330
fax: 516-543-7901
e-mail: lichess@aol.com

Museums/Libraries

Bernice & Floyd Sarisohn
Long Island Chess Museum
P.O. Box 166
Commack, NY 11725-0166
ph: 516-543-1330
fax: 516-543-7901
e-mail: lichess@aol.com
Private museum of over 850 chess sets and chess related art and collectibles; viewing by appointment only.

Josie De Falla, Dir.
Maryhill Museum of Art
35 Maryhill Museum Drive
Goldendale, WA 98620-4601
ph: 509-773-3733
fax: 509-773-6138
e-mail: MaryHill@gorge.net
web: http://www.maryhillmuseum.org/
Collection contains over 200 antique and unusual sets from around the world.

CHILDREN'S THINGS

(see also BOOKS; DOLLS; DOLL HOUSES & FURNISHINGS; DR. SEUSS ITEMS; HANDKERCHIEFS, Children's; MINIATURES; PERAMBULATORS; RIDING TOYS; TOYS)

Auction Services

Jim & Shari McMasters
McMasters Doll Auctions
P.O. Box 1755
Cambridge, OH 43725-6755
ph: 800-842-3526 or 740-432-4419
fax: 740-432-3191
e-mail: mcmasters@jadeinc.com
web: http://www.angelfire.com/oh/mcmastersauctions/
Specializes in auctioning antique and collectible dolls and doll related items such as teddy bears, children's dishes, toys, children's books, etc.

Collectors

Mary Young
P.O. Box 9244
Dayton, OH 45409-9244
Wants to buy children's tin tea sets from Ohio Art and Wolverine, school readers (primarily first and second grade readers) from the 1920s to 1960s, 1930-1960s coloring and punch-out books.

Dealers

Marjorie Jeffreys
Going to Pieces
P.O. Box 390
Cibolo, TX 78108
ph: 210-659-2458
Buys and sells old games, toys, blocks and children's dishes and children's baking items.

Baby Rattles

Collectors

Marcia Hersey
P.O. Box 976
Ansonia Station
New York, NY 10023-0976
ph: 212-877-5328 or 212-874-3946
Wants to buy baby rattles: gold, silver, wood, celluloid, plastic, etc.

Dealers

Jennifer Sykes
Jennifer Sykes Antiques
9018 Balboa Blvd. #595
Northridge, CA 91325-2610
ph: 818-993-1916
fax: 818-993-7612
e-mail: Veeda10@aol.com
Wants to buy Bakelite crib toys, pre-1970 sterling/celluloid/tin antique baby rattles, boudoir dolls.

Cups

Collectors

Deborah Gillham
47 Midline Ct.
Gaithersburg, MD 20878-1996
ph: 301-977-5727
e-mail: reamers@erols.com
web: http://www.reamers.org/
Wants whimsical children's cups with whistles or figurals on handles or with writing and child illustrations on cup.

Dishes

Clubs/Associations

Shelley Smith
Toy Dish Collectors Club
Newsletter: Tiny Times, The
P.O. Box 159
Bethlehem, CT 06751-0159
ph: 203-266-7496
fax: 203-266-7343
e-mail: toydish@aol.com
web: http://members.aol.com/toydish/
Collectors are interested in children's dishes, furniture, glass, toy kitchen and stores.

Collectors

Cindy Butler
607 Melody Lane
Bessemer, AL 35020
ph: 205-425-9340
e-mail: jdb007@aol.com
Wants to buy old child-size sets of china or porcelain dishes or tea sets.

Mary Young
P.O. Box 9244
Dayton, OH 45409-9244
Wants to buy children's tin tea sets from Ohio Art and Wolverine.

Doris M. Diabo
19953 Great Oaks Circle S.
Clinton Township, MI 48036-2440
ph: 810-463-5651
Wants to buy children's tea sets, especially Majolica; also R.S. Prussia, Wedgwood, Royal Doulton, Royal Rudolstadt, and other quality makers; send photo or photocopy of pattern & markings with price, # of pieces, condition and SASE.

F.J. Steffen
9705 Mill Creek Dr.
Eden Prairie, MN 55347
ph: 612-944-1041
Wants to buy children's dishes, furniture, kitchen and shops, etc.

Dealers

Shelley Smith
P.O. Box 159
Bethlehem, CT 06751-0159
ph: 203-266-7496
fax: 203-266-7343
e-mail: toydish@aol.com
web: http://members.aol.com/toydish/
Buys and sells toys, miniatures, Steiff, children's collectibles, and country smalls.

Abbie Kelly
P.O. Box 351
Camillus, NY 13031-0351
ph: 315-487-7451
e-mail: toydish@aol.com
web: http://members.aol.com/toydish/
Buys and sells doll dishes, toy glass, toy tea sets, doll furniture.

Anna Green
P.O. Box 92
Effort, PA 18330-0092
ph: 570-992-4566
Wants to buy children's dishes in pressed glass, Akro Agate, and depression glass; also china, tin litho, sets or individual pieces.

Louise M. Loehr
Louise's Old Things
163 W. Main St.
P.O. Box 208
Kutztown, PA 19530-0208
ph: 610-683-8370
fax: 610-683-6865
e-mail: louises@bellatlantic.net
Co-author of "Willow Pattern China." Specializing in willow, flow blue, and early children's china. Wants one piece or collections.

Experts

Cathy Cook
10 E. 13th St., #2D
New York, NY 10003-4467
ph: 212-691-2406
fax: 212-691-2406
e-mail: ccook710@aol.com
Collector, author, expert always looking for early 20th century tin litho dishes including those by Ohio Art, Chein Wolverine, etc.

Lorraine Punchard
8201 Pleasant Ave. So.
Minneapolis, MN 55420-2264
ph: 612-888-1079
fax: 612-888-8527
Author of "Playtime Kitchen Items and Table Accessories" (1993), "Playtime Pottery & Porcelain from the United Kingdom and the U.S." (1996), and "Playtime Pottery & Porcelain from Europe and Asia" (1996).

Handkerchiefs

Collectors

J.J. Murphy
920 Emerald St.
Madison, WI 53715-1614
ph: 608-257-3855
fax: 608-257-3730
e-mail: jjmurphy@facstaff.wisc.edu
Collector seeks 19th century printed children's kerchiefs and bandannas; special interest in moralistic, religious, instructional and black related examples (e.g. Uncle Tom's Cabin); condition important; serious sellers only, please.

CHINA

(see CERAMICS; DINNERWARE)

CHINESE ITEMS

(see FURNITURE [ANTIQUE], Chinese; ORIENTALIA)

CHIPS

(see GAMBLING COLLECTIBLES, Gambling Chips & Gaming Tokens)

CHRISTMAS COLLECTIBLES

(see also CATALOGS, Christmas; COLLECTIBLES [MODERN], Ornaments; COLLECTIBLES [MODERN], Christmas; ELVES; HOLIDAY COLLECTIBLES; LIGHT BULBS)

Auction Services

Robert J. Connelly, ASA
Bob & Sallie Connelly Auctions
666 Chenango St.
Binghamton, NY 13901-2015
ph: 607-722-9593 or 607-722-3555
fax: 607-722-1266
e-mail: connelly@clarityconnect.com
Conducts specialty Christmas sales.

Clubs/Associations

Robert Dalluge
Golden Glow of Christmas Past
Newsletter: Golden Glow of Christmas Past
6401 Winsdale St.
Minneapolis, MN 55427-4250
ph: 612-544-8933
e-mail: snowbaby@chesco.com
web: http://www.execpc.com/gmoe/gg-web2
Network of Christmas antique collectors focusing on 1870-1950; annual convention.

Collectors

Bob Merck
44 Newtown Turnpike
Weston, CT 06883-2118
fax: 203-761-8777
Wants pre-1940 figural glass or paper ornaments; Santa Claus figures, Santa blocks & games, figural glass light bulbs (need not work.)

Linda L. Vines
P.O. Box 43721
Upper Montclair, NJ 07043
ph: 973-748-4990
e-mail: lja@viconet.com
Wants to buy 1880-1940 German Santas, candy containers, glass and paper ornaments, early Christmas books, Snow Babies.

Greg Spatafore
103 Wilgate Rd.
Owings Mills, MD 21117-3325
ph: 800-866-5739 or 410-848-9295
Wants to buy old Christmas lighted decorations: bubble lights, candelabras, matchless stars, lighted plaques, unusual bulbs, etc.

Cindy Chipps
4027 Brooks Hill Rd.
Brooks, KY 40109-5002
ph: 502-955-9238
fax: 502-957-5027
e-mail: holauction@aol.com
web: http://members.aol.com/holauction/index.html
Wants figural light bulbs, Matchless Wonder Stars; also other Christmas items, electrical or mechanical.

Coleen Detzel
28 Lacresta Dr.
Florence, KY 41042-9663
ph: 606-647-6156
Wants older blown glass ornaments, older Santas; also any Christmas related items from the 1940s and 1950s.

J. W. & Treva Courter
3935 Kelley Rd.
Kevil, KY 42053-9431
ph: 270-488-2116
fax: 270-488-2116
e-mail: brtknight@aol.com
web: http://www.aladdinknights.org
Wants German Christmas glass figural ornaments, old Father Christmas and matchless Wonder Stars.

Janie Schmidt
P.O. Box 5706
Coralville, IA 52241
ph: 319-337-8270
e-mail: john-schmidt@juno.com
web: http://www.turtlesministry.com/
A 100% all-Christmas newsletter with Christmas related reader-written stories, poetry, recipes, ads, articles on collecting; readers invited to share their collections and stories; send $2 for a 6-page sample.

Susan Murphy
29668 Orinda Rd.
San Juan Capistrano, CA 92675-1211
ph: 949-364-4333
Wants to buy pre 1940s Christmas collectibles: Santa Claus, all ornaments, nativity sets, animals, celluloid toys, candy containers, etc.; please enclose SASE.

Sally Kimmel
1471 Lark Lane
Concord, CA 94521-2942
ph: 510-676-2857
e-mail: sallyraek@yahoo.com
Wants to buy elves, Santas, snowmen, angels, reindeer, toy soldiers, etc.; ornaments and decorations made out of plastic, paper cardboard, etc. made during the 1930s to 1970s; also wants Nativity scenes, sets and mangers.

Dealers

Georgeann High
Yesterday's Memories & More
296 Johnston Rd.
Bentleyville, PA 15314
ph: 724-239-4360 or 724-239-6001
fax: 724-239-6011
e-mail: yestrday@nauticom.net
web: http://www.nauticom.net/www/yestrday
Buys and sells Christmas ornaments: Hallmark, Enesco, German, Czech, early 20th century, handmade; Christmas lights and displays from the early 1900s through 1950s.

Bettie Petzoldt
178 Woolen Mill Rd.
New Park, PA 17352
ph: 717-382-1416
e-mail: philw3@erols.com
web: http://www.mindyourbusiness.com/ornaments/index.htm
Collect/buy/sell early Christmas ornaments: glass, diecut, Dresden, cotton, snow babies, lights, Santas; free monthly illustrated sales list available.

Kit Carter
Ticker Talker Toys
506 Briar Hill Rd.
Louisville, KY 40206
ph: 502-561-5030
Specializes in pre-1920 Christmas collectibles, especially papier-mache candy containers.

George Johnson
18 E. Hunter St.
Logan, OH 43138
ph: 614-385-4845
Always buying and selling Christmas ornaments; author of "Christmas Ornaments, Lights, and Decorations."

Jenny Tarrant
4 Gardenview Dr.
Saint Peters, MO 63376-3507
ph: 314-397-1763
e-mail: jennyjol@aol.com
Wants German Santas, bisque Santas, celluloid Santas, and Santa candy containers.

Mary Lou Holt
12510 Jackson
Grandview, MO 64030

Paul W. Schofield
Lion's Den Antiques
7988 Bethel Burley Rd. SE
Port Orchard, WA 98366
ph: 360-876-3364
fax: 360-876-5421
Buys, sells, appraises, and specializes in old Santas, candy containers, Halloween, Easter, Christmas, Easter, Dresden, figural lights.

Experts

Lissa & Richard Smith
3 Baldtop Heights
Danville, PA 17821
ph: 570-275-7796
Advisor to "Warman's Antiques & Collectibles Price Guide", authors of "Christmas Collectibles."

Margaret & Kenn Whitmyer
P.O. Box 30806
Columbus, OH 43230
e-mail: junquer9@idt.net
web: http://www.kandmantiques.com
Author of "Christmas Collectibles."

Dave Eppelheimer
47 Union Ave., SE
Grand Rapids, MI 49503
ph: 616-459-0474

Periodicals

Rita B. Bocher, Pub.
Newsletter: Creche Herald
117 Crosshill Rd.
Wynnewood, PA 19096-3511
ph: 610-649-7520
e-mail: crecher@op.net
web: http://www.op.net/~bocassoc/
A periodical for all who love, own or collect creches; Christmas events, art, collections, products; creche competitions, exchange for trading, selling, buying creches, figurines; send $3 for free sample,

Creches

Collectors

Rita B. Bocher, Pub.
117 Crosshill Rd.
Wynnewood, PA 19096-3511
ph: 610-649-7520
e-mail: crecher@op.net
web: http://www.op.net/~bocassoc/

Periodicals

Rita B. Bocher, Pub.
Newsletter: Creche Herald
117 Crosshill Rd.
Wynnewood, PA 19096-3511
ph: 610-649-7520
e-mail: crecher@op.net
web: http://www.op.net/~bocassoc/
Christmas events, art, collections, products; creche competitions, exchange for trading, selling, buying creches, figurines; send $3 for free sample,

Feather Trees

Repro. Sources

Karen Shields
Twins Feather Trees & Holiday Collectibles
1543 Pullan Ave.
Cincinnati, OH 45223-2164
ph: 513-681-9357
Limited productions of quality reproductions of feather trees and other Christmas items; Santa figures, Putz animals, fences; also Easter and Halloween; offers antique feather repair and restoration.

Mail Order Catalogs

Dealers

Judy Hesson
Hesson Collectables
1261 S. Lloyd
Lombard, IL 60148-4234
ph: 630-627-3298
fax: 630-627-3298
e-mail: jhesson@mediaone.net
Buys & sells Christmas mail order catalogs: Sears, Montgomery Ward, Penny, Aldens, Spiegel: 1900-1990; also other catalogs; send $4 for list of 900 for sale.

Mexican

Dealers

Ed Barry
Shop, The
116 E. Palace Ave.
Santa Fe, NM 87501-2011
ph: 505-983-4823 or 800-525-5764
Specializes in Mexican Christmas items.

Santa Claus

Collectors

Douglas M. Singleton
P.O. Box 416
Westmoreland, NY 13490-0416
ph: 315-336-7792
e-mail: archaic123@aol.com
Wants to buy Santa Clause pin back buttons from Department stores, banks, advertising products, etc.; also wants Santa pocket mirrors, whistles, spinners, etc.

Martha Tucker
21 Briar Hollow #803
Houston, TX 77027
ph: 713-877-1133
Has an extensive collection of over 2,500 Santas.

CHRONOMETERS

(see CLOCKS, Marine Chronometers)

CIGAR BOXES, LABELS & BANDS

(see also CIGAR STORE COLLECTIBLES; LABELS; PAPER COLLECTIBLES; SMOKING COLLECTIBLES; TOBACCO COLLECTIBLES)

Clubs/Associations

Cigar Label Collectors International
Newsletter: Stone Press
P.O. Box 66
Sharon Center, OH 44274-0066
ph: 216-930-2991
fax: 216-930-2991
For individuals who collect stone lithograph images that were designed to decorate cigar boxes; quarterly newsletter loaded with information on new discoveries, historical information, sales and auctions, plus ads for members.

Collectors

David & Barbara Freiberg
Cerebro
P.O. Box 327
East Prospect, PA 17317-0327
ph: 717-252-2400 or 800-69L-ABEL
fax: 717-252-3685
e-mail: cerebro@cerebro.com
web: http://www.cerebro.com
Wants cigar box, cigar bands, old advertising labels: fire cracker labels, baggage labels, US cigarette cards, sample books of labels.

Joseph Hruby
1511 Lyndhurst Rd.
Cleveland, OH 44124-2857
ph: 440-449-0977
Wants old cigar band collections in good condition.

James Mount
730 Tall Oaks Ave.
Lima, OH 45805
ph: 419-227-2320

Margo Toth
Up Down Tobacco Shop
1550 N. Wells St.
Chicago, IL 60610
ph: 312-337-8505

Dr. Tony Hyman
Treasure Hunt Publications
P.O. Box 3028
Pismo Beach, CA 93448-3028
ph: 805-773-6777 or 805-773-0117
fax: 805-773-8436
e-mail: thyman@fix.net
web: http://www.tobacciana.com
Collector, expert, author; wants pre-1920 cigar box labels, cans & all else related to cigar making, selling or smoking such as photos and historical ephemera; author of "Handbook of Cigar Boxes" and many articles on tobacco collectibles.

Dealers

Steven Gilbert
230 Forge Hill Rd.
Wrightsville, PA 17368
ph: 717-252-2023
e-mail: sgil2001@aol.com
web: http://members.aol.com/sgil2001
Collector and dealer of cigar box labels.

Jerry L. Striker
P.O. Box 372
Lititz, PA 17543
ph: 717-625-2031
fax: 717-625-4314
e-mail: segarman@aol.com
web: http://www.wildgrafx.com/
Wants to buy antique lithographed cigar box labels, cigar sample books, and other cigar related advertising.

David M. Beach
Paper Americana
P.O. Box 2026
Goldenrod, FL 32733-2026
ph: 407-657-7403
fax: 407-657-6382
e-mail: dbeach@ao.net
Wants to buy old cigar box labels.

Joe Davidson
Aaron's Archives
5185 Windfall Rd.
Medina, OH 44256-8703
ph: 330-723-7172
Buys and sells rare cigar labels.

Silas W. Bass
788 Cuchillo St.
Oceanside, CA 92057
ph: 760-726-9937
Wants to buy cigar labels.

Wayne Dunn
Cigar Label Art
P.O. Box 3902
Mission Viejo, CA 92691
ph: 714-582-7686
fax: 714-582-7947
e-mail: wayne@cigarlabelart.com
web: http://www.cigarlabelart.com
Buys, sells, collects, appraises, trades cigar labels; has over 1300 in stock; sells "Cigar Label Art Price Guide" and other cigar art books, also Cigar Label Art CD-ROM with 7000 labels in full 24 bit color.

Experts

Stephen C. Jones
P.O. Box 267
Homer, NY 13077-0267
ph: 607-753-8822
e-mail: stevejones@a-znet.com
Buy, sells, collects and specializes in cigar box labels; cigar box sample books, sample labels & proofs; also wants pre-1900 trade cards, cigarette cards, business cards, billheads, letterheads illustrating products sold; no cigar bands.

Joe & Sue Davidson
Aaron's Archives
5185 Windfall Rd.
Medina, OH 44256-8703
ph: 330-723-7172
Author and expert specializing in stone lithography especially cigar box labels; author of "The Art of the Cigar Label," "Smoker's Art."

Wayne Dunn
Cigar Label Art
P.O. Box 3902
Mission Viejo, CA 92691
ph: 714-582-7686
fax: 714-582-7947
e-mail: wayne@cigarlabelart.com
web: http://www.cigarlabelart.com
Buys, sells, collects, appraises, trades cigar labels; has over 1300 in stock; sells "Cigar Label Art Price Guide" and other cigar art books, also Cigar Label Art CD-ROM with 7000 labels in full 24 bit color.

Dr. Tony Hyman
Treasure Hunt Publications
P.O. Box 3028
Pismo Beach, CA 93448-3028
ph: 805-773-6777 or 805-773-0117
fax: 805-773-8436
e-mail: thyman@fix.net
web: http://www.tobacciana.com
Collector, expert, author; wants pre-1920 cigar box labels, cans & all else related to cigar making, selling or smoking such as photos and historical ephemera; author of "Handbook of Cigar Boxes" and many articles on tobacco collectibles.

Internet Resources

Terry Celano
ASTRALINC
128 W. Main
Brighton, MI 48116
ph: 810-494-2000
fax: 810-227-2450
e-mail: tcelano@ismi.net
web: http://www.astralinc.com/
A community web site where hundreds of people buy and sell antique cigar box labels, cigar boxes, and fruit crate labels.

Museums/Libraries

Dr. Tony Hyman
National Cigar Museum
P.O. Box 3000
Pismo Beach, CA 93448-3028
ph: 805-773-6777 or 805-773-0117
fax: 805-773-8436
e-mail: cigarmuseum@tobacciana.com
web: http://www.cigarnexus.com/nationalcigarmuseum

Periodicals

Ed Barnes
Newsletter: Cigar Label Gazette, The
P.O. Box 3
Lake Forest, CA 92630-0003
ph: 949-457-0737
e-mail: ed@cigarlabelgazette.com
web: http://www.cigarlabelgazette.com/
A bi-monthly newsletter specializing in collecting cigar label art; lists and reviews cigar label auctions; articles, terminology, book reviews, advertisements.

Repro. Sources

Jennifer Collins
Stone Mountain Press
12 Mauchly, Ste. B
Irvine, CA 92618
ph: 714-727-3939 or 888-552-7600
fax: 714-727-0526
e-mail: cigargirls@aol.com
web: http://www.stonepress.com
Has one of the largest collections of stone lithography in the U.S.; sells reproductions of cigar box labels.

CIGAR STORE COLLECTIBLES

(see also CIGAR BOXES, LABELS & BANDS; SMOKING COLLECTIBLES; TOBACCO COLLECTIBLES)

Collectors

Dr. Greg Zemenick
Dr. "Z"
1350 Kirts, Ste. 160
Troy, MI 48084-4852
ph: 248-642-8129 or 248-244-9430
fax: 248-244-9495
e-mail: drzzeezzi@aol.com
web: http://www.drzzeezzi.com/
Wants cigar store items: Indians, figures, cigar cutters, lighters, photos, blinking eye clocks, cast iron items: anything cigar store.

Mike Schwimmer
325 East Blodgett
Lake Bluff, IL 60044-2112
ph: 847-295-1901
Collector of cigar memorabilia; dealer in all forms of vintage advertising; buys and sells.

Russell Barnes
P.O. Box 141994
Austin, TX 78714-1994
ph: 512-835-9510
fax: 512-835-1276
e-mail: csindian@flash.net
Wants to buy pre-1910 cigar store Indians and other figures; wood or metal; also wants original pictures of cigar store Indians; willing to travel; please call collect; pays finders fees.

Museums/Libraries

New York Public Library, Arents Collections, The
455 5th Ave.
New York, NY 10016-0118
ph: 212-340-0833
web: http://www.nypl.org/branch/central_units/mm/midman.html

Cigar Cutters

Collectors

Howie Gross
407 Lincoln Rd.
Miami Beach, FL 33139
ph: 305-534-4757
fax: 305-538-5504
Wants to buy cigar cutters: desk, pocket, figural, counter advertising.

Experts

William J. Ennis
12220 14th Dr. S.E.
Everett, WA 98208-5929
ph: 425-337-5068
Collects any type of cigar cutter; has written several articles about cigar cutters and has done a complete USA patent search on cigar cutters.

CIGARETTE COLLECTIBLES

(see also ADVERTISING COLLECTIBLES, Trade Cards [Tobacco]; ADVERTISING COLLECTIBLES, Lucky Strike; ADVERTISING COLLECTIBLES, Philip Morris; LIGHTERS; MATCHCOVERS; MATCHBOXES & LABELS; MATCH SAFES; SMOKING COLLECTIBLES; TOBACCO COLLECTIBLES)

Collectors

Betty Bird
107 Ida St.
Mount Shasta, CA 96067-2629
ph: 530-926-4331 or 530-926-2231
Buy and sell smokers' sets, cigarette cases, match safes, etc.

Cards

(see ADVERTISING COLLECTIBLES, Trade Cards [Tobacco])

Cigarette Boxes

Dealers

Lenore Monleon
33 Fifth Ave.
New York, NY 10003-4338
ph: 212-475-7871 or 212-675-7771
Wants enamel and sterling match safes and cigarette boxes.

Packs

Clubs/Associations

Richard Elliott
Cigarette Pack Collectors' Association
Newsletter: Brandstand
61 Searle St.
Georgetown, MA 01833-2213
ph: 978-352-7377
e-mail: cigpack@aol.com
web: http://hometown.aol.com/cigpack/index.html
For those interested in cigarette packs, tins, boxes and related advertising items; especially obsolete U.S. brands.

Collectors

Richard Elliott
61 Searle St.
Georgetown, MA 01833-2213
ph: 978-352-7377
e-mail: cigpack@aol.com
web: http://hometown.aol.com/cigpack/index.html

Roll-Your-Own Papers

Collectors

Paul Scheuer
6753 Humbolt Ave.
Minneapolis, MN 55430-1533
ph: 612-561-7321
Collects Roll-Your-Own cigarette paper packets and related memorabilia; also wants old pipe cleaner containers.

Silks

Collectors

William Nielsen
1379 Main St.
Brewster, MA 02631-1723
ph: 508-896-7389
Wants U.S. cigarette silks, leathers, and inserts.

CIGARS

(see SMOKING COLLECTIBLES)

CIPHER MACHINES

(see SPY EQUIPMENT)

CIRCUS COLLECTIBLES

(see also CIRCUS EQUIPMENT, Miniature Models of; CLOWN COLLECTIBLES; PERFORMING ARTS)

Clubs/Associations

Irvin Mohler, Sec. Treas.
Circus Fans Association of America
Magazine: White Tops, The
P.O. Box 59710
Potomac, MD 20859
e-mail: b_taylor@mindspring.com
web: http://www.circusweb.com/CFA/
Focuses on circus history, current acts and activities, reviews of books about the circus, circus bands, etc.

Tom Bracewell
Society for the Preservation of Circus Art
P.O. Box 311192
Enterprise, AL 36331-1192
e-mail: skypilot@entercomp.com
Focus is to help preserve art unique to the circus.

Dave Price, Sec. Treas.
Circus Historical Society
Magazine: Bandwagon, The
4102 Idaho Ave.
Nashville, TN 37209
Members interested in the circus, past and present.

Collectors

Irvin C. Mohler
P.O. Box 59710
Potomac, MD 20859-9710
ph: 301-762-8272
e-mail: mohlerbros@aol.com

Tommy Sciortino
3723 Nebraska Ave.
Tampa, FL 33603
ph: 813-248-9911
Circus equipment and memorabilia, carousels, amusement devices, coin-ops; no circus toys.

Museums/Libraries

P.T. Barnum Museum
820 Main St.
Bridgeport, CT 06604
ph: 203-331-1104
fax: 203-339-4341
e-mail: barbara@barnum-museum.org
web: http://www.barnum-museum.org/

John & Mable Ringling Museum of Art
5401 Bayshore Rd.
Sarasota, FL 34243
ph: 941-359-5700
fax: 941-359-5745
e-mail: ringling@concentric.net
web: http://www.ringling.org/

Circus City Festival Museum
154 North Broadway
Peru, IN 46970-2234
ph: 765-472-3918
fax: 765-472-2826
e-mail: perucirc@perucircus.com
web: http://www.perucircus.com/info.htm
Filled with photos, miniatures and displays.

Fred Dahlinger, Dir. Coll.
Circus World Museum
426 Water St.
Baraboo, WI 53913-2560
ph: 608-356-8341
fax: 608-356-1800
e-mail: cwmlrc@chorus.net
web: http://www.circusworldmuseum.com/
The Museum collects all forms of circus ephemera, documentation, photography and sound recordings; particularly desirable are pre-1900 examples of posters, photographs, correspondence and business records.

Emmett Kelly Historical Museum
202 E. Main
Sedan, KS 67361-1629
ph: 316-725-3470
e-mail: stettler@horizon.hit.net
web: http://skyways.lib.ks.us/kansas/towns/Sedan/museum.html
This museum honors a native son, the famous clown Emmett Kelly (1898-1979) and his sad-faced character "Willie"; collection includes memorabilia of his circus career as well as many items related to local history.

Periodicals

Don Marcks
Newsletter: Circus Report
525 Oak St.
El Cerrito, CA 94530-3699
ph: 510-525-3332
A weekly newsletter devoted to the circus.

Ricketts Circus

Collectors

Bill Ricketts
P.O. Box 9605
Asheville, NC 28805-0605
ph: 828-669-2205 or 828-669-2668
fax: 828-669-2205
Wants to buy any posters, newspaper ads, etc. which advertise the Ricketts Circus (first circus in the US - Phila., PA.)

CIVIL RIGHTS

(see BLACK MEMORABILIA; PAPER COLLECTIBLES; POLITICAL COLLECTIBLES; SLAVERY ITEMS; SOCIAL CAUSES)

CIVIL WAR ARTIFACTS

(see also AMMUNITION & EXPLOSIVE ORDNANCE; BLACK MEMORABILIA; BOOKS, Reference [Civil War]; CIVIL WAR HISTORY; MEDICAL, DENTAL & PHARMACEUTICAL, Civil War; MILITARIA; PERSONALITIES [HISTORICAL], Abraham Lincoln; TREASURE HUNTING)

Appraisers

Courtney Wilson
American Military Antiques
8398 Court Ave.
Ellicott City, MD 21043-4514
ph: 410-465-6827
fax: 410-461-6820
Military antiques 1700-1900: appraiser, consultant, broker, dealer; arms, uniforms, equipment, memorabilia - especially Civil War.

Ronald R. Seagrave
Sergeant Kirkland's
912 Lafayette Blvd.
Fredericksburg, VA 22401-5617
ph: 540-899-5565
fax: 540-899-7643
e-mail: Civil-war@msn.com
Appraiser, consultant, and broker of military antiques from 1700 to 1900: autographs, documents, books, photographs; specializes in Civil War.

Auction Services

Ron Meininger
Antebellum Covers
P.O. Box 3494
Gaithersburg, MD 20885
ph: 888-268-3235 or 301-869-2623
fax: 301-869-2623
e-mail: antebell@antebellumcovers.com
web: http://www.antebellumcovers.com
Offers Civil War and 19th Century American Paper for sale through monthly auctions, net price lists and private treaty: soldier's letters, autographs, images, engravings, patriotic envelopes, images, general orders, slavery items.

Kurt R. Krueger
Krueger Auctions
P.O. Box 275
Iola, WI 54945-0275
ph: 715-445-3845
fax: 715-445-4100

Clubs/Associations

Rob Morgan
Civil War Collectors Society & the American Militaria Exchange
5970 Toylor Ridge Dr.
West Chester, OH 45069
ph: 513-874-0483
e-mail: RWMorgan@aol.com
web: http://www.civiwar-collectors.com/
Established to promote the preservation and collecting of material relating to our nation's rich military heritage, from pre-Revolutionary times to present day.

Collectors

Warren K. Tice
W. Tice & Company
8 Orchard Terrace
Essex Junction, VT 05452-3501
ph: 802-878-3835
e-mail: wtice@vbimail.champlain.edu
Wants to purchase U.S. Military, Confederate, and high quality decorative buttons; also wants to buy military antiques.

Gene Peters
'Tiques
P.O. Box 3267
Farmingdale, NY 11735-0679
ph: 516-842-9549
Wants documents, pictures, articles and artifacts relating to the African/Americans during the Civil War.

Julie Brighenti
1036 Rostraver Rd.
Belle Vernon, PA 15012
ph: 724-929-7311
Wants to buy Civil War memorabilia: swords, belt buckles, medals, badges, etc.

Ken Turner
Ken Turner's Civil War
P.O. Box 911
Ellwood City, PA 16117
e-mail: civilwar@ccia.com
web: http://www.ccia.com/~civilwar/cw.html
Civil War collector and historian, also some items for sale; web site has Civil War Classified Ad page, and Civil War Chatroom with experts answering your questions.

Gil Barrett
8322 Sperry Court
Laurel, MD 20723-1184
ph: 301-498-1412
Wants Civil War photos and memorabilia particularly Maryland Union, 6th and 8th Mass. Infantry, and Boston Light Artillery.

Barry Smith
P.O. Box 38306
Greensboro, NC 27438-8306
ph: 336-288-4375
fax: 336-282-6784
e-mail: bsmith1707@aol.com
Wants Union or Confederate Civil War memorabilia: letters, documents, autographs, photos, etc.

Lewis McSwain
1512 Carlson Ct.
Marietta, GA 30064
e-mail: lsmcswain@aol.com
web: http://members.aol.com/lsmcswain/
Specializes in excavated Civil War relics: buckles, plates, buttons, artillery and similar items.

Garl Fugitt
2430 Canterbury Chase
Murfreesboro, TN 37129
ph: 615-893-7762
Wants to buy Union and Confederate Civil War items: buckles, buttons, carte de visites, etc.

James Mejdrich
128 N. Knollwood Dr.
Wheaton, IL 60187
Wants Civil War photos, letters, diaries, and personal items.

Dean Roath
3050 Winnipeg Drive
Baton Rouge, LA 70819
e-mail: droath@intersurf.com
web: http://www.intersurf.com/~droath/
Collector of Civil War relics.

Jim Kopke
P.O. Box 4310
Dillon, CO 80435-4310
Wants to buy Civil War arms, uniforms, paper items, artifacts, pictures, etc.

Dealers

Bedford & Janet Hayes
Gunsight Antiques
P.O. Box 687
Standish, ME 04084-0687
ph: 207-839-3825
e-mail: info@gunsightantiques.com
web: http://www.gunsightantiques.com/
Specializing in quality items of the Civil War era; especially wants significant items belonging to Civil War soldiers from Maine.

Anna Pansini
P.O. Box 5031
South Hackensack, NJ 07606-4231
ph: 201-296-0419
e-mail: mcj@historyonline.net
web: http://www.historyonline.net
Buying and selling various Civil War items including books, pamphlets,

postcards, prints, audio cassettes, currency, postage stamps, videos, and commemorative medals; send SASE for price list/catalog.

Mike & Rose Klinepeter
Blue & Gray Relic Shop
HCR 81 Box 75
Big Cove Tannery, PA 17212-9603
ph: 717-294-3326
Original and reproductions mail order lists available; send 2 stamps for original and $1 for reproduction list.

Dale & Debra Anderson
Dale C. Anderson Co.
4 W. Confederate Ave.
Gettysburg, PA 17325
ph: 717-334-1031
Sells, appraises guns, swords, uniforms, headgear, relics, personal items, more; all offered in bi-monthly catalog ($12/yr); covers all periods 1775-1945; US & foreign; emphasis on Civil War/Indian Wars period; over 38 years experience.

Herbert Brown
Fields of Glory
55 York St.
Gettysburg, PA 17325
ph: 717-337-2837
e-mail: foglory@cvn.net
web: http://www.fieldsofglory.com/
Specializes in original, authentic Civil War antiques; also carries Civil War related books, prints, reproduction accouterments, and souvenirs.

Sam Small
Horse Soldier, The
777 Baltimore St.
Gettysburg, PA 17325
ph: 717-334-0347
fax: 717-334-5016
e-mail: info@horsesoldier.com
web: http://horsesoldier.com
Specializing in the sale of fine Civil War military antiques: firearms, edged weapons, photographs, documents, battlefield relics and more; all items backed by unconditional guarantee; appraisal and soldier research services available.

Howard A. Hoffman
Military Americana
97 Johnson Rd.
Bangor, PA 18013-9274
ph: 610-588-8853
fax: 610-588-2815

Clifford P. Catania
Joshua's Attic
518 Kimberton Road
Phoenixville, PA 19460
ph: 610-917-1167
web: http://www.joshuasattic.com/

Bob Buttafuso
Centreville Electronics
13810B Braddock Rd.
Centreville, PA 20121
ph: 703-631-0202
fax: 703-222-8625
e-mail: centelec@erols.com
web: http://www.cwrelics.com
Buys, sells, collects and specializes in dug Civil War relics including bullets, buckles, buttons, shells, fuses, spurs, etc.; all guaranteed to be authentic.

Ron Meininger
Antebellum Covers
P.O. Box 3494
Gaithersburg, MD 20885
ph: 888-268-3235 or 301-869-2623
fax: 301-869-2623
e-mail: antebell@antebellumcovers.com
web: http://www.antebellumcovers.com
Offers Civil War and 19th Century American Paper for sale through monthly auctions, net price lists and private treaty: soldier's letters, autographs, images, engravings, patriotic envelopes, images, general orders, slavery items.

Barbara Pengelly
Barb Pengelly, Autographs
13917 No. Meadow Road
Hagerstown, MD 21742
ph: 301-733-9070
fax: 301-416-7891
e-mail: BarbPengly@aol.com
web: http://www.civilwarmall.com/pengly.htm
Authenticate, appraise, buy and sell Civil War documents, letters, diaries, autographs, photos, imprints; member of UACC and of The Manuscript Society; premium paid for Civil War-related material; references available.

Picket Post, The
602 Caroline Street
Fredericksburg, VA 22401
ph: 540-371-7703
Caries a complete line of authentic Civil War memorabilia and metal detectors.

Rick Burton
Carolina Collectors Civil War Relics
P.O. Box 1177
Kernersville, NC 27285
ph: 336-771-0346
e-mail: ccrelics@collectorsnet.com
web: http://www.collectorsnet.com/ccrelics/
Collector and dealer specializes in authentic Civil War items including buttons, buckles, bullets and other Civil War artifacts; website has photo illustrated catalog online.

Brian & Maria Green
Brian & Maria Green, Inc.
P.O. Box 1816
Kernersville, NC 27285-1816
ph: 336-993-5100
fax: 336-993-1801
e-mail: bmgcivilwar@webtv.net
web: http://www.bmgcivilwar.com
Buy & sell Confederate States and Union autographs, letters and documents, especially military related; also photos, CDV's and other memorabilia.

R. Douglas Sanders
McGowan Book Company
P.O. Box 4226
Chapel Hill, NC 27515-4226
ph: 800-449-8406 or 919-968-1121
fax: 919-968-1644
e-mail: mcgowanbooks@mindspring.com
web: http://www.mcgowanbooks.com/
Specializes in Abraham Lincoln and the American Civil War: books, autographs, photographs, and objects of the period.

Jerry R. Robbins
P.O. Box 1349
Hampstead, NC 28443
ph: 800-686-0222
Wants to buy Civil Way and other types of militaria: old swords, flags, uniforms, hats, old daggers and knives, Bowie knives, German, US, Japanese, pistols, Winchester rifle, Civil War guns; also wants Civil War dug items.

Will Gorges
Will Gorges Civil War Items
3100 U.S. Highway 70 East
New Bern, NC 28560
ph: 252-636-3039
fax: 252-637-1862
e-mail: rebel@civilwarantiques.com
web: http://www.civilwarantiques.com/
Full time dealer buys, sells, collects and appraises authentic Civil War artifacts: firearms, accoutrements, edged weapons, dug items, documents, uniforms, coins, etc.; catalog available.

William Skelton
Highland's Vault
P.O. Box 55448
Birmingham, AL 35255-5548
ph: 205-939-1178 or 205-939-3166
Buys and sells Civil War paper items: newspapers (North and South), letters, photos, books, documents, reunion ribbons and medals.

James Mitchell
Ye Old Post Office Antiques & Militaria
P.O. Box 9
17070 Scenic Highway 98
Point Clear, AL 36564-0009
ph: 334-928-0108
e-mail: jim@confederateordinance.com
web: http://www.confederateordinance.com/
Specializes in Civil War arms, accessories, books, etc.

Larry W. Hicklen
Yesteryear Civil War Relics
3511 Old Nashville Highway
Murfreesboro, TN 37129-3094
ph: 615-893-3470
Send $5/yr. for five mail order lists of artifacts for sale: buys & sells CW muskets, pistols, sabers, buckles, buttons, letters, etc.

Paul & Linda Gibson
Gibson's Civil War Newspapers
P.O. Box 948
Bristol, TN 37621-0948
ph: 423-323-2427
fax: 423-323-8123
e-mail: gcivilwar@aol.com
Buys and sells Civil War era (1861-1865) newspapers as well as Civil War related letters, diaries, flags, uniforms, photos; CSA bonds, currency and interim deposit slips; slavery items.

Miles Huskey
Miles of History
P.O. Box 599
Sweetwater, TN 37874
ph: 423-337-2540
e-mail: huskey@usit.net
web: http://www.collectorsnet.com/miles
Collector, dealer and expert in Civil War items.

Rafael & Lori Eledge
Shiloh Civil War Relics
4730 Hwy. 22
Shiloh, TN 38376
ph: 901-689-4114 or 901-926-3900
e-mail: relics@shilohrelics.com
web: http://www.ShilohRelics.com
A 2300 square foot relic shop next to Shiloh National Park in West TN; buys, sells, trades on everything from bullets to full size cannons; also appraises.

Barry Anderson
Barry'd Treasure - Civil War Relics
P.O. Box 40256
Louisville, KY 40256
ph: 502-448-8772
e-mail: btreasur@iglou.com
web: http://www.iglou.com/btreasure/
Collector and dealer in authentic Civil War relics and related items; on-line catalog.

Ted Caldwell
Caldwell & Co. Civil War Antiques
816 Pleasant St.
Lebanon, IN 46052
ph: 765-482-0292 or 765-482-6280
e-mail: civilwr@in-motion.net
web: http://members.tripod.com/~OTC_50/index.html
Actively buy, sell, trade all military items from Revolutionary War through Indian War era; also rewraps leather grips on swords and sabers.

Terry Thomann
Great Lakes Civil War, Inc.
P.O. Box 353
Braidwood, IL 60408
ph: 815-458-2029
fax: 815-458-2428
e-mail: tthomann@ix.netcom.com
web: http://www.bmark.com/cw.show
Has over 35 years experience with Civil War artifacts, firearms, relics; can locate just about anything a collector or museum would like to add to a collection; hosts a major CW show each year in Westmont, IL.

Karl Sundstrom
2512 2nd Ave.
Riverside, IL 60546-1313
ph: 708-447-8673
e-mail: sndstro68@aol.com
Wants to buy all Civil War photographs especially CDVs, albumens, tintypes, ambrotypes, military daguerreotypes; also wants Corps unit badges, paper items, books, personal items; issues photo catalog 3 times per year.

William Butts
Main Street Fine Books & Manuscripts
206 N. Main St.
Galena, IL 61035-2244
ph: 815-777-3749
fax: 815-777-8950
e-mail: msfb@galenalink.com
web: http://www.wcinet.com/msfbooks
Open shop dealing in autographs and out-of-print books in most fields; specializing in all aspects of American history; books and autograph catalogs issued regularly; member of A.B.A.A.

Alex Peck
Antique Scientifica
P.O. Box 710
Charleston, IL 61920-0710
ph: 217-348-1009
e-mail: antiques@advant.net
Wants uniforms, insignia, guns, swords, diaries, photos, Corps badges, Bowie knives, medical instruments, hats, medals, belt plates, tokens, autographs, Lincoln items.

Charles Brecheisen
Trans-Mississippi Militaria
1004 Simon Drive
Plano, TX 75025-2501
ph: 972-517-8111
fax: 972-517-8111
e-mail: charlucv@flash.net
web: http://www.transmississippi.com
Buys, sells, trades anything to do with the Civil War, with a specialty in Civil War medical items: UCV, GAR, reunion items, paper, relics, photographs.

Experts

Ken & Jean Owings
Americana & Bookbinding
P.O. Box 389
Whitman, MA 02382
ph: 781-447-7850
fax: 781-447-3435
Civil War, Colonial American documents, books, autographs and related collectibles.

Richard Friz
Maddie's Muse
P.O. Box 472
Peterborough, NH 03458-0472
ph: 603-563-8155
e-mail: jmdfriz@top.monad.net
Author of "Official Price Guide to Civil War Collectibles."

Mike Woshner
2306 Spokane Ave.
Pittsburgh, PA 15210-4414
ph: 412-884-9299
e-mail: mwoshner@bellatlantic.net
Collects India-rubber and gutta-percha military and civilian artifacts; conducts patent research, publishes articles, displays artifacts and delivers presentations.

Robert P. Broadwater
861 Jefferson Ave.
Tyrone, PA 16686
ph: 814-684-0385
e-mail: milwriter1@aol.com
Author of books about the Civil War; contributor to "North South Trader's Civil War Collector's Price Guide."

Courtney Wilson
American Military Antiques
8398 Court Ave.
Ellicott City, MD 21043-4514
ph: 410-465-6827
fax: 410-461-6820
Military antiques 1700-1900: appraiser, consultant, broker, dealer; arms, uniforms, equipment, memorabilia - especially Civil War.

Craig Wofford
2101 Harrison Ave.
Orlando, FL 32804-5467
ph: 407-872-7425
Collects, appraises and specializes in Civil War memorabilia, Union or Confederate: photographs, letters, documents, diaries, uniforms, canteens, etc.; 25 years experience; free appraisals with SASE; references available.

Terry Thomann
Great Lakes Civil War, Inc.
P.O. Box 353
Braidwood, IL 60408
ph: 815-458-2029
fax: 815-458-2428
e-mail: tthomann@ix.netcom.com
web: http://www.bmark.com/cw.show
Has over 35 years experience with Civil War artifacts, firearms, relics; can locate just about anything a collector or museum would like to add to a collection; hosts a major CW show each year in Westmont, IL.

Internet Resources

Ken Turner
Ken Turner's Civil War
P.O. Box 911
Ellwood City, PA 16117
e-mail: civilwar@ccia.com
web: http://www.ccia.com/~civilwar/cw.html
Civil War collector and historian, also some items for sale; web site has Civil War Classified Ad page, and Civil War Chatroom with experts answering your questions.

Dean Roath
3050 Winnipeg Drive
Baton Rouge, LA 70819
e-mail: droath@intersurf.com
web: http://www.intersurf.com/~droath/
Website is dedicated to the detection, recovery, cleaning, and preservation of metallic artifacts from the American Civil War.

Aaron Harvey
Civil War On-Line
6727 Rose St.
Killeen, TX 76544
ph: 254-539-6924
fax: 254-539-6179
e-mail: stonewal@n-link.com
web: http://www.geocities.com/CapitolHill/8472/webring.html
A web site with lots of links to other Civil War sites on the Internet.

Carter Thompson
Civil War Mall, The
P.O. Box 5033
Pleasanton, CA 94566
ph: 510-462-5211
fax: 510-462-5211
e-mail: civwarmall@aol.com
web: http://www.civilwarmall.com
An on-line marketplace for buyers and sellers of Civil War books, prints, maps. ephemera, artifacts and collectibles.

Museums/Libraries

Grand Army of the Republic Civil War Museum & Library
4278 Griscom St.
Philadelphia, PA 19124-3954
ph: 215-289-6484
e-mail: garmuslib@aol.com
web: http://suvcw.org/garmus.htm
Civil War Museum & Library; artifacts, personal memorabilia, paintings, G.A.R. & S.U.V.C.W. records; open first Sunday or by appt.

Museum of the Confederacy, The
1201 East Clay St.
Richmond, VA 23219
ph: 804-644-7150
e-mail: info@moc.org
web: http://www.moc.org
One of the largest and most comprehensive collections of Confederate art, artifacts, and memorabilia.

Will Gorges, Dir.
New Bern Civil War Museum
3100 U.S. Highway 70 East
New Bern, NC 28560
ph: 252-636-3039
fax: 252-637-1862
e-mail: rebel@civilwarantiques.com
web: http://www.civilwarantiques.com/
Largest inventory of authentic Civil War items in the Southern U.S.; on-site museum and textile conservation studio; full appraisal services; large selection of historical reference books; full authentication services available.

Civil War Soldiers Museum
108 South Palafox Place
Pensacola, FL 32501
ph: 850-469-1900
fax: 850-469-9328
e-mail: info@cwmuseum.org
web: http://www.cwmuseum.org/
Provides an accurate, in-depth and enjoyable trip back to the Civil War through a diverse collection of artifacts, music, art, handcrafted figurines, and life-size camp scenes.

Dr. B.D. Patterson
Confederate Research Center, The Harold B. Simpson
P.O. Box 619
Hillsboro, TX 76645
ph: 254-582-2555
e-mail: thf@texashf.org
web: http://www.texashf.org/publications/sum96/scrapbook9607.html
Large collection of Civil War artifacts; museum provides information about Confederate soldiers & capsule histories of Confederate regiments.

Periodicals

Magazine: Artilleryman, The
RR 1 Box 36
Tunbridge, VT 05077-9707
ph: 802-889-3500 or 800-777-1862
fax: 802-889-5627
e-mail: mail@civilwarnews.com
web: http://www.civilwarnews.com/
Published quarterly, the only magazine exclusively for the 1750-1898 artillery enthusiast: artillery history, unit profiles, shell collecting, etc.

Antique Trader Publications, Inc.
Newspaper: Military Trader
P.O. Box 1050
Dubuque, IA 52004-1050
ph: 800-334-7165 or 800-482-4155
fax: 800-531-0880
e-mail: atpzines@aol.com
web: http://www.collect.com/militarytrader
Monthly publication focusing on military collectibles: articles, collecting, interviews with dealers, military toy column, book reviews, collectibles for sale, espionage.

Bullets

Clubs/Associations

Charles Haislip
Civil War Bullet Collecting Association, The
Newsletter: CWBCA Newsletter
1420 Champions Pines Lane
Augusta, GA 30909
e-mail: cwbullet@cwbullet.com
web: http://www.cwbullet.com/
A nonprofit organization to promote the hobby and education about collecting Civil War ammunition.

Experts

Charles Haislip
1420 Champions Pines Lane
Augusta, GA 30909
e-mail: cwbullet@cwbullet.com
web: http://www.cwbullet.com/
Expert, collector, appraiser of Civil War bullets.

Confederate

Experts

Lewis Leigh, Jr.
P.O. Box 4327
Leesburg, VA 20177
ph: 703-771-3081
fax: 703-771-1432
Wants to buy Confederate uniforms, swords, buttons, weapons, belts, soldiers' letters & diaries, hats and related items.

Confederate Bonds

Dealers

William Skelton
Highland's Vault
P.O. Box 55448
Birmingham, AL 35255-5548
ph: 205-939-1178 or 205-939-3166
Wants all U.S. currency before 1929 and all Confederate States of America currency and coins; also CSA bonds.

Paul & Linda Gibson
Gibson's Civil War Newspapers
P.O. Box 948
Bristol, TN 37621-0948
ph: 423-323-2427
fax: 423-323-8123
e-mail: gcivilwar@aol.com
Buys and sells Civil War era (1861-1865) newspapers as well as Civil War related letters, diaries, flags, uniforms, photos; CSA bonds, currency and interim deposit slips; slavery items.

Experts

Jule Dews
Stoneridge Institute
7703 Baltimore National Pike
Frederick, MD 21702-3557
ph: 301-473-8287
Author/publisher of "Windows of Confederate Finance - CSA Bearer Bonds;" $16 ppd.

Confederate Swords

Collectors

Steve Hess
P.O. Box 1747
Deland, FL 32720-1747
ph: 904-736-1067 or 904-756-6068

Currency

Dealers

William Skelton
Highland's Vault
P.O. Box 55448
Birmingham, AL 35255-5548
ph: 205-939-1178 or 205-939-3166
Wants all U.S. currency before 1929 and all Confederate States of America currency and coins; also CSA bonds.

Cy Phillips, Jr.
S C Coin & Stamp Co. Inc.
P.O. Drawer 661180
Arcadia, CA 91066-1180
ph: 818-445-8277 or 800-367-0779
fax: 818-445-8278
Wants Confederate stamps, Civil War tokens, medals, currency, encased postage, etc.

Internet Resources

Arthur W. Henrick
P.O. Box 61075
Sunnyvale, CA 94088-1075
e-mail: MajorAWH@aol.com
web: http://members.aol.com/webmasacwa/
Web site shows images of US/CSA currency; great site for students and reenactors

Medical

Museums/Libraries

National Museum of Civil War Medicine
Newsletter: Surgeon's Call
P.O. Box 470
Frederick, MD 21705-0470
ph: 301-695-1864
fax: 301-695-6823
e-mail: museum@civilwarmed.org
web: http://www.civilwarmed.org/
Contains the Gordon E. Dammann Collection which includes the only surviving Civil War surgeon's tent, medical chests, uniforms, stretchers, medical instruments, swords, books and personal effects.

Paper Items

Collectors

Jack Donahue
P.O. Box 610123
Flushing, NY 11361-0123
ph: 718-225-0446 or 800-248-5927
fax: 718-225-4067
e-mail: jvdonahue@yahoo.com
Wants Civil War autographs, letters, diaries, arms; also daguerreotypes, ambrotypes, tintypes, carte-de-visites; North and South.

Dealers

Bob & Pat Bartosz
P.O. Box 226
Wenonah, NJ 08090-0226
ph: 609-468-0866
e-mail: civilwarbnp@snip.net
Wants Civil War paper items, e.g. letters, diaries, bank checks, fire department items, early baseball, slave papers. Author of "The Civil War Letter of George R. White 19th Mass. Vol."

Photographs

Collectors

Peter Falk
P. Hastings Falk, Inc.
859 Boston Post Rd.
P.O. Box 833
Madison, CT 06443
ph: 203-245-2246
fax: 203-245-5116
e-mail: info@folkart.com
Wants important vintage Civil War photographs, especially of notable figures such as Abraham Lincoln, Grant, Lee, etc.

Tom Molocea
P.O. Box 100
North Lima, OH 44452-0100
ph: 330-549-3245 or 330-629-1864
e-mail: himages@cisnet.com
Wants to buy vintage Civil War photographs in any format; will buy single image or entire collection.

Dealers

Henry Deeks
P.O. Box 2260
Acton, MA 01720-6260
ph: 508-263-1861
Buys and sells Civil War photographs; issues a sales catalog twice a year.

Herbert Brown
Fields of Glory
55 York St.
Gettysburg, PA 17325
ph: 717-337-2837
e-mail: foglory@cvn.net
web: http://www.fieldsofglory.com/
Specializes in original, authentic Civil War antiques; also carries Civil WAr related books, prints, reproduction accouterments, and souvenirs.

David Cress
Images, Inc.
P.O. Box 21036
Charlotte, NC 28277
ph: 704-849-0740
e-mail: dcress@mindspring.com
web: http://www.civilwarimages.com
Internet site specializing in the sale of authentic Civil War photographs.

Karl Sundstrom
2512 2nd Ave.
Riverside, IL 60546-1313
ph: 708-447-8673
e-mail: sndstro68@aol.com
Wants to buy all Civil War photographs especially CDVs, albumens, tintypes, ambrotypes, military daguerreotypes; also wants Corps unit badges, paper items, books, personal items; issues photo catalog 3 times per year.

Dan Furtak
Shades of Blue & Gray
3543 S. Ferguson
Springfield, MO 65807
ph: 417-887-0009
e-mail: dugspring@worldnet.att.net
web: http://home.att.net/~dugspring/
Appraiser, collector, dealer in Civil War photography & ephemera; has over 150 Civil War images for sale, trade; always looking to buy Civil War photographs, especially of identified soldiers from MO, KS, AR; also wants CW autography.

Swords

Repro. Sources

Sudha Gupta
Legendary Arms, Inc.
P.O. Box 479
Three Bridges, NJ 08887-0479
ph: 800-528-2767 or 908-788-7330
fax: 908-788-8522
web: http://www.legendaryarms.com/
Offers line of reproduction knives and swords; Civil War swords include CSA Artillery, M1850 US Staff & Field, M1850 US Foot Officer, M1860 US Cavalry, CSA Foot Officer, CSA NCO, etc.

Tokens

Clubs/Associations

Dale Cade
Civil War Token Society
Journal: Civil War Token Journal
26548 Mazur Dr.
Rancho Palos Verdes, CA 90274
ph: 310-378-4182
e-mail: TC38thark@worldnet.att.net
web: http://home.att.net/~cwts/cwts.htm
Purpose is to promote the study of Civil War tokens along educational, historic and scientific lines.

Veterans

(see VETERAN ITEMS, Civil War)

CIVIL WAR HISTORY

(see also CIVIL WAR ARTIFACTS; LIVING HISTORY, Civil War)

Clubs/Associations

Civil War Society, The
Magazine: Civil War Magazine
P.O. Box 770
Berryville, VA 22611
ph: 800-247-6253 or 540-955-1176
fax: 540-955-1297
e-mail: cwmag@mnsinc.com
An international organization of Civil War enthusiasts; publishes full-color "Civil War" magazine bi-monthly.

Glenn Wiche
Chicago Civil War Round Table, The
Newsletter: Civil War Roundtable Newsletter
410 S. Michigan Ave., Ste. 1402
Chicago, IL 60605-1402
The nation's leading organization dedicated to the study of Civil War history.

Jerry L. Russell
Heritagepac
P.O. Box 7388
Little Rock, AR 72217
ph: 501-225-3996
e-mail: milhistory@aristotle.net
web: http://www.civilwarbuff.org
The nation's leading battlefield preservation organization.

Jerry L. Russell, NatCh.
Civil War Round Table Associates
Newsletter: Civil War Round Table Digest
P.O. Box 7388
Little Rock, AR 72217
ph: 501-225-3996
e-mail: milhistory@aristotle.net
web: http://www.civilwarbuff.org
The nation's leading battlefield preservation organization.

Jerry L. Russell
Confederate Historical Institute, The
Newsletter: CHI Dispatch
P.O. Box 7388
Little Rock, AR 72217
ph: 501-225-3996
e-mail: milhistory@aristotle.net
web: http://www.civilwarbuff.org
The only organization devoted to the study of the history of The Confederate States of America.

Dr. Stephen Engle
Society of Civil War Historians, The
Newsletter: SCWH Newsletter
P.O. Box 7388
Little Rock, AR 72217
ph: 501-225-3996
e-mail: milhistory@aristotle.net
web: http://www.civilwarbuff.org
The only organization for the teachers of Civil War history; Dr. Engle can be e-mailed at engle@acc.fau.edu.

Internet Resources

United States Civil War
e-mail: hsova@uscivilwar.com
web: http://www.uscivilwar.com/uscwhp2.cfm
Interactive home for Civil War enthusiasts.

Tom Atkinson
Atkinson Guide to Civil War Websites
e-mail: TAtkinson@brii.com
web: http://www.uscivilwar.com/USLinks1.cfm
Website has everything from calendars of events to reenactment information; even bugle calls; primarily for Civil War researchers and reenactors.

George H. Hoemann
American Civil War Homepage, The
719 Luttrell
Knoxville, TN 37920
ph: 423-974-5917
fax: 423-546-3182
e-mail: hoemann@utk.edu
Gathers together in one place hypertext links to the most useful identified electronic files about the American Civil War.

David Madden
United States Civil War Center
Raphael Semmes Dr.
Louisiana State University
Baton Rouge, LA 70803
ph: 504-388-3151
fax: 504-388-4876
e-mail: dmadden@cwc.lsu.edu
web: http://www.cwc.lsu.edu/index.htm
A great Civil War resource website.

Leah Jewett
U.S. Civil War Center
Louisiana State University
Raphael Semmes Drive
Baton Rouge, LA 70803
ph: 225-388-3151
fax: 228-388-4876
e-mail: lwood@lsu.edu
web: http://www.cwc.lsu.edu/
Mission is to promote the study of the war from perspectives of all professions, occupations, and academic disciplines; web site features links to 3000 Civil War related sites, including sites dealing with collectibles & antiques.

Misc. Services

National Archives & Records Administration
700 Pennsylvania Ave. NW
Washington, DC 20408
ph: 202-501-5403
e-mail: inquire@nara.gov
web: http://www.nara.gov/
For locating military records of Civil War veterans; regional offices located across the country.

Department of Veteran Affairs, Director of National Cemetery System
810 Vermont Ave. NW
Washington, DC 20420
web: http://www.cem.va.gov/
Contact to find out where a Civil War ancestor was buried during or after the Civil War.

Marie Varrelman Melchiori, CGRS, CGL
121 Tapawingo Rd. SW
Vienna, VA 22180-5964
ph: 703-938-8103
fax: 703-938-7279
e-mail: mvmcgrs@juno.com
Certified Genealogical Record Specialist in Civil War research; will help identify owners of historical items; will assist members of the legal profession locate missing heirs.

Periodicals

Newspaper: Civil War News, The
RR 1 Box 36
Tunbridge, VT 05077-9707
ph: 802-889-3500 or 800-777-1862
fax: 802-889-5627
e-mail: mail@civilwarnews.com
web: http://www.civilwarnews.com/
A current events newspaper published ten times per year for people with an active interest in Civil War history.

Anna Pansini
Distant Frontier Press
Journal: Mail Call Journal
P.O. Box 5031
South Hackensack, NJ 07606-4231
ph: 201-296-0419
e-mail: mcj@historyonline.net
web: http://www.historyonline.net
Published six times per year, each issue is filled with excerpts from letters, stories, diaries, journals, and poems written to, by or about Civil War soldiers.

Dave Gallagher
Newspaper: Civil War Courier, The
2503 Delaware Ave.
Buffalo, NY 14216
ph: 716-873-2594 or 800-418-1861
fax: 716-873-0809
A bi-monthly newspaper containing classified ads, articles, events, calendar, book reviews, reenactors, and goods/services for Civil War buffs.

Cowles Magazines, Inc.
Magazine: Civil War Times Illustrated
741 Miller Dr. SE, Ste. D2
Harrisburg, PA 20175
ph: 717-540-6617 or 800-829-3340
fax: 717-540-6706
e-mail: brentd@cowles.com
web: http://www.cowles.com/maglist.html
A bi-monthly magazine focusing on the historical aspects of the great conflict; a general interest magazine examining all aspects of the Civil War era, including personalities, battles, travel, art, artifacts and politics; bi-monthly.

Cowles Magazines, Inc.
Magazine: America's Civil War
741 Miller Dr. SE, Ste. D2
Harrisburg, PA 20175
ph: 717-540-6617 or 800-829-3340
fax: 717-540-6706
e-mail: brentd@cowles.com
web: http://www.cowles.com/maglist.html
A bi-monthly magazine with colorful articles on Civil War battles, personalities, units; also ads for Civil War related products, prints, books, models, etc.

Cowles Magazines, Inc.
Magazine: Columbiad
741 Miller Dr. SE, Ste. D2
Harrisburg, PA 20175
ph: 717-540-6617 or 800-829-3340
fax: 717-540-6706
e-mail: brentd@cowles.com
web: http://www.cowles.com/maglist.html
A quarterly journal covering the events, persons, and phenomena of the Civil War in detailed, analytical, but lively articles that meet scholarly

standards but are edited specifically for amateur rather than professional historians.

Nancy Dearing Rossbacher
Magazine: North South Trader's Civil War
P.O. Drawer 631
Orange, VA 22960-0370
ph: 540-67C-IVIL
fax: 540-672-7283
e-mail: nstcw@msn.com
web: http://www.nstcivilwar.com
Bi-monthly magazine for Civil War relic hunters, collectors, reenactors & historians.

Magazine: Blue & Gray Magazine
P.O. Box 28685
Columbus, OH 43228
ph: 800-248-4592 or 614-870-1861
fax: 614-870-7881
e-mail: AdvRep@aol.com
web: http://www.bluegraymagazine.com/
A bi-monthly full-color magazine focusing on the Civil War.

Theodore P. Savas
Regimental Studies, Inc.
Journal: Civil War Regiments
1475 S. Bascom Ave., Ste. 204
Campbell, CA 95008-0629
ph: 408-879-9039 or 800-848-6585
fax: 408-879-9327
e-mail: mhbooks@aol.com
A quarterly journal of the American Civil War; book reviews, The Preservation Report and The Regimental Bookshelf, unit-related articles.

Cavalry

Experts

Nick Nichols
Heartland House
Old Blue Ridge Turnpike
Rochelle, VA 22738
ph: 540-672-9267
fax: 540-672-9267
e-mail: neocelt@earthlink.net
Over 25 years of intensive research &scholarship on Civil War history; special emphasis on cavalry themes; extensive background in material culture, tactics, etc.; references provided on request; buys & collects cavalry-related items.

Repro. Sources

Nick Nichols
Heartland House
Old Blue Ridge Turnpike
Rochelle, VA 22738
ph: 540-672-9267
fax: 540-672-9267
e-mail: neocelt@earthlink.net
Museum-quality replica items for collectors & interpreters; exclusive line of Confederate central government issue horse furniture & accoutrements; also carries reference materials, etc.; conservation; consultations; catalog $4.

CIVILIAN CONSERVATION CORPS ITEMS

Clubs/Associations

Association of Civilian Conservation Corps Alumni
P.O. Box 16429
Saint Louis, MO 63125
ph: 314-487-8666
fax: 314-487-9488
e-mail: nacca@aol.com
web: http://pages.prodigy.com/naccca/home.htm
A group of over 10,000 members who served in the CCC from 1933 to 1942.

Collectors

Jake Eckenrode
310 Wallace Rd.
Bellefonte, PA 16823
ph: 814-355-8769
Wants CCC items from the 1930s.

Robert A. Fratkin
8280 Greensboro Dr., #200
Mc Lean, VA 22102
ph: 703-556-8101 or 202-483-0274
fax: 703-356-6492
e-mail: coxfdr@erols.com
Wants all CCC issued items.

Larry Jarvinen
313 Condon Rd.
Manistee, MI 49660
ph: 616-723-5063
Wants CCC or WPA marked items and early forestry or conservation related items; also wants USFS, FSR, FSF, and US marked items.

Thomas W. Pooler
P.O. Box 1861
Grass Valley, CA 95945-1861
ph: 530-268-1338
Wants all CCC material: medals, flags, rings, tokens, insignia (especially numbered company patches - will pay $25 for each numbered Unit sleeve patch.) Send description AND price.

Dealers

Ken Kipp
Allenwood Americana Antiques
P.O. Box 116
Allenwood, PA 17810-0116
ph: 570-538-1440
Established dealer with over 20 years experience; always buying and selling.

CLOCKS

(see also ART DECO; BOOKS, Reference [Clocks]; INSTRUMENTS & DEVICES, Scientific; NAUTICAL ANTIQUES, Marine Chronometers; NEON, Clocks; WATCHES)

Appraisers

Robert J. Connelly, ASA
Bob & Sallie Connelly Auctions
666 Chenango St.
Binghamton, NY 13901-2015
ph: 607-722-9593 or 607-722-3555
fax: 607-722-1266
e-mail: connelly@clarityconnect.com
Appraisers and brokers of American & European clocks.

Walter A. Dayett
Dayett's Clock Repair & Appraisals
75 Study Rd.
Littlestown, PA 17340-9746
ph: 717-359-4850
fax: 717-359-4850
e-mail: wdayett@desupernet.net
web: http://users.desupernet.net/wdayett/wdayett.html
Specializes in antique and contemporary clock sales and repair, primarily weight and spring driven movements; also specializes in clock appraisals.

Martha Tips, AAA, ISA CAPP
For All Time Enterprises
7012 Blackwood Dr.
Dallas, TX 75231-5706
ph: 214-348-0075 or 214-349-0095
fax: 214-349-0095
e-mail: timetalk@flash.net
Author of "Tips on Identifying and Appraising Clocks"; clock appraisals furnished on a fee-basis.

Auction Services

George Horan
Jones & Horan Auction Team
453 Mast Rd.
Goffstown, NH 03045
ph: 603-625-5314

Robert Schmitt
R.O. Schmitt Fine Arts
P.O. Box 1941
Salem, NH 03079
ph: 603-893-5915
fax: 603-893-9777
e-mail: roschmit@worldnet.att.net
web: http://www.pricelessads.com/roschmit/index.htm
Two antique clock auctions per year.

John McClain
York Town Auction Inc.
1625 Haviland Rd.
York, PA 17404
ph: 717-751-0211
fax: 717-767-7729
e-mail: yorktownauction@cyberia.com
Antique & specialty auctions, lecture & appraisal services; antiques also purchased; American & English furniture, related specialties & accessories, Americana, folk art, jewelry, art, clocks & watches, militaria, steins, Oriental rugs.

Clubs/Associations

Thomas J. Bartels, ExDir
National Association of Watch & Clock Collectors, Inc.
Magazine: Bulletin of the NAWCC
514 Poplar St.
Columbia, PA 17512-2130
ph: 717-684-8261
fax: 717-684-0878
e-mail: patti@nawcc.org
web: http://www.nawcc.org
The NAWCC is a non-profit and scientific association founded in 1943 and now serving the horological interests of 38,000 members worldwide.

American Watchmakers-Clockmakers Institute
Magazine: Horological Times
701 Enterprise Dr.
Harrison, OH 45030-1696
ph: 513-367-9800
fax: 513-367-1414
e-mail: awi-info@awi-net.org
web: http://www.awi-net.org
For those interested in horology as a profession or avocation; monthly technical magazine, technical bulletins, training, public relations, networking.

Doug Cowan
British Horology
110 Central Terrace
Cincinnati, OH 45215

Les McAlister, Pres.
National 400-Day Clock Chapter
716 Loretta Dr.
O Fallon, MO 63366

Mrs. P.V.. Hossbach
Antiquarian Horological Society, The
Magazine: Antiquarian Horology
New House, High Street
Ticehurst, East Sussex TN5 7AL
U.K.
ph: 01580-200155
fax: 01580-201323
e-mail: ahsoc@compuserve.com
web: http://ourworld.compuserve.com/homepages/ahsoc/
The world's leading organization in this field; the Society's aim is to serve all those interested in antique clocks, watches and other time-measuring instruments; publishes the quarterly journal, books, and monographs.

Tony Woolven
British Watch & Clock Collectors Association
Newsletter: Timepiece
5 Cathedral Lane
Truro, Cornwall TR1 2SQ
U.K.
ph: +44 01872 41953
e-mail: FMMatEZI@aol.com
Geared mainly to the collector, but also solicits membership from restorers and repairers.

British Horological Institute
Upton Hall, Upton
Newark, Nottingham NG23 5TE
U.K.
ph: (01636) 813795
fax: (01636) 812258
e-mail: clocks@bhi.co.uk
web: http://www.bhi.co.uk/
Education is a major part of the BHI; strong ties with institutions offering horological training; members have access to museum collection for study; membership open to anyone with an interest in timekeeping.

Collectors

Jerry Boxenhorn
Clock Exchange, The
2045 Legion St.
Bellmore, NY 11710-4914
ph: 516-221-7077
Wants to buy one clock or entire collections; also movements, parts, and all clock related items; especially wants Ansonia statue clocks, Ansonia Royal Bonn clocks, French bronze clocks, and any animated or unusual clocks.

Howard Prince
796 Hartwood Road
Hartwood, VA 22406-4108
ph: 540-752-2783
e-mail: ecnir@erols.com
Buys and sells American antique clocks.

Larry Spilkin
P.O. Box 5039
Southfield, MI 48086-5039
ph: 248-642-3722
Wants Lawson, Herman-Miller, Howard-Miller clocks.

Paul H. Hayashi, PE
18 Tarabrook Dr.
Orinda, CA 94563-3121
ph: 925-254-5074 or 925-253-1038
fax: 925-253-0592
Wants to buy precision wall regulators with different escapments.

Dealers

Robert C. Cheney
Robert C. Cheney Fine Antique Clocks
19 Brookfield Rd.
Brimfield, MA 01010
ph: 413-245-7017
Since 1900 the Cheney clock makers have provided consulting services, restoration, appraisals, and sales of fine antique clocks; by appointment.

John & Barbara Delaney
435 Main St.
Route 119
Townsend, MA 01474
ph: 978-597-2231
Largest selection of American tall case clocks in the country.

John Delaney
Delaney Antique Clocks
435 Main St., Route 119
Townsend, MA 01474
ph: 978-597-2231
e-mail: delaney@net1plus.com
web: http://www.delaneyantiqueclocks.com
In business for over 30 years; carries extensive selection of American tall case as well as antique wall and shelf clocks; located 50 miles northwest of Boston.

Bob Frishman
Bell-Time Clocks
53 Poor St.
Andover, MA 01810-2501
ph: 978-475-5001
e-mail: rjfjs@mediaone.net
web: http://www.bell-time.com/
Buys and sells clocks of all styles, ages, sizes and nationalities; also repairs and restores clocks.

Howard Zimmerman
Internet Clock Shop
732 Main Street
Boxford, MA 01921
ph: 978-352-6005
fax: 978-352-6005
e-mail: howard@antiqueclocks.com
web: http://www.antiqueclocks.com
Buys and sells American and European antique clocks, early American tallcase, mantel and wall clocks; also French antique marble, steeple, calendar, Ansonia, Chelsea, Waterbury, Gilbert, Seth Thomas, Japy Freres clocks.

Mounir Mazzawi
Oakshadows Hour
105 Plimpton St.
Walpole, MA 02081
e-mail: mmazzawi@worldnet.att.net
web: http://www.oakshadows.com
Buys and sells antique clocks: American, English, French, and others.

Debbie Woolley
Favorite Past-Times
6 Main Hill
Bridgton, ME 04009
ph: 207-647-5286
e-mail: woolley@maine-antiques.com
web: http://www.maine-antiques.com/fpt/Index/
Buys and sells keywind American mantle and kitchen clocks; will buy even if not working.

James Taylor
Taylor Time
P.O. Box 311
Woodstock, VT 05091
ph: 802-457-3757
fax: 802-457-3757
e-mail: taylor.time@taylor-time.com
web: http://www.taylor-time.com
Working with Bill Mather, has 40 years experience supplying rare quality antique clocks and reliable service; cleaning, bushing, overhaul of case and movement.

Larson's Clock Shop
P.O. Box 144
Westminster, VT 05158
Issues large catalog of clocks for sale.

Ed Kazemekas
35 Riverview Circle
Wolcott, CT 06716
ph: 203-879-1814

Charles F. Breuel
Charles Bruel Antiques
P.O. Box 261
Glenmont, NY 12077
ph: 518-439-6717
Specializing in American time pieces, furniture, unusual accessories; shows only.

Bruce A. Austin
c/o RIT/College Liberal Arts
92 Lomb Memorial Dr.
Rochester, NY 14623-5604
ph: 716-475-2879 or 716-387-9820
fax: 716-475-7732
e-mail: baagll@rit.edu
Buying American clocks manufactured between 1800 - 1915; especially interested in wall regulators.

Old Timers Antique Clocks
P.O. Box 392
Camp Hill, PA 17001-0392
ph: 717-761-1908
fax: 717-767-7446
e-mail: kenmark@webtv.com
web: http://www.antiqnet.com/oldtimers/
Wants to buy antique clocks; must be at least 100 years old, no reproductions, electrics, cuckoos, or grandfather clocks; if selling, seller must send clear photos and asking for each clock.

Walter A. Dayett
Dayett's Clock Repair & Appraisals
75 Study Rd.
Littlestown, PA 17340-9746
ph: 717-359-4850
fax: 717-359-4850
e-mail: wdayett@desupernet.net
web: http://users.desupernet.net/wdayett/wdayett.html
Specializes in antique and contemporary clock sales and repair, primarily weight and spring driven movements; also specializes in clock appraisals.

Patrick Managan
P.M. Clock & Watch Company
497 English Rd.
Bath, PA 18014
ph: 610-837-7326

Paul D. Phillips
Paul D. Phillips, Antiques
P.O. Box 147
Bryn Mawr, PA 19010
ph: 610-527-4577
fax: 610-527-4577
e-mail: pdp@pond.com
web: http://www.antiqueclocksandart.com
Buys, sells and appraises fine examples of American clocks from the 18th to 19th centuries; also sells period American furniture and works of art.

Gordon S. Converse
Gordon S. Converse & Co.
503 W. Lancaster Ave.
Strafford, PA 19087
ph: 610-964-7632 or 800-789-1001
fax: 610-964-1181
e-mail: gsc@pond.com
web: http://www.converseclocks.com/
Specializes in fine antique clocks including American, French, English, porcelain, banjo, Vienna regulators, ships clocks, skeleton clocks, mantel and tallcase; high quality color catalog issued periodically.

Douglas Whitesell
P.O. Box 1805
Middleburg, VA 22117
ph: 540-687-5550
Buys, sells and repairs clocks; does resilvering of dials.

Jill & Chuck Probst
Charles Edwin Antiques
P.O. Box 1340
Louisa, VA 23093-1340
ph: 540-967-0416
fax: 540-967-0416
e-mail: cei@charles-edwin.com
web: http://www.charles-edwin.com

Olivier Perrault
ClockWorld
3330 Pacific Ave., Ste. 404
Virginia Beach, VA 23451
ph: 757-428-8180
fax: 757-428-6253
e-mail: olivier@visi.net
web: http://www.clockworld.com
Repairs, buys and sells clocks; specializes in European clocks, cuckoo clocks, Trumpeter clocks, and Atmos clocks.

Larry Davenport
Roswell Clock & Antique Co.
955 Canton St.
Roswell, GA 30075
ph: 770-992-5232
fax: 770-587-4597
e-mail: roswellclock@mindspring.com
web: http://www.networkcommunity.com/roswellclock/
Carries large selection of antique clocks.

Mark Peer
Mark of Time
1518 Florida Blvd., #B
Bradenton, FL 34207-5854
ph: 800-277-5275 or 941-955-3211
e-mail: mpeer1@aol.com
web: http://www.markoftime.com/
Buys and sells antique clocks and entire clock collections.

David Pendley
Pendley's Clock Repair
4610 Murray Ln, #C
Chattanooga, TN 37416-2211
Repairs, restores, buys, sells old vintage antique clocks, member NAWCC.

C.L. Horton
201 Culpepper Rd.
Lexington, KY 40502
ph: 606-255-0287 or 606-266-4532
fax: 606-255-2162
Issues large catalog of clocks for sale.

Bruce Hannon
Investor's Antiques
1208 W. Union St.
Champaign, IL 61821
e-mail: b-hannon@uiuc.edu
web: http://www.shout.net/~smgorman/bruce/
Selling and repairing clocks since 1969; everything from tower clocks to pocket watches.

Tim Sweet
M.O.S.T. Watch & Clock Co.
3010 Forest Trail
San Angelo, TX 76904
ph: 915-947-8196
e-mail: timekeep@gte.net
web: http://www.tritco.com/most/most1.html
Dealer, collector, expert, auction and repair services, appraiser offering all aspects of antique clock and watch services; website has an Internet Horology Club.

Don Levison
Don Levison Antiques
P.O. Box 22262
San Francisco, CA 94122
ph: 415-753-0455
fax: 415-753-5206
e-mail: dlevison@juno.com
web: http://www.antiquehorology.com
Buys and sells antique and better quality pocket and wrist watches, clocks, music boxes, singing birds, and other small automata; also mercury barometers from the 17th century to present.

Steve Bogoff
Bogoff Antique Timepieces
P.O. Box 408
Mill Valley, CA 94942
ph: 415-383-8100
fax: 415-383-8112
e-mail: info@bogoff.com
web: http://www.bogoff.com
Buys, sells, appraises and has on-line catalog of complicated, rare, early, unusual, beautiful pocket watches, vintage wrist watches, small clocks, singing bird boxes and more.

Bob Setnik
Setniks In Time Again
815 Sutter St.
Folsom, CA 95630
ph: 916-985-2390 or 888-333-1715
fax: 916-985-4030
e-mail: setniks@cwo.com
web: http://setniksintimeagain.com
Over 35 years in service; sells and restores antique clocks and American Victorian antique furniture; all clocks completely original and thoroughly and properly restored; all with one year guarantee; ships world wide.

Adam Schoolsky
P.O. Box 23182
Portland, OR 97281-3162
ph: 503-579-3162
fax: 503-579-5046
e-mail: Adam@ArtDeco.com
web: http://www.ArtDeco.com
Buying one item or entire collections or estates; specializing in clocks with Art Deco styling, American weight regulators, complicated musical clocks; also buys clock/watch related advertising signs; expert clock restorations.

James Poag, GG, ISA CAPP
James O. Poag Jewellers, Ltd.
94 Frank Street
P.O. Box 39, Ontario N7G 3J1
Canada
ph: 519-245-1040 or 519-245-1580
fax: 519-245-6073
e-mail: james@poag.com
web: http://www.poags.com/
Retail clock, jewellery, china and gift stores; staff included 3 goldsmiths, 2 stone setters, watchmaker, clockmaker and ISA Certified Appraiser; largest selection of clocks in Ontario; in business since 1959.

Experts

Eric Chandlee Wilson
16 Bondsville Rd.
Thorndale, PA 19372
ph: 610-383-5597
Tallcase clock dealer specializing in Chester County, PA clocks and an expert on clocks by the Chandlee's.

Julian Gibbard
P.O. Box 1092
Harpers Ferry, WV 25425
ph: 304-725-2035
Specialist in long case clocks.

Joe Cohen
4250 Galt Ocean Dr., Apt. 9A
Oakland Park, FL 33308
ph: 954-561-2234
Specializing in 17th, 18th, and 19th century clocks and watches.

Internet Resources

Fortunat Mueller-Maerki
Horology - The Index
350 Park Ave.
New York, NY 10022
e-mail: horology@horology.com
web: http://www.horology.com
A comprehensive resource guide to clock, watch, horology, and timekeeping related sites on the Internet; 100 pages with 3000 links to dealers, brands, repair tips, museums, schools, periodicals, organizations, related people.

Museums/Libraries

Nancy Connelly
American Clock & Watch Museum
Journal: Timepiece Journal
100 Maple St.
Bristol, CT 06010-5034
ph: 860-583-6070
fax: 860-583-1862
web: http://www.pricelessads.com/acwmuseum/
Preserves the history of American horology, especially Connecticut and Bristol's role; large displays of clocks & watches.

Patricia Tomes, Cur.
National Association of Watch & Clock Collectors Museum, Inc., The
514 Poplar St.
Columbia, PA 17512-2130
ph: 717-684-8261
fax: 717-684-0878
e-mail: patti@nawcc.org
web: http://www.nawcc.org
The Watch & Clock Museum of the NAWCC strives to illustrate the history of timekeeping from the 1600's to the present with a collection of more than 8000 horological items.

National Museum of American History
14th & Constitution Ave. NW
Washington, DC 20560
ph: 202-357-2700
e-mail: webmaster@si.edu
web: http://www.si.edu/organiza/museums/nmah/nmah.htm

Carol Riehle
Bily Clock Exhibit/Antonin Dvorak Exhibit
323 Main St.
P.O. Box 258
Spillville, IA 52168-0258
ph: 319-562-3569 or 319-562-3457
fax: 319-562-4373
e-mail: webmaster@spillville.ia.us
web: http://www.spillville.ia.us/about.html
One-of-a-kind exhibit displaying clocks by the two Bily brothers; historical and educational display of handcarved clocks; housed in the building famous composer Antonin Dvorak lived in during his stay in 1893.

Museum of Timepieces & Mechanical Music
Stattsstrasse 18
Oberhofen am Thunersee, CH 3853
Switzerland
ph: +41 33 243 4377
e-mail: horology@horology.com
web: http://www.horology.com/horology/mumm.html

Periodicals

Steven G. Conover, Ed.
Newsletter: Clockmakers Newsletter
203 John Glenn Ave.
Reading, PA 19607
ph: 610-796-0969
e-mail: sconover@ptdprolog.net
web: http://www.dc-adnet.com/clockmakers/
Published since 1987; an eight-page, clocks-only newsletter for repairers and for collectors who restore their own clocks, old and new; photos, drawings, free classifieds; emphasis is on practical repairs rather than on theory.

Magazine: Watch & Clock Review
2403 Champa St.
Denver, CO 80205-2621
ph: 303-296-1600
fax: 303-295-2159
Monthly magazine primarily for new and vintage watch and clock retailers; features articles on watches, clocks and shops; also ads for buyers, sellers, and restorers.

Erika Daileda
Wise Owl Worldwide Publications
Magazine: Clocks
4314 West 238th St. - Dept. MACR
Torrance, CA 90505-4509
ph: 310-375-6258
fax: 310-375-0548
e-mail: wiseowl@sprintmail.com
A monthly English publication; the international monthly magazine for clock enthusiasts; feature articles on clock history and restoration from all over the world; horological news and views; clock questions and answers; great photos!

Nexus Special Interests
Magazine: Clocks Magazine
Nexus House, Azalea Drive
Swanley, BR8 8HY
U.K.
ph: +44 1322 660070
fax: +44 1322 667633
e-mail: Clocksmag@aol.com
web: http://members.aol.com/clocksmag/homepage.htm
The international monthly magazine for clock enthusiasts; feature articles on clock history and restoration from all over the world; horological news and views; clock questions and answers.

Repair Services

Leon Trefler
Trefler & Sons Antique Restoring Studio, Inc.
99 Cabot St.
Needham, MA 02494
ph: 781-444-2685
fax: 781-444-0659
e-mail: trefler@trefler.com
web: http://www.trefler.com/
Restoration of porcelain and painted faces as well as porcelain and wood clock cases.

Burt Dial Company
Rt. 107 N
Raymond, NH 03077
ph: 603-895-2879
Specializes in reverse painting on glass for clock tablets and doors, and in the restoring of clock dials.

James Taylor
Taylor Time
P.O. Box 311
Woodstock, VT 05091
ph: 802-457-3757
fax: 802-457-3757
e-mail: taylor.time@taylor-time.com
web: http://www.taylor-time.com
Working with Bill Mather, has 40 years experience supplying rare quality antique clocks and reliable service; cleaning, bushing, overhaul of case and movement.

Jim Mulhern
Medford Clock Shop
3 Union Street
Medford, NJ 08055
ph: 609-953-0014
fax: 609-953-0411
e-mail: medclock@aol.com
web: http://www.medfordclock.com
Specializes in the repair of all types of antique clocks; also antique mercury and aneroid barometers repaired and restored; mercury barometer tubes made to fit old barometers.

Garrett Moore
Garrett's Clock Sales & Repair
24 Main St.
Clinton, NJ 08809
ph: 908-735-0496
web: http://www.fnets.com/garrettsclocksales.htm
Buys, sells and restores clocks - new and old.

Philip M. Poniz
European Watch & Casemakers, Ltd.
P.O. Box 1314
Highland Park, NJ 08904-1314
ph: 732-777-0111
fax: 732-777-0118
e-mail: horology@webspan.net
Restoration of watches, clocks, and music boxes; museum experience; can make any part and restore any watch; clients include Sotheby's, Cartier, collectors in USA, Asia and Europe; appraises, researches, lectures on watch making, fakes.

Roger Gordon
Gordon's Gallery of Clocks
R.R. #1, Box 100
Cooperstown, PA 16317
ph: 814-374-4886
fax: 814-374-4899
e-mail: rgordon@csonline.net
web: http://www.csonline.net/rgordon/
Authentic antique clock restorations and repair; 20 years experience; uses only the highest quality standards in restoring heirloom clocks; also specializes in complete case and clock face restorations.

Walter A. Dayett
Dayett's Clock Repair & Appraisals
75 Study Rd.
Littlestown, PA 17340-9746
ph: 717-359-4850
fax: 717-359-4850
e-mail: wdayett@desupernet.net
web: http://users.desupernet.net/wdayett/wdayett.html
Specializes in antique and contemporary clock sales and repair, primarily weight and spring driven movements; also specializes in clock appraisals.

Joel J. Lynn
Joel Lynn, Clock Repair & Restoration
4100 W St. NW
Washington, DC 20007
ph: 202-333-5541
e-mail: jlynn43375@aol.com
Complete clock restoration including parts fabrication; offers in-home service.

James Horner
Horner Clock Services
310-C East Market Street
Leesburg, VA 20176
ph: 703-771-4636
Repair to complete restoration of clocks from the 17th century to present.

Joel Vernick
Antique Clock Repair
10807 Kenilworth Ave.
P.O. Box 81
Garrett Park, MD 20896-0081
ph: 301-933-0654 or 301-933-4689
fax: 301-933-4689
Over 30 years experience in clock repair.

Harvey Flemister
512 Highgate Terrace
Silver Spring, MD 20904-6314
ph: 301-622-3686
Many years experience in the repair, service and restoration of antique clocks.

John Stephens
Clock Doc
429 St. Johns St.
Havre De Grace, MD 21078-2818
ph: 410-939-3334
Area's largest selection of antique clocks; also offers on-site repair facility.

Kenzie Smith
Clock Shop, The
119 East St.
Frederick, MD 21701
ph: 301-698-8252
Repairs and restores all mechanical clocks and watches; references upon request.

Clyde M. Berger, Jr.
Hand Crafted Products Co.
8 Fulton Ave.
P.O. Box 458
Walkersville, MD 21793-0458
ph: 301-898-3057
fax: 301-845-2119
e-mail: cberg@erols.com

Douglas Whitesell
P.O. Box 1805
Middleburg, VA 22117
ph: 540-687-5550
Buys, sells and repairs clocks; does resilvering of dials.

Olivier Perrault
ClockWorld
3330 Pacific Ave., Ste. 404
Virginia Beach, VA 23451
ph: 757-428-8180
fax: 757-428-6253
e-mail: olivier@visi.net
web: http://www.clockworld.com
Repairs, buys and sells clocks; specializes in European clocks, cuckoo clocks, Trumpeter clocks, and Atmos clocks.

Dennis Kaye
Advanced Clock Service
1922 Cassowary Lane
Apex, NC 27502
ph: 919-363-9510
fax: 919-387-6666
e-mail: dwk@pophost.com
Clock dealer, expert and appraiser; repair and restoration of any type clock including Atmos and 400 day clocks; especially wants any item marked "Tiffany."

Len Hambleton
Reversen Time Inc.
6005 Bunchberry Court
Raleigh, NC 27616-5454
ph: 919-981-7323
e-mail: hamblesl@mindspring.com
web: http://www.europeanwatchworks.com/rt/index.html
Specializes in wooden clock case restoration, reviving and cleaning original finish, carving, scroll work, turnings or missing elements; museum objects conservator/cabinetmaker; please call after 6 PM EST.

Robert Terwilliger
2963 Bird Avenue
Miami, FL 33133-4501
ph: 305-447-4619
e-mail: bobt@shadow.net
web: http://www.shadow.net/~bobt/
Certified as a Master Clockmaker by the American Clock & Watchmaker's Institute.

David Pendley
Pendley's Clock Repair
4610 Murray Ln, #C
Chattanooga, TN 37416-2211
Repairs, restores, buys, sells old vintage antique clocks, member NAWCC.

Ron Hughes
Main Street Clock Repair
4923 Main St.
Downers Grove, IL 60515
ph: 630-810-1366
e-mail: clockmd@clockmd.com
web: http://www.clockmd.com/
Expert repair of modern and antique clocks.

Bruce Hannon
Investor's Antiques
1208 West Union St.
Champaign, IL 61821
ph: 217-333-0348
fax: 217-244-1785
e-mail: b-hannon@uiuc.edu
web: http://www.shout.net/~smgorman/bruce/
Has been repairing American and foreign clocks since 1970; NAWCC #41581.

Billy E. Young
Young's Ole Clock & Music Box Shop
3511 Rio Grande Circle
Dallas, TX 75233
ph: 214-331-8265
Buys, sells and restores.

Bob Setnik
Setniks In Time Again
815 Sutter St.
Folsom, CA 95630
ph: 916-985-2390 or 888-333-1715
fax: 916-985-4030
e-mail: setniks@cwo.com
web: http://setniksintimeagain.com
Over 35 years in service; sells and restores antique clocks and American Victorian antique furniture; all clocks completely original and thoroughly and properly restored; all with one year guarantee; ships world wide.

James Poag, GG, ISA CAPP
James O. Poag Jewellers, Ltd.
94 Frank Street
P.O. Box 39, Ontario N7G 3J1
Canada
ph: 519-245-1040 or 519-245-1580
fax: 519-245-6073
e-mail: james@poag.com
web: http://www.poags.com/
Retail clock, jewellery, china and gift stores; staff included 3 goldsmiths, 2 stone setters, watchmaker, clockmaker and ISA Certified Appraiser; largest selection of clocks in Ontario; in business since 1959.

Suppliers

Rick Dunnuck, VP
S. LaRose, Inc.
3223 Yanceyville St.
P.O. Box 21208
Greensboro, NC 27420-1208
ph: 336-621-1936
fax: 336-621-0706
e-mail: slarose@worldnet.att.net
web: http://www.slarose.com
Supplier of clock and watch parts.

Butterworths Clocks, Inc.
1715 Pearlview Ct.
Muscatine, IA 52761
ph: 319-263-7659 or 800-258-5418
fax: 888-599-8463
Largest distributor of mechanical clock movements in the U.S.; grandfather units, wall and mantle units, Hermle movements, Kieninger, German movements.

KLOCKIT
P.O. Box 636
Lake Geneva, WI 53147
ph: 800-556-2548
e-mail: klockit@klockit.com
web: http://www.klockit.com/
Mail order source for clock movements, hands, faces, hardware, music boxes, barometers, parts, tools, etc.

Turncraft Clocks Inc.
P.O. Box 100
Mound, MN 55364
ph: 800-544-1711 or 612-471-9573
fax: 612-471-8579
web: http://www.nonni.com/woodhobby/TurnCraft/default.htm
Mail order source of fine clock movements, kits, parts and supplies.

Southwest Clock Supply
P.O. Box 394
Carthage, MO 64836-0394
ph: 417-358-1865 or 800-654-8629
fax: 417-358-7446

Steven Berger
Timesavers
P.O. Box 12700
Scottsdale, AZ 85267-2700
ph: 480-483-3711 or 800-552-1520
fax: 480-483-6116
e-mail: clocks@timesavers.com
web: http://www.timesavers.com/
Sells new clock parts, tools, books and kits; inventories 1000s of keys, pendulums, dials, hands, ultrasonic cleaners, springs, quartz and mechanical movements, tools, cleaning solutions and lubricants.

Anniversary (400-Day)

Repair Services

Mike Murray
Mike's Clock Clinic
1326 Stanford Street
Santa Monica, CA 90404-2502
ph: 310-828-6707
fax: 310-828-7381
e-mail: z4murray@webcom.com
web: http://www.webcom.com/z4murray/
Specializing in the repair and dating of Atmos, 400 day (anniversary), and plug-in electric clocks.

Art

Clubs/Associations

Doris Westerholm, Pres.
Horological Art
3021 Fisher Ave.
Hopewell, VA 23860
A specialty chapter within the National Association of Watch & Clock Collectors, Inc.; focuses on clocks, watches and time keeping devices in art, i.e. art incorporating clock themes but having no movements.

Art Deco

Dealers

John Sakas
P.O. Box 4124
South Hackensack, NJ 07606-4124
ph: 201-794-0437
fax: 201-794-8359
Specializing in Catalin, Deco, mirror radios; also in Art Deco clocks.

Experts

Ira Raskin
Try To Remember
5120 Wilson Ln.
Bethesda, MD 20814-2436
ph: 301-652-1695
fax: 301-986-4528
e-mail: iraskin@aol.com
Buys and sells Art Deco radios and clocks of the 1920s to 1950s; also repairs electric clocks.

Mark Stein
Radiomania
2109 Carterdale Rd.
Baltimore, MD 21209
fax: 410-466-0815
e-mail: radioman@crosslink.net
web: http://www.radiomania.com
Expert in 20th century Moderne clocks.

Character/Comic

Collectors

David Welch
P.O. Box 714
Murphysboro, IL 62966-0714
ph: 618-687-2282
fax: 618-684-2243
e-mail: PezDude1@aol.com
Wants pre-1980 watches/clocks relating to sports, TV, cartoon, comic, movie characters with original boxes ONLY; also wants empty boxes; no political, please.

Computer Programs For

Man./Prod./Dist.

John Christians
ClockWare
4130 Terrace Drive
Anchorage, AK 99502
ph: 907-243-8894
e-mail: watch@alaska.net
web: http://www.alaska.net/~watch/
Horological software for collectors or businesses; keep track of your collections with easy-to-use software; print reports for quick reference.

Cuckoo

Collectors

Steve Elliott
1600 Tennessee St.
Vallejo, CA 94590
ph: 707-552-8400 or 707-642-1949
fax: 707-552-0881
Wants to buy carved wooden cuckoo clocks.

Dials

Repair Services

Martha Smallwood
Dial House, The
2287 Buchanan Highway
Dallas, GA 30132-5712
ph: 770-445-2877
fax: 770-443-5426
Antique clock dials only; preserved, restored or replaced; call or write before shipping.

Electric

Clubs/Associations

Martin Swetsky, Pres.
Electric Horology Society, Chapter 78 NAWCC
Journal: Electric Horology Society Journal
15 Hummingbird Lane
Whiting, NJ 08759
ph: 732-350-2084
e-mail: swetsky@prodigy.net
A specialty chapter within the National Association of Watch & Clock Collectors, Inc.; purpose is to inform members of the various types of battery/electrical clocks from the earliest inception to present.

Elmer G. Crum, FNAWCC
Midwest Electric Horology Group
18220 Oak Way Dr.
Hudson, FL 34667-6333
ph: 727-868-0181
e-mail: electrichorology@juno.com
A specialty chapter within the National Association of Watch & Clock Collectors, Inc.; purpose is to inform members of the various types of battery/electrical clocks from the earliest inception to present.

L.E. Sizemore, Pres.
Western Electrics
19412 Mayall St.
Northridge, CA 91324
A specialty chapter within the National Association of Watch & Clock Collectors, Inc.; purpose is to inform members of the various types of battery/electrical clocks from the earliest inception to present.

Experts

Elmer G. Crum, FNAWCC
18220 Oak Way Dr.
Hudson, FL 34667-6333
ph: 727-868-0181
e-mail: electrichorology@juno.com
Collects, repairs, appraises and specializes in early battery and electric clocks; from time of their inception to present including watches; lectures on electric horology; a Fellow of the NAWCC.

Mike Murray
Mike's Clock Clinic
1326 Stanford Street
Santa Monica, CA 90404-2502
ph: 310-828-6707
fax: 310-828-7381
e-mail: z4murray@webcom.com
web: http://www.webcom.com/z4murray/
Specializing in the repair and dating of Atmos, 400 day (anniversary), and plug-in electric clocks.

Repair Services

Mike Murray
Mike's Clock Clinic
1326 Stanford Street
Santa Monica, CA 90404-2502
ph: 310-828-6707
fax: 310-828-7381
e-mail: z4murray@webcom.com
web: http://www.webcom.com/z4murray/
Specializing in the repair and dating of Atmos, 400 day (anniversary), and plug-in electric clocks.

Electric (Atmos)

Experts

Mike Murray
Mike's Clock Clinic
1326 Stanford Street
Santa Monica, CA 90404-2502
ph: 310-828-6707
fax: 310-828-7381
e-mail: z4murray@webcom.com
web: http://www.webcom.com/z4murray/
Specializing in the repair and dating of Atmos, 400 day (anniversary), and plug-in electric clocks.

European

Experts

Frank Vitale
Brielle Galleries
707 Union Ave.
Brielle, NJ 08730
ph: 723-528-9300 or 888-274-3553
fax: 723-528-8319
e-mail: info@brielle.com
web: http://www.brielle.com/
Foremost collector and dealer of 17th, 18th, and 19th century European clocks.

European (French)

Dealers

Robert Beaver
Classic Touch Antiques
P.O. Box 27
Newport, RI 02840-0001
ph: 401-849-1717 or 401-846-9663
fax: 401-849-1717
Buys and sells all types of French and English clocks, including clock movements, cases, etc.

Alfred L. Chatelain
L'Epoque Romantique/Antique Quest
P.O. Box 4376
Clifton Park, NY 12065
ph: 518-373-0910
fax: 518-373-0910
e-mail: nracnyfr@albany.net
web: http://www.albany.net/~nracnyfr/
Dealers and collectors of quality French clocks.

Military

Clubs/Associations

William R. Bricker
Society of Military Horologists
4 Hull Cove
Jamestown, RI 02835
A specialty chapter within the National Association of Watch & Clock Collectors, Inc.; focuses on time keeping devices as applied to military use.

Novelty Animated

Collectors

Carole Kaifer
P.O. Box 232
Bethania, NC 27010-0232
ph: 336-924-9672
e-mail: kaifer@earthlink.net
Novelty clocks are spring-powered and pendulum operated from 1930s to 1950s; wants to buy clocks by Lux, Keebler, Westclox, Columbia Time, Oswald, and Mi-Ken.

Experts

Sam & Anna Samuelian
P.O. Box 504
Edgemont, PA 19028-0504
ph: 610-566-7248
fax: 610-566-7285
e-mail: sms@bee.net
web: http://www.smsnoveltiques.com/
Buys, sells, restores novelty electric animated clocks; leading buyers and sellers with largest collection in the world from 1920s-1980s; can reproduce parts; book in the offing.

Sundials

Clubs/Associations

Fred Sawyer, Pres.
North American Sundial Society
Journal: Compendium
8 Sachem Drive
Glastonbury, CT 06033
e-mail: Fred_Sawyer@compuserve.com
web: http://www.shadow.net/~bobt/nass/nass.htm
An international association of people from a wide variety of disciplines who are interested in the study, development, history and preservation of sundials and the art of dialing.

Collectors

Cal Frye
125 E. Oak St.
Kent, OH 44240-3825
ph: 330-678-7006
fax: 330-678-7006
e-mail: cj_frye@bigfoot.com
web: http://Phoenix.kent.edu/~cfrye
Wants oddball slide rules: circular, cylindrical, special-purpose, or big (classroom-sized); also wants pocket/portable sundials.

Dealers

David & Yola Coffeen
Tesseract
P.O. Box 151
Hastings On Hudson, NY 10706-0151
ph: 914-478-2594
fax: 914-478-5473
e-mail: coffeen@aol.com
Issues a series of well illustrated catalogs of early scientific instruments: astronomy, microscopy, sundials, surveying, calculation, computation, adding, navigation, etc.; always interested in buying single items of collections.

R.C. & Faye Blankenhorn
Gemmary, The
P.O. Box 2560
Fallbrook, CA 92088
ph: 760-728-3321 or 760-728-3322
fax: 760-728-3322
e-mail: rcb@gemmary.com
web: http://www.gemmary.com/rcb/
Antique scientific instruments: 18th & 19th C. mathematical, philosophical, optical instruments, microscopes, telescopes, globes, orreries, sundials, compasses, surveying, navigating, drawing, medical, laboratory.

Experts

Robert Terwilliger
2963 Bird Avenue
Miami, FL 33133-4501
ph: 305-447-4619
e-mail: bobt@shadow.net
web: http://www.shadow.net/~bobt/
Unique concepts and designs for exceptional, uncommon, and site-specific sundials.

Man./Prod./Dist.

Robert Terwilliger
2963 Bird Avenue
Miami, FL 33133-4501
ph: 305-447-4619
e-mail: bobt@shadow.net
web: http://www.shadow.net/~bobt/
Unique concepts and designs for exceptional, uncommon, and site-specific sundials.

Tower

Clubs/Associations

Donn Lathrop
Tower Clock Chapter of the NAWCC
180 Sawmill Road
New Providence, PA 17560-9410
ph: 717-786-4528
fax: 815-371-3312
e-mail: Donnl@aol.com
web: http://members.aol.com/indexnawcc/134.html
A specialty chapter within the National Association of Watch & Clock Collectors, Inc.; focusing on tower clocks.

Willard

Museums/Libraries

John R. Stephens, Curator
Willard House & Clock Museum, Inc.
11 Willard St.
North Grafton, MA 01536-2011
ph: 508-839-3500
web: http://www.pricelessads.com/willardhouse/index.html
Largest known collection of Willard clocks and memorabilia.

CLOISONNE

(see also ORIENTALIA)

Dealers

Joseph Belperio
1303 Hawthorne Ct.
Sewell, NJ 08080
ph: 609-256-0791
Specializes in fine quality Japanese Satsuma and cloisonne.

Bill Eberhardt
Harry A. Eberhardt & Son
2010 Walnut St.
Philadelphia, PA 19103-5608
ph: 610-568-4144
Specializes in Japanese cloisonne and fine Satsuma.

Museums/Libraries

George Walter Vincent Smith Art Museum
220 State St.
Springfield, MA 01103-1703
ph: 413-263-6800
fax: 413-263-6814
e-mail: jhanna@spfldlibmus.org
web: http://www.quadrangle.org/GWVS.htm
Recognized collections of American paintings; Orientalia including Japanese arms & armor, screens, lacquers, textiles and ceramics; Islamic rugs; and the largest collection of Chinese cloisonne in the western world

CLOTHES SPRINKLERS

Collectors

Craig Dinner
P.O. Box 4399
Long Island City, NY 11104-0399
ph: 718-729-3850 or 802-365-7181
Wants to buy ceramic laundry sprinkler bottles.

Al Little
151 Highway 173
Antioch, IL 60002
ph: 847-395-7752
fax: 847-395-7703
Buy, sells and trades laundry sprinkle bottles.

Dealers

Carol Silagyi
C.S. Antiques & Jewelry
P.O. Box 151
Wyckoff, NJ 07430
ph: 201-934-6528
Wants figural ceramic clothes sprinklers; Cardinal, American bisques, Japanese, etc.

Estelle Sharp
ESCO Enterprises, Inc.
441 E. River Oaks Dr.
Baton Rouge, LA 70815-4063
ph: 225-924-5089
fax: 225-924-5089
Buys and sells clothes sprinklers.

CLOTHING & ACCESSORIES

(see also BRIDAL COLL.; BUTTONS; BUTTON HOOKS; CLOTHES SPRINKLERS; COMPACTS; COMBS & HAIR ACCESS.; CUFF LINKS; DRESSER ITEMS; LIVING HISTORY; LUGGAGE; PURSES; REPAIR/ RESTOR./CONSER., Textiles; SEWING ITEMS & GO-WITHS; TEXTILES)

Appraisers

Stephanie Kline Morehouse
894 South Bronson Ave.
Los Angeles, CA 90005-3605
ph: 323-939-2240 or 323-931-4987
fax: 323-931-4987
e-mail: MorehouseB@aol.com
Specializes in costumes, clothing, textiles, film costumes, couture; IRS related appraisals of large donations of costumes and clothing to charities and institutions; member, Appraisers Association of America.

Periodicals

Ornament, Inc.
Magazine: Ornament
P.O. Box 2349
San Marcos, CA 92079-2349
ph: 760-599-0222
fax: 760-599-0228
e-mail: ornament@cts.com
web: http://www.ornamentmagazine.com/
A quarterly magazine focusing on craft and art items of personal adornment in any media or form: fiber, glass, metal, ancient historic/ ethnic ornament; ethnographic and tribal jewelry; also reviews of museum exhibits and publications.

1960s

Collectors

Steve Hannan
141 East Central St.
Natick, MA 01760-3625
Wants to buy 1960s leather clothing, mini-skirts, micro-skirts, and hotpants; no suede, please; also wants leather clothing from 1970 to present, including dresses and lingerie.

Boots

Collectors

D. Seagraves
111 Cleveland Rd. #78
Pleasant Hill, CA 94523
ph: 925-934-4848
Wants to buy 1950s women's rubber boots.

Collars & Cuffs

(see CUFF LINKS)

Costumes (Historical)

(see also CLOTHING & ACCESSORIES, Costumes; CLOTHING & ACCESSORIES, Vintage; MOVIE MEMORABILIA; LIVING HISTORY; SCIENCE FICTION, Costuming)

Clubs/Associations

Costume Society of America, The
Newsletter: CSA News
55 Edgewater Dr.
P.O. Box 73
Earleville, MD 21919-0073
ph: 410-275-1619x or 800-CSA-9447
fax: 410-275-8936
e-mail: webmaster@costumesocietyamerica.com
web: http://www.costumesocietyamerica.com/
Dedicated to advancing the global understanding of all aspects of dress and appearance; also publishes the journal "Dress."

Costume Society, The
Journal: Costume
St. Paul's House
Warwick Lane, London EC4P 4BN
U.K.
Formed to promote the study and preservation of significant examples of costume history and development; publishes an illustrated journal and newsletters; organizes an annual symposium; visits collections; study days.

Sue Tibbles
Costume Guild of UK
Newsletter: Cutting Edge
6 Blacksmiths Meadow
Oak Leys
Oxford, Oxforshire OX4 5YF
U.K.
e-mail: set@bodley.ox.ac.uk
web: http://www.ireadh.demon.co.uk/cguk/index.html
"Cutting Edge" features forthcoming events and items of special interest including other recommended societies or suppliers; also publishes the magazine "The Mantle."

Internet Resources

WWW.Costumes.Org
e-mail: Tara@costumes.org
web: http://www.costumes.org/
Amazing costume resource web site: chat rooms, history of fashion and dress, wigs, timeline of costume history with images from ancient Babylon to modern, costume links, makeup classes, costume shops on the web, supplies, and more.

Man./Prod./Dist.

Time Warp Custom & Vintage Attire
P.O. Box 9186
Schenectady, NY 12305-0186
ph: 518-347-1126
fax: 518-347-1126
e-mail: timewarp@timewarp.com
web: http://www.timewarp.com/
Buys/sells/appraises vintage clothing, jewelry, accessories; reproduces vintage and historical clothing for museums, reenactment, theater, ballroom dancing, etc.; also restores, repairs and alters clothing, textiles and costume jewelry.

Kathe Reynolds
Creative Clothes
330 N. Church St.
Thurmont, MD 21788-1640
ph: 301-695-5340
Researches, designs, creates clothing for men, women, and children; especially 18th and 19th century historical costumes.

Saundra Ros Altman
Past Patterns
P.O. Box 2446
Richmond, IN 47375-2446
ph: 765-962-3333
fax: 765-962-3773
e-mail: pastpat@thepoint.net
Sells clothing patterns from the years 1830-1949 in woman's sizes 8-20; also men and children's patterns available; free information.

Sarah Fox
Somewhere in Time
P.O. Box 263
Breaux Bridge, LA 70517
ph: 318-983-9364 or 318-893-7824
fax: 318-232-3001
Costume design, period and contemporary; research, sketches, swatches, construction; offers clothing and accessories 1850-1960; wants handbags, jewelry, buttons; supplier/ stylist/costumer for film, television, videos.

Heidi Marsh
Heidi Marsh Patterns
3494 N Valley Rd.
Greenville, CA 95947-9604
Men's, women's, and children's patterns from the Civil War era; many taken from Godey's Lady Book diagrams and patterns; catalog $3.

Denim

Dealers

Marc Luers
Tatters
2928 Lyndale Ave. South
Minneapolis, MN 55408-2110
ph: 612-823-5285
fax: 612-823-6887
e-mail: tattersinc@aol.com
Wants old denim as well as pre-1960 Japanese, Korean, and European satin and velveteen reversible souvenir jackets; also buys any other interesting vintage clothing.

Jeannine Orzechowski
American Vintage Blues
1036-22nd Street
Rock Island, IL 61201
ph: 309-236-9792
fax: 309-788-4847
e-mail: avblues@aol.com
web: http://vintageblues.com/
Specializes in pre-1970s denim, new/ old stock.

Experienced Denim
P.O. Box 239
Fayetteville, AR 72702-0239
ph: 501-444-7541 or 800-336-4694
fax: 501-521-8331
e-mail: exd@edenim.com
web: http://www.edenim.com/
Wants '30s-'50s Levis, denim wear of all types, '40s-'50s gabardine shirts & jackets, Hawaiian and bowling shirts; also vintage fabrics, textiles, bedspreads, tablecloths with Western or Mexican theme; vintage mens wear, casual clothing.

Blue Denim Clothing Co.
3213 Jeannie Ln.
Muskogee, OK 74403
ph: 918-683-1589
Wants to buy vintage Levis, Lee, Wrangler: jeans, jackets, men's 501 Blue Jeans, vintage workwear advertising, pre-1960 sweatshirts, vintage Air Jordans and pre-1980 Nike shoes, Buddy Lee Dolls, banners, denim shirts, etc.

David Bailey
Bailey's Antiques & Thrift
517 Kapahulu Ave.
Honolulu, HI 96815-3854
ph: 808-734-7628
e-mail: baileysantqiues@webtv.net
Buys and appraises pre-1960 Levis, pre-1960 Aloha Shirts, and Hawaiiana; pre-1960 Levis have a capital "E", hence "Big E" on small red tag at side of left breast pocket (jackets) and right rear pocket (pants).

Larry McKaugham
Heller's Far West Clothing
1000 Lenora, Ste. 116
Seattle, WA 98121
ph: 206-233-9014 or 800-328-5384
e-mail: hellers@halcyon.com
web: http://www.hellerscafe.com/
Wants to buy 1930s and 1940s denim buckleback pants, vintage running and basketball shoes from 1970s and 1980s.

Husky Boy Vintage
4441 S. Meridian, Ste. 471
Puyallup, WA 98373-5959
ph: 800-HUSKY-BO or 253-472-6341
e-mail: steve@huskyboy.com
Wants to buy Nike Air Jordan 1985-1991 and 1970s-1980s Nike shoes and sportswear; also buying vintage denim workwear, i.e. Levi's, Lee, etc. and vintage military flight jackets.

Experts

Jeff Mark
P.O. Box 5178
Santa Monica, CA 90409-5178
ph: 800-666-9553 or 310-396-9767
fax: 310-396-2666
America's largest buyer of and leading authority on Levi & Lee brand old blue jeans, jackets, and advertising display materials; especially wants older (pre-1970) button-fly jeans.

Museums/Libraries

Levi Strauss & Co. Museum
250 Valencia St.
San Francisco, CA 94103
ph: 415-565-9159
Open by appointment; located in the oldest jeans factory still in operation.

Hats

Collectors

Daniell Ware
1199 S. Main Rd.
Vineland, NJ 08360
ph: 609-794-8300
fax: 609-794-8300
Long time collector wants to buy millinery items: hat stands, hat blocks, signs, trade cards, ladies hats, hat boxes, beaded and mesh purses from 1800s to 1940s.

Dealers

Janine Smith
Hats by Janine
87367 Green Hill Rd.
Eugene, OR 97402-9170
Buys and sells hats; large selection from 1900-1960; also restores vintage hats and makes reproductions of period hats.

Museums/Libraries

Colonial Williamsburg Millinery Shop
P.O. Box C
Williamsburg, VA 23185
ph: 757-229-1000 or 800-HISTORY
e-mail: webmaster@cwf.org
web: http://www.history.org

Suppliers

Manny's Millinery
26 W. 38th St.
New York, NY 10018-6227
ph: 212-840-2235 or 212-840-2236
Sells hatmaking supplies in small quantities for refurbishing old ones or making new hats.

Lingerie

Museums/Libraries

Frederick's of Hollywood Lingerie Museum & Celebrity Lingerie Hall of Fame
6608 Hollywood Blvd.
Los Angeles, CA 90028
ph: 323-466-8506
web: http://www.fredericks.com/museum/
Contains famous underfashions beginning with lingerie and bras from 1946.

Mannequins

Collectors

Gwen Daniel
18 Belleau Lake Ct.
O Fallon, MO 63366-3144
ph: 314-978-3190
e-mail: gdaniel@mail.win.org
Wants Victorian through 1950s mannequins; heads only or full mannequins; send photos first if possible.

Suppliers

Goldsmith, Inc.
10-09 43rd Ave.
Long Island City, NY 11101
Sells Victorian and Edwardian mannequins.

Neckties

Clubs/Associations

Barry Hautala
Kollectors of Nasty Old Ties (K.N.O.T.)
1860 Greentree Dr.
Plover, WI 54467
ph: 715-344-4779
fax: 715-342-4909
e-mail: baha22@coredcs.com
web: http://www.geocities.com/RodeoDrive/4026/
A place for accumulators and enthusiasts of vintage neckties; specializing in the colorful and unusual tie designs of the late 1940s and early 1950s; buy, sell or trade ties at the "Trading Post."

Collectors

Al Guerra
636 Tulip Ave.
Stewart Manor, NY 11001-3755
Collector of rare ties; specializes in 1940s-1950s hand-painted men's neckties; also other vintage, souvenir/commemorative ties such as political, World's Fair, fraternal, advertising, pin-up, and cowboy/western. Include SASE for reply.

Barry Hautala
1860 Greentree Dr.
Plover, WI 54467
ph: 715-344-4779
fax: 715-342-4909
e-mail: baha22@coredcs.com
web: http://www.geocities.com/RodeoDrive/4026/
Collector of vintage neckties; specializing in the colorful and unusual tie designs of the late 1940s and early 1950s.

Dealers

John Marshall
For Love or Money
16693 NW Meadowgrass Ct.
Beaverton, OR 97006
e-mail: john@europa.com
web: http://www.europa.com/~john/
Buys and sells vintage neck ties.

Experts

Dr. Ron Spark
P.O. Box 43414
Tucson, AZ 85733-3414
ph: 520-323-8714
fax: 520-324-5341
Author of "Fit-To-Be-Tied" (Abbeville, 1988) specializes in 1940s neckties; inquiries always invited.

Parasols

Repair Services

Abbie Orem
265 N. Union St.
Russianville, IN 46979-9602
ph: 765-883-5108
Recovers parasols; call first to discuss the project.

Patterns

Book Sellers

Fred Struthers
R.L. Shep Publications
P.O. Box 2706
Fort Bragg, CA 95437
ph: 707-964-8662
fax: 707-964-8662
e-mail: fsbks@mcn.org
web: http://www.mcn.org/e/fsbks/
Publishes reprints of dressmaking/tailoring manuals and needlework books.

Collectors

Joy Emery
84 Estelle Dr.
West Kingston, RI 02892
Devoted collector who is compiling a complete database of tissue patterns.

Dealers

Nancy Garcelon
Antique & Otherwise
10 Hastings Ave.
Millbury, MA 01527
ph: 508-754-2267
Buys and sells used books on costume, sewing, knitting, crochet; vintage patterns and pattern catalogs; send for free list.

Bette S. Feinstein
Hard-to-Find Needlework Books
96 Roundwood Rd.
Newton, MA 02164-1217
ph: 617-969-0942
fax: 617-969-0942
e-mail: hardtofind@needleworkbooks.com
web: http://www.needleworkbooks.com/
Buys and sells vintage fashion magazines, old and new books on many types of needlework.

Saundra Ros Altman
Past Patterns
P.O. Box 2446
Richmond, IN 47375-2446
ph: 765-962-3333
fax: 765-962-3773
e-mail: pastpat@thepoint.net
Carries a large selection of copies of sewing patterns from 1900 to 1950 in original sizes.

Shoes

Dealers

Wishing Corner, The
9201 S.E. Foster Rd.
Portland, OR 97266
ph: 503-771-1549
e-mail: Shoesbydi@aol.com
web: http://www.hilndr.com/wishing/
Huge stock of over 10,000 pairs of vintage shoes from 1940s to 1970s; never ben worn; 40's pumps and granny shoes, 70's platforms, 6-'s slings, 50's saddles, etc.

Museums/Libraries

Brockton Shoe Museum
216 No. Pearl St.
Brockton, MA 02401
ph: 508-583-1039
e-mail: gerryb@brocktonma.com
web: http://www.brocktonma.com/bhs/shoe.html
Claims to be the only authentic shoe museum in America.

Shoe Museum, Temple University School of Podiatric Medicine
8th & Race Streets
Philadelphia, PA 19107
ph: 215-629-0300
e-mail: pcpmnet@pcpm.edu
web: http://www.pcpm.edu/shoemus.htm
Collection contains over 700 examples of shoes, dating back to Egyptian burial sandals c. 2000 B.C.

Bata Shoe Museum
327 Bloor Street West
Toronto, Ontario M5S 1W7
Canada
ph: 416-979-7799
fax: 416-979-0078
e-mail: mta@mtarch.com
web: http://www.mtarch.com/bsm.html
A five-story building with over 130,000 visitors each year; collection includes more than 10,000 pieces of footwear and related artifacts spanning 4,500 years and representing every culture in the world.

Shoes (Oversize)

Clubs/Associations

Danny Eskenazi, Pres.
Society for Preservation of Oversize Footwear (SPOOF)
169 Broadway East
Seattle, WA 98102
ph: 206-932-6621
fax: 206-932-1449
e-mail: k7ss@wolfenet.com
Wants to buy big display shoes.

Suspender Buckles

Experts

Robert James Lloyd
158 Brookside Blvd.
Newark, DE 19711
Collects and studies suspenders and garter belts.

T-shirts

Collectors

Rich Cacioppo
44 Brookside Terrace
North Caldwell, NJ 07006
ph: 973-364-1765
fax: 973-364-1766
Interested in the history of imprinted T-shirts.

Vintage

(see also BRIDAL COLL.; BUTTONS; BUTTON HOOKS; CLOTHES SPRINKLERS; COMPACTS; COMBS & HAIR ACCESS.; CUFF LINKS; DRESSER ITEMS; LIVING HISTORY; LUGGAGE; PURSES; REPAIR/ RESTOR./CONSER., Textiles; SEWING ITEMS & GO-WITHS; TEXTILES)

Appraisers

Leon Castner, ISA CAPP
National Appraisal Consultants
P.O. Box 482
Hope, NJ 07844
ph: 800-323-5996 or 908-459-5996
fax: 908-459-4899
e-mail: castner@garden.net
web: http://www.nacvalue.com
Expert witness on several high level fashion claims including insurance loss, fair market value; has written articles regarding collectible fashion clothing.

Auction Services

Amory Spizzirri, Client Svc.
William Doyle Galleries
175 E. 87th St.
New York, NY 10128-2205
ph: 212-427-2730
fax: 212-369-0892
e-mail: info@doylegalleries.com
web: http://www.doylegalleries.com
Holds over 50 auctions annually of furniture and decorations, paintings and sculpture, jewelry, books and prints, couture and textiles, 20th century art & design, majolica, Lalique, Asian works of art and other specialty categories.

Robert J. Connelly, ASA
Bob & Sallie Connelly Auctions
666 Chenango St.
Binghamton, NY 13901-2015
ph: 607-722-9593 or 607-722-3555
fax: 607-722-1266
e-mail: connelly@clarityconnect.com
Conducts specialty vintage clothing and fabric auctions.

Clubs/Associations

Textile & Costume Guild, c/o Fullerton Museum Center
Newsletter: Textures
301 North Pomona Ave.
Fullerton, CA 92632
ph: 714-738-6545
Guild meets 2nd Sat. of the month Sept.-June; extensive costume collection; women's and mens from 1820s to the present.

Collectors

Lydia M. Jackson-Fryer
608 Winans Way
Baltimore, MD 21229-1430
ph: 410-233-6231
fax: 410-233-6231
e-mail: lcfryer@erols.com
Wants to buy vintage clothing female size 18 or plus size; also male 44 regular.

Cheryl Melnick
P.O. Box 790
Cupertino, CA 95015
ph: 408-559-7799 x222
e-mail: webmistress@hand-fan.org
web: http://www.hand-fan.org
Serious collector wants to buy vintage clothing and accessories for personal collection and for reenacting to teach living history to others as a volunteer: clothing, parasols, hand-held fans, hats, accessories.

Dealers

Carol Moyse
Collage Antiques
ph: 301-831-6314
fax: 301-831-9617
e-mail: ccmoyse@aol.com
web: http://www.antiqnet.com/collage/
A 20-year business specializing in vintage apparel from 1880 through 1950: wearable clothing, hats, antique jewelry, beaded and mesh purses, alligator and crocodile purses and accessories.

Daveda Howe
Davenport & Co.
146 Bowdoin St.
Springfield, MA 01109
ph: 413-781-1505 or 413-781-6746
e-mail: dandt2@map.com
web: http://www.davenportandco.com
Buys and sells fine vintage clothing from the 1840s to 1960s.

Deborah Burke
Antique & Vintage Dress Gallery
P.O. Box 600353
Boston, MA 02460-0003
ph: 781-891-9659
e-mail: antiquedress@mediaone.net
web: http://www.antiquedress.com
A constantly changing gallery of clothing and accessories for sale featuring the elegance of original clothing from the 1800s to present; Victorian ensembles, Edwardian whites, 1920s beaded dresses, bridal gowns, hats, purses, etc.

Linda Dalenberg
Timeless Pieces
246 West Main St.
Hillsboro, NH 03244-5239
ph: 603-464-5621 or 603-464-6747
e-mail: timeless@cocknet.com
Wants to buy antique dolls, doll clothes, and doll accessories; also wants adult and children's vintage clothing, estate linens, and pre WWII toys.

Fay Knicely
Antique Apparel
P.O. Box 1
Acworth, NH 03601-0001
ph: 603-835-2295
fax: 603-835-2295
e-mail: fay@sover.net
Over 30 years buying and selling a wide range of antique and vintage clothing, accessories, and related goods; open by appointment; maintains sales outlet at Peewee's Market, downtown Claremont, NH.

Nancy Haugh
Victorian Whites
7 Winterbrook Ct.
York, ME 03909
ph: 207-363-8111

M. Weiss
Bee's Knees Kennebunkport
P.O. Box 732
Kennebunkport, ME 04046
ph: 207-967-3512
e-mail: tbkkpt@biddeford.com
web: http://www.biddeford.com/~tbkkpt/
A boutique of vintage & contemporary designer clothing, accessories and collectibles from 1900 to present; specializes in custom designs for Heirloom Bears, porcelain dolls and fine art folding screens.

Judith A. Young
Yesterday's Threads
206 Meadow St.
Branford, CT 06405-3634
ph: 203-481-6452
fax: 203-483-7550
Buys and sells women's, men's and childrens' clothing and accessories from mid-1800s through 1960s; call for information about upcoming vintage clothing shows.

Pahaka September
Pahaka
19 Fox Hill
Upper Saddle River, NJ 07458-1314
ph: 201-327-1464
Buys and sells women's, men's and children's clothing 1800s-1950s; also jewelry, hats, shoes, fashion accessories, and patterns; by appointment or mail order; sorry, no catalog; in business for over 20 years.

Sid Warshafsky
240 Overlook Rd.
Woodstock, NY 12498
ph: 914-246-9363
Wants to buy vintage clothing, jewelry, hats, accessories: Christian Dior, Chanel, Yves St. Laurant, Gucci, Hermes bags, Louis Vuitton, Pucci, Fortuny, Halston, etc.; veils, collars, umbrellas, curtains, shawls.

Laura Russell
Cats Pajamas, The
Rd 1, Box 27A
Millville, PA 17846
ph: 717-458-5233
e-mail: catspjs@sunlink.net
web: http://catspajamas.web2010.com
The largest on-line vintage clothing supplier; carries mens, womens, and some childrens from Victorian through 1970s; can supply costumers and individuals; also carries all accessories including jewelry and some home decor.

Dottie Wordell
30-A Trolley Sq.
Wilmington, DE 19806
ph: 302-651-9331
fax: 302-429-8491
e-mail: Davidam@dca.net
Appraiser, dealer, collector and expert in vintage clothing and jewelry; see website for online catalog.

Kathleen Flynn
Carriage House Antiques
4212 Gallatin St.
Hyattsville, MD 20781-2049
ph: 301-779-3696
Always buying vintage fashions, accessories and jewelry; prefers Victorian though 1950s; especially wants antique purses, compacts, silver smalls, and costume jewelry.

Yvonne D. Smith
Yvon's Vintage Chic
7 North Court St.
Frederick, MD 21701-5413
ph: 301-694-5500
Wants pre-1950 vintage clothing, accessories, and jewelry; vintage bridal gowns, silk shawls, beaded and mesh purses, fine wearable vintage apparel, antique jewelry, vintage gifts.

Joyce & Judy
Krazy Cat Collectibles
P.O. Box 21727
Emmitsburg, MD 21727
ph: 301-309-2513
e-mail: KrazyCatCo@aol.com
Buys and sells exceptional quality vintage ladies accessories and jewelry: Lucite purses, vintage beaded bags, enamel compacts, etc.

Donna & Fiona Neary
Heritage Studio
P.O. Box 697
Fredericksburg, VA 22404
e-mail: gallery@heritagestudio.com
web: http://www.heritagestudio.com
Buys and sells authentic antique costume from the 18th and 19th centuries; man's, women's, children's garments and accessories.

Susan M. Black
Susan's Vintage Boutique
120 Mopar Lane
West End, NC 27376
ph: 910-295-6575
fax: 910-295-9109
e-mail: smblack@ac.net
web: http://www.tias.com/stores/susans
In business since 1984; specializes in vintage clothing and jewelry, 1800s and 1900s.

Priscilla Washed
Victorian Lady, The
102 South Main St.
P.O. Box 424
Waxhaw, NC 28173-0424
ph: 704-843-4467 or 800-786-1886
A Victorian specialty store featuring 19th century ladies decorative & fashion accessories; buys and sells purses; also sewing and needlework tools, vintage fashion, Victoriana, and combs; mail order; catalog $5.

Donna Barr
Victorian Elegance, A
3648 NW 67th Ave.
Gainesville, FL 32653-8801
ph: 352-377-0459
e-mail: designs@gator.net
web: http://victorianelegance.com/
Specializes in vintage clothing (including wedding gowns) from 1800s to 1970s; carries a full line of hats, shoes, accessories.

Maryce Garber
Antique Addict
1234 Grove St.
Clearwater, FL 33755
ph: 727-449-8336 or 727-464-2499
e-mail: anaddict@pascomall.com
web: http://www.pascomall.com/anaddict.htm
Carries male and female attire, accessories, costume jewelry, swing clothes; shop located at Oldsmar Flea Market, 180 Race Track, Oldsmar, FL.

Joanne Haug
Reflections of the Past
P.O. Box 40361
Bay Village, OH 44140-2263
ph: 440-835-6924
fax: 440-835-6924
e-mail: antiques@victoriana.com
web: http://www.victoriana.com/antiques/
Buys and sells antique and vintage clothing (1770-1930): bridal gowns, Civil War era dresser, christening gowns, Victorian corsets, hats, purses, parasols, shoes, hand-held fans; also bed and table linen.

Gayle Wilson
Gayle's Vintage Clothing & Accessories
3742 Kellogg Ave.
c/o Ferguson Antiques Mall
Cincinnati, OH 45226
ph: 513-321-7341 or 513-271-3722
e-mail: gayles1@earthlink.net
Buys and sells vintage clothing; men's, women's, children's, wedding gowns; also costume jewelry.

Marie Minnich
Sylvia's Attic
210 South First St.
Ann Arbor, MI 48104
ph: 734-971-0430
e-mail: minnich@msen.com
web: http://www.cyberantiquemall.com/vendors/sylvia/sylvia.html
Collector, dealer, expert specializing in 1800-1950 vintage clothing including vintage lingerie.

Barbara Stevens
Rare Wear at Farm Village Antique Mall
4490 Cricket Ridge Dr., #204
Holt, MI 48842
ph: 517-699-8372 or 517-337-4988
fax: 517-337-4560
e-mail: stevensg44@aol.com

Patricia O'Brien
Flapper Alley Ltd.
1518 North Farwell Ave.
Milwaukee, WI 53202
ph: 414-276-6252 or 414-332-3618
Wants to buy antique clothing and textiles from the 1920s and earlier; also fancy beaded bags; appraisal services available.

Carrie Homann
Carrie's Vintage Clothing
204 N. Neil
Champaign, IL 61820
ph: 217-352-3231
e-mail: carries@advancenet.net
web: http://www.advancenet.net/~carries
A complete range of 20th century stock through the 1970s.

Carol F. Obradovits
Caris Corp.
105 W. 69th Terrace
Kansas City, MO 64113-2537
ph: 816-361-1173
fax: 816-822-7502
Buys and sells women's, childrens' and men's clothing and accessories from the period 1890-1950; mail order only.

Diane McGee
Diane McGee Estate Clothing Company
5225 Jackson
Omaha, NE 68106-1331
ph: 402-551-0727
Mail order only; complete line from 1850s to 1960s.

Sarah Fox
Somewhere in Time
P.O. Box 263
Breaux Bridge, LA 70517
ph: 318-983-9364 or 318-893-7824
fax: 318-232-3001
Costume design, period and contemporary; research, sketches, swatches, construction; offers clothing and accessories 1850-1960; wants handbags, jewelry, buttons; supplier/stylist/costumer for film, television, videos.

Janene Fawcett
Vintage Clothing
1301 Pomona St.
Crockett, CA 94525
ph: 510-787-7274

Jules Kliot
Lacis
3163 Adeline St.
Berkeley, CA 94703-2401
ph: 510-843-7178
fax: 510-843-5018
Antique & historic textiles, lace from the 16th century, vintage garments and accessories; sells books and supplies for costume, lace and embroidery; also offers repairs and conservation services.

Eureka, I Found It! Antiques & Collectibles
P.O. Box 2192
Petaluma, CA 94953-2192
e-mail: eureka@erueka-i-found-it.com
web: http://www.eureka-i-found-it.com
An online dealer specializing in vintage textiles and clothing, toy and model steam engines, buttons, fans, Art Deco, costume jewelry, toy sewing machines.

Reed Wetter
Moon Zooom
813 Pacific Ave.
Santa Cruz, CA 95060-4433
ph: 831-423-8500 or 408-287-5876
fax: 831-423-8500

Nicole Sanders
Rusty Zipper Vintage Clothing
P.O. Box 700547
San Jose, CA 95170-0547
ph: 800-816-4699 or 503-909-0358
e-mail: rusty@rustyzipper.com
web: http://www.rustyzipper.com
An online vintage clothing store; specializes in 1940s through 1970s vintage clothing, patterns, books and accessories.

Lora Jabot
Jabot's Vintage Boutique
304 Henderson St.
Eureka, CA 95501
ph: 707-445-8220
e-mail: jabots@geocities.com
web: http://www.geocities.com/Eureka/Park/5956/
Authentic vintage apparel for men and women; Victorian through the 1970s including hats, shoes, purses, and accessories.

Sandy Thornton
Vintage Clothing Company
P.O. Box 20504
Keizer, OR 97307-0504
e-mail: retrothreds@aol.com
web: http://www.angelfire.com/co/retrothrds
Online shop carries hip retro wear from the 1960s and 1970s; inventory includes Fritzi, Rhodes, Russell, Gunne Sax, McClintock, Saks, mini & maxi dresses, peasant skirts and dresses, velvet and wool coats, etc.

Meg Andrews
Meg Andrews, Costumes & Textiles
23, Cowper Rd.
Harpenden, Hertfordshire AL5 5NF
U.K.
ph: 44 1582 460107
fax: 44 1582 461112
e-mail: 106020.2035@compuserve.com
web: http://www.victoriana.com
Specializes in 18th/19th cent. English costumes & accessories, 19th cent. paisley shawls, Arts & Crafts textiles incl. William Morris, Chinese court costumes and textiles, worldwide hangings, 18th/19th cent. samplers.

Experts

Evelyn Siefert Kennedy
Sewtique, Inc.
391 Long Hill Rd.
P.O. Box 1293
Groton, CT 06340-1293
ph: 860-445-7320 or 800-332-9122
fax: 860-445-1448
e-mail: sewtique@aol.com
web: http://members.aol.com/sewtique/home.htm
Specialist in restoration, preservation & conservation of apparel and textiles; full service by mail/phone or appt.; appraises textiles, laces, tapestries, etc.; removes spots & stains; teaches textile appraisal & restoration workshops.

Elizabeth S. Brown
45 Whippoorwill Way
Belle Mead, NJ 08502-5827
ph: 908-359-3395
fax: 908-874-7590
e-mail: wbrown@nerc.com
Lecturer, appraiser & costume consultant on various aspects of clothing collecting & conservation; uses own collection for lectures; also may buy after inspection; specializes in old patterns and garment drafting.

Time Warp Custom & Vintage Attire
P.O. Box 9186
Schenectady, NY 12305-0186
ph: 518-347-1126
fax: 518-347-1126
e-mail: timewarp@timewarp.com
web: http://www.timewarp.com/
Buys/sells/appraises vintage clothing, jewelry, accessories; reproduces vintage and historical clothing for museums, reenactment, theater, ballroom dancing, etc.; also restores, repairs and alters clothing, textiles and costume jewelry.

Roseann Ettinger
Remember When
21-23 W. Broad St.
Hazleton, PA 18201
ph: 570-454-8465 or 570-450-5542
Author of "50's Popular Fashions," "Fifties Forever," and "Twentieth Century Neckties."

Diane McGee
5225 Jackson
Omaha, NE 68106-1331
ph: 402-551-0727
Author of "A Passion for Fashion: Antique, Collectible, & Retro Clothes 1850-1950"; 200 pgs., over 190 photos; send $24.95 + $2 UPS.

Frances Grimble
Lavolta Press
20 Meadowbrook Dr.
San Francisco, CA 94132
ph: 415-566-6259
e-mail: lavolta@best.com
web: http://www.best.com/~lavolta/
Lavolta Press has published "After a Fashion," "The Edwardian Modiste," and "The Voice of Fashion"; Frances Grimble collects pre-1930 clothing, books and magazines with clothing patterns, and books and mags with dance instruction.

Kristina Harris
904 N. 65th St.
Springfield, OR 97478-7021
e-mail: kriswrite@aol.com
Lectures on collectible clothing and historical fashion; author of ten books on the subject, including "Vintage & Edwardian Fashions For Women: 1840-1919," and "Vintage Fashion for Women: 1920s-1940."

Terry McCormick
2009 23rd Ave. W, Apt 2
Seattle, WA 99899-4145
ph: 206-545-2945
Gives workshops on vintage clothing and hats.

Misc. Services

Lauriann Greene
Vintage Clothing Shopping Tours
1122 E. Pike St., Ste. 609
Seattle, WA 98122
ph: 206-324-8139 or 877-261-1500
e-mail: info@gildedagetours.com
web: http://www.gildedagetours.com
Offers vintage clothing shopping tours of France and England; small group, bilingual tour escort is vintage clothing expert; also lace tours of England, France and Belgium.

Museums/Libraries

Museum of Fine Arts, Boston
465 Huntington Ave.
Boston, MA 02115-5523
ph: 617-267-9300
e-mail: webmaster@mfa.org
web: http://www.mfa.org/home.html

Rhode Island School of Design Museum
224 Benefit St.
Providence, RI 02903-2723
ph: 401-454-6500
fax: 401-454-6556
e-mail: rbenefie@risd.edu
web: http://www.risd.edu/museum.html
Apparel, architecture, furniture, graphic design, industrial design, interior architecture, landscape architecture.

Wadsworth Atheneum
600 Main St.
Hartford, CT 06103
ph: 860-278-2670
fax: 860-527-0803
e-mail: info@wadsworthatheneum.org
web: http://www.wadsworthatheneum.org/
Regularly changing themed exhibitions display and interpret selections from an extensive collection of historic costumes and textiles.

Fashion Institute of Technology, Edward C. Blum Design Laboratory
227 West 27th St.
New York, NY 10001
ph: 212-760-7970
web: http://www.newmedia1.com/fitama.htm

Metropolitan Museum of Art, The Costume Institute
1000 Fifth Ave.
New York, NY 10028
ph: 212-570-3838
fax: 212-794-9316
web: http://www.metmuseum.org/

Phyllis Magidson
Museum of the City of New York
1220 5th Ave.
New York, NY 10029-5221
ph: 212-534-1672
fax: 212-534-5974
e-mail: mcny@mcny.org
web: http://www.mcny.org/mcny/
Specializes in street and theatrical costumes; access by appointment; research fee charged.

Museums at Stony Brook, The
Newsletter: News & Events
1208 Route 25A
Stony Brook, NY 11790-1992
ph: 516-751-0066
fax: 516-751-0353
e-mail: museums@longisland.com
web: http://www.museumsatstonybrook.org/
Large collection of American Art, decoys, horse-drawn vehicles, costumes, and miniature period rooms; museum shop.

Anne R. Fabbri, Dir.
Philadelphia College of Textiles & Science, The Goldey Paley Design Center
4200 Henry Ave.
Philadelphia, PA 19144
ph: 215-951-2860 or 800-951-7287
e-mail: webmaster@philacol.edu
web: http://www.philacol.edu/paey/index.html
A repository for many historical textiles and textile-related artifacts.

National Museum of American History
14th & Constitution Ave. NW
Washington, DC 20560
ph: 202-357-2700
e-mail: webmaster@si.edu
web: http://www.si.edu/organiza/museums/nmah/nmah.htm

Colleen Callahan
Valentine Museum
1015 East Clay
Richmond, VA 23219
ph: 804-649-0711
fax: 804-643-3510
e-mail: valmus@mindspring.com
web: http://www.valentinemuseum.com
Largest costume and textile collection in the South.

Western Reserve Historical Society
10825 East Blvd.
Cleveland, OH 44106-1703
ph: 216-721-5722
fax: 216-721-0645
e-mail: pomerleau@wrhs.org
web: http://www.wrhs.org/
Oldest cultural institution in Cleveland, with a research/genealogical library, costume wing, auto & aviation museum and restored mansion under one roof; special interest area in costume and textiles.

Indianapolis Museum of Art, Indiana Fashion Design Collection
1200 W. 38th St.
Indianapolis, IN 46208
ph: 317-923-1331
e-mail: ima@ima-art.org
web: http://www.ima-art.org/collections/textiles.html

Detroit Historical Museum
5401 Woodward Ave.
Detroit, MI 48202-4009
ph: 313-833-1805
web: http://www.detroithistorical.org/

Douglas Greenberg, Dir.
Chicago Historical Society
Clark St. at North Ave.
Chicago, IL 60614
ph: 312-642-4600
fax: 312-266-2077
e-mail: douglasg@chicagohistory.org
web: http://www.chicagohs.org/

Missouri Historical Society
P.O. Box 11940
Saint Louis, MO 63112-0040
ph: 314-746-4599
fax: 314-746-4548
web: http://www.livable.com/misshist.htm

Patricia L. McClain, Cur.
Museum of Vintage Fashion, Inc.
Newsletter: Decades
10 Lacassie Court
Lafayette, CA 94549
ph: 925-944-1896 or 925-938-3810
Research center, historical and vintage clothing (1736-1980), library;

terrace tea room and garden; ongoing exhibitions on and off site.

Museum of Costume
Assembly Rooms
Bennett St.
Batt, Somerset BA1 2QH
U.K.
ph: 0122-5477789 or 0122-5477752
fax: 0122-5444793
e-mail: costume_enquiries@bathnes.gov.uk
web: http://www.museumofcostume.co.uk/
The museum's collection includes all aspects of fashion from the 16th century to the present - handmade, ready-to-wear and designer.

Periodicals

Molly Turner
Molly's Vintage Promotions
Newsletter: Vintage Gazette, The
194 Amity St.
Amherst, MA 01002-2201
ph: 413-549-6446
e-mail: merrylees@aol.com
Quarterly newsletter focusing on vintage clothing.

Elyse Zorn Karlin, Ed.
Newsletter: Adornment
1333A North Avenue, Box 103
New Rochelle, NY 10804
ph: 914-637-0087 or 914-636-3784
fax: 914-637-0087
e-mail: ekarlin@usa.net
Quarterly newsletter covering ancient to contemporary studio and vintage jewelry, historic costume, antique buttons, and beads; contains articles, book reviews, terminology, extensive calendar, and more.

Jacqueline Horning
Newsletter: Lill's Vintage Clothing Newsletter
19 Jamestown Dr.
Cincinnati, OH 45241-1435
ph: 513-779-3708
Written for collectors and dealers of vintage clothing; bi-monthly.

Kristina Harris, Editor
Newsletter: Vintage Connection, The
904 N. 65th St.
Springfield, OR 97478-7021
e-mail: kriswrite@aol.com
For collectors of vintage and antique fashions; covers specific areas of the 19th and 20th centuries; reproductions, sources, dealers, how-to articles.

Repair Services

Time Warp Custom & Vintage Attire
P.O. Box 9186
Schenectady, NY 12305-0186
ph: 518-347-1126
fax: 518-347-1126
e-mail: timewarp@timewarp.com
web: http://www.timewarp.com/
Buys/sells/appraises vintage clothing, jewelry, accessories; reproduces vintage and historical clothing for museums, reenactment, theater, ballroom dancing, etc.; also restores, repairs and alters clothing, textiles and costume jewelry.

Suppliers

Greenburg & Hammer
24 W. 57th St.
New York, NY 10019
ph: 800-955-5135
fax: 212-765-8475
Supplier of mounting and displaying products for clothing: silk thread, hangers, ready-made torsos, steamers, Kraft wrapping paper.

Rita Marx
Cherish
205 W. 86th St.
New York, NY 10024
ph: 212-724-1748
fax: 212-480-1143
e-mail: cherish_ny@hotmail.com
Carries Orvus and other conservation supplies for the storage, cleaning and displaying of vintage textiles and clothing.

Baltimore Display
1900 Bayard St.
Baltimore, MD 21230
ph: 800-638-3764 or 410-685-3393
fax: 410-685-6877
A clothing store supply company selling display cases, racks, etc.; also sells "poly forms" for the display of vintage clothing.

Vintage (Black)

Museums/Libraries

Lois K. Alexander, Dir.
Black Fashion Museum, The
155 W. 126th St.
New York, NY 10027
ph: 212-666-1320
A textile and vintage fashion research center for students and collectors of costume history, art and design.

Joyce Bailey, Dir.
Black Fashion Museum, The
2007 Vermont Ave. NW
Washington, DC 20001-4029
ph: 202-667-0744 or 301-455-2212
fax: 301-306-9249
e-mail: bfmdc@aol.com
web: http://www.blackfamilies.com/community/groups/BlackFashion
A textile and vintage fashion research center for students and collectors of costume history, art and design.

Wearable Art

Appraisers

Sally A. Ambrose
P.O. Box 536
11156 North Rd.
Leavenworth, WA 98826-9512
ph: 509-548-7472
fax: 509-548-0240
e-mail: sally@televar.com
Specializes in the appraising of antique and contemporary American quilted textiles, as well as contemporary wearable art. Wearable art is not always quilted but may exhibit surface design in a variety of art media and embellishment.

CLOWN COLLECTIBLES

(see also CIRCUS COLLECTIBLES; COLLECTIBLES [MODERN], Clowns; COLLECTIBLES [MODERN], Figurines [Emmett Kelly, Jr.])

Emmett Kelly

Collectors

N.W. Neill, Jr.
P.O. Box 38
Ennice, NC 28623-0038
fax: 336-657-8084
e-mail: saddlemtn@skybest.com
Wants to buy Emmett Kelly SR/JR pieces, dolls, Circus items, books, photos; anything related to Emmett Kelly Senior or Junior.

Museums/Libraries

Emmett Kelly Historical Museum
202 E. Main
Sedan, KS 67361-1629
ph: 316-725-3470
e-mail: stettler@horizon.hit.net
web: http://skyways.lib.ks.us/kansas/towns/Sedan/museum.html

COAST GUARD

(see also NAUTICAL ANTIQUES; NAUTICAL ANTIQUES, Lighthouses)

Collectors

Bob Glick
Columbia Trading Company
1 Barnstable Rd.
Hyannis, MA 02601
ph: 508-778-2929
fax: 508-778-2922
e-mail: nautical@capecod.net
web: http://www.columbiatrading.com/

Dealers

James W. Claflin
Kenrick A. Claflin & Son
30 Hudson St.
Northborough, MA 01532
ph: 508-869-6955
Collectors and dealers in fine nautical antiques; specializing in U.S. Lighthouse Service, U.S. Lifesaving Service, U.S. Revenue Cutter Service, U.S. Coast Guard.

Adin Otto
253 Bonnybrook Rd.
Carlisle Barracks, PA 17013
Wants to buy U.S. Lifesaving Service, Lighthouse Service, Revenue Cutter Service, and Coast Guard items: photographs, uniforms, china, annual reports, etc.

Museums/Libraries

Robert Nason Davis, Cur.
Shore Village Museum
Newsletter: Shore Village Museum Newsletter
104 Limerock St.
Rockland, ME 04841-2945
ph: 207-594-0311 or 207-236-3206
fax: 207-594-9481
e-mail: knb@ime.net
web: http://www.tiac.net/users/buster/shorevillage/
Largest collection of lighthouse and Coast Guard artifacts in the U.S.; navigation instruments, ship models, scrimshaw, lighthouse models, and 5,000 lighthouse postcards from around the world; also lighthouses, Civil War, navigation, GAR.

Cindee Herrick
U.S. Coast Guard Museum
U.S. Coast Guard Academy
15 Mohegan Ave.
New London, CT 06320-4195
ph: 860-444-8511
e-mail: herrick@dcseq.uscga.edu
web: http://www.uscg.mil/hq/g-cp/museum/muse_info.html
History of the U.S. Coast Guard including the Lifesaving Service, Lighthouse Service, and Revenue Cutter Service.

U.S. Life-Saving Service

Clubs/Associations

U.S. Life-Saving Service Heritage Association, The
P.O. Box 75
Caledonia, MI 49316-0075
web: http://www.maine.com/lights/lssha.htm
Quarterly magazine on the Life-Saving Service and the Coast Guard, historic preservation activities, station tours, learn about shipwrecks, rescues and maritime history.

Dealers

James W. Claflin
Kenrick A. Claflin & Son
30 Hudson St.
Northborough, MA 01532
ph: 508-869-6955
Collectors and dealers in fine nautical antiques; specializing in U.S. Lighthouse Service, U.S. Lifesaving

Service, U.S. Revenue Cutter Service, U.S. Coast Guard.

Jacques Noel Jacobsen, Jr.
60 Manor Rd.
Staten Island, NY 10310-2698
ph: 718-981-0973
Buys and sells U.S. Lifesaving Service, U.S. Lighthouse Service, and lighthouse artifacts, photographs, books and ephemera; American military antiques 1840-1940 large illustrated catalog, 3 issues for $12 ($15 overseas).

U.S. Lighthouse Service

Collectors

Timothy Harrison
P.O. Box 1690
Wells, ME 04090
ph: 800-758-1444 or 207-646-0515
fax: 207-646-0516
e-mail: lhdigest@lhdigest.com
web: http://www.lhdigest.com
Wants to buy memorabilia from U.S. Lighthouse Service (USLHS) or U.S. Lighthouse Establishment (USLHE): badges, flags, dinnerware, buttons, uniforms, old photographs of keepers and their families, postcards, newspaper stories.

Dealers

James W. Claflin
Kenrick A. Claflin & Son
30 Hudson St.
Northborough, MA 01532
ph: 508-869-6955
Collectors and dealers in fine nautical antiques; specializing in U.S. Lighthouse Service, U.S. Lifesaving Service, U.S. Revenue Cutter Service, U.S. Coast Guard.

U.S. Revenue Cutter Service

Dealers

James W. Claflin
Kenrick A. Claflin & Son
30 Hudson St.
Northborough, MA 01532
ph: 508-869-6955
Collectors and dealers in fine nautical antiques; specializing in U.S. Lighthouse Service, U.S. Lifesaving Service, U.S. Revenue Cutter Service, U.S. Coast Guard.

COAT OF ARMS

(see BOOKS, Heraldry; HERALDRY)

COCA-COLA COLLECTIBLES

(see SOFT DRINK COLLECTIBLES, Coca-Cola)

CODE MACHINES

(see SPY EQUIPMENT)

COFFEE

(see also ELECTRICITY RELATED ITEMS, Appliances [Coffee Pots])

Collectors

Bill Park
12312 Starlight Lane
Bowie, MD 20715-2138
ph: 301-464-1608
e-mail: coffee5@erols.com
Wants to buy coffee containers of all types (condition important), but prefers 1-lb. screw-top and sample sizes; also wants other types of coffee memorabilia.

Nancy Pennington
1750 Keyes Rd.
Greenbrier, TN 37073
ph: 615-643-0290
fax: 615-643-0290
Wants coffee related collectibles such as coffee jars.

Arbuckles Bros. Coffee Co.

Collectors

Al Kruse
2536 Teslin St.
Juneau, AK 99801
ph: 907-789-1817
Wants to buy memorabilia relating to Arbuckles Bros. Coffee Company.

Experts

Greg Q. ArBuckle
Arbuckles' Coffee Museum
97 16th Ave. SW
Cedar Rapids, IA 52404-5948
ph: 319-363-1242
fax: 319-365-5115
Wants to buy memorabilia relating to Arbuckles Bros. Coffee Company.

Museums/Libraries

Greg Q. ArBuckle
Arbuckles' Coffee Museum
97 16th Ave. SW
Cedar Rapids, IA 52404-5948
ph: 319-363-1242
fax: 319-365-5115
Large displayed collection of Arbuckles Bros. Co. products: coffee tins, spice tins, tea tins, trade cards, company documents, billings, letters, covers, bottles, banners, signs, counter displays, magazine ads.

Mills & Grinders

Clubs/Associations

Joe MacMillan
Association of Coffee Mill Enthusiasts
Newsletter: Grinder Finder
657 Old Mountain Rd.
Marietta, GA 30064-1339
ph: 770-427-6434
e-mail: jillmacmillan2@juno.com

Collectors

Alex Caiola
84 Seneca
Emerson, NJ 07630-1243
ph: 201-967-9540
e-mail: actiques@aol.com
Wants 2-wheel coffee grinders; also grand union, Griswold, and golden rule grinders.

Terry Friend
839 Glendale Rd.
Galax, VA 24333
ph: 540-236-9027
e-mail: friend@tcia.net

Joe MacMillan
657 Old Mountain Rd.
Marietta, GA 30064-1339
ph: 770-427-6434
e-mail: jillmacmillan2@juno.com

Andrew E. Thomas
4681 North 84th Way
Scottsdale, AZ 85251-1864
ph: 888-255-0664 or 480-947-5693
fax: 480-994-4382
Wants coffee grinders.

Stu Johnson
710 Taylor Ave. #B
Alameda, CA 94501
ph: 510-523-1089
Wants to buy cast iron, double wheel coffee grinders in all sizes; no electric.

Repro. Sources

Cumberland General Store
#1 Highway 68
Crossville, TN 38555
ph: 931-484-8481 or 800-334-4640
fax: 931-456-1211
web: http://www.cumberlandgeneral.com/

Tins

Collectors

Hugh Pinney
1387 Madison
Santa Clara, CA 95050-4758
ph: 408-241-5417
Buys keywind coffee tins which are mint or near mint and free of rust or cancer, must have right tops! Also wants certain unopened keywind tins.

Dealers

Tim Schweighart
1123 Santa Luisa Dr.
Solana Beach, CA 92075-1614
ph: 619-481-8315
fax: 619-481-5699
Collector, appraiser, and dealer of coffee tins.

COFFINS

(see FUNERAL ITEMS)

COIN-OPERATED MACHINES

(see also AMUSEMENT PARK ITEMS; BOOKS, Reference [Coin-Operated]; GAMBLING COLLECTIBLES, Punchboards; POPULAR CULTURE; REPAIR/RESTORATION/CONSERVATION, Metal Items; SCALES; SOFT DRINK COLLECTIBLES, Soda Machines)

Auction Services

US Amusement Auctions
P.O. Box 4819
Louisville, KY 40204
ph: 502-451-1263
fax: 502-897-7771
e-mail: webmaster@usamusement.com
web: http://www.usamusement.com/
Specialized auctions of video games, slot machines, juke boxes, arcade games, collectibles, trade stimulators, etc.

Clubs/Associations

Frank Demayo
Coin Operators Collectors Association
Newsletter: C.O.C.A. Newsletter
1511 Holliston Trail
Fort Wayne, IN 46825
ph: 219-489-0053 or 800-258-8243
fax: 219-484-8605
e-mail: seeburgh@aol.com
Publishes a quarterly newsletter for collectors of gambling, penny arcade and vending machines.

Collectors

Andy Rudoff
P.O. Box 111
Oceanport, NJ 07757-0111
ph: 732-542-3712
fax: 732-542-3712
Wants pre-1945 coin operated machines: arcade machines, vending, slots, trade stimulators, and games; send description and price; photos very helpful.

Richard O. Gates
P.O. Box 187
Chesterfield, VA 23832-0187
ph: 804-748-0382 or 804-794-5146
fax: 804-748-6349
e-mail: rogates@mindspring.com
Wants coin-operated machines including jukeboxes, pinballs, trade

stimulators, slot machines, old gumball machines, Coca-Cola, Pepsi, R.C., Dr. Pepper machines and any signs or literature related to any of the above.

Lucky Riley
901 Lynne Ave.
Napoleon, OH 43545-1217

Mike Gorski
1770 Dover Rd.
Westlake, OH 44145
ph: 440-871-6071
Slot machines, old penny arcade machines; Wurlitzer 78 RPM jukeboxes, odd vending machines; Regina musical boxes, old coin-operated machines.

Frank Demayo
1511 Holliston Trail
Fort Wayne, IN 46825
ph: 219-489-0053 or 800-258-8243
fax: 219-484-8605
e-mail: seeburgh@aol.com
Wants coin-operated slot, gum, card, dice machines; also wants to buy automatons and key wound figures.

Richard McCoy
2719 Lakeview Ave.
St. Joseph, MI 49085
Wants slot machines, trade stimulators, gumball machines, pinball machines, arcade games, etc.

Richard Trautwein
Toys N Such
437 Dawson St.
Sault Sainte Marie, MI 49783-2119
ph: 906-635-0356
e-mail: rtraut@portup.com
Collector, dealer wants to buy coin-op machines such as slot machines, scales, gumball and other vending machines; also wants arcade games such as strength tester games and games of skill, etc.

Dave Ogden
P.O. Box 223
Northbrook, IL 60062-0223
ph: 847-564-2893
fax: 847-564-2893
e-mail: musical@flash.net
Wants to buy early coin-operated machines, gambling and slot machines.

Dealers

John S. Zuk
106 Orchard St.
Belmont, MA 02478
ph: 617-489-7540
fax: 617-484-4800
e-mail: jzuk@integral-inc.com
Buys, sells and repairs slot machines, jukeboxes, arcade machines, gumballs, neon clocks, etc.

Darrow's Fun Antiques
1101 1st Ave.
New York, NY 10021-8737
ph: 212-838-0730
fax: 212-838-3617
e-mail: george@fun-antiques.com
web: http://www.fun-antiques.com/
Buys & sells antique games, toys, ad signs, animated art, jukeboxes, slot machines, comic watches, bicycles & memorabilia of all types.

Steve Wager
Pennsylvania Gameroom Warehouse
520 Lehman St.
Lebanon, PA 17042
ph: 717-272-7052 or 888-443-4837
e-mail: gameroom@gameroomwarehouse.com
web: http://gameroomwarehouse.com
Buys and sells arcade amusements that have been fully-reconditioned for home or commercial use; full-color online catalog; two central-PA retail locations.

Ken Durham
909 26th St. NW
Washington, DC 20037-2029
e-mail: durham@gameroomantiques.com
web: http://www.GameRoomAntiques.com
Buy/sell/trade countertop coin-operated machines: trade stimulators, vending machines, arcade machines, punchboards; also sells large selection of books and service manuals on same; send $2 for list.

Harold Daniel
Quicksilver Oddities Antique Coin-Ops & Collectibles
2500 E. Grann Blanc Rd.
Grand Blanc, MI 48439
ph: 810-694-0787
With Greg Young wants slot machines 25 yrs. old or older; also antique coin-operated gaming devices, trade stimulators, vending machines, arcade games, and items with sports themes.

Jack Freund
Slots of Fun
P.O. Box 4
Springfield, WI 53176
ph: 414-642-3655
fax: 414-642-2632
Buys and sells counter top gum or nut machines, early cigar store trade stimulators, and cigar nippers; any coin operated game or machine; 25 years experience in the field; can identify and appraise old coin operated machines.

John Adorjan
Amusing Devices
1092 Randville Dr.
Palatine, IL 60067
ph: 847-274-3759
fax: 847-836-0104
e-mail: amusingd@ix.netcom.com
Specializes in any machine that takes a coin from 1899 to present: video games, pinball, bowling, mechanical, antique and more; sell, services, buys, trades.

Allan B. Pall
1118 North Harlem Ave.
River Forest, IL 60305
ph: 708-771-7446
web: http://www.coin-opclassics.com/Ads/A_Pall/a_pall.htm
Wants to buy coin-operated machines: gambling, trade stimulators, vending machines, arcade games, automatons, bird boxes, music boxes, nickelodeons, etc.

Home Arcade Corp.
1108 Front St.
Lisle, IL 60532-2258
ph: 630-964-2555
fax: 630-964-9367
web: http://www.homearcadecorp.com/
Sells restored vintage Coke machines; also juke boxes, phone booths, beer signs, tavern items, barber poles and other '50s memorabilia; send $5 for Coke Restoration Parts Catalog.

Walt Baxley
Be-Bop Jukeboxes & Gameroom Goodies
11441 Stemmons Frwy., Ste. 133
Dallas, TX 75229
ph: 972-243-5725
fax: 972-243-2179
e-mail: bebops@aol.com
web: http://www.2nd-sight.com/bebop
Southwest's largest retailer of antique and collectible jukeboxes, pool tables, and other gameroom items; sales, service, restoration, and party rentals.

Daina Pettit
Mr. Pinball
4805 Marabow Circle
Salt Lake City, UT 84117-5419
ph: 801-277-6296 or 801-277-0888
fax: 801-277-0888
e-mail: daina@mrpinball.com
web: http://www.xmission.com/~daina/pinball.html
Pinball machine collector, dealer, expert and restorer.

Dennis Clark
Off the Wall Antiques, Inc.
7325 Melrose Ave.
Los Angeles, CA 90046
ph: 323-930-1185
fax: 323-930-1595

Herb Silvers
Fabulous Fantasies
12602 Ventura Blvd.
Studio City, CA 91604
ph: 818-761-2255
fax: 818-752-4372
e-mail: pinball@fabfan.com
web: http://www.fabfan.com
Sells and restores vintage pinball and arcade games and all Gameroom furnishings; also reproduces many pinball machine backglass art and video game overlays; can also create custom upholstered pieces; offers gameroom design assistance.

Randy Hilberg
Collector's Nectar
Box 431
Morro Bay, CA 93443
ph: 805-772-2968
fax: 805-772-2968
e-mail: nectar@thegrid.net
Always buying coin-operated devices; offers complete restoration services; appraisals; no collection too big or too small to purchase or restore; the only lifetime guarantee in the business.

Mike Harrod
Trailside Treasures
365 Victor Street "S"
Salinas, CA 93907
e-mail: m.harrod@worldnet.att.net
web: http://home.att.net/~m.harrod/
Buy, sells and trades coin-operated machines; many coin-ops, plastic radios and other gameroom collectibles in stock.

Wild Bill's Casino
2318 N.W. Vaughn St.
Portland, OR 97210
ph: 503-658-3607
Buys, sells, trades, repairs, restores vintage amusement machines.

John Robertson
John's Jukes Ltd.
2343 Main St.
Vancouver, British Columbia V5T 3C9
Canada
ph: 604-872-5757
fax: 604-872-2010
e-mail: JRR@flippers.com
web: http://www.flippers.com
Sales and service of pinball, video games and jukeboxes; parts and schematics available; shop service for game boards; call about shipping for repair.

Experts

Bill Nesnay
P.O. Box 67
Atlantic Highlands, NJ 07716-0067
ph: 732-708-0660 or 732-349-5764
e-mail: coinop@bellatlantic.net
Specializes in and wants to buy baseball related coin-op machines: gumball, pinball, arcade, vending, and

trade stimulators; please no calls after 10 pm EST.

Bob Levy
Unique One, The
2802 Centre St.
Pennsauken, NJ 08109-5304
ph: 609-663-2554
e-mail: theuniqueone@att.net
Buys and sells coin-operated machines including slot machines and arcade games; advisor to "Warman's Antiques & Collectibles Price Guide."

Joseph S. Jancuska
619 Miller St.
Luzerne, PA 18709-1307
ph: 570-287-3478
Buys, sells, repairs and appraises slot machines, trade stimulators, gum & nut machines & other coin-operated machines.

Bill Enes
8520 Lewis Dr.
Shawnee Mission, KS 66227-3277
ph: 913-441-1492 or 913-441-1502
fax: 913-441-1502
e-mail: bille@unicom.net
Author of "Silent Salesmen - an Encyclopedia of Collectible Gum, Candy & Nut Machines."

Internet Resources

Rick's Gameroom
e-mail: ZanyMail@Zany-Pix.com
web: http://zany-pix.com/rix.htm
Jukeboxes, arcade machines, vending machines, weight scales, kiddie rides, soda fountain stuff, advertising signs, radios, classic cars, carousel animals, gasoline pumps.

Ken Durham
GameRoomAntiques
909 26th St. NW
Washington, DC 20037-2029
e-mail: durham@gameroomantiques.com
web: http://www.GameRoomAntiques.com
A World Wide Web site dedicated to game room collecting: pinball machines, juke boxes, Coke machines, etc.; monthly feature articles, book reviews, links to other game room resources.

Roy Baker
Coin-Op Connection
10132 Brentridge Court
Dallas, TX 75243
ph: 972-783-0767
fax: 972-783-0705
e-mail: roy@2nd-sight.com
web: http://2nd-sight.com/coin-op/
An internet resource for collectors, dealers and gameroom owners; focus is in jukeboxes and related items, but also covers advertising, salesman samples, pinballs, slot machines, etc.

Sally Georgeson
Pinmall
13159 SW Falcom Rise Dr.
Tigard, OR 97223
ph: 503-524-3119
fax: 503-524-0888
e-mail: pinmall@pinmall.com
web: http://www.pinmall.com
Lots of information on this website for gameroom enthusiasts: pinball, jukebox, billiards, cards, videos, and anything gameroom or coin-operated; information about collectors, players, manufacturers, repair companies, events; free ads.

Museums/Libraries

Marvin Yagoda
Marvin's Marvelous Mechanical Museum
31005 Orchard Rd.
Farmington, MI 48334
ph: 248-626-5020
fax: 248-626-7945
e-mail: adamant726@aol.com
web: http://www.marvin3m.com/

Periodicals

Magazine: Gameroom Magazine
P.O. Box 41
Keyport, NJ 07735-0041
ph: 732-739-1955
fax: 732-739-2834
e-mail: coinop@gameroommagazine.com
web: http://www.gameroommagazine.com
A great source of information for the collector and dealer of jukeboxes, pinballs, slot machines, Coke and other soda machines, arcade games, classic arcade video, and other gameroom collectibles.

Ken Durham
Newsletter: Coin Op
909 26th St. NW
Washington, DC 20037-2029
e-mail: durham@gameroomantiques.com
web: http://www.GameRoomAntiques.com
A bimonthly 8-page newsletter that features all coin machine categories with a special focus on what is new on the WWW for coin machine and gameroom collectors.

Rosanna Harris
Newspaper: Coin Drop International
5815 W. 52nd Ave.
Denver, CO 80212-7503
ph: 303-431-9266
fax: 303-431-6978
e-mail: info@royalbell.com
A bi-monthly publication with a major focus on vintage slot machines, jukeboxes, pinball machines, arcade machines, scales, coin operated music, shows, etc.

Daniel R. Mead
Mead Publishing Co.
Magazine: Loose Change
1551 South Commerce St.
Las Vegas, NV 89102-2703
ph: 702-387-8750
fax: 702-366-1599
A monthly magazine with articles on coin-operated gaming machines, and gambling and related subjects; contemporary and antique.

Magazine: Coin Slot International
P.O. Box 53
2 daltry Street
Oldham, Manchester OL1 4BB
U.K.
ph: 0161 624 3687
fax: 0161 665 1260
The U.K.'s premier weekly magazine for the coin-op industry.

Repair Services

Tony DeLucia
Antique Amusement Service
765 Shephard Ave.
Hamden, CT 06514
ph: 203-288-3797
e-mail: AntAmuSvc@webtv.net
Restoration and repair of jukeboxes, pinball machines, and other 1930s through 1960s coin-operated machines; over 20 years experience; large selection of restored machines always on hand.

Gary Taplin
Penny Arcade Restorations
28 Southfield Ave.
Stamford, CT 06902
ph: 203-357-1913
Restores all kinds of coin-operated machines: mechanical, electro-mechanical, pneumatics, part fabrication, cabinetry refinishing, marbleizing, graphics, marquees, papier mache, glass, carving, castings, polishing, plating.

Tony Miklos
Pinball Paramedic Repair Service
1372 Targat Road
East Greenville, PA 18041
ph: 215-541-4167
e-mail: tmiklos@netcarrier.com
Serving Eastern Pennsylvania from Allentown to Philadelphia; repairs pinballs, jukeboxes, slot machines, shuffle alleys, etc.; from antique to state-of-the-art; in business since 1979; no retail parts for sale.

Joseph S. Jancuska
619 Miller St.
Luzerne, PA 18709-1307
ph: 570-287-3478
Buys, sells, repairs and appraises slot machines, trade stimulators, gum & nut machines & other coin-operated machines.

John Adorjan
Amusing Devices
1092 Randville Dr.
Palatine, IL 60067
ph: 847-274-3759
fax: 847-836-0104
e-mail: amusingd@ix.netcom.com
Specializes in any machine that takes a coin from 1899 to present: video games, pinball, bowling, mechanical, antique and more; sell, services, buys, trades.

John Robertson
John's Jukes Ltd.
2343 Main St.
Vancouver, British Columbia V5T 3C9
Canada
ph: 604-872-5757
fax: 604-872-2010
e-mail: JRR@flippers.com
web: http://www.flippers.com
Sales and service of pinball, video games and jukeboxes; parts and schematics available; shop service for game boards; call about shipping for repair.

Repro. Sources

Mechanical Antiques & Amusements Co.
R.R. 7 Bateman Circle
Barrington, IL 60010
ph: 847-381-1234
Sells recreations of coin-operated machines such as Grandmother Predictions.

Suppliers

Rick Frink
2977 Eager
Howell, MI 48843-6711
Supplies reelstrips, pay cards, decals, instruction sheets, and mint wrappers for antique slot machines and some trade stimulators; send 7 1st class postage stamps for catalog; also buys and repairs antique machines.

Arcade Games

Dealers

TNT Amusements
1028 Shade Lane Rd.
Columbus, OH 43227
ph: 614-577-0111
e-mail: tntgame@netwalk.com
web: http://www.tntgame.com
Specializes in buying, selling, restoring quality arcade video games, pinball machines, jukeboxes.

Gumball Machines

Collectors

Don L. Reedy
13 South Carroll St.
Frederick, MD 21701-5606
ph: 301-663-4240 or 301-662-5503
fax: 301-694-9190
e-mail: shineit4u@aol.com
Buying pre-1940 cast iron or

porcelain gumball and peanut vending machines and parts.

Robert Couch
Mr. Gumball
6321 West Fletcher St.
Chicago, IL 60634
ph: 773-889-3115
Wants gumball and peanut machines from 1890 to 1960.

Dealers

Rich Brinkos
Antique Gumball Machines
948 Clyde Lane
Philadelphia, PA 19128-1136
ph: 215-482-1429 or 215-482-9099
Sells, restores, repairs and services gumball and peanut machines; globes, parts, vending products, stands; anything required to make a fully authentic period vending machine.

Richard Ackerberg
R & S Marketing
574 Mt. Holyoke Ave.
Pacific Palisades, CA 90272
ph: 800-235-5471 or 310-573-2007
fax: 310-230-2825
e-mail: ackra@aol.com
web: http://www.antiquegumball.com
Buys and sells antique gumball machines.

Repair Services

Rich Brinkos
Antique Gumball Machines
948 Clyde Lane
Philadelphia, PA 19128-1136
ph: 215-482-1429 or 215-482-9099
Sells, restores, repairs and services gumball and peanut machines; globes, parts, vending products, stands; anything required to make a fully authentic period vending machine.

Jukeboxes

(see also BOOKS, Reference [Jukeboxes])

Collectors

Joe Weber
604 Centre St.
Ashland, PA 17921-1332
ph: 570-875-4787 or 570-875-4401
Wants early Capehart & Wurlitzer jukeboxes which play 78 rpm records; will arrange pickup; all letters answered; will offer advise.

Mike Gorski
1770 Dover Rd.
Westlake, OH 44145
ph: 440-871-6071
Slot machines, old penny arcade machines; Wurlitzer 78 RPM jukeboxes, odd vending machines;Regina musical boxes, old coin-operated machines.

Roark Vane
6839 Havenside Dr.
Sacramento, CA 95831-2168
ph: 916-392-3864
e-mail: neonclock@aol.com
Wants to buy Wurlitzer, Rock-Ola or other 1929-1948 jukeboxes; also wants jukebox related accessories or related advertising items.

Dealers

John T. Johnston
6742 Fifth Ave.
Brooklyn, NY 11220-5418
ph: 718-833-8455
fax: 718-833-0560
Buys, sells, rents, trades and repairs slot and jukeboxes; wants to buy old jukeboxes, slot machines, vending, arcade, old gambling items, neons, cash registers, music boxes, phonographs, syrup dispensers.

Lloyd Thoburn
Lloyd's Jukeboxes
11311 Fieldstone Ln.
Reston, VA 20191-3905
ph: 703-620-3850
e-mail: llthoburn@aol.com
Buys jukeboxes in any condition; free phone appraisal of wholesale values; has over 100 jukeboxes in stock.

TNT Amusements
1028 Shade Lane Rd.
Columbus, OH 43227
ph: 614-577-0111
e-mail: tntgame@netwalk.com
web: http://www.tntgame.com
Specializes in buying, selling, restoring quality arcade video games, pinball machines, jukeboxes.

David Reed
Jukebox Central
841 West Main St.
Madison, OH 44057
ph: 440-428-6666
Buys, sells, collects and repairs jukeboxes and other coin-op equipment; also sells jukebox accessory equipment and parts.

Walt Baxley
Be-Bop Jukeboxes & Gameroom Goodies
11441 Stemmons Frwy., Ste. 133
Dallas, TX 75229
ph: 972-243-5725
fax: 972-243-2179
e-mail: bebops@aol.com
web: http://www.2nd-sight.com/bebop
Southwest's largest retailer of antique and collectible jukeboxes, pool tables, and other gameroom items; sales, service, restoration, and party rentals.

Randy Hilberg
Collector's Nectar
Box 431
Morro Bay, CA 93443
ph: 805-772-2968
fax: 805-772-2968
e-mail: nectar@thegrid.net
Always buying jukeboxes; offers complete restoration services; appraisals; no collection too big or too small to purchase or restore; the only lifetime guarantee in the business.

Experts

Rick Botts
2545 SE 60th Ct.
Des Moines, IA 50317-5049
ph: 515-265-8324
fax: 515-265-1980

Frank Zygmunt
Zygmunt & Associates
P.O. Box 542
Westmont, IL 60559-0542
ph: 630-985-2742 or 630-971-1015
fax: 630-985-5151
e-mail: zygm1015@aol.com
Buys and sells slot machines and jukeboxes; 200-300 slot machines & Wurlitzer jukeboxes in stock; also Wurlitzer One More Time distributor; also interested in music boxes, nickelodeons, and Coke machines.

Man./Prod./Dist.

Joseph Pankus
Wurlitzer Jukebox Company
1318 Estes St.
Gurnee, IL 60031
ph: 800-987-5480 or 847-662-1700
fax: 847-662-1212
e-mail: bubbles@wurlitzer-jukebox.com
web: http://www.wurlitzer-jukebox.com/
Web site contains a historical account of Wurlitzer, recent news stories, displaying old and current jukebox models, offering licensed products to be purchased, and inviting visitors to sent in stories about jukeboxes in their lives.

Periodicals

Ken Durham
Newspaper: Antique Amusements, Slot Machine & Jukebox Gazette
909 26th St. NW
Washington, DC 20037-2029
e-mail: durham@gameroomantiques.com
web: http://www.GameRoomAntiques.com
Semi-annual newspaper focusing on slot machines and jukeboxes; lots of ads, articles, shows, auctions; send SASE for info.

Rick Botts
Magazine: Jukebox Collector
2545 SE 60th Ct.
Des Moines, IA 50317-5049
ph: 515-265-8324
fax: 515-265-1980
A monthly magazine with large classified ad department, reprinted articles, repair information, shows, auctions, etc.

Michael F. Baute
Always Jukin'
Newspaper: Always Jukin'
1952 1st Avenue S. #6
Seattle, WA 98134-1406
ph: 206-652-4005
fax: 972-783-0705
e-mail: alwaysjuke@aol.com
web: http://www.alwaysjukin.com/
Largest circulation monthly jukebox publication; photos, show reports, ads, new products, restoring guides, etc.

Repair Services

Chance Tess
Pinball Wizard Sales & Service
39425 Atkinson Dr.
Sterling Heights, MI 48313-5018
ph: 810-978-0393
fax: 313-369-6377
Restores '50s and '60s Seeburg & Wurlitzer juke boxes.

David Headley
DH Distributors
P.O. Box 48623
Wichita, KS 67201-8623
ph: 316-684-0050
fax: 316-684-0050
Repairs and restores jukeboxes; chassis and cabinet restorations.

Electrons Past Vintage Electronics
ph: 801-262-3903
fax: 801-262-3903
e-mail: sales@jukin.com
web: http://www.jukin.com
Repairs old jukeboxes and radios.

Jukeboxes (Film)

Experts

Fred Bingaman
P.O. Box 370
Brownstown, IL 62418
ph: 618-427-2761
fax: 314-230-9559
e-mail: mr356@aol.com
Wants audio visual (film) jukeboxes (scopitones), and related advertising items, films, spare parts, etc.

Periodicals

Fred Bingaman
Newsletter: Scopitone Newsletter, The
P.O. Box 370
Brownstown, IL 62418
ph: 618-427-2761
fax: 314-230-9559
e-mail: mr356@aol.com

Parking Meters

Dealers

Ron Rogers
Gas Pumps & Parking Meters
ph: 418-673-1067
e-mail: impala1@bright.net
web: http://www.bright.net/~impala1/
Specializes in buying, selling and restoring old gas pumps and parking meters; also other gas station memorabilia such as oil cans, porcelain and tin signs; pedal cars, too.

Pinball Machines

Appraisers

Amy D. Moore
Thundercade, Inc.
RR1 Box 290
Pownal, VT 05261
ph: 802-823-0216 or 802-447-8558
fax: 802-447-8558
e-mail: pinball@together.net
web: http://www.suezcues.com/
Appraiser, dealer, repairer of pinballs and other coin-operated machines.

Clubs/Associations

Pinball Owners Association
P.O. Box 122
Cambridge, Cambridgeshire CB1 8AH
U.K.
ph: 01223 251477
fax: 01233 351730
e-mail: dmbl@pcmail.nerc-bas.ac.uk
web: http://ds.dial.pipex.com/poa/
500 members; over 20 years old; promotes the owning, restoration and playing of pinball machines; produces a magazine, organizes an annual convention and sells spares and collectibles; pinball ownership not necessary to join.

Collectors

Joe Iozzia
Chameleon Collectibles
P.O. Box 1005
Pomona, NJ 08240-1005
ph: 609-652-8504
fax: 609-652-8888
e-mail: pinflyers@aol.com
web: http://members.aol.com/Pinflyers/chameleon.html
Buys, sells, trades vintage coin-operated slot machines, pinball machines, video and arcade games; also related advertising flyers and brochures; will buy entire collections; hundreds of vintage items on the web site.

Bill Cowles
Vintage Pinballs
4255 Green Ave.
Los Alamitos, CA 90706
ph: 562-594-6489

Dealers

Steve Young
Pinball Resource, The
8 Commerce St.
Poughkeepsie, NY 12603
ph: 914-47307114
fax: 914-473-7116
e-mail: PBResource@idsi.net
Source for maintenance manuals, schematics, replacement parts and supplies to restore and maintain vintage pinball machines; manufacturer of replacement parts; sells pinball books and price guides.

Cynthia O'Brien
Classic Amusement Devices, Inc.
ph: 704-575-8900
e-mail: sales@classicamusement.com
web: http://www.classicamusement.com/
Buys, sells, leases and repairs pinball machines and video games.

Marc Mandeltort
Macro Specialties, Inc.
5290 Platt Springs Rd.
Lexington, SC 29073-9252
ph: 803-957-5500
fax: 803-957-6974
e-mail: tilt@ix.netcom.com
web: http://pinballmachine.com
Provides books, parts, supplies, manuals, schematics, etc. for pinball machine owners.

TNT Amusements
1028 Shade Lane Rd.
Columbus, OH 43227
ph: 614-577-0111
e-mail: tntgame@netwalk.com
web: http://www.tntgame.com
Specializes in buying, selling, restoring quality arcade video games, pinball machines, jukeboxes.

Chance Tess
Pinball Wizard Sales & Service
39425 Atkinson Dr.
Sterling Heights, MI 48313-5018
ph: 810-978-0393
fax: 313-369-6377
Pinball machine expert; buys, sells, trades and restores all makes and models of pinball machines; also repairs '50s and '60s Seeburg & Wurlitzer juke boxes.

Kent Tieche
Game Doc, The
8000 Wheatland Ave. #B
Sun Valley, CA 91352
ph: 800-766-3166 or 818-504-0440
fax: 818-504-1153
e-mail: KTieche@gamedoc.com
web: http://www.gamedoc.com
Sales, service and rentals of classic to new video games and pinball machines.

Herb Silvers
Fabulous Fantasies
12602 Ventura Blvd.
Studio City, CA 91604
ph: 818-761-2255
fax: 818-752-4372
e-mail: pinball@fabfan.com
web: http://www.fabfan.com
Sells and restores vintage pinball and arcade games and all Gameroom furnishings; also reproduces many pinball machine backglass art and video game overlays; can also create custom upholstered pieces; offers gameroom design assistance.

Harold Balde
Fungus Amungus
21 Wellington St.
Orangeville, Ontario L9W 2L2
Canada
ph: 519-942-3984
e-mail: kingpin@total.net
web: http://tilt.largo.fl.us/hbalde/
Collector and dealer of coin-operated machines, mostly pinballs but can also help with other coin-ops; will help new collectors with pricing and general info.

Experts

Gordon A. Hasse, Jr.
Silverball Amusements
140 East 95th St., 6-D
New York, NY 10128-1722
ph: 212-885-3619
Expert & collector of pinball machines with access to most of the country's collectors; fair value for properly graded Gottlieb & Williams wood-rail pinball machines 1948-1958; seeks quantity purchases but will buy one.

Marc Mandeltort
Macro Specialties, Inc.
5290 Platt Springs Rd.
Lexington, SC 29073-9252
ph: 803-957-5500
fax: 803-957-6974
e-mail: tilt@ix.netcom.com
web: http://pinballmachine.com
Provides books, parts, supplies, manuals, schematics, etc. for pinball machine owners.

Internet Resources

Daina Pettit
Mr. Pinball
4805 Marabow Circle
Salt Lake City, UT 84117-5419
ph: 801-277-6296 or 801-277-0888
fax: 801-277-0888
e-mail: daina@mrpinball.com
web: http://www.xmission.com/~daina/pinball.html
Web site contains large pinball-related classifieds as well as hundreds of repair tips; also "The Pinball Collector Register" - over 1,500 pinball collectors around the world that help, buy, sell, trade, repair.

Periodicals

Jim Schelberg, Ed.
Journal: pinGame journal
31937 Olde Franklin Dr.
Farmington, MI 48334-1731
ph: 248-626-5203
fax: 248-626-5203
e-mail: jim@pingamejournal.com
web: http://www.pingamejournal.com
Focuses on old as well as new pinball machines; articles on game development, repair and play; lots of buy and sell ads.

Repair Services

Steve Engel
Mayfair Amusement Company
60-41 Woodbine St.
Flushing, NY 11385-3234
ph: 718-417-5050
fax: 718-386-9049
e-mail: info@mayfairamusement.com
web: http://www.mayfairamusement.com/
Repair or replace most Bally and Williams circuit boards.

Bob Thurman
Bob's Servicing
154 Spindle Road
Hicksville, NY 11801
ph: 516-579-4746
e-mail: PFS7PINWIZ@aol.com
Repair of coin-operated, flipper pinball machines; over 25 years experience; electro-mechanical pinball machines a specialty; rates determined by travel from the New York City/Long Island, NY area.

Don Bryant
Bryant Antique Players
4819 Stallcup
Mesquite, TX 75150-1143
ph: 972-270-0135
fax: 972-613-1627
e-mail: aplayr@airmail.net
Sales, service and rebuilding of player pianos, pump organs, reproducing & coin-operated instruments, pin balls, & game room equipment; since 1975.

Bill Cowles
Vintage Pinballs
4255 Green Ave.
Los Alamitos, CA 90706
ph: 562-594-6489
Restores the old-style vintage pinball machines.

Kent Tieche
Game Doc, The
8000 Wheatland Ave. #B
Sun Valley, CA 91352
ph: 800-766-3166 or 818-504-0440
fax: 818-504-1153
e-mail: KTieche@gamedoc.com
web: http://www.gamedoc.com
Sales, service and rentals of classic to

new video games and pinball machines.

Suppliers

Steve Engel
Mayfair Amusement Company
60-41 Woodbine St.
Flushing, NY 11385-3234
ph: 718-417-5050
fax: 718-386-9049
e-mail: info@mayfairamusement.com
web: http://www.mayfairamusement.com/
Source for over 6,000 backglasses in stock.

Marc Mandeltort
Macro Specialties, Inc.
5290 Platt Springs Rd.
Lexington, SC 29073-9252
ph: 803-957-5500
fax: 803-957-6974
e-mail: tilt@ix.netcom.com
web: http://pinballmachine.com
Provides books, parts, supplies, manuals, schematics, etc. for pinball machine owners.

Tim Nabours
Nabours Novelty Inc.
320 Hwy. 55 West
P.O. Box 204
Maple Lake, MN 55358-0204
ph: 800-657-4657 or 320-963-5953
fax: 320-963-5953
Parts for Foosball and Pinball machines: rubber rings, coils, flipper rings, rebound rubbers, plastic pins, etc.; for Atari, Bally, Chicago Coin, Gottlieb, Game Plan, Williams, Stern, etc.; also carries complete pinballs and jukeboxes.

Scales

Dealers

Bill & Jan Berning
135 W. Main St.
Genoa, IL 60135-1101
ph: 815-784-3134
fax: 815-895-6328
e-mail: iweighu@yahoo.com
Buys, sell, repair, restore, collect, trade and operate coin-operated scales and most other scales; also sells original and reproduction parts; free parts catalog and adjustment information.

Repair Services

Bill & Jan Berning
135 W. Main St.
Genoa, IL 60135-1101
ph: 815-784-3134
fax: 815-895-6328
e-mail: iweighu@yahoo.com
Buys, sell, repair, restore, collect, trade and operate coin-operated scales and most other scales; also sells original and reproduction parts; free parts catalog and adjustment information.

Slot Machines

Collectors

Mike Gorski
1770 Dover Rd.
Westlake, OH 44145
ph: 440-871-6071
Slot machines, old penny arcade machines; Wurlitzer 78 RPM jukeboxes, odd vending machines;Regina musical boxes, old coin-operated machines.

Scott Fawcett
3835 Birch St.
Newport Beach, CA 92660-2616
ph: 949-756-8677 or 949-968-5000
Collector wants to buy unusual slot machines including Watling Rol-A-Top and other slot machines in tall floor model console stands; also wants Silver Dollar slot machines including Fey.

Fred & Marjie Ryan
Slot Closet
P.O. Box 83135
Portland, OR 97283-0135
ph: 503-286-3597 or 503-235-9559
Wants slot machines and related literature and advertisements.

Dealers

John T. Johnston
6742 Fifth Ave.
Brooklyn, NY 11220-5418
ph: 718-833-8455
fax: 718-833-0560
Buys, sells, rents, trades and repairs slot and jukeboxes; wants to buy old jukeboxes, slot machines, vending, arcade, old gambling items, neons, cash registers, music boxes, phonographs, syrup dispensers.

Slot Shop, The
P.O. Box 496
Simpsonville, KY 40067
ph: 800-228-SLOT or 502-722-0095
Buys, sells and trades antique slot machines.

Alan D. Sax
Nationwide Amusement/Slot Machine Brokers, Inc.
3239 R.F.D.
Long Grove, IL 60047
ph: 847-438-5900
e-mail: slots4you@aol.com

Hans Havlicek
Jennings Junction
4418 N. Elston
Chicago, IL 60630
ph: 773-736-6624
fax: 773-736-4390
Specializes in rebuilt and restored Jennings slot machines; replacement plastic for Sun Chiefs, console cabinets available, repro payout cards available separately, most all machines and parts; Jennings parts catalog available.

Tom Kolbrener
St. Louis Slot Machine Company
9400 Manchester Rd.
Saint Louis, MO 63119-1428
ph: 314-961-4612
e-mail: stlslot@aol.com
$3 for 32 page color catalog of fully-restored antique slot machines for sale.

Martin Roenigk
Mechantiques
The Crescent Hotel
75 Prospect St.
Eureka Springs, AR 72632
ph: 800-671-6333 or 501-253-9766
e-mail: mroenigk@aol.com
web: http://www.mechantiques.com
Slot machines and other coin-operated machines; also Wurlitzer 78 rpm jukeboxes.

Paul Z. Siegel
Royal Bell, Ltd.
5815 W. 52nd Ave.
Denver, CO 80212
ph: 303-431-9266
fax: 303-431-6978
Specializes in vintage, remanufactured and new slot machines.

Randy Hilberg
Collector's Nectar
Box 431
Morro Bay, CA 93443
ph: 805-772-2968
fax: 805-772-2968
e-mail: nectar@thegrid.net
Always buying slot machines; offers complete restoration services; appraisals; no collection too big or too small to purchase or restore; the only lifetime guarantee in the business.

Experts

Bob Levy
Unique One, The
2802 Centre St.
Pennsauken, NJ 08109-5304
ph: 609-663-2554
e-mail: theuniqueone@att.net
Buys and sells coin-operated machines including slot machines and arcade games; advisor to "Warman's Antiques & Collectibles Price Guide."

Richard Reddock
914 Isle Ct.
Bellmore, NY 11710-1545
ph: 516-826-2032 or 800-223-PNUT
e-mail: pnutfanclb@aol.com
Buys, sells, restores slot machines; author of "Price Guide to Antique Slot Machines."

Frank Zygmunt
Zygmunt & Associates
P.O. Box 542
Westmont, IL 60559-0542
ph: 630-985-2742 or 630-971-1015
fax: 630-985-5151
e-mail: zygm1015@aol.com
Buys and sells slot machines and jukeboxes; 150-200 slot machines & Wurlitzer jukeboxes in stock; also Wurlitzer One More Time distributor; also interested in music boxes, nickelodeons, and Coke machines.

Clark Phelps
Amusement Sales Co.
7610 South Main St.
Midvale, UT 84047
ph: 801-255-4731

Marshall Fey
Liberty Belle Saloon Saloon & Restaurant
4250 South Virginia St.
Reno, NV 89502-6011
ph: 775-825-1776
Collector of antique slot machines for 38 years; author of "Slot Machines - A Pictorial History of the First 100 Years," $29.95 ppd.

Bill Whelan
Slot Dynasty Restorations
P.O. Box 617
Daly City, CA 94017-2332
ph: 650-756-1189
Expert in slot machines and trade stimulators; has studied the history for over 30 years and has written many articles on the subject for trade magazines; has also helped other authors by supplying information and photos for their books.

Museums/Libraries

Marshall Fey
Liberty Belle Saloon & Slot Machine Collection
4250 South Virginia St.
Reno, NV 89502-6011
ph: 775-825-1776
Nations largest display of antique slot machines; also other antiques; free admission.

Periodicals

Ken Durham
Newspaper: Antique Amusements, Slot Machine & Jukebox Gazette
909 26th St. NW
Washington, DC 20037-2029
e-mail: durham@gameroomantiques.com
web: http://www.GameRoomAntiques.com
Semi-annual newspaper focusing on slot machines and jukeboxes; lots of ads, articles, shows, auctions; send SASE for info.

Repair Services

David Claxton
2952 Lynn Ave.
Billings, MT 59102-6640
ph: 406-656-0949
Buys, sells and trades slot machines; specializes in the repair of Mills, Jennings, and Pace slot machines.

Bill Whelan
Slot Dynasty Restorations
P.O. Box 617
Daly City, CA 94017-2332
ph: 650-756-1189
Specializes in the repair & restoration of antique slot machines as well as all other types of coin-operated gaming machines such as trade stimulators, arcade games & vending machines; also buys/sells/trades coin-operated gaming machines.

Suppliers

Tom Krahl
Antique Slot Machine Part Co.
140 N. Western Ave.
Carpentersville, IL 60110
ph: 847-428-8476
fax: 847-428-4471
Publishes a catalog of reproduction slot machine parts; also repairs.

Bernie Berten
9420 S. Trumbull Ave.
Evergreen Park, IL 60642-2224
ph: 708-499-0688
fax: 708-499-5797
Carries just about every spring needed by coin machines; also castings for antique slot machines.

Bill Whelan
Slot Dynasty Restorations
P.O. Box 617
Daly City, CA 94017-2332
ph: 650-756-1189
Sells reel strips and award & instruction cards for trade stimulators (counter model gambling machines); send LSASE w/99 cents postage for catalog.

Trade Stimulators

Experts

Bill Whelan
Slot Dynasty Restorations
P.O. Box 617
Daly City, CA 94017-2332
ph: 650-756-1189
Expert in slot machines and trade stimulators; has studied the history for over 30 years and has written many articles on the subject for trade magazines; has also helped other authors by supplying information and photos for their books.

Vending Machines

(see also SOFT DRINK COLLECTIBLES, Soda Machines)

Collectors

Don L. Reedy
13 South Carroll St.
Frederick, MD 21701-5606
ph: 301-663-4240 or 301-662-5503
fax: 301-694-9190
e-mail: shineit4u@aol.com
Buy, sell, trade gumball and peanut machines; also Coca-Cola advertising.

Mike Gorski
1770 Dover Rd.
Westlake, OH 44145
ph: 440-871-6071
Slot machines, old penny arcade machines; Wurlitzer 78 RPM jukeboxes, odd vending machines; Regina musical boxes, coin-operated machines.

Steve Perry
593 Lavina
Hemet, CA 92544
ph: 909-658-4620
Wants to buy old gum, peanut, and candy machines; even if incomplete or not working.

Dealers

Vintage Vending, Inc.
68 Stiles Road, Unit C
Salem, NH 03079
ph: 603-898-7676 or 888-242-6633
fax: 603-898-2080
e-mail: memories@vintagevending.com
web: http://www.vintagevending.com
Specializes in the sale of restored 1950s vending machines: soda, candy, Coke; also neon clocks and signs, soda bars, fountain dispensers, picnic coolers, gas pumps, pedal cars, juke boxes, bar stools, and other game room items.

Rich Brinkos
Antique Gumball Machines
948 Clyde Lane
Philadelphia, PA 19128-1136
ph: 215-482-1429 or 215-482-9099
Sells, restores, repairs and services gumball and peanut machines; globes, parts, vending products, stands; anything required to make a fully authentic period vending machine.

Craig Willardson
P.O. Box 8296
Spokane, WA 99203-0296
ph: 509-624-0772
e-mail: cwillardsn@aol.com
Collector, dealer and expert in early gum and peanut vending machines; will buy one machine of an entire collection; also interested in parts, broken and incomplete machines, and related literature.

Experts

Bill Enes
8520 Lewis Dr.
Shawnee Mission, KS 66227-3277
ph: 913-441-1492 or 913-441-1502
fax: 913-441-1502
e-mail: bille@unicom.net
Author of "Silent Salesmen - Encyclopedia of Collectible Gum, Candy, and Nut Machines"; buys and sells.

Repair Services

Rich Brinkos
Antique Gumball Machines
948 Clyde Lane
Philadelphia, PA 19128-1136
ph: 215-482-1429 or 215-482-9099
Sells, restores, repairs and services gumball and peanut machines; globes, parts, vending products, stands; anything required to make a fully authentic period vending machine.

COINS & CURRENCY

(see also ANTIQUITIES; BANKING, Bank Checks; BOOKS, Reference [Coins]; CIVIL WAR ARTIFACTS, Currency; CREDIT CARDS & CHARGE ITEMS; ELONGATED COINS; GOLD; MACERATED CURRENCY ITEMS; SILVER; STOCKS & BONDS; TOKENS; WOODEN MONEY)

Appraisers

Dr. Spencer Peck
P.O. Box 526
Oldwick, NJ 08858-0526
ph: 908-236-2880
One of only nine ASA accredited appraisers of rare coins, currency, tokens and medals for IRS, estate, insurance, trust, liquidation and equitable distribution purposes in the U.S.

Charles R. Hoskins
International Numismatic Society
P.O. Box 2091
Aston, PA 19014
ph: 610-494-2880
fax: 610-494-2270
Specializes in and appraises rare coins and currency.

Thomas J. Terpilak, GG, ASA, AAA
Metro Gem Consultants
7315 Wisconsin Ave.
Bethesda, MD 20814-3202
ph: 301-654-0838 or 301-654-8678
Professional numismatist and numismatic appraiser.

John L. Frank
John Frank Rare Coins
725 South Adams, Ste. 21
Birmingham, MI 48009-6916
ph: 248-644-8818
fax: 248-258-5058
Buys, sells, appraises rare coin & currency collections; liquidates for maximum value; certified in rare coin grading by Adelphi University Institute of Numismatics & Philatelic Studies; constructs rare coin portfolios; guest speaker.

Auction Services

Q. David Bowers
Bowers & Merena, Inc.
P.O. Box 1224
Wolfeboro, NH 03894-1224
ph: 800-458-4646 or 603-569-5095
fax: 603-569-5319
e-mail: bowersmerena@conknet.com
web: http://web.coin-universe.com/bowers/index.html
Specializes in coin auctions; member International Association of Professional Numismatists.

Lawrence Stack
Stack's Coin Galleries
123 West 57th St.
New York, NY 10019-2280
ph: 212-582-2580
fax: 212-245-5018
e-mail: info@stacks.com
web: http://www.stacks.com
Specializes in coin auctions.

Christie's
502 Park Ave.
New York, NY 10022
ph: 212-546-1000
fax: 212-980-8163
web: http://www.christies.com

John D. Compton
J.D. Compton Auctioneering
13833 Rockdale Rd.
Clear Spring, MD 21722
ph: 301-582-0727
fax: 301-582-6114
e-mail: COMPTONAUC@aol.com
Specializes in the auction sale of U.S. coins and currency; call toll-free in the U.S. 1-800-66-AUCTION.

Ron Playle
Playle's Online Auctions
P.O. Box 65918
West Des Moines, IA 50265
ph: 515-267-0213
fax: 515-267-0213
e-mail: ron@playle.com
web: http://www.playle.com/main.html
Buy and sell postcards, stamps, coins, antiques, collectibles online.

Kurt R. Krueger
Krueger Auctions
P.O. Box 275
Iola, WI 54945-0275
ph: 715-445-3845
fax: 715-445-4100
Specializing in the mail-bid auction of tokens, advertising, brewery items, Western Americana, postcards, World's Fair & Expo., autographs, sports, coins & currency, pinbacks,

military memorabilia, automotive, Disneyana, etc.

Joe Stephens
CCE-Auction
10681 Haddington #100
Houston, TX 77279
ph: 713-973-1616
e-mail: joe@atchou.com
web: http://www.cce-auction.com/
U.S. rare coin auction service via the Internet.

Hobby Markets Online, Inc.
375 Alabama Street, Ste. 410
San Francisco, CA 94110
ph: 415-252-6040 or 415-252-6040
fax: 415-252-6044
e-mail: hobbyinfo@hobbymarkets.com
web: http://www.Numismatists.com/
Online auction service for coin and currency collectors; participate in auctions from leading numismatic dealers and auction houses whose items range from beginner coins for the new collector to elite coins for the investor.

Spink & Son, Ltd.
5-7 King St.
St. James's, London SW1Y 6QS
U.K.
ph: 0171 930 7888
fax: 0171 839 4853
web: http://www.auctions.co.uk/antique/spink.htm
Auctioneers and dealers of coins (ancient to present), medals, orders, tokens, decorations and other numismatic items.

Clubs/Associations

George Van Trump, Jr.
Jefferson County Coin Club
Newsletter: JCCC Newsletter
6837 Murray Lane
Annandale, VA 22003

Young Numismatists of America
Newsletter: Young Numismatists Digest
2315 Poplar Lane
Anderson, SC 29621-3247
ph: 864-224-2084
e-mail: John536693@aol.com
web: http://membrs.aol.com/TheYNA/
Only nationwide club dedicated specifically to young numismatists.

Bradley S. Karoleff, Co.-Ed.
John Reich Collectors Society
Journal: John Reich Journal
P.O. Box 135
Harrison, OH 45030-0135
e-mail: Karoleffs4@aol.com
web: http://www.logan.com/jrcs/
The purpose of the JRCS is to encourage the study of numismatics, particularly US gold and silver coins minted before 1838.

Boyd Mattox
Fremont Coin Club, Inc.
231 Lincoln St.
Tecumseh, NE 68450-2116

Edward C. Rochette, ExDir
American Numismatic Association
Magazine: Numismatist, The
818 N. Cascade Ave.
Colorado Springs, CO 80903-3279
ph: 719-632-2646 or 800-367-9723
fax: 719-634-4085
e-mail: nulty@money.org
web: http://www.money.org
Worldwide assoc. of collectors of coins, paper money, medals, tokens; over 30,000 members; offers collector services/benefits; web site lists hundreds of coin and related clubs worldwide arranged by specialty or by state and country.

Robert Brueggeman, Ex. Dir.
Professional Numismatists Guild
3950 Concordia Lane
Fallbrook, CA 92028
ph: 760-728-1300
fax: 760-728-8507
e-mail: info@pngdealers.com
web: http://www.pngdealers.com
Send for free copy of "The Pleasure of Coin Collecting." Founded in 1955, the P.N.G. has more than 300 members in 35 states. Directory lists professional member numismatists who possess knowledge, responsibility, and integrity.

Bill Grant
San Bernardino County Coin Club
Newsletter: SBCCC Newsletter
P.O. Box 295
Patton, CA 92369-0295
ph: 909-864-7617
e-mail: mesared@aol.com
Program speakers, auctions, short general meeting; meets monthly at the San Bernadino County Museum in Redlands, CA; annual coin show.

Gordon Donnell
Pacific Coast Numismatic Society
1960 San Antonio
Berkeley, CA 94707-1620

International Association of Professional Numismatists
14, Rue de la Bourse
Brussels, B-1000
Belgium
ph: +32-2-513-3400
fax: +32-2-512-2528
e-mail: iapnsecret@compuserve.com
web: http://www.iapn.ch/
Object is to develop a healthy and prosperous numismatic trade conducted according to the highest ethical standards; membership limited to firms or departments of commercial institutions; all sales by members are fully guaranteed.

Canadian Numismatic Association
P.O. Box 226
Barrie, Ontario L4M 4T2
Canada
ph: 705-737-0845
fax: 705-737-0293
e-mail: cna@barint.on.ca
The national numismatic organization of Canada.

Collectors

Frederick Lingenfelser
814 Byram St.
Reading, PA 19606-1446
Wants pre-1950 coin auction catalogs, books, price lists, photographic plates of coins, and signed letters from coin dealers of yesteryear; also wants to buy any undamaged U.S. coins dated before 1816.

Byron Alan Johnson
Coin Library, The
619-B State Highway 32 East
Leesburg, GA 31763
ph: 912-759-6268
e-mail: Muckalee.Slope@juno.com
web: http://www.geocities.com/WallStreet/6671/
Visit "The Coin Library" for a great lesson in the history of American coinage.

John & Nancy Wilson
Wilson's Syngraphics
9353 SW 92nd Place Rd.
Ocala, FL 34481-6502
ph: 414-545-8636
e-mail: johnancy@aol.com
Wants any pre-1934 paper money issued in the U.S.; also wants any pre-1930 postcards depicting banks.

Dealers

Michael Sachar
B & M Coin Company
P.O. Box 4007
Peabody, MA 01961-4007
ph: 978-538-3183
e-mail: saetch@aol.com
web: http://www.csmonline.com/BandM/
Collector, dealer, appraiser; buys and sells RARE coins only.

Q. David Bowers
Bowers & Merena, Inc.
Magazine: Rare Coin Review
P.O. Box 1224
Wolfeboro, NH 03894-1224
ph: 800-458-4646 or 603-569-5095
fax: 603-569-5319
e-mail: bowersmerena@conknet.com
web: http://web.coin-universe.com/bowers/index.html
Buys and sells U.S. coins and currency; publishes Rare Coin Review bi-monthly, includes articles, price lists, coins for sale; member International Association of Professional Numismatists.

Allen G. Berman
Allen G. Berman Professional Numismatist
P.O. Box 605
Fairfield, CT 06430-0605
ph: 914-434-6090 or 914-434-6079
fax: 914-434-6079
e-mail: agberman@aol.com
Buying, selling and appraising foreign, ancient, medieval and rare U.S. coins since 1973; extensively published; consultant to auction houses; will consider purchase of items too early of esoteric for smaller "main line" dealers.

Jim Fehr
Ellesmere Numismatics
Newsletter: Winning Edge, The
P.O. Box 402
Brookfield, CT 06804-0402
ph: 203-794-1232 or 800-426-3343
Buys and sells PCGS and NGC certified U.S. coins; also publishes "The Winning Edge" every three weeks (call for free copy) which contains current market information as well as a listing of certified coins for sale.

Arthur & Ira Friedberg
Coin & Currency Institute, Inc.
P.O. Box 1057
Clifton, NJ 07014
ph: 9731-471-1441
fax: 973-471-1062
e-mail: coincurin@aol.com
Member International Association of Professional Numismatists.

Gene Yotka
H.F.Y. Rare Coin
2100 Hwy. 35
Sea Girt, NJ 08750
ph: 732-974-8855

Harvey Stack
Stack's Coin Galleries
123 West 57th St.
New York, NY 10019-2280
ph: 212-582-2580
fax: 212-245-5018
e-mail: info@stacks.com
web: http://www.stacks.com
United States, European, ancient, medieval coins; member International Association of Professional Numismatists.

Wade Hinderling
P.O. Box 606
Manhasset, NY 11030
ph: 516-365-3729
Buys and sells coins of the US and France; member International Association of Professional Numismatists.

William S. Panitch
William S. Panitch, Inc.
P.o. Box 3712
Albany, NY 12203-0712
ph: 518-489-4400
fax: 518-489-2776
e-mail: wpanitch@aol.com
Buys and sells U.S. and foreign coins, commemorative and award medals, paper money, etc.; also lectures and appraises.

Brad Shiff
Cybercoins
2930 W. Liberty Ave.
Pittsburgh, PA 15216
ph: 724-276-6782 or 412-531-3100
e-mail: coins@nauticom.net
web: http://www.nauticom.net/www/coins/
Shows you exactly what you are purchasing; carries coins (B.C. to modern US and World), stamps (US and World, currency (US and World), medals, tokens, newspapers from the 1700s.

James J. Reeves, Inc.
P.O. Box 219
Huntingdon, PA 16652
ph: 800-364-2948
fax: 814-641-2600
e-mail: Reeves5@vicon.net
web: http://www.JamesJReeves.com

C.E. Bullowa
Coinhunter
1616 Walnut St., Ste. 2112
Philadelphia, PA 19103-5364
ph: 215-735-5517
fax: 215-735-5517
Buys and sells U.S., ancient and foreign coins and books; appraisals; member International Association of Professional Numismatists.

Milton O. Lynn
Harford Coin Co.
2160 E. Joppa Rd., Ste. 101
Baltimore, MD 21234
ph: 410-665-1814 or 410-665-1815
fax: 410-665-1815
e-mail: oldtenor@erols.com
web: http://www.dmatech.com/harfordcoins/
Dealer, appraiser, expert in rare coins, currency, tokens and medals through 20th century.

Burton's Coins & Cards
5831 Buckeystown Pike
Frederick, MD 21701
ph: 301-663-3223

Mark E. Mitchell
3002 Winter Pine Ct.
Fairfax, VA 22031-1125
ph: 703-591-3150
fax: 703-385-3152
e-mail: info@mitchellarchives.com
web: http://www.mitchellarchives.com/
Buying and selling coin collections and accumulations.

Ron Gordon
San Juan Precious Metals Corp.
4818 San Juan Ave.
Jacksonville, FL 32210-3232
ph: 904-387-3466
fax: 904-387-5166
e-mail: support@ejewelry.com
web: http://www.ejewelry.com/sjpm/
Buys and sells all US and foreign coins and currency.

Steven Schor
P.O. Box 5521
Lighthouse Point, FL 33074-5521
ph: 954-571-8510
e-mail: lhnumis@gate.net
Buy, sell, trade all coins, tokens, medals and currency; wants better numismatic items for inclusion in brochure.

Ed Kuszmar
Florida Currency & Coins
P.O. Box 4049
Boca Raton, FL 33429
ph: 561-995-7985
fax: 561-995-7983
e-mail: EdKuszmar@aol.com
Buys and sells coins, currency, paper Americana, ephemera, and 1893 Columbia Exposition items; specializes in Confederate and obsolete currency; large and small size nationals, Colonial, fractional, error notes, precious metals, etc.

Jeff Z. Means
Enterprise Coins
P.O. Box 2338
Lutz, FL 33549
ph: 813-948-2505
fax: 813-948-2305
e-mail: john@coach.net
web: http://www.coach.net/coins
Dealer, collector, appraiser; specializes in purchasing and selling foreign coins.

Carlos A. Amaro
COINS et cetera
P.O. Box 76232
Ocala, FL 34481
ph: 352-854-4513
e-mail: c.etc@atlantic.net
web: http://www.atlantic.net/~c.etc/
Buys and sells US coins (certified and raw), collectible newspapers and financial documents such as checks, bonds, and stock certificates.

William Skelton
Highland's Vault
P.O. Box 55448
Birmingham, AL 35255-5548
ph: 205-939-1178 or 205-939-3166
Wants all U.S. currency before 1929 and all Confederate States of America currency and coins; also CSA bonds.

Greg Brown
B Squared Coins
2545 Hilliard Rome Rd., Box #205
Hilliard, OH 43026
ph: 614-529-8218
fax: 614-529-2945
e-mail: bsquared@columbus.rr.com
web: http://www.stratamar.com/bsquared/
A family run, on-line coin store; deals mainly in American coins but also sells some ancient classical coins; website has an online catalog, monthly auctions, coin related software, books, and links.

Kent Froseth
K.M. Froseth, Inc.
P.O. Box 23116
Minneapolis, MN 55423-0116
ph: 612-831-9550 or 800-648-7662
fax: 612-835-3903
US, foreign gold and silver coins; member Professional Numismatists Guild, International Association Professional Numismatists; also life member of ANA and CNA.

Edward Milas
Rare Coin Company of America, Inc.
6262 South Rte. 83, Ste. 102
Willowbrook, IL 60514
ph: 630-654-2580 or 800-774-2580
fax: 630-654-3556
e-mail: wmilas@rarcoa.com
web: http://www.rarcoa.com/
U.S., foreign type coins and paper money; member International Association of Professional Numismatists.

Harlan Berk
Harlan J. Berk, Ltd.
31 North Clark St.
Chicago, IL 60602
ph: 312-609-0016
fax: 312-609-1309
e-mail: info@harlanjberk.com
web: http://www.harlanjberk.com/
Buys and sells all coins 700 BC to present; classical antiquities; member International Association of Professional Numismatists.

John G. Ross
John G. Ross, Inc.
55 West Monroe St., Ste. 1070
Chicago, IL 60603
ph: 312-236-4088
fax: 312-236-6839
U.S. coins, coins of the world; member International Association of Professional Numismatists.

Dr. R.A. Hiett
Maple City Coin
P.O. Drawer 47
Monmouth, IL 61462-0047
ph: 309-734-3212
fax: 309-734-8083
e-mail: hiett@misslink.net
Buys and sells all coins and numismatic items; also knives, Indian artifacts, fishing lures, old pens, and many other miscellaneous items.

Blanchard & Co.
P.O. Box 61740
New Orleans, LA 70161-1740
ph: 888-524-2646
fax: 504-837-4884
e-mail: info@blanchardonline.com
web: http://www.blanchardonline.com
Dealers in rare coins and precious metals.

Darwin S. Marshall
MHG Services
1520 Grand
Texarkana, AR 71854-4452
ph: 870-773-2128
fax: 870-772-3703
Buys, sells, collects, auctions, and specializes in US and foreign coins.

Tina Vogel
Tina Vogel Collectibles
527 A. West Wheatland Rd.
Duncanville, TX 75137
fax: 214-342-2373
e-mail: tina@jcvcoin.com
web: http://www.jcvcoin.com/index.htm

Paul Simonetti
Heritage Rare Coin Galleries
1— Highland Park Village
Dallas, TX 75205-2788
ph: 214-528-3500
fax: 214-443-8406
e-mail: pauls@heritagecoin.com
web: http://www.heritagecoin.com/
One of the world's largest numismatic firms; serving collectors and dealers worldwide for almost 30 years.

Joe Stephens
Archives Coins
P.O. Box 79682
Houston, TX 77279
ph: 281-216-0359
e-mail: joe@archbbs.com
web: http://www.archc.com/
Buys and sells quality rare U.S. coins.

Chuck D'Ambra
Chuck D'Ambra Coins
P.O. Box 746481
Arvada, CO 80006
ph: 303-431-9333
e-mail: chuckd@telesphere.com
web: http://www.telesphere.com/ts/coins/
Buys, collects, specializes in coins; has a favorite Internet resource for coin collectors since 1993; lots of hobby info, including extensive Coin

Collecting GAQ, and a large selection of quality U.S. coins for sale.

Klaus J. Degler
Rocky Mountain Coin Exchange, Inc.
538 S. Broadway
Denver, CO 80209-4002
ph: 800-781-4653 or 307-777-4653
fax: 303-733-4946
e-mail: rmcoin@aol.com
web: http://www.rmcoin.com/
Appraises, buys, sells, collects and specializes in coins and currency.

John J. Ford, Jr.
P.O. Box 10317
Phoenix, AZ 85064
ph: 602-957-6443
fax: 602-957-1861
Collects and deals; U.S. colonial coins, US silver, gold medals; member International Association of Professional Numismatists; also specializes in counterfeit coins scales and detectors.

Donald M. Hardisty
Don's Collectibles
3020 E. Majestic Ridge
Las Cruces, NM 88011
ph: 505-522-3721
fax: 505-522-7909
e-mail: donsbossons@zianet.com
web: http://www.zianet.com/donsbossons/
Internationally recognized expert, collector, supplier, appraiser, and restoration artist recommended by Bossons; also specializes in Hummels and rare coins; member Inter. Bossons Collectors Society, MI Hummel Club, Amer. Numismatic Assoc.

Superior Galleries
9478 West Olympic Blvd.
Beverly Hills, CA 90212-4246
ph: 310-203-9855 or 800-421-0754
fax: 310-203-0496
e-mail: superior@superiorsc.com
web: http://www.superiorsc.com/
Has been a retail and auction source for dealers and collectors for over 70 years; specializes in stamps, coins, sports memorabilia, Hollywood memorabilia, space memorabilia, historic manuscripts and autographs.

Cy Phillips, Jr.
S C Coin & Stamp Co. Inc.
P.O. Drawer 661180
Arcadia, CA 91066-1180
ph: 818-445-8277 or 800-367-0779
fax: 818-445-8278
Tokens, medals, coins, currency, badges, expo. and fair items, scrap gold and silver.

Teller Numismatic Enterprises
16027 Ventura Blvd., Suit 606
Encino, CA 91436
ph: 818-783-8545
fax: 818-783-9083
e-mail: awwwa@earthlink.net
web: http://www.tellercoins.com
Gold and silver coins of the World; specialist in Russia, China, 19th Century Oriental coins, and choice foreign paper money; member International Association of Professional Numismatists.

Neil Osina
Best Variety Sports Cards & Coins
358 W. Foothill Blvd.
Glendora, CA 91740-3327
ph: 626-914-2273
fax: 626-914-6624
Wants to buy coins from the period 1792 through 1885; Life Member of all major associations; over 34 years experience.

Karl Stephens
Karl Stephens, Inc.
P.O. Box 3038
Fallbrook, CA 92088
ph: 760-731-6138
fax: 760-731-9132
e-mail: upua68a@prodigy.com
Foreign coins, medals, tokens, eastern Europe, US type and copper coins; member International Association of Professional Numismatists.

Richard Ponterio
Ponterio & Associates, Inc.
1818 Robinson Ave.
San Diego, CA 92103
ph: 800-854-2888 or 619-299-0400
fax: 619-299-6952
Coins, medals and banknotes of Mexico and Latin America, World paper money, gold coins and crowns, Ancient coins; member International Association of Professional Numismatists.

Brent Gutekunst
Coin Universe
6440 Lusk Blvd., Ste. D209
San Diego, CA 92121
ph: 619-643-1900
fax: 619-643-1905
e-mail: brent@collectors.com
web: http://coin-universe.com
The starting point for coin collecting on the Internet; get up-to-date collecting information on coin prices, population, counterfeits, articles and other numismatic data at Coin Universe; on-line auctions, chat rooms, coin marketplaces.

Howard Markham
Howard Markham Professional Numismatist
5225 Canyon Crest Dr., Bldg 200, Ste. 254
Riverside, CA 92507-6301
ph: 909-686-2122 or 800-953-3027
Buys all U.S. coins, gold coins, collections and accumulations; nationally recognized numismatist; will pay top dollar for rare coins; will travel to buy larger collections.

Freeman Craig
P.O. Box 4176
San Rafael, CA 94913-4176
ph: 415-883-5336
fax: 415-382-1008
e-mail: raccoonnet@earthlink.net
Expert in Latin American coinage in gold, silver and minor metals from 1536-1950 including medals; member International Association of Professional Numismatists.

Kagins
98 Main Street, #201
Belvedere Tiburon, CA 94920
ph: 888-8KAGINS or 415-435-2601
e-mail: kagins@earthlink.net
web: http://www.csmonline.com/kagins/
Specializes in early and rare U.S. copper, gold and silver coins; U.S. Colonials, patterns, paper currency, California fractional coinage, pioneer gold and patterns.

James F. Elmen
World-Wide Coins of California
P.O. Box 3684
Santa Rosa, CA 95402
ph: 707-527-1007
fax: 707-527-1204
e-mail: elmen@sonic.net
Specializes in world coins and medals from 1500 to present.

Alex Pancheco
Tipsico Coin LLC
P.O. Box 1128
North Bend, OR 97459-0306
ph: 541-756-7111
e-mail: tipsico@gte.net
Appraises, sells and buys all U.S. and world coins via a 44 page catalog; coin albums and supplies, plus gold and silver bullion are also offered; specialties include Morgan and Peace dollars, Lincoln and Indian cents.

Collectors Exchange Network
P.O. Box 305
Beecroft, NSW 2119
Australia
ph: 61 +2-9869 3550
e-mail: cen@collect.com.au
web: http://www.collect.com.au
Wants to buy rare coins, banknotes, artifacts and rare flutes; see the rare tortoise shell flute (the only one found so far!) and the world record (1994) banknote worth over $250,000.

Experts

Allen G. Berman
Allen G. Berman Professional Numismatist
P.O. Box 605
Fairfield, CT 06430-0605
ph: 914-434-6090 or 914-434-6079
fax: 914-434-6079
e-mail: agberman@aol.com
Co-author of "Warman's Coins & Currency"; author/editor of numerous books & articles on early coinage; leading authority on coins of Middle Ages and Papacy; recognized authority by periodicals & auction houses; ANA instructor.

Scott A. Travers
Scott Travers Rare Coin Galleries, Inc.
P.O. Box 171
F.D.R. Station
New York, NY 10150-1711
ph: 212-535-9135
e-mail: travers@inch.com
web: http://www.inch.com/~travers/travers3.htm
Author of "How to Make Money in Coins Right Now."

W. Crutchfield Williams, II
Crutchfield's Currency
P.O. Box 521
Kemah, TX 77565
ph: 281-334-3297
e-mail: CrutchfieldWilliams-CSA@worldnet.att.net
web: http://www.CrutchWilliams.com/
Buys, sells, appraises Confederate States of America and Southern state currency, broken bank notes, Republic of Texas collectibles (TEXANA), U.S. Federal issues, coins, tokens, and other related material; life member ANA, SPMC, IBNS.

Klaus J. Degler
Rocky Mountain Coin Exchange, Inc.
538 S. Broadway
Denver, CO 80209-4002
ph: 800-781-4653 or 307-777-4653
fax: 303-733-4946
e-mail: rmcoin@aol.com
web: http://www.rmcoin.com/
Professional Numismatist Guild #463, American Numismatic Assoc. Life-Member, Industry Council for Tangible Assets, consultant to the American Numismatic Assoc., Colorado Professional Numismatic Assoc. Pres.; expert witness experience.

Internet Resources

Numismatists Online
e-mail: coininfo@numismatists.com
web: http://www.numismatists.com

Numismatica
e-mail: Lloyd_Lim@limunltd.com
web: http://www.limunltd.com/numismatica/
A site dedicated to providing information about numismatics - the

study and collecting of coins, paper money, tokens, medals, and other similar objects: FAQ's, glossaries, biographies, news, articles, stories, reviews, trivia, etc.

Coin Collecting Home Page, The
e-mail: mikec@iquest.net
web: http://emporium.turnpike.net/M/mikec/

Bob Bakondi
Penny Lane
e-mail: rbakondi@olg.com
web: http://www.geocities.com/RodeoDrive/4044/
Lots of links to coin websites and resources worldwide.

Roxanne Goldberg
CoinMasters
P.O. Box 0166
Wyncote, PA 19095-0116
e-mail: president@coinmasters.org
web: http://www.coinmasters.org
An internet club built by coin collectors for coin collectors; CM is a world-wide online interactive clubhouse which focuses on ALL aspects of coin collecting; website is a huge source of numismatic information contributed by members.

U.S. Mint
Customer Care Center
Lanham, MD 20706-4331
ph: 202-283-2646
web: http://www.usmint.gov/
How coins are made, fun facts, history of the Mint, paper money, tour information,

Byron Alan Johnson
Coin Library, The
619-B State Highway 32 East
Leesburg, GA 31763
ph: 912-759-6268
e-mail: Muckalee.Slope@juno.com
web: http://www.geocities.com/WallStreet/6671/
Visit "The Coin Library" for a great lesson in the history of American coinage.

Stan Klein
Roko Design Group, Inc.
1712 SE 13th Street
Fort Lauderdale, FL 33316
ph: 954-954-0770
e-mail: rokogrp@aol.com
web: http://www.coinsite.com
A most informative website for coins and paper money: images, The Coin Doctor, articles about coins, list coins to buy/sell/trade in The Trading Room. links to research sites, coin dealers, etc.

Robert Johnson
GOLDSHEET Numismatic Directory
5560 Shasta Lane, Ste. 3
La Mesa, CA 91942-402
ph: 619-697-8541
e-mail: rjohnson@prodigy.net
web: http://goldsheet.simplenet.com/coins.htm
Comprehensive directory of Internet numismatic resources, bullion spot prices, coin supplies.

Brent Gutekunst
Coin Universe
6440 Lusk Blvd., Ste. D209
San Diego, CA 92121
ph: 619-643-1900
fax: 619-643-1905
e-mail: brent@collectors.com
web: http://coin-universe.com
The starting point for coin collecting on the Internet; get up-to-date collecting information on coin prices, population, counterfeits, articles and other numismatic data at Coin Universe; on-line auctions, chat rooms, coin marketplaces.

Brian R. Smith
Canadian Coin Reference Site, The
110 The Esplanade, Ste. 521
Toronto, Ontario M5E 1X9
Canada
e-mail: webmaster@torex.net
web: http://www.torex.net/
Website created primarily for the novice and intermediate coin enthusiast; website includes important numismatic reference material.

Man./Prod./Dist.

Kennedy Mint, Inc., The
12102 Pearl Rd.
Strongsville, OH 44136-3398
ph: 800-442-6468
fax: 440-572-3692
e-mail: comments@kennedymint.com
web: http://www.kennedymint.com/
Sells individual and proof sets of early and new commemorative U.S. coins; write for catalog - in addition to coins and coin sets for sale, it contains tools and storage devices for coin collectors.

Misc. Services

Numismatic Guaranty Corporation of America (NGC)
P.O. Box 1776
Parsippany, NJ 07054
ph: 973-984-6222
web: http://www.ngccoin.com/home.cfm
Grades coins and issues a guarantee of authenticity.

Charles R. Hoskins
International Numismatic Society
Newsletter: Numorum
P.O. Box 2091
Aston, PA 19014
ph: 610-494-2880
fax: 610-494-2270
The INS offers authentication and grading of rare coins and paper money to the public for a nominal fee.

ANACS
P.O. Box 182141
Columbus, OH 43218-2141
ph: 800-888-1861
fax: 614-791-9103
web: http://coincity.com/ANACS/default.htm
Grades coins and issues a guarantee of authenticity.

Professional Coin Grading Service (PCGS)
P.O. Box 9458
Newport Beach, CA 92658-9458
ph: 800-447-8848
web: http://pcgs.com/
Grades coins and issues a guarantee of authenticity.

Museums/Libraries

Newark Museum, The
49 Washington St.
P.O. Box 540
Newark, NJ 07101-0540
ph: 973-596-6550 or 800-7-MUSEUM
fax: 973-642-0459
Numismatics is a specialty area.

Mr. Leslie A. Elam, Dir.
American Numismatic Society, The
Newsletter: American Numismatic Society Newsletter, The
Broadway at 155th St.
New York, NY 10003
ph: 212-234-3130
e-mail: info@amnumsoc.org
web: http://www.amnumsoc2.org/index.htm
Has a major collection of American coins in addition to major and important collections of ancient, Latin American, Islamic, European, and other material; also publishes "American Journal of Numismatics" and "Numismatic Literature."

National Museum of American History, National Numismatic Collection
14th & Constitution Ave. NW
Washington, DC 20560
ph: 202-357-2700
e-mail: webmaster@si.edu
web: http://www.si.edu/organiza/museums/nmah/nmah.htm
The Hall of Monetary History and Medallic Art exhibits an amazing number of U.S. and foreign coins, tokens, medals, and paper money from earliest times to the present; the finest coin collection in the world.

Money Museum, Federal Reserve Bank of Richmond
701 East Byrd St.
Richmond, VA 23219
ph: 804-697-8108
fax: 804-697-8123
e-mail: fedbalt@rich.frb.org
web: http://www.rich.frb.org/generalinfo/tourinfo.html
Primitive monies, ancient coins, Colonial money, U.S. coins and paper money, Confederate currency, and U.S. commemorative coins are on display.

Edward C. Rochette, ExDir
Museum of the American Numismatic Association
818 N. Cascade Ave.
Colorado Springs, CO 80903-3279
ph: 719-632-2646 or 800-367-9723
fax: 719-634-4085
e-mail: nulty@money.org
web: http://www.money.org
A museum collection 400,000 items including American, ancient, Latin American, Islamic, European, and other coins; largest numismatic circulating library with books and A/V material free to members.

Old U.S. Mint Museum
5th & Mission Sts.
San Francisco, CA 94103-2906
ph: 415-744-6830
Collection of coins, numismatic items, and mining equipment and related items.

Bank of Canada Currency Museum
245 Sparks St.
Ottawa, Ontario K1A 0G9
Canada
ph: 613-782-8914
e-mail: museum-musee@bank-banque-canada.ca
web: http://www.bank-banque-canada.ca/
Eight galleries trace the history of money from barter to modern currency, with emphasis on Canada's monetary history; impressive coin and paper money exhibits.

Periodicals

Susan
Newsletter: Restrike, The
RFD 1 Box 530
Winthrop, ME 04364-9705
ph: 207-377-2540
e-mail: ressce@ctel.net
Buy, sell, trade with other collectors nationwide; published monthly.

Newsletter: Trader's Horn
P.O. Box 2781
Henderson, NC 27536
e-mail: thorn@gloryroad.net
A monthly newsletter serving the small to intermediate collector of coins, paper money, stamps, lottery tickets, tokens and other collecting area.

Newsletter: Silver & Gold Report
P.O. Box 109665
West Palm Beach, FL 33410
ph: 800-289-9222 or 561-627-3300
fax: 561-625-6685
e-mail: sgr@weissinc.com
web: http://www.wessinc.com
Financial advice newsletter in precious medals, and gold & silver bullion and coins.

Amos Press, Inc.
Newspaper: Coin World
P.O. Box 150
Sidney, OH 45365-0150
ph: 800-673-8311
fax: 937-498-0812
e-mail: kchen@coinworld.com
web: http://www.coinworld.com/
The weekly newspaper for the entire numismatic field; articles, ads, paper money, foreign and ancient coins, auctions, value guides, grading, etc.

Pat DuChene, PR
Krause Publications
Magazine: Coin Prices
700 E. State St.
Iola, WI 54990-0001
ph: 715-445-2214
fax: 715-445-4087
e-mail: info@krause.com
web: http://www.krause.com/
Provides complete current market prices for U.S. coins; values listed for up to 12 grades of preservation; frequently updated pricings; bi-monthly.

Pat DuChene, PR
Krause Publications
Magazine: Coins
700 E. State St.
Iola, WI 54990-0001
ph: 715-445-2214
fax: 715-445-4087
e-mail: info@krause.com
web: http://www.krause.com/
Leading monthly newsstand magazine provides in-depth features on U.S. coins with color photos; collector columns, articles, values, ads; the complete magazine for collectors.

Pat DuChene, PR
Krause Publications
Newspaper: Numismatic News
700 E. State St.
Iola, WI 54990-0001
ph: 715-445-2214
fax: 715-445-4087
e-mail: info@krause.com
web: http://www.krause.com/
A weekly guide to the coin collecting hobby serving active collectors of U.S. coins with timely news; values, ads, calendar.

Pat DuChene, PR
Krause Publications
Newsmagazine: World Coin News
700 E. State St.
Iola, WI 54990-0001
ph: 715-445-2214
fax: 715-445-4087
e-mail: info@krause.com
web: http://www.krause.com/
Monthly guide serving world coin collectors; news, historical features, huge ad section, coin values, show calendar.

Dennis R. Barker
CDN Publications
Newsletter: Certified Coin Dealer Newsletter (The "Bluesheet")
P.O. Box 7939
Torrance, CA 90504
ph: 310-515-7369
fax: 310-515-7534
e-mail: orders@graysheet.com
web: http://www.coinprices.com/
A weekly report on the certified coin market; unbiased wholesale information on rare coins for the coin hobby and business.

CDN Publications
Newsletter: Coin Dealer Newsletter (The "Greysheet")
P.O. Box 7939
Torrance, CA 90504
ph: 310-515-7369
fax: 310-515-7534
e-mail: orders@graysheet.com
web: http://www.coinprices.com/
A weekly report on the certified coin market; unbiased wholesale information on rare coins for the coin hobby and business.

CDN Publications
Newsletter: Currency Dealer Newsletter, The (The "Greensheet")
P.O. Box 7939
Torrance, CA 90504
ph: 310-515-7369
fax: 310-515-7534
e-mail: orders@graysheet.com
web: http://www.coinprices.com/
A monthly newsletter reporting on the currency market.

Barry Stuppler, Pub.
Magazine: Coin Connoisseur
P.O. Box 6494
Woodland Hills, CA 91365
ph: 888-264-6624 or 818-592-2800
fax: 818-594-8599
e-mail: barry@coinmag.com
web: http://www.coinmag.com/
The international magazine for coin collectors and investors.

Miller Enterprises, Inc.
Magazine: COINage
4880 Market St.
Ventura, CA 93003
ph: 805-644-3824

Trajan Publishing Corporation
Newspaper: Canadian Coin News
103 Lakeshore Rd., Ste. 202
St. Catharines, Ontario L2N 2T6
Canada
ph: 905-646-7744
fax: 905-646-0995
e-mail: bret@trajan.com
web: http://www.vaxxine.com/trajan/
All the news on Canadian coin collecting.

Trajan Publishing Corp.
Magazine: Les Monnaies
103 Lakeshore Rd., Ste. 202
St. Catharines, Ontario L2N 2T6
Canada
ph: 905-646-7744
fax: 905-646-0995
e-mail: bret@trajan.com
web: http://www.vaxxine.com/trajan/
North America's only French language periodical on the subject of coins, medals and paper money.

Repro. Sources

Ron Landis
Gallery Mint Museum
Newsletter: Gallery Mint Report
P.O. Box 706
Eureka Springs, AR 72632
ph: 501-253-5055
e-mail: gmm@arkansas.net
web: http://www.coin-gallery.com/gmm/
A mint and museum; reproductions of early American coins and commemorative medals, hobo nickels and tokens for collectors; preserves numismatic arts and coin-making techniques.

Coins (Ancient)

(see also ANTIQUITIES)

Auction Services

Alex G. Malloy
Alex G. Malloy, Inc.
P.O. Box 38
South Salem, NY 10590-0038
ph: 203-438-0396 or 203-438-9652
fax: 203-438-6744
e-mail: alexmalloy@aol.com
web: http://members.aol.com/AlexMalloy/agmalloy.htm
Issues fixed price lists and mail bid sales of ancient and medieval coinage, and of ancient art and antiquities for sale; co-author of "Warman's Coins & Currency" (1994 Wallace-Homestead).

Clubs/Associations

Barry Rightman
Ancient Coin Club
P.O. Box 227
Canoga Park, CA 91305-0227

Dealers

Jan Blamberg
Stack's Coin Galleries
123 West 57th St.
New York, NY 10019-2280
ph: 212-582-2580
fax: 212-245-5018
e-mail: info@stacks.com
web: http://www.stacks.com
Buys and sells European, ancient, medieval coins; member International Association of Professional Numismatists.

Alex G. Malloy
Alex G. Malloy, Inc.
P.O. Box 38
South Salem, NY 10590-0038
ph: 203-438-0396 or 203-438-9652
fax: 203-438-6744
e-mail: alexmalloy@aol.com
web: http://members.aol.com/AlexMalloy/agmalloy.htm
Issues fixed price lists and mail bid sales of ancient and medieval coinage, and of ancient art and antiquities for sale; co-author of "Warman's Coins & Currency" (1994 Wallace-Homestead).

Frank J. Wagner
Classica Antiquities
P.O. Box 509
Syracuse, NY 13201-0509
ph: 315-687-0036 or 315-457-7249
e-mail: clasant@servtech.com
web: http://www.servtech.com/~clasant/
For over 30 years buying/selling ancient and medieval Greek, Roman, Egyptian, Near Eastern coins and antiquities.

Edward J. Waddell, Jr.
Edward J. Waddell, Ltd.
444 N. Frederick Ave., Ste. 316
Gaithersburg, MD 20877
ph: 301-990-7446
fax: 301-990-3712
e-mail: sales@coin.com
web: http://www.coin.com
Greek, Roman, Byzantine and Medieval coins, antiquities and numismatic literature; member International Association of Professional Numismatists.

Carl & Jon Subak
Subak Inc.
22 West Monroe St.
Room 1506
Chicago, IL 60603
ph: 312-346-0609 or 312-346-0673
fax: 312-346-0150
e-mail: subakinc@interlync.com
Roman, Byzantine, medieval coins; member International Association of Professional Numismatists.

Wayne Sales
Wayne G. Sayles, Antiquarian
P.O. Box 911
Gainesville, MO 65655
ph: 417-679-2142
fax: 417-679-2524
e-mail: wayne@celator.com
web: http://www.celator.com/
Buys and sells ancient Greek, Roman, Byzantine, Islamic and related coins; authenticity guaranteed without limitation; 32 years experience in the field.

Jim Mason
Jim's Medieval Coins
4080 S. 570 E.
Salt Lake City, UT 84107
ph: 801-263-2350 or 801-581-8221
e-mail: mason_j@gse.utah.edu
web: http://members.tripod.com/~Charlemagne64/medieval.html
Specializes in medieval European coins, with an emphasis on Royal and Feudal French denier from the 8th to the 14th century.

Joel & Michael Malter
Malter Galleries, Inc.
17005 Ventura Blvd.
Encino, CA 91316-4128
ph: 818-784-7772 or 818-784-2181
fax: 818-784-4726
e-mail: rarearts@earthlink.net
web: http://www.maltergalleries.com/
Buys and sells ancient and medieval coins, classical antiquities, numismatic books and literature; member International Association of Professional Numismatists.

Frank L. Kovacs
P.O. Box 25300
San Mateo, CA 94402
ph: 650-574-2028
fax: 650-574-1995
Buys and sells ancient and Byzantine coins and antiquities; member International Association of Professional Numismatists.

Periodicals

Magazine: Celator, The
P.O. Box 911
Gainesville, MO 65655
ph: 417-679-2142
fax: 417-679-2524
e-mail: wayne@celator.com
web: http://www.celator.com/
A monthly magazine focusing on antiquities and ancient coins; ads, articles, auction reports, etc.

Coins (Copper)

Clubs/Associations

Rod Burress
Early American Coppers
Newsletter: Penny-Wise
P.O. Box 15782
Cincinnati, OH 45215
e-mail: info@eacs.org
web: http://www.eacs.org/
Interested in early American copper coinage.

Internet Resources

USCents.com
e-mail: USCents@aol.com
web: http://www.uscents.com/
Auctions of copper coins, feature articles, photo library, chat room, copper grading guide, rarity guide, glossary of copper terms, copper checklist, etc.

Coins (Encased)

(see also GOOD LUCK)

Auction Services

Bob Slawsky
P.O. Box 864
Windermere, FL 34786-0864
ph: 407-352-7807
fax: 407-352-BIDS
e-mail: WWGD54A@prodigy.com
Buys, sells, auctions tokens, medals, badges, small advertising items, political, World's Fair, Olympic items, encased coins, etc.

Collectors

R. Wells
5 Elm
Trenton, NJ 08611-2501
Wants encased coins; good luck, advertising, etc.; describe item, date on coin, price.

Coins (World Proof)

Clubs/Associations

Gail P. Gray, Sec.
World Proof Numismatic Association
Newsletter: Proof Collectors Corner
P.O. Box 4094
Pittsburgh, PA 15201-0094
ph: 412-782-4477
fax: 412-782-0227
WPNA is dedicated to the collector of proof and BU coinage; purpose is to bring forth the latest news on new coin issues, medals and books, etc.; special Master Price List is mailed out to all members containing over 1,000 proof coins.

Dealers

Edward J. Moschetti
Treasures of the World
P.O. Box 4094
Pittsburgh, PA 15201-0094
ph: 412-782-4477
fax: 412-782-0227
Medals in silver and gold proof condition; offering the Rarities Mint issues, plus Batman, Bugs Bunny, etc.

Commemorative Coins

Clubs/Associations

Society for U.S. Commemorative Coins
P.O. Box 302
Huntington Beach, CA 92648
Members dedicated to sharing the knowledge and enjoyment of collecting U.S. commemorative coins.

Computer Programs For

Man./Prod./Dist.

Tom Bilotta
Carlisle Development Corp.
Software: Coin Collectors Assistant
P.O. Box 291
Carlisle, MA 01741-0291
ph: 800-219-0257
e-mail: carlisleDC@aol.com
web: http://www.csmonline.com/carlisledc/
Coin Collectors Assistant is a collection management software program for coin collectors; linked automatically to "Coin World" values price database.

PrimaSoft PC, Inc.
Software: Coin Organizer
P.O. Box 456
Surrey, British Columbia V3T 5B7
Canada
ph: 800-371-7520 or 604-951-1085
fax: 604-951-7797
e-mail: support@primasoft.com
web: http://www.primasoft.com/coo.htm
A complete program that allows coin collectors, hobbyists, and clubs to organize, catalog, and manage their collections on their PCs.

Liberty Street Software
Software: CoinManage
3126 Lendnier Software
Mississauga, Ontario L4Y 4A1
Canada
ph: 888-REG-IT-80 or 888-282-5887
fax: 801-530-7161
e-mail: webmaster@libertystreet.com
web: http://www.libertystreet.com
A program to manage your coin collection.

Liberty Street Software
Software: CurrencyManage
3126 Lendnier Software
Mississauga, Ontario L4Y 4A1
Canada
ph: 888-REG-IT-80 or 888-282-5887
fax: 801-530-7161
e-mail: webmaster@libertystreet.com
web: http://www.libertystreet.com
A program to manage your collection of bank notes.

Croatian

Clubs/Associations

Eck Spahich, Ed.
Croatian Philatelic Society
Journal: Trumpeter, The
P.O. Box 696
Fritch, TX 79036-0696
ph: 806-857-0129
e-mail: ou812@arn.net
web: http://www.dalmatia.net/cps/
Focuses on the history of the stamps and numismatic items of all the Balkan states, past and present.

Errors

Clubs/Associations

Michael Ellis
Combined Organizations of Numismatic Error Collectors of America
Newsletter: Errorscope
Rt. 2, Box HI 504
Donalsonville, GA 31745
ph: 912-861-2089
fax: 912-861-2089
e-mail: coneca@surfsouth.com
web: http://hermes.csd.net/~coneca/
The only national numismatic organization devoted exclusively to the study of error and variety coinage; newsletter contains informative articles and a 16-page auction.

Collectors

George Van Trump, Jr.
6837 Murray Lane
Annandale, VA 22003

Dealers

Michael Ellis
Rt. 2, Box HI 504
Donalsonville, GA 31745
ph: 912-861-2089
fax: 912-861-2089
e-mail: coneca@surfsouth.com
web: http://hermes.csd.net/~coneca/
Numismatic collector/dealer since 1968; has specialized in error/variety coinage since 1987; recognized as an authority in the field; author of the column "The Error Chronicles" for "Numismatic News," the hobby's leading weekly paper.

Neil Osina
Best Variety Sports Cards & Coins
358 W. Foothill Blvd.
Glendora, CA 91740-3327
ph: 626-914-2273
fax: 626-914-6624
Wants to buy coin errors; Life Member of all major associations; over 34 years experience.

Experts

Michael Ellis
Rt. 2, Box HI 504
Donalsonville, GA 31745
ph: 912-861-2089
fax: 912-861-2089
e-mail: coneca@surfsouth.com
web: http://hermes.csd.net/~coneca/
Numismatic collector/dealer since 1968; has specialized in error/variety coinage since 1987; recognized as an authority in the field; author of the column "The Error Chronicles" for "Numismatic News," the hobby's leading weekly paper.

Stephen M. Sullivan
Capital Currency, Incorporated
P.O. Box 361632
Melbourne, FL 32936-1632
ph: 407-777-4604
e-mail: errors@palmnet.net
Appraiser, auctioneer, collector, dealer, expert in U.S. currency; full service dealer for rare U.S. currency; author of "The US Error Note Encyclopedia."

Periodicals

Arnold Margolis
Magazine: Error Trends Coin Magazine
P.O. Box 158
Oceanside, NY 11572-0158
ph: 516-764-8063
A monthly magazine focusing on coin errors.

Lincoln Cent

Clubs/Associations

Lincoln Cent Society
Newsletter: Centinel, The
P.O. Box 113
Winfield, IL 60190
ph: 630-462-8654
e-mail: rjulianj@ix.netcom.com
Dedicated to the study of the Lincoln cent.

Medieval

(see ANTIQUITIES; COINS & CURRENCY, Coins [Ancient])

Paper Money

Auction Services

R.M. Smythe & Company
26 Broadway, Ste. 271
New York, NY 10004-1701
ph: 212-943-1880 or 800-622-1880
fax: 212-908-4047
e-mail: info@rm-smythe.com
web: http://www.rm-smythe.com/
Conducts auctions of Colonial currency, Confederate currency, federal essay notes, proof vignettes, fractional and obsolete currency, stocks, bonds, coins and autographs.

Clubs/Associations

Arthur C. Matz
Latin American Paper Money Society
Newsletter: LANSA
3304 Milford Mill Rd.
Baltimore, MD 21244-2041
ph: 410-655-3109
e-mail: amatzlansa@aol.com
A booklet issued three times a year for those interested in Latin American and Iberia paper money.

Kevin Foley
Professional Currency Dealers Association
P.O. Box 573
Milwaukee, WI 53201
This organization is just for dealers, but send a SASE for a free list of respectable dealers; also send 59 cents for the booklet "How to Collect Paper Money."

International Bank Note Society
Journal: International Bank Note Society Journal
P.O. Box 1642
Racine, WI 53401-1642
ph: 414-554-6255
e-mail: milana@wi.net
Members interested in worldwide bank notes and paper currencies; journal published quarterly with articles, ads, etc.

Bob Cochran
Society of Paper Money Collectors, Inc.
Journal: Paper Money
P.O. Box 1085
Florissant, MO 63031-0085
e-mail: bob@spmc.org
web: http://www.spmc.org/
Interested in all aspects of collecting paper currency; welcomes opportunity to help non-collectors, but PLEASE send SASE for reply.

Dick Dunn, Sec/Treas
Canadian Paper Money Society
P.O. Box 562
Pickering, Ontario L1V 2R7
Canada
ph: 905-509-1146
e-mail: cpms@idirect.com

Collectors

Bob Cochran
P.O. Box 1085
Florissant, MO 63031-0085
e-mail: bob@spmc.org
Collector of U.S. paper money; also banking history.

Dealers

Jim Sciuto
GoldTek
P.O. Box 128
Methuen, MA 01844
ph: 978-374-2254 or 603-645-4717
fax: 978-373-1088
Wants old paper money: gold certificates, silver certificates, errors, star notes, red seals, etc.

Denly's of Boston
P.O. Box 1010
Boston, MA 02205
ph: 617-482-8477
fax: 617-357-8163
Buys and sells national currency, banknotes, fractional and Colonial currency.

Russell Kaye
P.O. Box 635
Shrub Oak, NY 10588
ph: 914-528-1496
e-mail: oldpaper@bestweb.net
Buys and sells old U.S. currency, 1700s through 1929; send photocopy of email of items for sale; especially interested in large size notes, National currency, broken banknotes and scrip.

William S. Panitch
William S. Panitch, Inc.
P.o. Box 3712
Albany, NY 12203-0712
ph: 518-489-4400
fax: 518-489-2776
e-mail: wpanitch@aol.com
Buys and sells U.S. and foreign coins, commemorative and award medals, paper money, etc.; also lectures and appraises.

Art Leister
Commercial Coin Co.
1611 Market St.
P.O. Box 607
Camp Hill, PA 17001-0607
ph: 717-737-8981 or 717-761-8264
Buys and sells national banknotes.

Stephen M. Sullivan
Capital Currency, Incorporated
P.O. Box 361632
Melbourne, FL 32936-1632
ph: 407-777-4604
e-mail: errors@palmnet.net
Appraiser, auctioneer, collector, dealer, expert in U.S. currency; full service dealer for rare U.S. currency; author of "The US Error Note Encyclopedia."

Tom Knebl, Inc.
P.O. Box 3689
Carson City, NV 89702-3689
ph: 775-265-6614
Wants all world bank notes; also U.S. large size notes and military currency; U.S. fractional currency; Colonial currency, etc.

Tom Sluszkiewicz
ATS Numismatics
P.O. Box 54521
Burnaby, British Columbia V5E 4J6
Canada
e-mail: ats@atsnotes.com
web: http://www.atsnotes.com
Buys and sells numismatic world banknotes, local and private paper money, collectibles bonds and stock certificates.

Experts

Ken D. Tanaka
Nova Online, Inc.
P.O. Box 231028
Portland, OR 97281-1028
ph: 503-469-0609
fax: 503-469-0609
e-mail: ggat@teleport.com
Specialist in all forms of paper money; offering evaluations and appraisals; also buys and sells paper money.

Internet Resources

Mark Mearns
World Banknote Collector's Club
Newsletter: World Banknote Collector's Club Newsletter
73 Hampton Lane
Solihull, West Midlands B19 2QD
U.K.
e-mail: banknote@geocities.com
web: http://www.users.dircon.co.uk/~m-mearns/banknote/
An online forum for all collectors and dealers of banknotes; free membership; free advertising to members and dealers (within reason); links to other sites and a periodical newsletter to all members; online only.

Periodicals

Pat DuChene, PR
Krause Publications
Newspaper: Bank Note Reporter
700 E. State St.
Iola, WI 54990-0001
ph: 715-445-2214
fax: 715-445-4087
e-mail: info@krause.com
web: http://www.krause.com/
Monthly news source and marketplace for collectors of U.S. and world paper money, notes, checks and related fiscal paper.

Token Publishing, Ltd.
Magazine: Coin News
P.O. Box 14
Honiton, Devon EX14 9YP
U.K.
ph: +44 1404 46972
fax: +44 1404 381895
e-mail: info@coin-news.com
web: http://www.coin-news.com/
A monthly English publication focusing on coins and paper money.

Paper Money (World)

Dealers

Donald Arnone
P.O. Box 240
Bohemia, NY 11716-0240
e-mail: Notalist@aol.com
On this website you will find some good information on collecting and grading paper money; member IBNS and the ANA.

Steve Eyer
P.O. Box 123 -MA
Mount Zion, IL 62549-0123
ph: 217-864-4321
fax: 217-864-3021
Buys and sells world coins and world banknotes.

Tracey L. Wolf
4694 Rio Poco Rd.
Reno, NV 89502-6336
e-mail: TLWolf@aol.com
web: http://members.aol.com/TLWolf/banknotes/index.htm
Buys and sells modern to rare banknotes from around the world; free price list to collectors either by mail or online.

Gary Snover
P.O. Box 9696
San Bernardino, CA 92427-0696
ph: 909-883-5849
fax: 909-886-6874
e-mail: snover@ix.netcom.com
Buys and sells world banknotes; send for free catalog; active buyer of all world paper money.

Yasha Beresiner
InterCol Gallery
43 Templars Crescent
London, N3 3QR
U.K.
ph: 0181-349-2207 or 0171-354-2599
fax: 0181-346-9539
e-mail: yasha@compuserve.com
web: http://www.intercol.co.uk
Buys and sells world banknotes, all playing cards, old maps, related books on Free Masonry.

Experts

Neil Shafer
P.O. Box 17138
Milwaukee, WI 53217
ph: 414-352-5962
fax: 414-352-5974
e-mail: nelsshaf@aol.com
Editor of "Standard Catalog of World Paper Money."

Play Money

Clubs/Associations

Jack Phillips
American Play Money Society
Newsletter: Fun Money
2044 Pine Lake Trail, NW
Arab, AL 35016
e-mail: japhillips@mindspring.com
web: http://www.geocities.com/Athens/Oracle/9738/
Dedicated to the promotion and research of play money and related exonumia.

Collectors

Richard & Wendy Clothier
881 S. Washington State Rd.
Becket, MA 01223
ph: 413-623-8866 or 413-558-9203
e-mail: clothier@prodigy.net
web: http://www.geocities.com/Athens/Parthenon/7338/
Author of "Play Money of American Children"; member of American Play Money Society.

Jack Phillips
2044 Pine Lake Trail, NW
Arab, AL 35016
e-mail: japhillips@mindspring.com
web: http://www.geocities.com/Athens/Oracle/9738/
Interested in learning about all types of play money including coins and currency in all types of materials including plastic, metal, cardboard, and paper.

Silver Dollars

Clubs/Associations

Jeff Oxman, Ed.
Society of Silver Dollar Collectors
Journal: S.S.D.C. Journal
P.O. Box 2123
North Hills, CA 91393
e-mail: jeffssdc@aol.com
web: http://www.geocities.com/TheTopics/4666/index1.html

Souvenir Cards

Clubs/Associations

Souvenir Card Collectors Society
Journal: Souvenir Card Journal
P.O. Box 4155
Tulsa, OK 74159-0155
ph: 918-664-6724
e-mail: dmarr5569@aol.com
Souvenir cards are 8 1/2" x 11" cards with engraved reproductions of philatelic or numismatic designs from original plates.

Supplies For

Suppliers

Lighthouse Publications
P.O. Box 705
Hackensack, NJ 07602-0705
ph: 201-342-1513
fax: 201-342-7142
e-mail: lighthouse-us.info@leuchtturn.com
web: http://www.leuchtturm.com/
Carries full line of products for the coin and stamp collector: albums, binders, blank pages, magnifiers, tongs, UV lamps.

Brooklyn Gallery Coin & Stamp
8725 Fourth Ave.
P.O. Box 146
Brooklyn, NY 11209-0146
ph: 718-745-5701
fax: 718-745-2775
e-mail: info@brooklyngallery.com
web: http://www.brooklyngallery.com/
Send $1.50 for 100+ page catalog.

Linder Publications, Inc.
P.O. Box 5056
Syracuse, NY 13220
ph: 315-437-0463 or 800-654-0324
fax: 315-437-4832
Sells collector's accessories for stamps, coins, telephone cards, postcards: ring binders, blank album pages, UV lamps, magnifiers, stamp tongs, clear pocket pages, protective covers, coin holders, etc.

COLLAR BUTTONS & PINS

(see CLOTHING & ACCESSORIES, Vintage; CUFF LINKS)

COLLECTIBLES

(see ANTIQUES & COLLECTIBLES; COLLECTIBLES [MODERN])

COLLECTIBLES (MODERN)

(see also ANIMATION FILM ART; DOLLS; ENESCO; FIGURINES; MINIATURES, Sculptures; PRINTS [MODERN]; STEIFF)

Clubs/Associations

Cowboy Collector Society, The, c/o Shade Tree Creations, Inc.
6210 NW 124th Place
Gainesville, FL 32606-1071
ph: 800-327-6923 or 824-524-0863

Collectors' Society of America
29352 Hoover Rd.
Warren, MI 48093
ph: 800-910-2762
fax: 800-910-2762 x329
e-mail: xtxt00e@prodigy.com
web: http://www.collectors-society.org
Monthly news and information about your favorite collectibles; provides information for collectors; publishes eight monthly newsletters; covers ornaments, figurines, crystal, dolls, cottages, plates, animation collectibles, etc.

Ralph Bloch
National Association of Limited Edition Dealers
35 E. Wacker Dr., Ste. 500
Chicago, IL 60601
ph: 800-446-2533 or 312-782-5252
fax: 312-236-1140
e-mail: naled@collectibles.net
web: http://www.naled.com

Hunter Haines
Collectibles & Platemakers Guild
77 W. Washington St., Ste. 1507
Chicago, IL 60602-2902
ph: 312-201-0262
fax: 312-201-8579
e-mail: cpgnews@aol.com

San Diego Plate & Collectible Club
P.O. Box 17625
San Diego, CA 92177
ph: 619-560-0595 or 619-467-9317
For collectors of modern limited edition collectibles including figurines, plates, lithographs, prints, dolls, cottages, miniatures, etc.

Dealers

Jim Darwiche
Touch of Class, A
ph: 800-726-1803
e-mail: touchoclass@wyoming.com
web: http://www.topgifts.com/
Specializes in G. Armani, Disney, Lladro, Lladro Goyescas, Legend, Swarovski, Wee Forest, and other contemporary collectibles.

Bob Dorman
New England Collectibles Exchange
Newsletter: New England Collectibles Exchange Newsletter
201 Pine Ave.
Clarksburg, MA 01247-4640
ph: 413-663-3643
fax: 413-663-5140
e-mail: nece@collectiblesbroker.com
web: http://www.collectiblesbroker.com
Monthly newsletters for collectors; list, buy, sell or trade limited editions and retired pieces; ads free for active members: Cherished Teddies, Anri, Cat's Meow, Dept. 56, Shelia's, Hummel, Disney Classics, Tom Clark, Boyds Bears, etc.

Collector's Cabinet
4 Pleasant St.
Natick, MA 01760
ph: 800-847-5283 or 508-653-7444
e-mail: collector@collectors-cabinet.com
web: http://www.collectorsuperstore.com/
A super store of modern collectibles: Disney, plates, figurines, dolls, Christmas, prints, Ashton Drake, Gorham, Hamilton, Bradford, Sandra Kuck, Edna Hibel, Lowell Davis, Perillo, Rockwell, Chilmark, Hummels, Titanic, etc.

Mary Gavrilles
Collector's Cabinet
4 Pleasant St.
Natick, MA 01760
ph: 800-84-PLATE or 800-847-5283
e-mail: collector@collectors-cabinet.com
web: http://www.collectors-cabinet.com/
On-line collectibles super store: limited edition plates, figurines, dolls, ornaments, lithographs, and more; over 1800 items pictured: Disney Classics, Hummels, Hibel, David Winter, Sandra Kuck, DeGrazia, Titanic, Bradford, etc.

Linda's Originals & The Yankee Craftsmen
230 Rt. 6A
Brewster, MA 02631
ph: 800-385-4758
All God's Children, Armani, Annalee Dolls, Byers Choice, Cat's Meow, Cherished Teddies, Dept. 56, Harbour Lights, Hummel, Krystonia, Lilliput Lane, Shelia's, Steinbeck, and more.

Maurice Nasser Co.
New London Shopping Center
New London, CT 06320
ph: 860-443-6523 or 800-243-0895

Elissa Cohen ISA CAPP, GG
Suburban Jewelers
126 East Front St.
Plainfield, NJ 07060-1202
ph: 908-756-1774
Authorized dealer of Lladro, Hummel, Precious Moments, Swarovski, All God's Children, Sarah's Attic, G. Armani, Miss Martha, Ebony Visions, Tom Clark, and other modern collectibles; buys, sells, trades.

Someone Special
1830 Route 70 East
Cherry Hill, NJ 08003
ph: 609-424-1914 or 800-237-7656
e-mail: info@someonespecial.com
web: http://www.someonespecial.com/
Web site has over 9,000 items, over 8,500 images, and over 1,300 pages: Armani, Boehm, Belleek, Cardew teapots, Chilmark pewter, Lowell Davis, Emmett Kelly Jr., Forma Vitrum, Hummels, Harbour Lights, Hibel, Maruri, Olszewski and more.

Irv Losman
Tiara Gifts
1675 Rockville Pike
Congressional Plaza
Rockville, MD 20852-1619
ph: 301-468-1122 or 800-74-TIARA
fax: 301-468-1352
e-mail: tiaragalleries@juno.com
web: http://tiaragalleries.com
Lladro, Herend, Waterford, Swarovski, David Winter, Chilmark, Hummels, Goebel miniatures, Sarah's Attic, Tom Clark, Armani, Dept. 56, Boehm, Connoisseur, Herend, EKJ.

Donny Biggs
Biggs Collectibles
5517 Lakeside Ave.
Richmond, VA 23228
ph: 804-266-7744 or 800-637-0704
fax: 804-266-7775
Carries lots of limited edition dolls (Ashton Drake dealer of the year); also Chilmark, Hummel, David Winter, Lladro, Jan Hagara, Lowell Davis, Maud Humphrey, Swarovski, etc.

Linda Ross Hughes
Best Collectibles
Newsletter: Best Collectibles
16151 Morganton Highway
P.O. Box 152
Morganton, GA 30560-0152
ph: 706-838-5920
fax: 706-838-4008
e-mail: bestcoll@mail.tds.net
web: http://www.bestcollectibles.com/
A secondary market for retired and limited edition collectibles featuring Byers' Choice, Dept. 56, Lefton, Cherished Teddies, Charming Tails, Dreamsicles, NASCAR, Walt Disney Classics and many others.

Mary Ann Lowery
Crystal Corner, Inc., The
317 Billy Dyar Blvd.
P.O. Box 756
Boaz, AL 35957-0756
ph: 256-593-6169
fax: 256-593-6560
e-mail: ccorner@netnav.com
web: http://www.crystalcorner.com/
Carries Boyd's Bears, Cherished Teddies, Bradford collectible plates, Hawthorne Villages, Ashton Drake dolls, etc.

Collectible Exchange, Inc.
P.O. Box 429
New Middletown, OH 44442
ph: 800-752-3208
fax: 330-542-9644
Offers a brokerage service; buy or sell your retired, limited edition collectibles: Anri, Cybis, Lowell Davis, Jan Hagara, Gartlan, Duncan Royale, Ispanky, Lladro, Swarovski, Emmett Kelly, Jr., Hummel, etc.

Graham's Crackers Inc.
5981 E. 86th St.
Indianapolis, IN 46250
ph: 317-842-5727
fax: 317-577-7777
e-mail: grmckerbox@aol.com
web: http://www.grahamcrackers.com/
Christopher Radko, Department 56, Fontanini, Steinbach and Ulbricht nutcrackers, Beyer's Choice.

Tom Hayes
Collectibles Showcase
Newsletter: Collectibles Showcase Newsletter
1047 Burnsville Center
Burnsville, MN 55306
ph: 612-892-0552 or 800-723-4072
fax: 612-892-1596
Largest collectibles store in U.S.; located in the Mall of America; thousands of collectibles; many lines discounted 20% or more including Lladro, David Winter, Lilliput Lane, Waterford; also Precious Moments, Hummel, Dept. 56.

Dan Crimmins
Primal Merchandise
P.O. Box 2047
Palatine, IL 60078-2047
ph: 847-776-2739
e-mail: danco1@compuserve.com
web: http://www.dancoconsulting.com
American Sweetheart Collection porcelain dolls, Maiku Collection of handpainted alabastrite American Indian theme sculptures, LaVerona Collection porcelain figurines, Land & Sea lighthouses & cottages, Liberty Bronze alabastrite sculpture.

British Collectibles
917 Chicago Ave.
Evanston, IL 60202
ph: 800-634-0431 or 847-570-4867
fax: 847-570-4871
Produces Toby Jugs designed by Francis Salmon and Kevin Pearson; carries a wide assortment of modern collectibles, focusing on British.

Sue Reeves
Eloise's Gifts & Antiques
722 South Goliad
Rockwall, TX 75087-3936
ph: 972-771-6371 or 800-771-6371
fax: 972-771-6371
Carries Cairn, All Gods, Armani, L. Davis, Dept. 56, Duncan Royale, EKJ, Hummel, Hagara, Sarahs, D. Winter, Lilliput Lane, Wee Forest, plates, Cat's Meow, Swarovski, ENESCO,, Byers, Lizzie High, Dreamsicles, Cherished Teddies, etc.

Ken Armke
OHI Exchange
Newsletter: OHI Exchange
553 Landa St.
New Braunfels, TX 78130
ph: 830-629-1191
fax: 830-606-1118
e-mail: Comments@OHIExchange.com
web: http://www.ohiexchange.com/
Acts as broker to match buyers and sellers of all limited edition collectibles such as collector plates, figurines, bells, ornaments, dolls, etc.; Dept. 56, David Winter, Lowell Davis, Hummel, Duncan Royale, etc.

Genevra Fox
Fox's Gifts & Collectables
7030 5th Ave.
Scottsdale, AZ 85251
ph: 602-947-0560 or 800-592-2555
Specializes in modern collectibles by Ted DeGrazia, Cat's Meow, J. Hagara, Dept. 56, and Bradford plates.

Eva Flynn
Eva Flynn Collectibles & Antiques
P.O. Box 1011
Carlsborg, WA 98324-1011
ph: 360-683-7725
e-mail: evaflynn@tenforward.com
web: http://www.clallam.com/eva/index.htm
Specializes in B&G/RC Christmas plates; search service for back issues for most major collectibles including Disney, Raggedy Ann, Peanuts, Rockwell, Hummels, Royal Doulton, doll plates, Ferrandiz, Veneto Flair, Rosenthal; send SASE.

Experts

Peggy Veltri
Collectors' Information Bureau
Newsletter: C.I.B. Report & Showcase, The
5065 Shoreline Rd., Ste. 200
Barrington, IL 60010-1700
ph: 847-842-2200
fax: 847-842-2205
e-mail: askcib@collectorsinfo.com
web: http://www.collectorsinfo.com/
CIB provides collectors with the most accurate and up-to-date information on limited edition plates, figurines, bells, graphics, ornaments, and dolls; publishes an annual "Collectibles Price Guide" and a quarterly newsletter.

Internet Resources

Steve Hart
Airmont OnLine
13 Park Ave.
Monsey, NY 10952
ph: 914-352-0789
e-mail: custserv@airmont.com
web: http://www.airmont.com
An on-line source for modern collectibles: Baccarat, Hummels, Lilliput Lane, Swarovski, David

Winter, Lalique, Lladro, Orrefors, Waterford, Lenox.

David J. Maloney, Jr., ISA CAPP
MaloneysOnline Antiques & Collectibles Resource Directory
P.O. Box 2049
Frederick, MD 21702-1049
ph: 301-695-8544
fax: 301-695-6491
e-mail: dave@maloney.com
web: http://www.maloneysonline.com/
Online resource information source for collectors, sellers, claims adjusters, etc.: includes experts, buyers, clubs, periodicals, repairers, museums/libraries, appraisers, auctioneers, matching services, dealers, etc.

Darryl Kirk
World Collectors Net
8 Aldous Court, Clifton Road
Kingston-upon-Thames, Surrey KT2 6PH
U.K.
ph: +44 (0) 181 5497103
fax: +44 (0) 181 5497103
e-mail: info@worldcollectorsnet.com
web: http://www.worldcollectorsnet.com/
An on-line resource that provides news, information, message boards, and chat rooms for a number of collectibles; also a free on-line Collectors Magazine featuring articles, clubs and magazines from around the world.

Man./Prod./Dist.

Hudson Creek
321 Central St.
Hudson, MA 01749
ph: 978-568-1401
fax: 978-568-8741
web: http://www.hudsoncreek.com/
Producers of collectible figurines, plates, Christmas ornaments; line include Chilmark limited edition collectibles, Hudson Pewter, Sebastian Miniatures, and c.p. smithshire Shirelings.

American Artists
66 Poppasquash Rd.
Bristol, RI 02809
ph: 800-828-0086 or 401-254-1191
fax: 401-254-8881
e-mail: american_art@ids.net
Manufactures and distributes limited edition plates, figurines and prints by artists such as Fred Stone, Donald Zolan and Susan Leigh.

Anna-Perenna, Inc.
35 River St.
New Rochelle, NY 10801
ph: 914-633-3777 or 800-627-2550
fax: 914-633-8727
Manufactures and publishes limited edition figurines, sculpture and plates by artists such as P. Buckley Moss.

Customer Service
Reco International Corp.
138 Haven Ave.
Port Washington, NY 11050
ph: 516-767-2400 or 800-221-5356
fax: 516-767-2409
e-mail: recoint@aol.com
web: http://www.reco.com/
Distributor of collector plates, bells, Christmas ornaments, dolls, figurines and graphics based in designs by noted artists such as John McClelland and Sandra Kuck, and Jody Beresma.

United States Historical Society
25 E. Main St.
Richmond, VA 23219
ph: 804-648-4736 or 800-788-4478
fax: 804-648-0002
e-mail: dolls@ushsdolls.com
web: http://www.ushsdolls.com/
Direct mail marketer of plates, figurines, dolls and Christmas ornaments in stained glass, pewter, porcelain and other materials.

James Measell
Fenton Art Glass Company, The
700 Elizabeth St.
Williamstown, WV 26187-1028
ph: 304-375-6122 or 800-249-4527
fax: 304-375-6459
e-mail: askfenton@fentonartglass.com
web: http://www.fentonartglass.com/
Manufactures collectible plates, figurines and bells.

Flambro Imports, Inc.
1530 Ellsworth Industrial Dr.
Atlanta, GA 30318-3752
ph: 800-355-2582 or 404-352-1381
fax: 404-352-2150
e-mail: flambro@flambro.com
web: http://www.flambro.com
Importer of collectible clowns (Emmett Kelly, Jr.) and circus-related items, plates, ornaments, figurines and miniatures.

Hamilton Collection, The
4810 Executive Park Court
Jacksonville, FL 32216-6069
ph: 800-228-2945
fax: 904-279-1339
Formerly The Hamilton Mint, produces collectible plates, figurines and dolls.

American Greetings Corp.
One American Rd.
Cleveland, OH 44144
ph: 216-252-7300 or 800-242-2732
fax: 216-252-6777
World's largest manufacturer of greeting cards and social expression products, gift wrap and accessories, Christmas ornaments, collector plates, etc.; licenses Holly Hobbie, Ziggy, Strawberry Shortcake, and the Care Bears.

Midwest Importers of Cannon Falls, Inc.
P.O. Box 20
Cannon Falls, MN 55009-0020
ph: 507-263-4261 or 800-377-3335
Imports and wholesales unique gifts from around the world - bells, paperweights, dolls, ornaments, figurines, German nutcrackers, etc.

ENESCO Corp.
225 Windsor Dr.
Itasca, IL 60143
ph: 630-875-5300 or 800-436-3726
fax: 630-875-5359
web: http://www.enesco.com/
Giftware company produces/designs fine gifts & collectibles: figurines, musicals, waterballs, etc. by Precious Moments and others.

Hollywood Limited Editions, Inc.
6990 Central Park Ave.
Lincolnwood, IL 60645
ph: 708-673-3250 or 800-323-1413
fax: 708-673-4037
Distributes an extensive line of collector plates, figurines, bells, ornaments and accessories.

Dave Grossman Creations
1608 N. Warson Rd.
Saint Louis, MO 63132
ph: 314-423-5600 or 800-325-1655
fax: 314-423-7620
e-mail: dgrea@aol.com
Producer of collectible plates, ornaments and figurines including Rockwell, Gone With the Wind, Wizard of Oz, and Emmett Kelly, Sr.

Robert M. Ready
World of Products
1410 Oak Tree Drive
Houston, TX 77055-4316
Colorful catalog full of modern collectibles, knickknacks, curios: figurines, lit cottages, night lights, miniature furniture, carousel horses, frames, wall decor, music boxes, brass and wood sculptures, music boxes, "Mandarin" ivory.

Michael McCarthy
Character Collectibles
10861 Business Drive
Fontana, CA 92337
ph: 909-822-9999
fax: 909-823-6666
Manufacturers of Barkley Crossing, Hippity Hollow, Mooseberry Farms, Red Hats of Courage, and Celestial Guardians limited edition collectible figurines.

Giftstar
630 A Airpark Rd.
Napa, CA 94558
ph: 888-893-2323 or 707-226-2323
fax: 707-226-6464
Produce collectibles: snowglobes, Brian Baker building wall hangings, etc.

Willitts Designs
1129 Industrial Ave.
Petaluma, CA 94975
ph: 800-358-9184 or 707-778-7211
fax: 707-769-0304
e-mail: dreif@willitts.com
web: http://www.willitts.com/
Produces The American Carousel limited edition collections by Tobin Fraley; also other collectibles including plates, figurines, etc.

Misc. Services

Unity Marketing
Newsletter: Collectibles Business
188 Cocalico Creek Rd.
Stevens, PA 17578
ph: 717-336-1600
fax: 717-336-1601
e-mail: mail@unitymarketingonline.com
web: http://www.unitymarketingonline.com/
Specializes in tracking the contemporary collectibles marketplace and in publishing market research studies.

Pam Danziger
Unity Marketing
Newsletter: Collectibles Business
188 Cocalico Creek Rd.
Stevens, PA 17578
ph: 717-336-1600
fax: 717-336-1601
e-mail: mail@unitymarketingonline.com
web: http://www.unitymarketingonline.com/
Specializes in tracking the contemporary collectibles marketplace and in publishing market research studies.

Periodicals

David M. Duke, Ed.
Magazine: Collector Editions
170 Fifth Ave. - 12th Floor
New York, NY 10010
ph: 212-989-8700 or 800-347-6969
fax: 212-645-8976
A biweekly consumer magazine covering contemporary collector plates, figurines, prints and glass objects; companies, artists, etc.

Geyer-McAllister Publications, Inc.
Magazine: Gifts & Decorative Accessories
345 Hudson St., 4th Floor
New York, NY 10014
ph: 212-519-7200
fax: 212-519-7431
Trade magazine for new gifts, decorative accessories, collectibles, stationery, gift baskets, and tabletop wares; buyer's resource directory guide available with subscription.

Linda Kruger, Ed.
Collectors News Co.
Magazine: Collectors News
506 Second St.
P.O. Box 156
Grundy Center, IA 50638
ph: 319-824-6981 or 800-352-8039
fax: 319-824-3414
e-mail: collectors@collectors-news.com
web: http://collectors-news.com
The monthly publication for antiquers & collectors; complete show & sale calendar, articles, expert advice, values, etc.; a special emphasis is always given to contemporary limited edition collectibles: what's new, artists, events.

Magazine: Joy of Collecting
1333 Grandview Parkway
Sturtevant, WI 53177
ph: 800-777-5582
Bi-monthly magazine for collectors of contemporary collectibles: figurines, plates, prints, dolls, bears, ornaments, and much more.

Pat DuChene, PR
Krause Publications
Magazine: Collector's mart magazine
700 E. State St.
Iola, WI 54990-0001
ph: 715-445-2214
fax: 715-445-4087
e-mail: info@krause.com
web: http://www.krause.com/
Bi-monthly magazine for limited edition art and collectibles: classifieds, articles, dealers ads, club notices, etc.

Peggy Veltri
Collectors' Information Bureau
Directory: Directory to Secondary Market Retailers
5065 Shoreline Rd., Ste. 200
Barrington, IL 60010-1700
ph: 847-842-2200
fax: 847-842-2205
e-mail: askcib@collectorsinfo.com
web: http://www.collectorsinfo.com/
Lists scores of dealers and exchanges to assist in liquidating, buying, locating, or trading your contemporary limited edition artwork: prints, figurines, plates, bells, ornaments, etc.

Rosie Wells
Rosie Wells Enterprises, Inc.
Magazine: Collectors' Bulletin
22341 E. Wells Rd.
Canton, IL 61520
ph: 309-668-2211 or 800-445-8745
fax: 309-668-2795
e-mail: Rosie@RosieWells.com
web: http://www.RosieWells.com
Articles about today's collectibles: Lowell Davis, Anri, Dept. 56, Precious Moments, Cherished Teddies, Hallmark ornaments, Jan Hagara, Maud Humphrey, David Winter and more.

Rosie Wells
Rosie Wells Enterprises, Inc.
Newsletter: Weekly Collectors' Gazette
22341 E. Wells Rd.
Canton, IL 61520
ph: 309-668-2211 or 800-445-8745
fax: 309-668-2795
e-mail: Rosie@RosieWells.com
web: http://www.RosieWells.com
News bits for Hallmark, Disney Classics, Disney Collectibles, Dreamsicles, Cherished Teddies, McDonald's, Barbie, Hot Wheels, Dept. 56, Snowbabies, Precious Moments, Memories of Yesterday, Steiff, Longaberger baskets, etc.

Tom Power
Magazine: Collector, The
4 Queens Parade Close
London, N11 3FY
U.K.
ph: +44 181 361 7787
e-mail: collector@globalnet.co.uk
55 page collectibles magazine published twice a year; lots of articles and items for sale; specialist dealer in modern collectibles such as Doulton, Beswick, David Winter, Lilliput Lane; call 800-514-8176, ext. 3328.

Bing & Grondahl

Dealers

Pat Owen
Viking Import House, Inc.
690 NE 13th St.
Ft. Lauderdale, FL 33304-1110
ph: 954-763-3388 or 800-327-2297
fax: 954-462-2317
e-mail: vikingimp@aol.com
Operates the VIDEX, a buy/sell service for any and all Royal Copenhagen and Bing & Grondahl collectibles.

Man./Prod./Dist.

Josephine Dillon
Royal Scandinavian
140 Bradford Dr.
West Berlin, NJ 08091
ph: 609-768-5400 or 800-431-1992
fax: 800-448-7553
Royal Copenhagen, Bing & Grondahl, Holmegaard, and Georg Jensen are the best of Scandinavian collectibles; manufactures dinnerware, cobalt blue underglaze collector plates, figurines, bells, dolls, ornaments and gift accessories.

Black Related

Dealers

Karl J. Graham
Graham Collection, The
1800 Belmont Rd. NW
Washington, DC 20009
ph: 202-232-0911
Comprehensive collection of quality new Black collectibles: Giuseppe Armani, Duncan Royale, All God's Children, Positive Image Collection, John Sandridge, Daddy Long Legs, Black Legends, Enesco, LuvLife, Norman Hughes, and more.

Buildings

(see also COLLECTIBLES [MODERN], Cottages)

Buildings (Brandywine)

Clubs/Associations

Truman Whiting
Brandywine Neighborhood Association
104 Greene Dr.
Yorktown, VA 23692-4800
ph: 800-336-5031 or 757-898-5031
fax: 757-898-6895
e-mail: heartbwine@aol.com
web: http://www.brandywinecollectibles.com
A company sponsored collectors club.

Man./Prod./Dist.

Truman Whiting
Brandywine Woodcrafts Inc.
104 Greene Dr.
Yorktown, VA 23692-4800
ph: 800-336-5031 or 757-898-5031
fax: 757-898-6895
e-mail: heartbwine@aol.com
web: http://www.brandywinecollectibles.com
Manufactures three types of miniature collectible houses and accessories in hand painted cast resin and full color prints on wood; all buildings can be personalizes with your choice of name on sign.

Buildings (Brian Baker)

Clubs/Associations

Brian Baker's Deja Vu Collectors' Club
Newsletter: Brian's Backyard
630 A Airpark Rd.
Napa, CA 94558
ph: 888-893-2323 or 707-226-2323
fax: 707-226-6464
A club for collector's of Brian Baker's architecturally-inspired wall sculptures.

Man./Prod./Dist.

Giftstar
630 A Airpark Rd.
Napa, CA 94558
ph: 888-893-2323 or 707-226-2323
fax: 707-226-6464
Produces Brian Baker's architecturally-inspired wall sculptures.

Buildings (Cat's Meow)

Clubs/Associations

Cat's Meow Collectors Club
Newsletter: Village Mews, The
2163 Great Trails Dr.
Wooster, OH 44691-3738
ph: 330-264-1377
fax: 330-263-0219
e-mail: cmv@fjdesign.com
web: http://www.catsmeow.com
For collectors of the Cat's Meow Village, a product line of two-dimensional miniature historical buildings and accessories.

Man./Prod./Dist.

F.J. Designs, Inc./The Cat's Meow Village
2163 Great Trails Dr.
Wooster, OH 44691-3738
ph: 330-264-1377
fax: 330-263-0219
e-mail: cmv@fjdesign.com
web: http://www.catsmeow.com
Manufacturer of the Cat's Meow Village, a product line of two-dimensional miniature historical buildings and accessories.

Buildings (My Friends & Me)

Man./Prod./Dist.

My Friends & Me
P.O. Box 8000
Spokane, WA 99203
4" to 6" hand-cast reproductions of historic homes.

Buildings (R.R. Creations)

Man./Prod./Dist.

R.R. Creations, Inc.
P.O. Box 8707
Pratt, KS 67124
ph: 800-779-3610
Makes two-dimensional miniature homes, lighthouses and buildings.

Buildings (Shelia's)

Clubs/Associations

Shelia's Collectors Society
Newsletter: Our House
1856 Belgrade Ave.
Charleston, SC 29407
ph: 843-766-0485 or 800-227-6564
fax: 843-556-0040
e-mail: shelias@sheilas.com
web: http://www.shelias.com
Miniature handpainted two-dimensional houses made of wood.

Man./Prod./Dist.

Shelia's Collectibles
1856 Belgrade Ave.
Charleston, SC 29407
ph: 843-766-0485 or 800-227-6564
fax: 843-556-0040
e-mail: shelias@sheilas.com
web: http://www.shelias.com
Miniature handpainted two-dimensional houses made of wood.

Buildings (Town Square)

Man./Prod./Dist.

Cavanaugh Group International
1000 Holcomb Woods Pkwy., #440-B
Roswell, GA 30078
ph: 800-895-8100 or 770-643-1175
fax: 770-643-1172
web: http://www.cavanaghgrp.com/
Manufacturer of high-quality porcelain buildings.

Christmas

Clubs/Associations

Cavanaugh's Coca-Cola Christmas Collectors' Society
P.O. Box 768090
Roswell, GA 30076
ph: 800-653-1221 or 770-643-1175
fax: 770-643-1172
web: http://www.cavanaghgrp.com/
Sells modern Coca-Cola collectibles with a Christmas theme.

Old World Christmas Collectors' Club
Newsletter: Old World Christmas Star Gazette
P.O. Box 8000
Spokane, WA 99203-0030
ph: 800-962-7669 or 509-534-9000
fax: 509-534-9098
web: http://www.oldworldchristmas.com/
Club members can purchase exclusive German holiday collectibles made of wood or glass.

Man./Prod./Dist.

Kurt S. Adler
Kurt S. Adler, Inc.
1107 Broadway
New York, NY 10010
ph: 212-924-0900 or 800-243-9627
fax: 212-807-0575
The nations leading importer, designer and supplier of Christmas ornaments, decorations and accessories.

Great American Taylor Collectibles Corp.
P.O. Box 428
Aberdeen, NC 28315
Manufacturer of old world Santas.

Knobstone Studio
5809 West Oak Hill Rd.
Scottsburg, IN 47170
ph: 812-752-7022
fax: 812-752-7022
Produces collectible old world Santas; each face is an original (not molded or cast), bodies are soft sculpture.

Old World Christmas Collectors' Club
P.O. Box 8000
Spokane, WA 99203-0030
ph: 800-962-7669 or 509-534-9000
fax: 509-534-9098
web: http://www.oldworldchristmas.com/
Distributes high-quality, collectible Christmas collectibles and decorations.

Christmas (Clothtique)

Clubs/Associations

Santa Claus Network
Newsletter: Santa Claus Network Newsletter
6 Perry Drive
Foxboro, MA 02035-1051
ph: 508-543-6667 or 508-543-5412
fax: 508-543-4255
e-mail: possdreams@aol.com
Members receive free Possible Dreams Clothique (stiffened cloth) Santa and more.

Possible Dreams Limited
6 Perry Drive
Foxboro, MA 02035-1051
ph: 508-543-6667 or 508-543-5412
fax: 508-543-4255
e-mail: possdreams@aol.com
Manufacturer of the Clothique (uses a centuries-old method of stiffening cloth) line of collectible Christmas ornaments and figurines such as angels and Santa Claus.

Clarissa Johnson

Man./Prod./Dist.

Clarissa Johnson
Clarissa's Creations
18111 Meyers
Detroit, MI 48235
ph: 313-341-7762
Produces original Afro American artwork: prints, collector plates, and note and greeting cards designed by Clarissa Johnson.

Clowns

Dealers

Just Clowning Around
12401 Folsom Blvd., #203
Rancho Cordova, CA 95742
ph: 916-687-7594
web: http://www.web-images.com/justclown/
Carries modern clown collectibles: Ron Lee, Emmett Kelly Jr., Red Skelton, Melody in Motion; crystal, pewter, hand painted pewter, bells, papier mache, statues with clocks, portraits, collector plates.

Clowns (Ron Lee)

Clubs/Associations

Ron Lee's Greatest Clown Collector's Club
Newsletter: Collectible News From Ron Lee
330 Carousel Parkway
Henderson, NV 89014
ph: 800-829-3928 or 702-434-1700
fax: 702-434-4310
web: http://www.ronlee.com/
For collectors of Ron Lee's fine white metal or pewter figurines with 24-karat gold plating and hand painting; on hand-cut onyx bases with gold beading.

Man./Prod./Dist.

Ron Lee's World of Clowns
330 Carousel Parkway
Henderson, NV 89014
ph: 800-829-3928 or 702-434-1700
fax: 702-434-4310
web: http://www.ronlee.com/
Manufacturer and sculpture of clown and circus-theme collectibles; fine white metal or pewter figurines with 24-karat gold plating and hand painting; on hand-cut onyx bases with gold beading.

Computer Programs For

Man./Prod./Dist.

Russ Wood
Collector's Marketplace
Software: Intelligent Collector Software
RD 1 Box 213B
Montrose, PA 18801-9779
ph: 570-278-2099
e-mail: cmonline@epix.net
Lists secondary market products, mainly Dept. 56; also David Winter, Lilliput Lane, Swarovski, Lladro, Precious Moments, Barbie, Disney Classics, Harbour Lights, Radko, and others; developer of Windows software for collectors.

Michael Belofsky
MSdataBase Solutions
Software: Collectibles Database for Collectors
614 Warrenton Terrace NE
Leesburg, VA 22076-2465
ph: 800-407-4147 or 703-777-5660
fax: 703-777-5440
e-mail: techsupport@collectorsoft.com
web: http://www.collectorsoft.com
Windows: How many items to you own? How much have you spent? How much insured for? What items do you want? Includes on-line price guides for Prec. Mom., Hallmark Orns., Swarovski, D56, Tender Touches, Cher. Teddies, Disney Classics, others.

Cottages

(see also COLLECTIBLES [MODERN], Buildings; COLLECTIBLES [MODERN], Dept. 65)

Dealers

Joe Schulte
Gift Music Book & Collectibles
420 Wallace St.
Chicago Heights, IL 60411
ph: 708-877-7099
e-mail: jntschulte@rocketmail.com
web: http://www.beisecurity.com/gift
Carries a full line of cottages and lighthouses: Department 56, Lefton, Spencer Collin, David Winter, Lilliput Lane, Forma Vitrum, Harbour Lights, Cottontail Lane, Creepy Hollow, Fontanini, Sheila, etc.; a non-profit music group.

Man./Prod./Dist.

Department 56, Inc.
Magazine: Quarterly
P.O. Box 44456
Eden Prairie, MN 55344-1056
ph: 800-548-8696
fax: 612-943-4500
web: http://www.department56.com
Produces "Snow Village", "Dickens' Village" and other lighted houses and accessories.

Cottages (David Winter)

Clubs/Associations

Enesco David Winter Cottages Collectors Guild
Magazine: Cottage Country
225 Windsor Dr.
Itasca, IL 60143
ph: 630-875-5300 or 800-436-3726
fax: 630-875-5359
web: http://www.enesco.com/
For David Winter Cottage collectors; membership includes "Cottage Country" magazine plus the "Squeek" & "Studio News" newsletters, members-only pieces, complimentary gift from David Winter.

Ann Hamlet
Cottage Exchange, The
Newsletter: Cottage Times, The
45 The Avenue
Leighton Bromswold, Cambridgeshire PE18 0SH
U.K.
ph: +44 (0)1480-891304
fax: +44 (0)1480-891895
e-mail: dwcellar@aol.com
web: http://www.worldcollectorsnet.com/CottageExchange/
The only U.K. club for David Winter Collectors; all retired David Winter pieces available; write for a price list and any other details regarding your favorite collectible.

Dealers

Paul Fruchey
1802 Lamar Lane
Napoleon, OH 43545
ph: 419-592-0024
Specialists in retired David Winter Cottages.

Stan Worrey
Colonial House Antiques
182 Front St.
Berea, OH 44017-1920
ph: 440-826-4169 or 800-344-9299
fax: 440-826-0839
e-mail: ywhorrey@aol.com
web: http://www.colonial-house-clltbs.com/
Specializes in David Winter and Lilliput Lane cottages; mail lists on request.

Experts

Bette Page
Front Parlor, The
300 Cemetery Rd.
Oakland, IL 61943
ph: 217-346-3533 or 800-346-5996
fax: 217-346-3533
e-mail: frntprlr@advant.com
Writes monthly column about David Winter cottages for the "Collectors' Bulletin."

Cottages (Forma Vitrum)

Man./Prod./Dist.

Forma Vitrum
Newsletter: Vitreville Voice
c/o Cavanaugh Group International
1000 Holcomb Woods Parkway
Roswell, GA 30076
ph: 800-537-7899
e-mail: formavit@mindspring.com
web: http://www.formavit.com/
Manufacturer of collectible lit glass cottages handcrafted by artist Bill Job.

Cottages (Fraser Int'l.)

Man./Prod./Dist.

Fraser International
7811 North Shepherd Dr., Ste.112
Houston, TX 77088
ph: 281-260-0090 or 800-878-5448
fax: 281-260-8131
Produces handcrafted miniature cottages.

Cottages (Hawthorne)

Man./Prod./Dist.

Hawthorne Villages
9210 N. Maryland Ave.
Niles, IL 60714
ph: 847-966-0070 or 800-772-4277
web: http://www.hawthorne.com/
A leading marketer of highly detailed architectural miniatures with an emphasis on sculptures inspired by traditional architecture.

Cottages (Hopkins Shop)

Man./Prod./Dist.

Hopkins Shop
1552 Highway 52
Moncks Corner, SC 29461
ph: 843-761-7626 or 800-356-1813
fax: 843-761-7634
Create the Village Lights, a series of lighted English and turn-of-the-century American style cottages.

Cottages (Lemax)

Clubs/Associations

Gaston Lee
Lemax Collectors Club
Newsletter: Collector's Club Journal
25 Pequot Way
Canton, MA 02021-2354
ph: 888-536-2988 or 781-821-4555
fax: 781-821-4455
e-mail: lemax@earthlink.net
A company-sponsored collectors' club.

Man./Prod./Dist.

Gaston Lee
Lemax, Inc.
25 Pequot Way
Canton, MA 02021-2354
ph: 888-536-2988 or 781-821-4555
fax: 781-821-4455
e-mail: lemax@earthlink.net
Produces the Lemax Dickensvale Collectible line of fine handcrafted porcelain cathedrals, quaint cottages, and accessories.

Cottages (Lilliput Lane)

Clubs/Associations

Enesco Lilliput Lane Collectors' Club
225 Windsor Dr.
Itasca, IL 60143
ph: 630-875-5300 or 800-436-3726
fax: 630-875-5359
web: http://www.enesco.com/
For collectors of Lilliput Lane miniature cottages.

Experts

Annette Power
4 Queens Parade Close
London, N11 3FY
U.K.
ph: +44 181 361 7787
e-mail: collector@globalnet.co.uk
Author of "The Collector's Handbook of Lilliput Lane Cottages."

Man./Prod./Dist.

ENESCO Corp.
225 Windsor Dr.
Itasca, IL 60143
ph: 630-875-5300 or 800-436-3726
fax: 630-875-5359
web: http://www.enesco.com/

Cottages (Pleasantville)

Clubs/Associations

Mary Lee Graham
Pleasantville 1893 Historical Preservation Society, c/o Flambro
Newsletter: Pleasantville Gazette
1530 Ellsworth Industrial Dr.
Atlanta, GA 30318-3752
ph: 800-355-2582 or 404-352-1381
fax: 404-352-2150
e-mail: collsoc@flambro.com
web: http://www.flambro.com
Bisque porcelain village figurines by Joan Berg Victor; sponsored by Flambro, Inc; gazette, Pleasantville Gazette lighted building, lapel pin, and retailer listing.

Cottages (Windy Meadows)

Clubs/Associations

Jan Richardson
Windy Meadows Pottery Collector Club, c/o Windy Meadows Pottery
1036 Valley Rd.
Knoxville, MD 21758
ph: 301-834-8857 or 800-527-6274
fax: 301-663-0612
Specializes in the original hand-constructed stoneware Windy Meadows candlehouses & cottages designed by Jan Richardson. A company-sponsored club.

Crystal

Man./Prod./Dist.

Crystallite
963 Transport Way
Petaluma, CA 94954
ph: 800-999-9856 or 707-765-0500
fax: 707-765-0600
Distributes Austrian crystal figurines by Charles Castelli and cold-cast porcelain fantasy figurines by Mark Newman and Randy Bowen.

Crystal (Crystal Reflection)

Man./Prod./Dist.

Crystal Reflection
150 Park Lane
Brisbane, CA 94005-1312
ph: 415-468-2520
fax: 415-468-2554
A leader in the design and production of 32% Austrian lead crystal collectibles.

Crystal (Crystal World)

Man./Prod./Dist.

Crystal World Co., The
120 Industrial Ave.
Little Ferry, NJ 07643
ph: 201-931-9500 or 800-445-4251
fax: 201-931-0220
e-mail: gift@crystalworld.com
web: http://www.crystalworld.com/
America's premier producer of full-cut, faceted crystal figurines; offers a wide selection of award-winning crystal gifts and collectibles, including Disney Showcase Collection, wildlife figures, Teddy Bears, famous buildings, etc.

Crystal (Iris Arc)

Clubs/Associations

Joelene Bowen
Iris Arc Crystal Collectors Society
Newsletter: Illuminations
114 East Haley St.
Santa Barbara, CA 93101-2347
ph: 805-963-3661 or 800-392-7546
fax: 805-965-2458
e-mail: info@irisarc.com
For collectors of Iris Arc full lead crystal collectibles including cottages, ornaments, figurines, miniatures, etc.

Man./Prod./Dist.

Joelene Bowen
Iris Arc Crystal
114 East Haley St.
Santa Barbara, CA 93101-2347
ph: 805-963-3661 or 800-392-7546
fax: 805-965-2458
e-mail: info@irisarc.com
Designs and manufactures full lead crystal collectibles including cottages, ornaments, figurines, miniatures, etc.

Crystal (Silver Deer)

Clubs/Associations

Silver Deer Collectors' Club
963 Transport Way
Petaluma, CA 94954
ph: 707-765-8311 or 800-729-3337
fax: 707-765-0770
A manufacturer-sponsored club offering members-only figurines, special club activities and promotions, and a quarterly newsletter with information about designers, product retirements and upcoming events.

Man./Prod./Dist.

Brian Danziger
Silver Deer, Ltd.
963 Transport Way
Petaluma, CA 94954
ph: 707-765-8311 or 800-729-3337
fax: 707-765-0770
Designs, manufactures and distributes limited edition crystal figurines and other giftware.

Crystal (Swarovski)

Auction Services

Cindy Morton
crystal-auction.com
600 Harbor Blvd.
Union City, NJ 07087
ph: 201-865-7777
fax: 201-865-7777
e-mail: info@crystal-auction.com
web: http://www.crystal-auction.com
Auction web site for collectors of Swarovski crystal.

Clubs/Associations

Swarovski Collectors Society, c/o Swarovski America, Ltd.
Newsletter: Swarovski Collector
1 Kenney Dr.
Cranston, RI 02920
ph: 800-556-6478 or 800-426-3088
fax: 401-463-8459
e-mail: manuela.sieberer@swarovski.com
web: http://www.swarovski.com/
Focuses on Austrian Swarovski crystal figurines and giftware. Sponsored by Swarovski America, Ltd.

Collectors

Jimer DeVries
9740 Campo Road, Ste. 134
Spring Valley, CA 91977-1415
ph: 619-462-2333
fax: 619-462-5517
e-mail: jimer@swanseekers.com
web: http://www.swanseekers.com
A long-time Swarovski collector; knowledgeable about manufacturing variations and values of current and retired Swarovski Silver Crystal including items not available at retail in USA.

Dealers

Cindy Morton
Morton's Crystal
600 Harbor Blvd.
Union City, NJ 07087
ph: 201-865-7777
fax: 201-865-7777
e-mail: mail@mortonscrystal.com
web: http://www.mortonscrystal.com/

Gregg Shienbaum
Illum
30 NE 1st Street
Miami, FL 33132
ph: 800-984-5586 or 305-373-3918
fax: 305-373-3803
e-mail: illum1@aol.com
web: http://www.illumcollectibles.com
Specializing in retired, hard-to-find Lladro and Swarovski; open stock of current items of Lladro, Swarovski, and Lalique.

Lladro Connection, A
30 NE 1st Street
Miami, FL 33132
ph: 800-984-5586
e-mail: illum1@aol.com
web: http://www.illumcollectibles.com/
Specializing in current and retired Swarovski and Lladro; also carries a complete line of Lalique and Kosta Boda.

David & Angie McIntosh
Crystal Exchange America
6505 Browns Run Rd.
Middletown, OH 45042
ph: 513-423-5272
fax: 513-423-8318
e-mail: angie@crystalexchange.com
web: http://www.crystalexchange.com
Collector, dealer, expert in Swarovski crystal; buys and sells; specializing in retired and limited edition pieces.

Robin Yaw
Crystal Connection, The
Newsletter: Crystal News
8510 N. Knoxville Ave., Ste. 218
Peoria, IL 61615-2034
ph: 309-692-2221
fax: 309-692-2221
e-mail: crystalconnection@worldnet.att.net
web: http://www.crystal.org
A comprehensive listing service for collectors worldwide interested in buying, selling, trading retired Swarovski crystal on the secondary market; free listings, registration, search, courier delivery and appraisal services; member ISA.

Clark Sanchez
Sanchez Collectibles
1555 East Glendale Ave.
Phoenix, AZ 85020
ph: 602-395-9974 or 602-277-1661
fax: 602-241-0702
e-mail: sanchcol@primenet.com
web: http://www.primenet.com/~sanchcol
Buys, sells, appraises, repairs Swarovski crystal; does not sell new pieces, only pre-owned pieces no longer being manufactured; list available for free by snail mail if a mailing address is provided.

Ben Swan
Golden Swan Collectibles
881 Lincoln Way
Auburn, CA 95603
ph: 530-823-7926 or 800-231-9055
fax: 530-823-1945
Offers a "search and find" and a listing service to collectors, buyers and sellers of Lladro figurines; also for Swarovski, Walt Disney Classics, and Disneyana Convention figurines.

Experts

Jane Warner, ISA
7613 W. Frederick-Garland Rd.
Union, OH 45322-9621
ph: 937-698-4508
fax: 937-698-4508
e-mail: jane@wbrb.com
web: http://www.wbrb.com/
Appraises and specializes in Swarovski crystal; author of four Warner books now available: "Warner's Blue Ribbon Book on Swarovski Silver Crystal" (plus Companion) and "Warner's Blue Ribbon Book on Swarovski" (plus Companion).

Robin Yaw
Crystal Connection, The
8510 N. Knoxville Ave., Ste. 218
Peoria, IL 61615-2034
ph: 309-692-2221
fax: 309-692-2221
e-mail: crystalconnection@worldnet.att.net
web: http://www.crystal.org
Buy, sell, trade appraises retired Swarovski crystal on the secondary market; free listings, registration, search, courier delivery and appraisal services; Accredited Member ISA, member BBB.

Clark Sanchez
Sanchez Collectibles
1555 East Glendale Ave.
Phoenix, AZ 85020
ph: 602-395-9974 or 602-277-1661
fax: 602-241-0702
e-mail: sanchcol@primenet.com
web: http://www.primenet.com/~sanchcol
Buys, sells, appraises, repairs Swarovski crystal; does not sell new pieces, only pre-owned pieces no longer being manufactured; list available for free by snail mail if a mailing address is provided.

Jimer DeVries
Swan Seekers Network
9740 Campo Road, Ste. 134
Spring Valley, CA 91977-1415
ph: 619-462-2333
fax: 619-462-5517
e-mail: jimer@swanseekers.com
web: http://www.swanseekers.com
A long-time Swarovski collector; knowledgeable about manufacturing variations and values of current and retired Swarovski Silver Crystal including items not available at retail in USA.

Internet Resources

Cindy Morton
Morton's Crystal
600 Harbor Blvd.
Union City, NJ 07087
ph: 201-865-7777
fax: 201-865-7777
e-mail: mail@mortonscrystal.com
web: http://www.mortonscrystal.com/
Extensive informational web site for collectors of Swarovski crystal; includes many items for sale.

Pat King
Swarovski Crystal Fanatics
fax: 770-460-6869
e-mail: pking100@bellsouth.net
web: http://clubs.yahoo.com/clubs/swarovskicrystalfanatics
Web site servicing Swarovski collectors from around the world; lots of useful information, message board, evening chats, photo galleries, and links for the avid collector;

Man./Prod./Dist.

Swarovski America Ltd.
1 Kenney Dr.
Cranston, RI 02920
ph: 800-556-6478 or 800-426-3088
fax: 401-463-8459
e-mail: manuela.sieberer@swarovski.com
web: http://www.swarovski.com/

Matching Services

Jimer DeVries
Swan Seekers Network
9740 Campo Road, Ste. 134
Spring Valley, CA 91977-1415
ph: 619-462-2333
fax: 619-462-5517
e-mail: jimer@swanseekers.com
web: http://www.swanseekers.com
Dedicated strictly to the Swarovski secondary market; buy, sell, trade or information about retired and current Swarovski Silver Crystal for collectors in USA and 38 other countries; over 7500 retired items listed.

Periodicals

Dean A. Genth
Newsletter: Crystal Report, The
1322 N. Barron St.
Eaton, OH 45320-1016
ph: 937-456-4151
fax: 937-456-7851
e-mail: dean@millershallmark.com
web: http://www.millershallmark.com
The international forum for collectors of retired Swarovski silver crystal: histories, secondary market reports and prices, information on variations, collector questions and answers, classified ads.

Jimer DeVries
Newsletter: Swan Seekers News
9740 Campo Road, Ste. 134
Spring Valley, CA 91977-1415
ph: 619-462-2333
fax: 619-462-5517
e-mail: jimer@swanseekers.com
web: http://www.swanseekers.com
Dedicated to the Swarovski secondary market; published three times per year; provides information about retired Swarovski crystal pieces: articles on connoisseurship, Q&A, collector profiles, sales, prices, wanted list.

Repair Services

Randy Edwards
Crystal Doctor, The
3633 Bramble Rd.
Jacksonville, FL 32210
ph: 904-781-9702
fax: 904-786-3346
e-mail: CrystalDoc@aol.com
web: http://www.crystalfoxgallery.com/cleaning.htm
Specializes in all restored Swarovski

items; uses only genuine Swarovski replacement parts and guarantees the price and value will be fully restored.

Danbury Mint

Man./Prod./Dist.

Danbury Mint, The
47 Richards Ave.
Norwalk, CT 06857
ph: 203-853-2000 or 800-243-4664
fax: 203-847-5251
A direct mail marketer of collector plates. Also produces miniatures, dolls, figurines and other collectibles.

Dept. 56

Clubs/Associations

Newsletter: Village Pride!
735 Don Mills Rd., Ste. 2306
Toronto, ON M3C 1T1
Canada
ph: 416-425-4972
fax: 416-425-4972
e-mail: d56pride@aol.com
web: http://members.aol.com/d56pride/intro.html
A monthly publication for collectors of Department 56 villages.

Collectors

Sue Coffee
10 Saunders Hollow Rd.
Old Lyme, CT 06371-1126
ph: 860-434-5641
fax: 860-434-2653
e-mail: SueCoffee@aol.com
web: http://www.suecoffee.com/
Buys and sells retired Dept. 56 snowbabies.

Dealers

Ken & Jamie Boucher
Northeast Collectors Exchange
145 W 5th St.
Bloomsburg, PA 17815-2119
ph: 800-231-6364 or 570-784-4377
A brokerage and listing service for retired collectibles; specializes in Dept. 56 Villages, Snowbabies and accessories.

Becky Carter
Becky Carter, Inc.
9605 Red Bird Lane
Alpharetta, GA 30202-7101
ph: 770-475-8138
Specializes in Department 56: all villages, accessories, ornaments, snowglobes; also offers a full-service collectibles exchange for Department 56 items.

Linda Ross Hughes
Best Collectibles
Newsletter: Best Collectibles
16151 Morganton Highway
P.O. Box 152
Morganton, GA 30560-0152
ph: 706-838-5920
fax: 706-838-4008
e-mail: bestcoll@mail.tds.net
web: http://www.bestcollectibles.com/
An independent exchange service specializing in listing and selling retired and limited edition collectibles for most major collectible lines.

Partridge Christmas Shop, The
105 Riverwalk
New Orleans, LA 70130
ph: 504-566-0149
Sells Heritage Village, Snow Village, Disney Parks Village.

Lynda W. Blakenship
Dickens' Exchange, Inc.
5150 Highway 22, Ste. C-16
Mandeville, LA 70471-2515
ph: 504-845-1954
fax: 504-845-1873
e-mail: de@dickensexchange.com
web: http://www.dickensexchange.com/
Carries a complete line of Dept. 56 villages and accessories; offers an exchange service to match buyer and seller of Dept. 56 ceramic cottages.

Experts

Peter & Jeanne George
Collectible Source, Inc., The
757 Park Ave.
Cranston, RI 02910-2137
ph: 401-467-9343
fax: 401-467-9359
e-mail: d56er@aol.com
web: http://www.villagechronicle.com/
Publishers of "The Village Chronicle."

Linda Harlan
303 Murfreesboro Rd.
Nashville, TN 37210-2834
ph: 800-388-2556 or 615-832-0564
fax: 615-244-1553
Collector specializing in Dept. 56 ceramic cottages and other Dept. 56 collectibles.

Man./Prod./Dist.

Department 56, Inc.
Magazine: Quarterly
P.O. Box 44456
Eden Prairie, MN 55344-1056
ph: 800-548-8696
fax: 612-943-4500
web: http://www.department56.com
Produces "Snow Village", "Dickens' Village" and other lighted houses and accessories.

Periodicals

Peter & Jeanne George
Collectible Source, Inc., The
Magazine: Village Chronicle, The
757 Park Ave.
Cranston, RI 02910-2137
ph: 401-467-9343
fax: 401-467-9359
e-mail: d56er@aol.com
web: http://www.villagechronicle.com/
The largest independent publication for Department 56 collectors; the latest news, tips, information, display ideas, informative articles; "All the News that's Lit to Print!"

Linda Harlan
Newsletter: Snowflake News
303 Murfreesboro Rd.
Nashville, TN 37210-2834
ph: 800-388-2556 or 615-832-0564
fax: 615-244-1553
A newsletter for Dept. 56 collectors: published bi-monthly, photos, club activities, upcoming activities, collector profiles.

Lynda W. Blakenship
Dickens' Exchange, Inc.
Magazine: Dickens' Exchange
5150 Highway 22, Ste. C-16
Mandeville, LA 70471-2515
ph: 504-845-1954
fax: 504-845-1873
e-mail: de@dickensexchange.com
web: http://www.dickensexchange.com/
A magazine for collectors of "Dept. 56" items: Dickens, Alpine, New England, Snow Village & Snowbabies; ads, articles, prices.

Paul & Mirta Burns
Newsletter: Vintages Classified
P.O. Box 34166
Granada Hills, CA 91344-9166
ph: 818-368-6765
fax: 818-360-6612
A monthly newsletter with buy and sell ads, articles, regional club news, photos of new releases.

Dolls

(see also DOLLS)

Auction Services

Nancy Farley
Auctions by Nancy
505 Trelawney Lane
Apex, NC 27502
ph: 919-362-7235
e-mail: info@auctionsbynancy.com
web: http://www.auctionsbynancy.com/
Conducts auction sales of collectible dolls.

Book Sellers

Scott Publications
30595 Eight Mile
Livonia, MI 48152-1798
ph: 800-458-8237 or 248-477-6650
fax: 248-477-6795
e-mail: 104137.1254@compuserve.com
Issues free catalog (specify dolls, ceramics or miniatures) of books offering an array of information on ceramics, china painting, doll crafting, doll collecting, and miniatures.

Clubs/Associations

Jeanne Niswonger
Modern Doll Club
Journal: Modern Doll Club Journal
305 West Beacon Rd.
Lakeland, FL 33803
ph: 941-682-8484
A corresponding club for doll collectors; members receive illustrated journal featuring research articles, doll stories, craft ideas for dolls, patterns, paper dolls, photos, etc.

Shelley Thornton, Sec.
National Institute of American Doll Artists
1600 South 22nd St.
Lincoln, NE 68502
ph: 402-474-7948
e-mail: shelley@forus.com
web: http://www.niada.org/
An organization of doll artists and supportive patrons whose purpose is to promote the art of the original, handmade doll.

Dealers

A. Mann
Doll Art Sale at Art of the Doll
39 Newbury St., Ste. 208
Boston, MA 02116
ph: 617-266-6266
e-mail: art@dollartsale.com
web: http://www.dollartsale.com/
Deals in one-of-a-kind and very small editions of dolls created by doll artists; website also has lots of fun pages for the artist and collector alike.

N. Mann
Mann Gallery
39 Newbury St., Ste. 208
Boston, MA 02116
ph: 617-266-6266
e-mail: artmann@worldnet.att.net
web: http://www.manngallery.com
Appraiser, collector and dealer in art dolls; mixed media figurative sculptures by artists from varied disciplines.

Doll Menagerie, The
127-6 Rouote 23
Hamburg, NJ 07419
ph: 973-209-2828
fax: 973-209-2030
e-mail: menagere@warwick.net
web: http://www.dollmenagerie.com
Specializing in collectible dolls from the finest artists and companies in the world; online catalog features over 60 of these artists and companies.

Nancy Pelham
Homestead Gift Shop
4 Hillwood Lane
Catskill, NY 12414
ph: 518-943-4371
e-mail: fluffy@capital.net
web: http://www.homestead-gift-shop.com
Sells new manufactured dolls from Hamilton, Georgetown, Daddy's Long Legs, Kingstate, Seymour Mann and others; also doll furniture.

Sharon Greenfield
Sharon's Dolls
Rte. 1, Box 235-R
Martinsburg, WV 25401
ph: 304-267-4882
Specializes in original artist and limited edition dolls.

Doll Market, The
4215 Highpoint Rd.
Greensboro, NC 27407
ph: 336-632-4600 or 800-432-DOLL
fax: 336-632-4466
Carries limited edition and collector dolls from scores of artists.

Jean's Dolls
616 12th St.
West Columbia, SC 29169
ph: 803-791-7421 or 803-799-1382
Sells wide range of contemporary artists dolls.

Littlest Princess Doll Shoppe, The
6365 Spalding Dr.
Norcross, GA 30092
ph: 770-446-8909
fax: 770-446-7103
Disney, Gunzel, limited editions, Alexander, Zook, Barbie, Annalee, Gotz, Royal, Susan Wakeen.

Celia's & Susan's Dolls & Collectibles
800 East Hallandale Beach Blvd.
Hallandale, FL 33009
ph: 954-458-0661
fax: 954-458-5609
Barbie, Lee Middleton, Susan Wakeen, Effanbee, Connie Walser Derek, Robin Woods, Madame Alexander, Gotz, R. John Wright, Julie Good-Kruger, Georgetown, Turner, Gunzel, Wendy Lawton, Fayzah Spanos, Zook, Himstedt, Steiff, etc.

Beckett's Doll House
646 High Street
Columbus, OH 43085-4106
ph: 614-848-9636
Madame Alexander, Annette Himstedt, Barbie, Effanbee, Pfaltzgraff, Ginny.

Lots of Dolls
215 Garfield Ave.
Milford, OH 45150
ph: 513-248-2151 or 800-755-6402
Sells older and contemporary artists dolls; Barbies, Robin Wood, Ashton Drake, Annalees, Steiff, Alexanders, Wendy Lawton, Annette Himstedt, Hartman, etc.

Internet Resources

Flossy Eddy
Flossy's Dolls & Collectibles
153 Sundance Dr.
Grand Junction, CO 81503
ph: 970-242-1358
e-mail: flossydolls@youfoundme.com
web: http://www.youfoundme.com/flossy.htm
Large online website for doll enthusiasts: Barbie, fast food toys, Beanie Babies, doll tips and terms, collectible dolls chat room, and more; dolls, free classifieds, collector books.

Rashida Young
DollLuvr's
15040 Bahama St.
North Hills, CA 91343
ph: 818-894-9331
fax: 818-893-3055
e-mail: DollLuvr01@aol.com
web: http://members.aol.com/DollLuvr01

Periodicals

Beth Schwartz, Ed.
House of White Birches
Magazine: Doll World
306 East Parr Rd.
Berne, IN 46711
ph: 219-589-8741 or 800-829-5865
fax: 219-589-8093
A bi-monthly magazine which covers many aspects of dolls and doll collecting: articles on doll history, patterns, interviews with doll artists, how-to articles, doll ID, etc.

Scott Publications
Magazine: Doll Crafter
30595 Eight Mile
Livonia, MI 48152-1798
ph: 800-458-8237 or 248-477-6650
fax: 248-477-6795
e-mail: 104137.1254@compuserve.com
Most complete magazine for creating and collecting beautiful dolls; filled with beautiful color photos of antique reproduction and modern dolls, patterns; informative articles by experts on how-to make, collect, costume and sculpt dolls.

Scott Publications
Magazine: Contemporary Doll Collector
30595 Eight Mile
Livonia, MI 48152-1798
ph: 800-458-8237 or 248-477-6650
fax: 248-477-6795
e-mail: 104137.1254@compuserve.com
Award-winning magazine covers the vast doll market for doll lovers; how-to collect, where to buy, restoring your dolls and display ideas; published bi-monthly; breathtaking color photos of dolls.

Scott Publications
Magazine: Ceramic Arts & Crafts
30595 Eight Mile
Livonia, MI 48152-1798
ph: 800-458-8237 or 248-477-6650
fax: 248-477-6795
e-mail: 104137.1254@compuserve.com
The "Bible" for the ceramic hobbyist since 1955; each monthly issue filled with projects and patterns, celebrity clips, new products, show listings, industry news, shoppers guides, book reviews, ads and classifieds.

Joe Jones
Jones Publishing, Inc.
Magazine: Dollmaking
P.O. Box 5000
Iola, WI 54945
ph: 715-445-5000 or 800-331-0038
fax: 715-445-4053
e-mail: jonespub@gglbbs.com
web: http://www.dollmakingartisan.com/
A bi-monthly magazine of dollmaking projects and plans for makers of porcelain and sculpted modern dolls; beautifully and lavishly illustrated.

Joe Jones
Jones Publishing, Inc.
Magazine: Doll Artisan
P.O. Box 5000
Iola, WI 54945
ph: 715-445-5000 or 800-331-0038
fax: 715-445-4053
e-mail: jonespub@gglbbs.com
web: http://www.dollmakingartisan.com/
A bi-monthly publication of reproduction porcelain dollmaking, projects, and plans illustrated with photos of antique and reproduction dolls.

Brian Savage
Fun Publications
Newspaper: Master Collector
225 Cattle Barron Parc Dr.
Fort Worth, TX 76108
ph: 800-772-6673 or 817-448-9863
fax: 817-448-9843
e-mail: brian@mastercollector.com
web: http://www.mastercollector.com
Ads-only newspaper; dolls (antique and modern collectible), toys, banks, models, cars, Matchbox, monsters, puzzles, political, toy trains, etc.; subscribers receive free 30 word ad each month; published monthly; reaches 20,000.

Dolls (American Girl)

Dealers

American Girl/Pleasant Company
8400 Fairway Place
Middleton, WI 53562
ph: 800-845-0005
e-mail: im_cs@americangirl.com
web: http://www.americangirl.com/
The "Fun For Girls" section of the American Girl web site features activities, games, puzzles, polls, advice, and more based on the American Girls Collection and American Girl magazine; web site intended for girls ages 8 and older.

Dolls (Annette Himstedt)

Clubs/Associations

Annette Himstedt Collector Club
Karl Schurz Strasse 27
Paderborn, D-33110
Germany
ph: +49 (0) 5251 521717
fax: +49 (0) 5251 521730
e-mail: annette.himstedt@owl-online.de
web: http://www.annettehimstedt.com/
Original artist dolls by Annette Himstedt.

Dolls (Ashton-Drake)

Dealers

Bobbi Stavros
12 Arlington Rd.
Burlington, MA 01803
ph: 781-273-0293
Specializing in Gene/Ashton Drake, current and discontinued.

Man./Prod./Dist.

Ashton-Drake Galleries, The
9200 Maryland Ave.
Niles, IL 60648-1397
ph: 847-581-8057 or 800-634-5164
fax: 847-966-3026
e-mail: custsrv@ashtondrake.com
web: http://www.ashtondrake.com/
Direct mail marketer of dolls by various designers such as Yolando Bello, Dianna Effner, Cindy M. McClure, and Kathy Hippensteel.

Dolls (Attic Babies)

Clubs/Associations

Attic Babies Collectors Club
P.O. Box 2475
Stillwater, OK 74076
ph: 918-352-4414 or 888-622-2437
e-mail: babies@galstar.com
web: http://www.ctechbis.com/Attic%20Babies2/ATTIC/CLUB.HTM

Man./Prod./Dist.

Attic Babies
P.O. Box 2475
Stillwater, OK 74076
ph: 918-352-4414 or 888-622-2437
e-mail: babies@galstar.com
web: http://www.ctechbis.com/Attic%20Babies2/ATTIC/CLUB.HTM
Manufacturer of Attic Babies dolls.

Dolls (Bradley)

Clubs/Associations

Joanna Harstein
Bradley's Collectibles Doll Club
Newsletter: Bradley Doll Club Newsletter
1400 North Spring St.
Los Angeles, CA 90012
ph: 323-221-4162
fax: 323-221-8272
Focuses on the collectible dolls issued by Bradley Collectibles. A manufacturer-sponsored club.

Dolls (Daddy's Long Legs)

Clubs/Associations

Daddy's Long Legs Collector's Club
Newsletter: Daddy's Long Legs Newsletter
300 Bank St.
Southlake, TX 76092-9972
ph: 817-488-4644 or 888-2-DADDYS
A club sponsored by the manufacturer, KVC, Inc.

Man./Prod./Dist.

KVC, Inc.
300 Bank St.
Southlake, TX 76092-9972
ph: 817-488-4644 or 888-2-DADDYS
Produces Daddy's Long Legs dolls.

Dolls (Effanbee)

Clubs/Associations

Effanbee Doll Cub
ph: 888-272-2363 or 804-458-0735
e-mail: pacenet@pacenetinc.com
web: http://www.effnbeedolls.com/directory_page.html

Man./Prod./Dist.

Effanbee Doll Company
ph: 888-272-2363 or 804-458-0735
e-mail: pacenet@pacenetinc.com
web: http://www.effnbeedolls.com/directory_page.html

Dolls (Federica Kasabasic)

Man./Prod./Dist.

Federica Dolls of Fine Art
4501 West Highland Rd.
Milford, MI 48380
ph: 800-421-3655 or 248-887-9575
fax: 248-887-9575
web: http://www.federicadollsco.com/
Produces dolls in the highest quality vinyl and porcelain.

Dolls (Georgetown Collection)

Man./Prod./Dist.

Georgetown Collection, Inc.
P.O. Box 9730
Portland, ME 04104-5030
ph: 800-626-3330
fax: 207-775-6457
A direct mail marketer of heirloom quality collectibles, including porcelain dolls and figurines.

Dolls (Good-Kruger)

Man./Prod./Dist.

Good-Kruger Dolls
5015 Lincoln Way #B
Kinzers, PA 17535-9709
Manufactures dolls designed by Julie Good-Kruger.

Dolls (Lee Middleton)

Clubs/Associations

Lee Middleton Collectors Club
Newsletter: Our Doll family
1301 Washington Blvd.
Belpre, OH 45714-2242
ph: 740-423-1717 or 800-238-2225
fax: 740-423-5983
e-mail: club@leemiddleton.com
web: http://www.leemiddleton.com/
For collectors of original porcelain and vinyl dolls designed by artists Lee Middleton and Reva Schick.

Man./Prod./Dist.

Becky Richardson
Lee Middleton Original Dolls, Inc.
1301 Washington Blvd.
Belpre, OH 45714-2242
ph: 740-423-1717 or 800-238-2225
fax: 740-423-5983
e-mail: club@leemiddleton.com
web: http://www.leemiddleton.com/
The sole manufacturer and producer of original porcelain and vinyl dolls designed by artists Lee Middleton and Reva Schick.

Dolls (Lenox)

Man./Prod./Dist.

Lenox Collections/Gorham
P.O. Box 519
Langhorne, PA 19047-0519
ph: 215-750-6900 or 800-225-1779
fax: 215-750-7362
e-mail: Lenox_Collections@b-f.com
web: http://www.lenoxcollections.com
Producers of the Lenox Collection/Gorham line of collectible porcelain dolls.

Lexington Hall Ltd., c/o The Wimbledon Collection
P.O. Box 21948
Lexington, KY 40522-1948
ph: 606-277-8531 or 606-277-8532
fax: 606-277-9231
The Wimbledon Collection, more widely known as Lexington Hall Dolls, produces high-quality porcelain dolls.

Dolls (Lizzie High)

Clubs/Associations

Lizzie High Society
Newsletter: Lizzie High Notebook
220 North Main St.
Sellersville, PA 18960
ph: 215-453-8200 or 800-763-0557
fax: 215-453-8155
web: http://www.lizziehigh.com/
Wooden folk art dolls by husband and wife Peter Wisber and Barbara Kafka Wisber.

Man./Prod./Dist.

Ladie & Friends
220 North Main St.
Sellersville, PA 18960
ph: 215-453-8200 or 800-763-0557
fax: 215-453-8155
web: http://www.lizziehigh.com/
Producers of the Lizzie High doll collection.

Dolls (Madame Alexander)

Clubs/Associations

Billie Stevens
Madame Alexander Doll Club
Newsletter: Review
P.O. Box 330
Mundeline, IL 60060
ph: 847-949-9200
fax: 847-949-9201
e-mail: office@madc.org
web: http://www.madc.org/
Members receive the "Madame Alexander Shopper" which is devoted to buying and selling Madame Alexander dolls and accessories.

Collectors

Elaine DeVylder
2 Weed Circle
Stamford, CT 06902-4414

Leah Sargent
74 The Oaks
Roslyn, NY 11576
ph: 800-421-9912 or 516-621-7517

Experts

Jane Sarasohn-Kahn
355 Friendship Dr.
Paoli, PA 19301-1206
ph: 610-296-5085
fax: 610-296-8278
e-mail: jskahn@aol.com
web: http://www.csmonline.com/barbie/barbcolm.html
Author of "Contemporary Barbie 1980 to Present," "Contemporary Barbie, 1998 Edition" (2nd edition), and "Notes From a Friend of the Barbie Doll" and "Regarding the Doll" monthly columns.

Man./Prod./Dist.

Alexander Doll Company, Inc.
615 West 131 St.
New York, NY 10027
ph: 212-283-5900
fax: 212-283-4901
e-mail: Design@alexdoll.com
web: http://www.alexanderdoll.com/
Manufactures, produces and/or distributes Madame Alexander dolls.

Dolls (Marie Osmond)

Man./Prod./Dist.

L.L. Knickerbocker Co., Inc.
25800 Commercentre Drive
Lake Forest, CA 92630
ph: 800-779-5335 or 949-595-7900
e-mail: vincentmon@knickerbocker.com
web: http://www.knickerbocker.com/

Dolls (Naber)

Periodicals

Newsletter: Naber Kids News Report
8915 S. Suncoast Blvd.
Homosassa, FL 34446
Monthly newsletter containing information for doll collectors and enthusiasts alike; focuses on Naber dolls.

Dolls (Nancy Ann Storybook)

Clubs/Associations

Judy Svoboda
Nancy Ann Clearing House
2504 Pioneer
Grand Island, NE 68801

Dolls (Phyllis Parkins)

Clubs/Associations

Phyllis Parkins
Phyllis' Collectors Club
Newsletter: PCC Newsletter
Rte. 4 Box 503
Rolla, MO 65401-9300
ph: 573-364-7849 or 800-874-7120
fax: 573-364-2448
web: http://www.thecollectables.com/
Focuses on the Phyllis Parkins' collectible dolls, treetop angels, and a line of Victorian jewelry and frames. Sponsored by The Collectables, Inc.

Man./Prod./Dist.

Collectables, The
Rte. 4 Box 503
Rolla, MO 65401-9300
ph: 573-364-7849 or 800-874-7120
fax: 573-364-2448
web: http://www.thecollectables.com/
Produces Phyllis Parkins' collectible dolls, treetop angels, and a line of Victorian jewelry and frames.

Dolls (Prestige)

Man./Prod./Dist.

Prestige Dolls
P.O. Box 1081
Gresham, OR 97030
ph: 503-667-1008
Produces limited edition happy-face dolls based on the designs of Caroline Kandt-Lloyd.

Dolls (Robin Woods)

Collectors

Elaine DeVylder
2 Weed Circle
Stamford, CT 06902-4414
Wants cloth or vinyl "Robin Woods" dolls.

Dolls (Seymour Mann)

Clubs/Associations

Seymour Mann Collectible Doll Club
P.O. Box 2046
Madison Square Station
New York, NY 10159
ph: 212-683-7262
e-mail: smanninc@aol.com
For collectors of the Seymour Mann Signature Collection of collectible dolls.

Man./Prod./Dist.

Seymour Mann, Inc.
230 Fifth Ave., Rm. 102
New York, NY 10010
ph: 212-683-7262
fax: 212-213-4920
Produces the Seymour Mann Signature Collection of collectible dolls, as well as a cat musical collection featuring cats in whimsical settings accompanied by popular tunes; also unique collectible teapots.

Dolls (Susan Wakeen)

Man./Prod./Dist.

Susan Wakeen Doll Company, Inc.
P.O. Box 1321
Litchfield, CT 06759-1321
ph: 860-567-0007
fax: 860-567-5334
e-mail: info@susanwakeendolls.com
web: http://www.susanwakeendolls.com/Default.htm
Manufactures collectible vinyl and porcelain dolls designed by Susan Wakeen.

Dolls (Terri Lee)

Clubs/Associations

Susan Girardot
Terri Lee Collectors Club
Newsletter: TL Love of a Lifetime
05432 State Route 119
Minster, OH 45865
ph: 419-628-3405
e-mail: gdot@bright.net
web: http://members.aol.com/Gdot2/
A newsletter for Terri Lee collectors; annual convention.

Collectors

Terry Bukowski
3010 Sunland Dr.
Alamogordo, NM 88310
ph: 505-427-4422
e-mail: bukowski@wazoo.com
Collector of Terri Lee dolls.

Periodicals

Terry Bukowski
Newsletter: Daisy Chain Newsletter
3010 Sunland Dr.
Alamogordo, NM 88310
ph: 505-427-4422
e-mail: bukowski@wazoo.com
A quarterly newsletter about Terri Lee dolls: color photos, articles, want and for sale ads, birthday club, and a Christmas card.

Dolls (Wendy Lawton)

Clubs/Associations

Lawton Collectors Guild
Newsletter: Lawton Collectors Guild Newsletter
P.O. Box 969
Turlock, CA 95381-0969
ph: 209-632-3655
fax: 209-632-6788
Original artist dolls by artist Wendy Lawton.

Man./Prod./Dist.

Lawton Doll Company
548 North First
Turlock, CA 95380-3804
ph: 209-632-3655
fax: 209-632-6788
Original artist dolls by artist Wendy Lawton.

Dolls (Wimbledon)

Man./Prod./Dist.

Wimbledon Collection
P.O. Box 21948
Lexington, KY 40522-1948
ph: 606-277-8531
fax: 606-277-9231

Dolls (Xavier Roberts)

(see DOLLS, Cabbage Patch Kids)

Dolls (Zook)

Man./Prod./Dist.

Debbie O'Neal
Johannes Zook Originals
1519 S. Badour Rd.
Midland, MI 48640
ph: 517-835-9388
Limited edition collectible vinyl dolls, 22" tall, which are sculpted after real children.

Donald Zolan

Collectors

Jo Hancock
Jo's Antiques & Collectibles
621 S. Main St.
Nashville, AR 71852-2707
ph: 870-845-1070
Sells Donald Zolan items, also Lenox collectibles, Cybis figurines, Pickard, Royal Bonn, and Art Glass by Moser, Loetz, Webb, etc.

Duncan Royale

Clubs/Associations

Duncan Royale Collectors Club
Newsletter: Royale Courier
1141 South Acacia Ave.
Fulerton, CA 92631
ph: 714-879-1360
fax: 714-879-4611
e-mail: duncan@duncanroyale.com
web: http://www.duncanroyale.com
Focuses on the collectible figurines, graphics and plates issued by Duncan Royale; sponsored by Duncan Royale Co.

Man./Prod./Dist.

Duncan Royale Co.
1141 South Acacia Ave.
Fulerton, CA 92631
ph: 714-879-1360
fax: 714-879-4611
e-mail: duncan@duncanroyale.com
web: http://www.duncanroyale.com
Produces collectible figurines, graphics, ornaments, and plates.

Eggs

Man./Prod./Dist.

eggspressions!
1635 Deadwood Ave.
Rapid City, SD 57702-0353
ph: 800-551-9138 or 605-342-4268
fax: 605-342-8699
Manufacturer of decorated porcelain eggs containing jewels, cute bunnies, foliage or other decorations.

Figurines

Dealers

Peggy Guy
Happy Pastime
P.O. Box 1225
Ellicott City, MD 21041-1225
ph: 410-203-1101
e-mail: hpastime@bellatlantic.net
web: http://www.happypastime.com/
Buys and sells; specializes in Royal Doulton, M.I. Hummel, Royal Copenhagen, Bing & Grondahl, Lladro, Goebel, Beswick, Royal Worcester.

Robert Goins
Replacements Ltd.
P.O. Box 26029
1089 Knox Road
Greensboro, NC 27420
ph: 800-737-5223 or 336-697-3000
fax: 336-697-3100
e-mail: replaceltd@aol.com
web: http://www.replacements.com
Carries post-1960 limited edition figurines in addition to china, crystal and flatware (obsolete, active and inactive.)

Stan Worrey
Colonial House Antiques
182 Front St.
Berea, OH 44017-1920
ph: 440-826-4169 or 800-344-9299
fax: 440-826-0839
e-mail: ywhorrey@aol.com
web: http://www.colonial-house-clltbs.com/
Specializes in old Royal Doultons, Hummels, David Winter & Lilliput Lane Cottages; mail list on request.

Joe Schulte
Gift Music Book & Collectibles
420 Wallace St.
Chicago Heights, IL 60411
ph: 708-877-7099
e-mail: jntschulte@rocketmail.com
web: http://www.beisecurity.com/gift
Carries a full line of figurines: Seraphim Angels, Swarovski, Precious Moments, Memories of Yesterday, Anri, Cherished Teddies, Fontanini, Lladro, Hummel, All God's Children, Sports Impressions, Emmett Kelly, Rockwell, etc.

Emily's Hallmark & Collectibles
14855 Clayton Rd.
Chesterfield, MO 63017
ph: 314-391-8755 or 800-726-0440
fax: 314-391-8755
web: http://www.collectibles.net/naled/emilys/
Sell modern figurines: Precious Moments, Armani, Lladro, Walt Disney Classics and Enchanted Places, Harbour Lights, Swarovski, David Winter cottages, Dept. 56, Cherished Teddies, etc.

Man./Prod./Dist.

H & G Studios
5660 Corporate Way
West Palm Beach, FL 33407
ph: 561-615-9900 or 800-777-1333
fax: 561-615-8400
Produces collectible plates, figurines, dolls and graphics by leading artists; exclusive distributor of M.I. Hummel music boxes in North America.

David Grossman Creations, Inc.
1608 North Warson Rd.
Saint Louis, MO 63132-1028
ph: 314-423-5600
fax: 314-423-7620
e-mail: dgcrea@aol.com
Creates and markets resin/porcelain sculptures and other collectible art.

Donna Lamb
United Design Corp.
P.O. Box 1200
Noble, OK 73068-1200
ph: 800-727-4883 or 405-872-3468
fax: 405-360-4442
e-mail: udc@ionet.net
web: http://www.united-design.com/
A producer of figurines by sculptors Donna Kennicutt, Suzan Bradford, Larry Miller, Ken Memoli and Penni Jo Jonas; publishes "PenniBear Post" newsletter twice a year and "The Legend of Santa Claus" newsletter once a year.

Periodicals

Cowles Magazines, Inc.
Magazine: Figurines & Collectibles
741 Miller Dr. SE, Ste. D2
Harrisburg, PA 20175
ph: 717-540-6617 or 800-829-3340
fax: 717-540-6706
e-mail: brentd@cowles.com
web: http://www.cowles.com/maglist.html
A vehicle for both the advertiser and the reader with a vehicle to sell and buy figurines; covers porcelain, resin, crystal, and pewter figurines - both new and old; secondary market information.

Scott Publications
Magazine: Figurines & Collectibles
30595 Eight Mile
Livonia, MI 48152-1798
ph: 800-458-8237 or 248-477-6650
fax: 248-477-6795
e-mail: 104137.1254@compuserve.com
Bi-monthly magazine showcasing contemporary collectibles, primarily figurines, for beginning as well as experienced collectors.

Figurines (All God's Children)

Clubs/Associations

Kathy Martin, Dir.
All God's Children Collector's Club
Magazine: All God's Children Collector's Edition
P.O. Box 5038
Gadsden, AL 35905-0038
ph: 256-492-0221
fax: 256-492-0261
Focuses on All God's Children figurines; offers members personal checklist and the opportunity to purchase members-only figurines.

Man./Prod./Dist.

Miss Martha Originals, Inc.
P.O. Box 5038
Glencoe, AL 35905
ph: 256-492-0221
fax: 256-492-0261
Manufacturer of nostalgic figurines cast from original sculptures by Martha Holocombe.

Figurines (Andrea by Sadek)

Collectors

A. Grisham
11101 Anderson, Ste. 203
Little Rock, AR 72212
ph: 501-868-1020

Figurines (Anri)

Clubs/Associations

Vicki Farris
ANRI Collectors Society
Newsletter: ANRI Collector Society Newsletter
P.O. Box 380760
Duncanville, TX 75138-0760
ph: 800-730-2674 or 972-283-8378
fax: 972-283-3522
e-mail: anriwood@aol.com
web: http://www.anri.com
Caters to collector; information on new products, exclusive figures for purchase, limited research on old pieces.

Collectors

Joe Iozzia
P.O. Box 1005
Pomona, NJ 08240-1005
ph: 609-652-8504
fax: 609-652-8888
e-mail: pinflyers@aol.com
web: http://members.aol.com/Pinflyers/anri.html
Buys and sells vintage Anri handcarved items made in Italy; buys entire collections; also bottle stoppers, nutcrackers, humidors, napkin rings, bar sets and more; only wants carved figural items from Italy.

Experts

Philly Rains
1401 Brentwood Dr.
Harrison, AR 72601
ph: 870-743-2040
fax: 870-743-2120
e-mail: phillyr@yournet.com
web: http://members.aol.com/corkskrue/philly.htm
Expert in old ANRI Italian wood carvings, 1912 through 1970s; non-limited editions only, including nutcrackers, bar sets, figurines, napkin rings, smoking accessories, and bottle stoppers; appraisals $25 per item; no limited editions.

Man./Prod./Dist.

Vicki Farris
ANRI U.S.
P.O. Box 380760
Duncanville, TX 75138-0760
ph: 800-730-2674 or 972-283-8378
fax: 972-283-3522
e-mail: anriwood@aol.com
web: http://www.anri.com
Import and distribution of high-end collectible ANRI wooden hand carved maple figurines; emphasis on Nativity sets and religious items, also animals, children, and chess sets.

Figurines (Armani)

Clubs/Associations

Giuseppe Armani Society
Magazine: Giuseppe Armani Review
300 Mac Lane
Keasbey, NJ 08832
ph: 732-417-0330 or 800-327-6264
fax: 732-417-0031
e-mail: miller_society@prodigy.com
web: http://www.the-society.com
For fans and collectors of the cold cast porcelain figurines of master sculptor Giuseppe Armani.

Dealers

A.D. & Pat Clay
Clemons-Eicken Fine European Imports
6166 N. Scottsdale Rd., #204
Scottsdale, AZ 85253
ph: 602-998-9042 or 800-250-5423
fax: 602-998-3755
Carries Lladro, Armani, Boehm, Lalique, Cybis.

Experts

Herb Miller
Miller Import Co.
300 Mac Lane
Keasbey, NJ 08832
ph: 732-417-0330 or 800-327-6264
fax: 732-417-0031
e-mail: miller_society@prodigy.com
web: http://www.the-society.com

Sid Perkins
Roberta's Place
4972 North Pine Rd.
Fort Lauderdale, FL 33351

Figurines (Bridal)

Man./Prod./Dist.

Today's Creations, Inc.
167 Main St.
Lodi, NJ 07644
ph: 800-5TO-DAYS
Manufacturer of hand-painted 8" high bridal figurines.

Figurines (Bunny Toes)

Man./Prod./Dist.

Pacific Rim Import Corp.
5930 Fourth Ave. S.
Seattle, WA 98108
ph: 800-425-5932
fax: 206-767-9179
Manufacturers of resin molded "Bunny Toes" figurines.

Figurines (Byers)

Clubs/Associations

Caroler Chronicle, The
4355 County Line Road
P.O. Box 158
Chalfont, PA 18914
ph: 215-822-6700
fax: 215-822-3847
e-mail: support@byerschoice.com
web: http://www.byerschoice.com/
For collectors of Byers caroling figurines.

Dealers

Linda's Originals & The Yankee Craftsmen
230 Rt. 6A
Brewster, MA 02631
ph: 800-385-4758
Buy and sell new and old Byers Choice Carolers dolls.

Linda Ross Hughes
Best Collectibles
Newsletter: Best Collectibles
16151 Morganton Highway
P.O. Box 152
Morganton, GA 30560-0152
ph: 706-838-5920
fax: 706-838-4008
e-mail: bestcoll@mail.tds.net
web: http://www.bestcollectibles.com/
A secondary market for retired and limited edition collectibles featuring Byers' Choice, Dept. 56, Lefton, Cherished Teddies, Charming Tails, Dreamsicles, NASCAR, Walt Disney Classics and many others.

Man./Prod./Dist.

Byers' Choice Ltd.
4355 County Line Road
P.O. Box 158
Chalfont, PA 18914
ph: 215-822-6700
fax: 215-822-3847
e-mail: support@byerschoice.com
web: http://www.byerschoice.com/
Manufacturer of caroling figurines reminiscent of the 19th century.

Museums/Libraries

Byers' Choice Museum
Wayside Country Store
1015 Boston Post Rd.
Marlboro, MA 01752
ph: 508-481-3458
fax: 508-485-4978
e-mail: comments@waysidecountrystore.com
web: http://waysidecountrystore.com/byers.htm

Figurines (Cairn)

Clubs/Associations

Cairn Collector Society, The
Newsletter: Cairn Collector Society Newsletter
P.O. Box 400
Davidson, NC 28036
ph: 704-892-5859
e-mail: info@cairnstudio.com
web: http://www.cairnstudio.com
Focuses on collectible figurines such as Dr. Tom Clark's Gnomes issued by Cairn Studio Ltd. Sponsored by Cairn Studio, Ltd.

Man./Prod./Dist.

Cairn Studio Ltd.
P.O. Box 400
Davidson, NC 28036
ph: 704-892-5859
e-mail: info@cairnstudio.com
web: http://www.cairnstudio.com
Manufactures gnomes and other character figurines by artist Dr. Tom Clark.

Museums/Libraries

Tom Clark Museum
P.O. Box 400
Davidson, NC 28036
ph: 704-892-5859
e-mail: info@cairnstudio.com
web: http://www.cairnstudio.com
Large collection of sculptures by noted artist, Dr. Tom Clark.

Figurines (Carousels by PJ)

Clubs/Associations

Jim Hennon
PJ's Carousel Collectors Club
Newsletter: PJ's Carousel Collectors Club Newsletter
P.O. Box 610
Newbern, VA 24126
ph: 540-674-4300
fax: 540-674-2356
Focuses on the miniature replica carousel animals from the turn of the century. Sponsored by PJ's, Inc.

Figurines (Carousels)

Dealers

Melody in Motion
Waco Products
3900 Schiff Dr.
Las Vegas, NV 89103
ph: 702-253-0450
fax: 775-348-4370
web: http://www.melodyinmotion.com/
Buys and sells retired Waco carousel figurines: Santas, Clowns, Madames, Willies.

Man./Prod./Dist.

Cape Collectibles
210 Old Dairy Rd., #A
Wilmington, NC 28405-3770
ph: 800-262-5447 or 910-452-7544
fax: 910-452-7721
Produces the Original Bedford Falls Village buildings and accessories; also the first copyrighted carousel horse collection in the world.

Figurines (Cherished Teddies)

Clubs/Associations

Enesco Cherished Teddies Collectors Club
P.O. Box 99
Itasca, IL 60143-0099
ph: 630-875-5300 or 800-436-3726
fax: 630-875-5359
web: http://www.enesco.com/
For collectors of Cherished Teddies resin figurines.

Figurines (Disney)

Clubs/Associations

Walt Disney Collectors Society, The
Magazine: Sketches
500 South Buena Vista St.
Burbank, CA 91521
ph: 818-567-5500 or 800-932-5749
For Disney collectors around the world; members get free animation sculpture, quarterly magazine, opportunity to buy "member only" figurines, and advance notice of new releases; for Walt Disney Classics call 800-WD-CLSIX.

Dealers

Ben Swan
Golden Swan Collectibles
881 Lincoln Way
Auburn, CA 95603
ph: 530-823-7926 or 800-231-9055
fax: 530-823-1945
Offers a "search and find" and a listing service to collectors, buyers and sellers of Lladro figurines; also for Swarovski, Walt Disney Classics, and Disneyana Convention figurines.

Figurines (Dreamsicles)

Clubs/Associations

James Farrell
Dreamsicles Collectors' Club
Newsletter: ClubHouse
1120 California Ave.
Corona, CA 91719-3324
ph: 800-437-5818 or 909-371-3025
fax: 909-371-0674
web: http://www.dreamsiclesclub.com/
A company-sponsored club for collectors of Dreamsicles collectible cherubs and animals; also sells Bumpkins and Ivy & Innocence figurines.

Man./Prod./Dist.

Cast Art Industries, Inc.
1120 California Ave.
Corona, CA 91719-3324
ph: 800-437-5818 or 909-371-3025
fax: 909-371-0674
web: http://www.dreamsiclesclub.com/

Figurines (Emmett Kelly, Jr.)

(see also CLOWN COLLECTIBLES)

Clubs/Associations

Mary Lee Graham
Emmett Kelly, Jr. Collectors' Society, c/o Flambro
Journal: EK Journal
1530 Ellsworth Industrial Dr.
Atlanta, GA 30318-3752
ph: 800-355-2582 or 404-352-1381
fax: 404-352-2150
e-mail: collsoc@flambro.com
web: http://www.flambro.com
Focuses on the Emmett Kelly, Jr. clown figurines. Sponsored by Flambro Imports, Inc.; journal, binder, pin, "members only" plaque; enrollment includes member's plaque, newsletter, lapel pin, registry, member's-only redemption coupon.

Emmett's Friends, c/o Frankenmuth Gallery
568 South Main St.
Frankenmuth, MI 48734
ph: 800-344-2917
e-mail: gallery@tir.com
web: http://www.frankenmuthgallery.com
Focuses on the clown figurines issued by Flambro Imports, Inc.; also Gantz, Snoopy, Armani, Pocket Dragons, Lenox, Thomas Kinkade.

Collectors

N.W. Neill, Jr.
P.O. Box 38
Ennice, NC 28623-0038
fax: 336-657-8084
e-mail: saddlemtn@skybest.com
Wants anything related to Emmett Kelly, Jr. or Emmett Kelly, Sr.: advertising, postcards, Flambro pieces, dolls, etc.

Figurines (Enchanted Kingdom)

Clubs/Associations

V. Rangel
Enchanted Kingdom Collector's Club
Newsletter: Enchanted Times
2607 Delhi Rd.
Charleston, SC 29406-9717
ph: 843-761-5313
fax: 843-572-3130
e-mail: vcarolina@Charleston.net
For fantasy and castle enthusiasts.

Figurines (Fontanini)

Clubs/Associations

Fontanini Collectors' Club
Newsletter: Fontanini Collector
555 Lawrence Ave.
Rosell, IL 60172-1599
ph: 630-529-3000 or 800-729-7662
fax: 630-529-1121
e-mail: questions@roman.com
web: http://www.roman.com/
For collectors of Fontanini nativity sets and plates; sponsored by Roman, Inc.

Man./Prod./Dist.

Roman, Inc.
555 Lawrence Ave.
Rosell, IL 60172-1599
ph: 630-529-3000 or 800-729-7662
fax: 630-529-1121
e-mail: questions@roman.com
web: http://www.roman.com/
Produces figurines, plates, lithographs, bells, dolls, music boxes, etc. Exclusive importer of Fontanini nativity sets and plates.

Figurines (Goebel)

Dealers

Lois & Ralph Behm
Lois' Collectibles of Antique Market III
413 W. Main St.
Saint Charles, IL 60174-1815
ph: 630-377-5599 or 847-831-5997
Buys and sells Goebel figurines including Friar Tuck (no Hummels); will buy entire collections.

Man./Prod./Dist.

Customer Service
Goebel United States
P.O. Box 10
Pennington, NJ 08534-0010
ph: 609-737-8700 or 800-366-4632
fax: 609-737-8685
Distributors of Goebel and other figurines.

Figurines (Goebel-Friar Tuck)

Clubs/Associations

Karen & Bob Furman
Friar Tuck Collectors Club
P.O. Box 262
Owego, NY 13827-0260
ph: 607-687-3243
e-mail: n2dfc@juno.com

Figurines (Goebel-Miniatures)

Experts

Dick Hunt
Hunt's Collectibles
114 Scenic Dr.
Flat Rock, NC 28731-9522
ph: 828-693-6150 or 800-621-8112
fax: 828-693-6150
e-mail: micro@miniature.com
web: http://www.miniature.com
Specializes in buying and selling Goebel Miniatures by Robert Olszewski; also author of "The Goebel Miniatures of Robert Olszewski."

Man./Prod./Dist.

Goebel Miniatures
P.O. Box 10
Pennington, NJ 08534-0010
ph: 609-737-8700 or 800-366-4632
fax: 609-737-8685
Produces fine handpainted limited edition Goebel miniature figurines.

Figurines (Great American)

Clubs/Associations

Great American Collector's Guild
Newsletter: Big Bear Tracks
P.O. Box 428
Aberdeen, NC 28315
ph: 910-944-7447 or 800-222-2309
fax: 910-944-7449
e-mail: jacktaylor@greatamerican.net
web: http://www.greatamerican.net/
Wood carving reproductions of Old World Santas, teddy bears, and houses; made of resin.

Figurines (Janco Studio)

Man./Prod./Dist.

Bert Anderson
Janco Studio
P.O. Box 30012
Lincoln, NE 68503
ph: 402-435-1430 or 800-490-1430
Produce very detailed figurines and Christmas ornaments.

Figurines (June McKenna)

Dealers

Brenda Higgins
Handmaiden, The
P.O. Box 392
Fiskdale, MA 01518
ph: 508-347-7757
Specializes in buying and selling works by artist June McKenna.

Man./Prod./Dist.

June McKenna Collectibles, Inc.
P.O. Box 1540
Ashland, VA 23005
ph: 804-798-2024
fax: 804-798-2618
e-mail: JunMcKenna@aol.com
web: http://www.jmckenna.com/
Designs, manufactures and distributes three dimensional highly detailed limited edition figurines including Black Folk Art Figurines and Christmas/Santa Figurines designed by June McKenna.

Figurines (Krystonia)

Clubs/Associations

Krystonia Collectors Club
Newsletter: Phargol Horn
125 W. Ellsworth Rd.
Ann Arbor, MI 48108-2206
ph: 313-663-1885 or 313-663-1989
fax: 313-663-2343
Focuses on the collectible Krystonia dragons, wizards, and storybooks. Sponsored by Precious Art/Panton, Inc.; "members' only" pieces available.

Man./Prod./Dist.

Precious Art/Panton Inter.
125 W. Ellsworth Rd.
Ann Arbor, MI 48108-2206
ph: 313-663-1885 or 313-663-1989
fax: 313-663-2343
Manufacturer of make-believe collectible Krystonia dragons, wizards, and storybooks.

Figurines (Lighthouses)

Clubs/Associations

Harbour Lights Collectors' Society
Newsletter: Legacy
1000 N. Johnson Ave.
El Cajon, CA 92020
ph: 800-365-1219 or 619-579-1820
fax: 619-579-1911
e-mail:
HarbourLights@HarbourLights.com
web: http://www.harbourlights.com
For collectors of Harbour Lights Hydrostone lighthouses.

Man./Prod./Dist.

Cheryl Spencer Collin Studio
2 Government St.
Kittery, ME 03904
ph: 207-439-6016
fax: 207-439-5787
Produces exquisite lighthouse recreations of incredible detail.

Bill Younger
Harbour Lights
1000 N. Johnson Ave.
El Cajon, CA 92020
ph: 800-365-1219 or 619-579-1820
fax: 619-579-1911
e-mail:
HarbourLights@HarbourLights.com
web: http://www.harbourlights.com
Manufacturer of Hydrostone lighthouses and a full line of lighthouse collectibles.

Figurines (Margaret Furlong)

Man./Prod./Dist.

Margaret Furlong Designs
210 State St.
Salem, OR 97301-3444
ph: 503-363-6004
fax: 503-371-0676
web: http://www.margaretfurlong.com/
Produces white-on-white porcelain angels, shell stars, hearts, snowflakes, wreaths, picture frames, and miniature chairs.

Figurines (Maruri)

Man./Prod./Dist.

Maruri USA
21510 Gledhill St.
Chatsworth, CA 91311-5878
ph: 818-717-9900 or 800-562-7874
fax: 818-717-9901
e-mail: maruriUS@pacbell.net
Producer and distributor of high quality porcelain plates and figurines.

Figurines (Maud Humphrey)

Clubs/Associations

Barbara Schrage
Maud Humphrey Bogart Collectors' Club
Newsletter: Victorian Times
225 Windsor Dr.
Itasca, IL 60143
ph: 630-875-5300 or 800-436-3726
fax: 630-875-5359
web: http://www.enesco.com/
Members receive symbol of membership figurine, quarterly newsletter, membership card, members' only offering, collection registry, catalog.

Figurines (Memories Of Yesdy')

Clubs/Associations

Enesco Memories of Yesterday Collectors' Society
Newsletter: Sharing Memories...
225 Windsor Dr.
Itasca, IL 60143
ph: 630-875-5300 or 800-436-3726
fax: 630-875-5359
web: http://www.enesco.com/
Members receive symbol of membership figurine, club newsletter, membership card, members' only offering, club binder.

Periodicals

Laryl Berry, Pub.
Berry Enterprises, Inc.
Newsletter: MOY Connection, The
3906 W. Ina Rd. #200-227
Tucson, AZ 85741-2295
ph: 520-744-1456
fax: 520-744-8989
For collectors of Memories of Yesterday figurines and other collectibles designed by Mabel Lucie Attwell; articles and classified listings for secondary market buying and selling.

Figurines (Michael Garman)

Man./Prod./Dist.

Michael Garman Productions, Inc.
2418 West Colorado Ave.
Colorado Springs, CO 80904
ph: 800-874-7144 or 719-471-1600
e-mail: info@chest.com
web: http://www.chest.com/garman/index.html
Manufactures three-dimensional sculptures of people who have shaped America: cowboys, aviators, soldiers, policemen, wino, heroes, etc.

Figurines (Myth & Magic)

Clubs/Associations

Myth & Magic Collectors Club
55-E East Beaver Creek Rd.
Richmond Hill, Ontario L4B 1EB
Canada
ph: 905-731-3232
fax: 905-731-0872
For collectors of Olde English pewter figurines, each of which incorporates a piece of Swarovski Crystal.

Myth & Magic Collectors Club
Vulcan Road
Solihull
West Midlands, B91 2JY
U.K.
ph: (0121) 7114128
fax: (0121) 7111086
For collectors of Olde English pewter figurines, each of which incorporates a piece of Swarovski Crystal.

Figurines (Patchville)

Man./Prod./Dist.

MCK Gifts, Inc.
P.O. Box 621848
Littleton, CO 80162-1848
ph: 800-755-6254
fax: 303-789-9379
Produces the world of Patchville - individually cast and delicately handpainted whimsical, lop-eared bunnie figurines.

Figurines (PenDelfin)

Clubs/Associations

Susan Beard
PenDelfin Family Circle
Newsletter: PenDelfin Times, The
Atlanta Gift Mart
230 Spring St. MW, Ste. 1238
Atlanta, GA 30303-1063
ph: 800-872-4876 or 404-523-3380
For collectors of PenDelfin miniature stoneware handpainted Rabbit Family members backdrop cottages, shops and landmarks.

Man./Prod./Dist.

PenDelfin Sales Inc.
Cameron Mill
Hoswin Street
Burnley, Lancashire BB10 1PP
U.K.
ph: 01282 459464
fax: 01282 432301
e-mail: boswell@pendelfin.co.uk
web: http://www.pendelfin.co.uk
Manufacturer of PenDelfin miniature stoneware handpainted Rabbit Family members backdrop cottages, shops and landmarks.

Figurines (Pocket Dragons)

Clubs/Associations

Pocket Dragons & Friends Collectors Club, c/o Flambro
Newsletter: Pocket Dragon Gazette
1530 Ellsworth Industrial Dr.
Atlanta, GA 30318-3752
ph: 800-355-2582 or 404-352-1381
fax: 404-352-2150
e-mail: collsoc@flambro.com
web: http://www.flambro.com
Members get Membership card, newsletter, lapel pin, exclusive members-only figurines, club-sponsored events.

Figurines (Red Mill)

Clubs/Associations

Karen S. McClung
Red Mill Collectors Society
Newsletter: RMCS Newsletter
1023 Arbuckle Rd.
Summersville, WV 26651
ph: 304-872-5237
fax: 304-872-5234
A manufacturer-sponsored club for collectors of Red Mill figurines made from crushed pecan shells.

Man./Prod./Dist.

Karen S. McClung
Red Mill Mfg., Inc.
1023 Arbuckle Rd.
Summersville, WV 26651-1747
ph: 304-872-5231 or 800-624-8280
fax: 304-872-5234
web: http://www.red-mill.com/
Manufactures Red Mill figurines made from crushed pecan shells.

Figurines (Ron Lee)

Man./Prod./Dist.

Ron Lee's World of Clowns
330 Carousel Parkway
Henderson, NV 89014
ph: 800-829-3928 or 702-434-1700
fax: 702-434-4310
web: http://www.ronlee.com/

Figurines (Sarah Schultz)

Clubs/Associations

Forever Friends Collectors Club
Magazine: From the Heart
126 1/2 W. Broad
P.O. Box 448
Chesaning, MI 48616
ph: 517-845-3990 or 800-437-4363
fax: 517-845-3477
e-mail: sarahattic@aol.com

Man./Prod./Dist.

Sarah's Attic
126 1/2 W. Broad
P.O. Box 448
Chesaning, MI 48616
ph: 517-845-3990 or 800-437-4363
fax: 517-845-3477
e-mail: sarahattic@aol.com
Manufactures collectible figurines designed by Sarah Schultz; "From the Heart" magazine is published twice a year; also publishes "The Forever Friends Club Newsletter" quarterly.

Figurines (Sebastian)

Clubs/Associations

Sebastian Miniatures Collectors Society
Newsletter: Sebastian Miniatures Collectors Society News
321 Central St.
Hudson, MA 01749
ph: 978-568-1401
fax: 978-568-8741
web: http://www.hudsoncreek.com/
Focuses on the Sebastian collectible figurines; members receive free miniature, annual value guide; also distributes the "Sebastian Exchange Quarterly" newsletter for secondary market information.

Paul J. Sebastian
Sebastian Exchange Collectors Association
Price Guide: Sebastian Exchange
P.O. Box 10905
Lancaster, PA 17605-0905
ph: 717-392-2978
Issues three newsletters each year covering the secondary market; also publishes annual Sebastian "Value Register Handbook."

Dealers

Jim Waite
Blossom Shop Collectibles
112 No. Main
Farmer City, IL 61842-1424
ph: 309-928-3222 or 800-842-2593
Buys and sells old and new Sebastian miniatures by P.W. and "Woody" Baston, private issues, commercial & Marblehead, MA.; sponsors Midwest Sebastian fair which includes an auction of hard-to-find pieces.

Figurines (Second Nature)

Man./Prod./Dist.

Second Nature Design
P.O. Box 50624
Phoenix, AZ 85076
ph: 480-961-3963 or 800-939-3963
fax: 480-961-4178
Creates affordable wildlife collectible figurines.

Figurines (Shade Tree)

Clubs/Associations

Shade Tree Cowboy Collector Society
Newsletter: Cowboy Times
6210 NW 124th Place
Gainesville, FL 32606-1071
ph: 800-327-6923 or 824-524-0863
For collectors of Bill Vernon's humorous cowboy figurines; wildlife images which seem to "evolve" from twisted pieces of driftwood.

Man./Prod./Dist.

Shade Tree Creations
6210 NW 124th Place
Gainesville, FL 32606-1071
ph: 800-327-6923 or 824-524-0863
Creators of sculptures designed by artists including Bill Vernon: dragons, Road kill, Shade Tree Cowboys, Treeples, Mini Nuts, The Series of Evolution.

Figurines (Silver Deer)

Clubs/Associations

Silver Deer Collectors' Club
963 Transport Way
Petaluma, CA 94954
ph: 707-765-8311 or 800-729-3337
fax: 707-765-0770
A manufacturer-sponsored club for collectors of cold-cast figurines; special club activities/promotions, members-only figurines, and a quarterly newsletter with information about designers, product retirements and upcoming events.

Man./Prod./Dist.

Brian Danziger
Silver Deer, Ltd.
963 Transport Way
Petaluma, CA 94954
ph: 707-765-8311 or 800-729-3337
fax: 707-765-0770
Designs, manufactures and distributes limited edition crystal figurines and other giftware.

Figurines (VickiLane)

Clubs/Associations

VickiLane Collectors Club
3233 NE Cadet Ave.
Portland, OR 97220
ph: 800-456-4259
fax: 503-747-1957
Focuses on collectible figurines designed by Vicki Anderson and others at VivkiLane.

Figurines (Wee Forest Folk)

Clubs/Associations

Wee Forest Folk Collector's Club
Newsletter: Folktales
2605 Hospital Road
Saginaw, MI 48603-2611
ph: 517-792-8478
fax: 517-792-8478
e-mail: WFFCClady1@aol.com
web: http://www.weeforestfolkclub.org/
Club provides information about Wee Forest Folk figurines, past and present; helps locate figurines from 1978 to present.

Collectors

Jeanne Fredericks
12364 Downey Ave.
Downey, CA 90242-3556
ph: 562-861-4781
e-mail: jeenrob@aol.com
Collector wants older, retired Wee Forest Folk figurines created by the Peterson family.

Dealers

Creative Hands
342 R.P. Coffin Rd.
Long Grove, IL 60047
ph: 847-634-0545 or 847-459-1922
Specializes in the endearing miniature figurines sculpted by Annette Peterson of Wee Forest Folk.

Dan Thompson
Thompson Studios
1414 W. Central, Ste. 24
Brea, CA 92821
ph: 714-749-2858
e-mail: habitat-hideaway@cybercitymall.com
web: http://www.cybercitymall.com/habitat-hideaway/
The Habitat Hideaway collection are exquisitely sculpted, hand cast and hand painted nature scenes designed to accessorize and display a collection of Wee Forest Folk.

Internet Resources

Bill Montague
Wee Forest Folk news - The Monthly Squeak
ph: 978-287-4800
fax: 978-287-4240
e-mail: Bill@concordmousetrap.com
web: http://concordmousetrap.com/squeak.html
Online newsletter for collectors of Wee Forest Folk.

WFF For Sale Ads Search
e-mail: wff_collector@yahoo.com
web: http://www.bizbio.com/forsale/wff/
A web site with retired or discounted Wee Forest Folks for sale.

Figurines (Wizards & Dragons)

Clubs/Associations

Mary Lee Graham
Wizards & Dragons Collectors Club, c/o Flambro
Newsletter: Land of Legend
1530 Ellsworth Industrial Dr.
Atlanta, GA 30318-3752
ph: 800-355-2582 or 404-352-1381
fax: 404-352-2150
e-mail: collsoc@flambro.com
web: http://www.flambro.com
Figurines of amazingly detailed dragons and wizards with splendid coloring and stones; designed by international artist Hap Henriskson.

Flowers (Capodimonte)

Man./Prod./Dist.

Napoleon U.S.A.
P.O. Box 860
Oaks, PA 19456-0860
ph: 610-666-1650
fax: 610-666-1379
U.S. distributor for Napoleon Capodimonte flowers with the crown/ "N" mark from Italy.

Folk Art

Man./Prod./Dist.

Vaillancourt Folk Art
145 Armsby Rd.
Sutton, MA 01590
ph: 508-865-9183
fax: 508-865-4140
e-mail: valfa@valfa.com
web: http://www.valfa.com/
Creates limited edition chalkware replicas cast from antique chocolate molds and ice cream forms.

Franklin Mint

Clubs/Associations

Franklin Mint Collectors Society
Newsletter: Franklin Mint Almanac, The
U.S. Route 1
Franklin Center, PA 19091-0001
ph: 800-523-7622 or 610-459-6480
fax: 610-459-6880
Focuses on the quality jewelry, crystal, collectibles, and sculpture issued by The Franklin Mint which sponsors the Society.

Collectors

Jim Crane
15 Clemson Ct.
Newark, DE 19711-4301
ph: 302-738-6031
Wants Franklin Mint items, books and ads.

Dealers

AAACRC
P.O. Box 8061
Saddle Brook, NJ 07662-8061
Wants silver coins, complete sets or single piece from Franklin Mint or any other mint.

Man./Prod./Dist.

Customer Service
Franklin Mint, The
U.S. Route 1
Franklin Center, PA 19091-0001
ph: 800-523-7622 or 610-459-6480
fax: 610-459-6880
Designs, manufactures and markets collectibles including jewelry, sculpture, dolls, figurines, bells, ornaments, arms replicas, etc.

Holly Hobbie

Collectors

Mary Winfrey
3202 Kilgrennan Ct.
Herndon, VA 22071
ph: 703-435-3788
Wants to buy pre-1990 adult luncheon and dinner sets, fabric, playing cards, adult tea sets, bicentennial glasses, Holly Hobbie porcelain dolls, music boxes, figurines, sterling silver plates, and Christmas tree ornaments.

Dealers

Wilma Schiebel
No Place Like Home Collectibles
HCR 63 Box 116C
Yellville, AR 72687-9512
ph: 870-436-5874
e-mail: grantiques@alltel.net
Buys and sells anything Holly Hobbie: plates, figurines, vases, cookie jars, dishware, tea sets, banks, dolls, eggs, lunch boxes, etc.; also wants California Raisins, Garfield, and Smurfs.

Man./Prod./Dist.

Sue Holiday
American Greetings Corp.
One American Rd.
Cleveland, OH 44144
ph: 216-252-7300 or 800-242-2732
fax: 216-252-6777
American Greetings produced Holly Hobbie items - including figurines, plates, bells, etc. - from 1974 through 1986. Items were reintroduced through the Summit Corp. in 1990-91; the "Summit" figurines have also now been retired.

Periodicals

Donna Stultz
Newsletter: Holly Hobbie Collectors Gazette
1455 Otterdale Mill Rd.
Taneytown, MD 21787-3032
ph: 410-775-2570
For the enthusiast of Holly Hobbie memorabilia; the bi-monthly newsletter has articles, information, free buy/sell/trade ads with subscription; holds annual convention for Holly Hobbie collectors; send SASE to join; $25 per year.

Jan Hagara

Clubs/Associations

Jan Hagara Collectors' Club/Jan Hagara Collectables
Newsletter: Official Jan Hagara Collectors' Club Newsletter
40114 Industrial Park
Georgetown, TX 78626-4704
ph: 512-863-9499 or 800-722-3996
fax: 512-869-2093
e-mail: info@hagaradolls.com
web: http://www.hagaradolls.com/Club.htm
For collectors of Hagara prints, figurines, porcelain dolls, miniatures. Sponsored by Jan Hagara Collectables, Inc.

Dealers

Mary Sower
Card Cupboard, The
116 W. Main St.
Coldwater, OH 45828-1773
ph: 419-678-2417
Maintains a price list for Jan Hagara collectibles; will try to find any retired Jan Hagara item for customers.

Man./Prod./Dist.

B & J Company, The
P.O. Box 67
Georgetown, TX 78627
ph: 512-863-8318 or 800-722-3996
fax: 512-863-0833
e-mail: info@hagaradolls.com
web: http://www.hagaradolls.com
Produces and distributes prints, porcelain dolls, cards and collector plates by Jan Hagara.

Lenox

Man./Prod./Dist.

Lenox Collections
P.O. Box 519
Langhorne, PA 19047-0519
ph: 215-750-6900 or 800-225-1779
fax: 215-750-7362
e-mail: Lenox_Collections@b-f.com
web: http://www.lenoxcollections.com
Direct mail marketing division of Lenox Corp. selling doll, ornament, figurines and giftware collectibles issued by Lenox.

Lithophanes

Man./Prod./Dist.

David N. Failing
Schmidt-Failing, Ltd.
10579 Miller Rd.
Utica, NY 13502-7005
ph: 315-724-1139 or 800-498-5866
fax: 315-724-0496
David Failing is the only American artist skilled in the creation of original porcelain lithophanes; all are signed, numbered & limited.

Lowell Davis

Clubs/Associations

Lowell Davis Farm Club, c/o Schmid, Inc.
Newsletter: Lowell Davis Farm Club Gazette
P.O. Box 636
Carthage, MO 64836
Focuses on the collectible plates and figurines designed by artist Lowell Davis. Sponsored by Schmid Co.

Experts

Rosie Wells
22341 E. Wells Rd.
Canton, IL 61520
ph: 309-668-2211 or 800-445-8745
fax: 309-668-2795
e-mail: Rosie@RosieWells.com
web: http://www.RosieWells.com
Author of "Lowell Davis Collectibles - The Official Secondary Market Price Guide."

Music Boxes

Man./Prod./Dist.

Splendid Music Box Co.
225 Fifth Ave.
New York, NY 10010-1102
ph: 212-532-9304
fax: 212-532-9334
Imports over 1000 types of music boxes from all over the world.

H & G Studios
5660 Corporate Way
West Palm Beach, FL 33407
ph: 561-615-9900 or 800-777-1333
fax: 561-615-8400
Sells Italian-made, wooden music boxes; containing images of exclusive original art; have Swiss Reuge musical movements.

Norman Rockwell

(see also ILLUSTRATORS, Norman Rockwell)

Experts

Mary Moline
P.O. Box 1-4444
South Lake Tahoe, CA 96151
ph: 530-543-1414
fax: 530-543-1414
e-mail: marymoline@aol.com
World authority on original Norman Rockwell art; author of "Norman Rockwell Collectibles Values Guide," "Norman Rockwell Encyclopedia" as well as six other books on the subject.

Ornaments

(see also CHRISTMAS COLLECTIBLES; HOLIDAY COLLECTIBLES)

Clubs/Associations

Treasury of Christmas Ornaments Collectors' Club
P.O. Box 277
Itasca, IL 60143-0277
ph: 630-875-5404
fax: 630-875-5359

Collectors

Maret Webb
4118 East Vernon Ave.
Phoenix, AZ 85008-2333
ph: 602-957-0653
fax: 602-957-1631
Wants Biederman brass ornaments; also will buy or trade for sterling ornaments by Wallace, Reed & Barton, Gorham, Swarovski and others; also wants to buy Swarovski ornaments.

Dealers

Alice Korman
Alice's Past & Presents Replacements
P.O. Box 465
Merrick, NY 11566-0465
ph: 516-379-1352
fax: 516-379-7302
e-mail: alicechina@aol.com
Specializes in Lenox, Gorham, Towle and other Christmas ornaments.

Joe Schulte
Gift Music Book & Collectibles
420 Wallace St.
Chicago Heights, IL 60411
ph: 708-877-7099
e-mail: jntschulte@rocketmail.com
web: http://www.beisecurity.com/gift
Carries a full line of ornaments: Carlton, Hallmark, Swarovski, Enesco, Roman, Radko, Hummel, Midwest, Kurt Adler, Precious Moments, Schmid, Bing & Grondahl, Royal Copenhagen, Anna Parenna, Anri, Goebel, Grossman, Rockwell, Hibel, etc.

Man./Prod./Dist.

Kirk Stieff Co. Outlet Store
800 Wyman Park Dr.
Baltimore, MD 21211
ph: 410-338-6080 or 800-531-7946
fax: 410-338-6097
Sterling, silverplate, stainless steel and pewter flatware, sterling and silverplate hollowware; pewter, jewelry; a division of Lenox Brands.

Periodicals

Newsletter: Christmas Times
1024 N. Hamilton Ave.
Lindenhurst, NY 11757
e-mail: voesack@interport.net
web: http://www.users.interport.net/~voesach/ctimes.htm
Monthly buy-sell publication.

Rosie Wells
Rosie Wells Enterprises, Inc.
Magazine: Ornament Collector, The
22341 E. Wells Rd.
Canton, IL 61520
ph: 309-668-2211 or 800-445-8745
fax: 309-668-2795
e-mail: Rosie@RosieWells.com
web: http://www.RosieWells.com
The magazine specializing in Ornament Collector news, especially in Hallmark, Enesco, Carlton ornaments; ads, articles, photos, etc.; many classified ads from collectors.

Ornaments (Buccellati)

Man./Prod./Dist.

Buccellati, Inc.
46 East 57th St.
New York, NY 10022
ph: 212-308-2900 or 800-223-7885
fax: 212-750-1323
web: http://www.buccellati.com/
Produces hundreds of entirely handmade ornaments annually using classical and baroque influences, gold, silver, precious and semi-precious stones

Ornaments (Carlton Cards)

Man./Prod./Dist.

Carlton Cards
One American Rd.
Cleveland, OH 44144
ph: 216-252-7300 or 800-242-2732
fax: 216-252-6777
Offers many ornaments including Jim Hensen's Muppets and lighted ornaments.

Ornaments (Cazenovia Abroad)

Man./Prod./Dist.

Glen Trush
Cazenovia Abroad, Ltd.
67 Albany St.
Cazenovia, NY 13035-1219
ph: 315-655-3433
fax: 315-655-4249
Offers a collection of over 50 full-size ornaments and almost as many miniature ornaments; also offers limited edition carousel figurines.

Ornaments (Christopher Radko)

Clubs/Associations

Christopher Radko Starlight Family of Collectors
Newsletter: Starlight
P.O. Box 533
Elmsford, NY 10523
ph: 800-717-2356
fax: 914-693-3770
e-mail: radko@sji-sjif.com
web: http://www.christopherradko.com/

Dealers

Captain Jack
2866 NW 82nd Ave.
Ankeny, IA 50021
ph: 515-964-8500
e-mail: captain@captainjack.com
web: http://www.radko.org/
Web site has images and prices for over 3000 Christopher Radko ornaments.

Experts

David Williams
Williams Nursery & The Gift House
524 Springfield Ave.
Westfield, NJ 07090
ph: 888-88R-ADKO or 908-232-4076
fax: 908-232-0079
e-mail: dwilliams1@home.com
web: http://www.radkoshop.com
A Christopher Radko Rising Star store; large selection of Radko ornaments; visit website for live ornament chat, bulletin board, and current inventory.

Man./Prod./Dist.

Christopher Radko
P.O. Box 533
Elmsford, NY 10523
ph: 800-717-2356
fax: 914-693-3770
e-mail: radko@sji-sjif.com
web: http://www.christopherradko.com/
Carries mouth blown Christmas ornaments and accessories for the home.

Ornaments (Danforth)

Man./Prod./Dist.

Danforth Pewterers
P.O. Box 828
Middlebury, VT 05753
ph: 877-326-3678
fax: 802-388-0099
e-mail: info@danforthpewter.com
web: http://www2.danforthpewter.com/
Specializes in Christmas ornaments; also original Danforth Pewter hollowware.

Ornaments (Enesco)

Clubs/Associations

Enesco Treasury of Christmas Ornaments Collectors' Club
Newsletter: Treasury Trimmings
P.O. Box 277
Itasca, IL 60143-0277
ph: 630-875-5300 or 800-436-3726
fax: 630-875-5359
web: http://www.enesco.com/
Members receive symbol of membership ornament, membership card, club newsletter, subscription to Treasury Trimmings, collector's guide, list of dealers.

Ornaments (Hallmark)

Clubs/Associations

California Ornament Collectors Club
Newsletter: California Ornament Collectors Newsletter
6 Ness Place
Marietta, OH 45750
ph: 740-373-3114
A club for collectors of Hallmark Christmas ornaments; the original and the largest such club for Hallmark collectors.

Nancy M. Soddy
Central Wisconsin Ornament Collectors Club
401 Novak St.
Mosinee, WI 54455-2030
ph: 715-693-4135
Members interested primarily in collecting Hallmark Christmas ornaments; some members have other areas of interest as well.

Hallmark Keepsake Ornament Collectors Club
Newsletter: Collector's Courier
P.O. Box 419034
Kansas City, MO 64141-6034
ph: 816-274-4000 or 800-523-5839
fax: 816-274-5061
Focuses on Hallmark Ornaments made of wood, acrylic, bone china, porcelain. A manufacturer-sponsored club.

Dealers

Kathy Parrott
Christmas in Vermont
51 Jalbert Rd.
Barre, VT 05641
ph: 802-479-2024
e-mail: katparrott@aol.com
Specializes in mail order Hallmark Christmas ornaments, Kiddie Car classics, Merry Christmas and other Hallmark collectibles; serving collectors worldwide since 1988; catalog 4 times per year, send $3 for copy.

Joan Ketterer
Carousel Collectibles
P.O. Box 97172
Pittsburgh, PA 15229
ph: 412-367-2352
e-mail: twelve-months@webtv.net
Buys and sells Hallmark ornaments.

Experts

Rosie Wells
22341 E. Wells Rd.
Canton, IL 61520
ph: 309-668-2211 or 800-445-8745
fax: 309-668-2795
e-mail: Rosie@RosieWells.com
web: http://www.RosieWells.com
Author of "Secondary Market Price Guide for Hallmark Ornaments and Merry Miniatures."

Internet Resources

Collecting Ornaments On Line
e-mail: smarr@abcs.com
web: http://www.daffodilgifts.com/club/cool.htm
A not-for-profit online collectors club designed to bring together collectors of Hallmark Keepsake Ornaments, to provide a "club" experience for all collectors, and to support a charity.

Man./Prod./Dist.

Hallmark Cards, Inc.
Consumer Affairs #216
P.O. Box 419034
Kansas City, MO 64141-6034
ph: 800-425-5627
web: http://www.hallmark.com/
Producer of Christmas ornaments and figurines.

Museums/Libraries

Prudencio/Hamrick Hallmark Ornament Museum
c/o The Party Shop
3418 Lake City Hwy.
Warsaw, IN 46580
ph: 219-267-8787
e-mail: PrtyShopDH@aol.com
web: http://www.thepartyshop.com/museum.htm
Displays over 2,800 Hallmark ornaments - one of every design produced since Hallmark debuted its line of Keepsake Ornaments in 1973.

Hallmark Visitors Center
P.O. Box 419580
Mail Drop 132
Kansas City, MO 64141-6580
ph: 816-274-5672 or 800-425-5627
web: http://www.hallmark.com

Periodicals

Joan Ketterer
Newsletter: Twelve Months of Christmas
P.O. Box 97172
Pittsburgh, PA 15229
ph: 412-367-2352
e-mail: twelve-months@webtv.net
A biweekly newsletter for new and long-time Hallmark collectors.

Ornaments (Silver)

Clubs/Associations

Hand & Hammer Collectors Club
Newsletter: Silver Tidings
2610 Morse Lane
Woodbridge, VA 22192
ph: 703-491-4866 or 800-SIL-VERY
fax: 703-491-2031
e-mail: deChip@hand-hammer.com
web: http://www.hand-hammer.com
Focuses on the sterling silver collectibles designed by Chip deMatteo. Sponsored by Hand & Hammer, Co.

Patti Flanigin, Treas./Mem.
Silver Ornament Society
Newsletter: Silver Ornament Society Newsletter
P.O.Box 903
Laramie, WY 82073-0903
fax: 307-745-3198
e-mail: a7flanigin@aol.com
Club promotes silver and silverplated Christmas ornament collecting; quarterly newsletter.

Collectors

Betty Overton
200 Avenida Santa Margarita
San Clemente, CA 92672
ph: 949-498-5330 or 949-498-4027
fax: 949-498-5330
e-mail: edwhiffen@aol.com
Wants sterling and silverplated Christmas ornaments which have been made by many silver companies since 1970.

Dealers

Gary Niederkorn
Gary Niederkorn Silver
Newspaper: Silver Edition
2005 Locust St.
Philadelphia, PA 19103-5606
ph: 215-567-2606
fax: 215-567-2606
Specializes in 19th and 20th cent. silver novelties, Christmas ornaments, napkin rings, Judaica, picture frames, etc.; also Tiffany, Jensen, Mexican.

Peg Zurkowski
Becker Brooks Antiques
8027 Ellingson Dr.
Chevy Chase, MD 20815
ph: 301-588-8558
fax: 301-608-2167
e-mail: pzrkwski@ix.netcom.com
Specializing in out-of-production sterling ornaments.

Experts

Peggy & Arthur Hart
Ornament Collector, The
101 E. Holly Ave., Ste. 3
Sterling, VA 20164-5402
ph: 703-444-6155
fax: 703-421-9386
e-mail: peggyphd@aol.com
web: http://members.aol.com/Peggyphd/Peggyshomepage.index.html
Experts on sterling silver Christmas ornaments and co-authors of "Sterling Ornaments, '96," and "Sterling Ornaments Update, '98", a complete guide for collectors of sterling silver Christmas ornaments.

Man./Prod./Dist.

Hand & Hammer Silversmiths
Newsletter: Silver Tidings
2610 Morse Lane
Woodbridge, VA 22192
ph: 703-491-4866 or 800-SIL-VERY
fax: 703-491-2031
e-mail: deChip@hand-hammer.com
web: http://www.hand-hammer.com
Manufacturer of sterling silver Christmas ornaments.

Periodicals

Kimlie Fox
Newsletter: Silver Lining, The
525 2nd Ave. NW
Hickory, NC 28601
ph: 704-322-6326
fax: 704-322-1281
A quarterly newsletter for sterling ornament collectors.

P. Buckley Moss

Clubs/Associations

P. Buckley Moss Society
Newsletter: Sentinel
601 Shenandoah Village Dr., Ste. 1C
Waynesboro, VA 22980
ph: 540-943-5678 or 804-725-7378
fax: 540-949-8408
e-mail: pbmsoc@cfw.com
web: http://www.bridgewater.edu/moss/pbm-soc/
Focuses on the collectible figurines, plates and graphics designed by P. Buckley Moss. Sponsored by The Moss Portfolio.

Man./Prod./Dist.

Moss Portfolio, The
HC69 Box 17118
Mathews, VA 23109
ph: 804-725-7378
fax: 804-725-3040
e-mail: mossportfolio@ccsinc.com
web: http://www.p-buckley-moss.com
Publisher and distributor of watercolors, original prints, offset lithographs, plates, dolls, and figurines by P. Buckley Moss.

Penni Anne Cross

Man./Prod./Dist.

Cross Gallery, Inc.
P.O. Box 4181
Jackson, WY 83001-4181
ph: 307-733-2200
fax: 307-733-1414
Offers plates, figurines, dolls, Christmas ornaments, and graphics designed by Penni Anne Cross.

Pickard

Man./Prod./Dist.

Pickard China Co.
782 Pickard Ave.
Antioch, IL 60002
ph: 847-395-3800
fax: 847-395-3827
e-mail: Finest@pickardchina.com
web: http://www.pickardchina.com/
In addition to dinnerware, manufactures collectible plates, bells, ornaments, steins and bowls.

Plates

(see also PLATES)

Clubs/Associations

Hunter Haines
Collectibles & Platemakers Guild
77 W. Washington St., Ste. 1507
Chicago, IL 60602-2902
ph: 312-201-0262
fax: 312-201-8579
e-mail: cpgnews@aol.com

International Plate Collectors Guild
Newsletter: Platter Platter
P.O. Box 487
Artesia, CA 90702-0487
ph: 213-924-6335
A monthly newsletter for plate collectors.

Dealers

Nancy Pelham
Homestead Gift Shop
4 Hillwood Lane
Catskill, NY 12414
ph: 518-943-4371
e-mail: fluffy@capital.net
web: http://www.homestead-gift-shop.com
Carries a variety of collector plates by several manufacturers as well as display easels and frames.

Village Plate Collector, The
120 Forrest Ave.
Cocoa, FL 32922
ph: 800-511-2935
fax: 407-636-0929
e-mail: loisvpc@aol.com
web: http://collectibles.net/naled/villageplate/

Joe Schulte
Gift Music Book & Collectibles
420 Wallace St.
Chicago Heights, IL 60411
ph: 708-877-7099
e-mail: jntschulte@rocketmail.com
web: http://www.beisecurity.com/gift
Carries a full line of collector plates: Hamilton, Bing & Grondahl, Diana Art, Eklund, Derk Hansen, H & G, Hollywood, Lynette Decor, Memories-Canada, Wedgwood, Rob Anders, Roman, Royal Copenhagen, Svend Jenses, Wild Wing, Kaiser, etc.

Bradford Exchange Trading Center, The
9333 N. Milwaukee Ave.
Niles, IL 60714
ph: 800-323-5577
e-mail: custsrv@bradex.com
web: http://www.bradex.com/
A brokerage service to match secondary market buyers and sellers of collector plates that are no longer in production.

Mickey Kaz
Collectibles Unlimited
P.O. Box 606
Woodland Hills, CA 91365-0606
ph: 818-703-6173
fax: 818-703-6173
e-mail: mickeyk@cris.com
web: http://www.geocities.com/Eureka/Park/7789/plates.html
Serving the world of plate collectors since 1977: plates, plate frames, stands, easels; will help you locate your plate regardless of its age.

Experts

Ross Ernst
Collectors Plates
7308 Izard
Omaha, NE 68114-3237
ph: 402-391-3469
Buys and sells Bradford plates, Royal Copenhagen (RC), Bing & Grondahl (B/G), P. Buckley Moss plates, Perillo, M.I. Hummel, Duncan Royale, Lilliput Lane, Hamilton Dolls, Ashton Drake Dolls, and old estate RC & B/G plates.

Man./Prod./Dist.

Bradford Exchange, The
9333 N. Milwaukee Ave.
Niles, IL 60714
ph: 800-323-5577
e-mail: custsrv@bradex.com
web: http://www.bradex.com/
Pioneered direct mail marketing of collector plates and created an organized secondary market trading exchange for collector plates.

Matching Services

Robert Goins
Replacements Ltd.
P.O. Box 26029
1089 Knox Road
Greensboro, NC 27420
ph: 800-737-5223 or 336-697-3000
fax: 336-697-3100
e-mail: replaceltd@aol.com
web: http://www.replacements.com
Carries collector plates in addition to china, crystal and flatware (obsolete, active and inactive.)

Museums/Libraries

Bradford Museum of Collector's Plates, The
9333 N. Milwaukee Ave.
Niles, IL 60714
ph: 800-323-5577
e-mail: custsrv@bradex.com
web: http://www.bradex.com/

Plates (Rockwell)

Clubs/Associations

Michael J.P. Collins, Pres.
Rockwell Society of America
Newsletter: Rockwell Society of America Newsletter
P.O. Box 705
Ardsley, NY 10502-0705
Founded in 1974 and dedicated to the appreciation of America's most famous artist, Norman Rockwell; specializing in original paintings, drawings, collectibles, e.g. Saturday Evening Post covers/magazines, illustrated books, etc.

Plates (Ron Anders)

Clubs/Associations

Lance J. Klass, Pres.
Rob Anders Collectors Society
5 Mountain Road
Concord, NH 03301-5479
ph: 603-228-1864 or 800-660-8345
fax: 603-228-1888
e-mail: porterfields@mediaone.net
web: http://www.porterfields.com/
The collector society for Rob Anders, voted America's "Best Plate Artist" for his award-winning mini plates on early childhood.

Man./Prod./Dist.

Lance J. Klass, Pres.
Porterfield's Fine Art in Limited Editions
5 Mountain Road
Concord, NH 03301-5479
ph: 603-228-1864 or 800-660-8345
fax: 603-228-1888
e-mail: porterfields@mediaone.net
web: http://www.porterfields.com/
Porterfield's, Fine Art in Limited Editions, specializes in producing the fine limited edition porcelain mini plates on early childhood by award-winning artist Rob Anders.

Prayer Ladies

Experts

April M. Tvorak
P.O. Box 94
Warren Center, PA 18851
ph: 570-395-3775
e-mail: april@epix.net
Wants to buy Mother-in-the-Kitchen (Prayer Ladies) ceramic figurines and accessories; imported in the 1960s by ENESCO; typically decorated with a motif of an older woman with hair in bun, head bowed, hands in prayer, and prayer on apron.

Steve Johnson
4003 Jefferson St.
Sioux City, IA 51108
Collector and consultant to "The Official Price Guide to Pottery and Porcelain."

Juarine Woolridge
418 Country Lane
Mount Vernon, MO 65712-1906
Collector and consultant to "The Official Price Guide to Pottery and Porcelain."

Precious Moments

Appraisers

Rosie Wells
Limited Edition Appraisers
22341 E. Wells Rd.
Canton, IL 61520
ph: 309-668-2211 or 800-445-8745
fax: 309-668-2795
e-mail: Rosie@RosieWells.com
web: http://www.RosieWells.com
Specializes in the appraisal of Precious Moments porcelain bisque collectibles.

Clubs/Associations

Enesco Precious Moments Collectors' Club
Newsletter: Goodnewsletter
P.O. Box 99
Itasca, IL 60143-0099
ph: 630-875-5300 or 800-436-3726
fax: 630-875-5359
web: http://www.enesco.com/
Members receive symbol of membership figurine, quarterly newsletter, membership card, members' only offerings, gift registry, club binder, annual local chapter national convention, Orient tour.

Enesco Precious Moments Birthday Club
Newsletter: Good News Parade
P.O. Box 689
Itasca, IL 60143-0689
ph: 630-875-5300 or 800-436-3726
fax: 630-875-5359
web: http://www.enesco.com/
For young collectors; this category of Precious Moments figurines feature animals and circus themes; members receive symbol of membership figurine, club newsletter, membership certificate, members' only offerings, birthday card.

Rosie Wells
Precious Moments Collectors
Magazine: Precious Collectibles
22341 E. Wells Rd.
Canton, IL 61520
ph: 309-668-2211 or 800-445-8745
fax: 309-668-2795
e-mail: Rosie@RosieWells.com
web: http://www.RosieWells.com
A glossy magazine with ads, articles, collector interviews, etc.; published exclusively for Precious Moments collectors; keeps track of numerous area Precious Moments collector clubs throughout the country.

Dealers

Limited Edition, The
2170 Sunrise Highway
Merrick, NY 11566
ph: 516-623-4400 or 800-645-2864
fax: 516-867-3701
e-mail: tle@thelimitededition.com
web: http://www.thelimitededition.com/
Specializes in suspended and retired Precious Moments figurines; also Dept. 56, and Christopher Radko.

Experts

Rosie Wells
22341 E. Wells Rd.
Canton, IL 61520
ph: 309-668-2211 or 800-445-8745
fax: 309-668-2795
e-mail: Rosie@RosieWells.com
web: http://www.RosieWells.com
Author of "Secondary Market Price Guide for Precious Moments"; specializing in Precious Moments bisque collection, dolls, pewter, etc. since 1983; offers appraisals of Precious Moments porcelain bisque collectibles.

Internet Resources

Hans J. Schindhelm
M.I. Hummel & Precious Moments Internet Sites Directory
P.O. Box 120
Briarcliff, NY 10510
ph: 914-734-8410
fax: 914-762-1719
e-mail: hummel2001@aol.com
web: http://members.aol.com/hummel2001
Free on-line directory of web pages and internet sites relating to M.I. Hummel and Precious Moments collectibles.

Misc. Services

Rosie Wells Enterprises, Inc.
22341 E. Wells Rd.
Canton, IL 61520
ph: 309-668-2211 or 800-445-8745
fax: 309-668-2795
e-mail: Rosie@RosieWells.com
web: http://www.RosieWells.com
Rosie's Instant Hot Top Line has news flashes & hot tips for Precious Moments collectors; message changes Thursdays at noon; call 900-740-7575; $2/min.

Precious Moments (Musicals)

Clubs/Associations

Enesco Musical Society
Newsletter: Musical Notes
225 Windsor Dr.
Itasca, IL 60143
ph: 630-875-5300 or 800-436-3726
fax: 630-875-5359
web: http://www.enesco.com/
For collectors of Enesco's musical collectibles; members receive color calendar, quarterly newsletter, membership certificate, members' only offering.

Reed & Barton

Man./Prod./Dist.

Reed & Barton
144 W. Britannia St.
Taunton, MA 02780
ph: 508-824-6611 or 800-822-1824
fax: 508-822-7269
Produces china, crystal, silver, silverplate, and stainless flatware, collectible plates, bells, dolls, ornaments and accessories.

Royal Copenhagen

Man./Prod./Dist.

Josephine Dillon
Royal Scandinavian
140 Bradford Dr.
West Berlin, NJ 08091
ph: 609-768-5400 or 800-431-1992
fax: 800-448-7553
Royal Copenhagen, Bing & Grondahl, Holmegaard, and Georg Jensen are the best of Scandinavian collectibles; manufactures dinnerware, cobalt blue underglaze collector plates, figurines, bells, dolls, ornaments and gift accessories.

Royal Doulton

(see also CERAMICS [ENGLISH], Doulton; CERAMICS [ENGLISH], Royal Doulton)

Clubs/Associations

Royal Doulton International Collectors Club
Magazine: Gallery
701 Cottontail Lane
Somerset, NJ 08873
ph: 732-356-7880 or 800-682-4462
fax: 732-764-4974
e-mail: usa@royal-doulton.com
Focuses on the Royal Doulton collectibles; members entitled to purchase "member only" figurines or character and Toby jugs; advance notice of introductions and withdrawals; a newsletter has free buy/sell ads for members.

Patricia O'Brien, Manager
Royal Doulton International Collectors Club
Magazine: Gallery
850 Progress Ave.
Scarborough, Ontario M1H 3C4
Canada
ph: 416-431-4202 or 800-268-4040
fax: 416-431-0089
Focuses on the Royal Doulton collectibles; members entitled to purchase "member only" figurines or character and Toby jugs; advance notice of introductions and withdrawals; a newsletter has free buy/sell ads for members.

Maria Murtagh
Royal Doulton International Collectors Club
Magazine: Gallery
Minton House
london Road
Stoke-on-Trent, Staffordshire ST4 7QD
U.K.
ph: (01782) 292127 or (01782) 292292
fax: (01782) 292099
e-mail: icc@royal-doulton.com
web: http://www.royal-doulton.com/
Focuses on the Royal Doulton collectibles; members entitled to purchase "member only" figurines or charter and Toby jugs; advance notice of introductions and withdrawals; a newsletter has free buy/sell ads for members.

Dealers

Arlene & Barry
Recollections
3823 Oceanside Rd. East
Oceanside, NY 11572
ph: 516-678-4652

Matching Services

Regina Negrotti
Tablescapes
P.O. Box 448
Cheshire, CT 06410
ph: 800-801-4084
e-mail: lenox@ntplx.net
web: http://www.tabletopdesigns.com/

Russian

Dealers

Natalie Bell
Open House Miniatures
402 Railroad Ave. W.
Allendale, SC 29810
Carries highest quality Russian miniatures available; also painted eggs, matreshkas (nesting dolls), icons, and Palekh boxes made by the Russian Association of Dollhouse & Miniature Masters (see examples at http://www.aha.ru/~vladin/).

Vitaly Shukin
Russian Shop - Maison Russe
1720 Ogden Ave.
Lisle, IL 60532-1230
ph: 630-963-5160
fax: 630-963-5170
e-mail: mail@TheRussianShop.com
web: http://www.TheRussianShop.com/
Imports unusual and one-of-a-kind Russian gifts and collectibles; experts in identifying authentic Russian lacquer boxes and nesting dolls; dealer in contemporary Russian porcelain; periodic catalogs; in business for 25 years.

Natasha Soboleva
Russian Treasure
2801 Leavenworth St.
San Francisco, CA 94133
ph: 415-346-1104
fax: 415-664-6561
e-mail: natasha@russiantreasure.com
web: http://www.russiantreasure.com
Sells contemporary Russian items: Matryoshka-babushka (nesting dolls), original Palekh, Fedoskino, Mstera lacquered papier-mache boxes, Faberge eggs, Baltic amber, chess sets.

Matvei Finkel
Siberian Wild Products
325 W. Brierwood Ave.
Spokane, WA 99218
ph: 509-467-5562
fax: 509-468-2184
e-mail: mfinkel@cet.com
web: http://www.russianmade.com/temp/
Sells hand crafted items from Siberia, the Russian Far East, and also from many parts of Moscow and Western Russia; nesting dolls, eggs, icons, lacquered boxes.

Internet Resources

Lynn Hinkle
Seven Sisters
5602 SW Fairlawn Rd.
Topeka, KS 66610-9442
ph: 785-862-6000
fax: 785-862-0537
e-mail: 7sisters@astrawow.com
A web site dedicated to helping Russian women sell their art; parent site www.astrawow.com/7sisters contains a web catalog for and about women and features collectible art and clothing made by women around the world: Russia China, US.

Man./Prod./Dist.

Marina's Russian Collection
507 North Wolf Rd.
Wheeling, IL 60090
ph: 847-808-0994
fax: 847-808-0997
Distributes Russian matryoshka (nesting dolls) and lacquered boxes.

Sculptures (Cain)

Clubs/Associations

Mike Kemp
Cain Studios Collectors Guild
Newsletter: Rick Cain Studios' Collectors Guild News
3500 NE Waldo Rd.
Gainesville, FL 32609
ph: 800-535-3949 or 352-377-7657
fax: 352-377-7038
A club for fans of artist Rick Cain; members receive free membership sculpture, redemption coupons, members-only sculptures, and more.

Sculptures (Chilmark)

Clubs/Associations

Chilmark Gallery
Newsletter: Chilmark Report
321 Central St.
Hudson, MA 01749
ph: 978-568-1401
fax: 978-568-8741
web: http://www.hudsoncreek.com/
Focuses on Chilmark pewter sculptures; "Chilmark Report" reports on new editions and artist appearances. "The Observer" keeps collectors up-to-date on secondary markets and values.

Repair Services

Isaura
CRC Workshop
16 Drumlin Hill
Groton, MA 01450
ph: 978-448-5252
Specializes in the complete restoration of Chilmark pewters made by the Lance Corp.; extremely knowledgeable about Lance materials, processes and techniques.

Sculptures (CPSmithshire)

Clubs/Associations

Pangaean Society, The
Newsletter: Shirespeak
321 Central St.
Hudson, MA 01749
ph: 978-568-1401
fax: 978-568-8741
web: http://www.hudsoncreek.com/
Focuses on Cindy Smity's collection of Shireling Figurines.

Sculptures (Don Polland)

Clubs/Associations

Polland Collectors Society, c/o Polland Studios
Newsletter: Collectors Review
P.O. Box 2468
Prescott, AZ 86302
ph: 520-778-1900
fax: 520-778-4034
Focuses on Don Polland's pewter sculpture collectible figurines. Sponsored by Polland Studios.

Man./Prod./Dist.

Donald J. Polland
Polland Studios
P.O. Box 2468
Prescott, AZ 86302
ph: 520-778-1900
fax: 520-778-4034
Focuses on Don Polland's pewter sculpture collectible figurines. Sponsored by Polland Studios (Gerard Corp.)

Sculptures (LEGENDS)

Clubs/Associations

Starlite Collectors Society
11908 Ventura Blvd.
Studio City, CA 91604
ph: 800-726-9660 or 818-761-7779
fax: 818-761-8889
e-mail: legends1@aol.com
Collectors of art sculptures in mixed media such as bronze, fine pewter and 24 karat gold vermeil made by Legends. A manufacturer-sponsored collector's club.

Man./Prod./Dist.

LEGENDS
11908 Ventura Blvd.
Studio City, CA 91604
ph: 800-726-9660 or 818-761-7779
fax: 818-761-8889
e-mail: legends1@aol.com
Producers of art sculptures in mixed media such as bronze, fine pewter and 24 karat gold vermeil.

Sculptures (Mark Hopkins)

Clubs/Associations

L. Susan Fife
Mark Hopkins Bronze Guild
Newsletter: Bronzeworks
21 Shorter Industrial Blvd.
Rome, GA 30165-1838
ph: 800-678-6564 or 706-235-8773
fax: 706-235-2814
Focuses on bronze castings by Mark Hopkins.

Man./Prod./Dist.

Russell Bower
Mark Hopkins Bronze Guild
21 Shorter Industrial Blvd.
Rome, GA 30165-1838
ph: 800-678-6564 or 706-235-8773
fax: 706-235-2814
Produces and sells fine bronze sculptures.

Sculptures (Rawcliffe)

Man./Prod./Dist.

Rawcliffe Corp.
155 Public St.
Providence, RI 02903
ph: 401-331-1645 or 800-343-1811
web: http://www.augusta.net/~pewter/rc-main.htm
Manufactures giftware and collectibles in fine pewter.

Sculptures (Sandicast)

Clubs/Associations

Steve Yaptangco
Sandicast Collectors Guild
Newsletter: Paw Press
P.O. Box 910079
San Diego, CA 92191-0079
ph: 619-695-9611 or 800-722-3316
fax: 619-695-0615
e-mail: guild@sandicast.com
web: http://www.sandicast.com/
For collectors of animal sculptures noted for their lifelike appearance and designed by artist Sandra A. Brue; annual members-only piece not available to the general public.

Man./Prod./Dist.

Steve Yaptangco
Sandicast, Inc.
P.O. Box 910079
San Diego, CA 92191-0079
ph: 619-695-9611 or 800-722-3316
fax: 619-695-0615
e-mail: guild@sandicast.com
web: http://www.sandicast.com/
Manufacturer of handcast and handpainted animal sculptures noted for their lifelike appearance and designed by artist Sandra A. Brue; Paw Press published semiannually.

Sculptures (Tom Clark)

(see also GNOMES)

Dealers

Bill Hart
GnomeHunter
6711 San Mateo Drive
West Chester, OH 45069
ph: 513-779-2968
fax: 513-731-0019
e-mail: info@gnomehunter.com
web: http://www.gnomehunter.com/
The source for Gnomes by Tom Clark.

Man./Prod./Dist.

Cairn Studio Ltd.
P.O. Box 400
Davidson, NC 28036
ph: 704-892-5859
e-mail: info@cairnstudio.com
web: http://www.cairnstudio.com
Manufactures gnomes and other character figurines by artist Dr. Tom Clark.

Skippy

Clubs/Associations

Joan Crosby Tibbetts, Pres.
Skippy Collectors Club, c/o Skippy, Inc.
8304 Tobin Rd., #14
Annandale, VA 22003
ph: 703-698-4346
fax: 703-698-4346
e-mail: JCTSkippy@aol.com
web: http://www.skippy.com/
Focuses on the Skippy print and doll collectibles. Sponsored by Skippy, Inc.

Spangler's Realm

Man./Prod./Dist.

Spangler's Realm Collectors Club, c/o Realms, Inc.
11733 Lackland Rd.
Maryland Heights, MO 63146
ph: 314-991-0793
fax: 314-991-0958
web: http://www.fantasticart.com/randal_spangler_fantasy_art.htm
Focuses on the Spangler's Realm line of figurines, bells, ornaments and prints. Sponsored by Realms, Inc.

Sports Related

(see also SPORTS COLLECTIBLES)

Dealers

Morgan Co., The
6301 Highbanks Rd.
Mascoutah, IL 62258
ph: 618-566-7568 or 800-422-4510
fax: 618-566-7518
Specializes in limited edition figurines and plates; Gartlan USA, Sports Impressions, etc.

Man./Prod./Dist.

Mark Bloomquist
S. A. M. Inc.
P.O. Box 77
Palo Alto, CA 94301
ph: 800-483-2643 or 650-369-0190
Manufactures sports related ceramic bobbing head dolls.

Sports Related (Gartlan)

Clubs/Associations

Tom Nardi
Collectors' League
Newsletter: Collectors' Quarterly
575 Hwy. 73 North
West Berlin, NJ 08091-2440
ph: 609-753-9229
fax: 609-753-9280
e-mail: info@gartlanusa.com
web: http://www.gartlanusa.com
Focuses on the Gartlan sports and entertainment collectibles; sponsored by Gartlan USA.

Man./Prod./Dist.

Tom Nardi
Gartlan USA
575 Hwy. 73 North
West Berlin, NJ 08091-2440
ph: 609-753-9229
fax: 609-753-9280
e-mail: info@gartlanusa.com
web: http://www.gartlanusa.com
Produces sports and entertainment collectibles including plates, figurines, graphics, ornaments, and baseballs.

Sports Related (Sports Imp.)

Man./Prod./Dist.

ENESCO Corp.
225 Windsor Dr.
Itasca, IL 60143
ph: 630-875-5300 or 800-436-3726
fax: 630-875-5359
web: http://www.enesco.com/
Distributor of Sports Impressions.

Sports Related (Start. Lineup)

Dealers

All-Star Sports Cards
P.O. Box 351
Syracuse, NY 13211
ph: 315-454-8700

Midwest Sports Collectibles
1027 Shayler Rd.
Cincinnati, OH 45245
ph: 513-752-4939
fax: 513-752-8960

Minnesota Connection, The
8393 213th St. West
Lakeville, MN 55044
ph: 612-469-1321
fax: 612-469-4477
Large dealer in Kenner's Starting Lineup figures.

D & J Collectibles
4256 W. 131st St.
Savage, MN 55378
ph: 612-882-9373
fax: 612-895-1084

Steins

(see also GLASSES, Drinking)

Clubs/Associations

Joyce M. Reyhons, Pres.
Advertising Cup & Mug Collectors of America
Newsletter: Cupletter, The
P.O. Box 680
Solon, IA 52333
ph: 319-644-3636
For collectors of special custom-made ceramic or plastic mugs, cups, and steins from advertisers, fund raisers, shows, conventions, or promotions; quarterly newsletter; send $2 plus LSASE for sample.

Anheuser-Busch Collectors Club
2700 South Broadway
Saint Louis, MO 63118
ph: 313-577-7465 or 800-305-2582
fax: 314-577-9656
web: http://www.budweiser.com/
For collectors of Anheuser-Busch steins and related collectibles.

Dealers

Sam & Samantha May
Sam's Steins & Collectibles
2207 Lincoln Highway East
Lancaster, PA 17602-1111
ph: 717-394-6404
fax: 717-394-6427
e-mail: SamsSteins@msn.com
For the collector of mugs and steins: Anheuser Busch, Strohs, Coors, Miller, Hamm's, Pabst, Yuengling, etc.; also German steins, Cavanaugh Coca-Cola bear figurines; send two first class stamps for list.

Bob Lamson
Bob Lamson Beer Steins, Inc.
509 N. 22nd St.
Allentown, PA 18104-4305
ph: 610-435-8611 or 800-435-8611

Wally Karutz
Great American Brewery Shoppe, The
128 N.Main St.
P.O. Box 4417
Salisbury, NC 28145-4417
ph: 704-642-1345 or 800-223-8197
fax: 704-642-1377
e-mail: wallyworld@collectorsteins.com
web: http://www.geocities.com/Eureka/Plaza/3544/
Carries large selection of Budweiser and other brewery steins and collectibles.

Larry Meyer
Kaiser Bill's
P.O. Box 177
Helen, GA 30545
ph: 800-922-2182 or 706-878-2182
fax: 706-878-2057
e-mail: kbills@orchid-isle.com
web: http://www.kaiserbills.com/
Displays over 1500 different beer steins including Budweiser, German, Coke, Civil War, wooden, and NASCAR steins; 1995's largest Anheuser-Busch dealer in the country.

Roy & Cordie Willis
Heartland of Kentucky Decanters & Steins
P.O. Box 428
Lebanon Junction, KY 40150
ph: 502-833-2827
fax: 502-833-3480
e-mail: heartlandky@ka.net
web: http://www.ka.net/heartlandky/
Hundreds of whiskey decanters by Jim Beam, Wild Turkey, Ski Country, McCormick and others; also beer steins, domestic or foreign; call ONLY 9-5 eastern time.

Bill Cress
P.O. Box 989
Alton, IL 62002-0989
ph: 618-466-3513
Buys and sells all of the new and lots of the old steins; quarterly lists of modern steins and mugs for sale.

Doug & Natalie Marks
Flash Collectibles
560 N. Moorpark Rd., Ste. 287
Thousand Oaks, CA 91360-3703
ph: 805-499-9222
fax: 805-376-5541
e-mail: flashcoll@aol.com
web: http://members.aol.com/flashcoll/
Buys and sells contemporary beer steins by mail order; specializes in American beer brands, Budweiser, Miller, Coors, Hamms, Pabst, Old Style, etc.

Jim & Linda Cheely
These Steins of Mine
2449 Hugo Rd.
Merlin, OR 97532
ph: 541-479-1971
e-mail: lcheely@cpros.com
web: http://www.cpros.com/~lcheely/
Buys, sells, trades Anheuser Busch Budweiser steins in the secondary market worldwide over the Internet.

Man./Prod./Dist.

M. Cornell Importers, Inc.
1462 18th St.
St. Paul, MN 55112
ph: 651-633-8690
fax: 651-636-3568
Focuses on importing hundreds of new conventional, miniature, character, and special-interest German steins each year; constantly introducing new artists, molds, color combinations, handles and lids.

Anheuser-Busch, Inc.
2700 South Broadway
Saint Louis, MO 63118
ph: 313-577-7465 or 800-305-2582
fax: 314-577-9656
web: http://www.budweiser.com/
Creates collector steins and plates of character and celebration, with classic and contemporary themes and styles.

Ken Armke
OHI Exchange
Newsletter: OHI Exchange
553 Landa St.
New Braunfels, TX 78130
ph: 830-629-1191
fax: 830-606-1118
e-mail: Comments@OHIExchange.com
web: http://www.ohiexchange.com/
OHI offers exclusive limited edition steins and mugs for the discerning collector.

Ted DeGrazia

Man./Prod./Dist.

Artists of the World
2915 N. 67th Place
Scottsdale, AZ 85251-6001
ph: 602-946-6361
fax: 602-941-8918
e-mail: a-o-w@primenet.com
web: http://www.a-o-w.com/
Produces collector plates, figurines, ornaments and miniatures based on the work of Ted DeGrazia.

Toby Jugs

Periodicals

RBT Antiques
Newsletter: Tobies to Tinies
1035 Lupine Dr.
Sunnyvale, CA 94086-8733
ph: 408-733-4755
Newsletter for Toby and Character Jug collectors.

Toby Jugs (Kevin Francis)

Clubs/Associations

Kevin Francis Toby Jug Collectors Guild
917 Chicago Ave.
Evanston, IL 60202
ph: 800-634-0431 or 847-570-4867
fax: 847-570-4871
Produces Toby Jugs designed by Francis Salmon and Kevin Pearson.

COLLEGE COLLECTIBLES

Collectors

Beisner
P.O. Box 580613
Minneapolis, MN 55458
Wants to buy college yearbooks from Kansas colleges; also wants to buy histories of college social sororities and fraternities; describe and price.

Experts

Kevin McCandless
P.O. Box 435
Champaign, IL 61824-0435
ph: 217-367-4466

Humor Magazines

Collectors

Michael Gessel
P.O. Box 748
Arlington, VA 22216-0748
ph: 703-542-0462
Wants magazines (bound or individual copies); also posters and anthologies.

Pins

Collectors

Beisner
P.O. Box 580613
Minneapolis, MN 55458
Wants to buy college social sorority and fraternity pins as well as other sorority or fraternity jewelry; send sketch or photocopy, and price.

COMBS & HAIR ACCESSORIES

(see also BARBERSHOP COLLECTIBLES; BEAUTY SHOP COLLECTIBLES; CLOTHING & ACCESSORIES, Vintage; DRESSER ITEMS, Hatpins & Hatpin Holders; HAIRWORK; GEMS & JEWELRY; SHAVING COLLECTIBLES)

Clubs/Associations

Belva Green, Ed.
Antique Comb Collectors Club International
Newsletter: Antique Comb Collector
90 Highland Ave., #1204
Tarpon Springs, FL 34689
ph: 727-942-7354
e-mail: comber@iserv.net
web: http://www.geocities.com/Heartland/Pointe/5350/
Organization dedicated to sharing research and information about antique and ornamental accessories for the hair from any culture; offers research, networking, networking, bi-annual convention.

Collectors

Mary Bachman
4901 Grandview
Ypsilanti, MI 48197-3762
ph: 313-434-2045
e-mail: bachman@provide.net
Author of "Collectors Guide to Hair Combs" (Collector Books).

Glenn L. Beall
32981 N. River Rd.
Libertyville, IL 60048-4259
ph: 847-549-9970
fax: 847-549-9935

Betty Miller
5285 Marble Dr.
Gold Junction, AZ 85219
ph: 480-983-4655

Dealers

Priscilla Washed
Victorian Lady, The
102 South Main St.
P.O. Box 424
Waxhaw, NC 28173-0424
ph: 704-843-4467 or 800-786-1886
A Victorian specialty store featuring 19th century ladies decorative & fashion accessories; buys and sells purses; also sewing and needlework tools, vintage fashion, Victoriana, and combs; mail order; catalog $5.

Experts

Belva Green
90 Highland Ave., #1204
Tarpon Springs, FL 34689
ph: 727-942-7354
e-mail: comber@iserv.net
Collector, historian, researcher, lecturer on combs, jewelry and accessories for the hair; editor for Antique Comb Collector Club International newsletter; manuscripts welcome; query with SASE.

Museums/Libraries

David Wilson
Leominster Historical Society, Field School Museum
17 School St.
Leominster, MA 01453
ph: 978-534-5375
One of the best comb collections in the U.S.

COMIC ART

(see CARTOON ART)

COMIC BOOKS

(see also CARTOON ART; CHARACTER COLLECTIBLES; COMIC ART; COMIC COLLECTIBLES; COWBOY HEROES; DISNEY COLLECTIBLES; FAN CLUBS; PREMIUMS; SCIENCE FICTION; SUPER HEROES; TRADING CARDS, Non-Sport)

Appraisers

Thomas Bauer
Nonstop Collectibles
6659 Sherbrooke, #25
Montreal, Quebec H4B 1N8
Canada
ph: 514-489-5499
e-mail: tom2@odyssee.net
web: http://www.odyssee.net/~tom2/index.html
Internet sales consultant and broker since 1993; active in online sales and marketing of comic books and other collectibles; will do qualified evaluations of your collection; list items for sale for 20% commission; good comic info.

Collectors

Gary Pimenta
64 Lakeside Dr.
Tiverton, RI 02878-3111
Wants to buy comic books based on TV shows and theatrical movies.

Peter Tilp
B & T Publications
P.O. Box 580
Summit, NJ 07901-0580
Wants to buy pre-1960 comic books.

Steve A. Geppi
Diamond Comic Distributors
1966 Greenspring Dr., Ste. 300
Lutherville Timonium, MD 21093-4161
ph: 410-560-7100
Golden Age, DC's, Timelys, Marvels, all 10 cent and 12 cent comics pre-1968; also baseball cards or related items.

Dealers

Philip M. Levine & Sons
P.O. Box 246
Three Bridges, NJ 08887
ph: 908-788-0532
fax: 908-788-1028
Buys and sells comic books, TV Guides, magazines, etc.

Metropolis Collectibles
873 Broadway, Ste. 201
New York, NY 10003
ph: 212-627-9691 or 800-229-6387
fax: 212-627-5947
Buys and sells vintage movie posters and comic books; free appraisals; finders fees paid.

Joshua Nathanson
ComicLink: The Internet Comic Book Exchange
4842 Glenwood St.
Flushing, NY 11363-0299
ph: 718-423-6079
fax: 718-423-9801
e-mail: buysell@comiclink.com
web: http://www.comiclink.com

Richard Semowich
56 John Smith Rd.
Binghamton, NY 13901
ph: 607-648-4025
Wants old comic books from 1933 to 1970; buying any size collection; contact for the best price.

Jon Warren
American Collectibles Exchange
P.O. Box 2512
Chattanooga, TN 37409
ph: 423-265-5515 or 800-880-4289
fax: 423-265-5506
e-mail: jonrwarren@aol.com
Wants comics, also wants cartoon art, Disney, Big Little Books, Pulp Magazines, Baseball and Non-Sport Cards.

Bill & Joanne Bruegman
Toy Scouts, Inc.
137 Casterton Ave.
Akron, OH 44303-1543
ph: 330-836-0668
fax: 330-869-8668
e-mail: toyscout@akron.infi.net
Wants to buy 1935-1965 super hero, horror, etc. 10 cent and 12 cent comics.

John Kula
Goldmine Collectibles
65 54th Street SW
Grand Rapids, MI 49548
ph: 616-534-7227 or 616-361-2352
fax: 616-534-0009
e-mail: comicman@grnet.com
web: http://www.GoldmineComics.com
Collector and expert buys, sells, trades comic, toys and other collectibles pertaining to Star Wars, Spawn, GI Joe, Transformers, X-Files, Babylon V, and other science fiction shows or movies.

Carl Bonasera
Al-American Comic Shops, Ltd.
3514 W. 95th St.
Evergreen Park, IL 60642
ph: 708-425-7555
Advisor to Alex Malloy's "Comic Values Annual"; specializes in 1950s-1990s comic books, magazines, science fiction digests and pulps.

Bruce Mohrhard
Mo's Comics & Stories Shop
4573 Gravois
Saint Louis, MO 63116
ph: 314-353-9500

Clint's Bookstore
3943 Main St.
Kansas City, MO 64111
ph: 816-561-2848
The place to find old, new and obscure comic books from the Golden Age to present.

Stan Gold
As Time Goes By
7042 Dartbrook Dr.
Dallas, TX 75240
ph: 972-239-8621 or 214-352-2765
fax: 972-239-9622
e-mail: record@unicomp.net
web: http://www.astimegoesby.com/
Wants to buy Golden Age, Silver Age, 1940s and 1950s horror/humor/war comic books, TV related and Western comics; also wants vintage comic related puzzles, books, records and toys.

Michael Dice
309 S Washington
Cortez, CO 81321
ph: 970-564-9018
e-mail: oldcomix@fone.net
Buys, sells, trades comic strips from Sunday papers, especially from bound newspapers; also wants pre-1955 comic books.

Dennis Schamp
Comic Gallery, The
4224 Balboa Ave.
San Diego, CA 92117
ph: 619-483-4853
Advisor to Alex Malloy's "Comic Values Annual."

David Smith
Rocket Comics
P.O. Box 30183
Seattle, WA 98103
ph: 206-784-7300
fax: 206-782-2844
e-mail: rocket@jetcity.com
web: http://www.jetcity.com/~rocket/
Dealer/expert buying and selling vintage comic books and pulp magazines since 1969; store has 2,500 sq. ft. of vintage comic books, pulp magazines, mass market magazines and paper books, and related paper collectibles.

Thomas Bauer
Nonstop Collectibles
6659 Sherbrooke, #25
Montreal, Quebec H4B 1N8
Canada
ph: 514-489-5499
e-mail: tom2@odyssee.net
web: http://www.odyssee.net/~tom2/index.html
Internet sales consultant and broker since 1993; active in online sales and marketing of comic books and other collectibles; will do qualified evaluations of your collection; list items for sale for 20% commission; good comic info.

Experts

Robert Overstreet
Overstreet Publications Inc.
11729 Mayfair Field Dr.
Lutherville Timonium, MD 21093-7011
ph: 410-561-3217

Ernst Gerber
Gerber Publishing
P.O. Box 201
Glenbrook, NV 89413
ph: 775-883-4100
fax: 775-887-1000
Author of "The Photo-Journal Guide to Comic Books."

Ken Mitchell
710 Conacher Dr.
Willowdale, Ontario M2M 3N6
Canada
ph: 416-222-5808
Buys and sells comic character collectibles (comic books, Sunday funnies, "Big Little Books", etc.) and other nostalgic paper including music (Pop) magazines and books from 1890 through 1960s.

Internet Resources

Joshua Nathanson
ComicLink: The Internet Comic Book Exchange
4842 Glenwood St.
Flushing, NY 11363-0299
ph: 718-423-6079
fax: 718-423-9801
e-mail: buysell@comiclink.com
web: http://www.comiclink.com
High quality comic book exchange

where dealers and collectors buy and sell pre-1980 comic books, collections, original comic art and related items; wide selection of Golden and Silver Age comics including some of the most valuable.

ComicWeb, The
P.O. Box 3416
Silver Spring, MD 20918-3416
e-mail: editor@comicweb.com
web: http://www.comicweb.com

Jonah Weiland
Comic Book Resources
10153 1/2 Riverside Dr., Ste. #604
North Hollywood, CA 91602
ph: 818-9895-6688
fax: 818-985-6668
e-mail: jonah@boilingpoint.com
web: http://www.comicbookresources.com/
The web site for comic book fans: news, interviews, commentary, discussions.

Museums/Libraries

Dave Smith
Walt Disney Archives
500 South Buena Vista St.
Burbank, CA 91521-3040
ph: 818-560-5424
Comprehensive Disney collection including complete U.S. and most foreign Disney comics; comics not available to researchers for preservation reasons; usage limited to approved projects.

Periodicals

Gary M. Carter
Gemstone Publishing, Inc.
Magazine: Overstreet's Comic Book Marketplace
1996 Greenspring Dr., Ste. 405
Lutherville Timonium, MD 21093-4117
ph: 888-375-9800 x249
fax: 410-560-6107
e-mail: pdeanna@diamondcomics.com
Monthly comic book price guide; values, latest hot titles, regional market reports, fully illustrated; full color, 130-150 pgs.

Gary M. Carter
Gemstone Publishing, Inc.
Magazine: Overstreet's Advanced Collector
1996 Greenspring Dr., Ste. 405
Lutherville Timonium, MD 21093-4117
ph: 888-375-9800 x249
fax: 410-560-6107
e-mail: pdeanna@diamondcomics.com
Quarterly magazine the specifically focuses on Golden Age & Silver Age comic books & collectibles.

Jon Warren
American Collectibles Exchange
Magazine: Comics Source
P.O. Box 2512
Chattanooga, TN 37409
ph: 423-265-5515 or 800-880-4289
fax: 423-265-5506
e-mail: jonrwarren@aol.com
A monthly comics magazine about collecting, learning, reminiscing, buying, selling, trading, visiting, and sharing stories.

Pat DuChene, PR
Krause Publications
Newspaper: Comics Buyer's Guide
700 E. State St.
Iola, WI 54990-0001
ph: 715-445-2214
fax: 715-445-4087
e-mail: info@krause.com
web: http://www.krause.com/
Only weekly newspaper serving comic fans, collectors & the entire comics industry; articles on comics of the past & present, news, columns by top writers, comics show calendar, monthly price guide supplements on comics & trading cards.

Pat DuChene, PR
Krause Publications
Magazine: Comics Retailer
700 E. State St.
Iola, WI 54990-0001
ph: 715-445-2214
fax: 715-445-4087
e-mail: info@krause.com
web: http://www.krause.com/
Contains business-related editorial to help retailers become more profitable; covers comics, games, video, books, toys, trading cars; columns written by retailers and business experts.

Dana Gabbard
Magazine: Duckburg Times
3010 Wilshire Blvd. #362
Los Angeles, CA 90010-1146
ph: 213-388-2364
Focuses on comics based on Walt Disney characters.

Fantagraphics Books
Magazine: Comics Journal, The
7563 Lake City Way
Seattle, WA 98115
ph: 206-524-1967 or 800-657-1100
e-mail: fbicomix@fantagraphics.com
web: http://www.tcj.com/
Monthly magazine for the comic book industry: news, interviews, comic reviews, etc.

Ken Mitchell
Newsletter: Comic Buyers Guide
710 Conacher Dr.
Willowdale, Ontario M2M 3N6
Canada
ph: 416-222-5808
A weekly publication.

Computer Programs For

Man./Prod./Dist.

Todd VerBeek
Radio Zero
Software: cDATA2000
1311 Lake Dr., #2
Grand Rapids, MI 49506
e-mail: TVerBeek@RZero.com
web: http://www.rzero.com/soft/
A database for comic book collectors.

Fawcett

Clubs/Associations

P.S. Hamerlinck
Fawcett Collectors of America
P.O. Box 24751
Minneapolis, MN 55424-0751
e-mail: WaltGrogan@aol.com
web: http://shazam.imginc.com/fca/
For collectors of Fawcett comics and Magazine Enterprise comics.

Magazine Enterprise

Clubs/Associations

P.S. Hamerlinck
Fawcett Collectors of America
P.O. Box 24751
Minneapolis, MN 55424-0751
e-mail: WaltGrogan@aol.com
web: http://shazam.imginc.com/fca/
For collectors of Fawcett comics and Magazine Enterprise comics.

Super Heroes

Dealers

Anton Kawasaki
Adventure Ink
475 Bedford Rd.
Pleasantville, NY 10570
ph: 914-741-2510
fax: 914-741-2510
e-mail: AdvntreInk@aol.com
Interested in super hero comic books.

Western

Experts

Robert Phillips
1703 North Aster Place
Broken Arrow, OK 74012
ph: 918-254-8205
fax: 918-252-9362
Has studied and collected Western comics and Western comic art for years; has written many articles on the subject and is currently writing a reference book to be published.

COMIC COLLECTIBLES

(see also CARTOON ART; CHARACTER COLLECTIBLES; COMIC ART; COMIC BOOKS; COWBOY HEROES; DISNEY COLLECTIBLES; FAN CLUBS; PREMIUMS; SCIENCE FICTION; SUPER HEROES)

COMIC STRIPS

Sunday Newspaper

(see also CARTOON ART; CHARACTER COLLECTIBLES; ELVES)

Dealers

Claude Held
Claude Held Collectibles
P.O. Box 515
Cheektowaga, NY 14225
ph: 716-634-4842
Wants to buy pre-1960 Sunday comic sections; also pulp magazines before 1950 (horror, spicy, science fiction, weird types), and pre-1950 E.R. Burroughs books with dust jackets.

Michael Dice
309 S Washington
Cortez, CO 81321
ph: 970-564-9018
e-mail: oldcomix@fone.net
Buys, sells, trades comic strips from Sunday papers, especially from bound newspapers; also wants pre-1955 comic books.

Experts

Ken Mitchell
710 Conacher Dr.
Willowdale, Ontario M2M 3N6
Canada
ph: 416-222-5808
Buys and sells comic character collectibles (comic books, Sunday funnies, "Big Little Books", etc.) and other nostalgic paper including music (Pop) magazines and books from 1890 through 1960s.

Internet Resources

Stu's Comic Strip Connection
e-mail: stu@stus.com
web: http://www.stus.com/
You gateway to 1,000+ comic strip resources on the Internet: funnies pages, search tools, original content, descriptions of over 1,300 online cartoons.

Museums/Libraries

San Francisco Academy of Comic Art
170 W. Cliff Dr., #15
Santa Cruz, CA 95060-5440
ph: 831-427-1737
fax: 831-427-1737
Millions of newspaper strips, bound files, major dailies from 1890-1960, pulps, all science fiction, crime fiction, film history, children's books, comic books; excellent copies made of all graphic material; dup material for trade.

Periodicals

Tom Heintjes
Bull Moose Publishing Co.
Magazine: Hogan's Alley
P.O. Box 47684
Atlanta, GA 30362-0684
ph: 770-458-2624
fax: 815-328-0889
e-mail: 71061.43@compuserve.com
web: http://www.cagle.com/hogan
Contains coverage of comic strips, comic books, animation, political cartooning, gag cartooning, illustration, children's books, and more.

COMMEMORATIVE ITEMS

(see ROYALTY COLLECTIBLES; SOUVENIR & COMMEMORATIVE ITEMS)

COMMUNISM

(see SOCIAL CAUSES)

COMPACT DISCS

(see also RECORDS)

Dealers

Princeton Record Exchange
20 S. Tulane St.
Princeton, NJ 08542
ph: 609-921-0881
e-mail: info@prex.com
web: http://www.prex.com
Buys and sells new and used CDs, LPs, and tapes: rock, jazz, alternative, imports, oldies, hip hop, soul, funk, new releases, classical, opera, etc.

Record Setter, The
742 Rt. 18 N.
East Brunswick, NJ 08816-4906
ph: 732-257-3888
fax: 732-257-2366
Specializing in used CDs and out-of-print albums; promoters of largest record collectors convention in the US.

Paul C. Mawhinney
Record-Rama Sound Archives
1130 Perry Highway
Pines Plaza
Pittsburgh, PA 15237-2132
ph: 724-367-7330
fax: 724-367-7388
e-mail: recrama@recordrama.com
web: http://www.recordrama.com
Carries over 2,500,000 vinyl sound recordings and over 200,000 compact discs; orders by phone.

Wax Trax
1225 N. 5th St.
Stroudsburg, PA 18360
ph: 570-421-3320
fax: 570-420-1006
Records, cassettes, compact discs; buys record collections; specializes in out-of-print records.

Mike Hawkinson
Disc Collector
P.O. Box 4000
Parker, CO 80134
ph: 303-841-3000 or 303-841-1118
fax: 303-840-9373
e-mail: cd@discol.com
web: http://www.discol.com/
Specializing in oldies from the '50s to '70s; one of the world's largest selections.

Experts

Paul Bergquist
6406 W. Olympic Blvd.
Los Angeles, CA 90048
Co-author with Jerry Osborne of "The Official Price Guide to Compact Discs" (House of Collectibles, 1994).

Jerry Osborne
P.O. Box 255
Port Townsend, WA 98368
ph: 360-385-1200
fax: 360-385-6572
e-mail: jpo@olympus.net
web: http://www.jerryosborne.com
Co-author with Paul Bergquist of "The Official Price Guide to Compact Discs" (House of Collectibles, 1994).

Periodicals

Peter Howard, Pub.
Howard Communications Inc.
Magazine: ICE Magazine
P.O. Box 3043
Santa Monica, CA 90408-3043
ph: 310-829-1291
fax: 310-829-2979
e-mail: emailice@aol.com
web: http://www.icemagazine.com/
ICE provides collectors and enthusiasts a monthly dose of unrivaled CD coverage: release schedules, first word on new albums, upcoming box sets, reissues, and industry news; published monthly.

COMPACTS

(see also CLOTHING & ACCESSORIES, Vintage; DRESSER ITEMS; PURSES)

Clubs/Associations

Roselyn Gerson
Compact Collectors Club
Newsletter: Powder Puff
P.O. Box 40
Lynbrook, NY 11563-0040
ph: 516-593-8746
fax: 516-593-0611
e-mail: compactldy@aol.com
An international club whose members collect compacts, vanities, necessaires, etc.; newsletter contains articles, buy/sell ads, etc.

British Compact Collector's Society
P.O. Box 131
Woking, Surrey GU24 9YR
U.K.
Please send initial inquiries by mail, please enclose a SASE.

Collectors

Sherry & Mike Miller
303 Holiday Dr. #130
Tuscola, IL 61953-2118
ph: 217-253-4991
e-mail: miller@tuscola.net
web: http://www.tuscola.net/~miller/
Wants ladies powder compacts in shape of objects (figural compacts), e.g. shaped like a bird, a guitar, or a padlock; many made from 1920s through early 1960s by companies like Volupte, Zell, and Elgin.

Lori Landgrebe
2331 E. Main St.
Decatur, IL 62521-2263
ph: 217-423-2254
Wants to buy ladies' compacts and compact purses; buying any colorful, Art Deco, enamel novelty and figural compacts; must be in good to mint condition.

Susan Murphy
29668 Orinda Rd.
San Juan Capistrano, CA 92675-1211
ph: 949-364-4333
Wants to buy older powder compacts and anything with a compact in it or a part of it such as purses, lighters; please enclose SASE.

Dealers

Susan Murphy
29668 Orinda Rd.
San Juan Capistrano, CA 92675-1211
ph: 949-364-4333
Buys and sells ladies powder compacts, any and all that are in good to mint condition; please enclose SASE.

Experts

Roselyn Gerson
P.O. Box 100
Malverne, NY 11565
ph: 516-593-8746
fax: 516-593-0611
Wants unusual gadget compacts: cane/compact, hatpin/compact, gun/compact; also compact advertising; author of "Ladies' Compacts of the 19th & 20th Centuries", a fully-illustrated identification & value guide.

Roseann Ettinger
Remember When
21-23 W. Broad St.
Hazleton, PA 18201
ph: 570-454-8465 or 570-450-5542
Author of "Compacts and Smoking Accessories."

Leslie Scatch
664 Milwood Ave.
Venice, CA 90291
ph: 310-821-8011
fax: 310-837-6109
e-mail: vintagevamp@sprynet.com
Vintage compact collector and expert.

Repair Services

Anton Laub Glass Corp.
1873 Second Ave.
New York, NY 10029-7453
ph: 212-734-4270 or 718-430-1901
Installation, beveling and resilvering of glass mirrors including the especially thin mirrors required for compacts.

Daniel De Tagle
de Tagle Goldsmith Shop
14400 Union Ave.
San Jose, CA 95124-2815
ph: 408-377-7000
Jeweler who repairs and replaces missing twist closures, hinges and frames on various articles including compacts; also goldsmith and manufacturer of custom and fine gold jewelry.

COMPUTERS

(see also ANTIQUES DEALERS & COLLECTORS, Computer Programs For; CALCULATORS; SLIDE RULES)

Appraisers

Paul Willigan, Pres.
NICE Network, Inc.
2126 Alpine Place
Cincinnati, OH 45206-2603
ph: 513-961-1052 or 800-837-NICE
fax: 513-961-0538
e-mail: paul@nicenetwork.com
web: http://www.nicenetwork.com/
Appraisers of high tech and high value electronic equipment including computers, PBX telephone systems, medical equipment, copiers, software, film printers, optical jukeboxes, mainframe computers, audio-visual systems, etc.

Clubs/Associations

David Greelish
Historical Computer Society
Newsletter: Classic Computing
1 Oakleigh Ct.
Richmond, VA 23233-3125
ph: 804-754-1951
e-mail: david@classiccomputing.com
web: http://www.classiccomputing.com/
A unique magazine for the computer history buff and collector; web site is dedicated to computer history nostalgia; features a books store, magazine, auction and other links, letters, collector values, and news.

Computer History Association of California
Newsletter: Analytical Engine, The
4159-C El Camino Way
Palo Alto, CA 94306-4010
ph: 650-856-9915
fax: 650-856-9914
e-mail: engine@chac.org
web: http://www.chac.org/
Focuses on the history of computers and the computer industry in California.

Collectors

Tom Copper
Tom's Small Engines
1416 Ralapen St.
Roxboro, NC 27573-4232
ph: 336-599-6908
e-mail: tcopper@interpath.com
web: http://home.interpath.net/tcopper/
Collector of obsolete personal computers, peripherals, software, manuals and literature for same; offers support for people still using older computers.

Paul Pierce
2933 NE 17th Ave.
Portland, OR 97212
ph: 503-281-6995
e-mail: pp@teleport.com
web: http://www.teleport.com/~prp/collect/
Specializes in older mainframes, minis, and representative examples of other types of computers.

Dealers

Steve Spevak
P.O. Box 3173
Winchester, VA 22604-2373
ph: 540-877-2561 or 540-665-7375
fax: 540-877-2561
Wants to buy bulk quantities of old computer circuit boards, telephone equipment circuit boards, boards from main frame computers preferred; also wants to buy bulk quantities of old vacuum tubes from old amplifiers, etc.

Experts

Thomas F. Haddock
P.O. Box 2626
Ann Arbor, MI 48106
Author of "A Collector's Guide to Personal Computers and Pocket Calculators: A Historical, Rarity, and Value Guide" (Books Americana, 1993).

Museums/Libraries

Lucia Lucc Quinn, Ex. Dir.
Computer Museum, The
300 Congress St.
Boston, MA 02210
ph: 617-426-2800 or 617-423-6758
e-mail: quinn@tcm.org
web: http://www.tcm.org/

Steve Plotkin
Real World Computer Museum
7 Creek Parkway
Marcus Hook, PA 19061
ph: 610-494-9000
fax: 610-494-2090
A regional computer museum dedicated to preserving and displaying computing and allied technologies, storage devices, semiconductor technology, computer art; seeking old computers and electronic relics, devices and related memorabilia.

George Keremedjiev, Dir.
American Computer Museum
234 East Babcock St.
Bozeman, MT 59715-4765
ph: 406-587-7545
fax: 406-587-9620
e-mail: bitenbyte@aol.com
web: http://www.compustory.com/index.htm
Comprehensive display of calculation devices spanning 4,000 years of history; from slide rules to micro chips.

David Weil, Cur.
Computer Museum of America at Coleman College
Newsletter: Circuit, The
7380 Parkway Dr.
La Mesa, CA 91942
ph: 619-465-8228
fax: 619-463-0162
e-mail: dweil@computer-museum.org
web: http://www.computer-museum.org/
Computer and data processing related exhibits chronicling the history of the modern computer over the past century.

San Francisco Computer Museum
110 McAllister, Ste. 409
P.O. Box 420914
San Francisco, CA 94142-0914
ph: 415-703-8362
fax: 415-703-8359
e-mail: erich@fog.com
web: http://www.fog.com/sfcm/

CONDOM TINS

(see PROPHYLACTICS, Tins)

CONJURING

(see MAGICIANS PARAPHERNALIA)

CONSERVATION

(see also REPAIR/RESTORATION/CONSERVATION)

Museums/Libraries

American Association of State & Local History
Newsletter: History News Dispatch
1717 Church St.
Nashville, TN 37203-2991
ph: 615-320-3203
fax: 615-327-9013
e-mail: history@aaslh.org
web: http://www.aaslh.org/
Supplies technical leaflets on such things as proper lighting techniques for collectors & small museums; write for list of leaflets and books on similar subjects that are offered for sale; the "Dispatch" monthly, "History News" bi-monthly.

CONSERVATORS

(see REPAIR/RESTORATION/CONSERVATION)

CONSTRUCTION EQUIPMENT

(see INDUSTRY RELATED ITEMS; MACHINERY & EQUIPMENT)

COOKBOOKS

(see also BOOKS; COOKIES & COOKIE SHAPING; FOOD COLLECTIBLES; MENUS)

Clubs/Associations

Bob & Jo Ellen Allen
Cook Book Collectors Club of America, Inc.
Newsletter: Cook Book Gossip
P.O. Box 56
Saint James, MO 65559-0056
ph: 573-265-8296
Focuses on cookbooks & advertising cook books and recipe publications by many companies such as Jell-O, Pillsbury, Betty Crocker, etc.

Barbara Gelink
Cook Book Collector's Club
Newsletter: Cook Book Collector's Club Newsletter
4756 Terrace Dr.
San Diego, CA 92116-2514
ph: 619-281-8962
e-mail: cookwithbabs@home.com
web: http://www.sandiegoinsider.com/community/groups/cookbook/
Club has been well received for over 3 years; membership includes 12 newsletters, local field trips and quest speakers; club has nationwide membership; newsletter reports on cookbook auction results, list of cookbooks for sale each month.

Collectors

Steve Armstrong
P.O. Box 1409
Florence, AL 35631-1409
Wants pre-1950 soft bound cookbooks, booklets, advertising recipe publications such as baking powder, JELL-O, flour, etc.; send complete description and price.

Sue Erwin
P.O. Box 32369
San Jose, CA 95152-2369
ph: 408-258-8657

Dealers

Louise Pennisi
Around the Kitchen
P.O. Box 840
Georgetown, CT 06829
ph: 203-438-2338
e-mail: louise@aroundthekitchen.com
web: http://www.aroundthekitchen.com
Buying and selling collectible cookbooks (19th & 20th century), cookery booklets (Pillsbury, Baker's Chocolate, Jell-O, etc.), antique kitchen instruction & recipe pamphlets; issues catalogs of items for sale.

Mary Barile
Heritage Publications
P.O. Box 335
Arkville, NY 12406
ph: 914-586-3810
fax: 914-586-2797
Offers out-of-print and rare cookbooks; also "Cookbooks Worth Collecting", an illustrated history and guide with prices to the world of American cookbooks; for collectors, dealers, sellers, etc.; send SASE for information.

Betty Gabbert
Cookbooks 'N Things
HCR 33 Box 58
Compton, AR 72624
ph: 501-420-3418
Issues periodic catalog of contemporary cookbooks for sale.

Susan B. Jiminez
Vintage Bookbookery, The
P.O. Box 3943
Albuquerque, NM 87190-3943
ph: 505-837-2569
fax: 505-872-0851
e-mail: kalesija@aol.com
web: http://www.bibliofind.com/vintagecookbookery.htm
Buys and sells vintage, collectible, and classic cookbooks, cooking pamphlets, and advertising recipe booklets.

Vintage Cookbookery
P.O. Box 3943
Albuquerque, NM 87190-3943
ph: 505-837-2569
e-mail: kalesija@aol.com
web: http://www.bibliofind.com/vintagecookbookery.htm

Janet Jarvits
Janet Jarvits, Bookseller
P.O. Box 11327
Burbank, CA 91510-1327
ph: 818-848-4630
fax: 818-848-6357
e-mail: cookbkjj@ni.net
web: http://abebooks.com/home/JJARVITS/
Sells out-of-print cookbooks, books on wine and beverages, and related magazines, ephemera, etc.; issues periodic catalogs listing items for sale; want list is available upon request; mail order.

Barbara Gelink
OTENTO Book Search
Newsletter: Old Cookbook News & Views
4756 Terrace Dr.
San Diego, CA 92116-2514
ph: 619-281-8962
e-mail: cookwithbabs@home.com
web: http://www.sandiegoinsider.com/community/groups/cookbook/
Specialist in out-of-print cookbooks; also a book finder for out-of-print cookbooks; places ads in national book magazines and has realized a 50% success rate; charges $2 per title to locate book which usually takes 2-3 weeks.

Experts

Bob & Jo Ellen Allen
231 E. James Blvd.
P.O. Box 85
Saint James, MO 65559-0085
ph: 314-265-8296
Wants cookbooks & advertising cook books and recipe publications by many companies such as Jell-O, Pillsbury, Betty Crocker, etc.; author of "A Guide to Collecting Cookbooks - A Value Guide."

Museums/Libraries

Schlesinger Library at Radcliffe College
10 Garden St.
Cambridge, MA 02138-3630
ph: 617-495-8647
e-mail: slref@radcliffe.edu
web: http://www.radcliffe.edu/schles/
50,000 volumes including repository of cookbooks and manuscript materials including many charity cookbooks; also women's history and psychology.

Culinary Institute of America Library
433 Albany Post Rd.
Hyde Park, NY 12538
ph: 914-452-9600
web: http://www.ciachef.edu/Library/linfo.html
Large cookbook collection including many hard-to-find modern cookbooks and videos.

Library of Congress, Rare Books & Special Collections Division
101 Independence Ave. SE
Washington, DC 20540-4860
ph: 202-707-4144 or 202-707-8000
fax: 202-707-4142
e-mail: rbsc@loc.gov
web: http://www.loc.gov
Houses the Katherine Bitting and Elizabeth Pennell collections of gastronomy and culinary publications including the musical cookbook in which recipes may be sung.

Periodicals

Sue Erwin
Newspaper: Cookbook Collectors' Exchange
P.O. Box 32369
San Jose, CA 95152-2369
ph: 408-258-8657
Lists cookbooks for sale or trade; voluntarily assist in locating items; non-commercial ads are free to collectors; articles, etc.

COOKIE JARS

(see also CERAMICS [AMERICAN PRODUCTION ARTWARE])

Clubs/Associations

Merla Davis, Treas.
American Cookie Jar Association
1600 Navajo Rd.
Norman, OK 73026
e-mail: davismj@ionet.net
web: http://cookiejarclub.com/

Collectors

John Krupienski
5200 Hilltop Dr.
P.O. Box AA6
Brookhaven, PA 19015-1200
ph: 610-874-3003
Wants to buy character shaped cookie jars.

Olga Andreau
Extinct Collectibles
P.O. Box 347911
Miami, FL 33234-7911
ph: 305-857-9234
e-mail: oandreu@aol.com
web: http://www.extinctcollectibles.com/

Ellen Supnick
2771 Oakbrook Manor
Fort Lauderdale, FL 33332
ph: 954-578-8787
Wants to buy figural cookie jars.

Peggy Vaught
Neardark
P.O. Box 32
Mendon, OH 45862
ph: 419-795-3404
e-mail: neardark@bright.net
Wants to buy cookie jars.

Carl & Gari McCallum
918 Rosewood
Wasco, CA 93280-1619
ph: 805-758-5630
Buy, sell, trade cookie jars; collects all types but prefers figural and advertising jars.

Dealers

Carol Silagyi
C.S. Antiques & Jewelry
P.O. Box 151
Wyckoff, NJ 07430
ph: 201-934-6528
Buys and sells cartoon, Storybook, etc. cookie jars by Abingdon, Brush, McCoy, RRP, Shawnee, Regal, etc.; also collects head/faces cookie jars - over 200 in collection.

Martin C. Sobin
Ye Olde Cookie Jar Trader
91 Fox Hollow Rd.
Sparta, NJ 07871-1107
ph: 201-729-9492
Wants to buy figural cookie jars in very good or better condition, especially interested in cookie jars made by Abingdon, Brush, and Shawnee.

Mark McMahon
Cookie Jars, Etc.
Chelsea Antiques Building
110 West 25th St., 8th Floor
New York, NY 10001
ph: 212-633-1923
fax: 212-924-8535
e-mail: peter@peterandmark.com
web: http://www.peterandmark.com
Buy, sell, trade cookie jars, banks, salt & peppers and PEZ.

Mel Cohen
Cooki-Jar
P.O. Box 700
Pomona, NY 10970-0700
ph: 914-354-8707
Serious cookie jar collector.

Judy Posner
4195 South Tamiami Trail, Ste. 183
Venice, FL 34293-5112
ph: 941-497-7149
fax: 941-493-8085
e-mail: jpc@tias.com
web: http://www.tias.com/stores/jpc/
Wants FIGURAL cookie jars: comic characters, Disney, Black Mammys, Chefs, Butlers, etc.; send for illustrated want list.

Jean & Bill Correll
Great Jars by Jean
1615 N Street
Bedford, IN 47421
ph: 812-279-2549

Lois & Ralph Behm
Lois' Collectibles of Antique Market III
413 W. Main St.
Saint Charles, IL 60174-1815
ph: 630-377-5599 or 847-831-5997
Buys and sells cookie jars; will buy entire collections.

Mercedes DiRenzo
Jazz'e Junque
3831 N. Lincoln
Chicago, IL 60613
ph: 773-463-7411
fax: 773-463-3687
e-mail: JazzyJunk@aol.com
web: http://www.jazzejunque.com
Buys and sells vintage and new cookie jars.

Neil Wegner
Have Treasure Will Travel
5737 35 Street
Red Deer, Alberta T4N 0S5
Canada
ph: 403-346-9706
e-mail: neil@cnnet.com
web: http://www.cyberattic.com/dealer/travel/
Sells vintage character, advertising and figural cookie jars; also related "go-withs."

Experts

Fred & Joyce Roerig
1501 Maple Ridge Rd.
Walterboro, SC 29488-9278
ph: 843-538-2487
fax: 843-538-4263
e-mail: ckejrn@lowcountry.com
Buys/sells/collects cookie jars; 20+ years experience; wants figural cookie jars not in books: Metlox, Twin Winton Jars & accessories, black Americana, ND School of Mines Mammy; author of "The Collector's Encyclopedia of Cookie Jars."

Ermagene Westfall
RR 1 Box 222
Richmond, MO 64085
Author of "An Illustrated Value Guide to Cookie Jars" and "An Illustrated Value Guide to Cookie Jars - Book II," 8 1/2" x 11"; with history, dates of companies, over 1000 cookie jars plus full color pictures; send SASE with all inquiries.

Internet Resources

Barbara Crews
Cookie Jars on The Mining Co.
4005 Spyglass Lane
Bethany, OK 73008
e-mail:
collectibles.guide@miningco.com
web: http://collectibles.miningco.com
The complete internet resource for cookie jar collecting; over 100 cookie jar web sites; weekly feature on different aspects of cookie jar collecting.

Misc. Services

Bill Kasting
Cookie Jar Matchmaker
P.O. Box 96
Kelso, MO 63758
e-mail: kazz@midwest.net
web: http://scribers.midwest/net/kazz/matchmaker.html
A web site dedicated to "matching" cookie jar lids and bases.

Museums/Libraries

Lucille Bromberek
Cookie Jar Museum, The
111 Stephen St.
Lemont, IL 60439
ph: 630-257-5012
Only Cookie Jar Museum in the world; over 2000 jars from U.S. and all over the world; also buys and sells.

Periodicals

Joyce Roerig
Newsletter: Cookie Jarrin'
1501 Maple Ridge Rd.
Walterboro, SC 29488-9278
ph: 843-538-2487
fax: 843-538-4263
e-mail: ckejrn@lowcountry.com
A bi-monthly newsletter with new information, current pricing, exciting discoveries, lots of photos; carefully researched for accuracy providing collectors and dealers with an unequaled professional quality newsletter.

COOKIES & COOKIE SHAPING

(see also COOKBOOKS; COOKIE JARS; KITCHEN COLLECTIBLES)

Clubs/Associations

Ruth Capper
Cookie Cutter Collectors Club
Newsletter: Cookie Crumbs
1167 Teal Rd. S.W.
Dellroy, OH 44620-9704
ph: 330-735-2839 or 202-966-0869
Focusing on cookie cutters, boards and rollers.

Collectors

Joyce Moorhouse
2763 310th St.
Cannon Falls, MN 55009

Priscilla Hinners
2711 Jaynia Place
Lemon Grove, CA 91945-1319
ph: 619-265-1046
e-mail: phinners@yahoo.com
Wants cookie/cake boards, cookie molds, multiple cutters, springerle, rollers.

Dealers

Bob & Kaaren Grossman
B & K Kitchen Primitives & Collectibles
354 Rte. 206
Chester, NJ 07930
ph: 908-879-7935
Specializes in pre-1900 cookie cutters and will mail-order all over the country.

Experts

Rosemary Henry
Newsletter: Cookies Newsletter
9610 Greenview Lane
Manassas, VA 20109-3320
ph: 703-361-5898
fax: 703-361-5898
e-mail: checkers@erols.com
web: http://www.cookiesnewsletter.com/
Buys/collects cookie shaping items and anything related to cookies: cutters, molds, presses, irons, photographs, postcards, ads, etc.

Periodicals

Rosemary Henry
Newsletter: Cookies Newsletter
9610 Greenview Lane
Manassas, VA 20109-3320
ph: 703-361-5898
fax: 703-361-5898
e-mail: checkers@erols.com
web: http://www.cookiesnewsletter.com/
For over 25 years, "Cookies" contains historical information about the shaping of cookies: flea market finds, new and old cutters, molds and stamps, tinsmiths, irons, presses, etc.; bi-monthly.

Milli Simerl
Newsletter: Around Ohio
508 N. Clinton
Defiance, OH 43512-1607
ph: 419-784-1545
Newsletter contains new cutter sources, old cutter research, area and national events, Q & A column; 20 years of back issues are available.

COPPER ITEMS

(see also ARTS & CRAFTS, Roycroft)

Repro. Sources

Steve Kayne
Kayne & Son Custom Forged Hardware
100 Daniel Ridge Rd.
Candler, NC 28715-9434
ph: 828-667-8868 or 828-665-1988
fax: 828-665-8303
e-mail: kaynehdwe@ioa.com
Steel, brass, bronze reproductions of locks, pulls, thumb latches, furniture & interior/exterior hardware, fireplace tools & accessories, lighting, kitchen utensils, etc.; also does repairs, restoration & conservation; $5 for two catalogs.

Stickley

Collectors

Terry Seger
880 Foxcreek Ln.
Cincinnati, OH 45233-1462
ph: 513-941-9689
Wants to buy Stickley Brothers copper; also large examples of Fulper pottery.

CORKPULLERS

(see CORKSCREWS)

CORKSCREWS

(see also BOTTLE OPENERS, Figural; WINES & WINE RELATED ITEMS)

Clubs/Associations

Milt Becker
Canadian Corkscrew Collectors Club
Newsletter: Quarterly Worm, The
P.O. Box 5295
Englewood, NJ 07631
ph: 201-567-1500
fax: 201-493-0685
e-mail: clarethous@aol.com
Worldwide membership; write for application form.

John Stanley
Just for Openers
Newsletter: Just for Openers Newsletter
P.O. Box 64
Chapel Hill, NC 27514
ph: 919-419-1546 or 919-966-5794
e-mail: jfo@mindspring.com
web: http://www.mindspring.com/~jfo
Just for Openers is a club for bottle and corkscrew collectors; quarterly newsletter.

Joseph C. Paradi
International Correspondence of Corkscrew Addicts
Newsletter: Bottle Scrue Times
670 Meadow Wood Road
Mississauga, Ontario L5J 2S6
Canada
ph: 905-823-3754 or 416-978-6924 x210
fax: 905-823-3775
e-mail: paradi@ie.utoronto.ca
web: http://www.corkscrewnet.com/
Membership limited to 50; members interested in corkscrews as well as wine paraphernalia such as decanters, wine strainers, funnels, etc.

Collectors

Milt Becker
P.O. Box 5295
Englewood, NJ 07631
ph: 201-567-1500
fax: 201-493-0685
e-mail: clarethous@aol.com
Wants any corkscrew or corkpuller; buys single items or entire collections; send photocopy of item and price.

Joe Young
P.O. Box 587
Elgin, IL 60121-0587
ph: 847-695-0108 or 847-254-8208
fax: 847-695-1679
e-mail: sagphu@aol.com
Wants to buy unusual corkscrews; also interested in combination tools with corkscrews; all correspondence answered.

Raj & Justine Kanodia
Corkscrew.Com
3717 Ortega Court
Palo Alto, CA 94303
e-mail: corky@corkscrew.com
web: http://www.corkscrew.com
Website has some great corkscrew information and photographs.

Dealers

Mike Gordon
M & R Gordon
57 Bundy Lane
Storrs, CT 06268
ph: 860-429-3834
fax: 860-429-3834
e-mail: gordon@neca.com
web: http://users.neca.com/gordon/med.html
Wants to buy any old or unusual corkscrew; please photocopy.

Paul P. Luchsinger
1126 Wishart St.
Hermitage, PA 16148-4410
ph: 724-346-2331
fax: 724-246-2331
e-mail: ppl@infonline.net
Buys, sells, collects old and unusual corkscrews as well as other wine related items.

Derek White
Corkscrew Pages, The
769 Sumter Drive
Morrisville, PA 19067
ph: 215-493-4143 or 609-860-5380
e-mail: dswhite@marketsource.com
web: http://www.taponline.com/cork/cs.html
Active collector and dealer of antique corkscrews; specialty is rare, unusual mechanical and pocket figural corkscrews; will buy single items as well s entire collections; also wants wine-related items: funnels, bin labels, etc.

Dean Walters
Vintage Antiques
P.O. Box 717
San Anselmo, CA 94979
ph: 415-459-6393
fax: 415-459-6317
e-mail: crkscrew@hooked.net
web: http://www.wenet.net/~crkscrew/
Since 1983 buying, selling, trading, appraising collectible corkscrews; online catalog changes four timer each year.

Joseph C. Paradi
670 Meadow Wood Road
Mississauga, Ontario L5J 2S6
Canada
ph: 905-823-3754 or 416-978-6924 x210
fax: 905-823-3775
e-mail: paradi@ie.utoronto.ca
web: http://www.corkscrewnet.com/
Will trade, buy or sell hand held corkscrews of any type, champagne taps, bar screws, cork pullers, corkers; also ladies' kits, necessaires, camping kits, cocktail shakers, etc. containing corkscrews; plus related ephemera.

Experts

Donald A. Bull
P.O. Box 596
Wirtz, VA 24184
ph: 540-721-1128
fax: 540-721-5468
e-mail: corkskrue@aol.com
Buys corkscrews or anything picturing corkscrews; author of "A Price Guide to Beer Advertising Openers and Corkscrews."

Mark Barlow
Winetiques
3107A Medlock Bridge Rd.
Norcross, GA 30071-1423
ph: 770-449-7610
fax: 770-449-1839
Buys, sells and specializes in corkscrews and all wine related items; from basic to unique patents.

Roger V. Baker
Baker's Lady Luck Emporium
P.O. Box 620417
Redwood City, CA 94062-0417
ph: 369-851-7188
Specializing in saloon collectibles: gambling, bar bottles, shaving mugs, razors, Bowie knives, daggers, barber items, match safes.

CORN COLLECTIBLES

Clubs/Associations

E. Eloise Alton, Ed.
Corn Items Collectors Association Inc.
Newsletter: Bang Board, The
613 N. Long St.
Shelbyville, IL 62565-1544
ph: 217-774-5002
Association collecting and studying anything having to do with corn, i.e. inventions, corn collectibles, etc.; large format newsletter with lots of pictures and articles.

Corn Shellers

Collectors

Robert Rauhauser
RR 2 Box 766
Thomasville, PA 17364-9622
Wants corn shellers: handheld, table mounted, box mounted; any unusual corn shellers; also popcorn shellers.

Don Monnier
P.O. Box 772
Sidney, OH 45365
ph: 937-492-1420
Wants hand held iron or primitive handmade style corn shellers.

Jim Moffet
P.O. Box 200
Modesto, IL 62667-0200
ph: 217-439-7358
Wants all styles of hand-held ear corn shellers.

CORONATION MEMORABILIA

(see POSTCARDS, Royalty Related; ROYALTY COLLECTIBLES, British)

COSTUME JEWELRY

(see GEMS & JEWELRY, Vintage & Costume)

COUNTERFEIT DETECTING ITEMS

Collectors

Donald Gorlick
P.O. Box 24541
Seattle, WA 98124-0541
ph: 206-824-0508
Wants counterfeit currency detectors, coin testers, scales, scanners, grids, books, reporters, recorders, magnifiers, Detectographs, etc.

COUNTRY STORE COLLECTIBLES

(see ADVERTISING COLLECTIBLES; BOTTLES; CIGAR BOXES, LABELS & BANDS; FARM COLLECTIBLES; LABELS; STRING HOLDERS; TIN CONTAINERS)

COVERED BRIDGES

Clubs/Associations

Russell J. Holmes
Theodore Burr Covered Bridge Society of Pennsylvania, Inc.
Magazine: Wooden Covered Spans
P.O. Box 2382
Lancaster, PA 17606-2382
ph: 717-428-1006
e-mail: rusholmes@worldnet.att.net
Society is committed to saving and preserving covered bridges; monthly meeting held for collectors of bridge related material; also publishes the newsletter "Pennsylvania Crossings."

Collectors

Marie Ward
2461 E High St., #A-7
Pottstown, PA 19464-3111
ph: 610-970-6299
Wants items relating to covered bridges.

COVERLETS

(see also FOLK ART; REPAIR/RESTORATION/CONSERVATION, Textiles; TEXTILES)

Clubs/Associations

Barbara Frisbie
Colonial Coverlet Guild of America
Newsletter: CCGA Newsletter
5617 Blackstone
La Grange, IL 60525-3420
ph: 708-352-3812
Members are interested in coverlets or antique textiles, their preservation and in the present revival of weaving.

Dealers

Carl McCann
Troy & Black, Inc.
P.O. Box 228
Red Creek, NY 13143-0228
ph: 315-754-8115
e-mail: tbrc@banet.net
Buys and sells high quality flow blue, Staffordshire figurines, American painted furniture, stoneware, redware, coverlets, samplers, and other American textiles, folk art, etc.

Misc. Services

Barbara Luck
Abby Aldrich Rockefeller Folk Art Center
P.O. Box 1776
Williamsburg, VA 23187
Will assist in identifying an unknown coverlet weaver.

Museums/Libraries

Museum of American Textile History
491 Dutton St.
Lowell, MA 01854-4221
ph: 978-441-0400
fax: 978-441-1412
web: http://valley.uml.edu/lowell/historic/museums/textile.html
Outstanding collection of textiles and textile making machinery and equipment; tools, machines, prints, photographs, business records, industry periodicals, textiles, swatches, sample books, trade catalogs, etc.

Repro. Sources

David C. Kline
Family Heir-Loom Weavers
775 Meadowview Dr.
Red Lion, PA 17356-8608
ph: 717-246-2431 or 717-246-2431
fax: 717-246-7439
e-mail: PatKline@familyheirloomweavers.com
web: http://www.familyheirloomweavers.com/
Makers of fancy jacquard coverlets, ingrain carpets & other historic textiles; send $4.00 for brochure.

Goodwin Weavers
P.O. Box 408
Blowing Rock, NC 28605
ph: 800-445-4437

COW COLLECTIBLES

(see also DAIRY COLLECTIBLES; ELSIE THE BORDEN COW ITEMS)

Clubs/Associations

Crol J. Peiffer
Cow Observers Worldwide
240 Wahl Ave.
Evans City, PA 16033-1053
ph: 724-538-5038
e-mail: moosletter@cow.net
web: http://www.cow.net/moosletter/
Organization for people who have a soft spot in their hearts for cows and cow collectibles.

Man./Prod./Dist.

Carol J. Peiffer, Pub.
Cowtree Collector
240 Wahl Ave.
Evans City, PA 16033-1053
ph: 724-538-5038
e-mail: moosletter@cow.net
web: http://www.cow.net/moosletter/
Distributor of original cow art and matted reproductions of humorous cow art; these "visual puns" include "Americow Graffiti," "A Line of Bull," "The Darkside of the MOO," "Beautiful Creamer," "Blue MOO" and more.

Periodicals

Carol J. Peiffer, Pub.
Cowtree Collector
Newsletter: MOOsletter, the
240 Wahl Ave.
Evans City, PA 16033-1053
ph: 724-538-5038
e-mail: moosletter@cow.net
web: http://www.cow.net/moosletter/
Quarterly newsletter with cow talk, cartoons, mail order sources for whatever has been produced using the cow theme ("COWllectibles"): stories on collectors, cow and dairy information, from the serious to the UDDERLY ridiculous.

Carol J. Peiffer, Pub.
Cowtree Collector
Directory: Cow Buying Guide
240 Wahl Ave.
Evans City, PA 16033-1053
ph: 724-538-5038
e-mail: moosletter@cow.net
web: http://www.cow.net/moosletter/
This directory contains the names, addresses and phone numbers of more than 300 individuals, companies, corporations and associations who buy and sell cow-related merchandise or who provide information on cows or the dairy industry.

COWBOY HEROES

(see also CHARACTER COLLECTIBLES; COMIC BOOKS, Super Heroes; MOVIE MEMORABILIA, Westerns; POPULAR CULTURE; PREMIUMS; TELEVISION SHOWS & MEMORABILIA, Westerns; TOY GUNS; WESTERN AMERICANA)

Clubs/Associations

Norman Kietzer
Westerns & Serials Fan Club
Magazine: Westerns & Serials
527 S. Front St.
Mankato, MN 56001-3718
e-mail: kietzer@mctcnet.net
web: http://www.angelfire.com/biz2/normankietzerpubs/
A club for collectors as well as non-collectors interested in westerns and serials of the silver screen; also interested in related memorabilia.

Collectors

Jim Babchak
313 East 85 #4B
New York, NY 10028
ph: 212-861-1356
Wants to buy old cowboy stuff including cowboy boots, shirts, horsehair bridles, spurs, chaps, children's costumes from the 1940s and 1950s, anything Roy Rogers, Hopalong Cassidy or Gene Autry.

Dealers

Barry Friedman
P.O. Box 55492
Valencia, CA 91385-0492
ph: 805-255-2365
Buys blankets and bedspreads with cowboy or Indian designs.

Jim & Shirley's Antiques
146 N. Glassell St.
Orange, CA 92866
ph: 714-639-9662 or 562-598-1914
Specializes in Hopalong Cassidy, and Roy Rogers and Dale Evans memorabilia.

Experts

Mario De Marco
152 Maple St.
West Boylston, MA 01583-1825
ph: 508-835-4085
Author and publisher of books on Charles Starrett, George "Gabby" Hayes, Tom Mix, Horse Bits and B Westerns, John Wayne, Don Barry, Tex Ritter and Fred Scott, Sagebrush heroes, William "Hoppy" Boyd, and others.

Periodicals

Antique Trader Publications, Inc.
Newspaper: Toy Trader
P.O. Box 1050
Dubuque, IA 52004-1050
ph: 800-334-7165 or 800-482-4155
fax: 800-531-0880
e-mail: jmkoenig@execpc.com
web: http://www.collect.com/toytrader
Monthly newspaper with information on how to buy, sell and trade all types of toys; market trends, the latest prices, "how-to" columns, listings of toy clubs and upcoming toy shows and auctions; also full of buy and sell ads.

Joe Caro
Newsletter: Cowboy Collector Newsletter, The
P.O. Box 7486
Long Beach, CA 90807-0486
ph: 714-840-3942
e-mail: hoppycnn@aol.com
web: http://www.hopalong.com
Articles and collector values on Hopalong Cassidy, Gene Autry, Roy Rogers, The Lone Ranger, etc.

Gene Autry

Clubs/Associations

Rosemarie Addison
Gene Autry Fan Club
4322 Heidelberg Ave.
Saint Louis, MO 63123-6812

Alf Hill
Gene Autry International Fan Club
Newsletter: Gene Autry International Fan Club Bulletin
20 Cranleigh Gardens
Stoke Bishop, Bristol BS9 1HD
U.K.

Museums/Libraries

Elvin Sweeten
Gene Autry Oklahoma Museum
Newspaper: Gene Autry Star Telegram
P.O. Box 67
Gene Autry, OK 73436
ph: 580-389-5335 or 580-294-3047
fax: 580-389-5139
e-mail: esweeten@brightok.net
web: http://www.cow-boy.com/museum.htm
Museum of Gene Autry memorabilia including photos, posters, etc.; also local memorabilia; the newspaper is an annual to promote the community & the man; very big with collectors world over; includes photos & stories relating to both.

Autry Western of Heritage Museum
Magazine: Spur
4700 Western Heritage Way
Los Angeles, CA 90027-1462
ph: 323-667-2000
fax: 323-660-5721
e-mail: rroom@autry-museum.org
web: http://www.autry-museum.org/
Collects items relating to the American West, including Western film memorabilia.

Hopalong Cassidy

Clubs/Associations

John Spencer, Pres.
Friends of Hopalong Cassidy International Fan Club
Newsletter: Hoppy Talk
4613 Araby Church Rd.
Frederick, MD 21701-7791
ph: 301-663-6539
e-mail: webmaster@hopalong.com
web: http://www.hopalong.com
Club organized to establish a museum in Cambridge, OH (boyhood home of William Boyd); newsletter contains, articles, buy/sell ads, etc.; newsletter published quarterly.

Collectors

Chris Swain
P.O. Box 513
Williamsburg, MA 01096
ph: 413-628-3213
e-mail: Bluejettoy@aol.com
Wants items relating to Hopalong Cassidy and Roy Rogers.

Harry L. Rinker
5093 Vera Cruz Rd.
Emmaus, PA 18049-9554
ph: 610-965-1122
fax: 610-965-1124
e-mail: rinker@fast.net
web: http://www.rinker.com
Seeking Hopalong Cassidy memorabilia.

Ron Pieczkowski
1707 Orange Hill Dr.
Brandon, FL 33510-2632
ph: 813-685-2338
Wants to buy Hopalong Cassidy collectibles; single items or entire collections.

Laura Bates
6310 Friendship Dr.
New Concord, OH 43762-9708
ph: 740-826-4850
Editor of "Hoppy Talk", the newsletter of the Friends of Hopalong Cassidy International Fan Club; coordinator of Hopalong Cassidy festival held each May in Cambridge, OH; curator of Hopalong Cassidy Museum.

Dealers

Howard R. Cherry
10th Street Antique Mall
127 South 10th Street
Cambridge, OH 43725
ph: 740-432-3364
e-mail: hcherry@cambridgeoh.com
web: http://www.cambridgeoh.com/users/hcherry/
Wants to buy Cowboy memorabilia: Roy Rogers, Gene Autry, Hopalong Cassidy.

Experts

Joe Caro
P.O. Box 7486
Long Beach, CA 90807-0486
ph: 714-840-3942
e-mail: hoppycnn@aol.com
web: http://www.hopalong.com
Leading expert on Hoppy memorabilia; author of "Collectors Guide to Hopalong Cassidy Memorabilia" (1992) and "Hopalong Cassidy Collectibles" (1997); available from author.

Jerry Rosenthal
Hopalong Cassidy Enterprises
18623 Ventura Blvd, #210
Tarzana, CA 91356
ph: 818-881-2081 or 800-711-4677
fax: 818-881-4557
e-mail: jerry@hopalong.com
web: http://www.hopalong.com/
Restoration of 66 Hopalong Cassidy motion pictures; new Hoppy collectibles.

Lone Ranger

Clubs/Associations

John Samorajczyk
Lone Ranger Fan Club
Newsletter: Pictorial Scrapbook
19205 Seneca Ridge Court
Gaithersburg, MD 20879-3135
ph: 301-869-1755

Collectors

John S. Fawcett
P.O. Box 1156
Waldoboro, ME 04572-1156
ph: 207-832-7398
Wants to buy 1930s to 1950s Lone Ranger items; wants everything.

Karl L. Rommel
1377 Cloverleaf Rd.
Lansing, MI 48906
ph: 517-484-7865
Wants all 1933-1955 "Lone Ranger" memorabilia; especially wants anything related to radio's Lone Ranger, Brace Beemer, and any sponsor items of the radio show.

Experts

Terry & Kay Klepey
P.O. Box 553
Forks, WA 98331-0553
ph: 360-327-3726 or 360-374-5717
e-mail: slvrbllt@olypen.com
Collector, dealer expert; buys, sells and collects Lone Ranger and related items: comics, toys, books, dolls, etc.; also interested in other 1950s Westerns.

Periodicals

Terry & Kay Klepey
Silver Bullet, The
Newsletter: Silver Bullet Newsletter
P.O. Box 553
Forks, WA 98331-0553
ph: 360-327-3726 or 360-374-5717
e-mail: slvrbllt@olypen.com
A quarterly newsletter for Lone Ranger enthusiasts and collectors; publishing for over 46 issues since 1988; will reply if SASE enclosed.

Red Ryder

Collectors

Gabby Talkington
4703 Upland Dr.
Richmond, CA 94803-3227
ph: 510-223-1142
fax: 510-233-3388
e-mail: oldlures@aol.com
Wants Red Ryder games, books, guns, puzzles, etc. for private collection.

Robert Fuller

Clubs/Associations

Janette Anderson
Robert Fuller Fan Club
Newsletter: Laramie Trail, The
407 West Rosemary Lane
Falls Church, VA 22046-3847
fax: 703-358-5402
The official fan club for western star, Robert Fuller.

Roy Rogers & Dale Evans

Clubs/Associations

Nancy Horsley, ExSec
Roy Rogers - Dale Evans Collectors Association
Newsletter: RRDECA Newsletter
P.O. Box 1166
Portsmouth, OH 45662-1166
ph: 740-353-0900 or 740-353-4002
Organized as a part of the Portsmouth Area Community Exhibits which maintains the Roy Rogers Hometown Exhibit in Portsmouth, Roy's boyhood hometown.

Collectors

Chris Swain
P.O. Box 513
Williamsburg, MA 01096
ph: 413-628-3213
e-mail: Bluejettoy@aol.com
Wants items relating to Hopalong Cassidy and Roy Rogers.

Laura Lee Gwaltney
3104 East 5th St.
Anderson, IN 46012
ph: 765-642-6318
Especially interested in Western paper items, but also collects anything to do with Roy Rogers & his family.

Don Mabbitt
P.O. Box 114
Sheldon, IL 60966-0114
ph: 815-429-3671
Wants to buy Roy Rogers and Dale Evans collectibles: cap guns, toys, and other memorabilia.

Janey Miller
1822 Chelle Ct.
Jefferson City, MO 65101-6003
ph: 573-635-5171
e-mail: millczy4rr@aol.com
Collects all memorabilia related to Roy Rogers and Dale Evans: audio, video, paper, toys, etc.

Experts

Robert Phillips
1703 North Aster Place
Broken Arrow, OK 74012
ph: 918-254-8205
fax: 918-252-9362
Has conducted pioneering research with Roy Rogers comics, has collected Roy Rogers memorabilia for over 30 years, conducted extensive research into the careers of Roy Rogers and Dale Evans; authored/edited book on subject.

Museums/Libraries

Roy Rogers Hometown Exhibit, c/o Chamber of Commerce
P.O. Box 509
Portsmouth, OH 45662
ph: 740-353-1116

Roy Rogers & Dale Evans Museum
15650 Seneca Rd.
Victorville, CA 92392
ph: 760-245-5503 or 760-243-4547
fax: 760-245-2009
e-mail: administrator@royrogers.com
web: http://www.royrogers.com/museum.html
The museum is now selling authentic collectibles from the 1940s and 1950s; all items are signed by Roy and/or Dale and come with a certificate of authenticity signed by Roy Rogers, Jr.

Tom Mix

Clubs/Associations

John Samorajczyk
Tom Mix Fan Club
Newsletter: Tom Mix Fan Club Newsletter
19205 Seneca Ridge Court
Gaithersburg, MD 20879-3135
ph: 301-869-1755
Membership includes four issues of the club newsletter.

Dealers

Paul E. Mix
P.O. Box 180182
Austin, TX 78718-0182
ph: 512-836-8005
fax: 512-835-1708
e-mail: paulmix@prodigy.net
Sells Tom Mix related booklets and photo catalogs; also collects, buys and sells Tom Mix memorabilia.

Experts

Mario De Marco
152 Maple St.
West Boylston, MA 01583-1825
ph: 508-835-4085
Author of "Photostory of The Screen's Greatest Cowboy - Tom Mix"; one of the very early publications on Tom Mix, soft cover, 100+ pages, loaded with rare photos and bio of Tom and some of the other associated stars; $10.50 ppd.

M.G. "Bud" Norris
1324 N. Hague Ave.
Columbus, OH 3204-2108
ph: 614-274-4646
Buys Tom Mix memorabilia; author of "The Tom Mix Book"; publicity director of the International Tom Mix Festival; consultant to the Tom Mix Museum, Dewey, OK.

Museums/Libraries

Tom Mix Museum
721 North Delaware
P.O. Box 190
Dewey, OK 74029-0190
ph: 918-534-1555
web: http://www.ok-history.mus.ok.us/mus-sites/masnum31.htm

COWBOY/COWGIRL COLLECTIBLES

(see COWBOY HEROES; WESTERN AMERICANA)

CRACKER JACK COLLECTIBLES

Clubs/Associations

Ann Brogley
Cracker Jack Collectors Association
Newsletter: Prize Insider, The
P.O. Box 16033
Philadelphia, PA 19114-0033
ph: 215-824-4698 or 215-824-2350
fax: 215-824-4698
e-mail: mostprod@erols.com
web: http://www.collectoronline.com/CJCA/
A nonprofit association dedicated to the collector of Cracker Jack and related memorabilia; share knowledge and correspondence; membership includes newsletter and membership card; holds annual convention.

Collectors

Larry White
108 Central St.
Rowley, MA 01969
ph: 978-948-8187
e-mail: larrydw@erols.com
Buys and sells Cracker jack toys; author of two books on Cracker Jacks.

Ann Brogley
P.O. Box 16033
Philadelphia, PA 19114-0033
ph: 215-824-4698 or 215-824-2350
fax: 215-824-4698
e-mail: mostprod@erols.com
web: http://www.geocities.com/Heartland/Hills/2081/
Founder of Cracker Jack Collectors Association; avid collector wants to buy Cracker Jack items; one item or

entire collections; all letters answered.

Wes Johnson
106 Bauer Ave.
Louisville, KY 40207-2559
Advanced collector wants tin, cast metal, plastic toy prizes, old paper items; also ANGELUS Marshmallows, CHECKERS Confection items.

Edwin Snyder
P.O. Box 156
Lancaster, KY 40444-0156
ph: 606-792-4816
e-mail: snyecco@aol.com
Wants to buy Cracker Jack, Checkers Confections, Chums, and related items, prizes and advertising.

Jonathan Hodges
P.O.Box 309
Kankakee, IL 60901
e-mail: Crackerjak@bigfoot.com
web: http://www.geocities.com/Heartland/Hills/6537/crackerjack.html

Barry Brandon
651 Linda Ln.
Bonner Springs, KS 66012-1809
ph: 913-441-8663
Wants Cracker Jack prizes: tin, cast metal, plastic and paper; also collects Angelus, Checkers, Reliable Confections.

Jeffrey Maxwell
Alphabet26 Web Site
213 East Wells Blvd.
Sapulpa, OK 74066-6439
ph: 918-227-0657 or 918-594-8280
fax: 918-594-8281
e-mail: alphabet26@aol.com
web: http://members.aol.com/Alphabet26
A website dedicated to the study of 1940 to 1960s plastic prizes from gum machines and Cracker Jacks with an alphabet theme.

Experts

Ron Toth, Jr.
72 Charles St.
Rochester, NH 03867-3413
ph: 603-335-2062
e-mail: timepass@worldpath.net
Collects and specializes in Cracker Jack memorabilia.

Jim Davis
Cracker Jack Box, The
135 Jefferson Heights Ave.
New Orleans, LA 70121-3207
ph: 504-733-3619
e-mail: jeepers@ix.netcom.com
web: http://pw2.netcom.com/~jeepers/CrackerJackBox.html

Internet Resources

Jonathan Hodges
P.O.Box 309
Kankakee, IL 60901
e-mail: Crackerjak@bigfoot.com
web: http://www.geocities.com/Heartland/Hills/6537/crackerjack.html
A tribute page to "the greatest snack ever made!"; lots of links to other sources, trivia, history of Cracker Jack.

Jim Davis
Cracker Jack Box, The
135 Jefferson Heights Ave.
New Orleans, LA 70121-3207
ph: 504-733-3619
e-mail: jeepers@ix.netcom.com
web: http://pw2.netcom.com/~jeepers/CrackerJackBox.html
This site is dedicated to Cracker Jack collecting: prizes, ads, mail-in and point-of-sale premiums, etc,; also includes history and other related information along with Cracker Jack resources and links.

Museums/Libraries

COSI Columbus
280 East Broad St.
Columbus, OH 43215
ph: 614-228-2674
web: http://cosi.org/
Contains a permanent exhibit of over 10,000 pieces of Cracker Jack memorabilia, including advertising ephemera, prizes and premiums.

CRAFTS

(see also BASKETS; LAPIDARY; RUGS, Hooked; REPAIR/RESTORATION/CONSERVATION, Woodworking [Suppliers]; STAINED GLASS)

Clubs/Associations

American Craft Association
21 South Eltings Corner Rd.
Highland, NY 12528
ph: 800-724-0859 or 914-863-5218
fax: 914-883-6130
An association offering trade and professional services to craft persons and craft retailers.

National Crafts Association
1945 E. Ridge Rd., Ste. 5178
Rochester, NY 14622-2467
ph: 800-715-9594 or 716-266-5472
fax: 716-785-3231
e-mail: nca@craftassoc.com
web: http://www.craftassoc.com/
Information source for the professional arts & crafts industry.

Fred Bair, Jr.
Society of Workers in Early Arts & Trades
Newsletter: Sweat Rag, The
606 Lake Lena Blvd.
Auburndale, FL 33823-2937
ph: 941-967-3262
fax: 941-967-3262
Members are largely those who do public demonstrations of early crafts, but membership is open to anyone; exchange knowledge of practices in crafts; promotes the finding, making and exchange of tools; annual directory.

Internet Resources

World Wide Arts Resource
761 Franklin Ave.
Columbus, OH 43205
e-mail: info@wwar.com
web: http://wwar.com/
On-line crafts resources: baskets, ceramics, costumes, dolls, embroidery, furniture, instruments, jewelry, miniatures, pottery, quilts, textiles, wood carving.

CraftWEB, c/o Opportunity Network
3701 Heary Blvd., #325
San Francisco, CA 94118
e-mail: kmcmahon@craftweb.com
web: http://www.craftweb.com
On-line resource for artisans who make unique, quality, handcrafted fine craft art: craftspeople, craft organizations, etc.; basketry, ceramics, glass, textiles, woodworking.

Misc. Services

Linda Gibbs
Victorian - An Era of the Past
10380 Miranda Ave.
Buena Park, CA 90620-4447
ph: 714-827-6488
Offers classes in the lost Victorian arts & crafts; ribbon embroidery, hearts, flowers, a touch of lace create old fashioned delights, one-of-a-kind items that will become your heirloom keepsakes; send SASE for info.

Museums/Libraries

American Craft Museum
40 West 53rd St.
New York, NY 10019
ph: 212-956-3535
web: http://www.gallery-guide.com/museum/ammcrft/archive/

Periodicals

American Craft Council
Magazine: American Craft
21 S. Eltings Courner Road
Highland, NY 12528
ph: 914-883-6100 or 800-836-3470
fax: 914-883-6130
e-mail: council@craftcouncil.org
web: http://www.craftcouncil.org/
Non-profit educational organization founded in 1943; offers juried craft fairs, maintains special library of 20th century crafts; offers seminars and services to professional crafts people; membership open to all.

Magazine: Crafts Report, The
P.O. Box 1992
Wilmington, DE 19899-1992
ph: 302-656-2209 or 800-777-7098
fax: 302-656-4894
e-mail: subscribe@assocgraphics.com
web: http://www.craftsreport.com
The business journal for the crafts industry.

Sanford Carr
Magazine: Sunshine Artist
2600 Temple Drive
Winter Park, FL 32789-1371
ph: 407-539-1399 or 800-804-4607
fax: 407-539-1499
e-mail: site@sunshineartist.com
web: http://www.sunshineartist.com/
Covering the art and craft event marketplace for more than 25 years; show listings, reviews, entry information, articles, suppliers.

Ornament, Inc.
Magazine: Ornament
P.O. Box 2349
San Marcos, CA 92079-2349
ph: 760-599-0222
fax: 760-599-0228
e-mail: ornament@cts.com
web: http://www.ornamentmagazine.com/
A quarterly magazine focusing on craft and art items of personal adornment in any media or form: fiber, glass, metal, ancient historic/ethnic ornament; ethnographic and tribal jewelry; also reviews of museum exhibits and publications.

Basketry

(see also BASKETS)

Internet Resources

Alan Beebe
Basketry Information
277 Raplh Vedder Rd.
Saugerties, NY 12477
e-mail: abeebe@ulster.net
web: http://www.ulster.net/~abeebe/basket.html
On-line resource containing books, magazines & newsletters, sources of materials, associations and guilds, classes, conventions and meetings, basketmakers' web pages, related web links, basketmakers' e-mail addresses.

Periodicals

Magazine: Fiberarts
50 College St.
Asheville, NC 28801

Jim Rutherford
Magazine: Basketry Bits
P.O. Box 8
Loudonville, OH 44842
ph: 419-994-3256

Magazine: Just Patterns
2417 Hancock St.
Port Huron, MI 48060
e-mail: jpmag@sun.tir.com
web: http://www2.justpatterns.com/justpatterns/
Published quarterly; patterns, suppliers, weavers, books, etc.

Glass

(see also GLASS; STAINED GLASS)

Periodicals

Jim Thingwold, Ed.
Magazine: Glass Line
120 S. Kroeger St.
Anaheim, CA 92805-4011
ph: 714-520-0121
fax: 714-520-4370
e-mail: jht@exo.com
web: http://www.hotglass.com/
Bi-monthly; glass working information, supplies, etc.; the number one publication for the hot glass artists; beads, hobby, glass art, sculptures, supplies, equipment, collectors.

Jewelry

(see also GEMS & JEWELRY)

Appraisers

Daloma Armentrout
Armentrout-Hawken Appraisal Associates
P.O. Box 160906
Austin, TX 78716-0906
ph: 512-288-1507
fax: 512-328-9411
Expert specializing in the appraisal of fine contemporary art jewelry and art metals crafts; author of "Art Jewelry & Metals - Makers, Markets, Meaning"; also collection consultant, and educator.

Metal

Clubs/Associations

Bob Mitchell
Society of North American Goldsmiths
Journal: Metalsmith
5009 Londonderry Dr.
Tampa, FL 33647-9910
ph: 813-977-5326
fax: 813-977-8462
e-mail: mitchel@artguidesource.com
web: http://www.artguidesource.com/
An association for jewelers and metal artisans; quarterly magazine devoted to the development and appreciation for the craft of fine metalsmithing: jewelry, decorative art, etc.

CRANBERRY INDUSTRY ITEMS

Collectors

Peter K. Meier
136 Hayward St.
Halifax, MA 02338-1804
ph: 781-293-3218
Wants to buy cranberry scoops and related items; paper goods, tools and implements related to the cranberry growing industry.

CREDIT CARDS & CHARGE ITEMS

(see also BANKING; CIVIL WAR ARTIFACTS, Currency; COINS & CURRENCY; MONEYCARDS; TELEPHONE CARDS; WOODEN MONEY)

Clubs/Associations

Bill Wieland, Pres.
American Credit Card Collectors Society
Journal: Charge
P.O. Box 2465
Midland, MI 48640
ph: 517-839-2026
fax: 517-839-2026
e-mail: tmcgrath@proaxis.com
web: http://www.proaxis.com/~tmcgrath/acccs.htm

Collectors

Robert A. Hendel
1385 York Ave. #16B
New York, NY 10021
ph: 212-772-9070 or 212-450-4733
fax: 212-450-5521
Wants to buy all types of plastic or paper cards; also wants metal charge plates; will pay premium for American Express and Diners Club cards; ship cards for appraisal and offer.

Gary Olsen
505 S. Royal Ave.
Front Royal, VA 22630
ph: 540-635-7157 or 540-635-7158
fax: 540-635-1818
e-mail: hpfrigko@interloc.com
Collecting since 1960s; will pay $1 each plus postage for any age, quantity or condition of expired credit cards; plastic, paper, metal.

Jerry Ballard
P.O. Box 1992
Midlothian, VA 23112-1992
ph: 804-744-7700
fax: 804-744-6600
Wants credit cards and charge coins; will pay $1 to $5 for each pre-1985 card; send photocopy or cards.

Jose Moreira
P.O. Box 520995
Medley, FL 33152-0995
ph: 305-717-9747
e-mail: jmoreira@aol.com
Wants old, expired, obsolete charge or credit cards; from anywhere, any vintage, any quantity; free appraisals, send photocopies of front and back.

Ron Kempner
P.O. Box 981
Wilmette, IL 60091
ph: 847-869-6757
Wants to buy credit cards, charge plates; paper or plastic; AMX, Diners, Carte Blanche most desirable.

T.L. Helgeson
Credit Card Collector, The
1791 W. Tennyson Dr.
Tucson, AZ 85746-1381
ph: 520-294-6865
fax: 520-573-1509
Wants to buy all types of credit and charge items: paper, plastic, metal, and celluloid from the late 1800s to 1990s; expired/closed account items only; send photocopy and description of what you have.

Experts

Lin Overholt
P.O. Box 8481
Saint Petersburg, FL 33738-8481
ph: 727-393-5397
e-mail: axvisamc@aol.com
web: http://members.aol.com/AXVISAMC/index.html
Author of "Standard Catalog of International Credit Cards."

Periodicals

Lin Overholt
Newsletter: Credit Cards & Phone Cards News
P.O. Box 8481
Saint Petersburg, FL 33738-8481
ph: 727-393-5397
e-mail: axvisamc@aol.com
web: http://members.aol.com/AXVISAMC/index.html
Quarterly publication for collectors of telephone tokens/cards, charge coins, charge plates, credit cards.

Cards

Internet Resources

Terry Stewart
Collector Link
71 John St. East
Waterloo, Ontario N2J 1G2
Canada
ph: 519-745-1745
e-mail: stewart@collector-link.com
web: http://www.collector-link.com/
Catalogs over 2,000 trading card related web sites for: baseball, hockey, basketball, football, other sports, non-sports, phone cards, credit-debit cards, business cards, postcards.

CRESTED WARE

(see CERAMICS [ENGLISH], Goss Pottery Co./Crested Ware)

CRIME

(see LAW ENFORCEMENT MEMORABILIA; MYSTERY/DETECTIVE ITEMS; OUTLAWS & LAWMEN; PERSONALITIES [CRIMINALS])

CRUCIFIXES

(see RELIGIOUS COLLECTIBLES, Crosses)

CRUETS

(see also GLASS, Pattern; GLASS, Art)

Experts

Elaine Ezell
Cruets, Cruets, Cruets
P.O. Box 1609
Pasadena, MD 21122-1609
ph: 410-255-6777 or 410-551-4101
Advanced collector and co-author with George Newhouse of "Cruets, Cruets, Cruets" (Vol I $29.95 and Vol II $32.95 from author); buys/sells art glass and colored Victorian cruets.

CRUISE SHIP ITEMS

(see OCEAN LINER COLLECTIBLES)

CRYPTOGRAPHIC DEVICES

(see SPY EQUIPMENT)

CRYSTAL

(see GLASS, Crystal; TABLEWARE)

CRYSTAL BALLS

(see UFO'S & UNEXPLAINED PHENOMENA)

CUBAN COLLECTIBLES

Collectors

Miquel A. De Dios
P.O. Box 8156
North Bergen, NJ 07047
e-mail: madios@hotmail.com
web: http://members.tripod.com/~madios/
Wants to buy Cuba-related collectibles and memorabilia; send description and price.

Dealers

Ayer Books
15921 SW 85th St.
Miami, FL 33193-3077
Wants books, Cuban authors,

magazines, movie posters that mention Cubans, Cuban memorabilia.

Museums/Libraries

Cuban Museum of Arts & Culture
1300 SW 12th Ave.
Miami, FL 33129-2500
ph: 305-858-8006

CUFF LINKS

(see also BELT BUCKLES; CLOTHING & ACCESSORIES, Vintage; GEMS & JEWELRY; TIE BARS, CLIPS & TACKS)

Clubs/Associations

Eugene R. Klompus
National Cuff Link Society
Newsletter: Link, The
P.O. Box 5700
Vernon Hills, IL 60061
ph: 847-816-0035
fax: 847-816-0035
e-mail: genek@cufflink.com
web: http://www.cufflink.com
For collectors of cuff links, tie bars, tie tacks, collar buttons, collar pins, shirt studs, stick pins, money clips, vintage collars/cuffs, belt buckles, and button covers; members get 6 free cuff link appraisals per year.

Collectors

Claude Jeanloz
Yield House Industries, Inc.
P.O. Box 2525
Conway, NH 03818
ph: 603-447-8500 or 413-659-3109
fax: 603-447-1717
Wants all types of cull links for cuff link museum: cuff links, cuff buttons, cuff jewelry, and cuff link memorabilia.

James S. McCormick
476 Windswept Dr.
Asheville, NC 28801
ph: 828-253-2660 or 828-254-0071

Dealers

Gail Busche
Archangel Antiques
334 East Ninth St.
New York, NY 10003-7924
ph: 212-260-9313
Buying antique buttons, cuff links, eye glasses, and vintage lighters; always seeking fine examples such as enamel Deco and Art Nouveau.

Michael A. Pratt, Sr.
Off the Cuff
687 Co. Rd. ""U""
Rt. 2 Box 73
Fremont, NE 68025-9635
ph: 402-721-4765
fax: 402-721-4765
e-mail: mp@mb3.net
web: http://www.mb3.net/display/
Buys and sells unique cuff links of all kinds; also sells display cases for cuff links and collectibles of all types.

Experts

Eugene R. Klompus
P.O. Box 5700
Vernon Hills, IL 60061
ph: 847-816-0035
fax: 847-816-0035
e-mail: genek@cufflink.com
web: http://www.cufflink.com
Buys, sells, collects, appraises cuff links; writes articles for collectors' publications; author of "Collectors Guide to Cuff Link Collecting"; expert spokesperson on cuff links and related miscellaneous jewelry.

Howard L. Bell, Jr.
P.O. Box 11695
Kansas City, MO 64138-0195
ph: 816-756-3888
fax: 816-753-7739
e-mail: hrdzebl@msn.com
Buys, sells, collects, appraises Cuff Jewelry: cuff links & buttons, bachelor's buttons, button covers, silk knots; author of "Cuff Jewelry; A Historical Account for Collector and Dealer"; writes articles and speaks on the topic.

Museums/Libraries

Cuff Link Museum
71 Hobbs St.
P.O. Box 2525
Conway, NH 03818
ph: 413-659-3109

CUP PLATES

(see also CERAMICS, Cups & Saucers; GLASS)

Collectors

Ernest Remondini
P.O. Box 890052
East Weymouth, MA 02189-0001
ph: 781-335-2716

Experts

John E. Bilane
2065 Morris Ave., Apt. 109
Union, NJ 07083-6015
ph: 908-686-3060
Buys and sells antique glass cup plates.

CURRENCY

(see COINS & CURRENCY)

CUTLERY

(see DIAMOND EDGE; KEEN KUTTER; KNIVES)

Here are some tips when contacting someone listed in this book:

■ When requesting information about a particular item, include a description (material, dimensions, maker's mark, model number, etc.) and a photo, sketch, or photocopy of the item in question.

■ Always ask if there are charges for samples or for the services requested.

■ When writing, please be sure to include a Large (#10 business size) Self-Addressed and Stamped Envelope (LSASE) if requesting a reply or the return of photographs.

■ Never call collect unless otherwise directed. When calling, be considerate of time zone differences and always ask if the party you are calling has time to talk. When leaving an answering machine message, always instruct the party to call you back collect.

DAGUERREOTYPES

(see PHOTOGRAPHS)

DAIRY COLLECTIBLES

(see also BOTTLE CAPS, Milk; BOTTLES, Milk; COW COLLECTIBLES; DAIRY QUEEN MEMORABILIA; ELSIE THE BORDEN COW ITEMS; FARM COLLECTIBLES; KITCHEN COLLECTIBLES; POGS)

Clubs/Associations

Thomas Gallagher
National Association of Milk Bottle Collectors, Inc.
Newsletter: Milk Route, The
4 Ox Bow Rd.
Westport, CT 06880-2602
ph: 203-227-5244
fax: 203-227-2206
e-mail: milkroute@yahoo.com
web: http://www.collectoronline.com/club-NAMBC-wp.html
Focuses on milk and dairy history and related memorabilia; membership includes the newsletter and directory of members; newsletter has articles, ads, show dates, information exchange, patents, events, etc.

Dr. Paul Dettloff, Sec.
Dairy & Cream Collectors Association
Newsletter: Dairy & Cream Newsletter
Rt. 3 Box 189
Arcadia, WI 54612
ph: 608-323-7470
For those interested in cream separators and other dairy items; newsletter contains articles, free ads for subscribers, photos, etc.

Collectors

Stephen Foster
94 Knobb Hill Rd.
Milford, CT 06460-7245
ph: 203-877-5802
Wants to buy milk bottles and "udder" dairy items.

Sam A. Stephens
319 Juniper St.
Warminster, PA 18974-4720
ph: 215-672-4814 or 215-443-4173
Collector of advertising items relating to cream separators and the dairy industry,

Nancy Pennington
1750 Keyes Rd.
Greenbrier, TN 37073
ph: 615-643-0290
fax: 615-643-0290
Wants to buy dairy items such as milk bottles, advertising, cow pitchers, and ice cream items.

Dealers

Ridgecrest Farm
43 Ridgecrest Dr.
Wilton, ME 04294
ph: 207-645-2443
Your "Maine" connection for dairy collectibles, milk bottles; buys and sells; send SASE for latest catalog of offerings; from Nov. 1 through April 30 contact at 22201 Scenic Ridge Ct., Mt. Dora, FL 32575 (352-735-3831).

Debbie Gillete
Route 11
Watertown, NY 13601
ph: 315-788-0587
e-mail: dlg@imcnet.net
web: http://www.imcnet.net/~dlg/
A milk bottle and dairy memorabilia collector specializing in pyro (painted label) bottles and other dairy collectibles and go-withs.

Ralph Riovo
686 Franklin St.
Alburtis, PA 18011-9578
ph: 610-966-2536
Adlactilist and dealer in milk and dairy memorabilia; wants milk bottles, dairy advertising and related memorabilia.

Experts

Thomas Gallagher
4 Ox Bow Rd.
Westport, CT 06880-2602
ph: 203-227-5244
fax: 203-227-2206
e-mail: milkroute@yahoo.com
web: http://www.collectoronline.com/club-NAMBC-wp.html

Tony Knipp
P.O. Box 105
Blooming Grove, NY 10914-0105
ph: 914-496-6841 or 914-938-4580

Leigh Giarde
LG Enterprises
P.O. Box 2243
Redlands, CA 92373-0741
ph: 909-792-8681
fax: 909-792-8681
e-mail: onlyleigh@cpl.net
Mail order sales and purchases of milk bottles and go-withs; author of "Glass Milk Bottles: Their Makers and Marks."

Museums/Libraries

Farmers' Museum, The
P.O. Box 800
Lake Road
Cooperstown, NY 13326
ph: 607-547-1450 or 888-547-1450
e-mail: nyshal@aol.com
web: http://www.farmersmuseum.org/

Periodicals

Mike & Naomi Hull
Newsletter: Milk Bottle News
Stonemasons
Burleigh
Stroud, Gloucester GL5 2PJ
U.K.
ph: 01453 884922
e-mail: mbnews@artisan.abel.co.uk
web: http://www.artisan.uk.com/mbnews/
A British newsletter for collectors of milk bottles and dairy related memorabilia.

Cream Separators

Collectors

Sam A. Stephens
319 Juniper St.
Warminster, PA 18974-4720
ph: 215-672-4814 or 215-443-4173
Collector of advertising items relating to cream separators and the dairy industry,

Dave Ogle
954 W. Monroe
Jackson, MI 49202-2036
ph: 517-688-4561
Wants to buy DeLaval, Sharples, or other cream separator advertising: calendars, signs, trays, match holders, fobs, etc.

Larry Schrof
25971 E. 1200 St.
Geneseo, IL 61254
ph: 309-441-5055
Wants DeLaval or other cream separator advertising.

Dealers

Bill Heuring
Hickory Bend Antiques & Collectibles
2995 Drake Hill Rd.
Jasper, NY 14855-9715
ph: 607-792-3343
fax: 607-792-3309
Cream separators and related dairy collectibles bought and sold.

Creamers

Collectors

Toni & Michael Fusco
2629 Oneida St.
Utica, NY 13501
ph: 315-724-8773

Dealers

Ken Clee
P.O. Box 11412
Philadelphia, PA 19111-0412
ph: 215-722-1979
e-mail: waxntoys@aol.com
web: http://members.aol.com/waxntoys/main/kidsmeal.htm
Wants to buy glass dairy creamers with names printed on creamers; will buy one or an entire collection.

Periodicals

Lloyd Bindscheattle
Newsletter: Creamers
P.O. Box 11
Lake Villa, IL 60046-0011
Collector and expert on dairy creamers; "Creamers" is a quarterly, 16 page newsletter dealing with glass, advertising, individual, dairy, coffee creamers; free ads.

Dairy Case Tags

Collectors

Betty R. Foley
129 Meadow Valley Rd., Trlr. 11
Ephrata, PA 17522-1843
ph: 717-738-4813
Wants porcelain dairy tags; these were attached to old wooden milk crates to advertise the names of the dairies; usually 1 1/2" x 5."

Isaly Dairy Company

Collectors

Brian A. Butko
2640 Sunset Dr.
West Mifflin, PA 15122-3565
Collects 1910-1980 souvenirs from this regional chain best known for their Klondike bars, chipped ham, and skyscraper cones: milk cartons, signs, china, calendars, menus, etc.; no bottles, please.

DAIRY QUEEN MEMORABILIA

Collectors

Charles Cook
1481 Rte. 23
Butler, NJ 07405
ph: 973-838-3043
Wants Dairy Queen memorabilia from the 1940s to 1950s: signs, containers, premiums, advertisements, cups, etc.

DANCE MEMORABILIA

(see STRIPTEASE; PERFORMING ARTS)

DATE NAILS

Clubs/Associations

Jerry Waits
Texas Date Nail Collectors Association
Newsletter: Nailer News
501 W. Horton
Brenham, TX 77833-2357
ph: 409-830-1495
Date nails are 1" to 2" long; dime-size heads are marked with number on top to show the year installed; driven into railroad ties, telephone poles, or other wood products; shows the year put in service; collect by years or sets.

Collectors

Jerry Waits
501 W. Horton
Brenham, TX 77833-2357
ph: 409-830-1495

DAY BOOKS

(see ACCOUNT BOOKS; PAPER COLLECTIBLES)

DEALERS

(see ANTIQUES DEALERS & COLLECTORS)

DECANTERS

Figural Whiskey

(see also BOTTLES)

Dealers

Rick Williams
Burgerjane's Cyber Saloon
e-mail: Burgerjane@aol.com
web: http://members.aol.com/burgerjane/home.html

Whiskey Bottles/Decanters by Ingrid
e-mail: ingridp@texas.net
web: http://lonestar.texas.net/~ingridp/

Roy & Cordie Willis
Heartland of Kentucky Decanters & Steins
P.O. Box 428
Lebanon Junction, KY 40150
ph: 502-833-2827
fax: 502-833-3480
e-mail: heartlandky@ka.net
web: http://www.ka.net/heartlandky/
Hundreds of whiskey decanters by Jim Beam, Wild Turkey, Ski Country, McCormick and others; also beer steins, domestic or foreign; call ONLY 9-5 eastern time.

Internet Resources

Cheryl Hendrix
Buck-A-Bottle Auction
P.O. Box 12423
Seattle, WA 98082
ph: 425-844-6432
e-mail: babauction@aol.com
web: http://www.buckabottle.com
Online auction service for decanters and other fine breweriana collectibles.

Figural Whiskey (Beam)

Clubs/Associations

Shirley Sumbles
International Association of Jim Beam Bottle & Specialties Club
Newsletter: Beam Around the World
2015 Burlington Ave.
Kewanee, IL 61443-8348
e-mail: info@beam-wade.org
web: http://www.beam-wade.org
A group of collectors world wide with clubs in most states in the US as well as in New Zealand, Japan and Germany; annual international convention.

Evergreen State Beam Club
P.O. Box 12423
Seattle, WA 98082-0243
ph: 206-365-8286
e-mail: beamclub@aol.com
web: http://www.beamclub.com/
Focuses on the hobby of collecting Jim Beam and other ceramics decanters; new members always welcome; web site offers buy and sell board, online auctions, pictorials of over 4,000 decanters, bottle FAQs.

Experts

Bernie V. Durance
B.V.D. on Bottles
1008 North Star Drive
Colorado Springs, CO 80906
ph: 719-577-9033
fax: 719-226-0731
e-mail: bvdurance@juno.com
Expert, dealer, collector of Jim Beam and other whiskey decanters; appraisals, identification, buy, sell, trade; writes monthly column.

Figural Whiskey (Ski Country)

Clubs/Associations

National Ski Country Bottle Club
Newsletter: Ski Country Collector, The
1224 Washington Ave.
Golden, CO 80401
ph: 303-279-3373
fax: 303-278-9556
e-mail: BLowry@fossco.com
web: http://www.fossco.com/
Designed as a source of information on collector decanters, old and new; newsletter features articles about a broad range of decanters with an emphasis on decanters by Ski Country.

DECORATED OBJECTS

(see FOLK ART; FURNITURE [ANTIQUE], Painted)

DECORATIVE ARTS

(see also "APPRAISERS" Appendix as well as Appraisers listed under specific categories throughout this Directory.)

Clubs/Associations

Gerald Ward, Pres.
Museum of Fine Arts, Boston
Newsletter: Decorative Arts Society Newsletter
465 Huntington Ave.
Boston, MA 02115-5523
ph: 617-267-9300
e-mail: webmaster@mfa.org
web: http://www.mfa.org/home.html

American Decorative Arts Forum
c/o M.H. deYoung Museum
Golden Gate Park
San Francisco, CA 94118
ph: 415-431-6930
A nonprofit organization that seeks to encourage the study, understanding, end enjoyment of American decorative arts.

Museums/Libraries

Deborah Waters
Museum of the City of New York
1220 5th Ave.
New York, NY 10029-5221
ph: 212-534-1672
fax: 212-534-5974
e-mail: mcny@mcny.org
web: http://www.mcny.org/mcny/
Access by appointment; research fee charged.

Daughters of the American Revolution Museum
1776 D St. NW
Washington, DC 20006-5392
ph: 202-879-3241 or 202-879-3208
fax: 202-628-0820
e-mail: museum@dar.org
web: http://www.dar.org/museum/

National Museum of American History Branch Library
Smithsonian Institution
Washington, DC 20560
ph: 202-357-2414
e-mail: webmaster@si.edu
web: http://www.si.edu/organiza/museums/nmah/nmah.htm
Books/journals/trade catalogs on material culture, decorative arts, domestic & community life, applied science, engineering, technology.

Sally Grant
Museum of Early Southern Decorative Arts
Journal: Journal of the Early Southern Decorative Arts
P.O. Box 10310
Winston Salem, NC 27108-0310
ph: 336-721-7360 or 888-653-7253
fax: 336-721-7367
e-mail: webmaster@oldsalem.org
web: http://www.mesda.org
Focuses on Southern decorative arts; has Research Center, Catalog of Early Southern Decorative Arts, and Index of Southern Artists.

Victoria & Albert Museum
Cromwell Rd.
London, SW7 2RL
U.K.
ph: +44 171 938 8500
web: http://www.vam.ac.uk/
The V&A is Britain's national museum of art and design; houses many of the world's greatest decorative art treasures from priceless Oriental carpets to Italian sculpture.

Periodicals

Decorative Arts Trust
Newsletter: Decorative Arts Trust Newsletter
106 Bainbridge St.
Philadelphia, PA 19147-2402
ph: 215-627-2859
fax: 215-925-1144
Study and preservation of American decorative arts; features private collections, museums, restorations, and preservation; Spring and Fall symposiums each year held at various, rich historic sites throughout the US; a non-profit group.

Paula Hooper
Museum of Early Southern Decorative Arts
Journal: Journal of the Early Southern Decorative Arts
P.O. Box 10310
Winston Salem, NC 27108-0310
ph: 336-721-7360 or 888-653-7253
fax: 336-721-7367
e-mail: webmaster@oldsalem.org
web: http://www.mesda.org
Focuses on Southern decorative arts; has Research Center, Catalog of Early Southern Decorative Arts, and Index of Southern Artists.

DECOYS

(see also ART, Wildlife; FISHING COLLECTIBLES; FOLK ART; SPORTING COLLECTIBLES)

Book Sellers

Dean Dashner
Hunting Rig
349 S. Green Bay Rd.
Neenah, WI 54956
ph: 920-725-4350 or 920-725-4421
e-mail: dashners@athenet.net
web: http://www.athenet/net/~dashners
Buys and sells decoys, duck calls, Ducks Unlimited Pinbacks, sporting books, old sporting magazines.

Periodicals

Robert Woollens
R.W. Publishing
Magazine: Sporting Collector's Monthly
P.O. Box 305
Camden, DE 19934-0305
ph: 302-678-0113
fax: 302-678-3387
e-mail: rwpub@prodigy.net
A monthly with hundreds of buy, sell and trade ads; fish and waterfowl decoys, hunting equipment, fishing gear, loading tools, wildlife art, decorative wildlife & fish carvings, and related books, catalogs, magazines, etc.

Canadian

Experts

Bernie Gates
30 D Chambers St.
P.O. Box 653
Smiths Falls, Ontario K7A 5B8
Canada
ph: 613-283-1168
fax: 613-283-1345
e-mail: uppercanadian@recorder.ca
web: http://www.uppercanadian.com/
Author of "Ontario Decoys III"; $23.95 Canadian.

Factory

Experts

Henry Fleckenstein
P.O. Box 577
Cambridge, MD 21613
ph: 410-221-0076
Author of "American Factory Decoys," "Decoys of the Mid-Atlantic Region," "Southern Decoys of Virginia & the Carolinas," "Shorebird Decoys," and "New Jersey Decoys."

Fish

Clubs/Associations

Frank R. Baron, Sec.
Great Lakes Fish Decoy Collectors & Carvers Association
35824 West Chicago
Livonia, MI 48150-2522
ph: 734-427-7768
Regular meetings and newsletter; long range goal is to establish a permanent display of spearfishing artifacts.

John E. Shoffner
American Fish Decoy Association
Newsletter: American Fish Decoy Forum, The
624 Merritt St.
Fife Lake, MI 49633-9142
ph: 616-879-3912
e-mail: kjohn@gtii.com
3 year old association is the largest fish decoy collectors association with approx. 160 members; newsletter has color photos.

Collectors

R.C. Egan
c/o Meade Johnson Co.
2404 Penn Ave.
Evansville, IN 47708
Wants to buy wooden ice fishing decoys and wooden painted bobbers.

Dealers

Ronald J. Fritz
5221 Camberlea Ave.
Zephyrhills, FL 33541
ph: 813-788-2312
Buying and selling old working fish decoys by carvers from Michigan, New York as well as from other areas.

Frank R. Baron
Great Lakes Ice Decoys
35824 West Chicago
Livonia, MI 48150-2522
ph: 734-427-7768
Buys, sells, trades fish decoys; quarterly list of decoys for sale; author of "Bud Stewart, Michigan's Legendary Lure Maker."

John E. Shoffner
624 Merritt St.
Fife Lake, MI 49633-9142
ph: 616-879-3912
e-mail: kjohn@gtii.com
Issues 6 lists a year with approx. 600 fish decoys and antique fishing tackle items for sale.

Art Kimball
North Haven Antiques
P6790 Wildcat Drive
P.O. Box 252
Boulder Junction, WI 54512
ph: 715-385-2862
Periodic lists with photos of investment grade guaranteed authentic older fish decoys for sale; has written and published four available books on fish decoys.

John Cook
Peace Antiques
HC 3 Box 13A
Remer, MN 56672-9602
ph: 218-566-2793
Has specialized in buying and selling fish and duck decoys for 20 years.

Experts

Ronald J. Fritz
5221 Camberlea Ave.
Zephyrhills, FL 33541
ph: 813-788-2312
Specialist in the fish decoy carvings of Michigan carvers Peterson, Nelson, Ramey, Hulbert & Bruning; author of book on subject.

Man./Prod./Dist.

Mikko
Mikko's Bait Shop
P.O. Box 100
Osakis, MN 56360-0100
ph: 800-252-1186
e-mail: gitand@midwestinfo.net
Wholesale fish decoys to dealers only.

Waterfowl

Auction Services

Ted Harmon
Decoys Unlimited
2320 Main St.
West Barnstable, MA 02668
ph: 508-362-2766

Frank M. Schmidt
Guyette & Schmidt, Inc.
P.O. Box 522
West Farmington, ME 04992
ph: 207-778-6256 or 207-625-8055
fax: 207-778-6501
The world's largest decoy auction firm; please note that an alternate fax number is 207-625-4742.

Clubs/Associations

Ted Harmon
New England Decoy Collectors Association
2320 Main St.
West Barnstable, MA 02668
ph: 508-362-2766

John L. Clayton, Jr.
New Jersey Decoy Collectors Association
1745 Silverton Road
Toms River, NJ 08753
ph: 732-255-6291

Nat Glanz
Long Island Decoy Collectors Association
P.O. Box 807
Smithtown, NY 11787
ph: 516-537-0153
One of the oldest decoy collecting clubs in the country.

Jim Trimble
East Coast Decoy Collectors Association
P.O. Box 305
Camden, DE 19934
ph: 302-678-0113
e-mail: rwpub@prodigy.net
An organization to promote decoy collecting, the history of decoys, their makers, and related waterfowling interests.

Chad Tragacis
Potomac Decoy Collectors Association
6813 Moon Rock Court
Alexandria, VA 22306
ph: 703-768-2949

Carolina Decoy Collectors Association
4 St. Mary's Place
Wilmington, NC 28403

Ron Ernst
Georgia Decoy Collectors Club
200 Springtime Dr.
Warner Robins, GA 31088
ph: 912-953-6342

Ohio Decoy Collectors & Carvers Association
P.O. Box 499
Richfield, OH 44286
Focuses on both vintage and contemporary decoys and their makers.

Dick Brust
Minnesota Decoy Collectors Association
P.O. Box 385333
Minneapolis, MN 55438-5333
ph: 651-636-7700
A support group to the MN Decoy Foundation, specializing in MN waterfowl decoys.

Midwest Decoy Collectors Association
P.O. Box 4110
Saint Charles, IL 60174
ph: 312-337-7957
fax: 312-337-9679
e-mail: mdc@midwestdecoy.org
web: http://www.midwestdecoy.org

Collectors

David A. Galliher
2500 W. Berwyn Rd.
Muncie, IN 47304-5113
ph: 317-289-2233 or 317-284-6668
fax: 317-289-2376
Wants to buy antique or old decoys from the Midwest area, especially by the carver Charles Perdew (deceased) from Henry, IL; publishing a book on Charles Perdew; 295 pgs, 400 illustrations, color, museum quality printing and binding.

Dealers

Russ & Karen Goldberger
RJG Antiques
P.O. Box 2033
Hampton, NH 03843-2033
ph: 603-926-1770
fax: 603-929-4267
e-mail: russ@rjgantiques.com
web: http://www.rjgantiques.com
Dealers, appraisers, experts in waterfowl decoys; specializes in quality working decoys, folk art, and

American furniture and accessories in their original painted surfaces.

Lisa Trayer
Brickerville Antiques & Decoys
117 E. 28th Div. Hwy (Rte. 322)
Lititz, PA 17543
ph: 717-627-2466
Specializes in old factory and working decoys; also sporting antiques related to hunting and fishing; buy/sell/trade old decoys, creels, fishing tackle, eel traps, gigs, old advertising, salesman sample decoys, shell boxes, shorebirds.

Henry H. Stansbury
939 Elkridge Landing Road
Linthicum Heights, MD 21090
ph: 410-691-9120 or 410-744-8376
e-mail: henry@asionline.com
web: http://www.asionline.com/henry.html

Andrea J. Shreiner
Initialed Duck Antiques & Collectibles
3812 Hamilton Ave.
Baltimore, MD 21206-3505
Buys, sells and collects waterfowl decoys.

John Cook
Peace Antiques
HC 3 Box 13A
Remer, MN 56672-9602
ph: 218-566-2793
Has specialized in buying and selling fish and duck decoys for 20 years.

Museums/Libraries

Peabody Essex Museum
Essex & Libert Streets
Salem, MA 01970
ph: 978-745-9500 or 800-745-4054
e-mail: pem@pem.org
web: http://www.pem.org

Heritage Plantation of Sandwich
P.O. Box 566
Sandwich, MA 02563
ph: 508-888-3300 or 508-888-1222
fax: 508-833-2916
e-mail: heritage@heritageplantation.org
web: http://www.heritageplantation.org/autos.htm
Contains an outstanding exhibit of decoys by carvers including Elmer Crowell and his memorabilia.

Shelburne Museum, Inc.
P.O. Box 10
Shelburne, VT 05482-0010
ph: 802-985-3346 or 800-253-0191
fax: 802-985-2331
e-mail: museinfo@together.net
web: http://shelburnemuseum.org/
37 historic structures and exhibit buildings; diverse collection of American folk, fine, decorative and utilitarian art.

Museums at Stony Brook, The
Newsletter: News & Events
1208 Route 25A
Stony Brook, NY 11790-1992
ph: 516-751-0066
fax: 516-751-0353
e-mail: museums@longisland.com
web: http://www.museumsatstonybrook.org/
Large collection of American Art, decoys, horse-drawn vehicles, costumes, and miniature period rooms; museum shop.

Havre de Grace Decoy Museum
Magazine: Canvasback, The
215 Giles St.
Havre De Grace, MD 21078
ph: 410-939-3739
fax: 410-939-3775
e-mail: maryjohn@earthlink.net
web: http://www.decoymuseum.com/
Privately funded, non-profit organization for the documentation and interpretation of waterfowl decoys as a uniquely American folk art.

Pete Lesher, Cur.
Chesapeake Bay Maritime Museum
Magazine: Water Gauge, The
P.O. Box 636
Saint Michaels, MD 21663-0636
ph: 410-745-2916
fax: 410-745-6088
e-mail: letters@cbmm.org
web: http://www.cbmm.org
A major regional maritime museum with a 5200 volume research library; collections include 10,000 objects, 9.000 photos, 1,200 ships' plans, 72 linear feet of manuscripts; decoys, oystering, lighthouses, charts, nautical, tools.

Doug Johnson
Ward Museum of Wildfowl Art (Ward Foundation)
Magazine: Wildfowl Art
909 S. Schumaker Dr.
Salisbury, MD 21801
ph: 410-742-4988
fax: 410-742-3107
web: http://ecusa.com/npo/wardmus/
Conducts seminars on carving and painting decoys; the "Decoy Express" service offers up-to-the-minute information via your fax machine about available carvings.

Refuge Waterfowl Museum
7059 Maddox Blvd.
P.O. Box 272
Chincoteague, VA 23336
ph: 757-336-6117

Periodicals

Stackpole, Inc.
Magazine: Wildfowl Carving Magazine
500 Vaughn St.
Harrisburg, PA 17110-2220
ph: 717-234-5091 or 800-233-9055
fax: 717-234-1359
e-mail: editor@wildfowl-carving.com
web: http://wildfowl-carving.com/about.htm
Quarterly magazine devoted exclusively to bird carving; complete "how-to" and reference information for professional and amateur carvers alike; ads, articles, competition photos, special annual "Competition" issue.

Joe Engers
Decoy Magazine
Magazine: Decoy Magazine
P.O. Box 787
Lewes, DE 19958
ph: 302-644-9001
e-mail: kareno@azlink.com
web: http://www.dbqinc.com/decoy/
Only bi-monthly magazine serving the decoy collecting market; classifieds, calendar, auction news, carver profiles, full color.

Repro. Sources

Duane Sylor
49 Horner Rd.
Angelica, NY 14709-8780
ph: 716-466-7700
Make and sells handcarved carved and painted duck and shorebird decoys; copies of original working decoys.

Waterfowl (Mason)

Experts

Russ Goldberger
RJG Antiques
P.O. Box 2033
Hampton, NH 03843-2033
ph: 603-926-1770
fax: 603-929-4267
e-mail: russ@rjgantiques.com
web: http://www.rjgantiques.com
Specializes in quality working decoys, folk art, and American furniture and accessories in their original painted surfaces; co-author with Alan G. Haid of "Mason Decoys, A Complete Pictorial Guide."

DENTAL

(see MEDICAL, DENTAL & PHARMACEUTICAL, Dental)

DESERT STORM

Collectors

Carl F. Planzer
50 Gates Ave.
Gillette, NJ 07933
fax: 732-424-7814
e-mail: carl@njsystems.com
Wants Desert Storm memorabilia: Marx Playsets, trading cards, games, propaganda, etc.

DETECTIVE ITEMS

(see BOOKS, Mystery; CHARACTER COLLECTIBLES, Sherlock Holmes; MAGAZINES, Mystery; MYSTERY/DETECTIVE ITEMS)

DIAMOND EDGE (SHAPLEIGH HARDWARE)

(see also HARDWARE; KEEN KUTTER [SIMMONS HARDWARE]; KNIVES; TOOLS; WINCHESTER COLLECTIBLES)

Auction Services

Bob Simmons
Simmons & Company Auctioneers
40706 E. 144th St.
Richmond, MO 64085
ph: 816-776-2936 or 800-646-2936
fax: 816-470-5016
e-mail: simmons_auction@raycounty.com
web: http://www.raycounty.com/simmons/
Conducts annual specialty auctions of Winchester, Keen Kutter (E.C. Simmons Hardware) and Diamond Edge (Shapleigh Hardware) collectibles; has a well-established reputation for expertise and high quality merchandise.

Clubs/Associations

Barbara Huhn, Mem.
Hardware Companies Kollectors' Club
Newsletter: Winchester Keen Kutter Diamond Edge Chronicles
432 S. Gore St.
Saint Louis, MO 63119
ph: 314-968-0304
e-mail: gramma@mvp.net
web: http://www.raycounty.com/simmons/clubs/newsletter.htm
A non-profit organization to serve as an interactive information distribution center for collectors of E.C. Simmons/Keen Kutter, Winchester Store (non-gun), A.F. Shapleigh/Diamond Edge, Hibbard, and other hardware store brands.

Experts

Bob Simmons
40706 E. 144th St.
Richmond, MO 64085
ph: 816-776-2936 or 800-646-2936
fax: 816-470-5016
e-mail: simmons_auction@raycounty.com
web: http://www.raycounty.com/simmons/
Collects and specializes in Diamond Edge (Shapleigh Hardware) items especially advertising, catalogs, store signs and displays, promotions, sporting goods, and household items made for this St. Louis firm from the late 1800s to 1940.

DIARIES

Collectors

Roy C. Kulp
P.O. Box 264
Hatfield, PA 19440-0264
ph: 215-362-0732
Wants to buy account books and day books by farmers, carpenters, blacksmiths, coffin & carriage makers, and weavers; also wants pre-1890 hand written travel diaries.

Dealers

Barbara & Richard DePalma
Deer Park Books
609 Kent Rd., Route 7
Gaylordsville, CT 06755
ph: 860-350-4140
fax: 860-350-4140
e-mail: DeerParkBk@aol.com
web: http://www.abebooks.com/home/BARBDE/
Fine books bought and sold; antiquarian books, modern first editions, children's and illustrated; also maps, autographs, etc.; all subjects; also wants handwritten diaries, travel journals, scrapbooks, albums.

DICE

(see also GAMBLING COLLECTIBLES)

Collectors

Jeff Lauderman
Diceman, The
P.O. Box 9293
Canoga Park, CA 91309
e-mail: jldice@ix.netcom.com
web: http://pw2.netcom.com/~jldice/diceman.htm
Buys and sells; has collection of over 5,000 pairs of casino dice.

Bill Whelan
P.O. Box 617
Daly City, CA 94017-2332
ph: 650-756-1189
Wants to buy dice with casino or location imprints; also color variations, shapes and sizes; any type of dice, and dice related items.

DIECUTS

(see PAPER COLLECTIBLES)

DIME NOVELS

(see BOOKS, Paperback)

DIMESTORE SOLDIERS

(see SOLDIERS, Toy)

DINERS & RELATED ITEMS

(see also RESTAURANT COLLECTIBLES)

Collectors

Daniel Zilka
110 Benevolent St.
Providence, RI 02906
ph: 410-331-8575 or 410-461-7932
fax: 401-351-0127
Wants to buy diner photographs, postcards, matchbook covers, diner magazines, diner stools, coffee urns, vintage restaurant equipment.

Brian A. Butko
2640 Sunset Dr.
West Mifflin, PA 15122-3565
Wants only souvenir items from factory-built diners which typically look like wooden or stainless steel train cars; roadside diners were especially popular with automobile tourists from 1920 to 1970.

John Richard Shoaf
RR 5, Box 147 (Rt. 73)
Morgantown, WV 26505
ph: 304-292-4837
DINERholic doing research on diners; charter member of the American Diner Museum.

Larry Spilkin
P.O. Box 5039
Southfield, MI 48086-5039
ph: 248-642-3722
Wants postcards and matchbook covers of drive-ins, diners, cafes, gas stations and 1930s-1950s motels, restaurant/bar, cabins and Art Deco streamline hotels.

Museums/Libraries

Daniel Zilka
American Diner Museum
110 Benevolent St.
Providence, RI 02906
ph: 410-331-8575 or 410-461-7932
fax: 401-351-0127
A museum showcasing numerous manufacturers and various aspects of the diner industry; extensive photograph and artifact collection and reference library; wants photos and other items relating to diner history.

Periodicals

Randolph Garbin
Coffee Cup Publications
Magazine: Roadside
P.O. Box 652
West Side Station
Worcester, MA 01602
ph: 508-791-1838
fax: 508-755-5319
e-mail: info@roadsidemagazine.com
web: http://www.roadsidemagazine.com
A quarterly journal for the diner owner; the only publication devoted to the appreciation and preservation of the American Diner.

Repair Services

Daniel Zilka
110 Benevolent St.
Providence, RI 02906
ph: 410-331-8575 or 410-461-7932
fax: 401-351-0127
Performs restoration work on historic diners.

Steve Harwin
Diversified Diners
2043 Random Rd. #302
Cleveland, OH 44106-5916
ph: 216-229-4003
fax: 216-229-4005
e-mail: steveincleve@hotmail.com
web: http://www.oh-diners.com/
Buys, sells and restores diners and related items; diner restoration consultant; also buys diner related memorabilia.

Suppliers

Bill Raymer
Restoration Resources
31 Thayer St.
Roxbury, MA 02118
ph: 617-542-3033
Supplies vintage parts for diners: stools, jukeboxes, etc.

DINNERWARE

(see also CERAMICS; CERAMICS [AMERICAN DINNERWARE]; CERAMICS [CONTINENTAL]; CERAMICS [ENGLISH]; CERAMICS [ORIENTAL]; FLATWARE; GLASS, Elegant; GLASS, Crystal; MODERNISM; REPAIR/RESTORATION/CONSERVATION; TABLEWARE)

Clubs/Associations

Echo's Discontinued China & Silver
Lonsdale Ct. #121
1433 Lonsdale Ave.
North Vancouver, British Columbia V7M 2H9
Canada
ph: 800-663-6004 or 604-980-8011
fax: 604-988-3611
e-mail: echos@sunshine.net
web: http://www.sunshine.net/echos
Buys and sells discontinued china and silver tableware.

Collectors

Deborah G. Taylor
Bluegrass Rainbow Collection
HA 645, Dept Clin Chem, UK Hospital
Lexington, KY 40502
ph: 606-271-4577 or 606-323-6521
e-mail: stefan.kwiatkowski@worldnet.att.net
web: http://home.att.net/~stefan.kwiatkowski/icons.index.htm
Collector of fine European dinnerware: RS Prussia, RS Tillowitz, Limoges, Meissen, Royal Copenhagen, etc.

Matching Services

Ross Simmons
#9 Ross Simmons Dr.
Cranston, RI 02920-4476
ph: 800-521-7677 or 800-553-2135
fax: 800-896-9191
e-mail: customerservices@ross-simmons.com
web: http://www.ross-simmons.com/
Sells new, active patterns of Royal Doulton, Minton, Wedgwood, Noritake, Villeroy & Boch, Royal Worcester, Lenox, etc.; several outlets on East coast.

China By Pattern International Matching Service
P.O. Box 129
Farmington, CT 06034-0129
ph: 203-678-7079
Send SASE to locate/match Castleton, Lenox, Spode, Doulton, Worcester, Minton, Coalport, Franciscan, Rosenthal, Syracuse, Wedgwood, Haviland, Noritake, Johnson Bros., etc.

Regina Negrotti
Tablescapes
P.O. Box 448
Cheshire, CT 06410
ph: 800-801-4084
e-mail: lenox@ntplx.net
web: http://www.tabletopdesigns.com/
A small, personal matching service with a constantly changing inventory; want lists are kept; send photocopy or photo when unsure of pattern name; specializes in Lenox.

Silver & China Exchange
P.O. Box 4601
Dept. MA
Stamford, CT 06907-0601
ph: 203-322-5963
Specializing in Lenox/Oxford china; over 250 different patterns in stock.

Paul & Pearl Hoffman
China Brokers, Ltd.
11 Westgate Ct.
Colts Neck, NJ 07722
ph: 732-866-6613 or 800-867-6613
Over 40,000 dinnerware patterns in stock; obsolete, inactive, active.

Alice Korman
Alice's Past & Presents Replacements
P.O. Box 465
Merrick, NY 11566-0465
ph: 516-379-1352
fax: 516-379-7302
e-mail: alicechina@aol.com
Matching and locating service for Lenox, Oxford, Chinastone, Temperware, Gorham, Dansk, Denby, Wedgwood, Adams, Midwinter, Coalport, Fitz & Floyd, Christian Dior, Mikasa, Noritake, Royal Doulton, Minton, Royal Worcester, Spode, others.

Pattern Finders, A
P.O. Box 206
Port Jefferson Station, NY 11776-0206
ph: 516-928-5158 or 800-216-2446
fax: 516-928-5170
e-mail: apattern@aol.com
Adams, Arabia, Aynsley, Castleton, Coalport, Denby, Enoch, Franciscan, Gorham, Haviland, Johnson Brothers, Lenox, Mikasa, Minton, Noritake, Oxford, Rosenthal, Royal Doulton, Royal Worcester, Spode, Syracuse, Wedgwood.

Sophia Papapanu
Sophia's China & Crystal
141 Sedgwick Rd.
Syracuse, NY 13203-1136
ph: 315-472-6834
e-mail: jap@dreamscape.com
web: http://www.sophiaschina-crystal.com/
Discontinued china and crystal patterns; over 19 years service; American, English, and other manufacturers; mail order or by special appointment; please send SASE with requests for information.

Constance Stolz
China Match & Crystal Match
72 Longacre Rd.
Rochester, NY 14621-1019
ph: 716-338-3781
e-mail: chinamat@frontiernet.net
Replacements of discontinued china and stoneware; Fitz & Floyd, Royal Doulton, Royal Worcester, Spode, Wedgwood; buy and sell.

Dick & Rosemarie Lewis
Dining Antiques
#6 Market Plaza
Reinholds, PA 17569
ph: 888-346-4642 or 717-484-0661
e-mail: diningan@ptdprolog.net
Specializes in matching Syracuse china, 9,000 pieces and 80 patterns in stock.

Michael Round Fine China & Crystal, Inc.
7845 Wisconsin Ave.
Bethesda, MD 20814
ph: 301-656-2626 or 800-467-6863
fax: 703-550-7881
e-mail: feedback@Mround.com
web: http://www.michaelround.com
Impressive website for matching china, crystal or flatware.

Cee Cee China
3904 Parsons Rd.
Chevy Chase, MD 20815
ph: 301-652-6226 or 800-619-6226
e-mail: ccchina@aol.com
Buys, sells and locates; specializing in discontinued Lenox, Oxford, and Syracuse china only.

China Matching, Inc.
420 Belle Grove Rd.
Middletown, VA 22645
ph: 540-869-1261
Discontinued china & crystal; Castleton, Haviland, Lenox and Wedgwood china; Fostoria & Lenox crystal.

Mildred G. Brumback
China & Crystal Matching, Inc.
420 Belle Grove Rd.
Dept. M
Middletown, VA 22645
ph: 540-869-1261
Send requests with SASE; specializes in Lenox and Castleton.

Van Ness China Company
1124 Fairway Dr.
Waynesboro, VA 22980
ph: 540-942-2827
Discontinued English bone china: Aynsley, Coalport, Minton, Royal Dounton, Royal Worcester, Spode, Wedgwood.

Harry Weitkemper
China Finders
1-B South Holy Ave.
Highland Springs, VA 23075
ph: 888-244-6239 or 804-328-2897
Buys and sells Castleton, Lenox, Doulton, Franciscan, Haviland, Spode, Wedgwood, Shelley, Minton, Noritake, Adams, Metlox, Vernon Kilns, and most major manufacturers.

Thurber's
2256C Dabeny Rd.
Richmond, VA 23230-3342
ph: 804-278-9080 or 800-848-7237
fax: 804-278-9480
Carries only active patterns; will locate old patterns.

Randy Foster
Replacements Ltd.
P.O. Box 26029
1089 Knox Road
Greensboro, NC 27420
ph: 800-737-5223 or 336-697-3000
fax: 336-697-3100
e-mail: replaceltd@aol.com
web: http://www.replacements.com
China, crystal and flatware (obsolete, active and inactive.)

D & J Locations
1601 E. Canal St.
Tarboro, NC 27886
ph: 252-823-5333 or 800-818-5565
Discontinued china: Gorham, Haviland, Lenox, Metlox, Mikasa, Minton, Noritake, Pickard, Royal Doulton, Spode, Wedgwood, and other major brands; buys, sells, locates.

Jean-Paul Iannantuoni
455 Concord Parkway N., #5500
Dept. CIC
Concord, NC 28027-6736
ph: 704-786-7758
fax: 704-795-7975
e-mail: AnteekBear@aol.com
web: http://www.freeyellow.com/members/royaldoulton/index.html
Dinnerware search service for all manufacturers but specializes in Arabia, Block China, Boda Nova, Christopher Stuart, Epoch, Gibson, International China, Longchamp, Midwinter, Monton, Newcor, Nikko, Murifield; appraisals by fee only.

China Cabinet, The
214 Hillside Dr.
P.O. Box 426
Clearwater, SC 29822
ph: 803-593-9655
Features a number of Metlox Potteries patterns.

China & Crystal Matchers, Inc.
2379 John Glenn Dr., Ste. #108-M
Atlanta, GA 30341-1924
ph: 770-455-1162 or 800-286-1107
fax: 770-452-8616
e-mail: chinacmi@bellsouth.net
All manufacturers; buys, sells, locates; member of the International Association of Dinnerware Matchers.

Bob Owens
Network Pattern Matching
2551 Indian Ford Rd.
Valdosta, GA 31601
ph: 888-242-0994 or 912-242-6600
fax: 912-242-6602
e-mail: info@networkpatternmatching.com
web: http://www.networkpatternmatching.com
NPM is a network of more than 100 fine china dealers who have combined their inventories into a listing of more than 50,000 patterns, with a comprehensive selection of pieces, prices and pictures on the site; easy and free searches.

Atlantic Silver & China
7405 N.W. 57th St.
Tamarac, FL 33319
ph: 800-368-3153 or 954-720-4559
fax: 954-720-4577
e-mail: info@atlanticsilver.com
web: http://www.atlanticsilver.com
Inactive Lenox, Noritake, Rosenthal, Royal Doulton, Wedgwood.

Paul Church
Replacement Service, A
500 Oregon Ave.
Saint Cloud, FL 34769
ph: 407-957-1719 or 800-337-9075
e-mail: chinacrystal@juno.com
Buys, sells, locates Lenox, Oxford, Temperware, Castleton, Franciscan fine china and earthenware.

Mary Ann Lowery
Crystal Corner, Inc., The
317 Billy Dyar Blvd.
P.O. Box 756
Boaz, AL 35957-0756
ph: 256-593-6169
fax: 256-593-6560
e-mail: ccorner@netnav.com
web: http://www.crystalcorner.com/
Royal Doulton, Fitz & Floyd, Gorham, Noritake, Mikasa, Haviland, etc.

Mara F. Sprott
Fulbreit China Locators
1688 Autumn Ave.
Memphis, TN 38112-5222
ph: 901-274-6868 or 901-346-7357
fax: 901-346-7416
e-mail: chinas@bellsouth.net
web: http://www.havilandchina.com
Carries Fiesta, Haviland & Co., Theodore Haviland, American and French Haviland, Johann Haviland, Charles Field Haviland, Homer Laughlin, Metlox; want lists maintained; shipment by UPS; send photocopy of front and back.

Bruce & Donna Johnston
Abby's Attic
28107 Eugene E. Ladner Rd.
Perkinston, MS 39573
ph: 601-255-2799
Buys, sells, locates Dansk,

Franciscan, Gorham, Lenox, Noritake and others.

Vintage Patterns IV
9303 McKinney Rd.
Loveland, OH 45140
ph: 513-489-6247
Wedgwood specialists; also Adams, Coalport; buys and sells; send SASE.

Allan & Cathy Griggs
Chinamates
1673 Lakecrest Dr.
Sullivan, IN 47882-9585
ph: 800-726-0345 or 812-268-6411
fax: 812-268-6411
e-mail: chinamates@viaduct.custom.net
Stocks, locates discontinued patterns only of china & crystal; Franciscan, Gorham, Lenox, Minton, Oxford, Adams, Johnson Brothers, Pickard, Royal Doulton, Wedgwood, etc.; member Fostoria Glass Soc. of Am.

Barron's
P.O. Box 994
Novi, MI 48376
ph: 800-538-6340
fax: 800-523-4456
e-mail: barronsdw@aol.com
web: http://www.barronsdinnerware.com/
Carries only active patterns.

Wilma R. Wolff
Wolff's
315 Chestnut
Atlantic, IA 50022
ph: 800-765-8948 or 712-243-4704
fax: 712-243-2936
Aynsley, Castleton, Denby, Fitz & Floyd, Flintridge, Franciscan, Gorham, Haviland, Lenox, Metlox, Mikasa, Minton, Noritake, Oxford, Red Wing, Rosenthal, Royal Doulton, Sango, Syracuse, Vernon Kilns, Vistosa, Wallace.

Heritage China of Iowa
P.O. Box 244
Palo, IA 52324
ph: 888-416-1595 or 319-227-3688
e-mail: dischina@aol.com
Buys and sells discontinued china: Dansk, Denby, Franciscan, Haviland, Homer Laughlin, Mikasa, Minton, Noritake, Royal Doulton, Sango, Wedgwood, Japanese patterns, etc.

Clintsman International
811 E. Geneva St.
Elkhorn, WI 53121
ph: 414-723-1990 or 800-781-8900
fax: 414-723-1991
All manufacturers: Adams, Denby, Gorham, Johnson Brothers, Lenox, Metlox, Mikasa, Noritake, Royal Doulton, Spode, Syracuse, Wedgwood, and others; buys and sells.

Jacquelynn Ives
Jacquelynn's China Matching Service
219 N. Milwaukee St.
Milwaukee, WI 53202-5818
ph: 414-272-8880 or 800-482-8287
fax: 414-272-0361
e-mail: jchinams@aol.com
web: http://www.jacquelynnschinamatch.com
English/American exclusively; discontinued Coalport, Castleton, Franciscan, Lenox, Minton, Spode, Royal Doulton, Wedgwood, Flintridge/Gorham, Royal Crown Derby, Royal Worcester, Pickard, Royal Winton, Royal Albert, etc.

China & Crystal Replacements
P.O. Box 187
5613 Country Road 19
Excelsior, MN 55331
ph: 612-474-6418 or 800-432-4448
Discontinued and active china, dinnerware and crystal bought and sold.

Audrey Rickard
China Trade Ltd.
2133 Birchwood Ave.
Wilmette, IL 60091-2305
ph: 847-256-7414 or 800-295-4200
fax: 847-256-5952
e-mail: Trick2@juno.com
Specializing in major manufacturers of discontinued china; also 18th and 19th century porcelain.

China Replacements
P.O. Box 508
High Ridge, MO 63049
ph: 800-562-2655 or 314-677-5577
fax: 314-376-6319
e-mail: chinarep@i1.net
web: http://www.iadm.com/chinarep/
Buys, sells, and locates all major brands of china; Lenox/Oxford, Royal Doulton, Royal Worcester/Spode, Denby, Castleton, Syracuse, Franciscan, Wedgwood, Noritake, Mikasa and many others.

Arlene Mauer, Pres.
International Association of Dinnerware Matchers
P.O. Box 656
High Ridge, MO 63049-0656
ph: 314-677-5577
e-mail: iadm@i1.net
web: http://www.iadm.com
IADM is a group of independent dinnerware matchers (china, crystal, and flatware) in the US & Canada organized to promote honesty and integrity within the profession; publishes a directory of members.

Dining Elegance, Ltd.
P.O. Box 4203
Saint Louis, MO 63163
ph: 314-865-1408
American Lenox/Oxford; most English manufacturers; French & American Haviland; French Ceralene-Raynaud; listing of patterns in stock sent upon request; $1.

Betty Stachurski
Betty's Crystal & China
P.O. Box 433
Lawrence, KS 66044-0433
ph: 913-842-8054
Aynsley, Castleton, Denby, Franciscan, Gorham, Adams, Midwinter, Coalport, Lenox, Oxford, Temperware, Royal Doulton, Minton, Royal Worcester, Spode, Royal Crown Derby, Metlox, Mikasa, Noritake and others.

Peggy Endicott
Bygone China Match
1225 W. 34th North
Wichita, KS 67204-4236
ph: 316-838-6010
fax: 316-838-6010
e-mail: bygonchina@aol.com
Large inventory of discontinued patterns in Dansk, Denby, Fitz/Floyd, Franciscan, Gorham, Haviland, Lenox, Metlox, Mikasa, Noritake, Royal Doulton, Sango china/pottery.

Barbara Coleman
Finders Keepers China Lady
1537 Metairie Rd.
Metairie, LA 70005-3938
ph: 504-455-1530 or 504-831-4514
fax: 504-885-2512
Stock or locate Doulton, Lenox/Oxford, Minton, Noritake, Pickard, Spode, Wedgwood; also other china and crystal.

Jo Hancock
Jo's Antiques & Collectibles
621 S. Main St.
Nashville, AR 71852-2707
ph: 870-845-1070
China and crystal matching; Lenox and other fine brands; 35 years experience collecting and selling Lenox items.

Locators, Inc.
2217 Cottondale Lane
Little Rock, AR 72202-2018
ph: 501-663-7787 or 800-367-9690
fax: 501-663-7787
e-mail: locators@worldnet.att.net
web: http://www.chinalocators.com
Carries out-of-production (discontinued) china and crystal, and discontinued as well as active sterling flatware patterns.

Teri Read
China Teacup, The
509 East Texas Avenue
Mart, TX 76664
ph: 254-876-3453
fax: 254-876-3533
e-mail: teacup@eramp.net
web: http://www.chinateacup.com/
All major brands: Castleton, Denby, Franciscan, Lenox, Gorham, Mikasa, Royal Doulton, Noritake, Spode, Syracuse, Wedgwood, etc.; buys and sells.

David Lackey Antiques & China Matching
2311 Westheimer
Houston, TX 77098-1317
ph: 281-942-7171
fax: 713-521-2546
Buys and sells major brands: Lenox, Castleton, Wedgwood, Noritake, Franciscan, Haviland, Spode, Royal Doulton.

Larry & Anne McDonald
A & A Dinnerware Locators
P.O. Box 50222
Austin, TX 78763-0222
ph: 512-264-1054 or 888-898-4202
fax: 512-264-2727
e-mail: 73612.470@compuserve.com
Locate/match discontinued china, earthenware, etc.; all major manufacturers: American, European, Japanese: Castleton, Adams, Doulton, Franciscan, Gorham, Lenox, Metlox, Mikasa, Noritake, Spode, Worcester; primarily mail order.

Chip
Chinatown LLC
815 East 2100 South
Salt Lake City, UT 84106
ph: 801-486-8282
e-mail: chip@chinatownllc.com
web: http://www.edish.com
Browse the online inventory of discontinued and current china a crystal dinnerware.

Olympus Cove Antiques & China Matching
179 E. 300 St.
Salt Lake City, UT 84111
ph: 800-284-8046 or 801-532-0431
e-mail: olympus@aros.net
web: http://www.olympuscove.com
Buys and sells discontinued china: Syracuse, Spode, Lenox, Franciscan, Castleton, Haviland, and much more.

Sara's China Closet
7749 E. Luke Lane
Scottsdale, AZ 85250
ph: 602-946-9145
Discontinued china patterns from most major English and American Manufacturers.

Beverly Hills Pattern Matching Service
270 N. Canon Drive, #1419
Beverly Hills, CA 90210
ph: 800-443-1122
fax: 818-707-0425
Discontinued patterns of china: Gorham, Lenox, Pickard, Royal Doulton, Minton, Royal Worcester-Spode, Sango.

Carol Ulrey
Unique Antiques
P.O. Box 15815
San Diego, CA 92175-5815
ph: 619-281-8650
fax: 619-282-8407
e-mail: culrey@webcc.net
Specializing in china matching: Haviland, old French and American; also Lenox china and crystal.

Joanne Cone
Joanne Cone Matching Service
34 Silverwood
Irvine, CA 92604
ph: 949-551-3173
e-mail: jochina@aol.com
Buys, sells, locates all major manufacturers (Mikasa specialist): Mikasa, Castleton, Denby, Franciscan, Johnson, Lenox, Metlox, Noritake, Royal Doulton, Spode, Syracuse, Wedgwood, etc.

China Traders Replacement Service
P.O. Box 1920
Simi Valley, CA 93062
ph: 805-578-3800 or 800-638-9955
fax: 805-578-3803
e-mail: lmarvideo@aol.com
web: http://www.chinatraders.com
Totally computerized discontinued china matching service; all major patterns; large inventory; friendly and knowledgeable staff.

Past & Present
14851 Avenue 360
Visalia, CA 93292
ph: 500-437-7666 or 415-258-1775
fax: 415-456-4333
e-mail: P-P@ix.netcom.com
web: http://www.china-crystal-flatware.com
Formal and casual: Castleton, Community, Denby, Doulton, Flintridge, Franciscan, Gorham, Hall, Haviland, Johnson Bros., Lenox, Mason's, Metlox, Mikasa, Noritake, Redwing, Rosenthal, Spode, Syracuse, Wedgwood, etc.

Silver Lane Antiques
P.O. Box 322
San Leandro, CA 94577-0032
ph: 510-483-0632
Buys and sells discontinued patterns by major American and English china and earthenware companies; Lenox, Spode, Minton, Franciscan, Syracuse, Wedgwood, Royal Copenhagen, Doulton, Ceralene, American Haviland, Rosenthal, Castleton, etc.

B. Diane Ayers
5th Generation Antiques
124 W. 8th Ave.
Chico, CA 95926-3240
ph: 530-895-0813
fax: 530-895-0813
Specializes in Haviland, Noritake, Lenox, Gorham, Royal Copenhagen; discontinued patterns from 1860 to present; photos required of older pieces; send SASE.

White's Collectables & Fine China, Etc.
616 E. First
P.O. Box 670
Newberg, OR 97132
ph: 503-538-7421
fax: 503-538-6886
e-mail: whites@whitescollectables.com
web: http://www.whitescollectables.com
Discontinued china: Castleton, Denby, Lenox, Oxford, Royal Doulton, Royal Worcester, Franciscan, Syracuse, Spode, Minton, and Wedgwood; also current patterns of major manufacturers.

Michael Lindsey
Vintage American Pottery
116 S. Washington St.
Seattle, WA 98104-2522
ph: 206-682-6162
fax: 206-405-3561
e-mail: oiljars@aol.com
Specializes in American made collectible and discontinued dinnerware only: Bauer, Franciscan, Hall, Heath, Metlox, Russel Wright, Red Wing, Vernon, Winfield, and many others.

Warren & Betty Roundhill
Patterns Unlimited International
Dept. CIC
P.O. Box 15238
Seattle, WA 98115-0238
ph: 206-523-9710
fax: 206-524-1252
Buy and sell china from England, France and USA; also appraises discontinued tableware patterns of all china, silver and glass.

William Ashley Ltd.
50 Bloor Street West
Toronto, Ontario M4W 3V1
Canada
ph: 416-964-2400 or 800-268-1122
Discontinued pattern service specializing in English china and crystal manufacturers.

Old China Patterns Ltd.
1560 Brimley Rd.
Scarborough, Ontario M1P 3G9
Canada
ph: 800-663-4533 or 416-299-8880
fax: 416-299-4721
e-mail: ocp@chinapatterns.com
web: http://www.chinapatterns.com
Canada's largest matching service; buys and sells internationally; since 1966; specializing in English china and crystal; charter member International Association of Dinnerware Matchers.

Tom & Annette Power
Tablewhere?
4 Queens Parade Close
London, N11 3FY
U.K.
ph: +44 181 361 7787
e-mail: collector@globalnet.co.uk
Specializing in discontinued tableware of most British manufacturers from 1900 to the present day; worldwide mail order service; VISA/MC/AMEX.

Periodicals

Cleo Kapilla
Joyful Ventures
Directory: Directory of Discontinued Tableware Services
P.O. Box 5297
Ocala, FL 34478-5297
ph: 352-622-4077
Publishes biennial directory listing over 50 matching services that sell and search for discontinued tableware items - china, crystal, and flatware.

Susan Ranta
Magazine: Set Your Table
P.O. Box 22481
Lincoln, NE 68542-2481
ph: 800-600-2127 or 402-423-4865
fax: 402-423-4865
e-mail: sranta@setyourtable.com
web: http://www.setyourtable.com
Whether its pottery, stoneware or china, Set Your Table lists more than 80 dealers who can help you find your missing pieces; dealer listings are indexed by manufacturer so you will know which dealers can help you.

Advertising

Collectors

Bruce Fernie
121 Newbury St.
Boston, MA 02116
ph: 617-859-8593
fax: 617-859-0043
Wants china, porcelain, dinnerware, and silverplated hotelware decorated with hotel, restaurant, cruise line, club, corporate, steamship, railroad, and diner custom logos, crests, names, and designs.

European

Matching Services

Joan Nackman
China Matching Service
56 Meadowbrook Country Club
St. Louis, MO 63011
ph: 314-227-3444
Buys, sells, locates discontinued china, specializing in Bavarian, German, Czechoslovakian, Austrian dinnerware; Heinrich, Villeroy & Boch, Hutschenreuther, Johann Haviland, Tirschenreuth; most European Chinas; also stocks Lenox china.

Haviland

(see also CERAMICS [CONTINENTAL], Haviland)

Appraisers

Virginia Cannon, ISA
China House, The
801 W. Eldorado
Decatur, IL 62522
ph: 217-428-7212 or 800-342-9536
fax: 217-864-4852
e-mail: 76573.376@compuserve.com
Matches, specializes in, and appraises French & American; carries large selection of Haviland patterns for sale by mail order or from the shop; also most other major brands.

Dealers

Frances M. Jepson
Jepson Haviland China
13211 Redhills Rd.
P.O. Box 295
Chinese Camp, CA 95309-0295
ph: 209-984-4432
Experienced, buys, sells, does identification; send photocopy of front and back of plate, color and description plus $7.50 and SASE; will refund if cannot identify; appraisals $75; member International Haviland Collectors Association.

Matching Services

Sailor's Wife, The
RR 3 Box 137
Gorham, ME 04038-9418
ph: 207-929-3009
Specializing in old French Haviland; matching service for Haviland & Co., Theodore Haviland and C.F.H. backmarks; some American Haviland; send Schleiger number or photocopy for identification.

China By Pattern International Matching Service
P.O. Box 129
Farmington, CT 06034-0129
ph: 203-678-7079
Send SASE to locate/match American and French Haviland dinnerware china as well as Johann Haviland (Bavaria); no charge to list or search for wanted items.

Jan Fenger
Presence of the Past
488 Main St.
Old Saybrook, CT 06475-2530
ph: 860-388-9021
fax: 860-388-2025
Haviland, Noritake; send Schleiger number or sample saucer with SASE.

Linda Kinnett
Kinnett Antiques
110 Lake Terrace Ct.
Hendersonville, TN 37075-5101
ph: 615-824-5987
fax: 615-264-8751
e-mail: china@bellsouth.net
A Haviland matching service with hundreds of patterns in stock; member of A.A.D.A.; in business for over 30 years.

Walker's Haviland Matching Service
P.O. Box 357
Athens, OH 45701
ph: 740-593-5631
Buys and sells French or American patterns of Haviland.

Scott's Haviland Matching Service
1911 Leland Ave.
Des Moines, IA 50315-4952
ph: 800-952-7857 or 515-285-2739
fax: 515-285-0744
e-mail: scottshaviland@worldnet.att.net
web: http://www.havilandchinabyscotts.com
Specializing in French, American, Bavarian, Charles Field, (Johann) Haviland; buy, sell, and identify; send Schleiger number or photocopy of front and of backstamp; please enclose phone number or fax number to which you would like a reply.

Grace Graves
Haviland Matching Service, Ltd.
219 N. Milwaukee St.
Milwaukee, WI 53202-5818
ph: 414-291-9111
fax: 414-291-9018
e-mail: hmsgraves@aol.com
Collector, dealer in porcelains and pottery by the Haviland families of Limoges, France; specialists in identifying and locating French & American Haviland patterns; use Schleiger number or send photocopy for pattern identification.

Old Toll Gate Antiques
209 3rd Ave. W
Milan, IL 61264-2443
ph: 309-787-2392
French and American Haviland; send Schleiger number or photocopy of front and back.

Mary Jane Jurgens
50 DuClaire Rd.
Decatur, IL 62521-5527
ph: 217-423-8303
e-mail: jurgens@springnet.com
Sells and appraises dinnerware with a specialty in Haviland.

Virginia Cannon, ISA
China House, The
801 W. Eldorado
Decatur, IL 62522
ph: 217-428-7212 or 800-342-9536
fax: 217-864-4852
e-mail: 76573.376@compuserve.com
Matches, specializes in, and appraises French & American; carries large selection of Haviland patterns for sale by mail order or from the shop; also most other major brands.

Kick L. Tex
Ann's Antiques
P.O. Box 7196
Springfield, IL 62791-7196
ph: 217-652-3862 or 217-546-4048
Appraises, matches and locates French Haviland; sells Haviland by mail; no charge for listing or searching; send pattern number or picture of saucer for identification.

Herbert Crosson
Crosson Antiques
835 N. 3rd Ave.
Minneapolis, KS 67467
ph: 785-392-2810
Specializes in Haviland china.

Millie Conner
Haviland Matching Service
1060 Crestline Dr.
Crete, NE 68333
ph: 402-826-2622
Carries Haviland & Co., and American and French Haviland; please send Schleiger number or photocopy of front and back.

Joanne Copeland
Sweet Nothings
5533 S. 20th St.
Lincoln, NE 68512
ph: 402-420-1620

Nora Travis
Haviland China Replacements
P.O. Box 6008-161
Cerritos, CA 90701
ph: 714-521-9283
fax: 714-521-9283
e-mail: travishrs@aol.com
web: http://www.angelfire.com/biz2/havilandchina/index.html
Specializing in French and American Haviland; will identify and locate your pattern if possible; large inventory; send Schleiger number or photocopy of your pattern; author of "Haviland China - Age of Elegance" (Schiffer.)

Carol Ulrey
Unique Antiques
P.O. Box 15815
San Diego, CA 92175-5815
ph: 619-281-8650
fax: 619-282-8407
e-mail: culrey@webcc.net
Specializing in china matching: Haviland, old French and American; also Lenox china and crystal.

Carol Williams
Lillian Johnson Antiques
405 Third St.
P.O. Box 1207
San Juan Bautista, CA 95045
ph: 831-623-4381
fax: 831-623-4381
Well-established French and American Haviland matching service; pattern predominantly from the WWI era; buys, sells, appraises.

Frances M. Jepson
Jepson Haviland China
13211 Redhills Rd.
P.O. Box 295
Chinese Camp, CA 95309-0295
ph: 209-984-4432
Buys and sells Haviland & Co., American Haviland, French Haviland, Theodore Haviland, Charles Field Haviland.

Auld Lang Syne
6311 Delta Ct.
Magalia, CA 95954-9535
ph: 800-709-8060
Over 30,000 patterns of Haviland; send photocopy of front and back, color and description plus SASE and $7.50 for identification.

Johnson Bros.

Matching Services

Mary J. Finegan
Marfine Antiques
P.O. Box 3618
Boone, NC 28607-8911
ph: 828-262-3441
Johnson Brothers dinnerware exclusively.

Lenox

Man./Prod./Dist.

Lenox China Shop
53 Commerce Dr.
Cranberry, NJ 08512
ph: 609-395-8054 or 800-367-7467
Retail showroom selling open stock on current stemware, dinnerware, and giftware patterns.

Lenox China & Crystal Consumer Service
100 Lenox Dr.
Lawrenceville, NJ 08648
ph: 609-896-2800 or 800-635-3669
web: http://www.lenox.com
Offers Matching Services List of dealers who offer replacements for current of discontinued Lenox items; also gives insurance estimates.

Matching Services

Regina Negrotti
Tablescapes
P.O. Box 448
Cheshire, CT 06410
ph: 800-801-4084
e-mail: lenox@ntplx.net
web: http://www.tabletopdesigns.com/
A small, personal matching service with a constantly changing inventory; want lists are kept; send photocopy or photo when unsure of pattern name; specializes in Lenox.

Lenox China Chasers
Tilton Rd.
Pomona, NJ 08240
ph: 800-423-8946 or 609-804-9020
fax: 609-965-8466
web: http://www.lenox.com/
Sells from remaining stocks of discontinued patterns of Lenox dinnerware; normally does not carry anything over a few years old.

Allan & Cathy Griggs
Chinamates
1673 Lakecrest Dr.
Sullivan, IN 47882-9585
ph: 800-726-0345 or 812-268-6411
fax: 812-268-6411
e-mail: chinamates@viaduct.custom.net
Stocks and located discontinued Lenox patterns; also Oxford; no giftware; call or write; SASE; mail order only.

Jo Hancock
Jo's Antiques & Collectibles
621 S. Main St.
Nashville, AR 71852-2707
ph: 870-845-1070
China and crystal matching; Lenox and other fine brands; 35 years experience collecting and selling Lenox items.

Carol Ulrey
Unique Antiques
P.O. Box 15815
San Diego, CA 92175-5815
ph: 619-281-8650
fax: 619-282-8407
e-mail: culrey@webcc.net
Specializing in china matching: Haviland, old French and American; also Lenox china and crystal.

Lesley Hall
Lesley's Lenox
3020 Issaquah Pine Lake Rd., Ste. 322
Issaquah, WA 98029
ph: 425-391-2330 or 800-553-6693
fax: 425-391-3383
web: http://www.lesleyslenox.com
Lenox only; extensive inventory of discontinued Lenox Fine China and Lenox casual chinas; mail or phone inquiries welcomed.

Mikasa

Man./Prod./Dist.

Mikasa
1 Mikasa Dr.
Secaucus, NJ 07096
ph: 201-867-9210 or 800-833-4681
fax: 201-867-0457
e-mail: service_center@mikasainc.com
web: http://www.mikasa.com/
Dinnerware, crystal giftware, flatware, linens; call for location of nearest Mikasa factory store.

Matching Services

Mikasa Factory Store
595 Revell Highway
Annapolis, MD 21401
ph: 410-757-8400
Over 300 patterns of Mikasa dinnerware; also glassware, flatware and gift items.

Cleo Kapilla
CK's China Trace
P.O. Box 5297
Ocala, FL 34478-5297
ph: 352-622-4077
A matching service for thousands of fine & casual discontinued pieces of Mikasa dinnerware; buys, sells, locates.

Mikasa Factory Store
Pacific Edge Outlet Center
312 Fashion Way
Burlington, WA 98233
ph: 360-757-7400
Over 300 patterns of Mikasa dinnerware; also glassware, flatware and gift items.

Noritake

Matching Services

Peggy Roush
Peggy's Matching Service, Ltd.
P.O. Box 476
Ocala, FL 32678-0476
ph: 352-629-3954
Deals exclusively in discontinued Noritake fine and casual china; over 1000 patterns in current inventory; buys and sells.

R.L. Watson
Matchers, The
181 Belle Meade
Memphis, TN 38117-3017
ph: 901-683-1337
fax: 901-682-9491
Noritake specialists; also Lenox, Royal Doulton, American Haviland, Oxford, Wedgwood, Franciscan, and other major factories; best to phone.

Noritake Co., Inc.
2635 Clearbrook Drive
Arlington Heights, IL 60005
ph: 800-562-1991
fax: 847-228-5104
e-mail: noriserv@aol.com
web: http://www.noritake.com/
Sells formal china, casual dinnerware, crystal, glassware, giftware from around the world.

Ms. China
P.O. Box 229
Monterey, CA 93942
ph: 800-688-6807 or 831-655-9984
fax: 831-655-0198
e-mail: info@ms-china.com
web: http://www.ms-china.com/
Noritake only; pre-war and newly discontinued china identification and matching service.

Rosenthal

Matching Services

Mary Zawaski
Vintage Patterns Unlimited
3571 Crestnoll Dr.
Cincinnati, OH 45211-1813
ph: 513-622-2543
Former Rosenthal representative dealing exclusively in Rosenthal; send photo of cup and dinner plate; mail order only.

Wedgwood

Matching Services

Vintage Patterns IV
9303 McKinney Rd.
Loveland, OH 45140
ph: 513-489-6247
Wedgwood specialists; also Adams, Coalport; buys and sells; send SASE.

Allan & Cathy Griggs
Chinamates
1673 Lakecrest Dr.
Sullivan, IN 47882-9585
ph: 800-726-0345 or 812-268-6411
fax: 812-268-6411
e-mail: chinamates@viaduct.custom.net
Stocks and locates Wed wood china and crystal; no giftware; call or write; SASE; mail order only.

Wedgwood China Cupboard, ABC
740 N. Honey Creek Pkwy.
Wauwatosa, WI 53213
ph: 414-259-1025
Wedgwood, Adams, Coalport, Midwinter; discontinued patterns bought and sold; large collection of Wedgwood in stock.

Gloria Voss Beyer
Beyer's Wedgwood China Cupboard
740 Honey Creek Parkway
Milwaukee, WI 53213
ph: 800-893-WWCC
Discontinued Wedgwood, Coalport, Midwinter, and Adams.

DINOSAURS

Clubs/Associations

Mike Fredericks
Prehistoric Times, The
<u>Newsletter: Prehistoric Times, The</u>
145 Bayline Circle
Folsom, CA 95630-8077
ph: 916-985-7986 or 916-985-2481
fax: 916-985-2481
e-mail: pretimes@aol.com
The Prehistoric Times is a fanzine dedicated to dinosaur collectors and enthusiasts, including info on all manner of collectibles and other items of interest for Dinophiles everywhere; 48+ pages; bi-monthly; nothing like it!

Collectors

April Rhodes
RR 1 Box 284-E
Sunbury, PA 17801-9618
Wants to buy anything dinosaur: advertising premiums, old books, games, etc.

Museums/Libraries

Dinosaur Valley Museum
362 Main St.
Grand Junction, CO 81501
ph: 970-245-7695
e-mail: museum@mwc.mus.co.us
web: http://www.mwc.mus.co.us/dinosaurs/

BYU Earth Science Museum
1683 North Canyon Rd.
P.O. Box 23300
Provo, UT 84602-3300
ph: 801-378-3680
fax: 801-378-7919
Features mounted dinosaur skeletons, a fossil touch table, a mural of the Jurassic period, and a working paleontology lab.

DIPPERS

(see SODA FOUNTAIN COLLECTIBLES, Ice Cream Dippers)

DIRECTORIES

(see ANTIQUES SHOP DIRECTORIES; FLEA MARKETS, Directories; TOURS/BUYING TRIPS)

DIRIGIBLES

(see AIRSHIPS)

DIRILYTE FLATWARE

(see FLATWARE)

DIRT

(see also SAND)

Museums/Libraries

Museum of Dirt
Planet Interactive
36 Drydock Ave.
Boston, MA 02210
ph: 617-574-4800
e-mail: dirt@planet.com
web: http://www.planet.com/dirtweb/dirt.html
A virtual museum of dirt, some with celebrity associations.

DISCONTINUED TABLEWARE PATTERNS

(see FLATWARE; DINNERWARE; GLASS, Elegant; GLASS, Crystal)

DISNEY COLLECTIBLES

(see also CHARACTER COLLECTIBLES; COLLECTIBLES [MODERN]; POPULAR CULTURE; POSTCARDS, Disney)

Appraisers

Robert G. Jason-Ickes
3600 Elizabeth Ave., SE #19-203
Olympia, WA 98501-7458
ph: 360-455-9914
Specializes in pre-1950 Disney collectibles; also lectures.

Clubs/Associations

Robert Crooker
Mouse Club East
<u>Newsletter: Mouse Club East Newsletter</u>
P.O. Box 3195
Wakefield, MA 01880-0774
ph: 781-246-3876
fax: 781-245-4511
e-mail: mouse_man@msn.com
web: http://www.mouseman.com/
Interested in Disney related collectibles.

Louis Boish
National Fantasy Fan Club for Disneyana Collectors & Enthusiasts
<u>Journal: Fantasyline Express</u>
P.O. Box 19212
Irvine, CA 92713-9212
ph: 949-731-4705
e-mail: info@nffc.org
web: http://www.nffc.org
To preserve the legacy of Walt Disney through collecting and preserving of Disney memorabilia, research and sharing of information; a monthly newsletter.

Kate Klein
Imagination Guild
Newsletter: ImaginEars
P.O. Box 907
Boulder Creek, CA 95006-0907
ph: 831-335-2755
fax: 831-335-0800
e-mail: disney@cruzio.com
For the beginner and advanced collector or for the Disney enthusiast; no pictures or ads, just news on collectibles and where to find them; also shows and information on the Parks and Studio; monthly newsletter.

Kim & Julie McEuen
Mouse Club, The
Newsletter: Mouse Club, The
2056 Cirone Way
San Jose, CA 95124
ph: 408-377-2590
fax: 408-379-6903
A club with a bi-monthly newsletter devoted to articles about Disneyana collecting; sponsors semi-annual show and sale of strictly Disneyana.

Collectors

Dan Calandriello
53-C Beacon Village
Burlington, MA 01803-3843
ph: 781-229-9009
e-mail: dan@coe.neu.edu
Wants 1930s to 1950s Disney collectibles: poster ads, cards, albums, games, etc.

John S. Fawcett
P.O. Box 1156
Waldoboro, ME 04572-1156
ph: 207-832-7398
Collects 1930s comic character items, Post Toasties Disney cereal boxes & other old Disneyana.

Bob Havey
P.O. Box 183
North Sullivan, ME 04664-0183
ph: 207-422-3083
fax: 207-422-3430
Disney collector buys all nice 1930s/40s items; excellent prices paid.

Charles Sanna
P.O. Box 27
Brooklyn, NY 11231
ph: 800-252-6261 or 718-448-7528
fax: 718-625-2895
Wants to buy all types of early Disney and comic collectibles.

Linda Trew Ahlfield
Divine Inc.
107 Col Dunovant Ct.
Bluffton, SC 29910
ph: 910-868-3259
e-mail: kagneys@aol.com
Wants to buy Mickey Mouse memorabilia; no records, please; include asking price.

Jim Conley
2758 Coventry Lane
Canton, OH 44708-1320
ph: 330-477-7725 or 330-499-9283
fax: 330-879-2950
Very interested in early Disney.

Dealers

Robert Crooker
Mouse Man Ink, The
P.O. Box 3195
Wakefield, MA 01880-0774
ph: 781-246-3876
fax: 781-245-4511
e-mail: mouse_man@msn.com
web: http://www.mouseman.com/
Buys and sells, specializing in pre-1941 Disney; large catalog available for $1.

Jane & John Carroll
2894 John Tyler Highway
Williamsburg, VA 23185-1335
ph: 757-258-9322
fax: 757-258-9552
Buys and sells Disneyana.

Joel J. Cohen, ISA
Cohen Books & Collectibles
P.O. Box 810310
Boca Raton, FL 33481-0310
ph: 561-487-7888
fax: 561-487-3117
e-mail: cohendisney@prodigy.net
web: http://www.cohendisney.com
Walt Disney specialist and collector; will find what you want; buys, sells, appraises Disneyana from Mickey Mouse to Snow White to Pocahontas; vintage as well as limited edition items, animation art, books, figurines, toys, etc.

Dan Goodsell
Tick Tock Toys
P.O. Box 342
Culver City, CA 90232
ph: 310-815-0465
Wants to buy vintage (1950s and 1960s) Disneyland memorabilia especially guide books, maps, souvenirs, toys, model kits, brochures, etc.

Thomas Bauer
Nonstop Collectibles
6659 Sherbrooke, #25
Montreal, Quebec H4B 1N8
Canada
ph: 514-489-5499
e-mail: tom2@odyssee.net
web: http://www.odyssee.net/~tom2/index.html
Internet sales consultant and broker since 1993; active in online sales and marketing of Disneyana, other collectibles; will do qualified evaluations of your collection; list items for sale for 20% commission; good comic info.

Experts

Doug & Pat Wengel
P.O. Box 305
Skillman, NJ 08558-0305
ph: 609-466-2461
fax: 609-466-8911
e-mail: wengel@njcc.com
web: http://pluto.njcc.com/~wengel
Buys, sells and specializes in vintage character collectibles, especially those with early images of Disney characters Mickey, Minnie, Horace and Clarabelle; offers matching service for Disney china dishes - Japanese, Bavarian, Paragon.

Ted Hake
Hake's Americana & Collectibles Auction
P.O. Box 1444
York, PA 17405-1444
ph: 717-848-1333
e-mail: Ted@hakes.com
web: http://www.hakes.com/
Always purchasing items for 8 mail-bid auctions per year covering hundreds of categories including toys, character collectibles, Disney, cowboy heroes, premiums, television, politicals, pin-back buttons, advertising and more.

Joel J. Cohen, ISA
Cohen Books & Collectibles
P.O. Box 810310
Boca Raton, FL 33481-0310
ph: 561-487-7888
fax: 561-487-3117
e-mail: cohendisney@prodigy.net
web: http://www.cohendisney.com
Walt Disney specialist and collector; will find what you want; buys, sells, appraises Disneyana from Mickey Mouse to Snow White to Pocahontas; vintage as well as limited edition items, animation art, books, figurines, toys, etc.

Tom Tumbusch
Tomart Publications
3300 Encrete Lane
Dayton, OH 45439-1944
ph: 937-294-2250
fax: 937-294-1024
e-mail: office@tomart.com
web: http://www.tomart.com
Buys Disneyana items; author of "Tomart's Illustrated Disneyana Catalog and Price Guide" series depicting 20,000 items in color.

Paul F. Anderson
3136 South 3200 West
Salt Lake City, UT 84119-2622
ph: 801-967-3955
fax: 801-967-3999
e-mail: pov@aros.net
web: http://venus.aros.net/~pov/
Collector, dealer and expert on Disney collectibles.

Phil Sears
24592 Via Carissa
Laguna Niguel, CA 92677-7034
ph: 949-643-1477
fax: 949-643-8376
e-mail: Sears@pacbell.net
web: http://www.phil-sears.com
Buys and sells vintage Walt Disney memorabilia, including Disneyland and Disney Studio collectibles; Walt Disney autograph specialist.

Museums/Libraries

Dave Smith
Walt Disney Archives
500 South Buena Vista St.
Burbank, CA 91521-3040
ph: 818-560-5424
Comprehensive Disney collection including complete U.S. and most foreign Disney comics; comics not available to researchers for preservation reasons; usage limited to approved projects.

Periodicals

Tom Tumbusch
Tomart Publications
Magazine: Tomart's Disneyana Digest
3300 Encrete Lane
Dayton, OH 45439-1944
ph: 937-294-2250
fax: 937-294-1024
e-mail: office@tomart.com
web: http://www.tomart.com
Published quarterly.

Antique Trader Publications, Inc.
Newspaper: Toy Trader
P.O. Box 1050
Dubuque, IA 52004-1050
ph: 800-334-7165 or 800-482-4155
fax: 800-531-0880
e-mail: jmkoenig@execpc.com
web: http://www.collect.com/toytrader
Monthly newspaper with information on how to buy, sell and trade all types of toys; market trends, the latest prices, "how-to" columns, listings of toy clubs and upcoming toy shows and auctions; also full of buy and sell ads.

Source Publications, Inc.
Magazine: Collectors' Showcase
7134 S. Yale, Ste. 720
Tulsa, OK 74136
ph: 918-491-9088
fax: 918-491-9946
e-mail: bwilkerson@sourcepub.com
web: http://www.cslive.com/
Bi-monthly full-color magazine focusing on contemporary and vintage character collectibles from animation film art, comics and entertainment studios like Disney Warner Bros., and many more.

Paul F. Anderson
Persistence of Vision Publishing
Magazine: Persistence of Vision
3136 South 3200 West
Salt Lake City, UT 84119-2622
ph: 801-967-3955
fax: 801-967-3999
e-mail: pov@aros.net
web: http://venus.aros.net/~pov/
Filled with rare and unusual Disney items, most with an historical slant; an unofficial journal celebrating the creative legacy of Walt Disney featuring articles on Disneyana, Walt Disney, the Theme Parks, films and collectibles.

Paul F. Anderson
Persistence of Vision Publishing
Newsletter: Disneyana Times, The
3136 South 3200 West
Salt Lake City, UT 84119-2622
ph: 801-967-3955
fax: 801-967-3999
e-mail: pov@aros.net
web: http://venus.aros.net/~pov/
Each issue features thousands of Disney collectibles.

Magazine: E Ticket
P.O. Box 800800
Santa Clarita, CA 91380-0880
fax: 818-368-8701
e-mail: e-ticket@deltanet.com
web: http://www.the-e-ticket.com/
For those interested in Disneyland, Walt Disney, Disney artists, rides and attractions at Disneyland, and Disney collectibles.

Don Schockow
Rainbow Ridge Productions
VHS: Disney TV
P.O. Box 1064
Ojai, CA 93024-1064
ph: 805-640-8101
fax: 805-640-8101
e-mail: disnyanatv@aol.com
web: http://www.disneyanatv.com/
"Disneyana TV" is a quarterly VHS television show covering everything Disney; from behind the scenes to future projects...it's all on Disneyana TV.

Ceramics

Dealers

Calvin L. Hackeman
8865 Olde Mill Run
Washington, DC 20010-6132
ph: 703-368-6982 or 703-847-7530
fax: 703-848-9583
e-mail: calcoolege@aol.com
Serious advanced collector and dealer in child's ceramics; interested in purchasing one piece or a complete set; interest is limited to child's china, salt & pepper shakers, cookie jars and ceramic planters.

Judy Posner
4195 South Tamiami Trail, Ste. 183
Venice, FL 34293-5112
ph: 941-497-7149
fax: 941-493-8085
e-mail: jpc@tias.com
web: http://www.tias.com/stores/jpc/
Wants Disney bisque figures, Disney dinnerware, character cookie jars & shakers; send $1 for catalog; send for wants list.

DIVING EQUIPMENT

(see NAUTICAL ANTIQUES, Diving; SCUBA)

DIXIE CUP LIDS

Collectors

Leonard Schneir
P.O.Box 266
Village Station
New York, NY 10014
ph: 212-966-4357
Wants one or an entire collection.

Leigh Giarde
P.O. Box 2243
Redlands, CA 92373-0741
ph: 909-792-8681
fax: 909-792-8681
e-mail: onlyleigh@cpl.net
President, circus, animal and movie star lids and premiums wanted.

DOCUMENTS

(see AUTOGRAPHS; BOOKS; PAPER COLLECTIBLES; MANUSCRIPTS)

DOILIES

(see TEXTILES, Needlework)

DOLL HOUSES & FURNISHINGS

(see also CHILDREN'S THINGS; DOLLS; MINIATURES)

Appraisers

Judy Owen, ISA
Antique Appraisers - Grand Traverse
10332 Stoneybeach Pointe
Traverse City, MI 49686-8584
ph: 231-946-2534
fax: 231-946-2573
e-mail: judy@antiqueappraisers.com
web: http://www.antiqueappraisers.com/
Specializing in doll houses and miniatures.

Clubs/Associations

Shelley Smith
Toy Dish Collectors Club
Newsletter: Tiny Times, The
P.O. Box 159
Bethlehem, CT 06751-0159
ph: 203-266-7496
fax: 203-266-7343
e-mail: toydish@aol.com
web: http://members.aol.com/toydish/
Collectors are interested in children's dishes, furniture, glass, toy kitchen and stores.

Sharon Unger
Dollhouse & Miniature Collectors
Newsletter: Dollhouse & Miniature Collectors Quarterly
P.O. Box 16
Bellaire, MI 49615
ph: 616-377-7397
Purpose is to promote commercial and handmade dollhouses considered antique & collectible (not contemporary pieces).

Russian Association of Dollhouses & Miniatures Masters
Box 9
Moscow, 109005
Russia
fax: 095-912-2007
e-mail: vladin@aha.ru
web: http://www.aha.ru/~vladin/
Icons, matryoshka, samovars, bast shoes, eggs, lacquered boxes, caskets, dollhouses, etc.

Collectors

Sharon Wilkins
1105 Burnham St.
Cocoa, FL 32922-6838
Wants to buy 1940s and 1950s doll houses.

Jerry A. Phelps
1500 Van Buren Boat Deck Rd.
Mount Eden, KY 40046
ph: 502-859-4063
Wants to buy old dollhouses with paper lithography on wood; also wants early clockwork toys.

Peggy Ell
218 Gratton
Burlington, IA 52601
ph: 319-752-7670
Collects commercial doll houses: tin, masonite, fiberboard, cardboard, paper, and any other material.

R.L. Rice
612 E. Front St.
Bloomington, IL 61701-5314
Wants to buy metal doll house furniture; one piece or an entire set; please state brand and price.

Dealers

Ann Mechan
P.O. Box 6686
Portsmouth, NH 03802
ph: 603-433-5650

Robert Dankanics
Dollhouse Factory, The
P.O. Box 456
Lebanon, NJ 08833-0456
ph: 908-236-6404
fax: 908-236-7899
Wants old dollhouses and miniatures.

Abbie Kelly
P.O. Box 351
Camillus, NY 13031-0351
ph: 315-487-7451
e-mail: toydish@aol.com
web: http://members.aol.com/toydish/
Wants to buy German kitchens and stores, doll dishes, doll accessories.

Museums/Libraries

Peabody Essex Museum
Essex & Libert Streets
Salem, MA 01970
ph: 978-745-9500 or 800-745-4054
e-mail: pem@pem.org
web: http://www.pem.org

Strong Museum, The
1 Manhattan Square
Rochester, NY 14607
ph: 716-263-2700
web: http://www.strongmuseum.org
Collection contains more than 500,000 objects: toys, doll houses, miniatures, household furnishings, and the world's most comprehensive collection of dolls.

Washington Dolls' House & Toy Museum
5236 44th St. NW
Washington, DC 20015
ph: 202-244-0024

Wrecker's Museum
322 Duval St.
Key West, FL 33040
ph: 305-294-9502
Houses nautical photos and memorabilia from the Key West wrecking era.

Art Institute of Chicago, Thorne Miniature Rooms
111 S. Michigan Ave.
Chicago, IL 60603
ph: 312-443-0849
e-mail: webmaster@artic.edu
web: http://www.artic.edu/aic/firstpage.html

Periodicals

Magazine: Doll Castle News
P.O. Box 247
Washington, NJ 07882-0247
ph: 908-689-7042 or 800-572-6607
fax: 908-689-6320
e-mail: dcn@dollcastlenews.com
web: http://www.dollcastlenews.com/
A bi-monthly magazine focusing on dolls, miniatures, doll houses and related items; ads, paper doll section, needlework, patterns, etc.

Scott Publications
Magazine: Miniature Collector
30595 Eight Mile
Livonia, MI 48152-1798
ph: 800-458-8237 or 248-477-6650
fax: 248-477-6795
e-mail: 104137.1254@compuserve.com
An international bi-monthly glossy publication devoted exclusively to contemporary and antique scale miniatures: artists, manufacturers, retailers, suppliers, collectors, room settings, etc.

Plastic

Collectors

Bobbie Segal
415 Julian Woods Lane
P.O. Box 39
Julian, PA 16844
ph: 814-355-2542
Wants plastic dollhouse furniture from the 1940s through the 1960s; by Renwal, Ideal, etc.

Dealers

Judy Mosholder
186 Pine Springs Camp Road
Boswell, PA 15531-2421
ph: 814-629-9277
e-mail: jlytwins@floodcity.net
web: http://www.homepage.floodcity.net/users/gtrains
Buys and sells dollhouses and plastic dollhouse furniture, especially Renwal, Ideal, and Marx; send LSASE for list of items for sale.

DOLLS

(see also AMERICAN INDIAN, Skookum Dolls; AMERICAN INDIAN, Kachina Dolls; BOOKS, Reference [Dolls]; CHARACTER COLLECTIBLES; CHILDREN'S THINGS; COLLECTIBLES [MODERN], Dolls; ELVES; DOLL HOUSES & FURNISHINGS; STEIFF; TEDDY BEARS; TOYS; TROLLS)

Appraisers

Darlene Joy Gengelbach
Darlene's Joys
4785 St. Paul Blvd.
Rochester, NY 14617
ph: 716-544-6997
fax: 716-266-4623
Doll appraisals, lectures, research, consultant, restoration, conservation; private or museums; presently working for two museums.

Stuart Holbrook
Theriault's Auction
P.O. Box 151
Annapolis, MD 21404-0151
ph: 410-224-3655 or 800-638-0422
fax: 410-224-2515
e-mail: webmaster@theriaults.com
web: http://www.ea.net/theriaults/
Chief appraiser and buyer for one of the nation's largest doll auction houses; one doll or entire collection can be appraised.

Cary Raesner, Ed.
House of White Birches
Magazine: Doll Collector's Price Guide
306 East Parr Rd.
Berne, IN 46711
ph: 219-589-8741 or 800-829-5865
fax: 219-589-8093
Offers free doll appraisals to subscribers.

R. Rebecca Moncrief, ISA
2007 Sea Cove Ct.
Houston, TX 77058-4228
ph: 281-333-3672
fax: 281-333-0201
e-mail: becky@ufdc.org
Specializes in antique dolls.

Barbara De Feo
Janara Antique Dolls
P.O. Box 662
Bonita, CA 91908-0662
ph: 619-482-8575
fax: 619-482-8575
e-mail: janara@pacbell.net
Appraisals and conservation of antique dolls; buys and sells at shows or by mail order; will buy one doll or entire collection, only pre-1975, please; member National Antique Doll Dealer's Association, UFDC, and NADDA; published author.

Julie J. Scott, ISA
Plumed Horse, The
P.O. Box 904
Bellevue, WA 98009
ph: 425-453-9822
Buys, consigns, sells, and appraises toys and dolls.

Norene Ott
Antique & Collectible Doll Appraisal of Seattle
P.O. Box 46134
Seattle, WA 98146-0134
ph: 206-246-2290 or 206-244-8007
fax: 206-244-8007
e-mail: seniorott@aol.com

Auction Services

Mildred Ewing
Skinner, Inc.
357 Main St.
Bolton, MA 01740-1104
ph: 978-779-6241
fax: 978-779-5144
e-mail: info@skinnerinc.com
web: http://www.skinnerinc.com
Established in 1964, Skinner Inc. is the fifth largest auction house in the US; has offices in Bolton and Boston, MA.

Withington, Inc.
590 Centr Road
Hillsboro, NH 03244
ph: 603-464-3232
e-mail: withington@conknet.com

Randy Inman
James D. Julia Auctioneers Inc.
Rt. 201, Skowhegan Rd.
P.O. Box 830
Fairfield, ME 04937
ph: 207-453-7125
fax: 207-453-2502
e-mail: jjulia@juliaauctions.com
web: http://www.juliaauctions.com
Conducts specialized auctions of toys and doll items and are one of the leaders in this field in North America.

Stuart Holbrook
Theriault's Auction
P.O. Box 151
Annapolis, MD 21404-0151
ph: 410-224-3655 or 800-638-0422
fax: 410-224-2515
e-mail: webmaster@theriaults.com
web: http://www.ea.net/theriaults/
One of the oldest and perhaps largest doll auction houses in America; will send "Doll Information Guide" pamphlet upon request and LSASE; doll auction color catalogs are $154 for 10 issues per year; holds over 50 doll auctions per year.

Dorothy Hunt
Sweetbriar
P.O. Box 37
Earleville, MD 21919-0037
ph: 410-275-2094
fax: 410-275-2213
e-mail: dorothy.hunt@dol.net
Auctions dolls and doll costumes; also offers doll seminars and appraisals.

Ann Hays, ISA CAPP
Hays & Associates, Inc.
120 South Spring St.
Louisville, KY 40206-1953
ph: 502-584-4297
fax: 502-585-5896
e-mail: annhays@haysauction.com
web: http://www.haysautcion.com/
Conducts specialty toy and doll auctions; Ann Hays is a Certified Appraiser of Personal Property with the International Society of Appraisers; director of auction house antique and collectible toy and doll department for over 25 years.

David M. Cobb
Cobb's Doll Auction
1909 Harrison Rd. N.
Johnstown, OH 43031-9539
ph: 740-964-0444
fax: 740-927-7701
Conducts quarterly antique doll, automata, bears, etc. auctions; send $22 for catalog; send address for advance notice flyer.

Jim & Shari McMasters
McMasters Doll Auctions
P.O. Box 1755
Cambridge, OH 43725-6755
ph: 800-842-3526 or 740-432-4419
fax: 740-432-3191
e-mail: mcmasters@jadeinc.com
web: http://www.angelfire.com/oh/mcmastersauctions/
Specializes in auctioning antique and collectible dolls and doll related items such as teddy bears, Barbie dolls and accessories, children's dishes, toys, children's books, etc.

Kurt R. Krueger
Krueger Auctions
P.O. Box 275
Iola, WI 54945-0275
ph: 715-445-3845
fax: 715-445-4100
Specializing in the mail-bid auction of tokens, advertising, brewery items, Western Americana, postcards, World's Fair & Expo., autographs, sports, coins & currency, pinbacks, military memorabilia, automotive, Disneyana, toys, dolls, etc.

Butterfield & Dunning
755 Church Rd.
Elgin, IL 60123
ph: 847-741-3483
fax: 847-741-3589
e-mail: info@butterfields.com
web: http://www.butterfields.com

Barbara Frasher
Frasher's Doll Auction
2323 South Mecklin
Oak Grove, MO 64075
ph: 816-625-3786
fax: 816-625-6079
Conducts doll specialty auctions.

Jon Baddeley
Sotheby's
34-35 New Bond St.
London, W1A 2AA
U.K.
ph: 44 171 293 5000
fax: 44 171 293 5989
web: http://www.sothebys.com/
Conducts specialty auctions of tinplate toys, diecasts, trains, antique dolls, teddy bears, automata.

Clubs/Associations

JoAnn Mathias, Treas.
Doll Doctor's Association
Newsletter: Doll Rx
6204 Ocean Front Ave.
Virginia Beach, VA 23451
ph: 757-428-1609 or 757-427-9131
e-mail: dolldoc@pilot.infi.net
An association for doll repair and restoration specialists.

Bettyanne Twigg
United Federation of Doll Clubs
Newsletter: Doll News
10920 N. Ambassador Dr., Ste. 130
Kansas City, MO 64153
ph: 816-891-7040 or 816-891-8417
fax: 816-891-8360
e-mail: twigg@ufdc.org
web: http://www.ufdc.org
Contact to locate a club in your area.

West Phoenix Doll Club
7154 N. 58th Dr.
Glendale, AZ 85301
ph: 602-931-1579

Collectors

Linda L. Vines
P.O. Box 43721
Upper Montclair, NJ 07043
ph: 973-748-4990
e-mail: lja@viconet.com
Wants to buy antique bisque head dolls in excellent condition; also doll clothes and accessories.

Kate Emburg
P.O. Box 1437
North Highlands, CA 95660-1437
ph: 916-331-7435 or 916-331-7352
e-mail: dolladopt@aol.com
Collector especially interested in Madame Alexander, hard plastic and composition dolls; will identify and appraise post-1900 dolls.

Marci Van Ausdall
P.O. Box 946
Quincy, CA 95971
ph: 530-283-2770
e-mail: dreams@psln.com
Wants to buy all original, excellent condition and mint-in-box fashion dolls and clothing from the 1950s-1960s such as Ideal Toni, Shirley Temple, Sweet Sue, Revelons, American Character Toni.

Dealers

Judith Armistead
Doll Works, The
P.O. Box 195
Lynnfield, MA 01940
ph: 781-334-5577
Interested in buying bisque, composition, cloth, snow babies, half dolls, and early cartoon characters.

Valerie Zakszewski
61 6th St.
Cambridge, MA 02141
ph: 800-897-2933 or 617-576-0796
e-mail: valerie-z@mediaone.net
Wants to buy dolls (bisque, hard plastic, Vogue Ginnys, cloth/rag dolls), doll accessories, doll houses, children's toys and tea sets, Steiff, Teddy Bears, etc.

Eileen Mosteller
Dollworks
62-C Franklin St., PMB #107
Westerly, RI 02891
ph: 401-596-4674
e-mail: eileen@dollworks.com
web: http://www.dollworks.com/
Buys/sells mint & mint-in-box 1930-1970 dolls, especially rare cloth, composition & hard plastic Madame Alexanders plus fabulous Ginnys, Jills, Mary Hoyers, Arranbees, Effanbees, Style Shows, Shirley Temples, Revelons, etc.; $2 for list.

Linda Dalenberg
Timeless Pieces
246 West Main St.
Hillsboro, NH 03244-5239
ph: 603-464-5621 or 603-464-6747
e-mail: timeless@cocknet.com
Wants to buy antique dolls, doll clothes, and doll accessories; also wants adult and children's vintage clothing, estate linens, and pre WWII toys.

Liz Olimpio
Aladdin Antiques
59 Governor's Rd.
Sanbornville, NH 03872
ph: 603-522-8503
fax: 603-522-8933
Buy, sells, repairs antique dolls and antique clothing.

Debra Gulea
Debra's Dolls
P.O. Box 705
Mullica Hill, NJ 08062
ph: 609-478-9778 or 609-694-2007
Antique dolls bought and sold; doll furniture, clothing; doll houses, and accessories also available; member of UFDC and NADDA; send for photo doll list.

Debra's Dolls
P.O. Box 705
Mullica Hill, NJ 08062
ph: 609-478-9778 or 609-694-2007

Roberta's Doll House
140 Caryl Ave.
Yonkers, NY 10705
ph: 800-569-9739 or 914-968-3033
fax: 914-968-4172
Website has a nice selection of antique dolls for sale.

Bonnie J. Cook
P.O. Box 134
East Greenbush, NY 12061
ph: 518-477-7272
Wants to buy American and European antique dolls.

Jacquie Henry
Antique Treasures, Toys & Dolls
2240 Academy St.
P.O. Box 17
Walworth, NY 14568-0017
ph: 315-986-1424
e-mail: jacqueline.henry@cwix.com
web: http://www.cyberattic.com/dealer/toysndolls
Buys and sells antique German and French bisque dolls, and mint condition 1950s hard plastic dolls in original clothes such as Toni, Arranbee, Madame Alexander, Ginnys, Gingers, and Nancy Ann Storybooks.

Sherri & Jack Dempsey
1009 East 38th St.
P.O. Box 10037
Erie, PA 16514
ph: 814-825-6381
e-mail: dnb@erie.net
Specializes in antique dolls and Marx toys; also doll restorations.

Nikki Kvitka
Nikel Enterprises, Inc.
4536 Custer Dr.
Harrisburg, PA 17110
ph: 717-236-7148
fax: 717-236-6807

Sidney W. Jeffrey
My Dolly Dearest
229 Grofftown Road
Lancaster, PA 17602
ph: 717-295-9454 or 800-295-9457
fax: 717-295-9454
e-mail: sidneyjeffrey@mydollydearest.com
web: http://www.mydollydearest.com
Doll dealer, collector, appraiser with a web site dedicated to the sale of dolls, bears, and accessories from antique to contemporary.

Dawn Herlocher
Dawn's Dolls
Maple Ave.
Mackeyville, PA 17750
ph: 570-726-6458
Specializing in fine quality Japanese Satsuma and cloisonne.

Erlene Reed
Aquataurian
1794 Verbena St., NW
Washington, DC 20012
ph: 202-829-7170
fax: 202-723-7274
e-mail: dollyasm@erols.com
web: http://www.townsqr.com/dolly/
Specializes in black and ethnic dolls: artist dolls, antique dolls and modern dolls; also wants figurines, collectible plates, art, black memorabilia, etc.; has thousands of dolls.

Dollmasters
P.O. Box 2319
Annapolis, MD 21404
ph: 800-966-3655
fax: 410-224-2515
e-mail: webmaster@theriaults.com
web: http://www.dollmasters.com
"The Dollmasters" is published quarterly and contains articles about doll market news as well as recent auction reports and doll related products and accessories.

Joyce & Judy
Krazy Cat Collectibles
P.O. Box 21727
Emmitsburg, MD 21727
ph: 301-309-2513
e-mail: KrazyCatCo@aol.com
Buys and sells dolls: antique bisque, composition, vinyl, pre-1972 Barbie, modern artist dolls, Campbell Kids, Liddle Kiddles, Glamour dolls like Miss Revlon; also wants clothing and accessories.

Walter LaValley
Bachelor II Dolls & Bears
247 S. Van Dorn St.
Wheaton Plaza
Alexandria, VA 22304
ph: 703-823-BEAR
fax: 703-823-1787
Specializes in dolls and bears.

Julia Melton
Melton's Antique Dolls
4201 Indian River Rd.
Chesapeake, VA 23325-3005
ph: 757-420-9226
fax: 757-420-1462

Elaine London
1571 E. Sandpiper Circle
Hollywood, FL 33026
ph: 954-435-0671
fax: 954-435-0671
e-mail: ontheroadagain@webtv.net
Buys and sells dolls; all types, modern and antique.

Treasure & Dolls
518 Indian Rocks Rd., N.
Belleair Bluffs, FL 33770
ph: 888-584-7277 or 727-584-7277
fax: 727-581-7846
e-mail: dolls@antiquedoll.com
web: http://www.antiquedoll.com
Buys and sells antique and collectible

dolls, teddy bears, Madame Alexander, Annalee, stuffed animals, half dolls, Barbie, plastic/vinyl dolls, porcelain dolls.

Robert Zacher
Heirloom Doll Shoppe/Hospital/ Museum
416 E. Broadway
Waukesha, WI 53186
ph: 414-544-4739

Gary Sowatzka
Sowatzka's Dolls & Collectables
330 Main Ave.
De Pere, WI 54115
ph: 920-336-1676
fax: 920-336-5456
e-mail: sowatdol@execpc.com
web: http://www.sowatzka.com/
Dolls for sale; doll repairs and doll restoration classes; web site has tips on collecting dolls.

Valerie LaBreche
Enchanted World Doll Museum
615 North Main
Mitchell, SD 57301-1945
ph: 605-996-9896
fax: 605-996-0210
Buys and sells antique and collectible dolls and accessory items; specializes in 1800 to early 1900s bisque and china dolls.

David & Brenda Greener
7313 Wind Chime Dr.
Fort Worth, TX 76133
ph: 817-292-0909
Buys, sells and appraises dolls; former doll show promoter.

Rod Barto
Bubba's Dolls
3312 Moonlight
El Paso, TX 79904
ph: 915-755-4744
e-mail: rod.barto@worldnet.att.net
web: http://www.geo-mall.com/rodbarto/bubbas-dolls/
Dolls, doll items, books, magazines, catalogs, stands, calendars, paper dolls, puzzles, clothes, etc.

Turn of the Century Antiques
1475 S. Broadway
Denver, CO 80210
ph: 303-722-8700 or 303-778-7077

Jeri Cotherman
Doll & Bear's Paradise, A
855 1/2 N. Cedar
Laramie, WY 82072
ph: 307-742-3429
e-mail: jercoth@aol.com
Restores dolls, stuffed animals; makes artist specialty bears; sells dolls and bears; buying dolls, patterns, old material, fur and fake fur.

Gert :Leonard
E & G Antiques
P.O. Box 296
San Dimas, CA 91773
ph: 909-599-2723

Barbara De Feo
Janara Antique Dolls
P.O. Box 662
Bonita, CA 91908-0662
ph: 619-482-8575
fax: 619-482-8575
e-mail: janara@pacbell.net
Appraisals and conservation of antique dolls; buys and sells at shows or by mail order; will buy one doll or entire collection, only pre-1975, please; member National Antique Doll Dealer's Association, UFDC, and NADDA; published author.

Carmel Doll Shop
P.O. Box 7198
Carmel, CA 93921
ph: 831-373-5131
fax: 831-655-5755

Pat Wilson
Koya Designs
3445-A Divisadero
San Francisco, CA 94123
ph: 415-929-9173
e-mail: plwilson@sirius.com
Wants to buy French dolls and doll accessories including antique dolls; will do search for collectors; has a French contact.

Gloria McCarty
Doll Cellar, The
23337 46th Ave., S.W.
Seattle, WA 98116
ph: 206-938-4446
web: http://www.doll-cellar.com/
Buys, sells, collects, appraises and repairs dolls.

Experts

Judith Izen
P.O. Box 623
Lexington, MA 02173
e-mail: jizenres@aol.com
web: http://members.aol.com/jizenres/homepage/index.html
A noted doll historian who has compiled histories of several American doll companies including Ideal, Vogue, Eegee, Deluxe Reading, Mattel; writing book on character dolls including Tiny Tears, Betsy McCall, Tressy, Toodles, Sweet Sue, etc.

Patricia Snyder
My Dear Dolly
P.O. Box 303
Sparta, NJ 07871-0303
ph: 201-729-8087
e-mail: dolly@sparta.csnet.net
web: http://www.mydeardolly.com
Wants old dolls, bodies, parts, doll clothing, accessories, doll dishes, snowbabies; publishes monthly list of dolls for sale; also appraises

Mary Gorham
Gems of the Doll World
9399 Shelly Lane
Cincinnati, OH 45242-7607
Writes "Gems of the Doll World" column about dolls. Send SASE along with drawing of mold marks and photographs for identification of your antique, not modern, dolls.

Carol Sumpter
Cardan's Doll Shop
3808 Loughborough
Saint Louis, MO 63116
ph: 314-351-7955
Buys, sells, collects, specializes in, and appraises dolls.

Don & Vella Painter
23483 Shephard Rd.
Clatskanie, OR 97016
ph: 888-763-5122 or 503-728-3503
e-mail: dollmaster@webdolls.com
web: http://www.webdolls.com/
Buys, sells, appraises, collects and repairs dolls: antiques, compositions, pull string and battery operated talkers, mechanical, toys, vinyl; also reroots hair.

Internet Resources

DollFinder
e-mail: DollFinder@aol.com
web: http://www.dollfinder.com/
Find up-to-date doll information, historical facts, buy/sell connections, conventions, shows, suppliers and manufacturers, stores and artists.

Flossy Eddy
Flossy's Dolls & Collectibles
153 Sundance Drive
Grand Junction, CO 81503
ph: 970-242-1358
e-mail: flossysdolls@youfoundme.com
web: http://www.youfoundme.com/flossy.htm
Huge website with free doll classified ads, chat room, guestbook, e-mail discussion group, free doll newsletter, collector books, dolls, toys and more.

Don & Vella Painter
WebDolls
23483 Shephard Rd.
Clatskanie, OR 97016
ph: 888-763-5122 or 503-728-3503
e-mail: dollmaster@webdolls.com
web: http://www.webdolls.com/
WebDolls is the ultimate on-line resource to find anything related to dolls: museums, artist listings, clubs, shows, classifieds, doll businesses, etc.

Misc. Services

Dwaine E. Gipe
Dollologist
1406 Sycamore Rd.
Montoursville, PA 17754-9519
ph: 570-323-9604
e-mail: dolldoc@uplink.net
Teaches four-day doll restoration seminar; brochure available; also sells step-by-step video covering use of modern restoration materials including air brush, sources provided, tools used, tricks.

JoAnn Mathias
G & M Doll Restoration Seminar
6204 Ocean Front Ave.
Virginia Beach, VA 23451
ph: 757-428-1609 or 757-427-9131
e-mail: dolldoc@pilot.infi.net
Teaching four-day seminars on restoration of bisque, composition, tin, china, papier mache, and felt dolls; partner is Dwayne Gipe of Montoursville, PA.

Museums/Libraries

Eleanor E. Thompson, Dir.
Wenham Museum
132 Main St.
Wenham, MA 01984-1520
ph: 978-468-2377
web: http://www.nosh.net/wenhammuseum/
Largest permanent display of toy soldiers in the U.S.; collection includes pre-war Britains, large and small scale Heyde, composition figures and more; also model train room with operating layouts.

Yesteryears Doll & Toy Museum
Newsletter: Yesteryears Museum News
Main & River Streets
P.O. Box 609
Sandwich, MA 02563
ph: 508-888-1711

Doll Museum, The
520 Thames St.
Newport, RI 02840-6711
ph: 401-849-0405
fax: 401-849-0405
e-mail: DollMuseum@aol.com
web: http://www.dollmuseum.com/
Featuring a fine collection of antique and modern dolls; museum toy shop carries antiques, collectibles, etc.; offers repairs and appraisals.

Curator
Fairfield Historical Society
636 Old Post Rd.
Fairfield, CT 06430-6647
ph: 203-259-1598
fax: 203-255-2716

Doll Castle Doll Museum
P.O. Box 247
Washington, NJ 07882-0247
ph: 908-689-7042 or 800-572-6607
fax: 908-689-6320
e-mail: dcn@dollcastlenews.com
web: http://www.dollcastlenews.com/
Houses hundreds of dolls and related items collected by the staff of "Doll Castle News."

Sheila Clark
Museum of the City of New York
1220 5th Ave.
New York, NY 10029-5221
ph: 212-534-1672
fax: 212-534-5974
e-mail: mcny@mcny.org
web: http://www.mcny.org/mcny/
Access by appointment; research fee charged.

Aunt Len's Doll & Toy Museum
6 Hamilton Terrace
New York, NY 10031
ph: 212-281-4143

Town of Yorktown Museum
1974 Commerce St.
Yorktown Heights, NY 10598
ph: 914-962-2811

Linda Greenfield
Victorian Doll Museum
4332 Buffalo Rd.
North Chili, NY 14514-1206
ph: 716-247-0130
A wonderland exhibiting over 2000 identified dolls from mid-1800s to present; puppet show, toy circus, doll houses, paper dolls, etc.

Strong Museum, The
1 Manhattan Square
Rochester, NY 14607
ph: 716-263-2700
web: http://www.strongmuseum.org
Collection contains more than 500,000 objects: toys, doll houses, miniatures, household furnishings, and the world's most comprehensive collection of dolls.

Marjorie Darrah
Mary Merritt Doll Museum, The
843 Benjamin Hwy.
Douglassville, PA 19518
ph: 610-385-3809
fax: 610-689-4538
Dolls on display range from a 17th century bone doll to French wax mini-manequins, bisque dolls, and Jumeaus.

Washington Dolls' House & Toy Museum
5236 44th St. NW
Washington, DC 20015
ph: 202-244-0024

National Museum of American History
14th & Constitution Ave. NW
Washington, DC 20560
ph: 202-357-2700
e-mail: webmaster@si.edu
web: http://www.si.edu/organiza/museums/nmah/nmah.htm

Angela Peterson Doll & Miniatures Museum
101 W. Green Dr.
High Point, NC 27260
ph: 336-885-3655
fax: 336-884-4352
e-mail: hpcvb@highpoint.org
web: http://www.highpoint.org
More than 1,600 dolls, 800 miniatures and 15 fully furnished dollhouses on display including Shirley Temple and Bob Timberlake Collection and an extraordinary creche doll display.

Edwina Gill
Mary Miller Doll Museum
1523 Glynn Ave.
Brunswick, GA 31520
ph: 912-267-7569
3,000 dolls, doll houses, miniatures from 90 countries; dolls dating from 1850 to present.

Ellen E. Mauer
Milan Historical Museum, Inc.
Newsletter: New Milan Ledger
P.O. Box 308
Milan, OH 44846-0308
ph: 419-499-2968
fax: 419-499-9004
web: http://www.milanohio.com/historical_museum.htm
A seven-building complex 500 yards from the birthplace of Thomas A. Edison; restored home, carriage shed, blacksmith shop, general store, collections from the 19th century.

Children's Museum - Detroit Public Schools
67 East Kirby
Detroit, MI 48202
ph: 313-873-8100
fax: 313-873-3384
web: http://dpsnet.detpub.k12.mi.us/museum/docs/index.htm

Valerie LaBreche
Enchanted World Doll Museum
615 North Main
Mitchell, SD 57301-1945
ph: 605-996-9896
fax: 605-996-0210
4000 antique & collectible dolls set in 400 unique displays; gift shop features dolls, doll books, paper dolls, doll accessories, and Dept. 56, Dickens and Snow Babies.

House of a Thousand Dolls
106 First St.
P.O. Box 136
Loma, MT 59460-0136
ph: 406-739-4338
Collection of toys and dolls from 1830 to present.

Eugene Field House & Toy Museum
Newsletter: Field Notes
634 So. Broadway St.
Saint Louis, MO 63102
ph: 314-421-4689
Birthplace and childhood home of Eugene Field, the children's poet; large collection of antique toys always on display.

Sandi Russell
Toy & Miniature Museum of Kansas City
5235 Oak St.
Kansas City, MO 64112-2877
ph: 816-333-2055 or 816-333-9328
fax: 816-333-2055
e-mail: bergr@umkc.edu
web: http://www.umkc.edu/tmm/
Museum housed in an elegant mansion features collections of miniatures, antique dolls' houses and antique toys.

Gay Nineties Button & Doll Museum
Rte. 4 Box 420
Berryville, AR 72616
ph: 870-253-8588 or 800-645-8588
fax: 870-253-5444

Eliza Cruce Hall Doll Museum
320 E. Street, N.W.
Ardmore, OK 73401
ph: 580-223-8290
fax: 580-223-2033

Francis & Clara Franks
Franks Antique Doll Museum
410 N. Grove St.
Marshall, TX 75670-3243
ph: 903-935-3065 or 903-935-3070

Denver Museum of Miniatures, Dolls & Toys
1880 Gaylord St.
Denver, CO 80206-1211
ph: 303-322-1053
fax: 303-322-3704
e-mail: ldsbc@aol.com
web: http://www.sni.net/start/dmmdt/
Displays miniatures, dolls and toys dating back to the 18th century.

Hobby City Doll & Toy Museum
1238 South Beach Blvd.
Anaheim, CA 92804
ph: 714-527-2323

Rosalie Whyel Museum of Doll Art
1116 108th Ave. NE
Bellevue, WA 98004
ph: 425-455-1116
fax: 425-455-4793
e-mail: dollart@dollart.com
web: http://www.ohwy.com/wa/r/rosawmda.htm

Kate Bines
Bethnal Green Museum of Childhood
Cambridge Heath Rd.
London, E2 9PA
U.K.
ph: 0181-980-2415
fax: 0181-983-5225
e-mail: k.bines@vam.ac.uk
web: http://www.vam.ac.uk/index3.html
A division of the Victoria & ALbert Museum; national collection of dolls, toys, games, puppets, and children's costumes.

Periodicals

Magazine: Doll Castle News
P.O. Box 247
Washington, NJ 07882-0247
ph: 908-689-7042 or 800-572-6607
fax: 908-689-6320
e-mail: dcn@dollcastlenews.com
web: http://www.dollcastlenews.com/
A magazine focusing on dolls, miniatures, doll houses and related items; ads, paper doll section, needlework, patterns, etc.

Stephanie Finnegan, Ed.
Magazine: Dolls - The Collectors Magazine
170 Fifth Ave. - 12th Floor
New York, NY 10010
ph: 212-989-8700 or 800-347-6969
fax: 212-645-8976
Full-color magazine covering antique and contemporary collector dolls and the artists that designed them; auction reports, current prices, museum collections.

Donna Kaonis, Ed.
Magazine: Antique Doll Collector
6 Woodside Ave., Ste 300
Northport, NY 11768
ph: 516-261-4100 or 888-800-2588
fax: 516-261-9684
e-mail: donnakaonis@worldnet.att.net
web: http://www.antiqueDollCollector.com/
Articles about antique dolls, vintage teddy bears, dolls' houses and miniatures; articles by leading doll experts, visits to major collections, coverage of shows and auctions; published bi-monthly.

Cowles Magazines, Inc.
Magazine: Doll Reader
741 Miller Dr. SE, Ste. D2
Harrisburg, PA 20175
ph: 717-540-6617 or 800-829-3340
fax: 717-540-6706
e-mail: brentd@cowles.com
web: http://www.cowles.com/maglist.html
Gives both the beginning & advanced collector information on antique, collectible and modern dolls; current collecting trends, popular manufacturers and artists, new product releases, events calendar, display ideas.

Martha Pullen Co.
Magazine: Sew Beautiful Magazine
518 Madison St.
Huntsville, AL 35801
ph: 800-547-4176 or 256-533-9586
fax: 256-533-9630
e-mail: pullenco@hiwaay.net
web: http://www.marthapullenco.com
The magazine about heirloom sewing, primarily children's clothing but also includes patterns for dolls.

Cary Raesner, Ed.
House of White Birches
Magazine: Doll Collector's Price Guide
306 East Parr Rd.
Berne, IN 46711
ph: 219-589-8741 or 800-829-5865
fax: 219-589-8093
A quarterly magazine that focuses on antique and collectible dolls, identification, fakes, auction results, ads, investing, teddy bears, etc.

Beth Schwartz, Ed.
House of White Birches
Magazine: Doll World
306 East Parr Rd.
Berne, IN 46711
ph: 219-589-8741 or 800-829-5865
fax: 219-589-8093
A bi-monthly magazine which covers many aspects of dolls and doll collecting: articles on doll history, patterns, interviews with doll artists, how-to articles, doll ID, etc.

Magazine: Antique & Collectible Dolls
218 W. Woodin Blvd.
Dallas, TX 75224
ph: 214-943-2107
A monthly magazine with ads and articles about dolls, auctions, and shows.

Brian Savage
Fun Publications
Newspaper: Master Collector
225 Cattle Barron Parc Dr.
Fort Worth, TX 76108
ph: 800-772-6673 or 817-448-9863
fax: 817-448-9843
e-mail: brian@mastercollector.com
web: http://www.mastercollector.com
Ads-only newspaper; dolls (antique and modern collectible), toys, banks, models, cars, Matchbox, monsters, puzzles, political, toy trains, etc.; subscribers receive free 30 word ad each month; published monthly; reaches 20,000.

Patsy Moyer
Newsletter: Patsy & Friends
P.O. Box 311
Deming, NM 88031
e-mail: sctrading@zianet.com
web: http://www.zianet.com/patsyandfriends/
Focuses on composition & travel dolls; author of "Doll Values" (3rd Ed.), and "Modern Collectible Dolls" (Vol. III).

Sandra Hood, Pub.
Newspaper: Antique & Collectables
P.O. Box 12589
500 Fesler St., Ste. 201
El Cajon, CA 92022
ph: 619-593-2925 or 619-593-2927
fax: 619-447-7187
e-mail: antiqunews@aol.com
web: http://www.collect.com/antiqueandcollectables
The largest monthly newspaper in Southern California covering the antiques & collectibles industry with focus sections on Nevada and Arizona; 72+ pages; events and show section, feature articles; columns, ads.

Ashdown Publishing
Magazine: Doll Magazine
Avalon Court, Star Road
Partridge Green, West Sussex RH13 8RY
U.K.
ph: +44 (0) 1403 711511 or 513-353-4052 (in U.S.)
fax: +44 (0) 1403 711521
e-mail: mark@ashdown.co.uk
web: http://www.dollmagazine.com/
An English doll publication.

Repair Services

Leon Trefler
Trefler & Sons Antique Restoring Studio, Inc.
99 Cabot St.
Needham, MA 02494
ph: 781-444-2685
fax: 781-444-0659
e-mail: trefler@trefler.com
web: http://www.trefler.com/
Restoration of porcelain and ceramic dolls.

Pat Travisano
Doll Lady Hospital, The
94 Pent Rd.
Branford, CT 06405-4013
ph: 203-488-6193
Repair all types of dolls; supplier of parts and reproduction service; costume work; sent parts to be matched; wigs, dresses, shoes, doll jewelry, hats, pinafores, etc.; all work done by appointment only; over 25 years experience.

New York Doll Hospital
787 Lexington Ave.
New York, NY 10021-8164
ph: 212-838-7527
Buy, restore antique dolls, Teddy Bears, mechanical toys.

Linda Greenfield
Victorian Doll Museum & Chili Doll Hospital
4332 Buffalo Rd.
North Chili, NY 14514-1206
ph: 716-247-0130
Recognized expert in doll restoration; repairs all types of dolls; restringing, leather body repair, replacement of cloth bodies.

Dwaine E. Gipe
Dollologist
1406 Sycamore Rd.
Montoursville, PA 17754-9519
ph: 570-323-9604
e-mail: dolldoc@uplink.net
Can solve most doll problems: paper mache, bisque, composition; conservation, restoration; reset eyes, wigs, missing parts, recoloring.

JoAnn Mathias
Beach Doll Hospital
6204 Ocean Front Ave.
Virginia Beach, VA 23451
ph: 757-428-1609 or 757-427-9131
e-mail: dolldoc@pilot.infi.net
Doll restoration of dolls made before 1950; specializing in bisque and composition repair.

JoAnn Mathias, Treas.
Doll Doctor's Association
Newsletter: Doll Rx
6204 Ocean Front Ave.
Virginia Beach, VA 23451
ph: 757-428-1609 or 757-427-9131
e-mail: dolldoc@pilot.infi.net
An association for doll repair and restoration specialists.

Doll Heaven
502 Broadway
New Haven, IN 46774-1404
ph: 219-493-6428
Doll restoration & repair; specializing in broken bisque and composition dolls; modern, antique, collector dolls; all materials.

Stacy Spicer
Stacy's Vintage Specialties
2610 Olive St.
Grand Forks, ND 58201
ph: 701-775-9982
e-mail: srspicer@corpcomm.net
web: http://www.corpcomm.net/~srspicer
Specializes in hair rerooting, facial retouches and repaints, green ear treatment, custom doll jewelry and custom designs; says all dolls can be saved; also buys, sells and trades; free estimates via e-mail.

Mary Gates
Doll Doctor, The
P.O. Box 334
Pontiac, IL 61764-0334
ph: 815-842-3442
Doll repairs; specializes in composition work; work shown in museums and sold in antique shops; also does custom dressing of old dolls using her own designs.

Jeri Cotherman
Doll & Bear's Paradise, A
855 1/2 N. Cedar
Laramie, WY 82072
ph: 307-742-3429
e-mail: jercoth@aol.com
Restores dolls, stuffed animals; makes artist specialty bears; sells dolls and bears; buying dolls, patterns, old material, fur and fake fur.

Darla Waters
Doll Restoration
1115 Bear Ave.
Idaho Falls, ID 83402
ph: 208-522-4255
Antique and bisque doll restoration; reconstruct broken parts, repaint, refurbish old wigs, reset eyes, redress; specializes in basket cases.

Don & Vella Painter
Homestead Doll Hospital
23483 Shephard Rd.
Clatskanie, OR 97016
ph: 888-763-5122 or 503-728-3503
e-mail: homstead@aone.com
web: http://www.webdolls.com/Homestead_Collectibles/
Buys, sells, appraises, collects and repairs dolls: antiques, compositions, pull string and battery operated talkers, mechanical, toys, vinyl; also reroots hair.

Gloria McCarty
Doll Cellar, The
23337 46th Ave., S.W.
Seattle, WA 98116
ph: 206-938-4446
web: http://www.doll-cellar.com/
Buys, sells, specializes in, and appraises dolls; also sells doll-related books.

Suppliers

Ron Lipstein
Dollspart Supply Co.
8000 Cooper Ave., Bldg. 28
Flushing, NY 11385-7734
ph: 718-326-4500 or 800-336-3655
fax: 718-326-4971
Sells full range of doll books and parts: eyes, wigs, bodies, clothing, tools, etc.

Banner Doll Supply Inc.
P.O. Box 32
Mechanicsburg, PA 17055
ph: 717-766-1503 or 800-637-8305
Bodies, displays, eyes & eyelashes,

footwear, hats, molds, paints, patterns, reference books, wigs.

Pacific International Corp.
4438 E. Lake Mead Blvd.
Las Vegas, NV 89115
ph: 702-452-2133
fax: 702-647-3170
Specializes in high quality glass eyes, wigs, eye lashes, doll stands, human hair and mohair wigs, molds, patterns, etc.

Advertising

(see also ADVERTISING COLLECTIBLES, Figures)

Experts

Mary Jane Lamphier
Quilted Keepsakes & Unique Dolls Exhibit
577 Main St.
Arlington, IA 50606-9712
ph: 319-633-5885
Buys, sells and trades advertising dolls and characters such as Jolly Green Giant, the Ronald McDonald collection, Campbell Soup Kids, etc.; author of "Zany Characters of the Ad World" (Collector Books, 1995).

Annalee

Clubs/Associations

Townsend Thorndike, Dir.
Annalee Doll Society
Magazine: Collector, The
P.O. Box 708
Meredith, NH 03253
ph: 800-433-6557 or 603-279-3333
fax: 603-279-6659
e-mail: customerservice@annalee.com
web: http://www.annalee.com
A collectors club sponsored by the Annalee Doll Co.; conducts annual Annalee doll auction; sells Annalees dolls on consignment.

Dealers

Annalee Antique & Collectible Doll Shoppe
Newsletter: Collector, The
P.O. Box 708
Meredith, NH 03253
ph: 800-433-6557 or 603-279-3333
fax: 603-279-6659
e-mail: customerservice@annalee.com
web: http://www.annalee.com
A company-sponsored shop; the monthly newsletter lists the Annalee dolls currently for sale; appraisals of Annalee dolls are available for $5 per doll; also offers restoration and repair services for Annalee dolls.

Sue Coffee
Laysville Hardware
10 Saunders Hollow Rd.
Old Lyme, CT 06371-1126
ph: 860-434-5641
fax: 860-434-2653
e-mail: SueCoffee@aol.com
web: http://www.suecoffee.com/
Buys, sells, collects, appraises; $4 for list of retired Annalee dolls or visit web site; specializes in 1950s and 1960s Annalee dolls; send description, condition, photo and telephone number or call with the doll in front of you.

Experts

Sue Coffee
10 Saunders Hollow Rd.
Old Lyme, CT 06371-1126
ph: 860-434-5641
fax: 860-434-2653
e-mail: SueCoffee@aol.com
web: http://www.suecoffee.com/
Secondary market Annalee specialist for CIB (Collectors Information Bureau) and for Collectors Mart Magazine.

Richard Rogers
15 Owen Dr.
Mahopac, NY 10541
ph: 914-621-3702
Buys Annalee dolls, all kinds and all years; especially wants 1950s to 1960s.

Man./Prod./Dist.

Annalee Mobilitee Dolls, Inc.
P.O. Box 708
Meredith, NH 03253
ph: 800-433-6557 or 603-279-3333
fax: 603-279-6659
e-mail: customerservice@annalee.com
web: http://www.annalee.com
Creates, produces and distributes posable felt dolls of distinction which contain wire armatures for flexibility and repositioning.

Museums/Libraries

Annalee Doll Museum
P.O. Box 708
Meredith, NH 03253
ph: 800-433-6557 or 603-279-3333
fax: 603-279-6659
e-mail: customerservice@annalee.com
web: http://www.annalee.com

Automatons

Clubs/Associations

Association des Amis des Automates Poupees et Jouets Anciens
Magazine: Coppelia
1, rue du Dahomey
Paris, 75011
France
ph: (33) 01 43 71 96 79
fax: (33) 01 43 71 88 51
Plans exhibitions, trips, and meetings centering around antique automata, dolls, and toys; magazine printed in both French and English.

Collectors

Frank Demayo
1511 Holliston Trail
Fort Wayne, IN 46825
ph: 219-489-0053 or 800-258-8243
fax: 219-484-8605
e-mail: seeburgh@aol.com
Wants coin-operated slot, gum, card, dice machines; also wants to buy automatons and key wound figures.

Dealers

Cindy Oakes
34025 W. 6 Mile
Livonia, MI 48152
ph: 734-591-3252
Wants bisque automatons or bisque dolls on music boxes; any condition; 1890-1900s.

Don Levison
Don Levison Antiques
P.O. Box 22262
San Francisco, CA 94122
ph: 415-753-0455
fax: 415-753-5206
e-mail: dlevison@juno.com
web: http://www.antiquehorology.com
Buys and sells antique and better quality pocket and wrist watches, clocks, music boxes, singing birds, and other small automata; also mercury barometers from the 17th century to present.

Barbie

Auction Services

Jim & Shari McMasters
McMasters Doll Auctions
P.O. Box 1755
Cambridge, OH 43725-6755
ph: 800-842-3526 or 740-432-4419
fax: 740-432-3191
e-mail: mcmasters@jadeinc.com
web: http://www.angelfire.com/oh/mcmastersauctions/
Specializes in auctioning antique and collectible dolls and doll related items such as teddy bears, Barbie dolls and accessories, children's dishes, toys, children's books, etc.

Ann Walcher
Ann Christina's Remember When Collectibles & Auctions
5465 Rowland Rd.
Minnetonka, MN 55343-4398
Buy, sells, trades, consigns, auctions Barbie and family items.

Clubs/Associations

Dora Lerch
Barbie Doll Collectors Club International
Newsletter: Barbie Newsletter
P.O. Box 586
White Plains, NY 10603-0586
ph: 914-362-4657 or 914-362-3258
fax: 914-362-3258
Ads, upcoming shows, show reports, identification tips, convention news, etc.

Amy Reed
Barbie Doll Lover's Club
399 Winfield Rd.
Rochester, NY 14622
ph: 716-266-4965
e-mail: AMYBLC@frontiernet.net
web: http://home.switchboard.com/amyblc
Club does appraisals of Barbie dolls; has an excellent library to consult; are not dealers, but rather collectors; appraisal fees go to Special Olympics; reasonable rates.

Kathryn E. Darden
Belle Meade Plantation Belles
P. O. Box 218427
Nashville, TN 37221-8427
e-mail: kathryn@dollpage.com
web: http://www.geocities.com/FashionAvenue/6487/clubinfo.html

Julie Carino
Windy City Collectors of Barbie Doll Club
P.O. Box 417518
Chicago, IL 60641
ph: 847-577-7543
e-mail: julester@home.com
web: http://members.home.net/julester/barbie.html
A Chicago-based Barbie doll club; one of the largest in the country; monthly meetings; bimonthly newsletter and other club benefits.

Collectors

Keri Jones
420 Winthrop St.
Taunton, MA 02780-2157
Wants to buy vintage Barbie dolls and clothing from the 1960s to early 1970s; send description and price.

David & Becky Beane
Beane's Antiques & Photography
92 River Rd.
Benton, ME 04901
ph: 207-453-6790
fax: 207-453-6790
e-mail: dbeane@mint.net
web: http://www.metigues.com/catgalog/beane.html
Collector of pre-1970 Barbie dolls, fashions and accessories; call or write with descriptions and prices.

Monica Castillo
310 - 70th Street Apt. 1E
Guttenberg, NJ 07093
ph: 201-861-2666

Amy Reed
399 Winfield Rd.
Rochester, NY 14622
ph: 716-266-4965
e-mail: AMYBLC@frontiernet.net
web: http://home.switchboard.com/amyblc

Irene Davis
27036 Withams Rd.
Oak Hall, VA 23416
ph: 757-824-5524
Wants dolls from 1959 to 1965; also clothes, cars and other Barbie related items; send photos for offer.

Dan Stapleton
8237 Banyan Blvd.
Orlando, FL 32819
ph: 407-345-1132
Wants to buy mint condition (not removed from box), Holiday Barbies.

Laura Cordery
P.O. Box 0215
Elfers, FL 34680-0215
e-mail: allura@gte.net
web: http://www.geocities.com/FashionAvenue/1046/Barbie.html
Enthusiast and collector of America's plastic princess, Barbie; over 50 in her collection; also an html programmer and web page designer.

Margie Schultz
P.O. Box 9371
Cincinnati, OH 45209
Wants to buy 1959-1972 Barbie dolls, clothes, cases, and houses.

Tim Gordon, ISA
1750 W. Kent
Missoula, MT 59801-5508
ph: 406-728-1812
e-mail: stacey1165@aol.com
Wants singles, collections, accessories, clothing, related dolls; offers appraisal services.

Tammy Rodrick
1509 N. 300th St.
Sumner, IL 62466-2117
Wants to buy Barbie dolls and other dolls, new or old; also wants old toys, especially toy dishes and child-size appliances.

Lois Burger
2323 Lincoln
Beatrice, NE 68310-3306
ph: 402-228-2797
Wants pre-1966 Barbie clothes, accessories, Ken, Midge, Skipper & their clothes; also anything Barbie related such as comics, cars.

Marcie Melillo
P.O. Box 27705
Denver, CO 80227
ph: 303-933-0233
fax: 303-932-0468
Always buying Barbie and family dolls, clothes, etc.; author of "The Ultimate Barbie Doll Book," contact for signed copies.

Dealers

Patty & Fred Meyer
Meyer's Toy World New Barbie Center
ph: 800-963-1963
e-mail: mtw111@aol.com
web: http://www.newbarbie.com/

Lisa Scherzer
54 Gates Court
Matawan, NJ 07747-9716
ph: 732-290-1407
fax: 732-290-0636
Specializing in Barbie.

Kristin Peterson
Must B Vintage
2908 Durbin Place
Virginia Beach, VA 23456
ph: 757-468-9841
e-mail: KPeter24@aol.com
web: http://members.aol.com/kpeter24/index.html
Dealer who also specializes in the repair and restoration of vintage Barbie dolls: hair restyling, retouching face paint, reconstruction of nose nips, eyelash ridges, missing digits, limb reattachment and more.

Marl B. Davidson
Marl & Barbie
10301 Braden Run
Bradenton, FL 34202-1744
ph: 914-751-6275
fax: 941-751-5463
e-mail: Marlbe@aol.com
web: http://www.marlbe.com/
Always buying Barbies; issues catalogs listing Barbies from 1959 through present including fashions, accessories, especially hard-to-find Barbie items; send $7.50 for sample catalog; carries full line of Ashton Drake Gene and Billy dolls.

Faye Leach
Faye's Dolls of Yesterday
434 Newman Ave.
Newport, KY 41075
ph: 606-781-1038
Specializing in Barbie.

Paul David
Newsletter: Paul David Exclusively Barbie
610 Blackwater Rd.
Chillicothe, OH 45601-9004
ph: 740-642-2747
fax: 740-642-2755
Carries all the latest Barbies and old stock and accessories; newsletter is 40 pages, hundreds of Barbies listed for sale, articles, news, what's new, limited editions, special editions, values, updated prices, gossip, etc.

Cindy Oakes
34025 W. 6 Mile
Livonia, MI 48152
ph: 734-591-3252
Buying 1960s and 1970s Barbie and Friends dolls, and clothing, Holiday Barbie and Special Editions; will purchase entire collections; paying up to $1000 for #1 Barbie.

Denise Davidson
Deni's Vintage Barbies
7321 Seymour Rd.
Owosso, MI 48867
ph: 517-723-4611
fax: 517-725-5696
e-mail: davidson@tir.com
web: http://www.tir.com/~davidson/
Extensive list of vintage Barbie and friends for sale; web site has comprehensive vintage Barbie and friends ID Guide for viewing; select clothing ID Guide for viewing at photo gallery; also has Modern Barbie sales list.

Deanna Overdorf
D's Dolls
4 Lakeridge Dr.
Adrian, MI 49221
ph: 517-264-1862 or 888-239-0176
fax: 517-264-1863
e-mail: jrodjc@msn.com
web: http://www.dsdolls.com
Specializes in vintage Barbie, Dawn, Liddle Kiddles and other fashion dolls from the 1960s and 1970s including cars, houses, clothes and other accessories.

Cheryl Shimp
Nick & Cherly's Toy Collectors Page
749 Nottingham Lane
Crystal Lake, IL 60014
ph: 815-455-3308
e-mail: ncshimp@mc.net
web: http://mc.net/ncshimp/
Buys, sells, collects and appraises vintage Barbie dolls and fashions; also other various vintage dolls from the 1940s through the 1960s.

Diamonds & Dolls by Miss Alice
511 St. Louis
Springfield, MO 65806
ph: 417-868-8111
Buys, sells, trades Barbies.

Judy Kuster
Bear Essentials Dolls, Bears & Collectible Toys
1344 Pine St.
Paso Robles, CA 93446
ph: 805-238-4469
e-mail: toys4u@thegrid.net
web: http://www.thegrid.net/bear/bear.htm
Offers vintage to present Barbie, GI Joe, action figures, Beanie Babies, Starting Lineup, Boyds Bears, Steiff, Muffy Vanderbear, Superman, Batman, Star Wars, Star Trek, and more.

Craig Dawson
Baddog Collectibles
115 Oakley Blvd.
Scarborough, Ontario M1P 3P8
Canada
ph: 416-751-3227
fax: 416-755-4977
e-mail: baddog@thebulletin.net
web: http://www.thebulletin.net
Buys, sells, trades 1959-1974 Barbie dolls and friends (Ken, Skipper, Francie, Christie, Stacey, Casey, Twiggy, Scooter, Allan, Ricky, Tutti, Midge and others); also interested in celebrity items from the 1960s to 1970s.

Experts

Jane Sarasohn-Kahn
355 Friendship Dr.
Paoli, PA 19301-1206
ph: 610-296-5085
fax: 610-296-8278
e-mail: jskahn@aol.com
web: http://www.csmonline.com/barbie/barbcolm.html
Author of "Contemporary Barbie 1980 to Present," "Contemporary Barbie, 1998 Edition" (2nd edition), and "Notes From a Friend of the Barbie Doll" and "Regarding the Doll" monthly columns.

Kathryn E. Darden
Newsletter: Millicent's Attic
P. O. Box 218427
Nashville, TN 37221-8427
e-mail: kathryn@dollpage.com
Regular columnist for "Barbie Bazaar" magazine; also known for her work in the doll collecting world as a free-lance writer, and doll show promoter; publishes bimonthly newsletter of interest to local Tennessee Barbie collectors.

Joe Blitman
5163 Franklin Ave.
Los Angeles, CA 90027-3601
ph: 323-953-6490
fax: 323-953-0888
e-mail: joebarbie@aol.com
web: http://www.joeslist.com/
Publisher of "Oh, You Beautiful Doll" Barbie videotape; author of "Barbie and her Mod, Mod, Mod, Mod World of Fashion," and "Francis and her Mod, Mod, Mod, Mod, World of Fashion" (Hobby House Books, 1996).

Internet Resources

Plastic Princess Page, The
e-mail: znu@sptddog.com
web: http://d.armory.com/~zednugirl/barbie.html
Great info about Barbies; plus list of local Barbie clubs around the country and world.

Barbie Club Online
e-mail: dlpy98a@prodigy.com
web: http://pages.prodigy.com/BCONLINE/

Sarah Locker
Barbie Doll Collecting from the Mining Company
e-mail: barbiedolls.guide@miningco.com
web: http://barbiedolls.miningco.com
Long-time collector offering a website for the Barbie collector: weekly features, specials, exhaustive collection of the best links online for serious Barbie enthusiasts of all ages.

Man./Prod./Dist.

Ann Parducci
Mattel Toys
300 Continental Blvd.
El Segundo, CA 90245-5012
ph: 800-624-1456
web: http://www.barbie.com
Manufacturer of Barbie dolls; website includes Collecting Barbie Dolls, Product Showcase (the showcase edition, collector edition, limited edition and children's collection), and Barbie Shoppe.

Periodicals

Jacqueline Horning
Journal: Barbie Talks Some More
19 Jamestown Dr.
Cincinnati, OH 45241-1435
ph: 513-779-3708
A 65-page journal with 13 years of vital information for the Barbie collector; the author is a dealer/collector herself; $12.95 ppd.

Barbie Bazaar, Inc.
Magazine: Barbie Bazaar
5617 6th Ave.
Kenosha, WI 53140-4101
ph: 414-658-1004
fax: 414-658-0433
e-mail: marlene@barbiebazaar.com
web: http://www.barbiebazzar.com/

Brian Savage
Fun Publications
Newspaper: Master Collector
225 Cattle Barron Parc Dr.
Fort Worth, TX 76108
ph: 800-772-6673 or 817-448-9863
fax: 817-448-9843
e-mail: brian@mastercollector.com
web: http://www.mastercollector.com
Ads-only newspaper; dolls (antique and modern collectible), toys, banks, models, cars, Matchbox, monsters, puzzles, political, toy trains, etc.; subscribers receive free 30 word ad each month; published monthly; reaches 20,000.

Barbara & Dan Miller
Magazine: Miller's Barbie Collector
West One Sumner, #1
Spokane, WA 99204-3661
ph: 509-747-0139
fax: 509-455-6115
A bi-monthly exclusively-Barbie publication with in-depth articles, full color photography, directory of clubs and events, prices, ads, etc.; call subscriptions to 800-874-5201.

Repair Services

Kristin Peterson
Must B Vintage
2908 Durbin Place
Virginia Beach, VA 23456
ph: 757-468-9841
e-mail: KPeter24@aol.com
web: http://members.aol.com/kpeter24/index.html
Dealer who also specializes in the repair and restoration of vintage Barbie dolls: hair restyling, retouching face paint, reconstruction of nose nips, eyelash ridges, missing digits, limb reattachment and more.

Suppliers

Steve Lundin
Action Figure Display Case Co.
P.O. Box 7954
Chicago, IL 60680
ph: 773-395-3395
fax: 773-395-3495
e-mail: actioncc@enteract.com
web: http://www.enteract.com/~actioncc
Manufactures high quality display cases for all 12" action figures; full color combat backgrounds or cityscapes for Barbie; perfect for gifts, home or office.

Betsy McCall

Experts

David & Marci Van Ausdall
P.O. Box 946
Quincy, CA 95971
ph: 530-283-2770
e-mail: dreams@psln.com
Buys, sells, appraises, specializes in Betsy McCall of all sizes as well as clothing and related merchandise (toys, paperdolls, etc.); one item or collection.

Periodicals

David & Marci Van Ausdall
Betsy's Fan Club
Newsletter: Betsy's Fan Club Newsletter
P.O. Box 946
Quincy, CA 95971
ph: 530-283-2770
e-mail: dreams@psln.com

Black

(see also BLACK MEMORABILIA)

Dealers

Erlene Reed
Aquataurian
1794 Verbena St., NW
Washington, DC 20012
ph: 202-829-7170
fax: 202-723-7274
e-mail: dollyasm@erols.com
web: http://www.townsqr.com/dolly/
Specializes in black and ethnic dolls: artist dolls, antique dolls and modern dolls; also wants figurines, collectible plates, art, black memorabilia, etc.; has thousands of dolls.

Periodicals

Laverne Hall
VELB Associates
Newsletter: Doll-E-Gram
P.O. Box 1212
Bellevue, WA 98009-1212
ph: 425-643-4154
The newsletter of the black doll collector.

Bobbing Head

(see also SPORTS COLLECTIBLES, Baseball)

Clubs/Associations

Barry Larkins
Bobbin Head Collectors Club
P.O. Box 9297
Daytona Beach, FL 32120
ph: 940-253-7040
fax: 904-253-1115
e-mail: bobbin1013@aol.com
web: http://www.nationalbonninheadclub.com/

Collectors

Nostalgia Man
1621 Walenta Ave.
Rosenberg, TX 77471
ph: 281-344-9906
e-mail: NostalgiaMan@beer.com
web: http://www.freeyellow.com/members/whoathatscool/WantedList.html
Wants to buy or trade character bobbin' heads or sports nodders from the 1970s or earlier.

Experts

Tim Hunter
4301 W. Hidden Valley Dr.
Reno, NV 89502-9537
ph: 775-856-4357
fax: 775-856-4354
e-mail: thunter885@aol.com
Buys, sells and specializes in sports and advertising bobbing head dolls; author of "The Bobbing Head Price Guide."

Man./Prod./Dist.

Mark Bloomquist
S. A. M. Inc.
P.O. Box 77
Palo Alto, CA 94301
ph: 800-483-2643 or 650-369-0190
Manufactures ceramic bobbing head dolls.

Cabbage Patch Kids

Clubs/Associations

Julie Edwards
Cabbage Patch Kids Collectors Club
Newsletter: Limited Edition
P.O. Box 714
Cleveland, GA 30528
ph: 706-865-2171
fax: 706-865-5862
Focuses on the Cabbage Patch Kids and Little People soft-sculpture collectibles by Xavier Roberts. Sponsored by Original Appalachian Artworks, Inc.

Man./Prod./Dist.

Original Appalachian Artworks, Inc.
Newsletter: Limited Edition
P.O. Box 714
Cleveland, GA 30528
ph: 706-865-2171
fax: 706-865-5862
Manufacturer of Cabbage Patch Kids dolls.

Periodicals

Marty Liston
Newsletter: Cabbage Line, The
8500 C.R. 21
Clyde, OH 43410
ph: 419-547-8367
Focuses mostly on mass-market dolls by Coleco, Hasbro and Mattel.

Ann Wilhite
Newsletter: Cabbage Connection, The
610 W. 17th
Fremont, NE 68025
ph: 402-721-0954
Focuses mostly on mass-market dolls by Coleco, Hasbro and Mattel.

Celebrity

Collectors

Joedi Johnson
P.O. Box 565
Billings, MT 59101-0565
ph: 406-248-4875
fax: 407-248-4875
e-mail: starbase@mcn.net
Wants to buy Mego 12" Cher doll and other girl dolls such as Diana Ross, Jaclyn Smith, Wonder Woman and others; also girl doll fashions and accessories.

Chatty Cathy

(see also TOYS, Talking [Pullstring])

Clubs/Associations

Melissa Gilkey-Mince
Chatty Cathy Collector's Club
Newsletter: Chatty News
P.O. Box 4426
Seminole, FL 33775-1426
e-mail: ChattynMe@aol.com
web: http://www.ttiniet.com/chattycathy/
For collectors of Chatty Cathy; share and learn all about Mattel's 1960s line of talking dolls; send SASE for information; quarterly club newsletter since 1989.

Collectors

Lisa Eisenstein
P.O. Box 140
Readington, NJ 08870-0140
e-mail: chatty@eclipse.net
Wants Chatty Cathy items: clothes, case, accessories; books and all other related items.

Marci Van Ausdall
P.O. Box 946
Quincy, CA 95971
ph: 530-283-2770
e-mail: dreams@psln.com
Wants to buy all original, excellent condition Chatty Family dolls, clothing, accessories, paper dolls, etc.

Repair Services

Kelly McIntyre
Chatty Cathy's Haven
19528 Ventura Blvd. #495
Tarzana, CA 91356-2917
ph: 818-881-3878
e-mail: cchaven@aol.com
web: http://www.chattycathyshaven.com
Repairs, buys and sells pullstring talkers.

Cloth

Periodicals

Judy Beswick
Magazine: Cloth Doll Magazine, The
P.O. Box 2167
Lake Oswego, OR 97035-0051
ph: 503-244-3539 or 800-695-7005
fax: 503-244-2370
e-mail: theclothdoll@earthlink.com
web: http://www.theclothdoll.com/
A quarterly magazine on cloth/fabric dolls: patterns, how-to articles, artist profiles, collector information, sources of supplies, book reviews, etc.

Clothing

Clubs/Associations

Doll Costumers Guild
7112 W. Grovers Ave.
Glendale, AZ 85308
Goal is to promote cooperation and interchange of ideas among those who are engaged or interested in doll costuming.

Misc. Services

William K. Jones
Carter & Jones, Inc.
4026 Melrose Ave.
Roanoke, VA 24017
ph: 800-476-4215 or 540-362-3751
fax: 540-563-0545
e-mail: asnake65@aol.com
Specialist in cleaning and restoring antique doll clothes and accessories.

Alma Bucid
Royal-T Cleaners
17942 Magnolia
Fountain Valley, CA 92708
ph: 714-963-6110
Offers an special cleaning service for doll clothing; personal inspection to determine best method of cleaning (dry or wet) based on age, stains and overall condition; calls client to discuss stains, age and cost; do not sent doll.

Dawn

Experts

Joedi Johnson
P.O. Box 565
Billings, MT 59101-0565
ph: 406-248-4875
fax: 407-248-4875
e-mail: starbase@mcn.net
Buying all Dawn collections, dolls, fashions and accessories; looking for additional material for second printing of her Dawn price and guidebook; especially interested in international items, promotions, store displays.

Dolls (Nancy Ann Storybook)

Collectors

Elaine M. Pardee
3613 Merano Way
Santa Rosa, CA 95843-5538

Ginny

Clubs/Associations

Ginny Doll Club
P.O. Box 338
Oakdale, CA 95361
ph: 877-848-0300
Club sponsored by the manufacturer, Vogue Doll Co.

Experts

Jeanne Niswonger
305 West Beacon Rd.
Lakeland, FL 33803
ph: 941-682-8484
Author of "That Doll, Ginny."

Golliwoggs

Clubs/Associations

Juliet Savage
International Golliwogg Collectors Club
Newsletter: IGCC Newsletter
P.O. Box 612
Woodstock, NY 12498
ph: 914-679-5769
fax: 914-679-5769
e-mail: ohgolli@aol.com
web: http://www.teddybears.com/golliwog/

Collectors

Beth B. Savino
Franklin Park Mall
5001 Monroe St.
Toledo, OH 43623
ph: 419-473-9801 or 800-862-8697
fax: 419-473-3947
e-mail: info@toystorenet.com
web: http://www.toystorenet.com
Golliwoggs are black characters dolls based on a series of British children's books originating in 1895 and written by American authoress Florence Upton.

Half

Collectors

Sharon Wilkins
1105 Burnham St.
Cocoa, FL 32922-6838
Wants half dolls; porcelain half dolls decorated a lady's dresser in the '20s and '30s.

Iaulanda's

Experts

Jamie Saloff
P.O. Box 339
Edinboro, PA 16412
ph: 814-734-5189
fax: 814-734-7162
e-mail: jlsaloff@erie.net
web: http://www.erie.net/~jlsaloff
Daughter of Iaulanda Turner Downey, creator of Iaulanda's Storyteller Dolls (high quality, handcrafted felt dolls made in the 1960s-'70s for the Christmas tree.)

Ideal

Clubs/Associations

Judith Izen
Ideal Toy Co. Collector's Club
Newsletter: Ideal Toy Co. Collectors Club Newsletter
P.O. Box 623
Lexington, MA 02173
e-mail: jizenres@aol.com
web: http://members.aol.com/jizenres/homepage/index.html

Collectors

Elizabeth Arnold
205 Penns Lane
Malvern, PA 19355
ph: 610-647-8468
Wants to buy Saucey Walker dolls by Ideal.

Kewpie

(see also ROSE O'NEILL COLLECTIBLES)

Clubs/Associations

International Rose O'Neill Club
P.O. Box 668
Branson, MO 65616

Collectors

Jeff Dykes
6 Wildwood Terrace
Glen Ridge, NJ 07028
ph: 973-748-4990
e-mail: lja@viconet.com
Wants to buy German bisque Kewpies - the "action" pieces such as Kewpie gardener, Kewpie with dog, Kewpie soldier; must be in excellent original condition; also wants Kewpies made of celluloids and Kewpie tea sets.

Kitty Watson
201 Dena Dr.
Guthrie, OK 73044-9043
ph: 405-282-2287
Wants to buy Kewpies, Scootles, and Rose O'Neill items, preferably "action" bisque, and metal pieces, signed.

Liddle Kiddles

Clubs/Associations

Heidi Neufield
Little Kiddle Club - East Coast
16 Weathervane Way
Marlboro, NJ 07746-1693
fax: 732-617-1104

Laura Miller
Liddle Kiddles Klub
Newsletter: Liddle Kiddles Klub Newsletter
3639 Fourth Ave.
La Crescenta, CA 91214-2441
A bi-monthly newsletter all about Liddle Kiddles (dolls by Mattel 1966-1971); classifieds; send SASE for more information or $3 for sample newsletter.

Collectors

Jill Salerno
245 Sunnyridge Ave., Unit #41
Fairfield, CT 06430-4646
ph: 203-332-1469
Wants to buy Liddle Kiddles by Mattel; old stock, mint on card, or childhood collections.

Linda Strumski
74 Pierpont RD E-7
Waterbury, CT 06705-3847
ph: 203-757-8103
e-mail: JSmicro633@aol.com
Collector wants to buy Liddle Kiddles dolls, accessories, cases, and related paper items.

Joedi Johnson
P.O. Box 565
Billings, MT 59101-0565
ph: 406-248-4875
fax: 407-248-4875
e-mail: starbase@mcn.net
Buying Kiddle collections, especially coloring books, riddle books, puzzles, vinyl wallet, magic slate and paper dolls; also buying Mattel Upsy Downsy dolls, accessories and books.

Dealers

Sharon Rialto
Rialto Movie Art
81 1/2 S. Washington St.
Seattle, WA 98104
ph: 206-622-5099

Experts

Paris Langford
Kollecting Kiddles
415 Dodge Ave.
Jefferson, LA 70121-3311
ph: 504-733-0676 or 504-733-0676
e-mail: bbean415@aol.com
Buy, sell, trade Liddle Kiddles by Mattel and other small dolls from 60s to 70s; send SASE for current list of offerings; author of "Liddle Kiddles Identification and Value Guide," (Collector Books, 1995).

Nisbet

Clubs/Associations

Howard & Sarah Wade
Peggy Nisbet International Collectors' Society
Newsletter: PNICS Newsletter
P.O. Box 325
Orrville, OH 44667-0325
ph: 330-682-8551
fax: 330-682-3655
e-mail: ukdolls@aol.com
Clearinghouse for information about Peggy Nisbet portrait and costume dolls and Nisbet bears from Britain, both primary and secondary markets.

Man./Prod./Dist.

Howard & Sarah Wade
Nisbet Dolls & Bears
P.O. Box 325
Orrville, OH 44667-0325
ph: 330-682-8551
fax: 330-682-3655
e-mail: ukdolls@aol.com
U.S. distributor for Peggy Nisbet dolls and Nisbet bears from Britain.

Paper

(see also PAPER COLLECTIBLES)

Clubs/Associations

Jenny R. Taliadoros
Original Paper Doll Artists Guild, The
Magazine: OPDAG's Paper Doll Studio News
P.O. Box 14
Kingfield, ME 04947-0014
ph: 207-265-2500
fax: 207-265-2500
e-mail: info@opdag.com
web: http://www.opdag.com
An organization of paper doll enthusiasts to promote the PD hobby; magazine has PD news, how-to's, paper dolls, artist features, etc.

Collectors

Loretta Willis
808 Lee Ave.
Tifton, GA 31794-4134
Deals with many paper doll and doll collectors who collect PD's as a hobby; wants PD movie stars, nostalgia, new & old for collection.

Mary Keiller
242 31st St. NW
Canton, OH 44709-3118
Wants to buy pre-1970 paper dolls either cut or uncut.

Shirley Hedge
Rte. 2 Box 52
Princeton, IN 47670-9601
ph: 812-385-4080
Wants any paper dolls printed in the "Chicago Tribune" - comics or otherwise; advertising paper dolls, antique sets, book, boxed or packaged sets printed prior to 1950; pre-1935 magazine sets; any sets from children's magazines.

Lynne Hough
1603 Kenilworth Pl
Aurora, IL 60506-5376
Wants to buy all types of paper dolls.

Jerry Brand
10612 W. 101st Terr.
Overland Park, KS 66214
ph: 913-888-4739
Wants to buy pre-1970 paperdolls, cut or uncut; no magazines; also wants Little Golden Books with paperdolls and older Katy Keen comics with paperdolls in them.

Dealers

Carolyn Thompson
P.O. Box 157
Orleans, MA 02653
ph: 508-896-6748

Jo Ann Reisler
360 Glyndon St., NE
Vienna, VA 22180-3537
ph: 703-938-2967
fax: 703-938-9057
e-mail: Reisler@clark.net
web: http://www.clark.net/pub/reisler

Barbara Gilland
Fond Memories
105 Darcee Court
Lawrenceville, GA 30245-7404
ph: 770-963-0324
Vintage paper dolls, reproduction paper dolls, contemporary artist paper dolls, newest paper dolls, many other paper items.

R. H. Stevens
R. H. Stevens Antiques
17838 South East Hwy. 452
Umatilla, FL 32784
ph: 352-821-3276
web: http://www.opdag.com/Stevens.html
Paper dolls wanted: cut or uncut; send $1 for list.

Janie Barrett
829 Kenilworth Terr.
Orlando, FL 32803
ph: 407-898-7095 or 888-234-5089
fax: 407-898-7095
e-mail: janiepds@aol.com
web: http://www.opdag.com/Barrett.html
Sends out about ten lists per year: celebrities, non-celebrities, oldies, magazine sheets, contemporary artists, reference books.

Judy M. Johnson
Judy's Place
115 Kreiger Dr.
P.O. Box 176
Skandia, MI 49885-0176
ph: 906-942-7865
fax: 906-942-7865
web: http://www.opdag.com/jmj.html
Author/artist artist buys, sells, collects and designs paper dolls and and Magicloth dolls; wants paper dolls, especially original art and unique or comic paper dolls; send 2 first class stamps for catalog (NOT SASE).

Peggy Ell
Peggy's Paper
218 Gratton
Burlington, IA 52601
ph: 319-752-7670
Buys and sells paper dolls, cut or uncut; send double-stamped LSASE for most recent list of paper dolls for sale.

Johana Gast Anderton
6408 North Flora
Kansas City, MO 64118-3609
ph: 816-468-0558
Specializes in original & antique paper dolls and other paper collectibles, antique dolls and teddy bears, original doll clothes, patterns; lecturer, author, paper doll artist; LSASE for information.

Kim Brecklein
Brecklein Paper Miniatures
7949 S. 161st W. Ave.
Sapulpa, OK 74066
ph: 918-224-7307 or 918-595-7522
e-mail: kbreck-12@ionet.net
web: http://www.breckpaperdoll.com/
Collects and deals in paper doll ladies and children with lavish historically accurate costumes from Renaissance, Victorian, Edwardian eras plus from the 1920s through 1950s.

Loraine Burdick
Journal: Celebrity Doll Journal
413 10th Ave. Ct. NE
Puyallup, WA 98372-2948
e-mail: lo.burdick@n2movies.com
Celebrity Doll Journal features research on collectibles and creators; also offers sales list of paper dolls.

Experts

Marta Krebs
13628 Middlevale Lane
Silver Spring, MD 20906-2123
ph: 301-460-1068
e-mail: rkrebs@erols.com
Buys and sells paper dolls; publisher of former "Paper Doll Update" newsletter - back issues available; author of "Royalty of Paper Dolls," "Advertising Paper Dolls," and several Dover books.

Mary Young
P.O. Box 9244
Dayton, OH 45409-9244
Buys, sells and specializes in paper dolls; puts together a for-sale list of paper dolls twice a year; welcomes questions; author of "Paper Dolls & Their Artists," "Magazine Paper Dolls" with price guide, and other books.

Emma Terry
P.O. Box 807
Vivian, LA 71082-0807
Publisher of the bi-monthly "Paper Doll News" newsletter.

Denis C. Jackson
P.O. Box 1958
Sequim, WA 98382-1958
ph: 360-452-3810
e-mail: ticn@olypen.com
web: http://www.olypen.com/ticn/
Author of "The Price & Identification Guide to Old Magazine Paperdolls", 3rd Edition; with a strong focus on the golden age of paper, 'teens through the 1960s; send LSASE for information.

Periodicals

Marilyn Henry, Ed.
Magazine: Paper Doll Review
P.O. Box 14
Kingfield, ME 04947-0014
ph: 207-265-2500
fax: 207-265-2500
e-mail: PDR@opdag.com
web: http://www.opdag.com/PDReview.html
Published quarterly; a paper doll printed in color in each issue; lots of paper doll photos, and articles about paper dolls and related items; send LSASE for subscription information.

Arlene Del Fava
Newsletter: Now & Then
67-40 Yellowstone Blvd.
Forest Hills, NY 11375-2614
Newsletter published three times a year; covers some new but mostly nostalgic paper dolls and their times; about 30 pages.

Loretta Willis
Newsletter: Loretta's Place Paper Doll Newsletter
808 Lee Ave.
Tifton, GA 31794-4134
Focuses on original artists' paper dolls and features artists work and paper dolls in each issue; also old paper dolls; 4 issues ("in color" paper doll on front page) per year for $15.

Loretta Willis
Newsletter: Yesterday's Paper Dolls
808 Lee Ave.
Tifton, GA 31794-4134
Identification guide newsletter that illustrates, identifies, and prices old nostalgic paper dolls; 4 issues per year for $12.

Emma Terry
Newsletter: Paper Doll News
P.O. Box 807
Vivian, LA 71082-0807
A bi-monthly newsletter sharing news of the paper doll world; review paper dolls and share all known information regarding paper dolls; promote paper doll artists and share addresses in every issue of "Paper Doll News".

Nan Moorehead
Newsletter: Golden Paper Doll & Toy Opportunities
P.O. Box 252
Golden, CO 80402-0252
Concentrates on antique and collectible paper dolls.

Sharon Hill
Newsletter: Cornerstone Paper Doll Journal
2216 S. Autumn Ln.
Diamond Bar, CA 91789

Beverly Wethington
Newsletter: Northern Lights Paperdoll News
P.O. Box 871189
Wasilla, AK 99687-1189
ph: 907-745-4334

Newsletter: Paper Doll Circle
28 Ferndown Gardens
Gobham, KT11 2BH
U.K.
Paper doll newsletter for enthusiasts worldwide; free sample issue on request.

Parts

Collectors

Dorothy Grinewitlki
2424 Shoreham Highland Dr.
St. Joseph, MI 49085
Wants bisque dolls, heads or parts; also complete dolls.

Pincushion

Dealers

Linda Gibbs
Heirloom Keepsakes
10380 Miranda Ave.
Buena Park, CA 90620-4447
ph: 714-827-6488
Will consider any vintage type pincushion dolls.

Experts

Susan Endo
P.O. Box 4051
Covina, CA 91723
ph: 626-339-6352
Author of "A Price Guide to Pincushion Dolls" and "2nd Price Guide to Pincushion Dolls"; both available from the author; always buying and selling quality pincushion dolls; send LSASE for current list with colored photo.

Raggedy Ann & Andy

Collectors

Kathleen Ray
28 Kathy Ann Rd.
Bass River, MA 02664
ph: 508-394-9668
Wants Raggedy Ann books and ephemera.

Katherine James
487 Oak Ridge Rd.
Dyersburg, TN 38024-6511
ph: 901-286-2025
e-mail: kjames@usit.net
Serious Raggedy Ann and Raggedy Andy collector.

Dealers

Gwen Daniel
18 Belleau Lake Ct.
O Fallon, MO 63366-3144
ph: 314-978-3190
e-mail: gdaniel@mail.win.org
Wants Raggedy Ann & Andy's, books and related items; also teddy bears, Lulu & Tubby, Nancy & Sluggo, Howdy Doody and Barbie.

Internet Resources

Charles & Cheryl Platt
Raggedy Ann & Andy Homepage
1565 Greentree Parkway
Macon, GA 31220
e-mail: charles@raggedyland.com
web: http://www.raggedyland.com/
Contains everything Raggedy Ann & Andy on the web: artwork, doll dealers, stamps, Raggedy Ann Festival, costumes, and catalog items.

Periodicals

Barbara Barth
Newsletter: Rags
P.O. Box 823
Atlanta, GA 30301
A quarterly newsletter devoted to the creations of Johnny Gruelle; ads, articles, photos, etc. for Raggedy Ann and other cloth dolls.

Strawberry Shortcake

Clubs/Associations

Peggy Jimenez
Strawberry Shortcake Collectors' Club
Newsletter: Berry-Bits
1409 72nd St.
North Bergen, NJ 07047-3827
ph: 201-868-7334

Periodicals

Jennifer Bowles
Doll Patch, The
Newsletter: Strawberryland Gazette
138 E. Main Cross
Greenville, KY 42345
ph: 502-338-5213 or 502-338-4318
e-mail: jenniferb@kih.net
web: http://www.comsource.net/~sscake/
A bi-monthly newsletter for Strawberry Shortcake collectors; free ads; color photos.

Toni

Clubs/Associations

Newsletter: Toni Dolls Newsletter
7431-A LeMunyan Rd.
Addison, NY 14801

Vogue

Collectors

Victoria Broadhurst
5009 Queen Victoria Rd.
Woodland Hills, CA 91364-4757
ph: 818-883-3127
fax: 818-887-3739
e-mail: mrscdrew@aol.com
Wants to buy Vogue dolls and accessories.

Experts

Judith Izen
P.O. Box 623
Lexington, MA 02173
e-mail: jizenres@aol.com
web: http://members.aol.com/jizenres/homepage/index.html
Co-author with Carol Stover of "Vogue Dolls" (1997); covers all Vogue dolls including Ginny, Jill, Ginnette, Li'l Imp, Baby Dear, Toddles, Jeff, Jan, etc.; send SASE for more information.

DOLPHINS

(see WHALES)

DOOR PUSH PLATES

Collectors

Betty R. Foley
129 Meadow Valley Rd., Trlr. 11
Ephrata, PA 17522-1843
ph: 717-738-4813
Wants porcelain door push (or pull) plates with advertising; attached to old wooden porch doors; Red Rose Tea, Chesterfields, etc.

DOORKNOBS

(see also HARDWARE; LOCKS)

Book Sellers

Maudie L. Eastwood
Antique Doorknob Publishing Company
17300 135th Ave. NW, #103
Woodinville, WA 98072-6839
ph: 425-483-5848
Books about doorknobs and other builders' hardware.

Clubs/Associations

Rich Kennedy, Sec.
Antique Doorknob Collectors of America, The
Newsletter: Doorknob Collector, The
P.O. Box 31
Chatham, NJ 07928-9931
ph: 973-635-6338
fax: 973-635-6993
e-mail: knobnews@aol.com
web: http://members.aol.com/knobnews/
A club for doorknob and related hardware collectors and enthusiasts;

conventions, seminars, banquets, trading sessions.

Collectors

Richard C. Hubbard
162 Poplar Ave.
Hackensack, NJ 07601
ph: 201-342-1274
e-mail: DoorKnobID@aol.com
Wants to buy old doorknobs; historical, figural or emblematic knobs; please describe and price.

Charles W. Wardell
P.O. Box 195
Trinity, NC 27370-0195
ph: 336-434-1145
Wants ornate doorknobs, escutcheon plates, store door handles, push plates, door knockers, doorbells, mail slots, etc.; 1870-1920.

Loretta & Raymond Nemec
P.O. Box 126
Eola, IL 60519-0126
ph: 630-357-2381
fax: 630-357-2391

Dealers

H. Weber Wilson
Oltz-Wilson Antiques
P.O. Box 506
Portsmouth, RI 02871
ph: 800-508-0022
fax: 401-683-1644
e-mail: hww@edgenet.net
web: http://www.antiqnet.com/webwilson/
Buys and sells vintage door hardware, especially doorknobs; also wants vintage plumbing items.

Experts

Maudie L. Eastwood
Antique Doorknob Publishing Company
17300 135th Ave. NW, #103
Woodinville, WA 98072-6839
ph: 425-483-5848
Researcher, expert, collector and consultant specializing in antique builders hardware and author of books on early American door and other builders hardware.

DOORKNOCKERS

Dealers

John & Nancy Smith
American Sampler
P.O. Box 371
Barnesville, MD 20838-0371
ph: 301-972-6250
Wants cast iron doorstops, figural bottle openers, doorknockers, paperweights, banks, bookends, etc.

DOORSTOPS

(see also CAST IRON ITEMS)

Auction Services

Bill Bertoia
Bill Bertoia Auctions
1881 Spring Rd.
Vineland, NJ 08631
ph: 609-692-1881
fax: 609-692-8697
e-mail: webmaster@billbertoiaauctions.com
web: http://www.billbertoiaauctions.com/
Specializing in the auctioning of antique toys, banks, trains, and doorstops.

Clubs/Associations

Jeanne Bertoia
Doorstop Collectors of America
1881 Spring Rd.
Vineland, NJ 08631
ph: 609-692-1881
fax: 609-692-8697
e-mail: jeanne@billbertoiaauctions.com

Collectors

Bill Price
Paperweight Potentate of Pittsburgh, The
P.O. Box 82501
Pittsburgh, PA 15218-0501
ph: 412-351-5297
fax: 724-271-4329
e-mail: paperwghts@aol.com
web: http://www.collectoronline.com/wb-paperweights.html
Wants to buy glass doorstops advertising businesses or with people's portraits; also wants glass paperweights advertising businesses or with people's portraits.

Dealers

John & Nancy Smith
American Sampler
P.O. Box 371
Barnesville, MD 20838-0371
ph: 301-972-6250
Wants cast iron doorstops, figural bottle openers, doorknockers, paperweights, banks, bookends, etc.

Experts

Jeanne Bertoia
1881 Spring Rd.
Vineland, NJ 08631
ph: 609-692-1881
fax: 609-692-8697
e-mail: jeanne@billbertoiaauctions.com
Collector and dealer of cast iron figural doorstops; wants to buy painted cast iron doorstops; author of "Doorstop Identification & Values."

Craig Dinner
P.O. Box 4399
Long Island City, NY 11104-0399
ph: 718-729-3850 or 802-365-7181
Advisor to "Warman's Antiques & Collectibles Price Guide."

DR. SEUSS COLLECTIBLES

Collectors

Michael Gessel
P.O. Box 748
Arlington, VA 22216-0748
ph: 703-542-0462
Wants Dr. Seuss books, pamphlets, posters, advertising, ephemera, original illustrations, anything related to Dr. Seuss.

Dealers

Helen & Marc Younger
Aleph-Bet Books, Inc.
218 Waters Edge
Valley Cottage, NY 10989
ph: 914-268-7410
fax: 914-268-5942
e-mail: helen@alephbet.com
web: http://www.alephbet.com/
Specializing in fine first editions of collectible and rare children's and illustrated books; always interested in buying books in fine condition; business established in 1978.

Daniel Hirsch
Daniel Hirsch Rare Books
P.O. Box 5096
Chapel Hill, NC 27514
ph: 919-542-1816
fax: 919-542-1817
e-mail: rhirsch@interserv.com
Wants Dr. Seuss posters, books, dolls, etc.; also wants fairy tale books, pop-ups, movable books.

Experts

Dallas Poague
LaLaLand Toys
2800 Idaho Ave. S.
St. Louis Park, MN 55426
ph: 612-920-8135 or 612-927-7484 x 142
e-mail: seussnavy@aol.com
web: http://www.seussnavy.com/
Collector of 1930s to 1980s Dr. Seuss items; one of the leading experts on Dr. Seuss.

DRAMA

(see PERFORMING ARTS)

DRAWINGS

(see also ART; PRINTS)

Misc. Services

Wendy Reaves, Cur.
National Portrait Gallery
Prints & Drawings
8th & F Streets N.W.
Washington, DC 20560
ph: 202-357-1356 or 202-357-1633
e-mail: npgweb@npg.si.edu
web: http://www.npg.si.edu
Will authenticate prints & drawings brought in for inspection; make an appointment first; may be able to work from good photographs.

DRESSER ITEMS

(see also BUTTON HOOKS; CLOTHING & ACCESSORIES, Vintage; COMPACTS; COMBS & HAIR ACCESSORIES)

Collectors

K. Hartman
7459 Shawnee Rd.
North Tonawanda, NY 14120
ph: 716-693-4143
Wants to buy Victorian, Art Nouveau, and Art Deco dresser dolls, powder boxes, dresser trays, pin trays, hatpin holders, hair receivers, and other dresser items of china, pottery, glass, or metal.

Hatpins & Hatpin Holders

Clubs/Associations

Lillian Schoephoerster
International Club for Collectors of Hatpins & Hatpin Holders
Newsletter: Points
1013 Medhurst Rd.
Columbus, OH 43220
ph: 614-451-7368
For collectors of hat pins and hatpin holders; also publishes an annual 32 page Pictorial Journal.

Virginia J. Woodbury
American Hatpin Society
Newsletter: American Hatpin Society Newsletter
20 Montecillo Dr.
Rolling Hills Estates, CA 90274-4249
ph: 310-326-2196
e-mail: hatpnginia@aol.com
web: http://www.collectiononline.com/AHS/
A society for hatpin & hatpin holder collectors and enthusiasts; meetings held quarterly; newsletter published quarterly.

Frank Round
Hatpin Society of Great Britain
25 Kingswood Dr.
Norton Canes, Staffordshire WS11 3TR
U.K.

Collectors

Lillian Schoephoerster
1013 Medhurst Rd.
Columbus, OH 43220
ph: 614-451-7368

Collector
P.O. Box 93
Canoga Park, CA 91305
Buys, sells, collects, specializes in, and appraises hatpins and hatpin holders; wants to buy very ornate Victorian hatpins; also free standing or wall-type hatpin holders.

Dealers

Debbie Woolley
Favorite Past-Times
6 Main Hill
Bridgton, ME 04009
ph: 207-647-5286
e-mail: woolley@maine-antiques.com
web: http://www.maine-antiques.com/fpt/Index/
Dealing in authentic hatpins from simple to elaborate; send email to be put on email advance notice of new hatpin items.

Gail & John Dunn
P.O. Box 234
Waterville, OH 43566
ph: 419-878-9515
Buys and sells vintage purses and hatpins.

Diane Richardson
Gold Hatpin, The
P.O. Box 993
Oak Park, IL 60303-0993
ph: 708-848-3247 or 708-445-0610
e-mail: goldhatpin@mediaone.net
Wants all types hatpins & holders: Satsuma, vanity, enameled, figural, fancy & the unusual; no repros.

Internet Resources

Frankie
Hatpin Resource Page for Collectors
e-mail: frankie854@aol.com
web: http://members.aol.com/frankie854/
Great resource with lots of information and links for hatpin collectors.

Linda Pullen
Thimbles, Needlework Tools & Hatpins
U.K.
e-mail: linda.pullen@virgin.net
web: http://freespace.virgin.net/linda.pullen/homepage.htm
Web site is a pictorial tour of hatpins, hatpin holders, thimbles, needlework tools and ladies compacts; recommended reading and on-line book store; makers and their marks; clubs and links to other sites.

DRIVE-IN-THEATER MEMORABILIA

Collectors

Brian A. Butko
2640 Sunset Dr.
West Mifflin, PA 15122-3565
Wants items relating to Drive-In theaters: toys, flyers, photos, articles, and souvenirs such as postcards and ashtrays.

Joe C. Copeland
P.O. Box 4221
Oak Ridge, TN 37831-4221
ph: 423-482-4215
e-mail: joenatca@juno.com
Wants collectibles and memorabilia related to drive-in-theaters.

DRUM & BUGLE CORPS

Collectors

Lawrence Hogan
36457 N. 83
Lake Villa, IL 60046
ph: 847-356-2875
Wants Drum & Bugle Corps records, tapes, videos and memorabilia.

DUCK CALLS

(see SPORTING COLLECTIBLES, Game Calls)

DUCK DECOYS

(see DECOYS, Waterfowl)

Here are some tips when contacting someone listed in this book:

■ When requesting information about a particular item, include a description (material, dimensions, maker's mark, model number, etc.) and a photo, sketch, or photocopy of the item in question.

■ Always ask if there are charges for samples or for the services requested.

■ When writing, please be sure to include a Large (#10 business size) Self-Addressed and Stamped Envelope (LSASE) if requesting a reply or the return of photographs.

■ Never call collect unless otherwise directed. When calling, be considerate of time zone differences and always ask if the party you are calling has time to talk. When leaving an answering machine message, always instruct the party to call you back <u>collect</u>.

EASTER COLLECTIBLES

(see HOLIDAY COLLECTIBLES; RUSSIAN ITEMS, Faberge)

ECCLESIASTICAL ITEMS

(see RELIGIOUS COLLECTIBLES)

EDGED WEAPONS

(see also ARMS & ARMOR; AMERICAN INDIAN; BAYONETS; SWORDS; KNIVES; MILITARIA)

Auction Services

Ronnie Roberts, ISA
SoldUSA.com
6407 Idlewild Rd., Bldg. 2, Ste 207
Charlotte, NC 28212
ph: 704-364-2900 or 877-SoldUSA
fax: 704-364-2322
e-mail: gun1898@aol.com
web: http://www.soldusa.com/

Collectors

Brian Wojtowicz
Antique Exchange, The
9 Kettle Creek Rd.
Toms River, NJ 08753
ph: 732-255-9277 or 800-927-8463
Private collector wants to buy Japanese swords and daggers, German swords and daggers, European swords and daggers; also wants Japanese sword guards, related awards and documents, medals and photos, etc.

Brian L. Ebosh
17738 Indian Hollow rd.
Grafton, OH 44044
ph: 440-355-8118
Wants Indian and pioneer metal axes: pipe tomahawks, spike, spontoon, Missouri, and related items.

Jim Manteris
P.O. Box 40
Manvel, TX 77578
ph: 281-489-8074
fax: 281-489-4784
e-mail: manteris1@webtv.net
Wants clubs, saps, billy clubs, blackjacks, brass knuckles, and old knives; also wants African and Asian weapons.

John S. Fischer
10950 W. Pico Blvd.
Los Angeles, CA 90064-2115
e-mail: jsfischer1@aol.com
Wants British and American edged weapons from WWI and WWII; no bayonets, please; state description, price and phone number.

Dealers

David L. Hartline
P.O. Box 775
Columbus, OH 43085-0775
Buys and sells edged weapons; has large library and over 30 years experience; specialty is pre-1920 Bowie knives; has had many articles published on edge weapons; answers every letter; does appraisals and will authenticate.

Experts

Daniel Morrison
11 Maple Ave.
Demarest, NJ 07627
ph: 201-784-8486
fax: 201-768-4957
e-mail: djmconsult@aol.com
Over 30 years of collecting, buying, selling military edged weapons; specializing in U.S. pieces; knowledgeable for identification and valuation; also interested in buying one or more pieces.

Internet Resources

Robert Edwards
Military Collectors Consortium, The
P.O. Box 190
22 S. Main St.
Keedysville, MD 21756
ph: 301-416-2758 or 301-416-2884
e-mail: milcolco@intrepid.net
web: http://www.intrepid.net/militaria/
Global resource for collectors of military firearms, edged weapons, and militaria from 1750-1970; appraisal, brokerage, and consulting services relating to arms and militaria; publishes monthly "Military Collectors Journal" online.

German

Collectors

Greg Souchik
P.O. Box 161
Custer City, PA 16725-0161
ph: 814-362-2642
fax: 814-362-7356
e-mail:
AlleghenyArsenal@compuserve.com
Wants to buy all WWII German and Japanese swords and daggers.

Dealers

Thomas T. Wittmann
Wittmann Antique Militaria
P.O. Box 350
Moorestown, NJ 08057
ph: 609-866-8733 or 609-231-0323
fax: 609-235-4954
e-mail: TWittm350@aol.com
web: http://www.wwiidaggers.com/
Buys and sells edged weapons: daggers, swords and certain bayonets; specializing in German 3rd Reich or Imperial period weapons; author of "Exploring the Dress Daggers of the German Army," Vol. 1 and other books.

Experts

Thomas T. Wittmann
Wittmann Antique Militaria
P.O. Box 350
Moorestown, NJ 08057
ph: 609-866-8733 or 609-231-0323
fax: 609-235-4954
e-mail: TWittm350@aol.com
web: http://www.wwiidaggers.com/
Buys and sells edged weapons: daggers, swords and certain bayonets; specializing in German 3rd Reich or Imperial period weapons; author of "Exploring the Dress Daggers of the German Army," Vol. 1 and other books.

LTC(Ret) Thomas Johnson
Johnson Reference Books & Militaria
312 Butler Road, Bldg. 403
Fredericksburg, VA 22405-2514
ph: 540-373-9150 or 540-371-2665
fax: 540-373-0087
e-mail: ww2daggers@aol.com
web: http://www.ww2daggers.com
Wants to buy German War booty; specific interest is in edged weapons (dress swords, daggers, bayonets); author of seventeen books about Imperial and 3rd Reich German edged weapons, and militaria.

EDUCATIONAL TOYS

(see TOYS, Construction Sets)

EGGCUPS

Clubs/Associations

Dr. Joan M. George
Eggcup Collectors Club
Newsletter: Eggcup Collectors' Corner
67 Stevens Ave.
Old Bridge, NJ 08857-2244
ph: 732-679-8924
fax: 732-679-6102
e-mail: drjgeorge@nac.net
A quarterly newsletter for eggcup collectors; buy, sell, trade ads; share information, review books, meetings of collectors arranged.

Experts

Pat Stott
180 Bigelow St.
Port Perry, Ontario L9L 1L6
Canada
Author of "The Collectors Book of Egg Cups."

Periodicals

Audrey Diamond
Newsletter: Eggcup World
Flat 5, Cherry Court
Cherry Close Parkstone
Poole, Dorset BH14 OLJ
U.K.

EIFFEL TOWER

(see SOUVENIR & COMMEMORATIVE ITEMS, Buildings [Eiffel Tower])

ELECTRICITY RELATED ITEMS

(see also AUDIO-VISUAL; CLOCKS, Electric; COIN-OPERATED MACHINES; FANS, Mechanical; INSULATORS; KITCHEN COLLECTIBLES; LAMPS & LIGHTING; LIGHT BULBS; MODERNISM; RADIOS; TELEGRAPH ITEMS; TELEVISIONS; TOASTERS, Electric; VACUUM CLEANERS; WASHING MACHINES)

Clubs/Associations

Harry Goldman
Tesla Coil Builders' Association
Newsletter: TCBA News
3 Amy Lane
Queensbury, NY 12804
ph: 518-792-1003
web: http://www.eskimo.com/~billb/tesla/tcba.html
TCBA is a clearinghouse on the history of electricity, wireless, electrotherapy, etc.; acts as consultants for high voltage historical equipment.

Collectors

Harvey Greenspan
15 Chatham Circle
Brookline, MA 02146
ph: 617-566-4191
Wants early electric motors, generators, dynamos and other pre-1900 electrical/mechanical instruments for science, industry, business.

Steve Leffel
1790 Edison St.
Green Bay, WI 54302
fax: 414-465-6505
e-mail: steve97979@yahoo.com
Wants to buy tube testers and other used test equipment.

Dealers

Jim & Felicia Kreuzer
New Wireless Pioneers
P.O. Box 398
Elma, NY 14059
ph: 716-681-3186
fax: 716-681-4540
e-mail: wireless@pce.net
Buys and sells 1850-1950 books, catalogs, magazines, autographs, and other literature dealing with early radio, wireless, pre-1940 television, medical, telegraphy, early computers, television, x-ray and electricity.

Ye Ole Electric Store
507 E. 6th Street
Beaumont, CA 92223
ph: 909-849-7539
For the collector, experimenter, hobbyist: tesla coils, old electrical therapy devices, small appliances, test instruments, radio and tech books, neon signs, old motors, fans, meters, tubes, trains, etc.

Hank Andreoni
Ye Olde Electric Store
250-D South Lyon Ave.
Hemet, CA 92543
ph: 909-849-7539
For the collector, experimenter, hobbyist, researcher: tech. books, electronic surplus, fans, neon signs, old motors, small appliances, test instruments, trains, tubes, radios, meters, old electrical therapy devices, Tesla coils, etc.

Museums/Libraries

Edison National Historic Site
Main St. at Lakeside Ave.
West Orange, NJ 07052
ph: 973-736-0550
fax: 973-736-8496
e-mail: EDIS_Webmaster@nps.gov
web: http://www.nps.gov/edis/home.htm
A museum with exhibits in all fields of Edison's contributions.

National Museum of American History
14th & Constitution Ave. NW
Washington, DC 20560
ph: 202-357-2700
e-mail: webmaster@si.edu
web: http://www.si.edu/organiza/museums/nmah/nmah.htm
The most extensive research facility in the U.S. for electric relics; trade catalogs, electric razors, refrigerators, TV's, radios, etc.

Edison Winter Home & Museum
2350 McGregor Blvd.
Fort Myers, FL 33901
ph: 941-334-3614
Contains Edison-related displays: appliances, early bulbs, and scientific equipment.

Laurence J. Russell, Curator
Thomas Edison Birthplace Museum
9 Edison Dr.
P.O. Box 451
Milan, OH 44846-0451
ph: 419-499-2135
fax: 419-499-3241
e-mail: rwheeler@accnorwalk.com
web: http://www.tomedison.org/
An Edison exhibit featuring phonographs, lamps, fans, photos, and other items related to Thomas Edison.

Bakken Library & Museum, The
3537 Zenith Ave. South
Minneapolis, MN 55416
ph: 612-927-6508
fax: 612-927-7265
e-mail: webmaster@thebakken.org
web: http://www.bakkenmuseum.org/
Collects medical electricity items (no violet rays needed); over 2000 artifacts relating to the historical role of electricity in life; also a collection of 11,000 rare books.

Madsen Electric Co. Museum
3251 E. Washington Blvd.
Los Angeles, CA 90023
ph: 323-269-2127

Appliances

Clubs/Associations

Jack Santoro
Old Appliance Club
Newsletter: Old Road Home, The
P.O. Box 65
Ventura, CA 93002
ph: 805-643-3532
fax: 805-643-3532
e-mail: jes@west.net
web: http://www.antiquestove.com/
An organization for dealers, owners, restorers, users and fans of American appliances; accent is placed on mostly antique and classic ranges 1920s-1950s, Monitor-top refrigerators; builds thermostats, applies new porcelain, restores.

Collectors

Daniel Zilka
110 Benevolent St.
Providence, RI 02906
ph: 410-331-8575 or 410-461-7932
fax: 401-351-0127
Wants to buy older coffee pots, percolators, waffle irons, mixers, vaculator coffee makers; performs restorations; seeking manufacturers' promotional material and brochures.

Dennis Thompson
P.O. Box 26067
Cleveland, OH 44126-0067
ph: 216-235-8548
e-mail: dthomp@stratos.net
web: http://members.stratos.net/dthomp/index.htm
Collects and researches early electric mixers, especially those with depression glass bottom jars; collection is on-line at website.

Mary Faria
P.O. Box 32321
San Jose, CA 95152-2321
ph: 408-258-0413 or 408-258-0416
e-mail: izmars@worldnet.att.net
Collects excellent condition small kitchen appliances, c. 1930s; especially wants toasters, mixers, juicers.

Dealers

Jim Barker
Toaster Master
P.O. Box 746
Allentown, PA 18102
ph: 610-439-0751
fax: 610-439-1925
Dealer, collector, authority on electric appliances.

Experts

K. M. Scotty Mitchell
Millchell
2112 Lipscomb
Ft. Worth, TX 76110-2047
ph: 817-923-3274
fax: 817-926-1970
e-mail: millchel@airmail.net
Collector of small electrical kitchen appliances (1893-1940): toaster, waffle irons, coffee makers and specialty items, etc.

Gary L. Miller
Millchell
2112 Lipscomb
Ft. Worth, TX 76110-2047
ph: 817-923-3274
fax: 817-926-1970
e-mail: millchel@airmail.net
Collector of small electrical kitchen appliances (1893-1940): toaster, waffle irons, coffee makers and specialty items, etc.

Appliances (Coffee Pots)

Collectors

Carole Lundy
3 Long Lane
Hummelstown, PA 17036-9545
ph: 717-566-6016
e-mail: boxerlines@earthlink.net
Wants to buy porcelain coffee pots made by Hall, Westinghouse, Robeson Rochester, and Porcelier.

Appliances (Porcelier)

Clubs/Associations

Shirley Hall
Porcelier Collectors Club
Newsletter: Porcelier Paper, The
21 Tamarac Swamp Rd.
Wallingford, CT 06492-5529
ph: 203-265-5791
e-mail: ThePPLady@aol.com
For collectors of Porcelier dinnerware, service pieces and all-ceramic small electrical kitchen appliances; bi-monthly newsletter features information and pictures of patterns, new finds, and research; free ads for members.

Collectors

Carole Lundy
3 Long Lane
Hummelstown, PA 17036-9545
ph: 717-566-6016
e-mail: boxerlines@earthlink.net
Wants to buy Porcelier brand electric coffee pots, toasters, waffle irons, sandwich grills, and related items.

Batteries (9-Volt)

Clubs/Associations

Cliff Watts
World 9-Volt Battery Collectors Club
51 Glendale Rd.
Brantfors, Ontario N3T 1P5
Canada
ph: 519-753-9049
e-mail: novtrans@worldchat.com
Members collect 9-volt batteries like those used in smoke detectors and transistor radios; looking for as many brands and graphic styles as possible; new or old.

Collectors

Cliff Watts
51 Glendale Rd.
Brantfors, Ontario N3T 1P5
Canada
ph: 519-753-9049
e-mail: novtrans@worldchat.com
Wants to buy 9-volt batteries like those used in smoke detectors and transistor radios; looking for as many brands and graphic styles as possible; new or old.

Battery Jars

Collectors

W.M. Dickey
P.O. Box 7323
Macon, GA 31209-7223
ph: 912-471-0902
fax: 912-471-0902
e-mail: dickey@email.msn.com
Wants to buy glass battery jars; used as containers to hold lead plates and acid; used in the home and industry until the late 1930s where electricity was not available.

Motors

Collectors

Steve Cunningham
3200 Ashland Dr.
Bedford, TX 76021-6502
ph: 817-267-9851 or 800-991-0165
fax: 817-267-0387
e-mail: cunning@cyberramp.net
web: http://www.cyberramp.net/~cunning/
Collects antique electric motors; from lemon-sized to medium-sized; these motors all have open frames where all

the workings are exposed; brand names include Weeded, Rex, Ajax, K&D, Voltamp, Perrett, Crocker-Wheeler.

Power Utilities Items

Collectors

Tommy Bolack
3901 Bloomfield Hwy.
Farmington, NM 87401
ph: 503-325-7873 or 503-525-4275
fax: 503-323-1434
Wants any early watthour meter: GE, Thompson, Edison-Chemical, Duncan, Fort Wayne, Sangamo, pre-pay meters of any type; also any other early or foreign types; also wants early transformers and electrical distribution items.

Museums/Libraries

Dayton Power & Light Company Museum
P.O. Box 1247-Courthouse Sq.
Dayton, OH 45401
ph: 937-224-6428 or 80-Way-ToGo
e-mail: teri.kerrigan@dplinc.com
Over 1000 electrical and non-electrical appliances and historical artifacts pertaining to the gas & electric utility industry.

Rocky Reach Dam, Gallery of Electricity
P.O. Box 1231
Wenatchee, WA 98801-1231
ph: 509-663-8121 or 888-663-8121
fax: 509-664-2870
e-mail: publicinfo@chelanpud.org
web: http://www.chelanpud.org/
The museum features communications and power relics.

ELECTRONICS

(see AUDIO-VISUAL; ELECTRICITY RELATED ITEMS; HI-FI EQUIPMENT; RADIOS; TELEGRAPH ITEMS; TELEVISIONS)

ELONGATED COINS

Clubs/Associations

Howard C. Sharkey
Elongated Collectors, The
Newsletter: TEC News
203 S. Gladiolus St.
Momence, IL 60954-1709
ph: 810-629-3041
e-mail: tec@hainesworld.com
web: http://www.money.org/clubs/tec.html
Focuses on elongated coins but includes all denominations plus tokens and foreign coins rolled under extreme pressure through steel rollers forming custom designed oblong souvenirs commemorating people, places, things, and events.

Collectors

Doug Fairbanks, Sr.
5937 Beadle Dr.
Jamesville, NY 13078-9534
ph: 315-469-4682
Wants to buy "Oldie" elongated coins (rolled-out pennies, etc.) from 1893 to 1965; please write, describe and price.

C. Meccarello
Elongated Coin Museum
1572 Bowmans Trail
Lakeland, FL 33809-5006
ph: 941-859-7194 or 941-859-7194
Buys, sells, collects OPA tokens, Bank postcard, elongated coins.

Dealers

Rich Hartzog
World Exonumia
P.O. Box 4143
Rockford, IL 61110-0643
ph: 815-226-0771
fax: 815-397-7662
e-mail: hartzog@exonumia.com
web: http://www.exonumia.com/
Wants any elongated coins, tokens, medals, exonumia: badges, buttons, World's Fair items, political items, banners, etc.

ELSIE THE BORDEN COW ITEMS

(see also COW COLLECTIBLES; DAIRY COLLECTIBLES)

Collectors

Susan Schwartz
291 E. 4th Street
Brooklyn, NY 11218
Wants Elsie the Cow novelties.

Richard Reddock
914 Isle Ct.
Bellmore, NY 11710-1545
ph: 516-826-2032 or 800-223-PNUT
e-mail: pnutfanclb@aol.com
Wants to buy all Elsie Cow items: clocks, signs, rubber Elsie doll, papier mache Elsie head, letter opener, drinking glasses.

Lynny Borden
307 Stonebebridge Drive
Longwood, FL 32779-3326
ph: 407-788-0780 or 407-788-0225
fax: 407-788-8161
e-mail: LadyBorden@webtv.net
Wants to buy all types of Borden & Elsie items: soda fountain containers, clocks, neon or lighted signs, mugs, glassware, cream top and unusual bottles, bowls, watches, lighters, Danbury Mint Borden vehicles, paperweights, belt buckles.

Tim Greener
5791 Blossom Lake Dr.
Seminole, FL 33772-7405
ph: 727-398-1518
Wants anything (except magazine ads) advertising Elsie the Cow or her family: clocks, signs, pins, watches, salt and pepper shakers, cookie jars, etc.

Robb Johnson
1155 Crescent Lake Rd.
Waterford Township, MI 48327
ph: 810-673-2804
Wants to buy Borden items.

Ron Selcke
P.O. Box 237
Bloomingdale, IL 60108-0237
ph: 630-543-4848
Wants Elsie games, cookbooks, comic books, cups, glasses, Christmas cards, books, pictures, blotters, postcards, clocks, signs, neon signs, Borden Milk bottles and creamers, Borden Milk postcards, Borden Condensed Milk trade cards.

Dealers

Marty Blank
P.O. Box 405
Flushing, NY 11365-0405
ph: 516-485-8071
e-mail: martyadver@aol.com
Wants to buy Elsie, Campbell Kids, Reddy Kilowatt, Coke, figural vinyl advertising and Country Store items.

ELVES

(see also GNOMES)

Collectors

Walter Dworkin
8 Rugby Rd.
Westbury, NY 11590
ph: 516-334-4674
Collects Pixieware - those oh-so-cute ceramic containers for condiments, liquor, hor d'oeuvres, salt and pepper, and oil and vinegar bade by the Holt-Howard company of Stamford, CT from 1958 to the early 1960s.

Sally Kimmel
1471 Lark Lane
Concord, CA 94521-2942
ph: 510-676-2857
e-mail: sallyraek@yahoo.com
Elf lover wants to buy elves and pixies: Christmas tree, wall, hanging, table decorations and ornaments and any other holiday (Easter, Valentines Day, St. Patrick's Day, etc.) elves, pixies, fairies and leprechauns - anything with elves!

EMBALMING ITEMS

(see FUNERAL ITEMS)

EMBROIDERY

(see MILITARIA, Silk Embroideries; TEXTILES)

ENAMELS

(see also BATTERSEA ENAMEL BOXES; BOXES; CLOISONNE; GLASS; METAL ITEMS; RUSSIAN ITEMS)

Clubs/Associations

Tom Ellis, Ed.
Enamelist Society, The
Magazine: Glass on Metal
P.O. Box 310
Newport, KY 41072
ph: 609-291-3800
fax: 606-291-1849
e-mail: enamel@craftweb.com
web: http://www.craftweb.com/org/enamel/enamel.htm
Over 1300 members worldwide with interests in all aspects of enameling - glass on metal; the magazine is published 5 times per year plus 2 bulletins; conventions, exhibitions.

ENDANGERED SPECIES

(see also ANIMAL COLLECTIBLES; ANIMAL TROPHIES; IVORY; NAUTICAL ANTIQUES; SCRIMSHAW; SPORTING COLLECTIBLES)

Misc. Services

World Wildlife Fund
1250 24th Street, NW
Washington, DC 20037
Check with TRAFFIC USA regarding regulations for importing and exporting wildlife or wildlife products; TRAFFIC USA is the wildlife trade monitoring program of the World Wildlife Fund.

Canadian

Misc. Services

Canadian Wildlife Service Headquarters, CITES Administrator
351 St. Joseph Blvd., 3rd Floor
Place Vincent Massey
Hull, Quebec K1A 0H3
Canada
ph: 819-953-1411
fax: 819-994-4065
Canadian HQ contact for inquiries regarding CITES (the Convention on International Trade in Endangered Species of Wild Fauna & Flora); an international agreement that protects endangered and threatened species of animals & plants.

Canadian Wildlife Service, Pacific & Yukon Region
P.O. Box 340
Delta, British Columbia V4K 3Y3
Canada
ph: 604-946-8643
fax: 604-946-8359
Regional Canadian contact for inquiries regarding CITES (the Convention on International Trade in Endangered Species of Wild Fauna & Flora); an international agreement that protects endangered and threatened species of animals & plants

Canadian Wildlife Service, Western & Northern Region
115 Perimeter Road
Saskatoon, Saskatchewan S7N 0X4
Canada
ph: 306-975-4290
fax: 306-975-4089
Regional Canadian contact for inquiries regarding CITES (the Convention on International Trade in Endangered Species of Wild Fauna & Flora); an international agreement that protects endangered and threatened species of animals & plants

Environment Canada, Canadian Wildlife Service, Ontario Region
70 Fountain St. E
Guelph, Ontario N1H 3N6
Canada
ph: 519-826-2100
fax: 519-826-2108
e-mail: enviroinfo@ec.gc.ca
web: http://www.cciw.ca/green-lane/wildlife/intro.html
Regional Canadian contact for inquiries regarding CITES (the Convention on International Trade in Endangered Species of Wild Fauna & Flora); an international agreement that protects endangered and threatened species of animals & plants

Canadian Wildlife Service, Atlantic Region
P.O. Box 1590
Sackville, New Brunswick E0A 3C0
Canada
ph: 506-364-5044
fax: 506-364-5062
Regional Canadian contact for inquiries regarding CITES (the Convention on International Trade in Endangered Species of Wild Fauna & Flora); an international agreement that protects endangered and threatened species of animals & plants

Canadian Wildlife Service, Quebec Region
C.P. 10100
Ste-Foy, Quebec G1V 4H5
Canada
ph: 418-649-6122
fax: 418-649-6475
Regional Canadian contact for inquiries regarding CITES (the Convention on International Trade in Endangered Species of Wild Fauna & Flora); an international agreement that protects endangered and threatened species of animals & plants

National Marine Fisheries Ser.

Misc. Services

Special Agent in Charge
NOAA/NMFS Office of Enforcement, Northeast Region
1 Blackburn Drive, Room 206
Gloucester, MA 01930
ph: 978-281-9213
fax: 978-281-9317
National Oceanic & Administration/ National Marine Fisheries Service enforcement office, Northeast Region; call to join the NOAA Fisheries Enforcement PARTNERS program to help find solutions to marine resource problems.

National Marine Fisheries Service, Office of Protected Resources (F/PR)
1335 East-West Highway
Silver Spring, MD 20910
ph: 301-713-2332
e-mail: Thomas.McIntyre@noaa.gov
web: http://www.nmfs.gov/
Contact for current information on endangered marine life (whales, fish, dolphins); for most other flora and fauna contact U.S. Fish & Wildlife Service; point of contact for issues relating to the Endangered Species Act.

Nat. Marine Fisheries Serv., Asst. Administrator for Fisheries, c/o Permit Div.
Office of Protected Resources & Habitat Prog.
1335 East-West Hwy., Rm 7324
Silver Spring, MD 20910
ph: 301-713-2289
Contact for permits and inquiries regarding The Marine Mammal Protection Act for all whales, dolphins, seals, and sea lions (i.e. marine mammals other than polar bears, manatees, otters, walruses and dungongs.)

Chief
NOAA/NMFS Office of Enforcement, Headquarters
8484 Georgia Ave., Ste. 415
Silver Spring, MD 20910
ph: 301-417-2300
fax: 301-427-2055
National Oceanic & Administration/ National Marine Fisheries Service Office of Enforcement, Headquarters; call to join the NOAA Fisheries Enforcement PARTNERS program to help find solutions to marine resource problems.

Special Agent in Charge
NOAA/NMFS Office of Enforcement, Southeast Region
9721 Executive Center Drive, Room 130
Saint Petersburg, FL 33702
ph: 727-570-5344
fax: 727-570-5343
National Oceanic & Administration/ National Marine Fisheries Service enforcement office, Southeast Region; call to join the NOAA Fisheries Enforcement PARTNERS program to help find solutions to marine resource problems.

Special Agent in Charge
NOAA/NMFS Office of Enforcement, Southwest Region
501 W. Ocean Boulevard, Ste. 4400-A
Long Beach, CA 90802
ph: 562-980-4050
fax: 562-980-4058
National Oceanic & Administration/ National Marine Fisheries Service enforcement office, Southwest Region; call to join the NOAA Fisheries Enforcement PARTNERS program to help find solutions to marine resource problems.

Special Agent in Charge
NOAA/NMFS Office of Enforcement, Northwest Region
7600 Sand Point Way NE
Seattle, WA 98115
ph: 206-526-6133
fax: 206-526-6528
National Oceanic & Administration/ National Marine Fisheries Service enforcement office, Northwest Region; call to join the NOAA Fisheries Enforcement PARTNERS program to help find solutions to marine resource problems.

Special Agent in Charge
NOAA/NMFS Office of Enforcement, Alaska Region
P.O. Box 21767
Juneau, AK 99802
ph: 907-586-7225
fax: 907-586-7200
National Oceanic & Administration/ National Marine Fisheries Service enforcement office, Alaska Region; call to join the NOAA Fisheries Enforcement PARTNERS program to help find solutions to marine resource problems.

State Conservation Agencies

Misc. Services

Commissioner
Massachusetts Department of Fisheries, Wildlife & Environmental Law Enforcement
100 Cambridge Street, Rm. 1901
Boston, MA 02202
ph: 617-727-1614
e-mail: Mass.Wildlife@state.ma.us
web: http://www.magnet.state.ma.us/dfwele/dpt_toc.htm
Each state has its own wildlife laws which may differ from Federal laws. Check with state and local authorities for restrictions on ownership or commercial transactions of protected wildlife.

Chief
Rhode Island Division of Fish & Wildlife
4808 Tower Hill Rd.
Wakefield, RI 02879
ph: 401-222-3075
fax: 401-783-4460
web: http://www.state.ri.us/dem/fish&w.htm
Each state has its own wildlife laws which may differ from Federal laws. Check with state and local authorities for restrictions on ownership or commercial transactions of protected wildlife.

Director
New Hampshire Fish & Game Department
2 hazen Drive
Concord, NH 03301
ph: 603-271-3211
e-mail: info@wildlife.state.nh.us
web: http://www.wildlife.state.nh.us/home.html
Each state has its own wildlife laws which may differ from Federal laws. Check with state and local authorities for restrictions on ownership or commercial transactions of protected wildlife.

Commissioner
Maine Department of Inland Fisheries & Wildlife
284 State Street
41 State House Station
Augusta, ME 04333-0041
ph: 207-289-8000
fax: 207-287-6395
e-mail: webmaster_ifw@state.me.us
web: http://www.state.me.us/ifw/homepage.htm
Each state has its own wildlife laws which may differ from Federal laws. Check with state and local authorities for restrictions on ownership or commercial transactions of protected wildlife.

Department of Fish & Wildlife, Vermont Agency of Natural Resources
103 South Main St.
Waterbury, VT 05671-0501
ph: 802-479-3242
fax: 802-241-3205c
e-mail: jhall@fpr.anr.state.vt.us
web: http://www.anr.state.vt.us/fw/fwhome/index.htm
Each state has its own wildlife laws which may differ from Federal laws. Check with state and local authorities for restrictions on ownership or commercial transactions of protected wildlife.

Commissioner
Connecticut Department of Environmental Protection
79 Elm Street
Hartford, CT 06106-5127
ph: 860-423-3000
fax: 860-424-4051
e-mail: dep.webmaster@po.state.ct.us
web: http://dep.state.ct.us/
Each state has its own wildlife laws which may differ from Federal laws. Check with state and local authorities for restrictions on ownership or commercial transactions of protected wildlife.

Director
New Jersey Division of Fish Game & Wildlife
P.O. Box 400
Trenton, NJ 08625-040
ph: 609-292-2765
e-mail: njdivfgw@eclipse.net
web: http://www.state.nj.us/dep/fgw/
Each state has its own wildlife laws which may differ from Federal laws. Check with state and local authorities for restrictions on ownership or commercial transactions of protected wildlife.

Director
Outdoors & Natural Resources, New York Department of Environmental Conservation
50 Wolf Road
Albany, NY 12233-4750
ph: 518-457-5690
fax: 518-457-0341
e-mail: fwinfo@gw.dec.state.ny.us
web: http://www.dec.state.ny.us/website/dfwmr/
Each state has its own wildlife laws which may differ from Federal laws. Check with state and local authorities for restrictions on ownership or commercial transactions of protected wildlife.

Executive Director
Pennsylvania Game Commission
2001 Elmerton Ave.
Harrisburg, PA 17110-9797
ph: 717-787-4250
e-mail: info@pgc.state.pa.us
web: http://www.pgc.state.pa.us/
Each state has its own wildlife laws which may differ from Federal laws. Check with state and local authorities for restrictions on ownership or commercial transactions of protected wildlife.

Director
Delaware Division of Fish & Wildlife
89 Kings Highway
Dover, DE 19901
ph: 302-739-5295
e-mail: lherman@dnrec.state.de.us
web: http://www.dnrec.state.de.us/fw/fwwel.htm
Each state has its own wildlife laws which may differ from Federal laws. Check with state and local authorities for restrictions on ownership or commercial transactions of protected wildlife.

Director
Maryland Department of Natural Resources
Tawes State Office Building
Annapolis, MD 21401
ph: 410-260-8200
e-mail: mddnr@erols.com
web: http://www.dnr.state.md.us/
Each state has its own wildlife laws which may differ from Federal laws. Check with state and local authorities for restrictions on ownership or commercial transactions of protected wildlife.

Executive Director
Virginia Department of Game & Inland Fisheries
4010 W. Broad Street
Richmond, VA 23230
ph: 804-367-1000
e-mail: dgifweb@dgif.state.va.us
web: http://www.dgif.state.va.us/
Each state has its own wildlife laws which may differ from Federal laws. Check with state and local authorities for restrictions on ownership or commercial transactions of protected wildlife.

Director
West Virginia Department of Natural Resources
State Capitol Complex, Bldg. 3
1900 Kanawha Blvd.
Charleston, WV 25305-0060
ph: 304-558-2784
e-mail: wildlife@dnr.state.wv.us
web: http://www.dnr.state.wv.us/
Each state has its own wildlife laws which may differ from Federal laws. Check with state and local authorities for restrictions on ownership or commercial transactions of protected wildlife.

Executive Director
North Carolina Wildlife Resources Commission
512 N. Salisbury Street
Raleigh, NC 27604-1188
ph: 919-733-3391
web: http://www.state.nc.us/Wildlife/
Each state has its own wildlife laws which may differ from Federal laws. Check with state and local authorities for restrictions on ownership or commercial transactions of protected wildlife.

Executive Director
South Carolina Department of Natural Resources
1000 Assembly St.
Columbia, SC 29201
ph: 803-734-3888
web: http://www.dnr.state.sc.us/
Each state has its own wildlife laws which may differ from Federal laws. Check with state and local authorities for restrictions on ownership or commercial transactions of protected wildlife.

Director
Georgia Department of Natural Resources
116 Rum Creek Dr.
Forsyth, GA 31029
ph: 912-994-1438
fax: 912-933-3050
web: http://www.ganet.org/dnr/wild/
Each state has its own wildlife laws which may differ from Federal laws. Check with state and local authorities for restrictions on ownership or commercial transactions of protected wildlife.

Director
Florida Game & Fresh Water Fish Commission
620 S. Meridian St.
Tallahassee, FL 32399-1600
ph: 850-488-2975
web: http://fcn.state.fl.us/gfc/gfchome.html
Each state has its own wildlife laws which may differ from Federal laws. Check with state and local authorities for restrictions on ownership or commercial transactions of protected wildlife.

Director
Division of Game & Fish, Alabama Department of Conservation & Natural Resources
64 N. Union St.
Montgomery, AL 36130
ph: 334-242-3467 or 334-242-3465
e-mail: jscott@dcnr.state.al.us
web: http://www.dcnr.state.al.us/agfd/
Each state has its own wildlife laws which may differ from Federal laws. Check with state and local authorities for restrictions on ownership or commercial transactions of protected wildlife.

Tennessee Wildlife Resource Agency
Ellington Agricultural Center
P.O. Box 40747
Nashville, TN 37204
ph: 615-781-6500
web: http://www.state.tn.us/twra/
Each state has its own wildlife laws which may differ from Federal laws. Check with state and local authorities for restrictions on ownership or commercial transactions of protected wildlife.

Director
Mississippi Department of Wildlife, Fisheries & Parks
P.O. Box 451
Jackson, MS 39205
ph: 601-362-9212
web: http://www.mdwfp.com/
Each state has its own wildlife laws which may differ from Federal laws. Check with state and local authorities for restrictions on ownership or commercial transactions of protected wildlife.

Commissioner
Kentucky Department of Fish & Wildlife Resources
#1 Game Farm Road
Frankfort, KY 40601
ph: 502-564-3400 or 800-858-1549
e-mail: info.center@mail.state.ky.us
web: http://www.state.ky.us/agencies/fw/kdfwr.htm
Each state has its own wildlife laws which may differ from Federal laws. Check with state and local authorities for restrictions on ownership or commercial transactions of protected wildlife.

Director
Ohio Division of Wildlife
1840 Belcher Dr.
Columbus, OH 43224-1329
ph: 614-265-6300 or 800-WILDLIFE
web: http://www.dnr.state.oh.us/odnr/wildlife/wildlife.html
Each state has its own wildlife laws which may differ from Federal laws. Check with state and local authorities for restrictions on ownership or commercial transactions of protected wildlife.

Director
Division of Fish & Wildlife, Indiana Department of Natural Resources
402 W. Washington St., Rm W273
Indianapolis, IN 46204
ph: 317-232-4080
e-mail: rmaharjan@dnr.state.in.us
web: http://www.state.in.us/dnr/
Each state has its own wildlife laws which may differ from Federal laws. Check with state and local authorities for restrictions on ownership or commercial transactions of protected wildlife.

Director
Michigan Department of Natural Resources
P.O. Box 30028
Lansing, MI 48909
ph: 517-373-1263
web: http://www.dnr.state.mi.us/
Each state has its own wildlife laws which may differ from Federal laws. Check with state and local authorities

for restrictions on ownership or commercial transactions of protected wildlife.

Director
Fish & Wildlife Division, Iowa Department of Natural Resources
Wallace State Office Building
900 E Grand
Des Moines, IA 50319-0034
ph: 515-281-4687
fax: 515-281-6794
e-mail: dsantam@max.state.ia.us
web: http://www.state.ia.us/government/dnr/index.html
Each state has its own wildlife laws which may differ from Federal laws. Check with state and local authorities for restrictions on ownership or commercial transactions of protected wildlife.

Secretary
Wisconsin Department of Natural Resources
P.O. Box 7921
Madison, WI 53707
ph: 608-226-7012
e-mail: meyerg@dnr.state.wi.us
web: http://www.dnr.state.wi.us/
Each state has its own wildlife laws which may differ from Federal laws. Check with state and local authorities for restrictions on ownership or commercial transactions of protected wildlife.

Director
Minnesota Department of Natural Resources
500 Lafayette Rd.
Saint Paul, MN 55146-4040
ph: 651-296-6157
e-mail: info@dnr.state.mn.us
web: http://www.dnr.state.mn.us/
Each state has its own wildlife laws which may differ from Federal laws. Check with state and local authorities for restrictions on ownership or commercial transactions of protected wildlife.

Secretary
South Dakota Department of Game, Fish & Parks
523 East Capitol Ave.
Pierre, SD 57501-3182
ph: 605-773-3381
e-mail: Wildinfo@gfp.state.sd.us
web: http://www.state.sd.us/gfp/
Each state has its own wildlife laws which may differ from Federal laws. Check with state and local authorities for restrictions on ownership or commercial transactions of protected wildlife.

Director
North Dakota Game & Fish Department
100 N. Bismark Expressway
Bismarck, ND 58501-5095
ph: 701-328-6300
fax: 701-328-6352
e-mail: ndgf@state.nd.us
web: http://state.nd.us/gnf/index.html
Each state has its own wildlife laws which may differ from Federal laws. Check with state and local authorities for restrictions on ownership or commercial transactions of protected wildlife.

Director
Montana Fish, Wildlife & Parks
1420 East Sixth
Helena, MT 59620
ph: 406-444-2950
web: http://www.fwp.state.mt.us/
Each state has its own wildlife laws which may differ from Federal laws. Check with state and local authorities for restrictions on ownership or commercial transactions of protected wildlife.

Director
Illinois Department of Natural Resources
524 South Second St.
Springfield, IL 62706
ph: 217-782-6302
e-mail: endspec@dnrmail.state.il.us
web: http://dnr.state.il.us/
Each state has its own wildlife laws which may differ from Federal laws. Check with state and local authorities for restrictions on ownership or commercial transactions of protected wildlife.

Director
Missouri Department of Conservation
P.O. Box 180
Jefferson City, MO 65102-0180
ph: 573-751-4115
fax: 573-751-4467
e-mail: internet@mail.conservation.state.mo.us
web: http://www.conservation.state.mo.us/
Each state has its own wildlife laws which may differ from Federal laws. Check with state and local authorities for restrictions on ownership or commercial transactions of protected wildlife.

Kansas Department of Wildlife & Parks
512 SE 25th Ave.
Pratt, KS 67124-8174
ph: 316-672-5911
e-mail: feedback@wp.state.ks.us
web: http://www.kdwp.state.ks.us/
Each state has its own wildlife laws which may differ from Federal laws. Check with state and local authorities for restrictions on ownership or commercial transactions of protected wildlife.

Director
Nebraska Game & Parks Commission
2200 N. 33rd St.
Lincoln, NE 68503
ph: 402-471-0641
e-mail: webmaster@ngpc.state.ne.us
web: http://ngp.ngpc.state.ne.us/gp.html
Each state has its own wildlife laws which may differ from Federal laws. Check with state and local authorities for restrictions on ownership or commercial transactions of protected wildlife.

Keith LaCaze
Louisiana Department of Wildlife & Fisheries Law enforcement Division
P.O. Box 98000
Baton Rouge, LA 70898-9000
ph: 225-765-2469
fax: 225-765-2832
e-mail: lacaze_bk@wlf.state.la.us
web: http://www.wlf.state.la.us/
Each state has its own wildlife laws which may differ from Federal laws. Check with state and local authorities for restrictions on ownership or commercial transactions of protected wildlife.

Director
Arkansas Department of Fish & Game
#2 Natural Resources Drive
Little Rock, AR 72205
ph: 501-223-6300
e-mail: lcpitcock@agfc.state.ar.us
web: http://www.agfc.state.ar.us/
Each state has its own wildlife laws which may differ from Federal laws. Check with state and local authorities for restrictions on ownership or commercial transactions of protected wildlife.

Director
Oklahoma Department of Wildlife Conservation
1801 N. Lincoln
Oklahoma City, OK 73105
ph: 405-521-3851
fax: 405-521-6535
e-mail: pmoore@odwc.state.ok.us
web: http://www.state.ok.us/~odwc/
Each state has its own wildlife laws which may differ from Federal laws. Check with state and local authorities for restrictions on ownership or commercial transactions of protected wildlife.

Executive Director
Texas Parks & Wildlife Department
4200 Smith School Rd.
Austin, TX 78744
ph: 512-389-4864
web: http://www.tpwd.state.tx.us/
Each state has its own wildlife laws which may differ from Federal laws. Check with state and local authorities for restrictions on ownership or commercial transactions of protected wildlife.

Colorado Division of Wildlife
Magazine: Colorado Outdoors
6060 Broadway
Denver, CO 80216
ph: 303-297-1192
e-mail: russ.bromby@state.co.us
web: http://www.dnr.state.co.us/wildlife/
Each state has its own wildlife laws which may differ from Federal laws. Check with state and local authorities for restrictions on ownership or commercial transactions of protected wildlife; source for hunting and fishing info.

Director
Wyoming Game & Fish Department
5400 Bishop Blvd.
Cheyenne, WY 82006
ph: 307-777-4600
fax: 307-777-4699
e-mail: bkisse@missc.state.wy.us
web: http://www.gf.state.wy.us/
Each state has its own wildlife laws which may differ from Federal laws. Check with state and local authorities for restrictions on ownership or commercial transactions of protected wildlife.

Commissioner
Idaho Department of Fish & Game
600 South Walnut Street
Boise, ID 83707
ph: 208-334-3736
e-mail: idginfo@idfg.state.id.us
web: http://www.state.id.us/fishgame/fishgame.html
Each state has its own wildlife laws which may differ from Federal laws. Check with state and local authorities for restrictions on ownership or commercial transactions of protected wildlife.

Director
Utah Department of Wildlife Resources
P.O. Box 146301
Salt Lake City, UT 84114-6301
ph: 801-538-7200
e-mail: nris.help@state.ut.us
web: http://www.nr.state.ut.us/
Each state has its own wildlife laws which may differ from Federal laws. Check with state and local authorities for restrictions on ownership or commercial transactions of protected wildlife.

Director
Arizona Game & Fish Department
2221 West Greenway Rd.
Phoenix, AZ 85023-4399
ph: 602-942-3000
web: http://www.gf.state.az.us/frames/index.html
Each state has its own wildlife laws which may differ from Federal laws. Check with state and local authorities for restrictions on ownership or commercial transactions of protected wildlife.

Director
New Mexico Department of Game & Fish
405 Galisteo
P.O. Box 25112
Santa Fe, NM 87504
ph: 505-827-7911 or 800-862-9310
fax: 505-827-7915
e-mail: web_adm@gmfsh.state.nm.us
web: http://www.gmfsh.state.nm.us/
Each state has its own wildlife laws which may differ from Federal laws. Check with state and local authorities for restrictions on ownership or commercial transactions of protected wildlife.

Director
Nevada Department of Wildlife
P.O. Box 10678
1100 Valley Road
Reno, NV 89520
ph: 702-688-1500
fax: 702-688-1595
e-mail: ndowinfo@govmail.state.nv.us
web: http://www.state.nv.us/cnr/nvwildlife/
Each state has its own wildlife laws which may differ from Federal laws. Check with state and local authorities for restrictions on ownership or commercial transactions of protected wildlife.

Director
California Department of Fish & Game
1416 Ninth St.
Sacramento, CA 95814
ph: 916-653-7664
e-mail: jedwards@hq.dfg.ca.gov
web: http://dfg.ca.gov/
Each state has its own wildlife laws which may differ from Federal laws. Check with state and local authorities for restrictions on ownership or commercial transactions of protected wildlife.

Director
Hawaii Division of Fish & Game
1151 Punchbowl Street
Honolulu, HI 96813
ph: 808-587-0344
fax: 808-587-0360
web: http://www.hawaii.gov/dlnr/Welcome.htmlc
Each state has its own wildlife laws which may differ from Federal laws. Check with state and local authorities for restrictions on ownership or commercial transactions of protected wildlife.

Director
Oregon Department of Fish & Wildlife
2501 SW First Ave.
Portland, OR 97207
ph: 503-872-5268
web: http://www.dfw.state.or.us/
Each state has its own wildlife laws which may differ from Federal laws. Check with state and local authorities for restrictions on ownership or commercial transactions of protected wildlife.

Director
Washington Department of Fish & Wildlife
600 Capitol Way North
Olympia, WA 98501-1091
ph: 360-902-2200
fax: 360-902-2230
e-mail: webmaster@dfw.wa.gov
web: http://www.wa.gov/wdfw/
Each state has its own wildlife laws which may differ from Federal laws. Check with state and local authorities for restrictions on ownership or commercial transactions of protected wildlife.

Commissioner
Alaska Department of Fish & Game
P.O. Box 25526
Juneau, AK 99802-5526
ph: 907-465-4100
fax: 907-465-2332
e-mail: marlat@fishgame.state.ak.us
web: http://www.state.ak.us/local/akpages/FISH.GAME/
Each state has its own wildlife laws which may differ from Federal laws. Check with state and local authorities for restrictions on ownership or commercial transactions of protected wildlife.

U.S. Fish & Wildlife Service

Experts

Special Agent John Brooks
U.S. Fish & Wildlife Service
185 West F Street, Ste. 440
San Diego, CA 92101-6025
ph: 619-557-5063
fax: 619-557-2997
e-mail: John_L_Brooks@fws.gov
web: http://www.fws.gov
Specializes in regulations regarding endangered species; will direct you in the realm of Federal wildlife laws as they relate to your business.

Misc. Services

Regional Director
U.S. Fish & Wildlife Service, Region 5
300 Westgate Center Drive
Hadley, MA 01035-9589
ph: 413-253-8200
e-mail: terri_edwards@mail.fws.gov
web: http://www.fws.gov/r5fws/
Regional U.S. Fish & Wildlife Service contact for inquiries regarding laws pertaining to endangered and threatened species of wild fauna and wild flora; covers CT, DE, DC, ME, MD, MA, NH, NJ, NY, PA, RI. VT, VA, WV.

U.S. Fish & Wildlife Service, Office of Endangered Species
4401 N. Fairfax Dr.
Arlington, VA 22203
ph: 703-358-2171
Contact for current information on endangered flora and fauna species, other than marine (in which case contact National Marine Fisheries Service); point of contact for issues relating to the Endangered Species Act and the Lacey Act.

U.S. Fish & Wildlife Service, Office of Management Authority
4401 N. Fairfax Drive, Room 430
Arlington, VA 22203
ph: 703-358-2104
Contact for permits and inquiries regarding The Convention on International Trade in Endangered Species of Wild Fauna & Flora (CITES).

U.S. Fish & Wildlife Service, Office of Management Authority
4401 N. Fairfax Drive, Room 430
Arlington, VA 22203
ph: 703-358-2104
Contact for permits and inquiries regarding The Marine Mammal Protection Act (only for certain marine animals, specifically polar bears, manatees, otters, walruses and dungongs); also regarding Elephants and ivory.

U.S. Fish & Wildlife Service, Division of Law Enforcement
P.O. Box 3247
Arlington, VA 22203-3247
ph: 703-358-1949
Check with the U.S. Fish & Wildlife Service about regulations for importing and exporting wildlife or wildlife products.

Regional Director
U.S. Fish & Wildlife Service, Region 4
1875 Century Blvd.
Atlanta, GA 30345
ph: 404-679-7292
fax: 404-679-7286
web: http://www.fws.gov/r4eao/
Regional U.S. Fish & Wildlife Service contact for inquiries regarding laws pertaining to endangered and threatened species of wild fauna and wild flora; covers AL, AR, FL, GA, KY, LA, MS, NC, SC, TN, Puerto Rico, U.S. Virgin Islands.

Asst. Reg. Dir. for Ext. Affairs Dir.
U.S. Fish & Wildlife Service, Region 3
One Federal Drive, 6th Floor
BHW Federal Building
Fort Snelling, MN 55111
ph: 612-725-5360
e-mail: r3_pao@fws.gov
web: http://www.fws.gov/r3pao/
Regional U.S. Fish & Wildlife Service contact for inquiries regarding laws pertaining to endangered and threatened species of wild fauna and wild flora; covers IL, IN, IA, MI, MN, MO, OH, WI.

Regional Director
U.S. Fish & Wildlife Service, Region 6
134 Union Blvd.
Lakewood, CO 80228
ph: 303-236-7917
e-mail: r6ea_web@fws.gov
web: http://www.r6.fws.gov/
Regional U.S. Fish & Wildlife Service contact for inquiries regarding laws pertaining to endangered and threatened species of wild fauna and wild flora; covers CO, KS, MT, NE, ND, SD, UT, WY.

Regional Director
U.S. Fish & Wildlife Service, Region 2
P.O. Box 1306
Albuquerque, NM 87103
ph: 505-766-2321
web: http://ifw2irm2.irm1.r2.fws.gov/
Regional U.S. Fish & Wildlife Service contact for inquiries regarding laws pertaining to endangered and threatened species of wild fauna and wild flora; covers AZ, NM, OK, TX.

Regional Director
U.S. Fish & Wildlife Service, Region 1
911 N.E. 11th Ave.
Portland, OR 97232-4181
ph: 503-231-6121
web: http://www.r1.fws.gov/
Regional U.S. Fish & Wildlife Service contact for inquiries regarding laws pertaining to endangered and threatened species of wild fauna and wild flora; covers CA, HI, ID, NV, OR, WA, American Samoa, Marinas Islands, Guam.

Chuck Young
U.S. Fish & Wildlife Service, Region 7
1011 E. Tudor Rd.
Anchorage, AK 99503
ph: 907-786-3909
fax: 907-786-3844
e-mail: chuck_young@fws.gov
web: http://www.r7.fws.gov/
Regional U.S. Fish & Wildlife Service contact for inquiries regarding laws pertaining to endangered and threatened species of wild fauna and wild flora; covers Alaska.

ENESCO

(see also COLLECTIBLES [MODERN]; COLLECTIBLES [MODERN], Ornaments [Enesco])

Experts

Steve Johnson
4003 Jefferson St.
Sioux City, IA 51108
Consultant to "The Official Price Guide to Pottery and Porcelain."

Juarine Woolridge
418 Country Lane
Mount Vernon, MO 65712-1906
Consultant to "The Official Price Guide to Pottery and Porcelain."

ENGINES

(see also BOATS, Engines; FARM MACHINERY; LAWN MOWERS; MAYTAG; MODELS; STEAM-OPERATED, Models & Equipment; TRACTORS; WASHING MACHINES)

Collectors

Tom Copper
Tom's Small Engines
1416 Ralapen St.
Roxboro, NC 27573-4232
ph: 336-599-6908
e-mail: tcopper@interpath.com
web: http://home.interpath.net/tcopper/
Collector of Maytag, Briggs & Stratton and other engines; repairs, rebuilds, and restores most small engines; locates parts and/or related supplies and services.

Ed & Karen Laginess
2211 W. Sigler Rd.
Carleton, MI 48117-9581
ph: 734-654-9269 or 734-241-9403
Wants to buy unusual flywheel engines and old spark plugs.

Experts

Charles Chiarchiaro
Owls Head Transportation Museum
Rte. 73 Box 277
Owls Head, ME 04854
ph: 207-594-4418
fax: 207-594-4410
e-mail: ohtm@midcoast.com
web: http://www.ohtm.org/
Mr. Chiarchiaro is an expert in pre-1910 internal combustion and steam engines, and related technologies.

Museums/Libraries

Rod Groenewold
Antique Gas & Steam Engine Museum, Inc.
Newsletter: Ignitor
2040 Santa Fe Ave.
Vista, CA 92083-1534
ph: 760-941-1791 or 800-587-2286
fax: 760-941-0690
e-mail: rod@netimes.net
web: http://www.agsem.com/
40-acre living history museum focused on the period (1840-1950). Collections include historic agricultural and industrial equipment. Reference library on-site. Biennial Threshing Bee and Antique Engine Shows.

Periodicals

Erika Daileda
Wise Owl Worldwide Publications
Magazine: Model Engineers' Workshop
4314 West 238th St. - Dept. MACR
Torrance, CA 90505-4509
ph: 310-375-6258
fax: 310-375-0548
e-mail: wiseowl@sprintmail.com
An English magazine published eight times per year; helps the amateur machinist get the most from his tools and equipment in the home engineering workshop.

Gasoline

Book Sellers

Alan C. King
King's Books
P.O. Box 86
Radnor, OH 43066-0086
ph: 614-595-3332
Carries tractor and gas engine manuals.

Clubs/Associations

Alvin Confer
Tri-State Gas Engine & Tractor Association, Inc.
9597 W. Division Rd.
Dunkirk, IN 47336
ph: 765-369-2656

Sharon Gotcher
North Texas Antique Tractor & Engine Club
308 Gwendola
Mc Kinney, TX 75070
ph: 972-562-8697
e-mail: ntextrac@cyberramp.net
web: http://www.cyberramp.net/~ntextrac/index.htm
Meet regularly to share knowledge and interest in the tractors, engines and farm equipment that mechanized our early 20th century farms.

Jerry MacMartin, WebMaster
Early Day Gas Engine & Tractor Association, Inc.
Newsletter: National, The
570 Corliss Way
Campbell, CA 95008
ph: 408-378-4259
fax: 408-378-1390
e-mail: jemm@prodigy.net
web: http://www.ave.net/~edgeta/
A national organization with 90 regional "Branches" interested in early gas engines and tractors.

Collectors

Rob Skinner
Rusty Iron Gallery
e-mail: rskinner@rustyiron.com
web: http://www.rustyiron.com/rustiron.html
Collects, restores and displays antique stationary engines and related farm equipment.

Dealers

David Rotigel
RD #4 Box 143
Greensburg, PA 15601
ph: 724-668-7897
e-mail: rotigel@westol.com
web: http://www.iup.edu/~xddc/
Buys, sells, trades stationary antique engines: farm, oil, steam.

Larry Sikes
Rock Ridge Farm - The Florida Tractor Connection
1813 NW 97th Terr.
Pompano Beach, FL 33071
ph: 954-527-7360
e-mail: lsikes@gate.net
web: http://www.gate.net/~lsikes/
Collects, restores, buys and sells antique tractors, stationary engines and farm equipment.

Internet Resources

Antique Gas Engine Homepage
e-mail: cprucha@iinc.com
web: http://www.iinc.com/~cprucha/index.htm

Kate Smalley
Antique Tractor Resource Page
P.O. Box 896
Branford, CT 06405
e-mail: anttrac@antiquetractors.com
web: http://www.antiquetractors.com
A complete reference site for collectors and restorers of antique tractors, stationary engines and farm equipment; also provides web sites and advertising services for businesses and individuals.

Jim Dunmyer
OldEngine.org
4440 Samaria Rd.
Temperance, MI 48182
ph: 734-854-8814
fax: 734-854-5308
e-mail: jim@toltbbs.com
web: http://www.oldengine.org/
An online site dedicated to lovers of old iron; many pictures taken at area shows.

Periodicals

Stemgas Publishing Co.
Magazine: Gas Engine Magazine
P.O. Box 328
Lancaster, PA 17608-0328
ph: 717-392-0733
fax: 717-392-1341
e-mail: weidman@pptnet.com
web: http://www.stemgas.com/
G.E.M. is the leading magazine for antique tractor and gas engine collectors; articles, ads, auctions, models, Maytag gas engines, restoration tips, histories, auctions, suppliers, parts, etc.; published monthly.

Repair Services

David Rotigel
RD #4 Box 143
Greensburg, PA 15601
ph: 724-668-7897
e-mail: rotigel@westol.com
web: http://www.iup.edu/~xddc/
Buys, sells, trades stationary antique engines: farm, oil, steam.

Suppliers

Bill Starkey
Starbolt Engine Supplies
3403 Buckeystown Pike
Adamstown, MD 21710
ph: 301-874-2821 or 301-694-6840
e-mail: starbolt4u@aol.com
Sells parts for old gas engines; mail order only; open evenings until 9 p.m.

Simpson Motors
3708 S. Amherst Hwy.
Madison Heights, VA 24572
ph: 804-929-4468
New and used Maytag engine parts, restoration supplies, engines, etc.; rebuild, restore, supply parts for early gasoline engines that powered early washing machines; no appliance parts; makes parts not otherwise available.

Steam

(see also TOYS, Steam/Hot Air)

Clubs/Associations

Berkshire Gas & Steam Engine Association, Inc.
729 Old Windsor Road
Dalton, MA 01226

Conrad Milster
International Stationary Steam Engine Society
Newsletter: ISSES Bulletin
178 Emerson Place
Brooklyn, NY 11205-3803
ph: 718-857-9524 or 718-636-3694
Members interested in the history, documentation and preservation of stationary steam engines throughout the world; publishes a quarterly "Bulletin" and an annual "Journal."

Collectors

Bruce Cynar
10023 St. Clair's Retreat
Fort Wayne, IN 46825
ph: 219-489-5004
e-mail: oldtchnlgy@aol.com
Wants steam engines (small but not toys), steam whistles, and steam gauges.

Museums/Libraries

Dixie Gun Work's Old Car & Steam Engine Museum
1412 Reelfoot Ave.
Union City, TN 38261
ph: 901-885-0561
fax: 901-885-0440
e-mail: dixiegun@iswt.com
web: http://www.dixiegun.com

EPHEMERA

(see ADVERTISING COLLECTIBLES; PAPER COLLECTIBLES)

EQUIPMENT

(see MACHINERY & EQUIPMENT; RAILROADS)

ERECTOR SETS

(see TOYS, Construction Sets [Erector])

EROTICA

(see also BATHING BEAUTIES, Nudies & Naughties; PIN-UP ART; PLAYBOY ITEMS; STRIPTEASE)

Auction Services

Robert Bessette
Green Dragon Arts
P.O. Box 588
Burlington, VT 05402-0588
ph: 802-862-1930
fax: 802-862-1930
e-mail: grdragon@together.net
Conducts auctions specializing in the sale of early erotica from 18th century to present; also underground adult comics and men's girlie magazines.

Gail Wolpin, ISA
Phoebus Auction Gallery
14-16 E. Mellen St.
Hampton, VA 23663
ph: 757-722-9210
fax: 757-723-2280
e-mail: bwelch@phoebusauction.com
web: http://www.phoebusauction.com
Conducts auctions of antiques, collectibles, estates, furniture, decorative and fine arts, etc.

Collectors

Bizarre Lady
P.O. Box 1252
Dayton, OH 45401
Wants to buy old erotica.

Mitch O'Connell
6425 N. Newgard
Chicago, IL 60626
Wants oddball and offbeat sexy and sexist kitsch and tasteless; artwork, gag gifts, figurines, postcards, photos, magazines, etc.

Hasco Enterprises
P.O. Box 857
Wynne, AR 72396-0857
Wants erotica, semi-nude: real photos featuring sexy lingerie, men magazines showing sexy women.

Dealers

Edward Swain
P.O. Box 7420
Wayne, PA 19087
ph: 610-688-2882
Erotic fine art: American, European, Asian; bought and sold.

Edward Swain
Edward Swain Erotic Fine Art
P.O. Box 7420
Wayne, PA 19087-7420
ph: 610-688-2882
fax: 610-688-2882
Buys and sells all types of erotic fine art and artifacts: American paintings, drawings, prints, sculpture and photos; European and Asian artists of the 18th-20th C.; no catalogs at this time but photos of specific items upon request.

Miss Naomi Antiques & Erotica
Box 1421
Lutz, FL 33549-1421
ph: 813-949-3412
fax: 813-949-3148
e-mail: misnaomi@gte.net
web: http://www.missnaomi.com/
Wants erotic art, all mediums, for wall or display.

Experts

Terry Arellano
EroticArt.com
P.O. Box 6276
2191 S. El Camino Real, Ste. 6
San Mateo, CA 94403-0991
ph: 888-887-3444 or 650-906-8003
fax: 650-577-1485
e-mail: Terry@eroticart.com
web: http://www.eroticart.com/main.html
Collector, dealer, expert, appraiser of fine erotic art.

Internet Resources

Terry Arellano
EroticArt.com
P.O. Box 6276
2191 S. El Camino Real, Ste. 6
San Mateo, CA 94403-0991
ph: 888-887-3444 or 650-906-8003
fax: 650-577-1485
e-mail: Terry@eroticart.com
web: http://www.eroticart.com/main.html
The international marketplace for buyers and sellers of erotic art.

ESTATE JEWELRY

(see GEMS & JEWELRY)

EXIT GLOBES

Collectors

Michael Bruner
2615 Echo Lane
Ortonville, MI 48462
ph: 248-627-6351
Wants exit globes in all style, shapes and colors.

EXONUMIA

(see COINS; BADGES; BOOKS, Reference [Exonumia]; FRATERNAL ORGANIZATION ITEMS; MEDALS, ORDERS & DECORATIONS; POLITICAL COLLECTIBLES; TOKENS; VETERAN ITEMS; WOODEN MONEY)

EXPOSITIONS

(see WORLD'S FAIRS & EXPOSITIONS)

EYE RELATED ITEMS

(see also MEDICAL, DENTAL & PHARMACEUTICAL; OPTICAL ITEMS)

Eyecups

Collectors

Ken Jermac
215 Westridge Ct.
Chapin, SC 29036-8725
ph: 803-345-9780
e-mail: jjermac@aol.com
Buys and trades eyecups and eye related items.

Dealers

Doris K. Bagwell, R.N.
Bagwell Antiques
5607 Concord Dr.
Jackson, MS 39211-4239
ph: 601-956-3508
fax: 601-956-4190
e-mail: DKay5607@aol.com
Wants to buy eye wash baths (eye cups).

Eyeglasses

Appraisers

J. William Rosenthal, MD, ISA
3434 Prytania St., Ste. 250
New Orleans, LA 70115-3551
ph: 504-891-1988 or 504-895-1673
fax: 504-845-1657
e-mail: JWRosenHar@aol.com
Buys, sells, specializes in and appraises visual aids, spectacles, lorgnettes, opera glasses; author of "Spectacles and Other Visual Aids: A History and Guide to Collecting."

Collectors

Charles Letocha
444 Rathton Rd.
York, PA 17403
ph: 717-846-0428
fax: 717-854-9728
Wants to buy antique spectacles, opthalmoscopes, spectacle catalogs, trade cards, etc.

W.H. Marshall
P.O. Box 1023
Melrose, FL 32666-1023
Wants to buy eye related antiques, optic trade signs, advertising, memorabilia, rare glasses, etc.

D & L
P.O. Box 1411
Cuyahoga Falls, OH 44224
Wants to buy pre-1935 eyeglasses of all kinds and quantities; send photos and/or descriptions.

John Boggs
P.O. Box 66833
Seattle, WA 98166-0833
Wants to buy eyeglasses from the 1960s or older including unused frames and especially round lens wire rim; minimum seven; also buying real ugly jewelry and cuff links.

Dealers

Ed Welch
RFD 3 Box 1290
Winslow, ME 04901
e-mail: metiques@mint.net
web: http://www.metiques.com/catalog/glasses.html
Specializes in eyeglasses, spectacles, related tools and optical equipment.

Gail Busche
Archangel Antiques
334 East Ninth St.
New York, NY 10003-7924
ph: 212-260-9313
Buying antique buttons, cuff links, eye glasses, and vintage lighters; always seeking fine examples such as enamel Deco and Art Nouveau.

Museums/Libraries

Optometry Museum, The
338 W. Tenth Ave.
Columbus, OH 43210
ph: 614-292-2788
Large collection of eyeglasses once owned by famous people; also spectacle styles on display as well as related items.

Here are some tips when contacting someone listed in this book:

■ When requesting information about a particular item, include a description (material, dimensions, maker's mark, model number, etc.) and a photo, sketch, or photocopy of the item in question.

■ Always ask if there are charges for samples or for the services requested.

■ When writing, please be sure to include a Large (#10 business size) Self-Addressed and Stamped Envelope (LSASE) if requesting a reply or the return of photographs.

■ Never call collect unless otherwise directed. When calling, be considerate of time zone differences and always ask if the party you are calling has time to talk. When leaving an answering machine message, always instruct the party to call you back collect.

FAIRIES

(see ELVES; GNOMES; TOOTH FAIRY)

FAIRINGS

Experts

Mel & Barbara Alpren
14 Carter Rd.
West Orange, NJ 07052-4612
ph: 201-731-9427
Advisor to "Warman's Antiques & Collectibles Price Guide."

Janice & Richard Vogel
4720 SE Fort King St.
Ocala, FL 34470-1501
ph: 352-694-5776
fax: 352-694-7330
e-mail: vogels@atlantic.net

Ray Begley
2 Lydiate Ash Road
Bromsgrove, Worcestershire B61 OHU
U.K.
ph: (44) 121 457 9181
fax: (44) 121 457 9212
e-mail: fairings@globalnet.co.uk
web: http://www.users.global.net.co.uk/~fairings/
Collector and expert in Conta & Boehme fairings and match holders/strikers.

FAIRS

(see CARNIVAL ITEMS; WORLD'S FAIRS & EXPOSITIONS)

FAIRY LAMPS

(see also LAMPS & LIGHTING, Miniature; PERFUME LAMPS)

Clubs/Associations

Jim & Pat Sapp
Fairy Lamp Club
Newsletter: Fairy Lamp Newsletter
6422 Haystack Rd.
Alexandria, VA 22310-3308
ph: 703-971-3229
fax: 703-971-8432
e-mail: sapp@erols.com
Fair lamp collector, editor of newsletter, member of Night Light Miniature Lamp Club, a club for collectors of candle burning lamps.

Collectors

George A. Coupe
1243 1st St. S.E.
Washington, DC 20003
ph: 202-554-1000 or 800-368-5466
fax: 202-863-0775
Wants to buy fairy lamps.

Jim & Pat Sapp
6422 Haystack Rd.
Alexandria, VA 22310-3308
ph: 703-971-3229
fax: 703-971-8432
e-mail: sapp@erols.com
Collector wants to buy Victorian era fairy lamps; editor of newsletter, member of Night Light Miniature Lamp Club.

Bob Ruf
4201 Palomino
Reno, NV 89509-2939
fax: 775-747-2675
Wants to buy fairy lamps.

FAN CLUBS

(see also AUTOGRAPHS, Celebrity; COMIC BOOKS; CHARACTER COLLECTIBLES; MOVIE MEMORABILIA; PERSONALITIES; PHOTOGRAPHS, Celebrity; SCIENCE FICTION; TELEVISION SHOWS & MEMORABILIA; SPORTS COLLECTIBLES)

Clubs/Associations

Linda Kay
National Association of Fan Clubs
Newsletter: Fan Club Monitor
P.O. Box 7487
Burbank, CA 91510-7487
ph: 818-763-3280
fax: 818-752-4848
e-mail: lknafc@aol.com
web: http://www.fanclubs.com/
An international organization dedicated to promoting fan clubs from around the world in all fields of entertainment; has directory of over 2,000 fan clubs.

Tenata Lima
International Collectors Friends Club
Magazine: Radical Collectors
Nossa Sra. Copacabana J089 Apt. 1101
P.O. Box 44028
Rio De Janeiro, 22062-970
Brazil
International club of fans and fan clubs.

Internet Resources

Fan Clubs for Classic Movie Stars
e-mail: classicfilm@miningco.com
web: http://classicfilm.tqn.com/library/weekly/aa050398.htm
Online source of fan clubs, both online clubs as well as snail mail clubs.

Periodicals

Harry Hopkins, Pub.
FANDATA Publications
Directory: FANDOM Directory
7614 Cervantes Ct.
Springfield, VA 22152-1608
ph: 703-913-5575 or 888-FAN-DATA
fax: 703-913-5575
e-mail: fandata@aol.com
web: http://members.aol.com/fandata/index.htm
Fandom Directory (R) lists over 20,000 fans, collectors, dealers, stores, clubs, and conventions worldwide: science fiction, TV shows, Star Trek, etc.; now in its 17th annual edition; your listing published free of charge upon request.

Hollywood Movie Archives
Directory: Fan Club Directory
P.O. Box 1566
Apple Valley, CA 92307-0030
ph: 760-247-6819 or 800-771-6746
e-mail: sales@accidental.com
web: http://24.0.45.221/archives/index.htm
How to start a fan club, where to join, movie associations, movie & TV fan clubs, authorized country music fan clubs, where to write movie & TV stars, teens, soap stars, rock and rap stars; where to write for stars' autographs.

FANS

Hand-Held

Clubs/Associations

Cynthia Fendel
Fan Association of North America
Journal: FANA Quarterly
e-mail: FanCollect@aol.com
Promotes fans as art objects and historical artifacts; supports fan research; guides members and non-members in fan collecting; encourages fan exhibits; has active grants program; holds annual conferences with lectures and displays.

Mrs. J.D. Milligan
Fan Circle International
Magazine: Fans
Cronk-Y-Voddy, Rectory Rd.
Coltishall, Norwich NR12 7HF
U.K.
e-mail: jdm@coltishall.freeserve.co.uk
web: http://ourworld.compuserve.com/homepages/helenakitt/
A worldwide society to promote the interest and knowledge in all aspects of fan collecting.

Collectors

Kathy Maxwell
e-mail: katmax@magna.com.au
web: http://www.magna.com.au/~katmax/
Great website to learn about fans in antiquity; 17th through 20th century fans, Japanese and Chinese fans, and more.

Gretchen Walberg
P.O. Box 101
Sunbury, PA 17801-0101
ph: 717-286-6225
fax: 717-286-6229
e-mail: info@fancards.com
Wants hand fans with depictions: American historical, ballooning, printed or painted, World's Fair, etc.

Dorothy Fowler
201 Palmetto Court W.
St. Simons Island, GA 31522

Colin Johnson
6138 Deacon Dr.
Windermere, FL 34786-8936
ph: 610-799-2072

Cynthia Fendel
e-mail: handfanpro@aol.com
web: http://www.handfanpro.com/
Wants to buy fans: folding, advertising, commemorative, novelty, etc.; send photo or photocopy and price; Fan Association of North America (FANA) representative on CompuServe.

Cheryl Melnick
P.O. Box 790
Cupertino, CA 95015
ph: 408-559-7799 x222
e-mail: webmistress@hand-fan.org
web: http://www.hand-fan.org
Serious collector wants to buy hand-held fans for personal collection and for reenacting to teach living history to others as a volunteer.

Dealers

Eureka, I Found It! Antiques & Collectibles
P.O. Box 2192
Petaluma, CA 94953-2192
e-mail: eureka@erueka-i-found-it.com
web: http://www.eureka-i-found-it.com
An online dealer specializing in vintage textiles and clothing, toy and model steam engines, buttons, fans, Art Deco, costume jewelry, toy sewing machines.

Experts

Mary S. Frazier, Cur.
Frazier at D.H.S./Wedgwood
P.O. Box 215
Dedham, MA 02027-0215
ph: 781-843-5091
e-mail: wedgwood@hotmail.com
web: http://www.angelfire.com/ma/wsb
Wrote only book on American hand fans; lectures extensively; author of "Hunt and Allen Fans."

Wendy Blue
2118 Van Buren Dr.
Whitehall, PA 18052
ph: 610-799-2072
e-mail: bluebrd@aol.com
Lectures, writes about fans; curates; wants to buy any type of good quality hand fan: fashion accessories (ivory, tortoise, folding, cockade, etc.); advertising, historical; good graphics & condition; send photo & description & SASE.

Cynthia Fendel
e-mail: handfanpro@aol.com
web: http://www.handfanpro.com/
Has over 25 years collecting, publishing articles, speaking, and assessing collections.

Grace R. Grayson
2133 Pine Knoll Dr. #16
Walnut Creek, CA 94595-2187
ph: 925-256-0949
A FAN-atic! Collects antique and contemporary fans; European, Oriental, ethnic, etc.; also fan related advertising and literature; lecturer, writer, curator.

Paul Van Saanen
Ch. de la Becque 50
Switzerland
ph: 0041219445022 or 0041219445320
fax: 0041219441243
e-mail: Paul.vanSaanen@urbanet.ch

John Brooker
Fan Attic, The
The Square, East Rudham
King's Lynn, Norfolk PE31 8RB
U.K.
ph: c
e-mail: fanmaker@perform.demon.co.uk
web: http://www.fanmaker.demon.co.uk/
Maker of fine hand-held fans; also restores fans.

Internet Resources

International Fan Collector's Guild, The
P.O. Box 790
Cupertino, CA 95015
ph: 408-559-7799 x222
fax: 408-558-2322
e-mail: webmistress@hand-fan.org
web: http://www.hand-fan.org
The official online resource for fan collectors: fan museum, art, fan jewelry, Victorian fans, fans for sale, resources, conservation, history, books, vintage fans and more; list your fans or fan-related items on this website for free.

Misc. Services

Cynthia Fendel
Hand Fan Productions
e-mail: handfanpro@aol.com
web: http://www.handfanpro.com/
A multi-faceted resource for those with an interest in antique and collectible hand fans: speaking engagements, assessing collections, providing wedding fans are a few of the services offered.

Museums/Libraries

Braintree Historical Society
31 Tenney Rd.
Braintree, MA 02184-6512
ph: 781-848-1640
fax: 781-380-0731
web: http://
www.braintreehistoricalsoc.org/
Collection of approximately 400 hand fans; primarily American.

Colonial Williamsburg
P.O. Box C
Williamsburg, VA 23185
ph: 757-229-1000 or 800-HISTORY
e-mail: webmaster@cwf.org
web: http://www.history.org
Specializes in early American furniture and the decorative arts.

John & Mable Ringling Museum of Art
5401 Bayshore Rd.
Sarasota, FL 34243
ph: 941-359-5700
fax: 941-359-5745
e-mail: ringling@concentric.net
web: http://www.ringling.org/
Holds collection of over 150 fans.

Mrs. h. E. Alexander, Dir.
Fan Museum, The
Newsletter: Friends Newsletter
12 Crooms Hill
Greenwich, London SE10 8ER
U.K.
ph: (0) 181 305-1441
fax: (0) 181 293-1889
web: http://www.fan-museum.org/
The museum brings together art, craftsmanship, education and research to provide a unique center of interest and enjoyment for the public; the only museum in the world devoted exclusively to fan making.

Repair Services

T. W. DeLeo
Cereus, Inc.
31 Brook Lane
Cortlandt Manor, NY 10567-6501
ph: 914-737-3769 or 914-739-0754
fax: 914-737-4333
Specializes in the conservation of hand fans: folding, pleated, brise, fixed; European or Oriental.

Mechanical

(see also ELECTRICITY RELATED ITEMS)

Clubs/Associations

Nancy J. Tausssig, Mem.
American Fan Collectors Association, The
Newsletter: Fan Collector, The
P.O. Box 5473
Sarasota, FL 34277-5473
ph: 941-388-5513 or 800-964-2322
fax: 941-388-2053
e-mail: membership@fancollectors.org
web: http://www.fancollectors.org/
Interested in water powered, steam, electric, and other types of mechanical fans; the AFCA sponsors an annual convention and publishes its newsletter for 400 members.

Collectors

Kevin Shail
30 Old Middle Rd.
Brookfield, CT 06804-1131
ph: 203-775-7015
fax: 203-775-2536
Interested in old mechanical fans, especially non-electric fans such as those driven by hot-air (kerosene), water power, or wind-ups; also wants early motors.

Rick Padron
1005 E. Idlewild Ave.
Tampa, FL 33604-6831
ph: 813-238-8535 or 800-320-FANS
Serious collector wants to buy pre-1920 fans.

Howard Hazelcorn
6731 Ashley Ct.
Sarasota, FL 34241-9696
ph: 941-921-1815
Specializes in early (1889-1905) battery type electric fans.

Hilly Griffin
P.O. Box 877
Grenada, MS 38901
ph: 601-675-8270 or 601-226-3032
fax: 601-226-3439
Wants odd or unusual looking fans.

Jim Daggs
617 Main Street
Ackley, IA 50601
ph: 515-847-2623 or 515-847-2700
fax: 515-847-3588
e-mail: ludaggs@cnsinternet.com
Author of "A Scrapbook of Fans" (1997).

Michael Breedlove
1875 SE Hwy. 96
Leon, KS 67074
ph: 316-742-9995
e-mail: MGB_1@msn.com

Guinn Rigsby
4306 Idlewild Ave.
North Little Rock, AR 72116-8276
ph: 501-753-4073
e-mail: Imafanman@aol.com
Wants to buy early antique fans with brass blades and brass cages, ornate castings, 6 blades, unusual oscillating mechanisms, art deco, unusual, or mint fans; also wants pre-1910 motors, and parts and advertising related to all.

Steve Cunningham
3200 Ashland Dr.
Bedford, TX 76021-6502
ph: 817-267-9851 or 800-991-0165
fax: 817-267-0387
e-mail: cunning@cyberramp.net
web: http://www.cyberramp.net/~cunning/
Buying antique electric table fans with brass blades and brass cages; also very old ornate ceiling fans (paddle type); especially interested in very old antique electric motors; also wants books and catalogs on these items.

Mike Roberts
4416 Foxfire Way
Fort Worth, TX 76133-6704
ph: 817-294-2133
Wants to buy any odd, unusual fan in any condition; also wants motors, parts, toys and anything fan related.

Roger Anthony
23214 Whispering Willow Dr.
Spring, TX 77373-6232
ph: 281-353-4576
Wants to buy pre-1912 antique mechanical fans; electrical fans with brass guard and brass blades; battery powered and bipolar (exposed coil) fans; unusual oscillators (flaps, gyro & vane fans, etc.); water powered and wind-up fans.

Dealers

Normand Mainville
Machine Age
354 Congress St.
Boston, MA 02210
ph: 617-482-0048

Phil Massie
Wind Wizards, The
1924 Hilton Ave.
Dover, PA 17315-3834
ph: 717-764-2359
Wants antique electric fans with brass blades, related advertising and ephemera, especially metal signs, books and publications on electricity and pre-1900 electrical lighting.

Donald E. Taussig
Sanders' Antique Mall
22 N. Lemon Ave.
Sarasota, FL 34236-5711
ph: 941-366-0400
fax: 941-388-2053
e-mail: sandersant@aol.com
Buys, sells, restores ceiling and desk fans pre-1900 through 1940s: electric, hot-air, water-powered, etc.

Experts

Scott MacClymonds
Classic Fans & Lighting
10525 Airline Dr.
Houston, TX 77037
ph: 713-448-4739 or 713-697-0069
fax: 713-448-0189
Wants to buy unusual pre-1939 electric, water, kerosene power fans with ornate castings, brass blades and cages, fancy ornamentation, unusual mechanisms, ceiling or desk.

Kurt House
Cowboy Collectibles
218 Country Wood
San Antonio, TX 78216-1607
ph: 210-490-2433
fax: 210-490-3433
e-mail: cowboyhous@aol.com
Author of "Antique Mechanical Fans"; repairs, sells/buys, antique mechanical fans including electrical, fuel-driven, etc.; specializes in the restoration of antique fans and the manufacturing of fans and fan parts; wants fan information.

Museums/Libraries

Michael Breedlove
American Fan Collectors Museum
Vornado Air Circulation Systems
415 E. 13th Street
Andover, KS 67002
ph: 316-733-0035 or 800-297-0883
e-mail: membership@fancollectors.org
web: http://www.fancollectors.org/
Over 350 fans on display including many rare and one-of-a-kind items, the oldest dating back to the mid-1800s; the most comprehensive collection of air moving devices in the world.

Repair Services

Sidney Lamb
1501 Kesser Dr.
Plano, TX 75025
ph: 972-517-4526
Motor rewinding; old motors and choke coils rewound.

FANTASY

(see HORROR; SCIENCE FICTION)

FARM COLLECTIBLES

(see also CORN COLLECTIBLES; ENGINES; FARM MACHINERY; ANIMAL COLLECTIBLES, Horses; TOYS, Diecast; TOYS, Farm; WATCH FOBS, Farm Related; TRACTORS; WEANERS, Calf & Cow; WINDMILL COLLECTIBLES)

Collectors

Ron Bennett
Locust Lane Antiques
R1 1870 Strong Rd.
Victor, NY 14564-9134
ph: 716-657-7505
e-mail: bbmimi@aol.com
Wants farm yard tools: corn shellers, hay trolleys & forks, walking ploughs, hog oilers, cast iron seats, tool boxes, seamless cotton bags, corn and grass seed bags.

Jim Moffet
P.O. Box 200
Modesto, IL 62667-0200
ph: 217-439-7358
Interested in buying farm items such as handheld corn shellers, horse hay forks, etc.

Gary Van Hoozer, Ed.
P.O. Box 812
Tarkio, MO 64491
ph: 660-736-4528
Collects and specializes in farm toys.

Dealers

Stephen G. Del Sordo
Heritage Resource Group
305 Oakley St.
Cambridge, MD 21613
ph: 410-228-8934
fax: 410-221-8061
e-mail: delsordo@shore.intercom.net
web: http://www.heritageresource.com/
A cultural resource management/ historic preservation firm that has contracts to locate, provide, authenticate artifacts for museums and collectors; areas of expertise include architecture, industry, domestic, agriculture, and maritime.

Experts

Philip C. Whitney
303 Fisher Rd.
Fitchburg, MA 01420-1548
ph: 978-342-1350
Specializes in pricing and identification of farm tools.

Museums/Libraries

Esther Munroe Smith, Lib.
Billings Farm Museum
P.O. Box 489
Woodstock, VT 05091
ph: 802-457-2355
e-mail: billings-farm@valley.net
Museum of farm life & technology of the late 19th century; darying, haying, general store, ice cutting, apple orchard, etc.

New York State Historical Association & The Farmers' Museum, Inc., The
P.O. Box 800
Lake Road
Cooperstown, NY 13326
ph: 607-547-1450 or 888-547-1450
e-mail: nysha1@aol.com
web: http://www.farmersmuseum.org/

Landis Valley Farm Museum
2451 Kissel Hill Rd.
Lancaster, PA 17601
ph: 717-569-0401
fax: 717-560-1247
web: http://www.landisvalleymuseum.org/

Carroll County Farm Museum
500 S. Center St.
Westminster, MD 21157-5615
ph: 410-848-7775 or 800-654-4645
fax: 410-876-8544
web: http://www.fieldtrip.com/md/0a848777.htm
Focuses on Victoriana in rural America.

Ron & Lois Smith
Neverrest Farm Family Museum
1911 Harper Rd.
Mason, MI 48854-9260
ph: 517-676-9391
Located on a working farm and open on a "by chance" or by appointment.

David Huey
Living History Farms
2600 N.W. 111th St.
Urbandale, IA 50322
ph: 515-278-2400 or 515-278-5286
fax: 515-278-9808
A 600-acre, open-air museum specializing in the past 300 years of Midwest agriculture; interpreters in period clothing work out of authentic buildings with historically accurate tools and machinery to recreate routines of early farmers.

W. Vernon, Dir.
National Agricultural Center & Hall of Fame
630 Hall of Fame Dr.
Bonner Springs, KS 66012
ph: 913-721-1075 or 913-721-3355
fax: 913-721-1075
web: http://www.aghallloffame.com/
Collection of a wide range of farming and farm family related items: plows, tools, implements, art, dishes, schoolhouse items, etc.

Periodicals

Richard Van Vleck
Greybird Publishing
Newsletter: Scientific, Medical & Mechanical Antiques
P.O. Box 412
Taneytown, MD 21787
ph: 301-447-2680
e-mail: smma@americanartifacts.com
web: http://americanartifacts.com/smma/
For collectors, dealers and researchers; recent articles include reaper knife grinders, grain cradles, early cow milkers, hand corn shellers and rope machines; free ads for subscribers.

Gary Van Hoozer, Ed.
Magazine: Farm Antiques News
P.O. Box 812
Tarkio, MO 64491
ph: 660-736-4528
For collectors, restorers, traders of all types/sizes of old (pre-1950) farm items: tractors, horse & other machinery, toys, etc.

Cast Iron Seats

Clubs/Associations

Eunice Friedly, Editor
Cast Iron Seat Collectors Association
Newsletter: CISCA Newsletter
P.O. Box 14
Ionia, MO 65335
ph: 660-285-3451
Club for collectors of cast iron seats from farm implements and machinery; newsletter contains articles, notices of meets and shows, auction sale results, collector profiles.

Haying Tools

Collectors

Robert Rauhauser
RR 2 Box 766
Thomasville, PA 17364-9622
Buys haying tools (forks, carriers & knives), corn items (shellers, planter lids, etc.), hog oilers, wrenches, horse mower tool box lids, etc.

Hog Oilers

Collectors

Robert Rauhauser
RR 2 Box 766
Thomasville, PA 17364-9622
Author of "Good-Bye Mr. Louse - Hog Oiler Patents 1903 to 1995."

Literature

Collectors

Clarence L. Goodburn
101 W. Main
Madelia, MN 56062-1439
ph: 507-642-3281
fax: 507-642-3281
e-mail: goodlit@praiorie.lakes.com
Wants to buy sales literature, calendars, magazines, hardback books, etc. about farm tractors and equipment, crawler tractors, heavy construction, mining equipment, logging equipment, and trucks.

David Yates
321 West Church St.
Genoa, IL 60135
ph: 815-784-3369
e-mail: deere@tbcnet.com
Wants to buy farm sales literature, all brands.

FARM MACHINERY

(see also AUTOMOBILIA; ENGINES; FARM COLLECTIBLES; HORSE-DRAWN VEHICLES; MACHINERY & EQUIPMENT; STEAM-OPERATED, Models & Equipment; TOYS, Farm; TRACTORS; WINDMILL COLLECTIBLES)

Appraisers

Jay Proost
American Society of Agricultural Appraisers, Inc.
P.O. Box 186
Twin Falls, ID 83303-0186
ph: 208-733-2323 or 208-734-7570
fax: 208-733-2326
e-mail: JProost@micron.net
Members of this association appraise livestock, horses and farm equipment.

Auction Services

Iron Horse Auction Co.
413 South Hancock St.
P.O. Box 1267
Rockingham, NC 28380
ph: 910-997-2248 or 800-997-2248
fax: 910-895-1530
e-mail: horse@infoave.net
web: http://www.auctionweb.com/ironhorse/
Conducts auctions specializing in the sale of antique steam engines, tractors and farm related items.

Bill Dean
Waverly Sale Co.
P.O. Box 355
Waverly, IA 50677
ph: 319-352-2804
fax: 319-352-5642
Specializes in the sale of old and new farm machinery and equipment.

Clubs/Associations

Susan Knaub
Early American Steam Engine & Old Equipment Society
P.O. Box 652
Red Lion, PA 17356
ph: 717-244-2912
Interested in old steam and gas powered equipment, especially engines, tractors and other farm machinery.

David Semmel
Antique Engine, Tractor & Toy Club, Inc.
Newsletter: AETTC Newsletter
5731 Paradise Rd.
Slatington, PA 18080-4028
ph: 610-767-4768
Organized in 1986 with over 500 members; dedicated to preservation and enjoyment of old time farm engines, tractors and related toys; newsletter three times per year.

David Schnakenberg
Farm Machinery Advertising Collectors
10108 Tamarack Drive
Vienna, VA 22182-1843
e-mail: schnakenbergdd@erols.com

Sharon Gotcher
North Texas Antique Tractor & Engine Club
308 Gwendola
Mc Kinney, TX 75070
ph: 972-562-8697
e-mail: ntextrac@cyberramp.net
web: http://www.cyberramp.net/~ntextrac/index.htm
Meet regularly to share knowledge and interest in the tractors, engines and farm equipment that mechanized our early 20th century farms.

Internet Resources

Kate Smalley
Antique Tractor Resource Page
P.O. Box 896
Branford, CT 06405
e-mail: anttrac@antiquetractors.com
web: http://www.antiquetractors.com
A complete reference site for collectors and restorers of antique tractors, stationary engines and farm equipment; also provides web sites and advertising services for businesses and individuals.

Spencer Yost
Antique Tractor Internet Service
3160 MacBrandon Ln.
Pfafftown, NC 27040
ph: 910-924-6109
e-mail: yostsw@atis.net
web: http://www.atis.net
The oldest and most complete website on the Internet that specializes in antique tractors and farm equipment; thousands of people access the site monthly to buy and sell and research farm equipment.

Misc. Services

Austin Farms Salvage
Rte. 4 Box 241
Butler, MO 64730
ph: 660-679-4080
fax: 660-679-6488
Send $20 for a directory listing names, addresses, phone numbers of 800 used agri-parts yards; for new used and antique farm equipment.

Museums/Libraries

Bucks County Historical Society
Newsletter: Penny Lots
84 S. Pine St.
Doylestown, PA 18901-4930
ph: 215-345-0210
fax: 215-230-0823
e-mail: bchs@philadelphia.libertynet.org
web: http://www.libertynet.org/bchs
Operates three Nat. Historical Landmarks; Mercer Museum has over 50,000 tools of Early American trades/crafts; Spruance Library has research material on trades & crafts; Fonthill Museum is a concrete castle laden with tiles & treasures.

Darwin Quandt
Makoti Threshers Association Museum
P.O. Box 53
Makoti, ND 58756
ph: 701-726-5643
Show each year first full weekend in October; come see antique machines run.

W. Vernon, Dir.
National Agricultural Center & Hall of Fame
630 Hall of Fame Dr.
Bonner Springs, KS 66012
ph: 913-721-1075 or 913-721-3355
fax: 913-721-1075
web: http://www.aghallloffame.com/
Collection of a wide range of farming and farm family related items: plows, tools, implements, art, dishes, schoolhouse items, etc.

Ontario Agricultural Museum
P.O. Box 38
Milton, Ontario L9T 2Y3
Canada
ph: 905-878-8151

Periodicals

Gerald Lestz
Stemgas Publishing Co.
Magazine: Iron Men Album, The
P.O. Box 328
Lancaster, PA 17608-0328
ph: 717-392-0733
fax: 717-392-1341
e-mail: weidman@pptnet.com
web: http://www.stemgas.com/
Published six times per year; carries articles, ads, auctions for steam traction machinery: tractors, threshers, steam engines, etc.

Stemgas Publishing Co.
Directory: Steam & Gas Engine Show Directory
P.O. Box 328
Lancaster, PA 17608-0328
ph: 717-392-0733
fax: 717-392-1341
e-mail: weidman@pptnet.com
web: http://www.stemgas.com/
The annual show directory guides old-time farming enthusiasts to over 900 shows in the U.S. and Canada; $8 postpaid.

Stemgas Publishing Co.
Directory: Farm Museum Directory
P.O. Box 328
Lancaster, PA 17608-0328
ph: 717-392-0733
fax: 717-392-1341
e-mail: weidman@pptnet.com
web: http://www.stemgas.com/
Over 200 listings, ads and pictures of farm museums and exhibits in 40 states and Canada; published in cooperation with The Association of Living Historical Farm and Agricultural Museums (ALHFAM).

Christina Gargano
Heartland Communications Group, Inc.
Magazine: Farmers Hot Line & Manufacturer's Editions
1003 Central Ave.
P.O. Box 1052
Fort Dodge, IA 50501
ph: 800-247-2000 or 515-955-1600
fax: 515-574-2233
e-mail: libbie@hlipublishing.com
web: http://www.hlipublishing.com
Regional and state editions are edited for buyers and sellers of farm equipment.

Christina Gargano
Heartland Communications Group, Inc.
Magazine: Farmers Hot Line Parts Edition
1003 Central Ave.
P.O. Box 1052
Fort Dodge, IA 50501
ph: 800-247-2000 or 515-955-1600
fax: 515-574-2233
e-mail: libbie@hlipublishing.com
web: http://www.hlipublishing.com
Directory for the largest selection and the best prices of new, used, rebuilt parts and attachments.

Christina Gargano
Heartland Communications Group, Inc.
Magazine: Hot Line Farm Equipment Guide
1003 Central Ave.
P.O. Box 1052
Fort Dodge, IA 50501
ph: 800-247-2000 or 515-955-1600
fax: 515-574-2233
e-mail: libbie@hlipublishing.com
web: http://www.hlipublishing.com
The only monthly locating and pricing guide for farm equipment.

Magazine: Engineers & Engines Magazine
2240 Oak Leaf St.
P.O. Box 2757
Joliet, IL 60434-2757
ph: 815-741-2240
fax: 815-741-2243
Bi-monthly magazine: tractors, gas, steam, farm machinery, railroad.

Shawn Rogers
Magazine: Rusty Iron Monthly
P.O. Box 342
Sandwich, IL 60548-0342
ph: 815-496-9267
e-mail: rusty@indianvalley.com
Focuses on the old iron marketplace: early gas and steam engines, tractors and related equipment; published monthly: classified ads for antique tractors and gasoline engines, collectibles, literature, etc.

Kurt Aumann
Magazine: Belt Pulley, The
20114 IL Rt. 16
P.O. Box 83
Nokomis, IL 62075
ph: 217-563-2612
Features farm machinery, all makes and models, 1900-1950; antique tractors, farm machinery and equipment; bi-monthly.

Gary Van Hoozer, Ed.
Magazine: Farm Antiques News
P.O. Box 812
Tarkio, MO 64491
ph: 660-736-4528
For collectors, restorers, traders of all types/sizes of old (pre-1950) farm items: tractors, horse & other machinery, toys, etc.

Leslie McDaniel, Ed.
Magazine: Farm Collector
1503 SW 42nd St.
Topeka, KS 66609
ph: 800-682-4704 or 800-678-4883
fax: 785-274-4305
e-mail: farmcollector@cjnetworks.com
web: http://farmcollector.com
Monthly magazine focusing on the preservation of vintage farm equipment covering everything from antique tractors to engines, windmills, cream separators, horse-drawn implements, steam engines, farm toys and pedal tractors.

Magazine: Old Machinery Magazine, The
P.O. Box 1200
Port Macquarie, New South Wales 2444
Australia
ph: (02) 65 850055
fax: (02) 65 850755
e-mail: tomm_mag@turboweb.net.au
web: http://www.turboweb.net.au/oldmachinerymag/
Australian bi-monthly magazine with 16 pages of color inserts, color covers, regular feature writers; published over 13 years; focuses on stationary engines, tractors, steam and various farm machinery.

Suzanne Wright
Kelsey Publishing Ltd.
Magazine: Stationary Engine
Cudham Tithe Barn
Berrys Hill
Cudham, Kent TN16 3AG
U.K.
ph: 01959 541444
fax: 01959 541400
e-mail: info@kelsey.co.uk
web: http://www.kelsey.co.uk
A 40-page British monthly magazine for the stationary engine enthusiast: news, restorations, history.

Kelsey Publishing Ltd.
Magazine: Farm & Horticultural Equipment Collector
Cudham Tithe Barn
Berrys Hill
Cudham, Kent TN16 3AG
U.K.
ph: 01959 541444
fax: 01959 541400
e-mail: info@kelsey.co.uk
web: http://www.kelsey.co.uk
A 16-page bi-monthly illustrated British magazine solely devoted to farm equipment and implement collecting; packed with information, pictures; plus articles covering barn machinery, sawing machinery, garden machinery, hand tools, etc.

International Harvester

Clubs/Associations

Allen Dummler, Mem. Sec.
International Harvester Collectors
Newsletter: Harvester Highlights
310 Busse Hwy., Ste. 250
Park Ridge, IL 60068-3251
ph: 847-823-8612
fax: 847-683-0207
e-mail: ihcclub@aol.com
An association of International Harvester equipment and memorabilia collectors and enthusiasts; sanctions regional chapters.

Collectors

Terry & Kay Klepey
P.O. Box 553
Forks, WA 98331-0553
ph: 360-327-3726 or 360-374-5717
e-mail: slvrbllt@olypen.com
Wants to buy International Harvester items: calendars, advertisements, tools, misc.

Periodicals

Daryl Miller
Newsletter: Red Power
P.O. Box 277
Battle Creek, IA 51006
ph: 712-365-4873
Bi-monthly periodical about International Harvester and their products.

Salesman Samples

Collectors

Allan Hoover
2133 14th St.
Peru, IL 61354-1670
ph: 815-223-1159 or 815-223-1160
fax: 815-223-1499
Wants samples of walking plows, hay mowers, hay rakes, balers, cultivators, binders, reapers, windmills, silos, pitch forks, etc.

FASHION

(see CLOTHING & ACCESSORIES)

FAST FOOD COLLECTIBLES

(see also FOOD COLLECTIBLES; GLASSES, Drinking; HAMBURGERS; PREMIUMS; RESTAURANT COLLECTIBLES)

Dealers

William M. Poe
POE-pourri
220 Dominica Circle E.
Niceville, FL 32578-4085
ph: 850-897-4163
fax: 850-987-2606
e-mail: McPoes@aol.com
Buys, sells, trades; specializes in McDonald's; buys old McDonald's collections and collections of PEZ and Smurfs; publishes 80-page catalog of All fast Food Toys ($3 in USA, $6 Inter.); $3 refundable with first order of $50.

Debi Chaltraw
Debi's Fast Food Toys
437 Leslie Dr.
Frankenmuth, MI 48734
e-mail: gabrielc@cris.com
web: http://www.concentric.net/~Gabrielc/
Buys, sells, trades fast food collectibles, mint-in-package or loose, sets or singles; web site contains the McDonald's Collectors Club home page.

DeAnna Mansoor
Scribbles Toys & Collectibles
P.O. Box 93
Copperas Cove, TX 76522
ph: 254-542-8121
fax: 254-542-4427
e-mail: deanna@sagelink.net
web: http://www.sagelink.net/deanna/
Specializes in fast food collectibles from around the world; also action figures, Star Wars, Beanie Babies, Plushes, Smurfs, Care Bears, Disney, PEZ, Flintstones.

Richard Eymann
2619 E. Lynne Ln.
Phoenix, AZ 85040-4724
ph: 602-243-7064
Buy, sell, trade fast food toys; most restaurants; some foreign toys; send SASE for list.

Camille Boone
ph: 702-564-7380
fax: 702-564-7380
e-mail: Booneclan@aol.com
web: http://members.aol.com/booneclan/
Buys, sells and collects fast food collectibles from the past and present.

Sandy Hall
Che & Sandy's Fast Food Toys
5954 11th Ave.
Sacramento, CA 95820
e-mail: Che_San@ns.net
web: http://www.ns.net/~Che_San/
Has extensive collection of fast food toys from most restaurants including many hard-to-find pieces.

Internet Resources

Rick & Daphne's Webguide for Fast Food Toy Collectors
Netherlands
e-mail: rick.van.der.geest@tip.nl
web: http://www1.tip.nl/~t150368/
Buys and sells PEZ and European fast food toys.

Periodicals

Nigel Thomas
Newsletter: Collecting Fast Food & Advertising Premiums
9 Ellacombe Rd.
Longwell Green, Bristol BS15 6BQ
U.K.
Published six times each year; covers British and mainland Europe promotions (no US), fast food and advertising premiums: McDonald's, Burger King, Pizza Hut, Kelloggs and many others.

Kentucky Fried Chicken

Museums/Libraries

Colonel Harland Sanders Museum, KFC Headquarters
1441 Gardiner Lane
Louisville, KY 40232-2070
ph: 502-456-8607 or 502-456-8353

McDonald's

Clubs/Associations

Dianne Arazy
Rochester McDonald's Collectors Club
1053 Paul Rd.
Churchville, NY 14546
ph: 716-889-5656
e-mail: siranpour@aol.com

Sharon Iranpour
Rochester McDonald's Collectors Club
24 San Rafael Dr.
Rochester, NY 14618-3702
ph: 716-381-9467
fax: 716-383-9248
e-mail: watcher1@rochester.rr.com
A chapter of the National association.

Bill & Pat Poe
Sunshine Chapter, McDonald's Collectors Club
Newsletter: Sunshine Express
220 Dominica Circle E.
Niceville, FL 32578-4085
ph: 850-897-4163
fax: 850-987-2606
e-mail: McPoes@aol.com
Membership is open to all; send SASE for membership form.

McDonald's Collectors Club
Newsletter: McDonald's Collectors Club News
1153 S Lee Street, Ste. 200
Des Plaines, IL 60016
e-mail: secretary@mcdclub.com
web: http://www.mcdclub.com/
For collectors of McDonald's memorabilia: Happy Meal toys and boxes, advertising, ephemera, glassware, pins, garments, etc., quarterly newsletter; this club has regional chapters.

Bill & Betty McCormick
Metro St. Louis MacDonald's Collectors Club
725 "A" Woodside Trails
Ballwin, MO 63021-6192
ph: 314-230-3181
e-mail: WMccorm418@aol.com
web: http://members.aol.com/wmccorm418/collect/

Collectors

Charles Wichmann
255 New Lenox Rd.
Lenox, MA 01240-2242
ph: 413-637-3334
e-mail: charmac@aol.com

Tenna Greenberg
5400 Waterbury Rd.
Des Moines, IA 50312
ph: 515-279-0741

Pat Longeran
P.O. Box 2262
Melrose Park, IL 60164
Major collector of McDonald's memorabilia.

David Tuttle
329 Callan Ave.
Evanston, IL 60202
ph: 847-475-8676

Barbara Saitta
5407 W. Berenice Ave.
Chicago, IL 60641
ph: 773-736-3298

Bill & Betty McCormick
725 "A" Woodside Trails
Ballwin, MO 63021-6192
ph: 314-230-3181
e-mail: WMccorm418@aol.com
web: http://members.aol.com/wmccorm418/collect/
Collectors of MacDonald's Happy Meal toys and related items since 1987.

Meredith Williams
P.O. Box 633
Joplin, MO 64802-0633
ph: 417-624-2518 or 417-781-3855
e-mail: willictn@clandjop.com
Wants to buy McDonald's items: buttons, postcards, displays, old uniforms, kids clothes, Happy Meal boxes, toys, annual reports, old and rare comic books, signs, etc.

Dealers

Chris Rucho
7 Colonial Hill Dr.
West Boylston, MA 01583
ph: 508-835-4141
e-mail: carucho@ziplink.net
web: http://www.ziplink.net/~carucho
Buys and sells McDonald's collectibles.

Ron Abler
Certified McNut, The
5516 Maplefield Place
Alexandria, VA 22310-1891
ph: 703-971-9590 or 703-971-3524
Buys/sells/trades McDonald's Happy Meal translites, point-of-purchase displays, cartons, and other items; specializes in MIP (mint in package) items; also interested in other fast food items; send LSASE for free buy/sell/trade list.

Experts

Terry & Joyce Losonsky
SKI Publishing
7506 Summer Leave Lane
Columbia, MD 21046-2455
e-mail: joyceusa@aol.com
Authors of "Collectors Guide to McDonald's Happy Meal Boxes and Premiums"; available from author for $7 plus $2 postage.

Matt Welch
P.O. Box 30444
Tucson, AZ 85751-0444
ph: 520-886-0505
e-mail: matwelch@aol.com
Wants to buy any unusual items from McDonald's restaurants: uniforms, glasses, paper items, souvenirs, pins & buttons, regional items, reports, books, displays, signage, items not made available to the public.

Gary Killops
Canada
e-mail: gkillops@netcore.ca
McDonald's researcher and collector of older McDonald's memorabilia; webmaster for the McDonald's Collectors Club web site; committed to preserving the history of the McDonald's Corporation.

Internet Resources

Werner Zemanek
McD-Collect
Lange Gasse 14/13a
Vienna, A-1080
Austria
ph: +43-1-403 32 68-0
fax: +43-1-403 32 68-88
e-mail: webringmaster@bigfoot.com
web: http://www.mcd-collect.at/
Site of The Official Austrian McDonald's Happy Meal Toys Museum; also McDonald gallery, news, rarities, trade and sell, club; English and Dutch versions.

Museums/Libraries

McDonald's Museum #1 Store, The
400 N. Lee St.
Des Plaines, IL 60016
ph: 847-297-5022
web: http://www.mcdonalds.com/corporate/info/museum/
The first McDonald's; limited openings; across the street is an active McDonald's restaurant with lots of memorabilia.

Ray A. Crock Museum, The
McDonald's Plaza
Oak Brook, IL 60523
ph: 630-623-2377
web: http://www.mcdonalds.com/corporate/info/museum/

Periodicals

Meredith Williams
Newsletter: Collecting Tips Newsletter
P.O. Box 633
Joplin, MO 64802-0633
ph: 417-624-2518 or 417-781-3855
e-mail: willictn@clandjop.com
A monthly newsletter filled with up-to-date information about old and new McDonald's restaurant collectibles; also buy, sell and trade ads; send two stamps plus SASE for sample copy.

McDonald's (Happy Meal Toys)

Dealers

Jim Christoffel
409 Maple
Elburn, IL 60119
ph: 630-365-2914
Buys and sells McDonald's Happy Meal Toys.

Experts

Ron Abler
Certified McNut, The
5516 Maplefield Place
Alexandria, VA 22310-1891
ph: 703-971-9590 or 703-971-3524
Publishes the "Pocket Guide to Happy Meat Toys 1975-1994", a loose-leaf pocket-sized checklist of all U.S. Happy Meal toys; updated annually.

Meredith Williams
P.O. Box 633
Joplin, MO 64802-0633
ph: 417-624-2518 or 417-781-3855
e-mail: willictn@clandjop.com
Author of "Tomart's Price Guide to McDonald's Happy Meal Collectibles - List - Pictures - Prices - All Happy Meals 1977-1995," $30.95 ppd. from the author.

Internet Resources

McDonald's Happy Meal Collectors
McDonald's Plaza
Oak Brook, IL 60523
web: http://www.mcdonalds.com/collectibles/happymeal/
McDonald's corporate Happy Meal Collector web site; learn about about Happy Meal start dates.

David Smith
HappyToy.com
3770 S Harlan
Denver, CO 80235
e-mail: thedeke@happytoy.com
web: http://www.HappyToy.com
Website features everything you need to know as a collector of McDonald's Happy Meal toys; archive image gallery of toys, current toy images, collectors links, toys of the world, inside info on upcoming Happy Meal promotions.

McDonald's (Pins)

Clubs/Associations

Michael Fountaine
McDonald's International Pin Club
Newsletter: MIPC Newsletter
P.O. Box 328
Coopersburg, PA 18036
ph: 800-647-2746 or 610-282-8964
fax: 610-282-8963
e-mail: mike@mipc.com
web: http://www.mipc.com/index2.html
For collectors of McDonald's lapel pins; newsletter published two times per year; catalog of over 500 McDonald's pins for sale; sponsors shows to meet other collectors.

FASTENERS

Collectors

Mel Kirsner
726 Deal Ct.
San Diego, CA 92109
ph: 619-488-9805
fax: 619-488-0919
e-mail: pellmel@sd.znet.com
Wants fasteners, bolts, nuts, washers or screw related items, pre-1950 only: advertising displays, promotional items, wooden boxes, metal tins, signs, catalogs, etc.

Museums/Libraries

Mel Kirsner
Mell's Fastener Museum
3128 Tera Alta
Julian, CA 92036
ph: 760-765-0569
fax: 619-488-0919
Not-for-profit museum of fasteners, bolts, nuts, washers or screw related items; advertising displays, promotional items, wooden boxes, metal tins, signs, catalogs, etc.; open by appointment only.

FEED SACKS

(see also TEXTILES; QUILTS)

Clubs/Associations

Jane Clark Stapel
Feedsack Club, The
Newsletter: Switches & Swatches
25 S Starr Ave., Apt. 16
Pittsburgh, PA 15202-3424
ph: 412-766-3996
e-mail: baglady111@aol.com
web: http://members.aol.com/baglady111/feedsackclub.html
Members buy, sell, trade and exhibit feedsacks which are used to make quilts, vests, baby quilts, doll quilts, miniatures, clothing and for decorating; lecture programs on request.

Collectors

Diane Holmes
Jasmine Quilt & Supplies
32 Crestview Dr.
Fleetwood, PA 19522
ph: 610-987-9622
fax: 619-987-0742
e-mail: JasmineQlt@aol.com
Collects feedsacks to make quilts from patterns she designs and publishes; quilt lecturer, instructor, designer.

Karen Bush
Birdsong Collections
409 Morningside Dr.
Richmond, MO 64085
ph: 816-470-8976
e-mail: Birdsong@worldnet.att.net
web: http://www.idahoquilt.com/karenbush.htm

Dealers

Sandra Sorgenfrie
R 2, Box 103
Winnebago, MN 56098
ph: 507-866-4688
Buys and sells feedsacks: flowers, stripes, plaids, doubles, triples.

Experts

Ron Bennett
R1 1870 Strong Rd.
Victor, NY 14564-9134
ph: 716-657-7505
e-mail: bbmimi@aol.com
Collector of all kinds of fabric bags; sells original feed sack prints; charm packs of 25 all different prewashed and ironed cut to 6" x 6" swatches for $14 ppd.; also vests made of original feed and seed bags with logos, animals, etc.

Jane Clark Stapel
25 S Starr Ave., Apt. 16
Pittsburgh, PA 15202-3424
ph: 412-766-3996
e-mail: baglady111@aol.com
web: http://members.aol.com/baglady111/feedsackclub.html
Specializes, lectures on feedsacks and their use in quilts, clothing and as decoration.

FENCE COLLECTIBLES

Posts

(see also BARBED WIRE)

Museums/Libraries

Post Rock Museum, The
202 West 1st St.
P.O. Box 473
La Crosse, KS 67548-0473
ph: 785-222-2719 or 785-222-3508
web: http://skyways.lib.ks.us/towns/LaCrosse/postrock.html
Documents the quarrying and use of limestone for fence posts and buildings in the Midwest; displays stone quarry tools; open mid-May through mid-September.

FIESTA

(see CERAMICS [AMERICAN DINNERWARE], Homer Laughlin/Fiesta)

FIGURINES

(see also ANIMAL COLLECTIBLES; BATHING BEAUTIES, Nudies & Naughties; BOSSONS; CERAMICS; COLLECTIBLES [MODERN]; REPAIR/RESTORATION/CONSERVATION; TOYS, Action Figures; TOYS, Playsets)

Collectors

Warren C. Galbus
756 Kerry Dr.
Winona, MN 55987-2119
ph: 507-452-1135
fax: 507-452-1135
Collector of figurines by Wallace Berrie, Sillisculpts and Supersculpts, @C&W Berrie Co., 1966; wants all colors and sizes including miniatures 1974-1976; also American Greetings and Paulas from the same time period.

Boehm

Appraisers

Stephen van Cline, CAPP
van Cline & Davenport, Ltd.
792 Franklin Ave.
Franklin Lakes, NJ 07417-1343
Minimum charge $25; letter request only, SASE.

Clubs/Associations

Boehm Porcelain Society, The
Magazine: Boehm Guild Advisory, The
25 Princess Diana Lane
Trenton, NJ 08638
ph: 609-392-2207 or 800-257-9410
fax: 609-392-1437
e-mail: boehmporcelain@att.net
web: http://www.boehmporcelain.com/
A Boehm manufacturer-sponsored club.

Collectors

Leon Reimert
121 Highland Dr.
Coatesville, PA 19320-1709
ph: 610-383-6969
e-mail: theboehmer@aol.com
Wants to buy Boehm porcelain dogs, horses, colts, and other animal figurines.

Dealers

Benjamin Gallery
1303 Pennsylvania Ave.
Hagerstown, MD 21742
ph: 301-797-4775
Carries large selection of Boehm porcelain figurines.

Gwendolyn R. Reasoner, Ph.D.
Re Vann Galleries
125 Arthur Lane
Hackberry, LA 70645-3001
ph: 609-345-7474 or 800-821-4278
e-mail: revanngal@aol.com
Largest Boehm dealer in the U.S.; specializes in the Boehm secondary market; also Cybis, Royal Worcester, Erte; also appraises.

A.D. & Pat Clay
Clemons-Eicken Fine European Imports
6166 N. Scottsdale Rd., #204
Scottsdale, AZ 85253
ph: 602-998-9042 or 800-250-5423
fax: 602-998-3755
Carries Lladro, Armani, Boehm, Lalique, Cybis.

Man./Prod./Dist.

Boehm Porcelain, Inc.
25 Princess Diana Lane
Trenton, NJ 08638
ph: 609-392-2207 or 800-257-9410
fax: 609-392-1437
e-mail: boehmporcelain@att.net
web: http://www.boehmporcelain.com/
Boehm manufacturer, repair/restoration; appraisals.

Repair Services

Boehm Porcelain, Inc.
25 Princess Diana Lane
Trenton, NJ 08638
ph: 609-392-2207 or 800-257-9410
fax: 609-392-1437
e-mail: boehmporcelain@att.net
web: http://www.boehmporcelain.com/
Boehm manufacturer, repair/restoration; appraisals.

Borsato

Appraisers

Allan Koskela
Borsato Collectors Archives
P.O. Box 186
Webster City, IA 50595
ph: 515-832-1131
Appraisals and consulting; appraisals minimum $25; catalog available; request information sheet by letter.

Clubs/Associations

Allan Koskela
Borsato Collectors Club
P.O. Box 186
Webster City, IA 50595
ph: 515-832-1131
World's largest database on Italian porcelain and artist, Antonio Borsato; newsletter, appraisal, largest Borsato library in the world.

Cybis

Dealers

Gwendolyn R. Reasoner, Ph.D.
Re Vann Galleries
125 Arthur Lane
Hackberry, LA 70645-3001
ph: 609-345-7474 or 800-821-4278
e-mail: revanngal@aol.com
Largest Boehm dealer in the U.S.; specializes in the Boehm secondary market; also Cybis, Royal Worcester, Erte; also appraises.

Man./Prod./Dist.

Cybis Porcelains
65 Norman Ave.
Trenton, NJ 08618-3003
ph: 609-392-6074
e-mail: info@cybisporcelain.com
web: http://www.cybisporcelain.com/
Creates fine porcelain sculptures; contact for purchasing or appraising limited or open edition figurines; also offers authentic Cybis restorations.

Dahl Jensen

Dealers

Peg Zurkowski
Becker Brooks Antiques
8027 Ellingson Dr.
Chevy Chase, MD 20815
ph: 301-588-8558
fax: 301-608-2167
e-mail: pzrkwski@ix.netcom.com
Buys and sells figurines designed by the Danish artist Dahl Jensen.

Hartland

Collectors

Steve McPherson
RR 2 Box 139-A
La Belle, MO 63447-9569
ph: 660-213-3994
Wants to buy statues by Hartland Plastics: western, baseball, football, religious; also buying Marx playsets.

Experts

Patrick Flynn
Minnie Memories
50 Eginton Rd.
Mankato, MN 56001-2607
ph: 507-387-6864
Author of "Bobbin Head Dolls/ Hartland Statues."

Hummel

(see also COLLECTIBLES [MODERN], Figurines [Goebel])

Auction Services

Cindy Isennock
Isennock Auctions & Appraisals, Inc.
4203 Norrisville Rd.
White Hall, MD 21161-9306
ph: 410-557-8052
fax: 410-692-6449
e-mail: isennock@starix.net
web: http://www.isennockauction.com/
Sells and appraises Hummel figurines.

Clubs/Associations

M.I. Hummel Club
Newsletter: Insights
Goebel Plaza, Rte. 31
P.O. Box 11
Pennington, NJ 08534-0011
ph: 609-737-8777 or 800-666-2582
fax: 609-737-1545
e-mail: memsrv@mihummel.com
web: http://www.mihummel.com/fs_m_club.html
Oldest collectors club of its kind; members receive information on Hummel figurines, plates & bells history & artistry; website with great resource information on Hummel identification and appraising.

Dorothy Dous, Pres.
Hummel Collector's Club, Inc.
Newsletter: Hummel Collector's Club Quarterly
1261 University Drive
Yardley, PA 19067-2857
ph: 215-493-6705 or 888-5-HUMMEL
fax: 215-321-7367
e-mail: hummels@bellatlantic.net
web: http://www.hummels.com
Specializing in M.I. Hummel items; fact-filled newsletter includes new releases, discontinued and older figurines, sale items and monthly figurine giveaway; also conducts monthly mail auctions of 2000-2500 items.

Tampa Area M.I. Hummel Club
114 W. Bloomingdale Ave.
Brandon, FL 33511
ph: 813-855-5680 or 813-654-1938
e-mail: cjohns@aol.com

Larry L. Jensen
Mountaineers, The
1524 S. Tucson St.
Aurora, CO 80012
ph: 303-751-3782
fax: 303-752-0970
One of the largest chapters of the M.I. Hummel Club.

Dealers

Don & Beth Woodworth
Dustables, Inc.
6558 Fourth Section Rd. #170
Brockport, NY 14420-2472
ph: 800-560-6996
fax: 716-494-1617
e-mail: service@dustables.com
Buys and sells M.I. Hummel figurines by mail order; checks, money orders, major credit cards accepted; free price list available upon request.

Arnie Berger
Yesterdays South, Inc.
P.O. Box 565097
Miami, FL 33256
ph: 800-368-5866 or 305-251-1988
fax: 305-254-5977
e-mail: aberger@yesterdayssouth.com
web: http://www.yesterdayssouth.com/
Send SASE for list of almost 1000 Doultons, Hummels, and Lladros for sale.

Cindy Oakes
34025 W. 6 Mile
Livonia, MI 48152
ph: 734-591-3252
Wants complete set of Hummel plates; also Hummel figurines from crown mark to present.

Larry L. Jensen
1524 S. Tucson St.
Aurora, CO 80012
ph: 303-751-3782
fax: 303-752-0970
Buys, sells, trades Hummel figurines; selling secondary market figurines at half price.

Donald M. Hardisty
Don's Collectibles
3020 E. Majestic Ridge
Las Cruces, NM 88011
ph: 505-522-3721
fax: 505-522-7909
e-mail: donshummels@zianet.com
web: http://www.zianet.com/donsbossons/
Internationally recognized expert, collector, supplier, appraiser, and restoration artist recommended by Bossons; also specializes in Hummels and rare coins; member Inter. Bossons Collectors Society, MI Hummel Club, Amer. Numismatic Assoc.

Experts

Dorothy Dous
1261 University Drive
Yardley, PA 19067-2857
ph: 215-493-6705 or 888-5-HUMMEL
fax: 215-321-7367
e-mail: hummels@bellatlantic.net
web: http://www.hummels.com
Buys, sells, collects, appraises, auctions and specializes in Hummels; runs the Hummel Collector's Club.

Carl F. Luckey
1973 Lingerlost Trail (Co Rd 471)
Killen, AL 35645
fax: 256-757-5803
e-mail: cluckey@mail.hiwaay.net
Mail contact only, please; send SASE for replier; author of books on Hummels, decoys, antique American fishing tackle, and depression glass.

Dean A. Genth
Miller's Gift Gallery
1322 N. Barron St.
Eaton, OH 45320-1016
ph: 937-456-4151
fax: 937-456-7851
e-mail: dean@millershallmark.com
web: http://www.millershallmark.com
Offers replacements and loss claim analysis; author of the "Price Guide to M.I. Hummel."

Internet Resources

Hans J. Schindhelm
M.I. Hummel & Precious Moments Internet Sites Directory
P.O. Box 120
Briarcliff, NY 10510
ph: 914-734-8410
fax: 914-762-1719
e-mail: hummel2001@aol.com
web: http://members.aol.com/hummel2001
Free on-line directory of web pages and internet sites relating to M.I. Hummel and Precious Moments collectibles.

Man./Prod./Dist.

M.I. Hummel
Goebel Plaza, Rte. 31
P.O. Box 11
Pennington, NJ 08534-0011
ph: 609-737-8777 or 800-666-2582
fax: 609-737-1545
e-mail: feedback@mihummel.com
web: http://www.mihummel.com/
Web site has price list for current Hummel figurines at http://www.mihummel.com/collection/pricelist_all.html.

Museums/Libraries

Doreen Schaeffer
Hummel Museum, The
199 Main Plaza
P.O. Box 311100
New Braunfels, TX 78131-1100
ph: 800-456-HUMM or 830-625-5636
fax: 830-625-5966
e-mail: hummel@nbtx.com
web: http://www.bullcreek.austin.tx.us/hummel/index.htm
Exhibits the world's largest collection of original drawings by M.I. Hummel; figurines and other Hummel items for sale in gift shop.

Repair Services

Dona Danziger
Clay Works, The
4058 S. Main St.
P.O. Box 352
Exmore, VA 23350
ph: 757-414-0567
fax: 757-414-0571
e-mail: clayworks@esva.net
web: http://www.esva.net/~clayworks
Crazing corrections - trademarked in 1995; this is a kiln-fired process for the Hummels which eliminates crazing; call for free information sheet.

Hummel Look-Alikes

Collectors

Joan Oates
685 S. Washington
Constantine, MI 49042-1407
ph: 616-435-8353
e-mail: koates@remc12.k12.mi.us
Interested in child-like, Hummel look-alikes marked "Designed by Erich

Stauffer" and numbered, made in Japan and imported by Arnart Imports, NY; these 4 1/2" to 10" figurines resemble Hummels, but are not.

Josef Originals

Dealers

Gray Menagerie, The
e-mail: mmmac9@idt.net
web: http://idt.net/~mmmac9/home.html
Specializes in Josef Originals, and other California pottery including Metlox, Franciscan, Howard Pierce, Sascha Brastoff, Hedi Schoop, Kay Finch, Freeman-McFarlin, Florence Ceramics, etc.

Jim Whitaker
P.O. Box 475
Lynnwood, WA 98046-0475
ph: 800-774-6910
e-mail: eclectic@gte.net

Periodicals

Jim Whitaker
Newsletter: Josef Originals Newsletter
P.O. Box 475
Lynnwood, WA 98046-0475
ph: 800-774-6910
e-mail: eclectic@gte.net
Newsletter is published quarterly.

Kaiser

Man./Prod./Dist.

Kaiser Porcelain Co.
R.R. #3
Shelburne, Ontario L0N 1S0
Canada
ph: 705-466-2246 or 800-267-5467
fax: 705-466-3542
e-mail: kaiser@bconnex.net
web: http://www.kaiser-porc.com
Porcelain dinnerware and bone china; artificial flowers, vases, figurines and wallplates, giftware and collectibles.

Lady

Collectors

Ann M. Kerr
P.O. Box 437
Sidney, OH 45365-0437
ph: 937-492-6369
fax: 937-492-6369
e-mail: raintree@bright.net
Always looking for fine quality lady figurines; must be signed and in perfect condition.

Lladro

Clubs/Associations

Lladro Collectors Society
Magazine: Expressions
1 Lladro Dr.
Moonachie, NJ 07074
ph: 201-807-1177 or 800-634-9088
fax: 201-807-1168
e-mail: lladrosociety@worldnet.att.net
web: http://www.lladro.com
Focuses on the collectible Lladro figurines. Sponsored by Lladro Co.

Dealers

Lladro Connection, A
30 NE 1st Street
Miami, FL 33132
ph: 800-984-5586
e-mail: illum1@aol.com
web: http://www.illumcollectibles.com/
Specializing in current and retired Swarovski and Lladro; also carries a complete line of Lalique and Kosta Boda.

Gregg Shienbaum
Illum
30 NE 1st Street
Miami, FL 33132
ph: 800-984-5586 or 305-373-3918
fax: 305-373-3803
e-mail: illum1@aol.com
web: http://www.illumcollectibles.com
Specializing in retired, hard-to-find Lladro and Swarovski; open stock of current items of Lladro, Swarovski, and Lalique.

Arnie Berger
Yesterdays South, Inc.
P.O. Box 565097
Miami, FL 33256
ph: 800-368-5866 or 305-251-1988
fax: 305-254-5977
e-mail: aberger@yesterdayssouth.com
web: http://www.yesterdayssouth.com/
Send SASE for list of almost 1000 Doultons, Hummels, and Lladros for sale.

Janet Gale Hammer
Lladro: A Retired Collection
550 Harbor Cove Circle
Longboat Key, FL 34228-3544
ph: 941-387-0102 or 800-332-8594
fax: 941-383-8865
e-mail: janet@lladrolady.com
web: http://lladrolady.com
Secondary market dealer specializing in Lladro.

Clark Sanchez
Sanchez Collectibles
1555 East Glendale Ave.
Phoenix, AZ 85020
ph: 602-395-9974 or 602-277-1661
fax: 602-241-0702
e-mail: sanchcol@primenet.com
web: http://www.primenet.com/~sanchcol
Buys, sells, appraises, repairs Lladros; does not sell new pieces, only pre-owned pieces no longer being manufactured; list available for free; will assist in identifying pieces and estimating their value.

A.D. & Pat Clay
Clemons-Eicken Fine European Imports
6166 N. Scottsdale Rd., #204
Scottsdale, AZ 85253
ph: 602-998-9042 or 800-250-5423
fax: 602-998-3755
Carries Lladro, Armani, Boehm, Lalique, Cybis.

Ben Swan
Golden Swan Collectibles
881 Lincoln Way
Auburn, CA 95603
ph: 530-823-7926 or 800-231-9055
fax: 530-823-1945
Offers a "search and find" and a listing service to collectors, buyers and sellers of Lladro figurines; also for Swarovski, Walt Disney Classics, and Disneyana Convention figurines.

Experts

Clark Sanchez
Sanchez Collectibles
1555 East Glendale Ave.
Phoenix, AZ 85020
ph: 602-395-9974 or 602-277-1661
fax: 602-241-0702
e-mail: sanchcol@primenet.com
web: http://www.primenet.com/~sanchcol
Buys, sells, appraises, repairs Lladros; does not sell new pieces, only pre-owned pieces no longer being manufactured; list available for free; will assist in identifying pieces and estimating their value.

Internet Resources

Lladro Message Board
e-mail: info@worldcollectorsnet.com
web: http://www.worldcollectorsnet.com/lladro/
Discuss, buy, trade Lladros with other collectors.

Man./Prod./Dist.

Lladro USA
1 Lladro Dr.
Moonachie, NJ 07074
ph: 201-807-1177 or 800-634-9088
fax: 201-807-1168
e-mail: lladrosociety@worldnet.att.net
web: http://www.lladro.com
Manufactures and distributes quality handcrafted porcelains from Valencia, Spain.

Museums/Libraries

Lladro Museum
43 West 57th St.
New York, NY 10019
ph: 212-838-9352
A manufacturer-sponsored museum and retail outlet.

Periodicals

Lladro USA
Newsletter: Lladro Antique News
1 Lladro Dr.
Moonachie, NJ 07074
ph: 201-807-1177 or 800-634-9088
fax: 201-807-1168
e-mail: lladrosociety@worldnet.att.net
web: http://www.lladro.com
Focuses on the current secondary market values of Lladro's 3,000 hard-paste porcelain figurines produced since 1941; also covers history of hard-paste porcelain (1000 AD to present) such as Meissen, Sevres, Nymphenburg, etc.

Morten Studio

Collectors

Gene Roberts
1500 Gilbert Rd.
Kennesaw, GA 30144
ph: 770-422-4143
Interested in buying anything Mortens: dogs, cats, livestock, wildlife, horses, bookends, head studies, plaques, people, birds; also wants Morten catalogs, history, any information.

Dealers

Denise Hamilton
899 Latta Brook Rd.
Elmira, NY 14901-9226
ph: 607-732-2550
Buys dogs collectibles: figurines, old dog postcards, jewelry with dogs in it, etc.; Borzoi (Russian Wolfhound), greyhound, all Morten Studio and Erphila dogs and animals.

Pen Delfin

Dealers

George Sparacio
Miscellania Antiques & Collectibles
272 Morris Ave.
Newfield, NJ 08344-0544
ph: 856-694-4167
fax: 856-694-4536
e-mail: mrvesta1@aol.com
web: http://members.aol.com/mrvesta1/
Dealer, expert wants to buy pre-1975 retired Pen Delfin figurines; will buy one or entire collection; quality items only.

Royal Doulton

(see CERAMICS [ENGLISH], Doulton; CERAMICS [ENGLISH], Royal Doulton; COLLECTIBLES [MODERN], Royal Doulton)

Royal Dux

Man./Prod./Dist.

Royal Bohemian Inc.
P.O. Box 1533
115 Industrial Dr., Ste. F
Saint Marys, GA 31558
fax: 800-890-1054
e-mail: mmb@royaldux.com
web: http://www.royaldux.com/
Manufacturer of Royal Dux figurines.

FILMS

(see also AUDIO-VISUAL; CAMERAS & CAMERA EQUIPMENT; MOVIE MEMORABILIA)

Appraisers

Larry Urbanski
Urbanski Film & Video
P.O. Box 438
Orland Park, IL 60462-0438
ph: 708-460-9082
fax: 708-460-9099
e-mail: larryu@interaccess.com
Film collection appraisals (8mm, 16mm, 35mm) for legal purposes and/ or insurance claims; 30 years experience; member of AMIA (Association of Moving Image Archivists).

Dr. Steve Johnson
Behavioral Images, Inc.
Newsletter: Ten Thousands Words
302 Leland St., Ste. 101
Bloomington, IL 61701-5646
ph: 309-829-3931 or 800-988-6427
fax: 309-829-9677
e-mail: sjohnson@mediavalue.com
web: http://www.mediavalue.com
Film, video, recordings, photographs, negatives; author of "Appraising Audio-visual Media; A Guide for Attorneys, Trust Officers, Insurance Professionals, & Archivists" (1993); $34.95 & $3 S&H; publishes newsletter ten times per year.

Clubs/Associations

Association of Moving Image Archivists, Nat. Ctr. for Film & Video Preservation
P.O. Box 27999
2021 N. Western Ave.
Los Angeles, CA 90027
ph: 213-856-7637

Vintage Film Club, The
Magazine: Flickers: The Collector's Guide to Vintage Film
11 Norton Rd.
Knowle, Bristol BS4 2EZ
U.K.
For those interested in vintage films, projectors, film books and magazines, and related items; magazine published three times per year with articles, display ads, and a large free classifieds marketplace insert for club members.

Dealers

Kathy & Bill Lozowski
K & B Film & Collectibles
50 32nd St.
Copiague, NY 11726
ph: 516-842-3446
Also sells commercials on 16mm film.

Larry Urbanski
Urbanski Film & Video
P.O. Box 438
Orland Park, IL 60462-0438
ph: 708-460-9082
fax: 708-460-9099
e-mail: larryu@interaccess.com
16mm film exchange and sales; specializing in cartoons, educational features, TV shows, and shorts; projectors and equipment available; 16mm and 35mm; also buys and trades film; send two stamps for catalog.

Chris Perry
Doctor 3D
7470 Church St., Ste. A
Yucca Valley, CA 92284-3248
ph: 760-365-0475
fax: 760-365-0495
Wants motion picture films of all kinds, especially pre-1928 silent movies and also any 3-D movies; 8mm films are not desirable unless they are complete movies and not shorter, condensed versions.

Repair Services

Sockets International
4454 Coldwater Canyon Ave., Ste. #303
Studio City, CA 91604
ph: 818-508-0464
Certified Tomakote agent; Tomakote keeps all film stock soft and pliable so there is no eventual drying-to-brittleness; contains a powerful anti-static agent to reduces friction during projection and acts to repel dirt.

Videos

Man./Prod./Dist.

Larry Urbanski
Moviecraft Inc.
P.O. Box 438
Orland Park, IL 60462-0438
ph: 708-460-9082
fax: 708-460-9099
e-mail: larryu@interaccess.com
Offers a nostalgic/historical line of home videos including TV shows, World Fair, automotive, rare cartoons, classics, unique contemporary releases, war newsreels and propaganda, special interest subjects, and feature films.

Periodicals

Newspaper: VideoMania
P.O. Box 47
Neshkoro, WI 54960-0047
Quarterly newspaper for video collectors: new releases, video cassettes, laser discs, movies, equipment.

Magazine: Video Movie Collector
P.O. Box 62067
Minneapolis, MN 55426
fax: 612-929-0522
The monthly publication for collectors of movies on video tape or disc: up-to-the-minute news and information for the movie on video collector; listings of hard-to-find titles, articles, reviews, etc.

FINANCIAL PAPER

(see BANKING; CIVIL WAR ARTIFACTS, Confederate Bonds; COINS & CURRENCY, Paper Money; PAPER COLLECTIBLES; SCRIP; STOCKS & BONDS)

FIRE FIGHTING MEMORABILIA

Auction Services

Chuck Deluca
Maritime Auctions
P.O. Box 322
York, ME 03909
ph: 207-363-4247
fax: 207-363-1416
e-mail: maritim2@ix.netcom.com
web: http://www.maritiques.com
Author of "Firehouse Memorabilia - A Collector's Reference"; two cataloged auctions per year in April and August.

Clubs/Associations

David Cerull
Fire Collectors Club
P.O. Box 992
Milwaukee, WI 53201-0992
Collectors of Fire Service medals.

International Fire Photographers Association
16446 Union Ave.
Harvey, IL 60426-6133

Collectors

Joe Kaminski
Firetiques
31 Terrace Gardens
Meriden, CT 06451
ph: 203-235-2242
e-mail: jjkaminski@snet.net
web: http://pages.cthome.net/firetiques/

M. Gimley
P.O. Box 244
Oakland, NJ 07436-0244
ph: 201-684-7698
e-mail: spiatti@bellatlantic.net
Wants items from the 1800s to 1920s: gold & silver badges, buckets, engine lights, helmets, lanterns, tintypes, statues of firemen, etc.

Ralph Jennings
675 Forest Creek Dr.
Ambler, PA 19002
ph: 215-646-7178
Interested in fire fighting and fire insurance related collectibles.

Jeb S. Fuller
9 Durey Ct.
Cartersville, GA 30120
ph: 770-387-9758
Wants to buy firehouse items: postcards, ads or photographs featuring firemen or fire trucks, old fire trucks, extinguishers, trumpets, badges, alarms, helmets, etc.

David Cerull
P.O. Box 992
Milwaukee, WI 53201-0992
Wants Fire Service medals from any country; send detailed description, rubbing or photocopy along with price.

Stan Zukowski
1867 Ellard Place
Concord, CA 94521
ph: 925-687-6426
Wants fire department antiques: fire alarm boxes, wood cased fire station bells, desk bells, keys, books, catalogs, parts; anything fire alarm related in any condition; also wants helmets, lanterns, trumpets, glass grenades, etc.

Dealers

Robert A. Fratkin
American Experience, The
8280 Greensboro Dr., #200
Mc Lean, VA 22102
ph: 703-556-8101 or 202-483-0274
fax: 703-356-6492
e-mail: coxfdr@erols.com
Buys and sells fire fighting memorabilia; willing to give telephone assistance in identifying and valuing; please have item in hand when calling.

Robert H. Harper
Cary Station Antiques
22 Spring St.
Cary, IL 60013
ph: 847-639-7434
Wants helmets, trumpets, presentation badges, painted leather buckets, lamps, parade hats, alarm equipment, etc.

Marvin Karsten
Old Tyme Fire Classics
6217 Crystal Dr.
Alta Loma, CA 91701-3411
ph: 909-987-5084
e-mail: firegoods@aol.com
web: http://members.aol.com/firegoods/firegoods/home.html
Dealer, collector, expert wants to buy

firehouse memorabilia: American fire helmets, wood cased fire alarm bells, street boxes, speaking trumpets, Gamewell equipment, fire insurance advertising, fire toys, fire lanterns.

Experts

H. Thomas & Pat Laun
Little Century
215 Paul Ave.
Syracuse, NY 13206-3220
ph: 315-437-4156 or 315-654-3244
e-mail: tlaun@txcny.rr.com
Buys and sells fire related antiques and collectibles, any number; supplies and manufactures parts for firematic items; also repairs; call 315-437-4156 in the winter, and 315-654-3244 in summer.

Germaine Broussard
8280 Greensboro Drive #200
Mc Lean, VA 22102-3807
ph: 703-556-8183 or 800-336-0156
fax: 703-356-6492
e-mail: coxfdr@erols.com
Buys, sells, appraises fire department memorabilia; one piece or collection; early ribbons are a specialty; will answer questions for new collectors; former firefighter and paramedic.

Museums/Libraries

Eugene I. Morris, Dir.
New England Fire & History Museum
Newsletter: Siren Soundings
1439 Main St. (Rte. 6A)
Brewster, MA 02631
ph: 508-896-5711 or 508-432-2450
One of the world's most varied collections of antique fire engines; 35 historic fire engines; Mr. Morris appraises and has written many articles relating to fire fighting, apothecary and blacksmithing material.

New York City Fire Museum, The
Newsletter: Burning Issues
278 Spring St.
New York, NY 10013-1405
ph: 212-691-1303
fax: 212-924-0403
web: http://nyfd.com/museum.html
Focuses on fire related art and artifacts from the mid-18th century to present.

R. Dennis Randall, Cur.
American Museum of Fire Fighting
125 Harry Howard Ave.
Hudson, NY 12534-1601
ph: 518-828-7695 or 800-479-7695
fax: 518-828-1092
web: http://www.firemuseumnetwork.org/
Focuses on the preservation of fire fighting history; over 71 antique engines dating from 1725 to 1974 are displayed along with over 3,000 pieces of related fire fighting memorabilia; admission free; since 1925.

Fire Museum of Maryland
1301 York Rd.
Lutherville, MD 21093
ph: 410-321-7500
fax: 410-769-8433
e-mail: firemu@home.com
web: http://www.firemuseummd.org/

Glenn Hartley, Sr.
Smokey's Fire Museum
2859 Marlin Dr.
Chamblee, GA 30341-5119
ph: 770-451-2651

Toledo Firefighters Museum
Newsletter: Hook & Letter, The
918 W. Sylvania Ave.
Toledo, OH 43612
ph: 419-478-3473
web: http://www.toledolink.com/~matgerke/~tfm/
Comprehensive collection of fire fighting antiques and 2000 volume library.

Oklahoma Firefighters Museum
2716 NE 50th St.
Oklahoma City, OK 73100
ph: 405-424-3440
e-mail: info@tulsaweb.com
web: http://tulsaweb.com/FIREMUS.HTM
Houses the large, colorful Ben Dancy shoulder patch collection of over 4,500 pieces.

Hall of Flame Museum of Firefighting
6101 East Van Buren St.
Phoenix, AZ 85008
ph: 602-275-3473
fax: 602-275-0896
e-mail: webmaster@Hallofflame.org
web: http://www.hallofflame.org/
Over 35,000 square feet of exhibits, with almost 90 fully restored pieces of fire apaparatus on display dating from 1725 to 1968; sponsored by the National Historical Fire Foundation.

San Francisco Fire Department Memorial Museum
655 Presidio Ave.
San Francisco, CA 94115
ph: 415-558-3546

Repair Services

H. Thomas & Pat Laun
Little Century
215 Paul Ave.
Syracuse, NY 13206-3220
ph: 315-437-4156 or 315-654-3244
e-mail: tlaun@txcny.rr.com
Repairs fire fighting antiques and collectibles; wood and metal parts fabricated.

Apparatus

(see also TRUCKS, Emergency)

Clubs/Associations

Gibson Road Antique Fire Association
1545 Gibson Road
Crum Lynne, PA 19022
ph: 215-245-1545
e-mail: grafa@firefighting.com
web: http://www.firefighting.com/grafa/
Monthly meetings; over 120 members with 80 pieces of antique and classic fire apparatus; dedicated to preserving and restoring all types of fire apparatus.

William A. Conn
Great Lakes International Antique Fire Apparatus Association
P.O. Box 2519
Detroit, MI 48231
ph: 248-684-1521

Society for the Preservation & Appreciation of Motor Fire Apparatus in America
5420 S. Kedvale Ave.
Chicago, IL 60632
ph: 773-585-1301
e-mail: connorsba@aol.com
web: http://www.spaamfaa.org/
Over 300 members in over 50 chapters; ownership of an antique piece of fire apparatus is not a requirement of membership.

Collectors

Bob Ward
2461 E High St., #A-7
Pottstown, PA 19464-3111
ph: 610-970-6299

Periodicals

Magazine: Fire Apparatus Journal
P.O. Box 141295
Staten Island, NY 10314-1295
ph: 718-448-5009
fax: 718-981-2359
e-mail: fireappjnl@aol.com
web: http://fireapparatusjournal.com/
Focuses on all sorts of fire fighting apparatus: trucks, boats; also related modeling.

Dr. Robert B. Marvin
R-Mac Publications
Magazine: Vintage Vehicle & Fire Engine Magazine
Rt. 3, Box 425
Jasper, FL 32052
ph: 904-792-2480
e-mail: rbm@isgroup.net
web: http://www.vintagevehicle.com/MASTOF97.htm

Fire Alarm Telegraphy

Collectors

Gary Carino
805 W. 3rd St.
Duluth, MN 55806-2201
ph: 218-722-6565
fax: 218-878-0488
Wants wood cased gongs by Gamewell or Moses G. Crane.

Experts

Steven Scher
3010 Grand Concourse
Bronx, NY 10458-1504
Wants to buy antique fire alarm gongs and telegraph items; advises other collectors about same; author of magazine articles and contributor to a book on fire alarm telegraphy; also historical advisor to the NYC Fire Museum.

Grenades

Collectors

Jerry Pajak
4457 285th St.
Toledo, OH 43611-1912
ph: 419-726-4325
Wants turn-of-the-century fire fighting hand grenade fire extinguisher bottles (empty or full) which were originally sealed with a cork or with cement.

Larry Meyer
4001 Elmwood
Berwyn, IL 60402-4146
ph: 708-749-1564
e-mail: lmeyer1212@aol.com

FIRE INSURANCE RELATED COLLECTIBLES

(see also INSURANCE COLLECTIBLES)

Collectors

Ralph Jennings
675 Forest Creek Dr.
Ambler, PA 19002
ph: 215-646-7178
Interested in fire fighting and fire insurance related collectibles.

Glenn Hartley, Sr.
2859 Marlin Dr.
Chamblee, GA 30341-5119
ph: 770-451-2651
Buys and sells at area fire musters and apparatus shows.

Museums/Libraries

Glenn Hartley, Sr.
Smokey's Fire Museum
2859 Marlin Dr.
Chamblee, GA 30341-5119
ph: 770-451-2651

Fire Marks

Clubs/Associations

Glenn Hartley, Sr.
Fire Mark Circle of the Americas, The
Newsletter: Fire Mark Circle of the Americas Newsletter, The
2859 Marlin Dr.
Chamblee, GA 30341-5119
ph: 770-451-2651
Contains club news, auction prices, and articles about fire marks; also publishes the "FMCA Journal"; published addendum and booklets on fire marks and automobile insurance tags; also "Signs of Insurance", a book on insurance co. signs.

FIREARMS

(see also ADVERTISING COLLECTIBLES, Firearms Related; AIRGUNS; ARMS & ARMOR; BOOKS, Reference [Firearms]; CIVIL WAR ARTIFACTS; MILITARIA; AMMUNITION & EXPLOSIVE ORDNANCE; POWDER HORNS; SPORTING COLLECTIBLES; TARGET SHOOTING MEMORABILIA; TOY GUNS; TRAPSHOOTING)

Appraisers

Robert A. Dewar
Robert A. Dewar & Assoc.
512 Canal St.
New Smyrna Beach, FL 32168
ph: 904-428-3331
e-mail: corol@ucnsb.net
Dealer and appraiser in both antique and modern firearms.

Joseph G. Balshone, GG, ISA
463 East Town St.
Columbus, OH 43215-4796
ph: 800-209-4367 or 614-224-2404
fax: 614-224-5630
e-mail: jbalshone@compuserve.com
Specializing in appraising post-1800 firearms.

Paul E. Jurgens
50 DuClaire Rd.
Decatur, IL 62521-5527
ph: 217-423-8303
e-mail: jurgens@springnet.com
Specializes in appraising firearms.

Jim Supica
Old Town Station, Ltd. Antique Arms
P.O. Box 14040
Lenexa, KS 66285
ph: 913-492-3000
fax: 913-492-3022
e-mail: OldTownSta@aol.com
web: http://www.ArmchairGunShow.com/
Buys and sells antique firearms; co-author of "Standard Catalog of S&W," contributing editor to "Blue Book of Gun Values" and "American Rifleman" magazine, pricing panel for "Std. Catalog of Firearms," and "Flayderman's Guide."

Auction Services

William Harvey Gun Auctions
P.O. Box 130
Amherst, NH 03031
ph: 603-672-1888
fax: 603-673-8617
e-mail: wpharvey@aol.com
web: http://www.firearmsauctions.com

James D. Julia Auctioneers Inc.
Rt. 201, Skowhegan Rd.
P.O. Box 830
Fairfield, ME 04937
ph: 207-453-7125
fax: 207-453-2502
e-mail: jjulia@juliaauctions.com
web: http://www.juliaauctions.com
One of the leading firearms auctioneers in North America.

Ronnie Roberts, ISA
SoldUSA.com
6407 Idlewild Rd., Bldg. 2, Ste 207
Charlotte, NC 28212
ph: 704-364-2900 or 877-SoldUSA
fax: 704-364-2322
e-mail: gun1898@aol.com
web: http://www.soldusa.com/

Kim Richardson
GunBroker.com
P.O. Box 19137
Atlanta, GA 31126
ph: 770-234-4174
fax: 770-234-4174
e-mail: admin@gunbroker.com/
web: http://www.gunbroker.com/
A premiere firearms auction on the Internet; allows the user to buy and sell guns, gun accessories, air guns, and archery equipment; extensive FFL Holder network assists with the legal transfer of firearms; free to buyers & sellers.

Larry Garner
Larry Garner Auctioneers
P.O. Box 323
Carrollton, OH 44615
ph: 800-452-8452
fax: 330-627-3788
e-mail: garner@raex.com
web: http://www.auctionweb.com
Specializes in the auction sale of modern and antique firearms.

Butterfield & Dunning
755 Church Rd.
Elgin, IL 60123
ph: 847-741-3483
fax: 847-741-3589
e-mail: info@butterfields.com
web: http://www.butterfields.com

Patrick Hogan
Rock Island Auction Company
1050 36th Ave.
Moline, IL 61265
ph: 309-797-1500 or 800-238-8022
fax: 309-797-1655
e-mail: riauction@aol.com

Jim Supica
Old Town Station, Ltd. Antique Arms
P.O. Box 14040
Lenexa, KS 66285
ph: 913-492-3000
fax: 913-492-3022
e-mail: OldTownSta@aol.com
web: http://www.ArmchairGunShow.com/
Conducts periodic military arms auction sales.

Clubs/Associations

Jack Ackerman
New York State Arms Collectors Association
24 South Mountain Terrace
Binghamton, NY 13902-3128
ph: 607-723-5668

Potomac Arms & Collectors Association
P.O. Box 1812
Wheaton, MD 20915
ph: 301-921-9673

Attn: Membership
National Rifle Association
Magazine: American Rifleman
11250 Waples Mill Rd.
Fairfax, VA 22030
ph: 800-NRA-3888
e-mail: membership@NRAhq.org
web: http://www.nrahq.org/

Ontario Arms Collectors' Association
P.O. Box 477
Richmond Hill, Ontario L4C 4Y8
Canada
ph: 905-883-6222
fax: 905-737-4571
e-mail: oaca4570@aol.com
web: http://fox.nstn.ca/~dvc14/oaca.html
Ontario's foremost association for collectors of firearms and edged weapons.

Collectors

Dr. Anthony Sapienza
East 106 Ridgewood Ave.
Paramus, NJ 07652
ph: 201-262-6310
fax: 201-262-3990
e-mail: siringo45@aol.com
Serious collector wants anything related to trick or exhibition shooting (Annie Oakley, Doc Carver, Gus Peret, etc.); wants posters, pinbacks, glass target balls, souvenir targets; plus shot items such as coins, playing or business cards.

Jim Kopke
P.O. Box 4310
Dillon, CO 80435-4310
Wants to buy antique firearms.

Dealers

New England Arms Co.
P.O. Box 278
Kittery Point, ME 03905
ph: 207-439-0593
fax: 207-439-6726
Largest display of modern and antique sporting arms on the East Coast: Purdey, Boss, Woodward, Holland & Holland, Sauer, Merkel, Browning, Dumoulin, Ferlib, Fabbri, Piotti, Rizzini, Arrazabalaga, Arrieta, etc.

Greg Souchik
TMP Co.
P.O. Box 161
Custer City, PA 16725-0161
ph: 814-362-2642
fax: 814-362-7356
e-mail: AlleghenyArsenal@compuserve.com
Buys all broken and old firearms including parts.

William A. Kelley, Jr.
Gun Center, The
5831 Buckeystown Pike
Frederick, MD 21701
ph: 301-694-6887
fax: 301-694-6887
A full service gun store offering special order services, gunsmithing, and firearms appraisals; buy, sell, trade, consignment.

Dave Condon
David Condon, Inc.
P.O. Box 7
109 East Washington St.
Merrifield, VA 22118
ph: 540-687-5642 or 540-689-1363
web: http://www.davidcondon.com/
Antique firearms bought and sold.

Bill Williams
Guncraft Sports Inc.
10737 Dutchtown Rd.
Knoxville, TN 37932-3208
ph: 423-966-4545
fax: 423-966-4500
e-mail: findit@guncraft.com
web: http://www.usit.net/hp/guncraft/
Serving the shooting public since 1947; a multi-faceted supplier of guns, accessories, appraisal services, training, gunsmithing, gun related books.

Dixie Gun Work's Old Car & Steam Engine Museum
1412 Reelfoot Ave.
Union City, TN 38261
ph: 901-885-0561
fax: 901-885-0440
e-mail: dixiegun@iswt.com
web: http://www.dixiegun.com
Specializes in the sale of black powder rifles.

Douglas R. Carlson
Antique American Firearms
P.O. Box 71035
Des Moines, IA 50325
ph: 515-224-6552
Wants antique American revolvers and derringers 1848-1898; offers antique firearms catalogs every 12 weeks.

Dean Williams
Antique & Collector Firearms
RR 7157
Spirit Lake, IA 51360
ph: 712-336-5634
Buys and sells, especially Colts, Remingtons, Winchesters, Smith & Wessons, flintlocks and derringer; offers quarterly antique firearms.

LeRoy Merz
LeRoy Merz Antique Guns
Rt. 1, Box 380
Fergus Falls, MN 56537
ph: 218-739-3255
fax: 218-739-2356

Randy Donley
Donley's Wild West Town & Museum
8512 S. Union Rd.
Union, IL 60180-9661
ph: 815-923-9000
fax: 815-923-2253
web: http://www.wildwesttown.com/
Buys, sells and collects antique firearms of all sorts.

Collectors Firearms
140 S Seminary St.
Galesburg, IL 61401-4805
ph: 309-342-5800
fax: 309-342-5730
e-mail: simpsonltd@misslink.net
web: http://www.simpsonltd.com/
Wants antique firearms, Civil War carbines and muskets, Colts, European muskets, Derringers, Winchester, etc.

Michael Wamsher
17732 W. 67th St.
Shawnee Mission, KS 66217
ph: 913-631-0686
Specializes in military firearms.

Jim Supica
Old Town Ltd. Antique Arms
P.O. Box 14040
Lenexa, KS 66285
ph: 913-492-3000
fax: 913-492-3022
e-mail: OldTownSta@aol.com
web: http://www.ArmchairGunShow.com/
Buys and sells antique firearms; co-author of "Standard Catalog of S&W," contributing editor to "Blue Book of Gun Values" and "American Rifleman" magazine, pricing panel for "Std. Catalog of Firearms," and "Flayderman's Guide."

Terry Porter
Fine Antique Arms
P.O. Box 59028
Mesquite, TX 75150
ph: 214-679-7410
fax: 972-681-8992
e-mail: Terry.Porter@FineAntiqueArms.com
web: http://www.fineantiquearms.com
Dealing in fine antique arms, rapiers, swords, pistols, guns, muskets.

John Spangler
John Spangler Professional Services, LC
P.O. Box 711282
Salt Lake City, UT 84171
ph: 801-947-9442
e-mail: hq@oldguns.net
web: http://oldguns.net
Serving collectors and students of firearms and military history; huge inventory on website; single pieces, entire collections, or deaccessioned museum inventory wanted; appraisals for estate, divorce.

Walt Moreau
P.O. Box 14764
San Francisco, CA 94114
ph: 415-861-8319
fax: 415-255-2335
e-mail: WMoreau130@aol.com
web: http://www.moreau.com
Dealer and collector of classic antique firearms; also Americana and Plains Indian art.

Marc Wade
Antique & Collectable Firearms & Militaria Headquarters
P.O. Box 95021
Gilroy, CA 95021
ph: 801-898-3827
e-mail: hq@oldguns.net
web: http://oldguns.net/Sma.htm
Buys, sells, appraises; interesting and useful information for collectors of antique and collectible firearms and militaria; questions answered, gun show listings, catalog, gun related software.

Experts

Courtney Wilson
American Military Antiques
8398 Court Ave.
Ellicott City, MD 21043-4514
ph: 410-465-6827
fax: 410-461-6820
Wants to buy collectible and antique firearms; all periods.

Bill Williams
Guncraft Sports Inc.
10737 Dutchtown Rd.
Knoxville, TN 37932-3208
ph: 423-966-4545
fax: 423-966-4500
e-mail: findit@guncraft.com
web: http://www.usit.net/hp/guncraft/
Serving the shooting public since 1947; a multi-faceted supplier of guns, accessories, appraisal services, training, gunsmithing, gun related books.

Jim Supica
Old Town Ltd. Antique Arms
P.O. Box 14040
Lenexa, KS 66285
ph: 913-492-3000
fax: 913-492-3022
e-mail: OldTownSta@aol.com
web: http://www.ArmchairGunShow.com/
Buys and sells antique firearms; co-author of "Standard Catalog of S&W," contributing editor to "Blue Book of Gun Values" and "American Rifleman" magazine, pricing panel for "Std. Catalog of Firearms," and "Flayderman's Guide."

Robert H. Balderson
2830 Arden Way, #110
Sacramento, CA 95825
ph: 916-484-7906
fax: 916-484-7906
Specializes and appraises firearms, Western Americana, and Native American weapons; author of "Official Price Guide to Antique and Modern Firearms."

Internet Resources

Ron Landsborough
Antique Firearm Network
3442 East Hazelwood St.
Phoenix, AZ 85018
ph: 602-954-0373
fax: 602-381-0438
e-mail: sysop@OldGuns.com
web: http://www.oldguns.com
Website has individual and dealer services devoted to the collector and shooter of antique and vintage firearms.

Ben Loving
Gun Room, The
531 Main St., Ste. #518
El Segundo, CA 90245
ph: 310-546-6484
fax: 310-564-6484
e-mail: ben@doublegun.com
web: http://www.doublegun.com
A website with many dealers and collectors offering firearms for sale and listing firearms wanted to purchase.

Rob Robles
antiqueguns.com
P.O. Box 1387
Morgan Hill, CA 95038-1387
web: http://www.antiqueguns.com
This site is devoted to antique firearms manufactured prior to 1898; dealers, gun shows, parts, ask the experts, classifieds.

Man./Prod./Dist.

Smith & Wesson
2100 Roosevelt Ave.
Springfield, MA 01104
ph: 413-781-8300 or 800-826-5481
e-mail: qa@smith-wesson.com
web: http://www.smith-wesson.com

Greg Souchik
Allegheny Arsenal, Inc.
P.O. Box 161
Custer City, PA 16725-0161
ph: 814-362-2642
fax: 814-362-7356
e-mail: AlleghenyArsenal@compuserve.com
Manufacturers of Guardian Gun Care products: gun wipe, lubricant, corrosive ammo neutralizer, and metal finishing products, gun blue and Parkerizing kits.

Museums/Libraries

Springfield Armory National Historic Park
1 Armory Square
Springfield, MA 01105-1204
ph: 413-734-8551
fax: 413-747-8062
e-mail: spar_superintendent@nps.gov
web: http://www.nps.gov/spar/index.html

American Precision Museum Association, Inc.
Newsletter: Tools & Technology
P.O. Box 679
196 Main St.
Windsor, VT 05089
ph: 802-674-5781
fax: 802-674-2524
e-mail: curator@americanprecision.org
web: http://americanprecision.org/
Collections include examples of all of the guns manufactured in the museum building over its long history as an armory; examples include Sharpes, Jennings, Palmer, Ball, Robbins & Lawrence, Enfield, and L.G.Y.

Bruce M. Moseley, Cur.
Fort Ticonderoga Museum
Newsletter: Bulletin of the Fort Ticonderoga Museum
P.O. Box 390
Ticonderoga, NY 12883
ph: 518-585-2821
fax: 518-585-2210
web: http://www.neinfo.net/new_england/new_york/attractions/fort-ticonderoga/
10,000 volume research library specializing in 19th century military history and the history of the Champlain Valley; museum depicts history of the area and the campaigns during the 7 Year War and the Revolutionary War.

National Firearms Museum
11250 Waples Mill Rd.
Fairfax, VA 22030
ph: 800-NRA-3888
e-mail: membership@NRAhq.org
web: http://www.nrahq.org/

Museum of Weapons & Early American History
81-C King St.
Saint Augustine, FL 32084
ph: 904-829-3727
Rich collection of firearms including flintlocks, percussion rifles, carbines; also swords, bayonets, assorted tools, and photographs; artifacts in the collection date from 1500 to 1900.

Randy Donley
Donley's Wild West Town & Museum
8512 S. Union Rd.
Union, IL 60180-9661
ph: 815-923-9000
fax: 815-923-2253
web: http://www.wildwesttown.com/

J.M. David Arms & Historical Museum
333 Lynn Riggs Blvd.
Claremore, OK 74018
ph: 918-341-5707
e-mail: silver@tulsawalk.com
web: http://www.state.ok.us/~jmdavis/
40,000 sq. ft. museum houses a diverse collection of firearms and related items, Western artifacts, Native American artifacts, Civil War era artifacts, music boxes and instruments, steins, swords, knives, John Rogers' statuary.

Periodicals

Natcom Publications
Magazine: Gun Journal
ph: 918-491-6100
e-mail: cs@natcom-publications.com
web: http://www.gunjournal.com
A monthly magazine for the firearms collector and enthusiast.

Magazine: Arms Collecting
P.O. Box 70
Alexandria Bay, NY 13607-0070
ph: 613-393-2980
Reaches collectors, museums and librarians in 35 countries.

Joseph P. Tartaro, Ed.
Newspaper: Gun Week
P.O. Box 488
Buffalo, NY 14209-0488
ph: 716-885-6408
fax: 716-884-4471
e-mail: gunweek@aol.com
web: http://www.saf.org/
Covers all aspects of the shooting sport: new products, hunting regulations, gun legislation, shows and collecting.

Joseph P. Tartaro, Ed.
Magazine: Gun News Digest
P.O. Box 488
Buffalo, NY 14209-0488
ph: 716-885-6408
fax: 716-884-4471
e-mail: gunweek@aol.com
web: http://www.saf.org/
Quarterly magazine; in-depth coverage of important issues that effect gun owners.

Peggy Tartaro, Ed.
Magazine: Women & Guns
P.O. Box 488
Buffalo, NY 14209-0488
ph: 716-885-6408
fax: 716-884-4471
e-mail: waguns@aol.com
web: http://www.saf.org/
The only magazine of its kind; written and edited by women for women.

Dave Mullin
Magazine: Gun Dealers Network Magazine
120 Franklin Ave., Ste. 195
Scranton, PA 18503
ph: 570-941-9740
fax: 570-346-6236
Two issues per month.

Andrew Mowbray, Pub.
Magazine: Man at Arms
11250 Waples Mill Rd.
Fairfax, VA 22030
ph: 800-NRA-3888
e-mail: membership@NRAhq.org
web: http://www.nrahq.org/
"Man at Arms" is the official arms collecting periodical of the NRA. A non-shooting magazine focusing on collectible firearms, arms and armor.

Petersen Companies, Inc.
Magazine: Guns & Ammo
3816 Industry Blvd.
Lakeland, FL 33811
ph: 941-644-0449 or 800-999-3269
e-mail: leeke@petersenpub.com
web: http://www.d-p-g.com/
The world's leading firearms sporting journal for 40 years; edited for recreational hunting and shooting enthusiasts.

Richard Binger
Stott's Creek Armory, Inc.
Calendar: Stott's Creek Calendar - "The Gun Show Bible"
Rte. 1 Box 70
Morgantown, IN 46160-9619
ph: 317-878-5489
This schedule calendar lists antique gun and knife shows in the US plus many in Canada and England; each schedule or calendar lists shows for 8 months; published three times a year so they overlap by 3 months each to keep current.

Magazine: Double Gun Journal, The
P.O. Box 550
East Jordan, MI 49727
ph: 616-536-7439
fax: 616-536-7450
The world's only periodical dedicated to double barrel shotguns and rifles.

Magazine: BIG Show Journal
P.O. Box 217
Iola, WI 54945
ph: 715-445-2708
e-mail: paul@xlcom.com
web: http://www.showjournal.com/
The guide to knife and gun shows nationwide.

Pat DuChene, PR
Krause Publications
Newsmagazine: Gun List
700 E. State St.
Iola, WI 54990-0001
ph: 715-445-2214
fax: 715-445-4087
e-mail: info@krause.com
web: http://www.krause.com/
Ad newspaper for buying/selling collectible firearms, parts & accessories; gunsmithing services; reloading supplies; archery and knives; over 50,000 alphabetized guns in each issue.

Pat DuChene, PR
Krause Publications
Magazine: Gun Show Calendar
700 E. State St.
Iola, WI 54990-0001
ph: 715-445-2214
fax: 715-445-4087
e-mail: info@krause.com
web: http://www.krause.com/
Largest listing of gun shows available; lists shows throughout the U.S. and Canada; listings updated quarterly.

World-Wide Gun Report, Inc.
Magazine: Gun Report, The
P.O. Box 38
Aledo, IL 61231-0038
ph: 309-582-5311 or 309-582-5312
fax: 309-582-5555
e-mail: gunrprt@netins.net
The monthly magazine serving the antique gun collector and dealer for over 40 years.

Repair Services

Doug Turnball
Doug Turnball Restoration
6426 Co. Rd. 30
P.O. Box 471
Holcomb, NY 14469
ph: 716-657-6338
fax: 716-657-6338
e-mail: dtrrest@aol.com
web: http://gunshop.com/dtrguns.htm
Specializes in the accurate recreation of historical metal finishes on period firearms: from polishing to final finish: case-coloring, charcoal blue, nitre blue.

Browning Company

Clubs/Associations

Anthony Vanderlinden, Sec.
Browning Collectors Association
5603-B West Friendly Ave., Ste. 166
Greensboro, NC 27410
ph: 336-349-5427
e-mail: belgianpistol@worldnet.att.net
web: http://www.castblast.com/brmember.htm

Colt

Clubs/Associations

Colt Collectors Association
P.O. Box 2241
Los Gatos, CA 95031-2241
fax: 408-353-3613
e-mail: ccacolt@aol.com
web: http://www.coltcollectorsassoc.com/
Founded in 1980 by a group of avid Colt collectors; promotes the collecting of all types of Colt firearms and memorabilia.

Collectors

John S. Fischer
Coltania
10950 W. Pico Blvd.
Los Angeles, CA 90064-2115
e-mail: jsfischer1@aol.com
Buys and sells Colt factory items: original catalogs, pamphlets, advertising & promotional, books, posters: anything Colt, his factory or guns.

Experts

John T. Ogle
P.O. Box 252
Ocean Springs, MS 39566-0252
Collects memorabilia of the Colt Firearms Companies; author of Krause "Price Guide to Colt COmpany Collectibles" (1998).

Connecticut Arms & Mfg. Co.

Collectors

Edward Clark
P.O. Box 1812
Wheaton, MD 20915
ph: 301-921-9673
Collecting and researching Hammond Bulldog single shot pistols manufac-

tured by the Connecticut Arms & Mfg. Co. from 1863 to 1868.

Garand (M1)

Clubs/Associations

Garand Collectors Association
P.O. Box 181
Richmond, KY 40476-0181
ph: 606-623-2795
e-mail: redberns@javanet.com
web: http://www.garandcollassoc.org/
For collectors of M1 and M14 rifles made by John Garand originally in the 1950s.

Periodicals

Anthony Pucci, Jr.
Orion 7 Enterprises, Inc.
Magazine: Garand Times
P.O. Box 1592
Rocky Point, NY 11778
ph: 516-744-5842 or 800-653-4272
fax: 516-821-8446
e-mail: orion7@pb.net
web: http://www.m1garandrifle.com/
A quarterly magazine for the M1 collector, enthusiast, and shooter.

German

Clubs/Associations

German Gun Collectors Associations
Journal: Der Waffenschmied
P.O. Box 385
Meriden, NH 03770
ph: 603-469-3471
fax: 603-469-3471
web: http://www.germanguns.com/
An organization to preserve the rich heritage of German hunting and sporting guns.

Chris Cox
Karabiner Collector's Network
Newsletter: KCN Newsletter
P.O. Box 5773
High Point, NC 27262
ph: 336-884-5566
Network for collectors of German militaria; German rifles and snipers, pistols and holsters, Mausers, German medals and badges, helmets and uniforms, books, photographs, cartridges and ammo, field gear, edged weapons, etc.

Dealers

Tom Heller
Heller Arms, Ltd.
P.O. Box 398
Saint Charles, MO 63302-0398
ph: 314-447-3006
Autoloading pistols bought, sold, and appraised; Luger, Walther, Mauser; carries parts for most German pistols, plus original factory magazines and accessories for most pistols.

Gunsmithing

Dealers

Richard Binger
Stott's Creek Armory, Inc.
Rte. 1 Box 70
Morgantown, IN 46160-9619
ph: 317-878-5489
Antique only; buys, sells and collects flintlocks and cartridge rifles and muskets.

Repair Services

William Kennedy
Kennedy Firearms
10 North Market St.
Muncy, PA 17756
ph: 570-546-6695
web: http://amatty.com/artisans/kennedy.htm
Muzzleloading gunsmith specializing in the restoration and recreation of black powder rifles; manufactures replacement metal parts, stocks and forearms for muskets, Sharps, Maynard & Gallager.

William A. Kelley, Jr.
Gun Center, The
5831 Buckeystown Pike
Frederick, MD 21701
ph: 301-694-6887
fax: 301-694-6887
Offers a full line of gunsmithing services: repair, hot blueing, custom metal and stock work, etc.

Ron E. Dilliott
Dilliott Gunsmithing, Inc.
657 Scarlett Rd.
Dandridge, TN 37725
ph: 423-397-9204
e-mail: kared76@aol.com
web: http://www.dilliottgunsmithing.com/
Repair and restoration of antique firearms; make obsolete parts; metal and wood refinishing; 35 years experience.

Richard Binger
Stott's Creek Armory, Inc.
Rte. 1 Box 70
Morgantown, IN 46160-9619
ph: 317-878-5489
Buys and sells muzzle loaders and cartridge rifles and muskets; specializing in gunsmithing and restoration.

Japanese Matchlocks

Collectors

Raymond Macy
P.O. Box 11
West Alexandria, OH 45381-0011
ph: 937-839-5721 or 937-839-5203
Wants Japanese swords, daggers, sword parts, matchlock guns, anything samurai.

Machine Guns

Dealers

J. Curtis Earl
5512 North Sixth St.
Phoenix, AZ 85102-1309
ph: 802-264-3166 or 208-336-9330
A knowledgeable dealer of machine guns. Issues catalogs that are of interest to the beginning collector and to the advanced collector. 28 years in business listing a vast inventory of Title-II items; illustrated brochure $6 ppd.

Mannlicher

Clubs/Associations

Don Henry
Mannlicher Collectors Association
Newsletter: Mannlicher Collector, The
P.O. Box 7144
Salem, OR 97303
ph: 503-472-7710
For collectors of the Continental firearms by Mannlicher.

Internet Resources

Mannlicher-Schoenauer
e-mail: kanotex@discover-net.net
web: http://discover-net.net/~kantoex/mannlicher/
Great informative web site for the Mannlicher-Schoenauer rifle collector.

Mossberg

Clubs/Associations

National Mossberg Collectors Association
Newsletter: NMCA News
P.O. Box 487
Festus, MO 63028-0487
ph: 314-937-6401
For the collector or sporting enthusiast interested in Mossberg firearms, optics, and history; special assistance given to members in locating obsolete parts and accessories; newsletter published bi-monthly.

Collectors

Art Snyder
110 White Oak Dr.
Butler, PA 16001-3446
ph: 724-287-0278
Buys, sells, trades all pre-1950 Mossberg firearms, especially hammerless pump action rifles and smooth bore Targo guns; also wants any related accessories or literature.

Victor Havlin
P.O. Box 487
Festus, MO 63028
ph: 314-937-6401

Man./Prod./Dist.

O.F. Mossberg & Sons, Inc.
7 Grasso Ave.
North Haven, CT 06473
ph: 203-230-5300
fax: 203-230-5420
e-mail: O.F.Mossberg@worldnet.att.net
web: http://www.mossberg.com/
World's largest manufacturer of pump-action shotguns.

Pistols

Clubs/Associations

Thompson Knox, Sr.
National Automatic Pistol Collectors Association
Newsletter: Auto Mag
716 Lemay Ferry Road
Saint Louis, MO 63125
ph: 314-638-6505
e-mail: lonewolf@inlink.com
For the automatic hand gun enthusiast.

Remington

Museums/Libraries

Remington Firearms Museum
P.O. Box 179
Ilion, NY 13357-0179
ph: 315-895-3200
fax: 315-895-3237
e-mail: webmaster@remington.com
Affiliated with the Remington Arms Company, Inc.

Rifles

Experts

Richard Binger
Stott's Creek Armory, Inc.
Rte. 1 Box 70
Morgantown, IN 46160-9619
ph: 317-878-5489
Specialist in antique firearms; Life Member NRA, American Single Shot Rifle Assn., National Muzzle Loading Rifle Assn., Ohio Gun Collectors Assn.

Rifles (Single Shot)

Clubs/Associations

Rudi Prusok
American Single Shot Rifle Association
Journal: American Single Shot Rifle News
625 Pine St.
Marquette, MI 49855-3723
ph: 906-225-1828
fax: 906-227-1819
Organization dedicated to the shooting and collecting of single shot rifles from the turn of the century: German Schuetzen, buffalo, benchrest, and long range traditions; also interested in related memorabilia; free journal sample.

Periodicals

Magazine: Single Shot Exchange, The
P.O. Box 1055
York, SC 29745-1055
ph: 803-628-5326
fax: 803-628-5326
e-mail: sshotex@oldguns.com
web: http://www.oldguns.com/sshotex/
The magazine for black powder cartridge, silhouette, and Schuetzen shooters and antique gun collectors; monthly buy-sell-trade publication includes historical articles, collector's information, product reviews, match schedules, and more.

Shotguns

Collectors

Pat McKune
P.O. Box 116
Two Harbors, MN 55616
ph: 218-525-2596
e-mail: sporting@sportingcollectibles.com
web: http://www.sportingcollectibles.com
Wants to buy shotguns and gun powder hunting related collectibles: prints, annual catalogs, calendars, cardboard advertising materials; anything the American shotgun makers and powder companies used to sell their wares.

Spanish

Internet Resources

Thomas L. Allen
Sociedad Largo
P.O. Box 138
Millville, UT 84326-0138
ph: 801-797-1324 or 801-752-7038
fax: 801-797-1364
e-mail: largo@n-link.com
web: http://www.n-link.com/~largo/index.htm
Internet-based club for collectors and shooters of Spanish firearms, particularly those of 9mm Largo (also known as 9mm Bergmann-Bayard) caliber.

Thompson/Center Arms Co.

Clubs/Associations

Joe Wright, Pres.
Thompson/Center Association
Magazine: One Good Shot
P.O. Box 792
Northborough, MA 01532
e-mail: TCA@aol.com
web: http://members.aol.com/TCA/
Members dedicated to the collecting of Thompson/Center products and related memorabilia.

Winchester

Clubs/Associations

Richard A. Berg
Winchester Arms Collectors Association, Inc., The
Journal: Winchester Arms Journal, The
P.O. Box 6754
Great Falls, MT 59406-6754
ph: 406-771-8948
fax: 406-771-0601
Anything and everything for the collectors of Winchester firearms, ammunition, sporting goods, hardware items, posters, and anything else made by Winchester.

Dealers

LeRoy Merz
LeRoy Merz Antique Guns
Rt. 1, Box 380
Fergus Falls, MN 56537
ph: 218-739-3255
fax: 218-739-2356
Wants to buy fine antique Winchesters.

Doug Clemence
Treasure Chest
436 North Chicago
Salina, KS 67401-2020
ph: 785-827-9371 or 785-825-4111
e-mail: clemence@midusa.net
Buys, sells, trades Winchester related items.

Museums/Libraries

Shozo Kagoshima, Dir. of Mkt.
Winchester Mystery House, Historic Firearms Museum
525 South Winchester Blvd.
San Jose, CA 95128
ph: 408-247-2000
fax: 408-247-2090
web: http://www.sfbayfun.com/winchest.html
Medium size display of firearms through the ages.

FIRECRACKERS

(see FIREWORKS MEMORABILIA)

FIREPLACE ITEMS

Chimney Sweep

Collectors

Homestead Chimney Sweep
P.O. Box 5182
Clinton, NJ 08809
ph: 732-730-8319
fax: 732-537-7642
Wants chimney sweep items including toys, dolls, pictures, jewelry, figurines, etc.

Firebacks

Repro. Sources

Patricia Euston
New England Firebacks
P.O. Box 268
161 Main St. South
Woodbury, CT 06798
ph: 203-263-5737
Makes and sells reproduction solid cast iron firebacks.

Wendy Stoughton
Country Iron Foundry
800 Laurel Oak Dr., Ste. 200
Dept. MAC99
Naples, FL 34108-2713
ph: 941-513-1400
fax: 941-513-0969
e-mail: sales@firebacks.com
web: http://www.firebacks.com/
Firebacks are decorative cast iron plates that protect the rear wall of the fireplace from heat damage; call for catalog of firebacks.

Fireboards

Repro. Sources

Hope Angier
Sheepscot Stenciling
RFD 1 Box 613
Alna, ME 04535
ph: 207-586-5692

Mantels

Dealers

Park Pigott
Mantels of Yesteryear
70 W. Tennessee Ave.
P.O. Box 908
Mc Caysville, GA 30555
ph: 706-492-5534
fax: 706-492-3758

Tools

Repro. Sources

Lemee's Fireplace Equipment
815 Bedford St.
Bridgewater, MA 02324-3007
ph: 508-697-2672
e-mail: lemeefirep@aol.com

Charles R. Messner
Colonial Lighting & Tinware Reproductions
316 Franklin St.
Denver, PA 17517-1240
ph: 717-336-6295 or 717-336-0424
Makes Early American tinware: cookie cutters, coffee pots, wall sconces, chandeliers (electric and non-electric), post lights.

Virginia Metalcrafters
1010 East Main St.
Waynesboro, VA 22980-5855
ph: 540-949-9400 or 800-368-1002
fax: 540-949-9446
e-mail: vametal@rica.net
web: http://www.vametal.com/
Makes and sells andirons, fireplace tools and fenders, chandeliers, candlesticks, sconces, garden sculpture.

Steve Kayne
Kayne & Son Custom Forged Hardware
100 Daniel Ridge Rd.
Candler, NC 28715-9434
ph: 828-667-8868 or 828-665-1988
fax: 828-665-8303
e-mail: kaynehdwe@ioa.com
Fireplace tools, cranes, oven doors, enclosures, andirons, kitchen utensils, etc.; also does repairs, restoration & conservation; $5 for two catalogs.

FIREWORKS MEMORABILIA

(see also TOYS, Cannons; TOY GUNS)

Collectors

Brian J. Zompanti
P.O. Box 3193
New Britain, CT 06050-3193
ph: 860-223-8872 or 860-225-5137
Wants to buy old firecracker packs, boxes, catalogs, labels, etc.

R.J. Scheurer
23 Cherry Ct.
Cresskill, NJ 07626-2409
Wants fireworks, 1850-1967 4th of July memorabilia, firecracker labels, packs, posters and catalogs.

Stuart Schneider
P.O. Box 64
Teaneck, NJ 07666-0064
ph: 201-261-1983
fax: 201-599-1950
e-mail: stuarts1031@erols.com
web: http://www.geocities.com/Yosemite/Geyser/7949/
Wants old firecracker pack labels from the turn of the century to the 1950s.

Barry Zecker
Collectors Exchange, Inc.
P.O. Box 217
Martinsville, NJ 08836-0217
ph: 908-253-3400
Wants firecracker packs, fireworks catalogs; boxes for Sparklers, caps, salutes, torpedoes; also price lists, flyers, salesman's samples, photos of old fireworks plants & employees; happy to appraise items you have; 42 years experience.

Rick Fuith
5429 N. Linder
Chicago, IL 60630
ph: 773-775-6792
Wants firecracker labels, packs, catalogs, anything on fireworks.

Bill Scales
130 Fordham Circle
Pueblo, CO 81005-1649
ph: 719-561-0603
Especially wants old firecracker packs, labels, catalogs, etc.

Dealers

Kevin Hurt
July 4th Antiques
P.O. Box 6185
Battlement Mesa, CO 81636
ph: 970-285-7041 or 970-285-9141
fax: 970-285-1302
e-mail: j4antiques@aol.com
web: http://sd.znet.com/~rjweaver/kevin.html
Collector, expert, appraiser buying old 4th of July memorabilia: old firecracker packs, labels, boxes, old fireworks, catalogs, posters, cap gun caps; free appraisals; also conducts periodic fireworks memorabilia auctions.

Experts

Hal Kantrud
Newsletter: Phoenix, The
Rt. 7 Box 52
Jamestown, ND 58401
ph: 701-252-5639
Wants old firecracker packs and labels plus other fireworks related items; published quarterly newsletter.

Museums/Libraries

Al Castellano, Jr.
Firework City, Inc.
1444 W. 18th St.
P.O. Box 548
Rochester, IN 46975-0548
ph: 219-223-1616
fax: 219-223-3666
Extensive collection; looking for old fireworks packs, labels, catalogs, price lists, posters, salesman samples, pictures or anything 4th of July; will trade any of the above for live fireworks; donated items will bear donor's name.

FISHING COLLECTIBLES

(see also AQUARIUMS; BOOKS, Reference [Fishing]; DECOYS, Fish; SPORTING COLLECTIBLES)

Appraisers

Dr. Michael Echols
AntiqueLures.com
6300 Whiskey Creek Dr.
Fort Myers, FL 33919
ph: 941-489-0587
fax: 941-481-5473
e-mail: drechols@coconet.com
web: http://www.antiquelures.com
Specializes in the appraisal of pre-1940 fishing lures.

Auction Services

Withington, Inc.
590 Centr Road
Hillsboro, NH 03244
ph: 603-464-3232
e-mail: withington@conknet.com

Bob Lang
Lang's Auction
31R Turtle Cove
Raymond, ME 04071-6531
ph: 207-655-4265
fax: 207-655-4265
web: http://www.auctions-on-line.com/langs/

Ronnie Roberts, ISA
SoldUSA.com
6407 Idlewild Rd., Bldg. 2, Ste 207
Charlotte, NC 28212
ph: 704-364-2900 or 877-SoldUSA
fax: 704-364-2322
e-mail: gun1898@aol.com
web: http://www.soldusa.com/

Lindy Egan
Lures Etc.
4052 Sequoia Ave.
Grove City, OH 43123
ph: 614-871-3162

Clubs/Associations

Florida Antique Tackle Collectors, Inc.
P.O. Box 420703
Kissimmee, FL 34742-0703

Michigan Lure Collectors Club
P.O. Box 79
Lennon, MI 48449
e-mail: mlca@geocities.com

National Fishing Lure Collectors Club
Newsletter: NFLCC Gazette
H.C. #33, Box 4012
Reeds Spring, MO 65737
e-mail: spurr@kingfisher.com
web: http://www.gorp.com/cl_angle/canecoun/nflcc.htm
3500 members; fosters awareness of fishing tackle collecting as a hobby; assists members in identification, location and valuing fishing tackle, etc.; 26 pg. newsletter published quarterly; also publishes NFLCC full color magazine.

Collectors

Mark R. Van Sciver
120 Elm Street AG-5
Beverly, NJ 08010
ph: 609-877-2271
e-mail: MARKV500@aol.com
web: http://members.aol.com/markv500/
Collector of antique tackle, specializing in saltwater.

Paul Webber
P.O. Box K
Stockton, NJ 08559-0350
ph: 609-397-8727

Don Bailen
6 Carol Ave.
Fredonia, NY 14063
ph: 716-679-7292
Collects old metal lures stamped "Haskell," "Chapman," "Comstock," and most other lures stamped with pre-1920 patent dates.

Sam G. Husselman
474 Johnston Dr.
Bethlehem, PA 18017-1815
ph: 610-866-7984
e-mail: husselman@enter.net
web: http://www.enter.net/~husselman/sam.html
Very familiar with the identification and pricing of most antique fishing lures and other fishing collectibles; his web page has original research and information on the Heddon Crazy Crawler and 210 lures, two of his specialties.

Philip W. Hartman
1 South Eighth Alley
P.O. Box 263
New Market, MD 21774
ph: 301-865-5651
fax: 301-865-0518
e-mail: Phil@newmarketmd.com
web: http://www.newmarketmd.com/grange.htm
Buys lures, reels (including German silver reels), tackle, bobbers, etc.; wrote the first article, "Fishing Pike Floats & Bobbers" in "Antique Angler" (Aug. 1985); expert on bobbers.

David A. Gladwell
P.O. Box 238
Bedford, VA 24523-0238
ph: 540-586-1488 or 540-586-9575
e-mail: dagladwell@aol.com
Wants old fishing tackle, especially lures or plugs, and advertisements.

Brian Shillito
5501 65th Ave. North
Pinellas Park, FL 33781
ph: 727-541-7540
Wants pre-1950 fishing lures and tackle.

Ron Gast
2306 Leeward Cove
Kissimmee, FL 34746
ph: 407-933-7435
e-mail: rkgast@magicnet.net
web: http://www.magicnet.net/~rkgast/
Collector of antique fishing tackle for over 20 years; especially interested in lures made in Florida and reels made in Kentucky; always interested in talking with people about their tackle.

Stephen Bassler, Jr.
Vanderbilt University
P.O. Box 4011-B
Nashville, TN 37235
ph: 615-421-9462 or 847-446-2334
e-mail: basslesj@vuse.vanderbilt.edu
web: http://www.vuse.vanderbilt.edu/~basslesj/lurepage.htm
Serious collector; interests range from baits, rods and reels, to miscellaneous equipment; wants Heddon, Creek Chub, Shakespeare, Pflueger, and others.

Lindy Egan
4052 Sequoia Ave.
Grove City, OH 43123
ph: 614-871-3162
Wants to buy most anything having to do with fishing.

Rich Treml
P.O. Box 1791
Dearborn, MI 48121

Raymond L. Carver
22325 B Drive South
Marshall, MI 49068-9722
ph: 616-781-5668
e-mail: spurr@kingfisher.com
web: http://www.gorp.com/cl_angle/canecoun/nflcc.htm
Author of "Bud Stewart - Michigan's Legendary Lure Maker."

Richard McCoy
2719 Lakeview Ave.
St. Joseph, MI 49085
Wants to buy all kinds of fishing tackle: sinkers, bobbers, plugs, lures, poles, reels, tackle boxes.

Ron Bash
P.O. Box 888271
Grand Rapids, MI 49588-8271
ph: 616-248-0571
fax: 616-248-0693
e-mail: wittbash@aol.com
Buy, sell, trade antique fishing tackle: lures, reels, etc.

Thomas Jacomet
1255 Crown Court
Mukwonago, WI 53149
ph: 414-363-9079 or 414-363-9528
e-mail: tjacomet@execpc.com
web: http://www.execpc.com/~tjacomet/lurelore.html
Collector and trader of old fishing tackle, specializing in Heddon River Runt Spooks; author of "Lure Lore," on-line bi-weekly articles on fishing tackle collectibles.

John & JoAnn Monk
P.O. Box 261123
Plano, TX 75026
ph: 972-672-5114
e-mail: jwmonk@airmail.net
Wants to buy pre-1950 fishing tackle: wooden lures, plastic lures, small fly rods, metal spoons and spinners, ice fishing decoys, wooden factory tackle

boxes, two-piece cardboard boxes for lures, etc.

Eric Fuchslocher
8050 Ventura Cyn Ave.
Panorama City, CA 91402
ph: 818-994-1492
Wants to buy old wooden fishing lures.

George S. Lawson, Jr.
P.O. Box 796
Capitola, CA 95010-0796
ph: 831-476-6475
e-mail: fishnstuff@aol.com
Collector of quality split bamboo fly rods, all types of reels, old wooden lures, vintage tackle catalogs, creels and pre-1940 fishing licenses; author of "Lawson's Price Guide to Old Fishing Reels."

Dealers

Martin J. Keane
Classic Rods & Tackle, Inc.
P.O. Box 288
Ashley Falls, MA 01222
ph: 413-229-7988
Buys and sells antique rods, reels, and exotic accessories; high grade rods and reels bought and appraised.

Bob Greenbaum
Bob & Shirley's Antiques
6151 Beverly Hills Rd.
Coopersburg, PA 18036-1872
ph: 610-282-4881
Wants all items related to the sport of fishing.

Neil Ghingold
Neil Ghingold Antiques
1230-32 Broad St.
Augusta, GA 30901-1116
ph: 706-722-3483
Wants to buy fishing collectibles.

Ed & Carolyn Corwin
P.O. Box 1119
Hastings, FL 32145-1119
ph: 904-692-2037
fax: 904-692-2037
e-mail: reelures@aol.com
Buys, sells and appraises; general information no charge; send SASE with request; include photos or photocopies if possible (lures can be photocopied); specializes in pre-1950 reels, creels, lures, tackle catalogs.

Nancy & Glenn Darst
Boston Store, The
P.O. Box 190394
Mobile, AL 36619
ph: 334-666-9265 or 334-666-2079
e-mail: gdarst@zebra.net
Buys and sells Boy Scout and Girl Scout hatchets, knives, and axes; also wants pre-1950 LLBean.

John E. Shoffner
624 Merritt St.
Fife Lake, MI 49633-9142
ph: 616-879-3912
e-mail: kjohn@gtii.com
Issues 6 lists a year with approx. 600 fish decoys and antique fishing tackle items for sale.

Phil White
14099 Lakeshore Dr.
Nampa, ID 83686
ph: 208-466-1746
e-mail: pandm@micron.net
web: http://www.webpak.net/~pandm/
Collector of fishing tackle and sporting collectibles, specializing in fishing reels, catalogs, and related paper items; author of two books on fishing collectibles and editor of two fishing tackle newsletters.

Mike Berry
Mike's Tackle Box
P.O. Box 5827
Bellingham, WA 98227
ph: 360-734-7379
e-mail: mike@mikestackle.com
web: http://www.mikestackle.com
Online catalog of collectible rods, reels, and lures which can be purchased over the Internet.

Experts

Gary Wood
Fishing Lure & Angling Collector
733 Myrtle Rd.
North Brunswick, NJ 08902-2549
ph: 732-821-7633
e-mail: woodrasp@aol.com
Buying and appraising old fishing lures, reels, floats, and related advertising; feel free to call and chat; "If it's got a hook, I'll take a look!"

Ed & Carolyn Corwin
P.O. Box 1119
Hastings, FL 32145-1119
ph: 904-692-2037
fax: 904-692-2037
e-mail: reelures@aol.com
Buys, sells and appraises; general information no charge; send SASE with request; include photos or photocopies if possible (lures can be photocopied); specializes in pre-1950 reels, creels, lures, tackle catalogs.

Doug Jobe
Doug's Old Fishing Lures
217 S. College St.
Batavia, IL 60510
ph: 630-879-5104
e-mail: luresdog@inil.com
web: http://www.inil.com/users/luresdog/
Antique fishing lure collector; buy/sell/trade and appraise; buying old fishing and hunting magazines and catalogs; always happy to just talk old fishing tackle.

Russ Gulledge
Old Tackle Collections
1941 Heather Lane
Pacific, MO 63069
ph: 314-271-8078
fax: 314-271-8078
e-mail: tackle99@aol.com
web: http://members.aol.com/tackle99/page1.htm
Expert, appraiser, collector Buys single lures or entire collections of pre-WWII fishing lures.

Mark Copeland
Fishing Unlimited Antique Tackle
1710 Effie
Pasadena, TX 77502
ph: 281-487-8111
e-mail: fishunl@usa.net
web: http://www.angelfire.com/tx/FishingUnlimited/
Collector, expert, appraiser, repairer of antique fishing tackle.

Phil White
14099 Lakeshore Dr.
Nampa, ID 83686
ph: 208-466-1746
e-mail: pandm@micron.net
web: http://www.webpak.net/~pandm/
Collector of fishing tackle and sporting collectibles, specializing in fishing reels, catalogs, and related paper items; author of two books on fishing collectibles and editor of two fishing tackle newsletters.

Robert Whitaker
2810 E. Desert Cove Ave.
Phoenix, AZ 85028-2620
ph: 602-992-7304
fax: 602-493-5598
e-mail: whitakr@futureone.com

Rick Edmisten
P.O. Box 686
North Hollywood, CA 91603-0686
ph: 818-763-9406
fax: 818-763-5974
e-mail: flc@antiqnet.com
web: http://www.flc.com/
Wants to buy pre-1940 wooden lures, quality reels, catalogs, some high grade rods, tackle boxes, art prints, etc.; collect calls O.K.; offers free appraisal of any and all fishing tackle from photos sent if SASE included.

Gabby Talkington
4703 Upland Dr.
Richmond, CA 94803-3227
ph: 510-223-1142
fax: 510-233-3388
e-mail: oldlures@aol.com
Longtime buyer/seller of vintage fishing tackle: wood fishing lures, reels, rods, advertising and catalogs; sale list available; free appraisals; life member National Fishing Lures Collectors Club.

Richard Streater
P.O. Box 393
Mercer Island, WA 98040-0393
ph: 206-232-9060
fax: 206-232-9060
e-mail: lureguru@aol.com
Collector of antique fishing lures and tackle; author of "The Fishing Lure Collector's Bible," available from the author; fishing gadgetry a specialty.

Internet Resources

Dr. Michael Echols
AntiqueLures.com
6300 Whiskey Creek Dr.
Fort Myers, FL 33919
ph: 941-489-0587
fax: 941-481-5473
e-mail: drechols@coconet.com
web: http://www.antiquelures.com
Information on pre-1940 fishing lures with a heavy emphasis on Heddon, Shakespeare, Flyrod lures, and early miscellaneous lures; over 516 web pages of photos, articles, color charts, catalogs, and advice on collecting antique lures.

Brian Cooper
Short Stop Collectible Tackle Site
5511 W 99 Terr
Shawnee Mission, KS 66207
ph: 816-225-3747 or 913-642-4316
Comprehensive auction and sales list for vintage tackle enthusiasts with detailed descriptions and photos of items; consignments accepted (subject to item by item approval.)

Classic Angler, The
256 Nashua Court
Grand Junction, CO 81503
ph: 970-243-8780
fax: 970-243-6503
e-mail: spurr@kingfisher.com
web: http://www.gorp.com/bamboo.htm
A comprehensive Internet site for aficionados of classic tackle: bamboo rods and old fishing tackle; for collectors, builders and restorers of bamboo rods.

Museums/Libraries

Gary Tanner, Ex. Dir.
American Museum of Fly Fishing
Magazine: American Fly Fisher, The
P.O. Box 42
Manchester, VT 05254
ph: 802-362-3300
fax: 802-362-3308
e-mail: amffish@sover.net
web: http://www.amff.com/
Non-profit educational institution dedicated to preserving the rich history of fly fishing and American angling; over 1,500 rods, 800 reels, 40,000 flies, 2,500 books, manuscripts, photos, etc.

Ted Dzialo
National Fresh Water Fishing Hall of Fame
Newsletter: Splash, The
One Fame Dr.
P.O. Box 33
Hayward, WI 54843-0033
ph: 715-634-4440
fax: 715-634-4440
web: http://www.oldcabin.com/freshwater/
Custodian of historical sport fishing artifacts; world record qualifier; clearinghouse for contemporary & historical fishing facts.

Periodicals

Brian McGrath, Ed.
Magazine: Fishing Collectibles Magazine
P.O. Box 2797
2 Oak Street
Kennebunkport, ME 04046
ph: 207-967-8044
fax: 207-967-2671
e-mail: mcgrath@cybertours.com
web: http://www.fishcollmag.com/
The magazine for anyone interested in fishing or fishing collectibles; covers all aspects of fishing collectibles including art, advertising, books, decoys, lures, paraphernalia, rods, reels, etc.; free appraisals.

Abenaki Publishers, Inc.
Magazine: American Angler Magazine
160 Benmont Ave.
P.O. Box 4100
Bennington, VT 05201-4100
ph: 802-446-1518 or 800-877-5305
fax: 802-447-2471
web: http://www.flyfishingmags.com/americanangler/
Contains occasional articles about vintage fishing collectibles.

Fly Fishing

Experts

Wolf's Sporting Adventure
9191 Baltimore Pike
Ellicott City, MD 21043
ph: 410-465-1112
Buys and sells high quality fly fishing equipment and other sporting gear; takes collectible equipment on consignment to sell.

Fly Fishing (Flies)

Experts

David Klausmeyer
New England Angler, The
P.O. Box 105
Steuben, ME 04680-0105
ph: 207-546-2018

Ice Fishing Spears

Experts

Marcel L. Salive, Ph.D.
1483 Dunster Lane
Potomac, MD 20854-6107
ph: 301-762-1909
e-mail: msalive@erols.com
Author of "Ice Fishing Spears" (MarJac Publishing).

Reels

Clubs/Associations

Roger Schulz, Mem.
Old Reel Collectors Association
Newsletter: Reel News, The
160 Shoreline Walk
Alpharetta, GA 30022
ph: 770-521-1877
e-mail: orca@micron.net
web: http://www.webpak.net/~orca/
Purpose is the further the knowledge about reels used in fishing from 1800 through 1970.

Phil White
Meisselbach Association, The
Newsletter: Meisselbach News
14099 Lakeshore Dr.
Nampa, ID 83686
ph: 208-466-1746
e-mail: pandm@micron.net
web: http://www.webpak.net/~pandm/page17.html
Formed in 1993 to provide information for those interested in collecting Meisselbach & Meisselbach-Catucci fishing reels.

Collectors

Royal E. Fox
64 Collfield
Staten Island, NY 10302-2416
ph: 949-448-8317
Wants spinning reels; working or not; parts, boxes, literature, brochures, manuals.

Michael Nogay
3501 Riverview Dr.
P.O. Box 2540
Weirton, WV 26062

Reels (Fly Fishing)

Experts

Jim Brown
97 Franklin St.
Stamford, CT 06901-1309
ph: 203-324-5441
Specializes in collecting American fly reels and fly rod lures; author of "Fishing Reel Patents of the U.S., 1838 - 1940" (1985) and "A Treasury of Reels" (1990).

Rods (Bamboo)

Collectors

Lee Pattison
6 Christview Dr.
Cuba, NY 14727-1202
ph: 716-968-2458
Wants old and new fishing tackle, large ocean reels, old wood tackle boxes, fishing books, tackle catalogs.

Udwary
629 Spencer Circle
Spartanburg, SC 29307-2507
Buys, sells, trades bamboo fly rods, pre-1965, 7', 7 1/2', 8' sizes; Edwards, Leonard, Thomas, High-Grade Granger, Hardy, Heddon, Phillipson; OK if in need of repair, but must be priced accordingly.

Experts

David Klausmeyer
P.O. Box 105
Steuben, ME 04680-0105
ph: 207-546-2018
Buys and sells quality bamboo fly rods; also manufacturers bamboo rods and provides expert appraisal services for quality bamboo fly rods.

Internet Resources

Classic Angler, The
256 Nashua Court
Grand Junction, CO 81503
ph: 970-243-8780
fax: 970-243-6503
e-mail: spurr@kingfisher.com
web: http://www.gorp.com/bamboo.htm
A comprehensive Internet site for aficionados of classic tackle: bamboo rods and old fishing tackle; for collectors, builders and restorers of bamboo rods.

Man./Prod./Dist.

Cal Harvey
Cal Harvey Custom Fly Rods
401 E. 12th
Littlefield, TX 79339
ph: 806-385-4298
e-mail: bldarter@camalott.com
web: http://members.tripod.com/~BradBanner/flyrod.html
Maker of custom fly rods since 1940.

Repair Services

Michael Sinclair
Cane Clinic, The
2100 Blake St.
Denver, CO 80205
e-mail: caneclinic@aol.com
Offers refinishing and restoration of bamboo rods.

FLAGS & FLAG RELATED COLLECTIBLES

(see also MILITARIA)

Clubs/Associations

David Martucci
North American Vexillological Association
Newsletter: NAVA News
PMB 225, 1977 N. Olden Ave.
Trenton, NJ 08618-2193
ph: 207-845-2857
e-mail: pres@nava.org
web: http://www.nava.org/
Dedicated to the promotion of vexillogy, the scientific & scholarly study of flag history and symbolism; publishes bi-monthly newsletter and annual "Raven" journal, annual meetings, publishes booklets, undertakes special projects.

Collectors

Jon Radel
3806 Candlelight Ct.
Alexandria, VA 22310-2248
e-mail: jon@radel.com
web: http://www.radel.com/
Collects flags, flag books, and other printed matted concerning flags, including postcards; older foreign and local flags, foreign publications of special interest. No common or 20th cent. U.S. flags or flag items, please.

Mark Sutton
2035 St. Andrews Circle
Carmel, IN 46032-9547
ph: 317-844-5648
Buys/trades old cloth American flags with 47 or less than 45 stars; wants original flags from 6" to HUGE; also unusual star patterns.

Dealers

Dallas & Ann Dutson
Flag Store, The
20089 Broadway
Sonoma, CA 95476
ph: 707-996-8140 or 888-GET-FLAG
fax: 707-996-8171
e-mail: flags@vom.com
web: http://www.flagemporium.com
Dealer, expert, vendor, manufacturer; the most complete flag site on the internet!

Experts

Robert Banks
Stars & Stripes
18901 Gold Mine Court
Brookeville, MD 20833-2711
ph: 301-774-7850
Seeking antique American flags with 43 stars or less; also wants unique or uncommon examples of any period.

Man./Prod./Dist.

Carrot-Top Industries, Inc.
328 Elizabeth Brady Rd.
P.O. Box 820
Hillsborough, NC 27278-0820
ph: 800-628-3524 or 919-732-6200
fax: 919-732-5526
e-mail: ct_industries@compuserve.com
web: http://www.carrot-top.com/
Sells new flags and related hardware: US, states and territories, international, flagpoles, mounting hardware, parade accessories, NASCAR, special interest flags, historical and military flags, globes, pennants, custom designed flags.

Military

Experts

Ben K. Weed
Colours, The
P.O. Box 4643
Stockton, CA 95204
e-mail: B.K.Weed@worldnet.att.net
web: http://members.tripod.com/~oldflagswanted/usa.html
Largest private collector of worldwide military flags; buys flags, parts and photos.

FLASHLIGHTS

Clubs/Associations

Bill Utley
Flashlight Collectors of America
Newsletter: Flashlight Newsletter
P.O. Box 4095
Tustin, CA 92781
ph: 714-730-1252
fax: 714-505-4067
e-mail: flashlights@worldnet.att.net
Eight page flashlight newsletter printed quarterly: articles of flashlight history, great finds, questions & answers, classified ads, old flashlight catalog reprints.

Collectors

John Treggiari
ph: 978-744-2897
fax: 978-744-5572
e-mail: micrometer@juno.com
Serious collector wants to buy old flashlights and related manufacturer catalogs and displays; flashlights need not be working; especially wants with patent dates prior to 1930; old flashlight batteries also purchased.

Stuart Schneider
P.O. Box 64
Teaneck, NJ 07666-0064
ph: 201-261-1983
fax: 201-599-1950
e-mail: stuarts1031@erols.com
web: http://www.geocities.com/Yosemite/Geyser/7949/
Buys odd and unusual or early flashlights and flashlight advertising; author of "Collecting Flashlights."

Bill Utley
P.O. Box 4095
Tustin, CA 92781
ph: 714-730-1252
fax: 714-505-4067
e-mail: flashlights@worldnet.att.net
Collector/historian wants old flashlights, flashlight advertising, flashlight catalogs and other flashlight related items; interested in almost any portable object containing a dry cell battery and a light bulb.

Dealers

Shaw
P.O. Box 5096
Southfield, MI 48086
Wants to buy 1920s-1960s vintage flash lights: brass, chrome, enamel, etc.

FLATWARE

(see also SILVER; SILVERPLATE; TABLEWARE)

Matching Services

Paul & Pearl Hoffman
China Brokers, Ltd.
11 Westgate Ct.
Colts Neck, NJ 07722
ph: 732-866-6613 or 800-867-6613

Wilma Saxton, Inc.
37 Celementon Rd. Box 395
Berlin, NJ 08009
ph: 609-767-8640 or 800-267-8029
fax: 609-768-7795
Matching service for sterling, silverplate, stainless, pewter, dirilyte; flatware and hollowware; also repairs and replating; write for free price list in your pattern.

Alice Korman
Alice's Past & Presents Replacements
P.O. Box 465
Merrick, NY 11566-0465
ph: 516-379-1352
fax: 516-379-7302
e-mail: alicechina@aol.com
Matching and locating service for stainless and silverplate flatware: Community, Oneida, Gorham, International, Reed & Barton, Towle, Wallace, National, Yamazaki, W.M. Frazer, Kirk, Mikasa, Sasaki, Lunt, others.

Tony Garfield
Yudin & Associates
P.O. Box 1980
Boothwyn, PA 19061
ph: 610-859-9698
fax: 610-859-0142
Community, Gorham, Holmes & Edwards, National, Oneida, 1847 Rogers, Wallace, silverplate.

Michael Round Fine China & Crystal, Inc.
7845 Wisconsin Ave.
Bethesda, MD 20814
ph: 301-656-2626 or 800-467-6863
fax: 703-550-7881
e-mail: feedback@Mround.com
web: http://www.michaelround.com
Impressive website for matching china, crystal or flatware.

Mary Ann Lowery
Crystal Corner, Inc., The
317 Billy Dyar Blvd.
P.O. Box 756
Boaz, AL 35957-0756
ph: 256-593-6169
fax: 256-593-6560
e-mail: ccorner@netnav.com
web: http://www.crystalcorner.com/
Specializes in stainless and silverplate flatware.

Sterling & Collectables
P.O. Box 1665
Mansfield, OH 44901
ph: 800-537-5783
Sterling, silverplate, stainless, dirilyte; all manufacturers; current and discontinued.

Dona Miller
Ann Arbor Dinnerware Exchange
P.O. Box 6054
Ann Arbor, MI 48106-6054
ph: 734-663-9883
fax: 734-663-5766
e-mail: aadinex@aadinex.com
web: http://www.aadinex.com
Offers new patterns including some previously unavailable in the US: Magnum and Vantage (now called Aztec) stainless, flatware from Norway, Georg Jensen; also some previously discontinued Oneida patterns.

Barron's
P.O. Box 994
Novi, MI 48376
ph: 800-538-6340
fax: 800-523-4456
e-mail: barronsdw@aol.com
web: http://www.barronsdinnerware.com/
Matches stainless, silverplate, and sterling flatware.

Clintsman International
811 E. Geneva St.
Elkhorn, WI 53121
ph: 414-723-1990 or 800-781-8900
fax: 414-723-1991
Stocks all manufacturers of discontinued patterns for sterling silver, silverplate, and stainless steel flatware: Christofle, Dansk, Dirilyte, Whiting, Gorham, Japan, Lunt, Mikasa Retroneau, Rosenthal, Stanley, Tiffany, etc.

China Replacements
P.O. Box 508
High Ridge, MO 63049
ph: 800-562-2655 or 314-677-5577
fax: 314-376-6319
e-mail: chinarep@i1.net
web: http://www.iadm.com/chinarep/
Matches all major brands of sterling, silverplate, and stainless.

Betty Stachurski
Betty's Crystal & China
P.O. Box 433
Lawrence, KS 66044-0433
ph: 913-842-8054
Stainless, silverplate and sterling: 1881 Rogers, 1847 Rogers Bros., Alvin, Christofle, Community, COntinental, Dansk, Fine Arts, Frank Smith, Fraser, Gorham, Harmony House, Heritage, International, Kirk-Stieff, Reed & Barton, etc.

Joanne Cone
Joanne Cone Matching Service
34 Silverwood
Irvine, CA 92604
ph: 949-551-3173
e-mail: jochina@aol.com
All manufacturers; stainless, silverplate and sterling silver; Oneida specialist, Fraser, Gense, Gorham, International, Lauffer, Mikasa, National, Noritake, Oxford Hall, Reed & Barton, Roberts, Towle, Wallace, etc.

Past & Present
14851 Avenue 360
Visalia, CA 93292
ph: 500-437-7666 or 415-258-1775
fax: 415-456-4333
e-mail: P-P@ix.netcom.com
web: http://www.china-crystal-flatware.com
Silverplate, sterling, stainless, Dirilyte; by Alvin, Easterling, Frank Smith, Fraser, Gorham, International, Jensen, Kirk, Lunt, Manchester, Oneida, Reed & Barton, Steiff, Tiffany, Towle, Wallace, Westmoreland, etc.

Juanita Mallorie
Sterling Shop, The
P.O. Box 595
Silverton, OR 97381-0595
ph: 503-873-6315
e-mail: juanita@sterlingshop.com
web: http://www.sterlingshop.com
Sterling and silverplate flatware matching service.

Grace Ann Kupferschmid
Matchmaker of Iowa
109 Discovery Bay St.
Sequim, WA 98382-9327
ph: 360-683-7517
e-mail: gakup@olypen.com
Major brands of discontinued stainless, pewter, gold electroplated including Lunt, Wallace-International, Gorham, Oneida, Reed & Barton,

Towle (including Lauffer, Supreme Cutlery), Fraser, Mikasa, Sasaki, Yamazaki,Dansk, Dalia, Kirk Stieff.

Periodicals

Susan Ranta
Magazine: Set Your Table
P.O. Box 22481
Lincoln, NE 68542-2481
ph: 800-600-2127 or 402-423-4865
fax: 402-423-4865
e-mail: sranta@setyourtable.com
web: http://www.setyourtable.com
Looking for stainless, sterling, silverplate, pewter, Set Your Table lists more than 80 dealers who can help you find your missing pieces; dealer listings are indexed by manufacturer so you will know which dealers can help you.

Suppliers

Dennis Blaine
Cutlery Specialties
22 Morris Lane
Great Neck, NY 11024-1707
ph: 516-829-5899 or 516-773-0071
fax: 516-773-8076
e-mail: Dennis13@aol.com
Preservation products for flatware: waxes, polishes, cleaners, glues, epoxies, adhesives, chamois, buffs, putty.

Silverplate

Matching Services

Michael Kucharski
Vintage Silver
33 LeMay Court
Williamsville, NY 14221-3628
ph: 716-631-0419
fax: 716-433-2850
e-mail: mikekuch@localnet.com
Buys and sells; specializes in matching 1890-1950 silverplated flatware; 20,000 pieces in stock; 100s of patterns.

John Benetti
Silver Scotty
420 Ashwood Rd.
Darlington, PA 16115
ph: 724-827-2188
fax: 724-827-2811

Silver Girls
168 Riverview Rd. SW
Eatonton, GA 31024-6836
ph: 912-968-5225
fax: 912-968-5225
Silverplated flatware; all major manufacturers of discontinued/ collectible patterns.

Phil & Angela Dreis
Antique Cupboard
3712 N. 92 St.
Milwaukee, WI 53222
ph: 800-637-4583
fax: 414-464-1616
e-mail: mail@antiquecupboard.com
web: http://www.antiquecupboard.com
Over 900 sterling and 1000 plated patterns in stock; buys and sells current and obsolete patterns and rare and unusual pieces; largest inventory in the Midwest.

Helen Lawler
Helen Lawler's Silverplate Matching Service
5400 East County Rd. #2
Blytheville, AR 72315
ph: 573-720-8502
Large inventory of silverplated flatware; call or write for your pattern listing with prices; antique and recently discontinued patterns.

Sterling Silver

Matching Services

Silver Lady Antiques
Echo Bridge Mall
381 Elliot St.
Newton, MA 02164
ph: 617-243-0900 or 781-784-9184
fax: 781-784-0628
Tiffany, Jensen, Gorham, Kirk flatware and hollowware.

Ross Simmons
#9 Ross Simmons Dr.
Cranston, RI 02920-4476
ph: 800-521-7677 or 800-553-2135
fax: 800-896-9191
e-mail: customerservices@ross-simmons.com
web: http://www.ross-simmons.com/
Sells new, active patterns for Gorham, Reed & Barton, Wallace, Towle, Lunt, Kirk-Stieff, International; several outlets on East coast.

Regina Negrotti
Tablescapes
P.O. Box 448
Cheshire, CT 06410
ph: 800-801-4084
e-mail: lenox@ntplx.net
web: http://www.tabletopdesigns.com/
A small, personal matching service with a constantly changing inventory; want lists are kept; send photocopy or photo when unsure of pattern name.

Silver & China Exchange
P.O. Box 4601
Dept. MA
Stamford, CT 06907-0601
ph: 203-322-5963
Sterling flatware only; no stainless or silverplate; computerized search service available.

R.S. Goldberg
R.S. Goldberg
67 Beverly Rd.
Hawthorne, NJ 07506-3201
ph: 800-252-6655 or 201-427-6555
e-mail: rssilver@aol.com
web: http://www.rsgoldberg.com/
Hundreds of patterns in stock; always buying and selling.

Nathan Horowicz
Nathan Horowicz Antiques
1050 2nd Ave., Gallery 82
New York, NY 10022
ph: 800-214-6320 or 212-755-6320
fax: 212-755-6438
Large assortment of flatware, tea sets, hollowware; Tiffany, Georg Jensen; all American and European manufacturers.

Pattern Finders, A
P.O. Box 206
Port Jefferson Station, NY 11776-0206
ph: 516-928-5158 or 800-216-2446
fax: 516-928-5170
e-mail: apattern@aol.com

Martin Spickler, PhD
Tova's Treasures
11410 Strand Dr., #207
Rockville, MD 20852-2938
ph: 301-984-5954
A specialized matching matching service for American sterling silver patterns.

Thurber's
2256C Dabeny Rd.
Richmond, VA 23230-3342
ph: 804-278-9080 or 800-848-7237
fax: 804-278-9480
Carries only active patterns; will locate old patterns.

Joe Batista
Replacements Ltd.
P.O. Box 26029
1089 Knox Road
Greensboro, NC 27420
ph: 800-737-5223 or 336-697-3000
fax: 336-697-3100
e-mail: replaceltd@aol.com
web: http://www.replacements.com
China, crystal and flatware (obsolete, active and inactive.)

Beverly H. Bremer
Beverly Bremer Silver Shop
3164 Peachtree Rd. NE
Atlanta, GA 30305
ph: 404-261-4009 or 800-270-4009
fax: 404-261-5742
web: http://www.beverlybremer.com
Appraises, buys, sells and matches sterling silver flatware, new and antique sterling silver hollowware & giftware; send for inventory of your sterling pattern or send photocopy of your pattern; no SASE required; answers all inquiries.

Atlantic Silver & China
7405 N.W. 57th St.
Tamarac, FL 33319
ph: 800-368-3153 or 954-720-4559
fax: 954-720-4577
e-mail: info@atlanticsilver.com
web: http://www.atlanticsilver.com
Inactive and active sterling silver flatware and hollowware; buys and sells.

Silver Queen
730 N. Indian Rocks Rd.
Belleair Bluffs, FL 33770
ph: 800-262-3134 or 727-581-6827
fax: 727-586-0822
e-mail: sqbc@tampabay.rr.com
web: http://www.silverqueen.com/
High quality, estate and new flatware; call or write for inventory list of your pattern; also buys sterling silver flatware; over 1500 patterns in stock.

Antique Silver House, The
8976 Seminole Blvd.
Seminole, FL 33772
ph: 813-392-7250 or 800-SIL-VER5

Debra Bonner
Colonial Silver Shoppe
20 Gaylan Court
Montgomery, AL 36109
ph: 800-675-4837 or 334-272-7282
Gorham, Wallace, International, Towle, Kirk-Stieff, Lunt.

Tim & Nancy Young
Alcove Antiques
9825 Concord Rd.
Brentwood, TN 37027
ph: 615-776-5152 or 800-525-8170
fax: 615-776-3039
e-mail: mail@alcoveantiques.com
web: http://www.alcoveantiques.com

Carol Lewis
Sterling & Collectables, Inc.
P.O. Box 1665
Mansfield, OH 44901
ph: 800-537-5783 or 419-756-8800
fax: 419-756-2990
A matching service for discontinued and current sterling tableware, both flatware and hollowware; also carries current and back years of sterling and crystal Christmas ornaments.

Sterling Buffet
143 S. Ireland Blvd.
Mansfield, OH 44906
ph: 800-537-5783 or 419-529-0505
e-mail: info@sterlingbuffet.com
web: http://www.sterlingbuffet.com

Benjamin Randolph
Eden Sterling
7672 Montgomery Rd.
Cincinnati, OH 45236
ph: 800-385-3336 or 513-792-9345
e-mail: info@edensterling.com
web: http://www.edensterling.com/
Website has online encyclopedia of the most often seen marks of American

coin silversmiths and sterling silver manufacturers.

Phil & Angela Dreis
Antique Cupboard
3712 N. 92 St.
Milwaukee, WI 53222
ph: 800-637-4583
fax: 414-464-1616
e-mail: mail@antiquecupboard.com
web: http://www.antiquecupboard.com
Over 900 sterling and 1000 plated patterns in stock; buys and sells current and obsolete patterns and rare and unusual pieces; largest inventory in the Midwest.

Ted Rickard
Silver Service
ph: 847-256-5900
fax: 847-256-5952
e-mail: trick2@juno.com
Specializing in matching discontinued American and English sterling silver flatware; also locates antique sterling silver flatware.

Audrey Rickard
China Trade Ltd.
2133 Birchwood Ave.
Wilmette, IL 60091-2305
ph: 847-256-7414 or 800-295-4200
fax: 847-256-5952
e-mail: Trick2@juno.com
Discontinued and antique sterling patterns: Gorham, Reed & Barton, Towle, Kirk Stieff, International, Tiffany, WAllace, Lunt, Dominick & Haff, Durgin, Alvin, Whiting, Tuttle, etc.

Dining Elegance, Ltd.
P.O. Box 4203
Saint Louis, MO 63163
ph: 314-865-1408
Sterling silver - full sets only.

Mark
Silverwarehouse
4311 NE Vivion Rd.
Kansas City, MO 64119-2890
ph: 816-454-1990
fax: 816-454-1605
e-mail: mark@silverwarehouse.com
web: http://www.silverwarehouse.com
Largest sterling flatware inventory in the country; buys/sells sterling; also polishes, repairs, reblades knives; big buyer of sterling silver flatware and hollowware; also stainless, silverplate, pewter, Dirilyte.

Madeleine Guice Nicoladis
Melange Sterling
5419 Magazine St.
New Orleans, LA 70115
ph: 800-513-3991 or 504-899-4796
fax: 504-899-4796
e-mail: sterlingmelange@msn.com
Specializes in active, inactive, and obsolete American, British and Continental sterling flatware: Alvin, Amston, Baker, Birks, Buccellati, Christofle, Concord, Dominick & Haff, Duhme, Durgin, Easterling, Georg Jensen, Tuttle, etc.

Helen & Duncan Cox
As You Like It Silver Shop
3025 Magazine St.
New Orleans, LA 70115-2232
ph: 800-828-2311 or 504-897-6915
fax: 504-895-4149
e-mail: ayliss@cris.com
web: http://www.cris.com/~ayliss/
Large inventory of active and inactive patterns; also tea services, goblets, mint juleps, etc.

Locators, Inc.
2217 Cottondale Lane
Little Rock, AR 72202-2018
ph: 501-663-7787 or 800-367-9690
fax: 501-663-7787
e-mail: locators@worldnet.att.net
web: http://www.chinalocators.com
Carries out-of-production (discontinued) china and crystal, and discontinued as well as active sterling flatware patterns.

Nancy's Silver Shop
21550 Oxnard Street, 3rd Floor
Woodland Hills, CA 91367
ph: 800-352-8927 or 818-703-5000
fax: 818-703-5082
e-mail: hello@nancysilver.com
web: http://www.nancysilver.com/
Matching service, silverware sets, baby gifts, silver flatware pattern finder.

Betty Overton
Betty's Sterling Silver Matching Service
200 Avenida Santa Margarita
San Clemente, CA 92672
ph: 949-498-5330 or 949-498-4027
fax: 949-498-5330
e-mail: edwhiffen@aol.com
Active, inactive, and obsolete sterling silver patterns; all manufacturers; send want lists and photocopy; also sterling silver hollowware and sterling silver ornaments from 1970 to present.

Barry Rosenstein
Sunset Sterling
4369 Valley Fair
Simi Valley, CA 93063
ph: 800-468-6966 or 805-522-4711
fax: 805-522-4892
Alvin, Amston, Dominick & Haff, Durgin, Easterling, Fine Arts, Gorham, International, Kirk-Stieff, Lunt, Manchester, National, Oneida, Reed & Barton, Royal Crest, State House, Towle, Wallace, Westmoreland, Frank Whiting, Whiting Mfg. Co.

Silver Lane Antiques
P.O. Box 322
San Leandro, CA 94577-0032
ph: 510-483-0632
American sterling flatware in complete sets or by the piece; tea services, trays, etc. also available; specializing in unique pieces for advanced collectors.

Brenda Clayton
Silver Thistle
14314 SW Allen Blvd. #217
Beaverton, OR 97005
ph: 503-235-3749
Rogers, International, Gorham, Holmes and Edwards, and others; send SASE with pattern, manufacturer or photocopy for identification.

FLEA MARKETS

(see also ANTIQUES SHOP DIRECTORIES; TOURS/BUYING TRIPS)

Directories

Periodicals

House of Collectibles
Guide: Official Directory to U.S. Flea Markets
201 East 50th St.
New York, NY 10022-7703
ph: 212-751-2600 or 800-733-3000
fax: 212-572-8700
e-mail: bfi@randomhouse.com
web: http://www.randomhouse.com/catalog/
Covers about 500 markets; provides quality information about each.

Dorothy Clark
Clark's Publications
Guide: Clark's Flea Market U.S.A.
419 Garcon Point Rd.
Milton, FL 32583-7359
ph: 850-623-0794
fax: 850-626-2088
e-mail: fleaUSA@aol.com
A national flea market directory issued quarterly; over 1,800 flea markets and swap meets listed; subscription.

Jim Goodridge
Goodridge Guides
Guide: Flea Market Shoppers Companion
P.O. Box 744
Arnold, MO 63010
ph: 314-296-0989
e-mail: fleamktusa@aol.com
web: http://members.aol.com/fleamktusa/index.html
Covers all 50 states; contains over 3,500 separate listings of flea markets across North America.

Directories (Foreign)

Periodicals

Peter Manston
Travel Keys
Guide: Manston's Flea Market Guides
P.O. Box 160691
Sacramento, CA 95816-0691
ph: 916-452-5200
Publishes a series of Flea Market Guides, for Britain, France and Germany; $9.95 plus $4.00 shipping; accepts credit card orders.

FLICKERS

Dealers

Joe Statkus
84 State Rd.
Eliot, ME 03903
ph: 207-439-7429
Carries a wide selection of flicker rings and specializes in hard-to-find flickers.

Gary Kraut
Alphaville
226 W. Houston St.
New York, NY 10014-4846
ph: 212-675-6850
fax: 212-741-2609
e-mail: alphavil@mindspring.com
web: http://www.alphaville.com
Sells ring, button, pin, key chain flickers; flickers are those specially coated dimestore images mounted on cardboard backings that "moved" or shifted scenes as if animated when moved or viewed from a different angle.

FLOORCLOTHS

Repro. Sources

Angie Nelson
Homeplace Collection
1882 Kennedy Farm Rd. N
Thomasville, NC 27360-8335
ph: 336-472-6396
fax: 336-472-6396
Offers handpainted canvas floorcloths and wall hangings; beautiful family tree design; new one-of-a-kind hand-carved painted or stained cowboys, Indians, mountain men, bears; 7' plus.

FLOWER "FROGS"

Collectors

William G. Sommer, MD
9 W. 10th St.
New York, NY 10011-8748
ph: 212-260-0999
Wants ceramic figural flower "frogs": dancing ladies or nudes American (Cowan, Fulper, Rookwood) or European (Germany, England.)

Christie McCann
3019 Winter Pine Ct.
Fairfax, VA 22031
ph: 703-385-0551
e-mail: olga@erols.com
web: http://www.erols.com/aaac
Collects, researches Depression glass flower frogs; wrote a small pamphlet to accompany a glass show display, copies available upon request.

Kescia Moore
2225 Casa Vista Dr.
Palm Harbor, FL 34683
ph: 727-784-9664
e-mail: r2kmoore@gte.net

Lew & Joyce Hendrick
6526 Spring Brook Rd., #208
Rockford, IL 61114
ph: 815-636-4627
e-mail: lew4@webtv.net
Wants to buy flower frogs.

Marcia Bradley
P.O. Box 460931
Papillion, NE 68046-0931
ph: 402-597-0322
e-mail: froggie@radiks.net
web: http://www.angelfire.com/ne/FrogPrints/
An avid flower frog collector; predominantly interested in pottery animal figures and colored glass blocks.

Susan Cox
800 Murray Dr.
El Cajon, CA 92020
ph: 619-697-5922
e-mail: antiqfever@aol.com
Wants American pottery flower frogs.

Internet Resources

Flower Frog Gazette
e-mail: BluebirdCT@aol.com
web: http://members.aol.com/bluefirdct/ffg.html
Great resource website for collectors of flower frogs.

FOBS

(see WATCH FOBS)

FOLK ART

(see also ART, Outsider; BOTTLES, Puzzle; CAROUSELS & CAROUSEL FIGURES; CIGAR STORE COLLECTIBLES; COVERLETS; DECOYS; EAGLES; FRAKTURS; POPULAR CULTURE; QUILTS; RUGS, Hooked; SAMPLERS; SCRIMSHAW; SILHOUETTES; TRAMP ART)

Auction Services

John McClain
York Town Auction Inc.
1625 Haviland Rd.
York, PA 17404
ph: 717-751-0211
fax: 717-767-7729
e-mail: yorktownauction@cyberia.com
Antique & specialty auctions, lecture & appraisal services; antiques also purchased; American & English furniture, related specialties & accessories, Americana, folk art, jewelry, art, clocks & watches, militaria, steins, Oriental rugs.

Steve Slotin
Slotin Folk Art Auction House
Newspaper: 20th Century Folk Art News
5967 Blackberry Lane
Buford, GA 30518
ph: 770-932-1000
fax: 770-932-0506
Leading venue for self-taught, Outsider, Folk Art and Southern folk pottery; published newspaper twice each year chronicling important happenings in the field of 20th century folk art as the most popular feature, New, True & Blue Artists.

Clubs/Associations

Richard Trump
Folk Art Association of the Southwest
3993 Old Santa Fe Trail
Santa Fe, NM 87501
ph: 505-984-8680

Mel Penner
American Folk Art Society, Inc.
597 Chippendale Ave.
Simi Valley, CA 93065-7023
Focuses on American folk art.

Collectors

Michael J. Hennigan
20816 E. Eleven Mile
Saint Clair Shores, MI 48081-1565
ph: 313-822-9730 or 810-779-9992
fax: 313-821-2766
e-mail: henn48230@aol.com
Wants to buy figures made by tradesmen to advertise their businesses, such as figures made from mufflers and parts, radiators, heating/cooling/furnace fixtures, plumbing parts, leaf or coil springs, etc.

Dealers

Russ & Karen Goldberger
RJG Antiques
P.O. Box 2033
Hampton, NH 03843-2033
ph: 603-926-1770
fax: 603-929-4267
e-mail: russ@rjgantiques.com
web: http://www.rjgantiques.com
Specializes in quality working decoys, folk art, and American furniture and accessories in their original painted surfaces.

Gary Guyette
Gary Guyette Antiques
P.O. Box 522
West Farmington, ME 04992
ph: 207-778-6256 or 207-625-8055
fax: 207-778-6501

Marguerite Riordan
Marguerite Riordan Antiques
8 Pearl St.
Stonington, CT 06378
ph: 860-535-2511 or 860-535-3431
fax: 860-535-3431
Specializes in Folk Art, American furniture, paintings and decorative accessories; by appointment.

Peter H. Tillou Fine Arts
109 Prospect St.
Litchfield, CT 06759-2503
ph: 860-567-5706

Frank Maresca
Ricco/Maresca Gallery
529 W. 20th Street, 3rd Floor
New York, NY 10011
ph: 212-627-4819
fax: 212-627-5117
e-mail: rmgal@aol.com
web: http://www.riccomaresca.com/
Deals in American self-taught, folk and outsider art.

American Hurrah Antiques
P.O. Box 919
New York, NY 10024-0546
ph: 212-535-1930
fax: 212-580-5501
Specializes in American folk art, American Indian, and antique quilts.

Ronald Korman
Muleskinner Antiques
10626 Main St.
Clarence, NY 14031
ph: 716-759-2661
e-mail: muletiques@aol.com
web: http://www.muleskinnerantiques.com
Buys and sells redware, antique lighting, fold art, game boards, primitives, weathervanes, early glass, decoys, trade signs, etc.

John C. Newcomer
York Town Auction Inc.
1625 Haviland Rd.
York, PA 17404
ph: 717-751-0211
fax: 717-767-7729

M. Finkel & Daughter
936 Pine St.
Philadelphia, PA 19107
ph: 215-627-7797
fax: 215-627-8199

Joe Adams
America, Oh Yes!
P.O. Box 3075
Hilton Head Island, SC 29938
ph: 843-785-2649
e-mail: folkart@hargray.com
web: http://ww.americaohyes.com/
Wants Folk Art paintings, carvings, quilts, crafts by Southern artisans (contemporary and antique.)

Donald E. Taussig
Sanders' Antique Mall
22 N. Lemon Ave.
Sarasota, FL 34236-5711
ph: 941-366-0400
fax: 941-388-2053
e-mail: sandersant@aol.com
Buys and sells decoys, antique lighting, trade signs, decorative accessories.

Matt Lippa
Artisans
P.O. Box 256
Mentone, AL 35984-0256
ph: 256-634-4037
fax: 256-634-4037
e-mail: artisans@folkartisans.com
web: http://www.folkartisans.com
Buy and sell folk art, outsider art, fine art; Internet WWW site offers links to additional dealers; also offers non-profit clubs and museums with an outlet to post notices, press releases, calendar items, etc. at no charge.

Ivan Gilbert, MD
Miran Art & Books
2824 Elm Ave.
Columbus, OH 43209
ph: 614-231-3707 or 614-818-3222
fax: 614-818-3223
e-mail: IGilbert@ahhinc.com

Louis Picek
Main Street Antiques & Art
110 West Main
P.O. Box 340
West Branch, IA 52358-0340
ph: 319-643-2065
Buys and sells folk art; offers a monthly list of items for sale.

Frank & Barbara Pollack
1214 Green Bay Rd.
Highland Park, IL 60035-4011
ph: 847-433-2213 or 847-433-2295
fax: 312-372-8343
e-mail: fpollack@compuserve.com
web: http://www.maineantiquedigest.com/adimg/pollack.htm
Buys and sells American primitives: paintings, furniture, toleware, folk art, textiles, etc.

Experts

David A. Schorsch
David A. Schorsch American Antiques Inc.
244 Main St.
Woodbury, CT 06798
ph: 203-263-3131
fax: 203-263-2622

Clifford Wallach
277 W. 10th St.
New York, NY 10014-2562
ph: 212-243-1007
fax: 212-929-1839
e-mail: tramprt@aol.com
Author of "Tramp Art, One Notch at a Time" published by Wallace-Irons;

buys, sells exceptional forms of tramp art and other folk art and outsider art.

Helaine Fendelman
Helaine Fendelman & Assoc.
1248 Post Rd.
Scarsdale, NY 10583-2153
ph: 914-725-0292
fax: 914-472-2266
e-mail: HFendelman@aol.com
Appraises and liquidates estates; author of the "Official Identification and Price Guide to American Folk Art."

Internet Resources

Matt Lippa
Artisans
P.O. Box 256
Mentone, AL 35984-0256
ph: 256-634-4037
fax: 256-634-4037
e-mail: artisans@folkartisans.com
web: http://www.folkartisans.com
Buy and sell folk art, outsider art, fine art; Internet WWW site offers links to additional dealers; also offers non-profit clubs and museums with an outlet to post notices, press releases, calendar items, etc. at no charge.

Museums/Libraries

Robert D. Farwell, Dir.
Fruitlands Museums, Inc.
102 Prospect Hill Rd.
Harvard, MA 01451
ph: 978-456-3924
web: http://www.miele-fleury.com/~fruitland/
A 19th century American art and history museum complex.

Museum of Fine Arts, Boston
465 Huntington Ave.
Boston, MA 02115-5523
ph: 617-267-9300
e-mail: webmaster@mfa.org
web: http://www.mfa.org/home.html

Yale University Art Gallery, Garvan Collection
P.O. Box 20871
New Haven, CT 06520-8271
ph: 203-432-0600 or 203-432-0601
web: http://www.yale.edu/artgallery/

Museum of American Folk Art
Columbus Ave. between 65th and 66th Sts.
New York, NY 10023
ph: 212-977-7170
e-mail: info@folkartmuse.org
web: http://www.folkartmuse.org/
Dedicated to exploring the diversity of American culture as expressed through folk art.

New-York Historical Society, The
Two West 77th St.
New York, NY 10024
ph: 212-873-3400
fax: 212-874-8706
e-mail: nyhs@interport.net
web: http://www.nyhistory.org
An unparalleled resource for the study and appreciation of American art, history, and culture.

Albany Institute of History & Art
125 Washington Ave.
Albany, NY 12210
ph: 518-463-4478

New York State Historical Association & The Farmers' Museum, Inc., The
P.O. Box 800
Lake Road
Cooperstown, NY 13326
ph: 607-547-1450 or 888-547-1450
e-mail: nysha1@aol.com
web: http://www.farmersmuseum.org/

Landis Valley Farm Museum
2451 Kissel Hill Rd.
Lancaster, PA 17601
ph: 717-569-0401
fax: 717-560-1247
web: http://www.landisvalleymuseum.org/

Bucks County Historical Society
Newsletter: Penny Lots
84 S. Pine St.
Doylestown, PA 18901-4930
ph: 215-345-0210
fax: 215-230-0823
e-mail: bchs@philadelphia.libertynet.org
web: http://www.libertynet.org/bchs
Operates three Nat. Historical Landmarks; Mercer Museum has over 50,000 tools of Early American trades/crafts; Spruance Library has research material on trades & crafts; Fonthill Museum is a concrete castle laden with tiles & treasures.

Museum of American Art of the Pennsylvania Academy of Fine Arts
118 N Broad St.
Philadelphia, PA 19102
ph: 215-972-7600
e-mail: pafa@pafa.org
web: http://www.pafa.org/museum/museum.html

Daughters of the American Revolution Museum
1776 D St. NW
Washington, DC 20006-5392
ph: 202-879-3241 or 202-879-3208
fax: 202-628-0820
e-mail: museum@dar.org
web: http://www.dar.org/museum/

National Museum of American History
14th & Constitution Ave. NW
Washington, DC 20560
ph: 202-357-2700
e-mail: webmaster@si.edu
web: http://www.si.edu/organiza/museums/nmah/nmah.htm

Abby Aldrich Rockefeller Folk Art Center
P.O. Box C
Williamsburg, VA 23185
ph: 757-229-1000 or 800-HISTORY
e-mail: webmaster@cwf.org
web: http://www.history.org

Paula Hooper
Museum of Early Southern Decorative Arts
Journal: Journal of the Early Southern Decorative Arts
P.O. Box 10310
Winston Salem, NC 27108-0310
ph: 336-721-7360 or 888-653-7253
fax: 336-721-7367
e-mail: webmaster@oldsalem.org
web: http://www.mesda.org
Focuses on Southern decorative arts; has Research Center, Catalog of Early Southern Decorative Arts, and Index of Southern Artists.

David Warren
Bayou Bend Collection & Gardens, The
P.O. Box 6826
Houston, TX 77265-6826
ph: 281-639-7750
fax: 281-639-7770
e-mail: hirsch@mfah.org
web: http://mfah.org/bayou.html
One of the nation's premier American decorative arts collections, housed in the former residence of Houston philanthropist Miss Ima Hogg; collection includes over 4,800 works of American art: furniture, textiles, paintings, etc.

Charlene Cerny, Dir.
Museum of International Folk Art
706 Camino Lejo
Santa Fe, NM 87505-7511
ph: 505-827-6350
fax: 505-827-6349
e-mail: ccerny@moifa.org
web: http://www.state.nm.us/moifa/
Home of the world's largest folk art collection from around the globe; over 125,000 artifacts from over 100 nations.

Periodicals

Museum of American Folk Art
Magazine: Folk Art
Columbus Ave. between 65th and 66th Sts.
New York, NY 10023
ph: 212-977-7170
e-mail: info@folkartmuse.org
web: http://www.folkartmuse.org/

Carvings

Repro. Sources

Vaughn Rawson
Whimsical Whittler, The
1745 W. Columbia Rd.
Mason, MI 48854-9259
ph: 517-676-4846
Specializes in reproduction folk art carvings.

Contemporary

Clubs/Associations

Ann Oppenhimer
Folk Art Society of America
Newsletter: Folk Art Messenger
P.O. Box 17041
Richmond, VA 23226-7041
ph: 804-285-4532 or 800-527-3655
fax: 804-285-4532
e-mail: fasa@folkart.org
web: http://www.folkart.org
Non-profit organization formed to discover, study, promote, preserve, exhibit, and document contemporary folk art, folk artists, and folk environments; newsletter published quarterly.

Museums/Libraries

Joan M. Bendetti, Lib.
Craft & Folk Art Museum
5800 Wilshire Blvd.
Los Angeles, CA 90036-4591
ph: 323-934-9684 or 323-937-5544
fax: 323-937-5576
Specializing in contemporary craft, design, folk art: clay, fiber, wood, glass, paper, costume, dolls, masks, etc.; artist's registry.

Periodicals

Florence Laffal, Ed.
Gallery Press
Newsletter: Folk Art Finder
117 North Main St.
Essex, CT 06426
ph: 860-767-0313
FAF is devoted to news and information on contemporary folk art; calendar, feature stories, readers exchange, new artists, ads, etc.; published quarterly.

Mexican

Experts

Donna McMenamin
5001 Woodway #1002
Houston, TX 77056-1718
ph: 713-622-7252
fax: 281-780-9723
e-mail: DMcMenamin@msn.com
web: http://www.donnamcmenamin.com
Author of "Popular Arts of Mexico 1850-1950"; buys and sells.

Paintings

Repro. Sources

Diane Ulmer Pedersen
36 Westland Farm Rd.
Sterling, MA 01564
Specializes in reproduction style folk art paintings: still lives on checkerboard, landscapes, scenes with (or w/o) scripture, children, portraits; all works are original compositions; original designs.

Stoneware

Dealers

Richard Hume
P.O. Box 281
Point Pleasant Beach, NJ 08742-0281
ph: 732-899-8707 or 732-295-9285

Theorems

Repro. Sources

Hope R. Angier
Sheepscot Stenciling
RFD 1 Box 613
Alna, ME 04535
ph: 207-586-5692

Tinware

Museums/Libraries

Barbara Livenstein
Cooper-Hewitt Museum National Museum of Design, Smithsonian Institution
2 East 91st St.
New York, NY 10128
ph: 212-860-8400 or 212-849-8349
e-mail: liven@ch.si.edu
web: http://www.si.edu/organiza/museums/design/ndm.htm

Weathervanes

Museums/Libraries

Heritage Plantation of Sandwich
P.O. Box 566
Sandwich, MA 02563
ph: 508-888-3300 or 508-888-1222
fax: 508-833-2916
e-mail: heritage@heritageplantation.org
web: http://www.heritageplantation.org/autos.htm

Repro. Sources

Lemee's Fireplace Equipment
815 Bedford St.
Bridgewater, MA 02324-3007
ph: 508-697-2672
e-mail: lemeefirep@aol.com

Brian Chabot
Cape Cod Cupula
78 State Rd., Rte. 6
North Dartmouth, MA 02747-2922
ph: 508-994-2119
fax: 508-997-2511
Sells reproduction weathervanes and custom-made copulas.

Copper House, The
1747 Dover Rd., RT 4
Epsom, NH 03234-4416
ph: 800-281-9798
fax: 603-736-9798
e-mail: lights@thecopperhouse.com
web: http://www.thecopperhouse.com/copper/
Handmade copper reproduction lighting fixtures and weathervanes. No imports. Catalog $4 deducted from purchase.

FOOD COLLECTIBLES

(see also BANANA COLLECTIBLES; CEREAL BOXES; COFFEE; COOKBOOKS; COOKIES & COOKIE SHAPING; FAST FOOD COLLECTIBLES; GROCERY STORE ITEMS; HAMBURGERS; MENUS; NUT RELATED COLLECTIBLES; POPCORN ITEMS; PREMIUMS, Cereal Box; RESTAURANT COLLECTIBLES)

Dealers

Louise Pennisi
Around the Kitchen
P.O. Box 840
Georgetown, CT 06829
ph: 203-438-2338
e-mail: louise@aroundthekitchen.com
web: http://www.aroundthekitchen.com
Buying and selling collectible cookbooks (19th & 20th century), cookery booklets (Pillsbury, Baker's Chocolate, Jell-O, etc.), antique kitchen instruction & recipe pamphlets; issues catalogs of items for sale.

Fake Food

Man./Prod./Dist.

Fake Food
P.O. Box 184
Telford, PA 18969
ph: 215-679-6152
fax: 215-679-3975
The first food-art product line of this kind in the country; pies, miniature fake food products, etc.

Ketchup

Collectors

Ralph Finch
34007 Hillside Ct.
Farmington, MI 48335-2513
Wants antique material relating to ketchup.

Mustard

Clubs/Associations

Mount Horeb Mustard Museum
109 E. Main St.
Mount Horeb, WI 53572
ph: 608-437-3986 or 800-438-6878
e-mail: curatorweb@mustardweb.com
web: http://www.mustardweb.com/
Over 3,000 mustard-related artifacts on display.

Collectors

Barry Levinson
c/o Mount Horeb Mustard Museum
109 E. Main St.
Mount Horeb, WI 53572
ph: 608-437-3986 or 800-438-6878
e-mail: curatorweb@mustardweb.com
web: http://www.mustardweb.com/
Collector of mustard-related items: mustard jars, advertising, knick-knacks, etc.

FORD MOTOR COMPANY ITEMS

Collectors

Cliff Moebius
484 Winthrop St.
Westbury, NY 11590
ph: 516-333-3797
fax: 516-333-1712
Wants Ford Motor Co. and Henry Ford memorabilia: joke books, postcards, books, photos, Christmas cards, records, sheet music, script pens, pins, china, silverware, menus, sales literature, etc.

Dealers

Tim O'Callaghan
305 St. Lawrence Rd.
P.O. Box 512
Northville, MI 48167
ph: 248-449-2652
e-mail: timothyo@ameritech.net
Author of Ford aviation book and video and numerous articles on Ford Motor Company; collects, buys, sells, trades Ford memorabilia: books, postcards, coins, badges, pins, etc.; always willing to answer questions.

FOSSILS

(see also ARCHAEOLOGY; MINERAL SPECIMENS; NATURAL HISTORY; PREHISTORIC ARTIFACTS; SKELETONS)

Auction Services

Jeremy Fuller
Mineral, Fossil & Gemstones Auctions Co.
997 N. Chapel Dr., Ste. #4
Bountiful, UT 84010
ph: 801-296-2516
fax: 801-292-5439
e-mail: info@minimarket.com
web: http://www.minmarket.com/
The first mineral, fossil, and gemstone "mall" auction of its kind on the Web.

Clubs/Associations

Karl Stuekerjuergen
Mid-American Paleontology Society
1503 265th Ave.
Cedar Rapids, IA 552656
ph: 319-837-6690

Fossil Collectors Club
2280 N. Greenville Ave.
Richardson, TX 75082
ph: 800-730-6060

Collectors

Scott Young
P.O. Box 8452
Port Saint Lucie, FL 34985-8452
ph: 561-878-5634
fax: 561-878-22009
e-mail: iceageman3@aol.com
Buys, sells, trades vertebrate fossils from around the world.

Dealers

Ken LeBlanc
PaleoPlace
60 E Fox Meadow Rd.
Leominster, MA 01453
ph: 978-537-3614
e-mail: rand50@tiac.net
web: http://www.paleoplace.com
PaleoPlace is "The Old Earth Catalog" for genuine fossils from around the world; the beauty of life from the ancient preserved in stone.

Al Prandi
Two Guys Fossils
1 Lynne's Way
East Bridgewater, MA 02333-2131
ph: 800-FOS-SILS
fax: 508-378-7081
e-mail: app@twoguysfossils.com
web: http://www.twoguysfossils.com
Insects in amber, dinosaurs.

Jerry & Sandy Sherman
Paleoworld Connection
P.O. Box 86
Spencerville, MD 20868-0086
ph: 301-476-9313 or 301-476-7531
e-mail: jerry.sherman@erols.com
web: http://www.paleoworld.com/
Deals in Native American, prehistoric artifacts and fossils worldwide.

Gene Harris
Art By God
50 Upper Alabama, Store No. 248
Underground Atlanta
Atlanta, GA 30303
ph: 404-577-7311 or 800-940-4449
fax: 305-573-9343
e-mail: artbygod@netside.net
Mineral specimens, fossils, gems, sea shells, animal mounts, animal pelts, insects/butterflies, snail shells, skulls.

J.F. Ray
P.O. Box 1364
Ocala, FL 32678-1364
Catalog sales of fossils; supplies museums, shops, schools; since 1962.

Gene Harris
Art By God
3705 Biscayne
Miami, FL 33137
ph: 305-573-3011 or 305-573-3691
fax: 305-573-9343
e-mail: artbygod@netside.net
Mineral specimens, fossils, gems, sea shells, animal mounts, animal pelts, insects/butterflies, snail shells, skulls.

Eric S. Kendrew
Fossil Store, The
4436 Tevalo Dr.
Valrico, FL 33594-7343
ph: 813-681-4330
Buy, sell, trade for fossils worldwide; prepare fossils; gives lectures; supplies schools and museums with fossils; expert underwater and land excavations; written articles on fossils; featured in many magazines and newspaper articles.

Jim & Susan Pendergraft
J & S Fossils
17 Jeff Rd.
Largo, FL 33774-2038
ph: 813-595-2661
fax: 813-595-8544
e-mail: Fossils@gte.net
web: http://home1.gte.net/fossils/jaws.htm
Supplies discerning collectors with fossil specimens from ancient sharks, whales, mastodons and mammoths; visit the web site to see a reconstruction from the gigantic miocene shark megalodon.

John & Karen Mediz
Copper City Rock Shop
566 Ash St.
Globe, AZ 85501
ph: 520-425-7885 or 520-425-4506
fax: 520-425-4506
Buys and sells mining artifacts; also wants to buy minerals and fossils, especially old collections.

Richard B. Troyanowski
Rich Relics
P.O. Box 432
Sandia Park, NM 87047-0432
ph: 505-281-2611 or 505-281-2329
Buys/sells prehistoric/historic Indian artifacts, cowboy, militaria, old world antiquities & coins, fossils & ethnographic collectibles.

Jesse Wellman
High Grade Treasures
P.O. Box 5470
Reno, NV 89513
e-mail: jesse@highgradetreasures.com
web: http://www.highgradetreasures.com
Field collects and purchases minerals and fossils to provide quality common and unusual specimens for the discriminating collector and hobby beginner.

Fossil Company, The
P.O. Box 1339
El Cerrito, CA 94530
ph: 510-233-8891
fax: 510-232-5614
e-mail: sales@fossil-company.com
web: http://www.fossil-company.com
Supplier of fine quality fossils, mineral specimens and crystals.

Internet Resources

Canadian Rockhound
Canada
e-mail: cdn_rockhound@hotmail.com
web: http://pangea.usask.ca/~dfs846/rockhound/
An on-line magazine providing interesting and educational stories on rock, fossil and mineral collecting, the art of lapidary, gems and faceting, and on the earth sciences as well.

Jeremy Fuller
Mineral Market
997 N. Chapel Dr., Ste. #4
Bountiful, UT 84010
ph: 801-296-2516
fax: 801-292-5439
e-mail: info@minimarket.com
web: http://www.minmarket.com/
On-line mineral and fossil auctions, dealer lists, on-line mineral and fossil museum.

Museums/Libraries

Fick Fossil & History Museum
700 W. 3rd St.
Oakley, KS 67748
ph: 758-672-4839
e-mail: cmullen@ruraltel.net
web: http://www.oakley-kansas.com/fick/

Periodicals

Magazine: Lapidary Journal
60 Chestnut Ave., Ste. 201
Devon, PA 19333-1312
ph: 610-293-1112 or 800-676-4336 (sub)
fax: 610-293-1717
e-mail: Ljmagazine@aol.com
web: http://www.lapidaryjournal.com
Covers gems, beads, jewelry, minerals, and fossils, for artisans and collectors, including profiles, step-by-step instructions, and a show calendar.

FOUNTAIN PENS

(see PENS)

FOURTH OF JULY ITEMS

(see FIREWORKS MEMORABILIA; HOLIDAY COLLECTIBLES)

FRAKTURS

(see also FOLK ART; STATE RELATED MEMORABILIA, Pennsylvania German Heritage)

Book Sellers

Russell D. Earnest
P.O. Box 1007
East Berlin, PA 17316-0507
Sells books on fraktur.

Dealers

Russell D. Earnest
P.O. Box 1007
East Berlin, PA 17316-0507
Buys and sells fraktur including printed fraktur, birth and baptism certificates, bookplates, fraktur-like watercolors, or other decorated manuscripts; send photo or clear photocopy; describe and state price.

Experts

Ron Lieberman
Family Album, The
RD 1 Box 42
Glen Rock, PA 17327-9707
ph: 717-235-2134
fax: 717-235-8765
e-mail: ronbiblio@delphi.com
web: http://www.auldbooks.com/biblio/clients/lieberman.html
Buys, sells and appraises German Americana: fraktur, books, manuscripts, artwork, etc.

Pstr. Frederick Weiser
55 Kohler School Rd.
New Oxford, PA 17350-9201
ph: 717-624-4106

Museums/Libraries

Free Library of Philadelphia
1901 Vine St.
Philadelphia, PA 19103
ph: 215-686-5322 or 215-686-5416
e-mail: webteam@library.phila.gov
web: http://www.library.phila.gov/
The Henry S. Borneman collection of Pennsylvania German Fraktur.

Repro. Sources

Sally Greene Bunce
1520 Makefield Rd.
Yardley, PA 19067-3150

FRAMES

(see also REPAIR/RESTORATION/CONSERVATION, Gilding)

Appraisers

Jerome S. Feig, CPF, ISA
Field Art Studio
24242 Woodward Ave.
Pleasant Ridge, MI 48069-1144
ph: 248-399-1320
fax: 248-399-7018
e-mail: jsfieldart@aol.com
Frame specialist and appraiser: restoration of art, frames, objects, gilding; period frame reproductions made; fine art and frame appraisals; conservation of picture frames.

Clubs/Associations

William Adair
International Institute for Frame Study
443 I Street NW
P.O. Box 50156
Washington, DC 20091
ph: 202-638-4660
fax: 202-347-4569
e-mail: bill@goldleafstudios.com
web: http://www.goldleafstudios.com
Established in 1992 as the first public archive devoted exclusively to the history of picture frames; archive has hundreds of photographs, drawings, out-of-print books, auction and frame makers' catalogs, articles, videos, etc.

Dealers

John Baker
50 Granite St.
Foxboro, MA 02035
ph: 508-543-4626
Wants to buy ornate gilt frames.

Eli Wilner
Eli Wilner & Co.
1525 York Ave.
New York, NY 10028
ph: 212-744-6521
fax: 212-628-0264
e-mail: info@eliwilner.com
web: http://www.eliwilner.com/index2.htm
Sells, buys and restores fine 19th and 20th century frames; author of

"Antique American Frames: Identification and Price Guide."

Mary Webster
Mary Webster Antique Picture Frames
12 Edwards St.
Binghamton, NY 13905
ph: 607-722-1483
e-mail: mwebster@lightlink.com
web: http://www.marywebster.com/
Carries large inventory of mainly American period frames in many styles including Federal, Victorian, Renaissance Revival, Eastlake, Aesthetic, Arts & Crafts, folk art; also frames for photographs and mirror frames; buys and sells.

Carol Payne
Carol's Antique Gallery
14455 Big Basin Way
Saratoga, CA 95070-6008
ph: 408-867-7055
Wants to buy stand-up frames of wood, silver, brass, ivory, enamel, etc.; send photocopy of front and back of frame plus description for a cash offer.

Experts

William Adair
Gold Leaf Studios, Inc.
443 I Street NW
P.O. Box 50156
Washington, DC 20091
ph: 202-638-4660
fax: 202-347-4569
e-mail: bill@goldleafstudios.com
web: http://www.goldleafstudios.com

Internet Resources

Art & Framing Headquarters
e-mail: webmaster@artframing.com
web: http://www.artframing.com/
Provides a centralized source for people who have an interest in the art and picture framing industry; vendors can promote their products; customers can purchase artwork or get items framed.

Scott Kublin
Art Directory
P.O. Box 1616
Rincon, GA 31326
ph: 912-826-6840
e-mail: admin@artframing.com
web: http://www.artframing.com
Centralized resource for businesses in the art and framing industry.

Periodicals

Magazine: Decor
330 N. Fourth St.
Saint Louis, MO 63102
ph: 314-421-5445 or 800-280-5445
fax: 314-421-1070
e-mail: decor@cpcmags.com
web: http://www.decomagazine.com/
Aimed at the frame shop/gallery owner; lots of articles about how to increase sales, gallery floor plans, advertising; occasionally covers some new trend in print making; also published annual Sources issues.

Repair Services

Susan B. Jackson
Harvard Art
49 Littleton County Rd.
Harvard, MA 01451-1729
ph: 978-456-9050
fax: 978-456-9050
e-mail: sbj@ma.ultranet.com
Restoration and conservation of period frames and other gilded objects; stabilization, replacement of missing pieces, gilding and toning to match the existing surface.

Alexandra Hadik
Gilder's Studio, The
34 Jarves St.
Sandwich, MA 02563-2039
ph: 508-833-0782
Custom gold leaf framing and conservation; also offers instruction in gold leaf.

William Adair
Gold Leaf Studios, Inc.
443 I Street NW
P.O. Box 50156
Washington, DC 20091
ph: 202-638-4660
fax: 202-347-4569
e-mail: bill@goldleafstudios.com
web: http://www.goldleafstudios.com
Frame repairs, gold leaf repair; also makes copies of antique frames in different sizes.

R. Wayne Reynolds
R. Wayne Reynolds, Inc.
3618 Falls Rd.
Baltimore, MD 21211
ph: 410-467-1800 or 410-467-1890
Specializes in the application of gold leaf; complete restoration services for gilded art objects, including furniture, frames, and mirrors.

Paul J. Buco
Fine Arts Services, Inc.
127 N. Front St.
Wilmington, NC 28401-3944
ph: 910-251-8859
Restoration of frames including oil and water gilding, recasting and replacement of lost ornament.

Jerome S. Feig, CPF, ISA
Field Art Studio
24242 Woodward Ave.
Pleasant Ridge, MI 48069-1144
ph: 248-399-1320
fax: 248-399-7018
e-mail: jsfieldart@aol.com
Frame specialist and appraiser: restoration of art, frames, objects, gilding; period frame reproductions made; fine art and frame appraisals; conservation of picture frames.

FRANK LLOYD WRIGHT

(see also ARCHITECTURE & RELATED ITEMS; ARTS & CRAFTS)

Clubs/Associations

Frank Lloyd Wright Foundation, Taliesin West
Magazine: FLLW Quarterly
12621 Frank Lloyd Wright Blvd.
Scottsdale, AZ 85259
ph: 602-860-2700
web: http://www.franklloydwright.org/

Collectors

Jerry A. McCoy
800 Thayer Ave.
Silver Spring, MD 20910-4504
ph: 301-565-2519
e-mail: ohiowa@erols.com
Wants anything related to architect Frank Lloyd Wright: autographs, books, furniture, drawings, etc.

Dealers

Michael FitzSimmons
Michael FitzSimmons Decorative Arts
311 West Superior St.
Chicago, IL 60610
ph: 312-787-6343
fax: 312-787-0496
Specializing in 20th century architecture and decorative arts especially Frank Lloyd Wright and the Prairie School of design; also Gustav Stickley and others.

J.B. Muns
Fine Arts Books & Musical Autographs
1162 Shattuck Ave.
Berkeley, CA 94707-2635
ph: 510-525-2420
fax: 510-525-1126
Specializes in Frank Lloyd Wright; catalogs issued since 1964; by appointment only.

Internet Resources

Lists of Frank Lloyd Wright Links
e-mail: usonia@hotmail.com
web: http://www.geocities.com/SoHo/1469/flwlinks.htm
Website contains Frank Lloyd Wright links to organizations, items for sale, Frank Lloyd Wright discussion groups, etc.

FRANKART

(see also ART DECO)

Collectors

Adrienne Leff
1550 S Dixie Hwy. #210
Coral Gables, FL 33146-3034
ph: 305-667-4214
fax: 305-668-2592
Buys, sells, trades and collects Frankart lamps, ashtrays, bookends and candlestick holders.

Jeff Leegood
DecoLectibles
P.O. Box 596553
Dallas, TX 75359-6653
ph: 214-824-7917
fax: 214-824-7917
e-mail: decolectibles@cyberramp.net
Buys all types of Frankart: nude figures, animals, etc.; Frankart made lamps, bookends, ashtrays, etc.; items were made in the '20s & '30s and are of cast metal; most pieces are marked; also buys other similar Art Deco figures.

Dealers

David Negley
David Negley's Gallery
438 W. 47th St., #1A
New York, NY 10036-2330
ph: 212-459-8954
e-mail: negleyd@sprynet.com
web: http://www.davids-deco.com/
Buys and sells all Frankart items

Experts

Walter Glenn
Geode, Ltd.
3393 Peachtree Rd.
Atlanta, GA 30326-1162
ph: 404-261-9346
Buys and sells Frankart, Inc. items; also advisor to collectors, dealers, auction houses, etc.

FRATERNAL ORGANIZATION ITEMS

(see also BADGES; VETERAN ITEMS; SOCIAL CAUSES)

Collectors

James Berkel
420 Arthur Ave.
Endicott, NY 13760
Wants Union and lodge badges 7" long with fringe on bottom; also wants any Improved Order of the Red Man badges or pins.

American Legion

Collectors

Bob Bowen
13516 Kingsman Rd.
Woodbridge, VA 22193
ph: 703-590-3945
Buy American Legion convention badges or related Legion memorabilia.

Elks

Collectors

David & Brenda Wendel
F.E.I.
P.O. Box 1187
Poplar Bluff, MO 63902-1187
ph: 573-686-1926
fax: 573-686-8450
e-mail: bwendel@ldd.net
Wants Elks Lodge memorabilia; BPOE badges, tankards, steins, souvenir plates, programs, jewelry, etc.

Knights Of Columbus

Museums/Libraries

Mary Lou Cummings, Cur.
Knights of Columbus Headquarters Museum
One Columbus Plaza
New Haven, CT 06510-3325
ph: 203-772-2130
fax: 203-777-0114
web: http://www.kofc-supreme-council.org
Museum and archives revealing the history, formation and activities of the K. of C. as an international, Catholic, service-oriented, fraternal organization with insurance benefits.

Lions

Collectors

Frank Johnson
73 West Johnston St.
Washington, NJ 07882-1332
Wants Lions Club pins and other memorabilia.

Tom Owen
P.O. Box 435
Marshfield, MO 65706-0435
ph: 417-468-2791
Wants to buy Lion's Club pins.

Masonic

Collectors

Dave
315 So. 4th St.
P.O. Box 522
Manhattan, KS 66505-0522
ph: 913-776-1433
Wants Masonic/Shriners jewelry, coins, tokens, books, paper items, memorabilia, anything Masonic needed for collection.

Dealers

Frank Everts
Frank Everts & Associates
11846 Donore
Dallas, TX 75218-1845
ph: 214-349-5577
fax: 214-553-0446
Collector of Masonic jewelry, fobs and pins (except Shrine); also manufactures Masonic jewelry.

Experts

Stanley W. Johnson
P.O. Box 462
Auburn, MA 01501-0462
ph: 508-799-6300
Specializes in the material culture of Freemasons including the obscure, cryptic, esoteric, enigmatic and genre; also Blue Lodge, Scottish Rite, York Rite, Royal Arch, Knights Templar, Shrine; member Museum Of Our National Heritage.

Museums/Libraries

Thomas W. Leavitt, Dir.
Museum of our National Heritage
33 Marrett Rd.
P.O. Box 519
Lexington, MA 02420-0519
ph: 781-861-6559
fax: 781-861-9846
e-mail: info@mnh.org
web: http://www.mnh.org/
Research library specializing in the history of Freemasonry and related fraternal organizations in the U.S.

Iowa Masonic Library & Museum
813 First St. SE
P.O. Box 279
Cedar Rapids, IA 52406-0279
ph: 319-365-1438
fax: 319-365-1439
e-mail: Grand_Lodge_IA@msn.com
web: http://www.gl-ia.org/museums.html
Collection displays a great number of Masonic relics.

Masonic Grand Lodge Library & Museum of Texas
715 Columbus Ave.
P.O. Box 446
Waco, TX 76703
ph: 254-753-7395
fax: 254-753-2944
e-mail: webmason@gltexas.org
web: http://www.gltexas.org/

Odd Fellows

Collectors

Greg Spiess
230 E. Washington St.
Joliet, IL 60433-1006
ph: 815-722-5639
fax: 815-722-0171
e-mail: spiessantq@aol.com
Wants to buy Odd Fellows items: steins, badges, medals, pins, ritual prints, coffins, banners, ark of covenants, flags, pedestals, heart in hand items, carvings with symbolism, supply catalogs.

FREAKS

(see MORBID & ODD ITEMS)

FRENCH FOREIGN LEGION

Collectors

David Stevens
Playboy Magazine
680 North Lake Shore Dr.
Chicago, IL 60611
ph: 773-751-8000
Wants to buy French Foreign Legion ephemera.

FRUIT JARS

(see also BOTTLES; JELLY CONTAINERS; INSULATORS)

Clubs/Associations

J. Carl Sturm, Pres.
Federation of Historical Bottle Collectors, Inc.
Magazine: Bottles & Extras
P.O. Box 1558
Southampton, PA 18966
ph: 215-953-1686
fax: 215-953-1104
e-mail: sives@antiquez.com
web: http://www.fohbc.com/
"Bottles & Extras" contains articles, pictures, letters, show dates, and show and auction reports in the field of antique bottles, insulators, fruit jars and associated items; check website for list of scores of clubs by region.

Norman & Junne Barnett
Midwest Antique Fruit Jar & Bottle Club
Newsletter: Midwest Glass Chatter, The
P.O. Box 38
Flat Rock, IN 47234
ph: 812-587-5560
Sponsors two fruit and bottle shows each year in Indianapolis.

Mason Bright
Ball Collectors Club
Newsletter: Ball Collectors Club Newsletter
497 Fox Drive
Monroe, MI 48161
ph: 734-241-0113 or 734-242-3430
fax: 734-242-3436
e-mail: balljars@cheerful.com
Focuses on collecting Ball fruit jars and GO-WITHS; newsletter includes information on Ball jars; lists jars for sale by members.

Collectors

Richard Dalton
30 Primrose Lane
Brick, NJ 08724
ph: 732-458-7650
Collects, buys, sells, trades old fruit jars or canning jars.

Art Snyder
110 White Oak Dr.
Butler, PA 16001-3446
ph: 724-287-0278
Buys/sells/trades all types of fruit jars especially Ball jars, odd closures, pint sizes, midgets and highly whittled quart size examples.

Claude Bellar
1750 Keyes Road
Greenbrier, TN 37073
ph: 615-643-0290
fax: 615-643-0290
e-mail: cbellar@aol.com

Harry Fisher
Rte. 1 Box 197
Owensville, MO 65066
ph: 573-437-4227
Wants Globe, Lightning, Masons amber, Millville Atmospherics and Improveds, Princess, Perfections, The Darling, Royal Amber, etc.; any unusual jars, please describe and price.

Scott Grandstaff
63742 Applegate Dr.
Happy Camp, CA 96039
ph: 530-493-2032

Dealers

John Hathaway
Hathaway's Antiques
3 Mills Rd.
Bryant Pond, ME 04219
ph: 207-665-2124
fax: 207-665-2124
e-mail: meidea@megalink.net
web: http://www.megalink.net/~meidea/
Buys and sells fruit jars; hundreds of rare jars to inexpensive jars in all categories; midgets and half pints; mail order a specialty.

Experts

Bill & Jill Meier
103 Canterbury Ct.
Carlisle, MA 01741-1860
ph: 978-369-0208
e-mail: bill@insulators.com
web: http://www.insulators.com/
Specialists in Hemingray, H.G. Co. and DEC 19 1871 insulators and other Hemingray items such as water bottles and H.G. Co. fruit jars; looking to expand collection; interested in sharing knowledge with others.

John Hathaway
Hathaway's Antiques
3 Mills Rd.
Bryant Pond, ME 04219
ph: 207-665-2124
fax: 207-665-2124
e-mail: meidea@megalink.net
web: http://www.megalink.net/~meidea/
Buys and sells fruit jars; hundreds of rare jars to inexpensive jars in all categories; midgets and half pints; mail order a specialty.

Mike Jordan
Jordan Antiques & Research Co.
8411 Porter Ln.
Alexandria, VA 22308-2140
ph: 703-360-8181
e-mail: bjordan@aol.com
web: http://members.aol.com/Potomacbtl/bottle2.htm
Buy, sells, appraises and specializes in rare, early American fruit jars; specializing in odd closures and colors.

Mason Bright
497 Fox Drive
Monroe, MI 48161
ph: 734-241-0113 or 734-242-3430
fax: 734-242-3436
e-mail: balljars@cheerful.com
Specialist and collector of BALL fruit jars; wants jars, letterheads, advertising items, GO-WITHS; has largest collection in the U.S.

Doug Leybourne
P.O. Box 5417
Muskegon, MI 49445-0417
ph: 616-744-2003
Author of "Red Book No. 8: The Collector's Guide to Old Fruit Jars," a price guide of over 5000 known jars; available from the author for $30 ppd.; also author of "The Fruit Jar Works," a 2-vol. encyclopedia, the set for $59 ppd.

Jerry McCann
Phoenix Press
5003 West Berwin
Chicago, IL 60630
ph: 773-777-0443
e-mail: fjar@aol.com
web: http://www.antiquebotl.com/mccann.htm
Wants to buy unusual fruit jars; publishes "Fruit Jar Annual," a price guide, for $30.

Periodicals

Tom Caniff
Newsletter: Fruit Jar New, The
1223 Oak Grove Ave.
Steubenville, OH 43952
ph: 740-282-8918
e-mail: tomcaniff@aol.com
Covers new finds, glass factory histories, jar news in general plus want ads, for-sale page and show dates.

FUNERAL ITEMS

(see also MORBID & ODD ITEMS)

Collectors

Rich Hartzog
World Exonumia
P.O. Box 4143
Rockford, IL 61110-0643
ph: 815-226-0771
fax: 815-397-7662
e-mail: hartzog@exonumia.com
web: http://www.exonumia.com/
Wants items showing or issued by funeral parlors; tokens, badges, medals, ribbons, and other small collectibles.

Museums/Libraries

National Museum of Funeral History
415 Barren Springs Dr.
Houston, TX 77090
ph: 281-876-3063 or 800-238-8861
web: http://www.roadsideamerica.com/attract/TXHOUfun.html
The nations largest collection of funeral service memorabilia: historic coffins, death wagons, embalming instruments, etc.; a creation of Service Corporation INternational, the world's largest funeral provider.

FURNITURE (ANTIQUE)

(see also ARTS & CRAFTS; ART DECO; ART NOUVEAU; GARDEN FURNITURE; MODERNISM; ORIENTALIA; REPAIR/RESTORATION/CONSERVATION, Furniture; SHAKER ITEMS; WALLACE NUTTING; WICKER; see also "REPAIR SERVICES" Appendix)

Appraisers

Nickolas Kotula, ASA
493 Simsbury Rd.
Bloomfield, CT 06002-1512
ph: 860-243-1646
fax: 860-243-8899
Appraiser, expert witness, lecturer, writer, author of articles in "Maine Antique Digest": "The Faking of Antique Furniture," and "Historical Cabinetmaking Construction."

Stephen van Cline, CAPP
van Cline & Davenport, Ltd.
792 Franklin Ave.
Franklin Lakes, NJ 07417-1343
Specializes in 18th & early 19th cent. furniture & accessories; appraisals, authentication, lectures, expert testimony; minimum charge $25; letter request only, SASE.

Bruce M. Schuettinger, ISA
Antique Restorations Ltd.
17 N. Alley
P.O. Box 244
New Market, MD 21774-0244
ph: 301-865-3009
fax: 301-865-3009
e-mail: schuettinger@erols.com
Expert specializing in the appraisal of antique period furniture.

Kathleen M. Bailey, ISA CAPP
Antique Appraisal & Estate Sale Services
9416 1st Ave., NE, #311
Seattle, WA 98115
ph: 425-746-2777
fax: 425-746-3793

Robert G. Jason-Ickes
3600 Elizabeth Ave., SE #19-203
Olympia, WA 98501-7458
ph: 360-455-9914
Specializes in 19th and 20th century furniture including "Depression" era furniture of the 1920s through 1940s; also lectures.

Dealers

Russ & Karen Goldberger
RJG Antiques
P.O. Box 2033
Hampton, NH 03843-2033
ph: 603-926-1770
fax: 603-929-4267
e-mail: russ@rjgantiques.com
web: http://www.rjgantiques.com
Specializes in quality working decoys, folk art, and American furniture and accessories in their original painted surfaces.

R. Jorgensen Antiques
502 Post Road
Wells, ME 04090
ph: 207-646-9444
fax: 207-646-4954
Family business on historical property selling 18th and 19th C. American, British and Continental period antique furniture and accessories; also fireplace equipment and clocks.

Wayne Pratt & Company
346 Main Street South
Woodbury, CT 06798
ph: 203-263-5676
fax: 203-266-4766
Fine American 18th and 19th century furniture with an emphasis on original condition and patina; also a selection of fine line-for-line handmade copies of authentic antiques.

Leigh Keno
Leigh Keno American Antiques
980 Madison Ave. at 76th St.
New York, NY 10021
ph: 212-734-2381
fax: 212-734-0707
Specializes in fine American antique furniture.

Emily Greenspan
Newel Art Galleries, Inc.
425 East 53rd St.
New York, NY 10022
ph: 212-758-1970
fax: 212-371-0166
e-mail: info@newel.com
web: http://www.newel.com/
One of the largest resources of quality antique furniture from the 17th to 20th centuries: Biedermeier, Art Nouveau, Art Deco, Neoclassic, Bamboo, and period French, English and Italian.

John C. Newcomer
York Town Auction Inc.
1625 Haviland Rd.
York, PA 17404
ph: 717-751-0211
fax: 717-767-7729

H.L. Chalfant Antiques
1352 Paoli Pike
West Chester, PA 19380-6263
ph: 610-696-1862
Specializes in American antique furniture.

G.K.S. Bush, Inc.
2828 Pennsylvania Ave. NW
Washington, DC 20007
ph: 202-965-0653
fax: 202-342-6560
Specializes in fine American antique furniture.

Bob O'Dell
Era of Elegance Antiques
Kennerly Rd.
Irmo, SC 29063
ph: 803-345-1689
Buys and sells period antiques from 1830-1890; by appointment; East coast only.

Deborah Smallwood
Seller of Dreams
P.O. Box 428
Powell, OH 43065
ph: 614-436-8393
Specializes in Victorian furniture, but also carries primitive and handpainted furniture; restoration and refinishing available.

Experts

Nickolas Kotula, ASA
493 Simsbury Rd.
Bloomfield, CT 06002-1512
ph: 860-243-1646
fax: 860-243-8899
Reaccredited Senior Member of the American Society of Appraisers, Personal Property, Furniture designation; author of articles in "Maine Antique Digest": "The Faking of Antique Furniture," and "Historical Cabinetmaking Construction."

Suzy McLennan Anderson
Heritage Antiques, Inc.
65 East Main St.
Holmdel, NJ 07733-2310
ph: 908-946-8801
fax: 908-946-1036
Authentication service offered for pre-1840 American furniture; also buys and sells.

Robert F. Weinhagen, Jr.
221 Cameron St.
Alexandria, VA 22314-3203
ph: 703-549-2560
Author of "Assume Nothing: A Manual For Buyers of American and English Antique Furniture".

J. Robert Boykin, III
Boykin Appraisals, Inc.
P.O. Box 7440
Wilson, NC 27895
ph: 252-237-1700
fax: 252-237-2314
e-mail: boykinappraisals@coastalnet.com
Specializing in American & English antique furniture, decorative arts, and appreciable residential contents.

Museums/Libraries

Society for the Preservation of New England Antiquities, The
141 Cambridge Street
Boston, MA 02114
ph: 617-227-3956
fax: 617-227-9204
web: http://www.spnea.org/
A museum of cultural history that preserves, interprets, and collects buildings, landscapes, and objects reflecting New England life from the 17th century to present.

Rhode Island School of Design Museum
224 Benefit St.
Providence, RI 02903-2723
ph: 401-454-6500
fax: 401-454-6556
e-mail: rbenefie@risd.edu
web: http://www.risd.edu/museum.html
Apparel, architecture, furniture, graphic design, industrial design, interior architecture, landscape architecture.

Bennington Museum, The
W. Main St.
Bennington, VT 05201
ph: 802-447-1571
fax: 802-442-8305
web: http://www.bennington.com/museum/
One of the finest regional art history museums in the country; works by Grandma Moses, American glass, VT furniture, Bennington pottery, the oldest Stars & Stripes in existence, the 1925 luxury touring car "The Wasp", and much more.

Winterthur Museum
ph: 800-448-3883 or 302-888-4600
e-mail: winterthur@udel.edu
web: http://www.udel.edu/winterthur/

Colonial Williamsburg
P.O. Box C
Williamsburg, VA 23185
ph: 757-229-1000 or 800-HISTORY
e-mail: webmaster@cwf.org
web: http://www.history.org
Specializes in early American furniture and the decorative arts.

Bernice Bienenstock Furniture Library
1009 North Main St.
High Point, NC 27262
ph: 336-883-4011
fax: 336-883-6579
e-mail: russ@furninfo.com
web: http://furninfo.com/associationlibrary.html
Comprehensive library covering furniture design, styles, periods, motifs, production, history, etc.

Henry Ford Museum
20900 Oakwood Blvd.
P.O. Box 1970
Dearborn, MI 48121-1970
ph: 313-982-6001 or 313-271-1620
fax: 313-271-9621
e-mail: webmaster@hfmgv.org
web: http://www.hfmgv.org/
Museum houses a collection of over one million three-dimensional artifacts, defined by the following general categories: agricultural and industrial production, transportation, communication, and domestic life.

Repair Services

Nickolas Kotula, ASA
493 Simsbury Rd.
Bloomfield, CT 06002-1512
ph: 860-243-1646
fax: 860-243-8899
Furniture conservator for museums and serious collectors; also does moving and insurance claims for fine furniture.

Howard Pletcher
Upshur Restoration
40 Mario St.
Buckhannon, WV 26201
ph: 304-473-0500 or 304-472-4353
fax: 304-473-1903
Over 15 years restoring antique furniture; also offers complete claim service to the moving and insurance industry; wide variety of third party services available; also offers architectural restoration and salvage.

Repro. Sources

Thomas E. McGarry
Birnam Wood Joinery, The
300 N. Mildred St.
Charles Town, WV 25414
ph: 304-728-0373 or 800-700-5959
fax: 304-728-6600
e-mail: info@benchmadefurniture.com
web: http://www.benchmadefurniture.com/
Specializes in the restoration of antiques including woven chairs of all kinds; restorations done by hand and restored to period appearance; custom reproductions of country styles from 1740-1840 made to standards of the originals.

American Antique Reproductions, Inc.
P.O. Box 72846
Chattanooga, TN 37407-5846
ph: 800-221-1988 or 423-867-1988
fax: 423-867-1788
e-mail: sales@americanantiques.com
web: http://www.americanantiques.com/
Wholesale only: handcrafted American oak furniture and mahogany reproduction furniture from Indonesia; also reproduction leaded glass table lamps, and reproduction American made ice cream table and chair sets, signs, prints, posters.

Antler & Horn

Collectors

J.A. Higgins
5017 Walnut
Kansas City, MO 64112-2758
ph: 816-931-4095
Wants to buy old horn furniture.

Experts

Alan Rogers
1012 Shady Dr.
Gladstone, MO 64188
ph: 816-436-9008
Has studied and collected Texas cattle horns, horn furniture, and related items for over 20 years; wants to buy old steer horns over 7' long, but not horns wrapped in tooled leather.

Beds

Dealers

Mendes Antiques
Rte. 44
52 Blanding Rd.
Rehoboth, MA 02769
ph: 508-336-7381
Specializing in antique four-poster beds, all sizes.

Belter

Dealers

Richard & Eileen Dubrow
Richard & Eileen Dubrow Antiques & Books
P.O. Box 128
Flushing, NY 11361-0128
ph: 718-767-9758
fax: 718-767-8172
Specializing in 19th century American cabinet maker furniture and decorative arts; will identify pieces as to maker by photo; also sells books (out of print and current) about 19th C. furniture and about furniture and decorative arts.

British

Experts

David P. Lindquist
Whitehall at the Villa
1213 E. Franklin St.
Chapel Hill, NC 27514-3307
ph: 919-942-3179 or 919-933-3305
fax: 919-942-6600
e-mail: whchnc@aol.com
Author of "The Official Price Guide to Antiques & Collectibles: English & Continental Furniture - With Prices"; co-author with Caroline Warren of "English and Continental Furniture - With Prices."

Chinese

Dealers

Evelyn's Antique Chinese Furniture, Inc.
381 Hayes St.
San Francisco, CA 94102-2440
ph: 415-255-1815
Offers a large inventory of Classic Chinese furniture and works of art from the Ming & Qing Dynasties.

Shen's Gallery
1368 Pacific Ave.
Santa Cruz, CA 95060
ph: 831-457-4422
Offers fine Oriental furniture and antiques; also ancient Chinese ceramics, carvings and statuary.

Colonial Revival

Experts

David P. Lindquist
Whitehall at the Villa
1213 E. Franklin St.
Chapel Hill, NC 27514-3307
ph: 919-942-3179 or 919-933-3305
fax: 919-942-6600
e-mail: whchnc@aol.com
Co-author with Caroline Warren of "Colonial Revival Furniture - With Prices."

Museums/Libraries

Judith Smith, PR
Reynolda House Museum of American Art
P.O. Box 11765
Winston Salem, NC 27116
ph: 336-725-5325
fax: 336-721-0991
e-mail: reynolda@reynoldahouse.org
web: http://www.reynoldahouse.org/
Magnificent former home of Richard J. Reynolds, founder of the R. J. Reynolds Tobacco Company; houses the finest fine art collection in the area.

Bernice Bienenstock Furniture Library
1009 North Main St.
High Point, NC 27262
ph: 336-883-4011
fax: 336-883-6579
e-mail: russ@furninfo.com
web: http://furninfo.com/associationlibrary.html
Comprehensive library covering furniture design, styles, periods, motifs, production, history, etc.

Grand Rapids Public Library Furniture Design Collection
60 Library Plaza, Northeast
Grand Rapids, MI 49503-3903
e-mail: rraz@grapids.lib.mi.us
web: http://www.grapids.lib.mi.us/

Christian G. Carron
Grand Rapids Public Museum
272 Pearl St. NW
Grand Rapids, MI 49504-5371
ph: 616-456-3977
fax: 616-456-3873
e-mail: staff@grmuseum.org
web: http://www.grmuseum.org/
Focus is on furniture made in the Grand Rapids area; exhibits, publications and research information relating to all styles of 19th and 20th century furniture manufactured in Grand Rapids.

Continental

Experts

David P. Lindquist
Whitehall at the Villa
1213 E. Franklin St.
Chapel Hill, NC 27514-3307
ph: 919-942-3179 or 919-933-3305
fax: 919-942-6600
e-mail: whchnc@aol.com
Author of "The Official Price Guide to Antiques & Collectibles: English & Continental Furniture - With Prices"; co-author with Caroline Warren of "English and Continental Furniture - With Prices."

French

Dealers

Nancy Kramer
Sparrows
4115 Howard Ave.
Kensington, MD 20895-2417
ph: 301-530-0175
fax: 301-530-0189
e-mail: NSKramer@aol.com
web: http://www.sparrows.com
Specializes in 19th and early 20th century French antique furniture and decorative arts.

Horn

(see FURNITURE [ANTIQUE], Adirondack; FURNITURE [ANTIQUE], Antler & Horn; WESTERN AMERICANA)

Kitchen Cabinets

Dealers

Marcy A. Rau
Marcy A. Rau Antiques & Collectibles
R.D. #2, Box 431
Dalton, PA 18414
ph: 570-378-2198
e-mail: marcyrau@hotmail.com
web: http://www.angelfire.com/biz/marcyrau/
Specializes in Hoosiers and "Hoosier" type kitchen cabinets.

Tom Loser
Uncle Tom's Antique Hoosier Cabinets & Parts
5680 W. McNeely St.
Ellettsville, IN 47429-9411
ph: 812-876-5060 or 800-892-5695
fax: 812-876-5045
e-mail: tomscab@ix.netcom.com
web: http://www.hoosiercabinets.com
Selling top quality oak Hoosier cabinets and cupboards; also originally cabinet glassware, flour bins, cabinet accessories, etc.; parts catalog $1; 45 minute documentary for $23.95.

Experts

Phyllis & Phil Kennedy
Phyllis Kennedy Hardware
10655 Andrade Drive
Zionsville, IN 46077
ph: 317-873-1316
fax: 317-873-8662
e-mail: philken@kennedyhardware.com
web: http://www.kennedyhardware.com
Author of "Hoosier Cabinets."

Suppliers

Phyllis & Phil Kennedy
Phyllis Kennedy Hardware
10655 Andrade Drive
Zionsville, IN 46077
ph: 317-873-1316
fax: 317-873-8662
e-mail: philken@kennedyhardware.com
web: http://www.kennedyhardware.com
Author of "Hoosier Cabinets;" stocks parts for Hoosier cabinets including flour sifters, cardboard door charts, metal tags, sugar bins, etc.; send for catalog.

Muff's Antiques
135 S. Glassell St.
Orange, CA 92866-1421
ph: 714-997-0243
fax: 714-997-1601
e-mail: muffs@earthlink.net
web: http://home.earthlink/~muffs/
Mail order source for kitchen cabinet hardware (Hoosiers) including hinges, labels, canisters, castors, and rolls; also 25 sizes of lids for jars, and salt & pepper canisters from Hoosier & Depression items; catalog $5.

Oak

Museums/Libraries

Christian G. Carron
Grand Rapids Public Museum
272 Pearl St. NW
Grand Rapids, MI 49504-5371
ph: 616-456-3977
fax: 616-456-3873
e-mail: staff@grmuseum.org
web: http://www.grmuseum.org/
Focus is on furniture made in the Grand Rapids area; exhibits, publications and research information relating to all styles of 19th and 20th century furniture manufactured in Grand Rapids.

Pie Safes

Experts

Dennis & Louise Paustenbach
65 Roan Place
Woodside, CA 94062
Authors of a book about pie safes.

Rustic

Dealers

Bert Savage
Rte. 126 Box 11
Center Strafford, NH 03815
ph: 603-269-7411
Wants to buy rustic furniture: Adirondack, Indiana Hickory, twig, birch bark, root, burl.

Christine Guille
Country & Cabin Antiques
256 Osbrook Pt.
Pawcatuck, CT 06379
ph: 860-599-1244
fax: 860-536-1267
e-mail: cwguille@aol.com
Wants quality Adirondack furniture and accessories: Old Hickory, Rittenhouse, birch bark, rustic lamps, coat racks, mirrors, Black Forest carved bears and clocks, miniature canoes, pond boats, camp signs, art and advertising.

Ralph Kylloe
Kylloe Antiques
P.O. Box 669
Lake George, NY 12845-0669
Specializes in buying and selling antiques for the cabin; old hickory, Adirondack, root, twig, antler furnishings, and rustic accessories; also creels, snowshoes, skis, sailboats, fishing nets, camp signs, birch bark frames, canoes, etc.

Bob Berman
441 S. Jackson St.
Media, PA 19063-3715
ph: 610-566-1516

Museums/Libraries

Adirondack Museum, The
Rte. 30
P.O. Box 99
Blue Mountain Lake, NY 12812-0099
ph: 518-352-7311
fax: 518-352-7653
web: http://www.adkmuseum.org/
Sponsors rustic furniture fair to showcase modern makers; has an extensive rustic furniture collection.

Soap Hollow

Museums/Libraries

Julie Robinson
Conemaugh Township Area Historical Society
100-104 South Main St.
P.O. Box 307
Davidsville, PA 15928
ph: 814-479-2211 or 814-479-2067
e-mail: contwpsc@ctcnet.net
web: http://www.ctcnet.net/ConemaughTwp/history.htm
Historical information on the furniture makers of Soap Hollow; lecture frequently on furniture style, hallmarks and stencils of the unique Mennonite craftsmen.

Stickley

Dealers

Dennis Lucier
1034 Mammoth Rd.
Dracut, MA 01826
ph: 978-957-0143
Buys and sells Gustav, L & JG Stickley mission oak furniture.

Jerry Cohen
Aurora Studios
109 Main St.
Putnam, CT 06260
ph: 860-928-1965 or 800-448-7828
fax: 860-928-1966
e-mail: Aurora@neca.com
web: http://www.artsncrafts.com
Original antique Stickley and other Mission style furniture makers; over 4,000 square feet furniture on display.

Bob Berman
441 S. Jackson St.
Media, PA 19063-3715
ph: 610-566-1516

Caren Fine
11603 Gowrie Ct.
Potomac, MD 20854-3623
ph: 301-299-6886 or 301-299-2116
Wants to buy Arts & Crafts items such as furniture and copper by Stickley, Dirk Van Erp, Roycroft, Limbert, Harden, Rohlfs, Wright; pottery, paintings, Nakashima furniture.

Museums/Libraries

Craftsman Farms Foundation, Inc.
2352 Rt. 10-W, Box 5
Morris Plains, NJ 07950
ph: 973-540-1165
fax: 973-540-1167
e-mail: setabit@njskylands.com
web: http://njskylands.com/hscrfarm.htm
Runs Stickley's National Landmark family home in Parsippany, NJ; sponsors Stickley exhibits and related catalogs.

Repro. Sources

L. & J.G. Stickley, Inc.
P.O. Box 480
Manlius, NY 13104-0480
ph: 315-682-5500
fax: 315-682-6306
web: http://www.stickley.com

Twig

(see FURNITURE [ANTIQUE], Adirondack)

Victorian

Auction Services

Rob Slawinski
Slawinski Auction Company
6192 Highway 9
Felton, CA 95018
ph: 831-335-9000
e-mail: antiques@slawinski.com
web: http://www.slawinski.com
One of the largest auctioneers in the country specializing in Victorian antiques including works by Herter, Belter, Meeks, Roux, J.J. Horner and others; monthly estate auctions also feature fine art & accessories.

Dealers

Joan Bogart
Jean Bogart Antiques
P.O. Box 265
Rockville Centre, NY 11571
ph: 516-764-5712 or 516-764-5743
fax: 516-764-0529
e-mail: joanbogart@aol.com
web: http://www.joanbogart.com/
Dealer, expert, appraiser specializing in Victorian furniture by Belter, Meeks, Horner, Herter, etc.; also specializes in Victorian lighting, gas chandeliers, astrals, kerosene lamps, epergnes, silverplate, majolica, Parian ware.

Steve Moon
New Moon Antiques
1606 11th St.
Monroe, WI 53566
ph: 608-325-9100
e-mail: newmoon@inwave.com
web: http://www.inwave.com/~newmoon/
Specializes in quality Victorian furniture.

Museums/Libraries

Newark Museum, Ballantine House
49 Washington St.
P.O. Box 540
Newark, NJ 07101-0540
ph: 973-596-6550 or 800-7-MUSEUM
fax: 973-642-0459

Henry Duffy, Curator
Lyndhurst
635 S. Broadway
Tarrytown, NY 10591-6401
ph: 914-631-4481 or 914-631-0046
fax: 914-631-5634
Furniture, paintings, decorative arts, library, archive; Gothic Revival mansion on 67 acre European-style park; tours, special events, catering for parties, gallery.

Wallace Nutting

Museums/Libraries

Wadsworth Atheneum
600 Main St.
Hartford, CT 06103
ph: 860-278-2670
fax: 860-527-0803
e-mail: info@wadsworthatheneum.org
web: http://www.wadsworthatheneum.org/
The collection of Wallace Nutting 17th century American furniture, the largest of its kind, includes a wide array of "Pilgrim-Century" housewares and tools; also has two fully-restored period rooms.

Wooton Desks

Clubs/Associations

Richard & Eileen Dubrow
Wooton Desk Owners Society, Inc.
Newsletter: Wooton Desk Owners Society Newsletter, The
P.O. Box 128
Flushing, NY 11361-0128
ph: 718-767-9758
fax: 718-767-8172
Archival records, authentication, and sales of Wooton desks.

FURS

Dealers

Farhad Radfar, ISA
MIR International Gallery, Inc.
332 n. Michigan Ave., 2nd Floor
Chicago, IL 60611
ph: 312-814-8510
fax: 312-814-8511
e-mail: mirgallery@aol.com
web: http://www.mirgallery.com/

Misc. Services

Richard A. Newman
Newman Fur Appraisers & Consultants, Inc.
11 Penn Plaza, 5th Floor
New York, NY 10001
ph: 212-564-4733
fax: 212-564-4735
e-mail: richn1@idt.net
Fur appraiser, consultant, all phases of the fur industry; damage claim consultant.

Museums/Libraries

Gail DeBuse Potter, Dir.
Museum of the Fur Trade
Magazine: MFT Quarterly
6321 Highway 20
Chadron, NE 69337-9501
ph: 308-432-3843
fax: 308-432-5963
e-mail: museum@furtrade.org
web: http://www.furtrade.org/
Dedicated to the study of the American fur trade from colonial times to the present; furs, traps, trade guns, trade goods, Indians; not involved with present day trapping.

Here are some tips when contacting someone listed in this book:

■ When requesting information about a particular item, include a description (material, dimensions, maker's mark, model number, etc.) and a photo, sketch, or photocopy of the item in question.

■ Always ask if there are charges for samples or for the services requested.

■ When writing, please be sure to include a Large (#10 business size) Self-Addressed and Stamped Envelope (LSASE) if requesting a reply or the return of photographs.

■ Never call collect unless otherwise directed. When calling, be considerate of time zone differences and always ask if the party you are calling has time to talk. When leaving an answering machine message, always instruct the party to call you back collect.

G-MAN

(see LAW ENFORCEMENT MEMORABILIA, FBI)

G.A.R. MEMORABILIA

(see VETERAN ITEMS, Civil War)

G.I. JOE

(see TOYS, Action Figures [G.I. Joe])

GAMBLING COLLECTIBLES

(see also COIN-OPERATED MACHINES, Slot Machines; DICE; MATCHCOVERS, Casino; PLAYING CARDS; SALOON & BAR COLLECTIBLES; TOKENS)

Collectors

Robert Eisenstadt
140 Cadman Plaza West, #26-C
Brooklyn, NY 11202
ph: 718-625-3553
e-mail: chipe@ix.netcom.com
web: http://www.megsinet.net/~wally/Robert/robert.htm
Collects and buys all kinds of gambling chips (casino, ivory, mother of pearl, clay poker chips, etc. but no light plastic chips); also wants gambling-related items such as equipment, books, catalogs, playing cards, etc.

John A. Greget
John A. Greget - Magic Lists
2631 E Claire Dr.
Phoenix, AZ 85032-4932
Buys and appraises gambling books or equipment.

Kitty & Russell Umbraco
P.O. Box 5331
Richmond, CA 94805-0331
ph: 510-235-1656
Wants to buy gambling collectibles including Faro, playing cards, etc.

Dealers

Larry Lubliner
Re-Finders
25303 Rutledge Crossing
Farmington Hills, MI 48335-1350
ph: 248-426-0066
fax: 248-426-9944
e-mail: joker1854@aol.com
Buys and sells gambling items including playing cards, poker chips, Faro, poker, roulette, dice; also wants related advertising items, sales catalogs, and books.

Internet Resources

Casinos & Gaming Web Guide - Collectors & Collectibles
e-mail: cynchittick@prodigy.com
web: http://pages.prodigy.com/CasinoGaming/collect.htm

Periodicals

Magazine: Gaming Times
4089 Spring Mountain Rd.
Las Vegas, NV 89102
ph: 702-876-6020
fax: 702-876-2175
e-mail: gaming@intermind.net
web: http://gamingtimes.com/
Monthly publication containing news and stories about chips, dice, casino memorabilia, and more; new chip releases, Atlantic City news, electronic chipping, dice department, casino news and histories.

Tom Pleau
Magazine: Coast to Coast's Casino Collectible Magazine
P.O. Box 7438
Laguna Niguel, CA 92607-7438
ph: 800-892-2629
fax: 949-362-9101

Gambling Chips & Gaming Tokens

Clubs/Associations

Michael Knapp
Casino Chips & Gaming Tokens Collectors Club
Magazine: Casino Chips & Token News
P.O. Box 340345
Columbus, OH 43234
ph: 614-451-0006 or 614-723-1092
fax: 614-723-1704
e-mail: ChipProf@aol.com
web: http://www.ccgtcc.com/
Collectors of casino chips and gaming tokens; ANA affiliation, yearly convention in Las Vegas, 100+ page quarterly newsletter; over 1600 members.

Collectors

Andrew R. Young III
5 Meadowbrook Rd.
East Longmeadow, MA 01028
ph: 413-525-8211
e-mail: ayoung@map.com
web: http://pages.map.com/~ayoung/
A collector of Las Vegas, Atlantic City, and Caribbean casino chips.

Charles Tomarchio
P.O. Box 8386
Turnersville, NJ 08012

Archie A. Black
P.O. Box 63
Brick, NJ 08723-0063
ph: 732-840-9390

George Davis
67 Franklin Ave.
Yonkers, NY 10705
ph: 914-963-6436
Wants to buy casino chips: Cuba, Puerto Rico, Caribbean, Atlantic City, Las Vegas, etc.

Robert Eisenstadt
140 Cadman Plaza West, #26-C
Brooklyn, NY 11202
ph: 718-625-3553
e-mail: chipe@ix.netcom.com
web: http://www.megsinet.net/~wally/Robert/robert.htm
Collects and buys all kinds of gambling chips (casino, ivory, mother of pearl, clay poker chips, etc. but no light plastic chips); also wants gambling-related items such as equipment, books, catalogs, playing cards, etc.

Neal Silverman
585 Merrick Rd.
Lynbrook, NY 11563
ph: 516-693-3333
fax: 516-693-7515
e-mail: neal@chequers.com
web: http://www.chequers.com
Wants to buy casino chips.

Nate Pincus
P.O. Box 693
Havertown, PA 19083-0693
ph: 610-642-6093
fax: 610-642-3641
e-mail: npincus@home.com
Collector of casino chips from all areas; buy, sell, trade.

John Benedict
P.O. Drawer 1423
Loxahatchee, FL 33470-1423
ph: 561-798-2520 or 800-844-3397
fax: 561-798-2520
e-mail: benedict@webtv.net
web: http://www.netmar.com/~creator/benedict/
Wants old casino chips and ivory poker chips.

John "Top" Newby, USMC Ret.
P.O. Box 5064
Inverness, FL 34450
ph: 352-637-4202
fax: 352-637-4202
e-mail: Top@TopUsmc.com
web: http://TopUsmc.com
Buys and trades casino chips; wants old chips that might be laying around from your travels around the world: Las Vegas, Atlantic City, foreign chips; call or send fax with descriptions.

Michael Knapp
P.O. Box 340345
Columbus, OH 43234
ph: 614-451-0006 or 614-723-1092
fax: 614-723-1704
e-mail: ChipProf@aol.com
Buys, collects and specializes in poker chips; author of books and articles about chips and chip collecting.

Greg Johnson
3344 S. Raible Ave.
Anderson, IN 46011
e-mail: gregj@netusa1.net
web: http://www.netusa1.net/~gregj
Buy, sell, trade casino chips.

Dave Brattain
P.O. Box 335
Zionsville, IN 46077
ph: 317-769-3257
Wants to buy old or unique gambling chips and sets, U.S. or foreign; premium paid for ivories.

Tom Dirnberger
8493 142nd St. West
Apple Valley, MN 55124

Michael Skelton
112 Simmons St.
Coppell, TX 75019

George Conrad
1101 Elm St.
Boulder City, NV 89005
ph: 702-293-9226
fax: 702-293-9221
e-mail: georgecon@aol.com
web: http://members.aol.com/georgecon/
Collector, trader, buyer, seller of Nevada casino chips.

Janice O'Neal
8122 W. Flamingo #66
Las Vegas, NV 89147
ph: 702-222-1998
fax: 702-362-4617
e-mail: Junkman2@prodigy.net
web: http://angelfire.com/ga/Junkman3/
Member and club historian for the Casino Chips & Gaming Tokens Collectors Club.

Mike & Dianne Draper
4970 Stagecoach Dr.
Silver Springs, NV 89429
ph: 702-629-9148
e-mail: antgamb@reno.quik.com
Collector of Nevada casino items, especially Harolds Club, Reno; also wants to buy native American Indian items.

Charles T. Rodgers
P.O. Box 4572
Lakewood, CA 90711-4572
ph: 562-634-8107
e-mail: ctcoins@aol.com

Scott Hartman
P.O. Box 387
Agoura Hills, CA 91376-0387
ph: 818-706-1986 or 800-LUCK-707
fax: 818-706-1986
e-mail: scott@chipman.com
web: http://www.chipman.com/
Largest shop on line casino chip catalog and reference guide, over 5600 chips in color.

Marv Weaver
P.O. Box 8595
Pittsburg, CA 94565-8595
e-mail: SPTokens@juno.com
web: http://ourworld.compuserve.com/homepages/mweaver/
Collector of Silver Strikes only; author of "Nevada Silver Premium Gaming Tokens Price Guide."

Dealers

Bob Mera
Gaming Emporium, The
3011 Boardwalk
Atlantic City, NJ 08401-6203
ph: 800-354-3075
Gambling books, tapes and casino related equipment and supplies.

Don Anthony
505 Halsey Road
North Brunswick, NJ 08902-2616
ph: 732-297-2422
e-mail: chip99e@prodigy.com
web: http://pages.prodigy.com/GamingChips/index.htm
Collects, sells, trades casino gaming chips; specializing on denominations from 25 cents to $10; has chips from all over the world, including Nevada, Atlantic City, river boats, Colorado, Australia, Aruba and many other locations.

John Rudden
Starchip Enterprises
P.O. Box 140557
Jamaica, NY 11414
ph: 718-738-8125
e-mail: starchip@compuserve.com
web: http://www.starchip.com
Collector and dealer buys, sells and trades casino chips and gaming tokens; free downloadable catalog; monthly contests; website had scanned images of chips, links, news and much more.

New York Chip Connection
2950 Hempstead Turnpike
Levittown, NY 11756
ph: 800-NYC-HIPS

Jim Smith
Chip Chamber, The
4220 Judd Road
Milan, MI 48160
ph: 734-439-2510
e-mail: jim@chipchamber.com
web: http://www.chipchamber.com/
Dealer in worldwide casino chips with emphasis on limited edition chips; member Casino Chip & Gaming Token Collector's Club.

Wilcox Enterprises
P.O. Box 395
Carthage, IL 62321-0395
ph: 217-357-3308
e-mail: rwc@acm.org
web: http://golden.adams.net/~rwc/wilcox/
Buys and sells chips, tokens, cards, matches and dice from river boats, Indian reservations, Deadwood, Colorado.

Greg Susong
P.O. Box 654
Wellington, KS 67152
ph: 316-326-2202
fax: 316-326-3893
e-mail: greg@chipguide.com
web: http://www.chipguide.com
Buys, sells casino chips of all kinds; specializes in chips from Riverboats and Indian casinos; website has an online guide, "Greg Susong's CyberGuide To Casino Chips," a state-by-state reference work for casino chip collectors.

Andy Jung
4800 Bissonet Dr.
Metairie, LA 70003-1136
e-mail: apjung@prodigy.net
web: http://pages.prodigy.net/apjung/chips.htm
Buys and sells mainly New Orleans area chips and tokens; also some Lake Charles, LA, MS, and Gulf Coast.

Allen Banick
Colorado Casino Chip Exchange
Newsletter: Colorado Casino Chip Newsletter
P.O. Box 260575
Highlands Ranch, CO 80163-0575
fax: 303-683-0433
e-mail: info@abanick.com
web: http://www.abanick.com
Collector and expert who buys, sells and trades collectible casino chips from all around the world; specializes in chips from Colorado, New Mexico, and South Dakota.

Gary Snover
P.O. Box 9696
San Bernardino, CA 92427-0696
ph: 909-883-5849
fax: 909-886-6874
e-mail: snover@ix.netcom.com
Send $1 for price list.

Tom Arestad
P.O. Box 1931
Lake Oswego, OR 97035

Dean Richmond
Casino Collectibles
P.O. Box 370
Yachats, OR 97498-0370
ph: 541-547-4471
fax: 541-547-4487
e-mail: jodean@pioneer.net
Full time dealer in casino collectibles since 1987; colored, monthly mail/fax bid auctions.

Experts

Travis H. D. Lewin
Syracuse Univ. College of Law
Syracuse, NY 13244-1030
ph: 315-443-1222 or 315-446-8678
fax: 315-443-5394
e-mail: thdlewin@law.syr.edu
web: http://web.syr.edu/~thlewin/
Collects, buys and trades ivory, mother-of-pearl, and clay composition poker chips and casino checks and tokens.

Michael Knapp
P.O. Box 340345
Columbus, OH 43234
ph: 614-451-0006 or 614-723-1092
fax: 614-723-1704
e-mail: ChipProf@aol.com
Buys, collects and specializes in poker chips; author of books and articles about chips and chip collecting.

Greg Susong
P.O. Box 654
Wellington, KS 67152
ph: 316-326-2202
fax: 316-326-3893
e-mail: greg@chipguide.com
web: http://www.chipguide.com
Buys, sells casino chips of all kinds; specializes in chips from Riverboats and Indian casinos; website has an online guide, "Greg Susong's CyberGuide To Casino Chips," a state-by-state reference work for casino chip collectors.

Dale Seymour
11170 Mora Dr.
Los Altos, CA 94024-6536
ph: 415-948-0948
fax: 415-941-3695
e-mail: seymourdg@aol.com
Wants old poker chips; ivory, clay, or casino; no paper, plain or plastic chips wanted. Author of book on same.

Internet Resources

Neal Silverman
Chequers
585 Merrick Rd.
Lynbrook, NY 11563
ph: 516-693-3333
fax: 516-693-7515
e-mail: neal@chequers.com
web: http://www.chequers.com
An on-line directory for casino chip collectors; presently over 400 members with e-mail addresses and homepages; site is full of information on the hobby submitted weekly by members; free to all collectors and dealers.

Periodicals

Magazine: Gaming Times
4089 Spring Mountain Rd.
Las Vegas, NV 89102
ph: 702-876-6020
fax: 702-876-2175
e-mail: gaming@intermind.net
web: http://gamingtimes.com/
Monthly publication containing news and stories about chips, dice, casino memorabilia, and more; new chip releases, Atlantic City news, electronic chipping, dice department, casino news and histories.

Punchboards

(see also COIN-OPERATED MACHINES; GAMES; PAPER COLLECTIBLES)

Dealers

Ken Durham
909 26th St. NW
Washington, DC 20037-2029
e-mail: durham@gameroomantiques.com
web: http://www.GameRoomAntiques.com
Buys and sells punchboards with gambling, sport, pin-up and other colorful decorations; send $2 for illustrated list; also buys in quantity.

Clark Phelps
Amusement Sales Co.
7610 South Main St.
Midvale, UT 84047
ph: 801-255-4731
Buys and sells punchboards.

Internet Resources

Marcus Stafford
punchboard.com
540 S. Mendenhal, Ste. 12-169
Memphis, TN 38117
ph: 901-274-1472
e-mail: marcus@punchboard.com
web: http://www.punchboard.com/
All about punchboards; loaded with tips for the collector of gambling memorabilia; includes historical information and an extensive photo gallery of vintage punchboards.

GAME ROOM AMUSEMENTS

(see BILLIARD RELATED ITEMS; BOOKS, Reference [Coin-Op.]; COIN-OP. MACHINES; GAMBLING COLLECTIBLES, Punchboards; LAMPS & LIGHTING, Traffic Lights; REPAIR/RESTORATION/ CONSERVATION, Metal Items; SCALES; SOFT DRINK COLLECTIBLES, Soda Machines)

GAMES

(see also BILLIARD RELATED ITEMS; BRIDGE; CHESS SETS; DICE; FRISBEES; GAMBLING COLLECTIBLES; MARBLES; PAPER COLLECTIBLES; PLAYING CARDS; PUZZLES; TOYS)

Appraisers

Lee Dennis
447 Park Ave., Apt. 12
Keene, NH 03431-6506
ph: 603-358-0060
Author of "Warman's Antique American Games, 1840 - 1940"; republished in 1991 with updated prices.

Auction Services

Withington, Inc.
590 Centr Road
Hillsboro, NH 03244
ph: 603-464-3232
e-mail: withington@conknet.com

Clubs/Associations

Robert R. Grew
Antique Toy Collectors of America, Inc., The
Newsletter: Toy Chest
c/o Carter, Ledyard & Milburn
Two Wall St. - 13th Floor
New York, NY 10005
ph: 212-238-8803
fax: 212-732-3232
e-mail: grew@clm.com
An organization focusing on antique toys and games; since membership is by invitation only for established collectors, there is a waiting list; bi-monthly newsletter available only to members.

H.M. Levy, Pres.
Gamers Alliance
Newsletter: Gamers Alliance Report
P.O. Box 197 -CIC
East Meadow, NY 11554-0197
e-mail: gamers@pipeline.com
Members receive quarterly reports with news, views and reviews on games plus FREE out-of-print catalogs, FREE research service, and more; send SASE for more information; also buys games - one or one thousand.

American Game Collectors Association
Newsletter: Game Times
P.O. Box 44
Dresher, PA 19025
e-mail: agca@agca.com
web: http://www.agca.com
Focuses on board and card games as well as puzzles, playing cards, tops, yo-yos, and action games; also publishes "Game Researchers' Notes" - reports on member's research.

Collectors

Joe Angiolilo
P.O. Box 44
Dresher, PA 19025

Dealers

Wizard of Os
57 Lakeshore Dr.
Marlborough, MA 01752
ph: 508-481-1087

Paul Fink
Fun & Games
P.O. Box 488
Kent, CT 06757-0488
ph: 860-927-4001
Buys and sells Victorian games, comic and cartoon games, TV & nostalgia games; dealer and mail order.

Darrow's Fun Antiques
1101 1st Ave.
New York, NY 10021-8737
ph: 212-838-0730
fax: 212-838-3617
e-mail: george@fun-antiques.com
web: http://www.fun-antiques.com/
Buys & sells antique games, toys, ad signs, animated art, jukeboxes, slot machines, comic watches, bicycles & memorabilia of all types.

Marjorie Jeffreys
Going to Pieces
P.O. Box 390
Cibolo, TX 78108
ph: 210-659-2458
Buys and sells old games, toys, blocks and children's dishes and children's baking items.

Maurice & Laya Jakubowicz
Affiche Francaise
Le Plateau
Bazincourt/Epte, 21740
France
ph: 33 (0)232 27 61 53
fax: 33 (0)232 27 10 12
e-mail: ml@affiche-Francaise.com
web: http://affiche-Francaise.com/
Large collection of "saussine" board games from 1880-1940.

Experts

Lee Dennis
447 Park Ave., Apt. 12
Keene, NH 03431-6506
ph: 603-358-0060
Author of "Warman's Antique American Games, 1840 - 1940"; former curator-owner of the country's largest collection of board games; continues to offer slide film presentation about games to clubs/ associations/Historical Societies.

Bob Cereghino
6400 Baltimore National Pike, Ste. 170A-319
Baltimore, MD 21228-3914
ph: 410-766-7593
e-mail: jwbc@juno.com

Earnest & Ida Long
Long's Americana
P.O. Box 90
Mokelumne Hill, CA 95245
ph: 209-286-1348
Specializes in toys, banks, games and other children's items; publishes "Dictionary of Toys, Vol I & II" and "Penny Lane."

Museums/Libraries

Peabody Essex Museum
Essex & Libert Streets
Salem, MA 01970
ph: 978-745-9500 or 800-745-4054
e-mail: pem@pem.org
web: http://www.pem.org

Washington Dolls' House & Toy Museum
5236 44th St. NW
Washington, DC 20015
ph: 202-244-0024

University of Waterloo Museum & Archive of Games
Dept. olf Recreation & Leisure Studies
Faculty of Applied Health Sci.
Waterloo, Ontario N2L 3G1
Canada
ph: 519-888-4424 or 519-885-4567
fax: 519-746-6776
e-mail: eavedon@healthy.uwaterloo.ca
web: http://www.ahs.uwaterloo.ca/~museum/index.html
2000 references: books, journals, reports, patent information, scholarly studies, and other printed materials concerning games and playing behavior; also many games, photos, advertisements, catalogs, and rules about games.

Periodicals

Peter Sarrett
Magazine: Game Report, The
1920 N. 49th St.
Seattle, WA 98103
ph: 206-547-3449
e-mail: editor@gamereport.com
web: http://www.gamereport.com/
A quarterly publication dedicated to board, card, dice, party, family, and strategy games (but not war games or role playing games): game reviews, articles, interviews, classifieds; website has online game auctions.

Bagatelle

Dealers

Harold Balde
Fungus Amungus
21 Wellington St.
Orangeville, Ontario L9W 2L2
Canada
ph: 519-942-3984
e-mail: kingpin@total.net
web: http://tilt.largo.fl.us/hbalde/
Collector and dealer in 1800s through 1940s bagatelles; will help new collectors with pricing and general information.

Baseball Related

Experts

Mark Cooper
Baseball Games & Memorabilia
816 Chauncey Rd.
Narberth, PA 19072
ph: 215-952-9153 or 610-667-7401
fax: 610-667-2341
e-mail: markbaseb@aol.com
A premier collector of 1860-1980 baseball games; has published the definitive text on the subject; will provide free information to all interested; always buying, selling, trading baseball games.

Board

Clubs/Associations

American Game Collectors Association
Newsletter: Game Times
P.O. Box 44
Dresher, PA 19025
e-mail: agca@agca.com
web: http://www.agca.com
Focuses on board and card games as well as puzzles, playing cards, tops, yo-yos, and action games; also publishes "Game Researchers' Notes" - reports on member's research.

Collectors

Bill Smith
56 Locust St.
East Douglas, MA 01516-2440
ph: 508-476-2015
Wants all board games; any age or theme.

Bernard Newman
2004 Delancy Place
Philadelphia, PA 19103-6510
ph: 800-523-3256
fax: 215-332-8586
e-mail: bnewman@erols.com
Wants pre-1930 board games, especially by McLoughlin, Parker, Bliss, Bradley, Ives; must be in excellent condition with excellent graphics.

Dealers

Debra Krim
P.O. Box 2273
Peabody, MA 01960-7273
ph: 978-535-3140
fax: 978-535-7522
e-mail: dlkrim@star.net
web: http://www.old-toys.com
Wants boxed & board games from 1843 to 1970: McLoughlin, Ives, Bliss and other companies; baseball and TV games; cartoon strip games.

Paul Fink
Fun & Games
P.O. Box 488
Kent, CT 06757-0488
ph: 860-927-4001
Buys and sells Victorian games, comic and cartoon games, TV & nostalgia games; dealer and mail order.

Bill & Joanne Bruegman
Toy Scouts, Inc.
137 Casterton Ave.
Akron, OH 44303-1543
ph: 330-836-0668
fax: 330-869-8668
e-mail: toyscout@akron.infi.net

Jeff Lowe
Jeff Lowe's ExtravaGAMEza
9674 V Plaza #29
Omaha, NE 68127
ph: 402-592-8186
e-mail: gamesguy1@aol.com
web: http://www.ewtech.com/games/
Collector and dealer with catalog of over 2500 games available for nominal postage charge.

Experts

Lee Dennis
447 Park Ave., Apt. 12
Keene, NH 03431-6506
ph: 603-358-0060
Author of "Warman's Antique American Games, 1840 - 1940"; former curator-owner of the country's largest collection of board games; continues to offer slide film presentation about games to clubs/ associations/Historical Societies.

Pat McFarland
P.O. Box 400
Averill Park, NY 12018-0400
ph: 518-674-8390
e-mail: greatgames@webtv.net
Buyer of American board games 1800s to 1940s; McLoughlin, Bliss, Ives, Doan, early Parker and Bradley; also wants game catalogs and ephemera; pre-1936 Monopoly; player related Baseball; The Landlord's Game; related information.

Bruce Whitehill
Big Game Hunter, The
620 Park Ave. #202
Rochester, NY 14607
ph: 716-442-8998
Buys, sells, collects; one of the world's foremost authorities on American games; author of "Games: American Games & Their Makers, 1822-1992, With Values" (Wallace-Homestead, 1992); book available from author for $23.00 ppd.

Rick Polizzi
4602 Morse Ave.
Sherman Oaks, CA 91423-3326
Co-author with Fred Shaeffer of "Spin Again: Board Games From the Fifties and Sixties."

Board (TV Show Related)

Experts

Norm Vigue
62 Bailey St.
Stoughton, MA 02072
ph: 781-344-5441
Author of "Name of the Game." Buys & sells board games from TV cartoons, comedies, westerns, adventure, comic strip, detective, etc.

Card

Experts

Lee Dennis
447 Park Ave., Apt. 12
Keene, NH 03431-6506
ph: 603-358-0060
Author of "Warman's Antique American Games, 1840 - 1940"; former curator-owner of the country's largest collection of board games; continues to offer slide film presentation about games to clubs/ associations/Historical Societies.

Bruce Whitehill
Big Game Hunter, The
620 Park Ave. #202
Rochester, NY 14607
ph: 716-442-8998
Buys/sells/collects; one of the world's foremost authorities on American games; author of "Games: American Games & Their Makers, 1822-1992, With Values" (Wallace-Homestead, 1992); book available from author for $23.00 ppd.

Checkers

Collectors

Henry A. Justice
30 Thomas Ct.
Stockbridge, GA 30281-2900
ph: 770-389-8527
Wants checkers: plastic, wood, etc.; loose, boxed, sets, with or without board.

Checker Book World
3520 Hillcrest, Apt. 4
Dubuque, IA 52002
Wants to buy old checker sets, books and memorabilia.

Experts

Don Deweber
John Caldwell-Irving Windt Library of Checkers
3520 Hillcrest, Apt. 4
Dubuque, IA 52002
Wants to buy old checker sets, checker books, and other checker memorabilia.

Museums/Libraries

International Checkers Hall of Fame
P.O. Box A
220 Lynn Ray Rd.
Petal, MS 39465
ph: 601-582-7090
Hosts international checkers competitions

Cribbage Boards

Clubs/Associations

Bette L. Bemis
Cribbage Board Collectors Society
Newsletter: Members of the Board
P.O. Box 170
Carolina, RI 02812-0170
ph: 401-364-7241
For collectors of cribbage boards; newsletter published quarterly.

Collectors

Al Tenebaum
3095 N. Course Dr., #401
Pompano Beach, FL 33069

Experts

Bette L. Bemis
P.O. Box 170
Carolina, RI 02812-0170
ph: 401-364-7241
Author of book "Collectible Cribbage Boards," as well as articles on cribbage board collecting published on the American Cribbage Congress website, http://www.cribbage.org.

Mah Jongg

Collectors

Allan & Lila Weitz
12 Van Every Cr.
Kirkland, Quebec H9J 2P5
Canada
ph: 514-697-3276
Wishing to share mah jongg information; buys, sells, trades old Chinese sets; will travel.

Experts

Jim May
Mah Jongg Cyber Museum
P.O. Box 4139
Hazelwood, MO 63042
e-mail: pungchow@aol.com
web: http://members.aol.com/pungchow/
Collector, dealer, expert in the ancient game of mah jongg; website has lots of great information about the game at this site, even an Mah Jongg Cyber Museum, and a personal collection and gift shop.

Internet Resources

Jim May
Mah Jongg Cyber Museum
P.O. Box 4139
Hazelwood, MO 63042
e-mail: pungchow@aol.com
web: http://members.aol.com/pungchow/
Collector, dealer, expert in the ancient game of mah jongg; website has lots of great information about the game at this site, even an Mah Jongg Cyber Museum, and a personal collection and gift shop.

Skill & Action

Experts

Bruce Whitehill
Big Game Hunter, The
620 Park Ave. #202
Rochester, NY 14607
ph: 716-442-8998
Buys/sells/collects skill & action games: Mouse Trap, Operation, spinner games, Pick-Up Sticks (Jack Straws), Tiddley Winks, marble games, ball games, table top billiards/ croquet/pinball (bagatelle), Twister, Hungry Hippo, etc.

Video Games

Clubs/Associations

Video Arcade Preservation Society
e-mail: keeper@vaps.org
web: http://www.vaps.org/
Web site has a Killer List of Video Games.

Collectors

Frank Polosky
Video Games
P.O. Box 9542
Pittsburgh, PA 15223-0542
Wants to buy video games: Sega, Apple, Atari, Commodore 64, Vic 20, Odyssey, Bally Astrocade, ColecoVision; also wants related books and magazines; wants all 8 bit games: Mappy, Space Cavern, Apollo, Sewer Sam; write before sending.

Waterfuls

Collectors

Garrett Perryman
56 Sunset Blvd.
Trenton, NJ 08690
ph: 609-587-4676
Wants to buy Waterfuls and Watergames; these are water-filled plastic toys designed as a game.

GANGSTER RELATED COLLECTIBLES

(see LAW ENFORCEMENT MEMORABILIA; PERSONALITIES [CRIMINAL]; PROHIBITION ITEMS)

GARDEN FURNITURE

Furniture & Ornaments

(see also ARCHITECTURAL ELEMENTS; CAST IRON ITEMS)

Dealers

New England Garden Ornaments
38 East Brookfield Rd.
North Brookfield, MA 01535-0235
ph: 508-867-4474
fax: 508-867-8409
e-mail: nego@bx.com
web: http://www.negardenornaments.com
Carries old and new garden architecture and ornamentation: sundials, statuary, planters, urns, wrought iron, pedestals, birdbaths, etc.

Experts

Elizabeth Schumacher
Garden Accents
4 Union Hill Rd.
West Conshohocken, PA 19428
ph: 610-825-5525
fax: 610-825-4817
e-mail: eschuatga@aol.com
Buys and sells best assortment of antique garden accessories: urns, planters, statuary, benches, fountains; bronze, iron, lead, etc.

Margaret Lindquist
Whitehall at the Villa
1213 E. Franklin St.
Chapel Hill, NC 27514-3307
ph: 919-942-3179 or 919-933-3305
fax: 919-942-6600
e-mail: whchnc@aol.com
Author of "The Official Price Guide to Garden Furniture and Accessories."

Repro. Sources

John C. Allen, Jr.
Robinson Iron
P.O. Box 1119
Alexander City, AL 35011-1119
ph: 256-329-8486 or 800-824-2157
fax: 256-329-8960
e-mail: sales@robinson-iron.com
web: http://www.robinson-iron.com/
Makes reproduction furniture and fountains; catalog $5.

GARDEN HOSE NOZZLES

(see WATER SPRINKLERS)

GAS STATION COLLECTIBLES

(see also AUTOMOBILIA; GAUGES; HIGHWAY COLLECTIBLES; LICENSE PLATES; TOYS, Trucks & Equipment; TRAILERS & RV'S)

Clubs/Associations

John Logsdon
Iowa Gas Swap Meet
2417 Linda Dr.
Des Moines, IA 50322-5200
ph: 515-251-8811
e-mail: IowaGasJon@aol.com
web: http://home.stlnet.com/~jimpotts/iowagas
An organization dedicated to the collecting of all oil, gas, petroleum and auto advertising including signs, globes, pumps, cans, bottles, and related memorabilia. The annual convention held each August is the largest of its kind.

Collectors

Ed Natale, Jr.
P.O. Box 222
Wyckoff, NJ 07481
ph: 201-848-8485
fax: 201-848-8485
Wants to buy gas station and petroliana signs, uniform pins and badges, oil cans, pre-WWII road maps; photos helpful.

Larry Spilkin
P.O. Box 5039
Southfield, MI 48086-5039
ph: 248-642-3722
Wants postcards and matchbook covers of drive-ins, diners, cafes, gas stations and 1930s-1950s motels, restaurant/bar, cabins and Art Deco streamline hotels.

Peter Capell
1838 West Grace St.
Chicago, IL 60613-2724
ph: 773-871-8735
e-mail: pcapell@netware.net
Collects gasoline company/service station items: pump globes, giveaways such as banks, thermometers, salt & pepper shaker sets in the shape of gas pumps.

Ben Eckart
1121 Hylton Heights
Manhattan, KS 66502
ph: 785-539-7562
fax: 785-539-0822
e-mail: enarco@flinthills.com
web: http://www.enarco.com
Collects anything from the National Refining Company, Cleveland, Ohio; produced White Rose gasoline and EN-AR-CO motor oil; signs, cans, maps, national news booklets, calendars, photographs, etc.

Jeffrey Herman
3333 N. Carson St.
Carson City, NV 89706
ph: 775-888-3333
fax: 775-883-4214
Wants to buy oil cans; also wants gas station collectibles such as signs, pumps, globes, etc.

Bill Allard
1801 S. Fernside Dr.
Tacoma, WA 98465-1310
ph: 253-565-2545

Ace Feek
P.O. Box 1358
Chelan, WA 98816
ph: 509-682-5345 or 800-573-8847 x55
Wants to buy oil company and service station cap badges: Mobile, Union Oil, Mohawk Gasoline, Texaco, Shell, Union 76, etc.

Ted Appleby
29 Baptiste Rd.
South Baptiste, Alberta T9S 1R7
Canada
ph: 780-675-5371
fax: 780-675-5205
Buy, sell, trade Canadian quart oil cans, gas pumps, globes and signs, clocks, thermometers, etc. from tire companies, farm implement dealers, automobile companies, etc.; Canadian oil can appraiser; author of "Oil Cans of Canada."

Experts

Mark Anderton
Collectors Auction Services
RR2, Box 431
Oil City, PA 16301
ph: 814-677-6070
fax: 814-677-6166
e-mail: manderton@mail.usachoice.net
web: http://www.caswel.com/
Co-author with Sherry Mullen of "Gas Station Collectibles" (Wallace-Homestead, 1994).

Wayne Henderson
338 Spartan Rd.
Wilmington, NC 28405
ph: 910-395-4279
fax: 910-793-0631
e-mail: PCMPublishing@worldnet.att.net
web: http://www.pcmpublishing.com/
World's largest collection of historical material concerning service stations and oil company collectibles; co-author of "Gasoline Pump Globes", the new comprehensive catalog of known gas pump globes with complete company histories.

Scott Anderson
Time Passages, Ltd.
P.O. Box 65596
West Des Moines, IA 50265-0596
ph: 515-223-5105 or 515-223-5104
fax: 515-223-5149
e-mail: timepass@netins.net
web: http://www.time-pass.com/
Author of "Check the Oil" (Wallace-Homestead).

Jim Potts
9925 Reavis Rd.
Saint Louis, MO 63123
e-mail: admin@oldgas.com
web: http://www.oldgas.com
Specializes in gas station collectibles.

Internet Resources

Jim Potts
Primarily Petroliana
9925 Reavis Rd.
Saint Louis, MO 63123
e-mail: admin@oldgas.com
web: http://www.oldgas.com
An Internet service bringing gas station memorabilia collectors, dealers, publishers and service providers together for the benefit of all; web site features event schedules and reports, articles and images, links and roster of collectors.

Periodicals

Tim Dye
Magazine: Tiger Hightest Magazine
e-mail: hightest@galstar.com
web: http://www.galstar.com/~hightest/
Focuses on gas station and oil can collectibles.

Jerry Keyser
Magazine: Check the Oil!
30 W. Olentangy St.
Powell, OH 43065-9764
ph: 614-848-5038 or 800-228-6224
fax: 614-436-4760
web: http://www.oldgas.com/info/cto.htm
Pumps, oil cans, signs, oil bottles, pens, pump globes; anything to do with the petroleum industry of days gone by.

Scott Benjamin, Co-Ed.
Newsletter: Petroleum Collectibles Monthly
P.O. Box 556
Lagrange, OH 44050-0556
ph: 440-355-6608
e-mail: scott@pcmpublishing.com
web: http://www.pcmpublishing.com/
Research on all phases of gasoline marketing; world's largest collection of historical material concerning service stations and oil company collectibles: cans, signs, paper, toys, gas pumps, globes, large ad section.

Conoco

Collectors

Paul A. Wilson
P.O. Box 290
Hondo, TX 78861
ph: 830-426-8663
fax: 830-426-8645
WAnts any Conoco collectibles: toy trucks, maps, tour aides, pumps, dolls, signs, oil cans, filters, gas pump globes, etc.

Experts

Todd Helms
1023 East 5th Ave.
Lancaster, OH 43130
ph: 740-681-6151 or 740-654-6179
fax: 740-681-6076
e-mail: thelms@greenapple.com
web: http://www.greenapple.com/~thelms/
Collects Conoco (Continental Oil Company) and Maryland-related oil company items such as signs, cans, maps, pumps, giveaways; especially interested in "Minuteman" era of Conoco (1913-1929); author of "The Conoco Collector's Bible."

Frontier

Collectors

Jim Hollabaugh
3800 Congress Parkway
P.O. Box 460
Richfield, OH 44286-0460
ph: 330-659-3888 or 800-662-6344
fax: 330-659-9410
Wants to buy Shell & Frontier petroliana: containers, globes, signs, toys, promotional items, shell pocket watches with fobs; specializes in Shell and Frontier.

Gulf Oil

Collectors

Charles Roach
3212 Tudor
Oklahoma City, OK 73122-1346
ph: 405-942-4520
Wants to buy Gulf Oil gas station collectibles: maps, signs, cans, giveaways, ads, paper items, letterheads; only Gulf Oil items, please.

Hess

Collectors

Bob Ford
4804 Bensalem Blvd.
Bensalem, PA 19020
ph: 215-638-0531
e-mail: modelts@icdc.com
web: http://www.icdc.com/~modelts/
Collects and sells Hess, Wilco, Servco, Texaco and other gasoline promotional toy trucks by Ertl and others; also collects Hess memorabilia.

Oil Cans

Clubs/Associations

Rita Abney
Oil Can Collectors Club
4213 Derby Lane
Evansville, IN 47715
e-mail: oilcanlady@aol.com
web: http://www.oilcancollectors.com/

Collectors

Rita Abney
4213 Derby Lane
Evansville, IN 47715
e-mail: oilcanlady@aol.com
web: http://www.oilcancollectors.com/

Robert Larson
3517 Vernal Ct.
Merced, CA 95340-0689
ph: 209-723-7828
Wants to buy oil cans (push the bottom type) and other lubrication devices such as grease guns, lubricators, grease cups and fittings.

Pumps & Globes

Collectors

Gary Hildman
3240 Sevier Rd.
Marcellus, NY 13108-9624
ph: 315-673-2535
fax: 315-673-2412
Wants gasoline pump globes and related items: inserts, glass and metal bodies; also wants porcelain, tin, and neon signs.

Kent Blaine
505 N. Mission Rd.
Winona, MS 38967-9534
ph: 601-624-2947 or 601-283-3524
Wants pre-1960 gas station items through 1950s; especially brass padlocks with oil company logos, e.g. Texaco, Pan Am, Crown, etc.; also wants 15" single globe lens; always has items for trade and for sale.

Scott Benjamin
411 Forest St.
Lagrange, OH 44050
ph: 440-355-6608
fax: 440-355-4955
e-mail: scottpcm@aol.com
web: http://www.pcmpublishing.com/
Wants gasoline globes, inserts, etched globes, aviation, Benzol and others.

Dealers

Ron Rogers
Gas Pumps & Parking Meters
ph: 418-673-1067
e-mail: impala1@bright.net
web: http://www.bright.net/~impala1/
Specializes in buying, selling and restoring old gas pumps and parking meters; also other gas station memorabilia such as oil cans, porcelain and tin signs; pedal cars, too.

Walt Feiger
Walt's Antiques
2513 Nelson Rd.
Traverse City, MI 49686-8557
ph: 231-223-7386 or 231-223-4123
Buys and sells gas pumps, globes, signs, auto memorabilia, and slot machines.

Repro. Sources

Benkin & Co.
16 E. Main
Tripp City, OH 45371
ph: 937-667-5975
Handmade antique-style gas pumps, wide selection of colors, 35 oil company globes to chose from; sold in kits or completely finished; write for flyer.

Suppliers

Scott Anderson
Time Passages, Ltd.
P.O. Box 65596
West Des Moines, IA 50265-0596
ph: 515-223-5105 or 515-223-5104
fax: 515-223-5149
e-mail: timepass@netins.net
web: http://www.time-pass.com/
Supplies restoration parts and supplies for vintage gasoline pumps.

Ted Appleby
29 Baptiste Rd.
South Baptiste, Alberta T9S 1R7
Canada
ph: 780-675-5371
fax: 780-675-5205
Restoration parts, supplies for vintage gas pumps; Canada's largest selection of Canadian globes, decals; castings, glass, I.D. tags, brass nozzles, hose, etc. for Gilbert 7 Barker and Clearvision single and 20 gallon twin; catalog $4.

Road Maps

Clubs/Associations

Mark Anderson, Sec.
Road Map Collectors of America
Newsletter: RMCA Newsletter
5832 NW 62nd Terrace
Oklahoma City, OK 73122
e-mail: dave@roadmaps.org
web: http://www.roadmaps.org
A club for researchers, collectors, dealers of North American road maps.

Collectors

Jeff Hubbard
2900 91st St.
Sturtevant, WI 53177-2013
ph: 414-886-0477
Buys and sells older Hotwheel cars and pre-1960 oil company highway maps.

David Schul
2214 Princeton Blvd.
Lawrence, KS 66049
ph: 785-864-5143
e-mail: dave@roadmaps.org
Looking for official road maps, road atlases, highway maps (all states and provinces) and pre-1940 road atlases (any publisher).

Peter Sidlow
5895 Duneville St.
Las Vegas, NV 89118
ph: 702-873-1818 or 702-498-1040
fax: 702-248-4288
e-mail: pedro666@earthlink.net
Wants early road maps; oil company or other issues; prefers colorful graphics.

Dealers

Michael Kelly
Paper Pandemonium
1321 Jack's Mountain Road
Fairfield, PA 17320
ph: 717-642-8019
e-mail: kellym@mail.cvn.net
web: http://www.tias.com/stores/pp
Carries large selection of vintage gas company road maps, state maps, wall maps for collectors.

Noel Levy
1109 Silentglade Rd.
Owings Mills, MD 21117-2455
ph: 410-363-9040
e-mail: megamapster@juno.com
Road map collector, expert, dealer; more than 6,000 different oil company, official state and miscellaneous road maps available on 30-page monthly catalog; dates range from 1908 to present; catalog $5 refundable with first purchase.

James Willinger
Wide World of Maps
2626 W. Glenrosa
Phoenix, AZ 85017
ph: 602-455-0616
fax: 602-433-0695
e-mail: azmapman@prodigy.net
web: http://www.maps4u.com
Buys sells and trades old maps and travel related brochures with a focus on the Southwestern states.

Experts

Doug Yorke
7 Conover Lane
Rumson, NJ 07760
Co-author with John Margolies of "Hitting the Road."

David Schul
2214 Princeton Blvd.
Lawrence, KS 66049
ph: 785-864-5143
e-mail: dave@roadmaps.org
Dealer and expert looking for official road maps, road atlases, highway maps (all states and provinces) and pre-1940 road atlases (any publisher).

Shell

Collectors

Jim Hollabaugh
3800 Congress Parkway
P.O. Box 460
Richfield, OH 44286-0460
ph: 330-659-3888 or 800-662-6344
fax: 330-659-9410
Wants to buy Shell & Frontier petroliana: containers, globes, signs, toys, promotional items, shell pocket watches with fobs; specializes in Shell and Frontier.

Texaco

Collectors

Richard Eaves
9838 Rustic Gate
La Porte, TX 77571
ph: 713-470-2191
Wants Texaco toys, literature, memorabilia.

Dealers

Cecil Buchanan
1589 Curfman Rd.
Greensboro, NC 27455
ph: 336-288-3780
fax: 336-288-2745
Wants to buy pre-1950 Texaco advertising items.

GAUGES

(see also GAS STATION COLLECTIBLES; INSTRUMENTS & DEVICES; STEAM-OPERATED, Models & Equipment)

Collectors

Jarvis
P.O. Box 2245
Lynnwood, WA 98036-8636
Wants tire pressure gauges having car names or other advertising on them.

Experts

Brian Lerohl
29048 486th Ave.
Fairview, SD 57027-6204
ph: 605-987-5378
fax: 605-987-5378
Appraiser, collector and historian of fluid pressure gauges, especially Bourdon tube and diaphragm type steam gauges; also does gauge repairs.

Repair Services

Brian Lerohl
29048 486th Ave.
Fairview, SD 57027-6204
ph: 605-987-5378
fax: 605-987-5378
Appraiser, collector and historian of fluid pressure gauges, especially Bourdon tube and diaphragm type steam gauges; also does gauge repairs.

GAVELS

Collectors

Bill Retskin
P.O. Box 18481
Asheville, NC 28814-0481
ph: 828-254-4487
fax: 828-254-1066
e-mail: bill@matchcovers.com
web: http://www.matchcovers.com
Wants to buy gavels: auctioneers', judicial, ceremonial, toy, giant, traditional size, miniature; prefers wood; please no mallets, meat tenderizers, or hammers.

GEMS & JEWELRY

(see also AMERICAN INDIAN, Jewelry; BEADS; BOOKS, Reference [Gems/Jewelry]; CHATELAINES; COMBS & HAIR ACCESSORIES; COMPACTS; CRAFTS, Jewelry; CUFF LINKS; GOLD; DRESSER ITEMS, Hatpins & Hatpin Holders; IVORY; JADE; LAPIDARY; MINERAL SPECIMENS; WATCHES)

Appraisers

Martin D. Haske, GG, ISA
Adamas Gemological Laboratory
P.O. Box 470828
Brookline Village, MA 02147-0828
ph: 617-232-5508
fax: 617-232-5508
e-mail: adamas@gis.net

Judith Fineblit Anderson, GG, ISA CAPP
Bijoux Extraordinaire, Ltd.
P.O. Box 1424
Manchester, NH 03105-1424
ph: 603-624-8672
e-mail: judi@jewelryexpert.com
web: http://www.jewelryexpert.com/
Appraises diamonds, colored gems, antique & period jewelry, and contemporary designer jewelry for insurance, estate, divorce, charitable donation, damage reports, expert witness testimony.

Katherine Vandygriff, GG,ISA CAPP
Katherine's
59 Colonial Daniels Dr.
Bedford, NH 03110
e-mail: Katherine@muscanet.com
Professional, independent gems & jewelry appraiser.

Trina McCandless
McCandless Custom Jewelry & Appraisal
567 Vauxhaul Street Ext.
Waterford, CT 06385
ph: 860-443-3039
e-mail: trina@unidial.com
ISA CAPP, GIA GG, NAJA, SNAG; specializes in gemology & gemstones, antique & period jewelry, custom jewelry; appraisals for estate, insurance, etc.

Jo Anne M. Whitteaker,ISA CAPP, GG
Independent Gemological Lab Appraisers & Consultants
23 W. Westfield Ave.
P.O. Box 4086
Roselle Park, NJ 07204-2252
ph: 908-241-8800 or 908-298-0121
e-mail: 3580@polygon.net
Professional gemological examinations, grading, appraisals, fraudulent claims investigations, expert witness; appraisals for casualty loss, insurance replacement, liquidation, damage, equitable distribution, donation, estate, etc.

Karen J. Russo, G.G.
Karen Jocelyn, Inc.
792 Partridge Dr.
P.O. Box 6795
Bridgewater, NJ 08807
ph: 908-526-8440
fax: 908-526-8348
Provides a full range of appraisal and consultation services for studio/art jewelry, antique/estate jewelry, mineral specimens, and collector gemstones; market research, identification, photography, provenance research, portable services.

Jerry Ehrenwald, GG, ISA
International Gemological Institute
579 5th Ave.
New York, NY 10017-1917
ph: 212-398-1700 or 212-398-1701
fax: 212-869-8047
e-mail: igi@interport.net
web: http://www.igi-usa.com
Devoted to identification, authentication and valuation of gems and jewelry from an unbiased point of view; no buying or selling.

Paul Cassarino ISA, GG
Gem Lab, The
4098 W. Henrietta Rd.
Rochester, NY 14623-5222
ph: 716-359-3900
fax: 716-359-8932
e-mail: paulcass@rochester.rr.com

Gemological Appraisal Association
658 Washington Road
Pittsburgh, PA 15228
ph: 412-344-5500
fax: 412-344-4910
The most comprehensive service available for the location, retrieval and reinstatement of valued possessions including art, antiques and collectibles.

Pennye Jones-Napier, FGA, ISA
Jewellery Appraisal Services
236 Walnut Street NW
Washington, DC 20012-2157
ph: 202-291-5575 or 202-251-0494
fax: 202-291-5345
e-mail: pennyenj@earthlink.net
web: http://www.triratna.com
Appraiser specializing in Studio/ Design jewelers, and contemporary and antique jewelry targeting the 19th and 20th centuries; also offers consultation services to auction houses worldwide.

Dan James, GG
Antique Jewelry Specialists
4212 Gallatin St.
Hyattsville, MD 20781-2049
ph: 301-779-3696
Graduate gemologist, appraiser, specialist in antique jewelry, diamonds and colored gemstones; Georgian to modern; gemological lab on premises for appraisals and evaluations; by appointment only.

Thomas J. Terpilak, GG, ASA, AAA
Metro Gem Consultants
7315 Wisconsin Ave.
Bethesda, MD 20814-3202
ph: 301-654-0838 or 301-654-8678
Gemological consultant and professional jewelry appraiser.

James Jolliff
National Association of Jewelry Appraisers, The
Newsletter: Jewelry Appraiser, The
P.O. Box 6558
Annapolis, MD 21401-0558
ph: 301-261-8270 or 410-266-0744
Members perform gem and jewelry, silver flatware and hollowware, and watch valuations exclusively; also watches and silver.

James Jolliff
P.O. Box 6558
Annapolis, MD 21401-0558
ph: 301-261-8270 or 410-266-0744
Appraises antique to contemporary gems and jewelry, silver flatware and hollowware, and watches exclusively.

Joette Humphrey, GG
Shelley's Auction Gallery
429 N. Main St.
Hendersonville, NC 28792-4903
ph: 704-698-8485 or 704-692-3615
fax: 704-693-4305
Buy, consign and auction antiques and collectibles with a heavy emphasis on antique jewelry and diamonds.

Rose & Lornie Mueller, ISA, GG
Lithos Jewelry
344 Corey Ave.
Saint Petersburg, FL 33706
ph: 727-367-9010
fax: 727-367-9011
e-mail: lithos@tampabay.rr.com
web: http://www.lithosjewelry.com
High-end jewelry dealer; trained and accredited appraisers.

Joseph G. Balshone, GG, ISA
Columbus Gemological Laboratories, Inc.
463 East Town St.
Columbus, OH 43215-4796
ph: 800-209-4367 or 614-224-2404
fax: 614-224-5630
e-mail: jbalshone@compuserve.com
Specializing in appraising gems & jewelry, post-1800 firearms, and vintage and modern writing instruments and accessories.

Pamela L. Hickman, ISA, GG
International Diamond & Gold Design
4026 E 82nd St.
Indianapolis, IN 46250-4209
ph: 317-578-4653
fax: 317-578-9335
Specializes in gems, jewelry, diamonds, colored stones, gold, platinum, pearls, and estate and custom jewelry.

Anne Hawken, GG, ASA
Anne Hawken Gems
P.O. Box 160906
Austin, TX 78716-0906
ph: 512-288-1507
fax: 512-328-9411
Buys, sells, brokers, and appraises fine and collectible gemstones; also collection consultant, expert witness, educator; Accredited Senior Appraiser (ASA), AGA-Certified Gem Laboratory.

Sharon Wakefield
Northwest Gemological Lab
P.O. Box 8243
Boise, ID 83707-2243
ph: 208-362-3938
fax: 208-362-2889
e-mail: sharon@gem-science.com
web: http://www.gem-science.com/Index.htm
Noted expert, appraiser, lecturer and author specializing in the appraisal of diamonds, gems and jewelry.

Larry Phillips, GG, ISA
Phillips & Associates
2430 Juan Tabo NE, Ste. 275
Albuquerque, NM 87112
ph: 505-299-7999
Master Gemologist Appraiser.

Barbara Pickett, GCA, MCA, GGAC
Antique Rose, The
P.O. Box 771
Lakewood, CA 90714-0771
ph: 562-425-4149
fax: 562-425-4149

Norman K. Monteau
AIG Labs/Monteau Gemological Services
21250 Califa St., #203
Woodland Hills, CA 91367
ph: 818-712-9750
fax: 818-712-9755
e-mail: aig-labs@pacbell.net
Offers appraisals and laboratory grading for diamonds and colored stones.

La Verne Larson, ISA, NJA, GG
Gemological & Appraisal Services
4796 Marblehead Bay Dr.
Oceanside, CA 92057-3409
ph: 760-9667-8497
e-mail: m-l-larson@worldnet.att.net
Accredited Member of the International Society of Appraisers; Member of the National Association of Jewelry Appraisers.

Nancy Stacy, GG, ISA CAPP
Jewels by Stacy Appraisals
712 Bancroft, #436
Walnut Creek, CA 94598
ph: 925-939-4367
e-mail: nancy@appraiser.net
web: http://www.jewelry-appraisal.com/
Appraisals for insurance scheduling and claims, equitable distribution, liquidation, estates, trusts, conservatorships, etc.; forensic gemologist; litigation support, experienced in expert testimony.

Christian Coleman, Ex. Dir.
International Society of Appraisers
Newsletter: Professional Appraisers Information Exchange
16040 Christensen Rd., Ste. 102
Seattle, WA 98188
ph: 206-241-0359 or 888-472-4732
fax: 206-241-0436
e-mail: ISA_HQ@compuserve.com
web: http://www.isa-appraisers.org
Largest association of professional personal property appraisers; members specialize in antiques & residential contents, gems & jewelry, fine art, and machinery & equipment; call for appraiser nearest you.

James Poag, GG, ISA CAPP
James O. Poag Jewellers, Ltd.
94 Frank Street
P.O. Box 39, Ontario N7G 3J1
Canada
ph: 519-245-1040 or 519-245-1580
fax: 519-245-6073
e-mail: james@poag.com
web: http://www.poags.com/
ISA appraiser certified in gems & jewelry, and in antique & period jewelry; also sells and restores new and estate jewelry; four goldsmiths on staff, as well as a GIA Graduate Gemologist.

Auction Services

Gloria Lieberman
Skinner, Inc.
357 Main St.
Bolton, MA 01740-1104
ph: 978-779-6241
fax: 978-779-5144
e-mail: info@skinnerinc.com
web: http://www.skinnerinc.com
Established in 1964, Skinner Inc. is the fifth largest auction house in the US; has offices in Bolton and Boston, MA.

Sotheby's
1334 York Ave.
New York, NY 10021
ph: 212-606-7000
fax: 212-606-7107
web: http://www.sothebys.com
Over 70 collecting areas are featured at Sotheby's auctions including toys, dolls, porcelain, furniture, silver, art, books; exhibitions are free and everyone is welcome; for a free copy of "Sotheby's Newsletter", call 212-606-7245.

John S. Weschler
Weschler's
909 E St. NW
Washington, DC 20004-2006
ph: 202-628-1281 or 800-331-1430
fax: 202-628-2366
web: http://www.weschlers.com/
Specializes in the auction sale of jewelry, coins, and watches.

Joette Humphrey, GG
Shelley's Auction Gallery
429 N. Main St.
Hendersonville, NC 28792-4903
ph: 704-698-8485 or 704-692-3615
fax: 704-693-4305
Buy, consign and auction antiques and collectibles with a heavy emphasis on antique jewelry and diamonds.

Joseph Mackley
Mackley & Company
9724 Kingston Pike, Ste. 1012
Knoxville, TN 37922
ph: 423-693-3097
e-mail: joseph@mackley.com
web: http://www.mackley.com
On-line and live auction sales of gems & jewelry, pocket watches, enameled jewelry, estate jewelry, silver, chiming watches, gold watch fobs, gold charms, etc.; also buys.

Joseph DuMouchelle
Joseph DuMouchelle Fine & Estate Jewelry Auctions
5 Kercheval
Grosse Pointe Farms, MI 48236
ph: 313-884-4800 or 800-475-4367
fax: 313-884-7662
e-mail: joelindy@earthlink.net
Specializes in the sale of fine and estate jewelry and small objects of art; large diamonds and colored stones, paintings, Oriental rugs, silver, antique furniture and sculpture, Russian objects of art.

Butterfield & Dunning
755 Church Rd.
Elgin, IL 60123
ph: 847-741-3483
fax: 847-741-3589
e-mail: info@butterfields.com
web: http://www.butterfields.com

Clubs/Associations

Manufacturing Jewelers & Silversmiths of America, Inc.
Magazine: American Jewelry Manufacturer
One State St., 6th Floor
Providence, RI 02908
ph: 401-274-3840 or 800-444-6572
fax: 401-274-02665
e-mail: mjsa@mjsainc.com
web: http://mjsa.polygon.net/
A national trade association for the jewelry manufacturing industry; for jewelry manufacturers, goldsmiths and silversmiths, casters, refiners, electroplaters, gemstone dealers, findings manufacturers, suppliers, sales reps.

International Colored Gemstone Association
3 East 48th St., 5th Floor
New York, NY 10017
ph: 212-688-8452
fax: 212-688-9006
e-mail: ica@gemstone.org
web: http://www.gemstone.org/
Represents the international gemstone industry (miners, cutters, wholesalers); working to increase the understanding, appreciation of colored gemstones worldwide; website with great information for the public; members are trade only.

Jacoby Carolyn
Jewelry Information Center
1185 Avenue of the Americas, 30th Floor
New York, NY 10036-2601
ph: 800-459-0130 or 212-398-2319
fax: 212-398-2324
e-mail: jic@jewelryinfo.org
web: http://www.jewelryinfo.org
A trade association founded in 1946 to provide public relations for the entire jewelry industry; provides consumers with information about fine jewelry, how to buy, how to care for it, its history, and new product trends.

Jewelers of America, Inc.
1185 Avenue of the Americas, 30th Floor
New York, NY 10046
ph: 800-223-0673 or 212-768-8777
fax: 212-768-8087
e-mail: jewelersam@aol.com
web: http://jewelers.org/
A national association of retail jewelers; part of their mission is to provide consumers with information and education about fine jewelry; website offers information on how to select a jeweler, consumer news, test your jewelry knowledge.

American Society of Jewelry Historians
Newsletter: ASJH Newsletter
1333A North Avenue, Box 103
New Rochelle, NY 10804
ph: 914-637-0087 or 914-636-3784
fax: 914-637-0087
e-mail: ekarlin@usa.net
Promotes education and appreciation of antique jewelry, crossing all periods from ancient to present; quarterly newsletter informs members of related lectures, exhibitions, and book reviews; also publishes a periodic journal.

Lucille Tempesta
Vintage Fashion & Costume Jewelry Club
Newsletter: VFCJ Newsletter
P.O. Box 265
Glen Oaks, NY 11004-0265
ph: 718-939-3095
fax: 718-939-7988
e-mail: VFCJ@aol.com
web: http://www.lizjewel.com/vf/

Bob Mitchell
Society of North American Goldsmiths
Journal: Metalsmith
5009 Londonderry Dr.
Tampa, FL 33647-9910
ph: 813-977-5326
fax: 813-977-8462
e-mail: mitchel@artguidesource.com
web: http://www.artguidesource.com/
An association for jewelers and metal artisans; quarterly magazine devoted to the development and appreciation for the craft of fine metalsmithing: jewelry, decorative art, etc.

Thomas P. Dorman, Ex. Dir.
American Gem Society
8881 West Saraha Ave.
Las Vegas, NV 89117
ph: 702-255-6500
fax: 702-255-7420
web: http://www.ags.org/
Founded in 1934 to protect consumers in their purchases of fine jewelry.

Gemological Institute of America
Journal: Gems & Gemology
5345 Armada Dr.
Carlsbad, CA 92008
ph: 760-603-4200
fax: 760-603-4266
web: http://www.gia.org

Accredited Gemologists Association
Journal: Cornerstone
3309 Juanita St.
San Diego, CA 92105
ph: 619-286-1603
fax: 619-286-7541
e-mail: aga@polygon.net
web: http://aga.polygon.net/
Professional association of gemstone experts, quality grading laboratories, appraisers, and dealers; all professional members are advanced, degree-holding gemologists, subscribing to a strong code of ethics and professional practice.

Myra McKeen
Canadian Jewellers Association
Newsletter: Jewellry World
27 Queen Street East, Ste. 600
Toronto, Ontario M5C 2M6
Canada
ph: 416-368-7616 or 800-580-0942
fax: 416-368-1986
e-mail: cja@canadianjewellers.com
web: http://canadianjewellers.com
A professional association with a membership that is obligated to maintain the highest level of personal integrity, honesty and business ethics.

W. Wight, Ed.
Canadian Gemmological Association
Magazine: Canadian Gemmologist, The
1767 Avenue Rd.
Toronto, Ontario M5M 3Y8
Canada
ph: 416-785-0962 or 877-244-3090
fax: 416-785-9043
e-mail: qwight@sympatico.ca
web: http://pangea.usask.ca/~dfs846/rmac/cga.html
A non-profit educational institution which teaches gemmology; founded in 1958; affiliated with the Gemmological Association and Gem Testing Laboratory of Great Britain; magazine published quarterly.

Canadian Institute of Gemmology
Newsletter: Gemmology Canada
P.O. Box 57010
Vancouver, British Columbia V5K 5G6
Canada
ph: 604-530-8569
fax: 604-530-8569
e-mail: wolf@kwantlen.bc.ca
web: http://cigem.ca/

Gemmological Association of Great Britain
27 Greville St., 1st Floor
London, EC1N 8SU
U.K.
ph: (171) 404-3334
fax: (171) 404-8843
Offers correspondence and in-residence classes in gemology.

Dealers

Judith Fineblit Anderson, GG, ISA CAPP
Bijoux Extraordinaire, Ltd.
P.O. Box 1424
Manchester, NH 03105-1424
ph: 603-624-8672
e-mail: judi@jewelryexpert.com
web: http://www.jewelryexpert.com/
Buys, sells, brokers fine quality antique and estate jewelry, contemporary designer jewelry, diamonds and colored gemstones; also custom design and restorations of antique jewelry; appraisal services; lecturer on jewelry.

Elissa Cohen ISA CAPP, GG
Suburban Jewelers
126 East Front St.
Plainfield, NJ 07060-1202
ph: 908-756-1774
Dealer and appraiser of modern and period jewelry, GIA Graduate Gemologist, Certified Member of the ISA, appraiser of diamonds, gemstones, pearls, jewelry.

S.J. Moore
5 E. Genesee St.
Skaneateles, NY 13152-1317
ph: 315-685-8758
fax: 315-685-1564
e-mail: moore90w@aol.com
Buys and sells fine jewelry and diamonds, ruby, sapphire, emeralds.

Dan James, GG
Antique Jewelry Specialists
4212 Gallatin St.
Hyattsville, MD 20781-2049
ph: 301-779-3696
Buys and sells diamonds and colored stone jewelry, antique to 1940s; including platinum, enameled and costume jewelry.

Kenneth M. Glass
Glyndon Jewelry
4880 Butler Rd.
Glyndon, MD 21071
ph: 410-526-4112
fax: 410-526-0344
Manufacturer and wholesaler of 10K, 14K, 18K and platinum vintage style earrings, pendants, rings, brooches, etc. with genuine stones; also restore and repair and will make models from your merchandise; to the trade only.

Tony Laughter
Perry's at SouthPark
SouthPark Mall
Charlotte, NC 28211
ph: 704-364-1391
Deals in fine, antique and estate jewelry; Accredited Member of the International Society of Appraisers.

John Almasi
Salon Gems
2901 Vassar St.
Melbourne, FL 32901
ph: 407-725-8740
e-mail: topblubaby@aol.com
Specializing in fine gemstones and gold products, including, but not limited to bullion, diamonds, alexandrite, and finished gold jewelry.

Ed London
Parke Lloyds International, Inc.
9408 NW 70 St.
Fort Lauderdale, FL 33321-3002
ph: 954-724-4274 or 954-726-4107
Wants to buy old jewelry.

Rose & Lornie Mueller, ISA, GG
Lithos Jewelry
344 Corey Ave.
Saint Petersburg, FL 33706
ph: 727-367-9010
fax: 727-367-9011
e-mail: lithos@tampabay.rr.com
web: http://www.lithosjewelry.com
High-end jewelry dealer; trained and accredited appraisers.

Robert E. Spomer
Gem Kingdom, The
P.O. Box 27088
Lakewood, CO 80227
ph: 303-986-1851
e-mail: gemkingdom@aol.com
web: http://members.aol.com/respomer/gk.htm
A professional gem cutter by trade, specializing in custom collector's gemstones and fancy-cut jewelry grade stones; also collects and mines minerals and gems, especially in Colorado; also collects Fairburn and other banded agates.

Anne Foster
1913 Hyde St.
San Francisco, CA 94109
ph: 415-776-8865
Wants Bakelite jewelry, bracelets, pins, necklaces, earrings, rings, etc.

Ray L. Elsey
Associate Jewelers Inc.
534 SW Third Ave.
Portland, OR 97204
ph: 800-224-8086
fax: 503-226-6787
e-mail: raylc@tradeshop.com
web: http://www.tradeshop.com/master/lobby.html
A union professional fine jewelry trade shop, designing, building and servicing fine jewelry since 1974; refined working drawings, custom wax carving, special order manufacturing, platinum manufacturing, Celtic design bands.

James Poag, GG, ISA CAPP
James O. Poag Jewellers, Ltd.
94 Frank Street
P.O. Box 39, Ontario N7G 3J1
Canada
ph: 519-245-1040 or 519-245-1580
fax: 519-245-6073
e-mail: james@poag.com
web: http://www.poags.com/
Retail clock, jewellery, china and gift stores; staff included 3 goldsmiths, 2 stone setters, watchmaker, clockmaker and ISA Certified Appraiser; largest selection of clocks in Ontario; in business since 1959.

Experts

Judith Fineblit Anderson, GG, ISA CAPP
Bijoux Extraordinaire, Ltd.
P.O. Box 1424
Manchester, NH 03105-1424
ph: 603-624-8672
e-mail: judi@jewelryexpert.com
web: http://www.jewelryexpert.com/
Buys, sells, brokers fine quality antique and estate jewelry, contemporary designer jewelry, diamonds and colored gemstones; also custom design and restorations; offers extensive consulting and appraisal services; lecturer on jewelry.

William D. Hoefer, FGA, GG
Hoefers' Gemological Services
5016 Alan Ave., Ste. B4
San Jose, CA 95124-5741
ph: 408-264-0670
fax: 408-264-0725
e-mail: editor@appraiserunderoath.com
web: http://www.appraiserunderoath.com/
Specializes in the appraisal of gemstones, diamonds, and contemporary jewelry; also offers expert testimony for attorneys, court, etc.

Internet Resources

John Kejr, Marketing Mngr.
Polygon, The Jewelry Industry WebCenter
First Bank Center, #201
P.O. Box 4806
Dillon, CO 80435
ph: 800-221-4425 or 970-468-1245
fax: 970-468-1247
e-mail: sales@polygon.net
web: http://www.polygon.net/
World's largest cluster of website-based on-line services for the jewelry industry; operated within a password-protected environment for trade-only communication; the public can find a local jeweler, and get tips for buying jewelry.

John Kejr, Marketing Mngr.
Tradelock.com
First Bank Center, #201
P.O. Box 4806
Dillon, CO 80435
ph: 800-221-4425 or 970-468-1245
fax: 970-468-1247
e-mail: sales@polygon.net
web: http://www.polygon.net/
The jewelry industry's most complete website search directory: equipment, designer jewelry, clocks and watches, materials, trade associations, publications, trade shows, etc.

Lorraine Venner
Jewelry Mall, A
1563 Solano Ave., Ste. 516
Berkeley, CA 94707
ph: 510-528-8072
e-mail: lorraine@jewelrymall.com
web: http://www.jewelrymall.com
Gemstone and jewelry store supplies, shows, birthstone information, arts/crafts malls, crystal therapy, diamond buyers guide, wholesale section, jewelry jokes; free links.

Ray L. Elsey
Gemology & Lapidary Pages, c/o Associate Jewelers Inc.
534 SW Third Ave.
Portland, OR 97204
ph: 800-224-8086
fax: 503-226-6787
e-mail: raylc@tradeshop.com
web: http://www.tradeshop.com/master/lobby.html
Great website for consumer information about gemstones; judging cut, color, clarity, carat; how gemstones are classified; gem substitutes; grading; caring for your gemstones; check out the jewelry Hall of Shame.

Tracey Phillips
T.A.M. Jewel Auction
26 Andover Drive
London, Ontario N6J 3W8
Canada
ph: 519-472-3171
e-mail: tam@tam.ca
web: http://www.tam.ca/jewelauction/
The only online auction exclusively for buying and selling vintage and collectible jewelry, beads, and handcrafted originals.

GemNet
P.O. Box 22
Victoria Street
Bourton-on-the-Water, The Cotswolds GL54 2ZA
U.K.
ph: +44 1451 810595
fax: +44 1451 810594
e-mail: info@gemnet.co.uk
web: http://www.gemnet.co.uk
International gem links, online forum, second hand jewelry, trade and press associations, watch buying sources.

Misc. Services

Jewelers Vigilance Committee
401 East 34th St., Ste. N13A
New York, NY 10016-8578
web: http://www.gis.net/~adamas/jvc.html
Has published "Recommended Minimum Guidelines for Insurance Replacement Cost Estimate Documentation foe Jewelers," see this website for the guidelines in full.

Rapaport Diamond Report RapNet
15 West 47th St.
New York, NY 10036
ph: 212-354-0575
fax: 212-840-0243
e-mail: rap@diamonds.com
web: http://www.diamonds.com/
Lings together all aspects of the jewelry industry to form an electronic community; a secured site for members of the trade only; provides instant access to diamond price data as well as continuously updated news; a fee service.

Howard Rubin
GemDialogue Systems, Inc.
P.O. Box 7683
Rego Park, NY 11374-7683
ph: 718-997-0231
fax: 718-997-9057
GemDialogue is a gemstone descriptive system for colored stones and fancy colored diamonds; it gives you visual comparison points for over 60,000 colors; a grading system is also included.

Periodicals

Magazine: American Jewelry Manufacturer
One State St.
Providence, RI 02908-5035
ph: 401-274-3840
fax: 401-274-0265
e-mail: 102262.223@compuserve.com
A monthly glossy trade publication; industry articles, ads for jewelry manufacturing goods and services.

Dan Kisch, Pub.
Magazine: National Jeweler
1 Penn Plaza
New York, NY 10019
ph: 212-615-2380 or 800-250-2430
fax: 212-279-3971
e-mail: dkisch@mfi.com
web: http://www.national-jeweler.com/
The most popular jewelry industry resource; up-to-the-minute news twice a month.

Martin Rapaport, Pres.
Magazine: Rapaport Diamond Report
15 West 47th St.
New York, NY 10036
ph: 212-354-0575
fax: 212-840-0243
e-mail: rap@diamonds.com
web: http://www.diamonds.com/
A weekly report of world wide activity relating to diamonds, colored stones and jewelry; price performances, cash asking prices, precious metal prices, actual transaction prices for diamonds and diamond jewelry, etc.

PTN Publishing Co.
Magazine: Modern Jeweler
455 Broad Hollow Rd., Ste. 21
Melville, NY 11747
ph: 516-845-2700
fax: 516-845-2797
Monthly trade magazine for the jewelry industry.

Chilton Company
Magazine: JCK - Jewelers' Circular-Keystone
201 King of Prussia Rd.
Wayne, PA 19089-0001
ph: 610-964-4480
fax: 610-964-4481
e-mail: mmiriam@cahners.com
web: http://www.jckgroup.com/
A monthly trade magazine focusing on new and antique gems, jewelry, and watches.

Bond Communications
Magazine: Professional Jeweler Magazine
1500 Walnut St., Ste. 1200
Philadelphia, PA 19102
ph: 215-731-2243
fax: 610-545-9629
e-mail: askus@professionaljeweler.com
web: http://www.professionaljeweler.com

Cindy Valerio
Magazine: Colored Stone
60 Chestnut Ave., Ste. 201
Devon, PA 19333-1312
ph: 610-293-1112 or 800-676-4336 (sub)
fax: 610-293-1717
e-mail: clrdstone@aol.com
The international reporter of the gemstone trade; features also include The Annual Buyers Guide, The Fall Show Guide, and the Tucson Show Guide - a guide to the largest US gemstone show held annually in Arizona; also book & video sales.

Gemworld International, Inc.
Magazine: Guide, The
650 Dundee Rd., Ste. 465
Northbrook, IL 60062
ph: 847-564-0555
fax: 847-564-0557
e-mail: gemguide@ix.netcom.com
Monthly price guides and related information on gems.

Magazine: Gems & Gemology
P.O. Box 2110
Santa Monica, CA 90407-2110
ph: 310-829-2991 or 800-421-7250
fax: 310-453-4478

Ornament, Inc.
Magazine: Ornament
P.O. Box 2349
San Marcos, CA 92079-2349
ph: 760-599-0222
fax: 760-599-0228
e-mail: ornament@cts.com
web: http://www.ornamentmagazine.com/
A quarterly magazine focusing on craft and art items of personal adornment in any media or form: fiber, glass, metal, ancient historic/ethnic ornament; ethnographic and tribal jewelry; also reviews of museum exhibits and publications.

Magazine: JQ Magazine
P.O. Box 299
585 Fifth Street West
Sonoma, CA 95476-6800
ph: 707-938-1082
fax: 707-935-6585
The journal for professional jewelers and jewelry designers.

Carol Besler, Ed.
Magazine: Canadian Jeweller
1448 Lawrence Ave. E., Ste. 302
Toronto, Ontario M4A 2V6
Canada
ph: 416-755-5199
fax: 416-755-9123
e-mail: canjewel@style.ca
web: http://canjewel.polygon.net/
A bi-monthly glossy magazine focusing on gems, jewelry and timepieces; trade shows, business news, products and services.

Repair Services

Richard P. Hegeman
Hegeman & Co.
361 S. Main St.
Providence, RI 02903-2912
ph: 401-831-6812
Cutters of all precious/semi-precious stones; specializing in the repair & restoration of all types of jewelry (antique and contemporary); gemstone replacements and repairs.

Pat Morse
Edelstein & Morse Antique Jewelry Repair
62 Canaan Back Road
Barrington, NH 03825
ph: 603-664-2205
fax: 603-664-9699
e-mail: pat@trunk.com
Specializes in the fine repair and restoration of antique jewelry, hollowware and small objects of art including gold, platinum, silver, gemstones, diamonds.

Antiques Restoration by Julian
Chelsea Antiques Building
110 West 25th St., #208
New York, NY 10001
ph: 212-647-0305 or 201-791-7875
Gold, silver and any metal subjects; lamps and small sculptures; jewelry and costume jewelry; gold and silver plating.

Byron Klein
A. Ludwig Klein & Son, Inc.
683 Sumneytown Pike
P.O. Box 145
Harleysville, PA 19438
ph: 215-256-9004 or 800-379-2929
fax: 215-256-9644
Specializing in the repair and restoration of all types of glass, china and porcelain as well as ivory, jade, brass, pewter.

Ray L. Elsey
Associate Jewelers Inc.
534 SW Third Ave.
Portland, OR 97204
ph: 800-224-8086
fax: 503-226-6787
e-mail: raylc@tradeshop.com
web: http://www.tradeshop.com/master/lobby.html
A union professional fine jewelry trade shop, designing, building and servicing fine jewelry since 1974; does remanufacturings and restorations; specializes in platinum.

Gilbertson & Co.
800 SW Morrison, 2nd Floor
Portland, OR 97205
ph: 503-274-2802

Amber

Dealers

Leslie Schwing
Amber Lady, The
P.O. Box 38109
Baltimore, MD 21231
ph: 410-342-1832
fax: 410-675-7565
e-mail: amberlady@amberlady.com
web: http://amberlady.com/amberlady/
Buys and sells amber, also repairs and manufactures amber jewelry; features genuine 40 million year old insects in polished honey colored amber; also offers more traditional amber jewelry such as neckware, earrings, etc.

Diamonds

Appraisers

Jeff Marcus
Marcus Jewelers
4047 Okeechobee Blvd.
West Palm Beach, FL 33409
ph: 561-689-2002 or 800-780-2357
fax: 561-689-2008
e-mail: jnmar689@aol.com
web: http://marcusjewelers.com
Staff of gemologists with over 115 years of combined experience in buying, selling and appraising diamonds.

Dealers

Rose Proler
Rose Proler, Inc.
5433 Westheimer, Ste. 1105
Houston, TX 77056-5300
ph: 713-627-3098 or 800-627-3098
fax: 713-627-0504
e-mail: texarose@msn.com
Specializes in rough and polished diamonds.

Periodicals

Martin Rapaport, Pres.
Rapaport Diamond Report
15 West 47th St.
New York, NY 10036
ph: 212-354-0575
fax: 212-840-0243
e-mail: rap@diamonds.com
web: http://www.diamonds.com/
Can subscribe to a monthly or to a weekly price report; these reports are considered the primary source of diamond price information by the jewelry trade.

Joseph W. Tenhagen
Newsletter: Diamond Value Index
36 NE 1st St., #419
Miami, FL 33132
ph: 305-374-2411
The industry's only diamond price guide which categorizes by cut grade.

Hair

(see GEMS & JEWELRY, Mourning; HAIRWORK)

Mourning

(see also HAIRWORK)

Clubs/Associations

C. M. Baker, Ed.
Association for Collectors of Mourning Jewelry
Newsletter: Mourning Edition, The
P.O. Box 641
Burlington, WI 53105
e-mail: ACMJ@hotmail.com
Club serves its members as a definitive resource for the collection, preservation and contextual study of mourning jewelry and related customs.

Collectors

C. M. Baker
P.O. Box 641
Burlington, WI 53105
e-mail: ACMJ@hotmail.com

Dealers

Darlene Tzavaras
Things Gone By
P.O. Box 325
Reedsville, WV 26547
ph: 304-864-5921
fax: 304-864-0519
e-mail: darlene@thingsgoneby.com
web: http://www.thingsgoneby.com
Specializes in sentimental and mourning jewelry of high quality and variety; also offers extensive inventory of other antique jewelry from the Georgian, Victorian, Edwardian, and Art Nouveau periods.

Opals

Clubs/Associations

Northwest Opal Association
e-mail: nwopal@geocities.com
web: http://www.geocities.com/Yosemite/Rapids/4964/

Experts

Paul B. Donning
Majestic Gems & Carvings
P.O. Box 1348
Estes Park, CO 80517
ph: 800-468-0324 or 970-586-2411
fax: 970-586-0996
Importer of rough opal; cutter and designer; author of three books on opals: "Opal Identification and Value", "Opal Adventures", and "Opal Cutting Made Easy."

Pearls

Periodicals

Richard Torrey, Editor
Pearl World - The International Pearling Journal
: Pearl World - The International Pearling Journal
5501 N 7th Ave., Ste. 331
Phoenix, AZ 85021-1755
ph: 602-678-5799
fax: 602-678-6799
e-mail: prlwrld@aol.com
web: http://www.pearlworld.com/
Covers whatever is happening in the pearling industry: statistics, market developments, auctions, interviews with cultivators and importers, coverage of major trade fairs, educational materials, history of pearling, etc.

Pearls (Majorican)

Man./Prod./Dist.

Majorica
366 5th Ave., Ste. 507
New York, NY 10001
ph: 800-223-7560
Distributor of Majorican simulated pearls; also sold through fine department stores such as Nieman-Marcus.

Pearls (Mikimoto)

Man./Prod./Dist.

Mikimoto America
730 Fifth Ave.
New York, NY 10036
ph: 212-586-7153
web: http://www.mikimoto.co.jp/

Stick Pins

Collectors

Elynore "Pet" Kerins
82 Briarwood
Terre Haute, IN 47803-1770
ph: 812-877-1264
Serious stickpin collector with over 2700 in many categories: cameos, pearls, enamel, mourning, carved, dogs, cats, other animals, advertising, political and patriotic, colored stones, diamonds, etc.

Experts

Elynore "Pet" Kerins
82 Briarwood
Terre Haute, IN 47803-1770
ph: 812-877-1264
Co-author with Jack Kerins of "Collecting Antique Stickpins - Identification & Value Guide."

Supplies For

(see ANTIQUES DEALERS & COLLECTORS, Supplies For; BLACKLIGHTS [UV LAMPS])

Suppliers

26th St. Supply House
P.O. Box 680
Bellmore, NY 11710
ph: 800-605-2626
fax: 516-781-7831
Loupes, illuminated magnifiers, gold & silver testing kits, diamond testers, electronic metal testers, scales of all kinds, black lights, Riker mounts, etc.

Kassoy
16 Midland Ave.
Hicksville, NY 11801
ph: 800-452-7769 or 516-942-0560
fax: 516-942-0402
e-mail: sales@kassoy.com
web: http://www.kassoy.com
Mail order source for tools, supplies and instruments for the jewelry trade: diamond testers, gold testers, loupes, gauges, diamond scales, gold scales, colorimeters, magnifiers, polishing equipment, watch repair tools, etc.

Robert Gitnick
R & D Supply Co.
1310 Apple Ave.
Silver Spring, MD 20910
ph: 301-588-7296
fax: 301-495-7312
Phone or mail order for jewelry tools and supplies: loupes, diamond testers, tweezers, gold test equipment, black lights, diamond measuring gauges, etc.

Brenda Sue Lansdowne
B'sue Boutiques
1441 North Market St. Ext.
East Palestine, OH 44413
ph: 330-426-2636
fax: 330-426-6905
e-mail: BSue1441@aol.com
Carries basic supplies for jewelry dealers and collectors: sunshine cloths, simichrome, loupes, ziplocks, mailing supplies, hypo-tube cement, arious pliers, tweezers, cutters, clamps, Jewelry Key; hatpin making supplies, beads, trays.

Indiana Jewelers Supply Inc.
31 E. Georgia, #202
Indianapolis, IN 46204-3621
ph: 317-632-6346 or 800-382-9973
Supplier of jewelers tools and equipment, and watch parts.

Swest Inc.
11090 North Stemmons Freeway
P.O. Box 59389
Dallas, TX 75229-1389
ph: 972-247-7744 or 800-527-5057
fax: 800-441-5162
e-mail: email@swestinc.com
web: http://swestinc.com
Mail order source for tools, supplies and instruments for the jewelry trade; for Eastern orders call Atlanta 800-241-5738: diamond testers, loupes, scales, gold testing kits, etc.

David D. Harleston
Lathrop's
6704 Ferris St.
Bellaire, TX 77401
ph: 713-665-2699
fax: 713-665-0214
Jeweler supplies and findings; loupes, scales, test kits.

John & Jaqueline Foutz
550 Silver & Supply
4187 US Highway 64
Kirtland, NM 87417
ph: 505-598-5322
fax: 505-598-0974
e-mail: sales@metalworks.com
web: http://www.metalworks.com/
Supplies metal and bead crafters with the finest possible jewelry supplies, tools, materials and services: sterling silver, .999 fine silver, silver filled, 14k gold, gold filled, nickel, copper, red and yellow brass, bead supplies, etc.

Prized Possessions
P.O. Box 1147
Fresno, CA 93715
ph: 559-275-6498
e-mail: jack@gemworld.com
web: http://www.gemworld.com
Gems, minerals, fossils, gemstone rough, equipment, supplies; provides opals, gemstones, collector stones, synthetics, cabbing and faceting rough, lapidary equipment and supplies, appraisals, etc.; extensive website.

Otto Frei - Jules Borel
P.O. Box 796
Oakland, CA 94604
ph: 510-832-0355 or 800-772-3456
fax: 800-900-3734
web: http://www.ofrei.com/
Carries complete line of clock parts.

Vintage & Costume

Appraisers

Neola Caveny, ISA, GIA GG
Neola Caveny Gem & Jewelry Appraisals
42 Pau Ole Street
Paia, HI 96779
ph: 808-579-9769
fax: 808-579-9769
e-mail: neola@tiki.net
Graduate Gemologist, GIA; Accredited Member, ISA; 22 years in the jewelry industry, 12 as an independent appraiser for retailers, attorneys, banks, and consumers; specializing in the appraisal of antique & period jewelry.

James Poag, GG, ISA CAPP
James O. Poag Jewellers, Ltd.
94 Frank Street
P.O. Box 39, Ontario N7G 3J1
Canada
ph: 519-245-1040 or 519-245-1580
fax: 519-245-6073
e-mail: james@poag.com
web: http://www.poags.com/
ISA appraiser certified in gems & jewelry, and in antique & period jewelry; also sells and restores new and estate jewelry; four goldsmiths on staff, as well as a GIA Graduate Gemologist.

Clubs/Associations

Lucille Tempesta
Vintage Fashion & Costume Jewelry Club
Newsletter: VF&CJ Newsletter
P.O. Box 265
Glen Oaks, NY 11004-0265
ph: 718-939-3095
fax: 718-939-7988
e-mail: VFCJ@aol.com
web: http://www.lizjewel.com/vf/
Over 1,000 members in 50 states and overseas; quarterly newsletter; conventions.

Pandora L. McKinnon, Ed.
Leaping Frog Antique Jewelry & Collectible Club
Newsletter: LFAJCC Newsletter
4841 Martin Luther King Blvd.
Sacramento, CA 95820-4932
ph: 916-452-6728
fax: 916-452-6728
e-mail: pandora@cwia.com
web: http://homepages.go.com/~jewels4u2/welcome2.html
Articles of interest regarding antique and collectibles jewelry and other collectible items such as hats, furs, smoking items, compacts, purses and more; annual convention.

Collectors

Jane Spies
ph: 330-380-8670
e-mail: Lark5000@aol.com
Specializes in photographic jewelry.

Elyse Zorn Karlin
1333A North Avenue, Box 103
New Rochelle, NY 10804
ph: 914-637-0087 or 914-636-3784
fax: 914-637-0087
e-mail: ekarlin@usa.net

Dena Share
4349 LaVale Ct.
Clemmons, NC 27012-9009
ph: 336-766-6579
fax: 336-766-5445
e-mail: denarc@aol.com
Interested in buying fine jewelry by Erte and Carrera Y Carrera.

Doris M. Diabo
19953 Great Oaks Circle S.
Clinton Township, MI 48036-2440
ph: 810-463-5651
Wants to buy butterfly pins (brooches) - designer names or not - especially those flashy with colored rhinestones; send photocopies, price, condition, SASE.

Patti Vahary
Curious Cat, The
41 Crosby Dr.
Battle Creek, MI 49014
ph: 616-965-0943
e-mail: pattiv0204@aol.com
Buys estate jewelry, especially costume signed work and 1800s style jewelry; also interested in Art Deco and jewelry from the 1920s through 1940s.

Daniel Brown
P.O. Box 149
Davenport, CA 95017-0149
ph: 831-426-0134 or 800-492-6786
Wants to buy old jewelry from A to Z; fine antique Victorian and Art Nouveau gold to Edwardian and Art Deco platinum; especially with fine colored stones; Taxco silver, especially Spratling, Aquilar, Davis, etc., pre-1940 Navajo pieces.

Dealers

Carol Moyse
Collage Antiques
ph: 301-831-6314
fax: 301-831-9617
e-mail: ccmoyse@aol.com
web: http://www.antiqnet.com/collage/
A 20-year business specializing in vintage apparel from 1880 through 1950: wearable clothing, hats, antique jewelry, beaded and mesh purses, alligator and crocodile purses and accessories.

Jackie Ling Wong
Eyecatchers
P.O. Box 1941
Lenox, MA 01240
e-mail: eyecatchrs@aol.com
web: http://eyecatchersjewelry.com
Collector/dealer specializing in signed and unsigned vintage and antique costume jewelry; Bakelite and designers such as Haskell and Trifari.

Marilyn Ostrow
Terezi Vintage Costume Jewelry
30 Suomi Street
Paxton, MA 01612-1212
ph: 508-756-8339
e-mail: TereziB@aol.com
web: http://members.aol.com/TereziJ/index.html
Vintage costume jewelry of the 9120s to 1960s; specializing in glitz! Also vintage glass beads; member of JewelCollect and Vintage Fashion & Costume Jewelry Club.

Elaine Kula
Antiquing On Line - Costume, Victorian & Estate Jewelry
P.O. Box 7905
Nashua, NH 03060
ph: 603-888-7464
fax: 603-888-5648
e-mail: webmistress@antiquingonline.com
web: http://www.antiquingonline.com
On-line catalog specializing in high quality designer, antique, and collectible vintage costume jewelry, Victorian jewelry, estate jewelry and accessories.

Rita Perloff
Remember When
52 Summer Street
Bristol, NH 03222
ph: 603-744-2191
e-mail: rewhen@lr.net
web: http://www.tias.com/stores/rewhen/
Specializes in costume jewelry ranging from Victorian era pieces to contemporary designs; features Mexican & Scandinavian sterling, pot metal figurals, and signed and unsigned jewelry in all categories.

Debbie Woolley
Favorite Past-Times
6 Main Hill
Bridgton, ME 04009
ph: 207-647-5286
e-mail: woolley@maine-antiques.com
web: http://www.maine-antiques.com/fpt/Index/

Elisha Morgan
Elisha Morgan & Associates
200 Piper Lane
South Royalton, VT 05068
ph: 800-444-4367 or 802-763-7649
fax: 802-651-9326
e-mail: rockman@aol.com
Dealer and purchaser of fine estate jewelry, gemstones, and vintage watches.

Deborah Robinson
Vintage Jewels Collectibles
190 West Middle Turnpike
Manchester, CT 06040
ph: 860-645-1525 or 860-533-9529
e-mail: Vinjewels@aol.com
web: http://www.theplace2b.com/VintageJewels/
Estate and signed vintage jewelry: pins, necklaces, bracelets, Trifari, Vendome, Hobe, Holycraft, Boucher, Weiss; 1930s Czech necklaces, Bakelite, compacts, Victorian rings, garnets, sapphires, diamonds; Deco, Victorian, 1940s.

Deborah J. Robinson
Vintage & Jewels Collectibles
190 West Middle Turnpike
Manchester, CT 06040
ph: 860-645-1525 or 860-646-9766
e-mail: vinjewels@aol.com
web: http://www.theplace2b.com/VintageJewels/
Specializes in costume jewelry: by Boucher, Carnegie, Coro, Eisenberg, Florenza, Har, Haskell, Hobe, Hollycraft, Kramer, Lisner, Napier, Ora, Regency, Schreiner.

Chris Peck
All That Glitters
3000 Fairfield Ave.
Bridgeport, CT 06605
ph: 203-333-5836
fax: 203-333-5840
Buys and sells fine estate jewelry, including diamonds; also appraises.

Suzanne W. Smith
Collectible Costume Jewelry
P.O. Box 431
Andover, NJ 07821
ph: 973-300-4101
e-mail: swsmith@costumejewelry.com
web: http://www.costumejewelry.com
Features signed and unsigned vintage and collectible jewelry.

Leigh Nacht
Bernard Nacht & Co., Inc.
589 Fifth Ave., Ste. 910
New York, NY 10017-1923
ph: 212-371-8100 or 800-348-3419
fax: 212-371-8284
e-mail: leigh5@mail.idt.net
Buys and sells antique, estate and period jewelry and objects as well as diamonds and gemstones.

Barry Weber
Edith Weber & Associates Antique Jewelry
994 Madison Ave.
New York, NY 10021
ph: 212-570-9668
fax: 212-570-9668
e-mail: barry@antique-jewelry.com
web: http://www.antique-jewelry.com
One of America's premier antique jewelry specialist dealers; featured at many of the country's charity auctions for over 30 years; retail store is located on Madison Ave. in Historic Upper East Side, Manhattan; great website.

A La Vieille Russie, Inc.
781 Fifth Ave.
New York, NY 10022
ph: 212-752-1727
fax: 212-223-6454
e-mail: alvr@aol.com
web: http://www.alvr.com
Specializes in fine Russian antiques: jewelry, snuff boxes, Faberge, silver, Russian icons, and other works of art.

Karima Parry
Plastic Fantastic
ph: 412-363-8888
fax: 412-363-8888
e-mail: info@plasticfantastic.com
web: http://www.plasticfantastic.com
One of the largest sites of its kind on the internet, offering over 300 pieces of vintage Bakelite, Lucite and celluloid jewelry; also selected signed designer costume jewelry; author of "Collecting Bakelite Bangles."

Collectible Costume Designer Jewelry
P.O. Box 631
Green Lane, PA 18054
ph: 215-234-2818
e-mail: char@theplace2b.com
web: http://www.theplace2b.com/jewelry/
Buys and sells vintage and costume jewelry; Website displays large collection of vintage necklaces, earrings, bracelets, brooches, compacts and other collectible items.

Isabelle & Liz Bryman
Liz Collectible Jewelry
ph: 215-781-1174
e-mail: ibryman@lizjewel.com
web: http://www.lizjewel.com
Online worldwide collectible costume jewelry shopping; home of JewelCollect Online Email Club.

Ronald Talley
Talley Jewelry, Inc.
Village Sq. Shopping Center
P.O. Box 245
Waldorf, MD 20604-0245
ph: 301-645-5144 or 301-870-9593
fax: 301-870-9593
Buys, sells, appraises, repairs, and restores jewelry.

Deborah G. Kosnett
Rhinestone Rainbow
24 Solitaire Court
Gaithersburg, MD 20878
ph: 301-990-9473
e-mail: dkos@radix.net
web: http://www.rhinestonerainbow.com
Specializing in vintage costume jewelry from the 1930s to the 1960s; designer, Lea Stein, Lucite, bakelite, rhinestones.

Linda Miller
Victorian Lady, The
P.O. Box 613
Jarrettsville, MD 21084
ph: 410-557-7071
e-mail: victorianldy@earthlink.net
web: http://www.pacificws.com/victorianlady/
Specializes in Victorian and vintage jewelry along with ladies things including purses, dolls, vanity items.

Bonnie Plimack
Goodtimes Collectibles
P.O. Box 10477
Baltimore, MD 21202
ph: 410-653-2223 or 410-685-4426
fax: 410-602-2097
e-mail: plimack@tias.com
web: http://www.tias.com/stores/goodtime/
Buying and selling costume jewelry for many years; specializes in Czech and pre-1950 jewelry; also has a large collection of compacts.

Drauga Gilmore
Portebello Square
28 A Allegheny Ave.
Baltimore, MD 21204
ph: 410-821-1163

Eugene Rooney, GG
Victorian Manor
P.O. Box 285
New Market, MD 21774
ph: 301-865-3083
Buys and sells antique and estate jewelry; repairs, restores, re-enameling, remounting, restring, and custom design jewelry.

Darlene Tzavaras
Things Gone By
P.O. Box 325
Reedsville, WV 26547
ph: 304-864-5921
fax: 304-864-0519
e-mail: darlene@thingsgoneby.com
web: http://www.thingsgoneby.com
Specializes in sentimental and mourning jewelry of high quality and variety; also offers extensive inventory of other antique jewelry from the Georgian, Victorian, Edwardian, and Art Nouveau periods.

Susan M. Black
Susan's Vintage Boutique
120 Mopar Lane
West End, NC 27376
ph: 910-295-6575
fax: 910-295-9109
e-mail: smblack@ac.net
web: http://www.tias.com/stores/susans
In business since 1984.

Gail Corwin
Bejeweled
476 Hwy. 70E
Beaufort, NC 28516
ph: 919-728-1331
e-mail: gail@bejeweled.com
web: http://www.bejeweled.com
Offers vintage and collectible jewelry; a variety of the finest antique, vintage and collectible costume jewelry by top designers and manufacturers; glitzy unsigned pieces and colorful vintage plastics.

Claire Doyle
BC Jewels & Collectibles
3405 Sweetwater Road, #836
Lawrenceville, GA 30044
ph: 770-381-7378
Buys and sells collectible costume and vintage jewelry; member of JewelCollect.

Marcia Oliver
Marcia's Putting On The Glitz!
4921 Athens Rd.
Carnesville, GA 30521-4316
ph: 706-245-9593
e-mail: marcia@vintagecostumejewelry.com
web: http://www.vintagecostumejewelry.com
Offers quality antique and collectible costume jewelry: Victorian, Deco, Bakelite, signed, unsigned; also carries purses, perfumes, compacts.

Peter Thurber
Ritzi & Thurber, Inc.
160 S. Beach St.
Daytona Beach, FL 32114
ph: 904-252-2552 or 904-226-8489
fax: 904-226-8490
e-mail: ritzi1881@earthlink.net
web: http://www.ritzi-thurber.com/
Founded in 1881, firm is one of the largest buyers of estate jewelry in Florida.

Gloria Quincy
Q-Tiques Vintage Jewelry & Collectibles
6475 Ferber Road
Jacksonville, FL 32277
ph: 904-745-0618
fax: 904-743-9159
e-mail: junebug@southeast.net
web: http://www.tias.com/stores/qtiques/
Specializes in costume designer jewelry, bakelite, and Mexican Silver.

Donna Barr
Victorian Elegance, A
3648 NW 67th Ave.
Gainesville, FL 32653-8801
ph: 352-377-0459
e-mail: designs@gator.net
web: http://victorianelegance.com/
Specializing in vintage jewelry, ranging from collectible costume to Victorian mourning and hair jewelry.

Wendy Hankins
Black Cat Collectibles
P.O. Box 864
Geneva, FL 32732
ph: 407-349-9150
e-mail: rh8421@gate.net
Specializing in collecting vintage and costume jewelry; features both designer pieces and unsigned pieces from the 1920s through the 1970s: rhinestones, sterling, copper, Bakelite, Lucite, celluloid; also carries estate jewelry.

Suzie Bell
Bells Jewels
2200 Winter Springs Blvd., Ste. 106-225
Oviedo, FL 32765-9344
ph: 407-366-4747
fax: 407-366-4747
e-mail: sbwb@worldnet.att.net
web: http://www.bellsjewels.com
Specializing in high quality vintage costume jewelry.

Cathy Corday
Vintage Jewelry & More
ph: 954-749-1374
e-mail: ccorday102@aol.com
web: http://members.aol.com/ccorday102/vintage.html
Buys and sells vintage costume jewelry and accessories; carries an assortment of signs as well as unsigned pieces; lots of rhinestones; also carries vintage purses.

Fred Hare
Headdress Jewelry & Accessories, Inc.
1135 9th Ave. N
Saint Petersburg, FL 33705
ph: 727-894-2280
fax: 727-894-2280
e-mail: headress@tampabay.rr.com
web: http://www.headress.com
Online catalog of antique and estate jewelry and vintage designer accessories.

Denise Kowal
Denise Kowal & Sons Jewelry
530 S. Orange Ave.
P.O. Box 1676
Sarasota, FL 34236
ph: 941-364-3384 or 941-364-3385
fax: 941-364-3385
e-mail: dkowalson@aol.com
Purchasing and selling fine antique, estate, custom and modern jewelry; Graduate Master Appraiser of Jewelry.

Patt Pugh
Patt's Gems
P.o. Box 681681
Prattville, AL 36068-1681
ph: 334-361-7933
e-mail: pattsgem@mindspring.com
web: http://www.pattsgems.com
Antique, vintage, contemporary and costume jewelry including signed, unsigned, rhinestone, Bakelite, Lucite, and enameled costume jewelry.

Patricia A. Witt, GG, CGA, ISA
Way-Fil Jewelry
1123 West Main St.
Tupelo, MS 38801-3453
ph: 601-844-2427
fax: 601-840-4791
e-mail: pattiwit@ebicom.net
Manufacturer, appraisals, repairs, buy/sell, consignments, estate disposal.

Lonny Rosen
Ooh Aah Antique Jewelry
492 S. Parkview Ave.
Columbus, OH 43209
ph: 614-237-6884
e-mail: oohaah@iwaynet.net
web: http://www.iwaynet.net/~oohaah
An online catalog of rare jewelry; specializes in Victorian, Mexican, Scandinavian, costume, fun and ethnic jewelry; includes Georg Jensen, William Spratling, Miriam Haskell, WW2 Sweetheart to early Native American.

Brenda Sue Lansdowne
B'sue Boutiques
1441 North Market St. Ext.
East Palestine, OH 44413
ph: 330-426-2636
fax: 330-426-6905
e-mail: BSue1441@aol.com
Actively dealing in vintage costume Victorian to 1970s for over ten years; dealer approvals are a specialty; any qualified dealer may receive a package - email or call for details.

Candace Silvasy
Silvasy & Tangeman Antiques
P.O. Box 6796
Cincinnati, OH 45206-0796
ph: 513-281-2827 or 513-312-2817
fax: 513-569-2602
International dealers; deals privately and in trade shows and antique fairs.

Ann Mills
Collections by Ann: Vintage Jewelry & Accessories
P.O. Box 102
Clawson, MI 48017
ph: 248-588-3474
e-mail: AM56@tias.com
web: http://www.tias.com/stores/anns/
Specializing in quality vintage jewelry, sterling sliver, and glittering evening bags.

Kathleen Kielkopf
AntiqueJewelry.com
2073 Ford Parkway
Saint Paul, MN 55116
ph: 800-328-1179 or 651-690-0842
fax: 651-698-0316
e-mail: kate@antiquejewelry.com
web: http://www.antiquejewelry.com/
Source for buying and selling estate and antique jewelry.

Peggy
Pegasus Antiques
162 West Hubbard
Chicago, IL 60610
ph: 847-338-0780
e-mail: peggy@antiqueshop.com
web: http://www.antiqueshop.com
Carries vintage costume jewelry.

Ron Geweniger
Old World Jewelers Ltd.
7438 W. North Ave.
Elmwood Park, IL 60707
ph: 708-456-7730 or 800-322-3871
e-mail: owltd@ix.netcom.com
web: http://www.antiqnet.com/oldworld/
Dealers in fine antique and estate jewelry and timepieces for over 20 years; featuring toy Swiss made watches; also new watches.

Kim & Larry Cummins
Just Jewelry
20 Burcham Dr.
East Saint Louis, IL 62208
ph: 618-398-2173
e-mail: kdcllc@stlnet.com
web: http://www.jstjewelry.com
Specializes in quality vintage costume jewelry from the 1920s through the 1970s: Boucher, Haskell, KJL, Schiaparelli, Trifari, Weiss, and other designers.

Janice Costiloe
Jan's Jewels
3325 Eastman Dr.
Oklahoma City, OK 73112
ph: 405-840-2341
fax: 405-840-1057
e-mail: jan@jansjewels.com
web: http://www.jansjewels.com
Buys and sells all kinds of vintage and antique jewelry: Lucite, Bakelite, celluloid, Victorian, rhinestone jewelry and much more.

Patty Armstrong
Costume Jewelry Showcase, The
e-mail: jewelry@graycat.com
web: http://www.graycat.com/jewelry/
An online source of collectible costume jewelry and other hard-to-find collectibles including ceramics, pottery, glassware, purses, clothing items and even toys; all items have pictures and descriptions.

Judi Scheele
Wink & A Smile Vintage, A
265 Village Tree Drive
Lewisville, TX 75067-6959
ph: 972-966-0092
fax: 972-317-7400
e-mail: judi@winksmile.com
web: http://www.winksmile.com
Offers a comprehensive collections of vintage and costume jewelry on the internet: designer, Bakelite, Deco, copper, sterling jewelry; also purses and handbags: beaded, Lucite, rare skin bags.

Jan Thomas
J'antiques & Collectibles
9307 Mercer Dr.
Dallas, TX 75228
ph: 214-320-0489
fax: 214-320-1660
e-mail: jthomas@jantiques.com
web: http://www.jantiques.com
Specializing in antique and vintage jewelry in all price ranges.

Jerry Forrest, GG, ISA CAPP
Jewelry Forest, The
9100 N. Central Expy., Ste. 185
Dallas, TX 75231-5901
ph: 972-368-5352 or 800-368-5376
e-mail: 102152.2165@compuserve.com
Custom jewelers and gemologists, AGS Accredited Gem Laboratory, Accredited Member, ISA.

George Stringfield
Illusion Jewels
101 Plum Creek Rd.
Longview, TX 75605
ph: 903-663-3415
e-mail: jewels@illusionjewels.com
web: http://www.illusionjewels.com
Buys and sells vintage and collectible costume jewelry dating from the mid 1800s to the 1980s; also carries accessories such as buttons, vintage sewing items, beads.

Billie & John McBride
South Texas Trading Company
P.O. Box 857
Port Aransas, TX 78373
ph: 512-749-6149
e-mail:
STFNandTRADING@centuryinter.net
web: http://www.tam.ca/southtexas/
Specializing in the sale of vintage and collectible costume jewelry, specializing in Bakelite and 20th century costume jewelry; will do searches; member of a 350 member online jewelry and have nationwide pickers available.

Christina Felps
Cat's Fancy, The
12221 Chisholm Valley Dr., #423
Round Rock, TX 78681
ph: 512-238-8037
e-mail: catfancy@io.com
web: http://www.io.com/~catfancy
Buys and sells vintage and costume jewelry; website contains an online store front; maintains wish list for customers wanting to add to their collection; also repairs and restores (replace pin shanks and clasps, match/replace stones.)

Greg DeMark
DeMark Jewelry & Antiques
1745 N. Main St.
Longmont, CO 80501
ph: 303-682-5321 or 303-678-0545
e-mail: demark@concentric.net
web: http://www.tias.com/stores/demark/
Specializes in antique and vintage jewelry, particularly in Victorian, Edwardian, Deco, Retro and modern jewelry in gold, silver, platinum; also costume jewelry.

Janet Lawwill
Sparkles
P.O. Box 36269
Tucson, AZ 85750
ph: 520-219-3712
fax: 520-219-3715
e-mail: Jewel@SparklePlenty.com
web: http://www.sparkleplenty.com
Buys and sells vintage costume jewelry: Victorian, Nouveau, Deco, rhinestones through the 1960s; cuff links, charms, buckles, shoe buckles, cameos, hair, sterling, gold; guides for cleaning, relating, storing, buying, and selling.

Patsy Comer
Patsy Comer's Antiques & Jewelry
7249 Reseda Blvd.
Reseda, CA 91335-3046
ph: 818-345-1631
fax: 818-345-1914
Buys and sells costume and fine jewelry from all eras including designer; also costume jewelry, gold and sterling; 1960s memorabilia such as peace signs, designer costume and 1960s and 70s jewelry; sells to the trade, does mail order

Leigh Leshner
Thanks for the Memories
P.O. Box 55113
Sherman Oaks, CA 91413-0113
ph: 818-981-7813
fax: 818-981-3466
e-mail: venture818@aol.com
web: http://www.tias.com/stores/memories/
Carries a large variety of antique and vintage jewelry covering all styles and periods.

Eve Lickver
P.O. Box 1778
San Marcos, CA 92079
ph: 760-761-0868
Buys and sells carved and figural Bakelite jewelry; also wants signed costume jewelry of 1920s through 1950s including sterling, copper, enamel.

Eve Lickver
P.O. Box 1778
San Marcos, CA 92079-1778
ph: 760-744-5686
Specializes in vintage jewelry: bakelite, sterling, designer, costume; showing at high quality antique shows including Atlantic City, NJ, and Hillsborough, CA.

Roni Campbell
Fabulous Finds Antiques & Collectibles
1450 N Santa Fe, Ste. C295
Vista, CA 92083
e-mail: virtvint@aol.com
web: http://members.aol.com/rnjustin/vintage.htm
A complete online antiques and collectibles shop featuring costume jewelry, and vintage clothing and accessories.

Susan Murphy
29668 Orinda Rd.
San Juan Capistrano, CA 92675-1211
ph: 949-364-4333
Wants to buy pre-1950 costume jewelry; please enclose SASE.

Pat Wilson
Koya Designs
3445-A Divisadero
San Francisco, CA 94123
ph: 415-929-9173
e-mail: plwilson@sirius.com
Wants to buy French and American costume jewelry from the 1920s to 1960s.

Yvonne Brooks
Family Jewels, The
572 Tahos Rd.
Orinda, CA 94563
ph: 925-254-4422
fax: 925-254-7706
e-mail: sandy@thefamilyjewels.coom
web: http://www.thefamilyjewels.com

Sheila Pamfiloff
Glitter Box, The
P.O.Box 35
Walnut Creek, CA 94596
ph: 510-937-7554
e-mail: pamfil@crl.com
web: http://www.crl.com/~pamfil/GLITTER.HTM
Specializing in vintage designer costume jewelry including Haskell, Schiaparelli, Hagler, Eisenberg, DeMario, Mazer, Boucher; also vintage Mexican sterling silver from the great designers of Taxco.

Janice Friedli
Gold Turtle & Co.
1315 W. Lockeford Street
Lodi, CA 95242
ph: 209-334-1909 or 209-334-5108
fax: 209-334-5108
e-mail: gturtle@inreach.com
web: http://www.tace.com/vendors/gturtle.html
Buys and sells vintage jewelry: Victorian cameos and other authentic Victorian era jewelry set with jet, coral, garnets, and mosaics.

Pandora L. McKinnon
Pandora's Jewelry Box
4841 Martin Luther King Blvd.
Sacramento, CA 95820-4932
ph: 916-452-6728
fax: 916-452-6728
e-mail: pandora@cwia.com
web: http://homepages.go.com/~jewels4u2/welcome2.html
Antique and collectible costume jewelry for sale.

Betty Bird
Memory Lane Antiques
107 Ida St.
Mount Shasta, CA 96067-2629
ph: 530-926-4331 or 530-926-2231
Buys and sells antique and collectible jewelry; prefers Victorian through 1950, especially signed pieces.

Randeen Cummings, ISA CAPP
Cummings & Associates
P.O. Box 5484
Eugene, OR 97405-0484
ph: 541-345-5856 or 541-485-3068
fax: 541-345-8192
e-mail: rmcummings@ibm.net
web: http://www.antiquesinn.com
Specializes in selling & appraising residential contents, fine art, estate jewelry, 18th & 19th century antiques, American Brilliant period cut glass; also specialized marketing for clients: consultations, estate, and Internet sales.

Hillary Parsons
Hillary's Antique Jewelry Store
8441 SE 68th Street #313
Mercer Island, WA 98040
ph: 206-232-5309
fax: 206-236-0142
e-mail: antiquejewelry@worldnet.att.net
web: http://www.pacificws.com/jewelry/
A large catalog of antique and vintage jewelry including Victorian, Art Deco, Art Nouveau and costume jewelry; website also contains monthly articles.

Terri Krantz
Lovejoys Antique Jewelry & Silver
P.O. Box 28366
Bellingham, WA 98228
fax: 360-715-3757
e-mail: tkrantz@nas.com
web: http://www.nas.com/lovejoy/love.html
Specializes in antique jewelry and silver with an emphasis on Victorian, Art Deco, and Art Nouveau.

Experts

Peter J. Shemonsky, GG, ISA
24 Horace St.
Boston, MA 02128-1534
ph: 617-569-1502
fax: 617-846-4767
e-mail: pshemonsky@aol.com

Peter J. Theriault, FGA, GG
Northeast Gemlab, Inc.
58 Bayview St.
Camden, ME 04843-2242
ph: 207-236-3933
fax: 207-236-3933
e-mail: gemlab@midcoast.com
web: http://www.antiquejewelrytimes.com
Independent gems and jewelry appraiser; publishes "The Art & Antique Service Directory", the "Redbook"; writes gemology column for "Maine Antique Digest" and "Antiques West."

Harrice Simons Miller
Harrice Miller Collection
40 West 25th St., Gallery #230
New York, NY 10010
ph: 212-242-0910
fax: 212-532-1394
e-mail: harrice@worldnet.att.net
Collectible costume jewelry appraiser, dealer and expert; author of "The Confident Collector: Costume Jewelry" and "Kenneth Jay Lane: Faking It"; consultant to Christie's, lecturer.

Judith Katz-Schwartz
Twin Brooks Antiques & Collectibles
P.O. Box 6572
New York, NY 10128-0006
ph: 212-876-3512
fax: 212-876-3512
e-mail: twinb@msjudith.net
web: http://www.msjudith.net
Buys, sells, appraisers signed and unsigned pieces of costume jewelry: brooches & pins, bracelets, earrings, rings, rhinestone jewelry, dress clips, Bakelite, sets, etc.

Gail Brett Levine, GG
Timeless, Inc.
P.O. Box 7683
Rego Park, NY 11374-7683
ph: 718-897-7305
fax: 718-997-9057
e-mail: 76766.614@compuserve.com
Graduate Gemologist, appraiser, lecturer, publisher of "Auction Market Resource For Gems & Jewelry", a semi-annual jewelry price, condition, quality report.

Time Warp Custom & Vintage Attire
P.O. Box 9186
Schenectady, NY 12305-0186
ph: 518-347-1126
fax: 518-347-1126
e-mail: timewarp@timewarp.com
web: http://www.timewarp.com/
Buys/sells/appraises vintage clothing, jewelry, accessories; reproduces vintage and historical clothing for museums, reenactment, theater, ballroom dancing, etc.; also restores, repairs and alters clothing, textiles and costume jewelry.

Roseann Ettinger
Remember When
21-23 W. Broad St.
Hazleton, PA 18201
ph: 570-454-8465 or 570-450-5542
Author of "Popular Jewelry 1840-1940," "Forties and Fifties Popular Jewelry," and "Popula Jewelry of the 60s, 70s, & 80s."

Arthur Guy Kaplan
P.O. Box 1942
Baltimore, MD 21203
ph: 410-752-2090 or 410-664-8350
fax: 410-783-2723
Author of "The Official Price Guide to Antique Jewelry."

Ann Pitman
314 Richmond Drive
Greenvile, SC 29617-1032
e-mail: apitman@bellsouth.net
Writes the "Jewelry Box" column on vintage and antique jewelry.

Elaine Luartes, GG
Athena Antiques
100 Beta Dr.
Franklin, TN 37064-3912
ph: 615-377-3442
Specializes in antique and estate jewelry; Board of Advisors, Warman's; wants jewelry emphasizing craftsmanship and design.

C. Jeanenne Bell, G.G., N.G.J.A.
Jewelry Box Antiques, Inc.
7325 Quivira Rd., Ste. 238
Shawnee Mission, KS 66216
ph: 913-962-0085 or 913-962-8533
e-mail: cjbell@msn.com
Vintage jewelry dealer and expert; author of "Collectors Encyclopedia of Hairwork Jewelry," and "Answers & Questions About Old Jewelry 1810-1950" 5th Edition.

Christie Romero
Center for Jewelry Studies
P.O. Box 424
Anaheim, CA 92815-0424
ph: 714-778-1828
fax: 714-778-3432
e-mail: CR4jewelry@aol.com
One of America's leading scholars on antique & vintage jewelry; author of "Warman's Jewelry - An Identification & Price Guide to 19th & 20th Century Fine & Costume Jewelry - 2nd Ed." (1998); host of video "Hidden Treasures"; lecturer.

Pandora L. McKinnon
Pandora's Jewelry Box
4841 Martin Luther King Blvd.
Sacramento, CA 95820-4932
ph: 916-452-6728
fax: 916-452-6728
e-mail: pandora@cwia.com
web: http://homepages.go.com/~jewels4u2/welcome2.html
Writes articles about jewelry and other accessories.

Hillary Parsons
Hillary's Antique Jewelry Store
8441 SE 68th Street #313
Mercer Island, WA 98040
ph: 206-232-5309
fax: 206-236-0142
e-mail: antiquejewelry@worldnet.att.net
web: http://www.pacificws.com/jewelry/
A large catalog of antique and vintage jewelry including Victorian, Art Deco, Art Nouveau and costume jewelry; website also contains monthly articles.

Internet Resources

Peter J. Theriault, FGA, GG
Antique Jewelry Times On-Line
58 Bayview St.
Camden, ME 04843-2242
ph: 207-236-3933
fax: 207-236-3933
e-mail: gemlab@midcoast.com
web: http://www.antiquejewelrytimes.com
An on-line magazine dedicated to antique jewelry and collectible watches; educational articles for dealers and collectors.

Robert S. Koppelman
JewelShow
1712 SE 13th St.
Fort Lauderdale, FL 33316
ph: 954-524-0770
fax: 954-524-1999
e-mail: rokogrp@ix.netcom.com
web: http://www.jewelshow.com
The ultimate locator and showcase for fine antique and estate jewelry, rare gems, unusual timepieces.

Man./Prod./Dist.

Ron Edelstein
Ron's Rhinestones
P.O. Box 2028
New York, NY 10159-2028
ph: 212-253-6299 or 800-299-2185
fax: 212-253-6299
e-mail: rhinestones@mindspring.com
web: http://www.ronrhinestones.com
Specializes in contemporary rhinestone jewelry of Austrian crystal made in the USA: earrings, necklaces, bracelets, hair ornaments, chokers, pins.

Misc. Services

Leigh Leshner
Venture Entertainment Group
P.O. Box 55113
Sherman Oaks, CA 91413-0113
ph: 818-981-7813
fax: 818-981-3466
e-mail: venture818@aol.com
web: http://www.tias.com/stores/memories/
Producers of the award winning video cassette series on vintage & costume jewelry from 1800s to 1960; a visual price guide for signed and unsigned costume jewelry by Trifari, Coro, Corocraft, Haskell, Hobe, Eisenberg, Chanel, etc.

Periodicals

Elyse Zorn Karlin, Ed.
Newsletter: Adornment
1333A North Avenue, Box 103
New Rochelle, NY 10804
ph: 914-637-0087 or 914-636-3784
fax: 914-637-0087
e-mail: ekarlin@usa.net
Quarterly newsletter covering ancient to contemporary studio and vintage jewelry, historic costume, antique buttons, and beads; contains articles, book reviews, terminology, extensive calendar, and more.

Davida Baron
Newsletter: Glittering Times
P.O. Box 656675
Flushing, NY 11365
ph: 718-969-2320
e-mail: glittering_times@bigfoot.com
For collectors and dealers of vintage costume jewelry.

Gail Brett Levine, GG
Timeless, Inc.
Magazine: Auction Market Resource for Gems & Jewelry
P.O. Box 7683
Rego Park, NY 11374-7683
ph: 718-897-7305
fax: 718-997-9057
e-mail: 76766.614@compuserve.com
A semi-annual publication providing data for a wide range of jewelry items including antique through contemporary, diamonds and colored stones; detailed text with photographs; offers research services to track fads, trends, etc.

Repair Services

Eugene Rooney, GG
Victorian Manor
P.O. Box 285
New Market, MD 21774
ph: 301-865-3083
Buys and sells antique and estate jewelry; repairs, restores, re-enameling, remounting, restring, and custom design jewelry.

John Leonard
John Leonard Jewelers
3525 S.W. Voyager St.
Port Saint Lucie, FL 34953
ph: 561-336-8516
e-mail: catalano@gate.net
Specializes in antique and vintage costume jewelry repair.

Suppliers

Matthew Ribarich
P.O. Box 10104
Costa Mesa, CA 92627
ph: 949-645-9017
fax: 949-645-9017
e-mail: MRstones4U@aol.com
web: http://www.sparkleplenty.com/matt/
Supplies a wide variety of antique and costume jewelry replacement stones including marcasites, rhinestones, imitation pearls, rose cut garnets and jade; over 1 million stones in inventory!

Matthew Ribarich
P.O. Box 10104
Costa Mesa, CA 92627
ph: 949-645-9017
fax: 949-645-9017
e-mail: MRstones4U@aol.com
web: http://www.sparkleplenty.com/matt/
Supplies a wide variety of antique and costume jewelry replacement stones including marcasites, rhinestones, imitation pearls, rose cut garnets and jade.

GENEALOGY

(see also HERALDRY; IMMIGRATION)

Misc. Services

Marie Varrelman Melchiori, CGRS
121 Tapawingo Rd. SW
Vienna, VA 22180-5964
ph: 703-938-8103
fax: 703-938-7279
e-mail: mvmcgrs@juno.com
Certified Genealogical Record Specialist in Civil War research; will help identify owners of historical items; will assist members of the legal profession locate missing heirs.

Family History Library, Genealogical Society of Utah
35 North West Temple St.
Salt Lake City, UT 84150
fax: 801-240-1584
e-mail: fhl@ldschurch.org

Museums/Libraries

Western Reserve Historical Society
10825 East Blvd.
Cleveland, OH 44106-1703
ph: 216-721-5722
fax: 216-721-0645
e-mail: pomerleau@wrhs.org
web: http://www.wrhs.org/
Oldest cultural institution in Cleveland, with a research/genealogical library, costume wing, auto & aviation museum and restored mansion under one roof; special interest area in genealogical research.

Periodicals

Magazine: Heritage Quest
P.O. Box 329
Bountiful, UT 84011
ph: 800-760-2455
e-mail: sales@agll.com
web: http://www.heritagequest.com
America's leading magazine for genealogists and family historians; published bi-monthly.

Newsletter: Ancestry Newsletter
P.O. Box 476
Salt Lake City, UT 84110
Published bi-monthly.

GERMAN ITEMS

(see ANTIQUES & COLLECTIBLES, German; MILITARIA; NAZI ITEMS; SWORDS, Nazi)

GHOSTS & HAUNTINGS

(see also HALLOWEEN COLLECTIBLES; HORROR; WITCHES)

Book Sellers

Chris Woodyard
Invisible Ink: Books on Ghosts & Hauntings
1811 Stonewood Dr.
Beavercreek, OH 45432-4002
ph: 937-426-5110
fax: 937-320-1832
e-mail: invisiblei@aol.com
web: http://www.invink.com
Collector of nonfiction books on ghosts & hauntings; also dealer in new and paranormal books; founder of Invisible Ink Collection at BGSU Popular Collection Library.

GILBERT

(see TOYS, Construction Sets; TRAINS, Toy [American Flyer])

GIRL SCOUT MEMORABILIA

(see also BOY SCOUT MEMORABILIA)

Collectors

Phyllis Palm
P.O. Box 5272
Hamden, CT 06518-0272
ph: 203-288-9190
e-mail: poohdingaling@worldnet.att.net
Wants to buy old Girl Scout uniforms (also uniform parts), insignia, dolls, etc.

D. Nordlinger Stern
385 Bayview Dr. NE
Saint Petersburg, FL 33704-2430
ph: 727-894-4000
fax: 727-894-1040
e-mail: dnordstern@aol.com
Wants girl scout memorabilia; please send list of items and prices.

Jerry King
8429 Katy Freeway
Houston, TX 77024-1903
ph: 713-465-2500
fax: 713-465-0824
e-mail: jerryksl@kinglok.com
Wants Girl Scout memorabilia: pre-1960 catalogs, postcards, magazines, handbooks, 1912-1920 uniforms, equipment, etc.; do not send items without prior arrangements.

Dealers

Roland Sayers
Southeastern Antiques & Collectibles
305 N. Main St.
Hendersonville, NC 28792
ph: 826-697-6064
fax: 826-883-9562
Wants to buy pre-1960 Boy Scout and Girl Scout collectibles.

Darrell Wessinger
Wessingers, The
17 Sandy Bank Dr.
Lexington, SC 29072-9185
ph: 803-356-0161 or 800-572-2427
fax: 803-957-4147
e-mail: Darrwess@aol.com
web: http://www.scsn.net/users/darrwess/
Specializing in Boy Scout and Girl Scout memorabilia; publishes several sales/auction lists each year.

Jack O'Brian
Memory Tree
P.O. Box 9462
Madison, WI 53715
ph: 414-261-6641
fax: 414-261-9461
Heavy buyer of brown and gray uniforms, cloth badges, medals with ribbons, early Brownie, Golden Eaglet, dolls, cookie (candy) containers, prof. badges; will help identify and date if inquiries are accompanied by a SASE.

Experts

Fran & Cal Holden
P.O. Box 264 - M264
Doylestown, OH 44230-0264
ph: 800-663-2793
Wants old or unusual pins, badges, medals; from Brownies, Senior Scouts, Roundups, Adult insignia, Councils, official literature, etc.; offers subscription sales lists to collectors of all sorts of Girl Scout memorabilia.

Roy More
Scout Patch Auction
2484 Dundee
Ann Arbor, MI 48103
ph: 734-663-6203
fax: 734-663-7227
e-mail: spa@msen.com
web: http://www.tspa.com
Collector, dealer, appraiser expert in Girl Scout memorabilia.

Museums/Libraries

Mrs. Ralph Zitelman
Zitelman Scout Museum
123 Beard St.
Danville, IL 61832-6009
ph: 217-442-6678
Worldwide Scouting: patches, books, uniforms & equipment including Boy and Girl Scouts, Brownies, Explorers, Scoutmasters, etc.

GLASS

(see also BOOKS, Reference [Glass]; CUP PLATES; CRAFTS, Glass; ENAMELS; GLASS KNIVES; GLASSES; KITCHEN COLLECTIBLES; POWDER JARS; REPAIR/RESTORATION/ CONSERVATION, Glass; SALOON & BAR COLLECTIBLES; TABLEWARE)

Appraisers

Dianne Gregg
Glassnob Antiques
10413 Gary Rd.
Potomac, MD 20854
ph: 301-299-6456
fax: 301-299-6456
e-mail: glassnob@aol.com
Appraiser specializing in European glass from the 18th-20th century, American art glass, and contemporary studio glass.

Linda H. Richard, ISA
Cajun Collection
3308 White Oak
Temple, TX 76502
ph: 254-774-8608
e-mail: cajun@vvm.com
web: http://www.vvm.com/~cajun/
Specializing in glass with emphasis on 1950s Modern glass, particularly American, Swedish, and Scandinavian; also collects glass from WV, including Morgantown, Pilgrim, Blenko, Kanawha, Seneca, Rainbow, and Bischoff.

Auction Services

James A. Megura
Skinner, Inc.
357 Main St.
Bolton, MA 01740-1104
ph: 978-779-6241
fax: 978-779-5144
e-mail: info@skinnerinc.com
web: http://www.skinnerinc.com
Established in 1964, Skinner Inc. is the fifth largest auction house in the US; has offices in Bolton and Boston, MA.

Ed Swann
James D. Julia Auctioneers Inc.
Rt. 201, Skowhegan Rd.
P.O. Box 830
Fairfield, ME 04937
ph: 207-453-7125
fax: 207-453-2502
e-mail: jjulia@juliaauctions.com
web: http://www.juliaauctions.com
Conducts specialized auctions of all types of quality glassware including Tiffany, Galle, Royal Flemish, fine quality cut glass, Victorian glass and early glassware; uses nationally recognized experts to catalog sales.

James Hagenbuch
Glass Works Auctions
P.O. Box 180
102 Jefferfson St.
East Greenville, PA 18041
ph: 215-679-5849
fax: 215-679-3068
e-mail: glswrk@enter.net
web: http://www.glswrk-auction.com/
Specializes in the auction of historical flasks, fruit jars, food & milk bottles, sodas, poisons, whiskeys, medicines, inks, barber bottles, bitters bottles, scent bottles, shaving mugs, target & range balls, etc.

Reyne Haines
Just Glass
405 Lafayette Ave.
Cincinnati, OH 45220
ph: 513-559-1405 or 513-961-5794
e-mail: reyne@justglass.com
web: http://www.justglass.com
An internet glass-only online auction service; offering constant auction auction for art glass, carnival, Depression, modern, studio, opalescent, pattern, etc.

Gene Harris Antique Auction Center, Inc.
203 South 18th Ave.
P.O. Box 476
Marshalltown, IA 50158
ph: 515-752-0600 or 800-862-6674
fax: 515-753-0226
e-mail: ghaac@marshallnet.com
web: http://www.marshallnet.com/ghaac
Specialized auctions of flint glass, Sandwich, Pittsburgh; also ceramics such as transferware, lustre, historical Staffordshire, etc.

Pacific Glass Auctions
1507 21st St., Ste. 203
Sacramento, CA 95814
ph: 916-443-3296 or 916-443-3210
fax: 916-443-3199
e-mail: info@pacglass.com
web: http://www.pacglass.com/
The largest antique bottle auction house currently on the internet.

Clubs/Associations

Glass Research Society of New Jersey
1501 Glasstown Rd.
Millville, NJ 08332-1566
ph: 609-825-6800 or 800-998-4552
fax: 609-825-2410
e-mail: mail@wheatonvillage.org
web: http://www.wheatonvillage.org/

Nancy Sheriff, Mem.
National American Glass Club, The, Ltd.
Newsletter: Glass Shards
P.O. Box 8489
Silver Spring, MD 20907-8489
e-mail: nagc@worldnet.att.net
web: http://home.att.net/~NAGC/
An international organization devoted to the study and appreciation of glass from antiquity to present; the semi-annual newsletter of the NEAGC covers glass exhibits, chapter activities, etc.; also publishes the Glass Club Bulletin.

Bill Donalson
Tallahassee Glass & Antiques Club
Newsletter: TGAC Newsletter
3808 Forsythe Way
Tallahassee, FL 32308-2532
ph: 904-893-9794
e-mail: donalsob@mail.tallahassee.cc.fl.us
Collectors of glass, china, pottery, silver and tools; meets 4th Tuesday from September through June.

Alvina Breckel
Greater Chicago Glass Collectors' Club
185 Fuller Lane
Winnetka, IL 60093
ph: 847-441-8626
e-mail: alvina@oakton.edu
A Chicago area chapter of the National American Glass Club; meets first Thursday of each month, Sept. through June; members interested in all types of glass.

Alvina Breckel
Greater Chicago Glass Collectors' Club
Newsletter: Glass Club Bulletin
339 Selborne Road
Riverside, IL 60546-1624
ph: 708-442-1624
e-mail: alvina@oakton.edu
A chapter of the National American Glass Club.

Lenette Heidman
Houston Glass Club
P.O. Box 1254
2728 First St.
Rosenberg, TX 77471-1254
ph: 281-342-4876 or 281-342-7722
e-mail: hgclub@webtv.net
Club specializes in depression and elegant glassware from the 1920s through 1950s; sponsors annual depression glass show in August in Rosenberg, TX; meets 2nd Tuesday of each month in Houston, TX.

Collectors

Tim Mason
Sweet Glass Antiques & Collectibles
719 Rawdon Rd.
Hillsvale, Nova Scotia B0N 1Z0
Canada
ph: 902-757-2780
e-mail: admason@ns.sympaatico.com
web: http://www3.ns.sympatico.ca/ns/admason/
Specializes in collecting glass from the 1930s to 1960s.

Dealers

Bud Marchant
Lil-Bud Antiques
142 Main St.
Yarmouth Port, MA 02675
ph: 508-362-8984

William Banks
Classical Glass
P.o. Box 364
Wiscasset, ME 04578
ph: 207-882-9393
e-mail: inventor@lincoln.midcoast.com
web: http://lincoln.midcoast.com/~inventor
Specializing in antique and collectible glassware and art pottery; author of a price guide on Victorian opalescent glass.

Christopher Woods
Historic Glasshouse
200 Mile Common Road
Easton, CT 06612
ph: 718-855-3776 or 203-254-2183
e-mail: info@antiquebottles-glass.com
web: http://www.antiquebottles-glass.com
One of the largest dealers in 17th - 19th century antique bottles and glass; website lists a wide variety of fine quality items for sale; professionally clean staining on glass items; will search for specific items; also appraises.

George Kamm
219 W. Market St.
Marietta, PA 17547
ph: 717-426-1761
fax: 717-426-1045
e-mail: marpwts@redrose.net
web: http://www.art-craftpa.com/kamm.html
Buys and sells antique and contempo-

rary glass paperweights; paperweight appraisals.

Barbara M. Lessig, ISA CAPP
Pleasant Valley Antiques
21000 Georgia Ave.
Brookeville, MD 20833-1138
ph: 301-924-2293
fax: 301-570-1625
e-mail: bmlessig@aol.com
Specialist in appraising and selling all types of glassware.

Stephen G. Del Sordo
Heritage Resource Group
305 Oakley St.
Cambridge, MD 21613
ph: 410-228-8934
fax: 410-221-8061
e-mail: delsordo@shore.intercom.net
web: http://www.heritageresource.com/
A cultural resource management/ historic preservation firm that has contracts to locate, provide, authenticate artifacts for museums and collectors; areas of expertise include architecture, industry, domestic, agriculture, and maritime.

Jim & Barbara Payne
Liberty Ridge Antiques
9634 St. Rt. 12 West
Findlay, OH 45840
ph: 419-422-7920
Specializes in buying and selling antique glassware, especially Findlay, Fostoria, Tiffin.

Experts

Frank Chiarenza
39 West Main St.
Meriden, CT 06451-4110
ph: 203-639-9778
Director of the Frank Chiarenza Museum of Glass, co-author with James Slater of "The Milk Glass Book," a frequent contributor to glass publications, and former president of the National Milk Glass Collectors Society.

Dianne Gregg
Glassnob Antiques
10413 Gary Rd.
Potomac, MD 20854
ph: 301-299-6456
fax: 301-299-6456
e-mail: glassnob@aol.com
Appraiser specializing in European glass from the 18th-20th century, American art glass, contemporary studio glass.

Internet Resources

Angela Bowey
Glass Museum On-Line
P.O. Box 113
Paihia Mall
Paihia, Bay of Islands 0252
New Zealand
ph: 649-402-8416
fax: 649-402-8538
e-mail: abowey@clear.net.nz
web: http://www.glass.co.nz/
Extensive on-line articles about glass; information message board; glass encyclopedia.

Man./Prod./Dist.

Joe Rice
House of Glass, Inc., The
7900 E State Road 28
Elwood, IN 46036-8449
ph: 765-552-6841
fax: 765-552-6854
Makes paperweights all signed by owner, Joe Rice; also makes all sorts of other solid glass: ashtrays, pears, ringholders, etc.

Museums/Libraries

Currier Gallery of Art, The
201 Myrtle Way
Manchester, NH 03104
ph: 603-669-6144
web: http://www.currier.org/

Miss Dorothy Lee Jones, Founder/Cur.
Jones Museum of Glass & Ceramics, The
35Douglas Mountain Rd.
East Sebago, ME 04029
ph: 207-787-3370 or 207-787-2800
fax: 207-787-2800
Unique museum: over 7500 examples of glass & ceramics ranging from ancient to modern; large holdings of blown, pressed, cut glass, 18th to 20th c.; American, British, Continental; glass paperweights, lamps, studio art glass; library.

Bennington Museum, The
W. Main St.
Bennington, VT 05201
ph: 802-447-1571
fax: 802-442-8305
web: http://www.bennington.com/museum/
One of the finest regional art history museums in the country; works by Grandma Moses, American glass, VT furniture, Bennington pottery, the oldest Stars & Stripes in existence, the 1925 luxury touring car "The Wasp", and much more.

Frank Chiarenza, Dir.
Frank Chiarenza Museum of Glass, The
39 West Main St.
Meriden, CT 06451-4110
ph: 203-639-9778
Museum displays an eclectic collection of American and European glass, mainly pressed, 1850 to present, including many animal covered dishes, historical and commemorative tablewares, lamps, inkwells, Victorian novelties, etc.

Wheaton Village Museum of American Glass
1501 Glasstown Rd.
Millville, NJ 08332-1566
ph: 609-825-6800 or 800-998-4552
fax: 609-825-2410
e-mail: mail@wheatonvillage.org
web: http://www.wheatonvillage.org/
Covers all types of American glass: Stiegel, Amelung, flasks, pressed, art glass, art nouveau, paperweights, lamps & lighting, cut glass, 20th century art glass, reproductions, pre-studio movement, contemporary studio glass, etc.

Corning Museum of Glass, The
Journal: Journal of Glass Studies
One Museum Way
Corning, NY 14830-2253
ph: 607-937-5371
fax: 607-937-3352
e-mail: cmg@cmog.org
web: http://www.pennynet.org/glmuseum/
Over 24,000 glass objects, innovative exhibits, videos, models; glass history, archaeology, and early manufacturing; great website with lots of information about glass.

Chrysler Museum, The
245 West Olney Road
Norfolk, VA 23510-1587
ph: 757-664-6200
fax: 757-664-6201
e-mail: museum@chrysler.org
web: http://www.chrysler.org
Fine collection of early to 20th century glass; also ancient to modern artifacts from all over the world.

Toledo Museum of Art, The
2445 Monroe St.
P.O. Box 1013
Toledo, OH 43697
ph: 419-255-8000 or 800-644-6862
web: http://www.toledomuseum.org/
Internationally-recognized collections of glass, paintings, and decorative and graphic arts.

Glass Museum at the Dunkirk Library
309 S. Franklin
Dunkirk, IN 47336-1209
ph: 765-768-6872
fax: 765-768-6872
e-mail: gayrife@netscape.net
Collection contains 25 leaded-glass windows, 25 hanging lamps and hundreds of hand-blown and hand-pressed glass creations.

Jan Smith, Curator
Bergstrom-Mahler Museum
165 N. Park Ave.
Neenah, WI 54956
ph: 920-751-4675
Extensive collection of glass paperweights, Bohemian Glass and Victorian Art Glass.

Historical Glass Museum
Newsletter: Looking Glass
1157 Orange Street
P.O. Box 921
Redlands, CA 92373
ph: 909-798-0868
web: http://rth.netgate.net/lookingglass/
A breathtaking display of American glassware.

Periodicals

James Hagenbuch
Magazine: Antique Bottle & Glass Collector
P.O. Box 180
102 Jeffersfon St.
East Greenville, PA 18041
ph: 215-679-5849
fax: 215-679-3068
e-mail: glswrk@enter.net
web: http://www.glswrk-auction.com/
A monthly magazine for the glass and bottle collector.

David Richardson
Antique Publications
Magazine: Glass Collector's Digest
217 Union St.
P.O. Box 553
Marietta, OH 45750-0553
ph: 800-533-3433 or 740-373-6146
fax: 740-373-6917
e-mail: info@antiquepublications.com
web: http://www.antiquepublications.com/
A bi-monthly magazine focusing on the glass collecting specialties; articles and ads feature lots of color photography.

Teri Steele, Ed.
Depression Glass Daze, Inc.
Newspaper: Daze, The
P.O. Box 57
Otisville, MI 48463-0057
ph: 810-631-4593 or 800-336-9927
fax: 810-631-4567
web: http://www.thedaze.com
A monthly newspaper catering to the dealers and collectors of glass, china and pottery from the 1920s and 1930s.

Ruth Grizel, Ed.
Newspaper: Glass Post, The
P.O. Box 205
Oakdale, IA 52319-0205
ph: 319-626-3216
fax: 319-626-3216
Monthly 18-20 page newsletter featuring classified ads for selling glass, collectibles like plates, china, pottery, dolls, etc.; subscription cost includes cost of ads for one year; all ads free to subscribers.

Akro Agate/Westite

Clubs/Associations

Roger Hardy
Akro Agate Collector's Club, Inc.
Newsletter: Clarksburg Crow
97 Milford St.
Clarksburg, WV 26301
ph: 304-624-4523 or 304-624-7600
e-mail: rhardy0424@aol.com
Focuses on Akro marbles, children's dishes and general line items.

Collectors

Albert Morin
668 Robbins Ave. #23
Dracut, MA 01826
ph: 978-454-7907
Wants either Akro Agate or Westite items.

Experts

Roger Hardy
West End Antiques
97 Milford St.
Clarksburg, WV 26301
ph: 304-624-4523 or 304-624-7600
e-mail: rhardy0424@aol.com
Author of "The Complete Line of Akro Agate, With Prices."

Anchor Hocking (Fire King)

Experts

April M. Tvorak
P.O. Box 94
Warren Center, PA 18851
ph: 570-395-3775
e-mail: april@epix.net
Author of "History and Price Guide to Fire-King," "Fire-King II", and "Fire-King '95," "Fire-King 5th Ed.-97 Values," "Fire-King Fever, 95-96 Values" updated values; please include a SASE with all correspondence.

Ancient

Collectors

Earl Jacobs
21540 West Eleven Mile Rd.
Southfield, MI 48076-3876
Interested in ancient glass - from its most early types through blown glass, cast, cone form and Islamic; interested in scholarship, acquisition, disposition and publication.

Animals

Periodicals

Ruth Grizel
Newsletter: Glass Animal Bulletin, The
P.O. Box 143
North Liberty, IA 52317-0143
ph: 319-626-2807
fax: 319-626-2807
Full color monthly magazine featuring glass animal figurines and covered animal dishes of all kinds; free classified ads to subscribers.

Art

(see also GLASS, Studio [Contemporary]; LAMPS & LIGHTING, Tiffany/Handel/Pairpoint; TIFFANY ITEMS)

Appraisers

Stephen van Cline, CAPP
van Cline & Davenport, Ltd.
792 Franklin Ave.
Franklin Lakes, NJ 07417-1343
Minimum charge $25; letter request only, SASE.

Brian Severn
Severn's Art Glass
150 Cleaveland Ave.
Pleasant Hill, CA 94523
e-mail: bsevern@earthlink.net
web: http://home.earthlink.net/~bsevern/artglass.htm
Dealer, collector, appraiser of art glass; offers antique, Art Nouveau, contemporary: Steuben, Loetz, Quezal, Durand, Tiffany, Orient & Flume, Lundberg Studios, PHOENIX Studios, Mashlach, Correia, perfumes and more.

Kathleen M. Bailey, ISA CAPP
Antique Appraisal & Estate Sale Services
9416 1st Ave., NE, #311
Seattle, WA 98115
ph: 425-746-2777
fax: 425-746-3793

Auction Services

Louise Luther
Skinner, Inc.
357 Main St.
Bolton, MA 01740-1104
ph: 978-779-6241
fax: 978-779-5144
e-mail: info@skinnerinc.com
web: http://www.skinnerinc.com
Established in 1964, Skinner Inc. is the fifth largest auction house in the US; has offices in Bolton and Boston, MA.

Early Auction Co.
123 Main St.
Milford, OH 45150
ph: 513-831-4833
fax: 513-831-1441
e-mail: RREarly@aol.com
web: http://www.SL2.com/EarlyAuctionCo.html
Specializes in art glass auctions.

James L. Jackson, ISA
Jackson's Auctioneers & Appraisers
2229 Lincoln St.
Cedar Falls, IA 50613
ph: 319-277-2256
fax: 319-277-1252
e-mail: jacksons@jacksonsauction.com
web: http://www.jacksonsauction.com
Conducts specialty auctions of Victorian, Art Nouveau and Art Deco glass, leaded and reverse painted lamps, etc.

Joy Luke
Joy Luke Auction Gallery
300 E. Grove St.
Bloomington, IL 61701-5232
ph: 309-828-5533
fax: 309-829-2266
e-mail: robert@joyluke.com
web: http://www.joyluke.com/
Conducts auctions specializing in fine art glass.

Clubs/Associations

Reyne Haines
Art Glass Discussion Group
405 Lafayette Ave.
Cincinnati, OH 45220
ph: 513-559-1405
fax: 513-651-0860
e-mail: reyne@tias.com
web: http://www.tias.com/stores/RHA/
Collectors talk about book reviews, auction information, reproduction information, buying and selling; no dues; e-mail access essential.

Collectors

John O. Burgess
10738 Harley Rd.
Lorton, VA 22079-3908
Wants to buy Burmese art glass from any source or time period.

Henry Tyler
13 Bellevue Dr.
Saint Petersburg, FL 33706-1201
Interested in Mount Washington, Crown Milano, Web art glass, English cameo.

Dealers

Valerie Sevene
Route 7 Antiques & Treasures
388 Shelburne Road
Burlington, VT 05401
ph: 802-859-0917
e-mail: sevene@together.net
Wants to buy Murano and other art glass.

Lenore Monleon
33 Fifth Ave.
New York, NY 10003-4338
ph: 212-475-7871 or 212-675-7771
Wants Galle, Lalique, silver overlay, Art Deco, Art Nouveau.

Joseph D. Cantara
Cantara/Galletti
ph: 718-352-7273
fax: 718-352-6661
e-mail: Deco11358@aol.com
web: http://www.antiqnet.com/da/tiffany.html
Buys, sells and specializes in art glass and in Tiffany items such as lamps, desk sets, glass and accessories; also buys and sells Art Deco - especially French & Austrian.

Dottie Freeman
P.O. Box 429
Chester Heights, PA 19017
ph: 610-459-5265 or 717-336-6622

Gerald Shultz
Antique Gallery, The
8523 Germantown Ave.
Philadelphia, PA 19118-3316
ph: 215-248-1700
fax: 215-247-8411
Galle, Daum, Moser, Lalique, Legras, Durand, Tiffany, Venetian, Quezal, Bohemian, Steuben.

Jim & Grace Greenwald, ISA
Greenwald Antiques
925 Walnut St.
Royersford, PA 19468
ph: 610-948-9391 or 610-948-1308

Alain Fournier
La Verrerie D'Art
P.O. Box 757
Bowie, MD 20718-0757
ph: 301-464-3251
e-mail: grafour@aol.com
Buys, sells and specializes in European art glass of the Art nouveau and Art Deco eras (1880-1940); Schneider, Daum, Muller Fres., Loetz, D'Avesn.

Caren Fine
11603 Gowrie Ct.
Potomac, MD 20854-3623
ph: 301-299-6886 or 301-299-2116
Wants glass and lamps by Renee Lalique, Tiffany, Galle, Handel, Quezal; also wants 1950s Italian glass.

L. Michael Boak
Initialed Duck Antiques & Collectibles
3812 Hamilton Ave.
Baltimore, MD 21206-3505
Buys, sells and collects Steuben, Mt. Washington, Webb, Libbey, Venetian, Stevens & Williams, Hobbs & Brockunier; wants American, English and Continental art glass.

Patricia Carta
Art Attic, Inc.
P.O. Box 811689
Boca Raton, FL 33481-1689
ph: 800-741-4017
e-mail: lct1890@aol.com
Buys and sells old art glass: Tiffany, Daum, Galle, etc.

Allan Dowling
Allan & Company Antiques Inc.
P.O. Box 254
Berea, OH 44017
ph: 440-238-8474
e-mail: adowling@pantek.com
web: http://www.webinsights.com/allanantiques/
Dealers and appraisers of art glass: Tiffany, Quezal, Loetz, Durand, Steuben, Moser and cameo; buy and

sell both American and European examples of art glass.

Reyne Haines
Vintage Glass
405 Lafayette Ave.
Cincinnati, OH 45220
ph: 513-559-1405
fax: 513-651-0860
e-mail: reyne@tias.com
web: http://www.tias.com/stores/RHA/
Buys and sells Tiffany glass, lamps, bronze, jewelry and windows; also buys art glass of the same period.

Mary L. Brinkman
Cedars Antiques, The
P.O. Box 215
Aurelia, IA 51005
ph: 712-434-2244
e-mail: mbrinkman@aurelia.k12.ia.us
web: http://www.csmonline.com/cedars/
Search or browse entire inventory and order online.

Fred Wishnie
Art Glass & Antiques by Wishful Things
207 E. Buffalo St.
Milwaukee, WI 53202
ph: 414-765-1117
fax: 414-765-1213
e-mail: luvglass@execpc.com
web: http://wishfulthings.com
Collector, dealer, expert, book seller specializing in American and European art glass from Victorian to contemporary; website features 300+ pieces with full color photos and descriptions.

Dr. David Schwab
Dr. David Schwab Antiques
18 Silman Ave.
Hammond, LA 70401-1083
ph: 504-429-0143
e-mail: ecoprof1@hotmail.com
Art glass collector, dealer, expert, appraiser; has been the glass business for 30 years and has extensive library; deals in art glass of all kinds and better production items such as elegant Depression era glass.

Brian Severn
Severn's Art Glass
150 Cleaveland Ave.
Pleasant Hill, CA 94523
e-mail: bsevern@earthlink.net
web: http://home.earthlink.net/~bsevern/artglass.htm
Dealer, collector, appraiser of art glass; offers antique, Art Nouveau, contemporary: Steuben, Loetz, Quezal, Durand, Tiffany, Orient & Flume, Lundberg Studios, PHOENIX Studios, Mashlach, Correia, perfumes and more.

Steve Hetherington
Glasstiques
P.O. Box 6177
Vacaville, CA 95696-6177
ph: 707-451-3688
e-mail: glasstiques@msn.com
web: http://www.bmark.com/glasstiques/
Wants to buy art glass: Rose Amber, Peachblow, Napoli, Crown Milano, Colonial Ware, Royal Flemish, Burmese, Lava, M.O.P., Verona, Alexandrite, Silveria, Agata, Pink Slag, Holly Amber, Amberina, Plated Amberina; also fairy lamps.

Kathleen M. Bailey, ISA CAPP
Antique Appraisal & Estate Sale Service - K. Bailey
9416 1st Ave., NE, #311
Seattle, WA 98115
ph: 425-746-2777
fax: 425-746-3793
Specializing in fine Art Glass; Tiffany, Steuben, Lalique, Moser, Webb, Galle, Daum, etc..

Experts

Louis O. St. Aubin, Jr.
Brookside Antiques "Art Glass Gallery"
44 North Water St.
New Bedford, MA 02740
ph: 508-993-4944
Museum consultant, expert, established in 1964, author of "Pairpoint Lamps. A Collectors Guide"; nationally known authority, lecturer, appraiser, auction house consultant; founder of the New Bedford Glass Museum.

Scott Roland
Glimmer Glass Antiques
P.O. Box 262
Schenevus, NY 12155-0262
ph: 607-638-9543
e-mail: glimmerglass.swr@worldnet.att.net
Buys, sells, specializes in and appraises Victorian glass, art glass, milk glass, water pitchers and tumblers, etc.

Clarence Maier
Burmese Cruet, The
P.O. Box 432
Montgomeryville, PA 18936-0432
ph: 215-855-5388
Specializes in Burmese, Crown Milano, and Royal Flemish art glass; advisor to "Warman's Antiques & Collectibles Price Guide" and to "Schroeder's Price Guide."

Mildred & Ralph Lechner
P.O. Box 554
Mechanicsville, VA 23111-0554
ph: 804-737-3347
Feature writers on antique glassware for "AntiqueWeek"; authors of "The World of Salt Shakers," Vols. 1, 2 & 3; Victorian art and pattern glass reproduction identification experts; collectors of art and pattern glass salt & pepper shakers.

Robin & June Greenwald
June Greenwald Antiques, Inc.
3096 Mayfield Rd.
Cleveland, OH 44118
ph: 215-932-5535
Nationally recognized art glass dealers.

Museums/Libraries

Wadsworth Atheneum
600 Main St.
Hartford, CT 06103
ph: 860-278-2670
fax: 860-527-0803
e-mail: info@wadsworthatheneum.org
web: http://www.wadsworthatheneum.org/
Collection of decorative art glass includes examples ranging from Roman times to Victorian America.

Ellen E. Mauer
Milan Historical Museum, Inc.
Newsletter: New Milan Ledger
P.O. Box 308
Milan, OH 44846-0308
ph: 419-499-2968
fax: 419-499-9004
web: http://www.milanohio.com/historical_museum.htm
A seven-building complex 500 yards from the birthplace of Thomas A. Edison; restored home, carriage shed, blacksmith shop, general store, collections from the 19th century.

Art (1950s)

Collectors

Dennis Boyd
P.O. Box 14642
Richmond, VA 23221-0642
ph: 804-560-0753
Wants 1950s art glass by Venini, Sarpaneva, Tapio Wirkkala, Kosta, Orrefors, Kaj Franck, Nutajari-Notsjo, Flysfors, Leerdam, Toso, Barovier, Seguso; any Italian or Scandinavian art glass (signed or unsigned.)

Art (Austrian)

Dealers

Eric's Antiques
381 Elliot St.
Newton Upper Falls, MA 02164
ph: 617-332-3744
Specializes in fine Austrian art glass.

Baccarat

(see also PAPERWEIGHTS)

Experts

R. Rosenberg
P.O. Box 554
Hicksville, NY 11802-0554
ph: 516-669-5321
fax: 516-333-4149
e-mail: rudyrr@worldnet.att.net
Wants to buy Verlys, also Val St. Lambert and Baccarat.

Matching Services

David Lackey Antiques & China Matching
2311 Westheimer
Houston, TX 77098-1317
ph: 281-942-7171
fax: 713-521-2546
Buy and sell most major brands: Fostoria, Lenox, Tiffin, Waterford, Stuart, Baccarat, etc.

Past & Present
14851 Avenue 360
Visalia, CA 93292
ph: 500-437-7666 or 415-258-1775
fax: 415-456-4333
e-mail: P-P@ix.netcom.com
web: http://www.china-crystal-flatware.com
Baccarat, Cambridge, Denby, Duncan & Miller, Fostoria, Franciscan, Gorham, Heisey, Imperial, Lalique, Lenox, Mikasa, Nancy Prentiss, Noritake, Orrefors, Sasaki, Tiffin, Towle, Val St. Lambert, Waterford, etc.

Black

Experts

Marlena Toohey
c/o Antique Publications
217 Union St.
P.O. Box 553
Marietta, OH 45750-0553
ph: 800-533-3433 or 740-373-6146
fax: 740-373-6917
e-mail: info@antiquepublications.com
web: http://www.antiquepublications.com/
Author of "A Collector's Guide to Black Glass."

Blenko

Museums/Libraries

Richard Blenko
Blenko Glass Visitor Center Museum & Wholesale Outlet
Newsletter: Antique Notes
P.O. Box 67
Milton, WV 25541-0067
ph: 304-743-9081
fax: 304-743-0547
e-mail: blenko@usa.net
web: http://blenkoglass.com/
Museum and outlet for nationally known blown glassware; also stained glass studio.

Bohemian

Collectors

Tom Price
10122 Windward Way N.
Jacksonville, FL 32256
ph: 904-646-9162 or 904-646-9357
e-mail: merprice3@aol.com
Wants to buy Bohemian glass; especially interested in glass made by Rossler.

Tom Bradshaw
325 Carol Dr.
Ventura, CA 93003-1710
Wants to buy 19th century Bohemian decorated drinking glasses, beakers, goblets, wine glasses, etc. that are engraved with scenes, people, animals, etc.; colored or clear glass.

Experts

Bob Truitt
5120 White Flint Dr.
Kensington, MD 20895-1037
ph: 301-929-2539
Author of "Collectible Bohemian Glass 1880-1940" (1995) and "Collectible Bohemian Glass Vol. II 1915-1945" (1998).

Boyd's Crystal Art

Dealers

Rick Morris
Rick's Black Lights & Art Glass
194 Stonefield Circle
Macon, GA 31206
ph: 912-781-5119
e-mail: southern@mindspring.com
web: http://www.mindspring.com/~southern1/blacklig.htm

Darrell Crim
Jody & Darrell's Glass Collectibles
P.O. Box 180833
Arlington, TX 76096-0833
ph: 817-467-5483

Man./Prod./Dist.

Boyd's Crystal Art Inc.
Newsletter: Boyd's Crystal Art Glass Newsletter
1203 Morton Ave.
P.O. Box 127
Cambridge, OH 43725
ph: 740-439-2077
fax: 740-432-1827
e-mail: 73250.2104@compuserve.com
web: http://www.boydglass.com/
Manufacturers many collectible glass items in a wide array of colors.

Periodicals

Jody Best
Newsletter: Jody & Darrell's Glass Collectibles Newsletter
P.O. Box 180833
Arlington, TX 76096-0833
ph: 817-467-5483
Published bi-monthly, focuses on Boyd's Crystal Art Glass and other contemporary glass collectibles; subscription includes an exclusive figurine produced by Boyd's Art Glass; articles, secondary market price information, classified ads.

Cambridge

Clubs/Associations

Charles A. Upton
National Cambridge Collectors, Inc.
Newsletter: Cambridge Crystal Ball
P.O. Box 416
Cambridge, OH 43725-0416
ph: 740-432-4245 or 740-432-6794
fax: 740-432-4245
e-mail: webmaster@cambridgeglass.org
web: http://www.cambridgeglass.org/
Preserves and studies the products of the Cambridge Glass Co., Cambridge, OH; please send a SASE when requesting information.

Collectors

Susan Leite
44 Glenwood Rd.
Brewster, MA 02631-2202
ph: 508-385-4905
Wants to buy Cambridge Etch #520 in pink.

Dealers

Penny Drucker
Mother Drucker's
P.O. Box 50261
Irvine, CA 92619-0261
ph: 888-637-8253 or 949-551-5529
fax: 949-551-2116
e-mail: Penny@Motherdruckers.com
web: http://www.motherdruckers.com/
Carries hard-to-find as well as common pieces of Cambridge glass.

Museums/Libraries

Cambridge Glass Museum, The
812 Jefferson Ave.
Cambridge, OH 43725
ph: 740-432-3045
Over 5000 pieces of Cambridge glass on display; also 100 pieces of Cambridge Art Pottery; private museum.

Charles A. Upton
Museum of the National Cambridge Collectors, Inc.
P.O. Box 416
Cambridge, OH 43725-0416
ph: 740-432-4245 or 740-432-6794
fax: 740-432-4245
e-mail: webmaster@cambridgeglass.org
web: http://www.cambridgeglass.org/
Preserves and studies the products of the Cambridge Glass Co., Cambridge, OH.

Candlewick

Clubs/Associations

Connie Doll, Mem.
National Candlewick Collector's Club, The
Newsletter: Candlewick Collector Newsletter, The
6534 South Ave.
Holland, OH 43528
ph: 419-866-6350
The newsletter is devoted to the Candlewick pattern, collectors, finds, prices, questions answered, look-alikes and repros. discussed.

Cliff McCaslin
National Imperial Glass Collectors Society
Newsletter: Glasszette
P.O. Box 534
Bellaire, OH 43906
ph: 816-436-7719
fax: 816-436-6955
e-mail: rocliff@unicom.net
web: http://www.imperialglass.org
Members interested in the history and glassware produced by the Imperial Glass Corp.; conducts an annual convention offering seminars, show and sale, and "members only" auction; establishing an Imperial museum.

Lucille R. Geisler, Treas/Mem
Michiana Association of Candlewick Collectors
Newsletter: Spyglass
17370 Battles Rd.
South Bend, IN 46614
ph: 219-291-9245

Collectors

Lucille R. Geisler
17370 Battles Rd.
South Bend, IN 46614
ph: 219-291-9245

Dealers

Kathy Burch
221 N. Maple
Ithaca, MI 48847-1025
ph: 517-875-3138
Buys and sells unusual pieces of Candlewick glass including colored pieces.

Penny Drucker
Mother Drucker's
P.O. Box 50261
Irvine, CA 92619-0261
ph: 888-637-8253 or 949-551-5529
fax: 949-551-2116
e-mail: Penny@Motherdruckers.com
web: http://www.motherdruckers.com/
Always changing inventory of color, cut, rare and common pieces; send LSASE for list.

Experts

Virginia R. Scott
275 Milledge Terrace
Athens, GA 30606-4937
ph: 706-548-5966
e-mail: vrsicw@aol.com
Researcher, author of "The Collector's Guide to Imperial Candlewick"; a very complete book illustrating almost every known Candlewick pattern piece, including colors, variations, cuttings; has look-alike and reproduction appendix.

Mary M. Wetzel-Tomalka
17370 Battles Rd.
South Bend, IN 46614
ph: 219-291-9245
Author of "Candlewick - The Jewel of Imperial."

Carnival

Auction Services

Tom Burns
Burns Auction Service
P.O. Box 608
Bath, NY 14810
ph: 607-776-7942
Sells Victorian and art glass, Nippon, Noritake, lamps, carnival glass.

Randy S. Burdette
Riverbend Auction
P.O. Box 800
103 South Monroe St.
Alderson, WV 24910
ph: 304-445-2897 or 800-726-2897
fax: 304-445-2900
e-mail: rivauction@newwave.net
web: http://www.riverbendauction.com

Cooper & Albrecht Auctions
202 South Mill St.
Clio, MI 48420

Seeck Auctions
17736 280th St.
Mason City, IA 50401-9096

Mickey Reichel Auction Service
516 3rd St.
Boonville, MO 65233

Woody Auction Company
P.O. Box 618
317 S. Forrest St.
Douglass, KS 67039
ph: 316-746-2694
fax: 316-746-2145

Clubs/Associations

Eva Backer
New England Carnival Glass Club
12 Sherwood Rd.
W Hartford, CT 06117-2738
ph: 860-233-3961

Mary Sharp
Keystone Carnival Glass Club
719 W. Brubaker Valley Rd.
Lititz, PA 17543
ph: 717-626-5521

Jackie Poucher, Sec.
Sunshine State Carnival Glass Association
9087 Baywood Park Dr.
Seminole, FL 33777
ph: 727-398-1866
e-mail: jackie@carnivalglass.net
web: http://www.carnivalglass.net/sscga/

Barbara Hobbs
Tampa Bay Carnival Glass Club
Newsletter: Tampa Bay Carnival Glass Club Newsletter
5501 101st Ave. N
Pinellas Park, FL 33782-3311
ph: 727-541-6164
Non-profit group, meetings, conventions, auctions, shows, monthly newsletter.

Cliff McCaslin
National Imperial Glass Collectors Society
Newsletter: Glasszette
P.O. Box 534
Bellaire, OH 43906
ph: 816-436-7719
fax: 816-436-6955
e-mail: rocliff@unicom.net
web: http://www.imperialglass.org
Members interested in the history and glassware produced by the Imperial Glass Corp.; conducts an annual convention offering seminars, show and sale, and "members only" auction; establishing an Imperial museum.

Larry Yung
American Carnival Glass Association
Newsletter: American Carnival Glass News
9621 Springwater Ln.
Miamisburg, OH 45342
Learn about highly collectible carnival glass; news, conventions; send SASE for full color brochure.

Lee Markley, Sec.
International Carnival Glass Association
Newsletter: Town Pump, The
P.O. Box 306
Mentone, IN 46539-0306
ph: 219-353-7678
e-mail: rjc4470@dcccd.edu
web: http://carnival.ksnews/com/icga/
Promotes interest in collecting old Carnival Glass; holds annual convention featuring displays, seminars and banquet.

Ellen Hemm, Sec.
Lincoln Land Carnival Glass Club
N 951 Highway 27
Conrath, WI 54731
ph: 715-532-5816

Karen Skinner
Gateway Carnival Glass Club
108 Riverwoods Cove
East Alton, IL 62024
ph: 618-259-1373

Ed Kramer, Sec.
Heart of America Carnival Glass Association
Newsletter: HOACGA Bulletin
4305 W 78th St.
Prairie Village, KS 66208
ph: 913-642-3587
Focuses on old carnival glass; members share information; monthly newsletter contains articles about OLD carnival glass, club meeting dates and secretary reports; members can advertise free of charge.

Paula Thompson
Texas Carnival Glass Club
260 Shoreline
Azle, TX 76020
ph: 817-238-9163

Marie McGee
San Joaquin Carnival Glass Club
3906 E. Acacia Ave.
Fresno, CA 93726
ph: 559-222-0796

Mary Christian
Northern California Carnival Glass Club
4324 Raiders Way
Modesto, CA 95355
ph: 209-521-9062

Jerry Reynolds
Pacific Northwest Carnival Glass Club
1305 N. Highlands Parkway, B-6
Tacoma, WA 98406
ph: 253-759-2263

Margaret Hunt
Canadian Carnival Glass Association
Newsletter: CCAA Newsletter
12 Dalhousie Crescent
London, Ontario N6G 2H7
Canada
Meetings are held every six weeks in the southwestern area of Ontario; holds annual convention; newsletter published every six weeks with articles, auction reports, sales, shows, etc.

Collectors

Eva Backer
12 Sherwood Rd.
W Hartford, CT 06117-2738
ph: 860-233-3961

Dick Hatscher
142 Walnut Hill Rd.
Bethel, CT 06801
ph: 203-743-1468
Wants to buy Carnival glass, any color or amount.

John O. Burgess
10738 Harley Rd.
Lorton, VA 22079-3908
Wants pre-1950 US carnival glass.

Barbara Hobbs
5501 101st Ave. N
Pinellas Park, FL 33782-3311
ph: 727-541-6164
Collects only old carnival glass, carnival glass hatpins, carnival glass bottles.

Larry Yung
9621 Springwater Ln.
Miamisburg, OH 45342

Cliff McCaslin
Rocliff Communications
8422 N. Park Ct.
Kansas City, MO 64155
ph: 816-436-7719
fax: 816-436-6955
e-mail: rocliff@unicom.net
Wants to buy several manufacturers of carnival glass, stretch and art glassware patterns including Northwood, Dugan-Diamond, Millersburg.

Dealers

W. J. Warren
38 Mosher Dr.
Tonawanda, NY 14150-5218
ph: 716-692-2886
e-mail: wwa38@aol.com
Buys and sells; wants all colors of carnival glass; one piece or a collection.

Charles & Marianne Wilson
Thistle hill B&B Inn
5541 Sperryvile Pike
Boston, VA 22713
ph: 540-987-9142

C. Lucille Britt
4305 W 78th St.
Prairie Village, KS 66208
ph: 913-642-3587
Buyer and seller of old carnival glass; active member of the Heart of American Carnival Glass Association.

Kevin Thorne
Eclectiques Carnival Glass
1470 Gamble Oaks Drive
Elizabeth, CO 80107
e-mail: eclectiq@qadas.com
web: http://www.qadas.com/eclectiq/
Buys and sells carnival glass; over 400 pieces online for sale; detailed description, iridescence available.

Gary Lickver
P.O. Box 1778
San Marcos, CA 92079-1778
ph: 760-744-5686
California's largest carnival glass dealer, collector; consistently at most quality indoor antique shows in California, Atlantic City, NJ and others; wants to buy one piece or entire collections.

Experts

Helen Greguire
Helen's Antiques
103 Trimmer Rd.
Hilton, NY 14468-9305
ph: 716-392-2704
Author of "Carnival Lighting", focusing on carnival glass used in lighting such as Gone With The Wind lamps, electric and kerosene lamp shades, chandeliers, etc.; the book is out of print but copies are still available from the author.

Donald Grizzle
Sanctified Cross-Eyed Bear, The
P.O. Box 1296
Huntsville, AL 35807-1296
ph: 256-534-9076 or 256-534-9049
e-mail: bearbook@isle.net
Publishes the most extensive sales references available for carnival glass: reports on over 30,000 actual sales during the past five years; clarifies upward and downward price trends.

Tom & Sharon Mordini
36 North Mernitz Ave.
Freeport, IL 61032
ph: 815-235-4407
fax: 815-232-3911
e-mail: tmordini@mwci.net
Publishes annual list of 5,000 carnival glass auction prices.

Kitty & Russell Umbraco
P.O. Box 5331
Richmond, CA 94805-0331
ph: 510-235-1656
Buys and sells; author of "Iridescent Stretch Glass."

Internet Resources

Fred Stone
Woodsland World Wide Carnival Glass Association
e-mail: fstone@woodsland.com
web: http://www.woodsland.com/carnivalglass/pages/wwwcga.htm
Online resource for carnival glass collectors.

Museums/Libraries

James Measell
Fenton Art Glass Company, The
700 Elizabeth St.
Williamstown, WV 26187-1028
ph: 304-375-6122 or 800-249-4527
fax: 304-375-6459
e-mail: askfenton@fentonartglass.com
web: http://www.fentonartglass.com/
Large attractive display of early Fenton and Upper Ohio Valley glass.

Carnival (Post-1960)

Clubs/Associations

Nora Proctor
Collectible Carnival Glass Association
Newsletter: CCGA Newsletter
2100 South Fairway Dr.
Joplin, MO 64804
ph: 417-623-3705
For collectors of newer carnival glass made after 1960; quarterly newsletter has articles about carnival glass, and for sale and want ads; annual convention with sale and seminars.

Collectors

Annette Bosselman
3101 Brentwood Circle
Grand Island, NE 68801-7217
ph: 308-382-6384

Dealers

John Valentine
Contemporary Carnival Glass
19930 SW 92nd Ave.
Miami, FL 33157
ph: 305-235-8704
e-mail: johnval@carnivalglass.net
web: http://www.carnivalglass.net/
Buys and sells; main focus in glass made from 1950s through 1990s; web site lists glass companies and a brief story of their history and samples of carnival glass; also books and glass clubs involved with contemporary carnival glass.

Wilma Thurston
2360 N. Old S.R. 9
Columbus, IN 47203-9430
ph: 812-546-5724

Coin

Experts

Tim Timmerman
11655 S.W. Allen Blvd. #31
Beaverton, OR 97005-4850
ph: 503-646-8300
Author of "U.S. Coin Glass" (dated 1892); 70 page book includes pictures and descriptions of 88 pieces and also a section on reproductions; available from author for $20.

Consolidated

Clubs/Associations

Tom Jiamachello
PHOENIX & Consolidated Glass Collectors' Club
Newsletter: PHOENIX & Consolidated Collectors News & Views
41 River View Dr.
Essex Junction, VT 05452
ph: 802-878-2692 or 412-561-3379
e-mail: TOPofVT@aol.com
web: http://www.collectoronline.com/club-PCGCC-wp.html
For collectors/dealers of art glass produced by PHOENIX GLASS Co. of Monaca, PA and Consolidated Lamp & Shade Co. of Coraopolis, PA; bi-monthly newsletter - market trends, repro. alerts, buy/sell ads, price reports, articles.

Collectors

Kevin & Barbara Kiley
23 Harvard Terrace
West Orange, NJ 07052
ph: 210-736-2997
Wants to buy Ruba Rombic, red & black Consolidated, Imperial & Fenton freehand.

Barbara Norman
P.O. Box 251382
West Bloomfield, MI 48325-1382
ph: 248-855-7766
fax: 248-855-5224
Wants to buy Ruba Rombic, red or cased pieces of PHOENIX or Consolidated Art Glass, Catalonian, and Muncie Ruba Rombic.

Experts

Jack D. Wilson
3926 N. Keeler Ave.
Chicago, IL 60641-2915
ph: 773-282-9553
e-mail: jdwilson1@earthlink.net
web: http://home.earthlink.net/~jdwilson1/
Author of "PHOENIX & Consolidated Art Glass: 1926-1980"; features in-depth research, 48 color pages illustrating over 750 items (out of print); wants original Consolidated catalogs & company literature.

Consolidated (Ruba Rombic)

Collectors

Paul Galli
ph: 408-730-4010
e-mail: paul.galli@lmco.com
Wants to buy Consolidated's Ruba Rombic pattern glass.

Experts

Jack D. Wilson
3926 N. Keeler Ave.
Chicago, IL 60641-2915
ph: 773-282-9553
e-mail: jdwilson1@earthlink.net
web: http://home.earthlink.net/~jdwilson1/
Wants to buy examples of the Ruba Rombic pattern of art glass made by the Consolidated Lamp & Glass Co. of Coraopolis, PA; author of "PHOENIX & Consolidated Art Glass: 1926-1980"; advisor to Schroeder's.

Crackle

Experts

Stan & Arlene Weitman
P.O. Box 1186
N. Massapequa, NY 11758
ph: 516-799-2619
fax: 516-797-3039
e-mail: scrackle@systec.com
web: http://www.tias.com/stores/crackleking/
Author of "Crackle Glass Identification & Value Guide Book 2."

Cranberry

Clubs/Associations

Pilgrim Cranberry Glass Collectors Club
Newsletter: PCGCC Newsletter
P.O. Box 395
Ceredo, WV 25507
ph: 304-453-3553
fax: 304-453-6849
e-mail: pilgrim@ezwv.com
web: http://www.pilgrimglass.com/
For those interested in Pilgrim cranberry glass; club sponsored by the world's largest cranberry glass and "cameo" art glass manufacturer; free catalogs, advance notice of new offerings.

Cranberry Opalescent

Collectors

Larry Nellans
15065 McGregor Blvd., Ste. #107
Fort Myers, FL 33908-1902
ph: 941-481-6665
fax: 941-481-7391
Advanced collector of cranberry opalescent Victorian glass; will pay highest prices for rare cranberry opalescent barber bottles, water pitchers, table sets, oil lamps, etc.

Crystal

(see also GLASS, Elegant; LAMPS & LIGHTING, Chandeliers; TABLEWARE)

Matching Services

China By Pattern International Matching Service
P.O. Box 129
Farmington, CT 06034-0129
ph: 203-678-7079
Locate and match all manufacturers of stemware and crystal; send SASE with manufacturer, size and shape wanted, quantity, and photocopy if available: Fostoria, Cambridge, Lenox, Waterford, etc.

Regina Negrotti
Tablescapes
P.O. Box 448
Cheshire, CT 06410
ph: 800-801-4084
e-mail: lenox@ntplx.net
web: http://www.tabletopdesigns.com/
A small, personal matching service with a constantly changing inventory; want lists are kept; send photocopy or photo when unsure of pattern name; specializes in Lenox.

Paul & Pearl Hoffman
China Brokers, Ltd.
11 Westgate Ct.
Colts Neck, NJ 07722
ph: 732-866-6613 or 800-867-6613

Alice Korman
Alice's Past & Presents Replacements
P.O. Box 465
Merrick, NY 11566-0465
ph: 516-379-1352
fax: 516-379-7302
e-mail: alicechina@aol.com
Matching and locating service for Lenox, Gorham, Mikasa, Orrefors, Franciscan, Noritake, Wedgwood, Royal Doulton, Tiffin, Towle, Galway, Cambridge, Fostoria, Denby, Royal Leerdam, Atlantis, Stuart, Val St. Lambert, Sasaki, others.

Pattern Finders, A
P.O. Box 206
Port Jefferson Station, NY 11776-0206
ph: 516-928-5158 or 800-216-2446
fax: 516-928-5170
e-mail: apattern@aol.com
All major brands of dinnerware and crystal stocked in huge inventory; locating service for hard to find patterns; Rosenthal specialists.

Sophia Papapanu
Sophia's China & Crystal
141 Sedgwick Rd.
Syracuse, NY 13203-1136
ph: 315-472-6834
e-mail: jap@dreamscape.com
web: http://www.sophiaschina-crystal.com/
Discontinued china and crystal patterns; over 19 years service; American, English, and other manufacturers; mail order or by special appointment; please send SASE with requests for information.

Constance Stolz
China Match & Crystal Match
72 Longacre Rd.
Rochester, NY 14621-1019
ph: 716-338-3781
e-mail: chinamat@frontiernet.net
Replacements of discontinued glass and crystal stemware; Fostoria, Gorham, Lenox, Noritake, Mikasa, Royal Doulton; buy and sell.

Michael Round Fine China & Crystal, Inc.
7845 Wisconsin Ave.
Bethesda, MD 20814
ph: 301-656-2626 or 800-467-6863
fax: 703-550-7881
e-mail: feedback@Mround.com
web: http://www.michaelround.com
Impressive website for matching china, crystal or flatware.

China Matching, Inc.
420 Belle Grove Rd.
Middletown, VA 22645
ph: 540-869-1261
Discontinued china & crystal; Castleton, Haviland, Lenox and Wedgwood china; Fostoria & Lenox crystal.

Mildred G. Brumback
China & Crystal Matching, Inc.
420 Belle Grove Rd.
Dept. M
Middletown, VA 22645
ph: 540-869-1261
Specializes in Fostoria and Lenox.

Thurber's
2256C Dabeny Rd.
Richmond, VA 23230-3342
ph: 804-278-9080 or 800-848-7237
fax: 804-278-9480
Carries only active patterns; will locate old patterns.

David Thompson
Replacements Ltd.
P.O. Box 26029
1089 Knox Road
Greensboro, NC 27420
ph: 800-737-5223 or 336-697-3000
fax: 336-697-3100
e-mail: replaceltd@aol.com
web: http://www.replacements.com
China, crystal and flatware (obsolete, active and inactive.)

D & J Locations
1601 E. Canal St.
Tarboro, NC 27886
ph: 252-823-5333 or 800-818-5565
Discontinued crystal: Fostoria, Franciscan, Gorham, Imperial, Lenox, Lotus, Mikasa, Noritake, Seneca, Tiffin, Wedgwood, and other major brands; buys, sells, locates.

China Cabinet, The
214 Hillside Dr.
P.O. Box 426
Clearwater, SC 29822
ph: 803-593-9655
Matches fine & casual crystal; Cambridge, Franciscan, Fostoria, Galway, Glastonbury, Gorham, Imperial, Lenox, Lotus, Mikasa, Noritake, Royal Doulton, Seneca, Tiffin, Towle, etc.

China & Crystal Matchers, Inc.
2379 John Glenn Dr., Ste. #108-M
Atlanta, GA 30341-1924
ph: 770-455-1162 or 800-286-1107
fax: 770-452-8616
e-mail: chinacmi@bellsouth.net
All manufacturers; buys, sells, locates; member of the International Association of Dinnerware Matchers.

Paul Church
Replacement Service, A
500 Oregon Ave.
Saint Cloud, FL 34769
ph: 407-957-1719 or 800-337-9075
e-mail: chinacrystal@juno.com
Buys, sells and locates Fostoria and Lenox crystal.

Mary Ann Lowery
Crystal Corner, Inc., The
317 Billy Dyar Blvd.
P.O. Box 756
Boaz, AL 35957-0756
ph: 256-593-6169
fax: 256-593-6560
e-mail: ccorner@netnav.com
web: http://www.crystalcorner.com/
Fostoria, Tiffin, Mikasa, Lenox, Imperial, Gorham, Franciscan, etc.

Allan & Cathy Griggs
Chinamates
1673 Lakecrest Dr.
Sullivan, IN 47882-9585
ph: 800-726-0345 or 812-268-6411
fax: 812-268-6411
e-mail: chinamates@viaduct.custom.net
Stocks and locates discontinued patterns only of china and crystal; Franciscan, Fostoria, Gorham, Lenox, Tiffin, Waterford crystal, Wedgwood, etc.; member Fostoria Glass Society of American.

Barron's
P.O. Box 994
Novi, MI 48376
ph: 800-538-6340
fax: 800-523-4456
e-mail: barronsdw@aol.com
web: http://
www.barronsdinnerware.com/

Heritage China of Iowa
P.O. Box 244
Palo, IA 52324
ph: 888-416-1595 or 319-227-3688
e-mail: dischina@aol.com
Crystal by Fostoria, Heisey, Imperial, Candlewick, Lenox, Noritake, Sasaki.

Clintsman International
811 E. Geneva St.
Elkhorn, WI 53121
ph: 414-723-1990 or 800-781-8900
fax: 414-723-1991
All manufacturers: Atlantis, Fostoria, Galway, Gorham, Imperial, Kosta, Lenox, Lotus, Mikasa, Noritake, Stuart, Tiffin, Waterford, Wedgwood, and others; buys and sells.

Gloria Voss Beyer
Beyer's Wedgwood China Cupboard
740 Honey Creek Parkway
Milwaukee, WI 53213
ph: 800-893-WWCC
Specializes in discontinued patterns of Wedgwood crystal.

N. Skaja
Crystal Connection
8661 West Midland Dr.
Greendale, WI 53219-1038
ph: 414-425-1321
A discontinued crystal matching service specializing in Cambridge, Lenox and Fostoria.

China & Crystal Replacements
P.O. Box 187
5613 Country Road 19
Excelsior, MN 55331
ph: 612-474-6418 or 800-432-4448
Discontinued and active china, dinnerware and crystal bought and sold.

China Replacements
P.O. Box 508
High Ridge, MO 63049
ph: 800-562-2655 or 314-677-5577
fax: 314-376-6319
e-mail: chinarep@i1.net
web: http://www.iadm.com/chinarep/
Matches Lenox, Fostoria, Tiffin, Cambridge, Gorham, Lotus, Stuart, Noritake, Mikasa, and many others.

Dining Elegance, Ltd.
P.O. Box 4203
Saint Louis, MO 63163
ph: 314-865-1408
List of patterns in stock available upon request; $1.

Betty Stachurski
Betty's Crystal & China
P.O. Box 433
Lawrence, KS 66044-0433
ph: 913-842-8054
Atlantis, Bryce, Cambridge, Dansk, Denby, Duncan & Miller, Fostoria, Glastonbury/Lotus, Heisey, Josair, Lenox, Mikasa, Noritake, Royal Doulton, Tiffin, Wedgwood, and others.

Peggy Endicott
Bygone China Match
1225 W. 34th North
Wichita, KS 67204-4236
ph: 316-838-6010
fax: 316-838-6010
e-mail: bygonchina@aol.com
Stock and locates Fostoria, Gorham, Lenox, Mikasa, and Tiffin crystal.

Barbara Coleman
Finders Keepers China Lady
1537 Metairie Rd.
Metairie, LA 70005-3938
ph: 504-455-1530 or 504-831-4514
fax: 504-885-2512
Stock or locate Doulton, Lenox/ Oxford, Minton, Noritake, Pickard, Spode, Wedgwood; also other china and crystal.

Locators, Inc.
2217 Cottondale Lane
Little Rock, AR 72202-2018
ph: 501-663-7787 or 800-367-9690
fax: 501-663-7787
e-mail: locators@worldnet.att.net
web: http://www.chinalocators.com
Carries out-of-production (discontinued) china and crystal, and discontinued as well as active sterling flatware patterns.

David Lackey Antiques & China Matching
2311 Westheimer
Houston, TX 77098-1317
ph: 281-942-7171
fax: 713-521-2546
Buy and sell most major brands: Fostoria, Lenox, Tiffin, Waterford, Stuart, Baccarat, etc.

Larry & Anne McDonald
A & A Dinnerware Locators
P.O. Box 50222
Austin, TX 78763-0222
ph: 512-264-1054 or 888-898-4202
fax: 512-264-2727
e-mail: 73612.470@compuserve.com
Locate/match discontinued crystal patterns; all major manufacturers: American, European, Japanese; primarily mail order.

Chip
Chinatown LLC
815 East 2100 South
Salt Lake City, UT 84106
ph: 801-486-8282
e-mail: chip@chinatownllc.com
web: http://www.edish.com
Browse the online inventory of discontinued and current china a crystal dinnerware.

Glass Urn, The
456 West Main St.
Mesa, AZ 85201-6523
ph: 480-833-2702 or 480-838-5936
Specializing in discontinued American made glass: Cambridge, Fostoria, Heisey, Tiffin, etc.; from 1890s to 1970s; open shop or mail order.

Past & Present
14851 Avenue 360
Visalia, CA 93292
ph: 500-437-7666 or 415-258-1775
fax: 415-456-4333
e-mail: P-P@ix.netcom.com
web: http://www.china-crystal-flatware.com
Baccarat, Cambridge, Denby, Duncan & Miller, Fostoria, Franciscan, Gorham, Heisey, Imperial, Lalique, Lenox, Mikasa, Nancy Prentiss, Noritake, Orrefors, Sasaki, Tiffin, Towle, Val St. Lambert, Waterford, etc.

Silver Lane Antiques
P.O. Box 322
San Leandro, CA 94577-0032
ph: 510-483-0632
Discontinued crystal available by most major manufacturers.

Old China Patterns Ltd.
1560 Brimley Rd.
Scarborough, Ontario M1P 3G9
Canada
ph: 800-663-4533 or 416-299-8880
fax: 416-299-4721
e-mail: ocp@chinapatterns.com
web: http://www.chinapatterns.com
Canada's largest matching service; buys and sells internationally; since 1966; specializing in English china and crystal; charter member International Association of Dinnerware Matchers.

Periodicals

Susan Ranta
Magazine: Set Your Table
P.O. Box 22481
Lincoln, NE 68542-2481
ph: 800-600-2127 or 402-423-4865
fax: 402-423-4865
e-mail: sranta@setyourtable.com
web: http://www.setyourtable.com
From Anchor Hocking to Westmoreland crystal, Set Your Table lists more than 80 dealers who can help you find your missing pieces; dealer listings are indexed by manufacturer so you will know which dealers can help you.

Curved

(see also REPAIR/RESTORATION/ CONSERVATION, Glass)

Suppliers

Hudson Glass
219 North Division St.
Peekskill, NY 10566-2716
ph: 800-431-2964 or 914-737-2124
fax: 914-737-4447
Sells bent glass for china cabinets; convex picture frame glass; also carries restoration/old house glass in stock; sells stained glass tools and supplies (no stained glass repair); stained glass supply catalog available for $3.

B.J.'s Custom Curve Glass Co.
49 South Monroe St.
Monroe, MI 48161
ph: 734-241-4629

B & L Antiqurie, Inc.
P.O. Box 453
Lexington, MI 48450-0453
ph: 800-840-1110 or 810-359-8623
fax: 810-359-7498
Bent glass, convex portrait glass, antique flat glass, beveled mirror shapes, domes, and other specialty glass products for over 30 years.

Don King
King's Repair
403 E. Montgomery
Knoxville, IA 50138
ph: 515-842-6394
Curved glass for china cabinets; all sizes; will ship.

Central Glass Products
405 West Hamon Ave.
Pocola, OK 74902-3702
ph: 918-436-2401 or 888-236-8452
fax: 888-236-8452
e-mail: info@bentglass.com
web: http://www.bentglass.com/
Custom bent glass for furniture, solariums, architecture and limousines; bent, laminated, insulated; specialty is antique seeded glass for cabinet manufacturers and replacement dealers.

Patrick McCluskey
PECO Glass Bending
P.O. Box 777
Smithville, TX 78957
ph: 512-237-3600
Bends glass for antique china cabinets and similar items.

Cut

Clubs/Associations

Kathy Emerson
American Cut Glass Association
Newsletter: Hobstar, The
P.O. Box 482
Ramona, CA 92065-0482
ph: 768-789-2715
fax: 768-789-7112
e-mail: acgakathy@aol.com
web: http://www.geocities.com/WallStreet/1921/
Focuses on the Brilliant Period (1880-1915) of American glass.

Collectors

Mike & Lynda Carrigan
RR2 Box 128
New Freedom, PA 17349
ph: 717-235-7159
Collects Brilliant Period cut glass.

Charles Blanton
118 Magothy Bridge Rd.
Severna Park, MD 21146-1221
ph: 410-647-2841
Advanced collector wants one piece or entire collection.

Dealers

Frank W. Larned
Bagwells Flowers & Antiques, Inc.
312 S. Peninsula Dr.
Daytona Beach, FL 32118
ph: 904-252-7687
Specializes in American Brilliant Period cut glass.

Randeen Cummings, ISA CAPP
Cummings & Associates
P.O. Box 5484
Eugene, OR 97405-0484
ph: 541-345-5856 or 541-485-3068
fax: 541-345-8192
e-mail: rmcummings@ibm.net
web: http://www.antiquesinn.com
Specializes in selling & appraising residential contents, fine art, estate jewelry, 18th & 19th century antiques, American Brilliant period cut glass; also specialized marketing for clients: consultations, estate, and Internet sales.

Experts

Joan & Dick Randles
From the Cutter's Wheel Antiques
P.O. Box 285
Webster, NY 14580-0285
ph: 716-671-3760
Specializes, buys and sells American Brilliant period cut glass and engraved glass; members ACGA; eves and weekends best time to call.

Chet Cassel
910 Pheasant Run
Newark, DE 19711
ph: 302-737-3819
Buys, sells (retail/wholesale) and collects examples of fine cut glass.

Bill & Louise Boggess
4016 Martin Dr.
San Mateo, CA 94403-3623
ph: 650-345-5230
Authors of "Identifying American Brilliant Cut Glass" "Collecting American Brilliant Cut Glass," and "Reflection on American Brilliant Cut Glass."

Martha Louise Swan
3930 SE 162nd Ave., Unit 61
Portland, OR 97236-7006
ph: 503-669-8697
Author of "American Cut & Engraved Glass: The Brilliant Period in Historical Perspective (1876-1916)", 3rd revision (Krause), updated price guide, available from author.

Misc. Services

Dean & Sharon DeOgny
Sentimental Journey Antiques
121 S. Washington Ave., Ste. 810
Minneapolis, MN 55401
ph: 612-332-3270
fax: 612-630-9496
Produces a series of videos about cut glass: signatures, assembly line cutting, details of cutting, pattern names, why stoppers are not interchangeable, figured blanks, what to do with broken pieces, etc.

Museums/Libraries

Hank
Dorflinger Glass Museum
e-mail: loftus@ezaccess.net
web: http://www.dorflinger.org/
A tribute to the life and accomplishments of Christian Dorflinger, known throughout the world as the creator of fine crystal and exquisite cut glass.

High Museum of Art, The
1280 Peachtree St.
Atlanta, GA 30309
ph: 404-733-4400
fax: 404-733-4502
web: http://www.high.org/

Lightner Museum
P.O. Box 334
75 King St.
Saint Augustine, FL 32085
ph: 904-824-2874

Czechoslovakian

Appraisers

Peggy Sebek, ISA, AAA
Century Appraisals, Inc.
3255 Glencairn Rd.
Shaker Heights, OH 44122-3407
ph: 216-991-2356
fax: 216-991-2935
e-mail: peggylane@worldnet.att.net
Accredited Member of the International Society of Appraisers, Member of the Appraisers Association of America.

Clubs/Associations

Kathy Foster
Czechoslovakian Collectors Guild International
Newsletter: CCGI Newsletter
P.O. Box 901395
Kansas City, MO 64190-1395
ph: 816-891-9115 or 888-910-2424
fax: 816-891-0988
e-mail: ccgi@kc.net
For collectors of anything Czechoslovakian and Bohemian: glass, pottery, art.

Dealers

Czech Cottage
100 16th Ave. SW
Cedar Rapids, IA 52404-2955
ph: 319-366-4937
fax: 319-366-4937
e-mail: czechcottage@uswest.net
web: http://www.czechcottage.com/
Carries a large selection of traditional Bohemian glass and porcelain from the Czech Republic.

Gillian Hine
Gillian Hine Antiques
858 W. Armitage, Box 241
Chicago, IL 60614
ph: 773-281-4186
Buys and sells Czech and German glass and pottery.

Experts

Charles & Barbara Plummer
11417 Sherrie Lane
Silver Spring, MD 20902

Joseph Mattis
Black Swan
P.O. Box 925
Spencer, WV 25276

Andries van Dam
Andries van Dam Fine Art & Antiques
74 Ridgelake Drive
Columbia, SC 29209
ph: 803-695-3099
fax: 803-695-4987
e-mail: lavand@worldnet.att.net
web: http://www.web-pac.com/mall/vandam/
Dealer and expert in Czech glass of Josef Drahonovsky.

Polly Enloe, ISA
Century Antiques & Appraisals, Inc.
212 Miller St.
Lafayette, LA 70503
ph: 318-232-5100
Specializes in and appraises Czechoslovakian glass.

Museums/Libraries

Bob Truitt
Friends of the Glass Museum at Novy Bor
5120 White Flint Dr.
Kensington, MD 20895-1037
ph: 301-929-2539
Organizes symposiums and other research and educational functions focusing on the glassware produced or decorated in the Novy Bor region of Czechoslovakian; supports the Glass Museum at Novy Bor, Czechoslovakia.

Periodicals

Magazine: New Glass Review
Ciklova 3,
Praha 2
Prague, 128 00
Czech Republic
ph: 42 2 6926207
Brief, well illustrated articles in English covering all aspects of Czechoslovakian and Slovak glass; production glass, art glass, plus artists; Bohemian glass, novelties, new trends & technologies; also china & ceramics.

Dalzell-Viking

Man./Prod./Dist.

Dalzell-Viking Glass
P.O. Box 459
New Martinsville, WV 26155
ph: 304-455-2900
fax: 304-455-5984
Has outlet store adjacent to factory; also in Cambridge, OH.

Degenhart

Clubs/Associations

Friends of Degenhart
Newsletter: Heartbeat
65323 Highland Hills Rd.
P.O. Box 186
Cambridge, OH 43725-0186
ph: 740-432-2626
Open to all Degenhart collectors and supporters; free museum admission, 5% discount on most purchases, newsletter, annual "Gathering."

Museums/Libraries

Degenhart Paperweight & Glass Museum, Inc.
65323 Highland Hills Rd.
P.O. Box 186
Cambridge, OH 43725-0186
ph: 740-432-2626
History of glass in the Ohio valley; video, exhibits, research library, gift shop.

Depression

Clubs/Associations

W. Walker
North Jersey Dee Geer's
P.O. Box 741
Oradell, NJ 07649
ph: 201-384-6703

Long Island Depression Glass Club
P.O. Box 148
West Sayville, NY 11796
ph: 516-421-5065
e-mail: dgemma@webspan.net
web: http://www.antiquehaven.com/club/lidgs.htm

Gerald Manitone
Depression Glass Club of Greater Rochester
Newsletter: Bits & Pieces
P.O. Box 10362
Rochester, NY 14610
ph: 716-288-4290

Millie Downey
Land of Sunshine Depression Glass Club
Newsletter: LSDGC Newsletter
P.O. Box 560275
Orlando, FL 32856-0275
ph: 407-298-3355 or 407-855-5502
Purpose of the club is to preserve the history of Depression glass and to encourage new collectors and familiarize the public with glassware of the era.

Joe Baxa
Western Reserve Depression Glass Club
5168 Lake Vista Dr.
Solon, OH 44139
ph: 440-248-4570

J. Ryan
Buckeye Dee Geer's
2501 Campbell St.
Sandusky, OH 44870

Jeff Settell
Iowa Depression Glass Association
Newsletter: ISGA Newsletter
5871 Vista Dr., Apt. 725
West Des Moines, IA 50266
ph: 515-223-9364

20-30-40's Society, Inc.
Newsletter: Society Page, The
P.O. Box 856
La Grange, IL 60525-0856
ph: 815-495-9576
e-mail: centralgw@indianvalley.com
Formed in 1972; devoted to collecting and learning about Depression-era glassware; annual glass show every March.

Don C. Baker
St. Louis Depressioners Glass Club
2040 Flight Dr.
Florissant, MO 63031
ph: 314-839-2874
e-mail: DonCbaker@juno.com
Club meets monthly in Kirkwood, MO.

Sarah VanDalsem, Mem.
National Depression Glass Association, The
Newsletter: News & Views
P.O. Box 8264
Wichita, KS 67209-0264
ph: 918-241-1205
e-mail: firekingok@aol.com
web: http://www.glassshow.com/NDGA/
A central organization for depression glass collectors; sponsors an annual show and sale in July.

Gary Greenawalt
Greater Tulsa Depression Era Glass Club
P.O. Box 470763
Tulsa, OK 74147-0763
e-mail: garyg74112@aol.com

A. Nicholson
Big "D" Pression Glass Club
10 Winding Creek Trail
Garland, TX 75043

Anita Wood
Permian Basin Depression Glass Club
1412 Alamosa St.
Odessa, TX 79763
ph: 915-337-1297
e-mail: dganita@aol.com

Walter Lemiski
Canadian Depression Glass Association
Newsletter: CDGA Newsletter
119 Wexford Road
Brampton, Ontario L6Z 2T5
Canada
ph: 905-846-2835
e-mail: cdga@home.com
web: http://www.members.home.net/cdga/
Formed in 1976, members receive the CDGA Newsletter with ads, articles, finds, a dealer directory, show reports, book reviews, repro alerts and more.

Collectors

Anita Wood
1412 Alamosa
Odessa, TX 79763
ph: 915-337-1297

Mary Faria
P.O. Box 32321
San Jose, CA 95152-2321
ph: 408-258-0413 or 408-258-0416
e-mail: izmars@worldnet.att.net
Wants to buy pink or apple green depression glass in non-etched designs for kitchen, soda fountain, desk ware, barware, perfume, vanity and bath ware; especially wants pink straw holder, desk blotter sets, apple green rolling pin.

Dealers

Susan Leite
44 Glenwood Rd.
Brewster, MA 02631-2202
ph: 508-385-4905
Wants to buy all pink, green and jadite (creamy green) depression glass; must be undamaged.

Fred & Linda Suzman
Suzman's Antiques
P.O. Box 301
Rehoboth, MA 02769
ph: 508-252-5729
e-mail: suzmanf@ride.ri.net
Buys and sells Depression glass and Fiestaware.

Jay Adams
248 Lakeview Ave., Ste. 208
Clifton, NJ 07011
ph: 973-365-5970
fax: 973-471-5323
e-mail: jadams7811@aol.com
Specializing in Depression era glass and china: also wants to buy elegant glass such as Cambridge, Tiffin, Fostoria and others; send SASE with wants; will search and keep want list on file; best to call 6-11 EST; mail order only.

Gerald Manitone
P.O. Box 10362
Rochester, NY 14610
ph: 716-288-4290
Buys, sells, and collects Depression glass.

Seth Price
Antiques Nook, The
402 Benfield Road
Severna Park, MD 21146
ph: 410-544-5607
e-mail: sprice@clark.net
web: http://www.clark.net/pub/aaccspri/home.html
Buys and sells elegant depression glass; Adam to Windsor; mail order or internet sales; no shop.

Millie Downey
Millie's Glass & China
P.O. Box 560275
Orlando, FL 32856-0275
ph: 407-298-3355 or 407-855-5502
Wants to buy Depression glass; collects many patterns.

Anne Shatrau
Auntie Q's Antiques & Collectibles
P.O. Box 3411-AQ
Albany, OR 97321-0716
ph: 541-928-6180
fax: 541-928-0202
e-mail: dg@auntieqs.com
web: http://www.auntieqs.com
Specializes in depression glass and post Depression-era glassware.

Experts

Gene Florence
P.O. Box 22186
Lexington, KY 40522-2186
ph: 606-266-4615 or 352-742-3380
e-mail: jafo@iglou.com
web: http://www.geneflorence.com
Author of several books about Depression glass.

Margaret & Kenn Whitmyer
P.O. Box 30806
Columbus, OH 43230
e-mail: junquer9@idt.net
web: http://www.kandmantiques.com
Specializing in Depression era bedroom and bathroom glassware. Author of "Bedroom & Bathroom Glassware of the Depression Years."

Nadine Pankow
P.O. Box 207
Willow Springs, IL 60480

Kay Larsson
20825 102nd Ave., SE
Kent, WA 98031

Internet Resources

Anne Shatrau
DG Shopper Online
P.O. Box 3411
Albany, OR 97321-0716
ph: 541-928-6180
fax: 541-928-0202
e-mail: editor@dgshopper.com
web: http://www.dgshopper.com
The Internet's first Depression Era glassware magazine and marketplace; daily chat, weekly sales, monthly articles, online price guides; free one week trial; website also includes book sellers, periodicals and dealers.

Periodicals

Teri Steele, Ed.
Depression Glass Daze, Inc.
Newspaper: Daze, The
P.O. Box 57
Otisville, MI 48463-0057
ph: 810-631-4593 or 800-336-9927
fax: 810-631-4567
web: http://www.thedaze.com
A monthly newspaper catering to the dealers and collectors of glass, china and pottery from the 1920s and 1930s.

Domes

Suppliers

B & L Antiqurie, Inc.
P.O. Box 453
Lexington, MI 48450-0453
ph: 800-840-1110 or 810-359-8623
fax: 810-359-7498
Bent glass, convex portrait glass, antique flat glass, beveled mirror shapes, domes, and other specialty glass products for over 30 years.

D. Roberts
139 W. Montana Ave.
Glendale Heights, IL 60139
ph: 630-690-0848
fax: 630-690-2756
e-mail: deroberts@super-highway.net
web: http://www.geocities.com/RodeoDrive/2504/glassdomes.html
Leading supplier of show cases and shadow boxes for collectibles; also carries a wide selection of glass domes.

Duncan & Miller

Clubs/Associations

National Duncan Glass Society
Journal: National Duncan Glass Journal
525 Jefferson Ave.
P.O. Box 965
Washington, PA 15301
ph: 724-225-9950
e-mail: museum@nb.net
web: http://www.duncan-glass.com/lobby.htm
Focuses on the glassware produced by the Duncan & Miller Glass Co.

Collectors

Cliff McCaslin
Rocliff Communications
8422 N. Park Ct.
Kansas City, MO 64155
ph: 816-436-7719
fax: 816-436-6955
e-mail: rocliff@unicom.net
Wants to buy Duncan and Duncan-Miller glass; all patterns.

Museums/Libraries

Duncan Miller Glass Museum
525 Jefferson Ave.
P.O. Box 965
Washington, PA 15301
ph: 724-225-9950
e-mail: museum@nb.net
web: http://www.duncan-glass.com/lobby.htm
Museum has over 1400 pieces of Duncan glass in five display rooms; annual show and sale in July.

Durand

Dealers

Edward J. Meschi
129 Pinyard Rd.
Monroeville, NJ 08343-1870
ph: 609-358-7293
fax: 609-358-7789
e-mail: emfinearts@yahoo.com
Buys and sells Durand art glass; wants original sales catalogs for Durand Art Glass which operated under the name of Vineland Flint Glass Co. in the 1920s; author of "Durand - The Man and His Glass."

Early American

Auction Services

Norman C. Heckler
Norman C. Heckler & Company
79 Bradford Corner Rd.
Woodstock Valley, CT 06282-2002
ph: 860-974-1634
fax: 860-974-2003
e-mail: heckler@neca.com
web: http://www.heckler auction.com/
Specializes in the sale of early glass and bottles; Heckler & Co. sold a single bottle for $66,000 at auction in 1993.

Clubs/Associations

Walter B. Moore
Early American Glass Traders
RD 5 Box 638
Milford, DE 19963-9805
ph: 302-422-0932
e-mail: wmoore53@aol.com
Association of collectors of early American pressed glass who are interested in improving their collections by trading or selling their duplicates amongst themselves.

Collectors

Calvin L. Hackeman
8865 Olde Mill Run
Washington, DC 20010-6132
ph: 703-368-6982 or 703-847-7530
fax: 703-848-9583
e-mail: calcoolege@aol.com
Serious advanced collector of Hawaiian Ley by Higbee; wants hard to find or unusual pieces; also interested in purchasing colored Flint Glass, especially Sandwich items.

Experts

Jamie Houdeshell
16255 Normandy South
Perrysburg, OH 43551
ph: 419-872-1966
Buys, sells, appraises and specializes in antique bottles and early American glass.

Museums/Libraries

Sandwich Glass Museum
Newsletter: Cullet, The
129 Main St.
P.O. Box 103
Sandwich, MA 02453-0103
ph: 508-888-0251
The museum preserves and displays the glass manufactured in Sandwich 1825-1907.

Periodicals

David & Linda Arman
Magazine: China & Glass Quarterly
P.O. Box 39
Portsmouth, RI 02871-0039
ph: 401-841-8403
fax: 401-841-8403
e-mail: info@oaklandpublications.com
web: http://oaklandpublications.com/new%20pubs.html
Deals with the fields of English ceramics 1750-1865 (Historical Staffordshire, Pratt Ware, Lustre, Figures, transferware) and Early American glass 1750-1880 (blown three mold, freeblown, pattern molded, pressed, paperweights.)

Elegant

(see also GLASS, Cambridge; GLASS, Crystal; GLASS, Duncan & Miller; GLASS, Fostoria; GLASS, Heisey; GLASS, Imperial; GLASS, Tiffin)

Dealers

Jay Adams
248 Lakeview Ave., Ste. 208
Clifton, NJ 07011
ph: 973-365-5970
fax: 973-471-5323
e-mail: jadams7811@aol.com
Specializing in Depression era glass and china: wants to buy elegant glass such as Cambridge, Tiffin, Fostoria and others; send SASE with wants; will search and keep want list on file; best to call 6-11 EST.; mail order only.

Christie McCann
Always Available Antiques & Collectibles
3019 Winter Pine Ct.
Fairfax, VA 22031
ph: 703-385-0551
e-mail: olga@erols.com
web: http://www.erols.com/aaac
Specializes in elegant, Depression and kitchen glassware.

Allan & Cathy Griggs
Chinamates
1673 Lakecrest Dr.
Sullivan, IN 47882-9585
ph: 800-726-0345 or 812-268-6411
fax: 812-268-6411
e-mail: chinamates@viaduct.custom.net
Stocks and locates Fostoria, Gorham, Lenox, Wedgwood crystal; send wants; SASE; mail order only; members of Fostoria Glass Society of America.

Kelly O'Kane
Elegant American Glass
P.O. Box 16303
Saint Paul, MN 55116-0303
e-mail: eag@wavefront.com
web: http://www.visi.com/~eag
Author of "Tiffin Glassmasters: the Modern Years," which identifies all artware production at Tiffin from 1938 to 1984; dealer in elegant American glass (all major companies), and collector of Tiffin Modern glass.

Constance Crow
Crow's Nest Antiques - CyberGlass Shop
1601 S. IH 35, Ste. 400
Round Rock, TX 78664
ph: 512-218-4290 or 512-918-1709
fax: 512-310-0680
e-mail: cnest@antiquetexas.com
web: http://www.antiquetexas.com/crow/
Specializes in elegant glassware from the depression era: Heisey, Cambridge, Fostoria, Tiffin, Morgantown, etc.; has large inventory of rare and not-so-rare American elegant glassware.

Experts

Genevieve Belson
Junk General Store, The
Trade Mart - Booth 10
2121 Sam Houston Tollway
Houston, TX 77043
ph: 713-468-2608
web: http://www.trademartantiques.com/junkgeneral.htm
Specializes in 20th century glassware; Fostoria, Cambridge, Tiffin, Depression era, etc.

Matching Services

China By Pattern International Matching Service
P.O. Box 129
Farmington, CT 06034-0129
ph: 203-678-7079
Locating crystal & glassware: Fostoria, Cambridge, etc.

Florence & Jay Solito
Solito
54 Old Stafford Rd.
Tolland, CT 06084
ph: 860-872-3294
Tiffin, Morgantown, Imperial, Fostoria, Depression glass, Cambridge, and other elegant glassware.

Fran Jay
Fran Jay's Glass
10 Church St.
Lambertville, NJ 08530-2102
ph: 609-397-1571
e-mail: kelly@glassshow.com
web: http://www.GlassShow.com
Cambridge, Depression glass, Fenton, Fostoria, Heisey, and other elegant glass companies; daily hours, also mail order.

Harry Weitkemper
China Finders
1-B South Holy Ave.
Highland Springs, VA 23075
ph: 888-244-6239 or 804-328-2897
Candlewick, Fostoria, Cambridge, Tiffin, Libby, etc.

Jerry Gallagher
Red Horse Inn Antiques
420 1st Ave. N.W.
Plainview, MN 55964-1213
ph: 507-534-3511
e-mail: Morgantown@aol.com
Specializes in matching glass by Cambridge, Fostoria, Morgantown, Heisey, Tiffin, Duncan and Fry; no European glass companies in stock.

Wayne Carpenter
Country Store, The
2156 S. 7th Street
Lincoln, NE 68502-3301
ph: 402-476-2254
Cambridge, Duncan Miller, Fenton, Fostoria, Heisey, Imperial, Tiffin, Westmoreland, Depression glass.

Joanne Copeland
Sweet Nothings
5533 S. 20th St.
Lincoln, NE 68512
ph: 402-420-1620
Specializes in Heisey, Tiffin, Fostoria, Cambridge, Hawkes.

Milbra's Crystal
P.O. Box 784
Cleburne, TX 76033-0784
ph: 817-645-6066 or 817-294-9837
e-mail: longseat@flash.net
web: http://www.dealersdirect.com/Dealer/LongSeate/
Crystal matching: Fostoria, Tiffin, Lenox & others; buy and sell; requests kept on file; send SASE for reply.

Michael Krumme
P.O. Box 48225
Los Angeles, CA 90048-0025
ph: 323-874-4527
e-mail: mkrumme@pacbell.net
Send detailed want list; searches for Cambridge, Heisey, Fostoria, Duncan-Miller, New Martinsville, Fenton, Tiffin, Imperial, Morgantown, and Paden City Glass; specializes in obscure and less-collected etched patterns.

Periodicals

Teri Steele, Ed.
Depression Glass Daze, Inc.
Newspaper: Daze, The
P.O. Box 57
Otisville, MI 48463-0057
ph: 810-631-4593 or 800-336-9927
fax: 810-631-4567
web: http://www.thedaze.com
A monthly newspaper catering to the dealers and collectors of glass, china and pottery from the 1920s and 1930s.

European

Auction Services

Ron Fox
Ron Fox Auctions
P.O. Box 4026
Farmingdale, NY 11735
ph: 516-661-8387
fax: 516-376-0916
e-mail: oz@webspan.net
Conducts periodic auctions of European glass: Bohemian and Germanic, cut and enameled.

Dealers

Ron Fox
P.O. Box 4026
Farmingdale, NY 11735
ph: 516-661-8387
fax: 516-376-0916
e-mail: oz@webspan.net
Wants old European glass: transparent or opaque enamel, wheel cut, engraved, overlay, iridescent, etc.

Fenton

Clubs/Associations

Fenton Art Glass Collectors of America, Inc.
Newsletter: Butterfly Net, The
P.O. Box 384
Williamstown, WV 26187
ph: 304-375-6196
fax: 304-375-4679
e-mail: dnielsen@csinet.net
web: http://www.collectoronline.com/club-FAGCA.html
FAGCA is a non-profit educational corporation dedicated to learning about Fenton art glass.

Bob Stein
National Fenton Glass Society
Newsletter: Fenton Flyer, The
P.O. Box 4008
Marietta, OH 45750-7008
ph: 614-374-3345
e-mail: nfgs@ee.net

Jack R. Skaw
Pacific Northwest Fenton Association
Newsletter: Fenton Nor'Wester
P.O. Box 881
Tillamook, OR 97141
ph: 503-254-7038
e-mail: The_Wizard@glasscastle.com
web: http://www.glasscastle.com/pnwfa.htm
Annual convention each June in Springfield, OR; check web page for membership details.

Collectors

Connie Fry
C. Frye & Company
ph: 330-745-7104 or 330-535-2500
fax: 330-745-9304
e-mail: murmaid44@aol.com
Avid collector of old and new Fenton glass.

John O. Burgess
10738 Harley Rd.
Lorton, VA 22079-3908
Wants pre-1970 Fenton art glass.

Dealers

Darcie Smith
17 Lobue Lane
Cheektowaga, NY 14225
ph: 716-685-0060
e-mail: puppet531@aol.com
web: http://www.puppetsglass.com/
Buys and sells Fenton art glass; also Westmoreland.

Jack R. Skaw
Glass Castle, The
8055 SE Taylor Ct.
Portland, OR 97215
ph: 503-254-7038
e-mail: The_Wizard@glasscastle.com
web: http://www.glasscastle.com
Buys and sells Fenton Art Glass both old and new; website is a fun place to visit.

Experts

Margaret & Kenn Whitmyer
P.O. Box 30806
Columbus, OH 43230
e-mail: junquer9@idt.net
web: http://www.kandmantiques.com
Author of two books on Fenton glassware.

Ferill J. Rice
302 Pheasant Run
Kaukauna, WI 54130-1802
ph: 414-788-4123 or 414-766-9176
Advisor to "Warman's Antiques & Collectibles Price Guide" and "Warman's Garage Sale & Flea Market Annual."

Man./Prod./Dist.

Ann Stull
Fenton Art Glass Company Gift Store
420 Caroline Ave.
Williamstown, WV 26187
ph: 304-375-7772
fax: 304-375-6459
Retail outlet for replacement pieces still in stock; also many discontinued items still available for purchase; knowledge of old Fenton glass.

James Measell
Fenton Art Glass Company, The
Newsletter: Glass Messenger
700 Elizabeth St.
Williamstown, WV 26187-1028
ph: 304-375-6122 or 800-249-4527
fax: 304-375-6459
e-mail: askfenton@fentonartglass.com
web: http://www.fentonartglass.com/
Manufacturer of unique art glass such as Burmese and Rosalene; currently manufactures plates, figurines, bells, ornaments and a "Connoisseur Collection."

Periodicals

Ferill J. Rice
Newsletter: Butterfly Net
302 Pheasant Run
Kaukauna, WI 54130-1802
ph: 414-788-4123 or 414-766-9176
Published six times per year; advisor to "Warman's Antiques & Collectibles Price Guide" and "Warman's Garage Sale & Flea Market Annual."

Findlay

Clubs/Associations

Marilyn Jackson
Collectors of Findlay Glass
Newsletter: Melting Pot
P.O. Box 256
Findlay, OH 45839-0256
ph: 419-424-0332
Club for members to share information about Findlay Glass and the current activity in the marketplace; quarterly newsletter.

Dealers

Jennifer Payne
Gifts In Time
540 S. Main St.
Findlay, OH 45840
ph: 419-422-7227
fax: 419-422-3824
Buys and sells Findlay pattern glass.

Fire-King

Clubs/Associations

Dane & Debbie Dane
Fire-King Collectors Club
1406 E. 14th St.
Des Moines, IA 50316
ph: 515-265-6667
e-mail: ddj100@aol.com

Flowers

Museums/Libraries

Botanical Museum of Harvard University, The Blaschka Collection
26 Oxford St.
Cambridge, MA 02138
ph: 617-495-2326
fax: 617-495-5667
Lifelike handcrafted glass replicas of plants and flowers.

Fostoria

Clubs/Associations

Clifford Bucy
Fostoria Glass Society of America, The
Newsletter: Facets of Fostoria
P.O. Box 826
Moundsville, WV 26041-0826
ph: 304-845-9188 or 304-845-2170
e-mail: mailme@fostoriaglass.org
web: http://www.fostoriaglass.org/

Melvin Murray
Fostoria Glass Association
109 N. Main St.
Fostoria, OH 44830
e-mail: mmurray419@aol.com

Theresa Ujfalusi
Fostoria Glass Collectors
Newsletter: Fostoria Reflections
P.O. Box 1625
Orange, CA 92668
ph: 949-770-4088
e-mail: fgcglass@aol.com
web: http://www.jcweise.com/fgc.htm
A nonprofit organization dedicated to the study and preservation of Fostoria glass as well as all American handmade glassware.

Dealers

Allan & Cathy Griggs
Chinamates
1673 Lakecrest Dr.
Sullivan, IN 47882-9585
ph: 800-726-0345 or 812-268-6411
fax: 812-268-6411
e-mail: chinamates@viaduct.custom.net
Stock and locate Fostoria glassware; mail order only; call or write; SASE; send wants; member of Fostoria Glass Society of America.

Penny Drucker
Mother Drucker's
P.O. Box 50261
Irvine, CA 92619-0261
ph: 888-637-8253 or 949-551-5529
fax: 949-551-2116
e-mail: Penny@Motherdruckers.com
web: http://www.motherdruckers.com/
Carries large selection of Fostoria glassware.

Experts

Ann M. Kerr
P.O. Box 437
Sidney, OH 45365-0437
ph: 937-492-6369
fax: 937-492-6369
e-mail: raintree@bright.net
Author of a book on Fostoria glass.

Juanita Williams
P.O. Box 1624
Jacksonville, OR 97530
e-mail: juanita@webvenues.com
web: http://www.webvenues.com/fostoria/

Matching Services

China By Pattern International Matching Service
P.O. Box 129
Farmington, CT 06034-0129
ph: 203-678-7079
Send SASE to locate/match Fostoria and other stemware and crystal pieces. No charge to list/search for wanted items. Send quantity, shape, photocopy, size, etc.

Charlotte Krauch
Charlotte's Glass Reflections
1516 Florida Blvd.
Bradenton, FL 34207
ph: 800-221-2953 or 941-756-1940
Specializes in Fostoria glassware; all discontinued patterns; locating service; send wants; SASE for reply.

Fostoria Registry
1060 Crestline Dr.
Crete, NE 68333
ph: 402-826-2622
Matching service for Fostoria from 1940 to 1982; locating service for items in stock; SASE required for reply.

Museums/Libraries

Clifford Bucy
Fostoria Glass Museum
P.O. Box 826
Moundsville, WV 26041-0826
ph: 304-845-9188 or 304-845-2170
e-mail: mailme@fostoriaglass.org
web: http://www.fostoriaglass.org/

Gay Fad Studios

Experts

Donna McGrady
154 Peters Ave.
Lancaster, OH 43130-3658
ph: 740-653-0376
Collects and specializes in glassware decorated from 1945-1964 by the Gay Fad Studios of Lancaster, Ohio; Gay Fad was known for applying hand decorations to many pieces of glass including Fire King.

Goofus

Experts

Steve Gillespie
400 Martin Blvd.
Kansas City, MO 64118
ph: 888-452-5554
fax: 816-452-5554
e-mail: goofus@mid-west.net
Publisher of the "Goofus Glass Gazette", dealer and collector of goofus glass for over 30 years; developer of a Goofus Glass Museum; goofus glass advisor to price guides, books; writing an illustrated book on goofus glass & its history.

John Martin Davis, Jr.
2705 Swiss Ave.
Dallas, TX 75204
ph: 214-823-9367
Writing a book about goofus glass.

Internet Resources

David & Maureen Ballentine
639 E. Amelia St.
Orlando, FL 32803
e-mail: gballens@sundial.net
web: http://sundial.net/~gballens/
The only known internet website dedicated specifically to Goofus glass; subscribe online to an goofus glass email newsletter.

Periodicals

Steve Gillespie
Newsletter: Goofus Glass Gazette
400 Martin Blvd.
Kansas City, MO 64118
ph: 888-452-5554
fax: 816-452-5554
e-mail: goofus@mid-west.net
Quarterly newsletter for goofus collectors; educational articles, free classifieds with subscription.

Gorham

Man./Prod./Dist.

Gorham, Inc.
100 Lenox Dr.
Lawrenceville, NJ 08648
ph: 609-896-2800 or 800-635-3669
web: http://www.lenox.com
Sterling and stainless steel flatware, sterling and silverplated hollowware; fine china, crystal stemware, giftware and dolls; a division of Lenox Brands.

Greentown

Clubs/Associations

National Greentown Glass Association
Newsletter: National Greentown Glass Association Newsletter
P.O. Box 107
Greentown, IN 46936-0107
ph: 765-628-7363
web: http://birch.palni.edu/%7Elhurst/gplhome/glassass.htm
Annual meetings are held 2nd Saturday in June at the National

Greentown Glass Museum, Greentown, IN.

Collectors

LeAnne Milliser
19596 Glendale Ave.
South Bend, IN 46637-1814
ph: 219-272-1184

Dealers

Jerry Garrett
Jerry's Antiques & Postcards
1807 West Madison St.
Kokomo, IN 46901-1829
ph: 765-457-5256
Buys and sells Greentown glass as well as chocolate glass made by other National Company factories.

Experts

Jim & Mira Houdeshell
JMJ Antiques
1801 N. Main St.
Findlay, OH 45840-3815
ph: 419-423-2895 or 419-424-4551
fax: 419-424-6974

Museums/Libraries

Gary Buckley
Greentown Glass Museum
112 N. Meridian
P.O. Box 161
Greentown, IN 46936-0161
ph: 765-628-6206
web: http://birch.palni.edu/%7Elhurst/gplhome/musmhist.htm
An exhibit from the old Indiana Tumbler & Goblet Co. (1894-1903.)

Grand Rapids Public Museum
272 Pearl St. NW
Grand Rapids, MI 49504-5371
ph: 616-456-3977
fax: 616-456-3873
e-mail: staff@grmuseum.org
web: http://www.grmuseum.org/
Large collection of Greentown Glass; publisher of the book "Greentown Glass - the Indiana Tumbler & Goblet Company."

Hazel-Atlas

Collectors

Kenneth G. Sloan
5707 S. Kenwood
Chicago, IL 60637-1718
ph: 773-752-4247
Wants to buy Hazel-Atlas company catalogs, re-use containers and packers, especially tumblers.

Heisey

Clubs/Associations

"Butch" Jones
National Capital Heisey Collectors
Newsletter: Heisey Herald
P.O. Box 23
Clinton, MD 20735
ph: 301-505-0041
Purpose is to study and preserve Heisey glassware; meetings held second Monday of each month except July and August; programs on Heisey patterns, pieces, colors, etc.

Heisey Collectors of America, Inc.
Newsletter: Heisey News, The
169 W. Church St.
Newark, OH 43055
ph: 740-345-2932
fax: 740-345-9638
e-mail: heisey@infinet.com
web: http://www.ahheisey.com/mus.htm
Every production color and pattern is on display in the King House, built in 1831.

Bay State Heisey Collectors Club
169 W. Church St.
Newark, OH 43055
ph: 740-345-2932
e-mail: heisey@infinet.com
web: http://www.ahheisey.com

Collectors

Ralph & Sandra McKelvey
P.O. Box 102
Plymouth, OH 44865
ph: 419-935-0338
Collectors of Heisey glass; also sells books about Heisey.

Cliff McCaslin
Rocliff Communications
8422 N. Park Ct.
Kansas City, MO 64155
ph: 816-436-7719
fax: 816-436-6955
e-mail: rocliff@unicom.net
Wants to buy glassware by Heisey.

Dealers

Rhoda & David Curley
ph: 800-972-2775
e-mail: mostlyheisey@webtv.com
web: http://sony.inergy.com/mostlyheisey/
Specializing in Heisey glassware since 1970.

Ward Stewart
Stewart's Antiques
1000 Coolidge
Lafayette, LA 70503-2336
ph: 318-232-2957

Robert Henicksman
Classic Glass
916 Q St.
Sacramento, CA 95814
ph: 916-448-0840
Buys and sells all patterns of Heisey glass; also maintains want lists and will search for customer needs.

Museums/Libraries

National Heisey Glass Museum, The
169 W. Church St.
Newark, OH 43055
ph: 740-345-2932
fax: 740-345-9638
e-mail: heisey@infinet.com
web: http://www.ahheisey.com/mus.htm
Owned and operated by Heisey Collectors of America; hundreds of patterns of glass made by A.H. Heisey & Co. 1895-1957 on display.

Imperial

Clubs/Associations

Cliff McCaslin
National Imperial Glass Collectors Society
Newsletter: Glasszette
P.O. Box 534
Bellaire, OH 43906
ph: 816-436-7719
fax: 816-436-6955
e-mail: rocliff@unicom.net
web: http://www.imperialglass.org
Members interested in the history and glassware produced by the Imperial Glass Corp.; conducts an annual convention offering seminars, show and sale, and "members only" auction; establishing an Imperial museum.

Collectors

Kathy Doub
5359 Iron Pen Place
Columbia, MD 21044-1811
ph: 410-995-1254
e-mail: capguns-igmg@erols.com

Cliff McCaslin
Rocliff Communications
8422 N. Park Ct.
Kansas City, MO 64155
ph: 816-436-7719
fax: 816-436-6955
e-mail: rocliff@unicom.net

Dealers

Cliff McCaslin
Rocliff Communications
8422 N. Park Ct.
Kansas City, MO 64155
ph: 816-436-7719
fax: 816-436-6955
e-mail: rocliff@unicom.net
Wants to buy all patterns of Imperial glass.

Penny Drucker
Mother Drucker's
P.O. Box 50261
Irvine, CA 92619-0261
ph: 888-637-8253 or 949-551-5529
fax: 949-551-2116
e-mail: Penny@Motherdruckers.com
web: http://www.motherdruckers.com/
Always changing inventory of color, cut, rare and common pieces; send LSASE for list.

Experts

Myrna & Bob Garrison
Collector's Loot
3816 Hastings Dr.
Arlington, TX 76013-1900
ph: 817-275-6342
fax: 817-275-6342
e-mail: 73074.3655@compuserve.com
Authors of "Imperial Cape Cod Tradition to Treasure", 2nd Edition, $16.45 ppd. plus $1.16 tax for TX residents; and of "Imperial's Boudoir, Etcetera", 1996, $29.95 ppd. plus #2.09 for TX residents; available from authors.

Misc. Services

Cliff McCaslin
Rocliff Communications
8422 N. Park Ct.
Kansas City, MO 64155
ph: 816-436-7719
fax: 816-436-6955
e-mail: rocliff@unicom.net
Offers videotapes on popular glassware patterns of the Depression era, Imperial Candlewick, Imperial Slag, Imperial Cape Cod.

Italian

(see also MODERNISM)

Clubs/Associations

William Scott Bata
Murano Glass Society
32040 Mt. Hermon Rd.
Salisbury, MD 21804
ph: 410-546-5881
fax: 410-546-5881
e-mail: willmurano@aol.com
web: http://www.Murano.netnz.com/bulletinboard.html

Collectors

Tom Fry
C. Frye & Company
ph: 330-745-7104 or 330-535-2500
fax: 330-745-9304
e-mail: murmaid44@aol.com
Avid collector of Italian glass including Murano glass clowns; plans to travel to Murano and write book on the subject; has extensive collection of clowns.

Dealers

Vetri Italian Glass
P.O. Box 191
Fort Lee, NJ 07024
ph: 201-969-0373
fax: 201-969-0373
Carries a large selection of Italian glass; also sells books on Italian glass.

William Scott Bata
Glassfinders
32040 Mt. Hermon Rd.
Salisbury, MD 21804
ph: 410-546-5881
e-mail: willmurano@aol.com
web: http://ourworld.compuserve.com/homepages/glassfinder
Collector, expert, dealer specializes in Venetian and Italian glass from the island of Murano; 19th century to present day; buying and selling.

David Huffman
P.O. Box 26151
Charlotte, NC 28221-6151
ph: 800-327-9654 or 704-598-7720
e-mail: batant@ix.netcom.com
Wants to buy Italian glass.

Kenneth P. Lesko
Kenneth Paul Lesko 20th Century Decorative Arts
P.O. Box 16099
Rocky River, OH 44116-0099
ph: 216-356-0275
fax: 216-331-1280
e-mail: kplesko@aol.com
web: http://members.aol.com/kplesko/kplesko.html
Specialist in Italian glass 1920-1970; wants to buy Venini, Matinuzzi, Scarpa, Seguso, Barovier, Cenedese, A. Toso/Dino Martens, MVM Cappelin, CVM, Avem, Salir, Nason, Fratelli Toso, Salviati, Vistosi, A. Barbini.

Ara Tavitian
Retro Gallery
524 1/2 N. La Brea Ave.
Los Angeles, CA 90036-2016
ph: 213-936-5261
fax: 213-936-5262
e-mail: retroglass@aol.com
web: http://www.retroglass.com/
Art glass from the 1940s through the 1960s; specializing in Italian and Scandinavian glass.

Experts

Howard Lockwood
P.O. Box 191
Fort Lee, NJ 07024-0191
ph: 201-692-9780
fax: 201-692-9780
Buys, sells and specializes in Venini and other Italian glass.

Dan Ripley
Dan Ripley Antiques
907 E. Michigan St., Ste. 102
Indianapolis, IN 46202
ph: 317-955-5900
fax: 317-630-9384
e-mail: dnripley@iei.net
web: http://www.danripley.com
A most experienced dealer; specializes in Italian and Scandinavian glass and ceramics; thousands of pieces sold privately and at auction; guest speaker at International Society of Appraisers' convention.

Periodicals

Howard Lockwood
Newsletter: VETRI: Italian Glass News
P.O. Box 191
Fort Lee, NJ 07024-0191
ph: 201-692-9780
fax: 201-692-9780
Quarterly newsletter for the collector, museum curator, and dealer in 20th century Italian glass.

Kosta Boda

Dealers

Lladro Connection, A
30 NE 1st Street
Miami, FL 33132
ph: 800-984-5586
e-mail: illum1@aol.com
web: http://www.illumcollectibles.com/
Specializing in current and retired Swarovski and Lladro; also carries a complete line of Lalique and Kosta Boda.

Man./Prod./Dist.

Kosta Boda USA Ltd. (Div. of Orrefors)
140 Bradford Dr.
Berlin, NJ 08009
ph: 609-768-5400
fax: 609-768-9726
e-mail: orrefors@franzenfalk.se
web: http://www.orrefors.se/ofkb/eng/
Swedish full lead crystal glassware, giftware and accessories.

Lalique

Auction Services

Amory Spizzirri, Client Svc.
William Doyle Galleries
175 E. 87th St.
New York, NY 10128-2205
ph: 212-427-2730
fax: 212-369-0892
e-mail: info@doylegalleries.com
web: http://www.doylegalleries.com
Holds over 50 auctions annually of furniture and decorations, paintings and sculpture, jewelry, books and prints, couture and textiles, 20th century art & design, majolica, Lalique, Asian works of art and other specialty categories.

Clubs/Associations

Lalique Collectors Society
Newsletter: Lalique
400 Veterans Blvd.
Carlstadt, NJ 07072-2704
ph: 800-274-7825
fax: 201-939-4492
e-mail: info@lalique.com
web: http://www.lalique.com/lcs.htm
Focuses on the collectibles issued by Lalique North America.

Collectors

Jeff Myers
P.O. Box 26151
Charlotte, NC 28221-6151
ph: 800-327-9654 or 704-598-7720
e-mail: batant@ix.netcom.com
Wants to buy R. LALIQUE glass; also wants Galle, Daum and Tiffany glass.

Dealers

Shai H. Bandmann
Paul Stamati Gallery
1050 2nd Ave.
New York, NY 10022
ph: 212-754-4533
fax: 718-271-6958
e-mail: mail@rene-lalique.com
web: http://rene-lalique.com/
A leading dealer and expert in works by Rene Lalique.

David Huffman
P.O. Box 26151
Charlotte, NC 28221-6151
ph: 800-327-9654 or 704-598-7720
e-mail: batant@ix.netcom.com
Wants to buy R. LALIQUE glass; also wants Loetz, Daum, and Italian glass.

Lladro Connection, A
30 NE 1st Street
Miami, FL 33132
ph: 800-984-5586
e-mail: illum1@aol.com
web: http://www.illumcollectibles.com/
Specializing in current and retired Swarovski and Lladro; also carries a complete line of Lalique and Kosta Boda.

A.D. & Pat Clay
Clemons-Eicken Fine European Imports
6166 N. Scottsdale Rd., #204
Scottsdale, AZ 85253
ph: 602-998-9042 or 800-250-5423
fax: 602-998-3755
Carries Lladro, Armani, Boehm, Lalique, Cybis.

Experts

Nicholas Dawes
67 East 11th St.
New York, NY 10003-4613
ph: 212-473-5111
fax: 212-353-3845
e-mail: nmdawes@aol.com
web: http://www.pbs.org/wgbh/pages/roadshow/appraisers/dawes.html
Buys, sells and specializes in pre-war works by Rene Lalique; author of "Lalique Glass" (Crown Publishers, 1986).

Carole Hibel
Art & Antiques
131-B Broadview Road
Woodstock, NY 12498
ph: 914-679-2966 or 800-426-3357
fax: 914-679-9101
Wants to buy R. Lalique art glass.

Randy Monsen
Monsen & Baer Inc.
P.O. Box 529
Vienna, VA 22183-0529
ph: 703-938-2129
fax: 703-242-1357
e-mail: monsenbaer@erols.com
Wants perfume bottles by Lalique; prefers pre-1940 pieces by Rene Lalique but will consider later pieces; premium prices paid for early bottles with their original boxes.

Man./Prod./Dist.

Lalique North America, Inc.
400 Veterans Blvd.
Carlstadt, NJ 07072-2704
ph: 201-939-4199
e-mail: info@lalique.com
web: http://www.lalique.com/
French porcelain, crystal, stemware, dinnerware and giftwares; distributor of Lalique porcelain, crystal, jewelry, silk scarves, and "parfum" in U.S. (crystal patterns are never discontinued.)

Lenox

Man./Prod./Dist.

Lenox China & Crystal Consumer Service
100 Lenox Dr.
Lawrenceville, NJ 08648
ph: 609-896-2800 or 800-635-3669
web: http://www.lenox.com
Offers Matching Services List of dealers who offer replacements for current of discontinued Lenox items; also gives insurance estimates.

Lenox Shop
P.O. Box 1115
Mt. Pleasant, PA 15666
ph: 800-842-3681
Factory where crystal is made. Call to place custom orders for inactive pattern replacements.

Matching Services

Carol Ulrey
Unique Antiques
P.O. Box 15815
San Diego, CA 92175-5815
ph: 619-281-8650
fax: 619-282-8407
e-mail: culrey@webcc.net
Specializing in china matching: Haviland, old French and American; also Lenox china and crystal.

Lesley Hall
Lesley's Lenox
3020 Issaquah Pine Lake Rd., Ste. 322
Issaquah, WA 98029
ph: 425-391-2330 or 800-553-6693
fax: 425-391-3383
web: http://www.lesleyslenox.com
Lenox only; specializing in discontinued patterns of Lenox elegant stemware, casual crystal and barware; brochure available;

founding member of Haviland Collectors International Foundation.

Lotton

Dealers

Lotton Glass Gallery
900 N. Michigan Ave.
Chicago, IL 60601
ph: 312-664-6203

Man./Prod./Dist.

Lotton Glass Studio
24760 Country Lane
Crete, IL 60417
ph: 800-661-0950

Mary Gregory

Experts

Bob Truitt
5120 White Flint Dr.
Kensington, MD 20895-1037
ph: 301-929-2539
Author of "Mary Gregory Glassware."

Milk

Clubs/Associations

Helen Storey
National Milk Glass Collectors Society
Newsletter: Opaque News
46 Almond Dr.
Hershey, PA 17033-1759
ph: 717-534-8585
fax: 717-520-0965
e-mail: hdstorey@aol.com
Dedicated to the study, collection and preservation of milk glass items.

Collectors

John Vosevich
7418 Apple Cross
Plainfield, IN 46168
ph: 317-272-4959

June & Stan Sohl
P.O. Box 2291
Salina, KS 67402
ph: 785-823-1320 or 785-823-6627

Arlene Johnson
1113 Birchwood Dr.
Garland, TX 75043

Experts

Frank Chiarenza
39 West Main St.
Meriden, CT 06451-4110
ph: 203-639-9778
Director of the Frank Chiarenza Museum of Glass, co-author with James Slater of "The Milk Glass Book," a frequent contributor to glass publications, and former president of the National Milk Glass Collectors Society.

Barbara Joyce Kaye
P.O. Box 20346
Cherokee Station
New York, NY 10021-0065
Author of "White Gold: A Primer for Previously Unlisted Milk Glass, Book 1" (out of print) and "White Gold: A Primer for Previously Unlisted Milk Glass, Book II."

April M. Tvorak
P.O. Box 94
Warren Center, PA 18851
ph: 570-395-3775
e-mail: april@epix.net
Buys and sells pink milk glass including Jeanette, Cambridge, Fenton, Westmoreland, etc.

Myrna & Bob Garrison
Collector's Loot
3816 Hastings Dr.
Arlington, TX 76013-1900
ph: 817-275-6342
fax: 817-275-6342
e-mail: 73074.3655@compuserve.com
Authors of "Imperial's Vintage Milk Glass", 1992; available from the authors for $18.70 ppd. plus $1.32 tax for TX residents; also authors of "Imperial's Boudoir, Etcetera," $29.95 ppd. plus $2.09 tax for TX residents.

Phyllis Osjecki
Phyllis'
P.O. Box 792
Canyonville, OR 97417
ph: 541-839-4135 or 541-839-6151
Buys, sells, and appraises milk glass.

Museums/Libraries

Houston Museum of Decorative Arts, The
201 High St.
Chattanooga, TN 37403
ph: 423-267-7176
e-mail: houston@chattanooga.net
web: http://www.chattanooga.net/houston/
Contains one of the world's finest collections of antique glass and ceramics.

Moser

Experts

Gary Baldwin
Touch of Glass, A
P.O. Box 213
Simpsonville, MD 21150-0213
ph: 410-997-8425 or 410-765-2439
Buys, sells and collects European enameled glass; co-author with Lee Carno of "Moser - Artistry in Glass."

Man./Prod./Dist.

Bohemia-Moser
110 00 Praha 1, NA
Prikope, 12
Czechoslovakia
The Moser factory.

Mount Washington

Clubs/Associations

Mount Washington Art Glass Society
Magazine: Mount Washington Art Glass Newsletter, The
P.O. Box 24094
Fort Worth, TX 76124-1094
ph: 817-457-3246 or 817-457-9315
fax: 817-451-9357
A national society dedicated to the appreciation, preservation and study of the art glass wares made by the Mount Washington Glass Co. from 1870 to 1900.

Collectors

Henry Tyler
13 Bellevue Dr.
Saint Petersburg, FL 33706-1201

Phillip T. Egelston
P.O. Box 748
Jonesboro, IL 62952-0748
ph: 618-833-2862
Consultant, broker, author, expert; founding editor "The Mount Washington Art Glass Review"; has written a book on Mother-of-pearl satin glass featuring 40 patterns plus information on decoration, reproduction, rarity.

Old Morgantown

Clubs/Associations

Old Morgantown Glass Collectors' Guild
Newsletter: Topics
P.O. Box 894
Morgantown, WV 26507-0894
ph: 304-292-9400
e-mail: reillyjoanne@hotmail.com
Dedicated to the education of members and the preservation of Old Morgantown glass through the establishment of a museum in Morgantown, WV.

Jerry Gallagher
Morgantown Collectors of America, Inc.
Newsletter: Morgantown Newscaster, The
420 1st Ave. N.W.
Plainview, MN 55964-1213
ph: 507-534-3511
e-mail: Morgantown@aol.com
The M.C.A. goals are to research and preserve the history of The Old Morgantown Glass Company, West Virginia.

Orrefors

Man./Prod./Dist.

Orrefors, Inc.
140 Bradford Dr.
Berlin, NJ 08009
ph: 609-768-5400
fax: 609-768-9726
e-mail: orrefors@franzenfalk.se
web: http://www.orrefors.se/ofkb/eng/
Crystal stemware and giftware, bar accessories, Christmas ornaments, and art glass.

Paden City

Experts

Michael Krumme
P.O. Box 48225
Los Angeles, CA 90048-0025
ph: 323-874-4527
e-mail: mkrumme@pacbell.net
Author/researcher seeks any printed information regarding the Paden City Glass Mfg. Co. of Paden City, WV; 1916-1952 catalogs, trade journal ads, previously published articles; please price & describe; no Paden City Pottery Co., please.

Pairpoint

Man./Prod./Dist.

Valerie Kelly
Pairpoint Glass Works
851 Sandwich Rd.
P.O. Box 515
Sagamore, MA 02561
ph: 508-888-2344 or 800-899-0953
fax: 508-888-3537
Blowing room open to visitors; catalog $2 (refundable.)

Pattern

Clubs/Associations

Fred Phelps
Early American Pattern Glass Society
Newsletter: News Journal, The
P.O. Box 266
Colesburg, IA 52035
ph: 319-365-8894 or 319-856-2025
fax: 319-856-5800
e-mail: petcoff@earthlink.net
web: http://home.earthlink.net/~petcoff/EAPGS.html
Devoted solely to pattern glass.

Collectors

Fred Phelps
P.O. Box 217
Colesburg, IA 52035-0217
ph: 319-856-2025
Specializes in early American pattern glass.

Dealers

Phyllis Petcoff
Phyllis Petcoff Antique Glassware
7885 Columbia Street
Dyer, IN 46311
ph: 219-365-8894
e-mail: petcoff@earthlink.net
web: http://home.earthlink.net/~petcoff/
Buys and sells primarily American glassware dating from 1850 through 1920; also some out-of-print books on the subject.

Glenda Ridgway
P.O. Box 231
Anna, IL 62906
ph: 618-833-7971

Bill & Elaine Henderson
EAPG Inc.
1220 Monroe, NE
Albuquerque, NM 87110
ph: 505-268-0819
fax: 505-266-7204
e-mail: ElaineEAPG@aol.com
web: http://www.patternglass.com/
Pattern matching service exclusively for early American pattern glass tableware, 1850-1910; sellers may list their inventory in a computer database at no charge; free computer searches for collectors.

Experts

Dori Miles
Pattern Glass Historian
B20
Crown Point, NY 12928
ph: 518-597-3432
e-mail: dori@Capital.Net
Buys, sells, appraises, collects, specializes in pattern glass; over 13,000 pieces in stock; lid and base matching service; want lists wanted; former pattern glass editor for Warman's; contributing editor for Glass Collectors Digest.

John & Alice Ahlfeld
2634 Royal Rd.
Lancaster, PA 17603
ph: 717-397-7313
fax: 717-397-7931
e-mail: ahlfelds@aol.com
Advisor to "Warman's Antiques & Collectibles Price Guide."

Mildred & Ralph Lechner
P.O. Box 554
Mechanicsville, VA 23111-0554
ph: 804-737-3347
Feature writers on antique glassware for "AntiqueWeek"; authors of "The World of Salt Shakers," Vols. 1, 2 & 3; Victorian art and pattern glass reproduction identification experts; collectors of art and pattern glass salt & pepper shakers.

Periodicals

David Richardson
Antique Publications
Magazine: Glass Collector's Digest
217 Union St.
P.O. Box 553
Marietta, OH 45750-0553
ph: 800-533-3433 or 740-373-6146
fax: 740-373-6917
e-mail: info@antiquepublications.com
web: http://www.antiquepublications.com/
A bi-monthly magazine focusing on the glass collecting specialties; articles and ads feature lots of color photography.

Pattern (Moon & Star)

Clubs/Associations

Barbara Jeffries, Treas.
Society of Moon & Star Pattern Glass
200 East Olson Rd.
Midland, MI 48640
ph: 517-631-2543

PHOENIX

Clubs/Associations

Tom Jiamachello, Sec.
PHOENIX & Consolidated Glass Collectors' Club
Newsletter: PHOENIX & Consolidated Collectors News & Views
41 River View Dr.
Essex Junction, VT 05452
ph: 802-878-2692 or 412-561-3379
e-mail: TOPofVT@aol.com
web: http://www.collectoronline.com/club-PCGCC-wp.html
For collectors/dealers of art glass produced by PHOENIX GLASS Co. of Monaca, PA and Consolidated Lamp & Shade Co. of Coraopolis, PA; bi-monthly newsletter - market trends, repro. alerts, buy/sell ads, price reports, articles.

Collectors

Kathy Hansen
1621 Princess Ave.
Pittsburgh, PA 15216-3738
ph: 412-561-3379
e-mail: hansen@pps.pgh.pa.us
Wants to buy PHOENIX GLASS vases, bowls, boxes, oil lamps, light shades, catalogs, ads, photos, postcards, Reuben-Line, Vollden Ware; compiling history of the PHOENIX GLASS Co., Monaca, PA, 1880 to present; seeks PG employees, collectors.

Barbara Norman
P.O. Box 251382
West Bloomfield, MI 48325-1382
ph: 248-855-7766
fax: 248-855-5224
Wants to buy Ruba Rombic, red or cased pieces of PHOENIX or Consolidated Art Glass, Catalonian, and Muncie Ruba Rombic.

Mark Lawyer
P.O. Box 3847
Edmond, OK 73083-3847
ph: 405-341-0020
e-mail: mcdd@flash.net

Scott Montroy
P.O. Box 11166
Fort Worth, TX 7611001166
ph: 817-927-5119
e-mail: connix@flash.net
web: http://www.flash.net/~connix
Previous editor of the "PHOENIX & Consolidated Glass Collectors News & Views" newsletter; current owner and moderator of the Internet email discussion group, "PHOENIX & Consolidated Art Glass Discussion List."

Dealers

Susan Frost
806 Rosedale Terrace
Austin, TX 78704-3159
ph: 512-447-2575 or 512-447-0407
e-mail: Reuter@io.com
web: http://www.io.com/~reuter/
Buys and sells PHOENIX & Consolidated glass.

Experts

Kathy Hansen
1621 Princess Ave.
Pittsburgh, PA 15216-3738
ph: 412-561-3379
e-mail: hansen@pps.pgh.pa.us
Wants to buy PHOENIX GLASS vases, bowls, boxes, oil lamps, light shades, catalogs, ads, photos, postcards, Reuben-Line, Vollden Ware; compiling history of the PHOENIX GLASS Co., Monaca, PA, 1880 to present; seeks PG employees, collectors.

Jack D. Wilson
3926 N. Keeler Ave.
Chicago, IL 60641-2915
ph: 773-282-9553
e-mail: jdwilson1@earthlink.net
web: http://home.earthlink.net/~jdwilson1/
Author of "PHOENIX & Consolidated Art Glass: 1926-1980"; features in-depth research, 48 color pages illustrating over 750 items (out of print); wants original Consolidated catalogs & company literature.

Pilgrim

Clubs/Associations

Pilgrim Art Glass Club
Newsletter: PAGC Notebook
P.O. Box 395
Ceredo, WV 25507
ph: 304-453-3553
fax: 304-453-6849
e-mail: pilgrim@ezwv.com
web: http://www.pilgrimglass.com/
Focuses on Pilgrim cameo/art glass.

Pilgrim Cranberry Glass Collectors Club
Newsletter: PCGCC Newsletter
P.O. Box 395
Ceredo, WV 25507
ph: 304-453-3553
fax: 304-453-6849
e-mail: pilgrim@ezwv.com
web: http://www.pilgrimglass.com/
For those interested in Pilgrim cranberry glass; club sponsored by the world's largest cranberry glass and "cameo" art glass manufacturer; free catalogs, advance notice of new offerings.

Man./Prod./Dist.

Shelly Adkins
Pilgrim Glass Corp.
P.O. Box 395
Ceredo, WV 25507
ph: 304-453-3553
fax: 304-453-6849
e-mail: pilgrim@ezwv.com
web: http://www.pilgrimglass.com/
The world's largest cranberry glass and "cameo" art glass manufacturer.

Post-WWII

Matching Services

April M. Tvorak
P.O. Box 94
Warren Center, PA 18851
ph: 570-395-3775
e-mail: april@epix.net
Buys, sells, matches any glassware from 1940-1970; please include SASE with all correspondence.

Periodicals

April M. Tvorak
Newsletter: 50's Flea!!!, The
P.O. Box 94
Warren Center, PA 18851
ph: 570-395-3775
e-mail: april@epix.net
Members interested in 1940s-1970s glass and other items; the yearly covers any kitchen glass subject from 1940-1970; free for members; please include SASE with all correspondence.

Pressed

Museums/Libraries

Schminck Memorial Museum
128 South E St.
Lakeview, OR 97630-1721
ph: 541-947-3134
Large collection of American pressed glass, 1830-1920.

Reed & Barton

Man./Prod./Dist.

Reed & Barton
144 W. Britannia St.
Taunton, MA 02780
ph: 508-824-6611 or 800-822-1824
fax: 508-822-7269
Produces china, crystal, silver, silverplate, and stainless flatware,

collectible plates, bells, dolls, ornaments and accessories.

Riverside

Experts

Cliff Gorham
Heartlights
P.O. Box 2962
Springfield, MO 65801
ph: 800-833-2007
fax: 417-473-6466
Author of "Riverside Glasswork of Wellsburg, WV 1879-1907," available from author for $35 ppd.; focuses on Riverside bar accessories, vases, bowls, decorative objects, presentation awards.

Rose Bowls

Clubs/Associations

Johanna & Sean Billings
Rose Bowl Collectors Club
Newsletter: Rose Bowl Collectors Club Newsletter
P.O. Box 244
Danielsville, PA 18038-0244
ph: 610-760-8134 or 610-760-1814
fax: 610-760-8142
e-mail: bankie@concentric.net
web: http://www.facets.net/facets/freeserv-edu/rosebowl/
Free sample newsletter; club helps collectors identify and appreciate both old and new rose bowls; newsletter buy and sell ads free to members.

Collectors

Johanna & Sean Billings
P.O. Box 244
Danielsville, PA 18038-0244
ph: 610-760-8134 or 610-760-1814
fax: 610-760-8142
e-mail: bankie@concentric.net
web: http://www.facets.net/facets/freeserv-edu/rosebowl/
Author of several articles on rose bowls.

Sandwich

Museums/Libraries

Sandwich Glass Museum
Journal: Acorn, The
129 Main St.
P.O. Box 103
Sandwich, MA 02453-0103
ph: 508-888-0251
The museum contains and studies glass associated with the Sandwich Factory era.

Scandinavian Art

Appraisers

William L. Geary
P.O. Box 2247
Colorado Springs, CO 80901-2247
ph: 719-527-0810
fax: 719-527-0810
e-mail: nordglass@aol.com
Appraiser of American, European art glass with a specialty in Scandinavian art glass; member of Appraisers Association of America; producer of video "Lyricism of Swedish Glass."

Dealers

Anita L. Grashof
Gallerie Ani'tiques
Stage House Village
Park & Front Streets
Scotch Plains, NJ 07076
ph: 908-322-4600 or 201-377-3032
fax: 973-765-9565
Buys, sells, appraises Swedish (Orrefors, Kosta, glass by Gate, Hald, Lindstand) and Finish (Karhula, Littala, glass by Wirkkala, Sarpaneva) art glass; also Finnish (Tittala, Karhula, Wirkkala, Sarpaneva).

Ara Tavitian
Retro Gallery
524 1/2 N. La Brea Ave.
Los Angeles, CA 90036-2016
ph: 213-936-5261
fax: 213-936-5262
e-mail: retroglass@aol.com
web: http://www.retroglass.com/
Art glass from the 1940s through the 1960s; specializing in Italian and Scandinavian glass.

Shoes

Clubs/Associations

Earlene Freeman
Miniature Shoe Collectors Club
P.O. Box 2390
Apple Valley, CA 92308-0045
ph: 760-868-5814

Collectors

J.P. (Phil) Jamieson
2546 Sinclair Road
Victoria, British Columbia V8N 1B8
Canada
ph: 250-477-3034
e-mail: jpj2@home.com
Collector of glass shoes and glass slippers, U.S. or European; also interested in glass hens-on-nests and Carnival glass.

Experts

Libby Yalom
Shoe Lady, The
P.O. Box 7146
Adelphi, MD 20787-7146
ph: 301-422-2026
fax: 301-422-0713
e-mail: libbyshoes@aol.com
Wants to buy glass and china slippers, shoes and boots; author of "Shoes of Glass" and "Shoes of Glass II" (Antique Publications.)

Silver Overlay

Dealers

John Marshall
For Love or Money
16693 NW Meadowgrass Ct.
Beaverton, OR 97006
e-mail: john@europa.com
web: http://www.europa.com/~john/
Buys and sells silver overlay and silver deposit on glass.

Souvenir & Commemorative

(see SOUVENIR & COMMEMORATIVE ITEMS)

St. Louis

(see PAPERWEIGHTS)

Steuben

Dealers

Jeff E. Purtell
P.O. Box 28
Amherst, NH 03031-0028
ph: 603-673-4331 or 800-973-4331
fax: 603-673-1525
Buys and sells Steuben animals, exhibition pieces, etc.

Experts

Stephen Milne
Stephen Milne Collection
45 Tudor City Place, Ste. 210
New York, NY 10017-7615
ph: 212-687-4420 or 800-322-7337
fax: 212-687-4420
e-mail: cardrstubn@aol.com
Buys and sells the finest Carder Steuben; the Stephen Milne Collection has been praised by the Smithsonian Inst., and acclaimed in publications such as the NY Times, San Francisco Business Times, House Beautiful, and on national TV.

Man./Prod./Dist.

Steuben Glass
717 Fifth Ave.
New York, NY 10022
ph: 212-752-1441 or 800-447-9876
fax: 212-753-1354
web: http://www.nycbest.com/steuben.htm
Bar accessories, vases, bowls, lead crystal, decorative objects, presentation awards.

Museums/Libraries

Robert F. Rockwell, III
Rockwell Museum, The
111 Cedar St.
Corning, NY 14830
ph: 607-937-5386
fax: 607-974-4536
e-mail: Rmuseum@stny.lrun.com
web: http://www.stny.lrun.com/RockwellMuseum/
Largest public exhibition (2,000+ examples) of Frederick Carder's Steuben Glass, 1903-1932, and Carder's later glass sculpture; also permanent exhibitions of Western art, firearms, Native American artifacts, antique toys.

Stretch

Clubs/Associations

David Sheltar
Stretch Glass Society
Newsletter: SGS Newsletter
P.O. Box 901
Hampshire, IL 60140
e-mail: bugdoc@columbus.rr.com
For collectors of iridescent stretch glass made by such companies as Fenton, Imperial and Northwood; annual convention late April; newsletter contains articles submitted by membership; line drawings of shapes by company.

Dealers

Calvin L. Hackeman
8865 Olde Mill Run
Washington, DC 20010-6132
ph: 703-368-6982 or 703-847-7530
fax: 703-848-9583
e-mail: calcoolege@aol.com
Collects, buys and sells stretch glass.

William Crowl
1500 Avery St.
Parkersburg, WV 26101
ph: 304-422-5042
Buys and sells unusual shapes and colors of stretch glass; one piece or entire collection.

Experts

Kitty & Russell Umbraco
P.O. Box 5331
Richmond, CA 94805-0331
ph: 510-235-1656
Buys and sells; author of "Iridescent Stretch Glass."

Studio (Contemporary)

Clubs/Associations

Jerry Cloninger
American Scientific Glassblowers Society
Magazine: Fusion
302 Red Bud Lane
Thomasville, NC 27360
ph: 336-882-0174
fax: 336-882-0172
e-mail: jerry.cloninger@chemistry.gatech.edu
web: http://www.science.wayne.edu/~asgs/asgshome.htm
A professional organization of scientific glassblowers and vendors associated with the glassblowing industry.

Penny Berk, Ex. Dir.
Glass Art Society
Journal: GAS News
1305 4th Ave. Ste. 711
Seattle, WA 98101-2401
ph: 206-382-1305
fax: 206-382-2630
e-mail: glassartsoc@earthlink.net
web: http://www.glassart.org
An international organization to encourage excellence and to advance the appreciation, understanding and development of the glass arts.

Dealers

Sally Hansen
Glass Gallery
4720 Hampden Lanec
Bethesda, MD 20814-2910
ph: 301-657-3478
fax: 301-657-3478
e-mail: salgall@worldnet.att.net
web: http://www.artresources.com/guide/featured.main.ihtml?c=15
A pioneer in the contemporary glass movement since 1971; retails one-of-a-kind contemporary glass sculptures and wall pieces; emphasizes glass as an art form.

Betsy Lane
2002 Jimmy Durante Blvd.
Del Mar, CA 92014
ph: 619-581-1088

Misc. Services

Creative Glass Centre of America
1501 Glasstown Rd.
Millville, NJ 08332-1566
ph: 609-825-6800 or 800-998-4552
fax: 609-825-2410
e-mail: cgca@wheatonvillage.org
web: http://www.wheatonvillage.org/
Located in Wheaton Village, CGCA awards 12 fellowships per year to gifted students; provides glass artists with time and resources necessary to work without the restrictions imposed by the high cost of glass production.

Marge Levy, Ex. Dir.
Pilchuck Glass School
315 Second Avenue South
Seattle, WA 98104-2618
ph: 206-621-8422
fax: 206-621-0713
e-mail: pilchuck-info@pilchuck.com
web: http://www.pilchuck.com
Largest and most comprehensive center for artists who create with glass.

Periodicals

Uta Klotz, Ed.
Kunsthandwerk & Design
Magazine: Neu Glaz (New Glass)
Rudolf - Diesel - Str. 5-7
Frechen, 50226
Germany
ph: +49 2234 1866 21
fax: +49 2234 1866 90
Many well illustrated bilingual articles on contemporary European as well as U.S. studio glass; reports worldwide.

Sulphides-Cameos In Glass

Museums/Libraries

Alex Vance, ExDir
Bergstrom-Mahler Museum
165 N. Park Ave.
Neenah, WI 54956
ph: 920-751-4675

Tiffin

Clubs/Associations

Ruth Hemminger, Pres.
Tiffin Glass Collectors' Club
Newsletter: Tiffin Glassmasters
P.O. Box 554
Tiffin, OH 44883-0554
ph: 419-447-5505
web: http://www.visi.com/~eag/club.html
Established in 1985 to study and preserve the fine glassware produced from 1892-1984 by the Tiffin Glass Company, Tiffin, OH; holds glass shows and fund raisers to benefit the Tiffin Glass Museum; monthly meetings in Tiffin.

Collectors

Cliff McCaslin
Rocliff Communications
8422 N. Park Ct.
Kansas City, MO 64155
ph: 816-436-7719
fax: 816-436-6955
e-mail: rocliff@unicom.net
Collects all patterns of Tiffin glassware (US Glass Company - Factory R).

Experts

Kelly O'Kane
Elegant American Glass
P.O. Box 16303
Saint Paul, MN 55116-0303
e-mail: eag@wavefront.com
web: http://www.visi.com/~eag
Author of "Tiffin Glassmasters: the Modern Years," which identifies all artware production at Tiffin from 1938 to 1984; dealer in elegant American glass (all major companies), and collector of Tiffin Modern glass.

Toy

(see CHILDREN'S THINGS)

Val St. Lambert

Experts

R. Rosenberg
P.O. Box 554
Hicksville, NY 11802-0554
ph: 516-669-5321
fax: 516-333-4149
e-mail: rudyrr@worldnet.att.net
Wants to buy Verlys, also Val St. Lambert and Baccarat.

Matching Services

Past & Present
14851 Avenue 360
Visalia, CA 93292
ph: 500-437-7666 or 415-258-1775
fax: 415-456-4333
e-mail: P-P@ix.netcom.com
web: http://www.china-crystal-flatware.com
Baccarat, Cambridge, Denby, Duncan & Miller, Fostoria, Franciscan, Gorham, Heisey, Imperial, Lalique, Lenox, Mikasa, Nancy Prentiss, Noritake, Orrefors, Sasaki, Tiffin, Towle, Val St. Lambert, Waterford, etc.

Vaseline

Clubs/Associations

Dave Peterson, Ed.
Vaseline Glass Collectors, Inc.
Newsletter: Glowing Report
P.O. Box 125
Russellville, MO 65074
ph: 405-949-1561 or 573-782-4620
e-mail: vgci@hotmail.com
web: http://www.icnet.net/users/davepeterson/

Verlys

Experts

R. Rosenberg
P.O. Box 554
Hicksville, NY 11802-0554
ph: 516-669-5321
fax: 516-333-4149
e-mail: rudyrr@worldnet.att.net
Wants to buy Verlys, also Val St. Lambert and Baccarat.

Carole & Wayne McPeek
McPeek Antiques & Books
1211 Pembroke Rd.
Newark, OH 43055-1627
ph: 740-344-7846
e-mail: wmcr@alltec.net
Authors of "Verlys of America Decorative Art, 1935-1951" (1992); advisor to "Warman's Antiques & Collectibles Price Guide"; author of "Verlys of France" (1993).

Waterford

Man./Prod./Dist.

Waterford/Wedgwood USA Inc.
P.O. Box 1276
Wall, NJ 07719
ph: 732-938-5800 or 800-444-1997
fax: 732-938-6915
web: http://www.wedgwood-usa.com/
Crystal stemware.

Wave Crest

Appraisers

Peggy Sebek, ISA, AAA
Century Appraisals, Inc.
3255 Glencairn Rd.
Shaker Heights, OH 44122-3407
ph: 216-991-2356
fax: 216-991-2935
e-mail: peggylane@worldnet.att.net
Accredited Member of the International Society of Appraisers, Member of the Appraisers Association of America.

Clubs/Associations

Wave Crest Collectors Club
P.O. Box 2013
Santa Barbara, CA 93120
e-mail: cardons@msn.com

Dealers

Ward Stewart
Stewart's Antiques
1000 Coolidge
Lafayette, LA 70503-2336
ph: 318-232-2957

Lyn Livingston, ISA CAPP
Remember When Antiques & Collectibles
2809 NW Expressway, Ste. 150
Oklahoma City, OK 73132
ph: 405-722-1475 or 405-721-7034
fax: 405-415-2114
e-mail: LynL@keytech.com
web: http://www.WhatsItsWorth.com/
Desires exchange of ideas, identification tips and impressions on C.F. Monroe glass with other collectors; also buys and sells.

Westmoreland

Clubs/Associations

Terry Porterfield, Pres.
National Westmoreland Glass Collectors Club
P.O. Box 100
Grapeville, PA 15634
e-mail: tap15666@webtv.net
web: http://www.glassshow.com/clubs/NWGCC/west.html

Mickey Lockwood
Westmoreland Glass Society
Newsletter: Westmoreland Glass Society Newsletter
1144 42 Ave.
Vero Beach, FL 32960
ph: 561-567-4603
fax: 561-563-0385
e-mail: lockwoom@irene.net
web: http://www.glassshow.com/Clubs/Wgsi/wgsi.html
Sponsors annual Westmoreland Glass convention, auction and souvenir limited edition items.

Collectors

Daniel Sperry
P.O. Box 949
Denville, NJ 07834-0949
Wants to buy Westmoreland glass, especially Ruby Stain; also wants Westmoreland catalogs.

Jim Fisher
513 Fifth Ave.
Coralville, IA 52241
ph: 319-354-5011

Dealers

Cynthia Pergantides
MediaSpecialists Westmoreland Gallery On-Line
28 Revell Ave.
Northampton, MA 01060
ph: 413-586-7571 or 413-584-1034
fax: 413-584-1034
e-mail: milkglass@mediaspec.com
web: http://www.mediaspec.com/GNET/wmoreland
Buys, sells, specializes in Westmoreland glass; checkout the on-line catalog.

Betty J. Viecelli
Viecelli Antiques & Collectibles
615 Gaskill Ave.
Jeannette, PA 15644
ph: 724-863-3677 or 724-527-2222

Experts

Ruth Grizel
P.O. Box 143
North Liberty, IA 52317-0143
ph: 319-626-2807
fax: 319-626-2807
Author of two books about Westmoreland Glass.

John & Carol Wiese
P.O. Box 1311
Orange, CA 92856
ph: 714-744-6977
e-mail: wsco1889@jcwiese.com
web: http://www.jcwiese.com
Buy, sell, trade Westmoreland glass; main collection consists of Paneled Grape and decorated and etched Specialty Co. pieces; also collects original Westmoreland catalogs from 1889 to 1983.

Museums/Libraries

Phillip Rosso
Rosso's Westmoreland Glass Museum
1725 Trimble Ave.
Port Vue, PA 15133
ph: 412-678-7352 or 412-678-7352
fax: 412-672-0593
e-mail: RossoWhol1@aol.com
web: http://home.att.net/~Rossos_Wholesale_Glass/
Over 4,000 pieces on display; original photos, tools, molds, etc.; also wholesales glass.

Periodicals

Ruth Grizel, Ed.
Newsletter: Original Westmoreland Collectors Newsletter, The
P.O. Box 143
North Liberty, IA 52317-0143
ph: 319-626-2807
fax: 319-626-2807
Full color monthly publication for Westmoreland glass collectors and dealers; features classified section, plus articles and photos; sponsors yearly glass convention; over 1,400 subscribers worldwide.

Wheaton

Clubs/Associations

Lois Clark
Classic Wheaton Club
Newsletter: Classic Wheaton Club Newsletter
c/o Creative Wheaton Collectibles
P.O. Box 59
Downingtown, PA 19335
ph: 610-692-4474
e-mail: cwc@cwcusa.com

Whimsies

Clubs/Associations

Lon Knickerbocker
Whimsey Club, The
Newsletter: Whimsical Notions
2 Hessler Ct.
Dansville, NY 14437
ph: 716-335-6506
For collectors of hand blown glass whimsies such as ink pens, smoke bells, flip flops, witch balls, canes, rolling pins, etc.

Collectors

Jeff & Mary Waterhouse
4544 Cairo Dr.
Whitehall, PA 18052

Experts

Joyce Blake
1220 Stolle Rd.
Elma, NY 14059
ph: 716-652-7752
Advisor to "Warman's Antiques & Collectibles Price Guide"; author of "Glasshouse Whimsies," available from author.

Whimsies (Pens)

(see also PENS)

Experts

Lon Knickerbocker
2 Hessler Ct.
Dansville, NY 14437
ph: 716-335-6506
Collects glass ink pens; advisor to "Warman's Antiques & Collectibles Price Guide."

GLASS KNIVES

Collectors

Brenda Macomber
RD 3 Box 201-K
Delta, PA 17314-9588
ph: 717-456-6116
e-mail: cruzegal@aol.com
Wants Depression-era glass knives, daggers, and butter spreaders.

Wilbur Peterson
711 Kelly Dr.
Lebanon, TN 37087
ph: 615-444-4303

Doug Heaton
8723 Artesia Blvd.
Bellflower, CA 90706
Wants to buy glass knives; give price and description; all letters answered.

Adrienne S. Escoe
4448 Ironwood Ave.
Seal Beach, CA 90740-2926
ph: 562-430-6479 or 562-598-1585
e-mail: escoebliss@earthlink.net
Wants to buy rare glass knives (used for fruit and cake, given away at World's Fairs and Expositions as souvenirs) especially forest green, amber and rare crystal.

GLASSES

(see also BREWERIANA; EYE RELATED ITEMS, Eyeglasses; FAST FOOD COLLECTIBLES; SPORTS COLLECTIBLES, Thoroughbred Racing; STEINS; SWANKYSWIGS)

Dealers

Gail Busche
Archangel Antiques
334 East Ninth St.
New York, NY 10003-7924
ph: 212-260-9313
Buying antique buttons, cuff links, eye glasses, and vintage lighters; always seeking fine examples such as enamel Deco and Art Nouveau.

Drinking

Auction Services

Pete Kroll
Glasses, Mugs & Steins Auction
P.O. Box 207
Sun Prairie, WI 53590-0207
ph: 608-837-4818
fax: 608-825-4205
e-mail: pkroll@chorus.net
web: http://www.gmskroll.com/
Produces a semi-annual mail auction featuring collectible advertising glasses, mugs & steins: beer, soda, horse racing, cartoon, Disney, root beer, Budweiser, whiskey shot glasses, whiskey pitchers, etc.

Tom Hoder
Tom Hoder Collectables
444 S. Cherry
Itasca, IL 60143-2109
ph: 630-773-2635
Conducts mail/phone-bid auctions of cartoon, character, and horse racing drinking glasses three times each year (January, April, and October.)

Clubs/Associations

Keith Cooper
Promotional Glass Collectors Association
2654 S.E. 23rd
Albany, OR 97321
ph: 541-967-7586
e-mail: spacemouse@prodigy.net
Association of promotional drinking glass collectors - cartoon, character, sports, soft drink, root beer, advertising, Disney, etc.; regional and national meetings; buy, sell, trade.

Collectors

Matt Maloney
390 S. Broadway
Lindenhurst, NY 11757

Tim Russell
245 East St., Apt. 101
Honeoye Falls, NY 14472-1235

Mark E. Chase
3991 Bethel Rd.
New Wilmington, PA 16142
ph: 724-946-2838
fax: 724-946-9012

Steve Zehr
P.O. Box 74
Fogelsville, PA 18051

Carl Sehnert
4595 Limestone Lane
Memphis, TN 38141-7870
ph: 901-794-8723

Ed Dunwoody
3055 Handview Dr.
Rochester, MI 48306
ph: 248-362-1750 or 810-659-9322

Tom Hoder
444 S. Cherry
Itasca, IL 60143-2109
ph: 630-773-2635
Specializing in cartoon, character and horse racing drinking glasses.

Bev Chapman
P.O. Box 638
Lindsay, CA 93247-0638
Major collector of drinking glasses.

Keith Cooper
2654 S.E. 23rd
Albany, OR 97321
ph: 541-967-7586
e-mail: spacemouse@prodigy.net
Collector of drinking glasses decorated with any type of picture or advertisement.

Dealers

Dale & Debbie Morrison
1810 Ferry St.
Easton, PA 18042
ph: 610-250-0242
Wants to buy cartoon, super heroes, sports drinking glasses.

Jimmy Driver
Glasses Galore
934 Greenbriar Dr.
Harrisonburg, VA 22801
ph: 540-434-5193
e-mail: glasgalore@aol.com
Buy, sell, trade cartoon and promotional drinking glasses: Pepsi, Coke, Sports, Disney, McDonald's, and other fast foods; also Kentucky Derby glasses.

Jay Honan
4349 Robertson Rd.
Stuart, FL 34997
ph: 561-286-8845
Buys, sells and trades cartoon and character drinking glasses.

Pat & Larry Aikins
P & L Collectibles
Rt. 5, Box 5174
Athens, TX 75751
ph: 903-675-3765
fax: 903-677-3643
e-mail: Texasboxer@aol.com
web: http://www.mrlunchbox.com/
Buys and sells collectible drinking glasses.

Experts

Mark E. Chase
P.O. Box 308
Slippery Rock, PA 16057
ph: 724-946-2838
fax: 724-946-9012
e-mail: cgn@glassnews.com
web: http://www.glassnews.com/
Buys and sells cartoon, sports, and fast-food drinking glasses: Disney, super heroes from '30s to present; author of books on same.

Mark E. Chase
3991 Bethel Rd.
New Wilmington, PA 16142
ph: 724-946-2838
fax: 724-946-9012
Author of "Drinking Glass Collectibles," and "Contemporary Fast-Food & Drinking Glass Collectibles," co-editor of "Collector Glass News"; wants to buy cartoon, sports and fast-food drinking glasses from the '30s to the present.

William Friedberg
462 Hillcreek Rd.
Shepherdsville, KY 40165
ph: 502-957-4039
e-mail: buddy431@gateway.net
Author of Bill Friedberg's drinking glass collector's price guide "Racing into the 21st Century Special "Millenium" Edition," 1999 - 2000; $13.50 ppd. from author; color photographs; Ky. Derby, Preakness, Belmont, Breeder's Cup and more.

Pete Kroll
Glasses, Mugs & Steins Auction
P.O. Box 207
Sun Prairie, WI 53590-0207
ph: 608-837-4818
fax: 608-825-4205
e-mail: pkroll@chorus.net
web: http://www.gmskroll.com/
Buys and sells collectible advertising glasses, mugs, & steins.

Lynn Geyer
Lynn Geyer Advertising Auctions
300 Trail Ridge
Silver City, NM 88061-6071
ph: 505-538-2341
fax: 505-388-9000
Conducts semi-annual mail/phone bid specialized auctions on all aspects of breweriana and soda-pop; also contemporary steins, mugs & drinking glasses.

Periodicals

Mark E. Chase
Newsletter: Collector Glass News
P.O. Box 308
Slippery Rock, PA 16057
ph: 724-946-2838
fax: 724-946-9012
e-mail: cgn@glassnews.com
web: http://www.glassnews.com/
Information for the collector of cartoon, fast food, sports and promotional glassware; each issue features articles, classified ads, new issues, and an auction; co-author with Michael J. Kelly of "Collectible Drinking Glasses."

Dave & Kathy Nader
Newsletter: Root Beer Float
P.O. Box 571
Lake Geneva, WI 53147
For collectors of root beer and root beer collectibles of all types, styles and ages.

Shot

Auction Services

Lawrence Powers
Shot Glass Exchange
P.O. Box 219
Western Springs, IL 60558-0219
ph: 708-246-1559
fax: 708-246-1559
Created in 1989 to provide an open national market for buyers and sellers of whiskey tumblers and shot glasses via the semi-annual mail-bid auction; color photos and bid tab provided for each catalog; sells books on shot glasses.

Clubs/Associations

Mark Pickvet
Shot Glass Club of America, The
Newsletter: Shot of News
5071 Watson Dr.
Flint, MI 48506
Members collect shot glasses; the newsletter is published monthly and contains articles about new and old shot glasses, where to obtain them, membership directories, etc.

Collectors

Carl F. Pflanzer
50 Gates Ave.
Gillette, NJ 07933
fax: 732-424-7814
e-mail: carl@njsystems.com
Wants to buy shot glasses, advertising spirits glasses, and foreign shot glasses.

Experts

Mark Pickvet
5071 Watson Dr.
Flint, MI 48506
Author of "Shot Glasses: An American Tradition" (Antique Publications.)

Spirit (Advertising)

Collectors

Carl F. Pflanzer
50 Gates Ave.
Gillette, NJ 07933
fax: 732-424-7814
e-mail: carl@njsystems.com
Wants to buy shot glasses, advertising spirits glasses, and foreign shot glasses.

GLIDERS

(see AIRPLANES, Sailplanes)

GLOBES

(see also ATLASES; EXIT GLOBES; GAS STATION COLLECTIBLES, Pumps & Globes; GAS STATION COLLECTIBLES, Road Maps; INSTRUMENTS & DEVICES; MAPS & CHARTS)

Dealers

George D. Glazer
28 East 72nd St.
New York, NY 10021
ph: 212-535-5706
fax: 212-988-3992
e-mail: worldglobe@aol.com
web: http://www.georgeglazer.com
Buys and sells terrestrial and celestial globes, armillary spheres, orreries, and maps; American, British, Continental; floor-standing, table, and miniature globes; former attorney now specializes in broad range of antique globes.

James E. Hess
49 N. Water St.
P.O. Box 412
Lititz, PA 17543
ph: 717-626-5002
fax: 717-626-8858
e-mail: heritage@carto.com
web: http://www.carto.com
One of the largest map and atlas, and globe dealers in the world; buys, sells, collects, appraises.

James E. Hess
Heritage Map Museum
55 N. Water Street
Lititz, PA 17543
ph: 717-626-5002
fax: 717-626-8858]
e-mail: heritage@carto.com
web: http://www.carto.com
Buys, sells, auctions, and appraises 15th to 19th century maps, atlases, and globes; offers retail sales, appraisals, collections consultations, and quarterly international auctions.

John Forster
Barometer Fair
P.O. Box 25502
Sarasota, FL 34277
ph: 941-923-6136
fax: 941-923-6136
e-mail: barometer@glimmer.com
Buys, sells, restores all antique barometers; also deals in antique maps, globes, compasses, telescopes and other scientific instruments.

Murray Hudson
Murray Hudson - Antiquarian Books, Maps, Prints & Globes
109 S. Church St.
P.O. Box 163
Halls, TN 38040-0163
ph: 901-836-9057 or 800-748-9946
fax: 901-836-9017
e-mail: mapman@usit.net
web: http://www.murrayhudson.com
Buys/sells pre-1900 antique maps

(especially pocket, wall, Civil War and railroad maps) & books with maps (e.g. atlases, travel guides, geographies, land surveys, etc.); esp. of S.E. & S.W. US; also wants pre-1950 world globes.

Jonathan Blackman
Yellow Room, The
511 N. Robertson Blvd.
Los Angeles, CA 90048
ph: 310-274-3190
fax: 310-274-0129
e-mail: Globemeister@msn.com
web: http://www.telecomputers.com/globes/
Specializes in globes, maps and scientific instruments; great resource information on the website.

GNOMES

(see also COLLECTIBLES [MODERN], Sculptures [Tom Clark]; ELVES)

Clubs/Associations

Liz Spera
International Gnome Club, The
Newsletter: Gnome News
22841 Kings Court
Hayward, CA 94541-4326
ph: 510-888-1808
fax: 510-889-0343
e-mail: gnomegnet@aol.com
web: http://www.ndia.ndirect.co/uk/club/

GO-KARTS

Clubs/Associations

Kart Expo International
P.O. Box 101
Wheaton, IL 60189
ph: 630-653-7368
fax: 630-653-2637
Conducts annual Kart Expo International.

GOLD

(see also COINS & CURRENCY; GEMS & JEWELRY)

Dealers

Blanchard & Co.
P.O. Box 61740
New Orleans, LA 70161-1740
ph: 888-524-2646
fax: 504-837-4884
e-mail: info@blanchardonline.com
web: http://www.blanchardonline.com
Dealers in rare coins and precious metals.

Judy Brown
P.O. Box 5368
Frazier Park, CA 93222
ph: 805-242-5411
Mail order only dealer of gold and silver smalls: boxes, chatelaines, match safes, sewing items, Victorian or earlier frames and silverplate items; long time dealer.

Beth Scott
Affordable Jewelry & Precious Metals
304 SW Washington St.
Portland, OR 97204
ph: 800-690-4995 or 503-224-7520
fax: 503-227-4204
e-mail: sight@ajpm.com
web: http://www.ajpm.com
Gold, silver and platinum bullion dealers.

Misc. Services

Big Ten, Inc.
P.O. Box 321231
Cocoa Beach, FL 32932-1231
ph: 407-783-4595
web: http://www.goldmaps.com/
Big Ten's gold maps are used by thousands of families for gold panning and outdoor recreation when vacationing, RVing, camping, hiking, biking, backpacking, etc.

Periodicals

Newsletter: Silver & Gold Report
P.O. Box 109665
West Palm Beach, FL 33410
ph: 800-289-9222 or 561-627-3300
fax: 561-625-6685
e-mail: sgr@weissinc.com
web: http://www.wessinc.com
Financial advice newsletter in precious medals, and gold & silver bullion and coins.

Scrap

Dealers

Jim Sciuto
GoldTek
P.O. Box 128
Methuen, MA 01844
ph: 978-374-2254 or 603-645-4717
fax: 978-373-1088
Buys scrap gold and silver: class rings, wedding bands, gold coins, gold watches, gold plated circuit boards, gold solder, gold wire, gold teeth; also scrap sterling silver flatware, coins, bars, silver flake, silver anodes, etc.

Greg Walsh
32 River View Lane
P.O. Box 747
Potsdam, NY 13676-0747
ph: 315-265-9111 or 800-371-9286
fax: 315-265-9222
e-mail: gwalsh@northnet.org
web: http://www.walshauction.com/
Wants to buy gold and silver rings, coins, estate jewelry, pocket watches, diamonds, sterling silver items, scrap gold, broken or damaged jewelry, dental gold, etc.; 24-hour turn around; ship on approval or call for quote; since 1979.

Michael A. Merrill
Michael A. Merrill, Inc.
Crestar Bank Building
2045 York Rd.
Timonium, MD 21093
ph: 410-453-9400
e-mail: merrill@home.com
web: http://www.pm-connect.com/mmerrill/
Buying precious metals from the public, dealers since 1974; buys scrap gold, diamonds, old gold, dental gold, school rings, gold & silver numismatic coins, sterling silver (Kirk & Steiff), Franklin Mint, platinum, palladium, exotics.

Jaime Raskansky
Gold & Silver Traders
723 Main St., Ste. 101B
Houston, TX 77002
ph: 713-520-5111 or 713-223-0777
fax: 713-223-0707
e-mail: gstforex@msn.com
Buys and sells gold and silver scrap and bullion.

Cy Phillips, Jr.
S C Coin & Stamp Co. Inc.
P.O. Drawer 661180
Arcadia, CA 91066-1180
ph: 818-445-8277 or 800-367-0779
fax: 818-445-8278
Tokens, medals, coins, currency, badges, expo. and fair items, scrap gold and silver.

GOLD LEAF

(see REPAIR/RESTORATION/CONSERVATION, Gilding)

GOLD RUSH MEMORABILIA

Collectors

Chester Jaffee
P.O. Box 5369
Berkeley, CA 94705
Wants items relating to the California Gold Rush 1848-1858.

Dealers

Cy Phillips, Jr.
S C Coin & Stamp Co. Inc.
P.O. Drawer 661180
Arcadia, CA 91066-1180
ph: 818-445-8277 or 800-367-0779
fax: 818-445-8278
Wants gold rush items; also historical trail items; old west town tokens.

Museums/Libraries

George Fox, Cur.
Amador County Museum
108 Court St.
Jackson, CA 95642
ph: 209-223-6386
Mailing address is as above; physical location is at 225 Church St. Jackson, CA.

Klondike Gold Rush National Historical Park, Seattle Unit
P.O. Box 517
Skagway, AK 99840
ph: 907-983-2921
fax: 907-983-9249
e-mail: KLGO_Ranger_Activities@nps.gov
web: http://nos.gov/klgo/

Klondike Gold Rush National Historical Park, Skagway Unit
P.O. Box 517
Skagway, AK 99840
ph: 907-983-2921
fax: 907-983-9249
e-mail: KLGO_Ranger_Activities@nps.gov
web: http://www.nps.gov/klgo/

Angela Wheelock
Yukon Archives
Box 2703
Whitehorse, Yukon Territory Y1A 2C6
Canada
ph: 867-667-5321 or 800-661-0408 x5321
fax: 403-393-6243
e-mail: Angela.Wheelock@gov.yk.ca
web: http://www.yukoncollege.yk.ca/archives
Responsible for acquiring, preserving, displaying documentary sources related to the Yukon including the Klondike gold rush; 100,000 photos, 12,000 maps, newspapers, 1,600 hours of sound recordings, etc.

Dawson City Museum & Historical Society
P.O. Box 303
Dawson City, Yukon Territory Y0B 1G0
Canada
ph: 867-993-5291
fax: 867-993-5839
e-mail: dcmuseum@yknet.yk.ca
web: http://users.yknet.yk.ca/dcpages/Museum.html
Maintains an extensive collection of records and photographs and provides research services; has over 7,000 photos.

GOOD LUCK ITEMS

(see also COINS & CURRENCY, Coins [Encased])

Collectors

J.A. Higgins
5017 Walnut
Kansas City, MO 64112-2758
ph: 816-931-4095
Wants items with "Good Luck" on them.

GRANITEWARE

(see also KITCHEN COLLECTIBLES)

Clubs/Associations

Pam Johnson
Mayflower Chapter of the National Graniteware Society
681 Congress St.
Duxbury, MA 02332
ph: 781-834-8773
For collectors of graniteware (also known as enamelware or agateware).

Gary Boggio
National Graniteware Society
Newsletter: National Graniteware News
420 E. High St.
Hennepin, IL 61327
ph: 815-925-7264
fax: 815-925-7264
e-mail: nwind@ivnet.com
For collectors to share information about graniteware.

Collectors

Dan Allers
P.O. Box 10013
Cedar Rapids, IA 52410-0013
ph: 319-393-0252

Dealers

Rita Mueller
Grange Hall Antiques
1 South Eighth Alley
P.O. Box 263
New Market, MD 21774
ph: 301-865-5651
fax: 301-865-0518
e-mail: Rita@newmarketmd.com
web: http://www.newmarketmd.com/grange.htm
Quality Steiff animals from 1950s through 1980s; always buying one piece or entire collection: teddy bears, Schuco, Hermann, Steiff; also fine country graniteware from Germany available; mail orders and layaways.

Bob Techav
Techav's Antiques
705 8th Ave.
De Witt, IA 52742
ph: 319-659-8365
e-mail: grannite@netins.net
Buys and sells graniteware; all types and all colors.

Experts

Helen Greguire
Helen's Antiques
103 Trimmer Rd.
Hilton, NY 14468-9305
ph: 716-392-2704
Author of "The Collector's Encyclopedia of Granite Ware."

Gregg Ellington
Upper Loft Antiques
47 Columbus St.
Wilmington, OH 45177
ph: 937-382-4311
Buys, sells, trades and collects graniteware and American ceramics including mochaware, yellowware, spongeware, etc.

Pamela & Allan Luttig
Blue Boar Antiques
P.O. Box 423
Grand Ledge, MI 48837
ph: 517-626-6432

Gary & Lorraine Boggio
North Wind Antiques
420 E. High St.
Hennepin, IL 61327
ph: 815-925-7264
fax: 815-925-7264
e-mail: nwind@ivnet.com
Buy, sell and specializes in graniteware.

French

Dealers

David T. Pikul
Chuctanunda Antique Company, The
1 Fourth Ave.
Amsterdam, NY 12010-3803
ph: 518-843-3983
fax: 518-843-3983
e-mail: dtpikul@telenet.net
web: http://www.enameledware.com/
Sells French and European enameled ware: coffee pots, canisters, utensil racks, etc.; colorful and highly decorative; free color brochure available.

GRAVESTONES

Clubs/Associations

Association for Gravestone Studies
Newsletter: AGS Quarterly
278 Main St., Ste. 207
Greenfield, MA 01301-3230
ph: 413-772-0836
e-mail: ags@javanet.com
web: http://gemini.berkshire.net/ags
Mission is to foster appreciation for gravestones and cemeteries through study and preservation; offers information and restoration referrals for gravestones; NOTE: Respect gravestones; they are sacred and not collectible!

GREETING CARDS

(see HOLIDAY COLLECTIBLES; PAPER COLLECTIBLES; POSTCARDS; VALENTINES)

GROCERY STORE ITEMS

(see CEREAL BOXES; FOOD COLLECTIBLES; PREMIUMS, Cereal Box)

GUIDES

(see ANTIQUE SHOP DIRECTORIES; FLEA MARKET GUIDES; TOURS/BUYING TRIPS)

GUINNESS WORLD RECORDS

Museums/Libraries

Guinness World of Records Museum
2780 Las Vegas Blvd., South
Las Vegas, NV 89109-1102
ph: 702-792-3766
fax: 702-792-0530
web: http://www.lasvegas.com/lv/guinness/
This unique museum brings the Guinness Book of World Records to three-dimensional life via life-sized replicas, computerized databanks and color videos.

GUITARS

(see MUSICAL INSTRUMENTS, String [Guitars]; TOYS, Guitar)

GUM

(see BUBBLE GUM CARDS; BUBBLE GUM & CANDY WRAPPERS; TRADING CARDS, Non-Sport)

GUMBALL MACHINES

(see COIN-OPERATED MACHINES, Vending Machines)

GUNFIGHTERS

(see WESTERN AMERICANA)

GUNS

(see ADVERTISING, Firearms Related; AIRGUNS; ARMS & ARMOR; CIVIL WAR ARTIFACTS; FIREARMS; MILITARIA; TOY GUNS; TRAPSHOOTING; WESTERN AMERICANA)

Here are some tips when contacting someone listed in this book:

■ When requesting information about a particular item, include a description (material, dimensions, maker's mark, model number, etc.) and a photo, sketch, or photocopy of the item in question.

■ Always ask if there are charges for samples or for the services requested.

■ When writing, please be sure to include a Large (#10 business size) Self-Addressed and Stamped Envelope (LSASE) if requesting a reply or the return of photographs.

■ Never call collect unless otherwise directed. When calling, be considerate of time zone differences and always ask if the party you are calling has time to talk. When leaving an answering machine message, always instruct the party to call you back collect.

HAIR ACCESSORIES

(see BARBERSHOP COLLECTIBLES; BEAUTY SHOP COLLECTIBLES; CLOTHING & ACCESSORIES, Vintage; COMBS & HAIR ACCESSORIES; DRESSER ITEMS, Hatpins & Hatpin Holders; GEMS & JEWELRY; SHAVING COLLECTIBLES)

HAIRWORK

(see also BARBERSHOP COLLECTIBLES; BEAUTY SHOP COLLECTIBLES; COMBS & HAIR ACCESSORIES; GEMS & JEWELRY, Mourning; SHAVING COLLECTIBLES)

Clubs/Associations

Ruth Gordon
Hair Art International
Newsletter: H.A.I.R. Line
24629 Cherry St.
Dearborn, MI 48124-3103
ph: 313-277-2479
H.A.I.R. is an acronym for Hair Art International Restorers, a society interested in hair art: collectors, hair workers, and others interested in the art of making beautiful things out of human and animal hair.

Marlys Fladeland
Victorian Hairwork Society
P.O. Box 1617
Pleasant Grove, UT 84062
ph: 801-785-7210
fax: 801-785-6235
e-mail: marlys@hairwork.com
web: http://www.hairworksociety.org
A website for networking anyone who is interested in the art of Victorian hairwork; includes articles on hairwork, instructions on braiding, items for sale, and much more; dealers, collectors, historians welcome.

Collectors

Jerry Denzler
P.O. Box 127
Marengo, IA 52301-0127
ph: 319-642-3528 or 319-642-7777
Wants to buy human hair jewelry and other items made of hair or with hair such as framed mourning wreaths, postcards, buttons, purses; also wants samples of tablework and equipment used in weaving hair.

Dealers

Vince Tartaglione
T-Graphix
P.O. Box 2116
Patterson, NJ 07509-2116
ph: 973-450-8948
Buys hair and hair related items: video, photographs, books, ads, labels, haircutting; long hair or no hair; Rapunzel, Sutherland Sisters; also buys braids, ponytails.

Nancy Robertson
Hair Art
1519 N.E. 51st Terrace
Kansas City, MO 64118-6046
ph: 816-454-9601
e-mail: hairart@swbell.net
web: http://www.hairwork.com/hairart
Collector, expert, reproduction source for Victorian hairwork; makes both wreaths and jewelry items; does custom work for the public; especially interested in antique wreaths and cutwork; demonstrates at living history festivals.

Marlys Fladeland
P.O. Box 1617
Pleasant Grove, UT 84062
ph: 801-785-7210
fax: 801-785-6235
e-mail: marlys@hairwork.com
web: http://www.hairwork.com
Collects, buys and sells Victorian hairwork.

Experts

Ruth Gordon
Cherished Memories
24629 Cherry St.
Dearborn, MI 48124-3103
ph: 313-277-2479
Practices the art of Victorian hairweaving to create jewelry; reproduces hairweaving catalog of pins, earrings, watchfobs, shadow-boxes, bell jars, etc.; lectures, magazine articles.

Wreaths

Museums/Libraries

Leila Cohoon
Leila's Hair Museum, College of Cosmology
815 West 23rd St.
Independence, MO 64055
ph: 816-252-HAIR
e-mail: Lcohoon@aol.com
web: http://www.hairwork.com/leila/
An interesting display of various items made from human hair and dating back to the 1800s; over 150 wreathes and 500 pieces of hair jewelry.

HALLMARK

(see COLLECTIBLES [MODERN], Ornaments [Hallmark])

HALLOWEEN COLLECTIBLES

(see also ANIMAL COLLECTIBLES, Cats; GHOSTS & HAUNTINGS; HOLIDAY COLLECTIBLES; HORROR; WITCHES)

Collectors

Mark Bergin
P.O. Box 3073
Peterborough, NH 03458-3073
ph: 603-924-2079
fax: 603-924-2022
Wants Jack-o'-lanterns, candy containers, nodders, any figures, die-cuts, crepe paper, noise makers, postcards, anything Halloween.

Bob Merck
44 Newtown Turnpike
Weston, CT 06883-2118
fax: 203-761-8777
WAnts pre-1950 jack-o'-lanterns, other lanterns, candy containers; also photos of old Halloween parties and people in costume.

Linda L. Vines
P.O. Box 43721
Upper Montclair, NJ 07043
ph: 973-748-4990
e-mail: lja@viconet.com
Wants to buy pre-1950 decorations including candy containers, jack-o'-lanterns, witches, black cats, skeletons.

Tom Rutledge
3015 Bever Ave., SE
Cedar Rapids, IA 52403-3028
ph: 319-399-1427
Wants only pre-1950 Halloween collectibles including decorations, postcards, candy containers, lanterns, invitations, papier-mache items, plaster of Paris items, etc.; also old mail order catalogs and flyers featuring Halloween.

Tom Pritchard
4905 Drew Ave. So.
Minneapolis, MN 55410
ph: 800-473-3815 or 612-926-3815
fax: 612-926-3815
e-mail: HalloweenT@aol.com
Wants to buy Halloween collectibles: jack-o'-lanterns, noisemakers, candy containers, nodders, hard plastic, German diecuts, pumpkin tea set pieces, Bogie books, etc.

Dawn Kroma
P.O. Box 143
Brookfield, IL 60513-0143
ph: 708-387-0334 or 708-387-0334
fax: 708-387-0334
e-mail: BooNews@aol.com

David Welch
P.O. Box 714
Murphysboro, IL 62966-0714
ph: 618-687-2282
fax: 618-684-2243
e-mail: PezDude1@aol.com
Wants Don Post rubber monster masks (sold through Famous Monster magazines only); also '50s-'60s monster, TV, movie, comic, and cartoon costumes; must be in original boxes; $500 for Captain Action.

Gwen Daniel
18 Belleau Lake Ct.
O Fallon, MO 63366-3144
ph: 314-978-3190
e-mail: gdaniel@mail.win.org

Dealers

Leila Dunbar
Dunbar's Gallery
76 Haven St.
Milford, MA 01757-3821
ph: 508-634-8697 or 508-634-8097
fax: 508-634-8698
Mail order Americana - no reproductions; buys, sells and specializes in vintage character and comic toys, banks, advertising, automobilia, and Halloween related items.

Hugh Alan Luch Collections, The
P.O. Box 111
Wenonah, NJ 08090
ph: 609-464-9751
Buys and sells illustrator and holiday collectibles with emphasis on Maxfield Parrish and Halloween.

Diane Richardson
Gold Hatpin, The
P.O. Box 993
Oak Park, IL 60303-0993
ph: 708-848-3247 or 708-445-0610
e-mail: goldhatpin@mediaone.net
Wants old German Halloween items: veggie people, candy containers, diecuts, hard plastic toys, jewelry, lanterns, noisemakers, etc.

Jenny Tarrant
4 Gardenview Dr.
Saint Peters, MO 63376-3507
ph: 314-397-1763
e-mail: jennyjol@aol.com
Wants Halloween items, papier-mache candy containers, Jack O'Lanterns, Halloween party books, party decorations and favors, Halloween postcards, plastic toys.

Paul W. Schofield
Lion's Den Antiques
7988 Bethel Burley Rd. SE
Port Orchard, WA 98366
ph: 360-876-3364
fax: 360-876-5421
Buys, sells, appraises, and specializes in old Santas, candy containers, Halloween, Easter, Christmas, Easter, Dresden, figural lights.

Experts

Chris Russell
Halloween Queen
P.O. Box 499
Winchester, NH 03470-0499
ph: 603-239-8875
fax: 603-239-8875
Author of "Halloween - An American Holiday" (Schiffer).

Stuart Schneider
Hudson Valley Graphics
Newsletter: Pens
P.O. Box 64
Teaneck, NJ 07666-0064
ph: 201-261-1983
fax: 201-599-1950
e-mail: stuarts1031@erols.com
web: http://www.geocities.com/Yosemite/Geyser/7949/
Wants to buy Halloween decorations from the turn-of-the-century to 1960, especially trick-or-treat bags, party invitations, and Dennisons products; author of "Halloween in America."

Internet Resources

Halloween Collectibles
e-mail: halween@aol.com
web: http://members.aol.com/halween/

Periodicals

Chris Russell
Halloween Queen
Newsletter: Trick or Treat Trader, The
P.O. Box 499
Winchester, NH 03470-0499
ph: 603-239-8875
fax: 603-239-8875
For the collector of Halloween related memorabilia; published quarterly; almost 14 years old.

Dawn Kroma
Kromazone Media
Newsletter: BooNews
P.O. Box 143
Brookfield, IL 60513-0143
ph: 708-387-0334 or 708-387-0334
fax: 708-387-0334
e-mail: BooNews@aol.com
Quarterly, full color subscription based newsletter for Halloween enthusiasts; provides information and networking regarding old and modern Halloween collectibles, reproductions, history, photos, interviews, events, shows, etc.

HAMBURGERS

(see also FAST FOOD COLLECTIBLES; FOOD COLLECTIBLES)

Collectors

Harry Sperl
Hamburger Harry
1000 North Beach Street
Daytona Beach, FL 32117
ph: 904-254-8753
fax: 904-255-2460
e-mail: harry@burgerweb.com
web: http://www.burgerweb.com

Museums/Libraries

Harry Sperl
Hamburger Museum
1000 North Beach Street
Daytona Beach, FL 32117
ph: 904-254-8753
fax: 904-255-2460
e-mail: harry@burgerweb.com
web: http://www.burgerweb.com
Collection contains more than 500 different hamburgers and related material: hamburger banks, badges, biscuit jars, clocks, hats, trays, erasers, salt & pepper shakers, music boxes, pencil holders, pillows, signs, posters, cups, etc.

HANDBAGS

(see PURSES)

HANDS

Wooden

Collectors

Donald Gorlick
P.O. Box 24541
Seattle, WA 98124-0541
ph: 206-824-0508
Wants wooden hands with articulated fingers; may be a glove stretcher mold for sizing gloves; wooden with fingers and thumb that move.

HARDWARE

(see also ARCHITECTURAL ELEMENTS; ARCHITECTURE & RELATED ITEMS; CATALOGS, Trade; DIAMOND EDGE; DOORKNOBS; FASTENERS; KEEN KUTTER [SIMMONS HARDWARE]; PLUMBING; REPAIR/ RESTORATION/CONSERVATION, Woodworking; TOOLS; WINCHESTER COLLECTIBLES)

Appraisers

Rilla Simmons, CAGA
Simmons & Company Auctioneers
40706 E. 144th St.
Richmond, MO 64085
ph: 816-776-2936 or 800-646-2936
fax: 816-470-5016
e-mail: simmons_auction@raycounty.com
web: http://www.raycounty.com/simmons/
Appraises Keen Kutter (Simmons Hardware), Diamond Edge (Shapleigh Hardware), Winchester tools.

Auction Services

H. Weber Wilson
Web Wilson's Antique Hardware Auction
P.O. Box 506
Portsmouth, RI 02871
ph: 800-508-0022
fax: 401-683-1644
e-mail: hww@edgenet.net
web: http://www.antiqnet.com/webwilson/
Conducts two phone/fax auctions per year of quality builders' hardware including door knobs, bells, shutter pulls, plates, etc.

Clubs/Associations

Barbara Huhn, Mem.
Hardware Companies Kollectors' Club
Newsletter: Winchester Keen Kutter Diamond Edge Chronicles
432 S. Gore St.
Saint Louis, MO 63119
ph: 314-968-0304
e-mail: gramma@mvp.net
web: http://www.raycounty.com/simmons/clubs/newsletter.htm
A non-profit organization to serve as an interactive information distribution center for collectors of E.C. Simmons/ Keen Kutter, Winchester Store (non-gun), A.F. Shapleigh/Diamond Edge, Hibbard, and other hardware store brands.

Collectors

Larry Eastley
46460 Hwy. 10
Hardin, MO 64035
ph: 660-398-4617
e-mail: eastley@iland.net
Collector of Keen Kutter, Diamond Edge, Winchester Store (non-gun), Simmons & Shapleigh and other hardware store brands.

Dealers

Ed Donaldson
Hardware Restorations
1488 York Rd.
Carlisle, PA 17013-9237
ph: 717-249-3624
fax: 717-249-5647
e-mail: ed@eddonaldson.com
web: http://eddonaldson.com
Sells restored hardware and hardware replacement parts.

Experts

H. Weber Wilson
Web Wilson's Antique Hardware Auction
P.O. Box 506
Portsmouth, RI 02871
ph: 800-508-0022
fax: 401-683-1644
e-mail: hww@edgenet.net
web: http://www.antiqnet.com/webwilson/

Repro. Sources

Period Furniture Hardware Co., Inc.
Charles Street Station
P.O. Box 314
Boston, MA 02114
ph: 617-227-0758
fax: 617-227-2987
Supplies fine quality reproduction hardware for furniture and the home; specializes in solid brass fittings and accessories; 120 page catalog available for $5.

Barbara Horton Rockwell
Horton Brasses Inc.
P.O. Box 120
Cromwell, CT 06416
ph: 860-635-4400
fax: 860-635-6473
e-mail: barb@horton-brasses.com
web: http://www.horton-brasses.com
Sells authentic period reproduction hardware of the finest quality. Manufactured of solid brass or handforged black iron in CT factory.

John M. Fisher
18th Century Hardware Co., Inc.
131 East 3rd St.
Derry, PA 15627-1607
ph: 724-694-2708
fax: 724-694-9587
Clean, polish & repair brass items; makes, sells reproduction hardware; clean and electrify brass lamps; offers catalog; will duplicate any style or pattern.

Bill Ball
Ball & Ball Antique Hardware Reproduction & Restorations
463 W. Lincoln Highway
Exton, PA 19341
ph: 800-257-3711 or 610-363-7330
fax: 610-363-7639
e-mail: billball@ptd.net
web: http://www.ballandball-us.com/
Sells reproduction hardware; 18th century reproduction brass and iron chandeliers, sconces, candle stands and candlesticks; also offers a recasting service.

Paxton Hardware Ltd.
P.O. Box 256
Upper Falls, MD 21156-0256
ph: 410-592-8505 or 800-241-9741
fax: 410-592-2224
e-mail: paxton@ix.netcom.com
web: http://www.paxtonhardware.com/
Supplies authentic solid brass, hard-

to-find reproduction hardware in period styles: pulls, knobs, hinges, locks, casters, table hardware, bed hardware.

Robert Hershberger
Hershberger's Hardware
1411 Township Rd. 178
Baltic, OH 43804
ph: 330-893-2464 or 800-734-8044
fax: 330-698-3200
Catalog of specialty products for antiques and woodworking such as spool cabinet decals, high chair trays, antique telephone parts, Hoosier cabinet parts, lamp parts; $4 for 64 page catalog (refundable).

Phyllis & Phil Kennedy
Phyllis Kennedy Hardware
10655 Andrade Drive
Zionsville, IN 46077
ph: 317-873-1316
fax: 317-873-8662
e-mail: philken@kennedyhardware.com
web: http://www.kennedyhardware.com
Hardware for antique furniture, ice boxes, Hoosier cabinets and trunks; manufacturer of flour bins and sifters for Hoosier cabinets; pulls, bails, knobs, latches, char seats and caning, hinges, locks and keys, coat hooks, etc.

Scott's-Becker's Hardware Inc.
1411 S. 3rd St.
Ozark, MO 65721-9188
ph: 800-247-2594 or 417-581-6525
fax: 417-485-3067
Carries hardware for antique furniture: trunk hardware, bed parts, kitchen cabinets, Hoosier, pulls, latches, hinges, locks keys.

B & M Hardware Co.
4868 Carediff Bay Dr.
Oceanside, CA 92057-3413
ph: 800-783-2212
Sells brass antique reproduction hardware - Chippendale, Victorian, Mission; also glass knobs and handles, oak knobs and handles, etc.; send for free catalog.

Muff's Antiques
135 S. Glassell St.
Orange, CA 92866-1421
ph: 714-997-0243
fax: 714-997-1601
e-mail: muffs@earthlink.net
web: http://home.earthlink/~muffs/
Has thousands of pieces of hardware in stock both new and old for restoration of furniture and homes from antique to modern: door plates, locks/keys, knobs, light fixtures, electric and oil lamps; catalog $5.

Mary Ann Aldrich
Thor's Hardware
1740 Myers Street
Oroville, CA 95966
ph: 530-533-9121 or 530-533-7614
fax: 530-533-9180
e-mail: oldthings@cncnet.com
web: http://www.lumarmall.com/thors/thors.htm
Supplier of antique reproduction hardware, including locks, hinges, ice box hardware, trunk hardware, Victorian, Eastlake, Mission and Waterfall furniture hardware; also bar railing, door hardware and lighting.

HEALTH & BEAUTY

Devices To Restore

Collectors

Olg Lindan
1404 Dorsh Rd.
Cleveland, OH 44121-3840
ph: 216-382-7113
Wants old electrotherapeutic and controversial healing devices and related literature; also wants medical, scientific instruments.

HEBRAICA

(see JUDAICA)

HERALDRY

(see also BOOKS, Heraldry; GENEALOGY)

Clubs/Associations

David R. Wooten
American College of Heraldry, The
P.O. Box 1899
Little Rock, AR 72203-1899
fax: 501-834-4038
e-mail: ballywoodn@aol.com
web: http://users.aol.com/ballywoodn/acheraldry.html
A private body for the recording of arms in the U.S.; lots of great links to other heraldry related sites.

Heraldry Society, The
P.O. Box 32
Maidenhead, Berkshire SL6 3FD
U.K.
e-mail: hersoc@londwill.demon.co.uk
web: http://www.kwtelecom.com/heraldry/hersoc/
Exists to increase and extend interest in and knowledge of heraldry, armory, chivalry, genealogy and allied subjects.

Experts

Will Chandler
Chandler Art Consulting Services
3605-B Fifth Ave.
San Diego, CA 92103-4219
ph: 619-542-0118

Internet Resources

James P. Wolf
Heraldry on the Internet
e-mail: jawolf@earthlink.net
web: http://www.digiserve.com/heraldry/
Great online resource for heraldry information: heraldic glossary, castles, medieval resources, dictionaries, organizations, genealogical research tips and techniques.

Misc. Services

College of Arms, The
Queen Victoria St.
London, EC4V 4BT
U.K.
ph: +44 171 248 2762
fax: +44 171 248 6448
web: http://www.kwtelecom.com/heraldry/collarms/
Charged with maintaining the system of heraldry; online website includes how it all began, heralds in modern times, granting of arms today, tracing your family.

HERITAGE RESOURCES

(see also AMERICAN INDIAN; ARCHAEOLOGY; PREHISTORIC ARTIFACTS)

Clubs/Associations

National Conference of State Historic Preservation Offices
Hall of States, Suite 342
444 North Capitol Street, NW
Washington, DC 20001-1512

National Institute for the Conservation of Cultural Property
3299 K St. NW, Ste. 602
Washington, DC 20007
ph: 800-422-4612 or 202-625-1495
fax: 202-625-1485
web: http://www.heritagepreservation.org/PROGRAMS/SOS/sosmain.htm
Provides national leadership to promote & facilitate the conservation and preservation of the nation's heritage, including works of art, anthropological artifacts, documents, historic objects, architecture and natural science specimens.

Center for Archaeology in the Public Interest
Magazine: Public Archaeology Review
Department of Anthropology
425 University Blvd., IUPUI
Indianapolis, IN 46202-5140
ph: 317-274-1406
fax: 317-274-2347

Misc. Services

Repatriation Coordin'tr
American Indian Ritual Object Repatriation Foundation
463 East 57th St.
New York, NY 10022-3003
ph: 212-980-9441
fax: 212-421-2746
e-mail: RepatFdn@aol.com
web: http://www.repatriationfoundation.org
A non-federally funded intercultural partnership committed to assisting in the return of ceremonial material to American Indian Nations and to educating the public about the importance of repatriation.

Licensing Officer
National Trust for Historic Preservation
Magazine: Preservation Magazine
1785 Massachusetts Ave., NW
Washington, DC 20036
ph: 202-588-6000
fax: 202-588-6292
e-mail: resource@nthp.org
web: http://nthp.org/
Licenses some of America's leading home furnishings, decorative arts, giftware and collectibles manufacturers to reproduce objects related to Nat. Trust sites, and American history & culture; educates public about historic preservation.

Naval Historical Center, Office of the Senior Historian
Washington Navy Yard
901 M Street SE
Washington, DC 20374-5060
ph: 202-433-7229 or 202-433-7230
fax: 202-433-3593
Department of Navy ship and aircraft wrecks remain government property; questions and information concerning historic U.S. Navy aircraft and shipwrecks should be addressed to the Naval Historical Center.

Museums/Libraries

National Museum of Natural History, Anthropology Department
Smithsonian Institution
Washington, DC 20560
web: http://www.mnh.si.edu/
Contact about "Anthro Notes", a bulletin for teachers.

National Park Service

Misc. Services

National Park Service, Northeast Regional Office
200 Chestnut Street, 5th Floor
Philadelphia, PA 19106
ph: 215-597-7013
fax: 215-597-0815
e-mail: NEFA_Field_Director@nps.gov
Technical assistance, publications, training, Secretary of the Interior's Report on Federal Archeology, National Archeological Database (NADB), Listing of Education in Archeology Projects (LEAP), Regional Office Programs.

National Register of Historic Places, National Register, History & Education
National Park Service, DOI
P.O. Box 37127, Mail Stop 2280
Washington, DC 20013-7127
ph: 202-343-9500
fax: 202-343-1836
e-mail: nr_reference@nps.gov
web: http://www.cr.nps.gov/nr/nrhome.html
For information on the National Register of Historic Places and "Teaching With Historic Places."

Richard Waldbauer
National Park Service, DOI, Archeology & Ethnography Program
1849 C Street NW
Washington, DC 20240
ph: 202-343-4113
fax: 202-523-1547
e-mail: richard_waldbauer@nps.gov
Can convey information concerning the federal archaeological program from a land management perspective.

David Tarler
National Park Service, DOI, Archeology & Ethnography Program
1849 C Street NW
Washington, DC 20240
ph: 202-343-1108
fax: 202-523-1547
e-mail: david_tarler@nps.gov
Can convey information concerning both criminal and civil federal law relating to heritage resources from both a lawyer's and archeologist's perspective.

Tim McKeown
NAGPRA Team Leader, Archeology & Ethnography Program, National Park Service
1849 C Street NW
Washington, DC 20240
ph: 202-343-4101
fax: 202-523-1547
e-mail: tim_mckeown@nps.gov
web: http://www.cast.uark.edu/products/NAGPRA/
Can convey information concerning Native American human remains, funerary objects, sacred objects, and objects of cultural patrimony as defined by the Native American Graves Protection & Repatriation Act (NAGPRA).

National Park Service, National Capital Region
1100 Ohio Srive, SW
Washington, DC 20242
ph: 202-619-7000
fax: 202-619-7220
e-mail: Terry_Carlstrom@nps.gov
Technical assistance, publications, training, Secretary of the Interior's Report on Federal Archeology, National Archeological Database (NADB), Listing of Education in Archeology Projects (LEAP), Regional Office Programs.

National Park Service, Southeast Regional Office
100 ALabama St. SW
NPS/Atlanta Federal Center
Atlanta, GA 30303
ph: 404-562-3100
fax: 404-562-3263
e-mail: Jerry_Belson@nps.gov
Technical assistance, publications, training, Secretary of the Interior's Report on Federal Archeology, National Archeological Database (NADB), Listing of Education in Archeology Projects (LEAP), Regional Office Programs.

National Park Service, Midwest Region
1709 Jackson St.
Omaha, NE 68102
ph: 402-221-3471 or 402-221-3471
fax: 402-221-3461
e-mail: Bill_Schenk@nps.gov
Technical assistance, publications, training, Secretary of the Interior's Report on Federal Archeology, National Archeological Database (NADB), Listing of Education in Archeology Projects (LEAP), Regional Office Programs.

National Park Service, Intermountain Region
12795 West Alameda Parkway
P.O. Box 25287
Denver, CO 80225-0287
ph: 303-969-2500
fax: 303-696-2785
e-mail: IMFA_Field_Director@nps.gov
Technical assistance, publications, training, Secretary of the Interior's Report on Federal Archeology, National Archeological Database (NADB), Listing of Education in Archeology Projects (LEAP), Regional Office Programs.

National Park Service, Pacific West Region
600 Harrison St., Ste. 600
San Francisco, CA 94107-1372
ph: 415-427-1300
fax: 415-744-4043
e-mail: PWFA_Regional_Director@nps.gov
Technical assistance, publications, training, Secretary of the Interior's Report on Federal Archeology, National Archeological Database (NADB), Listing of Education in Archeology Projects (LEAP), Regional Office Programs.

National Park Service, Alaska Regional Office
2525 Gambell Street, Rm. 107
Anchorage, AK 99503-2892
ph: 907-257-2687
fax: 907-257-2533
e-mail: AKRO_Regional_Director@nps.gov
Technical assistance, publications, training, Secretary of the Interior's Report on Federal Archeology, National Archeological Database (NADB), Listing of Education in Archeology Projects (LEAP), Regional Office Programs.

State Archaeologists

Misc. Services

Senior Archaeologist, Dept. of Planning & Natural Resources, Div. of Archaeology
396-1 Anna's Retreat
Foster Building
Charlotte Armalie, VI 00802
ph: 809-774-8605
fax: 809-774-5416
e-mail: webmaster@gov.vi
web: http://www.gov.vi/
Provides information on laws, procedures, current research, education programs, and other aspects of archaeology for this state or possession.

Puerto Rico State Historic Preservation Office
La Fortaleza
P.O. Box 82
San Juan, PR 00901
ph: 787-721-3737
fax: 787-723-0957
web: http://nasa.uconn.edu/prosa.html
Provides information on laws, procedures, current research, education programs, and other aspects of archaeology for this state or possession.

State Archaeologist, D-SHPO, Massachusetts Historical Commission
220 Morrissey Blvd.
Dorchester, MA 02125
ph: 617-727-8470
fax: 617-727-5128
web: http://nasa.uconn.edu/massosa.html
Provides information on laws, procedures, current research, education programs, and other aspects of archaeology for this state or possession.

Principal/State Archaeologist, Rhode Island Historic Preservation Commission
Old State House
150 Benefit St.
Providence, RI 02903
ph: 401-277-2678
fax: 401-277-2968
web: http://nasa.uconn.edu/riosa.html
Provides information on laws, procedures, current research, education programs, and other aspects of archaeology for this state or possession.

New Hampshire State Archaeologist, Division of Historical Resources
Walker Building
P.O. Box 2043
Concord, NH 03302-2043
ph: 603-271-3483
fax: 603-271-3558
web: http://nasa.uconn.edu/nhosa.html
Provides information on laws, procedures, current research, education programs, and other aspects of archaeology for this state or possession.

Archaeologist, Maine Historic Preservation Commission
55 Capitol St.
State House Station 65
Augusta, ME 04333
ph: 207-287-2132
fax: 207-287-2335
web: http://nasa.uconn.edu/meosa.html
Provides information on laws, procedures, current research, education programs, and other aspects of archaeology for this state or possession.

State Archaeologist, Division for Historic Preservation
National Life, Drawer 20
Montpelier, VT 05633-0501
ph: 802-828-3050
fax: 802-828-3206
web: http://nasa.uconn.edu/vtosa.html
Provides information on laws, procedures, current research, education programs, and other aspects of archaeology for this state or possession.

State Archaeologist, Connecticut State Museum of Natural History
U-23 University of Connecticut
Storrs Mansfield, CT 06269-3023
ph: 860-486-5248
fax: 860-486-4460
e-mail: nbell@uconnvm.uconn.edu
web: http://nasa.uconn.edu/connosa.html
Provides information on laws, procedures, current research, education programs, and other aspects of archaeology for this state or possession.

New Jersey State Archaeologist, New Jersey State Museum
205 W. State St., CN 530
Trenton, NJ 08625
ph: 609-292-8594
fax: 609-599-4098
web: http://nasa.uconn.edu/njosa.html
Provides information on laws, procedures, current research, education programs, and other aspects of archaeology for this state or possession.

Archaeologist, New York State Museum
3122 Cultural Education Center, Rm. 3124
Empire State Plaza
Albany, NY 12224
ph: 518-486-2015
e-mail: rdkdelmar@aol.com
web: http://nasa.uconn.edu/nyosa.html
Provides information on laws, procedures, current research, education programs, and other aspects of archaeology for this state or possession.

Chief, Pennsylvania Division of Archaeology & Protection
P.O. Box 1026
Harrisburg, PA 17120-1026
ph: 717-738-9926
fax: 717-783-1073
web: http://nasa.uconn.edu/paosa.html
Provides information on laws, procedures, current research, education programs, and other aspects of archaeology for this state or possession.

State of Delaware, Department of State, Division of Historical/Cultural Affairs
15 The Green
Dover, DE 19901-3611
ph: 302-736-5685
fax: 302-739-6711
e-mail: fstocum@state.de.us
web: http://nasa.uconn.edu/delosa.html
Provides information on laws, procedures, current research, education programs, and other aspects of archaeology for this state or possession.

Archaeologist, Washington DC Historic Preservation Office
614 H Street, NW - Rm. 305
Washington, DC 20001
ph: 202-727-7360
fax: 202-727-7211
web: http://nasa.uconn.edu/dcosa.html
Provides information on laws, procedures, current research, education programs, and other aspects of archaeology for this state or possession.

Maryland Office of Archaeology, Division of Historical/Cultural Programs
100 Community Place
Crownsville, MD 21032-2032
ph: 410-514-7600
fax: 410-987-4071
web: http://nasa.uconn.edu/mdos.html
Provides information on laws, procedures, current research, education programs, and other aspects of archaeology for this state or possession.

Catherine Slusser
State Archaeologist, Department of Historic Resources
2801 Kensington Ave.
Richmond, VA 23221
ph: 804-367-2323
fax: 804-367-2391
e-mail: cslusser@dhr.state.va.us
web: http://www.dhr.state.va.us/
Provides information on laws, procedures, current research, education programs, and other aspects of archaeology for this state or possession.

Senior Archaeologist, West Virginia Division of Culture/History
The Cultural Center
1900 Kanowha Blvd. East
Charleston, WV 25305-0300
ph: 304-558-0220
fax: 304-558-2779
web: http://nasa.uconn.edu/wvosa.html
Provides information on laws, procedures, current research, education programs, and other aspects of archaeology for this state or possession.

North Carolina State Archaeologist
109 E. Jones St.
Raleigh, NC 27601-2807
ph: 919-733-7342
fax: 919-715-2671
e-mail: sclaggett@ncsl.dcr.state.nc.us
web: http://nasa.uconn.edu/ncosa.html
Provides information on laws, procedures, current research, education programs, and other aspects of archaeology for this state or possession.

Bruce Rippeteau
Director/State Archaeologist, SC Institute of Archaeology/Anthropology
University of South Carolina
1321 Pendleton St.
Columbia, SC 29201-0071
ph: 803-777-8170 or 803-734-0567
fax: 803-254-1338
e-mail: rippeteau@sc.edu
web: http://www.cla.sc.edu/sciaa/sciaa.html
Provides information on laws, procedures, current research, education programs, and other aspects of archaeology in and for South Carolina; maintains archaeological collections, site files; accepts private giving for research.

Georgia State Archaeologist
Martha Munro, Rm. 308
West Georgia College
Carrollton, GA 30118
ph: 770-836-6455 or 770-836-6767
e-mail: david_crass@mail.dnr.state.ga.us
web: http://nasa.uconn.edu/faosa.html
Provides information on laws, procedures, current research, education programs, and other aspects of archaeology for this state or possession.

James Miller
State Archaeologist, Florida Division of Historical Resources
500 S. Bronough St.
Tallahassee, FL 32399-0250
ph: 850-487-2299
fax: 850-414-2207
e-mail: jmiller@mail.dos.state.fl.us
web: http://www.flheritage.com/
Provides information on laws, procedures, current research, education programs, and other aspects of archaeology for this state or possession.

Chief, Archaeological Services Division, Alabama Historical Commission
468 S. Perry St.
Montgomery, AL 36130
ph: 334-242-3184
fax: 334-240-3477
e-mail: TMaher@mail.preserveala.org
web: http://nasa.uconn.edu/alaosa.html
Provides information on laws, procedures, current research, education programs, and other aspects of archaeology for this state or possession.

TN State Archeologist, Dept. of Environment & Conservation, Div. of Archaeology
5103 Edmonson Pike
Nashville, TN 37211-5129
ph: 615-741-1588
fax: 615-741-7329
e-mail: nfielder@mail.state.tn.us
web: http://nasa.uconn.edu/tnosa.html
Provides information on laws, procedures, current research, education programs, and other aspects of archaeology for this state or possession.

Chief, Mississippi Department of Archives & History
P.O. Box 571
Jackson, MS 39205
ph: 601-359-6940
fax: 601-359-6955
web: http://nasa.uconn.edu/missosa.html
Provides information on laws, procedures, current research, education programs, and other aspects of archaeology for this state or possession.

Kentucky State Archaeologist, Department of Anthropology
University of Kentucky
Lexington, KY 40506-0024
ph: 606-258-5735
web: http://nasa.uconn.edu/kentosa.html
Provides information on laws, procedures, current research, education programs, and other aspects of archaeology for this state or possession.

Deputy SHPO, Ohio Historic Preservation Office, Ohio Historical Society
567 East Hudson St.
Columbus, OH 43211-1030
ph: 614-297-2470
fax: 614-297-2546
e-mail: davidsn@freenet.columbus.oh.us
web: http://nasa.uconn.edu/ohosa.html
Provides information on laws, procedures, current research, education programs, and other aspects of archaeology for this state or possession.

Indiana Dept. of Natural Resources, Div. of Historic Preservation/Archaeology
402 W. Washington, Rm. W274
Indianapolis, IN 46204
ph: 317-232-1646
fax: 317-232-8036
e-mail: rick_jones_at_dnrlan@ima.isd.state.in.us
web: http://nasa.uconn.edu/inosa.html
Provides information on laws, procedures, current research, education programs, and other aspects of archaeology for this state or possession.

John R. Halsey
State Archaeologist, Michigan Historical Center
717 W. Allegan St.
Lansing, MI 48918
ph: 517-373-6358
fax: 517-373-0851
web: http://nasa.uconn.edu/michosa.html
Provides information on laws, procedures, current research, education programs, and other aspects of archaeology for this state or possession.

Iowa State Archaeologist, University of Iowa
700 CLSB
Iowa City, IA 52242
ph: 319-384-0732
fax: 319-384-0768
e-mail: bill-green@uiowa.edu
web: http://nasa.uiowa.edu/~osa
Provides information on laws, procedures, current research, education programs, and other aspects of archaeology for this state or possession.

Archaeologist, State Historical Society of Wisconsin
816 State St.
Madison, WI 53706
ph: 608-264-6495
fax: 608-264-6404
web: http://www.shsw.wisc.edu/arch/
Provides information on laws, procedures, current research, education programs, and other aspects of archaeology for this state or possession.

Minnesota State Archaeologist
Fort Snelling History Center
Saint Paul, MN 55111
ph: 612-725-2411
fax: 612-725-2429
web: http://nasa.uconn.edu/minnosa.html
Provides information on laws, procedures, current research, education programs, and other aspects of archaeology for this state or possession.

South Dakota State Archaeologist, State Archaeological Research Center
2425 E. St. Charles St.
P.O. Box 1257
Rapid City, SD 57709-1257
ph: 605-394-1936
fax: 605-394-1941
e-mail: jhaug@silver.sdsmt.edu
web: http://nasa.uconn.edu/sdosa.html
Provides information on laws, procedures, current research, education programs, and other aspects of archaeology for this state or possession.

Chief Archaeologist, State Historical Society of ND, Arch. & Hist. Pres. Div.
North Dakota Heritage Center
612 E. Boulevard Ave.
Bismarck, ND 58505-0830
ph: 701-328-2672
fax: 701-328-3710
web: http://nasa.uconn.edu/ndosa.html
Provides information on laws, procedures, current research, education programs, and other aspects of archaeology for this state or possession.

State Archaeologists, Montana Historical Society
1410 8th Ave.
P.O. Box 20102
Helena, MT 59620
ph: 406-444-7715
fax: 406-444-6575
web: http://nasa.uconn.edu/mtosa.html
Provides information on laws, procedures, current research, education programs, and other aspects of archaeology for this state or possession.

State Archaeologist, Preservation Services Div., IL Historic Preservation Agency
500 East Madison St.
Springfield, IL 62701
ph: 217-785-4999
fax: 217-782-8161
web: http://nasa.uconn.edu/ilosa.html
Provides information on laws, procedures, current research, education programs, and other aspects of archaeology for this state or possession.

Senior Archaeologist, Missouri Historic Preservation Program
P.O. Box 176
Jefferson City, MO 65102
ph: 573-751-7958
fax: 573-526-2852
web: http://nasa.uconn.edu/moosa.html
Provides information on laws, procedures, current research, education programs, and other aspects of archaeology for this state or possession.

Kansas State Archaeologist
120 W. Tenth
Topeka, KS 66612
ph: 785-296-4781
fax: 785-296-1005
web: http://nasa.uconn.edu/kans.html
Provides information on laws, procedures, current research, education programs, and other aspects of archaeology for this state or possession.

Curator of Anthropology, Nebraska State Historical Society
1500 R. St.
P.O. Box 82554
Lincoln, NE 68501
ph: 402-471-4787
fax: 402-471-3100
web: http://nasa.uconn.edu/neosa.html
Provides information on laws, procedures, current research, education programs, and other aspects of archaeology for this state or possession.

Louisiana State Archaeologist, Division of Archaeology
Capitol Annex Building
P.O. Box 44247
Baton Rouge, LA 70804
ph: 504-342-8170
fax: 504-342-8173
e-mail: teubanks@crt.state.la.us
web: http://nasa.uconn.edu/luosa.html
Provides information on laws, procedures, current research, education programs, and other aspects of archaeology for this state or possession.

State Archaeologist, Arkansas Archeological Survey
P.O. Box 1249
Fayetteville, AR 72702-1249
ph: 501-575-3556
fax: 501-575-5453
e-mail: hadavis@comp.uark.edu
web: http://nasa.uconn.edu/arkosa.html
Provides information on laws, procedures, current research, education programs, and other aspects of archaeology for this state or possession.

State Archaeologist, University of Oklahoma, Oklahoma Archaeology Survey
111 East Chesapeake, Rm. 102
Norman, OK 73019
ph: 405-325-7211
fax: 405-325-7604
web: http://nasa.uconn.edu/okosa.html
Provides information on laws, procedures, current research, education programs, and other aspects of archaeology for this state or possession.

State Archaeologist, Texan Historical Commission
Box 12276, Capitol Station
Austin, TX 78711
ph: 512-463-8882
fax: 512-463-2530
e-mail: pmercado-allinger@access.texas.gov
web: http://nasa.uconn.edu/txosa.html
Provides information on laws, procedures, current research, education programs, and other aspects of archaeology for this state or possession.

State Archaeologist, Colorado Historical Society
1300 Broadway
Denver, CO 80203
ph: 303-886-2736
fax: 303-866-4464
e-mail: daleh@lynx.sni.net
web: http://nasa.uconn.edu/colosa.html
Provides information on laws, procedures, current research, education programs, and other aspects of archaeology for this state or possession.

State Archaeologist, Department of Anthropology
Box 3413
University Station
Laramie, WY 82071
ph: 307-766-5301
fax: 307-766-4052
e-mail: mmiller@uwyo.edu
web: http://nasa.uconn.edu/wyosa.html
Provides information on laws, procedures, current research, education programs, and other aspects of archaeology for this state or possession.

Idaho State Archaeologist
210 Main St.
Boise, ID 83703
ph: 208-334-3847
fax: 208-334-2775
web: http://nasa.uconn.edu/idosa.html
Provides information on laws, procedures, current research, education programs, and other aspects of archaeology for this state or possession.

Utah State Archaeologist, Division of State History
310 Rio Grande
Salt Lake City, UT 84101
ph: 801-533-3527
fax: 801-533-3503
e-mail: kjones@history.state.ut.us
web: http://nasa.uconn.edu/utosa.html
Provides information on laws, procedures, current research, education programs, and other aspects of archaeology for this state or possession.

Curator of Archaeology, Arizona State Museum
University of Arizona
Tucson, AZ 85721
ph: 520-621-2556
fax: 520-621-2976
e-mail: pfish@u.arizona.edu
web: http://nasa.uconn.edu/arizosa.html
Provides information on laws, procedures, current research, education programs, and other aspects of archaeology for this state or possession.

New Mexico State Archaeologist, Historic Preservation Division
Villa Rivera Bldg.
228 E. Palace Ave.
Santa Fe, NM 87503
ph: 505-827-6320
fax: 505-827-6338
e-mail: gdean@lvr.state.nm.us
web: http://nasa.uconn.edu/nmosa.html
Provides information on laws, procedures, current research, education programs, and other aspects of archaeology for this state or possession.

Nevada State Historic Preservation Office
100 N. Stewart Street
Carson City, NV 89710
ph: 775-684-3448
fax: 775-684-3441
e-mail: blprudic@clan.lib.nv.us
web: http://www.clan.lib.nv.us
Provides information on laws, procedures, current research, education programs, and other aspects of archaeology for this state or possession.

California Office of Historic Preservation
1416 9th St.
Sacramento, CA 95814
ph: 916-653-6624
fax: 916-653-9824
e-mail: calshpo@mail2.quiknet.com
web: http://ohp.cal-parks.ca.gov
Provides information on laws, procedures, current research, education programs, and other aspects of archaeology for this state or possession.

Head Archaeologist, Hawaii State Historic Preservation Division
33 S King Street, 6th Floor
Honolulu, HI 96813
ph: 808-587-0012
fax: 808-587-0018
web: http://nasa.uconn.edu/hiosa.html
Provides information on laws, procedures, current research, education programs, and other aspects of archaeology for this state or possession.

Guam Department of Parks & Recreation
Building 13-8 Tiyan
P.O. Box 2950
Agana, GU 96910
ph: 671-475-6290
fax: 671-477-2822
e-mail: vicapril@ns.gov.gu
web: http://nasa.uconn.edu/guamosa.html
Provides information on laws, procedures, current research, education programs, and other aspects of archaeology for this state or possession.

Archaeologist, Historic Preservation Office, Oregon State Parks & Recreation
1115 Commercial St., NE
Salem, OR 97310-1001
ph: 503-378-5001
fax: 503-378-6447
web: http://nasa.uconn.edu/orosa.html
Provides information on laws, procedures, current research, education programs, and other aspects of archaeology for this state or possession.

State Archaeologist, Dept. of Community, Trade & Economic Development
P.O. Box 48343
Olympia, WA 98504-8343
ph: 360-407-0771
fax: 360-407-6217
e-mail: robw@cted.wa.gov
web: http://nasa.uconn.edu/waosa.html
Provides information on laws, procedures, current research, education programs, and other aspects of archaeology for this state or possession.

State Archaeologist
State of Alaska Office of History & Archaeology
3601 C Street, #1278
Anchorage, AK 99503-5921
ph: 907-269-8721 or 907-269-8727
fax: 907-269-8908
e-mail: bobsh@dnr.state.ak.us
web: http://nasa.uconn.edu/akosa.html
Provides information on laws, procedures, current research, education programs, and other aspects of archaeology for this state or possession.

HI-FI EQUIPMENT

(see also AUDIO-VISUAL; PHONOGRAPHS; RADIOS; RECORDS)

Collectors

Jeffrey Viola
784 Eltone Rd.
Jackson, NJ 08527
ph: 201-928-0666
Wants to buy old tubes and tube-type Hi-fi & stereo equipment by such manufacturers as Marantz, Mcintosh, Fisher, Dynaco, Eico, Harman Kardon, Heathkit, Acrosound, Western Electric, Altec Lansing, Fairchild, others; no Japanese equipment.

Summer McDaniel
One Edgewood Place
North Brunswick, NJ 08902
ph: 732-249-3738
Wants to buy 1940s-1960s audio equipment; theater or home hi-fidelity amplifiers, speakers, horns, tube collections, microphones, etc.

Sonny Goldson
1413 Magnolia Lane
Midwest City, OK 73110
ph: 405-737-3312
fax: 405-737-3355
Wants commercial tube hi-fi sound equipment: speakers, horns, and tubes; McIntosh, Altec, Jensen, Marantz, Heath, Dynaco, James Lansing, Western Electric, Fisher, Scott, Eico, Electrovoice, Tannoy, RCA, etc.

Maury Corb
12325 Ashcroft
Houston, TX 77035
ph: 281-728-4343
fax: 281-723-1301
Wants to buy old, new or used electronics and sound equipment: speakers, amps, turntables, horns, misc. by Western Electric, RCA, McIntosh, Altec, Jensen, Marantz, Ev, Dynaco, JBL, etc.

HIGHWAY COLLECTIBLES

(see also AUTOMOBILIA; GAS STATION COLLECTIBLES; HOTEL COLLECTIBLES; DINERS & RELATED ITEMS; SOUVENIR & COMMEMORATIVE ITEMS; TRAILERS & RV'S)

Collectors

Laurel Kane
148 Old Kings Highway North
Darien, CT 06820
ph: 203-655-3893
fax: 203-655-2581
e-mail: laruelrk66@aol.com
Advanced collector of postcards and other U.S. highway-related memorabilia such as maps, travel guides, and motel guides; especially wants those related to Route 66; buys, sells, trades.

Decals

Dealers

Richard Schneider
Lost Highway Art Co.
P.O. Box 164
Bedford Hills, NY 10507-1064
ph: 914-234-6016
fax: 914-234-2761
Buys and sells souvenir water-dip decals: states, parks, cities, attractions, etc., wants singles or collections or inventories.

Repro. Sources

Richard Schneider
Lost Highway Art Co.
P.O. Box 164
Bedford Hills, NY 10507-1064
ph: 914-234-6016
fax: 914-234-2761
Large variety of vintage travel images available for graphic artists or reproduced on mugs, magnets and t-shirts.

Lincoln Highway

Collectors

Brian A. Butko
2640 Sunset Dr.
West Mifflin, PA 15122-3565
Collects souvenirs of what was the first auto road in the U.S. to cross the country; interested in Lincoln Highway ephemera such as books, pennants, and materials from early businesses along the route only.

Lynn Christian
1114 Wilson Ave.
Ames, IA 50010-5570
ph: 515-232-2222
Wants old "Lincoln Highway" related items.

Route 66 Items

Clubs/Associations

Route 66 Association of Illinois
2743 Veterans Parkway, #166
Springfield, IL 62704
ph: 847-392-0860 or 847-577-2501
e-mail: teague66@eosinc.com
web: http://www.il66assoc.org/idx_1a.htm
Organization focusing on protecting and promoting Rt. 66 (The Mother Road) and collecting items relating thereto.

International Route 66 Association
2700 Kiowa S.
Lake Havasu City, AZ 86403
e-mail: info@route66.com
web: http://www.route66.com

Museums/Libraries

Texas Old Route 66 Association Museum and Hall of Fame
100 Kingsley St.
P.O. Box 290
Mclean, TX 79057-0290
ph: 806-779-2225 or 806-779-3164
e-mail: barbwiremueum@centramedia.com
1800 sq. ft. of 450 authentic Route 66 artifacts; Route 66 gift shop.

Bob Lundy
Route 66 Museum & Gift Shop
2400 San Dimas Cnayon Rd., #318
La Verne, CA 91750
ph: 909-592-2090 or 800-JOG-RT66
e-mail: rte66@citivu.com
web: http://www.citivu.com/rc/rte66/rte66.html

Periodicals

Paul Taylor
: Route 66 Magazine
326 W. Route 66
Williams, AZ 86046
ph: 520-635-4322
A glossy magazine loaded with news, photos and plenty of Route 66 nostalgia.

Signs & Traffic Devices

Periodicals

Jeff Francis
Newsletter: Signpost
P.O. Box 41381
Saint Petersburg, FL 33743-1381
ph: 727-345-6627
fax: 727-343-8977
e-mail: gobucs13@aol.com
An association focusing on the research and preservation of traffic devices, markers and signs.

HIPPIE ITEMS

(see SOCIAL CAUSES)

HISTORICAL AMERICANA

(see also AUTOGRAPHS; GLASS, Commemorative; IMMIGRATION; MANUSCRIPTS; MILITARIA; PAPER COLLECTIBLES; POLITICAL COLLECTIBLES; SOCIAL CAUSES; VETERAN ITEMS)

Auction Services

Rex Stark
Rex Stark Americana
P.O. Box 1029
Gardner, MA 01440-6029
ph: 978-630-3237
fax: 978-630-2388
Conducts mail auctions of quality historical Americana: political, early military, advertising, sports, etc.

Bob Moffatt
P.O. Box 281
Auburn, MA 01501-0281
ph: 508-832-9707
fax: 508-832-2992
Conducts mail bid auctions of tokens, badges, and other historical Americana.

East Coast Books
P.O. Box 849
Wells, ME 04090
ph: 207-646-3584
fax: 207-646-0416
Specializes in mail-bid auctions of historically significant autographs, manuscripts and letters, art works on paper.

Remember When Antiquities
P.O. Box 1829
Wells, ME 04090-1829
Wants autographs, books, historical ephemera, sports memorabilia for consignment auctions; free quarterly auction catalogs.

Donald Ackerman
Provenance Galleries, Inc.
P.O. Box 3487
Wallington, NJ 07057
ph: 973-779-8785
fax: 973-744-1517
Conducts periodic mail catalog auctions featuring historical Americana such as political items, early photography, autographs, Civil War, broadsides, etc.

Caroline Birenbaum
Swann Galleries, Inc.
104 E. 25th St.
New York, NY 10010-2977
ph: 212-254-4710
fax: 212-979-1017
e-mail: swann@swanngalleries.com
web: http://www.swanngalleries.com/
Oldest/largest U.S. auctioneer specializing in rare books, autographs & manuscripts, maps, atlases, photographs, and works of art on paper including vintage posters.

Robert H. Snyder
Cohasco, Inc.
P.O. Box 821
Yonkers, NY 10702-0821
ph: 914-476-8500
fax: 914-476-8573
e-mail: cohascodpc@earthlink.net
web: http://home.earthlink.net/~cohascodpc/index.html
Mail bid auctions of paper and Americana: medallic art, Civil War, presidential ephemera and letters, music, old newspapers, prints, maps, political, financial, aviation, Judaica, legal, Lincolniania, personalities, royalty, sports, etc.

Ted Hake
Hake's Americana & Collectibles Auction
P.O. Box 1444
York, PA 17405-1444
ph: 717-848-1333
e-mail: Ted@hakes.com
web: http://www.hakes.com/
Always purchasing items for 8 mail-bid auctions per year covering hundreds of categories including toys, character collectibles, Disney, cowboy heroes, premiums, television, politicals, pin-back buttons, advertising and more.

Robert Coup
Historicana
P.O. Box 348
Leola, PA 17540-0348
ph: 717-656-7780
fax: 717-656-8233
e-mail: POLBANDWGN@aol.com
Specializes in mail-bid auctions of character collectibles, Disneyana, political items & historical Americana; sample catalog $2.

C. Wesley Cowan
747 Park Ave.
Terrace Park, OH 45174
ph: 513-248-8122
fax: 513-248-2566
Sells historical Americana: photographic images, political items, manuscripts, autographs, etc.

Al Anderson
Anderson Auction
P.O. Box 644
Troy, OH 45373-0644
ph: 937-339-0850
fax: 937-339-8620
e-mail: aaauctn@erinet.com
web: http://www.erinet.com/aaauctn
Specializes in mail-bid auctions of political items and historical Americana.

Tom Slater
Political Gallery, The
1315 W. 86th St.
Indianapolis, IN 46260
ph: 317-257-0863
fax: 317-254-9167
Specializing in mail-bid auctions of Disneyana, historical Americana, toys, political items, and other collectibles.

U.I. "Chick" Harris
Harris Auctions
P.O. Box 20614
Saint Louis, MO 63139-0614
ph: 314-352-8623
Collector/specialist in all types of political Americana; conducts specialized mail-auctions of political and historical Americana.

Early American History Auction
P.O. Box 3341
La Jolla, CA 92038
ph: 619-459-4159
fax: 619-459-4373
e-mail: auctions@earlyamerican.com
web: http://www.earlyAmerican.com
Autographs, currency, coins, Americana, Civil War, Lincoln, slavery, weapons, maps.

Collectors

Sheldon Lerman
7505 Osler Dr.
Baltimore, MD 21204-7736
ph: 410-321-1514 or 410-828-1928
fax: 410-825-5710
Wants to buy historical documents, Presidential and historical signatures.

Cary Demont
P.O. Box 16013
Minneapolis, MN 55416
ph: 612-522-0957
e-mail: Caryd8@aol.com
Serious collector looking for historical ephemera including political campaign items of all kinds, the woman's suffrage movement, prohibition and Carrie Nation items, Civil War period broadsides, and interesting Wild West material.

Dealers

Rex Stark
Rex Stark Americana
P.O. Box 1029
Gardner, MA 01440-6029
ph: 978-630-3237
fax: 978-630-2388
Buys & sells historical Americana; wants 1770-1870 Amer. historical pottery; offers catalog of historical/political Americana for sale.

University Archives
600 Summer St.
Stamford, CT 06901-1403
ph: 800-237-5692 or 203-975-9291
fax: 203-348-3560
Buying and selling fine historical autographs, manuscripts, documents, autographed books and autographed photographs of notable people including U.S. presidents, Revolutionary and Civil War, literary, aviation, science, art, and music.

Peter Hlinka
Peter Hlinka Historical Americana
P.O. Box 310
New York, NY 10028-0017
ph: 718-409-6407
Buys, sells, and appraises historical Americana; publishes a large catalog of militaria, military insignia, war relics, related books, and other historical Americana; also foreign.

Donald Blincoe
Uncle Davey's Americana
6140 St. Augustine Rd.
Jacksonville, FL 32217
ph: 904-730-8932 or 904-777-6478
fax: 904-730-8932
e-mail: uncledv@collectorsnet.com
web: http://www.collectorsnet.com/uncledv/
Expert who buys, sells, appraises vintage historical U.S. military related items from 1740 to 1885: weapons, documents, currency, coins, autographs, slavery, photos, books, newspapers, jewelry, clothing, maps, letters, etc.

Robert Richshafer
2929 First Ave. #L
San Diego, CA 92103
ph: 619-294-7950
e-mail: robrich5683@webtv.net
For 30 years a source of photographs, historic newspapers, broadsides, pamphlets, Americana, documents, ledgers, advertising, prints for collectors, dealers and museum.

Steve Schmale
Out West
2231 Creekside Rd.
Santa Rosa, CA 95405-8022
ph: 707-838-1859 or 707-575-5406
e-mail: outweststv@aol.com
Buys and sells better vintage postcards since 1976; approval service; strong in Western states views; always buying better cards and real photos; also wants railroad paper, stereoviews, photos, brochures, trade cards; member IFPD.

Charles Zeder
Zeder's Antiques
1320 SW 10th Street
North Bend, WA 98045
ph: 425-888-6697
Deals in 19th century ephemera, Civil War items, stock certificates, bonds, fruit box labels, 19th century advertising.

Ruth A. Miller Knott
Paperpeneur, The
2601 Kittias Highway
Ellensburg, WA 98926
ph: 509-962-8840
fax: 509-962-3609
e-mail: ruthie@ellensburg.com
Offers a unique selection of paper ephemera, historical documents, and collectibles: advertising, Americana,

agriculture, Colonial, maritime, transportation, fraternal; does research and will answer questions.

Internet Resources

Library of Congress, American Memory
101 Independence Ave. SE
Washington, DC 20540
ph: 202-707-8000
e-mail: ndlpcoll@loc.gov
web: http://memory.loc.gov/ammem/
Historical collections from the National Digital Library: Washington's Papers, Lincoln's Papers, baseball cards, photos, prints, maps, motion pictures, sound recordings.

Making of America
University of Michigan
209 Graduate Libary
Ann Arbor, MI 48103-1205
ph: 313-764-1148
fax: 313-764-0259
e-mail: moa-feedback@umich.edu
web: http://www.umdl.umich.edu/moa/
The MOA Collection is a digital library of primary sources in American social history from the antebellum period through reconstruction: 1,600 books, 50,000 journals with 19th century imprints; all scanned in their entirety.

HITCHING POSTS

Collectors

Bob Maclin
1436 Lakewood
Lexington, KY 40502
ph: 606-269-4450
Interested in corresponding with others who are interested in hitching posts.

HOBBY HORSES

(see RIDING TOYS, Rocking Horses)

HOBBY TOYS

(see TOYS, Construction Sets)

HOBO COLLECTIBLES

(see also TRAMP ART)

Clubs/Associations

Buzz Potter
National Hobo Association
Newsletter: Hobo Times
P.O. Box 706
Nisswa, MN 56468
e-mail: hobousa@uslink.net
web: http://uslink.net/~hobousa/
Hobo tails, hobo calendar of events, hobo poetry, news and notes; sponsors hobo gatherings.

HOLIDAY COLLECTIBLES

(see also CHRISTMAS COLLECTIBLES; COLLECTIBLES [MODERN], Ornaments; ELVES; HALLOWEEN COLLECTIBLES; VALENTINES; ST. PATRICK)

Auction Services

Cindy Chipps
Holiday Auction, The
4027 Brooks Hill Rd.
Brooks, KY 40109-5002
ph: 502-955-9238
fax: 502-957-5027
e-mail: holauction@aol.com
web: http://members.aol.com/holauction/index.html
Holds bi-monthly mail auction of a wide variety of holiday items from the common to the very rare; send for free catalog.

Collectors

Ann C. Bergin
P.O. Box 105
Amherst, NH 03031-0105
fax: 508-649-6807
e-mail: acbergin@aol.com
Wants items relating to holidays, and ceremonies of life (Christenings, baptisms, weddings, confirmations, graduations, birthdays, etc.)

Linda L. Vines
P.O. Box 43721
Upper Montclair, NJ 07043
ph: 973-748-4990
e-mail: lja@viconet.com
Wants to buy pre-1950 holiday decoration including German Christmas, Halloween, Easter and patriotic candy containers, pumpkins, and Santas.

Trish Claar
2621 Manor Court
Owings, MD 20736-9145
ph: 301-855-6531
Wants 1950s and 1960s Holiday collectibles, especially Christmas.

Kit Carter Weilage
506 Briar Hill Rd.
Louisville, KY 40206
ph: 502-561-5030
Buys and sells Christmas collectibles, specializing in German-made Santa candy containers.

Dealers

Chris Savino
P.O. Box 419
Breesport, NY 14816-0419
ph: 607-739-3106
fax: 607-739-3106
e-mail: csavino@extrope.net
Wants Holiday items including Christmas, Halloween, Easter; Santas, papier mache items such as ornaments, party favors, decorations, candy containers; tin toys, devils, skulls, witches; items made in Germany, Japan or USA.

Bettie Petzoldt
178 Woolen Mill Rd.
New Park, PA 17352
ph: 717-382-1416
e-mail: philw3@erols.com
web: http://www.mindyourbusiness.com/ornaments/index.htm
Wants pre-1940 Christmas items: unusual, collectible (figural) Christmas ornaments, snow babies, lights, Santas; other holiday items too.

Jenny Tarrant
Holly-Daze
4 Gardenview Dr.
Saint Peters, MO 63376-3507
ph: 314-397-1763
e-mail: jennyjol@aol.com
Wants German Santas, Halloween candy containers, Jack O'Lanterns, German rabbits, and George Washington composition candy containers.

Experts

Lissa & Richard Smith
3 Baldtop Heights
Danville, PA 17821
ph: 570-275-7796
Advisor to "Warman's Antiques & Collectibles Price Guide", authors of "Christmas Collectibles."

Easter

Dealers

Paul W. Schofield
Lion's Den Antiques
7988 Bethel Burley Rd. SE
Port Orchard, WA 98366
ph: 360-876-3364
fax: 360-876-5421
Buys, sells, appraises, and specializes in old Santas, candy containers, Halloween, Easter, Christmas, Easter, Dresden, figural lights.

HOLLOWWARE

(see SILVER; SILVERPLATE)

HOLLYWOOD POSTERS

(see MOVIE MEMORABILIA, Movie Posters; PHOTOGRAPHS, Celebrity)

HOLOGRAMS

Man./Prod./Dist.

Excalibur
P.O. Box 14478
Philadelphia, PA 19115
ph: 610-342-6913
Promo cards, non-sports and adult trading cards.

NeoVisions Productions
P.O. Box 74277
Los Angeles, CA 90004
ph: 213-387-0461
fax: 213-387-0461
Holograms for home and industry: Star Wars, Star Trek, Deep Space Nine, Next Generation, Aliens, MAD, Jurassic Park, dozens of collectible licensed holographic items: pens, pencils, badges, bookmarks, keychains, stickers, etc.

HOLSTERS

(see TOY GUNS; WESTERN AMERICANA)

HOLT HOWARD

Collectors

Trish Claar
2621 Manor Court
Owings, MD 20736-9145
ph: 301-855-6531
Holt Howard items are usually ceramic, always whimsical.

HOMESPUN

(see TEXTILES)

HOOSIER CABINETS

(see FURNITURE [ANTIQUE], Kitchen Cabinets)

HORNS & WHISTLES

(see also NAUTICAL ANTIQUES; SPORTING COLLECTIBLES, Game Calls; STEAM-OPERATED, Models & Equipment)

Clubs/Associations

Harry D. Barry
Air Horn & Steam Whistle Enthusiasts
Newsletter: Horn & Whistle
275 Windswept Dr.
North East, PA 16428
ph: 814-725-8150
Purpose is to preserve, increase, and disseminate knowledge concerning horns, whistles, sirens, and bells in industrial, marine, transportation, signaling, and warning applications.

James C. Fitch
Call & Whistle Collectors Association
Newsletter: Whistle Notes
2839 E. 26th Place
Tulsa, OK 74114-4309
ph: 918-747-3202
e-mail: jfitch@noria.com
Club for collectors of game calls, antique whistles, bo's'n pipes, flutes, bird calls, advertising whistles, toy whistles, and folk art whistles.

Collectors

Harry D. Barry
275 Windswept Dr.
North East, PA 16428
ph: 814-725-8150
Collects steam whistles and horns which were and are used on locomotives, ships, factories, boilers, etc.

Sirens

Collectors

Bill Cary
1104 Clinton St.
Rome, NY 13440-2516
ph: 315-336-7623
Wants to buy hand-cranked sirens; working or not working, parts, brackets, etc.

HORROR

(see also GHOSTS & HAUNTINGS; MORBID & ODD ITEMS; MOVIE MEMORABILIA; SCIENCE FICTION; WITCHES)

Collectors

Rich Zelachowski
220 Centre Ave.
Secaucus, NJ 07094
ph: 201-319-9339
e-mail: richz@tiac.net
Wants to buy horror collectibles: toys, games, props, models, autographs, books, magazines, posters, robots, records, etc.

Dracula

Clubs/Associations

Dr. M. Jeanne Youngson
Count Dracula Fan Club
Journal: Dracula News
29 Washington Square West
New York, NY 10011-9180
ph: 212-982-6754
Club keeps members of the CDFC up on everything happening in the world of the undead; also publishes other newsletters.

Museums/Libraries

Dr. M. Jeanne Youngson
Count Dracula Permanent Collection of Vampire Memorabilia
29 Washington Square West
New York, NY 10011-9180
ph: 212-982-6754
Figurines, posters, games, pulps, autographed photos of Lugosi, Hamilton Deane, Karloff, Langella, Kinski, Price, Cushing, Lanchester, etc., original art, early playbills; also Frankenstein and Wolfman memorabilia.

Frankenstein

Museums/Libraries

Dr. M. Jeanne Youngson
Count Dracula Permanent Collection of Vampire Memorabilia
29 Washington Square West
New York, NY 10011-9180
ph: 212-982-6754
Figurines, posters, games, pulps, autographed photos of Lugosi, Hamilton Deane, Karloff, Langella, Kinski, Price, Cushing, Lanchester, etc., original art, early playbills; also Frankenstein and Wolfman memorabilia.

Wolfman

Museums/Libraries

Dr. M. Jeanne Youngson
Count Dracula Permanent Collection of Vampire Memorabilia
29 Washington Square West
New York, NY 10011-9180
ph: 212-982-6754
Figurines, posters, games, pulps, autographed photos of Lugosi, Hamilton Deane, Karloff, Langella, Kinski, Price, Cushing, Lanchester, etc., original art, early playbills; also Frankenstein and Wolfman memorabilia.

HORSE RACING

(see SPORTS COLLECTIBLES, Thoroughbred Racing)

HORSE-DRAWN VEHICLES

(see also FARM COLLECTIBLES; FARM MACHINERY; ANIMAL COLLECTIBLES, Horse-Related)

Auction Services

Paul Martin, Jr.
Martin Auctioneers, Inc.
14 S. Holland Rd.
P.O. Box 477
Intercourse, PA 17534-0477
ph: 717-768-8108
fax: 717-768-7714
Specializes in the sale of horse drawn carriages, buggies, hitch wagons, tack and other horse-related items; buys and sells through private transactions and public auction; will buy complete collections or single pieces.

Larry Garner
Larry Garner Auctioneers
P.O. Box 323
Carrollton, OH 44615
ph: 800-452-8452
fax: 330-627-3788
e-mail: garner@raex.com
web: http://www.auctionweb.com
Conducts auctions of horse-drawn carriages, buggies, hitch wagons, tack and other horse-related items.

Shipshewana Auction, Inc.
P.O. Box 185
Shipshewana, IN 46565
ph: 219-768-41129
Conducts an annual (May/June) auction of horse-drawn vehicles and related items.

Sweeney's Auction Services
739 7th Ave. SE
Waukon, IA 52172
ph: 319-568-4577

Dealers

Horse-Drawn Carriages
P.O. Box 1392
Santa Rosa, CA 95402-1392
Wants horse-drawn wagons, fifth wheel wagons, light delivery wagons, stagecoaches, etc.

Periodicals

Draft Horse Journal, Inc.
Magazine: Draft Horse Journal
P.O. Box 670
Waverly, IA 50677
ph: 319-352-4046
fax: 319-352-2232
e-mail: horshoes@horseshoes.com
web: http://www.horseshoes.com
A trade magazine of the Draft Horse and Mule Industry; present day uses along with historical material; horses, mules, and equipment advertised.

Magazine: Driving Digest Magazine
2533 North Carson Street, Ste. 2990
Carson City, NV 89706
ph: 775-841-3768
fax: 775-883-2384
A magazine for horsemen interested in competitive driving of a single horse, pairs and four-in-hands.

Repro. Sources

Cumberland General Store
#1 Highway 68
Crossville, TN 38555
ph: 931-484-8481 or 800-334-4640
fax: 931-456-1211
web: http://
www.cumberlandgeneral.com/

Carriages

Auction Services

Paul Martin, Jr.
Martin Auctioneers, Inc.
14 S. Holland Rd.
P.O. Box 477
Intercourse, PA 17534-0477
ph: 717-768-8108
fax: 717-768-7714
Specializes in the sale of horse drawn carriages, buggies, hitch wagons, tack and other horse-related items; buys and sells through private transactions and public auction; will buy complete collections or single pieces.

Clubs/Associations

Jill Ryder, Ed. Dir.
Carriage Association of America, The
Journal: Carriage Journal, The
177 Pointers-Auburn Rd.
Salem, NJ 08079
ph: 609-935-1616
fax: 609-935-4955
e-mail: carrassc@jaguarsystems.com
web: http://www.caaonline.com/
Founded in 1960; devoted to the knowledge, collecting, restoring, driving and research of horse-drawn vehicles; more than 3,500 members in 25 countries.

American Driving Society
Newsletter: Whip, The
P.O. Box 160
Metamora, MI 48455
ph: 810-664-8666
fax: 810-664-2405
e-mail:
info@americandrivingsociety.org
web: http://
www.americandrivingsociety.org/
Promotes the sport of carriage driving and horse training for sport and pleasure; articles, ads, competitions, carriage maintenance.

Mrs. Jenny Dillon, Sec.
British Driving Society, The
Newsletter: British Driving Society Newsletter
27 Dugard Place
Barford, Warwick CV35 8DX
U.K.
ph: 01926 624420 or +44 1926 624420
fax: 01926 624633
web: http://www.images.mcmail.com/
bds/index.htm
Focuses on carriage driving and horse training.

Museums/Libraries

Museums at Stony Brook, The
Newsletter: News & Events
1208 Route 25A
Stony Brook, NY 11790-1992
ph: 516-751-0066
fax: 516-751-0353
e-mail: museums@longisland.com
web: http://
www.museumsatstonybrook.org/
Large collection of American Art,

decoys, horse-drawn vehicles, costumes, and miniature period rooms; museum shop.

Susan Green
Carriage Museum of America Library
P.O. Box 417
Bird In Hand, PA 17505
ph: 717-656-7019
A research library that serves as a source for historically accurate technical information on horse-drawn vehicles and related subjects.

Rose Hill Manor
1611 N. Market St.
Frederick, MD 21701
ph: 301-694-1650

Henry Ford Museum
20900 Oakwood Blvd.
P.O. Box 1970
Dearborn, MI 48121-1970
ph: 313-982-6001 or 313-271-1620
fax: 313-271-9621
e-mail: webmaster@hfmgv.org
web: http://www.hfmgv.org/
Over 100 horse-drawn vehicles.

Periodicals

Magazine: Driving West Magazine
P.O. Box 395
Jamul, CA 91935
ph: 619-669-1046 or 760-787-0433
fax: 619-669-3904
e-mail: drivingwst@aol.com
web: http://www.drivingwest.com/
A bi-monthly magazine with a calendar of events, listings of local clubs as well as information about carriage driving in the Western US and Canada.

Repair Services

Ivan Burkholder
Woodlyn Coach Co.
4410 TR 628
Millersburg, OH 44654
ph: 330-674-9124
Specializes in the repair and complete restoration of horse drawn carriages, buggies and wagons; also builds new hitch wagons.

Old World Wheel Works
41 N. Business Park
1033 E. Mt. Pleasant Rd.
Evansville, IN 47711
ph: 800-877-3622
Specializes in the repair and restoration of horse drawn carriages and buggies; reproductions, custom made-to-order parts.

Suppliers

Ivan Burkholder
Woodlyn Coach Co.
4410 TR 628
Millersburg, OH 44654
ph: 330-674-9124
Carries buggy restoration and supply parts; send for catalog.

HORSES

(see also ANIMAL COLLECTIBLES, Horse Related; LIVESTOCK)

Appraisers

Jay Proost
American Society of Agricultural Appraisers, Inc.
P.O. Box 186
Twin Falls, ID 83303-0186
ph: 208-733-2323 or 208-734-7570
fax: 208-733-2326
e-mail: JProost@micron.net
Members of this association appraise livestock, horses and farm equipment.

Auction Services

Professional Auction Services, Inc.
P.O. Box 1399
Leesburg, VA 20177
ph: 800-240-7900 or 703-777-6975
fax: 703-777-5580
e-mail: pasinc@aol.com
web: http://professionalauction.com/
One of America's leading show horse auction companies.

HOTEL COLLECTIBLES

(see also HIGHWAY COLLECTIBLES; NIGHTCLUB MEMORABILIA; SOUVENIR & COMMEMORATIVE ITEMS; TRAILERS & RV'S)

Collectors

Larry Spilkin
P.O. Box 5039
Southfield, MI 48086-5039
ph: 248-642-3722
Wants postcards and matchbook covers of drive-ins, diners, cafes, gas stations and 1930s-1950s motels, restaurant/bar, cabins and Art Deco streamline hotels.

Hyatt Hotels

Collectors

Michael Hickey
1512 Chasewood Dr.
Austin, TX 78727
ph: 512-989-0188
fax: 512-989-0112
e-mail: Mike_Hickey@msn.com
Collects anything to do with Hyatt Hotels & Resorts (has over 1600 Hyatt items!)

Tourist Cabins

Collectors

Brian A. Butko
2640 Sunset Dr.
West Mifflin, PA 15122-3565
Wants to buy books, brochures, guides and souvenirs from tourist courts that had individual cabins; no postcards please.

HOUSEWARES

(see ELECTRICITY RELATED ITEMS, Appliances; KITCHEN COLLECTIBLES)

HUMIDORS

(see SMOKING COLLECTIBLES)

HUMMELS

(see COLLECTIBLES [MODERN], Figurines [Goebel]; FIGURINES, Hummel)

HUNTING

(see ANIMAL TROPHIES; LICENSES, Hunting & Fishing; SPORTING COLLECTIBLES; TRAPS)

HYMNALS

(see also BOOKS; SHEET MUSIC)

Collectors

Christian Williams
8 Elm Rd.
Scarsdale, NY 10583
ph: 914-723-8739
Wants to buy old hymnals; prefers Victorian era with picture on cover; also small Sunday school books; send title, date, condition and price; all offers considered.

Here are some tips when contacting someone listed in this book:

■ When requesting information about a particular item, include a description (material, dimensions, maker's mark, model number, etc.) and a photo, sketch, or photocopy of the item in question.

■ Always ask if there are charges for samples or for the services requested.

■ When writing, please be sure to include a Large (#10 business size) Self-Addressed and Stamped Envelope (LSASE) if requesting a reply or the return of photographs.

■ Never call collect unless otherwise directed. When calling, be considerate of time zone differences and always ask if the party you are calling has time to talk. When leaving an answering machine message, always instruct the party to call you back collect.

I

ICE CREAM MEMORABILIA

(see ICE INDUSTRY; MOLDS, Ice Cream; SODA FOUNTAIN COLLECTIBLES)

ICE INDUSTRY

Collectors

Tom & Lucia Lucia
2145 Wilbraham Rd.
Springfield, MA 01129-1806
e-mail: icebox@tiac.net
web: http://www.tiac.net/users/icebox/
Wants to buy ice business memorabilia: ice cards, advertising, ice tools, ice picks with ice company names, photos, etc.; send asking price and description.

Joe Pedro
9 Whitcomb Ave.
Ayer, MA 01432-1627
ph: 978-772-2971
Wants ice memorabilia: signs, paper, tokens, photos, badges, watches, fobs, tools, delivery bags, picks, axes; anything to do with the ice business.

City Ice Co.
475 N. Main St.
Janesville, WI 53545
ph: 608-754-6619
Wants ice harvesting tools and ice items: plows, markers, fork bars, chisels, splitting bars, pictures, books, catalogs on ice harvesting.

Somers
4524 Rialto Place
Stockton, CA 95207
Wants ice tongs, picks, signs, bottles, scales, crushers, shavers; anything to do with the ice business.

Experts

Philip C. Whitney
Whitney Historic Programs
303 Fisher Rd.
Fitchburg, MA 01420-1548
ph: 978-342-1350
Specializes in demonstrating the art of antique ice harvesting and the matching of buyers and sellers of ice harvesting equipment; owner of the largest mobile collection of ice harvesting equipment in the country.

Museums/Libraries

Ice House Museum
303 Franklin Street
Cedar Falls, IA 50613
ph: 319-266-5149

ICONS

(see also RUSSIAN ITEMS)

Appraisers

Tad Sviderskis
Icon Painting, Restoration, Expertise & Appraisal Company, Inc.
730 Fifth Ave., 9th Floor
New York, NY 10019-4105
ph: 800-510-9799
fax: 570-643-8730
e-mail: sviders@aol.com
Specializing in appraisals of 14th to 19th century Russian and Greek icon painting; provides documented reports in compliance with the Uniform Standards of Professional Appraisal Practice; serving collectors and museums.

Dealers

Don E. Springer
Slava Gallery
P.O. Box 2893
Fairfax, VA 22301
ph: 703-323-6185 or 800-210-0113
e-mail: don@slavagal.com
web: http://www.slavagal.com
Collector, dealer, expert in icons: Russian, Orthodox Church, Eastern Church, Byzantine; also offers icon restoration service.

James L. Jackson, ISA
Jackson's Sacred Heart
2229 Lincoln St.
Cedar Falls, IA 50613
ph: 319-277-2256
fax: 319-277-1252
e-mail: jacksons@jacksonsauction.com
web: http://www.jacksonsauction.com
Specializing in quality 17th, 18th and 19th century Russian icons and related items; quarterly full color catalog offering Russian icons and related items.

Experts

Tad Sviderskis
Icon Painting, Restoration, Expertise & Appraisal Company, Inc.
730 Fifth Ave., 9th Floor
New York, NY 10019-4105
ph: 800-510-9799
fax: 570-643-8730
e-mail: sviders@aol.com
Specializing in professional conservation, restoration treatment of ancient icon painting; consolidation of deteriorated paint layer, grounding, cleaning of grime & darkened varnish; services televised nationwide; video tape available.

James L. Jackson, ISA
Jackson's Sacred Heart
2229 Lincoln St.
Cedar Falls, IA 50613
ph: 319-277-2256
fax: 319-277-1252
e-mail: jacksons@jacksonsauction.com
web: http://www.jacksonsauction.com
Has written and lectured widely on Russian icons, and has traveled extensively throughout Russia and the former Soviet Union studying Russian icons.

Museums/Libraries

Dr. Gary Vikan
Walters Art Gallery
600 N. Charles St.
Baltimore, MD 21201
ph: 410-547-9000
e-mail: lwolfe@thewalters.org
web: http://www.thewalters.org/
One of only a few museums worldwide to present a comprehensive history of art from the third millennium B.C. to the early 20th century.

Repair Services

Tad Sviderskis
Icon Painting, Restoration, Expertise & Appraisal Company, Inc.
730 Fifth Ave., 9th Floor
New York, NY 10019-4105
ph: 800-510-9799
fax: 570-643-8730
e-mail: sviders@aol.com
Specializing in professional conservation, restoration treatment of ancient icon painting; consolidation of deteriorated paint layer, grounding, cleaning of grime & darkened varnish; services televised nationwide; video tape available.

Don E. Springer
Slava Gallery
P.O. Box 2893
Fairfax, VA 22301
ph: 703-323-6185 or 800-210-0113
e-mail: don@slavagal.com
web: http://www.slavagal.com
Collector, dealer, expert in icons: Russian, Orthodox Church, Eastern Church, Byzantine; also offers icon restoration service.

ILLUSTRATORS

(see also ART; BOOKS, Illustrated; MAGAZINES; PAPER COLLECTIBLES, Illustrated; PERSONALITIES [ARTISTS]; PIN-UP ART; PRINTS)

Auction Services

Illustration House
96 Spring St., 7th Floor
New York, NY 10012-3923

Collectors

Charles Martignette
P.O. Box 293
Hallandale, FL 33008
ph: 305-454-3474
American illustration art historian wants to buy original illustration artwork: original paintings and drawings, magazine front-cover art, magazine story illustrations, advertising art; please send photos, dimensions, price.

Tim Isaacson
1002 Clinton
Oak Park, IL 60304-1824
ph: 708-383-5646
e-mail: TFIsaacson@aol.com
Wants to buy original illustrator art: paintings & interior illustrations used for magazine covers, paperback books, pulp magazines, The Shadow, comic book art pages, daily & Sunday comic strip funnies, science fiction, detective, etc.

Wendy Hoffman
Wendy Hoffman Gallery
8305 Rosewood
Shawnee Mission, KS 66207-1742
ph: 913-649-1717
e-mail: wendysart@aol.com
Wants to buy art by illustrators Fox, Parrish, Gutmann, Humphrey; Esquire magazines with Vargas gatefolds; pin-up calendars/prints by Elvgren, Moran, Mozert and Armstrong; sporting calendars/prints by Goodwin, Stick, etc.

Dealers

Joan Jenkins
45 Brown's Lane
Old Lyme, CT 06371
ph: 860-434-1852
Buys and sells illustrator art by Parrish, Fox, Thompson, Pressler, Hare, Goodwin, Stick, Gutmann, Becker, Harris and Indian Maidens.

Judy Goffman Cutler
Judy Goffman Fine Art
18 East 77th Street
New York, NY 10021
ph: 212-744-5190
fax: 212-744-0128
e-mail: art@amerillus.com
web: http://www.amerillus.com/
Specializing in paintings, watercolors and drawings from the "Golden Age" of American illustration 1880-1940.

Matt Iarocci
Matt's
P.O. Box 290H
Scarsdale, NY 10583-8790
ph: 914-472-6361
e-mail: matt173838@aol.com
Buys and sells original illustrator art; done for magazine covers, stories, pulps, ads, calendars, posters, comics, etc.; subjects include Western,

adventure, fashion, pin-up, horror, sports, movies, travel.

Jo Ann Reisler
360 Glyndon St., NE
Vienna, VA 22180-3537
ph: 703-938-2967
fax: 703-938-9057
e-mail: Reisler@clark.net
web: http://www.clark.net/pub/reisler
Wants to buy original illustrator art.

Danny Eskenazi
Jack Hammer Ltd.
169 Broadway East
Seattle, WA 98102
ph: 206-932-6621
fax: 206-932-1449
e-mail: k7ss@wolfenet.com
Buys and sells original 20th century illustration art.

Museums/Libraries

Society of Illustrators Museum of American Illustration
128 E. 63rd. St.
New York, NY 10021
ph: 212-838-2560
fax: 212-838-2561
e-mail: society@societyillustrators.org
web: http://www.societyillustrators.org/
Permanent collection of the Society is the home for hundreds of works of art by many of the greatest names in American painting and illustration.

Periodicals

Joan Jenkins
Newsletter: Calendar Art Collectors' Newsletter
45 Brown's Lane
Old Lyme, CT 06371
ph: 860-434-1852
Illustrated articles about Parrish, Fox, Thompson, VanNortwick, Garratt, Whitroy, Grossman, Icart-type, Gutmann, Becker, Fangel, Kenyon, Hibel, "Cupid" prints, Pressler, Eggleston, Leyendecker, Phillips, Indian Maiden prints.

Doug Watson
Magazine: Paper Collectors' Marketplace
470 Main St.
P.O. Box 128
Scandinavia, WI 54977-0128
ph: 715-467-2379
fax: 715-467-2243
e-mail: pcmpaper@gglbbs.com
web: http://www.pcmpaper.com/
Monthly magazine for collectors of paper memorabilia including autographs, paperbacks, postcards, advertising, photographica, magazines; all types of paper ephemera.

Denis C. Jackson, Ed.
Newsletter: Illustrator Collector's News, The
P.O. Box 1958
Sequim, WA 98382-1958
ph: 360-452-3810
e-mail: ticn@olypen.com
web: http://www.olypen.com/ticn/
A bi-monthly publication for collectors of magazines and other paper illustrations; free classifieds for subscribers; send LSASE for information; old prints, calendars.

Arthur Szyk

Clubs/Associations

Irvin Ungar
Arthur Szyk Society, Inc.
Newsletter: Arthur Szyk Newsletter
1200 Edgehill Drive
Burlingame, CA 90410
ph: 650-343-9588
fax: 650-579-6014
e-mail: szyksociety@szyk.com
web: http://www.syzk.com/
Arthur Szyk (1894-1951, artist, miniaturist, illuminator,illustrator) is regarded as the greatest miniature painter and illustrator of his times; newsletter published six timer per year.

Bessie Pease Gutmann

Clubs/Associations

Gutmann Collectors Club
24A E. Roseville Road
Lancaster, PA 17601
Focuses on the works of Bessie Pease Gutmann.

Collectors

George & Janice Parola
43 Oakfield Ave.
Freeport, NY 11520-1935
ph: 516-868-8439
fax: 516-379-1534
e-mail: georgejanp@aol.com
Wants Bessie Pease Gutmann prints, magazine covers, postcards, calendars, etc.

Warren Wissemann
521 South Dyre Ave.
West Islip, NY 11795
ph: 516-587-7633
Wants prints by Bessie Pease Gutmann, Eda Doench, Bessie Collins Pease, and Meta Grimball.

Eleanor Popelka
530 S. Chicot Ave.
West Islip, NY 11795-4206
ph: 516-587-8260
e-mail: popedel@msn.com
Collector of prints, postcards, magazine covers, books and calendars illustrated by Bessie Pease Gutmann, Meta Grimball, and Eda Doench; no reproductions, please.

Dr. Victor J.W. Christie
Cheshire Cat, The
1050 West Main St.
Ephrata, PA 17522
ph: 717-738-4032
e-mail: smiller@redrose.net
Wants to buy prints, illustrated books, postcards, calendars, etc. done by the artists Bessie Pease Gutmann, Meta M. Grimball, ad Eda S. Doench.

Jim & Sharon Eckert
P.O. Box 62
Anchor, IL 61720-0062
ph: 309-723-4241
e-mail: anchorsb@dave-world.net
Wants Wallace Nutting, Bessie Pease Gutmann prints.

Dealers

Edward J. Meschi
129 Pinyard Rd.
Monroeville, NJ 08343-1870
ph: 609-358-7293
fax: 609-358-7789
e-mail: emfinearts@yahoo.com
Buying paintings, calendars, original works of art.

Coles Phillips

Experts

Denis C. Jackson
P.O. Box 1958
Sequim, WA 98382-1958
ph: 360-452-3810
e-mail: ticn@olypen.com
web: http://www.olypen.com/ticn/
Covered magazines from 1900 to 1926; author of "The Price & ID Guide to Coles Phillips", 2nd Edition; send LSASE for information.

Fern Bisel Peat

Collectors

Cathy Cook
10 E. 13th St., #2D
New York, NY 10003-4467
ph: 212-691-2406
fax: 212-691-2406
e-mail: ccook710@aol.com
Collector interested in buying, selling and trading books, paper dolls, puzzles, tin-lithographed toys, etc. by children's illustrator Fern Bisel Peat.

Experts

David W. Peat
1225 Carroll White
Indianapolis, IN 46219-3907
ph: 317-357-6895
Wants books, tin toys, other metal or paper children's items from 1927-1947 illustrated by my aunt, Fern Bisel Peat.

Periodicals

Peggy Welch Mershon
Newsletter: Fern Bisel Peat Newsletter
20 S. Linden Rd., Apr. 112
Mansfield, OH 44906
ph: 419-524-5992
e-mail: marwelmer@aol.com
Fern Bisel Peat (1893-1971) is a highly regarded illustrator of children's books (Saalfield, Harter), toys (Ohio Art), and magazines (Children's Play Mate); newsletter published quarterly and dedicated to the legacy of Fern Bisel Peat.

Grace Drayton

Experts

G.L. Wine
649 Bayview Dr.
Akron, OH 44319-1502
Researcher who specializes in the life and art of Campbell Kids' creator, Grace G. Drayton.

Harrison Fisher

(see also POSTCARDS)

Clubs/Associations

Deena M. Zachritz, Dir.
Harrison Fisher Society, The
Newsletter: Harrison Fisher Society Newsletter
123 N Glassell
Orange, CA 92666
ph: 714-633-5206
fax: 714-633-5726
The Society gathers and researches references and works by or about Harrison Fisher.

Experts

Naomi Welch
Images of the Past
309 Playa Blvd., Ste. 110
La Selva Beach, CA 95076-1737
fax: 831-689-0318
e-mail: naomi@harrisonfisher.com
web: http://www.harrisonfisher.com/
Collector, dealer, expert specializes in Harrison Fisher; author of two books, published in 1999, entitled "The Complete Works of Harrison Fisher Illustrator," and "American & European Postcards of Harrison Fisher Illustrator."

Hy Hintermeister

Clubs/Associations

Carole Schwartz
Hy Hintermeister Collectors Group
Newsletter: Hy H Notes
5 Pasture Road
Whitehouse Station, NJ 08889-3357
ph: 908-236-9675
e-mail: HYHNOTESed@worldnet.att.net
Brings together collectors of Hintermeister illustration art.

Collectors

Hugh Hetzer
209 Homevale Rd.
Reisterstown, MD 21136
ph: 410-833-5170
e-mail: hhetzer@prodigy.net

Dealers

Jo Havens-Wright
Wright Enterprises
610 N. Delaware Ave.
Roswell, NM 88201-2135
ph: 505-623-8053
e-mail: johavens@dfn.com
web: http://www.dfn.com/~johavens
Specializes in Hy Hintermeister and William M. Thompson prints but also carries others.

J.C. & F.X. Leyendecker

Experts

Denis C. Jackson
P.O. Box 1958
Sequim, WA 98382-1958
ph: 360-452-3810
e-mail: ticn@olypen.com
web: http://www.olypen.com/ticn/
Specializes in illustrators from 1890s through 1950s; author of "The Price Guide to JC & FX Leyendecker" 2nd edition; send LSASE for information.

Joan Walsh Anglund

Experts

Ann C. Bergin
P.O. Box 105
Amherst, NH 03031-0105
fax: 508-649-6807
e-mail: acbergin@aol.com

Periodicals

Ann C. Bergin
Newsletter: Joan Walsh Anglund Collectors News
P.O. Box 105
Amherst, NH 03031-0105
fax: 508-649-6807
e-mail: acbergin@aol.com
An annual newsletter containing information on children's book illustrator Joan Walsh Anglund; free buy, sell ad for subscribers.

Kate Greenaway

Clubs/Associations

Dr. James Lewis Lowe, Dir.
Kate Greenaway Society
P.O. Box 8
Norwood, PA 19074
ph: 610-485-8572

Maxfield Parrish

Collectors

John Crawford
3442 Manor Hill
Cincinnati, OH 45220
ph: 513-221-6050
Wants Maxfield Parrish illustrations, especially magazine items.

John Buonaguidi
540 Reeside Ave.
Monterey, CA 93940-1828
ph: 831-375-7345
Wants to buy Maxfield Parrish collectibles including calendars, posters, books, advertising items, paintings, prints, etc. - anything Parrish!

Dealers

John S. Zuk
106 Orchard St.
Belmont, MA 02478
ph: 617-489-7540
fax: 617-484-4800
e-mail: jzuk@integral-inc.com
Buys and sells Maxfield Parrish prints, books, and originals (pen & ink, watercolor, etc.); premium paid for Edison Mazda calendars, lamp testers, etc.

Hugh Alan Luch Collections, The
P.O. Box 111
Wenonah, NJ 08090
ph: 609-464-9751
Buys and sells illustrator and holiday collectibles with emphasis on Maxfield Parrish and Halloween.

Edward J. Meschi
129 Pinyard Rd.
Monroeville, NJ 08343-1870
ph: 609-358-7293
fax: 609-358-7789
e-mail: emfinearts@yahoo.com
Buys and sells Maxfield Parrish prints and paintings.

Barb & Dan Fromer
Fromer's Antiques
P.O. Box 224
New Market, MD 21774-0224
ph: 301-831-6712
Buys and sells Maxfield Parrish prints.

John Walkowiak
3452 Humbolt Ave. S.
Minneapolis, MN 55408-3332
ph: 612-824-0785
Maxfield Parrish prints, books, calendars, advertising, reference items, posters, and other items bought and sold.

William T. Byrne
1625 Broadway, Ste. 2450
Denver, CO 80202-4624
ph: 303-744-9403
Seeking mint condition Maxfield Parrish calendars, prints, posters, books, letters, originals, playing cards, games, puzzles, signs, novelty and ad items.

Michelle Ferretta
Maxfield Parrish Collectibles
1314 Oak St.
Alameda, CA 94501-4506
ph: 510-522-1823
e-mail: mpferretta@aol.com
web: http://collect.com/maxfield/
Dealer, expert buys and sells Maxfield Parrish; in business over 23 years; large collection in stock; vintage prints, books, calendars, advertising, estate items, original artwork.

Experts

Bill Holland
William Holland Fine Arts
1554 Paoli Pike
West Chester, PA 19380
ph: 610-344-9848
fax: 610-344-06651
e-mail: bill@hollandarts.com
web: http://www.hollandarts.com/
Buys and sells Parrish art prints, calendars, posters, advertising items, books, and magazine covers; author of "The Collectible Maxfield Parrish", $60 ppd.

John Goodspeed Stuart
Parrish House, The
1740 Marion St.
Denver, CO 80218-1121
ph: 303-831-0055
fax: 303-831-4901
e-mail: jgstuart@aol.com
web: http://www.parrish-house.com
Buys, sells, appraises and specializes in Maxfield Parrish prints, books, etc.; send for free price list; author of "Young Maxfield Parrish" and "The Art of MAxfield Parrish."

Denis C. Jackson
P.O. Box 1958
Sequim, WA 98382-1958
ph: 360-452-3810
e-mail: ticn@olypen.com
web: http://www.olypen.com/ticn/
Maxfield Parrish prints, calendars, books, magazines; author of "The Price and Identification Guide to Maxfield Parrish" 11th edition; send LSASE for information.

Misc. Services

Laurence S. Cutler
Maxfield Parrish Family Trust, The
P.O. Box 687
Holderness, NH 03245-0687
ph: 603-968-3067
fax: 603-968-3068
Dedicated to keeping the work of Maxfield Parrish before the public eye; licenses the right to use images produced by Maxfield Parrish.

Norman Rockwell

(see also COLLECTIBLES [MODERN], Norman Rockwell)

Clubs/Associations

Michael J.P. Collins, Pres.
Rockwell Society of America
Newsletter: Rockwell Society of America Newsletter
P.O. Box 705
Ardsley, NY 10502-0705
Founded in 1974 and dedicated to the appreciation of America's most famous artist, Norman Rockwell; specializing in original paintings, drawings, collectibles, e.g. Saturday Evening Post covers/magazines, illustrated books, etc.

Dealers

Marshall Stoltz
Rockwell Gallery Collection of Norman Rockwell Art
P.O. Box 126
Huntingdon Valley, PA 19006-0126
ph: 215-922-4345
fax: 215-969-6466
e-mail: stoltzmarsh@juno.com
web: http://www.rockwellsite.com/
Sells new prints and posters based on the works of Norman Rockwell.

Experts

Denis C. Jackson
P.O. Box 1958
Sequim, WA 98382-1958
ph: 360-452-3810
e-mail: ticn@olypen.com
web: http://www.olypen.com/ticn/
Magazines and paper items from 1914 to present; author of "The Price Guide to Norman Rockwell", 4th edition; send LSASE for information.

Museums/Libraries

Norman Rockwell Museum at Stockbridge, The
Route 183
Stockbridge, MA 01262
ph: 413-298-4100 or 800-298-9450
e-mail: info@nrm.org
web: http://www.nrm.org
Exhibiting the world's largest collection of original Rockwell art, the museum preservers and studies the life, art and spirit of Rockwell's work.

Joyce Devore
Museum of Norman Rockwell Art
227 S. Park
Reedsburg, WI 53959-1945
ph: 608-524-2123 or 800-524-2123
fax: 608-524-0611
e-mail: nrmusrdb@mwt.net
web: http://www.rockwellart-reedsburg.com/
Private museum with gift shop.

Palmer Cox

Experts

Wayne Morgan
69 Main Street East
Grimsby, Ontario L3M 1N5
Canada
ph: 905-945-5754
fax: 905-945-5754
e-mail:
morgan.modculture@sympatico.ca
Advice on Palmer Cox (1840-1924) author/illustrator famous for The Brownie's books and others; illustrator Dudley Ward (1879-1935)(developed The Dingbats for commercial use); illustrators of Mounties in popular culture, ephemera, prints.

Philip Boileau

Clubs/Associations

Karen Gamlin
Philip Boileau Collector's Society
Newsletter: PBCS Newsletter
1025 Redwood Blvd.
Redding, CA 96003
ph: 530-241-2166
e-mail: Gamlin@aol.com
web: http://members.aol.com/PBoileauCC/
Members are collectors of illustrations, art, drawings, postcards by Philip Boileau (1863-1917).

Experts

Karen Gamlin
1025 Redwood Blvd.
Redding, CA 96003
ph: 530-241-2166
e-mail: Gamlin@aol.com
web: http://members.aol.com/PBoileauCC/
Buys, sells, collects and specializes in illustrations by Philip Boileau (1863-1917).

R. Atkinson Fox

Clubs/Associations

Sharon Gergen
R. Atkinson Fox Society
Newsletter: Fox Tales
8141 Main
Kansas City, MO 64114

Collectors

Frances L. Woodworth
P.O. Box 358
Janesville, IA 50647
ph: 319-987-2168

Sharon Gergen
8141 Main
Kansas City, MO 64114-2401
ph: 816-361-7539

Sherri Fountain
1511 W. 4th Ave.
Hutchinson, KS 67501
ph: 316-663-4293

Pat Gibson
38280 Guava Dr.
Newark, CA 94560
ph: 510-792-0586
Always looking for any R.A. Fox prints, calendars, oils, postcards, and anything with his work on it.

Experts

Rita Mortenson
727 North Spring
Independence, MO 64050
R. Atkinson Fox (1860-1927) was a Canadian artist. Rita Mortenson is author of "R. Atkinson Fox: His Life and Work" (Vol. I & II.); SASE required for reply.

IMMIGRATION

Collectors

Kathy Sheeran
P.O. Box 520251
Miami, FL 33152-0251
Wants photos, documents and passports from pre-1950 immigrants to the US; also wants buttons and ribbons from immigrant groups (A.O.H., Sons of Italy, etc.); also Ellis Island and anti-immigrant items.

IMPLEMENT SEATS

(see FARM COLLECTIBLES, Cast Iron Seats)

INAUGURATION ITEMS

(see PERSONALITIES [HISTORICAL]; POLITICAL COLLECTIBLES; WHITE HOUSE MEMORABILIA)

INDIA

(see ART, Asian)

INDIAN ITEMS

(see AMERICAN INDIAN)

INDIAN WARS ITEMS

(see also AMERICAN INDIAN; MILITARIA; MILITARY HISTORY)

Clubs/Associations

Jerry L. Russell, NatCh.
Order of the Indian Wars, The
Newsletter: Order of the Indian Wars Communique
P.O. Box 7388
Little Rock, AR 72217
ph: 501-225-3996
e-mail: milhistory@aristotle.net
web: http://www.civilwarbuff.org
The only national organization devoted to the study & preservation of Indian Wars history.

Collectors

Thomas W. Pooler
P.O. Box 1861
Grass Valley, CA 95945-1861
ph: 530-268-1338
Wants to buy INDIAN WARS medals and insignia; also wants National and United Indian War Veterans medals, convention ribbons, pins, flags, photos, etc.

INDONESIA

(see also ART, Asian; ORIENTALIA; PHILIPPINES)

Appraisers

Elisabeth Weikert Douglas
China Coast Oriental Art Appraisal Services
11266 Taylor Draper Lane, Apt. 2024
Austin, TX 78759-3972
ph: 512-288-3043
fax: 512-345-8420
e-mail: wien@texas.net
Active in the field of Asian art and antiques for over 20 years; owned and operated antiques export service in Bangkok, Thailand; owned and operated Oriental art and antiques shop in Washington DC.

Dealers

Antik Indonesia
Jl. Kemuning 4-B no. 8
RT.013 RW.06, Pejaten Timur
Jakarta, 12510
Indonesia
ph: +62-21-794-9435
fax: +62-21-723-4676
e-mail: kamajaya@alabanza.com
web: http://www.alabanza.com/kamajaya/antik/
Specializes in antiques from Indonesia: bead, stone, books, banknotes, clocks, furniture, mask, statue, stamps, textiles, costume, ceramics, brass and metal work, weapons.

Borneo

Experts

Michael G. Price
P.O. Box 468
Michigan Center, MI 49254
ph: 517-764-4517
e-mail: mgprice@acd.net
Wants Philippine picture postcards, photos, magazines, books, maps; also wants items from nearby islands such as Borneo.

INDUSTRIAL DESIGN

(see MODERNISM)

INDUSTRY RELATED ITEMS

(see also BEEKEEPING MEMORABILIA; CONSTRUCTION EQUIPMENT; CRANBERRY INDUSTRY; FARM MACHINERY; FASTENERS; ICE INDUSTRY; LOGGING; MACHINERY & EQUIPMENT; MILLING; MINING; MODERNISM; SCRIP; SOCIAL CAUSES; TOOLS; WHISKEY INDUSTRY ITEMS)

Appraisers

Robert L. Johnson
Whistles in the Woods Museum Services
P.O. Box 309
Chickamauga, GA 30707-0309
ph: 706-375-4326
e-mail: oldgoat@voy.net
Consultants specializing in 1750 - early 20th century historic machinery; power-generation, tools, machines, scientific & technical instruments, mining, milling, transportation, logging & lumbering, steam engines, etc.

Clubs/Associations

Elton W. Hall, Ex. Dir.
Early American Industries Association, The
Newsletter: Shavings, The
167 Bakersville Rd.
South Dartmouth, MA 02748-4198
ph: 508-993-4198
e-mail: 70610.2041@compuserve.com
web: http://www.eaiainfo.org/
Interested in old tools, implements, utensils, vehicles, "Whatsits"; and to discover, identify and preserve same; also publishes the magazine "Chronicle."

Museums/Libraries

Keith R. Gill
Museum of Science & Industry
57th St. & Lake Shore Dr.
Chicago, IL 60637
ph: 773-684-1414
fax: 773-684-5580
Archives contains documents &

photos of the 1893 Columbian Exposition.

INFANT FEEDERS

(see also BOTTLES)

Clubs/Associations

Jo Ann Todd
American Collectors of Infant Feeders
Newsletter: Keeping Abreast
5161 West 59th St.
Indianapolis, IN 46254-1107
ph: 317-291-5850
Founded in 1973 for those interested in feeding infants and the devices used therefore: nursers, baby bottles, infant/invalid feeders; book, "A Guide to American Nursing Bottles" is now available.

Collectors

Jo Ann Todd
5161 West 59th St.
Indianapolis, IN 46254-1107
ph: 317-291-5850
Wants infant/invalid feeders; nursers, baby bottles, etc.; made of horn, wood, pewter, silver, glass, plastic or pottery.

INK BLOTTERS

(see BLOTTERS; INKWELLS & INKSTANDS; PAPER COLLECTIBLES; PENS)

INKWELLS & INKSTANDS

(see also BOTTLES; BLOTTERS; LETTER OPENERS; PAPER COLLECTIBLES; PENCILS; PENS; SEALS, Wax)

Clubs/Associations

Vince McGraw
Society of Inkwell Collectors, The
Newsletter: Stained Finger, The
5136 Thomas Ave. So.
Minneapolis, MN 55410-2241
ph: 612-922-2792
fax: 612-920-7835
e-mail: soic@concentric.net
web: http://www.soic.com
Features articles about inkwells, pens and writing accessories; has catalog offering books about inkwells, and replacement inserts, quills, rocker blotters, etc; newsletter published quarterly.

Bevy & Ray Jaegers
St. Louis Inkwell Collectors Society
P.O. Box 29396
Saint Louis, MO 63126-0396
e-mail: USPsiSquad@aol.com

Kevin Prime, Mem.
Writing Equipment Society
178 Foster Hill Road
Bedford, MK41 7TB
U.K.
ph: 012324 271453
Devoted to the conservation and study of writing instruments and accessories: pens of all types and materials, pencils, nibs, inkwells, stamp boxes, quill cutters, scriveners' knives, seals, writing slopes, blotters, paper knives, etc.

Collectors

Robert Kwalwasser
168 Camp Fatima Rd.
Renfrew, PA 16053-9104
ph: 724-789-7766
fax: 724-789-9771
e-mail: robert@tcis.net
Wants to buy traveling inkwells.

Lew Poggiali
7421 Pakepark Dr.
West Chester, OH 45069

Elaine Hinkle Crittenden
Calligraphy Heaven
14902 Preston Rd., Ste. 216
Dallas, TX 75240-9103
ph: 972-934-1055
fax: 972-934-1055
Buys inkwells and related items such as blotters, desk sets, dip pen points, etc.

John E. Kochenburger
1304 Robertson St.
Fort Collins, CO 80524-4258
ph: 304-484-0274
Collects a variety of inkstands, inkwells, ink bottles and "go-withs"; also buys and sells.

Dealers

Gene Bensen
AntiqueLine, Inc.
771 West End Ave.
New York, NY 10025
ph: 212-749-2526
fax: 212-749-1686
e-mail: antqline@i-2000.com
web: http://www.antiqueline.com
Specializes in inkwells, desk accessories, bookends, and fountain pens for the home or office.

Geraud Schultz
Antique Gallery, The
8523 Germantown Ave.
Philadelphia, PA 19118
ph: 215-248-1700
fax: 215-247-8411
Buys and sells inkwells: ceramic, brass, glass, traveling, figural.

Sam Fiorella
Pendemonium
15231 Larkspur Lane
Dumfries, VA 22026-1075
ph: 703-670-8549
fax: 703-670-3785
e-mail: sam@pendemonium.com
web: http://www.pendemonium.com
Buys and sells fountain pens, inkwells, ink bottles, pen stands, blotters, pen catalogs, magazine covers and advertisements; write for current "Writing Collectibles" catalog, it's FREE!

Bill Thompson
502 Woodhaven Rd.
Centerville, GA 31028-1327
Buys and sells anything related to writing; inkwells, rocker blotters, letter openers, lap desks, etc.

Sandra & L. "Buck" Van Tine
Lora's Memory Lane
13133 N. Caroline St.
Chillicothe, IL 61523-9115
ph: 309-579-3040
fax: 309-579-2696
e-mail: lorasink@aol.com
Buys and sells inkwells, inkstands, and ink related items.

Carol Payne
Carol's Antique Gallery
14455 Big Basin Way
Saratoga, CA 95070-6008
ph: 408-867-7055
Wants to buy inks of any material; sometimes considers broken ones for parts; also wants desk items like letter racks, wax seals, blotters, pens, pen stands, pen wipers, etc.

Experts

Veldon Badders
692 Martin Rd.
Hamlin, NY 14464-9744
ph: 716-964-3360
Author of "Collector's Guide to Inkwells."

Ray & Bev Jaegers
P.O. Box 29396
Saint Louis, MO 63126-0396
e-mail: USPsiSquad@aol.com
Experts and historians.

INSECTS

Museums/Libraries

Frost Entomological Museum, Pennsylvania State University
501 ASI Building
University Park, PA 16802
ph: 814-863-2863
fax: 814-865-3048
e-mail: kck@psu.edu
web: http://www.ento.psu.edu/home/Frost/

Butterflies

Internet Resources

Butterfly Website
e-mail: butterfly@mgfx.com
web: http://mgfx.com/butterfly/
The most complete information on butterfly gardening, farming, ecology and education; lots of links to all sorts of butterfly resources including collections.

Cockroaches

Museums/Libraries

Michael Bohdan
Combat Cockroach Hall of Fame, The Pest Shop Inc.
2231-B West Fifteenth St.
Plano, TX 75075
ph: 972-519-0355
e-mail: vwbug@swbell.net
web: http://www.pestshop.com/
Come see dressed up cockroaches like Roach Pero or Liberoachi!

Ticks

Museums/Libraries

Dr. James E. Keirans, Curator
U.S. National Tick Collection, Institute of Anthropodology & Parasitology
Georgia Southern University
Landrum, Box 8056
Statesboro, GA 30460
ph: 912-681-5564
fax: 912-681-0559
e-mail: jkeirans@gasou.edu
web: http://www2.gasou.edu/iap/ustick.htm
Collection of over one million ticks - the smallest fits on the head of a pin, the largest is the size of a quarter; history of each includes location collected and the "host" organism.

INSTRUMENTS & DEVICES

(see also ARCHITECTURE & RELATED ITEMS; ASTRONOMICAL ITEMS; BAROMETERS; GAUGES; GLOBES; MEDICAL, DENTAL & PHARMACEUTICAL; MICROSCOPES; NAUTICAL ANTIQUES; OFFICE EQUIPMENT; SCALES; SLIDE RULES; SPY EQUIPMENT; SURVEYING INSTRUMENTS; THERMOMETERS)

Dealers

Bob Elsner
Heights Antiques
29 Clubhouse Ln.
Boynton Beach, FL 33436-6056
ph: 561-736-1362
fax: 561-736-1914
e-mail: rjelsner@aol.com
Barometer expert who buys, sells, appraises and repairs all types of barometers: gimbaled, mercury, aneroid, altimeters, barographs; antique and reproduction.

Compasses

Dealers

David S. Bennett
Bennett Antiques
15800 26th Ave. N.
Minneapolis, MN 55447-1940
Wants to buy military compasses, pocket variety of WWI, WWII and earlier; pocket compasses in wooden boxes; old sport compasses; Boy Scout and Girl Scout pocket compasses; also pocket transits.

Egg Related

Collectors

John Weber
50 Erobi Ln.
Iowa City, IA 52240
ph: 319-354-6920
Wants to buy egg scales, egg washers, egg graders; single, multiple, dial, balance; for turkey, duck, chicken eggs, any kind; also wants figurines, etc. depicting children hatching from eggs.

Scientific

Appraisers

Prof. Thomas Perera
Telegraph & Scientific Instrument On-Line Cyber-Museum
Department of Psychology
Montclair State University
Upper Montclair, NJ 07043
ph: 973-655-7083
e-mail: pererat@alpha.montclair.edu
web: http://www.chss.montclair.edu/~pererat/telegraph.html
On-line museum dedicated to the preservation of telegraph history, lore, and instrumentation; downloadable images; telegraph history, bibliography, and related links; e-mail appraisals available.

Auction Services

Sotheby's
1334 York Ave.
New York, NY 10021
ph: 212-606-7000
fax: 212-606-7107
web: http://www.sothebys.com
Over 70 collecting areas are featured at Sotheby's auctions including toys, dolls, porcelain, furniture, silver, art, books; exhibitions are free and everyone is welcome; for a free copy of "Sotheby's Newsletter", call 212-606-7245.

VERNONScope & Co.
5 Ithaca Rd.
Candor, NY 13743
Two scientific antique instrument auctions each year: telescopes, microscopes, surveying, nautical, meteorologic equipment offered.

Jon Baddeley
Sotheby's
34-35 New Bond St.
London, W1A 2AA
U.K.
ph: 44 171 293 5000
fax: 44 171 293 5989
web: http://www.sothebys.com/
Conducts regular auctions of scientific instruments.

Book Sellers

John Ptak
J.F. Ptak Science Books
1531 33rd St. NW
Washington, DC 20007
ph: 202-337-0945
fax: 202-234-3511
e-mail: jfptak@access.digex.net
web: http://www.access.dignex.net/~jfptak
Specializes in books about science and scientific instruments.

Clubs/Associations

Zeiss Historica Society
Journal: Zeiss Historica Society Journal
300 Waxwing Drive
Cranbury, NJ 08512
ph: 540-981-1036
e-mail: msmall@roanoke.infi.net
web: http://www.netins.net/showcase/crye/zi-hist.htm
Dedicated to the study & exchange of information on the history of Carl Zeiss Optical Co. and Zeiss-Ikon, its people and products (cameras, accessories, and optical equipment of all types) from 1846 to present; semi-annual journal.

Dr. Sam Koslov
Maryland Microscopical & Scientific Instrument Society
1531 33rd St. NW
Washington, DC 20007
ph: 202-337-0945
fax: 202-234-3511
e-mail: jfptak@access.digex.net
web: http://www.access.dignex.net/~jfptak
Focuses on instruments and devices: medical, surveying, photographic, microscopical, navigational, horological, astronomical, etc.

Howard Dawes
Scientific Instrument Society
P.O. Box 15
Pershore, Worcestershire WR10 2RD
U.K.
A British organization that travels extensively; quarterly journal with polished articles.

Collectors

Thomas B. Perera
11 Squire Hill Rd.
Caldwell, NJ 07006-4718
ph: 973-226-9185
e-mail: pererat@alpha.montclair.edu
web: http://www.w1tp.com/
Wants to buy early scientific instruments; has been collecting for over 40 years.

Dr. Allan Wissner
P.O. Box 102
Ardsley, NY 10502-0102
ph: 914-693-4628
e-mail: wissner@bestweb.net
web: http://www.bestweb.net/~wissner/
Wants microscopes, medical, scientific instruments: Zentmayer, Grunow, Bullock, McAllister, Gundlack, McIntosh, Tolles, Queen, Pike.

Paul Ferraglio
3332 W. Lake Rd.
Canandaigua, NY 14424-2441
ph: 716-394-7663
fax: 716-394-5424
e-mail: p4alyo@aol.com
Buys old scientific instruments: microscopes, surveying instruments, mineralogical & other optical instruments in any condition; also books & catalogs; also wants parts.

W. Feely
1172 Lindsay La.
Jenkintown, PA 19046-1839
ph: 215-884-5640
fax: 215-884-8660
Wants unusual drafting and navigation equipment, coast artillery manuals and memorabilia.

Dr. Sam Koslov
1531 33rd St. NW
Washington, DC 20007
ph: 202-337-0945
fax: 202-234-3511
e-mail: jfptak@access.digex.net
web: http://www.access.dignex.net/~jfptak
Wants to buy medical, surveying, photographic, microscopical, navigational, horological, astronomical, etc. instruments & devices.

Jon Lewin
622 Raleigh Ave., Apt. 3
Norfolk, VA 23507-2034
ph: 757-625-6732
Wants to buy floor-standing electro-medical machines, electro-static generators, leyden jars, oddly-shaped vacuum tubes or x-ray tubes, hand-operated vacuum pumps, glass-legged tables and stools, glass-handled rods, astronomical models.

John M. Shannon
7319 West Cedar Circle
Lakewood, CO 80226-2019
ph: 303-232-1534
e-mail: rovers@aol.com
Wants to buy assay balances (wood and glass encased with small pans) - both laboratory and portable; also wants brass scientific instruments.

Paul H. Hayashi, PE
18 Tarabrook Dr.
Orinda, CA 94563-3121
ph: 925-254-5074 or 925-253-1038
fax: 925-253-0592
Buys old scientific instruments: surveying, microscopes, barometers, calculators, drafting sets, chronometers, navigational devices, etc.

Robert De Cesaris
7429 Bree Ann Ct.
Citrus Heights, CA 95610-2455
ph: 916-356-5769
e-mail: rdecesar@pcocd2.intel.com
Serious collector of slide rules, early mechanical adders and calculators; special interests include circular, cylindrical or other unusual slide rules and lever set calculators right up to the Curta calculator.

Dealers

David L. Isabelle
MediaSpecialies
28 Revell Ave.
Northampton, MA 01060
ph: 413-586-7571 or 413-584-1034
fax: 413-584-1034
e-mail: websites@mediaspec.com
web: http://www.mediaspec.com/GNET/mediaspecialties/
Specializing in medical, scientific, optical, cameras, images, and cinema.

Paul Madden
Weather Store, The
146 Main Street
P.O. Box 729
Sandwich, MA 02563
ph: 800-646-1203
e-mail: pmadden@wxstore.com
web: http://www.wxstore.com
Specializes in weather instruments ranging from marine related antiques to weathervanes.

David & Yola Coffeen
Tesseract
P.O. Box 151
Hastings On Hudson, NY 10706-0151
ph: 914-478-2594
fax: 914-478-5473
e-mail: coffeen@aol.com
Issues a series of well illustrated catalogs of early scientific instruments: astronomy, microscopy, sundials, surveying, calculation, computation, adding, navigation, etc.; always interested in buying single items of collections.

James & Norvell Kennedy
James Kennedy Antiques, Ltd.
905 W. Main St.
Durham, NC 27701-2054
ph: 919-682-1040 or 800-236-1868
fax: 919-683-9633
e-mail: kantiques@earthlink.net
web: http://www.antiqnet.com/kennedy
Specialist in scientific, medical, and nautical antiques and prints.

John Forster
Barometer Fair
P.O. Box 25502
Sarasota, FL 34277
ph: 941-923-6136
fax: 941-923-6136
e-mail: barometer@glimmer.com
Buys, sells, restores all antique barometers; also deals in antique maps, globes, compasses, telescopes and other scientific instruments.

Alex Peck
Antique Scientifica
P.O. Box 710
Charleston, IL 61920-0710
ph: 217-348-1009
e-mail: antiques@advant.net
Wants to buy early microscopes, telescopes, telegraphs, globes, electrical, patent models, surveying instruments, scales, nautical, demonstration items.

Jonathan Blackman
Yellow Room, The
511 N. Robertson Blvd.
Los Angeles, CA 90048
ph: 310-274-3190
fax: 310-274-0129
e-mail: Globemeister@msn.com
web: http://www.telecomputers.com/globes/
Wants to buy brass telescopes, solar system models (orrery, tellurium, planetarium), and nautical items including passenger steam ship items, and compasses.

Al & Bobbie Roberts
Rational Past, The
221 Oceano Dr.
Los Angeles, CA 90049-4123
ph: 310-476-6277
fax: 310-476-6278
e-mail: rational_past@mindspring.com
Organizer of West Coast Scientific & Technical Antique and Collectible Shows (Los Angeles in the winter and San Francisco are in late summer.)

R.C. & Faye Blankenhorn
Gemmary, The
P.O. Box 2560
Fallbrook, CA 92088
ph: 760-728-3321 or 760-728-3322
fax: 760-728-3322
e-mail: rcb@gemmary.com
web: http://www.gemmary.com/rcb/
Antique scientific instruments: 18th & 19th C. mathematical, philosophical, optical instruments, microscopes, telescopes, globes, orreries, sundials, compasses, surveying, navigating, drawing, medical, laboratory.

Rod & Becky Cardoza
West Sea Company
2495 Congress St.
San Diego, CA 92110-2820
ph: 619-296-5356
fax: 619-296-1097
Buys, sells all types of marine paintings, scrimshaw, ships' carvings, ship models, navigational and scientific instruments, sailor handcrafts, campaign furniture, hard hat diving, antique marine photography, nautical books, ceramics.

Lynn Harding
Antique Instruments of the Professions & Sciences
103 West Aliso St.
Ojai, CA 93023-2603
ph: 805-646-0204
fax: 805-646-0204
Specializes in buying and selling antique scientific and technological instruments: orreries, steam, calculating, optics, electrical, golfing, tennis, medical, microscopes, scales & weights, measuring, books, tools, drafting, surveying.

Gloria Dekter
Ashton-Blakey Antiques & Collectibles
6021 Yonge St., Ste. 895
Toronto, Ontario M2M 3W2
Canada
ph: 905-886-5122
fax: 905-886-8566
e-mail: ashtonb@netcom.ca
web: http://www.ashton-blakey-antiques.com
A complete internet shop specializing in vintage wrist watches, antique pocket watches, watch fobs, chains; web site contains images of all items; also specializes in scientific instruments.

Experts

Thomas B. Perera
11 Squire Hill Rd.
Caldwell, NJ 07006-4718
ph: 973-226-9185
e-mail: pererat@alpha.montclair.edu
web: http://www.w1tp.com/
Maintains internet telegraph and scientific instrument museum and collector's guide.

Dale R. Beeks
Perceptions Scientifica
P.O. Box 117
Mount Vernon, IA 52314-0117
ph: 800-880-5178 or 319-895-0506
e-mail: dbeeksci@aol.com
Buys fine microscopes; old scientific, surveying, technical, medical and precision instruments; pre-1900 typewriters, calculating devices, medical items & quackery.

Internet Resources

Prof. Thomas Perera
Telegraph & Scientific Instrument On-Line Cyber-Museum
Department of Psychology
Montclair State University
Upper Montclair, NJ 07043
ph: 973-655-7083
e-mail: pererat@alpha.montclair.edu
web: http://www.chss.montclair.edu/~pererat/telegraph.html
On-line museum dedicated to the preservation of telegraph history, lore, and instrumentation; downloadable images; telegraph history, bibliography, and related links; e-mail appraisals available.

Richard Van Vleck
Scientific Medical & Mechanical Antiques
P.O. Box 412
Taneytown, MD 21787
ph: 301-447-2680
e-mail: smma@americanartifacts.com
web: http://americanartifacts.com/smma/
Items for sale and wanted, U.S. Patents search, SMMA articles and regular features, auction announcements, scientific instrument show schedules, books for the collector, links to related sites.

R.C. & Faye Blankenhorn
Gemmary, The
P.O. Box 2560
Fallbrook, CA 92088
ph: 760-728-3321 or 760-728-3322
fax: 760-728-3322
e-mail: rcb@gemmary.com
web: http://www.gemmary.com/rcb/
On-line catalog of items for sale, conservation products, restoration materials, archival supplies, recommended scientific instrument reference books, other useful web sites.

Museums/Libraries

National Museum of American History Branch Library
Smithsonian Institution
Washington, DC 20560
ph: 202-357-2414
e-mail: webmaster@si.edu
web: http://www.si.edu/organiza/museums/nmah/nmah.htm
Books/journals/trade catalogs on material culture, decorative arts, domestic & community life, applied science, engineering, technology.

Periodicals

David & Yola Coffeen
Tesseract
Journal: Rittenhouse
P.O. Box 151
Hastings On Hudson, NY 10706-0151
ph: 914-478-2594
fax: 914-478-5473
e-mail: coffeen@aol.com
A bi-annual periodical to facilitate communication among collectors, curators & historians of scientific instruments; provides a forum for information about instruments made and/or sold in America.

Richard Van Vleck
Greybird Publishing
Newsletter: Scientific, Medical & Mechanical Antiques
P.O. Box 412
Taneytown, MD 21787
ph: 301-447-2680
e-mail: smma@americanartifacts.com
web: http://americanartifacts.com/smma/
A bi-monthly newsletter about scientific, medical and mechanical devices; microscopy, surveying, scales, navigation, surgical, quackery, steam, electrical, agriculture, astronomy, calculators, etc.; ads, auction reports, article.

INSULATORS

(see also BOTTLES; TELEPHONES)

Appraisers

John McDougald
P.O. Box 1003
Saint Charles, IL 60174
ph: 630-513-1544
fax: 630-513-8278
e-mail: crnjewels@aol.com
web: http://www.insulators.com/personal/cmcdoug.htm
Buys, sells, appraises glass insulators.

Clubs/Associations

Bill & Jill Meier
Yankee Polecat Insulator Club, The
Newsletter: YPIC Newsletter
103 Canterbury Ct.
Carlisle, MA 01741-1860
ph: 978-369-0208
e-mail: bill@insulators.com
web: http://www.insulators.com/
Oldest continuing insulator club in the country; members throughout New England and surrounding areas; annual show, swap meets.

Kevin Lawless, Sec.
Capital District Insulator Club
Newsletter: Pilgrim Hat, The
41 Crestwood Dr.
Schenectady, NY 12306-3433
ph: 518-355-5688 or 518-356-0300
fax: 518-356-1947
e-mail: cdic@insulators.com
web: http://www.insulators.com/clubs/cdic.htm
Club for collectors of antique electrical insulators; membership based in Northeast U.S.; annual show; regular club swaps and meetings.

J. Carl Sturm, Pres.
Federation of Historical Bottle Collectors, Inc.
Magazine: Bottles & Extras
P.O. Box 1558
Southampton, PA 18966
ph: 215-953-1686
fax: 215-953-1104
e-mail: sives@antiquez.com
web: http://www.fohbc.com/
"Bottles & Extras" contains articles, pictures, letters, show dates, and show and auction reports in the field of antique bottles, insulators, fruit jars and associated items; check website for list of scores of clubs by region.

Chesapeake Bay Insulator Club
7651 Wesley Road
Silver Spring, MD 20109-3321
ph: 703-361-5996
e-mail: cbic@insulators.com
web: http://www.insulators.com/clubs/cbic.htm
Services most of the mid-Atlantic area and meets quarterly in the Baltimore-Washington DC area; holds shows/sales in March and a swap meet in September.

Keith Roloson
Dixie Jewels Insulator Club
Newsletter: Dixie Jewels Newsletter
6220 Carriage Ct.
Cumming, GA 30040-9111
ph: 770-781-5021 or 770-750-6429
e-mail: kroloson@mindspring.com
web: http://www.insulators.com/clubs/djic.htm
Newsletter published quarterly; complimentary back issue available upon request; includes calendar of upcoming shows, show reports, insulator hunt plans, research articles, and more.

Jacque Linscott
Central Florida Insulator Collectors Club
Newsletter: CFICC Newsletter
3557 Nicklaus Drive
Titusville, FL 32780-5356
ph: 407-264-3934 or 407-267-9170
e-mail: bluebellwt@aol.com
web: http://www.insulators.com/clubs/cfic.htm

Joe J. Beres, Mem.
National Insulator Association
Newsletter: Drip Point
1315 Old Mill Path
Broadview Heights, OH 44147-3276
ph: 440-526-3478
e-mail: jjjb@aol.com
web: http://www.nia.org/
An organization for those interested in collecting electrical insulators and other artifacts connected with related industries.

Alan Stastny
National Trails Insulator Club
6332 Clark Road
West Manchester, OH 45382
ph: 937-678-4745
e-mail: ntic@insulators.com
web: http://www.insulators.com/clubs/ntic.htm

Ed Peters
North Western Insulator Club
5424 Dufferin Drive
Savage, MN 55378
ph: 612-447-2422
e-mail: nwric@insulators.com
web: http://www.insulators.com/clubs/nwric.htm

Rick Soller
Greater Chicago Insulator Club
Newsletter: GCIC Newsletter
34273 Homestead Rd.
Gurnee, IL 60031-4206
ph: 847-855-9136 or 847-543-2958
fax: 847-548-3383
e-mail: rick-soller@clc.cc.il.us
web: http://www.insulators.com/clubs/gcic.htm
Hosts shows, swap meets and hunts.

Dennis & Jeanne Weber
Missouri Valley Insulator Club
3609 Jackson
Saint Joseph, MO 64501-1940
ph: 816-364-1312
e-mail: lwhitl7251@aol.com
web: http://www.insulators.com/clubs/mvic.htm

Elton Gish
Lone Star Insulator Club
Newsletter: Lone Star Lines
P.O. Box 1317
Buna, TX 77612-1317
ph: 409-994-5662 or 409-989-7161
fax: 409-989-7407
e-mail: lsic@insulators.com
web: http://www.insulators.com/clubs/lsic.htm
Meets monthly on the 3rd Friday in Houston, TX; educational programs offered at each meeting.

Matt Poage
Triple Ridge Insulator Club
12771 Eudora Dr.
Denver, CO 80241
ph: 303-453-1895
e-mail: tric@insulators.com
web: http://www.insulators.com/clubs/tric.htm

Steve Marks
Grand Canyon State Insulator Club
Newsletter: Arizona Telegraph Times
21639 North 74th Way
Scottsdale, AZ 85255
ph: 602-640-9245
fax: 602-664-2051
e-mail: gcsic@insulators.com
web: http://www.insulators.com/clubs/gcsic.htm
Members receive membership certificate, permission to ride with the Kelly posse in search of insulators, attend club meetings for trade-in, swap-in, buy-in and sell-in; newsletter published quarterly.

Tom Katonak
Enchantment Insulator Club
1024 Camino de Lucia
Corrales, NM 87048-8314
ph: 505-898-5592
e-mail: eic@insulators.com
web: http://www.insulators.com/clubs/eic.htm
Specialty area includes telegraph, telephone, and power insulators; glass and porcelain; experts in identification and evaluation.

Ron Norton
Central/Southern Counties Insulator Club
P.O. Box 1423
Port Hueneme, CA 93044
ph: 805-488-7445
e-mail: cscic@insulators.com
web: http://www.insulators.com/clubs/cscic.htm

Dale Huber
Nor-Cal Insulator Club
22800 Canyon Way
Colfax, CA 95713
ph: 530-346-2901
e-mail: ncic@insulators.com
web: http://www.insulators.com/clubs/ncic.htm

Collectors

Dario Dimare
1 Elda Rd.
Framingham, MA 01701-4335
ph: 508-877-4444 or 508-877-0958
fax: 508-877-4474
e-mail: dario@dariodesigns.com
Buys, sells, appraises glass insulators; one piece or entire collection; wants threadless and good colored glass such as cobalt blue, purple, yellow, citron, 7-Up green, and amber; also wants pre-1900 telegraph maps, books and catalogs.

John DeSousa
5 Brownstone Rd.
East Granby, CT 06026-9705
ph: 860-658-0353

Dick Bowman
1253 LaBaron Circle
Webster, NY 14580-9529
ph: 716-872-4015
Wants to buy quality insulators, especially threadless insulators.

Allen Klapaska
6242 Glen Arm Rd.
Hydes, MD 21082
ph: 410-592-6416

John Hunsaker
7651 Wesley Rd.
Manassas, VA 22110-3321
ph: 703-361-5996

Keith Roloson
6220 Carriage Ct.
Cumming, GA 30040-9111
ph: 770-781-5021 or 770-750-6429
e-mail: kroloson@mindspring.com
web: http://www.insulators.com/clubs/djic.htm
Interested in all glass and porcelain insulators; seeks Southeastern threadless-pinhole styles; specializes in radio antenna "strain" insulators, early (1860-1890) telegraph styles; also offers free appraisals.

Jim Meyer
3310 State Rd. 40
Ormond Beach, FL 32174-2537
ph: 904-677-0530
fax: 904-673-9883
Wants to buy better insulators.

Mark Reutebuch
3125 Redwing Ln.
Rapid City, SD 57701
ph: 605-393-9707
Buys, sells, trades glass and wooden insulators.

Ross Baird
P.O. Box 937
Fort Worth, TX 76101
ph: 817-236-5580
Wants to buy glass insulators embossed Boston Bottle Works, Cal. Elec. Works, Emminger, Seilers, Harloe, Chester, E.C.M. & Co. (color), Combination Safety.

Steve Marks
21639 North 74th Way
Scottsdale, AZ 85255
ph: 602-640-9245
fax: 602-664-2051
e-mail: gcsic@insulators.com
Interested in buying better insulators; one or an entire collection.

Dealers

Doug MacGillvary
79 New Bolton Rd.
Manchester, CT 06040
ph: 860-649-0477
fax: 860-649-0477
Glass & porcelain insulators, collections or singles bought/sold/traded; a reputation built on over twenty-five years of honest dealing.

Larry Novak
7651 Wesley Road
Silver Spring, MD 20109-3321
ph: 703-361-5996
e-mail: cbic@insulators.com
web: http://www.insulators.com/clubs/cbic.htm
Buys and sells glass insulators and related items such as most telegraph-

related items and many railroad collectibles; advertising and catalogs related insulators are also wanted.

Experts

Bill & Jill Meier
103 Canterbury Ct.
Carlisle, MA 01741-1860
ph: 978-369-0208
e-mail: bill@insulators.com
web: http://www.insulators.com/
Specialists in Hemingray, H.G. Co. and DEC 19 1871 insulators and other Hemingray items such as water bottles and H.G. Co. fruit jars; looking to expand collection; interested in sharing knowledge with others.

Kevin Lawless
41 Crestwood Dr.
Schenectady, NY 12306-3433
ph: 518-355-5688 or 518-356-0300
fax: 518-356-1947
e-mail: cdic@insulators.com
web: http://www.insulators.com/clubs/cdic.htm
Buys and sells all types of antique insulators; glass, porcelain, threadless, foreign, colored, rare, common, singles or collections.

Keith Roloson
6220 Carriage Ct.
Cumming, GA 30040-9111
ph: 770-781-5021 or 770-750-6429
e-mail: kroloson@mindspring.com
web: http://www.insulators.com/clubs/djic.htm
Interested in all glass and porcelain insulators; seeks Southeastern threadless-pinhole styles; specializes in radio antenna "strain" insulators, early (1860-1890) telegraph styles; also offers free appraisals.

Jacqueline C. Linscott
3557 Nicklaus Dr.
Titusville, FL 32780-5356
ph: 407-267-9170
e-mail: bluebellwt@aol.com
Wants "eared" glass electrical insulators; especially CD#250-CD#270; also those with rare colors of embossing errors; sells book solely devoted to insulators; willing to assist the novice collector with insulator information & ID.

Michael Bruner
2615 Echo Lane
Ortonville, MI 48462
ph: 248-627-6351
Wants rare or unusual style insulators; single or entire collections; also wants related telephone/telegraph items such as signs, catalogs.

John & Carol McDougald
P.O. Box 1003
Saint Charles, IL 60174
ph: 630-513-1544
fax: 630-513-8278
e-mail: crnjewels@aol.com
web: http://www.insulators.com/personal/cmcdoug.htm
Buys, sells, trades insulators & telephone related items & lightning rod balls and weathervanes; authors of "Insulators-A History and Guide to North Amer. Glass Pintype Insulators, Vol. 1 & 2"; $68.50 both vols. & current price guide.

Elton Gish
P.O. Box 1317
Buna, TX 77612-1317
ph: 409-994-5662 or 409-989-7161
fax: 409-989-7407
e-mail: lsic@insulators.com
web: http://www.insulators.com/clubs/lsic.htm
Wants 1890-1930 unipart or multipart porcelain insulators; author of "Multipart Porcelain Insulators," "Biography of Fred M. Locke - The Father of Porcelain Insulators", "Value Guide for Porcelain Insulator."

Michael G. Guthrie
1209 West Menlo
Fresno, CA 93711-1477
ph: 559-435-6127
e-mail: mgg17@cvip.fresno.com
web: http://www.insulators.com/
Author of "A Handbook for the Recognition & Identification of Fake, Altered and Repaired Insulators"; Treasurer for the National Insulator Association.

Paul Keating
1705 S. 41st St.
Tacoma, WA 98405-1610
ph: 253-474-9659
Author of an "Milholland Price Guide", an insulator price guide; published about every two years; currently $15 ppd., 159 pages, with historical notes, full descriptions, and average mint price.

Internet Resources

Bill & Jill Meier
Glass Insulators
103 Canterbury Ct.
Carlisle, MA 01741-1860
ph: 978-369-0208
e-mail: bill@insulators.com
web: http://www.insulators.com/
Great website: general information, photo albums, clubs, shows, reference material.

Patti Norton
P.O. Box 1423
Port Hueneme, CA 93044
ph: 805-488-7445
e-mail: rrtp@ix.netcom.com
Ads, stories, interesting articles.

Periodicals

Carol McDougald
Magazine: Crown Jewels of the Wire
P.O. Box 1003
Saint Charles, IL 60174
ph: 630-513-1544
fax: 630-513-8278
e-mail: mcd@crownjewelsofthewire.com
web: http://www.crownjewelsofthewire.com/
76-page monthly magazine of insulator and telephone history; glass, porcelain; foreign columns; classified ads, show dates, etc.

Foreign

Experts

Marilyn Albers
14715 Oak Bend Dr.
Houston, TX 77079-6418
ph: 281-497-4146 or 281-497-3320
fax: 281-497-3957
e-mail: marilynAFI@aol.com
Co-author of "Glass Insulators From Outside North America," "Worldwide Porcelain Insulators," "Price Guide for Glass Insulators from Outside North America" (1996); specialist in foreign insulators.

INSURANCE MEMORABILIA

(see also FIRE INSURANCE RELATED COLLECTIBLES)

Collectors

Byron Gregerson
P.O. Box 713
Modesto, CA 95353-0713
ph: 209-523-3300
fax: 209-523-3399
e-mail: ByronGregerson@worldnet.att.net
Collector wants pre-1930 auto and fire (no life insurance items, please) insurance memorabilia especially advertising signs: reverse-painting-on-glass, tin & lithography.

State Farm

Collectors

Ken Jones
100 Manor Dr.
Columbia, MO 65203
ph: 573-445-7171

INTERNET AUDIO/VIDEO PROGRAMMING

Internet Resources

AnnOnline Smart Talk
e-mail: jon@annonline.com
web: http://www.annonline.com/
Search archives for key words "antiques" and "collectibles" to locate internet audio interviews with Harry Rinker, Christopher Radko, Jack Santoro, William "Tripp" Kline and others.

CollectingChannel Live on Broadcast.com
e-mail: collecting@broadcast.com
web: http://www.broadcast.com/specialinterest/collecting/
Antiques & collectibles related internet video programs.

CollectingChannel Video Archives
e-mail: info@collectingchannel.com
web: http://www.collectingchannel.com/media/videoarchive.html
Video segments of collector shows.

INTERNET CLASSIFIEDS FOR COLLECTORS

(see also ANTIQUES & COLLECTIBLES; AUCTIONS, Internet)

Internet Resources

Net Collectibles
e-mail: info@netcollectibles.com
web: http://www.netcollectibles.com
An online mall dedicated to bringing together buyers and sellers of antiques and collectibles.

Classifieds2000, a Division of Excite
e-mail: suggestions@classifieds2000.com
web: http://www.classifieds2000.com/
Internet classified ad categories include vehicles, general merchandise, antiques and collectibles; also Hot Auctions for art, antiques, Beanie Babies, books and magazines, coins and stamps, comic books, porcelain, glass, etc.

Collectit.net Classifieds
e-mail: info@collectit.net
web: http://www.collectit.net/classifieds/
Brought to you by Krause Publications, one of the world's largest hobby publishers; includes the classified ads from more than 30 collectibles periodicals that Krause published.

Michael Almeida
DealerNet, Inc.
P.O. Box 2952
Woburn, MA 01888-1752
ph: 781-942-4626 or 781-944-6514
fax: 781-942-2626
e-mail: collectorweb@collectorweb.com
web: http://www.collectorweb.com
Internet web based services for collectors & dealers: page development & maintenance, management of monthly sales/auctions, database marketing, qualified buyers.

International Arts, Antiques & Collectibles Forum
1095 Washington St.
P.O. Box 69
Norwood, MA 02062
ph: 781-762-4209
fax: 781-762-8708
e-mail: hschlesi@tiac.net
web: http://www.the-forum.com/

Andy Kaufman
Real Time Antiques Market
P.O. Box 383
Manchester, NH 03105-0383
ph: 603-624-5600
e-mail: andy@grolen.com
web: http://www.rtam.com
An Internet site where buyers sign up for categories and are instantly notified the moment a dealer posts them on the Internet; will design web sites for dealers.

Sam & Sally Pennington
Maine Antique Digest, Inc.
Newspaper: Maine Antique Digest
911 Main St.
P.O. Box 1429
Waldoboro, ME 04572-1429
ph: 207-832-7534
fax: 207-832-7341
e-mail: mad@maine.com
web: http://maineantiquedigest.com/
The major monthly newspaper on antiques, art and Americana; photos with prices, dealers.

Erik J. Wheeler
Collector Online
P.O. Box 159
Burlington, VT 05402-0159
ph: 802-658-5411 or 800-546-2941
fax: 802-879-3843
e-mail: info@collectoronline.com
web: http://www.collectoronline.com/
Established in 1995, is one of the oldest and largest dealer communities online providing resources and buying/selling opportunities; free inventory management system for collectors and dealers allows for unlimited number of items.

Brian Stanton
Antique Alley Internet Mall
56 Valleywood Road
Cos Cob, CT 06807
ph: 716-928-1993
e-mail: webmaster@bmark.com
web: http://bmark.com/aa/
Online resources to find buyers and sellers of antiques and collectibles; online search capability; multi-dealer antique mall featuring thousands of antiques pictured to browse and buy.

Susan Kopsch, Cust. Serv.
Internet Antique Shop, The
16 Heath Place
Garden City, NY 11530
ph: 248-288-9074 or 888-OLD-STUF
e-mail: info@tias.com
web: http://www.tias.com/
An on-line source of antiques and collectibles.

Arts & Antiques Network
National Press Bldge., Ste. 2003
Washington, DC 20045
ph: 703-553-0472
fax: 703-243-6012
e-mail: webmaster@newsolutions.com
web: http://www.aanconnect.com
Internet source for information on the arts, antiques, collectibles, and cultural heritage.

Larry L. Krug
Collectors.Org
18222 Flower Hill Way, #299
Gaithersburg, MD 20879-5300
ph: 301-926-8663
fax: 301-926-7648
e-mail: info@collectors.org
web: http://www.collectors.org
An information web site for collector clubs and collectors, show calendar, theft reports, industry news, events calendar, auctioneer listings; official web site for the National Association of Collectors.

World-Wide Collectors Digest
2 Railroad Ave., Ste. 203
Glyndon, MD 21071
ph: 410-581-1110
fax: 410-363-8698
e-mail: prod@wwcd.com
web: http://www.wwcd.com/
Collectibles Internet site: trading cards, memorabilia, non-sports, comic books, figurines, toys and trains, phone cards, stamps and coins, milk caps and POGS, collector supplies.

Cindy Tipton
Collectibles.com
5388 Hickory Hollow Parkway
Antioch, TN 37013-8084
ph: 888-365-7467 or 615-263-8563
fax: 615-263-8084
e-mail: collectibles@sath.com
web: http://www.collectibles.com/
Web site for collectors; from sports figurines and jewelry to die casts, crystal, and plush toys; hard-to-find one-of-a-kind items; chat rooms and clubs for collectors, message boards, auctions; secure ordering.

Robert Bates
NetCollect.com
1055 Ridgecrest Drive
Goodlettsville, TN 37072
ph: 615-859-5236
fax: 615-859-5238
e-mail: Robwork@gono.com
web: http://www.netcollect.com
Internet member-based online auction and trade site.

Kathy Kamnikar
Antique Networking, Inc.
1350 West Fifth Ave., Ste. 300
Columbus, OH 43212
ph: 614-481-5750
fax: 614-481-5751
e-mail: kathy@antiqnet.com
web: http://www.antiqnet.com
Internet on-line database that networks buyers and sellers of antiques locally, nationally, internationally.

Kathy Kamnikar
BuyCollectibles.Com
1350 West Fifth Ave., Ste. 300
Columbus, OH 43212
ph: 614-481-5750
fax: 614-481-5751
e-mail: kathy@antiqnet.com
web: http://www.buycollectibles.com
Internet on-line database that networks buyers and sellers of collectibles locally, nationally, internationally.

Joanne Haug
Victoriana - Resources for Victorian Living
P.O. Box 40361
Bay Village, OH 44140-2263
ph: 440-835-6924
fax: 440-835-6924
e-mail: antiques@victoriana.com
web: http://www.victoriana.com/antiques/
Resources for Victorian living: articles, museum links, 19th century links, over 30 Victorian shops, advertising, etc.

Marie Minnich
CyberAntiqueMall
P.O. Box 6107
Ann Arbor, MI 48106
ph: 734-971-0430
e-mail: info@cyberantiquemall.com
web: http://www.cyberantiquemall.com
An on-line educational community for lovers of antiques and collectibles.

Collector's Super Mall Online
P.O. Box 1050
Dubuque, IA 52004-1050
ph: 800-482-3158 or 800-480-6169
fax: 800-531-0880
e-mail: randylte@mwci.net
web: http://www.collect.com
The largest on-line source of information and merchandise for collectors; classified ads, mall stores, directory listings, show and auction calendars, market news; for more information send e-mail or call.

Lori Unruh
American Collectors Network
525 South Old 81
Mc Pherson, KS 67460
ph: 316-241-7267
e-mail: lori@midusa.net
web: http://www.acollectorsnet.com
A great place to find what you want: glassware, paper items, sports memorabilia, military items, dolls, toys.

George Guiver
Collectible Trust
1270 W. Whitten St.
Chandler, AZ 85224
ph: 602-814-1586
e-mail: avaj4@home.com
A website for buyers and sellers of collectibles in a variety of categories; no fee for listing items until the items sell.

Buyer's Index - The Search Engine for Buyers
1045 Via Mill Cumbres
Solana Beach, CA 92075
ph: 619-793-085
fax: 619-793-0629
e-mail: info@buyersindex.com
web: http://www.buyersindex.com/
Search 13,000 web shopping sites and North American mail order catalogs with over 96 million product offerings for individuals and businesses including antiques and collectibles.

Tom Johnson
Ruby Lane
1576 Waller Street
San Francisco, CA 94117
ph: 888-782-9586 or 415-864-4563
fax: 415-840-0039
e-mail: help@rubylane.com
web: http://www.rubylane.com/
Search over 1.7M items in 2,000 categories.

Ken Davis
Curioscape.com
P.O. Box 15894
Seattle, WA 98115
ph: 206-527-1533
e-mail: pither@blarg.net
web: http://www.curioscape.com
Thousands of internet based shops and sites dealing with antiquing and collecting; buy, sell, investigate online.

Walter Onori
Swappers & Collectors Pages
Via Oderisi da Gubbio 224
Rome, RM 00146
Italy
e-mail: support@swappersandcollectors.com
web: http://swappersandcollectors.com
Everything for the on-line collector: chats, links, lists, newsgroups, bookstore, free ads.

Sophie Bickford
Interactive Collector
Corsellis Montford Plc., Bolton House
194 Old Brompton Rd.
London, SW5 0AW
U.K.
ph: +44 (0) 171 370 0400
fax: +44 (0) 171 370 0488
e-mail: s.bickford@icollector.com
web: http://www.icollector.com/
An on-line site for buying and selling fine arts, antiques and collectibles.

International Collectors Network
Inglesbatch, Brimpton
Reading, Berkshire RG7 4ST
U.K.
ph: +44 (0) 118 971 2745
fax: +44 (0) 118 971 4195
e-mail: info@icn.co.uk
web: http://www.icn.co.uk/

Ashleigh Ogier, G.M.
Arthema Limited
338 Old York Road
London, London SW18 1SS
U.K.
ph: 0181 870 9389
fax: 0181 870 4673
e-mail: email@arthema.com
web: http://www.arthema.com/
Items for sale and wanted listings plus valuation service, international events listings, directories of 30 categories of arts related businesses, internet site design tailored to the art and antiques industry.

INVALID FEEDERS

(see also BOTTLES; INFANT FEEDERS)

Collectors

Ken Odiorne
Rte. 2 Box 22
Bertram, TX 78605
ph: 512-355-2542
Wants invalid feeders: "cup", "boat" or "Aladdin's" lamp shapes; no plain white in "cup" or "boat" shapes unless unusual shape or mark.

IRONS

Pressing

(see also KITCHEN COLLECTIBLES; WATER SPRINKLERS; TRIVETS)

Clubs/Associations

Lynette Conrad, Sec./Treas.
Mid-West Sad Iron Collectors Club
Newsletter: Pressing News
24 Nob Hill Dr.
Saint Louis, MO 63138-1458
ph: 314-741-4171
e-mail: dpmcd@elnet.com
web: http://www.raycounty.com/simmons/clubs/more.html
Quarterly newsletter, membership directory, annual meeting.

Vi Swanson
Washington-Oregon Iron Collectors Club
1539 NE 100th St.
Seattle, WA 98125-7617
ph: 206-523-0953

Julia Morgan
British Iron Collectors Club
19 Churchill Road
Frome, Somerset BA11 4ED
U.K.
ph: 01373-46-49-11
e-mail: a.stead@rhbnc.ac.uk

Collectors

Harry Poster
P.O. Box 1883
South Hackensack, NJ 07606-0483
ph: 201-794-9606
fax: 201-794-9553
e-mail: hposter@att.net
web: http://www.harryposter.com
Buys unusual pressing irons; wants glass irons and other very unusual irons (glass irons were WWII vintage, made of Pyrex and metal); also buy store advertising, plus catalogs and brochures from manufacturers of unusual irons.

William "Buck" Carson
936 Dove Island Rd.
Newton, NJ 07860-4512
ph: 973-383-4894
fax: 973-300-5946
e-mail: bcarson@garden.net
Editor of the "Pressing News," the newsletter of the Midwest Sad Iron Collectors Club.

Jerry Jankowski
754 34th Pl.
West Des Moines, IA 50265-3126
ph: 515-223-8757
e-mail: jankowski@uswest.net

Paul & Lynette Conrad
24 Nob Hill Dr.
Saint Louis, MO 63138-1458
ph: 314-741-4171
e-mail: dpmcd@elnet.com
web: http://www.raycounty.com/simmons/clubs/more.html

Jay Poirier
5964 S. Lee Way
Littleton, CO 80127
ph: 303-973-4255
fax: 303-288-1790
Wants mint or near mint gasoline, kerosene, or alcohol fueled pressing irons; also wants parts.

Carole Meeker
5702 Vacation Blvd.
Somerset, CA 95684-9324
ph: 530-620-7019
fax: 530-620-7020
e-mail: clm@inforum.net
Wants to buy rare and unusual small patented mechanical antiques, early American technology and occupational-related photography, advertising and catalogs.

Experts

David & Sue Irons
Dave Irons Antiques
223 Covered Bridge Rd.
Northampton, PA 18067
ph: 610-262-9335
fax: 610-262-2853
Buys and sells; issues semi-annual catalog of irons for sale; advisor to "Warman's" and "Schroeder's"; author of "Irons by Irons" (106 pgs/ $43.45 ppd.), "Pressing Iron Patents" (70 pgs/$25 ppd.), "More Irons by Irons" (160 pgs/$45 ppd.).

Periodicals

Carol & Jimmy Walker
Magazine: Iron Talk
P.O. Box 68
Waelder, TX 78959-0068
ph: 830-788-7166 or 800-532-IRON
fax: 830-788-7275
e-mail: jimmy@irontalk.com
web: http://www.irontalk.com/
Know today's prices, markets, trends, collectors' articles on gasoline irons, box irons, sad irons, fluters, little irons, heaters, sprinkle bottles and more.

ISRAEL

(see JUDAICA)

IVER JOHNSON ARMS & CYCLE WORKS

Experts

Charles W. Best
11523 Pine Valley Dr.
Franktown, CO 80116-8708
ph: 303-660-2318
e-mail: Budbest@aol.com
Advanced collector and historian for Iver Johnson Arms & Cycle Works of Fitchburg, MA; interested in any Iver Johnson product including guns, tools, bicycles, motorcycles, signs, advertising and memorabilia.

IVORY

(see also ENDANGERED SPECIES; GEMS & JEWELRY; NAUTICAL ANTIQUES; NETSUKE; ORIENTALIA; SCRIMSHAW)

Clubs/Associations

Robert E. Weisblut
International Ivory Society
Newsletter: International Ivory Society Newsletter
11109 Nicholas Dr.
Silver Spring, MD 20902-3532
ph: 301-649-4002
e-mail: ivorysoc@digizen.net
web: http://www.ivoryinfo.com/
Provides a basis for people interested in ivory to network worldwide and learn to identify ivory and its history, care, and current pricing.

Collectors

Bill Simmons
8955 NW 19th St.
Coral Springs, FL 33071-6109
ph: 954-340-0734
e-mail: wsim1206@aol.com
Wants all ivory: Chinese, Japanese, African, Eskimo, netsukes, carvings, tusks.

David Warther II
David Warther Carving Museum
2561 Crestview Dr. NW
Dover, OH 44622-7405
ph: 330-852-3455 or 330-343-1868
Purchases estate elephant tusks for ongoing ivory carving art project; only wants tusks from African elephants and they must be estate tusks within the U.S.

Dealers

Brian J. Kiracofe
Newport Scrimshander, The
14 Bowen's Wharf
Newport, RI 02840
ph: 401-849-5680 or 800-635-5234
fax: 401-849-9306
e-mail: newportscrimshaw@juno.com
web: http://www.scrimshanders.com
Carries an extensive collection of European and Far Eastern carved ivory antiques.

R. Cronin
207 Silver Palm
Melbourne, FL 32901-3143
Wants to buy ivory: whale, walrus, elephant, any kind; raw and carved; please state asking price.

David Boone
Boone's Trading Company
P.O. Box BB
Brinnon, WA 98320
ph: 360-796-4330 or 800-423-1945
fax: 360-796-4551
Buys and sells legal ivory, scrimshaw, furs and skulls: scrimshaw, netsuke, Eskimo artifacts, carvings, walrus, hippo, warthog, mammoth, jewelry, pistol grips, ivory beads, old trade beads, scrimshaw supplies and reproductions.

John Edward Cunningham
1525 E. Berkley
Springfield, MO 65804-3203
ph: 417-889-7702
Ivory, highly detailed and handcarved; genuine ivory replacement parts for Art Deco and Japanese figurines; also ivory and mother-of-pearl inlays; will travel for large restorations.

Experts

Ed Tripp
Collector's World
139 Main St.
Cooperstown, NY 13326
ph: 607-547-5509
fax: 607-547-5483

Robert E. Weisblut
11109 Nicholas Dr.
Silver Spring, MD 20902-3532
ph: 301-649-4002
e-mail: ivorysoc@digizen.net
web: http://www.ivoryinfo.com/
Wants to buy books about ivory: care, identification, collections, the ivory trade, etc.

Museums/Libraries

David Warther II
David Warther Carving Museum
2561 Crestview Dr. NW
Dover, OH 44622-7405
ph: 330-852-3455 or 330-343-1868
Purchases estate elephant tusks for ongoing ivory carving art project; only wants tusks from African elephants and they must be estate tusks within the U.S.

Periodicals

Joan L. Cervi
Newsletter: Netsuke & Ivory Carving Newsletter-Video
3203 Adams Way
Ambler, PA 19002-3741
ph: 215-628-2026
fax: 215-628-2026
e-mail: jcnetsuke@aol.com
A wholesaler who offers VHS videos and a monthly newsletter about imported netsuke, ivory carvings and other Orientalia.

Repair Services

David Warther II
David Warther Carving Museum
2561 Crestview Dr. NW
Dover, OH 44622-7405
ph: 330-852-3455 or 330-343-1868
Restores wood and ivory carvings and turnings; specialty is in small objects in ivory: chess sets, finials, small turned items, insulators, handles, and finials of ivory on sterling hollow-ware.

Here are some tips when contacting someone listed in this book:

■ When requesting information about a particular item, include a description (material, dimensions, maker's mark, model number, etc.) and a photo, sketch, or photocopy of the item in question.

■ Always ask if there are charges for samples or for the services requested.

■ When writing, please be sure to include a Large (#10 business size) Self-Addressed and Stamped Envelope (LSASE) if requesting a reply or the return of photographs.

■ Never call collect unless otherwise directed. When calling, be considerate of time zone differences and always ask if the party you are calling has time to talk. When leaving an answering machine message, always instruct the party to call you back collect.

J-K

JACOULET

(see PRINTS, Woodblock [Jacoulet])

JADE

(see also GEMS & JEWELRY; ORIENTALIA)

Periodicals

Friends of Jade
Journal: Bulletin of the Friends of Jade
5004 Ensign St.
San Diego, CA 92117
fax: 619-581-1511
The "Bulletin" is an annual comprehensive source of of jade information.

JAMES BOND

(see CHARACTER COLLECTIBLES, Spy Memorabilia [James Bond])

JAPANESE ITEMS

(see ART, Oriental; ARMS & ARMOR, Japanese; BOOKS, Reference [Japanese Items]; FIREARMS, Japanese Matchlocks; OCCUPIED JAPAN; MILITARIA; ORIENTALIA, Japanese Items; PRINTS, Woodblock [Japanese])

JARS

(see ADVERTISING COLLECTIBLES, Counter Jars; BOTTLES; BISCUIT BARRELS/JARS/TINS; CANDY CONTAINERS, Jars; FRUIT JARS; JELLY CONTAINERS; TOBACCO COLLECTIBLES, Jars)

JELL-O MEMORABILIA

Collectors

Lee Davis
4150 Old Orchard Rd.
York, PA 17402-3319
ph: 717-757-7267
Collects only pre-1912 JELL-O recipe books.

Ron Schieber
P.O. Box 72057
Akron, OH 44372
ph: 330-836-9442
e-mail: dschiebe@neo.rr.com
web: http://www.tradecards.com/pages/rsListsForm.html

Experts

Bob Allen
231 E. James Blvd.
P.O. Box 85
Saint James, MO 65559-0085
ph: 314-265-8296

JELLY CONTAINERS

(see also FRUIT JARS)

Clubs/Associations

Art Snyder, Treas.
Jelly Jammers
Newsletter: Jelly Jammers' Journal
110 White Oak Dr.
Butler, PA 16001-3446
ph: 724-287-0278
Jelly Jammers focuses on collecting jelly jars, glasses, molds, cups, mugs and samples or miniatures, and on the education of its members; newsletter published quarterly.

Collectors

Art Snyder
110 White Oak Dr.
Butler, PA 16001-3446
ph: 724-287-0278
Buys/sells/trades all types of jelly glasses, jars, molds and cups, especially patented examples; also wants all related material.

Margaret Shaw
6086 W Boggstown Rd.
Boggstown, IN 46110-9731
ph: 317-835-7121
e-mail: emshaw@in.net

Janice Andres
1951 St. Rd. 28 East
Lafayette, IN 47905

JEWELRY

(see ART DECO; GEMS & JEWELRY)

JOHNSON SMITH CO.

Collectors

Stan & Mardi Timm
Uniquely Racine
6001 Leeward Lane
Racine, WI 53402-9783
ph: 414-639-2304 or 414-639-3312
e-mail: mtimm@aol.com
Wants to buy Johnson Smith Co. catalogs and items sold by the company; writing book about the company and would be interested in any anecdotes, stories or experiences with the company and its products.

JUDAICA

(see also ART, Jewish; STAMP COLLECTING, Holly Land; TEXTILES, Needlework [Judaic])

Appraisers

Y.M. "Max" Rottenberg
Hebraica & Judaica Consultant
1524 56 Street
Brooklyn, NY 11219
ph: 718-435-7691

Auction Services

Daniel E. Kestenbaum
Kestenbaum & Company
20 West 20th Street
New York, NY 10011
ph: 212-366-1197
fax: 212-366-1368
Specializes in the sale of Judaica and Hebraica.

Sotheby's
1334 York Ave.
New York, NY 10021
ph: 212-606-7000
fax: 212-606-7107
web: http://www.sothebys.com
Over 70 collecting areas are featured at Sotheby's auctions including toys, dolls, porcelain, furniture, silver, art, books; exhibitions are free and everyone is welcome; for a free copy of "Sotheby's Newsletter", call 212-606-7245.

Book Sellers

Gary Broder
Broder's Rare & Used Books
205 Columbia Blvd.
Waterbury, CT 06710
ph: 203-755-1114
fax: 203-575-9308
e-mail: bookssss@aol.com
web: http://members.aol.com/bookssss/
Rare and used books on the web; great searchable web pages with a wide selection of books with Judaica a specialty; books in English, Yiddish, and Hebrew.

Clubs/Associations

Israel I. Bick, Pres.
Judaica Collectors Society
Newsletter: Judaica Collectors Society Newsletter
P.O. Box 854
Van Nuys, CA 91408-0854
ph: 818-997-6496
fax: 818-988-4337
e-mail: iibick@aol.com
web: http://www.bick.net
Dealing with and promoting the knowledge of all things related to Judaica and the state of Israel.

Collectors

Stanley Fried
195 Froehlich Farm Blvd.
Woodbury, NY 11797-2931
ph: 516-364-1112
fax: 516-625-4220

Cheryl Weitzman
P.O. Box 790
Cupertino, CA 95015
ph: 408-559-7799 x222
e-mail: cheryl@sessionware.com
web: http://protector.sessionware.com/showcases2/
Volunteer curator of historical displays, Congregation Kol Emeth, Palo Alto, CA; seeks Judaica for private collection and to create Jewish history displays at the synagogue.

Cheryl Melnick
P.O. Box 790
Cupertino, CA 95015
ph: 408-559-7799 x222
e-mail: webmistress@hand-fan.org
web: http://www.hand-fan.org
Seeks the loan, donation or sale of items of Jewish interest (Judaica) to add to the display at the Congregation Kol Emeth Jewish Historic Displays.

Dealers

Judaix Art
P.O. Box 248
Monsey, NY 10952-0248
ph: 914-352-0359
Wants pre-1950 Judaica: menorahs, illustrated books, boxes, children's items, posters.

Alan Scop
Menorah Antiques, Ltd.
1318 Avenue J.
Brooklyn, NY 11230-3635
ph: 718-692-3683
fax: 718-692-0084
Buys and sells Judaica: postcards, posters, prints, photos, menorahs, spice boxes, kiddush cups, esrog boxes, Holocaust memorabilia.

Gary Niederkorn
Gary Niederkorn Silver
Newspaper: Silver Edition
2005 Locust St.
Philadelphia, PA 19103-5606
ph: 215-567-2606
fax: 215-567-2606
Specializes in 19th and 20th cent. silver novelties, jewelry, napkin rings, Judaica, picture frames, etc.; also Tiffany, Jensen, Mexican.

Allan & Ita Fogel
Twin Tankard Antiques
P.O. Box 4847
Silver Spring, MD 20904
ph: 301-236-9391
fax: 301-236-0427
e-mail: pewter@twintankard.com
web: http://www.twintankard.com
Specializes in European pewter; also buys and sells Russian and Judaica.

Israel I. Bick
Bick International
P.O. Box 854
Van Nuys, CA 91408-0854
ph: 818-997-6496
fax: 818-988-4337
e-mail: iibick@aol.com
web: http://www.bick.net
Wants to buy Jewish postcards, Hollywood memorabilia, stamps, coins, documents, currency, photos, bonds, religious articles, everything from the 1933-1945 Holocaust era.

Historicana
1200 Edgehill Dr., Ste. D
Burlingame, CA 94010
ph: 650-343-9578
Wants to buy Jewish rare books, manuscripts, documents, works by Arthur Szyk.

Experts

Lael Bower
507 Michigan Ave.
Grayling, MI 49738
ph: 517-348-6984 or 810-378-5785
Wants to buy Christian and Judaic collectibles; co-author with Penny Forstner of "Guide to Collecting Christian and Judaic Artifacts."

Arthur M. Feldman
1815 St. Johns Ave.
Highland Park, IL 60035-3215
ph: 847-432-8858
fax: 847-266-1199
Buys, sells and specializes in Judaica; former Director, Jewish Museum of Chicago; former Curator at Smithsonian; former Visiting Curator at the Victoria & Albert Museum.

Museums/Libraries

Sylvia Herskowitz
Yeshiva University Museum
2520 Amsterdam Ave.
New York, NY 10033
ph: 212-960-5390
fax: 212-960-5406
web: http://www.jewishculture.org/jewishmuseums/yum.htm
Exhibits and programs relating to Jewish themes, featuring fine and decorative art, textiles and costumes, photography, manuscripts, contemporary crafts and sculpture.

Jewish Museum, The
1109 5th Ave.
New York, NY 10128
ph: 212-423-3200
fax: 212-423-3232
web: http://www.jewishmuseum.org/

Museum of Jewish Heritage
18 First Place
New York, NY 10280
ph: 212-968-1800
fax: 212-968-1368
web: http://www.jewishculture.org/jewishmuseums/mjh.htm

National Museum of American Jewish History
55 N. 5th St.
Philadelphia, PA 19106-2197
ph: 215-923-3811
fax: 215-923-0763
e-mail: nmajh@nmajh.org
web: http://www.nmajh.org/
Established in 1976; dedicated exclusively to collecting, preserving and interpreting artifacts pertaining to the American Jewish experience; over 10,000 artifacts from the history of more than 300 years of American Jewish life.

B'nai B'rith Klutznick National Jewish Museum
1640 Rhode Island Ave. NW
Washington, DC 20036-3278
ph: 202-857-6583
fax: 202-296-1092
web: http://www.jewishculture.org/jewishmuseums/klutz.htm
The only museum in Washington, DC offering the sweep of Jewish culture and history; exhibits and programs on ethnography, history, and art which examines the contributions of Jewish culture to human civilization.

Barry Kessler
Jewish Museum of Maryland
15 Lloyd St.
Baltimore, MD 21202
ph: 410-732-6400
fax: 410-732-6451
e-mail: jhsm@charm.net
web: http://www.jhsm.org/

Marcia Zerivitz, Ex. Dir.
Sanford L. Ziff Jewish Museum of Florida
301 Washington Ave.
Miami Beach, FL 33139-6965
ph: 305-672-5044
fax: 305-672-5933
e-mail: mzerivitz@aol.com
web: http://www.jewishmuseum.com/

Sylvia Plotkin Judaica Museum
10460 N. 56th St.
Paradise Valley, AZ 85253
ph: 480-951-0232
fax: 480-951-7150
web: http://www.jewishculture.org/jewishmuseums/plotkin.htm

Judah L. Magnes Memorial Museum
2911 Russell St.
Berkeley, CA 94705
ph: 510-849-2710
fax: 510-849-3673
e-mail: magnes-pr@eb.jfed.org
web: http://www.jfed.org/magnes/magnes.htm
Third largest Jewish museum in the U.S.; permanent collections, changing exhibitions, library, archives, educational and outreach programs.

Holocaust

Collectors

Phil Froom
U.K.
ph: (44) 411 415616
e-mail: PhilFroom@compuserve.com
Collector of Holocaust related paperwork and items; has a large collection of related ephemera; always interested in buying items; also has items to trade with collectors having similar interests.

Museums/Libraries

Museum of Jewish Heritage
18 First Place
Battery Park City
New York, NY 10004-1484
ph: 212-968-1800
web: http://www.mjhnyc.org/
Dedicated to the Jewish history of the 20th century with a focus on the Holocaust.

United States Holocaust Memorial Museum
100 Raoul Wallenberg Place SW
Washington, DC 20024-2150
ph: 202-488-0400
e-mail: web_administrator@ushmm.org
web: http://www.ushmm.org/
America's national institution for the documentation, study, and interpretation of Holocaust history; serves as this country's memorial to the millions of people murdered during the Holocaust.

C.A.N.D.L.E.S. Holocaust Museum
1532 S. Third St.
Terre Haute, IN 47802
ph: 812-234-7881
fax: 812-235-2665
e-mail: Candles@abcs.com
web: http://users.abcs.com/candles/
Purpose of C.A.N.D.L.E.S. (Children of Auschwitz Nazi Deadly Lab Experiments Survivors) is to educate the public about the horrors of the Holocaust, and to tell the story of the children who survived.

JUGS

(see CERAMICS, Jugs; CERAMICS, Stoneware; SALOON & BAR COLLECTIBLES, Whiskey Pitchers;)

KALEIDOSCOPES

(see also OPTICAL TOYS)

Clubs/Associations

Cozy Baker
Brewster Society
Newsletter: Brewster Society Newsletter
9020 McDonald Dr., #B
Bethesda, MD 20817-1940
ph: 301-365-1855
fax: 301-365-2284
A club for designers, collectors and lovers of kaleidoscopes; sponsors an annual kaleidoscope convention.

Collectors

Coleen Detzel
28 Lacresta Dr.
Florence, KY 41042-9663
ph: 606-647-6156
Wants to buy quality kaleidoscopes, especially unusual and older pieces.

Dealers

Lucille Malitz
Lucid Antiques
P.O. Box KH
Scarsdale, NY 10583
ph: 914-636-7825 or 914-636-5171
fax: 914-636-7825
e-mail: kromscope@aol.com
Invented by Sir David Brewster in the middle of the 19th century, early kaleidoscopes were beautifully crafted scientific instruments, made of ivory, brass and shagreen leather; some silver plated & contained ampules of colored liquid.

Martin Roenigk
Mechantiques
The Crescent Hotel
75 Prospect St.
Eureka Springs, AR 72632
ph: 800-671-6333 or 501-253-9766
e-mail: mroenigk@aol.com
web: http://www.mechantiques.com
Buys and repairs high quality kaleidoscopes from the 1800s made of wood, leather, brass by Bush, Brewster, Bate, Carpenter, etc.

William P. Carroll
ACR Books
P.O. Box 4294
Whittier, CA 90607-4294
ph: 562-693-8421
fax: 562-945-6011
Buys, sells and collects modern, top quality kaleidoscopes and, at times, antique kaleidoscopes.

Eric Sinizer
Light Opera Retail Gallery
174 Grant Ave.
San Francisco, CA 94108-5405
ph: 415-956-9866
fax: 415-956-5624

Experts

Cozy Baker
9020 McDonald Dr., #B
Bethesda, MD 20817-1940
ph: 301-365-1855
fax: 301-365-2284

Man./Prod./Dist.

Jan & Shel Haber
Hand of the Craftsman
Five South Broadway
Nyack, NY 10960
ph: 914-358-6622 or 914-358-3366
fax: 914-735-7669
e-mail: hand@tco.com
web: http://www.kaleidoscopesUSA.com
Showing virtually every contemporary collectible American kaleidoscope by over 50 of the best American designers.

KEEN KUTTER (SIMMONS HARDWARE)

(see also DIAMOND EDGE; HARDWARE; KNIVES; TOOLS; WINCHESTER COLLECTIBLES)

Auction Services

Bob Simmons
Simmons & Company Auctioneers
40706 E. 144th St.
Richmond, MO 64085
ph: 816-776-2936 or 800-646-2936
fax: 816-470-5016
e-mail: simmons_auction@raycounty.com
web: http://www.raycounty.com/simmons/
Conducts annual specialty auctions of Winchester, Keen Kutter (E.C. Simmons Hardware) and Diamond Edge (Shapleigh Hardware) collectibles; has a well-established reputation for expertise and high quality merchandise.

Clubs/Associations

Barbara Huhn, Mem.
Hardware Companies Kollectors' Club
Newsletter: Winchester Keen Kutter Diamond Edge Chronicles
432 S. Gore St.
Saint Louis, MO 63119
ph: 314-968-0304
e-mail: gramma@mvp.net
web: http://www.raycounty.com/simmons/clubs/newsletter.htm
A non-profit organization to serve as an interactive information distribution center for collectors of E.C. Simmons/ Keen Kutter, Winchester Store (non-gun), A.F. Shapleigh/Diamond Edge, Hibbard, and other hardware store brands.

Collectors

John M. Otte
800 N. Moulton St.
Perryville, MO 63775
ph: 573-547-6386
e-mail: aaotte@ldd.net
Interested in Keen Kutter advertising items that were given away by hardware stores; also interested in rare Keen Kutter tools and postcards with Keen Kutter logo or name on them.

Larry Eastley
46460 Hwy. 10
Hardin, MO 64035
ph: 660-398-4617
e-mail: eastley@iland.net
Collector of Keen Kutter, Diamond Edge, Winchester Store (non-gun), Simmons & Shapleigh and other hardware store brands.

Frank Miller
960 Kirkwood Lane
La Habra, CA 90631
ph: 714-870-5902
Wants Keen Kutter memorabilia.

Experts

Jerry & Elaine Heuring
28450 US Highway 61
Scott City, MO 63780
ph: 573-264-3947
e-mail: jheuring@igateway.net
web: http://users.igateway.net/~jheuring/
Authors of "Keen Kutter Collectibles: An Illustrated Price Guide."

Bob Simmons
40706 E. 144th St.
Richmond, MO 64085
ph: 816-776-2936 or 800-646-2936
fax: 816-470-5016
e-mail: simmons_auction@raycounty.com
web: http://www.raycounty.com/simmons/
Collects and specializes in Keen Kutter (E.C. Simmons Hardware) items especially advertising items and unusual items (household, sporting goods, catalogs, signs) made for this St. Louis firm from the late 1800s to 1940.

KENTUCKY DERBY

(see SPORTS COLLECTIBLES, Thoroughbred Racing)

KEY CHAINS

Clubs/Associations

Dr. Edward H. Miles
License Plate Key Chain & Mini License Plate Collectors
Newsletter: DAV Keychain & Chauffeur Badge Collectors News
888 Eighth Ave.
New York, NY 10019-5704
ph: 212-765-2660
Focuses on miniature Disabled American Veterans key chains, chauffeurs' badges, gum cards featuring license plates, windshield stickers, mini license plates.

Collectors

Edward Foley
129 Meadow Valley Rd., Trlr. 11
Ephrata, PA 17522-1843
ph: 717-738-4813
Wants to buy or trade DAV key chain tags 1941 - 1960.

John Vahary, Jr.
41 Crosby Dr.
Battle Creek, MI 49014
ph: 616-965-0943
e-mail: johnjr1222@aol.com
Collects key chains in any form, shape or color, especially those with advertising.

KEYS

(see also KEY CHAINS; KEY FOBS; LOCKS; RESTRAINT DEVICES; SAFES)

Clubs/Associations

Bob Heilemann
West Coast Lock Collectors
Newsletter: West Coast Lock Collectors Newsletter
1427 Lincoln Blvd.
Santa Monica, CA 90401-2732
ph: 310-454-7295 or 310-230-3004
e-mail: locksmann@aol.com
Call evenings; no collect calls, please.

Collectors

Joseph Biunno
129 West 29th St.
New York, NY 10001
ph: 212-629-5630
fax: 212-268-4577
Wants furniture locks and keys; barrel, skeleton, door, drawer, old or new; also wants escutcheons in all styles and sizes.

Bruce Axler
Ansonia Station
P.O. Box 1288
New York, NY 10023-1288
ph: 212-362-4429
fax: 212-579-1274
Wants pocket items, i.e. items/gadgets designed to fit in the pocket: tools, knives, lighters, compacts, folding cups, items which look like a pocket watch but are not, calculators, leather items, matchsafes, candle safes, travel items.

Mark Lyons
544 Crest Dr.
Encinitas, CA 92024-4145
ph: 760-431-5397
fax: 760-431-1515
Wants unusual keys, original handcuff keys, keys to the city, padlock keys, jail/prison keys; also wants old locks and handcuffs.

KITCHEN COLLECTIBLES

(see also APPLE PARERS; CAST IRON ITEMS; CATALOGS; CERAMICS; COOKIES & COOKIE SHAPING; COOKIE JARS; DAIRY COLLECTIBLES; ELECTRICITY RELATED ITEMS, Appliances; GRANITEWARE; IRONS; MOLDS; PIE BIRDS; RANGES; SPOONS; STOVES; STRING HOLDERS)

Clubs/Associations

Bob Grossman, Pres.
Kollectors of Old Kitchen Stuff
354 Route 206 North
Chester, RGross1831@aol.com 07930
ph: 908-879-7935
fax: 908-879-0976

Collectors

Trish Claar
2621 Manor Court
Owings, MD 20736-9145
ph: 301-855-6531
Wants 1950s and 1960s kitchen collectibles, gadgets and furniture.

Phyllis Moffet
P.O. Box 200
Modesto, IL 62667-0200
ph: 217-439-7358
Interested in buying old kitchen items: egg beaters, nutmeg grinders, apple parers, etc.

Reid Cooper
32942 Josheroo Ct.
Temecula, CA 92592
ph: 909-302-3348
e-mail: rcoop4129@aol.com
Kitchen collector seeking to purchase tin advertising egg separators or tea strainers in good or better condition; also wants to buy other tin or iron kitchen implements with advertising; please describe fully and price.

Carole Meeker
5702 Vacation Blvd.
Somerset, CA 95684-9324
ph: 530-620-7019
fax: 530-620-7020
e-mail: clm@inforum.net
Wants to buy rare and unusual small patented mechanical antiques, early American technology and occupa-

tional-related photography, advertising and catalogs.

Dealers

Bob & Kaaren Grossman
B & K Kitchen Primitives & Collectibles
354 Rte. 206
Chester, NJ 07930
ph: 908-879-7935
Specializing in tin, copper, Japanned ware and mechanicals for household, hotel and bakery use.

Jerry Harmyk
Kitschen
380 Bleecker St.
New York, NY 10014
ph: 212-727-0430
Buys and sells kitchen collectibles from the 1920s through 1970s.

Stephen G. Del Sordo
Heritage Resource Group
305 Oakley St.
Cambridge, MD 21613
ph: 410-228-8934
fax: 410-221-8061
e-mail: delsordo@shore.intercom.net
web: http://www.heritageresource.com/
A cultural resource management/ historic preservation firm that has contracts to locate, provide, authenticate artifacts for museums and collectors; areas of expertise include architecture, industry, domestic, agriculture, and maritime.

Tom Lawson
Buckeye Appliance
714 W. Fremont
Stockton, CA 95203-2702
ph: 209-464-9643
Specializes in the sales, parts and restoration of antique gas stoves; also sells kitchen collectibles, Hoosiers, 1950s chrome dinettes, and porcelain-top tables.

Jennifer & Co. Antiques & Collectives
P.O. Box 884
Groveland, CA 95321
ph: 209-962-7112
web: http://www.yosemitegold.com/jennifer/kitchen.html
Specializes in much-sought-after kitchen collectibles.

Butter Churns

Dealers

Wendell W. Stream
Churn Castle Antiques
809 Maple Ave.
Woodward, IA 50276
ph: 515-438-4142
e-mail: xisp142@netins.net
web: http://www.netins.net/showcase/churns/
Appraiser, dealer and collector of butter churns; website has information on most kinds of butter churns.

Egg Separators

Collectors

Don Thornton
1345 Poplar Ave.
Sunnyvale, CA 94087-3770
ph: 408-737-0434
fax: 408-737-0191
e-mail: offbeatbks@aol.com
web: http://www.vena.com/authors/1013bi.html
Wants old tin or aluminum egg separators, with advertising.

Egg Timers

Collectors

Lance V. Kuntzman
21 Perry
South Dartmouth, MA 02748-1803
ph: 508-994-5934
e-mail: tomcaper@aol.com
Wants to buy unusual or figural egg timers with sand glass attached.

Jeannie Greenfield
310 Parker Rd.
Stoneboro, PA 16153-2810
ph: 724-376-2584
Wants figural egg timers; any condition.

Phyllis Eisenach
3759 SW Whispering Sound Dr.
Palm City, FL 34990-7735
ph: 561-223-8275
e-mail: eisenach@webtv.net
Specializes in figural egg timers; interested particularly in German Goebel and Japanese ceramic figures with glass timer attached.

Dealers

Pat Klein
Nostalgia Unlimited
P.O. Box 262
East Berlin, CT 06023
ph: 860-828-3973
fax: 860-828-1544
e-mail: pklein262@yahoo.com

Eggbeaters

Collectors

Craig Dinner
P.O. Box 4399
Long Island City, NY 11104-0399
ph: 718-729-3850 or 802-365-7181
Wants early or unusual egg beaters.

Dana & Darlene DeMore
4645 Laurel Ridge Dr.
Harrisburg, PA 17110-3446
ph: 717-545-7320
Wants to buy old eggbeaters; one or entire collection.

Clay Tontz
4043 Nora Ave.
Covina, CA 91722
ph: 626-338-9976

Reid Cooper
Mixer Mania
32942 Josheroo Ct.
Temecula, CA 92592
ph: 909-302-3348
e-mail: rcoop4129@aol.com
Advanced collector/researcher buying pre-1920 U.S. made eggbeaters, mayonnaise mixers, cream whips and stoneware beater bowls in top working order and/or condition; no electrics, plastic, or stainless; send price, photo or sketch.

Experts

Don Thornton
1345 Poplar Ave.
Sunnyvale, CA 94087-3770
ph: 408-737-0434
fax: 408-737-0191
e-mail: offbeatbks@aol.com
web: http://www.vena.com/authors/1013bi.html
Wants old eggbeaters and related memorabilia and paper items, especially old catalogs; author of "Beat This, The Eggbeater Chronicles," (1994) and "The Eggbeater Book," (1983).

Flour Sifters

Collectors

Dana & Darlene DeMore
4645 Laurel Ridge Dr.
Harrisburg, PA 17110-3446
ph: 717-545-7320
Wants to buy mechanical flour sifters.

Frisbie Pie Pans

Collectors

Victor Malafronte
909 Marina Village Pkwy., #321
Alameda, CA 94501
ph: 510-814-9639
Wants to buy Frisbie pie pans (made by the Frisbie Pie Co., Bridgeport, CT); will pay up to $5 each if in good condition.

Ice Shavers

Collectors

Don Thornton
1345 Poplar Ave.
Sunnyvale, CA 94087-3770
ph: 408-737-0434
fax: 408-737-0191
e-mail: offbeatbks@aol.com
web: http://www.vena.com/authors/1013bi.html
Wants old ice shavers, cast iron planes and bowls.

Lemon Squeezers

Collectors

Stanley D. Watson
2959 Hundred Oaks Ave.
Baton Rouge, LA 70808-1536
ph: 504-383-1594
e-mail: sdwatson@earthlink.net
Wants to buy cast iron lemon squeezers with glass or porcelain bowls.

Mixers

Collectors

Norman Hagey
Mr. Sunbeam
19672 Steavens Creek #424
Cupertino, CA 95014-2465
ph: 408-973-8129
Wants to buy old Sunbeam mixers only: complete mixers, attachments, bowls, toasters, and information on model numbers and types; books, pamphlets about Sunbeam mixers.

Nutmeg Grinders

Collectors

Dana & Darlene DeMore
4645 Laurel Ridge Dr.
Harrisburg, PA 17110-3446
ph: 717-545-7320
Wants to buy mechanical nutmeg grinders.

Pie Crimpers/Jaggers

Collectors

Priscilla Hinners
2711 Jaynia Place
Lemon Grove, CA 91945-1319
ph: 619-265-1046
e-mail: phinners@yahoo.com
Wants all types of pie crimpers (jaggers): ceramic, ivory, metal, unusual wooden, etc.

Pot Scrubbers

Collectors

Don Thornton
1345 Poplar Ave.
Sunnyvale, CA 94087-3770
ph: 408-737-0434
fax: 408-737-0191
e-mail: offbeatbks@aol.com
web: http://www.vena.com/authors/1013bi.html
Wants old pot scrubbers - the ugly chain-mail variety.

Reamers

Clubs/Associations

Deborah Gillham
National Reamer Collectors Association
Newsletter: NRCA Quarterly Review
47 Midline Ct.
Gaithersburg, MD 20878-1996
ph: 301-977-5727
e-mail: reamers@erols.com
web: http://www.reamers.org/
A non-profit organization with over

350 members devoted to promoting citrus and juice reamer and squeezer collecting; interested in reamers of all materials - porcelain, glass, wood, metal, etc.

Winnie Cerbin, Sec.
Mid-American Reamer Collectors
Newsletter: Juicy Journal
2262 Clay St.
Austinburg, OH 44010-9753
ph: 440-275-9753
Club is an affiliate of the National Reamers Collectors Association; membership in the NRCA is required for Regional Club membership.

John Brown, Pres.
Southwest Reamer Collectors Association
2824 Willing
Fort Worth, TX 76110
ph: 817-923-2026
Club is an affiliate of the National Reamers Collectors Association; membership in the NRCA is required for Regional Club membership.

Terry McDuffee
Western Regional Reamer Collectors Association
1478 W. Cypress Ave.
Redlands, CA 92373-5613
ph: 909-739-9534
fax: 909-335-8354
Club is an affiliate of the National Reamers Collectors Association; membership in the NRCA is required for Regional Club membership.

Collectors

Bobbie & Alan Bryson
1 St. Eleanoras Ln.
Tuckahoe, NY 10707-1307
ph: 914-779-1405
e-mail: napkindoll@aol.com
Wants figural reamers; Bobbie is co-author of the pictorial reference guide "Collectibles For The Kitchen, Bath & Beyond" (Antique Trader Books).

Judy Smith
1702 Lamont St., NW
Washington, DC 20010
ph: 202-332-3020
fax: 202-234-6653
e-mail: judy@quilt.net
web: http://www.quiltart.com/judy/glass.html
Interested in unusual glass, china and metal reamers and other Depression era kitchen glassware; webmaster for National Reamer Collector's Association (http://www.reamers.org/).

Deborah Gillham
47 Midline Ct.
Gaithersburg, MD 20878-1996
ph: 301-977-5727
e-mail: reamers@erols.com
web: http://www.reamers.org/
Membership chairman for the National Reamer Collectors Association.

Ray Maxwell
222 Cooper Ave.
Elgin, IL 60120-2128
ph: 847-695-6284
e-mail: antiquemax@n2antiques.com
Collects all reamers; especially interested in glass reamers from the Depression era.

Jim Pulliam
1925 Ashley Dr.
Edmond, OK 73034
ph: 405-340-8710

Terry McDuffee
1478 W. Cypress Ave.
Redlands, CA 92373-5613
ph: 909-739-9534
fax: 909-335-8354
Buys and sells reamers, juicers and kitchen glassware; rare and unusual items wanted; please price and describe.

Dealers

John & Peggy Hoy
Monrovia West Antique Mall
925 West Foothill Blvd.
Monrovia, CA 91016-1915
ph: 626-355-5081
Avid collectors and dealers specializing in reamers, jadite.

Experts

Dee Long
112 S. Center
Lacon, IL 61540-1306
ph: 309-246-8996 or 309-246-5278
e-mail: merle.long@juno.com

Ed & Mary Walker
13550 Addison St.
Sherman Oaks, CA 91423
ph: 949-793-9534
Authors of three volumes about reamers.

Rolling Pins

Collectors

Priscilla Hinners
2711 Jaynia Place
Lemon Grove, CA 91945-1319
ph: 619-265-1046
e-mail: phinners@yahoo.com
Wants all types of rolling pins: Nailsea, Meissen, Harker, ceramic, glass, stoneware, advertising, metal, unusual wooden, springerle, and other types of rollers.

Rugbeaters

Collectors

Bill Carroll
RR 1, Box 62
Hope, ND 58046-9760
ph: 701-945-2416
fax: 701-945-2772
e-mail: BillND29@ictc.com
web: http://www.collectoronline.com/booths/booth-74/
Collects rug beaters and related items such as catalogs and samples.

Sausage Stuffers

Collectors

Dale Schmidt
610 Howell Prairie Rd. SE
Salem, OR 97301-9097
ph: 503-364-0499
fax: 503-585-3071
e-mail: jschm62655@aol.com
Wants all types; complete or parts.

Wire Ware

Repro. Sources

Mathews Wire, Inc.
654 West Morrison
Frankfort, IN 46041-1670
ph: 800-826-9650
fax: 765-659-1059
e-mail: mwire@mathewswire.com
web: http://www.mathewswire.com
Wholesale supplier of wire reproductions; egg baskets, display racks, etc.; also reproduction toys and advertising signs.

KITES

Clubs/Associations

American Kitefliers Association
Newsletter: Kiting
352 Hungerford Dr.
Rockville, MD 20850-4117
ph: 800-252-2550
e-mail: aka@aka.kite.org
web: http://www.kite.org/
Non-profit volunteer organization of 4500 kitefliers in 29 countries; educates the public in the art, history, technology, and practice of building and flying kites; directory includes member/merchants nationwide.

Experts

Valerie Govig
P.O. Box 446
Randallstown, MD 21133-0446
ph: 410-922-1212
fax: 410-922-4262
e-mail: kitelines@compuserve.com
Editor of "Kite Lines Magazine."

Man./Prod./Dist.

Andrew Gelinas
Burlesque Kites
18 W. 3rd. St.
Bethlehem, PA 18015-1222
ph: 610-867-3313 or 610-867-1665
fax: 610-867-4999
e-mail: silvertiger@enter.net
Specializes in handmade parachuting Teddy Bears and other fine parafauna; also sells parafauna supplies, 'chutes, releases, etc.; also imports "hand-painted" art on silk that flies - 30" to 10' birds, insects, dragons, pandas, etc.

Museums/Libraries

World Kite Museum & Hall of Fame
112 - 3rd St. NW
P.O. Box 964
Long Beach, WA 98631-0964
ph: 360-642-4020
e-mail: jkite@willapabay.org
web: http://www.funbeach.com/Attrac9.html
Collection contains more than 600 kites from around the world; exhibits change annually.

Japan Kite Museum
Fifth Floor, Taimeiken Bldg.
1-12-10 Nihonbashi, Chuo-ku
Japan
ph: 03-3275-2704
fax: 03-3273-0575
web: http://www.tako.gr.jp/eng/museums_e/tokyo_e.html
Exhibits mainly typical Japanese traditional kites.

Periodicals

Valerie Govig, Ed.
Magazine: Kite Lines Magazine
P.O. Box 446
Randallstown, MD 21133-0446
ph: 410-922-1212
fax: 410-922-4262
e-mail: kitelines@compuserve.com
A quarterly publication with articles, ads, etc. relating to kites, kite making, kite history and kite flying; also sells a large line of books relating to kites; will help make connections with kite buyers and sellers.

Suppliers

Frank Gramkowski
High Fly Kite, Co.
30 West End Ave.
Haddonfield, NJ 08033
ph: 609-429-6260
fax: 609-429-0142
e-mail: frang@voicenet.com
Mail order kite specialists; kites, lines, reels and handles, kite building supplies and parts, etc.

World of Kites
525 S. Washington
Royal Oak, MI 48067
ph: 248-398-5900
fax: 609-429-0142
The kite flier's pro shop: kites, lines, reels and handles, accessories; Oriental, sportsman's, custom, stunters and fighters.

KITS

(see also MODELS; SCIENCE FICTION)

Dealers

Trader Rick's Collectible Toy Cars
P.O. Box 161
Newark, IL 60541
ph: 815-695-9484
Wants to buy toy cars and model cars; also built or unbuilt car kits.

Periodicals

Magazine: Modeler's Resource, The
4120 douglas Blvd., #306-292
Granite Bay, CA 95746-5936
ph: 916-784-9517
fax: 916-784-8384
e-mail: modres@quiknet.com
web: http://www.modelersresource.com/
Bi-monthly magazine with up-to-date information on what's new in the vehicular and figure kit market.

Figures

Clubs/Associations

Gordy Dutt
International Figure Kit Club
Magazine: KitBuilders Magazine
P.O. Box 201
Sharon Center, OH 44274-0201
ph: 330-239-1657
fax: 330-239-2991
e-mail: Gordys_kitbuilders@juno.com
web: http://www.gordyskitbuilders.com/
Published four times a year, this magazine deals mostly with plastic, vinyl, and resin figure or Sci/Fi type model kits from the 1950s to present.

Dealers

Gordy Dutt
Gordy's
P.O. Box 201
Sharon Center, OH 44274-0201
ph: 330-239-1657
fax: 330-239-2991
e-mail: Gordys_kitbuilders@juno.com
web: http://www.gordyskitbuilders.com/
Buys and sells plastic, vinyl, and resin figure or Sci/Fi type model kits from the 1950s to present; also toys from the late '50s to the early '70s.

John F. Green
John F. Green, Inc.
P.O. Box 55787
Riverside, CA 92517
ph: 909-684-5300 or 800-807-4759
fax: 909-684-8819
e-mail: ML@greenmodels.com
web: http://www.greenmodels.com
Sells, buys, trades plastic model kits from and of science fiction, TV, figures, space movies, etc.; old and new; send for free sales catalog.

Experts

Terry J. Webb
P.O. Box 30885
Columbus, OH 43230-0885
ph: 614-882-2125
fax: 614-882-6012
web: http://www.amazingmodeler.com/
Internationally renowned expert on the Garage Kit hobby; author of "Reverence of the Garage Kit That Ate My Wallet."

Gordy Dutt
Gordy's
P.O. Box 201
Sharon Center, OH 44274-0201
ph: 330-239-1657
fax: 330-239-2991
e-mail: Gordys_kitbuilders@juno.com
web: http://www.gordyskitbuilders.com/

Periodicals

Terry J. Webb
Amazing Publications & Communications Inc.
Magazine: Amazing Figure Modeler
P.O. Box 30885
Columbus, OH 43230-0885
ph: 614-882-2125
fax: 614-882-6012
web: http://www.amazingmodeler.com/
A quarterly magazine that focuses on the international garage and model figure kit market.

Newsletter: Garage, The
330 Merriman Rd.
Akron, OH 44303-1552
Focuses on vinyl and resin-poured kit modeling: classic horror figures, sci-fi monsters, movie stars, classical beauties; new and exciting kits being produced each year.

Plastic

Clubs/Associations

Jerry Hall
International Plastic Modelers Society USA
Journal: IPMS/USA Modelers Journal
P.O. Box 6138
Warner Robins, GA 31095-6138
ph: 912-922-7132 or 912-452-3744
fax: 912-452-3744
e-mail: ehall@hom.net
web: http://ipmsusa.org/
Journal includes review of new kits and accessories, scratch-building, convention articles, IPMS news, etc.

John W. Burns
Society for the Preservation & Encouragement of Scale Model Kit Collecting
Magazine: Kit Collectors Clearinghouse
3213 Hardy Dr.
Edmond, OK 73013-5319
ph: 405-341-4640
e-mail: cheersjwb@aol.com
A bi-monthly magazine for kit collectors; buy and sell ads, re-issue notices, information on new kits, vacuum-formed and resin kits, etc.

Bob Keller
Kit Collectors International
P.O. Box 38
Stanton, CA 90680-0038
ph: 714-826-5216
e-mail: prsdog@aol.com
web: http://members.aol.com/PRSdog/kitshow.html
Sponsors the "Kit Collectors Exposition & Sale" three times each year. The world's largest model kit collectors swap meet and show; buys and sells collections.

Collectors

Wally Krocsko
P.O. Box 307
Atlasburg, PA 15004-0307
ph: 724-947-5671
Buys, sells, trades plastic model kits; must enclose a LSASE to get a reply to buy/sell/trade inquiries; please call evenings.

John Krupienski
5200 Hilltop Dr.
P.O. Box AA6
Brookhaven, PA 19015-1200
ph: 610-874-3003

Jim Crane
15 Clemson Ct.
Newark, DE 19711-4301
ph: 302-738-6031
Wants Aurora, Revell, Monogram plastic kits; built or unbuilt; any condition; wants figures, planes, boats and catalogs.

Experts

John W. Burns
3213 Hardy Dr.
Edmond, OK 73013-5319
ph: 405-341-4640
e-mail: cheersjwb@aol.com
Author of "Collectors Value Guide for Scale Model Plastic Kits," and "In Plastic: WWII Aircraft Kits"; willing to buy unbuilt plastic model kits of all subjects.

Plastic (Aurora)

Dealers

Rocky Sorrentino
Art 'N' Things
133 S. Andersen Ave.
Fairview, NJ 07022
ph: 201-943-2288
Buys and sells original Aurora figure model kits, reproduction boxes and battery-operated clocks.

Experts

Bill & Joanne Bruegman
Toy Scouts, Inc.
137 Casterton Ave.
Akron, OH 44303-1543
ph: 330-836-0668
fax: 330-869-8668
e-mail: toyscout@akron.infi.net
Author of "Aurora History and Price Guide."

David Welch
P.O. Box 714
Murphysboro, IL 62966-0714
ph: 618-687-2282
fax: 618-684-2243
e-mail: PezDude1@aol.com
Specializing in Aurora figure kits; buying any pre-1977 TV, science fiction, comic, movie, monster related kits; must have original boxes unless factory promos; contributor to "O'Brien's Collecting Toys" and Tomart's "Garage Sale Gold."

KKK

(see KU KLUX KLAN COLLECTIBLES)

KNIFE RESTS

Collectors

Beverly Ales
495 Linden Way
Pleasanton, CA 94566-6879
ph: 925-846-5297
fax: 925-846-5297

Periodicals

Beverly Ales
Newsletter: Knife Rests of Yesterday & Today
495 Linden Way
Pleasanton, CA 94566-6879
ph: 925-846-5297
fax: 925-846-5297
Sponsors conference for collectors of knife rests.

KNIVES

(see also ARMS & ARMOR; BLACKSMITHING ITEMS; BOOKS, Reference [Knives]; DIAMOND EDGE; EDGED WEAPONS; KEEN KUTTER; KNIFE RESTS)

Clubs/Associations

Cindy Taylor
Northeast Cutlery Collectors Association
P.O. Box 624
Mansfield, MA 02048
ph: 508-226-5157
e-mail: cklevine@worldnet.att.net
web: http://www.donb.com/ncca/

Ruth Trout, Sec.
Allegheny Mountain Knife Collectors Association
P.O. Box 23
Hunkers, PA 15639
ph: 724-925-2713

Keystone Blade Association
P.O. Box 46
Lewisburg, PA 17837
ph: 717-523-3211

Susquehanna Knife Collectors Association
839 Beaver Lane
Reading, PA 19606

Glenn Smit
Chesapeake Bay Knife Club, Inc.
Newsletter: CBKC Newsletter
939I Beards Hill Rd.
Aberdeen, MD 21001
ph: 410-343-0380 or 410-686-5529
Club meets monthly on the second Monday; visits to local knifemakers' shops are scheduled; members' interests are varied, but all are cutlery related.

Ernie Cook
Northern Virginia Knife Collectors
P.O. Box 501
Falls Church, VA 22040
ph: 703-790-1960

Shenandoah Valley Knife Collectors
P.O. Box 843
Harrisonburg, VA 22801

John Riddle
Old Dominion Knife Collectors
4236 Lakeridge Circle
Troutville, VA 24175-2540
ph: 540-977-0242

Mason Dixon Knife Club
P.O. Box 2726
Martinsburg, WV 25401-5526

Tar Heel Cutlery Club
2730 Tudor Rd.
Winston Salem, NC 27106
ph: 336-725-1016

Palmetto Cutlery Club
P.O. Box 1356
Greer, SC 29652
ph: 864-877-0303

Chattachoochee Cutlery Club
P.O. Box 568
Tucker, GA 30085

Jimmy Green
Three Rivers Knife Club
783 NE Jones Mill Rd.
Rome, GA 30165-9075
ph: 706-235-0581 or 706-234-2540

Deep South Knife Collectors
P.O. Box 9001
Pensacola, FL 32513-9001
ph: 850-477-2202
fax: 850-477-2202

Mitch Weiss
Art Knife Collector's Association
Newsletter: Art Knife Trader
2211 Lee Rd.
Winter Park, FL 32789
ph: 407-740-8778
fax: 407-740-8283
e-mail: mitch@artknife.com
web: http://artknife.com/

Louie Prothman
Florida Knife Collectors Association
5321 Holden Rd.
Cocoa, FL 32927
ph: 407-636-1876

Gary G. Nichols
Heart of Dixie Cutlery Club
4141 Camp Coleman
Trussville, AL 35173-2818
ph: 205-655-7789

Fight'n Rooster Cutlery Club
Newsletter: FRCC Newsletter
P.O. Box 936
Lebanon, TN 37087
ph: 615-444-8070
web: http://www.fightnrooster.com/

Soddy Daisy knife Collectors Association Club
P.O. Box 1224
Soddy Daisy, TN 37379
ph: 423-842-2663

National Knife Collectors Association
Magazine: National Knife Magazine
P.O. Box 21070
Chattanooga, TN 37421-0700
ph: 800-548-3907 or 423-892-5007
fax: 423-899-9456
e-mail: nkca@aol.com
web: http://members.aol.com/nkca/
Each month receive "National Knife Magazine" (focuses mainly on new knives but also carries some articles about old knives); free admission to NKCA sanctioned shows; annual club knife.

North East Tennessee Knife Club
P.O. Box 562
Kingsport, TN 37660

Memphis Knife Collectors
1439 Elmgrove Rd.
Burlison, TN 38015
ph: 901-476-3834

Kentucky Cutlery Association
4914 Bluebird Ave.
Louisville, KY 40213
ph: 502-267-9456

G.T. Williams
Central Kentucky Knife Club
P.O. Box 55049
Lexington, KY 40555
ph: 502-863-4919

Mahoning Valley Knife Collectors
1900 McCloskey
Columbiana, OH 44408

Western Reserve Cutlery Association
P.O. Box 355
Dover, OH 44622

James Webb
Johnny Appleseed Knife Collectors
668 Lenox Ave.
Mansfield, OH 44906
ph: 419-747-7551

Fort City Knife Collectors Club
P.O. Box 31396
Cincinnati, OH 45231-0396

Ed Etchason
Indiana Knife Collectors
P.O. Box 101
Fountaintown, IN 46130-0101
ph: 317-835-7487

Patrick Donovan
Wolverine Knife Collectors Club
Newsletter: Wolverine Knife Collectors Newsletter
P.O. Box 52
Belleville, MI 48112-0052
ph: 810-247-5883
Michigan's largest knife collectors club; members are expert in most knife collecting categories; annual show is one of the largest in the Midwest; affiliated with the National Knife Collectors Association.

Mack McDonald
Marble Plus Knife Club
P.O. Box 228
Gladstone, MI 49837
ph: 906-428-1075

Hawkeye Knife Collectors Club
800 Knob Hill Dr.
Des Moines, IA 50317-7810
ph: 515-266-4976

Bob Schrap
Badger Knife Club, Inc.
Newsletter: Badger Knife Club Newsletter
P.O. Box 511
Elm Grove, WI 53122-0511
ph: 414-479-9765 or 515-771-6472
fax: 414-784-2996
e-mail: RSchrap@aol.com
Club for all knife collectors; custom, factory, military, antique knives; for knife collectors, makers and dealers.

North Star Blade Collectors
P.O. Box 20523
Bloomington, MN 55420
web: http://hps.com/Organizations/Blades.html

Willard C. Patrick, Pres.
Professional Knifemakers Association, Inc.
2906 N. Montana Ave., Ste. 30027
Helena, MT 59601
ph: 406-458-6552
e-mail: wilamar@ixi.net
An association for knifemakers.

Louie Jamison, Pres.
American Edge Collectors Association
Newsletter: AECA Newsletter
24755 Hickory Ct.
Crete, IL 60417
ph: 708-868-7784 or 708-672-8838

L. Lutz
Soy Knife Collectors
P.O. Box 532
Warrensburg, IL 62573

Larry Hancock
Jefferson County Custom Knife Club
12193 E. Turner Dr.
Mount Vernon, IL 62864
ph: 618-242-4514
e-mail: lhancock@benton103.frnkln.kiz.il.us

Gateway Area Knife Club
310 Andrews Trail
Saint Peters, MO 63376

Kansas Knife Collectors Association
P.O. Box 1125
Wichita, KS 67201
ph: 316-838-0540

Knife Collectors Club, Inc., The
1705 N. Thompson
Springdale, AR 72764
ph: 501-751-7341
fax: 501-751-4520
e-mail: agrussell@arkansasusa.com
web: http://www.k-c-c.com/

Ft. Smith Knife Club
3907 Kenner Chapel Road
Rudy, AR 72952
ph: 501-474-4474

Mike Ramsey, Sec.
Sooner Knife Collectors Club
1813 SW 30th St.
Moore, OK 73160
ph: 405-799-8698

Mike Moeskau
Gulf Coast Knife Club
P.O. Box 265
Pasadena, TX 77501-0265
ph: 713-479-3072

Tom Gilroy, Pres.
Rocky Mountain Blade Collectors
P.O. Box 324
Westminster, CO 80230-0324
ph: 303-426-9004
e-mail: rmbcknife@aol.com
web: http://members.aol.com/rmbcknife/

Knifemaker's Guild, The
7148 W. Country Gables Dr.
Peoria, AZ 85381
ph: 602-878-3064
fax: 602-878-3964
web: http://www.kmg.org/index.html
Recognized as the organization of the finest custom handmade knifemakers in the world, where more than 250 members display and offer for sale handcrafted knives of the finest quality at an annual show.

Joseph G. Cordova
American Blacksmith Society
P.O. Box 977
Peralta, NM 87042-0977
ph: 505-869-3912
fax: 505-869-2509
e-mail: abs@rt66.com
An international society composed of knifemakers who use the forging method to make the blade and of collectors who appreciate the forged blade.

Joseph G. Cordova
American Bladesmith Society
P.O. Box 977
Peralta, NM 87042-0977
ph: 505-869-3912
fax: 505-869-2509
e-mail: abs@rt66.com
web: http://www.americanbladesmith.com/
For knifemakers and knife enthusiasts.

Lowell Shelhart
Southern California Blades Knife Collectors Club
P.O. Box 1140
Lomita, CA 90717
ph: 310-530-8412

Bay Area Knife Collectors Association
P.O. Box 223
Fremont, CA 94537
ph: 510-683-9122
e-mail: cgc@ccnet.com
web: http://www.cgcweb.com/bakca/

Oregon Knife Collectors
P.O. Box 2091
Eugene, OR 97402
ph: 541-484-5564
e-mail: okca@oregonknifeclub.org
web: http://www.oregonknifeclub.org/

Paul Johnston, Sec./Treas.
Canadian Knifemakers Guild
RR #2
Marmora, Ontario K0K 2M0
Canada
ph: 613-472-5644
e-mail: cdnguild@ckg.org
web: http://www.ckg.org/
Goal is to increase public awareness of knifemakers, not as makers of weapons, but as skilled and versatile crafts people producing high quality implements which happen to be knives.

Collectors

Bruce Axler
Ansonia Station
P.O. Box 1288
New York, NY 10023-1288
ph: 212-362-4429
fax: 212-579-1274
Wants pocket items, i.e. items/gadgets designed to fit in the pocket: tools, knives, lighters, compacts, folding cups, items which look like a pocket watch but are not, calculators, leather items, matchsafes, candle safes, travel items.

Kenneth D. Smith
55 Howard Ave.
Staten Island, NY 10301-4404
Wants to buy Fairbairn-Sykes fighting knives with personalized Wilkinson blades.

Bill Campesi
P.O. Box 140
Merrick, NY 11566-0140
ph: 516-546-9630
Buy, sell, trade all cutlery and related advertising: catalogs, postcards, cutlery display items; pocket, sheath, Bowie knives.

Gerald A. Shaw
1928 Causton Bluff Rd.
Savannah, GA 31404-1310
ph: 912-232-0771
Wants knives by Remington, Boker, Winchester, CASE, Russell, Western, Ka-Bar, etc.; also wants razors, knife books, daggers, hunting knives, pocket knives, etc.

Gordon White
P.O. Box 181
Cuthbert, GA 31740
ph: 912-732-6982
Wants to buy M.S.A., Marbles, Scagel, and R.H. Ruana knives and hatchets; also Loveless, Morseth, Randall, and Remington sheath knives; any Heiser, V.L. & A., or A&F Co. marked knives or ax sheaths.

Guy Manwaring
P.O. Box 361
Tecumseh, MI 49286-0361
ph: 517-423-4466
fax: 517-423-4466
Collects knives: pocket, Bowie, hunting, American switchblades, etc.; also wants old magazine ads for knives or Keen Kutter hardware, cardboard pocket knife boxes, countertop displays, postcards, catalogs, any cutlery items.

A.L. Hunt
P.O. Box 711
Excelsior Springs, MO 64024
ph: 816-637-8464
Wants to buy military knives & bayonets from WI, WWII, Korea, Vietnam: Special Forces stilettos & bolos, Seals dive knives, USMC recon knives & KA Bars, presentation knives, trench knives, M-4s, M-6s, bayonets, Randalls, EKS.

Tom Gilroy
P.O. Box 324
Westminster, CO 80230-0324
ph: 303-426-9004
e-mail: rmbcknife@aol.com
web: http://members.aol.com/rmbcknife/
Has collected and traded knives for over 30 years.

Murray White
1200 Shamir Cr.
Mississaugua, Ontario L5C 1L1
Canada
ph: 905-275-8320
fax: 905-275-0492
e-mail: phymur@home.com

Dealers

Bob Albrecht
Bob's Antiques & Curios
P.O. Box 108
Collinsville, CT 06022
ph: 860-747-0009
e-mail: hugybear@esslink.com
Wants Connecticut made folding knives, especially Ebenizer Wing, Southington Cutlery (Empire, Winsted, etc.) and Northfield; also collect other folding knives.

Dennis Blake
Cutlery Specialties
22 Morris Lane
Great Neck, NY 11024-1707
ph: 516-829-5899 or 516-773-0071
fax: 516-773-8076
e-mail: Dennis13@aol.com
Buys, sells, trades, designs knives and other related cutlery items.

Tom Clark
Blue Ridge Knives
166 Adwolfe Rd.
Marion, VA 24354-9351
ph: 540-783-6143
fax: 540-783-9298
Will purchase entire knife collections or by the piece; interested in antique, commemorative, custom hardware, or entire business inventories; immediate payment; also wholesales current factory knives.

Rhett & Janie Stidham
Stidham's Knives
P.O. Box 570
Roseland, FL 32957
ph: 561-589-0618
fax: 561-589-3162
e-mail: rstidham@gate.net
web: http://www.kmg.org/stidham/
Over 29 years in business; specializes in older makers and in particular Loveless, Horn, Moran, Cronk, Hibben, Draper, Lile, Cooper, and Scagel; buys and sells at all major shows; buys collections large and small; specializes in Bowie knives.

Parkers' Knife Collector Service
6715 Heritage Business Court
P.O. Box 23522
Chattanooga, TN 37422
ph: 800-247-0599 or 423-892-0448
Distributes all kinds of knives including Winchester, antique Case, Remington, Club knives, Marbles, Fightn' Rooster, New German knives, antique knives, Bulldog Brand Pit Bull collector knives, prototypes, etc.

J. Bruce Voyles
Heritage Antique Knives
P.O. Box 22007
Chattanooga, TN 37422
ph: 423-894-8319
fax: 423-892-7254
e-mail: jbruce77@aol.com
Buys, sells, collects, appraises and specializes in all kinds of knives including store closing inventories, Bowie knives, old pocket knives, antique, current, commemorative, advertising; also store displays, knife memorabilia, etc.

Steve Koontz
Riverside Cutlery Co.
P.O. Box 278
Kodak, TN 37764-0278
ph: 423-453-9558
fax: 423-453-2682
e-mail: rvrside@up2me.com
Specializes in new and old cutlery; over 1,000 rare and collectible knives.

Experts

J. Bruce Voyles
P.O. Box 22007
Chattanooga, TN 37422
ph: 423-894-8319
fax: 423-892-7254
e-mail: jbruce77@aol.com
Former publisher of "Blade Magazine" and "Edges, The Journal of American Knife Collecting"; author of 16 books on knives including price guides; edits the Knives entry of the "World Book Encyclopedia"; member Cutlery Hall of Fame.

Charles H. Price
c/o Knife World
P.O. Box 3395
Knoxville, TN 37927-3395
ph: 423-397-1955
fax: 423-397-1969
Author of "The Official Price Guide to Collector Knives."

Jim Weyer
Weyer International
2740 Nebraska Ave.
Toledo, OH 43607-3245
ph: 419-534-2020
e-mail: law-weyerinternational@msn.com
Author of the "Knives: Points of Interest" book series which focuses on custom made knives.

Charles D. Stapp
7037 Haynes Rd.
Georgetown, IN 47122-8610
ph: 812-923-3483
e-mail: dennyjoyce@aol.com
Wants pre-1965 folding and non-folding knives; free appraisals; provide photocopy or tracing and send with SASE.

Alex Peck
Antique Scientifica
P.O. Box 710
Charleston, IL 61920-0710
ph: 217-348-1009
e-mail: antiques@advant.net
Collects early Bowie knives, American or English, especially with a motto and Civil War era; also California knives, knives by Rose, Goulding, Schively, Bell, Rees.

Charles H. Clements, III
1741 Dallas St.
Aurora, CO 80010-2018
ph: 303-364-0403
fax: 303-739-9824
e-mail: gryphons@worldnet.att.net
Appraises and specializes in arms & armor, hunting, gaming, military and leisure material for men, frontier, fur-trade and Indian artifacts, etc.

Bernard Levine
P.O. Box 2404
Eugene, OR 97402-0124
ph: 541-484-0294
Identification and appraisal, museum consultation, expert witness, research, writing; author of "Levine's Guide to Knives and Their Values."

Internet Resources

Larry Burton
Knife Trader, The
e-mail: burtonld@chattanooga.net
web: http://www.chattanooga.net/~burtonld/knife.html
Great resource web site for knife collectors.

Russell L. Horn
International Knife Directory
1878 Galaxy Way
Redding, CA 96002
ph: 530-226-9488
e-mail: ikd@horn-net.com
web: http://www.horn-net.com/ikd
Internet site for knife enthusiasts: custom makers, manufacturers, retailers, suppliers, specialists, shows, classifieds, organizations, ads, and more.

Museums/Libraries

National Knife Museum, The
Magazine: National Knife Magazine
7201 Shallowford Rd.
P.O. Box 21070
Chattanooga, TN 37421
ph: 423-892-5007
e-mail: burtonld@chattanooga.net
web: http://bertha.chattanooga.net/~burtonld/nkm.html
Collection includes over 15,000 knives from the Bronze Age to present; owned and operated by the National Knife Collectors Association.

Periodicals

Newspaper: Knife World
P.O. Box 3395
Knoxville, TN 37927-3395
ph: 423-397-1955 or 800-828-7751
fax: 423-397-1969
e-mail: knifepub@knifeworld.com
web: http://www.knifeworld.com
A monthly newspaper with ads, shows, knife makers, knife artistry, knife making supplies, knife books, articles of interest to collectors and knife historians; has knife identification and value columns.

Magazine: BIG Show Journal
P.O. Box 217
Iola, WI 54945
ph: 715-445-2708
e-mail: paul@xlcom.com
web: http://www.showjournal.com/
The guide to knife and gun shows nationwide.

Pat DuChene, PR
Krause Publications
Magazine: Blade
700 E. State St.
Iola, WI 54990-0001
ph: 715-445-2214
fax: 715-445-4087
e-mail: info@krause.com
web: http://www.krause.com/
A monthly magazine focusing on all aspects of knives, razors, pocket knives, knife making, care, sharpening, etc.

Pat DuChene, PR
Krause Publications
Magazine: Blade Trade
700 E. State St.
Iola, WI 54990-0001
ph: 715-445-2214
fax: 715-445-4087
e-mail: info@krause.com
web: http://www.krause.com/
Directed at the retailer who sells cutlery; provides important tips and product knowledge on how to sell cutlery; full range of cutlery is covered.

Repair Services

Wendell Carson's Knife Exchange
1041 CR 59
New Albany, MS 38652
Factory authorized knife repair center; Case, KaBar, Queen, Bulldog, LL Bean, and others.

Suppliers

Texas Knifemakers Supply
P.O. Box 79402
Houston, TX 77279
ph: 713-461-8632
An extensive selection of micarta, steel, pakkawood, exotic woods, brass, books, stag horn, bone handle fasteners, rod tubing, ox horn, belt sanders, belts, buffing wheels, rouge, epoxy, heat treating ovens, custom sheaths.

Bowie

Clubs/Associations

Paul L. Holmer
Antique Bowie Knife Association
Newsletter: Antique Bowie Journal
Buley Library, S. Ct. State U
501 Crescent St.
New Haven, CT 06515-1330
ph: 203-248-6318
fax: 203-392-5740
The ABKA exists to serve collectors and students of antique Bowie-type knives; the Journal is published four times per year and an annual meeting features a board to authenticate members' knives.

Collectors

David Wallach
P.O. Box 150285
San Rafael, CA 94915-0285
ph: 415-777-0123 or 415-883-7121
fax: 415-284-5364
e-mail: vcsrs@aol.com
Wants to buy find old Bowie knives.

Dealers

Rhett & Janie Stidham
Stidham's Knives
P.O. Box 570
Roseland, FL 32957
ph: 561-589-0618
fax: 561-589-3162
e-mail: rstidham@gate.net
web: http://www.kmg.org/stidham/
Over 29 years in business; specializes in older makers and in particular Loveless, Horn, Moran,Cronk, Hibben, Draper, Lile, Cooper, and Scagel; buys and sells at all major shows; buys collections large and small; specializes in Bowie knives.

David L. Hartline
P.O. Box 775
Columbus, OH 43085-0775
Buys and sells edged weapons; has large library and over 30 years experience; specialty is pre-1920 Bowie knives; has had many articles published on edge weapons; answers every letter; does appraisals and will authenticate.

Experts

Paul L. Holmer
P.O. Box 6091
Hamden, CT 06517-0091
ph: 203-392-5746
fax: 203-392-5740
e-mail: holmer@scsu.ctstateu.edu
Always interested in talking with collectors or students and sharing information; has special interest in knives (e.g. Bowie, folding dirks, silver-mounted American daggers) made in the northeastern states during the 19th century.

Buck

Clubs/Associations

W. Murray Andrews
Buck Collectors Club, Inc.
P.O. Box 3
Enon, OH 45323-0003
ph: 937-767-7613
fax: 937-767-1773
e-mail: wma@mics.net
For collectors of both fixed blade and folding pocket knives produced by Buck Knives, Inc. and their founders; Andrews is a former newsletter editor and has written for some periodicals pertaining to Buck knives.

Case

Collectors

Tony Foster
5926 Willard Dr.
Charleston, SC 29406
ph: 843-554-7090
Wants to buy case pocketknives, especially 10 Dot and older.

Frank Miller
960 Kirkwood Ln.
LaHabra, CA 90631
ph: 714-870-5902
fax: 714-879-9049
e-mail: fshnfrank@aol.com
Wants CASE knives in mint condition: Doctors, Peanuts, Toothpicks, Melon Tasters, Flyfishermen and Appaloosa; also CASE memorabilia.

Military

Collectors

Rickie Marquette
P.O. Box 343133
Homestead, FL 33034-0133
ph: 305-246-5431 or 305-245-2323
fax: 305-245-9295
Wants to buy military fighting knives, especially John Ek, Scagel, Randall, and Gerber knives; also Special Forces, S.O.G. knives, presentation pieces, and edged weapons in general.

Miniature

Clubs/Associations

Terry Kranning
Miniature Knifemakers' Society
1900 W. Quinn Rd.
Pocatello, ID 83202-2801
ph: 208-237-9047
Promotes the collecting and making of miniature knives.

Collectors

Jim
6831 Colton Blvd.
Piedmont, CA 94611-1347
ph: 510-339-1147
Wants quality old miniature (1" or less) folding knives.

Pocket

Collectors

Steve Deer
1503 Albin Pond
Greencastle, IN 46135
ph: 765-653-9437
Wants tricky openers; also picture handled carnival or punchboard knives.

Dealers

Rhett & Janie Stidham
Stidham's Knives
P.O. Box 570
Roseland, FL 32957
ph: 561-589-0618
fax: 561-589-3162
e-mail: rstidham@gate.net
web: http://www.kmg.org/stidham/
Over 29 years buying and selling antique pocket knives, hunting knives, Bowie knives and custom knives as a full time business; does 25 knife shows per year; founders and owners of the Randall Knife Society; buy collections large & small.

Harrell Braddock, Jr.
1412 Los Colinos
Graham, TX 76450-4447
ph: 940-549-2607
Buys and sells all pocket knives, any condition, any number; send SASE for list of knives for sale.

Randall

Clubs/Associations

Rhett & Janie Stidham
Randall Knife Society of America
Newsletter: Randall Knife Society Newsletter
P.O. Box 539
Roseland, FL 32957
ph: 561-589-0618
fax: 561-589-3162
e-mail: rstidham@gate.net
web: http://www.randallknifesociety.com/
Formed with the approval of the Randall Made Knives, Orlando, FL; over 2000 members; newsletter on old and new knives, military Randall's, Randall history, latest shop news, ads, etc.

Man./Prod./Dist.

Randall Made Knives
4857 S. Orange Blossom Trail
Orlando, FL 32839
ph: 407-855-8075
fax: 407-855-9054
e-mail: grandall@randallknives.com
web: http://www.randallknives.com/

Sheaths

Suppliers

Bob Schrap
Custom Leather Knife Sheath Co.
7024 W. Wells St.
Milwaukee, WI 53213
ph: 414-771-6472 or 414-784-0863
fax: 414-784-2996
e-mail: RSchrap@aol.com
Maker of custom leather knife sheaths.

Switchblade/Automatic

Collectors

Sheldon
P.O. Box 1775
Warren, MI 48089
Long time collector wants to buy vintage and antique switchblades; American, Italian, or foreign; working or broken.

Periodicals

Magazine: Automatic Knife Resource Guide & Newsletter
2269 Chestnut Street, Ste. 212
San Francisco, CA 94123
ph: 415-664-2105
Issued quarterly; photos, in-depth articles, maintenance and repair tips, latest trends, resources of ALL kinds of automatic knives, free classified ads and more.

KU KLUX KLAN COLLECTIBLES

(see also SOCIAL CAUSES)

Collectors

Roger Henry
RR 1 Box 192
Smithshire, IL 61478-9801
Wants KKK books and other KKK items.

Dealers

Roy Winfield
Winfield Historical
P.O. Box 305 - WOB
West Orange, NJ 07052-0305
ph: 973-672-2236

Historical Collections
P.O. Box 42
Waynesboro, PA 17268-0042
ph: 717-762-3068
Wants KKK material and items.

Here are some tips when contacting someone listed in this book:

■ When requesting information about a particular item, include a description (material, dimensions, maker's mark, model number, etc.) and a photo, sketch, or photocopy of the item in question.

■ Always ask if there are charges for samples or for the services requested.

■ When writing, please be sure to include a Large (#10 business size) Self-Addressed and Stamped Envelope (LSASE) if requesting a reply or the return of photographs.

■ Never call collect unless otherwise directed. When calling, be considerate of time zone differences and always ask if the party you are calling has time to talk. When leaving an answering machine message, always instruct the party to call you back collect.

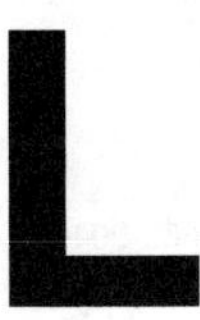

LABELS

(see also ADVERTISING COLLECTIBLES; AIRLINE MEMORABILIA; BANANA COLLECTIBLES, Stickers; BREWERIANA, Labels; CIGAR BOXES, LABELS & BANDS; MATCHBOXES & LABELS; PAPER COLLECTIBLES)

Clubs/Associations

Joe Davidson
American Antique Graphics Society
5185 Windfall Rd.
Medina, OH 44256-8703
ph: 330-723-7172
Members interested in graphic arts prints: from medieval, natural history to cigar labels, can labels, fruit labels.

Dealers

Stephen Zeigfinger
Athens Antique Prints
RR 3 Box 169A Route 35
Chester, VT 05143
ph: 802-869-2722
e-mail: oldlabel@sover.net
web: http://www.sover.net/~oldlabel/
Buys and sells many categories of antique food and tobacco labels all in mint condition.

Steve Zeigfinger
Athens Antique Prints
193 Rt. 35
Athens, VT 05143
ph: 802-869-2722
e-mail: oldlabel@sover.net
web: http://www.sover.net/~oldlabel/
Sells original antique labels that have been scavenged from abandoned packing houses: food, cigar, seed.

Bill Weinberger
21 Luddington Road
West Orange, NJ 07052
e-mail: weinberb@anchorcon.com
Buys and sells hotel & baggage labels, Cinderella stamps, Poster Stamps, and all other labels with the exception of Christmas seals and can/fruit/vegetable labels.

David & Barbara Freiberg
Cerebro
P.O. Box 327
East Prospect, PA 17317-0327
ph: 717-252-2400 or 800-69L-ABEL
fax: 717-252-3685
e-mail: cerebro@cerebro.com
web: http://www.cerebro.com
Wants cigar labels, pictorial cigar bands, fruit crate labels, firecracker labels, can labels, and other graphically pleasing labels.

Paul Jarmusz
Vintage Original Fruit Crate Labels
2845 D St. N.E.
Salem, OR 97301-1600
ph: 503-371-0868
fax: 503-371-0868
e-mail: mail@labelcollector.com
web: http://www.labelcollector.com
Buys and sells fruit crate or vegetable crate labels, old can labels, beer labels, soda labels, medical labels, cosmetic labels, etc.; unused stock found from old packing houses, canneries, produce businesses.

Paul Klym
Cubehouse Collectible Labels
202-1531 Beach Ave.
Vancouver, British Columbia V6G 1Y5
Canada
ph: 604-687-4249
e-mail: pklym@cubehouse.com
web: http://www2.viaweb.com/labels01/
On-line gallery of antique fruit crate labels and salmon can labels; specializing in authentic Canadian labels.

Bread Package Ends

Experts

Christopher Benjamin
P.O. Box 4020
Saint Augustine, FL 32085-4020
fax: 904-826-1600
Author of "Bread End Labels, Illustrated Price Guide."

Fruit Crate

Clubs/Associations

Jerry Chicone
Florida Citrus Label Collectors Association
P.O. Box 547636
rlando, FL 32854-7636
ph: 407-877-1044
fax: 407-877-1137

Noel Gilbert, Sec.
Citrus Label Society, The
Newsletter: Citrus Peal
131 Miramonte Dr.
Fullerton, CA 92635
ph: 714-871-2864
Members concentrate on the collection of citrus fruit crate labels and on the history of the citrus fruit industry.

Carole Crim
Fruit Crate Label Society
Journal: Box End, The
Rt 2, Box 695
Chelan, WA 98816
ph: 509-682-5879
fax: 509-682-5879
Newsletter published six times per year; the club for collectors of fruit crate labels; to promote agrilithography.

Collectors

Michael Urban
2029 N. Mitchell St.
Phoenix, AZ 85006-2126
ph: 602-252-8615
Buys early citrus labels.

Dealers

Gerry Haskins
Haskins House
P.O. Box 44
Gainesville, FL 32602-0044
ph: 352-466-4789

Thomas P. "Pat" Jacobsen
California Fresh Fruit Label Exchange
P.O. Box 791
Weimar, CA 95736
ph: 530-637-5923
fax: 530-637-5923
e-mail: pjacobsen@fruitcratelabels.com
web: http://www.fruitcratelabels.com
Buys and sells fruit crate labels.

Jerry & Rocky Hensley
P.O. Box 86
Burbank, WA 99323
ph: 509-544-9513
Wants to buy fruit crate labels: apple, pear, orange, lemon, cherry, peach, apricot, grape and tomato.

Experts

Lloyd Crim
Rt 2, Box 695
Chelan, WA 98816
ph: 509-682-5879
fax: 509-682-5879
Buys, sells, appraises, and specializes in fruit crate labels and the history of apple growing and processing.

Internet Resources

Terry Celano
ASTRALINC
128 W. Main
Brighton, MI 48116
ph: 810-494-2000
fax: 810-227-2450
e-mail: tcelano@ismi.net
web: http://www.astralinc.com/
A community web site where hundreds of people buy and sell antique cigar box labels, cigar boxes, and fruit crate labels.

Thomas P. "Pat" Jacobsen
California Fresh Fruit Label Exchange
P.O. Box 791
Weimar, CA 95736
ph: 530-637-5923
fax: 530-637-5923
e-mail: pjacobsen@fruitcratelabels.com
web: http://www.fruitcratelabels.com
Site has images, trading, history of fruit crate labels.

Periodicals

K.H. Foster, Ed.
Newsletter: Please Stop Snickering
4113 Paint Rock Dr.
Austin, TX 78731-1320
ph: 512-346-8253
web: http://www3.shore.net/~lloydc/snicker.html
Bi-monthly newsletter for produce seal (label) collectors; banana seals, asparagus hangtags, apple stickers, broccoli aprons, tissue wrappers, and any kind of fruit or vegetable identification.

Thomas P. "Pat" Jacobsen
Newsletter: Pacific Label News, The
P.O. Box 791
Weimar, CA 95736
ph: 530-637-5923
fax: 530-637-5923
e-mail: pjacobsen@fruitcratelabels.com
web: http://www.fruitcratelabels.com
A bimonthly newsletter.

Luggage

(see also AIRLINE MEMORABILIA, Baggage I.D. Labels; PAPER COLLECTIBLES)

Collectors

Leigh Giarde
P.O. Box 2243
Redlands, CA 92373-0741
ph: 909-792-8681
fax: 909-792-8681
e-mail: onlyleigh@cpl.net
Wants Scandinavian hotel labels and USA travel decals.

Dealers

Bill Weinberger
21 Luddington Road
West Orange, NJ 07052
e-mail: weinberb@anchorcon.com
Buys and sells hotel & baggage labels, Cinderella stamps, Poster Stamps, and all other labels with the exception of Christmas seals and can/fruit/vegetable labels.

Pat Sweeney
Pat Sweeney Ephemera
511 Woods End
Portage, MI 49002
ph: 616-381-9416
e-mail: pse@tias.com
web: http://www.tias.com/stores/pse/
Specializes in paper ephemera

including cigar labels, sheet music, hotel luggage labels, vintage posters.

LABOR UNION ITEMS

(see BADGES; BUTTONS, Pin-Back; MINING RELATED ITEMS; PINS; POLITICAL COLLECTIBLES; SOCIAL CAUSES, Labor Unions)

LADY HEAD VASES

(see CERAMICS, Head Vase Planters)

LAMPS & LIGHTING

(see also ART DECO; CAMPING EQUIPMENT, Coleman; ELECTRICITY RELATED ITEMS; FAIRY LAMPS; FLASHLIGHTS; LIGHT BULBS; MINING RELATED ITEMS, Lamps; PERFUME LAMPS; RAILROAD COLLECTIBLES, Signal Lamps)

Appraisers

Randy Knox
714 E Brown Ave.
Bellefontaine, OH 43311
ph: 937-599-3367
e-mail: ran51@webtv.net
Specializes in lamps from the 1930s and 1940s.

Auction Services

Ed Swann
James D. Julia Auctioneers Inc.
Rt. 201, Skowhegan Rd.
P.O. Box 830
Fairfield, ME 04937
ph: 207-453-7125
fax: 207-453-2502
e-mail: jjulia@juliaauctions.com
web: http://www.juliaauctions.com
Conducts specialized auctions of fine glass and lamps of all types including miniature lamps, early lighting devices, fluid lamps, art glass such as Tiffany, Handel, Pairpoint, etc.

Clubs/Associations

Amanda Sherwin
Rushlight Club Inc., The
Journal: Rushlight, The
P.O. Box 75
Southampton, NY 11969
fax: 516-287-1738
e-mail: info@rushlight.org
web: http://www.rushlight.org/
One of the oldest organizations focusing on early lighting including lighting devices and fuels; journal published quarterly; also publishes the "Flickerings" newsletter; three meetings a year, heavily devoted to serious study.

Hugh F. Hicks, Cur.
Incandescent Lamp Collectors Association, The, c/o Museum of Lighting
717 Washington Place
Baltimore, MD 21201-5235
ph: 410-752-8586

AAlan Goulding
Historical Lighting Society of Canada
Newsletter: HLS Newsletter
P.O. Box 561, Postal Station R
Toronto, Ontario M4G 4E1
Canada
ph: 416-724-0703 or 905-824-4117
e-mail: goulding@idirect.com
web: http://historical-lighting.idirect.com
A social club organized by Catherine Thuro on 1981; primary interest is kerosene lamps and lighting from 1850 to the 1930s; two meetings per year.

Historical Lighting Club
Causeway House
1 Dane Street
Bishops Stortford, Hertfordshire CM233BT
U.K.
ph: +44 (0) 1752 221980
e-mail: caunteris@aol.com

John Hadley
British Lighting Society
Newsletter: Midnight Oil, The
Digby
1, Carmarthen Close
Winsford, Cheshire CW7 1LP
U.K.
ph: 01606-553739

Collectors

Bruce Axler
Ansonia Station
P.O. Box 1288
New York, NY 10023-1288
ph: 212-362-4429
fax: 212-579-1274
Wants to buy pocket, portable, and travel lighting devices and fire appliances: cap lighters, pocket lamps, folding candlesticks, matchsafes, candle safes, lamps in cases.

Carole Lundy
3 Long Lane
Hummelstown, PA 17036-9545
ph: 717-566-6016
e-mail: boxerlines@earthlink.net
Wants to buy porcelain or ceramic light fixtures: ceiling lights or wall sconces.

Anthony Glab
6708 Duluth Ave.
Baltimore, MD 21222
e-mail: glab@aol.com
Wants CARBIDE miners and bicycle lamps; no railroad lanterns.

David O. Benson
Lamps & Lanterns
1106 Mill Hill Landing Rd.
Richmond Hill, GA 31324
ph: 912-727-4680
e-mail: antiquelam@aol.com
web: http://www.antiquelamps.net/
Specializes in angle lamps.

Lynn Goldfinger
P.O. Box 4962
Burlingame, CA 94011-4962
ph: 650-342-7829
fax: 650-343-3269
e-mail: goldie1943@aol.com
Wants whimsical lamps from the 1940s through 1960s: moss lamps, spinners, anything unusual.

Peter Blundell
P.O. Box 6
Vernon, British Columbia V1T 6M1
Canada
ph: 250-542-4540
e-mail: peterblundell@bc.sympatico.ca
Involved in research since 1969; a founding member of the Historical Lighting Society of Canada; primarily interested in North American kerosene lighting.

Dealers

Chris Osborne
City Lights
2226 Massachusetts Ave.
Cambridge, MA 02140
ph: 617-547-1490
fax: 617-497-2074
e-mail: lights@citylights.nu
web: http://www.citylights.nu
Antique lighting from 1850-1930 including ceiling fixtures, wall sconces and table and floor lamps; specialists in 1870 neo-Grecian white metal and brass fixtures and 1880 aesthetic fixtures with porcelain components.

Dan Johnson
Continuum: Quality Antique Lighting
#7 Rte. 28
Orleans, MA 02653
ph: 508-255-8513
fax: 508-255-8515
e-mail: dan@oldlamp.com
web: http://www.oldlamp.com
Carries hundreds of restored antique lamps and lighting fixtures.

Judy Oppert
Victorian Lighting, Inc.
29 York St.
P.O. Box 1067
Kennebunk, ME 04043-1067
ph: 207-985-6868
Buys and sells antique lighting, 1840-1930; gas, kerosene and early electric, chandeliers, wall sconces, table lamps, floor lamps and outdoor lighting; fixtures and shades.

JoAnne Fuerst
Pine Bough Antiques
Main Street
P.O. Box 46
Northeast Harbor, ME 04662-0046
ph: 207-276-5079
Quarter century as scholar, dealer, author, with broad knowledge of pre-1860 lighting devices.

Ray Christensen
Metzger's Lamps & Lighting
15 South Main St.
W Hartford, CT 06107
ph: 860-232-1843
fax: 860-232-5267
e-mail: rayp10@aol.com
Buys and sells 1880-1930 antique lamps and lighting.

Trudy Chatlos
Chester Antique Center
32 Grove St.
P.O. Box 253
Chester, NJ 07930
ph: 908-879-4331
fax: 908-766-0386
Carries large selection of quality period lighting, hanging fixtures, table and floor lamps; wants to buy unrestored period fixtures.

Sayed Antiques & Art
19 Stonehedge Lane
Madison, NJ 07940
ph: 973-301-0894
fax: 973-301-0895
e-mail: sayed@sayed.com
web: http://www.sayed.com
Museum quality sand casting, fancy engraving and chasing, specializes in lighting and architectural fixtures, complete fixture or parts reproduced; references available.

Hugo A. Ramirez, Pres.
Hugo Ltd.
233 East 59th St.
New York, NY 10022-1425
ph: 212-750-6877
fax: 212-750-7346
A leading authority on 19th cent. lighting; restorer and supplier to U.S. Senate, Treasury Dept., Nantucket Hist. Soc., Gracie Mansion NYC, Metropolitan Museum NYC; restores and conserves to factory original finish all by hand.

Peter B. Gregory
Gatehouse, The
P.O. Box 195
Morris, NY 13808-0195
ph: 607-263-5855 or 607-263-5746
fax: 607-263-5746
Wants to buy early lighting, kerosene lamps.

Fred Neece, Jr.
1307 Hadtner St.
Williamsport, PA 17701-3707
ph: 570-323-4679
fax: 570-323-5293
Wants to buy candle, kerosene, and gas lamps, lighting fixtures, chandeliers, pieces, parts, shades, etc.

Marco Astrologo
SPQR Lamps & Lighting Unlimited
3232 Brookview Place
Elkins Park, PA 19027-2807
ph: 215-782-8288
Buys and sells art glass lamps.

Stephen G. Del Sordo
Heritage Resource Group
305 Oakley St.
Cambridge, MD 21613
ph: 410-228-8934
fax: 410-221-8061
e-mail: delsordo@shore.intercom.net
web: http://www.heritageresource.com/
A cultural resource management/ historic preservation firm that has contracts to locate, provide, authenticate artifacts for museums and collectors; areas of expertise include architecture, industry, domestic, agriculture, and maritime.

Richard Dudley
A-Bit-of-Antiquity
1412 Forest Lane
Woodbridge, VA 22191-3024
ph: 703-491-2878
e-mail: dudleyre@erols.com
web: http://www.erols.com/dudleyre/
Huge inventory of table, piano, student, hanging, bracket and banquet lights; many new and old parts for oil lamps; buys and sells.

David & Phyllis Helphenstine
David's Brass Works
P.O. Box 111
Washington, KY 41096
ph: 606-759-7423
Buys, sells, repairs lamps of all sorts; custom lamp repair, rewire, polish, lacquered, complete antique lamp restoration, glass lampshades, hand painted and artist signed shades, custom shades.

Tom & Linda Millman
231 S. Main St.
Bethel, OH 45106-1327
ph: 513-734-6884
fax: 513-734-6884
Wants to buy early metal and colored glass kerosene lamps; figural glass electric lamps; parts for kerosene lamps; original shades for both kerosene and electric; send description and price.

Robert Daly
Robert Daly's Historic Lighting Restoration Sales & Service
10341 Jewell Lake Ct.
Fenton, MI 48430-2418
ph: 810-629-4934
fax: 810-714-1009
e-mail: ldaly1@aol.com
Buying, selling and restoration of old kerosene, gas and electric lighting fixtures (chandeliers & sconces); especially interested in 1800 to 1920 style lighting; iron, brass and tin.

Bohnet Electric Co.
2918 N. Grand River Ave.
Lansing, MI 48906-3808
ph: 517-482-2654
Stained glass lighting, antique lighting, fabric and fringed lamp shades, table and floor lamps, hanging lamps, crystal lighting, crystal prisms, ceiling fans; also lamp repairing and parts, lighting glassware, glass fringe.

Karl Kester
Karlucci Studios
1255 Lincoln Ave.
Saint Paul, MN 55105
ph: 651-690-2975
e-mail: karlucci@gte.net
web: http://home1.gte.net./karlucci/index.htm
Buys, sells, restores antique lighting; this homepage gives information about the history of lighting and architectural styles in the US; regularly updated listing with pictures of fixtures and lamps for purchase on-line.

Harry Johannsen
Country Look, The
77 W. Isabel St.
Saint Paul, MN 55107
ph: 651-474-0050 or 651-293-1734

Scott MacClymonds
Classic Fans & Lighting
10525 Airline Dr.
Houston, TX 77037
ph: 713-448-4739 or 713-697-0069
fax: 713-448-0189
Wants to buy art glass lighting, especially by Quezal.

Michael Dalio
Light Years Antiques & Restorations
8006 Grandview Ave.
Arvada, CO 80002-2404
ph: 303-422-4379
Extensive inventory of antique, reproduction lighting fixtures, parts, shades, etc. consisting of floor, table, and desk lamps also chandeliers, wall sconces, exterior lighting & street lights; also does custom plating and appraisals.

John D. McKenna
McKenna Bros. Wholesale
801-803 W Cucharras St.
Colorado Springs, CO 80905
ph: 719-630-8732
Buys, sells and trades gas, fluid and electric lighting devices 1850-1930.

Ross Levine
Levine Antique Lighting
555 Main St.
San Rafael, CA 94901
ph: 415-455-8657
e-mail: levine@dnai.com
web: http://www.dnai.com/~levine/
Collector, expert, and dealer in original antique lighting; also offers lighting repair and restoration services.

Greg Davidson
Greg Davidson Antiques
1020 1st Ave.
Seattle, WA 98104-1008
ph: 206-625-0406
Carries an outstanding selection of original Victorian chandeliers, wall sconces and other lighting devices; gas, electric, kerosene, Tiffany, Handel, Pairpoint, etc.

Don & Doreen Jewell
Spring House Antiques
RR 6
Barrie, Ontari L4M 5P5
Canada
ph: 705-722-3950
Wants to buy early lighting.

Michael Peiffer
Assorted Treasures
1969 Oak Bay Ave.
Victoria, British Columbia V8R 1E3
Canada
ph: 250-370-1926
e-mail: mjek@home.com
web: http://www.bc-ziz.com/assortedtreasures/
Specializes in vintage ceiling fixtures, wall sconces, table and floor lamps as well as reproduction lighting.

Experts

Robert Daly
Robert Daly's Historic Lighting Restoration Sales & Service
10341 Jewell Lake Ct.
Fenton, MI 48430-2418
ph: 810-629-4934
fax: 810-714-1009
e-mail: ldaly1@aol.com
Buying, selling and restoration of old kerosene, gas and electric lighting fixtures (chandeliers & sconces); especially interested in 1800 to 1920 style lighting; iron, brass and tin.

Michael Dalio
Light Years Antiques & Restorations
8006 Grandview Ave.
Arvada, CO 80002-2404
ph: 303-422-4379
Restores, designs, builds, fabricates lighting fixtures: Denver Mint, Stanley Hotel, Scottish Rites Temple, Love Oil Company; provides lighting fixtures for movies, commercials and plays; consultant.

Internet Resources

Geoff Inglis
234 Parrish Road
Honeoye Falls, NY 14472
ph: 716-624-2638
e-mail: inglis@envmed.rochester.edu
web: http://www.maxcomp.com/~inglis/
Great internet resource page for lamps and lighting collectors: events, organizations, museums, web sites, books; focus on antique lighting from the 1850s to 1910.

Periodicals

Tom Barnard
Newsletter: Light Revival
35 West Elm Ave.
Quincy, MA 02170-2423
ph: 617-773-3255
Quarterly newsletter for collectors and dealers of medium-priced lamps with a focus on late 19th and early 20th century lighting.

Repair Services

Richard Dermody
Brass n' Bounty
68 Front St.
Marblehead, MA 01945-3275
ph: 617-631-3864 or 617-631-6204
e-mail: dermodys@mediaone.net
web: http://www.brassandbounty.com
Restores brass chandeliers, sconces, floor and table lamps; also refinishes metal, rewires.

Tom Barnard
Light Revival
Newsletter: Light Revival
35 West Elm Ave.
Quincy, MA 02170-2423
ph: 617-773-3255
Committed to the restoration of 1890-1930 period lighting; seeks out and restores quality fixtures and lamps, especially turn-of-the-century gas & electric lighting devices.

Leon Trefler
Trefler & Sons Antique Restoring Studio, Inc.
99 Cabot St.
Needham, MA 02494
ph: 781-444-2685
fax: 781-444-0659
e-mail: trefler@trefler.com
web: http://www.trefler.com/
Repairs, cleaning, rewire.

Stephen W. Conant
Conant Custom Brass
266-270 Pine St.
Burlington, VT 05401-4737
ph: 802-658-4482 or 800-832-4482
fax: 802-864-5914
e-mail: store@conantcustombrass.com
web: http://www.conantcustombrass.com/
Offers metal restoration and repair; specializes in repairing antique brass lighting fixtures.

Ray Christensen
Metzger's Lamps & Lighting
15 South Main St.
W Hartford, CT 06107
ph: 860-232-1843
fax: 860-232-5267
e-mail: rayp10@aol.com
Repairs all types of lamps and lamp shades, new and antique; family-owned since 1925; no job too large or too small.

Hugo A. Ramirez, Pres.
Hugo Ltd.
233 East 59th St.
New York, NY 10022-1425
ph: 212-750-6877
fax: 212-750-7346
A leading authority on 19th cent. lighting; restorer and supplier to U.S. Senate, Treasury Dept., Nantucket Hist. Soc.; restores and conserves to factory original finish (no plating or polishing, all hand restoration).

Jeffery Venturella
Architectural Emporium
207 Adams Ave.
Canonsburg, PA 15317
ph: 724-222-8586 or 724-746-3861
e-mail: salesml@architectural-emporium.com
web: http://architectural-emporium.com
Carries a full line of architectural antiques; specializes in restoring antique lighting, chandeliers, and sconces.

David & Carol Baker
Baker's Metal & Wood Shop
11956 Augustine Herman Hwy.
P.O. Box 68
Kennedyville, MD 21645-0068
ph: 410-778-6681
fax: 410-348-5966
Polishing/lacquering/repairing gas/electric/oil lighting; new and old parts available, prisms, shades, etc.; rewiring, gilding, leafing, antiquing in bronze and brass; repair candlesticks; also architectural and fireplace items.

Don L. Reedy
Brass & Copper Polishing Shop, The
13 South Carroll St.
Frederick, MD 21701-5606
ph: 301-663-4240 or 301-662-5503
fax: 301-694-9190
e-mail: shineit4u@aol.com
Repair and restore antique lighting; 1000s or antique and new lamp parts and supplies in stock; replacement glass shades and chimneys.

Kip Young
Copper Kettle Metal Polishing
158 1/2 South Potomac St.
Hagerstown, MD 21740
ph: 301-791-4555
Specialists in antique lamps and lighting sales, repairs and restorations; metal polishing, fabrication of missing metal parts; also specializes in crystal chandelier repair.

Richard Dudley
A-Bit-of-Antiquity
1412 Forest Lane
Woodbridge, VA 22191-3024
ph: 703-491-2878
e-mail: dudleyre@erols.com
web: http://www.erols.com/dudleyre/
Expert restoration, repair, deplating & polishing of gas and electric lamps; specializing in oil lighting; carries old parts & shades; also buys and sells old lamps and lamp parts.

David & Phyllis Helphenstine
David's Brass Works
P.O. Box 111
Washington, KY 41096
ph: 606-759-7423
Buys, sells, repairs lamps of all sorts; custom lamp repair, rewire, polish, lacquered, complete antique lamp restoration, glass lampshades, hand painted and artist signed shades, custom shades.

Rick Charpie
Crystal Clear Chandelier Care
9602 W. 156th St.
Overland Park, KS 66221-9709
ph: 913-681-6700 or 800-373-7804
fax: 913-897-7608
Crystal & glass chandeliers a specialty: repair/cleaning/restoration, electrification of gas or candle devices, replacement of parts & prisms, buys whole or broken chandeliers and old trade catalogs, chandelier consultant, etc.

Antique Lighting Restoration & Sales Co.
316 E. 11th St.
Little Rock, AR 72202
e-mail: oldlight@arkansas.net
web: http://www.oldlight.com/
Commercial, church, government, residential restoration, repair, sales of antique and old lighting fixtures; chandelier installation, maintenance, cleaning.

Jay Core
Antique Lighting Restoration & Sales Co.
10612 Lathrop Dr.
Dallas, TX 75229
ph: 888-299-5267 or 214-352-2007
fax: 214-904-2564
e-mail: oldlight@hotmail.com
web: http://www.oldlight.com
Antique lighting restoration and sales since 1958; commercial, church, government, residential; also has offices in Little Rock, AR.

Hal Resnikoff
Lighting Restoration Center
15029 N. Cave Road
Phoenix, AZ 85032
ph: 602-867-2681
fax: 602-867-2683
e-mail: lightman@cwix.com
Complete repair and restoration service for all types of lighting; specializing in authentic restoration of all vintage lighting fixtures; sales of original parts as well as very high quality reproductions.

Dorothy West
Glass Painting by Dorothy
251 Starlight Ave.
London, Ontario N5W 4X8
Canada
ph: 519-455-5742
fax: 519-455-2941
e-mail: dwest@execulink.com
web: http://www.execulink.com/~dwest/
Expert restores Victorian painted oil lamps; custom shade matched to your original base; glass paint is used and the shades are kiln fired so paint will not wash off; has blank ball shades and half shades available; some other parts.

Repro. Sources

Copper House, The
1747 Dover Rd., RT 4
Epsom, NH 03234-4416
ph: 800-281-9798
fax: 603-736-9798
e-mail: lights@thecopperhouse.com
web: http://www.thecopperhouse.com/copper/
Handmade copper reproduction lighting fixtures and weathervanes. No imports. Catalog $4 deducted from purchase.

Renovator's Supply
P.O. Box 2515
Conway, NH 03818
ph: 800-659-2211 or 603-447-8500
fax: 603-447-1717
Offers catalog of Victorian reproduction accessories, lighting, hardware, bath fixtures, and door, window and cabinet hardware.

Ray Christensen
Metzger's Lamps & Lighting
15 South Main St.
W Hartford, CT 06107
ph: 860-232-1843
fax: 860-232-5267
e-mail: rayp10@aol.com
Has huge stock of reproduction lighting and parts plus catalog orders.

Hugh C. Pribell
Early Lighting Specialties
24219 West Main St.
Columbus, NJ 08022-1917
ph: 609-298-9125
e-mail: hugh1nj@aol.com
Reproduction early lighting burners and cut glass shades: camphene fluid burners, whale oil burners, Noyes 1855 patent lamp extinguishers for camphene fluid burners, brass fluid burner with coronets, betty lamps, other brass burners.

Mitch Smith
Mitchell K. Smith - Blacksmith
1155 Erbs Quarry Road
Lititz, PA 17543
ph: 717-581-7416
fax: 717-519-0799
e-mail: mksmith@theblacksmith.com
web: http://www.theblacksmith.com
Reproduction of 18th century iron chandeliers, sconces, candle stands and candlesticks.

John Blowers
Olde Mill House Shoppe
105 Strasburg Pike
Lancaster, PA 17602
ph: 717-299-0678
fax: 717-299-5822
Dealer in reproduction colonial and country indoor and outdoor lighting.

Jack Cunningham
American Period Lighting, Inc.
3004 Columbia Ave.
Lancaster, PA 17603-4001
ph: 717-392-5649
fax: 717-509-3127
Sells complete line of reproduction period style lighting fixtures including lanterns, post lights, and chandeliers; also offers restoration of antiques lighting fixtures.

Paxton Hardware Ltd.
P.O. Box 256
Upper Falls, MD 21156-0256
ph: 410-592-8505 or 800-241-9741
fax: 410-592-2224
e-mail: paxton@ix.netcom.com
web: http://www.paxtonhardware.com/
Authentic reproductions of oil lamps and lamp parts including glass, fabric, and parchment shades.

Cumberland General Store
#1 Highway 68
Crossville, TN 38555
ph: 931-484-8481 or 800-334-4640
fax: 931-456-1211
web: http://www.cumberlandgeneral.com/
Aladdin, Dietz; send $4 for catalog.

Bill Wiebold
Pewter Reproduction Works
5950 Park Rd. #3
Madeira, OH 45243
ph: 513-831-2815 or 800-321-2541
fax: 513-831-2815
Makes replicas of pewter oil lamps, bull's-eye lamps, candlesticks, baby bottles, and funnels; complete with antique patina, nicks, dents, bends; all reproductions permanently marked as such.

Jim Kelly
Rejuvenation Lamp & Fixture
1100 SE Grand Ave.
Portland, OR 97214
ph: 503-231-1900
fax: 503-230-0537
e-mail: JKelly@rejuvenation.com
web: http://www.rejuvenation.com
Manufactures reproduction lighting fixtures: Victorian, Arts & Crafts, etc.; send for free 72 page catalog; also repairs lighting fixtures.

Suppliers

Lamp Glass
2230 Massachusetts Ave.
Cambridge, MA 02140
ph: 617-497-0770
fax: 617-497-2074
e-mail: lamps@lampglass.nu
web: http://www.lampglass.nu/
A unique retail store specializing in replacement glass lamp shades; over one hundred in stock: Gone-With-The-Wind globes, student shades, chimneys, hurricanes, banker's shades, cased glass, prisms, glass shades, sconce glass, etc.

Ray Christensen
Metzger's Lamps & Lighting
15 South Main St.
W Hartford, CT 06107
ph: 860-232-1843
fax: 860-232-5267
e-mail: rayp10@aol.com
Sells and manufactures parts for new and old lamps.

Kirk Lane Co.
2541 Pearle Buck Rd.
Bristol, PA 19007
ph: 215-785-1251 or 800-355-5475
fax: 215-785-1651
Source for lamp parts including sockets, bases, harps, finials, chimneys, shades, etc.

Mike Barnes
B & P Lamp Supply, Inc.
843 Old Morrison Highway
McMinnville, TN 37110
ph: 931-473-3016 or 800-822-3450
fax: 931-473-3014
Wholesale distributor of early style lamp parts including oil burners, chimneys, shades, lamp cord, and wiring devices; mail order to the trade only.

Steve Kaye
Brass Light Gallery
131 South First St.
Milwaukee, WI 53204
ph: 414-271-8300 or 800-243-9595
fax: 800-505-9404
e-mail: comments@brasslight.com
web: http://www.brasslight.com/home.htmlc
Specializes in parts for gas wall sconces and chandeliers, and for early electric lamps; also does lamp repairs including metal work.

Aladdin

Clubs/Associations

J. W. "Bill" Courter
Aladdin Knights, The
Newsletter: Mystic Light, The
3935 Kelley Rd.
Kevil, KY 42053-9431
ph: 270-488-2116
fax: 270-488-2116
e-mail: brtknight@aol.com
web: http://www.aladdinknights.org
Purpose is to preserve Aladdin kerosene and electric lamps and Aladdin advertising history and memorabilia; sponsors annual national lamp and lighting show.

Dealers

Jim & Sheri Van Es
222 W. Washington St.
Charles Town, WV 25414
ph: 304-725-1673 or 703-435-9045
e-mail: wdnshu@aol.com
Buys, sells, and repairs Aladdin lamps, glass and parts.

Experts

J. W. "Bill" Courter
3935 Kelley Rd.
Kevil, KY 42053-9431
ph: 270-488-2116
fax: 270-488-2116
e-mail: brtknight@aol.com
web: http://www.aladdinknights.org
Wants Aladdin and "angle" lamps; author of "Aladdin Collectors Manual & Price Guide Kerosene Mantle Lamps."

Man./Prod./Dist.

Aladdin Mantle Lamp Company
P.O. Box 100255
Nashville, TN 37224
e-mail: support@aladdinlamps.com
web: http://www.aladdinlamps.com/

Repair Services

Richard Dudley
A-Bit-of-Antiquity
1412 Forest Lane
Woodbridge, VA 22191-3024
ph: 703-491-2878
e-mail: dudleyre@erols.com
web: http://www.erols.com/dudleyre/
Expert restoration, repair, deplating & polishing of gas and electric lamps; specializing in oil lighting; carries old parts & shades; also buys and sells old lamps and lamp parts.

Suppliers

Bruce B. Phillips
Phillips Lamp Shades Ltd.
172 Main St.
Toronto, Ontario M4E 2W1
Canada
ph: 416-691-7372
fax: 416-691-7360
Parts & expert repairs for Aladdin lamps; wicks, chimneys, mantles, holders, decorated glass shades, electric adapters; parts catalog $5; dealing in lighting since 1925.

Angle

Collectors

David O. Benson
Lamps & Lanterns
1106 Mill Hill Landing Rd.
Richmond Hill, GA 31324
ph: 912-727-4680
e-mail: antiquelam@aol.com
web: http://www.antiquelamps.net/
Specializes in angle lamps.

G. Millman
231 S. Main St.
Bethel, OH 45106-1327
ph: 513-734-6884
fax: 513-734-6884
Wants to buy wall-mounted cast-metal angle lamps (glass desired, but not necessary); also old angle chimneys and elbows; send description and price.

Experts

J. W. "Bill" Courter
3935 Kelley Rd.
Kevil, KY 42053-9431
ph: 270-488-2116
fax: 270-488-2116
e-mail: brtknight@aol.com
web: http://www.aladdinknights.org
Wants Aladdin and "angle" lamps; author of "Aladdin Collectors Manual & Price Guide Kerosene Mantle Lamps."

Bellova

Collectors

Bruce Bleier
73 Riverdale Rd.
Valley Stream, NY 11581
ph: 516-791-4353
fax: 516-792-0519
e-mail: emeralite@aol.com
Buys and sells Bellova and Emeralite lamps.

Candlesticks

Collectors

William G. Hodges
Ridgefield, Inc.
12509 Patterson Ave.
Richmond, VA 23233-6414
ph: 703-768-6562

Dealers

Bruce A. Sikora
P.O. Box 163
Bay Shore, NY 11706
ph: 516-665-0665
fax: 516-665-0634
Buys, sells, and specializes in 15th through 18th century lighting.

Lois A. Temple
Temple & Co.
110 Bittersweet N.E.
Ada, MI 49301
ph: 616-676-3659 or 616-776-2515
fax: 616-752-2500
Interested in antique wooden candlesticks and candle stands, including wooden pieces with petal, glass, or ceramic components.

Betty Bird
107 Ida St.
Mount Shasta, CA 96067-2629
ph: 530-926-4331 or 530-926-2231
Wants to buy brass candlesticks, silver, bronze, pewter candleholders; also wants glass candleholders, fairy lamps and miniature lamps of all sorts.

Carriage

Collectors

Larry Sluiter
4053 S. Springfield Rd.
Freeport, IL 61032-9510
ph: 815-362-6002
Wants coach, hearse, and carriage lamps in pairs; also wants horse-drawn carriages.

Chandeliers

Experts

Rick Charpie
Crystal Clear Chandelier Care
9602 W. 156th St.
Overland Park, KS 66221-9709
ph: 913-681-6700 or 800-373-7804
fax: 913-897-7608
Crystal & glass chandeliers a specialty: repair/cleaning/restoration,

electrification of gas or candle devices, replacement of parts & prisms, buys whole or broken chandeliers and old trade catalogs, chandelier consultant, etc.

Repair Services

Kip Young
Copper Kettle Metal Polishing
158 1/2 South Potomac St.
Hagerstown, MD 21740
ph: 301-791-4555
Specialists in antique lamps and lighting sales, repairs and restorations; metal polishing, fabrication of missing metal parts; also specializes in crystal chandelier repair.

Suppliers

Lighting Designers
1500 Rockville Pike
Rockville, MD 20852
ph: 301-468-7300
e-mail: mkogod@mauriceelectric.com
Carries large selection of crystal chandeliers.

Emeralite

Collectors

Bruce Bleier
73 Riverdale Rd.
Valley Stream, NY 11581
ph: 516-791-4353
fax: 516-792-0519
e-mail: emeralite@aol.com
Buys and sells Emeralite and Bellova lamps.

Jerry Propst
P.O. Box 45
Janesville, WI 53547-0045
ph: 608-752-2816
fax: 608-752-7691
Buys and sells Emeralite, Amrolite and Bellova shades and lamp bases; also literature on same; when writing, please include a LSASE if requesting a reply.

Gas

Dealers

Federico Santi
Drawing Room of Newport, The
152 Spring St.
Newport, RI 02840-6806
ph: 401-841-5060
fax: 401-848-0953
e-mail: zsolnay@drawrm.com
web: http://www.drawrm.com
Buys and sells high style 19th century gas lighting and gas shades.

Experts

Dan Mattausch
Cortelyou House
260 Maryland Ave., NE
Washington, DC 20002
ph: 202-544-4415
fax: 202-544-4415
e-mail: NMattausch@technautics.com
Researching and collecting gaslight burners, igniters, galleries, and mantles; also any related new-old-stock, packaging, catalogs, or advertising; wants anything that comes off a gaslight fixture when it is electrified.

Kerosene

Collectors

Geoff Inglis
234 Parrish Road
Honeoye Falls, NY 14472
ph: 716-624-2638
e-mail: inglis@envmed.rochester.edu
web: http://www.maxcomp.com/~inglis/
Interested in kerosene lamps from 1850s to 1910, especially in mechanical lamps, i.e. a lamp that has to be wound up.

Dealers

Carleton L. Cotting
1441 Crowell Rd.
Vienna, VA 22182-1512
ph: 703-759-5646
Collects, buys and sells oil lamps - miniature and full size.

Experts

Dennis Hearn
www.Oillamp.Com
Radio City Station
P.O. Box 1555
New York, NY 10101-1555
ph: 212-307-9397
e-mail: dhearn@oillamp.com
web: http://www.oillamp.com/
Has appeared as an expert on the subject of oil lamps in the pages of national magazines and on television; lecturer and feature article contributor to trade publications; lamp designer on Broadway stage.

Fil Graff
Lamp Shop at Lamplighters Farm, The
10111 Lincoln Way West
Saint Thomas, PA 17252-9513
ph: 717-369-3577
e-mail: fgraff@epix.net
web: http://www.dapllc.com/lampguild
Expert, dealer, collector of Aladdin kerosene lamps, other kerosene and gasoline lamps, and early electric lamps; old patent old flat wick or round wick burners and chimneys, gas lighting fixtures, lamp glass; also offers repair services.

Internet Resources

Dennis Hearn
www.Oillamp.Com
Radio City Station
P.O. Box 1555
New York, NY 10101-1555
ph: 212-307-9397
e-mail: dhearn@oillamp.com
web: http://www.oillamp.com/
The information and market resource for anyone interested in oil lamps.

Fil Graff, Sec.
International Guild of Lamp Researchers
10111 Lincoln Way West
Saint Thomas, PA 17252-9513
ph: 717-369-3577
e-mail: fgraff@epix.net
web: http://www.dapllc.com/lampguild
An excellent website to get your questions about antique lamps (liquid fueled) answered.

Lanterns

Dealers

Dennis Kuhl
A-n-D Antiques
4052 Altura Drive
Oceanside, CA 92056-4315
ph: 760-941-6816
Wants to buy pre-1940 lanterns.

Experts

Anthony Hobson
238 Schoolhouse Rd.
Ghent, NY 12075-4028
ph: 518-392-3732
fax: 518-392-3742
e-mail: cathtone@aol.com
Specializes in and appraises railroad, marine, fire, carriage, farm, and other lanterns; author of "Lanterns That Lit Our World."

Lava Lamps

Internet Resources

Lava World Int'l.
e-mail: Lavamaster@Lavaworld.com
web: http://www.lavaworld.com/
Creators of the Lava Lite take you on a journey through time; Lava Lite FAQs, graphics and links to other sites.

Miniature

(see also FAIRY LAMPS; PERFUME LAMPS)

Clubs/Associations

Bob Culver
Night Light Miniature Lamp Club
Newsletter: Night Light Newsletter
38619 Wakefield Ct.
Northville, MI 48167-9060
ph: 248-473-8575
e-mail: rculver107@aol.com
The goal of Night Light is to further the hobby of collecting miniature oil lamps; newsletter published quarterly.

Dealers

Betty Bird
107 Ida St.
Mount Shasta, CA 96067-2629
ph: 530-926-4331 or 530-926-2231
Wants fairy lamps and miniature lamps of all sorts.

Motion

Collectors

Bill & Linda Montgomery
ph: 503-652-2992
e-mail: cpm@hevanet.com
Authors of "Montgomery's Animated Motion Lamps: A Price Guide" (L-W Book Sales, 1991).

Amy Kanis
5000 W. 96th St.
Indianapolis, IN 46268
ph: 317-873-2727
Wants 1930s-60s revolving lamps, i.e. plastic or glass w/light bulb-heat propelled inner cylinder; all applications desired.

Dealers

Jim Whitaker
P.O. Box 475
Lynnwood, WA 98046-0475
ph: 800-774-6910
e-mail: eclectic@gte.net
Buys and sells motion (revolving) lamps.

Experts

Sam & Anna Samuelian
P.O. Box 504
Edgemont, PA 19028-0504
ph: 610-566-7248
fax: 610-566-7285
e-mail: sms@bee.net
web: http://www.smsnoveltiques.com/
Buys, sells, restores motion lamps: Econolite, L.A. Goodman, Scene-In-Action, Roto-Vue, etc.; leading buyers and sellers with largest collection in the world from 1920s-1980s; can reproduce parts; book in the offing.

Neon

(see also NEON)

Collectors

Len Davidson
2140 Mount Vernon St.
Philadelphia, PA 19130-3134
ph: 215-232-0478
fax: 215-232-0478
e-mail: LNDavidson@aol.com
Wants to buy antique neon signs.

Stephen Seltzer
7912 Georgia Ave.
Silver Spring, MD 20910-4837
ph: 301-565-2444 or 301-565-3339
fax: 301-565-2228
e-mail: eseltzer@aol.com
Wants to buy neon signs - new and antique - working or not.

Dealers

Dennis Clark
Off the Wall Antiques, Inc.
7325 Melrose Ave.
Los Angeles, CA 90046
ph: 323-930-1185
fax: 323-930-1595
Wants to buy figural neon signs; die cut and animated preferred; porcelain or painted; send photos.

Museums/Libraries

Len Davidson
Neon Museum of Philadelphia
2140 Mount Vernon St.
Philadelphia, PA 19130-3134
ph: 215-232-0478
fax: 215-232-0478
e-mail: LNDavidson@aol.com
Museum restores & displays antique neon signs.

Museum of Neon Art
501 W. Olympic Blvd.
Los Angeles, CA 90015
ph: 213-489-9918
e-mail: celeff@earthlink.net
web: http://www.museneon.org/
A non-profit, cultural and educational organization which exhibits, documents and preserves contemporary fine art in electric media; founded in 1981.

Repair Services

Volcano Neon
P.O. Box 668
Volcano, HI 96785
ph: 808-967-7648
fax: 808-967-7648
e-mail: neon@pobox.com
web: http://www.v-neon.com/
Specializes in restoring and repairing historic neon signs for clients around the world; also makes accurate reproductions, and designs custom neon signs, lighting, art, and gifts.

Shades

Man./Prod./Dist.

Kristina Krause
Victorian Rapture Company
198 Garibaldi Rd.
Winnsboro, SC 29180-6788
Custom makes high Victorian shades; 16" beaded fringe patterns & 85 frame choices to order; also covers old frames and supplier of reproduction Victorian lighting, jewelry (14K plated), bronzes, perfume bottles.

Deborah Smallwood
Seller of Dreams
P.O. Box 428
Powell, OH 43065
ph: 614-436-8393
Custom makes all types of lamp shades; specializes in Victorian shades; lamp rewiring also available.

Faith Kovach
201 W. Alyea St.
P.O. Box 522
Hebron, IN 46341-0522
ph: 219-996-2924
Makes Victorian lamp shades made with silk, satin lace and fringes.

Daniel Primo
Lampshades of Antique
P.O. Box 1507
Medford, OR 97501-0112
ph: 541-826-9737
fax: 541-826-1086
e-mail: contact@lampshader.com
web: http://www.lampshader.com/
Designers, manufacturers, vendor for elegant lampshades for restaurants, hotels, movies, casinos, antiques, lighting stores; extensive selection of fabrics, laces & trim; also repairs and restores.

Repair Services

Daniel Primo
Lampshades of Antique
P.O. Box 1507
Medford, OR 97501-0112
ph: 541-826-9737
fax: 541-826-1086
e-mail: contact@lampshader.com
web: http://www.lampshader.com/
Designers, manufacturers, vendor or elegant lampshades for restaurants, hotels, movies, casinos, antiques, lighting stores; extensive selection of fabrics, laces & trim; also repairs and restores.

Tiffany/Handel/Pairpoint

Collectors

Harvey Weinstein
22 Halifax Dr.
Morganville, NJ 07751
ph: 201-536-4467 or 800-321-0204
e-mail: weinsteingal@earthlink.net
Wants lamps and glass by Tiffany, Galle, Daum Nancy, Handel, Lotz, Pairpoint, Lalique, etc.

Alan Grodsky
642 Franklin Ave.
Garden City, NY 11530-5729
ph: 800-431-8256 or 800-835-0008
Buys, sells Pairpoint puffies and painted scenic lamps; also Tiffany and Handel painted lamps and accessories.

Mark Kaplan
135 W. Penn St.
Long Beach, NY 11561-4040
ph: 800-626-1752
Wants Pairpoint puffies, painted scenes; also Handel painted lamps and accessories.

Robert Ogorek
6400 Davidson Rd.
Burton, MI 48509
ph: 810-743-5358
Serious collector of Tiffany lamps.

Dr. Neil Superfon
2121 W. Indian School Rd.
Phoenix, AZ 85015-4908
ph: 602-277-1449 or 800-258-0216
fax: 602-263-8523
e-mail: npsuperdern@worldnet.att.net
Wants Handel, Galle, Pairpoint, Tiffany lamps and glass.

Dealers

Joseph D. Cantara
Cantara/Galletti
ph: 718-352-7273
fax: 718-352-6661
e-mail: Deco11358@aol.com
web: http://www.antiqnet.com/da/tiffany.html
Buys, sells and specializes in art glass and in Tiffany items such as lamps, desk sets, glass and accessories; also buys and sells Art Deco - especially French & Austrian.

Tom & Linda Millman
231 S. Main St.
Bethel, OH 45106-1327
ph: 513-734-6884
fax: 513-734-6884
Wants to buy complete reverse painted or stained glass lamps or shades: by Handel, Pairpoint, Pittsburgh, Jefferson, Tiffany, Wilkerson, Moe Bridges, Chicago Mosaic, etc.; all items must be signed or otherwise identifiable.

Bob Ogorek
Plantation Galleries, Inc.
6400 Davison Road
Burton, MI 48509-1612
ph: 810-743-5258
fax: 810-743-5791
e-mail: Plantgall@aol.com
web: http://plantationgalleries.com/
Specializes in the buying and selling of art glass lamp shades.

Experts

Sheila & Edward Malakoff
276 Princeton Dr.
River Edge, NJ 07661-1031
ph: 201-487-1989
fax: 201-489-0179
e-mail: pairpointlamps@juno.com
Authors of "Pairpoint Lamps."

Carole Hibel
Art & Antiques
131-B Broadview Road
Woodstock, NY 12498
ph: 914-679-2966 or 800-426-3357
fax: 914-679-9101
Buys, sells, collects, appraises Tiffany, Pairpoint, Handel lamps; author of "Handel Lamps - Painted Shades & Glassware."

Carl Heck
Carl Heck Decorative Antiques
P.O. Box 8416
Aspen, CO 81612-8416
ph: 970-925-8011
fax: 970-925-8100
web: http://www.carlheck.com/
Specializes in lamps by Tiffany, Pairpoint, Handel, Galle, etc.

Museums/Libraries

Edward Malakoff
Pairpoint Lamp Museum
276 Princeton Dr.
River Edge, NJ 07661-1031
ph: 201-487-1989
fax: 201-489-0179
e-mail: pairpointlamps@juno.com
Author of "Pairpoint Lamps."

Repair Services

Joan Meyer
104 Colwyn Lane
Bala Cynwyd, PA 19004
ph: 610-664-3174
Repairs Tiffany lamps; expert craftsmanship, only uses Tiffany glass, damaged shades purchased.

Repro. Sources

Dale Tiffany, Inc.
230 5th Ave.
New York, NY 10001
ph: 212-213-2738
fax: 212-213-2673
Sells brand new solid bronze Tiffany replica lamp bases; 30 different Tiffany bases available including urn turtleback, four-sided turtleback, lion's paw, snake base, and roots telescope.

Asher Shahar
3146 J.P. Curcie Dr., Bldg. 3-A
Hallandale, FL 33009
ph: 954-981-7440
fax: 954-981-7440
Sells 2, 3, 12, and 18 light Lily Lamps and many other Tiffany reproductions.

Traffic Lights

Collectors

Jeff Saltzman
Jeff's Streetlight Site
e-mail: jeffsaltzman@iname.com
web: http://members.tripod.com/streetlights/
Street light enthusiast; also interested in general highway and transit related things; website has photo gallery,

roadside fixture links, transit links, and other road and highway stuff.

Suppliers

Bill Andreas
Lights To Go!
P.O. Box 533
Derby, KS 67037
ph: 316-788-4911
e-mail: ltg@trafficlights.com
web: http://www.trafficlights.com
Sells traffic light control sequencer for antique or collectible traffic lights; compact unit installs in any traffic light to make it operational.

LANDMARK REPLICAS

(see SOUVENIR & COMMEMORATIVE ITEMS, Buildings)

LANTERNS

(see LAMPS & LIGHTING; MINING RELATED ITEMS, Lamps; RAILROAD COLLECTIBLES, Signal Lamps)

LAPIDARY

(see also GEMS & JEWELRY; MARBLE & STONE; MINERAL SPECIMENS)

Clubs/Associations

Jeff Ursillo
Gem & Mineral Society of Palm Beaches
Newsletter: Rockhound, The
1240 NW 22nd Ave.
Delray Beach, FL 33445
ph: 561-278-1120
fax: 561-272-3828
e-mail: bnmjeff@aol.com
An educational organization teaching members various lapidary techniques.

Rollin' Rock Club
Magazine: Rollin' Rock Club Newsletter
6004 Cohoke Dr.
Arlington, TX 76018-2366
web: http://www.ghgcorp.com/gpenning/roll2.htm
Interest is in lapidary: cutting, shaping and polishing of stones.

Jay DePuy
Ute Mountain Gem & Mineral Society
P.O. Box 385
Cortez, CO 81321

Faceters Guild of Northern California
4270 Silver Crest Ave.
Sacramento, CA 95821
ph: 916-486-0168
e-mail: lklomp@cnetech.com
web: http://www.cnetech.com/lklomp/rockpage.htm

Dealers

Dad's Rock Shop
P.O. Box 10649
4508 S. Hwy. 95, Sts. G-H
Fort Mohave, AZ 86427
ph: 520-763-3311 or 800-844-3237
fax: 520-763-3335
e-mail: dadsrocks@dadsrockshop.com
web: http://www.dadsrockshop.com/
Dealers in lapidary equipment and supplies, rock carving material, rockhound books, and much more.

Susan McCune, ISA
GemFacets
20649 Keswick St.
Winnetka, CA 91306-2028
ph: 818-348-6701
fax: 818-348-6701
Active in the lapidary arts field; represents lapidary artists.

Internet Resources

Canadian Rockhound
Canada
e-mail: cdn_rockhound@hotmail.com
web: http://pangea.usask.ca/~dfs846/rockhound/
An on-line magazine providing interesting and educational stories on rock, fossil and mineral collecting, the art of lapidary, gems and faceting, and on the earth sciences as well.

Misc. Services

Suzanne Wagner
William Holland School of Lapidary Arts
P.O. Box 980
Young Harris, GA 30582-0980
ph: 706-379-2126
e-mail: lapidary@stc.net
web: http://www.stc.net/~lapidary
Offers classes in the lapidary arts.

Museums/Libraries

Lizzadro Museum of Lapidary Art
220 Cottage Hill Ave.
Elmhurst, IL 60126-3351
ph: 630-833-1616
e-mail: webmaster@elmhurst.org
web: http://www.elmhurst.org/lizzmus.html
Large collection of hard stone carvings (especially Chinese jade carvings), rocks, minerals, and a unique gift shop.

Periodicals

Magazine: Lapidary Journal
60 Chestnut Ave., Ste. 201
Devon, PA 19333-1312
ph: 610-293-1112 or 800-676-4336 (sub)
fax: 610-293-1717
e-mail: Ljmagazine@aol.com
web: http://www.lapidaryjournal.com
Covers gems, beads, jewelry, minerals, and fossils, for artisans and collectors, including profiles, step-by-step instructions, and a show calendar.

Repair Services

Richard P. Hegeman
Hegeman & Co.
361 S. Main St.
Providence, RI 02903-2912
ph: 401-831-6812
Cutters of all precious/semi-precious stones; specializing in the repair & restoration of all types of jewelry (antique and contemporary); gemstone replacements and repairs.

LARKIN SOAP COMPANY

Collectors

Jerome P. Puma
78 Brinton St.
Buffalo, NY 14214-1175
ph: 716-838-5674
e-mail: jpp@buffnet.net
web: http://members.ebay.com/aboutme/jpp/
Would like any items pertaining to the Larkin Soap Co. of Buffalo, NY: catalogs, calendars, other paper items and Larkin items; also any item dealing with the Larkin administration building designed by Frank Lloyd Wright.

LAW ENFORCEMENT MEMORABILIA

(see also BADGES; OUTLAWS & LAWMEN; RESTRAINT DEVICES; WESTERN AMERICANA)

Collectors

Jim Manteris
P.O. Box 40
Manvel, TX 77578
ph: 281-489-8074
fax: 281-489-4784
e-mail: manteris1@webtv.net
Wants clubs, saps, billy clubs, blackjacks, brass knuckles, and old knives; also wants African and Asian weapons.

Experts

Lt. Talbert Kanigher, Ret.
Tal's Nostalgia
P.O. Box 6294
Burbank, CA 91505-6294
ph: 818-848-6469
fax: 818-848-6469
Collecting for over 30 years; interested in anything pertaining to outlaws, lawmen, police, gangsters, murderers.

FBI

Collectors

Dick Guttler
P.O. Box 2114
Garden City, NY 11531-9998
ph: 516-935-7218
fax: 516-935-7218
Wants G-Man, Melvin Purvis, Gangbusters, books, badges, toys, collectibles.

Barry O'Neill
6500 Ridge Rd.
Mount Airy, MD 21771
ph: 301-829-2050
Wants G-Man, Melvin Purvis, FBI collectibles.

Police & Sheriff

Clubs/Associations

Sgt. James Post
International Police Historical Society
15677 Highway 62 West
Eureka Springs, AR 72632
ph: 501-253-4948
fax: 501-253-4949
e-mail: jcasey@policeguide.com
web: http://www.policeguide.com/IPHS/iphs.html
Focus is to encourage the preservation of appropriate police material relating to the history of the police.

Collectors

Hervey P. Cote
P.O. Box 2053
Westford, MA 01886-5053
ph: 978-692-2161
Collector of police memorabilia including badges, uniforms, hats, Bobby helmets, etc.; especially interested in older badges and memorabilia from MA and New England.

Bob Fischer
P.O. Box 9763
Baldwin, MD 21013
Wants to buy old police badges.

Daryl Weseloh
P.O. Box 606
Delavan, IL 61734-0606
ph: 309-497-9322
e-mail: weseloh@accessus.net
Wants to buy all sorts of police uniform articles, equipment, police toys, badges, shoulder patches, etc.

Walt Gist
4190 Juniper Creek Rd.
Reno, NV 89509
ph: 775-747-2888
fax: 775-747-0926
Wants to buy law enforcement memorabilia including paper, photos, badges, etc.; has over 39 years experiencing collecting.

Donald G. Robinson
United States Marshals Posse
P.O. Box 590487
San Francisco, CA 94159
ph: 415-386-1565
fax: 415-386-2316
Wants to buy police and sheriff memorabilia.

Richard A. Perry
Perry's Cyber - P.I.G. page
3149 C Street
Sacramento, CA 95816-3328
ph: 916-448-6960
fax: 916-444-3011
e-mail: satcong@tomatoweb.com/perry
web: http://www.tomatoweb.com/perry/
Collector and dealer in police memorabilia; antique CA badges, patches, US Marshal badges, patches and highly detailed customized Road Champs models.

Dealers

Baird Co.
P.O. Box 7240
Moreno Valley, CA 92303-7240
ph: 909-943-4180
fax: 909-943-8491
e-mail: bedoya2@aol.com
web: http://www.bairdco.com
Publishes lists of law enforcement memorabilia available; also conducts specialty mail auctions of same.

Experts

Chip Greiner
P.O. Box 125
Bogota, NJ 07603
e-mail: rrbadges@aol.com
Specializes in Railroad Police; produced a one hour cable TV special on the topic the the History Channel.

Gene Matzke
Gene's Badges & Emblems
2345 S. 28th
Milwaukee, WI 53215-2925
ph: 414-383-8995
fax: 414-645-8288
e-mail: badgeone@asapnet.net
Wants police/fire/sheriffs & related law enforcement badges; also old cabinet police photos, handcuffs, leg irons and related items.

George E. Virgines
P.O. Box 13761
Albuquerque, NM 87192-3761
ph: 505-292-3853
Consultant, historian and author of "Badges of Law and Order" and "Police Collectibles Pictorial Guide"; collector of lawmen badges.

Internet Resources

Darrell Haynes
Police Emblem Collectors Page
P.O. Box 9072
Wichita, KS 67277-0072
e-mail: emblems@dtc.net
web: http://www2.dtc.net/~emblems/emblems.html
Great resource web site for those interested in collecting police emblems: Capitol City, Native American, Tribal police, State Shape, Highway Patrol, Foreign police, Federal Police (US Government), etc.

Museums/Libraries

New York City Police Museum
235 E. 20th St.
New York, NY 10003
ph: 212-477-9753
Devoted to exhibits of police memorabilia and crime-related items such as Al Capone's machine gun.

Suffolk County Police Department Museum
30 Yaphank Ave.
Yaphank, NY 11980
ph: 516-345-6011
e-mail: lscharf@nais.com
web: http://bern.nais.com/clients/scpd/historic.shtml

Jim Gordon
American Police Hall of Fame & Museum
Magazine: Chief of Police and Police Times
3801 Biscayne Blvd.
Miami, FL 33137
ph: 305-573-0202
fax: 305-573-9819
web: http://www.aphf.org/
Over 11,000 items on display; equipment, uniforms, firearms, etc. from the 1700s; wants anything related to law enforcement.

Florence Panson, Dir.
American Police Center & Museum
1717 S. State St.
Chicago, IL 60616
ph: 312-431-0005
fax: 312-939-1122
web: http://www.policemuseum.com/cops.htm
An educational museum with over 10,000 sq. ft. of exhibits and viewing; guided tours are available; free parking; wheelchair accessible.

Sgt. James Post
Last Precinct Police Museum, The
15677 Highway 62 West
Eureka Springs, AR 72632
ph: 501-253-4948
fax: 501-253-4949
e-mail: jcasey@policeguide.com
web: http://www.policeguide.com/police-museum.htm
Over 150 years of law enforcement history, movie memorabilia, police toys, advertising, badges, weapons, uniforms; also four decades of police cars and motorcycles.

Periodicals

Mike R. Bondarenko, Ed.
Newsletter: Police Collectors News
2392 US Highway 12
Baldwin, WI 54002
ph: 715-684-2216
fax: 715-684-3098
e-mail: jcasey@policeguide.com
web: http://www.p-c-news.com/
The premier vehicle for the Police Emblem collector.

Prison Related

Collectors

Larry Franklin
3238 Hutchison Ave.
Los Angeles, CA 90034
ph: 310-559-4461
Collects all American manufactured handcuffs, non-medical restraints in any form: handcuffs, leg irons, Oregon boots, manacles, slave irons, thumb cuffs, etc.; also wants toys or patent models of same.

Museums/Libraries

San Quentin Prison Museum
Building 106, Delores Way
P.O. Box 205
San Quentin, CA 94964
ph: 415-454-8808
web: http://www.turnpike.net/~mystery/tmg/san_quentin.html

LAWMEN

(see LAW ENFORCEMENT MEMORABILIA, Police & Sheriff; OUTLAWS & LAWMEN; WESTERN AMERICANA)

LAWN FURNITURE & ORNAMENTS

(see GARDEN FURNITURE, Furniture & Ornaments)

LAWNMOWERS

Museums/Libraries

Ian Britstone
British Lawnmower Museum
106-114 Shakespeare St.
Southport, Lancashire PR8 5AJ
U.K.
ph: (0044) (0) 1704 501336
fax: (0044) (0) 1704 500564
e-mail: gf86@dial.pipex.com
web: http://www.lawnmowerworld.co.uk/lmuseum/
Over 100 machines on display including those of the rich and famous.

LEAD SOLDIERS

(see SOLDIER, Toy)

LEADED WINDOWS

(see STAINED GLASS)

LEATHER

(see also ANIMAL COLLECTIBLES, Horses; ANIMAL COLLECTIBLES, Mules; KNIVES, Sheaths; LUGGAGE; OUTLAWS & LAWMEN; PURSES; SADDLES; SPORTS COLLECTIBLES, Equipment; TRUNKS)

Clubs/Associations

Dan Preston
Saddle, Harness & Allied Trades Association
Newsletter: Harness Shop News, The
1101-A Broad St.
Oriental, NC 28571
ph: 252-249-3414 or 251-249-3409
fax: 252-249-3409
e-mail: thsn@always-online.com
web: http://www.HarnessShopNews.com/
Specialist in scientific, medical, and nautical antiques and prints.

Collectors

Bill Mackin
1137 Washington St.
Craig, CO 81625-1613
ph: 970-824-6717 or 970-824-6360
fax: 970-824-7175
Wants pre-1940s cowboy and tack items: guns, cartridge belts, chaps, law badges, neckerchiefs, brands and brand books, spurs, knives, quirts, cowboy boots, hats, neckerchiefs, vests, cuffs, gauntlets, gun and saddle catalogs, etc.

Periodicals

Dan Preston
Magazine: Harness Shop News, The
1101-A Broad St.
Oriental, NC 28571
ph: 252-249-3414 or 251-249-3409
fax: 252-249-3409
e-mail: thsn@always-online.com
web: http://www.HarnessShopNews.com/
Professional leather workers, saddle makers, shoe and saddle repairmen, holster manufacturers, harness makers, boot makers; ads, calendar of events.

Magazine: Leather Crafters & Saddlers Journal, The
331 Annette Court
Rhinelander, WI 545012902
ph: 715-362-5393
fax: 715-362-5391
An instructional, how-to journal with leather projects using illustrations

from for the professional to the novice; news from the business world of leather, important ads to locate tools, leather, machinery, allied materials.

Designers Network
Newsletter: DNN Newsletter
P.O. Box 98
Fort Stanton, NM 88323-0098

Repair Services

Bruce Hamilton
R. Bruce Hamilton, Furniture Restoration
P.O. Box 815
West Newbury, MA 01985-0815
ph: 978-363-2638
fax: 978-363-2638
Repairs and replaces leather and cloth table tops; brochure available; 20th year.

Maria Pukownik
Fine Art & Paper Conservation
1045 Orrtanna Rd.
Orrtanna, PA 17353
ph: 717-337-0668
fax: 717-337-1093
e-mail: pukownik@cvn.net
Surface cleaning, softening of cockled and distorted leather, stabilizing and flattening, calligraphy, conservation of wax seals and other materials.

Gary Martin
Metro Leather Furniture Restoration
202 Lane Court, Ste. E
Sterling, VA 20166
ph: 703-450-6850 or 800-553-3872
fax: 703-471-1776
Cleans, repairs, refinishes, colors leather furniture, auto leather, etc.

Suppliers

C. S. Osborne & Co.
104 Jersey St.
Harrison, NJ 07029
ph: 973-483-3232
fax: 973-484-3621
Supplier of fine leather working tools for over 160 years.

Wickett & Craig of American
120 Copper Rd.
Curwensville, PA 16833
ph: 800-TAN-NERY
Leather supplier.

Smucker's Harness Shop
2014 Main St.
Narvon, PA 17555
ph: 717-445-5956
fax: 717-445-7752
Carries complete line of leather working supplies including solid brass and plated brass bells for harnesses and decorative purposes.

Mast Harness Hardware
115E C.R. 500N
Arthur, IL 61911
ph: 217-543-3463
Specializing in hardware, tools, leather oils, sleigh bells, and machines for the harness maker.

Bill Confer
Hereford Bi-Products, Inc.
P.O. Box 2257
Hereford, TX 79045
ph: 800-858-4384
American made rawhide for saddle & tree makers, braiders and craftsmen.

Charles L. Hardtke, Inc.
11040 Argal Ct.
El Paso, TX 79935
ph: 915-590-0088
Specializing in fine leathers from around the world: kangaroo, calf, cowhide, water buffalo, kid & goat, ostrich, alligator, pangolin, stringray, snake skins, etc.

Charles H. Clements, III
Charles Clements Leathercraft
1741 Dallas St.
Aurora, CO 80010-2018
ph: 303-364-0403
fax: 303-739-9824
e-mail: gryphons@worldnet.att.net
Makes cases, luggage, specialty items for Rodeo, Circus, Safari, Fashion/Commercial, Advertising/Cinema, etc.

R. Stephen Dorsey
Pecard
P.O. Box 263
Eugene, OR 97440-0263
Sells the very best antique leather preservative - moisturizes, preserves, colorless, softens, odorless, long lasting, safe; 6 oz. sample tube $9.50 ppd.; other, larger sizes available.

LETTER OPENERS

Experts

Diane Levin
880 North Lake Shore Dr. #3C
Chicago, IL 60611-1701
ph: 312-337-4913
Buys and sells old, vintage letter openers; please include a SASE if requesting a reply; wants old letter openers, especially celluloid figurals; no advertising; seeks contact with other collectors as there is no club or newsletter.

LETTERHEADS

(see PAPER COLLECTIBLES, Billheads)

LETTERS (FAMILY)

(see MANUSCRIPTS; PAPER COLLECTIBLES)

LEVIS

(see CLOTHING & ACCESSORIES, Denim)

LICENSE PLATE ATTACHMENTS

Automobile

Collectors

Edward Foley
129 Meadow Valley Rd., Trlr. 11
Ephrata, PA 17522-1843
ph: 717-738-4813
Wants cast or steel license plate attachments (bolts to top of a plate): cities, beaches, tourist meccas, oil company, porcelain, etc.

LICENSE PLATES

(see also AUTOMOBILIA; BICYCLES & RELATED MEMORABILIA; GAS STATION COLLECTIBLES; LICENSE PLATE ATTACHMENTS)

Collectors

Josh Friedman
445 Cushing St.
Hingham, MA 02043
ph: 781-740-1660
e-mail: friedman@cache.cow.net
web: http://cache.cow.net/~friedman/
Collector of automobile license plates, old and new, both from North America and abroad; website provides information and hot links for license plate collectors.

William Caswell
3 Buxton Place
Concord, NH 03303-1219
ph: 603-753-8244
e-mail: wscaswell@aol.com

Trent Culp
P.O. Box 550
Misenheimer, NC 28109-0550
ph: 704-279-6242
Collects license plates from all states: porcelain, early tin, motorcycle, Presidential Inauguration, early Alaskan & Hawaiian, etc.

Dan Segal
Great License Plate Trade Page, The
P.O. Box 98263
Lyman, WA 98263
ph: 919-613-1665
e-mail: dms10@acpub.duke.edu
web: http://www.duke.edu/~dms10/plates.html
Great website for finding license plates or for getting questions answered.

Dealers

Ed English
PlatesUSA.com
4 Moors Circle
Scituate, MA 02066
fax: 781-545-5799
e-mail: getplates@aol.com
web: http://www.PlatesUSA.com
Internet license plate webstore; license plates stocked from all 50 states plus Canada; pictures on web site of each plate style.

Greg Glaude
130 Coomer Hill Rd.
Dayville, CT 06241
e-mail: ggplates@neca.com
web: http://www.geocities.com/MotorCity/8772/
Specializing in collecting, trading and selling U.S. license plates; web site has listing of Motor Vehicle Administration addresses to obtain sample plates (some of which are free!)

Drew Steitz
PL8S Magazine
P.O. Box 222
East Texas, PA 18046-0222
ph: 610-791-7979
fax: 610-791-7979
e-mail: pl8seditor@aol.com
web: http://www.pl8s.com
Collects, buys, sells and trades all types of license plates: porcelain, leather, U.S. or Canada, foreign, errors, blanks, tests, political, low number, motorcycle, movie props or prototypes, etc.

Billy Moore
3128 Kline Dr.
Virginia Beach, VA 23452-6226
e-mail: moore@exis.net
web: http://wwwp.exis.net/~moore/us.htm
Collector and dealer of modern special issue U.S. graphic license plates; also will trade for interesting foreign plates; specializes in VA graphic plates - for sale or trade.

Jeff Francis
P.O. Box 41381
Saint Petersburg, FL 33743-1381
ph: 727-345-6627
fax: 727-343-8977
e-mail: gobucs13@aol.com

Chuck Batey
1115 Theresa St.
Stuart, FL 34996-3610
ph: 561-283-1881 or 561-283-5335
fax: 561-287-0943
Buys and sells license plates from 1920 to 1997.

Walt Feiger
Walt's Antiques
2513 Nelson Rd.
Traverse City, MI 49686-8557
ph: 231-223-7386 or 231-223-4123
Wants all kinds of older Michigan license plates.

Denny Williams
Denny's Trading Company
4038 Saltspring Dr.
Ferndale, WA 98248
ph: 360-380-1670
fax: 360-380-1477
e-mail: denny4plat@aol.com
web: http://www.iphome.com/iat/enter.html
License plate dealer, appraiser, expert; very active member of numerous collector clubs; deals world wide in license plates; one or 1000 at a time.

Leonard Heller
Automobile License Plates
2909 280 St. NW
Stanwood, WA 98292
ph: 360-629-4692
e-mail: LPL8MAN@whidbey.net
web: http://www.whidbey.net/licenseplate/
Dealer in automobile and motorcycle license plates from the U.S., Canada, Australia and over 100 other countries available to collectors; web site contains hundreds of license plate graphics; snail mail price lists available.

Dwayne Spark
Nostalgia Plus
8441 Sublaines
Anjou, Quebec H1K 2C1
Canada
ph: 514-352-6892
fax: 514-352-1856
Wants to buy current passenger license plates and commemorative from US States and Canadian Provinces; prefers to buy in lots of 50 or more plates.

Experts

Tom Smith
License Plate Collectibles
3064 River Road West
P.O. Box 238
Goochland, VA 23063
ph: 804-556-3598
fax: 804-556-6224
e-mail: tomvsmith@aol.com
web: http://www.erols.com/plates/lp/collect/
Collector, dealer, expert in license plates worldwide; many plates available for sale or trade; technical consultant to the movie industry for the use of authentic license plates in productions.

Denny Williams
Denny's Trading Company
4038 Saltspring Dr.
Ferndale, WA 98248
ph: 360-380-1670
fax: 360-380-1477
e-mail: denny4plat@aol.com
web: http://www.iphome.com/iat/enter.html
License plate dealer, appraiser, expert; very active member of numerous collector clubs; deals world wide in license plates; one or 1000 at a time.

Internet Resources

Josh Friedman
Platesmenistan
445 Cushing St.
Hingham, MA 02043
ph: 781-740-1660
e-mail: friedman@cache.cow.net
web: http://cache.cow.net/~friedman/
Collector of automobile license plates, old and new, both from North America and abroad; website provides information and hot links for license plate collectors.

Periodicals

Stephen Tuday
Newsletter: Plate Trader, The
21 Ridge Run SE, Apt. D
Marietta, GA 30067-2806
ph: 770-421-0864
A bi-monthly newsletter dedicated to the promotion of the hobby by encouraging the trading of plates instead of buying them; subscribers are entitled to FREE advertising every month.

Automobile

Clubs/Associations

Gary Brent Kincade, Sec.
Automobile License Plate Collectors Association, Inc.
Newsletter: ALPCA Newsletter
P.O. Box 7
Horner, WV 26372
ph: 304-842-3773
e-mail: pl8mail@alpca.org
web: http://www.alpca.org
A non-profit organization to promote interest in the collecting of motor vehicle license plates and to share information among members.

Dealers

Conrad Hughson
Self Help Services
P.O. Box 399
Brattleboro, VT 05302-0399
ph: 802-387-4223
e-mail: chughson@sover.net
Collector of U.S. and Canadian license plates since 1952; will buy entire collections of early plates; many duplicates; appraisal service available; consignment sales of license plates and related collectibles; since 1952.

Experts

Chuck Crisler
P.O. Box 114
Ponchatoula, LA 70454-0114
e-mail: cc@lp1.com
web: http://www.lp1.com/
Author of "License Plates Values."

Periodicals

Drew Steitz
Magazine: PL8S - The License Plate Collector's Hobby Paper
P.O. Box 222
East Texas, PA 18046-0222
ph: 610-791-7979
fax: 610-791-7979
e-mail: pl8seditor@aol.com
web: http://www.pl8s.com
A bi-monthly hobby magazine dedicated to the license plate collecting hobby; license plate photos, puzzles, cartoons, giveaways, games, ads, and lots more.

Automobile (Delaware)

Collectors

Dave Lincoln
P.O. Box 331
Yorklyn, DE 19736-0331
ph: 610-444-4144
e-mail: tagbarn@msn.com
Collector seeks Delaware plates of all types, variety, and vintage for comprehensive display and forthcoming book. Largest DELAWARE collection extant; finders fees paid; references available; information requests are welcome.

Automobile (Porcelain)

Collectors

Tom Mills
30 Bay Path Rd.
Spencer, MA 01562-1602
ph: 508-885-9550
Wants to buy porcelain license plates and signs; best to write and send photos first.

Stephen S. Uss
60 Homecrest Ave.
Yonkers, NY 10703
ph: 914-423-0442
Wants early porcelain, leather and tin auto or motorcycle license plates; also chauffeurs badges and dashboard registration discs.

Dave Lincoln
P.O. Box 331
Yorklyn, DE 19736-0331
ph: 610-444-4144
e-mail: tagbarn@msn.com
Active hobbyist interested in expired plates from anywhere; any type, any number, any vintage; 30 years collecting; sells or swaps extras; collecting and researching PORCELAIN-ENAMEL plates - information wanted; postage costs refunded.

Jim Crilly
8261 141st St. N.
Seminole, FL 34646-2835
ph: 727-393-7295
e-mail: jascrilly@aol.com
Collects state and city porcelain license plates; also wants 1940 B.F. Goodrich license plate key chain tags from AZ, AR, NV, NM, and SC.

Government

Experts

Jake Eckenrode
310 Wallace Rd.
Bellefonte, PA 16823
ph: 814-355-8769
Wants old U.S. Government license plates from any agency including old Civilian Conservation Corps (CCC) signs, and Pennsylvania licenses (vehicle, hunting, fishing, dog); author of "Collector's Guide to Pennsylvania Licenses."

Miniature

Clubs/Associations

Dr. Edward H. Miles
License Plate Key Chain & Mini License Plate Collectors
Newsletter: DAV Keychain & Chauffeur Badge Collectors News
888 Eighth Ave.
New York, NY 10019-5704
ph: 212-765-2660
Focuses on miniature Disabled American Veterans key chains, chauffeurs' badges, gum cards featuring license plates, windshield stickers, mini license plates.

Collectors

Virginia Young
15463 McNeill Rd.
Sterling, NY 13156-4212
ph: 315-947-5840 or 315-947-5782
fax: 315-947-6905
e-mail: gifts@sterlingfestival.com
Wants DAV and BFG miniature license keychain tags; also gum and cereal plates depicting license plates; all years, all state; especially looking for older, Western or Southern states, or a 1943 round DAV tag.

Edward Foley
129 Meadow Valley Rd., Trlr. 11
Ephrata, PA 17522-1843
ph: 717-738-4813
Wants B.F. Goodrich keychain license plates from all states, 1939 - 1942; many painted brass with B.F. Goodrich on back; 1 3/4" x 3/4."

LICENSES

(see also AUTOMOBILIA; LICENSE PLATES)

Collectors

Ken Mitzel
5225 N. George
Manchester, PA 17345-9400
ph: 717-266-2783
Wants to buy hunting & fishing licenses, dog licenses, bicycle licenses, sidepath licenses, PA Dept. of Forestry & Waters licenses and badges.

Animal

Clubs/Associations

William Bone
International Society of Animal License Collectors
Newsletter: Paw Prints
928 SR 2206
Clinton, KY 42031
ph: 270-653-6060
e-mail: tagman@ibm.net
Animal license collectors united for the exchange of hobby material; annual convention in various areas of the U.S.; Sec./Treas. of the International Society of Animal License Collectors; editor of "Paw Prints."

Collectors

Henry Keyes
P.O. Box 1683
Cedar Rapids, IA 52406
ph: 319-355-2427 or 319-366-1323
fax: 319-366-2427
e-mail: tagcentral@aol.com
Has a collection of over 7000 licenses.

Experts

William Bone
928 SR 2206
Clinton, KY 42031
ph: 270-653-6060
e-mail: tagman@ibm.net
Has published a book on pre-1900 animal license tags; Sec./Treas. of the International Society of Animal License Collectors; editor of "Paw Prints."

Dog

Collectors

James C. Case
10189 Crane Rd.
Lindley, NY 14858-9719
ph: 607-524-6606
e-mail: hftlicense@aol.com
Wants log licenses and dog tags dated before 1920; especially interested in pre-1917 tags from New York state.

Jerome Schaeper, Jr.
705 Philadelphia St.
Covington, KY 41011-1252
ph: 606-581-3729
Collects and appraises early dog (canine) license tags, especially pre-1920, from any state or country.

Driver

Collectors

Albert Velocci
62 Cherrywood Dr.
Hillside Manor, NY 11040
Wants to buy divers licenses and vehicle registrations; also wants any early automobile related paper.

Driver (PA Licensed Operator)

Collectors

Edward Foley
129 Meadow Valley Rd., Trlr. 11
Ephrata, PA 17522-1843
ph: 717-738-4813
Wants PA Licensed Operator badges 1910-1929. The 1910 is keystone shape, 1911-1928 oval, 1929 is round; also special Licensed Driver.

Hunting & Fishing

Clubs/Associations

Fred Woodland
Michigan Hunting & Fishing License Collectors Club
480 Maiden Lane
Pleasant Lake, MI 49272
ph: 517-769-6276
e-mail: woodys@voyager.net

Collectors

Eric T. Hado
145 Summit Avenue, #106
Summit, NJ 07901
ph: 973-912-7735
fax: 973-376-5813
e-mail: ericth@hotmail.com
Wants hunting, fishing, and trapping license buttons from New Jersey and New York state (mainly pre-WWII); also wants metal "no hunting/no-trespassing" signs from NJ and NY.

James C. Case
10189 Crane Rd.
Lindley, NY 14858-9719
ph: 607-524-6606
e-mail: hftlicense@aol.com
Wants hunting, fishing, trapping licenses and license buttons as well as guide badges from all states (mainly pre-1945.)

Ron Brownawell
331 Old State Rd.
Shermans Dale, PA 170907
ph: 717-582-2088
Wants hunting and fishing licenses: especially PA related; also pin-back type licenses from all states and Canada.

Ken Mitzel
5225 N. George
Manchester, PA 17345-9400
ph: 717-266-2783
Wants old hunting and fishing licenses from all states and Canada; game warden, fish warden, fire warden; duck stamps, animal calls, dog licenses; also conservation, guide, forestry and other badges and related items.

Howard Share
4349 LaVale Ct.
Clemmons, NC 27012-9009
ph: 336-766-6579
fax: 336-766-5445
e-mail: HowSha43@aol.com
Wants to buy state hunting and fishing licenses, especially from the Southern states and Hawaii; will also trade.

Dealers

Walt Feiger
Walt's Antiques
2513 Nelson Rd.
Traverse City, MI 49686-8557
ph: 231-223-7386 or 231-223-4123
Buys old Michigan hunting or fishing licenses.

Frank's Antiques
7242 Heil Ave.
Huntington Beach, CA 92647
ph: 714-847-0707
fax: 717-843-5645
e-mail: franks@franksupply.com
web: http://www.franksupply.com
Wants hunting, fishing, trapping license buttons, any state; also Ducks Unlimited buttons; gun company or fishing tackle company buttons, posters.

Experts

Jake Eckenrode
310 Wallace Rd.
Bellefonte, PA 16823
ph: 814-355-8769
Wants old U.S. Government license plates from any agency including old Civilian Conservation Corps (CCC) signs, and Pennsylvania licenses (vehicle, hunting, fishing, dog); author of "Collector's Guide to Pennsylvania Licenses."

Robert F. Miller
401 Old Rt 6
Ulysses, PA 16948
ph: 814-435-2140
Collects and appraises; author of "A Guide to Collecting Pennsylvania Hunting and Fishing Licenses", 1992 edition; $6 plus $2 P&H; also collects PA Game Commission items, patches and posters.

LIDS

(see also POT LIDS)

Suppliers

Charles Bodiker
Lid Lady, The
7790 East Ross Rd.
New Carlisle, OH 45344-9624
ph: 937-845-1266
Carries replacement lids for ceramic, glass, metal, and plastic vessels and containers.

LIGHT BULBS

(see also CHRISTMAS COLLECTIBLES; ELECTRICITY RELATED ITEMS; LAMPS & LIGHTING; PERSONALITIES [INVENTORS], Thomas Alva Edison)

Collectors

Rob M. Simon
245 N. Stewart
Lombard, IL 60148-2026
ph: 630-620-4770
e-mail: rsimon2424@aol.com
Wants to buy pre-1900 light bulbs and anything pertaining to light bulbs.

Experts

Carolyn T. Little
725 Esla Dr.
Chula Vista, CA 91910
Collects and specializes in light bulbs; wants light bulbs with tips or unusual light bulbs, Glow Lamps (neon) with figurals inside, meters, sockets, bulbs with figural or decorative filaments, Edison, Westinghouse, Reddy Kilowatt, etc.

Museums/Libraries

Hugh F. Hicks, Cur.
Mount Vernon Museum of Incandescent Lighting
717 Washington Place
Baltimore, MD 21201-5235
ph: 410-752-8586
Museum with display of electric light bulbs depicting the entire industry which spans 110 years.

Carolyn T. Little
Light Bulb Museum
1655 Morena Blvd.
San Diego, CA 92110
ph: 619-276-1500

Glow Lights

Clubs/Associations

Cindy Chipps
Glowlight Collectors Club
4027 Brooks Hill Rd.
Brooks, KY 40109-5002
ph: 502-955-9238
fax: 502-957-5027
e-mail: holauction@aol.com
web: http://members.aol.com/holauction/index.html
A club for beginners to advanced collectors dedicated to collecting Glow Lights and related items.

Experts

Cindy Chipps
4027 Brooks Hill Rd.
Brooks, KY 40109-5002
ph: 502-955-9238
fax: 502-957-5027
e-mail: holauction@aol.com
web: http://members.aol.com/holauction/index.html
Buys/sells Glow Lights; made by Aerolux, Birdseye, Luxram and others; also wants advertising for same; author of book on Glow Lights.

LIGHTERS

(see also CIGARETTE COLLECTIBLES; SMOKING COLLECTIBLES)

Clubs/Associations

Pocket Lighter Preservation Guild & Historical Society, Inc.
Newsletter: Flint & Flame
380 Brooks Dr., Ste. 209A
Hazelwood, MO 63042
ph: 314-731-2411
fax: 314-731-2903
web: http://studioshowroom/zippo/plpg1.htm
An organization to help promote, maintain and preserve interest in the hobby of lighter collecting; newsletter published bi-monthly.

Judith Sanders, Ed.
On the LIGHTER Side International Lighter Collectors
Newsletter: On The Lighter Side
P.O. Box 1733
Quitman, TX 75783-1733
ph: 903-763-2795
fax: 903-763-4953
web: http://www.vintagevault.com/otls.html
Members collect cigar & cigarette lighters & research lighter history; bi-monthly newsletter; send SASE for information.

Christian Wenger
Spark International
P.O. Box 1656
Olten, 4600
Switzerland
ph: ++41622963381
fax: ++41622963381
e-mail: intSpark@aol.com
web: http://members.aol.com/IntSpark/welcome.html
International lighter collector's club; world wide bilingual (English/German) operation; quarterly newsletter, web services and annual conventions; members are from all around the world.

Lighter Club of Great Britain
30 Heathfield Road
Croydon, Surrey CRO 1EU
U.K.
ph: 011-44-688-7673

Collectors

Barry D. Hoffman
7 Stonemeadow
Westwood, MA 02090
ph: 617-267-9000 or 781-326-3333
fax: 781-266-6666
e-mail: pakistan@tiac.net
Wants to buy Ronson, Zippo and Dunhill cigarette lighters; also offers free appraisal service.

Wes & Elaine Hart
963 Westhaven St.
Columbus, OH 43228
ph: 614-870-7141
Wants to buy "trench" lighters and other vintage or unique lighters; also pre-1960 Zippo pocket lighters with advertising, and Zippo table lighters.

John E. Shoffner
624 Merritt St.
Fife Lake, MI 49633-9142
ph: 616-879-3912
e-mail: kjohn@gtii.com

Karen L. Cairo
Cairo Lighters
P.O. Box 1054
Addison, IL 60101-8054
ph: 630-543-9120
fax: 630-834-4051
e-mail: lightergod@aol.com
Wants to buy cigar and cigarette lighters made in U.S. or in Europe; prefers pre-1970 items: pocket or table models, figural, complicated mechanisms, case and lighter sets, solid gold lighters with watches, advertising displays, etc.

Leonard Shafer
3202 West Magnolia Blvd.
Burbank, CA 91505-2905
ph: 818-846-5655
Wants to buy Ronson, Zippo and Dunhill cigarette lighters.

Christian Wenger
Saelistgrasse 131
Olten, 4600
Switzerland
ph: +41622963381
fax: +41622963381
e-mail: c.wenger@spectraweb.ch
Lighter collector and expert wants to buy high quality pre-WWII lighters: Dunhill, Cartier, Ronson, Evans, Carlton, Elgin, Douglas, Lincoln, etc.

Dealers

Peter Stanton
57 Earle St.
Central Falls, RI 02863
ph: 401-725-0055
Wants Ronson, Dunhill, Zippo.

Richard Weinstein
International Vintage Lighter Exchange
30 W. 57th St.
New York, NY 10019
ph: 212-586-0947
fax: 212-586-1296
e-mail: vinlighter@aol.com
web: http://www.vintagelighters.com
Specializes in the sales, repairing and purchasing of vintage lighters such as Zippo, Dunhill, Ronson, Evans, Thorens, Marathon, Cartier, Tiffany, Occupied Japan, and lighters of precious metals and with watches.

Shaw
P.O. Box 5096
Southfield, MI 48086
Wants to buy table model cigarette lighters: Dunhill, Ronson, Evans, Thorens, etc.

Ron Bash
P.O. Box 888271
Grand Rapids, MI 49588-8271
ph: 616-248-0571
fax: 616-248-0693
e-mail: wittbash@aol.com
Buys, sells and trades cigarette lighters: Zippo, Ronson, Dunhill, Evans, Trench.

Michael A. Pratt, Sr.
Lighter Chest, The
687 Co. Rd. ""U""
Rt. 2 Box 73
Fremont, NE 68025-9635
ph: 402-721-4765
fax: 402-721-4765
e-mail: mp@mb3.net
web: http://www.mb3.net/display/
Buys and sells unique cigarette lighters links of all kinds; also sells display cases for cuff links and collectibles of all types.

Experts

Ira Pilossof
Vintage Lighters, Inc.
P.O. Box 1325
Fair Lawn, NJ 07410-8325
ph: 201-797-6595 or 888-454-4483
fax: 201-797-8642
e-mail: vintageltr@aol.com
web: http://www.deco-echoes.com/vintage/
Avid collector, dealer and specialist in cigarette lighters; wants to buy any unusual lighter from the 1880s-1940s, especially Dunhill, Ronson, add Zippo lighters; also with lighters watches and any related memorabilia.

Jack Seiderman
1631 N.W. 114 Ave.
Hollywood, FL 33026-2539
ph: 954-438-0928
fax: 954-438-0928
Buys, sells, & collects collectible lighters, accessories, advertising, catalogs, books, brochures, instruction sheets, etc.; author of "Lighter Encyclopedia" (soon to be published).

Jeff Mogilner
Racine & Laramie, Ltd.
2737 San Diego Ave.
San Diego, CA 92110-2731
ph: 619-291-7833
fax: 619-297-6653
web: http://sandiego.sidewalk.com/link/10622
Wants to buy antique & unusual lighters: Ronson (LVA, AMW, Art Metal Works), Dunhill, Zippo; U.S. Navy ships, air squadrons, US Marine lighters; also repairs lighters

Man./Prod./Dist.

Zippo Manufacturing Company
1932 Zippo Drive
Bradford, PA 16701
ph: 814-368-2700
web: http://www.zippomfg.com/standard/
Offers a free "Zippo Collector's Guide" to vintage Zippo lighters; website has Zippo trivia and collector's and museum pages.

Repair Services

Richard Weinstein
International Vintage Lighter Exchange
30 W. 57th St.
New York, NY 10019
ph: 212-586-0947
fax: 212-586-1296
e-mail: vinlighter@aol.com
web: http://www.vintagelighters.com
Specializes in the sales, repairing and purchasing of vintage lighters such as Zippo, Dunhill, Ronson, Evans, Thorens, Marathon, Cartier, Tiffany, Occupied Japan, and lighters of precious metals and with watches.

Ronson

Experts

Urban K. Cummings
P.O. Box 1482
Palo Alto, CA 94302
Author of "Ronson: The World's Greatest Lighter" (Bird Dog Books, 1993).

Zippo

Collectors

Frank Briola
P.O. Box 44022
Pittsburgh, PA 15205-0222
ph: 412-937-8787 or 800-372-6509
e-mail: americana@mail.com
Wants to buy Zippo lighters.

Dealers

Jerry Korn
Lighters Galore Plus
P.O. Box 534
San Marcos, CA 92079
ph: 800-853-3941 or 760-734-1414
fax: 760-744-6666
e-mail: info@pipeshop.com
web: http://www.pipeshop.com
Collector, dealer, appraiser, expert specializes in collectible Zippo lighters and handcarved Meerschaum pipes; also carries many other hard-to-find smoking accessories.

LIGHTING

(see LAMPS & LIGHTING)

LIGHTNING BALLS & RODS

(see LIGHTNING PROTECTION COLLECTIBLES)

LIGHTNING PROTECTION COLLECTIBLES

Collectors

John Gephart
1 Firestone Ct.
Fairfield, OH 45014
ph: 513-858-3368
fax: 513-595-2661
Lightning rods, balls, arrows, vanes, all related catalogs, paper and advertising.

Larry Bergman
N33015 Square Bluff Road
Whitehall, WI 54773-9148
ph: 715-985-3310
Wants to buy lightning rod items: balls, arrows, vanes, pendants.

Mike Sovereign
1S777 Westview
Lombard, IL 60148
Wants lightning rod items including balls, arrows, vanes, advertising, paper, etc.

Experts

Michael Bruner
2615 Echo Lane
Ortonville, MI 48462
ph: 248-627-6351
Wants lightning rod balls, catalogs, installation tags, rods, braces, etc.; co-author of "The Complete Book of Lightning Rod Balls."

Rod Krupka
2615 Echo Lane
Ortonville, MI 48462
ph: 248-627-6351
Collector, dealer, expert; buys, sells lightning rod balls, weathervanes, related catalogs and ads; co-author of "The Complete Book of Lightning Rod Balls."

Russell Barnes
P.O. Box 141994
Austin, TX 78714-1994
ph: 512-835-9510
fax: 512-835-1276
e-mail: csindian@flash.net
Author of the "Lightning Rod Collectibles Price Guide," available from the author for $32.95 ppd.

Periodicals

Newsletter: Crown Point, The
P.O. Box 23
Winfield, IL 60190
ph: 630-876-1316
e-mail: crownpoint@ntsource.com
Devoted to the history of lightning protection and the collecting of related items: lightning rod balls, pendants, weathervanes, points, etc.

LIMITED EDITION COLLECTIBLES

(see COLLECTIBLES [MODERN])

LINCOLN

(see PERSONALITIES [HISTORICAL], Abraham Lincoln)

LINENS

(see TEXTILES, Lace & Linens)

LITERATURE

(see AUTOGRAPHS; BOOKS; MANUSCRIPTS; PERSONALITIES [LITERARY])

LITHOPHANES

(see also COLLECTIBLES [MODERN], Lithophanes)

Collectors

Donald Gorlick
P.O. Box 24541
Seattle, WA 98124-0541
ph: 206-824-0508
Wants "Berlin transparencies": looks like bisque but when turned to light it has a picture in it; in tea sets, lamp shades, beer steins.

Dealers

Lucille Malitz
Lucid Antiques
P.O. Box KH
Scarsdale, NY 10583
ph: 914-636-7825 or 914-636-5171
fax: 914-636-7825
e-mail: kromscope@aol.com
These 19th century porcelain plaques, made with the lost wax process; when illuminated from the back they depict famous paintings or portraits of popular personalities of the times because of the varying thickness of the porcelain.

LIVESTOCK

(see also ANIMAL COLLECTIBLES; HORSES)

Appraisers

Jay Proost
American Society of Agricultural Appraisers, Inc.
P.O. Box 186
Twin Falls, ID 83303-0186
ph: 208-733-2323 or 208-734-7570
fax: 208-733-2326
e-mail: JProost@micron.net
Members of this association appraise livestock, horses and farm equipment.

LIVING HISTORY

(see also CLOTHING & ACCESSORIES, Costumes; MILITARY HISTORY)

Clubs/Associations

Darrell K. English
Living History Association
Newspaper: Living Historian
P.O. Box 1389
Wilmington, VT 05363
ph: 802-464-5569
e-mail: info@livinghistoryassn.org
web: http://www.livinghistoryassn.org/
One of the largest group of reenactors in the country; members dress up according to the era, and act our battles, home life, balls, etc.; catalog of merchandise, lectures, school programs, teaches workshops, etc.; quarterly magazine.

Internet Resources

Living History Online
P.O. Box 77
Fairfax, VA 22030
ph: 703-913-6319 or 703-758-5838
e-mail: 72774.2240@compuserve.com
web: http://www.LivingHistoryOnline.com/
Your best online source for living history events and articles.

Periodicals

Magazine: Artilleryman, The
RR 1 Box 36
Tunbridge, VT 05077-9707
ph: 802-889-3500 or 800-777-1862
fax: 802-889-5627
e-mail: mail@civilwarnews.com
web: http://www.civilwarnews.com/
Published quarterly, the only magazine exclusively for the 1750-1898 artillery enthusiast: artillery history, unit profiles, shell collecting, etc.

Magazine: Smoke & Fire News
P.O. Box 166
Grand Rapids, OH 43522-0166
ph: 419-832-0303
e-mail: dmeyers@smoke-fire.com
web: http://www.smoke-fire.com
Contains national listings of living history events; emphasis on the 18th century and Rendezvous period primarily in the Midwest; good coverage on War of 1812 era; numerous ads, classifieds, reenacting articles.

Magazine: Backwoodsman Magazine
P.O. Box 627
Westcliffe, CO 81252
e-mail: bwmmag@ris.net
web: http://purelight.com/bwmmag/home.htm
The magazine for the twentieth century frontiersman specializing in muzzleloading, woodslore, survival, homesteading, history, Indian lore and much more.

Suppliers

Collector's Armoury
3000 South Eads St.
Arlington, VA 22202-4027
ph: 800-544-3456 or 703-684-6111
fax: 703-683-5486
Offers museum quality reproductions: Civil War swords, knives, pistols and field gear; non-firing Western pistols, rifles and collectibles; medieval, Samurai and military swords; historic miniature Gatling guns and cannons.

Ron Eberhart
Western Trading Post
P.O. Box 9070
Denver, CO 80209-0070
ph: 303-777-7750
fax: 303-698-1387
A complete Indian craft supply store; has everything from beads and buckskins to tipis and tomahawks,

Civil War Reenactors

Clubs/Associations

Arthur W. Henrick
American Civil War Association, Union Brigade
P.O. Box 61075
Sunnyvale, CA 94088-1075
e-mail: WebMasACWA@aol.com
web: http://www.acwa.org/
Union/CSA reenactors don authentically reproduced clothing and uniforms, shoulder period muskets, cook over open fires, sleep in canvas tents, participate in battle reenactments and some even speak in the dialect of the era.

Mark Weiner
American Civil War Association, Confederate Brigade
P.O. Box 83333
San Jose, CA 95155
e-mail: AdjCSAACWA@aol.com
web: http://www.reenact.org/acwa/
Confederate reenactors don authentically reproduced clothing and uniforms, shoulder period muskets, cook over open fires, sleep in canvas tents, participate in battle reenactments and some even speak in the dialect of the era.

Internet Resources

Bill Cyders
P.O. Box 5614
Novato, CA 94948
ph: 415-474-2377
e-mail: bcyders@midas.org
web: http://marin.org/npo/cwar/home/
Great internet site with lots of Civil War reenactor web sites.

Periodicals

Dan Preston
Magazine: Harness Shop News, The
1101-A Broad St.
Oriental, NC 28571
ph: 252-249-3414 or 251-249-3409
fax: 252-249-3409
e-mail: thsn@always-online.com
web: http://www.HarnessShopNews.com/
Original McClellans, sources for military hardware, accoutrements, and reproductions; professional leather workers, saddle makers, saddle & shoe repairmen, holster manufacturers, harness makers, boot makers; ads, calendar of events.

Jeff H. Grzelak
Department of the South
Newspaper: Hilton Head Dispatch
7214 Laurel Hill Rd.
Orlando, FL 32818-5233
ph: 407-295-7510
Carries the latest information on all Southeastern Civil War events: shows, reenactments, book fairs; for historians, reenactors, buffs in S.E.

William Holschuh, Pub.
Newspaper: Camp Chase Gazette
P.O. Box 707
Marietta, OH 45750
ph: 740-373-1865 or 800-449-1865
fax: 740-374-5710
e-mail: CampChase@compuserve.com
web: http://www.cybergate.net/~civilwar/
For 17 years the voice of the Civil War reenactor: recruiting, events, equipment, etc.; website has links to many Civil War sites, including reenactors.

Magazine: Civil War Lady, The
622 3rd Ave. S.W.
Pipestone, MN 56164
ph: 507-825-3182
fax: 507-825-3182
The best Civil War bi-monthly reenacting magazine for women: fashion news & articles, research, reenacting tips, child rearing, ads, etc.

Patrick Publishing
Magazine: Reenactor's Journal
P.O. Box 1864
Varna, IL 61375
ph: 309-463-2123
fax: 309-463-2188
A concise, to-the-point monthly magazine for reenactors of the War Between the States; for military or civilian reenactor.

Suppliers

Regimental Quartermaster, The
P.O. Box 553
Hatboro, PA 19040
ph: 215-672-6891
fax: 215-672-9020
e-mail: regtqm@aol.com
web: http://members.aol.com/regtqm/
Civil War reproduction Muskets, Revolvers, Swords, Uniforms, Leather Goods, Buckles, Buttons, Accouterments, Accessories, etc.; send $2 for list.

Southern Exposure
710 Caroline St.
Fredericksburg, VA 22401
ph: 540-899-6464
fax: 540-373-2469
e-mail: sutler@erols.com
web: http://www.staleyssundries.com/
Carries American Revolution and Civil War era gifts, flags, music, accessories, accouterments, etc.

WWII Reenactors

Internet Resources

WW2 German Army Reenacting Page
e-mail: Soldaten@aol.com
web: http://members.aol.com/soldaten/main.htm
Specializing in WWII German army reenacting.

LOBBY CARDS

(see MOVIE MEMORABILIA; PAPER COLLECTIBLES)

LOCKS

(see also BANKS; DOORKNOBS; HARDWARE; KEYS; RESTRAINT DEVICES; SAFES)

Clubs/Associations

Charles Chandler
American Lock Collectors Association
Newsletter: American Lock Collectors Association Newsletter
36076 Grennada
Livonia, MI 48154-5278
ph: 313-522-0920
fax: 313-522-0920
e-mail: cwchandler@aol.com
Club newsletter reports on coming lock shows, also articles on locks, keys, handcuffs; prices, unusual items, historical information.

Bob Heilemann
West Coast Lock Collectors
Newsletter: West Coast Lock Collectors Newsletter
1427 Lincoln Blvd.
Santa Monica, CA 90401-2732
ph: 310-454-7295 or 310-230-3004
e-mail: locksmann@aol.com
Call evenings; no collect calls, please.

Collectors

Alene Saap
400 Calaf St., Ste. 80
San Juan, PR 00918-1314
ph: 787-758-5606 or 787-782-0020
Wants antique or unusual padlocks with key.

Richard C. Hubbard
162 Poplar Ave.
Hackensack, NJ 07601
ph: 201-342-1274
e-mail: DoorKnobID@aol.com
Interested in old US key or combination padlocks, embossed RR locks, figural shapes and unusual mechanisms or early patent dates.

Joseph Biunno
129 West 29th St.
New York, NY 10001
ph: 212-629-5630
fax: 212-268-4577
Wants furniture locks and keys; barrel, skeleton, door, drawer, old or new; also wants escutcheons in all styles and sizes.

Al Cahill
13 Loudon Dr., Apt. 4
Fishkill, NY 12524-1816
Wants to buy old and unusual padlocks; also wants brass figural doorknobs.

Tom Gallian
P.O. Box 545
906 West Broad
Dunn, NC 28334
ph: 910-892-9104
Serious collector wants collectible padlocks.

Franklin Arnall
Collector, The
P.O. Box 253
Claremont, CA 91711-0253
ph: 909-621-2461
Wants to buy antique padlocks: brass railroad and express, odd miniatures, any unusual cast iron of brass; any quantity.

Mark Lyons
544 Crest Dr.
Encinitas, CA 92024-4145
ph: 760-431-5397
fax: 760-431-1515
Wants antique pad locks or collectible and unusual locks and keys; also wants jail and prison locks.

Daniel C. Zolezzi
2211 Froude St.
San Diego, CA 92107-1721
ph: 619-223-7440
Wants to buy old padlocks, keys and locks.

Dealers

Joseph & Pamela Tanner
Wheeler-Tanner ESCAPES
3024 E. 35th Ave.
Spokane, WA 99223-4504
ph: 509-448-8457
fax: 509-448-8457
e-mail: JnPwLrTnr@aol.com
Wants padlocks of all sizes and shapes; figural, combination, round pancake types, railroad, Winchester, Wells Fargo, Express Co's., etc.

Experts

Bob Heilemann
1427 Lincoln Blvd.
Santa Monica, CA 90401-2732
ph: 310-454-7295 or 310-230-3004
e-mail: locksmann@aol.com
Collector and historian of antique padlocks; also repairs and restores padlocks; call evenings; no collect calls, please.

Museums/Libraries

Thomas Hennessy, Cur.
Lock Museum of America
Newsletter: Lock Museum of America Newsletter
230 Main St., Rte. 6
Terryville, CT 06786-0104
ph: 860-589-6359
fax: 860-589-6359
web: http://www.untangled.com/lock/

Repair Services

Muff's Antiques
135 S. Glassell St.
Orange, CA 92866-1421
ph: 714-997-0243
fax: 714-997-1601
e-mail: muffs@earthlink.net
web: http://home.earthlink/~muffs/
Specializes in the repairing and rekeying of antique locks.

LODGE BADGES

(see FRATERNAL ORGANIZATION ITEMS)

LOGGING RELATED ITEMS

(see also SCRIP)

Museums/Libraries

Ashland Logging Museum, Inc.
P.O. Box 348
Ashland, ME 04732
ph: 207-435-6039

Lumberman's Museum
P.O. Box 300
Patten, ME 04765
ph: 207-528-2650
e-mail: jimwalk@mainerec.com
web: http://www.mainerec.com/logger.html

Carol Riggs, Dir.
Texas Forestry Museum
P.O. Box 1488
Lufkin, TX 75902-1488
ph: 409-632-9535
e-mail: cets@sfasu.edu
web: http://www.cets.sfasu.edu/TFM.html
One of the largest museums of its kind in the U.S.: offers a historic look at early logging, lumberjacks, and sawmill towns.

LONE SCOUT MEMORABILIA

Collectors

Fran & Cal Holden
P.O. Box 264 - M264
Doylestown, OH 44230-0264
ph: 800-663-2793
Wants to buy Lone Scout (1915-1925) memorabilia (sometimes marked "LSA"): old pins, badges, medals, uniforms, literature, etc.

LOOMS

(see COVERLETS; SPINNING WHEELS)

LORGNETTES

(see EYE RELATED ITEMS, Eyeglasses)

LOTTERY TICKETS

Instant (Used)

Clubs/Associations

Eric White
Lottery Collectors Society
Newsletter: Lotologist, The
1080 North Main St.
Conyers, GA 30012
ph: 770-924-3491 or 770-483-8927
e-mail: lotteryfan@aol.com
Unites lottery collectors and provides services such as newsletters, ticket catalog, and trading roster.

Collectors

Bill Pasquino
1824 Lyndon Ave.
Lancaster, PA 17602-4711
ph: 717-393-0843
e-mail: wpsquino@aol.com
Wants losing instant lottery tickets; instant rub off lottery tickets from the 1970s and early 1980s.

Scott Simon
301 Goodman Dr.
Paducah, KY 42003
ph: 502-441-7008
e-mail: sdsimon@apex.net
web: http://www.apex.net/users/sdsimon/
Always looking to buy scratch-offs and paper tickets from US and abroad.

LUGGAGE

(see also CLOTHING & ACCESSORIES, Vintage; LEATHER; LABELS, Luggage; TRUNKS)

Dealers

Lilit Eclectiques
483 Broome St.
New York, NY 10013
ph: 212-966-0650
Carries designer trunks, bags and steamers from 18th century to 1920s.

Louis Vuitton

Collectors

Brian J. Vazquez
25 Comstock Hill Rd.
Norwalk, CT 06850
ph: 203-846-3767
Wants to buy Louis Vuitton trunks and luggage.

Dealers

Ron Coolk
R. Cook & Co.
44 North Federal Highway
Dania, FL 33004
ph: 954-922-1118
e-mail: info@rcookco.com
One of the nation's largest dealers of vintage Louis Vuitton trunks, wardrobes and suitcases.

Duane S. Bietz
Les Meilleurs
6461 S.E. Thorburn
Portland, OR 97215-1378
ph: 503-238-6888
fax: 503-233-1602
e-mail: dbietz@aol.com
Collects and sells hard luggage and trunks; specialty pieces, cosmetic, cigar, liquor, shoe, hat, collar, and car trunks; any Louis Vuitton memorabilia and promotional items; email or write with photos for appraisals or to sell.

Man./Prod./Dist.

Louis Vuitton
49 E. 57th St.
New York, NY 10022
ph: 212-371-6111
e-mail: jargento@lvna.com
web: http://www.vuitton.com/

LUMBERING

(see LOGGING RELATED ITEMS)

LUNCH BOXES

Collectors

Peter Reginato
60 Green St.
New York, NY 10012
ph: 212-925-9787
Wants lunch boxes from 1950s through 1970s.

Dennis Visco
11 Aldrich St.
Huntington Station, NY 11746-2632
ph: 516-549-2719
fax: 516-421-5215
Wants to buy lunch boxes (metal or vinyl) from the 1950s to the 1960s.

David Reed
841 West Main St.
Madison, OH 44057
ph: 440-428-6666
Wants Jetsons, Lost in Space, Westerns, TV Shows, Space: metal and vinyl.

Andy Galbus
Pak-Rat
900 8th St. NW
Kasson, MN 55944-1079
e-mail: lhpakrat@means.net
Wants to buy lunch boxes.

Fred & Jan Carlson
P.O. Box 2
Hillsboro, OR 97123-0002
ph: 503-648-8477
fax: 503-642-2534
Wants to buy lunch pails and thermoses.

Tom Hattrup
P.O. Box 246
Moxee, WA 98936
ph: 509-457-4027
Wants to buy lunch boxes; Toppie the Elephant, NHL, Our Friends, and others.

Dealers

Jim Cassidy
P.O. Box 157
West Boylston, MA 01583
ph: 508-829-2985
fax: 508-829-3415
e-mail: lunchbox@cassidyframes.com
web: http://www.cassidyframes.com/box/
Has been buying, collecting, selling, trading lunch boxes and thermoses since 1991.

Allen Woodall
2 Shalom Pl.
Columbus, GA 31904-2847
ph: 706-322-0516
fax: 706-322-0515
e-mail: awoodall@fiac.net

Mark Walters
Ricky Smith Toys
6159 N 9th Ave.
Pensacola, FL 32504-8204
ph: 850-857-1343
fax: 850-477-8508

Tomel
3464 Hazelton Ave.
Rochester, MI 48307
ph: 248-853-0785
e-mail: simone7@sprintmail.com

Terri Ivers
Terri's Toys & Nostalgia
206 E. Grande Ave.
Ponca City, OK 74601
ph: 580-762-8697 or 580-762-5174
fax: 580-765-2657
e-mail: toylady@poncacity.net
Buys and sells metal and vinyl lunch boxes, and metal or plastic thermoses from the late 1940s to the present; the most desirable are from the 1950s through 1984; also wants Western, space, and character related collectibles.

Experts

Bill Henry
Box-O-Rama
104 Davidson Lane
Oak Ridge, TN 37830-7705
ph: 423-483-0769
fax: 423-482-1581
Buys, sells, and trades lunch boxes; promoter of Box-O-Rama, the only show devoted exclusively to Lunch Boxes; show is usually on the second weekend in August and includes a sale and auction.

Pat & Larry Aikins
P & L Collectibles
Rt. 5, Box 5174
Athens, TX 75751
ph: 903-675-3765
fax: 903-677-3643
e-mail: Texasboxer@aol.com
web: http://www.mrlunchbox.com/
Author of "Pictorial Price Guide to Vinyl & Plastic Lunch Boxes" and "Pictorial Price Guide to Metal Lunch Boxes" (L-W Book Sales); wants to buy lunch boxes, thermos bottles: metals, soft vinyls, promotional, odd shaped plastics boxes.

LURAY

(see CERAMICS [AMERICAN DINNERWARE], Taylor, Smith & Taylor/LuRay)

LURES

(see FISHING COLLECTIBLES)

Here are some tips when contacting someone listed in this book:

■ When requesting information about a particular item, include a description (material, dimensions, maker's mark, model number, etc.) and a photo, sketch, or photocopy of the item in question.

■ Always ask if there are charges for samples or for the services requested.

■ When writing, please be sure to include a Large (#10 business size) Self-Addressed and Stamped Envelope (LSASE) if requesting a reply or the return of photographs.

■ Never call collect unless otherwise directed. When calling, be considerate of time zone differences and always ask if the party you are calling has time to talk. When leaving an answering machine message, always instruct the party to call you back collect.

M

M&M/MARS CANDY

Clubs/Associations

Ken Clee
M&M Collector's Club
Newsletter: MMCC Newsletter
P.O. Box 11412
Philadelphia, PA 19111-0412
ph: 215-722-1979
e-mail: waxntoys@aol.com
web: http://www.mnmclub.com/
Collector's club not affiliated with Mars/M&M; quarterly newsletter, annual convention.

Collectors

Frederick Kraut
120 Covington Drive
Warwick, RI 02886-1936
ph: 401-738-2277
e-mail: uki845@aol.com
Big collector of M&M items, memorabilia and clothing; also carries pre-1975 baseball cards and baseball memorabilia.

Dealers

Ken Clee
P.O. Box 11412
Philadelphia, PA 19111-0412
ph: 215-722-1979
e-mail: waxntoys@aol.com
web: http://members.aol.com/waxntoys/main/kidsmeal.htm
Buys and sells anything related to Mars M&M candy, including NASCAR, dispensers, toppers, advertising & displays.

MACERATED CURRENCY ITEMS

Collectors

Bertram M. Cohen
Great American Co.
169 Marlborough St.
Boston, MA 02116-1830
ph: 617-247-4754
fax: 617-247-9093
e-mail: marblebert@aol.com
web: http://members.aol.com/marblebert/
Wants items made from macerated U.S. money 1880-1940, original advertisements for macerated currency items, and any magazine articles regarding macerated money.

Donald Gorlick
P.O. Box 24541
Seattle, WA 98124-0541
ph: 206-824-0508
Wants macerated currency - items made up of ground-up money pulp; usually souvenir items, statues, plates, animals; often with a tag.

MACHINE AGE

(see MODERNISM)

MACHINERY & EQUIPMENT

(see also AIRPLANES; CONSTRUCTION EQUIPMENT; FARM MACHINERY; INDUSTRY RELATED ITEMS; LAWN MOWERS; RAILROADS; TOOLS; WASHING MACHINES)

Appraisers

Michael Saperstein, ISA
Paul E. Saperstein Co., Inc.
148 State St., Ste. 520
Boston, MA 02109
ph: 617-227-6553
fax: 617-227-4538
e-mail: msaperstein@pesco.com
web: http://www.pesco.com
Machinery & equipment appraisers and auctioneers.

Equipment Appraisers Association of North America
1370 Langport Dr.
Pittsburgh, PA 15241-3605
ph: 412-221-1097 or 800-637-5614
fax: 412-221-7658
A professional appraisal society representing all aspects of the industrial equipment industries; actual market experience is a requirements for all designated member appraiser.

Association of Machinery & Equipment Appraisers (AMEA)
315 S. Patrick St.
Alexandria, VA 22314-3501
ph: 800-537-8629 or 703-836-7900
fax: 703-836-9303
e-mail: amea@amea.org
web: http://www.amea.org
Association of machinery and equipment appraisers; publishes directory of appraisers who are used machinery dealers and/or auctioneers actively involved in the used machinery marketplace.

C.D. Gallimore, ISA, CAI
AMC Appraisal Co. Inc.
P.O. Box 306
Concord, NC 28026-0306
ph: 800-938-2121
fax: 704-782-2399
e-mail: 104427.3455@compuserve.com

Phillip D. Peck, ISA
Revpro Appraisal Service
4021 Indian Run Dr.
Baton Rouge, LA 70816-3571
ph: 504-755-7002
fax: 504-755-0302
e-mail: 102432.1674@compuserve.com

James Pharr, ISA
James Pharr Machinery Co.
P.O. Box 38385
Shreveport, LA 71133
ph: 318-636-6050
fax: 318-636-6608
e-mail: jamespharr@worldnet.att.net
Buys and sells earth moving equipment.

Noel L. Novak, MVS, ISA, ASA
Donahue & Associates
17251 East 17th St., Ste. D
Tustin, CA 92780-1951
ph: 714-508-7780
fax: 714-508-7789
Specializes in the appraisal of fixtures, equipment and inventory.

Christian Coleman, Ex. Dir.
International Society of Appraisers
Newsletter: Professional Appraisers Information Exchange
16040 Christensen Rd., Ste. 102
Seattle, WA 98188
ph: 206-241-0359 or 888-472-4732
fax: 206-241-0436
e-mail: ISA_HQ@compuserve.com
web: http://www.isa-appraisers.org
Largest association of professional personal property appraisers; members specialize in antiques & residential contents, gems & jewelry, fine art, and machinery & equipment; call for appraiser nearest you.

Auction Services

Larry Mitchell
Superior Asset Management
P.O. Box 792427
San Antonio, TX 78279-2427
ph: 210-499-0777
fax: 210-495-1319
e-mail: info@saami.com
web: http://www.saami.com
Specializes in the auction sale machinery and equipment, oil rigs, classic cars.

Museums/Libraries

American Precision Museum Association, Inc.
Newsletter: Tools & Technology
P.O. Box 679
196 Main St.
Windsor, VT 05089
ph: 802-674-5781
fax: 802-674-2524
e-mail: curator@americanprecision.org
web: http://americanprecision.org/
Housed in the original Robbins & Lawrence Armory and Machine Shop, the museum features the largest collection of historic precision machine tools in the nation.

Periodicals

National Auto Research
Magazine: Black Book Official Auction Report
2620 Barrett Rd.
P.O. Box 758
Gainesville, GA 30503
ph: 770-532-4111 or 800-554-1026
fax: 770-532-4792
web: http://hearstcorp.com/bpub14.html
Publishes weekly, monthly, bimonthly, annual guides (Black Books) containing new and used car and truck values for the automotive and finance industries including used and new car dealers, bankers, wholesale buyers, credit unions.

Marcia Gruver, Ed.
Randall Publishing Co.
Magazine: Equipment World
3200 Rice Mine Road, N.E.
Tuscaloosa, AL 35406
ph: 205-349-2990 or 800-633-5953
fax: 205-750-8070
e-mail: wfair@randallpub.com
web: http://www.topbid.com/
Monthly magazine with articles about new equipment on the market.

Randall Publishing Co.
Magazine: Top Bid
3200 Rice Mine Road, N.E.
Tuscaloosa, AL 35406
ph: 205-349-2990 or 800-633-5953
fax: 205-750-8070
e-mail: mgruver@randallpub.com
web: http://www.randallpub.com/
Monthly auction report listing machinery & equipment prices realized as well as an upcoming auction schedule.

Christina Gargano
Heartland Communications Group, Inc.
Magazine: Contractors Hot Line Equipment Guide
1003 Central Ave.
P.O. Box 1052
Fort Dodge, IA 50501
ph: 800-247-2000 or 515-955-1600
fax: 515-574-2233
e-mail: libbie@hlipublishing.com
web: http://www.hlipublishing.com
Lists construction equipment manufacturer's addresses, basic equipment specs., original selling prices, current market values; published annually; information source for buyers, sellers, dealers, auctioneers, appraisers.

Christina Gargano
Heartland Communications Group, Inc.
Magazine: Hot Line's Parts Connection
1003 Central Ave.
P.O. Box 1052
Fort Dodge, IA 50501
ph: 800-247-2000 or 515-955-1600
fax: 515-574-2233
e-mail: libbie@hlipublishing.com
web: http://www.hlipublishing.com
Directory for the largest selection and best prices of new, used, rebuilt parts and attachments for construction equipment.

Christina Gargano
Heartland Communications Group, Inc.
Magazine: Industrial Machine Trade
1003 Central Ave.
P.O. Box 1052
Fort Dodge, IA 50501
ph: 800-247-2000 or 515-955-1600
fax: 515-574-2233
e-mail: libbie@hlipublishing.com
web: http://www.hlipublishing.com
The only weekly nationwide publication that links active buyers and sellers of new and used industrial machinery.

Christina Gargano
Heartland Communications Group, Inc.
Magazine: Mine & Quarry Hot Line
1003 Central Ave.
P.O. Box 1052
Fort Dodge, IA 50501
ph: 800-247-2000 or 515-955-1600
fax: 515-574-2233
e-mail: libbie@hlipublishing.com
web: http://www.hlipublishing.com
Offers the buyers and sellers of aggregate equipment a direct way to reach thousands of highly qualified customers in their specific industry.

Dataquest Incorporated
Magazine: Green Guide
251 River Oaks Pkwy.
San Jose, CA 95134
ph: 408-468-8000 or 800-669-3282
fax: 408-954-1780
e-mail: help@gartner.com
web: http://www.gartner.com/
Professionally researched market values on construction equipment; average resale values to 20 years old; 3,000 equipment models, all types; original and current prices, serial numbers for years of manufacture, basic specs.

Dataquest Incorporated
Magazine: Serial Number Guide
251 River Oaks Pkwy.
San Jose, CA 95134
ph: 408-468-8000 or 800-669-3282
fax: 408-954-1780
e-mail: help@gartner.com
web: http://www.gartner.com/
Lists year of manufacture by maker and model.

Catalogs

(see also CATALOGS, Trade)

Collectors

Marvin McKinley
1652 State Rte. 511
Ashland, OH 44805-9214
ph: 4109-289-1706
Wants old sales catalogs and manuals for machinery, steam engines, gas engines, windmills, farm machinery, buggies, sleighs, etc.

Dealers

Eldon Bryant
Broken Kettle Book Service
702 East Madison St.
Fairfield, IA 52556-3649
e-mail: bkettle@kdsi.net
Wants old sales catalogs and manuals for machinery, steam engines, gas engines, windmills, farm machinery, buggies, sleighs, etc.

Construction

Auction Services

Walter Vilsmeier
Vilsmeier Auction Company, Inc.
1044 Bethlehem Pike, Rt. 309
Montgomeryville, PA 18936
ph: 215-699-5833 or 800-243-6289
e-mail: auction@vilsmeier.com
web: http://www.vilsmeier.com/
Specializes in the sale of used machinery and equipment; tractor crawlers, loader backhoes, air compressors, graders, etc.

Forke Brothers
P.O. Box 21960
Lincoln, NE 68542-1960
ph: 402-421-3631
fax: 402-421-1738
e-mail: ScottB@Forkebros.com
web: http://www.forkebros.com
Specializes in the sale of used machinery and equipment; tractor crawlers, loader backhoes, air compressors, graders, etc.

Clubs/Associations

Historical Construction Equipment Association
P.O. Box 328
Grand Rapids, OH 43522
ph: 419-832-4232
fax: 419-832-4034
e-mail: info@bigtoy.com
web: http://www.bigtoy.com
Dedicated to preserving the history of all types of construction, surface mining and dredging equipment.

Road Making

Clubs/Associations

D.J. Crampton, Mem.
Road Roller Association
Newsletter: Rolling
6 Norwood Close
Mackworth, Derby DE22 4GA
U.K.
ph: +44 1904 331926
e-mail: dean@drayner.demon.co.uk
web: http://www.drayner.demon.co.uk/rra.html
Caters specifically to those interested in the science of road making and road repair and in the associated equipment involved with these operations, including steam and motor rollers.

Woodworking

Experts

Mr. Dana Martin Batory
402 E. Bucyrus St.
Crestline, OH 44827-1506
Wants catalogs, photographs, advertising, manuals, reminiscences, etc. pertaining to woodworking machinery and/or their manufacturers; author of "Vintage woodworking machinery - An Illustrated Guide to Four Manufacturers" (Astragal Press).

MAGAZINES

(see also AQUARIUMS, Magazines; BOOKS; COLLEGE COLLECTIBLES, Humor Magazines; ILLUSTRATORS; MYSTERY/DETECTIVE ITEMS; PAPER COLLECTIBLES; PERIODICALS; SPORTING COLLECTIBLES, Magazines; TELEVISION SHOWS & MEMORABILIA, TV Guide)

Collectors

Bob Havey
P.O. Box 183
North Sullivan, ME 04664-0183
ph: 207-422-3083
fax: 207-422-3430
Wants many magazines from the 1800s to 1950: Movie Magazine, Vogue, Pictorial Review, Esquire, Good Housekeeping, McCall's, etc.

Gary Olsen
505 S. Royal Ave.
Front Royal, VA 22630
ph: 540-635-7157 or 540-635-7158
fax: 540-635-1818
e-mail: hpfrigko@interloc.com
Wants pre-1970 Life, Look, Colliers, Post, etc. especially with WWI and/or WWII stories and articles.

Dealers

Gary Borkan
Vintage Magazine Gallery
P.O. Box 870
Melrose, MA 02176
e-mail: garyborkan@aol.com
web: http://members.aol.com/maggallery/
Specializes in antique magazines which have high quality cover graphics and are in excellent condition; included are 1930s Fortunes, Vogues, Jugend, etc.; illustrated and for sale on the web site.

Charles Zayic
Magazine Man, The
P.O. Box 57
Ellsworth, ME 04605-0057
ph: 207-667-7342
e-mail: magman@acadianet.com
Wants old magazines from the teens and 1920s; especially Ladie's Home Journal, Pictorial Review, Woman's Home Companion, McCall's, Delineator, Modern Priscilla, and Needlecraft.

Michael Kelly
Paper Pandemonium
1321 Jack's Mountain Road
Fairfield, PA 17320
ph: 717-642-8019
e-mail: kellym@mail.cvn.net
web: http://www.tias.com/stores/pp
Collector and dealer carries a large selection of early magazines with famous people covers: LIFE, LOOK, TIME, and others.

Stan Gold
As Time Goes By
7042 Dartbrook Dr.
Dallas, TX 75240
ph: 972-239-8621 or 214-352-2765
fax: 972-239-9622
e-mail: record@unicomp.net
web: http://www.astimegoesby.com/
Wants to buy Life 1936-1972, Post, Time, Playboy 1953-1965, Sports Illustrated 1954-1970s, TV Guides 1947-1970s, vintage movie magazines, aviation, men's adventure, automotive, sports, pin-up magazines 1920s to 1960s, world's fair pre 1940.

Mike Sandusky
Million Magazines
1760 Calle del Vaso
Tucson, AZ 85737
ph: 800-877-9887 or 520-297-0006
fax: 520-544-7878
e-mail: magazin@primenet.com
web: http://www.primenet.com/~magazin/
Over one million magazines in stock dating back to 1843 and to present; over 750,000 pieces of magazine art available in most categories; in the trade since 1976; databases and indexes available for research.

Magazine Baron
1236 S. Magnolia Ave.
Anaheim, CA 92804
ph: 714-527-0358
fax: 714-527-5634
e-mail: bkbaron1@interloc.com
Buys and sells back issue magazines: movies from 1914 to present, 1000s of Sports Illustrated, 50s to 90s Playboy, fashion, pulps, teen magazines, aviation, art, historical, hobbies.

Ken Mitchell
710 Conacher Dr.
Willowdale, Ontario M2M 3N6
Canada
ph: 416-222-5808
Appraises, collects, buys and sells 1890 to 1970s comic books, newspapers, comic strips, "Big Little" books, popular music/jazz books/magazines/tapes; pulp magazines, original comic art, radio and cereal premiums.

Experts

Mike Sandusky
Million Magazines
1760 Calle del Vaso
Tucson, AZ 85737
ph: 800-877-9887 or 520-297-0006
fax: 520-544-7878
e-mail: magazin@primenet.com
web: http://www.primenet.com/~magazin/
Over one million magazines in stock dating back to 1843 and to present; over 750,000 pieces of magazine art available in most categories; in the trade since 1976; databases and indexes available for research.

Denis C. Jackson
P.O. Box 1958
Sequim, WA 98382-1958
ph: 360-452-3810
e-mail: ticn@olypen.com
web: http://www.olypen.com/ticn/
Buys, sells, collects and specializes in OLD magazines; author of "The Masters Price & Identification Guide to Old Magazines" 4th edition 1999; 1st through 4th editions cover 1,200 publishers from 1800 to present; LSASE for information.

Periodicals

Doug Watson
Magazine: Paper Collectors' Market-place
470 Main St.
P.O. Box 128
Scandinavia, WI 54977-0128
ph: 715-467-2379
fax: 715-467-2243
e-mail: pcmpaper@gglbbs.com
web: http://www.pcmpaper.com/
Monthly magazine for collectors of autographs, paperbacks, postcards, advertising, photographica, magazines; all types of paper ephemera.

Denis C. Jackson, Ed.
Newsletter: Illustrator Collector's News, The
P.O. Box 1958
Sequim, WA 98382-1958
ph: 360-452-3810
e-mail: ticn@olypen.com
web: http://www.olypen.com/ticn/
A monthly publication for collectors of magazines and other paper illustrations; free classifieds for subscribers; send LSASE for information; free magazines guide offer.

Automotive

Dealers

Dave Allen
Imperial Palace Auto Collection
3535 Las Vegas Blvd., So.
Las Vegas, NV 89109
ph: 702-731-3311
web: http://www.ipautocollection.com/
Buys and sells out-of-print motorcycle and automotive magazines: "Hot Rod," "Motor Trend," "Speed Age," "Road Track," also all half-size magazines.

Covers & Tear Sheets

Dealers

Mary Ann Hahn
Second Hand Mary Ann's
103 Ocean Point Road
Boothbay Harbor, ME 04538
ph: 207-633-2426
fax: 207-633-2586
e-mail: maryann@gwi.net
Buys and sells magazine covers and tear sheets of any advertisement or illustration.

Charles Zayic
Magazine Man, The
P.O. Box 57
Ellsworth, ME 04605-0057
ph: 207-667-7342
e-mail: magman@acadianet.com
Buys and sells vintage magazines ads, 11"x14", full page color originals, mixed subjects, 1920s, 1930s, 1940s and 1950s; send SASE for list.

Life

Dealers

Charles Zayic
Magazine Man, The
P.O. Box 57
Ellsworth, ME 04605-0057
ph: 207-667-7342
e-mail: magman@acadianet.com
Buys and sells Life magazines 1936 through 1972; maintains active inventory of over 5,000 copies for sale, send SASE for list.

Dwayne Spark
Nostalgia Plus
8441 Sublaines
Anjou, Quebec H1K 2C1
Canada
ph: 514-352-6892
fax: 514-352-1856
Wants to buy Life magazines from 1970 and earlier in small or large quantities.

Experts

Denis C. Jackson
P.O. Box 1958
Sequim, WA 98382-1958
ph: 360-452-3810
e-mail: ticn@olypen.com
web: http://www.olypen.com/ticn/
Author of "Life Magazines", major illustrators from 1898 to 1930s.

MAD

Auction Services

Michael Lerner
32862 Springside Lane
Solon, OH 44139-2067
ph: 440-349-3776
e-mail: mlerner@wviz-nt1.wviz.org
Buys and sells MAD memorabilia.

Collectors

Roland Coover
1537 E. Strasburg Rd.
West Chester, PA 19380-6380
ph: 610-692-3112
e-mail: rlcoover@aol.com
Wants anything related to MAD magazine or Alfred E. Neuman: jewelry, presidential campaign kits, Halloween costume, clothing, straight jacket, postcards, toys, etc.; no paperbacks or magazines, please.

Casey Nicholson
415 Vancleave Ave.
Ocean Springs, MS 39564
ph: 601-872-8864 or 601-872-4280

Gary Kritzberg
P.O. Box 47
Yorkville, IL 60560
ph: 630-553-7653
Wants MAD Magazine collectibles: magazines, comics, toys, shirts, records, hardback books, jewelry, pins, buttons, etc.

Experts

Michael Lerner
32862 Springside Lane
Solon, OH 44139-2067
ph: 440-349-3776
e-mail: mlerner@wviz-nt1.wviz.org
Buys and sells MAD memorabilia.

Internet Resources

Doug Gilford
MAD Cover Site
e-mail: gilford@e-z.net
web: http://e-z.net/~gilford/themadcoversite/
A resource for collectors and fans of MAD Magazine.

Men's

(see also PLAYBOY ITEMS)

Men's (Girlie)

Experts

Denis C. Jackson
P.O. Box 1958
Sequim, WA 98382-1958
ph: 360-452-3810
e-mail: ticn@olypen.com
web: http://www.olypen.com/ticn/
Author of "The Price & Identification Guide to Men's (Girlie) Magazines", 4th edition; also issues 6 sale catalogs/year of magazines for sale; send LSASE for information.

Men's (Playboy)

Dealers

Passaic Books
267 Passaic St.
Passaic, NJ 07055
ph: 973-778-0416
fax: 973-778-6823
e-mail: info@passaicbooks.com
web: http://www.passaicbooks.com/
Sells a price guide devoted strictly to "Playboy" magazines; $10.95 postpaid.

Ken Ritchie
P.O. Box 22604
Memphis, TN 38122

Clint's Bookstore
3943 Main St.
Kansas City, MO 64111
ph: 816-561-2848
One of the largest national dealers in back issues of Playboy.

Experts

Douglas L. Tracy
Centerfold Shop, The
1220 23rd St., Ste. 2-M
San Diego, CA 92102-1960
ph: 619-235-6010
fax: 619-235-8005
Dealer, expert, specializing in Playboy magazines from the 1950s since 1968; mail order only; 24 page catalog $8 (refundable); stock of 50,000 issues; strict grading; internationally recommended by Playboy Enterprises, Inc.; buy pre-1964.

Denis C. Jackson
P.O. Box 1958
Sequim, WA 98382-1958
ph: 360-452-3810
e-mail: ticn@olypen.com
web: http://www.olypen.com/ticn/
Author of "The Price & Identification Guide to Playboy Magazines", 1995 2nd Edition; send LSASE for information.

Monster

Collectors

Steve Dolnick
P.O. Box 69
East Meadow, NY 11554-0069
ph: 516-486-5085
fax: 516-458-5085
Buys, sells and trades monster magazines: wants Famous Monsters, Vampirella, Monsters Parade, World Famous Creatures, Little Shoppe of Horrors, and other monster magazines and fanzines.

Motorcycle

Dealers

Dave Allen
Imperial Palace Auto Collection
3535 Las Vegas Blvd., So.
Las Vegas, NV 89109
ph: 702-731-3311
web: http://www.ipautocollection.com/
Buys and sells out-of-print motorcycle and automotive magazines: "Hot Rod," "Motor Trend," "Speed Age," "Road Track," also all half-size magazines.

Movie

(see also MOVIE MEMORABILIA)

Dealers

Pauline Harry
11493 Spring Hill Blvd.
Brooksville, FL 34609

Mary Wagner
419 W. King St.
Aberdeen, WA 98520

Experts

Denis C. Jackson
P.O. Box 1958
Sequim, WA 98382-1958
ph: 360-452-3810
e-mail: ticn@olypen.com
web: http://www.olypen.com/ticn/
Author of "The Old Movie, Television, Soap Opera, Radio Magazines Price & Identification Guide", 1st edition, 1994, 1914 through 1994.

Periodicals

Ray Stewart
Magazine: Magazines of the Movies
45 Killybawn Rd., Saintfield
Ballynahinch
Co Down, N. Ireland BT24 7JP
U.K.
Published each May; informs collectors of all screen periodicals available today; aimed at film/TV magazine collectors; professionally printed publication with illustrations of magazine covers, reviews, etc.

Music Related

Dealers

Jim Weaver
405 Dunbar
Pittsburgh, PA 15235-5218
e-mail: weaverjim@aol.com
Wants music magazines from the 1950s to early 1980s: "Billboard" and "Cashbox".

Mystery

Collectors

Jack Deveny
6805 Cheyenne Trail
Edina, MN 55439-1158
ph: 612-941-2457
e-mail: plane@itol.net
Wants Spider, Shadow, Doc Savage, Spicy, Detective, Mystery, Horror, Terror, etc.

Dealers

Peggy Ell
Peggy's Paper
218 Gratton
Burlington, IA 52601
ph: 319-752-7670
Buys and sells mystery magazines such as Alfred Hitchcock and Ellery Queen mystery magazines; also wants hardback mystery books.

National Geographic

Collectors

William Barr
6341 Werk Rd.
Cincinnati, OH 45248-2924
ph: 513-451-6174
Buys and sells pre-1916 National Geographic Magazines, maps, publications.

Norman Hagey
19672 Steavens Creek #424
Cupertino, CA 95014-2465
ph: 408-973-8129
Wants National Geographic magazines from the late 1800s and early 1900s including magazines bound in books; has over 3,000 magazines and many old National Geographic maps.

Dealers

B. Spiker
245 New Rd.
Southampton, PA 18966
ph: 215-364-8471
Buys and sells; free search.

Jeanne K. Bauxbaum
Baxbaum Geographics
P.O. Box 3746
Wilmington, DE 19807
ph: 302-994-2663
Buys and sells National Geographic from 1888-1920 only.

Don Smith
Don Smith's National Geographic Magazines
3930 Rankin St.
Louisville, KY 40214-1748
ph: 502-366-7504
Wants magazines from 1888; buying and selling; author of "National Geographic Magazines (1888-1996) For Collectors" price guide booklet.

Randolph M. Moss
Eclectic Books
2740 Hannah Place
Friday Harbor, WA 98250
ph: 360-378-5732
e-mail: eclecticbk@aol.com
Buys and sells National Geographic: pre-1915 magazines, bound sets, reprint, books; all publications by The National Geographic Society.

Office Related

Collectors

Darryl Rehr
P.O. Box 641824
Los Angeles, CA 90064
ph: 310-477-5229
fax: 310-268-8420
e-mail: dcrehr@earthlink.net
web: http://home.earthlink.net/~dcrehr/
Wants pre-1920 magazines & articles relating to old office equipment: "System", "Business Man's Monthly", "Phonographic World", etc.

Puck & Judge

Collectors

Bob Putnam
9140 Conversation Way
Springfield, VA 22153
ph: 703-644-9711
Wants to buy "Puck" and "Judge" periodicals, especially political cartoons pages, dating from 1876 to 1910; whole issues preferred; also wants to buy cartoons by Thomas Nast (1840-1902.)

Dealers

Mary Ann Hahn
Second Hand Mary Ann's
103 Ocean Point Road
Boothbay Harbor, ME 04538
ph: 207-633-2426
fax: 207-633-2586
e-mail: maryann@gwi.net
Buys "Puck & Judge" periodicals as well as Brown Book, The Truth, Verdict & Vim prior to 1910.

Pulp

(see also ART, Pulp; BOOKS, Paperback; SCIENCE FICTION/ FANTAST/HORROR)

Clubs/Associations

Ron Hanna
Secret Society of the Sanctum, The
Newsletter: Secret Sanctum
17803 Superior St., #204
Northridge, CA 91325
Newsletter features new pulp fiction, articles, and artwork; critically acclaimed with award-winning writers (Nick Carr, Will Murray); newsletter published bi-monthly.

Collectors

Jack Deveny
6805 Cheyenne Trail
Edina, MN 55439-1158
ph: 612-941-2457
e-mail: plane@itol.net
Wants Spider, Shadow, Doc Savage, Spicy, Detective, Mystery, Horror, Terror, etc.

Doug Ellis
13 Spring Lane
Barrington, IL 60010-9009
ph: 773-763-8763
Wants to buy all pulp magazines, especially adventure genre pulps, pulps published by Clayton, and "spicy" pulps; also issues sale catalogs from time to time.

Dealers

Jerry Peters
Chestnut Hollow, Ltd.
6060 Bordman Rd.
P.O. Box 6
Almont, MI 48003-0006
ph: 810-798-3158
Wants pulp magazines from the 1900s to 1950s: The Shadow, Doc Savage, weird tales, amazing stories, astounding, astonishing, planet stories, The Spider, spicy detective, thrilling wonder stories, detective stories, G-man, adventure.

David Smith
Rocket Comics
P.O. Box 30183
Seattle, WA 98103
ph: 206-784-7300
fax: 206-782-2844
e-mail: rocket@jetcity.com
web: http://www.jetcity.com/~rocket/
Dealer/expert buying and selling vintage comic books and pulp magazines since 1969; store has 2,500 sq. ft. of vintage comic books, pulp magazines, mass market magazines and paper books, and related paper collectibles.

Experts

Ray Walsh
Curious Book Shop
307 E. Grand River
East Lansing, MI 48823-4324
ph: 517-332-0112
Dealer/expert; owner of three book shops in Michigan; hosts radio call-in show about books and paper collectibles; writes columns; send a SASE for reply when writing.

Internet Resources

ThePulp.Net
e-mail: editor@thepulp.net
web: http://thepulp.net/
Pulp links, forums, chats; The Shadow, Doc Savage, The Spider, and more.

Museums/Libraries

San Francisco Academy of Comic Art
170 W. Cliff Dr., #15
Santa Cruz, CA 95060-5440
ph: 831-427-1737
fax: 831-427-1737
Millions of newspaper strips, bound files, major dailies from 1890-1960, pulps, all science fiction, crime fiction, film history, children's books, comic books; excellent copies made of all graphic material; dup material for trade.

Periodicals

Doug Ellis
Tattered Pages Press
Magazine: Pulp Vault
13 Spring Lane
Barrington, IL 60010-9009
ph: 773-763-8763
Irregularly published magazine devoted to pulps; approx. 128 pgs, 8 1/2x11, perfect-binding; reprints fiction stories from pulps; articles about the pulps; recollections of the pulp era; priced per issue; no subscriptions.

Pulp (Doc Savage)

Periodicals

Howard Wright
Green Eagle Publications
Newsletter: Bronze Gazette, The
2900 Standiford Ave., #136
Modesto, CA 95350-0167
The only publication devoted exclusively to the invincible Man of Bronze, Doc Savage.

Radio & Wireless

(see also TELEGRAPH ITEMS)

Collectors

Paul Thompson
315 Larkspur Dr.
Santa Maria, CA 93455-1625
ph: 805-934-2778
Wants radio and wireless magazines before 1940.

Scandal/Cult/R 'N' R

Experts

Alan Betrock
Shake Books
449 12 St.
Brooklyn, NY 11215-5167
ph: 718-499-6941
e-mail: alanshake@webtv.com
Author of "Unseen America - The Greatest Cult Exploitation Magazines 1950-1966," "Illustrated Price Guide to Cult Magazines, 1945-1969," and "Hitsville: The Greatest Rock 'n Roll Magazines, 1954-1968."

Toy

Collectors

Christmas Catalog Collector, The
175 East Delaware, #7403
Chicago, IL 60611-1731
ph: 800-879-6948 or 312-337-3123
fax: 312-266-7982
Collector eager to buy pre-1970 back copies of toy industry magazines such as "Playthings" and "Toys and Novelties;" also wants toy and Christmas catalogs.

TV Guide

Dealers

Philip M. Levine & Sons
P.O. Box 246
Three Bridges, NJ 08887
ph: 908-788-0532
fax: 908-788-1028
Buys and sells comic books, TV Guides, magazines, etc.

Rick Brown
Synergy
6031 Winterset
Lansing, MI 48911
ph: 517-887-1255 or 517-887-8027
e-mail: info@historybuff.com
web: http://www.historybuff.com
Appraises, auctions, collects and specializes in TV Guide magazines; buying and selling Pre-National and National editions 1948-1986.

TV Guide Specialists
P.O. Box 20
Macomb, IL 61455-0020
ph: 309-833-1809
Buys and sells TV Guide and newspaper TV magazines, 1948-1997.

MAGIC LANTERNS & SLIDES

(see also CAMERAS & CAMERA EQUIPMENT; OPTICAL ITEMS; TOYS, Optical)

Clubs/Associations

Ralph Shape
Magic Lantern Society of the U. S. & Canada
Magazine: Magic Lantern Gazette
3757 South 194th St.
Seattle, WA 98188
ph: 206-592-8270
fax: 206-592-8269
e-mail: maglanso@satx.net
web: http://www.magiclanternsociety.org/

Collectors

Daniel Gerber
6115 Shady Oak Lane
Bethesda, MD 20817
ph: 301-229-2702
Wants to buy magic lanterns and optical toys.

Sherry L. Werdon
400 N. Washington
Lowell, MI 49331-1465
ph: 616-897-9580
Wants unusual magic lanterns or mechanical lantern slides; also round and extra large slides and wooden viewers, pantoscope, etc.

Jack Judson, Jr.
1419 Austin Hwy.
San Antonio, TX 78209
ph: 210-805-0011
fax: 210-822-1226
e-mail: castle@magiclanterns.org
web: http://www.magiclanterns.org
Wants to buy magic lanterns and slides.

Dealers

Bryan W. Ginns
2109 Cty. Rte. 21
Valatie, NY 12184-6001
ph: 518-392-5805
fax: 518-392-7925
e-mail: the3dman@aol.com
Wants large collections of stereo views, old cameras, daguerreotypes, magic lanterns, optical toys; anything relating to photographics.

Ronald Krueger
R.W. Krueger's
P.O. Box 741
Oak Park, IL 60303-0741
ph: 708-788-8235
Collects glass slides used to advertise movies (coming attraction slides); also wants song slides.

Experts

Jack Judson, Jr.
1419 Austin Hwy.
San Antonio, TX 78209
ph: 210-805-0011
fax: 210-822-1226
e-mail: castle@magiclanterns.org
web: http://www.magiclanterns.org
Has extensive knowledge, collection/museum, and research facilities focusing on the magic lantern and other optical devices.

Museums/Libraries

Jack Judson, Jr.
Magic Lantern Castle Museum
1419 Austin Hwy.
San Antonio, TX 78209
ph: 210-805-0011
fax: 210-822-1226
e-mail: castle@magiclanterns.org
web: http://www.magiclanterns.org
Open by appointment; one man's collection of optical projection devices and items relating to the science of optics and optical projection.

MAGICIANS PARAPHERNALIA

(see also MORBID & ODD ITEMS; PERFORMING ARTS; POSTERS; RESTRAINT DEVICES; WITCHES)

Clubs/Associations

Edward Hill
New England Magic Collectors Association
3 Chandler St.
North Providence, RI 02911-2210
ph: 401-231-1215
e-mail: ride0167@ride.ri.net
Association of serious collectors of magic who reside in the New England area; three meetings/year; all collectors welcome as guests.

David Meyer
Magic Collector's Association
Magazine: Magicol
P.O. Box 511
Glenwood, IL 60425-0511
An association for collectors of all kinds of memorabilia related to magic as a performing art; magazine published quarterly.

Collectors

Joseph Gargano
P.O. Box 170
Lake Hiawatha, NJ 07034
ph: 973-538-2501
Wants to buy original, old pre-1940 posters and lithographs of magicians; please state condition and price.

Mark Whipple
102 Clarette Rd.
Pittsburgh, PA 15237
ph: 412-366-9459
Collects anything to do with magic and magicians: tricks, books, magazines, posters, etc.

Ken Trombly
1825 K St. NW, #901
Washington, DC 20006
ph: 800-673-8158 or 202-887-5000
fax: 202-457-0343
e-mail: trombly@erols.com
Wants magic posters, Mysto Magic sets, magic books and Houdini items; also wants broadsides and old photos of magicians; will pay top dollar or will trade from his collection.

Dan Stapleton
8237 Banyan Blvd.
Orlando, FL 32819
ph: 407-345-1132
Collector only, not a dealer; wants to buy old magic kits (pre-1965), magic lithographs and posters (pre-1950).

Ron Allesi
P.O. Box 54502
Cincinnati, OH 45254
ph: 513-697-6143 or 513-438-2894
e-mail: rallesi@sprynet.com
Buying, selling and trading used and antique magic equipment, posters, books and anything else pertaining to magic.

LaVerne Anderson
944 35th St.
Des Moines, IA 50312-3102
ph: 515-274-4443 or 515-274-9196
fax: 515-274-9196
Wants old magic books and magic tricks.

Andy Gross
P.O. Box 6134
Beverly Hills, CA 90212-1134
ph: 310-362-4372 or 818-765-1305
fax: 310-820-3308
e-mail: apedoll69@aol.com
web: http://www.lamagictoy.com/
Wants old magic tricks, kits, books, posters.

Michael Jaffe
P.O. Box 61484
Vancouver, WA 98666-1484
ph: 360-695-6161 or 800-782-6770
fax: 360-695-1616
e-mail: mjaffe@gstis.net
Wants to buy magic, magicians, escape artists, ventriloquists, jugglers; also related photo cards, advertising cards.

Dealers

David Winkler
Winkler's Warehouse of Wonders
24 Doyle Road
Oakdale, CT 06370-1052
ph: 860-859-3474
fax: 860-859-3135
e-mail: david.winkler@snet.net
web: http://www.magichq.com/
Buys, sells collectible and pre-owned magic items of all types, plus books, periodicals, anything magic related; web site features large list of used magic items and books; always seeking to buy.

Kenna Thompson
KT Magic, Inc.
P.O. Box 260
Hebron, KY 41048
ph: 606-689-7080
fax: 606-689-0227
e-mail: kennat@earthlink.net
web: http://www.ktmagic.com/
Buys, sells & appraises Magic, collectible, vintage, antique and rare: apparatus, books, lithograph posters (especially Strobridge), broadsides, sets, photos and autographs, memorabilia, collector item magic, Houdini, Kellar, Thurston.

Ed Verba
Magic Old & New
7655 Lexington Green
Cleveland, OH 44130
ph: 440-243-2424 or 440-243-2350
e-mail: everba@ameritech.com
Dealer in new and old magic (conjuring); used books, videos, illusions, antique magic, ephemera, and memorabilia; quarterly mailings of items for sale; no charge for mailing for first two years; many items on consignment.

Frank Herman
710 Anchor Way
Carlsbad, CA 92008
ph: 760-434-2254
Buys and sells magician related items: autographs, posters, programs, Mysto Magic sets, toys; also mentalists, escape artists, ventriloquists, fire eaters, spiritualists; plus all related books and apparatus; all offering lists answered.

Experts

Mario Carrandi
Mario Carrandi Inc. Antiquarian Magic & Collectibles
122 Monroe Ave.
Belle Mead, NJ 08502-4608
ph: 908-874-0630
fax: 908-874-4892
e-mail: mario@carrandimagic.com
web: http://www.carrandimagic.com/
Buys, sells, appraises and specialize in all categories of magic; one of the oldest and largest dealer in the field.

Herb Jacobs
P.O. Box 5390
Pompano Beach, FL 33074-5390
ph: 954-943-4213
Buys, sells, appraises and specializes in magic and conjuring memorabilia.

Dan Bradbury
Bradbury Books & Beyond
3318 Karnes Blvd.
Kansas City, MO 64111
ph: 816-531-2468
fax: 816-531-2468
e-mail: dbjb@sky.net
web: http://www.bradburybooks.com/
Buys and sells books (primarily out-of-print and used) and ephemera related to magic (conjuring) and its allied arts and entertainments: history and bibliography of magic, advertising, instructions, programs, books on performing.

John A. Greget
John A. Greget - Magic Lists
2631 E Claire Dr.
Phoenix, AZ 85032-4932
Buys and appraises magic books, posters, magazines, ephemera, equipment, etc.; singles or collection.

Museums/Libraries

Elaine Lund
American Museum of Magic
107 E. Michigan
P.O. Box 5
Marshall, MI 49068
ph: 616-781-7666
e-mail: chamber@marshallmi.org
web: http://marshallmi.org/tours/virtual/magic.html
Museum with holdings of approximately 250,000 items, all on magic.

Periodicals

Magazine: Magic Magazine
7380 South Eastern, Ste. #124-179
Las Vegas, NV 89123
ph: 702-798-4893
fax: 702-798-0220
e-mail: editor@magicmagazine.com
web: http://www.magicmagazine.com/

Phil Temple, Pub.
Newsletter: Magic Set Collector's Newsletter
P.O. Box 561
Novato, CA 94949-0561
ph: 415-897-5130
fax: 415-897-5130
e-mail: ptemple@webtv.net
A bi-monthly newsletter.

Houdini

Collectors

Sidney Radner
1050 Northampton St.
Holyoke, MA 01040-1321
ph: 413-532-6009 or 413-533-3000
fax: 413-536-9634
Wants items related to Houdini: posters, playbills, books, ephemera, etc.; honorary curator of the Houdini Historical Center.

Kevin Connolly
257 E Woodland Rd.
New Milford, NJ 07646-2321
ph: 201-262-9693
e-mail: houdini26@aol.com
Wants anything Houdini or about magic: books, posters, autographs, tricks, tokens, sets, apparatus, etc.

Ken Trombly
1825 K St. NW, #901
Washington, DC 20006
ph: 800-673-8158 or 202-887-5000
fax: 202-457-0343
e-mail: trombly@erols.com
Wants magic posters, Mysto Magic sets, magic books and Houdini items; also wants broadsides and old photos of magicians; will pay top dollar or will trade from his collection.

Arthur Moses
4205 Hildring Dr. East
Fort Worth, TX 76109-4717
ph: 817-921-2840
e-mail: aem102@aol.com
Wants to buy Houdini and related items: books, articles, posters, photos, autographs, personal effects, programs, pamphlets, playbills, scrapbooks, letters, lobby cards, films, etc.

Dealers

A. Peter Monticup
MagicTricks.Com
101 14th Street
Charlottesville, VA 22903
ph: 804-293-5788
e-mail: monticup@magictricks.com
web: http://www.magictricks.com

Michael Griffin
International Handcuff Exchange
356 W. Powell Rd.
Powell, OH 43065-9650
ph: 614-846-0585
Buys/sells Houdini memorabilia and old collectible magic; also handcuffs, leg irons, etc.; list of items for sale available.

Joseph & Pamela Tanner
Wheeler-Tanner ESCAPES
3024 E. 35th Ave.
Spokane, WA 99223-4504
ph: 509-448-8457
fax: 509-448-8457
e-mail: JnPwLrTnr@aol.com
Wants Houdini & other escape artist

items: autographs, posters, letters, postcards, books, photos, playbills, equipment, etc.

Internet Resources

A. Peter Monticup
MagicTricks.Com
101 14th Street
Charlottesville, VA 22903
ph: 804-293-5788
e-mail: monticup@magictricks.com
web: http://www.magictricks.com
Great Houdini web site: research, read and learn about the most famous magician in history: biography, odditorium, seances, photo gallery, etc.

Museums/Libraries

Houdini Museum
1433 N. Main Ave.
Scranton, PA 18508
ph: 714-342-5555
e-mail: magicusa@microserve.net
web: http://www.microserve.net/~magicusa/houdini.html
The only museum dedicated to Harry Houdini.

Kimberly Louagie, Curator
Houdini Historical Center
Magazine: Mystifier, The
330 East College Ave.
Appleton, WI 54911-5715
ph: 920-733-8445
e-mail: ochs@foxvalleyhistory.org
web: http://www.houdinihistory.org/
Dedicated to the gathering, interpretation, and dissemination of information and artifacts related to the life and career of Harry Houdini; collection features the Sidney H. Radner collection of Houdini memorabilia.

MAGNETS (REFRIGERATOR)

Collectors

Louise J. Greenfarb
307 John Henry Drive
Henderson, NV 89015-1610
ph: 702-433-5628
e-mail: mgntldy@aol.com
Has held Guiness record since 1995 for owning over 28,500 different refrigerator magnets; a display of 7,000 are on display at the Guiness Museum in Las Vegas, NV; has a network of "magpal" traders world wide.

MAILBOXES

Collectors

Charles W. Wardell
P.O. Box 195
Trinity, NC 27370-0195
ph: 336-434-1145
Wants 1870-1940 cast iron mailboxes; these boxes were fancy in design and served on homes and shops; usually with many coats of paint.

MANUALS & INSTRUCTION BOOKLETS

(see PAPER COLLECTIBLES)

MANUSCRIPTS

(see also AUTOGRAPHS; BOOKS; HISTORICAL AMERICANA; PAPER COLLECTIBLES)

Clubs/Associations

David R. Smith, Ex. Dir.
Manuscript Society, The
Magazine: Manuscripts
350 N. Niagara St.
Burbank, CA 91505-3648
e-mail: manuscrip@aol.com
web: http://www.manuscript.org
An organization of collectors, dealers, librarians, archivists, scholars and others interested in autographs and manuscripts.

Dealers

Robert Lucas
Robert F. Lucas Antiquarian Books
P.O. Box 63
Blandford, MA 01008
ph: 413-848-2061
e-mail: books@lucasbooks.com
web: http://www.lucasbooks.com
Mail order, on-line sales of antiquarian books; also a wide variety of ephemera including autographs, letters, broadsides, trade cards, photos, pamphlets, newspapers, diaries, account books, etc. especially from 19th century America.

George & Julie Perron
Old Paperphiles, The
P.O. Box 135
Tiverton, RI 02878-0135
ph: 401-624-9420
fax: 401-624-4204
Buys and sells paper collectibles: books, autographs, sheet music, postcards, photos, stereoviews, documents, old letters; issues periodic catalog of items for sale.

University Archives
600 Summer St.
Stamford, CT 06901-1403
ph: 800-237-5692 or 203-975-9291
fax: 203-348-3560
Buying and selling fine historical autographs, manuscripts, documents, autographed books and autographed photographs of notable people including U.S. presidents, Revolutionary and Civil War, literary, aviation, science, art, and music.

Gary J. Zimet
Moments in Time, Inc.
5 Cardinal Dr.
Washingtonville, NY 10992
ph: 914-497-7373
fax: 914-496-6367
Wants to buy rare letters and manuscripts: Washington, Adams, Jefferson, Lincoln, M.L. King, Malcolm X, Churchill, Disney, Ruth, Lee, Grant, Custer, etc.

Carmen D. Valentino
Rare Books & Manuscripts
2956 Richmond St., Drawer 19
Philadelphia, PA 19134-5720
ph: 215-739-6056
Antiquarian bookseller specializing in rare books, manuscripts, documents, early newspapers, handwritten diaries, account books and ledgers, ephemera, broadsides; pre-WWI.

Pennsylvania

Experts

Ron Lieberman
Family Album, The
RD 1 Box 42
Glen Rock, PA 17327-9707
ph: 717-235-2134
fax: 717-235-8765
e-mail: ronbiblio@delphi.com
web: http://www.auldbooks.com/biblio/clients/lieberman.html
Buys, sells, appraises all Pennsylvania related books, manuscripts, artwork, etc.

MAPS & CHARTS

(see also ATLASES; GAS STATION COLLECTIBLES, Road Maps; GLOBES; NAUTICAL ANTIQUES, Maps & Charts; PAPER COLLECTIBLES; PRINTS; STAMP COLLECTING, Maps & Charts; TRAILERS & RV'S)

Auction Services

James E. Hess
49 N. Water St.
P.O. Box 412
Lititz, PA 17543
ph: 717-626-5002
fax: 717-626-8858
e-mail: heritage@carto.com
web: http://www.carto.com

Joke Vrijenhoek
Paulus Swaen Internet Auction
P.O. Box 1238
Indian Rocks Beach, FL 33785
ph: 727-596-8734
fax: 727-596-8734
e-mail: paulus@swaen.com
web: http://www.swaen.com
Buys and sells old maps; conducts interactive map auctions on the Internet; offices in U.S. and The Netherlands.

Marti Griggs
Old World Auctions
671 Highway 179, Ste. E-3
Sedona, AZ 86336
ph: 520-282-3944 or 800-664-7757
fax: 520-282-3945
e-mail: marti@oldworldauctions.com
web: http://www.oldworldauctions.com
Auction specialists in maps, atlases, globes and antique prints; also repairs, buys, sells, and takes consignments.

Clubs/Associations

Siegfried Feller
Cartomania
8 Amherst Rd.
Amherst, MA 01002-9739
ph: 413-253-3115
Purpose is to provide and exchange information and news by/from/for collectors of maps in various formats.

David Cobb
Boston Map Society
Harvard College Library
Cambridge, MA 02138
ph: 617-495-2417
fax: 617-496-0440
e-mail: cobb@husc.harvard.edu
web: http://icg.harvard.edu/~maps/hpbms.htm
Brings together people with an interest in collecting, studying, using and preserving maps.

John Green, Treas.
Washington Map Society
Newsletter: Portolan
3016 Edgewater Dr.
Edgewater, MD 20037
e-mail: maphunter@aol.com
web: http://www.cyberia.com/pages/jdocktor/washmap.htm
For people interested in cartography and in collecting maps.

Eric Riback
NorthEast Map Organization (NEM)
Newsletter: NEMO Newsletter
2504 Hillwood Place
Charlottesville, VA 22901
ph: 804-975-2180
fax: 804-975-2280
e-mail: eriback@mapville.com

Maureen Farrell
Northern Ohio Map Society
c/o Map Department, Cleveland Public Library
325 Superior Ave.
Cleveland, OH 44111
ph: 216-623-2880
fax: 216-902-4978
e-mail: Maureen.Farrell@cpl.org
web: http://www.csuohio.edu/CUT/MapSoc/NOMS.htm

Sharon Hill
Map Society of Wisconsin
P.O. Box 399
Milwaukee, WI 53201
ph: 414-229-6282
fax: 414-229-3624
e-mail: slh@gml.lib.uwm.edu

Chicago Map Society, The
Newsletter: Mapline
60 West Walton St.
Chicago, IL 60610-7324
ph: 312-943-9090
web: http://www.newberry.org/smith/chicago.htm
Oldest map society in North America.

International Map Trade Association
P.O. Box 1789
Kankakee, IL 60901
ph: 815-939-4627
fax: 815-933-8320
e-mail: imta@maptrade.org
web: http://www.maptrade.org
Fostering and promoting the sales, usage, awareness and understanding of maps and map related products; for map retailers, map publishers, globe manufacturers, travel produce manufacturers, bookstores, educators and collectors.

Katherine R. Goodwin
Texas Map Society
c/o Special Collections Division
UTA Libraries
Arlington, TX 76019-0497
ph: 817-272-5329
fax: 817-272-3360
e-mail: goodwin@library.uta.edu
web: http://nicanor.acu.edu/~armstrongl/geography/txmapsoc.htm

William J. Warren
California Map Society
1109 Linda Glen Dr.
Pasadena, CA 91105
ph: 626-792-9152
fax: 626-568-4945
e-mail: wjwarren@aol.com
web: http://www.raremaps.com/cms/
Anyone with an interest in maps may join; members are mainly nonacademic types, many are collectors, some are dealers in maps and antiquarian books; two meetings per year and a quarterly newsletter.

Jenny Harvey
International Map Collectors Society
Journal: IMCoS Journal
27 Landford Rd.
Putney, London SW15 1AQ
U.K.
ph: +44 (0) 181 789 7358 or +44 (0) 135 469 2023
fax: +44 (0) 181 788 7819
e-mail: jeh@harvey27.demon.co.uk
web: http://www.harvey27.demon.co.uk/imcos/
Members from 22 countries worldwide who are a mix of collectors, academics, dealers and others who love old maps; members have access to important national and international map collections not normally available to the public.

Collectors

Norman D. Leckert
P.O. Box 363
Bethel, VT 05032-0363
ph: 802-234-5657 or 800-717-2021
fax: 802-234-6104
Wants pre-1900 atlases and maps.

Dealers

Siegfried Feller
Cartomania
8 Amherst Rd.
Amherst, MA 01002-9739
ph: 413-253-3115
Buys and sells maps and map related memorabilia.

Amherst Antiquarian Maps
P.O. Box 12
Amherst, MA 01004-0012
ph: 413-256-8900
fax: 413-256-6291
e-mail: navigateur@aol.com
General stock of antique maps and charts.

Reg Lombard
Lombard Antiquarian Maps & Prints
P.O. Box 281
Cape Elizabeth, ME 04107
ph: 207-799-1889
fax: 207-799-9593
e-mail: lamp@cybertours.com
web: http://www.cybertours.com/~lamp/
Specializes in fine maps, charts, rare botanical, natural history and architectural prints; also maps, prints, and books relating to Napoleon I.

G.B. Manasek, Inc.
P.O. Box 1204
Norwich, VT 05055
ph: 802-649-1722
fax: 802-649-2256
e-mail: manasekinc@aol.com
Buys maps and atlases from almost any region; also star maps, city plans and sea charts; folding (pocket), wall and roller maps of states, countries, continents and the world; offers appraisals on a fee-for-services basis.

Charles Neuschafer
New World Maps, Inc.
Apple Hill Road
Bennington, VT 05201-9544
ph: 802-442-2846
e-mail: maps@sover.net
web: http://pages.prodigy.com/maproom/
Buys and sells antique and collectible maps and charts; author of a column on map collecting in "Paper Collectors' Marketplace."

Christopher Watters
Cartographics of Vermont
P.O. Box 645
East Middlebury, VT 05740-0645
ph: 802-388-6229
e-mail: watters@middlebury.edu
Buys and sells all forms of separately issued 19th c. American maps including: wall and pocket maps, school exercise maps, family and school atlases, government and commercial publications related to exploration, games & quiz maps, etc.

Latitudes
P.O. Box 66
Essex, CT 06426-0066
ph: 860-767-3001 or 860-526-2100
Dealer/collector buys and sells unusual format maps (folding, strip, ribbon of rivers, canals), wall maps (CT & MA counties & entire US), harbor charts (USCS, Blunt, Eldridge, New England), coast pilot books, Nantucket, Block Island.

Lynn Vigeant
Maps of Antiquity
160 Midland Ave.
Montclair, NJ 07042
ph: 973-744-4364
Buys and sells historical, decorative maps, 19th century and earlier.

George D. Glazer
28 East 72nd St.
New York, NY 10021
ph: 212-535-5706
fax: 212-988-3992
e-mail: worldglobe@aol.com
web: http://www.georgeglazer.com
Buys and sells 19th century atlases and maps; emphasis is on United States; star and celestial charts; also American historical and color plate antiquarian books.

High Ridge Books, Inc.
P.O. Box 286
Rye, NY 10580
ph: 914-967-3332
fax: 914-967-6056
e-mail: highridg2@usa.pipeline.com
web: http://www.highridgebooks.com/
Wants to buy 19th century American cartography; atlases, wall maps, sea charts, pocket maps.

Michael Tokman
A-ha! Books, Inc.
3 Cedar Lane
Ithaca, NY 14850
ph: 607-257-9200
fax: 607-257-1540
e-mail: ahabooks@lightlink.com
web: http://www.lightlink.com/tokman/
Buys and sells rare, antiquarian and out-of-print books, autographs, and maps; online catalog, book search service.

James E. Hess
49 N. Water St.
P.O. Box 412
Lititz, PA 17543
ph: 717-626-5002
fax: 717-626-8858
e-mail: heritage@carto.com
web: http://www.carto.com
One of the largest map and atlas, and globe dealers in the world; buys, sells, collects, appraises.

James E. Hess
Heritage Map Museum
55 N. Water Street
Lititz, PA 17543
ph: 717-626-5002
fax: 717-626-8858]
e-mail: heritage@carto.com
web: http://www.carto.com
Buys, sells, auctions, and appraises 15th to 19th century maps, atlases, and globes; offers retail sales, appraisals, collections consultations, and quarterly international auctions.

Heritage Antique Maps
551 Christopher Ln.
Doylestown, PA 18901-3127
ph: 215-340-9662
fax: 215-340-9662
e-mail: maps1@HeritageAntiqueMaps.com
web: http://www.HeritageAntiqueMaps.com/
Interested in purchasing maps.

Christopher W. Lane
Philadelphia Print Shop, Ltd., The
8441 Germantown Ave.
Philadelphia, PA 19118
ph: 215-242-4750
fax: 215-242-6977
e-mail: PhilaPrint@PhilaPrintShop.com
web: http://www.philaprintshop.com
Buys, sells, appraises prints, maps, related rare books and atlases; also bookstore of reference books related to antique prints and maps; also paper conservation and restoration, museum quality framing.

Judith Blakely
Old Print Gallery, The
1220 31st St. NW
Washington, DC 20007-3422
ph: 202-965-1818
fax: 202-965-1869
e-mail: oldprintgallery@erols.com
web: http://www.oldprintgallery.com/
Wants antique maps and prints: American or foreign, 16th to 19th centuries.

Baldwin's Old Prints & Maps
P.O. Box 3515
Norfolk, VA 23514
ph: 757-625-1888
e-mail: maps@baldwinsmaps.com
web: http://www.baldwinsmaps.com/
Specializes in prints, maps and charts; U.S. Coast Survey charts, historical

prints, biblical/religious maps, U.S. Civil War maps, etc.

Luke & Patricia Vavra
Cartographic Arts
P.O. Box 2202
Petersburg, VA 23804-1502
ph: 804-861-6770
fax: 804-861-3021
e-mail: carto@dogstar.com
web: http://www.dogstar.com/carto/
Buys and sells only antique maps and charts; no reproductions.

Joel Kovarsky
Prime Meridian: Antique Maps & Books
385 Thistle Trail
Danville, VA 24540
ph: 804-799-0218
fax: 804-799-0218
e-mail: jsk@gamewood.net
web: http://www.bibliocity.com/home/PM
Buys and sells antiquarian maps and related books; specializes in southeastern USA and Africa; browsing and secured ordering available at online website.

Bernard Rogers, Jr.
Appalachian Arts
22 Swiss Lane
Blue Ridge, GA 30513
ph: 706-632-8974
fax: 706-632-8974
e-mail: aarts@athens.net
web: http://www.oldcharts.com
Specializes in 19th century antique state, city, and world maps, antique nautical charts, and antique decorative prints.

John Forster
Barometer Fair
P.O. Box 25502
Sarasota, FL 34277
ph: 941-923-6136
fax: 941-923-6136
e-mail: barometer@glimmer.com
Buys, sells, restores all antique barometers; also deals in antique maps, globes, compasses, telescopes and other scientific instruments.

Murray Hudson
Murray Hudson - Antiquarian Books, Maps, Prints & Globes
109 S. Church St.
P.O. Box 163
Halls, TN 38040-0163
ph: 901-836-9057 or 800-748-9946
fax: 901-836-9017
e-mail: mapman@usit.net
web: http://www.murrayhudson.com
Buys/sells pre-1900 antique maps (especially pocket, wall, Civil War and railroad maps) & books with maps (e.g. atlases, travel guides, geographies, land surveys, etc.); esp. of S.E. & S.W. US; also wants pre-1950 world globes.

Mary & George Ritzlin
George Ritzlin Maps & Prints
473 Roger Williams Ave.
Highland Park, IL 60035-4704
ph: 847-433-2627
fax: 847-433-6389
Buys and sells antique maps and atlases 1500-1900; cartographic references; books on early travel and exploration; pre-WWII Baedekers; illuminated medieval manuscripts; natural history prints; antique fashion plates.

Jonathan Blackman
Yellow Room, The
511 N. Robertson Blvd.
Los Angeles, CA 90048
ph: 310-274-3190
fax: 310-274-0129
e-mail: Globemeister@msn.com
web: http://www.telecomputers.com/globes/
Specializes in globes, maps and scientific instruments; great resource information on the website.

Barry Lawrence Ruderman
Barry Lawrence Ruderman Antique Maps
6141 Soledad Mountain Road
La Jolla, CA 92037
ph: 858-551-8500
fax: 858-456-4095
e-mail: blr@raremaps.com
web: http://www.raremaps.com/
Large Internet gallery featuring 15th through 19th century antique maps from all parts of the world, specializing in Americana.

Steve & Laurie Armistead
Deja View Antique Maps & Prints
P.O. Box 61722
Vancouver, WA 98666
ph: 360-696-3252
e-mail: sarmis@teleport.com
web: http://www.teleport.com/~sarmis/dejaview/index.htm
Specializes in antique maps and atlases.

Bruce Magnotti
Aesthetic Image
309 West Fifth Ave.
Ellensburg, WA 98926
ph: 509-962-5204
e-mail: aesthetic@tias.com
web: http://www.tias.com/stores/aesthetic/
Buys and sells rare prints, maps and illustrated books.

Alec Parley
Beach Antique Maps & Prints
3 Firstbrooke Road
Toronto, Ontario M4E 2L2
Canada
ph: 416-694-8119
fax: 416-694-2462
e-mail: beachmp@ican.net
web: http://home.ican.net/~beachmp/
Sells genuine engraved antique maps and prints dating from 1540 to 1895; every item in stock is over 100 years old.

Yasha Beresiner
InterCol Gallery
43 Templars Crescent
London, N3 3QR
U.K.
ph: 0181-349-2207 or 0171-354-2599
fax: 0181-346-9539
e-mail: yasha@compuserve.com
web: http://www.intercol.co.uk
Buys and sells world banknotes, all playing cards, old maps, related books on Free Masonry.

W.D.J. Bennett
Postaprint
Taidswood House
Iver Heath, Bucks SL0 0PQ
U.K.
ph: +44 1 895 833 720
fax: +44 1 895 834 890
e-mail: Postaprint@btinternet.com
web: http://www.postaprint.co.uk/
Antiquarian books, maps, prints, historic engravings, and atlases; has an online database of over 200,000 antique maps, steel, copper or wood engravings available for searching; items date from 1550 to 1899; library of scanned images.

Richard Nicholson
Richard Nicholson of Chester
Stoneydale, Pepper Street
Christleton
Chester, Cheshire CH3 7AG
U.K.
ph: (44)(1) 244 336004
fax: (44)(1) 244 336138
e-mail: richard@maps.u-net.com
web: http://www.antiquemaps.com
Large selection of antique maps of the British Isles and other parts of the world.

Experts

Charles Neuschafer
New World Maps, Inc.
Apple Hill Road
Bennington, VT 05201-9544
ph: 802-442-2846
e-mail: maps@sover.net
web: http://pages.prodigy.com/maproom/
Active dealer in antique and collectibles maps; belongs to several professional map associations; writes a regular column on maps for "Paper Collectors Marketplace."

Joke Vrijenhoek
Paulus Swaen Old Maps & Prints
P.O. Box 1238
Indian Rocks Beach, FL 33785
ph: 727-596-8734
fax: 727-596-8734
e-mail: paulus@swaen.com
web: http://www.swaen.com
Buys and sells old maps; conducts interactive map auctions on the Internet; offices in U.S. and The Netherlands.

Art-Emporium
Camford Square
Corner Douglas & Dorsey Sts.
milton, Queensland 4064
Australia
ph: +61 7 3368 2637
fax: +61 7 3368 2847
e-mail: printco@art-emporium.com
web: http://www.art-emporium.com/maps/
Website with great resource information on identifying and appraising Hummel figurines.

Museums/Libraries

David Cobb
Harvard Map Collection
Harvard College Library
Cambridge, MA 02138
ph: 617-495-2417
fax: 617-496-0440
e-mail: cobb@husc.harvard.edu
web: http://icg.harvard.edu/~maps/hpbms.htm
One of the largest and oldest collections of cartographic materials in the U.S.

James E. Hess
Heritage Map Museum
49 N. Water St.
P.O. Box 412
Lititz, PA 17543
ph: 717-626-5002
fax: 717-626-8858
e-mail: heritage@carto.com
web: http://www.carto.com
The only museum in the world dedicated to the 15th through 19th century original maps; a commercial enterprise, map services include auctioning, buying, selling, consulting and educational services.

Periodicals

Patrick M. O'Brien
Compass, The
Newsletter: Antique Map & Print Quarterly
P.O. Box 254
West Simsbury, CT 06092
ph: 860-651-5962
This free newsletter is designed to stimulate interest in the collection of antique maps and prints; articles, shows & exhibition schedules, map and chart values, free ads as space permits; write for information about a free subscription.

Edward D. Aster, Pub.
Aster Publishing Corporation
Magazine: Mercator's World
845 Williamette St.
Eugene, OR 97401-2918
ph: 800-840-3810 or 541-345-3800
fax: 541-302-9872
e-mail: edaster@westecpark.com
web: http://www.mercatormag.com
Examines the art, history, culture, and

science/technology of cartography, geography, and exploration—past and present; collecting maps, globes, charts; profiles explorers, adventurers, cartographers, navigators.

Repro. Sources

Lily Wall
American Dream Mall
3350 NW Boca Raton Blvd.
Boca Raton, FL 33431
ph: 800-431-7100
e-mail: custserv@americandreammall.com
web: http://www.americandreammall.com
Specializes in the sale of antique map reproductions.

Folding

Dealers

Paul Mahoney
Old Map Gallery, The
1746 Blake St.
Denver, CO 80202
ph: 303-296-7725
fax: 303-296-7725
e-mail: oldmapgallery@denver.net
web: http://www.oldmapgallery.com
Wants atlases and folding pocket maps.

Map Related Memorabilia

Clubs/Associations

Siegfried Feller
Association of Map Memorabilia Collectors
Newsletter: Cartomania
8 Amherst Rd.
Amherst, MA 01002-9739
ph: 413-253-3115
For collectors & lovers of maps: on postcards, stamps/envelopes, postmarks/cancels, labels, fabrics, trays/plates, etc.

MARBLE & STONE

(see also LAPIDARY; MINERAL SPECIMENS; NATURAL HISTORY; SCULPTURES)

Internet Resources

Walter S. Arnold
ph: 847-568-1188
fax: 847-568-1187
e-mail: walter@stonecarver.com
web: http://www.stonecarver.com/marble.html
An amazing website; everything you ever wanted to know about marble; hundreds of names of marbles within family groups and accompanying images; also marble history, tools, techniques and more.

Richard Zenobio
Natural-Stone.com
P.O. Box 1932
Paso Robles, CA 93447
ph: 805-237-9713
fax: 805-237-9713
e-mail: nstone@natural-stone.com
web: http://www.natural-stone.com
Internet marketplace for stone products, including materials, stone giftware, semi-precious stone knobs and accent tiles, fireplaces, etc.; information about the stone industry and stone companies; restoration products, sources, etc.

Periodicals

Alex Bachrach, Pub.
Magazine: Stone World
299 Market St., 3rd Floor
Saddle Brook, NJ 07663
ph: 201-291-9001
fax: 201-291-9002
e-mail: stoneworld@aol.com
web: http://www.stoneworld.com
The premier magazine for stone and tile related products and services; web sites has lots of links for stone and machinery suppliers.

Alex Bachrach, Pub.
Magazine: Contemporary Stone Design
299 Market St., 3rd Floor
Saddle Brook, NJ 07663
ph: 201-291-9001
fax: 201-291-9002
e-mail: stoneworld@aol.com
web: http://www.stoneworld.com

Repair Services

Absolute Granite & Restoration Co.
ph: 415-437-1966
fax: 650-637-1228
e-mail: absolutegranite@hotmail.com
web: http://www.datamania.com/AbsoluteGranite/
Marble fabrication and repair; specializing in the restoration of antique stone and terra-cotta.

Dimitri Nedelcu
Universal Fine Art Restoration
267 Derby Ave.
Orange, CT 06477-1319
ph: 203-795-8849
Museum quality restorations of marble/stone carvings: statuary, capitals and columns, ornamentation, compete fireplaces, reliefs, furniture, animals, busts; also repairs wood carvings, antiques, paintings.

David Modine
Jack T. Irwin, Inc.
601 East Gude Dr.
Rockville, MD 20852
ph: 301-762-5800
fax: 301-294-9726
Cuts and repairs marble tops.

Ron Leatherman
Leatherman Services
509 Mairo
Austin, TX 78748
ph: 512-282-1556 or 512-799-7871
fax: 512-282-1562
e-mail: ron@kdi.com
web: http://leathermanservices.com/
Restores marble, granite, miscellaneous stone, plaster and wood art objects, ornate picture frames, obsolete ceramic or porcelain tile; 25 years experience.

MARBLES

Auction Services

Robert S. Block
Block's Box
P.O. Box 51
Trumbull, CT 06611-0051
ph: 203-261-0057 or 203-926-8448
fax: 203-261-7033
e-mail: blockschip@aol.com
web: http://www.blocksite.com/
Conducts mail-bid and Internet auctions of marbles received from collectors, dealers, estates, museums and others; also conducts live Internet marble auctions.

Lloyd & Chris Huffer
Gold Medal Videos
Star Route
Damascus, PA 18415
ph: 570-224-4012
Conducts twice-yearly auctions by video.

Danny & Gretchen Turner
Running Rabbit Video Auctions
P.O. Box 701
Waverly, TN 37185-0701
ph: 931-296-3600
fax: 931-296-1732
e-mail: marbles@waverly.net
web: http://www.runningrabbit.com
Conducts marble mail auctions using VHS video tape/catalog or full color catalog. Quality marbles are shown on well-detailed 2 hr. tape. Excellent educational tool!

Clubs/Associations

Beverly Brule
Marble Collectors Unlimited
Newsletter: Marble Mart/Newsletter
P.O. Box 206
Northborough, MA 01532-0206
ph: 508-393-2923
The newsletter is published for and by members of MCU; contains items of interest such as meets, auctions, member buy/sell/trade ads, etc.

Stanley Block
Marble Collectors Society of America
Newsletter: Marble Mania
P.O. Box 222
Trumbull, CT 06611-0222
ph: 203-261-3223
e-mail: Blockschip@aol.com
web: http://blocksite.com/mcc/mcsa.htm
Established to gather and disseminate information and to perform services to further the hobby of marbles and marble collecting.

Jim Ridpath
National Marble Club of America
Newsletter: National Marble Club of America Newsletter
440 Eaton Rd.
Drexel Hill, PA 19026-1205
ph: 610-622-4444
To keep marble collectors informed, to encourage children to once again play the game, to advise members on all aspects of marbles including about books and publications about marbles and buying/selling marbles; offers appraisals.

Roger Dowdy
Blue Ridge Marble Club
Newsletter: Marble Circle News
2401 Brookmont Ct.
Richmond, VA 23233
ph: 804-754-8371
fax: 804-754-8379
e-mail: rdowdy-cp@mindspring.com
For collectors, dealers, and shooters.

Cape Fear Marble Club
1212-A Columbus Cr.
Wilmington, NC 28403

Brian Estepp
Buckeye Marble Collectors Club
Newsletter: BMC Newsletter
10380 Taylor Road SW
Reynoldsburg, OH 43068
ph: 614-863-5350
Active club sponsoring annual convention in Columbus, OH; newsletter contains articles, buy/sell ads, calendar of events, etc.

Tulsa Marble Collectors
5635 S. Quebec
Tulsa, OK 74135

Sherry Ellis
California Marble Collectors Society
Newsletter: Mainly Marbles
P.O. Box 6913
San Pedro, CA 90734-6913
ph: 310-548-4906
fax: 310-833-3892
e-mail: sellis9439@aol.com
Marble shows; buy, sell, trade antique and machine made marbles.

Larry Vandyke
Sea-Tac Marble Collectors Club
Newsletter: Marble Monitor
P.O. Box 793
Monroe, WA 98272
ph: 360-794-5266
e-mail: stmcc@marbleclub.com
web: http://www.marbleclub.com

Canadian Marble Collectors Association
10B Murdock St.
Georgetown, Ontario L7G 3L6
Canada

Collectors

Beverly Brule
P.O. Box 206
Northborough, MA 01532-0206
ph: 508-393-2923
Buy/sell/trade marbles and marble related items.

David & Becky Beane
Beane's Antiques & Photography
92 River Rd.
Benton, ME 04901
ph: 207-453-6790
fax: 207-453-6790
e-mail: dbeane@mint.net
web: http://www.metigues.com/catgalog/beane.html
Buys, sells and trades marbles; will travel for collections.

Jack Whistance
288 Rte. 28
Kingston, NY 12401
ph: 914-338-4397
Wants old handmade marbles: swirls, onion skins, Lutz, slags, opaques, micas, sulphides, etc.; also wants pre-1940's machine made marbles.

Tom Nelligan
Navarre Road
Canton, OH 44706
ph: 330-477-1032
e-mail: stratus@neo.rr.com
web: http://home.neo.rr.com/marbles/
Marble collector would be happy to help anyone who needs information.

Yvonne Marie Holmberg
7229 Pine Island Dr., NE
Comstock Park, MI 49321-9534
ph: 616-784-1715
Wants to buy all pre-1940 glass marbles except sulphides; pays full current market value.

Bill Tinkcom
2406 West Madison
Sioux Falls, SD 57104
ph: 605-331-5740
Wants to buy all kinds of marbles and marble type items such as marble games and old time marble boxes or bags.

Dealers

Bertram M. Cohen
Great American Co.
169 Marlborough St.
Boston, MA 02116-1830
ph: 617-247-4754
fax: 617-247-9093
e-mail: marblebert@aol.com
web: http://members.aol.com/marblebert/
Marbles bought and sold, especially "art glass" marbles; also wants postcards showing children playing with marbles; organizes the Northeast Marble Meet in October of each year (Columbus Day weekend).

Bill Sweet
P.O. Box 4736
Rumford, RI 02916-0736
ph: 401-434-4548
Marble dealer, collector and appraiser.

Jerry Biern
Rare Marbles, etc.
65 Crest Drive
Cranston, RI 02921-3313
ph: 401-826-3933
fax: 401-826-4460
e-mail: raremarble@aol.com
Buys and sells rare, antique marbles; free appraisals backed with data from previous sales.

Kevin Stump
P.O. Box 237
Merrimack, NH 03054
e-mail: Kevin_Stump@hotmail.com
web: http://www.angelfire.com/ct/marbles/index.html
Buys and sells antique and collectible marbles.

Ardyth & John Stimson
AJS Marbles & Records
P.O. Box 8052
Glen Ridge, NJ 07028
e-mail: ajs@viconet.com
Buys, sells, collects machine-made or antique marbles; will trade, buy or sell; also deals in old records, especially jazz, R&B, 33/45/778 rpm.

Charles Eson
Hawkeye Collectibles
128 Western Ave.
Altamont, NY 12009
ph: 578-861-6256
Buys and sells antique and machine made collectible marbles; also sells plastic display cases for marbles and other collectibles.

Gloria Munsell
Allenwood Americana Antiques
P.O. Box 116
Allenwood, PA 17810-0116
ph: 570-538-1440
Buying and selling marbles and marble games, etc.

Elliot Pincus
Elliot's Marbles
P.O. Box C
Jenkintown, PA 19046
ph: 215-886-7421

Wayne E. Sanders
2202 Livingston St.
Jefferson City, MO 65109-0850
ph: 573-636-7515
Buys, sells and collect antique handmade marbles and collectible machine-made marbles; no contemporary marbles; looking for single ribbon cores, clouds and unusual or colored figure sulphides; send $1 for list of marbles for sale.

Michael A. Pratt, Sr.
Marble Emporium, The
687 Co. Rd. ""U""
Rt. 2 Box 73
Fremont, NE 68025-9635
ph: 402-721-4765
fax: 402-721-4765
e-mail: mp@mb3.net
web: http://www.mb3.net/display/
Buys and sells marbles of all kinds; also sells display cases for cuff links and collectibles of all types.

Dan Packard
Lone Star Marbles & Collectibles
125 Remington Hills
Eustace, TX 75124
ph: 903-479-3644
fax: 903-479-3644
e-mail: lsmc125@aol.com
web: http://packards.com/page11.html
Contemporary art glass marbles is their specialty, but they also carry a large selection of antique marbles both handmade and machine-made; carries contemporary art glass marbles from over 75 artisans worldwide.

Experts

Stanley & Bob Block
Block's Box
P.O. Box 51
Trumbull, CT 06611-0051
ph: 203-261-0057 or 203-926-8448
fax: 203-261-7033
e-mail: blockschip@aol.com
web: http://www.blocksite.com/
Buys, sells, and specializes in marbles; experts on identification and valuation of marbles; offers 18-page list of marbles currently available; send LSASE with 52 cents postage.

Cathy C. Runyan
Marble Lady, The
7812 N.W. Hampton Rd.
Kansas City, MO 64152-4940
ph: 816-587-8687
fax: 816-587-8687
e-mail: marbleldy@aol.com
Author of "Knuckles Down - A Fun Guide to Marble Play"; helps people identify & value their marbles; also teaches, demonstrates & lectures about marbles and marble playing; interested in handmades, machine made, and marble memorabilia.

Larry Castle
Castle Fair
3387 Polk Ave.
Ogden, UT 84403
ph: 801-393-8131
e-mail: marblelc8@aol.com
Advanced collector and nationally recognized expert with over 10 years experience with marbles; buys, appraises and repairs marbles.

Internet Resources

Stanley & Bob Block
Marble Collectors Corner
P.O. Box 51
Trumbull, CT 06611-0051
ph: 203-261-0057 or 203-926-8448
fax: 203-261-7033
e-mail: blockschip@aol.com
web: http://www.blocksite.com/
An information and exchange center for anyone who is interested in marble collecting, marble making or marble playing; tons of information.

Repair Services

Larry Castle
Castle Fair
3387 Polk Ave.
Ogden, UT 84403
ph: 801-393-8131
e-mail: marblelc8@aol.com
Restores and regrinds glass marbles; over ten years experience and more that 6000 marbles restored.

Suppliers

Michael Cosentino
Marble Show-Case
6936 N. Overhill Ave.
Chicago, IL 60631
fax: 773-594-9479
e-mail: mikecoz@aol.com
web: http://marbleshowcase.com/
Sells display cases for marbles and other small collectibles; also sells and appraises marbles.

Michael A. Pratt, Sr.
Marble Emporium, The
687 Co. Rd. ""U""
Rt. 2 Box 73
Fremont, NE 68025-9635
ph: 402-721-4765
fax: 402-721-4765
e-mail: mp@mb3.net
web: http://www.mb3.net/display/
Manufactures unique inexpensive cases to display, organize, and protect small collectibles of all types including marbles; send SASE for more information.

MARDI GRAS ITEMS

Collectors

Michael Reese II
P.O. Box 5704
South San Francisco, CA 94083-5704
ph: 415-641-5920
e-mail: creole@shutmymouth.com
web: http://www.shutmymouth.com
Wants anything relating to New Orleans ad Mardi Gras: invitations, medals, call out gifts, etc.

New Orleans

Collectors

Marilyn & Celeste Bordelon
1750 St. Charles Ave., Ste. 303
New Orleans, LA 70130
ph: 504-596-6550
Wants to buy pre-1950 New Orleans Mardi Gras items: ball invitations, dance cards, admit, newspaper print of floats, carnival bulletins, programs, pendants, pins, buttons, favors, postcards, medal or rhinestone badges.

Experts

Arthur Hardy
Arthur Hardy Enterprises, Inc.
602 Metairie Rd., Ste. C
Metairie, LA 70005-4009
ph: 504-838-6111
fax: 504-838-0100
e-mail: mardihardy@aol.com
web: http://mardigrasneworleans.com/arthur/
Buys, collects and specializes in Mardi Gras memorabilia such as ball invitations, post cards, carnival bulletins (parade papers), photos, illustrated feature articles, brochures, etc.; author of the annual "Mardi Gras Guide."

Museums/Libraries

Mardi Gras World
23 Newton St.
New Orleans, LA 70114
ph: 504-361-7821 or 800-362-8213
e-mail: briankern@mardigrasworld.com
web: http://www.mardigrasworld.com/

Periodicals

Arthur Hardy
Arthur Hardy Enterprises, Inc.
Magazine: Arthur Hardy's Mardi Gras Guide
602 Metairie Rd., Ste. C
Metairie, LA 70005-4009
ph: 504-838-6111
fax: 504-838-0100
e-mail: mardihardy@aol.com
web: http://mardigrasneworleans.com/arthur/
Published annually on December 31st: Mardi Gras history, stories about collectibles, interviews, parade routes, etc.

Arthur Hardy
Arthur Hardy Enterprises, Inc.
Newsletter: Arthur Hardy's Carnival Times Newsletter
602 Metairie Rd., Ste. C
Metairie, LA 70005-4009
ph: 504-838-6111
fax: 504-838-0100
e-mail: mardihardy@aol.com
web: http://mardigrasneworleans.com/arthur/

MARINE ARTIFACTS

(see NAUTICAL ANTIQUES)

MARINE CORPS ITEMS

Collectors

Dick Weisler
53-07 213th St.
Flushing, NY 11364-1823
ph: 718-428-9829 or 718-626-7110
fax: 718-726-2011
Wants recruiting posters, sheet music, belt buckles, cigarette lighters, steins, trucks, toy soldiers, documents, trench art, etc.

Stan Clark
915 Fairview Ave.
Gettysburg, PA 17325-2905
ph: 717-337-1728
fax: 717-337-0581
Wants Marine Corps items: books (unit histories, memoirs, campaigns, etc.), postcards, tapestries, recruiting, letters, documents, embroideries, prints, photographs, scrap books, toy soldiers, etc.

Bruce Updegrove
52 Woodside Lane
Boyertown, PA 19512
ph: 610-369-1798
Interested in pre-1946 Marine Corps items; also want women's uniforms of WWII.

LtCol J.K. Williams, USMC (Ret'd.)
6025 Makely Dr.
Fairfax Station, VA 22039-1324
ph: 703-250-8421 or 202-371-8880
fax: 202-371-8258
Wants U.S. Marine Corps WWI-era recruiting posters, photos, bus/trolley cards, tin signs, brochures, advertisements, etc.

Harold Dylhoff
23511 Paulson's Rd.
Gobles, MI 49055-8651
ph: 616-628-4051
e-mail: hdylxrds@aol.com
Wants to buy letters and postal history from U.S. Marine Corp (WWI through WWII), including postmarks from bases, camps and other locations; send photocopies and LSASE for reply.

MARIONETTES

(see PUPPETS)

MARITIME ANTIQUES

(see NAUTICAL ANTIQUES)

MASCOTS

(see AUTOMOBILIA, Hood Ornaments)

MATCH SAFES

(see also CIGARETTE COLLECTIBLES; CIGAR STORE COLLECTIBLES; LIGHTERS; MATCHBOXES & LABELS; MATCHCOVERS; TOBACCO COLLECTIBLES)

Clubs/Associations

George Sparacio
International Match Safe Association
Newsletter: IMSA Newsletter
P.O. Box 791
Malaga, NJ 08328-0791
ph: 856-694-4167
fax: 856-694-4536
e-mail: IMSAoc@aol.com
FOcuses on pocket match safes; newsletter published quarterly; annual meetings featuring buying/selling session, information and networking opportunities.

Collectors

George Sparacio
P.O. Box 791
Malaga, NJ 08328-0791
ph: 856-694-4167
fax: 856-694-4536
e-mail: mrvesta1@aol.com
web: http://members.aol.com/mrvesta2/
Buys, sells and trades pocket match safes; especially interested in fancy, figural and unusual match safes; also interested in pre-1915 match safe related catalogs, advertisements and ephemera; will answer all correspondence.

Dealers

Lenore Monleon
33 Fifth Ave.
New York, NY 10003-4338
ph: 212-475-7871 or 212-675-7771
Wants enamel and sterling match safes and cigarette boxes.

MATCHBOOKS

(see MATCHCOVERS)

MATCHBOXES

(see also MATCHCOVERS; MATCH SAFES; TOYS, Diecast [Matchbox])

Clubs/Associations

Linda Clavette
New Moon Matchbox & Label Club
Newsletter: New Moon News
P.O. Box 192
Cascade, MD 21719-0192
e-mail: Clavette@mail.cvn.net
Newsletter is published 5 times per year.

Collectors

Fredrik Karlsson
Sweden
e-mail: fredrik.karlsson@ida.utb.hb.se
web: http://enterprise.hb.se/~match/
Collects Swedish match related items such as matchboxes, matchbox labels, match holders and match related literature.

MATCHCOVERS

(see also MATCHBOXES; MATCH SAFES; PAPER COLLECTIBLES)

Clubs/Associations

Ellen Gutting, Membr.
Liberty Bell Matchcover Club
Newsletter: Liberty Bell Crier
5001 Albridge Way
Mount Laurel, NJ 08054-2652
ph: 609-231-4602
Members are interested in the collecting of matchcovers & matchboxes; hosts annual national convention; holds shows, auctions, bi-monthly meetings with displays and trading.

Bill Retskin
American Matchcover Collecting Club, The
Journal: Front Striker Bulletin, The
P.O. Box 18481
Asheville, NC 28814-0481
ph: 828-254-4487
fax: 828-254-1066
e-mail: bill@matchcovers.com
web: http://www.matchcovers.com
Devoted to the study and collecting of older matchcovers; the publication includes a matchcover mail auction and covers history and current status of the matchbook industry as well as the matchcover collecting hobby.

Terry Rowe, Mem.
Rathkamp Matchcover Society
Newsletter: RMS Bulletin
432 N. Main St.
Urbana, OH 43078-1608
e-mail: rmsed@psyber.com
web: http://www.psyber.com/~rmsed/
Membership is open to all matchcover and matchbox collectors; annual

convention, six bulletins per year, tips, list of local clubs, web page ads.

Annie Johnson
Windy City Matchcover Club
Newsletter: Windy City Matchcover News
257 E. First St., Apt. 4
Elmhurst, IL 60126
e-mail: Ltlb1t@aol.com

Nancy Bailey
Angelus Matchcover Club
12707 Montague St.
Pacoima, CA 91331-4138
e-mail: sjbnab@aol.com
Publishes bi-monthly newsletter.

Emily Hiller, Treas.
Long Beach Matchcover Club
Newsletter: Matchcover Beachcomber
2501 West Sunflower, H-5
Santa Ana, CA 92704-7503
ph: 714-540-8220
fax: 714-252-5265

Mike Prero
Sierra-Diablo Matchcover Club
12659 Echard Way
Auburn, CA 95603
fax: 978-389-0396
e-mail: Rmsed@psyber.com
web: http://www.psyber.com/~rmsed/sierra/
Second largest regional matchcover club in the country; monthly color newsletter.

Richard W. Lauck
Pacific Northwest Matchcover Collector's Club
9424 Odin Way
Bothell, WA 98011-1164
ph: 425-486-4501
e-mail: rlauck@halcyon.com
web: http://www.halcyon.com/rlauck/pnmcc.html
Membership is open to all collectors of matchcovers, matchboxes, and matchbooks.

Jerry Craig
Trans-Canada Matchcover Club
44 Invermarge Dr.
Scarborough, Ontario M1C 3M4
Canada

Arthur Alderton, Mem.
British Matchbox Label & Booklet Society
122 High Street
Melbourn, Cambridgeshire SG8 6AL
U.K.
e-mail: de9531@ida.utb.hb.se
web: http://enterprise.shv.hb.se/~match/bmfl&bs/

Collectors

Joe DeGennaro
309 East 87th St., Apt. 6E
New York, NY 10128
ph: 212-876-1730 or 212-975-4108
fax: 212-975-8424
e-mail: jtdegennaro@cbs.com

Marc Edelman
882 Hargrave St.
Philadelphia, PA 19152-1511
ph: 215-969-6258
e-mail: matchman@gateway.net

Mike Landis
P.O. Box 814
Adamstown, PA 19501
ph: 888-248-2291
e-mail: landis2@desupernet.net
Buys and sells matchcovers; full books and especially feature matches; call toll free.

John C. Williams
1359 Surrey Rd., Dept. CH
Vandalia, OH 45377-1646
ph: 937-890-8684

Calvin J. Meider
441 Lake St.
Excelsior, MN 55331-1901
ph: 651-926-2142

Dean Hodgdon
2920 E. 77th St.
Tulsa, OK 74136-8723
ph: 918-494-0225 or 918-665-6512
e-mail: d.hodgdon@worldnet.att.net
web: http://home.att.net/~d.hodgdon

Neil Hospers
4000 Edgehill Rd.
Fort Worth, TX 76116
ph: 817-738-8181

Susan Cox
800 Murray Dr.
El Cajon, CA 92020
ph: 619-697-5922
e-mail: antiqfever@aol.com
Wants to buy matches, book type, old only; matches inside, unused and boxes a plus; good condition.

Mike Prero
12659 Eckard Way
Auburn, CA 95603
fax: 978-389-0396
e-mail: Rmsed@psyber.com

Richard W. Lauck
9424 Odin Way
Bothell, WA 98011-1164
ph: 425-486-4501
e-mail: rlauck@halcyon.com
web: http://www.halcyon.com/rlauck/pnmcc.html
Wants to buy 1930s to 1950s matchcovers and matchbooks.

Experts

Bill Retskin
P.O. Box 18481
Asheville, NC 28814-0481
ph: 828-254-4487
fax: 828-254-1066
e-mail: bill@matchcovers.com
web: http://www.matchcovers.com
Author of "The Matchcover Resource Book and Price Guide," and "The Matchcover Collectors Price Guide - 1st Edition."

Wray Martin
221 Upper Paradise
Hamilton, Ontario L9C 5C1
Canada
ph: 905-383-0454

Casino

Clubs/Associations

Richard D. Hagerman
Casino Matchcover Collectors Club
Newsletter: Gambling Gazette
5001 Albridge Way
Mount Laurel, NJ 08054-2652
ph: 609-231-4602
Members are dedicated to the collection of all casino and gaming establishment matchbooks and matchboxes which are displayed and traded at regular meetings throughout the US and Canada; monthly newsletter.

Collectors

Richard D. Hagerman
5001 Albridge Way
Mount Laurel, NJ 08054-2652
ph: 609-231-4602
Buys older matchcovers from Atlantic City hotels, restaurants; and Atlantic City businesses other than casinos.

MATCHING SERVICES

(see DINNERWARE; FLATWARE; GLASS, Elegant; GLASS, Crystal)

MAYTAG

(see also WASHING MACHINES)

Clubs/Associations

Mark A. Shulaw
Maytag Collectors Club Eastern Division
452 County Road 33
Bluffton, OH 45817-9601
ph: 419-358-7076
e-mail: frappi@wcoil.com
A chapter of the national Maytag Collectors Club; dedicated to the preservation and restoration of all types of Maytag items, anything built by Maytag.

Nate & Charlene Stoller
Maytag Collectors Club
Newsletter: Maytag Collectors Club Newsletter
960 Reynolds Dr.
Ripon, CA 95366
ph: 209-956-5244 or 209-529-5300
e-mail: nate@maytagclub.com
web: http://www.maytagclub.com/
Over 250 members nationwide collecting all types of Maytag items; lots of ads for Maytag engines, meat grinders, washers, new and used parts, gaskets, replacement decals, etc.

Collectors

Tom Copper
Tom's Small Engines
1416 Ralapen St.
Roxboro, NC 27573-4232
ph: 336-599-6908
e-mail: tcopper@interpath.com
web: http://home.interpath.net/tcopper/
Collector of Maytag, Briggs & Stratton and other engines; repairs, rebuilds, and restores most small engines; locates parts and/or related supplies and services.

Les Parker
1513 Hanover St.
Raleigh, NC 27608
ph: 919-828-1221

Mark A. Shulaw
452 County Road 33
Bluffton, OH 45817-9601
ph: 419-358-7076
e-mail: frappi@wcoil.com
Buying anything Maytag: cans, engines, washer accessories, literature, tools, new old stock and used engine parts, promotional items, almost anything that is Maytag; will answer questions; please send SASE with inquiries.

Man./Prod./Dist.

Orville Butler, Hist.
Maytag Company Archives
1 Dependability Sq.
Newton, IA 50208
ph: 515-792-7000
fax: 515-791-8793
Private company archives include paper artifacts, production records, old catalogs; will help identify or date your Maytag machine.

Museums/Libraries

Hans J. Brosig, Dir.
Maytag Exhibit, Jasper County Historical Museum
1700 South 15th Ave. West
P.O. Box 834
Newton, IA 50208-0834
ph: 515-792-9118
A museum about Jasper County, Iowa; contains a large artifact collection of the Maytag Company: washing machines, seed cleaners, ironers,

dryers, advertising & promotional items.

Suppliers

Simpson Motors
3708 S. Amherst Hwy.
Madison Heights, VA 24572
ph: 804-929-4468
New and used Maytag engine parts, restoration supplies, engines, etc.; rebuild, restore, supply parts for early gasoline engines that powered early washing machines; no appliance parts; makes parts not otherwise available.

MEDALLIC SCULPTURES

(see also MEDALS, ORDERS & DECORATIONS; SCULPTURES)

Auction Services

Bob Slawsky
P.O. Box 864
Windermere, FL 34786-0864
ph: 407-352-7807
fax: 407-352-BIDS
e-mail: WWGD54A@prodigy.com
Buys, sells, auctions tokens, medals, badges, small advertising items, political, World's Fair, Olympic items, encased coins, etc.

Clubs/Associations

American Medallic Sculpture Association
Newsletter: Members Exchange
56 North Plant Road, Ste. 1-685
Newburgh, NY 12550
e-mail: info@amsamedals.org
web: http://www.amsamedals.org/
A group of sculptors, collectors, suppliers, producers and scholars interested in high relief medallic sculptures; annual exhibitions; newsletter published bi-monthly, "Medallic Sculpture" magazine published annually.

MEDALS

(see BADGES; COINS & CURRENCY; MEDALS, ORDERS & DECORATIONS; MILITARIA, Insignia; RELIGIOUS COLLECTIBLES; TOKENS; VETERAN ITEMS)

MEDALS, ORDERS & DECORATIONS

(see also HISTORICAL AMERICANA; MEDALLIC SCULPTURES; VETERAN ITEMS; MILITARIA; MILITARIA, Russian; TOKENS)

Auction Services

David M. Gale
C & D Gale
2404 Berwyn Rd.
Wilmington, DE 19810-3525
ph: 302-478-0872
fax: 302-478-6866
e-mail: cdgale@dol.net
web: http://www.cdgale.com/catalog/exonumia.htm
Conducts mail bid auctions of medals, tokens, religious items, trade checks, miscellaneous items, Civil War tokens and other exonumia; issues fixed-price exonumia catalogs.

Jeffrey B. Floyd
Floyd, Johnson & Paine, Inc.
P.O. Box 9791
Alexandria, VA 22304-0469
ph: 703-461-9582
fax: 703-461-3059
e-mail: fjp4floyd@aol.com
Conducts four sales per year of orders, medals and decorations.

Floyd, Johnson & Paine, Inc.
6427 W. Irving Park Rd., Ste. 160
Chicago, IL 60634-2437
ph: 312-777-0499

Roy Butler
Wallis & Wallis
West Street Auction Galleries
Lewes, East Sussex BN7 2NJ
U.K.
ph: 01273-480208
fax: 01273-476562
e-mail: wallisandwallis@mcmail.com
web: http://www.wallisandwallis.co.uk/
Britain's specialist auctioneers of arms, armor, militaria and military orders.

Spink & Son, Ltd.
5-7 King St.
St. James's, London SW1Y 6QS
U.K.
ph: 0171 930 7888
fax: 0171 839 4853
web: http://www.auctions.co.uk/antique/spink.htm
Auctioneers and dealers of coins (ancient to present), medals, orders, tokens, decorations and other numismatic items.

Clubs/Associations

Mr. Leslie A. Elam, Dir.
American Numismatic Society, The
Newsletter: American Numismatic Society Newsletter, The
Broadway at 155th St.
New York, NY 10003
ph: 212-234-3130
e-mail: info@amnumsoc.org
web: http://www.amnumsoc2.org/index.htm
Has a major collection of American coins in addition to major and important collections of ancient, Latin American, Islamic, European, and other material; also publishes "American Journal of Numismatics" and "Numismatic Literature."

David E. Schenkman, Ed.
Token & Medal Society
Journal: Token & Medal Society Journal
P.O. Box 366
Bryantown, MD 20617-0366
ph: 301-274-3441
e-mail: turtlehill@olg.com
Promotes and stimulates "exonumia", the study of non-government issue tokens and medals; an organization of collectors and researchers of tokens, medals and related items.

Edward C. Rochette, ExDir
American Numismatic Association
Magazine: Numismatist, The
818 N. Cascade Ave.
Colorado Springs, CO 80903-3279
ph: 719-632-2646 or 800-367-9723
fax: 719-634-4085
e-mail: nulty@money.org
web: http://www.money.org
Worldwide assoc. of collectors of coins, paper money, medals and tokens; over 30,000 members; offers collector services and benefits.

Cameron Ward
Canadian Society of Military Medals & Insignia
Journal: Journal, The
64 Edgemont St. South
Hamilton, Ontario L8K 2H5
Canada
ph: 905-547-1815 or 905-547-8293

General Secretary
Orders & Medals Research Society
123 Turnpike Link
Croydon, CRO 5NU
U.K.
e-mail: phil@ihug.co.nz
web: http://homepages.ihug.co.nz/~phil/omrs.htm
Promotes and fosters a general interest in the study of orders, decorations and medals and all matter related thereto; assists members in their researches.

Collectors

Stanley Steinberg
P.O. Box 8733
Lowell, MA 01853-8733
Wants tokens and all engraved awards and medals: military, political, merchant advertising, agriculture, schools & colleges, historical, city and town, associations, expositions, lifesaving awards, etc.

Dr. Paul Rohe
P.O. Box 122
Martinville, NJ 08336-0122

Howard Averbach
1919 Delaware Ave.
Pittsburgh, PA 15218-1801
ph: 412-441-6904
Wants to buy quality U.S. Military campaign medals and decorations; no reproductions.

Rickie Marquette
P.O. Box 343133
Homestead, FL 33034-0133
ph: 305-246-5431 or 305-245-2323
fax: 305-245-9295
Wants to buy American medals and orders, especially named and/or numbered pieces, valor awards, and Southern Crosses of Honor.

Jerome Schaeper, Jr.
705 Philadelphia St.
Covington, KY 41011-1252
ph: 606-581-3729
Collects, appraises United Confederate reunion badges, WWI homecoming medals and Civil War dog tags.

Alan Harrow
2292 Chelan Dr.
Los Angeles, CA 90068-2621
ph: 323-874-3474
Primarily interested in military campaign and gallantry medals of most countries, especially US and Great Britain, as well as related documents; also wants civilian medals for heroism.

Dealers

Peter Hlinka
Peter Hlinka Historical Americana
P.O. Box 310
New York, NY 10028-0017
ph: 718-409-6407
Buys, sells, and appraises historical Americana; publishes a large catalog of militaria, war medals, military insignia, war relics, related books, and other historical Americana; also foreign.

Medals of America
1929 Fairview Road
Fountain Inn, SC 29644
ph: 800-308-0849
e-mail: ffoster@usmedals.com
web: http://www.usmedals.com
One of America's largest insignia dealers: all US military badges, medals, patches, and books; publishes an annual catalog of items for sale.

Steve Johnson
Steve Johnson Medals & Militaria
P.O. Box 4706
Aurora, IL 60507
ph: 630-851-0744
fax: 630-851-0866
Large dealer; issues 3 to 4 catalogs per year.

Dan Farek
P.O. Box 1212
Bellaire, TX 77402-1212
ph: 713-666-2629
fax: 713-666-2629
e-mail: danjfa@swbell.net
Dealer in military medals of the

world; issues list of items for sale for $8/yr.; sample list $1.

Cy Phillips, Jr.
S C Coin & Stamp Co. Inc.
P.O. Drawer 661180
Arcadia, CA 91066-1180
ph: 818-445-8277 or 800-367-0779
fax: 818-445-8278
Tokens, medals, coins, currency, badges, expo. and fair items, scrap gold and silver.

Sydney Vernon
P.O. Box 890280
Temecula, CA 92589-0280
ph: 909-698-1646
fax: 909-698-7091
e-mail: svernon@aol.com
web: http://home.earthlink.net/~svernon/
Dealer since 1967 in orders, medals and decorations of the world; both military and civilian.

Sydney Vernon
P.O. Box 890280
Temecula, CA 92589-0280
ph: 909-698-1646
fax: 909-698-7091
e-mail: svernon@inland.net
web: http://home.earthlink.net/~svernon/
Dealer in orders, medals & decorations since 1967; offers hundreds of items, including books, in mail order sales catalogs 5 to 6 times each year.

S.G. Yasinitsky
Medal Exchange, The
P.O. Box 777
Millbrae, CA 94030-0777
e-mail: omsa1@ix.netcom.com
Appraiser, dealer and specialist in medals, orders and decorations; founder of the Orders & Medals Society of America; writer of numerous articles on the subject.

Ackley Unlimited
P.O. Box 82144
Portland, OR 97282-0144
ph: 503-659-4681
fax: 503-659-4681
Buys, sells, trades orders, decorations and medals.

Michael Rice
Michael Rice Collectibles
P.O. Box 286
Saanichton, British Columbia V8M 2C5
Canada
ph: 250-652-9412
e-mail: mrice@pacificcoast.net
Wants pre-1946 medals and badges from all English speaking countries; military (except US), fraternal, sports, academic, memberships, etc.; approvals or photocopies welcome; will make offer; send 2 stamps to ensure reply; call evenings.

Madeline Colman
Southern Medals
16 Broom Grove
Knebworth, Herts. SG3 6BQ
U.K.
ph: 01438 811657
fax: 01438 813320
e-mail: crcolman@globalnet.co.uk
web: http://www.blacklight.co.uk/southernmedals.htm
Buys and sells medals, orders and decorations: campaign, gallantry, casualty, long service, miniatures, WWI, WWII, foreign.

Experts

Jeffrey B. Floyd
P.O. Box 9791
Alexandria, VA 22304-0469
ph: 703-461-9582
fax: 703-461-3059
e-mail: fjp4floyd@aol.com
Buys, sells, trades, specializes in all military medals & decorations; specializing in Imperial German, British and American awards; all periods.

Sydney Vernon
P.O. Box 890280
Temecula, CA 92589-0280
ph: 909-698-1646
fax: 909-698-7091
e-mail: svernon@aol.com
web: http://home.earthlink.net/~svernon/
Author of "Vernon's Collectors' Guide to Medals & Decorations" III edition; catalog of Orders, Medals & Decorations available for a subscription fee.

Sydney Vernon
P.O. Box 890280
Temecula, CA 92589-0280
ph: 909-698-1646
fax: 909-698-7091
e-mail: svernon@inland.net
web: http://home.earthlink.net/~svernon/
Author of "Vernon's Collectors' Guide to Orders, Medals & Decorations (with valuations," and "The Medal Collector's Companion."

S.G. Yasinitsky
Medal Exchange, The
P.O. Box 777
Millbrae, CA 94030-0777
e-mail: omsa1@ix.netcom.com
Appraiser, dealer and specialist in medals, orders and decorations; founder of the Orders & Medals Society of America; writer of numerous articles on the subject.

Museums/Libraries

Edward C. Rochette, ExDir
Museum of the American Numismatic Association
Magazine: Numismatist, The
818 N. Cascade Ave.
Colorado Springs, CO 80903-3279
ph: 719-632-2646 or 800-367-9723
fax: 719-634-4085
e-mail: nulty@money.org
web: http://www.money.org
A museum collection including 400,000 items; collection includes medals, orders and decorations from all countries and time periods.

John Langton, Jr.
Military Medal Museum & Research Center
448 N. San Pedro St.
San Jose, CA 95110-2232
ph: 408-298-1100
Send for free "History of the U.S.S. Washington" of WWII fame.

Periodicals

Token Publishing, Ltd.
Magazine: Medal News
P.O. Box 14
Honiton, Devon EX14 9YP
U.K.
ph: +44 1404 46972
fax: +44 1404 381895
e-mail: info@medal-news.com
web: http://www.medal-news.com/
A monthly English publication focusing on military history, medals, and badge collecting.

British

Collectors

Phil Froom
U.K.
ph: (44) 411 415616
e-mail: PhilFroom@compuserve.com
Wants to buy British campaign medals and decorations; from Waterloo to the Falklands and Gulf wars.

Medal of Honor

Clubs/Associations

Ronald D. Drake, Ex. Dir.
Congressional Medal of Honor Society, The
40 Patriots Point Rd.
Mount Pleasant, SC 29464
ph: 843-884-8662
fax: 843-884-1471
e-mail: medal@awod.com
web: http://www.awod.com/gallery/probono/cmhs/

Museums/Libraries

National Medal of Honor Museum of Military History
400 Georgia Ave.
Chattanooga, TN 37403
ph: 423-267-1737
fax: 423-266-7771
e-mail: dsmith0344@worldnet.att.net
web: http://www.smoky.com/medalofhonor/

MEDICAL, DENTAL & PHARMACEUTICAL

(see also BOOKS, Medical & Dental; CIVIL WAR ARTIFACTS, Medical; EYE RELATED ITEMS; HEALTH & BEAUTY; INSTRUMENTS & DEVICES, Scientific; OPTICAL ITEMS; STAMP COLLECTING, Medical; VETERINARY MEDICINE ITEMS)

Appraisers

Peggy Landt
LHL Services
9065 La Serena Drive
Fair Oaks, CA 95628
ph: 916-962-0592
e-mail: peggy@jps.net
Complete soda fountain and pharmacy appraisal services.

Clubs/Associations

Dr. M. Donald Blaufox, MD, PhD
Medical Collectors Association
Newsletter: Medical Collectors Newsletter
Montefiore Medical Park
1695 A Eastchester Rd., #1695A
Bronx, NY 10461-2374
ph: 718-405-8454
fax: 718-824-0625
e-mail: blaufox@aecom.un.edu
The association meets once a year and issues its newsletter semi-annually.

John Ptak
Maryland Microscopical & Scientific Instrument Society
1531 33rd St. NW
Washington, DC 20007
ph: 202-337-0945
fax: 202-234-3511
e-mail: jfptak@access.digex.net
web: http://www.access.dignex.net/~jfptak
Focuses on instruments and devices; medical, surveying, photographic, microscopical, navigational, horological, astronomical, etc.

Collectors

Norman B. Meadow
225 E. 64th St.
New York, NY 10021
ph: 212-628-0032
Wants pre-1900 medical and surgical instruments or medical books; all specialties: eye, obstetrics, surgery,

ear, dental, etc.; one instrument or an operating room full.

Dr. Allan Wissner
P.O. Box 102
Ardsley, NY 10502-0102
ph: 914-693-4628
e-mail: wissner@bestweb.net
web: http://www.bestweb.net/~wissner/
Wants microscopes, medical, scientific instruments: Zentmayer, Grunow, Bullock, McAllister, Gundlack, McIntosh, Tolles, Queen, Pike.

Dr. F. Terry Hambrecht
14015 Manorvale Rd.
Rockville, MD 20853
e-mail: fh2@cu.nih.gov

Richard Van Vleck
Greybird Publishing
P.O. Box 412
Taneytown, MD 21787
ph: 301-447-2680
e-mail: smma@americanartifacts.com
web: http://americanartifacts.com/smma/
Wants medical and scientific antiques of all sorts; especially microscopes, eye-related instruments, laboratory and demo devices.

Jon Lewin
622 Raleigh Ave., Apt. 3
Norfolk, VA 23507-2034
ph: 757-625-6732
Buying medical & scientific items: bleeding instruments, wood/bone-handled surgical tools, phrenology heads, electric or violet ray quack boxes, electric belts, microscopes, 19th C. medical books, eye-massagers, ear trumpets, etc.

Jerry A. Phelps
1500 Van Buren Boat Deck Rd.
Mount Eden, KY 40046
ph: 502-859-4063
Wants pre-1900 medical and apothecary antiques, especially colored pontiled medicine bottles, bleeding items, leeching jars; also pre-1900 country store items and advertising items.

Atled Delta, Ph.D.
2911 N.W. 122nd, Ste. 262
Oklahoma City, OK 73120-1900
ph: 405-751-0859
Wants to buy any medical or sick room device having a black, hard rubber nozzle/tip that penetrates any body orifice such as rubber douche syringes (bag or bulb); also pre-1950 enema equipment.

Dale B. Peterson
Past Times Treasures
22762 Woodridge Drive
Claremore, OK 74017
ph: 918-341-5475
e-mail: cpeters2@webzone.net
web: http://www.webzone.net/cpeters2/
Actively seeking drug store and country store show globes, pedestal candy jars, old shelf stock, advertising, and especially counter top containers used for serving or displaying candy, gum, nuts, etc.; appraisals given.

Colin R. Voorneveld, MD
27 Roncesvalles Ave., #408
Toronto, Ontario M6R 3B2
Canada
ph: 416-516-4751
e-mail: 72774.257@compuserve.com
Avid collector specializing in pre-1900 medical and pharmaceutical antiques; actively seeks medical instruments, spectacles, historic medicine, etc.

Dealers

C. Keith Wilbur, M.D.
Doctor's Bag, The
397 Prospect St.
Northampton, MA 01060-2047
ph: 413-584-1440
Buys, sells, appraises apothecary, medical, dental, surgical, optical & quack instruments, equipment, advertising, books, etc.; catalogs available 3 to 4 times a year; author of "Antique Medical Instruments" and other books.

Mike Gordon
M & R Gordon
57 Bundy Lane
Storrs, CT 06268
ph: 860-429-3834
fax: 860-429-3834
e-mail: gordon@neca.com
web: http://users.neca.com/gordon/med.html
Wants to buy pre-WWII medical and dental items: diagnostic, surgical, bloodletting instruments, tooth extractors, opthalmic devices, obstetric forceps, hearing aids, phrenological heads and quack items.

Lucille Malitz
Lucid Antiques
P.O. Box KH
Scarsdale, NY 10583
ph: 914-636-7825 or 914-636-5171
fax: 914-636-7825
e-mail: kromscope@aol.com
Interested in the most collectible medical and dental antiques dating from the 19th century before the period of sterilization.

Eric P. Kane
285 Sills Rd., Bldg #7
Patchogue, NY 11772
ph: 516-475-2144
fax: 516-475-1588
e-mail: epk@aol.com
Wants to buy medical antiques from the Civil War and earlier: medical instruments, cased sets, especially marked "USA Hospital/Medical Dept.", medical texts, and associated materials such as medicine bottles, tins, etc.

Rod Harmic
Harmic's Antique Gallery
550 Rose Dale Lane
Dover, DE 19904
ph: 302-736-1174 or 302-736-1266
e-mail: rodney.harmic@dol.net
web: http://www.harmic.com
Wants to buy medical antiques.

J. Glen & Violet Moore
Main Street Antiques
47 W. Main St.
P.O. Box 627
New Market, MD 21774
ph: 301-865-3710
Buys and sells early medical devices, quack devices, signs and curiosities; eye, vet, dentist and other fields; patent medicines; appointments preferred.

Willisia Holbrook
Armbrook Antiques
531 Doub Rd.
Lewisville, NC 27023
ph: 888-393-8025 or 336-945-9477
fax: 336-945-9914
e-mail: olestuff@armbrookantiques.com
web: http://www.armbrookantiques.com
Buys and sells early medical and pharmaceutical antiques; specializes in pre-1930s items; web site has full online catalog including descriptions and photos.

James & Norvell Kennedy
James Kennedy Antiques, Ltd.
905 W. Main St.
Durham, NC 27701-2054
ph: 919-682-1040 or 800-236-1868
fax: 919-683-9633
e-mail: kantiques@earthlink.net
web: http://www.antiqnet.com/kennedy
Specialist in scientific, medical, and nautical antiques and prints.

Dr. John S. Gimesh, M.D.
Stein's Antiques
202 Stedman St.
P.O. Box 53788
Fayetteville, NC 28305-3788
ph: 910-484-2219
e-mail: steinmed@foto.infi.net
Buys and sells medical, dental, apothecary items, spectacles, books, etc.

Doris K. Bagwell, R.N.
Bagwell Antiques
5607 Concord Dr.
Jackson, MS 39211-4239
ph: 601-956-3508
fax: 601-956-4190
e-mail: DKay5607@aol.com
Buys and sells any medical related items: surgical, instruments, supplies, books, etc.

Al & Bobbie Roberts
Rational Past, The
221 Oceano Dr.
Los Angeles, CA 90049-4123
ph: 310-476-6277
fax: 310-476-6278
e-mail: rational_past@mindspring.com
Organizer of West Coast Scientific & Technical Antique and Collectible Shows (Los Angeles in the winter and San Francisco are in late summer.)

Experts

L.C. & C.G. Richardson
Mortar & Pestle Antiques
1176 South Dogwood Dr.
Harrisonburg, VA 22801-1535
ph: 540-434-1506
e-mail: dcknlill@gte.net
Buys, sells and specializes in medical and pharmaceutical antiques; authors of "A Book on Apothecary Antiques and Collectibles" (Old Fort Press.)

Paul Wherry
Pharmatiques
20 West North St.
Columbus, OH 43085-4133
ph: 614-885-1322
Collects and appraises pharmacy antiques.

Dale R. Beeks
Perceptions Scientifica
P.O. Box 117
Mount Vernon, IA 52314-0117
ph: 800-880-5178 or 319-895-0506
e-mail: dbeeksci@aol.com
Buys fine microscopes; old scientific, surveying, technical, medical and precision instruments; pre-1900 typewriters, calculating devices, medical items & quackery.

Dr. Robert E. Kravetz, M.D.
c/o Administration, Phoenix Baptist Hospital
2000 W. Bethany Home Rd.
Phoenix, AZ 85015
ph: 602-246-5319
fax: 602-433-6646
Medical museum curator, collector and historian; deals mainly with 18th and 19th century medical & pharmaceutical antiques.

Richard M. Wiehopf, Cur.
University of Arizona College of Pharmacy, History of Pharmacy Museum
P.O. Box 210207
Tucson, AZ 85721-0207
ph: 520-626-3036
fax: 520-626-4063
e-mail: wiedhopf@pharmacy.arizona.edu
web: http://www.pharmacy.arizona.edu/museum
Collector and expert specializing in pharmaceutical collectibles.

Internet Resources

Thomas E. Jones
Scientific & Medical Antiques
ph: 901-682-5182
e-mail: thjones@utmem1.utmem.edu
web: http://www.utmem.edu/personal/thjones/sci_ant.htm
Contains critical evaluations of books, periodicals, shops, businesses, and other medical and scientific resources; a depository of information about medical, dental, and scientific devices.

U.S. National Library of Medicine (NLM)
8600 Rockville Pike
Bethesda, MD 20894
ph: 888-346-3656 or 301-594-5983
e-mail: publicinfo@nlm.nih.gov
web: http://www.nlm.nih.gov/
Image library of nearly 60,000 images in prints and photograph collection; search by keyword or browse.

Richard Van Vleck
Scientific Medical & Mechanical Antiques
P.O. Box 412
Taneytown, MD 21787
ph: 301-447-2680
e-mail: smma@americanartifacts.com
web: http://americanartifacts.com/smma/
Items for sale and wanted, U.S. Patents search, SMMA articles and regular features, auction announcements, scientific instrument show schedules, books for the collector, links to related sites.

Dr. Michael Echols
Medical Antiques
6300 Whiskey Creek Dr.
Fort Myers, FL 33919
ph: 941-489-0587
fax: 941-481-0100
e-mail: drechols@coconet.com
web: http://www.antiquelures.com/medical/med.htm
An extensive website which specializes in pre-1900 medical, surgical, and dental instruments; extensive information on medical antique collecting with hundreds of photos from a personal collection; also has a wanted-to-buy list.

Museums/Libraries

Gretchen Worden, Dir.
Mutter Museum, College of Physicians of Philadelphia
19 South 22nd St.
Philadelphia, PA 19103-3097
ph: 610-563-3737 x242
fax: 215-561-6477
e-mail: muttref@collphyphil.org
web: http://www.collphyphil.org/muttpg1.shtml
Collection consists of antique medical instruments and equipment primarily from the 19th and 20th centuries, and rare anatomical specimens and medical curiosities such as 2,000 swallowed objects removed from food and air passages.

Alan Hawk, Collection Mngr.
National Museum of Health & Medicine of the Armed Forces Institute of Pathology
Bldg. 54
Walter Reed Medical Center
Washington, DC 20306
ph: 202-782-2200
fax: 202-782-3573
e-mail: hawk@afip.osd.mil
web: http://bubba.afip.org/
Historical collections containing over 1100 artifacts documenting the history of medicine; actively seeking medical instruments.

Hugh Mercer Apothecary Shop
1020 caroline St.
Fredericksburg, VA 22401-3814
ph: 703-373-3362

Country Doctor Museum, The
P.O. Box 34
Bailey, NC 27807
ph: 252-235-4165
fax: 252-291-2756

McDowell House & Apothecary Shop
125 S. Second St.
Danville, KY 40422-1801
ph: 606-236-2804
web: http://www.danville-ky.com/BoyleCounty/mcdowell.htm
Has an outstanding apothecary shop museum.

James M. Edmonson, PhD
Dittrick Museum of Medical History
11000 Euclid Ave.
Cleveland, OH 44106-1714
ph: 216-368-3648
fax: 216-368-6421
e-mail: jme3@po.cwru.edu
web: http://www.cwru.edu/chsl/hist_div.htm
Collection of 75,000 artifacts: medical history, diagnostic instruments, microscopes, surgical and obstetric instruments, etc.

Bakken Library & Museum, The
3537 Zenith Ave. South
Minneapolis, MN 55416
ph: 612-927-6508
fax: 612-927-7265
e-mail: webmaster@thebakken.org
web: http://www.bakkenmuseum.org/
Collects medical electricity items (no violet rays needed); have 2000 artifacts; 10,000 books.

International Museum of Surgical Science
1524 North Lake Shore Dr.
Chicago, IL 60610
ph: 312-642-6502
e-mail: info@imss.org
web: http://www.imss.org/

Dr. Robert E. Kravetz, M.D.
Medical Museum
c/o Administration, Phoenix Baptist Hospital
2000 W. Bethany Home Rd.
Phoenix, AZ 85015
ph: 602-246-5319
fax: 602-433-6646
Mailing address is as above; physical location is at 6025 N. 20th Ave., Phoenix, AZ.

Richard M. Wiehopf, Cur.
University of Arizona College of Pharmacy, History of Pharmacy Museum
P.O. Box 210207
Tucson, AZ 85721-0207
ph: 520-626-3036
fax: 520-626-4063
e-mail: wiedhopf@pharmacy.arizona.edu
web: http://www.pharmacy.arizona.edu/museum
Spanning all four floors of the Pharmacy building, the museum contains a collection of over 60,000 bottles, original drug containers, books, display cases, and artifacts from 1880 to 1930.

Sue Gold
Wellcome Institute for the History of Medicine Library
183 Euston Rd.
London, NW1 2BE
U.K.
ph: +44 171 611 8582
fax: +44 171 611 8369
e-mail: library@wellcome.ac.uk
web: http://www.wellcome.ac.uk/library/

Periodicals

Richard Van Vleck
Greybird Publishing
Newsletter: Scientific, Medical & Mechanical Antiques
P.O. Box 412
Taneytown, MD 21787
ph: 301-447-2680
e-mail: smma@americanartifacts.com
web: http://americanartifacts.com/smma/
For collectors, dealers, researchers; recent articles include formaldehyde disinfectors, galvanic spectacles and electric dumbbells; free ads for subscribers.

Civil War

Dealers

Alex Peck
Antique Scientifica
P.O. Box 710
Charleston, IL 61920-0710
ph: 217-348-1009
e-mail: antiques@advant.net
Wants surgical and bloodletting instruments, any Civil War (and pre-1890) medical gear, USA Hosp. Dept., etc.; anything Civil War.

Dental

Collectors

William Winburn, Jr.
1502 Showalter Rd.
Grafton, VA 23692
ph: 757-898-8246
fax: 757-898-6689
Dental instruments especially extracting; also contents of old dental offices.

Ralph Nix
P.O. Box 655
Red Bay, AL 35582-0655
ph: 256-356-2997
e-mail: ralphn@getaway.net
web: http://www.shavingmug.com
Wants dental antiques such as fancy wooden dental cabinets, four-leg dental chairs, wood or ivory handled instruments, foot engines, etc.

Dr. Barry Janov
2454 Depmster St., Ste. 416
Des Plaines, IL 60016-5320
Collector of early dental tools and related memorabilia.

Museums/Libraries

Dr. Scott D. Swank
Dr. Samuel D. Harris National Museum of Dentistry
31 South Greene St.
Baltimore, MD 21201-1504
ph: 410-706-0600
fax: 410-706-8313
e-mail: sswank@dentalmuseum.umaryland.edu
web: http://www.dentalmuseum.umaryland.edu/
Opened in 1996 with 7,000 sq. ft. of exhibit spaces, archives, reference library; collections consist of dental advertising art, pre-1950 dentist's directories (e.g. Polk's, Beecher's), trade catalogs, etc.

Dr. John Harris Dental Museum
P.O. Box 344
Bainbridge, OH 45612
ph: 740-634-2228
Mailing address is as above, but located in Bainbridge, OH.

Museum of Dentistry
295 S. Flower St.
Orange, CA 92668
ph: 714-634-8944
fax: 714-978-2686

Drug Store

Appraisers

Jim McMahon
James L. McMahon & Sons
635 Gilbert Hwy.
Fairfield, CT 06430-1646
ph: 203-226-3430
Buys, sells, collects, and appraises antique apothecary (pharmacy) and medical items.

Clubs/Associations

American Institute of the History of Pharmacy
University of Wisconsin
425 North Charter St.
Madison, WI 53706
ph: 603-262-5378
A non-profit national organization devoted to advancing knowledge and understanding of the place of pharmacy in history; supports both public and private collections of manuscript material and artifacts related to the profession.

Collectors

Mart James
487 Oak Ridge Rd.
Dyersburg, TN 38024-6511
ph: 901-286-2025
e-mail: kjames@usit.net
Wants to buy label-under-glass apothecary bottles, show globes, porcelain and show jars, medicine advertising, drug store window display pieces, etc.

Andrew E. Thomas
4681 North 84th Way
Scottsdale, AZ 85251-1864
ph: 888-255-0664 or 480-947-5693
fax: 480-994-4382
Buying apothecary antiques and drug store collectibles; show globes, drug jars, drug mills, mortars and pestles, balances and scales, displays, pill tiles, labels and label cabinets; specialty is show globes.

Dealers

Jim McMahon
James L. McMahon & Sons
635 Gilbert Hwy.
Fairfield, CT 06430-1646
ph: 203-226-3430
Buys, sells, collects, and appraises antique apothecary (pharmacy) and medical items.

Museums/Libraries

Eugene I. Morris, Dir.
New England Fire & History Museum
Newsletter: Siren Soundings
1439 Main St. (Rte. 6A)
Brewster, MA 02631
ph: 508-896-5711 or 508-432-2450
"The Schmidt Apothecary Shop" contains the largest collection of pharmaceutical bottles, original medicines and prescriptions; library contains many volumes dealing with pharmaceutical history.

Hearing Aids

Collectors

Jon Kolger
6906 Meade Dr.
Colleyville, TX 76034-6416
ph: 817-329-5262
e-mail: jkolger@gte.net
Wants to buy all sorts of primitive hearing-aid devices such as conversation tubes, ear trumpets, early battery-powered hearing-aids, etc.

Patent Medicines

Collectors

Mark S. McNee
Nostrums & Quackery
1009 Vassar Dr.
Kalamazoo, MI 49001-4483
ph: 616-343-8393
Collector for 20 years wants pre-1910 patent medicine bottles, tins, packages, and pills; also wants to buy advertising items and contents of old drug stores.

Harold Dylhoff
23511 Paulson's Rd.
Gobles, MI 49055-8651
ph: 616-628-4051
e-mail: hdylxrds@aol.com
Wants to buy Hadacol patent medicine memorabilia, almanacs, flyers, Captain Hadacol comics, Col. LeBlanc items; send photocopies and LSASE for reply.

Dan Cowman
43 Shallow Pond Place
Spring, TX 77381-3224
ph: 713-367-2935
fax: 281-292-0637
Wants to buy any items relating to patent medicines: almanacs, trade cards, billheads, labeled bottles, boxes, packages, tins, plasters, advertising, druggist trade catalogs, tin and paper patent medicine advertising signs, etc.

Dealers

Gary Hofe
Gypsy's Treasures
Rt 4, Box 665
Berkeley Springs, WV 25411
ph: 304-258-1617
Wants to buy medicine bottles; patent medicines from 1800s to mid 1900s; S&D, Merck, J&J, Lilly and others; also spice, talc, other tins and general advertising; mail order and shows.

Phrenology Busts

Collectors

Jon Lewin
622 Raleigh Ave., Apt. 3
Norfolk, VA 23507-2034
ph: 757-625-6732
Wants to buy phrenology heads, instruments or machines for measuring the head, fortune telling hands marked with zones, and related books, signs, etc.

Quackery

(see also HEALTH & BEAUTY, Devices to Restore)

Collectors

Jon Lewin
622 Raleigh Ave., Apt. 3
Norfolk, VA 23507-2034
ph: 757-625-6732
Wants to buy "electric" or "violet ray" quack boxes, "electric" belts, "electric" medals, "electric" brushes, big floor standing electrostatic generators; also wants books, advertisements, other items relating to medical quackery.

Jeff Behary
Electrotherapy Museum, The
16797 60th Lane N.
Loxahatchee, FL 33470
e-mail: jeff_behary@hotmail.com
web: http://www.lvstrings.com/quack.htm
Collects turn of the century electrotherapy devices: magneto-electric machines, Faradic medical batteries, violet rays, ultra violet ozone lamps, carbon arc lamps, Tesla coils, induction coils, high frequency apparatus.

O. Lindan
1404 Dorsh Rd.
Cleveland, OH 44121-3840
ph: 216-382-7113
Wants old electrotherapeutic and controversial healing devices and related literature; also wants medical, scientific instruments.

Ed Keller
1205 Imperial Dr.
Pittsburg, KS 66762-6123
Wants quack medical devices, cure-all devices, and old electrotherapeutic gadgets which shock, spark, buzz, light up or remain silent; no violet-rays, please; please send name, brief description and price.

Museums/Libraries

O. Lindan
Lindan Hist. Coll. of Electrotherapeutic & Controversial Medical Devices, The
1404 Dorsh Rd.
Cleveland, OH 44121-3840
ph: 216-382-7113
Focuses on old electrotherapeutic and controversial healing devices and related literature.

Robert W. McCoy, Dir.
Museum of Questionable Medical Devices
219 S.E. Main St.
Minneapolis, MN 55414-2149
ph: 612-545-1113 or 612-379-4046
fax: 612-540-9999
e-mail: quack@mtn.org
web: http://www.mtn.org/quack/
Nation's largest display of quack devices, from the AMA, FDA, St. Louis Science Center, Bakken Library and the National Council Against Health Fraud; publishes copies of old posters & advertising brochures dealing with medical quackery.

Bakken Library & Museum, The
3537 Zenith Ave. South
Minneapolis, MN 55416
ph: 612-927-6508
fax: 612-927-7265
e-mail: webmaster@thebakken.org
web: http://www.bakkenmuseum.org/
Collects medical electricity items (no violet rays needed); have 2000 artifacts; 10,000 books; maintains a special collection of quack devices.

Diablo Valley College Museum
321 Golf Club Rd.
Pleasant Hill, CA 94523
ph: 925-685-1230

Stethoscopes

Collectors

Chris Papadopoulos,MD
1107 Chaterleigh Circle
Baltimore, MD 21286-1755
ph: 410-825-9157
Wants antique and unusual stethoscopes; please send photos and price.

Experts

Erik Soiferman
Medical Antiques Online
823 Primrose Lane
Wynnewood, PA 19096
ph: 610-664-0551
fax: 610-668-9949
e-mail: erik@antiquemed.com
web: http://www.antiquemed.com/
Expert on the history of the stethoscope; collector of binaural stethoscopes; extensive online collection.

MEDICINE RELATED ITEMS

(see MEDICAL, DENTAL & PHARMACEUTICAL)

MENUS

(see also COOKBOOKS; PAPER COLLECTIBLES; RESTAURANT COLLECTIBLES)

Collectors

Barbara & Richard DePalma
Deer Park Books
609 Kent Rd., Route 7
Gaylordsville, CT 06755
ph: 860-350-4140
fax: 860-350-4140
e-mail: DeerParkBk@aol.com
web: http://www.abebooks.com/home/BARBDE/
Collector of 19th century menus, preferably American; will purchase single menu or entire collection.

Museums/Libraries

Strong Museum, The
1 Manhattan Square
Rochester, NY 14607
ph: 716-263-2700
web: http://www.strongmuseum.org
Has a small collection of 100 menus dating back to the 1840s; fully cataloged on a computer database.

Cornell University Hotel School Library
G80 Statler Hall
Cornell University
Ithaca, NY 14853-6902
ph: 607-255-3673
fax: 607-255-0021
e-mail: djb4@cornell.edu
web: http://www.nestlelib.cornell.edu/
Over 10,000 menus from the 1850s through the 1940s.

National Restaurant Association
1200 17th St. NW
Washington, DC 20036
ph: 202-331-5900
e-mail: info@dineout.org
web: http://www.restaurant.org/
Computer cataloged collection of thousands of menus from the 1930s to present.

MERMAIDS

Collectors

Jennifer Sykes
9018 Balboa Blvd. #595
Northridge, CA 91325-2610
ph: 818-993-1916
fax: 818-993-7612
e-mail: Veeda10@aol.com
Wants to buy mermaid items: wall plaques, figurines.

Wayne Babcock
4846 Carpenteria Ave.
Carpinteria, CA 93013-1935
ph: 805-684-8148
Collects mermaid figurines, clocks, artwork; any mermaid items.

Dealers

Stephanie M. Schnatz
17 Tallow Ct.
Baltimore, MD 21244-2516
ph: 410-944-0819
e-mail: chelsealady@hotmail.com
Buys and sells any printed materials with mermaids, mermen, merbabies on them; also wants antique merpeople in porcelain, silver, metal, china, wood, ivory, linens, lace, jewelry, etc.; items must be pre-1930.

METAL DETECTING

(see TREASURE HUNTING)

METAL ITEMS

(see also ALUMINUM, Hammered; BRASS ITEMS; BRONZES; CAST IRON ITEMS; CHROME; COPPER ITEMS; GOLD, Scrap; PLATINUM, Scrap; SILVER, Scrap; REPAIR/ RESTORATION/CONSERVATION, Metal Items)

Museums/Libraries

Judy Wallace
National Ornamental Metal Museum
Newsletter: Museum News
374 Metal Museum Drive
Memphis, TN 38106
ph: 901-774-6380
fax: 901-774-6382
web: http://www.memphisguide.com/NOMN.html
Conservation and restoration services available to the public and private sector; changing exhibits of historic and contemporary metalwork, classes, metalsmithing demonstrations.

Repro. Sources

Steve Kayne
Kayne & Son Custom Forged Hardware
100 Daniel Ridge Rd.
Candler, NC 28715-9434
ph: 828-667-8868 or 828-665-1988
fax: 828-665-8303
e-mail: kaynehdwe@ioa.com
Steel, brass, bronze reproductions of locks, pulls, hinges, thumb latches, furniture & interior/exterior hardware, fireplace tools & accessories, military accoutrements, etc.; also does repairs, restoration; $5 for two catalogs.

Suppliers

Glenn Hayes
Right Stuff Company, The
6246 Mission Road
Shawnee Mission, KS 66205-3253
ph: 913-722-4002 or 877-4-POLISH
fax: 913-722-6819
e-mail: info@rtstuf.com
web: http://www.rtstuf.com
Sells Cape Cod Metal Polishing Cloths: moist cotton cloths that remove tarnish on silver, gold, brass, copper, pewter, aluminum - all metals' pleasant vanilla scent; anti-tarnish formula so shine lasts longer.

Heintz Art Metal

Collectors

David Surgan
328 Flatbush Ave., Ste. 123
Brooklyn, NY 11238-4302
ph: 718-638-3768
fax: 718-638-3768
Dealer, exhibit curator, avid collector of Heintz Art Metal Shop items including vases, bowls, lighting, boxes, bookends, picture frames, etc.

METALSMITHS

(see CRAFTS; METAL ITEMS; REPAIR/RESTORATION/ CONSERVATION, Metal Items)

METEORITE COLLECTIBLES

(see ASTRONOMICAL ITEMS, Meteorites)

METTLACH

(see STEINS)

MICROSCOPES

(see also INSTRUMENTS & DEVICES, Scientific; OPTICAL ITEMS)

Clubs/Associations

Manuel del Cerro, MD
Microscope Historical Society
14 Tall Acres Dr.
Pittsford, NY 14534
Interested in the antique microscopes, parts, and history.

John Ptak
Maryland Microscopical & Scientific Instrument Society
1531 33rd St. NW
Washington, DC 20007
ph: 202-337-0945
fax: 202-234-3511
e-mail: jfptak@access.digex.net
web: http://www.access.dignex.net/~jfptak
Focuses on instruments and devices; medical, surveying, photographic, microscopical, navigational, horological, astronomical, etc.

David Hirsch, Treas.
Los Angeles Microscope Society, The
11815 Indianapolis St.
Los Angeles, CA 90066
One of the largest and most active societies in the U.S.

Fritz Schulze
Historical Microscopical Society of Canada
Newsletter: HMSC Bulletin
RR #2
Priceville, Ontario NOC 1K0
Canada
ph: 519-369-2855
fax: 519-369-2855
e-mail: glenelly@wcl.on.ca
web: http://www.geocities.com/CapeCanaveral/Hangar/5485/
Members are hobby microscopists and collectors of optical instruments and related books, etc.; some do repairs and restorations, some buy and sell.

Collectors

Paul Ferraglio
3332 W. Lake Rd.
Canandaigua, NY 14424-2441
ph: 716-394-7663
fax: 716-394-5424
e-mail: p4alyo@aol.com
Wants to buy antique brass microscopes, scientific and surveying instruments in any condition; also wants related books and catalogs; also wants parts.

Richard Van Vleck
Greybird Publishing
P.O. Box 412
Taneytown, MD 21787
ph: 301-447-2680
e-mail: smma@americanartifacts.com
web: http://americanartifacts.com/smma/
Seeking pre-1900 American microscopes by Zentmayer, Tolles, Gundlach, McIntosh, McAllister, Bulloch, Grunow, Spencer, Baush & Lomb and others.

Paul H. Hayashi, PE
18 Tarabrook Dr.
Orinda, CA 94563-3121
ph: 925-254-5074 or 925-253-1038
fax: 925-253-0592
Wants to buy pre-1900 microscopes.

Dealers

C. Keith Wilbur, M.D.
Doctor's Bag, The
397 Prospect St.
Northampton, MA 01060-2047
ph: 413-584-1440
Buys, sells, appraises apothecary, medical, dental, surgical, optical & quack instruments, equipment, advertising, books, etc.; catalogs available 3 to 4 times a year; author of "Antique Medical Instruments" and other books.

Experts

Dale R. Beeks
Perceptions Scientifica
P.O. Box 117
Mount Vernon, IA 52314-0117
ph: 800-880-5178 or 319-895-0506
e-mail: dbeeksci@aol.com

Randy D. Watson, M.D.
545 SE Oak, Ste. D
Hillsboro, OR 97123-4147
ph: 503-297-7424 or 503-640-1614
fax: 503-681-0925
e-mail: gate@teleport.com
Advanced collector wants all microscopes; antique and toy; also wants related books; says "I never met a microscope I didn't like!"; has private museum of over 2500 microscopes and 200 meteorites.

Internet Resources

Moody Medical Library
Univ. of Texas Medical Branch
Galveston, TX 77555-1035
e-mail: ref@utmb.edu
web: http://www.utmb.edu/mml/scopes/welcome.htm
Museum with a collection of 40 microscopes on display; website has resources for makers, anatomy of a microscope, toy microscopes, replicas, and more.

Museums/Libraries

Adrianne Noe, Dir.
National Museum of Health & Medicine, Billings Microscope Collection
Bldg. 54
Walter Reed Medical Center
Washington, DC 20306
ph: 202-782-2200
fax: 202-782-3573
e-mail: noe@afip.osd.mil
web: http://bubba.afip.org/
Approx. 1000 microscopes and 700 accessories; documents histological techniques by the inclusion of microtomes, accessories & microslides.

MILITARIA

(see also ARMS & ARMOR; AVIATION; BADGES; CANNONS; CIVIL WAR; FIREARMS; FLAGS; FRENCH FOREIGN LEGION; INDIAN WARS; KNIVES; MEDALS, ORDERS & DECORATIONS; MILITARY HISTORY; NAZI ITEMS; AMMUNITION; POSTERS; SWORDS; TRENCH ART; VETERAN ITEMS; VIETNAM ITEMS)

Auction Services

Anthony B. Lawson
Anthony B. Lawson, Inc.
P.O. Box 7051
Oakland, NJ 07436
ph: 201-337-5584 or 800-BID-2WIN
Auction sales of historical antiques, militaria, orders & medals: edged weapons, American militaria, helmets, flags, uniforms, edged weapons, arms & armor; also sells art, collectibles and autographs from all nations, all periods.

Raymond J. Zyla
Mohawk Arms Inc.
P.O. Box 399
Utica, NY 13503-0399
ph: 315-724-1234
fax: 315-724-5003
e-mail: sales@militaryrelics.com
web: http://www.militaryrelics.com
Three auctions per year: original historical militaria, personality items, daggers, swords, medals, award documents, uniforms, headgear, art items, presentation pieces, etc.

Stephen Flood, Pres.
AAG, International Militaria Mail Auction
1226-B Sans Souci Parkway
Wilkes Barre, PA 18702-1230
ph: 570-822-5300 or 570-822-5300
fax: 570-822-9992
web: http://www.aag-militaria.com/
Specializing in mail-bid auctions of militaria from Revolutionary War to Vietnam with emphasis on WWII, guns, Nazi, Japanese swords; all countries; 3 catalogs with over 7,000 items for $35; a large, fine auction house.

Gilbert Shatto
Militaria Collectibles Auction Haus
900 Hilton Dr.
Fayetteville, NC 28311-2540
ph: 910-822-2706
fax: 910-822-2706
e-mail: auctionhaus@msn.com
web: http://www.militaria-collectibles.com
This interactive Auction Haus features a wide assortment of rare historical militaria collectibles from all over the world.

Roger S. Steffen
Roger S. Steffen Historical Militaria
P.O. Box 280
Newport, KY 41076
ph: 606-431-4499
Conducts periodic mail bid militaria auctions: firearms, military art, rare books, medals, uniforms, photos, etc.

Manion's Auction House
P.O. Box 12214
Kansas City, KS 66112-0214
ph: 913-299-6692
fax: 913-299-6792
e-mail: collecting@manions.com
web: http://www.manions.com
The largest auction service in the U.S. handling military related antiques and items from U.S, Germany, Japan & all other countries.

Roy Butler
Wallis & Wallis
West Street Auction Galleries
Lewes, East Sussex BN7 2NJ
U.K.
ph: 01273-480208
fax: 01273-476562
e-mail: wallisandwallis@mcmail.com
web: http://www.wallisandwallis.co.uk/
Britain's specialist auctioneers of arms, armor, militaria and military orders.

Bosley's Military Auctioneers
42 West St.
Marlow, Buckinghamshire SL7 2NB
U.K.
ph: 01 628 488 188
fax: 01 628 488 111
Military auctioneers and appraisers.

Clubs/Associations

Rickie Marquette
Militaria Collectors Society of Florida
Newsletter: Frontal Dispatch, The
P.O. Box 343133
Homestead, FL 33034-0133
ph: 305-246-5431 or 305-245-2323
fax: 305-245-9295
Purpose is to promote the knowledge, study and preservation of military relics, and to support militaria collectors in the pursuit of their hobby; meets monthly; promotes shows; buy, sell, trade.

Rob Morgan
Civil War Collectors Society & the American Militaria Exchange
5970 Toylor Ridge Dr.
West Chester, OH 45069
ph: 513-874-0483
e-mail: RWMorgan@aol.com
web: http://www.civiwar-collectors.com/
Established to promote the preservation and collecting of material relating to our nation's rich military heritage, from pre-Revolutionary times to present day.

American Society of Military History
Los Angeles Patriotic Hall
1816 S. Figueroa
Los Angeles, CA 90015
ph: 213-746-1776
Society of men and women dedicated to developing programs to perpetuate and maintain the great American military heritage; library has over 25,000 titles and 10 periodical subscriptions.

Mike Hanlon, Mem.
Great War Society, The
Magazine: Relevance
P.O. Box 4585
Stanford, CA 94309
e-mail: medwardh@hotmail.com
web: http://www.mcs.com/~mikei/tgws/
Encourages discussion, learning, scholarship and independent research on the events surrounding the First World War.

Collectors

Darrell K. English
P.O. Box 1389
Wilmington, VT 05363
ph: 802-464-5569
e-mail: info@livinghistoryassn.org
web: http://www.livinghistoryassn.org/
Wants to buy any and all militaria: Revolution through WWII; U.S. and foreign; medals, uniforms, insignia, headgear, edged weapons.

Warren K. Tice
W. Tice & Company
8 Orchard Terrace
Essex Junction, VT 05452-3501
ph: 802-878-3835
e-mail: wtice@vbimail.champlain.edu
Wants to purchase U.S. Military, Confederate, and high quality decorative buttons; also wants to buy military antiques.

Kenneth D. Smith
55 Howard Ave.
Staten Island, NY 10301-4404
Wants to buy WWII OSS memorabilia, relics and documents; also buys espionage items, cryptographic and code/cipher machines, devices, books and manuals; any era, any nation.

Gene Christian
3849 Bailey Ave.
Bronx, NY 10463-2503
ph: 718-548-0243
Wants Foreign Legion, Devils Isl.; Shanghai, Tientsin Volunteer Corps - police - fire; China (Marines, 15th Inf., gunboats, White Russians, Fr. Forces, Warlords), P.A.A. China Clipper, Imperial Chinese headdress; animal rescue, truant officer.

Charles Dubsky
686 North Dupont Blvd. #328
Milford, DE 19963
ph: 302-422-7766
fax: 302-424-1928

Don Carter
P.O. Box 142164
Gainesville, FL 32614-2164
ph: 352-376-6668
fax: 352-376-6668
Wants to buy German weapons, daggers, swords, and unusual items (will travel); also wants Japanese militaria and other WWII militaria.

Don Johnson
5110 S. Greensboro Pike
Knightstown, IN 46148-9596
ph: 765-345-5758
e-mail: djohnson@comsys.net
Writes column for "Military Trader."

Pat Olson
4533 Rutledge Ave.
Minneapolis, MN 55436-1418
ph: 612-927-0560
e-mail: ptbasil@aol.com
Wants military war souvenirs from all countries and all periods: daggers, swords, uniforms, helmets, flags, papers, badges, wings, patches, medals, squadron insignia.

Charles G. Kratz, Jr.
17821 Golfview
Homewood, IL 60430-1210
ph: 708-799-8478 or 312-951-0336
Wants old military cannons (only full-size, authentic type) in any condition; also want U.S. artillery clothing and equipment such wooden artillery carriages and ammunition chests.

Ron L. Willis
2110 Fox Ave.
Moore, OK 73160-4217
ph: 405-793-9604 or 405-521-3484
Wants U.S. Navy - any period -

patches, wings, uniforms, books, documents, edged weapons, photos, plaques, flags, etc.

Ed Royse
112 N. Broadway St.
Walters, OK 73572
ph: 580-357-8000
fax: 580-875-2063
e-mail: edroyse@juno.com
Wants to buy US military collectibles, US Army firearms, swords, knives and accoutrements from Civil War to present; also wants US WWI and WWII posters, patriotic, recruiting, Red Cross, propaganda.

Jim Kopke
P.O. Box 4310
Dillon, CO 80435-4310
Wants to buy nearly anything from the Civil War through the Indian Wars.

David J. DeLaurant
1505 N. Lafayette
Fresno, CA 93728-1123
ph: 559-488-3229 or 559-233-1492
e-mail: dlaurant@sjvls.lib.ca.us
Serious student of post-1914 military helmets & other body armor items from all nations; communicates with other body armor collectors via the "Body Armor Reporter", a quarterly newsletter; will identify armor free - send SASE.

Dealers

Blue Cape Antiques
620 Great Rd., Rte. 119
Littleton, MA 01460
ph: 978-486-4709
Wants to buy military collectibles; US, German, Japanese.

George P. van Duinwyk
Articles of War
358 Boulevard
Middletown, RI 02842
ph: 401-846-8503
e-mail: dutch5@ids.com
Buys, sells, appraises, collects and specializes in antique militaria.

Tom & Dave's Militaria
P.O. Box 725
Wyoming, RI 02898
e-mail: pir3@aol.com
web: http://members.aol.com/pir3/tom.html
WWII militaria dealers specializing in American, German and Japanese military collectibles and the stories behind them; want to buy helmets, uniforms, edged weapons, and anything that a soldier would have carried or used.

Military Specialties, Inc.
2543 Berlin Tnpk.
Newington, CT 06111
ph: 860-666-4275
fax: 860-666-1939
e-mail: morforles@aol.com
Buys and sells German, U.S., Japanese, British military souvenirs from WWII: helmets, hats, uniforms, swords, daggers, knives, medals, patches, insignia, firearms, etc.

Jacques Noel Jacobsen, Jr.
60 Manor Rd.
Staten Island, NY 10310-2698
ph: 718-981-0973
American military antiques 1840-1940 large illustrated catalog, 3 issues for $12 ($15 overseas).

Eric P. Kane
285 Sills Rd., Bldg #7
Patchogue, NY 11772
ph: 516-475-2144
fax: 516-475-1588
e-mail: epk@aol.com
Wants to buy Civil War and earlier antique guns and militaria, uniforms, photographs; also wants books on guns.

Raymond J. Zyla
Mohawk Arms Inc.
P.O. Box 399
Utica, NY 13503-0399
ph: 315-724-1234
fax: 315-724-5003
e-mail: sales@militaryrelics.com
web: http://www.militaryrelics.com

Dale & Debra Anderson
Dale C. Anderson Co.
4 W. Confederate Ave.
Gettysburg, PA 17325
ph: 717-334-1031
Sells, appraises guns, swords, uniforms, headgear, relics, personal items, more; all offered in bi-monthly catalog ($12/yr); covers all periods 1775-1945; US & foreign; emphasis on Civil War/Indian Wars period; over 38 years experience.

Kathleen Miller
Kat's Militaria
906 Chambers Ridge
York, PA 17402
ph: 717-840-4156
Buying anything military, from Roman Empire to Desert Storm; buy small items like dog tags or large items like tanks; buying and selling for over 30 years; free phone estimates, but prefer to work from photos.

Ken Kipp
Allenwood Americana Antiques
P.O. Box 116
Allenwood, PA 17810-0116
ph: 570-538-1440
Established militaria dealer and Veteran with over 20 years experience; especially interested in WWI and WWII memorabilia; buys and sells.

Terry Hannon, Pres.
Phoenix Militaria, Inc.
P.O. Box 245
Lyon Station, PA 19536-9986
ph: 610-682-1010 or 800-446-0909
fax: 610-682-1066
e-mail: TerryHannon@msn.com
web: http://www.phoenixmilitaria.com
Buys/sells general militaria; also sells militaria collecting books & periodicals.

Randy Gravenor
E.R.G. Militaria
P.O. Box 299
Delmar, DE 19940
ph: 410-835-2280
Over 12 years old and has rare, unusual military collectibles; always buying items of interest.

LTC(Ret) Thomas Johnson
Johnson Reference Books & Militaria
312 Butler Road, Bldg. 403
Fredericksburg, VA 22405-2514
ph: 540-373-9150 or 540-371-2665
fax: 540-373-0087
e-mail: ww2daggers@aol.com
web: http://www.ww2daggers.com
Wants to buy German War booty; specific interest is in edged weapons (dress swords, daggers, bayonets); author of seventeen books about Imperial and 3rd Reich German edged weapons, and militaria.

Newton Carter
King's Own, The
P.O. Box 46
Wallace, NC 28466
ph: 910-285-5506
fax: 910-285-8042
e-mail: kingsown@duplinnet.com
web: http://www.thekingsown.com
Produces a catalog with over 1000 British and American military antiques; Queen Victorian period through WWII; send $3.

Andrew Lipps
Wartime Collectables
P.O. Box 165
539 Dekalb St.
Camden, SC 29020
ph: 803-424-5273
fax: 803-424-5273
e-mail: wartime@camden.net
web: http://collectorsnet.com/wartime/
Buys and sells authentic military items from the Civil War to the Vietnam War with an emphasis on U.S. material from Spanish American War to WWII; authentic material only.

P & K Military Collectables
407 Whitaker St.
Savannah, GA 31401
ph: 912-234-5277

Ron Gordon
San Juan Precious Metals Corp.
4818 San Juan Ave.
Jacksonville, FL 32210-3232
ph: 904-387-3466
fax: 904-387-5166
e-mail: support@ejewelry.com
web: http://www.ejewelry.com/sjpm/
Wants German, US, Japanese, Vietnam military items: helmets, flags, uniforms, badges, swords, coins, daggers, etc.

Donald Blincoe
Uncle Davey's Americana
6140 St. Augustine Rd.
Jacksonville, FL 32217
ph: 904-730-8932 or 904-777-6478
fax: 904-730-8932
e-mail: uncledv@collectorsnet.com
web: http://www.collectorsnet.com/uncledv/
Expert who buys, sells, appraises vintage historical U.S. military related items from 1740 to 1885: weapons, documents, currency, coins, autographs, slavery, photos, books, newspapers, jewelry, clothing, maps, letters, etc.

Frank & Bill Muir
Grande Armee Military Antiques
Via Gucci 256 Worth Ave.
Palm Beach, FL 33480
ph: 800-278-8212
e-mail: gama@safari.net
web: http://www.grandearmee.com/
Buys and sells armor, medals and orders, regimental tankards, edged weapons, aviation models, helmets and headgear, toy soldiers, GI Joe and Action Man, firearms, military miniatures, etc

Donald E. Taussig
Sanders' Antique Mall
22 N. Lemon Ave.
Sarasota, FL 34236-5711
ph: 941-366-0400
fax: 941-388-2053
e-mail: sandersant@aol.com
Buys and sells military related swords, medals.

William Skelton
Highland's Vault
P.O. Box 55448
Birmingham, AL 35255-5548
ph: 205-939-1178 or 205-939-3166
Wants to buy all military collectibles from Civil War through WWII.

Steffen's Historical Militaria
14 Mornan Rd.
Newport, KY 41076-9723
ph: 606-431-4499
Antique firearms, accouterments, swords, helmets, orders, medals; Revolutionary War, Civil War, WWI, WWII, Korean War, Vietnam War; American, Imperial German and Third Reich, British, French, Russian.

John W. Poling
John W. Poling: Military & Political Collectibles
5998 South Ridgeview Rd.
Anderson, IN 46013-9774
ph: 765-778-2714
Mail order dealer in military collectibles (helmets, uniforms, medals, war souvenirs); issues periodic catalog of items for sale; send $2 for latest catalog; most prices in catalog well below current retail.

Ted Caldwell
Caldwell & Co. Civil War Antiques
816 Pleasant St.
Lebanon, IN 46052
ph: 765-482-0292 or 765-482-6280
e-mail: civilwr@in-motion.net
web: http://members.tripod.com/~OTC_50/index.html
Actively buy, sell, trade all military items from Revolutionary War through Indian War era; also rewraps leather grips on swords and sabers.

Last Square, The
5944 Odana Rd.
Madison, WI 53719
ph: 800-750-4401 or 608-278-4401
fax: 608-278-4402
e-mail: orders@lastsquare.com
web: http://www.lastsquare.com
A military/militaria art & books/ historical miniatures dealer catering to all aspects of the military history hobby; from collectible art to large-scale hand-painted figures to wargaming miniatures.

Hayes Otoupalik
14000 Highway 93 N.
Missoula, MT 59802
ph: 406-549-4817
Wants to buy all American military items from 1845 to 1945: Civil War, Indian and Spanish American Wars, blue wool uniforms and caps, WWI doughboy uniforms and helmets, WWII flyers jackets, paratrooper uniforms, patch collections, etc.

Randy Donley
Donley's Wild West Town & Museum
8512 S. Union Rd.
Union, IL 60180-9661
ph: 815-923-9000
fax: 815-923-2253
web: http://www.wildwesttown.com/
Buys and sells souvenirs and relics from all wars: uniforms, helmets, medals, weapons, guns, swords, etc.

John Spangler
Antique & Collectible Firearms & Militaria Headquarters
P.O. Box 711282
Salt Lake City, UT 84171
ph: 801-947-9442
e-mail: hq@oldguns.net
web: http://oldguns.net
Appraises, buys, sells, specializes in firearms & militaria; website has interesting and useful information for collectors of antique and collectible firearms and militaria; questions answered, gun show listings, catalog.

Warren Anderson
America West Archives
P.O. Box 100
Cedar City, UT 84721-0100
ph: 435-586-9497 or 435-586-7323
e-mail: awa@netutah.com
web: http://www.americawestarchives.com/
Buys and sells pre-1900 U.S. military documents, letters, autographs, photos, especially interested in Civil War, Indian Wars, and military documents from the Western U.S.; author of "Owning Western History."

Stewart's Military Antiques
108 W. Main St.
Mesa, AZ 85201
ph: 602-834-4004
Buys and sells helmets, medals, insignia, uniforms, photos, swords, and other military collectibles from 1860 to 1945.

Barrett Behnke
Barrett's Toys & Collectibles
7063 E. Blue Lake Dr.
Tucson, AZ 85715
ph: 520-290-2864
Buys and sells U.S. militaria from the Civil War to present; also general military items of all countries.

Robert C. Thomas, Jr.
1926 W. Trask Ave.
Santa Ana, CA 92706-1363
ph: 714-971-2258
fax: 714-971-1531
e-mail: milathomas@aol.com
Buys and sells military collectibles; collects WWII U.S. Airborne related items.

Military Antiques & Museum
300 Petaluma Blvd. North
Petaluma, CA 94952
ph: 707-763-2220
fax: 707-763-5964
e-mail: warstuff@sonic.net
web: http://www.sonic.net/~warstuff/
Military antiques from the Civil War to WWII; U.S., Japanese, German, Italian, French; books, video and audio tapes, uniforms, badges, medals, edged weapons, headgear, antique firearms, posters.

Marc Wade
Antique & Collectable Firearms & Militaria Headquarters
P.O. Box 95021
Gilroy, CA 95021
ph: 801-898-3827
e-mail: hq@oldguns.net
web: http://oldguns.net/Sma.htm
Buys, sells, appraises; interesting and useful information for collectors of antique and collectible firearms and militaria; questions answered, gun show listings, catalog, gun related software.

Kelley's Military Antiques
P.O. Box 1442
San Martin, CA 95046
e-mail: suggestions@militaryantiques.com
web: http://www.militaryantiques.com
Great website with lots of resource information.

Geoff Pollard
Geoff Pollard Militaria
P.O. Box 89
Lytham St. Annes, Lancshire FY8 3UQ U.K.
ph: 01253 721070
Specializes in German and WWII memorabilia.

Experts

Stephen Flood, Pres.
AAG, International Militaria Mail Auction
1226-B Sans Souci Parkway
Wilkes Barre, PA 18702-1230
ph: 570-822-5300 or 570-822-5300
fax: 570-822-9992
web: http://www.aag-militaria.com/
Buys and sells militaria from Revolutionary War to Vietnam with emphasis on WWII; all countries; issues a catalog approximately every six months; a large, fine auction house.

Richard Hovis
Timeframes Inc.
P.O. Box 3679
Washington, DC 20007-0179
ph: 202-333-7849
fax: 202-333-0938
Buys, trades, sells, consults, appraises, and specializes in original and authentic militaria, especially on 1776-1950 U.S. Navy uniforms, photographs, paper and memorabilia.

Courtney Wilson
American Military Antiques
8398 Court Ave.
Ellicott City, MD 21043-4514
ph: 410-465-6827
fax: 410-461-6820
Military antiques 1700-1900: appraiser, consultant, broker, dealer; arms, uniforms, equipment, memorabilia - especially Civil War.

Robert Edwards
Military Collectors Consortium, The
P.O. Box 190
22 S. Main St.
Keedysville, MD 21756
ph: 301-416-2758 or 301-416-2884
e-mail: milcolco@intrepid.net
web: http://www.intrepid.net/militaria/
Dealer, collector and expert in military firearms, edged weapons, and militaria from 1750 to 1970; appraises, brokers, consults.

Sheperd Paine
6427 W. Irving Park Rd., Ste. 160
Chicago, IL 60634-2437
ph: 312-777-0499
Wants British, French and German pre-1914 uniforms, helmets, swords; familiar with military items from most countries & periods.

David C. Williams
Lost Cause Relics
2237 Brookhollow Dr.
Abilene, TX 79605-5507
ph: 915-692-1858
e-mail: dcjew@swbell.net
Collector and dealer in U.S. medals and medal groupings of all periods; also military photography, documents, uniforms, aviation items, etc.; Special Forces (Green Berets) a specialty.

Internet Resources

Olive Drab
e-mail: chuck@olive-drab.com
web: http://www.olive-drab.com/
Web site where you will find original materials on many military subjects and links: military vehicles, military movies and books, vehicle/parts dealers, organizations, surplus dealers, military photos and clip art, etc.

Jonathan Gawne
Militaria.com
P.O. Box 2925
Framingham, MA 01703
e-mail: jgawne@militaria.com
web: http://www.militaria.com/gij.html
A place for military collectors and military historians; home of the "G.I. Journal", with information on some of the best military magazines, books, collectibles, and militaria sites.

Military Mall, The
365 Boundary Ave.
Bethpage, NY 11714
ph: 516-579-7400
This site includes a large number of links to militaria-related sites: daggers, swords, helmets, medals, uniforms, accoutrements, flags, military toys, military shows, bronzes, restoration, reenactment, etc.

Robert Edwards
Military Collectors Consortium, The
P.O. Box 190
22 S. Main St.
Keedysville, MD 21756
ph: 301-416-2758 or 301-416-2884
e-mail: milcolco@intrepid.net
web: http://www.intrepid.net/militaria/
Global resource for collectors of military firearms, edged weapons, and militaria from 1750-1970; appraisal, brokerage, and consulting services relating to arms and militaria; publishes monthly "Military Collectors Journal" online.

Steve Baker
Antique Militaria & Collectibles Network
106 Osprey Ct.
Morehead City, NC 28557
ph: 252-393-7821
e-mail: ddesign@collectorsnet.com
web: http://www.collectorsnet.com
A network dedicated to militaria dealers of all eras; put your list on-line for as little as $21.50 per month and advertise to over 12,000 visitors per day.

Chris Arnold
Militaria Collector's Exchange, The
124 Mary Lane
Jacksonville, AR 72076
ph: 501-988-2565
fax: c
e-mail: tmcx@infinet.com
web: http://www.tmcx.com/
An internationally recognized website devoted to the preservation and collecting of military relics; great website with just about everything related to militaria.

Chris Arnold
Military Collectors' Exchange, The
P.O. Box 1129
Jacksonville, AR 72078
ph: 501-988-2565
e-mail: chrisa@aristotle.net
web: http://www.tmcx.com/
TMCX is designed to assist both beginner and advanced collectors of militaria; feature articles, free ads, international advertisers; webmaster, Chris Arnold, is a recognized expert on U.S. steel combat helmets.

John Spangler
Antique & Collectible Firearms & Militaria Headquarters
P.O. Box 711282
Salt Lake City, UT 84171
ph: 801-947-9442
e-mail: hq@oldguns.net
web: http://oldguns.net
Impressive site with loads of helpful information for the beginning or advanced collector as well as highly detailed catalog listings (many with photos) of militaria: guns, swords, bayonets, modern firearms; also consignments & repairs.

Museums/Libraries

Greg Souchik
Allegheny Arms & Armor Museum, Inc.
P.O. Box 161
Custer City, PA 16725-0161
ph: 814-362-2642
fax: 814-362-7356
e-mail: AlleghenyArsenal@compuserve.com
Firearms, cannons, all types of historical military material.

George W. Marinos
Battlefield Military Museum
900 Baltimore Pike
P.O. Box 3192
Gettysburg, PA 17325-0192
ph: 717-334-6568
Wants war relics - U.S., German, any country and any war; guns, swords, medals, helmets, belts, buckles, flags, etc.

U.S. Marine Corps Museum/Library
Marine Corps Historical Center
Washington Navy Yard, Bldg. 58
Washington, DC 20374-0580
ph: 202-433-3483
fax: 202-433-4691
web: http://www.usmc.mil/

Naval Historical Center
901 M St. SE
Washington, DC 20374-5060
ph: 212-433-4882
fax: 202-433-8200
web: http://www.history.navy.mil/

Director
U.S. Army Transportation Museum
Bldg. 300, Besson Hall
Ft. Eustis, VA 23604-5259
ph: 757-878-1115
fax: 757-878-5656
e-mail: atzfptm@eustis.army.mil
web: http://www.eustis.army.mil/dptmsec/museum.htm
Collects, exhibits and interprets the history of U.S. Army transportation activities from the Revolutionary War to present.

Parris Island Museum, The
Commanding General, Attn: MCRD ERR
Box 19001
Beaufort, SC 29905-9001
ph: 843-525-2951
fax: 843-525-3065
web: http://www.parrisisland.com/musem.htm
Museum features large exhibit halls of the history of recruit training, 20th century Marine Corps history, and the history of Parris Island.

National Infantry Museum
U.S. Army Infantry School
ATSH-OTN Building 396
Fort Benning, GA 31905-5593
ph: 706-545-2958 or 706-545-6762
fax: 706-545-5158
web: http://www-benning.army.mil/fbhome/INFmuseum.htm

Richard L. Uppstrom, Dir.
U.S. Air Force Museum
1100 Spaatz Street
Dayton, OH 45433-7102
ph: 937-255-3286
fax: 937-255-3910
e-mail: champpa.rr@usafa.af.mil
web: http://129.48.104.231/museum/
World's largest aviation museum with 10 1/2 acres of aircraft and other exhibits under roof.

Randy Donley
Donley's Wild West Town & Museum
8512 S. Union Rd.
Union, IL 60180-9661
ph: 815-923-9000
fax: 815-923-2253
web: http://www.wildwesttown.com/
Large display of souvenirs and relics from all wars: uniforms, helmets, medals, weapons, guns, swords, etc.

Liberty Memorial Museum, The
Newsletter: Signals
100 West 26th St.
Kansas City, MO 64108
ph: 816-221-1918

Periodicals

Jonathan Gawne
Magazine: G.I. Journal
P.O. Box 2925
Framingham, MA 01703
e-mail: jgawne@militaria.com
web: http://www.militaria.com/gij.html
Covers all aspects of WWI and WWII that apply to the common soldier; a large percentage of readers are collectors of military artifacts, and thus many articles are geared to them; author of several books on the subject.

Terry Hannon, Ed.
Phoenix Militaria, Inc.
Directory: American Militaria Sourcebook & Directory
P.O. Box 245
Lyon Station, PA 19536-9986
ph: 610-682-1010 or 800-446-0909
fax: 610-682-1066
e-mail: TerryHannon@msn.com
web: http://www.phoenixmilitaria.com
A complete listing of militaria dealers, service companies and organizations.

Cowles Magazines, Inc.
Magazine: Military History
741 Miller Dr. SE, Ste. D2
Harrisburg, PA 20175
ph: 717-540-6617 or 800-829-3340
fax: 717-540-6706
e-mail: brentd@cowles.com
web: http://www.cowles.com/maglist.html
A guide through history focusing on armed conflicts; incisive accounts of land, naval and air warfare in world history from ancient to modern times; published bi-monthly.

Cowles Magazines, Inc.
Magazine: World War II
741 Miller Dr. SE, Ste. D2
Harrisburg, PA 20175
ph: 717-540-6617 or 800-829-3340
fax: 717-540-6706
e-mail: brentd@cowles.com
web: http://www.cowles.com/maglist.html
A bi-monthly magazine; the ultimate authority on WWII: weapons, personalities, tactics.

Chris George
War of 1812 Consortium, The Star Spangled Banner Flag House & 1812 Museum
Magazine: Journal of the War of 1812 & the Era 1800 to 1840
844 E. Pratt St.
Baltimore, MD 21202
ph: 410-223-1638 or 410-243-5635
e-mail: cgeorge@jhsph.edu
web: http://www.cronab.demon.co.uk/jour.htm
For those interested in the early years of our history.

Antique Trader Publications, Inc.
Newspaper: Military Trader
P.O. Box 1050
Dubuque, IA 52004-1050
ph: 800-334-7165 or 800-482-4155
fax: 800-531-0880
e-mail: atpzines@aol.com
web: http://www.collect.com/militarytrader
Monthly publication focusing on military collectibles: articles, collecting, interviews with dealers, military toy column, book reviews, collectibles for sale, espionage.

Thomas O. Berndt, Pub.
Magazine: Militaria International
P.O. Box 43400
Minneapolis, MN 55443-0400
ph: 888-428-1942 or 612-428-4345
fax: 612-428-7575
e-mail: militintl@aol.com
web: http://members.aol.com/militintl/
A monthly worldwide magazine with articles, features and photos; for all types of collectible militaria: uniforms and field gear, weapons, vehicles and parts, travel and museums, clubs and organizations, sale and show information.

Magazine: Der Gauleiter
3800 Taft Park
Metairie, LA 70002
ph: 504-887-6709
fax: 504-456-1092
A monthly publication offering collectors and dealers an outlet for buying and selling militaria.

Newsmagazine: Military
2122 28th St.
P.O. Box 189490
Sacramento, CA 95818
ph: 800-366-9192 or 916-457-8990
fax: 916-457-7339
e-mail: military@ns.net
web: http://www.milmag.com/
Monthly newsmagazine with articles, ads, etc.; many articles on military aviation.

Service Publications
Newsletter: Military Artifact
55 Abingdon Drive
Nepean, Ontario K2H 7M5
Canada
ph: 613-820-7350
fax: 613-820-1288
e-mail: service@magi.com
web: http://infoweb.magi.com/~service/home/se09000.htm
A quarterly newsletter dedicated to collectible artifacts of the British Empire, Commonwealth and specifically Canada; covers the period of the Crimea to Korea, 1854 to 1953.

Histoire et Collections
Magazine: Militaria Magazine
19, Ave de la Republique
Paris, 75011
France
A French monthly magazine written in French featuring pristine examples of existing memorabilia, supported with historical photos.

Imperial War Museum
Magazine: Imperial War Museum Review
Mail Order Department
Duxford, Cambridge CB2 4QR
U.K.
e-mail: mail@iwm.org.uk
web: http://www.iwm.org.uk/
A richly illustrated journal from the UK's museum of 20th century conflict; covering war history and art; primary source material covering documents, films, posters, photographs; invaluable for the historian, student or teacher.

Beaumont Publishing
Magazine: Armourer Magazine, The
25 Westbrook Dr.
Macclesfield, Cheshire SK10 3AQ
U.K.
ph: +44 1625 431583
fax: +44 1625 431583
e-mail: editor@armourer.u-net.com
web: http://www.armourer.u-net.com/
Bi-monthly English magazine; has everything for the militaria, arms, armor and weapon enthusiast and collector and those with an interest in WWI, WWII, and military history; ads, articles on ordnance, bayonets, medals, insignia, etc.

Repro. Sources

Collector's Armoury
3000 South Eads St.
Arlington, VA 22202-4027
ph: 800-544-3456 or 703-684-6111
fax: 703-683-5486
Offers museum quality reproductions: Civil War swords, knives, pistols and field gear; non-firing Western pistols, rifles and collectibles; medieval, Samurai and military swords; historic miniature Gatling guns and cannons.

Anti-Axis

Collectors

Ken Fleck
496 2nd St.
Highspire, PA 17034-1505
ph: 717-939-8441
fax: 717-939-0064
Wants to buy WWII Anti-Axis items depicting anti-Hitler, anti-Mussolini, anti-Tojo, etc. sentiments: toys, games, coin-ops, banks, ashtrays, paper, textiles, etc.

Martin Jacobs
P.O. Box 22026
San Francisco, CA 94122-0026
ph: 415-661-7552
e-mail: MJacobs784@aol.com
Collector seeks WWII memorabilia from the Homefront 1941-1945; will purchase any size collection; wants victory pins, Cinderella stickers and stamps, envelope art, war propaganda, Anti-Axis art, matchcovers, postcards, etc.

British

Clubs/Associations

J. Barker
Military Heraldry Society
Magazine: Formation Sign, The
37 Wolsey Close
Southall, Middlesex UB2 4NQ
U.K.
ph: 0181 574 4425
Formed in 1951 for collectors of cloth formation signs: shoulder sleeve insignia, shoulder titles, regimental and unit flashes, etc.

Paul Smith, Mem.
Crown Imperial
10 Woodlands Ave.
Tadcaster, North Yorkshire LS24 9LE
U.K.
web: http://www.pwstubbs.force9.co.uk/crownimp/journal.htm
Formed in 1973 to study the history, traditions and regalia of the forces of the crown and other insignia; members have a strict policy against dealing in reproduction or restrikes or fake badges and insignia.

A.N. McClenaghan
Indian Military Historical Society
Magazine: Durbar
33 High Street
Huntingdon, Cambridgeshire PE18 0JP
U.K.
web: http://ozemail.com.au/~clday/imhs.htm
Formed in 1983 to bring together those interested in the military history of the Indian Subcontinent; a forum for the dissemination of knowledge of uniforms, medals, badges, buttons and other militaria of Service units.

Experts

Brian Whitely
British Regalia Imports
P.O. Box 1416
Palm Harbor, FL 34682-1416
ph: 727-736-6750
fax: 727-736-6585
e-mail: execucom@gte.net
British and Scottish regimental insignia and accessories: cap badges, rank badges, uniform buttons, patches, wings, garrison belts, berets, blazer crests, ties, officers' swagger canes, swords, flags, medals, maps, etc.

German

Clubs/Associations

J.J Daub
Imperial German Military Collectors Association
Journal: Kaiserzeit
82 Atlantic St.
Keyport, NJ 07735-1857
ph: 908-739-1799 or 816-455-3214
Military collectors and historians with a wide range of interests in all aspects of the Imperial German military (pre-1919).

Chris Cox
Karabiner Collector's Network
Newsletter: KCN Newsletter
P.O. Box 5773
High Point, NC 27262
ph: 336-884-5566
Network for collectors of German militaria; German rifles and snipers, pistols and holsters, Mausers, German medals and badges, helmets and uniforms, books, photographs, cartridges and ammo, field gear, edged weapons, etc.

Collectors

John Telesmanich
P.O. Box 62
White Plains, NY 10604-0062
ph: 914-949-5519
e-mail: teles1@aol.com
Wants WWII or earlier German daggers, swords, medals, uniforms, helmets, flags, books, documents, patches, belt buckles, postcards, etc.

Phil Froom
U.K.
ph: (44) 411 415616
e-mail: PhilFroom@compuserve.com
WAnts to buy WWII German Wehrpasses and Soldbucher to SS units, especially concentration camp officials.

Dealers

Diane Schreiber
Brandenburg Historica
342A Winchester St., Ste. 121B
Keene, NH 03431-3936
ph: 603-352-1961
e-mail: info@brandenburghistorica.com
web: http://www.brandenburghistorica.com/
Buys and sells German militaria: civil, police & paramilitary organizations, decorations and badges of the German Armed Forces 1871-1945, German military marches and soldiers' songs on cassette, historical and reference material.

Albert Steckler
Military Collectibles
674 Hampton Ave.
Southampton, PA 18966
ph: 215-357-4107
Wants to buy original German helmets from both WWI and WWII; also wants to buy German holsters, daggers, swords, medals, and uniforms from both wars.

Marc J. Cohen
P.O. Box 220153
Hollywood, FL 33022-0153
ph: 954-565-9754
Wants to buy German war souvenirs: helmets, uniforms, medals, gas masks, buttons, canteens, badges, hats, belts, buttons, bayonets, patches, daggers, flags, knives, etc.

Ronald J. Weinand
Weinand Militaria
P.O. Box 323
Quincy, IL 62306-0323
ph: 217-223-2322
fax: 217-223-2552
e-mail: relic@bcl.net
web: http://www.warrelic.com
Appraiser, collector, dealer specializing in German militaria; author of "German Helmets 1933-1945," and "NPEA Daggers and Associated Knives."

Gus Villarreal
7300 Glen Hart
San Antonio, TX 78239
ph: 210-656-4597
Specializing in Waffen SS, army panzer, arm, army tropical & Luftwaffe, headgear items, helmets, visors, overseas caps & M43 caps, SS totenkopf collar tabs, cufftitles & uniforms, SS helmets, etc.

Mark Sansom
German Militaria & Collectibles
U.K.
e-mail: sansom@globalnet.co.uk
web: http://www.users.globalnet.co.uk/~sansom/

Experts

Richard J. Kimmel
P.O. Box 19
Bayville, NJ 08721-1412
ph: 732-269-8581
e-mail: cc1954@adelphia.net
Author of "The Phenomenon of Third Reich Badge Collecting: From the Hocus Bogus to True Genuine"; wants WWII combat cameras: military versions with subdued olive drab and black finish only.

Ronald J. Weinand
Weinand Militaria
P.O. Box 323
Quincy, IL 62306-0323
ph: 217-223-2322
fax: 217-223-2552
e-mail: relic@bcl.net
web: http://www.warrelic.com
Appraiser, collector, dealer specializing in German militaria; author of "German Helmets 1933-1945," and "NPEA Daggers and Associated Knives."

German (East)

Clubs/Associations

Lee Stewart
Society of East German Militaria Collectors
Magazine: SEGMC Magazine
P.O. Box 2153
Reston, VA 20195-0153
ph: 703-715-0683
Source for information on history, uniforms, and insignia of former East German forces; quarterly newsletter.

Helmets

Dealers

Casey Hubbke
Papa Hoth Militaria
5945 West Parker Road, Ste. 3027
Plano, TX 75093
ph: 972-473-6736
fax: 972-473-7278
e-mail: hubblegroup@msn.com
Collectors and dealers in military helmets; also restores helmets, but not original period pieces; buys all types of helmets and helmet parts.

Insignia

(see also BADGES; MEDALS, ORDERS & DECORATIONS; PATCHES; VETERAN ITEMS)

Clubs/Associations

George Duell, Jr.
American Society of Military Insignia Collectors
Journal: Trading Post
526 Lafayette Ave.
Palmerton, PA 18071-1621
ph: 610-826-5067
fax: 610-826-5067
web: http://www.asmic.org/
Dedicated to the collection and preservation of U.S. military cloth and metal insignia; newsletter available only to members and contains members' buy/sell ads; approximately 3000 members; send for application and dues information.

Chute & Dagger
P.O. Box 7201
Arlington, VA 22207-7201
fax: 703-534-7634
e-mail: hfp@ix.netcom.com
Parachute and Special Force insignia collectors.

Collectors

Hank McGonagle
26 Broad St.
Newburyport, MA 01950-2103
ph: 978-462-2354
e-mail: mcgonag@seacoast.com
Wants to buy medals and cloth shoulder insignia; all nations and eras.

Paul Belschner
11303 Woodson Ave.
Kensington, MD 20895-1431
Buys and trades military shoulder insignia (patches).

Don Sexton
400 Flamingo Circle
Greeneville, TN 37743-6126
ph: 423-639-4725
fax: 423-639-3960
President of the American Society of Military Insignia Collectors.

Dealers

H.J. Saunders
H.J. Saunders U.S. Military Insignia, Inc.
5025 Tamiami Trail East
Naples, FL 34113-4126
ph: 941-775-2100 or 800-442-3133
fax: 941-774-3323
e-mail: hjs1usmi@naples.net
web: http://www.naples.net/clubs/zmilins.htm
America's largest retail insignia company; offering over 12,500 different U.S. military insignia items from WWII; insignia; shoulder patches, aviation wings, National Guard, Special Forces, squadron patches; also 150 books on insignia.

J. Polder
Aeroemblem
P.O. Box 6206
Wichita Falls, TX 76311-6202
ph: 940-855-0988 or 940-855-8606
fax: 940-855-0072
e-mail: AEROEMBLEM@aol.com
web: http://www.aeroemblem.com
Has been in the business of trading, buying and selling Air Force patches since the 1950s.

McGrogan's Military Patches
P.O. Box 502
Orofino, ID 83544-0502
ph: 208-476-7751
e-mail: macpatch@clearwater.net
web: http://www.comportcs.com/mcgrogan/
1000s of submarine, ship, Navy, Marine, Air Force, Army and Air Borne patches in stock.

Experts

Mario De Marco
152 Maple St.
West Boylston, MA 01583-1825
ph: 508-835-4085
Have book on Naval ships and aircraft, insignias and history; also Naval and Marine; price $9 each ppd.

David C. Williams
Lost Cause Relics
2237 Brookhollow Dr.
Abilene, TX 79605-5507
ph: 915-692-1858
e-mail: dcjew@swbell.net
Collector and dealer in U.S. medals and medal groupings of all periods; also military photography, documents, uniforms, aviation items, etc.; Special Forces (Green Berets) a specialty.

Internet Resources

Richard Operhall
U.S. Air Force Patch Collectors Homepage
e-mail: roperha@concentric.net
web: http://www.concentric.net/~Roperha/
A web site dedicated to the U.S. Air Force patch/insignia collector; patches for sale, where to buy patches, etc.

Insignia (British)

Dealers

Ian Kelly
Major Ian G. Kelly Militaria
P.O. Box 18
South District Office, Manchester M14 6BB
U.K.
e-mail: Ian_G_Kelly_Militaria@compuserve.com
web: http://ourworld.compuserve.com/homepages/Ian_G_Kelly_Militaria/
Buys and sells original post WWII British military and police badges; send 2 international postal response coupons for free substantial catalog: caps and collar insignia, trade and proficiency badges, shoulder titles, etc.

Experts

Ian Kelly
Major Ian G. Kelly Militaria
P.O. Box 18
South District Office, Manchester M14 6BB
U.K.
e-mail: Ian_G_Kelly_Militaria@compuserve.com
web: http://ourworld.compuserve.com/homepages/Ian_G_Kelly_Militaria/
Buys and sells original post WWII British military and police badges; send 2 international postal response coupons for free substantial catalog: caps and collar insignia, trade and proficiency badges, shoulder titles, etc.

Japanese

(see ARMS & ARMOR; FIREARMS, Japanese Matchlocks; ORIENTALIA, Japanese Items)

Manuals

Dealers

George Kastner
Daddy Warbooks
P.O. Box 6397
Los Osos, CA 93412-6397
ph: 805-528-1614
Wants to buy military books and manuals from 1900-1965.

Medals

(see also MEDALS, ORDERS & DECORATIONS)

Clubs/Associations

John E. Lelle, Sec.
Orders & Medals Society of America
Newsletter: Medal Collector, The
P.O. Box 484
Glassboro, NJ 08028-0484
e-mail: dlriley@hop-uky.campus.mci.net
web: http://www.omsa.org/
Interested in collecting and studying military and civil orders, decorations and medals of all countries.

Nuclear

Collectors

Danial Saks
Ground Zero
365 Hill St.
San Francisco, CA 94114
ph: 415-826-8337
Wants items related to nuclear warfare and testing: Manhattan Project, Pacific Tests, Nevada Tests, WWII.

Museums/Libraries

Shelley Renee
National Atomic Museum, Kirtland Air Force Base
P.O. Box 5400
Albuquerque, NM 87115
ph: 505-284-3243
e-mail: srenee@sandia.gov
web: http://www.sandia.gov/museum/main.htm
Exhibits cover the complete history of U.S. nuclear development.

Polish

Clubs/Associations

Polish Military Collectors Association
Magazine: Hetman
591 Humboldt St.
Brooklyn, NY 11222
ph: 718-441-5478
e-mail: hetman@hetman.org
web: http://www.hetman.org/pages/theclub.htm
A private club for collectors of Polish antiques, Polish art, and Polish militaria.

Experts

John Scott Mathews
SLm Consulting
1051 E. Kent Place
Chandler, AZ 85225
ph: 602-978-7185
e-mail: JScottMathews@netscape.net
Thirty years collecting experience in Polish militaria: headgear, uniforms, badges, medals, flags, bayonets and swords; professional historian employed as a professor at a major institution of higher learning.

Russian

(see also RUSSIAN ITEMS)

Dealers

Igor Moiseyev
Atlantic Crossroads, Inc.
P.O. Box 290715
Brooklyn, NY 11229-5904
ph: 718-332-5889
fax: 718-332-5904
Sells 1918-1980s Russian military and civilian decorations, documented award groups, WWII and 1950s uniforms and field gear, historical documents, reference books, military badges and insignia; offers appraisals, research, translations.

Robert Natanzon
Original Soviet Militaria
2536 Hubbard St.
Brooklyn, NY 11235-6223
ph: 718-769-1446
fax: 718-769-5617
e-mail: rob1329@aol.com
web: http://www.find-russian-antiques.com/
Specializes in Russian militaria, icons, crosses, silver, etc.

Silk Embroideries

Collectors

Howard Averbach
1919 Delaware Ave.
Pittsburgh, PA 15218-1801
ph: 412-441-6904
Wants to buy patriotic/military silk embroideries purchased as souvenirs by U.S. soldiers and sailors in the Orient; embroidered ships, flags, eagles, mottoes; wallhangings only; no pillowcases or clothing.

Spanish-American War

Collectors

Morris Pickerell, Jr.
103 South Crawford St.
Tompkinsville, KY 42167
ph: 800-826-4499 or 502-678-5848
fax: 502-678-7888
Wants to buy anything relating to Admiral George Dewey, the Spanish-American War, including battleship Maine.

Submarine Related

Collectors

Ken Blazier
2937 Elda St.
Duarte, CA 91010-1431
Wants WWII submarine memorabilia.

U-Boats

Clubs/Associations

Harry Cooper
Sharkhunters International Inc.
Magazine: KTB Magazine (Kriegs Tag Buch)
P.O. Box 1539
Hernando, FL 34442
ph: 352-637-2917
fax: 352-637-6289
web: http://uboat.europe.is/about/sharks.htm
Locates and preserves the history of the German and Italian U-Boat forces; recognized leading authority on the subject; Sharkhunters is the largest research center in the Western hemisphere on German U-Boat history.

Museums/Libraries

Keith R. Gill
Museum of Science & Industry
57th St. & Lake Shore Dr.
Chicago, IL 60637
ph: 773-684-1414
fax: 773-684-5580

Uniforms

Clubs/Associations

Company of Military Historians
Newsletter: Military Collector & Historian
North Main St.
Westbrook, CT 06498
ph: 860-399-9460
fax: 860-399-9320

Gil Sanow, II, Ed.
Association of American Military Uniform Collectors
Newsletter: Footlocker
P.O. Box 1876
Elyria, OH 44036
ph: 440-365-5321
e-mail: aamucfl@aol.com
web: http://www.naples.net/clubs/aamuc/info.html
Members are interested in improving their personal collections and in sharing information, ideas and knowledge about U.S. military uniforms.

Louis Wendruck
Military & Police Uniform Association
Magazine: Military & Police Uniform Association Newsletter
P.O. Box 69A04 - Dept. Mal
West Hollywood, CA 90069-0066
ph: 323-650-5112
e-mail: gayboylaca@writeme.com
web: http://members.tripod.com/~mpua/
A club for men into the uniform lifestyle including military, police, WWII, SS and boots; magazine has photos, stories, buy/sell ads.

Collectors

Joe Weber
604 Centre St.
Ashland, PA 17921-1332
ph: 570-875-4787 or 570-875-4401
Wants to buy Victorian, WWI (especially aviation), and WWII (especially CBI theater-made uniforms); all countries (US, Britain, German, France, Russia.)

Dealers

Experienced Denim
P.O. Box 239
Fayetteville, AR 72702-0239
ph: 501-444-7541 or 800-336-4694
fax: 501-521-8331
e-mail: exd@edenim.com
web: http://www.edenim.com/
Wants to buy vintage fatigue wear, denim wear, khaki pants, nylon flight jackets, tanker boots, etc.

Vehicles

Clubs/Associations

S. Sebring
Red Ball Military Transport
400 Ave. C
Stroudsburg, PA 18360
ph: 717-421-2950

Joe McClain
Indiana Chapter of the Military Vehicle Preservation Association
2330 Crystal St.
Anderson, IN 46012-1726
ph: 765-649-8265
fax: 765-642-0262
web: http://www.indol.com/ads/visitor/armormuseum.html

Kay Willard
Military Vehicle Preservation Association
Newsletter: Army Motors & Supply Line
P.O. Box 520378
Independence, MO 64052-0378
ph: 816-737-5111
fax: 816-737-5423
e-mail: mvpa-hq@mvpa.org
web: http://www.mvpa.org
Since 1976, an international organization dedicated to the preservation of military transport from trucks to tanks.

Lani Geisler, Treas.
Inland Empire Military Vehicle Preservation Association
4960 Pinto Place.
Norco, CA 91760
ph: 909-734-1854
A world-wide organization dedicated to the preservation and restoration of military vehicles.

Frank Von Rosenstiel
Ontario Military Vehicle Association
1248 Dartmoor St.
Oshawa, Ontario L1K 2K2
Canada
ph: 905-721-0840

Nigel Godfrey, Mem. Sec.
Military Vehicle Trust, The
Magazine: Windscreen
P.O. Box 6
Fleet, Hants. GU13 9PE
U.K.
fax: +44 (0) 1264 392951
e-mail: nigelgodfrey@mvt.org.uk
web: http://www.mvt.org.uk/

Dealers

David W. Uhrig
David W. Uhrig Military Vehicles Sales & Appraisals
P.O. Box 726
Chillicothe, OH 45601
ph: 740-772-1540
fax: 740-772-1540
e-mail: mvs@bright.net
web: http://brightnet.horizontel.com/MVS/
Buys, sells, brokers, appraises military vehicles.

Jack Tomlin
Tomlin Ordnance Depot
P.O. Box 778
Tooele, UT 84074
ph: 801-882-0420
fax: 801-882-5042
Buys and sells all sorts of military

vehicles from trailers to tanks.

Museums/Libraries

Joe McClain
Historical Military Armor Museum
2330 Crystal St.
Anderson, IN 46012-1726
ph: 765-649-8265
fax: 765-642-0262
web: http://www.indol.com/ads/visitor/armormuseum.html
One of the most complete collections of Light U.S. Tanks; plus a dozen prototypes of various vehicles; 30,000 sq. ft. of displays; collection has armored vehicles from WWI through Desert Storm.

Periodicals

SBI, Inc.
Magazine: Military Vehicles
12-Q3 Indian Head Rd.
Morristown, NJ 07960
ph: 973-285-0716
fax: 973-285-5934
e-mail: mvehicle@aol.com
web: http://members.aol.com/MVehicle/home.htm
A bi-monthly magazine for military vehicle (wheeled & tracked) enthusiasts.

Magazine: MV Magazine
North House
Northside
Patrington, East Yorkshire HU12 0PB
U.K.
ph: 01964 631244
fax: 01964 631576
e-mail: mv@tradingnorthwest.demon.co.uk
web: http://www.tradingnorthwest.demon.co.uk/military.vehicles/
A bi-monthly British publication for military vehicle collectors and enthusiasts: restoration tips, tales, news, contacts, photos, illustrations.

Repair Services

John A. Headley, Jr.
Doncar Equipment Co.
P.O. Box 133
Flanders, NJ 07836
ph: 973-927-0940
Restores military vehicles.

Suppliers

Daniel Janquitto
Canvas Beach Works
P.O. Box 137
Island Heights, NJ 08732
ph: 732-929-3168
Provides parts for WWII military vehicles such as Jeeps.

Peter Bella Jeep Parts
242 D Silas Carter Rd.
Manorville, NY 11949

Vehicles (Armored)

Internet Resources

Olive Drab
e-mail: chuck@olive-drab.com
web: http://www.olive-drab.com/
Web site where you will find original materials on many military subjects; links to military vehicles, military movies and books, vehicle/parts dealers, organizations, surplus dealers, military photos and clip art, etc.

Museums/Libraries

Bill Gasser
American Armoured Foundation, Tank & Ordnance War Memorial Museum
2383 5th Ave.
Ronkonkoma, NY 11779
ph: 516-588-0033
fax: 516-981-4992
e-mail: aaf.tank.museum@erols.com
web: http://www.aaftankmuseum.com/
Museum of armored vehicles, weapons and militaria dedicated in the honor of all veterans.

Patton Museum of Cavalry & Armor
P.O. Box 208
Fort Knox, KY 40121-0208
ph: 502-624-3812
fax: 502-624-6968
e-mail: museum@ftknox-emh3.army.mil
web: http://147.238.100.101/museum/
Established to preserve historical materials relating to Cavalry and Armor and to make these properties available for public use.

American Military Museum
Whittier Narrows Rec. Area
1918 North Rosemead Blvd.
El Monte, CA 91732
ph: 626-442-1776
Maintained by the American Society of Military History; contains the largest collection of tanks and military vehicles in the U.S.

WWI Items

Collectors

Randy Trawnik
8226 Douglas, #415
Dallas, TX 75225
ph: 214-941-2445
fax: 214-739-8361
e-mail: dallaseye@airmail.net
Wants WWI German spiked helmets, uniforms, etc.; wants in any condition; also identification and restoration.

Dealers

Dale & Debra Anderson
Dale C. Anderson Co.
4 W. Confederate Ave.
Gettysburg, PA 17325
ph: 717-334-1031
Sells, appraises guns, swords, uniforms, headgear, relics, personal items, more; all offered in bi-monthly catalog ($12/yr); covers all periods 1775-1945; US & foreign; emphasis on Civil War/Indian Wars period; over 38 years experience.

Ken Greenfield
Der Rittmeister Militaria
P.O. Box 2456
Woodstock, GA 30188
ph: 770-926-8110
e-mail: rittmeister@mindspring.com
web: http://www.mindspring.com/~rittmeister/
Specializes in German Imperial WWI collectibles with an emphasis on aviation-related items.

WWI Items (Posters)

(see also POSTERS)

Collectors

Ken Khuans
155 Harbor Dr. #4812
Chicago, IL 60601-7378
ph: 312-642-0554
Collector wants WWI posters; also books relating to WWI posters.

Dealers

Maurice & Laya Jakubowicz
Affiche Francaise
Le Plateau
Bazincourt/Epte, 21740
France
ph: 33 (0)232 27 61 53
fax: 33 (0)232 27 10 12
e-mail: ml@affiche-Francaise.com
web: http://affiche-Francaise.com/
Buys and sells posters, mainly French, some foreign; catalog sent on request.

Experts

George Theofiles
Miscellaneous Man
P.O. Box 1776
New Freedom, PA 17349-0191
ph: 717-235-4766
fax: 717-235-2853
Collects, buys and sells; since 1970 offering catalogs of rare posters and early advertising and ephemera on hundreds of subjects; descriptive flyer available; author of "American Posters of World War I".

WWII Items

Auction Services

Adrian Forman
Forman International Auctions
P.O. Box 25
Minehead, Somerset TA24 8YX
U.K.
ph: 01643 862511
For original military and historical pieces; specialist in German Third Reich era: awards, militaria, books, documents, ephemera; four auctions per year.

Collectors

Richard Harrow
8523 210 St.
Jamaica, NY 11427
ph: 718-740-1088
fax: 718-740-1088
Wants any item relating to WWII: allied forces, anti-fascist propaganda, Jewish Holocaust, soldier benevolent aid, etc.

Daniel Lee
P.O. Box 1142
Brentwood, TN 37024-1142
ph: 615-370-3220 or 615-429-5336
e-mail: 6lees@sprintmail.com
Federally licensed firearms collector seeking Third Reich era (WWII) items, especially Mauser, Luger, Walther manufactured and related accessories.

Harry Fisher
Rte. 1 Box 197
Owensville, MO 65066
ph: 573-437-4227
Wants WWII items: books, magazines, unit records (especially 8th Air Force memorabilia), etc.; please describe and price.

Dealers

Jerry Rubackin
Jerry's Cards & Collectibles
P.O. Box 1271
Framingham, MA 01701-0207
ph: 508-788-5197
fax: 508-788-5197
Buys and sells WWII fighter aces autographs and other WWII military signatures; also want autographed material by the crew of the Enola Gay which dropped the first atomic bomb on Hiroshima.

Dale & Debra Anderson
Dale C. Anderson Co.
4 W. Confederate Ave.
Gettysburg, PA 17325
ph: 717-334-1031
Sells, appraises guns, swords, uniforms, headgear, relics, personal items, more; all offered in bi-monthly catalog ($12/yr); covers all periods 1775-1945; US & foreign; emphasis on Civil War/Indian Wars period; over 38 years experience.

Anthony Jessen
Jessen's Relics, Inc.
P.O. Box 9523
Birmingham, AL 35220
ph: 205-681-6382
fax: 205-680-9171
Specializing in German WWII relics, some US and other nations, 400 to 500 German insignia each catalog: medals, badges, pins, buckles, flags, cloth insignia, visor hats, helmets and uniforms, field gear, edged weapons; catalog $10.

Don Gillis
WWII Productions
4750 S. Padre Island Dr.
Corpus Christi, TX 78411
ph: 512-854-3541
e-mail: wwii@trip.net
web: http://www.historicalmilitaria.com
Buys, sells, collects WWII militaria.

Wolfe-Hardin
6490 Bixby Hill Rd.
Long Beach, CA 90815
ph: 562-596-6610
fax: 562-596-0086
Buys and sells top quality items; especially interested in SS Allach, china documents, regimental embroidery, trumpet banners, poletops, streamers, gorgets, cased medals, orders and decorations, edged weapons, headgear, etc.

WWII Items (Homefront)

Collectors

Martin Jacobs
P.O. Box 22026
San Francisco, CA 94122-0026
ph: 415-661-7552
e-mail: MJacobs784@aol.com
Collector seeks WWII memorabilia from the Homefront 1941-1945; will purchase any size collection; wants victory pins, Cinderella stickers and stamps, envelope art, war propaganda, Anti-Axis art, matchcovers, postcards, etc.

WWII Items (Paratroop)

Collectors

Ed Hicks
819 Hope Mills Rd.
Fayetteville, NC 28304-2224
ph: 910-425-7000
Airborne collector/historian wants to buy WWII Paratroop and Elite militaria: jump jackets, pants, boots, M1C helmets, A-2 leather jackets, fighting and jump knives, T-5 parachutes, unit histories, all related equipment.

WWII Items (Photographs)

Collectors

Scott A. Swanson
50 Gloucester St.
Boston, MA 02115-3141
ph: 617-536-8013
Wants photos of American, European soldiers, sailors; all fronts, all branches; albums, single snapshots, photos taken by soldiers rather than official or press; no printed cards or reproductions; also German and P.O.W.

WWII Items (Posters)

(see also POSTERS)

Collectors

John Stachmus
RR 1 Box 110
Homer, IL 61849
ph: 217-896-2859
Collector wants WWII posters.

Dealers

Jim Meehan
Meehan Military Collectibles
P.O. Box 477
New York, NY 10028-0018
ph: 212-734-5683
fax: 212-535-4249
e-mail: meehan@interport.net
web: http://www.posterfair.com/mm/storefront.htm

Maurice & Laya Jakubowicz
Affiche Francaise
Le Plateau
Bazincourt/Epte, 21740
France
ph: 33 (0)232 27 61 53
fax: 33 (0)232 27 10 12
e-mail: ml@affiche-Francaise.com
web: http://affiche-Francaise.com/
Buys and sells posters, mainly French, some foreign; catalog sent on request.

Experts

George Theofiles
Miscellaneous Man
P.O. Box 1776
New Freedom, PA 17349-0191
ph: 717-235-4766
fax: 717-235-2853
Catalogs issued.

MILITARY HISTORY

(see also AVIATION, Military; AVIATION MEMORABILIA; BOOKS, Collector [Militaria]; CIVIL WAR HISTORY; INDIAN WARS; LIVING HISTORY; MARINE CORPS ITEMS; MILITARIA; SOLDIERS, Toy; VIETNAM ITEMS)

Book Sellers

Richard S. Gardner
Battery Press, Inc., The
P.O. Box 198885
Nashville, TN 37219-8885
ph: 615-298-1401
fax: 615-298-1401
e-mail: batterybks@aol.com
web: http://www.sonic.net/~bstone/battery/
Carries books about WWI and WWII; specializes in aviation, military and naval titles.

Clubs/Associations

Company of Military Historians
Newsletter: Military Collector & Historian
North Main St.
Westbrook, CT 06498
ph: 860-399-9460
fax: 860-399-9320
Military collection from 1775 to present; library, exhibits, educational programs.

Internet Resources

Jonathan Gawne
Militaria.com
P.O. Box 2925
Framingham, MA 01703
e-mail: jgawne@militaria.com
web: http://www.militaria.com/gij.html
A place for military collectors and military historians; home of the "G.I. Journal", with information on some of the best military magazines, books, collectibles, and militaria sites.

Misc. Services

Meredith Vezina
Traditions Military History
102 West 6th Ave.
Escondido, CA 92025
ph: 800-277-1977 or 760-735-9313
fax: 760-432-9043
e-mail: cservice@militaryvideo.com
web: http://www.militaryvideo.com/
Sells hard-to-find government-produced films originally recorded in the 1930s through 1980s on 16 and 35 mm film by combat camera teams; films have been transferred to video.

Museums/Libraries

Massachusetts National Guard Military Museum & Archives
Worcester Armory
44 Salisbury St.
Worcester, MA 01609
ph: 508-797-0334 or 508-757-2410
web: http://www.state.ma.us/guard/Museum/museum.htm
Military history museum and archive related to the history of the Massachusetts National Guard from 1638 to present.

Bruce M. Moseley, Cur.
Fort Ticonderoga Museum
Newsletter: Bulletin of the Fort Ticonderoga Museum
P.O. Box 390
Ticonderoga, NY 12883
ph: 518-585-2821
fax: 518-585-2210
web: http://www.neinfo.net/new_england/new_york/attractions/fort-ticonderoga/
10,000 volume research library specializing in 19th century military history and the history of the Champlain Valley; museum depicts history of the area and the campaigns during the 7 Year War and the Revolutionary War.

Virginia War Museum
9285 Warwick Blvd.
Newport News, VA 23607
ph: 757-247-8523 or 757-247-8522
fax: 757-247-8627
Museum interprets U.S. military history from 1775 to present; featuring over 60,000 artifacts.

Periodicals

Magazine: Artilleryman, The
RR 1 Box 36
Tunbridge, VT 05077-9707
ph: 802-889-3500 or 800-777-1862
fax: 802-889-5627
e-mail: mail@civilwarnews.com
web: http://www.civilwarnews.com/
Published quarterly, the only magazine exclusively for the 1750-1898 artillery enthusiast: artillery history, unit profiles, shell collecting, etc.

Cowles Magazines, Inc.
Magazine: MHQ: The Quarterly Journal of Military History
741 Miller Dr. SE, Ste. D2
Harrisburg, PA 20175
ph: 717-540-6617 or 800-829-3340
fax: 717-540-6706
e-mail: brentd@cowles.com
web: http://www.cowles.com/maglist.html
A quarterly magazine containing a wide variety of articles on military history.

Erika Daileda
Wise Owl Worldwide Publications
Magazine: Regiment
4314 West 238th St. - Dept. MACR
Torrance, CA 90505-4509
ph: 310-375-6258
fax: 310-375-0548
e-mail: wiseowl@sprintmail.com
An English magazine published 9 timer per year; regimental and unit histories presented through pictorial records; weapons, vehicles, accoutrements, uniforms, medals and decorations, equipment, model soldiers, etc.

Erika Daileda
Wise Owl Worldwide Publications
Magazine: Military Illustrated
4314 West 238th St. - Dept. MACR
Torrance, CA 90505-4509
ph: 310-375-6258
fax: 310-375-0548
e-mail: wiseowl@sprintmail.com
A monthly English publication; all periods of military history from ancient to WWII; in-depth research, rare photos, specially commissioned artwork make this magazine one of the finest reference sources for collectors and enthusiasts.

Cavalry

Clubs/Associations

Patricia S. Bright
U.S. Cavalry Association & U.S. Cavalry Memorial Research Library
Journal: Cavalry Journal
P.O. Box 2325
Fort Riley, KS 66442-0325
ph: 785-784-5759
fax: 785-784-5797
e-mail: cavalry@flinthills.com
web: http://www.wtvi.com/cavalry
Mission is to preserve for posterity the history, equipment, and traditions of the U.S. Cavalry from its inception as a horse mounted force during the Revolutionary War into the 21st century; sponsors the U.S. cavalry Museum.

Museums/Libraries

Terry Van Meter
U.S. Cavalry Museum
P.O. Box 2160
Fort Riley, KS 66442-0160
ph: 785-239-2737
e-mail: vanmeter@riley-emh1.army.mil
Preserves and displays the uniforms, weapons and equipment used by cavalry soldiers from the Revolutionary War through WWII.

Unit Histories

Collectors

Bill Baumann
P.O. Box 319
Esperance, NY 12066-0319
ph: 518-875-6753
Collects military unit history books from all American wars (i.e. Civil War, Spanish American War, WWI, WWII, Korea, Vietnam); also wants unit photos, holiday menus, albums, posthumous decorations; specializes in black militaria.

Museums/Libraries

U.S. Military History Institute
22 Ashburn Drive
Carlisle Barracks
Carlisle, PA 17013-5008
ph: 717-245-3611
e-mail: MHI-HR@awc.carlisle.army.mil
web: http://carlisle-www.army.mil/usamhi/
Specialized library to research military history including unit histories; department of the U.S. Army War College; the Army's central repository for historical materials; collects, preserves, and makes available military history.

U.S. Army Center of Military History
103 Third Avenue
Ft. McNair, DC 20319-5058
ph: 202-272-0310
e-mail: cmhonline@hqda.army.mil
web: http://www.army.mil/cmh-pg/
Specialized library to research military unit histories.

U.S. Marine Corps Museum/Library
Marine Corps Historical Center
Washington Navy Yard, Bldg. 58
Washington, DC 20374-0580
ph: 202-433-3483
fax: 202-433-4691
web: http://www.usmc.mil/
Specialized library to research military unit histories.

Library of Congress
101 Independence Ave. SE
Washington, DC 20540
ph: 202-707-5000 or 202-707-8000
e-mail: lcinfo@loc.gov
web: http://www.loc.gov
Specialized library to research military unit histories.

U.S. Army Military Police Corps Regimental Museum
Bldg. 3182
Anniston, AL 36205-5000
ph: 256-848-3522
fax: 256-848-6139
Gift shop provides military police memorabilia on site and by mail order.

Jerry G. Burgess, Dir.
U.S. Army Women's Corps Museum
Newsletter: WAC Newsletter
Bldg. 10777
3rd St. & 5th Ave.
Fort McClellan, AL 36205-5000
ph: 205-848-3512 or 205-848-5559
fax: 205-848-7323
e-mail: jerry_burgess@prodigy.com
web: http://www.mcclellan.army.mil/wac.htm
Cannot buy, sell or appraise items; can only provide information to collectors and researchers.

MILLING

Appraisers

Robert L. Johnson
Whistles in the Woods Museum Services
P.O. Box 309
Chickamauga, GA 30707-0309
ph: 706-375-4326
e-mail: oldgoat@voy.net
Consultants specializing in 1750 - early 20th century historic machinery; power-generation, tools, machines, scientific & technical instruments, mining, milling, transportation, logging & lumbering, steam engines, etc.

Book Sellers

Sidney Halma
Mill Book Store
P.O. Box 1055
Newton, NC 28658
ph: 704-465-0383 or 704-465-0928
fax: 704-465-9813
e-mail: eamedit@aol.com
web: http://www.spoom.org
Sells books relating to milling; many reprints.

Clubs/Associations

Sidney Hamla
Society for the Preservation of Old Mills (SPOOM)
Magazine: Old Mill News
P.O. Box 1055
Newton, NC 28658
ph: 704-465-0383 or 704-465-0928
fax: 704-465-9813
e-mail: eamedit@aol.com
web: http://www.spoom.org
Organization focuses on the milling industry: mills, millwrights, equipment, techniques; ads, mills for sale, millwrights, stones, etc.; in existence for over 20 years; over 2000 members.

Collectors

Fred Foley
1333 Randolph Ave.
Saint Paul, MN 55105-2957
ph: 612-690-0993 or 612-699-0859
fax: 612-699-0859
e-mail: FredFromMN@webtv.net
Collector seeks pre-1940 flour milling memorabilia: calendars, signs, thermometers, flour bags with graphics, trade cards, store advertising displays; anything related to the milling industry.

Museums/Libraries

Hanford Mills Museum
P.O. Box 99
East Meredith, NY 13757
ph: 607-278-5744 or 800-295-4992
fax: 607-278-5840
e-mail: hanford4@hanfordmills.org
web: http://www.catskillguide.com/hanford.htm

Bobbins & Spools

Dealers

David W. Harris
Joel S. Perkins & Son, Inc.
P.O. Box 299
South Strafford, VT 05070-0209
ph: 802-889-3260
fax: 802-889-3316
e-mail: jsperk@sover.net
web: http://www.joelsperkins.com/
Textile mill supplies, bobbins, spools, shuttle, mill memorabilia.

Man./Prod./Dist.

Dirk & Ann Poole
Ma's Bobbin Works, Inc.
P.O. Box 667
Newcastle, ME 04553-0667
ph: 207-563-1210 or 800-782-8581
fax: 207-633-2313
web: http://www.woodenbobbins.com/
Manufactures a wide assortment of items (candle holders, lamps, etc.) from old textile mill bobbins.

MINERAL SPECIMENS

(see also FOSSILS; GEMS & JEWELRY; GOLD; LAPIDARY; MARBLE & STONE; MINING RELATED ITEMS; NATURAL HISTORY; SAND)

Auction Services

Jeremy Fuller
Mineral, Fossil & Gemstones Auctions Co.
997 N. Chapel Dr., Ste. #4
Bountiful, UT 84010
ph: 801-296-2516
fax: 801-292-5439
e-mail: info@minimarket.com
web: http://www.minmarket.com/
The first mineral, fossil, and gemstone "mall" auction of its kind on the Web.

Clubs/Associations

Mineralogical Society of America
Magazine: American Mineralogist
1015 Eighteenth St. NW, Ste. 601
Washington, DC 20036-5274
ph: 202-775-4344
fax: 202-775-0018
e-mail: j_a_speer@minsocam.org
web: http://www.minsocam.org
Members are interested in mineralogy, crystallography, and petrology; promotes, through education and research, the understanding and application of mineralogy by industry, universities, government and the public.

Carolyn Weinberger
Gem Cutters Guild of Baltimore, Inc.
Newsletter: Gem Cutters News
P.O. Box 302
Glyndon, MD 21071-0302
e-mail: cweinber@bcpl.net
For those interested in the study of earth sciences and the practice of lapidary arts and crafts.

Gem & Mineral Society of the Virginia Peninsula
P.O. Box 6424
Hidenwood Station
Newport News, VA 23606
e-mail: vapen@widowmaker.com
web: http://www.widowmaker.com/~finn/vapen/index.html

Duncan Heron
Carolina Geological Society
P.O. Box 90234
Durham, NC 27708-0234
ph: 919-684-5321
fax: 919=684-5833
e-mail: heron@geo.duke.edu
web: http://www.geo.duke.edu/cgsinfo.htm

Steve Henegar
Middle Tennessee Gem & Mineral Society
Newsletter: Mid Tenn Gem'ers
P.O. Box 1256
Murfreesboro, TN 37133-1256
ph: 615-896-1472
e-mail: steve.henegar@nashville.com
web: http://www.nashville.com/~Rockhound/MTGMS.htm
Dedicated to the study and enjoyment of the earth sciences; monthly meetings 3rd Thursday, Farm Bureau Bldg., 818 South Church St.; annual gems & mineral show.

John Watkins
Southeast Federation of Mineralogical Societies
299 Edwards School Rd.
Loudon, TN 37774
e-mail: Riesling4@aol.com
web: http://www.ces.clemson.edu/~frsias/sfms.html
Brings together those clubs and societies devoted to the study of earth sciences and the practice of lapidary arts and crafts in the Southeast part of the US.

Knoxville Gem & Mineral Society
P.O. Box 50291
Knoxville, TN 37950-0291
web: http://www.kornet.org/kgms/

Evansville Lapidary Society
1304 North Willow Road
Evansville, IN 47711
ph: 812-425-GEMS
e-mail: mylines@evansville.net
web: http://www.evansville.net/~mylines/els.html

Hellgate Mineral Society
P.O. Box 3015
Missoula, MT 59807
e-mail: Macsgems@aol.com
web: http://www.freeyellow.com/members2/macsgems/

American Federation of Mineralogical Societies
P.O. Box 26523
Oklahoma City, OK 73126-0523
e-mail: afms@afmed.org
web: http://www.amfed.org/
A non-profit educational federation of seven similar regional organizations of gem, mineral and lapidary societies.

Granvil Pennington
Clear Lake Gem & Mineral Society
P.O. Box 58072
Houston, TX 77258
ph: 281-481-1591
fax: 281-481-2002
e-mail: gpenning@ghgcorp.com
web: http://www.ghgcorp.com/gpenning/
The club web site gives those individuals interested in rocks, minerals, faceting and lapidary a source for information on the earth sciences and supporting organizations.

Clark County Gem Collectors, The
P.O. Box 89125
Las Vegas, NV 89125
e-mail: admin@ccgc.org
web: http://www.ccgc.org
An educational and social club for those who enjoy collecting and learning about rocks, gems, minerals, fossils, and the lapidary arts.

Dr. Rodney Burroughs, Pres.
Fluorescent Mineral Society, Inc.
P.O. Box 572694
Tarzana, CA 91357
A society for professional mineralogists, gemologists, amateur collectors, and anyone else sharing an interest in minerals that glow under invisible ultraviolet light.

Dr. Rodney Burroughs
Fluorescent Mineral Society
Newsletter: UV Waves
P.O. Box 572694
Tarzana, CA 91357-2694
e-mail: 71543.3343@compuserve.com
Over 400 members worldwide specialize in the collection and study of fluorescent minerals.

Garth Bricker
Fallbrook Gem & Mineral Society
Newsletter: Lithoshpere
P.O. 62
Fallbrook, CA 92088-0062
ph: 760-728-1333
e-mail: gbricker@sd.znet.com
web: http://www.inetworld.net/rbusch/fgms/
Amateur gem and mineral society, free gem and mineral museum.

Everett Rock & Gem Club
P.O. Box 1615
Langley, WA 98260
e-mail: sheeeeesh@msn.com
web: http://www.geocities.com/Yosemite/Trails/3085/

Collectors

Stephen Seltzer
7912 Georgia Ave.
Silver Spring, MD 20910-4837
ph: 301-565-2444 or 301-565-3339
fax: 301-565-2228
e-mail: eseltzer@aol.com
Wants to buy specimen size minerals and fossils for display.

Gary E. Fleck
P.O. Box 2886
Hot Springs National Park, AR 71914-2886
ph: 501-623-4098
fax: 501-623-4098
Wants to buy mineral collections, natural rock crystals, cutting rough rock.

Robert E. Spomer
Gem Kingdom, The
P.O. Box 27088
Lakewood, CO 80227
ph: 303-986-1851
e-mail: gemkingdom@aol.com
web: http://members.aol.com/respomer/gk.htm
A professional gem cutter by trade, specializing in custom collector's gemstones and fancy-cut jewelry grade stones; also collects and mines minerals and gems, especially in Colorado; also collects Fairburn and other banded agates.

Dealers

John Betts
John Betts Fine Minerals
215 West 98 Street, No. 2F
New York, NY 10025
ph: 212-678-1942
fax: 212-242-7020
e-mail: jhbnyc@aol.com
web: http://members.aol.com/jhbnyc/home.htm
Wide range of natural history collectibles: fossils, crystals, minerals, books on earth sciences; specializes in large, aesthetic mineral crystal specimens from around the world; have sold to museums, collectors and decorators.

Les Tolonen
Keweenaw Agate Shop
P.O. Box 20
Copper Harbor, MI 49918
ph: 906-289-4491

Deb & Dave McClain
Mac's Gems
2204 South 8th St.
Missoula, MT 59801
ph: 406-549-7003
e-mail: Macsgems@aol.com
Offers Montana gems and crystals: sapphire, garnets, agate, quartz crystals, and very large smoky quartz points; also Canadian ammolite, ammetrine, Brazilian amethyst, and much more.

R. Kelley Laughlin
Kelrocks
324 W. Lincoln Hwy.
De Kalb, IL 60115
ph: 815-748-7425
e-mail: kelrocks@webtv.net
web: http://www.angelfire.com/biz/kelrocks/
Mineral specimens, finished and unfinished gemstones, custom silver jewelry; specimens collected by experienced agents who can provide precise information for systematic collectors.

Jayne Horak
Crystal Springs Mining & Jewelry
P.O. Box 40
Royal, AR 71968
ph: 501-991-3557
fax: 501-991-3281

Joe Pfeiffer
XTAL Publishing
P.O. Box 253
Sandy, UT 84091-0253
ph: 801-571-5453
e-mail: joep@antiquesecrets.com
web: http://www.antiquesecrets.com/
Buy, sell, trade books on mining, geology, mineralogy; USGS publications, rockhound books, any old geology literature and paper or memorabilia related to mining and minerals; publisher of "A System of Mineral Collecting."

John & Karen Mediz
Copper City Rock Shop
566 Ash St.
Globe, AZ 85501
ph: 520-425-7885 or 520-425-4506
fax: 520-425-4506
Buys and sells mining artifacts; also wants to buy minerals and fossils, especially old collections.

Jesse Wellman
High Grade Treasures
P.O. Box 5470
Reno, NV 89513
e-mail: jesse@highgradetreasures.com
web: http://www.highgradetreasures.com
Field collects and purchases minerals and fossils to provide quality common and unusual specimens for the discriminating collector and hobby beginner.

Gem & Mineral Exploration Company, The
4141 Ball Road #373
Cypress, CA 90630
e-mail: gameco@gemandmineral.com
web: http://www.gemandmineral.com/

George Campbell
OsoSoft Mineral Collection
2122 9th St., Ste. 202
Los Osos, CA 93402
ph: 805-528-1759
fax: 805-528-3074
e-mail: osomin@compuserve.com
web: http://www.osomin.com
Buys and sells high quality mineral specimens.

Fossil Company, The
P.O. Box 1339
El Cerrito, CA 94530
ph: 510-233-8891
fax: 510-232-5614
e-mail: sales@fossil-company.com
web: http://www.fossil-company.com
Supplier of fine quality fossils, mineral specimens and crystals.

Peter Chesko
Castle Rocks
P.O. Box 565
201 N. Shasta Blvd.
Mount Shasta, CA 96067
ph: 530-926-5804
fax: 530-926-6392
e-mail: castlerx@jps.net
web: http://www.jps.net/castlerx/
Collect, evaluate, sell rare mineral specimens from Afghanistan, Brazil, Pakistan, Russia and many other parts of the world; carries the finest tourmaline, aquamarine, garnet, chrome diopside, epidote, rhodochrosite, and many others.

Tome & Sue Robertson
Robertson's Rock Works
1785 Tumalo Dr. SE
Salem, OR 97301
ph: 503-363-9678
fax: 503-364-3750

Doug Miller
Northern Lights Minerals
#106-186, 3120 8th St. E.
Saskatoon, SK S7H 0W2
Canada
ph: 306-373-5013
fax: 306-477-1727
e-mail: mildg@sk.sympatico.ca
web: http://www.minerals.sk.ca
Specializes in fine quality Canadian mineral specimens.

Experts

Dr. Abraham Rosenzweig
Rosenzweig Associates
P.O. Box 16187
Tampa, FL 33687-6187
ph: 813-988-0880
fax: 813-989-8091
e-mail: rosetwig@aol.com
Consultant specializing in mineralogy and gemology.

Internet Resources

Canadian Rockhound
Canada
e-mail: cdn_rockhound@hotmail.com
web: http://pangea.usask.ca/~dfs846/rockhound/
An on-line magazine providing interesting and educational stories on rock, fossil and mineral collecting, the art of lapidary, gems and faceting, and on the earth sciences as well.

Scott Shrader
Gems, Minerals & Fossils Webring
e-mail: sshrader@mindspring.com
web: http://www.geocities.com/Yosemite/2352/gmf.html
Webring has scores of links to rockhound web sites.

Smithsonian Gem & Mineral Collection, National Museum of Natural History
10th St. & constitution Ave.
Washington, DC 20560
ph: 202-357-1300
A Smithsonian website with a great selection of mineral specimen images with descriptions.

Elizabeth "Boo" Commean
624 Terra West Drive
Freeport, IL 61032
ph: 815-235-7345
e-mail: Boo@commean.com
web: http://www.commean.com/rocks/
Collector whose website lists free-for-entry collecting sites for rock, mineral and fossil specimens, state geological information, field trip reports on sites, listings of quarries, rock clubs, and other information for the rockhound.

Jeremy Fuller
Mineral Market
997 N. Chapel Dr., Ste. #4
Bountiful, UT 84010
ph: 801-296-2516
fax: 801-292-5439
e-mail: info@minimarket.com
web: http://www.minmarket.com/
On-line mineral and fossil auctions, dealer lists, on-line mineral and fossil museum.

Bob Keller
Bob's Rock Shop
227 West Rillito Street
Tucson, AZ 85705
ph: 520-624-1899
fax: 520-624-1891
e-mail: bkeller@rockhounds.com
web: http://www.rockhounds.com
The Internet's first 'zine for mineral collectors, lapidary hobbyists, and rockhounds.

Museums/Libraries

Mineralogical Museum of Harvard University
26 Oxford St.
Cambridge, MA 02138
ph: 617-495-2326
fax: 617-495-5667

Earth & Mineral Sciences Museum & Art Gallery, Pennsylvania State University
122 Streidle Bldg.
Pollock Rd.
University Park, PA 16802
ph: 814-865-6427
fax: 814-863-7708
e-mail: sicree@geosc.psu.edu
web: http://www.ems.psu.edu/Museum/
Displays of minerals, materials, gemstones, and art work related to mining; displays of old lamps and other mining artifacts.

Daniel Lazar, Ex. Dir.
Colburn Gem & Mineral Museum
Newsletter: Touchstone
P.O. Box 1617
Asheville, NC 28802-1617
ph: 828-254-7162
fax: 828-251-5652
web: http://www.main.nc.us/colburn/
Features gems and minerals from North Carolina and around the world.

Arizona Mining Museum
1502 W. Washington
Phoenix, AZ 85007
ph: 602-255-3795 or 800-446-4259
fax: 502-255-3777
web: http://www.miningrendezvous.com/ammm/

Periodicals

Heldref Publications
Magazine: Rocks & Minerals
1319 18th St., NW
Washington, DC 20036-1826
ph: 800-365-9753 or 202-396-6267
fax: 202-296-5149
e-mail: rm@heldref.org
web: http://www.heldref.org/
America's oldest popular magazine about minerals; bi-monthly; mineralogy, geology, and paleontology.

Lanny R. Ream
Newsletter: Mineral News
P.O. Box 2043
Coeur D Alene, ID 83816-2043
ph: 208-664-2448
e-mail: lream@mineralnews.com
web: http://www.mineralnews.com/
A monthly newsletter for mineral collectors; contains news and information on minerals and mineral localities; show reports, new discoveries, new collecting opportunities; abstracts of new minerals; show information.

Magazine: Mineralogical Record, The
P.O. Box 35565
Tucson, AZ 85750
ph: 520-297-6709
fax: 520-544-0815
e-mail: minrec@aol.com
web: http://www.minrec.org/
Each bimonthly issue packed with in-depth articles about minerals and mineral localities; lavishly illustrated with beautiful color photos of some of the world's finest mineral specimens; prominent collectors, mineral museums, etc.

Miller Enterprises, Inc.
Magazine: Rock & Gem
4880 Market St.
Ventura, CA 93003
ph: 805-644-3824
A monthly magazine.

Suppliers

Carl W. Haywood
Rockman McLean Trading Co.
P.O. Box 7174
Loveland, CO 80537-0174
ph: 970-622-0869
fax: 970-622-0869
e-mail: rockman@rocksnstuff.com
web: http://www.rocksnstuff.com
Sells earth science supplies for classroom and collector: starter rock, mineral, fossil, and ore collections; handbooks, display cases, magnifiers, etc.

Prized Possessions
P.O. Box 1147
Fresno, CA 93715
ph: 559-275-6498
e-mail: jack@gemworld.com
web: http://www.gemworld.com
Gems, minerals, fossils, gemstone rough, equipment, supplies; provides opals, gemstones, collector stones, synthetics, cabbing and faceting rough, lapidary equipment and supplies, appraisals, etc.; extensive website.

Fluorescent

Clubs/Associations

Fluorescent Mineral Society
Newsletter: UV Waves
P.O. Box 572694
Tarzana, CA 91357-2694
e-mail: president@uvminerals.org
web: http://www.uvminerals.org/
Founded in 1971, an international organization of professional mineralogists, gemologists, amateur collectors, and others who study and collect fluorescent minerals.

MINIATURES

(see also ART, Portraits [Miniature]; BOOKS, Miniature; BOTTLES, Miniature; BOTTLES, Puzzle; CHILDREN'S THINGS; DOLL HOUSES & FURNISHINGS; IRONS, Pressing [Miniature]; MODELS, Cars; PIANOS, Miniature; TRUCKS, Miniature)

Appraisers

Judy Owen, ISA
Antique Appraisers - Grand Traverse
10332 Stoneybeach Pointe
Traverse City, MI 49686-8584
ph: 231-946-2534
fax: 231-946-2573
e-mail: judy@antiqueappraisers.com
web: http://www.antiqueappraisers.com/
Specializing in doll houses and miniatures.

Clubs/Associations

International Guild of Miniature Artisans
Newsletter: Cube & Hotline, The
P.O. Box 2320
Malta, NY 12020
ph: 800-711-IGMA or 518-885-5744
fax: 518-885-2543
e-mail: info@igma.org
web: http://www.igma.org/
Dedicated to the recognition of excellence in the field of miniatures.

Miniatures Industry Association of America
P.O. Box 2188
Zanesville, OH 43702-2188
ph: 614-452-4541
fax: 614-352-2552
e-mail: info@offinger.com
web: http://www.miaa.com
A trade organization; purpose is to promote the common interests of the miniatures industry; approximately 400 company members; website has some good information about miniatures with links to related sites.

Miniatures Industry Association of America
Newsletter: MIAA Member News
P.O. Box 3388
Zanesville, OH 43702-3388
ph: 740-452-4541
fax: 740-452-2552
e-mail: miaa.info@offinger.com
web: http://www.miaa.com/

John Purcell
National Association of Miniature Enthusiasts
Magazine: Miniature Gazette
P.O. Box 69
Carmel, IN 46032
ph: 317-571-8094
fax: 317-571-8105
e-mail: name@miniatures.org
web: http://www.miniatures.org/
N.A.M.E. serves the miniature collector and builder; the monthly magazine contains articles, ads, dealer listings, etc.

Cottage Industry Miniaturists Trade Association, Inc.
P.O. Box 42849
Chicago Ridge, IL 60805-0849
ph: 773-233-5522
fax: 773-233-5506
e-mail: janatcimta@aol.com
web: http://www.cimta.com/
Non-profit organization whose membership is limited to handcrafters of dollhouse miniatures.

Miniature Enthusiasts Across Canada
1133 Sixth Line
Oakville, Ontario L6H 1W6
Canada
ph: 905-294-0902
e-mail: meac@miniature.net
web: http://www.miniature.net/meac/
An association for people interested in dollhouse miniatures.

Collectors

Betty Bird
107 Ida St.
Mount Shasta, CA 96067-2629
ph: 530-926-4331 or 530-926-2231
Wants to buy tiny toys, doll house items, and salesman's samples.

Dealers

Natalie Bell
Open House Miniatures
402 Railroad Ave. W.
Allendale, SC 29810
Carries highest quality Russian miniatures available; also painted eggs, matreshkas (nesting dolls), icons, and Palekh boxes made by the Russian Association of Dollhouse & Miniature Masters (see examples at http://www.aha.ru/~vladin/).

Misc. Services

Kay Fisher
College of Miniature Knowledge
13757 Upper Cow Creek Rd.
Azalea, OR 97410
ph: 541-837-3743
Organizes instructional classes in miniature craftsmanship.

Museums/Libraries

Museums at Stony Brook, The
Newsletter: News & Events
1208 Route 25A
Stony Brook, NY 11790-1992
ph: 516-751-0066
fax: 516-751-0353
e-mail: museums@longisland.com
web: http://
www.museumsatstonybrook.org/
Large collection of American Art, decoys, horse-drawn vehicles, costumes, and miniature period rooms; museum shop.

Toy & Miniature Museum of Delaware
P.O. Box 4053
Route 141
Wilmington, DE 19807
ph: 302-427-8697
fax: 302-427-8654
e-mail: toys@thomes.net
web: http://www.thomes.net/toys/
Collections include dollhouses, miniatures, dolls, toys, trains, boats, and planes; both European and American; 18th to 20th centuries.

Delaware Toy & Miniature Museum
P.O. Box 4053
Wilmington, DE 19807
ph: 302-427-8697
fax: 302-427-8654
e-mail: toys@thomes.net
web: http://www.thomes.net/toys/
A historical reference of antique and contemporary dollhouses, miniatures and sample furniture as well as dolls, toys, trains, boats and planes, both European and American from the 18th to 20th centuries.

Washington Dolls' House & Toy Museum
5236 44th St. NW
Washington, DC 20015
ph: 202-244-0024

Art Institute of Chicago, Thorne Miniature Rooms
111 S. Michigan Ave.
Chicago, IL 60603
ph: 312-443-0849
e-mail: webmaster@artic.edu
web: http://www.artic.edu/aic/
firstpage.html

Sandi Russell
Toy & Miniature Museum of Kansas City
5235 Oak St.
Kansas City, MO 64112-2877
ph: 816-333-2055 or 816-333-9328
fax: 816-333-2055
e-mail: bergr@umkc.edu
web: http://www.umkc.edu/tmm/
Museum housed in an elegant mansion features collections of miniatures, antique dolls' houses and antique toys.

Laura Douglas, Ex. Dir.
Denver Museum of Miniatures, Dolls & Toys
1880 Gaylord St.
Denver, CO 80206-1211
ph: 303-322-1053
fax: 303-322-3704
e-mail: ldsbc@aol.com
web: http://www.sni.net/start/dmmdt/
Displays miniatures, dolls and toys dating back to the 18th century.

Carole & Barry Kay Museum of Miniatures
5900 Wilshire Blvd.
Los Angeles, CA 90036
ph: 323-937-6464 or 323-937-7766
fax: 323-937-2126
e-mail: carolekaye@aol.com
web: http://museumofminiatures.com
14,000 square feet containing hundreds of exhibits, most done in remarkable 1/12 scale.

Periodicals

Magazine: Doll Castle News
P.O. Box 247
Washington, NJ 07882-0247
ph: 908-689-7042 or 800-572-6607
fax: 908-689-6320
e-mail: dcn@dollcastlenews.com
web: http://www.dollcastlenews.com/
A magazine focusing on dolls, miniatures, doll houses and related items; ads, paper doll section, needlework, patterns, etc.

Scott Publications
Magazine: Miniature Collector
30595 Eight Mile
Livonia, MI 48152-1798
ph: 800-458-8237 or 248-477-6650
fax: 248-477-6795
e-mail: 104137.1254@compuserve.com
An international bi-monthly glossy publication devoted exclusively to contemporary and antique scale miniatures: artists, manufacturers, retailers, suppliers, collectors, room settings, etc.

Sybil Harp
Kalmbach Publishing Co.
Magazine: Dollhouse Miniatures
P.O. Box 1612
21027 Crossroads Circle
Waukesha, WI 53187
ph: 414-796-8776 or 800-533-6644
fax: 414-796-1615
e-mail: customerservice@kalmbach.com
web: http://www.dhminiatures.com/
Monthly magazine with techniques, how-to's, projects, plans, collections, artists profiles, reviews of miniature shows, extensive calendar of events, etc.

Magazine: Dolls & Miniatures
1040 Bentoak Lane
San Jose, CA 95129
e-mail: dollsmini@aol.com
web: http://members.aol.com/
dollsinmin/
Quarterly magazine featuring the work of talented miniature doll and bear artisans and collectors; also covers accessories for the well-dressed doll and many other dollhouse items.

Ashdown Publishing
Magazine: Dolls House World
Avalon Court, Star Road
Partridge Green, West Sussex RH13 8RY
U.K.
ph: +44 (0) 1403 711511 or 513-353-4052 (in U.S.)
fax: +44 (0) 1403 711521
e-mail: mark@ashdown.co.uk
web: http://www.dollshouseworld.com/
Britain's top selling miniatures magazine.

EMF Publishing
Magazine: Doll Houses & Miniatures Scene
EMF House
5-7 Elm Park
U.K.
ph: 01903 244900
fax: 01903 506626
e-mail: dolltedemf@aol.com
web: http://members.aol.com/dolltedemf/
Every issue packed with ideas, features, free competitions and much more.

Repro. Sources

Duane Sylor
49 Horner Rd.
Angelica, NY 14709-8780
ph: 716-466-7700
Makes & sells authentically crafted 1/2 scale traditionally painted furniture accurately copying Early American examples; great for dolls, teddies, tots.

Dishes

Clubs/Associations

Shelley Smith
Toy Dish Collectors Club
Newsletter: Tiny Times, The
P.O. Box 159
Bethlehem, CT 06751-0159
ph: 203-266-7496
fax: 203-266-7343
e-mail: toydish@aol.com
web: http://members.aol.com/toydish/
Collectors are interested in children's dishes, furniture, glass, toy kitchen and stores.

Military

(see also SOLDIERS, Toy; TOYS, Playsets)

Appraisers

Barry Carter
Knightstown Antiques Mall
136 W. Carey St.
Knightstown, IN 46148-1111
ph: 765-345-5665
e-mail: bcarter@spitfire.net
Buys, sells, appraises and specializes in toy soldiers and military miniatures; consultant for AntiqueWeek; promoter of the Indiana Toy Soldier Show (last Sunday in March.)

Auction Services

Glenn Butler
Wallis & Wallis
West Street Auction Galleries
Lewes, East Sussex BN7 2NJ
U.K.
ph: 01273-480208
fax: 01273-476562
e-mail: wallisandwallis@mcmail.com
web: http://www.wallisandwallis.co.uk/
Britain's specialist auctioneers of diecast & tin plate toys & models including model soldiers.

Clubs/Associations

Miniature Figure Collectors of America
Newsletter: Guidon, The
102 St. Paul's Rd.
Ardmore, PA 19003-2811
ph: 610-649-4144
Non-profit corporation; members interested in military history, miniature figures of military personnel in uniform, dioramic scenes, painting, casting, conversion of miniature figures; annual exhibition, competition and show each May.

Andy Hansen
Military Miniature Society of Illinois
Newsletter: Scabbard, The
529 S. Burno Dr.
Palatine, IL 60067-6711
e-mail: rsarnowski@aol.com
web: http://members.aol.com/RSarnowski/MMSI.HTML
Sponsors an annual exhibition on the 3rd Saturday in October; features the best work from the U.S., Canada and Europe.

Wayne Morrissey
Historical Miniature Figure Society of Colorado
2413 Skysail Court
Longmont, CO 80503
ph: 303-651-2187
web: http://users.lanminds.net/~waynem/

Ontario Model Soldier Society
43 Saugeen Crescent
Scarborough, Ontario M1K 3M8
Canada
e-mail: CY771@Torfree.net
web: http://www.cris.com/~Paitchis/
Provides a meeting place and a means of exchange of information among those interested in creating, painting, war gaming, collecting and displaying model and toy soldiers and small figures, and history thereof.

Recruitment Officer
British Model Soldier Society
75 Mill Road
Woodford
Kettering, Nortants. NN14 4HL
U.K.
e-mail: Model.Soldiers@btinternet.com
web: http://www.btinternet.com/~MODEL.SOLDIERS/
The largest and longest established association of model soldier enthusiasts.

Dealers

Jim Hillestad
Toy Soldier, The
RR 1, Box 379
Cresco, PA 18326
ph: 570-629-7227
fax: 570-629-9205
e-mail: jimhill@ptd.net
web: http://www.The-Toy-Soldier.com
Deals in all major toy soldier makers, furniture-quality display cases, Michael Sutty bone china military sculptures, regimental drums, bugles and more; also has a 3,000 sq. ft. museum of figures and dioramas.

Barry Carter
Knightstown Antiques Mall
136 W. Carey St.
Knightstown, IN 46148-1111
ph: 765-345-5665
e-mail: bcarter@spitfire.net
Buys, sells, appraises and specializes in toy soldiers and military miniatures; consultant for AntiqueWeek; promoter of the Indiana Toy Soldier Show (last Sunday in March.)

Mark Avery
Avalon Court, Star Road
Partridge Green, West Sussex RH13 8RY
U.K.
ph: +44 (0) 1403 711511 or 513-353-4052 (in U.S.)
fax: +44 (0) 1403 711521
e-mail: mark@ashdown.co.uk
web: http://www.ashdown.co.uk/magazfr.htm
Toy soldier dealer and expert; specializes in antique and modern toy soldiers and 54mm collectors figures; also sells books and special edition figurines for the discerning collector.

Man./Prod./Dist.

Dr. Paul Rohe
Museum Quality Miniatures
P.O. Box 122
Martinville, NJ 08336-0122
Produces the world's finest quality, detailed and accurate miniatures (54mm) painted to absolute perfection; most popular are Knights and Civil War themes; wholesale and resale.

Periodicals

Hank Olsen
Newsletter: Mini Soldier Gazette
P.O. Box 15
Eatontown, NJ 07724
e-mail: olsenh@doim6.monmouth.army.mil

Erika Daileda
Wise Owl Worldwide Publications
Magazine: Military Modelling
4314 West 238th St. - Dept. MACR
Torrance, CA 90505-4509
ph: 310-375-6258
fax: 310-375-0548
e-mail: wiseowl@sprintmail.com
A monthly English publication; for modelers, enthusiasts and historians.

MINING RELATED ITEMS

(see also INDUSTRY RELATED ITEMS; MINERAL SPECIMENS; SCRIP; SOCIAL CAUSES; STOCKS & BONDS, Mining Related)

Appraisers

Robert L. Johnson
Whistles in the Woods Museum Services
P.O. Box 309
Chickamauga, GA 30707-0309
ph: 706-375-4326
e-mail: oldgoat@voy.net
Consultants specializing in 1750 - early 20th century historic machinery; power-generation, tools, machines, scientific & technical instruments, mining, milling, transportation, logging & lumbering, steam engines, etc.

Collectors

Len Gaska
e-mail: gaska@nilenet.com
web: http://ra.nilenet.com/~gaska/

David C. Crawford
3421 Fremont St.
Rockford, IL 61103
ph: 815-637-6720
Wants to buy all mining items: oil, safety, and carbide lamps; blasting cap tins, photos, postcards; United Mine Workers of America, Western Federation of Miners, and local union ribbons, banners, and patches.

John M. Shannon
7319 West Cedar Circle
Lakewood, CO 80226-2019
ph: 303-232-1534
e-mail: rovers@aol.com
Wants to buy mining memorabilia including assay balances (wood and glass encased with small pans) - both laboratory and portable; also wants brass scientific instruments.

Manfred Stutzer
Madenburgstr. 6
Ludwigshafen, 67065
Germany
ph: 0621-5792432
fax: 0621-5792433
e-mail: mkstu@t-online.de
web: http://home.t-online.de/home/mkstu/hptmt.htm
Wants to buy miner's flame safety

lamps, mining artifacts, and mining medals.

Dealers

Leo Stambaugh
Powder Cache Antiques
P.O. Box 779
Georgetown, CO 80444-0779
ph: 800-651-2848 or 303-569-2109
e-mail: leocolo@bewellnet.com
Wants to buy mining books, catalogs, photos, equipment, maps; anything mining related and pre-1930.

Warren Anderson
America West Archives
P.O. Box 100
Cedar City, UT 84721-0100
ph: 435-586-9497 or 435-586-7323
e-mail: awa@netutah.com
web: http://www.americawestarchives.com/
Buys and sells pre-1920 mining related documents including letters, maps, photos, checks, stock certificates, prospectuses, etc.; author of "Owning Western History."

John & Karen Mediz
Copper City Rock Shop
566 Ash St.
Globe, AZ 85501
ph: 520-425-7885 or 520-425-4506
fax: 520-425-4506
Buys and sells mining artifacts; also wants to buy minerals and fossils, especially old collections.

Experts

Andy Martin
3030 N. Sarsparilla Pl.
Tucson, AZ 85749
ph: 520-760-0337
fax: 520-806-3227
e-mail: martin@mmsi.com
web: http://www.nmt.edu/~tromero/caps/tins.html
Mining collectibles collector, dealer, expert; author of the "Blasting Cap Tin Catalog" (available from author); has considerable expertise with cap tins, candle boxes, dynamite boxes, and other relics found in abandoned mines.

Museums/Libraries

Earth & Mineral Sciences Museum & Art Gallery, Pennsylvania State University
122 Streidle Bldg.
Pollock Rd.
University Park, PA 16802
ph: 814-865-6427
fax: 814-863-7708
e-mail: sicree@geosc.psu.edu
web: http://www.ems.psu.edu/Museum/
Displays of minerals, materials, gemstones, and art work related to mining; displays of old lamps and other mining artifacts.

National Mining Hall of Fame & Museum
P.O. Box 981
120 W. 9th
Leadville, CO 80461
ph: 719-486-1229
fax: 719-486-3927
web: http://www.leadville.com/miningmuseum/index.htm

Bisbee Mining & Historical Museum
P.O. Box 14
Bisbee, AZ 85603
ph: 520-432-7071
e-mail: bisbeemuseum@theriver.com
web: http://azstarnet.com/public/nonprofit/bisbeemuseum/

Old Mint Museum
5th & Mission Sts.
San Francisco, CA 94103-2906
ph: 415-744-6830
Collection of coins, numismatic items, and mining equipment and related items.

Periodicals

Magazine: Eureka! The Journal of Mining Collectibles
e-mail: ttown@cybertrails.com
web: http://ra.nilenet.com/~gaska/eureka.html

Ted Bobrink
Newsletter: Mining Artifact Collector, The
34612 Avenue B
Yucaipa, CA 92399-4185

Cap Tins

Experts

Andy Martin
3030 N. Sarsparilla Pl.
Tucson, AZ 85749
ph: 520-760-0337
fax: 520-806-3227
e-mail: martin@mmsi.com
web: http://www.nmt.edu/~tromero/caps/tins.html
Mining collectibles collector, dealer, expert; author of the "Blasting Cap Tin Catalog" (available from author); has considerable expertise with cap tins, candle boxes, dynamite boxes, and other relics found in abandoned mines.

Coal Mining

Collectors

William Blake
506 Driftwood Dr. Lot A
Charleston, WV 25306-6306
ph: 304-925-3780
Coal mine items wanted; all categories: carbide lights, safety lamps, oil wicks, etc.

Museums/Libraries

Museum of Anthracite Mining
Pine & 17th St.
Ashland, PA 17921
ph: 570-875-4708

National Coal Museum, The
3197 Route 37 North
P.O. Box 369
West Frankfort, IL 62896
ph: 618-YES-COAL
fax: 618-932-2347
e-mail: yescoal@midwest.net
web: http://www.spiderbytes.com/coalmuseum/
Tour an actual coal mine 600 feet underground.

Colorado

Collectors

George Foott
120 W. Park Ave.
Salida, CO 81201
Wants to buy early Western mining memorabilia (especially Colorado): photographs, maps, promotional pamphlets, books, mining directories, miners' candleholders; also wants Old West cattle brand books, saddle catalogs, cowboy items.

Lamps

(see also LAMPS & LIGHTING)

Clubs/Associations

Henry A. Pohs
Old Mine Lamp Collectors Society of America
Newsletter: Underground Lamp Post, The
4537 Quitman St.
Denver, CO 80212-2535
ph: 303-455-3922
Focuses on old non-electric mining lamps and related items.

Collectors

Brian Williamson
4690 Springgate Dr.
Powder Springs, GA 30073
ph: 770-439-7003
Buys, sells, restores and specializes in older carbide mining lamps, especially those made by Justrite, Baldwin, Autolite, etc.; also interested in lamp parts and in British mining lamps.

John W. Coons
9757 S. Isabel Ct.
Littleton, CO 80126-4717
ph: 303-791-6496
e-mail: jcoons1552@aol.com
Wants to buy mining lamps, candlestick holders, carbide lamps.

Manfred Stutzer
Madenburgstr. 6
Ludwigshafen, 67065
Germany
ph: 0621-5792432
fax: 0621-5792433
e-mail: mkstu@t-online.de
web: http://home.t-online.de/home/mkstu/hptmt.htm
Wants to buy miner's flame safety lamps, mining artifacts, and mining medals.

Experts

Henry A. Pohs
4537 Quitman St.
Denver, CO 80212-2535
ph: 303-455-3922
Mine lighting historian; buys, sells, trades old non-electric mining lamps and related items; author of two books on the subject.

MIRRORS

(see POCKET MIRRORS; REPAIR/RESTORATION/CONSERVATION, Mirrors)

MISSILES

(see ROCKETS; SPACE COLLECTIBLES)

MISSION STYLE

(see ARTS & CRAFTS; COPPER ITEMS, Stickley; FURNITURE [ANTIQUE], Stickley)

MIXERS

(see KITCHEN COLLECTIBLES, Eggbeaters; KITCHEN COLLECTIBLES, Mixers)

MOBILE HOMES

(see also TRAILERS & RV'S)

Auction Services

Florida's Manufactured Home Auctions & Wholesale
P.O. Box 61
Candler, FL 32111
ph: 352-288-2328
fax: 352-288-9108
e-mail: florida@mobilehome.com
web: http://florida.mobilehome.com/
Buys and sells manufactured homes online.

MODEL KITS

(see KITS)

MODELS

(see also AIRLINE MEMORABILIA, Models [Desk]; AIRPLANES, Model; BOATS, Model; KITS; MILITARY HISTORY; NAUTICAL ANTIQUES, Models [Ships]; SOLDIERS, Toy; STEAM-OPERATED; TOYS, Diecast; TOYS, Transportation; TRAINS, Model)

Dealers

Toys for Collectors
P.O. Box 1406
North Attleboro, MA 02763
ph: 508-695-0588 or 508-695-6966
fax: 508-699-8649
e-mail: gklarwasse@aol.com
If you collect models of cars, trucks, fire trucks, construction equipment, cranes, buses, race cars, NASCARS, etc. this is the source for better quality 1/43 scale models as well as 1/50, 1/18 and 1/14 scale models.

Colleen Lewis
Buffalo Road Hobby
10120 Main St.
Clarence, NY 14031-2049
ph: 716-759-7541
fax: 716-759-7462
web: http://www.toyline.com/clubs/pcc
Dealer, collector, appraiser, distributor of construction scale models; also diecast scale model military vehicles, aircraft, ships, soldiers; also replacement parts for old models.

Lelan Kuhlmann
M & L Records & Models
6504 Ravenna Ave.
Seattle, WA 98115
ph: 206-522-8189
e-mail: mlrecmod@halcyon.com
web: http://www.halcyon.com/mlrecmod/
Seattle storefront with an online catalog having over 22,000 LPs and 2,000 models, rare and used.

Periodicals

Kalmbach Publishing Co.
Magazine: FineScale Modeler
P.O. Box 1612
21027 Crossroads Circle
Waukesha, WI 53187
ph: 414-796-8776 or 800-533-6644
fax: 414-796-1615
e-mail: customerservice@kalmbach.com
web: http://www.finescale.com
For those interested in the scaled-down universe including aircraft, military vehicles, ships, cars or dioramas; how-to tips and techniques, new project ideas and step-by-step instructions that make modeling more fun.

Newspaper: Collectors Gazette
Fleck Way
Thornaby
Stockton-on-Tees, Cleveland TS17 9JZ
U.K.
ph: +44 (0) 1642 762335
fax: +44 (0) 1642 762401
e-mail: info@icn.co.uk
web: http://www.icn.co.uk/cg.html
Published 10 times per year for toy and model collectors worldwide; covers tinplate toys, obsolete and modern diecast cars (Corgi, Dinky, Matchbox, EFE, Lledo, Days Gone, etc.) and models, trains, airplanes, ships, dolls, etc.

Suppliers

Ernie Weinberg
Superior Aircraft Materials
12020 Centralia Ave. #G
Hawaiian Gardens, CA 90716-1064
ph: 562-865-3220
fax: 562-860-0327
e-mail: balsa@ix.netcom.com
Specializes in supplying wood materials (balsa, spruce, plywood) for the model builder.

Aircraft

(see also AVIATION MEMORABILIA; KITS; TOYS, Airplane Related; TOYS, Diecast)

Clubs/Associations

Don E. Vineyard, Sec.
International Miniature Aircraft Association, Inc.
205 S. Hilldale Rd.
Salina, KS 67401

Collectors

Charles Martignette
P.O. Box 293
Hallandale, FL 33008
ph: 305-454-3474
Wants to buy travel agency and airport counter displays of model airplanes; please send length, width, height and asking price along with photographs.

Man./Prod./Dist.

Arlene Scherff
Arch, Inc.
Newsletter: Flying Times News
7 Hyatt Road
P.O. Box 458
Branchville, NJ 07826-0458
ph: 973-702-0440
fax: 973-702-2699
e-mail: molly@interpow.net
web: http://www.archtheworld.com/
Manufacturer of highly detailed diecast model airplanes.

Periodicals

Erika Daileda
Wise Owl Worldwide Publications
Magazine: Aeromodeller
4314 West 238th St. - Dept. MACR
Torrance, CA 90505-4509
ph: 310-375-6258
fax: 310-375-0548
e-mail: wiseowl@sprintmail.com
Great Britain's favorite model aircraft magazine; a monthly featuring reviews, plans and news from the world of aircraft modeling and flight.

Erika Daileda
Wise Owl Worldwide Publications
Magazine: Plastic Kit Constructor
4314 West 238th St. - Dept. MACR
Torrance, CA 90505-4509
ph: 310-375-6258
fax: 310-375-0548
e-mail: wiseowl@sprintmail.com
A U.K. quarterly magazine for plastic model aircraft modelers.

Aircraft (Flying)

(see also AIRPLANES, Model [Remote Control])

Periodicals

Harold H. Carstens
Carstens Publications
Magazine: Flying Models
108 Phil Hardin Road
P.O. Box 700
Newton, NJ 07860-0700
ph: 973-383-3355 or 800-474-6995
fax: 973-383-4064
e-mail: carstens@carstens-publications.com
web: http://www.carstens-publications.com/mainindex.html

Ron Firth
PAMAG Publications Ltd.
Magazine: Flying Model Designer & Constructor
3 Lowfield Court
Sark Road
Heeley, Sheffield S2 4HG
U.K.
ph: 0114 255 0641
e-mail: ronald.firth@ukonline.co.uk
A quarterly magazine for flying model aircraft modelers.

Cars

(see also AUTOMOBILIA; KITS; NASCAR; TOYS, Cars; TOYS, Diecast; TOYS, Transportation)

Clubs/Associations

Ben Lawson
Northland Toy Club
Newsletter: Northland News
8 N. Gate Dr.
Albany, NY 12203-5102
Focuses on all kinds of model vehicles.

Ray Denney
Model Car Collectors Association
Journal: Model Car Collectors Association Journal
5113 Sugar Loaf Dr. SW
Roanoke, VA 24018
ph: 540-744-8109
web: http://www.vintagekarts.com/MCCA/MCCA.htm
Dedicated to the promotion & enjoyment of the model car hobby; a bi-monthly journal features kit reviews, how-to's, free member ads.

Peter H. Foss
Michigan Model Car Collectors
Newsletter: MMCC Newsletter
33290 W. 14 Mile Rd. #454
West Bloomfield, MI 48322-3549
ph: 248-682-0272
fax: 248-682-5782
A regional chapter of The Toy Car Collectors Club.

Tucson Miniature Auto Club
Newsletter: Tucson Miniature Auto Club
1111 E. Limberlost Dr., #164
Tucson, AZ 85719-1062
ph: 520-293-3178 or 800-484-1097 pin 2984

Jay Olins
Diecast Car Collectors Club
Newsletter: PDCCC Newsletter
P.O. Box 670226
Los Angeles, CA 90067-1126
ph: 213-500-4355
e-mail: jay@diecast.org
web: http://www.diecast.org/
For collectors of Danbury Mint and Franklin Mint models and all other precision die cast models; published bi-monthly newsletter with photos and reviews of new models, classifieds, etc.; website is "Diecast Car Collectors' Zone."

Bill Goddard
1/87th Scale Vehicle & Equipment Club, The
P.O. Box 382
Brentwood, CA 94513-0382
Covers intermodal, modern truck, vintage vehicles and equipment, military, logging, carnival, emergency, construction, bus and coach, maintenance and automobiles, all in 1/87th scale.

Collectors

Ken Katz
354 Townline Rd.
Commack, NY 11725-1423
ph: 516-462-5808
fax: 516-499-0366
e-mail: kennyskars@aol.com
Wants models of automotive vehicles: plastic, friction, built or unbuilt kits, promotional models.

Bill Whelan
P.O. Box 617
Daly City, CA 94017-2332
ph: 650-756-1189
Wants to buy 1/25 scale promotional Corvette and Corvette models; also buys, sells and trades other makes of model cars; no list available.

Dealers

Dean Klein
Distinctive Die-Cast Inc.
P.O. Box 656
Tallman, NY 10982
ph: 914-357-3382
Specializing in Dinky and Corgi diecast toys.

Tailfin Productions
2014 Green Juniper Ln.
Brandon, FL 33511
ph: 813-684-3785
Buys and sells model car kits from the 1950s to present; promos, original auto art, and relate items.

Trader Rick's Collectible Toy Cars
P.O. Box 161
Newark, IL 60541
ph: 815-695-9484
Wants to buy toy cars and model cars; also built or unbuilt car kits.

MODELAUTO
P.O. Box SM2
Leeds, LS25 5XA
U.K.
ph: 0113-2686685
fax: 01977-681991
e-mail: hotline@modelauto.co.uk
web: http://www.modelauto.co.uk
Worldwide mail order specializing in 1:43 and 1:50 scales, but other models stocked as well; see advertisement in "Model Auto Review."

Man./Prod./Dist.

ExotiCar Model Company
2-8 New York Ave.
Framingham, MA 01701
ph: 508-620-6784 or 800-348-9159
fax: 508-620-6786
e-mail: pitcrew@exoticarmodel.com
web: http://www.exoticarmodel.com
The complete one-stop source for the automobile enthusiast; the largest US distributor for 1/18 scale; also carries 1/24th, 1/43rd and 1/12th scale models; also sells automobile clothing and accessories.

EWA Miniature Cars USA, Inc.
205 US Hwy. 22
Dunellen, NJ 08812
ph: 732-424-0200 or 732-424-7811
fax: 732-424-7814
e-mail: ewa@ewacars.com
web: http://www.ewacars.com
Carries North America's largest inventory of scale model automobiles - over 90,000 in stock from 350 manufacturers including many rare and hard-to-find pieces.

Periodicals

Magazine: Diecast Digest Magazine
P.O. Box 12510
Knoxville, TN 37912-0510
ph: 423-922-1091
fax: 423-922-1614
e-mail: ghubbs@vic.com
web: http://www.diecastdigest.com/
A monthly magazine focusing on diecast model cars including NASCAR and Formula 1; articles, advertising, models.

Kalmbach Publishing Co.
Magazine: Scale Auto Enthusiast
P.O. Box 1612
21027 Crossroads Circle
Waukesha, WI 53187
ph: 414-796-8776 or 800-533-6644
fax: 414-796-1615
e-mail: customerservice@kalmbach.com
web: http://www.scaleautomag.com
Covers the complete automotive modeling hobby including the newest and most successful kit building techniques, collector's market insight, new kit and product releases, and today's greatest modelers.

Jeff Atkinson
Newsletter: Traders Horn
1903 Schoettler Valley Rd.
Chesterfield, MO 63017-5203
ph: 314-532-3871
e-mail: thorn@gloryroad.net
The oldest, largest bi-monthly periodical dedicated to the sales, trading of diecast toy vehicles, promotional models, model kits; obsolete, rare, current automotive & other transportation miniatures and related memorabilia; all scales.

Magazine: Model Auto Review
P.O. Box SM2
Leeds, LS25 5XA
U.K.
ph: 0113-2686685
fax: 01977-681991
e-mail: hotline@modelauto.co.uk
web: http://www.modelauto.co.uk
MAR is a bi-monthly glossy magazine with many color and b/w photos; covering model cars, trucks, buses, military vehicles.

Link House Magazines
Magazine: Model Collector
Link House, Dingwall Avenue
Croydon, Surrey CR9 2TA
U.K.
ph: +44 (0) 181 686 2599
fax: +44 (0) 181 781 6535
e-mail: modelcollector@lhm.co.uk
web: http://www.linkhouse.co.uk/modelcollector/
A glossy monthly English with detailed articles about old and new model cars, buses, trucks, motorcycles, trains, etc.; new releases; lots of advertisements.

Cars (Dinky)

Clubs/Associations

Jerry Fralick
Dinky Toy Club of America
Newsletter: DTCA Newsletter
P.O. Box 11
Highland, MD 20777
ph: 301-854-2217
fax: 301-854-2217
e-mail: MrDinky@erols.com
web: http://www.erols.com/dinkytoy/
For Dinky collectors.

Engines

Collectors

Joel Balsam
#4 Pickwick Hills Dr.
Huntington Station, NY 11746-1241
ph: 516-271-3267
Wants to buy pre-1955 model airplane, car, and boat engines; also wants model race cars and other related items.

Bill Bickel
3121 W. Cavedale Dr.
Phoenix, AZ 85027-7637
ph: 623-582-0211
e-mail: billob@uswest.net
Wants to buy or trade for old model plane engines and gas powered race cars; also wants gas powered planes and cars that were originally sold as ready-to-run toys; incomplete or damaged items and parts also wanted.

Periodicals

Robert A. Washburn, Ed.
Magazine: Strictly I.C.
24920 43th Ave. S.
Kent, WA 98032
fax: 253-946-5253
A bi-monthly periodical of information promoting the design and construction of internal combustion miniature model engines in the home shop.

Trucks & Equipment (Winross)

Clubs/Associations

Winross Collectors Club of America
Newsletter: Winross Collectors Club of America Newsletter
18 W. Main St.
P.O. Box 444
Mount Joy, PA 17552-0444
ph: 717-653-7327
fax: 717-653-1247
e-mail: winrosclub@aol.com
web: http://members.aol.com/WinrosClub/index.html
The purpose of this organization is to share and preserve the common interest of dedication to the collection and preservation of 1/64-inch scale Winross trucks; monthly newsletter.

Collectors

Jim Brandt
TruckHobby.com
280 Meadow Lane
Lebanon, PA 17042
ph: 717-273-5776
e-mail: jim@truckhobby.com
web: http://www.truckhobby.com
Avid collector of Winross trucks since 1987.

Man./Prod./Dist.

Winross
Newsletter: Collector Series
12 Tobey Village Office Park
Pittsford, NY 14534
ph: 800-227-2060 or 716-381-5638
fax: 716-381-5884
web: http://www.winross.com/

MODERNISM

(see also ART, Outsider; ART DECO; CERAMICS [AMERICAN], Russel Wright Designs; ELECTRICITY RELATED ITEMS, Appliances; GLASS, Italian; POPULAR CULTURE; SOCIAL CAUSES)

Auction Services

David Rago
David Rago Auctions Inc.
333 North Main St.
Lambertville, NJ 08530
ph: 609-397-9374 or 609-397-1802
fax: 609-397-9377
e-mail: info@ragoarts.com
web: http://www.ragoarts.com
Specializing in the sale of 20th century decorative and applied arts from 1920 to present.

Don Treadway
Treadway Gallery
2029 Madison Rd.
Cincinnati, OH 45208
ph: 513-321-6742 or 800-526-0491
fax: 513-871-7722
e-mail: info@treadwaygallery.com
web: http://www.treadwaygallery.com
Special auction sales of 1950s/Modern design.

Peter Loughrey
L.A. Modern Auctions
P.O. Box 462006
Los Angeles, CA 90046
ph: 323-845-9456
fax: 323-845-9601
e-mail: info@lamodern.com
web: http://www.lamodern.com/
Auctions twice a year specializing in 20th Century decorative arts with an emphasis on works by Designers; publishes full-color catalogs for each auction.

Collectors

John M. England, Jr.
P.O. Box 393
Lincolnshire, IL 60069
ph: 847-823-5287
fax: 847-823-5287
e-mail: triodes@sprintmail.com
Buys, collects, and sells machine age design, Art Deco and Moderne furnishings, radios.

Dealers

Jim Medeiros
Twentieth Century Designs
P.O. Box 3386
Fayville, MA 01745-0386
ph: 508-370-7330
e-mail: info@fiestajim.com
web: http://www.fiestajim.com
Jim Medeiros and his partner Ken Paruti Specialize in modern American dinnerware and pottery, kitchen and barware, Jadite, Deco, Fifties, etc.

Dennis Bradbury
Deco Reflections
44 Market St.
Amesbury, MA 01913-2424
ph: 978-388-6250
fax: 978-388-6250
Specializing in items from the 20th century: Chase chrome, Manhattan glass, kitchen appliances, toasters, blenders, lamps & lighting, clocks, dinnerware, furniture, and costume jewelry.

Normand Mainville
Machine Age
354 Congress St.
Boston, MA 02210
ph: 617-482-0048
Buys and sells vintage modern furniture and decorative arts from the '30s to the '50s: desks, chairs, lamps, vases, ceramics, radios, telephones, ashtrays, sofas, clocks, fans, irons, mirrors, toys, globes, toasters, blenders, etc.

Steven Caitai
New Era Antiques
7304 5th Ave., Ste. 112
Brooklyn, NY 11209
ph: 718-232-0889
fax: 718-232-0889
web: http://www.neweraantiques.com/
Specializing in 1920 to 1950 industrial design, Art Deco, electrical antiques, vintage radios, televisions, World's Fair, lighting, Chase chrome, and American Moderne style.

City Barn Antiques
362 Atlantic Ave.
Brooklyn, NY 11217
ph: 718-855-8566
Buys and sells mid-century modern furniture, lighting and accessories: Herman Miller, Knoll, Conanc Ball, Heywood-Wakefield, Widdicomb, John Stuart, Simmons, Chase, Frankart.

Carole Hibel
Art & Antiques
131-B Broadview Road
Woodstock, NY 12498
ph: 914-679-2966 or 800-426-3357
fax: 914-679-9101
Buying 1950s Heywood-Wakefield furniture, period lighting, ceramics, pottery, etc.

Catch It All
159 N. 3rd St.
Philadelphia, PA 19106
ph: 215-627-0299

Ken Forster
5501 Seminary Rd., Ste. 1311 South
Falls Church, VA 22041
ph: 703-379-1142
Dealer in American art pottery and tiles, specializing in American tiles from 1860 to 1940; also Art Nouveau, Art Deco, Georg Jensen silver, and American Modernism.

Daniel Donnelly Modern Design Studio
520 N. Fayette St.
Alexandria, VA 22314
ph: 703-549-4672
web: http://www.machineage.com/donnelly/

Boomerang Modern
3301 South Dixie Highway
West Palm Beach, FL 33405
ph: 561-835-1865
e-mail: boomer@flinet.com
web: http://www.boomerangmodern.com
Buys and sells 20th century modern design items; top quality Knoll, Herman-Miller, Heywood-Wakefield; American and European.

Suite Lorain
7105 Lorain Ave.
Cleveland, OH 44102
ph: 216-281-1959
Specializes in Deco to 1950s: vintage fabric, kitchen kitsch, ceramics and glass, lighting, Herman Miller, Heywood-Wakefield, Eames, Saarinen, Herman Miller, clocks, televisions, radios.

Steve Hachen
2109 Luray Ave.
Cincinnati, OH 45206-2630
ph: 513-221-1959
Wants 1950s accessories and designer furniture by Herman Miller, Charles Eames, George Nelson, Knoll, Harry Bertoia, Russell Wright, Eero Saarinen, Isamu Noguchi.

Don Treadway
Treadway Gallery
2029 Madison Rd.
Cincinnati, OH 45208
ph: 513-321-6742 or 800-526-0491
fax: 513-871-7722
e-mail: info@treadwaygallery.com
web: http://www.treadwaygallery.com
Wants to buy mid-20th century "modern design" furniture and decorative arts by designers Charles and Ray Eames, Kem Weber, Gio Ponti, George Nakashima, Isamu Noguchi, George Nelson, Herman Miller, Lloyd Manufacture, Troy, etc.

Lee Hay
Weird & Wonderful
P.O. Box 14898
Cincinnati, OH 45250-0898
ph: 513-621-6034
fax: 513-621-6448
e-mail: heywood@sprintmail.com
Wants to buy Peter Max, 1960's protest items, books on 1930-1970 designers; strange one-of-a-kind items from the 1930s through the 1970s.

Connie Zeigler
Durwyn Smedley Antiques
431 Massachusetts Ave.
Indianapolis, IN 46204
ph: 317-822-0102
e-mail: smedley@iquest.net
web: http://www.smedley.com/smedley/
Buys and sells 20th Century design: Arts & Crafts era, Art Deco, Mid-Century Modern, upscale 50's; art pottery from all eras and designer dinnerware; the first Indiana antique shop in the World Wide Web.

Steve Savitt
Josie's
545 Ridge Rd.
Wilmette, IL 60091-2439
ph: 847-256-7646
fax: 847-256-7004
Specializes in Art Deco, 20th Century Modern, art pottery, art glass and jewelry; no reproductions.

Don Colclough
Mr. Modern
2148 W. Belmont Ave.
Chicago, IL 60618-6414
ph: 800-775-5078 or 708-848-7496
fax: 708-848-9124
e-mail: mrmodern@aol.com
Specialist in Art Deco lighting, both commercial and residential, Heywood-Wakefield furniture, and period hardware.

Zig Zag
3419 North Lincoln Ave.
Chicago, IL 60657
ph: 773-525-1060
Buys, sells, and rents Art Deco and Moderne furnishings, Bakelite jewelry, industrial design, radios, purses, etc.

Urban Artifacts
2928 N. Lincoln
Chicago, IL 60657-4109
ph: 773-404-1008
Buys and sells vintage modern furniture and decorative arts from the '40s to the '70s.

Kathryn Wiese
Retrospective Modern Designs
3225 Yellowstone Dr.
Lawrence, KS 66047
ph: 785-832-0972
e-mail: modern@hialoha.net
web: http://www.retrospective.net/
Mid-century modern dinnerware & home designs sold exclusively on the internet and by phone; featuring Russel Wright, Ben Seibel, Eva Zeisel, Metlox Poppytrail, Franciscan, Chase, Sascha Brastoff, Vernon and more; no storefront sales.

20th Century Classics
3017-B Routh St.
Dallas, TX 75201
ph: 214-880-0020
fax: 214-351-6208
Wants 20th century collectibles: Knoll, H. Miller, Juhl, Artlo, Noguchi, Venini, etc.

Citi Modern
2928 Main St.
Dallas, TX 75226
ph: 214-651-9200
Buys and sells 1950s and 1960s modern, futurist, Heywood-Wakefield, microphones, lighting, Bakelite, industrial design.

Aqua
1415 S. Congress
Austin, TX 78704-2434
ph: 512-916-8800
fax: 512-916-8800
Herman Miller, ethnic, 20th century modern, architectural.

Jet Age
250 Oak St.
San Francisco, CA 94102
ph: 415-864-1950
Buys and sells classic modern furnishings from the 1930s to 1960s; Art Deco, '30s and '40s modern, Eames, Nelson, Noguchi, Saarinen, Bertoia, Aalto, Herman-Miller, Knoll, etc.

Peter & Deborah Keresztury
Deco to 50s
149 Gough Street
San Francisco, CA 94102-5919
ph: 415-553-4500
Wants to buy furniture, accessories, rugs, art, fabric, jewelry, and decorative objects of the 20th century.

Wrinkled Bohemia
1125 Pike
Seattle, WA 98101
ph: 206-464-0850
Buys and sells mid-20th century furniture, dishware, and decorative arts by Russell Wright, Eva Zeisel, Charles and Ray Eames, Ken Weber, Noguchi, George Nelson, Herman Miller, Knoll Associates, Paul McCobb, Heywood-Wakefield, etc.

Biff Brayman
Laguna
5828 Roosevelt Way
Seattle, WA 98105
Specializes in 20th century dinnerware.

Experts

Jan Lindenberger
P.O. Box 7224
Colorado Springs, CO 80933
ph: 719-591-9558
fax: 719-591-9558
Buys and sells '50s and '60s memorabilia; author of "'50s-'60s Memorabilia - Information & Price Guide" (Schiffer Pub., 1993).

Steve Cabella
Modern "i", The
500 Red Hill Ave.
San Anselmo, CA 94960-2409
ph: 415-456-3960
Collecting modern furniture, products and design facts for over 20 years; specialize in the work of Ray and Charles Eames; also always buying 50s modernist craft jewelry and ceramics; settle estates of artists, architects, designers.

Museums/Libraries

Annabel Hanson
Walter Gropius House, Society for the Preservation of New England Antiquities
68 Baker Bridge Rd.
Lincoln, MA 01773
ph: 781-259-8098 or 781-227-3957
fax: 781-227-9204
Designed and lived in by architect Walter Gropius (founder of the German design school known as Bauhaus), SPNEA's Gropius House is open to the public; house tours run regularly; admission charged.

Periodicals

Scott Cheverie
Deco Echoes Publications
Magazine: Echoes Magazine
P.O. Box 155
Cummaquid, MA 02637
ph: 508-362-3822 or 800-695-5768
fax: 508-362-6670
e-mail: hey@deco-echoes.com
web: http://www.deco-echoes.com
Glossy, elegantly designed quarterly dedicated to the styles & designs of the mid-20th C.; emphasis on 1920s-1960s eras including Art Deco, Streamline Moderne, Biomorphic '50s, Abstract '60s styles and movements from kitsch to high-end.

David Rago
Magazine: Modernist Magazine, The
333 North Main St.
Lambertville, NJ 08530
ph: 609-397-9374 or 609-397-1802
fax: 609-397-9377
e-mail: info@ragoarts.com
web: http://www.ragoarts.com
A quarterly publication focusing on modernism and the Machine Age.

Heywood-Wakefield

Dealers

Kathy Burch
Tri-State Antique Center
47 W. Pike
Canonsburg, PA 15317
ph: 724-745-9116
fax: 724-745-4769
e-mail: info@tri-stateantiques.com
web: http://tri-stateantiques.com
Extensive internet gallery featuring Heywood-Wakefield and other mid-20th century modern designer furniture.

Boomerang Modern
3301 South Dixie Highway
West Palm Beach, FL 33405
ph: 561-835-1865
e-mail: boomer@flinet.com
web: http://www.boomerangmodern.com
Buys and sells 20th century modern design items; top quality Knoll, Herman-Miller, Heywood-Wakefield; American and European.

Lee Hay
Weird & Wonderful
P.O. Box 14898
Cincinnati, OH 45250-0898
ph: 513-621-6034
fax: 513-621-6448
e-mail: heywood@sprintmail.com
Wants to buy Heywood-Wakefield advertising pieces, catalogs, and furniture.

Don Colclough
Mr. Modern
2148 W. Belmont Ave.
Chicago, IL 60618-6414
ph: 800-775-5078 or 708-848-7496
fax: 708-848-9124
e-mail: mrmodern@aol.com
Specializes in Heywood-Wakefield as well as other modern furnishings.

Bill Lewis
Spotlight on Modern
The Antique Center on Broadway
1235 S. Broadway
Denver, CO 80210-1503
ph: 303-744-1857
e-mail: Spotmodern@aol.com
web: http://members.aol.com/spotmodern/
Specialists in vintage Heywood-Wakefield furniture and other 1950s mid-century modern.

Cadillac Jack
2820 Gilroy St.
Los Angeles, CA 90039
ph: 800-775-5078
Featuring the largest selection of Heywood-Wakefield furniture in the country; total restoration available; buy, sell, trade.

Experts

Lee Stanley
Antique Store, An
1450 W. Webster Ave.
Chicago, IL 60614-3050
ph: 773-935-6060
fax: 773-871-6660
Buys, sells, appraises Heywood-Wakefield furniture and original catalogs, signs, advertising, etc.; also wants Dunbar and Widdicomb furniture catalogs, brochures, etc.

Peter Max

Collectors

Bill Triola
1114 E. Mt. Hope Ave.
Lansing, MI 48910
ph: 517-332-1203 or 517-484-5414
fax: 517-484-3480

Dealers

Lee Hay
Weird & Wonderful
P.O. Box 14898
Cincinnati, OH 45250-0898
ph: 513-621-6034
fax: 513-621-6448
e-mail: heywood@sprintmail.com
Wants to buy Peter Max memorabilia.

MOLDS

(see also KITCHEN COLLECTIBLES)

Butter

Collectors

Priscilla Hinners
2711 Jaynia Place
Lemon Grove, CA 91945-1319
ph: 619-265-1046
e-mail: phinners@yahoo.com
Wants butter molds, stamps, multiple prints, rollers.

Dealers

Carleton L. Cotting
1441 Crowell Rd.
Vienna, VA 22182-1512
ph: 703-759-5646
Collects, buys and sells butter molds and stamps.

Candy

Collectors

Priscilla Hinners
2711 Jaynia Place
Lemon Grove, CA 91945-1319
ph: 619-265-1046
e-mail: phinners@yahoo.com
Wants candy molds, chocolate, maple sugar, rollers, etc.

Museums/Libraries

Wilbur Chocolate's Candy Americana Museum
48 N. Broad St.
Lititz, PA 17543-1026
ph: 717-626-3249 or 888-294-5287
web: http://www.800padutch.com/wilbur.html

Chocolate

Experts

Lorry & Bruce Hanes
Dad's Follies
40 Kingston Ct.
Gibsonville, NC 27249-3353
ph: 336-449-0494
fax: 336-449-9670
e-mail: dadsfollie@aol.com
Buys, sells, and specializes in ice cream molds; carries large inventory of tin and pewter chocolate and ice cream molds.

Ice Cream

Experts

Lorry & Bruce Hanes
Dad's Follies
40 Kingston Ct.
Gibsonville, NC 27249-3353
ph: 336-449-0494
fax: 336-449-9670
e-mail: dadsfollie@aol.com
Buys, sells, and specializes in ice cream molds; carries large inventory of tin and pewter chocolate and ice cream molds.

Allan Mellis
Mr. Ice Cream
1115 West Montana
Chicago, IL 60614-2220
ph: 773-327-9123
fax: 773-327-9456
e-mail: mellis@enteract.com
Wants postcards, pewter molds, ice cream trays, and ice cream-related watch fobs, magazines, valentines, buttons, ice cream and soda fountain real photo postcards, trade cards, pre-1920 ephemera, and supply catalogs.

MONEY

(see BANKING; CIVIL WAR ARTIFACTS, Currency; COINS & CURRENCY; CREDIT CARDS & CHARGE ITEMS; MONEYCARDS; TELEPHONE CARDS; WOODEN MONEY)

MONEY CLIPS

(see CUFF LINKS)

MONEYCARDS

(see also BANKING; CIVIL WAR ARTIFACTS, Currency; COINS & CURRENCY; CREDIT CARDS & CHARGE ITEMS; TELEPHONE CARDS; WOODEN MONEY)

Periodicals

Magazine: Moneycard Collector
911 Vandemark Road
Sidney, OH 45365-0783
ph: 937-498-0879 or 800-645-7456
fax: 937-498-0876
Special interest magazine providing news and information for collectors, issuers, manufacturers and users of telephone and other types of debit cards.

MONSTER COLLECTIBLES

(see CHARACTER COLLECTIBLES; COMIC BOOKS; HORROR; SCIENCE FICTION; TELEVISION SHOWS & MEMORABILIA; MOVIE MEMORABILIA; TOYS, Monsters; UFO'S & UNEXPLAINED PHENOMENA)

MONUMENT REPLICAS

(see SOUVENIR & COMMEMORATIVE ITEMS, Buildings)

MORBID & ODD ITEMS

(see also CIRCUS COLLECTIBLES; FUNERAL ITEMS; GHOSTS & HAUNTINGS; RIPLEY'S BELIEVE IT OR NOT!; SKELETONS; SCIENCE FICTION; SHRUNKEN HEADS; UFO'S & UNEXPLAINED PHENOMENA; WITCHES)

Dealers

A. Peter Monticup
MagicTricks.Com
101 14th Street
Charlottesville, VA 22903
ph: 804-293-5788
e-mail: monticup@magictricks.com
web: http://www.magictricks.com
Buys and sells sideshow, freak show and carnival items and curiosities; souvenir photos, autographs, sideshow banners, giant's rings, posters, memorabilia, sideshow illusions and actual exhibits.

Museums/Libraries

Gretchen Worden, Dir.
Mutter Museum, College of Physicians of Philadelphia
19 South 22nd St.
Philadelphia, PA 19103-3097
ph: 610-563-3737 x242
fax: 215-561-6477
e-mail: muttref@collphyphil.org
web: http://www.collphyphil.org/muttpg1.shtml
Collection consists of antique medical instruments and equipment primarily from the 19th and 20th centuries, and rare anatomical specimens and medical curiosities such as 2,000 swallowed objects removed from food and air passages.

Harvey Lee Boswell
Palace of Wonders Museum
P.O. Box 446
Elm City, NC 27822-0446
Wants to buy anything strange, odd and unusual: Tibetan items, 2-headed calf, shrunken head, mummy, skeleton, tombstones, antique funeral items, mounted reptiles/fish/animals, circus & carnival sideshow items, jungle weapons, etc.

MORMON ITEMS

Dealers

Warren Anderson
America West Archives
P.O. Box 100
Cedar City, UT 84721-0100
ph: 435-586-9497 or 435-586-7323
e-mail: awa@netutah.com
web: http://www.americawestarchives.com/
Buying and selling documents, letters, autographs and other types of printed ephemera related to Mormonism; author of "Owning Western History."

MOTOR SCOOTERS

(see also MOTORCYCLES)

Collectors

Howard Murrill
826 DeWitt Dr.
Lenoir City, TN 37772-5514
ph: 423-986-3042
e-mail: hmurrill@ix.netcom.com
Wants unrestored motor scooters and parts, especially Cushman, Silver Pigeon, Vespa, Powell, Autoglide, Salsbury, Fuji Rabbit, Zun Dap, Doodlebug; must be 30 years old or older; also need cycle license plates, Cushman signs.

Cushman

Clubs/Associations

Tom O'Hara, Sec.
Cushman Club of America
Magazine: Cushman Club of America Member Magazine
P.O. Box 661
Union Springs, AL 36089-0661
ph: 334-738-3874
fax: 334-738-2711
web: http://frontpage.bitshop.com/cushman.htm
Dedicated to the preservation and restoration of Cushman Motor Scooters.

Mike Mitchell
5628 Logan Ave. So.
Minneapolis, MN 55419
ph: 612-441-7059
Dedicated to the preservation of Cushman motor scooters.

MOTORCYCLES

(see also AUTOMOBILIA; MAGAZINES, Motorcycle; MOTOR SCOOTERS)

Auction Services

Jerry Wood
J. Wood Co. Auctioneers
P.O. Box 852
Searsport, ME 04974-0852
ph: 207-567-4250 or 901-795-8895
fax: 207-567-4252
e-mail: jwoodandco@mindspring.com

Clubs/Associations

American Motorcycle Association
13515 Yarmouth Dr.
Pickerington, OH 43147
ph: 614-856-1900 or 800-AMA-JOIN
e-mail: afitch@ama-cycle.org
web: http://www.ama-cycle.org/
Has over 200,000 members.

Dick Winger, Mem.
Antique Motorcycle Club of America
Magazine: Antique Motorcycle, The
P.O. Box 300
Sweetser, IN 46987-0300
ph: 765-384-5421 or 800-782-2622
fax: 765-384-7002
web: http://ww1.comteck.com/~amc/
A club of 6000 members worldwide dedicated to the preservation, restoration and enjoyment of antique motorcycles; have approximately 8-10 shows and swap meets, and road rides around the country each year.

Joyce Lee
Vintage Motor Bike Club
537 W. Huntington St.
Montpelier, IN 47359
ph: 765-728-5318

Women on Wheels
Magazine: WOW Magazine
P.O. Box 26
Fall River, WI 53932-0026
ph: 800-322-1969 or 608-337-4676
fax: 608-337-4419
e-mail: wowheels@yahoo.com
web: http://www.geocities.com/MotorCity/Shop/4171/Wow.htm
Has over 65 chapters in the US and Canada; over 1500 members.

Washington Classic Motorcycle Club
8615 N. Meridian Ave.
Seattle, WA 98103

Collectors

Ken Kiczynski
1075 W. Chestnut St.
Union, NJ 07083-6767
ph: 908-688-9475
Wants to buy old motorcycles, motorcycle toys, parts, literature, memorabilia, anything motorcycle.

Ed Natale, Jr.
P.O. Box 222
Wyckoff, NJ 07481
ph: 201-848-8485
fax: 201-848-8485
Wants motorcycle related item: club/gang items such as photos, pins; also oil cans, tools, literature, advertising, clothing, pre-1970s license plates, trinkets, etc.; photos helpful.

Kevin Flanagan
P.O. Box 503
Rockaway, NJ 07866-0503
ph: 201-328-3027
Wants to buy motorcycles, parts, literature, memorabilia, motorcycle toys, pre-1950, motorcycle watch fobs and stick pins.

Herb Glass
RD 1 Box 506A
Pine Bush, NY 12566-9778
ph: 914-361-3657
Wants to buy antique American pre-1920 motorcycles, motorcycle literature and motorcycle advertising items: factory sales catalogs, manuals, magazines, pins, fobs, trophies, medals, etc.

Bob "Sprocket" Eckardt
P.O. Box 172
Gansevoort, NY 12866-0172
ph: 518-584-2405
Buys motorcycle memorabilia: literature, posters, toys, trophies, medals, fobs, pennants, programs, photos, jerseys, F.A.M., AMA, Gypsy tour items, advertising items, clocks, signs, showroom items; anything to do with motorcycles.

Chris Savino
P.O. Box 419
Breesport, NY 14816-0419
ph: 607-739-3106
fax: 607-739-3106
e-mail: csavino@extrope.net
Wants to buy motorcycle literature, pins, awards, motorcycles, clothing toys, shop signs, old parts inventory, motorcycle license plates, dealer plates, anything related to motor scooters and motorcycles!

Jack C. Bishop
209 Tebbs Road
Montgomery, PA 17752-9733
ph: 570-547-2578
fax: 570-547-2578
e-mail: jackcbishop@yahoo.com
A collector of pre-1970 European and antique American motorcycles, clothing, pins, literature, and advertising; wants motorcycle related pins, hats, signs, literature, oil cans - anything related to motorcycles.

Jack C. Bishop
209 Tebbs Road
Montgomery, PA 17752-9733
ph: 570-547-2578
fax: 570-547-2578
e-mail: jackcbishop@yahoo.com
A collector of pre-1970 European and antique American motorcycles, clothing, pins, literature, and advertising.

Richard L. Weiss
1885 Klines Mill Rd.
Breinigsville, PA 18031
ph: 610-285-4122
e-mail: mrsdlw@prodigy.net
Specialized wants: Smith, Briggs & Stratton, Merkel, Steffy motor wheels; Whizzer & pre-1940 American motorcycles; whole or parts.

Dealers

Chris Savino
P.O. Box 419
Breesport, NY 14816-0419
ph: 607-739-3106
fax: 607-739-3106
e-mail: csavino@extrope.net
Wants to purchase any motor scooters made in America: Cushman, Sears Allstate, Salsbury, Doodlebug, Motoscoot, etc.; also need Whizzers or Mustangs; parts and scooters in any condition wanted; also motorcycle literatures and memorabilia.

David Gaylin
Motor Cycle Days
P.O. Box 9686
Rosedale, MD 21237
ph: 410-665-6295
Author of "Triumph Motorcycles in America," (1993) and "Triumph Motorcycle Restoration Guide," (1997); always seeking original motorcycle literature, art, especially from British and Japanese makers; also wants motorcycle movie posters.

Clarke's Classic Cycles
4969 NW 72nd Way
Bell, FL 32619-3851
Buys and sells British and American classic motorcycles and scooters.

Gainsville Cycle
2509 Linebaugh Rd.
Xenia, OH 45385-9512
Buys and sells modern and classic motorcycles including German, Italian, British and Japanese.

Al Bogg
Al Bogg Motorscooters & Motorcycles
P.O. Box 839
Poplar Bluff, MO 63902
ph: 573-785-0172 or 573-785-0385
fax: 573-785-0015
e-mail: albogg@sheltonbbs.com
web: http://www.albogg.com/
Specializes in classic, vintage and antique motorcycles, motor scooters and bicycles.

Mick Stamm
Antique & Vintage Motorcycles
3401 S. 1st
Abilene, TX 79605-1708
ph: 915-676-8788
American motorcycles, parts, advertising items, Harley/Indian dealer items, signs, clocks, mirrors, original boxed parts, oil/paint cans, clothing, toys, jewelry, ash trays, literature, pins, awards, ribbons, fobs, license plates.

Internet Resources

Motorcycle Museum Online, The
e-mail: mmo@tower.org
web: http://www2.tower.org/museum/main.html
Contains information in individual motorcycle marques and manufacturers.

Motorcycle Museum Online
e-mail: mmo@tower.org
web: http://www2.tower.org/museum/
Collects, archives, and displays information regarding the rich history of the production of motorized 2- and 3-wheeled vehicles; center of information on little-known marques as well the better known manufacturers.

Museums/Libraries

Motorcycle Hall of Fame Museum
13515 Yarmouth Dr.
Pickerington, OH 43147
ph: 614-856-1900 or 800-AMA-JOIN
e-mail: afitch@ama-cycle.org
web: http://www.ama-cycle.org/
Museum belongs to the American Motorcycle Association.

Rocky Mountain Motorcycle Museum & Hall of Fame
308 E. Arvada
Colorado Springs, CO 80906-1439
ph: 719-633-5392
web: http://travelassist.com/mag/a20.html
A non-profit Colorado corporation dedicated to the preservation of early American motorcycling and the pioneers of the sport.

Periodicals

Buzz Kanter, Pub.
TAM Communications, Inc.
Magazine: Old Bike Journal
6 Prowitt St.
Norwalk, CT 06855-1204
ph: 203-855-0008
fax: 203-852-9980
e-mail: buzz@americaniron.com
web: http://www.americaniron.com
For collectors and others interested in older motorcycles; the best seller in its field throughout North America; average of 700-1000 classified ads per issue; 17 issues per year.

Buzz Kanter, Pub.
TAM Communications, Inc.
Magazine: American Iron Magazine
6 Prowitt St.
Norwalk, CT 06855-1204
ph: 203-855-0008
fax: 203-852-9980
e-mail: buzz@americaniron.com
web: http://www.americaniron.com
For collectors and others interested in American motorcycles, specifically Harleys and Indians.

Luis Hernandez
Magazine: Motorcycle Shopper Magazine
1353 Herndon Ave.
Deltona, FL 32725-9046
ph: 407-860-1989 or 800-982-4599
fax: 407-574-1014
web: http://www.motorcycleshopper.com/
A comprehensive buy-sell-trade monthly magazine distributed worldwide; covers all brands of motorcycles and all aspects of the sport and hobby.

Magazine: Walneck's Classic Cycle Trader
P.O. Box 9059
Clearwater, FL 34618-9059
ph: 727-712-0035 or 800-548-8889
fax: 727-712-0034
e-mail: webmaster@traderonline.com
web: http://www.traderonline.com
Buy, sell, trade; color photos, road tests, bikes and parts;published monthly.

Kelley Blue Book
Price Guide: Kelley Blue Book
5 Oldfield
Irvine, CA 92618
ph: 949-770-7704
fax: 949-837-1904
e-mail: kelley@kbb.com
web: http://www.kbb.com/indexv.html
Website offers current trade-in values for all makes and model cars for the past 21 years; also publishes printed value guides for cars, RV's, motorcycles, snowmobiles, motor homes, travel trailers, personal watercraft, etc.

Steve Ferguson, Ed.
National Automobile Dealers Association
Price Guide: N.A.D.A. Official Used Car Guide
P.O. Box 7800
Costa Mesa, CA 92628
ph: 800-544-6232
fax: 714-556-8715
e-mail: nada@nada.org
web: http://www.nada.org/
A series of value guides for domestic and foreign cars, trucks, vans, RV's, mobile homes, motorcycles, snowmobiles, and boats, small and large; also Heavy Duty Trucks and Aircraft Book, car clubs & organizations, museums.

Magazine: Canadian Biker Magazine
P.O. Box 4122
Victoria, British Columbia V8X 2X4
Canada
ph: 604-384-0333 or 800-667-5667
e-mail: canbike@islandnet.com
web: http://www.canadianbiker.com/

Brown Bear Publishing, Ltd.
Magazine: Classic Bike
Royex House
Aldermanbury
London, EC2V 7HR
U.K.
web: http://classicbike.subscriptions.co.uk

Repair Services

Antique Motorcycle Restoration
14611 N. Nebraska Ave.
Tampa, FL 33613
ph: 813-972-9297
fax: 813-979-9475
Complete ground-up restoration; painting, sheet metal repair, sand blasting, engine repair, transmission repair, welding.

Randy Hilberg
Collector's Nectar
Box 431
Morro Bay, CA 93443
ph: 805-772-2968
fax: 805-772-2968
e-mail: nectar@thegrid.net
Always buying antique motorcycles, scooters; offers complete restoration services; appraisals; master

technician; all makes and models; no collection too big or too small to purchase or restore; the only lifetime guarantee in the business.

Don Doody
North West Classic Motorcycles
P.O. Box 774
Lynden, WA 98264
fax: 604-530-5077
Sells and repairs antique Harley and Indian motorcycles.

BMW

Clubs/Associations

Kathy Harmacek, Mem.
Yankee Beemers, Inc.
Newsletter: Boxer Shorts
116 Turnpike Rd., #7
Chelmsford, MA 01824
e-mail: kathyh@eudoramail.com
web: http://www.angelfire.com/ma/beemernews/

Roland Slabon, Ed
Vintage BMW Motorcycle Owners, Ltd.
Newsletter: Vintage BMW Bulletin
P.O. Box 67
Exeter, NH 03833
ph: 603-772-9799
e-mail: vintage_editor@juno.com
web: http://www.greatanswers.com/vintagebmw/

British

Clubs/Associations

British Iron Association of Connecticut
Newsletter: British Iron Association of Connecticut Newsletter
P.O. Box 610
Canton, CT 06019

British (Triumph)

Clubs/Associations

John W. Healy
Triumph International Owners Club/British Motorcycle Association
Newsletter: TIOC/BMA Newsletter
P.O. Box 6676
Holliston, MA 01746-6676
ph: 508-429-4221
fax: 508-429-6213
e-mail: JohnTIOC@aol.com
web: http://tioc.com/
Dedicated to the riding, restoration and racing of Triumph motorcycles; 3,000 members; annual rally in various parts of the US; newsletter includes rallies, ads, classifieds, and varying social and technical articles.

Triumph International Owners Club
Magazine: Vintage Bike
P.O. Box 6676
Holliston, MA 01746-6676
ph: 508-429-4221
fax: 508-429-6213
e-mail: JohnTIOC@aol.com
web: http://tioc.com/

Harley-Davidson

Man./Prod./Dist.

Harley-Davidson Motor Company
3700 W. Juneau Ave.
p.O. Box 653
Milwaukee, WI 53208
ph: 414-342-4680
web: http://www.harley-davidson.com

Periodicals

Buzz Kanter, Pub.
TAM Communications, Inc.
Magazine: Thunder Alley
6 Prowitt St.
Norwalk, CT 06855-1204
ph: 203-855-0008
fax: 203-852-9980
e-mail: buzz@americaniron.com
web: http://www.americaniron.com
Every issue packed with articles which offer everything from hands-on technical explanations, complete with clear photos and diagrams, to profiles and reviews of the parts and people that make up the go-fast Harley world.

Magazine: American Rider
2575 Vista Del Mar Dr.
Ventura, CA 93001
ph: 805-667-4100 or 800-926-0484
web: http://www.ridermagazine.com/
A quarterly magazine for the Harley-Davidson enthusiast; historical profiles, technical information, racing coverage, club news, road tests, product evaluations, etc.

Indian

Clubs/Associations

Don Doody
Laughing Indian Riders
Newsletter: Laughing Indian Riders Newsletter
P.O. Box 774
Lynden, WA 98264
fax: 604-530-5077

Dealers

Starklite Cycle
21230 Gold Valley Rd.
Perris, CA 92570
ph: 909-780-0421
fax: 909-780-0857
e-mail: sales@starklite.com
web: http://www.starklite.com
World's largest supplier of quality antique Indian (made from 1901-1953) motorcycle parts, accessories and complete restorations.

Museums/Libraries

Esta Manthos, Dir.
Indian Motocycle Museum & Hall of Fame
33 Hendee St.
P.O. Box 90003 Mason Sq. Sta.
Springfield, MA 01139-3003
ph: 413-737-2624
e-mail: webmaster@sidecar.com
web: http://www.sidecar.com/indian/

Periodicals

Buzz Kanter, Pub.
TAM Communications, Inc.
Magazine: Indian Motorcycle Illustrated
6 Prowitt St.
Norwalk, CT 06855-1204
ph: 203-855-0008
fax: 203-852-9980
e-mail: buzz@americaniron.com
web: http://www.americaniron.com
Special interest magazine dedicated to Indian motorcycles, once the most popular motorcycle in the world.

Japanese

Clubs/Associations

Don Brown
Classic Japanese Motorcycle Club
Newsletter: Classic Japanese Motorcycle Club Newsletter
3139 Hawkcrest Circle
San Jose, CA 95139
ph: 408-238-9458
fax: 408-531-1157
e-mail: doncjmc@aol.com
Dedicated to having fun with pre-1984 Japanese motorcycles; newsletter has information, technical help, and the largest Japanese motorcycle want ad section; free want ads!

Vintage Japanese Motorcycle Club
Newsletter: Vintage Japanese Motorcycle Club Newsletter
P.O. Box 515
Dartford, Kent DA1 3RE
U.K.
e-mail: vjmc@vjmc.com
web: http://www.vjmc.com/
Welcomes collectors, riders, restorers, and racers of vintage Japanese motorcycles; 18 year old club; 6,500+ members; make contact with others involved in all aspects of vintage and classic Japanese motorcycles.

Moto Guzzi

Clubs/Associations

Moto Guzzi National Owners Club
P.O. Box 98
Olmitz, KS 67564
ph: 316-285-7344
Focuses on the collection and restoration of Moto Guzzi motorcycles and related items.

Sidecars

Periodicals

Jim Dodson, Ed.
Magazine: Hack'd
P.O. Box 813
Buckhannon, WV 26201-0813
ph: 304-472-6146
fax: 304-472-7027
e-mail: hackd@neumedia.net
web: http://www.sidecar.com/HACKD/
The magazine for and about sidecarists.

Suzuki

Clubs/Associations

Suzuki Owners Club
30 Lavender Place
Carterton
Oxford, Oxfordshire OX18 3XR
U.K.
e-mail: webmaster@suzuki-club.co.uk
web: http://www.suzuki-club.co.uk/
For owners of Suzuki motorcycles.

Whizzer

Collectors

Robert J. Lee
P.O. Box 465
Franklin, TN 37065
e-mail: rjustinlee@juno.com

Ron Klaus
35769 Simon Dr.
Clinton Township, MI 48035
ph: 810-791-5594

Don Hooper
9645 Sylvia Ave.
Northridge, CA 91324-1756
ph: 818-772-1721
fax: 818-772-4647
e-mail: vntgplbg@aol.com
Wants to buy Whizzer bikes, parts, tanks, accessories, literature, etc.

MOTTOES (PICTURE POEMS)

Clubs/Associations

Howard & Sarah Wade
Mad About Mottoes
Newsletter: Mad About Mottoes Newsletter
P.O. Box 325
Orrville, OH 44667-0325
ph: 330-682-8551
fax: 330-682-3655
e-mail: ukdolls@aol.com

Collectors

Howard & Sarah Wade
P.O. Box 325
Orrville, OH 44667-0325
ph: 330-682-8551
fax: 330-682-3655
e-mail: ukdolls@aol.com
Has extensive collection of mottoes and picture poems by Buzza, P.F. Volland, Cincinnati Art Publishers, Mottograph, Buckbee-Grehn, and Gibson.

MOUNTS

(see ANIMAL TROPHIES)

MOVIE MEMORABILIA

(see also AUDIO-VISUAL; AUTOGRAPHS; BROADCASTING; COWBOY HEROES; DISNEY COLLECTIBLES; FAN CLUBS; FILMS; HORROR; MAGAZINES, Movie; PERSONALITIES [MOVIE STARS]; PHOTOGRAPHS, Celebrity; SCIENCE FICTION; TELEVISION SHOWS & MEMORABILIA)

Appraisers

John Kisch
Separate Cinema
P.O. Box 114
Hyde Park, NY 12538-0114
ph: 914-452-1998
fax: 914-454-7131
e-mail: johnkisch@aol.com
Appraises movie memorabilia of all kinds.

Auction Services

Alexandra Peters
Phillips Fine Art & Auctioneers
406 East 79th St.
New York, NY 10022
ph: 212-570-4830
fax: 212-570-2207
e-mail: phillips@philmail.demon.co.uk
web: http://www.phillips-auctions.com
Solicits items for sale in their London office; specializes in the sale of jewelry, paintings, prints, silver, coins, stamps, toys (especially lead soldiers), and movie memorabilia.

Heather Holmberg
Holmberg Auctions
3727 W. magnolia Blvd., #247
Burbank, CA 91505
ph: 818-557-7435
fax: 818-557-7436
e-mail: heather@collectible.com
web: http://www.collectible.com
Specializes in the auctioning of motion picture and entertainment memorabilia.

Butterfield & Butterfield
220 San Bruno Ave.
San Francisco, CA 94103-5018
ph: 415-861-7500
fax: 415-861-8951
e-mail: info@butterfields.com
web: http://www.butterfields.com/
Specialties include posters, toys, decorative arts, furniture, photography, etc.; the largest full service auction in the west.

George Baker
Baker's Eclectibles
P.O. Box 580466
Modesto, CA 95358
ph: 290-537-5221
fax: 209-531-0233
e-mail: georgeb1@thevision.net
web: http://www.collectorsmart.com/
Buys, sells, appraises, auctions authentic autographs and movie memorabilia, music collectibles, art, trading cards, etc.; monthly autograph, coin/currency/token, and general auctions; 25 years in service; member UACC, TAMS.

Miles Barton
Sotheby's
34-35 New Bond St.
London, W1A 2AA
U.K.
ph: 44 171 293 5000
fax: 44 171 293 5989
web: http://www.sothebys.com/
Conducts regular auctions of movie memorabilia.

Book Sellers

Hollywood Movie Archives
P.O. Box 1566
Apple Valley, CA 92307-0030
ph: 760-247-6819 or 800-771-6746
e-mail: sales@accidental.com
web: http://24.0.45.221/archives/index.htm
Sells hard-to-find movie information for the collector & movie buff; star's birthdays and addresses, fan club directories, old theaters, where stars are buried, where to find movie memorabilia, movie star stamps, etc.; brochure available.

Collectors

Bob Havey
P.O. Box 183
North Sullivan, ME 04664-0183
ph: 207-422-3083
fax: 207-422-3430
Wants to buy 1930s-1940s posters, lobby cards, advertising, magazines; anything movie related.

Van Polla
16-64 155 St.
Whitestone, NY 11357
ph: 718-746-0911
fax: 718-746-0911
Wants to buy Hollywood memorabilia: posters, lobby cards, photos, sheet music, magazines, animation art, TV & radio items, etc.

Bill Simmons
8955 NW 19th St.
Coral Springs, FL 33071-6109
ph: 954-340-0734
e-mail: wsim1206@aol.com
Wants all movie memorabilia, autographs, posters, photos; especial wants anything on Chuck Connors including baseball and basketball items.

Scott Weiss
1158 26th St., #489
Santa Monica, CA 90403
ph: 310-442-0040
fax: 310-442-5530
e-mail: sweiss5905@aol.com
Wants to buy movie and TV promotional and advertising specialty gift items such as pin-back buttons, badges, cloisonne pins, cloth usher ribbons, paperweights, tokens, snow domes, ashtrays, statues, clocks, radios, flashlights, lighters.

Talbert Kanigher
Tal's Nostalgia
P.O. Box 6294
Burbank, CA 91505-6294
ph: 818-848-6469
fax: 818-848-6469
Wants movie autographs, photographs, etc.; collecting movie memorabilia for over 40 years.

Dealers

Jon Allan
Elmer's Nostalgia, Inc.
3 Putnam St.
Sanford, ME 04073-2024
ph: 207-324-2166

Dennis & Mary Luby
Casey's Collectible Corner
HCR 31 Box 30
No. Blenheim, NY 12131
ph: 607-588-6464
e-mail: caseyscc@aol.com
web: http://www.csmonline.com/caseys/
Buys and sells collectible toys: comic characters, TV shows and personalities; also space and monster toys, sports collectibles, etc.

John Kachmar
Techno-Fantasy Traders
779 Carissa Dr.
West Palm Beach, FL 33411-3412
ph: 561-798-5978
fax: 561-798-5978

Sandra McGovern
Global Music Enterprises
P.O. Box 450763
Kissimmee, FL 34745-0763
ph: 407-396-4176
fax: 407-396-4176
e-mail: globaltreasures@webtv.net
Buys and sells vintage sheet music and movie/movie star memorabilia, Marilyn Monroe, pin-ups; send want lists or email requests.

Bruce Hubbard IV
Williams Collection, The
260 Ridgeview Drive
Wayzata, MN 55391
ph: 612-473-9591
e-mail: bedlum@aol.com
web: http://members.aol.com/bedlum/
Large movie prop dealer; drama, horror, Sci-fi, action; deals only in authentic movie props and wardrobe; no common posters, concert tickets, common movie items, or T-shirts.

Peggy
Silver Screen
6332 Clayton Ave.
Saint Louis, MO 63139
ph: 314-781-0077
fax: 314-781-2208
e-mail: peggy@vintagefilm.com
web: http://www.vintagefilm.com
Inventory constantly changing; check website for stock; call 800-317-6957 for orders ONLY.

Randi L. Massingill
Eye of the Beholder
1125 W. Baseline, #2F
Mesa, AZ 85210
ph: 602-732-9235
fax: 602-732-9590
e-mail: randi@ntpage.com
web: http://www.geocities.com/Hollywood/Bungalow/7284/eyeofbeholder.html
Runs a search service of collectors of movie memorabilia; specializes in selling movie magazines, posters, teen magazines, movie stills, television items, and celebrity items.

Kristopher Orr
Hollywood Book City Collectables
6631 Hollywood Blvd.
Los Angeles, CA 90028
ph: 323-466-2525 or 800-4CINEMA
fax: 323-962-6742
e-mail: hwdbookcity@earthlink.net
web: http://hollywoodbookcity/
Buys and sells books, autographed celebrity pictures, movie and television scripts, and other movie memorabilia.

Larry Edmunds Book Shop
6644 Hollywood Blvd.
Los Angeles, CA 90028-6219
ph: 323-463-3273
fax: 323-463-4245
Sells movie memorabilia, stills, posters, books and TV and movie scripts.

Book City Collectibles
6627 Hollywood Blvd.
Los Angeles, CA 90028-6285
ph: 323-466-0120 or 323-962-7411
fax: 323-962-6742
Sells movie memorabilia, books and TV and movie scripts.

Myron Ross
Heroes & Legends
P.O. Box 9088
Calabasas, CA 91372
ph: 818-346-9220
e-mail: heroesross@aol.com
Wants character memorabilia, books, comic books, Fanzines, movie memorabilia, etc.; science fiction or fantasy, rock 'n roll, autographs.

Israel I. Bick
Bick International
P.O. Box 854
Van Nuys, CA 91408-0854
ph: 818-997-6496
fax: 818-988-4337
e-mail: iibick@aol.com
web: http://www.bick.net
Buy, sell, trade and appraises Princess Diana, Hollywood, Beatles, Churchill, Lincoln, James Dean, Disney, Elvis, Marilyn Monroe, Bruce Lee, movies, Sherlock Holmes,

Judaica, space, Star Trek, Streisand, etc.

Heather Holmberg
Heather Holmberg Auctions
3727 W. Magnolia Blvd., #247
Burbank, CA 91505
ph: 818-557-7435
fax: 818-557-7436
e-mail: heather@collectible.com
web: http://www.collectible.com
Buys, sells, auctions movie posters, props and costumes, autographs, letters and documents, photographs, original art; also rock 'n' roll, animation, postcards, ephemera.

Eddie Brandt's Saturday Matinee
5006 Vineland Ave.
North Hollywood, CA 91601
ph: 818-506-4242 or 818-506-7722
fax: 818-506-5649
A great source for stills, posters, and lobby cards.

Reel Clothes & Props
12132 Ventura Blvd.
Studio City, CA 91604
ph: 818-508-7762
e-mail: sales@reelclothes.com
web: http://www.reelclothes.com
Sells off clothing and props from movies and TV.

Chris Perry
Doctor 3D
7470 Church St., Ste. A
Yucca Valley, CA 92284-3248
ph: 760-365-0475
fax: 760-365-0495
Buys glass slides that were used in movie theaters; prefers pre-1940 slides but buys slides from all eras; these slides measure 4"x3 1/4"; also buys all 3D movie memorabilia (says "3D" or "3-Dimension" on it).

Sylvia Bongiovanni
P.O. Box 1673
Anaheim, CA 92815
Buys and sells movie and TV memorabilia: books, magazines, lobby cards, etc.

J. Dyson
P.O. Box 10013
Fullerton, CA 92838
Sells movie and TV memorabilia by mail order; sends a list upon request; provide name of star or show you are interested in; enclose SASE.

Ann Daman
Big Picture Movie Posters & Collectibles
e-mail: bigpix@dnai.com
web: http://www.big-pix.com
Movie posters, press kits, banners, standees, buttons and other miscellaneous movie memorabilia from the 1960s to present.

William Rumpf
Memorabilia Mine
P.O. Box 21026
San Jose, CA 95151
ph: 408-270-1072
fax: 408-270-1072
e-mail: sirwgr@memomine.com
web: http://www.memomine.com/
Movie memorabilia collector, dealer, expert and appraiser.

George Baker
CollectorsMart
P.O. Box 580466
Modesto, CA 95358
ph: 290-537-5221
fax: 209-531-0233
e-mail: georgeb1@thevision.net
web: http://www.collectorsmart.com/
Buys, sells, appraises, auctions authentic autographs and movie memorabilia, music collectibles, art, trading cards, etc.; monthly autograph, coin/currency/token, and general auctions; 25 years in service; member UACC, TAMS.

Loraine Burdick
Quest-Eridon Books
413 10th Ave. Ct. NE
Puyallup, WA 98372-2948
e-mail: lo.burdick@n2movies.com
Buys/sells movie magazines, theater advertising, memorabilia, stills, clippings on specific stars by request, Shirley Temple, pre-1960.

Thomas Bauer
Nonstop Collectibles
6659 Sherbrooke, #25
Montreal, Quebec H4B 1N8
Canada
ph: 514-489-5499
e-mail: tom2@odyssee.net
web: http://www.odyssee.net/~tom2/index.html
Internet sales consultant and broker since 1993; active in online sales and marketing of movie memorabilia, other collectibles; will do qualified evaluations of your collection; list items for sale for 20% commission; good comic info.

STARticles
58 Stewart St., Studio 301
Totonto, Ontario M5V 1H6
Canada
ph: 416-504-8286
e-mail: info@starticles.com
web: http://www.starticles.com/
Hollywood props, wardrobe used in films, gold records, signed guitars, stage worn items, autographs, sports items, movie "star articles."

Eric G. Lilley
2 Holly Close, Crookham Park
Crookhan Common
Thatcham, Berkshire RG19 8QZ
U.K.
ph: 01635-869694
Buys and sells memorabilia from the "Golden Era" of Hollywood (1930s to 1950s): American Westerns, swash bucklers, dancers, dramatic stars, British stars: posters, photographs, autographs, films, rare books, etc.

Experts

Richard C. De Thuin
875 West End Ave., Apt. 11F
New York, NY 10025-4954
e-mail: Rdethuin@aol.com
Welcomes written inquiries; please keep inquiries to a max of two items and include both condition and a photograph; SASE required for reply which will be dictated by volume of mail received; please be patient.

Richard Alan Davis
Bijou Dream
9500 Old Georgetown Rd.
Bethesda, MD 20814-1724
ph: 301-530-5904
fax: 301-530-8532
e-mail: rdavis9500@aol.com
No photographs of movie stars.

Richard L. Wilson
Norma's Jeans
3511 Turner Lane
Chevy Chase, MD 20815-3213
ph: 301-652-4644
fax: 301-907-0216
Buys, sells, collects and appraises entertainment costumes, props, promo items; also belongings of famous people, historical relics and artifacts; issues periodic catalog of celebrity items for sale.

Museums/Libraries

Library & Museum of the Performing Arts
40 Lincoln Center Plaza
New York, NY 10023-7498
ph: 212-870-1630
e-mail: performingarts@nypl.org
web: http://www.nypl.org/research/lpa/lpa.html
Houses one of the world's most extensive combination of circulating, reference, and rare archival collections in the field: historic recordings, autograph manuscripts, sheet music, stage designs, press clippings, programs, posters, etc.

American Museum of the Moving Image
35 Avenue at 36 Street
Astoria, NY 11106
ph: 718-784-4520 or 718-784-0077
fax: 718-784-4681
e-mail: info@ammi.org
web: http://www.ammi.org/
The only museum in the US devoted to the art, history, technology of film, television, video, interactive media; collection includes costumes, dolls, movie posters, magazines, TV sets, movie cameras, and other items of film & TV history.

Debbie Reynolds Hollywood Movie Museum
305 Convention Central Drive
Las Vegas, NV 89101
ph: 702-734-0177 or 800-633-1777
web: http://www.lasvegashost.com/lvh_t1.htm
Largest private collection of movie memorabilia in the world; 3,000 costumes, 36,000 square feet of props and furniture; highlights include Judy Garland's pinafore dress from "The Wizard of Oz" and much, much more.

American Film Institute, The
2021 N. Western Ave.
Los Angeles, CA 90027
ph: 323-856-7600
fax: 323-467-4578
e-mail: info@afionline.org
web: http://www.afionline.org/

Periodicals

George A. Carpinone, Ed.
Magazine: Celebrity Collector Magazine
P.O. Box 1115
Boston, MA 02117-1115
ph: 617-426-7724
fax: 617-426-7724
Interviews with classic movie stars, TV stars, and fan club presidents; exploration of Hollywood memorabilia collecting and collection care; contributions by readers; classified ads; beautifully designed as a collectible on glossy paper.

Magazine: Chiller Theatre
P.O. Box 23
Rutherford, NJ 07070

Magazine: Cineaste
200 Park Ave., S.
New York, NY 10003-1503
ph: 212-982-1241
fax: 212-982-1241
e-mail: cineaste@cineaste.com
web: http://www.cineaste.com/
A quarterly magazine on the art and politics of the cinema; interviews, articles, and reviews of films, videos and books; funded by the New York State Council on the Arts.

Jon Warren
American Collectibles Exchange
Magazine: Collecting Hollywood Magazine
P.O. Box 2512
Chattanooga, TN 37409
ph: 423-265-5515 or 800-880-4289
fax: 423-265-5506
e-mail: jonrwarren@aol.com
Articles and stories for film fans and memorabilia collectors.

Magazine: American Movie Classics
P.O. Box 469082
Marion, OH 469082
ph: 888-262-4700
e-mail: info@amctv.com
web: http://www.amctv.com/amcmagazine.html

Brian A. Bukantis
Arena Publishing, Inc.
Newspaper: Movie Collector's World
17230 13 Mile Rd.
Roseville, MI 48066-1916
ph: 810-774-4311
fax: 810-774-5450
e-mail: mcwarena@aol.com
web: http://www.mcwonline.com/MCW.html
Largest leading biweekly movie memorabilia collecting publication existing; posters, stills, videos, etc. offered in each issue; over 525 consecutive biweekly issues published.

Antique Trader Publications, Inc.
Newspaper: Big Reel
P.O. Box 1050
Dubuque, IA 52004-1050
ph: 800-334-7165 or 800-482-4155
fax: 800-531-0880
e-mail: atpzines@aol.com
web: http://www.collect.com/bigreel
A monthly tabloid for movie and television memorabilia collectors and fans: ads, news, current & nostalgic feature articles, obits, etc.

Bob King
Classic Images
Newspaper: Classic Images
301 East 3rd St.
Muscatine, IA 52761
ph: 319-263-2331
fax: 319-262-8042
web: http://www.classicimages.com
Monthly tabloid featuring articles and advertisements directed at film buffs; classic screen biographies, filmographies, interviews, and historical articles on the film industry.

Bob King
Classic Images
Magazine: Films of the Golden Age
301 East 3rd St.
Muscatine, IA 52761
ph: 319-263-2331
fax: 319-262-8042
web: http://www.classicimages.com
For classic movie buffs; beautifully produced stories and art will take you back to Hollywood's Golden Age; 100 pages in each issue; published quarterly.

Doug Watson
Magazine: Paper Collectors' Marketplace
470 Main St.
P.O. Box 128
Scandinavia, WI 54977-0128
ph: 715-467-2379
fax: 715-467-2243
e-mail: pcmpaper@gglbbs.com
web: http://www.pcmpaper.com/
Monthly magazine for collectors of autographs, paperbacks, postcards, advertising, photographica, magazines; all types of paper ephemera.

Randy Skretvedt
Past Times Nostalgia Network
Newsletter: Past Times
7308-H Filmore Dr.
Buena Park, CA 90620
ph: 714-527-5845
fax: 714-527-5845
e-mail: skretved@ix.netcom.com
A quarterly newsletter covering music, movies, and radio programs from the 1920s, '30s, and '40s.

Jordan Young
Past Times Nostalgia Network
Directory: Nostalgia Entertainment Sourcebook
7308-H Filmore Dr.
Buena Park, CA 90620
ph: 714-527-5845
fax: 714-527-5845
e-mail: skretved@ix.netcom.com
Complete resource guide to classic movies, vintage radio, old time music, and theater: programs, sheet music, equipment, where to replace and repair, where to rent or buy old movies, theater posters.

Ev Phillips
Oddesy Publications
Magazine: Pop Culture Collecting
510-A S. Corona Mall
Corona, CA 91720-1420
ph: 909-371-7137 or 800-99-ODYSSEY
fax: 909-371-7139
e-mail: DBTOGI@aol.com
web: http://www.odysseygroup.com/collect.htm
A monthly magazine focusing on collecting autographs, movie memorabilia, movie posters, television, rock & roll, props, costumes, sports, space collectibles, animation art and more.

George Lucas

Clubs/Associations

Dan Madsen
Lucasfilm Fan Club
Newsletter: Lucasfilm Fan Club Newsletter
P.O. Box 111000
Aurora, CO 80042
ph: 303-341-1813 or 800-878-3326
web: http://www.starwars.com/
Quarterly newsletter.

Gone With The Wind

(see also PERSONALITIES [LITERARY], Margaret Mitchell)

Clubs/Associations

Vivien Leigh Fan Club
5 Highpoint Rd.
Perkasie, PA 18944

Collectors

Robert Buchanan
277 W. 22nd St.
New York, NY 10011-2755
ph: 212-989-3917
Wants any GWTW items; also any Vivien Leigh and Clark Gable.

June Crawford
Katie Scarlett's Place
55 E. Patrick St.
Frederick, MD 21701
ph: 301-662-3111

John Wiley, Ed.
1347 Greenmoss Dr.
Richmond, VA 23225-4112
ph: 804-330-5484
fax: 804-771-3054
Wants to buy early copies of the novel in dust jackets and limited editions (US and foreign); Margaret Mitchell items (personal effects, business cards, etc.), movie & stage version items (programs, scarves, novelties, scripts, etc.)

Herb Bridges
P.O. Box 192
Sharpsburg, GA 30277-0192
ph: 404-253-4934
e-mail: herb-gwtw@mindspring.com
Seeks the many GWTW movie tie-in items which were produced in the 1940s: figurines, dolls, games, jewelry, perfume bottles, powder boxes, book ends, candy boxes, handkerchiefs, stationary boxes; also GWTW posters, programs, banners.

Kenneth Nix
307 Rosewood Dr.
Dublin, GA 31021-4133
ph: 912-275-0281 or 912-272-4335
fax: 912-272-4972
e-mail: knix@nlamerica.com
Especially wants merchandising tie-ins associated with both the book and film versions of GWTW. "Scarlett's Chocolates" candy box, neckties, scarves, handkerchiefs, puzzles, games, etc.; publisher of "Gone With The Wind Marketplace."

Barb Kieffer
P.O. Box 43406
Cincinnati, OH 45243
ph: 513-530-5633
Wants to buy Gone With The Wind collectibles, especially cast iron bookends and magazines featuring Scarlett and Rhet.

Dealers

J. Faye Bell
Gone With the Wind Memorabilia
1701 S. Alexander St.
Plant City, FL 33567
ph: 813-752-7700
fax: 813-754-8211
e-mail: GWTWfaye@aol.com
web: http://www.gwtwmemories.com/
Buying and selling GWTW; has thousands of items; two locations - one in Plant City, FL and one in Cypress Gardens, FL where there is also a large exhibit of hundreds of GWTW collectibles from her private collection.

Museums/Libraries

Margaret Mitchell House & Museum
990 Peachtree St.
Atlanta, GA 30309
ph: 404-249-7012 or 404-249-7015
e-mail: jinw@gwtw.org
web: http://www.gwtw.org/
Memorabilia from around the world has been collected and offered in over 6,000 square feet of displays, artwork and artifacts that are of interest to the serious historian as well as the curious traveler.

Periodicals

John Wiley, Ed.
Newsletter: Scarlett Letter, The
1347 Greenmoss Dr.
Richmond, VA 23225-4112
ph: 804-330-5484
fax: 804-771-3054
Published quarterly; honors both book and film; keeps collectors up-to-date on all aspects of GWTW; articles, auction results, ads, etc.

Horror Films & Literature

(see HORROR; SCIENCE FICTION)

Indiana Jones

Dealers

Cindy Oakes
34025 W. 6 Mile
Livonia, MI 48152
ph: 734-591-3252
Wants Indiana Jones dolls, figurines, playsets, etc.

Movie Posters

Collectors

Ed Royse
112 N. Broadway St.
Walters, OK 73572
ph: 580-357-8000
fax: 580-875-2063
e-mail: edroyse@juno.com
Wants to buy movie posters, B Westerns, any Audie Murphy of John Wayne movie posters.

Gene Arnold
2234 South Blvd.
Houston, TX 77098-5225
ph: 713-528-1880
Wants any old movie posters or 11" x 14" lobby cards.

Dealers

Arnold Movie Poster Company
ph: 713-524-9000
e-mail: info@movieposters.com
web: http://www.movieposters.com/
Buys and sells old movie posters; in business since 1965; carries a wide variety of original posters covering the obscure to the well-known; also has access to newer movie posters.

Class Act Movie Posters
ph: 800-380-6405 or 630-960-2465
e-mail: clssact@email.msn.com
web: http://www.movieposters.net/

Movie Poster Shop, The
e-mail: 103075.526@compuserve.com
web: http://www.moviepostershop.com/
Over 60,000 different posters and photographs to choose from.

Rudy Franchi
Nostalgia Factory, The
51 North Margin St.
Boston, MA 02113
ph: 617-720-2211 or 800-479-8754
e-mail: posters@nostalgia.com
web: http://www.nostalgia.com
Always buying all forms of movie advertising from 1900 to present; posters, lobby cards, stills, press books, press kits, inserts, etc.

Q. David Bowers
Bowers & Merena, Inc.
P.O. Box 1224
Wolfeboro, NH 03894-1224
ph: 800-458-4646 or 603-569-5095
fax: 603-569-5319
e-mail: bowersmerena@conknet.com
web: http://web.coin-universe.com/bowers/index.html
Wants American film posters from 1895-1915.

Alan Levine
P.O. Box 1577
Bloomfield, NJ 07003
ph: 973-743-5288
Buys and sells movie posters and lobby cards.

Marc Zydiak
Star Archives
P.O. Box 285
Westfield, NJ 07091-0285
ph: 908-654-6505

Poster World
9 Bolton Place
Fair Lawn, NJ 07410
ph: 201-791-1073
Specializing in movie posters from 1940 through 1970.

Metropolis Collectibles
873 Broadway, Ste. 201
New York, NY 10003
ph: 212-627-9691 or 800-229-6387
fax: 212-627-5947
Buys and sells vintage movie posters and comic books; free appraisals; finders fees paid.

Jerry Ohlinger
Jerry Ohlinger's Movie Material Store, Inc.
242 W. 14th St.
New York, NY 10011-7206
ph: 212-989-0869
fax: 212-989-1660
Buys and sells motion picture photos and posters from 1920 to present; also TV photos; research services available; free lists available; complete lists of 100,000 black & white photos or of 100,000 color photos are $4 each.

Sam Sarowitz
Posteritati
241 Centre St., Suite 5F
New York, NY 10013-3224
ph: 212-226-2207
fax: 212-226-2102
e-mail: sam@posteritati.com
web: http://www.posteritati.com
Wants movie posters, lobby cards; 1900-1970s; small or large collections bought; immediate cash available; call, fax or write.

Joe Burtis
Motion Picture Arts Gallery
133 E. 58th St., 10th Floor
New York, NY 10022
ph: 212-223-1009
fax: 212-371-0809
e-mail: info@mpagallery.com
web: http://www.mpagallery.com/
Buys and sells posters, lobby cards, etc.

Todd Richard Feiertag
Poster City
P.O. Box 94
Orangeburg, NY 10962-0094
ph: 201-869-1692 or 800-272-3323
Buys and sells movie posters; entire collections purchased; free appraisals; will travel anywhere.

John Hazelton
235 Horton Highway
Mineola, NY 11501
ph: 800-224-6394

George Theofiles
Miscellaneous Man
P.O. Box 1776
New Freedom, PA 17349-0191
ph: 717-235-4766
fax: 717-235-2853
Collects, buys and sells vintage film posters; since 1970 offering catalogs of rare posters and early advertising and ephemera on hundreds of subjects. Descriptive flyer available.

Bill Fisher
How Sweet It Was
16104 Delaire Landing Road
Philadelphia, PA 19114
ph: 888-3-POSTER
fax: 215-551-4068
e-mail: fisherb@voicenet.com
web: http://www.phillynews.com/clients/bill/
Sells linen-backed and restored posters from the past.

Rick's Movie Graphics & Posters
P.O. Box 23709
Gainesville, FL 32602
ph: 352-373-7202 or 800-252-0425
fax: 352-373-2589
e-mail: ricks@ricksmovie.com
web: http://www.ricksmovie.com/

Marty Davis
Vintage Film Posters
15875 Van Aken Blvd., Ste. 304C
Cleveland, OH 44120-5384
ph: 216-751-8888
fax: 216-751-8885
Buys and sells movie posters, all sizes and periods; also related movie memorabilia; specialist in silent era, especially Chaplin, Keaton and Lloyd.

John Green
Movie Poster Page
2729 Cranbrook Road
Ann Arbor, MI 48104
ph: 734-973-7303
fax: 734-973-7304
e-mail: john@musicman.com
web: http://www.musicman.com/mp/mp.html
Buys and sells vintage as well as new movie posters; also repairs and restores.

Celebrity Graphics
P.O. Box 385
Flushing, MI 48433-0385
ph: 810-659-8751
fax: 810-659-8751
e-mail: mhess@tir.com
Wants movie posters, lobby cards, any vintage, any quantity.

Dwight M. Cleveland
P.O. Box 10922
Chicago, IL 60610-0922
ph: 773-525-9152
fax: 773-525-2969
Buys, sells and collects movie posters, lobby cards, 1-sheets, 3-sheets, window cards, glass slides, studio annuals, motion picture heralds, etc.; highest prices paid.

Bruce Hershenson
Hershenson-Allen Archive
P.O. Box 874
West Plains, MO 65775-0874
ph: 417-256-9616
fax: 417-257-6948
e-mail: mail@brucehershenson.com
web: http://www.brucehershenson.com
Wants high quality original posters from major pre-1970 Hollywood films; publisher of 18 books of full-color reproductions of movie posters; sells posters through sales lists and annual auctions.

Cyber-cinema
P.O. Box 1944
Tempe, AZ 85280-1944
e-mail: info@cyber-cinema.com
web: http://www.cyber-cinema.com
Specializes in new releases and classic movie reprints.

Erik Dorr
Hollywood Movie Posters & Autographs
557 E. Saraha Ave., Ste. 108
Las Vegas, NV 89104
ph: 702-735-8170
Las Vegas' largest selection of movie memorabilia: posters, autographs, photos and stills; buys, sells, trades.

Hollywood Movie Posters
6727 Hollywood Blvd.
Los Angeles, CA 90028
ph: 323-463-1792

Harry Lemay
LeMay Movie Posters
P.O. Box 480879
Los Angeles, CA 90048
ph: 323-935-4053 or 800-565-3629
fax: 323-933-4465
e-mail: LeMayCo@aol.com
web: http://www.csmonline.com/lemay/

CINEMAGIC
852 Fifth Ave., Ste. #317
San Diego, CA 92101
ph: 619-291-2500
fax: 619-295-7626
e-mail: cinemagic@classicmovieposters.com
web: http://www.classicmovieposters.com
Buys and sells original movie posters and lobby cards from the 1930s through the early 1980s.

James Dietz
J.S. Dietz Vintage Movie Posters
2726 Shelter Island Dr.
San Diego, CA 92106
ph: 619-223-1563
fax: 619-223-8944
e-mail: jsdietz@earthlink.net
web: http://www.jimdietz.com/poster.html
Collector, dealer, expert, appraiser has one of the oldest and largest

internet sites for pre-1970 vintage US and foreign movie posters.

Ann Daman
Big Picture Movie Posters & Collectibles
e-mail: bigpix@dnai.com
web: http://www.big-pix.com
Movie posters, press kits, banners, standees, buttons and other miscellaneous movie memorabilia from the 1960s to present.

Thom March
Movie Memories
P.O. Box 660541
Sacramento, CA 95825
ph: 916-921-5016
e-mail: posters5@webtv.net
web: http://www.moviememories.com
Specializes in rare original vintage U.S. movie posters of the silver screen.

Robert Candel
Movie Poster Shop
1314 S. Grand Blvd., #2-156
Spokane, WA 99202
ph: 403-250-7588
fax: 403-250-7589
e-mail: 103075.526@compuserve.com
web: http://www.movieapostershop.com
15,000 original movie posters from 1925 to present; 20,000 photos, posters and reproductions.

Hollywood Canteen, The
1516 Danforth Ave.
Toronto, Ontario M4J 1N4
Canada
ph: 416-461-1704
Buys and sells movie posters and movie books.

Experts

Jon Warren
American Collectibles Exchange
P.O. Box 2512
Chattanooga, TN 37409
ph: 423-265-5515 or 800-880-4289
fax: 423-265-5506
e-mail: jonrwarren@aol.com
Author of "Warren's Movie Poster Price Guide."

Cinemonde - Movie Poster Center
1932-J Polk St.
San Francisco, CA 94109-3006
ph: 415-776-9988 or 615-742-3048
fax: 415-776-1424
e-mail: cinemonde@earthlink.net
web: http://home.earthlink.net/~cinemonde/
Buys, sells, specializes in movie posters; has an office in Nashville, TN.

Periodicals

John Kisch
Price Guide: Movie Poster Price Database
P.O. Box 114
Hyde Park, NY 12538-0114
ph: 914-452-1998
fax: 914-454-7131
e-mail: johnkisch@aol.com
An annual price guide.

Jon Warren
American Collectibles Exchange
Newsletter: Movie Poster Update, The
P.O. Box 2512
Chattanooga, TN 37409
ph: 423-265-5515 or 800-880-4289
fax: 423-265-5506
e-mail: jonrwarren@aol.com

Repro. Sources

Moviead Corp.
3111 University Dr., #320
Pompano Beach, FL 33065
ph: 800-327-4989
Full color poster reproductions in one sheet sizes, 27" x 41".

Movie Posters (Black)

Dealers

John Kisch
Separate Cinema
P.O. Box 114
Hyde Park, NY 12538-0114
ph: 914-452-1998
fax: 914-454-7131
e-mail: johnkisch@aol.com
Buys, sells and collects black movie posters; publishes "Movie Poster Price Data Base" twice a year with prices, dealers, and lists.

Movie Posters (Silent Movies)

Dealers

Ronald Krueger
R.W. Krueger's
P.O. Box 741
Oak Park, IL 60303-0741
ph: 708-788-8235
Buys, sells, and trades silent movie related posters, stills, portraits, magazines, glass slides, etc.; especially wants Mary Miles Minter and Valentino.

Oscars

Collectors

Jon Warren
P.O. Box 2512
Chattanooga, TN 37409
ph: 423-265-5515 or 800-880-4289
fax: 423-265-5506
e-mail: jonrwarren@aol.com
Wants to buy Oscars; from insignificant technical award to major aware.

Scripts

Collectors

Grayson D. Cook
Grayson D. Cook, Bookseller
367 W. Ave. 42
Los Angeles, CA 90065-3905
ph: 213-227-8899
Wants to buy screenplays and movie scripts; prefers original studio production copies; will consider agency copies or photocopies; please send description (title, writer, and draft).

Serials

Periodicals

Linda S. Downey
World of Yesterday Productions
Journal: Cliffhanger
104 Chestnut Wood Drive
Waynesville, NC 28786-6514
ph: 828-648-5647
Periodic journal focusing on serials.

Silent Films

Experts

Richard Alan Davis
Bijou Dream
9500 Old Georgetown Rd.
Bethesda, MD 20814-1724
ph: 301-530-5904
fax: 301-530-8532
e-mail: rdavis9500@aol.com
Wants silent movie items: posters, lobby cards, programs, stills, Star Garment Co. hangers with head/shoulder of movie stars.

Periodicals

Gene Vazzana
Newsletter: Silent Film Monthly, The
501 Maryland Ave., #J
Oakmont, PA 15139-1569
e-mail: vazzana@bellatlantic.net
Devoted to the silent film era; contains articles and reviews of silent films and the men and women who made them - recounted in thoughtful, interesting articles by writers who know their subject.

Star Wars

Clubs/Associations

Guillermo Rivera
Chicago Area Star Wars Collectors Club
e-mail: Cesba@aol.com
web: http://members.aol.com/Cesba/index.html
Star Wars collecting information; buying and selling.

Official Star Wars Fan Club
Magazine: Star Wars Insider
P.O. Box 111000
Aurora, CO 80042
ph: 303-341-1813 or 800-878-3326
web: http://www.starwars.com/
Publishes full-color magazine and official catalog, "The Jawa Trader."

Collectors

Martin Thurn
20982 Home Crest Ct.
Ashburn, VA 20147-4015
e-mail: MartinThurn@iname.com
web: http://www.pitt.edu/~thurn/SWB/

David Welch
P.O. Box 714
Murphysboro, IL 62966-0714
ph: 618-687-2282
fax: 618-684-2243
e-mail: PezDude1@aol.com
Wants 1977-1984 complete items with original packaging only; especially interested in Kenner Action Figure related items; paying over $2000 for rarer items; no books, records or comics, please.

Dealers

Cindy Oakes
34025 W. 6 Mile
Livonia, MI 48152
ph: 734-591-3252
Wants Star Wars figures, jewelry, vehicles, autographs.

411 Toys
16054 Sherman Way
Van Nuys, CA 91406
ph: 818-786-9760 or 888-411-TOYS
fax: 818-786-4655
web: http://www.411toys.com

Brian Rachfal
P.O. Box 7772
San Jose, CA 95150-3766
ph: 408-298-9070 or 408-629-3980
Wants to buy Star Wars action figures and related items.

David Roberts
D & S Sci-fi Toy World
4701 NE 72nd Ave. #J222
Vancouver, WA 98661
ph: 360-891-7822
fax: 360-604-5746
e-mail: dnstoys@spiritone.com
web: http://members.aol.com/dnsroberts/index.htm
Specializes in Star Wars, Star Trek, Aliens and other sci-fi movie related toys and collectibles.

Experts

L.I. Kyro
6030 Magnolia
Saint Louis, MO 63139
Expert, collector, historian, authority on Star Wars.

Nick J. Lehrling
Teleco Group
P.O. Box 18536
Tucson, AZ 85731
ph: 520-749-3897 or 520-749-2621
fax: 520-749-3897
e-mail: nicksdaman@aol.com
web: http://members.aol.com/NICKSDAMAN/index.html
Star Wars collector and expert.

Internet Resources

Official Star Wars Web Site - Lucasfilm, Inc.
web: http://www.starwars.com

Gus Lopez
Star Wars Collectors Archives
e-mail: lopez@halcyon.com
web: http://www.toysrgus.com/
A virtual tour of some of the finest Star Wars collections in the world; an exhaustive archive of Star Wars information and photographs.

Star Wars (Art)

Experts

William Plumb
5646 Terrace Drive
Rocklin, CA 95765-1741
ph: 916-632-3267
e-mail: disneyp@mindsync.com
web: http://www.origartgallry-starwars.com/
Collects all Star Wars original art: drawings, sketches, paintings; plans on opening a museum of original Star Wars art.

The Godfather

Collectors

Lynn Goldfinger
P.O. Box 4962
Burlingame, CA 94011-4962
ph: 650-342-7829
fax: 650-343-3269
e-mail: goldie1943@aol.com
Wants to buy unusual and hard-to-find The Godfather (I and II) and related actor memorabilia: promo items, photos, costumes, props, etc.

Trade Publications

Collectors

George Reed
7216 Kindred St.
Philadelphia, PA 19149-1124
ph: 215-725-3003
Wants illustrated movie advertising trade books, coming attraction folios, pamphlets, etc., in color or black and white; also exhibitors/trade magazines and publications, pressbooks and souvenir programs, and related material.

Westerns

(see also COWBOY HEROES)

Clubs/Associations

Milo Holt
Old Time Western Film Club
Newsletter: Old Time Western Film Newsletter
P.O. Box 142
Siler City, NC 27344-0142
ph: 919-737-3460
Interested in promoting the showing of old westerns and in the collecting of memorabilia relating thereto; meets every other month for Western film festival; 500 on mailing list.

Western Film Preservation Society, Inc., Raleigh Chapter
Newsletter: Western Film Preservation Society Newsletter
1012 Vance St.
Raleigh, NC 27608

Norman Kietzer
Westerns & Serials Fan Club
Magazine: Westerns & Serials
527 S. Front St.
Mankato, MN 56001-3718
e-mail: kietzer@mctcnet.net
web: http://www.angelfire.com/biz2/normankietzerpubs/
A club for collectors as well as non-collectors interested in westerns and serials of the silver screen; also interested in related memorabilia.

Alan Dobrey
Western Film Appreciation Club of Alberta
Newsletter: Western Film Appreciation Society Bulletin
9826 171A Ave.
Edmonton, Alberta T5X 3Y4
Canada
ph: 403-456-3769
Dedicated to keeping the Western films of yesteryear (1930s to 1950s) alive through the screening and promoting of these films; holds monthly meetings; open to the public.

Barrie Hanfling
Westerns - N.Z. Chapter
Magazine: Westerns
79 Tiroroa Ave.
Te Atatu South, Aucklane 1008
New Zealand
Publishes bi-monthly magazine on old Westerns, both "A" and "B".

Eric G. Lilley, Pres.
Boys Hollywood
2 Holly Close, Crookham Park
Crookhan Common
Thatcham, Berkshire RG19 8QZ
U.K.
ph: 01635-869694
Focuses on the great Hollywood Western film stars of the 1930s to 1950s: Roy Rogers, Gene Autry, William Boyd.

Dealers

Jerry Ohlinger
Jerry Ohlinger's Movie Material Store, Inc.
242 W. 14th St.
New York, NY 10011-7206
ph: 212-989-0869
fax: 212-989-1660
Buys and sells motion picture photos and posters from 1920 to present; also TV photos; research services available; free lists available; complete lists of 100,000 black & white photos or of 100,000 color photos are $4 each.

Periodicals

Janette & Bob Anderson
Magazine: Trail Dust
407 West Rosemary Lane
Falls Church, VA 22046-3847
fax: 703-358-5402
Glossy magazine devoted to both television and feature-length westerns.

Linda S. Downey
World of Yesterday Productions
Journal: Under Western Skies
104 Chestnut Wood Drive
Waynesville, NC 28786-6514
ph: 828-648-5647
Focuses on the old west of the Silver Screen & TV.

Colin Momber
Magazine: Wrangler's Roost
23 Sabrina Way
Bristol, BS9 1ST
U.K.
ph: 0117-9684776
A 32-page periodical published three times per year; longest running fanzine in the western field; printed on gloss paper and is directed at enthusiasts of the old "B" Western movies.

Westerns (Italian)

Periodicals

Tom Betts
Newsletter: Westerns...All' Italiana!
P.O. Box 25042
Anaheim, CA 92825-5042
fax: 714-836-9040
Quarterly newsletter focusing on Italian Westerns.

MOVIE PROJECTORS

(see CAMERAS & CAMERA EQUIPMENT, Movie; FILMS; MAGIC LANTERNS)

MOVING & STORAGE ASSOCIATIONS

(see also REPAIR/RESTORATION/CONSERVATION)

Clubs/Associations

Household Goods Forwarders Association of America
2320 Mill Road, Ste. 102
Alexandria, VA 22314
ph: 703-684-3780
fax: 703-684-3784
e-mail: hhgfaa@aol.com
web: http://www.hhgfaa.org/
World's largest union of moving and shipping companies in the world; business links, Congressional addresses, industry terms, industry abbreviations, etc.

Estelle Tredway
American Moving & Storage Association
Magazine: Moving World, The
1611 Duke St.
Alexandria, VA 22314-3406
ph: 703-706-4984 or 703-683-7410
fax: 703-683-7525
e-mail: amsa1@erols.com
web: http://www.amconf.org/
Provides educational and certification programs for the moving & storage industry; approx. 3500 members worldwide who provide goods & services to those who are relocating; actively involved in government and military affairs.

Chuck Naylor, Ex. Dir.
Claims Prevention & Procedure Council
Newsletter: CPPC Newsletter
P.O. Box 1367
Englewood, FL 34295-1367
ph: 941-473-2772
fax: 941-473-2775
e-mail: claimsnet@aol.com
web: http://www.claimsnet.org/
A moving industry related organization of repairmen, van lines, appraisers, insurance companies, lawyers and claims adjusters.

MOXIE

(see SOFT DRINK COLLECTIBLES, Moxie)

MR. PEANUT

(see PLANTERS PEANUTS ITEMS)

MUGS

(see BARBERSHOP COLLECTIBLES, Shaving Mugs; COLLECTIBLES [MODERN], Steins; GLASSES, Drinking; RESTAURANT COLLECTIBLES; STEINS)

MUSIC

(see also AUTOGRAPHS, Music Related; BOOKS, Reference [Music]; DRUM & BUGLE CORPS; MUSIC BOXES; MUSICAL INSTRUMENTS; PERFORMING ARTS; PERSONALITIES [MUSICIANS]; PHONOGRAPHS; PIANO ROLLS; ROCK 'N' ROLL COLLECTIBLES; RECORDS; SHEET MUSIC; TICKETS)

Clubs/Associations

James Henderson
Sonneck Society for American Music & Music in America
Newsletter: Sonneck Society Bulletin
P.O. Box 476
Canton, MA 02021-0476
ph: 781-828-8450
fax: 781-828-8915
e-mail: acadsvc@aol.com
Promotes the dissemination of accurate information on all aspects of American music and music in America; also publishes "American Music", a quarterly journal addressing music in America.

James Henderson
Music Library Association
Magazine: Notes
P.O. Box 487
Canton, MA 02021-0487
ph: 781-828-8450
fax: 781-828-8915
e-mail: acadsvc@aol.com
For music scholars, teachers, performers, librarians: scholarly articles, reviews, CR reviews, music publishers' information; also ads for records, scores, books, journals and other services.

Dealers

Leland Stein
Roundup Records
Newsletter: Record Roundup
1 Camp St.
Cambridge, MA 02140-1194
ph: 617-661-6308 or 800-443-4727
fax: 617-868-8769
e-mail: info@rounder.com
web: http://www.rounder.com
Mail order CDs, LPs, cassettes; specializing in hard to find blues, country, R&B, Rock 'N' Roll, jazz, bluegrass, etc.; "Record Roundup" is a bi-monthly catalog/newsletter.

Bob Luliucci
MusicandVideo.com
One Surey Lane
Allendale, NJ 07401
ph: 201-236-9107
fax: 201-236-2916
e-mail: riuliu6832@aol.com
web: http://www.musicandvideo.com/
Web site updated weekly; items for sale include rare records, CDs, sheet music, music laser discs, designed guitars, concert tickets, rock books, DVDs, memorabilia and industry record awards; memorabilia featuring thousands of artists.

Periodicals

Pat DuChene, PR
Krause Publications
Magazine: Goldmine
700 E. State St.
Iola, WI 54990-0001
ph: 715-445-2214
fax: 715-445-4087
e-mail: info@krause.com
web: http://www.krause.com/
A biweekly magazine containing articles, ads about records & recording artists from 1940s to present; the record & CD marketplace.

1960s

Dealers

Charles F. Rosenay
Liverpool Productions
315 Derby Ave.
Orange, CT 06477
ph: 203-891-8131
e-mail: rosenay@aol.com
Buys and sells '60s music and memorabilia relating to the Beatles, British Invasion, Monkees and Beach Boys.

Big Band

Collectors

John L. Mickolas
172 Liberty St.
Trenton, NJ 08611-2631
ph: 609-530-5568 or 609-599-9672
Wants Glenn Miller, Bunny Berigan, autographs, recordings, photos, sheet music, magazines, films, anything related.

Mark Rosenblum
10776 Blackley St.
Temple City, CA 91780-3501
ph: 626-453-8890
Wants big band memorabilia: concert posters, programs, advertising, magazines, ballroom tickets pertaining to Miller, Goodman, Dorsey, James, Ellington, etc.

Country

Museums/Libraries

Country Music Hall of Fame & Museum, Country Music Foundation
4 Music Square, East
Nashville, TN 37203
ph: 615-256-1639 or 615-256-1639
web: http://
www.countrymusichalloffame.com/

Periodicals

Disc Collector Publications
Newsletter: Disc Collector
P.O. Box 315
Cheswold, DE 19936-0315
ph: 302-674-3632
Focuses on bluegrass and old time country music.

Cowboy (Bob Wills)

Experts

Robert Phillips
1703 North Aster Place
Broken Arrow, OK 74012
ph: 918-254-8205
fax: 918-252-9362
Researched heavily the life, career and music of The Father of Western Swing Music, Bob Wills; collects Bob Wills music and memorabilia.

Dixieland & Ragtime

Collectors

Don Hoffman
P.O. Box 4231
Salinas, CA 93912-4231
ph: 831-449-7311
Wants to buy blues, jazz, ragtime, minstrel, Dixieland related items: posters, tickets, programs, autographs, videos, broadsides, antique photos, souvenirs, ephemera, memorabilia, books, booklets, souvenirs; describe and price, please.

Periodicals

Richard Zimmerman, Ed.
Maple Leaf Club
Newsletter: Rag Times, The
15522 Ricky Ct.
Grass Valley, CA 95949-6672
A bi-monthly newsletter with everything about ragtime - past and present; since 1967.

Jazz & Blues

Auction Services

George Wilson
AllJazz
1079 Stuart Rd.
Princeton, NJ 08540
ph: 800-303-6557
e-mail: gwilson@alljazz.com
web: http://www.alljazz.com/
Conducts auction sales of jazz, personality, blues, C&W records including 78s, LPs, CDs, etc.; over 20,000 items per year.

Clubs/Associations

George Wilson
New Jersey Jazz Society
1079 Stuart Rd.
Princeton, NJ 08540
ph: 800-303-6557
e-mail: gwilson@alljazz.com
web: http://www.alljazz.com/njjs/
njjsinfo.htm
Mission is to promote and preserve interest in jazz; many members are collectors of jazz related music and records.

American Federation of Jazz Societies, Inc.
2787 Del Monte St.
West Sacramento, CA 95691
ph: 916-372-5277
fax: 916-372-3479
e-mail: dhampton@worldmall.com
web: http://worldmall.com/wmcc/afjs/
Serving jazz societies, individuals, musicians, and the music industry.

Collectors

Stanley King
260 Fifth Ave.
New York, NY 10001-6408
ph: 212-447-1880
fax: 212-447-0728
Wants to jazz band and jazz musician memorabilia: photos, posters, advertisements, postcards, contracts, letters, etc.

Don Hoffman
P.O. Box 4231
Salinas, CA 93912-4231
ph: 831-449-7311
Wants to buy blues, jazz, ragtime, minstrel, Dixieland related items: posters, tickets, programs, autographs, videos, broadsides, antique photos, souvenirs, ephemera, memorabilia, books, booklets, souvenirs; describe and price, please.

Chuck Moore
P.O. Box 280
Gladstone, OR 97027
ph: 503-654-9994
fax: 503-656-7603
Wants Jazz LP's, singles, 78's; also older books, magazines, sheet music on jazz.

Dealers

Gary Alderman
G's Jazz
P.O. Box 9164
Madison, WI 53715-0164
ph: 608-274-3527
fax: 608-277-1999
Wants to buy jazz LP's, jazz literature, jazz photos, autographs, etc.

Rock 'N' Roll

(see also AMERICAN BANDSTAND)

Auction Services

Stephen Maycock
Sotheby's
34-35 New Bond St.
London, W1A 2AA
U.K.
ph: 44 171 293 5000
fax: 44 171 293 5989
web: http://www.sothebys.com/
Conducts regular auctions of Rock 'N Roll memorabilia.

Clubs/Associations

Dave Frees
American Bandstand 1950's Fan Club
Magazine: Bandstand Boogie
P.O. Box 131
Adamstown, PA 19501-0131
ph: 717-738-2513
Focuses on "American Bandstand" from the 1950s and 1980s; magazine published twice a year; sells "Dave's Collectables Catalog" (50s through 80s photos, magazines, etc.) for $1 - free to members.

Museums/Libraries

Rock & Roll Hall of Fame & Museum
One Key Plaza
Cleveland, OH 44114
ph: 800-493-ROLL
e-mail: director@rockhall.com
web: http://www.rockhall.com/

Periodicals

Gene Bondy
Magazine: Rock & Roll Radio Archives
677 - 49th St.
Brooklyn, NY 11220
fax: 718-438-0399
Newsletter about rock 'n roll radio from the 1950s through 1970s: music, singers, oldies, etc.

MUSIC BOXES

(see also DOLLS, Automatons; MUSICAL INSTRUMENTS, Mechanical)

Clubs/Associations

Rick Cooley
Musical Box Society International
Magazine: Journal of Mechanical Music
700 Walnut Hill Rd.
Hockessin, DE 19707
e-mail: cotps@aol.com
web: http://www.mbsi.org
Members collect, study, preserve all types of instruments that mechanically produce music: musical boxes, orchestrions, band organs, player pianos, musical clocks, automata, etc.; "News Bulletin" contains Mart for buying & selling.

Alan Wyatt, Sec.
Musical Box Society of Great Britain
Journal: Music Box, The
P.O. Box 299
Waterbeach, Cambridge CB4 8DT
U.K.
e-mail:
mbsgb@kreedman.globalnet.co.uk
For collectors, dealers and enthusiasts of all types of mechanical music boxes, large and small; journal published quarterly.

Collectors

Sherlock S. Holmes, D.D.
P.O. Box 3
Worcester, MA 01613-0003
ph: 508-754-9907
e-mail: mail@SherlockHolmes.com
web: http://www.SherlockHolmes.com
Wants to buy pre-1950 WORKING music boxes; cylinder type, disk type, etc.; please send complete details including asking price.

Stephen Leonard
121 McKinley Ave.
Albertson, NY 11507
ph: 516-742-0979
e-mail: lentoydag@aol.com
Wants to buy antique mechanical toys, daguerreotypes, and music boxes.

John W. Hess
244 Bernaski Rd.
Amsterdam, NY 12010-7827
ph: 518-843-6117
Wants to buy Vogue picture disc records, horn phonographs, music boxes, roller organs; also wants parts, empty cabinets, horns; any condition, any material.

Frank Rider
1062 Alber St.
Wabash, IN 46992-1003
ph: 219-563-5030

Dave Ogden
P.O. Box 223
Northbrook, IL 60062-0223
ph: 847-564-2893
fax: 847-564-2893
e-mail: musical@flash.net
Wants disc and cylinder music boxes; Regina; also monkey organs and any self playing musical instruments.

Dealers

Porter Music Box Co., Inc.
Rte. 66, Box 424
Randolph, VT 05060
ph: 800-635-1938
fax: 802-728-9699
Repairs and sells antique music boxes; also manufactures copperplated discs for Regina, Polyphone, and Porter music boxes in 11", 12 1/4", and 15 1/2" sizes.

Al Meekins
Meekins Music Box Co.
P.O. Box 161
Collingswood, NJ 08108
ph: 609-858-6421
fax: 609-858-1642
e-mail: ameek37754@aol.com
web: http://www.finest1.com/antiques/
Buys, sells, restores antique music boxes.

Rita Ford Music Boxes
19 E 65th St.
New York, NY 10021
ph: 212-535-6717
fax: 212-772-0992
Buys, sells, repairs antique music boxes.

Music To My Ears
P.O. Box 13101
Mc Graw, NY 13101
e-mail:
AntiqueMusicBox@compuserve.com
web: http://ourworld.compuserve.com/homepages/AntiqueMusicBox/
Specializes in heirloom quality antique music boxes of all sizes, shapes and styles.

R.C. Bornand
Bornand Music Box Company
801 Zinnia Ln.
Fort Lauderdale, FL 33317
ph: 954-791-3837

Jim Brady
Brady Sales & Restorations of Pianos & Music Boxes
2725 E. 56th St.
Indianapolis, IN 46220
ph: 317-259-4307
fax: 317-259-4340
e-mail: jlbrady@mindspring.com
web: http://www.mindspring.com/~jlbrady/
Music boxes wanted; any type or condition; also jukeboxes.

Doug Negus
Phonograph Phanatic
215 Mason St.
Sutherland, IA 51058-7606
ph: 712-446-2270 or 712-446-3746
e-mail: negus@nwidt.com
Music boxes, phonographs, cylinder records, pianos, NO piano rolls, older mechanical musical instruments, pre-1930; any parts or repairables wanted.

Martin Roenigk
Mechantiques
The Crescent Hotel
75 Prospect St.
Eureka Springs, AR 72632
ph: 800-671-6333 or 501-253-9766
e-mail: mroenigk@aol.com
web: http://www.mechantiques.com
Wants all types of mechanical music instruments: music boxes, player organs, coin pianos, singing birds, Wurlitzer 78 rpm jukeboxes, etc.

Rick Wilkins
Olden Year Musical Museum
P.O. Box 381951
Duncanville, TX 75138
ph: 972-298-5587
e-mail: 1museum@cyberramp.com
Buys, sells, repairs and appraises all types of windup automated musical machines including Victrolas, Gramophones, music boxes, grind organs, etc.

Margaret Marcus
Music Box Shop, The
7236 E 1st Ave.
Scottsdale, AZ 85251
ph: 602-945-0428 or 800-932-2745
fax: 602-200-9365
e-mail: musicboxshop@home.com
web: http://www.themusicboxshop.com
Buys, sells, appraises, repairs music boxes; over 3000 music boxes: Reuge, Sankyo, Porter, Hummel.

Experts

William H. Edgerton
P.O. Box 88
Darien, CT 06820-0588
ph: 203-655-0566
fax: 203-655-8066
e-mail: wedgerton@aol.com
Buys, sells, repairs pianos and rolls, musical boxes, player organs, nickelodeons, and automata.

Nancy Fratti
P.O. Box 210
Whitehall, NY 12887-0210
ph: 518-282-9770
fax: 518-282-9800
Specializes in, buys, sells and restores antique cylinder and disc musical boxes, restoration supplies; restoration school, books, discs, recordings of automatic musical instruments; catalog available for $6.

Ken Danckaert
231 Kennedy Ct.
Severna Park, MD 21146-3039
ph: 410-544-0260
e-mail: kend@lemur.org
Collects, buys, sells, appraises, and repairs music boxes, phonographs, and organettes; in business since 1972; an expert who gives lectures, presentations and videos.

David & Carol Beck
75 Waters Edge Lane
Newnan, GA 30263-3579
ph: 770-304-9066
Specializes in cylinder and disc music boxes; offers quality repair of cylinder and disc music boxes.

Marty Persky
6514 N. Trumball
Chicago, IL 60645-3835
ph: 847-675-6144
fax: 847-675-6160
e-mail: persky@worldnet.att.net
Specializes in disc and cylinder music boxes.

Christian Eric
Antique Music Box Restoration
1825 Placentia Ave.
Costa Mesa, CA 92627-3565
ph: 949-548-1542
fax: 949-631-9996
e-mail: musicbox@email.com
web: http://www.antique-music-box.com/
Specialists in antique musical boxes, emphasis on early cylinder, miniature and sur plateau mechanisms; author on subject; buys, sells and repairs.

Museums/Libraries

Lockwood-Mathews Mansion Museum
295 West Ave.
Norwalk, CT 06850
ph: 203-838-9799
fax: 203-838-1434
e-mail: lockwood-mathews@norwalk.ct.us
web: http://norwalk.ct.us/mansion/

Museum of Musical Instruments, The Schubert Club
302 Landmark Center
75 W. 5th St.
Saint Paul, MN 55102
ph: 651-292-3267
fax: 651-292-4317
e-mail: schubert@schubert.org
web: http://www.schubert.org/
More than 100 pianofortes, harpsichords, clavichords and organs spanning more than 425 years; also various musical instruments from around the world, automatic musical instruments and phonographs; early composer & musician letters.

Musical Museum, The
3525 State Highway 258 E.
Wichita Falls, TX 76308-7037
ph: 940-691-7809
e-mail: Quashnock@aol.com
web: http://sponsor.globalknowledge.nl/ros/

Repair Services

Donald Tendrup
7 Ashland Ct.
Holtsville, NY 11742
ph: 516-758-4755
Music box repairs; over 30 years experience; complete machine shop on premises; cylinder repining, main springs, governor work, comb work, gear work, etc.

Chet Ramsay
Chet Ramsay Antiques
2460 Strasburg Rd.
Coatesville, PA 19320-4339
ph: 610-384-0514
Wants all types of pre-1912 music boxes; buy, sell and repair; also wants parts.

George Paladics
1840 Colonial Dr.
Green Cove Springs, FL 32043-8004
European craftsman repairs or restores antique music boxes; capable of making necessary parts.

Emerson E. Whitacre
Mechanical Music Man
7550 President Court
Dayton, OH 45414-3671
ph: 937-898-6044 or 937-898-0865
Repairs, adjusts and cleans disc music boxes, cylinder music boxes, antique phonographs, etc.

Jim Brady
2725 East 56th St.
Indianapolis, IN 46220
ph: 317-259-4307 or 317-849-1469
Buys, sells and restores automatic musical instruments: music boxes; tooth replacement, comb dampening, governor work, cylinder repining, new gears, sound board restoration, case refinishing, tuning, inlay repair, etc.

Mechanical Musicologist
420 W. State St.
Belle Plaine, MN 56011
ph: 612-873-6704
fax: 612-873-6704
Repairs all types of music boxes.

K.R. Powers
K.R. Powers Antique Music Boxes
28 Alton Circle
Rogers, AR 72756-9252
ph: 501-263-2643
Disc and cylinder music box restoration, sales and repairs.

Billy E. Young
Young's Ole Clock & Music Box Shop
3511 Rio Grande Circle
Dallas, TX 75233
ph: 214-331-8265
Buys, sells and restores.

Christian Eric
Antique Music Box Restoration
1825 Placentia Ave.
Costa Mesa, CA 92627-3565
ph: 949-548-1542
fax: 949-631-9996
e-mail: musicbox@email.com
web: http://www.antique-music-box.com/
Specialists in antique musical boxes, emphasis on early cylinder, miniature and sur plateau mechanisms; fine precision restoration; all facets of restoration personally undertaken in house; also buys and sells.

Birds & Bird Boxes (Singing)

Dealers

Don Levison
Don Levison Antiques
P.O. Box 22262
San Francisco, CA 94122
ph: 415-753-0455
fax: 415-753-5206
e-mail: dlevison@juno.com
web: http://www.antiquehorology.com
Buys and sells antique and better quality pocket and wrist watches, clocks, music boxes, singing birds, and other small automata; also mercury barometers from the 17th century to present.

Steve Bogoff
Bogoff Antique Timepieces
P.O. Box 408
Mill Valley, CA 94942
ph: 415-383-8100
fax: 415-383-8112
e-mail: info@bogoff.com
web: http://www.bogoff.com
Buys, sells, appraises and has on-line catalog of complicated, rare, early, unusual, beautiful pocket watches, vintage wrist watches, small clocks, singing bird boxes and more.

Cylinder

Experts

Alan Bies
357 N. Oak Post Rd.
Houston, TX 77008
ph: 281-686-5669
Specializes in cylinder music boxes.

Steve Boehck
357 N. Oak Post Rd.
Houston, TX 77008
ph: 281-686-5669
Specializes in cylinder music boxes.

David Wells
P.O. Box 280368
Lakewood, CO 80228-0368
ph: 303-985-4481
fax: 303-985-4481
Specializes in the restoration of cylinder music boxes since 1978.

Repair Services

David Wells
P.O. Box 280368
Lakewood, CO 80228-0368
ph: 303-985-4481
fax: 303-985-4481
Specializes in the restoration of cylinder music boxes since 1978.

Disc

Experts

Coulson Conn
432 Old Forge Rd.
Media, PA 19063-5511
ph: 610-459-0367
Collects rare and particularly melodic disc and other musical boxes, and is a clearinghouse of information about disc music boxes.

Susan & Al Choffnes
Collector's World, Inc.
2 High Terrace
Bannockburn, IL 60015-1585
ph: 847-948-1472
fax: 847-948-1486
e-mail: cworld@aol.com
web: http://members.aol.com/cworldinc
Buys, sells and specializes in disc music boxes: Regina, large German glass front upright music boxes, table models, console models, Stella, Mira; also cylinder music boxes, mechanical organs and pianos.

Barry Johnson
1305 Hoover St.
Menlo Park, CA 94025-4218
ph: 650-964-0685
Specializes in disc music boxes; also makes new discs for music boxes.

MUSICAL INSTRUMENTS

(see also CAROUSELS & CAROUSEL FIGURES; DRUM & BUGLE CORPS; MUSIC; MUSIC BOXES)

Auction Services

Kerry Keane
Skinner, Inc.
357 Main St.
Bolton, MA 01740-1104
ph: 978-779-6241
fax: 978-779-5144
e-mail: info@skinnerinc.com
web: http://www.skinnerinc.com
Established in 1964, Skinner Inc. is the fifth largest auction house in the US; has offices in Bolton and Boston, MA.

Christie's
502 Park Ave.
New York, NY 10022
ph: 212-546-1000
fax: 212-980-8163
web: http://www.christies.com

Graham Wells
Sotheby's
34-35 New Bond St.
London, W1A 2AA
U.K.
ph: 44 171 293 5000
fax: 44 171 293 5989
web: http://www.sothebys.com/
Conducts regular auctions of vintage musical instruments.

Clubs/Associations

Jeannine E. Abel, Sec.
American Musical Instrument Society
Newsletter: Newsletter & Journal of the AMIS
RD 3 Box 205-B
Franklin, PA 16323-9319
ph: 814-374-4119
fax: 814-374-4563
Inter. organization founded to promote the study of the history, design and use of musical instruments; all periods and cultures; also publishes the "Journal of the AMIS".

Dealers

William D. Voiers
William D. Voiers Fine Musical Instruments
P.O. Box 23
North Egremont, MA 01252-0023
ph: 413-528-3321 or 800-788-3521
fax: 413-528-5801
Dealer, collector, appraiser of the violin family of instruments: violins, violas, cellos, bows, banjos, ukuleles, guitars and mandolins; electric or acoustic; also saxes, brasses, drums, percussion; also buys, sells, collects and trades.

Dominic S. Cucinotti
Dominic's Music
1682A Beacon St.
Brookline, MA 02445
ph: 617-734-9300 or 877-744-5722
fax: 617-734-1059
e-mail: dominic@world.std.com
web: http://dominicsmusic.com/
Buys, sells, and repairs musical instruments.

Guitars Unlimited
151 Morehouse St.
Bridgeport, CT 06605
ph: 203-221-0040
fax: 203-366-6416
e-mail: guitarsulimited@msn.com
Wants to buy musical instruments such as guitars, amps, saxophones, violins, mandolins, banjos; also wants related catalogs, signs, clocks, etc.

Ron Sassano
Black Rock Music Center LLC
3004 Fairfield Ave.
Bridgeport, CT 06605
ph: 203-331-0040 or 203-384-2207
fax: 203-366-6416
e-mail: SSassano@erols.com
web: http://www.blackrockmusiccenter.com/
Buys and sells all types of musical instruments, new or old: guitars and amps, violins, mandolins, banjos, ukes, cellos; also wants related memorabilia, catalogs, and anything to do with instrument manufacturers.

John G. McAuliffe
ARDAGH Vintage Musical Instruments
P.O. Box 810
Carmel, NY 10512
ph: 914-225-1746 or 800-217-1746
Buys, sells, collects, appraises buy fine violins, violas, cellos, bows, guitars, banjos, mandolins, ukes, harps, concertinas, wood flutes, ivory flutes, glass flutes, silver flutes by Powell, Haynes, Badger, etc.

Louis J. Porsi, Jr.
King Louie Music
115 Marbeteh Ave.
Carlisle, PA 17013-1626
ph: 717-258-1177
e-mail: luigibosco@webtv.net
web: http://members.aol.com/kingloumus/index.htm
Vintage musical instruments including drums, guitars and basses, microphones, amplifiers, etc.; also instrument catalogs, banners, advertising pieces, salesman promos and dealer items.

Frederick W. Oster
Vintage Instruments
1529 Pine St.
Philadelphia, PA 19102-4623
ph: 215-545-1100
fax: 215-735-3634
e-mail: vintageFO@aol.com
web: http://ww.vintage-instruments.com/
Since 1975; dealer, appraiser, consultant; rare & antique musical instruments; specializing in violins, violas, cellos, bows; American fretted instruments - guitars, mandolins, banjos; antique wind instruments, etc.; SASE for reply.

Mickie Zekley
Lark in the Morning
P.O. Box 1176
Mendocino, CA 95460
ph: 707-964-5569
fax: 707-964-1979
e-mail: larkinam@larkinam.com
web: http://www.larkinam.com
Mail order musician's service specializing in hard-to-find musical instruments, music and instructional materials.

Experts

Sid Glickman
Antique Musical Instrument Service
314 Park Hill Ave.
Yonkers, NY 10705
ph: 914-591-5001
e-mail: sidglick@earthlink.net
Buys and sells all types of musical instruments, especially antique and ethnic; availability lists to collectors; send SASE for copy; free estimates to dealers and collectors; also answers questions about musical instruments.

Frederick W. Oster
Vintage Instruments
1529 Pine St.
Philadelphia, PA 19102-4623
ph: 215-545-1100
fax: 215-735-3634
e-mail: vintageFO@aol.com
web: http://ww.vintage-instruments.com/
Since 1975; dealer, appraiser, consultant; rare & antique musical instruments; specializing in violins, violas, cellos, bows; American fretted instruments - guitars, mandolins, banjos; antique wind instruments, etc.; SASE for reply.

Museums/Libraries

Yale University Collection of Musical Instruments
409 Prospect Street
New Haven, CT 06511
ph: 203-432-5180
fax: 203-432-5296
e-mail: ruth.lackstrom@yale.edu
web: http://www.yale.edu/ism/facilities.html
Collection contains over 1,000 instruments.

University of Michigan, Stearns Collection of Musical Instruments
Newsletter: Stearns Newsletter, The
Earl V. More School Of Music Building
1100 Baits Drive
Ann Arbor, MI 48109-2085
ph: 734-763-4389
web: http://www.hvcn.org/info/libscmi.html
A collection of over 2000 musical instruments from around the world.

Musical Museum, The
3525 State Highway 258 E.
Wichita Falls, TX 76308-7037
ph: 940-691-7809
e-mail: Quashnock@aol.com
web: http://sponsor.globalknowledge.nl/ros/

Kenneth G. Fiske Museum of the Claremont Colleges
450 North College Way
Claremont, CA 91711-4491
ph: 909-621-8307
e-mail: arrice@rocketmail.com
web: http://www.cuc.claremont.edu/fiske/welcome.htm
One of the most diverse collections of musical instruments in the U.S.; contains over 1,400 American, European and ethnic instruments dating from the 17th century to present.

Periodicals

Christina Gargano
Heartland Communications Group, Inc.
Magazine: Midwest Musicians Hot Line
1003 Central Ave.
P.O. Box 1052
Fort Dodge, IA 50501
ph: 800-247-2000 or 515-955-1600
fax: 515-574-2233
e-mail: libbie@hlipublishing.com
web: http://www.hlipublishing.com
The monthly buy, sell and trade magazine by performing musicians for performing musicians in the Midwest.

String Letter Publishing, Inc.
Price Guide: Musical Instrument Auction Price Guide
P.O. Box 151049
San Rafael, CA 94915
ph: 415-485-6946 or 800-827-6837
fax: 415-485-0831
e-mail: custserv@stringletter.com
web: http://www.stringsmagazine.com/
Lists values for musical instruments that are sold at auction; string instruments, wind instruments, pianos, etc.

Repair Services

Frederick W. Oster
Vintage Instruments
1529 Pine St.
Philadelphia, PA 19102-4623
ph: 215-545-1100
fax: 215-735-3634
e-mail: vintageFO@aol.com
web: http://ww.vintage-instruments.com/
Since 1975; dealer, appraiser, consultant; rare & antique musical instruments; specializing in violins, violas, cellos, bows; American fretted instruments - guitars, mandolins, banjos; antique wind instruments, etc.; SASE for reply.

Accordions

Collectors

Fran Barnes
25 Fifth Ave. 9B
New York, NY 10003-4310
ph: 212-505-2720
Wants images and figurines of small guys playing the accordion or squeeze box.

Jared Snyder
524 B Glen Echo Rd.
Philadelphia, PA 19119
ph: 215-247-8996
Wants anything accordion related: photographs, illustrations, postcards, etc. with emphasis on button accordions and exotic locales.

Drums

Dealers

Ned Ingberman
Vintage Drum Center
2243 Ivory Dr.
Libertyville, IA 52567-8533
ph: 800-729-3111 or 515-693-3611
fax: 515-693-3101
e-mail: vintagedrum@lisco.com
web: http://www.vintagedrum.com/
Wants to buy pre-1980 drums, and cymbals; also wants drum catalogs.

Experts

Dan Paul
Paul-Mueller Percussion Studio
3049 W. 71st St.
Indianapolis, IN 46268-2241
ph: 317-293-5057 or 317-842-6165
fax: 317-842-6165
Percussion instrument specialist, collector and appraiser; drums and related memorabilia including catalogs and magazines.

Repair Services

Dan Paul
Paul-Mueller Percussion Studio
3049 W. 71st St.
Indianapolis, IN 46268-2241
ph: 317-293-5057 or 317-842-6165
fax: 317-842-6165
Restorations of all percussion instruments including drums, xylophones, marimbas, timpani, traps, etc.

Harmonicas

Clubs/Associations

Bob Williams
Society for the Preservation & Advancement of the Harmonica
P.O. Box 865
Troy, MI 48099-0865
fax: 248-542-5793
e-mail: HarpSPAH@aol.com
web: http://members.aol.com/harmonica/
Maintains a database of over 3000 harmonicas from all over the world.

Harland Crain
Harmonica Collectors International
741 Cedar Field Ct.
Chesterfield, MO 63017
ph: 314-434-8875
fax: 314-567-0755
e-mail: hcrain@harleysharps.com
web: http://www.harleysharps.com
Serves harmonica collectors interests around the world.

Collectors

Alan G. Bates
495 Dogwood Dr.
Hockessin, DE 19707-9358
ph: 302-239-4296 or 800-597-7012
fax: 302-239-0306
e-mail: harmonicas@compuserve.com
web: http://antiqueharmonicas.com/
Seeking many makes and models, especially those that don't look like ordinary harmonicas (e.g. have bells or trumpets, fancy side plates, etc.); also wants harmonica catalogs, advertising, display stands,

Harland Crain
741 Cedar Field Ct.
Chesterfield, MO 63017
ph: 314-434-8875
fax: 314-567-0755
e-mail: hcrain@harleysharps.com
web: http://www.harleysharps.com
Harmonica collector, dealer, expert, repair service; collects harmonicas and any related items such as displays, posters, catalogs, books and booklets, price lists, signs, ads, etc.

Rick Nielsen, ISA
1132 Westmoor Place
Saint Louis, MO 63131
ph: 314-997-7963
e-mail: rn1132@aol.com
web: http://members.aol.com/Rn1132
Serious harmonica collector and expert.

Horns

Dealers

Charles Fail Music, Inc.
4710G Ecton Dr.
Marietta, GA 30066-1095
ph: 404-591-0645 or 770-926-3960
fax: 404-591-9893
e-mail: cfail@mindspring.com
web: http://www.charlesfail.com
Wants to buy saxophones, any age or condition; also wants to buy old brass and woodwind band instruments.

Play-It-Again, Bob
1235 W. Murray Dr.
Springfield, MO 65810
ph: 800-755-8289
Wants saxophones, double French horns, old Cornets, and other antique brass and reed instruments; also wants trumpets, trombones, clarinets, oboes, bassoons, English horns, etc.

Repair Services

Brass & Reed Music Center, Inc.
675 Mason Ave.
Daytona Beach, FL 32117
ph: 904-252-5544
fax: 904-253-4171
Specializes in the repair and restoration of brass wind band instruments, violins and guitars and other fretted instruments.

Horns (Brass)

Collectors

Jim Kopke
P.O. Box 4310
Dillon, CO 80435-4310
Wants to buy antique and unusual horns, other instruments, and related items.

Dealers

David Reed
841 West Main St.
Madison, OH 44057
ph: 440-428-6666
Buys, sells and collects saxophones and band instruments: silver plated or brass; any condition; also wants parts, early sax sales brochures, etc.

Robb Stewart
Robb Stewart Brass Instruments
140 E. Santa Clara St., #18
Arcadia, CA 91006-3204
ph: 626-447-1904
fax: 626-447-1904
Will buy all brass instruments, especially pre-1880 and high quality later instruments; also wants interesting woodwinds; offers restoration, repair and conservation of brass instruments; send for free price guide and sale list.

Museums/Libraries

Ralph Dudgeon
Streitwieser Foundation Trumpet Museum, Landesmusikdirektion
Schloss Kremsegg
Kremseggerstrasse 59
Kremsmunster, 4550
Upper Austria
ph: 0 75 83/247
e mail:
dudgeonr@snycorva.cortland.edu
A major collection over 750 brass instruments; also prints, recordings, books, figurines, sheet music, etc.; seeking additions including old brass instruments, band photos, uniforms and recordings.

Mechanical

Clubs/Associations

Rick Cooley
Musical Box Society International
Magazine: Journal of Mechanical Music
700 Walnut Hill Rd.
Hockessin, DE 19707
e-mail: cotps@aol.com
web: http://www.mbsi.org
Members collect, study, preserve all types of instruments that mechanically produce music: musical boxes, orchestrions, band organs, player pianos, musical clocks, automata, etc.; "News Bulletin" contains Mart for buying & selling.

I. Savins
Australian Collectors of Mechanical Musical Instruments
Newsletter: Bulletin
19 Waipori Street
St. Ives
Sydney, NSW 2075
Australia
ph: 61 2 9449 5296
e-mail: acmmi@collector.org
web: http://www.zip.com.au/~job/

Jurgen Hocker
Society of Self-Playing Musical Instruments
Journal: Das Mechanische Musikinstrument
Heiligenstock 46
Bergisch Gladbach, D-51465
Germany
ph: 49-2202-932524
fax: 49-2202-932526
e-mail: Juergen.Hocker@t-online.de
web: http://www.geocities.com/Vienna/2831/Gsmev_e.htm
Has the aim of investigating, maintaining and encouraging the cultural tradition of self-playing musical instruments.

Collectors

Frank Rider
1062 Alber St.
Wabash, IN 46992-1003
ph: 219-563-5030

Dealers

John S. Zuk
106 Orchard St.
Belmont, MA 02478
ph: 617-489-7540
fax: 617-484-4800
e-mail: jzuk@integral-inc.com
Buys, sells and repairs musical boxes, phonographs, and related mechanical music machines.

Danilo Konvalinka
Musical Wonder House Museum, The
18 High St.
P.O. Box 604
Wiscasset, ME 04578-0604
ph: 207-882-7163 or 800-336-3725
e-mail:
musicbox@musicalwonderhouse.com
web: http://
www.musicalwonderhouse.com/
Buys & sells music boxes, wind-up phonographs, player pianos & rolls, cylinder records, complete or parts; full repair services: combwork, gearwork, spring repairs.

Wayne Edmonston
2177 Bishop Estates Rd.
Jacksonville, FL 32259-3019
ph: 904-287-5996
fax: 904-287-4131
Wants to buy music boxes of all types, player grand pianos, coin-operated machines, Wurlitzer 78 rpm jukeboxes, nickelodeons and orchestrions, violin machines, monkey and band organs, and other automatic musical machines.

Doug Negus
Phonograph Phanatic
215 Mason St.
Sutherland, IA 51058-7606
ph: 712-446-2270 or 712-446-3746
e-mail: negus@nwidt.com
Music boxes, phonographs, cylinder records, pianos, NO piano rolls, older

mechanical musical instruments, pre-1930; any parts or repairables wanted.

Martin Roenigk
Mechantiques
The Crescent Hotel
75 Prospect St.
Eureka Springs, AR 72632
ph: 800-671-6333 or 501-253-9766
e-mail: mroenigk@aol.com
web: http://www.mechantiques.com
Largest business in the US specializing in mechanical musical instruments; buys disc & cylinder music boxes, horn phonographs, player organs, carousel organs, musical clocks & watches, monkey organs, coin pianos, mechanical birds, etc.

Ragtime Automated Music
4218 Jesup Rd.
Ceres, CA 95307
ph: 209-667-5525
fax: 209-668-8922
e-mail: ragtimewest@earthlink.net
web: http://www.ragtimewest.com
Carousel organs, nickelodeons, musical counters, custom parade vehicles, automated player pianos.

Experts

William H. Edgerton
P.O. Box 88
Darien, CT 06820-0588
ph: 203-655-0566
fax: 203-655-8066
e-mail: wedgerton@aol.com
Buys, sells, repairs pianos and rolls, musical boxes, player organs, nickelodeons, and automata.

Marty Persky
6514 N. Trumball
Chicago, IL 60645-3835
ph: 847-675-6144
fax: 847-675-6160
e-mail: persky@worldnet.att.net
Specializes in automatic musical instruments.

Museums/Libraries

Danilo Konvalinka
Musical Wonder House Museum, The
18 High St.
P.O. Box 604
Wiscasset, ME 04578-0604
ph: 207-882-7163 or 800-336-3725
e-mail: musicbox@musicalwonderhouse.com
web: http://www.musicalwonderhouse.com/
America's unique Music Museum in an 1852 sea captain's mansion; antique music boxes, player pianos, wind-up phonographs; restored pieces in rooms furnished with antiques of the period; founded 1963; instruments bought, sold, repaired.

Neil Ratliff
Music Library, University of Maryland
Hornbrake 3210
College Park, MD 20742
ph: 301-405-9217
fax: 301-314-7170
e-mail: ml160@umail.umd.edu
web: http://www.lib.umd.edu/UMCP/MUSIC/music.html

Marvin Yagoda
Marvin's Marvelous Mechanical Museum
31005 Orchard Rd.
Farmington, MI 48334
ph: 248-626-5020
fax: 248-626-7945
e-mail: adamant726@aol.com
web: http://www.marvin3m.com/

Repair Services

Danilo Konvalinka
Musical Wonder House Museum, The
18 High St.
P.O. Box 604
Wiscasset, ME 04578-0604
ph: 207-882-7163 or 800-336-3725
e-mail: musicbox@musicalwonderhouse.com
web: http://www.musicalwonderhouse.com/
Buys & sells music boxes, wind-up phonographs, player pianos & rolls, cylinder records, complete or parts; full repair services: combwork, gearwork, spring repairs.

Mechanical (Band Organs)

(see also CAROUSELS & CAROUSEL FIGURES; MUSICAL INSTRUMENTS, Organs)

Clubs/Associations

Ken Smith
American Band Organ Association
3766 Mann Rd.
Blacklick, OH 43004
Members interested building, rebuilding, and playing band, fairground, and monkey organs.

Dealers

Danie Horenberger
Brass Ring Entertainment
11001 Peoria St.
Sun Valley, CA 91352
ph: 818-394-0028
fax: 818-394-0062
e-mail: sales@carousell.com
web: http://www.carousell.com
20 years experience, sales, restoration, parts, service.

Alan S. Erb, P.E. (M.E.)
Erb Engineering
P.O. Box 124
Mt. Eden, CA 94557-0124
ph: 510-783-5068
fax: 510-783-5068
web: http://www.quikpage.com/E/erbc
Expert buys, sells, restores, music boxes, coin-op pianos, organs and parts; offers the finest pipework including reed pipes; also makes custom made organs and calliopes to any customer specification (commercial use, home use, etc.)

Experts

Mike Kitner
735 Factory St.
Carlisle, PA 17013-1855
ph: 717-249-3851
Specializes in band organs.

Jerry Biasella
286 W. 14th Pl.
Chicago Heights, IL 60411
ph: 708-756-3307
Specializes in band organs.

Art Reblitz
Reblite Restorations Inc.
P.O. Box 7392
Colorado Springs, CO 80933-7392
e-mail: orchestrion@juno.com
Specializes in the restoration of orchestrions and band organs; also music arranging for these instruments.

Repair Services

Art Reblitz
Reblite Restorations Inc.
P.O. Box 7392
Colorado Springs, CO 80933-7392
e-mail: orchestrion@juno.com
Specializes in the restoration of orchestrions and band organs; also music arranging for these instruments.

Alan S. Erb, P.E. (M.E.)
Erb Engineering
P.O. Box 124
Mt. Eden, CA 94557-0124
ph: 510-783-5068
fax: 510-783-5068
web: http://www.quikpage.com/E/erbc
Expert buys, sells, restores, repairs organs and parts; offers the finest pipework including reed pipes; also makes custom made organs and calliopes to any customer specification (commercial use, home use, etc.)

Repro. Sources

Stinson Organ Co.
4691 Co. Rd. 91
Bellefontaine, OH 43311
ph: 937-593-5709
fax: 937-593-5553
Makes new band organs.

Organs

(see also MUSIC BOXES; MUSICAL INSTRUMENTS, Mechanical [Band Organs])

Clubs/Associations

Michael Fellenzer, Ex. Sec.
American Theatre Organ Society
P.O. Box 551081
Indianapolis, IN 46205-1081
ph: 317-251-6441
fax: 317-251-6443
e-mail: felenzer@in.net
web: http://www.atos.org

James Quashnock
Reed Organ Society, Inc.
Magazine: Reed Organ Society Quarterly
3525 State Highway 258 E.
Wichita Falls, TX 76308-7037
ph: 940-691-7809
e-mail: Quashnock@aol.com
web: http://sponsor.globalknowledge.nl/ros/
Focuses to all aspects of reed organs: music, construction, historical value, repair, etc.

Dr. Hans van Oost, Gen. Sec.
Dutch Mechanical Organ Society - Kring van Draaiorgelvriended (KDV)
Naaldwijkseweg 262-264
PW's-Gravenzande, 2691
The Netherlands
ph: (31) 174 41 54 38
fax: (31) 174 41 54 38
e-mail: havo@kabelfoon.nl
web: http://www.caiw.nl/~havo/en_idx2.htm
For those interested in self-playing organs: street organs, fairground organs, dance hall organs, orchestrions.

John Page, Mem.
Fair Organ Preservation Society
Magazine: Key Frame, The
43 Woolmans
Fullers Slade, Milton Keynes MK11 2BA
U.K.
ph: +44 1908 263717
fax: +44 1908 263717
e-mail: memsec@fops.ndirect.co.uk
web: http://www.ndirect.co.uk/~fops/
For the enthusiast of fair organs and mechanical music instruments.

Andrew Paterson, Mem. Sec.
Cinema Organ Society
Journal: Cinema Organ
80 Merrylee Road
Newlands, Glasgow G43 2QZ
U.K.
e-mail: john@leemingj.demon.co.uk
web: http://www.mrc-bsu.cam.ac.uk/COS/

Dealers

Gary Besteman
Pump & Pipe Shop, The
7945 Kraft Ave.
Caledonia, MI 49316
ph: 616-891-8743
Specializes in the restoration, buying

and selling of reed organs; also buys parts.

Don Bryant
Bryant Antique Players
4819 Stallcup
Mesquite, TX 75150-1143
ph: 972-270-0135
fax: 972-613-1627
e-mail: aplayr@airmail.net
Sales, service and rebuilding of player pianos, pump organs, reproducing & coin-operated instruments, pin balls, & game room equipment; since 1975

Internet Resources

Jerrell Kautz
Theatre Organ Home Page
2250 Holly Trail
Houston, TX 77054
ph: 713-797-6173
e-mail: jkautz@theatreorgans.com
web: http://theatreorgans.com/
An organization for those interested in theatre pipe organs and Hammond and other electronic organs.

Periodicals

Fred Pelton
Newsletter: Reed Organ Newsletter, The
4328 Rolling Acres Dr., SE
Grand Rapids, MI 49512
ph: 616-977-7297
Published every two months with articles, restoration tips, stories, classifieds.

Repair Services

Gary Besteman
Pump & Pipe Shop, The
7945 Kraft Ave.
Caledonia, MI 49316
ph: 616-891-8743
Specializes in the restoration, buying and selling of reed organs; also buys parts.

Pianos

(see also PIANOS, Miniature)

Dealers

Legay Piano Resales
ph: 925-735-8625
e-mail: pianos@webcom.com
web: http://www.legacypiano.com/
Specializes in the sales of pre-owned Steinway pianos.

Roger's Piano
879 Washington St.
Hanover, MA 02339
ph: 781-826-0453
fax: 781-826-1212
e-mail: roger@usedsteinways.com
web: http://usedsteinways.com/
Buys, sells and restores find quality vintage Steinway pianos; also other makers of similar handcrafted quality pianos.

Pyrianos Collection, Inc., The
P.O. Box 1655
Greenwich, CT 06836
ph: 203-661-2566
fax: 203-661-2566
e-mail: mmw@pyrianos.com
web: http://www.pyrianos.com/
Specializes in the acquisition, restoration, and sales of vintage Steinway & Sons pianos.

Leopold Holder
New York Piano Center, Inc.
121 W. 19th Street, 7th Floor
New York, NY 10011-4114
ph: 212-229-2600
fax: 212-229-2668
e-mail: lholder@compuserve.com
A thoroughly complete piano rebuilding, restoration and refinishing workshop; also offers other services such as sales, rentals and appraisals of vintage pianos.

Ted Snyder
Old Towne Piano SHop
2 N. Market St.
P.O. Box 852
Frederick, MD 21705-0852
ph: 301-695-6150
e-mail: info@townpiano.com
web: http://www.townpiano.com
Sells used piano (like-new, refurbished, rebuilt, restored) and piano accessories; also does piano restorations.

Mike Evola
Evola Music
48800 Van Dyke
Utica, MI 48317
ph: 810-726-6570
fax: 810-726-0416
e-mail: pianoman@evola.com
web: http://www.evola.com/
Buys, sells, restores, appraises pianos: Baldwin, Bosendorfer, Wurlitzer, PianoDisc, Schimmel, Estonia, Yamaha Claviona, Chickering, Knabe, Mason & Hamlin.

Internet Resources

Piano World
38 Parky Dr.
Enfield, CT 06082
ph: 860-745-5826
fax: 860-741-2625
e-mail: pianos@email.com
web: http://www.pianoworld.com/
Great web site for piano related information: how old is your piano?, tuners, CD's, books, dealers, for sale, restoring, care, moving, supplies, organs.

Piano Technicians Guild
3930 Washington
Kansas City, MO 64111-2963
ph: 816-753-7747
fax: 816-531-0070
e-mail: ptg@ptg.org
web: http://www.ptg.org
Website offers an incredible collection of piano resources: dealers, industry, literature, merchandise, piano museum, organs, research, software, teachers, technicians.

Man./Prod./Dist.

Steinway & Sons
1 Steinway Place
Long Island City, NY 11105
ph: 800-366-1853
e-mail: info@steinway.com
web: http://www.steinway.com
Great website with music links, links to Steinway artists, caring for your Steinway, Steinway Restoration Center, find out the weight and age of a Steinway, sizes of "modern" grand pianos, Steinway patents, and more.

Museums/Libraries

Museum of the American Piano
211 West 58th St.
New York, NY 10019
ph: 212-246-4646
e-mail: Pmuseum@pianomuseum.com
web: http://www.pianomuseum.com/museum/

Museum of Musical Instruments, The
Schubert Club
302 Landmark Center
75 W. 5th St.
Saint Paul, MN 55102
ph: 651-292-3267
fax: 651-292-4317
e-mail: schubert@schubert.org
web: http://www.schubert.org/
More than 100 pianofortes, harpsichords, clavichords and organs spanning more than 425 years; also various musical instruments from around the world, automatic musical instruments and phonographs; early composer & musician letters.

Periodicals

Marienne Uszler
Sparrow Hawk Press
Magazine: Piano & Keyboard
P.O. Box 2626
San Anselmo, CA 94979
ph: 800-233-3690
fax: 415-458-2955
e-mail: muszler@pianoandkeyboard.com
web: http://www.pianoandkeyboard.com/PKHome.html
A bi-monthly magazine of interviews, memories, insights, practical knowledge, music to play, piano history, legend & lore; for piano teachers, beginning through advanced students, educators, musicologists, amateur piano players.

Repair Services

Roger's Piano
879 Washington St.
Hanover, MA 02339
ph: 781-826-0453
fax: 781-826-1212
e-mail: roger@usedsteinways.com
web: http://usedsteinways.com/
Buys, sells and restores find quality vintage Steinway pianos; also other makers of similar handcrafted quality pianos.

Pyrianos Collection, Inc., The
P.O. Box 1655
Greenwich, CT 06836
ph: 203-661-2566
fax: 203-661-2566
e-mail: mmw@pyrianos.com
web: http://www.pyrianos.com/
Specializes in the acquisition, restoration, and sales of vintage Steinway & Sons pianos.

Leopold Holder
New York Piano Center, Inc.
121 W. 19th Street, 7th Floor
New York, NY 10011-4114
ph: 212-229-2600
fax: 212-229-2668
e-mail: lholder@compuserve.com
A thoroughly complete piano rebuilding, restoration and refinishing workshop; also offers other services such as sales, rentals and appraisals of vintage pianos.

Ted Snyder
Old Towne Piano SHop
2 N. Market St.
P.O. Box 852
Frederick, MD 21705-0852
ph: 301-695-6150
e-mail: info@townpiano.com
web: http://www.townpiano.com
Sells used piano (like-new, refurbished, rebuilt, restored) and piano accessories; also does piano restorations.

Dan Hall
Hall Piano Co., Inc.
901 David Dr.
Metairie, LA 70003
ph: 504-733-8863
fax: 504-736-0109

Dan Reed
Piano Arts
1909 Lilac Court
Richardson, TX 75080
ph: 972-699-7463
fax: 972-644-1304

Pianos (Player)

(see also PIANO ROLLS)

Clubs/Associations

Bill Chapman, Mem.
Automatic Musical Instrument Collectors Association (AMICA)
Magazine: AMICA News Bulletin
2150 Hastings Court
Santa Rosa, CA 95405-8377
ph: 707-570-2258
e-mail: shazam@sonic.net
web: http://www.amica.org/
Purpose is to foster preservation and appreciation of instruments and recordings of roll-actuated instruments, especially player pianos and organs.

J.J.I.M. ten Horn, Sec.
Nederlandse Pianola Vereniging (Dutch Pianola Association)
Newsletter: Pianola Bulletin
Eikendreef 24
HR OSS, NL-5342
The Netherlands
ph: (0412) 623369
fax: (0412) 623369

Everson Whittle, Sec.
North West Player Piano Association, The
Journal: NWPPA Journal
47 Raikes Road
Preston, Lancashire PR1 5EQ
U.K.
ph: 01772 792795
Association dealing in all aspects of Mechanical Music, repair of instruments, and interest in the hobby.

Dealers

David M. Hall, Sr.
P.O. Box 161
Uxbridge, MA 01569
ph: 508-278-2874
Player piano sales and service since 1959; pickup and deliver on the East Coast with own trucks.

Don Bryant
Bryant Antique Players
4819 Stallcup
Mesquite, TX 75150-1143
ph: 972-270-0135
fax: 972-613-1627
e-mail: aplayr@airmail.net
Sales, service and rebuilding of player pianos, pump organs, reproducing & coin-operated instruments, pin balls, & game room equipment; since 1975.

Mr. Kim Bunker
Orange Coast Piano
1251 S. Wright
Santa Ana, CA 92705
ph: 714-836-7368
fax: 714-543-0835
e-mail: ocpiano@pacbell.net
web: http://www.forpianos.com/
Buys, sells and restores player pianos.

Internet Resources

John Tuttle
John Tuttle "Self-Playing Pianos"
407 19th Ave.
Bricktown, NJ 08724
ph: 732-840-8787
e-mail: john@player-care.com
web: http://www.player-care.com/
Dedicated to player and reproducing pianos: service, repair, rebuilding; also sells new QRS and Tempola music rolls on-line; lots of technical information and information about used rolls and roll auctions.

Michael Waters
Player Piano
Austraila
e-mail: mwaters@ruralnet.net.au
web: http://www.pianoworld.com/
Great resource web site for player pianos: restoration, societies, links, roll manufacturers.

Museums/Libraries

International Piano Archives at Maryland, Neil Ratliff Music Library
Hornbrake 3210
College Park, MD 20742
ph: 301-405-9217
fax: 301-314-7170
e-mail: ml160@umail.umd.edu
web: http://www.lib.umd.edu/UMCP/MUSIC/music.html

Repair Services

John Tuttle
John Tuttle "Self-Playing Pianos"
407 19th Ave.
Bricktown, NJ 08724
ph: 732-840-8787
e-mail: john@player-care.com
web: http://www.player-care.com/
Dedicated to player and reproducing pianos: service, repair, rebuilding; also sells new QRS and Tempola music rolls on-line; lots of technical information and information about used rolls and roll auctions.

Jeff Morgan
833 S. Front St.
Allentown, PA 18103-3384
ph: 610-797-3381
fax: 610-797-3381
Consultant, expert who specializes in the repair, restoration and technical history of reproducing pianos.

Mel Septon
9045 N. Karlov Ave.
Skokie, IL 60076
ph: 847-679-3455
Specializes in the repair of reproducing pianos.

W. Gilstrap
Player Action Rebuilding
1374 E. Chestnut St.
Canton, IL 61520-2365
Rebuilds all makes of player pianos actions: Gulbransen, Schulz, Standard, etc.; packing crate supplied for stacks.

Bill Singleton
1101 South Kingshighway
Saint Louis, MO 63110
Specializes in the repair of reproducing pianos.

Craig Brougher
Brougher Restorations
3500 Claremont Ave.
Independence, MO 64052
ph: 816-254-1693
e-mail: craigbr@mindspring.com
Complete restoration facilities for reproducers, orchestrions and fine grand pianos; also case and veneer repairs.

Alan S. Erb, P.E. (M.E.)
Erb Engineering
P.O. Box 124
Mt. Eden, CA 94557-0124
ph: 510-783-5068
fax: 510-783-5068
web: http://www.quikpage.com/E/erbc
Expert buys, sells, restores, repairs nickelodeon/coin-op pianos, parts; offers the finest pipework.

Suppliers

Player Piano Co., Inc.
704 East Douglas
Wichita, KS 67202-3506
ph: 316-263-3241 or 316-263-1714
fax: 316-263-5480
Complete line of player piano restoration supplies, service manuals, music rolls; catalog if mailed free upon request.

Picks

Collectors

Alan Ralph
Guitar-Picks.com
2311 East 9th Ave. N
Tampa, FL 33605
e-mail: alanr666@yahoo.com
web: http://www.guitar-picks.com/
Collecting picks since 1991.

Carl Oates
2003 Avenue L
Galveston, TX 77550
ph: 409-762-9995
fax: 409-762-9996
e-mail: lynchrox@aol.com
web: http://hometown.aol.com/lynchrox/coates.html
Trades guitar picks with other collectors and makes purchases for his own collection; looking for imprinted guitar picks from bands and individual musicians: actual sage used, mint, promotional, fan club picks.

Dennis Chase
Picknet
7637 S. Goosesberry Way
Tucson, AZ 85747
e-mail: Tucrock@aol.com
Avid collector of picks; always willing to talk with others having a similar interest.

Experts

Will Hoover
92-1553-B Aliinui Dr.
Kapolei, HI 96707
ph: 808-679-0114
Author of "Picks! The Colorful Saga of Vintage Celluloid Guitar Plectrums."

Internet Resources

Hand Pick'd
e-mail: bdaleiden@hotmail.com
web: http://members.tripod.com/~bdaleiden/

Steve Leavitt
Pick Net
e-mail: StevieLeavitt@juno.com
web: http://home.att.net/~StevieLeavitt/
Brings collectors who want to trade picks together; not four buyers or sellers of picks - just traders.

Jeff White
Universal Guitar Pick Trader, The
28 K Corniche Dr.
Dana Point, CA 92629
ph: 949-487-7050
e-mail: jeffwhite@earthlink.net
web: http://home.earthlink.net/~jeffwhite/
Great web site with lots of pick information and resources for the pick collector; many celebrity, promo and vintage picks to trade.

Periodicals

Newsletter: Pick Tips
1833 Peck Road, #18
Monrovia, CA 91016
ph: 626-357-9271
Newsletter about vintage picks (plectrums).

String

Appraisers

Fritz Reuter
Fritz Reuter & Sons, Inc.
3917 W. Touhy Ave.
Chicago, IL 60645-1027
ph: 847-677-7255 or 847-677-7257
fax: 847-677-7256
e-mail: freuter@fritz-reuter.com
web: http://www.fritz-reuter.com
Master violin makers and dealers; international consultants and expert appraisers; specializes in string instruments (violins, violas, cellos, bows); also repairs and restores string instruments.

Collectors

Richard Schwartz
24550 Hawthorne Dr.
Cleveland, OH 44122-2314
ph: 216-464-0183
e-mail: richs48969@aol.com
Wants to buy older violins, violas, cellos, basses, bows, etc.; also wants books and catalogs about string instruments.

Dealers

Jim Bollman
Music Emporium, Inc., The
165 Massachusetts Ave.
Lexington, MA 02173-4039
ph: 617-860-0049
fax: 617-860-0051
e-mail: musicemp@tiac.net
Wants old guitars, ukuleles, banjos, mandolins, concertinas, wooden flutes or other stringed instruments in any condition.

R.D. Kress
503 W. Lakeshore Dr. #503A1
Port Clinton, OH 43452-9324
Wants violas, cellos, violins, string basses.

Fritz Reuter
Fritz Reuter & Sons, Inc.
3917 W. Touhy Ave.
Chicago, IL 60645-1027
ph: 847-677-7255 or 847-677-7257
fax: 847-677-7256
e-mail: freuter@fritz-reuter.com
web: http://www.fritz-reuter.com
Master violin makers and dealers; international consultants and expert appraisers; specializes in string instruments (violins, violas, cellos, bows); also repairs and restores string instruments.

Periodicals

String Letter Publishing, Inc.
Magazine: Strings
P.O. Box 151049
San Rafael, CA 94915
ph: 415-485-6946 or 800-827-6837
fax: 415-485-0831
e-mail: custserv@stringletter.com
web: http://www.stringsmagazine.com/
The bi-monthly magazine for players and makers of bowed instruments; articles, profiles, instrument making and repair, music schools, ads; also publishes annual auction Price Guide and annual Resource Guide.

String (Fretted)

Appraisers

Stanley M. Jay
Mandolin Brothers, Ltd.
Newsletter: Vintage News, The
629 Forest Ave.
Staten Island, NY 10310-2515
ph: 718-981-3226 or 718-981-8585
fax: 718-816-4416
e-mail: mandolin@ix.netcom.com
web: http://www.mandoweb.com
Buy guitars, banjos & mandolins by fine American brands: Gibson, C.F. Martin, National, Dobro, D'Angelico, Fender, Gretsch, Rickenbacker, Paramount, Vega, B&D, Epiphone, Stromberg, S.S. Stewart; free telephone appraisals; repairs.

Steve Underwood, ISA
Appraisals & Consulting by F. Steven Underwood
2516 Larwood Dr.
Charleston, WV 25302-4318
ph: 304-345-4089
Independent, professional appraisals of electric and acoustic guitars, banjos, mandolins, etc. for insurance, estate valuation, tax, legal, and other matters; Member, International Society of Appraisers; does not appraise violins.

George Gruhn
Gruhn Guitars, Inc.
400 Broadway
Nashville, TN 37203-3931
ph: 615-256-2033
fax: 615-255-2021
e-mail: gruhn@gruhn.com
web: http://www.gruhn.com/
Buys, sells, appraises, and specializes in American vintage or custom-made fretted instruments; issues monthly catalog of over 1500 vintage guitars, mandolins and banjos.

Stan Werbin
Elderly Instruments
1100 N. Washington
Lansing, MI 48906
ph: 517-372-7890 or 517-372-7880
fax: 517-372-5155
e-mail: swerbin@elderly.com
web: http://www.elderly.com
Collector, dealer, expert, appraiser specializes in American made fretted stringed instruments including guitars, banjos, mandolins: by Martin, Gibson, Vega, B&D, D'Angelico, Stromberg, Maurer, Fender, etc.

Collectors

K. Wiley
719 Baldwin SE
Grand Rapids, MI 49503-4470
ph: 616-451-8410
e-mail: quillion1@aol.com
Wants older (pre-1970) guitars, banjos, ukuleles, mandolins; pieces, junkers, basket cases; also buying tube amplifiers.

Dealers

Stanley M. Jay
Mandolin Brothers, Ltd.
Newsletter: Vintage News, The
629 Forest Ave.
Staten Island, NY 10310-2515
ph: 718-981-3226 or 718-981-8585
fax: 718-816-4416
e-mail: mandolin@ix.netcom.com
web: http://www.mandoweb.com
Buy guitars, banjos & mandolins by fine American brands: Gibson, C.F. Martin, National, Dobro, D'Angelico, Fender, Gretsch, Rickenbacker, Paramount, Vega, B&D, Epiphone, Stromberg, S.S. Stewart; free telephone appraisals; repairs.

Stan Werbin
Elderly Instruments
1100 N. Washington
Lansing, MI 48906
ph: 517-372-7890 or 517-372-7880
fax: 517-372-5155
e-mail: swerbin@elderly.com
web: http://www.elderly.com
Collector, dealer, expert, appraiser specializes in American made fretted stringed instruments including guitars, banjos, mandolins: by Martin, Gibson, Vega, B&D, D'Angelico, Stromberg, Maurer, Fender, etc.

Experts

David E. Schenkman
Turtle Hill Banjo Co.
P.O. Box 265
Bryantown, MD 20617-0265
ph: 301-274-3441
e-mail: turtlehill@olg.com
Buying vintage stringed instruments: banjos, guitars, mandolins, and ukuleles; especially wants instruments made by Gibson, Martin, Fairbanks, B & D, Bacon, Vega, Paramount, Weymann, etc.

George Gruhn
Gruhn Guitars, Inc.
400 Broadway
Nashville, TN 37203-3931
ph: 615-256-2033
fax: 615-255-2021
e-mail: gruhn@gruhn.com
web: http://www.gruhn.com/
Buys, sells, appraises, and specializes in American vintage or custom-made fretted instruments; issues monthly catalog of over 1500 vintage guitars, mandolins and banjos.

Repair Services

Stanley M. Jay
Mandolin Brothers, Ltd.
Newsletter: Vintage News, The
629 Forest Ave.
Staten Island, NY 10310-2515
ph: 718-981-3226 or 718-981-8585
fax: 718-816-4416
e-mail: mandolin@ix.netcom.com
web: http://www.mandoweb.com
Buy guitars, banjos & mandolins by fine American brands: Gibson, C.F. Martin, National, Dobro, D'Angelico, Fender, Gretsch, Rickenbacker, Paramount, Vega, B&D, Epiphone, Stromberg, S.S. Stewart; free telephone appraisals; repairs.

Brass & Reed Music Center, Inc.
675 Mason Ave.
Daytona Beach, FL 32117
ph: 904-252-5544
fax: 904-253-4171
Specializes in the repair and restoration of brass wind band instruments, violins and guitars and other fretted instruments.

Repro. Sources

John & Ann Rawdon
Dulcimers by JR
10068 Stonecreek Rd.
Newcomerstown, OH 43832-9118
ph: 614-498-7753
Builders of fine quality lap and hammered dulcimers; price lists upon request; some wholesale, ask for details.

String (Guitars)

Collectors

Sonny Goldson
1413 Magnolia Lane
Midwest City, OK 73110
ph: 405-737-3312
fax: 405-737-3355
Wants to buy old guitars, amplifiers and effects: Gibson, Fender, VOX, Gretsch, Ricken Backer, Mosrite, Silvertone, Guico, Harmony, Martin, Epiphone, National, Valco.

Dealers

Southworth Guitars
7854 Old Georgetown Rd.
Bethesda, MD 20814
ph: 301-718-1667
fax: 301-718-0391

East Coast Guitars
8 Oak Grove Pl.
Dublin, VA 24084-2533

Guitar Emporium
1610 Bardstown Rd.
Louisville, KY 40205
ph: 502-459-4153
fax: 502-454-3661

Gordy's Music
3341 Hilton Rd.
Ferndale, MI 48200
ph: 248-546-7447
fax: 248-546-5249

Steve Evans
Jacksonville Guitar Center
1105 Burman Dr.
Jacksonville, AR 72076-4386
ph: 501-982-4933
e-mail: jvilguitar@aol.com
web: http://members.aol.com/jvilguitar
Buys, collects, and specialized in

stencil-painted cowboy guitars, toy guitars, and vintage guitars.

Guitar Heaven
150 Longbrook Way
Pleasant Hill, CA 94523
ph: 800-797-5750
Wants to buy pre-1970 old guitars: Fender, Gibson, Gretsch, Guild and Martins only.

Guitarville
19258 15th NE
Seattle, WA 98155
ph: 206-363-8188
fax: 206-363-0478

Experts

Mike Longworth
C.F. Martin Guitar & Co.
510 Sycamore St.
Nazareth, PA 18064-1000
ph: 610-759-2937 or 800-759-3827
fax: 610-759-2340
web: http://www.mguitar.com/
Historian, Martin Guitar Co.; curator (ret.) of Martin Museum; author of "Martin Guitars, A History"; offers appraisals and authoritative letters on Martin instruments.

Internet Resources

GuitarBase GuitarMall
3107 Douglas Road
Flushing, NY 11363-1043
ph: 718-229-4289
fax: 718-229-3061
e-mail: info@gbase.com
web: http://www.gbase.com/
Great web site for guitar enthusiasts: search dealer database for guitars for sale, guitar links.

Man./Prod./Dist.

C.F. Martin Guitar & Co.
510 Sycamore St.
Nazareth, PA 18064-1000
ph: 610-759-2937 or 800-759-3827
fax: 610-759-2340
web: http://www.mguitar.com/
Offers Woodworker's Guitar Makers Connection for Woodworkers & Luthiers; tools, materials, parts for the fretted instrument maker; factory tours M-F; Guitar Makers Connection catalog $2 ppd.

Periodicals

Magazine: Guitar Digest
ph: 740-592-4614
e-mail: alexmack@frognet.net
web: http://www.guitardigest.com/
The magazine for guitar players and collectors.

Magazine: 20th Century Guitar
135 Oser Ave.
Hauppauge, NY 11788
ph: 516-273-1674 or 800-291-9687
fax: 516-434-9057
e-mail: tcguitar@tcguitar.com
web: http://www.tcguitar.com/
A bi-monthly magazine covering the vintage guitar market; up-to-date reports on technical information, guitar prices, shows, photo classifieds, as well as interesting, off-beat interviews with celebrity musicians who collect.

Magazine: Bluegrass Unlimited
P.O. Box 111
Broad Run, VA 20137-0111
ph: 540-349-8181 or 800-258-4727
fax: 540-341-0011
e-mail: info@bluegrassmusic.com
web: http://www.bluegrassmusic.com/
Bluegrass Festival calendar, artist interviews, personal appearance calendar, some articles about vintage guitars; classified ads with man instruments.

Vintage Guitar Inc.
Magazine: Vintage Guitar Magazine
P.O. Box 7301
Bismarck, ND 58507
ph: 701-255-1197
fax: 701-255-0250
e-mail: vintage@vguitar.com
web: http://www.vguitar.com
Guitar related articles, ads, parts, supplies, books, music, used and new guitars for sale, amps, price guides, guitar factories, repairs, interviews, guitar cases.

Vintage Guitar Inc.
Magazine: VG Classics
P.O. Box 7301
Bismarck, ND 58507
ph: 701-255-1197
fax: 701-255-0250
e-mail: vintage@vguitar.com
web: http://www.vguitar.com
A quarterly glossy magazine dedicated to vintage guitars and other stringed instruments; also publishes "The Official Vintage Guitar Magazine Instrument Price Guide."

Miller Freeman, Inc.
Magazine: Guitar Player
600 Harrison St.
San Francisco, CA 94107
ph: 650-655-4308 or 800-289-9839
e-mail: guitarplayer@neodata.com
web: http://www.guitarplayer.com/
Monthly glossy magazine serving the guitar playing community; some articles about collectible vintage guitars.

String Letter Publishing, Inc.
Magazine: Acoustic Guitar
P.O. Box 767
San Anselmo, CA 94979-0767
ph: 415-485-6946 or 800-827-6837
fax: 415-485-0831
e-mail: custserv@stringletter.com
web: http://www.acousticguitar.com/
The magazine acoustic guitars.

String (Violin Family)

Appraisers

Robert Portukalian
Providence Violin Shop
1279 North Main St.
Providence, RI 02904
ph: 401-521-5145
Violin appraiser, dealer, expert; wants quality handcrafted or factory-made violins.

Collectors

Richard Schwartz
24550 Hawthorne Dr.
Cleveland, OH 44122-2314
ph: 216-464-0183
e-mail: richs48969@aol.com
Wants to buy older violins, violas, cellos, basses, bows, etc.; also wants books and catalogs about string instruments.

Dealers

Ron Midgett
Easthampton Violin Company
15 Lovefield St.
Easthampton, MA 01027-1167
ph: 413-527-8033 or 800-207-2400
e-mail: violins@javanet.com
web: http://www.worldinmotion.com/violins.html
Wants violins, violas, cellos; American or European; especially wants violins made by Massachusetts makers.

William D. Voiers
William D. Voiers Fine Musical Instruments
P.O. Box 23
North Egremont, MA 01252-0023
ph: 413-528-3321 or 800-788-3521
fax: 413-528-5801
Dealer, collector, appraiser of the violin family of instruments: violins, violas, cellos, bows, banjos, ukuleles, guitars and mandolins; electric or acoustic; also saxes, brasses, drums, percussion; also buys, sells, collects and trades.

Robert Portukalian
Providence Violin Shop
1279 North Main St.
Providence, RI 02904
ph: 401-521-5145
Violin appraiser, dealer, expert; wants quality handcrafted or factory-made violins.

Peter Zaret
Peter Zaret Violins
861 W 46th St.
Norfolk, VA 23508-2009
ph: 800-222-2998 or 757-423-3336
fax: 757-423-3340
e-mail: zaret@exis.net
Sells all sizes of new and old violins including violins made in China and Eastern Europe; also deals in violas, cellos and their bows; instruments & bows by contemporary luthier also available; expert repairs & bow rehairing.

John Montgomery
John Montgomery, Inc.
509 Hillsborough St.
Raleigh, NC 27603-1729
ph: 919-821-4459
fax: 919-821-4459
Dealer in the violin family of instruments; violin maker and restorer.

Al Stancel
Casa Del Sol Violins, Ltd.
4302 East 62nd St.
Indianapolis, IN 46220-4568
ph: 800-423-0236 or 317-257-9923
Buys, sells, and restores old violins; also makes and sells new violins; especially wants French bows and Italian violins.

Experts

William L. Monical
William L. Monical, Inc., Dealers & Restorers of Fine Violins
288 Richmond Terrace
Staten Island, NY 10301-1512
ph: 718-816-7878 or 718-816-7176
fax: 718-816-7711
Specializes in bowed string instruments of modern & Baroque violin and viola da gamba families: sales, restoration, appraisals, cases.

Internet Resources

Violink
Italy
e-mail: info@graffiti.it
web: http://www.violink.com/
Lots of information about violins, fiddles, etc.: conferences, violin and bow makers, violin making schools, organizations, dealers, shops, museums, books, journals.

Periodicals

Magazine: Strad, The
P.O. Box 648
Harrow, Middlesex HA1 2EE
U.K.
ph: +44 (0)20 8863 4040 or +44 (0)20 8863 2020
fax: +44 (0)20 8863 2444
e-mail: thestrad@orphpl.com
web: http://www.thestrad.com/
A monthly magazine covering all aspects of violin-family stringed instruments: playing, making,

teaching; includes great performers, teachers and luthiers, news, reviews; US subscriptions call 1-800-688-6247.

Repair Services

Brass & Reed Music Center, Inc.
675 Mason Ave.
Daytona Beach, FL 32117
ph: 904-252-5544
fax: 904-253-4171
Specializes in the repair and restoration of brass wind band instruments, violins and guitars and other fretted instruments.

MYSTERY/DETECTIVE ITEMS

(see also BOOKS, Mystery; CAMERAS & CAMERA EQUIPMENT, Subminiature; CHARACTER COLLECTIBLES, Sherlock Holmes; CHARACTER COLLECTIBLES, Spy Memorabilia; MAGAZINES, Mystery; SPY EQUIPMENT)

Collectors

Beverley Furlow-Cleary
1555 N. Arcadia Ave.
Tucson, AZ 85712-4010
ph: 520-323-1709
e-mail: beverleyf@aol.com
Buys, sells, and appraises collectible mystery/detective items: books, vintage clothing and hats.

MYSTICAL ARTS

(see UFO'S & UNEXPLAINED PHENOMENA)

Here are some tips when contacting someone listed in this book:

■ **When requesting information about a particular item, include a description (material, dimensions, maker's mark, model number, etc.) and a photo, sketch, or photocopy of the item in question.**

■ **Always ask if there are charges for samples or for the services requested.**

■ **When writing, please be sure to include a Large (#10 business size) Self-Addressed and Stamped Envelope (LSASE) if requesting a reply or the return of photographs.**

■ **Never call collect unless otherwise directed. When calling, be considerate of time zone differences and always ask if the party you are calling has time to talk. When leaving an answering machine message, always instruct the party to call you back collect.**

N-O

NAPKIN DOLLS

Collectors

Bobbie & Alan Bryson
1 St. Eleanoras Ln.
Tuckahoe, NY 10707-1307
ph: 914-779-1405
e-mail: napkindoll@aol.com
A napkin dolls is a ceramic figurine of a girl with slits in her skirt for holding a folded napkin; Bobbie is co-author of the pictorial reference guide "Collectibles For The Kitchen, Bath & Beyond"; 150 photos of napkin dolls plus ads.

NAPKIN RINGS

Figural

Collectors

Steve Aaronson
P.O. Box 7522
Northridge, CA 91327
ph: 818-368-6052
e-mail: bjaaronson@aol.com
Wants to buy American silverplate figural napkin rings; old only.

Maria E. Raymond
Plow & Pen, Inc.
P.O. Box 251
Robbins, CA 95676-0251
ph: 530-735-6596
fax: 530-735-6112
e-mail: M_Raymond@compuserve.com
Interested in buying Meriden Company napkin rings only.

Dealers

Sandra Whitson
Van Anda's Antiques
P.O. Box 272
Lititz, PA 17543-0272
ph: 717-626-4978
fax: 717-626-7625
Buys and sells fine quality Victorian figural napkin rings; co-author of "Figural Napkin Rings" (1996), a collector's identification and value guide.

NASA

(see SPACE COLLECTIBLES)

NATIVE AMERICAN ARTS

(see AMERICAN INDIAN)

NATURAL HISTORY

(see also ANIMAL COLLECTIBLES; ASTRONOMICAL ITEMS; BOOKS, Reference [Natural History]; CAVE RELATED ITEMS; FOSSILS; HERITAGE RESOURCES; LAPIDARY; MARBLE & STONE; MINERAL SPECIMENS; SEASHELLS)

Auction Services

Alexandra Peters
Phillips Fine Art & Auctioneers
406 East 79th St.
New York, NY 10022
ph: 212-570-4830
fax: 212-570-2207
e-mail: phillips@philmail.demon.co.uk
web: http://www.phillips-auctions.com
Conducts specializes auction sales of natural history items including seashells.

Book Sellers

Frank J. Mikesh
1356 Walden Rd.
Walnut Creek, CA 94596-3158
ph: 510-934-9243
fax: 510-947-6113
e-mail: natscibooks@netvista.net
web: http://www.netvista.net/~natscibooks/
Interested in out-of-print natural history, hunting, fishing, sporting, and wildlife books, and related art.

Museums/Libraries

Amy Chionchio, Marketing
Milwaukee Public Museum
800 W. Wells St.
Milwaukee, WI 53233
ph: 414-278-2702
e-mail: amy@mpm.edu
web: http://www.mpm.edu/
A museum of human and natural history.

Meteorites

Dealers

RA Langheinrich Meteorites & Fossils
290 Brewer Road
Ilion, NY 13357
ph: 732-764-0879
fax: 732-764-0879
e-mail: meteorite@compuserve.com
web: http://www.nyrockman.com
Numerous links to websites focusing on archaeology, ancient history, ancient medicine, ancient Greek, Roman and Egyptian cultures, ancient coins, etc.

NAUTICAL ANTIQUES

(see also ART, Marine; BOATS; COAST GUARD; DIVING EQUIPMENT; INSTRUMENTS & DEVICES; MAPS & CHARTS; IVORY; OCEAN LINER MEMORABILIA; OUTBOARD MOTORS; SCRIMSHAW; SEASHELLS; SHIPPING; SHIP RELATED; STEAMBOAT COLLECTIBLES; TITANIC MEMORABILIA; WHALES & DOLPHINS; WHALING)

Appraisers

Peter C. Sorlien, ASA
Accredited Appraisers
17 1/2 State St.
Marblehead, MA 01945-3536
ph: 781-631-5956
fax: 781-631-6550
e-mail: appraisr@shore.net
Professional nautical antiques appraisals; experience with divorce, donation, estate, insurance, litigation, and tax matters; does not buy or sell.

Auction Services

Chuck Deluca
Maritime Auctions
P.O. Box 322
York, ME 03909
ph: 207-363-4247
fax: 207-363-1416
e-mail: maritim2@ix.netcom.com
web: http://www.maritiques.com
Three catalog auctions per year in March, July and October.

Clubs/Associations

National Maritime Historical Society
Magazine: Sea History
5 John Walsh Boulevard
Peekskill, NY 10566
ph: 914-737-7378
web: http://www.seahistory.org/
Preservation (full-rigger ship, brigantine, schooner, tug boat), education to heighten the maritime awareness of young Americans across the country, and publication of the magazines "Sea History" and the monthly newsletter "Gazette."

Harry D. Barry
Air Horn & Steam Whistle Enthusiasts
Newsletter: Horn & Whistle
275 Windswept Dr.
North East, PA 16428
ph: 814-725-8150
Purpose is to preserve, increase, and disseminate knowledge concerning horns, whistles, sirens, and bells in industrial, marine, transportation, signaling, and warning applications.

Collectors

Bob Glick
Columbia Trading Company
1 Barnstable Rd.
Hyannis, MA 02601
ph: 508-778-2929
fax: 508-778-2922
e-mail: nautical@capecod.net
web: http://www.columbiatrading.com/
Wants to buy all marine items; items relating to lighthouses, Coast Guard, naval, yachting, marine architecture, marine engineering, boating, sailing, marine engines, outboard motors, boat building, ship building, etc.

Stephen Seltzer
7912 Georgia Ave.
Silver Spring, MD 20910-4837
ph: 301-565-2444 or 301-565-3339
fax: 301-565-2228
e-mail: eseltzer@aol.com
Wants to buy authentic brass items salvaged form ships.

Dealers

James W. Claflin
Kenrick A. Claflin & Son
30 Hudson St.
Northborough, MA 01532
ph: 508-869-6955
Collectors and dealers in fine nautical antiques; specializing in U.S. Lighthouse Service, U.S. Lifesaving Service, U.S. Revenue Cutter Service, U.S. Coast Guard.

Andrew Jacobson
Andrew Jacobson Marine Antiques
P.O. Box 437
Ipswich, MA 01938
ph: 978-356-5583
fax: 978-356-8705
e-mail: marineantiques@nii.net
web: http://www.marineantiques.com/
Fine marine artifacts, paintings, models, half-hulls, antique scrimshaw, navigational instruments, photography, out-of-print books, manuscript material.

Richard Dermody
Brass n' Bounty
68 Front St.
Marblehead, MA 01945-3275
ph: 617-631-3864 or 617-631-6204
e-mail: dermodys@mediaone.net
web: http://www.brassandbounty.com
Buys and sells navigation instruments, telescopes, binnacles, compasses, sextants, clocks, barometers; also yachting items.

Ed Lefkowicz
Edward J. Lefkowicz, Inc.
500 Angell St.
Providence, RI 02906
ph: 800-201-7901
fax: 401-277-1459
e-mail: seabooks@saltbooks.com
web: http://www.saltbooks.com
Appraiser and dealer specializes in rare books and manuscripts relating

to the sea, the islands, and nautical science: voyages, naval, navigation, polar, the Pacific, sea charts.

John F. Rinaldi
Nautical Antiques
P.O. Box 765
Kennebunkport, ME 04046-0765
ph: 207-967-3218
fax: 207-967-2918
Buys and sells marine antiques, antique scrimshaw, paintings, naval items; fully illustrated catalog for $5.

Bernhard W. Sound
Jonesport Nautical Antiques
Cogswell & Main St., Box 401
Jonesport, ME 04649
ph: 207-497-5655
fax: 207-497-5954
e-mail: bsund@NauticalAntiques.com
web: http://www.NauticalAntiques.com
Specializes in nautical art, nautical antiques, and nautical reproductions: carries compasses, engine order telegraphs, diving helmets, binnacles, charts, items for restaurant decoration, and other items of interest.

James & Ann Marenakos
Quester Gallery
77 Main St.
P.O. Box 446
Stonington, CT 06378
ph: 860-535-3860
fax: 860-535-3533
e-mail: questergal@snet.net
web: http://www.artnet.com/quester.html
Buys, sells, consults on 19th & 20th century marine paintings, ships models, bronzes, campaign furniture, etc.

J. Tobin
Antique & Classic Boats
12 Carstead Dr.
Slingerlands, NY 12159
ph: 518-439-0477
fax: 518-439-0477

Stevens Bunker
China Sea Marine Trading Company
903 South Ann Street Wharf
Baltimore, MD 21231
ph: 410-276-8220
fax: 410-276-8220
e-mail: Chinaseas@hotmail.com
web: http://www.chinaseas.com/
Carries a unique jumble of maritime artifacts, antiques and curios gathered from around the world.

Robert Shourot
Coastal Diving Operations
10297 Rainbow Rd.
Carrollton, VA 23314-4109
ph: 757-826-3945
fax: 757-826-7879
Specialty is nautical artifacts and diving antiques including pumps, helmets, bells, steam gauges, engine telegraphs, portholes, lights, etc.

Daniel Alex Haase
Haase's Nautical Antiques & Furnishings
6150 Virginia Beach Blvd.
Norfolk, VA 23502-2702
ph: 757-461-2465 or 757-461-6150
Makers of resin-covered hatch cover tables; buys and sells nautical antiques: brass lights, ship's wheels, sextants, etc.; also specializes in restoring nautical antiques.

James & Norvell Kennedy
James Kennedy Antiques, Ltd.
905 W. Main St.
Durham, NC 27701-2054
ph: 919-682-1040 or 800-236-1868
fax: 919-683-9633
e-mail: kantiques@earthlink.net
web: http://www.antiqnet.com/kennedy
Specialist in scientific, medical, and nautical antiques and prints.

Raymond & Lyn Newman
Martifacts, Inc.
P.O. Box 350190
Jacksonville, FL 32235-0190
ph: 904-645-0150
fax: 904-645-0150
e-mail: martifacts@aol.com
web: http://www.martifacts.com/
Buys/sells authentic brass and/or wood nautical items salvaged from ships: lights, compasses, clocks, bells, hatch covers, sextants, etc.

John McSwain
Marine Antiques & Maritime Artifacts
4155 Hwy. 11
Deland, FL 32724-9745
ph: 904-734-8786
fax: 904-738-5629
Specializes in deep sea diving, gauges, antique outboard motors 1900-1955, boating equipment and accessories.

Jack P. Berten
Antiques of Merit
2400 SW 30th Ave.
Hallandale, FL 33009
ph: 954-456-1657 or 954-763-3223
fax: 954-767-3528
Specializes in 18th, 19th and early 20th century marine antiques.

Marc J. Cohen
P.O. Box 220153
Hollywood, FL 33022-0153
ph: 954-565-9754
Buys, sells and collects antique "hard hat" diving gear: helmets, hoses, shoes, knives, weights, belts, dresses, pumps, tools, catalogs, books, pictures, and other related "hard hat" diving equipment items.

Bob Elsner
Heights Antiques
29 Clubhouse Ln.
Boynton Beach, FL 33436-6056
ph: 561-736-1362
fax: 561-736-1914
e-mail: rjelsner@aol.com
Barometer expert who buys, sells, appraises and repairs all types of barometers: gimbaled, mercury, aneroid, altimeters, barographs; antique and reproduction.

Bruce Littler
Olde Nautical Shoppe
25 Causeway Blvd.
Clearwater, FL 33727
ph: 727-441-3036
fax: 727-443-5032
e-mail: oldnaut@aol.com
web: http://
www.oldenauticalshoppe.com/
Carries a large selection nautical antiques, ship artifacts, scientific instruments, navigation instruments, vintage fishing tackle, antique marine art, ship and boat models, weather instruments, ship clocks, etc.

Donald E. Taussig
Sanders' Antique Mall
22 N. Lemon Ave.
Sarasota, FL 34236-5711
ph: 941-366-0400
fax: 941-388-2053
e-mail: sandersant@aol.com
Buys and sells ship models, helmets, instruments, maps, clocks, bells, etc.

Gordon Stanley
Maritime Gallery
P.O. Box 40
Fulton, TX 78358-0040
ph: 512-729-4026 or 512-729-3691
web: http://www.gordonstanley.com/
Specializes in 1800s to 1900s maritime artifacts; shows at high quality antique shows.

Al & Bobbie Roberts
Rational Past, The
221 Oceano Dr.
Los Angeles, CA 90049-4123
ph: 310-476-6277
fax: 310-476-6278
e-mail: rational_past@mindspring.com
Organizer of West Coast Scientific & Technical Antique and Collectible Shows (Los Angeles in the winter and San Francisco are in late summer.)

Maidhof Bros. International
1891 San Diego Ave.
San Diego, CA 92110
ph: 800-SEA-JUNK
e-mail: nautical@electriciti.com
web: http://www.seajunk.com/
Carries Old ship relics from dead and dying ships of the world: real ship furniture, nautical lamps & lanterns, brass hardware, seagoing clocks and barometers, portholes, ships' wheels, etc.

Rod & Becky Cardoza
West Sea Company
2495 Congress St.
San Diego, CA 92110-2820
ph: 619-296-5356
fax: 619-296-1097
Buys, sells all types of marine paintings, scrimshaw, ships' carvings, ship models, navigational and scientific instruments, sailor handcrafts, campaign furniture, hard hat diving, antique marine photography, nautical books, ceramics.

Kenneth Brown
Franks Fisherman
366 Jefferson St.
San Francisco, CA 94133
ph: 415-775-1165
fax: 415-776-6549
e-mail: franksfish@earthlink.net
Fine selection of authentic nautical antiques including diving helmets, scrimshaw and whaling artifacts, ship models and scientific instruments; buys, sells, consignments, rentals; located two blocks from SF Maritime Museum.

Kathryn Retzer
Kathryn's Collectibles
2650 Emma Dr.
Pinole, CA 94564
ph: 800-424-3339 or 510-741-9976
fax: 510-741-1689
e-mail: shipnsea@aol.com
web: http://members.aol.com/Shipnsea/
kathryns.htm
Collectors and dealers in all types of nautical antiques with a special interest in deep sea diving equipment and naval items.

Fred Von Wiegen
Ship Store Galleries
P.O. Box 1058
Kapaa, HI 96746-1058
ph: 808-822-4999
Buys and sells 18th and 19th century shipboard items: old maps and charts, models, scrimshaw; particularly Pacific vessels and South Sea items.

James W. Coulson
Cuttysark of Bellevue
10235 Main St.
Bellevue, WA 98004-6121
ph: 425-453-1265
fax: 425-451-8779
Buys and sells a general line of marine items: flags, marine antiques, models, clocks, etc.

A. Rex Bennett
Anchor Antiques Co.
5129 No. Pearl St.
Tacoma, WA 98407
ph: 253-752-1134
Specializes in diver's helmets and old oil lamps.

Experts

Sara Conklin
Nautical Appraisals
239 Sierra Pt. Rd.
Brisbane, CA 94005-1664
ph: 415-467-6249
fax: 415-467-6249
e-mail: sconklin2@earthlink.com
Appraises maritime items and collections: ship models, scrimshaw, navigational instruments, figurehead carvings, marine art, paper & ephemera archival collections, telescopes, shipwrecks, diving equip., ocean liner memorabilia, whaling.

Internet Resources

John Kohnen
Mother of All Maritime Links, The
e-mail: jkohnen@cyber-dyne.com
web: http://www.cyber-dyne.com/~jkohnen/boatlink.html
Web site contains an incredible number of links to other nautical sights; boat builders and dealers, canoes, Coast Guard, diving, events, navies, hardware, lighthouses, modeling, nautical history, sailing, steamboats, etc.

Bill Momsen
Nautical Brass Online
P.O. Box 3966
Fort Myers, FL 33918-3966
e-mail: nbrass@peganet.com
web: http://members.aol.com/nbrass/ezine.htm
Provides free on-line information about nautical antiques.

Museums/Libraries

Peabody Essex Museum
Magazine: American Neptune
Essex & Libert Streets
Salem, MA 01970
ph: 978-745-9500 or 800-745-4054
e-mail: pem@pem.org
web: http://www.pem.org

Mystic Seaport Museum
75 Greenmanville Ave.
P.O. Box 6000
Mystic, CT 06355-0990
ph: 860-572-0711 or 888-9SEAPORT
e-mail: administration@mysticseaport.org
web: http://www.mysticseaport.org
General focus is 19th century seafaring America: scrimshaw, figureheads, instruments, maritime art, carvings, etc.

U.S. Naval Academy Museum
118 Maryland Ave.
Annapolis, MD 21402-5034
ph: 410-293-2180
fax: 410-293-5220
e-mail: jsharmon@nadn.navy.mil
web: http://www.nadn.navy.mil/Museum/
Focuses on the heritage of the U.S. Navy; ship models, paintings, prints, flags, uniforms, swords, medals, sculptures, rare books, photographs, instruments and gear, personal memorabilia.

Pete Lesher, Cur.
Chesapeake Bay Maritime Museum
Magazine: Weather Gauge, The
P.O. Box 636
Saint Michaels, MD 21663-0636
ph: 410-745-2916
fax: 410-745-6088
e-mail: letters@cbmm.org
web: http://www.cbmm.org
A major regional maritime museum with a 10,00 volume research library; collections include 7,500 objects, 12,000 photos, 1,200 ships' plans, 100 linear feet of manuscripts; decoys, oystering, lighthouses, charts, nautical, tools.

Mariners' Museum, The
100 Museum Dr.
Newport News, VA 23606
ph: 757-596-2222 or 800-581-7245
e-mail: info@mariner.org
web: http://www.mariner.org

Keith R. Gill
Museum of Science & Industry
57th St. & Lake Shore Dr.
Chicago, IL 60637
ph: 773-684-1414
fax: 773-684-5580

Maritime Museum of Monterey
5 Custom House Plaza
Monterey, CA 93940-2430
ph: 831-375-9259
fax: 831-665-3054
e-mail: mhaamm@mbay.net
web: http://www.mhaamm.org/

San Francisco Maritime National Historical Park, Museum & Library
Bldg. E, Fort Mason Center
San Francisco, CA 94123
ph: 415-556-9870 or 415-556-9871
fax: 415-556-3540
e-mail: safr_maritime_library@nps.gov
web: http://www.nps.gov/safr/local/lib/libtop.html

Periodicals

Robert R. McKenna, Ed.
Magazine: Nautical Collector
One Whale Oil Row
New London, CT 06320
ph: 860-444-0127
fax: 860-444-0129
e-mail: nautworld@aol.com
An authoritative bi-monthly magazine on the antiques, collectibles, art, artifacts, literature and memorabilia associated with the seas, lakes and waterways.

Cowles Magazines, Inc.
Magazine: Nautical World
741 Miller Dr. SE, Ste. D2
Harrisburg, PA 20175
ph: 717-540-6617 or 800-829-3340
fax: 717-540-6706
e-mail: brentd@cowles.com
web: http://www.cowles.com/maglist.html
Covering the arts, allure and traditions of the sea.

Repair Services

Richard Dermody
Brass n' Bounty
68 Front St.
Marblehead, MA 01945-3275
ph: 617-631-3864 or 617-631-6204
e-mail: dermodys@mediaone.net
web: http://www.brassandbounty.com
Repairs nautical instruments such as compasses, sextants, telescopes; polishes and lacquers marine hardware and lights.

James P. Connor
J.P. Connor & Co.
P.O. Box 305
Devon, PA 19333-0305
ph: 610-644-1474
fax: 610-993-0760
Specialist in antique and modern marine chronometers, deck watches, ship's clocks, barometers, and sextants; buys and sells, appraisals, evaluating, dating; catalog available; repair and restoration services also available.

Diving

(see also SCUBA)

Clubs/Associations

Nick Baker, Sec.
Historical Diving Society
Magazine: Underwater Contractor Magazine
23 Brompton Drive
Brierley Hill, West Midlands DY5 3N7
U.K.
ph: (44) 1384 896079
fax: (44) 1384 896079
e-mail: 101463.726@compuserve.com
web: http://www.resort-guide.co.uk/subsea/hds/
Dedicated to the preservation, study and promotion of our diving heritage; enables individuals, organizations and divers interested in the historical aspect of diving to make academic, social and practical contacts on a national level.

Dealers

Leon Lyons
Helmets of the Deep
P.O. Box 190
Saint Augustine, FL 32085-0190
ph: 904-824-9588
e-mail: amoebus102@aol.com
Collects all types and material of deep sea diving equipment; wrote and published the book "Helmets of the Deep", available from author.

Diving Helmets

Collectors

Dan Cramer
P.O. Box 447
Swartz Creek, MI 48473-0447
ph: 810-635-4957
Wants deep sea diving helmets and related items.

L.D.
P.O. Box 60063
Phoenix, AZ 85082
Wants to buy deep sea diving helmets, especially U.S. Navy Mark V.

Dealers

Larry Pitman
Pioneer Peddler Antiques
5424 Bryan Station Rd.
Paris, KY 40361-9062
ph: 606-299-5022
fax: 606-299-4522
e-mail: zanzibar@uky.campuscw.net
Wants diving helmets.

Repair Services

Diving Equipment & Supply Co.
240 N. Milwaukee St.
Milwaukee, WI 53202
ph: 414-272-2371
Old helmets repaired and reconditioned; in business since 1937.

Figureheads & Ships Carvings

Experts

Sara Conklin
Nautical Appraisals
239 Sierra Pt. Rd.
Brisbane, CA 94005-1664
ph: 415-467-6249
fax: 415-467-6249
e-mail: sconklin2@earthlink.com
Managed the collections of the National Maritime Museum in San Francisco for ten years and is an expert in appraising figureheads and other ship carvings such as trailboards, sternboards, beakboards, and billetheads.

Fishing Floats

Collectors

John Honl
P.O. Box 1201
Kailua Kona, HI 96745-1201
ph: 808-325-9905
e-mail: jonhonl@konacoast.net
Buys and trades glass fishing floats; looking to buy floats with embossing; also wants odd shapes and colors.

Stu Farnsworth
P.O. Box 847
Wilsonville, OR 97070
Has written articles about glass

fishing floats for the "Antique Trader Weekly."

Experts

Stu Farnsworth
P.O. Box 847
Wilsonville, OR 97070-0847
ph: 503-393-9115
Wants to buy glass fishing floats; unusual colors such as pink, lavender, purple, black, cobalt blue, red, orange, etc.; also wants rolling pin floats with writing on side, European floats with embossed markings or characters; no repros.

Lighthouses

Clubs/Associations

Lighthouse Preservation Society, The
4 Middle Street
Newburyport, MA 01950
ph: 978-499-0011 or 800-727-BEAM
fax: 978-499-0026
web: http://www.maine.com/lights/lps.htm
Catalyst for the preservation of lighthouses up and down the nation's coasts.

Timothy Harrison
New England Lighthouse Foundation
P.O. Box 1690
Wells, ME 04090
ph: 800-758-1444 or 207-646-0515
fax: 207-646-0516
e-mail: lhdigest@lhdigest.com
web: http://www.lhdigest.com
Mission is to act as an agency to encourage Historic Preservation, to foster and support local lighthouse initiatives, and to improve public awareness and appreciation of and access to all of New England's lighthouses.

United States Lighthouse Society
Magazine: Keeper's Log
244 Kearney St., 5th Floor
San Francisco, CA 94108
ph: 415-362-7255 or 415-362-7464
web: http://www.maine.com/lights/uslhs.htm
Nonprofit historical/educational society; maintains comprehensive library and archives on lighthouse matters, conducts regional and foreign lighthouse tours, conducts research, hosts photography contests, has state chapters.

Collectors

Bob Glick
Columbia Trading Company
1 Barnstable Rd.
Hyannis, MA 02601
ph: 508-778-2929
fax: 508-778-2922
e-mail: nautical@capecod.net
web: http://www.columbiatrading.com/
Wants to buy items relating to lighthouses.

Timothy Harrison
P.O. Box 1690
Wells, ME 04090
ph: 800-758-1444 or 207-646-0515
fax: 207-646-0516
e-mail: lhdigest@lhdigest.com
web: http://www.lhdigest.com
Wants to buy memorabilia from U.S. Lighthouse Service (USLHS) or U.S. Lighthouse Establishment (USLHE): badges, flags, dinnerware, buttons, uniforms, old photographs of keepers and their families, postcards, newspaper stories.

J. Carol Duncan
Keeper's Lighthouse Establishment
1027 Garden St.
Santa Barbara, CA 93101-1416
ph: 805-963-9129 or 805-965-1174
fax: 805-962-5054
e-mail: jcduncan@aol.com
Wants to buy lighthouse artifacts and antiques: lamps, lanterns, oil cans, maps, photographs, lighthouse keeper items, lighthouse ephemera, Fresnel lens (whole or in parts); also wants to buy Coast Guard items.

Man./Prod./Dist.

Lighthouse Depot
P.O. Box 427
Wells, ME 04090-0427
ph: 800 758 1444
fax: 207-646-0516
e-mail: lhdigest@lhdigest.com
web: http://www.biddeford.com/~lhdigest/catalog/home.html
Issues catalog containing new items having the lighthouse motif: clocks, lamps, figurines, clothing, lighthouse replicas, prints, steins, jewelry boxes, glassware, watches, candles, key fobs, snow globes, etc.

Museums/Libraries

Pete Lesher, Cur.
Chesapeake Bay Maritime Museum
Magazine: Water Gauge, The
P.O. Box 636
Saint Michaels, MD 21663-0636
ph: 410-745-2916
fax: 410-745-6088
e-mail: letters@cbmm.org
web: http://www.cbmm.org
A major regional maritime museum with a 5200 volume research library; collections include 10,000 objects, 9.000 photos, 1,200 ships' plans, 72 linear feet of manuscripts; decoys, oystering, lighthouses, charts, nautical, tools.

Periodicals

Timothy Harrison
Newspaper: Lighthouse Digest
P.O. Box 1690
Wells, ME 04090
ph: 800-758-1444 or 207-646-0515
fax: 207-646-0516
e-mail: lhdigest@lhdigest.com
web: http://www.lhdigest.com
America's only monthly Lighthouse newspaper; issues catalog of a large selection of contemporary lighthouse collectibles.

Maps & Charts

Dealers

W.J. Auburn
Chartifacts
P.O. Box 8954
Richmond, VA 23225-0654
ph: 804-272-7120
e-mail: chart@richmond.infi.net
Buys and sells U.S. Coast Survey maps, charts, sketches, recons; primarily 1850-1871, both original lithographs and selected reprints; issues 1) East Coast, ME to GA, and 2) Gulf and West Coasts, FL to WA catalogs.

Marine Chronometers

Dealers

Marine Antiques & Timepieces
8028 - 238th SW
Edmonds, WA 98020
ph: 425-774-8159
Specializes in Elgin and Hamilton marine chronometers, military timepieces and parts; also other antique and modern marine instruments.

Experts

James P. Connor
J.P. Connor & Co.
P.O. Box 305
Devon, PA 19333-0305
ph: 610-644-1474
fax: 610-993-0760
Specialist in antique and modern marine chronometers, deck watches, ship's clocks, barometers, and sextants; buys and sells, appraisals, evaluating, dating; catalog available; repair and restoration services also available.

Repair Services

Philip M. Poniz
European Watch & Casemakers, Ltd.
P.O. Box 1314
Highland Park, NJ 08904-1314
ph: 732-777-0111
fax: 732-777-0118
e-mail: horology@webspan.net
Restoration of watches, clocks, and music boxes; museum experience; can make any part and restore any watch; clients include Sotheby's, Cartier, collectors in USA, Asia and Europe; appraises, researches, restores chronometers.

Phillip Howard
4220 Virginia Beach Blvd.
Virginia Beach, VA 23452
ph: 757-481-7633
fax: 757-481-1784
Sells marine chronometers (send SASE for list); also repairs and restores; buys chronometers, working or not.

Merchant Marine

Collectors

Ian A. Millar
1806 Bantry Trail
Kernersville, NC 27284-4306
ph: 336-869-1123
Wants memorabilia of the WWI Merchant Marine (U.S. or England): pins, badges, caps, uniforms, medals, awards, photos, etc.; send price.

Museums/Libraries

Harvey Lee Boswell
Palace of Wonders Museum
P.O. Box 446
Elm City, NC 27822-0446
Wants Merchant Marine and U.S. Maritime Service items: flags, uniforms, photos, medals, etc.

Models (Sailboats)

Clubs/Associations

Bruce Bollenbach
Rocky Mountain Shipwrights
Newsletter: Scuttlebutt, The
8046 Lee Court
Arvada, CO 80005
ph: 303-424-7578
e-mail: BDBoll@aol.com
A club for those interested in ship models, especially wooden sailing models; for beginners or advanced; newsletter posted on the internet at http://www.naut-res-guild.org/newsletr/nl-rms.html.

Models (Ship)

Clubs/Associations

Eugene L. Larson
Nautical Research Guild, Inc.
Journal: Nautical Research Journal
9223 Presidential Drive
Alexandria, VA 22309
e-mail: genenrg@Naut-Res-Guild.org
web: http://www.naut-Res-Guild.org
Has been linking researchers, collectors, builders of the highest quality ship models for nearly 50 years; focuses on the story of the ship, the technologies of marine transportation, the shipwrights and sailors.

Dealers

Arrangements Inc., Marine Div.
P.O. Box 126
Mount Kisco, NY 10549-0126
ph: 914-238-1300
Buys, sells, custom builds, appraises, and restores ship models.

Experts

R. Michael Wall
American Marine Model Gallery, Inc.
12 Derby Square
Salem, MA 01970-3704
ph: 978-745-5777
fax: 978-745-5778
e-mail: wall@shipmodel.com
web: http://www.shipmodel.com
Buys, sells, appraises and specializes in model ships; representing the finest work of internationally acclaimed model makers; all models fully documented; 92 pg. illustrated catalog $10.

Sara Conklin
Nautical Appraisals
239 Sierra Pt. Rd.
Brisbane, CA 94005-1664
ph: 415-467-6249
fax: 415-467-6249
e-mail: sconklin2@earthlink.com
Managed the collections of the National Maritime Museum in San Francisco for ten years & is an expert in appraising ship models, ships-in-bottles, marine art, scrimshaw, figureheads, paper ephemera, instruments, whaling, diving equipment.

Internet Resources

Eugene L. Larson
Nautical Research Guild, Inc.
Journal: Nautical Research Journal
9223 Presidential Drive
Alexandria, VA 22309
e-mail: genenrg@Naut-Res-Guild.org
web: http://www.naut-Res-Guild.org
Has been linking researchers, collectors, builders of the highest quality ship models for nearly 50 years; focuses on the story of the ship, the technologies of marine transportation, the shipwrights and sailors.

Periodicals

Jeffrey A. Phillips
Magazine: Model Ship Builder
P.O. Box 128
Cedarburg, WI 53012-0128
ph: 414-377-7888
fax: 414-377-7888
A bi-monthly magazine covering all aspects of building museum-quality model ships including also book, product, and museum reviews.

Repair Services

R. Michael Wall
American Marine Model Gallery, Inc.
12 Derby Square
Salem, MA 01970-3704
ph: 978-745-5777
fax: 978-745-5778
e-mail: wall@shipmodel.com
web: http://www.shipmodel.com
Offers complete professional restoration services, custom models, cases, appraisals.

Rick Fortenberry
Cape Cod Scale Watercraft
1335 Rt. 134
Box 1459
East Dennis, MA 02641-1459
ph: 508-385-4019
fax: 508-385-4019
e-mail: whaler@aol.com
web: http://www.capecod.net/shipmodel/
Construction, restoration, acquisition and display of fine watercraft models.

Al August
44 Cambridge Dr.
Mashpee, MA 02649-2219
ph: 508-477-4169
e-mail: al_august@hotmail.com
Ship model repair; also buys and sells wood ship models old or new in any condition; will buy total or partial wrecks, hulls, kits; will give repair or restoration quotes from good photos; also will buy and sell through photos.

Shipwrecks

Experts

Sara Conklin
Nautical Appraisals
239 Sierra Pt. Rd.
Brisbane, CA 94005-1664
ph: 415-467-6249
fax: 415-467-6249
e-mail: sconklin2@earthlink.com
Managed the collections of the National Maritime Museum in San Francisco for ten years and is an expert in appraising shipwreck material such as vessel fragments and related objects.

Telescopes

Dealers

Daniel J. Vaughn
Spyglass, The
618 Main St.
Chatham, MA 02633
ph: 508-945-9686
Buys, sells, repairs and restores telescopes (especially mounted scopes); world's largest dealer.

NAZI ITEMS

(see also EDGED WEAPONS; MILITARIA; SWORDS, Nazi)

Collectors

J. Burnet
P.O. Box 1472
Massapequa, NY 11758-0908
Wants to buy WWII Nazi relics: flags, helmets, badges, etc.; also wants Adolf Hitler memorabilia: postcards, cigarette cards and albums, silverware, etc.; anything pertaining to Hitler.

K. Wiley
719 Baldwin SE
Grand Rapids, MI 49503-4470
ph: 616-451-8410
e-mail: quillion1@aol.com
Wants Japanese swords, daggers, sword parts. Also German 3rd Reich daggers, swords, bayonets. References available.

Dealers

Brent's Military Antiques
P.O. Box 9255
Greensboro, NC 27429-0255
ph: 336-288-5061
e-mail: bsmith1181@aol.com
Wants WWII Nazi military items: swords, daggers, helmets, medals, hats, uniforms, autographs, etc.

Dr. R.A. Hiett
Maple City Coin
P.O. Drawer 47
Monmouth, IL 61462-0047
ph: 309-734-3212
fax: 309-734-8083
e-mail: hiett@misslink.net
Wants any Nazi or SS related items.

Experts

Col. Terance L. Kelly
P.O. Box 3443
Scottsdale, AZ 85271-3443
Internationally known collector of Nazi era German paraphernalia.

Repro. Sources

Hutchinson House
P.O. Box 41021
Chicago, IL 60641
Sells large selection of reproduction Nazi medals and badges; also war mementos from other countries; illustrated catalog $1.

NEEDLEWORK

(see TEXTILES)

NEON

(see also BREWERIANA; COIN-OPERATED MACHINES; LAMPS & LIGHTING, Neon)

Collectors

Roark Vane
6839 Havenside Dr.
Sacramento, CA 95831-2168
ph: 916-392-3864
e-mail: neonclock@aol.com
Wants to buy vintage neon clocks, small advertising neon signs, neon light bulbs, or other unusual illuminated advertising signs; also signs with "bubble tubes" - glass tubes or letters are filled with a liquid that "bubbles."

Periodicals

Magazine: Gameroom Magazine
P.O. Box 41
Keyport, NJ 07735-0041
ph: 732-739-1955
fax: 732-739-2834
e-mail: coinop@gameroommagazine.com
web: http://www.gameroommagazine.com
A great source of information for the collector and dealer of jukeboxes, pinballs, slot machines, Coke and other soda machines, arcade games, classic arcade video, and other gameroom collectibles.

Clocks

Collectors

Van Stueart
2240 Hwy 27 N
Nashville, AR 71852
ph: 870-845-4864 or 800-577-1810
e-mail: sodaman@iosa.com
Buys and trades all types of advertising neon clocks; also wants Cleveland type neon thermometers.

Dealers

Wayne Woodrum
Wayne's Neon Clocks
10955 Lower Valley Pk.
Medway, OH 45341
ph: 937-849-6727
fax: 937-849-6658
Old, new, parts.

David A. Dyer
Neon Clock
246 Third Ave.
New Lenox, IL 60451
ph: 815-485-5573
fax: 815-485-0483
Old neon clocks bought and sold.

Robert Newman
10809 Charnock Rd.
Los Angeles, CA 90034-6606
ph: 310-559-0539
Wants to buy neon and lighted clocks, with or without advertising.

Repair Services

Tom Arrington
Neon Specialties
P.O. Box 2292
Chapel Hill, NC 27515-2292
ph: 919-932-5747
fax: 919-932-1782
Reproduction and restoration of vintage neon clocks.

NETSUKE

(see also ORIENTALIA)

Clubs/Associations

International Netsuke Society
Journal: International Netsuke Society Journal
P.O. Box 161269
Altamonte Springs, FL 32716
ph: 407-772-1906
fax: 407-772-1907
e-mail: odanuki@worldnet.att.net
web: http://www.netsuke.org/
Over 600 members in 25 countries; celebrates 20th anniversary in 1995.

Dealers

Michael Spindel
Gallery of Fine Netsuke
163 Third Avenue, Ste. 295
New York, NY 10003
ph: 212-353-3666
fax: 212-353-3667
e-mail: mspindel@mindspring.com
web: http://www.spindel.com/
Specializes in contemporary and antique netsuke.

Bill Egleston
509 Brentwood Rd.
Marshalltown, IA 50158-3727
ph: 800-798-4579
fax: 515-752-4570
Specializing in mail order sale of Oriental art, jade, cloisonne, netsuke, etc.; send for catalog.

Periodicals

Joan L. Cervi
Newsletter: Netsuke & Ivory Carving Newsletter-Video
3203 Adams Way
Ambler, PA 19002-3741
ph: 215-628-2026
fax: 215-628-2026
e-mail: jcnetsuke@aol.com
A wholesaler who offers VHS videos and a monthly newsletter about imported netsuke, ivory carvings and other Orientalia.

NEWSBOY ITEMS

(see also NEWSPAPERS)

Clubs/Associations

B. J. Hughes
Newspaper Memorabilia Collectors Network
P.O. Box 797
Watertown, NY 13601-0797
Newsletter published quarterly; members interested in old newspapers as well as newsboy related memorabilia.

Mark Peters
Newspaper Memorabilia Collectors Network
Newsletter: NMCN Newsletter
504 Boynton Ave.
Berkeley, CA 94707-1704
ph: 510-525-7972
fax: 510-525-7972
e-mail: marpet24@aol.com
For collectors of items relating to newspaper promotion and circulation, and newsboy items.

Collectors

Mark Peters
504 Boynton Ave.
Berkeley, CA 94707-1704
ph: 510-525-7972
fax: 510-525-7972
e-mail: marpet24@aol.com
Wants to buy newsboy memorabilia including badges, buttons, ephemera, figurines, photos, books, etc.; anything related to newsboys.

Experts

Tony Lee
P.O. Box 134
Monmouth Junction, NJ 08852-0134
ph: 201-429-1531
Collector and dealer of badges and other credentials issued to newsboys, as well as the buttons, ribbons, aprons and hats they wore to advertise the newspapers they sold.

NEWSPAPERS

(see also COMIC STRIPS, Sunday Newspaper; PAPER COLLECTIBLES; PERIODICALS; NEWSBOY ITEMS)

Auction Services

Robert Raynor
Historical Collectible Auctions
P.O. Box 975
Burlington, NC 27215
ph: 336-570-2803
fax: 336-570-2748
e-mail: info@hcaauctions.com
web: http://www.hcaauctions.com/
Buys, sells historic newspapers from 1760 through 1945; also conducts periodic mail/phone bid auctions of old collectible newspapers.

Rick Brown
History Buff's Auction
6031 Winterset
Lansing, MI 48911
ph: 517-887-1255 or 517-887-8027
e-mail: info@historybuff.com
web: http://www.historybuff.com
Consignors with historical ephemera wanted for major auctions held several times each year on the Internet.

Clubs/Associations

B. J. Hughes
Newspaper Memorabilia Collectors Network
P.O. Box 797
Watertown, NY 13601-0797
Newsletter published quarterly; members interested in old newspapers as well as newsboy related memorabilia.

Collectors

Gene Peters
'Tiques
P.O. Box 3267
Farmingdale, NY 11735-0679
ph: 516-842-9549
Wants 18th and 19th C. newspapers and articles documenting the African-American experience.

B. J. Hughes
P.O. Box 797
Watertown, NY 13601-0797

Joe Weber
604 Centre St.
Ashland, PA 17921-1332
ph: 570-875-4787 or 570-875-4401
Wants to buy pre-1890 newspapers, especially those discussing important events; also papers from Pennsylvania; will advise others.

Dealers

Phil Barber
Historic Newspapers & Early Imprints
P.O. Box 8694
Boston, MA 02114-0036
ph: 617-492-4653
fax: 617-868-1534
e-mail: barber10@channel1.com
web: http://www.channel1.com/barbernews/
Buying and selling fine paper collectibles since 1979; specializes in historic newspapers from the period 1775 to 1865; also early Bible leaves, and ephemera dating 1440 to 1940.

Eric Caren
Caren Archives, The
P.O. Box 185
Lincolndale, NY 10540-0185
ph: 914-248-8038
fax: 914-248-6439
e-mail: info@historicalnews.com
web: http://www.historicalnews.com/
Buys and sells Americana, Western, rare Newspapers.

Kyle Rothgeb
Yesterday's News
67 Chapel St.
Kingston, NY 12401
ph: 914-339-8930
e-mail: greywoulfe@aol.com
web: http://members.tripod.com/~greywoulfe/index2.html
Collector and dealer of old and rare newspapers dating from the late 1700s to present; has written a manual, "Yesterday's News," for other collectors to explain the proper way of storing and displaying newspapers.

Michael Kelly
Paper Pandemonium
1321 Jack's Mountain Road
Fairfield, PA 17320
ph: 717-642-8019
e-mail: kellym@mail.cvn.net
web: http://www.tias.com/stores/pp
Buys and sells whole newspapers and front pages only of famous historical events; also old comic sections.

Timothy Hughes
Timothy Hughes Rare & Early Newspapers
P.O. Box 3636
Williamsport, PA 17701-8636
ph: 570-326-1045
fax: 570-326-7606
e-mail: tim@rarenewspapers.com
web: http://www.rarenewspapers.com
Buys and sells old newspapers; Colonial era through 1965; catalog of offerings for $2.

Bob Morris
706 Pawnee St.
Bethlehem, PA 18015-1432
ph: 610-865-9052
Wants to purchase bound volumes of newspapers; Colonial to 1900; also wants Harpers's.

Steve Goldman
Stephen Goldman Historical Newspapers
P.O. Box 359
Parkton, MD 21120
ph: 410-357-8204
e-mail: info@historicalnews.com
web: http://www.historicalnews.com/
Buys and sells historical newspapers, large or small quantities, bound volumes, single issues; from 18th, 19th, or 20th centuries.

Mark E. Mitchell
Original Historic Newspapers, Letters & Documents
3002 Winter Pine Ct.
Fairfax, VA 22031-1125
ph: 703-591-3150
fax: 703-385-3152
e-mail: info@mitchellarchives.com
web: http://www.mitchellarchives.com/
Buys and sells 1620-1945 original high quality newspapers and periodicals; including Amer. Rev., Civil War, Harper's Weekly.

Robert Raynor
Vintage Cover Story
P.O. Box 975
Burlington, NC 27215
ph: 336-570-2803
fax: 336-570-2748
e-mail: info@hcaauctions.com
web: http://www.hcaauctions.com/
Buys, sells historic newspapers from 1760 through 1945; also conducts periodic mail/phone bid auctions of old collectible newspapers.

Experts

Rick Brown
6031 Winterset
Lansing, MI 48911
ph: 517-887-1255 or 517-887-8027
e-mail: info@historybuff.com
web: http://www.historybuff.com
Collects, appraises and specializes in old newspapers.

Internet Resources

Rick Brown
History Buff's Home Page/Online
6031 Winterset
Lansing, MI 48911
ph: 517-887-1255 or 517-887-8027
e-mail: info@historybuff.com
web: http://www.historybuff.com
On-line magazine with over 600 files of information about old and historic newspapers; files include price guide, collector primer, reprint guide and much more.

Museums/Libraries

Newseum
1101 Wilson Blvd.
Arlington, VA 22209
ph: 703-284-3725 or 888-NEWSEUM
e-mail: newseum@freedomforum.org
web: http://www.newseum.org
World's only interactive museum of news, news gathering, news reporting, journalism; showcases hundreds of objects associated with news events and news people, historic broadcasts, newspapers and magazines.

Harpers Weekly

Dealers

Dale W. Rose
104 Tern Court
Wilmington, DE 19808
ph: 302-239-3150
"Harpers Weekly" specialist offers original engravings: Civil War through 1897; all sports, city views, firemen, Indians, Santas, Presidents and other political.

NICKELODEONS

(see CAROUSELS & CAROUSEL FIGURES; MUSICAL INSTRUMENTS, Mechanical [Band Organs])

NIGHT LIGHTS

(see FAIRY LAMPS; LAMPS & LIGHTING, Miniature; PERFUME LAMPS)

NIGHTCLUB MEMORABILIA

Collectors

Bruce Fernie
121 Newbury St.
Boston, MA 02116
ph: 617-859-8593
fax: 617-859-0043
Wants nightclub and high life memorabilia, '20s-'50s; ashtrays, china, barware, tablephotos, matches, menus, ads, glassware, etc; anything from the Stork Club, El Morocco, The Copa, etc.

T. M.
1015 S. Cedar Rd.
Minneapolis, MN 55405
ph: 612-374-1162
Wants to buy memorabilia from American nightclubs that featured entertainment and/or gambling, 1930-1960.

NIPPER

(see PHONOGRAPHS, Nipper)

NIPPON

(see also CERAMICS [ORIENTAL], Nippon)

NORMAN ROCKWELL

(see ILLUSTRATORS, Norman Rockwell; COLLECTIBLES [MODERN], Norman Rockwell)

NUMISMATICS

(see COINS & CURRENCY; MEDALS, ORDERS & DECORATIONS; SOUVENIR CARDS; TOKENS)

NURSES

(see also RED CROSS)

Collectors

M. Brunswick
P.O. Box 9729
Baltimore, MD 21286-9729
e-mail: brunswickm@hotmail.com
Wants books illustrating baby and child care, home nursing, basic nursing treatments and procedures, sick care, home health, nursing school manuals and films, etc.; prefer 1900-1970, especially photo-illustrated; also foreign.

Dealers

UHR Books
P.O. Box 306
Hollis Center, ME 04042
ph: 207-929-5100
e-mail: uhrbooks@uhrbooks.com
web: http://www.uhrbooks.com
Wants nurse and nursing related items: old books, postcards, magazines, sheet music, prints, posters, photos, dolls, diplomas, letters, diaries, pins and caps.

NUT RELATED COLLECTIBLES

Museums/Libraries

Elizabeth Tashjian
Nut Museum, The
303 Ferry Rd.
Old Lyme, CT 06371-1615
ph: 860-434-7616
web: http://www.roadsideamerica.com/nut/CTOLDmus.html
Focuses on the hard-shell fruit.

Nutcrackers

Clubs/Associations

Steinbach/KSA Collectible Nutcracker Club
1107 Broadway
New York, NY 10010
ph: 212-924-0900 or 800-243-9627
fax: 212-807-0575
Collectors of contemporary German hand-carved wooden figurals.

Susan Otto
Nutcracker Collectors' Club
12204 Fox Run Drive
Chesterland, OH 44026
ph: 440-729-2686

Collectors

Nutcrackers, Etc.
P.O. Box 6337
Tyler, TX 757116337
ph: 903-531-9747 or 903-597-8090
fax: 903-597-4035
Wants to buy ornamental and figural nutcrackers, plus carved wooden heads and figurals.

Claudia J. Davis
East 4400 English Point Rd.
Hayden, ID 83835
ph: 208-772-6801
fax: 208-772-5311
World's largest nutcracker collection; bronze, iron, ivory, brass, porcelain, wood.

Experts

James E. Anthony
6300 Indian Creek Dr.
Fort Worth, TX 76116
ph: 817-732-4724 or 817-279-7056
fax: 817-279-7057
e-mail: anthony6@flash.net
Nutcracker collector and expert.

NUTS & BOLTS

(see FASTENERS)

OCCUPIED GERMANY

Clubs/Associations

Larry L. Krug
Occupied Germany Collectors Club
18222 Flower Hill Way, #299
Gaithersburg, MD 20879-5300
ph: 301-926-8663
fax: 301-926-7648
e-mail: info@amres.com
web: http://www.amres.com
Collectors of items produced in Germany following World War II and marked "U.S. Zone," "British Zone," or "French Zone."

Collectors

Larry L. Krug
Americana Resources, Inc.
18222 Flower Hill Way, #299
Gaithersburg, MD 20879-5300
ph: 301-926-8663
fax: 301-926-7648
e-mail: info@amres.com
web: http://www.amres.com

OCCUPIED JAPAN

Clubs/Associations

Florence Archambault
Occupied Japan Club, The
Newsletter: Upside Down World of an O.J. Collector, The
29 Freeborn St.
Newport, RI 02840-1821
ph: 401-846-9024
e-mail: florence@aiconnect.com
Focuses on Japanese-made items marked "Occupied Japan"; newsletter includes free buy/sell ads, up-to-date price information, lots of photos, and more; newsletter published bi-monthly; send SASE for more information.

Collectors

Margaret Bolbat
8714 Alicia St.
Philadelphia, PA 19115-4103
ph: 215-671-1766
e-mail: ojane@starlinx.com
Advanced collector looking for quality bisque and porcelain, large bisque birds, American children, objects with Mioj Hokutosha mark, books pamphlets, maps or paper marked "Printed in Occupied Japan.

Linda Trew Ahlfield-Bruhn
Divine Inc.
107 Col Dunovant Ct.
Bluffton, SC 29910
ph: 910-868-3259
e-mail: kagneys@aol.com
Wants figurines only: Pixies, any figurines over 6# high, ethnic figurines, mermaids and dancers; no cups, plates, fans or metal items.

Dealers

Stephanie Seguin
Occupied Attic, The
1 Gleneagles Blvd.
Ballston Lake, NY 12019
ph: 518-899-5030
fax: 518-899-7841
e-mail: occupied-attic@usa.net
Buys and sells Occupied Japan items; also a member of the OJ Club; deals mostly with unusual items, e.g. sewing machines, rugs, dinnerware sets, tea sets, toys, large figurines and bisque; deals in US and in Japan.

Bradford W. Crumb
Occupied with Toys & Antiques
1129 Fairlane Drive
Aliquippa, PA 15001-1735
ph: 412-375-5773 or 412-913-8114
fax: 412-375-6243
e-mail: occtoys@bigfoot.com
web: http://idt.net/~occtoy19/
Specializes in Occupied Japan collectibles and wind-up toys from the 1920s through 1950s.

Experts

Florence Archambault
29 Freeborn St.
Newport, RI 02840-1821
ph: 401-846-9024
e-mail: florence@aiconnect.com
Author of "Occupied Japan Collectibles."

OCEAN LINER COLLECTIBLES

(see also DINNERWARE, Advertising; NAUTICAL ANTIQUES; SHIPPING; SHIP RELATED; STEAMBOAT COLLECTIBLES; TITANIC MEMORABILIA; TRANSPORTATION COLLECTIBLES)

Clubs/Associations

Sue Ewen
Steamship Historical Society of America, Inc.
Magazine: Steamboat Bill
300 Ray Dr., Ste. #4
Providence, RI 02906
ph: 401-274-0805
web: http://www.sshsa.org/
For those interested in maritime history; publishes high quality quarterly magazine; has photo bank of thousands of negatives of powered vessels, national and regional meetings.

Charles Ira Sachs
Oceanic Navigation Research Society, Inc.
Journal: Ship To Shore
P.O. Box 8005
Universal City, CA 91618-8005
ph: 818-985-1345
fax: 818-985-1345
e-mail: onrs@earthlink.net
web: http://www.titanic.org/
Studies the history of ocean liner travel with a focus on the transatlantic service from 1840 to present; quarterly journal focuses on a topic or ship using rare illustrations and memorabilia to highlight this romantic era of travel.

Collectors

Ken Schultz
P.O. Box M753
Hoboken, NJ 07030
ph: 201-656-0966
fax: 201-418-8640
Wants all items relating to ocean liners: brochures, deck plans, souvenirs, postcards, models, menus, etc.

Frederick Lingenfelser
814 Byram St.
Reading, PA 19606-1446
Wants to buy pre-1945 ocean liner collectibles: post cards, letters, ship blue prints, deck plans, books, tickets, brochures, dinnerware, souvenirs, models, menus, etc.; especially wants Titanic items.

Dave Cooper
2900 Faulkland Rd.
Wilmington, DE 19808-2514
ph: 302-999-9940
e-mail: dcooper@synerfac.com
Collects White Star Line china, silver, souvenirs (no paper, please).

Randy Ridgely
447 Oglethorpe Ave.
Athens, GA 30606-2236
ph: 706-549-9264
e-mail: erie@negia.net
Wants railroad, steamship and airline items.

Robert L. Loewenthal
10161 SW 1st Court
Fort Lauderdale, FL 33324-2226
ph: 954-474-4246
fax: 954-382-1213
e-mail: bobship@earthlink.net
Wants to buy ocean liner memorabilia: postcards, china, silver, deck plans, models, posters, books, paper, etc.

New Steamship Consultants
P.O. Box 30088
Mesa, AZ 85275-0088
e-mail: ships@oceanliner.com
web: http://www.oceanliner.com/
Wants ocean liner deck plans, brochures, menus, etc.; world's largest buyers of all ships and lines; quote or send on approval.

Bill Gardner
P.O. Box 1031
Desert Hot Springs, CA 92240-0914
ph: 760-251-4546
Wants old liner cabin plans, view booklets, posters, pictures, reference books, etc. that promote ship travel.

Dave Lathom
P.O. Box 5053
Bellingham, WA 98227-5053
ph: 360-676-0715
e-mail: china@telcomplus.net
Wants to buy U.S. and Canadian steamship china and memorabilia, especially Pacific Coast, Northwest, and Great Lakes and river operations.

E.S. Radcliffe
3732 Colonial Lane SE
Port Orchard, WA 98366-1846
ph: 206-876-8615
Wants pre-1940 ocean liner related items: brochures, labels, cards, tableware, books, souvenirs and all paper items.

Dealers

Richard C. Faber, Jr.
230 E. 15th St.
New York, NY 10003
ph: 212-228-7353
fax: 212-477-9392
Wants booklets, china, deck plans, models, souvenirs, posters, etc. from Lusitania, Titanic, Normandie, Queen Mary, Andrea Doria, etc.

George Theofiles
Miscellaneous Man
P.O. Box 1776
New Freedom, PA 17349-0191
ph: 717-235-4766
fax: 717-235-2853
Buys and sells posters and ocean liner ephemera.

David Rhinehart
ShipShape
1041 Tuscany Place
Winter Park, FL 32789-1017
ph: 407-644-2892
fax: 407-644-1833
e-mail: shipshape@shipshape.com
web: http://www.shipshape.com
Buy, sell ocean liner (cruise ship) china, silver, models, deck plans, souvenirs, ephemera.

Robert L. Loewenthal
10161 SW 1st Court
Fort Lauderdale, FL 33324-2226
ph: 954-474-4246
fax: 954-382-1213
e-mail: bobship@earthlink.net
Wants ocean line memorabilia: postcards, china, books, pictures, silverplate, posters, deck plans, models, etc.

Ered Matthew
Cabin Class Collectibles
P.O. Box 740474
Dallas, TX 75374-0474
ph: 972-235-8639
e-mail: ematt@msn.com
web: http://www.cabinclass.com
Buys and sells fine ocean liner memorabilia on the Internet.

New Steamship Consultants
P.O. Box 30088
Mesa, AZ 85275-0088
e-mail: ships@oceanliner.com
web: http://www.oceanliner.com/

Experts

Charles Ira Sachs
TransAtlantic Research
P.O. Box 8005
Universal City, CA 91618-8005
ph: 818-985-1345
fax: 818-985-1345
e-mail: onrs@earthlink.net
web: http://www.titanic.org/
Buys/sells/specializes/lectures on ocean liner and zeppelin history & memorabilia from the high seas (i.e. none from coastal or river steamers)

dating from 1840 to 1960s; posters, postcards and related material for collectors/museums.

Sara Conklin
Nautical Appraisals
239 Sierra Pt. Rd.
Brisbane, CA 94005-1664
ph: 415-467-6249
fax: 415-467-6249
e-mail: sconklin2@earthlink.com
Managed the collections of the National Maritime Museum in San Francisco for ten years and is an expert in appraising Titanic and other ocean liner objects and related paper ephemera and archival collections.

Museums/Libraries

South Street Seaport Museum
207 Front St.
New York, NY 10038
ph: 212-748-8600
e-mail: webmaster@SouthStSeaport.org
web: http://www.southstseaport.org/

Periodicals

R.D. Roland
R.S. & T. Ry. Co.
Ad Paper: Main Line Journal, The
P.O. Box 121
Streamwood, IL 60107-0121
A bi-monthly "ad" paper exclusively for buying and selling railroad collectibles as well as airline and steamship memorabilia; subscribers receive FREE ads.

ODDITIES

(see MORBID & ODD ITEMS; GUINNESS WORLD RECORDS; RIPLEY'S BELIEVE IT OR NOT)

OFFICE EQUIPMENT

(see also ADDING MACHINES; CALCULATORS; CLOCKS, Time; INSTRUMENTS & DEVICES; PAPER CLIPS; PENCIL SHARPENERS; PENS; PENCILS; TYPEWRITERS)

Clubs/Associations

Darryl Rehr, Ed.
Early Typewriter Collectors Association
Magazine: ETCetera
P.O. Box 641824
Los Angeles, CA 90064
ph: 310-477-5229
fax: 310-268-8420
e-mail: dcrehr@earthlink.net
web: http://home.earthlink.net/~dcrehr/
An international club for collectors of old office equipment; provides contact with worldwide network of over 500 members; free ads.

Internationales Forum Historische Burowelt
Magazine: Historische Burowelt
P.O. Box 50 11.19
Koln, D-50971
Germany
ph: 941-925-0385
fax: 941-925-0487
Quarterly magazine in German for members of the I.F.H.B. only; in non-German speaking countries with English summaries only.

Collectors

William Feigin
Dualoy, Inc.
45 W. 34th St., Ste. 811
New York, NY 10001-3008
ph: 212-736-3360
fax: 212-594-8327
Wants to buy very old check writers, check perforators, staplers in working condition.

Uwe H. Breker
6731 Ashley Ct.
Sarasota, FL 34241-9696
ph: 941-925-0385
fax: 941-925-0487
e-mail: auction@breker.com
web: http://www.breker.com/
Wants to buy office equipment, typewriters, calculators, pre-1900 printing presses and equipment, adding machines, pencil sharpeners, office literature and magazines.

Bob Titus
P.O. Box 265
Pomeroy, OH 45769-0265
ph: 740-992-5052
Wants to buy early typewriters (Hammond, Peoples, World, etc.); also wants early adding machines by Burroughs and Comptometer.

Don Bryant
Bryant Office Machine Repairs
4819 Stallcup
Mesquite, TX 75150-1143
ph: 972-270-0135
fax: 972-613-1627
e-mail: aplayr@airmail.net
Collector since 1956.

Larry Wilhelm
P.O. Box 1922
Wichita Falls, TX 76307-1922
Wants to buy old calculators, adding machines or devices, typewriters, check writers, etc.

Carole Meeker
5702 Vacation Blvd.
Somerset, CA 95684-9324
ph: 530-620-7019
fax: 530-620-7020
e-mail: clm@inforum.net
Wants to buy rare and unusual small patented mechanical antiques, early American technology and occupational-related photography, advertising and catalogs.

Dealers

William Feigin
Dualoy, Inc.
45 W. 34th St., Ste. 811
New York, NY 10001-3008
ph: 212-736-3360
fax: 212-594-8327
Buys and sells very old check writers, check perforators, staplers in working condition.

GiGi Konwin
Olde Office, The
68-845 Perez Road, Ste. 30
Cathedral City, CA 92234
ph: 800-246-8558 or 760-346-8653
fax: 760-346-6479
e-mail: info@thisoldeoffice.com
web: http://www.thisoldeoffice.com
Complete online catalog of vintage office equipment including typewriters, adding machines, check protectors and other office items.

Experts

Trent Condellone, Esq.
P.O. Box 2741
Springfield, MO 65801-2741
ph: 417-868-8274
fax: 417-831-7688
e-mail: TCondellone@worldnet.att.net
web: http://home.att.net/~tcondellone
Buys, collects and specializes in adding machines, calculating devices, teletypes, clipless stand machines, and any advertising pieces, manuals, parts, tools, etc. relating to the above.

OIL COMPANY MEMORABILIA

(see GAS STATION COLLECTIBLES)

OIL DRILLING COLLECTIBLES

Museums/Libraries

Oil Museum
821 West Main St.
Hill City, KS 67642-1937
ph: 785-674-5621
web: http://www.ruraltel.net/gced/oil.htm

OINTMENT POTS

(see POT LIDS)

OLD SLEEPY EYE

Clubs/Associations

Jim Martin
Old Sleepy Eye Collectors Club of America
Newsletter: Sleepy Eye Newsletter
P.O. Box 12
Monmouth, IL 61462-0012
ph: 309-734-2703
e-mail: oseclub@maplecity.com
web: http://www.maplecity.com/~oseclub/
Based in Monmouth, IL, home of Western Stoneware Co., the plant where Sleepy Eye pottery was produced; club dedicated to the collecting and preservation of items related to the Sleepy Eye Milling Co. of Sleepy Eye, MN.

OLYMPIC GAMES COLLECTIBLES

(see also PINS; SPORTS COLLECTIBLES; STAMP COLLECTING, Sports Related)

Collectors

Harvey & Sandy Dolin
Harvey Dolin & Co.
5 Beekman St.
New York, NY 10038-2206
ph: 212-267-0216
Wants to buy Olympic items.

Kenneth Nix
307 Rosewood Dr.
Dublin, GA 31021-4133
ph: 912-275-0281 or 912-272-4335
fax: 912-272-4972
e-mail: knix@nlamerica.com
Wants Olympic memorabilia from the Atlanta, 1996 Games; especially wants media pins and badges, and Atlanta Session badges.

Jim Greensfelder
5825 Squire Hill Ct.
Cincinnati, OH 45241-6021
ph: 513-489-6750
fax: 513-489-6757
e-mail: medal_man@fuse.net
Wants to buy, sell or trade Olympic pins, medals, torches, automobile items, clothing, banners, uniforms, badges, mugs, steins, anything.

Jim Clark
6100 Walnut Street
Kansas City, MO 64113-2236
ph: 816-361-4311
Wants anything related to the Olympics: pins, dolls, coins, toys, mascots, displays, and anything marked with the Olympic rings.

Alan Polsky
4086 Hayvenhurst Dr.
Encino, CA 91436-3645
e-mail: OLYARP@aol.com
Wants any original Olympic Games

memorabilia including medallions, badges worn by athletes, press and officials, programs, pins, torches, etc.

John & Virginia Torney
P.O. Box 2387
Huntington Beach, CA 92647-0387
ph: 714-840-7778
e-mail: vjtorney@earthlink.net
Olympic Games memorabilia wanted; all years; winter and summer games; wants medals, badges, torches, pins, flags, diplomas, documents, programs, uniforms, etc.

Dealers

Ray Smith
P.O. Box 254
Elizabeth, NJ 07207-0254
ph: 908-354-5224
fax: 908-352-1576
e-mail: cgs918@aol.com
Buys and sells Olympic memorabilia: posters, pins, medals, ephemera, wire photos, programs, cigarette cards, uniforms, autographs, tickets, etc.

Internet Resources

U.S. Olympic Committee Online
One Olympic Plaza
Colorado Springs, CO 80909-5760
ph: 719-578-4948
fax: 719-632-02504
e-mail: usoc.online@usoc.org
web: http://www.usoc.org/
The U.S. Olympic Committee offers many licensed items with all purchases from their Online Store.

Pins & Buttons

Clubs/Associations

Don Bigsby
Olympic Pin Collector's Club
1386 5th St.
Schenectady, NY 12303
ph: 518-355-9445
The largest pin trading club in North America.

Rowan Fay
International Pin Collectors Club
Newsletter: IPCC Newsletter
602 Chenango St.
Binghamton, NY 13901-2029
ph: 607-724-4583 or 607-723-7421
fax: 607-723-3687
e-mail: rhfay@juno.com
Interested in all sorts of pins: Olympic, Coca Cola, sports, Desert Storm, media, etc.

Collectors

Don Bigsby
1386 5th St.
Schenectady, NY 12303
ph: 518-355-9445

Dealers

Rowan Fay
602 Chenango St.
Binghamton, NY 13901-2029
ph: 607-724-4583 or 607-723-7421
fax: 607-723-3687
e-mail: rhfay@juno.com
Buys and sells Olympic memorabilia and pins.

Rick Amari
Wreckme's Olympic Pin Trader
111 Misty Oak Place
Gahanna, OH 43230
ph: 614-471-1112
fax: 614-471-3606
e-mail: wreckme@usa.net
web: http://wreckme.simplenet.com
Great web site for Olympic pin traders and enthusiasts; site includes over 400 pins (with photos) from all Olympics from 1980 through 2004; new pins added every week; links to pin discussion groups, pin auctions, pin information.

Bill Nelson
Newsletter: Bill Nelson Newsletter, The
P.O. Box 41630
Tucson, AZ 85717-1630
ph: 520-629-0868 or 800-368-8434
fax: 520-629-0387
web: http://www.billnelsonnewsletter.com
Monthly newsletter with news, tips, and sources for collectors of Olympic, Sport, Disney, Coca Cola pins; over a million pins inventory; established in 1985.

OPENERS

(see BOTTLE OPENERS; CAN OPENERS; CORKSCREWS)

OPTICAL ITEMS

(see also BINOCULARS; CAMERAS & CAMERA EQUIPMENT; EYE RELATED ITEMS; INSTRUMENTS & DEVICES; KALEIDOSCOPES; MEDICAL, DENTAL & PHARMACEUTICAL; MAGIC LANTERNS & SLIDES; MICROSCOPES; STANHOPES; STEREO VIEWERS & STEREOVIEWS; 3-D PHOTOGRAPHICA; TOYS, Optical)

Appraisers

J. William Rosenthal, MD, ISA
3434 Prytania St., Ste. 250
New Orleans, LA 70115-3551
ph: 504-891-1988 or 504-895-1673
fax: 504-845-1657
e-mail: JWRosenHar@aol.com
Buys, sells, specializes in and appraises visual aids, spectacles, lorgnettes, opera glasses; author of "Spectacles and Other Visual Aids: A History and Guide to Collecting."

Auction Services

Bryan W. Ginns
2109 Cty. Rte. 21
Valatie, NY 12184-6001
ph: 518-392-5805
fax: 518-392-7925
e-mail: the3dman@aol.com
Conducts mail sales specializing in optical items such as cameras, magic lantern slide projectors, stereographica, polyorama pantoptiques, praxinoscopes, zeotropes, kinoras, coin-operated mutoscopes, etc.

Clubs/Associations

J. William Rosenthal, MD, ISA
Ocular Heritage Society
3434 Prytania St., Ste. 250
New Orleans, LA 70115-3551
ph: 504-891-1988 or 504-895-1673
fax: 504-845-1657
e-mail: JWRosenHar@aol.com
Annual meetings, sale, lectures.

Collectors

Valda J. Tull
467 West Market St.
York, PA 17404

Jon Lewin
622 Raleigh Ave., Apt. 3
Norfolk, VA 23507-2034
ph: 757-625-6732
Wants to buy eye-massagers (looks like binoculars with rubber bulb intended to squirt air at eyes), collections of old eye glasses (with telescoping ear pieces, no nose pads), microscopes, kaleidoscopes, and anything optical and exotic.

Maret Webb
4118 East Vernon Ave.
Phoenix, AZ 85008-2333
ph: 602-957-0653
fax: 602-957-1631
Wants to buy antique spyglasses, telescopes, microscopes.

Dealers

C. Keith Wilbur, M.D.
Doctor's Bag, The
397 Prospect St.
Northampton, MA 01060-2047
ph: 413-584-1440
Buys, sells, appraises apothecary, medical, dental, surgical, optical & quack instruments, equipment, advertising, books, etc.; catalogs available 3 to 4 times a year; author of "Antique Medical Instruments" and other books.

Al & Bobbie Roberts
Rational Past, The
221 Oceano Dr.
Los Angeles, CA 90049-4123
ph: 310-476-6277
fax: 310-476-6278
e-mail: rational_past@mindspring.com
Organizer of West Coast Scientific & Technical Antique and Collectible Shows (Los Angeles in the winter and San Francisco are in late summer.)

ORDNANCE

(see AMMUNITION & EXPLOSIVE ORDNANCE)

ORIENTALIA

(see also ARMS & ARMOR; ART, Asian; ART, Oriental; BRONZES; CERAMICS [ORIENTAL]; CLOISONNE; FURNITURE [ANTIQUE], Chinese; INDONESIA; IVORY; JADE; PHILIPPINES; NETSUKE; PRINTS, Woodblock [Japanese]; SILVER, Chinese; SNUFF BOTTLES)

Appraisers

Patricia Graham
Asian Art Research & Appraisals
1641 Rhode Island St.
Lawrence, KS 66044
ph: 785-841-1477
fax: 785-841-1477
e-mail: p-graham@ukans.edu
Serves as a consultant on Asian fine arts to private collections, businesses, and museums; does IRS, estate and insurance appraisals; specializes in Japanese paintings, prints and ceramics; also Chinese, and Korean.

Elisabeth Douglas, ISA
China Coast, The
11266 Taylor Draper Lane, #2024
Austin, TX 78759
ph: 512-288-3043 or 512-789-7507
fax: 512-345-8420
e-mail: wien@texas.net
Specializes in the appraisal of Oriental art including Chinese, Japanese, Korean, Southeast Asian, and Indian; fine art as well as folk art.

Elisabeth Weikert Douglas
China Coast Oriental Art Appraisal Services
11266 Taylor Draper Lane, Apt. 2024
Austin, TX 78759-3972
ph: 512-288-3043
fax: 512-345-8420
e-mail: wien@texas.net
Active in the field of Asian art and antiques for over 20 years; owned and operated antiques export service in Bangkok, Thailand; owned and operated Oriental art and antiques shop in Washington DC.

Scott Singer, ISA
411 W. Galer St.
Seattle, WA 98119
ph: 206-285-0394
fax: 206-283-5264
Specializes in Asian art, furniture, porcelain, pottery, ceramics.

Auction Services

Stuart Slavid
Skinner, Inc.
357 Main St.
Bolton, MA 01740-1104
ph: 978-779-6241
fax: 978-779-5144
e-mail: info@skinnerinc.com
web: http://www.skinnerinc.com
Established in 1964, Skinner Inc. is the fifth largest auction house in the US; has offices in Bolton and Boston, MA.

John H. Schofield
Eldred's
P.O. Box 796
East Dennis, MA 02641-0796
ph: 508-385-3116
fax: 508-385-7201
e-mail: eldreds@capecod.net
web: http://www.eldreds.com/
Specialists with annual week-long series of auction dedicated to Orientalia for over 25 years.

Sotheby's
1334 York Ave.
New York, NY 10021
ph: 212-606-7000
fax: 212-606-7107
web: http://www.sothebys.com
Over 70 collecting areas are featured at Sotheby's auctions including toys, dolls, porcelain, furniture, silver, art, books; exhibitions are free and everyone is welcome; for a free copy of "Sotheby's Newsletter", call 212-606-7245.

Christie's
502 Park Ave.
New York, NY 10022
ph: 212-546-1000
fax: 212-980-8163
web: http://www.christies.com

Lynn Martin
Freeman/Fine Arts of Philadelphia
1808 Chestnut St.
Philadelphia, PA 19103
ph: 610-563-9275 or 610-563-9453
fax: 610-563-8236
web: http://www.artlibrary.com/freeman/
America's oldest auction house: Continental, English and American furniture, paintings, silver and decorative arts; Oriental rugs, rare books, fine jewelry, Orientalia.

Isadore M. Chait
I.M. Chait Gallery
9330 Civic Center Drive
Beverly Hills, CA 90210
ph: 310-285-0182
fax: 310-285-9740
e-mail: IMChait@chait.com
web: http://www.chait.com
Appraiser, auctioneer, expert in Oriental antiques and art; monthly auctions of approximately 450 mostly period lots; also has a retail store; specializes in Han, T'ang, Sung, Ming, Ching, and other dynasties.

Butterfield & Butterfield
220 San Bruno Ave.
San Francisco, CA 94103-5018
ph: 415-861-7500
fax: 415-861-8951
e-mail: info@butterfields.com
web: http://www.butterfields.com/
Specialties include posters, toys, decorative arts, furniture, photography, etc.; the largest full service auction in the west.

McClain Auctions
825 Halekauwila St.
Honolulu, HI 96813-5315
ph: 808-538-7227 or 808-596-3900
fax: 808-545-7007

Clubs/Associations

Byla Simon Kunis, ISA, Pres.
Oriental Art Society of Chicago
P.O. Box 59863
Chicago, IL 60659-0863
ph: 773-761-2907
fax: 773-761-0789
Brings together and enriches members through viewing, sharing knowledge and information about Orientalia; programs and field trips.

Dealers

Circle of the Moon Antiques
219P Berlin Rd., Ste. 160
Cherry Hill, NJ 08034
ph: 609-428-3546
fax: 609-428-9282
e-mail: info@circleofthemoon.com
web: http://www.circleofthemoon.com

Jeffrey L. Andracht
Oriental Antiques Shop Miracle Ventures Inc.
P.O. Box 75
Flushing, NY 11363
ph: 718-225-1461
fax: 718-822-1461
e-mail: Samuari66@aol.com
web: http://hometown.aol.com/Samuari66/orientalantiques.html
An on-line shop specializing in Chinese, Japanese and Korean antiques including Imari, Kutani, Satsuma, woodblock prints, metalwares, etc.; always interested in purchasing items.

Sandra Andracht
P.O. Box 94
Flushing, NY 11363-0094
ph: 718-229-6593
e-mail: Orientalia@aol.com
web: http://members.aol.com/Orientalia/index.html
Buys and sells Oriental antiques: Asian, Japanese, Chinese, Korean, Southeast Asia.

Bob Miller
P.O. Box 640245
Flushing, NY 11364-0245
ph: 718-776-7409
Buys and sells antique Chinese, Korean, and Japanese items; included are ceramics, hardstone, snuff bottles, woodblock prints, ivory carvings, metalware, weapons, lacquer, inro, ojimes, bronzes, silver, jewelry, and Japanese cloisonne.

Jim Staggs
J & L Antiques
P.O. Box 1616
Rockville, MD 20849-1616
ph: 301-424-7218

Susan Akins
Oriental Antiques by Susan Akins
3740 Howard Ave.
Kensington, MD 20895-3347
ph: 301-946-4609
web: http://www.kensingtonantiquerow.com/orientalantiquesbysusan/
All Asian countries: China, Japan, Indonesia, S.E. Asia, India, etc.; specializing in fine porcelains, furniture, ivories, carvings, hangings, ancient artifacts.

Joe Arnold
East & Beyond, Ltd.
6727 Curran St.
Mc Lean, VA 22101
ph: 703-448-8200
fax: 703-821-1272
e-mail: EandBeyond@aol.com
web: http://www.eandbeyond.com
A three-story gallery specializing in antiques from China, Japan and Korea: furniture, boxes, benches, chairs, porcelain, and textiles.

Sharon & Arno Ziesnitz
7835 Painted Daisy Dr.
Springfield, VA 22152
ph: 703-451-1033
fax: 703-569-4221
e-mail: ziesnitz@aol.com
Lecturers, authors, consultants want fine works of art: netsuke, inro, ojime, sword accessories, cloisonne, Satsuma, ivory and wood carvings, Chinese snuff bottles, Japanese traveling shrines, and Japanese metalworks.

Bill Egleston
509 Brentwood Rd.
Marshalltown, IA 50158-3727
ph: 800-798-4579
fax: 515-752-4570
Specializing in mail order sale of Oriental art, jade, cloisonne, netsuke, etc.; send for catalog.

Byla Simon Kunis, ISA
Oriental Treasures Antiques
159 W. Kenzie St.
Chicago, IL 60610-4514
ph: 773-761-2907 or 312-527-0533
fax: 773-761-0789
Specializes in Chinese and Japanese antiques: textiles, ivory, jade, lacquer, metal; also appraises.

Isadore M. Chait
I.M. Chait Gallery
9330 Civic Center Drive
Beverly Hills, CA 90210
ph: 310-285-0182
fax: 310-285-9740
e-mail: IMChait@chait.com
web: http://www.chait.com
Appraiser, auctioneer, expert in Oriental antiques and art; specializes in Han, T'ang, Sung, Ming, Ching, and other dynasties; also sells Japanese woodblock prints, netsuke, jades, ivory, snuff bottle, furniture, Tibetan, SE Asia.

Marsha L. Vargas
Oriental Corner, The
280 Main St.
Los Altos, CA 94022
ph: 650-941-3207
fax: 650-941-3297
e-mail: mvargas@theorientalcorner.com
web: http://www.theorientalcorner.com
Buys and sells fine quality Asian works of art: Japanese netsuke, lacquer, Chinese ceramics and snuff bottles.

Robyn Buntin
Robyn Buntin of Honolulu
848 So. Beretania St.
Honolulu, HI 96813
ph: 808-523-5913
fax: 808-536-6305
e-mail: rbuntin@lava.net
web: http://www.robynbuntin.com/
Buys and sells extraordinary Chinese and Japanese items such as netsuke, scholar's table items, paintings, prints, screens, jade and lacquer ware.

Victor Topper
Topper Gallery
2900 John Street, Ste. 402
Markham, Ontario L3R 5G3
Canada
ph: 905-513-8070 or 416-633-4518
fax: 905-513-6628
e-mail: toppart@pathcom.com
web: http://www.topperart.com/
Chinese art, Japanese art, Buddhistic art, pre-Columbian, Judaica, Inuit art, Northwest Coast Indians; early Chinese bronze vessels, snuff bottles, early Jade carvings.

Peter
Oriental Art Collection
Blk 3, New Bugis St., #01-21
Singapore, 188867
Singapore
ph: 3369208
e-mail: boyseen@cyberway.com.sg
web: http://members.xoom.com/Edward/Lu/
Specializes in Oriental fine arts from: wood carvings, jade, paintings, netsuke, ivory, bronzes.

Experts

Patricia M. Grove
PMG Antique Appraisal Research
3 Ober St.
Beverly, MA 01915-4639
ph: 978-927-2979
Collects, researches and appraises decorative and fine arts of the China, Japan, India and Russia export trades, 17th through mid-19th centuries: paintings, silver, ivory, tortoise carvings, furniture, fans, lacquer.

Sandra Andracht
P.O. Box 94
Flushing, NY 11363-0094
ph: 718-229-6593
e-mail: Orientalia@aol.com
web: http://members.aol.com/Orientalia/index.html
Author of "Oriental Antiques Art - An Identification and Value Guide", (Wallace-Homestead), "Collector's Value Guide to Oriental Decorative Arts) (Antique Trader Books).

Dr. Daphne L. Rosenzweig
Rosenzweig Associates
P.O. Box 16187
Tampa, FL 33687-6187
ph: 813-988-0880
fax: 813-989-8091
e-mail: rosetwig@aol.com
Consultant and appraiser dealing with Oriental Art; author of "Selected Works from the Fine Arts Group of Later Chinese Painting"; specializes in Chinese art, and Japanese prints and ceramics.

Richard R. Silverman
838 N. Doheny Dr. #1102
West Hollywood, CA 90069-4851
ph: 310-271-1896 or 310-273-3838
fax: 310-273-3843
Specializes in Japanese prints and ceramics; netsuke and inro; also Thai, Burmese, Indian and Nepalese items; call 12:00 noon to 12:00 midnight PST; International Society of Appraiser Certified Appraiser in netsuke.

Museums/Libraries

Charles Jones
University of Chicago's Oriental Institute Museum
ph: 773-702-9537
e-mail: cejo@midway.uchicago.edu
web: http://www-oi.uchicago.edu/OI/MUS/OI_Museum.html

George Walter Vincent Smith Art Museum
220 State St.
Springfield, MA 01103-1703
ph: 413-263-6800
fax: 413-263-6814
e-mail: jhanna@spfldlibmus.org
web: http://www.quadrangle.org/GWVS.htm
Recognized collections of American paintings; Orientalia including Japanese arms & armor, screens, lacquers, textiles and ceramics; Islamic rugs; and the largest collection of Chinese cloisonne in the western world

Arthur M. Sackler Gallery
Smithsonian Institution
1050 Independence Ave. SW
Washington, DC 20560
ph: 202-357-3200
e-mail: edsonmi@asia.si.edu
web: http://www.si.edu/organiza/museums/freer/start.htm
The Chinese Dept. will authenticate your Chinese works of art; call to make an appointment; limit 5 items per visit, 10 items per year; may be able to work from good photographs.

Art Institute of Chicago
111 S. Michigan Ave.
Chicago, IL 60603
ph: 312-443-0849
e-mail: webmaster@artic.edu
web: http://www.artic.edu/aic/firstpage.html
Galleries of Chinese, Japanese, and Korean art contain 20,000 works covering nearly 5,000 years representing a variety of media from China, Japan, Korea, Southeast Asia, India, and the Near and Middle East.

Pacific Asia Museum
Newsletter: Pacific Asia Museum Member Newsletter
46 N. Los Robles Ave.
Pasadena, CA 91101
ph: 626-449-2742
fax: 626-449-2754
web: http://www.sppsr.ucla.edu/dup/courses/s97/comdev/pamuseum/
Preserves, presents, and interprets to the public the arts and culture of the Pacific Islands and Asia.

Asian Art Museum of San Francisco, The Avery Brundage Collection
Golden Gate Park
San Francisco, CA 94118-4598
ph: 415-379-8800
e-mail: info@asianart.org
web: http://www.asianart.org

Periodicals

Sandra Andracht
Journal: Orientalia Journal
P.O. Box 94
Flushing, NY 11363-0094
ph: 718-229-6593
e-mail: Orientalia@aol.com
web: http://members.aol.com/Orientalia/index.html
A bi-monthly newsletter about all types of Chinese and Japanese art; areas covered include pottery, porcelain, wood, metal, paintings, prints, textiles, netsuke, Satsuma, Chinese & S.E. Asian bronzes, Oriental rugs, cloisonne, etc.

Repair Services

Isadore M. Chait
I.M. Chait Gallery
9330 Civic Center Drive
Beverly Hills, CA 90210
ph: 310-285-0182
fax: 310-285-9740
e-mail: IMChait@chait.com
web: http://www.chait.com
Restorers of all types of Asian antiques: ceramics, paper, wood, metal, etc.

Repro. Sources

Joan L. Cervi
Arts of Asia
3203 Adams Way
Ambler, PA 19002-3741
ph: 215-628-2026
fax: 215-628-2026
e-mail: jcnetsuke@aol.com
Importer of statues, netsuke, snuff bottles, etc., etc., wholesale prices; annual catalog with updates $5; annual video $5.

Manny Shaool
Manny's Oriental Rugs
72 W. Washington St.
Hagerstown, MD 21740
ph: 301-797-7434
Importer of Oriental ivory, porcelain, reverse paintings, rugs; also Remington recast bronzes, clocks, lacquered furniture.

Chinese Antiques & Art
9615 Las Tunas Dr.
Temple City, CA 91780-2109
ph: 626-286-8696 or 626-286-8698
fax: 626-286-8338
Carries porcelain, bronze, lacquer ware, jade, cloisonne, antique furniture, ivory, antique clocks, carvings and much more.

Chinese Items

Dealers

Michael Yip
Han Palace Fine Arts
11665 Powell Street
San Francisco, CA 94108
ph: 415-788-5338
fax: 415-788-5233
e-mail: yip@hanpalace.com
web: http://www.hanpalace.com/
A private antique gallery in San Francisco specializing in high quality authentic Chinese antiques.

Jadestone Gallery
10922 N.E. St. Johns Rd.
Vancouver, WA 98686
ph: 360-573-2580 or 800-854-JADE
fax: 360-573-4834
e-mail: artinfo@jadestonegallery.com
web: http://www.jadestonegallery.com/
Specializes in Chinese art and antiquities: Neolithic, tomb sculptures, pottery and porcelain, fine jade and other carvings.

Misc. Services

Arthur M. Sackler Gallery
Smithsonian Institution
1050 Independence Ave. SW
Washington, DC 20560
ph: 202-357-3200
e-mail: edsonmi@asia.si.edu
web: http://www.si.edu/organiza/museums/freer/start.htm
The Chinese Dept. will authenticate your Chinese works of art; call to make an appointment; limit 5 items per visit, 10 items per year; may be able to work from good photographs.

Japanese

Appraisers

Elisabeth Weikert Douglas
China Coast Oriental Art Appraisal Services
11266 Taylor Draper Lane, Apt. 2024
Austin, TX 78759-3972
ph: 512-288-3043
fax: 512-345-8420
e-mail: wien@texas.net
Active in the field of Asian art and antiques for over 20 years; owned and operated antiques export service in Bangkok, Thailand; owned and operated Oriental art and antiques shop in Washington DC.

Dealers

Michael R. Berstein, Esq.
ph: 212-533-9935
fax: 212-533-0325
e-mail: netsukeninro@worldnet.att.net
web: http://www.netsuke-inro.com
Deals exclusively in Japanese art, specializing in netsuke, inro, pipe cases, ojime, tsuba and lacquer; has sold works which now appear in the collections of major museums and the most prominent private collectors.

Michael R. Bernstein
Fine Japanese Art
201 E. 19th St., 12E
New York, NY 10003
ph: 212-533-9935
fax: 212-533-0325
e-mail: netsukeninro@worldnet.att.net
web: http://www.netsukeinro.com/
Specialist in netsuke, info, lacquer, pipe cases, ojime, tsuba, and Japanese metalwork.

Lars Nordin
Meiji Art
Bjornbergsv.3
Saltsjo-boo
Stockholm, 132 39
Sweden
ph: +46 8 7478529
fax: +46 8 7478529
e-mail: oni@meijiart.se
web: http://www.meijiart.se
Specializes in Japanese art such as netsuke, inro, cloisonne and metalwork.

Japanese Items

(see also ARMS & ARMOR, Japanese; BOOKS, Reference [Japanese Items]; FIREARMS, Japanese Matchlocks; OCCUPIED JAPAN; PRINTS, Woodblock [Japanese])

Auction Services

John H. Schofield
Eldred's
P.O. Box 796
East Dennis, MA 02641-0796
ph: 508-385-3116
fax: 508-385-7201
e-mail: eldreds@capecod.net
web: http://www.eldreds.com/
Specialists with annual week-long series of auction dedicated to Orientalia for over 25 years.

Collectors

Alistair C.G. Seton
Daruma Magazine
Sumiyoshidai 10-11A
Higashinada-ku
Kobe, 658-0062
Japan
ph: +81-78-851-6654
fax: +81-78-851-0402
e-mail: aliseton@gol.com
web: http://www.darumamagazine.com/
Collector of Japanese art and antiques.

Dealers

Richard Murphy
Asahi Japan Collectibles
19 Timberwood Road
Kensington, CT 06037
ph: 888-282-4452 or 860-828-3106
fax: 860-828-3106
e-mail: info@asahi-jc.com
web: http://www.asahi-jc.com/
Provides customers world wide with high quality Japanese culture related goods: kimono, Ukiyo-E art, Japanese dolls, Buddha, etc.

Robert & Vinka Berg
Ichiban Japanese Antiques
P.O. Box 395
Marion, CT 06444-0395
ph: 860-272-7392
e-mail: info@ichibanantiques.com
web: http://www.ichibanantiques.com/
Japanese bronzes and Ningyo (festival dolls), Japanese & Chinese ceramics, Japanese woodblock prints from the 19th and 20th centuries.

Denis Szeszler
Antique Oriental Art
P.O. Box 714
New York, NY 10028-0044
ph: 212-427-4682
fax: 212-860-4426
Specializes in antique netsuke and related works of art: inro and other sagemono, pipe cases, yatate, okimono, etc.; buys and sells; researches and appraises.

Yoneyama
Ginza, "Things Japanese"
1721 Connecticut Ave., NW
Washington, DC 20009-1108
ph: 202-331-7991
Specialty gift store 95% Japanese imports/collectibles/decorative accessories: fine china, sake sets, tea sets, kimono & happi coats, futons/frames, bonsai/ikebana, origami, toys, dolls/cases, shoji screens & lamps, prints, lanterns, etc.

Imari, Inc.
200 Gate Five Road
Sausalito, CA 94965
ph: 415-332-0245
fax: 415-332-3621
Specializes in Japanese antiques and screens.

Tansu Ltd.
Skopos Mills
Bradford Road
Batley, West Yorkshire WF17 6LZ
U.K.
ph: 44-1924-422391
fax: 44-1924-443856
e-mail: tansu@tias.com
web: http://www.tias.com/stores/tansu
Specializes in Tansu.

Experts

Dr. Daphne L. Rosenzweig
Rosenzweig Associates
P.O. Box 16187
Tampa, FL 33687-6187
ph: 813-988-0880
fax: 813-989-8091
e-mail: rosetwig@aol.com
Consultant and appraiser dealing with Oriental Art; author of "Selected Works from the Fine Arts Group of Later Chinese Painting"; specializes in Chinese art, and Japanese prints and ceramics.

Misc. Services

Barbara Brooks
Arthur M. Sackler Gallery
Smithsonian Institution
1050 Independence Ave. SW
Washington, DC 20560
ph: 202-357-3200
e-mail: edsonmi@asia.si.edu
web: http://www.si.edu/organiza/museums/freer/start.htm
The Japanese Dept. will authenticate your Japanese works of art; call to make an appointment; limit 5 items per visit, 10 items per year; may be able to work from good photographs.

Museums/Libraries

Annie Van Assche, Cur.
Morikami Museum & Japanese Gardens
4000 Morikami Park Rd.
Delray Beach, FL 33446-2305
ph: 561-495-0233
fax: 561-499-2557
e-mail: avanassc@co.palm-beach.fl.us
web: http://www.morikami.org/
Focuses on Japanese utilitarian objects of everyday use; also contains a comprehensive collection of Japanese textiles, folk crafts, tea ceremony utensils, and folding screens; 5,000 artifacts on permanent display; 4,500 books in library.

Periodicals

Alistair C.G. Seton
Magazine: Daruma Magazine
Sumiyoshidai 10-11A
Higashinada-ku
Kobe, 658-0062
Japan
ph: +81-78-851-6654
fax: +81-78-851-0402
e-mail: aliseton@gol.com
web: http://www.darumamagazine.com/
English language quarterly full-color magazine devoted solely to Japanese art and antiques.

Japanese Items (Tsuba)

Internet Resources

Jim Gilbert
Tsuba
e-mail: jggilbert@earthlink.net
web: http://home.earthlink.net/~jggilbert/tsuba.htm
THE place for tsubas (handguards mounted on Japanese swords) and related information.

Korean Items

Dealers

Jeffrey L. Andracht
Oriental Antiques Shop Miracle Ventures Inc.
P.O. Box 75
Flushing, NY 11363
ph: 718-225-1461
fax: 718-822-1461
e-mail: Samuari66@aol.com
web: http://hometown.aol.com/Samuari66/orientalantiques.html
An on-line shop specializing in Chinese, Japanese and Korean antiques including Imari, Kutani, Satsuma, woodblock prints, metalwares, etc.; always interested in purchasing items.

Sandra Andracht
P.O. Box 94
Flushing, NY 11363-0094
ph: 718-229-6593
e-mail: Orientalia@aol.com
web: http://members.aol.com/Orientalia/index.html
Buys and sells Oriental antiques: Asian, Japanese, Chinese, Korean, Southeast Asia.

Joe Arnold
East & Beyond, Ltd.
6727 Curran St.
Mc Lean, VA 22101
ph: 703-448-8200
fax: 703-821-1272
e-mail: EandBeyond@aol.com
web: http://www.eandbeyond.com
A three-story gallery specializing in antiques from China, Japan and Korea: furniture, boxes, benches, chairs, porcelain, and textiles.

Lacquer

Experts

Janet Francine Cobert
Fine Art of Asia
P.O. Box 2976
Beverly Hills, CA 90213
ph: 310-470-2176
fax: 818-986-5584
Specializes in and appraises Oriental lacquer.

Repair Services

Janet Francine Cobert
Fine Art of Asia
P.O. Box 2976
Beverly Hills, CA 90213
ph: 310-470-2176
fax: 818-986-5584
Restores Oriental lacquer and ceramic wares.

Near East Items

Misc. Services

Arthur M. Sackler Gallery
Smithsonian Institution
1050 Independence Ave. SW
Washington, DC 20560
ph: 202-357-3200
e-mail: edsonmi@asia.si.edu
web: http://www.si.edu/organiza/museums/freer/start.htm
The Near East Dept. will authenticate your Near East works of art; call to make an appointment; limit 5 items per visit, 10 items per year; may be able to work from good photographs.

South & Southeast Asia

Collectors

John Rudak
32 Princess Lane
North Stonington, CT 06359-1117
ph: 860-599-8489
Wants Buddhist and Hindu art of Southeast Asia; all representations desired.

Dealers

Art of the Past
1242 Madison Ave.
New York, NY 10128-0515
ph: 212-860-7070
fax: 212-876-5373
Specializing in paintings, sculptures, textiles, Islamic and other works of art from India, Tibet, Nepal, and Southeast Asia.

Misc. Services

Arthur M. Sackler Gallery
Smithsonian Institution
1050 Independence Ave. SW
Washington, DC 20560
ph: 202-357-3200
e-mail: edsonmi@asia.si.edu
web: http://www.si.edu/organiza/museums/freer/start.htm
The South & Southeast Dept. will authenticate your South & Southeast Asian works of art; call to make an appointment; limit 5 items/visit, 10 items/year; may be able to work from good photographs.

OSBORNE IVOREX

Collectors

Andy Jackson
501 Falcon Lane
West Chester, PA 19382-5716
ph: 610-692-0269 or 610-272-7900
Wants wall plaques, figurines, calendars and advertising brochures; will buy, sell or trade.

Experts

John Smith
28 Garfield Road
Bitterne
Southampton, Hampshire S019 4BU
U.K.
ph: 01703 331582
e-mail: ivorex@compuserve.com
web: http://ourworld.compuserve.com/homepages/ivorex/
Collector and dealer of Osborne Ivorex plaques; all subjects covered; web site packed with history and information on the subject.

OUTBOARD MOTORS

(see also BOATS; NAUTICAL ANTIQUES; TOYS, Boats & Outboards)

Clubs/Associations

Antique Outboard Motor Club
Magazine: Antique Outboarder
P.O. Box 69
Sussex, WI 53089
e-mail: webmaster@aomci.org
web: http://www.aomci.org/aomc.htm

Collectors

Bob Glick
Columbia Trading Company
1 Barnstable Rd.
Hyannis, MA 02601
ph: 508-778-2929
fax: 508-778-2922
e-mail: nautical@capecod.net
web: http://www.columbiatrading.com/
Buys old and antique outboard motors.

Richard Mussehl
Antique Outboard Motor Man
320 W. 20th St.
Erie, PA 16502
ph: 800-354-6089
Wants old rowboat motors by Waterman, Clarke, Amphion, etc.

Dealers

John McSwain
Marine Antiques & Maritime Artifacts
4155 Hwy. 11
Deland, FL 32724-9745
ph: 904-734-8786
fax: 904-738-5629
Specializes in deep sea diving, gauges, antique outboard motors 1900-1955, boating equipment and accessories.

Walter Pawlikowski
Superior Antiques
4022 E 2nd St.
Superior, WI 54880-4209
ph: 715-398-3665
Buys, collects antique outboards, marine engines, and antique boat equipment or related fishing equipment, boat models and outboard toys literature on pre-1940 items; offers free appraisals on antique outboards; historical writer.

Experts

Walter Pawlikowski
Superior Antiques
4022 E 2nd St.
Superior, WI 54880-4209
ph: 715-398-3665
Buys, collects antique outboards, marine engines, and antique boat equipment or related fishing equipment, boat models and outboard toys literature on pre-1940 items; offers free appraisals on antique outboards; historical writer.

Suppliers

Arthur DeKalb
51 Van Alstyne Dr.
Pulaski, NY 13142
ph: 315-298-3410
web: http://members.aol.com/ArtDeKalb/
Antique outboard catalogs, parts, instructions and service manuals for most brands.

OUTDOOR COLLECTIBLES

(see ANIMAL TROPHIES; ART, Sporting; CAMPING EQUIPMENT; DECOYS; FISHING COLLECTIBLES; LICENSES, Hunting & Fishing; SPORTING COLLECTIBLES; TARGET SHOOTING MEMORABILIA; TRAP SHOOTING; TRAPS)

OUTHOUSES

Collectors

J. W. "Bill" Courter
3935 Kelley Rd.
Kevil, KY 42053-9431
ph: 270-488-2116
fax: 270-488-2116
e-mail: brtknight@aol.com
web: http://www.aladdinknights.org
Wants items relating to outhouses: post cards, books, old photographs, plans, catalogs, models, etc.

OUTLAWS & LAWMEN

(see also LAW ENFORCEMENT MEMORABILIA, Police & Sheriff; WESTERN AMERICANA)

Clubs/Associations

Hank Clark
National Association for Outlaw & Lawman History
Newsletter: NOLA Newsletter & Quarterly
P.O. Box 812
Waterford, CA 95386-0812
ph: 209-874-2640
fax: 209-874-5750
Members interested in Western outlaw and lawmen history and artifacts; sponsors annual Rendezvous.

Collectors

Dr. Anthony Sapienza
East 106 Ridgewood Ave.
Paramus, NJ 07652
ph: 201-262-6310
fax: 201-262-3990
e-mail: siringo45@aol.com
Serious collector wants photographs, autographs, documents, Wanted posters and postcards, original Western Law officers' badges, invitations to hangings, telegrams, etc.

Bill Mackin
1137 Washington St.
Craig, CO 81625-1613
ph: 970-824-6717 or 970-824-6360
fax: 970-824-7175
Author of "Cowboy and Gunfighter Collectibles" with 1993-94 updated price guide; sells books for Old West collectors by mail and at shows; over 45 years collecting; wants nice gun leather and cowboy gear; appraises, consults, lectures.

OVENS

(see RANGES)

OYSTER RELATED COLLECTIBLES

Clubs/Associations

Andrea H. Sullivan
Oyster Plate & Collectibles Society International
Newsletter: OPCS Newsletter
P.O. Box 632
Brigantine, NJ 08203-0632
ph: 609-226-3989 or 215-342-6450
fax: 410-378-9431
e-mail: oystersociety@geocities.com
web: http://www.geocities.com/Heartland/Bluffs/1570

Collectors

Donald C. Bell
89 Canoe Brook Rd.
Trumbull, CT 06611
ph: 203-268-7380
Wants old oyster cans, bottles, boxes, barrels, advertising and related items; no oyster plates, please.

Sheldon Katz
18 Cliffside Drive
Port Jefferson, NY 11777
ph: 516-928-1800

Carlton G. Riggin
Rt. 617
Marionville, VA 23408
ph: 757-442-5321
fax: 757-442-5321
Wants to buy old oyster cans and containers, oyster advertising,

envelopes and letterheads, postcards, trade cards, and other oyster related items.

Jan & Dick Wilson
Seasonal Seafoods
P.O. Box 356
Bay Center, WA 98527
ph: 360-875-5519
fax: 360-875-5937
e-mail: jan_dick@willapabay.org
web: http://willapabay.org/~jan_dick/
Collectors of oyster plates.

Dealers

Vivian & James Karsnitz
1428 Jerry Lane
Manheim, PA 17545-9353
ph: 717-665-4202
Buys and sells oyster cans, advertising and related items; authors of "Oyster Plates" and "Oyster Cans" (Schiffer, 1993.)

Oscar Schabb
P.O. Box 1377
Brooklandville, MD 21022-1377
ph: 410-486-2436
fax: 410-486-0653
Buys, sells, trades and collects old oyster cans and memorabilia; also wants 1# peanut butter pails, pocket tobacco tins, coffee tins with good graphics.

OZ

(see WIZARD OF OZ)

Here are some tips when contacting someone listed in this book:

■ When requesting information about a particular item, include a description (material, dimensions, maker's mark, model number, etc.) and a photo, sketch, or photocopy of the item in question.

■ Always ask if there are charges for samples or for the services requested.

■ When writing, please be sure to include a Large (#10 business size) Self-Addressed and Stamped Envelope (LSASE) if requesting a reply or the return of photographs.

■ Never call collect unless otherwise directed. When calling, be considerate of time zone differences and always ask if the party you are calling has time to talk. When leaving an answering machine message, always instruct the party to call you back collect.

P

PADLOCKS

(see LOCKS)

PAINT CANS

Collectors

Irene Davis
27036 Withams Rd.
Oak Hall, VA 23416
ph: 757-824-5524
Wants to buy old paint cans, paint advertising displays, or retail items; send photos for offer.

PAINTINGS

(see ART)

PAMPHLETS

(see PAPER COLLECTIBLES)

PAPER CLIPS

Collectors

John T. Ogle
P.O. Box 252
Ocean Springs, MS 39566-0252
Wants to buy paper clips and notched bookmarks: antique, foreign, plastic, novelty, advertising; also wants early paper clip advertising.

PAPER COLLECTIBLES

(see also ADVERTISING COLLECTIBLES; AUTOGRAPHS; BLOTTERS; BOOKS; BUSINESS CARDS; CALENDARS; CARDS; CATALOGS; HISTORICAL AMERICANA; MAPS & CHARTS; MAGAZINES; NEWSPAPERS; POSTCARDS; POSTERS; REPAIR/ RESTORATION/CONSERVATION, Paper Items; SHEET MUSIC)

Appraisers

Ken Sowman
Vista Group, The
229 Foster Dr.
Barrie, Ontaria LN4 3X9
Canada
ph: 705-739-0482
fax: 705-739-7544
e-mail: ksowman@bconnex.net
Appraises, deals in all kinds of paper collectibles; any subject, any age.

Auction Services

Russell Mascieri
Victorian Images
P.O. Box 284
Marlton, NJ 08053
ph: 609-985-7711
fax: 609-985-8513
e-mail: RMascieri@aol.com
web: http://www.tradecards.com/vi

Robert H. Snyder
Cohasco, Inc.
P.O. Box 821
Yonkers, NY 10702-0821
ph: 914-476-8500
fax: 914-476-8573
e-mail: cohascodpc@earthlink.net
web: http://home.earthlink.net/~cohascodpc/index.html
In business over 50 years, specializing in paper collectibles, autographs, documents, Americana, ephemera, etc.; mail auction catalogs issued.

Dale Sorenson
Waverly Auctions, Inc.
4931 Cordell Ave.
Bethesda, MD 20814-2508
ph: 301-951-8883
fax: 301-718-8375
e-mail: wavauc@clark.net
web: http://www.waverlyauctions.com
Specializes in the auction of graphic art, books, paper, atlases, prints, postcards, autographs, and other paper ephemera.

Harold Trainor
P.O. Box 13055
Fort Pierce, FL 34979
ph: 561-878-7376
fax: 561-878-3676
Conducts mail bid auctions of tokens, medals, pins, paper items, World's Fair and Exposition, beer & whiskey items, celluloid mirrors, political, fire department, Centennial items, automobilia, railroadiana, airline collectibles.

Joseph Millard
Grandma's Trunk
P.O. Box 404
Northport, MI 49670
ph: 616-386-5351
e-mail: maxfield@traverse.com
web: http://www.antiquepaper.com
Trade cards, rewards of merit, valentines, etc.

Kurt R. Krueger
Krueger Auctions
P.O. Box 275
Iola, WI 54945-0275
ph: 715-445-3845
fax: 715-445-4100
Specializing in the mail-bid auction of paper collectibles: stocks & bonds, advertising, books, letters, manuscripts, children's books, prints, photographs, historical Americana, posters, etc.

Butterfield & Dunning
755 Church Rd.
Elgin, IL 60123
ph: 847-741-3483
fax: 847-741-3589
e-mail: info@butterfields.com
web: http://www.butterfields.com
Premier mid-American auction firm selling antiques, fine art, jewelry, American Indian art, and real estate.

Michael Hickey
Accumulations & Collections
1512 Chasewood Dr.
Austin, TX 78727
ph: 512-989-0188
fax: 512-989-0112
e-mail: Mike_Hickey@msn.com
Conducts six auctions per year; directs auctions to a database of collectors who are interested in paper collectibles.

Clubs/Associations

Ephemera Society of America Inc., The
Newsletter: Ephemera News
P.O. Box 95
Cazenovia, NY 13035-0095
ph: 315-655-9139
fax: 315-655-9139
e-mail: info@ephemerasociety.org
web: http://www.ephemerasociety.org/
The major organization for collectors and dealers of paper collectibles; focuses on the preservation and study of ephemera (short-lived printed matter); also publishes "The Ephemera Journal."

Ephemera Society of Australia, The
P.O. Box 479
Warragul, Victoria 3820
Australia

Wolaskowitz Frederick
Ephemera Society of Austria, The
Journal: Ephemera Journal
Baumlegarten 5
Hoehst, A-6973
Austria
ph: 0043 5578 76903
Members collect mostly coffee cream lids (peel offs) and lids from hone, lemon, jam, marmalade containers; also collect packaging items and advertising collectibles and promotion items from food and drink; want contact with US collectors.

Ephemera Society of Canada, The
Newsletter: Ephemera Canada
36 Macauley Dr.
Thornhill, Ontario L3T 5S5
Canada
ph: 416-492-5958
fax: 416-492-5958
e-mail: ephemera@tht.net
Dedicated to the preservation, study and display of Canada's printed heritage.

Ephemera Society of England, The
Journal: Ephemerist, The
8 Galveston Rd.
London, SW15 2SA
U.K.
ph: 0181 874 3363
fax: 0181 874 3363
web: http://www.manacled.demon.co.uk/phaistos/ephsoc.htm

Collectors

Paul R. Lafavore
1211-I 10th St. Blvd. NW
Hickory, NC 28601
ph: 828-323-8221
e-mail: lafavore@twave.net
Collecting 19th century or earlier broadsides or handbills relating to photography, medicine, or the state of Maine.

Tom Rutledge
3015 Bever Ave., SE
Cedar Rapids, IA 52403-3028
ph: 319-399-1427
Wants rare and antiquarian books, paper, manuscripts, documents, calendars, postcards, valentines, trade cards, maps, atlases, autographs, railroadiana, cook books, posters, rewards of merit, and children's books.

James E. Kattner
P.O. Box 11132
Spring, TX 77391
ph: 281-986-6916 or 281-376-4826
Wants to buy Texas saloon letterheads, envelopes, advertising cards, photographs, and other saloon paper collectibles; also wants same from pre-1919 Texas liquor dealers.

Dealers

Robert Lucas
Robert F. Lucas Antiquarian Books
P.O. Box 63
Blandford, MA 01008
ph: 413-848-2061
e-mail: books@lucasbooks.com
web: http://www.lucasbooks.com
Mail order, on-line sales of antiquarian books; also a wide variety of ephemera including autographs, letters, broadsides, trade cards, photos, pamphlets, newspapers, diaries, account books, etc. especially from 19th century America.

Jerry Rubackin
Jerry's Cards & Collectibles
P.O. Box 1271
Framingham, MA 01701-0207
ph: 508-788-5197
fax: 508-788-5197
Buys and sells WWII fighter aces autographs and other WWII military signatures; also want autographed material by the crew of the Enola Gay which dropped the first atomic bomb on Hiroshima.

George & Julie Perron
Old Paperphiles, The
P.O. Box 135
Tiverton, RI 02878-0135
ph: 401-624-9420
fax: 401-624-4204
Buys and sells paper collectibles: books, autographs, sheet music, postcards, photos, stereoviews, documents, old letters; issues periodic catalog of items for sale.

Deborah Lavoie
Deborah Leavoie Fine Books & Paper Treasures
P.O. Box 117
New Boston, NH 03070-0117
ph: 603-487-2369
fax: 603-487-2333
e-mail: rare@worldnet.att.net
web: http://abebooks.com/home/RARE/
Buys/sells rare and antiquarian books, paper, letters, documents, catalogs, newspapers, postcards, trade cards, diaries, ledgers, atlases, maps, etc.

Kit Barry
Kit Barry Ephemera
88 High Street Box S-I
Brattleboro, VT 05301
ph: 802-254-3634
web: http://www.tradecards.com/kb/
Specializes in fine ephemera, scarce and rare, including trade cards, billheads, labels, and posters; also sells a complete line of ephemera supplies: plastic pages, matchbook pages, rigid print holders, soft plastic sleeves, et.

Old Paper Archive, The
122 West 25th St.
New York, NY 10001-7401
ph: 212-645-3983
Specializing in antique prints, ads, books, movie posters, sports, postcards, photographica, magazines.

Stephen Cohen
Cohen's Collectibles
Ccelsea Antiques Building
110 West 25th St., Room 305
New York, NY 10001-7401
ph: 212-675-5300
fax: 212-675-5300
e-mail: kingcohen@msn.com
web: http://www.ephemera-king.com/
Photographs, autographs, steamship, airline, World's Fair, travel, black heritage, Judaica, sheet music, film memorabilia, postcards, trade catalogs; only open shop for ephemera in Manhattan.

Judith Katz-Schwartz
Twin Brooks Antiques & Collectibles
P.O. Box 6572
New York, NY 10128-0006
ph: 212-876-3512
fax: 212-876-3512
e-mail: twinb@msjudith.net
web: http://www.msjudith.net
Buys, sells, appraises postcards, photos, old magazines, valentines, advertising fans, cookbooks and pamphlets, 39 World's Fair, advertising trade cards, blotters, die cuts, calendars, etc.

George Theofiles
Miscellaneous Man
P.O. Box 1776
New Freedom, PA 17349-0191
ph: 717-235-4766
fax: 717-235-2853
Issues periodic catalog of paper items for sale including labels, poster stamps, etc.

Ridgley G. Hill
Beaver Tree Ephemera
5039 Ijamsville Rd.
Ijamsville, MD 21754
ph: 301-865-0335
Buys and sells paper Americana, specializing in western travel, railroad, land promotion, bird's-eye views, trade catalogs, trade cards; will also consider all other categories of collectible paper ephemera.

Pat Sweeney
Pat Sweeney Ephemera
511 Woods End
Portage, MI 49002
ph: 616-381-9416
e-mail: pse@tias.com
web: http://www.tias.com/stores/pse/
Specializes in paper ephemera including cigar labels, sheet music, hotel luggage labels, vintage posters.

Hugh Passow
306 Main St.
Eau Claire, WI 54701
ph: 715-832-2494
fax: 715-832-1863
e-mail: mgallery@execpc.com
Wants large folio pre-1920 books, scrap albums, quantities of pre-1940 magazines, old prints, miscellaneous paper items.

Bindy Bitterman
Eureka! Antiques
705 W. Washington
Evanston, IL 60202-2214
ph: 847-869-9090
Specializes buying and selling early paper advertising, catalogs, calendars, etc.; a small shop - they send no lists but write detailed individual letters; SASEs get first attention.

Susan Nicholson
Greater Chicago Productions
P.O. Box 595
Lisle, IL 60532
ph: 630-964-5240
e-mail: deltiology@aol.com
Buys and sells rare and unusual postcards, Victorian valentines, periodicals, advertising trade cards, etc.

Ann White
Once Upon a Memory
P.O. Box 4765
Lincoln, NE 68504
ph: 402-473-2960
fax: 402-474-3623
e-mail: resumeann@aol.com
web: http://www.tias.com/stores/once/
Buys and sells paper collectibles: pin-ups, original art, lithographs, advertising items, books, fans, anything paper.

Vivian Briggs
Briggs Antiques
4443 Linwood Place
Riverside, CA 92506
ph: 909-781-3121
fax: 909-781-3121
e-mail: drago120@aol.com
web: http://www.tias.com/stores/briggs/
Buys and sells paper collectibles: checks, stocks, autographs, receipts, invoices, etc. from 1850s through early 1900s.

Ron & Carol Haglund
Yesterday's Paper
31815 Camino Capistrano, Ste. 11
San Juan Capistrano, CA 92675-3212
ph: 949-248-0945 or 949-583-9838
fax: 949-583-1899
e-mail: ydayspaper@aol.com
Buys and sells anything made of old paper: books, maps, prints, comics, catalogs, stock certificates, sheet music, posters, newspapers, documents, Disneyana, magazines, etc.

David Yager
Old Paper
P.O. Box 271
La Honda, CA 94020
e-mail: admin@old-paper.com
web: http://www.old-paper.com
Website has over 6,000 collectible paper items for sale; sorted by date, city, category, company name; items priced.

Ada Fitzsimmons
Paper Pile
P.O. Box 337
San Anselmo, CA 94979-0337
ph: 415-454-5552
fax: 415-454-2947
e-mail: apaperpile@aol.com
web: http://www.paperpilecollectibles.com
Shop and mail order dealer of all kinds of paper items and ephemera; specialties are postcards, magazines, advertising trade cards, valentines, poster stamps and stickers, sheet music, advertising, handmade/primitive paper items, etc.

Tom Osjecki
Phyllis' Philatelics
P.O. Box 792
Canyonville, OR 97417
ph: 541-839-4135 or 541-839-6151
Buys, sells and specializes in postcards, paper Americana, stamps and covers; over 25,000 covers and postcards listed by state or topic.

Ruth A. Miller Knott
Paperpeneur, The
2601 Kittias Highway
Ellensburg, WA 98926
ph: 509-962-8840
fax: 509-962-3609
e-mail: ruthie@ellensburg.com
Offers a unique selection of paper ephemera, historical documents, and collectibles: advertising, Americana, agriculture, Colonial, maritime, transportation, fraternal; does research and will answer questions.

Ken Sowman
Vista Group, The
229 Foster Dr.
Barrie, Ontaria LN4 3X9
Canada
ph: 705-739-0482
fax: 705-739-7544
e-mail: ksowman@bconnex.net
Appraises, deals in all kinds of paper collectibles; any subject, any age.

Albert Van den Bosch
Collectomania
Stenenbrug 14
Antwerp, Flanders 2140
Netherlands
ph: 003 343 365952 or 003 232 711588
fax: 003 232 711583
e-mail: Albert.vandenBosch@ping.be
web: http://www.ping.be/card/index.html
Buys and sells European trade cards; also calendars, menus and all other European ephemera.

Hava Getz
HGIMAGES
P.O. Box 6
Markfield, Leicestershir LE67 9TX
U.K.
ph: 44 1530 244354
fax: 44 1530 244354
e-mail: hgimages@dircon.co.uk
web: http://www.hgimages.dircon.co.uk
Has a large selection of playing cards and card games for sale on the web; also carries large selection of ephemera including cigar box labels and old cigarette packets.

Experts

A. David Rutstein
As Time Goes by Ephemera & Nostalgia Shop
P.O. Box 73
Great Barrington, MA 01230-0073
ph: 413-528-3002
e-mail: davidr@bcn.net
Buys and sells paper collectibles and ephemera, especially WWI posters, Victorian scrapbooks, sheet music, Judaica, baseball, ethnic, non-sports trading cards, etc.; has spoken extensively on WWI propaganda and on sheet music.

Norman E. Martinus
Nostalgia Gallery, Inc.
3501 N Croatan Hwy.
Kill Devil Hills, NC 27948-8350
ph: 252-441-1881 or 252-261-2002
Co-author with Harry Rinker of "Warman's Paper" (Wallace-Homestead, 1994); wants to buy pre-1940 surfing paper, Wright Bros., paper related to spiders, US Coast Guard Stations in N.C.

Ray Walsh
Curious Book Shop
307 E. Grand River
East Lansing, MI 48823-4324
ph: 517-332-0112
Dealer/expert; owner of three book shops in Michigan; hosts radio call-in show about books and paper collectibles; writes columns; send a SASE for reply when writing.

Ken Prag
Ken Prag Paper Americana
P.O. Box 14817
San Francisco, CA 94114-0817
ph: 415-586-9386
e-mail: kprag@planeteria.net
Eager to buy old stocks and bonds, quality picture postcards, western stereoviews, old timetables and brochures, etc.

Internet Resources

Printed Ephemera Collection, Library of Congress
101 Independence Ave. SE
Washington, DC 20540
ph: 202-707-8000
e-mail: ndlpcoll@loc.gov
web: http://memory.loc.gov/ammem/rbpehtml/pehome.html
The Printed Ephemera Collection is a rich repository of Americana; 28,000 primary source items dating from the 17th century; website preview has 50 digitized images: posters, notices, advertisements, proclamations, leaflets, etc.

John Lobota
Antique Paper & Ephemera X-change
P.O. Box 15493
West Palm Beach, FL 33416-5493
ph: 561-697-0055
e-mail: papertique@apex-ephemera.com
web: http://www.apex-ephemera.com
Buy, sell, trade your paper collectibles; APEX offers over 80 categories of paper collectibles; free classifieds for collectors; bulletin boards, search and more.

Misc. Services

Deborah Lavoie
Deborah Leavoie Fine Books & Paper Treasures
P.O. Box 117
New Boston, NH 03070-0117
ph: 603-487-2369
fax: 603-487-2333
e-mail: rare@worldnet.att.net
web: http://abebooks.com/home/RARE/
Offers shrinkwrapping services for dealers, collectors, or auctioneers for display and protection; shrinkwraps prints, ephemera and paper of all shapes and sizes on white foam board or on cardboard.

Museums/Libraries

Crane Museum of Papermaking
30 South St.
Dalton, MA 01226
ph: 413-648-2600
e-mail: info@crane.com
web: http://www.crane.com/about/ac_sets/set_ac_museum.html
Operated by the Crane Paper Company.

American Antiquarian Society
185 Salisbury St.
Worcester, MA 01609
ph: 508-755-5221
fax: 508-753-3311
e-mail: library@mwa.org
web: gopher://mark.mwa.org/
A learned society founded in 1812; maintains a research library of American history and culture in order to collect, preserve, and make available for study the printed record of the U.S.; 3 million books, maps, pamphlets, etc.

Periodicals

Dennis M. Sater, Ed.
Newspaper: Paper & Advertising Collector (P.A.C.)
P.O. Box 500
Mount Joy, PA 17552-0500
ph: 717-492-2540 or 800-800-2833
fax: 717-653-6165

Doug Watson
Magazine: Paper Collectors' Marketplace
470 Main St.
P.O. Box 128
Scandinavia, WI 54977-0128
ph: 715-467-2379
fax: 715-467-2243
e-mail: pcmpaper@gglbbs.com
web: http://www.pcmpaper.com/
Monthly magazine for collectors of autographs, paperbacks, postcards, advertising, photographica, magazines; all types of paper ephemera.

Ada Fitzsimmons, Ed.
Paper Pile Press
Magazine: Paper Pile Quarterly
P.O. Box 337
San Anselmo, CA 94979-0337
ph: 415-454-5552
fax: 415-454-2947
e-mail: apaperpile@aol.com
web: http://www.paperpilecollectibles.com
A quarterly magazine with many ads for both buyer and seller; also contains feature articles about collectibles, book reviews, auction reviews, show/auction calendar.

Magazine: Intercard's Magazine
Via Valfre
Torino, 4-10121
Italy
Covers advertising, movie posters, postcards, calendars, political and historical documents, autographs, and all paper collectibles.

Arcade Cards

Clubs/Associations

Bob Schulhof
Arcade Collectors International
Newsletter: Penny Arcade
3621 Silver Spur Lane
Acton, CA 93510-1268
ph: 661-269-2841
fax: 661-272-9864
e-mail: omega@ptw.com
Ads, news, research, price lists, check list of arcade cards, especially Exhibit Supply Co. & Nutoscope Co.

Experts

Bob Schulhof
3621 Silver Spur Lane
Acton, CA 93510-1268
ph: 661-269-2841
fax: 661-272-9864
e-mail: omega@ptw.com

Billheads

Collectors

Joseph F. Loccisano
Historic Photographs & Paper Americana
2264 Nicholson Square Dr.
Lancaster, PA 17601-3966
ph: 717-560-5182
Wants to buy billheads and business letterheads (1850s - 1920s) that graphically show products, buildings, logos, etc.; send photo with asking price.

Canadian

Dealers

Michael Rice
Michael Rice Collectibles
P.O. Box 286
Saanichton, British Columbia V8M 2C5
Canada
ph: 250-652-9412
e-mail: mrice@pacificcoast.net
Wants pre-1940 Canadian and English picture postcards, and other pre-1940 Canadian interesting paper memorabilia; stock certificates, photographs, steamship souvenirs, posters, autographs; all queries answered; call evenings.

Certificates

Repro. Sources

Sally Green Bunce
1520 Makefield Rd.
Yardley, PA 19067-3150

Mark Sutton
Victorian Certificates
2035 St. Andrews Circle
Carmel, IN 46032-9547
ph: 317-844-5648
Reproduces Victorian-era certificates; add your own photos & calligraphy; commemorate weddings, anniversaries, births or baptisms.

Dance Cards

Dealers

Federico Santi
Drawing Room of Newport, The
152 Spring St.
Newport, RI 02840-6806
ph: 401-841-5060
fax: 401-848-0953
e-mail: zsolnay@drawrm.com
web: http://www.drawrm.com
Buys, sells, and collects late 19th century and early 20th century dance cards; prefers fancy examples; can buy from photo or photocopy.

Historical

Auction Services

Remember When Antiquities
P.O. Box 1829
Wells, ME 04090-1829
Wants autographs, books, historical ephemera, sports memorabilia for

consignment auctions; free quarterly auction catalogs.

Collectors

Gary Ronk
6247 Cove Rd.
Roanoke, VA 24019-1715
ph: 540-562-2368
Wants to buy early deeds, indentures, land grants, etc., especially those that have revenue stamps or seals.

Illustrated

Periodicals

Denis C. Jackson, Ed.
Newsletter: Illustrator Collector's News, The
P.O. Box 1958
Sequim, WA 98382-1958
ph: 360-452-3810
e-mail: ticn@olypen.com
web: http://www.olypen.com/ticn/
A bi-monthly for collectors and dealers of old art prints, calendars, books, magazines, pin-ups, posters and original artwork and old paper relating to illustrators 1800s-1990s.

Napkins

Experts

Moira Jaffe
255 W. 88 St.
New York, NY 10024
e-mail: jaffer@earthlink.net
Interested in pre-1950 decorative and commemorative napkins.

Radio Related

(see also RADIOS)

Dealers

Jim & Felicia Kreuzer
New Wireless Pioneers
P.O. Box 398
Elma, NY 14059
ph: 716-681-3186
fax: 716-681-4540
e-mail: wireless@pce.net
Buys and sells 1850-1950 books, catalogs, magazines and other literature dealing with early radio, wireless, x-ray and electricity.

Southern

Dealers

Henry Barnet
516 Maverick Circle
Spartanburg, SC 29307-3707
ph: 864-579-2112
e-mail: yourtowninc@compuserve.com
Buys, sells, appraises paper, photos, documents, maps, autographs, and prints associated with The Old South or New South.

Western

(see also WESTERN AMERICANA)

Auction Services

Warren Anderson
America West Archives
P.O. Box 100
Cedar City, UT 84721-0100
ph: 435-586-9497 or 435-586-7323
e-mail: awa@netutah.com
web: http://www.americawestarchives.com/
Buys and sells paper Americana associated with the Western US: old documents, letters, photos, stocks, maps, autographs, prints, etc.; author of "Owning Western History."

PAPERDOLLS

(see DOLLS, Paper)

PAPERWEIGHTS

(see also GLASS)

Auction Services

Stanley Block
Block's Box
P.O. Box 51
Trumbull, CT 06611-0051
ph: 203-261-0057 or 203-926-8448
fax: 203-261-7033
e-mail: blockschip@aol.com
web: http://www.blocksite.com/
Conducts mail-bid auctions of paperweights received from collectors, dealers, estates, museums and others.

Lawrence H. Selman
L.H. Selman, Ltd.
761 Chestnut St.
Santa Cruz, CA 95060-3751
ph: 800-538-0766 or 831-427-1177
fax: 831-427-0111
e-mail: lselman@got.net
web: http://www.paperweight.com/
Conducts periodic auctions of fine paperweights.

Clubs/Associations

Libby Helprin, Pres
New England Paperweight Collectors
500 Partridge Hill Rd.
Stowe, VT 05672
ph: 802-253-8676
NEPCA holds meetings to provide members the opportunity to learn more about paperweights by offering educational programs and to purchase paperweights from dealers.

Andrew Dohan
Delaware Valley Chapter, Paperweight Collectors Association
Newsletter: DVC-PCA Newsletter
49 East Lancaster Ave.
Malvern, PA 19355-2120
ph: 610-722-5800 or 610-688-8718
fax: 610-647-5476
e-mail: Dohan@juno.com
Full program meetings four times a year; color photography quarterly newsletter.

Brian Landis
MD-DC-VA Paperweight Collectors
P.O. Box 665
Jessup, MD 20794
e-mail: Brian_Landis@msn.com

Joann Eck
Indiana Paperweight Collectors
135 North 9th St.
Zionsville, IN 46077-1217
ph: 317-873-2194

Rosanne Milius
Evangeline Bergstrom Paperweight Collectors
1305 Maricopa Dr.
Oshkosh, WI 54904-8150

Leo C. McNamee III
Paperweight Collectors Association of Chicago
Newsletter: PCAC Newsletter
535 Delkir Court
Naperville, IL 60565-4165
ph: 630-369-2242

Leo McNamee III
Chicago Paperweight Collectors
535 Delkir Ct.
Naperville, IL 60565-4166
ph: 630-369-2242

Alvin R. Bates, Pres.
Paperweight Collectors' Association, Inc.
Newsletter: Paperweight Collectors' Bulletin
P.O. Box 40
Barker, TX 77413-0040
e-mail: lrayb@juno.com
web: http://www.collectoronline.com/paperweight/PCA.html
1600 member association of paperweight collectors; antique and modern; dealers, artists, makers of contemporary weights.

Bob White
Paperweight Collectors Association of Texas
Newsletter: Paperweight, The
2900 Sussex Gardens Lane
Austin, TX 78748-2020
ph: 512-282-0061
e-mail: white-rr@juno.com
web: http://www.main.org/pcatx/
Three or four meetings and five or six newsletters per year.

Janis Cadwallader
San Diego Paperweight Collectors
P.O. Box 881463
San Diego, CA 92168
ph: 619-292-5617
e-mail: janisc@thegroup.net
web: http://w3.thegroup.net/~janisc/pca/index.html

Lawrence H. Selman
International Paperweight Society
Newsletter: Paperweight News
761 Chestnut St.
Santa Cruz, CA 95060-3751
ph: 800-538-0766 or 831-427-1177
fax: 831-427-0111
e-mail: lselman@got.net
web: http://www.paperweight.com/
The purpose of the society is to uncover knowledge about the history and making of glass paperweights (antique and contemporary), to bring together collectors from around the world, and to organize displays of glass paperweights.

Larry Manning
Northern California Paperweight Collectors Association
6041 Monteverde Dr.
San Jose, CA 95121

Michel-Pierre Grenier
Montreal Paperweight Collectors
3275 Sherbrooke St. East, #2
Montreal, Quebec H1W 1C3
Canada
ph: 514-523-9580

Phyllis Helfand
Ontario Paperweight Collectors
16 Tanburn Place
Don Mills, Ontario M3A 1X5
Canada
ph: 416-447-4659

Peter Pommerencke
Paperweight Club of Deutchland
Postfach 1733
Planegg, D-82145
Germany

Cambridge Paperweight Circle
Newsletter: CPC Newsletter
34 Huxley Rd.
Welling, Kent DA16 2EW
U.K.
ph: 0181 303 4663
The only paperweight club in the U.K. with members worldwide; newsletter covers paperweight activity, auctions, and new books.

Collectors

Andrew Dohan
49 East Lancaster Ave.
Malvern, PA 19355-2120
ph: 610-722-5800 or 610-688-8718
fax: 610-647-5476
e-mail: Dohan@juno.com
Collector buys antique pre-1900s glass paperweights: French, American, English, Bohemian, Russian; buying one or entire collection; surface wear & minor chips to base not a problem; write or call first with description.

James Lefever
P.O. Box 1263
Beltsville, MD 20704
ph: 410-828-0776
e-mail: MrGlass@redrose.net

Barry Schultheiss
P.O. Box 6259
High Point, NC 27262
ph: 336-841-6966
fax: 336-841-6987
e-mail: barrysppwt@aol.com

Alvin Bates
19302 Marlstone Ct.
Houston, TX 77094-3082
ph: 713-579-7413
e-mail: alrayb@juno.com
Paperweight collector; also editor of the Paperweight Collectors Association of Texas newsletter.

Aleen Burfening
21405 North 142nd Drive
Sun City West, AZ 85375
ph: 623-546-4405
e-mail: jwburf@aol.com

Tom Bradshaw
325 Carol Dr.
Ventura, CA 93003-1710
Wants to buy antique glass paperweights; French, American, Bohemian, English, and others; wants millefiori, flower, butterflies, snakes, etc.; also modern fine pieces by Ysart, Kaziun, Stankard, and other makers.

Margaret Gunn
10110 Longview
Atwater, CA 95301
ph: 209-394-7724

Dealers

Stanley Block
Block's Box
P.O. Box 51
Trumbull, CT 06611-0051
ph: 203-261-0057 or 203-926-8448
fax: 203-261-7033
e-mail: blockschip@aol.com
web: http://www.blocksite.com/
Buys and sells antique French and modern Kaziun paperweights.

Leo Kaplan
Leo Kaplan, Ltd.
967 Madison Ave.
New York, NY 10021
ph: 212-249-6766 or 212-249-7574

George Kamm
George Kamm Paperweights
219 W. Market St.
Marietta, PA 17547
ph: 717-426-1761
fax: 717-426-1045
e-mail: marpwts@redrose.net
web: http://www.art-craftpa.com/kamm.html
Buys and sells antique and contemporary glass paperweights; paperweight appraisals.

Lawrence H. Selman
L.H. Selman, Ltd.
Newsletter: Paperweight News
761 Chestnut St.
Santa Cruz, CA 95060-3751
ph: 800-538-0766 or 831-427-1177
fax: 831-427-0111
e-mail: lselman@got.net
web: http://www.paperweight.com/
World's largest dealer in fine paperweights, both antique and contemporary; mail order company selling directly or through paperweight auctions offered twice yearly; call for free brochure.

Experts

Dan McNamara
P.O. Box 163 - 163
Boston, MA 02113-0002
ph: 617-846-9465
Buys and sells antique glass paperweights; has identified and cataloged paperweights for numerous museums; will identify paperweights for others who send photo and SASE.

Louis O. St. Aubin, Jr.
Brookside Antiques "Art Glass Gallery"
44 North Water St.
New Bedford, MA 02740
ph: 508-993-4944
Museum consultant, expert, established in 1964, author of "Pairpoint Lamps. A Collectors Guide"; nationally known authority, lecturer, appraiser, auction house consultant; founder of the New Bedford Glass Museum.

Paul H. Dunlop
Dunlop Collection, The
P.O. Box 6269
Statesville, NC 28687-6269
ph: 800-227-1996 or 704-871-2626
fax: 704-871-2329
Leading paperweight dealers; buys and sells all top quality antique and contemporary glass paperweights, paperweight books and related items; author of "The Jokelson Collection of Antique Cameo Incrustation."

George N. Kulles
13441 Little Creek Dr.
Lockport, IL 60441-8686
ph: 708-301-0996
Buys, appraises and repairs antique paperweights.

Steve Cole
Steve Cole Antiques
23897 Corte Emerado
Murrieta, CA 92562
ph: 909-600-0335
fax: 909-600-0445
e-mail: stevecole@dconn.com
web: http://www.paperweightsonline.com/
Buy, sell, collect, trade glass paperweights from around the world; collections can be consigned for sale or appraised; member of the National Paperweight Collector's Association and numerous local collector groups; will answer questions.

Lawrence H. Selman
L.H. Selman, Ltd.
761 Chestnut St.
Santa Cruz, CA 95060-3751
ph: 800-538-0766 or 831-427-1177
fax: 831-427-0111
e-mail: lselman@got.net
web: http://www.paperweight.com/
Buys and sells antique paperweights; also repairs and polishes paperweights. Author of "Art of the Paperweight."

Man./Prod./Dist.

Joe Rice
House of Glass, Inc., The
7900 E State Road 28
Elwood, IN 46036-8449
ph: 765-552-6841
fax: 765-552-6854
Makes paperweights all signed by owner, Joe Rice; also makes all sorts of other solid glass: ashtrays, pears, ringholders, etc.

Museums/Libraries

Wheaton Village Museum of American Glass
1501 Glasstown Rd.
Millville, NJ 08332-1566
ph: 609-825-6800 or 800-998-4552
fax: 609-825-2410
e-mail: mail@wheatonvillage.org
web: http://www.wheatonvillage.org/
Covers all types of American glass: Stiegel, Amelung, flasks, pressed, art glass, art nouveau, paperweights, lamps & lighting, cut glass, 20th century art glass, reproductions, pre-studio movement, contemporary studio glass, etc.

Corning Museum of Glass, The
One Museum Way
Corning, NY 14830-2253
ph: 607-937-5371
fax: 607-937-3352
e-mail: cmg@cmog.org
web: http://www.pennynet.org/glmuseum/
Over 24,000 glass objects, innovative exhibits, videos, models; glass history, archaeology, and early manufacturing; great website with lots of information about glass.

Degenhart Paperweight & Glass Museum, Inc.
65323 Highland Hills Rd.
P.O. Box 186
Cambridge, OH 43725-0186
ph: 740-432-2626
Over 1000 paperweights on exhibit; video, research library, gift shop.

Alex Vance, ExDir
Bergstrom-Mahler Museum
165 N. Park Ave.
Neenah, WI 54956
ph: 920-751-4675
The museum houses one of the world's finest collections of glass paperweights.

Repair Services

Edward Poore
Crystal Workshop
P.O. Box 475
Sagamore, MA 02561-0475
ph: 508-888-1621 or 888-869-0867
fax: 508-888-9298
e-mail: crystalw@capecod.net
Repairs and recutting of damaged glass paperweights; impact fractures removed; recutting of faceted weights and star bottom done when needed; 30 years experience; contact for free detailed brochure.

Art Cut Glass Studio
RD 1 -10 Fawn Drive
Matawan, NJ 07747
ph: 732-583-7648
Restores fine antique glass such as Lalique, Steuben, Baccarat, Galle; also resurfaces paperweights.

George N. Kulles
13441 Little Creek Dr.
Lockport, IL 60441-8686
ph: 708-301-0996
Restores and polishes damaged paperweight surfaces; author of "Identifying Antique Paperweights - Millifiore and Lampwork."

Larry Castle
Castle Fair
3387 Polk Ave.
Ogden, UT 84403
ph: 801-393-8131
e-mail: marblelc8@aol.com
Over ten years experience; all work is hand held using water-cooled diamond equipment to heal fractures.

Advertising

Collectors

Bill Price
Paperweight Potentate of Pittsburgh, The
P.O. Box 82501
Pittsburgh, PA 15218-0501
ph: 412-351-5297
fax: 724-271-4329
e-mail: paperwghts@aol.com
web: http://www.collectoronline.com/wb-paperweights.html
Wants to buy old glass advertising paperweights featuring businesses, World's Fair, buildings, machinery, factories, banks, portraits of people or anything; bottom must be milk glass or glass or glaze-like.

John Andreae
P.O. Box 156
Granger, IN 46530-0156
ph: 219-272-2337
fax: 219-271-1146
e-mail: jkandreae@aol.com
Wants glass paperweights with advertising on them.

Charles Goodman
636 W. Grant Ave.
Charleston, IL 61920-3226
ph: 217-345-6771
Wants any shape, size or form; preferably glass paperweights with milk glass bottoms; any theme including railroads, steamship, airlines, insurance, banks, most anything.

Glenn Fletcher
Wood Room, The
1070 State Highway 46 East
New Braunfels, TX 78130-2850
ph: 830-625-5384
Advanced collector wants standing promotional metal paperweights displaying cars, trucks, buildings, RR, ships, tools; also figural animals, human, medical or representing product advertising; must have company logo, name, or trademark.

Cast Iron

Dealers

Richard Tucker
Argyle Antiques
P.O. Box 262
Argyle, TX 76226-0262
ph: 940-464-3752
fax: 940-464-7293
e-mail: lead1234@gte.net
Buys and sells cast iron advertising paperweights; no reproductions or repaired items.

PAPERWEIGHTS (MODERN)

Clubs/Associations

Caithness Collectors Club
Newsletter: Caithness Report, The
Bldg. 12
141 Lanza Ave.
Garfield, NJ 07026-3530
ph: 973-340-3330 or 800-452-7987
fax: 973-340-9415
e-mail: caithglas@aol.com
web: http://www.caithnessglass.co.uk
Focuses on paperweights; also publishes the "Reflections" magazine.

Alvin R. Bates
Paperweight Collectors' Association, Inc.
Newsletter: Paperweight Collectors' Bulletin
P.O. Box 40
Barker, TX 77413-0040
e-mail: lrayb@juno.com
web: http://www.collectoronline.com/paperweight/PCA.html
1600 member association of paperweight collectors; antique and modern; dealers, artists, makers of contemporary weights.

Dealers

George J. Grupe
Grupe Paperweight Collection, The
3 North Bishop St.
San Angelo, TX 76901-3301
ph: 915-653-0640 or 915-655-0158
Buys and sells contemporary studio art glass and contemporary paperweights by noted artists.

Eric Sinizer
Light Opera Retail Corp.
174 Grant Ave.
San Francisco, CA 94108-5405
ph: 415-956-9866
fax: 415-956-5624
Specializes in contemporary glass paperweights and other studio glass.

Dennis H. Gould
34 Huxley Rd.
Welling, Kent DA16 2EW
U.K.
ph: 0181 303 4663
Specialist dealer in modern European paperweights; interested in exchanging modern American artists for U.K. makers.

Experts

Paul H. Dunlop
Dunlop Collection, The
P.O. Box 6269
Statesville, NC 28687-6269
ph: 800-227-1996 or 704-871-2626
fax: 704-871-2329
Leading paperweight dealers; buys and sells all top quality antique and contemporary glass paperweights, paperweight books and related items; author of "The Jokelson Collection of Antique Cameo Incrustation."

Man./Prod./Dist.

Caithness Glass Inc.
Bldg. 12
141 Lanza Ave.
Garfield, NJ 07026-3530
ph: 973-340-3330 or 800-452-7987
fax: 973-340-9415
e-mail: caithglas@aol.com
web: http://www.caithnessglass.co.uk
The largest producer of museum-quality glass paperweights in the world in both traditional and modern styles.

Ron & Sherry Blankenship
Baron Creek Glassworks
Rt. 2, Box 176
Westville, OK 74965
ph: 918-778-3243
Elegant studio art glass with an emphasis on intricacy and beauty.

PASSPORTS

Collectors

Dan M. Jacobson
P.O. Box 277101
Sacramento, CA 95827-7101
United States and overseas.

PATCHES

(see also BADGES; BOY SCOUT MEMORABILIA; FIRE FIGHTING MEMORABILIA; LAW ENFORCEMENT MEMORABILIA; MILITARIA, Insignia; GIRL SCOUT MEMORABILIA)

PATENT MODELS

Collectors

Alan Rothschild
P.O. Box 1347
Syracuse, NY 13201
ph: 315-655-9367
e-mail: Maxertaxer@aol.com
Wants to buy patent models and Patent Office documents.

Skip Gladwin
11900 SE Shell Ave.
Hobe Sound, FL 33455
ph: 561-546-1500
fax: 561-746-8336
e-mail: rfg101842@aol.com
Collects U.S. Patent Models; requests information on models or literature pertaining to models; will assist in answering questions about patent models and can recommend others who might be able to help.

Museums/Libraries

U.S. Patent & Trademark Museum
2121 Crystal Drive
Arlington, VA 22202
ph: 703-305-8341
web: http://www.uspto.gov/web/offices/ac/ahrpa/opa/museum/welcome.html
Strives to educate the public about the patent and trademark systems, and the important role intellectual property protection plays in our nation's social and economic health.

Patent Model Museum
400 North 8th St.
Fort Smith, AR 72901
ph: 501-782-9014 or 501-782-1555
fax: 501-782-1555
Collection contains over 80 miniature models and pictures of 19th century inventions.

PATENTS, TRADEMARKS & COPYRIGHTS

Internet Resources

United States Copyright Office, The Library of Congress
101 Independence Ave. SE
Washington, DC 20559-6000
e-mail: copyinfo@loc.gov
web: http://lcweb.loc.gov/copyright
Copyright basics, registration procedures, copyright records, application forms, form letters, copyright law, Federal regulations, international copyright, related resources.

Misc. Services

U.S. Government Printing Office, Superintendent of Document
P.O. Box 371954
Pittsburgh, PA 15250-7954
ph: 202-512-1800
fax: 202-512-2250
e-mail: gpoaccess@gpo.gov
Send $4 for "General Information Concerning Patents."

United States Patent & Trademark Office, Copy Sales
Box 9
Washington, DC 20231
ph: 703-305-4350 or 800-786-9199
fax: 703-305-8759
e-mail: ptcs@uspto.gov
web: http://www.uspto.gov/
Send $3 for copy of a patent.

Richard Van Vleck
Greybird Publishing
P.O. Box 412
Taneytown, MD 21787
ph: 301-447-2680
e-mail: smma@americanartifacts.com
web: http://americanartifacts.com/smma/
Patent search and copy service for items in your collection; a copy of any patent from 1790 to present will be provided, including full text and illustrations; cost is $15 for the first search and $9 for each additional search.

U.S. Patent & Trademark Office, Scientific Library, Foreign Patents Division
2021 Jefferson Davis Highway
Arlington, VA 22202
ph: 703-308-1076 or 800-786-9199
fax: 703-308-1000
e-mail: ptcs@uspto.gov
web: http://www.uspto.gov/web/offices/pac/dapp/sir/stic/newstic.html
Can obtain copies of foreign patents for $10.

PAWNBROKERS

Clubs/Associations

National Pawnbrokers Association
2050 Stemmons, Ste. 107
P.O. Box 420028
Dallas, TX 75342-0028
ph: 214-745-4746 or 800-235-5400
fax: 214-745-1459
e-mail: npamembers@aol.com
web: http://npa.polygon.net/
Contributes to the professional and personal development of member pawnbrokers through enhancement of the images/perceptions of the industry, by advocating pawnbrokers rights, responsibilities and issues, and by representing the industry.

Periodicals

Brian K. Burkart, Pub.
BKB Publications Inc.
Magazine: Today's Pawnbroker
98 Greenwich Ave., #1FL
New York, NY 10011-7743
ph: 212-807-6558
fax: 212-807-1821
e-mail: bkbpub1@ix.netcom.com
Trade news and articles, ads, refining companies, buyers of jewelry and coins, trade shows, etc.

PEACE MOVEMENT ITEMS

(see also MODERNISM, 1960s Memorabilia)

PEANUT MACHINES

(see COIN-OPERATED MACHINES, Vending Machines)

PEANUTS

(see CHARACTER COLLECTIBLES, Peanuts Characters; PLANTERS PEANUTS ITEMS; TOM'S PEANUTS)

PEARL HARBOR

(see also MILITARIA)

Collectors

Martin Jacobs
P.O. Box 22026
San Francisco, CA 94122-0026
ph: 415-661-7552
e-mail: MJacobs784@aol.com
Collector seeks WWII memorabilia from the Homefront 1941-1945; will purchase any size collection; wants victory pins, Cinderella stickers and stamps, envelope art, war propaganda, Anti-Axis art, matchcovers, postcards, etc.

Experts

Harvey & Sandy Dolin
Harvey Dolin & Co.
5 Beekman St.
New York, NY 10038-2206
ph: 212-267-0216
Wants any item pertaining to Pearl Harbor, WWI and WWII.

PEDAL CARS

(see RIDING TOYS)

PEEP SHOWS

(see STANHOPES)

PENCIL SHARPENERS

Collectors

Craig Dinner
P.O. Box 4399
Long Island City, NY 11104-0399
ph: 718-729-3850 or 802-365-7181
Wants pre-1920 mechanical pencil sharpeners.

Robert Kwalwasser
168 Camp Fatima Rd.
Renfrew, PA 16053-9104
ph: 724-789-7766
fax: 724-789-9771
e-mail: robert@tcis.net
Wants old pencil sharpeners, pocket and desk types.

Martha Crouse
4516 Brandon Lane
Beltsville, MD 20705-2601
ph: 301-937-2343
e-mail: mecrouse@aol.com
Wants to buy old pencil sharpeners; figural, celluloid, hand held; wants one or entire collections.

Bernice Kraker
9800 McMillan Ave.
Silver Spring, MD 20910-1149
ph: 301-589-2544
Wants only hand-held, figural sharpeners made from metal, celluloid, or Bakelite from German, USA and Japan from 1920s to 1940s; wants no plastic or common bronzed metal types; description important; answers all mail and glad to share.

Jay Bolante
3058 North Honore St.
Chicago, IL 60657-2050
ph: 773-327-5091
Collects and wants to buy mechanically operated pencil sharpeners.

Clay Tontz
4043 Nora Ave.
Covina, CA 91722
ph: 626-338-9976
Please send SASE if requesting a reply.

Roger Graham
Every Era Antiques
855 57th St.
Sacramento, CA 95819-3300
ph: 916-456-1767
e-mail: roger@every-era.com
web: http://www.every-era.com
Wants pre-1925 cast iron mechanical pencil sharpeners: Little Shaver, Mills, Stimpson, Dixon, Planetary, Perfect Pointer, Gem, Webster, Jupiter, Angell.

Experts

Bernice Kraker
9800 McMillan Ave.
Silver Spring, MD 20910-1149
ph: 301-589-2544
Wants only hand-held, figural sharpeners made from metal, celluloid, or Bakelite from German, USA and Japan from 1920s to 1940s; wants no plastic or common bronzed metal types; description important; answers all mail and glad to share.

PENCILS

(see also OFFICE EQUIPMENT; PENCIL SHARPENERS; PENS; SPORTS COLLECTIBLES, Golf Pencils)

Clubs/Associations

Boris Rice
Pen Collectors of America
Newsletter: PENnant
P.O. Box 821449
Houston, TX 77282-1449
ph: 281-496-7152 or 281-496-2290
fax: 281-496-2290
e-mail: p_c_a@compuserve.com
web: http://ourworld.compuserve.com/homepages/P_C_A/
Association of fountain pen collectors; maintains library of materials for pen collectors; disseminates information, holds regular meetings; promotes collecting as a hobby and using pens.

Louise Hiltz
American Pencil Collectors Society
Newsletter: Pencil Collector, The
640 Evergreen Drive
Mountain View, WY 82939
web: http://ernie.bgsu.edu/~dmartin/apcs.htm
Members focus on the collecting of pens & pencils: unsharpened lead pencils with advertisements or addresses, old mechanical pencils.

Kevin Prime, Mem.
Writing Equipment Society
178 Foster Hill Road
Bedford, MK41 7TB
U.K.
ph: 012324 271453
Devoted to the conservation and study of writing instruments and accessories: pens of all types and materials, pencils, nibs, inkwells, stamp boxes, quill cutters, scriveners' knives, seals, writing slopes, blotters, paper knives, etc.

Collectors

Bruce Axler
Ansonia Station
P.O. Box 1288
New York, NY 10023-1288
ph: 212-362-4429
fax: 212-579-1274
Wants pocket items, i.e. items/gadgets designed to fit in the pocket: tools, knives, lighters, compacts, folding cups, items which look like a pocket watch but are not, calculators, leather items, matchsafes, candle safes, travel items.

Bill Lean
3351 Jeffrey Lane
Eau Claire, WI 54703
ph: 715-832-4301

Andrew Westberg
916 Wall St.
Mankato, MN 56003
ph: 507-344-0643
e-mail: westberg@mctcnet.net
web: http://www.mctcnet.net/~westberg/pencil.htm
Collects advertising pencils, mechanical, bullet, golf and carpenter pencils.

Susan Cox
800 Murray Dr.
El Cajon, CA 92020
ph: 619-697-5922
e-mail: antiqfever@aol.com
Wants old, unsharpened pencils with advertising on them.

Dealers

David Nishimura
Vintage Pens & Lighters
P.O. Box 41452
Providence, RI 02940-1452
ph: 401-351-7607
fax: 401-351-1168
e-mail: info@vintagepens.com
web: http://www.vintagepens.com
Buys and sells all sorts of vintage fountain pens and pencils; specializes in European and Japanese pens, especially those with enamel or lacquer decoration; also offers repair service.

Experts

Marc L. Ames
539 Lyme Rock Rd.
Bridgewater, NJ 08807-1670
ph: 908-526-7676
fax: 908-575-0880
e-mail: magames@ix.netcom.com
Wants to buy mechanical pencils, as well as pre-1950 advertising pencils.

Judith & Cliff Lawrence
Pen Fanciers Club
1169 Overcash Dr.
Dunedin, FL 34698-5537
ph: 727-734-4742
e-mail: PenFanC@aol.com
Buys, sells and specializes in old fountain pens, dip pens and mechanical pencils.

Internet Resources

Doug Martin
Pencil Pages, The
17797 W. Toussaint N.
Graytown, OH 43432
ph: 419-862-2380
e-mail: doug@pencilpages.com
web: http://www.pencilpages.com
Web site contains general information of use to pencil collectors, and can aid collectors in contacting one another.

Clips

Dealers

Lee Trout
17 Westdell Dr.
St. Louis, MO 63136-1936
Wants to buy pencil clips that have advertising on them; also wants advertising wood pencils, but prefers unsharpened pencils.

PENS

(see also BLOTTERS; GLASS, Whimsies [Pens]; INKWELLS & INKSTANDS; OFFICE EQUIPMENT; PENCILS)

Appraisers

Joseph G. Balshone, GG, ISA
Columbus Gemological Laboratories, Inc.
463 East Town St.
Columbus, OH 43215-4796
ph: 800-209-4367 or 614-224-2404
fax: 614-224-5630
e-mail: jbalshone@compuserve.com
Specializing in appraising gems & jewelry, post-1800 firearms, and vintage and modern writing instruments and accessories.

Jim Gaston
Jim Gaston Vintage Fountain Pens & Dip Pens
1777 River Road
Lakeview, AR 72642
ph: 870-431-5206 or 870-431-5204
fax: 870-431-5216
e-mail: gaston@mtnhome.com
web: http://www.jimgaston.com/
Wants to buy vintage fountain pens, dip pens; will purchase entire collections, or appraiser single pen(s) or collections; also repairs.

Victor Topper
Topper Gallery
2900 John Street, Ste. 402
Markham, Ontario L3R 5G3
Canada
ph: 905-513-8070 or 416-633-4518
fax: 905-513-6628
e-mail: toppart@pathcom.com
web: http://www.topperart.com/
Pen appraiser, dealer collector specializing in pens of various materials made from 1890 to 1990: Waterman, Mont Blanc, etc.

Clubs/Associations

Boris Rice
Pen Collectors of America
Newsletter: PENnant
P.O. Box 821449
Houston, TX 77282-1449
ph: 281-496-7152 or 281-496-2290
fax: 281-496-2290
e-mail: p_c_a@compuserve.com
web: http://ourworld.compuserve.com/homepages/P_C_A/
Association of fountain pen collectors; maintains library of materials for pen collectors; disseminates information, holds regular meetings; promotes collecting as a hobby and using pens.

Rick Propas, Sec.
Pan Pacific Pen Club, The
43739 Montrose Ave.
Fremont, CA 94538-6058
ph: 707-996-9720 or 510-623-8351
e-mail: rickp@mediacity.com

Canadian Association of Writing Instrument Collectors
1057 Steeles Avenue West, Ste. 642
North York, Ontario M2R 2S9
Canada
e-mail: dszpiro@vax2.concordia.ca
web: http://www.hemsingad.com/cwic.html
A not-for-profit club for writing instrument collectors and enthusiasts.

Kevin Prime, Mem.
Writing Equipment Society
178 Foster Hill Road
Bedford, MK41 7TB
U.K.
ph: 012324 271453
Devoted to the conservation and study of writing instruments and accessories: pens of all types and materials, pencils, nibs, inkwells, stamp boxes, quill cutters, scriveners' knives, seals, writing slopes, blotters, paper knives, etc.

Collectors

Arvin & Ann Chaikin
e-mail: arvann@pacificrim.net
web: http://www.pacificrim.net/~arvann/
Collects vintage fountain pens and shares the hobby with friends all over the world; website has additional pen links and connections; especially interested in Chilton pens, Crocker, Sears (not the store), Parker, Sheaffer, Conklin.

Dan McNamara
P.O. Box 163 - 163
Boston, MA 02113-0002
ph: 617-846-9465
Buying fancy metal or overlay pens; will help identify fountain pens for others who send photo and SASE.

David & Becky Beane
Beane's Antiques & Photography
92 River Rd.
Benton, ME 04901
ph: 207-453-6790
fax: 207-453-6790
e-mail: dbeane@mint.net
web: http://www.metigues.com/catgalog/beane.html
Collector of quality fountain pens, showcases, advertisements, and other pen related items: LeBouef, Waterman, Parker, Chilton and any quality pen wanted.

Gary Lehrer
16 Mulberry Rd.
Woodbridge, CT 06525-1717
ph: 203-389-5295 or 800-484-1081
fax: 203-389-4515
Wants pens of any age and condition; single items or large collections; call collect; write or send pens and pencils (insured); also offers fountain pen repair service.

Richard Carvell
249 Sportsmans Ave.
Freeport, NY 11520-5635
ph: 516-623-1325 or 800-767-7367
Wants old fountain pens; any large size pen; any ornate pens; also gold filled & silver filigree; pre-1910 pearl overlay and solid gold; also wants to buy pen ephemera.

George J. Samuels
10122 Cape Anne Dr.
Columbia, MD 21046
ph: 410-997-4421
Wants to buy fountain pens, regular or cartridge; any condition.

Howard Share
4349 LaVale Ct.
Clemmons, NC 27012-9009
ph: 336-766-6579
fax: 336-766-5445
e-mail: HowSha43@aol.com
Wants to buy high quality fountain pens, especially the oversized men's pens or the fancy pens with overlays or filigrees of gold silver, or mother-of-pearl.

Judson H. Bell
10124 Inverness Way
Port Saint Lucie, FL 34986-3210
Buys high quality fountain pens and parts, 1880-1940; prefer sterling and 14k overlays; one or entire collection; also desires pens and information about Eisenstadt Mfg. Co., St. Louis.

Stephen Berger
7759 Seminary Ridge
Columbus, OH 43235
ph: 614-885-6083
fax: 614-436-8695
e-mail: chinku@worldnet.att.net
Wants to buy pens by Parker, Waterman, Conklin, Wahl-Eversharp, Chilton, Schnell.

Jim Beattie
3730 Augusta Lane
Elkhart, IN 46517
ph: 219-522-3467
fax: 219-875-6617
e-mail: indianapen@cyberlink-inc.com
Wants quality old fountain pens or parts, 1870-1970; also does repairs.

Rich Hartzog
World Exonumia
P.O. Box 4143
Rockford, IL 61110-0643
ph: 815-226-0771
fax: 815-397-7662
e-mail: hartzog@exonumia.com
web: http://www.exonumia.com/
Wants silver and silver overlay fountain pens.

Bob Arnell
P.O. Box 313
Grandview, MO 64030-0313
ph: 816-966-0544 or 816-213-4999
e-mail: bobstuff11@excite.com
Wants to buy fountain pens.

Dealers

Peter Stanton
57 Earle St.
Central Falls, RI 02863
ph: 401-725-0055
Wants to buy fountain pens, especially Waterman, Parker, Wahl Ever Sharp, Chilton, LeBoeuf, Montblanc, Triad, Conklin, Sheaffer, Carter.

David Nishimura
Vintage Pens & Lighters
P.O. Box 41452
Providence, RI 02940-1452
ph: 401-351-7607
fax: 401-351-1168
e-mail: info@vintagepens.com
web: http://www.vintagepens.com
Buys collections, parts, and all pen-related material; full repair and restoration services available; maintains an extensive informational website and on-line catalog.

Geoffrey Berliner
Catalog: Pen Finder Quarterly
928 Broadway, Ste. 604
New York, NY 10010
ph: 800-444-PENS or 212-614-3020
fax: 212-614-3025
e-mail: BerlinerPn@aol.com
web: http://www.berlinerpen.com
Buys and sells vintage and contemporary pens; restorations; newsletter is a monthly glossy color catalog designed to help dealers and collectors buy and sell vintage pens.

Charles M. Yassky
424 Madison Ave., 8th Floor
New York, NY 10017-1106
ph: 800-969-2345
fax: 212-826-6214
Active buyer of fountain pens and related advertising material; wants fountain pens by Wahl, Waterman, Parker, Conklin, etc.

Richard Weinstein
Authorized Repair Service
30 W. 57th St.
New York, NY 10019
ph: 212-586-0947
fax: 212-586-1296
e-mail: vinlighter@aol.com
web: http://www.vintagelighters.com
Wants to buy unusual old fountain pens in precious metal or plastic by Parker, Waterman, Wahl, Eversharp, Conklin, Chilton, Esterbrook, etc.

Gene Bensen
AntiqueLine, Inc.
771 West End Ave.
New York, NY 10025
ph: 212-749-2526
fax: 212-749-1686
e-mail: antqline@i-2000.com
web: http://www.antiqueline.com
Specializes in inkwells, desk accessories, bookends, and fountain pens for the home or office.

Frank Briola
P.O. Box 44022
Pittsburgh, PA 15205-0222
ph: 412-937-8787 or 800-372-6509
e-mail: americana@mail.com
Wants to buy fountain pens.

Jim Monroe
Monroe's Pen Shop
P.O. Box 508
Edgemont, PA 19028
ph: 888-666-7637
fax: 877-666-7637
e-mail: Jim@penshop.com
web: http://www.penshop.com/
Avid pen collector; web site serves pen collectors world wide featuring consignments, repairs, pen locator, magazine subscriptions, vintage fountain pens; also offers a large selection of new and limited edition pens.

Fahrney's Pens
8329 Old Marlboro Pike, B-13
Upper Marlboro, MD 20772
ph: 800-624-7367 or 301-568-6550
fax: 301-736-2926
Carries contemporary pen catalog; also does repairs.

Sam Fiorella
Pendemonium
15231 Larkspur Lane
Dumfries, VA 22026-1075
ph: 703-670-8549
fax: 703-670-3785
e-mail: sam@pendemonium.com
web: http://www.pendemonium.com
Buys and sells fountain pens, inkwells, ink bottles, pen stands, blotters, pen catalogs, magazine covers and advertisements; write for current "Writing Collectibles" catalog, it's FREE!

Judith & Cliff Lawrence
Pen Fanciers Club
1169 Overcash Dr.
Dunedin, FL 34698-5537
ph: 727-734-4742
e-mail: PenFanC@aol.com
Issues catalog with articles on fountain pens and mechanical pencils; vintage fountain pens, mechanical pencils & pen parts for sale; quarterly catalog; send $5 for sample copy.

Terry Mawhorter
Gentle Ben's Antiques
P.O. Box 3324
Zanesville, OH 43702
ph: 740-454-2314
e-mail: linklady@cyberzane.net
Has been buying and selling pens since 1983.

Thomas Zoss
Zoss Communications, Inc.
230 South Tuxedo Dr.
South Bend, IN 46615
ph: 219-288-1422
fax: 219-288-1422
e-mail: tzoss@zoss.com
web: http://www.zoss.com/pens.htm
Broker of pen-related items, moderator of Internet mailing list of pen collectors and experts; website offers a free mailing list where people from all over the world ask questions, buy and sell, and explore fountain pen collecting.

Michael Clague
Clague's Antiques & Collectibles
515 North 7th Street
Estherville, IA 51334
ph: 712-362-2343
e-mail: mpcac@ncn.net
web: http://www.ncn.net/~mpcac/
Buys and sells fountain pens and mechanical pencils; will furnish references; offers a five day return privilege.

Michael A. Pratt, Sr.
Pen Palace, The
687 Co. Rd. “"U"”
Rt. 2 Box 73
Fremont, NE 68025-9635
ph: 402-721-4765
fax: 402-721-4765
e-mail: mp@mb3.net
web: http://www.mb3.net/display/
Buys and sells unique pens of all kinds; also sells display cases for cuff links and collectibles of all types; also can make old pens modern so they can be use cartridge ink without altering the pen's appearance in any way.

Mark Wright
P.O. Box 6007
Humble, TX 77325
ph: 800-774-8555 or 281-359-6868
Wants unusual fountain pens and related pen catalogs and pen paper ephemera.

John Marshall
For Love or Money
16693 NW Meadowgrass Ct.
Beaverton, OR 97006
e-mail: john@europa.com
web: http://www.europa.com/~john/
Buys and sells antique and collectible fountain pens mostly Sheaffer and Parker, occasionally more unusual pens.

Simon Gray
Battersea Pen Home
Catalog: Battersea Pen Home Quarterly
P.O. Box 4361
London, SW11 4PT
U.K.
ph: 44-171-652-4695
fax: 44-171-652-4695
e-mail: info@penhome.co.uk
web: http://www.penhome.co.uk
Specialists in buying, selling and restoring vintage fountain pens including Montblanc, Waterman, Conklin, Sheaffer, Parker, Pelikan and all major brands. Organizer of the annual London Pen Show.

Experts

Marc L. Ames
539 Lyme Rock Rd.
Bridgewater, NJ 08807-1670
ph: 908-526-7676
fax: 908-575-0880
e-mail: magames@ix.netcom.com
Wants to buy vintage fountain pens (Waterman, Parker, Sheaffer, Wahl, Eversharp, Chilton Carter, etc.); matching and non-matching pencils, as well as pre-1950 advertising pencils.

Max Davis
New York Vintage Pen Company
Newsletter: Journal of Vintage Pens
Chelsea Antiques Building
110 West 25th St., Gallery 307
New York, NY 10001-7401
ph: 212-243-7090 or 800-641-4884
fax: 212-769-9199
e-mail: maxpen@aol.com
web: http://www.nypen.com/
Buys and sells vintage pens, pencils, ink, ink bottles, Victorian pencils, pen stands, desk sets, vintage dip pens; does repairs; newsletter available for $12/year; also publishes a free "Journal of Vintage Nibs."

Bert Heiserman
9434 Royal Bonnet Terrace
Gaithersburg, MD 20879-2489
ph: 301-681-5893
Buys, sells, restores and specializes in old fountain pens including those made by Parker, Waterman, Sheaffer, Conklin, Swan, Wahl-Eversharp, Mont Blanc, Holland, etc.

Judith & Cliff Lawrence
Pen Fanciers Club
1169 Overcash Dr.
Dunedin, FL 34698-5537
ph: 727-734-4742
e-mail: PenFanC@aol.com
Buys, sells and specializes in old fountain pens, dip pens and mechanical pencils.

Jack Price
Vintage Fountain Pens
3481 North High St.
Columbus, OH 43214
ph: 614-267-8468 or 614-267-7978
fax: 614-267-8468
e-mail: jproto1@aol.com
Buys, sells, restores antique pens.

Ray & Bev Jaegers
P.O. Box 29396
Saint Louis, MO 63126-0396
e-mail: USPsiSquad@aol.com
Experts and historians.

Glen Benton Bowen
Fountain Pen Hospital - Texas
P.O. Box 6007
Kingwood, TX 77325-6007
ph: 281-359-4363
fax: 281-359-4468
e-mail: webmaster@penworld.com
web: http://www.penworld.com
Repairs, buys and sells; offers a consignment catalog, PENFINDER, containing the world's most valuable and rare pens; author of book about pens.

Anthony Davis
Rainbow Creations
P.O. Box 8935
Universal City, CA 91618-8935
ph: 818-762-3540
fax: 818-762-2503
e-mail: antiqphoto@earthlink.net
web: http://www.19cphoto.com
Specializes in the fountain pen by such makers Parker, Waterman, Sheaffer, Conklin, Wahl, and other.

Bernard Gagnon
29 Marguerite d'Youville
Gatineau, Quebec J8T IR8
Canada
ph: 819-568-0581
Writes column about fountain pens for "The Upper Canadian" newspaper.

Simon Gray
Battersea Pen Home
P.O. Box 4361
London, SW11 4PT
U.K.
ph: 44-171-652-4695
fax: 44-171-652-4695
e-mail: info@penhome.co.uk
web: http://www.penhome.co.uk
Specialists in buying, selling and restoring vintage fountain pens including Montblanc, Waterman, Conklin, Sheaffer, Parker, Pelikan and all major brands. Organizer of the annual London Pen Show.

Internet Resources

Lynn Brant
Pen Lovers - The Internet Fountain Pen Homepage
e-mail: LBrant@msn.com
web: http://www.penlovers.com

Thomas Zoss
Zoss Communications, Inc.
230 South Tuxedo Dr.
South Bend, IN 46615
ph: 219-288-1422
fax: 219-288-1422
e-mail: tzoss@zoss.com
web: http://www.zoss.com/pens.htm
Broker of pen-related items, moderator of Internet mailing list of pen collectors and experts; website offers a free mailing list where people from all over the world ask questions, buy and sell, and explore fountain pen collecting.

Bill Acker
Bill Acker's Fountain Pen Page
P.o. Box 338
Henderson, TX 75653
ph: 903-657-0558
e-mail: 74040.1175@compuserve.com
web: http://www.billspens.com
Website includes information on brands, repair information, literature, shows, pen links.

Fountain Pen Paradise, LLC
678 Wells Road
Boulder City, NV 89055
ph: 702-294-6582
fax: 702-294-6538
e-mail: feedback@fountainpens.com
web: http://www.fountainpens.com
Newsletter, many brands of pens for sale, online collections, pen information, etc.

Glenn Marcus
Glenn's Pens
#6, 216 9th Street
New Westminster, British Columbia V3M 3V3
Canada
ph: 604-522-3134
e-mail: gmarcus@istar.ca
web: http://home.istar.ca/~gmarcus/review1.shtml
Website has directory and reviews of pen stores from around the world.

Periodicals

Stuart Schneider
Hudson Valley Graphics
Newsletter: Pens
P.O. Box 64
Teaneck, NJ 07666-0064
ph: 201-261-1983
fax: 201-599-1950
e-mail: stuarts1031@erols.com
web: http://www.geocities.com/Yosemite/Geyser/7949/
A quarterly newsletter focusing on fountain pens.

Terry Monzo
World Publications
Magazine: Pen World Magazine
P.O. Box 6007
Kingwood, TX 77325-6007
ph: 281-359-4363
fax: 281-359-4468
e-mail: webmaster@penworld.com
web: http://www.penworld.com
Premier magazine for fountain pens and fine writing instruments; bi-monthly glossy color magazine to provide histories of pen companies and their products; full color reproductions of worlds most valuable pens; some articles on old pens.

Repair Services

Fountain Pen Hospital
Newsletter: Vintage Pen Quarterly
10 Warren St.
New York, NY 10007-2211
ph: 212-964-0580 or 800-253-7367
fax: 212-227-5916
Repairs fountain pens; also sells books, new and vintage pens, and accessories.

Thom D'Amico
Fine Italian Hand, A
P.O. Box 624
Putnam Valley, NY 10579
ph: 914-528-4350
e-mail: afineitalianhand@pcrealm.net
Antique and classic writing instruments restored, repaired, replated, and recreated; special attention to nibs.

Simon Gray
Battersea Pen Home
P.O. Box 4361
London, SW11 4PT
U.K.
ph: 44-171-652-4695
fax: 44-171-652-4695
e-mail: info@penhome.co.uk
web: http://www.penhome.co.uk
Specialists in buying, selling and restoring vintage fountain pens including Montblanc, Waterman, Conklin, Sheaffer, Parker, Pelikan and all major brands. Organizer of the annual London Pen Show.

Suppliers

Pen Sac Company, The
P.O. Box 4470
Carlsbad, CA 92018
ph: 760-735-2501 or 888-PENSACS
fax: 760-735-2502
e-mail: PenSacs@aol.com
Manufactures ink sacs for vintage fountain pens; has almost 50 different sizes; can supply ink sacs for practically every vintage pen.

Fr. Terence Koch
P.O. Box 128
Los Altos, CA 94023-0128
Sells pen parts, tools and repair information.

Floaty

Collectors

Cheryl Vincent
e-mail: escher@primenet.com
web: http://www.primenet.com/~escher/

Elizabeth Spatz
e-mail: espatz@earthlink.net
web: http://home.earthlink.net/~espatz/floaty/
Website has lots of links to other collectors.

Beverly Broadstone
Go With The Flo-at!
22925 Arlington Ave., Ste. 10
Torrance, CA 90501
ph: 310-325-0039
e-mail: bonzilla@concentric.net
web: http://members.tripod.com/~floatypens/
Trades and collects float pens; website has a list of pens for trade as well as collector information and resources.

Karen Rolstad
1 Via Honrado
Rancho Santa Margarita, CA 92688
e-mail: rolstad@pacbell.net
web: http://home.pacbell.net/rolstad/penpal.html
Collector and trader of float pens.

Internet Resources

Luis Aquila
Floaty Pens of the World
e-mail: aguila@interlog.com
web: http://www.interlog.com/~aguila/
Website has lots of images of floaty pens from around the world.

Man./Prod./Dist.

Ideal Motion Promotion, The
e-mail: floatpen@floatpens.com
web: http://www.floatpens.com/
Importers of Eskesen floating action products such as floaty pens, a.k.a. floating action pens, photoramic pens, floating view pens, view pens, motion pens, magic motion pens.

Sharon Jones
Global Shakeup
235 East Colorado Blvd., #178
Pasadena, CA 91101
ph: 323-256-8325
fax: 323-259-8988
e-mail: feedback@snowdomes.com
web: http://www.snowdomes.com/
Features a huge selection of American and European glass and plastic snowdomes including figurals, comic characters, locations, advertising, limited edition, science fiction, and much more; also float pens; 28-page catalog $2.

Sandy Medorf
Floaty Industries
2219 West Olive Ave., Dept. 260
Burbank, CA 91506
ph: 800-883-3627
fax: 818-566-4420
e-mail: floaty@floaty.com
web: http://www.floaty.com/
Website has a store of exclusive floaty products and you can e-mail or call to request a free mail order catalog.

Periodicals

Diana Andra
Newsletter: Float About
1676 Millsboro Rd.
Mansfield, OH 44906-3374
ph: 419-529-8876
fax: 419-529-3354
e-mail: DiAndra@FloatAbout.com
web: http://www.FloatAbout.com
Floaty pens contain an image or other object that floats in a small chamber of liquid.

Nibs

Collectors

John Gwin
1845 Anderson Dr.
Las Cruces, NM 88001
ph: 505-522-2171
Since 1995 has collected antique steel pen nibs, the boxes/tins in which they came, and relate advertising, equipment and ephemera.

Repair Services

John Mottishaw
Classic Fountain Pens
P.O. Box 46723
Los Angeles, CA 90046
ph: 323-655-2641
fax: 323-651-0265
e-mail: john@nibs.com
web: http://www.nibs.com
Offers a complete fountain pen point (or nib) repair service including custom tipping, crack repair, and straightening; most other pen repairs provided as well (mail order business only offering return insured UPS shipping.)

PERAMBULATORS

(see also CHILDREN'S THINGS)

Museums/Libraries

Janet L. Pallo
Victorian Perambulator Museum
26 East Cedar St.
Jefferson, OH 44047
ph: 440-576-9588
Only Victorian perambulator museum in the U.S.; over 100 examples along with related items such as sleighs, dolls, etc.

PERFORMING ARTS

(see also MAGICIANS PARAPHERNALIA; MUSIC; NIGHTCLUB MEMORABILIA; POPULAR CULTURE; PUPPETS; SHEET MUSIC; STRIPTEASE; VAUDEVILLE MEMORABILIA; VENTRILOQUIST ITEMS)

Collectors

Don Hoffman
P.O. Box 4231
Salinas, CA 93912-4231
ph: 831-449-7311
Wants to buy minstrel, vaudeville, ragtime items: posters, broadsides, cabinet cards, CDV's, tintypes, daguerreotypes, ambrotypes, programs, tickets, antique photos, autographs, books, booklets, memorabilia; please describe and price.

Dealers

Jonathan & Lisa Reynolds
Dramatis Personae - Booksellers
P.O. Box 1070
Sheffield, MA 01257-1070
ph: 413-229-7735
fax: 413-229-7735
Sale of antiquarian books, prints, ephemera, autographs, and manuscripts relating to theater, drama, circus, conjuring, puppetry, and popular entertainers; also select theatrical antiques; issues 4-5 catalogs per year.

Museums/Libraries

Consortium of Popular Culture Collections
Popular Culture Library
Bowling Green State University
Bowling Green, OH 43403-0001
ph: 419-372-2450
fax: 419-372-7996
e-mail: ascott@bgnet.bgsu.edu
web: http://www.bgsu.edu/colleges/library/pcl/cpccm.html
Consortium composed of Bowling Green State U., Kent State U., Michigan State U., and Ohio State U.; the largest academic library collections of primary research material in comic art, popular fiction, popular music, performing arts.

Gilbert & Sullivan

Collectors

David Trutt
3711 North Round Rock Dr.
Tucson, AZ 85750-2082
ph: 520-751-4215
e-mail: davettt@aol.com
Wants Gilbert & Sullivan items: books, posters, antiques, collectibles; any item relating to W.S. Gilbert, Arthur Sullivan, or their operas.

Opera Mementos

Dealers

Roger Gross
Roger Gross, Ltd.
225 East 57th St.
New York, NY 10022-2822
ph: 212-759-2892
fax: 212-838-5425
e-mail: rogergross@earthlink.net
web: http://www.rgrossmusicautograph.com/
Buys and sells signed photos of singers, instrumentalists, conductors and composers; letters, musical quotes; classical music and operatic books, memorabilia, ephemera, unsigned photos, etc.

Museums/Libraries

Nordica Homestead Museum
Holly Rd.
Farmington, ME 04938
ph: 207-778-2042
Home of Maine's homegrown international opera diva, Lillian Norton, born in 1857.

Lester DeQuaine, Dir.
Rosa Ponselle Museum, The
39 West Main St.
Meriden, CT 06451-4110
ph: 203-639-9778
Museum is open daily; buys and sells artifacts of Rosa Ponselle's life and opera world she new; museum store sells Ponselle books and CDs.

Marcella Sembrich Opera Museum
4800 Lakeshore Dr.
Bolton Landing, NY 12814-0417
ph: 518-644-9839
web: http://www.adirondack.net/orgs/arccleader/marcella.html

Theatrical Memorabilia

Collectors

D. Eliot
400 W. 43rd St. #25T
New York, NY 10036-6312
Wants theater souvenirs; pre-1920; especially commemorative items, e.g. 50th performance, 100th, etc.

Dealers

Lacy E. Long
199 Tarrytown Rd.
Manchester, NH 03103
ph: 603-622-5449
Buys, sells and trades theatrical memorabilia, holds periodic telephone auctions, sends out monthly price lists.

Chuck Haley
Sherlock's
13926 Double Girth Ct.
Matthews, NC 28105-4068
ph: 704-847-5480
Primarily interested in post-1940 Broadway and related items.

Museums/Libraries

Marty Jacobs
Museum of the City of New York
1220 5th Ave.
New York, NY 10029-5221
ph: 212-534-1672
fax: 212-534-5974
e-mail: mcny@mcny.org
web: http://www.mcny.org/mcny/
Access by appointment; research fee charged.

Lennis Moore
Theatre Museum of Repertoire Americana
1887 Threshers Rd.
Mount Pleasant, IA 52641
ph: 319-385-8937 or 319-385-9432
Largest American collection of 1850s-1950s middle plains Tent, Opera House, Repertoire Theatre and Chautauqua memorabilia, with Research Library and data base.

PERFUME LAMPS

(see also BOTTLES, Perfume & Scent; FAIRY LAMPS; LAMPS & LIGHTING, Miniature)

Collectors

Sandy Katz-Leegood
P.O. Box 596553
Dallas, TX 75359-6653
ph: 214-824-7917
fax: 214-824-7917
e-mail: decolectibles@cyberramp.net
Interested in all types of perfume lamps (similar to night lights, but has well/container to add/hold perfume; also small holes on top preventing exploding and allows perfume to escape); porcelain, glass, ceramic, French, Robj, etc.

Dealers

Tom & Linda Millman
231 S. Main St.
Bethel, OH 45106-1327
ph: 513-734-6884
fax: 513-734-6884
Wants to buy perfume lamps: Goebel, DeVilbiss, Fulper, Robj, Aladin, Aerozon, Aroma, and other foreign and domestic manufacturers.

PERIODICALS

(see also "GENERAL INTEREST PERIODICALS" Appendix in the back of this book as well as Periodicals listed under specific categories throughout this Directory.)

Internet Resources

David J. Maloney, Jr., ISA CAPP
MaloneysOnline Antiques & Collectibles Resource Directory
P.O. Box 2049
Frederick, MD 21702-1049
ph: 301-695-8544
fax: 301-695-6491
e-mail: dave@maloney.com
web: http://www.maloneysonline.com/
Online resource information source for collectors, sellers, claims adjusters, etc.: includes experts, buyers, clubs, periodicals, repairers, museums/libraries, appraisers, auctioneers, matching services, dealers, etc.

PERSONALITIES

(see also AUTOGRAPHS; AUTOGRAPHS, Celebrity; FAN CLUBS; MOVIE MEMORABILIA; PHOTOGRAPHS, Celebrity; POLITICAL COLLECTIBLES; SPORTS COLLECTIBLES)

Wills of

Repro. Sources

Celebrity Collectibles
2303 N. 44th St., #4-175
Phoenix, AZ 85008
Sells copies of celebrity wills: Lucille Ball, Marilyn Monroe, Al Jolson, Jack Benny, the Three Stooges, Robert Reed - and 600 more.

PERSONALITIES (ARTISTS)

(see also ART; CARTOON ART, Walt Kelly; ILLUSTRATORS)

Daniel Chester French

Museums/Libraries

Chesterwood
4 Williamsville Road
P.O. Box 827
Stockbridge, MA 01262
ph: 413-298-3579
web: http://www.berkshireweb.com/chesterwood/index.html

Edna Hibel

Clubs/Associations

Ralph Burg, Pres.
Edna Hibel Society
Magazine: Hibeletter
P.O. Box 9721
Coral Springs, FL 33075-9721
ph: 561-848-9633 or 954-731-6699
fax: 954-978-3088
e-mail: HibelSoc@aol.com
A fellowship to honor the art and achievements of internationally famous artist Edna Hibel; magazine published quarterly.

Man./Prod./Dist.

Andy Plotkin, Ph.D.
Edna Hibel Studio
Newsletter: Hibelleter
P.O. Box 10907
Riviera Beach, FL 33419-4967
ph: 561-655-2410 or 800-771-3362
fax: 561-848-9640
e-mail: hibel@worldnet.att.net
web: http://www.hibel.com/
Publishes and distributes fine arts, collectibles, reproductions, gift items, and fashion and accessories designed by Edna Hibel, America's best loved artist.

Museums/Libraries

Andy Plotkin, Ph.D.
Hibel Museum of Art
Newsletter: Hibelleter
P.O. Box 10907
Riviera Beach, FL 33419-4967
ph: 561-655-2410 or 800-771-3362
fax: 561-848-9640
e-mail: hibel@worldnet.att.net
web: http://www.hibel.com/
Oversees the world's oldest artist fellowship, and the world's only non-profit public museum dedicated to the art of a living American woman.

Grant Wood

Collectors

Jerry A. McCoy
800 Thayer Ave.
Silver Spring, MD 20910-4504
ph: 301-565-2519
e-mail: ohiowa@erols.com
Wants anything relating to Grant Wood: autographs, lithographs, etc.

Saint-Gaudens

Museums/Libraries

Saint-Gaudens National Historic Site
RR 3, Box 73
Cornish, NH 03745
ph: 603-675-2175
fax: 603-675-2701
e-mail: saga@valley.net
web: http://www.sgnhs.org/
Home of one of America's greatest sculptures.

Salvador Dali

Museums/Libraries

Kathleen A. White
Salvador Dali Museum
Newsletter: Dali Newsletter
1000 Third St. South
Saint Petersburg, FL 33701
ph: 727-823-3767 or 800-442-DALI
fax: 727-894-6068
e-mail: daliweb@mindspring.com
web: http://www.daliweb.com/
Permanent home of the world's most comprehensive collection of Dali's works; oil and watercolor paintings, drawings, graphics, etc.; also a library with over 5,000 books on Dali and Surrealism.

PERSONALITIES (ENTERTAINERS)

(see also RADIO SHOWS, Old Time)

Abbott & Costello

Clubs/Associations

Chris Costello
Abbott & Costello Fan Club
Newsletter: Abbott & Costello Quarterly, The
P.O. Box 2084
North Hollywood, CA 91610-0084
ph: 818-566-4062
fax: 818-558-3799
e-mail: 102437.104@compuserve.com
web: http://www.city-net.com/abbottandcostellofc/
Promotes the legacy of Abbott & Costello along with selling A&C Fan Club products and merchandise; sells A&C products on their web site.

Collectors

Eugene Kirschenbaum
723 E. 84th St.
Brooklyn, NY 11236

Al Jolson

Clubs/Associations

International Al Jolson Society, Inc.
Magazine: Jolson Journal, The
P.O. Box 473
Stevenson, MD 21153-0473
ph: 888-4JOLSON
e-mail: ajr@ari.net
web: http://www.jolson.org/
Dedicated to perpetuating the memory "THE WORLD'S GREATEST ENTERTAINER!" - AL JOLSON; also publishes The Jolson News newsletter.

British

Periodicals

Bill King
Goody Press, The
Newsletter: Anglofile
P.O. Box 33515
Decatur, GA 30033-0515
ph: 404-633-5587
fax: 404-321-3109
web: http://www.the-beatles.com/beatlepg/anthadd/bfan.htm
Anglofile keeps tabs on British entertainment and entertainers and when and where they're appearing in the U.S.

Carpenters

Collectors

Bob Mason
381 Mayfair Drive South
Brooklyn, NY 11234
ph: 718-444-4749
Wants Karen & Richard Carpenter memorabilia.

Dean Martin

Clubs/Associations

Dean Martin Fan Center
Newsletter: Dean Martin Fan Center Newsletter
P.O. Box 660212
Arcadia, CA 91066-0212
e-mail: admin@deanmartinfancenter.com
web: http://deanmartinfancenter.com/
Magazine-style newsletter published quarterly: articles, news, question and answer, auction section, editorials, lots of photos.

Dean Martin Association, The
P.O. Box 80
Uckfield, East Sussex TN22 1ZR
U.K.
e-mail: dma@cableinet.co.uk
web: http://wkweb4.cableinet.co.uk/dma/
Promotes and publicizes the Dean Martin legacy.

Collectors

Andrea Fuller
RD 1 Box 240
Morgantown, PA 19543
Wants to buy photos, 45s, memorabilia, lobby cards, magazines, etc.

Neil T. Daniels
P.O. Box 660203
Arcadia, CA 91066-0203
e-mail: webdir@deanmartinfancenter.com
web: http://deanmartinfancenter.com/
Wants to buy anything Dino: records, photos, programs, videos, reel-to-reel tapes, acetates, toys, novelties, comics, posters, oddball items, etc.

Eddie Cantor

Clubs/Associations

Michelle Malik
Eddie Cantor Appreciation Society
Newsletter: ECAS Newsletter
14611 Valley Vista Blvd.
Sherman Oaks, CA 91403
e-mail: ecantor@aol.com
web: http://members.aol.com/ecantor/
Members receive a newsletter, biographical information, and a black-and-white photograph of the 1930s-1940s singer/entertainer.

Esther Phillips

Clubs/Associations

Dave Frees
Esther Phillips "Memory Lane" Fan Club
P.O. Box 131
Adamstown, PA 19501-0131
ph: 717-738-2513
The first memorial for blues/jazz artist, "Little" Esther Phillips.

Frank Sinatra

Clubs/Associations

Sinatra Society of America
Newsletter: Sinatra Society of America Newsletter
P.O. Box 2705
North Hollywood, CA 91610-0705
e-mail: fssociety@aol.com
web: http://members.aol.com/BrianC101/SSA.htm

Collectors

Bill Brooks
31 Thorns Lane
Highland, NY 12528-1213
ph: 914-691-7370

Scott Sayers
1800 Nueces
Austin, TX 78701
ph: 512-478-3483
fax: 512-473-2447
Wants any Frank Sinatra related collectibles including records, toys, books, etc.; issues an auction list quarterly.

Dealers

Footlight Records
113 East 12th Street
New York, NY 10003
ph: 212-533-1572
fax: 212-673-1496
e-mail: footlight1@aol.com
web: http://www.footlight.com
Offers large selection of Sinatra records, tapes and CDs.

Experts

Peter Barbato
917 South Bishop St.
Chicago, IL 60607-4019
ph: 312-733-7943 or 312-746-5369
Buys, collects, appraises Frank Sinatra memorabilia; author of "Sinatra: 50th Anniversary Collector's Guide, 1935-1985"; serious Sinatra collectors; collecting for over 35 years; no calls after 9 p.m. CST; large collection now for sale.

Fred Astaire

Collectors

M. Russell
1425 4th St. SW, A206
Washington, DC 20024-2240
Wants to buy Fred Astaire costumes, signed letters, contracts, and other memorabilia.

Girl Groups

Clubs/Associations

Louis Wendruck
Girl Groups Fan Club
Newsletter: Girl Groups Gazette
P.O. Box 69A04 - Dept. Mal
West Hollywood, CA 90069-0066
ph: 323-650-5112
e-mail: gayboylaca@writeme.com
web: http://members.tripod.com/~ggfc/
Fan Club for the 1960s and 1970s female singers and singing groups of Rock 'n Roll; sells related t-shirts, photos, videos, records, postcards, memorabilia.

Jack Benny

Clubs/Associations

Laura Lee, Pres.
International Jack Benny Fan Club
Newsletter: Jack Benny Times, The
9461 Skyline Blvd.
Piedmont, CA 94611-1738
ph: 925-933-3879
fax: 925-210-3699
Forum for acquisition and trading of memorabilia relating to Jack Benny & his associates; also JB audio tape lending library.

Johnny Mathis

Collectors

Steve Luth
1116 48th St.
Sacramento, CA 95819
Buys anything related to Johnny Mathis.

Lily Langtry

Collectors

Cummings
P.O. Box 622
Saint Helena, CA 94574-0622
Wants any Lily Langtry related memorabilia; stage posters, sheet music, newspaper and magazine articles, etc.

Marilyn Monroe

Clubs/Associations

Jamie Leigh
Marilyn Monroe Fan Club, The
e-mail: Monroe1Fan@aol.com
web: http://members.aol.com/Monroe1Fan/fanclub.html
An on-line club Marilyn Monroe fans; lots of links to related sites.

Marx Brothers

Collectors

Ira Dolnick
241 Golf Mill center #718
Niles, IL 60714
e-mail: ijdds@aol.com
Wants anything relating to the Marx Brothers: magazines, lobby cards, sheet music, etc.

Internet Resources

Frank Bland
Marx Brotherhood
e-mail: webmaster@whyaduck.com
web: http://www.whyaduck.com/
Web site offers Marx Brothers career info, pictures, sounds, games, and more.

Sonja Henie

Collectors

Ann J. Bates
Trout Point
5660 Keefe Road
Land O' Lakes, WI 54540
ph: 715-547-3836
e-mail: ajb@newnorth.net
Long time, active collector of all Sonja Henie memorabilia.

PERSONALITIES (FAMOUS)

Charles A. Lindbergh

(see also AVIATION)

Clubs/Associations

Janet & Dick Hoerle, ExSec
C.A.L./N-X-211 Collectors Society
Newsletter: Spirit of St. Louis
727 Youn Kin Parkway, South
Columbus, OH 43207-4788
ph: 614-497-9517
Organized to perpetuate the memory of the man and the machine; interested in items concerning Charles A. Lindbergh (1902-1974) and the aeroplane, The Spirit of St. Louis (N-X-211}.

Collectors

Stanley King
260 Fifth Ave.
New York, NY 10001-6408
ph: 212-447-1880
fax: 212-447-0728
A life long interest in collecting Lindbergh related material.

Lou Lufker
Lufker Airport Flight Museum
115 Montauk Highway
East Moriches, NY 11940
ph: 516-878-6302
e-mail: flymuseum@aol.com
Wants Lindbergh memorabilia; anything about Lindy or the Spirit of St. Louis.

Robert A. Fratkin
8280 Greensboro Dr., #200
Mc Lean, VA 22102
ph: 703-556-8101 or 202-483-0274
fax: 703-356-6492
e-mail: coxfdr@erols.com
Wants all Lindbergh memorabilia except books; will appraise by phone, email or with SASE.

Doug Studer
16 Orchard Terrace
Cold Spring, KY 41076
ph: 606-441-2754
Wants Lindbergh and Spirit of St. Louis items.

Janet & Dick Hoerle
727 Youn Kin Parkway, South
Columbus, OH 43207-4788
ph: 614-497-9517
Collects items related to Charles A. Lindbergh and the aeroplane, The Spirit of St. Louis (N-X-211}.

Lyndon Sheldon
2019 Essex
Colorado Springs, CO 80909-1423
ph: 719-597-7066
Buys, sells and trades Charles A. Lindbergh/Spirit of St. Louis memorabilia.

Dealers

Irene Brostow
92 Normandy Rd.
Colonia, NJ 07067-1010
e-mail: IBrostow@aol.com
Wants to buy anything related to Charles Lindbergh; no newspapers

Museums/Libraries

Missouri Historical Society
P.O. Box 11940
Saint Louis, MO 63112-0040
ph: 314-746-4599
fax: 314-746-4548
web: http://www.livable.com/misshist.htm

Dionne Quintuplets

Clubs/Associations

Fay & Jimmy Rodolfos
Dionne Quint Collectors
Newsletter: Quint News
P.O. Box 2527
Woburn, MA 01888-1027
ph: 781-933-2219
A 21-page quarterly newsletter containing articles, columns and classified ads; also reproduction alerts of newly produced items such as signs, pocket mirrors, and paper and composition dolls.

Collectors

Fay & Jimmy Rodolfos
P.O. Box 2527
Woburn, MA 01888-1027
ph: 781-933-2219
Wants Dionne quintuplet items.

Ethelyn Hulit
236 Cape Rd.
Standish, ME 04084-6232
ph: 207-642-3091
Wants to buy Dionne quintuplet items including games, china, paper, advertising, cloth, wooden, plaster

items, real photos, sketches, paintings, unusual items; will reply.

Marceil Drake
RR 3
Roanoke, IN 46783-8903
ph: 219-672-2475
Wants Dionne quintuplet items: games, china, toys, paper advertising, etc.; anything related to Dionne quintuplets or Quintland.

Lois Helen Brown
708 E. Broadway
Logansport, IN 46947-3158
ph: 219-753-3323 or 765-473-3983
Wants Dionne quintuplet and related items such as postcards, games, china, paper, advertising, etc.

Museums/Libraries

Sharon Clark-Berard
Dionne Quints Home & Museum, North Bay Chamber of Commerce
P.O. Box 747
North Bay, Ontario P1B 8J8
Canada
ph: 705-472-8480
fax: 705-472-8027
e-mail: nbcc@enfi.com
web: http://www.northbaychamber.com/dionnequ.htm

William Randolph Hearst

Collectors

Robert A. LeGresley
P.O. Box 1199
Lawrence, KS 66044-8199
ph: 785-331-0782 or 785-749-5458
fax: 785-331-0782
e-mail: rlegres@aol.com
Wants to buy original autographs, manuscripts, books and printed material on Hearst and his family.

PERSONALITIES (HISTORICAL)

(see also POLITICAL COLLECTIBLES; WHITE HOUSE COLLECTIBLES)

Abraham Lincoln

Collectors

Donald Ackerman
P.O. Box 3487
Wallington, NJ 07057
ph: 973-779-8785
fax: 973-744-1517
Devoted collector eager to buy Lincoln memorabilia: campaign flags, ribbons, banners, posters, photographic badges, glass, china.

Cary Demont
P.O. Box 16013
Minneapolis, MN 55416
ph: 612-522-0957
e-mail: Caryd8@aol.com
Wants Lincoln related items: campaign badges, photographic badges, ribbons, banners, political flags, posters and the unusual; also wants the same for any of Lincoln's contemporaries.

Dealers

Steve H. Nowlin
History Makers, Inc.
4040 E. 82nd St.
Indianapolis, IN 46250
ph: 800-424-9259 or 317-842-5828
fax: 317-842-5845
e-mail: steven@indy.net
web: http://www.a1.com/history/

Chuck Hand
310 Monterey St.
Paris, IL 61944
ph: 217-463-4555
fax: 217-463-4555
Extensive catalog of Lincoln ephemera, books, and related material issued every year.

Experts

Stuart Schneider
P.O. Box 64
Teaneck, NJ 07666-0064
ph: 201-261-1983
fax: 201-599-1950
e-mail: stuarts1031@erols.com
web: http://www.geocities.com/Yosemite/Geyser/7949/
Collects and authenticates Lincoln photographs taken and printed while Lincoln was still living (first generation photographs); author of "Collecting Lincoln."

Museums/Libraries

Lincoln Homestead State Park
5549 Lincoln Park Rd.
Springfield, KY 40069
ph: 606-336-7461
web: http://www.state.ky.us/agencies/parks/linchome.htm

Abraham Lincoln Birthplace National Historical Site
2995 Lincoln Farm Rd.
Hodgenville, KY 42748
ph: 502-358-3137
web: http://www.nps.gov/abli/

Lincoln Museum, The
200 E. Berry St.
Fort Wayne, IN 46802
ph: 219-455-3864
web: http://www.thelincolnmuseum.org/

Lincoln Boyhood National Memorial
P.O. Box 1816
Lincoln City, IN 47552
ph: 812-937-4541
web: http://www.nps.gov/libo/

Lincoln Log Cabin State Historic Site
Rte. 1 Box 175
Lerna, IL 62440
ph: 217-345-6489
web: http://www.state.il.us/HPA/LINCLOG.HTM

Lincoln's New Salem Historic Site
Rte. 1 Box 244A
Petersburg, IL 62675-9729
ph: 217-632-4000
fax: 217-632-4010
e-mail: newsalem@fgi.net
web: http://www.state.il.us/HPA/II.HTM
Reconstructed village where Lincoln lived from 1831 to 1837.

Lincoln Home National Historical Site
413 South Eighth St.
Springfield, IL 62701-1905
ph: 217-492-4241
e-mail: Timothy_Good@nps.gov
web: http://www.nps.gov/liho/
At the park's center stands the two-story home of Abraham Lincoln, the only home he over owned.

Lincoln Tomb State Historic Site
Oak Ridge Cemetery
Springfield, IL 62702
ph: 217-782-2717
web: http://www.state.il.us/HPA/LINCTOMB.HTM

Periodicals

Jonathan H. Mann
Magazine: Rail Splitter, The
P.O. Box 275
New York, NY 10044-0205
ph: 212-980-7031 or 212-691-1224
fax: 212-741-8756
e-mail: splitter@interport.net
web: http://www.railsplitter.com/
Dedicated to the study and preservation of materials relating to Abraham Lincoln; assists in appraising Lincoln/Civil War and related collectibles; publishes quarterly journal on new finds and market activity.

Eleanor Roosevelt

Dealers

M. McGovern
Home Grown
1012 Manoa Rd.
Wynnewood, PA 19096
ph: 610-649-6316
fax: 610-649-2369
Wants to buy signed Eleanor Roosevelt documents.

George Washington

Museums/Libraries

Stacey Swigart, Cur.
Valley Forge Historical Society Museum, The
P.O. Box 122
Valley Forge, PA 19481-0122
ph: 610-783-0535
fax: 610-783-0957
web: http://www.ushistory.org/valleyforge/
Focuses on Washington artifacts from the period of the American War for Independence.

Mount Vernon Ladies' Association
P.O. Box 110
Mount Vernon, VA 22121
ph: 703-780-2000
e-mail: library@mountvernon.org
web: http://www.mountvernon.org

Lafayette

Collectors

Andrew B. Golbert
RR 1 Box 1820
North Ferrisburg, VT 05473
ph: 802-453-2525
Wants any Lafayette ephemera, particularly relating to his visit to the U.S. in 1824-25: ribbons, medals, tokens, prints, books, etc.

Napoleon

Appraisers

Pierre Bovis
AZ-Tex Cowboy Trading Co., The
P.O. Box 13345
Tucson, AZ 85732-3345
ph: 520-318-9512
fax: 520-318-0023
e-mail: boris@azstarnet.com
Buy, sells, appraises cowboy memorabilia, primitive arts, American Indian arts, Napoleonic artifacts.

Clubs/Associations

Robert M. Snibbe
Napoleonic Society of America
Newsletter: Member's Bulletin
1115 Ponce De Leon Blvd.
Clearwater, FL 34616-1040
ph: 727-586-1779
fax: 727-581-2578
e-mail: napoleonic1@juno.com
web: http://www.napoleonic-society.com
Founded in 1983 to provide a means of communicating and sharing views on Napoleon as a man and as a military genius; also memorabilia.

Collectors

W.R. Morat
3942 Park Ave.
Memphis, TN 38111-6666
ph: 901-458-2633
fax: 901-458-6202
Wants Napoleon or his family & marshals; books, pictures, statues,

paintings, plates, tables, miniatures, letters, manuscripts, newspapers, swords, ink wells, etc.; especially in America after exile.

James Hilty
Balcony Row
216 S. Broad St.
Holly, MI 48442
ph: 248-634-1400
Wants items of Napoleonic history; manuscripts, letters, diaries, maps, documents, books, etc.

Sir Winston S. Churchill

Clubs/Associations

Lorraine C. Horn, Bus. Mngr.
Churchill Societies, International
Magazine: Finest Hour
135 S. LaSalle St.
Chicago, IL 60603
ph: 800-621-1917
fax: 312-726-9474
e-mail: dcraighorn@msn.com
web: http://www.winstonchurchill.org/society.htm
Educational/charitable assoc. devoted to preserving the memory, thought, writings, of Sir Winston S. Churchill (1874-1965.)

Churchill Center, The
Magazine: Finest Hour
1847 Stonewood Drive
Baton Rouge, LA 70816
ph: 888-972-1874
e-mail: Malakand@conknet.com
web: http://www.winstonchurchill.org/center.htm
Devoted to the promotion of all aspects of Churchill studies, including a broad academic program of seminars, lectures and symposia; publishes specialty handbooks on Churchill-related stamps, books and memorabilia.

PERSONALITIES (INVENTORS)

Thomas Alva Edison

Collectors

John W. Hess
244 Bernaski Rd.
Amsterdam, NY 12010-7827
ph: 518-843-6117
Wants to buy or trade any Edison related merchandise: inventions, antique phonographs, cylinders, advertising, prototypes; also original documents, photographs, etc.

Steven Ramm
420 Fitzwater St.
Philadelphia, PA 19147-3109
ph: 610-922-7050 or 610-545-3290
e-mail: steveramm@aol.com
Wants items related to Thomas Alva Edison, such as books, articles, stock certificates, products from various Edison companies; no magazine ads please.

Carolyn T. Little
725 Esla Dr.
Chula Vista, CA 91910
Wants miniature busts, Edison commemoratives, Edison memorabilia, etc.

Experts

David C. Heitz
Edison Connection, The
P.O. Box 518
New Hope, PA 18938
ph: 215-862-5717
Wants to buy Thomas A. Edison memorabilia: autographs, stock certificates, company letters, advertising, anything Edison; no magazine ads please.

Museums/Libraries

Edison National Historic Site
Main St. & Lakeside Aves.
West Orange, NJ 07052
ph: 973-736-0550
fax: 973-736-8496
e-mail: edis_archives@nps.gov
web: http://www.nps.gov/edis/
Edison's home and laboratory.

David C. Heitz
Edison Connection, The
P.O. Box 518
New Hope, PA 18938
ph: 215-862-5717
Edison Museum open by appointment only - school groups, clubs, Seniors Groups are all welcome; lectures and demonstrations about Edison; no charge.

Laurence J. Russell, Curator
Thomas Edison Birthplace Museum
9 Edison Dr.
P.O. Box 451
Milan, OH 44846-0451
ph: 419-499-2135
fax: 419-499-3241
e-mail: rwheeler@accnorwalk.com
web: http://www.tomedison.org/
An Edison exhibit featuring phonographs, lamps, fans, photos, and other items related to Thomas Edison.

PERSONALITIES (LITERARY)

(see also LITERATURE)

Charles Dickens

Collectors

Gerald DiMinico
105 Park St.
Montclair, NJ 07042-2905
ph: 973-744-2092
Wants Charles Dickens material; seeking primarily prints, lithographs or original art work pertaining to Dickens' books.

Edgar Allan Poe

Museums/Libraries

Edgar Allan Poe House & Museum
417 E. Fayette St., Room 1037
Baltimore, MD 21202
ph: 410-396-7932
web: http://www.comnet.ca/~forrest/museum1.html

Edgar Rice Burroughs

(see also CHARACTER COLLECTIBLES, Tarzan)

Clubs/Associations

George McWhorter
Burroughs Bibliophiles
Magazine: Burroughs Bulletin
Burroughs Memorial Collection
University of Louisville
Louisville, KY 40292-0001
ph: 502-852-8729 or 502-852-6752
fax: 502-852-8734
International club interested in Edgar Rice Burroughs; the "Gridley Wave" newsletter is published monthly; the "Burroughs Bulletin" is a quarterly magazine; annual convention since 1960 with buying, selling, speakers.

Collectors

Butch Smith
P.O. Box 390
Fort Worth, TX 76101
ph: 800-443-7381
Wants books by Edgar Rice Burroughs.

Emily Dickinson

Dealers

Robert Lucas
Robert F. Lucas Antiquarian Books
P.O. Box 63
Blandford, MA 01008
ph: 413-848-2061
e-mail: books@lucasbooks.com
web: http://www.lucasbooks.com
Mail order, on-line sales of antiquarian books, ephemera; specializing in books, ephemera by & about Emily Dickinson and Henry D. Thoreau, 19th century Americana, and manuscript Americana; member ABAA; online essay on book collecting.

Henry Thoreau

Dealers

Robert Lucas
Robert F. Lucas Antiquarian Books
P.O. Box 63
Blandford, MA 01008
ph: 413-848-2061
e-mail: books@lucasbooks.com
web: http://www.lucasbooks.com
Mail order, on-line sales of antiquarian books, ephemera; specializing in books, ephemera by & about Emily Dickinson and Henry D. Thoreau, 19th century Americana, and manuscript Americana; member ABAA; online essay on book collecting.

Horatio Alger, Jr.

(see also BOOKS, Horatio Alger, Jr.)

Clubs/Associations

Horatio Alger Society
Newsletter: Newsboy, The
P.O. Box 70361
Richmond, VA 23255
e-mail: alger-l@listserv.wuacc.edu
web: http://www.wuacc.edu/sobu/broach/algerres.html
To further the philosophy of Horatio Alger, Jr. and to encourage the spirit of Strive & Succeed.

Internet Resources

Bill Roach
Horatio Alger, Jr. Resources Web Site & Listserv
School of Business
Washburn University
Topeka, KS 66621
ph: 785-231-1010 x1748 or 785-231-1010 x1306
fax: 785-231-1063
e-mail: zzroac@acc.wuacc.edu
web: http://www.wuacc.edu/sobu/broach/algerres.html
Provides a forum for discussing the work and world of Horatio Alger; submissions on the novels, short stories, and/or poetry are welcome; works that deal with Alger or the philosophical or historical significance of his writing.

Jack London

Museums/Libraries

Jack London State Historic Park
2400 London Ranch Road
Glen Ellen, CA 95442
ph: 707-938-5216
e-mail: ajstumpf@earthlink.com
web: http://parks.sonoma.net/JLPark.html
House of Happy Walls museum wants Jack London books, magazines, letters and other memorabilia.

Lewis Carroll

Clubs/Associations

Ellie Luchinsky, Sec.
Lewis Carroll Society of North America
Newsletter: Knights Letter, The
18 Fitzharding Place
Owings Mills, MD 21117
ph: 410-356-5110
e-mail: eluchin@erols.com
web: http://www.lewiscarroll.org
Many members also collect books and other Lewis Carroll related materials.

Margaret Mitchell

(see also MOVIE MEMORABILIA, Gone With The Wind)

Collectors

John Wiley, Ed.
1347 Greenmoss Dr.
Richmond, VA 23225-4112
ph: 804-330-5484
fax: 804-771-3054
Wants to buy early copies of Gone With The Wind in dust jackets & limited editions (U.S. & foreign); original Macmillan promotional material (catalogs, counter displays, etc.); Margaret Mitchell items (personal effects, business cards.)

Mark Twain

Dealers

Chuck Haley
Sherlock's
13926 Double Girth Ct.
Matthews, NC 28105-4068
ph: 704-847-5480

Experts

Kevin MacDonnell
MacDonnell Rare Books
9307 Glenlake Dr.
Austin, TX 78730
ph: 512-345-4139
e-mail: macbooks@jump.net
Wants to buy Mark Twain memorabilia: photos, autographs, advertising statues, relics, books, postcards, dinner menus, recordings, lecture tickets, etc.; published author of articles about Mark Twain.

Museums/Libraries

Mark Twain House
351 Farmington Ave.
Hartford, CT 06105
ph: 860-247-0998 or 860-493-6411
fax: 860-246-1577
e-mail: david_bush@hartnet.org
web: http://www.hartnet.org/~twain/
Now a historic house museum, this 19-toom Picturesque Gothic home was built for Samuel Clemens (aka Mark Twain) in 1874 and was the Clemens family residence until 1891; extensive photo archive and collections relating to Mark Twain.

Henry Sweets, Dir.
Mark Twain Home & Museum
Newsletter: Fence Painter, The
208 Hill St.
Hannibal, MO 63401
ph: 573-221-9010
Museum operates Mark Twain's boyhood home, J.M. Clemens Law Office, Grant's Drug Store, and three museum buildings; the newsletter contains historical notes on mark Twain and Hannibal, MO as well as museum news.

Randolph Caldecott

Clubs/Associations

Owen Reichert, Pres.
Randolph Caldecott Society
112 Crooked Tree Trail
Moultrie Trails, RR #4
Saint Augustine, FL 32086
e-mail: reicheg@mail.stjohns.k12.fl.us
web: http://macserver.stjohns.k12.fl.us/others/rc.html
Wants Charles Dickens material.

Shakespeare

Collectors

Tom
P.O. Box 288
Mount Olive, NC 28365
Interested in items related to William Shakespeare and/or the characters in his plays: Staffordshire and other figures, busts, bookends, plaques, engravings, paintings, pictures, plates, mugs, etc.

Sir Arthur Conan Doyle

Collectors

Robert C. Hess
559 Potter Blvd.
Brightwaters, NY 11718-1615
ph: 516-665-8365
e-mail: two21@aol.com
Wants Sherlock Holmes/Sir Arthur Conan Doyle items: figurines, sculpture, statuary, dolls, original artwork, illustrations, etc.

Zane Grey

Clubs/Associations

Carolyn Timmerman, Sec.
Zane Grey's West Society
Newsletter: Zane Grey Review
708 Warwick Ave.
Fort Wayne, IN 46825-5653
ph: 219-484-2904
e-mail: webmaster@zanegreysws.org
web: http://www.zanegreysws.org
Members are collectors of Zane Grey books and memorabilia.

PERSONALITIES (MILITARY)

Audie Murphy

Clubs/Associations

Stan H. Smith, Ed.
Audie Murphy National Fan Club
Newsletter: Audie Murphy National Fan Club Newsletter
8313 Snug Hill Lane
Potomac, MD 20854-4057

Gen. George S. Patton

Clubs/Associations

Charles M. Province, Pres.
George S. Patton, Jr. Historical Society
Newsletter: Patton Blade, The
3116 Thorn St.
San Diego, CA 92104-4618
ph: 619-282-4404
fax: 619-282-1920
e-mail: mike.province@uniontrib.com
web: http://members.aol.com/PattonsGHQ/homeghg.html
Founded in 1970 for the purpose of perpetuating the history of the achievements of General Patton and the men who served with him.

Museums/Libraries

Katie Talbot
Patton Museum of Cavalry & Armor
P.O. Box 208
Fort Knox, KY 40121-0208
ph: 502-624-3812
fax: 502-624-6968
e-mail: museum@ftknox-emh3.army.mil
web: http://147.238.100.101/museum/
The "Patton Gallery" and the Emert L. "Red" Davis Library contains Gen. George S. Patton, Jr. artifacts and reference materials.

PERSONALITIES (MOVIE STARS)

(see also AUTOGRAPHS, Celebrity; MOVIE MEMORABILIA)

Periodicals

George A. Carpinone, Ed.
Magazine: Celebrity Collector Magazine
P.O. Box 1115
Boston, MA 02117-1115
ph: 617-426-7724
fax: 617-426-7724
Interviews with classic movie stars, TV stars, and fan club presidents; exploration of Hollywood memorabilia collecting and collection care; contributions by readers; classified ads; beautifully designed as a collectible on glossy paper.

Ava Gardner

Museums/Libraries

Melody Godwin
Ava Gardner Museum
Newsletter: Ava Advocate
205 S. 3rd St.
P.O. Box 1182
Smithfield, NC 27577
ph: 919-934-5830 or 919-934-0887
fax: 919-934-5830
e-mail: jmivey@ipass.net
web: http://www.avagardner.org/museum
Collection of posters, costumes, photographs and personal items relating to the famous Hollywood movie star, Ava Gardner.

Bette Davis

Collectors

James L. Harmon
P.O. Box 25
Banks, OR 97106
ph: 503-324-7041
Want to buy Bette Davis movie posters, lobby cards, magazines, unusual paper items; original and vintage material only.

Clint Eastwood

Collectors

Fred & Jan Carlson
P.O. Box 2
Hillsboro, OR 97123-0002
ph: 503-648-8477
fax: 503-642-2534
Wants to buy Rawhide and Clint Eastwood items including comics, books, records, tapes, posters, etc.

Errol Flynn

Clubs/Associations

Eric G. Lilley, Pres.
International Errol Flynn Society
Magazine: Sword Magazine
2 Holly Close, Crookham Park
Crookhan Common
Thatcham, Berkshire RG19 8QZ
U.K.
ph: 01635-869694
Founded 1977, over 6000 members in 23 countries; an international club devoted to Errol Flynn.

Greta Garbo

Collectors

Rick Rann
P.O. Box 877
Oak Park, IL 60303-0877
ph: 708-442-7907
e-mail: ukczech@aol.com
Wants to buy Greta Garbo movie posters, lobby cards, glass slides, magazines, coming attraction flyers, books, and pressbooks from 1920s to 1940s.

James Dean

Clubs/Associations

Sylvia Bongiovanni
We Remember Dean International
Newsletter: We Remember Dean International Newsletter
P.O. Box 1673
Anaheim, CA 92815
Formed in respectful memory of actor James Dean; bi-monthly newsletter includes Dean articles, current news, where to buy memorabilia, etc.

Museums/Libraries

David Loehr
James Dean Memorial Gallery
425 North Main St.
P.O. Box 55
Fairmount, IN 46928-0055
ph: 765-948-3326
fax: 765-948-3389
e-mail: dl@jamesdeangallery.com
web: http://www.jamesdeangallery.com/
Houses the world's largest collection of memorabilia dealing with James Dean; wants James Dean plates, posters, records, novelties, photos, autographs, etc.

James Doohan

Collectors

Jan Benham
2457 Raymond SE
Grand Rapids, MI 49507-3923
ph: 616-247-0072
e-mail: jabenham@aol.com
Wants to buy photographs, news clippings, unique collectibles on the actor James Doohan ("Scotty" on StarTrek).

Jimmy Stewart

Museums/Libraries

Jimmy Stewart Museum
P.O. Box 1
Indiana, PA 15701
ph: 724-349-6112 or 800-83-JIMMY
fax: 724-349-6140
e-mail: curator@jimmy.org
web: http://www.jimmy.org/

John Wayne

Periodicals

Mario De Marco
Newsletter: John Wayne, The All-American Hero
152 Maple St.
West Boylston, MA 01583-1825
ph: 508-835-4085
Has a number of books on other western and serial stars; send large SASE for book list.

Tim Lilley
Journal: Trail Beyond, The
540 Stanton Ave.
Akron, OH 44301-1554
ph: 330-724-9225
e-mail: BigTrailak@aol.com
Published annually on the films of John Wayne: John Wayne movie reviews, items for sale, feature articles.

Laurel & Hardy

Collectors

Gino Dercola
10134 Cape Ann Dr.
Columbia, MD 21046
ph: 301-596-6547
Wants Laurel & Hardy toys, games, novelties, dolls, comics, etc.

Jan Benham
2457 Raymond SE
Grand Rapids, MI 49507-3923
ph: 616-247-0072
e-mail: jabenham@aol.com
Wants to buy Laurel & Hardy memorabilia such as dolls, toys, costumes, cookie jars, etc.

Marilyn Monroe

Collectors

Ann Bartoli
1230 Woodridge Ct.
Princeton, IL 61356-8622
ph: 815-875-8925
Wants to buy magazines with Marilyn on the cover (American and foreign), sheet music, press books; especially wants older magazines including pre-national TV Guides; also Sunday sections newspapers like NY Daily News.

Dealers

Cindy Oakes
34025 W. 6 Mile
Livonia, MI 48152
ph: 734-591-3252
Wants dolls, jewelry, autographs, etc.

Carl Kidder
3219 E. County Rd. "N"
Milton, WI 53563
ph: 608-868-4185
fax: 608-868-6808
e-mail: ckidder@jvlnet.com
web: http://www.jvlnet.com/bus/marilynhelp.htm
Collects, buys, sells, appraises and specialize in Marilyn Monroe memorabilia.

Experts

Dawn E. Reno
3280 Shingler Terrace
Deltona, FL 32738-5351
ph: 904-532-1960
fax: 904-532-1960
e-mail: DawnReno@juno.com
Author of "The Marilyn Monroe Phenomena" (Chilton, 1996).

Carl Kidder
3219 E. County Rd. "N"
Milton, WI 53563
ph: 608-868-4185
fax: 608-868-6808
e-mail: ckidder@jvlnet.com
web: http://www.jvlnet.com/bus/marilynhelp.htm
Collects, buys, sells, appraises and specialize in Marilyn Monroe memorabilia.

Denis C. Jackson
P.O. Box 1958
Sequim, WA 98382-1958
ph: 360-452-3810
e-mail: ticn@olypen.com
web: http://www.olypen.com/ticn/
Author of "The Price & Identification Guide to Marilyn Monroe" 2nd edition, 1992; lists mens' magazines, movie magazines, paper, books, etc.; send LSASE for information.

Internet Resources

Peggy Wilkins
Marilyn Monroe
e-mail: mozart@uchicago.edu
web: http://glamournet.com/legends/Marilyn
Web site listing many resources relating to Marilyn Monroe: fan clubs, videos, recent publications, films, etc.

Mary Miles Minter

Experts

Ronald Krueger
P.O. Box 741
Oak Park, IL 60303-0741
ph: 708-788-8235
Always buying photos, posters, lobby cards, postcards, glass slides, theater handbills or anything related to this silent film actress; also interested in making contact with other Minter collectors.

Shirley Temple

Clubs/Associations

ShirleyTempleFans.com
fax: 781-344-7782
e-mail: admin@shirleytemplefans.com
web: http://www.shirleytemplefans.com/

Shirley Temple Collectors by the Sea
Newsletter: Lollipop News
P.O. Box 6203
Oxnard, CA 93031
web: http://www.shirleytemplefans.com/clubs/stclub.htm

Collectors

Gen Jones
294 Park St.
Medford, MA 02155-2668
ph: 781-395-8598
e-mail: genjones@world.std.com
Serious collector wants anything related to Shirley Temple.

Rita Dubas
8811 Colonial Rd.
Brooklyn, NY 11209

W.C. Fields

Clubs/Associations

Ted Wioneck, Jr.
W.C. Fields Fan Club
P.O. Box506
Stratford, NJ 08084-0506
e-mail: fieldsfanc@aol.com
web: http://www.webtrec.com/wcfields
The official W.C. Fields fan club; members receive an 8" x 10" photo of W.C. Fields, membership card, W.C. Fields films list, discounts on related memorabilia.

PERSONALITIES (MUSICIANS)

(see also ROCK 'N' ROLL COLLECTIBLES)

Beatles

Clubs/Associations

B. Whatmough
Working Class Hero Beatles Club
Newsletter: Working Class Hero, The
3311 Niagara St.
Pittsburgh, PA 15213-4223
Non-profit organization for and by true Beatles fans; three newsletter per year covers news, pictures and articles about the Beatles; please send SASE for information.

Beatles Connection
Newsletter: Beatles Connection
P.O. Box 1066
Miami, FL 33780-1066

London Beatles Fan Club, The
Magazine: Off The Beatle Track
4 Oaklands
Constance Rd.
London, TW2 7JQ
U.K.
ph: 44 +181 8989 3606
web: http://members.xoom.com/londonbeatle/

Collectors

Marc Zydiak
P.O. Box 285
Westfield, NJ 07091-0285
ph: 908-654-6505
Wants to buy rare Beatles items: Butcher Album covers, important autograph material, original photographs, etc.

Herb Van Vliet
35 Roberta Dr.
Howell, NJ 07731
ph: 732-458-3950
fax: 732-785-9585
e-mail: herbvan@idt.net
Wants to buy Beatles memorabilia: toys, records, memorabilia and rock concert ticket stubs 1955-1975.

Michael Summers
3258 Harrison St.
Paducah, KY 42001
Wants to buy Beatles memorabilia: fan club items from the 1960s, trading cards, dolls, puzzles, toys, glasses, jewelry; everything Beatles except records.

Gretchen Dziadosz
333 Grentree Lane NE
Ada, MI 49301-9796
e-mail: gretchen@aol.com
Wants original 1960s items only: games, dolls, other memorabilia; please write (include SASE if you want reply) or e-mail; please include asking price.

Dealers

Hein's Rare Collectibles
P.O. Box 179
Little Silver, NJ 07739-0179
ph: 732-219-1988
fax: 732-219-5940
Now buying original Beatles: autographs, motion displays, bongos, guitars, record players, full and used concert tickets, kaboodle kits, costumes, color forms, kits, dolls, school supplies, Yellow Submarine items, lunch boxes, records.

Cindy Oakes
34025 W. 6 Mile
Livonia, MI 48152
ph: 734-591-3252
Wants original 1960s items only: porcelain Beatles, Remco Beatles, cloth Beatles dolls, Beatles nodders, Beatles blowup dolls, etc.

Experts

Joseph Hilton
6 Wheelwright Dr.
Durham, NH 03824-6607
ph: 603-659-3987
e-mail: JHilton@aol.com
Collecting original 1960s items only: Beatles lunch boxes, games, toys, Yellow Submarine items, promo displays, anything Beatles.

Charles F. Rosenay
315 Derby Ave.
Orange, CT 06477
ph: 203-891-8131
e-mail: rosenay@aol.com
Editor of Beatles Fan Club magazine; produces Beatles conventions; trades and sells memorabilia by mail; recognized expert.

Bob Gottuso
BOJO
P.O. Box 1403
Cranberry Twp., PA 16066
ph: 724-776-0621
fax: 724-776-0621
Buys, sells, trades, and collects 1960's Beatles items; send $2 for 20-page sales catalog filled with Beatles and Yellow Sub items.

Marty Eck
P.O. Box 764
Elburn, IL 60119
ph: 630-365-5468
Toys, dolls, guitars, record player, hair spray, records, concert tickets, movie items, magazines; co-author of book on same.

Rick Rann
P.O. Box 877
Oak Park, IL 60303-0877
ph: 708-442-7907
e-mail: ukczech@aol.com
Wants to buy toys, dolls, guitars, record player, hair spray, records, concert tickets, movie items, magazines; co-author of book on The Beatles.

Jeff Augsburger
507 Normal Ave.
Normal, IL 61761-2412
ph: 309-452-9376
fax: 309-664-1771
e-mail: Beatles@dave-world.net
Buys, collects, sells Beatles memorabilia: toys, dolls, guitars, record player, hair spray, records, concert tickets, movie items, magazines; co-author of book on same.

Museums/Libraries

Jeff Augsburger
Beatles Mobile Museum, The
507 Normal Ave.
Normal, IL 61761-2412
ph: 309-452-9376
fax: 309-664-1771
e-mail: Beatles@dave-world.net
Has the largest collection of Beatles memorabilia in the US; actively buying for the collection; will buy one item or 1,000.

Periodicals

Bill King
Goody Press, The
Magazine: Beatlefan
P.O. Box 33515
Decatur, GA 30033-0515
ph: 404-633-5587
fax: 404-321-3109
web: http://www.the-beatles.com/beatlepg/anthadd/bfan.htm
A bi-monthly magazine for Beatles fans; a news-oriented, professional publication; articles, books for sale, ads, etc.

Matt Hurwitz
Magazine: Good Day Sunshine
P.O. Box 661008
Los Angeles, CA 90066-9608
ph: 310-391-0778
fax: 301-390-7475
e-mail: gds1964@aol.com
web: http://www.gooddaysunshine.net/
A leading Beatles magazine in the U.S.

Joe Pope
Magazine: Strawberry Fields Forever
P.O. Box 880981
San Diego, CA 92168
Oldest Beatles fanzine in the world.

Def Leppard

Collectors

Tammy Clack
101 Queensbury Circle
Goose Creek, SC 29445-5524
ph: 843-863-0857
e-mail: tammy5145@aol.com
web: http://members.aol.com/Tammy5145/
Wants to buy rare, important and promo records and memorabilia relating to the rock band Def Leppard; also Phil, Collen & Girl.

Duran Duran

Dealers

Tammy Clack
Strange Behavior Discs & Collectibles
101 Queensbury Circle
Goose Creek, SC 29445-5524
ph: 843-863-0857
e-mail: tammy5145@aol.com
web: http://members.aol.com/Tammy5145/
Wants to buy Duran Duran items, single items or collections.

Elvis

Auction Services

Elvis Auctions
P.O. Box 255
Port Townsend, WA 98368
ph: 360-385-1200
fax: 360-385-6572
e-mail: jpo@olympus.net
web: http://www.jerryosborne.com
Conducts periodic auctions of Elvis memorabilia.

Clubs/Associations

Susan Still
Elvis Forever TCB Fan Club
Newsletter: Elvis Forever TCB Fan Club Newsletter
P.O. Box 1066
Miami, FL 33780-1066

Collectors

Burt Atwood
894 Greenway Rd.
Woodbridge, CT 06525-2413
Buyer of rare Elvis memorabilia.

Eddie Hammer
735 Roosevelt Ave.
Carteret, NJ 07008-2318
ph: 732-969-2232
fax: 732-969-2232
Authority on current releases of Elvis recordings; writes "Elvis News" column for "DISCoveries"; largest Elvis collection in the world; buy, sell, trade anything Elvis.

B.J. Garton
401 N. 5th St.
Millville, NJ 08332
Wants ELvis memorabilia from the 1950s through 1970s; 1956 items, 45s, picture sleeves, movie, Las Vegas, sheet music, etc.

Dealers

Ed Wall
Big Boys Toys
449R Western Ave.
Gloucester, MA 01930-3526
ph: 978-283-4406 or 978-283-8384
e-mail: jukin@tiac.net
web: http://www.tiac.net/users/jukin/
Buys, sells and trades Elvis memorabilia.

Peter Weldon
815 2nd Ave.
Troy, NY 12182
ph: 518-235-6795
Issues catalog containing Elvis albums, 45s, EPs, picture sleeves, colored vinyl, picture discs, magazines, books, memorabilia, etc.

Tod Hutchinson
P.O. Box 915
Griffith, IN 46319-0915
ph: 219-923-8334
fax: 219-923-8334
e-mail: Toddtcb@aol.com
Specialize in Elvis collectibles, records, movie posters, etc.

Cindy Oakes
34025 W. 6 Mile
Livonia, MI 48152
ph: 734-591-3252
Wants dolls, jewelry, autographs, etc.

Dwayne Spark
Nostalgia Plus
8441 Sublaines
Anjou, Quebec H1K 2C1
Canada
ph: 514-352-6892
fax: 514-352-1856
Buys and sells Elvis memorabilia.

Sid Shaw
Elvisly Yours
1 Piccadilly Circus
London, E1 6JN
U.K.
ph: 44-0207-734-2001
fax: 44-0207-734-2001
e-mail: elvisly@globalnet.co.uk
web: http://www.elvisly-yours.com
The world's leading supplier of Elvis Presley memorabilia with over 400 different Elvis souvenirs - inexpensive, good quality and excellent designs; now in their 20th year; totally independent of Elvis Presley Enterprises.

Experts

Eddie Hammer
735 Roosevelt Ave.
Carteret, NJ 07008-2318
ph: 732-969-2232
fax: 732-969-2232
Authority on current releases of Elvis recordings; writes "Elvis News" column for "DISCoveries"; largest Elvis collection in the world; buy, sell, trade anything Elvis.

Sean O'Neal
6218 Braden Run
Bradenton, FL 34202
ph: 941-727-8316
fax: 941-756-9437
e-mail: colonelsnow@prodigy.net
Buys, sells, trades vintage Elvis Presley memorabilia; looking for personal items, unpublished photographs, film footage, unreleased sound recordings, 1956 novelty items, Las Vegas memorabilia; also holds quarterly Elvis auction.

Jerry Osborne
P.O. Box 255
Port Townsend, WA 98368
ph: 360-385-1200
fax: 360-385-6572
e-mail: jpo@olympus.net
web: http://www.jerryosborne.com
Author of "The Official Price Guide to Elvis Presley Records and Memorabilia" (House of Collectibles).

Museums/Libraries

Graceland
P.O. Box 16508
Memphis, TN 38186
ph: 800-238-2000
fax: 901-344-3119
e-mail: graceland@memphisonline.com
web: http://www.elvis-presley.com

Billy Beeny
Elvis Is Alive Museum
P.O. Box 377
Wright City, MO 63390
ph: 314-745-3154
web: http://ns.egyptian.net/~leftypen/elvis.htm
Cafe/arcade/museum filled with Elvis photos, memorabilia and printed material related to the controversy.

Eric Clapton

Collectors

Diane Smith
P.O. Box 262
Glenolden, PA 19036
Wants items relating to Eric Clapton (no guitars, please); wants strange or unusual items signed or unsigned; send description and photo; will return photo if SASE included.

KISS

Clubs/Associations

Gary Conn, Jr.
Kissaholics
Magazine: Kissaholics Magazine
P.O. Box 22334
Nashville, TN 37202
e-mail: gconnjr@aol.com
An internationally recognized KISS fan club and magazine geared toward the KISS fan and collector.

Collectors

Bob Gottuso
BOJO
P.O. Box 1403
Cranberry Twp., PA 16066
ph: 724-776-0621
fax: 724-776-0621
Buys and sells memorabilia related to KISS, the 1970s rock band: original Kiss toys, dolls, household items, etc.; send SASE for sales list.

Liberace

Museums/Libraries

Sandra L. Harris, Ex. Dir.
Liberace Foundation for the Performing & Creative Arts/Liberace Museum
Newsletter: Liberace Museum Newsletter
1775 E. Tropicana Ave.
Las Vegas, NV 89119-6529
ph: 702-798-5595
fax: 702-798-7386
e-mail: sharris@liberace.org
web: http://www.liberace.org/
A non-profit Foundation, Museum, Archives, and gift shop with proceeds funding scholarships in the Arts; collection includes Liberace pianos, furnishings, costumes, cars, jewelry, film, photographs, and recordings.

Merle Travis

Periodicals

Dave Stewart
Newsletter: Cannonball Rag
P.O. Box 1474
Corinth, MS 38834
ph: 601-287-4136
Dedicated to the life and music of Merle Travis.

Monkees

Clubs/Associations

Charles F. Rosenay
Liverpool Productions' Monkees Buttonmania Club
315 Derby Ave.
Orange, CT 06477
ph: 203-891-8131
e-mail: rosenay@aol.com
Produces Monkees conventions.

Collectors

Rick Rann
P.O. Box 877
Oak Park, IL 60303-0877
ph: 708-442-7907
e-mail: ukczech@aol.com
Wants to buy 1960s Monkees memorabilia: toys, dolls, concert tickets, magazines, books, fan club items, etc.

Tex Ritter

Clubs/Associations

Sharon L. Sweeting
Tex Ritter Fan Club
Newsletter: Gringo, The
828 Wandering Creek Dr.
Bothell, WA 98011
12 page newsletter packed with news, reports, clippings, a trading post, discography, and more relating to Tex Ritter.

PETROLIANA

(see GAS STATION COLLECTIBLES)

PEWTER

(see also REPAIR/RESTORATION/CONSERVATION, Metal Items)

Clubs/Associations

Louise Graver, Mem.
Pewter Collectors Club of America
504 W. Lafayette St.
West Chester, PA 19380-2210
Association of private collectors and interested parties; annual national as well as regional meetings; semi-annual newsletter.

Collectors

Bill Burkett
P.O. Box 2488
Sun City, AZ 85372-2488
ph: 623-974-4535 or 800-507-7234
fax: 623-974-4323
Collector of old American made pewter items; preferred items will contain "touch" marks including initials or a name and possibly a city name; please no new items; note that OLD items will NOT be marked "Pewter."

Dealers

Abbott's Arcade of Antiques
e-mail: DwAbbott@aol.com
web: http://members.aol.com/dwabbott/pewter2.htm
Buys and sells old pewter.

Allan & Ita Fogel
Twin Tankard Antiques
P.O. Box 4847
Silver Spring, MD 20904
ph: 301-236-9391
fax: 301-236-0427
e-mail: pewter@twintankard.com
web: http://www.twintankard.com
Specializes in European pewter; also buys and sells Russian and Judaica.

Museums/Libraries

Currier Gallery of Art, The
201 Myrtle Way
Manchester, NH 03104
ph: 603-669-6144
web: http://www.currier.org/

Repro. Sources

Ron Kusins
Pewter Crafter of Cape Cod
933 Rt. 6A
Yarmouth Port, MA 02675-5100
ph: 508-362-3407
fax: 508-362-3407
Handcrafted American pewter holloware in traditional and contemporary designs.

Bill Wiebold
Pewter Reproduction Works
5950 Park Rd. #3
Madeira, OH 45243
ph: 513-831-2815 or 800-321-2541
fax: 513-831-2815
Makes replicas of pewter oil lamps, bull's-eye lamps, candlesticks, baby bottles, and funnels; complete with antique patina, nicks, dents, bends; all reproductions permanently marked as such.

PEZ

(see also CANDY CONTAINERS)

Clubs/Associations

Dennis Martin
Fliptop Pezervation Society
Newsletter: Fliptop PEZervation Society News
1368 Dearing Downs Circle
Birmingham, AL 35080

Collectors

M. Koenigsberg
700 Boulevard East #7D
Weehawken, NJ 07087
ph: 201-863-0868
Wants to buy PEZ collections.

Richard Belyski
P.O. Box 124
Sea Cliff, NY 11579-0124
ph: 516-676-1183
fax: 516-676-1183
e-mail: peznews@juno.com
web: http://www.peznews.com/
Buys, sells, trades and collects PEZ candy containers.

Brian Suppin
1309 Susan Ave.
Croydon, PA 19021
ph: 215-785-2442 or 215-785-2754
e-mail: Fendereh@aol.com
A PEZ collector for over 3 years.

Maureen Winer
5900 Brackenridge Ave.
Baltimore, MD 21212
ph: 410-435-5226
Interested in buying all PEZ containers.

Charles Beesley
P.O. Box 400
Saint Michaels, MD 21663-0400
ph: 410-745-9206
fax: 410-822-5460
Wants PEZ candy dispensers; one item or entire collection - anything PEZ.

Richard Geary
P.O. Box 622
Madison, OH 44057

Jill Cohen
13900 Shker Blvd., #714
Cleveland, OH 44120
ph: 216-283-5993
e-mail: pezamania@msn.com
web: http://www.pezmania.com/
Organizer of the PEZ-A Mania Convention, held annually in Cleveland, OH.

Marcia Marshall
Pezheads
ph: 330-929-9588
e-mail: gotfriends@aol.com
PEZ collector seeks to build private collection.

Todd Hanson
PEZ Trade & Buy
ph: 507-452-1388
e-mail: whanson@luminet.net
web: http://www.angelfire.com/biz/pez/
Always looking to buy or trade PEZ.

Michael Newman
4600 Monarca Dr.
Tarzana, CA 91356
ph: 818-345-7804
e-mail: n82678m@aol.com

Sally Kimmel
1471 Lark Lane
Concord, CA 94521-2942
ph: 510-676-2857
e-mail: sallyraek@yahoo.com
Wants to buy pre 1960s PEZ dispensers (the ones without feet); also other PEZ items.

Dealers

Mark McMahon
Cookie Jars, Etc.
Chelsea Antiques Building
110 West 25th St., 8th Floor
New York, NY 10001
ph: 212-633-1923
fax: 212-924-8535
e-mail: peter@peterandmark.com
web: http://www.peterandmark.com
Buy, sell, trade cookie jars, banks, salt & peppers and PEZ.

Graham Trievel
P.O. Box 1625
West Chester, PA 19380
ph: 610-701-9193

Diane Davison
Indispensable PEZ
1517 Reisterstown Rd., Ste. 101
Baltimore, MD 21208
ph: 410-486-0900
fax: 410-486-0901
e-mail: lawgal@usa.net
web: http://mail.bcpl.lib.md.us/~ddavison/home.html
Buys, sells, collects and specializes in PEZ dispensers.

David A. Hull
Small Town Coins & Collectibles
7498 E. Davison Rd.
Davison, MI 48423-2014
ph: 810-658-1992
fax: 810-658-2977
Has 100s of old PEZ for sale; wants to buy singles or entire collections.

Michele Lorenz
5367 East Hidden Lake Dr.
East Lansing, MI 48823
ph: 517-332-3534
fax: 517-347-1522
e-mail: mgl@voyager.net
Buys and sells PEZ candy containers.

Troy Huffer
Pez Sactum, The
7723 N. 18th Ave.
Phoenix, AZ 85021-7021
ph: 602-994-8383
e-mail: pezsanctum@rocketmail.com
web: http://members.xoom.com/pezsanctum/
PEZ expert/collector/dealer with a website to buy, trade, sell PEZ dispensers over the Internet; also contains the latest Pez News.

Gary Doss
Burlingame Museum of Pez Memorabilia
214 California Dr.
Burlingame, CA 94010
ph: 650-347-2301
fax: 650-347-3840
e-mail: gary@spectrumnet.com
web: http://www.burlingamepezmuseum.com
Buys and sells current and collectible PEZ candy dispensers; the museum, located 20 minutes south of San Francisco, features the largest public display of PEZ candy dispensers in the world.

Bob Tipton
1526 S. Ray St.
Spokane, WA 99223
ph: 509-534-8557
e-mail: tipton@pezworld.com
web: http://www.pezworld.com

Experts

Chris MacTaggart
ph: 724-941-3863
e-mail: chris@mactaggart.com
Send email to be added to an Internet email mailing list for PEZ collectors.

Steven L. Glew
5611 Lehman Rd.
Dewitt, MI 48820
ph: 517-669-5931
fax: 517-669-3581
Buys, sells and specializes in PEZ.

David Welch
P.O. Box 714
Murphysboro, IL 62966-0714
ph: 618-687-2282
fax: 618-684-2243
e-mail: PezDude1@aol.com
Wants anything relating to PEZ for collection and book research; paying over $3000 for certain items; author of "A Pictorial Guide to Plastic Candy Dispensers" and "Collecting PEZ."

John Devlin
"The Cool PEZ Man"
5441 Oakville Center, Ste. 119
Saint Louis, MO 63129-3554
ph: 314-416-0333
Buys, sells, collects, and trades PEZ candy containers; runs the annual National PEZ Collectors Convention (not affiliated with the Pez Company.)

Robert Yarak
30216 Matisse Drive
Rancho Palos Verdes, CA 90275
ph: 310-377-2364
fax: 310-377-2629
e-mail: Spectres@aol.com
web: http://members.aol.com/spectres/
PEZ collector since 1976 always willing to help with any questions regarding PEZ candy dispensers; also buys.

Caleb Melvin
PEZ Corner, The
416 S. Alder
Port Angeles, WA 98362
ph: 360-452-4458 or 360-457-3624
e-mail: pezcorner@hotmail.com
web: http://www.geocities.com/EnchantedForest/Dell/5561/pezpage.html
PEZ Expert and collector.

Bob Tipton
Wonderful World of PEZ Collector's Association
1526 S. Ray St.
Spokane, WA 99223
ph: 509-534-8557
e-mail: tipton@pezworld.com
web: http://www.pezworld.com
One stop source for all your PEZ Dispenser questions.

Internet Resources

Original World Famous Pez Home Page
e-mail: pez@pobox.com
web: http://www.io.com/~pault/

Ultimate PEZ Resource, The
e-mail: Popapez1@aol.com
web: http://www.geocities.com/Area51/6759/menu.html
Lots of great PEZ information, free PEZ email newsletters, PEZ links.

Chris Dieterly
PEZ by Chris Dieterly
104 Laurel Court
Quakertown, PA 18951
ph: 215-529-5529
fax: 215-529-4653
e-mail: PEZbyChris@webtv.net
web: http://members.tripod.com/~Dieterly/

Caleb Melvin
PEZ Corner, The
416 S. Alder
Port Angeles, WA 98362
ph: 360-452-4458 or 360-457-3624
e-mail: pezcorner@hotmail.com
web: http://www.geocities.com/EnchantedForest/Dell/5561/pezpage.html
One stop internet resource for PEZ info: pictures, new releases, etc.

Man./Prod./Dist.

Pez Candy, Inc.
web: http://www.pez.com
Website has list of all PEZ containers ever made.

Misc. Services

Richard Geary
P.O. Box 622
Madison, OH 44057
Author of "PEZ Collectibles I" and PEZ Collectibles II"; organizes the annual PEZ-A Mania collectors' convention.

Museums/Libraries

Gary Doss
Burlingame Museum of Pez Memorabilia
214 California Dr.
Burlingame, CA 94010
ph: 650-347-2301
fax: 650-347-3840
e-mail: gary@spectrumnet.com
web: http://www.burlingamepezmuseum.com
Buys and sells current and collectible PEZ candy dispensers; the museum, located 20 minutes south of San Francisco, features the largest public display of PEZ candy dispensers in the world.

Periodicals

Richard Belyski
Newsletter: PEZ Collector's News
P.O. Box 124
Sea Cliff, NY 11579-0124
ph: 516-676-1183
fax: 516-676-1183
e-mail: peznews@juno.com
web: http://www.peznews.com/
Newsletter for collectors of PEZ candy dispensers; great web site of PEZ resources, history, factory tour, and more.

PHARMACY

(see MEDICAL, DENTAL & PHARMACEUTICAL)

PHILATELICS

(see STAMP COLLECTING)

PHILIPPINES

(see also ART, Asian; ORIENTALIA; INDONESIA)

Collectors

Roy Stephens
201 West Shore Rd.
Great Neck, NY 11024-1638
ph: 516-829-8827
fax: 718-281-2055
Wants Indonesian and Philippine art: paintings, wood carvings, inlaid chests, batik, textiles, brass, krises, betel nut boxes, swords and other weapons.

Experts

Michael G. Price
P.O. Box 468
Michigan Center, MI 49254
ph: 517-764-4517
e-mail: mgprice@acd.net
Wants Philippine picture postcards, photos, magazines, books, maps; also wants items from nearby islands such as Borneo.

PHONOGRAPHS

(see also BOOKS, Reference [Phonographs]; HI-FI EQUIPMENT; MUSICAL INSTRUMENTS, Mechanical; PERSONALITIES [INVENTORS], Thomas Alva Edison; RECORDS)

Appraisers

Charlotte Mager
Waves
110 W. 25th St., 10th Floor
New York, NY 10001
ph: 212-989-9284
fax: 201-461-7121
e-mail: c1wave@aol.com
web: http://www.wavesradio.com
Established in 1976, buys, sells, repairs, appraises and rents radios, phonographs, TVs, microphones, telephones, fans, neon clocks and signs, and related advertising and literature.

Book Sellers

Yesterday Once Again
P.O. Box 6773
Huntington Beach, CA 92615-6773
ph: 714-963-2474
fax: 714-963-1558
e-mail: yesterdayonceagain@yahoo.com
Carries a large selection of books dealing with early phonographs and related ephemera.

Clubs/Associations

John & Linda Gramm
Hudson Valley Antique Radio & Phonograph Society
Newsletter: HARPS Newsletter
P.O. Box 1, Rt. 207
Campbell Hall, NY 10916
ph: 914-427-2602 or 914-496-5130
web: http://members.aol.com/JBishop701/Harps.html
For antique radio and phonograph collectors who want to share information, equipment and related items with others having similar interests; monthly meetings feature educational demonstrations and mini swap meets.

Allen Koenigsberg
Antique Phonograph Collectors Club
Newsletter: Antique Phonograph Monthly
502 E. 17th St.
Brooklyn, NY 11226-6606
ph: 718-941-6835
fax: 718-941-1408
e-mail: AllenAmet@aol.com
web: http://members.aol.com/allenamet/PhonoBooks.html

Steve Dando
Buckeye Radio & Phonograph Club
Newsletter: Soundings
4572 Mark Trail
Akron, OH 44321-1462
ph: 330-666-7222
Members exchange expertise in restoration of vintage radios and phonographs; club holds annual mall show (displaying radios and phonographs) and picnic.

Phil Stewart, Ed.
Michigan Antique Phonograph Society, Inc.
Newsletter: In The Groove
60 Central St.
Battle Creek, MI 49027
e-mail: pgstewart@aol.com
web: http://www.lrbcg.com/pogo/MAPS.html
A highly recommended newsletter contains articles, member ads about antique phonographs, records and music boxes; MAPS Membership & Resource Directory published every other year.

C.F. Crandell, Pres.
Vintage Radio & Phonograph Society, Inc.
Newsletter: Reproducer, The
P.O. Box 165345
Irving, TX 75016-5345
ph: 214-337-2823 or 972-315-2553
e-mail: billhar@flash.net
web: http://www.flash.net/~billhar/vrpsinfo.htm
Purpose is to preserve early radios, phonographs, and related material and to conduct historical research of same; also publishes "Soundwaves" newsletter.

Karyn Sitter
California Antique Phonograph Society
18242 Timberlane
Yorba Linda, CA 92686
ph: 714-777-2486

Jim M. Whitty, Historian
Wolverine Antique Music Society
252 Mill St.
Silverton, OR 97381
e-mail: whitty@hevanet.com
web: http://www.teleport.com/~rfrederi/

Bill Pratt
Canadian Antique Phonograph Society
Journal: Antique Phonograph News
122 Major St.
Toronto, Ontario M5S 2L2
Canada
ph: 416-924-8207
e-mail: caps@rose.com
web: http://www.rose.com/~caps/
Members interested in sound recording and its history: phonographs, gramophones; also related ephemera and memorabilia; journal has original articles, repair tips and how-to's, auction results, ads.

Don Moore, Hon. Treas.
City of London Phonograph & Gramophone Society
Woodbine Cottage
Brigg Road, Fonaby
Caistor, Lincoln LN7 6RX
U.K.
e-mail: clpgs@aol.com
web: http://members.aol.com/clpgs/clpgs.htm

Federation of Recorded Music Societies
67 Galleys Bank Kidsgrove
Staffordshire, ST7 4DE
U.K.
e-mail: the-frms@netcentral.co.uk
web: http://www.musicweb.force9.co.uk/music/frms/index.htm

Collectors

Aaron Cramer
2056 E. 28th St.
Brooklyn, NY 11229
Has written columns about phonographs, or talking machines; discovered the world's oldest recording.

John W. Hess
244 Bernaski Rd.
Amsterdam, NY 12010-7827
ph: 518-843-6117
Wants to buy Vogue picture disc records, horn phonographs, music boxes, roller organs; also wants parts, empty cabinets, horns; any condition, any material.

Alvin Heckard
RD 1 Box 88
Lewistown, PA 17044-9801
ph: 717-248-7071 or 717-248-2816
Wants wind-up type phonographs (outside horn type only, please), parts, literature and advertising.

Bernie Seinberg
714 Moredon Rd.
Bensalem, PA 19020
ph: 215-886-6124
fax: 215-638-2265
e-mail: phonoman-bernie@worldnet.att.net
Wants Edison, RCA, Victor, and Columbia tabletop phonographs; also phonograph related advertising, trade cards, displays, needle tins, record dusters, puzzles, fans, pins, buttons, badges, mirrors, etc.

Steven Ramm
420 Fitzwater St.
Philadelphia, PA 19147-3109
ph: 610-922-7050 or 610-545-3290
e-mail: steveramm@aol.com
Specializes in phonographs and pre-1930 records; wants to buy sheet music, postcards, and advertising with illustrations of phonographs, records, or Thomas A. Edison; also wants cylinder rolls in playable condition.

David Giovannoni
ph: 301-869-1501
fax: 301-258-0420
e-mail: DGio@ARAnet.com
Advanced collector looking for certain phonographs and records from 1890s through 1920s; call if you have 78s, cylinder records, antique phonographs, or related items for sale; if

on-line, join the CompuServe Collectibles Forum!

John Greenstreet
1409 Cherry St.
Baltimore, MD 21226-1230
ph: 410-355-4437
fax: 410-354-2039
e-mail: jgreenst@bcpl.net

Stuart Stein
P.O. Box 303
Frederick, MD 21705-0303
ph: 301-663-8369
fax: 301-663-8202
e-mail: steincpa@ix.netcom.com
Wants disc type wind up phonographs with horns.

Mike Ellingson
1412 2nd Ave. S.
Fargo, ND 58103-1612
ph: 701-280-1413
e-mail: mikellingson@webtv.net
web: http://members.ebay.com/aboutme/phonomike/
Has most phonographs he needs for his personal collection, but is willing to help you determine what your phonograph is worth; will try to answer any antique phonograph question 10:00 a.m. to 10:00 p.m. CST M-F.

Loran T. Hughes
936 Fairfield Circle
Central Point, OR 97502
ph: 541-664-7997
e-mail: oldecrank@aol.com
web: http://www.teleport.com/~lthughes/
Collector of pre-1930 wind-up phonographs; also want to buy early phonograph literature, especially instruction manuals.

Dealers

Rob Lomas
Edison Shop, The
e-mail: edisonshop@enter.net
web: http://www.edisonshop.com

Howard Embleton
Vintage Sounds & Antiques
P.O. Box 77262
Sussex, NJ 07461
ph: 973-786-7955 or 973-875-9227
e-mail: vsphonos@warwick.net
web: http://members.xoom.com/vsphonos
Buys, sells, repairs windup phonographs: Edison, Victor, Columbia and others wanted for sale; parts available for most phonographs; also buys and sells cylinders, 78 records, and related memorabilia; work guaranteed; free estimates.

Charlotte Mager
Waves
110 W. 25th St., 10th Floor
New York, NY 10001
ph: 212-989-9284
fax: 201-461-7121
e-mail: c1wave@aol.com
web: http://www.wavesradio.com
Established in 1976, buys, sells, repairs, appraises and rents radios, phonographs, TVs, microphones, telephones, fans, neon clocks and signs, and related advertising and literature.

Bruce & Charlotte Mager
Waves
Chelsea Antiques Building
110 West 25th St., 10th Floor
New York, NY 10001-7401
ph: 212-989-9284
fax: 201-461-7121
e-mail: c1wave@aol.com
web: http://www.wavesradio.com/
Over 20 years experience specializing in vintage radios, phonographs, telegraphy, televisions, assorted electrical and mechanical apparatus, and related advertising memorabilia, books and pamphlets.

Allen Koenigsberg
502 E. 17th St.
Brooklyn, NY 11226-6606
ph: 718-941-6835
fax: 718-941-1408
e-mail: AllenAmet@aol.com
web: http://members.aol.com/allenamet/PhonoBooks.html
Author of the "Patent History of the Phonograph."

Dennis Valente
Antique Phonograph Supply Co.
P.O. Box 123
Rt. 23
Davenport Center, NY 13751
ph: 607-278-5136
fax: 607-278-5136
e-mail: apsco@antiquephono.com
web: http://www.antiquephono.com
Buys, collects, sells, specializes and appraises phonographs; carries a comprehensive line of restoration parts, services, and books for the restoration of turn-of-the-century mechanical, wind up talking machines and phonographs.

Tim Fabrizio
Terra Firma Antiques
P.O. Box 10307
Rochester, NY 14610-0307
ph: 716-244-5546
fax: 716-244-7601
e-mail: phonophan@aol.com
web: http://members.aol.com/phonophan/
Buys and sells talking machines, mechanical music, records and related books and ephemera; also sells phonograph parts and supplies.

Peter S. Liebert
Nipperhead Antique Phonographs
e-mail: peter@nipperhead.com
web: http://www.nipperhead.com/
Buying and selling phonographs; web site serves the phonograph community by offering information pertaining to antique phonographs, gramophones, Victor, Edison, Columbia, Nipper.

Rose & Gracey's Antiques
5806 South First St.
Arlington, VA 22204
ph: 703-998-6208
e-mail: info@TalkingMachines.com
web: http://www.TalkingMachines.com
Specializes in restored pre-1929 spring-driven phonographs and talking machines; in business since 1986.

Doug Negus
Phonograph Phanatic
215 Mason St.
Sutherland, IA 51058-7606
ph: 712-446-2270 or 712-446-3746
e-mail: negus@nwidt.com
Music boxes, phonographs, cylinder records, pianos, NO piano rolls, older mechanical musical instruments, pre-1930; any parts or repairables wanted.

Shawn Borri
Shawn Borri's Oldtime Talking Machine Co.
26594, 2600N Ave.
La Moille, IL 61330-9801
ph: 815-638-2243
fax: 815-638-2243
e-mail: sborri@softfarm.com
web: http://members.tripod.com/~Edison_1/index.html
Expert knowledge on early hand-cranked phonographs, Victrolas, and other talking machines; author of "The Antique Phonograph Corner"; also offers repair and restoration services as well as appraisals.

Rick Wilkins
Olden Year Musical Museum
P.O. Box 381951
Duncanville, TX 75138
ph: 972-298-5587
e-mail: 1museum@cyberramp.com
Buys, sells, repairs and appraises all types of windup automated musical machines including Victrolas, Gramophones, music boxes, grind organs, etc.

Yesterday Once Again
P.O. Box 6773
Huntington Beach, CA 92615-6773
ph: 714-963-2474
fax: 714-963-1558
e-mail: yesterdayonceagain@yahoo.com
Equipped to supply almost any part necessary to restore the old handcranked phonographs; also sells accessories such as steel phonograph needles, paper record sleeves, books, instruction manual reprints, and related items.

Experts

John P. Andolina, Jr.
Early Sound Man, The
28 Glen Oaks Dr.
Rochester, NY 14624-1405
ph: 716-247-3056
Over 24 years experience in the collecting, repair, and research of crank type phonographs and related items; buys, sells, collects, repairs; also supplies original and reproduction parts and related items; Edison reproducers in stock.

Ken Danckaert
231 Kennedy Ct.
Severna Park, MD 21146-3039
ph: 410-544-0260
e-mail: kend@lemur.org
Collects, buys, sells, appraises, and repairs music boxes, phonographs, and organettes; specialist in coin-operated phonographs; in business since 1972; an expert who gives lectures, presentations and videos.

Howard Hazelcorn
6731 Ashley Ct.
Sarasota, FL 34241-9696
ph: 941-921-1815
Collector and author of "Collectors Guide to Columbia Spring-Wound Cylinder Phonographs."

Randy & Larry Donley
Donley's Wild West Town & Museum
8512 S. Union Rd.
Union, IL 60180-9661
ph: 815-923-9000
fax: 815-923-2253
web: http://www.wildwesttown.com/
Experts in antique phonographs; buys, sells, collects and repairs.

Shawn Borri
Shawn Borri's Oldtime Talking Machine Co.
26594, 2600N Ave.
La Moille, IL 61330-9801
ph: 815-638-2243
fax: 815-638-2243
e-mail: sborri@softfarm.com
web: http://members.tripod.com/~Edison_1/index.html
Expert knowledge on early hand-cranked phonographs, Victrolas, and other talking machines; author of "The Antique Phonograph Corner"; also offers repair and restoration services as well as appraisals.

Steve Oliphant
5255 Allott Ave.
Van Nuys, CA 91401-5902
ph: 818-789-2339 or 818-865-1400
fax: 818-865-1450
e-mail: jlo55@aol.com
Adviser and dealer of old phono-

graphs; buys entire collections or individual pieces.

Internet Resources

Peter S. Liebert
Nipperhead Antique Phonographs
e-mail: peter@nipperhead.com
web: http://www.nipperhead.com/
Serving the phonograph community for over 50 years; a premiere web site for information pertaining to antique phonographs, gramophones, Victor, Edison, Columbia, Nipper; repair instructions, resource listings, online catalogs, more.

Steve Adams
RadioGallery.com
P.O. Box 90
Moody, AL 35004
ph: 205-640-2701
fax: 205-640-2701
e-mail: radios@RadioGallery.com
web: http://www.radiogallery.com
RadioGallery.com features classified ads with color photos of antique and collectible radios, phonographs, and other radio-related items for sale; free wanted and "help" ads; free notices of radio club events.

Rick Salsman
Antique Phonograph Gallery Online
2645 San Pablo Ave.
Berkeley, CA 94702
ph: 510-849-0818
fax: 510-849-2855
e-mail: RSalsman@inkyfingers.com
web: http://www.inkyfingers.com/Record.html
Web site has several personal collections of antique phonographs and related items; also an index of machines by category.

Tim Gracyk
9180 Joy Lane
Granite Bay, CA 95746-9682
e-mail: tgracyk@garlic.com
web: http://www.garlic.com/~tgracyk/
Great resource website phonographs and phonograph records/cylinders.

Loran T. Hughes
936 Fairfield Circle
Central Point, OR 97502
ph: 541-664-7997
e-mail: oldecrank@aol.com
web: http://www.teleport.com/~lthughes/
Great list of phonograph links: organizations and museums, publications and history, newsgroups and mailing lists, dealers in phonograph ephemera, parts, sales & service, recordings, turntables, and other phonograph related sites.

Museums/Libraries

Edison National Historic Site
Main St. at Lakeside Ave.
West Orange, NJ 07052
ph: 973-736-0550
fax: 973-736-8496
e-mail: EDIS_Webmaster@nps.gov
web: http://www.nps.gov/edis/home.htm
A museum with exhibits in all fields of Edison's contributions.

Madeline Dunn
Johnson Victrola Museum
c/o Delaware State Visitor's Center
406 Federal St., Box 1401
Dover, DE 19903
ph: 302-739-4266
fax: 302-739-3943
Museum is a tribute to Eldridge Reeves Johnson, inventor and businessman who founded the Victor Talking Machine Company; extensive collection of talking machines, Victrolas, "Nipper", early recordings, equipment, Johnson memorabilia.

Randy & Larry Donley
Donley's Wild West Town & Museum
8512 S. Union Rd.
Union, IL 60180-9661
ph: 815-923-9000
fax: 815-923-2253
web: http://www.wildwesttown.com/
Large exhibit of Edison phonographs, cylinder and disc music machines, and other music memorabilia.

Periodicals

Martin F. Bryan, Ed.
New Amberola Phonograph Co. The
Magazine: New Amberola Graphic, The
37 Caledonia St.
St. Johnsbury, VT 05819
A quarterly publication for collectors of early phonographs & records from the years 1895-1935; articles, book reviews, ads, auctions, etc.

Newsletter: Jerry's Musical Newsletter
4624 West Woodland Rd.
Minneapolis, MN 55424-1553
ph: 612-926-7775
fax: 612-926-7775
e-mail: jerryclare@aol.com
Focuses on phonograph toys, memorabilia, needle tins, books, etc.

James Cranshaw
Horn Speaker, The
Newspaper: Horn Speaker, The
P.O. Box 1193
Mabank, TX 75147-1193
ph: 903-848-0304
fax: 903-848-0596
e-mail: cranshaw@gte.net
web: http://home.navisoft.com/horn/ths2.htm
A newspaper for collectors and historians interested in antique radios and phonographs.

Repair Services

Victrola
206 Cliff St.
Saint Johnsbury, VT 05819
ph: 800-239-4188
e-mail: victrola@together.net
web: http://www.angelfire.com/vt/victrola
Victrola sales and repair.

Rod Lauman
Victrola Repair Service
206 Cliff St.
Saint Johnsbury, VT 05819-1002
ph: 802-748-4893 or 800-239-4188
e-mail: victrola@together.net
web: http://homepages.together.net/~victrola
Repairs Victrolas and wind-up phonographs; repairs done via U.P.S.; mainsprings, parts, needles also available; call between 10 a.m. and 10 p.m. EST.

Howard Embleton
Vintage Sounds & Antiques
P.O. Box 77262
Sussex, NJ 07461
ph: 973-786-7955 or 973-875-9227
e-mail: vsphonos@warwick.net
web: http://members.xoom.com/vsphonos
Buys, sells, repairs windup phonographs: Edison, Victor, Columbia and others wanted for sale; parts available for most phonographs; also buys and sells cylinders, 78 records, and related memorabilia; work guaranteed; free estimates.

Floyd Silver
Antique Phonograph Center
P.O. Box 2574
Vincentown, NJ 08088-2574
ph: 609-859-8617
e-mail: fsilver@compuserve.com
Antique phonograph sales and service; complete restorations of Edison, Victor and Columbia phonographs.

Dennis Valente
Antique Phonograph Supply Co.
P.O. Box 123
Rt. 23
Davenport Center, NY 13751
ph: 607-278-5136
fax: 607-278-5136
e-mail: apsco@antiquephono.com
web: http://www.antiquephono.com
Buys, collects, sells, specializes and appraises phonographs; carries a comprehensive line of restoration parts, services, and books for the restoration of turn-of-the-century mechanical, wind up talking machines and phonographs.

John P. Andolina, Jr.
Early Sound Man, The
28 Glen Oaks Dr.
Rochester, NY 14624-1405
ph: 716-247-3056
Wants to buy outside horn phonographs, Edison, Victor, Columbia, others; records, brown wax cylinders, Berliner, Vogue picture discs, concert cylinders, need tins, record dusters, "Nipper"; also does repairs and adjustments.

Emerson E. Whitacre
Mechanical Music Man
7550 President Court
Dayton, OH 45414-3671
ph: 937-898-6044 or 937-898-0865
Repairs, adjusts and cleans disc music boxes, cylinder music boxes, antique phonographs, etc.

Wyatt's Musical Americana
P.O. Box 601
Lakeport, CA 95453-0601
ph: 707-263-5013
fax: 707-263-8823
web: http://www.pacific.net/~oldcrank/
Carries large supply of antique phonographs parts; also specializes in the repair and restoration of all types of windup phonographs; send $4 for 64 page catalog listing over 1,500 parts.

Suppliers

J.J. Papovich
53 Magnolia Ave.
Pitman, NJ 08071
ph: 856-464-6741
Supplies parts for old phonographs.

Dennis Valente
Antique Phonograph Supply Co.
P.O. Box 123
Rt. 23
Davenport Center, NY 13751
ph: 607-278-5136
fax: 607-278-5136
e-mail: apsco@antiquephono.com
web: http://www.antiquephono.com
Buys, collects, sells, specializes and appraises phonographs; carries a comprehensive line of restoration parts, services, and books for the restoration of turn-of-the-century mechanical, wind up talking machines and phonographs.

Jim Dalton, Sr.
Dalton & Dalton
P.O. Box 487
Muncie, IN 47305-0487
ph: 317-288-9488
e-mail: rockys@iquest.net
Has an assortment of over 2000 phonograph needles for sale; covers nearly every make and model of the past 35 years.

Nipper

Collectors

Bernie Seinberg
714 Moredon Rd.
Bensalem, PA 19020
ph: 215-886-6124
fax: 215-638-2265
e-mail: phonoman-bernie@worldnet.att.net
Wants any pre-1950s items picturing the R.C.A. dog, Nipper.

Dealers

Yesterday Once Again
P.O. Box 6773
Huntington Beach, CA 92615-6773
ph: 714-963-2474
fax: 714-963-1558
e-mail: yesterdayonceagain@yahoo.com
Largest selection of "Nipper" available: dogs, accessories, books, and more.

Internet Resources

Allen Koenigsberg
502 E. 17th St.
Brooklyn, NY 11226-6606
ph: 718-941-6835
fax: 718-941-1408
e-mail: AllenAmet@aol.com
web: http://members.aol.com/allenamet/PhonoBooks.html
Online information about Nipper and the story of "His Master's Voice."

PHOTOGRAPHICA

(see 3-D PHOTOGRAPHICA; CAMERAS & CAMERA EQUIPMENT; OPTICAL ITEMS; PHOTOGRAPHS; PHOTOGRAPHY; STANHOPES; STEREO VIEWERS & STEREOVIEWS)

PHOTOGRAPHS

(see also 3-D PHOTOGRAPHICA; AUDIO-VISUAL; CAMERAS & CAMERA EQUIPMENT; MOVIE MEMORABILIA; PHOTOGRAPHY; REPAIR/RESTORATION/ CONSERVATION, Archival Supplies For; REPAIR/RESTORATION/ CONSERVATION, Paper Items; STEREO VIEWERS & STEREOVIEWS)

Appraisers

Larry Gottheim
Fine Early Photographs
78 Rockland Ave.
Yonkers, NY 10705
e-mail: behold@be-hold.com
web: http://www.be-hold.com
Specializes in appraising vintage photographs, daguerreotypes, tintypes, stereo views; entire collections as well as important single items, especially rare and unique items with little published record of sales.

Julia Nelson-Gal
826 Alvarado
San Francisco, CA 94114-3116
ph: 415-641-8004
fax: 415-641-8053
Specialist in appraisals of 19th and 20th century photographs and photographic literature; will authenticate and broker sales.

Auction Services

Caroline Birenbaum
Swann Galleries, Inc.
104 E. 25th St.
New York, NY 10010-2977
ph: 212-254-4710
fax: 212-979-1017
e-mail: swann@swanngalleries.com
web: http://www.swanngalleries.com/
Oldest/largest U.S. auctioneer specializing in rare books, autographs & manuscripts, maps, atlases, photographs, and works of art on paper including vintage posters.

Denise Bethel
Sotheby's
1334 York Ave.
New York, NY 10021
ph: 212-606-7000
fax: 212-606-7107
web: http://www.sothebys.com

Christie's
502 Park Ave.
New York, NY 10022
ph: 212-546-1000
fax: 212-980-8163
web: http://www.christies.com

Larry Gottheim
BE-HOLD, Inc.
78 Rockland Ave.
Yonkers, NY 10705
e-mail: behold@be-hold.com
web: http://www.be-hold.com
Conducts mail-bid auctions of vintage photographs, daguerreotypes, tintypes, stereo views, especially of historic and aesthetic importance; well illustrated informative catalogs $50 for 3 issues plus auction results.

Butterfield & Butterfield
220 San Bruno Ave.
San Francisco, CA 94103-5018
ph: 415-861-7500
fax: 415-861-8951
e-mail: info@butterfields.com
web: http://www.butterfields.com/

Tim McIntyre
Tim McIntyre's Antique Photographs
137 Nile St.
Stratford, Ontario N5E 4E1
Canada
ph: 519-273-5360
fax: 519-273-7310
e-mail: timoni@orc.ca
web: http://www.orc.ca/~timoni/
Buys, sells, auctions 19th and early 20th century photographs, especially stereoviews, CDVs, cabinet cards, ambrotypes, tintypes, daguerreotypes and larger formats; conducts periodic phone/mail auctions.

John Saddy
Jefferson Stereoptics
50 Foxborough Grove
London, Ontario N6K 4A8
Canada
ph: 519-641-4431
fax: 519-641-2899
e-mail: john.saddy.3d@sympatico.ca
web: http://www3.sympatico.ca/john.saddy.3d/home.htm
Wants photography from early daguerreotypes to View-Master including antique stereo cards, cartes des visites, cabinet cards, cased images; specializes in consignments, but will also buy outright.

Clubs/Associations

Prof. Andrew Davidhazy, Webmaster
Photographic Historical Society, Inc., The
Newsletter: PHS Newsletter
P.O. Box 39563
Rochester, NY 14604
ph: 716-475-2592
fax: 716-475-7750
e-mail: andpph@rit.edu
web: http://www.rit.edu/~andpph/tphs.html
For those with an interest in the history of photography; conducts monthly meetings and a tri-annual symposium.

Association of International Photography Art Dealers
1609 Connecticut Ave. NW #200
Washington, DC 20009-1034
ph: 202-986-0105
fax: 202-986-0448
web: http://www.artline.com/association/ipa/ipa.html
Dedicated to creating and maintaining high standards in the business of exhibiting, buying, selling photographs as art.

Michigan Photographic Historical Society
Newsletter: Photogram, The
P.O. Box 2278
Birmingham, MI 48012-2278
ph: 313-882-1113 or 245-549-6026
e-mail: pmotz@worldnet.att.net

Chicago Photographic Collectors Society
Newsletter: CPCS Bulletin
P.O. Box 303
Grayslake, IL 60030
ph: 773-262-5979 or 847-223-4348
e-mail: info@chicagophotographic.org
web: http://www.chicagophotographic.org/
A non-profit organization since 1971; over 200 U.S. and foreign members; sponsors two trade shows a year in the Chicago area; "CPCS Bulletin" is published monthly; also publishes the journal "By Daylight" periodically.

Michael Pritchard, Editor
Photographic Collectors Club of Great Britain
Magazine: Photographica World
1B Church Street Industrial Estate
Haydon Bridge
Hexham, Northumberland NE47 6JG
U.K.
ph: (0044) (0)1434 688129
e-mail: pccgb@lightwave.demon.co.uk
web: http://www.lightwave.demon.co.uk/pccgb/pccgb.htm
Club aims to promote the study and collection of photographic equipment and images by publications, meetings, auctions and shows; covers cameras, lenses, photographers, optical toys, stereoscopes, magic lanterns, and related areas.

Collectors

Norman D. Leckert
P.O. Box 363
Bethel, VT 05032-0363
ph: 802-234-5657 or 800-717-2021
fax: 802-234-6104
Wants to buy old photographs and daguerreotypes; especially wants photos by E.S. Curtis (Curtis photographed the American Indians._

George Sullivan
330 East 33rd St.
New York, NY 10016-9466
ph: 212-689-9745
e-mail: gsullbooks@aol.com
Wants to buy cased images by Mathew Brady.

Larry Berke
28 Marksman Ln.
Levittown, NY 11756-5110
ph: 516-796-7280
Wants to buy photographs (daguerreotypes, stereoviews, tintypes, CDVs, cards) and 19th or 20th photos and unusual century cameras.

Karl L. Jannen
106 Bishops Rd.
Smithtown, NY 11787-1427
ph: 516-265-3654
Wants to buy early photographs showing humor or suggesting an amusing caption; nothing sensational expected — any smile-provoker

qualifies; will pay up to $25 per; send photocopy first, please; will reply promptly.

Gary Ronk
6247 Cove Rd.
Roanoke, VA 24019-1715
ph: 540-562-2368
Wants to buy CDVs of soldiers, animals, buildings, outdoor; tax stamped or any unusual is preferred.

Randy Beach
313 Julia St.
New Smyrna Beach, FL 32168
ph: 904-427-7444
Wants to buy daguerreotypes, ambrotypes, tintypes, postmortems, animals.

David L. Hartline
P.O. Box 775
Columbus, OH 43085-0775
Wants Western photographs, Annie Oakley, Buffalo Bill, Indian, etc.; also images of Black soldiers, military forts and regiments; will answer all letters.

Betty Davis
5291 Ravenna Rd.
Newton Falls, OH 44444-9440
ph: 330-872-0318 or 330-872-0386
fax: 216-872-0386
e-mail: noahsattic@neosplice.com
Collector wants interesting, unusual images (cased, tin, paper, etc.) of pre-1930 albums, horse-drawn vehicles, soldiers, Indians, occupations, toys, sports, motorcycles, store fronts, cowboys, blacks, etc.; no snapshots; send photocopy.

Bill Becker
P.O. Box 7076
Huntington Woods, MI 48070
e-mail: wmb@wwwnet.net
Seeking attractive photographs of all types that have interesting historical content; daguerreotypes, early glass stereo views, French tissue (hold-to-light) stereos with hidden balloons, ships, trains; Indians, Shakers, etc.

Norman Kulkin
727 N. Fuller Ave.
Los Angeles, CA 90046-7504
ph: 323-653-6929
fax: 323-651-0640
e-mail: pixidom@aol.com
web: http://www.pixidom.com/
Buy, sell, trade vintage photographs: ambrotypes, tintypes, stereoviews, specialty is daguerreotypes; also early 19th century paper photos, early 20th century photos; also photographica including cameras.

Jeff Mark
P.O. Box 5178
Santa Monica, CA 90409-5178
ph: 800-666-9553 or 310-396-9767
fax: 310-396-2666
Wants old photographs from 1850-1900; prefers from Old America: cowboys, Indians, miners, slaves, occupationals (fireman, police, etc.), baseball, sports; especially wants larger old photos.

Don Hoffman
P.O. Box 4231
Salinas, CA 93912-4231
ph: 831-449-7311
Wants old photographs, images, prints, stereoviews, CDV's, cabinet cards, calotypes, daguerreotypes, ambrotypes, negatives about sports, boxing, jazz, blues, minstrel, vaudeville, general Americana subjects; please describe and price.

David Wallach
P.O. Box 150285
San Rafael, CA 94915-0285
ph: 415-777-0123 or 415-883-7121
fax: 415-284-5364
e-mail: vcsrs@aol.com
Wants to buy photographs, images, antique daguerreotypes, ambrotypes, tintypes; interested in military, Indian, armed civilians, nudes.

Don Callies
Mirror Images
205 N L St., Apt. 4
Aberdeen, WA 98520-6104
Wants early daguerreotypes, ambrotypes, melainotypes, ferrotypes, cabinet photos of American Indians, Civil War, Mexican War, military, gunboats, ships, sailors, Western Americana, gold rush, miners, lawmen, outlaws, cowboys, etc.

Dealers

Mack Lee
Lee Gallery
1 Mount Vernon St.
Winchester, MA 01890-2703
ph: 781-729-7445
fax: 781-729-4592
e-mail: leegall@tiac.net
web: http://www.leegallery.com/
Buys, sells, and appraises fine 19th and 20th century photographs and daguerreotypes.

David & Becky Beane
Beane's Antiques & Photography
92 River Rd.
Benton, ME 04901
ph: 207-453-6790
fax: 207-453-6790
e-mail: dbeane@mint.net
web: http://www.metigues.com/catgalog/beane.html
Actively buying early photography including but not limited to daguerreotypes, ambrotypes, tintypes, and all related forms of photographica.

George D. Glazer
28 East 72nd St.
New York, NY 10021
ph: 212-535-5706
fax: 212-988-3992
e-mail: worldglobe@aol.com
web: http://www.georgeglazer.com
Buys and sells vintage photographs, mostly photojournalist, of popular subjects such as skiing, golf, landscapes and views, fashion, Grand Tour views of Italy.

Larry Gottheim
Fine Early Photographs
78 Rockland Ave.
Yonkers, NY 10705
e-mail: behold@be-hold.com
web: http://www.be-hold.com
Buys and sells by appointment and mail; specializes in vintage photographs, daguerreotypes, tintypes, stereo views, especially of historic and aesthetic importance; publishes well illustrated informative catalog, $50 for 3 issues.

Nicholas M. Graver
276 Brooklawn Dr.
Rochester, NY 14618-2923
ph: 716-244-4818
e-mail: ngraver1@rochester.rr.com
Buys early and unusual daguerreotypes, stereo views, cartes de visites, early Kodak (round) photos, Civil War photos, family albums, photographers at work, ambrotypes, tintypes; speech & hearing (19th c. deaf & dumb) related.

Joseph F. Loccisano
Historic Photographs & Paper Americana
2264 Nicholson Square Dr.
Lancaster, PA 17601-3966
ph: 717-560-5182
Wants to buy American photographs from 1870s to 1930s; prefers 5" x 7" or larger; interiors or exteriors of businesses, stores, shops, saloons, amusement arcades, factories, etc.; also buys pre-1910 photos of circus people; send photos.

Bruce Lancaster
AntiquePhoto.com
P.O. Box 151541
Chevy Chase, MD 20825
fax: 301-718-1875
e-mail: lancaster@antiquephoto.com
web: http://www.antiquephoto.com
An online marketplace for antique and historic photographs and related literature; conducts periodic photograph auctions.

Ivan Gilbert, MD
Miran Art & Books
2824 Elm Ave.
Columbus, OH 43209
ph: 614-231-3707 or 614-818-3222
fax: 614-818-3223
e-mail: IGilbert@ahhinc.com

Tom Molocea
Historic Images
P.O. Box 100
North Lima, OH 44452-0100
ph: 330-549-3245 or 330-629-1864
e-mail: himages@cisnet.com
Buys photos of all categories and all formats; single images to entire collections.

Don Leone
Remains to be Seen
608 W. Main
Collinsville, IL 62234
ph: 618-344-6927
e-mail: info@remainstobeseen.com
web: http://www.remainstobeseen.com
Purveyor of photographs and photograph cases.

Jennifer Moss
Photografique
11901 Santa Monica Blvd., #644
Los Angeles, CA 90025
ph: 310-442-0976
e-mail: jamoss@photografique.com
web: http://www.photografique.com
Antique and collectible photographs for sale and reprint; specializes in images from the 1840s through 1940s.

Jeffrey Fraenkel
Fraenkel Gallery
49 Geary St.
San Francisco, CA 94108
ph: 415-981-2661
fax: 415-981-4014
With co-owner Frish Brandt specializes in 19th and 20th century photography.

Richard C. Frey, ISA
R.T.L.H. Enterprises
1275 East Ave.
Chico, CA 95926-1020
ph: 530-343-4528 or 800-567-7854
fax: 530-343-9380
e-mail: RFREYRTLH@aol.com
Wants to buy 19th and 20th century photographs; prefers American Indian, art subjects, Oriental, and albums.

Dave Morris
3388 Merlin Rd., Ste. 351
Grants Pass, OR 97526
ph: 541-955-8411
e-mail: dave@wattpottery.com
web: http://www.wattpottery.com
Wants to buy photographs, CDV's, stereoviews, cabinet cards; prefer Civil War era.

Tim McIntyre
Tim McIntyre's Antique Photographs
137 Nile St.
Stratford, Ontario N5E 4E1
Canada
ph: 519-273-5360
fax: 519-273-7310
e-mail: timoni@orc.ca
web: http://www.orc.ca/~timoni/
Buys, sells, auctions 19th and early

20th century photographs, especially stereoviews, CDVs, cabinet cards, ambrotypes, tintypes, daguerreotypes and larger formats; conducts periodic phone/mail auctions.

John Saddy
Jefferson Stereoptics
50 Foxborough Grove
London, Ontario N6K 4A8
Canada
ph: 519-641-4431
fax: 519-641-2899
e-mail: john.saddy.3d@sympatico.ca
web: http://www3.sympatico.ca/john.saddy.3d/home.htm
Wants photography from early daguerreotypes to View-Master including antique stereo cards, cartes des visites, cabinet cards, cased images; specializes in consignments, but will also buy outright.

Experts

Marv B. Chait
P.O. Box 1979
Evanston, IL 60204-1979
ph: 312-262-5979
e-mail: Marv5555@aol.com

Anthony Davis
Rainbow Creations
P.O. Box 8935
Universal City, CA 91618-8935
ph: 818-762-3540
fax: 818-762-2503
e-mail: antiqphoto@earthlink.net
web: http://www.19cphoto.com
Collector/dealer wants images of all subjects particularly early flat mounts, stereo daguerreotypes, autochromes (early color photography), ambrotypes, albumen, CDVs, platinum prints; all subjects; will buy entire collections.

Julia Nelson-Gal
826 Alvarado
San Francisco, CA 94114-3116
ph: 415-641-8004
fax: 415-641-8053
Specialist in appraisals of 19th and 20th century photographs and photographic literature; will authenticate and broker sales.

Misc. Services

Library of Congress, Prints & Photographs Reading Room
Library of Congress
James Madison Bldg., Rm LM-339
Washington, DC 20540-4730
ph: 202-707-6394 or 202-707-8000
e-mail: lcinfo@loc.gov
web: http://www.lcweb.loc.gov/rr/print/
Has a collection of over 13,000,000 images: prints, photographs, drawings, posters, and architectural and engineering drawings.

Mary Panzer
National Portrait Gallery, Catalog of American Portraits
Photo Dept.
8th & F Streets N.W.
Washington, DC 20560
ph: 202-357-2578
fax: 202-785-2565
e-mail: npgweb@npg.si.edu
web: http://www.npg.si.edu/inf/cap.htm
Will examine photographs brought in for inspection; make an appointment first; may be able to work from good photos of the items; no monetary values given.

Gordon's Art Reference, Inc.
Price Guide: Gordon's International Photography Price Annual
306 West Coronado Rd.
Phoenix, AZ 85003
ph: 602-253-6948 or 800-892-4622
fax: 602-253-2104
e-mail: info@gordonart.com
web: http://www.gordonart.com
Database of over 5,000 entries organized by photographer and print title; includes information about negative and print dates; notes if item is signed, dated, or annotated; now on CD-ROM.

Periodicals

Journal: Art On Paper
39 E 78th St., #501
New York, NY 10021-0213
ph: 212-988-5959
fax: 212-988-6107
e-mail: info@artonpaper.com
web: http://www.artonpaper.com
Published bi-monthly, this journal reports on the entire print and photograph market and is considered a must by print collectors and dealers; also contains scholarly articles and reviews, and auction results.

Photographic Arts Center, The
Newsletter: Photograph Collector, The
301 Hill Ave.
Langhorne, PA 19047
For photograph collectors, dealers and curators; also publishes "The Photographic Art Market," an annual compilation of auction prices.

Photographic Arts Center, The
Directory: Photograph Collector's Resource Directory
301 Hill Ave.
Langhorne, PA 19047
The Directory lists photograph conservators, restorers, appraisers, and galleries and museums that exhibit photography

Repair Services

Take Two Photocraft
202 Massachusetts Ave.
Arlington, MA 02174
ph: 781-643-0000
web: http://www.std.com/Newbury/Take-Two/
Digitally retouches photos using computers; restore faded, torn and creased old photographs; even remove someone from a photo!

David Mishkin
Just Black & White
P.O. Box 4628
54 York Ave.
Portland, ME 04112
ph: 800-827-5881
e-mail: photos@maine.com
web: http://www.maine.com/photos
Specializes in photographic copies, enhancements from faded originals and restorations; can lighten dark tintypes or provide sepia toning; can provide archival (lasts 100 years+) negatives or prints; in business for over 15 years.

Maria Pukownik
Fine Art & Paper Conservation
1045 Orrtanna Rd.
Orrtanna, PA 17353
ph: 717-337-0668
fax: 717-337-1093
e-mail: pukownik@cvn.net
Surface cleaning, mending tears and creases, removal/replacing of decayed backing board, B/W photographic copies of restored original.

Daniel Moyer
After Image Visual Services
121 Sweet Ave.
Moscow, ID 83843-2386
ph: 208-882-6386
fax: 208-895-3803
Uses computers to digitally restore damaged photographs.

Suppliers

John A. Dunphy
University Products, Inc.
517 Main St.
P.O. Box 101
Holyoke, MA 01041-0101
ph: 413-532-3372 or 800-628-1912
fax: 800-532-9281
e-mail: jadunphy@universityproducts.com
web: http://www.universityproducts.com
Carries safe products for the long term storage of postcards, posters, stamps, documents, photographs, textiles, costumes; acid free archival supplies, and materials for conservation and preservation; send for free catalog.

Ansel Adams

Dealers

Edward Carter Gallery Ltd.
560 Broadway, 4th Floor
New York, NY 10012
ph: 212-966-1933
fax: 212-966-2145
e-mail: ecarter@edwardcartergallery.com
web: http://www.edwardcartergallery.com/
Offers the world's largest available inventory of Ansel Adams' work.

Glenn Crosby
Ansel Adams Gallery, The
Village Mall
Yosemite National Park, CA 95389
ph: 800-568-7398 or 209-372-4413
web: http://www.anseladams.com/
Buys and sells Ansel Adams photographs.

Cases

Dealers

Gene Groves
P.O. Box 2471
Baton Rouge, LA 70821-2471
ph: 225-387-3221 or 225-927-2795
fax: 225-346-8049
e-mail: tpbr.gene@em2.com
Buys, sells and collects early photo cases 1840-1865; big size, mother-of-pearl, tortoise, patriotic, signed, wall frames, Union, Mascher, etc.

Celebrity

(see also AUTOGRAPHS, Celebrity; MOVIE MEMORABILIA; TELEVISION SHOWS & MEMORABILIA)

Dealers

Fred Sense Autographs
P.O. Box 310
Brockton, MA 02403
ph: 800-231-9758 or 508-586-1796
fax: 508-580-1632
Specializes in autograph celebrity photographs.

Scott Johnson
Celebrity Locators
P.O. Box 12
North Whitefield, ME 04353
ph: 207-832-6687
fax: 207-832-0546
e-mail: Scott@CelebrityLocators.com
web: http://www.CelebrityLocators.com
Specialist in putting fans in contact with celebrities; carries a variety of celebrity-related products; publisher of "The Big Book of Celebrity Addresses," and "The Autograph Collecting News" (a free email newsletter).

Doug Wirth
Hummerdude's
P.O. Box 4348
Dunellen, NJ 08812
ph: 732-424-9367
Buys and sells celebrity photos and autographs.

Movie Star News
134 West 18th St.
New York, NY 10011
ph: 212-620-8160
fax: 212-727-0634
Carries large variety of movie photos.

Arbe Bareis
Safka & Bareis Autographs
P.O. Box 886
Flushing, NY 11375
ph: 718-263-2276
fax: 718-263-2276
e-mail: sbautog@idt.net
web: http://www.safka-bareis.com/
Buys and sells signed and unsigned photographs in all categories, specializing in performing arts (film, opera, composers, musicians); free catalogs issued.

Robert M. Ready
Movie & TV Star Photos & Books
1410 Oak Tree Drive
Houston, TX 77055-4316
Sells over 2,000 B&W and color 8"x10" celebrity photographs from 1930s to present including Westerns, movie, TV stars; celebrity books are also available; catalog $5 (refundable); wholesale available to dealers.

Mike Gould
Hollywood Legends
6621A Hollywood Blvd.
Los Angeles, CA 90028
ph: 323-962-7411
fax: 323-962-6742
Specializes in signed photographs of contemporary movie stars; also autographs of television stars.

Kristopher Orr
Hollywood Book City Collectables
6631 Hollywood Blvd.
Los Angeles, CA 90028
ph: 323-466-2525 or 800-4CINEMA
fax: 323-962-6742
e-mail: hwdbookcity@earthlink.net
web: http://hollywoodbookcity/
Buys and sells books, autographed celebrity pictures, movie and television scripts, and other movie memorabilia.

Book City Collectibles
6627 Hollywood Blvd.
Los Angeles, CA 90028-6285
ph: 323-466-0120 or 323-962-7411
fax: 323-962-6742
Sells autographed celebrity photos, movie and TV scripts, and other Hollywood memorabilia.

S. & P. Parker's Movie Market
P.O. Box 3900
Dana Point, CA 92629-8900
ph: 949-488-8444
fax: 949-488-8445
Over 20,000 celebrity photographs to choose from.

Civil War

Internet Resources

Civil War Photographs, Library of Congress
101 Independence Ave. SE
Washington, DC 20540
ph: 202-707-8000
e-mail: ndlpcoll@loc.gov
web: http://memory.loc.gov/ammem/cwphome.html
Contains 1,118 photographs, most by Mathew Brady, including scenes of military personnel, preparations for battle, battle aftereffects; also includes portraits of both Confederate and Union officers, and a selection of enlisted men.

Daguerreotypes

Clubs/Associations

Daguerreian Society, The
Newsletter: Daguerreian Society Newsletter
3045 W. Liberty Ave., Ste. 7
Pittsburgh, PA 15216-2460
ph: 412-343-5525
fax: 412-563-5972
e-mail: DagSocPgh@aol.com
web: http://www.austinc.edu/dag
An organization dedicated to the history, art and science of the world's first form of photography - the daguerreotype; over 850 members worldwide; also publishes an annual journal in addition to the bi-monthly newsletter.

Collectors

Stephen Leonard
121 McKinley Ave.
Albertson, NY 11507
ph: 516-742-0979
e-mail: lentoydag@aol.com
Wants to buy antique mechanical toys, daguerreotypes, and music boxes.

Harold E. Boyer
2200 Clayton Rd.
Beaver Falls, PA 15010
ph: 724-843-4774
Wants to buy Daguerreian photo jewelry: daguerreotypes on all kinds of jewelry, on canes, and on other original/unusual pieces; also wants daguerreotypes in cases, especially those showing photo of jewelry.

Paul R. Lafavore
1211-I 10th St. Blvd. NW
Hickory, NC 28601
ph: 828-323-8221
e-mail: lafavore@twave.net
Collecting quality daguerreotype images of any subject, especially maker-marked Maine images; also collecting dageuerrian ephemera and broadsides.

Norman Kulkin
727 N. Fuller Ave.
Los Angeles, CA 90046-7504
ph: 323-653-6929
fax: 323-651-0640
e-mail: pixidom@aol.com
web: http://www.pixidom.com/
Buy, sell, trade vintage photographs: ambrotypes, tintypes, stereoviews, specialty is daguerreotypes; also early 19th century paper photos, early 20th century photos; also photographica including cameras.

Peter E. Palmquist
1183 Union St.
Arcata, CA 95521
Editor of the Daguerreian Society's "The Daguerreian Annual."

Gary Ewer
6406 E. 18th Ave.
Spokane, WA 99212-0102
ph: 509-535-9101

Dealers

Mack Lee
Lee Gallery
1 Mount Vernon St.
Winchester, MA 01890-2703
ph: 781-729-7445
fax: 781-729-4592
e-mail: leegall@tiac.net
web: http://www.leegallery.com/
Buys, sells, and appraises fine 19th and 20th century photographs and daguerreotypes.

Dennis Waters
Daguerreian Forum, The
P.O. Box 1073
Exeter, NH 03833-1073
ph: 603-772-9065
e-mail: dwaters@finedags.com
web: http://www.finedags.com/
Buys and sells daguerreotypes, thermoplastic cases, and related material.

Bryan W. Ginns
2109 Cty. Rte. 21
Valatie, NY 12184-6001
ph: 518-392-5805
fax: 518-392-7925
e-mail: the3dman@aol.com
Wants large collections of stereo views, old cameras, daguerreotypes, magic lanterns, optical toys; anything relating to photographics.

Gene Groves
P.O. Box 2471
Baton Rouge, LA 70821-2471
ph: 225-387-3221 or 225-927-2795
fax: 225-346-8049
e-mail: tpbr.gene@em2.com
Buys, sells, repairs and collects quality daguerreotypes: outdoors, occupationals, military, blacks, Louisiana, animals, signed, toys, large groups, etc.

Janos Novomeszky
8408 Kawala Dr.
Las Vegas, NV 89128-7170
Wants to buy fine daguerreotypes and pre-1880 photographic equipment; single pieces or entire collections.

Experts

Anthony Davis
Rainbow Creations
P.O. Box 8935
Universal City, CA 91618-8935
ph: 818-762-3540
fax: 818-762-2503
e-mail: antiqphoto@earthlink.net
web: http://www.19cphoto.com
Collector/dealer specializing in daguerreotypes of outdoor scenes, military, occupationals; also hand-tinted portraits, stereo daguerreotypes all categories; wants single items or entire collections; bi-monthly catalog $40 per year.

Internet Resources

Mark Koenigsberg
Daguerreotypes: 19th Century Photography
ph: 201-863-0868
e-mail: dagmark@worldnet.att.net
web: http://www.geocities.com/~daguerreotype/
Learn about daguerreotypes at this sites.

Daguerreotype Collection, Library of Congress
101 Independence Ave. SE
Washington, DC 20540
ph: 202-707-8000
e-mail: ndlpcoll@loc.gov
web: http://memory.loc.gov/ammem/daghtml/daghome.html
The collection consists of more than 650 photographs dating from 1839 to 1864 including portrait daguerreotypes and early architectural views.

Repair Services

Gene Groves
P.O. Box 2471
Baton Rouge, LA 70821-2471
ph: 225-387-3221 or 225-927-2795
fax: 225-346-8049
e-mail: tpbr.gene@em2.com
Professionally repairs daguerreotypes; replaces old and damaging glass which deteriorates with new safe glass.

Medical

Museums/Libraries

Michael Rhode, Archivist
Otis Historical Archives, National Museum of Health & Medicine
Bldg. 54
Walter Reed Medical Center
Washington, DC 20306
ph: 202-782-2200
fax: 202-782-3573
e-mail: rhode@afip.osd.org/
web: http://bubba.afip.org/
Federal government museum archives that collects photographic material related to the history of medicine, especially military medicine.

Military

Misc. Services

National Archives Still Picture Branch
8601 Adelphi Rd.
College Park, MD 20740
ph: 301-713-6660
Photos of movie stars in uniform while serving their country can be purchased.

Real War Photos
P.O. Box 728
Hammond, IN 46325-0728
ph: 219-931-3359
fax: 219-931-3359
Combat photographs taken by combat photographers can be obtained; catalogs available of Army, navy, Marines USAF, Civil War - send $3.

Periodicals

Magazine: Military Images
RD 1 Box 99A
Henryville, PA 18332-9726
ph: 570-629-9152
e-mail: milimage@uplink.net
web: http://www.civilwar-photos.com
Focuses on military images from 1839 to 1900; six issues per year; since 1979.

PHOTOGRAPHY

(see also 3-D PHOTOGRAPHICA; CAMERAS & CAMERA EQUIPMENT; PHOTOGRAPHS; STEREO VIEWERS & STEREOVIEWS)

Clubs/Associations

Thruman F. Naylor
Photographic Historical Society of New England, Inc.
Journal: New England Journal of Photographic History
P.O. Box 650189
West Newton, MA 02465-0189
ph: 617-731-6603 or 617-277-0207
fax: 617-277-7878
e-mail: alevesque@aol.com
800 member non-profit society; 60 page journal.

Gerald Fine
American Photographic Historical Society, Inc.
Magazine: Photographica
1150 Avenue of the Americas
New York, NY 10036
ph: 212-575-0483 or 732-617-3142
fax: 732-617-1360
e-mail: gfine@monmouth.com
web: http://www.superexpo.com/aphs/
International organization with educational meetings six times each year in NYC; conducts two fairs for the selling of antique cameras, equipment & photos; publishes "Photographica" quarterly and a monthly newsletter, "In Focus".

Prof. Andrew Davidhazy, Webmaster
Photographic Historical Society, Inc., The
Newsletter: PHS Newsletter
P.O. Box 39563
Rochester, NY 14604
ph: 716-475-2592
fax: 716-475-7750
e-mail: andpph@rit.edu
web: http://www.rit.edu/~andpph/tphs.html
For those with an interest in the history of photography; conducts monthly meetings and a tri-annual symposium.

Photographic Society of America
3000 United Founders Blvd., Ste. 103
Oklahoma City, OK 73112
ph: 405-843-1437
e-mail: RGorrill@compuserve.com
web: http://www.tiac.net/users/bcsbob/psa/

William P. Carroll
Western Photographic Collectors Association, Inc.
Magazine: Photographist, The
P.O. Box 4294
Whittier, CA 90607-4294
ph: 562-693-8421
fax: 562-945-6011
Non-profit organization dedicated to the dissemination of information on, and to stimulate interest in, all aspects of photographica.

Bob Wilson, Pres.
Photographic Historical Society of Canada
Magazine: Photographic Canadiana
P.O. Box 54620
Toronto, Ontario M5M 4N5
Canada
ph: 416-736-2100
fax: 416-736-5838
e-mail: phsc@onramp.ca
web: http://web.onramp.ca/phsc/
Collectors and historians interested in the apparatus, processes, images, and history of photography; photographica fairs held in March and October; auction in April/March.

Collectors

Rod Coddington
2233 N. Quantico St.
Arlington, VA 22205
ph: 703-532-3358
e-mail: rcoddington@krtinfo.com
web: http://www.imagemag.net/
Collector of early historic photographs, 1840 to 1920.

Dealers

J. Fernando Martinez
Alternative Photography
Joanot Martorell 14,30B
P.O. Box 132
Novelda, Alciante 04660
Spain
ph: 34 65600338 or 939 642461
fax: 34 6560038
Specializes in books, photography and small collectibles.

Internet Resources

Photo Shopper Online
e-mail: photoshopper-support@photoshopper.com
web: http://www.photoshopper.com/
An on-line mall with a vast selection of photo products, services, suppliers; see what equipment dealers and collectors what to buy from you; classified ads to buy or sell; forum to post and reply to messages with experts/collectors.

Prof. Andrew Davidhazy, Webmaster
PhotoForum
RIT School of Photographic Arts & Sciences
Lomb Memorial Drive
Rochester, NY 14623
ph: 716-475-2592
fax: 716-475-7750
e-mail: andpph@rit.edu
web: http://www.rit.edu/~andpph/photoforum.html
Online educational network established to serve the photographic and imaging communities in general with a medium for exchange of ideas; has an accessible databank of informational files about a wide variety of photo/imaging subjects.

Rod Coddington, Ed.
Image Magazine
2233 N. Quantico St.
Arlington, VA 22205
ph: 703-532-3358
e-mail: rcoddington@krtinfo.com
web: http://www.imagemag.net/
A quarterly online magazine devoted to the history, technology and aesthetics of photography and motion pictures, 1840 to 1920.

Misc. Services

David Silver
International Photographic Historical Association
Newsletter: INPHO News
P.O. Box 16074
San Francisco, CA 94116-0074
ph: 415-681-4356 or 415-731-5717
e-mail: silver@well.com
Corresponding research & resource center for those interested in studying/collecting cameras, photographs, or other objects pertaining to the history of photography; free appraisals and information services; speakers/presentation bureau.

Museums/Libraries

Thurman F. Naylor
Naylor Museum of Photography
P.O. Box 23
Waltham, MA 02254
ph: 617-731-6603 or 617-277-0207
fax: 617-277-7878
e-mail: jacknaylor@aol.com
A private museum with over 20,000 photographic items on display; by appointment.

International Center of Photography
1130 5th Ave.
New York, NY 10128
ph: 212-860-1776
fax: 212-722-3674
e-mail: education@icp.org
web: http://www.icp.org/

George Eastman House International Museum of Photography & Film
900 East Ave.
Rochester, NY 14607
ph: 716-271-3361
fax: 716-271-3970
e-mail: tbannon@geh.org
web: http://www.eastman.org/1_geninfo/1_index.htm
The museum includes the restored house and garden of George Eastman (1854-1932), founder of Eastman Kodak Co., and displays the art, technology, and impact of photography and motion pictures over 150 years.

Bill Becker
American Museum of Photography
P.O. Box 7076
Huntington Woods, MI 48070
e-mail: images@photographymuseum.com
web: http://www.photographymuseum.com/
A very well done virtual museum based on a 75,000 piece collection of images from the first 75 years of photography: photos, museum bookstore, early photographic processes, links to related sites, protecting & preserving photos.

National Museum of Photography, Film & Television
U.K.
ph: 01274 203305
e-mail: a.jarman@nmsi.ac.uk
web: http://www.nmsi.ac.uk/nmpft/
A popular British museum; collections contain exciting galleries outlining the past, present and future imaging technology.

Periodicals

Taylor & Francis Ltd.
Magazine: History of Photography
Rankine Road
Basingstoke, Hants RG24 8PR
U.K.
ph: +44(0) 1256 813000
fax: +44(0) 1256 479438
e-mail: webmaster@tandfdc.com
web: http://www.tandf.co.uk/JNLS/hph.htm
An international publication devoted exclusively to the history and criticism of the photograph; covers photography from the earliest times to the present day; published quarterly.

Suppliers

Dick Haviland
Film for Classics
P.O. Box 486
Jamaica, NY 11472-0486
ph: 716-624-4945
e-mail: joankay@frontiernet.net
web: http://www.simplyrochester.com/directory/photography/equipment.html
Provides film for collectors/users of classic and antique cameras all over the world.

PIANO ROLLS

(see also MUSICAL INSTRUMENTS, Pianos [Player])

Auction Services

Paul & Cindy Johnson
Piano Roll Shop, The
28 Prospect Hill
Burlington, VT 05401
ph: 802-660-8041
e-mail: pianorol@globalnetisp.com
Holds periodic auctions of player piano rolls and nickelodeon rolls; also produces new rolls of the best in ragtime and jazz as well as rolls for reproducing pianos.

Dan Wilke
QRS Music Rolls, Inc.
1026 Niagara St.
Buffalo, NY 14213-2007
ph: 716-885-0250 or 716-885-4600
fax: 716-885-7510
Offers bi-monthly auctions by mail of original antique 88-note and reproducing player piano rolls; buys collections of old rolls, but does not accept consignments.

Collectors

Deno Buralli
P.O. Box 6
Spring Grove, IL 60081
Reproducing rolls and standard 88-note rolls.

Dealers

John Tuttle
John Tuttle "Self-Playing Pianos"
407 19th Ave.
Bricktown, NJ 08724
ph: 732-840-8787
e-mail: john@player-care.com
web: http://www.player-care.com/
Dedicated to player and reproducing pianos: service, repair, rebuilding; also sells new QRS and Tempola music rolls on-line; lots of technical information and information about used rolls and roll auctions.

Sheet Music Center
Box 10
Old Bethpage, NY 11804
ph: 800-527-7626
e-mail: smctr@sheetmusiccenter.com
web: http://www.sheetmusiccenter.com
Buys and sells sheet music and piano rolls; FREE catalog to readers of "Maloney's Antiques & Collectibles Resource Directory", check it out at http://www.sheetmusiccenter.com/catalog.

Experts

Dan Wilke
1026 Niagara St.
Buffalo, NY 14213-2007
ph: 716-885-0250 or 716-885-4600
fax: 716-885-7510

Repro. Sources

Dan Wilke
QRS Music Rolls, Inc.
1026 Niagara St.
Buffalo, NY 14213-2007
ph: 716-885-0250 or 716-885-4600
fax: 716-885-7510
World's oldest manufacturer of player piano rolls; thousands of songs, old and new, by famous pianists of past and present.

Play-Rite Music Rolls
401 S. Broadway
Turlock, CA 95380
ph: 209-667-1996
fax: 209-667-8241
Sells new 10 to 16 tune "O" rolls for player pianos.

PIANOS

Dealers

Melvin Besbrode
Besbrode Piano
Galways Mill
Leeds, West Yorkshire LS11 9XE
U.K.
ph: 00 44 1132 448344 or 00 44 1132 663225
fax: 00 44 1132 456960
e-mail: melvin@legend.co.uk
web: http://www.piano-uk.com/
Piano dealer and appraiser specializing in Steinway, Bechstein, Erard, Pleyel artcased grand pianos; suppliers of all types of new and used pianos.

Miniature

(see also MINIATURES; MUSICAL INSTRUMENTS, Pianos)

Clubs/Associations

Janice E. Kelsh
Miniature Piano Enthusiast Club
Newsletter: Musically Yours!
633 Pennsylvania Ave.
Hagerstown, MD 21740-3769
ph: 301-797-7675
fax: 301-496-7383
e-mail: jkelsh@niaid.nih.gov
Established in 1990 to promote the hobby of miniature piano collecting; annual convention.

Collectors

Janice E. Kelsh
633 Pennsylvania Ave.
Hagerstown, MD 21740-3769
ph: 301-797-7675
fax: 301-496-7383
e-mail: jkelsh@niaid.nih.gov
Interested in obtaining miniature pianos of all kinds; also wants old postcards depicting pianos.

PICKLE CASTORS

Collectors

Virginia Young
15463 McNeill Rd.
Sterling, NY 13156-4212
ph: 315-947-5840 or 315-947-5782
fax: 315-947-6905
e-mail: gifts@sterlingfestival.com
Wants to buy pickle castors; frames must have a mark; especially interested in colored decorated jars or unusual castors; must be in very good condition.

PIE BIRDS

(see also KITCHEN COLLECTIBLES)

Clubs/Associations

Linda & Bobby Fields
Pie Bird Collectors Club
158 Bagsby Hill Lane
Dover, TN 37058-6248
ph: 931-232-5099
e-mail: fpiebird@compu.net
Hold annual Pie Bird Collectors convention.

Collectors

Jeannie Kolger
6906 Meade Dr.
Colleyville, TX 76034-6416
ph: 817-329-5262
e-mail: jkolger@gte.net
Wants to buy unusual old pie birds and pie vents, particularly Disney examples, Black Mammys and/or black chefs.

Dealers

Deborah Vanden Heuvel
Global Galleria, The
209 Riverwalk Circle
Cary, NC 27511
ph: 888-832-5616 or 919-859-5818
fax: 919-859-6396
e-mail: globalgal@tias.com
web: http://www.tias.com/stores/globalgal/
Has a large selection of whimsical English pie birds; always wants to buy more to add to inventory; straight from the English countryside.

Alan Pedel
Captivating Collectibles
Guineaford
Barnstaple, Devon EX31 4EA
U.K.
fax: 011-44-1271-322514
e-mail: ukpiebirds@btinternet.com
web: http://www.sosi.net/piebirds/
Rare and lovely pie birds such as Black Mammies, Clowns, Wizards, Teddy Bears, Roosters, Pigs, Rabbits, Frogs, Chefs, Blue Willow and Chintz vents.

Experts

Lillian Cole
14 Harmony School Rd.
Flemington, NJ 08822-2606
ph: 908-782-3198
Interested in the older foreign and U.S. pie birds either in singles or in collections; avid collector and historian/researcher.

Linda & Bobby Fields
158 Bagsby Hill Lane
Dover, TN 37058-6248
ph: 931-232-5099
e-mail: fpiebird@compu.net
Buy single birds or entire collections; have a large selection of traders; author of "Four & Twenty Blackbirds," 184 pages, 623 color photos, identification and value guide, $33.95 ppd.; available from author.

Periodicals

Lillian Cole
Newsletter: Pie Birds Unlimited
14 Harmony School Rd.
Flemington, NJ 08822-2606
ph: 908-782-3198
Nine issues of "Pie Birds Unlimited" (1990-1996) contained just about all that is presently known about pie birds; please SASE for information.

PIN-BACK BUTTONS

(see BUTTONS, Pin-Back)

PIN-UP ART

(see also EROTICA; PLAYBOY ITEMS)

Collectors

Louis K. Meisel
141 Prince St.
New York, NY 10012-5315
ph: 212-677-1340
fax: 212-533-7340
e-mail: gallery@meisels.com
web: http://home.att.net/~LKMgallery/LKM.html
Wants to buy pin-ups: oil paintings, pastels, watercolors, drawings.

David Kveragas
1943 Timberlane
Clarks Summit, PA 18411-9539
ph: 570-587-3429
Wants Vargas and Olivia illustrations; Vargas prior to his Playboy work, especially Shadowland mags, Ziegfeld Follies sheet music. Olivia items: catalogs, posters, greeting cards, etc.; offers made; also Rolf Armstrong items.

Charles Martignette
P.O. Box 293
Hallandale, FL 33008
ph: 305-454-3474
Wants pin-up and glamour art; original paintings.

John Crawford
3442 Manor Hill
Cincinnati, OH 45220
ph: 513-221-6050
Wants pin-up art by Vargas, Petty, Mozert, Elugren, others.

Jerry Peters
Chestnut Hollow, Ltd.
6060 Bordman Rd.
P.O. Box 6
Almont, MI 48003-0006
ph: 810-798-3158
Collecting pin-up photos, art and magazines; especially wants Vargas, Petty, Elvghrenn, Moran, Olivia; also wants old Playboy magazines and Bettie Page photos.

Ed Royse
112 N. Broadway St.
Walters, OK 73572
ph: 580-357-8000
fax: 580-875-2063
e-mail: edroyse@juno.com
Wants to buy Varga/Vargas pin-up art, Esquire calendars, playing cards, Esky cards, etc.

Dealers

Robert Bessette
Green Dragon Arts
P.O. Box 588
Burlington, VT 05402-0588
ph: 802-862-1930
fax: 802-862-1930
e-mail: grdragon@together.net
Buys and sells pin-up art works, calendars, fantasy and pin-up postcards, men's magazines, erotic books and paper books.

Experts

Denis C. Jackson, Ed.
P.O. Box 1958
Sequim, WA 98382-1958
ph: 360-452-3810
e-mail: ticn@olypen.com
web: http://www.olypen.com/ticn/
Author of "The Price and Identification Guide to Pin-Ups & Glamour Art", 1992; send LSASE for information; wants old prints, calendars, mutescope cards.

Periodicals

Steve Sullivan
Magazine: Glamour Girls: Then and Now
P.O. Box 34501
Washington, DC 20043-4501
ph: 703-641-0676
e-mail: stevesul@aol.com
web: http://www.ggtan.com/
Published approximately three timer per year; focuses on pin-up art: interviews and features on glamour girls from the 1950s to present in movies, TV, burlesque, and men's magazines.

Denis C. Jackson, Ed.
Newsletter: Illustrator Collector's News, The
P.O. Box 1958
Sequim, WA 98382-1958
ph: 360-452-3810
e-mail: ticn@olypen.com
web: http://www.olypen.com/ticn/
A bi-monthly publication for collectors of magazines and other paper illustrations; free classifieds for subscribers; send LSASE for information.

PINS

(see also BADGES; BUTTONS, Pin-Back; FAST FOOD COLLECTIBLES, McDonald's [Pins]; OLYMPIC GAMES COLLECTIBLES, Pins & Buttons; SOCIAL CAUSES; TIE BARS, CLIPS & TACKS)

Clubs/Associations

Rowan Fay
International Pin Collectors Club
Newsletter: IPCC Newsletter
602 Chenango St.
Binghamton, NY 13901-2029
ph: 607-724-4583 or 607-723-7421
fax: 607-723-3687
e-mail: rhfay@juno.com
Interested in all sorts of pins: Olympic, Coca Cola, sports, Desert Storm, media, etc.

Collectors

Mark & Anna
Mark's Pins
13727 Walbrooke Dr.
Tampa, FL 33624
e-mail: SprtyGrl12@aol.com
web: http://members.aol.com/SprtyGrl12/pins.html
Trades Olympic and Hard Rock Cafe pins.

Fred Swindall
2219 SE Salmon St.
Portland, OR 97214-3941
Wants pins, buttons, and badges: political pins, comic pins, advertising from tractors to cows, trucking co. badges, McDonald's, old and new movie promo pins, police and fire badges, Union ribbons, tokens, old Elks & Masonic badges, etc.

Gil & Marjorie Joanis
1329 14 St. East
Saskatoon, Saskatchewan S7H 0A6
Canada
ph: 306-665-9902
Buys, sells, trades metal pins, especially relating to curling (Brier, Scotch Cup, Silver Broom), media (CBC, SRC), figure skating (Worlds and other major events), Olympic Games; send photocopies;

Dealers

Bill Nelson
Newsletter: Bill Nelson Newsletter, The
P.O. Box 41630
Tucson, AZ 85717-1630
ph: 520-629-0868 or 800-368-8434
fax: 520-629-0387
web: http://www.billnelsonnewsletter.com
Monthly newsletter with news, tips, and sources for collectors of Olympic, Sport, Disney, Coca Cola pins; over a million pins inventory; established in 1985.

Award

Collectors

Bob Lucian
33 Merritts Road
Farmingdale, NY 11735-1820
ph: 516-293-3927
e-mail: bbluc@erols.net
Wants to buy corporate service pins; pins given to employees reaching 5-10-15-20+ years of service; also other corporate awards: watches, tie pins, cuff links, medals, etc.; prefers national or international companies.

PIONEERS

(see WESTERN AMERICANA)

PIPES

(see also CANES & WALKING STICKS; CHARACTER COLLECTIBLES, Sherlock Holmes; MATCH SAFES; SMOKING COLLECTIBLES; TOBACCO COLLECTIBLES)

Clubs/Associations

Sailorman Jack
New York Pipe Club
Newsletter: New York Pipe Club Newsletter
c/o S. Jack
440 East 81, Apt. 1C
New York, NY 10028
ph: 212-288-3832
Club meets on the first Tuesday of each month at 6 pm at Mary's of Madison Restaurant, 24 East 41 St., between 5th Ave. and Madison Ave.

Robert C. Hamlin
Pipe Collectors Club of America
Magazine: Pipe Smokers Pipeline
P.O. Box 5179
Woodbridge, VA 22194-5179
ph: 703-878-7655 or 703-878-3657
fax: 703-878-7657
e-mail: rch@pipeguy.com
web: http://www.pipesmoke.com/

Bill Unger, Sec/Treas
North American Society of Pipe Collectors
Newsletter: NASPC Newsletter
P.O. Box 9642
Columbus, OH 43209-9642
ph: 614-252-2904
e-mail: bill@naspc.org
web: http://www.naspc.org
A club of over 500 members dedicated to all aspects of pipe collecting and smoking; publishes a professional newsletter and produces a Fall swap/sell show in Columbus,s OH.

Neil Murray, Sec.
International Association of Pipe Smokers' Clubs
P.O. Box 930401
Wixom, MI 48393

Michael Reschke
Chicagoland Pipe Collectors Club
540 South Westmore
Lombard, IL 60148-3028
A local group of pipe collectors and smokers who gather once a month for an informal meeting and evening of fellowship; members have a common interest in pipes, cigars, and tobacciana.

P.C. Wiseman
Pipe Club of London, The
Journal: Journal of the Pipe Club of London, The
40 Crescent Drive
Petts Wood
Orpington, Kent BR5 1BD
U.K.
ph: 0168 983 7761
Premier pipe club in Great Britain; international in scope with over 500 members in 33 countries; promotes and protects the interests of pipe smokers; 12 meetings a year; free 26 page bi-annual Journal to all members.

Collectors

Charles H. Strom
100 Bleecker St.
New York, NY 10012-2205
ph: 212-998-8480
e-mail: charlie.strom@nyu.edu
Wants to buy ornately carved, top quality antique meerschaum pipes and cheroot holders.

Lee Pattison
6 Christview Dr.
Cuba, NY 14727-1202
ph: 716-968-2458
Wants antique meerschaum pipes carved and plain, briar pipes of more recent manufacture brand names: Charatan, Barling, Dunhill, Sasieni, Stanwell, Larson, Savinelli and others; also wants to buy tobacco jars and cigar store items.

Bob Spore
400 Riverside Dr.
Pasadena, MD 21122
ph: 410-437-2715
e-mail: bobspore@erols.com
Collector seeking pre-smoked briar pipes; sells and appraises pipe collections; member T.U.C.O.P.S., P.C.C.A.

Bob Spore
400 Riverside Dr.
Pasadena, MD 21122
ph: 410-437-2715
e-mail: bobspore@erols.com
Collector seeking pre-smoked briar pipes; sells and appraises pipe collections; member T.U.C.O.P.S., P.C.C.A.

Gary L. Donachy
801 W. Sunset
Steeleville, IL 62288-1015
ph: 618-965-3189
e-mail: foxnhare@egyptian.net
Wants to buy antique meerschaum and high grade briar pipes; also wants tobacco-related books, trade cards, and advertising.

Eric Fuchslocher
8050 Ventura Cyn Ave.
Panorama City, CA 91402
ph: 818-994-1492
Wants to buy carved wood and meerschaum pipes.

E.S. Radcliffe
3732 Colonial Lane SE
Port Orchard, WA 98366-1846
ph: 206-876-8615
Wants to buy cigar holders, cigarette holders, carved and ornamental pipes, meerschaum clay pipes.

Dealers

Chuck Haley
Sherlock's
13926 Double Girth Ct.
Matthews, NC 28105-4068
ph: 704-847-5480
Specializing in estate pipes and related smoking accessories.

Don Duco
Pikpenkabinet & Smokiana
Prinsengracht 488
KH Amsterdam, Pays Bas 1017
The Netherlands
ph: +31 20 42 11 779

Experts

Benjamin Rapaport
11505 Turnbridge Ln.
Reston, VA 20194-1220
ph: 703-435-8133
Wants antique meerschaum, opium, porcelain, Meissen, chinoiserie, Wedgwood, metal, cloisonne, champleve, early wood, etc. pipes.

James Kesterson
3881 Fulton Grove Rd.
Cincinnati, OH 45245-2504
ph: 513-752-0949
Wants smoked or new briar pipes: brands like Barling, Caminetto, Charatan, Comoy, Dunhill, GBD, Larsen, Sasieni, Savinelli, etc.

Museums/Libraries

Don Duco
Museum of Tobacco Pipes
Prinsengracht 488
KH Amsterdam, Pays Bas 1017
The Netherlands
ph: +31 20 42 11 779

Periodicals

SpecComm International, Inc.
Magazine: Pipes & Tobaccos
3000 Highwoodds Blvd., Ste. 300
Raleigh, NC 27604-1029
ph: 919-872-5040
fax: 919-876-6531
e-mail: mprice@pt-magazine.com
web: http://www.pt-magazine.com/
Articles about pipes, tobaccos, famous smokers, collectible pipes.

Neil Murray
Newsletter: Agricultural and Mechanical Gazette, The
P.O. Box 930401
Wixom, MI 48393
web: http://digiscape.com/a&mgazette/BriarPipes.html
Newsletter published 5 times a year.

Repair Services

Bill Braddock
Braddock Hand Made Pipes
P.O. Box 44021
Oklahoma City, OK 73144-1021
ph: 405-682-1558
fax: 405-682-1558
e-mail: kap50@aol.com
web: http://members.aol.com/kap50/
Restoration and repair of tobacco pipes; also buys, sells and appraises pipes; hand made pipes made from the highest quality plateau briar.

Clay

Clubs/Associations

Susanne Atkin, Ed.
Society for Clay Pipe Research
30 Ongrils Close
Pershore, Worcestshire WR10 1QE
U.K.
e-mail: 10074.2367@compuserve.com
Formed in the U.K. in 1984 with the aim to further enhance the study of clay tobacco pipes and their makers.

Collectors

Paul Jung
P.O. Box 817
Bel Air, MD 21014-0817
ph: 410-638-1475
e-mail: sjung93156@aol.com
Buys and collects clay pipes; researches the clay tobacco pipe industry in the U.S., Canada, and Europe; especially wants clay pipes marked France or Paris, or with name of an American city; has published books on smoking pipes.

Hookahs

Collectors

Jason Short
114 Avondale Dr.
Smyrna, TN 37167
ph: 617-459-4029
Wants Middle-Eastern and Indian hookahs for smoking tobacco (not interested in water pipes found in "head shops.")

Meerschaum

Collectors

Bernard Berlly
24 School House Ln.
Great Neck, NY 11020-1323
ph: 516-829-2777
fax: 516-829-2779
Wants antique carved meerschaum pipes.

Dealers

Jerry Korn
Lighters Galore Plus
P.O. Box 534
San Marcos, CA 92079
ph: 800-853-3941 or 760-734-1414
fax: 760-744-6666
e-mail: info@pipeshop.com
web: http://www.pipeshop.com
Collector, dealer, appraiser, expert specializes in collectible Zippo lighters and handcarved Meerschaum pipes; also carries many other hard-to-find smoking accessories.

Pipe Cleaners

Collectors

Paul Scheuer
6753 Humbolt Ave.
Minneapolis, MN 55430-1533
ph: 612-561-7321
Collects old pipe cleaner containers; also Roll-Your-Own cigarette paper packets and related memorabilia.

PIRATES

(see NAUTICAL ANTIQUES)

PISTOLS

(see FIREARMS; TOY GUNS)

PIXIES

(see CERAMICS, Pixieware; GNOMES; ELVES)

PLANNING ITEMS

(see also ARCHITECTURE & RELATED ITEMS; STATE RELATED MEMORABILIA; MAPS & CHARTS)

Dealers

Ken Kipp, AICP
Allenwood Americana Antiques
P.O. Box 116
Allenwood, PA 17810-0116
ph: 570-538-1440
Buys and sells city/town/regional planning items; early to current:

plans, maps, books, memorabilia of U.S. community planners.

PLANTERS PEANUTS ITEMS

Clubs/Associations

John Paglialunga
Peanut Pals
Newsletter: Peanut Papers
P.O. Box 652
Saint Clairsville, OH 43950-0652
ph: 740-695-4286
e-mail: pango2@yahoo.com
web: http://www.commserve.com/mrpeanut/ppals.html
Focuses on Planters Peanuts and Mr. Peanut history and memorabilia; national and regional conventions, newsletter, classified ads for members only.

Collectors

Joe Iozzia
P.O. Box 1005
Pomona, NJ 08240-1005
ph: 609-652-8504
fax: 609-652-8888
e-mail: pinflyers@aol.com
web: http://members.aol.com/Pinflyers/chameleon.html
Buying, selling, trading vintage Planters Mr. Peanut advertising items; will buy entire collections; wants any pre-1970 items.

Arleane Pawlowicz
5 Edgewood Road
Goshen, NY 10924-2303
ph: 914-294-3475
fax: 914-294-3475
e-mail: epphoto@frontiernet.net
Long time and avid collector of anything relating to Planters Peanuts.

Richard Reddock
914 Isle Ct.
Bellmore, NY 11710-1545
ph: 516-826-2032 or 800-223-PNUT
e-mail: pnutfanclb@aol.com
Wants to buy all types of Mr. Peanut tin displays, signs, paper items, ceramic oil and vinegar, metal letter openers.

Joyce Spontak
804 Hickory Grade Rd.
Bridgeville, PA 15017
ph: 412-221-7599
Has over 2000 Planters items in her collection.

Mike & Fran Nolan
1228 Oakdale Dr.
Sanatoga, PA 19464
ph: 610-718-9774
e-mail: fran247@aol.com
web: http://members.aol.com/fran247/
Avid collectors of Planters Mr. Peanut items from the early 1900s to present; lots of rare and unusual items; club info available; website has a For Sale/Trade page.

Glenn Grush
5344 North Collingwood Circle
Calabasas, CA 91302-3137
ph: 818-880-6200 or 800-653-3244
fax: 818-880-6500

Dealers

Judy Posner
4195 South Tamiami Trail, Ste. 183
Venice, FL 34293-5112
ph: 941-497-7149
fax: 941-493-8085
e-mail: jpc@tias.com
web: http://www.tias.com/stores/jpc/

Experts

Marty Blank
P.O. Box 405
Flushing, NY 11365-0405
ph: 516-485-8071
e-mail: martyadver@aol.com
Wants to buy unusual Mr. Peanut items, especially plastic toys, counter displays and older items; listed in "Planter's Peanut Collectibles" (Schiffer).

Judith & Bob Walthall
P.O. Box 4465
Huntsville, AL 35815
ph: 256-881-9198
Serious collectors specializing in Planter Peanut items; founded Peanut Pals in 1978; has done extensive research over the years; has had many articles published.

PLASTIC COLLECTIBLES

(see also BOXES; CELLULOID ITEMS; CHARMS; DOLLS HOUSES & FURNISHINGS; KITS; LUNCH BOXES; MODELS, Cars; SOLDIERS, Toy; TOYS; TOYS, Playsets; TRAINS, Toy [Plasticville]; TUPPERWARE)

Collectors

G. Marshall Naul
534 Stublyn Rd.
Granville, OH 43023
Interested in starting a club for collectors of plastic items.

Dealers

Abby Nash
Malabar Enterprises
172 Bush Lane
Ithaca, NY 14850
ph: 607-255-2905 or 607-266-0690
fax: 607-255-4179
e-mail: asn6@cornell.edu
Buying and selling 1920-1960 Bakelite and other plastic items.

Dee Battle
9 Orange Blossom Trail
Yalaha, FL 34797
ph: 352-324-3023
Expert and dealer in vintage plastics: Deco, watches, purses, radios.

Alicia & Jorge Valino
P.O. Box 1442
Montevideo, 11000
Uruguay
e-mail: vala@adinet.com.uy.
Wants to buy items made of Bakelite.

Experts

Jan Lindenberger
P.O. Box 7224
Colorado Springs, CO 80933
ph: 719-591-9558
fax: 719-591-9558
Buys and sells plastic collectibles; author of "Plastic Collectibles - Information & Price Guide" (Schiffer Pub., Ltd., 1992).

Museums/Libraries

Valerie A. Wilcox, Ed. Dir.
National Plastics Center & Museum
P.O. Box 639
210 Lancaster St.
Leominster, MA 01453
ph: 978-537-9529
fax: 978-537-3220
e-mail: vwilcox@polymers.com
web: http://npcm.plastics.com/welcome.html
An intriguing look at the snappy world of plastics, featuring the "Plastics Hall of Fame," "Rare Artifacts," "Modern Plastics Applications," and more.

Repair Services

Daniel Blake
Outsider Studios
Route 276, P.O. Box 63
Cedar Mountain, NC 28718
ph: 828-884-2619
Expert repair of Catalin and Plaskon repair: radio cases, boxes, jewelry; marbled or solid finishes; repairs of cracks, holes and warps; recast missing surfaces; recoloring of faded Catalin; undetectable repair technique.

PLASTICVILLE

(see TRAINS, Toy [Plasticville])

PLATES

(see also COLLECTIBLES [MODERN], Plates)

Danish

Dealers

Ed London
Parke Lloyds International, Inc.
9408 NW 70 St.
Fort Lauderdale, FL 33321-3002
ph: 954-724-4274 or 954-726-4107
Wants to buy Bing & Grondahl Christmas Plates from 1895 to 1963 and Royal Copenhagen Christmas Plates from 1908 to 1963.

PLATING

(see REPAIR/RESTORATION/CONSERVATION, Metal Items)

PLATINUM

Dealers

Beth Scott
Affordable Jewelry & Precious Metals
304 SW Washington St.
Portland, OR 97204
ph: 800-690-4995 or 503-224-7520
fax: 503-227-4204
e-mail: sight@ajpm.com
web: http://www.ajpm.com
Gold, silver and platinum bullion dealers.

Scrap

Dealers

Michael A. Merrill
Michael A. Merrill, Inc.
Crestar Bank Building
2045 York Rd.
Timonium, MD 21093
ph: 410-453-9400
e-mail: merrill@home.com
web: http://www.pm-connect.com/mmerrill/
Buying precious metals from the public, dealers since 1974; buys scrap gold, diamonds, old gold, dental gold, school rings, gold & silver numismatic coins, sterling silver (Kirk & Steiff), Franklin Mint, platinum, palladium, exotics.

PLAYBOY ITEMS

(see also EROTICA; MAGAZINES, Men's [Playboy]; PIN-UP ART)

Clubs/Associations

Tom Bonner
Playboy Collectors Association
P.O. Box 653
Phillipsburg, MO 65722-0653

Collectors

Ronnie Keshishian
P.O. Box 2654
Glendale, AZ 85311
ph: 623-435-2665
e-mail: ronniek@goodnet.com
web: http://www.goodnet.com/~ronniek/
Wants Playboy memorabilia: early calendars, special editions, puzzles, hand puppets, liquor caddies, femlin statues, rabbit dolls, club items, dinner plates, candles, menus, promo items, anything Playboy except magazines.

Charlie's
P.O. Box 593
Woodland Hills, CA 91365-0593
Wants Playboy calendars, pin-ups, 50s and 60s girlie magazines.

Autographs

Collectors

David Kveragas
1943 Timberlane
Clarks Summit, PA 18411-9539
ph: 570-587-3429
Wants Playboy Playmate autographs; also autographs of other women who have appeared in the magazine. Items must be on Playboy related pages, covers, etc.; photocopies appreciated; offers made.

PLAYER PIANOS

(see MUSICAL INSTRUMENTS, Pianos [Player])

PLAYING CARDS

(see also AIRLINE MEMORABILIA, Playing Cards; BRIDGE; CARDS; GAMBLING COLLECTIBLES; PAPER COLLECTIBLES; GAMES, Cards; RAILROAD COLLECTIBLES, Playing Cards)

Clubs/Associations

Rhonda Hawes, Sec.
52 Plus Joker
Magazine: Clear the Decks
204 Gorham Ave.
Hamden, CT 06514-3904
ph: 203-288-6584
e-mail: robertcard@aol.com
web: http://www.52PlusJoker.org
For those interested in collecting playing cards, antique and unusual decks; magazine is published quarterly.

American Game Collectors Association
Newsletter: Game Times
P.O. Box 44
Dresher, PA 19025
e-mail: agca@agca.com
web: http://www.agca.com
Focuses on board and card games as well as puzzles, playing cards, tops, yo-yos, and action games; also publishes "Game Researchers' Notes" - reports on member's research.

Barbara Lunaburg, Corres. Sec.
Chicago Playing Card Collectors, Inc.
Newsletter: Bulletin
1826 Mallard Lake Dr.
Marietta, GA 30068-1644
ph: 770-992-7478
e-mail: cpccink@aol.com
web: http://www.northshorepc.com/cpcc/toc.htm
Purpose of the club is to encourage and promote the hobby of playing card collecting and to explore the history of playing cards; newsletter offers buy/sell/trade ads, articles, etc.

Barbara Clark
International Playing Card Society
Journal: IPCS Journal
3570 Delaware Common
Indianapolis, IN 46220
ph: 317-251-5980
Members receive a journal six times per year, plus membership lists.

Major R.T. Welsh
English Playing Card Society, The
Newsletter: English Playing Card Society Newsletter
11 Pierrepont St.
Bath, Avon BA1 1LA
U.K.
ph: +44 (0)1225-465218
fax: +44 (0)1225-424993
e-mail: srpw@cwcom.net
web: http://www.epcs.mcmail.com/
For collectors, researchers, museums, archivists, manufacturers, etc. who are interested in English playing cards and card games; quarterly postal auction and sale of playing cards and card games; quarterly newsletter.

Collectors

Barbara Lunaburg
1826 Mallard Lake Dr.
Marietta, GA 30068-1644
ph: 770-992-7478
e-mail: cpccink@aol.com
Corresponding secretary of the Chicago Playing Card Collectors Club.

Robert Harrison
582 Woodlawn Ave.
Glencoe, IL 60022
ph: 708-835-0842

Bill Sachen
Waukegan Bridge Center
927 Grand Ave.
Waukegan, IL 60085-3709
ph: 847-662-7204
e-mail: futilewill@aol.com
web: http://members.aol.com/FutileWill/

Bernice De Somer
1559 West Pratt Blvd.
Chicago, IL 60626-4228
ph: 773-274-0250
Interested in playing cards, decks or single cards.

Bill Coomer
1024 South Benton
Cape Girardeau, MO 63703
ph: 573-334-0788
e-mail: grok52@ldd.net

Michael Gannaway
8127 Mesa Dr., Ste. B-391
Austin, TX 78759

Cary Basse
6927 Forbes Ave.
Van Nuys, CA 91406-4504
ph: 818-781-4856

Dealers

Glenn Currie
P.O. Box 1342
Concord, NH 03302-1342
ph: 603-228-3328
e-mail: glennkc@aol.com
Wants to buy antique or unusual decks of playing cards.

Larry Lubliner
Re-Finders
25303 Rutledge Crossing
Farmington Hills, MI 48335-1350
ph: 248-426-0066
fax: 248-426-9944
e-mail: joker1854@aol.com
Wants to buy pre-1930 playing cards and related advertising.

Yasha Beresiner
InterCol Gallery
43 Templars Crescent
London, N3 3QR
U.K.
ph: 0181-349-2207 or 0171-354-2599
fax: 0181-346-9539
e-mail: yasha@compuserve.com
web: http://www.intercol.co.uk
Buys and sells world banknotes, all playing cards, old maps, related books on Free Masonry.

Hava Getz
HGIMAGES
P.O. Box 6
Markfield, Leicstershir LE67 9TX
U.K.
ph: 44 1530 244354
fax: 44 1530 244354
e-mail: hgimages@dircon.co.uk
web: http://www.hgimages.dircon.co.uk
Has a large selection of playing cards and card games for sale on the web; also carries large selection of ephemera including cigar box labels and old cigarette packets.

Experts

David Galt
Games & Names
302 W. 78th St.
New York, NY 10024
ph: 212-769-2514
e-mail: gamepiece@msn.com
One of the premier playing card collectors in America.

Ray Hartz
120 Amberwood Ct.
Bethel Park, PA 15102-2262
Will pay top dollar for old, unusual playing card and game decks, complete and in excellent condition; U.S. or foreign.

Phil Bollhagen
7940 West Leroy Ave.
Greenfield, WI 53220
ph: 414-327-6220
e-mail: bollhagp@rocketmail.com
Has one of the largest collections of antique railroad playing card decks in the U.S.; wants to buy quality pre-1915 decks from all railroads; author of "The Great Book of Railroad Playing Cards"; railroad decks and singles.

Shami & Kathryn Maxwell
Parnell Publishing
P.O. Box 16432
Phoenix, AZ 85011-6432
ph: 602-279-2358
fax: 602-279-5754
Author of "Price Guide of Old & Unusual Playing Cards" and "Playing Cards - The Intentional Price Guide"; also recreates historical playing card decks.

Museums/Libraries

Cincinnati Art Museum
Eden Park
Cincinnati, OH 45202
ph: 513-721-5204
e-mail: cincyart@fuse.net
web: http://www.cincinnatiartmuseum.com/

Margery B. Griffith, Dir.
United States Playing Card Company Playing Card Museum
4590 Beech St.
Cincinnati, OH 45212
ph: 513-396-5700
fax: 513-396-6321
Resource for research materials dealing with playing cards; largest playing card collection in the world.

Repro. Sources

Shami & Kathryn Maxwell
Parnell Publishing
P.O. Box 16432
Phoenix, AZ 85011-6432
ph: 602-279-2358
fax: 602-279-5754
Recreates playing cards, faro and

Civil War; also makes faro equipment: casekeepers, layouts, dealing boxes.

PLUMBING

(see also ARCHITECTURAL ELEMENTS; CATALOGS; HARDWARE; OUTHOUSES)

Collectors

Don Hooper
9645 Sylvia Ave.
Northridge, CA 91324-1756
ph: 818-772-1721
fax: 818-772-4647
e-mail: vntgplbg@aol.com
Wants to buy high quality Victorian period antique bath tubs, toilets, sinks, showers, and nickel plated accessories.

Dealers

H. Weber Wilson
Oltz-Wilson Antiques
P.O. Box 506
Portsmouth, RI 02871
ph: 800-508-0022
fax: 401-683-1644
e-mail: hww@edgenet.net
web: http://www.antiqnet.com/webwilson/
Sells architectural antiques; garden ornaments, vintage plumbing, quality furniture, antique door hardware.

United House Wrecking
535 Hope St.
Stamford, CT 06906-1316
ph: 203-348-5371
fax: 203-961-9472
web: http://www.united-antiques.com
Sells architectural elements; stained and beveled glass, brass & copper, plumbing & lighting fixtures, Victorian gingerbread, etc.

Donald Hooper
Vintage Plumbing & Bathroom Antiques
5516 Cahuenga Blvd.
North Hollywood, CA 91601-2919
ph: 818-505-9315 or 818-772-1721
fax: 818-772-4647
Buys, sells, rents and repairs c. 1900 American bath fixtures such as unusual claw foot bathtubs, ornamental toilets, fancy pedestal sinks, rib-cage showers and more; over 20 years in business.

Museums/Libraries

American Sanitary Plumbing Museum, The
39 Piedmont St.
Worcester, MA 01610
ph: 508-754-9453
Collection includes bathtubs, sinks, toilets, plumbing books and tools.

Periodicals

Hanley-Wood, Inc.
Directory: Old-House Journal Restoration Directory
Two Main Street
Gloucester, MA 01930
ph: 800-234-3797
e-mail: jbutterf@hanley-wood.com
web: http://www.oldhousejournal.com/
Sourcebook listing companies large and small which manufacture and sell traditional hard-to-find items for the old house owner: sinks, siding, lumber, plumbing, stoves, etc.; also call 800-931-2931.

Bathroom Antiques

Dealers

Donald Hooper
Vintage Plumbing & Bathroom Antiques
5516 Cahuenga Blvd.
North Hollywood, CA 91601-2919
ph: 818-505-9315 or 818-772-1721
fax: 818-772-4647
Buys, sells, rents and repairs c. 1900 American bath fixtures such as unusual claw foot bathtubs, ornamental toilets, fancy pedestal sinks, rib-cage showers and more; over 20 years in business.

Repair Services

Premium Refinishing
300 Atlantic Ave.
Brooklyn, NY 11201
ph: 888-404-8827
e-mail: premium123@aol.com
Restores antique bathtubs and sinks to customer specifications; also sells reproductions of antique fixtures.

PLUSH

(see STEIFF; TEDDY BEARS; TOYS, Beanie Babies; TOYS, Plush)

POCKET KNIVES

(see KNIVES, Pocket)

POCKET MIRRORS

(see also ADVERTISING COLLECTIBLES)

Collectors

Burt Purmell
P.O. Box 3016
Troy, NY 12180
ph: 518-273-2454
Wants advertising pocket mirrors.

Howard Share
4349 LaVale Ct.
Clemmons, NC 27012-9009
ph: 336-766-6579
fax: 336-766-5445
e-mail: HowSha43@aol.com
Wants high quality advertising pocket mirrors, especially those picturing Blacks, nudes, or unusual products.

Jerome Schaeper, Jr.
705 Philadelphia St.
Covington, KY 41011-1252
ph: 606-581-3729
Collects and appraises colorful, graphic celluloid pocket mirrors.

James E. Kattner
P.O. Box 11132
Spring, TX 77391
ph: 281-986-6916 or 281-376-4826
Wants to buy mirrors with celluloid backs that picture pretty ladies and young girls which advertise saloons and bars, or that specify a redemption value such as "12 1/2" cents or "One Drink" at a merchant's establishment.

Dealers

Dave Beck
P.O. Box 435
Mediapolis, IA 52637-0435
ph: 319-394-3943
fax: 319-394-3943
Buys and sells advertising watch fobs, mirrors and pin-backs; send stamp for illustrated mail auction catalog.

POCKET-SIZE COLLECTIBLES

Collectors

Bruce Axler
Ansonia Station
P.O. Box 1288
New York, NY 10023-1288
ph: 212-362-4429
fax: 212-579-1274
Wants pocket items, i.e. items/gadgets designed to fit in the pocket: tools, knives, lighters, items which look like a pocket watch but are not, calculators, leather items, matchsafes, candle safes, travel items.

POGS

(see also BOTTLE CAPS, Milk; PREMIUMS; TRADING CARDS, Non-Sport)

Clubs/Associations

Worldwide Hawaiian Association of Milkcaps
P.O. Box 59256
San Jose, CA 95159-0256
ph: 408-236-3476
fax: 408-295-7507
web: http://www.microserve.net/vradio/sidesaddle/wham.html

Dealers

Kap City
2034 Green Acres Mall
Valley Stream, NY 11581
ph: 516-586-9634
web: http://www.wwcd.com/capcity/

Jerry Katz
Fun For All
P.O. Box 31806
Houston, TX 77231
ph: 713-729-5813
e-mail: fun-for-all@juno.com
Full sets of licensed milk caps and POGS; some singles to fill our your collection also available; send email for complete list of available items.

Dory Jones
Dory's MilkCap World
P.O. Box 8594
Honolulu, HI 96830
ph: 808-922-3344
fax: 808-922-8077
e-mail: milkcap1@webcom.com
web: http://www.webcom.com/milkcap1/
Has been selling milk caps for many years; all caps are officially licensed and trademarked; each set is complete and comes assembled in a protective vinyl collector sheet; also carries a large selection of single licensed caps.

Misc. Services

Jack L. Marcus
JM Productions
P.O. Box 2081
Sun City, CA 92586-2081
ph: 909-672-4455
Creates authentic hand drawn and numbered collectible milk caps; now over 5,000 and the numbers continue to grow; gives out one free collectible milk cap upon request.

Periodicals

Jack Mors
JM Productions
Newsletter: Radtoonz
P.O. Box 2081
Sun City, CA 92586-2081
ph: 909-672-4455
From the maker of the Juan Pollo milk cap series; a tabloid for kids; talks about milk caps and how to draw cartoons on them.

POINTS

(see AMERICAN INDIAN; PREHISTORIC ARTIFACTS, Arrowheads & Points)

POKER CHIPS

(see GAMBLING COLLECTIBLES, Gambling Chips & Gaming Tokens)

POLICE & SHERIFF

(see LAW ENFORCEMENT MEMORABILIA, Police & Sheriff)

POLITICAL COLLECTIBLES

(see also AUTOGRAPHS; BADGES; BUTTONS, Pin-Back; CANES & WALKING STICKS; CARTOON ART; CERAMICS, Political Related; HISTORICAL AMERICANA; PERSONALITIES [HISTORICAL]; PINS; PROHIBITION ITEMS; SOCIAL CAUSES; WHITE HOUSE COLLECTIBLES)

Appraisers

Mike Stakis
3 Brookside Ave., Room #3
Newburgh, NY 12550
ph: 914-568-0236 or 914-565-7378
Call or send photocopy of all political buttons for appraisal before you sell.

U.I. "Chick" Harris
P.O. Box 20614
Saint Louis, MO 63139-0614
ph: 314-352-8623
Collects, specializes in, and appraises all types of political Americana; conducts specialized mail-auctions of political and historical Americana.

Auction Services

Rex Stark
Rex Stark Americana
P.O. Box 1029
Gardner, MA 01440-6029
ph: 978-630-3237
fax: 978-630-2388
Conducts mail auctions of quality historical Americana: political, early military, advertising, sports, etc.

Ted Hake
Hake's Americana & Collectibles Auction
P.O. Box 1444
York, PA 17405-1444
ph: 717-848-1333
e-mail: Ted@hakes.com
web: http://www.hakes.com/
Always purchasing items for 8 mail-bid auctions per year covering hundreds of categories including toys, character collectibles, Disney, cowboy heroes, premiums, television, politicals, pin-back buttons, advertising and more.

Robert Coup
Historicana
P.O. Box 348
Leola, PA 17540-0348
ph: 717-656-7780
fax: 717-656-8233
e-mail: POLBANDWGN@aol.com
Specializes in mail-bid auctions of character collectibles, Disneyana, political items & historical Americana; sample catalog $2.

Bob Slawsky
P.O. Box 864
Windermere, FL 34786-0864
ph: 407-352-7807
fax: 407-352-BIDS
e-mail: WWGD54A@prodigy.com
Buys, sells, auctions tokens, medals, badges, small advertising items, political, World's Fair, Olympic items, encased coins, etc.

Al Anderson
Anderson Auction
P.O. Box 644
Troy, OH 45373-0644
ph: 937-339-0850
fax: 937-339-8620
e-mail: aaauctn@erinet.com
web: http://www.erinet.com/aaauctn
Specializes in mail-bid auctions of political items and historical Americana.

Tom Slater
Political Gallery, The
1315 W. 86th St.
Indianapolis, IN 46260
ph: 317-257-0863
fax: 317-254-9167
Specializing in mail-bid auctions of Disneyana, historical Americana, toys, political items, and other collectibles.

Kurt R. Krueger
Krueger Auctions
P.O. Box 275
Iola, WI 54945-0275
ph: 715-445-3845
fax: 715-445-4100

Robert M. Platt
Local, The
3810 Hyridge Dr.
Austin, TX 78759-7522
e-mail: lclare@pswtech.com
Specializing in the mail-bid auctions of pin-back political buttons of governors, congressional members, mayors, state officials, etc.

Clubs/Associations

Michael McQuillen
Indiana Political Collectors Club
Newsletter: IN A.P.I.C.
P.O. Box 50022
Indianapolis, IN 46250-0022
ph: 317-845-1721
e-mail: buttons@oaktree.net
web: http://www.collectors.org/apic/chapters/willkie.htm
Club meets two times per year with annual show; send SASE to be placed on show mailing list.

Joseph D. Hayes, Sec.
American Political Items Collectors (APIC)
Newsletter: Political Bandwagon, The
P.O. Box 340339
San Antonio, TX 78234-0339
ph: 210-945-2811
fax: 210-945-8232
e-mail: apic@texas.net
web: http://www.collectors.org/apic/
Dedicated to the collection, study, preservation of items relating to the political campaigns of the U.S.; also publishes the "Keynoter" magazine three times a year; ask about specialty and local chapters.

Collectors

Frank Consilvio
P.O.Box 552
Boston, MA 02128
e-mail: sales@ftctci.com

Dave Castaldi
c/o Genzyme Tissue Repair
64 Sidney St.
Cambridge, MA 02139-4170
ph: 617-494-8484
fax: 617-566-8344
e-mail: dlcjac@worldnet.att.net

Norwood H. Keeney, III
P.O. Box 1026
Georges Mills, NH 03751-1026
ph: 603-763-9157
e-mail: keeney@kear.tds.net
Wants items relating to Statesman John Hay (1838-1905), U.S. Secretary of State.

Donald Ackerman
P.O. Box 3487
Wallington, NJ 07057
ph: 973-779-8785
fax: 973-744-1517
Wants to buy presidential campaign items; wants one item or collection; over 35 years in the hobby; will make an offer if requested, or will make an honest attempt to tell you what you've got.

Robert Kwalwasser
168 Camp Fatima Rd.
Renfrew, PA 16053-9104
ph: 724-789-7766
fax: 724-789-9771
e-mail: robert@tcis.net
Wants political parade torches, tinder pistols.

Bob Cereghino
6400 Baltimore National Pike, Ste. 170A-319
Baltimore, MD 21228-3914
ph: 410-766-7593
e-mail: jwbc@juno.com
Wants advertising, entertainment and political pin-back buttons.

Chris Hearn
125 Morven Park Rd.
Leesburg, VA 22075
ph: 703-777-7181
Wants to buy political campaign items; political buttons, banners, flags, china, posters, ribbons; especially interested in Roosevelt and Women's Suffrage; also wants Presidential White House gift items and china.

Bob Putnam
9140 Conversation Way
Springfield, VA 22153
ph: 703-644-9711
Wants to buy all presidential campaign items: buttons, banners, posters and political cartoons.

John Gingerich
P.O. Box 358
Lexington, GA 30648-0358
ph: 706-743-3420
e-mail: lazydog2@earthlink.net
Wants political campaign items: buttons, ribbons, badges, posters, postcards, flags, 3-D items, etc.; also wants C.C.C., Bonus Army, United Confederate Veterans, Socialist Party, etc.; want lists sent on request; SASE please.

Peggy Dillard
P.O. Box 210904
Nashville, TN 37221-0904
ph: 615-646-1605
Send SASE and photocopy of political campaign items and receive free appraisal and offer in the mail.

Don Beck
P.O. Box 15305
Fort Wayne, IN 46885-5305
ph: 219-486-3010
Lincoln to Kennedy political pins, medals, flags, banners, autographs.

David Yount
3811 Oriole Dr.
Columbus, IN 47203
ph: 812-378-2980
Wants older political buttons, badges, ribbons, flags, posters, etc.; Lincoln items a priority.

Ken Hosner
5692 Comstock
Kalamazoo, MI 49001
ph: 616-345-5983
e-mail: mrbutton@cyberrealm.net
web: http://cyberrealm.net/~mrbutton/
Wants to buy presidential campaign items; over 30 years in the business.

Joe Doerring
P.O. Box 94444
Des Moines, IA 50394-0444
ph: 515-285-7702
e-mail: JDoerring@aol.com
Wants poster stamps and labels dealing with presidential campaigns,

women's suffrage, labor, and prohibition.

Millie Vaccarella
1955 Hythe St.
Roseville, MN 55113
ph: 651-631-2201
Wants to buy political buttons, banners, posters, canes, and any unusual item; interested in single items or large collections.

Paul Bengston
1225 N 7th St.
Minneapolis, MN 55411-4060
ph: 612-975-3955 or 612-287-0223
fax: 612-522-0025
e-mail: impb@uswest.net
web: http://members.aol.com/dawnlake/button_man.html
Wants pre-1964 political buttons, badges, ribbons, banners, tokens, flags, autographs, and related collectibles; send photocopy.

Cary Demont
P.O. Box 16013
Minneapolis, MN 55416
ph: 612-522-0957
e-mail: Caryd8@aol.com
Serious collector for over 35 years wants scarce and unusual campaign and presidential related items; pre-1964 campaign pins, badges, ribbons, posters, banners, political flags, postcards and 3-dimentional items.

David Yates
321 West Church St.
Genoa, IL 60135
ph: 815-784-3369
e-mail: deere@tbcnet.com
Wants to buy political campaign pin-backs.

Larry Leedom
7217 Via Rio Nido
Downey, CA 90241
ph: 562-927-5799
Wants 1840-1896 Presidential campaign ribbons, badges, pins and sulphides.

John Gearhart
3267 S.E. Hawthorne
Portland, OR 97214
ph: 503-255-8108 or 503-232-4099
Buttons, posters, ribbons, banners, etc.

Dealers

Rex Stark
Rex Stark Americana
P.O. Box 1029
Gardner, MA 01440-6029
ph: 978-630-3237
fax: 978-630-2388
Buys & sells political Americana; offers catalog of historical/political Americana for sale.

Paul Longo
Paul Longo Americana
P.O. Box 5510
Gloucester, MA 01930-0007
ph: 978-525-2290
Wants political pins, buttons, ribbons, banners, autographs, badges, etc.

Jon Allan
Elmer's Nostalgia, Inc.
3 Putnam St.
Sanford, ME 04073-2024
ph: 207-324-2166

Larry L. Krug
Americana Resources, Inc.
18222 Flower Hill Way, #299
Gaithersburg, MD 20879-5300
ph: 301-926-8663
fax: 301-926-7648
e-mail: info@amres.com
web: http://www.amres.com
Wants to buy political buttons/pins, ribbons, glassware and china, posters, autographs, and other memorabilia relating to U.S. presidents, the White House, and Camp David; has over 30 years of experience.

James M. Russell
7775 Forest Stream Club Rd.
Detour, MD 21757
ph: 410-775-2988
Buys, sells and collects any political collectibles including buttons, bandannas, textiles, pins, posters, etc.; especially interested in items relating to James G. Blaine and the election of 1884.

Tom Peeling
P.O. Box 6661
West Palm Beach, FL 33405-0661
ph: 561-585-1351
e-mail: trbuttons@aol.com
Collector and dealer of presidential/political campaign buttons, 3-D items, etc.; Theodore Roosevelt a special want.

John W. Poling
John W. Poling: Military & Political Collectibles
5998 South Ridgeview Rd.
Anderson, IN 46013-9774
ph: 765-778-2714
Mail order dealer in political collectibles; specializing in items from Alaska and Indiana; issues periodic catalog of items for sale; send $2 for latest catalog; most prices in catalog well below current retail.

Robert M. Levine
#2 Troll Court
Ballwin, MO 63011
ph: 314-394-4370
fax: 314-391-6618
Wants any political item; new or old; single or in quantity.

Ronald E. Wade
2100 Lafayette Dr.
Longview, TX 75601-3417
ph: 903-236-9615
e-mail: RonWadeGOP@aol.com
Political buttons/pins JFK and older, posters, 3-dimensional political items, e.g. clocks, glassware, bandannas, etc.; free appraisals, send photocopy with SASE.

Drew Julian
Drew Julian's Political Collectibles
P.O. Box 150363
Austin, TX 78715-0363
ph: 512-447-8785 or 512-441-2020
e-mail: djulian@io.com
web: http://www.io.com/political/

Earl F. Dodge
P.O. Box 2635
Denver, CO 80201
ph: 303-572-0646 or 303-237-4947
fax: 303-233-2099
e-mail: earldodge@home.com
web: http://www.buttonsbydodge.com/
15 years of buying and selling all political Americana: older items such as buttons, ferros, ribbons, etc.; specializes in Prohibition and Calvin Coolidge buy buy all types of political items; will make prompt offer if photocopies sent.

Gary L. Cohen
Political Memorabilia Marketplace
8665 West Flamingo, Ste. 2019
Las Vegas, NV 89147
ph: 702-933-2035
fax: 702-933-2038
e-mail: gary@politicalbuttons.com
web: http://www.politicalbuttons.com/
On-line resource with market information, auctions, sales, related links, and more; every aspect of buying, selling, trading political related collectibles; FREE appraisals given on any item of value; can come to you if necessary.

Vivian Briggs
Briggs Antiques
4443 Linwood Place
Riverside, CA 92506
ph: 909-781-3121
fax: 909-781-3121
e-mail: drago120@aol.com
web: http://www.tias.com/stores/briggs/
Buys and sells political collectibles: badges, paper items, ribbons, various souvenirs.

Experts

Richard Friz
Maddie's Muse
P.O. Box 472
Peterborough, NH 03458-0472
ph: 603-563-8155
e-mail: jmdfriz@top.monad.net
Author of "The Official Price Guide to Political Memorabilia."

Tony Lee
Le Politicals
P.O. Box 134
Monmouth Junction, NJ 08852-0134
ph: 201-429-1531
Collector and dealer in all types of political campaign memorabilia, from buttons and ribbons to badges and 3-D items; also president of the big Apple Chapter of the American Political Items Collectors group.

Mike Stakis
3 Brookside Ave., Room #3
Newburgh, NY 12550
ph: 914-568-0236 or 914-565-7378
Appraiser, expert, collector of political memorabilia; willing to help identify and value political buttons over the phone; have buttons handy when calling; also buys political buttons, single item or entire collections.

Robert A. Fratkin
8280 Greensboro Dr., #200
Mc Lean, VA 22102
ph: 703-556-8101 or 202-483-0274
fax: 703-356-6492
e-mail: coxfdr@erols.com
Nationally recognized expert and lecturer on political collectibles; willing to give telephone assistance in identifying and valuing items; send photo and SASE or have in front of you when calling.

Ed Krohn
P.O. Box 570699
Miami, FL 33257
ph: 305-237-2382
fax: 305-237-2635
e-mail: ekx@aressco.net
web: http://www.aressco.net/presidential/
Expert, appraiser, collector; author of "National Political Convention Tickets & Other Ephemera" catalog; illustrated catalog of tickets, programs and other ephemera for all National political conventions from 1856 to present.

Howard Hazelcorn
6731 Ashley Ct.
Sarasota, FL 34241-9696
ph: 941-921-1815
Collects and specializes in political textiles and posters; especially wants buttons and 3-D items.

Michael McQuillen
P.O. Box 50022
Indianapolis, IN 46250-0022
ph: 317-845-1721
e-mail: buttons@oaktree.net
web: http://www.collectors.org/apic/chapters/willkie.htm
Buys, sells, collects, appraises political collectibles; wants political items of any age: presidentials and local candidates from any state or election; writes the "Political

Parade" column for "AntiqueWeek"; send SASE for replies.

Museums/Libraries

Museum of American Political Life, University of Hartford
200 Bloomfield Ave.
W Hartford, CT 06117
ph: 860-768-4090
fax: 860-768-5159
web: http://www.hartford.edu/polmus/polmus1.html
The extraordinary collection of Mr. J. Doyle Dewitt donated to the University of Hartford forms the nucleus of the museum; 60,000 artifacts: posters, banners, textiles, prints, medals, pottery, glassware, ribbons, etc.

National Museum of American History
14th & Constitution Ave. NW
Washington, DC 20560
ph: 202-357-2700
e-mail: webmaster@si.edu
web: http://www.si.edu/organiza/museums/nmah/nmah.htm

Periodicals

Newspaper: Political Collector, The
P.O. Box 5171
York, PA 17405-5171
ph: 717-846-0418
web: http://www.collectors.org/displays/a-0114.htm
A monthly newspaper focusing on political collectibles.

Jeannine Coup
Newsletter: Political Bandwagon, The
P.O. Box 348
Leola, PA 17540-0348
ph: 717-656-7780
fax: 717-656-8233
e-mail: POLBANDWGN@aol.com
A monthly publication focusing on political collectibles; sample copy $1; contracts with American Political Items Collectors to publish for APIC membership.

Bill Clinton

Clubs/Associations

Philip J. Ross
Bill Clinton Political Items Collectors
Magazine: Arkansas Traveler, The
8226 McNeil St.
Vienna, VA 22180-6924
ph: 703-698-5883 or 703-698-0141
e-mail: politiphil@aol.com
web: http://www.collectors.org/apic/doc/chapters-specialty.htm
Serves political collectors specializing in memorabilia relating to Bill Clinton campaigns, Presidential and other stages of his career; editor of "The Arkansas Traveler, writes articles about political memorabilia for other magazines.

Calvin Coolidge

Collectors

Larry L. Krug
Americana Resources, Inc.
18222 Flower Hill Way, #299
Gaithersburg, MD 20879-5300
ph: 301-926-8663
fax: 301-926-7648
e-mail: info@amres.com
web: http://www.amres.com
Major collector for over 25 years of Calvin Coolidge campaign memorabilia and of items relating to the Coolidge administration.

Dealers

Earl F. Dodge
P.O. Box 2635
Denver, CO 80201
ph: 303-572-0646 or 303-237-4947
fax: 303-233-2099
e-mail: earldodge@home.com
web: http://www.buttonsbydodge.com/
15 years of buying and selling all political Americana: older items such as buttons, ferros, ribbons, etc.; specializes in Prohibition and Calvin Coolidge buy buy all types of political items; will make prompt offer if photocopies sent.

Canadian

Dealers

Michael Rice
Michael Rice Collectibles
P.O. Box 286
Saanichton, British Columbia V8M 2C5
Canada
ph: 250-652-9412
e-mail: mrice@pacificcoast.net
Particularly interested in Canadian pin-back buttons and paper election memorabilia; call evenings.

Dan Quayle

Museums/Libraries

Dan Quayle Center & Museum
815 Warren St.
P.O. Box 856
Huntington, IN 46750
ph: 219-356-6356
fax: 219-356-1455
e-mail: info@quaylemuseum.org
web: http://www.quaylemuseum.org/

Democratic

Clubs/Associations

Ben neill
Democratic Political Items Collectors (DPIC)
Newsletter: Democratic Spirit
P.O. Box 247
East Bend, NC 27018
ph: 336-699-3572
e-mail: dem1pols@yadtel.net
Purpose is to promote beneficial collaboration among collectors of any and all types of memorabilia related to Democratic candidates and/or Democratic Party; newsletter published three times a year.

Collectors

Susan Roman
16 Littlehale Rd.
Durham, NH 03824

Dwight D. Eisenhower

Collectors

John L. Pendergrass
P.O. Box 15729
Hattiesburg, MS 39404-5729

Museums/Libraries

Dwight D. Eisenhower Library
200 SE 4th St.
Abilene, KS 67410-2900
ph: 785-263-4751
fax: 785-263-4218
e-mail: library@eisenhower.nara.gov
web: http://www.eisenhower.utexas.edu/

Franklin D. Roosevelt

Clubs/Associations

Elizabeth Clare
Franklin D. Roosevelt Political Items Collectors
Newsletter: New Deal, The
3810 Hyridge Dr.
Austin, TX 78759-7522
e-mail: lclare@pswtech.com
web: http://www.collectors.org/apic/chapters/fdr-pic.htm
Provides a communications network among FDR collectors.

Collectors

Christopher Carroll
810 Verin Lane
Chula Vista, CA 91910-7830
e-mail: ccarroll@cvesd.k12.ca.us
Wants FDR items, especially 3-D items.

Museums/Libraries

Franklin Delano Roosevelt Library
511 Albany Rd.
Hyde Park, NY 12538-1999
ph: 914-229-8114
fax: 914-229-0872
e-mail: library@roosevelt.nara.gov
web: http://www.academic.marist.edu/fdr/

George Bush

Clubs/Associations

Ronald E. Wade
Bush Political Items Collectors
Newsletter: Bush Bandwagon
2100 Lafayette Dr.
Longview, TX 75601-3417
ph: 903-236-9615
e-mail: RonWadeGOP@aol.com

Museums/Libraries

George Bush Library
1000 George Bush Drive West
College Station, TX 77843
ph: 409-260-9554
fax: 409-260-9557
e-mail: library@bush.nara.gov
web: http://csdl.tamu.edu/bushlib/bushpage.html

Gerald R. Ford

Clubs/Associations

American Political Items Collectors (APIC), Gerald R. Ford Chapter
P.O. Box 340339
San Antonio, TX 78234-0339
ph: 210-945-2811
fax: 210-945-8232
e-mail: apic@texas.net
web: http://www.collectors.org/apic/
Dedicated to the preservation of political memorabilia of President Gerald R. Ford, the 38th President of the United States.

Museums/Libraries

Gerald R. Ford Library
1000 Beal Ave.
Ann Arbor, MI 48109-2114
ph: 734-741-2218
fax: 734-741-2341
e-mail: library@fordlib.nara.gov
web: http://www.lbjlib.utexas.edu/ford/index.htm

Gerald R. Ford Museum
303 Pearl St., NW
Grand Rapids, MI 49504-5343
ph: 616-451-9263
fax: 616-451-9570
e-mail: information.museum@fordmus.nara.gov
web: http://www.lbjlib.utexas.edu/ford/index.htm

Harry S. Truman

Clubs/Associations

Jim Cassidy
American Political Items Collectors (APIC), Harry S. Truman Chapter
Newsletter: Buckstopper, The
6 Arthur St.
Greenwich, CT 06831-5107
For those interested in the Truman Presidency, Truman's life, and related memorabilia.

Collectors

Mario Donald Thomas
860 18th Ave.
Salt Lake City, UT 84103-3719
ph: 801-532-5340
fax: 801-532-5340
Collects any items connected to President Harry S. Truman.

Museums/Libraries

Clay R. Bauske, Curator
Harry S. Truman Library & Museum
500 West U.S. Highway 24
Independence, MO 64050-1798
ph: 816-833-1400 or 816-833-1225
fax: 816-833-4368
e-mail: library@truman.nara.gov
web: http://www.trumanlibrary.org/

Herbert Hoover

Collectors

Joe Doerring
P.O. Box 94444
Des Moines, IA 50394-0444
ph: 515-285-7702
e-mail: JDoerring@aol.com
Wants items from both campaigns of Herbert Hoover: pinback buttons, ribbons, paper items, novelties, etc.

Museums/Libraries

Herbert Hoover Library
211 Parkside Dr.
P.O. Box 488
West Branch, IA 52358-0488
ph: 319-643-5301
fax: 319-643-5825
e-mail: library@hoover.nara.gov
web: http://hoover.nara.gov/

Jimmy Carter

Clubs/Associations

Roger Van Sickle
Carter Political Items Group
Newsletter: Carter Journal, The
614 PollyAnna Dr.
Delaware, OH 43015
Purpose is to preserve the memorabilia associated with the life, political administrations and family members of our nation's 39th president, Jimmy Carter; quarterly newsletter.

Museums/Libraries

Jimmy Carter Library
441 Freedom Parkway
One Copenhill Ave.
Atlanta, GA 30307-1498
ph: 401-331-3942
fax: 401-730-2215
e-mail: library@carter.nara.gov
web: http://cartercenter.galileo.peachnet.edu/

John F. Kennedy

Clubs/Associations

Harvey Goldberg, Ed.
Kennedy Political Items Collectors
Newsletter: Hyannisporter
P.O. Box 922
Clark, NJ 07066-0922
ph: 732-382-4652
fax: 732-382-1325
e-mail: heg@worldnet.att.net
web: http://www.collectors.org/apic/chapters/kpic.htm
KPIC is a world-wide organization for collectors of Kennedy political campaign items; members throughout the U.S. and Canada and as far away as Australia and Europe.

Collectors

Dave Lemon
25 Windstone Dr.
Findlay, OH 45840
Wants JFK related items: dolls, board games, Halloween bucket, PT109 kits, puppets, plates, busts, paperweights, book ends, figure dolls, thimbles, buttons, and badges; please send prices with list.

Experts

Harvey Goldberg, Ed.
P.O. Box 922
Clark, NJ 07066-0922
ph: 732-382-4652
fax: 732-382-1325
e-mail: heg@worldnet.att.net
web: http://www.collectors.org/apic/chapters/kpic.htm
Author of several books about Kennedy-related memorabilia and a noted expert on Kennedy materials; offers evaluations and liquidations of political collections.

Museums/Libraries

John Fitzgerald Kennedy Library & Museum
Columbia Point
Boston, MA 02125-3398
ph: 617-929-4500
fax: 617-929-4538
e-mail: library@kennedy.nara.gov
web: http://www.cs.umb.edu/jfklibrary/

Locals

Clubs/Associations

Ira Forman, Ed.
American Locals Political Items Collectors (ALPIC)
Newsletter: ALPIC Newsletter
1717 Webster St.
Washington, DC 20011
e-mail: Formanl@aol.com
Serves political collectors of state and local offices including governors, U.S. senators and Congressmen, mayors, sheriffs, etc.

Lyndon Baines Johnson

Museums/Libraries

Walt Roberts, Mngr.
Lyndon Baines Johnson Library
2313 Red River Rd.
Austin, TX 78705-5702
ph: 512-476-0029
fax: 512-478-9104
e-mail: library@johnson.nara.gov
web: http://www.lbjlib.utexas.edu/

Republican

Clubs/Associations

Jonathan A. Binkley
Republican Political Items Collectors
1786 Bucklew Drive
Toledo, OH 43613
ph: 419-472-1912
e-mail: bjbinkley@webtv.net

Richard Nixon

Clubs/Associations

Eldon Almquist
NIXCO (Nixon Political Collectors' Organization)
Newsletter: NIXCO News
975 Maunawili Circle
Kailua, HI 96734-4620
ph: 808-262-9837
fax: 808-834-1046
e-mail: eldon@aloha.net
web: http://www.aloha.net/~eldon/nixco1.htm
For those interested in collecting Richard Nixon memorabilia and in studying the political career of our 37th president.

Collectors

Eldon Almquist
975 Maunawili Circle
Kailua, HI 96734-4620
ph: 808-262-9837
fax: 808-834-1046
e-mail: eldon@aloha.net
web: http://www.aloha.net/~eldon/nixco1.htm
Wants to buy Nixon related pin-backs, jewelry and novelties; send SASE and photocopy of your items for response and free appraisal or offer.

Museums/Libraries

Nixon Presidential Materials Staff, National Archives at College Park
8601 Adelphi Rd.
College Park, MD 20740-6001
ph: 301-713-6950
fax: 301-713-9616
e-mail: nixon@arch2.nara.gov
web: http://metalab.unc.edu/lia/president/nixon.html

Sandy Quinn
Richard Nixon Library & Birthplace
18001 Yorba Linda Blvd.
Yorba Linda, CA 92686-3903
ph: 714-993-3393 or 714-993-5075
fax: 714-528-0544
e-mail: stedman@nixonfoundation.org
web: http://www.nixonfoundation.org/
Gift Shop and annual gifts catalog offers wide selection of Presidential and campaign memorabilia from contemporary administrations including Pres. Nixon; political memorabilia can be donated; library will buy selected items.

Ronald Reagan

Museums/Libraries

Ronald Reagan Presidential Library & Museum
40 Presidential Dr.
Simi Valley, CA 93065-0666
ph: 805-522-8444
fax: 805-522-9621
e-mail: library@reagan.nara.gov
web: http://www.webportal.com/reaganlibrary/
The museum store sells political items; store phone number is 805-522-9953.

Theodore Roosevelt

Clubs/Associations

Tom Peeling
Theodore Roosevelt Chapter of the American Political Items Collectors (APIC)
Newsletter: Bully Pulpit
P.O. Box 6661
West Palm Beach, FL 33405-0661
ph: 561-585-1351
e-mail: trbuttons@aol.com
web: http://www.collectors.org/apic/doc/chapters-specialty.htm
For collectors and scholars of the Theodore Roosevelt years and the political memorabilia associated with it.

Dealers

Tom Peeling
P.O. Box 6661
West Palm Beach, FL 33405-0661
ph: 561-585-1351
e-mail: trbuttons@aol.com
Collector and dealer of presidential/political campaign buttons, 3-D items, etc.; Theodore Roosevelt a special want.

Third Party & Hopefuls

Clubs/Associations

Jon Curtis, Ed.
Third Party & Hopefuls
Newsletter: Bullmoose, The
1901 Ridgeway, Apt. #8
De Pere, WI 54115
Collectors interested in the memorabilia associated with third party political candidates and political hopefuls.

Collectors

Joe Doerring
P.O. Box 94444
Des Moines, IA 50394-0444
ph: 515-285-7702
e-mail: JDoerring@aol.com
Collects items association with the Socialist, Communist, Union, and Prohibition parties.

Wendell L. Willkie

Clubs/Associations

Michael McQuillen
Wendell L. Willkie Political Items Collectors
Newsletter: Willkie World
P.O. Box 50022
Indianapolis, IN 46250-0022
ph: 317-845-1721
e-mail: buttons@oaktree.net
web: http://www.collectors.org/apic/chapters/willkie.htm
A group of collectors interested in buttons, ribbons, paper and all items related to Wendell Willkie's 1940 campaign; send SASE for replies.

POLYNESIAN COLLECTIBLES

Dealers

M.A. Blackburn
Antique Hawaiiana
2448 Lincoln Highway East
Lancaster, PA 17602
ph: 800-346-7847 or 717-295-9078
fax: 717-295-3494
e-mail: MBlackburn@aol.com
web: http://www.csmonline.com/blackburn/
Wants cultural art and artifacts from all the Polynesian islands; war clubs, items of personal adornment; also pre-1925 Hawaiian items.

POND BOATS

(see BOATS, Model)

POOL TABLES

(see BILLIARD RELATED ITEMS)

POP ART

(see MODERNISM)

POP CULTURE

(see MODERNISM)

POPCORN ITEMS

Collectors

Glenn Smith
3706 Westgate Rd.
Omaha, NE 68124
ph: 402-391-8876
Wants popcorn boxes and cans: 10 and 12 oz. size cans.

Jack Cory
7733 Spanish Bar Dr.
Las Vegas, NV 89113
ph: 702-364-1645
e-mail: kernelcory@earthlink.net
Wants to buy popcorn memorabilia, popcorn boxes, bags, cans, crates, brochures, catalogs, old machines and their parts, Cretor's steam engines and anything related to popcorn.

Museums/Libraries

Wyandot Popcorn Museum
Heritage Hall
169 E. Church St.
Marion, OH 43302
ph: 740-383-4255 or 740-389-2948
fax: 740-389-2066
e-mail: georgek@wyandotpopcornmus.com
web: http://www.wyandotpopcornmus.com/
Museum contains the world's largest collection of popcorn poppers and peanut roasters including all the classics: Cretors, Dunbar, Kingery, Holcomb and Hoke, Cracker Jack, Long-Eakin, Manley, Burch, Star, Bartholomew, Royal, and Advance.

POPULAR CULTURE

(see also ANTIQUES & COLLECTIBLES; CARTOON ART; MODERNISM; SOCIAL CAUSES; TELEVISION SHOWS & MEMORABILIA; TOYS, Action Figures)

Auction Services

Ted Hake
Hake's Americana & Collectibles Auction
P.O. Box 1444
York, PA 17405-1444
ph: 717-848-1333
e-mail: Ted@hakes.com
web: http://www.hakes.com/
Always purchasing items for 8 mail-bid auctions per year covering hundreds of categories including toys, character collectibles, Disney, cowboy heroes, premiums, television, politicals, pin-back buttons, advertising and more.

Clubs/Associations

Ephemera Society of America Inc., The
Newsletter: Ephemera News
P.O. Box 95
Cazenovia, NY 13035-0095
ph: 315-655-9139
fax: 315-655-9139
e-mail: info@ephemerasociety.org
web: http://www.ephemerasociety.org/
The major organization for collectors and dealers of paper collectibles; focuses on the preservation and study of ephemera (short-lived printed matter); also publishes "The Ephemera Journal."

Dealers

Gary Sohmers
Wex Rex Collectibles
280 Worcester Rd.
Framingham, MA 01701
ph: 978-568-0856 or 508-620-6181
fax: 508-562-1196
e-mail: wexres@aol.com
Specializes in Rock 'n Roll, movies, TV memorabilia, records, posters, magazines, autographs, toys, and other pop culture memorabilia from 1950s through 1970s.

Museums/Libraries

Consortium of Popular Culture Collections
Popular Culture Library
Bowling Green State University
Bowling Green, OH 43403-0001
ph: 419-372-2450
fax: 419-372-7996
e-mail: ascott@bgnet.bgsu.edu
web: http://www.bgsu.edu/colleges/library/pcl/cpccm.html
Consortium composed of Bowling Green State U., Kent State U., Michigan State U., and Ohio State U.; the largest academic library collections of primary research material in comic art, popular fiction, popular music, performing arts.

Russel B. Nye Popular Culture Collection, Michigan State University Libraries
Michigan State Univ. Libraries
Special Collections
East Lansing, MI 48825
ph: 517-355-3770
e-mail: scottr@pilot.msu.edu
web: http://www.lib.msu.edu/coll/main/spec_col/nye/
Includes a popular culture vertical file of related ephemera.

Periodicals

Ray B. Browne, Ed.
Popular Culture Association
Journal: Journal of American Culture
Popular Culture Center
Bowling Green State University
Bowling Green, OH 43403
ph: 419-372-7861 or 419-372-7867
fax: 419-372-8095
e-mail: rbrowne@bgnet.bgsu.edu
web: http://www.h-net.msu.edu/~pcaaca/popindex.html
The major center and source for the study of popular culture (media, music, folklore, ethnic popular culture, cartoons, performing arts, books, and more); maintains 200,000 volume reference library of clippings, leaflets, pamphlets, etc.

Baby Boomer

Auction Services

Gary Kraut
Alphaville
226 W. Houston St.
New York, NY 10014-4846
ph: 212-675-6850
fax: 212-741-2609
e-mail: alphavil@mindspring.com
web: http://www.alphaville.com
Along with partner Steve Karchin conducts phone auctions of 50s and 60s toys, games, and other memorabilia.

Dealers

Gary Kraut
Alphaville
226 W. Houston St.
New York, NY 10014-4846
ph: 212-675-6850
fax: 212-741-2609
e-mail: alphavil@mindspring.com
web: http://www.alphaville.com
Along with partner Steve Karchin buys and sells vintage 1940s, 50s, and 60s toys, games, and other memorabilia.

Toysensations
P.O. Box 218
Woodbury, NY 11797
ph: 516-338-4929 or 516-338-2701
fax: 516-681-3612
Specializes in selling toys from the 1940s through 1970s.

Ed & Kim McIntyre
Past-O-Rama
1122 East Ave.
Lancaster, CA 93535-4844
ph: 805-726-9983
Specializes in all sorts of baby-boomer memorabilia.

David Hendrickson
Kitsch-n-Stuff
P.O. Box 2271
Port Angeles, WA 98362
ph: 360-457-5589
fax: 360-457-3991
Specializes in "boomerabilia": collectibles from the mid 1940s through mid 1960s: kitchen items, dinnerware, chrome and Formica dinette sets, end tables, chairs, lamps, radios, small appliances, etc.

Man./Prod./Dist.

Gene Rees
Gino's Malt Shop Collection
P.O. Box 505
Bridgeville, PA 15017-0505
ph: 412-221-1495
fax: 412-221-1272
web: http://www.coin-opclassics.com/Ads/Rees/rees.htm
Sells 50s and 60s malt shop furniture, decor and accessories: booths, tables, chairs, stools, moldings, metal trim, lighting fixtures, quilted stainless sheets, counter accessories, etc.

Periodicals

Antique Trader Publications, Inc.
Newspaper: Toy Trader
P.O. Box 1050
Dubuque, IA 52004-1050
ph: 800-334-7165 or 800-482-4155
fax: 800-531-0880
e-mail: jmkoenig@execpc.com
web: http://www.collect.com/toytrader
Monthly newspaper with information on how to buy, sell and trade all types of toys; market trends, the latest prices, "how-to" columns, listings of toy clubs and upcoming toy shows and auctions; also full of buy and sell ads.

Magazine: Gearhead Magazine
P.O. Box 421219
San Francisco, CA 94142-1219
ph: 415-422-0595
web: http://www.nitronic.com/gearhead/
Marries articles about 1950s and 1960s hot rods with music.

PORCELAIN

(see CERAMICS; DINNERWARE; FIGURINES; OCCUPIED JAPAN; ORIENTALIA; REPAIR/ RESTORATION/CONSERVATION; TABLEWARE)

POSTAGE STAMPS

(see POSTAL SERVICE ITEMS; STAMP COLLECTING)

POSTAL SERVICE ITEMS

(see also POSTCARDS, Post Office Related; STAMP COLLECTING)

Auction Services

Jim Mehrer
Jim Mehrer's Postal History
2405 - 30th Street
Rock Island, IL 61201
ph: 309-786-6539
fax: 309-786-6551
e-mail: mehrer@postal-history.com
web: http://www.deltiology.com
Dealer, auctioneer conducts six postal history mail bid sales per year, each containing 3,000+ lots; also postcards, reference literature, collectors' supplies and more; website has dealers and show calendar sections.

Clubs/Associations

Bill DiPaolo
Modern Postal History Society
Journal: Modern Postal History Journal
404 Dorado Ct.
High Point, NC 27260
Focuses on the collection, documentation and study of postal history, practices and policies; emphasizing material from 1930 to date.

Collectors

Tom Mills
30 Bay Path Rd.
Spencer, MA 01562-1602
ph: 508-885-9550
Wants fire alarm and police boxes especially ones with dates cast into them; seeks cast iron signs and street letter pickup boxes marked "U.S. MAIL"; best to write and send photos.

Dr. Frank R. Scheer, Curator
Railway Mail Service Library
12 E. Rosemont Ave.
Alexandria, VA 22301-2325
ph: 703-549-4095
fax: 703-836-1955
e-mail: fscheer@erols.com
Wants to buy obsolete official postal artifacts from any country: postmarking handstamps, badges, mail locks, street letterboxes, mail route schedules, postal hand guns, etc.; no stamps, postmarked envelopes or modern collectibles.

Harold Dylhoff
23511 Paulson's Rd.
Gobles, MI 49055-8651
ph: 616-628-4051
e-mail: hdylxrds@aol.com
Wants to buy postal history items: ship cancels, covers from 1946 atomic bomb tests Bikini Atoll "Operation Crossroads", any material Air Force 509th connected with XRDs tests; send photocopies and LSASE for reply.

George Cross
P.O. Box 3923
Tustin, CA 92681
Wants to buy U.S. Post Office badges.

Dealers

Paul & Becky Huber
Fairwinds
26450 Moore Farm Lane
Onancock, VA 23417
ph: 757-787-1569
e-mail: fairwinds@esva.net
Dealers in naval and maritime postal history, postcards, historical documents and antiques; maintains an extensive stock and provides approval service; want lists appreciated.

Jim Mehrer
Jim Mehrer's Postal History
2405 - 30th Street
Rock Island, IL 61201
ph: 309-786-6539
fax: 309-786-6551
e-mail: mehrer@postal-history.com
web: http://www.deltiology.com
Dealer, auctioneer conducts six postal history mail bid sales per year, each containing 3,000+ lots; also postcards, reference literature, collectors' supplies and more; website has dealers and show calendar sections.

Internet Resources

Dr. Frank R. Scheer, Curator
Railway Mail Service Library
12 E. Rosemont Ave.
Alexandria, VA 22301-2325
ph: 703-549-4095
fax: 703-836-1955
e-mail: fscheer@erols.com
A FREE computer web page for postal history researchers interested in post items of the USA and other countries; replies to requests will be downloaded; upload articles to check technical information; send e-mail for current URL.

Museums/Libraries

Postal History Foundation, The
Newsletter: Heliograph
P.O. Box 40725
920 North First Ave.
Tucson, AZ 85719-0725
ph: 520-623-6652
e-mail: mman@primenet.com
web: http://www.primenet.com/~mman/phfmaon.htm
Houses artifacts, postmarks and covers dedicated to postal history.

Military

Clubs/Associations

George Cosentini
Military Postal History Society
Newsletter: MPHS Bulletin
12421 Banuelo COve
San Diego, CA 92130-2277
e-mail: apofpo@adnc.com
web: http://www.adnc.com/web2/~mphs/
Formed for the purpose of collecting and studying military mail of all periods: "Field Post" markings, censorship, occupation, internment, prisoner of war camp covers, and propaganda labels and leaflets; publishes books on the subject.

Collectors

Harold Dylhoff
23511 Paulson's Rd.
Gobles, MI 49055-8651
ph: 616-628-4051
e-mail: hdylxrds@aol.com
Collecting A.P.O.s (Army Post Office) especially from 1940s to 1950s; Alaska Highway construction, WWII Alaska Forts; also Canadian NWT postmarks and A.P.O.s; send photocopies and LSASE for reply.

Virginia

Collectors

Lewis Leigh, Jr.
P.O. Box 4327
Leesburg, VA 20177
ph: 703-771-3081
fax: 703-771-1432
Wants to buy postal history items especially pertaining to early Virginia: equipment & forms, old letters, documents, etc.

POSTCARDS

(see also BOOKS, Reference [Postcards]; ILLUSTRATORS; PAPER COLLECTIBLES)

Auction Services

Martin J. Shapiro
Postcards International
2321 Whitney Ave., Ste. 102
P.O. Box 185398
Hamden, CT 06518
ph: 203-248-6621
fax: 203-248-6628
e-mail: quality@vintagepostcards.com
web: http://www.vintagepostcards.com/
Buys and sells vintage picture postcards; offers the collector picture postcards or topical high quality postcards by auction, catalog or on approval; sample catalog is available upon request for $5.

John H. McClintock
Virginia Mail Auction
P.O. Box 1765
Manassas, VA 20108-1765
ph: 703-368-2757
e-mail: thewishbone@erols.com
web: http://www.playle.com/IFPD/
Conducts 4 to 5 illustrated postcard mail auctions per year; also promotes 8 postcard shows per year.

William Crawford
P.O. Box 2892
Hallandale, FL 33008
ph: 954-456-9671

Ron Playle
Playle's Online Auctions
P.O. Box 65918
West Des Moines, IA 50265
ph: 515-267-0213
fax: 515-267-0213
e-mail: ron@playle.com
web: http://www.playle.com/main.html
Buy and sell postcards, stamps, coins, antiques, collectibles online.

Roger Harvey
Card Source
170 Selwyn Lane
Buffalo Grove, IL 60089-4333
ph: 847-520-8145
fax: 847-520-8145
e-mail: RHarvey@thepostcard.com
web: http://www.thepostcard.com
Deals in antique, collectible and modern postcards; established the first postcard shop on the Internet/ world wide web; also appraises and auctions postcards.

Bob Coalbran
Card Mine, The
21 Pine View, Muxton
Telford, Shropshire TF2 8QX
U.K.
ph: 01952 410774
fax: 01952 411083
e-mail: bob.coalbran@cableinet.co.uk
web: http://wkweb4.cableinet.co.uk/card.mine/
A variety of unusual ephemera items are included within each of the regular Card Mine Auctions.

Clubs/Associations

Edith Costa
Granite State Postcard Collectors Club
P.O. Box 79
West Franklin, NH 03235
ph: 603-647-0634

Don Pocher
South Jersey Postcard Club
Newsletter: Postcard Courier
11 S. Lafayette St.
Cape May, NJ 08204-5301
ph: 609-884-3115
Club membership is open to all; meets 2nd Sunday of each month at Prince of Peace Lutheran Church, Marlton, NJ.

Dr. James Lewis Lowe, Dir.
Deltiologists of America
Magazine: Postcard Classics
P.O. Box 8
Norwood, PA 19074
ph: 610-485-8572
International postcard society for collectors, dealers, librarians, and archivist.

Hawai'i Postcard Club
P.O. Box 15563
Washington, DC 20003
e-mail: enelani@aol.com
web: http://www.stampshows.com/hpc.html

John H. McClintock, Dir
Postcard History Society
Newsletter: Postcard History Society Bulletin
P.O. Box 1765
Manassas, VA 20108-1765
ph: 703-368-2757
e-mail: thewishbone@erols.com
web: http://www.playle.com/IFPD/
Four quarterly newsletters, 4 to 8 pages each, keep you informed of deltiological (postcard) activities and research.

John H. McClintock, Sec
International Federation of Postcard Dealers, Inc.
Directory: Annual IFPD Directory
P.O. Box 1765
Manassas, VA 20108-1765
ph: 703-368-2757
e-mail: thewishbone@erols.com
web: http://www.playle.com/IFPD/
The Annual IFDP Directory of nearly 300 postcard dealers is free for $1.25 postage.

Jane Pepper
Gateway Post Card Club
P.O. Box 28941
Saint Louis, MO 63132
e-mail: jrpepper@inlink.com

Hal Ottaway
Wichita Postcard Club
P.O. Box 780282
Wichita, KS 67278-0282

Dalene Thomas
Denver Postcard Club
Newsletter: Denver Postcard Club News
8612 West Warren Lane
Denver, CO 80227-2352
ph: 303-986-6620
e-mail: dalene1@uswest.net
web: http://www.users.uswest.net/~dalene1/
Postcard collectors meet to buy, sell, trade cards; programs are presented to educate members about postcard collecting.

Joan Gentry, Pres.
Tucson Post Card Exchange Club
820 Via Lucitas
Tucson, AZ 85718-1046
ph: 520-297-0980
fax: 520-575-7010
e-mail: jgentry@primenet.com
web: http://www.tucson.com/tpcec/index.html
Club for postcard collectors in the southern Arizona region.

John Bateman, Sec.
Postcard Traders Association
Glanrhyd Station House
Manordeilo
Llandeilo, Dyfed SA19 7BP
U.K.
ph: +44 (0) 1550 777064
e-mail: info@postcard.co.uk
web: http://www.postcard.co.uk/
Represents foremost dealers and auctioneers, fair organizers and publishers in U.K & many worldwide; organizes annual "Picture Postcard Show" in London; website provides information on all aspects of postcards: fairs, clubs, dealers, etc.

Collectors

Mrs. G.M. Kirchgessner
421 Washington St.
Hoboken, NJ 07030

John H. McClintock
Postcard Society, Inc.
P.O. Box 1765
Manassas, VA 20108-1765
ph: 703-368-2757
e-mail: thewishbone@erols.com
web: http://www.playle.com/IFPD/
Promotes 8 postcard shows.

Ben Egerton
13009 Dover Rd.
Reisterstown, MD 21136-5512
Has been collecting postcards for over 20 years.

George Van Trump, Jr.
6837 Murray Lane
Annandale, VA 22003

Gary Olsen
505 S. Royal Ave.
Front Royal, VA 22630
ph: 540-635-7157 or 540-635-7158
fax: 540-635-1818
e-mail: hpfrigko@interloc.com
Wants postcards with maps, music themes, real estate subjects and/or famous "persons" autographs.

Calvin J. Meider
441 Lake St.
Excelsior, MN 55331-1901
ph: 651-926-2142

Jerry Abert
631 Broadway
East Alton, IL 62024
ph: 618-259-0901

Susan Frost
806 Rosedale Terrace
Austin, TX 78704-3159
ph: 512-447-2575 or 512-447-0407
e-mail: Reuter@io.com
web: http://www.io.com/~reuter/brehme.html
Specialist in photographs, postcards and Christmas cards by Hugo Brehme (Germany 1882 - 1954 Mexico).

Lee Aronsohn
16430 Westfall Place
Encino, CA 91436
ph: 818-905-0225
fax: 818-905-6334
e-mail: overpaid@metawire.com
Collects material relating to cartoonist Gary Trudeau and the "Doonesbury" comic strip; also wants humorous 3-D postcards marked "Eden Plastics," "Postplax," or "Cardell."

Lewis Baer
P.O. Box 621
Penngrove, CA 94951
e-mail: ursusmjr@metro.net
Writes postcard column for "Postcard Collector" magazine.

Dealers

Siegfried Feller
Cartomania
8 Amherst Rd.
Amherst, MA 01002-9739
ph: 413-253-3115

Martin J. Shapiro
Postcards International
2321 Whitney Ave., Ste. 102
P.O. Box 185398
Hamden, CT 06518
ph: 203-248-6621
fax: 203-248-6628
e-mail: quality@vintagepostcards.com
web: http://www.vintagepostcards.com/
Buys and sells vintage picture postcards; offers the collector picture postcards or topical high quality postcards by auction, catalog or on approval; sample catalog is available upon request for $5.

Barbara & Richard DePalma
Deer Park Books
609 Kent Rd., Route 7
Gaylordsville, CT 06755
ph: 860-350-4140
fax: 860-350-4140
e-mail: DeerParkBk@aol.com
web: http://www.abebooks.com/home/BARBDE/
Buys and sells early View cards as well as Art cards.

Max Davis
Postcards of the World
Chelsea Antiques Building
110 West 25th St., Gallery 307
New York, NY 10001-7401
ph: 212-243-7090 or 800-641-4884
fax: 212-769-9199
e-mail: maxpen@aol.com
web: http://www.nypen.com/
Buys and sells vintage postcards world wide.

Bob & Kay Schies
452 East Bissell Ave.
Oil City, PA 16301-2063
ph: 814-677-3182
Buying pre-1930 postcards, any amount.

Harry R. McKeon, Jr.
18 Rose Lane
Flourtown, PA 19031-1910
ph: 215-233-4094
e-mail: toyspost@aol.com
Send your postcards want list for large unpicked selection also Victorian trade cards.

Jay Miller
725 S. Schell St.
Philadelphia, PA 19147

Sheldon Dobres
S. Dobres Postcards
P.O. Box 1855
Baltimore, MD 21203-1855
ph: 410-486-6569 or 800-342-5983
fax: 410-486-6587
e-mail: sdpost@aol.com
Postcards bought and sold; top prices paid for all U.S. and foreign postcards.

Mary L. Martin, Ltd.
P.O. Box 787
Perryville, MD 21903
ph: 410-575-7768 or 410-939-2973
fax: 410-642-2053
Specializing in state views, signed artists, sports, transportation, political, Halloween, Santas, etc.

Joseph L. Mashburn
Colonial House
P.O. Box 609 - M
Enka, NC 28728-0609
ph: 828-667-1427
fax: 828-667-1111
e-mail: jmashb0135@aol.com
web: http://www.postcard-books.com
Buys and sells antique postcards; interested mainly in artist-signed beautiful ladies, children, fantasy, animals, blacks, nudes, real photos, sports; specializing in Harrison Fisher and Philip Boileau.

Betty Powell
P.O. Box 571
Columbus, OH 43085-0571
fax: 614-885-1962
e-mail: potteryplace@worldnet.att.net
Buys and sells U.S. postcards: artist signed, holidays, topicals, views.

Jerry Garrett
Jerry's Antiques & Postcards
1807 West Madison St.
Kokomo, IN 46901-1829
ph: 765-457-5256
Wants to buy old postcards.

Abbot's Postcards
1393 S. Woodward Ave.
Birmingham, MI 48009
ph: 248-644-8565
fax: 248-644-7038

Roger Harvey
Card Source
170 Selwyn Lane
Buffalo Grove, IL 60089-4333
ph: 847-520-8145
fax: 847-520-8145
e-mail: RHarvey@thepostcard.com
web: http://www.thepostcard.com
Deals in antique, collectible and modern postcards; established the first postcard shop on the Internet/ World Wide Web; also buys, sells, appraises and auctions postcards.

Jim Mehrer
Jim Mehrer's Postal History
2405 - 30th Street
Rock Island, IL 61201
ph: 309-786-6539
fax: 309-786-6551
e-mail: mehrer@postal-history.com
web: http://www.deltiology.com
Dealer, auctioneer conducts six postal history mail bid sales per year, each containing 3,000+ lots; also postcards, reference literature, collectors' supplies and more; website has dealers and show calendar sections.

Jim Taylor
P.O. Box 399
Neosho, MO 64850
ph: 417-451-4659
e-mail: jmtaylor@clandjop.com

Trenton Boyd
P.O. Box 517
Columbia, MO 65205-0517
ph: 573-882-2461 or 573-442-5235
fax: 573-882-2950
e-mail: vetlib@showme.missouri.edu
Interested in veterinary postcards including schools and military veterinary; also wants teratology cards that show animals with birth defects (e.g. five-legged calves); Red Cross dogs, Humane Association.

Ed Anderson
Kraze Ed
P.O. Box 1915
Temple City, CA 91780
ph: 626-309-7545
e-mail: krazeed@flash.net
web: http://www.web-pac.com/mall/kraze-ed/
Buys, sells, trades, collects postcards; also supplier of postcard protection sleeves and pages.

Steve Schmale
Out West
2231 Creekside Rd.
Santa Rosa, CA 95405-8022
ph: 707-838-1859 or 707-575-5406
e-mail: outweststv@aol.com
Buys and sells better vintage postcards since 1976; approval service; strong in Western states views; always buying better cards and real photos; also wants railroad paper, stereoviews, photos, brochures, trade cards; member IFPD.

Tom Osjecki
Phyllis' Philatelics
P.O. Box 792
Canyonville, OR 97417
ph: 541-839-4135 or 541-839-6151
Buys, sells and specializes in postcards, paper Americana, stamps and covers; over 25,000 covers and postcards listed by state or topic.

Dave Morris
3388 Merlin Rd., Ste. 351
Grants Pass, OR 97526
ph: 541-955-8411
e-mail: dave@wattpottery.com
web: http://www.wattpottery.com
Wants to buy pre-1930 U.S. postcards, especially real photo postcards; will buy collections.

Alicia & Jorge Valino
P.O. Box 1442
Montevideo, 11000
Uruguay
e-mail: vala@adinet.com.uy.

Experts

Martin J. Shapiro
Postcards International
2321 Whitney Ave., Ste. 102
P.O. Box 185398
Hamden, CT 06518
ph: 203-248-6621
fax: 203-248-6628
e-mail: quality@vintagepostcards.com
web: http://www.vintagepostcards.com/
Buys and sells vintage picture postcards; offers the collector picture postcards or topical high quality postcards by auction, catalog or on approval; sample catalog is available upon request for $5.

Dr. James Lewis Lowe, Dir.
P.O. Box 8
Norwood, PA 19074
ph: 610-485-8572

Roy Cox
P.O. Box 3610
Hamilton, MD 21214
Author of "How to Price and Sell Old Picture Postcards," available from the author for $9.95 ppd.

V. Lee Cox
Memory Lane Postcards, Inc.
P.O. Box 66
Keymar, MD 21757
ph: 410-775-0188 or 410-775-0190

Joseph L. Mashburn
Colonial House
P.O. Box 609 - M
Enka, NC 28728-0609
ph: 828-667-1427
fax: 828-667-1111
e-mail: jmashb0135@aol.com
web: http://www.postcard-books.com
Buys and specializes in high quality postcards; author and publisher of postcard price guides "The Postcard Price Guide", "The Artist-Signed Postcard Price Guide", and "Super Rare Postcards of Harrison Fisher"; write for prices.

Susan Nicholson
Greater Chicago Productions
P.O. Box 595
Lisle, IL 60532
ph: 630-964-5240
e-mail: deltiology@aol.com
Buys and sells rare and unusual postcards, Victorian valentines, periodicals, advertising trade cards, etc.

Ada Fitzsimmons
P.O. Box 337
San Anselmo, CA 94979-0337
ph: 415-454-5552
fax: 415-454-2947
e-mail: apaperpile@aol.com
web: http://www.paperpilecollectibles.com
Buys, sells, appraises, lectures and write about postcards.

Naomi Welch
Images of the Past
309 Playa Blvd., Ste. 110
La Selva Beach, CA 95076-1737
fax: 831-689-0318
e-mail: naomi@harrisonfisher.com
web: http://www.harrisonfisher.com/
Collector, dealer, expert specializes in Harrison Fisher; author of two books, published in 1999, entitled "The Complete Works of Harrison Fisher Illustrator," and "American & European Postcards of Harrison Fisher Illustrator."

Internet Resources

Dan
Postcard.Org
e-mail: dan@84.com
web: http://www.postcard.org/
Post card list members' web pages, auctions, postcards for sale, personal postcard pages, postcard supplies, clubs.

Jack D. Mount
Postcard Resources
e-mail: mount@bird.library.arizona.edu
web: http://www.library.arizona.edu/users/mount/postcard.html
Huge internet list of postcard resources: clubs, auctions, catalogs, directories, chatting, personal pages, dealers, FAQs, listserves and newsgroups, museums, publications, shows, events, exhibitions, webrings, trading lists, giveaways.

Steve Neis
Attic Antique Postcards & Images
115 Claytor St.
Lugoff, SC 29078
ph: 803-408-0486 or 888-731-4201
fax: 913-432-6103
e-mail: Postcard@web-pac.com
web: http://www.eantique.org/attic/
On-line shop for vintage postcards; also appraises, buys, sells, auctions, and collects postcards.

Roger Harvey
Postcard Collecting Worldwide
170 Selwyn Lane
Buffalo Grove, IL 60089
ph: 847-520-8145
fax: 847-520-8145
e-mail: postcard@mediaone.net
web: http://www.deltiology.org
Great starting place for postcard resources on the Web: links, exhibits, information, etc.

Steve Neis
Web-Pac Postcard Mall
10024 Burnham Dr. NW #3
Gig Harbor, WA 98335
ph: 253-851-9964
e-mail: web-pac@web-pac.com
web: http://www.web-pac.com/mall/

Terry Stewart
Collector Link
71 John St. East
Waterloo, Ontario N2J 1G2
Canada
ph: 519-745-1745
e-mail: stewart@collector-link.com
web: http://www.collector-link.com/
Catalogs over 2,000 trading card related web sites for: baseball, hockey, basketball, football, other sports, non-sports, phone cards, credit-debit cards, business cards, postcards.

Museums/Libraries

Katherine Hamilton-Smith
Curt Teich Postcard Archives, Lake County Museum
Journal: Image File
27277 Forest Preserve Dr.
Wauconda, IL 60084-2016
ph: 847-526-8638 or 847-526-7878
fax: 847-526-1545
e-mail: teicharc@nslsilus.org
web: http://www.co.lake.il.us/forest/ctpa.htm
Archive of North American postcards from 1898-1978; formerly industrial archives of Curt Teich Printing Co., Chicago; also postcard albums; provides full-color copies of postcards.

Periodicals

Antique Trader Publications, Inc.
Magazine: Postcard Collector
P.O. Box 1050
Dubuque, IA 52004-1050
ph: 800-334-7165 or 800-482-4155
fax: 800-531-0880
e-mail: atpzines@aol.com
web: http://www.collect.com/postcardcollector
The hobby's leading publication; best source to buy, sell, and learn about postcards and other paper collectibles; calendar of upcoming shows, postcard profiles, a collecting guide for moderns through the mail, and more.

Coteco, Inc.
Newspaper: Barr's Post Card News
70 South 6th St.
Lansing, IA 52151-9680
ph: 319-538-4500 or 800-397-0145
fax: 319-538-4038
e-mail: bpcn@salamander.com
web: http://www.bpcn.com
A weekly deltiology newspaper containing postcard events, shows, news, articles, club directory, current prices, ads, etc.

Gloria Jackson
Gloria's Corner
Newsletter: Gloria's Corner
P.O. Box 507
Denison, TX 75021-0507
ph: 903-463-4878
fax: 903-463-4878
e-mail: gmj@texoma.net
A bi-monthly newsletter about postcards published for over 11 years; trades, buying, selling, auctions, etc.

Brian & Mary Lund
Reflections of a Bygone Age
Magazine: Picture Postcard Monthly
15 Debdale Lane
Keyworth, Nottinghamshire NG12 5HT
U.K.
ph: 0115-9374079
fax: 0115-9376197
e-mail: reflections@argonet.co.uk
web: http://www.postcard.co.uk/ppm
Magazine designed for collectors of old picture postcards whatever your interest, theme or area; events, clubs, checklists, values, etc.; also includes a supplement of modern picture postcards from 1950; new issues, event, shops, values.

Bob Allan
Magazine: Postcard Magazine & Philatelic Corner
30 Grassholme
Woodthorpe, York Y02 2ST
U.K.
ph: 01904 333800
e-mail: Bob_Allan_2@compuserve.com

Suppliers

NuAce Company
131 Main St.
Reading, MA 01867-3900
ph: 781-944-4960
fax: 781-944-6101
Display and protect your first day covers or postcards in NuAce 23-ring binders; has twenty 3-pocket pages to hold standard covers or postcards.

RN Products
39 Monmouth St.
Red Bank, NJ 07701-1613
ph: 732-741-0626
fax: 732-741-0479
Postcard albums with 4 and 6 pocket crystal clear vinyl pages; send SASE for price list.

Linder Publications, Inc.
P.O. Box 5056
Syracuse, NY 13220
ph: 315-437-0463 or 800-654-0324
fax: 315-437-4832
Sells collector's accessories for stamps, coins, telephone cards, postcards: ring binders, blank album pages, UV lamps, magnifiers, stamp tongs, clear pocket pages, protective covers, coin holders, etc.

Morgan Co., The
6301 Highbanks Rd.
Mascoutah, IL 62258
ph: 618-566-7568 or 800-422-4510
fax: 618-566-7518
Pocket sheets and soft sleeves for archival safe storage.

Aviation Related

(see also AVIATION MEMORABILIA)

Dealers

Larry Myers
Postcard Post, The
2539 Millers Woods Road
Boonville, NY 13309-5020
e-mail: postcard@borg.com
web: http://www.borg.com/~postcard/
Expert, dealer, collector; buys and sells postcards, specializing in rare airline postcard; website has many illustrated postcard articles; also airline postcard sales and auctions.

Bank Related

Collectors

John & Nancy Wilson
Wilson's Syngraphics
9353 SW 92nd Place Rd.
Ocala, FL 34481-6502
ph: 414-545-8636
e-mail: johnancy@aol.com
Wants any pre-1934 paper money issued in the U.S.; also wants any pre-1930 postcards depicting banks.

Foreign

Dealers

Jerry Rubackin
Jerry's Cards & Collectibles
P.O. Box 1271
Framingham, MA 01701-0207
ph: 508-788-5197
fax: 508-788-5197
Buys early foreign postcards from Philippines and Hawaii: people, street scenes, advertising, costumes, real photo; no general views; need early atlases and Harpers Book of the Philippines.

Photo (Real)

Auction Services

Bob Ward
Antique Paper Guild
P.O. Box 5742
Bellevue, WA 98006-0242
ph: 425-643-5701
fax: 425-641-4363
e-mail: rwardapg@interserv.com
web: http://www.web-pac.com
Conducts periodic auctions specializing in pre-1935 real photo postcards; six mail/phone auction catalogs per year for $30, 8 1/2" x 11", profusely illustrated.

Experts

Bob Ward
Antique Paper Guild
P.O. Box 5742
Bellevue, WA 98006-0242
ph: 425-643-5701
fax: 425-641-4363
e-mail: rwardapg@interserv.com
web: http://www.web-pac.com
Specializes in pre-1935 real photo postcards, stereographs and photographica; also conducts specialized auctions of same; author of "Investment Guide to North American Real Photo Postcards," "Real Photo Postcards: The 'Life-Size' Edition."

Photo (Real) Canadian

Dealers

Michael Rice
Michael Rice Collectibles
P.O. Box 286
Saanichton, British Columbia V8M 2C5
Canada
ph: 250-652-9412
e-mail: mrice@pacificcoast.net
Active buyer of Canadian, U.S., English, foreign pre-1930 picture postcards; wants used or unused; especially wants "real photo" views of Western Canadian provinces and the Yukon Territory; cards may be sent on approval; will pay postage.

Piano Related

Collectors

Janice E. Kelsh
633 Pennsylvania Ave.
Hagerstown, MD 21740-3769
ph: 301-797-7675
fax: 301-496-7383
e-mail: jkelsh@niaid.nih.gov
Interested in obtaining miniature pianos of all kinds; also want postcards depicting pianos.

Post Office Related

Collectors

Dr. Frank R. Scheer, Curator
Railway Mail Service Library
12 E. Rosemont Ave.
Alexandria, VA 22301-2325
ph: 703-549-4095
fax: 703-836-1955
e-mail: fscheer@erols.com
Buys post office related postcards - any condition, era, location or country. Will send free list with buying prices. Also wants postcards with views of street letterboxes, postal vehicles, post office interiors, etc.

States

(see also STATE RELATED MEMORABILIA)

Collectors

Richard Pace
12556 Timber Hollow Place
Germantown, MD 20874-1561
ph: 202-708-2654 x2621 or 301-916-4913
A photographer who collects and wants to buy modern postcards depicting or related to the 50 States, the U.S. Territories, and the District of Columbia.

States (Florida)

Collectors

Steve Hess
P.O. Box 1747
Deland, FL 32720-1747
ph: 904-736-1067 or 904-756-6068
Buying Florida postcards: small town, depots, blacks; anything pre-1915 Florida.

States (Maryland)

Collectors

Jerry A. McCoy
800 Thayer Ave.
Silver Spring, MD 20910-4504
ph: 301-565-2519
e-mail: ohiowa@erols.com
Wants any postcards or memorabilia of Silver Spring, Maryland.

States (North Carolina)

Collectors

J. Robert Boykin, III
P.O. Box 7440
Wilson, NC 27895
ph: 252-237-1700
fax: 252-237-2314
e-mail: boykinappraisals@coastalnet.com
Buying pre-1930s North Carolina postcards; no mountains; prefers early or real photo.

States (Pennsylvania)

Collectors

Richard A. Wood
P.O. Box 22165
Juneau, AK 99802-2165
ph: 907-789-8450
fax: 907-789-8450
e-mail: akrare@alaska.net
web: http://www.alaska.net/~akrare/
Wants postcards of Penna. Pike County towns: Milford, Twin Lakes, Shohola, Parker's Glen, Walker Lake, Woodtown; also ALASKA postcards.

States (West Virginia)

Collectors

Randy Bryant
P.O. Box 62
Cannelton, WV 25036-0062
ph: 304-442-4480
Wants pre-1930 real photos and postcards of West Virginia: small towns, coal mining, lumbering, interiors, exteriors, lynchings, sports teams of WV coal towns; no scenic views (mountains, rivers, statues, etc.)

POSTERS

(see also ADVERTISING COLLECTIBLES, Posters; CARTOON ART; MAGICIANS PARAPHERNALIA; MARINE CORPS ITEMS; MILITARIA, WWI [Posters]; MILITARIA, WWII [Posters]; MOVIE MEMORABILIA, Movie Posters; PAPER COLLECTIBLES; PRINTS)

Auction Services

Terry Shargel
Poster Auctions International Inc
601 West 26th St., 13th Floor
New York, NY 1001
ph: 212-787-4000
fax: 212-604-9175
e-mail: jrennert@angel.net
web: http://www.posterauction.com
Conducts two poster-only auctions per year emphasizing original French advertising posters of the Belle Epoque; prices range from $1,000 to $65,000; resource for books on all aspects of poster art; catalogue available.

Caroline Birenbaum
Swann Galleries, Inc.
104 E. 25th St.
New York, NY 10010-2977
ph: 212-254-4710
fax: 212-979-1017
e-mail: swann@swanngalleries.com
web: http://www.swanngalleries.com/
Oldest/largest U.S. auctioneer specializing in rare books, autographs & manuscripts, maps, atlases, photographs, and works of art on paper including vintage posters.

R. Neil & Elaine Reynolds
Poster Mail Auction Co.
1015 King St.
Alexandria, VA 22314
ph: 703-882-3574
fax: 703-882-4765
Conducts 4 mail/telephone auctions per year of original vintage posters; 4 fully illustrated catalogs for $20.

Clubs/Associations

International Vintage Poster Dealers Association
P.O. Box 502
Old Chelsea Station
New York, NY 10113-0502
ph: 212-355-8391
fax: 212-355-8391
A trade association with strict standards and guidelines for all its members to insure the authenticity of the posters which they sell and to promote ethical and fair business practices.

Collectors

Dan Calandriello
53-C Beacon Village
Burlington, MA 01803-3843
ph: 781-229-9009
e-mail: dan@coe.neu.edu
Wants Disney posters, tobacco posters.

Ken Trombly
1825 K St. NW, #901
Washington, DC 20006
ph: 800-673-8158 or 202-887-5000
fax: 202-457-0343
e-mail: trombly@erols.com
Wants magic posters, Mysto Magic sets, magic books and Houdini items; also wants broadsides and old photos of magicians; will pay top dollar or will trade from his collection.

Dealers

International Vintage Poster Fair
e-mail: pfair@dti.net
web: http://www.posterfair.com/
The premier marketplace for buying original advertising posters; only original posters - no reproductions.

Nancy Steinbock
Nancy Steinbock Posters & Prints
60 Solon St.
Newton Highlands, MA 02461
ph: 800-438-1577
e-mail: nancy@nancysteinbockposters.com
web: http://www.nancysteinbockposters.com/
Buys and sells posters 1880-present; subjects: war, travel, circus, literary, political, product advertising, etc.; American or foreign.

George Dembo
P.O. Box 657
Chatham, NJ 07928-0657
ph: 973-701-0713
fax: 973-701-0713
Wants to buy vintage posters (1860-1960) in good condition; phone or write and send photos; wants one poster or a large collection.

Susan & Mario Carrandi
Carrandi Vintage Posters
122 Monroe Ave.
Belle Mead, NJ 08502-4608
ph: 908-874-0630
fax: 908-874-4892
e-mail: mario@carrandimagic.com
web: http://www.carrandimagic.com/
Buys and sells posters: French, circus, magic, Wild West, decorative.

Chisholm Larsson Gallery
145 8th Ave.
New York, NY 10011
ph: 212-741-1703
e-mail: info@chisholm-poster.com
web: http://www.chisholm-poster.com/
Deals in political, movie, circus, foreign posters; online catalog; also the only searchable database on the internet with thousands of titles and thumbnail images.

Louis Bixenman
Poster America
138 West 18th St.
New York, NY 10011-5403
ph: 212-206-0499
fax: 212-727-2495
e-mail: pfair@dti.net
web: http://www.posterfair.com
A leading gallery of original vintage advertising posters from Europe, Asia, and the Americas; charter member of the International Vintage Poster Dealers Assoc.; inventory dates from 1890-1980; art Nouveau, Belle Epoque, etc.

Debra Clifford
Vintage Poster Works
P.O. Box 88
Pittsford, NY 14534
ph: 716-218-9483
fax: 716-218-9035
e-mail: debra@vintageposterworks.com
web: http://www.vintageposterworks.com/
Buys and sells vintage posters including travel, military, advertising, French, European, magic, circus, and movie; online poster gallery, poster show, condition, grading and linen backing info; also sells books about vintage posters.

Martin Kramer
313 Arch St., Ste. 203
Philadelphia, PA 19106-1810
ph: 610-592-0103
fax: 610-592-0103
Wants to buy European and American posters; all types, including movie posters.

R. Neil & Elaine Reynolds
Fine Old Posters
1015 King St.
Alexandria, VA 22314
ph: 703-882-3574
fax: 703-882-4765
Buys and sells hundreds of original vintage posters.

Pam Brin
Pam Brin Gallery
8 Park Lane
Minneapolis, MN 55416-4340
ph: 612-920-3030
fax: 612-920-3031
e-mail: PGBallery@pbgallery.com
web: http://www.pbgallery.com
Buys and sells posters; has over 150 WWI posters; issues periodic list of items for sale.

Henry W. Taylor, Jr.
500 South Main St.
P.O. Box 2247
Ketchum, ID 83340-2247
ph: 208-726-5757
Wants to buy travel posters from the Western USA (especially Sun Valley,

IS or Yellowstone Park), travel posters from Bavaria (Germany) or the Austrian Tyrol, old movie posters (especially Idaho and Montana).

Ken Taylor
La Belle Epoque
11661 San Vicente, #3304
Los Angeles, CA 90049-5110
ph: 310-442-0054 or 310-207-4345
fax: 310-826-6934
e-mail: ktscicon@ix.netcom.com
Buys and sells vintage posters: travel, war, aviation, shipping, railway, advertising, Art Deco, Art Nouveau, sport, movie, etc.

Roger Graham
Every Era Antiques
855 57th St.
Sacramento, CA 95819-3300
ph: 916-456-1767
e-mail: roger@every-era.com
web: http://www.every-era.com
Specializing in vintage posters, especially travel, entertainment, and advertising posters from 1880-1950.

Maurice & Laya Jakubowicz
Affiche Francaise
Le Plateau
Bazincourt/Epte, 21740
France
ph: 33 (0)232 27 61 53
fax: 33 (0)232 27 10 12
e-mail: ml@affiche-Francaise.com
web: http://affiche-Francaise.com/
Buy and sell 1880-present vintage posters, mainly European, all subjects: advertising, travel, theater, sport, World War, cycles, political, etc.

Experts

Tony Fusco
Fusco & Four, Associates
One Murdock Terrace
Brighton, MA 02135-2817
ph: 617-787-2637
fax: 617-782-4430
e-mail: fuscofour@aol.com
Vintage posters 1800s to WWII plus selected modern art posters; author of "The Confident Collector Identification & Price Guide to Posters"; offers appraisal and brokerage services for vintage 1870-1940 poster collectors.

George Theofiles
Miscellaneous Man
P.O. Box 1776
New Freedom, PA 17349-0191
ph: 717-235-4766
fax: 717-235-2853
Collects, buys and sells; since 1970 offering catalogs of rare posters and early advertising and ephemera on hundreds of subjects. Descriptive flyer available.

Repair Services

Gary Goss
Funny Face Productions
320 Riverside Dr.
Northampton, MA 01060
ph: 413-586-0778
Fixes stains, missing pieces, faded areas and tears, remounts posters on Japanese paper and linen backs.

Phil Temple
Phil Temple Poster Mounting Service
P.O. Box 561
Novato, CA 94949-0561
ph: 415-897-5130
fax: 415-897-5130
e-mail: ptemple@webtv.net
Poster mounting service since 1980; posters museum-mounted on 100% cotton acid-free panels.

1960s

Dealers

J. Kastor
Psychedelic Solution
33 W 8th St., 2nd Floor
New York, NY 10011
ph: 212-529-2462
Carries reference books on 60s and 70s rock art and psychedelic posters; publishes price lists; also offers appraisals and consultations.

Eastern European

Dealers

Judy Sullivan
Eastern European Art Company
0061 Arapahoe
Carbondale, CO 81623-8713
ph: 970-963-8789
fax: 970-963-8789
Sells rare posters, mainly from Poland and dating from 1940s of American and foreign films, sports, music, political, circus, travel, theater, and gallery shows and gallery shows; posters have beautiful graphics and colors.

POSTMARKS

(see STAMP COLLECTING, Postmarks)

POT LIDS

Collectors

James Hagenbuch
P.O. Box 180
102 Jefferfson St.
East Greenville, PA 18041
ph: 215-679-5849
fax: 215-679-3068
e-mail: glswrk@enter.net
web: http://www.glswrk-auction.com/
Wants to buy American pot lids for private collection. (Pot lids are decorated lids from small ceramic containers from 1840s to 1880s; pot lids first appeared in England.)

Experts

Mark Priestley
Ointment Pot, The
Grendon Underwood
Aylesbury, Bicks HP18
U.K.
e-mail: qprman@aol.com
Buys, sells, collects, appraises Victorian ointment pots; also offers advice, expert comment on the subject; these are small, ceramic pots from the turn of the century and earlier claiming to cure all wounds and diseases.

POTTERY

(see CERAMICS; COOKIE JARS; DINNERWARE; FIGURINES; FLOWER "FROGS"; REPAIR/ RESTORATION/CONSERVATION; SALT & PEPPER SHAKERS; STEINS; TILES)

POWDER HORNS

(see also ARMS & ARMOR; FIREARMS)

Collectors

David A. Galliher
2500 W. Berwyn Rd.
Muncie, IN 47304-5113
ph: 317-289-2233 or 317-284-6668
fax: 317-289-2376
Wants very early powder horns (late 1700s to 1812), engraved and with historical significance.

Experts

William H. Guthman
Guthman Americana
P.O. Box 392
Westport, CT 06881
ph: 203-259-9763
Author of "Drums A'beating, Trumpets Sounding: Artistically Carved Powder Horns in the Provincial Manner, 1746-1781."

Jim Dresslar
Dresslar Publishing
P.O. Box 635
Bargersville, IN 46106
ph: 317-422-5147
Author of "Folk Art of Early America - The Engraved Powder Horn" (Dresslar Publishing), available from the author.

Repro. Sources

Michelle Ochonicky
Stone Hollow Studio
31 High Trail
Eureka, MO 63025
ph: 314-938-9570

POWDER JARS

Collectors

Darryl Rehr
P.O. Box 641824
Los Angeles, CA 90064
ph: 310-477-5229
fax: 310-268-8420
e-mail: dcrehr@earthlink.net
web: http://home.earthlink.net/~dcrehr/
Wants all kinds of frosted figural glass powder jars with animals or other figures on the lid; please send photo.

PRECOLUMBIAN

(see also PREHISTORIC ARTIFACTS)

Auction Services

Greg Manning
Greg Manning Auctions, Inc.
775 Passaic Ave.
West Caldwell, NJ 07006
ph: 973-882-0004 or 800-221-0243
fax: 973-882-3499
e-mail: gmauction@aol.com
web: http://www.gregmanning.com/
Since 1905, a leading auctioneer of Americana, glass, stoneware, and antiquities.

Howard Rose
Arte Primitivo
3 East 65th St., Ste. 2
New York, NY 10021
ph: 212-570-6999
fax: 212-570-1899
e-mail: arteprim@idt.net
web: http://www.arteprimitivo.com/
Specializes in Classical and Egyptian antiquities, pre-Columbian art, ethnographic art, Asian antiquities, and books; conducts absentee/ callback auctions biannually and publishes lavish color catalog with each auction.

Dealers

Norman Hurst, ISA
Hurst Gallery
53 Mount Auburn St.
Cambridge, MA 02138
ph: 617-491-6888
fax: 617-661-0439
e-mail: NHurst@compuserve.com
web: http://www.hurstgallery.com
Buys, sells, appraises, restores African, Oceanic, Native American, pre-Columbian and Asian art; has been apprising, authenticating, and dealing in pre-Columbian art of North and South America for over 25 years.

Dennis Mueller
Rangerdm Indian Artifacts & Collectibles
1112 Roanoke Ave.
Riverhead, NY 11901
ph: 516-369-9671 or 516-727-2486
e-mail: rangerdm@ieaccess.net
web: http://rangerdm.ieaccess.net
Buys and sells Indian artifacts: arrowheads, Indian art forms; also pre-Columbian artifacts such as beads, shell and stone effigies, and pottery.

Blackwater Gallery
4753 Summer Set
Rapid City, SD 57702
ph: 605-348-8684
fax: 605-342-6249
Buys and sells Precolumbian pottery from Panama, over 1000 years old; masks, figures.

John Buxton
Shango Galleries
6717 Spring Valley
Dallas, TX 75240
ph: 972-239-4620 or 972-239-9943
fax: 972-239-9766
e-mail: jbuxton@arttrak.com
web: http://www.arttrak.com
Buys, sells, and appraises African, Precolumbian, Oceanic, and American Indian art.

Joel & Michael Malter
Malter Galleries, Inc.
17005 Ventura Blvd.
Encino, CA 91316-4128
ph: 818-784-7772 or 818-784-2181
fax: 818-784-4726
e-mail: rarearts@earthlink.net
web: http://www.maltergalleries.com/

David Markarian
Markarian Ancient Artifacts
P.O. Box 2476
Rancho Mirage, CA 92270-1087
ph: 760-202-5000
e-mail: orion@inland.net
web: http://www.ancientart.org/
Buys and sells Precolumbian artifacts.

Experts

Dr. Elizabeth Benson
8314 Old Seven Locks Rd.
Bethesda, MD 20817

Museums/Libraries

Dumbarton Oaks Research Library & Collection
1703 32nd St. NW
Washington, DC 20007
ph: 202-339-6400
e-mail: DumbartonOaks@doaks.org
web: http://www.doaks.org/

Dr. Ramiro Matos
National Museum of Natural History
10th St. & Constitution Ave.
Washington, DC 20560
ph: 202-357-2700
web: http://www.mnh.si.edu/
Distinguished Peruvian archaeologist.

PREHISTORIC ARTIFACTS

(see also AMERICAN INDIAN; ARCHAEOLOGY; FOSSILS; HERITAGE RESOURCES; MINERAL SPECIMENS; PRECOLUMBIAN)

Auction Services

Hesse Galleries
53 Main St.
Otego, NY 13825
ph: 607-988-6322

Robert N. Converse
199 Converse St.
Plain City, OH 43064
ph: 614-873-5471

Michael Steele
5665 Oak St., Rt. 605
Westerville, OH 43081
ph: 740-984-4612

Lolli Brothers
Hwy. 63 South
Macon, MO 63552
ph: 660-385-2516

Bob Sleeper
Bob Sleeper Auction Center
90 Elm
Higginsville, MO 64037
ph: 816-587-0019

Book Sellers

Larry Garvin
Back to Earth
17 North LaSalle Dr.
Zanesville, OH 43701-6238
ph: 740-454-0874

Collectors

Bill Balinger
P.O. Box 296
North Lewisburg, OH 43060
ph: 937-747-2225
fax: 937-747-2784
Collector of prehistoric and native American Indian artifacts.

Lar Hothem
Hothem House
P.O. Box 458
Lancaster, OH 43130-0458
ph: 740-653-9030
Wants prehistoric American Indian artifacts, mainly from Ohio.

Scott Miller
1934 W. 69th Street N.
Wichita, KS 67204
ph: 316-755-1472
e-mail: smiller@southwind.net
web: http://www2.southwind.net/~smiller/arrow/ahead1.html
Specializes in prehistoric Kansas artifacts; surface hunts and has several distinctive finds including a 4 5/8" Scottsbluff Type I.

Dealers

Kevin Cordeiro
P.O. Box 579
Somerset, MA 02726
ph: 508-675-4886

Jerry & Sandy Sherman
Paleoworld Connection
P.O. Box 86
Spencerville, MD 20868-0086
ph: 301-476-9313 or 301-476-7531
e-mail: jerry.sherman@erols.com
web: http://www.paleoworld.com/
Deals in Native American, prehistoric artifacts and fossils worldwide.

Alton Martin
Artifacts, Etc.
P.O. Box 484
Cave Spring, GA 30124
ph: 770-487-3248
e-mail: artifactsetc@wwse.net
web: http://www.artifactsetc.com
Offers quality, investment grade, genuine American Indian prehistoric and historic artifacts: stone, flint, pottery; all legally obtained.

Scott Young
Scott Young Stone Age Artifacts & Fossils
P.O. Box 8452
Port Saint Lucie, FL 34985-8452
ph: 561-878-5634
fax: 561-878-22009
e-mail: iceageman3@aol.com
Appraiser, dealer buys, sells, trades American Indian relics, pre-historic pottery, points, tools, stone, shell, bone, etc.; also stone age artifacts world wide; pre-Columbian artifacts; one item or whole collection.

Bruce Cantrell
1223 Blossom Lane
Kingston, TN 37763
ph: 423-376-6451

W.T. Pinkston
466 W. Office St.
Harrodsburg, KY 40330
ph: 606-734-4213

Tom Davis
Tom Davis Artifacts
P.O. Box 386-272, Airport Rd.
Stanton, KY 40380
ph: 606-663-9871

Greg Shipley
6672 Maple St., Rt. 36
Cable, OH 43009
ph: 937-652-3020

Jim Justice
Quality Indian Artifacts
246 W. Ottawa St.
Richwood, OH 43344

W.B. Baughman
Mac-O-Chee Trading Co.
301 S. Taylor St.
West Liberty, OH 43357
ph: 937-465-4001

Larry Garvin
Back to Earth
17 North LaSalle Dr.
Zanesville, OH 43701-6238
ph: 740-454-0874

Ron Helman
1993 Dingman Slage Rd.
Sidney, OH 45365
ph: 937-492-2923

Gary Mumaw
9167 State Route 121
Versailles, OH 45380-9518
ph: 937-526-5687

Larry Lentz
First Mesa
P.O. Box 1256
South Bend, IN 46624
ph: 219-232-2095

Richard B. Troyanowski
Rich Relics
P.O. Box 432
Sandia Park, NM 87047-0432
ph: 505-281-2611 or 505-281-2329
Buys/sells prehistoric/historic Indian artifacts, cowboy, militaria, old world antiquities & coins, fossils & ethnographic collectibles.

Jerry Gaither
Tamarack Trading Co.
2785 Pacific Coast Hwy., Ste 333
Torrance, CA 90505
ph: 310-832-8996
Prehistoric and historic American Indian art and artifacts; all artifacts guaranteed; return within seven days for full refund if not satisfied; photos sent on request; full mail order service.

American Indian Artifacts
P.O. Box 60
Salinas, CA 93902-0060
ph: 805-238-6129

Experts

Len Weidner
Indian River Industries
13706 Robins Rd.
Westerville, OH 43082
ph: 614-965-2868 or 800-444-1280
fax: 614-965-5913
e-mail: janiew48@aol.com
web: http://members.aol.com/JanieW48/
Collector, dealer, and expert paying cash for Indian relics, both historic and prehistoric; author of many books on Indian relics.

Museums/Libraries

Anne Kaupp
National Museum of Natural History, Anthropology Public Information Office
Smithsonian
NHBMRC112
Washington, DC 20560
ph: 202-357-1592
web: http://www.mnh.si.edu/
With questions about found artifacts first try calling your State Archaeology department or the anthropology department of a local natural history museum.

Bob McWilliam
Museum of the Texas Amateur Archaeological Association
102 Hwy 27E #108
Ingram, TX 78025
ph: 803-367-7012
fax: 803-367-7012
e-mail: txcache@aol.com
web: http://www.arrowheads.com/taaa
A museum featuring ancient Indian artifacts from all over Texas; members of the TAAA put their collections on display on a rotating basis.

Periodicals

Gary L. Fogelman
Magazine: Indian-Artifact Magazine
RD 1 Box 240
Turbotville, PA 17772-9599
ph: 570-437-3698
fax: 570-437-3411
e-mail: iam@csrling.net
web: http://www.iampub.com/
An easy reading quarterly focusing on American Indian prehistory: artifacts, tools, lifestyles, customs, archaeology, book reviews; everything about collecting, buying, finding and enjoying Indian artifacts.

Bill Balinger
Magazine: Prehistoric Antiquities & Archaeological News
P.O. Box 296
North Lewisburg, OH 43060
ph: 937-747-2225
fax: 937-747-2784
Quarterly magazine about archaeology and antiquities; articles, ads, etc.

Repair Services

Dennis Bushley
Quality Restoration
113 Pine Forest Dr.
Selma, AL 36701
ph: 334-875-5299

Jerry Jenkins
Rte. 5 Box 472
Cynthiana, KY 41031
ph: 606-234-3350

Arrowheads & Points

Clubs/Associations

Robert Allen
Kolomoki Society
P.O. Box 665
San Antonio, FL 33576
web: http://www.artifactsetc.com/kolomoki.htm

Bob McWilliam
Texas Amateur Archeological Association
Magazine: Texas Cache
102 Hwy 27E #108
Ingram, TX 78025
ph: 803-367-7012
fax: 803-367-7012
e-mail: txcache@aol.com
web: http://www.arrowheads.com/taaa
A learning experience and adventure in archaeology, arrowhead hunting and collecting; photos and stories of Texas and Southwest points; national artifact show; archaeological digs.

Collectors

Bobby & Pat Maples
Rte. 4 Box 990
Waynesboro, TN 38485
ph: 931-722-5981

Phil Cummins
RR2 Box 505C
Augusta, KY 41002
ph: 606-756-3296

Ray Acra
323 Thomas Lane
Harrison, OH 45030
ph: 513-367-1744
Specializes in prehistoric lithics (stone items, e.g. arrowheads, points, clubs, bowls, etc.)

Larry Dyer
11175 S. 100 W.
Columbus, IN 47201
ph: 812-342-6398

Joe Lift
3616 Platte Ct.
Lafayette, IN 47905
ph: 765-447-2307

Ralph Strope
P.O. Box 952
Pekin, IL 61554
ph: 309-347-2570

Ed Meiners
219 Westwood
East Alton, IL 62024-1642
ph: 618-259-3764
One of the largest collectors in the US.

Kenneth Hamilton
416 South Walnut
Harrison, AR 72601
ph: 870-743-2175

Dan Stroud
P.O. Box 636
Maple, Ontario L6A 1S5
Canada

Dealers

Bob's Flint Shop
ph: 877-244-8998 or 970-241-7295
fax: 970-241-7516
e-mail: knowlton@gj.net
web: http://www.bobsarrowheads.com/
Buys, sells, trades, arrowheads and other prehistoric artifacts; also accepts consignment sales.

Artifacts, Inc.
e-mail: artifactsetc@wwse.net
web: http://www.artifactsetc.com/home.asp

Dennis Mueller
Rangerdm Indian Artifacts & Collectibles
1112 Roanoke Ave.
Riverhead, NY 11901
ph: 516-369-9671 or 516-727-2486
e-mail: rangerdm@ieaccess.net
web: http://rangerdm.ieaccess.net
Buys and sells Indian artifacts: arrowheads, Indian art forms; also pre-Columbian artifacts such as beads, shell and stone effigies, and pottery.

David Summers
Native American Artifacts
45 West Parkway
Victor, NY 14564-1243
ph: 716-924-5167
e-mail: naasummers@aol.com
One of the world's largest dealers in American Indian art and antiquities; buys and sells; specializing in Northeastern Indian specimens.

Roy Mitchell
3104 Glenmere Place, S.W.
Decatur, AL 35603
ph: 256-350-3103
Wants to buy Indian relics.

Arkansas Ozarks Arrowheads
P.O. Box 68
Saint Joe, AR 72675
ph: 870-439-2542
e-mail: xtreme@eritter.net
web: http://www.arrowheads.com/ozarks/
Dealing in only 100% authentic Indian artifacts; offers warranty; over 200 artifacts on-line.

Pat Dunnegan
Pat's Authentic Indian Artifacts
201 Harrison Ave.
Gustine, TX 76455
ph: 888-841-9386 or 915-667-7210
e-mail: teddun@itexas.net
web: http://www2.itexas.net/~teddun/
Online close-up photos of quality authentic American Indian artifacts offered for sale; also a selected list of related books; over 40 years in business.

Bear Creek Artifacts
P.O. Box 60201
San Angelo, TX 76906
ph: 915-944-7407
e-mail: cavallin@wcc.net
web: http://www.arrowheads.com/bearcreek/

Experts

Sam Williams
Arrowheads Dot Com
1211 W. Commerce
Eastland, TX 76448
ph: 254-629-2549 or 800-538-3490
fax: 254-631-0136
e-mail: sam@arrowheads.com
web: http://www.arrowheads.com/
Collector, dealer and expert specializing in arrowheads and other authentic American Indian artifacts.

Richard B. Troyanowski
Rich Relics
P.O. Box 432
Sandia Park, NM 87047-0432
ph: 505-281-2611 or 505-281-2329
Specializes in prehistoric lithics (stone items, e.g. arrowheads, points, clubs, bowls, etc.)

Internet Resources

Hugh Jarvis
Lithics Site, The
e-mail: hjarvis@acsu.buffalo.edu
web: http://wings.buffalo.edu/go?lithics
Great page with lots of links to all kinds of archaeological resources: lithics research projects, literary resources, related institutional sites, archaeological courses on lithics, artifact information, commercial concerns.

Sam Williams
Arrowheads Dot Com
1211 W. Commerce
Eastland, TX 76448
ph: 254-629-2549 or 800-538-3490
fax: 254-631-0136
e-mail: sam@arrowheads.com
web: http://www.arrowheads.com/
Informational resource and an on-line chat room for artifact enthusiasts; legal issues, arrowheads for sale, trader's corner, calendar of events,

arrowhead typology, products, arrowhead links.

PREMIUMS

(see also CEREAL BOXES; CRACKER JACK COLLECTIBLES; GROCERY STORE ITEMS; FAST FOOD COLLECTIBLES; PAPER COLLECTIBLES; POGS; TELEVISION SHOWS & MEMORABILIA)

Collectors

Chris Swain
P.O. Box 513
Williamsburg, MA 01096
ph: 413-628-3213
e-mail: Bluejettoy@aol.com
Wants radio show and cereal premiums from the 1930s through the 1950s.

Bob Havey
P.O. Box 183
North Sullivan, ME 04664-0183
ph: 207-422-3083
fax: 207-422-3430
Wants radio and cereal box premiums: rings, badges, decoders, etc. from Superman, Tom Mix, Buck Rogers, cowboys, etc.

Ed Pragler
P.O. Box 284
Wharton, NJ 07885-0284
ph: 201-875-8293
Wants to buy radio premiums, box top & cereal giveaways, comic character collectibles: rings, decoders, badges, paper items, manuals, maps, pinback buttons, cereal boxes, figurines, etc. from Buck Rogers, Capt. America, Flash Gordon, etc.

Dealers

Ken Mitchell
710 Conacher Dr.
Willowdale, Ontario M2M 3N6
Canada
ph: 416-222-5808
Appraises, collects, buys and sells 1890 to 1970s comic books, newspapers, comic strips, "Big Little" books, popular music/jazz books/ magazines/tapes; pulp magazines, original comic art, radio and cereal premiums.

Experts

Ted Hake
Hake's Americana & Collectibles Auction
P.O. Box 1444
York, PA 17405-1444
ph: 717-848-1333
e-mail: Ted@hakes.com
web: http://www.hakes.com/
Always purchasing items for 8 mail-bid auctions per year covering hundreds of categories including toys, character collectibles, Disney, cowboy heroes, premiums, television, politicals, pin-back buttons, advertising and more.

Cereal Box

(see also CEREAL BOXES)

Collectors

Roland Coover
1537 E. Strasburg Rd.
West Chester, PA 19380-6380
ph: 610-692-3112
e-mail: rlcoover@aol.com
Wants cereal items: cereal boxes, premiums, and store displays from the 1950s to 1980s; Cap'n Crunch, Quisp, Quake, Freakies, Frakenberry, King Vitamin; also wants items from kids products such as Bosco, Fizzies, candy, cookies, etc.

Kevin Meisner
5400 Cheshire Meadows Way
Fairfax, VA 22032-3216
ph: 703-527-3485
e-mail: slid-erkev@aol.com
Wants to buy Freakies stuff: cereal boxes, prizes from Freakies cereal, Freakies figures, Freakies boats, Freakies rings, Goody Goody Fruit Hat figure, and the Hamhose Good Friends Medal, magnets, flip-n-flys, fun dots, etc.

Aaron Sultan
3201 Arrowood Dr.
Raleigh, NC 27604
ph: 919-954-7111
Wants to buy cereal premiums and toys: Quisp, Cap'n Crunch, Freakies, Frakenberry, etc.

David Welch
P.O. Box 714
Murphysboro, IL 62966-0714
ph: 618-687-2282
fax: 618-684-2243
e-mail: PezDude1@aol.com
Wants giveaway or send-away items offered through cereal boxes and relating to TV, sports, comic, cartoon or movie characters, especially super heroes.

Steve Roden
P.O. Box 36B16
Los Angeles, CA 90036-1154
ph: 323-933-3158
fax: 323-933-3158
Wants to buy cereal boxes, back panels and premiums; also trading cards, bubble gum items, and radio premiums.

Dan Goodsell
P.O. Box 342
Culver City, CA 90232
ph: 310-815-0465
Interested in all 1950s to 1970s kid's food packaging and premiums such as cereal boxes.

Experts

Scott Bruce
P.O. Box 481
Cambridge, MA 02140-0004
ph: 617-492-5004
e-mail: scottbruce@flake.com
web: http://www.flake.com
Buy, sell, trade cereal prizes, displays and boxes from 1950s to 1970s; especially interested in character material such as Quisp, Quake, monsters and personalities.

Tom Tumbusch
Tomart Publications
3300 Encrete Lane
Dayton, OH 45439-1944
ph: 937-294-2250
fax: 937-294-1024
e-mail: office@tomart.com
web: http://www.tomart.com
Buys radio, cereal, comic book, etc. premiums, i.e. rings, badges, etc.; author of "Illustrated Radio Premium Catalog & Price Guide."

Comics

Collectors

John S. Fawcett
P.O. Box 1156
Waldoboro, ME 04572-1156
ph: 207-832-7398
Wants to buy comic book subscription giveaway premiums; radio show rings, decoders, etc.

Radio Show

(see also CHARACTER COLLECTIBLES; COWBOY HEROES; RADIO SHOWS, Old Time [Straight Arrow], SPACE COLLECTIBLES)

Collectors

Bruce Thalberg
23 Mountain View Dr.
Weston, CT 06883-1317
ph: 203-227-8175
Wants Lone Ranger, Sky King, Space Patrol, Tom Mix, Roy Rogers, The Shadow, Capt. Midnight, Terry & the Pirates, etc., especially pre-1965 rings; all novelty rings considered; photocopy helpful; please send SASE.

David Welch
P.O. Box 714
Murphysboro, IL 62966-0714
ph: 618-687-2282
fax: 618-684-2243
e-mail: PezDude1@aol.com
Wants giveaway or send-away items offered through radio programs and comic books relating to TV, sports, comic, cartoon or movie characters, especially super heroes.

Dealers

Jim Harmon
Jim Harmon, Producer
634 South Orchard Dr.
Burbank, CA 91506
ph: 818-843-5472
Buys, sells, trades radio premiums and tapes, comic books, and comic strips; author of "Radio Mystery & Adventure," "Great Radio Heroes," "Great Movie Serials," "The Godzilla Book," and "Monsters of the Movies" magazine.

Leon Rue
69-411 Ramon Rd., #1060
Cathedral City, CA 92234
ph: 714-998-6393
fax: 714-998-4839
e-mail: rue@pipeline.com
web: http://rue.home.pipeline.com/premiums.htm
Buys and sells radio show premiums such as from Capt. Midnight, Little Orphan Annie, Tom Mix, Amos & Andy, etc.; has over 400 to sell; digital pictures available for most.

Experts

Norm Vigue
62 Bailey St.
Stoughton, MA 02072
ph: 781-344-5441
Wants to buy rings, decoders, manuals, badges, store displays, etc.

Tom Tumbusch
Tomart Publications
3300 Encrete Lane
Dayton, OH 45439-1944
ph: 937-294-2250
fax: 937-294-1024
e-mail: office@tomart.com
web: http://www.tomart.com
Buys radio, cereal, comic book, etc. premiums, i.e. rings, badges, etc.; author of "Illustrated Radio Premium Catalog & Price Guide."

Radio Show (Jimmie Allen)

Collectors

Jack Deveny
6805 Cheyenne Trail
Edina, MN 55439-1158
ph: 612-941-2457
e-mail: plane@itol.net
Wants Jimmie Allen Flying Club wings, I.D. bracelets, knife, whistles, maps, blotters, membership cards, aircraft models, etc.

Rings

Collectors

Steve A. Geppi
Diamond Comic Distributors
1966 Greenspring Dr., Ste. 300
Lutherville Timonium, MD 21093-4161
ph: 410-560-7100
Wants to buy old and rare comic rings: Spider, Howdy Doody Jack-in-the-Box, Cisco Kid Secret Compart-

ment, Tom Mix Spinner, Radio Orphan Annie Altascope, Superman, Lone Ranger Meteorite, Valric the Viking, Joe Louis, etc.

Dealers

Robert Overstreet
Overstreet Publications Inc.
11729 Mayfair Field Dr.
Lutherville Timonium, MD 21093-7011
ph: 410-561-3217

Bruce Mohrhard
Mo's Comics & Stories Shop
4573 Gravois
Saint Louis, MO 63116
ph: 314-353-9500

Experts

Danny Fuchs
209-80 18th Ave., #4K
Bayside, NY 11360-1424
ph: 718-225-9030
fax: 718-225-3688
e-mail: superdf62@aol.com
"America's foremost Superman Collector"; co-author of "The Adventures of Superman Collecting."

Tom Tumbusch
Tomart Publications
3300 Encrete Lane
Dayton, OH 45439-1944
ph: 937-294-2250
fax: 937-294-1024
e-mail: office@tomart.com
web: http://www.tomart.com
Buys radio, cereal, and comic book, premiums, i.e. rings, badges, etc.; author of "Illustrated Radio Premium Catalog & Price Guide."

PRESIDENTIAL MEMORABILIA

(see PERSONALITIES [HISTORICAL]; POLITICAL COLLECTIBLES; WHITE HOUSE MEMORABILIA)

PRINTING EQUIPMENT

(see also BOOK ARTS; NEWSPAPERS; TYPEWRITERS)

Clubs/Associations

American Printing History Association
Newsletter: APHA Newsletter
P.O. Box 4922
Grand Central Station
New York, NY 10163-4922
web: http://wally2.rit.edu/cary/apha.html
Encourages the preservation of printing artifacts and source materials for printing history, as well as the development of museums and libraries to house them.

Collectors

Briar Press, The
P.O. Box 490
Briarcliff Manor, NY 10510
e-mail: bpress@aol.com
web: http://www.westnet.com/~bpress/
A private press with a collection of type, presses, printing equipment and ephemera; has a comprehensive web site: Online Letterpress Museum, resources, bookarts links for letterpress printers and enthusiasts.

Juergen Berndt
6731 Ashley Ct.
Sarasota, FL 34241-9696
ph: 941-925-0385
fax: 941-925-0487
e-mail: auction@breker.com
web: http://www.breker.com/
Wants to buy early printing presses, lithographic presses, typesetting hand presses, pre-1900 books on printing technology.

David W. Peat
1225 Carroll White
Indianapolis, IN 46219-3907
ph: 317-357-6895
Wants antique printers type, catalogs of printers type (typefounders specimen books), small presses, periodicals, stock certificates, medals, and other 19th cent. printing items.

James L. Weygand
P.O. Box 215
Nappanee, IN 46550-0215
ph: 219-773-4832
Wants tabletop printing presses, catalogs, instruction booklets, literature, equipment, accessories, etc.

Paul Aken
39221 N. Lewis
Beach Park, IL 60099-3344
ph: 847-746-8170 or 847-731-1945
e-mail: platenpress@iconnect.net
Wants printing items: presses, type, tools, books, manuals, catalogs, toy printing presses, multigraphs, litho stones, etc.

Dealers

Nancy Neale Silverman
Nancy Neale Typecraft
130 Ash Drive
Roslyn, NY 11576
ph: 516-621-7130 or 800-927-7469
fax: 516-621-7313
e-mail: typenancy@aol.com
web: http://www.acadia.net/typecraft/
Collector, dealer, expert, appraiser; specializes in antique printer's wood type and other printing artifacts; from June to October contact at P.O. Box 3, Bernard, ME 04612, phone 207-244-5192.

David Schwartz
Schwartz's Antique Printing
9214 New Albion Rd.
Little Valley, NY 14755-9771
ph: 716-938-9807
Wants to buy old printers type and cuts, type specimen books, old printing equipment & supply catalogs, books about printing, certificates and badges from printers unions; anything related to letter press printing.

Internet Resources

Briar Press, The
P.O. Box 490
Briarcliff Manor, NY 10510
e-mail: bpress@aol.com
web: http://www.westnet.com/~bpress/
A private press with a collection of type, presses, printing equipment and ephemera; has a comprehensive web site: Online Letterpress Museum, resources, bookarts links for letterpress printers and enthusiasts.

Museums/Libraries

International Printing Museum
315 East Torrance Blvd.
Carson, CA 90745
ph: 714-529-1832
e-mail: printmuseum@earthlink.net
Experience the development of the printing press, rare antique printing machines; offers printing equipment for sale on occasion.

Type Founding Items

Collectors

David W. Peat
1225 Carroll White
Indianapolis, IN 46219-3907
ph: 317-357-6895
Wants old type casting (founding) equipment: hand molds, mats (matrices) for casting antique type, Bruce type caster, catalogs.

PRINTS

(see also ART; ILLUSTRATORS; ILLUSTRATORS; MAPS & CHARTS; MOTTOES [PICTURE POEMS]; PAPER COLLECTIBLES; PERSONALITIES [ARTISTS]; POSTERS; PRINTS [MODERN]; REPAIR/RESTORATION/ CONSERVATION, Paper Items; WALLACE NUTTING)

Appraisers

Derek D. Cocovinis
DDC Fine Arts
P.O. Bbox 718
Montville, NJ 07045
ph: 973-316-0023
e-mail: ddcarts@earthlink.net
web: http://www.nobella.com/ddcarts/
Art sales and appraisals.

Christopher W. Lane
Philadelphia Print Shop, Ltd., The
8441 Germantown Ave.
Philadelphia, PA 19118
ph: 215-242-4750
fax: 215-242-6977
e-mail: PhilaPrint@PhilaPrintShop.com
web: http://www.philaprintshop.com
Gallery of antique prints and maps with related rare books and atlases; also bookstore of reference books related to antique prints and maps; appraisals, paper conservation and restoration.

Charles B. Goldstein, ISA CAPP
Charles Barry International
8 Hardwicke Place
Rockville, MD 20850-3010
ph: 301-340-6775
fax: 301-340-1726
Buys, sells, and appraises fine Old Master, 19th and 20th century, modern and contemporary, American and European prints; Certified Member, International Society of Appraisers; expert witness and trial consultant.

Melanie Smith, ISA
Seaside Art Gallery
P.O. Box 1
2716 Virginia Dare Trail S
Nags Head, NC 27959
ph: 252-441-5418 or 800-828-2444
fax: 252-441-8563
e-mail: seaside@interpath.com
web: http://www.seasideart.com
Accredited member of the International Society of Appraisers; specializes in fine art (paintings, graphics, sculpture) and animation art.

Jerry Bengis, ISA
9860 SW 122nd St.
Miami, FL 33176-4928
ph: 305-232-1143
fax: 305-251-1450
e-mail: yascha7@netrox.net
Fine art appraiser specializing in prints (especially Salvador Dali), graphics (Miro, Chagall, Picasso, Warhol), etchings, engravings, prints, bronzes.

Susan S. Pohle, ISA
Pigeon Creek Antiques
621 N. Main
Thiensville, WI 53092-1215
ph: 414-242-2054
Sells and appraises fine art prints, period furniture, lamps, toys, dolls.

Auction Services

Amory Spizzirri, Client Svc.
William Doyle Galleries
175 E. 87th St.
New York, NY 10128-2205
ph: 212-427-2730
fax: 212-369-0892
e-mail: info@doylegalleries.com
web: http://www.doylegalleries.com
Holds over 50 auctions annually of furniture and decorations, paintings and sculpture, jewelry, books and prints, couture and textiles, 20th century art & design, majolica, Lalique, Asian works of art and other specialty categories.

Clubs/Associations

Nancy Braun
American Historical Print Collectors Society
Magazine: Imprint
P.O. Box 201
Fairfield, CT 06430-0201
ph: 203-255-1627 or 914-795-5266
e-mail: cwood@mwa.org
web: http://www.ahpcs.org
Objectives are to the foster preservation, study and exhibition of historical American prints from the 17th through the 19th century; publishes "Imprint" magazine twice and "Newsletter" four times per year; scholarly meetings.

Dan Redmon
Print Club of New York
175 Fifth Ave., Ste. 2330
New York, NY 10010
Promotes prints and print making in New York.

International Fine Print Dealers Association
485 Madison Ave., 15th Floor
New York, NY 10022
ph: 212-759-4469
fax: 212-319-7752
e-mail: ifpda@printdealers.com
web: http://www.printdealers.com/
Membership of prestigious print dealers by election only; publishes membership directory.

Dr. Charles J. Semowich
Print Club of Albany
Newsletter: Print Club of Albany Newsletter
P.O. Box 6578
Albany, NY 12206-0578
ph: 518-432-9514
e-mail: pcaprint@crisny.org
web: http://crisny.org/not-for-profit/pcaprint/index.htm
Founded in 1933 for the purpose of promoting an appreciation of fine art prints among its members and community; each active member receives an original print; conducts lectures and workshops; holds artists papers in its archives.

Joe Davidson
American Antique Graphics Society
5185 Windfall Rd.
Medina, OH 44256-8703
ph: 330-723-7172
Members interested in graphic arts prints: from medieval, natural history to etchings, engravings.

Collectors

Joel Goleman
607 Chilton Hills Dr.
Elkins Park, PA 19027-1319
ph: 215-542-7700
e-mail: babsygo@webtv.net
Special interest in old master prints and Japanese woodblock prints; experienced as expert witness; teaches courses in print connoisseurship and curates print exhibitions.

Terry Ahlberg
1000 Irvine Blvd.
Tustin, CA 92680-3527
ph: 714-730-1000 or 949-654-1331
fax: 714-730-1752
e-mail: emailit@earthlink.net
Wants any prints or posters by artists Jo Mora (J.J. Mora), Till Goodan, Maynard Dixon, Frank Mechau, Ila McAfee, A.M. Cassandra.

Dealers

John Clement
36 Oakwood Ave.
Fitchburg, MA 01420-7421
ph: 978-345-5863
Specializes in American, European Old Master, and modern prints.

Robert Kipp
Art & Old Print Restorations
20 Macerick St.
Marblehead, MA 01945
ph: 781-639-7747
e-mail: robkipp@oldprints.com
web: http://www.oldprints.com
Print sales and restorations; specializing in 19th century prints.

Jim Messineo
JMW Gallery
144 Lincoln St.
Boston, MA 02111-2523
ph: 617-338-9097
fax: 617-338-7636
e-mail: jmwgallery@tiac.net
web: http://www.jmwgallery.com/
Buys, sells and specializes along with co-owner Mike Witt in the Arts & Crafts movement. Mission furniture: Lifetime, Limbert, Stickley; American Art Pottery 1875 to 1950s: Grueby, Newcomb, Marblehead, etc.; metalwork, Roycroft.

Tony Fusco
Fusco & Four, Associates
One Murdock Terrace
Brighton, MA 02135-2817
ph: 617-787-2637
fax: 617-782-4430
e-mail: fuscofour@aol.com
Specializing in 20th century European and American works on paper, 1900-1950, especially WPA, regionalists, and urban social realists; free quarterly illustrated lists.

Ernest S. Kramer
Ernest S. Kramer Fine Arts & Prints
P.O. Box 37
Wellesley Hills, MA 02181
ph: 781-237-3635
fax: 781-235-0112
Focuses on 19th and 20th century prints; always interested in purchasing singular works or collections of prints, drawings, watercolors or oil paintings.

Jim Martin
Martin Antiques
75 Meadowbrook Rd.
East Greenwich, RI 02818
e-mail: yankeetrader@home.com
web: http://members.home.com/yankeetrader
Offers vintage lithographs and prints by Mucha, Lefevre, Vernuil, Parrish, Stillwell, Phillips, Pognay, Cheret, Grasset and others.

Reg & Sally Lombard
Lombard Antiquarian Maps & Prints
P.O. Box 281
Cape Elizabeth, ME 04107
ph: 207-799-1889
fax: 207-799-9593
e-mail: lamp@cybertours.com
web: http://www.cybertours.com/~lamp/
Specializes in fine maps, charts, rare botanical, natural history and architectural prints.

Robert Bessette
Green Dragon Arts
P.O. Box 588
Burlington, VT 05402-0588
ph: 802-862-1930
fax: 802-862-1930
e-mail: grdragon@together.net
Has over 20,000 old prints to choose from; buys and sells 18th to early 20th century lithographs, etchings, woodcuts, chromolithographs, hand colored book plates, etc.

Jane Allinson
Allinson Gallery, Inc.
P.O. Box 646
Storrs, CT 06268-2022
ph: 860-429-2322
fax: 860-429-2825
e-mail: allinson@neca.com
web: http://www.allinsongallery.com
Buys and sells American & European fine prints, 1880-1960; also offers fine art appraisals; member of Appraisers Association of America, International Fine Print Dealers Association.

Marcy & Mindi Brahin
100 Sargent Rd.
Freehold, NJ 07728
ph: 732-462-7923
e-mail: Atprints@aol.com
Specializes in antique topical prints, especially 19th century matter Harpers & Leslie's weeklies, Civil War, baseball, Nast Santas and others.

Ellen Sragow
Sragow Gallery
73 Spring St.
New York, NY 10012-5800
ph: 212-219-1793
American prints, paintings and works on paper 1920s through 1940s.

Kenneth Newman
Old Print Shop, The
150 Lexington Ave. at 30th St.
New York, NY 10016
ph: 212-683-3950
fax: 212-779-8040
e-mail: info@oldprintshop.com
web: http://www.oldprintshop.com/
Wants 18th-20th century American prints; Currier & Ives, Endicott Hill, large folio American town views, marines, maps, historicals.

Sylvan Cole
Sylvan Cole Gallery
101 W. 57th St.
New York, NY 10019
ph: 212-333-7760
Specializes in buying and selling American prints from the period 1900-1970; a specialty area is James Abbott McNeil Whistler.

W. Graham Arader III
29 East 72nd St.
New York, NY 10021
ph: 212-628-3668
fax: 212-879-8714
e-mail: wgrahamaraderiii@email.msn.com
web: http://www.aradergalleries.com/
Buys & sells Audubon and other fine prints: Indians, natural history, sporting,, Currier & Ives, etc.; also maps, paintings and books; offices in Philadelphia, New York, San Francisco, and Houston.

George D. Glazer
28 East 72nd St.
New York, NY 10021
ph: 212-535-5706
fax: 212-988-3992
e-mail: worldglobe@aol.com
web: http://www.georgeglazer.com
Buys and sells antique prints: birds, botanicals, sporting (golf, tennis, skiing), architectural, fashion; works with interior designers and corporate art consultants.

Donald J. Bruckner
Bardon Antiques
37 August Lane
Hicksville, NY 11801-4419
ph: 516-931-5164
Wants to buy historical 19th century American lithographs; normally has 500-600 for sale.

Dr. Charles J. Semowich
Charles Semowich Fine Arts
242 Broadway
Rensselaer, NY 12144-2705
ph: 518-449-4756
e-mail: semowich@webtv.net
Buys and sells prints, especially American 20th century; also sells paintings and drawings.

Christopher W. Lane
Philadelphia Print Shop, Ltd., The
8441 Germantown Ave.
Philadelphia, PA 19118
ph: 215-242-4750
fax: 215-242-6977
e-mail: PhilaPrint@PhilaPrintShop.com
web: http://www.philaprintshop.com
Gallery of antique prints and maps with related rare books and atlases; also bookstore of reference books related to antique prints and maps; appraisals, paper conservation and restoration.

Barbara Dawson
P & C Art
3301 M St. NW
Washington, DC 20007
ph: 202-965-4630
Specializes in contemporary print artists; also carries the "Gum Shoe" line of polychrome ceramic figurines by Marcus Pierson.

Judith Blakely
Old Print Gallery, The
1220 31st St. NW
Washington, DC 20007-3422
ph: 202-965-1818
fax: 202-965-1869
e-mail: oldprintgallery@erols.com
web: http://www.oldprintgallery.com/
Wants antique prints: city views, historical scenes, Currier & Ives, Western, natural history, sporting, military and nautical scenes.

John Dupree
Creighton-Davis Gallery
3300 M St. NW
Washington, DC 20007-3513
ph: 202-333-3050
fax: 202-338-4470
Specializes in contemporary, old and modern print artists with national and international reputations.

art@home
4301 Massachusetts Ave., NW
Washington, DC 20016
ph: 202-364-0524
e-mail: villej@erols.com
web: http://www.art-at-home.com/
Carries prints from the Renaissance to present.

Monica Burdeshaw
Print Portfolio
4701 Sangamore Rd.
Bethesda, MD 20816
ph: 301-229-5800
Buys and sells fine prints.

Ray Moore
Heritage Historical Prints, Inc.
3772 Angelton Court
Burtonsville, MD 20866
ph: 301-890-4566 or 800-890-4566
fax: 301-890-5481
e-mail: hhpi@pop.erols.com
web: http://www.heritageprints.com/
Buys and sells 17th through 19th century prints; specializes in 17th through 19th century hand watercolored natural history lithographs; also offers restoration, conservation, framing, and documentation services.

Alan Bertaux
Framin' Place
10439 Stevenson Rd.
Stevenson, MD 21153
ph: 410-415-6666
e-mail: bertaux@erols.com
web: http://www.framin.com
Carries prints of the masters: Picasso, Miro, Matisse, Dali, etc.

Richard Kornemann
Museum Shop, Ltd.
20 N. Market St.
Frederick, MD 21701
ph: 301-695-0424 or 301-871-3855
fax: 301-698-5242
Specializes in Japanese ukiyoe woodblock prints, and 1930s era by Grant Wood, Whistler, T.H. Benton, WPA artists, etc.

David Allen
David Allen Fine Art
P.O. Box 5641
Arlington, VA 22205
Dealer and expert specializing in 19th & 20th century American prints.

Baldwin's Old Prints & Maps
P.O. Box 3515
Norfolk, VA 23514
ph: 757-625-1888
e-mail: maps@baldwinsmaps.com
web: http://www.baldwinsmaps.com/
Specializes in prints, maps and charts; U.S. Coast Survey charts, historical prints, biblical/religious maps, U.S. Civil War maps, etc.

John Sandberg
Yellowhouse Gallery
P.O. Box 554
2902 South Virginia Dare Trail
Nags Head, NC 27959
ph: 252-441-6928
e-mail: yelnag@pinn.net
web: http://
www.yellowhousegallery.com/
Established in 1969, offers a comprehensive collection of antique prints and maps; specialties are Civil War maps and prints; wood engravings by Winslow Homer, Thomas Nast and Frederic Remington; old orchids, birds, shells, fish prints.

Shirley & Al Bowers
Pablo Prints
206 Pablo Road
Ponte Vedra Beach, FL 32082
ph: 904-285-2962
e-mail: sbowers@aol.com
Specializes in McKenney & Hall prints, primarily Seminoles.

Robert Wieland
American Antique Prints
33 S. St. Andrews Dr.
Ormond Beach, FL 32174-3842
ph: 904-672-9972
fax: 904-677-7988
Member, American Historical Print Collectors Society.

National Wildlife Galleries
11000 Metro Parkway, Ste. 33
Fort Myers, FL 33912-1293
ph: 941-278-5665
fax: 941-936-2788
e-mail: art@artfinders.com
web: http://www.artlithos.com/
Specializes in highest quality quality wildlife art and non-wildlife limited edition prints and serigraphs: Thomas Kinkade, Bev Doolittle, Robert Bateman, Carl Benders, Charles Wysocki, Terry Redlin, Stephen Lyman and others.

Susan S. Pohle, ISA
Pigeon Creek Antiques
621 N. Main
Thiensville, WI 53092-1215
ph: 414-242-2054
Sells and appraises fine art prints, period furniture, lamps, toys, dolls.

Elaine Kwan
860 Cedar Lane
Northbrook, IL 60062-3538
ph: 847-564-1660 or 847-205-1459
fax: 847-564-1660
e-mail: elaine@artcollect.com
web: http://www.artcollect.com/
Buys and sells modern and contemporary art; resale; fine art appraiser; collections cataloging; member, Appraisers Association of America (AAA).

R. L. Butler, ISA
Galerie Vollard, Ltd.
P.O. Box 78155
Saint Louis, MO 63178-8155
ph: 314-773-3132
fax: 314-773-3132
Private dealer and appraiser in antique and contemporary prints: lithographs, etchings and silk-screens.

Sharon M. Gergen
Nostalgia Antiques
8141 Main
Kansas City, MO 64114-2401
ph: 816-361-7539
Buys and sells oil paintings, prints, illustrated books, pin-ups.

Jeff Measamer
Art Connections
8524 Highway 6 North, #258
Houston, TX 77095
ph: 281-861-0244
fax: 281-861-0266
e-mail:
ArtConnections@worldnet.att.net
web: http://www.houstonarts.com/
artconnections
Specializes in prints from 1750 to 1950.

Jeffery Measamer
Art Connections
8315 E. Copper Village Dr.
Houston, TX 77095
ph: 281-861-0244
fax: 281-861-0266
e-mail:
ArtConnections@worldnet.att.net
web: http://www.erols.com/villej/alldlr/
artconn/artconn.htm
Specialists in fine prints and drawings from 1750-1950; deals primarily in British prints and drawings; always has a wide selection of American and European works in stock.

Leila Lyons
Lyons Ltd. Antique PRints
75 Arbor Road
Menlo Park, CA 94025
ph: 650-325-9010 or 800-LYONS-LTD
fax: 650-325-8332
e-mail: lyonsltd@gte.net
web: http://www.dir-dd.com/lyons.html
Specializes in fine original etchings, engravings and lithographs dating from 1490 to 1920: botanicals, maps, city views, natural history, architecture, performing arts, fashion, and children's illustrations.

Priscilla Anne Lowry
Lowry-James Fine Antique Prints
P.O. Box 609
101 Athens
Langley, WA 98260
ph: 360-221-0477
fax: 360-221-0477
e-mail: fineprints@lowryjames.com
web: http://www.lowryjames.com/
Features Audubon, McKenney-Hall, Gould, George Brookshaw, Jane

Webb Loudon, botanical and ornithological prints, travel scenes, cartography, Native American portraiture.

Bruce Magnotti
Aesthetic Image
309 West Fifth Ave.
Ellensburg, WA 98926
ph: 509-962-5204
e-mail: aesthetic@tias.com
web: http://www.tias.com/stores/aesthetic/
Buys and sells rare prints, maps and illustrated books.

Elisabeth Legge
Elisabeth Legge Fine Antique Prints
37 Hazelton Ave.
Toronto, Canada M5R 2E3
Canada
ph: 416-972-1378
e-mail: elisl@netcom.ca
web: http://www.LeggePrints.com/
Specializes in and appraises original 15th through 19th century prints and manuscripts, specializing, but not restricted to, natural history; also offers traditional English framing and restoration.

W.D.J. Bennett
Postaprint
Taidswood House
Iver Heath, Bucks SL0 0PQ
U.K.
ph: +44 1 895 833 720
fax: +44 1 895 834 890
e-mail: Postaprint@btinternet.com
web: http://www.postaprint.co.uk/
Antique maps, prints, historic engravings, antiquarian atlases and books; has an online database of over 200,000 antique maps, steel, copper or wood engravings available for searching; items date from 1550 to 1899.

Experts

Joel Goleman
607 Chilton Hills Dr.
Elkins Park, PA 19027-1319
ph: 215-542-7700
e-mail: babsygo@webtv.net
Special interest in old master prints and Japanese woodblock prints; experienced as expert witness; teaches courses in print connoisseurship and curates print exhibitions.

William G. Hodges
Ridgefield, Inc.
12509 Patterson Ave.
Richmond, VA 23233-6414
ph: 703-768-6562
Specializes in buying and selling antique prints.

Misc. Services

Library of Congress, Prints & Photographs Reading Room
Library of Congress
James Madison Bldg., Rm LM-339
Washington, DC 20540-4730
ph: 202-707-6394 or 202-707-8000
e-mail: lcinfo@loc.gov
web: http://www.lcweb.loc.gov/rr/print/
Has a collection of over 13,000,000 images: prints, photographs, drawings, posters, and architectural and engineering drawings.

Wendy Reaves, Cur.
National Portrait Gallery
Prints & Drawings
8th & F Streets N.W.
Washington, DC 20560
ph: 202-357-1356 or 202-357-1633
e-mail: npgweb@npg.si.edu
web: http://www.npg.si.edu
Will authenticate prints & drawings brought in for inspection; make an appointment first; may be able to work from good photographs.

Gordon's Art Reference, Inc.
Price Guide: Gordon's Print Price Annual
306 West Coronado Rd.
Phoenix, AZ 85003
ph: 602-253-6948 or 800-892-4622
fax: 602-253-2104
e-mail: info@gordonart.com
web: http://www.gordonart.com
Print values: 1,400 pages of facts, figures, descriptions, prices; 37,000 actual prices realized; now on CD-ROM.

Museums/Libraries

Museum of Prints & Printmaking
P.O. Box 6578
Albany, NY 12206-0578
ph: 518-432-9514
e-mail: pcaprint@crisny.org
web: http://crisny.org/not-for-profit/pcaprint/index.htm
Shares space with the Print Club of Albany; open by appointment.

Periodicals

Newspaper: Journal of the Print World
1008 Winona Rd.
Meredith, NH 03253
ph: 603-279-6479
fax: 603-279-1337
A quarterly newspaper with articles, advertising and classifieds focusing on antique and contemporary prints and artists; features articles, ads, auction results, show reviews, calendar of events.

Journal: Art On Paper
39 E 78th St., #501
New York, NY 10021-0213
ph: 212-988-5959
fax: 212-988-6107
e-mail: info@artonpaper.com
web: http://www.artonpaper.com
Published bi-monthly; only international art magazine dedicated to works on paper; renowned for its coverage of prints, drawings, and photography.

Denis C. Jackson, Ed.
Newsletter: Illustrator Collector's News, The
P.O. Box 1958
Sequim, WA 98382-1958
ph: 360-452-3810
e-mail: ticn@olypen.com
web: http://www.olypen.com/ticn/
A bi-monthly publication for collectors of magazines and other paper illustrations; free classifieds for subscribers; send LSASE for information; new and old prints.

Repair Services

Robert Kipp
Art & Old Print Restorations
20 Macerick St.
Marblehead, MA 01945
ph: 781-639-7747
e-mail: robkipp@oldprints.com
web: http://www.oldprints.com
Print sales and restorations; specializing in 19th century prints.

George J. Cohenour
4301 Beaumont Rd.
Dover, PA 17315-2405
ph: 717-292-5345
Cleans, deacidifies, repairs and restores prints: American historical, antique and decorative, handcolored lithographs, chromolithographs, etchings, engravings, watercolors, etc.

Suppliers

Cronite Co., The
120 East Halsey Rd.
P.O. Box 6330
Parsippany, NJ 07054
ph: 973-887-7900
fax: 973-887-0015
e-mail: info@cronite.com
web: http://www.cronite.com/
Suppliers to engravers, etchers, and print makers for 100 years; plate printing inks and oils, steel/copper/zinc/brass plates, pantograph machines and supplies, etching acids/acid resists, photoengraving supplies, engraving tools.

Audubon

Dealers

Peter D. Cowen
225 Riverview Ave.
Waltham, MA 02466-1358
ph: 617-965-1985
fax: 617-965-1211
Wants to buy museum-quality Havell edition Audubon prints.

Bob Bascom
Bob Bascom Prints
P.O. Box 4327
Burlington, VT 05406
ph: 802-893-4082
Wants Audubon original prints; also other medium or large 19th century American prints.

Ed Kenney
Audubon Prints & Books
9720 Spring Ridge Ln.
Vienna, VA 22182-1449
ph: 703-759-5567 or 202-484-3334
Buys & sells natural history prints and books by John James Audubon; also prints by Wilson, Gould, Catesby, Bodmer, Catlin and others.

Taylor Clark
Taylor Clark Gallery
2623 Government St.
Baton Rouge, LA 70806-5408
ph: 225-383-4929
fax: 225-383-3043
Specializes in 18th, 19th, and 20th century oil paintings, watercolors, and prints, especially all editions of Audubon prints.

Museums/Libraries

John James Audubon State Park & Museum
P.O. Box 576
Henderson, KY 42419
ph: 270-826-2247 or 270-827-1893
fax: 270-826-2286
e-mail: jaudubon@henderson.net
web: http://go-henderson.com/audubon.htm
The world's largest gathering of John James Audubon memorabilia and one of the most extensive collections of his work in the world; four galleries present his life, work and legacy.

Cupid

Clubs/Associations

Juanita Ingles
Cupid Collectors Club
Newsletter: Cupid Capers
2116 Lincoln St.
Cedar Falls, IA 50613-3274
ph: 319-266-9902 or 319-273-8410
fax: 319-266-9902
e-mail: ingles@cedarnet.org
web: http://members.tripod.com/~CupidClub/Index-2.html
Purpose of this club is to promote the appreciation of Cupid prints of all types including the M.B. Parkinson

"Cupid Awake and Cupid Asleep" print.

Collectors

Cindy & Jerry Youngquist
P.O. Box 91
Gowrie, IA 50543

Juanita Ingles
2116 Lincoln St.
Cedar Falls, IA 50613-3274
ph: 319-266-9902 or 319-273-8410
fax: 319-266-9902
e-mail: ingles@cedarnet.org
web: http://members.tripod.com/~CupidClub/Index-2.html

Glen Tull
402 W. Montgomery
Creston, IA 50801
ph: 515-782-2335

Currier & Ives

Dealers

Bob Bascom
Bob Bascom Prints
P.O. Box 4327
Burlington, VT 05406
ph: 802-893-4082
Wants Currier and Ives original prints; also other medium or large 19th century American prints.

Donald J. Bruckner
Bardon Antiques
37 August Lane
Hicksville, NY 11801-4419
ph: 516-931-5164
Wants to buy historical 19th century American lithographs; normally has 500-600 for sale; especially interested in Currier & Ives.

George J. Cohenour
4301 Beaumont Rd.
Dover, PA 17315-2405
ph: 717-292-5345
Buys and sells original Currier & Ives lithographs; carries large selection and offers a free list; also offers cleaning and restoration service.

Robert Wieland
American Antique Prints
33 S. St. Andrews Dr.
Ormond Beach, FL 32174-3842
ph: 904-672-9972
fax: 904-677-7988
A dedicated collector and dealer in Currier & Ives prints for over 30 years; also buys & sells Kurz & Allison, and McKenny-Hall prints; quarterly itemized lists of prints available.

Experts

John & Barbara Rudisill
Rudisill's Alt Print Haus
P.O. Box 199
Worton, MD 21678-0199
ph: 410-778-9290
fax: 410-778-9310
Buys and sells original Currier & Ives prints; have written articles on the history of Currier & Ives and on identifying reproductions; send SASE for free list.

Museums/Libraries

Bob Shamis
Museum of the City of New York
1220 5th Ave.
New York, NY 10029-5221
ph: 212-534-1672
fax: 212-534-5974
e-mail: mcny@mcny.org
web: http://www.mcny.org/mcny/
Access by appointment; research fee charged.

Repair Services

Robert Kipp
Art & Old Print Restorations
20 Macerick St.
Marblehead, MA 01945
ph: 781-639-7747
e-mail: robkipp@oldprints.com
web: http://www.oldprints.com
A noted expert and authority on Currier & Ives prints; cleans, restores and conserves prints for clients throughout the U.S.; send for brochure; author of "Currier's Price Guide to Currier & Ives Prints."

Dali

Appraisers

Jerry Bengis, ISA
9860 SW 122nd St.
Miami, FL 33176-4928
ph: 305-232-1143
fax: 305-251-1450
e-mail: yascha7@netrox.net
Fine art appraiser specializing in prints (especially Salvador Dali), graphics (Miro, Chagall, Picasso, Warhol), etchings, engravings, prints, bronzes.

Bernard Ewell, ASA
Bernard Ewell Art Appraisals
318 E. Cache La Poudre
Colorado Springs, CO 80903-2905
ph: 719-632-5035 or 800-884-3254
fax: 719-633-0959
International expert on all Salvador Dali artworks.

Dealers

Janice King
Salvador Dali Gallery, The/Brana Fine Art Inc.
15332 Antioch St., Ste. 108
Pacific Palisades, CA 90272
ph: 310-459-8883 or 800-275-3254
fax: 310-454-2090

Experts

Albert Field
Salvador Dali Archives, The
2020 29th St.
Astoria, NY 11105
ph: 718-274-0407

Museums/Libraries

Joan R. Kropf, Curator
Salvador Dali Museum, The
Newsletter: Salvador Dali Museum Newsletter
1000 Third St. South
Saint Petersburg, FL 33701
ph: 727-823-3767 or 800-442-DALI
fax: 727-894-6068
e-mail: daliweb@mindspring.com
web: http://www.daliweb.com/
Permanent home to the world's most comprehensive collection of works exclusively by the late SPanish surrealist, Salvador Dali; 94 original oils, over 100 watercolors and drawings, holograms, objects of art and photographs.

French Boudoir

Dealers

Clifford P. Catania
David Chase Gallery
518 Kimberton Road
Phoenixville, PA 19460
ph: 610-917-1167
web: http://www.davidchase.net/
Wants Icart-like etchings by Ablett, Grellet, Felix, Helleu, Milliere, Robbe, Hardy, Meunier, etc.

Icart

Collectors

Adrienne Leff
1550 S Dixie Hwy. #210
Coral Gables, FL 33146-3034
ph: 305-667-4214
fax: 305-668-2592
Buys, sell and collects original Louis Icart etchings, oils and complete books.

Dr. Neil Superfon
2121 W. Indian School Rd.
Phoenix, AZ 85015-4908
ph: 602-277-1449 or 800-258-0216
fax: 602-263-8523
e-mail: npsuperdern@worldnet.att.net
Wants to buy Icart etchings.

Paul Kelly
24672 Belgreen Place
Lake Forest, CA 92630
ph: 949-770-1483
fax: 949-770-1483
Buys, sells and collects Louis Icart etchings, oils, and illustrated books.

Dealers

Edward J. Meschi
129 Pinyard Rd.
Monroeville, NJ 08343-1870
ph: 609-358-7293
fax: 609-358-7789
e-mail: emfinearts@yahoo.com
Buys and sells Louis Icart etchings, illustrated books, and oil paintings.

Clifford P. Catania
David Chase Gallery
518 Kimberton Road
Phoenixville, PA 19460
ph: 610-917-1167
web: http://www.davidchase.net/
Buys and sells original Icart etchings; assisting major collectors. Author of "Complete Etchings of Louis Icart" (1990-Schiffer Pub.)

Debra Freer
Freer & Associates, Fine Art & Antiques
P.O. Box 98327
Atlanta, GA 30359-2027
ph: 404-321-6369
fax: 404-636-8531
e-mail: DFreer@netscape.net
web: http://www.artnet.com/Freer/html
Buys and sells original Icart etchings, artwork and illustrated books; publishes quarterly newsletter "The Louis Icart Collector" which is available for $10/yr.

Experts

Carole Hibel
Art & Antiques
131-B Broadview Road
Woodstock, NY 12498
ph: 914-679-2966 or 800-426-3357
fax: 914-679-9101
Wants to buy Louis Icart etchings and paintings.

Bill Holland
William Holland Fine Arts
1554 Paoli Pike
West Chester, PA 19380
ph: 610-344-9848
fax: 610-344-06651
e-mail: bill@hollandarts.com
web: http://www.hollandarts.com/
Buys and sells Louis Icart etchings, oils and illustrated books; co-author of "Louis Icart - The Complete Etchings"; call for details or to order.

P. Bruce Marine
Cherub Antiques Gallery
2918 M. St. NW
Washington, DC 20007-3713
ph: 202-337-2224
fax: 202-337-2224
Nationally known author of articles, and leading expert in original Louis Icart etchings; also wants etchings and pastels by Paul Cesar Helleu.

Leroy Neiman

Dealers

Ralph Olsen
Hammer Graphics Gallery
33 W. 57th St.
New York, NY 10019
ph: 212-644-4405

Vanity Fair (Spy)

Collectors

Paul Davis
308 Landsende Rd.
Devon, PA 19333
ph: 610-644-1216
Wants Vanity Fair "Spy" caricature prints.

Ken Taylor
11661 San Vicente, #3304
Los Angeles, CA 90049-5110
ph: 310-442-0054 or 310-207-4345
fax: 310-826-6934
e-mail: ktscicon@ix.netcom.com
Wants to buy original Vanity Fair lithographs ("Spy" prints) published in England from 1869 to 1913.

Wallace Nutting

Collectors

Bob & Pam Franscella
2944 Ivanhoe Glen
Madison, WI 53711
ph: 608-274-4506
e-mail: franscella@aol.com

Jim & Sharon Eckert
P.O. Box 62
Anchor, IL 61720-0062
ph: 309-723-4241
e-mail: anchorsb@dave-world.net
Wants Wallace Nutting, Bessie Pease Gutmann prints.

Wildlife

Museums/Libraries

American Museum of Natural History
Central Park West & 79th St.
New York, NY 10024
ph: 212-769-5100
e-mail: webmaster@amnh.org
web: http://www.amnh.org/

Woodblock

Dealers

Steven Thomas
Steven Thomas, Inc.
P.O. Box 41
Woodstock, VT 05091-0041
ph: 802-457-1764 or 800-781-8028
fax: 802-457-1764
e-mail: stinc@sover.net
Dealer/expert wants to buy American, European and Canadian woodblock prints from 1895-1950; color or black and white; interested in strong images by major and minor artists alike; write for free 4 page illustrated want list.

Woodblock (American)

Dealers

Peter Falk
P. Hastings Falk, Inc.
859 Boston Post Rd.
P.O. Box 833
Madison, CT 06443
ph: 203-245-2246
fax: 203-245-5116
e-mail: info@folkart.com
Buys and sells color woodblock prints by American artists; 1890s to 1920s.

Woodblock (Jacoulet)

Auction Services

John H. Schofield
Eldred's
P.O. Box 796
East Dennis, MA 02641-0796
ph: 508-385-3116
fax: 508-385-7201
e-mail: eldreds@capecod.net
web: http://www.eldreds.com/
Specializes in the sale of 20th century Japanese-style woodblock prints by artist Paul Jacoulet.

Woodblock (Japanese)

(see also ART, Oriental; ORIENTALIA)

Auction Services

Paul Knuston
Asian Collection
4397 John's Point Rd.
Gloucester, VA 23061
ph: 800-693-2154 or 804-693-2154
fax: 804-693-2154
e-mail: asiancol@inna.net
web: http://www.woodblockprint.com
Offers over 100 18th and 19th century woodblock prints for sale on a bimonthly auction; full color catalog.

Yorie Ishihara
Ukiyo-E World GmbH
Johann Sebastian Bach Str. 11
Pullach, Bavaria 82049
Germany
ph: ++49-(0)89-79367709
fax: ++49-(0)89-79367708
e-mail: info@ukiyo-e-world.com
web: http://www.ukiyo-e-world.com/
An internet site for collectors of high quality Japanese woodblock prints; monthly online auction, gallery, forum, reference articles, links, Japanese calendar, newsletter by email.

Clubs/Associations

Rosemary Torre, Pres.
Ukiyo-E Society of America, Inc.
Newsletter: President's Newsletter
FDR Station
P.O. Box 665
New York, NY 10150-0665
Promotes the study/appreciation of Japanese woodblock prints through monthly meetings, seminars & exhibitions; also publishes Journal.

Collectors

John Clement
36 Oakwood Ave.
Fitchburg, MA 01420-7421
ph: 978-345-5863
Collector and expert; special interests include worldwide master works of art, particularly works on paper, including Japanese woodblock prints; also fine paintings.

Bob Vargas
P.O. Box 1284
Los Altos, CA 94023
ph: 650-949-3959
Wants 20th century and older Japanese woodblock prints.

Dave McClean
P.O. Box 8110-739
Blaine, WA 98230
ph: 604-882-9050
e-mail: dmcclean@home.com
web: http://members.home.net/dmcclean/prints.html
Specializes in contemporary 20th century Japanese woodblock prints; website includes a brief overview of shin hanga, sosaku hanga and contemporary Japanese prints; also a bibliography and list of relevant links.

Dealers

Valerie Zakszewski
61 6th St.
Cambridge, MA 02141
ph: 800-897-2933 or 617-576-0796
e-mail: valerie-z@mediaone.net
Specializes in works of art on paper.

Thomas J. Urso
Akitsu Gallery
P.O. Box 1762
Attleboro, MA 02703
ph: 508-223-3874
e-mail: akitsug@tiac.net
web: http://www.akitsugallery.com
Buys and sells fine Japanese woodblock prints.

Jane Allinson
Allinson Gallery, Inc.
P.O. Box 646
Storrs, CT 06268-2022
ph: 860-429-2322
fax: 860-429-2825
e-mail: allinson@neca.com
web: http://www.allinsongallery.com
Buys and sells 19th and 20th century Japanese woodblock prints.

Roni Neuer
Ronin Gallery
605 Madison Ave.
New York, NY 10022
ph: 212-688-0188
fax: 212-593-9808
e-mail: ronin@japancollection.com
web: http://www.japancollection.com/
Specializes in Japanese woodblock prints and publishes catalogs on specialty artists.

John Bradley
John Bradley Gallery
1020 Burlingham Rd.
Pine Bush, NY 12566
ph: 914-744-3642
Buys and sells Japanese woodblock prints.

Gilbert Luber Gallery
1220 Walnut St.
Philadelphia, PA 19107-5466
ph: 215-732-2996
fax: 610-546-2210
Specializes in Japanese woodblock prints; also carries general books on Japanese prints and art.

Shogun Gallery, Inc.
P.O. Box 5300
Gaithersburg, MD 20882
ph: 301-948-0899 or 800-926-4255
fax: 301-208-0725
e-mail: shogungallery@shogungallery.com
web: http://www.shoguninc.com
One of the largest dealers of original, museum-quality Japanese woodblock prints in the US; selection spans three centuries; website contains discussions about Japanese prints, exhibition schedule, price lists.

William Stein
Floating World Gallery
P.O. Box 148200
Chicago, IL 60614
ph: 312-587-7800
fax: 312-587-7888
e-mail: artwork@floatingworld.com
web: http://www.floatingworld.com
Seeking Japanese paintings and prints; antique to the present.

Richard Waldman
Art of Japan, The
P.O. Box 507
Mountain View, CA 94042-0507
ph: 650-964-4464 or 888-570-4464
fax: 650-964-9310
e-mail: rwaldman@theartofjapan.com
web: http://www.theartofjapan.com
Japanese print dealer specializing in 18th, 19th, and 20th century prints; Ukiyo-E, Shin Hanga and Sosaku Hanga; with emphasis on Shin Hanga and 19th century Ukiyo-E.

Elizabeth Danechild
Ukiyo-E Gallery
4736 Seventeenth St.
San Francisco, CA 94117-4329
ph: 415-731-5971
fax: 415-753-3415
Buys and sells Japanese color woodblock prints from the 18th to early 20th centuries; by appointment.

Peter Gilder
Arts & Designs of Japan
P.O. Box 22075
San Francisco, CA 94122
ph: 415-759-6233
fax: 415-759-9017
e-mail: gilder@best.com
web: http://www.artsanddesignsjapan.com/
Specialist in fine 17th through 20th century Japanese woodblock prints since 1973; buys, sells and appraises.

Carolyn Staley
Carolyn Staley Fine Prints
313 First Ave. South
Seattle, WA 98104-2505
ph: 206-621-1888
fax: 206-325-9047
Buys and sells fine Japanese woodblock prints, 16th - 20th century master prints, and decorative prints and maps.

G. C. Uhlenbeck
Hotei Japanese Prints
Breestraat 113a
CL Leiden, 23211
The Netherlands
ph: (071) 514 35 52/512 44 59
fax: (071) 514 14 88/512 38 55
e-mail: ukiyoe@xs4all.nl
web: http://www.nvva.nl/hotei/
Fine Japanese prints, paintings and illustrated books by appointment.

Experts

Paul R. Schweitzer
Schweitzer Japanese Prints, Inc.
6313 Lenox Rd.
Bethesda, MD 20817-6023
ph: 301-229-6574
fax: 301-229-0345
e-mail: olvino@earthlink.net
Buys, sells, appraises antique Japanese woodblock prints as well as contemporary Japanese graphics including woodblocks, etchings, etc.; also sells books about Japanese culture and graphics.

Internet Resources

Yorie Ishihara
Ukiyo-E World GmbH
Johann Sebastian Bach Str. 11
Pullach, Bavaria 82049
Germany
ph: ++49-(0)89-79367709
fax: ++49-(0)89-79367708
e-mail: info@ukiyo-e-world.com
web: http://www.ukiyo-e-world.com/
An internet site for collectors of high quality Japanese woodblock prints; monthly online auction, gallery, forum, reference articles, links, Japanese calendar, newsletter by email.

Hans Olof Johansson
Ukiyo-E: The Pictures of the Floating World
Sweden
e-mail: secutor@bahnhof.se
web: http://www.bahnhof.se/~secutor/ukiyo-e/
Website has lots of links to other Ukiyo-E (Japanese woodblock print) sites, and other sites relating to Japan and its culture and art.

Museums/Libraries

Honolulu Academy of Arts
900 S. Beretania St.
Honolulu, HI 96814-1495
ph: 808-532-88701 or 808-532-8700
e-mail: webmaster@honoluluacademy.org
web: http://www.honoluluacademy.org/
An encyclopedic museum of world art.

Yard-Long

Collectors

Al Little
151 Highway 173
Antioch, IL 60002
ph: 847-395-7752
fax: 847-395-7703
Buys and sells yard-long prints.

Sherry & Mike Miller
303 Holiday Dr. #130
Tuscola, IL 61953-2118
ph: 217-253-4991
e-mail: miller@tuscola.net
web: http://www.tuscola.net/~miller/
Wants to buy yard-long lithograph prints; only of lovely ladies dressed in 1900-1920s fashions; some have been trimmed to fit smaller frames; some have artist's name on front; most have advertising and small calendar on back.

Dealers

Kathy Wilkins
K.W.'s Antiques
1181 Stelzer Rd.
Howell, MI 48843
ph: 517-552-0012 or 517-548-9346
e-mail: kwilkins@livingonline.com
Calendar advertising distributed to consumers from the early 1900s to the 1920s are known as Yard-Long prints; these beautiful lithography prints are in a multitude of subjects ranging from polar bears to Victorian ladies.

Experts

Bill & June Keagy
Those Wonderful Yard-Long Prints & More
P.O. Box 106
Bloomfield, IN 47424-0106
ph: 812-384-3471
fax: 812-384-8824
e-mail: billjune@custom.com
Co-authors of the yard-long books, "Those Wonderful Yard-Long Prints and More" (1989), "More Wonderful Yard-Long Prints" (1992), and "Yard-Long Prints" Book III (1995); available from the author.

Charles & Joan Rhoden
Rhoden's Antiques
8693 N 1950 East Road
Georgetown, IL 61846-6264
ph: 217-662-8046 or 217-662-8440
fax: 217-662-8223
Buys and collects yard-long prints; co-author of "Those Wonderful Yard-Long Prints," Books I, II and III which are available from the author.

PRINTS (MODERN)

(see also ART; COLLECTIBLES [MODERN]; PRINTS)

Dealers

Tom & Rosemarie Prendergast
Pelican Art Galleries & Framers
One Nasturtium Ave.
Glenwood, NJ 07418
ph: 973-764-7149 or 561-283-6813
fax: 561-283-6813
Focuses on the collectible conservation prints, Duck Prints, equine prints, sport prints autographed by artist and player, and signed & numbered limited prints; deals with the secondary market

Allen's Creations, Inc. - Frame & Art Gallery
P.O. Box 452
Clemson, SC 29633-0452
ph: 864-654-3594 or 800-669-2731
e-mail: aci@innova.net
web: http://www.allenscreations.com/

National Wildlife Galleries
11000 Metro Parkway, Ste. 32
Fort Myers, FL 33912-1293
ph: 941-275-0500 or 800-DUCK-ART
fax: 941-936-2788
e-mail: stamps@nationalwildlife.com
web: http://www.nationalwildlife.com
Offers a large selection of Federal, State, International, and Junior Duck Stamps; also offers Federal, State, International and Junior Duck Stamp Prints.

Art Brokerage, Inc.
P.O. Box 3730
Ketchum, ID 83340
ph: 208-788-1484 or 208-788-1491
fax: 208-788-1492
e-mail: drose@earthlink.net
web: http://www.artbrokerage.com/
Buy and sell art including prints and sculpture on the internet.

Jonathan Farrow
Media Group, The
7510 W. Sunset Blvd., #553
Los Angeles, CA 90024
ph: 323-661-3382
e-mail: jfarrow@fineartsite.com
web: http://www.FineArtSite.com
Limited edition prints, original paintings, sculpture: Erte, Dali, Haring, Hockney, Indiana, Liechtenstein, Miro, Motherwell, Picasso, Rosenquist, Vasarely, Warhol, Hart, Kostabi, Max, Neiman, Rockwell, Yamagata.

Nielsen's Art
731 N. Columbia Ctr. #122
Kennewick, WA 99336
ph: 509-735-9420
fax: 509-783-4518
e-mail: nielsenj@nielsensart.com
web: http://www.nielsensart.com/
Advertises that they can get any limited edition print every done.

Man./Prod./Dist.

Greenwich Workshop, Inc.
1 Greenwich Place
Shelton, CT 06484-4618
ph: 203-925-0131
fax: 203-925-0262
web: http://www.greenwichworkshop.com/
Publishes aviation, Western, and fantasy art in limited edition print form.

Periodicals

Magazine: InformArt
204 Playhouse Corner
Southbury, CT 06488
ph: 203-262-9221 or 800-906-9600
fax: 203-262-9225
e-mail: westtown@wtco.net
A quarterly magazine focusing on modern limited edition prints (signed & numbered); ads, articles, new releases, secondary market values.

Magazine: Art Business News
270 Madison Ave.
New York, NY 10016-0601
web: http://www.artbusinessnews.com/
Focuses on the contemporary photoreproduction print market and the business aspect of art and framing, but includes timely information on tax changes and laws, as well as analysis of markets.

Magazine: Decor
330 N. Fourth St.
Saint Louis, MO 63102
ph: 314-421-5445 or 800-280-5445
fax: 314-421-1070
e-mail: decor@cpcmags.com
web: http://www.decomagazine.com/
Aimed at the frame shop/gallery owner; lots of articles about how to increase sales, gallery floor plans, advertising; occasionally covers some new trend in print making; also published annual Sources issues.

Adolf Sehring

Man./Prod./Dist.

American Artist Portfolio, Inc.
9625 Tetley Dr.
Somerset, VA 22972-2407
ph: 800-842-4445 or 540-672-0400
fax: 540-672-0286
Founded in 1988 to publish and market the works of realist artist Adolf Sehring.

Barbara Hails

Man./Prod./Dist.

Hails Fine Art
18319 Georgia Ave.
Olney, MD 20832-1435
ph: 301-774-6249 or 800-451-6411
Produces limited edition fine prints based on the pastels and oils of artist Barbara Hails; recently introduced canvas lithographs of her distinctive art.

Diane Graebner

Clubs/Associations

Diane Graebner Collector's Club
Newsletter: Diane Graebner Collector's Club Newsletter
P.O. Box 174
Millersburg, OH 44654-0174
ph: 800-626-4306
fax: 330-674-6666
e-mail: dgraebner@aol.com
Limited edition, paper prints depicting the Amish lifestyle.

Man./Prod./Dist.

Diane & Ted Graebner
Lynn's Prints
P.O. Box 174
Millersburg, OH 44654-0174
ph: 800-626-4306
fax: 330-674-6666
e-mail: dgraebner@aol.com
Producer of limited edition prints by Diane Graebner which depict Amish living.

Fred Stone

Man./Prod./Dist.

American Artists
66 Poppasquash Rd.
Bristol, RI 02809
ph: 800-828-0086 or 401-254-1191
fax: 401-254-8881
e-mail: american_art@ids.net

Jody Bergsma

Man./Prod./Dist.

Jody Bergsma Galleries
1344 King St.
Bellingham, WA 98226-6224
ph: 360-733-1101 or 800-237-4762
e-mail: bergsma@bergsma.com
web: http://www.bergsma.com/
Publishes and markets the works of artist Jody Bergsma.

Marty Bell

Clubs/Associations

Marty Bell Collector's Society
Newsletter: Sounds of Bells, The
9550 Owensmouth Ave.
Chatsworth, CA 91311-4801
ph: 818-700-0754 or 800-637-4537
fax: 818-709-7668
e-mail: info@martybell.com
web: http://www.martybell.com/
Focuses on the collectible prints of English thatched, tiled and slate roof cottages by Marty Bell.

Man./Prod./Dist.

Marty Bell Fine Art, Inc.
9550 Owensmouth Ave.
Chatsworth, CA 91311-4801
ph: 818-700-0754 or 800-637-4537
fax: 818-709-7668
e-mail: info@martybell.com
web: http://www.martybell.com/
Publishes limited edition lithographs from the original paintings of Marty Bell.

Thomas Kinkade

Clubs/Associations

Thomas Kinkade Collectors' Society, c/o Lightpost Publishing
Newsletter: Thomas Kinkade Collectors' Society Newsletter
521 Charcot Ave.
San Jose, CA 95131
ph: 408-324-2020 or 800-366-3733
fax: 408-232-4822
e-mail: customer_service@mediaarts.com
web: http://www.thomaskinkade.com/collector/society.shtml
Canvas lithographs and luminous archival paper prints.

Man./Prod./Dist.

Lightpost Publishing, Inc.
521 Charcot Ave.
San Jose, CA 95131
ph: 408-324-2020 or 800-366-3733
fax: 408-232-4822
e-mail: customer_service@mediaarts.com
web: http://www.thomaskinkade.com/
Widely known in the limited edition print field for its publishing of fine art prints by artist Thomas Kinkade.

PRISON RELATED ITEMS

(see LAW ENFORCEMENT MEMORABILIA)

PRISONER-OF-WAR ART

Straw

Dealers

Lucille Malitz
Lucid Antiques
P.O. Box KH
Scarsdale, NY 10583
ph: 914-636-7825 or 914-636-5171
fax: 914-636-7825
e-mail: kromscope@aol.com
Imprisoned by the British, French prisoners of war escaped boredom by fashioning ingenious items made of straw or ivory.

PROGRAMS

(see MOVIE MEMORABILIA; PAPER COLLECTIBLES; SPORTS COLLECTIBLES)

PROHIBITION ITEMS

(see also BREWERIANA; PERSONALITIES [CRIMINAL]; POLITICAL COLLECTIBLES; SALOON & BAR COLLECTIBLES; WHISKEY INDUSTRY ITEMS)

Clubs/Associations

Earl F. Dodge
Partisan Prohibition Historical Society
Newsletter: National Statesman, The
P.O. Box 2635
Denver, CO 80201
ph: 303-572-0646 or 303-237-4947
fax: 303-233-2099
e-mail: earldodge@home.com
web: http://www.prohibition.org/
Wants to buy all Prohibition related items

Collectors

Cary Demont
P.O. Box 16013
Minneapolis, MN 55416
ph: 612-522-0957
e-mail: Caryd8@aol.com
Wants early Prohibition, Temperance, and Carrie Nation related items; early badges, pins, postcards, posters, broadsides, banners, etc.

Dealers

Bob Lucian
33 Merritts Road
Farmingdale, NY 11735-1820
ph: 516-293-3927
e-mail: bbluc@erols.net
Buys and sells old pre-prohibition American beer items: mugs, steins, advertising signs, bottle openers, match safes, glasses, "giveaways", etc.; prefers items from the NYC and L.I. area; also wants prohibition items; call collect.

PROMOTERS

(see ANTIQUES SHOW PROMOTERS)

PROPHYLACTICS

Tins

Collectors

Bob Weissman
Neat Olde Things
P.O. Box 163
Stewartsville, NJ 08886
ph: 908-479-6494
fax: 908-479-1135
Wants condom tins in excellent condition.

Dennis & George
323 Sandpiper Lane
Delray Beach, FL 33483-7135
ph: 561-243-3072
Wants condom tins, especially Rough Rider, 3 Pirates, Akron Tourist Tubes.

Michael Dusek
1058 Lupin Dr. #5
Salinas, CA 93906
ph: 831-757-2526
Wants prophylactic/condom tins: Sphinx, Chariots, Napoleons, Carmen, etc.; also wants related advertising.

Experts

George Goehring
Dennis & George Collectibles
3407 Lake Montebello Dr.
Baltimore, MD 21218
ph: 410-889-3964
e-mail: dandgtins@aol.com
Co-author with Dennis O'Brien of "Remember Your Rubbers."

Vending Machines

Collectors

Mr. Condom
1635 Acorn Ano Rd.
Somerset, KY 42501
ph: 606-274-4848
e-mail: kyfarm@gte.net
Buys/sells collectible prophylactic and

feminine hygiene vending equipment and related items.

PSYCHEDELIC ITEMS

(see SOCIAL CAUSES, Hippie Items)

PUB JUGS

(see SALOON & BAR COLLECTIBLES, Whiskey Pitchers)

PUPPETS

(see also PERFORMING ARTS; VENTRILOQUIST ITEMS)

Clubs/Associations

Puppetry Guild of Greater Kansas City
Newsletter: PGGKC Newsletter
11711 Markham Rd.
Independence, MO 64052
ph: 816-252-7248
Send SASE for price list of Hazelle parts available.

Gayle Schluter
Puppeteers of America, Inc.
Magazine: Puppetry Journal
#5 Cricklewood Path
Pasadena, CA 91107-1002

Ontario Puppetry Association
Newsletter: Ontario Puppetry Association Newsletter
11 Arch Road
Mississaugua, Ontario L5M 1M4
Canada
ph: 905-826-7541
e-mail: webmaster@onpuppet.org
web: http://www.onpuppet.org/
Members include professional puppet performers and makers, collectors, and puppet enthusiasts.

Collectors

Andy Gross
P.O. Box 6134
Beverly Hills, CA 90212-1134
ph: 310-362-4372 or 818-765-1305
fax: 310-820-3308
e-mail: apedoll69@aol.com
web: http://www.lamagictoy.com/
Wants ventriloquist dummies and or any related items such as puppets, toys, games, photos, books, marionettes, and old pro & toy dummies, i.e. Jerry Mahoney, Knucklehead Smiff, Charlie McCarthy, Mortimer Snerd, Danny O'Day, Farfel, etc.

Experts

Bob Isaacson
1002 Clinton
Oak Park, IL 60304-1824
ph: 708-383-5646
Wants to buy professional ventriloquist figures and wooden dummies used by professional stage performers; please send photo.

Museums/Libraries

Bread & Puppet Museum
P.O. Box 153
Glover, VT 05839
ph: 802-525-3031
A large collection of gigantic puppets, masks and related graphics and paintings.

Library & Museum of the Performing Arts, Shelby Cullom Davis Museum
40 Lincoln Center Plaza
New York, NY 10023-7498
ph: 212-870-1630
e-mail: performingarts@nypl.org
web: http://www.nypl.org/research/lpa/lpa.html

Center for Puppetry Arts Museum
1404 Spring Street
Atlanta, GA 30309
ph: 404-873-3089
fax: 404-873-9907
web: http://www.puppet.org/museum.html
Library, videos, educational programs, exhibits, publications.

PURSES

(see also BEADS; CLOTHING & ACCESSORIES, Vintage; COMPACTS; DRESSER ITEMS)

Clubs/Associations

Molly Klumpfell
California Purse Collector's Club
Newsletter: California Purse Collectors' Club Newsletter
P.O. Box 572
Campbell, CA 95009
ph: 408-866-6250
Members from across the US learn how to collect antique purses, store them, identify styles/type/quality; historical info on pre-1940 purses; holds meetings to swap and sell in the San Francisco area.

Collectors

Kathy Glaeser
142 Cimarand Drive
Williamsville, NY 14221
ph: 716-639-7934
e-mail: ibuypurses@aol.com
Wants to buy Victorian era beaded purses with scenes, people, animals, Egyptian motifs, fine florals, jeweled frames, etc.; also wants White & Davis and Mandalian colored mesh purses, as well as fine petitpoint bags and unusual frames.

Lydia M. Jackson-Fryer
608 Winans Way
Baltimore, MD 21229-1430
ph: 410-233-6231
fax: 410-233-6231
e-mail: lcfryer@erols.com
Wants to buy antique purses: mesh, beaded, Bakelite, cloth, leather.

Ada Lyons
P.O. Box 190
Saint Augustine, FL 32085-0190
ph: 904-824-9588
e-mail: amoebus102@aol.com
Wants to buy vintage beaded purses and enamel mesh purses: Mandalian, Whiting & Davis bags, or unsigned purses.

Vallerie Roberts Shutterly
Victorian Touch
P.O. Box 4
Micanopy, FL 32667
ph: 352-466-4022
fax: 351-591-2872
Wants to buy gorgeous antique purses with jeweled frames, scenes of people, romantic couples, landscapes, castles, flowers, gardens, Egyptian, Persian rug designs; one-of-a-kind beaded, petitpoint, embroidered, or tapestry.

Barbara Hobbs
5501 101st Ave. N
Pinellas Park, FL 33782-3311
ph: 727-541-6164
Wants to buy beaded purses.

Purses
P.O. Box 6019
Chesterfield, MO 63006
ph: 314-227-0634
Wants scenic and figural beaded purses; also wants hand tooled Art Nouveau leather bags.

Jennifer Sykes
Jennifer Sykes Antiques
9018 Balboa Blvd. #595
Northridge, CA 91325-2610
ph: 818-993-1916
fax: 818-993-7612
e-mail: Veeda10@aol.com
Wants purses and vanity bags: mesh, enamel, bead, Bakelite, or celluloid; also wants girlie items such as mugs, ashtrays, figurines, novelties, etc.

Molly Klumpfell
Purse Snatchers
P.O. Box 572
Campbell, CA 95009
ph: 408-866-6250
Wants to buy pre-1930 antique purses in good to excellent condition; wants unusual purses such as scenic beaded, carpet bags; also buys collections; send clear photo, or zerox copies with complete description; will respond in 5 days.

Leslie Holms
P.O. Box 596
Los Gatos, CA 95031-0596
ph: 408-354-1626
fax: 408-395-0803
Wants to buy pre-1930s beaded purses with scenes of people and places, abstracts, Persian carpet motifs; also wants enameled mesh, bright colors, bold designs; damaged purses are OK.

Dealers

Debbie Woolley
Favorite Past-Times
6 Main Hill
Bridgton, ME 04009
ph: 207-647-5286
e-mail: woolley@maine-antiques.com
web: http://www.maine-antiques.com/fpt/Index/
Specializing in enameled mesh purses.

Priscilla Washed
Victorian Lady, The
102 South Main St.
P.O. Box 424
Waxhaw, NC 28173-0424
ph: 704-843-4467 or 800-786-1886
A Victorian specialty store featuring 19th century ladies decorative & fashion accessories; buys and sells purses; also sewing and needlework tools, vintage fashion, Victoriana, and combs; mail order; catalog $5.

Wendy Hankins
Black Cat Collectibles
P.O. Box 864
Geneva, FL 32732
ph: 407-349-9150
e-mail: rh8421@gate.net
Buys and sells fashion accessories including compacts, vanity bags, carryalls, and vintage purses from the 1920s to the 1970s: beaded, suede, faille, snakeskin, etc.

Cindy Butler
607 Melody Lane
Bessemer, AL 35020
ph: 205-425-9340
e-mail: jdb007@aol.com
Collector and dealer in vintage beaded scenic/figural purses; selling beaded, mesh, petite point and tapestry purses.

Gail & John Dunn
P.O. Box 234
Waterville, OH 43566
ph: 419-878-9515
Buys and sells vintage purses and hatpins.

Veronica Trainer
Bayhouse
P.O. Box 40442
Bay Village, OH 44140-0442
ph: 440-871-8584
Buys and sells purses by mail order; advisor to "Schroeder's Antiques Price Guide"; specializes in beaded

and enameled mesh purses; paying top dollar for scenics and purses with jeweled and ornate frames; also wants damaged purses.

Marion Spitzley
Spitzley Data & Graphics
1118 Nottingham
Grosse Pointe, MI 48230
ph: 313-824-9435
e-mail: esmee@io.com
web: http://www.io.com/~esmee/bag_lady/bag_lady.htm
Specializes in Lucite and Bakelite handbags and jewelry, but has a general knowledge of all types of purses: beaded, mesh, leather as well as 20th century jewelry and compacts.

Diane Richardson
Gold Hatpin, The
P.O. Box 993
Oak Park, IL 60303-0993
ph: 708-848-3247 or 708-445-0610
e-mail: goldhatpin@mediaone.net
Wants all types of beaded and mesh purses made before 1940, especially those with small beads, scenes, elaborate frames, etc.; also buys purse frames.

Anita Davis
P.O. Box 7238
Little Rock, AR 72217
Large selection of vintage purses and jewelry from the 1920s to 1970s; from the sublime to the ridiculous.

Experts

Roselyn Gerson
P.O. Box 100
Malverne, NY 11565
ph: 516-593-8746
fax: 516-593-0611
Author of "Vintage Vanity Bags & Purses."

Roseann Ettinger
Remember When
21-23 W. Broad St.
Hazleton, PA 18201
ph: 570-454-8465 or 570-450-5542
Author of "Handbags."

Sherry & Mike Miller
303 Holiday Dr. #130
Tuscola, IL 61953-2118
ph: 217-253-4991
e-mail: miller@tuscola.net
web: http://www.tuscola.net/~miller/
Wants to buy painted ring mesh & enameled flat mesh purses made in the 1920s and 1930s with ornate framed and compact/mesh bag combinations, or with painted designs; must be in mint or near-mint condition; also wants ads for mesh purses.

Suzi Mounts
Perfect Purse, The
15466 Los Gatos Blvd. 109-315
Los Gatos, CA 95032
ph: 408-559-4172

Jeannette Schoolsky
P.O. Box 23182
Portland, OR 97281-3162
ph: 503-579-3162
fax: 503-579-5046
e-mail: Purses@ArtDeco.com
Purse expert and collector wants to buy cut steel mesh and glass beaded purses; especially seeking any purse depicting a scenery, or any with birds, people, animals, etc.; one item or entire collection; also does purse repairs.

Museums/Libraries

Museum of Fine Arts, Boston
465 Huntington Ave.
Boston, MA 02115-5523
ph: 617-267-9300
e-mail: webmaster@mfa.org
web: http://www.mfa.org/home.html
An outstanding collection of purses.

Bette Johnson
Whiting & Davis Handbag Museum
200 John Dietsch Blvd.
North Attleboro, MA 02763
ph: 508-699-7639
Vintage mesh handbags and memorabilia from the late 1800s to present; also early mesh machine on display.

Repair Services

Suzi Mounts
Suzi's Purse Restoration, The
15466 Los Gatos Blvd. 109-315
Los Gatos, CA 95032
ph: 408-559-4172
Professionally repairs pre-1940 antique purses; specializes in relining, fringing, and reframing beaded purses; can also repair metal ring mesh purses, and broken clasps; call first to discuss your needs. Send purse for exact quote.

Plastic

Collectors

Melba Becker
2408 Las Verdes St.
Las Vegas, NV 89102
ph: 800-553-9490
Wants to buy plastic handbags from the 1940s and 1950s.

PUZZLES

(see also BOTTLES, Puzzle; GAMES; PAPER COLLECTIBLES)

Clubs/Associations

American Game Collectors Association
Newsletter: Game Times
P.O. Box 44
Dresher, PA 19025
e-mail: agca@agca.com
web: http://www.agca.com
Focuses on board and card games as well as puzzles, playing cards, tops, yo-yos, and action games; also publishes "Game Researchers' Notes" - reports on member's research.

Crosswords

Collectors

Will Shortz
55 Great Oak Lane
Pleasantville, NY 10570-2010
ph: 914-769-9128
e-mail: wshortz@aol.com
Wants to buy crossword puzzles: books and magazine.

Jigsaw

Collectors

Mark Cappitella
MGC's Custom Hand Cut Wooden Jigsaw Puzzles
57 Husted Station Road
Elmer, NJ 08318
ph: 888-604-7654 or 609-453-7654
e-mail: mark@mgcpuzzles.com
web: http://www.mgcpuzzles.com
Makes custom jigsaw puzzles; great online puzzle website.

Jim Rohacs
9721 Lomond Dr.
Manassas, VA 22110-3104
ph: 703-369-5578
Wants pre-1950s puzzles.

Liz & Dick Wilmes
38W567 Brindlewood Ave.
Elgin, IL 60123-7976
ph: 847-697-9679
fax: 847-742-1054
e-mail: Bblocks@cris.com
Especially interested in Depression era advertising jigsaw puzzles; please send SASE for reply.

Dave Cooper
Clarendon, Parsonage Road
Herne Bay, Kent CT6 5TA
U.K.
e-mail: jigsaw666@aol.com
web: http://members.aol.com/jigsaw666/index.html
Collector of wooden and old card jigsaw puzzles and maker of new wooden puzzles to order from customers' own prints; buy, sell, swap puzzles; researching information regarding U.K. jigsaws and wants to expand knowledge of U.S. puzzles.

Dealers

Robert J. Bergeron
CIA Group, The
2054 E. Balboa Dr.
Tempe, AZ 85282-4005
ph: 480-838-6266
fax: 480-839-5266
e-mail: www.zagzaw@worldnet.att.net
Collects, buys, sells jigsaw puzzles, specializing in Zag-Zaw wooden puzzles by Raphael Tuck, particularly the Dickens 1812-1912 series and all of Tuck's catalogs; Centenary a.k.a. Carriage Series in 2 sizes and 16 prints.

Experts

Bob Armstrong
15 Monadnock Rd.
Worcester, MA 01609
ph: 508-799-0644
fax: 508-793-5882
e-mail: raahna@oldpuzzles.com
web: http://www.oldpuzzles.com
Old wood jigsaw puzzles, adult cut, pre-1950; collects, restores, displays, sells, answers information via website; author of "Jigsaw Puzzle Cutting Styles," Game Researchers' Notes Issue No. 25, AGCA.

Anne D. Williams
Economics Dept.
Bates College
Lewiston, ME 04240
ph: 207-783-8732
e-mail: awilliam@bates.edu
Wants jigsaw puzzles, related ephemera, and company catalogs and information; wood, diecut, etc.; author of "Jigsaw Puzzles" (1990), "Cutting A Fine Figure" (1996), many articles about puzzles; special interest in small-scale makers.

Chris McCann
658 MacElroy Rd.
Ballston Lake, NY 12019-2202
ph: 518-877-7303
Researcher of cardboard jigsaw puzzles from 1930s to 1960s; has computer database of more than 10,000 titles from 18 major collections; 7800 titles have been identified with artist name; would like to hear from other collectors; author.

Harry L. Rinker
Puzzle Pit, The
5093 Vera Cruz Rd.
Emmaus, PA 18049-9554
ph: 610-965-1122
fax: 610-965-1124
e-mail: rinker@fast.net
web: http://www.rinker.com
Wants wooden or cardboard jigsaw puzzles with advertising, mystery, personality, cartoon character, depression era, or WWII theme.

Jigsaw (Wood)

Collectors

Gordon Hayter
751 Terraine Ave.
Long Beach, CA 90804-4405
ph: 562-498-2769
Collector of adult, wood, interlocking jigsaw puzzles.

Mechanical

Collectors

Cary Basse
6927 Forbes Ave.
Van Nuys, CA 91406-4504
ph: 818-781-4856

Experts

Jerry Slocum
P.O. Box 1635
Beverly Hills, CA 90213-1635
ph: 310-273-2270
fax: 310-274-3644
Wants mechanical & dexterity puzzles, trick locks, trick matchsafes, folding puzzles, advertising string puzzles, puzzle trade cards, checkerboard puzzles, catalogs with puzzles, puzzle books.

Mechanical (Rubik's Cubes)

Collectors

Peter M. Beck
Just Puzzles
P.O. Box 267
Wharton, NJ 07885
ph: 973-625-4191
e-mail: just_puzzles@yahoo.com
web: http://www.freeyellow.com/members4/justpuzzles/
Wants to buy any type of Rubik's cube memorabilia; buys and sells all forms of mechanical puzzles; send SASE for brochure.

Paper

Collectors

Will Shortz
55 Great Oak Lane
Pleasantville, NY 10570-2010
ph: 914-769-9128
e-mail: wshortz@aol.com
Wants to buy paper puzzles, also puzzle books and magazines.

PYROBILIA

(see FIREWORKS MEMORABILIA)

PYROGRAPHY ITEMS

Collectors

John Lewis
912 W. 8th St.
Loveland, CO 80537-5208
ph: 970-667-2960
e-mail: john4real@aol.com
Wants quality "burnt wood" items such as plaques, boxes and furniture; also wants catalogs, wood burning kits, and books on pyrography.

Dealers

Linda Gibbs
10380 Miranda Ave.
Buena Park, CA 90620-4447
ph: 714-827-6488
Wants wooden boxes with flower designs, beautiful ladies, etc., 1800s-1900s; please send SASE and photos.

Experts

Carole & Richard Smyth
Carole Smyth Antiques
P.O. Box 2068
Huntington, NY 11743-0861
ph: 516-673-8666
Authors of "The Burning Passion - A Study & Price Guide," now available from the authors for $22.95 ppd.

Here are some tips when contacting someone listed in this book:

■ When requesting information about a particular item, include a description (material, dimensions, maker's mark, model number, etc.) and a photo, sketch, or photocopy of the item in question.

■ Always ask if there are charges for samples or for the services requested.

■ When writing, please be sure to include a Large (#10 business size) Self-Addressed and Stamped Envelope (LSASE) if requesting a reply or the return of photographs.

■ Never call collect unless otherwise directed. When calling, be considerate of time zone differences and always ask if the party you are calling has time to talk. When leaving an answering machine message, always instruct the party to call you back collect.

Q-R

QUILTS

(see also FEED & GRAIN BAGS; FOLK ART; REPAIR/RESTORATION/ CONSERVATION, Textiles; TEXTILES)

Appraisers

American Quilter's Society
Magazine: American Quilter
P.O. Box 3290
Paducah, KY 42002-3290
ph: 800-626-5420 or 270-898-7903
fax: 270-898-8890
e-mail: aqsquilt@apex.net
web: http://www.aqsquilt.com
Publishes list of certified quilt appraisers.

Terri Ellis, ISA
1205 Mistletoe Dr.
Fort Worth, TX 76110-1018
ph: 817-926-9424
e-mail: tquilts@cyberramp.net
Certified quilt appraiser by the American Quilter's Society; Accredited Member of the ISA; also buys and sells vintage textiles.

Deborah Roberts
1071 San Pablo
Costa Mesa, CA 92626
ph: 714-557-5258
e-mail: quiltevals@aol.com
web: http://quilt.com/appraiser/
Historian, appraiser, specializing in buying and selling antique hooked rugs, quilts and quilt-related textiles; certified by the American Quilter's Society; wish list available; also lectures on quilts.

Bette G. Bell, ISA CAPP
Guildmark Appraisal & Estate Sale Services, LLC
P.O. Box 952
Edmonds, WA 98020
ph: 425-775-5650
fax: 425-670-6957
e-mail: stashn33@gte.net
Appraises quilts, cut glass, pottery and a general line of antiques; also handles estate sales throughout the NW; Certified Member of the International Society of Appraisers.

Sally A. Ambrose
P.O. Box 536
11156 North Rd.
Leavenworth, WA 98826-9512
ph: 509-548-7472
fax: 509-548-0240
e-mail: sally@televar.com
Specializes in the appraising of antique and contemporary American quilted textiles, as well as contemporary wearable art. Wearable art is not always quilted but may exhibit surface design in a variety of art media and embellishment.

Clubs/Associations

National Quilting Association, Inc., The
Magazine: Quilting Quarterly
P.O. Box 393
Ellicott City, MD 21043-0393
ph: 410-461-5733
fax: 410-461-3693
e-mail: nqa@erols.com
web: http://www.his.com/~queenb/nqa/nqa.index.html
Purpose is to stimulate, maintain and record interest in all matters pertaining to the making, collecting and preserving of quilts.

American Quilter's Society
Magazine: American Quilter
P.O. Box 3290
Paducah, KY 42002-3290
ph: 800-626-5420 or 270-898-7903
fax: 270-898-8890
e-mail: aqsquilt@apex.net
web: http://www.aqsquilt.com
Members receive bi-monthly newsletter, discount admission to Annual National AQS Quilt Show, discounts on quilting books, American Quilter Magazine; also publishes list of certified quilt appraisers.

American Quilt Study Group
Newsletter: Blanket Statements
P.O. Box 4737
Lincoln, NE 68504-0737
ph: 402-472-5361
fax: 402-472-5428
e-mail: AQSG2@unl.edu
web: http://catsis.weber.edu/aqsg
Goal is to develop a responsible and accurate body of information about quilts and their makers; membership open to any person having an interest in the history of quilt making; also publishes the annual journal, "Uncoverings."

Dealers

Lawrence Miller
Marie Miller Antique Quilts
Route 30
P.O. Box 968
Dorset, VT 05251
ph: 802-867-5969
fax: 802-867-0324
e-mail: quiltslr@vermontel.com
web: http://www.antiquequilts.com
Buys, sells, appraises quilts; has over 300 from 1820 to 1930s: applique, pieced, crazy quilts, crib, doll, Amish and Mennonite, and quilt tops; see the on-line catalog; also sells quilt hangers and Ensure, a quilt wash.

American Hurrah Antiques
P.O. Box 919
New York, NY 10024-0546
ph: 212-535-1930
fax: 212-580-5501
Specializes in American folk art, American Indian, and antique quilts.

Tom Vonah
Tom's Quilts
3 White Oak Lane
Southampton, NY 11968
ph: 516-726-6881
e-mail: tomsquilts@aol.com
web: http://www.starfaceinc.com
Sells antique quilts, tops, blocks, and sewing notions; stocks over 200 quilts from the 1870s to 1940s; website has about 100 photos.

Kris Driessen
Hickory Hill Antique Quilts
P.O. Box 273
Esperance, NY 12066
ph: 518-875-6133
fax: 518-875-9141
e-mail: oldquilt@albany.net
web: http://www.HickoryHillQuilts.com
Offers antique quilt tops, blocks by catalog; also offers vintage and reproduction fabrics, as well as restoration supplies and Quilt Heritage reference books.

Antique Quilt Source, The
385 Springview Road
Carlisle, PA 17013-0372
ph: 717-245-2054
e-mail: grafb@pa.net
web: http://www.antiquequiltsource.com/
Over 19 years in business buying and selling antique quilts.

Stella Rubin
12300 Glen Rd.
Potomac, MD 20854-1023
ph: 301-948-4187
fax: 301-948-0460
Buys and sells quality quilts; also Mexican silver jewelry.

Quilts Unlimited
444 A Duke of Gloucester St.
Williamsburg, VA 23185
ph: 757-253-8700
e-mail: quilts@rlc.net
web: http://www.quiltsunlimited.com/
Images, dates, descriptions, prices of quilts in inventory are available on the website.

Deborah Vanden Heuvel
Global Galleria, The
209 Riverwalk Circle
Cary, NC 27511
ph: 888-832-5616 or 919-859-5818
fax: 919-859-6396
e-mail: globalgal@tias.com
web: http://www.tias.com/stores/globalgal/
Carries a large selection of Antique and Experienced American Quilts; many pieces of museum quality.

Matt Lippa
Artisans
P.O. Box 256
Mentone, AL 35984-0256
ph: 256-634-4037
fax: 256-634-4037
e-mail: artisans@folkartisans.com
web: http://www.folkartisans.com
Buy and sell folk art, outsider art, fine art; Internet WWW site offers links to additional dealers; also offers non-profit clubs and museums with an outlet to post notices, press releases, calendar items, etc. at no charge.

Frank Geeslin
American Quilts!
P.O. Box 200
Upton, KY 42784
ph: 502-531-1619 or 877-531-1619
fax: 502-531-3745
e-mail: frank@AmericanQuilts.com
web: http://www.AmericanQuilts.com/
Over 1500 American-made quilts: new and antique, custom-made, baby and doll, quilt tops, applique, cutter quilts, quilt clothing, contemporary and traditional quilts; also repairs; buying extraordinary quilts or tops.

Barbara Woodford
Historic American Quilts
4775 S. River Road
Hanover, IL 61041-9523
ph: 815-777-2009
fax: 815-777-4130
e-mail: woodford@ix.netcom.com
web: http://www.historic-american.com/woodford/
Dealer and collector of high-quality antique quilts, principally from the 19th century.

Diane J. Reese
Antique Quilts & Vintage Textiles
6212 S. 177th St.
Omaha, NE 68135
e-mail: silvareese@aol.com
web: http://www.ultranet.com/~kiwi/diane.html
Buys and sells antique quilts, quilt tops, quilt squares from 1880 to 1945; also antique fabric, feedsacks, lace and hand crochet trims, needlework magazines, etc.

Mary Ann Walters
Log Cabin Antiques
4200 Peggy Lane
Plano, TX 75074
ph: 972-881-2818
e-mail: logcabin@flash.net
web: http://www.flash.net/~logcabin/
Buys and sells quilts, specializing in 19th and early 20th century quilts in excellent condition; on-line catalog features scores of quilts currently for sale with pictures, descriptions, and prices.

Deborah Roberts
1071 San Pablo
Costa Mesa, CA 92626
ph: 714-557-5258
e-mail: quiltevals@aol.com
web: http://quilt.com/appraiser/
Historian, appraiser, specializing in buying and selling antique hooked rugs, quilts and quilt-related textiles; certified by the American Quilter's Society; wish list available; also lectures on quilts.

Sally Hale
Covered Wagon Quiltworks
710 S.E. Dora
Troutdale, OR 97060
ph: 503-665-6178
e-mail: thale@teleport.com
web: http://www.coveredwagonquiltworks.com
Specializes in American-made 19th and early-20th century quilts from all areas of the country.

Experts

Suzy McLennan Anderson
Heritage Antiques, Inc.
65 East Main St.
Holmdel, NJ 07733-2310
ph: 908-946-8801
fax: 908-946-1036
Authenticates, buys, sells, appraises, lectures; author of "The Collectors Guide to Quilts."

Merry May
Schoolhouse Enterprises
P.O. Box 305
Tuckahoe, NJ 08250-0305
ph: 609-628-2256
fax: 609-628-3048
e-mail: cluesew@jerseycape.com
Has taught quilt making since 1988; quilt historian since 1989; offers lectures and workshops; writes articles for publications; interested in feedsacks; produces quilt patterns; designs and makes custom-made quilts; does not appraise.

Ardis & Robert James
Ardis & Robert James Quilt Collection, The
80 Ludlow Dr.
Chappaqua, NY 10514
ph: 914-666-3774
fax: 212-824-1102
e-mail: bobjames@eassets.com
Buys, sells, exhibits, lends, lectures and writes about quilts; collection featured in several publications.

Yvonne Khin
9423 Longs Mill Rd.
Rocky Ridge, MD 21778
ph: 301-898-0091
Author of "Collector's Dictionary of Quilt Names and Patterns" (1980.)

Internet Resources

World Wide Quilting Page
e-mail: QHomePage@quilt.com
web: http://quilt.com/MainQuiltingPage.html
All sorts of links to contemporary quilt resources; also to some resources for antique quilts.

Misc. Services

Quilter's Design Studio QuiltSoft
P.O. Box 19946
San Diego, CA 92159-0946
ph: 619-583-2970
fax: 619-583-2692
e-mail: quiltsoft@aol.com
Quilt design computer program for Windows or for Macintosh; copy, rotate, and flip blocks; print templates, calculate yardage, unlimited colors.

Museums/Libraries

New England Quilt Museum
18 Shattuck St.
Lowell, MA 01852
ph: 978-452-4207
fax: 978-452-5405
e-mail: mps@tiac.net
web: http://www.nequiltmuseum.org/default.htm

Shelburne Museum, Inc.
P.O. Box 10
Shelburne, VT 05482-0010
ph: 802-985-3346 or 800-253-0191
fax: 802-985-2331
e-mail: museinfo@together.net
web: http://shelburnemuseum.org/
37 historic structures and exhibit buildings; diverse collection of American folk, fine, decorative and utilitarian art.

National Museum of American History, Division of Textiles
14th & Constitution Ave. NW
Washington, DC 20560
ph: 202-357-2700
e-mail: webmaster@si.edu
web: http://www.si.edu/organiza/museums/nmah/nmah.htm

Yvonne Khin
Doll & Quilts Barn
9423 Longs Mill Rd.
Rocky Ridge, MD 21778
ph: 301-898-0091
Quilt museum offering quilt repairs, enlarging, duplicating, quilting classes, storage, and research.

Virginia Quilt Museum
301 South Main St.
Harrisonburg, VA 22801
ph: 540-433-3818
fax: 540-433-3818
e-mail: ceknight@postoffice.worldnet.att.net
web: http://www.folkart.com/~latitude/museums/m_vqm.htm
A resource center for the study of the role of quilts and quilting in the cultural life of society; collections include works by both early and contemporary quilt artisans.

Victoria Faoro
Museum of the American Quilter's Society
Newsletter: Friends of MAQS Newsletter
215 Jefferson St.
P.O. Box 1540
Paducah, KY 42001-1540
ph: 502-442-8856
fax: 502-442-5448
e-mail: MAQSmus@apex.net
web: http://www.aqsquilt.com/aqs/maqs.html
World's largest quilt museum; changing displays of new and antique quilts; gift and book shop carries over 400 titles related to quilts and textiles.

Quilters Hall of Fame
P.O. Box 681
Marion, IN 46952-0681
ph: 765-664-9333
fax: 765-664-9333
web: http://www.west.net/~rperry/qhf.html

James J. Prochaska, P.E. - Dir.
Rocky Mountain Quilt Museum
1111 Washington Ave.
Golden, CO 80401
ph: 303-277-0377 or 303-215-9001
fax: 303-215-1636
e-mail: rmqm@att.net
web: http://www.rmqm.org
A non-profit conservator of historic and contemporary quilts; collection includes over 150 quilts; six special exhibitions each year.

American Museum of Quilts & Textiles of San Jose
Newsletter: Connections
60 South Market St.
San Jose, CA 95113
ph: 408-971-0323
fax: 408-971-7226
e-mail: webmaster@sjquiltmuseum.org
web: http://www.sjquiltmuseum.org/
Non-profit, public benefit museum with regularly changing exhibits of traditional, contemporary and historical quilts and textiles; museum store.

Periodicals

Leman Publications
Magazine: Quilter's Newsletter
P.O. Box 4101
Golden, CO 80402
ph: 303-420-4272 or 800-477-6089
fax: 303-420-7358
web: http://www.quiltersnewsletter.com/
The magazine for quilt lovers; a glossy magazine published ten times per year; articles, appraisals, patterns, frames, old and new quilts, quilt history, fabric clubs, ads, calendar, techniques, supplies, shows, etc.

Leman Publications
Magazine: Quiltmaker
P.O. Box 4101
Golden, CO 80402
ph: 303-420-4272 or 800-477-6089
fax: 303-420-7358
web: http://www.quiltersnewsletter.com/
A bi-monthly magazine for today's quilters; a pattern magazine featuring original quilt art in addition to full color photographs of quilts; step-by-step instructions, yardage, and more.

Repair Services

Margaret & Audrey Ruhland Antiques
P.O. Box 245
North Gower, Ontario K0A 2T0
Canada
ph: 613-489-3298
Specializes in the repair of quilts and hooked rugs.

Suppliers

Kris Driessen
Hickory Hill Antique Quilts
P.O. Box 273
Esperance, NY 12066
ph: 518-875-6133
fax: 518-875-9141
e-mail: oldquilt@albany.net
web: http://www.HickoryHillQuilts.com
Offers antique quilt tops, blocks by catalog; also offers vintage and reproduction fabrics, as well as restoration supplies and Quilt Heritage reference books.

Miniature

Man./Prod./Dist.

Kate Adams
Kate Adams Designs
P.O. Box 3025
Kennebunkport, ME 04046
ph: 800-553-3766 or 207-967-5077
fax: 207-967-0972
Makes miniature quilts framed as wall decorations.

RACING

(see AIRPLANES, Racing; AUTO RACING MEMORABILIA; AUTOMOBILES, Racing; GO-KARTS; SPORTS COLLECTIBLES, Thoroughbred Racing; TOYS, Cars [Racing])

RADIO SHOWS

Dealers

Art Bilski
Art's Antique Radios
208 Green Mountain Dr.
Bolingbrook, IL 60440
ph: 630-739-1060
fax: 630-739-1060
e-mail: oldradio99@ntsource.com
web: http://www.ntsource.com/~oldradio99
Consultation, repair, sales and purchases of old tube style radios; will buy your old radios or will refer you to another resource who will buy.

Repair Services

Art Bilski
Art's Antique Radios
208 Green Mountain Dr.
Bolingbrook, IL 60440
ph: 630-739-1060
fax: 630-739-1060
e-mail: oldradio99@ntsource.com
web: http://www.ntsource.com/~oldradio99
Consultation, repair, sales and purchases of old tube style radios; will buy your old radios or will refer you to another resource who will buy.

Old Time

(see also AUDIO-VISUAL; BROADCASTING; PERSONALITIES [ENTERTAINERS]; PREMIUMS, Radio Show; RADIOS)

Clubs/Associations

Robert D. Gariepy
Nostalgia Theater Club
P.O. Box 1585
Haverhill, MA 01831-2285
ph: 978-372-9942
Golden age of radio, TV, and movies: records, videos, books, tapes, CDs.

Gerald Eskin, Rec. Sec.
Radio Collectors of America
Newsletter: RCA Newsletter
28 Wolfe St., Unit #1
West Roxbury, MA 02132-3234
ph: 617-323-0938
Purpose is to collect, preserve and enjoy old radio shows. Does not collect old radios, the emphasis is strictly on radio shows.

Richard Olday
Old Time Radio Club
Newsletter: OTRC Newsletter
100 Harvey Dr.
Lancaster, NY 14086-2840
ph: 716-684-1604
A nationally oriented local chapter.

Gene Leitner
Golden Radio Buffs of Maryland, Inc.
Newsletter: On the Air
301 Jeanwood Ct.
Baltimore, MD 21222-2857
ph: 410-477-2550 or 410-477-3051
e-mail: grbmd@aol.com
web: http://members.aol.com/grbmd/
International club interested in old time radio also has an Old Time radio exhibit in the Baltimore Museum of Industry,, Baltimore, MD; lots of radios, artifacts, pictures, etc.; OTR tape lending library for members.

Jack French
Metro Washington Old Time Radio Club
Newsletter: Radio Recall
5137 Richardson Dr.
Fairfax, VA 22032-2810
ph: 703-978-1236
e-mail: OTRpiano@erols.com

Janis DeMoss, Mem.
North American Radio Archives
Newsletter: NARA News
134 Vincewood Dr.
Nicholasville, KY 40356
ph: 606-885-1031
e-mail: aston@cosmoaccess.net
International club dedicated to the enjoyment of classic radio shows from the 1930s to present; has a printed materials as well as over 3000 cassettes to loan out.

Robert W. Newman
Radio Listener's Lyceum
Journal: RLL on the Air
11509 Islandale Drive
Forest Park, OH 45240-2319
ph: 513-825-3662
e-mail: rto5@juno.com
web: http://www.starshines-place.com/otrmain.htm
Cassette library contains thousands of the classic old-time radio programs; publishers of "RLL on the Air", a quarterly informative journal about old-time radio and those who participated in it; please send SASE with requests.

Barry Hill
Old Time Radio Collectors Association of England (North American Division)
Rte. 1 Box 197
Belpre, OH 45714
ph: 740-423-4010
fax: 740-423-4010
e-mail: orca@eurekanet.com
Preserve English-spoken radio shows broadcasts around the world and makes them available for the enjoyment of the members.

Gordon Spiering
Milwaukee Area Radio Enthusiasts
16670 Harmony Ct.
New Berlin, WI 53151-6524
ph: 414-784-4642
e-mail: spiering@execpc.com
Local group interested in old time radio programs; meets every other month; guest speakers and discussions about OTR; book and tape library; newsletter.

Nancy Warner
Illinois Old Radio Shows Society
Newsletter: Chicago Star
10 S. 540 County Line Rd.
Hinsdale, IL 60521
Over 4,000 hours of old radio shows in a lending library; also scripts, articles and comic books on radio topics.

Richard R. king
Radio Historical Association of Colorado
Newsletter: Return With Us Now
P.O. Box 1908
Englewood, CO 80150-1908
ph: 303-761-4139
e-mail: dick.king@worldnet.att.net
web: http://www.old-time.com/ffiles/rhac.zip
Club rents over 13,000 old time radio shows to members for a nominal charge.

River City Radio Club
P.O. Box 163464
Sacramento, CA 95816-9464
Trading, collecting, selling and more; 10,000 episodes; access by personal computer with modem - call BBS at 916-451-0473 (8-n-1); on-line club services and catalogs; 24 hours; no fees; free membership.

Collectors

David L. Easter
1900 Angleside Rd.
Fallston, MD 21047-1739
ph: 410-877-2949
e-mail: david_easter@compuserve.com
Interested in all old time radio shows, especially in science fiction program; American, BBC or South African.

Herb Brandenburg
4114 Montgomery Rd.
Cincinnati, OH 45212-3612
ph: 513-841-1267

Fred B. Korb, Jr.
725 Cardigan Ct.
Naperville, IL 60565-1202
ph: 630-416-8968
e-mail: skorb@ameritech.net
Looking for any new programs in circulation; member of O.R.C.A.T.S; personal library contains approximately 50,000 programs; trades shows on a limited basis.

Jack Mann
3883 Madrona Dr. SE, #204
Port Orchard, WA 98366
ph: 360-769-6275
e-mail: jmann@sincom.com
web: http://www.pe.net/~rnovak/jack.htm
A great online resource for Old Time Radio fans and show collectors; over 250 links for everything related to OTR.

Dealers

Erstwhile Radio
P.O. Box 2284
Peabody, MA 01960-7284
Send $3 for catalog listing nearly 5,300 old time radio shows: The Whistler, Suspense, Jack Benny, Sherlock Holmes, The Lone Ranger, Fiber McGee & Molly, Lux Radio Theater, etc.; mail order only.

Heritage Radio Classics
P.O. Box 16
Chestnut Hill, MA 02167
fax: 617-965-9984
e-mail: HERITAGE@aol.com
web: http://members.aol.com/HERITAGE4/
Super quality old-time radio shows from the 1930s to 1950s on TDK cassettes: Jack Benny, The Shadow, The Lone Ranger, Our Miss Brooks, The Great Gildersleeve, Lux Radio Theatre, Suspense and 100s more; catalog $1.50 refundable.

Can Corner, The
P.O. Box 1173 - MA
Marcus Hook, PA 19061-7173
Jack Benny, Amos & Andy, Big Band specials, WWII broadcasts, old commercials for Chevrolet, Nash & Studebaker, etc.; send for list; mail order.

Lawrence Rao
1009 Autumn Woods Ln. #106
Virginia Beach, VA 23454
Sells vintage radio broadcasts on audio-only VHS Hi-fi cassettes; broadcasts are also available on standard analog-Dolby cassettes; Vintage Radio catalog $6 ppd. refundable on first order.

Charlie Garant
P.O. Box 331
Greeneville, TN 37744-0331

Bob Burchett
Hello Again, Radio
P.O. Box 6176
Cincinnati, OH 45206-0176
ph: 606-282-0333
fax: 606-282-1999
Free catalog of Old Time radio shows on cassette.

Radio Vault
P.O. Box 9032
Grand Rapids, MI 49509-0032
ph: 616-531-7398
Old radio shows on cassettes; catalog $5.

Experts

Jack French
5137 Richardson Dr.
Fairfax, VA 22032-2810
ph: 703-978-1236
e-mail: OTRpiano@erols.com
Collecting, researching, and writing about the Golden Age of radio for over 20 years; former editor of "NARA News", current editor of "Radio Recall"; lecturer on old time radio, juvenile westerns, female detectives, soap operas, etc.

Internet Resources

William Pfeiffer
Old Time Radio Roundtable
e-mail: listmaster@broadcast.airwaves.com
web: http://www.airwaves.com/otr.html
Interactive e-newsletter dedicated to the collection, preservation and enjoyment of Old Time Radio programs, their stars and stories; it's like an Old Time Radio Club delivered daily to your email box.

Jack Mann
3883 Madrona Dr. SE, #204
Port Orchard, WA 98366
ph: 360-769-6275
e-mail: jmann@sincom.com
web: http://www.pe.net/~rnovak/jack.htm
A great online resource for Old Time Radio fans and show collectors; over 250 links for everything related to OTR.

Museums/Libraries

Library of Congress, Recorded Sound Reference Center
101 Independence Ave. SE
Washington, DC 20540-4698
ph: 202-707-7833
fax: 202-707-8464
e-mail: rsrc@loc.gov
web: http://www.loc.gov
Recorded sound collection includes old time radio broadcasts; copies can be made if you get permission from the rights holders.

American Library of Radio & TV, Thousand Oaks Library
1401 East Janss Rd.
Thousand Oaks, CA 91362
ph: 805-449-2660
fax: 805-449-2675
e-mail: bbauer@mx.tol.lib.ca.us
web: http://www.tol.lib.ca.us/1specoll.html
Research collection of scripts, sound recordings, books, pamphlets, and correspondence relating to old-time radio; available for research use at facility only.

Arthur S. Schreiber, CEO
National Broadcasters Hall of Fame & Museum
18600 Jamboree Rd., Apt. 321
Irvine, CA 92612
ph: 949-757-1337

Periodicals

Jay A. Hickerson
Friends of Old-Time Radio
Newsletter: Hello Again
P.O. Box 4321
Hamden, CT 06514-0321
ph: 203-248-2887
fax: 203-281-1322
e-mail: jayhick@aol.com
For collectors of old-time radio shows; sponsors an annual convention; send SASE for sample copy of newsletter.

Bob Burchett, Ed.
Audio Classic Press
Magazine: Old Time Radio Digest
10280 Gunpowder Rd.
Florence, KY 41042-8253
ph: 606-282-0333
fax: 606-282-1999
Published four times per year.

Rob Imes
Newsletter: Tune In
1844 E. Longmeadow
Trenton, MI 48183-1776
Forum for fans of new and old radio plays; share ideas, express creativity with original scripts, detailed information about programs compiled from research of readers; recent issues involve The Witch's Tale and The Shadow.

Jordan Young
Past Times Nostalgia Network
Directory: Nostalgia Entertainment Sourcebook
7308-H Filmore Dr.
Buena Park, CA 90620
ph: 714-527-5845
fax: 714-527-5845
e-mail: skretved@ix.netcom.com
Complete resource guide to classic movies, vintage radio, old time music, and theater: programs, equipment, where to replace and repair, where to rent or buy old movies, theater posters.

Repro. Sources

Old Time Radio Co.
P.O. Box 9032
Grand Rapids, MI 49509-0032
ph: 616-531-7398

Old Time (Lum 'n' Abner)

Clubs/Associations

Tim Hollis, ExSec
National Lum 'n' Abner Society
Newsletter: Jot 'Em Down Journal, The
#81 Sharon Blvd.
Dora, AL 35062
ph: 205-648-6110
fax: 205-674-0190
e-mail: jtemple@inu.net
web: http://www.inu.net/stemple/

Museums/Libraries

Lon & Kathy Stucker
Lum and Abner Museum
4562 Hwy. 88 West
General Delivery
Pine Ridge, AR 71966
ph: 870-326-4442
fax: 870-326-4442
web: http://www.lum-abner.com/
On National Register of Historic Places.

Old Time (Straight Arrow)

Clubs/Associations

Bill Harper
POW-WOW
Newsletter: POW-WOW
P.O. Box 24751
Minneapolis, MN 55424-0751
e-mail: WaltGrogan@aol.com
web: http://shazam.imginc.com/fca/
POW-WOW is the definitive source for information on the Nabisco Straight Arrow Promotion 1948-1954; dedicated to the memory of the real Straight Arrow - Howard Culver (1919-1984) and announcer/narrator Frank Bingham (1914-1988.)

Old Time (Vic & Sade)

Clubs/Associations

Barbara Schwarz
Friends of Vic & Sade
Newsletter: FVS Newsletter
7232 N. Keystone Ave.
Lincolnwood, IL 60646-2025
ph: 708-679-2706
Devoted fans of VIC & SADE focusing on searching for and sharing recorded episodes as well as information on the program and cast.

RADIOS

(see also ART DECO; AUDIO-VISUAL; BROADCASTING; ELECTRICITY RELATED ITEMS; PAPER COLLECTIBLES, Radio Related; PREMIUMS, Radio Shows; RADIO SHOWS, Old Time; TELEGRAPH ITEMS; TELEVISIONS)

Appraisers

Charlotte Mager
Waves
110 W. 25th St., 10th Floor
New York, NY 10001
ph: 212-989-9284
fax: 201-461-7121
e-mail: c1wave@aol.com
web: http://www.wavesradio.com
Established in 1976, buys, sells, repairs, appraises and rents radios, phonographs, TVs, microphones, telephones, fans, neon clocks and signs, and related advertising and literature.

Auction Services

Ronald Baker
Antique Radio Auction House
1600 Whitman, Ste. 100
Wheaton, IL 60187
ph: 630-665-5279
fax: 630-462-1750
e-mail: service@virtualauctions.com
web: http://www.virtualauctions.com/
Sells radios at auction; also buys direct.

Book Sellers

Joe Pfeiffer
Zapper Technologies
P.O. Box 253
Sandy, UT 84091-0253
ph: 801-571-5453
e-mail: joep@antiquesecrets.com
web: http://www.antiquesecrets.com/
Buys, sell, trade old books on early electronics, microphones, tubes, radio, antique electronics, telegraph; also early manuals and catalogs.

Clubs/Associations

George Kaczowka
New England Antique Radio Club
Newsletter: Escutcheon
P.O. Box 201
Spofford, NH 03462
ph: 617-923-2665
e-mail: gsk@oldradios.com
web: http://www.oldradios.com/clubs/nearc.htm

John Ellsworth
Connecticut Vintage Radio Collectors Club
Newsletter: Connecticut Wireless Gazette
563 West Avon Rd.
Avon, CT 06001
ph: 860-675-9916
fax: 860-675-9916
e-mail: radioclctr@aol.com
web: http://members.aol.com/radioclctr/
Museum, library, swap meets spring and fall.

John Dilks
New Jersey Antique Radio Club
Newsletter: NJARC Newsletter
125 Warf Road
Egg Harbor Twp., NJ 08234-8501
ph: 609-927-3873
e-mail: oldradio@worldnet.att.net
web: http://www.eht.com/oldradio/

Richard G. Brill
International Antique Radio Club, Div. of RGB Enterprises
P.O. Box 5367
Old Bridge, NJ 08857
ph: 732-607-0299
fax: 732-679-8024
e-mail: rgbent@aol.com
Welcomes information and schematics on all antique foreign radios; radios from the 1930s to 1960s; specializes in foreign radios; needs info on former Eastern European country radios like Tesla, Goplana, etc.

John & Linda Gramm
Hudson Valley Antique Radio & Phonograph Society
Newsletter: HARPS Newsletter
P.O. Box 1, Rt. 207
Campbell Hall, NY 10916
ph: 914-427-2602 or 914-496-5130
web: http://members.aol.com/JBishop701/Harps.html
For antique radio and phonograph collectors who want to share information, equipment and related items with others having similar interests; monthly meetings feature educational demonstrations and mini swap meets.

Chris Bacon
Greater New York Vintage Wireless Association
52 Uranus Rd.
Rocky Point, NY 11778-8842
ph: 516-821-7618

Allen W. Tomisman
Antique Radio Club of Schenectady
33 Bailey Ave.
Latham, NY 12110
ph: 518-785-3117

Gary Parzy
Niagara Frontier Wireless Association
Newsletter: NFWA Newsletter
135 Autumnwood
Cheektowaga, NY 14227

Bruce Kelley
Antique Wireless Association
Newsletter: Old Timer's Bulletin
59 Main St.
Holcomb, NY 14469-9336
ph: 716-657-6260 or 716-657-7489
e-mail: n2rsm@frontiernet.net
web: http://www.ggw.org/freenet/a/awa/
One of the world's largest and oldest historical radio collector organizations; purpose is to document and preserve the history of radio, telegraph and television artifacts.

Richard J. Harris, Sec.
Pittsburgh Antique Radio Society
407 Woodside Road
Pittsburgh, PA 15221
e-mail: schaefer@nb.net
web: http://www.nb.net/~schaefer/pars.html

Bill Overbeck
Delaware Valley Historic Radio Club
Newsletter: Oscillator, The
P.O. Box 847
Havertown, PA 19803
ph: 610-789-8199
e-mail: Billoradio@aol.com
web: http://pw2.netcom.com/~firstake/dvhrc.htm
Open to anyone with an interest in vintage radios.

Ken Mellgren, VP
Radio History Society, Inc.
13 Bitterroot Ct.
Rockville, MD 20853
e-mail: ken_mellgren@msn.com
web: http://www.radiohistory.org/
An IRS-recognized tax-exempt nonprofit organization set up primarily to establish a national vintage radio and television museum and library in Bowie, MD.

Barry Zimmerman, Treas./Mem.
Mid-Atlantic Antique Radio Club
Magazine: Radio Age
5825 Woodwinds Cr.
Frederick, MD 21702-7579
ph: 301-696-5561
e-mail: bcbelanger@aol.com
web: http://www.maarc.org/
Published monthly since 1975 for collectors interested in the history of radio and television; restoration, articles by early experts; free buy and sell ads; free sample.

Carl R. Shirley
Carolina Antique Radio Society
824 Fairwood Rd.
Columbia, SC 29209

Dennis G. Williams
Florida Antique Wireless Group
Newsletter: FAWGhorn News
321 East Evans Street
Orlando, FL 32804
ph: 407-895-0146
e-mail: oldradio@magicnet.net
web: http://www.clge.com/radiorelics/fawg.html
A group devoted to collecting old radios.

Bill Moore
Southern Vintage Wireless Association
Newsletter: SVWA Newsletter
3049 Box Canyon Rd.
Huntsville, AL 35803-1379
ph: 256-880-1207
e-mail: Bill_Moore@mevatec.com
Interested in antique radios; looking for Pilor and Lafayette radios and related advertising.

Randy Guttery
Mississippi Historical Radio & Broadcasting Society
Newsletter: MHRBS Newsletter
2412 C St.
Meridian, MS 39301
web: http://www.cybertron.com/~comcents/mhr/mhrlp.html

Steve Dando
Buckeye Radio & Phonograph Club
Newsletter: Soundings
4572 Mark Trail
Akron, OH 44321-1462
ph: 330-666-7222
Members exchange expertise in restoration of vintage radios and phonographs; club holds annual mall show (displaying radios and phonographs) and picnic.

Antique Radio Collectors of Ohio
Newsletter: ARCO Newsletter
P.O. Box 292292
Dayton, OH 45429
ph: 937-385-3855 or 937-253-4330
Newsletter published quarterly; holds several meetings and swap meets each year.

Society for the Preservation of Antique Radio Knowledge (SPARK)
Newsletter: SPARK Newsletter
c/o WQRP Radio
P.O. Box 482
Dayton, OH 45439

Dr. Edmund E. Taylor
Indiana Historical Radio Society
Newsletter: IHRS Bulletin
245 N. Oakland Ave.
Indianapolis, IN 46201-3360
ph: 317-638-1641
e-mail: IndianaHistoricalRadio@worldnet.att.net
web: http://home.att.net/~indianahistoricalradio/
Society of antique radio collectors who meet quarterly in Indiana; sponsors swap-meets, auctions, museum projects, contests.

Jim Clark
Michigan Antique Radio Club
Newsletter: Chronicle
3520 Okemos Rd., #6
Okemos, MI 48864
ph: 517-349-7187
fax: 517-349-7186
e-mail: jc072651@aol.com
web: http://www.antiqueradios.com/marc/
Preserves the history and enhance the knowledge of radio, TV and related disciplines with special emphasis on contributions made from the state of Michigan.

Dave Wiggert
Western Wisconsin Antique Radio Collectors Club
Newsletter: Radio Recollections
1611 Redfield St.
La Crosse, WI 54601

Northland Antique Radio Club
Newsletter: NARC Newsletter
P.O. Box 18362
Minneapolis, MN 55418
e-mail: farme007@tc.umn.edu
web: http://www.geocities.com/TelevisionCity/4544/index.html

Northland Antique Radio Club
P.O. Box 18362
Minneapolis, MN 55418
e-mail: farme007@tc.umn.edu
web: http://www.geocities.com/TelevisionCity/4544

Jeff Aulik
Antique Radio Club of Illinois
Newsletter: ARCI Newsletter
1708 Parkview Ave.
Rockford, IL 61107
ph: 815-399-1902
e-mail: caschwark@aol.com
web: http://members.aol.com/arci31280/arci.htm

Charles Haynes
Belleville Area Antique Radio Club
219 W. Spring
Marissa, IL 62257

Robert Lane, Pres.
Mid-American Antique Radio Club
Newsletter: Broadcaster, The
10332 Mowhawk Lane
Shawnee Mission, KS 66206-2525
ph: 913-648-5296
fax: 913-341-1610
e-mail: personal@shots.com
Historical preservation and collecting ratios with two auctions a year, April and October.

Steve Morton
Nebraska Antique Radio Collectors Club
Newsletter: NARCC Newsletter
905 West First
North Platte, NE 69101

Oklahoma Vintage Radio Collectors
Newsletter: OKVRC Broadcast News
P.O. Box 71-1197
Oklahoma City, OK 73172

C.F. Crandell, Pres.
Vintage Radio & Phonograph Society, Inc.
Newsletter: Reproducer, The
P.O. Box 165345
Irving, TX 75016-5345
ph: 214-337-2823 or 972-315-2553
e-mail: billhar@flash.net
web: http://www.flash.net/~billhar/vrpsinfo.htm
Purpose is to preserve early radios, phonographs, and related material and to conduct historical research of same.

David Moore
Houston Vintage Radio Association
Newsletter: Grid Leak, The
P.O. Box 31276
Houston, TX 77231-1276
e-mail: wd11@mindspring.com
web: http://www.clarc.org/HVRA/
Monthly meetings and electronic seminars, annual convention, swap meets, Christmas celebration, and two MEGA auctions.

Larry Weide, Ed.
Colorado Radio Collectors
Newsletter: Flash!, The
5270 East Nassau Circle
Englewood, CO 80110
ph: 303-758-8382
e-mail: lweide@ibm.net
Holds bi-monthly meetings and swap meets; annual auction, public displays, presentations, get-togethers/picnic.

Bill Lettow
Arizona Antique Radio Club, Inc.
Newsletter: AARC News
2025 E. LaJolla Dr.
Tempe, AZ 85282-5910
Has swap meets in Phoenix and Tucson, regular meetings and exhibits, quarterly journal.

Ed Brady, Treas.
New Mexico Radio Collectors Club
Newsletter: New Mexico Radio Collectors Club Newsletter
1333 White Rim Pl. NE
Albuquerque, NM 87112
e-mail: DJAdamson@aol.com
web: http://members.aol.com/djadamson5/nmrcc/nmrcc.html

Robert Schoenbeck
Southern California Antique Radio Society
Magazine: California Antique Radio Gazette
9301 Texhoma Ave.
Northridge, CA 91325-2330

California Historical Radio Society, North Valley Chapter
Newsletter: NVC-CHRS Newsletter
P.O. Box 31659
San Francisco, CA 94131
ph: 415-821-9800
web: http://www.antiqueradios.com/chrs/chrs.html

California Historical Radio Society
Journal: CHRS Journal
P.O. Box 31659
San Francisco, CA 94131-0659
ph: 415-978-9100
e-mail: mhadams@got.net
web: http://www.antiqueradios.com/chrs/
Members focus on vintage radios and other old electronics.

Waldo T. Boyd, Sec.
Society of Wireless Pioneers Inc.
P.O. Box 86
Geyserville, CA 95441
e-mail: k6dzy@netdex.com
web: http://web.mountain.net/~carto/sowp001.htm
Dedicated to collecting, researching, recording, preserving the history of communications, particularly wireless and radio telegraphy.

Sacramento Historical Radio Society
P.O. Box 162612
Sacramento, CA 95816-9998

Northwest Vintage Radio Society
Newsletter: NVRS Call Letter
P.O. Box 82379
Portland, OR 97282-0379
ph: 503-654-7387 or 503-281-6585
e-mail: wren@peak.org
web: http://www.peak.org/~wren/links.html

Harold Hagen
Puget Sound Antique Radio Association
Newsletter: Horn of Plenty
P.O. Box 7251
Seattle, WA 98133
ph: 425-747-1323
e-mail: hhagen@eskimo.com
web: http://www.eskimo.com/~hhagen/psara.html
Dedicated to the preservation, restoration of antique radio & wireless equipment; maintains a museum that is open to the public; activities include swap meets, auction, and monthly meetings featuring lectures, demonstrations.

Ottowa Vintage Radio Club
P.O. Box 84084, Pinecrest
Ottawa, Ontario K2C 3Z2
Canada
ph: 613-828-5152

Kenneth R. Allison, Ed.
Canadian Vintage Radio Society
Newsletter: Radio Waves
182 Street, #9515
Edmonton, Alberta V4N 3V8
Canada
ph: 604-882-0709
e-mail: krallison@lightspeed.bc.ca
Membership across Canada, USA, Europe, New Zealand, Australia, and Japan.

Mike Barker
British Vintage Wireless Society
Magazine: BVWS Bulletin
59 Dunsford Close
Hillside Park
Swindon, Wiltshire SN1 4PW
U.K.
ph: 01793 536040
e-mail: mike_barker@mitel.com
web: http://www.bvws.org.uk/

Collectors

George Kaczowka
P.O. Box 103
Boylston, MA 01505
ph: 508-869-6376
e-mail: gsk@oldradios.com
web: http://www.oldradios.com/gsk/
Collector of antique radios from the 1930s, and early transistor radios from the 1950s and 1960s; over 20 years experience.

Steve Fullmer
110 Delmage Rd.
Swansea, MA 02777
e-mail: sfullmer@ici.net
web: http://www.ici.net/cust_pages/sfullmer/sfullmer.html
Specializes in collecting wood radios.

Harry Poster
Vintage TV's
P.O. Box 1883
South Hackensack, NJ 07606-0483
ph: 201-794-9606
fax: 201-794-9553
e-mail: hposter@att.net
web: http://www.harryposter.com
Buying Art Deco and other unusual and old radios; also wants colorful Bakelite and Catalin, mirror, chrome & black, clear plastic, and other unusual sets; early battery & crystal radios, breadboard, speakers, horns; entire shops bought.

Jim McKinnon
605 North Bridge St.
Bridgewater, NJ 08807
An avid collector specializing in early battery and AC table radios.

Radio
P.O. Box 51
Alplaus, NY 12008-0051
ph: 518-399-0080
Wants to buy old radios made by Zenith, FADA, Emerson, Crosley, Bendix, Detrola, Grebe, Atwater Kent, and most others; early battery sets, crystal sets, cathedrals, and colorful plastics; single pieces or entire collections.

John Rohrer
John's Antique Radios
567 Railroad St.
Windber, PA 15963
e-mail: jrradio@twd.net
web: http://galaxy.twd.net/oldradio/
Collector of old radios; website has pictures of old radios, links to antique radio pages, parts for sale.

Alvin Heckard
RD 1 Box 88
Lewistown, PA 17044-9801
ph: 717-248-7071 or 717-248-2816
Wants wood table model radios, colored Bakelite and plastic radios; also any parts, tubes, literature, service manuals, advertising, etc.

Gerald Schneider
3101 Blueford Rd.
Kensington, MD 20895-2726
ph: 301-929-8593
Wants to buy vintage radios, radio equipment, parts, and related literature; specialization in radios with Oriental-style cabinets, and radio/furniture combinations (radio lamps, bed headboards with radios, tables with radios, etc.)

Richard O. Gates
P.O. Box 187
Chesterfield, VA 23832-0187
ph: 804-748-0382 or 804-794-5146
fax: 804-748-6349
e-mail: rogates@mindspring.com
Wants to buy 1930s and 1940s Catalin radios with names such as FADA, Emerson, Garod, etc.; also wants Charlie McCarthy, Hopalong Cassidy, and Sparton mirrored radios.

Edward K. Bell
5311 Woodsdale Rd.
Raleigh, NC 27606-3341
ph: 919-851-1517
fax: 919-851-1517
e-mail: ekbell@mindspring.com
Wants to buy old radios: pre-1926 battery sets, crystal sets, interesting plastics, cathedrals, advertising, horn speakers, old tubes, etc. Will buy entire collections.

Gary B. Schneider
9511 Sunrise Blvd. #J-23
North Royalton, OH 44133-3410
ph: 440-582-3094 or 216-251-3714
fax: 216-251-3714
e-mail: gbsptop@aol.com
Wants pre-1940 radio items: radios, tubes, parts, speakers; also technical radio magazines, catalogs, books, advertising, etc.

Steve Dando
4572 Mark Trail
Akron, OH 44321-1462
ph: 330-666-7222

Jerry Rose
Jerry's Antique Radio
4738 Branstetter Rd.
Nashville, IN 47448
ph: 812-988-4353
fax: 812-988-4347
e-mail: jerry.rose@usa.net
web: http://www.geocities.com/~jrose3/
Collects old radios and related items.

Larry Spilkin
P.O. Box 5039
Southfield, MI 48086-5039
ph: 248-642-3722
Wants Catalin & Bakelite radios especially colored, marbleized or Art Deco styles.

Doug Heimstead
1349 Hillcrest Dr.
Fridley, MN 55432
A collector with a special interest in unusual and mirror radios from both well-known and obscure manufacturers.

Dr. Barry Janov
2454 Depmster St., Ste. 416
Des Plaines, IL 60016-5320
Wants to buy early radios, microphones, speakers and related items.

William Ross
875 Gordon Terrace
Winnetka, IL 60093
ph: 847-441-6462 or 312-364-8722
e-mail: bross@interaccess.com
Interested in old radios and TVs; also related premiums; organizes Radiofest, a major antique radio meet.

"Flip" Livingston
Remember When Antiques & Collectibles
2809 NW Expressway, Ste. 150
Oklahoma City, OK 73132
ph: 405-722-1475 or 405-721-7034
fax: 405-415-2114
e-mail: flip1308@webtv.net
Wants to buy Zenith and Philco radios from 1936 to 1942; also wants transistor radios from the 1950s and 1960s; also tubes, speakers, radio cabinets.

Paul Thompson
315 Larkspur Dr.
Santa Maria, CA 93455-1625
ph: 805-934-2778
Wants Atwater Kent "breadboard" radios and parts for same; also early battery radios, crystal sets, parts, speakers, tubes and magazines.

Pete Petersen
5214 120th Ave. SE
Bellevue, WA 98006-2826
ph: 425-747-1323
e-mail: wy7z@juno.com
Collector of antique radios and related memorabilia.

John Jenkins
15736 NE 143 Place
Woodinville, WA 98072
ph: 425-936-8856
fax: 425-489-9566
e-mail: johnj@halcyon.com
web: http://www.halcyon.com/johnj/radios/
Long time collector of pre-1930 radios and wireless items; web site is a virtual Museum with hundreds of images of items in his collection; also repairs radios.

Dealers

John Sakas
P.O. Box 4124
South Hackensack, NJ 07606-4124
ph: 201-794-0437
fax: 201-794-8359
Specializing in Catalin, Deco, mirror radios; also in Art Deco clocks.

Richard G. Brill
RGB Enterprises
P.O. Box 5367
Old Bridge, NJ 08857
ph: 732-607-0299
fax: 732-679-8024
e-mail: rgbent@aol.com
Welcomes information and schematics on all antique foreign radios; radios from the 1930s to 1960s; specializes in foreign radios; needs info on former Eastern European country radios like Tesla, Goplana, etc.

Charlotte Mager
Waves
110 W. 25th St., 10th Floor
New York, NY 10001
ph: 212-989-9284
fax: 201-461-7121
e-mail: c1wave@aol.com
web: http://www.wavesradio.com
Established in 1976, buys, sells, repairs, appraises and rents radios, phonographs, TVs, microphones, telephones, fans, neon clocks and signs, and related advertising and literature.

Bruce & Charlotte Mager
Waves
Chelsea Antiques Building
110 West 25th St., 10th Floor
New York, NY 10001-7401
ph: 212-989-9284
fax: 201-461-7121
e-mail: c1wave@aol.com
web: http://www.wavesradio.com/
Over 20 years experience specializing in vintage radios, phonographs, telegraphy, televisions, assorted electrical and mechanical apparatus, and related advertising memorabilia, books and pamphlets.

Antica
P.O. Box 41
Eastchester, NY 10709-0041
ph: 914-337-7176
fax: 914-337-7176
Wants Deco radios: colorful plastic, mirrored, chrome, wood by Air King, Detrola, Emerson, FADA, Kadette, Motorola, Sparton, etc.; also wants radios from 1900s to 1920s: Marconi, Western Electric, commercial and broadcasting.

Allen W. Tomisman
33 Bailey Ave.
Latham, NY 12110
ph: 518-785-3117

Gary Formica
Radio Research
823 91st Street
Niagara Falls, NY 14304
ph: 716-283-2274 or 716-283-2651
Buys and sells radios and related items.

John & Kathy Slusser
Radio Daze
P.O. Box 144
Mendon, NY 14506
ph: 716-624-9755
fax: 716-624-7857
e-mail: info@radiodaze.com
web: http://www.radiodaze.com
Specialists in antique and novelty tube and transistor radios; offers professional repair and restoration services; buys and sells radios, vacuum tubes, parts, literature, magazines, and advertising; major E.H. Scott radio collector.

Chris Savino
P.O. Box 419
Breesport, NY 14816-0419
ph: 607-739-3106
fax: 607-739-3106
e-mail: csavino@extrope.net
Buying plastic color radios from the 1930s to 1950s; by makers such as Air King, Addison, Arvin, Crosley, De Wald, Emerson, Espey, Fada, Garod, GE, RCA, Sentinel, Sonora, Sparton, and Stewart Warner; AM tabletop radios only.

Donald M. Maurer
Maurer Radio-TV Service
29 South 4th St.
Lebanon, PA 17042
ph: 717-272-2481
e-mail: dmradios@aol.com
web: http://members.aol.com/dmradios/index.html
Supplier of hard-to-find radio and TV tubes, new old stock and in original boxes; also buying vintage tube/transistor radios and pre-1960 TV Guides; send SASE for price lists and inquiries.

John Okolowicz
624 Cedar Hill Rd.
Ambler, PA 19002-1504
ph: 215-542-1597
e-mail: grillecloth@compuserve.com
web: http://www.grillecloth.com
Buys, sells, trades pre-1950 radios and TV's in unusual or ornate plastic or wooden cabinets; especially those made by Emerson, Stromberg Carlson, or Detrola; also sells 40 types of antique radio reproduction grille cloth.

John E. Kendall
Vintage Electronics
P.O. Box 436
Fallston, MD 21047-0436
e-mail: maloney@vintage-electronics.com
web: http://www.vintage-electronics.com
Wants radios from the 1920s through 1960s; buys, sells tube and transistor radios, unusual TV's and other early odd electronics; also related items such as books, schematics, tubes, parts, advertising, odd test equipment.

Tommy Meers
GARMCo
fax: 404-297-8161
e-mail: garmco@mindspring.com
web: http://www.garm.com/garmradio.htm
Buys and sells vintage electronics including antique tube, crystal and transistor radios, phonographs (record players), microphones, televisions and related collectibles; on Internet since 1996; worldwide insured shipping.

Antique Radios, Inc.
P.O. Box 6352
Jackson, MI 49204-6352
ph: 517-787-2985
Manufacturer of power supplies for pre-1930s battery radios; complete electrical restoration of early 20's through 40's radios (no cabinet work); no list of radios available; appraisals on a fee-basis.

Merrill Mabbs
Classic Radio Gallery
709 Pluma Drive
Rapid City, SD 57702
e-mail: mmabbs@cpu.net
web: http://cpu.net/classicradio
Specializes in early 1930s to 1940s radios; schematics available for most US made radios from the 1920s to the 1950s; has an online virtual radio museum at the web site; also repairs.

Dick Morgan
Radio Man, The
3630 Cavalier Dr.
Garland, TX 75042-7503
ph: 972-272-3581
fax: 972-272-1831
e-mail: theradioman@att.net
Buys, sells, trades antique radios; also sells tubes for antique radios.

John D. McKenna
Radio King, The
801-803 W Cucharras St.
Colorado Springs, CO 80905
ph: 719-630-8732
Buys, sells, restores 1930-1950 vacuum tube radios, especially Zenith wood radios.

Joe Pfeiffer
Zapper Technologies
P.O. Box 253
Sandy, UT 84091-0253
ph: 801-571-5453
e-mail: joep@antiquesecrets.com
web: http://www.antiquesecrets.com/
Buy, sell, trade tube and transistor radios, early Hi-Fi, old tubes, microphones, HAM gear, books, manuals, catalogs, telegraph items, test equipment, radio ads and collectibles, Nipper and Reddy Kilowatt items.

Helen Wood
Wood's Antiques & Collectibles
2110 Heights Cr.
Alamogordo, NM 88310
ph: 505-434-0887
fax: 505-434-2546
e-mail: woods@zianet.com
web: http://www.zianet.com/woods
Offers online sales and help with antique/collectible computers and radios.

Henry Rogers
Virginia City Radio Museum
P.O. Box 511
109 "F" Street
Virginia City, NV 89440
ph: 775-847-9047
e-mail: hands@radioblvd.com
web: http://www.radioblvd.com
Buys, sells, and restores 1915 to 1950s antique radios.

Steve Oliphant
5255 Allott Ave.
Van Nuys, CA 91401-5902
ph: 818-789-2339 or 818-865-1400
fax: 818-865-1450
e-mail: jlo55@aol.com
Dealer in old phonographs and radios; buys entire collections or individual pieces.

Mike Harrod
Trailside Treasures
365 Victor Street "S"
Salinas, CA 93907
e-mail: m.harrod@worldnet.att.net
web: http://home.att.net/~m.harrod/
Buy, sells and trades coin-operated machines; many coin-ops, plastic radios and other gameroom collectibles in stock.

Adam Schoolsky
P.O. Box 23182
Portland, OR 97281-3162
ph: 503-579-3162
fax: 503-579-5046
e-mail: Adam@ArtDeco.com
web: http://www.ArtDeco.com
Buying one item of entire collections or estates; specializing in radios from 1910-1950 with Art Deco wood, plastic, mirrored cabinets; also buying any radio related advertising signs, banners, clocks, etc.; expert restorations.

Malcom Bennett
Vintage Radios
Shirley, Munns Lane
Hartlip.
Sittingbourne, Kent ME9 7SY
U.K.
ph: 01795 842616
e-mail: mfb@valve.demon.co.uk
web: http://www.valve.demon.co.uk
Purveyor and collector of vintage/antique radios and valves (tubes); also service data and components; plus full repair restoration services offered.

Experts

Marty & Sue Bunis
Radio Man, The
32 West Main St.
Bradford, NH 03221
ph: 603-938-5051
fax: 603-938-2430
e-mail: m_bunis@conknet.com
web: http://www.conknet.com/~m_bunis/
Collects and appraises old and unusual radios, especially novelty sets and 1950s/1960s transistors; authors of "Collector's Guide to Antique Radios."

Bob Eslinger
Antique Radio Restoration & Repair
20 Gary School Rd.
Pomfret Center, CT 06259-1212
ph: 860-928-2628
fax: 860-928-2628
e-mail: radiodoc@neca.com
web: http://users.neca.com/radiodoc
Professional restorations for all tube type antique table and console radios, communication receivers and music amplifiers; complete overhauls; lacquer sprayed hand rubbed and polished cabinet refinishing; also appraises, buys & sells.

Gerald Schneider
3101 Blueford Rd.
Kensington, MD 20895-2726
ph: 301-929-8593

Mark Stein
Radiomania
2109 Carterdale Rd.
Baltimore, MD 21209
fax: 410-466-0815
e-mail: radioman@crosslink.net
web: http://www.radiomania.com
Publisher of "Machine Age to Jet Age," Vol. 1 & 2 which picture over 4,000 radios; largest vintage radio retailer in US; website catalog offers over 200 radios at any time; internationally renowned expert on 1930s to 1950s US radios.

Gary B. Schneider
9511 Sunrise Blvd. #J-23
North Royalton, OH 44133-3410
ph: 440-582-3094 or 216-251-3714
fax: 216-251-3714
e-mail: gbsptop@aol.com
Founding publisher of "Antique Radio Classified"; author of "1988 Official Price Guide to Antiques - Radio Classification."

John M. England, Jr.
P.O. Box 393
Lincolnshire, IL 60069
ph: 847-823-5287
fax: 847-823-5287
e-mail: triodes@sprintmail.com
Buys, collects, sells, appraises radios and equipment made by Stromberg-Carlson of Rochester, NY; also wants to buy Stromberg-Carlson Co. radios, Scott radios, mirrored radios, plus related literature, magazines, ephemera.

David Lane
2515 W. 88th St.
Leawood, KS 66206
ph: 913-341-1610
Co-author of "Transistor Radios - a Collector's Encyclopedia and Price Guide."

Robert Lane
10332 Mowhawk Lane
Shawnee Mission, KS 66206-2525
ph: 913-648-5296
fax: 913-341-1610
e-mail: personal@shots.com
Co-author of "Transistor Radios - a Collector's Encyclopedia and Price Guide."

Mike Adams
112 Crescent Ct.
Scotts Valley, CA 95066-2815
ph: 408-924-4545
fax: 408-924-4543
Specialty area is radio and broadcast history; produced "Radio Collector" series for PBS TV; writes for "Antique Radio Classified."

Jonathan F. Winter
Bellingham Antique Radio Museum
1421 Saint Paul
Bellingham, WA 98226
ph: 360-671-4663
e-mail: jwinter@pacificrim.net
web: http://www.antique-radio.org/radio.html

Internet Resources

Antique Radio Collector, The
e-mail: wrldradio@aol.com
web: http://members.aol.com/wrldradio/
The international Internet magazine for collectors of antique radios and communications equipment; ads, news, radio club addresses.

Antique Radio Resource Page
e-mail: caschwark@aol.com
web: http://members.aol.com/caschwark/
Parts and supplies, restoration books and information, internet resources, online collections and museums, homebrew construction project.

Don Adamson
Antique Radio Page
e-mail: djadamson@aol.com
web: http://members.aol.com/djadamson/arp.html
Website has a gallery of radios from 1920s to 1960s; also reference books, articles, web sites, and a directory of information about 1500 antique radios from web sites around the world.

Tom Sundstrom
Radio Netherlands' Antique & Old Time Radio Page
P.O. Box 2275
Vincentown, NJ 08088-2275
ph: 609-859-2447
fax: 609-859-3226
e-mail: trs@trsc.com
web: http://www.rnw.nl/realradio/links/html/antique_index.html
A world-wide comprehensive compilation of several hundred web sites about antique and old-time radio; with descriptions, grouped by categories; a free service.

Richard Lancaster
Nostalgia Air
P.O. Box 2328
Melbourne, FL 32902-2328
e-mail: info-mo@nostalgiaair.org
web: http://www.nostalgiaair.org
Dedicated to the preservation, conservation and free dissemination of antique and vintage radio and electronics technical information, schematics, technical information, tube references, manuals, articles, vintage publications.

Steve Adams
RadioGallery.com
P.O. Box 90
Moody, AL 35004
ph: 205-640-2701
fax: 205-640-2701
e-mail: radios@RadioGallery.com
web: http://www.radiogallery.com
RadioGallery.com features classified ads with color photos of antique and collectible radios, phonographs, and other radio-related items for sale; free wanted and "help" ads; free notices of radio club events.

Warren Parks
Warren's Antique Radio Restoration Homepage
4470 S. Lemay Ave. #508
Fort Collins, CO 80525
e-mail: park7963@verinet.com
web: http://www.verinet.com/~park7963/radio.html
Website provides tips, hints, how-to and links on restoring and repairing antique radios: case histories, explanations of the restoration process and lots of pictures.

Phil Nelson
Phil's Old Radios
16104 167th Avenue NE
Woodinville, WA 98072
e-mail: philnelson@antigueradio.org
web: http://antiqueradio.org/
Comprehensive web site for antique radios; large online gallery with color photos, free ads for collectors, extensive information about restoration of old radios, special section for beginning collectors, links, and more.

Museums/Libraries

Robert Merriam
New England Wireless & Steam Museum, Inc.
1300 Frenchtown Road
East Greenwich, RI 02818
ph: 401-884-1710 or 401-885-0545
fax: 401-884-0683
e-mail: newsm@ids.net
web: http://users.ids.net/~newsm/

Connecticut Vintage Radio & Communications Museum, Inc.
1173 Main St.
East Hartford, CT 06108
ph: 860-675-9916
Displays include radio, television, motion picture and telephone equipment, as well as advertising and other communications related memorabilia.

Museum of Television & Radio
25 West 52nd St.
New York, NY 10019
ph: 212-621-6800 or 212-621-6600
web: http://www.mtr.org
Museum had two locations, one in New York city and one in Los Angeles.

Bruce Kelley
Antique Wireless Association's Electronic Communication Museum
59 Main St.
Holcomb, NY 14469-9336
ph: 716-657-6260 or 716-657-7489
e-mail: n2rsm@frontiernet.net
web: http://www.ggw.org/freenet/a/awa/
Open limited hours May through October; call or write before visiting; please enclose SASE if requesting a reply.

Richard Post
Museum of Radio & Technology, Inc.
1640 Florence Ave.
Huntington, WV 25701
ph: 304-525-8890
e-mail: postr@ohiou.edu
web: http://oak.cats.ohiou.edu/~post/MRT/
Great displays of old radios from the 1930s to 1950s.

Indiana Historic Radio Museum
800 Lincolnway South
Ligonier, IN 46767-0353
ph: 888-417-3562 or 219-894-9000
e-mail: olradio@ligtel.com
web: http://home.att.net/~indianahistoricalradio/ihrp6mus.htm
Features radios from the 1920s through the 1960s, specialty radios, novelty radios, WWII radios including one from Nazi Germany, telegraph keys.

Pavek Museum of Broadcasting
3515 Raleigh Ave.
Minneapolis, MN 55416
ph: 612-926-8198
fax: 612-926-9761
e-mail: sraymer@pavekmuseum.org
web: http://www.pavekmuseum.org/
Houses one of the world's finest collections of antique radio, television, and broadcast equipment.

Keith R. Gill
Museum of Science & Industry
57th St. & Lake Shore Dr.
Chicago, IL 60637
ph: 773-684-1414
fax: 773-684-5580

Henry Rogers
Virginia City Radio Museum
P.O. Box 511
109 "F" Street
Virginia City, NV 89440
ph: 775-847-9047
e-mail: hands@radioblvd.com
web: http://www.radioblvd.com
Museum of antique radios from 1915 through 1950s; also radio accessories, photographs, vacuum tubes and history; antique radio restoration service also available.

Museum of Television & Radio
465 N. Beverly Dr.
Beverly Hills, CA 90210
ph: 310-786-1000
web: http://www.mtr.org
Museum had two locations, one in New York city and one in Los Angeles.

Jonathan F. Winter
Bellingham Antique Radio Museum
1421 Saint Paul
Bellingham, WA 98226
ph: 360-671-4663
e-mail: jwinter@pacificrim.net
web: http://www.antique-radio.org/radio.html
Private collection held as a museum; open to the public Wed. through Sat; specializing in pre-1927 radios; many of the examples on display are able to be played and examined.

Periodicals

John V. Terrey
Magazine: Antique Radio Classified
P.O. Box 2
Carlisle, MA 01741
ph: 978-371-0512
fax: 978-371-7129
e-mail: arc@antiqueradio.com
web: http://www.antiqueradio.com
Antique radio's largest monthly about old radios, Art Deco, TV's, ham equip. - '40s, '50s, books, telegraph, etc.; lots of ads.

Magazine: Gameroom Magazine
P.O. Box 41
Keyport, NJ 07735-0041
ph: 732-739-1955
fax: 732-739-2834
e-mail: coinop@gameroommagazine.com
web: http://www.gameroommagazine.com
A great source of information for the collector and dealer of jukeboxes, pinballs, slot machines, Coke and other soda machines, arcade games, classic arcade video, and other gameroom collectibles.

James Cranshaw
Horn Speaker, The
Newspaper: Horn Speaker, The
P.O. Box 1193
Mabank, TX 75147-1193
ph: 903-848-0304
fax: 903-848-0596
e-mail: cranshaw@gte.net
web: http://home.navisoft.com/horn/ths2.htm
A newspaper for collectors and historians interested in antique radios and phonographs.

Joe Pfeiffer
XTAL Publishing
Directory: International Dir. of Antique Radio Collectors
P.O. Box 253
Sandy, UT 84091-0253
ph: 801-571-5453
e-mail: joep@antiquesecrets.com
web: http://www.antiquesecrets.com/
Lists radio collectors, dealers, historians, publications, stores, services, repairs, restorations, museums, clubs; free listings, display ads available.

Repair Services

Bob Eslinger
Antique Radio Restoration & Repair
20 Gary School Rd.
Pomfret Center, CT 06259-1212
ph: 860-928-2628
fax: 860-928-2628
e-mail: radiodoc@neca.com
web: http://users.neca.com/radiodoc
Professional restorations for all tube type antique table and console radios, communication receivers and music amplifiers; complete overhauls; lacquer sprayed hand rubbed and polished cabinet refinishing; also appraises, buys & sells.

Stan Watkins
5326 Doncaster Dr.
Charlotte, NC 28211
ph: 704-362-2147
e-mail: stwradio@concentric.net
web: http://www.cris.com/~stwradio/

Daniel Blake
Outsider Studios
P.O. Box 63
Cedar Mountain, NC 28718-0063
ph: 828-884-2619
Repair and restoration of Catalin radios, Plaskon.

Ed Romney
Romney Publishing
P.O. Box 487
Drayton, SC 29333
ph: 864-597-1882
e-mail: Romney@edromney.com
web: http://www.edromney.com
Fix your own cameras! Romney offers camera repair manuals, courses, tools and restoration supplies for most cameras, old or new: Leica Graflex, Rolleiflex, Nikon, Canon and many more; also books on repairing old radios.

John Pelham
John Pelham's Antique Radio Repair
ph: 770-623-0533
e-mail: jpelham@mindspring.com
web: http://jpelham.home.mindspring.com/arr.htm
Offers electronic repair and restoration service for most U.S.-made

antique radios from the 1930s to present; guarantees all work.

Al Welch
Antique Radios
2248 S 33 Street
Milwaukee, WI 53215
ph: 414-383-9908
e-mail: awelch@execpc.com
web: http://www.execpc.com/~awelch/
Buy, repair and trade antique radios; prefers 1930s Zeniths, Grunows, pre-war plastics or 1950s Crosleys; any 1930s radio is of interest; will supply information or suggestions on repair of old radios.

Merrill Mabbs
Classic Radio Gallery
709 Pluma Drive
Rapid City, SD 57702
e-mail: mmabbs@cpu.net
web: http://cpu.net/classicradio
Specializes in early 1930s to 1940s radios; schematics available for most US made radios from the 1920s to the 1950s; has an online virtual radio museum at the web site; also repairs.

David B. Johnson
2336 S. Kenilworth Ave.
Berwyn, IL 60402
ph: 708-484-2743
Vintage TV and radio repair and restorations; both electronics and cosmetics.

Clinton Blais
Antique Radio Restorations
109 S Oak St.
O Fallon, IL 62269-2000
ph: 618-632-7423
Collects and restores old radios; electronic consultant; also manufactures reproductions radio dials.

David Headley
DH Distributors
P.O. Box 48623
Wichita, KS 67201-8623
ph: 316-684-0050
fax: 316-684-0050
Repairs and restores tube-type radios and audio equipment; chassis and cabinet restorations for tube-type radios; schematics.

John Jenkins
15736 NE 143 Place
Woodinville, WA 98072
ph: 425-936-8856
fax: 425-489-9566
e-mail: johnj@halcyon.com
web: http://www.halcyon.com/johnj/radios/
Long time collector of pre-1930 radios and wireless items; web site is a virtual Museum with hundreds of images of items in his collection; also repairs radios.

Malcom Bennett
Vintage Radios
Shirley, Munns Lane
Hartlip.
Sittingbourne, Kent ME9 7SY
U.K.
ph: 01795 842616
e-mail: mfb@valve.demon.co.uk
web: http://www.valve.demon.co.uk
Purveyor and collector of vintage/antique radios and valves (tubes); also service data and components; plus full repair restoration services offered.

Suppliers

Electron Tube Enterprises
P.O. Box 8311
Essex, VT 05451
ph: 802-879-0611
fax: 802-879-7764
e-mail: etetubes@vbimail.champlain.edu
web: http://members.aol.com/etetubes/
Dealers in surplus electron tubes; free catalog available; over 2000 different types in stock; both new and used tubes available.

Michael Tannenbaum
A.G. Tannenbaum
P.O. Box 386
Ambler, PA 19002
ph: 215-540-8055
fax: 215-540-8327
e-mail: k2bn@agtannenbaum.com
web: http://www.agtannenbaum.com
Provides electronic service data for new and antique electronic equipment of all types from pre-1930s radios to latest electronic equipment; sells copies of manufacturer's documentation; collector books, hard to find parts.

John Okolowicz
624 Cedar Hill Rd.
Ambler, PA 19002-1504
ph: 215-542-1597
e-mail: grillecloth@compuserve.com
web: http://www.grillecloth.com
Source for over 40 reproduction grille cloth patterns for antique radios from 1920-1940.

Old Tyme Radio Co.
2445 Lyttonsville Rd., Ste. 317
Silver Spring, MD 20910-1932
ph: 301-585-8776 or 301-587-5280
fax: 301-587-5280
Carries hard-to-find radio parts: vintage tubes, AK style battery cable, hook up wire, audio transformers, vintage headphones, etc.; also vintage radio repair service and vintage radio data packages; send LSASE for flyer.

J.W.F. Puett
Puett Electronics
Newsletter: Antique Radio Topics
P.O. Box 28572
Dallas, TX 75228-0572
ph: 214-321-0927 or 214-327-8721
Mail order business in its 19th year servicing the antique radio collector; sells anything for old radios. Send for catalog.

Antique Electronic Supply
6221 S. Maple Ave.
Tempe, AZ 85283-2856
ph: 602-820-5411
fax: 800-706-6789
e-mail: info@tubesandmore.com
web: http://www.tubesandmore.com/
Large catalog carrying tubes, supplies, capacitors, transformers, chemicals, test equipment, wire, parts, tools, books, old fabric lamp cords, etc.

Larry Bordonaro
Old Time Replications
5744 Tobias
Van Nuys, CA 91411-3349
ph: 818-786-2500
fax: 818-909-0241
e-mail: oldtimerep@aol.com
Supplies replacement knobs, push-buttons, escutcheons, plastic grills, handles, etc.

Mike Tobin
Rock-Sea Enterprises
323 E. Matilija St., #110-241
Ojai, CA 93023
ph: 805-646-7362
e-mail: dials@juno.com
web: http://members.aol.com/RockSeaEnt/
Manufacturer of dial scales for antique radios; specializing in plastic and card/foil dial scales as replacements for any radio including glass and metal dials.

Art Deco

Collectors

John M. England, Jr.
P.O. Box 393
Lincolnshire, IL 60069
ph: 847-823-5287
fax: 847-823-5287
e-mail: triodes@sprintmail.com
Buys and sells Art Deco radios, clocks, machine age design.

Dealers

Carl Ratner
550 Lamoka Ave.
Staten Island, NY 10312
ph: 718-317-1838
e-mail: artdeco@nyct.net
Buys, sells, trades, and restores Art Deco radios from the 1930s and 1940s.

Atwater Kent

Internet Resources

Vane Warner
1513 Meadow Way Ct.
Mansfield, TX 76063
ph: 817-473-0455
e-mail: vanew@airmail.net
web: http://web2.airmail.net/vanew/
This web site is devoted to providing information about Atwater Kent radios and the man who created them; pictures, schematics, advertising, and web links dealing with Atwater Kent radios.

Hallicrafters

Clubs/Associations

Hallicrafters Collectors Association
P.O. Box 521
Morgantown, IN 46160
e-mail: webmaster@hallicrafters.org
web: http://www.hallicrafters.org/
Promote the collecting, use and care of Hallicrafters Company radios and products; membership is open to all.

Speakers

Repair Services

Lakes Loudspeaker Service
4400 W. Hillsboro Blvd.
Coconut Creek, FL 33073
ph: 800-367-7757
Loudspeaker rebuilding service.

Transistor

Collectors

Bob Davidson
310 Main St.
Concord, MA 01742-2319
ph: 508-369-2007
e-mail: m31@channel1.com
Wants to buy Japanese pocket transistor radios.

John Treggiari
ph: 978-744-2897
fax: 978-744-5572
e-mail: micrometer@juno.com
Serious collector wants to buy small transistor radios made in U.S.A. or in Japan 1950s to early 1960s; radios need not be working; radios molded in bright colors especially wanted; also wants catalogs and related items.

Richard Lambert
166 East 34th St.
New York, NY 10016
ph: 212-684-6564
Wants to buy 1950s and 1960s transistor radios; Emerson, Regency, Zenith, Sony, etc.

Arnold Hornstein
21 Golden Hill Ct.
Baltimore, MD 21228
Wants transistor radios made in Japan or in the U.S.

Gary Willoughby
5930 W. Jefferson
Los Angeles, CA 90016
ph: 310-559-0706
fax: 562-836-6518
Wants early pocket-sized one or two transistor radios; some say "Boy's Radio" on back.

Darryl Rehr
Transistor Collectors
P.O. Box 641824
Los Angeles, CA 90064-6824
ph: 310-477-5229
fax: 310-268-8420
e-mail: dcrehr@earthlink.net
web: http://www.earthlink.net/~dcrehr/trans1.html
Buying attractive radios 1954-1963; send photocopy and SASE for reply; no chips or cracks, please.

Eric Wrobbel
20802 Exhibit Ct.
Woodland Hills, CA 91367-5205
ph: 818-884-2282
e-mail: ewrobbel@aol.com
Wants shirt-pocket or coat-pocket size transistor radios, working or not; made in the U.S. or in Japan; call or write with radio brand name and model number, or send photocopy of front of radio; also wants toy crystal radios.

Mike Kramer
P.O. Box 3257
Vallejo, CA 94590-0676
ph: 800-568-8883 or 800-446-6581
fax: 707-642-2456
Wants to buy shirt pocket size Japanese transistor radios; also wants Catalin table model radios.

Mike Brooks
7335 Skyline
Oakland, CA 94611-1121
ph: 510-339-1751
e-mail: deborahwb@aol.com
Wants to buy early American and Japanese transistor radios including boys' models, earphone only, and other miniature sets; also wants toy pocket crystal radios from the 1920s to 1960s.

Dealers

Bob Roberts
P.O. Box 152
Guilderland, NY 12084-0152
e-mail: hbv2020@compuserve.com
Wants to buy novelty transistor radios, e.g. Atlas Battery, Brut cologne, Budweiser, Pepsi, Coke, McDonald's, etc.; also wants telephones in unusual shapes, e.g. gas pumps, food items, cartoon characters, cars, movie related, TV, etc.

Experts

Gary Arnold
615 Oak St.
Marion, NC 28752
ph: 704-652-6893
e-mail: garnold@icu2.net
web: http://www.geocities.com/eureka/8761/index.html
Buys, sells and trades novelty radios; tube or transistor; website shows many for sale and wanted.

Bill Burkett
P.O. Box 2488
Sun City, AZ 85372-2488
ph: 623-974-4535 or 800-507-7234
fax: 623-974-4323
Buyer of 1950s transistor radios; especially interested in shirt-pocket or coat pocket size radios made by Mitchell, Raytheon, Regency, or Toshiba; solar-powered radios by Admiral or Hoffman and any size plastic or cabinet radio.

Periodicals

Marty & Sue Bunis
Newsletter: Transistor Network
32 West Main St.
Bradford, NH 03221
ph: 603-938-5051
fax: 603-938-2430
e-mail: m_bunis@conknet.com
web: http://www.conknet.com/~m_bunis/
A monthly newsletter featuring pictures, articles and classified ads - all exclusively about transistor radios.

Tubes For

Clubs/Associations

Ludwell Sibley, Ed.
Tube Collectors Association
Newsletter: Tube Collector
P.O. Box 1181
Medford, OR 97501
ph: 541-855-5207
e-mail: philbert@pacbell.net
web: http://www.eht.com/oldradio/tubecollectors/
Collectors group focused on the collecting of radio and wireless tubes.

Collectors

Leo Gibbs
Radio Tubes
701 Brookfield Rd.
Dayton, OH 45429-3323
ph: 937-299-3965
Wants pre-1925 antique radio tubes.

Dealers

Richard Bergeron
Electron Tube Enterprise
P.O. Box 8311
Essex, VT 05451
ph: 802-879-1844
fax: 802-879-7764
e-mail: etetubes@vbimail.champlain.edu
web: http://members.aol.com/etetubes
Specializes in old vacuum tubes for radios, TVs, amplifiers, radio HAM gear, etc.; both new and older, pretested, used tubes are available; in business for over 10 years.

James P. Cross
Vacuum Tubes, Inc.
3246 Floridale Lane
Cincinnati, OH 45239-6203
ph: 513-385-3855
fax: 513-385-3855
e-mail: vactubes@cinternet.net
web: http://www.cinternet.net/~vactubes/
Carries a full line of vacuum tubes for audiophiles, radio enthusiasts, industry, and collectors.

Dick Morgan
Electronic Communications
3630 Cavalier Dr.
Garland, TX 75042-7503
ph: 972-272-3581
fax: 972-272-1831
e-mail: ec.inc@att.net
Collector and dealer wants all types of radio tubes; prefer new in box, old stock tubes and new and used antique tubes.

Suppliers

David Headley
DH Distributors
P.O. Box 48623
Wichita, KS 67201-8623
ph: 316-684-0050
fax: 316-684-0050
Buys and sells receiving, transmitting and industrial vacuum tubes.

RAILROAD COLLECTIBLES

(see also BOOKS, Railroad; DINNERWARE, Advertising; RAILROADS; STREETCAR LINE COLLECTIBLES; TRAINS, Model; TRAINS, Toy; TRANSPORTATION COLLECTIBLES)

Clubs/Associations

Sam Ferrara, Treas.
Key, Lock & Lantern, Inc.
Newsletter: Key, Lock & Lantern
P.O. Box 66
Penfield, NY 14526
e-mail: lantrnsite@aol.com
web: http://members.aol.com/klnlsite/
Since 1966 providing railroadiana collectors with camaraderie, education, and enjoyment; quarterly journal contains articles, information, and photos on subjects of interest to collectors of railroad artifacts.

National Railway Historical Society
P.O. Box 58547
Philadelphia, PA 19102-8547
ph: 610-557-6606
fax: 610-557-6740
e-mail: services@nrhs.com
web: http://www.nrhs.com/

Greg Gneier
American Southwestern Railway Association
P.O. Box 39846
Los Angeles, CA 90039
ph: 213-668-0104
e-mail: asra@compuserve.com
web: http://mcscom.com/asra/
Non-profit educational organization formed in 1982 for the purpose of preserving the history of American railroading; collects and preserves railroad artifacts.

Richard Wright
Railroadiana Collectors Association
Newsletter: Express
P.O. Box 4894
Diamond Bar, CA 91765-0084
ph: 909-681-4647 or 909-364-6620
e-mail: wrights.rrstation@gte.net
Over 1400 members; focuses on railroadiana; newsletter carries articles and photos; annual convention.

Railway & Locomotive Historical Society
Journal: Railroad History
P.O. Box 193552
San Francisco, CA 94119
e-mail: pcc@mp1.com
web: http://www.mp1.com/
National organization devoted to railroad history.

Canadian Railroad Historical Association - Toronto & York Division
P.O. Box 5849
Station A
Toronto, Ontario M5W 1P3
Canada

Collectors

Harold Schreibman
P.O. Box 121
Mountain Dale, NY 12763-0121
ph: 914-434-6662 or 718-225-9480
e-mail: harloo414@aol.com
Railroad timetables, annual passes, badges, depot items, calendars.

Nestle's Railroadiana
RD 2, Box 105
Greenwich, NY 12834-9425
ph: 518-692-2867
Buys and sells all sorts of railroadiana and trolley memorabilia: timetables, guides, maps, advertising info., menus, old books and magazines, etc.

Randy Ridgely
447 Oglethorpe Ave.
Athens, GA 30606-2236
ph: 706-549-9264
e-mail: erie@negia.net
Wants railroad china, silver, paper, etc.; also steamship and airline items.

Miles Hess
P.O. Box 942
Fitzgerald, GA 31750
Wants to buy railroad telegraph keys, sounders, and telegraph bugs, etc.

Seth Bramson
330 N.E. 96th St.
Miami, FL 33138-2718
ph: 305-757-1016
fax: 305-895-8178
Buys railroad and trolleyana; postage paid on approvals.

Richard Hebel
233 Dietrich Crescent Dr.
Lawrenceburg, IN 47025
ph: 812-537-0150
e-mail: bhebel@seidata.com
Collector buying railroad items: lanterns, globes, china, silver, brass locks, etc.

Greg Gneier
American Southwestern Railway Association
P.O. Box 39846
Los Angeles, CA 90039
ph: 213-668-0104
e-mail: asra@compuserve.com
web: http://mcscom.com/asra/
Collector and museum preservation of railroad artifacts; especially interested in dining car and passenger train related items: china, silverware, menus, promotional items; specializing in Union Pacific, Santa Fe, & Southern Pacific.

Richard Wright
P.O. Box 4894
Diamond Bar, CA 91765-0084
ph: 909-681-4647 or 909-364-6620
e-mail: wrights.rrstation@gte.net
Wants railroad items such as china, silverware, lanterns, etc.; all inquires answered.

Dealers

Fred N. Arone
Depot Attic, The
3 Vista Place
Hartsdale, NY 10530-1202
ph: 914-693-5858
fax: 914-674-6030
Buys and sells pre-1960 railroadiana: paper ephemera, books, hardware, silverware and chinaware, timetables, lanterns, brass locks, posters and display advertising, calendars, passes, porcelain signs, hat badges, playing cards, etc.

Dave Nestle
Nestle's Railroadiana
RD 2, Box 105
Greenwich, NY 12834
ph: 518-692-2867
Buys and sells old railroad time tables, guides, passes, badges, post cards, magazines, advertising, etc.

L. Michael Boak
Initialed Duck Antiques & Collectibles
3812 Hamilton Ave.
Baltimore, MD 21206-3505
Buys, sells and collects primarily B&O railroad memorabilia.

Steve Schmale
Out West
2231 Creekside Rd.
Santa Rosa, CA 95405-8022
ph: 707-838-1859 or 707-575-5406
e-mail: outweststv@aol.com
Buys and sells better vintage postcards since 1976; approval service; strong in Western states views; always buying better cards and real photos; also wants railroad paper, stereoviews, photos, brochures, trade cards; member IFPD.

Scott Arden
Antiques & Artifacts
20457 Highway 126
Noti, OR 97461-9706
ph: 541-935-1619
Leading RR mail order dealer for 28 years; catalog $1; buys and sells fine old transportation items, mostly non-paper; consignment.

Raul Roy
P.D.R.'s Train Shop
3874 Winlake Cres.
Burnaby, British Columbia V5A 2G5
Canada
ph: 604-420-1292
fax: 604-420-1292
e-mail: proy@direct.ca
web: http://www.direct.ca/adz/pdr/pdr.html
Trades, buys, sells railroad memorabilia, collectibles: cloth crests, RR pins, etc.

Experts

Alan Altman
Golden Spike Enterprises Inc.
P.O. Box 422
Williamsville, NY 14221
ph: 716-689-9074

Richard C. Barrett
Railroad Research Publications
3400 Ridge Rd. West, Ste. 5-266
Rochester, NY 14626-3458
ph: 716-227-6903
Publisher of books on railroad collectibles and railroad history.

Sue & Bill Knous
Railroad Memories
1903 S. Niagara St.
Denver, CO 80224
Authors of "The Railroad Detective, a Guide to Replica & Counterfeit Railroad Collectibles."

Brad Lomazzi
1300 Liberty Ct.
Roseville, CA 95747-7440
ph: 916-782-6587
Dealer and expert in railroad collectibles; author of "Railroad Timetables, Travel Brochures & Posters," and "Railroad Collectibles - A History and Price Guide."

Internet Resources

High Iron Exchange
712 W. 18th Ave.
Hutchinson, KS 67502
ph: 316-662-1562
fax: 316-662-1562
e-mail: agent@highiron.com
web: http://www.highiron.com/
Online marketplace devoted to buying and selling model railroad equipment and related railroad and transportation collectibles.

Museums/Libraries

Ralph Justen
National Railroad Museum
Newsletter: Railines
2285 S. Broadway
Green Bay, WI 54304-7245
ph: 414-435-7623 or 414-435-7245
e-mail: staff@nationalrrmuseum.org
web: http://www.nationalrrmuseum.org
One of the oldest railroad museums in the country; 75+ pieces of rolling stock; world's largest steam locomotive; seasonal train rides; well stocked gift shop.

Howard Page
Old Depot Railroad Museum, The
651 West Hwy., #12
P.O. Box 99
Dassel, MN 55325-0099
ph: 320-275-3876
An old Great Northern depot filled with railroad artifacts: bells & whistles, uniforms, signs, signals, advertising toys & models, two cabooses, freight car, section car, track bicycle, pictures, calendars, etc.

Railroad & Pioneer Museum
710 Jack Basin
Temple, TX 76504-5372
ph: 254-778-6873

Periodicals

R.D. Roland
R.S. & T. Ry. Co.
Ad Paper: Main Line Journal, The
P.O. Box 121
Streamwood, IL 60107-0121
A bi-monthly "ad" paper exclusively for buying and selling railroad collectibles as well as airline and steamship memorabilia; subscribers receive FREE ads.

B & O Items

Collectors

Charles Boice
7003 Charles Ridge Rd.
Baltimore, MD 21204-3608
ph: 410-321-7149 or 301-897-8850
Wants to buy Baltimore & Ohio R.R. memorabilia and china.

Dealers

John R. Hickman
Railroad Antiques
772 Tiffany Dr.
Gaithersburg, MD 20878-1821
ph: 301-926-5818
Baltimore & Ohio R.R. memorabilia and china; also other transportation memorabilia from steamships and airlines.

Repro. Sources

B & O Railroad Museum
901 Pratt St.
Baltimore, MD 21223
ph: 410-752-2490
fax: 410-752-2499
e-mail: webinfo@borail.org
web: http://www.borail.org/
Sells B & O railroad china and other B & O related items.

China

Collectors

Robert D'Achille
3972 NY Rt. 26
Whitney Point, NY 13862-2708
ph: 607-862-3914
e-mail: rdachill@stny.rr.com
Wants any railroad china especially Railroad-marked; must be in good condition (no hairlines, cracks or chips, etc.)

Dealers

Alan Altman
Golden Spike Enterprises Inc.
P.O. Box 422
Williamsville, NY 14221
ph: 716-689-9074
Wants to buy railroad china, especially by Buffalo or Syracuse China.

Experts

Gerry & Christie Geisler
Great Delaware & New England Antiques Trading Company
P.O. Box 1065
Chatham, NJ 07928
ph: 973-635-0756

Douglas W. McIntyre
20 Cleveland Place
Lockport, NY 14094-3104
ph: 716-433-2235
Author of "The Official Guide to Railroad Dining Car China."

Museums/Libraries

B & O Railroad Museum, Chessie Shop
901 Pratt St.
Baltimore, MD 21223
ph: 410-752-2490
fax: 410-752-2499
e-mail: webinfo@borail.org
web: http://www.borail.org/
Shop sells B&O railroad china.

Dining Car Items

Collectors

Peter Tilp
B & T Publications
P.O. Box 580
Summit, NJ 07901-0580
Wants railroad dining car items and related railroad collectibles: china, silverware, flatware, glassware, napkins, menus, etc.

Dealers

Charles Goodman
636 W. Grant Ave.
Charleston, IL 61920-3226
ph: 217-345-6771
Wants railroad dining car china, silverware, flatware, glassware, napkins, menus, and related items; offers catalog of items for sale.

Hat Badges

Experts

Jim Younger
4628 Old Dragon Path
Ellicott City, MD 21042-5970
ph: 410-964-1949
e-mail: jmyr@erols.com
Wants railroad hat badges (from all railroads and in all occupations), hats, uniforms, and brotherhood (RR Unions) lapel pins.

Paper Items

Collectors

Carl Loucks
P.O. Box 484
North Haven, CT 06473-0484
ph: 203-288-3765
fax: 203-234-2729
Wants railroad timetables, brochures, guides, maps, menus; also trolley, air and bus.

Passes

Collectors

George Johnson
P.O. Box 1449
Lexington, VA 24450-1449
ph: 540-464-4326
fax: 540-464-4326
Wants to buy pre-1940 timetables for railroad, trolley, airline, and bus; also wants passes, catalogs, and postcards of small town depots.

Ed Lewis
P.O. Box 505
Aberdeen, NC 28315
ph: 910-692-7457
fax: 910-944-9738
Collector wants to buy railroad timetables and passes from small railroads.

Playing Cards

Experts

Phil Bollhagen
7940 West Leroy Ave.
Greenfield, WI 53220
ph: 414-327-6220
e-mail: bollhagp@rocketmail.com
Has one of the largest collections of antique railroad playing card decks in the U.S.; wants to buy quality pre-1915 decks from all railroads; author of "The Great Book of Railroad Playing Cards"; railroad decks and singles.

Porters

Museums/Libraries

A. Philip Randolph/Pullman Porter Museum
web: http://www.wimall.com/pullportermu/
The museum collection includes photographs and memorabilia that documents the struggle between corporate power and the disenfranchised workers.

Posters

Collectors

Charles G. Kratz, Jr.
17821 Golfview
Homewood, IL 60430-1210
ph: 708-799-8478 or 312-951-0336
Wants original railroad posters produced for American and Canadian companies; also original railroad paintings and any material relating to Chicago & Eastern Illinois Railroad.

Signal Lamps

Experts

David Dreimiller
33200 Brainbridge Rd., Ste. #4
Solon, OH 44139
ph: 440-569-7415
Author of "Signal Lights" which covers railroad signal lamps and lanterns; also buys lanterns and manufacturer's sales literature; will assist in lamp/lantern identification and appraisal.

Internet Resources

Paul Koren
Railroad Lantern Collecting Website
e-mail: lantrnsite@aol.com
web: http://members.aol.com/lantrnsite/

Timetables

Collectors

Collector
4000 N. Upland
Arlington, VA 22207
Wants to buy all pre-1910 railroad passes and timetables.

Ed Lewis
P.O. Box 505
Aberdeen, NC 28315
ph: 910-692-7457
fax: 910-944-9738
Collector wants to buy railroad timetables and passes from small railroads.

Uniforms

(see BUTTONS, Railroad/Transit Uniforms)

RAILROADS

(see also BOOKS, Railroad; RAILROAD COLLECTIBLES; STEAM-OPERATED, Models & Equipment; TRAINS, Model; TRAINS, Toy)

Clubs/Associations

National Railway Historical Society
P.O. Box 58547
Philadelphia, PA 19102-8547
ph: 610-557-6606
fax: 610-557-6740
e-mail: nrhs@compuserve.com
web: http://www.rrhistorical.com/nrhs/

New York Central System Historical Society, Inc.
Magazine: Central Headlight
P.O. Box 58994
Philadelphia, PA 19102-8994
ph: 610-687-1207
Publishes quarterly magazine; information, drawings, photos available; research sources; inquiries welcome.

M. Diane Elliott, Ex. Dir.
American Association of Private Railroad Car Owners
Magazine: Private Varnish
421 New Jersey Ave., SE
Washington, DC 20003
ph: 202-547-5696
fax: 202-547-5697
e-mail: deaaprco@tmn.com
web: http://www.aaprco.com
For enthusiasts and owners of private railroad cars.

Chesapeake & Ohio Historical Society, Inc.
Magazine: Chesapeake & Ohio Historical Magazine
P.O. Box 79
Clifton Forge, VA 24422
ph: 540-862-2210
Monthly articles on history of the C&O RR and predecessors (PM RR in Mich., HV RR in Ohio, etc.), as well as successor CSX Transportation.

Motor Car Collectors of America
Newsletter: Speeder
5 Bay View Hills
Wever, IA 52658
e-mail: mayfieldeb@worldnet.att.net
web: http://walden.mo.net/~jdobcek/mcca.htm
Members interested in the preservation and operation of railroad track cars, handcars, motor cars and velocipedes.

Steve Brist
Tourist Railway Association, Inc.
Magazine: TrainLine
P.O. Box 1022
Madison, WI 53701
ph: 800-67-TRAIN or 608-273-3470
fax: 608-271-4339
e-mail: office@train.org
web: http://www.train.org/
Formed in 1972 to encourage creative railroading; membership open to railway museums, clubs, tourist railroads, product suppliers, railroad publishers, private car owners, excursion operators, etc.

Collectors

Robert Gormley
334 Brownsburg Rd.
Newtown, PA 18940-9626
ph: 215-598-3520
Wants switchback and Mt. Pisqah, Mauch Chunk, PA railroad collectibles and souvenirs.

Dealers

D.F. Barnhardt
D.F. Barnhardt & Associates
Magazine: Railroad & Tourist Rail Magazine
8344 W. Franklin St.
P.O. Box 1088
Mount Pleasant, NC 28124-1088
ph: 704-436-9393
fax: 704-436-9399
web: http://www.trains-trams-trolleys.com/
Sells rolling stock; magazine advertises equipment for sale and contains stories that focus on the use of old time trains in tourist locations such as parks and amusement centers.

David Thebodo
Flange R.R. Equipment Co.
P.O. Box 2019
Fairfield, IA 52556-8019
ph: 515-472-2020
Buys and sells railroad rolling stock: cabooses, Fairmont motorcars, passenger cars, box cars, bunk cars, flatcars, baggage cars, coaches, and other railroad equipment.

Experts

Robert L. Johnson
Whistles in the Woods Museum Services
P.O. Box 309
Chickamauga, GA 30707-0309
ph: 706-375-4326
e-mail: oldgoat@voy.net
Consultants specializing in narrow-gauge, steam, industrial, logging and mining railroads; American, foreign (European, Australian); also inclines, aerial tramways, garden and large scale model railroads.

Internet Resources

www.rrhistorical.com
e-mail: webmaster@rrhistorical.com/
web: http://www.rrhistorical.com/
Great first stop for railroad historical information: links to railroad history, clubs, historical and technical societies, museums, clip art, model railroad manufacturers, etc.

Shane Lambert
Coulee Web
P.O. Box 271
La Crosse, WI 54602-0271
ph: 608-784-5445 or 608-782-3496
e-mail: couleeweb@iname.com
web: http://www.rrdepot.com/Miscellaneous/webring.html
The Railroad Web Ring is designed to bring together web sites that contain information about prototype railroads, model railroading, rail fanning, railroad museums, and railroad historical societies/

Museums/Libraries

Museum of Transportation at Larz Anderson Park
15 Newton St.
Brookline, MA 02146
ph: 617-522-6547
web: http://www.mot.org/

New York Museum of Transportation
P.O. Box 136
6393 East River Road
West Henrietta, NY 14586
ph: 716-533-1113
e-mail: crhauf@frontiernet.net
web: http://www.nymt.mus.ny.us/

California State Railroad Museum
111 “”I”” Street
Sacramento, CA 95814-2265
ph: 916-445-7387
fax: 916-327-5655
e-mail: csrmf@csrmf.org
web: http://www.csrmf.org/

Periodicals

Harold H. Carstens
Carstens Publications
Magazine: Railfan & Railroad
108 Phil Hardin Road
P.O. Box 700
Newton, NJ 07860-0700
ph: 973-383-3355 or 800-474-6995
fax: 973-383-4064
e-mail: carstens@carstens-publications.com
web: http://www.carstens-publications.com/mainindex.html

Harold H. Carstens
Carstens Publications
Magazine: Railroad Model Craftsman
108 Phil Hardin Road
P.O. Box 700
Newton, NJ 07860-0700
ph: 973-383-3355 or 800-474-6995
fax: 973-383-4064
e-mail: carstens@carstens-publications.com
web: http://www.carstens-publications.com/mainindex.html

D.F. Barnhardt
D.F. Barnhardt & Associates
Magazine: Railroad & Tourist Rail Magazine
8344 W. Franklin St.
P.O. Box 1088
Mount Pleasant, NC 28124-1088
ph: 704-436-9393
fax: 704-436-9399
web: http://www.trains-trams-trolleys.com/
Magazine advertises equipment for sale and contains stories that focus on the use of old time trains in tourist locations such as parks and amusement centers.

Kalmbach Publishing Co.
Magazine: Trains
P.O. Box 1612
21027 Crossroads Circle
Waukesha, WI 53187
ph: 414-796-8776 or 800-533-6644
fax: 414-796-1615
e-mail: customerservice@kalmbach.com
web: http://www.trains.com
For the railroad buff: capture the power, history and drama of railroading; learn about railroad empires, see the newest high-tech locomotives, enjoy award-winning photography.

Flying Scotsman

Collectors

Paul R. Dowie
P.O. Box 472
Chester Springs, PA 19425-0472
ph: 610-827-7561
e-mail: lner4472fs@aol.com
Collects anything related to LNER 4472 "Flying Scotsman" (both the locomotive and the train of the same name): photos (especially with second/water tender), recordings, china and flatware from the F.S. train; books, posters, models.

RANGES

(see also CAST IRON ITEMS; KITCHEN COLLECTIBLES; STOVES)

Clubs/Associations

Macy Stern
Antique Stove Association
Newsletter: Stove Parts Needed Newsletter
5515 Almeda Rd.
Houston, TX 77004-7443
ph: 713-521-0934 or 713-528-1297
fax: 713-521-0889
For those interested in antique stoves and related items; you must join to receive the benefits which are for members only.

Jack Santoro
Old Appliance Club
Newsletter: Old Road Home, The
P.O. Box 65
Ventura, CA 93002
ph: 805-643-3532
fax: 805-643-3532
e-mail: jes@west.net
web: http://www.antiquestove.com/
An organization for dealers, owners, restorers, users and fans of American appliances; accent is placed on mostly antique and classic ranges 1920s-1950s, Monitor-top refrigerators; builds thermostats, applies new porcelain, restores.

Dealers

Erickson's Antique Stoves, Inc.
P.O. Box 2275
At the Depot
Littleton, MA 01460
ph: 978-486-3589
Antique gas coal and wood stoves and ranges; bought, sold, restored.

Paul Schoenharl
Rectanus Stove Co.
1328 Aster Pl.
Cincinnati, OH 45224-3208
ph: 513-541-0450
Buys, sells and restores antique stoves and ranges (pre 1930) with emphasis on antique gas ranges 1882-1930; also lectures and writes magazine articles about early kitchen stoves.

Macy Stern
Macy's Texas Stove Works
5515 Almeda Rd.
Houston, TX 77004-7443
ph: 713-521-0934 or 713-528-1297
fax: 713-521-0889
Buys, sells, brokers, repairs, and restores old ranges; also sells parts and publishes "Classic Ranges" newspaper.

Jack Santoro
J.E.S. Enterprises
P.O. Box 65
Ventura, CA 93002
ph: 805-643-3532
fax: 805-643-3532
e-mail: jes@west.net
web: http://www.antiquestove.com/
Superior range restoration: mechanical systems rebuilt, genuine porcelain finishes, safety valves, Bakelite refinished, clocks & timers rebuilt, brilliant electroplating, oven controls, movie prop rentals.

Museums/Libraries

Paul Schoenharl
Cincinnati Stove Museum
1328 Aster Pl.
Cincinnati, OH 45224-3208
ph: 513-541-0450
Small museum of stoves and ranges; no admission.

Periodicals

Macy Stern
Macy's Texas Stove Works
Newspaper: Classic Ranges
5515 Almeda Rd.
Houston, TX 77004-7443
ph: 713-521-0934 or 713-528-1297
fax: 713-521-0889
The only newsletter for classic range owners and buyers; ranges/ovens and stoves for sale, ranges wanted to buy, parts for sale, restoration services, articles, old advertisements, etc.

Repair Services

Jack Santoro
J.E.S. Enterprises
P.O. Box 65
Ventura, CA 93002
ph: 805-643-3532
fax: 805-643-3532
e-mail: jes@west.net
web: http://www.antiquestove.com/
Superior range restoration: mechanical systems rebuilt, genuine porcelain finishes, safety valves, Bakelite refinished, clocks & timers rebuilt, brilliant electroplating, oven controls, movie prop rentals.

RATIONING RELATED ITEMS

(see also MILITARIA, WWII Items)

Clubs/Associations

Thomas B. Smith
Society of Ration Token Collectors
Newsletter: Ration Board, The
618 Jay Drive
Gallipolis, OH 45631-1314
Society collects, trades, sells paper & token home front ration items (for food, clothing, gasoline, tires, etc.); send SASE for info.

Collectors

Lee Poleske
P.O. Box 871
Seward, AK 99664-0871
Wants OPA tokens and other WWII ration items.

RAY GUNS

(see TOYS, Space & Robot [Ray Guns])

RAZORS

(see BARBERSHOP COLLECTIBLES; SHAVING COLLECTIBLES)

RECORD JACKETS

(see PAPER COLLECTIBLES; RECORDS)

RECORDED SOUND

(see also COMPACT DISCS; RADIO SHOWS, Old Time; RECORDS)

Clubs/Associations

Peter Shambarger, ExDir
Association for Recorded Sound Collections, Inc.
Journal: ARSC Journal
P.O. Box 543
Annapolis, MD 21404-0543
ph: 410-757-0488 or 410-956-5600
fax: 410-349-0175
e-mail: peters@umd5.umd.edu
web: http://www.arsc-audio.org/
Dedicated to the preservation and study of recordings in the fields of music and speech: Edison cylinders, rare discs, oral history, etc.; publishes the ARSC Journal twice a year and the ARSC Newsletter four times per year.

Dealers

Don Kyle
Soundtracks!
P.O. Box 107
Venice, CA 90294-0107
ph: 310-226-2883
fax: 323-417-4937
e-mail: sndtrx@earthlink.net
web: http://home.earthlink.net/~sndtrx
Buys and sells soundtracks; original cast, children's, Disney and personality LPs; sells via mail order and at conventions; also trades and buys collections.

RECORDS

(see also BOOKS, Reference [Records]; AUDIO-VISUAL; COMPACT DISCS; DRUM & BUGLE CORPS; HI-FI EQUIPMENT; MUSIC; PHONOGRAPHS; RECORDED SOUND; ROCK 'N' ROLL COLLECTIBLES)

Appraisers

Scott Neuman
Forever Vinyl
P.O. Box 526
Lakehurst, NJ 08733
ph: 732-505-3646
fax: 732-505-5337
e-mail: info@vinlyweb.com
web: http://vinylweb.com/
Buys, sells, trades rare and hard-to-find vinyl records and albums, 45s picture sleeves; most anything to do with music; over 500,000 items in stock; over 20 years in business; appraise for estate, insurance, etc.

John Vogel
Phonograph Record Appraisals & Search Service
1083 Research Blvd., Ste. 204
Rockville, MD 20850
ph: 301-251-7850
fax: 301-294-8057
e-mail: jdvee@aol.com
Appraises single records or entire collections; also offers a finders service to locate rare items for collectors; will help locate buyers for your collections.

Steven Smolian
Smolian Sound Preservation Studios
1 Worman's Mill Court #4
Frederick, MD 21701
ph: 301-694-5134
fax: 301-694-5179
Record collections appraised for tax donation, estate & insurance loss purposes; all formats - 78s, 45s, LPs, cylinders, radio disks, etc.; rock, classical, country, old news broadcasts; over 20 years appraising major archives.

Steve Underwood, ISA
Appraisals & Consulting by F. Steven Underwood
2516 Larwood Dr.
Charleston, WV 25302-4318
ph: 304-345-4089
Independent, professional appraisals for insurance, estate valuation, tax, legal, and other matters; Member, International Society of Appraisers.

Auction Services

Floyd Silver
Antique Phonograph Center
P.O. Box 2574
Vincentown, NJ 08088-2574
ph: 609-859-8617
e-mail: fsilver@compuserve.com
Conducts special mail auctions of rare and unusual 78 rpm Edison diamond discs and cylinder records; $2 for catalog.

Clubs/Associations

Record Collectors Guild
e-mail: the_rcguild@hotmail.com
web: http://members.tripod.com/~theRCGuild/
A community of record collectors interested in the pursuit of knowledge and the collecting of vinyl records.

Richard Phillips
Association of Independent Record Collectors
Newsletter: AIRC Newsletter
P.O. Box 222
Northford, CT 06472-0222
ph: 203-484-2023
e-mail: dipdadip@aol.com

Bill Pratt
Canadian Antique Phonograph Society
Journal: Antique Phonograph News
122 Major St.
Toronto, Ontario M5S 2L2
Canada
ph: 416-924-8207
e-mail: caps@rose.com
web: http://www.rose.com/~caps/
Members interested in sound recording and its history: phonographs, gramophones; also related ephemera and memorabilia; journal has original articles, repair tips and how-to's, auction results, ads.

Collectors

Dave A. Reiss
3920 Eve Dr.
Seaford, NY 11783-1553
ph: 516-785-8336
Collects 78 rpm's, 1900 to 1930s: popular, classical, jazz, personalities, dance records, gospel, country & western, ethnic.

Dealers

Gerald Wilson
Select Circle Records
3 Dandy Dr.
Cos Cob, CT 06807
ph: 203-661-8421
Specializes in Frank Sinatra.

Ardyth & John Stimson
AJS Marbles & Records
P.O. Box 8052
Glen Ridge, NJ 07028
e-mail: ajs@viconet.com
Buys, sells, collects machine-made or antique marbles; will trade, buy or sell; also deals in old records, especially jazz, R&B, 33/45/778 rpm.

Rod Baum
Rare Records
1432 Queen Anne Rd.
Teaneck, NJ 07666
ph: 201-833-4883
fax: 201-833-4874

Allen Radwill
23 Hunters Lane
Vincentown, NJ 08088-2837
ph: 609-953-5473
250,000 items related to rock & roll, rhythm & blues, soul, gospel, television, movies: records, sheet music, magazines; no CDs or videos.

Princeton Record Exchange
20 S. Tulane St.
Princeton, NJ 08542
ph: 609-921-0881
e-mail: info@prex.com
web: http://www.prex.com
Buys and sells new and used CDs, LPs, and tapes: rock, jazz, alternative, imports, oldies, shows, new releases, soundtracks, classical, opera, etc.

Scott Neuman
Forever Vinyl
P.O. Box 526
Lakehurst, NJ 08733
ph: 732-505-3646
fax: 732-505-5337
e-mail: info@vinlyweb.com
web: http://vinylweb.com/
Buys, sells, trades rare and hard-to-find vinyl records and albums, 45s picture sleeves; most anything to do with music; over 500,000 items in stock; over 20 years in business; appraise for estate, insurance, etc.

Robert Hess
155 West 72nd St., #404
New York, NY 10023
ph: 212-579-0689
e-mail: hfis646942@aol.com
web: http://www.coachnet.com/music
Wants 1948-1965 LP records (33 1/3 rpm): V-Discs, picture discs, Jazz, R&B, R 'n R, Blues, pop, soundtracks, Latin; also related books, photos, posters, magazines, etc.; also sells LPs, 45s, 78s, sheet music; by appointment or mail.

Larry Augistover
Augie's 45 RPM Records
P.O. Box 932
Bellmore, NY 11710
e-mail: augustl@mail.earthlink.net
web: http://home.earthlink.net/~augustl/45_RPM_Sale.html
Collector and dealer with huge collection of 45 RPM records; web site is organized by artist name.

D & J Records
212 E. Main St.
Carnegie, PA 15106
ph: 412-279-8888
fax: 412-279-5538
Over 1 million 45s in stock; music from 1940s to 1990s.

Fred Bohn
Attic Record Store, Inc.
513 Grant Ave.
Pittsburgh, PA 15209-2657
ph: 412-821-8484
fax: 412-821-5179
e-mail: fbohn@ibm.net
Over 4 million phonograph records in stock; buys collections of 45s, 78s, and LPs; no amount too large.

Jay Notartomaso
Musical Energi
59 N. Main St.
Wilkes Barre, PA 18701
ph: 717-829-2929
fax: 717-829-2929
e-mail: energi@epix.net
Buys and sells CDs, records, tapes, videos and books; specializes in hard to find music; large selection of gifts too.

Nina's Discount Oldies
P.O. Box 77
Narberth, PA 19072
ph: 800-336-4627
Over 3 million records in stock; 12" and current hits available; mail order with music from 1950s through 1990s.

Ken Clee
P.O. Box 11412
Philadelphia, PA 19111-0412
ph: 215-722-1979
e-mail: waxntoys@aol.com
web: http://members.aol.com/waxntoys/main/kidsmeal.htm
Wants to buy 45s in bulk, old store stock, DJ collections or radio station stock; also has 45s for sale.

Mike Landis
P.O. Box 814
Adamstown, PA 19501
ph: 888-248-2291
e-mail: landis2@desupernet.net
Buys and sells 1950s-1960s black vocal groups; call toll free!

Tom Engle
P.O. Box 1802
Hyattsville, MD 20788-0802
ph: 410-750-3730
fax: 410-750-9537
e-mail: deepgroove@mindspring.com
Wants to buy jazz, classical LPs, rock 'n' roll, R&B 450s, LPs, posters, and related memorabilia.

Jay Norman
Fast Hits Music
P.O. Box 3052
Gaithersburg, MD 20885
ph: 301-838-0366
fax: 301-838-0274
e-mail: fasthits@aol.com
web: http://www.fasthits.com
Specializes in newly manufactured 45s, oldies and newies.

Steven Smolian
Smolian Sound Preservation Studios
1 Worman's Mill Court #4
Frederick, MD 21701
ph: 301-694-5134
fax: 301-694-5179
Wants large LP and 78rpm collections; classical and jazz music a specialty; also appraises records for donation purposes.

Memory Lane Records
Newspaper: Record Finder
P.O. Box 1047
Glen Allen, VA 23060-1047
ph: 804-266-1154 or 804-264-0300
fax: 804-264-9660
e-mail: sales1@recordfinders.com
web: http://www.recordfinders.com/
A monthly newspaper for the record collector: articles, ads, mail-bid record auctions; also sells record collections on consignment.

Walter Smith
Record Finder
8417 Glazebrook Ave.
Richmond, VA 23228
ph: 804-266-1154 or 804-2646-0300
fax: 804-264-9660
e-mail: sales1@recordfinders.com
web: http://www.recordfinders.com
One of the largest resources online for out-of-print, collectible oldies; primary format vinyl 45s, 78s, LPs, plus paper memorabilia; line of collectors' supplies, books, and stereo equipment; can transfer from CD to vinyl or tape.

Records Unlimited
2126 Wards Rd.
Lynchburg, VA 24502-5312
ph: 804-832-0729
fax: 804-239-7519
Buys and sells LPs, 45s from all periods; also new and used CDs and cassettes.

Revolution Records & CDs
1620A Alton Rd.
South Beach, FL 33139
ph: 305-673-6464
LPs, 45s, 12" singles, CDs, cassettes, box sets, videos, picture discs, sheet music, collectibles.

Douglas Allen
Bananas Records, Tapes & CDs
2226 16th Ave. N.
Saint Petersburg, FL 33713-5624
ph: 813-327-4616 or 800-823-4113
fax: 813-343-0775
e-mail: bananagram@aol.com
web: http://www.musicfinder.com/
Over two million out of print records, CDs, LPs, 45s, 78s; books on music, sheet music; posters, memorabilia; 7,000 sq. ft. warehouse of records in all categories.

NVI Classical Records
2195 Woods Edge Dr., #4
Memphis, TN 38134
ph: 901-388-4168
fax: 901-377-6875
e-mail: orders@nviclassical.com
web: http://www.nviclassical.com/
International dealers in rare, out-of-print classical LPs and 78s; mail order and via e-commerce only; also buys collections of classical LPs only.

Shelly G. Callies
4072 Scenic Rd.
Campbellsport, WI 53010
ph: 920-533-5593
Buying records, LPs, 45s, 78s, CDs; also magazines, books, and memorabilia relating to music and musicians; herself a musician collecting many kinds of recorded music, especially jazz.

Dusty Groove America
1180 N. Milwaukee Ave.
Chicago, IL 60622-4019
ph: 773-645-12100
e-mail: jp@dustygroove.com
web: http://www.dustygroove.com/

John Telizyn
Sparky's Mail Order
3724 N. Page
Chicago, IL 60634
ph: 773-625-8732
Specializes in buying and selling vinyl records.

Record Ron's Good & Plenty
1129 Decatur St.
New Orleans, LA 70116
ph: 504-524-9444
Pop, jazz, R&B, soul, blues, gospel, oldies, zydeco, comedy, doo wop, Dixieland, big bands, spoken word, Broadway shows, country & western; LPs, 45s, CDs, tapes, sheet music, music memorabilia.

Nitebird Sounds
P.O. Box 643
Stuttgart, AR 72160-0643

Stan Gold
As Time Goes By
7042 Dartbrook Dr.
Dallas, TX 75240
ph: 972-239-8621 or 214-352-2765
fax: 972-239-9622
e-mail: record@unicomp.net
web: http://www.astimegoesby.com/
Wants all formats from 78s to LPs; 1940s to 1960s jazz, rock and R&B 1950s to 1960s; also exotic/lounge, personalities, picture discs, classical, blues, folk, and related advertisements.

Kevin Bakos
Sound Exchange
1718 Westheimer
Houston, TX 77098
ph: 800-445-0500 or 713-666-5555
fax: 713-524-9532
e-mail: kevin@soundexchange.com
web: http://www.soundexchange.com
Buys and sells new and used LPs, CD, and tapes; rare, important and independent music; also does appraisals.

L.R. (Les) Docks
Shellac Shack
P.O. Box 691035
San Antonio, TX 78269-1035
ph: 210-492-6021
fax: 210-492-6489
Buying vintage popular records, especially 78's: jazz, blues, hillbilly, pop, rockabilly, etc.; wants list (a 72-page profusely illustrated booklet, including thousands of actual prices paid) for $2 (refundable.)

Paula Major
Paula's House of Music
8205 Geneva Ave.
Lubbock, TX 79423-2823
ph: 806-793-0111
fax: 806-793-0111
e-mail: paula@houseofmusic.com
web: http://www.houseofmusic.com
Thousands of vinyl albums, 45s and 12" singles from the 1950s to 1980s; specializing in 1950s and 1960s music; worldwide shipping; secure online ordering; in business since 1991; strict Goldmine grading, full money back guarantee.

Randy's Record Shop
157 East 900 S.
Salt Lake City, UT 84111
ph: 801-532-4413
Thousands of LPs, CDs, 45s, cassettes and collectibles.

Vinyl Vendors
1800 S. Robertson Blvd., #279
Los Angeles, CA 90035
e-mail: paul@vinylvendors.com
web: http://www.vinylvendors.com
Huge selection of vinyl records.

Jerry Bouquard
California Albums
P.O. Box 3426
Los Angeles, CA 90078
ph: 323-461-9806
fax: 323-461-4862
e-mail: calalbums@earthlink.net
web: http://www.californiaalbums.com
Well-stocked LP record dealer; 60 categories to browse.

Philip Smith
House of Records
3328 Pico Blvd.
Santa Monica, CA 90405
ph: 310-450-1222
fax: 310-450-5425
Buys, sells, trades new, used and collectible records.

American Pie Records
614 N. Milpas
Santa Barbara, CA 93103
ph: 805-965-2161
Specializing in 1960s and 1960s vinyl; no punk, heavy metal, rap, CDs or tapes - only real records.

Record Man, The
1322 El Camino Real
Redwood City, CA 94063
ph: 650-368-9065
fax: 650-368-2968
e-mail: recman@ix.netcom.com
LPs, 45s, EPs, picture discs, 78s, CDs, cassettes, reel-to-reels, videos, memorabilia, posters, books, magazines, sheet music.

Ed Leimbacher
MisterE Books & Records
1501 Pike Place Market #432
Seattle, WA 98101
ph: 206-622-5182 or 206-463-3986
fax: 206-622-2697
e-mail: mistere@wolfenet.com
web: http://www.wolfenet.com/~mistere/
Collector, dealer and expert specializes in vinyl records from all eras; especially looking for great jazz, blues, Reggae and early Rock to purchase.

Lelan Kuhlmann
M & L Records & Models
6504 Ravenna Ave.
Seattle, WA 98115
ph: 206-522-8189
e-mail: mlrecmod@halcyon.com
web: http://www.halcyon.com/mlrecmod/
Seattle storefront with an online catalog having over 22,000 LPs and 2,000 models, rare and used.

Experts

Paul C. Mawhinney
Record-Rama Sound Archives
1130 Perry Highway
Pines Plaza
Pittsburgh, PA 15237-2132
ph: 724-367-7330
fax: 724-367-7388
e-mail: recrama@recordrama.com
web: http://www.recordrama.com
Expert in recorded sound, albums, compact discs, 45 rpm records; search services; DJ supplies, record and disc cleaning supplies, reference material on history of recorded sound; author of "MusicMaster: The 45 RPM Record Directory."

Douglas Allen
Bananas Records, Tapes & CDs
2226 16th Ave. N.
Saint Petersburg, FL 33713-5624
ph: 813-327-4616 or 800-823-4113
fax: 813-343-0775
e-mail: bananagram@aol.com
web: http://www.musicfinder.com/
Over two million out of print records, CDs, LPs, 45s, 78s; books on music, sheet music; posters, memorabilia; 7,000 sq. ft. warehouse of records in all categories.

L.R. (Les) Docks
Shellac Shack
P.O. Box 691035
San Antonio, TX 78269-1035
ph: 210-492-6021
fax: 210-492-6489
Author of "American Premium Record Guide" (Books Americana).

John Tefteller
World's Rarest Records
P.O. Box 1727
Grants Pass, OR 97528
Writes "On the Record" column about collectibles records.

Jerry Osborne
Osborne Enterprises
P.O. Box 255
Port Townsend, WA 98368
ph: 360-385-1200
fax: 360-385-6572
e-mail: jpo@olympus.net
web: http://www.jerryosborne.com
Author of "The Official Price Guide to Records" (House of Collectibles).

Internet Resources

Edward Odel
Hot Platters
P.O. Box 4213
Thousand Oaks, CA 91359-1213
ph: 805-492-3682
fax: 805-492-3682
e-mail: HotPlatter@aol.com
web: http://www.HotPlatters.com
On-line music store; all categories of LPs, 45s, 78s, tapes, books, magazines, CDs, posters, videos, sheet music, paper goods, rock and movie memorabilia; new additions section added twice monthly; printed catalog $2.

Periodicals

Martin F. Bryan, Ed.
New Amberola Phonograph Co. The
Magazine: New Amberola Graphic, The
37 Caledonia St.
St. Johnsbury, VT 05819
A quarterly publication for collectors of early phonographs & records from the years 1895-1935; articles, book reviews, ads, auctions, etc.

Don Mennie, Pub.
Newspaper: Record Collectors Monthly
P.O. Box 75
Mendham, NJ 07945-0075
ph: 973-543-9520
fax: 973-543-6033
Covers collectible records primarily from 1950 to 1968; 45's, LP's, some 78's; Rock 'N' Roll, R & B, vocal groups, pop music of the era. Information about records, record companies, artists; NOT a price guide; irregularly published.

: 78 Quarterly
P.O. Box 283
Key West, FL 33041
e-mail: joelslot@inlink.com
web: http://www.bluesworld.com/78QSubs
An English publication; focus is 78 rpm records, particularly blues and jazz.

Antique Trader Publications, Inc.
Newsmagazine: DISCoveries
P.O. Box 1050
Dubuque, IA 52004-1050
ph: 800-334-7165 or 800-482-4155
fax: 800-531-0880
e-mail: jmkoenig@execpc.com
web: http://www.collect.com/discoveries
The record collector's magazine; articles on artists, ads for 10s of thousands of CD's & related music memorabilia from 1930s to present; in-depth coverage of a variety of music, stars, and eras; music memorabilia wanted and for sale.

Pat DuChene, PR
Krause Publications
Magazine: Goldmine
700 E. State St.
Iola, WI 54990-0001
ph: 715-445-2214
fax: 715-445-4087
e-mail: info@krause.com
web: http://www.krause.com/
A biweekly magazine containing articles, ads about records & recording artists from 1940s to present; the record & CD marketplace.

Suppliers

Andy's Record Supplies
48 Colonial Rd.
Providence, RI 02906
ph: 401-421-9453
fax: 401-421-0841
Japanese resealable mylar sleeves, poly sleeves, CD replacement cases, cardboard jackets, mailers, blister packs, storage boxes, cassette replacement cases, white plastic divider cards, quality paper sleeves.

Bags Unlimited
7 Canal St.
Rochester, NY 14608-1910
ph: 800-767-2247 or 716-436-9006
fax: 716-328-8526
e-mail: bags@frontiernet.net
web: http://www.frontiernet.net/~bags/
Sells record collector supplies: poly and paper sleeves, mailers, filler pads, album jackets, storage boxes, divider cards, etc.

Something Special Enterprises
P.O. Box 74
Allison Park, PA 15101
ph: 412-487-2626
fax: 412-487-3369
CD jewel cases, storage boxes and shippers; 45 rpm record sleeves, LP albums and sleeves, white paper sleeves, record and CD dividers; also regular comic bags, newspaper bags, magazine bags, baseball card holders, sheet music bags.

Jack Price
Cabco Products
3481 North High St.
Columbus, OH 43214
ph: 614-267-8468 or 614-267-7978
fax: 614-267-8468
e-mail: jproto1@aol.com
Catalog of replacement sleeves, jackets, covers, boxes, CD supplies, video supplies, storage boxes, frame displays, record holders, etc.

Big Band

Experts

L.R. (Les) Docks
Shellac Shack
P.O. Box 691035
San Antonio, TX 78269-1035
ph: 210-492-6021
fax: 210-492-6489
Expert, dealer and avid collector of 1920s-1930s jazz and big band 78s.

Children's

Experts

Peter Muldavin
173 W. 78th St., Apt. 5-F
New York, NY 10024-6711
ph: 212-362-9606
e-mail: kiddie78s@aol.com
web: http://members.aol.com/kiddie78s/
Expert, researcher, collector in Kiddie Records (78s and occasionally 45s);

wants to buy any label, any year; should be in original covers; will make cassette recordings of hard-to-find kiddie records; compiling discography.

Computer Programs For

Man./Prod./Dist.

FNProgramvare
Software: CATraxx
Pb 721 Krapfoss
Moss, N-1536
Norway
e-mail: info@fnprg.com
web: http://www.fnprg.com/catraxx/catraxx.html
Catalog information about the artist, album title, format, release date, company, label, catalog number, condition, playing time, purchase price, current value, song titles, songwriters, producers, studios, musicians, and instruments.

Cylinder Records

Collectors

Steven Ramm
420 Fitzwater St.
Philadelphia, PA 19147-3109
ph: 610-922-7050 or 610-545-3290
e-mail: steveramm@aol.com
Specializes in phonographs and pre-1930 records; wants to buy sheet music, postcards, and advertising with illustrations of phonographs, records, or Thomas A. Edison; also wants cylinder rolls in playable condition.

Gospel

Collectors

Arthur Crowley
207 Hamilton Rd.
Teaneck, NJ 07666-6367
ph: 201-833-0152
e-mail: arcrow@worldnet.att.net
Wants to buy Gospel 78rpm records from the mid 1940s and 1950s on Chess, Downbeat, Gotham, Nashboro, VJ, and other labels.

Jazz & Blues

Clubs/Associations

Ed Nickel
International Association of Jazz Record Collectors
Journal: IAJRC Journal
P.O. Box 518
Wingate, NC 28174
web: http://www.geocities.com/BourbonStreet/3910/
Promotes exchange of information and research on jazz, its musicians and recordings.

George Buck
Collectors Record Club
Newsletter: JazzBeat Magazine
1206 Decatur St.
New Orleans, LA 70116
ph: 504-525-1776
fax: 504-523-2629
Catalog is dedicate to the documentation and preservation of traditional jazz.

Collectors

Frederick Cohen
55 Park Ave.
New York, NY 10016
Wants Jazz records: 10" and 12" jazz LPs (33 1/3 rpm) on labels such as Blue Note, Prestige, Riverside, Debut, etc., must be in excellent condition; will travel for large collections; also jazz memorabilia and books wanted.

Dealers

Robert Hess
155 West 72nd St., #404
New York, NY 10023
ph: 212-579-0689
e-mail: hfis646942@aol.com
web: http://www.coachnet.com/music
Wants to buy jazz and R&B records; has been collecting for 30 years; also wants original jazz art including sheet music, statues, books, etc.; by appointment or mail.

Larry Raye
Cadence Building
Redwood, NY 13679
ph: 315-287-2852
fax: 315-287-2860
e-mail: cadence@cadencebuilding.com
web: http://www.cadencebuilding.com
Buys and sells old and new jazz and blues LPs and CDs, books, etc.; handles/distributes over 900 different labels.

Experts

L.R. (Les) Docks
Shellac Shack
P.O. Box 691035
San Antonio, TX 78269-1035
ph: 210-492-6021
fax: 210-492-6489
Expert, dealer and avid collector of 1920s-1930s jazz and big band 78s.

Periodicals

Larry Raye
Magazine: Cadence
Cadence Building
Redwood, NY 13679
ph: 315-287-2852
fax: 315-287-2860
e-mail: cadence@cadencebuilding.com
web: http://www.cadencebuilding.com
A monthly Jazz & Blues journal featuring interviews, oral histories, news and complete coverage of the entire record scene; the most complete coverage of jazz & blues, improvising music in the world.

Gene Joslin
Magazine: Joslin's Jazz Journal
P.O. Box 213
Parsons, KS 67357
ph: 316-421-4114
fax: 316-423-1554
e-mail: mail@jazzjournal.com
web: http://www.jazzjournal.com/
JJJ is the ultimate marketplace for original 78's, LP's, radio transcriptions, video tapes, and associated literature and memorabilia; a quarterly with articles, photos, collector wants, free subscriber ads, etc.

Rock 'N' Roll

Collectors

Richard Phillips
Radio Disc-Jockey
Flyer: Rockin' Richard 50's - 60's Entertainment Guide
P.O. Box 222
Northford, CT 06472-0222
ph: 203-484-2023
e-mail: dipdadip@aol.com
Collectors show (3) hours long (2) cassettes available for $20 ppd.; features extremely rare recordings; guest collectors chat and discuss rare recordings; make check or money order to Richard Phillips; list of shows with first order.

Dealers

Marc J. Cohen
P.O. Box 220153
Hollywood, FL 33022-0153
ph: 954-565-9754
Buys and sells 1950s and early 1960s rock and roll records: Bill Haley and the Comets, Chuck Berry, Ricky Nelson, Coasters, Bobby Darin, Buddy Holly, Fats Domino, Platters, Everly Brothers, Drifters, Elvis, Connie Francis, etc.

Soundtracks

Dealers

Footlight Records
113 East 12th Street
New York, NY 10003
ph: 212-533-1572
fax: 212-673-1496
e-mail: footlight1@aol.com
web: http://www.footlight.com
Specialty areas are cast recordings, soundtracks and vocalists.

Soundtrack Album Retailers
P.O. Box 487
New Holland, PA 17577
ph: 717-656-0121

Paul Aguirre
Intermission Talk
P.O. Box 472076
San Francisco, CA 94109-1221
ph: 415-775-4160
e-mail: SabuSabu@sirius.com
Mail order vinyl record dealer; specializes in records from stage, movies and television; rare movie, TV soundtracks, and stage recording.

Periodicals

Lukas Kendall
Newsletter: Film Score Monthly
5455 Wilshire Blvd., Ste. 1500
Los Angeles, CA 90036
ph: 323-937-9890
fax: 323-937-9277
e-mail: lukas@filmscoremonthly.com
web: http://www.filmscoremonthly.com/
Focuses on original movie soundtracks.

Vogue Picture

Collectors

Marc Grobman
94 Paterson Rd.
Fanwood, NJ 07023

John W. Hess
244 Bernaski Rd.
Amsterdam, NY 12010-7827
ph: 518-843-6117
Wants to buy Vogue picture disc records, horn phonographs, music boxes, roller organs; also wants parts, empty cabinets, horns; any condition, any material.

Paul Manganaro
P.O. Box 535
Coopersburg, PA 18036
Wants to buy 78 rpm picture records by Vogue, Mercury, RCA, etc.

Michelle Pollitt
Vogue Lady, The
P.O. Box 339
Orefield, PA 18069-0339
Wants to buy Vogue and all types of collectible picture records.

Berie Seinberg
714 Moredon Rd.
Bensalem, PA 19020
ph: 215-886-6124
fax: 215-638-2265
e-mail: phonoman-bernie@worldnet.att.net
Wants to buy picture records, 78 rpm, from Vogue and Victor; also any picture records from the 1930s through 1950s.

John Widmar
5800 3rd Ave., Apt. 515
Kenosha, WI 53140-4237
ph: 414-654-6802
Wants to buy Vogue picture records, 45s and 78s from the 1950s; send list

of what you have for site; list label number, artist, and record speed.

John Coates
324 Woodland Dr.
Stevens Point, WI 54481-9285
ph: 715-341-6113
e-mail: jcoaates@coredcs.com
Advanced Vogue picture record collector.

RED CROSS

(see also NURSES)

Collectors

Dick Lavin
2908 Cleave Dr.
Falls Church, VA 22042
ph: 703-533-8402
Wants to buy Red Cross medals, patches, pins, posters, tabs, and sheet music; please send photo or call.

Experts

Shirley Powers
7964 Sartan Way N.E.
Albuquerque, NM 87109-3128
ph: 505-821-2735
fax: 505-821-0245
e-mail: powerss@crossnet.org
web: http://www.angelfire.com/nm/collectarc
Collects and documents American Red Cross pins, posters, and uniforms; publisher of "The Collector's Guide to Red Cross Pins."

RED WING POTTERY

(see CERAMICS [AMERICAN], Stoneware [Red Wing Pottery]; CERAMICS [AMERICAN ART POTTERY], Red Wing; CERAMICS [AMERICAN DINNERWARE], Red Wing)

REDDY KILOWATT

(see ADVERTISING COLLECTIBLES, Figures [Reddy Kilowatt])

RELIGIOUS COLLECTIBLES

(see also ART, Asian; JUDAICA; HYMNS; MEDALS, ORDERS & DECORATIONS; MORMON ITEMS; STAMP COLLECTING, Religion Related)

Appraisers

Leon Castner, ISA CAPP
National Appraisal Consultants
P.O. Box 482
Hope, NJ 07844
ph: 800-323-5996 or 908-459-5996
fax: 908-459-4899
e-mail: castner@garden.net
web: http://www.nacvalue.com
Extensive appraisal experience in valuing stained glass, religious interiors (churches, seminaries), and related religious articles for insurance, charitable contribution, or claims purposes.

James C. Voors
Court of King James
515 West Wayne St.
Fort Wayne, IN 46802-2123
ph: 219-426-3234
Specializes in ecclesiastical furnishings, i.e. sacred vessels, church art, vestments and other church textiles, church furnishings, statuary, paintings, objets d'art.

Clubs/Associations

Emilio C. Botticelli
Foundation International for Restorers of Religious Medals
Newsletter: M.A.R.C., The
P.O. Box 2652
Worcester, MA 01603-2652
ph: 508-752-0612
All types of old religious medals; club focuses on medal history, values, varieties, makers, rarity, countries of origin, etc.

Collectors

Emilio C. Botticelli
P.O. Box 2652
Worcester, MA 01603-2652
ph: 508-752-0612
Wants to buy any and all types of old religious medals in any metal; also old Vatican medals.

Jim Osella
145 Adams Ave.
Bridgeville, PA 15017
ph: 412-746-2451 or 724-745-1333
fax: 412-746-2451
e-mail: osella@usaor.net
Wants to buy religious collectibles.

James D. Stambaugh, Dir.
Graham Center Museum
500 East College Ave.
Wheaton, IL 60187-1909
ph: 630-752-5909
fax: 630-752-5916
e-mail: BGCMus@wheaton.edu
web: http://www.wheaton.edu/BGC/museum/
Evangelism, revival, missions, 19th & 20th century prints & ephemera, postcards, artifacts, anything to do with the advancement of Evangelical Christianity in America.

Greg Spiess
230 E. Washington St.
Joliet, IL 60433-1006
ph: 815-722-5639
fax: 815-722-0171
e-mail: spiessantq@aol.com
Wants to buy church furnishings, religious stained glass, altars, pews, railings, confessionals, pulpits, baptismals, lighting, architectural renderings and blueprints, stained glass cartoons, furnishings catalogs.

J.A. Higgins
5017 Walnut
Kansas City, MO 64112-2758
ph: 816-931-4095
Wants to buy Buddha and Hindu statues.

Ernie Reda
3997 Latimer Ave.
San Jose, CA 95130-1568
ph: 408-378-7786
Accepting donation for the future Museum of All Religions; has collection of over 10,000 crosses and thousands of religious items from all over the world; Guiness Book of World Records.

Dealers

Lawrence Skilling
Antique Church Furnishings
Rivernook Farm
Sunnyside
Walton on Thames, Surrey KT12 2ET
U.K.
ph: 00 44 1932 252736
e-mail: antchurch@aol.com
web: http://www.freeride.co.uk/antique-church
A church antiques and architectural salvage business dealing in anything that can be found in a pre-WWII church: fonts, crosses, pews, furniture, etc.

Experts

Lael Bower
507 Michigan Ave.
Grayling, MI 49738
ph: 517-348-6984 or 810-378-5785
Wants to buy Christian and Judaic collectibles; co-author with Penny Forstner of "Guide to Collecting Christian and Judaic Artifacts."

Ann Ball
4726 Creekbend
Houston, TX 77035
ph: 713-526-7171 or 713-721-2981
fax: 713-721-2788
e-mail: AnnAlert@aol.com
Catholic writer and author; will provide help in identifying Catholic saints and miscellaneous sacramentals in various collectibles and in art.

Internet Resources

Resurrection Art
939 N. Clinton Ave
Dallas, TX 75208
web: http://www.geocities.com/Athens/Parthenon/1501/
This web site links collectors of previously cherished religious art and sacred items; creates a network of those skilled in the art of restoration.

Repair Services

Mueller Kaiser Plating Co.
5815 Hampton Ave.
Saint Louis, MO 63109
ph: 314-832-3553
Fine metal finishing in silver, gold, bronze, copper and brass; flatware, tea services, antiques and church ware including chalices, ciboria, crosses, candelabra, sanctuary lamps, vases, alms basins, flagons, book stands, etc.

Church Pews

Repair Services

Don Mullen
Oak Grove Restorations, Inc.
299B Broad St.
Manchester, CT 06040
ph: 860-646-1951
fax: 860-646-0770
e-mail: DohnM@aol.com
web: http://www.nvionline.com/donmullen
Furniture restoration service specializing in church pew restorations; since 1972.

Crosses

Collectors

Ernie Reda
3997 Latimer Ave.
San Jose, CA 95130-1568
ph: 408-378-7786
Accepting donation for the future Museum of All Religions; has collection of over 10,000 crosses and thousands of religious items from all over the world; Guiness Book of World Records.

Holy Cards

Clubs/Associations

Chuck Thompson
Psalm Card Collectors & Traders
Newsletter: Psalm Card Collectors, Readers & Traders
10802 Greencreek Dr., Ste. 703
Houston, TX 77070-5367
Members focus on collecting the 23rd and other found on greeting cards, pocket cards, postcards, and bookmarks; publishes a directory of collectors twice a year.

Collectors

Fr. Eugene J. Carrella
St. Adalbert Roman Catholic Church
337 Morningstar Rd.
Staten Island, NY 10707
ph: 718-442-8476
fax: 718-727-1241
e-mail: Eujoe@aol.com
Holy card collector and expert.

Rita Adams
3001 Stratford Hills Lane
Austin, TX 78746
ph: 512-328-6728
fax: 512-328-7274
e-mail: ritadams@eden.com
Buys and trades old small religious/ holy cards, Catholic or Protestant; serious inquiries only, please.

Experts

Brent Devitt
Saints Unlimited
821 Ingalls Road
Menomonie, WI 54751
ph: 715-235-1293
e-mail: bjdevitt@win.bright.net
web: http://members.xoom.com/bjdevitt/
Collector, expert, providing online information about collecting both antique and contemporary; Holy cards, Bible Lessons and small paper icons; online images, tips, and links.

Internet Resources

Yvonne
Bible Cards
e-mail: yvonne@ic.mankato.mn.us
web: http://www.internet-connections.net/web/antiques/paper/biblecards.html
Web site with great information on Holy Cards.

Jehovah's Witnesses

Collectors

Jeffrey Neumann
9960 Mt. Eaton
Wadsworth, OH 44281-9028
ph: 330-334-1784
Wants pre-1930 literature, books, booklets, magazines, memorabilia relating to Pastor Russell, Watchtower, Tower Publishing, International Bible Students Association, and Jehovah's Witnesses.

Rosaries

Museums/Libraries

Sharon Tiffany, Ex. Dir.
Don Brown Rosary Collection, Skamania Interpretive Center
P.O. Box 396
Stevenson, WA 98648
ph: 800-991-2338 or 509-427-5141
fax: 509-427-7429
web: http://www.rosaryworkshop.com/4000Rosaries.htm
The Historical Society interprets the human history surrounding and the natural events that created Columbia Gorge.

Televangelism

Collectors

J.B.
P.O. Box 740877
Dallas, TX 75374-0877
Wants collectibles relating to Televangelism: mailers, videos, from Jim Bakker, Swaggart, Tilton, Popoff, etc.

REMOTE CONTROL

(see AIRPLANES, Model [Remote Control]; BOATS, Model [Remote Control]; MODELS, Cars [Remote Control])

REPAIR/RESTORATION/ CONSERVATION

(see also "REPAIR SERVICES" Appendix in the back of this book for repair firm members of the Claims Prevention & Procedures Council [CPPC], as well as Repair Services listed specific categories throughout this Directory.)

Clubs/Associations

Andrea Daley
Association of Restorers
P.O. Box 447
2545 St. Rt 29
Salisbury Center, NY 13454
ph: 315-429-3094 or 800-260-1829
fax: 315-429-7265
e-mail: restorer@ntcnet.com
web: http://www.assoc-restorers.com/
An association for repairers and restorers of furniture, ceramics, glass, textiles, etc.

Internet Resources

Walter Henry
Conservation Online, Stanford University Libraries
Preservation Dept. Meyer #416
650 Escondido Mall
Stanford, CA 94305-3209
e-mail: whenry@lindy.stanford.edu
web: http://palimpsest.stanford.edu/
Resources for professionals involved with the conservation of museum, library, and archive materials.

Misc. Services

Allan Koskela
Allan Koskela Restorations
P.O. Box 186
Webster City, IA 50595
ph: 515-832-1131
Learn repair for invisible, ultra violet protected restorations on china, pottery, porcelain, bisque, composition, cold casts and ceramics; suitable for majolica, flow blue, Hummel, Lladro, Roseville, Weller, Hull, Royal Doulton, etc.

Allan Koskela
Nationwide Restoration Classes on Video
P.O. Box 186
Webster City, IA 50595
ph: 515-832-1131
Instructional videos available: "Repairing China, Pottery & Porcelain," "Airbrush Basics," "Color-Matching for the Restorer of Pottery & Porcelain," "Paintings: Cleaning & Repair," "Glass Cleaning & Repairing (Audio Tape)".

Periodicals

Eric Herman, Ed.
McCloskey Communications, Inc.
Magazine: Professional Refinishing
P.O. Box 306
Woodland Hills, CA 91365
ph: 818-715-9776
fax: 818-715-9059
e-mail: main@ProRefinishing.com
web: http://www.ProRefinishing.com
Glossy, full color magazine for the wood restoration industry; how-to, ads, supplies, tools, etc.

Repair Services

Leon Trefler
Trefler & Sons Antique Restoring Studio, Inc.
99 Cabot St.
Needham, MA 02494
ph: 781-444-2685
fax: 781-444-0659
e-mail: trefler@trefler.com
web: http://www.trefler.com/
Specializes in the repair and conservation of art objects: ceramics, paintings, furniture, frames, crystal, porcelain, marble, ivory, cloisonne, metals, jade, etc.

Dimitri Nedelcu
Universal Fine Art Restoration
267 Derby Ave.
Orange, CT 06477-1319
ph: 203-795-8849
Repairs and restores marquetry, stone & wooden statuary, stone & wood capitals and columns, antique fireplaces, furniture, stone & wooden busts, icons, porcelain, paintings, guilding, picture frames,

Patricia Little
Restorations by Patricia
420 Centre St.
Nutley, NJ 07110
ph: 973-235-0234 or 973-235-0732
e-mail: morganlafay@worldnet.att.com
Specialty in restoring plaster and religious statuary; also proficient in ceramics, china, pottery, porcelain, crystal, glass; repair of cracks, chips and replacements; Lladro, Hummel, Dept. 56, Royal Doulton, Swarovski, Armani, etc.

Ronald L. Aiello
Antique Restorations
1313 Mt. Holly Rd.
Burlington, NJ 08016-3773
ph: 609-387-2587
fax: 609-747-9340
e-mail: raiello@icdc.com
web: http://members.tripod.com/~chinarepair/homepage3.htm
Repairs and restores china, porcelain, pottery, dolls, objets d'art; specializes in professional repairs to figurines: Character and Toby Jugs, Lambeth, Burslem, Kingsware, stoneware, Flambe, etc.; 18 years full time experience.

Antiques Restoration by Julian
Chelsea Antiques Building
110 West 25th St., #208
New York, NY 10001
ph: 212-647-0305 or 201-791-7875
Gold, silver and any metal subjects; lamps and small sculptures; jewelry and costume jewelry; gold and silver plating.

Marina Pastor
Hess Restorations
200 Park Ave. South
New York, NY 10003
ph: 212-260-2255 or 212-979-1143
Since 1945 specializing in repairs and restorations of most objects of art; highly recommended by museums and leading galleries; ceramics, glass, ivory, porcelain, sculptures.

Walter C. Kahn, PE
1017 Constable Dr., S.
Mamaroneck, NY 10543-4702
ph: 914-381-3200
fax: 914-381-3200
Professional restoration of porcelain, china, glass, and pottery; also jade and ivory carvings and object d'art since 1972; life member of ASM, TMA, ASME, and SNDT.

Len Paradise, CR
Loss Recovery Systems, Inc.
10 Dwight Park Dr.
Syracuse, NY 13209-1029
ph: 315-451-9111
fax: 315-451-9222
Certified Restorer #94; repairs, cleans and restores following fire and flood loss, tree loss, smoke damage, structural collapse, etc.

Richard Michael Gramly, PhD
Great Lakes Artifact Repository
79 Perry St.
Buffalo, NY 14203-3037
ph: 716-849-0149
fax: 716-852-0093
Stores, sells, and conserves artifacts from all parts of the world in a secure, fireproof, climate-controlled working room and vault; examining room with drafting and photographic facilities; cataloguing of incoming collections, etc.

Byron Klein
A. Ludwig Klein & Son, Inc.
683 Sumneytown Pike
P.O. Box 145
Harleysville, PA 19438
ph: 215-256-9004 or 800-379-2929
fax: 215-256-9644
Specializing in the repair and restoration of all types of glass, china and porcelain as well as ivory, jade, brass, pewter.

David Sim
Nonomura Studios
3432 Connecticut Ave. NW
Washington, DC 20008-1308
ph: 202-363-4025
fax: 202-244-1541
Specializes in Korean, Japanese, Chinese antiques; restores china, glassware, screens, scrolls, ivory, paintings, jade, lamps, etc.

Sidney Williston
Mario's Conservation Services
1738 14th St. NW
Washington, DC 20009-4309
ph: 202-234-5795
Restorers/conservators of decorative arts objects: china, glass, plaster, lacquer, metal, ivory, icons, frames, gold leaf, glass grinding and drilling.

Richard Kornemann
Museum Shop, Ltd.
20 N. Market St.
Frederick, MD 21701
ph: 301-695-0424 or 301-871-3855
fax: 301-698-5242
Highly-recommended conservator of oils, paper (etchings, lithographs, engravings, maps), icons, Oriental art, photos, 23k gold leaf, etc.

Joseph Howell
Pleasant Valley Restoration
1725 Reed Rd.
Knoxville, MD 21758-1118
ph: 301-432-6022
fax: 301-432-2721
e-mail: jhowell371@aol.com
Restoration, cleaning, and consultation services for china, glass, porcelain, marble, ivory, and other objets d'art; fine art and antique repair; custom color matching and air brushing.

Mildred R. Shepherd
Shepherd Studio
5527 Third St., South
Arlington, VA 22204-1115
ph: 703-671-1789
Since 1970, conservation/restoration of art objects; specializing in porcelain, glass, pottery, plaster, stoneware, ivory, jade; for private clients and museums.

Gilbert Kerry Hall
Rikki's Studio Inc.
2809 Bird Ave.
Miami, FL 33133
ph: 305-624-1688
Restorers and conservators of crystal, paintings, porcelains (European and Oriental), coromandel and objets d'art.

Juergen Berndt
6731 Ashley Ct.
Sarasota, FL 34241-9696
ph: 941-925-0385
fax: 941-925-0487
e-mail: auction@breker.com
web: http://www.breker.com/
Specializes in the repair and restoration of antique mechanical devices such as typewriters, calculators, telephones, telegraphs, sewing machines, etc.; a specialty is the repair of cast iron cracks.

Adrienne Kreinberg
Dunhill Restorations
2309 Lee Rd.
Cleveland, OH 44118-3413
ph: 216-291-1771
Restores porcelain figurines, etc.

Douglas A. Eisele
Old World Restorations, Inc.
5729 Dragon Way
Cincinnati, OH 45227
ph: 513-271-5459
web: http://www.restorationart.com
Fine restoration and conservation of paintings, porcelain, glass, china, art pottery, metals, crystal, frames, ivory, gold leaf, photographs, etc.; nationwide service; free estimates; call or write for more information and brochures.

Allan Koskela
Allan Koskela Restorations
P.O. Box 186
Webster City, IA 50595
ph: 515-832-1131
Repairs most natural materials: ivory, jade, quartz, onyx, malachite, marble, lapis, gemstones; also carvings, figures, art objects, sculpture, clock cases; scientific color matching system; also conducts classes.

Susan Johnson
Furniture Doctor, The
4465 Harbor Lane
Minneapolis, MN 55446
ph: 612-557-6519
fax: 612-557-6573
Repairs all periods of furniture, antiques and household items.

David Jasper
D & J Glass & Art Clinic, Inc.
26707 466th Ave.
Sioux Falls, SD 57106
ph: 605-361-7524 or 800-361-7524
fax: 605-361-7216
Four generations of restorers; glass, porcelain, painting, dolls, figurines, ivory, lamps, etc.

Tom Redford
4311 NE Vivion Road, 3rd Floor
Kansas City, MO 64119-2890
ph: 816-454-1990
fax: 816-454-1605
e-mail: repair@silverwarehouse.com
Silver restoration, metal repair, glass restoration, porcelain restoration.

John Edward Cunningham
Fine Art Restoration
1525 E. Berkley
Springfield, MO 65804-3203
ph: 417-889-7702
Restoration artist; porcelains, ivory, jade, gold leaf, oil paintings, and frames; registered Boehm and Royal Worcester restorer.

Ron Leatherman
Leatherman Services
509 Mairo
Austin, TX 78748
ph: 512-282-1556 or 512-799-7871
fax: 512-282-1562
e-mail: ron@kdi.com
web: http://leathermanservices.com/
Restores marble, granite, miscellaneous stone, plaster and wood art objects, ornate picture frames, obsolete ceramic or porcelain tile; 25 years experience.

Mary Steffen
Wilderness Sculptures
1421 West Basin Ave.
P.O. Box 968
Pahrump, NV 89041
ph: 775-751-8582
e-mail: ka@fly-by-net.com
Restores porcelain, oil paintings, furniture, frames, glass, metals, and jewelry.

Dr. Lawrence Vescera
Pick Up the Pieces
711 West 17th St., Unit C-12
Costa Mesa, CA 92627-4334
ph: 714-645-9953 or 800-934-9278
fax: 714-645-8381
Repairs many types of materials including porcelain, glass, crystal collectibles, figurines, ceramics, marble, enamels, ivory, alabaster, antiques and paintings.

Butterfield & Butterfield Restoration Department
220 San Bruno Ave.
San Francisco, CA 94103-5018
ph: 415-861-7500
fax: 415-861-8951
e-mail: info@butterfields.com
web: http://www.butterfields.com/
Services include repair, restoration and refinishing of furniture and decorative arts: marquetry & parquetry, veneer, carved wood furniture, bronzes, ceramics, porcelain.

Suppliers

Ronald L. Aiello
Antique Restorations
1313 Mt. Holly Rd.
Burlington, NJ 08016-3773
ph: 609-387-2587
fax: 609-747-9340
e-mail: raiello@icdc.com
web: http://members.tripod.com/~chinarepair/homepage3.htm
Repair and restoration supplies available.

Restorite Systems
P.O. Box 7096
West Trenton, NJ 08628-0096
ph: 609-530-1526
Products for restoration and conservation of porcelain, pottery, and glass; sells a complete kit for repairing breaks and chips; also "How-to" videos available; send for free catalog.

Van Dykes Supply Company
P.O. Box 278
Woonsocket, SD 57385-0278
ph: 800-558-1234 or 605-796-4425
fax: 605-796-4085
web: http://www.vandykes.com/
Supplies for woodworkers and antique restorers: isen glass, curved & bubble glass, roll top accessories, Hoosier accessories, carvings & moldings, furniture components, over 1000 brass/glass/wooden hardware items.

Archival Supplies For

(see also ANTIQUES DEALERS & COLLECTORS, Supplies For)

Suppliers

John A. Dunphy
University Products, Inc.
517 Main St.
P.O. Box 101
Holyoke, MA 01041-0101
ph: 413-532-3372 or 800-628-1912
fax: 800-532-9281
e-mail: jadunphy@universityproducts.com
web: http://www.universityproducts.com
Carries safe products for the long term storage of postcards, posters, stamps, documents, photographs, textiles, costumes; acid free archival supplies, and materials for conservation and preservation; send for free catalog.

John Coutu
Rising Paper Co., Division of Fox River
P.O. Box 565
Housatonic, MA 01236-0565
ph: 413-274-3345
fax: 413-274-6684
General line of archival supplies including mat boards, framing and photographic supplies, mounting boards.

Nielsen & Bainbridge
17 S. Middlesex Ave.
Cranbury, NJ 08512
ph: 609-395-5550 or 800-927-8227
e-mail: info@nielsen-bainbridge.com
web: http://www.nielsen-bainbridge.com/
General line of archival supplies including mat boards, document storage boxes, framing and photographic supplies.

TALAS
568 Broadway
New York, NY 10012-3225
ph: 212-219-0770
fax: 212-219-0735
Archival supplies for artists, restorers, collectors, bookbinders, conservators, calligraphers, museums, vintage clothing restorers, archives, libraries, etc.

Document Preservation Center
P.O. Drawer 821
Yonkers, NY 10702-0821
ph: 914-476-8500
fax: 914-476-8573
e-mail: cohascodpc@earthlink.net
web: http://cohascoDPC.com/
Sells acid-free products: boxes, paste, binders, board, folders, tapes, tissue, paper, wrapping paper, etc.

Robert H. Snyder
Cohasco, Inc. - Document Preservation Center
P.O. Box 821
Yonkers, NY 10702-0821
ph: 914-476-8500
fax: 914-476-8573
e-mail: cohascodpc@earthlink.net
web: http://home.earthlink.net/~cohascodpc/index.html
Sells acid-free products: protectors, boxes, tissues, tapes, wrapping paper, paste, board, and various types of binders.

Light Impressions Corp.
P.O. Box 940
Rochester, NY 14603-0940
ph: 800-828-6216
fax: 800-828-5539
General line of archival supplies including mat boards, document storage boxes, framing and photographic supplies.

Brodart Company
P.O. Box 300
Mc Elhattan, PA 17748
ph: 800-820-4377 or 570-769-3265
fax: 800-283-6087
e-mail: supplies@brodart.com
web: http://www.brodart.com
Offers a comprehensive catalog of library and archival products, from acid-free folders to open shelving systems.

Kathy Hollinger
Conservation Resources International
8000 H Forbes Place
Springfield, VA 22151-2203
ph: 703-321-7730 or 800-634-6932
fax: 703-321-0629
e-mail: criusa@conservationresources.com
web: http://www.conservationresources.com/
Archival supplies for works of art on paper; document and photographic storage materials; chemicals; conservation tools; environmental monitoring supplies.

Hollinger Corporation
P.O. Box 8360
Fredericksburg, VA 22404
ph: 800-634-0491 or 540-898-7300
fax: 800-947-8814
Archival supplies for works of art on paper, textiles, quilts and stamps; document and photographic storage materials.

James Saunders
E. Gerber Products
P.O. Box 906
Minden, NV 89423
ph: 775-883-4100
Restoration supplies, instructional video, for restoring paper collectibles such as magazines baseball cards, comics, original art; manufacturer of Mylar sleeves for comics artwork, posters; also carries acid free boxes.

Art

Repair Services

Peter Kostoulakos
15 Sayles St.
Lowell, MA 01851-1625
ph: 978-453-8888
Conservation of oil paintings on canvas or solid supports; oil paintings cleaned and restored; by appointment.

Henry Lie
Center for Conservation & Technical Studies, The
Fogg Art Museum
Harvard University
Cambridge, MA 02138
ph: 617-495-2392
Provides conservation and restoration services for fine arts, including works of art on paper, paintings, objects and sculpture.

Art Conservation Services, Inc.
30 Ipswich St., Studio 101
Boston, MA 02215
ph: 617-247-2757
Paintings restored; treatment of paintings on canvas, wood panel and paper; expertly cleaned, patched and lined.

Leon Trefler
Trefler & Sons Antique Restoring Studio, Inc.
99 Cabot St.
Needham, MA 02494
ph: 781-444-2685
fax: 781-444-0659
e-mail: trefler@trefler.com
web: http://www.trefler.com/
Cleaning and restoration of tears, punctures; also restores frames.

John Squadra
Fine Art Restoration
RFD 2 Box 1440
Brooks, ME 04921-9643
ph: 207-722-3464
fax: 207-722-3475
Will send a written estimate from a photo of your damaged painting; upon approval, will UPS a wooden crate to you for shipment; work guaranteed.

Oscar & Debra Perez
Vigues Art Studio
54 Flanders Rd.
Woodbury, CT 06798-2103
ph: 203-263-4088
fax: 203-266-9118
e-mail: vigues@wtco.com
Conservation, restoration of oil paintings (cleaning, lining, touch up and repair), frames (gold leaf repairs, casting of missing parts) and paper (cleaning, repairs of prints, books, documents); also porcelain, glass & china repair.

Applebaum & Himmelstein
444 Central Park West
New York, NY 10025
ph: 212-666-4630
fax: 212-316-1039
Treats silk textiles, paintings and objects.

Leonard E. Sasso
21 Salem Lane
South Salem, NY 10590
ph: 914-248-8289
Master restorer of oil paintings & water colors; all periods; American, European, Old Masters; over 25 years experience; references available.

Sydney L. Germansky
Europa Master Gallery
16 A Lafayette Ave.
Suffern, NY 10901-5406
ph: 914-368-2707
Restorers of art, fine antiques, antique jewelry, old photographs.

Alexander Katlan
Alexander Katlan Conservation Inc.
5638 Main St.
Flushing, NY 11355-5046
ph: 718-445-7458
Conservation of paintings and panels, both European and American; author of "American Artists' Materials, Vol I: Suppliers Directory, 19th C." (Noyes Press 1987), and "Vol. II: A Guide to Stretchers, Panels, Millboards & Stencil Marks."

Romayne Shay McMahon, ISA
Veronique's Antiques
124 S. Market St.
Mechanicsburg, PA 17055-6329
ph: 717-697-4924
fax: 717-697-4924

Maria Pukownik
Fine Art & Paper Conservation
1045 Orrtanna Rd.
Orrtanna, PA 17353
ph: 717-337-0668
fax: 717-337-1093
e-mail: pukownik@cvn.net
Cleaning, old varnish removal, consolidation of flaking paint, relining, structural reinforcement of wooden panels, retouching, revarnishing.

Byron Klein
A. Ludwig Klein & Son, Inc.
683 Sumneytown Pike
P.O. Box 145
Harleysville, PA 19438
ph: 215-256-9004 or 800-379-2929
fax: 215-256-9644
Specializing in the repair and restoration of all types of glass, china and porcelain as well as ivory, jade, brass, pewter.

American Institute for Conservation of Historic & Artistic Works
Directory: AIC Directory
1717 K St. NW, Ste. 20
Washington, DC 20006
ph: 202-452-9545
fax: 202-452-9328
e-mail: InfoAic@aol.com
web: http://aic.stanford.edu/
Purpose is to advance the knowledge and practice of the conservation of cultural property; the AIC Directory lists competent conservators of paper, textiles, photographs, furniture, and more - over 2000 members.

Justine S. Wimsatt
Wimsatt & Associates Art Conservation Studio, Inc.
4230 Howard Ave.
Kensington, MD 20895-2418
ph: 301-493-4250
fax: 301-493-9563
e-mail: justine@artconservation.com
web: http://www.artconservation.com
For 20 years has provided professional restoration of paintings, murals, icons, frames and related objects.

H.I. Gates
118 E. Church St.
Frederick, MD 21701-5404
ph: 301-663-3717
fax: 301-663-5961
e-mail: samurai_gates@yahoo.com
Conservator of paintings.

Margaret Bardwell
Bardwell Conservation, Ltd.
11373 Park Dr.
Fairfax, VA 22030
ph: 703-385-8451
Conservation and restoration of paintings executed on canvas, metal or wood (including icons); also frames and small painted furniture.

Chris Carpenter
Renaissance Group Inc., The
P.O. Box 9283
Tampa, FL 33674
ph: 813-238-0617
fax: 813-238-0617
e-mail: RensGrpInc@aol.com
Specializes in the cleaning, stabilizing, and restoration of oil paintings; also specializes in the sale of old master paintings.

Antique & Art Restoration By Wiebold
413 Terrace Place
Terrace Park, OH 45174-1164
ph: 513-831-2541 or 800-321-2541
fax: 513-831-2815
e-mail: wiebold@eos.net
web: http://www.wiebold.com
Expert restoration of oil paintings, frames, mirrors, wooden artifacts, ivory, antiquities, etc.

Cornelia & Marcell Illozan
Fine Arts Conservation
P.O. Box 923
Wilmette, IL 60091
ph: 847-256-8595

Cher Goodson
Art Restorations, Inc.
7803 Inwood Rd.
Dallas, TX 75209
ph: 214-350-0811
Professional restoration of porcelains, ceramics, crystal, paintings (cleaning, lining, mending), frames (reconstruction, gold leaf, custom finishes), metal objects, plating, marble, lacquer ware, cloisonne, ivory, tortoise, etc.

Ellen D. Kennedy
Kennedy & Associates Art Conservation
6211 Royalton, #D
Houston, TX 77081
ph: 281-664-0606 or 800-437-8909
Specializes in the preservation of paintings, murals, frames, and related objects; over 25 years experience.

Scott M. Haskins
Fine Art Conservation Laboratories
P.O. Box 23557
Santa Barbara, CA 93121
ph: 805-564-3438
fax: 805-568-1178
e-mail: artdoc@earthlink.net
web: http://home.earthlink.net/~artdoc/
Specializes in the preservation of paintings, murals, works of art on paper and period frames.

Carol Carney
Gainsborough Products Company
281 Lafayette Cir.
Lafayette, CA 94549-4316
ph: 925-283-4187 or 800-227-2186
fax: 925-283-3343
web: http://catalog.com/ftrader/gains.htm
Complete line of oil painting restoration supplies since 1974, including manual cleaning solvents, varnish removers, lining compound, putty, canvas, ultraviolet lights as well as professional restoration services & classes.

Suzanne Adams, CPF
Art Restoration & Appraisals
16425 Trail Dr.
Redding, CA 96001
ph: 530-246-4868
fax: 530-246-4868
e-mail: charlieb@snowcrest.net

Canadian Conservation Institute
1030 Innes Rd.
Ottawa, Ontario K1G 0C8
Canada
ph: 613-998-3721
fax: 613-998-4721
e-mail: cci-icc_services@pch.gc.ca
web: http://www.cci-icc.gc.ca
CCI will work with you to develop cost-effective solutions for solving complex conservation problems; created in 1972 to promote the proper care and preservation of Canada's cultural heritage; works with museums, institutions.

Suppliers

Peter Millar
Quill, Hair & Ferrule, Ltd.
P.O. Box 23927
Columbia, SC 29224-3927
ph: 800-421-7961 or 803-788-4499
fax: 803-736-4731
e-mail: pmillar@paint-info.com
Professional restoration supplies: Japan & oil colors, brushes, abalone & mother-of-pearl, aluminum, copper, composition, gold leaf, burnishing tools, imported gold sizes, non-tarnish iridescent & metallic pigments, etc.

Carol Carney
Gainsborough Products Company
281 Lafayette Cir.
Lafayette, CA 94549-4316
ph: 925-283-4187 or 800-227-2186
fax: 925-283-3343
web: http://catalog.com/ftrader/gains.htm
Complete line of oil painting restoration supplies since 1974, including manual cleaning solvents, varnish removers, lining compound, putty, canvas, ultraviolet lights as well as professional restoration services & classes.

Cane & Basketry

Internet Resources

WeaveNet
25 Florida St.
Long Beach, NY 11561
web: http://www.weavenet.com/
This web site provides a complete source of basketry, weaving and caning information; restoration supplies, ash strips, chair cane, dyes, patterns, raffia, seagrass, weaving guilds and associations, etc.

Repair Services

Susan Dilworth
Iron Bridge Farm Antiques
2953 Appleton Rd.
Elkton, MD 21921-2176
ph: 410-398-0954

Mickey Johnson
Mickey's Chair
233 Byrnes Dr.
Waterloo, IA 50701
ph: 319-232-5934
e-mail: mlj091554@aol.com
Specializes in antique/modern caning and rush seating; over 20 years in business; also sells caning supplies.

Suppliers

Connecticut Cane & Reed Co.
P.O. Box 762
Manchester, CT 06045
ph: 860-646-6586 or 800-227-8498
fax: 860-649-2221
e-mail: ctcanereed@msn.com
web: http://www.canereed.com/
Largest selection of materials and books; source for cane, wicker and basket supplies; all types of materials to reseat a chair.

H.H. Perkins Co.
10 South Bradley Rd.
Woodbridge, CT 06525
ph: 203-389-9501

Lilian Cummings
Canecraft
RD 1 Box 126-A (Rte 443)
Andreas, PA 18211-9784
ph: 570-386-2441
Sells cane, reed and rushing material for seating chairs, making baskets, and repairing wicker furniture; also instruction books.

Paige W. Beasley
Carolina Caning Supply
111 Fairfax Lane
Cary, NC 27513
ph: 800-346-0142 or 919-467-7773
Chair caning and repair supplies.

Peerless Rattan Wrap n Post
624 S Burnett Rd.
Springfield, OH 45505-2722
ph: 937-323-7353
fax: 937-323-0003
web: http://www.weavenet.com/supp.htm#PEERLESS
Source for cane, wicker, splints, fiber rush, seagrass, and basket supplies.

Cane & Basket Supply Co.
1283 S. Cochran Ave.
Los Angeles, CA 90019
ph: 323-939-9644
fax: 323-939-7237
e-mail: cabasu@2cowherd.net
web: http://www.2cowherd.net/cabasu/
Source for cane, wicker and basket supplies.

Mike Frank
Franks Cane & Rush Supply
P.O. Box 3025
Huntington Beach, CA 92605-3025
ph: 714-847-0707
fax: 714-843-5645
e-mail: gacg74b@prodigy.com
Quality supplier of unusual supplies for the craftsman; mainly wicker repair and basketry; sorry, no restoration of repairs.

Michael Frank
Frank's Cane & Rush Supply
7242 Heil Ave.
Huntington Beach, CA 92647
ph: 714-847-0707
fax: 717-843-5645
e-mail: franks@franksupply.com
web: http://www.franksupply.com
Carries high quality natural seat weaving supplies.

Ceramics

Misc. Services

Gerlinde M. Kornmesser
Porcelain Restoration Workshop
8217 W. Ballard Rd.
Niles, IL 60714
ph: 847-724-3059 or 847-375-8105
fax: 847-724-3060
e-mail: antiquesGK@aol.com
web: http://members.aol.com/AntiquesGK/
China mending and restoration course; instructor on the campus of Lawrence University, Appleton, WI; practicing restorer and AIC member Gerlinde M. Kornmesser is successor to Morla Tsossen, founder and developer of the course.

Shirley Vickers
Shirley Vickers School of China Repair
P.O. Box 688
Pine, AZ 85544-0688
ph: 520-476-3703
fax: 520-476-3703
e-mail: shirley@shirleyvickers.com
web: http://www.shirleyvickers.com
Course lasts 7 days for those wishing

to go into the repair business; also suited for collectors and dealers.

Repair Services

Sharon Smith Abbott
Fine Wares Restoration
P.O. Box 753
Bridgton, ME 04009-0753
ph: 207-647-2093
e-mail: abbttfwr@megalink.net
Restores ceramic & glass art objects for private collectors and museums; references of museum clients on request.

Christine Peltier
CP Restoration
6 South 3rd Ave.
Taftville, CT 06380-1428
ph: 860-886-1870 or 800-882-1870
fax: 860-887-9097
e-mail: cprest@snet.net
web: http://www.cac-bbs.com/cprest/
Restores damaged china or porcelain based on severity of damage and method of repair - not on the value of the article.

Oscar & Debra Perez
Vigues Art Studio
54 Flanders Rd.
Woodbury, CT 06798-2103
ph: 203-263-4088
fax: 203-266-9118
e-mail: vigues@wtco.com
Conservation, restoration of oil paintings (cleaning, lining, touch up and repair), frames (gold leaf repairs, casting of missing parts) and paper (cleaning, repairs of prints, books, documents); also porcelain, glass & china repair.

Patricia Little
Restorations by Patricia
420 Centre St.
Nutley, NJ 07110
ph: 973-235-0234 or 973-235-0732
e-mail: morganlafay@worldnet.att.com
Specialty in restoring plaster and religious statuary; also proficient in ceramics, china, pottery, porcelain, crystal, glass; repair of cracks, chips and replacements; Lladro, Hummel, Dept. 56, Royal Doulton, Swarovski, Armani, etc.

Ronald L. Aiello
Antique Restorations
1313 Mt. Holly Rd.
Burlington, NJ 08016-3773
ph: 609-387-2587
fax: 609-747-9340
e-mail: raiello@icdc.com
web: http://members.tripod.com/~chinarepair/homepage3.htm
Repairs and restores china, porcelain, pottery, dolls, objets d'art; specializes in professional repairs to figurines: Character and Toby Jugs, Lambeth, Burslem, Kingsware, stoneware, Flambe, etc.; 18 years full time experience.

Jonathan Mark Gershen
Jonathan Mark Gershen Porcelain, Pottery & Glass Restoration
1463 Pennington Rd.
Ewing, NJ 08618-2656
ph: 609-882-9417
fax: 609-530-0660
Second generation restorer and long time member of the AIC; clients include museums, collectors and dealers worldwide; free brochure available upon request.

Yolanda DiSalvo
Yolanda Studio
2365 Huckleberry Rd.
Lakehurst, NJ 08733-3423
Also purchases damaged items of fine porcelain.

Jareth Holub
Decorative Arts Restoration & Conservation
224 W. 29th St., 12th. Fl.
New York, NY 10001
ph: 212-564-8669 or 212-247-8657
fax: 212-843-3742
Specializes in the restoration & conservation of ceramics (porcelain, terra-cotta, bisque, etc.); over 20 yrs. experience; everything from pre-Columbian to Art Pottery; also marble, jade, ivory, cloisonne, tortoise shell; free estimates.

Hans J. Schindhelm
Ceramic Restorations of Westchester, Inc.
8 John Walsh Blvd.
Peekskill, NY 10566-5330
ph: 914-734-8410
fax: 914-762-1719
e-mail: siegmar@aol.com
web: http://members.aol.com/hummel2001/CROW/
Repair and restoration service for any brand of porcelain and ceramic collectibles, antiques and art objects.

Roger J. Krokey
Terra Nuova
38 Cedar Heights Rd.
Rhinebeck, NY 12572
ph: 914-876-3753
Located 100 miles north of New York City; complete restoration of ceramic items.

Romayne Shay McMahon, ISA
Veronique's Antiques
124 S. Market St.
Mechanicsburg, PA 17055-6329
ph: 717-697-4924
fax: 717-697-4924

Grady Stewart
Grady Stewart Expert Porcelain Restorations
2019 Sansom St.
Philadelphia, PA 19103-4416
ph: 215-567-2888
Offering repairs for museums, dealers, collectors; highest quality repairs of fine porcelain, pottery, and stoneware.

Bill Eberhardt
Harry A. Eberhardt & Son
2010 Walnut St.
Philadelphia, PA 19103-5608
ph: 610-568-4144
America's oldest repair firm.

Byron Klein
A. Ludwig Klein & Son, Inc.
683 Sumneytown Pike
P.O. Box 145
Harleysville, PA 19438
ph: 215-256-9004 or 800-379-2929
fax: 215-256-9644
Specializing in the repair and restoration of all types of glass, china and porcelain as well as ivory, jade, brass, pewter.

Sidney Williston
Mario's Conservation Services
1738 14th St. NW
Washington, DC 20009-4309
ph: 202-234-5795
Restorers/conservators of decorative arts objects: china, glass, plaster, lacquer, metal, ivory, icons, frames, gold leaf, glass grinding and drilling.

Mary Landess
Mary Landess Restorations
3102 Beverly Rd.
Baltimore, MD 21214
ph: 410-319-8684 or 410-267-7708
fax: 410-269-5909
e-mail: 104334.273@compuserve.com
Repairs porcelain, pottery, chins and some glass; will mend broken parts together, make missing parts, and match colors using quality materials from England.

Joseph Howell
Pleasant Valley Restoration
1725 Reed Rd.
Knoxville, MD 21758-1118
ph: 301-432-6022
fax: 301-432-2721
e-mail: jhowell371@aol.com
Restoration, cleaning, and consultation services for china, glass, porcelain, marble, ivory, and other objets d'art; fine art and antique repair; custom color matching and air brushing.

Mildred R. Shepherd
Shepherd Studio
5527 Third St., South
Arlington, VA 22204-1115
ph: 703-671-1789
Since 1970, conservation/restoration of art objects; specializing in porcelain, glass, pottery, plaster, stoneware, ivory, jade; for private clients and museums.

McHugh's Restoration Inc.
3461 W. Cary St.
Richmond, VA 232221
ph: 804-353-9596 or 804-353-9412
e-mail: mchughs@aol.com
China mending and restoration service; repairs chips, crank, and fabricates missing pieces; Boehm restorer; official Lladro and Hummel restorer.

Dona Danziger
Clay Works, The
4058 S. Main St.
P.O. Box 352
Exmore, VA 23350
ph: 757-414-0567
fax: 757-414-0571
e-mail: clayworks@esva.net
web: http://www.esva.net/~clayworks
Acquired skills working for Boehm, Goebel and the Franklin Mint; restorations of all types of fine porcelain and art pottery; specializes in Hummels; missing parts made; fully insured.

Richard Beggs
Pottery Restoration
9553 White Trail Trail
Kernersville, NC 27284-8741
ph: 336-595-2753 or 336-993-6971
e-mail: rtbeg@webtv.net
Specializing in invisible restoration of all types of ceramics, especially American art pottery, e.g. Rookwood, Weller, Roseville, Hull; also cookie jars and Fiestaware.

Jody Leak
Leak Enterprises
12500 SE Highway 301
Belleview, FL 34420-4410
ph: 352-245-8862
fax: 352-245-8862
e-mail: ogwen@aol.com
Specializing in the restoration of objets d'art, either antique or contemporary including Lladro, Boehm, Cybis, Hummel, Meissen, Orientalia, and all quality porcelain and ceramics.

Tice Goodson
Rte. 5, Box 985
Batesville, MS 38606
ph: 800-221-9177

Lester E. Sender
Galerie Nouvelle
23500 Mercantile Rd.
Cleveland, OH 44122-5914
ph: 216-595-0000
fax: 216-595-1111
Full cleaning and restoration of paintings, old and new; full repair and restoration of porcelain and pottery figurines, plates, objects; member A.I.C., Washington, DC.

Antique & Art Restoration By Wiebold
413 Terrace Place
Terrace Park, OH 45174-1164
ph: 513-831-2541 or 800-321-2541
fax: 513-831-2815
e-mail: wiebold@eos.net
web: http://www.wiebold.com
Restoration of all types of art pottery, fine porcelain, ceramics, glass, crystal, sculpture, antiquities, etc.

Anne R. Hackmann
2550 Kodiak Dr.
East Lansing, MI 48823-7208
ph: 517-351-2011
fax: 517-337-7234
e-mail: stanhack1@juno.com
Offers museum quality repair and restoration of antiques and ceramic art objects; specializing in Boehm and Stangl birds; please call or write before shipping.

Carol Coulter
Coulter's China Repair
2240 Scenic River Dr. S
Brainerd, MN 56401-8074
ph: 218-825-0283
Specializes in porcelain repair and restoration (Boehm, Lladro, Hummel, Dresden Lace); invisible repairs; mail order; free estimates.

Corey & Jo Ann Keller
Keller China Restoration
4825 Windsor Dr.
Rapid City, SD 57702-0125
ph: 605-342-6756
e-mail: kellerchina@juno.com
Professional repair of cracks, chips and missing parts on antique china, porcelain, dolls, Hummels, and porcelain lace; authorized restorers for the Lladro Society.

William & Michelle Marhoefer
Broken Art Restoration
1841 West Chicago Ave.
Chicago, IL 60622
ph: 312-226-8200 or 815-472-3900
fax: 815-472-3930
Museum quality invisible repair specializing in the professional restoration of porcelain, pottery, ceramics, wood, ivory, stone, art objects; Chicago Institute Masters Degree, qualified restorers since 1980; call for shipping instructions.

Craig Dodge Restorations
1326 W. Lark Industrial Park
Fenton, MO 63026
ph: 314-349-8009
fax: 314-326-1366
e-mail: cdrest@primary.net
web: http://www.cdrest.com/
Authorized Lladro restorationist; also restores Boehm, Kaiser, Hummel, Capodimonte, Royal Dounton, etc.

Bric-A-Brac, Inc.
8120 Nelson St.
New Orleans, LA 70118
ph: 504-861-8888
e-mail: plakotos@cnrf.nola.navy.mil
web: http://st11.yahoo.com/4948/ind.html

Linda Norris
Antique Restoration
1304 W. Virginia St.
Mc Kinney, TX 75069
ph: 972-529-2614
Specializes in the repair and restoration of fine pottery, porcelain, and figurines.

Nadia Wassef
303 Detering
Houston, TX 77007
ph: 713-880-0108
fax: 713-880-3544
e-mail: nfwassef@msn.com
Does stained glass, crystal and porcelain repair; email or snail mail photos to find out about restoration possibilities; repair and return ship.

Sue Thiessen
25115 Cemetery Rd.
Middleton, ID 83644-5103
ph: 208-585-3243
Specializing in restoring model horses, Roseville, and other pottery; also collector of Hagen Renaker horse and animal figurines.

Billie Coleman
China & Crystal Clinic
1808 N. Scottsdale Rd.
Tempe, AZ 85281
ph: 602-430-3286

Andy Goldschmidt
Ceramicare
P.O. Box 1812
Corrales, NM 87048
ph: 505-898-2728
e-mail: agoldschmidt@earthlink.net
web: http://home.earthlink.net/~agoldschmidt/wizzg.html
Repairs and restores ceramic art; specializing in Native American Indian pottery - prehistoric, historic and contemporary.

Casey Reed
Material Culture
1727 Dietz Plaza, NW
Albuquerque, NM 87107
ph: 505-344-8492
fax: 505-344-8492
e-mail: Casey@material-culture.com
web: http://material-culture.com/PuebloPotteryRestoration.htm
Conservation and restoration of Pueblo pottery; application of traditional and unique methodologies to preserve the past; also collects and appraises Pueblo pottery.

Cheleen Morgan
Antiques, Etc.
1270 Autumn Wind Way
Henderson, NV 89012
ph: 702-270-9910
Specializing in museum-quality restorations of pottery, porcelain, china, ceramics and hand painted items.

Mark J. Dorian
101 West Olive
Fresno, CA 93728

Suppliers

Restorite Systems
P.O. Box 7096
West Trenton, NJ 08628-0096
ph: 609-530-1526
Products for restoration and conservation of porcelain, pottery, and glass; sells a complete kit for repairing breaks and chips; also "How-to" videos available; send for free catalog.

Allan Koskela
Allan Koskela Restorations
P.O. Box 186
Webster City, IA 50595
ph: 515-832-1131
Sells repair supplies including fillers, glazes, lacquers, resins and cleaners; no heat needed; how-to video, "Repairing Pottery & Porcelain" recommended by Harry L. Rinker; restoration classes 6 times a year, with glueless repairing.

Figurines

(see REPAIR/RESTORATION/CONSERVATION; REPAIR/RESTORATION/CONSERVATION, Ceramics)

Furniture

(see also HARDWARE; REPAIR/RESTORATION/CONSERVATION, Woodworking; WOOD; "REPAIR SERVICES" Appendix of this book as well as Repair Services listed under REPAIR/RESTORATION/CONSERVATION and other specific categories throughout this Directory)

Experts

Lew Larason
2 E. Butler Ave.
Chalfont, PA 18914-3014
Writes syndicated antique furniture repair column.

Man./Prod./Dist.

Minuteman Furniture Restoration Systems & Supplies
115 North Monroe St.
Waterloo, WI 53594-1124
ph: 800-733-1776
fax: 920-478-3966
Free catalog features complete line of wholesale furniture restoration supplies, systems and equipment.

Repair Services

Leon Trefler
Trefler & Sons Antique Restoring Studio, Inc.
99 Cabot St.
Needham, MA 02494
ph: 781-444-2685
fax: 781-444-0659
e-mail: trefler@trefler.com
web: http://www.trefler.com/
Repair, restoration, conservation of all furniture; specializing in all hand finish work, custom color matching and preserving original finishes.

Don Mullen
Oak Grove Restorations, Inc.
299B Broad St.
Manchester, CT 06040
ph: 860-646-1951
fax: 860-646-0770
e-mail: DohnM@aol.com
web: http://www.nvionline.com/donmullen
Furniture restoration service specializing in church pew restorations; since 1972.

Alex Zhitnisky
Al's Furniture Restorers, Inc.
425 Ella T. Grasso Blvd.
New Haven, CT 06519
ph: 203-865-1885
fax: 203-562-5868
Specializes in the repair and restoration of furniture, reupholstery, brass repair, etc.; trained in Russia.

Dan Manning
Manning Claim Services
P.O. Box 212
Allendale, NJ 07401
ph: 201-825-8450
fax: 201-825-8301
web: http://www.premiereservicegoup.com/manning.html
Specializing in cargo claims handling, and furniture and antiques repair services.

Jim Murphy
Jim Murphy - Furniture & Paint
19 North President Ave.
Lancaster, PA 17603
ph: 717-299-9964
All types of paint work on reproduction or antique furniture: vinegar painting, grain painting and "fanciful" color work available.

Andrew Gelinas
Burlesque Repair Service
18 W. 3rd. St.
Bethlehem, PA 18015-1222
ph: 610-867-3313 or 610-867-1665
fax: 610-867-4999
e-mail: silvertiger@enter.net
Specializing in cargo claims handling and repair services for moving,

insurance, retail companies; full shop facilities; 22 years experience.

David A. Glassberg
Shop Furniture Repair Service & Custom, Restoration & Design, Inc, The
52 Street Road
Newtown Square, PA 19073
ph: 610-240-4822 or 800-746-7489
e-mail: info@shopguy.com
A specialist in antique restoration and repair; furniture, breakables, frames.

Michael Shur
Refinishing Touch, A
604 Hillcrest Ave.
Edgemoor, DE 19809
ph: 302-762-3684
fax: 302-762-4191
Specializing in cargo claims handling, and furniture and antiques repair services.

Joseph Miller
Joseph Miller Furniture Restoration
4811 Catharpin Rd.
Gainesville, VA 20155
ph: 703-754-7598
fax: 703-754-3955
e-mail: furnfoto@aol.com
Refinishing, repairing, caning.

Gene Shontere
Shontere Restoration, Inc.
P.O. Box 1805
Bowie, MD 20717-1805
ph: 301-753-6051
fax: 301-743-2128
e-mail: shontere@erols.com
Specializing in furniture restoration of all types; complete insurance and transit claims service.

Bob Neiderlander
Yesteryear Antique Farms Inc.
7420 Hawkins Creamery Rd.
Laytonsville, MD 20882
ph: 301-948-3979
Repairs and restores new and antique furniture.

Steve Rogowsky
Frederick Refinishing Center
117 S. Bentz St.
Frederick, MD 21701
ph: 301-663-0105
Commercial and residential furniture and antiques; repairs, refinishing, restorations, touch-up; water/fire/ moving damage claim work.

John Pyle
Glade Valley Furniture Repair
10464 Glade Rd.
Walkersville, MD 21793-9715
ph: 301-898-3795
fax: 301-898-3795
Moving claims service.

Mike Hartsky
AAA Professional Claim Services
12860 Parapet Way
Herndon, VA 22071-1725
ph: 800-548-3131
fax: 800-323-2948
e-mail: AAAclaim@idt.net
web: http:// www.furniturecaresolutions.com/
Offers nationwide furniture repairs and restorations, fire and water damage, upholstery and vinyl repair and restoration, fabric and leather repair, antique glass and mirror replacement; marble repair, appliance and clock service.

Bill Kala
Transportation Related Services of Virginia
154 Mountain Laurel Court
Fredericksburg, VA 22406
ph: 540-752-7546 or 540-752-7599
fax: 540-752-7599
e-mail: WKKala@aol.com
Offers claims services for household goods and residence damage to include inspections and repairs; also millwork, touch-up and refurbishing for churches and commercial establishments.

Bill Ivey
William Ivey Fine Furniture
2710 W. Cary St.
Richmond, VA 23220
ph: 804-358-7545
Conservation, restoration and design of furniture.

Thomas E. McGarry
Birnam Wood Joinery, The
300 N. Mildred St.
Charles Town, WV 25414
ph: 304-728-0373 or 800-700-5959
fax: 304-728-6600
e-mail: info@benchmadefurniture.com
web: http:// www.benchmadefurniture.com/
Specializes in the restoration of antiques including woven chairs of all kinds; restorations done by hand and restored to period appearance; custom reproductions of country styles from 1740-1840 made to standards of the originals.

Larry Hinshaw
Custom Restorations, Inc.
3230 Piper Lane
Charlotte, NC 28208
ph: 704-357-9929
fax: 704-357-0560
e-mail: info@custom-restorations.com
web: http://www.custom-restorations.com
Quality furniture repair, restoration and refinishing; on-line catalog of restoration supplies.

Restoration Center
P.O. Box 988
Danielsville, GA 30633
ph: 800-332-2747
fax: 800-332-2017
e-mail: hot-line@ix.netcom.com
web: http://www.furniture-hotline.com/
Use their Hot Line to contact an authorized Restoration Center specialist for moving damage claims, insurance casualty damages, furniture manufacturers and distributors, adjusters, relocation departments, retailers, corporations.

Dick Adams, ISA CAPP
Specialists of the South, Inc.
544 East Sixth St.
Panama City, FL 32401-3066
ph: 850-785-2577
fax: 850-872-8662
e-mail: 76652.31@compuserve.com
Specializing in furniture restorations & repairs, upholstery, refinishing; designated restoration center for northwest Florida; repairs for individuals, and the moving and insurance industries; also repairs rugs, porcelain, glass, silver.

Richard Raines
Furniture Medic of Broward/Palm Beach FL
3725 Hollywood Blvd.
Hollywood, FL 33021
ph: 954-981-9663
fax: 954-981-9663
e-mail: Furnituremedic@hotmail.com
web: http://www.laker.net/fmedic/
Furniture restoration and repair: burn-ins, scratches, dents, broken chairs, broken legs, nail polish damage, fire and water damage, pet damage; moving claims, insurance, estimates, Furniture Medic.

Ernest Littlejohn
Retouchables, The
9330 Grove Rd.
Cordova, TN 38018
ph: 901-383-1603
Repair, refinish, restore furniture; also caning; specializing in antiques.

Furniture Medic Corporate Office
860 Ridge Lake Blvd.
Memphis, TN 38120
ph: 700-408-7378
e-mail: Pat.Nelson@worldnet.att.net
web: http://www.furnituremedic.com/
Corporate headquarters for Furniture Medic; franchises of furniture repair firms nationwide.

Blake Soule'
Soule' Furniture Restorations, Inc.
5145 Raleigh-LaGrange Rd., Ste. 102
Memphis, TN 38134-5603
ph: 901-377-3646
fax: 901-377-3615
e-mail: bsoule1@aol.com
Specializes in furniture repair: on site spot repair, fire and water damage, moving damage, office furniture refinishing and touch up, antique restorations, retail stores.

Jim & Helen Roose
Mt. Pleasant Restoration Shop
Township Rd. 100, House #222
P.O. Box 245
Mount Pleasant, OH 43939
ph: 740-769-7565
Furniture repair, hand stripping, refinishing, caning, custom millwork, furniture made to order; over 28 years experience.

Bob Kovach
201 W. Alyea St.
P.O. Box 522
Hebron, IN 46341-0522
ph: 219-996-2924
Antique restorations, veneer work, wicker repair.

Michigan Antique Preservation Company
2034 Eureka Road
Wyandotte, MI 48192
ph: 313-283-5700
fax: 313-283-4312
e-mail: mapco@ili.net
Furniture conservators; repair and restoration of everyday furniture as well as fine antiques; member of American Institute for Conservation.

Robert Thomas
Furniture Medic #1791
2177 Avon Industgrial Drive
Rochester, MI 48309
ph: 248-853-9886
fax: 248-853-2959
e-mail: furnituremedic@ameritech.net
The Thomas family has been in the furniture industry since 1989; experienced in the repair, restoration, and conservation of all wooden furniture.

David Colglazier
Original Woodworks
360 North Main St.
Stillwater, MN 55082-5024
ph: 651-430-3622
e-mail: orgwood@iaxs.net
web: http://home.iaxs.net/orgwood/
A full service shop specializing in wooden antique restorations including furniture and architectural elements requiring extensive restoration and repairs, especially veneers.

William W. Ingram
Refinishing Touch, Ltd., The
950 N. Rand Road, Unit #103
Wauconda, IL 60084-1179
ph: 847-526-3113
A full service shop specializing in furniture repair, hand stripping, refinishing and antique restoration; also caning, veneers, and custom wood finishes.

Duane Mitch
Mercury Furniture Service
1017 W. Highland Ave.
Elgin, IL 60123
ph: 847-608-9553
fax: 847-608-9553
Refinishing, repairs, restoration.

James Bandy
Furniture Medic
2528 W. 183rd St.
Homewood, IL 60430
ph: 708-957-79109
fax: 708-957-8530
e-mail: www.furnmed@interaccess.com
web: http://www.imawa.com/furnmed
On-site repair, scratches and dents, gouges, scuffs and scrapes, broken joints, chair regluing, refinish and restorations.

Dave Kummerow
Image Restoration Services Inc.
P.O. Box 489
127 West Locust St.
Belvidere, IL 61008
ph: 815-547-5919
fax: 815-547-6413
e-mail: www.kummerowdl@aol.com
Restoration on and collector of Victorian era furniture and period pieces; complete repair and conservation including reproduction and replacement of parts.

Don Kistner
Kistner's Full Claims Service, Inc.
520 20th Street
Rock Island, IL 61201
ph: 309-7786-5868
fax: 309-794-0559
e-mail: Kistner.c@mcleodusa.net
web: http://www.kistners-service.simplenet.com/
Full claims service serving the eastern Iowa and northwestern Illinois area; furniture repair and touch up, manufacturing of new parts, furniture stripping, refinishing, marble repair, porcelains, etc.

Jack Craig
Craig's Limited Inc.
P.O. Box 487
Festus, MO 63028
ph: 314-937-6401
web: http://www.mossberg.com/collectors.htm
Antique & fine furniture restoration, stripping, refinishing, repair; over 20 years experience; licensed and insured; free phone estimates.

Wood Works Inc., The
7710 West 63rd Street
Shawnee Mission, KS 66202
ph: 913-362-2432
fax: 913-362-0588
e-mail: tim@movingclaims.com
web: http://www.movingclaims.com/
Furniture repair and refinishing, moving claims, woodworking, kitchen refacing, shutters, etc.

Ray Spencer
Spencer Corporation
23220 Maple Valley Highway SE, Unit 3B
Maple Valley, WA 98038
ph: 425-413-1660
fax: 425-413-1659
e-mail: Spencercorp@msn.com
Specializing in cargo claims handling and in complete repair services.

Ron Lawrence
Town & Country Claim Service, Inc.
18421 Driftwood Drive East
Sumner, WA 98390
ph: 253-826-0322
fax: 253-826-0324
e-mail: TwnCntryInc@msn.com
Transit damage specialist; specializes in the repair and restoration of fine furniture and antiques.

Furniture & Upholstery

Repair Services

Renaissance Furniture Repair
RD 4 Box 266-A
Wynantskill, NY 12198
ph: 518-283-5317
fax: 518-283-5380
Specializing in cargo claims handling, and furniture and antiques repair services.

Tom Kuhns
West Interior Services, Inc.
P.O. Box 540
Natrona Heights, PA 15065-0740
ph: 724-224-2215
fax: 724-226-3233
e-mail: tomjr@westinteriorservices.com
web: http://www.westinteriorservices.com/
Specializes in moving or insurance claims; furniture repair, refinishing & restoration, architectural refinishing; fire, smoke, water damage.

Timothy P. Hughes
MSS Furniture Service
211 Commerce Dr.
Montgomeryville, PA 18936-9641
ph: 800-433-1159 or 215-393-1900
fax: 800-835-0338
e-mail: timh@mss1.com
web: http://www.mss1.com/
Specializing in cargo claims handling, fire and water damage repairs, and furniture and antiques repair services; wood repairs and refinishing, woodworking and cabinetry, custom upholstery, antique restoration, china, metal repairs.

Charles Jourdant
Jourdant Furniture Repair
611 Alabama Ave.
North Beach, MD 20714-9602
ph: 301-855-6563 or 800-479-5427
fax: 410-257-0752
Specializing in cargo claims handling; furniture, upholstery and museum quality antique restorations.

L. Philip Oliver
Oliver's
24610 Frederick Rd.
P.O. Box 659
Clarksburg, MD 20871-0659
ph: 301-428-3336
fax: 301-428-9282
Specializes in moving or insurance claims; complete line of furniture upholstery, repair, refinishing and restoration.

Pete Simonetti
Artisian Restoration, Inc.
P.O. Box 72035
Baltimore, MD 21237
ph: 410-682-3700
fax: 410-682-3738
A complete furniture claims service specializing in cargo claims and fire water damage for insurance industry; repairs, refinishing, antique restoration, upholstery, touch-up, third party services; MD's largest furniture service.

Richard M. Montalbano
Montalbano Majestic International
3000 St. Charles Road
Bellwood, IL 60104-1544
ph: 708-547-1010
fax: 708-547-1032
e-mail: info@montalbanofurniture.com
web: http://www.montalbanofurniture.com

Al Zajec
Bay Area Restoration
850 Airport St., #3
Moss Beach, CA 94038-9683
ph: 650-728-1662
fax: 650-728-1663
Offers total restoration of antiques and furniture; crystal chandelier parts and restoration; insurance casualty loss and moving industry claims adjusters.

Suppliers

John K. Burch Co.
1818 Underwood Blvd.
Delran, NJ 08075
ph: 800-257-9112
fax: 609-461-7093
Mail order source for upholstering supplies; also fabric books.

Naomi Taylor
Douglas Industries, Inc.
412 Boston Ave.
Egg Harbor City, NJ 08215
ph: 800-257-8551
Source for foam and fabrics.

Jack Raskin
Jack Raskin Upholstery
845 Timber Lane
Dresher, PA 19025-1811
ph: 800-523-3213
Supplier to custom upholsterers.

Minute-Man Upholstery Supply Company of North Carolina
1905 South Elm St.
High Point, NC 27260
ph: 800-457-0029 or 336-882-4100
fax: 336-885-6890
e-mail: mkmsales@infoave.net
Mail order source for upholstering supplies.

Furniture (Antique Only)

Misc. Services

Society for the Preservation of New England Antiquities, The Conservation Center
185 Lyman St.
North Waltham, MA 02154
ph: 781-891-4882
fax: 781-893-7832
web: http://www.spnea.org/
Performs wood and finish/coatings analysis; also offers conservation treatment of furniture and objects.

Repair Services

Wade Holtzman
104 Bolton Rd.
Harvard, MA 01451
ph: 978-456-6850
e-mail: antique@tiac.net
web: http://www.tiac.net/users/antique
Professionally trained in England; over 22 years experience.

Bruce Hamilton
R. Bruce Hamilton, Furniture Restoration
P.O. Box 815
West Newbury, MA 01985-0815
ph: 978-363-2638
fax: 978-363-2638
Antique & fine furniture restoration; French polish, cleaning and restoration of existing finishes, false graining, removal of water stains & marks, leather work, veneering, carving, etc.; 20th century lacquer finishes repaired.

John Sutton
John Sutton Antique Restorations
14 North Henry St.
Brooklyn, NY 11222
ph: 718-389-6101
e-mail: yellowhouse39@earthlink.net
Specializes in the restoration of 17th and 18th century English, French and American furniture.

Tom Matthews
Furniture Restoration Services
204 Smith Road
Eaton, NY 13334
ph: 315-684-7716
fax: 315-684-7716
e-mail: Wefinish@dreamscape.com
web: http://wefinish.com
A small shop allowing for consistent and high quality work; also does more contemporary furniture as well.

Eugene E. Landon
144 Quaker State Rd.
Montoursville, PA 17754
ph: 570-433-3476
fax: 570-433-3476
Specializing in the restoration, conservation and replication of antique wooden furniture and artifacts.

Lawrence Bodine
Bodine Conservations
299 W. Mr. Pleasent Ave.
Ambler, PA 19002
ph: 215-646-1030
e-mail: LDBodine4@aol.com
Conservation, restoration and reproduction of antique American and European furniture including carving, marquetry, veneering, boulle, gold leaf conservation and historic finish conservation and restoration.

Stephen Rice
Heritage Restorations
4233 Howard Ave. #F
Kensington, MD 20895-2419
ph: 301-493-4458
European trained craftsmen specializing in wooden objets d'art & antique furniture restoration; duplicating finishes, inlays, etc.

Walter Raynes
4900 Wetheredsville
Baltimore, MD 21207-6625
ph: 410-448-3515
fax: 410-448-0855
Specializes in the restoration and conservation of antique furniture only; also builds reproduction of antique furniture.

Arnold Begleiter
Begleiter Antique Restorations
6801 Reisterstown Rd.
Baltimore, MD 21215
ph: 410-764-7467
fax: 410-486-2473

Bruce M. Schuettinger, ISA
Antique Restorations Ltd.
17 N. Alley
P.O. Box 244
New Market, MD 21774-0244
ph: 301-865-3009
fax: 301-865-3009
e-mail: schuettinger@erols.com
Conservators and consultants of wooden artifacts, specializing in the preservation of original finishes, painted or gilt decoration, and structural elements.

R.B. White
White Rose Manor, Ltd.
1972 Pineview Dr.
Kent, OH 44240
ph: 330-678-7929
Antique restoration and repair; studied at Sotheby's of New York and London.

Nemie Merkley
Merkley's Fine Wood Finishing Co.
111 Hausfeldt Lane
New Albany, IN 47150
ph: 812-944-7946 or 502-722-7727
fax: 812-944-7946
e-mail: merkleys1@aol.com
Family-owned and operated antique restoration and refinishing business; specializes in reproduction of missing parts; a full service restoration/ refinishing business.

Peter Storey Pentz
P.O. Box 58408
Seattle, WA 98138
ph: 206-251-0909
fax: 206-251-0682
Specializes in the restoration of period antique wooden objects.

Gilding

(see also FRAMES)

Repair Services

Susan B. Jackson
Harvard Art
49 Littleton County Rd.
Harvard, MA 01451-1729
ph: 978-456-9050
fax: 978-456-9050
e-mail: sbj@ma.ultranet.com
Restoration and conservation of period frames and other gilded objects; stabilization, replacement of missing pieces, gilding and toning to match the existing surface.

Romayne Shay McMahon, ISA
Veronique's Antiques
124 S. Market St.
Mechanicsburg, PA 17055-6329
ph: 717-697-4924
fax: 717-697-4924

William Adair
Gold Leaf Studios, Inc.
443 I Street NW
P.O. Box 50156
Washington, DC 20091
ph: 202-638-4660
fax: 202-347-4569
e-mail: bill@goldleafstudios.com
web: http://www.goldleafstudios.com
Gilding of anything gold leafed: frames, sculpture, sconces, etc.

R. Wayne Reynolds
R. Wayne Reynolds, Inc.
3618 Falls Rd.
Baltimore, MD 21211
ph: 410-467-1800 or 410-467-1890
Specializes in the application of gold leaf; complete restoration services for gilded art objects, including furniture, frames, and mirrors.

Richard Kornemann
Museum Shop, Ltd.
20 N. Market St.
Frederick, MD 21701
ph: 301-695-0424 or 301-871-3855
fax: 301-698-5242
23k gold leafing of antiques, picture frames, signs, etc.; also complete art and frame restoration.

Ken Brown
Kenneth Brown Studio, The
2703 Stokes Ferry Rd.
Salisbury, NC 28146
ph: 704-633-0604
fax: 704-633-5664
Restoration and conservation of gilded objects: frames, mirrors, furniture, etc.; also custom made frames and reproductions.

Susan Saye, Ex. Dir.
Society of Gilders
Newsletter: Society of Gilders Newsletter
P.O. Box 920490
Norcross, GA 30092
ph: 770-452-1113
fax: 770-452-1112
Promotes traditional gilding skills, techniques and knowledge; gives workshops and lectures on the art of gilding.

Jerome S. Feig, CPF, ISA
Field Art Studio
24242 Woodward Ave.
Pleasant Ridge, MI 48069-1144
ph: 248-399-1320
fax: 248-399-7018
e-mail: jsfieldart@aol.com
Frame specialist and appraiser: restoration of art, frames, objects, gilding; period frame reproductions made; fine art and frame appraisals; conservation of picture frames.

Marlene Matalon
10410 Willowisp
Houston, TX 77035
ph: 713-721-8404
fax: 281-729-5756
Conservator of gilded objects; uses these steps: 1) examination 2) written evaluation & estimate 3) technical analysis 4) care and maintenance recommendations 5) conservation using safest techniques for the object being conserved.

Glass

(see also GLASS, Curved)

Repair Services

Leon Trefler
Trefler & Sons Antique Restoring Studio, Inc.
99 Cabot St.
Needham, MA 02494
ph: 781-444-2685
fax: 781-444-0659
e-mail: trefler@trefler.com
web: http://www.trefler.com/
Repair of all glass items; removal of chips on glass.

Edward Poore
Crystal Workshop
P.O. Box 475
Sagamore, MA 02561-0475
ph: 508-888-1621 or 888-869-0867
fax: 508-888-9298
e-mail: crystalw@capecod.net
Repairs stemware, cut glass, and art glass; chips removed; recutting, stoppers fitted; contact for free detailed brochure; also engraved glass panels from old houses reproduced; new designs cut to order; 30 years experience.

Sharon Smith Abbott
Fine Wares Restoration
P.O. Box 753
Bridgton, ME 04009-0753
ph: 207-647-2093
e-mail: abbttfwr@megalink.net
Restores ceramic & glass art objects for private collectors and museums; references of museum clients on request.

Sylvio Bettio
Sylvio's
44 Longhill Dr.
Clifton, NJ 07013
ph: 973-777-0288
fax: 973-779-7659
e-mail: Sylvio11@aol.com
Repairs chipped glass and crystal.

Art Cut Glass Studio
RD 1 -10 Fawn Drive
Matawan, NJ 07747
ph: 732-583-7648
Restores fine antique glass such as Lalique, Steuben, Baccarat, Galle; also resurfaces paperweights.

Jonathan Mark Gershen
Jonathan Mark Gershen Porcelain, Pottery & Glass Restoration
1463 Pennington Rd.
Ewing, NJ 08618-2656
ph: 609-882-9417
fax: 609-530-0660
Second generation restorer and long time member of the AIC; clients include museums, collectors and dealers worldwide; free brochure available upon request.

Flemington Cut Glass
156 Main St.
Flemington, NJ 08822
ph: 908-782-3017

Glass Restorations
1597 York Ave.
New York, NY 10028
ph: 212-517-3287
fax: 212-517-3287

Anton Laub Glass Corp.
1873 Second Ave.
New York, NY 10029-7453
ph: 212-734-4270 or 718-430-1901
Installation, beveling and resilvering of glass and mirrors; also fabrication of reproduction antique mirrors.

Antique Workshop Inc.
150 Aerial Way
Syosset, NY 11791
ph: 516-933-6213
Repairs and restorations; chipped crystal repaired, chips removed from glass statues, cut glass, stoneware, and all glass items.

Ernest Kionke
Dropped Shop, The
34 Elm St.
East Aurora, NY 14052
ph: 716-652-7053
e-mail: ernie102@juno.com

Michael Andras
244 East Lake Rd.
Bear Rocks, PA 15610
ph: 724-547-6419
e-mail: andras@cvzoom.net
Custom hand engraving using vintage equipment, stone or diamond wheel.

Byron Klein
A. Ludwig Klein & Son, Inc.
683 Sumneytown Pike
P.O. Box 145
Harleysville, PA 19438
ph: 215-256-9004 or 800-379-2929
fax: 215-256-9644
Specializing in the repair and restoration of all types of glass, china and porcelain as well as ivory, jade, brass, pewter.

Henry Chaudron
Chaudron Glass & Mirror Co., Inc.
1801 Lovegrove St.
Baltimore, MD 21202-2815
ph: 410-685-1568
Resilvers mirrors; also specializes in cutting, hand-beveling plate glass, and stone wheel engraving.

Mildred R. Shepherd
Shepherd Studio
5527 Third St., South
Arlington, VA 22204-1115
ph: 703-671-1789
Since 1970, conservation/restoration of art objects; specializing in porcelain, glass, pottery, plaster, stoneware, ivory, jade; for private clients and museums.

Jim & Sheri Van Es
222 W. Washington St.
Charles Town, WV 25414
ph: 304-725-1673 or 703-435-9045
e-mail: wdnshu@aol.com
Grinds and repairs chips on glass.

Ray Errett
Ray Errett - Glass Restoration
101 Mohican Trail
Wilmington, NC 28409-3418
ph: 910-792-1807
e-mail: jrerrett@bellsouth.net
Restores glass figurines, sculpture crystal, cut glass, grinding, polishing; semi retired, Corning Museum of Glass.

Don & Joyce McCurley
McCurley Glass Repair
5011 Memorial Dr.
Sebring, FL 33870-1087
ph: 813-471-9814
fax: 941-471-3359
Repairs glass and crystal; chip removal, polishing, sawing, bells made from goblets; stopper specialist - carries large stock of replacement stoppers for bottles; also prism replacement.

David Jasper
D & J Glass & Art Clinic, Inc.
26707 466th Ave.
Sioux Falls, SD 57106
ph: 605-361-7524 or 800-361-7524
fax: 605-361-7216
Four generations of restorers; glass, porcelain, painting, dolls, figurines, ivory, lamps, etc.

Josef Puehringer
Crystal Cave, The
1141 Central Ave.
Wilmette, IL 60091
ph: 847-251-1160
fax: 847-251-1172
European trained craftsmen will restore your treasures with expert care; call or write for free estimates.

Jerry Lewis
Bevel Glass Works, Inc.
900 Hacienda
Belville, TX 77418
ph: 409-865-5711
Makes replacement beveled glass and mirrors, engraved glass and mirrors, shelves with plate grooves, etc.

Michael Blair
Restorations by Michael, Inc.
Golden, CO 80403
ph: 303-384-9121
e-mail: mblair5028@aol.com

Wayne Montano
Montano's Antique Glass Repair
P.O. Box 290003
Phelan, CA 92329
ph: 760-868-6598
fax: 760-868-6598
e-mail: info@montanosglassrepair.com
web: http://www.montanosglassrepair.com/
In business since 1982; repairs about 10,000 pieces per year; repairs on site at antique shows throughout California; also teaches professional glass repair at their shop.

Mike Maher
Dr. Chips
88154 Chita Loop
Springfield, OR 97478
ph: 541-747-6532
Restoration of glass and fine crystal; also porcelain, pottery restoration; gluing, making new parts when necessary, refinishing to match original; ships nationwide.

Suppliers

Restorite Systems
P.O. Box 7096
West Trenton, NJ 08628-0096
ph: 609-530-1526
Products for restoration and conservation of porcelain, pottery, and glass; sells a complete kit for repairing breaks and chips; also "How-to" videos available; send for free catalog.

Allan Koskela
Allan Koskela Restorations
P.O. Box 186
Webster City, IA 50595
ph: 515-832-1131
Sells glass repair materials including Diamond Hand Pads, fillers, glues and cleaners; instructional videos on Lampworking, to make glass beads, jewelry, figurines, etc.; highly recommended by many publications including Glass Art.

Ivory

Repair Services

Byron Klein
A. Ludwig Klein & Son, Inc.
683 Sumneytown Pike
P.O. Box 145
Harleysville, PA 19438
ph: 215-256-9004 or 800-379-2929
fax: 215-256-9644
Specializing in the repair and restoration of all types of glass, china and porcelain as well as ivory, jade, brass, pewter.

Mildred R. Shepherd
Shepherd Studio
5527 Third St., South
Arlington, VA 22204-1115
ph: 703-671-1789
Since 1970, conservation/restoration of art objects; specializing in porcelain, glass, pottery, plaster, stoneware, ivory, jade; for private clients and museums.

Mattresses

Man./Prod./Dist.

Tucker Mattress Company
3926 Lawrenceville Hwy.
Tucker, GA 30085
ph: 770-938-1176
Manufacturer of customized mattresses for antique beds, adjustable beds, brass beds; also for boats, RV's and campers.

Scott Lipps
Sleep-Tite Mattress Company
1355 E. Second St.
Franklin, OH 45005
ph: 800-859-3703 or 513-746-2556
fax: 513-746-9101
e-mail: comfort@sleeptite.com
web: http://www.sleeptite.com/
Specializes in custom made mattresses and box springs for hard-to-fit antique beds.

Mattresses Unlimited
840 Pleasant Valley Dr.
Springboro, OH 45066
ph: 800-326-5668
Carries any size mattress for antique beds.

Metal Items

(see also SILVER)

Periodicals

James R. Walker, Dir.
Institute of Metal Repair, The
Newsletter: Repairing Metalware
P.O. Box 2907
Escondido, CA 92033-2907
ph: 760-432-8942
fax: 760-747-1477
e-mail: 71477.1742@compuserve.com
Promotes knowledge, skill, and understanding of the metalware repair trade; publishes repair techniques and other information, sells specialty repair tools and supplies; flatware, sculpture/statuary, duplicating parts, etc.

James R. Walker, Dir.
Institute of Metal Repair, The
Directory: IMR Sourcebook
P.O. Box 2907
Escondido, CA 92033-2907
ph: 760-432-8942
fax: 760-747-1477
e-mail: 71477.1742@compuserve.com
A source book for restoration, repair, replication and preservation of metal items; contains sources for replacement parts (original & reproduced), metal repairers/restorers, tips/techniques, schools, organizations, etc.

Repair Services

Walter Allen
Specialty Castings
19 Mill Rd.
Boxford, MA 01921
ph: 978-887-9783
Reproduces items for collectors by casting in cast iron, bronze, brass or aluminum; all items created through the lost wax process; also mold making, parts modification, and shrinkage compensation.

Fleming's
24 Elm Street
Cohasset, MA 02025
ph: 781-383-0684
Metal repair and restoration; replating, dent removal, breaks repaired; pewter, silver, copper, polishing, plating, repairing, lacquering.

Leon Trefler
Trefler & Sons Antique Restoring Studio, Inc.
99 Cabot St.
Needham, MA 02494
ph: 781-444-2685
fax: 781-444-0659
e-mail: trefler@trefler.com
web: http://www.trefler.com/
Repairs and polishes brass.

Joseph J. Pistilli
Orum Silver Co., Inc.
51 S. Vine St.
P.O. Box 805
Meriden, CT 06450-0805
ph: 203-237-3037
fax: 203-237-3037
e-mail: Orum@ct1.nai.net
web: http://w3.nai.net/~maddog/orum.htm
Repairing, restoring, replating of antique and old silver, gold, nickel; brass & copper plating; cleaning, buffing, polishing.

Zophy's Fine Silver Plating
4702 Park St.
Peterboro, NY 13134
ph: 315-684-3062
Fine restoration for over 40 years of copper, brass, sterling, pewter.

Romayne Shay McMahon, ISA
Veronique's Antiques
124 S. Market St.
Mechanicsburg, PA 17055-6329
ph: 717-697-4924
fax: 717-697-4924
Fine metals refinishing: replating, cleaning, polishing, lacquering, repairing; silver, brass, copper, pewter, bronze; chandeliers, lamps, etc. rewired and restored; brass beds a specialty.

Boris Paskvan
Awesome Metal Restorations, Inc.
4233-G Howard Ave.
Kensington, MD 20895-2449
ph: 301-897-3266
fax: 301-530-8428
European expert restores gold, gilt, bronze, silver, silver plating, icons, metal accessories, sculptures, etc. for museums, homes, insurance; repairs, solders, fabricates duplicates parts, replates, rewires, retins, polishes, lacquers.

Abercombie & Co.
9159A Brookeville Rd.
Silver Spring, MD 20910
ph: 301-585-2385
fax: 301-587-5708
e-mail: abernco@comm-plus.net
web: http://www.silverplaters.com
Replates silverplate; repairs all sorts of metal; silver, brass, copper; also welding.

American Alloy Foundry
112-118 S. Eden Street
Baltimore, MD 21231
ph: 410-276-1930
Custom castings to replace broken or missing parts.

Pete Markey
Creative Metal Design
7935 Edgewood Church Rd.
Frederick, MD 21702-2713
ph: 301-473-5995
fax: 301-473-5995
Specializes in ornamental ironwork, hand forged originals; metal repairs; made the Statue of Liberty gates.

David Nelson
Jarnel Iron & Forge
221 Rowland Ave.
Hagerstown, MD 21740
ph: 301-733-0441
fax: 301-733-0919
Recasts replacement parts in various metals; also iron work.

Kip Young
Copper Kettle Metal Polishing
158 1/2 South Potomac St.
Hagerstown, MD 21740
ph: 301-791-4555
Specialists in antique lamps and lighting sales, repairs and restorations; metal polishing, fabrication of missing metal parts; also specializes in crystal chandelier repair.

Alexander Bigler
Equestrian Forge
P.O. Box 1950
Leesburg, VA 22075
ph: 703-777-2110
fax: 703-777-3949
Recasts replacement parts in various metals; also casts portrait sculptures.

Steve Kayne
Kayne & Son Custom Forged Hardware
100 Daniel Ridge Rd.
Candler, NC 28715-9434
ph: 828-667-8868 or 828-665-1988
fax: 828-665-8303
e-mail: kaynehdwe@ioa.com
Steel, brass, bronze reproductions of locks, pulls, hinges, thumb latches, furniture & interior/exterior hardware, fireplace tools & accessories, military accoutrements, etc.; also does repairs, restoration; $5 for two catalogs.

Alfred L. Crabtree
Brass & Silver Workshop, The
758 St. Andrew Blvd.
Charleston, SC 29407
ph: 843-571-4342
fax: 843-571-7417
Museum quality restoration and conservation of most fine metal decorative arts; emphasis on 17th, 18th and 19th century brass and silver; also purchases Southern coin silver and unusual sterling items.

Estes-Simmons Silverplating, Ltd.
1050 Northside Dr., NW
Atlanta, GA 30318
ph: 404-875-9581 or 800-645-4193
fax: 404-873-4826
e-mail: info@estes-simmons.com
web: http://www.estes-simmons.com/
Repairs silver, silverplate, gold, pewter, brass and copper; also replates silver, gold, brass, nickel, copper.

Memphis Plating Works
682 Madison Ave.
Memphis, TN 38103
ph: 901-526-3051
Gold, silver, copper, brass, nickel and chrome plating; restoration of chandeliers, floor lamps, brass beds, fern tables, tea sets, trays, vanity sets, etc.; repairs teapot feet, spouts, missing parts, flatware, etc.

Antique & Art Restoration By Wiebold
413 Terrace Place
Terrace Park, OH 45174-1164
ph: 513-831-2541 or 800-321-2541
fax: 513-831-2815
e-mail: wiebold@eos.net
web: http://www.wiebold.com
Silver repair and replating; restoration of bronzes, brass, copper, pewter, lead, combs, brushes, knife blades, mirrors, chandeliers, glass, etc.

Jerry Propst
P.O. Box 45
Janesville, WI 53547-0045
ph: 608-752-2816
fax: 608-752-7691
Repairs silver back hair brushes; when writing, please include a LSASE if requesting a reply.

Roger A. Sundblom
Specialized Repair Service
1125 E. Wisconsin Ave.
Appleton, WI 54911-3905
ph: 920-993-9993
e-mail: metlmstr@execpc.com
web: http://www.execpc.com/~metlmstr
Repairs all metal items; also designs and fabricates replacement metal parts; machining, welding (tig, heliarc, oxyacetylene, silver brazing, casting in yellow and red brass, etc.; if it can't be repaired, will remake from scratch!

Jerry Muradian
T & G Plating Service
721 Amsterdam St.
Woodstock, IL 60098
ph: 815-338-5020
fax: 815-338-5028
e-mail: jmuradian@cwix.com
web: http://www.chrome-plating.com
Specializes in chrome plating.

Glenn Taylor
Courtesy Metal Polishing
635 N. Addison Rd.
Villa Park, IL 60181
ph: 630-832-1862
All metals polished and buffed: motorcycle, automobile, marine parts, antique juke boxes and slot machines.

Mueller Kaiser Plating Co.
5815 Hampton Ave.
Saint Louis, MO 63109
ph: 314-832-3553
Fine metal finishing in silver, gold, bronze, copper and brass; flatware, tea services, church ware, antiques, and other items.

Danny O'Brien, ISA
Star Forge & Anvil
1816 E. 135th St.
Grandview, MO 64030
ph: 816-763-4741
Custom forgings and ornamental iron repair.

Craig Bierman
Speed & Sport Chrome Plating
404 Broadway
Houston, TX 77012
ph: 281-921-0235
Specializing in chrome plating of antique jukeboxes, Coke machines, slot machines, pedal cars, etc.

Carmelo Tringali
Colonial Silver
1219 Forest Ave.
Pacific Grove, CA 93950
ph: 831-375-0355
Recommended for silverplating and replating.

Tim Maple
Omega Silver Smithing Inc.
11130 117th Pl. NE
Kirkland, WA 98033
ph: 425-822-3727
Expert repair and restoration of fine silver, bronze, silverplate, spelter, brass, pewter and copper; from tea sets to brass beds, chandeliers, new knife blades, mirrors and combs; full service restoration.

Suppliers

Jax Chemical Company, Inc.
78-11 267th St.
Floral Park, NY 11004
ph: 718-347-0057
fax: 718-668-0057
Sells metal finishing solutions: green patina, pewter black, black darkener, gold finish, silver and copper plating solutions; also brass, copper, gold and marble cleaners.

Delphi Stained Glass
3380 E. Jolly Rd.
Lansing, MI 48910
ph: 800-248-2048 or 517-394-4631
fax: 517-394-5364
e-mail: webmaster@delphiglass.com
web: http://www.delphiglass.com/
Sells stained glass supplies; gives lessons; large mail order business; also sells chemical solutions to repair damaged patina on brass and other metals.

Mirrors

Repair Services

Anton Laub Glass Corp.
1873 Second Ave.
New York, NY 10029-7453
ph: 212-734-4270 or 718-430-1901
Installation, beveling and resilvering of glass and mirrors; also fabrication of reproduction antique mirrors.

Sundial Schwartz
159 E. 118th St.
New York, NY 10035
ph: 212-289-4969 or 800-876-4776
fax: 212-996-3236
Custom resilvering and antiquing of mirror and glass.

Romayne Shay McMahon, ISA
Veronique's Antiques
124 S. Market St.
Mechanicsburg, PA 17055-6329
ph: 717-697-4924
fax: 717-697-4924
Offers glass grinding and resilvering.

Henry Chaudron
Chaudron Glass & Mirror Co., Inc.
1801 Lovegrove St.
Baltimore, MD 21202-2815
ph: 410-685-1568
Resilvers mirrors; also hand-bevels plate glass.

Painted Finishes

Repair Services

Ruby Newman
Roundabout Restoration Studio
P.O. Box 823
Forest Knolls, CA 94933-0823
ph: 415-488-9213
fax: 415-488-9213
Restoration and recreating of classic finishes; all painted surfaces including furniture, mirror frames, carousel carvings, etc.: trompe l'oeil, contemporary murals, classical faux marbles, wood grain, gold leaf, wall treatments.

Paper Items

(see also PRINTS; REPAIR/RESTORATION/CONSERVATION, Archival Supplies For)

Repair Services

Henry Lie
Center for Conservation & Technical Studies, The
Fogg Art Museum
Harvard University
Cambridge, MA 02138
ph: 617-495-2392
Provides conservation and restoration services for fine arts, including works of art on paper, paintings, objects and sculpture.

Bridgitte Boyadjian
43 Fern St.
Lexington, MA 02173-6024
ph: 781-862-9395
fax: 781-862-9395
Paper restoration and conservation; fine prints, drawings, watercolors and manuscripts.

Oscar & Debra Perez
Vigues Art Studio
54 Flanders Rd.
Woodbury, CT 06798-2103
ph: 203-263-4088
fax: 203-266-9118
e-mail: vigues@wtco.com
Conservation, restoration of oil paintings (cleaning, lining, touch up and repair), frames (gold leaf repairs, casting of missing parts) and paper (cleaning, repairs of prints, books, documents); also porcelain, glass & china repair.

Kenneth Newman
Old Print Shop, The
150 Lexington Ave. at 30th St.
New York, NY 10016
ph: 212-683-3950
fax: 212-779-8040
e-mail: info@oldprintshop.com
web: http://www.oldprintshop.com/
Paper conservator: preservation, restoration, cleaning, deacidification, encapsulation.

George J. Cohenour
4301 Beaumont Rd.
Dover, PA 17315-2405
ph: 717-292-5345
Cleans, deacidifies, repairs and restores prints: American historical, antique and decorative, handcolored lithographs, chromolithographs, etchings, engravings, watercolors, etc.

Maria Pukownik
Fine Art & Paper Conservation
1045 Orrtanna Rd.
Orrtanna, PA 17353
ph: 717-337-0668
fax: 717-337-1093
e-mail: pukownik@cvn.net
Watercolors, charcoal and pastel, drawings, colored engravings, autographs, maps; cleaning, leaf casting, tears and cracks mending, flattening, retouching, dry mounting removal.

Marilyn Kemp Weidner, FAIC
612 Spruce St.
Philadelphia, PA 19106-4114
ph: 215-627-2303 or 215-627-0188
Conservation treatment for art & artifacts on paper, collection surveys and care consultations; extensive expertise and experience in the treatment of pastels, watercolors, drawings, maps, manuscripts, and problems with works on paper.

Christopher W. Lane
Philadelphia Print Shop, Ltd., The
8441 Germantown Ave.
Philadelphia, PA 19118
ph: 215-242-4750
fax: 215-242-6977
e-mail: PhilaPrint@PhilaPrintShop.com
web: http://www.philaprintshop.com
Gallery of antique prints and maps with related rare books and atlases; also bookstore of reference books related to antique prints and maps; appraisals, paper conservation and restoration, museum quality framing.

American Institute for Conservation of Historic & Artistic Works
Directory: AIC Directory
1717 K St. NW, Ste. 20
Washington, DC 20006
ph: 202-452-9545
fax: 202-452-9328
e-mail: InfoAic@aol.com
web: http://aic.stanford.edu/
Purpose is to advance the knowledge and practice of the conservation of cultural property; the AIC Directory lists competent conservators of paper, textiles, photographs, furniture, and more - over 2000 members.

James Von Ruster
Old Print Gallery, The
1220 31st St. NW
Washington, DC 20007-3422
ph: 202-965-1818
fax: 202-965-1869
e-mail: oldprintgallery@erols.com
web: http://www.oldprintgallery.com/
Paper conservator: preservation, restoration, cleaning, deacidification, encapsulation.

Janice & Dennis Dobson
Dobson Studios
810 N. Daniel St.
Arlington, VA 22201-1944
ph: 703-243-7363
fax: 703-243-2382
e-mail: ddobson@erols.com
Conservator of Oriental screens, scrolls and wood block prints; repairs and conservation to other paper items as well.

Christine Smith, Pres.
Conservation of Art on Paper, Inc.
2805 Mt. Vernon Ave., Ste. B
Alexandria, VA 22301-1125
ph: 703-836-7757
Conservation of fine art and historic artifacts on paper and parchment; also Japanese woodblock prints; conservation treatments, collection surveys, lectures, workshops, vault storage.

Paul J. Buco
Fine Arts Services, Inc.
127 N. Front St.
Wilmington, NC 28401-3944
ph: 910-251-8859
Restoration/conservation of art on paper: tears and paper loss repairs, deacidification, encapsulation.

David L. Swift
6436 Brownlee Dr.
Nashville, TN 37205
ph: 615-352-0308
Paper conservator: preservation, restoration, cleaning, deacidification, encapsulation.

John Pofelski
Resurrection Book & Paper Conservation
P.O. Box 582
330 West Georgetown St. #200A
Wood Dale, IL 60191-0582
ph: 708-616-8990

Marlene Matalon
10410 Willowisp
Houston, TX 77035
ph: 713-721-8404
fax: 281-729-5756
Conservator of art on paper; uses these steps: 1) examination 2) written evaluation & estimate 3) technical analysis 4) care and maintenance recommendations 5) conservation

using safest techniques for the object being conserved.

Phil Temple
Phil Temple Poster Mounting Service
P.O. Box 561
Novato, CA 94949-0561
ph: 415-897-5130
fax: 415-897-5130
e-mail: ptemple@webtv.net
Paper conservation and poster mounting (linen backing).

Shawn Leubner, Conservator
Sierra Restoration Services
P.O. Box 1884
Nevada City, CA 95959-1884
ph: 530-478-0499
e-mail: paperrest@aol.com
Professional paper restoration and conservation service; over 18 years of archival experience; specializes in comic book and original art restoration; call or email to have free information package sent to you.

Suppliers

Light Impressions Corp.
P.O. Box 940
Rochester, NY 14603-0940
ph: 800-828-6216
fax: 800-828-5539
General line of archival supplies including mat boards, document storage boxes, framing and photographic supplies.

Porcelain

(see REPAIR/RESTORATION/CONSERVATION, Ceramics)

Reverse Painting On Glass

Repair Services

Ingrid Sanborn
Ingrid Sanborn & Daughters
85 Church St.
West Newbury, MA 01985-1018
ph: 978-363-2253
fax: 978-363-2049
e-mail: sanborn@greennet.net
web: http://www.isd.pair.com
Specializes in the restoration of reverse paintings on glass and antique painted finishes; philosophy is to preserve as much of the original finish as possible and restore only those areas that have been lost or damaged.

Textiles

Repair Services

Textile Conservation Center, Museum of American Textile History
491 Dutton St.
Lowell, MA 01854-4221
ph: 978-441-0400
fax: 978-441-1412
web: http://valley.uml.edu/lowell/historic/museums/textile.html
TCC provides evaluation, treatment and educational services that pertain to the conservation and preservation of historic textiles.

Evelyn Siefert Kennedy
Sewtique, Inc.
391 Long Hill Rd.
P.O. Box 1293
Groton, CT 06340-1293
ph: 860-445-7320 or 800-332-9122
fax: 860-445-1448
e-mail: sewtique@aol.com
web: http://members.aol.com/sewtique/home.htm
Specialist in restoration, preservation & conservation of apparel and textiles; full service by mail/phone or appt.; appraises textiles, laces, tapestries, etc.; removes spots & stains; teaches textile appraisal & restoration workshops.

Stephen & Carol Huber
40 Ferry Rd.
Old Saybrook, CT 06475
ph: 860-388-6809
fax: 860-388-6809
Specializes in the repair and conservation of antique needlework.

Applebaum & Himmelstein
444 Central Park West
New York, NY 10025
ph: 212-666-4630
fax: 212-316-1039
Treats silk textiles, paintings and objects.

Patsy Orlofsky
Textile Conservation Workshop
3 Main St.
South Salem, NY 10590
ph: 914-763-5805
Textile conservation lecturer and consultant; also does conservation and repairs of all types of textiles.

Testfabrics, Inc.
415 Delaware Ave.
P.O. Box 26
West Pittston, PA 18643
ph: 570-603-0432
fax: 570-603-0433
Provides textile conservation services.

M. Finkel & Daughter
936 Pine St.
Philadelphia, PA 19107
ph: 215-627-7797
fax: 215-627-8199
Antique textile restoration for collectors, museums and dealers; specializes in mounting and repairing of antique samplers, quilts, needlework, hooked rugs and table rugs.

Linda Tomlin
Details in Design, A Needle Art Studio
4901 C. Helen Potts Pl.
Williamsburg, VA 23188
ph: 757-253-2483
fax: 757-253-2483
Linens and lace restoration, conservation; embroidered textiles; also reproduction embroidery for linens: Arts & Crafts, and 18th and 19th century period designs; sells marked linen kits on Irish linen for embroiderers.

Mini-Magic
3910 Patricia Drive
Columbus, OH 43220
ph: 614-457-3687
fax: 614-459-2306
Cleaning and repairing; conservation supplies.

Frances K. Faile
Frances K. Faile Textile Conservation
928 W. Lewiston Ave.
Ferndale, MI 48220
ph: 248-545-4699
Specializing in the care of antique samplers and needlework, Oriental embroideries, quilts, woven coverlets, hooked rugs, costume accessories, and all types of flat textiles; cleaning, repair & structural stabilization, framing.

Elizabeth L. Barbatelli
Linens Limited, Inc.
240 North Milwaukee St.
Milwaukee, WI 53202
ph: 414-223-1123 or 800-637-6334
fax: 414-223-1126
Expert specializing in the repair, restoration and cleaning of linens; restores both new and antique linens using old world European laundry techniques that are superior to simple laundering.

Bryce Reveley
Gentle Arts
936 Arabella
P.O. Box 15636
New Orleans, LA 70155
Cleaning and repairing of textiles.

Emily Sanford
Sanford Restoration Works
2102 Speyer Ln.
Redondo Beach, CA 90278
ph: 310-374-7412
fax: 310-798-2792
Restoration of antique textiles including oriental rugs, American Indian weavings, quilts, needlepoint, embroideries, and tapestries.

Suppliers

Rita Marx
Cherish
205 W. 86th St.
New York, NY 10024
ph: 212-724-1748
fax: 212-480-1143
e-mail: cherish_ny@hotmail.com
Carries Orvus soap and other conservation supplies including padded hangers, acid-free boxes and tissues, etc. for the storage, cleaning and displaying of vintage textiles and clothing.

Testfabrics, Inc.
415 Delaware Ave.
P.O. Box 26
West Pittston, PA 18643
ph: 570-603-0432
fax: 570-603-0433
Sells delicate clamps for textile repair and restoration.

Nancy's Notions
333 Beichl Ave.
P.O. Box 683
Beaver Dam, WI 53916-0683
ph: 920-887-0391 or 800-833-0690
fax: 920-887-0391
web: http://www.nancysnotions.com/
Carries Orvus brand quilt soap.

June Roth-Splain
Lily-White Linens
1496 Rolling Acres
Argyle, TX 76226-6330
ph: 940-240-8800 or 940-565-9611
fax: 940-383-8809
Lily-White Linens is a product that can be safely used on antique linens and quilts for stain and spot removal; safe for the environment.

Wicker

Repair Services

Veterans Chair Caning & Repair
442 10th Ave.
New York, NY 10001
ph: 212-564-4560
fax: 212-564-4560
web: http://www.caning.baweb.com/
Antique wicker restoration and repair; 13 years experience, by the piece or by the load; all expert work; no covering up.

Joan O. Silbermann
Antique Wicker Works
8002 McKenstry Dr.
Laurel, MD 20723-1152
ph: 410-792-4842
Sales, restorations, repairs.

Suppliers

Paige W. Beasley
Carolina Caning Supply
111 Fairfax Lane
Cary, NC 27513
ph: 800-346-0142 or 919-467-7773
Chair caning and repair supplies.

Woodblock

Suppliers

Ann Fremon
Refinishing Store, The
1943 N. Cleve-Mass Road
p.O. Box 498
Bath, OH 44210
ph: 330-668-2631
fax: 330-666-0586
e-mail: ann@refinish.com
web: http://www.refinish.com/
A source of finishing products waxes, cleaners easily used by professionals and first time restorers alike; all tested for ease of use and results; also carries hard-to-find products such as Butchers Wax and Goddards Polishes.

Woodworking

(see also HARDWARE; REPAIR/ RESTORATION/CONSERVATION, Furniture; WOOD; "REPAIR SERVICES" Appendix of this book as well as Repair Services listed under REPAIR/RESTORATION/ CONSERVATION and other specific categories throughout this Directory)

Misc. Services

Bess Naylor
Olde Mill Cabinet Shoppe
1660 Camp Betty Washington Road
York, PA 17402
ph: 717-755-8884
fax: 717-755-5688
e-mail: bnaylor@cyberia.com
web: http://www.oldemill.com
Offers one and two day courses on wood finishing, antique restoration, carving, furniture construction and several other topics; specialty wood finishing supplies including dyes, shellacs, pigments, milk paints, etc.

Suppliers

Trendlines
135 American Legion Hwy.
Revere, MA 02151
ph: 800-767-9999 or 617-853-0900
fax: 617-853-0226
e-mail: customer_service@trend-lines.com
web: http://www.trend-lines.com/
Mail order source for a good mix of woodworking tools.

Tremont Nail Company
P.O. Box 111
Wareham, MA 02571
ph: 617-295-0038
Carries twenty different styles of historic cut nails.

Brookstone
17 Riverside St.
Nashua, NH 03062-1373
ph: 800-351-7222
e-mail: brkcust@brookstonecompany.com
web: http://brookstoneonline.com/
Mail order source for hard to find tools and devices.

Barbara Horton Rockwell
Horton Brasses Inc.
P.O. Box 120
Cromwell, CT 06416
ph: 860-635-4400
fax: 860-635-6473
e-mail: barb@horton-brasses.com
web: http://www.horton-brasses.com
Sells authentic period reproduction hardware of the finest quality. Manufactured of solid brass or handforged black iron in CT factory.

Micro Mark
340 Snyder Ave.
Berkeley Heights, NJ 07922-1505
ph: 908-464-6764
fax: 908-665-9383
e-mail: micromark@worldnet.att.net
Mail order source for small tools only, e.g. X-Acto, knives, Dremel, airbrushes, micro-sanders, etc.; 80-pg. catalog $1.

Garrett Wade Company, Inc.
161 Ave. Of The Americas
New York, NY 10013-1299
ph: 800-221-2942 or 212-807-1155
fax: 800-566-9525
e-mail: mail@garrettwade.com
web: http://www.garrettwade.com/
Reproduction English solid brass hardware; also 220 page catalog of the world's finest specialty woodworking tools: planes, chisels, etc.

Constantine
2050 Eastchester Rd.
Bronx, NY 10461
ph: 800-223-8087
fax: 718-792-2110
e-mail: glendoc@constantines.com
web: http://www.constantines.com
A complete line of tools, hardware, finishing supplies, marquetry kits, books, moldings, parts, veneers, hardwoods, etc.

Mohawk Finishing Products
4715 State Highway 30
Amsterdam, NY 12010
ph: 800-545-0047 or 518-843-1380
fax: 518-842-3551
e-mail: mohawkinfo@mohawk-finishing.com
web: http://www.mohawk-finishing.com/
Major supplier of finishing tools, supplies and materials.

Woodworker's Supply, Inc.
7703 Perry Highway
Pittsburgh, PA 15237
ph: 800-645-9292 or 724-367-4330
fax: 800-853-9663
web: http://www.woodcrafterssupply.com/
Mail order source for hand tools, machinery, hardware, and finishes; also stores located in Erie, PA and Altoona, PA.

John M. Fisher
18th Century Hardware Co., Inc.
131 East 3rd St.
Derry, PA 15627-1607
ph: 724-694-2708
fax: 724-694-9587
Clean, polish & repair brass items; makes, sells reproduction hardware; clean and electrify brass lamps; offers catalog; will duplicate any style or pattern.

Bess Naylor
Olde Mill Cabinet Shoppe
1660 Camp Betty Washington Road
York, PA 17402
ph: 717-755-8884
fax: 717-755-5688
e-mail: bnaylor@cyberia.com
web: http://www.oldemill.com
Offers one and two day courses on wood finishing, antique restoration, carving, furniture construction and several other topics; specialty wood finishing supplies including dyes, shellacs, pigments, milk paints, etc.

Bill Ball
Ball & Ball Antique Hardware Reproduction & Restorations
463 W. Lincoln Highway
Exton, PA 19341
ph: 800-257-3711 or 610-363-7330
fax: 610-363-7639
e-mail: billball@ptd.net
web: http://www.ballandball-us.com/
Sells reproduction hardware; 18th century reproduction brass and iron chandeliers, sconces, candle stands and candlesticks; also offers a recasting service.

Industrial Abrasives Co.
P.O. Box 14955
Reading, PA 19612-4955
ph: 800-451-1861
fax: 610-378-4868
e-mail: indabrasives@msn.com
web: http://www.industrialabrasives.com/
Carries a large line of sand paper and other abrasives.

Paxton Hardware Ltd.
P.O. Box 256
Upper Falls, MD 21156-0256
ph: 410-592-8505 or 800-241-9741
fax: 410-592-2224
e-mail: paxton@ix.netcom.com
web: http://www.paxtonhardware.com/
Supplies authentic solid brass, hard-to-find reproduction hardware in period styles: pulls, knobs, hinges, locks, casters, table hardware, bed hardware.

Woodcraft
5300 Briscoe Road
P.O. Box 1686
Parkersburg, WV 26102
ph: 304-428-4866 or 800-225-1153
fax: 304-428-8271
e-mail: custserv@woodcraft.com
web: http://www.woodcraft.com/
Mail order source for complete line of woodworking tools, supplies and books.

Highland Hardware
1045 N. Highland Ave., NE
Atlanta, GA 30306
ph: 800-241-6748 or 404-872-4466
fax: 404-876-1941
e-mail: custservice@highland-hardware.com
web: http://www.highland-hardware.com
Mail order source for hand tools, machinery, workbenches, books, videos, and supplies; call 888-500-4466 for free catalog.

Power Kleen Corp.
101 Bayview Blvd.
Oldsmar, FL 34677
ph: 813-854-2648 or 800-844-2648
fax: 813-854-3133
Wholesale chemicals and supplies for refinishers; paint and varnish removers, lacquer thinner, mineral spirits.

A & H Brass & Supply
126 W. Main St.
Johnson City, TN 37601
ph: 423-928-8220 or 800-638-4252
fax: 423-928-8360
Carries a wide selection of hardware, caning supplies, trunk parts, fiberboard seats, etc.

Bob Morgan Woodworking Supplies
1121 Bardstown Rd.
Louisville, KY 40204
ph: 502-456-2545
Mail order source for hundreds of veneers, faces, flexibles, inlays, burls, tiger oak, etc. for restoring antique furniture; send for free catalog.

Cherry Tree Toys, Inc.
P.O. Box 369
Belmont, OH 43718
ph: 614-484-4363 or 800-848-4363
web: http://www.cherrytree-online.com/
Mail order source for children's toys, doll houses, whirligig kits, parts, books and supplies.

Robert Hershberger
Hershberger's Hardware
1411 Township Rd. 178
Baltic, OH 43804
ph: 330-893-2464 or 800-734-8044
fax: 330-698-3200
Catalog of specialty products for antiques and woodworking such as spool cabinet decals, high chair trays, antique telephone parts, Hoosier cabinet parts, lamp parts; $4 for 64 page catalog (refundable).

Leichtung Workshops
4944 Commerce Parkway
Cleveland, OH 44128
ph: 800-321-6840
fax: 216-464-6764
Mail order source for hand tools, supplies and small kits.

Shopsmith Tool Guide
6530 Poe Ave.
Dayton, OH 45414
ph: 800-543-7586 or 800-762-7555
fax: 800-722-3965
e-mail: shpsmith@aol.com
web: http://www.shopsmith.com
Mail order source for hand tools and supplies. Visit local Shopsmith Store or order by phone.

Phyllis & Phil Kennedy
Phyllis Kennedy Hardware
10655 Andrade Drive
Zionsville, IN 46077
ph: 317-873-1316
fax: 317-873-8662
e-mail: philken@kennedyhardware.com
web: http://www.kennedyhardware.com
Hardware for antique furniture, ice boxes, Hoosier cabinets and trunks; manufacturer of flour bins and sifters for Hoosier cabinets; pulls, bails, knobs, latches, char seats and caning, hinges, locks and keys, coat hooks, etc.

Doug Poe
Doug Poe Antiques
4213W 500N
Huntington, IN 46750
ph: 800-348-5004
fax: 219-356-4358
Carries antique restoration hardware: stamped-brass pulls, diecast brass knobs, casters, teardrop pulls, brass keys, cupboard latches, etc.

Woodsmith Store
2625 Beaver Ave.
Des Moines, IA 50310
ph: 800-929-8854 or 515-255-8979
fax: 515-282-6741
e-mail: woodstor@augusthome.com
web: http://www.augusthome.com/woodstor.htm
Mail order source for woodworking tools, hardware, and project plans and supplies.

David Colglazier
Restore-it Supply Co.
360 North Main St.
Stillwater, MN 55082-5024
ph: 651-430-3622
e-mail: orgwood@iaxs.net
web: http://home.iaxs.net/orgwood/
Brass, bronze, steel, iron hardware for furniture, architecture, trunks, carved wooden racetrack moldings for drawer front, etc.; custom casting available' also catalogs for AABCO, Leo Hardware, Ritter & Son.

Van Dykes Supply Company
P.O. Box 278
Woonsocket, SD 57385-0278
ph: 800-558-1234 or 605-796-4425
fax: 605-796-4085
web: http://www.vandykes.com/
Mail order source for refinishing supplies; large catalog of reproduction simulated and solid wood carvings, hardware, pulls, knobs, leather seats, old fashioned nails, isen glass, etc.; also issues catalog of taxidermy supplies.

WSI Distributors - Antique Restoration Supplies
405 N. Main St.
Saint Charles, MO 63301-2034
ph: 800-447-9974 or 314-946-5811
fax: 314-946-5832
e-mail: wsi@fastrans.net
Wholesale source for furniture & trunk hardware, cane & weaving materials, fiber chair seats, veneer, wood ornaments, Zap glues, and much more; over 1200 items for professional furniture restorers. Sorry, dealers only.

Gay Barton
Briwax Midwest, Inc.
20 Nonsuch Rd.
Lake Ozark, MO 65049-9307
ph: 573-365-4698 or 800-562-5855
Briwax is a restorative compound used mainly for restoring antique furniture and floors.

Scott's-Becker's Hardware Inc.
1411 S. 3rd St.
Ozark, MO 65721-9188
ph: 800-247-2594 or 417-581-6525
fax: 417-485-3067
Carries hardware for antique furniture: trunk hardware, bed parts, kitchen cabinets, Hoosier, pulls, latches, hinges, locks keys.

Woodworker's Supply, Inc.
5604 Alameda Place NE
Albuquerque, NM 87113
ph: 505-821-1511 or 800-645-9292
fax: 505-821-7331
Mail order source for wood finishing tools, supplies and brass hardware.

Mother of Pearl & Sons Trading Company
12328 Ventura Blvd.
Studio City, CA 91604
ph: 818-505-8057
fax: 818-505-0467
web: http://www.cybermall2000.com/stores/pearl/
Sells traditional restoration products; call or write for catalog.

Muff's Antiques
135 S. Glassell St.
Orange, CA 92866-1421
ph: 714-997-0243
fax: 714-997-1601
e-mail: muffs@earthlink.net
web: http://home.earthlink/~muffs/
Mail order source for kitchen cabinet hardware (Hoosiers) including hinges, labels, canisters, castors, and rolls; also ice box parts, locks, keys (specializes in rekeying antique locks), window hardware, and much, much more; catalog $5.

Harbor Freight Tools
3491 Mission Oaks Blvd.
Camarillo, CA 93011-6010
ph: 800-423-2567 or 805-388-3000
fax: 805-388-0760
e-mail: webmaster@harborfreight.com
web: http://www.harborfreight.com/
Absolutely the lowest prices on quality name brand tools, equipment, machinery for both the home and professional workshop; free catalog.

Woodline the Japan Woodworker
1731 Clement Ave.
Alameda, CA 94501-1204
ph: 510-521-1810 or 800-537-7820
fax: 510-521-1864
e-mail: fdamsen@ix.netcom.com
Mail order source for highest quality woodworking tools from Japan.

American Home Supply
191 Lost Lake Lane
P.O. Box 697
Campbell, CA 95009
ph: 408-246-1962
fax: 408-296-2450
Carries the largest selection of antique reproduction hardware on the West Coast; has a 99.9% stock rate.

Anglo American Brass Company
P.O. Box 9487
San Jose, CA 95157
ph: 800-AABRASS or 408-246-0203
fax: 408-248-1308
Publishes a hardware catalog; brass hardware, household hinges, glass knobs, brass casters, nickel plate ice box hardware, wooden casters.

Ritter & Son Hardware
38001 Old Stage Rd.
P.O. Box 578
Gualala, CA 95445-9984
ph: 800-445-5044 or 707-884-3363
fax: 800-445-5043
e-mail: flora@mcn.org
Supplier of furniture restoration hardware: carved oak gingerbread, Hoosier hardware, cast & stamped brass pulls, handles, etc.; dealers only.

Bridge City Tool Works, Inc.
1104 N.E. 28th Ave.
Portland, OR 97232
ph: 503-282-6997 or 800-253-3332
fax: 503-287-1085
e-mail: bridgecitytools@uswest.net
web: http://www.bridgecitytools.com/
Mail order source for fine woodworking hand tools.

RESTAURANT COLLECTIBLES

(see also CERAMICS; DINERS & RELATED ITEMS; FAST FOOD COLLECTIBLES; FOOD COLLECTIBLES; MENUS)

Collectors

Sandra Obuck
517 Krause St.
Ann Arbor, MI 48103
ph: 734-996-9002
e-mail: dover@mail.ic.net
web: http://ic.net/~dover/mugs2.htm
Wants to buy Howard Johnson's restaurant collectible items: china, menus, paper items, anything having to do with Howard Johnson's; also wants coffee mugs with restaurant logos.

Glenn Grush
5344 North Collingwood Circle
Calabasas, CA 91302-3137
ph: 818-880-6200 or 800-653-3244
fax: 818-880-6500
Wants restaurant memorabilia: Bob's Big Boy, Coon Chicken Inn; nodders, ceramic display pieces, tableware with logos, etc.

Dave Lathom
P.O. Box 5053
Bellingham, WA 98227-5053
ph: 360-676-0715
e-mail: china@telcomplus.net
Wants restaurant china from ice cream parlors, lunch rooms, hamburger stands, grills, diners, sandwich stands, cafes, coffee shops, greasy spoons.

Dealers

Steve Colby
Off The Deep End
712 East St.
Frederick, MD 21701-5239
ph: 301-698-9006
e-mail: chilimon@offthedeepend.com
web: http://www.offthedeepend.com/
Wants to buy old restaurant and diner items.

Internet Resources

Chris Trent
Little Spoon's Virtual Museum of Restaurant Ware
2801 Ocean Park Blvd. #243
Santa Monica, CA 90405
ph: 310-827-6510
e-mail: ltlspoon@aol.com
web: http://www.littlespoon.com/
An online resource and virtual museum of collectible vitrified restaurant chinas.

Big Boy

Collectors

Steve Soelberg
29126 Laro Dr.
Agoura Hills, CA 91301-1635
ph: 818-889-9909
Wants Big Boy collectibles such as lamps, lunch boxes, cookie jars, counter displays, buttons, nodders, menus, ash trays, salt/peppers, etc.; items must have the Big Boy logo on them; no vinyl banks, please; the older the better.

Glenn Grush
5344 North Collingwood Circle
Calabasas, CA 91302-3137
ph: 818-880-6200 or 800-653-3244
fax: 818-880-6500
A leading buyer and collector wants Big Boy restaurant items: cups, plates, menus, ceramic banks, lamps, figural ashtrays, menus, salt and peppers, display items, anything with Big Boy logo.

Chicken In The Rough

Collectors

Ted Hirt
4929 Butterworth Pl.
Washington, DC 20016
Wants memorabilia and information about "Chicken in the Rough" restaurant chain.

Howard Johnson's

Collectors

Jeffrey C. McCurty
P.O. Box 882
Pleasant Valley, NY 12569-0882
ph: 914-635-3566
e-mail: Jeffrey.McCurty@omr.state.ny.us
Wants 1930-1980 Howard Johnson's dishes, tins, candy boxes, toys, soda cans, employee patches/service awards; will seriously consider any items.

Sandra Obuck
517 Krause St.
Ann Arbor, MI 48103
ph: 734-996-9002
e-mail: dover@mail.ic.net
web: http://ic.net/~dover/mugs2.htm
Wants to buy Howard Johnson's restaurant collectible items: china, menus, paper items, anything having to do with Howard Johnson's; also wants coffee mugs with restaurant logos.

Sambo's

Collectors

Jeff Kline
616 Masselin Ave. #306
Los Angeles, CA 90036-3733
ph: 323-934-3117
fax: 323-934-7141
Wants anything related to Sambo's/No Place Like Sam's restaurants including signage, fixtures, china, employee items, mascots, menus, etc.

RESTRAINT DEVICES

(see also KEYS; LOCKS; MAGICIANS PARAPHERNALIA; LAW ENFORCEMENT MEMORABILIA)

Collectors

Mark Lyons
544 Crest Dr.
Encinitas, CA 92024-4145
ph: 760-431-5397
fax: 760-431-1515
Wants to buy law enforcement and magicians keys, handcuffs, leg irons, thumbcuffs, slave irons, ball and chains, and toy cuffs; American and foreign; old or new; also Wells Fargo strong boxes & locks.

Experts

Yossie Silverman
1855 Folsom St.
MCB-401
San Francisco, CA 94114
e-mail: yossie@mail.blacksteel.com
web: http://www.blacksteel.com/hcs.html
Collects and specializes in handcuffs and other restraint devices.

Handcuffs & Leg Shackles

Dealers

Joseph & Pamela Tanner
Wheeler-Tanner ESCAPES
3024 E. 35th Ave.
Spokane, WA 99223-4504
ph: 509-448-8457
fax: 509-448-8457
e-mail: JnPwLrTnr@aol.com
Specialize in handcuffs, leg shackles, balls & chains, restraints, padlocks, locks & locking devices of all kinds (including railroad.)

Peter D. McCahon
Handcuff Collection, The
60 St. Augustines Ave.
South Croydon, CR2 6JJ
U.K.
ph: (++) 44 0181 688 3114
e-mail: petermccahon@compuserve.com
Collector and dealer in all forms of handcuffs, leg irons, and manacles; interest limited solely to antique, police and magical related items.

Experts

Michael Griffin
International Handcuff Exchange
356 W. Powell Rd.
Powell, OH 43065-9650
ph: 614-846-0585
Buys/sells all types of handcuffs, leg irons, locks, magicians escape items, old or new; offers large quarterly list of items for sale.

REVERE GIFTWARE

Experts

Douglas M. Singleton
P.O. Box 416
Westmoreland, NY 13490-0416
ph: 315-336-7792
e-mail: archaic123@aol.com
Appraises and specializes in Revere Giftware made of chrome, copper and brass prior to 1942: cocktail shakers, condiment sets, goblets, magazine holders, pitchers, trays, etc.; no pots and/or pans, please.

REVERSE PAINTINGS ON GLASS

(see ART, Paintings [Reverse on Glass]; REPAIR/RESTORATION/ CONSERVATION, Reverse Painting on Glass)

REVOLUTIONARY WAR ITEMS

Collectors

Larry Jarvinen
313 Condon Rd.
Manistee, MI 49660
ph: 616-723-5063
Wants muskets, lamps, pipes, chests, swords, polearms, tools, silverware, compasses, bayonets, canteens, etc.

Alex Peck
Antique Scientifica
P.O. Box 710
Charleston, IL 61920-0710
ph: 217-348-1009
e-mail: antiques@advant.net
Wants uniforms, insignia, guns, swords, diaries, medical instruments, hats, medals, belt plates.

REVOLVING LAMPS

(see LAMPS & LIGHTING, Motion)

REWARDS OF MERIT

(see PAPER COLLECTIBLES; SCHOOL RELATED MEMORABILIA)

RIDING TOYS

(see also AUTOMOBILIA; BICYCLES & RELATED MEMORABILIA; GO-KARTS)

Experts

Edmund Weinberg
Atlantic Highlands Animal Hospital
77 Memorial Parkway
Atlantic Highlands, NJ 07716-1451
ph: 732-291-4400 or 732-741-2542
Collects and specializes in riding toys, velocipedes, wagons, wheel toys, and rocking horses.

Repair Services

Carl Kriewall
C & N Reproductions, Inc.
1341 Ashover Ct.
Bloomfield Hills, MI 48304
ph: 248-852-1998
fax: 248-852-1999
e-mail: ckcn@ix.netcom.com
web: http://www.pedalcar.com
Manufacturers parts and kits for pedal cars and pedal planes, especially the Pursuit plane.

Pedal Vehicles

Clubs/Associations

Bruce Beimers
National Pedal Vehicle Association
1720 Rupert, N.E.
Grand Rapids, MI 49505
ph: 616-361-9887
Focuses on pedal cars.

Collectors

Frank Martin
7669 Winterberry Dr.
Youngstown, OH 44512-4723
ph: 330-758-4470
e-mail: martin7669@aol.com
web: http://members.aol.com/Martin7669/
Wants any literature related to pedal vehicles: catalogs, old photos, advertisements, etc.; wants to buy postwar pedal cars in original excellent condition; also prewar pedal cars in any condition; also wants old tricycles.

Nate Stoller
960 Reynolds Dr.
Ripon, CA 95366
ph: 209-956-5244 or 209-529-5300
e-mail: nate@maytagclub.com
web: http://www.maytagclub.com/
Wants to buy or trade pre-1960 pedal cars.

Dealers

Matthew Vaznaian
Juvenile Automobiles
291 High Street
Woonsocket, RI 02895
ph: 401-762-9661 or 401-766-9661
Buys and sells antique pedal cars.

David A. Hull
Small Town Coins & Collectibles
7498 E. Davison Rd.
Davison, MI 48423-2014
ph: 810-658-1992
fax: 810-658-2977
Has over 100 antique (1920-1970) pedal cars for sale; also buys pedal cars.

Michael Ballengee
Smilin' Jack's Pedal Cars
5405 W. Glendale Ave.
Glendale, AZ 85301
ph: 602-847-3879

Experts

Sanford Weltman
39 Branford Rd.
Rochester, NY 14618-1707
ph: 716-442-8810 or 716-473-2498
20 year veteran collector/buyer of pedal vehicles and large riding toys; buys pre-WWII pedal cars, pedal planes, or pedal trucks; also will buy post-WWII up to 1950s; any condition; has parts; does not resell; please send photos.

George Medinilla
Pedal Cars by George Medinilla
14714 1/2 Chadron Ave.
Gardena, CA 90249-3505
ph: 310-679-8688
e-mail: medinilla1@rocketmail.com
web: http://www.palosverdes.com/pedalcars/
Pedal car collector, dealer, expert, repair and restoration service; also makes reproduction pedal cars, planes and boats; information books available; "How to Restore a Pedal Car" video.

Internet Resources

George Medinilla
Pedal Cars by George Medinilla
14714 1/2 Chadron Ave.
Gardena, CA 90249-3505
ph: 310-679-8688
e-mail: medinilla1@rocketmail.com
web: http://www.palosverdes.com/pedalcars/
Appraisal, pedal car news, restoration tips, classified ads, etc.

Periodicals

John Rastall
Newsletter: Wheel Goods Trader, The
P.O. Box 435
Fraser, MI 48026-0435
ph: 810-949-6282
fax: 810-949-6282
web: http://www.wgtpub.com/
Magazine for collectors pedal cars, pedal airplanes; classifieds, calendar, etc.

Blue Diamond Classics
Newsletter: Peddler, The
300 Speedway Circle
Lincoln, NE 68502
ph: 402-474-4411
fax: 402-736-3733
e-mail: info@bluediamondclassics.com
web: http://www.bluediamondclassics.com/

Repair Services

Chad Mapes
Chad Mapes Pedal Car Restoration
3216 Wayne St.
Endwell, NY 13760
ph: 607-754-7952
fax: 607-786-3549
Specializes in the restoration of pedal cars.

Ron Hanley
Mini-Motors
130 Main
Hobart, NY 13788
ph: 607-538-9926
Handcrafted "one-of-a-kind" pedal cars manufactured; can hand craft body parts and fenders for pedal cars.

Portell Restorations
P.O. Box 91
Hematite, MO 63047
ph: 314-937-8192
Restorer and manufacturer of pedal cars and parts.

Blue Diamond Classics
300 Speedway Circle
Lincoln, NE 68502
ph: 402-474-4411
fax: 402-736-3733
e-mail: info@bluediamondclassics.com
web: http://www.bluediamondclassics.com/
Pedal cars, car graphics, parts and repairs.

Mike Harfield
Elantec
16 Blackbrook Road
Fareham, Hampshire PO15 5DJ
U.K.
ph: +44 (0) 1329 285198
fax: +44 (0) 1329 285198
e-mail: bharfield@aol.com
web: http://members.aol.com/bharfield/elantec/home.htm
Reproduction and restoration of Eureka pedal cars and spares; special commissions also undertaken.

Repro. Sources

Tony Duran
Nostalgia Warehouse
3317 S. Shady Lane
Arlington, TX 76001
ph: 817-572-5012
e-mail: tonyduran@nostalgiawarehouse.com
web: http://www.nostalgiawarehouse.com/
Sells reproduction pedal cars; also automobilia, gameroom collectibles, HotWheels and other toy cars, Coke machines, pinball machines, etc.

Bob Lowry
Foss Company, The
1224 Washington Ave.
Golden, CO 80401
ph: 303-279-3373
fax: 303-278-9556
e-mail: BLowry@fossco.com
web: http://www.fossco.com/
Sells reproduction pedal cars.

Mike Harfield
Elantec
16 Blackbrook Road
Fareham, Hampshire PO15 5DJ
U.K.
ph: +44 (0) 1329 285198
fax: +44 (0) 1329 285198
e-mail: bharfield@aol.com
web: http://members.aol.com/bharfield/elantec/home.htm
Reproduction and restoration of Eureka pedal cars and spares; special commissions also undertaken.

Suppliers

Matthew Vaznaian
Juvenile Automobiles
291 High Street
Woonsocket, RI 02895
ph: 401-762-9661 or 401-766-9661
Smallest pedal car parts supplier in the world: tires, wheels, hubcaps, hood ornaments, bells, bumpers, steering wheels, headlights, pods, windshields, etc.; send $6 for catalog.

J.D. Dorsey
Texas Pedal Car Peddler Inc.
213 Stone Drive
Fort Worth, TX 76108
ph: 817-238-8363
320 page catalog/reference book for $8.

Rocking Horses

Dealers

Sandy Paul & Gary Franklin
3818 South 9th St.
Arlington, VA 22204-1530
ph: 703-892-8666
Buy, sell, restore; call or write for a complete list of antique carousel figures and rocking horses.

Experts

Edmund Weinberg
Atlantic Highlands Animal Hospital
77 Memorial Parkway
Atlantic Highlands, NJ 07716-1451
ph: 732-291-4400 or 732-741-2542
Collects and specializes in riding toys, wheel toys, and rocking horses.

Patricia Mullins
P.E.I. International
6001 Johns Rd., Ste. 148
Tampa, FL 33634
ph: 813-855-4213
Author of "The Rocking Horse."

Repair Services

Marsha A. Schloesser
Carousel Workshop, The
218 High St.
De Land, FL 32720
ph: 904-738-4229
web: http://www.carousel.net/workshop/
Dealer and lecturer; buys, sells, restores carousel figures; also gliding & rocking horses.

Sleds

Collectors

Art Bransky
1840 Siegfriedale Rd.
Breinigsville, PA 18031-2246
ph: 610-285-6180
Collects and restores children's sleds, bobsleds, and any unusual sledding related items from the past 100 years; a frequent museum exhibitor and serious collector.

Dealers

Lyle Palmiter
Canacadea Sled Shop
676 Tinker Town Rd.
Alfred Station, NY 14803
ph: 607-587-9450
e-mail: sledman@infonblvd.net
Buys old sleds regardless of condition; parts accepted.

Experts

Joan Palicia
15 Canton Rd.
Wayne, NJ 07470
ph: 201-831-0527
Flexible Flyer memorabilia, membership cards, models, pins, advertising, sleds; anything Flexible Flyer; author of "Flexible Flyer and other Great Sleds for Collectors."

Repair Services

Art Bransky
1840 Siegfriedale Rd.
Breinigsville, PA 18031-2246
ph: 610-285-6180
Collects and restores children's sleds, bobsleds, and any unusual sledding related items from the past 100 years; a frequent museum exhibitor and serious collector.

RINGS

Character/Comic

(see PREMIUMS, Rings)

RIPLEY'S BELIEVE IT OR NOT!

(see also MORBID & ODD ITEMS)

Clubs/Associations

Jan & Mick Ivanovich
Ripley's Believe It or Not! Collectors Club
Newsletter: RBION Newsletter
1433 Wyoming Ave., Apt. H
Billings, MT 59102-5351
For fans and collectors of Ripley's memorabilia; newsletter published quarterly.

Collectors

Dan Paulun
215 South Maple
West Lafayette, OH 43845-1138
ph: 740-545-9743
Wants anything Ripley: blotters, calendars, posters, museum & odditorium postcards and booklets, newspaper & magazine ads, etc.

Glen Carlisle
2163 Goshen Hill Rd. SE
New Philadelphia, OH 44663-6789
ph: 330-339-3859
Wants "Ripley's Believe It or Not" hardback books; also memorabilia from museum, Odditorium programs, giant rings, etc.; also humorous books about epitaphs, privies, preachers, funeral directors.

Museums/Libraries

Ripley's Believe It Or Not! Museum
175 Jefferson St.
San Francisco, CA 94113
ph: 415-771-6188
fax: 415-771-1246
e-mail: sanfran@ripleys.com
web: http://www.ripleysf.com/ripley/odd/odd.html
There are 17 Ripley's Believe It Or Not! museums across the U.S. and Canada.

Church of One Tree/Robert L. Ripley Museum
492 Sonoma Ave.
Santa Rosa, CA 95401
ph: 707-524-5233
Collection is housed in the church Ripley once worshiped; contains his personal papers and related memorabilia; church is built from one tree - the whole church including the wooden furniture inside as well.

RIVERBOAT COLLECTIBLES

(see STEAMBOAT COLLECTIBLES)

ROADSIDE MEMORABILIA

(see HIGHWAY COLLECTIBLES; HOTEL COLLECTIBLES; SOUVENIR & COMMEMORATIVE ITEMS)

ROBJ

Collectors

Charles Sorkin
19 Chatsworth Ave.
Larchmont, NY 10538-2903
ph: 914-235-4718
Wants Robj porcelains: figural bottles, inkwells, powder jars, statuettes; any piece marked "Robj"; call collect.

Jeff Leegood
DecoLectibles
P.O. Box 596553
Dallas, TX 75359-6653
ph: 214-824-7917
fax: 214-824-7917
e-mail: decolectibles@cyberramp.net
Seeks Robj perfume lamps, incense burners, statues, powder boxes, and liquor bottles; made in porcelain, ceramic, glass during the 1920s; most marked ROBJ, Paris France; also wants other similar Art Deco perfume lamps.

Experts

Randy Monsen
Monsen & Baer Inc.
P.O. Box 529
Vienna, VA 22183-0529
ph: 703-938-2129
fax: 703-242-1357
e-mail: monsenbaer@erols.com

ROBOTS

(see TOYS, Space & Robot)

ROCK 'N' ROLL COLLECTIBLES

(see also AUTOGRAPHS; MAGAZINES, Scandal/Cult/R 'N' R; MUSIC, Rock 'N' Roll; PERSONALITIES [MUSICIANS]; RECORDS; SHEET MUSIC)

Dealers

Terri Ivers
Terri's Toys & Nostalgia
206 E. Grande Ave.
Ponca City, OK 74601
ph: 580-762-8697 or 580-762-5174
fax: 580-765-2657
e-mail: toylady@poncacity.net
Buys and sells Beatles, Kiss, Monkees, Elvis original memorabilia such as guitars, drums, vehicles (Yellow Submarine, Monkeemobile, etc.).

Myron Ross
Heroes & Legends
P.O. Box 9088
Calabasas, CA 91372
ph: 818-346-9220
e-mail: heroesross@aol.com
Wants character memorabilia, books, comic books, Fanzines, movie memorabilia, etc.; science fiction or fantasy, rock 'n roll, autographs.

Experts

Greg Moore
P.O. Box 586
Aumsville, OR 97325
Author of "Here It Is! A Price Guide to Rock & Roll Collectibles"; music memorabilia from the 1950s to present including Beatles, Monkees, Elvis, KISS, California Raisins, Banana Splits, Archies, Partridge Family, and more.

ROCKETS

(see KITS; MODELS, Rockets; SCIENCE FICTION; SPACE COLLECTIBLES)

ROCKHOUNDS

(see LAPIDARY; MINERAL SPECIMENS)

ROGERS GROUPS

Clubs/Associations

George Humphrey
Rogers Group, The
Newsletter: Newsletter of the Rogers Group
4932 Prince George Ave.
Beltsville, MD 20705-1907
ph: 301-937-7899
fax: 703-556-5616
Focuses on the life and works of John Rogers (1829-1904), American sculptor.

Collectors

Bruce Bleier
73 Riverdale Rd.
Valley Stream, NY 11581
ph: 516-791-4353
fax: 516-792-0519
e-mail: emeralite@aol.com
Buys and sells John Rogers statuary.

Sangiorgi
35 Mildred Ave.
Cortland, NY 13045
ph: 607-753-6574
Wants to buy John Rogers groups; please describe and price.

Dealers

George P. Lentros
179A Main St.
Ashland, MA 01721-1153
ph: 508-881-1160 or 508-881-1635
fax: 508-881-6475
e-mail: pglentros@aol.com
Collector and dealer; buys and sells John Rogers Groups: appraises and consults on any collection; contact with wants and any Groups to sell.

Carme Pederson
Carmen's Garden of Treasures
114 E. 32nd St.
New York, NY 10016-5506
ph: 212-683-9197

Experts

Michael Semendinger
497 South Wellwood Ave.
Lindenhurst, NY 11757
ph: 516-957-8953
e-mail: mdsdaisy@webtv.net
Active collector with 35 John Rogers groups.

George Humphrey
4932 Prince George Ave.
Beltsville, MD 20705-1907
ph: 301-937-7899
fax: 703-556-5616
Interested in the life and works of John Rogers (1829-1904), American sculptor; wants to purchase Rogers groups for his collection.

Museums/Libraries

John Rogers Studio & Museum of the New Canaan Historical Society
13 Oenoke Ridge
New Canaan, CT 06840-4104
ph: 203-966-1776
fax: 203-972-5917
e-mail: newcanaan.historical@snet.net
web: http://nchistory.org/

Lightner Museum
P.O. Box 334
75 King St.
Saint Augustine, FL 32085
ph: 904-824-2874

ROLLER COASTERS

(see also AMUSEMENT PARK ITEMS)

Clubs/Associations

American Coaster Enthusiasts, Inc.
Magazine: Rollercoaster!
P.O. Box 2412
Shawnee Mission, KS 66201
e-mail: bpeters@aceonline.org
web: http://www.aceonline.org/
Promotes the preservation, appreciation and enjoyment of the roller coaster; 4700 members in 48 states and 17 countries.

Collectors

Peter Dusza
305 Mathew St.
Santa Clara, CA 95050
ph: 408-988-8161 or 408-723-0722
fax: 408-988-2206
e-mail: pdusza@ix.netcom.com
Wants to buy roller coaster souvenirs and memorabilia: coffee cups, drinking and shot glasses, pins, patches, post cards, posters, and buttons.

ROSE O'NEILL COLLECTIBLES

(see also DOLLS, Kewpie)

Clubs/Associations

International Rose O'Neill Club
P.O. Box 668
Branson, MO 65616

Experts

Denis C. Jackson
P.O. Box 1958
Sequim, WA 98382-1958
ph: 360-452-3810
e-mail: ticn@olypen.com
web: http://www.olypen.com/ticn/
Author of "The Price & Identification Guide to Rose O'Neill", 2nd edition; covering magazine covers, advertising, paper items from Puck, etc.; send LSASE for information.

ROYALTY COLLECTIBLES

(see also POSTCARDS, Royalty Related; RUSSIAN ITEMS; SOUVENIR & COMMEMORATIVE ITEMS)

Clubs/Associations

Steven N. Jackson
Commemorative Collector's Society
Newsletter: Members Journal
Lumless House, Gainsborough Road
Winthrope
Near Newark, Nottinghamshire NG24 2NR
U.K.
ph: 01636-671377
Members interested in commemorative items including commemorative pieces for Royal events and personages (both U.S. and worldwide): ceramics, glass, printed tins, textiles, and ephemera.

Collectors

Frank J. Buono
P.O. Box 1535
Binghamton, NY 13902
ph: 607-724-4444 or 800-527-8893
fax: 607-723-1656
Wants to buy royalty items: Victoria 1887, 1897 Jubilees, Edward & Alexandra 1901.

Dealers

Pat Klein
Nostalgia Unlimited
P.O. Box 262
East Berlin, CT 06023
ph: 860-828-3973
fax: 860-828-1544
e-mail: pklein262@yahoo.com

British

Collectors

Edward J. Sperling
Britannia Past
215 Beach Ave.
Kennebunk, ME 04043
ph: 207-967-5989
Buys and sells by mail order British Royalty commemoratives: china, glass, silver, paper, textile, etc.

Dealers

Anita L. Grashof
Gallerie Ani'tiques
Stage House Village
Park & Front Streets
Scotch Plains, NJ 07076
ph: 908-322-4600 or 201-377-3032
fax: 973-765-9565
Buys, sells and appraises British Royal commemoratives from Queen Victoria through Prince William.

Douglas H. Flynn
126 East Main St.
P.O. Box 294
Lititz, PA 17543-0294
ph: 717-627-4567
fax: 717-627-7727
e-mail: doug4brc@aol.com
web: http://www.antiquejunction.com/dougflynn/
Buys and sells British Royalty items; also publishes five or six catalogs per year; co-author of "British Royalty Commemoratives," $23.95 ppd.

Now & Then Antiques
401 Main St.
Laurel, MD 20707

Audrey B. Zeder
British Royalty Commemoratives
1320 SW 10th Street
North Bend, WA 98045
ph: 425-888-6697
Buys, sells, British Royal commemorative items for all royalty events; deals in royalty ceramics, tins, textiles, ephemera and souvenirs; for sale list available for $3.

Experts

Douglas H. Flynn
126 East Main St.
P.O. Box 294
Lititz, PA 17543-0294
ph: 717-627-4567
fax: 717-627-7727
e-mail: doug4brc@aol.com
web: http://www.antiquejunction.com/dougflynn/
Co-author with Alan H. Bolton of "British Royalty Commemoratives, 19th and 20th Century Royal Events in Britain Illustrated by Commemoratives" (Schiffer).

Audrey B. Zeder
British Royalty Commemoratives
1320 SW 10th Street
North Bend, WA 98045
ph: 425-888-6697
Author of "British Royal Commemoratives."

Internet Resources

British Monarch Official Web Site, The U.K.
web: http://www.royal.gov.uk/
The British Monarchy Official Web Site.

Italian

Collectors

Mario Donald Thomas
860 18th Ave.
Salt Lake City, UT 84103-3719
ph: 801-532-5340
fax: 801-532-5340
Buys any items connected to the Italian royal families.

Russian

Experts

Timothy A. Miller
ARTCo
P.O. Box 33191
Decatur, GA 30030-0191
ph: 404-292-6097
fax: 404-292-6097
e-mail: artco@mindspring.com
web: http://www.stic.net/users/artco/
Buys, sells, brokers, appraises quality Russian antiques: civil, military, religious items from Russia 1700s to 1917; periodic auction catalogs.

ROYCROFT

(see ARTS & CRAFTS, Roycroft)

RUBA ROMBIC

(see GLASS, Consolidated)

RUBBER ITEMS

Collectors

Mike Woshner
2306 Spokane Ave.
Pittsburgh, PA 15210-4414
ph: 412-884-9299
e-mail: mwoshner@bellatlantic.net
Collector, researcher, historian, lecturer; author of "India-Rubber and Gutta-Percha in the Civil War Era" (1999).

M. Brunswick
P.O. Box 9729
Baltimore, MD 21286-9729
e-mail: brunswickm@hotmail.com
Wants rubber goods, manuals, films; hot water bottle outfits, rubber syringes, bulbs, enamel cans, etc.: pre-1965 or foreign; also books, accessories, boxes, ads, catalogs, photos on use, etc.; also nursing, child care, sick care.

George Briese
12204 Woodlark Ct.
Manassas, VA 22111
Wants rubber hot water bottles, combination or fountain syringe outfits, douche or enema squeeze bulb syringes, folding syringes, syringe hoses and fittings related to pre-1965 health care rubber goods.

Atled Delta, Ph.D.
2911 N.W. 122nd, Ste. 262
Oklahoma City, OK 73120-1900
ph: 405-751-0859
Wants to buy any medical or sick room device having a black, hard rubber nozzle/tip that penetrates any body orifice such as rubber douche syringes (bag or bulb); also pre-1950 enema equipment.

Museums/Libraries

Goodyear World of Rubber
1201 East Market St.
Akron, OH 44316
ph: 330-796-2044 or 800-321-2136
e-mail: pa@goodyear.com
web: http://www.goodyear.com/

Clothing

Collectors

Standish H. Smith
P.O. Box 292
Villanova, PA 19085
Wants rubber raincoats, hats, rain suits, capes; any color; or photographs of firemen, policemen, fishermen, etc. wearing same.

M. Brunswick
P.O. Box 9729
Baltimore, MD 21286-9729
e-mail: brunswickm@hotmail.com
Wants to buy ladies rubber undergarments, solid or perforated girdles, corsets, Playtex, Kleinetts, etc.; also wants women's rubber boots and shoes (no black unless unusual).

RUBIK'S CUBES

(see PUZZLES, Mechanical [Rubik's Cubes])

RUGS

(see also AMERICAN INDIAN, Navajo)

Clubs/Associations

Stephanie Kline Morehouse
Textile Group of Los Angeles, Inc.
894 South Bronson Ave.
Los Angeles, CA 90005-3605
ph: 323-939-2240 or 323-931-4987
fax: 323-931-4987
e-mail: TGLAinc@aol.com
Non-profit society formed in 1979 to provide a further the interest in all and any type of carpets, textiles or related arts; regular meetings, lectures, viewing private collections; textile design, conservation, history.

Dealers

Allan Arthur
Cyber Rug Center
25 Bennett Street
Atlanta, GA 30309
ph: 800-686-7030 or 404-350-9560
e-mail: aarthur@cyberrug.com
web: http://www.cyberrug.com/
Buys and sells Kelim & flat woven rugs, Pre-Columbian, Coptic, Asian textiles, European rugs and tapestries, Kashmir shawls, American folk art rugs, Oriental rugs, Art Deco rugs; hundreds of images.

Experts

J. Barry O'Connell
RugNotes
12700 Ardennes Ave.
Rockville, MD 20851
ph: 301-468-2131
e-mail: Barry@oconnell.net
web: http://www.oconnell.net/rugnotes
A virtual magazine dealing with Oriental rugs, Persian carpets, Tribal rugs, etc.; covers rugs and the people who buy, sell, and collect them.

Man./Prod./Dist.

Dan Wax
Taylor Made Custom Rugs
121 Mansfield Circle
Lexington, SC 29073-8080
ph: 803-356-3182
fax: 803-808-6395
e-mail: dwax@netside.com
Specializing in handmade custom designed carved rugs; any design or idea can be reproduced into a beautiful rug for floor or wall.

Repro. Sources

David C. Kline
Family Heir-Loom Weavers
775 Meadowview Dr.
Red Lion, PA 17356-8608
ph: 717-246-2431 or 717-246-2431
fax: 717-246-7439
e-mail:
PatKline@familyheirloomweavers.com
web: http://
www.familyheirloomweavers.com/
Makers of fancy jacquard coverlets, ingrain carpets & other historic textiles; carpets in the Abe Lincoln home & various other sites.

Hooked

(see also FOLK ART; REPAIR/ RESTORATION/CONSERVATION, Textiles; TEXTILES)

Dealers

Deborah Roberts
1071 San Pablo
Costa Mesa, CA 92626
ph: 714-557-5258
e-mail: quiltevals@aol.com
web: http://quilt.com/appraiser/
Specializing in buying and selling antique hooked rugs, quilts and quilt-related textiles; certified by the American Quilter's Society; wish list available; also lectures on quilts.

Experts

Jessie A. Thurbayne
P.O. Box 2540
Westwood, MA 02090
ph: 781-769-4798
Author of "Hooked Rugs: History and the Continuing Tradition, 1991", available from the author.

Internet Resources

Rug Hooker's Network, The
101 cliff Nelson Rd.
Kingston, GA 30145
ph: 770-607-9713
fax: 770-607-9713
e-mail:
mailbox@rughookersnetwork.com
web: http://
www.rughookersnetwork.com/
Web site for rug hookers: suppliers, designers, locate a local teacher, workshops & events, exhibits and competitions.

Periodicals

Cathy Hart
Stackpole, Inc.
Magazine: Rug Hooking Magazine
500 Vaughn St.
Harrisburg, PA 17110-2220
ph: 717-234-5091 or 800-233-9055
fax: 717-234-1359
e-mail:
webmaster@rughookingonline.com
web: http://www.rughookingonline.com
Published five times yearly; provides how-to information as well as features on outstanding or historically significant hand-hooked rugs; special annual "Celebrations" is also published by the editors of "Rug Hooking" magazine.

Repair Services

Linda Eliasom
513 Sykes Hollow Rd.
Pawlet, VT 05761
ph: 802-325-3026
Repairs hooked rugs.

Margaret & Audrey Ruhland Antiques
P.O. Box 245
North Gower, Ontario K0A 2T0
Canada
ph: 613-489-3298
Specializes in the repair of hooked rugs and quilts.

Stephanie Harvey-Clark
Rug Lady, The
3 Melville Ave.
Halifax, Nova Scotia B3P 1C9
Canada
ph: 902-479-0796
Cleaning, binding, restoration of holes, wall mounting; all work done by hand.

Suppliers

Jean L. Edmonds
Sea Holly Hooked Rug Shop
1906 North Bayview Dr.
Kill Devil Hills, NC 27948
ph: 252-441-8961
e-mail: jean@seahollyhooked.com
web: http://seahollyhooked.com/
Traditional rug hooking; sells finished pieces, patterns, wool and other supplies and equipment; also teaches classes and workshops.

Oriental

Appraisers

Alan F. Butler
P.O. Box 2818
Durham, NC 27715-2818
ph: 919-489-9342

Samuel Abraham
Abrahams Oriental Rugs
5120 Woodway, Ste. 6010
Houston, TX 77056
ph: 713-622-4444
fax: 713-622-8928
e-mail: abrahams.rugs@worldnet.att.net
web: http://www.abrahamsrugs.com/
Specializes in appraising Oriental rugs, Persian rugs, European tapestries, and contemporary rugs.

Brian Morehouse
Brian Morehouse Fine Art
894 South Bronson Ave.
Los Angeles, CA 90005-3605
ph: 323-939-2240 or 323-931-4987
fax: 323-931-4987
e-mail: MorehouseB@aol.com
Member, Appraisers Association of America; collector, appraiser, author, dealer and expert on rugs and Oriental carpets.

Auction Services

Jo Kris
Skinner, Inc.
357 Main St.
Bolton, MA 01740-1104
ph: 978-779-6241
fax: 978-779-5144
e-mail: info@skinnerinc.com
web: http://www.skinnerinc.com
Established in 1964, Skinner Inc. is the fifth largest auction house in the US; has offices in Bolton and Boston, MA.

Michael B. Grogan
Grogan & Company Auctioneers
22 Harris St.
Dedham, MA 02026
ph: 781-461-9500
fax: 781-461-9625
e-mail: grogans@groganco.com
web: http://www.groganco.com/

Sotheby's
1334 York Ave.
New York, NY 10021
ph: 212-606-7000
fax: 212-606-7107
web: http://www.sothebys.com
Over 70 collecting areas are featured at Sotheby's auctions including toys, dolls, porcelain, furniture, silver, art, books; exhibitions are free and everyone is welcome; for a free copy of "Sotheby's Newsletter", call 212-606-7245.

Lynn Martin
Freeman/Fine Arts of Philadelphia
1808 Chestnut St.
Philadelphia, PA 19103
ph: 610-563-9275 or 610-563-9453
fax: 610-563-8236
web: http://www.artlibrary.com/freeman/
America's oldest auction house: Continental, English and American furniture, paintings, silver and

decorative arts; Oriental rugs, rare books, fine jewelry, Orientalia.

Book Sellers

Dennis Marquand
Dennis B. Marquand Books
P.O. Box 1187
Culver City, CA 90232-1187
ph: 310-313-0177
fax: 310-915-9922
e-mail: dmarquand@aol.com
web: http://www.rugbooks.com
Specialize in books on ethnographic textiles from around the world with a focus on Oriental rugs, embroideries, textiles from Central Asian, Navajo, Tibet, Guatemala, Africa.

Clubs/Associations

International Hajji Baba Society, Inc.
6500 Pinecrest
Annandale, VA 22003
ph: 703-960-0343
fax: 703-683-7545
e-mail: wdswan@erols.com
A non-profit association of rug & textile collectors & enthusiasts; sponsors several lectures each year featuring experts on Oriental rugs; the events are held in the Washington DC area and are academic, not social or commercial.

Michael F. Wiley
Rug & Textile Society of Indiana
8940 Sassafras Ct.
Indianapolis, IN 46260
ph: 317-872-3494
fax: 317-872-3832
e-mail: mwiley@oaktree.net
Dedicated to studying, collecting and discussing rugs and textiles of central Asia and Asia Minor; programs presented 8 times each year at the Indianapolis Museum of Art; open to novice and expert alike.

Dealers

Robert Davidson
Davidson Oriental Rugs
P.O. Box 650114
West Newton, MA 02165-0114
ph: 617-630-9996 or 800-746-4320
Buys all used, old and antique Oriental rugs; all sizes and condition.

Cynthia Cooper
Main Street Antiques
81 Albany Turnpike, Rte 44
Canton, CT 06019
ph: 860-693-4478 or 860-677-5423
fax: 860-677-5423
e-mail: cyncooper@imagine.com

Solomon Bassalely
Eliko Oriental Rugs
102 Madison Ave., Fl. 4
New York, NY 10016-7417
ph: 212-725-1600 or 800-733-5456
fax: 212-725-1885
Appraises, buys, sells, and repairs Oriental rugs.

Jacobsen Oriental Rugs
401 N. Salina Street
Syracuse, NY 13202
ph: 315-422-7832
fax: 315-422-6909
e-mail: rugpeople@jacobsenrugs.com
web: http://jacobsenrugs.com
In business since 1924; more than 6,000 handwoven Oriental rugs in stock; also repairs.

Peter Shihadeh
Worldwide Rug Market, The
116 Cricket Ave.
Ardmore, PA 19003
ph: 610-649-2000
fax: 610-649-6463
e-mail: peter@orientalrugs.com
web: http://www.orientalrugs.com/

Woven Treasures
221 South St.
Philadelphia, PA 19146
e-mail: P.Yathrebi@woventreasures.com
web: http://www.woventreasures.com/
Specializes in fine Oriental rugs.

David Zahirpour
David Zahirpour Oriental Rugs
4918 Wisconsin Ave. NW
Washington, DC 20016
ph: 202-338-4141 or 202-244-1800
Specialist in Oriental rugs; cleans and repairs; hand washing, stain removal, carpet reweaving and restoration, appraisals, etc.

Phil Wallick
Phil Wallick Tribal Rugs
P.O. Box 61
Simpsonville, MD 21150
ph: 410-381-5124 or 410-381-6373
fax: 410-381-6373
e-mail: philw3@erols.com
web: http://www.tribalrugs.com
Oriental rug collector and dealer; website has an online catalog specializing in collector pieces with high color resolution color images; also has links to other Oriental rug sites.

Gerald W. Thompson
Gerald W. Thompson Oriental Rugs
P.O. Box 193
Shepherdstown, WV 25443-0193
ph: 304-876-2218
fax: 304-876-3640
e-mail: kayethom@aol.com
Specialist in antique and semi-antique oriental rugs with 25 years experience; also does repairs, appraisals, padding, and lecturing; also buying and selling of Oriental rugs.

John Lucas
Oglukian Oriental Rugs
4600 Oglukian Rd.
Charlotte, NC 28226-5124
ph: 704-366-1972
Appraisals, cleaning, repair of handmade rugs.

Bob Anderson
Aaron's Oriental Rug Gallery
1217 Broadway
Fort Wayne, IN 46802-3303
ph: 219-422-5184
Buys, sells, trades and appraises Oriental rugs; the Midwest's finest selection.

Larry Bergman
Coulee Oriental Rugs
N33015 Square Bluff Road
Whitehall, WI 54773-9148
ph: 715-985-3310
Wants to buy older hand knotted rugs, both throw rugs and room size rugs; especially wants rugs made before 1940.

Farhad Radfar, ISA
MIR International Gallery, Inc.
332 n. Michigan Ave., 2nd Floor
Chicago, IL 60611
ph: 312-814-8510
fax: 312-814-8511
e-mail: mirgallery@aol.com
web: http://www.mirgallery.com/

Tom Stacy
TurkoTek
728 Indiana
Lawrence, KS 66044
ph: 784-843-7680
e-mail: tgstacy@sprynet.com
web: http://www.turkotek.com/
Buys, sells, appraises, specializes and sells books about Oriental rugs.

Samuel Abraham
Abrahams Oriental Rugs
5120 Woodway, Ste. 6010
Houston, TX 77056
ph: 713-622-4444
fax: 713-622-8928
e-mail: abrahams.rugs@worldnet.att.net
web: http://www.abrahamsrugs.com/
Buying and selling Oriental rugs since 1974; Orientals, needlepoint rugs, new Kilims, new Pakistani and Persian rugs, Kashmir silk rugs.

Jimmy Vitanza
Peregrine Galleries
508 Brinkerhoff Ave.
Santa Barbara, CA 93101-3441
ph: 805-963-3134
fax: 805-963-3134

Harold & Janice Bedoukian
Ararat Rug Company
3457 Park Ave.
Montreal, Quebec H2X 2H6
Canada
ph: 514-288-1218
fax: 514-288-1210
e-mail: araratrug@compuserve.com
Specializes in antique and used Oriental carpets; has a large selection of oversized rugs in stock; also expert cleaning and restoration facilities.

Experts

Joyce C. Ware
534B Heritage Village
Southbury, CT 06488-1535
ph: 203-264-8424
fax: 203-264-8424
e-mail: jware@mail1.nai.net
Collector, lecturer, and author of "The Official Identification and Price Guide to Oriental Rugs."

Sharon Kerwick
1715 N.E. 25th St.
Ft. Lauderdale, FL 33305-1408
ph: 954-565-9031
fax: 954-564-0648

Ellen Amirkhan
Oriental Rug Cleaning Co., Inc.
3907 Ross Ave.
Dallas, TX 75204-5248
ph: 214-821-9135
fax: 214-821-9136
Oriental and specialty rugs custom cleaned; rug repairing (Oriental and specialty); Oriental rug appraising.

Val Arbab, ISA CAPP
P.O. Box 684
La Jolla, CA 92038-0684
ph: 619-453-4686
fax: 619-457-3647
e-mail: valarbab@worldnet.att.net
Appraises all oriental rugs and textiles; also buys, sells and brokers collectible and old decorative rugs.

Internet Resources

Ron O'Callaghan
Oriental Rug Review
Sinclair Hill Rd.
New Hampton, NH 03256
ph: 603-744-9191
e-mail: ronocal@lr.net
web: http://www.rugreview.com/orr.htm
Formerly a glossy magazine published bi-monthly and focusing primarily on old rugs; book reviews, auctions, ads, detailed articles, etc.; now an on-line reference source.

J. Barry O'Connell
RugNotes
12700 Ardennes Ave.
Rockville, MD 20851
ph: 301-468-2131
e-mail: Barry@oconnell.net
web: http://www.oconnell.net/rugnotes
A virtual magazine dealing with

Oriental rugs, Persian carpets, Tribal rugs, etc.; covers rugs and the people who buy, sell, and collect them.

Tom Stacy
TurkoTek Journal
728 Indiana
Lawrence, KS 66044
ph: 784-843-7680
e-mail: tgstacy@sprynet.com
web: http://www.turkotek.com/
A web site devoted to collectible Oriental rugs; has rugs and books about rugs for sale; also an on-line magazine, a discussion forum, and educational content.

Man./Prod./Dist.

Peerless Imported Rugs
3033 North Lincoln Ave.
Chicago, IL 60657
ph: 800-621-6573
fax: 773-525-4055
Sells new oriental rugs and oriental style rugs.

Museums/Libraries

Weaving Art Museum & Research Institute
e-mail: info@weavingartmuseum.org
web: http://weavingartmuseum.org/
Focuses on the masterpiece weavings produced in the eastern Mediterranean region.

Periodicals

Ron O'Callaghan
Asian Trade
Magazine: Oriental Rug Review
Sinclair Rd.
New Hampton, NH 03256
ph: 603-744-9191
e-mail: ronocal@lr.net
web: http://www.rugreview.com/orr.htm
A bi-monthly journal of Oriental rugs and other textiles.

Museum Books, Inc.
Magazine: Rug News
90 John St., 5th Floor
New York, NY 10038
ph: 212-587-1340
fax: 212-587-1344
e-mail: rugnews@rugnews.com
web: http://www.rugnews.com
Contains articles about the construction and quality of new Oriental rugs, primarily; also auction reports, shows, buy & sell ads.

HALI Publications, Ltd.
Magazine: HALI
Kingsgate House
Kingsgate Place, London NW6 4TA
U.K.
ph: 44 171 328 9341 or 44 171 328 1998
fax: 44 171 372 5924
e-mail: hali@centaur.co.uk
"HALI" is the leading bi-monthly international publication in the field of carpet and textile art; an invaluable encyclopedic source of information with original research articles, reviews of museum collections, etc.; high color.

Repair Services

Solomon Bassalely
Eliko Oriental Rugs
102 Madison Ave., Fl. 4
New York, NY 10016-7417
ph: 212-725-1600 or 800-733-5456
fax: 212-725-1885
Appraises, buys, sells, and repairs Oriental rugs.

Hayko Restoration & Conservation
857 Lexington Ave., 2nd Floor
New York, NY 10021
ph: 212-717-5400
fax: 212-717-4854
web: http://www.hayko.com/
Restoration and conservation of antique rugs; 20 years experience with carpets and tapestries; at your home or in the studio; references on request.

Jacobsen Oriental Rugs
401 N. Salina Street
Syracuse, NY 13202
ph: 315-422-7832
fax: 315-422-6909
e-mail: rugpeople@jacobsenrugs.com
web: http://jacobsenrugs.com
In business since 1924; more than 6,000 handwoven Oriental rugs in stock; also repairs.

David Zahirpour
David Zahirpour Oriental Rugs
4918 Wisconsin Ave. NW
Washington, DC 20016
ph: 202-338-4141 or 202-244-1800
Specialist in Oriental rugs; cleans and repairs; hand washing, stain removal, carpet reweaving and restoration, appraisals, etc.

Frank Shaia
Shaia Oriental Rugs
1325 Jamestown Rd.
Williamsburg, VA 23185
ph: 757-220-0400
fax: 757-229-3406
e-mail: rugs@shaia.com
web: http://www.shaia.com/
Expert Oriental rug repairs and restorations; reweave, reknot, overcast, selvedge; also cleaning and appraisals.

Emily Sanford
Sanford Restoration Works
2102 Speyer Ln.
Redondo Beach, CA 90278
ph: 310-374-7412
fax: 310-798-2792
Specializing in antique village and nomadic weavings.

Harold & Janice Bedoukian
Ararat Rug Company
3457 Park Ave.
Montreal, Quebec H2X 2H6
Canada
ph: 514-288-1218
fax: 514-288-1210
e-mail: araratrug@compuserve.com
Specializes in antique and used Oriental carpets; has a large selection of oversized rugs in stock; also expert cleaning and restoration facilities.

RUSSEL WRIGHT

(see also CERAMICS [AMERICAN], Russel Wright Designs)

Collectors

Dennis Boyd
P.O. Box 14642
Richmond, VA 23221-0642
ph: 804-560-0753
Wants Russel Wright dinnerware (American Modern, Highlight, Iroquois, and other patterns); also wants Russel Wright stainless flatware, glassware, aluminum, Bauer, etc.

Dealers

Helene Guarnaccia
52 Coach Lane
Fairfield, CT 06430
ph: 203-374-6034

Edward E. Stump
Raccoons Tale
6 High St.
Mullica Hill, NJ 08062-9540
ph: 609-478-4488
e-mail: ractrale@fast.net
Wants Russel Wright items: china dinnerware, modern, Iroquois, sterling & highlights; also anything unusual.

Lee Hay
Weird & Wonderful
P.O. Box 14898
Cincinnati, OH 45250-0898
ph: 513-621-6034
fax: 513-621-6448
e-mail: heywood@sprintmail.com
Wants to by Russel Wright dishes, silverware, furniture; also Bauer pottery.

Connie Zeigler
Durwyn Smedley Antiques
431 Massachusetts Ave.
Indianapolis, IN 46204
ph: 317-822-0102
e-mail: smedley@iquest.net
web: http://www.smedley.com/smedley/
Buys, sells, appraises all works by Russel Wright or Mary Wright including dinnerware, furniture, pottery, lighting, metalwork, textiles, glassware, books, and other related items.

RUSSIAN ITEMS

(see also CAMERAS & CAMERA EQUIPMENT, Russian; COLLECTIBLES [MODERN], Russian; MILITARIA, Russian; ROYALTY COLLECTIBLES, Russian; STAMP COLLECTING, Russian; TOYS, Russian)

Auction Services

Timothy A. Miller
ARTCo
P.O. Box 33191
Decatur, GA 30030-0191
ph: 404-292-6097
fax: 404-292-6097
e-mail: artco@mindspring.com
web: http://www.stic.net/users/artco/
Buys, sells, brokers quality Russian antiques: civil, military, religious items from Russia 1700s to 1917; periodic auction catalogs.

Collectors

Productive Arts
100 Hayes Dr., Unit C
Cleveland, OH 44131
ph: 800-533-3244
fax: 216-398-8691
Wants to buy Soviet items: magazines, books, posters and ephemera.

Dealers

Natalya A. Fadeicheva
Russia: Business & Personal Connections
48 Coniston Ave.
Waterbury, CT 06708-1926
ph: 203-757-4891
Fine woolen scarves/shawls, birch paintings, nested Russian dolls (matryoshka), jewelry, lacquered boxes and eggs, polished stone boxes, hand carved wooden toys, serving trays (zhostovo).

Anita L. Grashof
Gallerie Ani'tiques
Stage House Village
Park & Front Streets
Scotch Plains, NJ 07076
ph: 908-322-4600 or 201-377-3032
fax: 973-765-9565
Buys, sells and appraises Russian commemoratives in brass, copper, silver and porcelain.

Russian House
253 Fifth Ave.
New York, NY 10016
ph: 212-685-1010
fax: 212-685-1046
e-mail: russia@russianhouse.net
web: http://www.russianhouse.com/
Carries large selection of the best selection of fine Russian books and gifts: lacquered miniatures, icons, amber jewelry, nesting dolls,

porcelain, hand-painted shawls, Faberge-style eggs.

A La Vieille Russie, Inc.
781 Fifth Ave.
New York, NY 10022
ph: 212-752-1727
fax: 212-223-6454
e-mail: alvr@aol.com
web: http://www.alvr.com
Specializes in fine Russian antiques: jewelry, snuff boxes, Faberge, silver, Russian icons, and other works of art.

Robert Natanzon
Fine Russian Antiques
2536 Hubbard St.
Brooklyn, NY 11235-6223
ph: 718-769-1446
fax: 718-769-5617
e-mail: rob1329@aol.com
web: http://www.find-russian-antiques.com/
Specializes in Russian icons, crosses, silver, militaria, etc.

Allan & Ita Fogel
Twin Tankard Antiques
P.O. Box 4847
Silver Spring, MD 20904
ph: 301-236-9391
fax: 301-236-0427
e-mail: pewter@twintankard.com
web: http://www.twintankard.com
Specializes in European pewter; also buys and sells Russian and Judaica.

Timothy A. Miller
ARTCo
P.O. Box 33191
Decatur, GA 30030-0191
ph: 404-292-6097
fax: 404-292-6097
e-mail: artco@mindspring.com
web: http://www.stic.net/users/artco/
Buys and sells Imperial Russian items: enamels, metal, art; civil, military, religious, etc.; send photo or photocopy and price, please.

Cynthia O'Grady
Russian Samovar
HC 63, Box 8
Pettigrew, AR 72752
ph: 501-677-2192 or 501-575-1852
Buys and sells the finest in antique Russian Christmas decorations and other Russian antiques.

Mitch Siegler
Sovietski Collection
3450 Kurtz St., Ste. C
San Diego, CA 92110
ph: 800-442-0002 or 619-294-2000
e-mail: fulcrum@sovietski.com
web: http://www.sovietski.com
Importer of Russian antique documents, coins, vintage artifacts, nautical instruments and aviation collectibles.

Andre Ruzhnikov
Andre Ruzhnikov Russian Art & Antiques
P.O. Box 1261
Palo Alto, CA 94302-1261
ph: 650-858-0469
fax: 650-858-1008
Large inventory of Russian icons, silver, enamels, paintings, watercolors, decorative arts and Faberge; always interested in buying collections of fine Russian antiques; appraisals, consultation, and restoration services available.

Experts

Patricia M. Grove
PMG Antique Appraisal Research
3 Ober St.
Beverly, MA 01915-4639
ph: 978-927-2979
Collects, researches and appraises decorative and fine arts of the China, Japan, India and Russia export trades, 17th through mid-19th centuries: paintings, silver, ivory, tortoise carvings, furniture, fans, lacquer.

Benedict J. Hastings
2006 Columbia Rd. N.W.
Washington, DC 20009
ph: 202-483-8575
Specializes in fine silver, Russian decorative arts, Russian icons, 18th and 19th century porcelain, military medals, decorations and orders.

Mimi Levine
Mimi & Steve Levine Antiques, Inc.
6205 Marilyn Drive
Alexandria, VA 22310
ph: 703-971-3941
e-mail: mimilev@erols.com
Experts in Russian porcelain, both Imperial and private factories.

James L. Jackson, ISA
Jackson's Auctioneers & Appraisers
2229 Lincoln St.
Cedar Falls, IA 50613
ph: 319-277-2256
fax: 319-277-1252
e-mail: jacksons@jacksonsauction.com
web: http://www.jacksonsauction.com
Has written and lectured widely on Russian icons, and has traveled extensively throughout Russia and the former Soviet Union studying Russian icons.

Museums/Libraries

Hillwood Museum & Gardens
Journal: Hillwood Studies
4155 Linnean Ave. NW
Washington, DC 20008
ph: 202-686-8500
fax: 202-966-7846
e-mail: hwdadmin@erols.com
web: http://www.hillwoodmuseum.org/
Most comprehensive collection of Russian art outside the former USSR; plus gift shop and 25 acres of gardens, greenhouses, and auxiliary buildings.

Repro. Sources

Robert Whiteside
Whiteside Jewelers
7805 Inwood Rd.
Dallas, TX 75209
ph: 214-358-0089
Specializes in recreating Faberge style jewelry and objects of art using original techniques including 19th century machinery to reproduce engine-turned enamel ware.

Enamels

Experts

Mel & Barbara Alpren
14 Carter Rd.
West Orange, NJ 07052-4612
ph: 201-731-9427
Advisor to "Warman's Antiques & Collectibles Price Guide."

Faberge

Auction Services

Joseph DuMouchelle
Joseph DuMouchelle Fine & Estate Jewelry Auctions
5 Kercheval
Grosse Pointe Farms, MI 48236
ph: 313-884-4800 or 800-475-4367
fax: 313-884-7662
e-mail: joelindy@earthlink.net
Specializes in the sale of fine and estate jewelry and small objects of art; large diamonds and colored stones, paintings, Oriental rugs, silver, antique furniture and sculpture, Russian objects of art.

Dealers

Philip M. Poniz
European Watch & Casemakers, Ltd.
P.O. Box 1314
Highland Park, NJ 08904-1314
ph: 732-777-0111
fax: 732-777-0118
e-mail: horology@webspan.net
Restoration of watches, clocks, and music boxes; museum experience; can make any part and restore any watch; clients include Sotheby's, Cartier, collectors in USA, Asia and Europe; appraises, researches, restores Faberge.

Museums/Libraries

Forbes Magazine Galleries
62 Fifth Ave.
New York, NY 10011-8882
ph: 212-206-5549 or 212-620-2200
web: http://www.tfaoi.com/newsmu/nmus172.htm
Collection of Russian Faberge eggs.

Walters Art Gallery
600 N. Charles St.
Baltimore, MD 21201
ph: 410-547-9000
e-mail: lwolfe@thewalters.org
web: http://www.thewalters.org/
One of only a few museums worldwide to present a comprehensive history of art from the third millennium B.C. to the early 20th century.

Virginia Museum of Fine Arts, Lillian Thomas Pratt Collection
2800 Grove Ave.
Richmond, VA 23221-2466
ph: 804-367-0844
fax: 804-367-9393
e-mail: webmaster@vmfa.state.va.us
web: http://dit1.state.va.us/vmfa/index.html
Fine arts museum covering the entire range of history of art.

Lacquer Boxes

Dealers

Russian Collection Inc.
RR1 Box 5
Intervale, NH 03845
ph: 800-575-8049
fax: 603-356-5540
e-mail: russian@ncia.net
web: http://www.russiancollect.com/
One of the largest selections of lacquer boxes outside Russia.

Tradestone International
803 Light Street
Baltimore, MD 21230
ph: 410-752-8085
e-mail: ajstone@erols.com
web: http://www.lacquerbox.com/
Specializes in new and antique Russian lacquer boxes.

Art at the Power House
2000 Sycamore St.
Cleveland, OH 44113
ph: 216-696-1942
fax: 216-623-3884
e-mail: artpower@yahoo.com
web: http://www.voiceoftheflats.org/artpower/html/russian_laquer.html

Experts

Eric Sinizer
Light Opera Retail Corp.
174 Grant Ave.
San Francisco, CA 94108-5405
ph: 415-956-9866
fax: 415-956-5624
Appraises, buys, sells, rights catalogs.

Samovars

Collectors

Jerome M. Marks
Jerome M. Marks Agency
120 Corporate Woods, Ste. 206
Rochester, NY 14623-1455
ph: 716-475-0220
fax: 716-475-0208
Wants to buy older Russian samovars;

also wants any samovar related literature; if selling, please send photo, description, condition, measurements, and asking price.

Dealers

Mehmet Nabi Israfil
Fil Caravan Inc.
240 Eat 56th St., Ste. 2E
New York, NY 10022
ph: 212-421-5972
fax: 212-421-5976
e-mail: filcaravan@worldnet.att.net
web: http://www.citysearch.com/nyc/filcaravan
Established in 1976, has large selection of authentic Russian samovars; has provided samovars to collectors worldwide; provides samovar restoration service as well as a limited supply of spare parts.

RV'S

(see TRAILERS & RV'S)

Here are some tips when contacting someone listed in this book:

■ When requesting information about a particular item, include a description (material, dimensions, maker's mark, model number, etc.) and a photo, sketch, or photocopy of the item in question.

■ Always ask if there are charges for samples or for the services requested.

■ When writing, please be sure to include a Large (#10 business size) Self-Addressed and Stamped Envelope (LSASE) if requesting a reply or the return of photographs.

■ Never call collect unless otherwise directed. When calling, be considerate of time zone differences and always ask if the party you are calling has time to talk. When leaving an answering machine message, always instruct the party to call you back <u>collect</u>.

SABERS

(see SWORDS)

SACKS

(see CORN COLLECTIBLES; FEED SACKS; MILLING)

SAD IRONS

(see IRONS, Pressing)

SADDLES

(see also ANIMAL COLLECTIBLES, Horses; LEATHER; WESTERN AMERICANA)

Clubs/Associations

Dan Preston
Saddle, Harness & Allied Trades Association
Magazine: Harness Shop News, The
1101-A Broad St.
Oriental, NC 28571
ph: 252-249-3414 or 251-249-3409
fax: 252-249-3409
e-mail: thsn@always-online.com
web: http://www.HarnessShopNews.com/
Members are makers of saddles, chaps, harnesses, whips, holsters; carving & tooling, luggage making & repair, other leather goods, sewing machine maintenance.

Collectors

Bill Mackin
1137 Washington St.
Craig, CO 81625-1613
ph: 970-824-6717 or 970-824-6360
fax: 970-824-7175
Author of "Cowboy and Gunfighter Collectibles" with 1993-94 updated price guide; sells books for Old West collectors by mail and at shows; over 45 years collecting; wants nice gun leather and cowboy gear; appraises, consults, lectures.

Dealers

Sharon Myers
J&S Oldwestern Store, Saddle Shop & Museum
RR 1, Box 315-c-nt
Warsaw, MO 65355
ph: 660-438-2631
fax: 660-438-6517
e-mail: oldwest@iland.net
web: http://www.cowgirls.com/dream/oldwest
Over 200 antique saddles, hibacks, side-saddles, military, charro, etc.; Admission to museum if free; also 1300 Western collectibles for sale; 55 page catalog for $5.

Periodicals

Dan Preston
Magazine: Harness Shop News, The
1101-A Broad St.
Oriental, NC 28571
ph: 252-249-3414 or 251-249-3409
fax: 252-249-3409
e-mail: thsn@always-online.com
web: http://www.HarnessShopNews.com/
Professional leather workers, saddle makers, shoe and saddle repairmen, holster manufacturers, harness makers, boot makers, equipment manufacturers; ads, calendar of events.

Side

Clubs/Associations

Linda A. Bowlby, Pres.
World Sidesaddle Federation, Inc., The
Magazine: Aside World
P.O. Box 1104
Bucyrus, OH 44820-1104
ph: 419-284-3176
fax: 419-284-3176
e-mail: WorldSFI@aol.com
web: http://members.aol.com/worldsfi/sidesadl.htm
A non-profit organization for promoting the use of the sidesaddle; provides sources of equipment and information on the use of the sidesaddle.

Collectors

Martha Coe Friddle
Hundred Oaks, Inc.
P.O. Box 886
Graham, NC 27253
ph: 818-376-8124 or 919-279-6201
fax: 919-376-8124
Dealer for new and used Western, English and period side saddles; certified instructor; saddle appraisal service available; wants to buy side saddles and related items such as books, sandwich cases, etc.

SAFARI

(see also ART, African & Tribal)

Collectors

James Podraza
RD 2 Box 626
Ruffs Dale, PA 15679
ph: 724-446-9433
Wants to buy African safari books, spears, weapons, cultural items.

SAFES

(see also ANTIQUES DEALERS & COLLECTORS, Supplies For; BANKS, Safe Shaped; LOCKS)

Clubs/Associations

Bob Heilemann
West Coast Lock Collectors
Newsletter: West Coast Lock Collectors Newsletter
1427 Lincoln Blvd.
Santa Monica, CA 90401-2732
ph: 310-454-7295 or 310-230-3004
e-mail: locksmann@aol.com
Call evenings; no collect calls, please.

Collectors

Larry Egelhoff
4175 Millersville Rd.
Indianapolis, IN 46205-2966
ph: 317-846-7228
e-mail: egelhoffl@juno.com
Collector and appraiser interested in key or combination safes.

SALMON RELATED COLLECTIBLES

Collectors

Harold Fossum
P.O. Box 210127
Auke Bay, AK 99821
ph: 907-780-4472
Wants old salmon labels from all U.S. states especially Alaska; also from Yukon, N.W. Territories; also wants related postcards, trade tokens, etc.

Dealers

Oscar Schabb
P.O. Box 1377
Brooklandville, MD 21022-1377
ph: 410-486-2436
fax: 410-486-0653
Buys, sells, trades and collects old salmon cans and related memorabilia; also wants old key wind metal tennis ball cans and horse racing glasses.

SALOON & BAR COLLECTIBLES

(see also ADVERTISING COLLECTIBLES; ALCOHOLICS ANONYMOUS ITEMS; BOTTLES; BREWERIANA; GAMBLING COLLECTIBLES; GLASSES; PROHIBITION ITEMS; WHISKEY INDUSTRY ITEMS)

Collectors

James E. Kattner
P.O. Box 11132
Spring, TX 77391
ph: 281-986-6916 or 281-376-4826
Wants to buy Texas saloon, bar and liquor advertisement items such as shot glasses, matchsafes, miniature and larger jugs, pocket mirrors with celluloid backs illustrating pretty ladies, corkscrews, old dice, tokens, coin purses.

John Goetz
P.O. Box 1570
Cedar Ridge, CA 95924
ph: 530-272-4644
Wants saloon bottles: label under glass, bottles, flasks, mugs, bottles and flasks with silver overlay, bottles with multicolored enamel pictures; also wants beer trays or signs.

Dealers

Deborah & Paul Inglis
Bootleggers Nostalgia
P.O. Box 165
South Hadley, MA 01075-0165
ph: 413-533-0419
fax: 413-533-0419
e-mail: bootleggers.nostalgia@worldnet.att.net
Buys pitchers, ashtrays, back bar statues, change receivers, and drip plates advertising Scotch whisky or other types of liquor.

Greg Spiess
Spiess Architectural Antiques
230 E. Washington St.
Joliet, IL 60433-1006
ph: 815-722-5639
fax: 815-722-0171
e-mail: spiessantq@aol.com
Buys saloon fixtures, back and front bars, liquor cabinets, saloon doors, dividers, etc.; also wants saloon catalogs and related saloon fixture advertising such as Brunswick, Passow & Sons, American, Rothschilds, Merle & Heany, etc.

Experts

Steve Visakay
Stephen Visakay Cocktail Shakers
P.O. Box 1517
West Caldwell, NJ 07007-1517
ph: 914-352-5640 or 201-575-0040
fax: 914-352-5640
e-mail: svisakay@aol.com
Author of "Vintage Bar Ware," (Collector Books), an identification and value guide dedicated to cocktail shakers, stemware, ice buckets, serving trays, recipe books, paper collectibles, cocktail picks, swizzle sticks, etc.

Roger V. Baker
Baker's Lady Luck Emporium
P.O. Box 620417
Redwood City, CA 94062-0417
ph: 369-851-7188
Specializing in saloon collectibles: gambling, bar bottles, shaving mugs, razors, Bowie knives, daggers, barber items, match safes.

Cocktail Shakers

Collectors

Andrew E. Thomas
4681 North 84th Way
Scottsdale, AZ 85251-1864
ph: 888-255-0664 or 480-947-5693
fax: 480-994-4382

Experts

Steve Visakay
Stephen Visakay Cocktail Shakers
P.O. Box 1517
West Caldwell, NJ 07007-1517
ph: 914-352-5640 or 201-575-0040
fax: 914-352-5640
e-mail: svisakay@aol.com
Offers free appraisals, identification and history of the maker of your cocktail shaker; please enclose SASE for reply.

Museums/Libraries

Cocktail Shaker Museum
150 Aerial Way
Syosset, NY 11791
ph: 516-933-6213

Corkstoppers

Collectors

Joe Iozzia
P.O. Box 1005
Pomona, NJ 08240-1005
ph: 609-652-8504
fax: 609-652-8888
e-mail: pinflyers@aol.com
Wants to buy figural handcarved wood people, animals, elves, pirates, monks, etc.; nutcrackers, cigarette boxes, book sends, ashtrays, pipe holders, figurines, bottle stoppers, humidors, and unusual figural handcarved items.

Philly Rains
1401 Brentwood Dr.
Harrison, AR 72601
ph: 870-743-2040
fax: 870-743-2120
e-mail: phillyr@yournet.com
web: http://members.aol.com/corkskrue/philly.htm
Expert in old ANRI Italian wood carvings, 1912 through 1970s; non-limited editions only, including nutcrackers, bar sets, figurines, napkin rings, smoking accessories, and bottle stoppers; appraisals $25 per item; no limited editions.

Pourers

Collectors

Perry Porter
1811 NE 80th St.
Seattle, WA 98115
ph: 206-524-4401
Buys and trades liquor bottle pourers (spouts) having advertising on them; wants Jack Daniels' collector decanters, antique whiskey jugs or bottles; also wants interesting Wild Turkey, Old Crow, and Beefeaters items.

Swizzle Sticks

Clubs/Associations

Ray P. Hoare
International Swizzle Stick Collectors Association
Newsletter: Swizzle Stick News
P.O. Box 1117
Bellingham, WA 98227-1117
ph: 604-936-7636
fax: 604-654-1224
e-mail: vera.issca@ibm.net
web: http://www.theplant.com/issca/
Ray Hoare is co-founder of the International Swizzle Stick Collectors Association; sponsors convention every other year.

Collectors

Joe Smith
4407 Seminole
Pasadena, TX 77504
Wants to buy advertising swizzle sticks; plastic, metal, glass, wood, Bakelite, laminated cardboard.

Bob Akin
7351 Picardie Lane
Las Vegas, NV 89123
ph: 702-361-0844

Ray P. Hoare
P.O. Box 1117
Bellingham, WA 98227-1117
ph: 604-936-7636
fax: 604-654-1224
e-mail: vera.issca@ibm.net
web: http://www.theplant.com/issca/
Ray Hoare is co-founder of the International Swizzle Stick Collectors Association; sponsors convention every other year.

Whiskey Pitchers

Auction Services

Pete Kroll
Glasses, Mugs & Steins Auction
P.O. Box 207
Sun Prairie, WI 53590-0207
ph: 608-837-4818
fax: 608-825-4205
e-mail: pkroll@chorus.net
web: http://www.gmskroll.com/
Produces a semi-annual mail auction featuring collectible advertising glasses, mugs & steins: beer, soda, horse racing, cartoon, Disney, root beer, Budweiser, whiskey shot glasses, whiskey pitchers, etc.

Clubs/Associations

Deborah & Paul Inglis
Pub Jug/Whiskey Pitcher Collectors
Newsletter: Pub Jug Trader, The
P.O. Box 165
South Hadley, MA 01075-0165
ph: 413-533-0419
fax: 413-533-0419
e-mail: bootleggers.nostalgia@worldnet.att.net
Bi-monthly publication dedicated to buying, selling and trading of whiskey pitchers/pub jugs and related items.

Tom Duhn
Whisky Pitcher Collectors Association of America
Newsletter: Black & White
19341 West Tahoe Dr.
Mundelein, IL 60060-4061
ph: 847-566-9512
fax: 847-566-8303
e-mail: thdpubjug1@aol.com
An international collector's club; annual convention/show; members buy, sell and trade pub jugs, liquor advertising, water jugs, whisky pitchers.

Collectors

Ed Miller
351 River Isle
Bradenton, FL 34208-9048
ph: 941-758-5207
Wants pub jugs, advertising, ceramic water pitchers for personnel collection.

Tom Duhn
19341 West Tahoe Dr.
Mundelein, IL 60060-4061
ph: 847-566-9512
fax: 847-566-8303
e-mail: thdpubjug1@aol.com
Buys, sells and trades pub jugs, liquor advertising, water jugs, whisky pitchers.

A.R. Blakeman
Elsecar Heritage Centre
Nr Barnsley, S. Yorks S74 8HJ
U.K.
e-mail: sales@bbrauctions.co.uk
web: http://www.bbracutions.co.uk/
Wants pottery whiskey pitchers, especially with colored tops or colored transfer decorations; will trade.

Dealers

Deborah & Paul Inglis
Bootleggers Nostalgia
P.O. Box 165
South Hadley, MA 01075-0165
ph: 413-533-0419
fax: 413-533-0419
e-mail: bootleggers.nostalgia@worldnet.att.net
Buys pitchers, ashtrays, back bar statues, change receivers, and drip plates advertising Scotch whisky or other types of liquor.

SALT & PEPPER SHAKERS

Collectors

Trish Claar
2621 Manor Court
Owings, MD 20736-9145
ph: 301-855-6531
Interested in advertising and Holiday related salt and pepper shaker sets.

Judy Posner
4195 South Tamiami Trail, Ste. 183
Venice, FL 34293-5112
ph: 941-497-7149
fax: 941-493-8085
e-mail: jpc@tias.com
web: http://www.tias.com/stores/jpc/
Wants figural salt & pepper shakers: Black Americana, Disneyana, Ceramic Art Studio, Regal China, advertising figurals, etc.

Coleen Detzel
28 Lacresta Dr.
Florence, KY 41042-9663
ph: 606-647-6156
Wants to buy novel, unique salt and pepper shakers, especially Holt Howard of any kind.

Tracy Nader
2322 Ninth St., N.W.
Canton, OH 44708
ph: 330-454-3060
e-mail: mnader@aol.com
web: http://members.aol.com/mnader/private/tracy.html
Salt & pepper shaker collector for over 5 years; member of the Ohio chapter of Novelty Shaker Collectors Club; website is dedicated to "collector helping collectors."

Dealers

Vera & Steve Skorupski
P.O. Box 572
Plainville, CT 06062
ph: 860-828-4097

Helene Guarnaccia
52 Coach Lane
Fairfield, CT 06430
ph: 203-374-6034
Send requests.

Carol Silagyi
C.S. Antiques & Jewelry
P.O. Box 151
Wyckoff, NJ 07430
ph: 201-934-6528
Wants to buy collections of salt and pepper shakers.

Mark McMahon
Cookie Jars, Etc.
Chelsea Antiques Building
110 West 25th St., 8th Floor
New York, NY 10001
ph: 212-633-1923
fax: 212-924-8535
e-mail: peter@peterandmark.com
web: http://www.peterandmark.com
Buy, sell, trade cookie jars, banks, salt & peppers and PEZ.

Joyce & Judy
Krazy Cat Collectibles
P.O. Box 21727
Emmitsburg, MD 21727
ph: 301-309-2513
e-mail: KrazyCatCo@aol.com
Wants to buy salt and pepper shakers of all kinds: animals, characters, couples, nodders; especially wants cat and dog s&p's.

Charlene Green
P.O. Box 250421
West Bloomfield, MI 48325-0421
ph: 810-610-7703
fax: 248-661-1266
e-mail: spcollect@aol.com
web: http://members.aol.com/spcollect/
Buys and sells novelty and figural salt and pepper shakers; Parkcraft and other states sets, Goebels, Ceramic Arts Studio, Van Telligan Huggies, Shawnee, Nodders, advertising sets; website is always under construction and changing.

Lois & Ralph Behm
Lois' Collectibles of Antique Market III
413 W. Main St.
Saint Charles, IL 60174-1815
ph: 630-377-5599 or 847-831-5997
Buys and sells salt and pepper shakers; will buy entire collections.

Estelle Sharp
ESCO Enterprises, Inc.
441 E. River Oaks Dr.
Baton Rouge, LA 70815-4063
ph: 225-924-5089
fax: 225-924-5089
Buys and sells nodder salt & pepper shakers.

Wilma Schiebel
No Place Like Home Collectibles
HCR 63 Box 116C
Yellville, AR 72687-9512
ph: 870-436-5874
e-mail: grantiques@alltel.net
Wants salt and pepper shaker pairs or singles: advertising, black Americana, figural, characters, novel, unique, fruit and vegetables with faces, etc.

Peggy Cole
134 E. Laveta
Orange, CA 92666-1908
ph: 714-997-7379
Wants nodder and black Americana figural salt & pepper shakers; mini's, Felix the Cat, Garfield.

Experts

Larry Carey
Salt & Pepper Man, The
P.O. Box 329
Mechanicsburg, PA 17055-0329
ph: 717-766-0868
e-mail: snpman@itech.net
Buys novelty salt and pepper shaker collections; co-author of five books on s&p's, "1001, 1002, 1003, 1005, and 1005 Salt & Pepper Shakers."

Mildred & Ralph Lechner
World of Salt Shakers
P.O. Box 554
Mechanicsville, VA 23111-0554
ph: 804-737-3347
Feature writers on antique glassware for "AntiqueWeek"; authors of "The World of Salt Shakers," Vols. 1, 2 & 3; Victorian art and pattern glass reproduction identification experts; collectors of art and pattern glass salt & pepper shakers.

Art Glass

Clubs/Associations

Mr. & Mrs. William Avery
Antique & Art Glass Salt Shaker Collector's Society
Newsletter: Pioneer, The
2832 Rapidan Trail
Maitland, FL 32751-5013
ph: 407-629-1168
e-mail: shakers@cbantiques.com
web: http://www.cbantiques.com/ssc/
Promotes and encourages the collection and study of salt shakers of the Antique Victorian and Art Glass type; quarterly newsletter.

Dealers

Janice C. Eldridge
64 Burt Rd.
Springfield, MA 01118-1848
ph: 413-783-4629
e-mail: eldride@ix.netcom.cm
Wants to buy art glass, colored Victorian glass salt and pepper shakers.

Novelty

Clubs/Associations

Lula Fuller
Novelty Salt & Pepper Shakers Club
Newsletter: Novelty Salt & Pepper Shakers Club Newsletter
P.O. Box 677388
Orlando, FL 32867-7388
ph: 407-678-1219
fax: 407-678-1240
e-mail: jlfuller1@aol.com
web: http://members.aol.com/jlfuller1/jdf1.htm
Focuses on novelty salt and pepper shakers; also anything picturing shakers; offers "singles matching service" for members; newsletter published quarterly.

Collectors

Irene Thornburg
581 Joy Rd.
Battle Creek, MI 49017-8450
ph: 616-963-7954 or 616-964-9024
e-mail: itburg@aol.com
Wants to buy unusual novelty shakers to add to collection.

SALTS

Open

Clubs/Associations

Mimi Waible
New England Society of Open Salts Collectors
Newsletter: Salt Talk
P.O. Box 177
Sudbury, MA 01776-0177
ph: 978-443-3613
fax: 617-893-4760
e-mail: mimiAHW@aol.com
Meets semi-annually usually in Marlborough, MA.

Lee Anne Gominer, Sec.
Open Salt Collectors of the Atlantic Region
Newsletter: OSCAR Newsletter
56 Northview Dr.
Lancaster, PA 17601
Meets quarterly at or near members' homes.

Dealers

Betty Bird
Memory Lane Antiques
107 Ida St.
Mount Shasta, CA 96067-2629
ph: 530-926-4331 or 530-926-2231
Buying fancy open salts and/or salt spoons; prefer art glass, colored glass and silver; any number; also condiment sets.

Experts

Daniel Snyder
30 Main St.
Leroy, NY 14482
ph: 716-768-6470
fax: 716-768-6663
e-mail: dasnyder@hfent.com
Specializes in master open salts.

Ed & Kay Berg
Delaware Salt Box
401 Nottingham Rd.
Newark, DE 19711-7404
ph: 302-731-5749
e-mail: desaltbox@cs.com
Buys, sells, and specializes in open salts; issues lists of open salts for sale about 4 times per year; writes columns on open salts for club newsletters; can provide information about open salt clubs.

Periodicals

Ed & Kay Berg
Delaware Salt Box
Newsletter: Salty Comments
401 Nottingham Rd.
Newark, DE 19711-7404
ph: 302-731-5749
e-mail: desaltbox@cs.com
The newsletter covers research on open salt dishes.

SALVATION ARMY ITEMS

Collectors

Nathan Johnson
P.O. Box 23526
Belleville, IL 62223-0526
ph: 618-277-9330
Wants to buy Salvation Army/William Booth family related items including posters, postcards, cabinet cards, medals, badges, magazine covers, jewelry, FDC's, sheet music, etc.

Museums/Libraries

George Scott Railton Heritage Center
2130 Bayview Ave.
Toronto, Ontario M4N 3K6
Canada
ph: 416-481-4441
fax: 416-481-6096
e-mail: rjbowles@sallynet.org
web: http://www.sallynet.org/services/f1056.htm

SAMPLERS

(see also FOLK ART; REPAIR/RESTORATION/CONSERVATION, Textiles; TEXTILES)

Collectors

Donna Litwin
P.O. Box 5865
Trenton, NJ 08638-0865
ph: 609-275-1427 or 609-275-0996
fax: 609-275-1427
Buys, sells, appraises American samplers; please send photo and price of items for sale; Accredited Member of the International Society of Appraisers.

Denise Hamilton
899 Latta Brook Rd.
Elmira, NY 14901-9226
ph: 607-732-2550
Buying pre-1900 samplers and other old needlework.

Dealers

Carl McCann
Troy & Black, Inc.
P.O. Box 228
Red Creek, NY 13143-0228
ph: 315-754-8115
e-mail: tbrc@banet.net
Buys and sells high quality flow blue, Staffordshire figurines, American painted furniture, stoneware, redware,

coverlets, samplers, and other American textiles, folk art, etc.

Experts

Suzy McLennan Anderson
Heritage Antiques, Inc.
65 East Main St.
Holmdel, NJ 07733-2310
ph: 908-946-8801
fax: 908-946-1036
Authenticates, buys, sells, appraises, lectures; author of "The Collectors Guide to Quilts."

Museums/Libraries

Barbara Livenstein
Cooper-Hewitt Museum National Museum of Design, Smithsonian Institution
2 East 91st St.
New York, NY 10128
ph: 212-860-8400 or 212-849-8349
e-mail: liven@ch.si.edu
web: http://www.si.edu/organiza/museums/design/ndm.htm

SAMURAI ITEMS

(see ARMS & ARMOR, Japanese [Swords]; ORIENTALIA, Japanese Items)

SAND

(see also DIRT)

Clubs/Associations

Nicholas D'Errico
International Sand Collectors Society
Newsletter: Sand Paper, The
P.O. Box 117
North Haven, CT 06473-0117
ph: 203-239-5488
fax: 203-239-5488
e-mail: iscs@juno.com
Founded in 1969; serious and whimsical collections for purposes of keepsake, analysis, bon hommarie; collector of sand, ore, or minerals; divisions include Beach Sands, Microscopy, Educators; all ages and sand related interests welcome.

Collectors

William Diefenbach
43 Highway Ave.
Old Greenwich, CT 06870
Has a collection of over 450 vials of sand.

Jean-Pierre Seys
Sand Collection
France
e-mail: james38@multimania.com
web: http://www.multimania.com/james38/sandcollection.shtm
Has a collection of 1200 samples of sand from over 100 different countries.

Fred Madiot
71, Rue du Courdray
Nantes, 44000
France
ph: 02 40 29 36 80
e-mail: Fmadiot@oceanet.fr
web: http://www.geocities.com/Pipeline/Curb/4028/
Collects sand from all over the world.

SANDPAPER

Museums/Libraries

3-M Sandpaper Museum
201 Waterfront Dr.
P.O. Box 313
Two Harbors, MN 55616-0313
ph: 218-834-4898
The birthplace of 3M (Minnesota Mining & Manufacturing); part of the Lake County Historical Society; displays of how sandpaper is made.

SANTA CLAUS

(see CHRISTMAS COLLECTIBLES; COLLECTIBLES [MODERN], Christmas)

SCALES

(see also COIN-OPERATED MACHINES; INSTRUMENTS & DEVICES, Scientific)

Clubs/Associations

Bob Stein, Pres.
International Society of Antique Scale Collectors
Magazine: Equilibrium
300 West Adams, Ste 821
Chicago, IL 60606
ph: 312-263-7500
fax: 312-263-7748
e-mail: bobstein@isac.org
web: http://www.isasc.org/
Club focuses on antique scales; several hundred members worldwide; the "Equilibrium" magazine is published quarterly and contains articles on scales & scale manufacturers.

Collectors

Gerald Neufeld
50 Saratoga Dr.
Cranbury, NJ 08512-2936
ph: 212-730-0445 or 609-936-8688
fax: 212-730-0447
e-mail: jneufeld2@home.com
Wants to buy unusual scales; send description and picture.

John M. Shannon
7319 West Cedar Circle
Lakewood, CO 80226-2019
ph: 303-232-1534
e-mail: rovers@aol.com
Wants to buy assay balances (wood and glass encased with small pans) - both laboratory and portable; also wants brass scientific instruments.

Henri Slaets
Elf Novemberstraat 20
Mechelen, N2800
Belgium
ph: (0)-54 -3635
e-mail: h.slaets@iname.com
Collecting and trading antique and ethnic scales and weights: old 17th, 18th, 19th century coin-weighted boxes, apothecary scales, Chinese, Japanese, African asahti, Burmese; opium, drug, pearl scales; Precolumbian bone and wood scales.

Dealers

John J. Ford, Jr.
P.O. Box 10317
Phoenix, AZ 85064
ph: 602-957-6443
fax: 602-957-1861
Collects and deals in counterfeit coin scales and detectors.

Repro. Sources

Sturbridge Yankee Workshop
90 Blueberry Rd.
Portland, ME 04102-1989
ph: 800-343-1144
fax: 207-774-2561
web: http://www.st3.yahoo.net/sturbridgeyankee/

Toy

Collectors

Donald Gorlick
P.O. Box 24541
Seattle, WA 98124-0541
ph: 206-824-0508
Wants old toy scales; small tin scales like the old penny toys; any small toy scale but not the pencil sharpener type scales.

SCHOOL RELATED MEMORABILIA

Collectors

Lee Dennis
447 Park Ave., Apt. 12
Keene, NH 03431-6506
ph: 603-358-0060
Wants early schoolhouse memorabilia from 1840-1880: unusual slates, pencil boxes, lunch boxes, sheet music depicting schoolhouses, book holders, etc,

Tedd Levy
P.O. Box 2217
Norwalk, CT 06850-2217
e-mail: teddlevy@aol.com
Wants pre-1920 items related to public schools, teaching, students, playgrounds, school buses, etc. including postcards, photos, journals, documents, correspondence, certificates and some 19th C books (none after 1860); prompt replies.

Diplomas

Collectors

Bob Hut
P.O. Box 1495
Grand Central Station
New York, NY 10163-1495
ph: 800-321-7687
Wants only pre-1865 diplomas from institutions of higher learning.

SCIENCE FICTION

(see also ANIMATION ART; CARTOON ART; CHARACTER COLLECTIBLES; COMIC BOOKS; FAN CLUBS; HORROR; KITS; MOVIE MEMORABILIA; POPULAR CULTURE; SPACE COLLECTIBLES; SUPER HEROES; TELEVISION SHOWS & MEMORABILIA; TOYS, Science Fiction; UFO'S & UNEXPLAINED PHENOMENA)

Clubs/Associations

Dale L. Ames
Galaxy Patrol
Newsletter: Galaxy Patrol Newsletter
144 Russell Street
Worcester, MA 01610
ph: 508-755-3830
e-mail: gp@telegram.infi.net
Focuses on memorabilia relating to radio and TV show space heroes.

Gordy Dutt
International Figure Kit Club
Magazine: KitBuilders Magazine
P.O. Box 201
Sharon Center, OH 44274-0201
ph: 330-239-1657
fax: 330-239-2991
e-mail: Gordys_kitbuilders@juno.com
web: http://www.gordyskitbuilders.com/
Published four times a year, this magazine deals mostly with plastic, vinyl, and resin figure or Sci/Fi type model kits from the 1950s to present.

William Center
National Fantasy Fan Federation
Newsletter: National Fantasy Fan
1920 Division St.
Murphysboro, IL 62966
National science fiction and fantasy club.

Debbie Keais
San Diego's Science Fiction Society
Newsletter: Interphase
P.O. Box 15373
San Diego, CA 92117-0303
ph: 619-286-0401
Local club interested in science fiction, fantasy, movies, gaming, costuming and conventions.

Collectors

Dale L. Ames
144 Russell Street
Worcester, MA 01610
ph: 508-755-3830
e-mail: gp@telegram.infi.net
Interested in collectibles associated with science fiction TV & radio shows & recordings of the programs themselves; also sic-fi comics.

Dealers

Jon Warren
American Collectibles Exchange
P.O. Box 2512
Chattanooga, TN 37409
ph: 423-265-5515 or 800-880-4289
fax: 423-265-5506
e-mail: jonrwarren@aol.com
Specializes in Science Fiction and Fantasy items.

Experts

Allen Shevy
P.O. Box 9421
Tampa, FL 33674-9421
ph: 813-933-7424
e-mail: wofshevy@gate.net
web: http://www.zipmail.com/wofmag
Collects, appraises and specializes in science fiction collectibles: movies, comic books, TV, music, toys, games, etc.

Internet Resources

Stephen Walker
Starland
P.O. Box 24955
Denver, CO 80224-0955
ph: 303-757-0955
fax: 303-757-4958
e-mail: starland@starland.com
web: http://starland.com
Science fiction movie and television news, information, and collectibles.

Museums/Libraries

Los Angeles Science Fantasy Society Library
11513 Burbank Blvd.
North Hollywood, CA 91601-2309
ph: 818-760-9234
e-mail: suggest@lasfs.org
web: http://www.lasfs.org/
A club collection primarily for members' use, with 12,500 volumes and over 125 magazine titles; public use by appointment.

University of California, J. Lloyd Eaton Collection of Science Fiction
Special Collections Library Dep.
P.O. Box 5900
Perris, CA 92571-5900
ph: 909-787-3233 or 909-787-6385
fax: 909-787-4673
e-mail: George.Slusser@ucr.edu
web: http://lib-www.ucr.edu/spec_coll/eaton.html
A comprehensive research resource for science fiction, fantasy and horror; over 75,000 volumes of hardbacks and paperbacks, related boy's books, pulp magazines, comic books, video and audio library, manuscripts, etc.

Periodicals

Andrew I. Porter, Editor
Magazine: Science Fiction Chronicle
P.O. Box 022730
Brooklyn, NY 11202-2730
ph: 718-643-9011
fax: 718-522-3308
e-mail: SF_Chronicle@compuserve.com
Monthly Science Fiction, fantasy and horror newsmagazine; news stories, interviews, columns, book buyers' forthcoming guide, market reports (updated every 4 months), 500+ book and small press reviews, author sales, etc.

Roxanne Toser
Roxanne Toser Non-Sport Enterprises, Inc.
Magazine: Non-Sport Update
4019 Green St.
P.O. Box 5858
Harrisburg, PA 17110-0858
ph: 717-238-1936
fax: 717-238-3220
e-mail: feedback@nonsportupdate.com
web: http://www.nonsportupdate.com/
The foremost quarterly publication for non-sport card collectors; original artwork covers, glossy paper, lots of articles by the experts, great variety of ads, separate 32-page "pop-out" price guide and free cards.

Harry Hopkins, Pub.
FANDATA Publications
Directory: FANDOM Directory
7614 Cervantes Ct.
Springfield, VA 22152-1608
ph: 703-913-5575 or 888-FAN-DATA
fax: 703-913-5575
e-mail: fandata@aol.com
web: http://members.aol.com/fandata/index.htm
Fandom Directory (R) lists over 20,000 fans, collectors, dealers, stores, clubs, and conventions world-wide: science fiction, TV shows, Star Trek, etc.; now in its 17th annual edition; your listing published free of charge upon request.

Allen Shevy
World of Fandom
Magazine: World of Fandom Magazine
P.O. Box 9421
Tampa, FL 33674-9421
ph: 813-933-7424
e-mail: wofshevy@gate.net
web: http://www.zipmail.com/wofmag
Covers movies, comic books, TV, music, toys, games; many exclusive interviews and stories; 108 pages, 4-color glossy covers.

Antique Trader Publications, Inc.
Newspaper: Toy Trader
P.O. Box 1050
Dubuque, IA 52004-1050
ph: 800-334-7165 or 800-482-4155
fax: 800-531-0880
e-mail: jmkoenig@execpc.com
web: http://www.collect.com/toytrader
Monthly newspaper with information on how to buy, sell and trade all types of toys; market trends, the latest prices, "how-to" columns, listings of toy clubs and upcoming toy shows and auctions; also full of buy and sell ads.

Bjo Trimble
Magazine: Space-Time Continuum
601 E. Foothill Blvd.
Monrovia, CA 91016-2403
The major news magazine for Sci-Fi media fans; published bi-monthly; latest news on upcoming Sci-Fi and fantasy films, animation, collecting, Disney, fan clubs, Lucasfilm, space news, Spielberg; TV shows, movies, media, celebrities.

Costuming

Clubs/Associations

International Costumer's Guild
Newsletter: Costumer's Quarterly
P.O. Box 94538
Pasadena, CA 91109
e-mail: icg@costume.org
web: http://www.costume.org/
International club interested in science fiction, fantasy, comic and historical costuming.

Jana Keeler
Greater Bay Area Costumer's Guild, The
Newsletter: Costumer's Scribe, The
5214-F Diamond Heights Blvd., #320
San Francisco, CA 94131
ph: 415-974-9333
e-mail: tryst@toreadors.com
web: http://www.toreadors.com/costume
Local chapter of the International Costumer's Guild; lots of information and networking for costume lovers in the area; includes a list of sewing circles, and costume wearing events.

Monsters (Japanese)

Periodicals

Ed Godziszewski
Newsletter: Japanese Giants
P.O. Box 357
Wilmette, IL 60091
Devoted exclusively to Japanese monsters.

Journal: Monster Attack Team
P.O. Box 821631
Fort Worth, TX 76182-1631
The Japanese monster superhero and fantasy fanzine.

Daikaiju Enterprises
Newsletter: G-FAN
P.O. Box 3468
Steinbach, Manitoba ROA 2AO
Canada
ph: 204-326-7754
fax: 204-326-7754
e-mail: letters@g-fan.com
web: http://www.g-fan.com
Devoted to Japanese live action Sci-Fi, with particular emphasis on Godzilla.

SCIENTIFIC INSTRUMENTS

(see INSTRUMENTS & DEVICES)

SCIENTIFIC TOYS

(see TOYS, Construction Sets)

SCOOPS

(see SODA FOUNTAIN COLLECTIBLES, Ice Cream Dippers)

SCOOTERS

(see RIDING TOYS)

SCOTTISH COLLECTIBLES

(see also ART, Scottish; BOOKS, Scottish)

Dealers

Sir Alasdair T. Munro, BT.
Alba Antiques
P.O. Box 940
Waitsfield, VT 05673-0940
ph: 802-496-2213
Buys and sells antiques of Scottish origin or association: Mauchline ware, Tartanware, Scottish dress, dirks, powder horns, pistols, swords, Victorian Scottish silver jewelry, oil paintings, watercolors, prints, etc.

Mauchline Ware

Clubs/Associations

Janet Hawkins
Mauchline Ware Collectors' Club
Journal: Journal of the Mauchline Ware Collectors Club
2131 1st Ave. SE, #314
Cedar Rapids, IA 52402-6360
ph: 319-362-2643
For collectors of Mauchline Ware, a wooden ware, souvenirs and furniture from Scotland decorated with transfer prints and photographs; will provide membership application for mailing to the parent club in England.

Barry Kottler
Mauchline Ware Collectors' Club
Journal: Journal of the Mauchline Ware Collectors Club
Unit 37, Romsey Industrial Estate
Greatbridge Rd.
Romsey, Hampshire SO51 0HR
U.K.
ph: +44 (0) 1903 775120
fax: +44 (0) 1794 830284
For collectors of Mauchline Ware, a wooden ware, souvenirs and furniture from Scotland decorated with transfer prints and photographs; also tartan and fern ware.

Collectors

Janet Hawkins
2131 1st Ave. SE, #314
Cedar Rapids, IA 52402-6360
ph: 319-362-2643

Dealers

Sir Alasdair T. Munro, BT.
Alba Antiques
P.O. Box 940
Waitsfield, VT 05673-0940
ph: 802-496-2213
Buys and sells antiques of Scottish origin or association: Mauchline ware, Tartanware, Scottish dress, dirks, powder horns, pistols, swords, Victorian Scottish silver jewelry, oil paintings, watercolors, prints, etc.

Experts

David Trachtenberg
c/o Keith
237 Eldridge St., #24
New York, NY 10002
ph: 212-643-1797
e-mail: djustint@aol.com
Co-author of "The Collector's Guide to Mauchline Ware."

Thomas Keith
237 Eldridge Street, #24
New York, NY 10002
ph: 212-533-8842
e-mail: tekny@aol.com
Co-author of "The Collector's Guide to Mauchline Ware."

SCOUTING MEMORABILIA

(see BOY SCOUT MEMORABILIA; CAMPING EQUIPMENT; GIRL SCOUT MEMORABILIA; LONE SCOUT MEMORABILIA)

SCRAP

(see GOLD, Scrap; PLATINUM, Scrap; SILVER, Scrap; GEMS & JEWELRY)

SCRAPBOOKS

(see ALBUMS; PAPER COLLECTIBLES)

SCRIMSHAW

(see also ENDANGERED SPECIES; FOLK ART; IVORY; NAUTICAL ANTIQUES; WHALING)

Dealers

Albert L. Doucette
Whale's Tale Scrimshanders
42 North Water St.
New Bedford, MA 02740-6335
ph: 508-997-4233 or 508-758-3065
fax: 508-997-0752
e-mail: adouce476@aol.com
web: http://www.whalestale.com
Specializes in contemporary ivory carvings and scrimshaw; appraisals, manufacturing, reproductions, repair and restoration.

Brian J. Kiracofe
Newport Scrimshander, The
14 Bowen's Wharf
Newport, RI 02840
ph: 401-849-5680 or 800-635-5234
fax: 401-849-9306
e-mail: newportscrimshaw@juno.com
web: http://www.scrimshanders.com
Carries an extensive collection of scrimshaw items, whaler folk art c. 1870.

Experts

Albert L. Doucette
Whale's Tale Scrimshanders
42 North Water St.
New Bedford, MA 02740-6335
ph: 508-997-4233 or 508-758-3065
fax: 508-997-0752
e-mail: adouce476@aol.com
web: http://www.whalestale.com
Specializes in contemporary ivory carvings and scrimshaw; appraisals, manufacturing, reproductions, repair and restoration.

Sara Conklin
Nautical Appraisals
239 Sierra Pt. Rd.
Brisbane, CA 94005-1664
ph: 415-467-6249
fax: 415-467-6249
e-mail: sconklin2@earthlink.com
Appraises maritime items and collections: ship models, scrimshaw, navigational instruments, figurehead carvings, marine art, paper & ephemera archival collections, telescopes, shipwrecks, diving equip., ocean liner memorabilia, whaling.

Museums/Libraries

Curator
Kendall Whaling Museum, The
Newsletter: KWM Newsletter
27 Everett St.
P.O. Box 297
Sharon, MA 02067-0297
ph: 781-784-5642
e-mail: staff@kwm.org
web: http://www.kwm.org
International collection of whaling artworks & artifacts specializing in paintings 1600-present, scrimshaw, tools, gear, prints, ship models, etc.; world's largest collection of scrimshaw; numerous publications; guide to fakes.

New Bedford Whaling Museum
18 Johnny Cake Hill
New Bedford, MA 02740-6317
ph: 508-997-0046
fax: 508-994-4350
e-mail: whaling@ma.ultranet.com
web: http://www.whalingmuseum.org/
A whaling and local historical museum.

Cold Spring Harbor Whaling Museum
P.O. Box 25
Cold Spring Harbor, NY 11724
ph: 516-367-3418
web: http://www.cshl.org/cshm/whale.htm

San Francisco Maritime National Historical Park, Museum & Library
Bldg. E, Fort Mason Center
San Francisco, CA 94123
ph: 415-556-9870 or 415-556-9871
fax: 415-556-3540
e-mail: safr_maritime_library@nps.gov
web: http://www.nps.gov/safr/local/lib/libtop.html

SCRIP

(see also LOGGING RELATED ITEMS; MINING RELATED ITEMS; STOCKS & BONDS; TOKENS)

Clubs/Associations

Sheila Medd
National Scrip Collectors Association
Newsletter: Scrip Talk
110 Braddock St.
Crossville, TN 38555-9113
e-mail: sgmedd@multipro.com
web: http://www.miningusa.com/mh-t/nsca/nsca.htm
Promotes collecting of coal, lumber & all mining scrip (metal & paper scrip used as a medium of wages in industries such as coal mining), merchant tokens, & mining artifacts including mining lamps.

Periodicals

Walter Caldwell
Newsletter: Token Talk
P.O. Box 29
Fayetteville, WV 25840
ph: 304-574-0105
e-mail: wcaldcw8519@aol.com
Periodical about coal, lumber & all mining scrip (metal & paper scrip used as a medium of wages in industries such as coal mining), merchant tokens, & mining artifacts including mining lamps.

Pat DuChene, PR
Krause Publications
Newspaper: Bank Note Reporter
700 E. State St.
Iola, WI 54990-0001
ph: 715-445-2214
fax: 715-445-4087
e-mail: info@krause.com
web: http://www.krause.com/
Monthly news source and marketplace for collectors of U.S. and world paper money, notes, checks and related fiscal paper.

Depression

Experts

Neil Shafer
P.O. Box 17138
Milwaukee, WI 53217
ph: 414-352-5962
fax: 414-352-5974
e-mail: nelsshaf@aol.com
Co-author of "Standard Catalog of Depression Scrip of the United States"; the 1930s including Canada and Mexico.

SCUBA

(see also NAUTICAL ANTIQUES, Diving)

Collectors

Mark Howell
25151 Windwood Ln.
Lake Forest, CA 92630
ph: 949-770-4920
fax: 949-837-6209
Wants scuba diving equipment from the 1950s: regulators, tanks, fins, masks, old photos, repair manuals, spare parts, sales catalogs, old diving books.

SCULPTURES

(see also ART; BRONZES; FOLK ART; GARDEN FURNITURE; MARBLE & STONE; MEDALLIC SCULPTURE; MINIATURES, Sculptures; ROGERS GROUPS; WOOD, Carvings)

Appraisers

Judith S. Jordan
Perrinart Associates
140 Scarborough Rd.
Briarcliff Manor, NY 10510-2006
ph: 914-762-1438 or 802-869-2784

Charles B. Goldstein, ISA CAPP
Charles Barry International
8 Hardwicke Place
Rockville, MD 20850-3010
ph: 301-340-6775
fax: 301-340-1726
Buys, sells, and appraises 20th century, modern and contemporary sculpture; Certified Member, International Society of Appraisers; expert witness and trial consultant.

William Lavendusky, M.S., ISA
William Lavendusky, Fine Art
3345 So. Harvard, Bldg. 100
Tulsa, OK 74135
ph: 918-747-5336
fax: 918-742-3425
Dealer and appraiser of paintings and sculpture; specialist in 19th century French animal bronzes.

Clubs/Associations

New England Wood Carvers
P.O. Box 561
Lexington, MA 02173
e-mail: rtrudel@tiac.net
web: http://www24.pair.com/rtrudel/newc.html
Promotes and encourages woodcarving, wood sculpture and whittling as art forms.

National Sculpture Society
Magazine: Sculpture Review
1177 Avenue of the Americas
New York, NY 10036
ph: 212-764-5645
fax: 212-764-5651
e-mail: NSS1893@aol.com
web: http://www.sculptor.org/NSS/
Oldest organization of professional sculptors in the US; purpose is to promote excellence in figurative and realist sculpture throughout the U.S.

Kelly Borsheim
Texas Society of Sculptors
P.O. Box 49291
Austin, TX 78765-9291
ph: 512-371-7606
e-mail: tsos@flash.net
web: http://www.flash.net/~tsos/
This site features the works of member sculptors in any medium including terra-cotta, stone and bronze; lists information about shows and festivals, and provides links to lots of sculpture-related sites.

Dealers

Steve Newman
112 Revonah Ave.
Stamford, CT 06905
ph: 203-327-9216
Buys and sells bronze, marble and wood sculpture: 19th century American Neoclassic figures, busts and reliefs; 19th and 20th century animal sculptures; garden fountains and figures.

Robin & June Greenwald
June Greenwald Antiques, Inc.
3096 Mayfield Rd.
Cleveland, OH 44118
ph: 215-932-5535
Buys and sells 19th and early 20th century bronze and marble sculptures.

Experts

Henry Swiggum, ISA
4246 Glencove Trl
Saint Paul, MN 55214-5517
ph: 612-891-1514
fax: 612-891-1514
Specialist in bronzes and marble sculptures, prints, paintings, and Oriental art.

Man./Prod./Dist.

Robin Trudel
Pine Tree Studios
271 Bouchard Ave.
Dracut, MA 01826-2229
e-mail: rtrudel@tiac.net
web: http://www24.pair.com/rtrudel/pinetree
Provides wooden sculptures of all sizes, specializing in small statuary including all the popular saints; member of NWCA and NEWC.

Cindy Bissessar
Cindy Arts
148/801 Elizabeth Street
263 Clarence Street
Sydney, 2000
Australia
ph: 61 2 9261 5880 or 61 2 9285 1726
fax: 61 2 9285 1710
e-mail: bssssr@ibm.net

Museums/Libraries

Jan Ramierz
Museum of the City of New York
1220 5th Ave.
New York, NY 10029-5221
ph: 212-534-1672
fax: 212-534-5974
e-mail: mcny@mcny.org
web: http://www.mcny.org/mcny/
Special paintings and sculpture collections; access by appointment; research fee charged.

Repair Services

Boris Paskvan
Awesome Metal Restorations, Inc.
4233-G Howard Ave.
Kensington, MD 20895-2449
ph: 301-897-3266
fax: 301-530-8428
European expert restores gold, gilt, bronze, silver, silver plating, icons, metal accessories, sculptures, etc. for museums, homes, insurance; repairs, solders, fabricates duplicates parts, replates, rewires, retins, polishes, lacquers.

Repro. Sources

Gothic Arts
2706 Devine St.
Columbia, SC 29205
ph: 803-765-1188 or 800-284-5435
fax: 803-779-9779
e-mail: J.Musselman@mindspring.com
web: http://www.GothicArts.com
Offers the finest quality reproductions of art objects ranging from traditional classic statuary to European gargoyles.

Erte

Dealers

Charles Huller
Benedetti Gallery
52 Prince St.
New York, NY 10012
ph: 212-226-2238
fax: 212-431-8106
Specializing in sculpture by Erte with over 60 sculptures on display; also sculptures by Felix deWeldon (creator of Iwo Jima War Memorial and over 2000 other monuments), Robazza, Falai, Brescianine, Li Causi; art by Anthony Quinn.

Gwendolyn R. Reasoner, Ph.D.
Re Vann Galleries
125 Arthur Lane
Hackberry, LA 70645-3001
ph: 609-345-7474 or 800-821-4278
e-mail: revanngal@aol.com
Largest Boehm dealer in the U.S.; specializes in the Boehm secondary market; also Cybis, Royal Worcester, Erte; also appraises.

Outdoor

Clubs/Associations

Save Outdoor Sculpture Proj., Nat. Instit. for the Conserv. of Cultural Property
3299 K St. NW, Ste. 602
Washington, DC 20007
ph: 800-422-4612 or 202-625-1495
fax: 202-625-1485
web: http://www.heritagepreservation.org/PROGRAMS/SOS/sosmain.htm
Non-profit organization that works to preserve and increase awareness about outdoor sculpture, works of art, anthropological artifacts, documents, historic objects, architecture and natural science specimens.

SEALS

(see also BOY SCOUT MEMORABILIA, Seals; SEALS & STAMPS; STAMP COLLECTING)

Christmas & Charity

Clubs/Associations

Florence H. Wright, Sec.
Christmas Seal & Charity Stamp Society, The
Newsletter: Seal News
P.O. Box 18615
Rochester, NY 14618
ph: 716-461-9792
Focuses on stamp and metered seals such as tuberculosis, veterans, fraternal and civic, Jewish, ethnic, pets, wildlife, medical, Easter, etc. seals.

SEALS & STAMPS

Periodicals

Scott Publications
Magazine: Stamp Arts & Crafts
30595 Eight Mile
Livonia, MI 48152-1798
ph: 800-458-8237 or 248-477-6650
fax: 248-477-6795
e-mail: 104137.1254@compuserve.com
Focuses on sharing new products and techniques about rubber stamp collecting; a bi-monthly magazine includes club news, shop profiles, feature articles, comprehensive directory of shops and shows.

Wax

Collectors

Sherlock S. Holmes, D.D.
P.O. Box 3
Worcester, MA 01613-0003
ph: 508-754-9907
e-mail: mail@SherlockHolmes.com
web: http://www.SherlockHolmes.com
Wants to buy wax seals; seals are used to impress a design in melted wax on the back of an envelope or at the bottom of a signed contract; made of metal, porcelain, glass, etc.; all types wanted.

Irwin & Eileen Prince
142 Fairway Dr.
Indianapolis, IN 46260-4218
ph: 317-255-1913 or 317-334-9200
fax: 317-228-3355
e-mail: noitall@inetdirect.net
Wants wood, sterling, bronze, agate, glass, crystal, ivory, bone, mother-of-pearl, etc. desk-type (non-fob type) sealing wax seals; send photos and price or call for an evaluation.

SEASHELLS

(see also NAUTICAL ANTIQUES; NATURAL HISTORY)

Clubs/Associations

San Diego Shell Club
e-mail: sdsc@molluscs.net
web: http://www.molluscs.net/SanDiegoShellClub/

Carol Simpson, Ed.
Palmetto Shell Club
Newsletter: Laddergram, The
121 Williams Way
Chapin, SC 29036
ph: 803-781-6530
e-mail: Epitonium@axs2k.net
web: http://molluscs.net/Palmetto_Shell_Club.htm

Mary Brady, Mem.
Georgia Shell Club, Inc.
Newsletter: Whelk Wavelength, The
3886 Rains Court
Atlanta, GA 30319
web: http://museum.nhm.uga.edu/GSC/

Astronaut Trail Shell Club
4812 Union Cypress Place
Melbourne, FL 32904
ph: 407-724-4585
fax: 407-724-4585
e-mail: ejpower@ix.netcom.com
web: http://pw1.netcom.com/~ejpower/atsc.html

Mark & Peta Bethke
Greater Miami Shell Club
Newsletter: Mollusk, The
3001 South Ocean Dr.
Hollywood, FL 33019
ph: 954-929-5967
e-mail: ferreter@gate.net
Members interested in collecting land and marine shells from all over the world; some shells are very rare and command thousands of dollars; regular meetings and shows held to display member collections.

St. Pete Shell Club, Inc.
P.O. Box 4919
Saint Petersburg, FL 33743-9191
e-mail: dejavu1@erols.com
web: http://www.geocities.com/RainForest/Vines/3910/

Glen Deuel, Ed.
North Alabama Shell Club
Newsletter: Nautiloid, The
8011 Camille Dr. SE
Huntsville, AL 35802
ph: 256-881-4067
e-mail: gmdeuel@hiwaay.net
web: http://fly.hiwaay.net/~dwills/nasc.html

Lynn Scheu, Editor
Conchologists of America
Journal: American Conchologist
1222 Holsworth Ln.
Louisville, KY 40222-6616
ph: 502-423-0469 or 502-458-5719
fax: 502-426-4336
e-mail: amconch@ix.netcom.com
web: http://coa.acnatsci.org/conchnet/
Amateurs, professionals interested in the study, collection, conservation of seashells; grants to deserving malacology students & qualified workers; annual convention with lectures, field trips, exhibits, dealers' bourse, auction.

Judy Lewis Caldeira
North Texas Conchological Society
2117 Via Estgrada
Carrollton, TX 75006
e-mail: jcaldeira@earthlink.net
web: http://home.earthlink.net/~jcaldeira/ntcs.html

Lindsey T. Groves, Treas.
Conchological Club of Southern California
c/o Malacology
900 Exposition Blvd.
Los Angeles, CA 90007
ph: 213-744-3377 or 213-744-3376
e-mail: groves@mizar.usc.edu
web: http://www.lam.mus.ca.us/~ccsc/
Oldest shell club in the country.

Guam Shell Club, The
P.O. Box 4482
Agana, GU 96910
web: http://www.geocities.com/CapeCanaveral/Lab/5501/GSCl.html

Mike Cortie
Conchological Society of Southern Africa
7 Jan Booysen Str.
Annlin, Pretoria 0182
South Africa
ph: 11-709-4485
e-mail: achatina@iafrica.com
web: http://www.molluscs.net/ConchSocSoAfrica.html

Collectors

Mique & C.E. Pinkerton
Mique's Molluscs
7078 Westmoremand Dr.
Warrenton, VA 20817-4451
ph: 540-347-3839
fax: 540-347-9740
e-mail: miques.molluscs.shells@erols.com
Collector and dealer in specimen seashells (also includes land and freshwater mollusks); appraisals on collections for estate settlements; sells collections on consignment; member Conchologists of America and NC Shell Club.

Mark & Peta Bethke
3001 South Ocean Dr.
Hollywood, FL 33019
ph: 954-929-5967
e-mail: ferreter@gate.net
Collector specializing in "cone shells"; when alive this animal is the deadliest animal in the world — fast-acting poison kills its victim within minutes.

Tony Lothian
12 Bluebeard Point
Hattiesburg, MS 39402
ph: 601-264-8598
fax: 601-264-0325
e-mail: tlothian@netdoor.com
web: http://www2.netdoor.com/~tlothian
A collector of sea shells for over 35 years; has over 500 species and 1200 shells.

Bret Raines
P.O. Box 3209
Victorville, CA 92393
ph: 760-949-1938
e-mail: mtp@molluscs.net
web: http://www.molluscs.net/
Shell appraiser, collector, dealer, expert and auctioneer.

Dealers

Richard L. Goldberg
Worldwide Specimen Shells
P.O. Box 6088
Columbia, MD 21046
ph: 410-379-6583
fax: 410-379-6583
e-mail: worldwide@erols.com
web: http://www.erols.com/worldwide
Collector, expert, and retail mail order specimen shell dealer since 1977.

Charles Cardin
Specimen Shells
105 Ckickadee Ct.
Daytona Beach, FL 32119
ph: 800-758-2885
fax: 904-756-6306
e-mail: ccshell@ibm.net
Dealer, expert, appraiser of exotic seashells for the serious collector; from $1.00 to $5,000; worldwide specimens; thousands of species in stock; also shell books, shelling tours to Asia; 25 years experience.

David Myers
Shell World
5684 International Drive
Orlando, FL 32819
ph: 407-370-3344 or 888-9-SHELLS
fax: 407-370-3145
e-mail: david@shellworld.com
web: http://www.shellworld.com/
One of the largest selections of sea shells, corals, and nautical and tropical decorative items on the internet; over 22 years in business; ships worldwide.

John Bernard
Shelloak
32 Old Homestead Hwy.
Crossville, TN 38555
ph: 931-484-7167
e-mail: shelloak@tnaccess.com
web: http://www.molluscs.net/shelloak.htm
Appraises and sells specimen seashells for the collector.

Mary Taylor
Broken Siphon
16784 Danbury Ave
Hesperia, CA 92345
ph: 760-947-3709
e-mail: olividae@hotmail.com
web: http://www.molluscs.net/Broken_Siphon/list.htm
Website offers the serious and casual seashell collector a place to view and purchase specimen quality shells; also shells for the collector who does not need a gem (perfect) specimen but rather a very good shell at a reasonable price.

Experts

Mique & C.E. Pinkerton
Mique's Molluscs
7078 Westmoremand Dr.
Warrenton, VA 20817-4451
ph: 540-347-3839
fax: 540-347-9740
e-mail: miques.molluscs.shells@erols.com
Collector and dealer in specimen seashells (also includes land and freshwater mollusks); appraisals on collections for estate settlements; sells collections on consignment; member Conchologists of America and NC Shell Club.

Bret Raines
P.O. Box 3209
Victorville, CA 92393
ph: 760-949-1938
e-mail: mtp@molluscs.net
web: http://www.molluscs.net/
Shell appraiser, collector, dealer, expert and auctioneer.

Internet Resources

Richard L. Goldberg
Worldwide Specimen Shells
P.O. Box 6088
Columbia, MD 21046
ph: 410-379-6583
fax: 410-379-6583
e-mail: worldwide@erols.com
web: http://www.erols.com/worldwide
Collector, expert, and retail mail order specimen shell dealer since 1977; highly illustrated site for learning about and purchasing shells.

Bret Raines
Molluscan Trading Post
P.O. Box 3209
Victorville, CA 92393
ph: 760-949-1938
e-mail: mtp@molluscs.net
web: http://www.molluscs.net/
Network of shell dealers and collectors; free classifieds, dealer's lists, shell auctions, list of collectors and clubs, chat rooms, online forum, and links to related shell sites; free webpages for any shell club in the world!

Guido T. Poppe
Conchology
Stanislas Leclefstraat 8
Berchem, 2600
Belgium
ph: 32(2)217-01-10
fax: 32(2)217-36-28
e-mail: guido.poppe@conchology.uunethost.be
web: http://www.conchology.uunethost.be/
A comprehensive website for seashells: seashell gallery, shell links, collecting shells, and much more all about seashells.

Museums/Libraries

Discovery Seashell Museum
P.O. Box 121
2717 Asbury Ave.
Ocean City, NJ 08226
ph: 609-398-2316
web: http://www.fieldtrip.com/nj/93982316.htm

Delaware Museum of Natural History
4840 Kennett Pike
P.O. Box 3937
Wilmington, DE 19807-0937
ph: 302-658-9111 or 302-658-5004
fax: 302-658-2610
web: http://www.delmnh.org/
Has seashell research collection; accepts donations of shells having locality data; loans material to bona fide researchers at research institutes.

Bailey-Matthews Shell Museum
3075 Sanibel-Captiva Rd.
Sanibel, FL 33957
ph: 941-395-2233
fax: 941-395-6706
web: http://www.coconet.com/sanibel-captiva/bm_shell.html

Shellorama Shell Museum (The Mikado Collection)
Mauritius
e-mail: mikado@intnet.mu
web: http://www.mikado.com/shellM.html

Periodicals

Wes Thorsson, Ed.
Hawaiian Shell News
122 Waialeale Ste.
Honolulu, HI 96825-2020
ph: 808-395-3581
e-mail: thorsson@hits.net
web: http://www.hits.net/~hsn/

Maria Antonietta Fontana Angioy
Magazine: La Conchiglia (The Shell)
Italy
e-mail: conchiglia@pronet.it
web: http://www.evolver.it/
Published four times each year in both English and Italian.

SEEDS

Collectors

Jean Riley
R 2, Box 2067
Equinunk, PA 18417
ph: 570-224-6330
e-mail: fiddlinaround@ezaccess.net
Wants to buy late 1800s to early 1900s seed catalogs, particularly Peter Henderson's, Childs, Mandeville & King; also wants seed packets.

SERVICE STATION COLLECTIBLES

(see GAS STATION COLLECTIBLES)

SEWING ITEMS & GO-WITHS

(see also BUTTONS; CLOTHING & ACCESSORIES, Vintage; TEXTILES)

Collectors

Michelle Revoir
2121 North Bayshore Dr. #716
Miami, FL 33137
ph: 305-573-6855
e-mail: OhRevoir@iname.com
Collector of antique and vintage clothing buttons and sewing items of all kinds.

Sherry L. Werdon
400 N. Washington
Lowell, MI 49331-1465
ph: 616-897-9580
Wants to buy figural tape measures; also wants unusual sewing items such as figural pin cushions, thimble holders, etc.

Wynneth Mullins
P.O. Box 381807
Duncanville, TX 75138-1807
ph: 972-780-8278
e-mail: thimble_guild@msn.com
Wants sewing thimbles and other sewing related tools.

Beth Szescila, ISA CAPP
9546 Enstone Circle
Spring, TX 77379-6605
ph: 281-376-4338
fax: 281-251-0608
e-mail: BethSzescila@compuserve.com
Collects sewing items; looking for sets of sewing tools, preferably in their original containers; also interested in 18th and 19th century sewing boxes in good condition, particularly those with sewing tools.

Dealers

Lillian Colern
Nimble Thimble
2117 Buffalo Rd.
Rochester, NY 14624
ph: 716-594-1237
Buys and sells small sewing items; thimbles, toy sewing machines, trade cards, etc.

Priscilla Washed
Victorian Lady, The
102 South Main St.
P.O. Box 424
Waxhaw, NC 28173-0424
ph: 704-843-4467 or 800-786-1886
A Victorian specialty store featuring 19th century ladies decorative & fashion accessories; buys and sells purses; also sewing and needlework tools, vintage fashion, Victoriana, and combs; mail order; catalog $5.

Barbara Cooney
Cooney's Collectibles
729 Indian Beach Circle
Sarasota, FL 34234-5740
ph: 941-355-1843
e-mail: bcooney9@aol.com
Specializes in figural tape measures, all types of needlework tools, especially the unusual, chatelaines and toy sewing machines; buy, sell and do mail order.

Beth Pulsipher
Prairie Home Antiques
P.O. Box 373
Schoolcraft, MI 49087-0373
ph: 616-679-2062
Buys, sells and specializes in unusual and rare needlework tools, ,thimbles, needle cases, lace bobbins, pincushions, silk winders, sewing clamps, tape measures, etc.; sells by mail; available for lectures and seminars.

Diane Richardson
Gold Hatpin, The
P.O. Box 993
Oak Park, IL 60303-0993
ph: 708-848-3247 or 708-445-0610
e-mail: goldhatpin@mediaone.net
Wants needle cases, sterling thimbles, scissors, unusual darning eggs, sewing birds, thread winders, figural tape measures, tatting shuttles, tool sets, the unusual.

C. Marziotto
P.O. Box 50623
Henderson, NV 89016-0623
Buys and sells fine quality needlework tools and related accessories; also toy sewing machines.

Darners

Collectors

Wayne Muller
P.O. Box 903
Pacific Palisades, CA 90272-0903
Wants to buy darners.

Experts

Wayne Muller
Darn It!
P.O. Box 903
Pacific Palisades, CA 90272-0903
Lecturer, author of "Darn It!: The History and Romance of Darners: A Price Guide;" comprehensive history of darners and darning; 370 full color photos, descriptions, background, prices.

Periodicals

Linda A. Swierczewski
Newsletter: Darn Newsletter, That
461 Brown Briar Circle
Horsham, PA 19044
ph: 215-441-0872

Machines

Clubs/Associations

Sharon Tedrow
International Sewing Machine Collectors Society
Magazine: ISMACS News
551 Kelmore St.
Moss Beach, CA 94038
ph: 650-728-3021
e-mail: webmaster@ismacs.net
web: http://ismacs.net/
U.S. contact for the English-based collectors club; the world's only society for collectors of antique sewing machines.

Graham Forsdyke
International Sewing Machine Collectors Society
Magazine: ISMACS News
158 Hampton Road
Chingford, London E1 9UB
U.K.
ph: 181 529 0394
fax: 181 926 4492
e-mail: graham@ismacs.u-net.com
web: http://www.ismacs.net
An English-based collectors club; the world's only society for collectors of antique sewing machines.

Collectors

Krisi Santilla
ph: 301-869-6025
e-mail: santilla@umd5.umd.edu
web: http://www.erols.com/santilla/
Collects anything related to Singer

sewing machines, including ephemera, banks, advertising, boxed attachments, Singer publications, award and promotional items, etc.; also other brand toy and full-size sewing machines.

Peter Frei
P.O. Box 500
Brimfield, MA 01010-0500
ph: 800-942-8968 or 413-245-4660
web: http://www.peterfrei.com/
Wants to buy hand powered vacuum cleaners, pre-1875 sewing machines, typewriters, calculators, and adding machines.

Mark & Linda Heminway
21 Misty Ridge Road
New Windsor, NY 12553
ph: 914-496-5606
e-mail: mljjhem@frontiernet.net
web: http://www.frontiernet.net/~mljjhem/
Collects and sells antique sewing machines, primarily Singer, as well as related parts and accessories; also collects quality "toy" sewing machines.

Jerry Propst
P.O. Box 45
Janesville, WI 53547-0045
ph: 608-752-2816
fax: 608-752-7691
When writing, please include a LSASE if requesting a reply.

Frank Smith
804 West Abram
Arlington, TX 76013
ph: 817-275-0971
e-mail: arlprosv@onramp.net
web: http://rampages.onramp.net/~arlprosv/museum.htm

Alan Quinn
U.K.
e-mail: alan@meiboku.demon.co.uk
web: http://www.demon.co.uk/quinn/
Collector of pre-1968 sewing machines, specializing in those made by Singer and the Jones Sewing Machine Company.

Dealers

Jim W. Slaten
Antique Sewing Machine Museum
3400 Park Boulevard
Oakland, CA 94610-2834
ph: 510-261-0413 or 800-474-8433
e-mail: jws@pacbell.net
Buys and sells antique sewing machines; also publishes the book "Antique American Sewing Machines - A Value Guide"; sells books relating to all phases of sewing machine interest.

Maggie Snell
158 Hampton Road
Chingford, London E1 9UB
U.K.
ph: 181 529 0394
fax: 181 926 4492
e-mail: graham@ismacs.u-net.com
web: http://www.sew-sales.com/
Collects, buys and sells antique sewing machines as part of a mechanical-antique business; great web site with a virtual Maggie Snell collection, fact files about makers, collection of featherweights and toy machines, and much more.

Experts

Elizabeth S. Brown
45 Whippoorwill Way
Belle Mead, NJ 08502-5827
ph: 908-359-3395
fax: 908-874-7590
e-mail: wbrown@nerc.com
Wants pre-1920 American sewing machines or early electric machines, early sewing tools and paper patterns for men or women, and garment drafting tools.

Carter Bays
143 Spring Lake Rd.
Columbia, SC 29206-2106
ph: 800-332-2297 or 888-PRE-1875
e-mail: bays@cs.sc.edu
web: http://kbs.net/tt/zone/carter/carter.html
One of the nation's leading sewing machine collectors; wants only pre-1875 machines; no oak machines; no Wheeler & Wilson; no Wilcox & Gibbs; author of "The Encyclopedia of Early American Sewing Machines."

Charles Law
1514 Keolu Dr.
Kailua, HI 96734
fax: 808-262-0362
e-mail: claw@geocities.com
Author of "The Encyclopedia of Antique Sewing Machines," the premier source for information on antique and vintage sewing machines.

Maggie Snell
48 Nightingale House
Thomas More Street, London E1 9UB
U.K.
ph: 171 488 0474 or 181 529 0394
fax: 171 481 9097
e-mail: maggie@ismacs.u-net.com
web: http://ismacs.net
Appraiser, auctioneer, buyer, seller, and specialist in antique sewing machines.

Internet Resources

Campbell's Guide to Toy Sewing Machines
e-mail: quilts@erols.com
web: http://www.erols.com/quilts/index.htm
Provides electronic service data for new and antique electronic equipment of all types from pre-1930s radios to latest electronic equipment; sells copies of manufacturer's documentation; collector books, hard to find parts.

Melissa Bishop
475 Mill Rd.
Coram, NY 11727-4137
e-mail: mbishop@needles.com
web: http://kbs.net/tt/faq/

Charles Law
Online Antique Sewing Machine Resource
1514 Keolu Dr.
Kailua, HI 96734
fax: 808-262-0362
e-mail: claw@geocities.com

Museums/Libraries

Frank Smith
Frank Smith's Sewing Machine Museum
804 West Abram
Arlington, TX 76013
ph: 817-275-0971
e-mail: arlprosv@onramp.net
web: http://rampages.onramp.net/~arlprosv/museum.htm
America's first sewing machine museum.

Jim W. Slaten
Antique Sewing Machine Museum
3400 Park Boulevard
Oakland, CA 94610-2834
ph: 510-261-0413 or 800-474-8433
e-mail: jws@pacbell.net
Buys and sells antique sewing machines; also publishes the book "Antique American Sewing Machines - A Value Guide"; sells books relating to all phases of sewing machine interest.

Repair Services

Cathy & Stephen Racine
Simple Machine, The
18 Masonic Home Rd. - Rt. 31
P.O. Box 234
Charlton, MA 01507-0234
ph: 508-248-6632
Buys, sells, repairs and restores old treadle sewing machines and antique hand crank sewing machines; also carries parts, belts, needles, bobbins and manuals.

Machines (Miniature & Toy)

Clubs/Associations

Claire Toschi
Toy Stitchers
Newsletter: Toy Stitchers Newsletter
623 Santa Florita Ave.
Millbrae, CA 94030-1203
ph: 650-589-6754
Acts as a clearinghouse for the exchange of factual details, tips, advice and information on toy sewing machines; collectors buy, sell, trade TSM's through ads.

Collectors

Lanelle Hodnett
2965 Avenue Z
Brooklyn, NY 11235-1658
ph: 718-891-3489
Collects all types of miniature and toy sewing machines, as well as any sewing machine motifs (especially Singer); also wants related items.

Dana & Darlene DeMore
4645 Laurel Ridge Dr.
Harrisburg, PA 17110-3446
ph: 717-545-7320
Wants to buy miniature and toy sewing machines.

Jay Bolante
3058 North Honore St.
Chicago, IL 60657-2050
ph: 773-327-5091
Collects and wants to buy antique toy and adult sewing machines.

Dealers

Jude Allen
Vintage Collection
356 Main St.
Half Moon Bay, CA 94019
ph: 650-712-0366
fax: 650-654-0842
Buys and sells linen and lace; also old yardage, buttons, quilts, sewing implements, sewing machines and miniature sewing machines.

Eureka, I Found It! Antiques & Collectibles
P.O. Box 2192
Petaluma, CA 94953-2192
e-mail: eureka@erueka-i-found-it.com
web: http://www.eureka-i-found-it.com
An online dealer specializing in vintage textiles and clothing, toy and model steam engines, buttons, fans, Art Deco, costume jewelry, toy sewing machines.

Carole Meeker
5702 Vacation Blvd.
Somerset, CA 95684-9324
ph: 530-620-7019
fax: 530-620-7020
e-mail: clm@inforum.net
Wants to buy rare and unusual small patented mechanical antiques, early American technology and occupational-related photography, advertising and catalogs.

Bob Bannen
Featherweight & TSM Sales
207/475 The West Mall
Etobicoke, Ontario M9C 4Z3
Canada
ph: 416-695-3975
e-mail: bbannen@idirect.com
web: http://webhome.idirect.com/~bbannen/homepage.htm
Collects, repairs, buys and sells vintage sewing machines, specializing in Singer Featherweights and all makes and models of toy sewing machines; also supplies Featherweight 221 reproduction decal sets; dealers invited.

Experts

Darryl & Roxana Matter
P.O. Box 65
Portis, KS 67474
ph: 785-346-5647
Authors of "Collector's Guide to Toy Sewing Machines" (Green Gate Books.)

Needle Books

Internet Resources

Connie McGinnis
Rosie's Needle Book Museum
111 E. 7th St.
Metropolis, IL 62960
ph: 618-524-2418
e-mail: rosierider@yahoo.com
web: http://www.geocities.com/Wellesley/Garden/7484
Visit Rosie's website to view the needle book exhibit, to learn about needle books, or to obtain price information; nothing for sale; just sharing the collection.

Thimbles

Clubs/Associations

Wynneth Mullins
Thimble Guild, The
Newsletter: Thimble Guild
P.O. Box 381807
Duncanville, TX 75138-1807
ph: 972-780-8278
e-mail: thimble_guild@msn.com

Kay Connors, Mem.
Thimble Collectors International
Newsletter: TCI Bulletin
2594 E Upper Hayden Lake Rd.
Hayden, ID 83835
ph: 208-762-9520
e-mail: Kconntex@aol.com
TCI introduces members to various aspects of thimble collecting; promotes research & scholarship; quarterly newsletter and booklets on thimbles and related needlework; regional chapters; biennial convention; send LSASE for information.

Collectors

Mary Innes Wagner
564 Linden St.
Rochester, NY 14620
ph: 716-271-8816
fax: 716-244-2673
Wants to buy all types of thimbles, especially antique, needle holders.

Sarah Locker
9706 North 111th East Avenue
Owasso, OK 74055-4335
ph: 918-272-7285
e-mail: thimblecollector@alphabetsoup.net
web: http://www.alphabetsoup.net/lockerfamily/thimbles.htm
A favorite among young and old, thimbles are a wonderful, inexpensive, and history-laden collectible; join the growing number of thimble collectors on the web and start your collection today.

Ray Conners
5285 North 15th St.
Cour D'Alene, ID 83815-9615
e-mail: Kconntex@aol.com

Dealers

Leslie Trobaugh
Thimble Boutique, The
P.O. Box 2894
Sherman, TX 75091-2894
e-mail: lmedenterprises@texoma.net
web: http://members.tripod.com/~lmed/boutique.html
Specializes in all varieties of collectible thimbles, both old and new; porcelain, china, sterling, gold, advertising; if not in stock can locate; also carries displays and showcases to display your thimbles.

Melinda Hum
Thimble Talk
11828 Ranchero Bernardo Rd., Ste. #123-10
San Diego, CA 92128
ph: 760-487-2016
Send $1.00 for catalog.

Experts

Estelle Zalkin
7524 West Treasure Dr.
Miami, FL 33141-4118
ph: 305-864-3012
Author of "Zalkin's Handbook of Thimbles and Sewing Implements" (Chilton Book Co.)

Internet Resources

Sarah Locker
Thimbles!
9706 North 111th East Avenue
Owasso, OK 74055-4335
ph: 918-272-7285
e-mail: thimblecollector@alphabetsoup.net
web: http://www.alphabetsoup.net/lockerfamily/thimbles.htm
Offers free thimbles newsletter.

Periodicals

Lorraine M. Crosby
Newsletter: Thimbletter
93 Walnut Hill Rd.
Newton Highlands, MA 02161-1836
ph: 617-969-9358
An informal bi-monthly newsletter, letters from subscribers, Q & A, for sale or trade, ads, new sources, misc. information.

SEX

(see BATHING BEAUTIES, Nudies & Naughties; EROTICA; PIN-UP ART; PLAYBOY ITEMS; STRIPTEASE)

SHAKER ITEMS

(see also FURNITURE [ANTIQUE])

Auction Services

David D. Newell
David D. Newell - Shaker Literature
39 Steady Lane
Ashfield, MA 01330
ph: 413-628-3240
fax: 413-628-3833
Buys, sells, appraises, auctions printed and manuscript items by/about Shakers and other like sects; also wants related photographica and ephemera; consignments available; catalog and mailing list placement $5.

Willis Henry
Willis Henry Auctions, Inc.
22 Main St.
Marshfield, MA 02050
ph: 781-834-7774 or 800-244-8466
fax: 781-826-3520
e-mail: wha@willishenry.com
web: http://www.willishenry.com/
Specializes in the sale of American antiques of all kinds, particularly Shaker, American Indian and early American.

Clubs/Associations

Ned Pratt
Shaker Heritage Society
Journal: Watervliet Shaker Journal, The
1848 Shaker Meeting House
Albany-Shaker Rd.
Albany, NY 12211
ph: 518-456-7890
web: http://www.shakerworkshops.com/waterv.htm

Karen campbell
Western Shaker Study Group
1700 Penbrooke Trail
Dayton, OH 45459
e-mail: shakerwssg@mindspring.com
web: http://www.shakerwssg.org/
Many members have expertise in various areas of Shaker collecting.

Collectors

Steve Miller
Six Park Place
New Britain, CT 06052
ph: 860-561-3342
fax: 860-223-6316
Wants Shaker bottles, booklets, paper, etc.

Dealers

David D. Newell
David D. Newell - Shaker Literature
39 Steady Lane
Ashfield, MA 01330
ph: 413-628-3240
fax: 413-628-3833
Buys, sells, appraises printed and manuscript items by/about Shakers and other like sects; also wants related photographica and ephemera; consignments available; catalog and mailing list placement $5.

Doug Hamel
Douglas H. Hamel Antiques
56 Staniels Rd.
Chichester, NH 03234
ph: 603-798-5912
fax: 603-798-5447
e-mail: Doug@ShakerAntiques.com
Buys and sells quality Shaker items; helping to build major private and public collections for 30 years.

Richard Vandall
American Decorative Arts
RFD #1, Box 239
Canaan, NH 03741-9746
ph: 603-523-4276
fax: 603-523-4888
Buying and selling Shaker goods; prompt complete service, confidential to the seller; family business, second generation; shipping service available.

Experts

David A. Schorsch
David A. Schorsch American Antiques Inc.
244 Main St.
Woodbury, CT 06798
ph: 203-263-3131
fax: 203-263-2622

Gary D. Gardner
200 College St.
Hodgenville, KY 42748-1404
ph: 502-358-3222
Collector, researcher of furniture, tools, textiles, and crafts produced by Shaker communities during the 19th century; also books written/printed by Shakers, especially S. Union, Pleasant Hill.

Museums/Libraries

Hancock Shaker Village
P.O. Box 927
Pittsfield, MA 01202-0927
ph: 413-443-0188
fax: 413-447-9357
e-mail: info@hancockshakervillage.org
web: http://www.hancockshakervillage.org/
A 200-year-old Shaker site encompassing 20 restored buildings housing the largest and finest collection of Shaker furnishings & artifacts in an original Shaker site.

Janie Chester Young
Canterbury Shaker Village
288 Shaker Rd.
Canterbury, NH 03224
ph: 603-783-9511 or 800-982-9511
e-mail: csv@newww.com
web: http://www.shakers.org
Archives open by appointment; collectors' seminars, craft workshops, demonstrations, museum book store and gift shop, exhibitions, 25 antique Shaker buildings on 694 acres.

Erin Budis
Shaker Museum & Library, The
88 Shaker Museum Rd.
Old Chatham, NY 12136
ph: 518-794-9100
fax: 518-794-8621
e-mail: shakeroldchat@taconic.net
web: http://www.shakermuseumoldchat.org/
The premier Shaker collection housing 24 galleries of furniture masterpieces, oval boxes, baskets, ingenious tools and machinery reflecting the "order, harmony, and utility" of Shaker design.

Shaker Village of Pleasant Hill
3501 Lexington Rd.
Harrodsburg, KY 40330-9218
ph: 606-734-5411 or 800-734-5611
web: http://www.shakervillageky.org/

Shaker Museum at South Union
P.O. Box 30
South Union, KY 42283
ph: 502-542-4167 or 800-811-8279
fax: 502-542-7558
e-mail: shakmus@logantele.com
web: http://www.longantele.com/~shakmus/

Cathie Winans, Dir.
Shaker Historical Museum, The
Journal: Journal, The
16740 S. Park Blvd.
Cleveland, OH 44120-1641
ph: 216-921-1201 or 216-295-2344
e-mail: shakhist@wviz.org
Collection and display of artifacts and furniture designed and used by the North Union Shaker Settlement (now known as Shaker Heights); materials about local history including early developers of Shaker Heights.

Periodicals

K.C. & Alana Parkinson
Magazine: Shakers World
P.O. Box 1276
Manchester, CT 06045
ph: 860-643-9258
e-mail: shakersworld@msn.com
A quarterly magazine focusing on the Shakers and their work products; articles, ads, Shaker news, Shaker events, study groups, auction reviews, Shaker books for sale.

Baskets

Repro. Sources

John E. McGuire
Baskets & Bears
398 S. Main St.
Geneva, NY 14456-2614
ph: 315-787-1251

Darryl & Karen Arawjo
P.O. Box 477
Bushkill, PA 18324-0477
ph: 570-588-6957
Reproduction of Nantucket, Shaker and Appalachian baskets in hand-split white oak; brochure available.

Furniture

Repro. Sources

Brian Braskie
North Woods Chair Shop
237 Old Tilton Rd.
Canterbury, NH 03224-2224
ph: 603-783-4595
fax: 603-783-3328

SHAPLEIGH HARDWARE

(see DIAMOND EDGE [SHAPLEIGH HARDWARE])

SHARPENERS

(see PENCIL SHARPENERS; PENCILS)

SHAVING COLLECTIBLES

(see also BARBERSHOP COLLECTIBLES)

Experts

Phillip Krumholz
P.O. Box 4050
Peoria, IL 61607-0050
ph: 309-697-1120
Acknowledged expert on razors; author of "The Complete Gillette Collectors Handbook" as well as two other books on shaving collectibles and Barberiana.

Museums/Libraries

Lester DeQuaine, Dir.
National Shaving & Barbershop Museum
39 West Main St.
Meriden, CT 06451-4110
ph: 203-639-9778
Displays barbershop and shaving furnishings and artifacts with on-site theater, sidewalk cafe, and museum store which buys and sells related collectibles and books including razor blade price guide.

Razor Sharpeners

Collectors

Jay Bolante
3058 North Honore St.
Chicago, IL 60657-2050
ph: 773-327-5091
Collects and wants to buy mechanical gadgets use to sharpen razor blades; also wants wind-up or battery operated shavers and unusual safety razors.

Cary Basse
6927 Forbes Ave.
Van Nuys, CA 91406-4504
ph: 818-781-4856
Wants to buy safety razors, blade sharpeners, blades.

Razors

Collectors

D. Perkins
6335 W. 62nd St.
Indianapolis, IN 46278-1906
ph: 317-293-9962
Wants early fancy or odd safety razors in tins or sets; also fancy handled straight razors.

Dealers

Sigmund Wohl
Razor's Edge, The
P.O. Box 429
Bronxville, NY 10708-0429
ph: 914-476-5939
fax: 914-376-4160
e-mail: swohl@compuserve.com
Buys and sells barber and shaving collectibles, fancy and unusual razors, and related advertising.

Experts

Charles D. Stapp
7037 Haynes Rd.
Georgetown, IN 47122-8610
ph: 812-923-3483
e-mail: dennyjoyce@aol.com
Free appraisals with SASE; provide photocopy or tracing; especially wants fancy straight razors and complete safety razor in box.

Hank Belasco
7939 Chastain Place
Reseda, CA 91335-2106
ph: 818-344-8790
Wants fancy or unusual straight razors; also wants safety razors, sharpeners, and blank blades; sent list and prices.

Razors (Safety)

Clubs/Associations

William Will, Dir.
Safety Razor Collectors Guild
P.O. Box 885
Crescent City, CA 95531-0885
Promotes interest in collecting and preserving safety-razors, blades and related items; please include SASE with inquiries.

Collectors

Lester Dequaine
155 Brewester St.
Bridgeport, CT 06605-3149
ph: 203-335-6833
Wants to buy early safety razors; also wants related advertisements, catalogs, instruction sheets, mechanical blade sharpeners, razor blade blanks, figural shaving mugs, figural handle shaving brushes, counter & window displays.

Clay Tontz
4043 Nora Ave.
Covina, CA 91722
ph: 626-338-9976

Experts

Howard Hazelcorn
6731 Ashley Ct.
Sarasota, FL 34241-9696
ph: 941-921-1815
Author of "Hazelcorn's Guide to Kampfe's Star Safety Razors."

Robert Waits
594 Endicott Dr.
Sunnyvale, CA 94087-4426
e-mail: rwaits@juno.com
Author of "Safety Razor Reference Guide" and "Safety Razor Reference Guide - First Supplement"; these are not price guides.

SHAWLS

Kashmir (Paisley)

(see also TEXTILES)

Collectors

Stephanie M. Schnatz
17 Tallow Ct.
Baltimore, MD 21244-2516
ph: 410-944-0819
e-mail: chelsealady@hotmail.com
Wants to buy paisley shawls and scraps; please, no dry rot.

Dealers

Allan Arthur
Cyber Rug Center
25 Bennett Street
Atlanta, GA 30309
ph: 800-686-7030 or 404-350-9560
e-mail: aarthur@cyberrug.com
web: http://www.cyberrug.com/
Buys and sells Kelim & flat woven rugs, Pre-Columbian, Coptic, Asian textiles, European rugs and tapestries, Kashmir shawls, American folk art rugs, Oriental rugs, Art Deco rugs; hundreds of images.

Experts

Val Arbab, ISA CAPP
P.O. Box 684
La Jolla, CA 92038-0684
ph: 619-453-4686
fax: 619-457-3647
e-mail: valarbab@worldnet.att.net
Appraises all oriental rugs, Kashmir shawls and textiles.

SHEET MUSIC

(see also HYMNS; MOVIE MEMORABILIA; MUSIC; PAPER COLLECTIBLES; PERFORMING ARTS; ROCK 'N' ROLL COLLECTIBLES)

Auction Services

Beverly A. Hamer
Hamer Sheet Music Sales
P.O. Box 75
East Derry, NH 03041
ph: 603-432-3528
Wants old collectible sheet music; publishes a set price list and conducts auctions of collectible sheet music; free search service.

Norcross
209 Township Line
Upper Darby, PA 19082
Conducts sheet music auctions; many old tunes in mint condition.

Paul A. Riseman
2205 South Park Ave.
Springfield, IL 62704-4335
ph: 217-787-2634
fax: 217-787-0062
e-mail: riseman@riseman.com
Send for free sheet music auction catalogs in the following categories: movie, broadway, rags, jazz, blues, rock, Berlin, Gershwin, transportation, sports, political, etc.

Lois Cordey
5623 N. 64th Ave.
Glendale, AZ 85301
ph: 602-931-2835
Conducts periodic sheet music auctions.

Clubs/Associations

James Henderson
Sonneck Society for American Music & Music in America
Newsletter: Sonneck Society Bulletin
P.O. Box 476
Canton, MA 02021-0476
ph: 781-828-8450
fax: 781-828-8915
e-mail: acadsvc@aol.com
Promotes the dissemination of accurate information on all aspects of American music and music in America; also publishes "American Music", a quarterly journal addressing music in America.

Sam Teicher
New York Sheet Music Society
P.O. Box 354
Hewlett, NY 11557
ph: 516-295-0719
fax: 516-569-1493
e-mail: samuelt313@aol.com
For collectors of all kinds of sheet music with an emphasis on popular music from 1890 to 1950.

Lois Cordey, Ed.
Remember That Song
Newsletter: Remember That Song
5623 N. 64th Ave.
Glendale, AZ 85301
ph: 602-931-2835
Sheet music collectors contribute informative articles and illustrations; illustrated newsletter covering every aspect of old-time popular music collecting; focuses on sheet music from 1840 to 1940; auctions; members get free ads.

Mayilyn Brees, Sec.
National Sheet Music Society, Inc.
Newsletter: Song Sheet
1597 Fair Park Ave.
Los Angeles, CA 90041
Membership includes bi-monthly newsletter and yearly directory; members get free 40 word listings in each.

Mary Brawley
City of Roses Sheet Music Collectors Club
2211 Northeast 53rd Ave.
Portland, OR 97213
Sponsors an annual sheet music sale and show.

Collectors

Roger Hankins
1550 Worcester Rd., #110
Framingham, MA 01702
ph: 508-872-7173
Wants film and show tunes by Berlin & Wenrich.

Stanley King
260 Fifth Ave.
New York, NY 10001-6408
ph: 212-447-1880
fax: 212-447-0728
Wants to buy sheet music: jazz, K.K.K. music, political music, and songsters.

Gary Olsen
505 S. Royal Ave.
Front Royal, VA 22630
ph: 540-635-7157 or 540-635-7158
fax: 540-635-1818
e-mail: hpfrigko@interloc.com
Wants sheet music with covers depicting sports, WWI, or first names in the titles.

Jim Wiemers
5312 Seiler Rd.
Dorsey, IL 62021-1700
ph: 618-377-6379
Hosts the annual Sheet Music Show in mid-June in Collinsville, IL; collector for over 25 years.

Margaret Horning
13447 SE Brush St.
Portland, OR 97236-3323
ph: 503-761-3817

Dealers

Beverly A. Hamer
Beverly A. Hamer Sheet Music Sales
P.O. Box 75
East Derry, NH 03041
ph: 603-432-3528
Expert, collector, dealer wants old collectible sheet music; publishes a set price list and conducts auctions of collectible sheet music; free search service.

Wayland Bunnell
199 Tarrytown Rd.
Manchester, NH 03103-2723
ph: 603-668-5466
e-mail: wtarrytown@aol.com
Wants unpicked box lots of sheet music, or individual pieces in any subject category; wholesale, retail, consignment.

Allen Radwill
23 Hunters Lane
Vincentown, NJ 08088-2837
ph: 609-953-5473
250,000 items related to rock & roll, rhythm & blues, soul, gospel, television, movies: records, sheet music, magazines; no CDs or videos.

Robert Hess
155 West 72nd St., #404
New York, NY 10023
ph: 212-579-0689
e-mail: hfis646942@aol.com
web: http://www.coachnet.com/music
Wants to buy jazz and R&B records; has been collecting for 30 years; also wants original jazz art including sheet music, statues, books, etc.; by appointment or mail.

Sheet Music Center
Box 10
Old Bethpage, NY 11804
ph: 800-527-7626
e-mail: smctr@sheetmusiccenter.com
web: http://www.sheetmusiccenter.com
Buys and sells sheet music and piano rolls; FREE catalog to readers of "Maloney's Antiques & Collectibles Resource Directory."

Tom Morgan
110 Monte Vista Ave.
Charlottesville, VA 22903-4117
ph: 804-296-9346
e-mail: tom@ric.com
web: http://www.jass.com/tom/
Author of "From Cakewalk to Concert Halls"; associate editor of the "African American Volume of the Dictionary of Twentieth Century Culture"; always looking for sheet music with photos of African Americans.

Roger Burgoon
107 S. Mulberry
Statesboro, GA 30458

Sandra McGovern
Global Music Enterprises
P.O. Box 450763
Kissimmee, FL 34745-0763
ph: 407-396-4176
fax: 407-396-4176
e-mail: globaltreasures@webtv.net
Buys and sells vintage sheet music and movie/movie star memorabilia, Marilyn Monroe, pin-ups; send want lists or email requests.

Jeannie Peters
Mt. Washington Antiques
3742 Kellogg Ave.
c/o Ferguson Antiques Mall
Cincinnati, OH 45226-1514
ph: 513-231-6584 or 513-321-0919
Buys, sells and specializes in sheet

music; over 200,000 available for sale; send want list, please.

Robert Johnson
Portobello Unit #126
5 Embarcadero West
Oakland, CA 94607

Jeanne Koch
Kookie Kollectorium
4312 SE Flavel St.
Portland, OR 97206-8426
ph: 503-771-2024
e-mail: jkoch@aol.com
Send want lists.

Experts

Sandy Marrone
113 Oakwood Dr.
Cinnaminson, NJ 08077
ph: 609-829-6104
e-mail: smusandy@aol.com
Sheet music collector for over 25 years; appraises and lectures; has contacts throughout the hobby; willing to answer questions and give advice about sheet music; would prefer discussing by phone but will answer mail if SASE enclosed.

Lois Cordey
5623 N. 64th Ave.
Glendale, AZ 85301
ph: 602-931-2835
Collects, appraises and specializes in sheet music.

Lynn Wenzel
29 Latham Lane
Berkeley, CA 94708-1513
ph: 510-527-0096 or 510-528-9548
fax: 510-528-9458
e-mail: lwhandow@ix.netcom.com
Co-author with Carol Binkowski of "I Hear American Singing"; features writer for antique and collectible publications nationwide under the syndicated name "Handed Down."

Radko Tichavsky
Cornalina 5349, Paseo Res. 5
Nuevo Leon, Montery 640 00
Mexico
Specializes in Mexican sheet music from the 1850-1913 period.

Internet Resources

American Sheet Music Collection, Library of Congress
101 Independence Ave. SE
Washington, DC 20540
ph: 202-707-8000
e-mail: ndlpcoll@loc.gov
web: http://memory.loc.gov/ammem/smhtml/smhome.html
The American Sheet Music Collection contains tens of thousands of pieces of sheet music registered for copyright during the post-Civil War era, 1870 to 1885: popular songs, piano music, sacred music, secular choral music, etc.

Museums/Libraries

American Antiquarian Society
185 Salisbury St.
Worcester, MA 01609
ph: 508-755-5221
fax: 508-753-3311
e-mail: library@mwa.org
web: gopher://mark.mwa.org/
A learned society founded in 1812; maintains a research library of American history and culture in order to collect, preserve, and make available for study the printed record of the U.S.; 3 million books, maps, pamphlets, etc.

Broadcast Music, Inc. (BMI)
320 West 57th St.
New York, NY 10019
ph: 212-586-2000
web: http://www.wheelofun.com/bmi.html
A nationwide music performance rights organization, licenses for more than 120,000 songwriters and composers and more than 60,000 music publishers; significant sheet music collection.

Periodicals

Kirk Miller, Ed.
Music Group, The
Magazine: Sheet Music Magazine
333 Adams St.
Bedford Hills, NY 10507
ph: 800-759-3036 or 914-244-8500
fax: 914-244-8560
e-mail: kirkmiller@yestermusic.com
Focuses on playable sheet music; some dealer ads for vintage sheet music.

Richard Zimmerman, Ed.
Maple Leaf Club
Newsletter: Rag Times, The
15522 Ricky Ct.
Grass Valley, CA 95949-6672
A bi-monthly newsletter with everything about ragtime - past and present; since 1967; also sheet music ads and articles.

Rock 'N' Roll

Collectors

Jim Weaver
405 Dunbar
Pittsburgh, PA 15235-5218
e-mail: weaverjim@aol.com
Wants 1950s-1960s rock 'n' roll photo cover sheet music; send lists and offers.

SHEFFIELD

(see also SILVER; SILVERPLATE)

Appraisers

James C. Voors
Court of King James
515 West Wayne St.
Fort Wayne, IN 46802-2123
ph: 219-426-3234
Specializes in Sheffield fused plate, first and second periods, especially with heraldry; also in 19th century Victorian silverplate (Elkington, Creswick, James Dixon, etc.) and in sterling, hallmarked, and Continental silver.

SHELLS

(see AMMUNITION & EXPLOSIVE ORDNANCE, Shell Casings; SEASHELLS; TRENCH ART)

SHIP RELATED

(see also NAUTICAL ANTIQUES; SHIPPING; STEAMBOAT COLLECTIBLES; TITANIC MEMORABILIA)

Experts

Sara Conklin
Nautical Appraisals
239 Sierra Pt. Rd.
Brisbane, CA 94005-1664
ph: 415-467-6249
fax: 415-467-6249
e-mail: sconklin2@earthlink.com
Managed the collections of the National Maritime Museum in San Francisco for ten years & is an expert in appraising ship models, ships-in-bottles, marine art, scrimshaw, figureheads, paper ephemera, instruments, whaling, diving equipment.

U.S.S. Constitution

Dealers

Tim O'Callaghan
305 St. Lawrence Rd.
P.O. Box 512
Northville, MI 48167
ph: 248-449-2652
e-mail: timothyo@ameritech.net
Wants USS Constitution "Old Ironsides" items, especially items made from the ship in the 1920s and sold to raise money for restoration; also wants postal covers from her 1931-1934 cruise around the US; other related items considered.

Museums/Libraries

U.S.S. Constitution Museum
P.O. Box 1812
Boston, MA 02129
ph: 617-426-1812
e-mail: info@ussconstitutionmuseum.org
web: http://www.ussconstitutionmuseum.org/

Warships

Clubs/Associations

International Naval Research Organization
Magazine: Warship International
5905 Reinwood Drive
Toledo, OH 43613
web: http://www.primenet.com/~inro/
Dedicated to the study of post-1860 naval vessels: histories, elements of ballistics, design, careers, etc.; magazine issued quarterly.

Collectors

Stan Dickinson
307 1/2 E. Lake St., Apt. B
Petoskey, MI 49770
ph: 616-347-1022
Collects prints or pictures of Spanish American War era, including U.S. Navy war ships.

SHIPPING

(see also NAUTICAL ANTIQUES; SHIP RELATED; STEAMBOAT COLLECTIBLES)

Canadian

Dealers

Michael Rice
Michael Rice Collectibles
P.O. Box 286
Saanichton, British Columbia V8M 2C5
Canada
ph: 250-652-9412
e-mail: mrice@pacificcoast.net
Looking for paper items from Canadian steamships and paddle wheelers, particularly menus, passenger lists, deck plans & similar items; also wants any envelopes used on board with appropriate postal markings such as "Posted on Board", etc.

Chesapeake Bay Steamship

Collectors

James Tigner, Jr.
P.O. Box 700
Fairfield, PA 17320-0770
e-mail: antqpapr@mail.cvn.net
Collector wants to buy memorabilia relating to the Chesapeake Bay area steamship lines: time tables, brochures, tickets, menus, photographs, etc.

Great Lakes Related

Dealers

Kenneth Benjamin
Island Shipyard, The
P.O. Box 599
Put In Bay, OH 43456-0599
ph: 419-285-2585
fax: 419-285-2585
e-mail: ksb@kenben.com
Specializes in genuine Great Lakes nautical antiques and ship models.

Michael Kujat
Anchor In Antiques
2122 W. U.S. 2
Saint Ignace, MI 49781-9647
ph: 906-643-8112 or 906-643-9917
Specializes in Great Lakes nautical items.

Experts

James A. Baumhofer
P.O. Box 4302
Saint Paul, MN 55104-0302
Great Lakes ships, books, pictures, photos; Green's or other directories.

SHIPS-IN-BOTTLES

(see NAUTICAL ANTIQUES, Models [Ships-In-Bottles])

SHIRT STUDS

(see CLOTHING & ACCESSORIES, Vintage; CUFF LINKS)

SHMOOS

Dealers

Barry Lutsky
31 Longfield Dr.
Neshanic, NJ 08853
ph: 201-369-7367
e-mail: shmoomania@aol.com
Buys, sells, trades anything Shmoo: figurines, salt & peppers, ash trays, clocks, vinyl, 3D, paper, etc.

SHOE HORNS

Dealers

Charles & Joan Rhoden
Rhoden's Antiques
8693 N 1950 East Road
Georgetown, IL 61846-6264
ph: 217-662-8046 or 217-662-8440
fax: 217-662-8223
Wants unusual shoe horns.

SHOESHINE STANDS

(see BARBERSHOP COLLECTIBLES; SHOE HORNS)

SHOULDER PATCHES

(see BADGES; MILITARIA; PATCHES)

SHRUNKEN HEADS

(see MORBID & ODD ITEMS; SKELETONS)

SIGNS

(see ADVERTISING COLLECTIBLES; BREWERIANA; GAS STATION COLLECTIBLES; HIGHWAY COLLECTIBLES; LAMPS & LIGHTING, Neon; MARINE CORPS ITEMS)

SILHOUETTES

(see also FOLK ART)

Collectors

Lester E. Sender
23500 Mercantile Rd.
Cleveland, OH 44122-5914
ph: 216-595-0000
fax: 216-595-1111
Buys and sells pre-1920 American and Continental silhouettes.

Experts

Alda Horner
3700 Dean Dr., Unit #3301
Ventura, CA 93003
ph: 805-642-7953
Author, consultant, and dealer.

Museums/Libraries

Peabody Essex Museum
Essex & Libert Streets
Salem, MA 01970
ph: 978-745-9500 or 800-745-4054
e-mail: pem@pem.org
web: http://www.pem.org

National Portrait Gallery
8th & F Streets N.W.
Washington, DC 20560-0001
ph: 202-357-2866
fax: 202-786-2565
web: http://www.npg.si.edu

Repro. Sources

Ellen Mischo
Profiles
P.O. Box 412
Leesburg, VA 22075-0412
ph: 703-771-7342
Makes and sells authentic 18th and 19th century reproduction silhouettes.

Glass

Experts

Shirley R. Mace
Shadow Enterprises
P.O. Box 1602
Mesilla Park, NM 88047-1602
ph: 505-524-6717
fax: 505-523-0940
e-mail: shadow-ent@zianet.com
Author of "Silhouette Collectibles on Glass" (1992) and price guide to silhouette collectibles; painted black on reverse of glass; sold in dimestores from the 1920s to 1950s; often with advertising and attached thermometers or calendars.

SILK EMBROIDERIES

(see also STEVENGRAPHS; TEXTILES)

SILVER

(see also BOOKS, Reference [Silver]; FLATWARE; GLASS, Silver Overlay; GEMS & JEWELRY; REPAIR/RESTORATION/CONSERVATION, Metal Items; SHEFFIELD; SILVERPLATE; SPOONS; TABLEWARE)

Appraisers

Linda Dawson
Dawson's
128 American Rd.
Morris Plains, NJ 07950
ph: 973-984-6900
fax: 973-984-6956
e-mail: dawson1@idt.net
web: http://www.dawsonsauction.com/
Accredited Senior Appraiser in the American Society of Appraisers and silver specialist on the "Antiques Roadshow."

James C. Voors
Court of King James
515 West Wayne St.
Fort Wayne, IN 46802-2123
ph: 219-426-3234
Specializes in Sheffield fused plate, first and second periods, especially with heraldry; also in 19th century Victorian silverplate (Elkington, Creswick, James Dixon, etc.) and in sterling, hallmarked, and Continental silver.

Dewey W. Smith, ASA
Dewey W. Smith, ASA Antique Appraisals
7346 S. Alton Way #10-G
Littleton, CO 80120-2327
ph: 303-930-9899
fax: 303-930-9919
e-mail: dwsmithasa@aol.com

Kathleen M. Bailey, ISA CAPP
Antique Appraisal & Estate Sale Services
9416 1st Ave., NE, #311
Seattle, WA 98115
ph: 425-746-2777
fax: 425-746-3793

Auction Services

Stuart Slavid
Skinner, Inc.
357 Main St.
Bolton, MA 01740-1104
ph: 978-779-6241
fax: 978-779-5144
e-mail: info@skinnerinc.com
web: http://www.skinnerinc.com
Established in 1964, Skinner Inc. is the fifth largest auction house in the US; has offices in Bolton and Boston, MA.

Michael B. Grogan
Grogan & Company Auctioneers
22 Harris St.
Dedham, MA 02026
ph: 781-461-9500
fax: 781-461-9625
e-mail: grogans@groganco.com
web: http://www.groganco.com/

Christie's
502 Park Ave.
New York, NY 10022
ph: 212-546-1000
fax: 212-980-8163
web: http://www.christies.com

John McClain
York Town Auction Inc.
1625 Haviland Rd.
York, PA 17404
ph: 717-751-0211
fax: 717-767-7729
e-mail: yorktownauction@cyberia.com
Antique & specialty auctions, lecture & appraisal services; antiques also purchased; American & English furniture, related specialties & accessories, Americana, folk art, jewelry, art, clocks & watches, militaria, steins, Oriental rugs.

Clubs/Associations

Jeffrey Herman, Ex. Dir.
Society of American Silversmiths
P.O. Box 704
Chepachet, RI 02814
ph: 401-567-7800
fax: 401-567-7801
e-mail: sas@silversmithing.com
web: http://www.silversmithing.com
Answers questions on silversmithing techniques, conservation and restoration, maker's mark identification and all other silver-related inquiries.

International Association of Silver Art Collectors
Newsletter: Silver Bugle, The
P.O. Box 28415
Seattle, WA 98118-8415
Newsletter published six times per year.

Collectors

Bruce Johnson
P.O. Box 8773
Asheville, NC 28814-8773
ph: 828-628-1915
fax: 828-628-4070
e-mail: bj1912@aol.com
Wants to buy silver marked DODGE or ASHEVILLE SILVERCRAFT.

Bill Simmons
8955 NW 19th St.
Coral Springs, FL 33071-6109
ph: 954-340-0734
e-mail: wsim1206@aol.com
Wants most sterling flatware and hollowware, especially Tiffany, Georg Jensen, and early Gorham.

Dealers

Spencer Gordon
Spencer Marks
P.O. Box 303
East Walpole, MA 02032
ph: 508-668-6990
e-mail: sg3@worldnet.att.net
web: http://www.spencermarks.com
Fine American and English antiques and silver; also books about antiques.

Steve Duffy
Sea Eagles Sterling
20 Bridle Dr.
Winsted, CT 06098-3422
ph: 860-379-5749
fax: 860-379-5749
Specializes in active, inactive, and obsolete sterling silver flatware.

John C. Foy
P.O. Box 476
Fanwood, NJ 07023-0476
ph: 908-654-3867
Buys and sells antique American coin silver, American sterling silver and souvenir spoons, and English sterling silver; also sells books on silver.

Nathan Horowicz
Nathan Horowicz Antiques
1050 2nd Ave., Gallery 82
New York, NY 10022
ph: 800-214-6320 or 212-755-6320
fax: 212-755-6438
Large assortment of flatware, tea sets, hollowware; Tiffany, Georg Jensen; all American and European manufacturers.

Fortunoff
681 5th Ave. at 54th St.
New York, NY 10022
ph: 212-758-6660
fax: 212-715-5906
e-mail: service@fortunoff.com
web: http://www.dir-dd.com/fortunoff.html/
Focuses on 19th and 20th century American, English, coin and Chinese silver; has over 1000 pieces in stock including tea sets, tureens, centerpieces, candlesticks, vases, pitchers, flatware and more.

Lauren Stanley Gallery
300 E. 51st St.
New York, NY 10022
ph: 212-888-6732
fax: 212-486-2503
e-mail: info@laurenstanley.com
web: http://www.laurenstanley.com/
Specializing in American silver from 1840 to 1900: Shiebler, Tiffany, Gale, Wood & Hughes, Whiting, Gorham, Krider, Dominick & Haff, Duhme, Wendt, Kidney & Johnston, Kirk, Coles, and others; Medallion pattern flatware a specialty.

Gary Niederkorn
Gary Niederkorn Silver
Newspaper: Silver Edition
2005 Locust St.
Philadelphia, PA 19103-5606
ph: 215-567-2606
fax: 215-567-2606
Specializes in 19th and 20th cent. silver novelties, Christmas ornaments, napkin rings, Judaica, picture frames, etc.; also Tiffany, Jensen, Mexican.

Gerald Shultz
Antique Gallery, The
8523 Germantown Ave.
Philadelphia, PA 19118-3316
ph: 215-248-1700
fax: 215-247-8411
Interested in sterling silver and Victorian silverplate (no flatware): Jensen, Tiffany, Stone, Kirk, etc.

Rita Lang
Silver 2000
"Sara's Fancy"
Middleburg, VA 20117-3110
ph: 540-687-4604
fax: 540-687-4604
e-mail: silver2000@erols.com
web: http://www.silver2000.com
Expert and dealer in early American silver.

Caren Fine
11603 Gowrie Ct.
Potomac, MD 20854-3623
ph: 301-299-6886 or 301-299-2116
Wants to buy silver objects by Liberty, Tiffany, Georg Jensen, Spratling, Shreve & Co., Jarvie, Kalo, Lebolt; jewelry by F.G. Nale, Edward Oakes; Judaica.

Pikesville Jewelry & Coin Exchange
1350 Reisterstown Rd.
Baltimore, MD 21208-3803
ph: 410-653-3430
fax: 410-653-8463

Beverly H. Bremer
Beverly Bremer Silver Shop
3164 Peachtree Rd. NE
Atlanta, GA 30305
ph: 404-261-4009 or 800-270-4009
fax: 404-261-5742
web: http://www.beverlybremer.com
Appraises, buys, sells and matches sterling silver flatware, and new and antique sterling silver hollowware & giftware; large shop; sterling silver only; want lists kept; mail order; totally computerized.

Peter Thurber
Ritzi & Thurber, Inc.
160 S. Beach St.
Daytona Beach, FL 32114
ph: 904-252-2552 or 904-226-8489
fax: 904-226-8490
e-mail: ritzi1881@earthlink.net
web: http://www.ritzi-thurber.com/
Founded in 1881, firm purchases all types of silver and Sheffield, from scrap sterling to fine English, French and Russian presentation pieces; very interested in purchasing American coin silver and any type of Art Nouveau sterling.

Atlantic Silver & China
7405 N.W. 57th St.
Tamarac, FL 33319
ph: 800-368-3153 or 954-720-4559
fax: 954-720-4577
e-mail: info@atlanticsilver.com
web: http://www.atlanticsilver.com
Inactive and active sterling silver flatware and hollowware; buys and sells.

Debra Bonner
Colonial Silver Shoppe
20 Gaylan Court
Montgomery, AL 36109
ph: 800-675-4837 or 334-272-7282
Gorham, Wallace, International, Towle, Kirk-Stieff, Lunt.

Robin & June Greenwald
June Greenwald Antiques, Inc.
3096 Mayfield Rd.
Cleveland, OH 44118
ph: 215-932-5535
Buys and sells 19th and 20th century silver; offers a matching service.

Ted Rickard
Silver Service
ph: 847-256-5900
fax: 847-256-5952
e-mail: trick2@juno.com
Specializing in matching discontinued American and English sterling silver flatware; also locates antique sterling silver flatware.

Mark
Silverwarehouse
4311 NE Vivion Rd.
Kansas City, MO 64119-2890
ph: 816-454-1990
fax: 816-454-1605
e-mail: mark@silverwarehouse.com
web: http://www.silverwarehouse.com
Buys, sells, repairs silverware and hollowware of all types; also silver books, silverware chests, silver care products, online resources, appraisals, repairs.

Connie & Bill McNally
McNally Co. Antiques, The
P.O. Box 1048
6033 Paseo Delicias
Rancho Santa Fe, CA 92067
ph: 858-756-1922
fax: 858-756-9928
e-mail: mcnally@silvermag.com
Buys, sells, collects and specializes in 18th and 19th century furnishings, silver and objets d'art.

Judy Brown
P.O. Box 5368
Frazier Park, CA 93222
ph: 805-242-5411
Mail order only dealer of gold and silver smalls: boxes, chatelaines, match safes, sewing items, Victorian or earlier frames and silverplate items; long time dealer.

Argentum - The Leopard's Head
414 Jackson St., Ste. 101
San Francisco, CA 94111
ph: 415-296-7757
fax: 415-296-7233
e-mail: info@argentum-theleopard.com
web: http://www.argentum-theleopard.com
Antique silver from all periods bought and sold; large shop; full catalog with prices available online; specializing in 18th c. English silver, early American and Victorian silver; no pattern matching except Shreve & Co., San Francisco.

Beth Scott
Affordable Jewelry & Precious Metals
304 SW Washington St.
Portland, OR 97204
ph: 800-690-4995 or 503-224-7520
fax: 503-227-4204
e-mail: sight@ajpm.com
web: http://www.ajpm.com
Gold, silver and platinum bullion dealers.

Juanita Mallorie
Sterling Shop, The
P.O. Box 595
Silverton, OR 97381-0595
ph: 503-873-6315
e-mail: juanita@sterlingshop.com
web: http://www.sterlingshop.com
Sterling and silverplate flatware matching service.

Kathleen M. Bailey, ISA CAPP
Antique Appraisal & Estate Sale Service - K. Bailey
9416 1st Ave., NE, #311
Seattle, WA 98115
ph: 425-746-2777
fax: 425-746-3793
Specializes in unusual sterling 18th through 20th century silver.

Experts

V. Stephen Vaughan
c/o E.B. Horn Co.
429 Washington St.
Boston, MA 02108
ph: 617-542-3902
Specializes in 19th century American silver; vast library of period research materials.

Benedict J. Hastings
2006 Columbia Rd. N.W.
Washington, DC 20009
ph: 202-483-8575
Specializes in fine silver, Russian decorative arts, Russian icons, 18th and 19th century porcelain, military medals, decorations and orders.

Gwendolyn L. Kelso
Rampant Lion, The
P.O. Box 5887
Washington, DC 20016-1487
ph: 202-364-2431
fax: 202-364-2431
Silver expert, appraiser, dealer; also silver reference service with extensive library; sells books about silver for appraisers, collectors, museums.

Jennifer F. Goldsborough
1688 Coventry Place
Annapolis, MD 21401
ph: 401-841-2634
American silver expert, lecturer, curator.

Suzy Van Massenhove
Fox in Flanders, A
3703 Whispering Lane
Falls Church, VA 22041
ph: 703-256-3094

Gary D. Gardner
200 College St.
Hodgenville, KY 42748-1404
ph: 502-358-3222
Expert, collector specializing in pre-1870 Southern coin grade silver crafted by silversmiths in the South; wants to purchase & research, especially KY, TN, VA, hollowware and pre-1830 spoons, ledgers, receipts, inventories for study.

Rod Tinkler
Silver Vault, The
P.O. Box 421
Barrington, IL 60011-0421
ph: 847-381-3101
fax: 847-381-3101
e-mail: SilverVlt@aol.com
Buy, sell, trade, and appraises American, English and Continental silver.

Internet Resources

SM Publications
353 West 56th St., MS7A
New York, NY 10019
ph: 212-246-5060 or 212-246-5216
e-mail: info@SMPub.com
web: http://www.smpub.com/
An Internet resource center for silver collectors, dealers and appraisers: books on silver marks, evaluating silver, identification; for flatware hollowware, silversmiths, silver jewelry, silver antiques; also covers gold.

David R. Clarke
Antidata, SilverMine
4 Mortimer Buildings
Bridge Street, Nailsworth GL6 0AA
U.K.
ph: (44)(0) 1453 836735
e-mail: a.data@virgin.net
web: http://freespace.virgin.net/a.data/index.htm
SilverMine is a stand-alone hypertext program to aid in the identification and study of marks struck on British silver; also contains brief details of some 250 American silver makers.

Museums/Libraries

Museum of Fine Arts, Boston
465 Huntington Ave.
Boston, MA 02115-5523
ph: 617-267-9300
e-mail: webmaster@mfa.org
web: http://www.mfa.org/home.html

Currier Gallery of Art, The
201 Myrtle Way
Manchester, NH 03104
ph: 603-669-6144
web: http://www.currier.org/

Wadsworth Atheneum
600 Main St.
Hartford, CT 06103
ph: 860-278-2670
fax: 860-527-0803
e-mail: info@wadsworthatheneum.org
web: http://www.wadsworthatheneum.org/
Collections include the Elizabeth B. Miles Silver Collection and the Philip H. Hammerslough Collection of American Silver.

Yale University Art Gallery
P.O. Box 20871
New Haven, CT 06520-8271
ph: 203-432-0600 or 203-432-0601
web: http://www.yale.edu/artgallery/

David Warren
Bayou Bend Collection & Gardens, The
P.O. Box 6826
Houston, TX 77265-6826
ph: 281-639-7750
fax: 281-639-7770
e-mail: hirsch@mfah.org
web: http://mfah.org/bayou.html

Periodicals

Nanette Monmonier-Schweitzer
Price Guide: Silver Update, The
P.O. Box 2157
Ellicott City, MD 21041-2157
ph: 410-750-3282
fax: 410-418-5128
Provides prices for current American and popular foreign sterling silver flatware manufacturers; published three timer each year.

Nanette Monmonier-Schweitzer
Price Guide: Sterling Silver Hollowware Update, The
P.O. Box 2157
Ellicott City, MD 21041-2157
ph: 410-750-3282
fax: 410-418-5128
Provides illustrations and prices for current American sterling silver hollowware.

Newsletter: Silver & Gold Report
P.O. Box 109665
West Palm Beach, FL 33410
ph: 800-289-9222 or 561-627-3300
fax: 561-625-6685
e-mail: sgr@weissinc.com
web: http://www.wessinc.com
Financial advice newsletter in precious medals, and gold & silver bullion and coins.

Connie McNally
Silver Magazine Inc.
Magazine: Silver Magazine
P.O. Box 9690
Rancho Santa Fe, CA 92067-4690
ph: 800-756-1054 or 858-756-1054
fax: 858-756-9928
e-mail: silver@silvermag.com
web: http://www.silvermag.com/
Top quality bi-monthly magazine for silver collectors; English, Continental, and Colonial silver; well illustrated articles.

Repair Services

Stephen Smithers
Smithers Restorations
1057 Hawley Rd.
Ashfield, MA 01330-9626
ph: 413-625-2994
Restoration of fine early silver and brass; design and making of hand hammered silver hollowware and brass lighting (chandeliers, lanterns, sconces, candlesticks); also demonstrations, silversmithing talks for museums and civic groups.

Beth A. Perry
Beth A. Perry, Hand Engraving
115 Newbury Street, #502
Boston, MA 02116
ph: 617-859-8805
fax: 617-247-4940
Hand engraving, inscriptions, coats-of-arms, monogramming, logos, custom designs, engraver of fine jewelry and tableware for 16 years; call or send sample for estimate to copy old engraving of any style or to create new design.

Jeffrey Herman
Jeffrey Herman Silver Restoration & Conservation
P.O. Box 704
Chepachet, RI 02814-0704
ph: 401-567-7800 or 800-584-2352
fax: 401-567-7801
e-mail: jherman@silversmithing.com
web: http://www.silversmithing.com/jherman/
Museum quality silver restoration and conservation; 14 years in business; founder Society of American Silversmiths; listed with Jewelers Board of Trade; website has complete list of services, pricing, and special silver care guide.

Joseph J. Pistilli
Orum Silver Co., Inc.
51 S. Vine St.
P.O. Box 805
Meriden, CT 06450-0805
ph: 203-237-3037
fax: 203-237-3037
e-mail: Orum@ct1.nai.net
web: http://w3.nai.net/~maddog/orum.htm
Repairing, restoring, replating of antique and old silver, gold, nickel; brass & copper plating; cleaning, buffing, polishing.

Zophy's Fine Silver Plating
4702 Park St.
Peterboro, NY 13134
ph: 315-684-3062
Fine restoration for over 40 years of copper, brass, sterling, pewter.

Abercombie & Co.
9159A Brookeville Rd.
Silver Spring, MD 20910
ph: 301-585-2385
fax: 301-587-5708
e-mail: abernco@comm-plus.net
web: http://www.silverplaters.com
Replates silverplate; repairs all sorts of metal; silver, brass, copper; also welding.

Harry Stock
Coventry Silversmiths
228 S. Washington St.
Alexandria, VA 22314
ph: 703-684-6821
Silver plating and restoration: combs, brushes, mirrors, knife blades replaced.

Estes-Simmons Silverplating, Ltd.
1050 Northside Dr., NW
Atlanta, GA 30318
ph: 404-875-9581 or 800-645-4193
fax: 404-873-4826
e-mail: info@estes-simmons.com
web: http://www.estes-simmons.com/
Repairs silver, silverplate, gold, pewter, brass and copper; also replates silver, gold, brass, nickel, copper.

Robert Kaynes
Senti-Metal Company, The
1919 Memory Lane, Dept. 39CA97
Columbus, OH 43209
ph: 800-345-8112 or 614-252-0353
fax: 614-252-4602
e-mail: bronzeinfo@bronshoe.com
web: http://www.antiqnet.com/SentiMetal/
Will restore your silver at factory-direct prices; brings back life to old, worn silver heirlooms; quadruple silverplating is covered by 25 year warranty; write for FREE catalog.

Paul Trageser
Paul Trageser Metalsmith
10330 Howard Rd.
Harrison, OH 45030
ph: 513-367-6226
Finest quality silver repairs.

Silverwarehouse
4311 NE Vivion Rd.
Kansas City, MO 64119-2890
ph: 816-454-1990
fax: 816-454-1605
e-mail: mark@silverwarehouse.com
web: http://www.silverwarehouse.com
Expert knife reblading, silverware repair, polishing, full-time silversmiths on staff; also sells loose knife blades; also stainless, silverplate, pewter, Dirilyte.

Carmelo Tringali
Colonial Silver
1219 Forest Ave.
Pacific Grove, CA 93950
ph: 831-375-0355
Recommended for silverplating and replating.

Tim Maple
Omega Silver Smithing Inc.
11130 117th Pl. NE
Kirkland, WA 98033
ph: 425-822-3727
Expert repair and restoration of fine silver, bronze, silverplate, spelter, brass, pewter and copper; from tea sets to brass beds, chandeliers, new knife blades, mirrors and combs; full service restoration.

Repro. Sources

Stephen Smithers
1057 Hawley Rd.
Ashfield, MA 01330-9626
ph: 413-625-2994
Design and making of hand hammered silver hollowware & brass lighting (chandeliers, lanterns, sconces, candlesticks); also restoration of fine early silver and brass; demonstrations, silversmithing talks for museums and civic groups.

Suppliers

Jeffrey Herman
Herman's Best Silver Care Products
P.O. Box 704
Chepachet, RI 02814-0704
ph: 401-567-7800 or 800-584-2352
fax: 401-567-7801
e-mail: jherman@silversmithing.com
web: http://www.silversmithing.com/jherman/
Supplies and instructions for caring for silver.

Baltimore

Dealers

Patrick Duggan
Imperial Half Bushel
831 N. Howard St.
Baltimore, MD 21201
ph: 410-462-1192
Specializes in Baltimore, Maryland silver.

Chinese

Experts

Stuart Slavid
9 Gryzboska Circle
Farmingham, MA 01702
ph: 508-620-2531
e-mail: wedghead@pop.ma.ultranet.com
Interested in Chinese silver.

Christofle

Man./Prod./Dist.

Christofle
web: http://www.christofle.com
Manufacturer of fine silver flatware and hollowware, porcelain, table linens and crystal; web site lists retail outlets worldwide.

Georg Jensen

Dealers

Soren Jensen
Chelsea Antique Bldg, Shop 306
110 W. 25th St.
New York, NY 10001
ph: 212-645-3671
fax: 212-924-5375
e-mail: soren@interport.net
web: http://www.jensensilver.com
Specializes in vintage Georg Jensen silver; also other Scandinavian designers, silversmiths and jewelers.

Gary Niederkorn
Gary Niederkorn Silver
Newspaper: Silver Edition
2005 Locust St.
Philadelphia, PA 19103-5606
ph: 215-567-2606
fax: 215-567-2606
Specializes in hollowware and flatware matching for Georg Jensen silver and other Danish makers.

Ken Forster
5501 Seminary Rd., Ste. 1311 South
Falls Church, VA 22041
ph: 703-379-1142
Dealer in American art pottery and tiles, specializing in American tiles from 1860 to 1940; also Art Nouveau, Art Deco, Georg Jensen silver, and American Modernism.

Matching Services

Caryl Rose Unger
Imagination Unlimited
4302 Alton Rd., Ste. 820
Miami, FL 33140-2893
ph: 305-534-2214
fax: 305-538-0914
e-mail: info@imaginationunlimited.com
web: http://www.imaginationunlimited.com
Specializes in Georg Jensen silver; offers a Jensen silver matching service; buys and sells Jensen silver: single pieces or sets, jewelry, serving pieces, hollowware, and other Danish silver; reprints of their Jensen articles available.

Gorham

Man./Prod./Dist.

Gorham, Inc.
100 Lenox Dr.
Lawrenceville, NJ 08648
ph: 609-896-2800 or 800-635-3669
web: http://www.lenox.com
Sterling and stainless steel flatware, sterling and silverplated hollowware; fine china, crystal stemware, giftware and dolls; a division of Lenox Brands.

International

Man./Prod./Dist.

International Silver Co.
175 McClellan Hwy.
Boston, MA 02128
ph: 617-561-2200
fax: 617-569-8484
web: http://www.wallacesilver.com/html/main/corporate.html

Kirk Stieff

Dealers

Michael A. Merrill
Michael A. Merrill, Inc.
Newsletter: Silver Letter, The
Crestar Bank Building
2045 York Rd.
Timonium, MD 21093
ph: 410-453-9400
e-mail: merrill@home.com
web: http://www.pm-connect.com/mmerrill/
Kirk & Steiff specialists; pattern matching, bridal registry, silver replating, appraisals; newsletter lists and pictures items for sale including sterling silver and books about silver.

Man./Prod./Dist.

Kirk Stieff Co. Outlet Store
800 Wyman Park Dr.
Baltimore, MD 21211
ph: 410-338-6080 or 800-531-7946
fax: 410-338-6097
Sterling, silverplate, stainless steel and pewter flatware, sterling and silverplate hollowware; pewter, jewelry; a division of Lenox Brands.

Lunt

Man./Prod./Dist.

Lunt Silversmiths
298 Federal St.
Greenfield, MA 01301
ph: 413-774-2774 or 800-242-2774
fax: 413-774-5349
e-mail: info@lunt-silversmiths.com
web: http://www.lunt-silversmiths.com/
Sterling and plated flatware and hollowware.

Mexican

Collectors

Jill A. Crawford
Crawford Design
7377 Birdview Ave.
Malibu, CA 90265
ph: 310-457-8076
fax: 310-457-3453
Interested in buying Spratling and other Mexican silver.

Dealers

Gary Niederkorn
Gary Niederkorn Silver
Newspaper: Silver Edition
2005 Locust St.
Philadelphia, PA 19103-5606
ph: 215-567-2606
fax: 215-567-2606
Specializes in 19th and 20th cent. silver novelties, Christmas ornaments, napkin rings, Judaica, picture frames, etc.; also Tiffany, Jensen, Mexican.

Gloria Quincy
Q-Tiques Vintage Jewelry & Collectibles
6475 Ferber Road
Jacksonville, FL 32277
ph: 904-745-0618
fax: 904-743-9159
e-mail: junebug@southeast.net
web: http://www.tias.com/stores/qtiques/
Specializes in costume designer jewelry, bakelite, and Mexican Silver.

Susan Morton
Mexican Silver Shop
2542 S. IH-35, Ste. 200-238
Round Rock, TX 78664
ph: 512-930-0124
e-mail: disorderlygirl@noisyboy.com
web: http://www.noisyboy.com
Specializes in silver items and other metalware from Mexico, pre-1960.

Jimmy Vitanza
Peregrine Galleries
508 Brinkerhoff Ave.
Santa Barbara, CA 93101-3441
ph: 805-963-3134
fax: 805-963-3134

Sheila Pamfiloff
Glitter Box, The
P.O.Box 35
Walnut Creek, CA 94596
ph: 510-937-7554
e-mail: pamfil@crl.com
web: http://www.crl.com/~pamfil/GLITTER.HTM
Specializing in vintage designer costume jewelry including Haskell, Schiaparelli, Hagler, Eisenberg, DeMario, Mazer, Boucher; also vintage Mexican sterling silver from the great designers of Taxco.

Experts

Carole A. Berk
Carole A. Berk, Ltd.
4918 Fairmont Ave.
Bethesda, MD 20814
ph: 800-382-2413 or 301-656-0355
fax: 301-652-5859
e-mail: cab@caroleberk.com
web: http://www.caroleberk.com/
Specializes in 20th century decorative art: Clarice Cliff, Keith Murray, Charlotte Rhead, Mexican silver, Bakelite, and costume jewelry; co-author of "Mexican Silver."

Nielloware

Internet Resources

Charles Dittell
Siam Sterling Nielloware Site, The
e-mail: cdittel@gate.net
web: http://www.gate.net/~cdittel/
Nielloware is silver and black Thai sterling silver pieces popular in the 1950s through 1970s.

Old Newbury Crafters

Man./Prod./Dist.

Jeanne Pritchard
Old Newbury Crafters
36 Main St.
Amesbury, MA 01913-2807
ph: 978-388-0983 or 800-343-1388
fax: 978-388-8430
e-mail: info@silvercrafters.com
web: http://www.silvercrafters.com/
Sterling silver flatware and hollowware, pewter giftware.

Oneida

Man./Prod./Dist.

Oneida Silversmiths
Kenwood Station
Oneida, NY 13421-2829
ph: 315-361-3000
e-mail: sales@oneida.com
web: http://www.oneida.com/
Sterling silver, silverplate, gold electroplate, stainless steel, flatware; stainless and silverplate hollowware, crystal stemware and hollowware.

Reed & Barton

Man./Prod./Dist.

Reed & Barton
144 W. Britannia St.
Taunton, MA 02780
ph: 508-824-6611 or 800-822-1824
fax: 508-822-7269
Produces china, crystal, silver, silverplate, and stainless flatware, collectible plates, bells, dolls, ornaments and accessories.

Scrap

Dealers

Jim Sciuto
GoldTek
P.O. Box 128
Methuen, MA 01844
ph: 978-374-2254 or 603-645-4717
fax: 978-373-1088
Buys scrap gold and silver: class rings, wedding bands, gold coins, gold watches, gold plated circuit boards, gold solder, gold wire, gold teeth; also scrap sterling silver flatware, coins, bars, silver flake, silver anodes, etc.

Greg Walsh
32 River View Lane
P.O. Box 747
Potsdam, NY 13676-0747
ph: 315-265-9111 or 800-371-9286
fax: 315-265-9222
e-mail: gwalsh@northnet.org
web: http://www.walshauction.com/
Wants to buy gold and silver rings, coins, estate jewelry, pocket watches, diamonds, sterling silver items, scrap gold, broken or damaged jewelry, dental gold, etc.; 24-hour turn around; ship on approval or call for quote; since 1979.Dup

Michael A. Merrill
Michael A. Merrill, Inc.
Crestar Bank Building
2045 York Rd.
Timonium, MD 21093
ph: 410-453-9400
e-mail: merrill@home.com
web: http://www.pm-connect.com/mmerrill/
Buying precious metals from the public, dealers since 1974; buys scrap gold, diamonds, old gold, dental gold, school rings, gold & silver numismatic coins, sterling silver (Kirk & Steiff), Franklin Mint, platinum, palladium, exotics.

Jaime Raskansky
Gold & Silver Traders
723 Main St., Ste. 101B
Houston, TX 77002
ph: 713-520-5111 or 713-223-0777
fax: 713-223-0707
e-mail: gstforex@msn.com
Buys and sells gold and silver scrap and bullion.

Cy Phillips, Jr.
S C Coin & Stamp Co. Inc.
P.O. Drawer 661180
Arcadia, CA 91066-1180
ph: 818-445-8277 or 800-367-0779
fax: 818-445-8278
Tokens, medals, coins, currency, badges, expo. and fair items, scrap gold and silver.

Towle

Man./Prod./Dist.

Mark Roland
Towle Silversmiths
175 McClellan Highway
P.o. Box 9114
Boston, MA 02128-9114
ph: 617-561-2200 or 617-568-1300
fax: 617-568-8134
web: http://www.towlesilver.com/
Sterling silver, silverplate, stainless steel, goldplate, barware.

Wallace

Man./Prod./Dist.

Wallace Silversmiths
175 McClellan Hwy.
Boston, MA 02128
ph: 617-561-2200
fax: 617-569-8484
web: http://www.wallacesilver.com/html/main/corporate.html
Sterling silver, silverplate, stainless steel, pewter flatware and hollow-ware.

SILVERPLATE

(see also FLATWARE; SHEFFIELD; SILVER; REPAIR/RESTORATION/CONSERVATION, Metal Items; TABLEWARE)

Appraisers

James C. Voors
Court of King James
515 West Wayne St.
Fort Wayne, IN 46802-2123
ph: 219-426-3234
Specializes in Sheffield fused plate, first and second periods, especially with heraldry; also in 19th century Victorian silverplate (Elkington, Creswick, James Dixon, etc.) and in sterling, hallmarked, and Continental silver.

Dealers

Paul Severino
Silver & Such
ph: 703-573-0509
e-mail: severinop@aol.com
Specializes in Victorian and Art Nouveau silverplate, hollowware and flatware.

Periodicals

Nanette Monmonier-Schweitzer
Price Guide: Silverplated Hollowware Update, The
P.O. Box 2157
Ellicott City, MD 21041-2157
ph: 410-750-3282
fax: 410-418-5128
Provides illustrations and prices for current American silverplated hollowware manufacturers.

Connie McNally
Silver Magazine Inc.
Magazine: Silver Magazine
P.O. Box 9690
Rancho Santa Fe, CA 92067-4690
ph: 800-756-1054 or 858-756-1054
fax: 858-756-9928
e-mail: silver@silvermag.com
web: http://www.silvermag.com/
Top quality bi-monthly magazine for silver collectors; English, Continental, and Colonial silver; well illustrated articles.

SILVERPLATED FLATWARE

(see FLATWARE)

SILVERWARE

(see FLATWARE)

SIMMONS HARDWARE

(see KEEN KUTTER [SIMMONS HARDWARE])

SINGING BIRDS

(see MUSIC BOXES, Birds & Bird Boxes [Singing])

SKATING

(see SPORTS COLLECTIBLES, Ice Skating; SPORTS COLLECTIBLES, Roller Skating; SPORTS COLLECTIBLES, Skateboards)

SKELETONS

(see also ANIMAL TROPHIES; FOSSILS; HAIRWORK; MORBID & ODD ITEMS)

Dealers

Antique Workshop Inc.
150 Aerial Way
Syosset, NY 11791
ph: 516-933-6213
Wants stuffed real animals, heads, birds; also skulls and skeletons.

Bone Room, The
1569 Solano
Berkeley, CA 94707-2116
ph: 510-526-5252
Wants to buy ivory, skeletons, tusks, skulls, fossils, insect collections, shrunken heads, etc.

SLAVERY ITEMS

(see also BLACK MEMORABILIA)

Collectors

Danny Drain
Slave Mart Museum "Preserving the Past"
P.O. Box 340569
Jamaica, NY 11434
ph: 718-529-2876
fax: 718-529-2876
e-mail: Slavemart@aol.com
web: http://www.slavemart.com/
Wants any slave related items: documents, letters, photographs, slave tokens, slave passes, slave chains and locks, collars, paintings, bills of sale, slave tags, etc.

Gene Peters
'Tiques
P.O. Box 3267
Farmingdale, NY 11735-0679
ph: 516-842-9549
Wants documents, pictures, and artifacts relating to American slavery.

James C. Allen
1187 Wildcreek Trail NE
Atlanta, GA 30324
ph: 404-321-5784 or 888-211-1663
Wants memorabilia and objects from the slave era through the Civil War Movement; also lynching postcards and photos.

Slave Tags

Collectors

Rich Hartzog
World Exonumia
P.O. Box 4143
Rockford, IL 61110-0643
ph: 815-226-0771
fax: 815-397-7662
e-mail: hartzog@exonumia.com
web: http://www.exonumia.com/
Wants slave tags, and other Black tokens and medals.

SLIDE RULES

(see also CALCULATORS; COMPUTERS; INSTRUMENTS & DEVICES, Scientific)

Clubs/Associations

Wayne Lehnert, Sec.
Oughtred Society
Journal: Journal of the Oughtred Society
P.O. Box 99077
Emeryville, CA 94662
ph: 925-754-9337
e-mail: 75770.231@compuserve.com
web: http://www.comcen.com.au/~adavie/slide/oughtred.html
For people interested in the history and collection of slide rules; annual meetings feature slide rule exhibits and exchanges of information.

Collectors

Andrew Davie
e-mail: adavie@mad.scientist.com
web: http://www.comcen.com.au/~adavie/slide/
Expert, collector, runs the Slide Rule Trading Post on the Internet.

W. Feely
1172 Lindsay La.
Jenkintown, PA 19046-1839
ph: 215-884-5640
fax: 215-884-8660
Wants slide rules: linear, circular or cylindrical; also books on slide rules, pre-1945 Army Field Manuals, and K&E, Gurley, Buff, Dietzgen, or Burger catalogs.

Cal Frye
125 E. Oak St.
Kent, OH 44240-3825
ph: 330-678-7006
fax: 330-678-7006
e-mail: cj_frye@bigfoot.com
web: http://Phoenix.kent.edu/~cfrye
Wants oddball slide rules: circular, cylindrical, special-purpose, or big (classroom-sized); also wants pocket/portable sundials.

Robert Otnes
2160 Middlefield Rd.
Palo Alto, CA 94301-4022
ph: 650-324-1821
e-mail: bobotnes@mediacity.com
A leading collector of calculating machines and slide rules.

Paul H. Hayashi, PE
18 Tarabrook Dr.
Orinda, CA 94563-3121
ph: 925-254-5074 or 925-253-1038
fax: 925-253-0592
Wants to buy old engineering instruments, slide rules, drafting sets, graphical integrators, planimeters.

Rodger Shepherd, MD
10592 Englewood Dr.
Oakland, CA 94605-5014
ph: 510-632-1680
Treasurer of The Oughtred Society, a club for slide rule collectors.

Wayne Lehnert
P.O. Box 99077
Emeryville, CA 94662
ph: 925-754-9337
e-mail: 75770.231@compuserve.com
web: http://www.comcen.com.au/~adavie/slide/oughtred.html
Secretary of The Oughtred Society, a club for slide rule collectors.

Osborne I. Price
8338 Colombard Ct.
San Jose, CA 95135

Robert De Cesaris
7429 Bree Ann Ct.
Citrus Heights, CA 95610-2455
ph: 916-356-5769
e-mail: rdecesar@pcocd2.intel.com
Actively seeking slide rules and other mechanical calculating devices: especially interested in circular slide rules, special purpose and special function rules, 20" rules, pocket watch type like Boucher, Sperry, Fowler, and others.

Dealers

Charles E. McCallum
Temple & Co.
110 Bittersweet N.E.
Ada, MI 49301
ph: 616-676-3659 or 616-776-2515
fax: 616-752-2500
Interested in slide rules, including circular and cylindrical models, as well as catalogs, and manuals/books on slide rule operations.

Experts

George Duckworth
12602 North 20 Ave.
Phoenix, AZ 85029-2610
ph: 520-582-4626
Author of "Slide Rule Collector's Guide," available from author.

Internet Resources

Andrew Davie
Slide Rule Trading Post
e-mail: adavie@mad.scientist.com
web: http://www.comcen.com.au/~adavie/slide/
THE Internet website for collectors of slide rules; information, pictures, software free for download, a forum and classified adds; links to other Internet sites related to slide rules and mechanical and electronic calculating.

SLOT CARS

(see TOYS, Cars [Racing])

SMOKEY BEAR ITEMS

Collectors

Pete Nowicki
1531 39th Ave.
San Francisco, CA 94122-3015
ph: 415-566-7506
e-mail: portfire86@aol.com
Collector seeks all licensed Smokey Bear items for collection: toys, dolls, posters, etc.

SB Collector
P.O. Box 9007
Bend, OR 97708-9007
Serious collector buying Smokey Bear items.

SMOKING COLLECTIBLES

(see also ADVERTISING COLLECTIBLES, Trade Cards [Tobacco]; CIGAR BOXES, LABELS & BANDS; CIGARETTE COLLECTIBLES; CIGAR STORE COLLECTIBLES; LIGHTERS; MATCHBOXES & LABELS; MATCHCOVERS; MATCH SAFES; PIPES; TOBACCO COLLECTIBLES)

Collectors

Lee Pattison
6 Christview Dr.
Cuba, NY 14727-1202
ph: 716-968-2458
Wants antique meerschaum pipes carved and plain, briar pipes of more recent manufacture brand names: Charatan, Barling, Stanwell, Larson, Dunhill, Savinelli and others; also wants to buy tobacco jars and cigar store items.

Les Franics
129 South Van Buren St.
Rockville, MD 20850
ph: 301-762-3003
Buys and sells tobacco cards and cigar related collectibles: silks, felts, cutters, tobacco jars, tobacco tags, books and ephemera.

D. Nordlinger Stern
385 Bayview Dr. NE
Saint Petersburg, FL 33704-2430
ph: 727-894-4000
fax: 727-894-1040
e-mail: dnordstern@aol.com
Wants tobacco memorabilia, particularly W. Duke and Duke's Mixture.

Cindy Porman
22044 Roosevelt Rd.
South Bend, IN 46614
ph: 219-291-6414
Wants Copenhagen Snuff, Weyman & Sons, Weyman Bros., Skoal Snuff, and Key Snuff tobacco items including crocks, pocket tins, store displays, metal and paper signs, and related advertising items.

Millie Vaccarella
1955 Hythe St.
Roseville, MN 55113
ph: 651-631-2201
Interested in buying old tobacco tins, especially pocket tins in good condition.

Dealers

Charles S. Levi
19 South Wabash
Chicago, IL 60603-3171
ph: 312-372-1306
fax: 312-372-1416
Buy and sells all things related to smoking: books, pipes, gadgets, literature, etc.

Susan Allan-Harshman
Past & Present Men's Club, The
11054 Ventura Blvd. #278
Studio City, CA 91604
ph: 818-314-1200
fax: 818-985-1835
e-mail: cigarantiques@earthlink.net
web: http://www.cigarantiques.com
Website includes over 6,000 items of men's antiques including smoking items, gambling and drinking collectibles; also has two stores in California.

Experts

Benjamin Rapaport
11505 Turnbridge Ln.
Reston, VA 20194-1220
ph: 703-435-8133
Wants antiquarian tobacciana: domestic & foreign literature, pipes & pipe smoking, snuff & its accoutrements, cigars & accessories, smoking technology, ephemera & lithography, pipe tampers, and tobacco jars and boxes.

Museums/Libraries

Duke Tobacco History Corporation
2828 Duke Homestead Rd.
Durham, NC 27705-2726
ph: 919-477-5498 or 919-479-7093
fax: 919-479-7092
e-mail: maggot@sunsite.unc.edu
web: http://metalab.unc.edu/maggot/dukehome2/
A non-profit support group for the Duke Homestead State Historic Site; collects materials relevant to the preservation of tobacco history: pipe, smoking, cigarette, advertising, etc.

Holders

Collectors

Jay Opperman
78 Clinton Ave.
Montclair, NJ 07042-2116
ph: 973-509-0195
fax: 973-509-0881
Wants to buy superb examples of exquisite antique meerschaum pipes and cigar holders.

Snuff Boxes

Collectors

Eli Hecht
Mineli Assoc.
19 Evelyn Lane
Syosset, NY 11791-5806
ph: 516-921-1837
Wants to buy snuff boxes, nautical items, and inkwells.

SNACK SETS

Collectors

Delores Long
P.O. Box 908
Hallock, MN 56728-0908
ph: 218-843-2700
e-mail: ssslady@mailexcite.com
Collector of glass or ceramic snack plates with matching cups; will buy or trade for snack plates with matching cups; please send SASE with photo, photocopy plate, asking price.

Periodicals

Delores Long
Newsletter: Snack Set Searchers' Newsletter
P.O. Box 908
Hallock, MN 56728-0908
ph: 218-843-2700
e-mail: ssslady@mailexcite.com
A bi-monthly publication devoted to providing information and a trading medium for collectors of snack sets (also known as toast or tea sets).

SNOW BABIES

Experts

Linda L. Vines
P.O. Box 43721
Upper Montclair, NJ 07043
ph: 973-748-4990
e-mail: lja@viconet.com
Buys, sells and trades German bisque snow babies; authored "Snow Babies" in "Collectors Showcase" magazine; Snow Babies advisor to "Schroeder's"; lecturer and appraiser.

SNOWDOMES

Clubs/Associations

Nancy McMichael
Snowdome Collectors Club
Newsletter: Snow Biz Newsletter
P.O. Box 53262
Washington, DC 20009-9262
"Snow Biz" aims to enhance the knowledge, enjoyment and collections of snowdome/waterglobe enthusiasts; quarterly newsletter.

Collectors

Miriam Bein
113 Cedar Rd.
Watchung, NJ 07060
ph: 908-561-0808 or 908-233-0115
fax: 908-232-7311
e-mail: mbein@ix.netcom.com
web: http://pw1.netcom.com/~mbein/domer.html
Serious collector of snowdomes; especially seeking plastic souvenir and location domes with place names; also wants advertising, Disney, commemoratives, and figurals; has snowdomes to sell and trade with other collectors.

Michael Muntner
Snowdome Mall, The
P.O. Box 30
Cabin John, MD 20818-0030
ph: 301-365-4784
fax: 301-365-4525
e-mail: trylon@erols.com
web: http://www.muntner.com/snowdome.htm
Wants snow domes (water globes), glass or plastic; souvenir (e.g. cities), tourist traps, events (e.g. Olympics), product advertising, and figural; will buy individual pieces or entire collections; also have domes for sale and trade.

Diane Davison
1517 Reisterstown Rd., Ste. 101
Baltimore, MD 21208
ph: 410-486-0900
fax: 410-486-0901
e-mail: lawgal@usa.net
web: http://mail.bcpl.lib.md.us/~ddavison/home.html

Ian Luria
2620 N 2nd Rd.
Arlington, VA 22201
e-mail: TINpinkey@aol.com
web: http://members.aol.com/TINpinkey/snowdome/welcome.htm

Fiona Neary
P.O. Box 697
Fredericksburg, VA 22404
ph: 540-374-1872
e-mail: fiona@heritagestudio.com
web: http://www.heritagestudio.com
Buys and sells old snowdomes of various themes: religions, military, snowbaby, animal, people, destination, and others; website has lots of examples from the collection as well as for sale.

Judy Posner
4195 South Tamiami Trail, Ste. 183
Venice, FL 34293-5112
ph: 941-497-7149
fax: 941-493-8085
e-mail: jpc@tias.com
web: http://www.tias.com/stores/jpc/

Linda Muether
7895 Watson Rd.
Saint Louis, MO 63129
ph: 314-961-1119
fax: 314-845-9942
e-mail: lmuether@aol.com
web: http://members.aol.com/lmuether/collect/index.htm

Henk van Ingen
Wilgengriend 138
Almere, Flevoland 1356 Jl
The Netherlands
e-mail: handm@snowdome.demon.nl
web: http://www.snowdome.demon.nl
Snowdome collector from The Netherlands presenting a regularly updated snowdome homepage with lots of information about snowdomes.

Dealers

Helene Guarnaccia
52 Coach Lane
Fairfield, CT 06430
ph: 203-374-6034
Buys and sells snowdomes; author of "Snowdomes, A Price Guide."

Experts

Nancy McMichael
P.O. Box 53262
Washington, DC 20009-9262
"Snow Biz" aims to enhance the knowledge, enjoyment and collections of snowdome/waterglobe enthusiasts; quarterly newsletter.

Carol Beilstein
1719 Primrose Dr.
El Cajon, CA 92020
e-mail: C1urchn@aol.com
web: http://members.aol.com/C1urchn/web/snowdome.htm
Snowdome collector and expert;

website displays many old glass snowglobes from the 1930s and 1940s, includes listings of references on snowdomes, information on snowglobe companies as well as links to other snowdome websites.

Man./Prod./Dist.

Bill Carmichael
Olde Tyme Companies
1300 Loomis
Des Moines, IA 50315-1863
ph: 515-282-4064
fax: 515-282-1763
e-mail: oldetyme@ix.netcom.com
web: http://www.mallofiowa.com/oldetyme/
Manufacturers snowdomes for wholesale; also repairs snowdomes.

Herb Rabbin
P.O. Box 421205
Los Angeles, CA 90042
ph: 213-258-1776
fax: 213-258-1776
e-mail: hrabbin@earthlink.net
web: http://home.earthlink.net/~hrabbin/
This site is a resource for collectors (and friends and relatives) who have broken domes by accident and need to have them repaired or refurbished; also does custom domes fabricated from 1 to 1500 in glass or plastic.

Sharon Jones
Global Shakeup
235 East Colorado Blvd., #178
Pasadena, CA 91101
ph: 323-256-8325
fax: 323-259-8988
e-mail: feedback@snowdomes.com
web: http://www.snowdomes.com/
Features a huge selection of American and European glass and plastic snowdomes including figurals, comic characters, locations, advertising, limited edition, science fiction, and much more; also float pens; 28-page catalog $2.

Repair Services

Herb Rabbin
P.O. Box 421205
Los Angeles, CA 90042
ph: 213-258-1776
fax: 213-258-1776
e-mail: hrabbin@earthlink.net
web: http://home.earthlink.net/~hrabbin/
This site is a resource for collectors (and friends and relatives) who have broken domes by accident and need to have them repaired or refurbished; also does custom domes fabricated from 1 to 1500 in glass or plastic.

Suppliers

National Artcraft Company
7966 Darrow Road
Twinsburg, OH 44087
ph: 800-793-0152
Sells replacement glass globes, bases, gaskets, snow, music boxes and more; everything you need to make or repair glass snowglobes.

Location

Experts

Chloe Ross
7553 Norton Ave. Apt. 4
Los Angeles, CA 90046-5500
ph: 213-874-3044
e-mail: trstrap@aol.com
Seeking all plastic (NO GLASS) souvenir location or advertising snowshakers/snowdomes; any size or condition; need not have water or snow; prefer uncracked but small leaks OK; must have inside plaque; no holidays; wants LA; all answered.

SNOWGLOBES

(see SNOWDOMES)

SNOWMOBILES

Clubs/Associations

Vintage Snowmobile Club of America
Newsletter: Vintage Snowmobiler, The
P.O. Box 392
Fultonville, NY 12072
e-mail: vsca@vsca.com
web: http://www.vsca.com
Caters to collectors and restorers of antique and unusual snowmobiles from the early days to 1980; over 1500 members across the US and Canada; over 6000 snowmobiles registered in the VSCA database; regional Ride-Ins annually.

Antique Snowmobile Club of America
Newsletter: Iron Dog Tracks
201 3rd St. SE, #1
Independence, IA 50644-2820

Internet Resources

Mikael Sterner
Sledding.com
Lasarettsgatan 10
Varnamo, S-331 30
Sweden
ph: +46 370 165 80
e-mail: editor@sledding.com
web: http://www.sledding.com
Lots of information on snowmobiling at this website

Museums/Libraries

New Hampshire Snowmobile Museum Association
P.O. Box 1856
Concord, NH 03302-1856
e-mail: nhsnowmuseum@mail.tds.net
web: http://www.statenh.com/snowmobilemuseum/

Periodicals

Kelley Blue Book
Price Guide: Kelley Blue Book
5 Oldfield
Irvine, CA 92618
ph: 949-770-7704
fax: 949-837-1904
e-mail: kelley@kbb.com
web: http://www.kbb.com/indexv.html
Website offers current trade-in values for all makes and model cars for the past 21 years; also publishes printed value guides for cars, RV's, motorcycles, snowmobiles, motor homes, travel trailers, personal watercraft, etc.

Steve Ferguson, Ed.
National Automobile Dealers Association
Price Guide: N.A.D.A. Official Used Car Guide
P.O. Box 7800
Costa Mesa, CA 92628
ph: 800-544-6232
fax: 714-556-8715
e-mail: nada@nada.org
web: http://www.nada.org/
A series of value guides for domestic and foreign cars, trucks, vans, RV's, mobile homes, motorcycles, snowmobiles, and boats, small and large; also Heavy Duty Trucks and Aircraft Book, car clubs & organizations, museums.

SNUFF BOTTLES

(see also ORIENTALIA; SMOKING COLLECTIBLES)

Clubs/Associations

John Ford, Pres.
International Chinese Snuff Bottle Society
Journal: Chinese Snuff Bottle Journal
2601 North Charles St.
Baltimore, MD 21218-4514
ph: 410-467-9400
fax: 410-243-3451
e-mail: ICSBS@worldnet.att.net
web: http://www.snuffbottle.org/
Members interested in "Chinese" snuff bottles.

Collectors

Richard Sindler
859 1/2 N. Howard St.
Baltimore, MD 21201
ph: 410-728-3377
Wants to buy snuff bottles; send photo and price.

SOCIAL CAUSES

(see also BLACK MEMORABILIA; BUTTONS, Pin-Back; IMMIGRATION; INDUSTRY RELATED ITEMS; KU KLUX KLAN COLLECTIBLES; MINING RELATED ITEMS; POLITICAL COLLECTIBLES; POPULAR CULTURE; PROHIBITION ITEMS; SLAVERY ITEMS; VIETNAM)

Auction Services

Dick Oestreicher
P.O. Box 407
Dallas, NC 28034
Conducts mail/phone auctions of American social history and social movements: Blacks, Women, Ethnics, Labor, Left, Anti-War, 1960s, Social Movements.

Collectors

Dick Oestreicher
P.O. Box 407
Dallas, NC 28034
Wants items relating to history and social movements: Blacks, Women, Ethnics, Labor, Left, Anti-War, 1960s, Social Movements.

Sylvia Marcotte-Cloutier
Sylvia Charles of Blythe
218 W. Hobson Way
Blythe, CA 92225-1619
ph: 619-922-3456
fax: 619-922-5651
Wants 1960 to 1970 material relating to Viet Nam, counterculture organizations, Civil Rights: diaries, letters, signed books, letters from military men sent home; documents, photos of sit-ins, marches, riots, demonstrations, etc.

Dealers

Dr. Pamela Oestreicher
American Social History & Social Movements
P.O. Box 55066
Pittsburgh, PA 15207
ph: 412-421-5230
fax: 412-421-0903
e-mail: ashsm@netscape.net
Produces a catalog of about 1000 cause items for sale, many from 19th century as well as 1960s through 1970s; African American, Civil War, political, West, women, labor; social movements: suffrage, KKK, anti-war, prohibition, etc.

Beatnik

Dealers

Skyline Books
P.O. Box T
Forest Knolls, CA 94933-0720
ph: 415-488-9491
e-mail: skylinbk@ix.netcom.com
web: http://www.abaa-booknet.com/usa/skyline/
Wants hippie, the Beat generation, '60s counterculture, drugs, student

activism, psychedelia; books, pamphlets, posters, handbills, ephemera, etc.

Hippie Items

(see also WOODSTOCK)

Collectors

Ronald Krueger
R.W. Krueger's
P.O. Box 741
Oak Park, IL 60303-0741
ph: 708-788-8235
Wants 1960s psychedelic hippie art: underground newspapers, rock, pro-drug, anti-war posters, handbills, pamphlets, books, Peter Max.

Dealers

Skyline Books
P.O. Box T
Forest Knolls, CA 94933-0720
ph: 415-488-9491
e-mail: skylinbk@ix.netcom.com
web: http://www.abaa-booknet.com/usa/skyline/
Wants hippie, the Beat generation, '60s counterculture, drugs, student activism, psychedelia; books, pamphlets, posters, handbills, ephemera, etc.

Labor Unions

Clubs/Associations

Michael Black
American Political Items Collectors (APIC) Labor History Chapter
Newsletter: Solidarity Forever!
P.O. Box 407
Dallas, NC 28034
Purpose is to publicize and preserve American labor history and to provide communication among collectors of labor movement memorabilia and ephemera; send SASE for more information.

Collectors

Scott Molloy
550 Usquepaugh Rd.
West Kingston, RI 02892-1924
ph: 401-782-3614
fax: 401-792-2954
Wants labor and left-wing items: badges, ribbons, pins, photos, flyers, books, pamphlets, posters, knick-knacks; wants Knights of Labor, Railroad unions, I.W.W., AFL-CIO, etc.

Dan Neuspiel
8 Anthony Road
White Plains, NY 10605
ph: 914-946-3523
e-mail: dneuspiel@compuserve.com
Collects pin-back labor union buttons, especially pre-1950.

Joe Doerring
P.O. Box 94444
Des Moines, IA 50394-0444
ph: 515-285-7702
e-mail: JDoerring@aol.com
Wants pre-1940 Industrial Workers of the World (IWW) items: pinback buttons, ribbons, paper items, etc.

Pat Kehoe
3455 S. 83rd St.
Milwaukee, WI 53219-3840
ph: 414-541-2538
e-mail: kehoe@execpc.com
Wants labor union buttons, ribbon badges, shop signs, especially 1960s and older; topics covering: 8-hour day, labor day, strikes, membership, etc.; famous labor union leaders memorabilia of Jimmy Hoffa, Eugene Debs, John L. Lewis.

Suffrage Items

Clubs/Associations

Ronnie Lapinsky
Woman Suffrage & Political Issues Chapter, APIC
7921 Ivymount Terrace
Potomac, MD 2085403721
Collectors of items relating to woman suffrage.

Collectors

Andy Avery
P.O. Box 471
Jamaica, VT 05343-0471
ph: 802-874-4207
Wants women's suffrage items: pins, ribbons, postcards, ceramics, papers, pennants, fans, stamps, cards, etc.; interested in most any souvenir memorabilia with a special interest in women's suffrage.

Cary Demont
P.O. Box 16013
Minneapolis, MN 55416
ph: 612-522-0957
e-mail: Caryd8@aol.com
Wants early women's suffrage items and Votes for Women material: pinback buttons, badges, posters, banners, pennants, costumes, postcards, and unusual 3-dimentional items; also wants Carrie Nation material of all kinds.

Steve Sobel
5132 Topeka Dr.
Tarzana, CA 91356-3921
ph: 818-705-4063
fax: 818-705-1123
Wants woman suffrage/votes for women materials: buttons, ribbons, posters, etc.

Maya Lee
1797 N. Arrowhead Ave.
San Bernardino, CA 92405-4111
ph: 909-882-4656
Wants to buy Votes for Women, suffrage, early feminist items: flags, jewelry, posters, sashes, ribbons, pins, banners, photos, books, etc.

John Gearhart
3267 S.E. Hawthorne
Portland, OR 97214
ph: 503-255-8108 or 503-232-4099

Internet Resources

Woman Suffrage Association Collection, Library of Congress
101 Independence Ave. SE
Washington, DC 20540
ph: 202-707-8000
e-mail: ndlpcoll@loc.gov
web: http://memory.loc.gov/ammem/naw/nawshome.html
Collection consists of books, pamphlets, and other artifacts documenting the suffrage campaign, 1848 to 1921.

SODA FOUNTAIN COLLECTIBLES

(see also MOLDS, Ice Cream; SOFT DRINK COLLECTIBLES)

Appraisers

Peggy Landt
LHL Services
9065 La Serena Drive
Fair Oaks, CA 95628
ph: 916-962-0592
e-mail: peggy@jps.net
Complete soda fountain and pharmacy appraisal services.

Clubs/Associations

Donald D. Snyder
Ice Screamers, The
Newsletter: Ice Screamer, The
P.O. Box 465
Warrington, PA 18976-0465
ph: 215-343-2676
e-mail: icescreamer@juno.com
For anyone who likes ice cream, who wants to learn more about the history of ice cream or who collects ice cream/soda fountain memorabilia.

Betty Davis, Pres.
National Association of Soda Jerks
Newsletter: Fiz Biz
P.O. Box 115
Omaha, NE 68101-0115
ph: 402-341-6965 or 712-322-8685
Dedicated to the preservation of nostalgia and of the history related to the soda fountain and soda jerks; recipes, soda fountain visits, nostalgic remembrances, etc.

Collectors

Beth & Mike Snyder
2415 Opal Rd.
York, PA 17404

Ed Marks
P.O. Box 5387
Lancaster, PA 17606-5387
ph: 717-569-8286 or 717-569-5663
fax: 717-569-8680
e-mail: paka@paonline.com
Wants ice cream ephemera, books, pamphlets, and any other printed material relating to ice cream.

Mary & Gus Brunner
2209 Township Rd.
Quakertown, PA 18951-3344
ph: 610-346-6650
Wants to buy ice cream scoops, tip trays, and other ice cream memorabilia.

William A. Shaner, Jr.
403 N. Charlotte St.
Pottstown, PA 19464-5311
ph: 610-326-0165
e-mail: was403@webtv.net
Wants ONLY Burdans Ice Cream items such as trays, signs, ads, and paper.

Mort & Bobbe Burness
11406 Nairn Rd.
Silver Spring, MD 20902

Devall & Barbara Sollers
P.O. Box 132
Monkton, MD 21111

Coleen Detzel
28 Lacresta Dr.
Florence, KY 41042-9663
ph: 606-647-6156
Wants c. 1940s soda fountain and ice cream items: dispensers, fountains, malt mixers, signs, neons, bars, stools, tables, booths, etc.; also wants diner items c. 1940s and 1950s including furniture.

Experts

Harold & Joyce Screen
2804 Munster Rd.
Baltimore, MD 21234-1131
ph: 410-661-6765
e-mail: hscreen@home.com
Historian wants: "Soda Fountain" pre-1925 trade magazines, fountain equipment & pre-1930 supply catalogs, interior view photos of pre-1910 soda fountains; will reply to queries if accompanied by a SASE; appraisals for fee.

Allan Mellis
Mr. Ice Cream
1115 West Montana
Chicago, IL 60614-2220
ph: 773-327-9123
fax: 773-327-9456
e-mail: mellis@enteract.com
Wants better ice cream and soda fountain postcards, especially real photo, advertising, interiors, artist signed and comic; the image must be primarily ice cream related; no

postcards that have only a small ice cream sign.

Man./Prod./Dist.

Gene Rees
Gino's Malt Shop Collection
P.O. Box 505
Bridgeville, PA 15017-0505
ph: 412-221-1495
fax: 412-221-1272
web: http://www.coin-opclassics.com/Ads/Rees/rees.htm
Sells 50s and 60s malt shop furniture, decor and accessories: booths, tables, chairs, stools, moldings, metal trim, lighting fixtures, quilted stainless sheets, counter accessories, etc.

Ice Cream Dippers

Collectors

Billy Sprague
3611 Westbrook Ave.
Nashville, TN 37205-2327
ph: 615-292-4559
e-mail: billyscoop@aol.com
Wants to buy unusual ice cream dippers.

Chris Potts
8104 Fontana
Prairie Village, KS 66208
ph: 913-642-8269
Wants to buy unusual ice cream scoops.

Danny & Denise Saleh
1520 Clubview
Tyler, TX 75701
ph: 903-595-6465
Wants to buy ice cream scoops (dippers).

Steve Elliott
1600 Tennessee St.
Vallejo, CA 94590
ph: 707-552-8400 or 707-642-1949
fax: 707-552-0881
Wants to buy old ice cream scoops.

Dealers

Charles Cook
1481 Rte. 23
Butler, NJ 07405
ph: 973-838-3043
Buys and sells ice cream scoops.

Experts

Wayne Smith
P.O. Box 418
Walkersville, MD 21793-0418
ph: 301-845-6066
Author of "Ice Cream Dippers," an illustrated history and collectors guide to early ice cream dippers; $22.45 from author; send LSASE for free brochure entitled "An Introduction to Collecting Ice Cream Dippers."

Malt Mixers

Collectors

Ken Rodoni
368 Luella Ave.
Calumet City, IL 60409
ph: 708-862-2667
fax: 708-862-9134
Collector wants old malt mixers by Hamilton Beach, Arnold, Gilchrist, etc.

SODA POP

(see SOFT DRINK COLLECTIBLES)

SOFT DRINK COLLECTIBLES

(see also BOTTLES; COIN-OPERATED MACHINES, Vending Machines; SODA FOUNTAIN COLLECTIBLES)

Clubs/Associations

Cola Club, The
P.O. Box 158715
Nashville, TN 37215
e-mail: cola@interport.net
web: http://www.nostalgiapubs.com/ppals/colaclub.html
Focuses on vintage, pre-1970 soda artifacts and soda advertising: Coca-Cola, Orange Crush, 7-up, Whistle, Pepsi, Royal Crown, Chero-Cola, Cleo-Cola, Moxie, Hires, Nesbit, Nu-Grape, Dr. Pepper, Nehi, Grapette, etc.

Collectors

Carolyn Hammond
P.O. Box 343
Black Mountain, NC 28711-0343
ph: 704-669-6262
Wants to buy soft drink collectibles: Pepsi, Coca-Cola, Dr. Pepper, Moxie, and Nu-Grape; signs, posters, calendars, trays, etc.

Wallace A. Newkirk
229 Tangelo Ave.
Fern Park, FL 32730-2811
ph: 407-834-2101
fax: 407-834-3101
WAnts to buy old bottles, defunct brands of bottles from the U.S. only.

Jim Carr
H.C. 30, Box 49-D
Brownwood, TX 76801
ph: 915-752-6818
Wants to buy older Coca-Cola, Pepsi, and 7-Up items; all types and any condition.

Dealers

Dan Morean
www.breweriana.com
13 Greenleaf St.
Malden, MA 02148
ph: 781-324-3330 or 781-322-3725
fax: 781-324-3320
e-mail: dan@breweriana.com
web: http://www.breweriana.com
Collects MA soda or beverage bottles and collectibles, buys and sells all else.

Louis DiDona
Lou's Breweriana Unlimited
623 Center Street
Bethlehem, PA 18018-4035
ph: 610-866-2373
fax: 610-866-2373
e-mail: lou@lousbreweriana.com
web: http://www.lousbreweriana.com/
Specializes in fine collectible soda advertising and soda bottles; also in beer advertising items and beer cans; website has large database of items for sale.

Wayne Merritt
5 Hanson Ct.
Greenville, SC 29615-4331
ph: 864-297-3999
fax: 804-297-3999
Wants to buy soft drink collectibles: Coca-Cola, Pepsi-Cola; bottles, signs, calendars, paper items, colored soda bottles, displays, posters, etc.; please state price and condition in first letter.

Lois & Ralph Behm
Lois' Collectibles of Antique Market III
413 W. Main St.
Saint Charles, IL 60174-1815
ph: 630-377-5599 or 847-831-5997
Buys and sells Coca-Cola and Pepsi collectibles.

Matt Holmes
Soda Pop Shop, The
119 S. Chambery
Olathe, KS 66061
ph: 913-764-9214
e-mail: shopkeep@sodashop.com
web: http://www.sodashop.com
A one-stop soda collectibles store on the internet; carries only licensed merchandise from all favorite sodas: Pepsi, Coke, 7UP, Dr. Pepper, Mountain Dew, Grapette, etc.

Matt Holmes
Soda Pop Shop, The
P.O. Box 13382
Shawnee Mission, KS 66212
e-mail: webmaster@sodashop.com
web: http://www.sodashop.com
Carries a wide variety of contemporary soda collectibles; all licensed by their respective companies.

Tim Smokoff
Pop Shoppe, The
9208 128th St. Ct. NW
Gig Harbor, WA 98329
ph: 888-323-COKE
fax: 888-323-COKE
e-mail: tim@popshoppe.com
web: http://www.popshoppe.com
Buys, sells, trades, conducts auctions, and shares information about Soda Pop Collecting; specializing in Coke, Hires, Moxie and Orange Crush; also tracks 7-Up, Squeeze, Dads Rootbeer and Pepsi.

Harold Balde
Fungus Amungus
21 Wellington St.
Orangeville, Ontario L9W 2L2
Canada
ph: 519-942-3984
e-mail: kingpin@total.net
web: http://tilt.largo.fl.us/hbalde/
Dealer of soda collectibles; specialty is Coca-Cola and Orange Crush items such as trays, bottles, clans, and paper material.

Experts

Craig & Donna Stifter
P.O. Box 6514
Naperville, IL 60540-6514
ph: 630-789-5780 or 630-939-7479
e-mail: cocacola@enteract.com
Wants to buy older Coca-Cola, Pepsi-Cola, Dr. Pepper, Orange-Crush, Hire Root Beer and other brand soda memorabilia; writes columns for several antiques periodicals; also interested in items pertaining to country (general) stores.

Tim Smokoff
Pop Shoppe, The
9208 128th St. Ct. NW
Gig Harbor, WA 98329
ph: 888-323-COKE
fax: 888-323-COKE
e-mail: tim@popshoppe.com
web: http://www.popshoppe.com
Buys, sells, trades, conducts auctions, and shares information about Soda Pop Collecting; specializing in Coke, Hires, Moxie and Orange Crush; also tracks 7-Up, Squeeze, Dads Rootbeer and Pepsi.

Periodicals

Dan Kwate
Magazine: Club Soda
P.O. Box 489
Troy, ID 83871-0489
ph: 208-835-2306
fax: 208-835-2307
e-mail: dkwate@clubsoda.net
web: http://www.clubsoda.net
Articles about all types of soda collectibles: vending machines, signs, bottles, etc.; features include company histories, restoration tips, show and auction reviews, and free classified ads.

Blair Matthews
Playing With Words
Magazine: Soda Pop Dreams
1020 Rose St.
Cambridge, Ontario N3H 2G3
Canada
ph: 519-650-3969
fax: 519-650-2547
e-mail: playing@pww.on.ca
web: http://www.pww.on.ca/dreams.htm
A publication for the amateur and experienced soda pop collector, and for those who enjoy soda pop beverages; free classifieds to those who subscribe (limited time only) online; published five times each year.

7-Up

Collectors

Gwen Daniel
18 Belleau Lake Ct.
O Fallon, MO 63366-3144
ph: 314-978-3190
e-mail: gdaniel@mail.win.org

Don Fiebiger
1970 Las Lomitas Dr.
Hacienda Heights, CA 91745-4128
ph: 562-693-6484
Serious collector buying all categories of pre-1960 7-Up memorabilia: pencils, tie bars, service pins, matchcovers, ash trays, bottles, calendars, signs, clocks, neons, "Fresh-Up" Freddie dolls, tin cars/ trucks, seltzer bottles, etc.

Brian Adamson
6732 Arlington St.
Vancouver, British Columbia V5S 3N9
Canada
Wants 7-Up related collectibles: thermometers, calendars, signs, etc.; also wants Pepsi and Orange Crush items.

Applied Color Label Bottles

Clubs/Associations

Rick Sweeney
Painted Soda Bottle Collectors Association
Newsletter: Soda Net
9418 Hilmer Dr.
La Mesa, CA 91942
ph: 619-461-4354
e-mail: ACLsRus@msn.com
web: http://www.collectoronline.com/PSBCA/PSBCA.html
The only national organization for "painted" (silkscreened) soda bottle collectors.

Collectors

Ed Kassay
P.O. Box 4
Calimesa, CA 92320
ph: 909-795-5551
Wants to buy and trade painted label soda bottles from the 1940s through 1960s; also wants soda crown caps, especially if unused.

Experts

Gary Brent Kincade
P.O. Box 7
Horner, WV 26372
ph: 304-842-3773
e-mail: pl8mail@alpca.org
web: http://www.alpca.org

Thomas Marsh
914 Franklin Ave.
Youngstown, OH 44502
ph: 800-845-7930
Author of "Official Guide to Collecting Applied Color Label Soda Bottles." Applied color label (ACL) bottles (heyday was 1930s-1970s) had silkscreened labels, as opposed to a glued-on paper label or an embossed label.

Victoria Herberta
P.O. Box 8154
Houston, TX 77004-8154
ph: 713-523-0303
Buys and sells painted-labed soda bottles; over 2,000 different applied color label bottles in stock; author of "American Goes Pop."

Periodicals

Soda Mart - Can World
Newsletter: Painted-Label Soda Bottles
1055 Ridgecrest Dr.
Goodlettsville, TN 37072
ph: 615-859-5236 or 877-859-4929
fax: 615-859-5238
e-mail: mbca@gono.com
web: http://gono.com/vir-mus/museum.htm
An annual periodical that focuses on soda bottles having painted, silk-screened or enameled labels.

Coca-Cola

(see also ADVERTISING COLLECTIBLES, Tin Vienna Art Plates)

Auction Services

Allan Petretti
Nostalgia Publications
21 S. Lake Dr.
Hackensack, NJ 07601
ph: 201-488-4536
e-mail: cola@interport.net
web: http://www.nostalgiapubs.com
Conducts semi-annual mail-bid auctions of Coca-Cola related advertising items; catalogs are $10 for subscription.

Clubs/Associations

Coca-Cola Collectors Club
Newsletter: Coca-Cola Collectors News
P.O. Box 49166
Atlanta, GA 30359-1166
fax: 404-728-9882
e-mail: webmaster@cocacolaclub.org
web: http://cocacolaclub.org
International communications with over 7,000 collectors, markets for buying/selling/trading, special monthly merchandise offerings for members, monthly newsletter with free classified.

Chris Wenzel
Florida West Coast Chapter of the Coca-Cola Collectors Club International
1007 Emerald Dr.
Brandon, FL 33511-6521
ph: 813-685-7242
fax: 813-645-0305
e-mail: tampa009@aol.com
Contact with questions about the club or about Coca-Cola memorabilia.

Collectors

Steve Sands
Steve's Coca-Cola Collection & Mini-Museum
1315 Washington St.
Weymouth, MA 02189-2333
ph: 781-335-6352
fax: 781-331-2472
e-mail: cckid@mediaone.net
web: http://www.77.cyberhost.net/cckid/
Collects anything having to do with Coca-Cola.

Drew Steitz
Coke Bottles of the World Website, The
P.O. Box 222
East Texas, PA 18046-0222
ph: 610-791-7979
fax: 610-791-7979
e-mail: pl8seditor@aol.com
web: http://www.pl8s.com/coke.htm
Wants to buy Coca-Cola bottles and cans from around the world; also looking for other international soft drink and bottled waters.

Scott Rosenman
1 E. Lexington St., Ste. 509
Baltimore, MD 21202
ph: 410-837-5897
Wants Coca-Cola and Pepsi-Cola items; pre-1960 and in excellent condition.

DaClassic1's Coca-Cola Collector's Corner
4025 Chapman
Sterling Heights, MI 48310
ph: 248-265-3075
e-mail: DaClassic1@aol.com
web: http://members.aol.com/daclassic1/home1.htm

Robb Johnson
1155 Crescent Lake Rd.
Waterford Township, MI 48327
ph: 810-673-2804

Keith Johnson
236 N. Catherine
Ithaca, MI 48847
e-mail: keithjo@edcen.ehhs.cmich.edu
web: http://edcen.ehhs.cmich.edu/~keithjo/cokexmas.html
Wants to buy Coca-Cola Christmas collectibles.

Dealers

John Forrest
Cola Shop, The
137 Cherry St.
Black Mountain, NC 28711
ph: 704-669-4019
Buys and sells Coca-Cola memorabilia; fountain on site.

Richard Mix
Mix International
P.O. Box 558
Marietta, GA 30061-0558
ph: 770-422-9083
fax: 770-422-5649
e-mail: mixintl@aol.com
web: http://www.bottleworld.com/
Coca-Cola collector, dealer, expert; noted world-wide expert on Coca-Cola memorabilia; has authored numerous books and articles on the subject; owns the world's largest collection of Coca-Cola bottles.

Dick & Kay Thompson
320 E. Washington St.
Pontiac, IL 61764
ph: 815-842-2586

Dwayne Spark
Nostalgia Plus
8441 Sublaines
Anjou, Quebec H1K 2C1
Canada
ph: 514-352-6892
fax: 514-352-1856
Buys and sells Coca-Cola memorabilia (old and new): cans, bottles, signs, Life ads, phone cards.

Experts

Allan Petretti
Nostalgia Publications
21 S. Lake Dr.
Hackensack, NJ 07601
ph: 201-488-4536
e-mail: cola@interport.net
web: http://www.nostalgiapubs.com
Author of "Petretti's Coca-Cola Collectibles Price Guide" - 10th edition, and "Petretti's Soda-Pop Collectibles Price Guide."

Randy S. Schaeffer
611 N. 5th St.
Reading, PA 19601-2201
ph: 610-373-3333 or 610-683-4401
e-mail: schaeffe@kutztown.edu
Advanced collector seeking the old, rare and unusual in Coca-Cola collectibles; also provides expert appraisals and evaluations.

William E. Bateman
611 N. 5th St.
Reading, PA 19601-2201
ph: 610-373-3333 or 610-683-4412
e-mail: bateman@kutztown.edu
Advanced collector seeking the old, rare and unusual in Coca-Cola collectibles; also provides expert appraisals and evaluations.

Bill Ricketts
Nostalgia Store, The
P.O. Box 9605
Asheville, NC 28805-0605
ph: 828-669-2205 or 828-669-2668
fax: 828-669-2205
Buys, sells and trades Coca-Cola memorabilia: trays, signs, posters, calendars, bottles, novelty items, etc.

Richard Mix
P.O. Box 558
Marietta, GA 30061-0558
ph: 770-422-9083
fax: 770-422-5649
e-mail: mixintl@aol.com
web: http://www.bottleworld.com/
Noted world-wide expert on Coca-Cola memorabilia; has authored numerous books and articles on the subject; owns the world's largest collection of Coca-Cola bottles.

Chris Wenzel
1007 Emerald Dr.
Brandon, FL 33511-6521
ph: 813-685-7242
fax: 813-645-0305
e-mail: tampa009@aol.com
Does Coca-Cola research for movie companies.

Thom Thompson
123 Shaw Ave.
Versailles, KY 40383-1157
ph: 606-873-8787 or 606-255-2727
fax: 606-255-2727
Serious collector and researcher of Coca-Cola collectibles since 1970; interested in buying older collectibles including posters, trays, coupons, calendars, knives, openers, fobs, etc.; especially chewing gum items; free appraisals.

Craig & Donna Stifter
P.O. Box 6514
Naperville, IL 60540-6514
ph: 630-789-5780 or 630-939-7479
e-mail: cocacola@enteract.com
Wants to buy older Coca-Cola, Pepsi-Cola, Dr. Pepper, Orange-Crush, Hire Root Beer and other brand soda memorabilia; writes columns for several antiques periodicals; also interested in items pertaining to country (general) stores.

Internet Resources

DaClassic 1's Coca-Cola Collector's Corner
4025 Chapman
Sterling Heights, MI 48310
ph: 248-265-3075
e-mail: DaClassic1@aol.com
web: http://members.aol.com/daclassic1/home1.htm
Internet Web Site homepage dedicated to providing facts, information and fun for Coke fans and collectors of Coca-Cola memorabilia.

Man./Prod./Dist.

Coca-Cola Catalog Store
P.O. Box 182264
Chattanooga, TN 37422
Carries a wide assortment of current Coca-Cola material.

Museums/Libraries

Coca-Cola Company Archives
P.O. Drawer 1734
Atlanta, GA 30301
ph: 800-GET-COKE or 404-676-3491
fax: 404-676-7701
Request information about your Coca-Cola collectibles directly from the Company; will answer questions about ingredients, recycling, products, packaging, promotions, advertising, history, and much, much more.

Philip F. Mooney, Cur.
World of Coca-Cola Pavilion, The
55 Martin Luther King Dr.
Atlanta, GA 30303-3505
ph: 404-676-5151
fax: 404-676-5432
web: http://www.cocacola.com/museum/
A 45,000 square foot attraction containing high-tech, interactive exhibits and archival materials from the company's 109-yr. history.

Biedenharn Candy Company & Museum of Coca-Cola Memorabilia
1107 Washington St.
Vicksburg, MS 39180
ph: 601-638-6514
fax: 601-636-5010
e-mail: bccmusem@bellsouth.net
web: http://www.cdiguide.com/ms/601/e_tou/biedenha.html

Channing Hardy
Schmidt's Coca-Cola Museum
P.O. Box 848
Elizabethtown, KY 42701-0848
ph: 502-769-3320 x237
fax: 502-769-3323
Contains the world's largest private collection of Coca-Cola memorabilia; will buy Coke items from 1890 to 1970, especially unusual paper items, toys, cut-outs, etc.

Periodicals

Magazine: Gameroom Magazine
P.O. Box 41
Keyport, NJ 07735-0041
ph: 732-739-1955
fax: 732-739-2834
e-mail: coinop@gameroommagazine.com
web: http://www.gameroommagazine.com
A great source of information for the collector and dealer of jukeboxes, pinballs, slot machines, Coke and other soda machines, arcade games, classic arcade video, and other gameroom collectibles.

Coca-Cola Machines

(see COIN-OPERATED MACHINES, Vending Machines; SOFT DRINK COLLECTIBLES, Soda Machines)

Dr. Pepper

Clubs/Associations

Dr. Pepper 10-2-4 Collector's Club
Newsletter: Lions Roar
3100 Monticello, Ste. 890
Dallas, TX 75205
ph: 214-520-5777
fax: 214-520-5795
web: http://www.drpep.com/clubpage.htm
The 10-2-4 club is a national organization of people dedicated to the study of the history and collecting of Dr. Pepper Co. memorabilia.

Collectors

Gwen Daniel
18 Belleau Lake Ct.
O Fallon, MO 63366-3144
ph: 314-978-3190
e-mail: gdaniel@mail.win.org

Ed Royse
112 N. Broadway St.
Walters, OK 73572
ph: 580-357-8000
fax: 580-875-2063
e-mail: edroyse@juno.com
Wants to buy pre-1951 (script logo) Dr. Pepper signs, cardboards, clocks, trays, calendars, promotional material, etc.

Bob Thiele
620 Tinker
Pawhuska, OK 74056-4039
ph: 918-287-3845
e-mail: rthiele@mmind.net
Wants early and unusual Dr. Pepper items: celluloid, early paper, tokens, jewelry, pins, pencils, clothing, fountain pens, etc.; also items from founding co. - "Artesian Mfg. & Bottling Co." (AM&B Co.), Waco, TX or other cities.

Wilton A. Lanning, Jr.
6433 Summit Ridge St.
Waco, TX 76710-1143
ph: 254-776-3130 or 254-772-2434
fax: 254-776-3153
Collector of Dr. Pepper, Circle A and Artesian Mfg. & Bottling memorabilia: bottles, signs, thermometers, advertising, etc.

Experts

Bill Ricketts
Pepper's Deli
P.O. Box 9605
Asheville, NC 28805-0605
ph: 828-669-2205 or 828-669-2668
fax: 828-669-2205
Buy/sell/trade, collects and specializes in pre-1960 Dr. Pepper advertising items; especially interested in old trays, signs, calendars; anything Dr. Pepper; will buy single items, duplicates, collections, or accumulations.

Craig & Donna Stifter
P.O. Box 6514
Naperville, IL 60540-6514
ph: 630-789-5780 or 630-939-7479
e-mail: cocacola@enteract.com
Wants to buy older Coca-Cola, Pepsi-Cola, Dr. Pepper, Orange-Crush, Hire Root Beer and other brand soda memorabilia; writes columns for several antiques periodicals; also interested in items pertaining to country (general) stores.

Museums/Libraries

Dr. Pepper Museum & Free Enterprise Institute
Newsletter: Bottlecaps
300 S. 5th St.
Waco, TX 76701-2115
ph: 254-757-1025 or 800-527-7096
fax: 254-757-2221
e-mail: dp-info@drpeppermuseum.com
web: http://www.drpeppermuseum.com/
The museum focuses on the soft drink industry; gift shop.

Grapette

Clubs/Associations

Van Stueart
Grapette Collectors Club
Newsletter: Grapette Collectors Club Newsletter
2240 Hwy 27 N
Nashville, AR 71852
ph: 870-845-4864 or 800-577-1810
e-mail: sodaman@iosa.com
For collectors of Grapette soda collectibles.

Collectors

Van Stueart
2240 Hwy 27 N
Nashville, AR 71852
ph: 870-845-4864 or 800-577-1810
e-mail: sodaman@iosa.com
Wants Grapette items: soda fountain

glasses, cardboard signs, light-up clocks, tin signs, neon clocks, calendars, flange signs, porcelain signs.

Dealers

Don Hunter
16502 Barcelina
Friendswood, TX 77546-3304
ph: 713-482-4098
Buys and sells Grapette items: drinking glasses, poster signs, shirt patches, shirt pins, pencils, clowns, elephants; "Grapette Price Guide" available for $29.95.

Howdy

Collectors

Don Fiebiger
1970 Las Lomitas Dr.
Hacienda Heights, CA 91745-4128
ph: 562-693-6484
Buys early Howdy soda items (note: no connection to "Howdy Doody").

Moxie

Clubs/Associations

Ira Seskin
New England Moxie Congress
Newsletter: Nerve Food News
445 Wyoming Ave.
Millburn, NJ 07041-2131
e-mail: Iraseski@xensei.com
web: http://www.xensei.com/users/iraseski/
Provides a clearinghouse for all information and memorabilia relating to Moxie, supports Maine Moxie weekends, promotes the consumption of Moxie; annual meeting of NEMC 2nd weekend in July in Kennebunkport, ME at Trolley Museum.

Collectors

Jan Bacci
82 Wyman Rd.
Braintree, MA 02184-4721
ph: 781-848-1095
Advanced collector interested in rare and early Moxie items for personal collection.

Misc. Services

Frank Anicetti
Kennebec Fruit Company - The Moxie Festival
2 Main St.
Lisbon Falls, ME 04252
ph: 207-353-8173
Each year sponsors a Moxie Festival in Lisbon Falls, ME; offers contemporary Moxie collectibles.

Orange Crush

Experts

Craig & Donna Stifter
P.O. Box 6514
Naperville, IL 60540-6514
ph: 630-789-5780 or 630-939-7479
e-mail: cocacola@enteract.com
Wants to buy older Coca-Cola, Pepsi-Cola, Dr. Pepper, Orange-Crush, Hire Root Beer and other brand soda memorabilia; writes columns for several antiques periodicals; also interested in items pertaining to country (general) stores.

Painted-Label Soda Bottles

(see SOFT DRINK COLLECTIBLES, Applied Color Label Bottles)

Pepsi-Cola

Clubs/Associations

Phyllis Dragovich
Ozark Mountain Pepsi Collectors Club
9101 Columbus Ave. S.
Bloomington, MN 55420
ph: 612-854-5817
e-mail: spdrago@wavetech.net
Local club for collectors of Pepsi memorabilia.

Pepsi-Cola Collectors Club
Newsletter: Pepsi Express
P.O. Box 817
Claremont, CA 91711
ph: 909-946-6026
fax: 909-946-4786
web: http://www.pepsigifts.com/pcccinfo.html

Collectors

Scott Rosenman
1 E. Lexington St., Ste. 509
Baltimore, MD 21202
ph: 410-837-5897
Wants Coca-Cola and Pepsi-Cola items; pre-1960 and in excellent condition.

Gwen Daniel
18 Belleau Lake Ct.
O Fallon, MO 63366-3144
ph: 314-978-3190
e-mail: gdaniel@mail.win.org

Dealers

Bill Ricketts
Nostalgia Store, The
P.O. Box 9605
Asheville, NC 28805-0605
ph: 828-669-2205 or 828-669-2668
fax: 828-669-2205
Wants to buy Pepsi-Cola items: advertising, trays, signs, posters, calendars, novelty items, bottles, etc.; please describe and price.

Experts

Bob Stoddard
P.O. Box 1275
Covina, CA 91722
ph: 909-459-3875
Author of "Introduction to Pepsi Collecting."

Museums/Libraries

Pepsi-Cola Company Archives
180 Interstate North Pkwy., Ste. 300
Atlanta, GA 30339
ph: 770-618-8325
fax: 770-618-8118
web: http://www.pepsi.com/

Root Beer

Collectors

Jerome Gundrum
27 Portman St.
Windsor, CT 06095
ph: 860-688-2472
e-mail: DrRootbeer@aol.com
web: http://www.rootbeer.com
Wants to buy root beer advertising items.

Bob Averill
1942 W. Market St.
Pottsville, PA 17901-2043
ph: 800-637-6484 or 570-628-3084
Wants root beer advertising items: tin, porcelain or cardboard signs, dispensers, mugs, bottles, trade cards, postcards, or anything root beer.

Experts

Tom Morrison
2930 Squaw Valley Dr.
Colorado Springs, CO 80918-1826
ph: 719-598-1754
e-mail: tnmor@earthlink.net
Interested in anything unique, unusual or odd that says "Root Beer." Author of "Root Beer Advertising and Collectibles" (Schiffer) and "More Root Beer Advertising and Collectibles" (Schiffer), both all-color price guides.

Root Beer (Hires)

Collectors

Steve Sourapas
1212 9th Ave. West #2
Seattle, WA 98119-3445
ph: 206-282-9922
fax: 206-782-1039
e-mail: sandswt@foxcomm.net
Advanced collector seeks pre-1930 good to mint condition items.

Experts

Craig & Donna Stifter
P.O. Box 6514
Naperville, IL 60540-6514
ph: 630-789-5780 or 630-939-7479
e-mail: cocacola@enteract.com
Wants to buy older Coca-Cola, Pepsi-Cola, Dr. Pepper, Orange-Crush, Hire Root Beer and other brand soda memorabilia; writes columns for several antiques periodicals; also interested in items pertaining to country (general) stores.

Smile

Collectors

Michael Urban
2029 N. Mitchell St.
Phoenix, AZ 85006-2126
ph: 602-252-8615
Buys early SMILE soda items.

Soda Machines

(see also COIN-OPERATED MACHINES, Vending Machines)

Clubs/Associations

Club Soda
P.O. Box 489
Troy, ID 83871
ph: 208-835-2306
fax: 208-835-2307
e-mail: dkwate@clubsoda.net
web: http://www.clubsoda.net/
For those interested in vintage vending machines and other soda pop hardware; monthly newsletter with show and auction reports, collector profiles, Q&A column, soda company history, new finds, free classified ads.

Collectors

Richard O. Gates
P.O. Box 187
Chesterfield, VA 23832-0187
ph: 804-748-0382 or 804-794-5146
fax: 804-748-6349
e-mail: rogates@mindspring.com
Wants coin-operated machines including Coca-Cola, Pepsi, Dr. Pepper, R.C., etc. machines, light-ups, advertising items and literature related to any of the above.

Dealers

Remember When Collectibles
6570 Memorial Dr.
Stone Mountain, GA 30083
ph: 404-879-7878
Specializing in vintage Coca-Cola machines and jukeboxes.

Bill Mock
2640 SW 29th Way
Fort Lauderdale, FL 33312
ph: 954-584-8958
Buys, sells, restores Coca-Cola vending machines.

Home Arcade Corp.
1108 Front St.
Lisle, IL 60532-2258
ph: 630-964-2555
fax: 630-964-9367
web: http://www.homearcadecorp.com/
Sells restored vintage Coke machines; also juke boxes, phone booths, beer signs, tavern items, barber poles and

other '50s memorabilia; send $5 for Coke Restoration Parts Catalog.

Periodicals

Dan Kwate
Magazine: Club Soda
P.O. Box 489
Troy, ID 83871-0489
ph: 208-835-2306
fax: 208-835-2307
e-mail: dkwate@clubsoda.net
web: http://www.clubsoda.net
Articles about all types of soda collectibles: vending machines, signs, bottles,etc.; features include company histories, restoration tips, show and auction reviews, and free classified ads.

Repair Services

Hobbs Country Store
P.O. Box 158
Galveston, IN 46932
ph: 219-699-7505
Custom restorer of only Coca-Cola vending machines.

Suppliers

Fun-Tronics
P.O. Box 448
Middletown, MD 21769
ph: 301-371-5246
Specializing in restoration supplies for vintage Coke machines.

Jeff Walters
Memory Lane Sodaware
P.O. Box 506
Camino, CA 95709
ph: 530-644-1924
Sells restoration parts for classic soda machines: rubber, decals, locks; $4 for catalog.

Soft Drink Cans

Clubs/Associations

Rich Simmons, Dir.
National Pop Can Collectors
Newsletter: Can-O-Gram
19201 Sherwood Green Way
Gaithersburg, MD 20879
ph: 301-869-4899
fax: 301-601-9322
e-mail: cokecans@aol.com
Worldwide network of collectors focusing on soda cans & bottles as well as other soda memorabilia; articles, free ads and roster; regional trade sessions so members can meet and trade in person; club roster provided to each member.

Collectors

Rich Simmons
19201 Sherwood Green Way
Gaithersburg, MD 20879
ph: 301-869-4899
fax: 301-601-9322
e-mail: cokecans@aol.com

Jerry Glader
1017 Villa Gran Way
Fenton, MO 63026
ph: 314-343-9433
e-mail: jerry@primary.net
web: http://www.angelfire.com/mo/JerryBeerCans/
Collects Coca-Cola, Pepsi, and 7-Up cans and specializes in one can from every country in the world and cans from Africa.

Museums/Libraries

Museum of Beverage Containers & Advertising, The
1055 Ridgecrest Dr.
Goodlettsville, TN 37072
ph: 615-859-5236 or 877-859-4929
fax: 615-859-5238
e-mail: mbca@gono.com
web: http://gono.com/vir-mus/museum.htm
The largest collection of soda and beer cans in the world; buy, sell, trade beer & soda advertising items.

Squirt

Collectors

Jan Vonburg
3749 E. Gill Dr.
Denver, CO 80209-3510
ph: 303-777-9388
Wants Squirt picnic coolers, soda machines, clocks, decals, 6 pack holders, etc.

Vernors Ginger Ale

Experts

Keith Wunderlich
P.O. Box 300572
Waterford, MI 48330
ph: 248-682-6134
e-mail: kw5owat@moa.net
Avid collector of Vernors Ginger Ale advertising and memorabilia; also Vernors historian and will help identify and date Vernors items.

Whistle Soda

Collectors

Andy Fulks
P.O. Box 92
Whitestown, IN 46075
ph: 765-482-1861 or 317-769-1861
fax: 765-482-1848
e-mail: ajf5577@aol.com
web: http://fcsutler.com/fcwanted.html
Serious collector of Whistle Soda and Cleo Cola advertising items: signs, calendars, die cuts, etc.

SOLDIERS

Toy

(see also MINIATURES, Military; TOYS; TOYS, Playsets)

Appraisers

Barry Carter
Knightstown Antiques Mall
136 W. Carey St.
Knightstown, IN 46148-1111
ph: 765-345-5665
e-mail: bcarter@spitfire.net
Buys, sells, appraises and specializes in toy soldiers and military miniatures; consultant for AntiqueWeek; promoter of the Indiana Toy Soldier Show (last Sunday in March.)

Auction Services

Henry Kurtz
Henry Kurtz Ltd.
163 Amsterdam Ave., Ste. 136
New York, NY 10023
ph: 212-642-5904
fax: 212-874-6018
Specializes in the sale of jewelry, paintings, prints, silver, coins, stamps, toys (especially lead soldiers), and movie memorabilia.

Glenn Butler
Wallis & Wallis
West Street Auction Galleries
Lewes, East Sussex BN7 2NJ
U.K.
ph: 01273-480208
fax: 01273-476562
e-mail: wallisandwallis@mcmail.com
web: http://www.wallisandwallis.co.uk/
Britain's specialist auctioneers of diecast & tin plate toys & models including model soldiers.

Clubs/Associations

Arley Pett, Past-Pres.
North East Toy Soldier Society
Newsletter: North East Toy Soldier Society Newsletter
12 Beach Rd.
Gloucester, MA 09130-3214
ph: 978-283-2612
fax: 978-283-2612
e-mail: apett92117@aol.com
Monthly meetings usually in the Boston area; sponsors two toy soldier sales/shows in Boston area each year.

Frank Burns
South Florida Toy Soldiers Club, Inc.
715 S.W. 15 Street
Boynton Beach, FL 33426
ph: 561-734-3842 or 561-732-7295
fax: 561-734-3842
e-mail: Majortoyman@webtv.net
web: http://commnity.gopbi.com/ToySoldiers/
Club host annual show every February in West Palm Beach, FL.

John Giddings
Toy Soldier Collectors of America
Newsletter: Communique
5340 40th Ave. N
Saint Petersburg, FL 33709
ph: 727-527-1430
An information center for all toy soldier collectors worldwide.

Collectors

Bill Lango
P.O. Box 4809
North Bergen, NJ 07047-4809
ph: 973-831-8900
fax: 973-831-8912
e-mail: toysold@bellatlantic.net
web: http://www.toysoldierreview.com/
Interested in Barclay vehicles, animals and soldiers from original and new molds.

Peter & Kathy Paul
1673A Town Point Rd.
Cambridge, MD 21613-3579
ph: 410-476-4627
Wants old toy soldiers; lead, iron, composition, rubber; any quantity.

David W. Francis
148 King St.
Wadsworth, OH 44281
ph: 330-335-3717
fax: 330-335-3617
e-mail: fphadv@bright.net
Wants to buy toy soldiers of all types.

Dealers

John A. Rollins
Toy Soldiers
P.O. Box 486
South Wellfleet, MA 02663
ph: 508-349-1715

Arley Pett
Arley L. Pett Antiques
12 Beach Rd.
Gloucester, MA 09130-3214
ph: 978-283-2612
fax: 978-283-2612
e-mail: apett92117@aol.com
Collects, buys, sells and appraises toy soldiers and civilians, lead farm, zoo, circus, hunt, railroad figures, military vehicles and related items such as miniature gardens; manages two toy shows per year for NETSS.

Jamie & Jenny Delson
Toy Soldier Company, The
100 Riverside Drive
New York, NY 10024
ph: 201-792-6665
fax: 201-792-2626
e-mail: jdelson@toysoldierco.com
web: http://toysoldierco.com/
Large mail order resource for modern toy soldiers; stocks unpainted and painted plastic figures in 54mm, 60mm, and 70mm scales, unpainted plastic figures in HO scale,a nd painted metal figures in 54mm scale; send $5 for catalog of stock.

Ron Ruddell
London Bridge Collector's Toys, Ltd.
401 Chestnut St.
Emmaus, PA 18049

Jim Hillestad
Toy Soldier, The
RR 1, Box 379
Cresco, PA 18326
ph: 570-629-7227
fax: 570-629-9205
e-mail: jimhill@ptd.net
web: http://www.The-Toy-Soldier.com
Deals in all major toy soldier makers, furniture-quality display cases, Michael Sutty bone china military sculptures, regimental drums, bugles and more; also has a 3,000 sq. ft. museum of figures and dioramas.

Michael & Norene Rosso
Stockade Miniatures, Inc.
4 North 6th St.
Stroudsburg, PA 18360
ph: 570-424-8507
fax: 570-424-8503
e-mail: mrosso@ptd.net
web: http://www.stockade-miniatures.com/
Deals in quality new and old toy soldiers from around the world; want lists accepted for old items.

Allen W. Smith
102 N. Cherry St.
Falls Church, VA 22046-3518
ph: 703-237-2164
Wants dimestore toy soldiers: lead, rubber, composition, paper; Auburn, Marx, Manoil, Barclay, Built-Rite, etc.; any number.

Stone Castle Imports
P.O. Box 141
Bardstown, KY 40004
ph: 502-897-0207
fax: 502-897-6415
e-mail: castle@toysoldiers.cc
web: http://www.toysoldiers.cc/
Carries a wide variety of toy soldiers and playsets.

Joseph Saine
Joseph Saine Toy Soldiers
P.O. Box 50506
Toledo, OH 43605-0506
ph: 419-691-0008
Buys and sells lead, composition, and plastic toy soldiers; any soldier or figure; issues periodic listings.

Barry Carter
Knightstown Antiques Mall
136 W. Carey St.
Knightstown, IN 46148-1111
ph: 765-345-5665
e-mail: bcarter@spitfire.net
Buys, sells, appraises and specializes in toy soldiers and military miniatures; consultant for AntiqueWeek; promoter of the Indiana Toy Soldier Show (last Sunday in March.)

Rick Berry
Michigan Toy Soldier & Figure Co.
405 S. Washington
Royal Oak, MI 48067
ph: 248-586-1022
fax: 248-398-4436
e-mail: otr@mich.com
web: http://www.michtoy.com
Buys and sells new and old toy soldiers of all types; web site contains one of the most comprehensive listings of information on the hobby available.

David S. Bennett
Bennett Antiques
15800 26th Ave. N.
Minneapolis, MN 55447-1940
Wants American dimestore toy soldiers made by Barclay, Manoil, Gray Ives, Jones, etc.

Pam & Bill Brunton
Brunton's Barracks
415 South Montezuma
Prescott, AZ 86303-4223
ph: 520-778-1915
fax: 520-717-1698
e-mail: bruntonw@primenet.com
Dealer, appraiser, manufacturer of lead, composition and plastic toy soldiers.

Paul Kemkemian
Ani Toy Soldiers
626 S. Myrtle Ave.
Monrovia, CA 91016
ph: 626-303-3990
fax: 818-360-2003
e-mail: tk777@prodigy.net
web: http://www.anitoysoldiers.com
Sells handmade and handpainted lead military soldiers.

Bob Fisher
Old Toy Soldier Home, The
977 S. Santa Fe, Ste. #11
Vista, CA 92083
ph: 760-758-5481
fax: 760-758-5481
e-mail: info@oldtoysoldierhome.com
web: http://www.oldtoysoldierhome.com/
A retail store dedicated to the toy soldier hobby; has over 15,000 figures on view covering all areas of history from ancient to modern times: Britain's and Mignot both new and old, Ducal, Imperial King & Country.

Bob Fisher
Old Toy Soldier Home, The
977 S. Santa Fe #11
Vista, CA 92083-6911
ph: 760-758-5481
fax: 760-758-5481
e-mail: info@oldtoysoldierhome.com
web: http://oldtoysoldierhome.com
Buys and sells toy soldiers: Britains, Mignot (old and new), dime store, composition, new makers, King & Country, Ducal, AQM, Trophy, Imperial; has over 20,000 figures on display.

Pinehill's Tin Soldier Factory
Pine Hill, RR #1
Clinton, Ontario N0M 1L0
Canada
e-mail: pinehill@odyssey.on.ca
web: http://www.odyssey.on.ca/~pinehill/factory/
Sells kits and books for the toy soldier hobbyist.

Mark Avery
Avalon Court, Star Road
Partridge Green, West Sussex RH13 8RY
U.K.
ph: +44 (0) 1403 711511 or 513-353-4052 (in U.S.)
fax: +44 (0) 1403 711521
e-mail: mark@ashdown.co.uk
web: http://www.ashdown.co.uk/magazfr.htm
Toy soldier dealer and expert; specializes in antique and modern toy soldiers and 54mm collectors figures; also sells books and special edition figurines for the discerning collector.

Experts

Chris Keller
219 Ridge Rd.
Carlisle, PA 17013-9275
ph: 717-258-3573 or 814-867-5434
e-mail: cbk108@psu.edu
Buying and selling antique W. Britains and dimestore collections; free appraisals; 12 years experience.

K. Warren Mitchell
1008 Forward Pass
Pataskala, OH 43062-7505
ph: 740-927-1661
Buys, sells, appraises and specializes in all kinds of old toy soldiers especially Britains, "dimestore", Mignot, Heyde (no plastic toys, please.) Author of articles on toy soldiers.

Man./Prod./Dist.

Joseph DiVincenzo
Nickolson Miniatures
17877 St. Clair Ave.
Cleveland, OH 44110
ph: 216-531-7334
e-mail: nickolson@nickolson-toy-soldiers.com
web: http://www.nickolson-toy-soldiers.com/
Manufactures traditional high gloss toy soldiers depicting the British Empire, the Indian Army under British rule, WWII American and German paratroopers.

Bill Hocker
Wm Hocker Toy Soldiers
1605 Arch St.
Berkeley, CA 94709
ph: 510-841-4458
fax: 510-644-3433
e-mail: bill@wmhocker.coom
web: http://www.wmhocker.com
Manufacturer of collectible metal toy soldiers; web site has many resources for the toy soldier collector.

Judiann & Bob O'Connell
Northcoast Miniatures
311 Biyle Drive
Eureka, CA 95503
ph: 707-443-8915
e-mail: oconnell@humboldt1.com
web: http://www.54mmtoysoldier.com/info/
Manufactures metal 54mm scale cannons, wagons, and figures: Napoleonic era, Civil War era, Victorian Village, Early Americana, Nativity; fine line of wagons available.

Periodicals

Bill Lango
Magazine: Toy Soldier Review
P.O. Box 4809
North Bergen, NJ 07047-4809
ph: 973-831-8900
fax: 973-831-8912
e-mail: toysold@bellatlantic.net
web: http://www.toysoldierreview.com/
A worldwide quarterly magazine for the toy soldier enthusiast.

Paul Stadinger
STAD'S
Magazine: Plastic Warrior
815 North 12th St.
Allentown, PA 18102-1318
ph: 610-770-1140 or 610-433-7728
fax: 610-770-1740
e-mail: pestad@browser.net
A British bi-monthly focusing on leading European plastic figures, firms (Britains, Timpo, etc.), reviews, Q&A, letters, news, ads, etc.

Magazine: Toy Soldiers & Collectibles
P.O. Box 301
Libertytown, MD 21762-0301
ph: 301-898-7686
e-mail: ilewis4566@aol.com
web: http://www.angelfire.com/bix/ToySoldierMag/
Quarterly magazine covers Marx, Imex, Accurate, A Call to Arms, CTS, Timpo, Hat Industries, and other brands of plastic toy soldiers.

Antique Trader Publications, Inc.
Newspaper: Military Trader
P.O. Box 1050
Dubuque, IA 52004-1050
ph: 800-334-7165 or 800-482-4155
fax: 800-531-0880
e-mail: atpzines@aol.com
web: http://www.collect.com/militarytrader
Monthly publication focusing on

military collectibles: articles, collecting, interviews with dealers, military toy column, book reviews, collectibles for sale, espionage.

Jo & Steve Sommers
OTSN, Inc.
Magazine: Old Toy Soldier
209 North Lombard
Oak Park, IL 60302
ph: 708-383-6525
fax: 708-383-2182
e-mail: dimestores@aol.com
web: http://www.oldtoysoldier.com/
A quarterly publication published since 1976; articles cover the full range of toy soldier topics and makers; packed with articles on Britains, American Dimestore, Lineol, Elastolin; book reviews, shows, ads; some civilian lines, too.

Mark Avery
Ashdown Publishing
Magazine: Toy Soldier & Model Figure Magazine
Avalon Court, Star Road
Partridge Green, West Sussex RH13 8RY
U.K.
ph: +44 (0) 1403 711511 or 513-353-4052 (in U.S.)
fax: +44 (0) 1403 711521
e-mail: mark@ashdown.co.uk
web: http://www.toy-soldier.com/
An English full color magazine and website devoted to collectors of antique and modern toy soldiers and 54mm collectors figures; also sells books and special edition figurines for the discerning collector.

SOUTH PACIFIC

(see ART, Oceanic; POLYNESIAN COLLECTIBLES)

SOUVENIR & COMMEMORATIVE ITEMS

(see also CERAMICS, Souvenir & Commemorative; DISNEY COLLECTIBLES, Disneyland Souvenirs; GLASS, Souvenir & Commemorative; HISTORICAL AMERICANA; MILITARIA, Silk Embroideries; ROYALTY COLLECTIBLES; SPOONS, Souvenir; STATE RELATED MEMORABILIA)

Auction Services

Richard Vogel
Vogels, The
4720 SE Fort King St.
Ocala, FL 34470-1501
ph: 352-694-5776
fax: 352-694-7330
e-mail: vogels@atlantic.net
Bi-monthly mail order souvenir auctions: china, glass, spoons, mauchline, paper, World's Fair, fraternal.

Collectors

David Ringering
Belle Ringer Antiques
1480 Tumalo Dr. SE
Salem, OR 97301
ph: 503-585-8253
Wants to buy Rowland & Marsellus rolled edge, 10" souvenir/historical plates; also any other c. 1890-1935 pictorial souvenirs with scenes of cities, towns, etc.; also wants German metal tumblers with American/ Canadian scenes.

Dealers

Gary Leveille
5 Brook Lane
Great Barrington, MA 01230
ph: 413-528-5490
e-mail: garyleve@aol.com
Wants to purchase antique souvenirs: souvenir china, glass, postcards.

Buildings

Clubs/Associations

Dixie Trainer
Souvenir Building Collectors Society
Newsletter: Souvenir Building Collector
P.O. Box 70
Nellysford, VA 22958-0070
ph: 804-361-1739
e-mail: souvenirbu@aol.com
Aims to educate and entertain collectors of three-dimensional souvenir buildings and monuments worldwide; annual convention; newsletter published three times a year; free newsletter sample on request.

Collectors

Barry D. Hoffman
7 Stonemeadow
Westwood, MA 02090
ph: 617-267-9000 or 781-326-3333
fax: 781-266-6666
e-mail: pakistan@tiac.net
Wants to buy metal souvenir buildings, all types: paperweight, bank, inkwells, etc.; wants anything that looks like a recognizable building model; free appraisals.

Bill Trainer
P.O. Box 70
Nellysford, VA 22958-0070
ph: 804-361-1739
e-mail: souvenirbu@aol.com
Wants to buy three-dimensional, metal replicas of famous buildings and monuments.

Mark Dittenbir
641 S. Shore Dr.
Kalamazoo, MI 49002
ph: 616-327-4227
Wants to buy metal replicas of landmark skyscrapers, cathedrals, bank buildings, etc. such as Chrysler Building, Capitol Records Building.

Fred Schwartz
RR 1 Box 135
Hull, IL 62343
ph: 217-432-5796 or 217-432-5502
Wants to buy small metal buildings, can be banks or paperweights or anything else.

Dave Forman
1914 11th St. #3
Santa Monica, CA 90404-4558
ph: 310-396-1272
fax: 310-392-1400
Wants to buy potmetal souvenir building replicas of banks, S&Ps, etc. of famous buildings, landmarks, monuments, etc.

Margarete Majua
Ace Architects
332 2nd St.
Oakland, CA 94607
ph: 510-286-2290 or 925-283-3218
fax: 510-452-1175
e-mail: ace@aceland.com
Wants to buy souvenir buildings; found in the form of banks, souvenirs, paperweights, inkwells, salt & pepper shakers, World's Fair memorabilia, pencil sharpeners, etc.

Dealers

Barbara Strand
Dullsville
143 E. 13th St.
New York, NY 10003
ph: 212-505-2505
Specializes in souvenir buildings.

Bob Kneisel
1278 Mare Vista Ave.
Pasadena, CA 91104-2951
ph: 626-797-2707
Buys and sells miniature buildings; souvenir buildings, banks, monuments, statues; metal and other materials.

Man./Prod./Dist.

Dixie Trainer
Souvenir Building Network, The
P.O. Box 70
Nellysford, VA 22958-0070
ph: 804-361-1583
fax: 804-361-9151
e-mail: souvenirbu@aol.com
Sells U.S. and foreign souvenir buildings via catalog; free copy on request; produces custom replicas of buildings of buildings for real estate developers, banks and museums.

Anthony Tremblay
Microcosms
809 N. Rose St.
Burbank, CA 91505
ph: 818-558-7952
This company casts high-quality and affordable mini replicas of a number of buildings, including modern, classical and ancient structures.

Niagara Falls

Internet Resources

Niagara Falls, Canada Visitor & Convention Bureau
e-mail: nfcvcb@tourismniagara.com
web: http://www.tourismniagara.com/nfcvcb/
Links, to Niagara Falls attractions.

Museums/Libraries

Niagara Falls Museum
5651 River Road
Niagara Falls, Ontario L2E 6V8
Canada
ph: 905-356-2151

Pillows

Collectors

J.J. Murphy
920 Emerald St.
Madison, WI 53715-1614
ph: 608-257-3855
fax: 608-257-3730
e-mail: jjmurphy@facstaff.wisc.edu
Wants lithograph pillow tops: turn-of-the-century color lithographs on cloth; approximately 22 inches square; all subjects; condition important.

Dealers

Susan & Michelle Horowitz
Quilted Corner, The
124 Fourth Ave.
New York, NY 10003-4903
ph: 212-505-6568
e-mail: michelle@quiltedcorner.com
web: http://www.quiltedcorner.com/
Carries a wide assortment of vintage linens, tablecloths, napkins, tea towels, souvenir pillows, drapes and textiles.

Summer Resort Items

Collectors

David W. Francis
148 King St.
Wadsworth, OH 44281
ph: 330-335-3717
fax: 330-335-3617
e-mail: fphadv@bright.net
Wants 1880-1930 summer resort souvenirs: Atlantic City, Coney Island, Cedar Point, etc. - post cards, booklets, pennants, tickets, etc.

Tablecloths

Collectors

Chloe Ross
7553 Norton Ave. Apt. 4
Los Angeles, CA 90046-5500
ph: 213-874-3044
e-mail: trstrap@aol.com
Wants tablecloths with maps, graphics or states, amusement parks, locations; may be worn and some stains OK; no

AK or CA; especially wants east coast, Midwest, New England or FL; buy or trade.

Universal Theatres

Collectors

Edwin Snyder
P.O. Box 156
Lancaster, KY 40444-0156
ph: 606-792-4816
e-mail: snyecco@aol.com
Wants to buy penny toys, pocket mirrors, dexterity games, compasses, small portrait plaques, mini books, etc. given away to children attending movies in the 1920s and 1930s; all toys marked "Souvenir of Universal Theatres - Chicago".

Yosemite

Collectors

Neal Austinson
P.O. Box 1691
Windsor, CA 95492-1691
ph: 707-837-9685
Wants old Yosemite items: photographs, souvenirs, etc.

SOVIET

(see RUSSIAN ITEMS)

SPACE COLLECTIBLES

(see also ASTRONOMICAL ITEMS; AUTOGRAPHS, Astronaut; BOOKS, Reference [Space Collectibles]; CHARACTER COLLECTIBLES; PREMIUMS; ROCKETS; SCIENCE FICTION; TELEVISION SHOWS & MEMORABILIA; TOYS, Space & Robot)

Auction Services

Superior Galleries
9478 West Olympic Blvd.
Beverly Hills, CA 90212-4246
ph: 310-203-9855 or 800-421-0754
fax: 310-203-0496
e-mail: superior@superiorsc.com
web: http://www.superiorsc.com/
Has been a retail and auction source for dealers and collectors for over 70 years; specializes in stamps, coins, sports memorabilia, Hollywood memorabilia, space memorabilia, historic manuscripts and autographs.

Book Sellers

Lee & Peggy Price
Knollwood Books
P.O. Box 197
Oregon, WI 53575-0197
ph: 608-835-8861
fax: 608-835-8421
e-mail: books@tdsnet.com
Issues quarterly catalogs; buys and sells out-of-print books on astronomy, meteorology, and space exploration; also books about microscopes, old scientific instruments, optics, and related areas.

Clubs/Associations

David Brandt
National Space Society
Magazine: Ad Astra
600 Pennsylvania Ave. SE, Ste. 201
Washington, DC 20003-4316
ph: 202-543-1900 or 800-376-ORBIT
fax: 202-546-4189
e-mail: nsshq@nss.org
web: http://www.nss.org/
International organization promoting space development; 80 local and international chapters; holds annual Space Development Conference and regional conferences.

International Space Hall of Fame
The Space Center
P.O. Box 533
Alamogordo, NM 88310
ph: 505-437-2840
fax: 505-434-2245
e-mail: spacepr@zianet.com
web: http://www.zianet.com/space/

Collectors

Michael Mitchell
RR 1, Box 4440
Kents Hill, ME 04349
ph: 207-897-6855
Collects space related memorabilia: newspapers headlining space missions, photographs, books; non-flown items.

Harvey & Sandy Dolin
Harvey Dolin & Co.
5 Beekman St.
New York, NY 10038-2206
ph: 212-267-0216
Wants to buy items relating to the space programs.

Larry McLaughlin
17 Seventh Ave.
Smithtown, NY 11787-4508
ph: 516-265-9224
e-mail: larrymak@erols.com
Wants space items from Apollo, Mercury, or Gemini; also wants NASA logos.

Dennis Kelly
P.O. Box 9942
Spokane, WA 99209
ph: 509-456-8488
e-mail: dennisk@ior.com
Wants items from space programs Apollo, Mercury, Gemini; also anything with NASA logo or serial numbers, autographs, X15, X20, high altitude equipment, helmets, miscellaneous gear.

Dealers

Gregg Linebaugh
AVD Services
P.O. Box 604
Glenn Dale, MD 20769
ph: 301-249-3895
Buys and sells artifacts that have flown in space and to the moon; actual space craft hardware, space suits, videos, books, patches, medallions, flags, and other unusual items; sponsors two Space Memorabilia shows each year.

J.W. Sigh
Ultimate Space Place, The
P.O. Box 541107
Merritt Island, FL 32954
ph: 407-454-4236
e-mail: questions@thespaceplace.com
web: http://www.thespaceplace.com/

Russsell Herron
Space Center, The
603 Val Lena
Houston, TX 77024
ph: 713-467-0264
fax: 713-973-0456
e-mail: imagine5@flash.net
web: http://imagine5.com
Historic and collectible items from the history of space exploration including official NASA mission patches, rare and hard-to-find scale models of historic spacecraft, art, photographs, autographs, commemoratives, and books.

Experts

Stuart Schneider
P.O. Box 64
Teaneck, NJ 07666-0064
ph: 201-261-1983
fax: 201-599-1950
e-mail: stuarts1031@erols.com
web: http://www.geocities.com/Yosemite/Geyser/7949/
Items flown in space, toys, toy ray guns, Russian items, Sputnik, Welcome Back astronaut buttons, coin banks, artwork, etc.; author of "Collecting the Space Race" (1993).

Tom N. Tumbusch
Tomart Publications
3300 Encrete Lane
Dayton, OH 45439-1944
ph: 937-294-2250
fax: 937-294-1024
e-mail: office@tomart.com
web: http://www.tomart.com
Aliens, Flash Gordon, Empire Strikes Back, Star Wars, Star Trek, Captain Video; action figures, comic books, and all related memorabilia; author of "Space Adventure Collectibles"; only inquiries accompanied by a SASE will be answered.

Museums/Libraries

Jim Johnson
U.S. Space & Rocket Center
One Tranquility Base
Huntsville, AL 35805-3371
ph: 256-837-3400

International Space Hall of Fame, The Space Center
Magazine: SpaceLog
P.O. Box 533
Alamogordo, NM 88310-0533
ph: 505-437-2840 or 800-545-4021
fax: 505-437-7722
e-mail: space@zianet.com
web: http://www.zianet.com/space/
The ISHF is a four-story museum which chronicles the history of man's exploration of space; from earliest rockets to space shuttle.

Apollo XI Memorabilia

Collectors

Ronald Ulrich
114 East Benton
Mt. Olive, IL 62069
Wants Apollo XI (first moon landing) items; plates, cups, dishes, coins, books, glasses, etc.

SPAM

(see ADVERTISING COLLECTIBLES, Hormel)

SPECTACLES

(see EYE RELATED ITEMS, Eyeglasses; OPTICAL ITEMS)

SPIES

(see CHARACTER COLLECTIBLES, Spy Memorabilia; SPY EQUIPMENT; TELEVISION SHOWS & MEMORABILIA, Private Eye)

SPINNING WHEELS

Museums/Libraries

Museum of American Textile History
491 Dutton St.
Lowell, MA 01854-4221
ph: 978-441-0400
fax: 978-441-1412
web: http://valley.uml.edu/lowell/historic/museums/textile.html
Outstanding collection of textiles and textile making machinery and equipment; tools, machines, prints, photographs, business records, industry periodicals, textiles, swatches, sample books, trade catalogs, etc.

Barbara Muret
Oklahoma's Yarn Spinning Museum
117 W. 7th Ave.
Stillwater, OK 74074
ph: 405-377-7195
e-mail: muret@cowboy.net
web: http://www.cowboy.net/~muret/
Send 52 cent LSASE for free color photograph brochure of replicas to help you identify your wheel and its missing parts; or you can order antique replicas in working order.

Periodicals

Florence Feldman-Wood
Newsletter: Spinning Wheel Sleuth, The
P.O. Box 422
Andover, MA 01810-0008
ph: 978-475-8790
e-mail: ffw@netway.com
A quarterly newsletter exploring all aspects of spinning wheels; feature articles include types of wheels, American and European, histories of wheels, biographies of wheel makers, and much more; for hand spinners, collectors, and museums.

Repair Services

Mick Holloway
P.O. Box 453
Winchester, IN 47394-0453
ph: 765-584-1971
Complete restoration of flax wheels and wool wheels; minors' heads and flyers repaired; distaffs turned and dressed with flax fiber; all parts custom fit; 22 years experience.

Suppliers

Barbara Muret
Fleece & Unicorn
Seventh Avenue Center
123 West 7th Ave.
Stillwater, OK 74074-4665
ph: 405-377-7105
Designer of yarn and fibers; international services, exceptional selections of doll hair and craft yarns.

Miniature

Collectors

Lanelle Hodnett
2965 Avenue Z
Brooklyn, NY 11235-1658
ph: 718-891-3489
Wants to buy miniature spinning wheels and motifs.

SPIRITUALISM

(see UFO'S & UNEXPLAINED PHENOMENA)

SPOON WARMERS

Dealers

Vivian & James Karsnitz
1428 Jerry Lane
Manheim, PA 17545-9353
ph: 717-665-4202
Buying and selling spoon warmers.

SPOONS

(see also KITCHEN COLLECTIBLES; SILVER; SOUVENIR & COMMEMORATIVE ITEMS; SPOON WARMERS)

Clubs/Associations

Terry & Mary Haines
Silver Spoon Club of Great Britain, The
Journal: Finial, The
Glenleigh Park
St. Austell, Cornwall PL26 7JD
U.K.
ph: 01726-65269
fax: 01726-65269
International postal club for experienced or beginner collectors of antique and other fine silver spoons and associated silver cutlery; worldwide membership; "The Finial" contains specialist articles and member's news and views; auctions.

Souvenir

(see also SOUVENIR & COMMEMORATIVE ITEMS)

Auction Services

Richard Vogel
Vogels, The
4720 SE Fort King St.
Ocala, FL 34470-1501
ph: 352-694-5776
fax: 352-694-7330
e-mail: vogels@atlantic.net
Bi-monthly mail order souvenir auctions: china, glass, spoons, mauchline, paper, World's Fair, fraternal.

Chris McGlothlin
780 Rock Springs Rd.
Kingsport, TN 37664
ph: 423-239-6776
e-mail: McSpoons@aol.com
web: http://hometown.aol.com/mcspons/home.html

Clubs/Associations

Erwin Goldman, PR
Northeastern Spoon Collectors Guild
Newsletter: Cauldron, The
8200 Boulevard East
North Bergen, NJ 07047-6039
ph: 201-662-1342
fax: 201-662-1342
NSCG is dedicated to the perpetuation of the spoon collecting hobby.

Bill Boyd
American Spoon Collectors
Newsletter: Spooners Forum
7408 Englewood Lane
Raytown, MO 64133-6913
ph: 816-356-7423
fax: 816-356-7423

Mary Bengston
Dallas Souvenir Spoon Collectors Club
9748 Broken Bow Rd.
Dallas, TX 75238

Trudy Geer
Southern California Souvenir Spoon Collectors Club
3832 Denwood Ave.
Los Alamitos, CA 90720

Bob Corson, Liaison
Washington State Spoon Collectors
1992 S. Elger Bay Road, Box 151
Stanwood, WA 98292

Collectors

Erwin & Dorothy Goldman
8200 Boulevard East
North Bergen, NJ 07047-6039
ph: 201-662-1342
fax: 201-662-1342

Chris McGlothlin
780 Rock Springs Rd.
Kingsport, TN 37664
ph: 423-239-6776
e-mail: McSpoons@aol.com
web: http://hometown.aol.com/mcspons/home.html

John W. Coons
9757 S. Isabel Ct.
Littleton, CO 80126-4717
ph: 303-791-6496
e-mail: jcoons1552@aol.com
Wants souvenir spoons: enamel bowls, blacks, mining, hotels, libraries, skylines, etc.

Dealers

Spoon Search
e-mail: spoons@spoonsearch.com
web: http://www.spoonsearch.com

Doris K. Bagwell, R.N.
Bagwell Antiques
5607 Concord Dr.
Jackson, MS 39211-4239
ph: 601-956-3508
fax: 601-956-4190
e-mail: DKay5607@aol.com
Collects, buys and sells quality sterling silver souvenir spoons, especially enamel bowls, blacks, embossed, and engraved.

T.K. Treadwell
4201 Nagle Rd.
Bryan, TX 77801-3938
ph: 409-846-0209
e-mail: 71222.1571@compuserve.com

Gary Lickver
P.O. Box 1778
San Marcos, CA 92079-1778
ph: 760-744-5686
Wants to buy sterling silver souvenir spoons 1890-1930; especially full bowl enamels, American and European.

Experts

Bill Boyd
7408 Englewood Lane
Raytown, MO 64133-6913
ph: 816-356-7423
fax: 816-356-7423
Wants souvenir spoons with embossed, enameled or engraved handles and bowls; also World's Fair subjects, full-figured people, etc.

Chuck Wasserman
11723 W. 101st
Shawnee Mission, KS 66214
ph: 913-492-5005
Expert and serious collector of 1904 St. Louis World's Fair memorabilia; specializes in spoons, ceramics, and glass; especially foreign exhibit material such as jasperware, Haviland Limoges, Nippon, and moriage.

SPORTING COLLECTIBLES

(see also ANIMAL TROPHIES; ART, Sporting; ART, Wildlife; CAMPING EQUIPMENT; DECOYS; ENDANGERED SPECIES; FIREARMS; FISHING COLLECTIBLES; FURNITURE [ANTIQUE], Rustic; LICENSES, Hunting & Fishing; TARGET SHOOTING MEMORAB.; TICKETS; TRAP SHOOTING; TRAPS)

Auction Services

Gerard Giguere
Giguere Auction Co.
P.O. Box 1272
Windham, ME 04062
ph: 207-892-3800
fax: 207-892-3800
Conducts sporting auctions: fishing, hunting, decoys, sporting art, taxidermy.

Frank & Frank
422 Lakewood-Farmingdale Rd.
Howell, NJ 07731
ph: 732-938-2988
fax: 732-938-2988
Auctions, buys and sells decoys, sporting collectibles, wildlife/sporting art.

Ronnie Roberts, ISA
SoldUSA.com
6407 Idlewild Rd., Bldg. 2, Ste 207
Charlotte, NC 28212
ph: 704-364-2900 or 877-SoldUSA
fax: 704-364-2322
e-mail: gun1898@aol.com
web: http://www.soldusa.com/

Kurt R. Krueger
Krueger Auctions
P.O. Box 275
Iola, WI 54945-0275
ph: 715-445-3845
fax: 715-445-4100
Specializing in the mail-bid auction of hunting, fishing, shooting, and trapping memorabilia.

Book Sellers

David E. Foley
David E. Foley - Sporting Books
76 Bonnyview Rd.
West Hartford, CT 06107
ph: 860-561-0783
Buys and sells fine sporting books: angling, hunting, firearms, shooting, archery, natural history.

Connecticut River Bookstore
P.O. Box 461
East Haddam, CT 06423
ph: 860-873-8881
Rare and out of print books and ephemera on hunting, fishing, natural history, guns.

Judith & Jim Bowman
Judith Bowman Books
Pound Ridge Rd.
Bedford, NY 10506
ph: 914-234-7543
Buys and sells rare and out-of-print books and ephemera on angling, hunting, related natural history, guns, dogs, old tackle and gun catalogs, etc.

Dean Dashner
Hunting Rig
349 S. Green Bay Rd.
Neenah, WI 54956
ph: 920-725-4350 or 920-725-4421
e-mail: dashners@athenet.net
web: http://www.athenet/net/~dashners
Buys and sells decoys, duck calls, Ducks Unlimited Pinbacks, sporting books, old sporting magazines.

Wilderness Adventures
P.O. Box 627
Gallatin Gateway, MT 59730
ph: 800-925-3339 or 406-763-4900
e-mail: books@wildadv.com
web: http://www.wildadv.com
World's largest selection of hunting and fishing books for the collector and enthusiast.

Collectors

Bert Lindsay
315 Broad St.
Manchester, CT 06040-4036
ph: 860-649-8473
Wants to buy sporting antiques and artifacts from 19th to mid-20th century; sporting event programs, tickets, autographs, signed items, documents, equipment, photographs, prints, etc.

Ron Willoughby
1072 Rte. 171
Woodstock, CT 06281-2134
ph: 860-974-1226
fax: 860-974-3190
e-mail: swillo@neca.com
web: http://www.neca.com/swillo
Wants to buy shotshell boxes, gun company posters and calendars, glass target balls and traps, gunpowder cans, animal traps, and related items; a very serious buyer; free appraisals; estate purchases.

Bill Bramlett
P.O. Box 1105
Florence, SC 29503-1105
ph: 803-393-7390 or 843-665-3165
e-mail: bbramlett@webtv.net
Wants 1890-1931 firearms-related advertising items such as calendars, signs and posters that advertise firearms, shotgun shells, gunpowders; also wants Edmund Osthaus and G. Muss-Arnolt bird dog and duck hunting art, prints, pictures.

Tommie Lee Horsley
P.O. Box 728
Jackson, AL 36545
ph: 334-246-5000
e-mail: Lee@Dixienet.com
Wants duck and turkey calls, hunting magazines and photographs, hunting books, Old turkey china such as plates or platters, old hunting and gun company advertising, WInchester fishing items, lures, etc.

Lynn "Dr. Duck" Troute
Lynn Troute Decoys
3808 Kingsley Dr.
Springfield, IL 62707-7250
ph: 217-787-3595
fax: 217-726-1801
e-mail: duckstamps@aol.com
Wants to buy duck stamps, duck decoys, duck calls, licenses, Illinois deer and turkey harvest pins, Ducks Unlimited buttons, and all hunting and fishing artifacts.

Bob Simmons
40706 E. 144th St.
Richmond, MO 64085
ph: 816-776-2936 or 800-646-2936
fax: 816-470-5016
e-mail: simmons_auction@raycounty.com
web: http://www.raycounty.com/simmons/
Collects all types of sporting goods, fishing tackle and related advertising from SImmons Hardware Co., St. Louis, MO; also items from Winchester-Simmons Hardware Co., Diamond Edge (Shapleigh), and Keen Kutter.

Bill Smith, Sr.
6326 Lakewood Park
San Antonio, TX 78239
ph: 800-982-9507
Wants to buy fishing and hunting items.

Dealers

Mary Ann Hahn
Second Hand Mary Ann's
103 Ocean Point Road
Boothbay Harbor, ME 04538
ph: 207-633-2426
fax: 207-633-2586
e-mail: maryann@gwi.net
Buys and sells old fishing and hunting magazines prior to 1939.

Henry Fleckenstein
P.O. Box 577
Cambridge, MD 21613
ph: 410-221-0076
Buys and sells, sporting collectibles: decoys, rare books, shell boxes, powder tins, ammo advertising, sporting magazines and books, reels, lures, bobbers, game calls, old licenses, knives, fish decoys.

Len Codella
Heritage Sporting Collectibles
2201 S. Carnegie Dr.
Inverness, FL 34450
ph: 352-637-5454
fax: 352-637-5420
Wants to buy bamboo rods, reels, tackle, etc.

Tony Laws
Woods & Water, Inc.
1019 McFarland Blvd.
Northport, AL 35476
ph: 205-333-1214
fax: 205-339-9573
Buys and sells sporting art: paintings, prints, drawings, classic firearms, rods & reels, sporting bronzes, wood carvings, advertising art, catalogs, brochures, books.

Robert Krause
Ravenwood Gallery
38745 Butternut Ridge Rd.
Elyria, OH 44035
ph: 440-458-4929
Wants to buy paintings, prints, etchings, calendars, and posters relating to hunting and fishing, birds, dogs, guns, ammunition and power companies; also duck and crow calls, decoys, sporting books, bamboo fly rods, rods, reels, etc.

Dean Dashner
Hunting Rig
349 S. Green Bay Rd.
Neenah, WI 54956
ph: 920-725-4350 or 920-725-4421
e-mail: dashners@athenet.net
web: http://www.athenet/net/~dashners
Buys and sells decoys, duck calls, Ducks Unlimited Pinbacks, sporting books, old sporting magazines.

Joseph & Donna M. Tonelli
29046 377th Ave.
P.O. Box 459
Lake Andes, SD 57356
ph: 605-337-2301 or 815-664-4580
e-mail: tonelli47@hotmail.com
web: http://www.edecoy.com/
Collector, dealer of quality hunting and fishing collectibles: duck decoys, fish decoys, vintage tackle and reels, gun advertising, sporting advertising, shotshell boxes, powder tins; author of "Top of the Line Hunting Collectibles."

Experts

Ralf Coykendall
P.O. Box 29
East Dorset, VT 05253-0029
ph: 802-362-5707
Writes a sporting collectibles column for "AntiqueWeek"; will answer questions if accompanied by a SASE; author of "Coykendall's Sporting Collectibles Price Guide" Vol. I, II and III.

Vivian & James Karsnitz
Vivian Karsnitz Antiques
1428 Jerry Lane
Manheim, PA 17545-9353
ph: 717-665-4202
Buys, sells sporting collectibles: decoys, shotshells, 2-pc. shotshell boxes, prints (especially Lynn Bogue Hunt), early sporting magazines, glass target balls, etc.; authors of "Sporting Collectibles" (Schiffer, 1992.)

Joseph & Donna M. Tonelli
29046 377th Ave.
P.O. Box 459
Lake Andes, SD 57356
ph: 605-337-2301 or 815-664-4580
e-mail: tonelli47@hotmail.com
web: http://www.edecoy.com/
Collector, dealer of quality hunting and fishing collectibles: duck decoys, fish decoys, vintage tackle and reels, gun advertising, sporting advertising, shotshell boxes, powder tins; author of "Top of the Line Hunting Collectibles."

Periodicals

Ralf Coykendall
Coykendall's Sporting Collectibles Newsletter
P.O. Box 29
East Dorset, VT 05253-0029
ph: 802-362-5707

Robert Woollens
R.W. Publishing
Magazine: Sporting Collector's Monthly
P.O. Box 305
Camden, DE 19934-0305
ph: 302-678-0113
fax: 302-678-3387
e-mail: rwpub@prodigy.net
A monthly with hundreds of buy, sell and trade ads; fish and waterfowl decoys, hunting equipment, fishing gear, loading tools, wildlife art, decorative wildlife & fish carvings, and related books, catalogs, magazines, etc.

Pat DuChene, PR
Krause Publications
Magazine: Trapper & Predator Caller, The
700 E. State St.
Iola, WI 54990-0001
ph: 715-445-2214
fax: 715-445-4087
e-mail: info@krause.com
web: http://www.krause.com/
A monthly magazine about hunting, trapping and predator calling, and animal damage control.

Pat DuChene, PR
Krause Publications
Magazine: Turkey & Turkey Hunting
700 E. State St.
Iola, WI 54990-0001
ph: 715-445-2214
fax: 715-445-4087
e-mail: info@krause.com
web: http://www.krause.com/
For serious, technical, year-round, gun and bow turkey hunters; features emphasize success and enjoyment of the sport; some articles on related collectibles.

Archery

Auction Services

Kim Richardson
GunBroker.com
P.O. Box 19137
Atlanta, GA 31126
ph: 770-234-4174
fax: 770-234-4174
e-mail: admin@gunbroker.com/
web: http://www.gunbroker.com/
A premiere firearms auction on the Internet; allows the user to buy and sell guns, gun accessories, air guns, and archery equipment; extensive FFL Holder network assists with the legal transfer of firearms; free to buyers & sellers.

Clubs/Associations

Professional Bowhunters Society
P.O. Box 246
Terrell, NC 28682
ph: 704-664-2534
fax: 704-664-7471
e-mail: Bowhunters@worldnet.att.net
web: http://www.bowsite.com/pbs/

Collectors

Lowell Hobbs
P.O. Box 226
Lynnville, IN 47619-0226
Wants pre-1970s bows and archery equipment; wood or modern recurves and longbows, all metal bows, books magazines, catalogs, old photos, quivers, arrows, accessories.

Leslie Bolyard
787 Westbrooke Dr.
South Lyon, MI 48178-1665
ph: 248-486-3494 or 248-696-6531
Wants to buy archery hunting memorabilia including wood long bows, wood arrows, leather back quivers, folk art with animal/hunting theme, rustic furniture, and accessories.

Periodicals

Larry Fischer
Magazine: Traditional Bowhunter
P.O. Box 15583
Boise, ID 83715-5583
ph: 208-853-0555
fax: 208-853-9925
e-mail: realbows@aol.com
web: http://www.tradbow.com
Periodically carries articles and ads about bowhunting and periodically about vintage hunting equipment.

Game Calls

Book Sellers

Dean Dashner
Hunting Rig Books
349 S. Green Bay Rd.
Neenah, WI 54956
ph: 920-725-4350 or 920-725-4421
e-mail: dashners@athenet.net
web: http://www.athenet/net/~dashners
Buys and sells decoys, duck calls, Ducks Unlimited Pinbacks, sporting books, old sporting magazines.

Clubs/Associations

William R. Bailey, Mem.
Callmakers & Collectors Association of America
Newsletter: CCAA Newsletter
137 Kingswood Dr.
Clarksville, TN 37043
ph: 931-647-9092
e-mail: mrprinting@aol.com
web: http://www.quackin.com/ccaa/
Purpose is to promote interest in and knowledge of the history of callmaking in America; annual meeting, quarterly swap meets, trade, buy, sell.

James C. Fitch
Call & Whistle Collectors Association
Newsletter: Whistle Notes
2839 E. 26th Place
Tulsa, OK 74114-4309
ph: 918-747-3202
e-mail: jfitch@noria.com
Club for collectors of game calls, antique whistles, bo's'n pipes, flutes, bird calls, advertising whistles, toy whistles, and folk art whistles.

Collectors

Robert Christensen
Duck Call Collectors Homepage
e-mail: outdoors@mc.net
web: http://user.mc.net/~outdoors/duckcalls/

Jim Fleming
518 Heather Place
Nashville, TN 37204
ph: 615-292-1463

Richard Tull
Rick's Antique Duck Calls
6310 Sea Haven Dr.
Hixson, TN 37343
e-mail: webmaster@oldcalls.com
web: http://www.oldcalls.com/

Experts

Howard Harlan
Heavy Duty Duck Call Company
303 Murfreesboro Rd.
Nashville, TN 37210-2834
ph: 800-388-2556 or 615-832-0564
fax: 615-244-1553
Expert and collector wants to collect all types of game calls as well as related historical information; author of "Duck Calls, An Enduring American Folk Art," and "Turkey Calls, An Enduring American Folk Art."

Internet Resources

Richard Tull
Rick's Antique Duck Calls
6310 Sea Haven Dr.
Hixson, TN 37343
e-mail: webmaster@oldcalls.com
web: http://www.oldcalls.com/
Web site is a great duck call resource: pictures,values, forum and more.

Magazines

Collectors

Hy Wood
10381 E. Shady Lane
Suttons Bay, MI 49682
ph: 616-271-3898
fax: 616-271-5013
e-mail: highwood@gtii.com
web: http://www.traversecity.com/highwood/
Wants to buy pre-1940 sporting & outdoor magazines such as Field & Stream, Outdoor Life, Sports Afield; also wants 1950s and 1960s gun magazines and accumulations of gun and fishing tackle catalogs.

Dealers

Lewis & Wilma Razek
Highwood Bookshop
P.O. Box 1246
Traverse City, MI 49684-1246
ph: 616-271-3898
e-mail: highwood@traversecity.com
web: http://traversecity.com/highwood/
Specializes in back issues of outdoor magazines on hunting, fishing, guns, collecting waterfowl decoys, collecting of old fishing tackle.

Skateboards

Collectors

Wayne Babcock
4846 Carpenteria Ave.
Carpinteria, CA 93013-1935
ph: 805-684-8148
Collects pre-1925 skateboards, skateboard magazines, trophies, and patches.

SPORTS COLLECTIBLES

(see also ART, Sports; AUTO RACING MEMORABILIA; AUTOGRAPHS; CAPS; COLLECTIBLES [MODERN], Sports Related; DOLLS, Bobbing Head; FAN CLUBS; POSTCARDS; SPORTS HISTORY; TICKETS; TRADING CARDS, Non-Sport; TRAPSHOOTING)

Appraisers

Robert J. Connelly, ASA
Bob & Sallie Connelly Auctions
666 Chenango St.
Binghamton, NY 13901-2015
ph: 607-722-9593 or 607-722-3555
fax: 607-722-1266
e-mail: connelly@clarityconnect.com
Gives litigation support; appeared on the TV show "Personal FX, The Collectibles Show" for four years; had own radio show for 14 years.

Mark Jordan
4709 Colleyville Blvd., Ste. 580-245
Colleyville, TX 76034
ph: 817-281-8455
fax: 817-281-3050
e-mail: mrjspts@aol.com
web: http://www.markjordon.com/Appraisals.htm
A nationally recognized sports collectibles authentication authority: over 27 years as autograph collector/dealer; principal authenticator for the National Sports Gallery in Washington, DC; auction house consultant.

Auction Services

Leland's
36 East 22nd St., 7th Floor
New York, NY 10010
ph: 212-254-2555
fax: 212-254-2389
e-mail: lelands@msn.com
web: http://www.lelandsauctions.com/
Conducts specialty sports auctions.

Christie's East
219 E. 67th St.
New York, NY 10021
ph: 212-606-0400
web: http://www.christies.com

B & E Collectibles
950 Broadway
Thornwood, NY 10594
ph: 914-769-1304

Coach's Corner
47 N. Front St.
Souderton, PA 18964
ph: 215-721-9162

Ron Oser
Ron Oser Enterprises
P.O. Box 101
Huntingdon Valley, PA 19006-0101
ph: 215-947-6575
fax: 215-938-7348
e-mail: ronoserent@aol.com
web: http://members.aol.com/ronoserent
Auctioneers of distinctive sports cards and memorabilia: 1880s-1960s baseball cards, early tobacco and gum cards, display advertising pieces, autographed baseballs, written letters, game-used uniforms, balls, gloves, etc.

Just Encase
1653 S. 27th St.
Philadelphia, PA 19145
ph: 610-271-0250

Jay's Sports Connection
724 York Road
Towson, MD 21204
ph: 410-296-6556

John D. Compton
J.D. Compton Auctioneering
13833 Rockdale Rd.
Clear Spring, MD 21722
ph: 301-582-0727
fax: 301-582-6114
e-mail: COMPTONAUC@aol.com
Specializes in the sale of sports collectibles; call toll-free in MD 1-800-499-3344.

Brian Collard
Bricol Enterprises
334 East Lake Road, Ste. 252
Palm Harbor, FL 34685
ph: 727-787-9577

Tom Slater
Political Gallery, The
1315 W. 86th St.
Indianapolis, IN 46260
ph: 317-257-0863
fax: 317-254-9167

Novak Enterprises
5205 Greystone Dr., Apt. 103
Inver Grove Heights, MN 55077-1743

North Shore Sports
853 Sanders Road
Northbrook, IL 60062
ph: 847-459-1980

Pat Quinn
Sports Collectors Store
1040 LaGrange Rd.
La Grange, IL 60525

Superior Galleries
9478 West Olympic Blvd.
Beverly Hills, CA 90212-4246
ph: 310-203-9855 or 800-421-0754
fax: 310-203-0496
e-mail: superior@superiorsc.com
web: http://www.superiorsc.com/
Has been a retail and auction source for dealers and collectors for over 70 years; specializes in stamps, coins, sports memorabilia, Hollywood memorabilia, space memorabilia, historic manuscripts and autographs.

Hobby Markets Online, Inc.
375 Alabama Street, Ste. 410
San Francisco, CA 94110
ph: 415-252-6040 or 415-252-6040
fax: 415-252-6044
e-mail: hobbyinfo@hobbymarkets.com
web: http://www.SportsTrade.com/
Online auction service for rare sports memorabilia; find sports cards, autographed bats, historic game-related jerseys and other collectibles from yesteryear's sports legends and today's sports heroes.

Sports Warehouse
P.O. Box 388
Wilsonville, OR 97070
ph: 503-682-8765
fax: 503-682-6912
e-mail: sportswhse@aol.com
Deals exclusively with game-used uniforms and equipment; main focus is baseball, but also carries basketballs, football, and some paper items.

Collectors

Bob, Ken & Mike Adelson
Adelson Sports
13610 N. Scottsdale
Scottsdale, AZ 85254-4037
ph: 602-596-1913
fax: 602-596-1914
e-mail: adelson@goodnet.com
web: http://www.adelsonsports.com/
Wants to buy sports memorabilia: yearbooks, ticket stubs, pennants, baseball, football, hockey, basketball, boxing; all items from all sports.

Goodwin Goldfaden
P.O. Box 48677
Bicentennial Station
Los Angeles, CA 90048-0677
ph: 818-986-4914
Buy, sell, trade all sports related items: baseball, football, basketball, boxing, wrestling, billiards, track & field, body building, other sports; books magazines, programs other sports collectibles from 1860 to present.

John Buonaguidi
540 Reeside Ave.
Monterey, CA 93940-1828
ph: 831-375-7345
Wants any sports related item: baseball cards, World Series programs; autographed baseballs and photos, boxing posters, advertising, etc.; especially interested in museum-quality items for soon-to-open sports museum.

Dealers

Paul Longo
Paul Longo Americana
P.O. Box 5510
Gloucester, MA 01930-0007
ph: 978-525-2290
Wants baseball and other sports memorabilia: sports cards, balls, autographs, uniforms, pennants, yearbooks, statues, silks, etc.

Sportsworld
429 Broadway
Everett, MA 02149
ph: 617-387-6177
New England's largest sports memorabilia shop.

Alan Rosen
Mr. Mint
70 Chestnut Ridge Road
Montvale, NJ 07645
ph: 201-307-0700

Bob Rothschild
5 Fillmore Dr.
Clarksburg, NJ 08510
ph: 609-259-9338

Les Wolff, ISA
P.O. Box 650037
Flushing, NY 11365-0037
ph: 718-454-3956
e-mail: lwolff1823@aol.com
Buys, sells, trades sports memorabilia; specializes in all types of sports auctions fund raisers; specializing in autographs.

Mark Lassman
2664 N. University Dr.
Fort Lauderdale, FL 33322
ph: 954-742-6773
fax: 954-742-6596
e-mail: cardshop@gate.net
Wants to buy all sports cards and bubble gum cards; also sports memorabilia, publications, any autographed items.

Richard Kohl
Strike Zone
1840 N. Federal Highway
Boynton Beach, FL 33435
ph: 800-344-9103
fax: 561-364-8765
Wants to buy all types of sports memorabilia: baseball, football, basketball, and hockey cards; bats, balls, and gloves; photographs and autographs; jerseys and ball caps; letters, books and mags; Olympic memorabilia; boxing, etc.

Mark F. Emerson
4040 Poste Lane Road
Columbus, OH 43221
ph: 614-771-7272 or 614-431-5800
fax: 614-431-4100
e-mail: mark@max-ermas.com
Appraiser, dealer, collector, wants to buy old golf programs, tickets, badges, pairing sheets, passes, photos, autographs of deceased players.

Stephen Hansrote
Griffin Trading Company
159 Howell St.
Dallas, TX 75207
ph: 214-747-9234
fax: 214-747-0660
e-mail: griffintc@aol.com
web: http://members.aol.com/griffintc/website.htm
Buying and selling 19th and 20th century American and European sports equipment, clothing and trophies.

Sports World Collectibles
897 Oak Park Blvd., Ste 272
Pismo Beach, CA 93449
ph: 805-474-7999

Gary Spoerle
Milestone Collectibles
P.O. Box 607
Troutdale, OR 97060-0607
ph: 503-695-3413
fax: 503-695-5406
Wants to buy baseball, golf, fishing and other sports memorabilia.

Experts

Jerome "MiMi" Alongi
961 South Lake Dr.
Du Quoin, IL 62832
ph: 618-542-4133
fax: 618-542-4133
e-mail: alongid@accessus.net
Collector and dealer specializing in the appraisal of baseball cards and

sports memorabilia; writes weekly sports column "MiMi's Dugout."

Misc. Services

Steve Bass
Sports Collector's Radio Show
527 Third Ave. #294
New York, NY 10016
ph: 212-573-8100
fax: 212-573-8100
e-mail: sportradio@aol.com
Talk show on New York's WGBB (1240 AM); heard Sunday 12-1 PM and 9-10 PM; explores all aspects of sports collecting; advice and insights from well-known collectors & dealers; cards, autographs - all types of sports memorabilia.

Museums/Libraries

New England Sports Museum
1175 Soldiers Field Rd.
Boston, MA 02134
ph: 617-787-7678
Not open to the public but archives may be researched by appointment.

Periodicals

Tuff Stuff Publications, Inc.
Magazine: Tuff Stuff
P.O. Box 3070
Richmond, VA 23228
ph: 804-266-0140 or 800-899-8833
fax: 804-264-4205
e-mail: tsonline@tuffstuffpubs.com
web: http://www.tuffstuffonline.com/subscribe.html
The complete monthly sports price guide publication including baseball, football, basketball, auto racing and hockey: 95% sports cards, Kenner's Starting Lineup sports figures, sports autographs.

Pat DuChene, PR
Krause Publications
Newsmagazine: Sports Collectors Digest
700 E. State St.
Iola, WI 54990-0001
ph: 715-445-2214
fax: 715-445-4087
e-mail: info@krause.com
web: http://www.krause.com/
A weekly newsmagazine for collectors of sports memorabilia; everything from baseball cards to game-worn uniforms.

Pat DuChene, PR
Krause Publications
Newsletter: Trade Fax
700 E. State St.
Iola, WI 54990-0001
ph: 715-445-2214
fax: 715-445-4087
e-mail: info@krause.com
web: http://www.krause.com/
Published each Monday and Thursday morning; contains breaking hobby news from shows, manufacturers, and other sources; $500 per year.

Hugh Murphy, PR
Beckett Publications, Inc.
Magazine: Beckett Sports Collectibles & Autographs
15850 Dallas Parkway
Dallas, TX 75248
ph: 972-448-9018 or 800-840-3137
e-mail: hmurphy@beckett.com
web: http://www.beckett.com/
Focuses on sports autographs and memorabilia; includes autograph, memorabilia and Minor League and draft pick sports card price guides.

Ed Kobak
Global Sports Productions, Ltd.
Directory: Sports Address Bible, The
1223 Broadway, Ste. 102
Santa Monica, CA 90404-2770
ph: 310-454-9480
fax: 310-454-6590
e-mail: sportsaddresses@hotmail.com
A worldwide reference guide (496 pages) with over 10K listings of sports addresses, phone and fax numbers, and contact person for Leagues, teams, organizations, and publications; major, minor, semi-pro, amateur, international, college.

Ed Kobak
Global Sports Productions, Ltd.
Directory: International Sports Directory
1223 Broadway, Ste. 102
Santa Monica, CA 90404-2770
ph: 310-454-9480
fax: 310-454-6590
e-mail: sportsaddresses@hotmail.com
435 page directory: listings for Olympic organizations and committees, national sports governing bodies, Olympic and multi-sport games committees, teams/clubs sports for foreign leagues & teams, collecting periodicals and societies.

Ed Kobak
Global Sports Productions, Ltd.
Directory: Athlete & Sport Personality Address Book, The
1223 Broadway, Ste. 102
Santa Monica, CA 90404-2770
ph: 310-454-9480
fax: 310-454-6590
e-mail: sportsaddresses@hotmail.com
Over 17K sports athlete/personality names and addresses from all sports; includes current athletes, Hall of Famers and former athletes, Negro League Baseball players, broadcasters/announcers, coaches, managers, etc.

Baseball

Auction Services

Rob Lifson
Robert Edward Auctions
P.O. Box 1923
Hoboken, NJ 07030
ph: 201-792-9324 or 800-766-9324
Conducts specialty baseball memorabilia auctions: baseball cards, Babe Ruth & Lou Gehrig items, tobacco cards, uncut sheets, buttons, autographs, display pieces, postcards, gum cards, world series items, original artwork, documents, etc.

Clubs/Associations

Robert E. Schmierer
Eastern Pennsylvania Sports Collectors Club
P.O. Box 3037
Maple Glen, PA 19002
ph: 215-643-0910
fax: 215-643-2697

Society for American Baseball Research
Journal: Baseball Research Journal
812 Huron Rd. E., #719
Cleveland, OH 44115
ph: 216-575-0500
fax: 216-575-0502
e-mail: info@sabr.org
web: http://www.sabr.org/
SABR's objectives are to facilitate and disseminate baseball research information and to establish an accurate historical account of baseball; membership is open to all who have an interest in baseball history.

Collectors

Rob Lifson
P.O. Box 1923
Hoboken, NJ 07030
ph: 201-792-9324 or 800-766-9324
Wants to buy baseball material: cards, buttons, photographs, World Series items, documents, advertising, postcards, tobacco cards, etc.

Ken Felden
2 Hemlock Lane
Marlboro, NJ 07746
ph: 732-536-5974
fax: 732-972-1976
Collector wants to buy baseball related antiques: cards (1880s-1930s), advertising, fans, pins, tins, scorecards and programs, photos, tickets (1860-1920), games, sheet music, early trophies and statuary, posters, etc.

Bill Simmons
8955 NW 19th St.
Coral Springs, FL 33071-6109
ph: 954-340-0734
e-mail: wsim1206@aol.com
Wants to buy baseball memorabilia: anything autographed including balls, bats, and gloves; old photos, postcards, cards, programs, statues, movie stuff, pens, lighters, etc.

Dan Busby
P.O. Box 50188
Indianapolis, IN 46250
ph: 765-674-3301
fax: 765-674-3302
Wants to buy post-season baseball tickets and baseball press pins.

William Mastro
12410 Ridge Rd.
Palos Park, IL 60464
ph: 708-361-2117
Advanced collector wants baseball cards and baseball memorabilia: advertising displays, pinback buttons, player uniforms, original early photos, programs, yearbooks, bats, autographs, games, early books, sheet music, etc.

Dealers

David Hall
Hall's Nostalgia
21-25 Mystic St.
P.O. Box 408
Arlington, MA 02174
ph: 800-367-4255 or 781-646-7757
Buys and sells all major sport collectibles (sport cards, publications, autographs, etc.); oldest sports store on the East Coast; opened in 1976; appraises sports memorabilia.

Tom & Jill Kaczor
1550 Franklin Rd.
Langhorne, PA 19047
ph: 215-968-5776 or 215-946-6044
fax: 215-946-6056
Serious collectors who want all sorts of baseball memorabilia: early bats, gloves, photos, board games, fans, sheet music, advertising pieces with players in them, stadium artifacts, score cards, programs, signed balls, trophies, etc.

Bob McCann
108 Village Green Dr.
Gilbertsville, PA 19525
ph: 610-367-1827
Wants to buy quality Baseball memorabilia.

Pat Quinn
Sports Collectors Store
1040 LaGrange Rd.
La Grange, IL 60525

Experts

Mark Cooper
Baseball Games & Memorabilia
816 Chauncey Rd.
Narberth, PA 19072
ph: 215-952-9153 or 610-667-7401
fax: 610-667-2341
e-mail: markbaseb@aol.com
A premier collector of 1860-1980 baseball games; has published the definitive text on the subject; will provide free information to all interested; always buying, selling, trading baseball games.

Phil Wood
P.O. Box 204
Reisterstown, MD 21136-0204
ph: 410-833-WOOD
Editor of "Diamond Duds," a bi-monthly newsletter on game-used major league baseball uniforms;

monthly memorabilia columnist in "Tuff Stuff" magazine.

Dennis Goldstein
1531 Beechcliff Dr. NE
Atlanta, GA 30329-3825
Baseball historian looking for early photographs, books, programs, memorabilia.

Museums/Libraries

National Baseball Hall of Fame & Museum, Inc.
P.O. Box 590
25 Main Street
Cooperstown, NY 13326
ph: 607-547-7200
fax: 607-547-2044
e-mail: info@baseballhalloffame.org
web: http://www.baseballhalloffame.org/

Periodicals

Pat DuChene, PR
Krause Publications
Magazine: Fantasy Baseball
700 E. State St.
Iola, WI 54990-0001
ph: 715-445-2214
fax: 715-445-4087
e-mail: info@krause.com
web: http://www.krause.com/
Complete guide to fantasy baseball league; every major league player ranked from scrub to star; hottest hobby with more than 1M players.

Kaufman Communications
Magazine: Sweet Spot
816 Congress Ave., Ste. 1280
Austin, TX 78701
ph: 512-708-1999
e-mail: ckaufman1@compuserve.com
web: http://www.sweetspotnews.com
Bimonthly publication focusing on baseball and baseball collectibles.

Magazine: Diamond Angle, The
706 South Alu
Wailuku, HI 96793
ph: 808-244-7704
e-mail: tdaflow@aloha.net
web: http://www.aloha.net/~tdaflow/
A journal feature articles, book reviews, trivia, lore, monthly card columns; sells cards plus has nationwide dealer ads.

Baseball (Books)

Collectors

R. Plapinger
P.O. Box 1062
Ashland, OR 97520-0063
ph: 541-488-1220
Wants any book about baseball: non-fiction, fiction, adult, juvenile, especially turn-of-the-century; send SASE for list of most wanted.

Dealers

Andy Moursund
Georgetown Book Shop
7770 Woodmont Ave.
Bethesda, MD 20814
ph: 301-907-6923
Specializes in baseball team history books.

R. Plapinger
R. Plapinger Baseball Books
P.O. Box 1062
Ashland, OR 97520-0063
ph: 541-488-1220
Specializes in catalog sales of baseball team history books.

Baseball (Washington Senators)

Clubs/Associations

Richard Bruce
Washington Senators Baseball Association
Newsletter: Save the Senators
11417 St. Rd. 535
Orlando, FL 32836
ph: 407-239-4482
Specializes in preservation of Washington Senators baseball club memorabilia, research and preservation ti include specialty in autographs.

Collectors

Richard Bruce
11417 St. Rd. 535
Orlando, FL 32836
ph: 407-239-4482
Buys, sells, collects and specializes in memorabilia relating to the Washington Senators baseball team.

Baseball Cards

Collectors

Marc L. Ames
539 Lyme Rock Rd.
Bridgewater, NJ 08807-1670
ph: 908-526-7676
fax: 908-575-0880
e-mail: magames@ix.netcom.com
Wants to buy all pre-1965 baseball cards; also wants any autographed cards to date.

Chuck Moore
P.O. Box 280
Gladstone, OR 97027
ph: 503-654-9994
fax: 503-656-7603
Wants baseball cards, publications, memorabilia; also older football and basketball memorabilia.

Dealers

Peggy Wolffrum
6201 Gabriel St.
Bowie, MD 20720
ph: 301-390-6243
e-mail: pegbbcds@erols.com
web: http://www.erols.com/pegbbcds/index.htm
Buys, sells, trades baseball cards ranging from 1988 to present; star players as well as common cards available for sale; good selection at prices below Beckett.

Larry Fritsch
Larry Fritsch Cards, Inc.
735 Old Wassau Road
P.O. Box 863
Stevens Point, WI 54481
ph: 715-344-8687
fax: 715-344-1778
e-mail: Larry@fritschcards.com
web: http://www.fritschcards.com/
Over 55 million cards in stock; buys and sells.

Pat Yeary
Pat & Larry's Baseball Cards
3708 W. Pioneer Parkway
Arlington, TX 76013-2901
ph: 817-265-0006
Buy, sell, trade baseball, football, basketball cards; specializing in sports trading cards since 1960s.

Texas Sportscard Company
2816 Center St.
Deer Park, TX 77536
ph: 281-476-9964
e-mail: fred@txsportcard.com
web: http://www.txsportcard.com/

David Levin
Dave's Vintage Baseball Cards
3101 Summertime Lane
Culver City, CA 90230
ph: 310-280-0292
e-mail: baseball@gfg.com
web: http://www.gfg.com/baseball/
Comprehensive listings of vintage baseball cards for sale on the internet; also football, basketball, hockey and boxing cards; all pre-1975; Topps, Fleer, Bowman, Leaf, Philly, Parkhurst, Wheaties, Post, Hostess, Kelloggs, etc.

Internet Resources

Baseball Cards 1887-1914, Library of Congress
101 Independence Ave. SE
Washington, DC 20540
ph: 202-707-8000
e-mail: ndlpcoll@loc.gov
web: http://memory.loc.gov/ammem/bbhtml/bbhome.html
The collection presents a Library of Congress treasure - 2,100 early baseball cards dating from 1887 to 1914.

Man./Prod./Dist.

Fleer Corp.
1120 Route 73, Ste. 300
Mount Laurel, NJ 08054-5113
e-mail: info@flrsbx.com
web: http://www.fleerskybox.com/
A baseball card company.

Leaf, Inc. (Donruss)
P.O. Box 2038
Memphis, TN 38101
A baseball card company.

Upper Deck Co. LLC, The
5909 Sea Otter Pl.
Carlsbad, CA 92008-6621
ph: 760-929-6500 or 800-873-7332
fax: 760-929-6500
web: http://www.upperdeck.com/
A baseball card company.

Museums/Libraries

Metropolitan Museum of Art, The Jefferson Burdich Collection
1000 Fifth Ave.
New York, NY 10028
ph: 212-570-3838
fax: 212-794-9316
web: http://www.metmuseum.org/

National Baseball Hall of Fame & Museum, Inc.
P.O. Box 590
25 Main Street
Cooperstown, NY 13326
ph: 607-547-7200
fax: 607-547-2044
e-mail: info@baseballhalloffame.org
web: http://www.baseballhalloffame.org/

Larry Fritsch
Larry Fritsch Collection, The
735 Old Wassau Road
P.O. Box 863
Stevens Point, WI 54481
ph: 715-344-8687
fax: 715-344-1778
e-mail: Larry@fritschcards.com
web: http://www.fritschcards.com/

Periodicals

Pat DuChene, PR
Krause Publications
Newsmagazine: Sports Collectors Digest
700 E. State St.
Iola, WI 54990-0001
ph: 715-445-2214
fax: 715-445-4087
e-mail: info@krause.com
web: http://www.krause.com/
A weekly newsmagazine for collectors of sports memorabilia; everything from baseball cards to game-worn uniforms.

Pat DuChene, PR
Krause Publications
Magazine: Sports Cards Magazine & Price Guide
700 E. State St.
Iola, WI 54990-0001
ph: 715-445-2214
fax: 715-445-4087
e-mail: info@krause.com
web: http://www.krause.com/
Full color monthly magazine featuring baseball, basketball, hockey and football cards from all eras; news, columns, feature stories, price guides; ads for cards and related items.

Pat DuChene, PR
Krause Publications
Newspaper: Card Trade
700 E. State St.
Iola, WI 54990-0001
ph: 715-445-2214
fax: 715-445-4087
e-mail: info@krause.com
web: http://www.krause.com/
Card industry's official trade journal, touching on topics pertinent the sports hobby professional.

Hugh Murphy, PR
Beckett Publications, Inc.
Magazine: Beckett Baseball Card Monthly
15850 Dallas Parkway
Dallas, TX 75248
ph: 972-448-9018 or 800-840-3137
e-mail: hmurphy@beckett.com
web: http://www.beckett.com/
A monthly baseball card price guide, articles, ads, show calendar.

Baseball Gloves

Clubs/Associations

Joe Phillips
Glove Collector Club, The
Newsletter: Glove Collector, The
14057 Rolling Hills Lane
Dallas, TX 75240-3807
ph: 972-699-1808
fax: 972-699-9851
e-mail: glovecol@onramp.net
A bi-monthly newsletter containing buy/sell/trade ads and articles about old baseball gloves; also the club is a source for glove price guides and glove reference books.

Experts

David Bushing
2171 Homewood Ave.
Libertyville, IL 60048-2123
ph: 847-816-6847
Author of "Vintage Baseball Glove Price Guide."

Repro. Sources

Joe Phillips
14057 Rolling Hills Lane
Dallas, TX 75240-3807
ph: 972-699-1808
fax: 972-699-9851
e-mail: glovecol@onramp.net
Deals in re-issue USA made baseball gloves.

Baseball Uniforms

Collectors

Gary Hong, Pub.
603 Concerto Lane
Silver Spring, MD 20901
ph: 301-593-6763
fax: 301-681-1476
e-mail: ghong@erols.com
Interested in game-worn major league baseball uniforms.

Basketball

Museums/Libraries

Naismith Memorial Basketball Hall of Fame
1150 W. Columbus Ave.
P.O. Box 179
Springfield, MA 01101-0179
ph: 413-781-6500
fax: 413-781-1939
web: http://www.hoophall.com/

Basketball Cards

Dealers

Robert Cosner
Bob's Baseball Cards
20978 E. Berry Place
Aurora, CO 80015
ph: 303-693-3852
e-mail: Bobplus@aol.com
web: http://www.Bobsbaseballcards.com
Buys and sells baseball cards; vintage and newer baseball stars and commons; website has monthly specials and free stuff.

Periodicals

Pat DuChene, PR
Krause Publications
Magazine: Sports Cards Magazine & Price Guide
700 E. State St.
Iola, WI 54990-0001
ph: 715-445-2214
fax: 715-445-4087
e-mail: info@krause.com
web: http://www.krause.com/
Full color monthly magazine featuring baseball, basketball, hockey and football cards from all eras; news, columns, feature stories, price guides; ads for cards and related items.

Hugh Murphy, PR
Beckett Publications, Inc.
Magazine: Beckett Basketball Card Magazine
15850 Dallas Parkway
Dallas, TX 75248
ph: 972-448-9018 or 800-840-3137
e-mail: hmurphy@beckett.com
web: http://www.beckett.com/
Articles, ads, basketball card price guide.

Bowling

Collectors

Walt Sill
557 Forest Retreat Rd.
Hendersonville, TN 37075
ph: 615-824-4646
fax: 615-822-6852
Wants to buy pre-1940 bowling items: wooden balls and pins, photos, equipment, posters, trophies, clocks, mugs, plaques, ribbons, bags, china, advertising, medals, etc.

Chuck Lande
11460 Audelia, Apt. #376
Dallas, TX 75243
ph: 817-589-3828
Wants bowling memorabilia of any kind.

Museums/Libraries

International Bowling Hall of Fame & Museum
111 Stadium Plaza
Saint Louis, MO 63102
ph: 314-231-6340 or 800-966-BOWL
web: http://www.bowlingmuseum.com/
Collection includes artifacts covering the history of bowling.

Boxing

Clubs/Associations

Frederick Ryan
Boxiana & Pugilistica Collectors International
Newsletter: BPCI Newsletter
P.O. Box 83135
Portland, OR 97283-0135
ph: 503-286-3597 or 503-235-9559

Collectors

Lou Manfra
27 Rochelle St.
Staten Island, NY 10304
ph: 718-979-9556
Wants to buy boxing memorabilia: autographs, photos, documents, tickets, posters, programs, books, figurines.

Bob Bryla
1912 Sunset Ave.
Utica, NY 13502-5636
ph: 315-733-1846
fax: 315-733-7518
e-mail: bryfour@dreamscape.com
Wants items relating to boxing and wrestling: strength books, magazines, programs, dolls, games, medals, pennants, bottles, etc. from 1860 to present.

Shawn Murphy
P.O. Box 103
Fithian, IL 61844-0103
Wants boxing memorabilia including programs, posters, tickets, books, souvenirs.

Don Hoffman
P.O. Box 4231
Salinas, CA 93912-4231
ph: 831-449-7311
Wants to buy boxing (all fighters) autographs, posters, tickets, programs, 8mm & 16mm films, old photos, silks, broadsides, cabinet cards, books, photo buttons, lithographs, banners, equipment, Golden Gloves, pins, etc.; describe & price.

Frederick Ryan
Arena Archives
P.O. Box 83135
Portland, OR 97283-0135
ph: 503-286-3597 or 503-235-9559
Boxing archivist, lifelong collector; owner of the "Grand Ave. Gym", organizer of the Annual Boxing memorabilia show held annually in Portland; wants tickets, programs, fight films, posters, literature, awards, mementos.

Lyle Whiteman
1526 Alki Ave. SW
Seattle, WA 98116
ph: 206-938-5746
fax: 206-938-0155
e-mail: LSWhiteman@aol.com
Wants to buy old boxing memorabilia.

Dealers

Richard R. Regan
293 Winter St. #5
Hanover, MA 02339-2528
ph: 617-826-3537
e-mail: foregolf@tiac.net
Wants to buy boxing posters & broadsides, books, prints, cigarette cards, programs, autographed photos, early equipment; anything related to boxing.

Seidman Productions, Inc.
P.O. Box 96
Clementon, NJ 08021
ph: 609-627-1356
Wants to buy boxing memorabilia: old and new programs, posters, tickets, pins, autographs, and any rare pieces or collections.

Jerome Shochet
6144 Oakland Mills Rd., CIC
Sykesville, MD 21784-6916
ph: 410-795-5879
Buys and sells boxing memorabilia of all kinds.

Bill Pollock
4267 Fox Hollow Circle
Casselberry, FL 32707-5240
ph: 407-695-9140
e-mail: pollockwk@mindspring.com
Wants boxing programs, tickets, autographs, pins, pre-1980 posters, buttons, trophies, estates of professional boxers, boxing pennants, and any items from restaurants owned by pro boxers (Jack Dempsey's, Lew Tendler's, etc.)

Museums/Libraries

International Boxing Hall of Fame
1 Hall of Fame Dr.
Canastota, NY 13032
ph: 315-697-7095
e-mail: publisher@ibhof.com
web: http://www.ibhof.com/

Periodicals

Don Scott
Magazine: Boxing Collectors News
3316 Luallen Dr.
Carrollton, TX 75007-3916
ph: 972-492-8518
e-mail: donscott@boxingcollectors.com
web: http://www.boxingcollectors.com
Articles, addresses and ads for boxing memorabilia; nine years of monthly publishing, 16-32 pages, editor/ publisher is columnist for "Ring" magazine; also offers appraisals.

Cards

(see also ADVERTISING COLLECTIBLES, Trading Cards; CARDS; SPORTS COLLECTIBLES, Baseball Cards; SPORTS COLLECTIBLES, Basketball Cards, SPORTS COLLECTIBLES, Football Cards, etc.)

Auction Services

Greg Manning
Greg Manning Auctions, Inc.
775 Passaic Ave.
West Caldwell, NJ 07006
ph: 973-882-0004 or 800-221-0243
fax: 973-882-3499
e-mail: gmauction@aol.com
web: http://www.gregmanning.com/
Conducts four to six mail/phone bid auctions per year containing primarily sports and non-sports cards; also autographs and varied memorabilia.

David Festberg
David Festberg Auctions
11 Stewart Ave.
Huntington, NY 11743-2708
ph: 516-271-3939
Buys and sells all types of pre-1970 trading cards; also non-sports trading cards.

Hager Group, Inc., The
P.O. Box 952974
Lake Mary, FL 32795
ph: 407-788-3865
One of the largest vintage sportscard dealers in the world.

Collectors

Kiska Reynolds
P.O. Box 411402
Enterprise, AL 36331-1402
ph: 334-393-2001
e-mail: kiska@strikeoutking.com
web: http://www.strikeoutking.com
Collects all sports trading cards and collectibles, especially Nolan Ryan items and rare and hard-to-find oddball items.

Peter Dean
2295 Benson Ave.
Santa Cruz, CA 95065-1670
ph: 831-457-4332
Wants to buy 1960s and early 1970s cards, all sports: baseball, football, basketball, hockey.

Dealers

Teletrade Sports
27 Main Street
Kingston, NY 12401-3853
ph: 800-232-1132

Burton's Coins & Cards
5831 Buckeystown Pike
Frederick, MD 21701
ph: 301-663-3223

David Levin
Dave's Vintage Baseball Cards
3101 Summertime Lane
Culver City, CA 90230
ph: 310-280-0292
e-mail: baseball@gfg.com
web: http://www.gfg.com/baseball/
Comprehensive listings of vintage baseball cards for sale on the internet; also football, basketball, hockey and boxing cards; all pre-1975; Topps, Fleer, Bowman, Leaf, Philly, Parkhurst, Wheaties, Post, Hostess, Kelloggs, etc.

Neil Osina
Best Variety Sports Cards & Coins
358 W. Foothill Blvd.
Glendora, CA 91740-3327
ph: 626-914-2273
fax: 626-914-6624
Wants to buy sports cards and autographed items; Life Member of all major associations; over 10 years experience.

Derrick Jones
Derrick's Sports Cards
2177 Pine St.
Quincy, CA 95971
ph: 530-283-2883
e-mail: dwjones@hotmail.com
web: http://www.angelfire.com/ca/derricksportscards/
Great website to buy, trade and and sell sports cards and sports-related memorabilia: baseball cards, basketball cards, football cards, Wheaties cereal boxes, Corinthian headliners, SLU's, coins, magazines, and other sports-related items.

Internet Resources

Terry Stewart
Collector Link
71 John St. East
Waterloo, Ontario N2J 1G2
Canada
ph: 519-745-1745
e-mail: stewart@collector-link.com
web: http://www.collector-link.com/
Catalogs over 2,000 trading card related web sites for: baseball, hockey, basketball, football, other sports, non-sports, phone cards, credit-debit cards, business cards, postcards.

Misc. Services

Professional Sports Authenticator
P.O. Box 6189
Newport Beach, CA 92658
ph: 800-325-1121
web: http://www.PSAcard.com/
Offers third party authentication and grading services for sports cards

Periodicals

Susan
Magazine: Sports Card Economizer
RFD 1 Box 530
Winthrop, ME 04364-9705
ph: 207-377-2540
e-mail: ressce@ctel.net
Monthly magazine with articles and ads for sports cards and sports memorabilia collectors; buy, sell, trade nationwide; sample $1.

Pat DuChene, PR
Krause Publications
Magazine: Sports Collectors Digest's Price Guide Weekly
700 E. State St.
Iola, WI 54990-0001
ph: 715-445-2214
fax: 715-445-4087
e-mail: info@krause.com
web: http://www.krause.com/
The sport card industry's first source for pricing on new card products, pricing updates, and industry trends.

Baron Bredesky
Trajan Publishing Corporation
Newspaper: Canadian Sportscard Collector
103 Lakeshore Rd., Ste. 202
St. Catharines, Ontario L2N 2T6
Canada
ph: 905-646-7744
fax: 905-646-0995
e-mail: newsroom@trajan.com
web: http://www.vaxxine.com/trajan/

Crew Rowing

Collectors

Peter Falk
P. Hastings Falk, Inc.
859 Boston Post Rd.
P.O. Box 833
Madison, CT 06443
ph: 203-245-2246
fax: 203-245-5116
e-mail: info@folkart.com
Wants 19th century cigarette & trade cards, posters, broadsides, stereoviews, prints, sheet music, & books on rowing.

Curling

Collectors

David Sgriccia
5216 Sherry Ln.
Howell, MI 48843
ph: 517-546-3857
e-mail: david@ismi.net
Wants to buy curling stones, memorabilia, trophies, books, prints, etc.

Museums/Libraries

Turner's Curling Museum
P.O. Box 370
Weyburn, Saskatchewan S4H 2K6
Canada
ph: 306-842-3604 or 306-848-3283
web: http://www.compusmart.ab.ca/nplooy/turner.htm

Equipment

Experts

David Bushing
Vintage Sports Equipment
2171 Homewood Ave.
Libertyville, IL 60048-2123
ph: 847-816-6847
Wants to buy old sports equipment: bats, gloves, catchers gear, old leather football helmets, old pennants, etc.; writes a sports collectibles column for "AntiqueWeek."

Football

Dealers

Athleticards
5638 Lake Murray Blvd., Ste. 110
La Mesa, CA 91942-1929
ph: 619-461-3451
fax: 619-461-2938
e-mail: oddballFB1@aol.com
Wants to buy items relating to pro football: advertising displays, postcards, equipment, posters, records, team-issued photos, bread labels, bottle caps, books, toys, games, glassware, bottles, cans, programs/ magazines, pennants, etc.

Museums/Libraries

Pro Football Hall of Fame
2121 George Halas Dr. NW
Canton, OH 44708
ph: 330-456-8207
web: http://www.footballhalloffame.com/

Football Cards

Periodicals

Pat DuChene, PR
Krause Publications
Magazine: Sports Cards Magazine & Price Guide
700 E. State St.
Iola, WI 54990-0001
ph: 715-445-2214
fax: 715-445-4087
e-mail: info@krause.com
web: http://www.krause.com/
Full color monthly magazine featuring baseball, basketball, hockey and football cards from all eras; news, columns, feature stories, price guides; ads for cards and related items.

Hugh Murphy, PR
Beckett Publications, Inc.
Magazine: Beckett Football Card Magazine
15850 Dallas Parkway
Dallas, TX 75248
ph: 972-448-9018 or 800-840-3137
e-mail: hmurphy@beckett.com
web: http://www.beckett.com/
Includes ads, show calendar, articles and football card price guide.

Golf

Auction Services

Kevin C. McGrath
Sporting Antiquities
44 Oakland St.
Melrose, MA 02176
ph: 781-662-6588
fax: 781-662-2643
e-mail: kmcgrath@wn.net
Sells antique golf collectibles through auction and private sales; buys high quality golf paintings, prints, clubs, books, balls, etc.; subscription to well-illustrated catalogs $24/yr; also appraises golf collectibles for a fee.

Jon Baddeley
Sotheby's
34-35 New Bond St.
London, W1A 2AA
U.K.
ph: 44 171 293 5000
fax: 44 171 293 5989
web: http://www.sothebys.com/
Conducts regular auctions of golfing memorabilia.

Book Sellers

Rhod McEwan
Rhod McEwan Golf Books
Glengarden
Ballater, Aberdeenshire AB35 5UB
Scotland
ph: 013397-55429
fax: 013397-55995
e-mail: rhodmcewan@easynet.co.uk
Specialist full-time dealer in rare, used, and out-of-print golf books; also golf ephemera and original paintings; always looking to purchase; member Antiquarian Bookseller's Association (UK) and Golf Collector's Society.

Clubs/Associations

Golf Collectors Society
Journal: Bulletin, The
P.O. Box 241042
Cleveland, OH 44124
ph: 216-861-1615
fax: 216-861-1630
e-mail: KKuhl@aol.com
web: http://www.golfcollectors.com
An international society for the preservation of the treasures and traditions of the Royal and Ancient game; largest in the world.

Collectors

Art DiProspero
Highlands Golf
25 Rolling Ridge Rd.
Monroe, CT 06468
ph: 203-268-2349
Wants wooden shaft golf clubs, early trophies, pre-1920 golf books, golf bronzes, modern "classic" clubs, golf paintings & prints, balls, golf memorabilia, early golf magazines and programs, etc.

P.M. Romano
32 Sterling Dr.
Lake Grove, NY 11755
ph: 516-585-9017
Wants golf memorabilia: programs, balls, score cards, wooden shafted clubs, post cards, photos, autographs, statues, china, trophies, ceramics.

Norman Boughton
P.O. Box 93262
Rochester, NY 14692
ph: 716-292-5550 or 716-292-0128
e-mail: nordel@rochester.infi.net
Wants to buy golf memorabilia including golf markers (used to mark a spot on the green), any material; especially those identifiable to a particular course or golfer.

Tom Hanley
905 Devere Dr.
Silver Spring, MD 20903
ph: 301-445-4597 or 301-681-9253
Wants golf collectibles: wood shaft clubs, old golf balls, classic putters, major championship memorabilia.

Mark F. Emerson
4040 Poste Lane Road
Columbus, OH 43221
ph: 614-771-7272 or 614-431-5800
fax: 614-431-4100
e-mail: mark@max-ermas.com
Appraiser, dealer, collector, wants to buy old golf programs, tickets, badges, pairing sheets, passes, photos, autographs of deceased players.

D. Perkins
6335 W. 62nd St.
Indianapolis, IN 46278-1906
ph: 317-293-9962
Wants wooden shaft golf clubs, early trophies or any antique sports related item.

Frank R. Zadra
N5830 Cty. Hwy. H.
Spooner, WI 54801
ph: 715-635-2791
Wants old golf related items: unusual golf clubs, old balls, books, bronzes, quality china and ceramics, and miscellaneous related items; has been collecting for over 35 years.

Scott Sayers
1800 Nueces
Austin, TX 78701
ph: 512-478-3483
fax: 512-473-2447
Wants to buy golf related autographs and memorabilia.

Dealers

Richard R. Regan
293 Winter St. #5
Hanover, MA 02339-2528
ph: 617-826-3537
e-mail: foregolf@tiac.net
Wants to buy wood shaft clubs, books, statues, china, paintings, prints, balls, scorecards, programs, autographs, sales catalogs, trophies, miniature golf clubs & games, pinball machines, cigarette & post cards; any golf related item.

George Lewis
George Lewis/Golfiana
P.O. Box 291
Mamaroneck, NY 10543
ph: 914-835-5100
fax: 914-835-1715
e-mail: george@golfiana.com
web: http://www.golfiana.com
Golf appraiser, dealer, expert specializing in golf collectibles since 1988.

Allen Wallach
Heritage Hickory Golf Collectibles
300 Edge Hill Rd.
Glenside, PA 19038
ph: 215-886-8875
fax: 215-886-3463
e-mail: heritagehickory@home.com
web: http://www.heritagehickory.com/
Collector, expert, dealer buying and selling all types of antique golf collectibles; specializes in golf balls, wood shafted golf clubs, books on golf, tees, art, trophies, pottery, and all other aspects of golf collectibles.

Neil Ghingold
Neil Ghingold Antiques
1230-32 Broad St.
Augusta, GA 30901-1116
ph: 706-722-3483
Wants to buy golfing collectibles.

Gordon Page
Hickory Sticks
34643 Sunward Loop
Zephyrhills, FL 33541
ph: 813-780-8841
e-mail: gpage@innet.com
web: http://www.webcom.com/oldgolf/mu/gpage.html
A well known dealer of antique golf collectibles specializing in antique wood shaft golf clubs; participates in many of the Golf Collectors Society shows throughout the U.S.; has a website that lists early golf collectibles.

Barbara Stevens
Queen of Clubs at Farm Village Antique Mall
4490 Cricket Ridge Dr., #204
Holt, MI 48842
ph: 517-699-8372 or 517-337-4988
fax: 517-337-4560
e-mail: stevensg44@aol.com

David N. Berkowitz
P.O. Box 842
Palatine, IL 60078-0842
ph: 847-934-4108
fax: 847-934-4107
e-mail: antiqglf@mediaone.net
web: http://www.golfsgoldenyears.com/
Buys and sells old golf items: balls, books, ceramics, tees, memorabilia, vintage golf autographs, wood shafted clubs, silver, trophies, etc.

Bob Lucas
P.O. Box 364
Geneva, IL 60134-0364
ph: 630-232-2665
fax: 630-262-1935
e-mail: antqgolf@aol.com
Old golf items, wood-shafted clubs, books, prints, china, etc.

Leo M. Kelly, Jr.
Old Chicago Golf Shop
4977 Arquilla Dr.
Richton Park, IL 60471-1643
ph: 708-747-1045
fax: 708-747-1055
e-mail: Ochicago@ix.netcom.com
web: http://www.oldgolf.com/
Dealer, appraiser and collector of pre-1930s golf antiques, memorabilia, and collectibles.

Al Moore
Moore's of Omaha
9230 Burt St., #214
Omaha, NE 68114
ph: 402-392-2964
e-mail: almor@home.com
web: http://members.home.com/almor/
Wants old golf related items: caddy badges, wood shaft clubs, books, signature golf balls, etc.; also wants WWII Navy PT boat memorabilia.

Barry O'Brien
Barry O'Brien's Golf Clubs & Collectibles
P.O. Box 22145
Lincoln, NE 68542
ph: 402-560-8956
e-mail: bds@navix.net
web: http://www.solu.net/barry/
Buys, sells, trades practically anything related to golf; specializes in Wooden Shaft Golf Clubs and classic golf clubs from the 1940s through the 1960s.

Chuck Furjanic
Golf Collectibles
P.O. Box 165892
Irving, TX 75016
ph: 972-594-7802 or 800-882-4825
fax: 972-257-1875
e-mail: furjanic@directlink.net
web: http://www.golfforallages.com/
Buys and sells golf collectibles, balls, books, autographs, wood shaft clubs and other golf memorabilia; issues monthly comprehensive Golf Collectibles Catalogue; will buy large collections.

Douglas MacKenzie
Antique Golf Clubs of Scotland - DMC Ltd.
2 La Belle Place
Glasgow, G3 7LH
Scotland
ph: +44 141 333 9400
fax: +44 141 333 9490
e-mail: douglas@dmcsoft.com
web: http://www.dmcsoft.com/antiquegolf/
Buy an antique golf club: great gift for the golf nut, club prize or corporate gift.

Robert Thomson
Antique Golf
10 Glasgow Road
Glasgow, G3 7LH
U.K.
ph: 0141-889-1860
fax: 0141-889-1880
e-mail: info@antiquegolf.com
web: http://www.antiquegolf.com
Premier golf dealer with on-line catalog.

Experts

John & Morton Olman
Old Golf Shop, Ltd.
P.O. Box 220
Pleasant Plain, OH 45162
ph: 513-877-2676
fax: 513-241-7855
Authors of the "Golf Antiques & Other Treasures of the Game" (1997); to order book call warehouse at 800-433-1000.

Leo M. Kelly, Jr.
Old Chicago Golf Shop
4977 Arquilla Dr.
Richton Park, IL 60471-1643
ph: 708-747-1045
fax: 708-747-1055
e-mail: Ochicago@ix.netcom.com
web: http://www.oldgolf.com/
Buys and sells golf related collectibles; issues a periodic catalog, "The Hickory Club Mart", packed with golf items for sale and having 40 to 70 B/W photos of antique golf collectibles; $35 for four issues; author of golf ball book.

Kevin McCandless
P.O. Box 435
Champaign, IL 61824-0435
ph: 217-367-4466

Museums/Libraries

World Golf Hall of Fame
ph: 904-940-8000 or 800-446-5301
web: http://www.wgv.com/wgv/main.nsf/allframesets/wgv200e.html

Golf Ball Markers

Collectors

Norman Boughton
P.O. Box 93262
Rochester, NY 14692
ph: 716-292-5550 or 716-292-0128
e-mail: nordel@rochester.infi.net
Wants golf markers (used to mark a spot on the green), any material; especially those identifiable to a particular course or golfer; also buys other golf memorabilia.

Golf Balls

Clubs/Associations

World Logo Ball Association
P.O. Box 91989
Long Beach, CA 90809
web: http://www.hyperhead.com/wlba2/default.asp

Collectors

Bruce
Golflogos Home Page
e-mail: golflogos@aol.com
web: http://www.geocities.com/Augusta/4360/

Roger Kleinschmidt
Golf Ball Art & Custom Displays
21218 St. Andrews Blvd., Ste. 620
Boca Raton, FL 33486
ph: 888-296-4133 or 561-417-5010
fax: 561-417-5010
e-mail: golfart@icanect.net
web: http://golfballart.com/
Buys, trades, collects, sells logo golf balls; also builds and sells a more functional rack for storing or displaying a golf ball collection.

Kirk Harney
Logo Ball Web Site, The
712 Lucy Goff Dr.
Rantoul, IL 61866
ph: 217-893-8406
e-mail: klharney@cu-online.com
web: http://www.cu-online.com/~klharney/
A website for those who collect Logo Golf Balls; filled with information and pictures of logos and collections.

Misc. Services

Roger Kleinschmidt
Golf Ball Art & Custom Displays
21218 St. Andrews Blvd., Ste. 620
Boca Raton, FL 33486
ph: 888-296-4133 or 561-417-5010
fax: 561-417-5010
e-mail: golfart@icanect.net
web: http://golfballart.com/
Builds golf ball display cases for collectors or to be given as awards of gifts; unique because of a new concept of attaching balls to a surface; made of oak or acrylic and of any size; takes up less wall or desk space.

Golf Clubs

Dealers

Robin W. Berg, Pub.
5407 Pennock Point Rd.
Jupiter, FL 33458-3496
ph: 561-744-2553
fax: 561-744-2374
e-mail: rokit8@aol.com
Dealer in fine collectible golfiana; buys, sells and appraises.

Barry O'Brien
Barry O'Brien's Golf Clubs & Collectibles
P.O. Box 22145
Lincoln, NE 68542
ph: 402-560-8956
e-mail: bds@navix.net
web: http://www.solu.net/barry/
Buys, sells, trades practically anything related to golf; specializes in Wooden Shaft Golf Clubs and classic golf clubs from the 1940s through the 1960s.

John Hawes
Antique Golf
40 Allendale Rd.
Brampton, Ontario L6W 2YB
Canada
ph: 905-796-3031 or 905-601-2631
e-mail: deepgrv@yesic.com
web: http://www.geocities.com/Augusta/4053/pg1.html
Has been collecting wood shaft golf clubs for over 10 years; buys, sells and trades.

Periodicals

Robin W. Berg, Pub.
Newsletter: Golfingly Yours
5407 Pennock Point Rd.
Jupiter, FL 33458-3496
ph: 561-744-2553
fax: 561-744-2374
e-mail: rokit8@aol.com
A 24-30 page "buy-sell-trade" newsletter for classic and antique golf buffs; woods, irons, putters, wedges, sets and singles, books, memorabilia.

Golf Clubs (British)

Experts

Peter Georgiady
6101 O'Briant Ct.
Greensboro, NC 27410-8606
ph: 919-665-6457
Author of "Compendium of British Club Makers," $55 ppd. and "Wood Shafter Golf Club Value Guide," $25 ppd.

Golf Pencils

(see also PENCILS)

Collectors

Golf Course Pencil Collectors
e-mail: janknez@aol.com
web: http://members.aol.com/janknez/pencil.html

Jim Mundy
128 Kingbrook Rd.
Linthicum Heights, MD 21090-1947
ph: 410-859-5835
e-mail: jimm@bellatlantic.net
web: http://members.bellatlantic.net/~jimm/index.html
Collects golf course pencils with the name of the course on them; has over 2700 different ones; will swap with other collectors.

Harness Racing

Museums/Libraries

Trotting Horse Museum
Newsletter: Hall of Fame Trotters News
P.O. Box 590
24 Main Street
Goshen, NY 10924
ph: 914-294-6330
fax: 914-294-3463

Hockey

Museums/Libraries

U.S. Hockey Hall of Fame
P.O. Box 657
Eveleth, MN 55734
ph: 218-744-5167
web: http://www.ushockeyhall.com/

Hockey Hall of Fame
BCE Place
30 Yonge Street
Toronto, Ontario M5E 1X8
Canada
ph: 416-350-7765
fax: 416-360-1316
e-mail: rellis@hhof.com
web: http://www.hhof.com/index.htm

Periodicals

Hugh Murphy, PR
Beckett Publications, Inc.
Magazine: Beckett Hockey Collector
15850 Dallas Parkway
Dallas, TX 75248
ph: 972-448-9018 or 800-840-3137
e-mail: hmurphy@beckett.com
web: http://www.beckett.com/
Articles, ads, show calendar and hockey card price guide.

Hockey Cards

Periodicals

Pat DuChene, PR
Krause Publications
Magazine: Sports Cards Magazine & Price Guide
700 E. State St.
Iola, WI 54990-0001
ph: 715-445-2214
fax: 715-445-4087
e-mail: info@krause.com
web: http://www.krause.com/
Full color monthly magazine featuring baseball, basketball, hockey and football cards from all eras; news, columns, feature stories, price guides; ads for cards and related items.

Ice Skating

Clubs/Associations

Professional Skaters Association, International
Magazine: Professional Skater
1821 2nd Street SW
Rochester, MN 55902
ph: 507-281-5122
fax: 507-281-5491
web: http://users.aol.com/skatepsa/homepage.html

Shirley Yates, Ex. Sec.
Amateur Speedskating Union of the United States
Magazine: Racing Blade, The
1033 Shady Lane
Glen Ellyn, IL 60137
ph: 630-790-3230
fax: 630-790-3235
e-mail: jeffrey@mit.edu
web: http://web.mit.edu/jeffrey/speedskating/asu.html

United States Figure Skating Association
Magazine: Skating
20 First St.
Colorado Springs, CO 80906
ph: 719-635-5200
fax: 719-635-9548
e-mail: usfsa1@aol.com
web: http://www.usfa.org/

Collectors

Lovena Harwood
P.O. Box 6139
Haverhill, MA 01831-6139
e-mail: lovena@netway.com
web: http://www.netway.com/~lovena/lovena.htm
Ice skating memorabilia collector; website has a bulletin board for posting for sale, buy or trade ads.

Karen Cameron
70-104 Scott St.
Meriden, CT 06450
ph: 203-238-3603
e-mail: kcam573014@aol.com
Collector of 18th and 19th century antique ice skates, especially those with a curly prow; also interested in books about the history of skating.

Keith Pendell
P.O. Box 761
Lake Arrowhead, CA 92352
ph: 909-337-8184
e-mail: kpendell@aol.com
Wants pre-1900 antique ice skates: swan's head, big turn up, brass blades; also china with skating motif, skater's lanterns, books, etc.; also wants ice show programs.

Dealers

Greg Walsh
32 River View Lane
P.O. Box 747
Potsdam, NY 13676-0747
ph: 315-265-9111 or 800-371-9286
fax: 315-265-9222
e-mail: gwalsh@northnet.org
web: http://www.walshauction.com/
Wants to buy antique ice skates of exceptional quality; appraises ice skates and relate material; corresponding with others.

Experts

Rick Palaima
37 Cedar Street
Mattapan, MA 02126
ph: 617-296-7777
e-mail: rjp001@ix.netcom.com
Wants to buy antique or modern figure skating collectibles; skating dresses, skates, and autographed items of any lady skaters, especially Oksana Baiul, Katarina Witt, Ekaterina Gordeeva, Sonja Henie, Josee Choiunard, Irina Slutskaya.

Periodicals

H. Kermit Jackson
Magazine: American Skating World
1816 Brownsville Rd.
Pittsburgh, PA 15210-3908
ph: 412-885-7600 or 800-245-6280
fax: 412-885-7615
web: http://www.americansk8world.com/
The only news monthly on figure skating.

Ice Skating (Ice Skates)

Clubs/Associations

Karen Cameron
Antique Ice Skate Collectors Club
70-104 Scott St.
Meriden, CT 06450
ph: 203-238-3603
e-mail: kcam573014@aol.com

Collectors

Ann J. Bates
Trout Point
5660 Keefe Road
Land O' Lakes, WI 54540
ph: 715-547-3836
e-mail: ajb@newnorth.net
Collector of antique ice skates.

Jerseys

Dealers

Grey Flannel Collectibles, Inc.
731 Middle Neck Rd.
Great Neck, NY 11024
ph: 800-242-7647 or 516-466-5533
fax: 516-466-5592
e-mail: gfcsports@aol.com
web: http://www.greyflannel.com
Leading dealers in game-used jerseys.

Jewelry

Collectors

M. B. Spragins
501 Adams St.
Huntsville, AL 35801
ph: 800-987-7464 x8424
Wants to buy sports rings: football, baseball, basketball, hockey, college, minor league; also professional Cotton Bowl Rolexes.

Experts

Mike Safran
Collectors' Collector, The
204 South Edisto Ave.
Columbia, SC 29205
ph: 803-771-6995
e-mail: collect1@scsn.net
Championship sports rings bought, sold, traded; from the Sugar Bowl to the Super Bowl, championship jewelry from all aspects of sports.

Lacrosse

Museums/Libraries

Steve Stenersen, Ex.Dir.
U.S. Lacrosse Museum & National Hall of Fame
Magazine: Lacrosse Magazine
113 West University Parkway
Baltimore, MD 21210-3301
ph: 410-235-6882
fax: 410-366-6735
e-mail: sstenersen@lacrosse.org
web: http://www.lacrosse.org
U.S. Lacrosse is the national governing body of men's and women's lacrosse; the Lacrosse Museum contains national lacrosse archives.

Little League

Museums/Libraries

Alan Robison
Peter J. McGovern Little League Museum
P.O. Box 3485
South Williamsport, PA 17701
ph: 570-326-3607
e-mail: publicrelations@littleleague.org
web: http://www.littleleague.org/museum/
Focuses on Little League Baseball/softball memorabilia; vintage baseball equipment; vintage magazine covers featuring youths and baseball.

Mountaineering

Book Sellers

Jim Havranek
Innominate Crux
58 Ramsey Ave.
Yonkers, NY 10701-5654
ph: 914-969-1554
fax: 914-969-1554
Mountaineering and Alpine related material; books, equipment, ephemera, and art; also Tibet and Mountainous Regions.

Nike Sportswear

Dealers

Larry McKaugham
Heller's Far West Clothing
1000 Lenora, Ste. 116
Seattle, WA 98121
ph: 206-233-9014 or 800-328-5384
e-mail: hellers@halcyon.com
web: http://www.hellerscafe.com/
Wants old Nike sportswear.

Husky Boy Vintage
4441 S. Meridian, Ste. 471
Puyallup, WA 98373-5959
ph: 800-HUSKY-BO or 253-472-6341
e-mail: steve@huskyboy.com
Wants to buy Nike Air Jordan 1985-1991 and 1970s-1980s Nike shoes and sportswear; also buying vintage denim workwear, i.e. Levi's, Lee, etc. and vintage military flight jackets.

Polo

Collectors

Dennis Amato
5 The Crow's Nest
Port Washington, NY 11050
ph: 212-605-2959
fax: 516-883-4602
Wants anything related to the sport of polo: books, magazines, programs, autographs, ephemera.

Rodeo

Clubs/Associations

Pro Bull Rider Fan Club
Magazine: Pro Bull Rider
6 South Tejon, Ste. 700
Colorado Springs, CO 80903
ph: 714-434-2579
fax: 719-471-4712
e-mail: fancorp@earthlink.net
web: http://www.pbrnow.com/
Merchandise, fashion, articles, behind the chutes, chutin' the bull, etc.

Professional Rodeo Cowboys Association
Magazine: ProRodeo Sports News
101 Pro Rodeo Dr.
Colorado Springs, CO 80919
ph: 719-593-8840
e-mail: prca@prorodeo.com
web: http://www.prorodeo.com/

Museums/Libraries

Pro Rodeo Hall of Fame & Museum of the American Cowboy
101 Pro Rodeo Dr.
Colorado Springs, CO 80919
ph: 719-528-4764 or 719-593-8840
e-mail: prca@prorodeo.com
web: http://www.prorodeo.com/html/1.8.halloffame.html

Periodicals

Magazine: Competitor News, The
28150 N. Holiday Lane
Athol, ID 83801
ph: 208-687-0473
fax: 208-623-2683
e-mail: compnews@comtch.iea.com
web: http://www.iea.com/~compnews/
Serving WA, OR, ID, MT, WY; keep up to date on rodeo, roping, cow horse, cutting, team penning, and barrel racing events.

Roller Skating

Clubs/Associations

Bill Wolf
USA Roller Skating
Magazine: US Roller Skating
4730 South St.
P.O. Box 6579
Lincoln, NE 68506-0579
ph: 402-483-7551 x20
fax: 402-483-1465
e-mail: bill4usars@yahoo.com
web: http://www.usarollerskating.com/
Governing body for amateur roller skating: speed skating, roller hockey, artistic skating.

Museums/Libraries

Michael Zaidman
National Museum of Roller Skating
Newsletter: Historical Roller Skating Overview
4730 South Street
P.O. Box 6579
Lincoln, NE 68506-0579
ph: 402-483-7551 x16
fax: 402-483-1465
e-mail: Rllrsktmus@aol.com
web: http://www.usarollerskating.com/museum.htm
Largest collection of historical roller skates dating to 1819; roller skating history as technology, sport, recreation and personalities; sells "The Evolution of the Roller Skate: 1820 - Present" by Scott Addison Wilhite.

Schedules

Collectors

Paul Jarrell
1800 Crumbley Rd.
McDonough, GA 30253
Specializes in buying and selling baseball schedules.

Skateboards

Collectors

Jack Koffron
8600 N. 53rd St.
Brown Deer, WI 53223
ph: 414-354-4850
fax: 414-765-1207
Wants to buy wooden skateboards with good graphics from the 1950s to 1970s; also wants hot rod car club jackets and license plaques from the 1940s to 1960s.

Snow Skiing

Collectors

Mark Miller
Mark Miller Collection, The
P.O. Box 3836
Park City, UT 84060
ph: 888-753-7807 or 435-649-1858
fax: 435-649-1858
e-mail: info@antiqueskis.com
web: http://www.antiqueskis.com
Has compiled the largest collection of antique wooden skis and snowshoes in the country.

Gary Schwartz
680 Hawthorne Dr.
Belvedere Tiburon, CA 94920-1412
ph: 415-256-9300
fax: 415-256-9400
e-mail: gary@woodrivermedia.com
web: http://www.picturesnow.com/
Wants pre-1940 books, company catalogs, magazines, post cards, sheet music, posters, photographs, etc. relating to skiing.

Museums/Libraries

E. John B. Allen
New England Ski Museum
Newsletter: NESM Newsletter
P.O. Box 267
Parkway Exit 2
Franconia, NH 03580-0267
ph: 603-823-7177
fax: 603-823-9505
e-mail: staff@skimuseum.org
web: http://www.skimuseum.org/
Museum contains library research materials, photo collections, etc.; available free to members or on a fee basis to the public.

U.S. National Ski Hall of Fame & Museum
P.O. Box 191
Ishpeming, MI 49849
ph: 906-485-6323
fax: 906-486-4570
e-mail: skihall@portup.com
web: http://www.exploringthenorth.com/fame/fame.html

Colorado Ski Museum - Ski Hall of Fame
Newsletter: Making Tracks
231 S. Frontage Rd.
P.O. Box 1976
Vail, CO 81657
ph: 970-476-1876
fax: 970-476-1879
e-mail: skimuse@vail.net
web: http://www.vailsoft.com/museum/
Traces 100 years of Colorado's ski heritage through displays containing equipment, artifacts and photographs.

Bill Clark, Dir.
Western America Skisport Museum
P.O. Box 729
Soda Springs, CA 95728
ph: 530-426-3313
Ski history, memorabilia, manuscript collection.

Soccer

Dealers

Andy Crossley
e-mail: MinorHeros@aol.com
web: http://pubweb.acns.nwu.edu/~csp191/memor.htm
Specializes in hard-to-find media guides, programs, and souvenirs; also in defunct rival and minor league teams.

Museums/Libraries

Albert L. Colone
National Soccer Hall of Fame, The
Newsletter: 90 Minutes
5-11 Ford Ave.
Oneonta, NY 13820
ph: 607-432-3351 or 607-432-3645
web: http://www.soccerhall.org/
Information on soccer history, especially American; wants all forms of memorabilia relating to soccer including photographs.

International Football Hall of Fame
U.K.
e-mail: info@ifhof.com
web: http://www.ifhof.com/

Periodicals

Magazine: Football Card Collector Magazine
P.O. Box 21709
London, E14 6NQ
U.K.
web: http://www.footballcards.co.uk/

Softball

Museums/Libraries

Ron Babb
Amateur Softball Association of America
Newsletter: Amateur Softball Hall of Fame Newsletter
2801 N.E. 50th St.
Oklahoma City, OK 73111
ph: 405-424-5266
fax: 405-424-3855
e-mail: info@softball.org
web: http://www.softball.org

National Softball Hall of Fame & Museum
2801 NW 50th St.
Oklahoma City, OK 73111-7200
ph: 405-424-5266
e-mail: info@softball.org
web: http://www.softball.org/

Surfing

Collectors

John Casper
2605 S. Peninsula Dr.
Daytona Beach, FL 32118-5603
ph: 904-767-2075
e-mail: sandab66@hotmail.com
Wants to buy 1960's and earlier surfing memorabilia including surfing magazines, books, advertising literature/items, decals, patches, films, original surf movie posters, clocks, board games, comics, trophies, 8' or longer boards, etc.

Wayne Babcock
4846 Carpenteria Ave.
Carpinteria, CA 93013-1935
ph: 805-684-8148
Collects old long surfboards, surfing trophies, magazines, photos, books, records, posters, and any pre-1968 surfing items; also wants any pre-1960 Hawaiian items; especially wants wooden surfboards and very old items.

Jim Winniman
2411 Lilikoi Rd.
Haiku, HI 96708
ph: 800-410-7648 or 808-572-2341
Buying anything relating to surfing of Duke Kahanamoku; old wooden surfboards or skateboards, surfing books, patches, posters, magazines, trophies, figurines, nodders, patches, stickers, buttons, toys, games, etc.

Museums/Libraries

International Surfing Museum
411 Olive
P.O. Box 782
Huntington Beach, CA 92648
ph: 714-960-3483
e-mail: intsurfing@earthlink.net
web: http://www.surfingmuseum.org/
Surfboards from 1900 to present.

Swimming

Museums/Libraries

Bob Duenkel
International Swimming Hall of Fame
1 Hall of Fame Dr.
Fort Lauderdale, FL 33316-1611
ph: 954-462-6536
fax: 954-525-4031
e-mail: museum@ishof.org
web: http://ishof.org/museum.htm
Seeks photos, memorabilia, etc. regarding the great athletes and history of the aquatic sports; swimming, diving, water polo, synchronized swimming, water safety, pools, etc.

Table Tennis

Clubs/Associations

Gerald Gurney
Tennis Collectors Society, The
Newsletter: Tennis Tennis Collector, The
Guildhall Orchard
Mary Lane North
Great Bromley Colchester, Essex CO7 7TU
U.K.
ph: 1206 230330
fax: 1206 230330
Purpose is to encourage research into the history of racket sports; to share information on collectible items; to publicize news of auctions; to put subscribers in touch with one another; informal with occasional meetings.

Tennis

Clubs/Associations

Gerald Gurney
Tennis Collectors Society, The
Newsletter: Tennis Collector, The
Guildhall Orchard
Mary Lane North
Great Bromley Colchester, Essex CO7 7TU
U.K.
ph: 1206 230330
fax: 1206 230330
Purpose is to encourage research into the history of racket sports; to share information on collectible items; to publicize news of auctions; to put subscribers in touch with one another; informal with occasional meetings.

Collectors

Sheldon Katz
18 Cliffside Drive
Port Jefferson, NY 11777
ph: 516-928-1800

Paul Dowling
2312 Riverbend Rd.
Allentown, PA 18103
ph: 610-220-6263
fax: 610-391-1556
e-mail: PAULD58103@aol.com
Wants to buy tennis ball cans (key-wind with metal lids); also wants tennis ball boxes, porcelain tennis figurines, and silver tennis items with a tennis motif.

Ken Benner
217 Hewett Rd.
Wyncote, PA 19095-1203
ph: 215-885-5876
fax: 215-885-4635
Wants to buy pre-1900 unusual racquets, photos, trophies, programs, tennis ball cans (metal lids), books, prints, etc.

Donald N. Jones
24 Marvalingrove
Savannah, GA 31406-6334
ph: 912-354-2133
Wants to buy tennis items: rackets, ball cans, and tennis ephemera.

Gary Plock
408 Clinton Rd.
Lexington, KY 40502
ph: 606-266-8538
Wants to buy old tennis rackets and metal tennis cans.

Larry Whitaker
2920 Jesse Ct.
San Jose, CA 95124
ph: 408-377-8120
e-mail: LWhita@aol.com
Wants to buy old tennis ball cans.

Dealers

Richard R. Regan
293 Winter St. #5
Hanover, MA 02339-2528
ph: 617-826-3537
e-mail: foregolf@tiac.net
Wants to buy tennis posters & broadsides, books, prints, cigarette cards, programs, autographed photos, early equipment such as balls, ball containers and rackets; anything related to tennis.

Don Brenner
2292 Fairoaks Rd.
Atlanta, GA 30333-1200
ph: 404-315-7782
Buys and sells Tennis memorabilia; programs, books, cards, magazines, autographs, tickets, trophies, etc.

Experts

Jeanne Cherry
Amaryllis Press
1402 San Vicente Blvd.
Santa Monica, CA 90402
ph: 310-395-3915
fax: 310-260-9425
e-mail: jcherry@lainet.com
web: http://www.tennisantiques.com/
Collects, buys, appraises and specializes in tennis collectibles; author of "Tennis Antiques & Collectibles," covering rackets, ball cans, books, ephemera, silver and ceramics.

Internet Resources

Rick Roth
Racquet Collector, The
4710 Hilltop Dr.
Pasco, WA 99301
ph: 509-543-9239
e-mail: reroth@theracquetcollector.com
web: http://www.theracquetcollector.com/
Online service for buyers and sellers of tennis related memorabilia: racquets, tennis balls and cans, art, books, prints, trophies, etc.

Museums/Libraries

Mark S. Young, II, Archivist
International Tennis Hall of Fame & Tennis Museum
194 Bellevue Ave.
Newport, RI 02840-3515
ph: 401-849-3990
fax: 401-849-8780
web: http://www.tennisfame.org/

Tennis Rackets

Collectors

Ralph Nix
P.O. Box 655
Red Bay, AL 35582-0655
ph: 256-356-2997
e-mail: ralphn@getaway.net
web: http://www.shavingmug.com
Wants early lawn tennis rackets and other tennis memorabilia.

Norman Hagey
19672 Steavens Creek #424
Cupertino, CA 95014-2465
ph: 408-973-8129
Wants old autographed tennis rackets and related equipment; has over 250 autographed tennis rackets.

Thoroughbred Racing

Appraisers

Joe Boone
Turf Legend Commemoratives
P.O. Box 14293
Louisville, KY 40214
ph: 502-361-8950
e-mail: jboone@ka.net
web: http://www.derbyglass.com
Buys, sells, trades, appraises and specializes in Kentucky Derby, Preakness, Belmont, or Breeders' Cup memorabilia: glasses, programs, pins, artwork, admission items, etc.

Collectors

Ken Grayson
P.O. Box 24586
Lexington, KY 40524-4586
ph: 606-278-7419
fax: 606-278-4268
Wants to buy Kentucky Derby, Belmont, Preakness, and Breeder's Cup glasses, programs, etc.

Coleen Detzel
28 Lacresta Dr.
Florence, KY 41042-9663
ph: 606-647-6156
Wants thoroughbred racing items pertaining to Kentucky Derby and Jim Beam Stakes; also Latonia Race Track items: glasses, programs, photos, tickets, etc.

Gary Gatanis
3283-B Cardiff
Toledo, OH 43606-1867
ph: 419-475-3192
Wants Kentucky Derby memorabilia including programs, advertising and glasses; also Dan Patch memorabilia.

Gary Medeiros
1319 Sayre St.
San Leandro, CA 94579
ph: 510-351-6193 or 800-227-6049
fax: 510-351-6193
e-mail: pharlap2@aol.com
Thoroughbred racing and Kentucky Derby memorabilia: programs, books, games, glasses, photos, passes, pins,

postcards; any thoroughbred related items considered; has written articles on collecting racing programs.

Dealers

Dick Hering
121 Spring Chase Lane
Rocky Point, NC 28457-7807
ph: 910-602-3388
fax: 910-602-6005
e-mail: drfager132@aol.com
web: http://members.aol.com/drfager132/auction.htm
Buy, sell, trade horse racing (thoroughbred) memorabilia, glasses, programs, pins, advertising signs, games, books, stocks, etc.; Kentucky Derby, Preakness, Belmont, etc.

Paul Gundy
Horse Racing Memorabilia
5610 Pebble Brook Lane
Boynton Beach, FL 33437
ph: 561-364-8403
e-mail: paulgundy@msn.com
web: http://www.derbystuff.com
Buys and sells drinking glasses, programs, books, magazines, decanters, posters, pins, trophies, track giveaways; anything to do with famous horses, races, tracks, jockeys, trainers, Kentucky Derby, Preakness, Belmont, Breeders' Cup.

Jim Settembre
5115 Woodstone Circle E.
Lake Worth, FL 33463-5819
ph: 561-964-5434 or 561-964-8230
fax: 561-964-1143
e-mail: bigred51@webtv.net
Wants Kentucky Derby, Breeder's Cup, Preakness, and Belmont Stakes glasses and programs; also wants to buy any related horse racing items; auction service also available.

Joe Boone
Turf Legend Commemoratives
P.O. Box 14293
Louisville, KY 40214
ph: 502-361-8950
e-mail: jboone@ka.net
web: http://www.derbyglass.com
Buys, sells, trades, appraises and specializes in Kentucky Derby, Preakness, Belmont, or Breeders' Cup memorabilia: glasses, programs, pins, artwork, admission items, etc.

Experts

William Friedberg
462 Hillcreek Rd.
Shepherdsville, KY 40165
ph: 502-957-4039
e-mail: buddy431@gateway.net
Author of Bill Friedberg's glass collector's price guide "Racing into the 21st Century Special "Millenium" Edition," 1999 - 2000; $13.50 ppd. from author; color photographs; Ky. Derby, Preakness, Belmont, Breeder's Cup and more.

Betty Hornback
Betty's Antiques
707 Sunrise Lane
Elizabethtown, KY 42701
ph: 502-765-2441 or 502-369-7279
Author of "Kentucky Derby Glass Price Guide;" specializes in Kentucky Derby glasses; sells nationwide; wants to buy pre-1974 glasses; send $2 for list of glasses for sale.

Tom Sporney
5871 Liberty Creek Drive E.
Indianapolis, IN 46254
e-mail: neYmo@in-motion.net
web: http://www.crt-stable.com/equillector/

Internet Resources

Tom Sporney
Equillector, The
5871 Liberty Creek Drive E.
Indianapolis, IN 46254
e-mail: neYmo@in-motion.net
web: http://www.crt-stable.com/equillector/
A guide for collectors of horse racing memorabilia; goal is to present realistic prices for items based on actual sales prices rather than arbitrary dealer prices, to aid in identifying items by giving descriptions and photos.

Museums/Libraries

National Museum of Racing & Hall of Fame
191 Union Ave.
Saratoga Springs, NY 12866
ph: 518-584-0400
fax: 518-584-4574
e-mail: webmaster@racingmuseum.org
web: http://www.racingmuseum.org/

Candace Perry
Kentucky Derby Museum, The
Newsletter: Inside Track
P.O. Box 3513
Louisville, KY 40201-3513
ph: 502-637-1111 or 800-273-3729
fax: 502-636-5855
e-mail: info@derbymuseum.org
web: http://www.derbymuseum.org
Cannot provide appraisals, but can help identify and research; located at 704 Central Ave., Louisville, KY 40208.

Track & Field

Collectors

Ed Kozloff
10144 Lincoln
Huntington Woods, MI 48070-1539
ph: 245-544-9099
fax: 245-544-4601
e-mail: racebreak@aol.com
Collector, expert on Olympic, running and track & field memorabilia; track & field, road races, Olympic material: medals, ribbons, trophies, annuals, books, magazines, etc.

Museums/Libraries

National Track & Field Hall of Fame
1 RCA Dome, Ste. 140
Indianapolis, IN 46225
ph: 317-261-0500
e-mail: usatfmedia@aol.com
web: http://www.usatf.org/

Weightlifting

Experts

David Chapman
656 32nd Ave. East
Seattle, WA 98112
ph: 206-329-7573
fax: 206-329-7573
Says there is more to weight training that fat Russian guys or Arnold Schwarzenegger; is interested in the early days of "physical culture" (1895-1950): wants photos, books, magazines, posters, etc.; has written extensively.

Museums/Libraries

Philip Redman
York Barbell Hall of Fame
330 Board Rd.
York, PA 17402
ph: 717-767-6481 or 800-358-9675
fax: 717-764-0044
e-mail: info@yorkbarbell.com
web: http://www.yorkbarbell.com/hall00.html
Weightlifting, body building, power lifting history and memorabilia.

Wrestling

Collectors

Tom Burke
31 Groveland St.
Springfield, MA 01108-2920
ph: 413-733-6015
e-mail: tbgblmat@javanet.com
Wants to buy Professional Wrestling postcards, programs, magazines, and related items from any era.

John Pantozzi
1000 Polk Ave.
Franklin Square, NY 11010-2018
ph: 516-488-7728
fax: 516-327-8984
Wants to buy wrestling related toys, dolls, pennants, patches, trading cards, pins, postcards, books, posters, movie posters, board games, ring gear, autographs, photos, scrapbooks, etc.

Bob Bryla
"Dr. Wrestling"
1912 Sunset Ave.
Utica, NY 13502-5636
ph: 315-733-1846
fax: 315-733-7518
e-mail: bryfour@dreamscape.com
Wants items relating to boxing and wrestling: strength books, magazines, programs, dolls, games, medals, pennants, bottles, etc. from 1860 to present.

Museums/Libraries

Myron Roderick
National Wrestling Hall of Fame
405 W. Hall Of Fame Ave.
Stillwater, OK 74075
ph: 405-377-5243
fax: 405-377-5244
America's shrine to the sport of amateur wrestling.

SPORTS HISTORY

Clubs/Associations

Chuck Hershberger, GM
Sports Hall of Oblivion
P.O. Box 69025
Pleasant Ridge, MI 48069-0025
ph: 248-543-9412
e-mail: wheresports@hotmail.com
The Sports Hall of Oblivion is an organization dedicated to preserving the memory of defunct sports teams (HS, College, semi-pro, pro.); also covering new and weird sports.

SPRINKLERS

(see CLOTHES SPRINKLERS; WATER SPRINKLERS)

SPY EQUIPMENT

(see also CAMERAS & CAMERA EQUIPMENT, Subminiature; CHARACTER COLLECTIBLES, Spy Memorabilia; MYSTERY/DETECTIVE ITEMS; TELEVISION SHOWS & MEMORABILIA, Private Eye)

Collectors

Kenneth D. Smith
55 Howard Ave.
Staten Island, NY 10301-4404
Wants to buy cryptographic and code machines, devices, books and manuals; any era, any nation.

Don Carter
P.O. Box 142164
Gainesville, FL 32614-2164
ph: 352-376-6668
fax: 352-376-6668
Wants to buy spy cameras and equipment.

Keith Melton
P.O. Box 2880
Jupiter, FL 33468-2880
Pays top dollar for all types of old Code machines: ENIGMA's, M-209's, M-94's, M-138's, cipher disks and wheels; also devices used by OSS, SOE, KGB, MOSSAD, British intelligence, etc.

Uwe H. Breker
6731 Ashley Ct.
Sarasota, FL 34241-9696
ph: 941-925-0385
fax: 941-925-0487
e-mail: auction@breker.com
web: http://www.breker.com/
Wants secret service communication machines and devices.

Mike & Gladys Kessler
25749 Anchor Circle
San Juan Capistrano, CA 92675-4002
ph: 949-661-3320
Buys and specializes in unusual 1880-1890s disguised or detective cameras; also Simon Wing cameras.

Museums/Libraries

Jack E. Ingram, Cur.
National Cryptologic Museum
DIRNSA
Attn: S542/Museum
Fort George G Meade, MD 20755
ph: 301-688-5849 or 301-688-5848
fax: 301-688-5847
web: http://www.nsa.gov:8080/museum/
Gov't. collection open free to the public; thousands of artifacts which collectively serve to sustain the history of the cryptologic profession: books, computers, cipher devices, Enigma, cryptanalysis, research library by appointment.

ST. PATRICK

(see ELVES)

Periodicals

Chuck Thompson
Newsletter: St. Patrick Notes
10802 Greencreek Dr., Ste. 703
Houston, TX 77070-5367
Legends, facts, quotes, stories, and other notes about St. Patrick; for fans of the Patron Saint of Ireland and collectors of St. Patrick memorabilia.

STAGECOACH ITEMS

(see WESTERN AMERICANA)

STAINED GLASS

(see also ARCHITECTURAL ELEMENTS; CRAFTS, Glass)

Clubs/Associations

Kathy Murdock, Ex. Admin.
Stained Glass Association of America
P.O. Box 22642
Kansas City, MO 64113
ph: 800-888-SGAA
fax: 816-361-9173
e-mail: sgaofa@aol.com
web: http://www.stainedglass.org/sgaamain.html
A non-profit association founded in 1903 to promote the development and advancement of the stained and decorative art glass craft.

Collectors

Bob Ward
2461 E High St., #A-7
Pottstown, PA 19464-3111
ph: 610-970-6299
Wants stained glass windows.

Dealers

Jim Osella
145 Adams Ave.
Bridgeville, PA 15017
ph: 412-746-2451 or 724-745-1333
fax: 412-746-2451
e-mail: osella@usaor.net
Wants to buy stained and beveled glass windows, one or a hundred.

Experts

H. Weber Wilson
Oltz-Wilson Antiques
P.O. Box 506
Portsmouth, RI 02871
ph: 800-508-0022
fax: 401-683-1644
e-mail: hww@edgenet.net
web: http://www.antiqnet.com/webwilson/
Author of books on stained glass; also sells architectural antiques.

Carl Heck
Carl Heck Decorative Arts
P.O. Box 8416
Aspen, CO 81612-8416
ph: 970-925-8011
fax: 970-925-8100
web: http://www.carlheck.com/
Specializes in antique stained and beveled glass and Tiffany windows; also leaded and reverse-painted lamps.

Internet Resources

Robert Daniels
Art Glass World
4002 W. State St.
Tampa, FL 33609
ph: 813-348-0605
fax: 813-872-6288
e-mail: general@artglassworld.com
web: http://www.artglassworld.com
The largest Internet stained glass resource in the world.

Man./Prod./Dist.

Stained Glass Resources, Inc.
15 Commercial Drive
Hampden, MA 01036
ph: 800-883-5052
fax: 413-566-2935

Rohlf's Studio, Inc.
783 South Third Ave.
Mount Vernon, NY 10550
ph: 800-969-4106 or 914-699-4848
fax: 914-699-7091
e-mail: Rohlf1@aol.com
web: http://www.RohlfStudio.com/

Durham Studios, Inc.
330 Eagle Ave.
West Hempstead, NY 11552
ph: 516-481-5656
fax: 516-481-7905

Hunt Stained Glass Studios, Inc.
1756 West Carson St.
Pittsburgh, PA 15219-1036
ph: 412-391-1796
fax: 412-391-1560

Willet Stained Glass Studios
10 East Moreland Ave.
Philadelphia, PA 19112
ph: 800-533-3960
fax: 215-247-2951

Althouse Glass Studios
316 W. Main St.
Kutztown, PA 19530
ph: 610-683-7806

Art in Glass, Inc.
414 Pine Ave.
Frederick, MD 21701-5764
ph: 301-663-1151 or 301-663-1152
fax: 301-620-7417
e-mail: carvedglass@artinglass.com
web: http://www.artinglass.com/
Specializing in custom stained glass designs for doors, sidelights, skylights, cabinets; also sandblast carving, etching, and repairs.

Ray Gregory
2708 Wyoming Ave.
Norfolk, VA 23513
ph: 757-855-4312
fax: 757-855-4312
Design and create stained glass for churches, synagogues, public buildings, restaurants and private homes; also repairs old stained glass windows.

Lynchburg Stained Glass Co.
P.O. Box 4453
Lynchburg, VA 24502
ph: 800-273-6161
fax: 804-526-6168

Stained Glass Associates
P.O. Box 1531
Raleigh, NC 27602-1531
ph: 919-266-2493
fax: 919-266-3601

Laws Stained Glass Studios, Inc.
145 Ebenezer Lane
Statesville, NC 28625
ph: 800-820-1292 or 704-876-3463
fax: 704-876-4238

Statesville Stained Glass, Inc.
136 Christopher Lane
Statesville, NC 28625
ph: 704-872-5147
fax: 704-872-7813
e-mail: ssglass@vnet.net

Advent Glass Works, Inc.
P.O. Box 174
Fort White, FL 32038
ph: 800-207-4875 or 904-497-2050
fax: 904-497-2941

Emmanuel Stained Glass Studios, Inc.
410 Maple Ave.
Nashville, TN 37210
ph: 800-326-2228 or 615-255-5446
fax: 615-255-5447
e-mail: emmanuel@voy.net

Goodson Glass Studios
615 Rutledge Pike
Blaine, TN 37709
ph: 423-933-6272
fax: 423-933-0063

Franklin Art Glass Studios, Inc.
222 East Sycamore St.
Columbus, OH 43206-2198
ph: 614-221-2972
fax: 614-221-5223

Whitney Stained Glass Studio, Inc.
2530 Superior Ave.
Cleveland, OH 44114
ph: 216-348-1616
fax: 216-348-1116

Ted Moss
Moss Stained Glass
2501 East 8th Street
Anderson, IN 46012
ph: 888-833-6677
fax: 765-643-0439

Shadetree Stained Glass Studio
417 Howard
Petoskey, MI 49770
ph: 616-347-1011
fax: 616-347-4826
e-mail: shadetre@freeway.net
web: http://www.shadetreestudios.com/

Gilbertson's Stained Glass Studio
400 Interchange Highway 120 North
Lake Geneva, WI 53147
ph: 414-248-8022
fax: 414-248-3044
e-mail: gsgs@genevaonline.com
web: http://www.stainedartglass.com

Conrad Schmitt Studios, Inc.
2405 S. 162nd Street
New Berlin, WI 53151
ph: 800-969-3033 or 414-786-3030
fax: 414-786-9036

Reinhart's Stained Glass Studios
506 W. Fifth St.
P.O. Box 604
Winona, MN 55987
ph: 800-533-4444

Kerble Stained Glass Studio, Inc.
2829 Bachman Drive
Dallas, TX 75220
ph: 214-357-5922
fax: 214-357-5922

Powell Brothers & Sons
4050 S. Howick St., Ste. 10E
Salt Lake City, UT 84107
ph: 800-484-5184 or 801-262-4002
fax: 801-262-4002
e-mail: jenkyn@aros.net
web: http://www.powellbrosglassart.com

Judson Studios
200 South Avenue 66
Los Angeles, CA 90042
ph: 800-445-8376
fax: 323-255-8529
e-mail: bjudson@flash.net
web: http://www.judsonstudios.com

Jean Myers
11 Willotta Dr.
Suisun City, CA 94585
ph: 707-864-3906
fax: 707-864-3467
e-mail: egoodell@aol.com

Museums/Libraries

Corning Museum of Glass, The
One Museum Way
Corning, NY 14830-2253
ph: 607-937-5371
fax: 607-937-3352
e-mail: cmg@cmog.org
web: http://www.pennynet.org/glmuseum/
Over 24,000 glass objects, innovative exhibits, videos, models; glass history, archaeology, and early manufacturing; Robert Sowers (stained glass artist, critic, author) collection of archival materials pertaining to stained glass.

Periodicals

Magazine: Glass Patterns Quarterly
8300 Hidden Valley Rd.
P.O. Box 69
Westport, KY 40077
ph: 502-222-5631 or 800-719-0769
fax: 502-222-4527
e-mail: Gpqmag@aol.com
web: http://www.glasspatterns.com/
Glossy quarterly magazine for the stained glass hobbyist: stained glass patterns, techniques, ads, etc.; also articles about sandblasting and etching glass, glass kiln firing, glass painting, lamps, windows, display cases, etc.

Richard Gross, Ed.
Magazine: Stained Glass
6 Southwest Secton St., Ste. 7
Lees Summit, MO 64063
e-mail: sgmagaz@kcnet.com
web: http://www.stainedglass.org/sglass.html
Primarily a trade magazine, but also contains articles and resources of interest to owners of old stained glass.

Magazine: Glass Art Magazine
P.O. Box 260377
Highlands Ranch, CO 80126-0377
ph: 303-791-8998
fax: 303-791-7739
e-mail: glassartm@aol.com
web: http://www.artglassworld.com/mag/glassart/
A bi-monthly magazine which includes glass industry news including upcoming museum and gallery exhibitions.

Repair Services

Nadia Wassef
303 Detering
Houston, TX 77007
ph: 713-880-0108
fax: 713-880-3544
e-mail: nfwassef@msn.com
Does stained glass, crystal and porcelain repair; email or snail mail photos to find out about restoration possibilities; repair and return ship.

Suppliers

Hudson Glass
219 North Division St.
Peekskill, NY 10566-2716
ph: 800-431-2964 or 914-737-2124
fax: 914-737-4447
Sells bent glass for china cabinets; convex picture frame glass; also carries restoration/old house glass in stock; sells stained glass tools and supplies (no stained glass repair); stained glass supply catalog available for $3.

Richard Blenko
Blenko Glass Company, Inc.
P.O. Box 67
Milton, WV 25541-0067
ph: 304-743-9081
fax: 304-743-0547
e-mail: blenko@usa.net
web: http://blenkoglass.com/
Supplies hand-blown "antique" glass for stained glass windows; colored handmade glassware, blown tableware, tumblers and stemware, vases, pitchers; custom mold work, awards and barware; stained glass studio.

Robert Danielss
Delphi Stained Glass
3380 E. Jolly Rd.
Lansing, MI 48910
ph: 800-248-2048 or 517-394-4631
fax: 517-394-5364
e-mail: webmaster@delphiglass.com
web: http://www.delphiglass.com/
Sells stained glass supplies; gives lessons; large mail order business; also sells chemical solutions to repair damaged patina on brass and other metals.

Steve
Stained Glass Web-Mart
2808 Broadway
Eureka, CA 95501
ph: 717-443-8157
e-mail: antiques@glassmart.com
web: http://www.glassmart.com
Stained glass tools and supplies online.

STAINLESS STEEL FLATWARE

(see FLATWARE)

STAMP BOXES

Collectors

Bob Morris
706 Pawnee St.
Bethlehem, PA 18015-1432
ph: 610-865-9052
Wants to buy stamp boxes and stamp holders; single item or collection; US or foreign; also wants stamp scales.

STAMP COLLECTING

(see also ADVERTISING COLLECTIBLES, Trading Cards; POSTAL SERVICE ITEMS; SEALS, Christmas & Charity; SEALS & STAMPS; STAMP BOXES; STAMP WETTERS; TRADING CARDS, Non-Sport)

Appraisers

Ray L. Coughlin
Coughlin's
P.O. Box 762
Washougal, WA 98671-0762
ph: 360-835-7990
fax: 360-835-7990
e-mail: coughlin@teleport.com
web: http://www.teleport.com/~coughlin/
Stamp expert, appraiser; buys and sells the stamps, postal stationary, postal history of the US Possessions, Canal Zone, pre-Castro Cuba, Guam, HI, Philippines (all eras), PR, The Tyukyu Islands, other places with US Postal facilities.

Auction Services

Stanley J. Richmond
Daniel F. Kelleher Company, Inc.
24 Farnsworth St., Ste. 605
Boston, MA 02210-1264
ph: 617-443-0033
fax: 617-443-0789
e-mail: kelleher@tiac.net
web: http://www.tiac.net/users/kelleher/
U.S. and BNA stamps at auction; also autographs and documents.

Greg Manning
Greg Manning Auctions, Inc.
775 Passaic Ave.
West Caldwell, NJ 07006
ph: 973-882-0004 or 800-221-0243
fax: 973-882-3499
e-mail: gmauction@aol.com
web: http://www.gregmanning.com/
Dealer and auctioneer in all philatelic properties.

Jacques C. Schiff, Jr.
Jacques C. Schiff, Jr. Inc.
195 Main St.
Ridgefield Park, NJ 07660-1620
ph: 201-641-5566
fax: 201-641-5705
Auctioneers of worldwide stamps and postal history; specialties include U.S. stamps, world stamps, U.S. and world postal history, errors and varieties; also purchase outright and sell consignments.

Robson Lowe
Christie's
502 Park Ave.
New York, NY 10022
ph: 212-546-1000
fax: 212-980-8163
web: http://www.christies.com

Elizabeth C. Pope
Robert A. Siegel Auction Galleries, Inc.
65 East 55th St.
New York, NY 10022-3219
ph: 212-753-6421
fax: 212-753-6429
e-mail: siegelstp@aol.com
web: http://www.siegelauctions.com/home.htm

Thomas Droege
Stamp Auction Central
20 West Colony, Ste. 120
Durham, NC 27705
ph: 919-403-9459
fax: 919-403-8199
e-mail: 73607.1717@compuserve.com
web: http://stampauctioncentral/auctions.htm
The most comprehensive resource for on-line stamp auction catalogs; over 70 stamp auction firms have provided complete on-line catalogs for over 350 sales and 600,000 lost since inception in Jan 1996.

Charles G. Firby Auctions
6695 Highland Rd., Ste. 107
Waterford, MI 48327-5333
ph: 248-666-5333
fax: 248-666-5020

Ron Playle
Playle's Online Auctions
P.O. Box 65918
West Des Moines, IA 50265
ph: 515-267-0213
fax: 515-267-0213
e-mail: ron@playle.com
web: http://www.playle.com/main.html
Buy and sell postcards, stamps, coins, antiques, collectibles online.

Bel-Aire Stamp Auctions
2589 Hamline Ave. North, Ste. D
Saint Paul, MN 55113
ph: 612-633-8553
fax: 612-633-8554
e-mail: belaire@stampguyz.com
web: http://www.stampguyz.com/belaire

Rasdale Stamp Company
36 South Street, Stuie 1102
Chicago, IL 60603
ph: 312-263-7334
fax: 312-263-1819
e-mail: rasdales@aol.com
web: http://www.rasdalestamps.com/
Frequent public and mail auctions of U.S. and world stamps.

Superior Galleries
9478 West Olympic Blvd.
Beverly Hills, CA 90212-4246
ph: 310-203-9855 or 800-421-0754
fax: 310-203-0496
e-mail: superior@superiorsc.com
web: http://www.superiorsc.com/
Has been a retail and auction source for dealers and collectors for over 70 years; specializes in stamps, coins, sports memorabilia, Hollywood memorabilia, space memorabilia, historic manuscripts and autographs.

Hobby Markets Online, Inc.
375 Alabama Street, Ste. 410
San Francisco, CA 94110
ph: 415-252-6040 or 415-252-6040
fax: 415-252-6044
e-mail: hobbyinfo@hobbymarkets.com
web: http://www.Philatelists.com/
Online auction service for stamps, covers, postal history collectors; auctions items from leading philatelic dealers and auction houses ranging from beginner stamps for the new collector to elite stamps for the investor.

Northwestern Philatelic Auctions, Inc.
304 Martin Street, Ste. 200
Penticton, British Columbia V2A 5K4
Canada
ph: 250-493-0145
fax: 250-493-4076
e-mail: northwestern@img.net
web: http://vvv.com/~northwest

Harmers of London
91 New Bond Street
London, W1A 4EH
U.K.
ph: 0171-629 0218
fax: 0171-495 0260
e-mail: auctions@harmers.demon.co.uk
web: http://www.harmers.com/
Harmers specializes in the sale of stamps, but also sells paper items such as autographs, manuscripts, maps, etc.

Book Sellers

David G. Phillips Company, Inc.
P.O. Box 611388
Miami, FL 33161-1388
ph: 305-895-0470
Deals in U.S. covers and philatelic literature; sells the basic important references for the U.S. stamp specialist.

Clubs/Associations

George Young
Rainbow Study Unit of the American Topical Association
Newsletter: Rainbow's Bend, The
P.O. Box 632
Tewksbury, MA 01876
Collectors of philatelic material concerning the spectrum: radar to gamma rays and all subtopics which are the different parts of the spectrum - astronomy, mineralogy, health, police, the sciences; also the aurorae on stamps.

American Stamp Dealers Association
3 School St., Ste. 205
Glen Cove, NY 11542-2548
ph: 516-759-7000
fax: 516-759-7014
e-mail: asda@erols.com
web: http://www.asdaonline.com/
Trade association representing stamp dealers; issues free list of dealers in your area and by your special area of interest; sponsors national and regional stamp shows; offers free brochures about stamp collecting, dealing, etc.

Charles Eson
Fort Orange Stamp Club
128 Western Ave.
Altamont, NY 12009
ph: 578-861-6256
Oldest continuously meeting stamp club in the U.S.; meets 2nd and 4th Tuesday of the month from September through May in Albany, NY.

American Philatelic Society
Magazine: American Philatelist
P.O. Box 8000
State College, PA 16803-8000
ph: 814-237-3803
fax: 814-237-6128
web: http://www.stamps.org/
The largest stamp collector organization in the US; provides services to 58,000 collectors in more than 100 countries; 700 local allied stamp clubs, 200 national "specialty groups", code of ethics, estate advice, expertizing.

Ellie Chapman, Ex. Sec.
Junior Philatelists of America
Journal: Philatelic Observer
P.O. Box 850
Boalsburg, PA 16827-0850
e-mail: JPAEllie@aol.com
web: http://www.jpastamps.org/
Organization for pre-adult collectors.

David Lee
Bureau Issues Association, Inc.
Journal: Specialist, The
P.O. Box 2641
Reston, VA 20195-0641
web: http://www.delphi.com/stamps/clubs/bia.html
For collectors of U.S. stamps; publisher of reference material on U.S. stamps.

John Hotchner, Ed.
American Association of Philatelic Exhibitors
Journal: Philatelic Exhibitor, The
P.O. Box 1125
Falls Church, VA 22041-0125
e-mail: JMHstamp@ix.netcom.com
Formed to provide a forum for stamp exhibitors to share and discuss ideas and techniques geared towards improving standards to exhibit preparation, judging, and show management; members are beginners through experienced stamp collectors.

Peter J. Roberts
Atlanta Stamp Collectors Club
Newsletter: Postmark Club
2442 King Point Dr.
Atlanta, GA 30338-5927
ph: 770-986-4214 or 404-894-0281
web: http://www.gsu.edu/~libpjr/atlstamps.htm

Dudley Bauerlein
CompuServe Stamp Chapter, American Philatelic Society
2117 Greenway Dr.
Winter Haven, FL 33881-1257
ph: 941-294-5279
fax: 941-299-2450
e-mail: 70661.3213@compuserve.com
Largest electronic stamp club in the world serving US and world wide collectors; 2 monthly stamp auctions; library with many files on stamp collecting; for CompuServe new member kit, dial toll free 800-848-8199 (GO COLLECT or GO STAMPS).

Carl Albrecht, Mem. Ch.
U.S. Philatelic Classics Society
Journal: Chronicle, The
P.O. Box 82252
Columbus, OH 43202
e-mail: calbrech@infinet.com
web: http://www.scruz.net/~eho/uspcs/
Focuses on stamps issued over one hundred years ago; old, rare and valuable stamps.

Wanda Miller
American Philatelic Congress
P.O. Box 8171
Cincinnati, OH 45208
e-mail: wandy001@aol.com
web: http://members.aol.com/TongaJan/APC.html
Provides a service to philately by editing, printing, and distributing to members a quality hardbound book of original research papers annually.

Carriers & Locals Society
P.O. Box 1574
Dayton, OH 45401-1574
Members interested in collecting and study of U.S. carriers and locals: U.S. official and semi-official carrier services, 19th century local posts, independent mails, package expresses of the 19th century, fakes & forgeries.

Indiana Stamp Club
Newsletter: Mule, The
P.O. Box 40792
indianapolis, IN 46240
e-mail: indypex@aol.com
web: http://hometown.aol.com/indypex/isc/
Largest stamp club in Indiana and home to INDYPEX, an APS World Series of Philately show.

Jerome C. Jarnick, Sec.
British North American Philatelic Society, Ltd.
Journal: BNA Topics
108 Duncan Dr.
Troy, MI 48098-4613
ph: 248-689-1966
fax: 248-689-1966
e-mail: alecunwin@email.msn.com
web: http://www.wep.ab.ca/bnaps/
BNAPS is devoted to the study of stamps and postal history of Canada

and the former colonies; also publishes the "BNA Portraits," a newsletter; annual convention.

Israel I. Bick, Ex. Dir.
International Stamp Collectors Society
Newsletter: Interstamps
P.O. Box 854
Van Nuys, CA 91408-0854
ph: 818-997-6496
fax: 818-988-4337
e-mail: iibick@aol.com
web: http://www.bick.net
Promoting understanding in the world through stamp collecting.

National Stamp Dealers Association
P.O. Box 7176
Redwood City, CA 94063
ph: 800-875-6633 or 650-364-6667
fax: 650-364-6972
e-mail: stamps@fortunesofwar.com
web: http://www.fortunesofwar.com/nsda.html

Collectors

Scott Kitchen
1301 Sunny Slope Rd.
Bridgewater, NJ 08807
Stamp collector; worldwide; tanks and chess.

Marc L. Ames
539 Lyme Rock Rd.
Bridgewater, NJ 08807-1670
ph: 908-526-7676
fax: 908-575-0880
e-mail: magames@ix.netcom.com
Wants to buy essays, proofs, specimens, samples and pre-1940 issues.

Roland Roehner
North Carolina Stamp Club
P.O. Box 1674
Nags Head, NC 27959
ph: 252-441-7510

Carl Albrecht, Mem.
U.S. Philatelic Classics Society, Inc.
Journal: Chronicle of the U.S. Classic Postal Issues
P.O. Box 82252
Columbus, OH 43202
e-mail: calbrech@infinet.com
web: http://www.scruz.net/~eho/uspcs/
Members focus on U.S. stamps from the period 1851 to 1857.

Tony Zollo, Pres.
International Society of Worldwide Stamp Collectors
Newsletter: Circuit, The
P.O. Box 150407
Lufkin, TX 75915-0407
ph: 409-633-2712
e-mail: zolloam@lcc.net
web: http://www.frontiernet.net/~stamptmf/iswsc/iswsc.html
Serves the interests of all worldwide stamp collectors.

Richard M. Simon
1846 27th Ave.
San Francisco, CA 94122-4212
ph: 415-566-3920
Wants to buy worldwide stamp, cover and postcard collections; member of the American Philatelic Society, Hong Kong Stamp Society, and Hong Kong Study Circle; specializing in US, British Commonwealth, and Asia.

James Yeaw
P.O. Box 1077
Rocklin, CA 95677
ph: 916-624-7281
fax: 916-624-9309
e-mail: jyeaw@interests.com
web: http://www.philately.com/

Dealers

Jack E. Molesworth
88 Beacon St.
Boston, MA 02108
ph: 617-523-2522
fax: 617-523-2265
Classic U.S. stamps and covers bought and sold.

Richard A. Champagne
P.O. Box 600372
Newtonville, MA 02460-0004
ph: 617-969-5719
Stocks U.S. classics; does important stamp shows; an entertaining speaker at show seminars.

Brookman Barrett & Worthen
10 Chestnut Dr.
Bedford, NH 03110
ph: 800-332-3383
fax: 603-472-8795
e-mail: brookman@xtdl.com
web: http://www2.xtdl.com/~brookman/
Dealers in stamps and covers.

Brookman Barrett & Worthen
10 Chestnut Dr.
Bedford, NH 03110
ph: 800-332-3383
fax: 603-472-8795
e-mail: brookman@xtdl.com
web: http://www2.xtdl.com/~brookman/

Jacques C. Schiff, Jr.
Jacques C. Schiff, Jr. Inc.
195 Main St.
Ridgefield Park, NJ 07660-1620
ph: 201-641-5566
fax: 201-641-5705
Buys, sells, auctions, and appraises U.S. and World stamps, errors and varieties.

Downtown Stamp Company
P.O. Box 329
Whitehouse, NJ 08888-0329
ph: 908-439-3663
fax: 908-439-2414
Services want lists for U.S. and world issues, including less expensive and moderately priced items.

Sam Malamud
Ideal Stamp Company
460 West 34th St.
New York, NY 10001
ph: 212-629-7979
fax: 212-629-3350
Buying and selling stamps of the world, especially U.S., British, Israel, and United Nations.

John A. Rerecic
J.R. Stamps
838 West End Ave., 1-A
New York, NY 10025-5365
ph: 212-663-6096 or 212-807-6477
e-mail: jrereci@aol.com
Operates a store open only on Saturdays and Sundays from 10 a.m. to 6 p.m. at 110 W 25th Street, Store #609, New York, NY 10001.

Harry Hagendorf
Columbian Stamp Company, Inc.
700 White Plains Rd.
Scarsdale, NY 10583
ph: 914-725-2290
fax: 914-572-2576
Dealer in rare stamps, including the famous 1918 inverted Jenny biplane.

Don Black
405 Tarrytown Rd., Ste. 402
White Plains, NY 10607
ph: 914-347-3971
fax: 914-347-3971
e-mail: don@donblack.com
web: http://www.donblack.com
Sells collectible world wide postage stamps and post cards.

Columbian Stamp Company
P.O. Box B
New Rochelle, NY 10804
ph: 914-725-2290
web: http://www.columbianstamp.com/
U.S. classics, including 19th century multiples.

Henry Gitner Philatelists, Inc.
P.O. Box 3077
Middletown, NY 10940
ph: 800-947-8267
fax: 914-343-0068
e-mail: hgitner@aol.com
web: http://www.hgitner.com
Specializes in classic U.S. stamps.

Henry Gitner
Henry Gitner Philatelists, Inc.
2-20 Low Ave., Ste. 311
P.O. Box 3077
Middletown, NY 10940
ph: 800-947-8267 or 914-343-5151
fax: 914-343-0068
e-mail: hgitner@hgitner.com
web: http://www.hgitner.com
One of America's most diverse stamp dealers with 15 rooms of stock; also offers valid postage for under face value.

Gary Posner
6340 Avenue N., Ste. 121
Brooklyn, NY 11234
ph: 718-251-1952 or 800-323-GARY
fax: 718-241-2801

Jack & Myrna Golden
Golden Philatelics
P.O. Box 484
Cedarhurst, NY 11516
ph: 516-791-1804
fax: 516-791-7846
e-mail: mgolden922@aol.com
Good stock of U.S. revenues, including cheaper but elusive varieties, bought and sold.

Ron Alfin
Alfin's Philatelic Connection
Newsletter: Newsletter, The
3 Williamsburgh Lane
Nesconset, NY 11767
ph: 516-737-1694
e-mail: ralfin@alfin.computerworks.net
web: http://alfin.computerworks.net/
Stamp trading and sales for the beginner to pro; website has valuable terminology for the beginner; some special introductory stamps available; trade with others in the club.

Alan Anderson
stampview.com
ph: 516-756-0167 or 718-248-7825
fax: 718-361-6550
e-mail: alan@stampview.com
web: http://www.stampview.com/
Sells stamps of the world, specializing in less common items, mostly via the Internet; appraisals also available; web site includes high resolution scans of many stamps offered for sale; accepts consignments to be placed on web site.

Charles Eson
Hawkeye Philatelics
128 Western Ave.
Altamont, NY 12009
ph: 578-861-6256
Specializing in U.S. coils, Revenues, used, Canada, Mexico, and Mediterranean countries.

Mystic Stamp Company
9700 Mill St.
Camden, NY 13316
ph: 800-835-3609
fax: 800-835-4919
Buys entire dealer stock, U.S. stamp collections, worldwide and topical stamp collections, rare individual stamps both U.S. and worldwide, mixed accumulations, U.S. and worldwide covers.

James J. Reeves, Inc.
P.O. Box 219
Huntingdon, PA 16652
ph: 800-364-2948
fax: 814-641-2600
e-mail: Reeves5@vicon.net
web: http://www.JamesJReeves.com

James Reeves
James Reeves Inc.
P.O. Box 219
Huntingdon, PA 16652-0219
ph: 800-364-2948
fax: 814-641-2600
e-mail: reeves5@vicon.net
web: http://www.jamesreeves.com/
In business for over 20 years.

Bob Morris
706 Pawnee St.
Bethlehem, PA 18015-1432
ph: 610-865-9052
Purchases U.S. and foreign stamps, envelopes and philatelic literature; will appraise in the PA, NJ, NY and DE area; will appraise stamp collections and cover collections in this region.

Dale
P.O. Box 539
Emmaus, PA 18049
ph: 610-433-3303
fax: 610-965-6089

Earl P.L. Apfelbaum, Inc.
2006 Walnut Street
Philadelphia, PA 19103-5608
ph: 215-567-5200 or 800-523-4648
fax: 215-567-5445
web: http://apfelbauminc.com/
One of the oldest and largest stamp firms in the world.

Patricia A. Kaufmann
Osborne-Kaurmann
522 Old State Road
Lincoln, DE 19960
ph: 800-933-6289 or 302-422-2656
fax: 302-424-1990
e-mail: trish@webuystamps.com
web: http://www.webuystamps.com/
Your American-European stamp connection; buying stamp and postal history collections on both sides of the Atlantic.

Maryland Stamp & Coins
7720 Wisconsin Ave.
Bethesda, MD 20815
ph: 301-654-8828 or 800-426-5723
fax: 301-942-8778
web: http://www.marylandstamps.com/

Martin L. Barron, Jr.
AmeriCom Philatelic
P.O. Box 587
New Market, MD 21774-0587
ph: 301-631-5362
e-mail: americom@fred.net
web: http://www.fred.net/americom/
Specializing in mint U.S. stamps from the Classic Period of 1890 to 1940.

Michael Rogers
Michael Rogers, Inc.
199 E. Welbourne Ave., Ste. 3
Winter Park, FL 32789
ph: 407-644-2290 or 800-843-2290
fax: 407-645-4434
e-mail: webmaster@michaelrogersinc.com
web: http://www.michaelrogersinc.com/
Carries full line of U.S. and foreign stamps; good selection of stamp collecting supplies.

Herman Herst, Jr.
P.O. Box 1583
Boca Raton, FL 33429-1583
ph: 800-321-6180 or 561-391-3223
Wants to buy old pre-1890 letters and envelopes, with or without stamps; toll free number to help you learn the value of what you have; 60 years in the business; Senior Member, ASA; free booklet to anyone sending SASE.

Joachim Steltzer
Steltzer International
5030 Champion Blvd., Ste. G-6 #116
Boca Raton, FL 33496-2496
ph: 561-852-1435
fax: 561-451-8774
Dealer and expert in stamps.

Jim Dalton, Sr.
Dalton & Dalton
P.O. Box 487
Muncie, IN 47305-0487
ph: 317-288-9488
e-mail: rockys@iquest.net
Stamp collections wanted, large or small; since 1949.

Jerry & Barbara Koepp
Stamps "n" Stuff
Governor Square
2700 University, Ste. 214
West Des Moines, IA 50266-1451
ph: 800-999-5964 or 515-224-1713
fax: 515-226-1651
e-mail: bkoepp@earthlink.net

Robert M. Weisz
4562 N. Austin Ave.
Chicago, IL 60630
ph: 773-545-2929
Buys, sells, appraises stamps and postcards.

John Rebello
Town & Country Stamps
P.O. Box 13542
North County, MO 63138
ph: 314-522-0289
Constantly buying large and small lots of stamps; will buy just about anything; sells mixtures and more expensive items also.

Raymond Weill
Raymond H. Weill Company
407 Royal St.
New Orleans, LA 70130
ph: 504-581-7373
Carries a good stock of U.S. stamps.

Paradise Valley Stamp Company
P.O. Box 8948
Scottsdale, AZ 85252-8948
ph: 602-9970-1733
fax: 602-970-0332
e-mail: pvscstamps@compuserve.com
web: http://www.stamp-one.com/pvsc

George C. Baxley
P.O. Box 807
Alamogordo, NM 88311
ph: 505-437-8707
fax: 505-434-1571
Buying and selling worldwide stamps and covers; specializing in Asia.

Cy Phillips, Jr.
S C Coin & Stamp Co. Inc.
P.O. Drawer 661180
Arcadia, CA 91066-1180
ph: 818-445-8277 or 800-367-0779
fax: 818-445-8278

Warren Sankey
United States Stamp Company
368 Bush St.
San Francisco, CA 94104
ph: 415-421-7398
fax: 415-421-3167
e-mail: usstamp@pacbell.net
web: http://www.usstampco.com/
Buys and sells worldwide and U.S. mint and used stamps; also carries supplies.

Ray L. Coughlin
Coughlin's
P.O. Box 762
Washougal, WA 98671-0762
ph: 360-835-7990
fax: 360-835-7990
e-mail: coughlin@teleport.com
web: http://www.teleport.com/~coughlin/
Stamp expert, appraiser; buys and sells the stamps, postal stationary, postal history of the US Possessions, Canal Zone, pre-Castro Cuba, Guam, HI, Philippines (all eras), PR, The Tyukyu Islands, other places with US Postal facilities.

Experts

William T. Crowe
Philatelic Foundation
501 5th Ave., Ste. 1901
New York, NY 10017-6107
ph: 212-867-3699
fax: 212-867-3984
e-mail: wtcrowe@aol.com

Internet Resources

StampUniverse.com
e-mail: suggestions@collectors.com
web: http://www.stampworld.com/
Provides a home base for stamp collectors, dealers, and stamp enthusiasts; site brings together a complete set of resources for collectors.

Philatelic.com
e-mail: webmaster@philatelic.com
web: http://www.philatelic.com

James T. McCusker
James T. McCusker, Inc.
804 Broadway
Raynham, MA 02767-1797
ph: 800-852-0076 or 508-822-7787
fax: 508-822-1230
e-mail: mail@jamesmccusker.com
web: http://www.jamesmccusker.com
Offers monthly philatelic auction with 1,500 lots offered weekly; indexes set up to search by topic and cachet maker.

Stampfinder
6175 NW 153rd St., Ste. 221
Hialeah, FL 33014
ph: 305-557-1135
fax: 309-557-1454
e-mail: USID@StampFinder.com
web: http://www.stampfinder.com
A multi-dealer buy site offering comparative side-by-side pricing of like items; search for stamps by topic, country or item; search for covers with full color images; download free inventory software; use the internet to buy/sell stamps.

Joseph R. Luft
Joseph Luft's Philatelic Resource Page
7621 West Willowbrook Dr.
Mequon, WI 53097
ph: 414-242-5120
fax: 414-358-8066
e-mail: joeluft@execpc.com
web: http://www.execpc.com/~joeluft/
Great links to stamp sites on the internet; stamp price lists, discount postage, philatelic resources of all kinds.

Roger Pearce
Stamp Ink
545 N. Mountain Ave., Ste. 109
Upland, CA 91786
ph: 909-861-9547
fax: 909-860-7557
e-mail: roger@stamplink.com
web: http://www.stamplink.com/
Jump-off platform to hottest internet stamp sites around the world.

Brent Gutekunst
Stamp Universe
6440 Lusk Blvd., Ste. D209
San Diego, CA 92121
ph: 619-643-1900
fax: 619-643-1905
e-mail: brent@collectors.com
web: http://stamp-universe.com
The starting point for stamp collecting on the Internet; on-line auctions, dealers, chat, listings, and much more.

James Yeaw
Ideal Solutions
P.O. Box 1077
Rocklin, CA 95677
ph: 916-624-7281
fax: 916-624-9309
e-mail: jyeaw@interests.com
web: http://www.philately.com/
Large internet site about stamps and stamp collecting.

Misc. Services

William T. Crowe
Philatelic Foundation
501 5th Ave., Ste. 1901
New York, NY 10017-6107
ph: 212-867-3699
fax: 212-867-3984
e-mail: wtcrowe@aol.com
An expertizing organization which will verify the genuineness of a rare stamp; write for list of fees; enclose a SASE.

A. Mercer Bristow
American Philatelic Society Expertizing Service
P.O. Box 8000
State College, PA 16803-8000
ph: 814-237-3803
fax: 814-237-6128
e-mail: ambristo@stamps.org
web: http://www.stamps.org/
Run jointly by the American Philatelic Society and the American Stamp Dealers Association; offers substantial discounts on fees to members of either organization for expertizing services; will evaluate stamps for a fee; send for info.

Citizens' Stamp Advisory Committee, c/o Stamp Development Branch
U.S. Postal Service
Washington, DC 20260
Welcomes suggestions from the private citizen for stamp ideas to honor famous (and not so famous) people, animals, historical events or sites, sports, occupations, and good causes; impressive stationery and long petitions help.

Museums/Libraries

Cardinal Spellman Philatelic Museum, Inc. at Regis College
235 Wellesley St.
Weston, MA 02193
ph: 781-894-6735
fax: 781-894-8056
This museum houses the personal collections of Cardinal Spellman, President Eisenhower, and Jascha Heifetz.

Collectors Club, The
Journal: Collectors Club Philatelist, The
22 East 35th St.
New York, NY 10016-3806
ph: 212-683-0559
fax: 212-481-1269
e-mail: collectorsclub@nac.net
web: http://www.collectorsclub.org/
Library has over 140,000 items and is one of the largest specialized philatelic library in the world.

American Philatelic Research Library
P.O. Box 8000
State College, PA 16803-8000
ph: 814-237-3803
fax: 814-237-6128
web: http://www.stamps.org/
The largest general philatelic library in the US that's open to the public.

National Museum of American History, National Philatelic Collection
14th & Constitution Ave. NW
Washington, DC 20560
ph: 202-357-2700
e-mail: webmaster@si.edu
web: http://www.si.edu/organiza/museums/nmah/nmah.htm

National Postal Museum
2 Massachusetts Ave., NE
Washington, DC 20560-0001
ph: 202-357-2700 or 202-357-2020
web: http://www.seedcstayva.com/postal.htm
23,000 square feet of exhibition space, 6,000 square foot research library, a stamp store and a museum shop.

Larry D. Sall
Wineburgh Philatelic Research Library, Univ. of TX at Dallas
P.O. Box 830643
Richardson, TX 75083-0643
ph: 972-883-2570
e-mail: sall@utdallas.edu
web: http://www.utdallas.edu/library/special/wprl.html
Contains over 5,000 stamp books, many journals, and auction catalogs.

Postal History Foundation, The
Journal: Heliograph
P.O. Box 40725
920 North First Ave.
Tucson, AZ 85719-0725
ph: 520-623-6652
e-mail: mman@primenet.com
web: http://www.primenet.com/~mman/phfmaon.htm
Houses artifacts, postmarks and covers dedicated to postal history.

Wells Fargo Bank History Museum, Wiltsee Memorial Collection of Western Stamps
420 Montgomery St.
San Francisco, CA 94163
ph: 415-396-2619
web: http://www.wellsfargo.com/about/museum/info/
This collection of Western stamps, franks, and postmarks includes over 235 different express companies and such fascinating items as Pony Express stamps and early California "ghost" town cancels.

Periodicals

William T. Crowe
Philatelic Foundation
Newsletter: Philatelic Focus
501 5th Ave., Ste. 1901
New York, NY 10017-6107
ph: 212-867-3699
fax: 212-867-3984
e-mail: wtcrowe@aol.com
Discusses the Philatelic Foundation and expertization.

Philatelic Communications Corp.
Magazine: Mekeel's & Stamps Magazine
P.O. Box 5050
White Plains, NY 10602
ph: 800-635-3351 or 914-997-7261
fax: 914-997-6096
e-mail: stampnews@aol.com
The world's oldest stamp weekly (founded in 1891) and the only stamp weekly in magazine format; "Mekeel's" now incorporates the former "Stamp Auction News."

Philatelic Communications Corp.
Magazine: U.S. Stamp News
P.O. Box 5050
White Plains, NY 10602
ph: 800-635-3351 or 914-997-7261
fax: 914-997-6096
e-mail: stampnews@aol.com
The only magazine for all U.S. stamp & cover collectors.

Michael Laurence, Ed.
Amos Press, Inc.
Newspaper: Linn's Stamp News
P.O. Box 29
Sidney, OH 45365-0029
ph: 937-498-0801 or 800-448-7293
fax: 800-340-9501
e-mail: linns@linns.com
web: http://www.linns.com
World's largest stamp marketplace with up-to-the-minute hobby news, reports on topics from trends in values, special interest collections to under-collected stamps; well-respected in the hobby; indispensable for the stamp collector.

Newsletter: Global Stamp News
110 N. Ohio Ave.
P.O. Box 97
Sidney, OH 45365-0097
ph: 937-492-3183
fax: 937-492-6514
e-mail: global@bright.net
Monthly newspaper with over 100 pages; articles, advertisements, etc.

Peter Martin
Amos Press, Inc.
Magazine: Scott's Stamp Monthly
P.O. Box 828
Sidney, OH 45365-0828
ph: 937-498-0802 or 800-5SC-OTT5
fax: 937-498-0808
e-mail: pmartin@amospress.com
web: http://www.scottonline.com
Magazine features notices of new stamp issues (using copyrighted Scott Numbering system) and other articles for the collector.

Pat DuChene, PR
Krause Publications
Newspaper: Stamp Collector
700 E. State St.
Iola, WI 54990-0001
ph: 715-445-2214
fax: 715-445-4087
e-mail: info@krause.com
web: http://www.krause.com/
Covers a wide variety of U.S. as well as foreign stamp news from the world over; articles, special features, and theme issues.

Pat DuChene, PR
Krause Publications
Newspaper: Stamp Wholesaler, The
700 E. State St.
Iola, WI 54990-0001
ph: 715-445-2214
fax: 715-445-4087
e-mail: info@krause.com
web: http://www.krause.com/
World's largest stamp dealer publication; used as a "Philatelic Phonebook" by the entire industry; articles and ads are written for the dealer.

Jacques Herrijgers
Newsletter: MiniPhil
1 Nachtegaallaan
Itterbeek, 1701
Belgium
A quarterly international advertising sheet for stamp collectors only; a bilingual publication (French and English.)

Paul Fiocca
Trajan Publishing Corp.
Newspaper: Canadian Stamp News
103 Lakeshore Rd., Ste. 202
St. Catharines, Ontario L2N 2T6
Canada
ph: 905-646-7744
fax: 905-646-0995
e-mail: bret@trajan.com
web: http://www.vaxxine.com/trajan/
Insightful, up-to-date philatelic articles, world-wide new releases, reports on finds, errors and auctions.

Link House Magazines
Magazine: Stamp Magazine
Link House, Dingwall Avenue
Croydon, Surrey CR9 2TA
U.K.
ph: +44 (0) 181 686 2599
fax: +44 (0) 181 781 6535
e-mail: stampmagazine@lhm.co.uk
web: http://www.linkhouse.co.uk/stamp.html
Britain's leading stamp publication; articles, G.B. covers, stamps, cancellations, postcards, auction news, stamp shows, etc.

Repair Services

Hans A. Sitt
FCI Stamp Restoration Service
306 Guelph Street
Kitchener, Ontario N2H 5X3
Canada
ph: 519-579-7208 or 519-579-7461
fax: 519-579-0288
e-mail: hanssitt@golden.net
Repair and restore postage stamps; regumming stamps, repairing thins and missing corners and reperforating; also cleans soiled stamps and can remove or improve most stains.

Air Mail Related

(see also AIRLINE MEMORABILIA)

Clubs/Associations

Jim Graue
American Air Mail Society
Journal: Airpost Journal, The
P.O. Box 110
Mineola, NY 11501-0110
ph: 509-924-4484 or 509-466-4602
fax: 509-466-4698
e-mail: sr1501@aol.com
web: http://ourworld.compuserve.com/homepages/aams/
Focuses on any stamps or covers relating to air mail; areas of specialty include Crash Mail, Lindberghiana, U.S. and foreign first flights, Rocket Mail, Balloon Mail, Glider Mail, Zeppelin Mail, Amelia Earhart, Concord, etc.

Albrecht Durer

Clubs/Associations

Jack Denys
Albrecht Durer Study Unit of the American Topical Association
Newsletter: Durer Journal
3 East Cadillac Dr.
Somerville, NJ 08876
Life and works of Albrecht Durer.

American Indian

Clubs/Associations

Charles Eson
American Indian Philatelic Society of the American Topical Association
Newsletter: Council Fire
128 Western Ave.
Altamont, NY 12009
ph: 578-861-6256
Native American cultures.

Americana

Clubs/Associations

Dennis Dengel, Sec. Treas.
Americana Unit of the American Topical Association
Newsletter: Americana Philatelic News
17 Peckham Rd.
Poughkeepsie, NY 12603-2018
fax: 781-459-0392
e-mail: info@americanunit.org
web: http://www.americanunit.org/
Group of stamp collectors interested in all phases of Americana on stamps of the world: American history, culture, and industry.

Archaeology

Clubs/Associations

M. Farrington
Old World Archaeological Study Unit of the American Topical Association
Newsletter: Old World Archaeologist
P.O. Box 145
Blackstone, MA 01504
Focuses on stamps featuring archaeology of the World, excluding North and South America.

Chris L. Moser
Meso American Archaeological Study Unit of the American Topical Association
Newsletter: Codex Filatelica
P.O. Box 1442
Riverside, CA 92502
ph: 909-782-5273
fax: 909-369-4970
e-mail: cmoser@ci.riverside.ca.us
Focuses on stamps featuring pre-Columbian cultures of the Americas.

Armenia

Clubs/Associations

Armenian Philatelic Association
8511 Beverly Park Place
Pico Rivera, CA 90660

Art

Clubs/Associations

Bernard Seckler, Pres.
Fine & Performing Arts Society, a Unit of the American Topical Association
Journal: Journal of Fine & Performing Arts Philately
10393 Derby Dr.
Laurel, MD 20723
e-mail: bersec@aol.com
web: http://www.philately.com/philately/fap.htm
For collectors and those interested in fine art and the performing arts on stamps.

Astronomy

Clubs/Associations

George Young
Astronomy Unit of the American Topical Association
Newsletter: Astrofax
P.O. Box 632
Tewksbury, MA 01876
ph: 978-851-8283
e-mail: george-young@msn.com
Astronomy, astrology, zodiac.

Australia

Clubs/Associations

Henry Bateman
Society of Australasian Specialists/Oceania
Newsletter: Informer, The
P.O. Box 4862
Monroe, LA 71211
e-mail: petyl@juno.com
web: http://members.aol.com/stampsho/saso.html

Biblical

Clubs/Associations

Rev. Frank Pieper
Biblical Topics Study Unit of the American Topical Association
Newsletter: Biblical Philately
P.O. Box 169
Emden, IL 62635
Old and New Testaments.

Bicycle

Clubs/Associations

Bill Hofmann
Bicycle Stamp Club of the American Topical Association
Newsletter: Bicycle Stamps
610 North Pin Oak Lane
Muncie, IN 47304
ph: 765-288-0648
e-mail: bicycle.stamps@worldnet.att.net
web: http://www.to.icl.fi/~majander/bsc.html
In addition to stamps, items of interest to members include other postal material and Cinderella items; subjects are bicycles used in racing, touring, play; venues, riders, use of bicycles in military, law enforcement, etc.

Biology

Clubs/Associations

Betty Rutherford
Biology Unit of the American Topical Association
Newsletter: Biophilately
4310 Indian Creek Rd.
Marion, IA 52302
Animal and plant life, present and prehistoric.

Black Related

Clubs/Associations

Sanford L. Byrd
Ebony Society of Philatelic Events & Reflections
P.O. Box 1864
Midland, MI 48641-1864
e-mail: esper@ibm.net
web: http://www.slsabyrd.com/esper.htm
Interested in collecting material related to all philatelic services that contribute to the long-term improvement and enhancement of black stamp collecting and black history makers, past and present.

Booklets

Clubs/Associations

Booklet Collectors Club
Newsletter: Interleaf, The
1016 E. El Camino Real, #107
Sunnyvale, CA 94087
Focuses on booklet panes (sheets) of the world.

Boy Scouting

Clubs/Associations

Lawrence E. Clay
Scouts on Stamps Society International of the American Topical Association
Journal: SOSSI Journal
P.O. Box 6228
Kennewick, WA 99336
ph: 509-735-3731
fax: 509-735-2789
e-mail: cclay@3-cities.com
web: http://www.sossi.org/

British

Clubs/Associations

Royal Philatelic Society, London
Journal: London Philatelist
41 Devonshire Place
London, W1N 1PE
U.K.
ph: 0171 486 1044
fax: 0171 486 0803

Dealers

Bill Martin
William Lawrence Philatelics
P.O. Box 991756
Redding, CA 96099-1756
ph: 530-223-5448
fax: 530-223-5448
e-mail: baldeagl2@earthlink.net
web: http://home.earthlink.net/~baldeagl2
Buys and sells collectible postage stamps of the British Empire.

Butterfly & Moth

Clubs/Associations

Charles V. Covell, Jr.
Butterfly & Moth Stamp Society of the American Topical Association
Newsletter: Swallowtail, The
2333 Brighton Dr.
Louisville, KY 40205

Canadian

Clubs/Associations

Andrew D. Parr, Administrator
Royal Philatelic Society of Canada
Journal: Canadian Philatelist, The
P.O. Box 929, Station ""Q""
Toronto, Ontario M4T 2P1
Canada
ph: 416-979-7474
fax: 416-979-1144
e-mail: rpsc@interlog.com
web: http://www.interlog.com/~rpsc/
Focus in on Canadian postal history; the journal is 80 pages, 6" x 8 3/4", published bi-monthly; accepts donations of philatelic material which is appraised and tax receipts issued to owners; journal "Opusculum" published every other year.

John Peebles
Canadiana Study Unit of the American Topical Association
Newsletter: Canadian Connection, The
P.O. Box 3262
Station "A"
London, Ontario N6A 4K3
Canada
e-mail: john.peebles@odyssey.on.ca
History, culture, and industry of Canada as seen on stamps of the world.

Museums/Libraries

Canadian Postal Archives
395 Wellington St.
Ottawa, Ontario K1A 0N3
Canada
ph: 613-992-6534
fax: 613-995-6297
Part of the National Archives of Canada; houses a library of 10,000 philatelic volumes, as well as a large collection of Canadian and international stamps.

Cancels

Clubs/Associations

Art Hadley
Machine Cancel Society
Journal: Machine Cancel Forum
3407 N 925 E
Hope, IN 47246-9717
e-mail: mail@swansongrp.com

Captain Cook

Clubs/Associations

Brain Sanford
Captain Cook Study Unit of the American Topical Association
Newsletter: Cook's Log
173 Minuteman Dr.
Concord, MA 01742
ph: 978-369-7741
e-mail: jeantm@ix.netcom.com
web: http://freespace.virgin.net/chris.jones/ccsu.htm
Interested in all aspects of the life and voyages of Captain James Cook, with philately as a significant but not dominant interest; main office in U.K.

Caribbean

Clubs/Associations

Peter Kaulback, Sec.
British Caribbean Philatelic Study Group
Journal: British Caribbean Philatelic Journal
108 Byron Ave.
Ottawa, Ontario K1Y 3J2
Canada
web: http://ourworld.compuserve.com/homepages/BCPSG/

Cats

Clubs/Associations

Susan Minniear
Cats on Stamps Unit of the American Topical Association
Newsletter: Cat Mews
910 East Russel Rd.
Sidney, OH 45365
Domestic and wild felines.

Chemistry & Physics

Clubs/Associations

Dr. Roland Hirsch
Chemistry & Physics Study Unit of the American Topical Association
Newsletter: Philatelia Chimica et Physica
20458 Water Point Lane
Germantown, MD 20874

Chess

Clubs/Associations

Anne Kasonic
Chess on Stamps Study Unit of the American Topical Association
Newsletter: Chesstamp Review
7624 Country Rd., #153
Interlaken, NY 14247
e-mail: reott@iglobal.net
web: http://www.iglobal.net/home/reott/stamps1.htm
Chess, other board games.

Chinese

Clubs/Associations

Paul H. Gault, Sec.
China Stamp Society, Inc., The
Magazine: China Clipper
P.O. Box 20711
Columbus, OH 43220
ph: 614-292-6009 or 614-292-2816
fax: 614-292-1685
e-mail: gault.1@osu.edu
web: http://www.chinastampsociety.org/index.htm

Christmas

Clubs/Associations

Linda Lawrence, Sec.
Christmas Philatelic Club of the American Topical Association
Journal: Yule Log
312 Northwood Dr.
Lexington, KY 40505-2104
ph: 606-293-0151
e-mail: stamplinda@aol.com
web: http://www.hwcn.org/link/cpc/
For those interested in collecting Christmas stamps from around the world: seals, covers, postcards and any related Christmas material.

Christmas & Charity

Clubs/Associations

Florence H. Wright, Sec.
Christmas Seal & Charity Stamp Society, The
Newsletter: Seal News
P.O. Box 18615
Rochester, NY 14618
ph: 716-461-9792
Focuses on stamp and metered seals such as tuberculosis, veterans, fraternal and civic, Jewish, ethnic, pets, wildlife, medical, Easter, etc. seals.

Christopher Columbus

Clubs/Associations

David Nye
Christopher Columbus Philatelic Society of the American Topical Association
Newsletter: Discovery
P.O. Box 1492
Frankenmuth, MI 48734-9539
Life and voyage of Christopher Columbus.

Colombia

Clubs/Associations

James A. Cross
Colombia/Panama Philatelic Study Group
Newsletter: COPACARTA
P.O. Box 2245
El Cajon, CA 92021
ph: 619-561-4959
e-mail: jimacross@juno.com

Commemorative

Collectors

Kim Malcom
6410 Sierra Dr. SE
Lacey, WA 98503
ph: 360-456-8424
Interested in U.S. commemorative stamps.

Computer Programs For

Man./Prod./Dist.

Roger S. Edelman
Software: Stamp Collector's Data Base
8505 River Rock Terrace, Ste. B
Bethesda, MD 20817-4321
ph: 800-321-SCDB or 301-320-2451
fax: 301-581-4591
e-mail: staff@scdbsoft.com
web: http://www.scdbsoft.com/

Changing Seasons Software, Inc.
Software: StampBase for Windows
5881 Roanoke Dr.
Madison, WI 53719
ph: 800-260-2739 or 608-273-2739
fax: 608-273-1965
e-mail: changingseasons@stampbase.com
web: http://www.stampbase.com/
Scott Catalog Number System, yearly catalog updates with market values, print your want lists, design customized inventory reports, store and display pictures of your stamps, and more.

Ninga Software Corporation
Software: Hobbysoft Stamp Keeper
882 Pepin Cres.
Victoria, British Columbia V8Z 6V6
Canada
ph: 800-656-4642 or 250-881-8355
fax: 250-881-8355
e-mail: ninga@islandnet.com
web: http://www.ninga.com/
Relevant stamp description, year of issue, denomination and price information, inventory, evaluate collections, annual market values updates, generates reports.

Confederate

Clubs/Associations

Ronald Teffs
Confederate Stamp Alliance
Magazine: Confederate Philatelist
19540 Yuma Street
Castro Valley, CA 94546
e-mail: rhbcsaps@flash.net
web: http://www.flash.net/~rhbcsaps/
Focuses on the mail and postal systems used during the Civil War period. The bi-monthly booklet contains extensively researched articles; an association (nonpolitical) of collectors of Confederate postage stamps and covers.

Dealers

Jack E. Molesworth
Confederate Philately, Inc.
88 Beacon St.
Boston, MA 02108
ph: 617-523-2522
fax: 617-523-2265
Buys and sells; has large and comprehensive stock of Confederate stamps, covers, and related items.

Brian & Maria Green
Brian & Maria Green, Inc.
P.O. Box 1816
Kernersville, NC 27285-1816
ph: 336-993-5100
fax: 336-993-1801
e-mail: bmgcivilwar@webtv.net
web: http://www.bmgcivilwar.com
Buy & sell Confederate States stamps, postally used envelopes & related material, military correspondences & Generals' letters, etc.

Costa Rica

Clubs/Associations

Society of Costa Rica Collectors, The
Newsletter: Oxcart, The
P.O. Box 14831
Baton Rouge, LA 70808
e-mail: hrmena@intersurf.com
web: http://www.intersurf.com/~hrmena/

Covers

Collectors

Lewis Leigh, Jr.
P.O. Box 4327
Leesburg, VA 20177
ph: 703-771-3081
fax: 703-771-1432
Wants to buy items pertaining to early Virginia postal history: old letters with interesting content, stampless covers, etc.

Dealers

Bob Morris
706 Pawnee St.
Bethlehem, PA 18015-1432
ph: 610-865-9052
Wants to purchase US and foreign covers; anything to 1960; stampless to WWII; large quantities wanted.

Tom Osjecki
Phyllis' Philatelics
P.O. Box 792
Canyonville, OR 97417
ph: 541-839-4135 or 541-839-6151
Buys, sells and specializes in postcards, paper Americana, stamps and covers; over 25,000 covers and postcards listed by state or topic.

Experts

James Kesterson
3881 Fulton Grove Rd.
Cincinnati, OH 45245-2504
ph: 513-752-0949
Wants 19th century U.S. stamps on envelopes (covers); also stampless and illustrated covers; any amount.

Periodicals

Brookman Barrett & Worthen
Magazine: Brookman's Coverline
10 Chestnut Dr.
Bedford, NH 03110
ph: 800-332-3383
fax: 603-472-8795
e-mail: brookman@xtdl.com
web: http://www2.xtdl.com/~brookman/
Bi-monthly magazine about covers: U.S. first day covers, Akron and Macon covers, Zeppelin covers, flight covers, WWII patriotic covers, catapult covers, Hawaii and Pacific Rim covers, etc.

Covers (First Day)

Auction Services

Michael Mellone
FDC Publishing Co.
P.O. Box 206
Stewartsville, NJ 08886-0206
ph: 908-479-4617
fax: 908-479-6158
e-mail: FDC@4-collectors.com
web: http://www.4-collectors.com
Conducts monthly mail auctions exclusively for First Day Covers; publishes price catalogs for first day covers.

Clubs/Associations

American First Day Cover Society
Journal: First Days
P.O. Box 65960
Tucson, AZ 85728-5960
ph: 520-321-9191
fax: 520-321-9494
e-mail: afdcs@aol.com
web: http://www.philately.com/society_news/afdcs.htm
First days, annual conventions, chapters, cover exchange, auctions, cachet information, awards, foreign information, expertizing, question box, archives, translation service, sales department, slide programs, USPS liaison.

Dealers

James T. McCusker
James T. McCusker, Inc.
804 Broadway
Raynham, MA 02767-1797
ph: 800-852-0076 or 508-822-7787
fax: 508-822-1230
e-mail: mail@jamesmccusker.com
web: http://www.jamesmccusker.com
One of the world's largest on-line retail offerings of U.S. first day covers complete with color illustrations; 50,000 different items expected on-line by 12/99.

Man./Prod./Dist.

Postal Commemorative Society
47 Richards Ave.
P.O. Box 57491
Norwalk, CT 06857-4910
ph: 203-853-2000
Sells a series of new first day covers.

Covers (Naval)

Clubs/Associations

Steve Shay, Sec.
Universal Ship Cancellation Society
Magazine: Log
747 Shard Ct.
Fremont, CA 94539
e-mail: djs@onramp.net
web: http://www.uscs.org/
Dedicated to the collection and study of Naval and maritime Postal History; interested in covers from ships and related installations.

Dogs

Clubs/Associations

Morris Raskin
Dogs On Stamps Study Unit of the American Topical Association
Journal: DOSSU Journal
202A Newport Rd.
Cranbury, NJ 08512-3920
ph: 609-655-7411
e-mail: mraskin@nerc.com
web: http://www.dossu.org/
Purpose is to further the collection and study of philatelic postal material that pertains to dogs.

Duck/Fish & Game

(see also PRINTS [MODERN]; STAMP COLLECTING, Revenue & Tax Stamps)

Clubs/Associations

Tony Monico
National Duck Stamp Collectors Society
Newsletter: Duck Tracks
P.O. Box 43
Harleysville, PA 19438-0043
e-mail: ndscs@hwcn.org
web: http://www.hwcn.org/links/ndscs
Promotes and encourages the collecting and study of migratory waterfowl hunting and conservation stamps: Federal/state/foreign duck stamps, first day covers, artist signed stamps, duck stamp prints.

Dealers

National Wildlife Philatelics
11000 Metro Parkway, Ste. 32
Fort Myers, FL 33912-1293
ph: 941-275-0500 or 800-DUCK-ART
fax: 941-936-2788
e-mail: stamps@nationalwildlife.com
web: http://www.nationalwildlife.com
Offers a large selection of Federal, State, International, and Junior Duck Stamps; also offers Federal, State, International and Junior Duck Stamp Prints.

Sport'en Art
1015 W. Jackson
Sullivan, IL 61951
ph: 800-382-5723 or 217-728-2361

Bob Dumaine
Sam Houston Philatelics
13310 Westheimer, Ste. 150
Houston, TX 77077-3506
ph: 281-493-6386 or 800-231-5926
fax: 281-496-1445
e-mail: rwhouduck@aol.com
Handles all types of collector stamps including United States and World Wide; specialty is Duck Stamps (also known as Hunting Permit stamps); holds several auctions each year; attends nation wide stamp shows; retail store; mail order.

Michael Jaffe
P.O. Box 61484
Vancouver, WA 98666-1484
ph: 360-695-6161 or 800-782-6770
fax: 360-695-1616
e-mail: mjaffe@brookmanstamps.com
web: http://www.brookmanstamps.com/
Issues catalog of state and federal duck stamps, and stamps issued by Indian reservations.

Experts

Lynn "Dr. Duck" Troute
Lynn Troute Decoys
3808 Kingsley Dr.
Springfield, IL 62707-7250
ph: 217-787-3595
fax: 217-726-1801
e-mail: duckstamps@aol.com
Buys, sells, collects, appraises and specializes in Federal and State duck stamps; also buying duck stamps, Illinois deer and turkey harvest pins, and old wooden decoys and other hunting and fishing artifacts.

David R. Torre
P.O. Box 4298
Santa Rosa, CA 95402
ph: 707-525-8785
fax: 707-546-4859
e-mail: drtorre@pacbell.net
Wants pictorial and non-pictorial waterfowl and fishing stamps; also

pre-1930 pictorial hunting & fishing licenses from any state.

Misc. Services

Anita Noguera
Federal Duck Stamp Office, U.S. Fish & Wildlife Service
1849 C. St., NW, Ste. 2058
Washington, DC 20240
ph: 202-208-4354
fax: 202-208-6269
e-mail: anita_noguera@mail.fws.gov
web: http://www.fws.gov/~r9dso/
Proceeds from the sale of Federal duck stamps go to the preservation of national wetlands.

Earth

Clubs/Associations

Fred Klein
Earth's Physical Features Study Unit of the American Topical Association
Newsletter: Nature's Wonders
515 Magdalena Ave.
Los Altos, CA 94022
e-mail: jyeaw@interests.com
web: http://www.philately.com/philately/earths_physical.htm
Earthquakes, environment, meteorology, mountains, oceanography, rivers, volcanoes.

Errors

Clubs/Associations

CWO McDevitt
Errors, Freaks & Oddities Collectors Club
Newsletter: EFO Collector
138 Lakemont Dr., East
Kingsland, GA 31548-6716
ph: 912-729-1573
fax: 912-729-1585
e-mail: cwouscg@aol.com

European

Clubs/Associations

Hank Klos
Europa Study Unit of the American Topical Association
Newsletter: Europa News
4N 512 South Church Rd.
Bensenville, IL 60106
All aspects of a United Europe.

French

Clubs/Associations

Walter Parshall, Sec.
France & Colonies Philatelic Society
Journal: France & Colonies Philatelist
103 Spruce St.
Bloomfield, NJ 07003
e-mail: d.r.stirrups@dundee.ac.uk
web: http://www.abel.co.uk/~stirrups/FCPS.HTM

Gay & Lesbian

Clubs/Associations

Joe Petronie
Gay & Lesbian History Stamp Club of the American Topical Association
Newsletter: Lambda Philatelic Journal
P.O. Box 575981
Dallas, TX 75251-5981
e-mail: glhsc@earthlink.net
web: http://home.earthlink.net/~glhsc/index.html

Gems & Jewelry

Clubs/Associations

George Young
Gems, Minerals, Jewelry Study Unit of the American Topical Association
Newsletter: Philagems International
P.O. Box 632
Tewksbury, MA 01876
ph: 978-851-8283
e-mail: george-young@msn.com
Gems, minerals, jewelry.

German

Clubs/Associations

Christopher Deterding, Sec. Treas.
Germany Philatelic Society
Journal: German Postal Specialist
P.O. Box 779
Arnold, MD 21012
web: http://www.gps.nu/
Members have an interest in stamps relating to Germany.

Burt Miller, Sec.
Germany Philatelic Society, Golden Gate Chapter
P.O. Box 911
Pacifica, CA 94044
e-mail: danziger@aol.com

Golf

Clubs/Associations

Kevin Hadlock
International Philatelic Golf Society of the American Topical Association
Newsletter: Tee Time
447 Skyline Dr.
Orange, CT 06477
Golf and golfing.

Graphics

Clubs/Associations

Dulcie Apgar, Sec.
Graphics Philately Association
Newsletter: Philateli-Graphics
P.O. Box 1513
Thousand Oaks, CA 91358-0513
History of printing and graphic arts as reflected in and on stamps and postal stationary of the world.

Guatemala

Clubs/Associations

Mae Vignola, Mem.
International Society of Guatemala Collectors, Inc.
Journal: El Quetzal
105 22nd Ave.
San Francisco, CA 94121-1216
ph: 415-386-0819
Quarterly journal; auction for members only held once a year.

Hawaii

Clubs/Associations

Hawaiian Philatelic Society
P.O. Box 10115
Honolulu, HI 96816-0115
ph: 808-521-5721
e-mail: bannan@pixi.com
web: http://stampshows.com/hps.html

Hong Kong

Clubs/Associations

Hong Kong Stamp Society
Journal: Hong Kong Philatelist
P.O. Box 206
Glenside, PA 19038-0206
web: http://www.erols.com/hkss/

Hungary

Clubs/Associations

Thomas Phillips
Society for Hungarian Philately
Newsletter: News of Hungarian Philately
P.O. Box 1162
Fairfield, CT 06432-1162
web: http://home.sprintmail.com/~aahoover/shp/shphome.htm

Israel

Clubs/Associations

Emil S. Dickstein, M.D.
Society of Israel Philatelists
Journal: Israel Philatelist
8358 Hitchcock Rd.
Youngstown, OH 44512
web: http://www.geocities.com/WallStreet/2785/

Experts

Israel I. Bick
P.O. Box 854
Van Nuys, CA 91408-0854
ph: 818-997-6496
fax: 818-988-4337
e-mail: iibick@aol.com
web: http://www.bick.net
A leading expert in the field of Holy Land stamp collecting specializing in Israel, Judaica and related materials.

Japanese

Clubs/Associations

Kenneth Kamholz, Sec.
International Society for Japanese Philately
Journal: Japanese Philately
P.O. Box 1283
Haddonfield, NJ 08033
e-mail: kamholz@uscom.com
web: http://www.west.net/~lmevans/isjp.html

Dealers

Frank L. Allard, Jr.
Nippon Philatelics
P.O. Drawer 7300
Carmel, CA 93921-7300
ph: 831-625-2643
fax: 831-624-4617
Buys and sells anything Japanese: postcards, mail, stamps, posters, postal stationary, First Day Covers, photos, etc.; price lists available for large SASE.

Journalists/Authors

Clubs/Associations

Louis Forster
Journalists, Authors & Poets on Stamps Unit of the American Topical Association
Newsletter: JAPOS Bulletin
7561 East 24th Court
Wichita, KS 67226
Journalists, authors, poets.

Liechtenstein

Clubs/Associations

Ralph Schneider, Ed.
Liechtenstudy USA
Newsletter: Liechtenstudy
P.O. Box 23049
Belleville, IL 62223
Provides a broad range of services to Liechtenstein collectors; postal history, auctions, etc.

Lighthouses

Clubs/Associations

Dalene Thomas
Lighthouse Stamp Society of the American Topical Association
Newsletter: Philatelic Beacon, The
8612 West Warren Lane
Denver, CO 80227-2352
ph: 303-986-6620
e-mail: dalene1@uswest.net
web: http://www.users.uswest.net/~dalene1/
Club promotes collecting stamps depicting lighthouses; bi-monthly journal discusses stamps, covers, postmarks and all philatelic items that picture lighthouses.

Lions

Clubs/Associations

John Bargus
Lions International Stamp Club of the American Topical Association
Newsletter: Philatelion
RR#1
Mill Bay, British Columbia V0R 2P0
Canada

Maps & Charts

Clubs/Associations

Miklos Pinther
Carto-Philatelists of the American Topical Association
Newsletter: Carto-Philatelist
206 Grayson Place
Teaneck, NJ 07666
Maps, globes, charts.

Masks

Clubs/Associations

Carolyn Weber, Sec./Treas.
Mask Study Unit of the American Topical Association
Newsletter: Mask Lore
P.O. Box 2542
Oxnard, CA 93034-2542
web: http://www.philately.com/philately/masks.htm
Discover the wide variety of masks on postage stamps and correspond with other collectors also interested in masks on stamps.

Masonic

Clubs/Associations

Otto Seding
Masonic Study Unit of the American Topical Association
Newsletter: Philatelic Freemason
1033 Hollytree Dr.
Cincinnati, OH 45231
web: http://www.philately.com/philately/masonic_stamp_clubs.htm
Freemasonry.

Mathematics

Clubs/Associations

Estelle Buccino
Mathematical Study Unit of the American Topical Association
Newsletter: Philamath
5615 Glenwood Rd.
Bethesda, MD 20817
Computers, mathematics.

Medical

Clubs/Associations

Dr. Frederick Skvara
Medical Subjects Unit of the American Topical Association
Journal: Scalpel & Tongs
P.O. Box 6228
Bridgewater, NJ 08807
e-mail: fcskvara@bellatlantic.net
Dentistry, nursing, physicians, Red Cross, veterinary medicine.

Meter Stamps

Collectors

Jack Mayer, Treas.
Meter Stamp Society
1379 Islewood Dr.
Anacortes, WA 98221
e-mail: joel5215@aol.com
For those interested in the segment of philately and postal history dealing with stamps produced by meters and similar equipment such as automat-stamp vending machines.

Mexico

Clubs/Associations

Kohn Kordich, Treas.
Mexico-Elmhurst Philatelic Society International
Journal: Mexicana
1014 37th St.
San Pedro, CA 90731

Mobile Post Office

Clubs/Associations

Douglas N. Clark
Mobile Post Office Society
Newsletter: Transit Postmark Collector
P.O. Box 51
Lexington, GA 30648-0051
ph: 706-743-5044
e-mail: dnc@alpha.math.uga.edu
web: http://www.eskimo.com/~rkunz/mposhome.html

Music Related

Clubs/Associations

Cathleen Osborne
Philatelic Music Circle of the American Topical Association
Newsletter: Baton, The
P.O. Box 1781
Sequim, WA 98382-1781
web: http://www.philately.com/philately/philatelic_music.htm
For collectors of music related philately.

Napoleon

Clubs/Associations

Ken Berry
Napoleon Age Philatelist of the American Topical Association
Newsletter: Campaign
7513 Clayton Dr.
Oklahoma City, OK 73132-5636
Life and time of Napoleon Bonaparte.

Pacific Islands

Clubs/Associations

John Ray
Pacific Islands Study Circle
Magazine: Pacifica
24 Woodvale Ave.
London, SE25 4AE
U.K.
e-mail: jray@dial.pipex.com
web: http://dspace.dial.pipex.com/jray/pisc.html
Caters to collectors of stamps and postal history of the smaller Pacific islands; Circle has group leaders who can offer advice on the philately of many islands; members dispose of surplus material in their postal auctions.

Panama Canal

Clubs/Associations

John C. Smith, Sec.
Canal Zone Study Group, The
Newsletter: Canal Zone Philatelist
408 Redwood Lane
Schaumburg, IL 60193-2748
e-mail: a.bentz@worldnet.att.net
web: http://stampshows.com/czsg.html

James A. Cross
Colombia/Panama Philatelic Study Group
Newsletter: COPACARTA
P.O. Box 2245
El Cajon, CA 92021
ph: 619-561-4959
e-mail: jimacross@juno.com

Perfins

Clubs/Associations

Floyd Walker, Ed.
Perfins Club
Newsletter: Perfins Bulletin
P.O. Box 3005
Alexandria, VA 22302
e-mail: edit2001@aol.com
web: http://members.aol.com/perfins/perfclub.htm
Perfins are little holes in the configuration of alphabet letters which are punched into stamps as a security, anti-theft measure.

Petroleum

Clubs/Associations

Feitze Papa
Petroleum Philatelic Society International of the American Topical Association
Newsletter: Petro-Philatelist, The
922 Meandor Dr.
Walnut Creek, CA 94598
e-mail: fpap@chevron.com
Oil, natural gas, petrochemical industry.

Polar

Clubs/Associations

Richard Julian
American Society of Polar Philatelists
Newsletter: Ice Cap News
1153 Fairview Dr.
York, PA 17403-3611
e-mail: rajulian@netrax.net
web: http://www.south-pole.com/p0000010.htm
Focuses on worldwide polar stamps, cancels, and covers.

Possessions of the U.S.

Clubs/Associations

United States Possessions Philatelic Society
Journal: Possessions
8100 Willow Stream Dr.
Sandy, UT 84092

Postal Stationery

Clubs/Associations

Executive Secretary
United Postal Stationery Society
Journal: Postal Stationery
P.O. Box 48
Redlands, CA 92373
For collectors of postal stationery, namely embossed stamped envelopes and government postal cards.

Poster

Clubs/Associations

Walter Schmidt
Poster Stamp Society
3654 Applegate Road
Jacksonville, OR 97530
fax: 541-899-8933
e-mail: pssoc@cdsnet.net

Collectors

Walter Schmidt
3654 Applegate Road
Jacksonville, OR 97530
fax: 541-899-8933
e-mail: pssoc@cdsnet.net
Collects stamps depicting posters from all over the world.

Dealers

Bill Weinberger
21 Luddington Road
West Orange, NJ 07052
e-mail: weinberb@anchorcon.com
Buys and sells hotel & baggage labels, Cinderella stamps, Poster Stamps, and all other labels with the exception of Christmas seals and can/fruit/vegetable labels.

Postmarks

Clubs/Associations

Post Mark Collectors Club
Newsletter: Bulletin
P.O. Box 4541
Virginia Beach, VA 23454-0541
e-mail: repoman696@aol.com
web: http://members.aol.com/postmarks/
National organization of post mark collector; supports the Margie Pfund Post Mark Museum in Bellevue, OH, and the Mittower Museum Foundation; annual convention and periodic newsletter.

Collectors

Joe Bussey
3405 Canterbury Ave.
Muskogee, OK 74403

Dealers

Bob Morris
706 Pawnee St.
Bethlehem, PA 18015-1432
ph: 610-865-9052
Wants to purchase US and foreign covers; anything to 1960; stampless to WWII; large quantities wanted.

Museums/Libraries

Post Mark Museum
P.O. Box 4541
Virginia Beach, VA 23454-0541
e-mail: repoman696@aol.com
web: http://members.aol.com/postmarks/

Railroad

Clubs/Associations

Oliver Atchison
Casey Jones Railroad Unit of the American Topical Association
Newsletter: Dispatcher
P.O. Box 31631
San Francisco, CA 94131-0631
ph: 415-648-8057
e-mail: casey_jones@gowebway.com
Trains, railroads, streetcars.

Dealers

Al Peterson
Rail Philatelist, The
P.O. Box 25505
Colorado Springs, CO 80936-5505
ph: 719-591-2341
e-mail: railphil@aol.com
web: http://www.collectors-mall/trp/
Carries everything philatelic relating to trains or trolleys: stamps, covers, postcards, cinderellas (labels and stickers), magazines, stock certificates, specialty material.

Reference (Stamps)

Book Sellers

Leonard H. Hartmann
Philatelic Bibliophile
P.O. Box 36006
Louisville, KY 40233-6006
ph: 502-451-0317
fax: 502-459-8538
e-mail: pbbooks@ibm.net
web: http://www.pbbooks.com/
A "Philatelic Bibliophile"; a source for virtually all important stamp books, in or out of print; sells new books from stock (no annual catalogs such as Scott's, S.G., Minkus, Yvert) from over 100 publishers; no drop shipping.

Religion Related

Clubs/Associations

Verna Shackleton
Collectors of Religion on Stamps
Magazine: COROS Chronicle
425 North Linwood Ave., #110
Appleton, WI 54914-3476
ph: 920-734-2417 or 920-734-6711
fax: 920-233-5604
e-mail: corosec@powernetonline.com
web: http://www.powernetonline.com/~corosec/coros1.htm
COROS Chronicle is published bimonthly.

Revenue & Tax Stamps

(see also BANK CHECKS; STAMP COLLECTING, Duck/Fish & Game)

Clubs/Associations

Harold A. Effner, Jr., Treas.
State Revenue Society
Newsletter: State Revenue Newsletter
27 Pine St.
Lincroft, NJ 07738
e-mail: haroldeffn@aol.com
web: http://www.hillcity-mall.com/SRS/
For collectors whose prime aim is the collection, identification and cataloging of state and local revenue philately.

Kenneth Trettin, Ed.
American Revenue Association
Newsletter: American Revenuer
P.O. Box 56
Rockford, IA 50468-0056
ph: 515-756-3542
fax: 515-756-3680
e-mail: hogman@netins.net
web: http://www.revenuer.org/
Interested in U.S. and foreign revenue and tax stamps and stamped paper.

Collectors

Kenneth Trettin
P.O. Box 56
Rockford, IA 50468-0056
ph: 515-756-3542
fax: 515-756-3680
e-mail: hogman@netins.net
web: http://www.revenuer.org/

Hermann Ivester
5 Leslie Circle
Little Rock, AR 72205-2529
ph: 501-225-8565 or 501-376-7788
fax: 501-376-8536
Collects all kinds of U.S. Federal, state and local revenue stamps including special tax stamps and cigar, cigarette, snuff and tobacco stamps; especially wants stamps on documents and packages.

Rotary Club

Clubs/Associations

Donald Fiery
Rotary on Stamps Unit of the American Topical Association
Newsletter: Rotary-on-Stamps
P.O. Box 333
Hanover, PA 17331
Rotary International.

Russian

Clubs/Associations

Gary A. Combs
Rossica Society of Russian Philately
Newsletter: Bulletin of the RSRP
8241 Chalet Ct.
Millersville, MD 21108
e-mail: gcombs@mail.erols.com
web: http://hercules.geology.uiuc.edu/~peterm/rossica.html

Samoa

Clubs/Associations

Mrty Miller
Fellowship of Samoa Specialists
Newsletter: Samoa Express, The
102-20 67 Drive
Forest hills, NY 11375-2809
e-mail: MMiller@LadasParry.com
web: http://hometown.aol.com/TongaJan/foss.html

Scandinavia

Clubs/Associations

Don Brent, Ex. Sec.
Scandinavian Collectors Club
Newsletter: Posthorn
P.O. Box 13169
El Cajon, CA 92020
e-mail: dbrent47@sprynet.com
web: http://www.nb.net/~downs/scc/scc.htm
A non-profit philatelic society devoted to research and of stamps and postal history relating to Denmark, Danish West Indies, Finland, Faroes, Greenland, Iceland, Karelia, North Ingermanland, Norway, Slesvig, and Sweden.

Ships

Clubs/Associations

Robert Stuckert
Ships on Stamps Unit of the American Topical Association
Newsletter: Watercraft Philately
2750 Highway 21 East
Paint Lick, KY 40461
e-mail: myron@uidaho.edu
web: http://baegis.ag.uidaho.edu/~myron/shipstamps/
All types of watercraft.

South Africa

Clubs/Associations

Philatelic Society for Greater South Africa
7227 Sparta Rd.
Sebring, FL 33872
e-mail: bobhisey@strato.net
web: http://www.homestead.com/psgsa

Souvenir Cards

Clubs/Associations

Michael Padwee
Souvenir Card Collectors Society, Metro Chapter
Newsletter: SCCS Metro Chapter Newsletter
P.O. Box 023138
Brooklyn, NY 11202-3138
ph: 718-499-4307
e-mail: mwpadwee@inch.com
Members are collectors of souvenir cards in the New York, New Jersey and Connecticut area; Michael Padwee is author of "Catalog of Locally Issued USPS Souvenir Cards."

Souvenir Card Collectors Society
Journal: Souvenir Card Journal
P.O. Box 4155
Tulsa, OK 74159-0155
ph: 918-664-6724
e-mail: dmarr5569@aol.com
Souvenir cards are 8 1/2" x 11" cards with engraved reproductions of philatelic or numismatic designs from original plates.

Space

Clubs/Associations

Carmine Torrisi, Sec.
Space Unit of the American Topical Association
Journal: Astrophile
P.O. Box 780241
Flushing, NY 11378
e-mail: ctorrisi@aol.com
web: http://stargate.1usa.com/stamps/
Hobbyists devoted to the collection and study of covers and stamps issued on space themes.

Sports Related

Clubs/Associations

Margaret Jones
Sports Philatelists International of the American Topical Association
Journal: Journal of Sports Philately
5310 Lindenwood Ave.
Saint Louis, MO 6319-1758
e-mail: laimins@concentric.net
web: http://www.geocities.com/Colosseum/Track/6279/
Promotes information on sports stamps, cancels; check lists & articles related to sports and the Olympics; Olympics, recreation, sports.

Stamps on Stamps

Clubs/Associations

Bill Critzer
Stamps on Stamps/Centenary Unit of the American Topical Association
Newsletter: SOS Journal
1360 Trinity Drive
Menlo Park, CA 94025
fax: 650-234-1136
e-mail: Willcrit@aol.com
web: http://ourworld.compuserve.com/homepages/soscu/
Stamps-on-stamps, stamp centenaries.

Supplies For

Suppliers

Lighthouse Publications
P.O. Box 705
Hackensack, NJ 07602-0705
ph: 201-342-1513
fax: 201-342-7142
e-mail: lighthouse-us.info@leuchtturn.com
web: http://www.leuchtturm.com/
Carries full line of products for the coin and stamp collector: albums, binders, blank pages, magnifiers, tongs, UV lamps.

Brooklyn Gallery Coin & Stamp
8725 Fourth Ave.
P.O. Box 146
Brooklyn, NY 11209-0146
ph: 718-745-5701
fax: 718-745-2775
e-mail: info@brooklyngallery.com
web: http://www.brooklyngallery.com/
Send $1.50 for 100+ page catalog.

Linder Publications, Inc.
P.O. Box 5056
Syracuse, NY 13220
ph: 315-437-0463 or 800-654-0324
fax: 315-437-4832
Sells collector's accessories for stamps, coins, telephone cards, postcards: ring binders, blank album pages, UV lamps, magnifiers, stamp tongs, clear pocket pages, protective covers, coin holders, etc.

Lincoln Coin & Stamp Company, Inc.
33 West Tupper
Buffalo, NY 14202
ph: 716-856-1884
fax: 716-856-4727
e-mail: sales@lincolncoinandstamp.com
web: http://www.lincolncoinandstamp.com/

Subway Stamp Shop, Inc.
2121 Beale Ave.
Altoona, PA 16601
ph: 800-221-9960 or 814-946-1000
fax: 814-946-9997
e-mail: hugh@subwaystamp.com
web: http://www.subwaystamp.com/
Supplies for the stamp and coin collector: albums, blank pages, cover protectors, clear sleeves, tongs, bags, illuminated magnifiers, SoftPRO stamp collectors software, coin boxes, currency holders, etc.

Potomac Supplies
7720 Wisconsin Ave.
Bethesda, MD 20815
ph: 301-654-8828 or 800-426-5723
fax: 301-942-8778
web: http://www.potomacsuplies.com/

John L. Tyler
Album Publishing Co. Inc.
P.O. Box 30063
Raleigh, NC 27622
ph: 919-571-4648
fax: 919-571-4215
Supplies for the stamp collector.

Michael Rogers
Michael Rogers, Inc.
199 E. Welbourne Ave., Ste. 3
Winter Park, FL 32789
ph: 407-644-2290 or 800-843-2290
fax: 407-645-4434
e-mail: webmaster@michaelrogersinc.com
web: http://www.michaelrogersinc.com/

Stuart Morrissey
Scott Publishing Co.
P.O. Box 828
Sidney, OH 45365-0828
ph: 937-498-0802 or 800-5SC-OTT5
fax: 937-498-0808
e-mail: pmartin@amospress.com
web: http://www.scottonline.com
Publisher of catalogs, albums and various stamp supplies.

Warren Sankey
United States Stamp Company
368 Bush St.
San Francisco, CA 94104
ph: 415-421-7398
fax: 415-421-3167
e-mail: usstamp@pacbell.net
web: http://www.usstampco.com/

Textiles

Clubs/Associations

Helen Cushman
Embroidery, Stitchery, Textile Unit of the American Topical Association
Newsletter: Textgile-Rama
1001 Center St., Apt. 9H
La Jolla, CA 92037
Embroidery, stitchery, textiles.

Tonga

Clubs/Associations

Tom Jackson
Tonga & Tin Can Mail Study Circle
Newsletter: Tin Canner
121 Mullingar Ct., #1A
Schaumburg, IL 60193-3258
ph: 847-352-5842
e-mail: tongajan@aol.com
web: http://members.aol.com/TongaJan/ttcmsc.html

Topical

Clubs/Associations

American Topical Association
Magazine: Topical Time
P.O. Box 50820
Albuquerque, AZ 87181-0820
ph: 505-323-8595
fax: 505-323-8795
e-mail: ATAStamps@aol.com
web: http://home.prcn.org/~pauld/ata/
Topicalists save stamps relating to a specific topic such as birds, space, buildings, transportation, etc.; affiliated with many specializing study units and clubs.

Ukrainian

Clubs/Associations

Ukrainian Philatelic & Numismatic Society
Newsletter: Ukrainian Philatelist, The
P.O. Box C
Southfields, NY 10975-0303

United Nations

Clubs/Associations

Blanton Clement
United Nations Philatelists of the American Topical Association
Newsletter: Journal of United Nations Philatelists
292 Springdale Terrace
Yardley, PA 19067
e-mail: who@tiac.net
web: http://www.unpi.com/
Worldwide U.N. related philately.

Windmills

Clubs/Associations

John Blocker
Windmill Study Unit of the American Topical Association
Newsletter: Windmill Whispers
7020 Mineola Rd.
Englewood, FL 34224
Molinology.

Wine

Clubs/Associations

James Crum
Wine on Stamps Study Unit of the American Topical Association
Newsletter: Enophilatelica
5132 Sepulveda
San Bernardino, CA 92404-1134

Women Related

Clubs/Associations

Phebe Royer
Women on Stamps Study Unit of the American Topical Association
Newsletter: Topical Woman
259 Middle Road
Falmouth, ME 04105

STAMP WETTERS

Collectors

Betty Franks
1831 Penthley Ave.
Akron, OH 44312-1915
ph: 330-784-2869
Wants old and unusual china or ceramic figural stamp wetters (stamp lickers) with or without sponges.

STAMPS

(see STAMP COLLECTING; SEALS & STAMPS)

STANHOPES

(see also OPTICAL ITEMS; PHOTOGRAPHS)

Appraisers

David L. Studebaker
300 Pease Road
Cle Elum, WA 98922
ph: 509-647-1916
e-mail: pspcs@geocities.com
web: http://www.geocities.com/Eureka/Park/3740/
Specializes in classic old cameras, colored cameras, subminiatures, stanhopes, old images, and photographs and daguerreotypes.

Collectors

Sheldon Katz
18 Cliffside Drive
Port Jefferson, NY 11777
ph: 516-928-1800

Brenda Macomber
RD 3 Box 201-K
Delta, PA 17314-9588
ph: 717-456-6116
e-mail: cruzegal@aol.com
Wants to buy stanhope souvenirs, charms, unusual items; especially seeking 1939 World's Fair and domestic scenes, and color views.

John Andreae
P.O. Box 156
Granger, IN 46530-0156
ph: 219-272-2337
fax: 219-271-1146
e-mail: jkandreae@aol.com

Mike & Gladys Kessler
25749 Anchor Circle
San Juan Capistrano, CA 92675-4002
ph: 949-661-3320
Wants to buy unusual items containing a microdot photograph in a tiny peephole: canes, walking sticks, parasols, sewing items, smoking paraphernalia, knives, jewelry, and souvenir items of all kinds.

Donald Gorlick
P.O. Box 24541
Seattle, WA 98124-0541
ph: 206-824-0508
Wants tiny viewers made of bone or metal sometimes found in crucifixes, pens, letter openers, needle holders, etc.

Dealers

Lucille Malitz
Lucid Antiques
P.O. Box KH
Scarsdale, NY 10583
ph: 914-636-7825 or 914-636-5171
fax: 914-636-7825
e-mail: kromscope@aol.com
These tiny photos, invented by Lord Stanhope in the 19th century, were found in many unusual souvenirs, such as pens, letter openers, sewing tapes, scissors, and charms.

STANLEY TOOLS

(see TOOLS, Stanley)

STAR TREK

(see SCIENCE FICTION; TELEVISION SHOWS & MEMORABILIA, Star Trek)

STATE RELATED MEMORABILIA

(see also PLANNING; POSTCARDS, States; SOUVENIR & COMMEMORATIVE ITEMS)

Auction Services

Richard Vogel
Vogels, The
4720 SE Fort King St.
Ocala, FL 34470-1501
ph: 352-694-5776
fax: 352-694-7330
e-mail: vogels@atlantic.net
Bi-monthly mail order souvenir auctions: china, glass, spoons, mauchline, paper, World's Fair, fraternal.

Alabama

Museums/Libraries

Alabama Department of Archives & History
624 Washington St.
P.O. Box 300100
Montgomery, AL 36130-0100
ph: 312-242-4363
fax: 312-240-3433
e-mail: dpendlet@archives.state.al.us
web: http://www.archives.state.al.us/

Alaska

Collectors

Richard Reisinger
2610 Holgate St.
Tacoma, WA 98402-1204
ph: 253-272-7092
Buys, trades pre-1960 Alaska, Yukon, and N.W. Territories travel brochures, ephemera, postcards, city directories, telephone books, tourist souvenirs, china, bottles, pins, badges, posters, paintings, license plates, calendars, etc.

Kaye Dethridge
P.O. Box 438
Sitka, AK 99835
ph: 907-747-8615
Wants to buy most items from Alaska's past: tokens, Alaska-Yukon-Pacific Expo material, etc.

Dealers

Richard A. Wood
Alaskan Heritage Bookshop
P.O. Box 22165
Juneau, AK 99802-2165
ph: 907-789-8450
fax: 907-789-8450
e-mail: akrare@alaska.net
web: http://www.alaska.net/~akrare/
Buys/sells books, maps, stereo views, prints, photos, souvenirs, Klondike, letters, paintings, ephemera, etc.; anything Alaska/Yukon/Klondike; also wants Louis Potter bronze sculptures (1904-05) of Alaska subjects.

Experts

Richard Reisinger
2610 Holgate St.
Tacoma, WA 98402-1204
ph: 253-272-7092
Buys, trades pre-1960 Alaska, Yukon, and N.W. Territories travel brochures, ephemera, postcards, city directories, telephone books, tourist souvenirs, china, bottles, pins, badges, posters, paintings, license plates, calendars, etc.

Richard A. Wood
Alaskan Heritage Bookshop
P.O. Box 22165
Juneau, AK 99802-2165
ph: 907-789-8450
fax: 907-789-8450
e-mail: akrare@alaska.net
web: http://www.alaska.net/~akrare/
Buys/sells books, maps, stereo views, prints, photos, souvenirs, Klondike, letters, paintings, ephemera, etc.; anything Alaska/Yukon/Klondike; also wants Louis Potter bronze sculptures (1904-05) of Alaska subjects.

Museums/Libraries

Alaska State Museum
395 Whittier St.
Juneau, AK 99801-1718
ph: 907-465-2901
fax: 907-465-2976
e-mail: bruce_kato@educ.state.ak.us
web: http://www.educ.state.ak.us/lam/museum/asmhome.html

Arizona

Collectors

Sam Michael
P.O. Box 8025
Mesa, AZ 85214-8025
ph: 602-962-6523
Wants to buy pre-1920 Arizona related items: calendar plates, documents, advertising, badges, pins, posters, photographs, tins, signs, broadsides, real photo postcards, tokens, etc.

Bob Temarantz
2824 N. Bentley Ave.
Tucson, AZ 85716-5513
ph: 520-326-6704
fax: 520-741-9751
Wants to buy Arizona related memorabilia including photographs, advertising items, signs, hand mirrors, tokens, broadsides, and other ephemera.

Museums/Libraries

Arizona Historical Society
929 E. 2nd Street
Tucson, AZ 85719-4980
ph: 520-628-5774
e-mail: azhist@azstarnet.com
web: http://www.azstarnet.com/~azhist/

Arkansas

Museums/Libraries

Old State House Museum
300 West Markham St.
Little Rock, AR 72201-1423
ph: 501-324-9685
fax: 501-324-9688
e-mail: info@dah.state.ar.us
web: http://www.heritage.state.ar.us/acc/

California

Collectors

Gil Schmidtmann
2346 Naples Ave.
Mentone, CA 92359-9569
ph: 909-794-1211
Wants San Bernardino County, CA pre-1930 stock certificates, postcards, postmarks, merchant tokens, badges, books, calendars, checks, currency, script, documents, newspapers, photos, promotional items, souvenir slates and spoons, etc.

Neal Austinson
P.O. Box 1691
Windsor, CA 95492-1691
ph: 707-837-9685
Wants old historical memorabilia including photographs of California and Yosemite.

Museums/Libraries

California Historical Society
678 Mission Street
San Francisco, CA 94105
ph: 415-357-1848
fax: 415-357-1850
e-mail: info@calhist.org
web: http://www.calhist.org/

Colorado

Dealers

Leo Stambaugh
Powder Cache Antiques
P.O. Box 779
Georgetown, CO 80444-0779
ph: 800-651-2848 or 303-569-2109
e-mail: leocolo@bewellnet.com
Buy, sell, trade Colorado historical photos, paper, medals, bottles, tokens, mining artifacts, paper and lamps, etc.; also wants mining items from any where.

Museums/Libraries

Colorado Historical Society
1300 Broadway
Denver, CO 80203-2137
ph: 303-866-3355
fax: 303-866-5739
web: http://www.gtownloop.com/chs.html

Connecticut

Museums/Libraries

Connecticut Historical Society
One Elizabeth St.
Hartford, CT 06105
ph: 860-236-5621
fax: 860-236-2664
e-mail: aaron_wartner@chs.org
web: http://www.hartnet.org/chs/

Delaware

Museums/Libraries

Historical Society of Delaware
505 Market Street
Wilmington, DE 19801
ph: 302-655-7161
fax: 302-655-7844
e-mail: hsd@hsd.org
web: http://hsd.org/

Florida

Collectors

Douglas Hendriksen
P.O. Box 21153
Kennedy Space Center, FL 32815
ph: 407-452-0633
e-mail: fl_collector@mpinet.net
Advanced collector wants to buy pre-1930 Florida items: photos, stereos, real photo and small town postcards, promotional pamphlets, paintings, souvenir china, license plates, RR and steamboat items; anything Florida.

Lee Harrison
3353 Higel Ave.
Sarasota, FL 34242
ph: 941-957-1600
Wants to buy pre-1940 Florida paper items: guides, promotional leaflets, land development, view books, railroad, hotel, tourist, steamboat, pocket or oil company maps, etc.; no postcards or prints, please.

Museums/Libraries

Florida Historical Society
1320 Highland
Melbourne, FL 32935
ph: 407-690-1971
fax: 407-690-0099
e-mail: Tebeaulib@aol.com
web: http://www.florida-historical-soc.org/

Georgia

Museums/Libraries

Georgia Historical Society
501 Whitaker Street
Savannah, GA 31499
ph: 912-651-2128
e-mail: www.ghs@georgiahistory.com
web: http://www.georgiahistory.com/

Hawaii

Collectors

Hunter, The
149 Stackhouse St.
South Dartmouth, MA 02748
ph: 508-993-8966
Wants pre-1960 Hawaiian vintage jewelry, menus, chalk and ceramic hula dancers, palm tree items, etched glass, TV lamps, shirts, tourist items, etc.

Gene Snyder
991 McLean St.
Dunedin, FL 34699-3532
Wants Hawaiian memorabilia: ukuleles, Matson menus, nudes on black velvet, 1950s shirts.

Jim Stiso
31925 Sunset Ave.
S. Laguna, CA 92677
ph: 949-499-3667
Wants to buy Hawaiiana: vintage paintings, prints, shirts, lamps, dolls, etc.

Wayne Babcock
4846 Carpenteria Ave.
Carpinteria, CA 93013-1935
ph: 805-684-8148
Wants to buy pre-1960 Hawaiian items including cruise line menus, bamboo framed floral prints by Mundorff, Tip Freeman and others; Hula girls, Hawaiian-made ukuleles, surfing items, poi pounders, koa wood items, Duke Kahanamoku.

Rick Ralston
99-969 Iwaena St.
Aiea, HI 96701-3249
ph: 800-486-9794 or 808-486-1243
fax: 808-486-1276
e-mail: ralston.hawaii@crazyshirts.com
web: http://www.ralstonantiques.com
Wants Hawaiian prints, paintings, early wooden bowls, hula girl lamps, dolls, etc.

Evan Olins
Hula Heaven
75-5744 Alii Dr.
Kailua Kona, HI 96740
ph: 808-329-7885
Wants pre-1960s Hawaiian shirts; also wants souvenir and hula girl items.

John Honl
P.O. Box 1201
Kailua Kona, HI 96745-1201
ph: 808-325-9905
e-mail: jonhonl@konacoast.net
Wants pre-1960 Hawaiian items including lamps, Hula girls, postcard, menus, etc.

Makani/Bailey
RR 2 Box 144
Kula, HI 96790
Wants to buy Hawaii related items: historical, pictorial, Hawaiian Royalty, ephemera, memorabilia.

Cedric Felix
42 Market St.
Wailuku, HI 96793
ph: 808-242-9211
Wants Hawaiian artifacts, wooden carvings, dolls, drums, whaling items, documents, photo albums, hula items, maps, etc.

Bernie Berman
755 Isenberg St., 305
Honolulu, HI 96826-4504
ph: 808-941-8639
Wants pre-1920 Hawaiiana, Oceania, Asian theater countries; postcards, photographs, advertising, memorabilia, broadsides, art books, historical, collectibles, postal covers, books, ephemera, screens, scrolls, prints, documents, etc.

Anne Moore
P.O. Box 604
Bingen, WA 98605-0604
ph: 509-493-4463
Wants all pre-1960 Hawaii memorabilia: Hula dolls, Hula lamps, ukuleles, books, menus, travel posters, paintings, prints, photos, postcards, clothing, artifacts, photos, sheet music, souvenirs, etc.

Dealers

M.A. Blackburn
Antique Hawaiiana
2448 Lincoln Highway East
Lancaster, PA 17602
ph: 800-346-7847 or 717-295-9078
fax: 717-295-3494
e-mail: MBlackburn@aol.com
web: http://www.csmonline.com/blackburn/
Wants Hawaiian artifacts, calabashes, menus, souvenirs, Hula dolls, lamps, ukuleles, quilts, vintage shirts, ceramics, perfume bottles, souvenir spoons, prints, engravings, jewelry, books, ephemera, missionary, royalty, diaries, etc.

Susan Mast
Susan Masst Enterprises
849 Almar Ave., #C-270
Santa Cruz, CA 95060
ph: 831-423-9786
fax: 831-423-7001
e-mail: sme@cruzio.com
web: http://www.cruzio.com/~alohasme/
Buys and sells vintage 1860 to 1950s Hawaiiana: Ming's jewelry, Hakata figures, hula lamps, menus, ephemera, books, Paradise of the Pacific magazine holiday issues, wood perfumes, hula prints and posters, photos, ukuleles, etc.

Museums/Libraries

Hawaiian Historical Society
560 Kawaiahao Street
Honolulu, HI 96813
ph: 808-537-6271
e-mail: bedunn@lava.net
web: http://www.hawaiianhistory.org/

Bishop Museum, The State Museum of Natural & Cultural History
1525 Bernice Street
Honolulu, HI 96817-0916
ph: 808-847-3511 or 888-777-7443
fax: 808-841-8968
e-mail: museum@bishop.bishop.hawaii.org
web: http://www.bishopmuseum.org/

Hawaii (Hawaiian Shirts)

Dealers

Experienced Denim
P.O. Box 239
Fayetteville, AR 72702-0239
ph: 501-444-7541 or 800-336-4694
fax: 501-521-8331
e-mail: exd@edenim.com
web: http://www.edenim.com/
Wants '30s-'50s Levis, denim wear of all types, any brand or condition, '40s-'50s gabardine shirts & jackets, Hawaiian and bowling shirts; also vintage fabrics, textiles, bedspreads, tablecloths with Western or Mexican theme.

David Bailey
Bailey's Antiques & Thrift
517 Kapahulu Ave.
Honolulu, HI 96815-3854
ph: 808-734-7628
e-mail: baileysantqiues@webtv.net
Buys and appraises pre-1960 Levis, pre-1960 Aloha Shirts, and Hawaiiana; pre-1960 Aloha Shirts can be identified by double-stitched seams around the armpit and along sides.

Danny Eskenazi
Jack Hammer Ltd.
169 Broadway East
Seattle, WA 98102
ph: 206-932-6621
fax: 206-932-1449
e-mail: k7ss@wolfenet.com
Wants to buy golden age (1930-1950s) Hawaiian shirts.

Idaho

Museums/Libraries

Idaho State Historical Society
1109 Main St., #250
Boise, ID 83702-5642
ph: 208-334-3987
fax: 208-334-2774
e-mail: skaraba@ishs.state.id.us
web: http://www2.state.id.us/ishs/

Illinois

Museums/Libraries

Illinois State Historical Society
1 Old State Capitol Plaze
Springfield, IL 62701-1507
ph: 217-782-2635 or 217-782-4286
fax: 217-524-8042
e-mail: ishs@eosinc.com
web: http://www.prairienet.org/ishs/

Indiana

Experts

Mark Roeder
305 Akron St.
Culver, IN 46511-1805
ph: 219-842-5141
Wants to buy anything related to Culver, IN and the Culver Military Academy; especially postcards, books, china, photos, and items of historical interest; author of book "A History of Culver and Lake Maxinkuckee."

Museums/Libraries

Indiana Historical Society
315 W. Ohio St.
Indianapolis, IN 46202-3299
ph: 317-232-1882
fax: 317-233-3109
e-mail: csmith@statelib.lib.in.us
web: http://www2.ihs1830.org/ihs1830/

Iowa

Museums/Libraries

State Historical Society of Iowa
600 East Locust
Des Moines, IA 50319-0290
ph: 515-281-5111
e-mail: jthomps1@max.state.ia.us
web: http://www.state.ia.us/government/idca/shsi/ht.htm

Kansas

Dealers

Billy & Jeane Jones
Dearing Country Antiques
309 Independence Ave.
P.O. Box 82
Dearing, KS 67340
ph: 316-948-6389
Want ceramic or glass souvenirs, plates, advertising items, calendars, vases, view cards - anything related to Dearing, Chanute, Coffeyville, Independence, Cherryvale, Iola, Fredonia, or Neodesha Kansas.

Museums/Libraries

Kansas State Historical Society
6425 SW Sixth Ave.
Topeka, KS 66615-1099
ph: 785-272-8681
fax: 785-272-8682
e-mail: webmaster@kshs.org
web: http://www.kshs.org/kshs1.html

Kentucky

Collectors

Ed McDermott
1415 McKendree
Kevil, KY 42053
ph: 502-488-3420
e-mail: emcdermott@brtc.net
Wants pre-1920 advertising items from Paducah, KY: signs, letterheads, labeled bottles, corkscrews, shot glasses, whiskey jugs, etc.

Museums/Libraries

Kentucky State Historical Society
P.O. Box 1792
Frankfort, KY 40602
ph: 502-564-3016
web: http://www.kyhistory.org/

Louisiana

Museums/Libraries

Louisiana Historical Society
c/o Louisiana State Museum
P.O. Box 2448
New Orleans, LA 70176-2448
ph: 504-568-6968 or 800-568-6968
fax: 504-568-4995
e-mail: lsm@crt.state.la.us
web: http://www.crt.state.la.us/crt/museum/lsmnet3.htm

Maine

Museums/Libraries

Maine Historical Society
c/o Center for Main History
485 Congress St.
Portland, ME 04101
ph: 207-774-1822
fax: 207-775-4301
web: http://www.mainehistory.com/

Maryland

Museums/Libraries

Maryland Historical Society
201 West Monument St.
Baltimore, MD 21201-4674
ph: 410-685-3750
fax: 410-385-2105
e-mail: web-comments@mdhs.org
web: http://mdhs.org/

Massachusetts

Museums/Libraries

Massachusetts Historical Society
1154 Boylston St.
Boston, MA 02215
ph: 617-536-1608
e-mail: admin@masshist.org
web: http://masshist.org/

Michigan

Museums/Libraries

Historical Society of Michigan
2117 Washtenaw Ave.
Ann Arbor, MI 48104-4599
ph: 734-769-1828 or 734-769-4267
fax: 734-769-1828
e-mail: hsofmich@leslie.k12.mi.us

Michigan Historical Center
717 West Allegan St.
Lansing, MI 48918-1800
ph: 517-373-3559
e-mail: webspinners@sosmail.state.mi.us
web: http://www.sos.state.mi.us/history/history.html

Dennis R. Boden, Ex. Dir
Jesse Besser Museum
491 Johnson St.
Alpena, MI 49707
ph: 517-356-2202
fax: 517-356-3133
e-mail: jbmuseum@northland.lib.mi.us
web: http://www.ogdennews.com/upnorth/museum/home.html
Special Great Lakes collections: Native Americans, Great Lakes maps, Great Lakes (NE Michigan) photographs.

Minnesota

Museums/Libraries

Minnesota Historical Society
345 Kellog Blvd. West
Saint Paul, MN 55102-1906
ph: 651-296-6126
fax: 651-296-6126
e-mail: webmaster@mnhs.org
web: http://www.mnhs.org/

Mississippi

Museums/Libraries

Mississippi Historical Society
Journal: Journal of Mississippi History
P.O. Box 571
Jackson, MS 39205-0571
ph: 601-359-6850
fax: 601-359-6975
e-mail: webmaster@mdah.state.ms.us
web: http://www.mdah.state.ms.us/mhistsoc.html

Missouri

Dealers

Trenton Boyd
P.O. Box 517
Columbia, MO 65205-0517
ph: 573-882-2461 or 573-442-5235
fax: 573-882-2950
e-mail: vetlib@showme.missouri.edu
Wants items from Missouri, except Kansas City and St. Louis.

Museums/Libraries

State Historical Society of Missouri
1020 Lowry Street
Columbia, MO 65201-7298
ph: 573-882-7083
fax: 573-884-4950
e-mail: shsofmo@umsystem.edu
web: http://www.system.missouri.edu/shs/
The preeminent research facility for the study of Missouri and Missourians; mission is to collect, preserve, make accessible, and publish material relating to the history of Missouri; does not hold memorabilia or artifacts.

Montana

Collectors

Tim Gordon, ISA
1750 W. Kent
Missoula, MT 59801-5508
ph: 406-728-1812
e-mail: stacey1165@aol.com
Wants any pre-1930 item marked "Montana": calendars, advertising, photos, post cards, history books, tokens, trade cards, etc.

Dealers

Idaho Street Antiques
110 East Idaho
Kalispell, MT 59911
ph: 406-755-1324
Buys and sells American Indian, National Park, and other photographic items relating to Montana.

Museums/Libraries

Montana Historical Society
225 North Roberts
Helena, MT 59620-1201
ph: 406-444-2694 or 800-243-9900
e-mail: mhspub@aol.com
web: http://www.his.state.mt.us/

Nebraska

Museums/Libraries

Nebraska State Historical Society
15th & P Streets
Lincoln, NE 68508
ph: 402-471-4754 or 800-833-6747
e-mail: ednshs@inetnebr.com
web: http://www.nebraskahistory.org/

Nevada

Collectors

Gil Schmidtmann
2346 Naples Ave.
Mentone, CA 92359-9569
ph: 909-794-1211
Wants pre-1930 stock certificates, postcards, postmarks, merchant tokens, badges, books, calendars, checks, currency, documents, newspapers, photos, promotional items, souvenir plates and spoons, etc.; also the same from Death Valley.

Museums/Libraries

Nevada Historical Society
1650 N. Virginia St.
Reno, NV 89503
ph: 775-688-1190
fax: 775-688-2917
e-mail:
plbandur@lahontan.clan.lib.nv.us
web: http://www.clan.lib.nv.us/docs/MUSEUMS/HIST/his-soc.htm

New Hampshire

Museums/Libraries

New Hampshire Historical Society, Inc.
30 Park St.
Concord, NH 03301
ph: 603-226-3189
e-mail: nhhsmus@aol.com
web: http://www.nhhistory.org/
One of New England's finest history museums with award-winning exhibitions giving an overview of 500 years of New Hampshire history.

New Jersey

Museums/Libraries

New Jersey Historical Society
52 Park Place
Newark, NJ 07102
ph: 973-596-8500
fax: 973-596-6957

New Jersey State Museum
205 West State Street
P.O. Box 530
Trenton, NJ 08625-0530
ph: 609-292-6464
fax: 609-599-4098
e-mail: feedback@sos.state.nj.us
web: http://www.state.nj.us/state/museum/musidx.html

New Mexico

Museums/Libraries

Museum of New Mexico
P.O. Box 2087
Santa Fe, NM 87501
ph: 505-827-6480
e-mail: sturt@nm-us.campus.mci.net
web: http://www.nmmnh-abq.mus.nm.us/mnm/mnm.html

New York

Museums/Libraries

New-York Historical Society
Two West 77th Street
New York, NY 10024
ph: 212-873-3400
fax: 212-874-8706
e-mail: nyhs@interport.net
web: http://www.nyhistory.org/

Adirondack Museum, The
Rte. 30
P.O. Box 99
Blue Mountain Lake, NY 12812-0099
ph: 518-352-7311
fax: 518-352-7653
web: http://www.adkmuseum.org/
Has extensive collection of paintings, prints, drawings, and historic photographs documenting the Adirondack region from 18th century through 20th century.

New York Historical Association
Lake Road, Route 80
Cooperstown, NY 13326
ph: 607-547-1400 or 888-547-1450
e-mail: carla@nysha.org
web: http://www.nysha.org/

New York (Brooklyn)

Collectors

Brian Merlis
P.O. Box 14
Lynbrook, NY 11563-0014
ph: 516-593-4505
Wants items relating to Brooklyn and Long Island: maps, LIRR, books, medals, prints, relics, badges, souvenirs, brochures, negatives, genealogy, histories, post cards, newspapers, artwork, atlases, letterheads, etc.

North Carolina

Collectors

J. Robert Boykin, III
P.O. Box 7440
Wilson, NC 27895
ph: 252-237-1700
fax: 252-237-2314
e-mail:
boykinappraisals@coastalnet.com
Wants to buy any pre-1930 items from North Carolina such as billheads, letterheads, postcards, history books, advertising, tokens, art, trade cards, bottles.

Museums/Libraries

North Carolina Museum of History
5 East Edenton St.
Raleigh, NC 27601-1011
ph: 919-715-0200
fax: 919-733-8655
web: http://nchistory.dcr.state.nc.us/museums/

North Dakota

Museums/Libraries

State Historical Society of North Dakota
612 East Boulevard Ave.
Bismarck, ND 58505-0830
ph: 701-328-2666
fax: 701-328-3710
e-mail: histsoc@state.nd.us
web: http://www.state.nd.us/hist/

Ohio

Museums/Libraries

Ohio Historical Society
1982 Velma Ave.
Columbus, OH 43211
ph: 614-297-2300
e-mail: webmaster@ohiohistory.org
web: http://www.ohiohistory.org/

Western Reserve Historical Society
10825 East Blvd.
Cleveland, OH 44106-1703
ph: 216-721-5722
fax: 216-721-0645
e-mail: pomerleau@wrhs.org
web: http://www.wrhs.org/
Oldest cultural institution in Cleveland, with a research/genealogical library, costume wing, auto & aviation museum and restored mansion under one roof; special interest area in genealogical research.

Oklahoma

Appraisers

Alvin Turner
Historical/Museum Services
115 N. Lazy Lane
Ada, OK 74820
ph: 580-436-5640
e-mail: aoturner@chickasaw.com
Collector and appraiser specializing in regional materials from Oklahoma and the American West.

Museums/Libraries

Oklahoma Historical Society
2100 N. Lincoln Blvd.
Oklahoma City, OK 73105
ph: 405-521-2491
web: http://www.ok-history.mus.ok.us

Oregon

Museums/Libraries

Oregon Historical Society
1200 SW Park Ave.
Portland, OR 97205-2483
ph: 503-222-1741
fax: 503-221-2035
e-mail: orhist@ohs.org
web: http://www.ohs.org/

Pennsylvania

Museums/Libraries

Historical Society of Pennsylvania
1300 Locust St.
Philadelphia, PA 19107-5699
ph: 215-732-6200
fax: 215-732-2680
e-mail: hsppr@aol.com
web: http://www.libertynet.org/pahist/
Holds many of the nation's most important historical documents; houses more than 500,000 books, 300,000 graphic works, and 15 million manuscript items; maintains one of the largest family history libraries in the nation.

Suppliers

State Museum of Pennsylvania
3rd & North Streets
P.O. Box 1026
Harrisburg, PA 17108-1026
ph: 717-772-4979 or 717-787-4980
e-mail: museum@statemuseumpa.org
web: http://www.statemuseumpa.org/

Pennsylvania German Heritage

Museums/Libraries

James McMahon
Hershey Museum
170 W. Hersheypark Dr.
Hershey, PA 17033-2727
ph: 717-534-3439
fax: 717-534-8940
web: http://www.hershey-museum.microserve.net/
Focused collection of objects detailing the town of Hershey history, regional PA German heritage, native American material culture.

Rhode Island

Museums/Libraries

Rhode Island Historical Society Library
1212 Hope St.
Providence, RI 02906
ph: 401-331-8575
fax: 401-751-7930

South Carolina

Dealers

Henry Barnet
516 Maverick Circle
Spartanburg, SC 29307-3707
ph: 864-579-2112
e-mail: yourtowninc@compuserve.com
Buys, sells and collects original artwork done by southern artists and those from South Carolina, especially from the Piedmont area; wants prints, ephemera, books, etc.

Museums/Libraries

South Carolina Historical Society
100 Meeting St.
Charleston, SC 29401
ph: 843-723-3225
fax: 843-723-8584
e-mail: info@schistory.org
web: http://www.schistory.org/

South Dakota

Museums/Libraries

South Dakota State Historical Society
900 Governors Drive
Pierre, SD 57501-2217
ph: 605-773-3458
fax: 605-773-6041
e-mail: David.Hartley@state.sd.us
web: http://www.state.sd.us/state/executive/deca/cultural/soc_gen.htm

Tennessee

Collectors

Claude Bellar
1750 Keyes Road
Greenbrier, TN 37073
ph: 615-643-0290
fax: 615-643-0290
e-mail: cbellar@aol.com
Wants Tennessee bottles, stoneware, advertising.

Paul A. Jarrett
611 West Main
Waverly, TN 37185
ph: 615-296-3151
Wants to buy pre-Prohibition Tennessee jugs (miniature or full size), embossed druggist bottles, pre-1920 business letterhead, merchant "good for" tokens.

Peggy Dillard
P.O. Box 210904
Nashville, TN 37221-0904
ph: 615-646-1605
Wants Tennessee postcards and historical items, especially Tennessee Centennial Exposition (1897) items.

Joe C. Copeland
P.O. Box 4221
Oak Ridge, TN 37831-4221
ph: 423-482-4215
e-mail: joenatca@juno.com
Wants to buy any Tennessee tokens and other memorabilia, city and county histories, pre-1950 phone books and city directories, Dun & Bradstreet directories, pins, medals, badges, crocks, whiskey jugs, gazetteers.

Museums/Libraries

East Tennessee Historical Society
P.O. Box 1629
Knoxville, TN 37901-1629
ph: 423-544-5732
fax: 423-544-4319
e-mail: eths@east-tennessee-history.org
web: http://www.east-tennessee-history.org

West Tennessee Historical Society
P.O. Box 111046
Memphis, TN 38111
e-mail: lgundersen@jscc.cc.tn.us
web: http://www.wths.tn.org/

Texas

Clubs/Associations

Texas Centennial Collector
P.O. Box 8072
Longview, TX 75607
fax: 903-757-3043
Free newsletter; no dues.

Collectors

James E. Kattner
P.O. Box 11132
Spring, TX 77391
ph: 281-986-6916 or 281-376-4826
Wants to buy Texas tokens from saloons, bars, military forts, post traders, lumber companies, drug stores, general stores, bakeries, etc.; also wants Texas, pocket mirrors, whiskey jugs and other Texas saloon advertisement items.

Museums/Libraries

Texas State Historical Association
2/306 Sid Richardson Hall
Austin, TX 78712
ph: 512-471-1525
fax: 512-471-1551
e-mail: comments@www.tsha.utexas.edu
web: http://www.tsha.utexas.edu/

Utah

Museums/Libraries

Utah State Historical Society
300 Rio Grande
Salt Lake City, UT 84101-1143
ph: 801-533-3500
fax: 801-533-3503
e-mail: ushs@history.state.ut.us
web: http://www.history.state.ut.us/

Vermont

Museums/Libraries

Vermont Historical Society
109 State Street
Montpelier, VT 05609-0901
ph: 802-828-2291
fax: 802-828-3638
e-mail: vhs@vhs.state.vt.us
web: http://www.cit.state.vt.us/vhs/

Virginia

Museums/Libraries

Virginia Historical Society
428 North Boulevard
Richmond, VA 23220
ph: 804-358-4901
e-mail: charles@vahistorical.org
web: http://www.vahistorical.org/

Washington

Collectors

Richard Reisinger
2610 Holgate St.
Tacoma, WA 98402-1204
ph: 253-272-7092
Wants 19th and early 20 century Puget Sound region (Seattle, Tacoma, Olympia, Mt. Rainier, etc.) travel brochures, ephemera, postal history, photos, view books, maps, tourist souvenirs, china, bottles, pins, badges, posters, etc.

Museums/Libraries

Washington State History Museum
1911 Pacific Ave.
Tacoma, WA 98402
ph: 253-272-3500 or 888-238-4373
e-mail: web@wshs.wa.gov
web: http://www.wshs.org/

Washington DC

Collectors

Jerry A. McCoy
800 Thayer Ave.
Silver Spring, MD 20910-4504
ph: 301-565-2519
e-mail: ohiowa@erols.com
Wants to buy real photo (B & W) postcards of 19th or early 20th century Washington DC.

Museums/Libraries

United States Capitol Historical Society
200 Maryland Ave., NE
Washington, DC 20002-5796
ph: 202-543-8919
fax: 202-544-8244
e-mail: uschs@uschs.org
web: http://www.uschs.org/

West Virginia

Museums/Libraries

West Virginia State Museum
c/o WV Div. of Culture & History
1900 Kanawha Bouolevard East
Charleston, WV 25305-0300
ph: 304-558-0220
e-mail: keller_m@wvlc.wvnet.edu
web: http://www.wvlc.wvnet.edu/culture/front.html

Wisconsin

Museums/Libraries

State Historical Society of Wisconsin
816 State St.
Madison, WI 53706
ph: 608-264-6400
web: http://www.shsw.wisc.edu/about/

Wyoming

Museums/Libraries

Wyoming State Museum
Barrett Building
2301 Central Ave.
Cheyenne, WY 82002
ph: 307-777-7022
fax: 307-777-5375
e-mail: WSM@missc.state.wy.us
web: http://commerce.state.wy.us/cr/wsm/index.htm

STATIONARY ENGINES

(see ENGINES, Gasoline)

STATUE OF LIBERTY COLLECTIBLES

(see also SOUVENIR & COMMEMORATIVE ITEMS)

Clubs/Associations

Iris & Mort November
Statue of Liberty Collectors' Club
Newsletter: Statue of Liberty Collectors' Club Newsletter
26601 Bernwood Rd.
Cleveland, OH 44122-7133
ph: 216-831-2646 or 216-831-0497
fax: 216-831-0497
e-mail: lbrtyclub@aol.com
web: http://www.statueoflibertyclub.com/
For collectors or enthusiasts with an interest in items relating to the Statue of Liberty; dues help support the Statue of Liberty Foundation.

Collectors

Jeffrey Eger
42 Blackberry Ln.
Morristown, NJ 07960-6404
ph: 973-455-1843
fax: 973-455-0186
Writer/author/Statue of Liberty historian looking for unusual early items relating to the statue's history.

Iris & Mort November
26601 Bernwood Rd.
Cleveland, OH 44122-7133
ph: 216-831-2646 or 216-831-0497
fax: 216-831-0497
e-mail: lbrtyclub@aol.com
web: http://www.statueoflibertyclub.com/
Collects items relating to the Statue of Liberty or its designer, Bartholdi.

Mike Brooks
7335 Skyline
Oakland, CA 94611-1121
ph: 510-339-1751
e-mail: deborahwb@aol.com
Buying early souvenir models, books, medals, advertising, donor certificates, unveiling invitations, Bartholdi related items, etc.

Dealers

Ronald Cutadean
1235 Kennedy Ave.
Louisville, CO 80027-1072
Buys, sells, trades Statue of Liberty items.

Experts

Harvey & Sandy Dolin
Harvey Dolin & Co.
5 Beekman St.
New York, NY 10038-2206
ph: 212-267-0216
Wants any item pertaining to the Statue of Liberty.

STEAM-OPERATED

Models & Equipment

(see also AUTOMOBILES, Steam; BOATS, Steam; ENGINES; FARM MACHINERY; GAUGES; HORNS & WHISTLES; INDUSTRY RELATED ITEMS; MACHINERY & EQUIPMENT, Road Making; RAILROADS; STEAMBOAT COLLECTIBLES; TOYS, Farm; TOYS, Steam/Hot Air)

Clubs/Associations

Northwest Steam Society
Newsletter: Steam Gage
3629 NW 64th St.
Seattle, WA 98107-2667
e-mail: halathome@aol.com
Interested in steam-operated models, equipment, and machinery; especially railroads.

John Cook, Mem. Sec.
National Traction Engine Trust
Magazine: Steaming
c/o "Dolfarni", Church Lane
Kirkby la Thorpe
Sleaford, Lincolnshire NG34 9NU
U.K.
e-mail: ntetuk@aol.com
web: http://members.aol.com/ntetuk/Ntet1.htm
Based i the U.K.; dedicated to the preservation of steam powered traction and stationary engines and ancillary equipment.

Collectors

D.E. Haskins
1237 Alleghany Ln.
Northbrook, IL 60062
ph: 847-498-3516
Wants old toy steam engines, parts and literature (no railroad, please).

Museums/Libraries

Hamilton Museum of Steam & Technology, The
900 Woodward Ave.
Hamilton, Ontario L8H 7N2
Canada
ph: 905-546-4797
fax: 905-546-4798
e-mail: hmstchin@interlynx.net
web: http://www.city.hamilton.on.ca/cultureandrecreation/steam.html
Exhibits of industrial history; children's activities.

Periodicals

Joe Rice, Ed.
Village Press
Magazine: Live Steam Magazine
P.O. Box 1810
Traverse City, MI 49685-1810
ph: 616-946-3712 or 800-447-7367
fax: 616-946-3289
e-mail: jrice@villagepress.com
web: http://www.villagepress.com/livesteam/
A magazine for the amateur machinist, or live steam hobbyist; steam locomotives, marine vessels, tractors, stationary steam engines, etc.; full scale or models.

George & Linda Broad
Magazine: Modeltec
P.O. Box 1226
Saint Cloud, MN 56302
ph: 320-654-0815
fax: 320-240-8690
e-mail: modeltec@cloudnet.com
web: http://www.4w.com/modeltec/
Monthly magazine for lovers of large-scale trains, live steam, hot air and antique gas engine models.

STEAMBOAT COLLECTIBLES

(see also BOATS; OCEAN LINER MEMORABILIA; SHIPPING; SHIP RELATED)

Clubs/Associations

Sue Ewen
Steamship Historical Society of America, Inc.
Magazine: Steamboat Bill
300 Ray Dr., Ste. #4
Providence, RI 02906
ph: 401-274-0805
web: http://www.sshsa.org/
For those interested in maritime history; publishes high quality quarterly magazine; has photo bank of thousands of negatives of powered vessels, national and regional meetings.

Tugboat Enthusiasts Society of the Americas
Magazine: Tug Bitts
308 Quince St.
Mount Pleasant, SC 29464-3420
ph: 843-881-1173
Published quarterly; covers steamboat & inland river history; packed with news, photos, articles on all types of tow boats, tugboats (harbor, ocean, military) and work boat salvage, restoration and history; a must for tugboat enthusiasts.

Steamboat Masters & Associations, Inc.
Journal: Egregious Steamboat Journal, The
P.O. Box 3046
Louisville, KY 40201-3046
ph: 502-778-6784
fax: 502-776-9006
e-mail: sbmaster@bellsouth.net
Offers a wide variety of research and consulting services; appraises steamboat collections; sell them through a bi-monthly journal of steamboat history and technical studies; a wealth of unpublished information and photos.

Mrs. J.W. Rutter
Sons & Daughters of Pioneer Rivermen
Magazine: S & D Reflector
126 Seneca Dr.
Marietta, OH 45750
With about 1,100 members, this organization is devoted to river history; magazine published quarterly; meets annually in Marietta, OH the third weekend of September.

Collectors

Tom Cottrell
17 Mattapoisett Ave.
Swansea, MA 02777-2810
ph: 508-674-4287
Wants to buy steamboat waybills and invoices.

Experts

Jack & Sandra Custer
P.O. Box 3046
Louisville, KY 40201-3046
ph: 502-778-6784
fax: 502-776-9006
e-mail: sbmaster@bellsouth.net
Experts, appraisers, dealers focusing on steamboats and steamboat collectibles; offers one-stop shopping for collectibles, artifacts, art prints, and resource books pertaining to steamboats.

Museums/Libraries

Steamship Historical Society Collection at the University of Baltimore Library
1420 Maryland Ave.
Baltimore, MD 21201-5779
ph: 410-625-3134
e-mail: ghaitsuka@ubmail.ubalt.edu
web: http://www.ubalt.edu/www/archives/ship.htm
A 10,000-volume library of books, periodicals, approx. 200,000 photographs, 25,000 printed postcards, ship plans, and a brochure collection devoted exclusively to the history of engine-powered vessels.

Inland Rivers Library at the Public Library of Cincinnati & Hamilton County
800 Vine St.
Cincinnati, OH 45202
ph: 513-369-6957
Specialty collections include rare book collection (history of the Ohio and Mississippi rivers and their tributaries as commercial transportation routes), clipping files, illustrations, maps, photos, manuscripts, blueprints, broadsides.

Ohio River Museum
601 Front St.
Marietta, OH 45750
ph: 740-373-3750 or 800-860-0145
fax: 740-860-3680
e-mail: webmaster@ohiohistory.org
web: http://www.ohiohistory.org/places/ohriver/
Features the "W.P. Snyder, Jr." (a 1918 stern-wheeler steamboat), and collections including geological, ecological, recreational and commercial history of the Ohio River from its origin to present.

Howard Steamboat Museum
1101 E. Market St.
P.O. Box 606
Jeffersonville, IN 47131-0606
ph: 812-283-3728
Steamboat artifacts and models, photographs, half-breadth models, tools; 1894 mansion tour; Victorian furnishings; Miss Mary Starr.

Fred. W. Woodward Riverboat Museum
2nd Street
P.O. Box 305
Dubuque, IA 52001
ph: 319-557-9545

Mississippi River Museum
400 E 3rd St.
P.O. Box 266
Dubuque, IA 52004-0266
ph: 319-557-9545
fax: 319-583-1241
Focuses on the "William M. Black" (1934 side-wheeler river boat); also collections relating to canoes, flatboats, steamboats, steam engines, and the Mississippi River.

Murphy Library at the University of Wisconsin, La Crosse
University of WI - La Crosse
1631 Pine Street
La Crosse, WI 54601
ph: 608-785-8511
fax: 608-785-8639
e-mail: specoll@mail.uwlax.edu
web: http://perth.uwlax.edu/MurphyLibrary/
40,000 photographs of inland river steamboats.

St. Louis Mercantile Library Association
510 Locust St.
Saint Louis, MO 63101-1845
ph: 314-621-0670
Specialty collections include the National Inland Waterways Collection consisting of books, manuscripts, maps, photographs, reports and pamphlets.

Periodicals

Journal: Waterways Journal, The
319 N. 4th St.
Saint Louis, MO 63102-1906
ph: 314-241-7354
fax: 314-241-4207
e-mail: waterwayj@socket.net
Weekly newspaper reporting on current events.

STEAMSHIP MEMORABILIA

(see OCEAN LINER MEMORABILIA; SHIPPING; SHIP REPLATED; STEAMBOAT COLLECTIBLES)

STEIFF

(see also DOLLS; TEDDY BEARS; TOYS)

Clubs/Associations

Steiff Club USA
Magazine: Steiff Club USA Magazine
31 East 28th St., 9th Floor
New York, NY 10016
ph: 212-779-2582 or 212-675-2727
fax: 212-779-2594
web: http://www.steiff-club.com
Contemporary plush teddy bears with trademark "button-in-ear"; a company-sponsored collectors club.

Beth B. Savino
Steiff Collectors Club
Newsletter: Collector Life
Franklin Park Mall
5001 Monroe St.
Toledo, OH 43623
ph: 419-473-9801 or 800-862-8697
fax: 419-473-3947
e-mail: info@toystorenet.com
web: http://www.toystorenet.com
Focus is on collecting Steiff toys; sells exclusive Steiff Limited Edition; also buys old Steiff.

Collectors

Jeff Dykes
6 Wildwood Terrace
Glen Ridge, NJ 07028
ph: 973-748-4990
e-mail: lja@viconet.com
Wants to buy any and all Steiff animals, especially teddy bears and rabbits, from 1890s to 1950s; prefer excellent condition with button and/or chest tag; send photo.

Dealers

Dale & Retha Tyo
Whispering Pines Antiques
280 Lawton Rd.
Hilton, NY 14468
ph: 716-637-4931

Old Friends Antiques
P.O. Box 754
Sparks, MD 21152
ph: 410-472-4632
fax: 410-472-3093
Specializing in Steiff bears and animals.

Rita Mueller
Grange Hall Antiques
1 South Eighth Alley
P.O. Box 263
New Market, MD 21774
ph: 301-865-5651
fax: 301-865-0518
e-mail: Rita@newmarketmd.com
web: http://www.newmarketmd.com/grange.htm
Quality Steiff animals from 1950s through 1980s; always buying one piece or entire collection: teddy bears, Schuco, Hermann, Steiff; also fine country graniteware from Germany available; mail orders and layaways.

Cheri Shivley
Cynthia's Country Store, Inc.
The Wellington Mall #15A
12794 W. Forest Hill Blvd.
West Palm Beach, FL 33414
ph: 561-793-0554
fax: 561-795-4222
e-mail: cynbears@aol.com
web: http://www.cynthiascountrystore.com/
Specializing in new, discontinued and antique Steiff, R. John Wright, and other manufacturers and artists bears.

E. Adorjan
Imaginary Friends
P.O. Box 40601
Denver, CO 80204
ph: 303-761-7234
e-mail: toyrep@aol.com
web: http://members.aol.com/toyrep/
Specializes repairs and restorations to Steiff and other stuffed toys and dolls; will is advise if toy would be better off if left as-is; references and before-and-after photos available; official restoration specialist with Steiff.

Karen Strickland
Rare Bears
17831 Chase St.
Northridge, CA 91325-3808
ph: 818-993-9361
fax: 818-341-9316
e-mail: rarebears@earthlink.net
web: http://www.rarebears.com/
Buys and sells Steiff, Schuco animals and vintage Teddy Bears; four quarterly listings for $20/yr.

Experts

Beth B. Savino
Toy Store, The
Franklin Park Mall
5001 Monroe St.
Toledo, OH 43623
ph: 419-473-9801 or 800-862-8697
fax: 419-473-3947
e-mail: info@toystorenet.com
web: http://www.toystorenet.com
Buys, sells and specializes in Steiff toys; sells exclusive Steiff Limited Edition; also buys old Steiff.

Man./Prod./Dist.

Steiff USA, L.P.
31 East 28th St., 9th Floor
New York, NY 10016
ph: 212-779-2582 or 212-675-2727
fax: 212-779-2594
web: http://www.steiff-club.com
Manufacturer of collectible plush stuffed Steiff animals.

Margarete Steiff GmbH
P.O. Box 1560
Giengen/Brenz, D-89530
Germany
ph: +49 7322 131 452
fax: +49 7322 131 476
web: http://www.steiff.com

Repair Services

E. Adorjan
Imaginary Friends
P.O. Box 40601
Denver, CO 80204
ph: 303-761-7234
e-mail: toyrep@aol.com
web: http://members.aol.com/toyrep/
Specializes repairs and restorations to Steiff and other stuffed toys and dolls; will is advise if toy would be better off if left as-is; references and before-and-after photos available; official restoration specialist with Steiff.

STEINS

(see also COLLECTIBLES [MODERN], Steins; GLASSES, Drinking)

Appraisers

George F. Adams
Steins Unlimited
Rt. 600 Box 7-B
Pamplin, VA 23958
ph: 804-248-6114
Buys, sells, appraises and repairs (pewter) steins; Mettlach, Villeroy Boch, other German, brewery, Bud, Millers, Coors, Strohs, old style, etc.

Auction Services

John McClain
York Town Auction Inc.
1625 Haviland Rd.
York, PA 17404
ph: 717-751-0211
fax: 717-767-7729
e-mail: yorktownauction@cyberia.com
Antique & specialty auctions, lecture & appraisal services; antiques also purchased; American & English furniture, related specialties & accessories, Americana, folk art, jewelry, art, clocks & watches, militaria, steins, Oriental rugs.

Gary Kirsner
Gary Kirsner Auctions
P.O. Box 8807
Coral Springs, FL 33075-8807
ph: 954-344-9856
fax: 954-344-4421
Six to seven cataloged auctions per year; steins and related items; also specialty auctions of Limited Edition and retired collectibles.

Andre Ammelounx
Stein Auction Company
P.O. Box 136
Palatine, IL 60078
ph: 847-991-5927
fax: 847-991-5947
Conducts live and mail bid catalog stein auctions.

Clubs/Associations

Rocky Mountain Steiners
e-mail: carolrooney@worldnet.att.net
web: http://home.att.net/~carolrooney/Rmsmain.htm

Les Hopper, Ed.
Bayou Stein Verein
Newsletter: Al E. Gator Sez
ph: 504-394-3530
fax: 504-392-8937
e-mail: leshopper@earthlink.net
web: http://www.steincollectors.org/chapters/bayou/

New England Steiners
65 Pierce Rd.
West Brookfield, MA 01585-3038
ph: 617-323-0018

Norman Pratore, Mem.
Stein Collectors International
Magazine: Prosit
P.O. Box 5005
Laurel, MD 20726-5005
ph: 301-498-7640
e-mail: tscheer@mcube.com
web: http://steincollectors.org/
Dedicated to the studious appreciation of the art, culture and manufacture of beer steins, mugs drinking vessel and related items; has its own stein museum; books, articles and video library; over 28 chapters worldwide.

Georgia Stein Collectors
3040 Sawtooth Dr.
Alpharetta, GA 30202-5400

Jim DeMars
Sun Steiners
Newsletter: Sun Steiner News
P.O. Box 11782
Fort Lauderdale, FL 33339-1782
ph: 954-772-4490
fax: 954-772-4490
e-mail: FLSteiners@aol.com
web: http://steincollectors.org/chapters/sunstein.html
Members collect beer steins; antique, brewery, character, Mettlach, etc.

Buckeye Stein Verein
2265 Bradley Rd.
Westlake, OH 44145-1737
ph: 419-841-3195

Lone Star Chapter of the Stein Collectors International
P.O. Box 555
Katy, TX 77482-0555
ph: 281-371-2646

Pacific Stein Sammler
Newsletter: die Kunde
P.O. Box 194
Oceanside, OR 97134-0194
ph: 503-842-5376
e-mail: layers@wa-net.com
web: http://home1.gte.net/johnp1/index.htm

Collectors

Dr. Paul Rohe
P.O. Box 122
Martinville, NJ 08336-0122
Wants to buy old steins.

Lester E. Hopper
3530 Mimosa Court
New Orleans, LA 70131-8305
ph: 504-394-3530
fax: 504-392-8937

Michael G. Anderson
6761 N. Placita Bella
Tucson, AZ 85718
ph: 520-299-3407
Wants steins: blown glass, regimental, military, Mettlach, etc.

Steve Elliott
1600 Tennessee St.
Vallejo, CA 94590
ph: 707-552-8400 or 707-642-1949
fax: 707-552-0881
Wants to buy antique beer steins.

Dealers

Heinz Roes
Heinz-N-Steins
231 Maple Ave.
Glen Burnie, MD 21061
ph: 410-760-0707
Buys and sells beer steins; military, Mettlach, character drinking vessels, cups, plaques, WWI, German, pipes, pictures, flasks, etc.; also occupational shaving mugs.

George F. Adams
Steins Unlimited
Rt. 600 Box 7-B
Pamplin, VA 23958
ph: 804-248-6114
Buys, sells, appraises and repairs (pewter) steins; Mettlach, Villeroy Boch, other German, brewery, Bud, Millers, COors, Strohs, old style, etc.

Bill Cress
P.O. Box 989
Alton, IL 62002-0989
ph: 618-466-3513
Buys and sells all of the new and lots of the old steins; quarterly lists of modern steins and mugs for sale.

Lester E. Hopper
3530 Mimosa Court
New Orleans, LA 70131-8305
ph: 504-394-3530
fax: 504-392-8937

Experts

Ron Fox
P.O. Box 4026
Farmingdale, NY 11735
ph: 516-661-8387
fax: 516-376-0916
e-mail: oz@webspan.net
Specializes in Mettlach steins.

John D. Stuart
Thirsty Knight Antiques
7-9 East Main St.
P.O. Box 48
New Market, MD 21774
ph: 301-831-9889 or 301-865-5053
Specializing in beer steins since 1972: Mettlachs, regimentals, characters, glass, porcelain, silver, pewter, faience, stoneware from 1500s to late 1800s.

Gary & Beth Kirsner
Glentiques, Ltd.
P.O. Box 8807
Coral Springs, FL 33075-8807
ph: 954-344-9856
fax: 954-344-4421
Wants quality steins: Mettlach, regimentals, character, glass, etc.; author of "The Beer Stein Book", (1990.)

Jim DeMars
P.O. Box 11782
Fort Lauderdale, FL 33339-1782
ph: 954-772-4490
fax: 954-772-4490
e-mail: FLSteiners@aol.com
web: http://steincollectors.org/chapters/sunstein.html

Les Paul
Les Paul, Steinologist
568 Country Isle M
Alameda, CA 94501-5614
ph: 510-523-7480
fax: 510-523-8755
Contact for free antique beer stein appraisal or information without obligation; photos are helpful, but he can usually tell you retail and a fair dealer offer over the phone; call with the stein in your hands.

Mettlach

Experts

Joe & Pat Hartzler
J & P Collectibles
89 Brook Hill Drive
Howell, NJ 07731
ph: 732-364-1354
Buys, sells and specializes in Mettlach steins; willing to share information.

STEREO VIEWERS & STEREOVIEWS

(see also 3-D PHOTOGRAPHICA; CAMERAS & CAMERA EQUIPMENT, Stereo Cameras; OPTICAL ITEMS; PAPER COLLECTIBLES; PHOTOGRAPHS)

Auction Services

Tim McIntyre
Tim McIntyre's Antique Photographs
137 Nile St.
Stratford, Ontario N5E 4E1
Canada
ph: 519-273-5360
fax: 519-273-7310
e-mail: timoni@orc.ca
web: http://www.orc.ca/~timoni/
Buys, sells, auctions 19th and early 20th century photographs, specializing in stereoviews, CDVs and cabinet cards.

Clubs/Associations

National Stereoscopic Association
Magazine: Stereo World
P.O. Box 14801
Columbus, OH 43214
ph: 614-263-4296
e-mail: nsa@nsa-3d.org
web: http://nsa-3d.org/
Members collect stereo views, stereoscopes, stereo cameras; View-Master reels, viewers, packets; all other 3-D collectibles; the glossy colorful magazine is published six timer per year.

Susan Pinsky
Stereo Club of Southern California
Newsletter: 3D News
P.O. Box 2368
Culver City, CA 90231-2368
ph: 310-837-2368
fax: 310-558-1653
e-mail: Reel3D@aol.com
web: http://home.earthlink.net/~campfire/
A club for people interested in sharing 3-D (stereo) photography; some equipment listed in club newsletter classifieds.

Collectors

Norman Kulkin
727 N. Fuller Ave.
Los Angeles, CA 90046-7504
ph: 323-653-6929
fax: 323-651-0640
e-mail: pixidom@aol.com
web: http://www.pixidom.com/
Buy, sell, trade vintage photographs: ambrotypes, tintypes, stereoviews, specialty is daguerreotypes; also early 19th century paper photos, early 20th century photos; also photographica including cameras.

Dealers

Bryan W. Ginns
2109 Cty. Rte. 21
Valatie, NY 12184-6001
ph: 518-392-5805
fax: 518-392-7925
e-mail: the3dman@aol.com

David Wood
daves-stereos
P.O. Box 838
Milford, PA 18337-0838
ph: 570-296-61767 or 914-856-5311 x397
fax: 914-856-5507
e-mail: wood@pikeonline.net
web: http://www.daves-stereos.com/
Collector and dealer wants stereoviews; wide range of interests, especially stereoviews by photographer L. Hansel who took views of PA (especially Pike County, PA) and New York.

Chris Perry
Doctor 3D
7470 Church St., Ste. A
Yucca Valley, CA 92284-3248
ph: 760-365-0475
fax: 760-365-0495
Can transfer stereoviews to 3D slides; also looking for views after 1900 and especially 1920 and after; no foreign travelogue of scenery; especially wants Hollywood, movie theaters, movie stars, World's Fair, magicians.

John Saddy
Jefferson Stereoptics
50 Foxborough Grove
London, Ontario N6K 4A8
Canada
ph: 519-641-4431
fax: 519-641-2899
e-mail: john.saddy.3d@sympatico.ca
web: http://www3.sympatico.ca/john.saddy.3d/home.htm
Specializes in stereoviews; buys, sells, and operates a specialized stereoview phone and mail auction; wants boxed sets, quality accumulations, View-Master and Tru-Vue; specializes in consignments.

Tim McIntyre
Tim McIntyre's Antique Photographs
137 Nile St.
Stratford, Ontario N5E 4E1
Canada
ph: 519-273-5360
fax: 519-273-7310
e-mail: timoni@orc.ca
web: http://www.orc.ca/~timoni/
Buys, sells, auctions 19th and early 20th century photographs, specializing in stereoviews, CDVs and cabinet cards.

Experts

Russell Norton
Photographic Antiques
P.O. Box 1070
New Haven, CT 06504-1070
ph: 203-562-7800
Buys, sells, trades, collects, specializes in stereo views; author of "Stereoviews Illustrated Vol. 1: 50 Early American;" $20 from author; full-size illustrations, great quality duotones.

John Waldsmith
Antique Graphics
302 Granger Rd.
Medina, OH 44256-8434
ph: 330-239-1944 or 330-239-2212
fax: 330-239-1944
e-mail: vansywalsy@aol.com
Wants stereoscopic views, View-Master reels, photographica; conducts mail/phone auctions on regular basis; also direct sales; author of "Stereo Views: An Illustrated History and Price Guide."

Chuck Reincke
Stereographica
2141 Sweet Briar Rd.
Tustin, CA 92780
ph: 714-832-8563
fax: 714-832-8563
Buy, sell stereo cards, View Master, Tru-Vue and viewers; prefer higher quality and more unusual items.

Misc. Services

Chris Perry
Doctor 3D
7470 Church St., Ste. A
Yucca Valley, CA 92284-3248
ph: 760-365-0475
fax: 760-365-0495
Can transfer a stereocard to an archival stereo slide.

Suppliers

David Starkman
Reel 3-D Enterprises, Inc.
P.O. Box 2368
Culver City, CA 90231-2368
ph: 310-837-2368
fax: 310-558-1653
e-mail: reel3d@aol.com
web: http://www.stereoscopy.com/reel3d
Offers a catalog with complete line of items for the modern 3-D enthusiast: books, stereo viewers, mounting supplies, etc.

Craig Daniels
StereoType
2006 Highway 101, #167
Florence, OR 97439-9723
ph: 541-997-8879
fax: 541-997-8879
e-mail: stereotype@winfinity.com
web: http://winfinity.com/streotype/3d.htm
Supplier/publisher/designer of custom direct-mailable stereo viewer packages, the conversion of ordinary pictures into stereo pairs (!), and general information on stereoscopic resources (old viewers).

Alaska

Collectors

Richard A. Wood
P.O. Box 22165
Juneau, AK 99802-2165
ph: 907-789-8450
fax: 907-789-8450
e-mail: akrare@alaska.net
web: http://www.alaska.net/~akrare/
Wants stereoviews of Alaska and Klondike; especially by Muybridge, Maynard, Brodeck, Haynes, etc.; also photographer L. Hensel views of PA (especially Pike County, PA) and NY.

STERLING SILVER FLATWARE

(see FLATWARE)

STEVENGRAPHS

Clubs/Associations

David L. Brown, Pres.
Stevengraph Collectors' Association
Newsletter: SCA Newsletter
2829 Arbutus Rd., #2103
Victoria, British Columbia V8N 5X5
Canada
ph: 250-477-9896
Approx. 140 members worldwide; focuses on the various jacquard woven silk works (Stevengraphs) by Thomas Stevens of Coventry, England but also has articles about other weavers.

Collectors

Frank J. Buono
P.O. Box 1535
Binghamton, NY 13902
ph: 607-724-4444 or 800-527-8893
fax: 607-723-1656
Wants to buy Stevengraphs woven silk pictures and postcards.

Dr. Mark Cottrill
Good Old Days, The
The Moat House
Lymm Hall
Lymm, Chesire WA13 0AJ
U.K.
ph: 01925-754097
Specializes in Stevengraphs, silk woven bookmarks and postcards; send for sales lists.

Dealers

Wayne R. Adams
RFD 1 Box 29
Canaan, NH 03741-9712
ph: 603-523-4276
fax: 603-523-4888
Buys and sells individual and complete collections of stevengraphs; looking for good quality; no bookmarks, please.

Experts

John High
415 E. 52nd St.
New York, NY 10022
ph: 212-758-1692
Advisor to "Warman's Antiques & Collectibles Price Guide."

Museums/Libraries

Paterson Museum
2 Market St.
Paterson, NJ 07501
ph: 973-881-3874

Herbert Art Gallery & Museum
U.K.
ph: 01203 832433
fax: 01203 832410
e-mail: coventry.museums@dial.pipex.com
web: http://www.coventry.org/coventrymuseums/
Has the largest collection of Stevengraphs in public hands; also has a very large silk ribbon collection.

STICK PINS

(see CLOTHING & ACCESSORIES, Vintage; CUFF LINKS; GEMS & JEWELRY, Stick Pins)

STILL PHOTOGRAPHS

(see MOVIE MEMORABILIA; PHOTOGRAPHS, Celebrity)

STOCK TICKERS

(see also TELEGRAPH ITEMS)

Collectors

Carl Ratner
550 Lamoka Ave.
Staten Island, NY 10312
ph: 718-317-1838
e-mail: artdeco@nyct.net
Buy, sell, trade antique stock tickers; interested in all types of machines, parts and accessories, but especially seeking Edison and Western Union tickers with glass domes.

Frank Guarino
P.O. Box 89
De Bary, FL 32713
ph: 407-668-5973

Charles Goodman
636 W. Grant Ave.
Charleston, IL 61920-3226
ph: 217-345-6771
Wants telegraph books, instruments, keys, sounders, relays, resonators, Western Union items; also old stock tickers by Western Union, Edison, Postal Telegraph or others, with or without domes also OK.

Jack Arnold
P.O. Box 2541
Reno, NV 89505-2541
ph: 775-786-0369 or 775-747-0311
fax: 702-787-8931
Wants Wall Street stock tickers (Western Union); also parts, stands, history, and repair books.

Dealers

Randy Donley
Donley's Wild West Town & Museum
8512 S. Union Rd.
Union, IL 60180-9661
ph: 815-923-9000
fax: 815-923-2253
web: http://www.wildwesttown.com/
Wants pre-1940 stock ticker tape machines made by Edison or Brunnell.

STOCKS & BONDS

(see also BANKING; CIVIL WAR ARTIFACTS, Confederate Bonds; COINS & CURRENCY, Paper Money; PAPER COLLECTIBLES; SCRIP; STOCK TICKERS)

Auction Services

R.M. Smythe & Company
26 Broadway, Ste. 271
New York, NY 10004-1701
ph: 212-943-1880 or 800-622-1880
fax: 212-908-4047
e-mail: info@rm-smythe.com
web: http://www.rm-smythe.com/
Conducts auctions of Colonial currency, Confederate currency, federal essay notes, proof vignettes, fractional and obsolete currency, stocks, bonds, coins and autographs.

Pierre Bonneau, Pres.
Stock Search International, Inc.
4761 W. Waterbuck Dr.
Tucson, AZ 85742
ph: 800-537-4523 or 520-579-5635
fax: 520-579-5639
e-mail: ssi@stocksearchintl.com
web: http://www.stocksearchintl.com/

Clubs/Associations

International Bond & Share Society
Newsletter: Scripophily
15 Dyatt Place
P.O. Box 430
Hackensack, NJ 07602-0430
ph: 201-489-2440
e-mail: IBSSociety@aol.com
web: http://www.scripophily.org/
Focus is to encourage and develop all aspects of scripophily, the collection and study of historic stocks, bonds and shares.

George Teas
Washington Historical Autograph & Certificate Organization (WHACO)
Newsletter: WHACO! News
P.O. Box 2428
Springfield, VA 22152-2428
ph: 703-866-0175
fax: 703-866-0175
e-mail: gteas@erols.com
web: http://www.whaco.com
Formed to bring collectors together to promote the hobby of antique stock and bond certificates and historical autographs; database of prices, featured articles, listings of dealers.

Piere Bonneau
Old Certificates Collector's Club
Newsletter: OCCC Newsletter
4761 W. Waterbuck Dr.
Tucson, AZ 85742
ph: 800-537-4523 or 520-579-5635
fax: 520-579-5639
e-mail: ssi@stocksearchintl.com
web: http://www.stocksearchintl.com/

Collectors

Fred Herrigel
P.O. Box 599
Millburn, NJ 07041-0599
Wants to buy obsolete stock certificates and pre-1920 postcard collections.

Richard Urmston
Centennial Documents
P.O. Box 5262
Clinton, NJ 08809-0262
ph: 908-703-6009
fax: 908-730-9566
e-mail: centdocs@postoffice.ptd.net
Wants stocks & bonds; send photocopy of items for sale; issues periodic catalog of items for sale.

Bob Schell
6804 Jeremiah Ct.
Fairfax, VA 22039
Wants obsolete and antique stocks and bonds, especially those with attractive artwork; also wants fancy old bill heads, invoices and stationary.

Ed London
Parke Lloyds International, Inc.
9408 NW 70 St.
Fort Lauderdale, FL 33321-3002
ph: 954-724-4274 or 954-726-4107
Wants to buy stocks & bonds, U.S. and foreign.

Dealers

Paul Longo
Paul Longo Americana
P.O. Box 5510
Gloucester, MA 01930-0007
ph: 978-525-2290
Wants pre-1910 stocks and bonds; any amount.

George H. La Barre
La Barre Galleries
P.O. Box 746
Hollis, NH 03049
ph: 603-882-2411
fax: 603-882-4979
e-mail: collect@glabarre.com
web: http://www.glabarre.com/
Specializes in collectible stocks and bonds, autographs, paper money; also deals with other areas of Americana; retail and wholesale to other dealers including large marketing companies; inventory includes over 5.7 million pieces in stock.

Scott J. Winslow
Scott J. Winslow Associates, Inc.
P.O. Box 10240
Nashua, NH 03110-0240
ph: 603-881-4071 or 800-225-6233
fax: 603-472-8773
Buys and sells stocks certificates, bonds and historical autographs; also conducts mail bid auctions of same.

Robert F. Kluge
American Vignettes
P.O. Box 155
Roselle Park, NJ 07204-0155
ph: 908-241-4209
fax: 908-241-4209

R.M. Smythe & Company
26 Broadway, Ste. 271
New York, NY 10004-1701
ph: 212-943-1880 or 800-622-1880
fax: 212-908-4047
e-mail: info@rm-smythe.com
web: http://www.rm-smythe.com/

D & D Scripophily International, Ltd.
P.O. Box 580063
Flushing, NY 11358
ph: 718-358-3447 or 800-941-0098
fax: 718-358-2849
Wants holed, cancelled, obsolete stock certificates.

Frank Hammelbacher
P.O. Box 660077
Flushing, NY 11366-0077
ph: 718-380-4009
fax: 718-380-9793
e-mail: morrico@compuserve.com
Deals in ephemera of all kinds, especially old stocks and bonds and Wild West posters.

Nick Johnson
1 Old Country Rd., Ste 300
Carle Place, NY 11514-1806
ph: 516-663-0606
fax: 516-663-0654
Dealer in 19th and 20th century stocks and bonds; certificate catalog is published 6 times a year for $2.35 which is refundable with first order.

Haley & Hannelore Garrison
Antique Stocks & Bonds
Drawer JH
Williamsburg, VA 23187-3632
ph: 800-451-4504 or 757-220-3838
fax: 757-220-0294
web: http://www.tiac.net/users/haley/

Barry Smith
P.O. Box 38306
Greensboro, NC 27438-8306
ph: 336-288-4375
fax: 336-282-6784
e-mail: bsmith1707@aol.com
Buys and sells stock certificates: railroad, sports, oil, financial, mining, etc.

David M. Beach
Paper Americana
P.O. Box 2026
Goldenrod, FL 32733-2026
ph: 407-657-7403
fax: 407-657-6382
e-mail: dbeach@ao.net
Buys and sells antique US stocks and bonds; wants to buy stocks signed by Jay Gould, James Fisk, Jr., Comm. Vanderbilt, Daniel Drew, Jay Cooke, Cyrus Field, Hetty Green and other Robber Barons.

Eric Drum
Collectible Stocks & Bonds
P.O. Box 266
Perrysburg, OH 43552
ph: 419-868-6539
fax: 419-868-6539
e-mail: oldstox@aol.com
web: http://www.oldstocks.com/
Collector, dealer buys and sells old stock certificates; one of the leaders in the hobby of scripophily, collecting stock and bonds; web site has online resource and catalog of offerings.

Collectors Gallery, Inc.
1530 Boise Ave., Ste. 109
Loveland, CO 80538
ph: 970-667-0651
e-mail: lommerse@cgi-stocks.com
web: http://www.ezlink.com/~lommerse/

Georgia Fox
Foxes' Den Antiques
P.O. Box 846
Sutter Creek, CA 95685-0846
ph: 209-267-0774
Wants old stocks & bonds, especially relating to gold mining in California or Nevada.

Tom Sluszkiewicz
ATS Numismatics
P.O. Box 54521
Burnaby, British Columbia V5E 4J6
Canada
e-mail: ats@atsnotes.com
web: http://www.atsnotes.com
Buys and sells numismatic world banknotes, local and private paper money, collectibles bonds and stock certificates.

Experts

Warren Anderson
America West Archives
P.O. Box 100
Cedar City, UT 84721-0100
ph: 435-586-9497 or 435-586-7323
e-mail: awa@netutah.com
web: http://
www.americawestarchives.com/
Buys and sells issued American stocks & bonds 1840-1930; especially mining, energy, transportation; offers mail order catalog; author of "Owning Western History."

Ken Prag
Ken Prag Paper Americana
P.O. Box 14817
San Francisco, CA 94114-0817
ph: 415-586-9386
e-mail: kprag@planeteria.net
Eager to buy old stocks and bonds, quality picture postcards, western stereoviews, old timetables and brochures, etc.

Misc. Services

Warren Anderson
America West Archives
P.O. Box 100
Cedar City, UT 84721-0100
ph: 435-586-9497 or 435-586-7323
e-mail: awa@netutah.com
web: http://
www.americawestarchives.com/
A professional stock tracer who researches stock certificates and bonds to determine whether they have value on the current stock market or to a collector of worthless securities; author of "Owning Western History."

Pierre Bonneau, Pres.
Stock Search International, Inc.
4761 W. Waterbuck Dr.
Tucson, AZ 85742
ph: 800-537-4523 or 520-579-5635
fax: 520-579-5639
e-mail: ssi@stocksearchintl.com
web: http://www.stocksearchintl.com/
Researches the background of companies no longer listed on any exchanges & help clients recover funds from what they think are worthless stocks; also ascertain the value of stocks as collectibles; research fee is $85.

Periodicals

Pat DuChene, PR
Krause Publications
Newspaper: Bank Note Reporter
700 E. State St.
Iola, WI 54990-0001
ph: 715-445-2214
fax: 715-445-4087
e-mail: info@krause.com
web: http://www.krause.com/
Monthly news source and marketplace

for collectors of U.S. and world paper money, notes, checks and related fiscal paper.

Financial History

Museums/Libraries

Anne Keane
Museum of American Financial History
Magazine: Financial History
15 Dyatt Place
P.O. Box 430
Hackensack, NJ 07602-0430
ph: 201-489-2440
e-mail: IBSSociety@aol.com
web: http://www.scripophily.org/
Dedicated to the development of the US capital markets and the people who made them famous; mission is to collect/preserve/display historical financial artifacts and to use them as an educational resource for schools & the public.

Mining Related

Dealers

Douglas McDonald
Gypsyfoot Enterprises, Inc.
P.O. Box 5833
Helena, MT 59604-5833
ph: 406-449-8076
fax: 406-443-8514
Buying all pre-1933 mining stocks; please send photocopies for offer.

Experts

Chuck Voelker
844 Fairground St.
Plymouth, MI 48170
ph: 734-451-5911
e-mail: usfmck3s@ibmmail.com
Collector and researcher of 19th and early 20th century mining stock certificates, especially Michigan related.

STONE

(see MARBLE & STONE)

STONE CARVINGS

(see SCULPTURES)

STOVES

(see also CAST IRON ITEMS; KITCHEN COLLECTIBLES; RANGES)

Clubs/Associations

Macy Stern
Antique Stove Association
Newsletter: Stove Parts Needed Newsletter
5515 Almeda Rd.
Houston, TX 77004-7443
ph: 713-521-0934 or 713-528-1297
fax: 713-521-0889
For those interested in antique stoves and related items; you must join to receive the benefits which are for members only.

Collectors

N.W. Neill, Jr.
Glascock Stove Co.
P.O. Box 38
Ennice, NC 28623-0038
fax: 336-657-8084
e-mail: saddlemtn@skybest.com
Historian wants cook stoves, heaters, etc. (complete or parts) made by the Glascock Stove Co. of Greensboro, NC; models include Carolina Beauty, Victor, Charter, Giant, Carolina Hot Blast, Blue Ridge, Plymouth, etc.

Dealers

Bob Brunelle
Brunelle Ent. Inc.
203 Union Rd.
Wales, MA 01081
ph: 413-245-7396
e-mail: Bob@oldstoves.com
web: http://www.oldstoves.com/
Collector and dealer wants to buy pre-1920 fancy antique stoves with tiles or mica windows, or ornate castings.

Erickson's Antique Stoves, Inc.
P.O. Box 2275
At the Depot
Littleton, MA 01460
ph: 978-486-3589
Antique gas coal and wood stoves and ranges; bought, sold, restored.

Mike Trainor
Mike's Stove Works
98 Webster St.
Haverhill, MA 01830-4123
ph: 978-373-0767
Buys, collects, sells and restores all types of coal, gas and wood stoves; old or new.

Barnstable Stove Shop
P.O. Box 472
West Barnstable, MA 02668
ph: 508-362-9913
Buys, sells and restores antique wood, coal and gas stoves; large parts inventory; 20 years in business; expert restoration work.

Edward Semmelroth
Antique Stoves
415 Fleming Rd.
Tekonsha, MI 49092
ph: 517-278-2214
e-mail: sales@antiquestoves.com
web: http://www.antiquestoves.com
Appraises, buys, sells, restores antique stoves and ranges, 1700s to 1950; museum quality restorations; over 200 in stock; wood, coal, gas; also cookware, custom plating.

Keokuk Stove Works
906 E. Co. Road 1120
Hamilton, IL 62341
ph: 212-847-2107
e-mail: sales@keokukstoveworks.com
web: http://www.keokukstoveworks.com
Buys and sells antique stoves and ranges.

Macy Stern
Macy's Texas Stove Works
5515 Almeda Rd.
Houston, TX 77004-7443
ph: 713-521-0934 or 713-528-1297
fax: 713-521-0889
Buys, sells, brokers, repairs, and restores old ranges; also sells parts and publishes "Classic Ranges" newspaper.

Ron Schaffer
Classic Stoves Emporium
480 San Juan St.
P.O. Box 153
Pagosa Springs, CO 81147
ph: 970-264-2710
Buys, sells and restores antique stoves; fabricates replacement parts as needed.

Experts

Clifford Boram
421 N. Main St.
Monticello, IN 47960
ph: 219-583-6465
Author of "How to Get Parts Cast for Your Antique Stove"; will answer questions, but only by phone. No mail inquiries, please; photocopies from 2000-volume archive of stove manufacturers' literature 1860-1935,

Periodicals

Macy Stern
Macy's Texas Stove Works
Newspaper: Classic Ranges
5515 Almeda Rd.
Houston, TX 77004-7443
ph: 713-521-0934 or 713-528-1297
fax: 713-521-0889
The only newsletter for classic range owners and buyers; ranges/ovens and stoves for sale, ranges wanted to buy, parts for sale, restoration services, articles, old advertisements, etc.

Art Wallace
Newsletter: Antique Stove Exchange, The
2729 SW 330th
Federal Way, WA 98023

Repair Services

Beatrice Bryant
Bryant Stove Works & Music Inc.
RR 2 Rich Rd.
P.O. Box 2048
Thorndike, ME 04986
ph: 207-568-3665
fax: 207-568-3666
Large collection on display; also sells parts and restores antique (1780s-1940s) cook stoves, parlor stoves, and gas stoves. In addition, restores player pianos.

Edward Semmelroth
Antique Stoves
415 Fleming Rd.
Tekonsha, MI 49092
ph: 517-278-2214
e-mail: sales@antiquestoves.com
web: http://www.antiquestoves.com
Appraises, buys, sells, restores antique stoves and ranges, 1700s to 1950; museum quality restorations; over 200 in stock; wood, coal, gas; also cookware, custom plating.

Tomahawk Foundry, Inc.
2337 29th St.
Rice Lake, WI 54868
ph: 715-234-4498
Makes replacement parts for cast iron stoves.

Tom Lawson
Buckeye Appliance
714 W. Fremont
Stockton, CA 95203-2702
ph: 209-464-9643
Specializes in the sales, parts and restoration of antique gas stoves; also sells kitchen collectibles, Hoosiers, 1950s chrome dinettes, and porcelain-top tables.

Majolica

Experts

Laura Sussi
37 via Garzarolli
Gorizia, 34170
Italy
ph: +39-0481-531343
fax: +39-0481-531343
e-mail: sagittarion@geocities.com
web: http://www.geocities.com/Paris/LeftBank/2153/
Specializes in majolica stoves (1750 to 1920) made during the former Austro-Hungarian Emperor; expert and collector wants to trade stoves and swap experiences in restoring.

Salesman Samples & Toys

Collectors

Andrew B. Golbert
RR 1 Box 1820
North Ferrisburg, VT 05473
ph: 802-453-2525
Wants to buy children's cast iron toy stoves and salesmen's sample stoves and furnaces.

Sally Swanson
3302 West 11th St.
Erie, PA 16505-3710
ph: 814-838-1866
Wants information on all cast iron toy stoves and salesman samples.

Karen Mullins
5679 Deerfield Rd.
Orlando, FL 32808-2802
ph: 407-297-9218
Wants to buy toy or salesman sample iron stoves, parts, cookware; also wants toy catalogs that have toy stoves listed.

Judy Owen, ISA
Antique Appraisers - Grand Traverse
10332 Stoneybeach Pointe
Traverse City, MI 49686-8584
ph: 231-946-2534
fax: 231-946-2573
e-mail: judy@antiqueappraisers.com
web: http://www.antiqueappraisers.com/
Wants to buy miniature stoves.

Ralph C. Hylton
245 Hughes Ford Rd.
Sullivan, MO 63080-1924
ph: 573-468-8418
Wants to buy salesman samples and toy stoves; complete or in parts; also wants small cookware.

Marilyn Wren
P.O. Box 3025
Blaine, WA 98231-3025

Experts

Ed Hullet
5200 N. Lorraine
Hutchinson, KS 67502-2727
ph: 316-662-9381
Buys, sells, restores, and appraises exclusively salesmen's sample stoves.

STREETCAR LINE COLLECTIBLES

(see also RAILROAD COLLECTIBLES)

Clubs/Associations

William M. Shapotkin, Mem.
Central Electric Railfans' Association
Newsletter: Trolley Sparks
P.O. Box 503
Chicago, IL 60690
ph: 312-346-3723
Interested in history and equipment of electric railroading: urban, rapid transit, suburban, trunk line and industrial electric railways.

Collectors

Nestle's Railroadiana
RD 2, Box 105
Greenwich, NY 12834-9425
ph: 518-692-2867
Buys and sells all sorts of railroadiana and trolley memorabilia: timetables, guides, maps, advertising info., menus, old books and magazines, etc.

Seth Bramson
330 N.E. 96th St.
Miami, FL 33138-2718
ph: 305-757-1016
fax: 305-895-8178
Buys railroad and trolleyana; postage paid on approvals.

Museums/Libraries

Seashore Trolley Museum
P.O. Box A
Kennebunkport, ME 04046-1690
ph: 207-967-2800
fax: 207-967-0867
e-mail: carshop@gwi.net
web: http://www.trolleymuseum.org/

Baltimore Streetcar Museum
1905 Falls Road
P.O. Box 4881
Baltimore, MD 21211
ph: 410-547-0264
e-mail: samsmeatm@aol.com
web: http://baltimoremd.com/streetcar/

STRING HOLDERS

Collectors

Bobbie & Alan Bryson
1 St. Eleanoras Ln.
Tuckahoe, NY 10707-1307
ph: 914-779-1405
e-mail: napkindoll@aol.com
Wants string holders; Bobbie is co-author of the pictorial reference guide "Collectibles For The Kitchen, Bath & Beyond" (Antique Trader Books) which has an entire chapter on string holders with over 400 photos and vintage ads.

Emma Kretchek
5726 Terrace Park Dr.
Dayton, OH 45429-6048
ph: 937-434-9126

Lewis Jones
665 Wirtz Rd.
Crown Point, IN 46307
ph: 219-663-7865
Wants to buy chalk or ceramic string holders; would also like to communicate with other collectors.

Al Little
151 Highway 173
Antioch, IL 60002
ph: 847-395-7752
fax: 847-395-7703
Buy, sells and trades string holders; single pieces or entire collections.

Dealers

John & Nancy Smith
American Sampler
P.O. Box 371
Barnesville, MD 20838-0371
ph: 301-972-6250
Wants ceramic, chalk, cast iron string holders.

Experts

Charles Reynolds
Reynolds Toys
2836 Monroe St.
Falls Church, VA 22042-2007
ph: 703-533-1322
e-mail: reynoldstoys@erols.com
web: http://www.reynoldstoys.com
Wants string holders made of metal, glass or wood; not interested in chalk or china types.

STRIPTEASE

Clubs/Associations

Exotic World Burlesque Hall of Fame & Nostalgia Museum
29053 Wild Road
Helendale, CA 92342
ph: 760-243-5261
web: http://aeve.com/exoticworld/

Collectors

Charles McCaghy
221 Williams St.
Bowling Green, OH 43402
ph: 419-352-7211
e-mail: cmccagh@bgnet.bgsu.edu
web: http://ernie.bgsu.edu/~cmccagh/
Purchases paper items related to stripping in US and Canada: burlesque theaters, carnivals, clubs; belly dancing, carnival girl shows, shake dancing, striptease, table dancing; photos, publications, postcards, programs.

Museums/Libraries

Burlesque Hall of Fame & Historical Museum
29053 Wild Road
Helendale, CA 92342
ph: 760-243-5261
web: http://aeve.com/exoticworld/

STUFFED TOYS

(see STEIFF; TEDDY BEARS; TOYS, Plush)

SUBWAY ITEMS

Museums/Libraries

New York Transit Museum
130 Livingston Street, 9th Floor, Box E
Brooklyn, NY 11201
ph: 718-694-1068 or 718-243-8601
fax: 718-722-4316
web: http://www.mta.nyc.ny.us/museum/index.html
Features displays, exhibits, archive information regarding the New York Subway System.

SUGAR PACKETS

Clubs/Associations

Norma Wordsworth
U.K. Sucrologitsts Club
U.K.
web: http://web.ukonline.co.uk/members/email.ukscsugar/
Collectors of the little packets of sugar you get when you order tea or coffee in a cafe or restaurant.

Collectors

Phillip Miller
Sugar Pack Collector's Page, The
e-mail: phillip@iquest.net
web: http://members.iquest.net/~phillip/

Mitzt Geiser
15601 Burkhart Rd.
Orrville, OH 44667-9618
ph: 330-682-7486

SUGAR SHAKERS

Collectors

Robert A. Hendel
1385 York Ave. #16B
New York, NY 10021
ph: 212-772-9070 or 212-450-4733
fax: 212-450-5521
Wants large and small collections; very interested in "diner" shakers.

Dealers

Glenda Ridgway
P.O. Box 231
Anna, IL 62906
ph: 618-833-7971

SUPER BOWL RINGS

(see SPORTS COLLECTIBLES, Jewelry)

SUPER HEROES

(see also COMIC BOOKS; POPULAR CULTURE; PREMIUMS; SCIENCE FICTION; TOYS, Super Hero)

Dealers

John Kachmar
Techno-Fantasy Traders
779 Carissa Dr.
West Palm Beach, FL 33411-3412
ph: 561-798-5978
fax: 561-798-5978

Periodicals

Antique Trader Publications, Inc.
Newspaper: Toy Trader
P.O. Box 1050
Dubuque, IA 52004-1050
ph: 800-334-7165 or 800-482-4155
fax: 800-531-0880
e-mail: jmkoenig@execpc.com
web: http://www.collect.com/toytrader
Monthly newspaper with information on how to buy, sell and trade all types of toys; market trends, the latest prices, "how-to" columns, listings of toy clubs and upcoming toy shows and auctions; also full of buy and sell ads.

Batman

Clubs/Associations

Fred Carini
Captain Action Society of Pittsburgh
Newsletter: Capt. Action News
516 Cubbage St.
Carnegie, PA 15106
ph: 412-276-6084
All Capt. Action club! Trading, buying, selling all Capt. Action items.

Don Kyle
Batman TV Series Fan Club
Newsletter: Batman TV Series Fan Club Newsletter
P.O. Box 107
Venice, CA 90294-0107
ph: 310-226-2883
fax: 323-417-4937
e-mail: sndtrx@earthlink.net
web: http://www.batfanclub.com/
Newsletter published quarterly averages 20-30 pages with photos; convention and cast updates; "Bat" related merchandise; also buys and sells Batman toys, paper, film, etc.; also includes Green Hornet as it was a crossover with Batman.

Collectors

David J. Anderson
5192 Dawes Ave.
Alexandria, VA 22311-1402
ph: 703-671-7422
fax: 703-578-1222
e-mail: dja@erols.com
Aggressively seeks Batman and Superman items.

Captain Midnight

Clubs/Associations

John Samorajczyk
Air Heroes Fan Club
19205 Seneca Ridge Court
Gaithersburg, MD 20879-3135
ph: 301-869-1755
This club honors Captain Midnight.

Phantom

Collectors

Robert J. Griffin
P.O. Box 76
Mattawan, MI 49071
ph: 616-387-3024
e-mail: griffinr@wmich.edu
Wants to buy memorabilia relating to The Phantom.

Rocketeer

Clubs/Associations

John Datz
Rocketeer Fan Club
Newsletter: Rocketeer Newsletter
10 Halick Ct.
East Brunswick, NJ 08816-1373

Superman

Collectors

David J. Anderson
5192 Dawes Ave.
Alexandria, VA 22311-1402
ph: 703-671-7422
fax: 703-578-1222
e-mail: dja@erols.com
Aggressively seeks Batman and Superman items.

Dealers

Danny Fuchs
209-80 18th Ave., #4K
Bayside, NY 11360-1424
ph: 718-225-9030
fax: 718-225-3688
e-mail: superdf62@aol.com
Buys and sells all types of pre-1960 Superman collectibles: toys, games, figurines, puzzles, novelties, premiums, etc. rare or unusual; also buying unusual/interesting collectibles from other comic book characters.

Experts

Danny Fuchs
209-80 18th Ave., #4K
Bayside, NY 11360-1424
ph: 718-225-9030
fax: 718-225-3688
e-mail: superdf62@aol.com
"America's foremost Superman Collector"; co-author of "The Adventures of Superman Collecting."

Periodicals

Jim Nolt
Newsletter: Adventures Continue, The
1935 Fruistville Pike, #105
Lancaster, PA 17601
ph: 717-560-6380
fax: 717-560-6380
e-mail: jimnolt@redrose.net
web: http://www.jimnoltenterprises.com/
Maintains a George Reeves (Superman) homepage on the world wide web.

SUPPLIERS

(see ANTIQUES DEALERS & COLLECTORS; CLOCKS; FIREARMS; KNIVES; MODELS; REPAIR/RESTORATION/ CONSERVATION; STAMP COLLECTING; TELEPHONES and other individual categories)

SURVEYING INSTRUMENTS

(see also INSTRUMENTS & DEVICES, Scientific)

Collectors

Stephen Buczko
27 Surrey Road
Salem, MA 01970
ph: 978-744-4683
Wants to buy surveying instruments.

Robert Miller
RD 2 Box 176
New Alexandria, PA 15670
Wants surveying instruments, catalogs, and related items.

Ron Kiser
70 Woodfin Pl. #214
Asheville, NC 28801
ph: 828-689-4845 or 828-258-1380
Wants to buy antique brass surveying instruments: transits, levels, alidades, plane tables, tripods, rods, chains, surveyor's compasses, pocket compasses, etc.

Michael S. Manier
100 E. Walnut
P.O. Box 110
Houston, MO 65483-0110
ph: 417-967-2777 or 417-962-5221
fax: 417-967-3026
Wants to buy compasses (both brass and wooden), wire-link measuring chains, theodolites, transits, levels, octants, sextants, quadrants, solar devices, calculating devices, and drawing instruments.

Paul H. Hayashi, PE
18 Tarabrook Dr.
Orinda, CA 94563-3121
ph: 925-254-5074 or 925-253-1038
fax: 925-253-0592
Buys high precision theodolites, levels, solar compasses, mining surveying instruments, solar transits, U.S. Coast & Geodetic instruments.

D. Sanders
P.O. Box 1980
Granite Falls, WA 98252
ph: 360-691-5063
Wants old surveying instruments: transits, compasses, unusual plumb bobs.

Dealers

Al & Bobbie Roberts
Rational Past, The
221 Oceano Dr.
Los Angeles, CA 90049-4123
ph: 310-476-6277
fax: 310-476-6278
e-mail: rational_past@mindspring.com
Organizer of West Coast Scientific & Technical Antique and Collectible Shows (Los Angeles in the winter and San Francisco are in late summer.)

Experts

Dale R. Beeks
Perceptions Scientifica
P.O. Box 117
Mount Vernon, IA 52314-0117
ph: 800-880-5178 or 319-895-0506
e-mail: dbeeksci@aol.com
Expert, appraiser, wants pre-1900 compasses, transits, unusual instruments, surveying ephemera; offers museum services.

SWANKYSWIGS

(see also GLASSES, Drinking)

Clubs/Associations

M. Fountain
Swankyswigs Unlimited
201 Alvena
Wichita, KS 67203
ph: 316-943-1925
e-mail: derby444@aol.com

Collectors

M.D. Fountain
201 Alvena
Wichita, KS 67203
ph: 316-943-1925
e-mail: derby444@aol.com
Avid collector with over 1500; Swankyswigs were decorated glasses originally filled with Kraft Cheese Spreads.

Gary Kane
15006 Brookpoint
Houston, TX 77062
ph: 281-488-1537
Wants to buy or trade swankyswigs with lids or labels, special issues, with advertisements.

Experts

Ian Warner
P.O. Box 93022
Brampton, Ontario LGY 4V8
Canada
ph: 905-453-9074
Specializing in Wade porcelain and swankyswigs.

SWAROVSKI

(see COLLECTIBLES [MODERN], Crystal [Swarovski])

SWORDS

(see also ARMS & ARMOR; ARMS & ARMOR, Japanese [Swords]; BAYONETS; CIVIL WAR ARTIFACTS; EDGED WEAPONS; MILITARIA; NAZI ITEMS)

Appraisers

Thomas Winter
817 Patton
Springfield, IL 62702-2430
ph: 217-523-8729
Collector/appraiser of swords; wants to buy quality Japanese swords & high quality or rare German and U.S. swords, daggers, fighting knives & any Samurai related items such as armor, matchlocks, etc.; send SASE for free evaluation.

Clubs/Associations

Leonard J. Garigliano
Association of American Sword Collectors, The
P.O. Box 288
Parsonsburg, MD 21849-0288
e-mail: lgarswds@shore.intercom.net

Dealers

Fred Coluzzi
Frederick's Swords
6919 Westview Dr.
Oak Forest, IL 60452-1566
ph: 708-687-3647
Buys and sells antique swords and daggers from all countries and all periods; issues 2 to 3 major catalogs per year: Japanese, US, German, Turkish, Moro, Indonesian, Philippine, Chinese.

Robert Miller
LionGate Arms & Armour
141 W. Moore Ave.
Gilbert, AZ 85233-1539
ph: 602-926-3962
e-mail: Hussar@earthlink.net
web: http://www.liongate-armsandarmour.com
Dealer and collector of antique edged weapons, specializing in Victorian and pre-Victorian weapons of England, France and Scotland.

Internet Resources

Kelley's Military Antiques
P.O. Box 1442
San Martin, CA 95046
e-mail: suggestions@militaryantiques.com
web: http://www.garlic.com/~kelley/swordid.htm
Great online sword resource: history, terminology, American, Japanese, European, detecting a reproduction.

Museums/Libraries

Bruce M. Moseley, Cur.
Fort Ticonderoga Museum
Newsletter: Bulletin of the Fort Ticonderoga Museum
P.O. Box 390
Ticonderoga, NY 12883
ph: 518-585-2821
fax: 518-585-2210
web: http://www.neinfo.net/new_england/new_york/attractions/fort-ticonderoga/
10,000 volume research library specializing in 19th century military history and the history of the Champlain Valley; museum depicts history of the area and the campaigns during the 7 Year War and the Revolutionary War.

Repair Services

Tom Nardi
Civil War Sword Rewrapping
P.O. Box 311
Windsor, CA 95492
ph: 707-838-1820
e-mail: nardi@cds1.net
web: http://www.garlic.com/~kelley/restoration.htm
Rewraps any Civil War of later sword just like the originals; work in most cases looks original; call only 10 am to 6 pm PST only.

Repro. Sources

Century International Arms Inc.
P.O. Box 714
Saint Albans, VT 05478
ph: 802-527-1252
fax: 802-527-0470
Reproduction of the finest military and edged weapons: US artillery saber, US Naval officer's sword, food officer sword, Souave bayonet, trooper sword, US Cavalry saber, Scottish sword, AK74 bayonet, etc.

Nazi

Collectors

K. Wiley
719 Baldwin SE
Grand Rapids, MI 49503-4470
ph: 616-451-8410
e-mail: quillion1@aol.com
Wants Japanese swords, daggers, sword parts. Also German 3rd Reich daggers, swords, bayonets. References available.

Wilkinson

Clubs/Associations

Wilkinson Collectors Society
c/o Wilkinson Sword Limited, Sword Centre
19/21 Brunel Road
London, W3 7UH
U.K.
ph: +44 181 749 2304
e-mail: comments@wilkinson-swords.com
web: http://www.wilkinson-swords.com/collectors.html
Members receive free access to gun and sword records, historical advisory service, visits to the Sword Centre, advance information on new projects, preferential number allocation on limited editions; a company-sponsored club.

Here are some tips when contacting someone listed in this book:

■ When requesting information about a particular item, include a description (material, dimensions, maker's mark, model number, etc.) and a photo, sketch, or photocopy of the item in question.

■ Always ask if there are charges for samples or for the services requested.

■ When writing, please be sure to include a Large (#10 business size) Self-Addressed and Stamped Envelope (LSASE) if requesting a reply or the return of photographs.

■ Never call collect unless otherwise directed. When calling, be considerate of time zone differences and always ask if the party you are calling has time to talk. When leaving an answering machine message, always instruct the party to call you back collect.

T

TABLEWARE

(see also CERAMICS; DINNERWARE; FLATWARE; GLASS, Elegant; GLASS, Crystal)

Man./Prod./Dist.

225 Fifth Avenue - The International Showcase
225 Fifth Ave.
New York, NY 10010
ph: 212-685-6377 or 800-235-3512
fax: 212-864-3203
Showplace for purveyors specializing in the sale of new giftware & decorative accessories; also tableware.

New York Merchandise Mart
41 Madison Ave.
New York, NY 10010
ph: 212-686-1203
fax: 212-779-7105
web: http://www.41madison.com/
Showplace for purveyors of new tableware including gifts, glassware, ceramicware, silverware and decorative accessories; sells exclusively to the trade.

Periodicals

Magazine: Gifts & Decorative Accessories
345 Hudson St., 4th Floor
New York, NY 10014
ph: 212-519-7200
fax: 212-519-7431
Trade magazine for new gifts, decorative accessories, collectibles, stationery, gift baskets, and tabletop wares; buyer's resource directory guide available with subscription.

Matching Services For

(see DINNERWARE; FLATWARE; GLASS, Elegant; GLASS, Crystal)

TARGET SHOOTING MEMORABILIA

(see also SPORTING COLLECTIBLES; TARGETS, Shooting Gallery; TRAPSHOOTING)

Clubs/Associations

Rudi Prusok
American Single Shot Rifle Association
Journal: American Single Shot Rifle News
625 Pine St.
Marquette, MI 49855-3723
ph: 906-225-1828
fax: 906-227-1819
Organization dedicated to the shooting and collecting of single shot rifles from the turn of the century: German Schuetzen, buffalo, benchrest, and long range traditions; also interested in related memorabilia; free journal sample.

Collectors

Dr. Anthony Sapienza
East 106 Ridgewood Ave.
Paramus, NJ 07652
ph: 201-262-6310
fax: 201-262-3990
e-mail: siringo45@aol.com
Serious collector wants anything related to trick or exhibition shooting (Annie Oakley, Doc Carver, Gus Peret, etc.); wants posters, pinbacks, glass target balls, souvenir targets; plus shot items such as coins, playing or business cards.

David L. Hartline
P.O. Box 775
Columbus, OH 43085-0775
Wants to buy all types of pre-1920 shooting medals, badges and trophies for marksmanship; will buy medals whether complete or not; prefers items that are engraved to winners; will answer all letters.

Rifle

Collectors

Allen Hallock
P.O. Box 7071
Corte Madera, CA 94976-7071
ph: 415-924-1967
e-mail: arh@earthlink.net
Wants American, German, Swiss "Schuetzen" memorabilia circa 1865-1915: medals, trophies, souvenirs, targets, photographs, match programs, posters, score books, steins, single-shot target rifles; anything "Schuetzen"; no military.

Target Balls

Collectors

Art Snyder
110 White Oak Dr.
Butler, PA 16001-3446
ph: 724-287-0278
Buys/sells/trades antique glass target balls, ball traps or throwers, glass house or sporting ads pertaining to same; anything related.

Ralph Finch
34007 Hillside Ct.
Farmington, MI 48335-2513
Wants glass target balls.

TARGETS

Shooting Gallery

(see also CAST IRON ITEMS; TARGET SHOOTING MEMORABILIA)

Experts

Richard Tucker
Argyle Antiques
P.O. Box 262
Argyle, TX 76226-0262
ph: 940-464-3752
fax: 940-464-7293
e-mail: lead1234@gte.net
Buys and sells figural cast iron items including shooting targets; no repros. or repaired items wanted; also wants catalogs, photographs and other shooting gallery memorabilia

TATTOO RELATED ITEMS

Museums/Libraries

Lyle Tuttle
Tattoo Art Museum, The
210 Clara Ave.
Ukiah, CA 95482
ph: 707-462-4406
fax: 707-462-4433
e-mail: lyletutt@pacific.net
web: http://lyletuttle.com/flash.htm
Largest collection of tattoo art and related antiques & collectibles; buys/sells machines, designs, artifacts, photos, paintings, etc.; the above is mailing address, studio is at 841 Columbus Ave., San Francisco, CA 94133, 415-775-4991.

TAXI RELATED COLLECTIBLES

Collectors

Nathan Willensky
Taxi Toys & Memorabilia
5 East 22nd St. #24C
New York, NY 10010-5329
ph: 212-982-2156
fax: 212-995-1065
e-mail: taxitoys@aol.com
Buy and trades anything Taxi - toys and memorabilia; Taxis only.

Henry Winningham
3205 S. Morgan St.
Chicago, IL 60608-6609
ph: 773-927-3796
Wants anything pre-1950 that's related to the Taxi industry.

TAXIDERMY

(see ANIMAL TROPHIES)

TEA RELATED COLLECTIBLES

(see also CERAMICS; KITCHEN COLLECTIBLES; ORIENTALIA, Japanese Items; SILVER)

Dealers

Alvin & Rose Harper
Harpers Antiques & Interiors
236 Second St.
Lewes, DE 19958-1326
ph: 302-645-9750
Buys and sells 19th and early 20th century tea accessories such as Staffordshire and ironstone teapots, sterling and plate silver, salesmen pottery samples, children's tea sets and furniture.

Tea Strainers

Dealers

Carol Payne
Carol's Antique Gallery
14455 Big Basin Way
Saratoga, CA 95070-6008
ph: 408-867-7055
Wants to buy silver and silverplated tea strainers, and other tea items such as tea caddies, tea caddy scoops, tea infusers, and toast racks; nothing dented, please.

Teapots

Experts

Geraud Schultz
Antique Gallery, The
8523 Germantown Ave.
Philadelphia, PA 19118
ph: 215-248-1700
fax: 215-247-8411
Buys, sells and specializes in tea pots: 18th through 20th century - English, American, French, Chinese; teapots and cadagans porcelain and creamware.

Tina M. Carter
882 South Mollison Ave.
El Cajon, CA 92020
ph: 619-440-5043
Author of "Teapots" - available from the author.

Museums/Libraries

Veilleuse-Theieres Collection
309 College Street
Trenton, TN 38382
ph: 901-855-2014
e-mail: webmaster@wtnnet.com
web: http://www.gibsoncountynet.com/arts-culture/default.html
Collection of 525 European "Veilleuse-Theieres" (French for "night-light teapots") sickroom and nursery teapots used also as night lights and for the mixture of medications.

Teapots (Cardew)

Clubs/Associations

Cardew Collectors' Club
1345 Campus Pkwy.
Neptune, NJ 07753
ph: 732-751-0500
web: http://www.cardewdesign.com/Pages/New2.40.html

Man./Prod./Dist.

Cardew Teapottery
Newton Road
Bovey Tracey, Devonshire TQ13 9DX
U.K.
ph: 01626 832172
fax: 01626 834773
web: http://www.cardewdesign.com/
Maker of the highly detailed and collectible tea pots designed by Paul Cardew.

TEDDY BEARS

(see also BOOKS, Reference [Teddy Bears]; DOLLS; SMOKEY BEAR ITEMS; STEIFF; TEDDY BEARS [MODERN]; TOYS)

Appraisers

Ann Miller, ISA
Bright-Miller Appraisals
19750 S.W. Peavine Mtn. Rd.
Mcminnville, OR 97128
ph: 503-472-1092
Appraises, collects old Teddy Bears, Raggedy Ann & Andy dolls and books; belongs to "Good Bears of the World" and "Teddy Bear Boosters"; life member of United Federation of Doll Collectors; teaches antiques at State Comm. College.

Clubs/Associations

Terri Stong
Good Bears of the World
Magazine: Bear Tracks
P.O. Box 13097
Toledo, OH 43613-0097
ph: 419-531-5365 or 419-475-3946
e-mail: terrie@tdi.net
web: http://www.goodbearsoftheworld.org
"Good Bears" spread love & understanding by giving away Teddy Bears to comfort every hurt, abused child or lonely, forgotten adult; quarterly newsletter.

Ann Miller
Teddy Bear Boosters Club
19750 S.W. Peavine Mtn. Rd.
Mcminnville, OR 97128
ph: 503-472-1092

Collectors

Jeff Dykes
6 Wildwood Terrace
Glen Ridge, NJ 07028
ph: 973-748-4990
e-mail: lja@viconet.com
Wants to buy teddy bears made of mohair wool from 1980s to 1950s, in very good condition (send photo); also wants all Steiff animals before 1960 with button and/or chest tags.

Tom Kuster
My Old Bear
5510 Stadium Dr.
Madison, WI 53705-4642
ph: 608-238-3460
Wants early Teddy Bears, 1900 to 1960s, and related items; also Three Bears books, Raggedy Ann and Andy dolls and books, miniature Teddy Bears.

Barbara Wolters
Magazine: Teddy Tribune, The
254 W. Sidney
St. Paul, MN 55107-3494
ph: 651-291-7571
10 issues of Teddy Tribune per year; everything about teddy bears; send for free brochure.

Bill Boyd
7408 Englewood Lane
Raytown, MO 64133-6913
ph: 816-356-7423
fax: 816-356-7423

Susan Murphy
29668 Orinda Rd.
San Juan Capistrano, CA 92675-1211
ph: 949-364-4333
Wants to buy old bears from early 1900s to 1950s; please enclose SASE.

Dealers

Rita Mueller
Grange Hall Antiques
1 South Eighth Alley
P.O. Box 263
New Market, MD 21774
ph: 301-865-5651
fax: 301-865-0518
e-mail: Rita@newmarketmd.com
web: http://www.newmarketmd.com/grange.htm
Quality Steiff animals from 1950s through 1980s; always buying one piece or entire collection: teddy bears, Schuco, Hermann, Steiff; also fine country graniteware from Germany available; mail orders and layaways.

Walter LaValley
Bachelor II Dolls & Bears
247 S. Van Dorn St.
Wheaton Plaza
Alexandria, VA 22304
ph: 703-823-BEAR
fax: 703-823-1787
Specializes in dolls and bears.

Cheri Shivley
Cynthia's Country Store, Inc.
The Wellington Mall #15A
12794 W. Forest Hill Blvd.
West Palm Beach, FL 33414
ph: 561-793-0554
fax: 561-795-4222
e-mail: cynbears@aol.com
web: http://www.cynthiascountrystore.com/
Specializing in new, discontinued and antique Steiff, R. John Wright, and other manufacturers and artists bears.

Beth B. Savino
Toy Store, The
Franklin Park Mall
5001 Monroe St.
Toledo, OH 43623
ph: 419-473-9801 or 800-862-8697
fax: 419-473-3947
e-mail: info@toystorenet.com
web: http://www.toystorenet.com
Focus is on collecting Steiff toys and teddy bears; sells exclusive Steiff Limited Edition; also buys old Steiff.

Myron Weis
Division Street Antiques
P.O. Box 374
Buffalo, MN 55313-0374
ph: 612-682-6453
Buys and sells a complete line of antiques with a specialty in Teddy Bears, Toys, and Folk Art.

World City, Inc.
6935 James Ave. South
Minneapolis, MN 55423-2147
Buys teddy bears; please send photo and asking price along with SASE for reply.

Experts

Patricia Snyder
My Dear Dolly
P.O. Box 303
Sparta, NJ 07871-0303
ph: 201-729-8087
e-mail: dolly@sparta.csnet.net
web: http://www.mydeardolly.com
Wants older bears, parts, bear accessories, books, dolly-teddies; also wants Santas, bunnies, cloth Raggedy dolls.

Marguerite Cantine
223 Southeast 37th Ave.
Ocala, FL 34471-3045
Author of "American Teddy Bear Reference, Identification and Price Guide"; appraises American-made Teddy Bears from 1902-1956.

Terry & Doris Michaud
Carrousel by Michaud
505 West Broad St.
Chesaning, MI 48616-1210
ph: 517-845-7881
fax: 517-845-6650
e-mail: dmmich217@aol.com
Teddy bear artists, authors and lecturers; write regular column about teddy bears for "Teddy Bear & Friends" magazine, "Collecting Figures" magazine, and for the British magazine, "Teddy Bear Times."

Man./Prod./Dist.

Bear-in-Mind, Inc.
Newsletter: Arctophile, The
53 Bradford St.
Concord, MA 01742-2901
ph: 978-369-1167
fax: 978-371-0762
e-mail: franbear78@aol.com
A catalog company devoted to the consumer of new Teddy Bear related items; the first mail order company for Teddy Bears; started in 1977; send $1 for 40 page catalog; $5 for subscription to "The Arctophile."

Misc. Services

Monica Murray
Jenks Teddy Bear Convention
P.O. Box 728
Jenks, OK 74037
ph: 918-299-5416
Holds annual teddy bear show and sale convention in Jenks, Oklahoma.

Museums/Libraries

George B. Black, Jr.
Teddy Bear Museum, The
2511 Pine Ridge Rd.
Naples, FL 34109
ph: 941-598-2711 or 800-681-2327
fax: 941-598-9239
e-mail: info@teddymuseum.com
web: http://www.teddymuseum.com/about.htm
Collects and displays teddy bears and related items from teddy bear artists; developing teddy bear archives from the antique to present.

Periodicals

Stephen L. Cronk, Ed.
Magazine: Teddy Bear Review
170 Fifth Ave. - 12th Floor
New York, NY 10010
ph: 212-989-8700 or 800-347-6969
fax: 212-645-8976

Cowles Magazines, Inc.
Magazine: Teddy Bear & Friends
741 Miller Dr. SE, Ste. D2
Harrisburg, PA 20175
ph: 717-540-6617 or 800-829-3340
fax: 717-540-6706
e-mail: brentd@cowles.com
web: http://www.cowles.com/maglist.html
Magazine dedicated to teddy bears and other plush friends; editorial coverage of bears - antique to modern artists; bear manufacturers, care and repair, display ideas, buying, selling, and insuring bears, new product arrivals, etc.

Sandra Hood, Pub.
Newspaper: Antique & Collectables
P.O. Box 12589
500 Fesler St., Ste. 201
El Cajon, CA 92022
ph: 619-593-2925 or 619-593-2927
fax: 619-447-7187
e-mail: antiqunews@aol.com
web: http://www.collect.com/antiqueandcollectables
The largest monthly newspaper in Southern California covering the antiques & collectibles industry with focus sections on Nevada and Arizona; 72+ pages; events and show section, feature articles; columns, ads.

Repair Services

Sally Winey
Winey Bear Care Clinic & Adoption Agency
P.O. Box 7
Saint Peters, PA 19470
ph: 717-774-7447 or 610-469-1020
Specializes in repairing collector teddy bears; also cleans stuffed animals.

E. Adorjan
Imaginary Friends
P.O. Box 40601
Denver, CO 80204
ph: 303-761-7234
e-mail: toyrep@aol.com
web: http://members.aol.com/toyrep/
Specializes repairs and restorations to Steiff and other stuffed toys and dolls; will is advise if toy would be better off if left as-is; references and before-and-after photos available; official restoration specialist with Steiff.

Jeri Cotherman
Doll & Bear's Paradise, A
855 1/2 N. Cedar
Laramie, WY 82072
ph: 307-742-3429
e-mail: jercoth@aol.com
Restores dolls, stuffed animals; makes artist specialty bears; sells dolls and bears; buying dolls, patterns, old material, fur and fake fur.

Nisbet

Clubs/Associations

Howard & Sarah Wade
Peggy Nisbet International Collectors' Society
Newsletter: PNICS Newsletter
P.O. Box 325
Orrville, OH 44667-0325
ph: 330-682-8551
fax: 330-682-3655
e-mail: ukdolls@aol.com
Clearinghouse for information about Peggy Nisbet portrait and costume dolls and Nisbet bears from Britain, both primary and secondary markets.

Man./Prod./Dist.

Howard & Sarah Wade
Nisbet Dolls & Bears
P.O. Box 325
Orrville, OH 44667-0325
ph: 330-682-8551
fax: 330-682-3655
e-mail: ukdolls@aol.com
U.S. distributor for Peggy Nisbet dolls and Nisbet bears from Britain.

TEDDY BEARS (MODERN)

Collectors

Kristin
Three Squires
6029 Flat Rock Rd. #429
Columbus, GA 31907
ph: 706-565-4931
e-mail: Kristin@knology.net
web: http://www.threesquires.com
Website has free bulletin board ads as well as contests.

Dealers

Mike Mellone
Essentially Bears
P.O. Box 25
Stewartsville, NJ 08886
ph: 908-479-4614
e-mail: fdc@4-collectors.com
web: http://www.4-collectors.com
Specializing in Puffkins, current and retired; also Ganz Bears and Keepsake Resin Bears.

Nancy Pelham
Homestead Gift Shop
4 Hillwood Lane
Catskill, NY 12414
ph: 518-943-4371
e-mail: fluffy@capital.net
web: http://www.homestead-gift-shop.com
Carries manufactured teddy bears from Boyds, Cottage Collectibles, Douglas, Mary Meyer, Orzek, and Ty; also artist bears by Quite A. Bear and Nostalgic Bears.

Judy Kuster
Bear Essentials Dolls, Bears & Collectible Toys
1344 Pine St.
Paso Robles, CA 93446
ph: 805-238-4469
e-mail: toys4u@thegrid.net
web: http://www.thegrid.net/bear/bear.htm
Offers vintage to present Barbie, GI Joe, action figures, Beanie Babies, Starting Lineup, Boyds Bears, Steiff, Muffy Vanderbear, Superman, Batman, Star Wars, Star Trek, and more.

Kitty Wilde
Bears by the Sea
680 Cypress Street
Pismo Beach, CA 93449
ph: 805-773-1952
fax: 805-773-5869
e-mail: info@bearsbythesea.com
web: http://www.bearsbythesea.com/
Specializing in Muffy and VanderBears, TY Plush and Beanie Babies, Boyds Plush Bears, Gund.

Niki Ferraro
Bear St.
P.O. Box 22009 Banker's Hall
135, 315-8th Ave. SW
Calgary, Alberta T2P 4J1
Canada
fax: 403-547-1018
e-mail: bearst@ibm.net
web: http://www.bearst.com
Specializes in Gund plush animals; Australian Animals, Christmas, Monkey Business, Signature Collection, baby GUND, Classic GUND, Jungle Cats, Pet Shop, Snuffles, Whimsical Friends, Puppets, Mohair Collection, Bunnies, Classic Pooh.

Internet Resources

Debbie Kesling
e-mail: debbie@cybearspace.com
web: http://www.cybearspace.com
Teddy bear designer maintains website with an incredible number of Teddy Bear links.

Periodicals

Andi Lucas, Ed.
Tuff Stuff Publications, Inc.
Magazine: Beans & Bears!
P.O. Box 3070
Richmond, VA 23228
ph: 804-266-0140 or 800-899-8833
fax: 804-264-4205
e-mail: beans@tuffstuffpubs.com
web: http://www.beansmagazine.com
Monthly magazine for collectors of bean bag collectibles including Ty, Warner Bros., Disney, Coca-Cola, etc.; also covers Teddy Bears collectibles; includes price guide for both bean bag and Teddy Bear collectibles.

Ashdown Publishing
Magazine: Teddy Bear Times
Avalon Court, Star Road
Partridge Green, West Sussex RH13 8RY
U.K.
ph: +44 (0) 1403 711511 or 513-353-4052 (in U.S.)
fax: +44 (0) 1403 711521
e-mail: mark@ashdown.co.uk
web: http://www.teddybeartimes.com/
Magazine with glossy color pages packed with news, information, ideas and inspiration for the growing bands of ardent teddy lovers.

EMF Publishing
Magazine: Teddy Bear Scene
EMF House
5-7 Elm Park
U.K.
ph: 01903 244900
fax: 01903 506626
e-mail: dolltedemf@aol.com
web: http://members.aol.com/dolltedemf/
Every issue packed with ideas, features, free competitions and much more.

Boyds

Experts

Laurie Anne Greez
P.O. Box 1393
Easton, MA 02334-1393
fax: 508-230-9517
e-mail: lag4boyds@aol.com
web: http://www.intheattic.com/lionstigersandboyds/
A professional writer whose Boyds expertise is widely respected.

Laurie Anne Greez
Newsletter: Lions, Tigers, & Boyds, Oh, My!!!
P.O. Box 1393
Easton, MA 02334-1393
fax: 508-230-9517
e-mail: lag4boyds@aol.com
web: http://www.intheattic.com/lionstigersandboyds/
Quarterly newsletter features articles relating to Boyds: Resin, Plus and Bear Necessity Lines; store exclusives, how to insure your Boyds, secondary market information, photos, contests, retailer's spotlight, etc.

Muffy Vanderbear

Clubs/Associations

Michelle Sterling
Muffy VanderBear Club
Newsletter: Fanfare
401 North Wabash, Ste. 500
Chicago, IL 60611-5646
ph: 773-329-0020 or 800-682-3427
fax: 773-329-1417
web: http://www.muffy.com/vbclub.htm
Muffy VanderBear, a seven-inch, golden pile plush stuffed dressed bear; the club provides information, services and limited edition bears exclusively to Club members.

TELECARDS

(see TELEPHONE CARDS)

TELEGRAMS

Collectors

Dr. Walter Brinker
Niedernfeld 2
Radevormwald, 42477
Germany
ph: 49-219540928
fax: 49-21956517
A collector of international telegram forms; has about 220 from 150 countries.

TELEGRAPH ITEMS

(see also BROADCASTING; BUMPER STICKERS, Radio Station; ELECTRICITY RELATED ITEMS; FIRE FIGHTING MEMORABILIA, Fire Alarm Telegraphy; INSULATORS; MAGAZINES, Radio & Wireless; RADIOS; STOCK TICKERS; TELEGRAMS)

Appraisers

Tom French
P.O. Box 66
Maynard, MA 01754
ph: 978-562-5573
fax: 978-562-3043
e-mail: tfrench@fiam.net
web: http://home.fiam.net/tfrench/artifax.htm
Can provide an informal opinion of value for old telegraph keys, sounders, etc.; send a letter including complete description, condition and photo if possible; please include a SASE; Vibroplex and McElroy instruments a specialty.

Clubs/Associations

Bill Myers
International Morse Preservation Society, The
Newsletter: IMPS Newsletter
e-mail: kk4kf@qsl.net
web: http://fists.org/
FISTS exists to promote amateur CW activity; newcomers welcome; awards, nets (including beginners' net), dial-a-sked for beginners, straight key activities, QSL bureau, newsletter,

Harry Goldman
Tesla Coil Builders' Association
Newsletter: TCBA News
3 Amy Lane
Queensbury, NY 12804
ph: 518-792-1003
web: http://www.eskimo.com/~billb/tesla/tcba.html
TCBA is a clearinghouse on the history of electricity, wireless, electrotherapy, etc.; acts as consultants for high voltage historical equipment.

Bruce Kelley
Antique Wireless Association
Newsletter: Old Timer's Bulletin
59 Main St.
Holcomb, NY 14469-9336
ph: 716-657-6260 or 716-657-7489
e-mail: n2rsm@frontiernet.net
web: http://www.ggw.org/freenet/a/awa/
One of the world's largest and oldest historical radio collector organizations; purpose is to document and preserve the history of radio, telegraph and television artifacts.

R.A. Iwasyk
Morse Telegraph Club, Inc.
Newsletter: Dots & Dashes
12350 W. Offner Rd.
Manhattan, IL 60442
For those with an interest in landline telegraphy; newspaper has articles having to do with stories and experiences of landline telegraphers, but also has some radiotelegraph articles as well.

Collectors

Peter Thomashow
301 E 17th St., Rm 1028
New York, NY 10003-3804
ph: 718-797-1024
Wants to buy old telegraphs.

Roger W. Reinke
Brasspounder
5301 Neville Ct.
Alexandria, VA 22310-1113
ph: 703-971-4095 or 800-348-0294
e-mail: brspndr@capcity.com
Wants telegraph instruments, stock tickers, and related items such as call boxes, signs, early paper; condition not important.

Howard Hazelcorn
6731 Ashley Ct.
Sarasota, FL 34241-9696
ph: 941-921-1815
Wants rare early items.

Dale R. Beeks
Perceptions Scientifica
P.O. Box 117
Mount Vernon, IA 52314-0117
ph: 800-880-5178 or 319-895-0506
e-mail: dbeeksci@aol.com
Wants pre-1900 telegraph keys, registers, and related items.

Charles Goodman
636 W. Grant Ave.
Charleston, IL 61920-3226
ph: 217-345-6771
Wants telegraph books, instruments, keys, sounders, relays, resonators, Western Union items; also old stock tickers by Western Union, Edison, Postal Telegraph or others, with or without domes also OK.

Dealers

Jim & Felicia Kreuzer
New Wireless Pioneers
P.O. Box 398
Elma, NY 14059
ph: 716-681-3186
fax: 716-681-4540
e-mail: wireless@pce.net
Buys and sells 1850-1950 books, catalogs, magazines, autographs, and other literature dealing with early radio, wireless, pre-1940 television, medical, telegraphy, early computers, television, x-ray and electricity.

Experts

Tom French
P.O. Box 66
Maynard, MA 01754
ph: 978-562-5573
fax: 978-562-3043
e-mail: tfrench@fiam.net
web: http://home.fiam.net/tfrench/artifax.htm
Wants to buy all kinds of telegraph instruments, including early railroad and Western Union keys and sounders, and modern semiautomatic Morse code keys; specialist in Martin, Vibroplex and McElroy keys (can identify and date).

Thomas B. Perera
11 Squire Hill Rd.
Caldwell, NJ 07006-4718
ph: 973-226-9185
e-mail: pererat@alpha.montclair.edu
web: http://www.w1tp.com/
Maintains internet telegraph and scientific instrument museum and collector's guide; author of "Perera's Telegraph Collector's Guide."

Internet Resources

Neal McEwen, K5RW
Telegraph Office, The
e-mail: nmcewen@metronet.com
web: http://fohnix.metronet.com/~nmcewen/ref.html
Lots of information about telegraphy, the history, links, instruments, etc.

Prof. Thomas Perera
Telegraph & Scientific Instrument On-Line Cyber-Museum
Department of Psychology
Montclair State University
Upper Montclair, NJ 07043
ph: 973-655-7083
e-mail: pererat@alpha.montclair.edu
web: http://www.chss.montclair.edu/~pererat/telegraph.html
On-line museum dedicated to the preservation of telegraph history, lore, and instrumentation; downloadable images; telegraph history, bibliography, and related links; e-mail appraisals available.

Museums/Libraries

Robert Merriam
New England Wireless & Steam Museum, Inc.
1300 Frenchtown Road
East Greenwich, RI 02818
ph: 401-884-1710 or 401-885-0545
fax: 401-884-0683
e-mail: newsm@ids.net
web: http://users.ids.net/~newsm/

American Radio Relay League Museum of Amateur Radio
225 Main St.
Newington, CT 06111-1494
ph: 860-666-1541
e-mail: hq@arrl.org

Bruce Kelley
Antique Wireless Association's Electronic Communication Museum
59 Main St.
Holcomb, NY 14469-9336
ph: 716-657-6260 or 716-657-7489
e-mail: n2rsm@frontiernet.net
web: http://www.ggw.org/freenet/a/awa/
Open limited hours May through October; call or write before visiting; please enclose SASE if requesting a reply.

Periodicals

John V. Terrey
Magazine: Antique Radio Classified
P.O. Box 2
Carlisle, MA 01741
ph: 978-371-0512
fax: 978-371-7129
e-mail: arc@antiqueradio.com
web: http://www.antiqueradio.com
Antique radio's largest monthly about old radios, Art Deco, TV's, ham equip. - '40s, '50s, books, telegraph, etc.; lots of ads.

John McDougald
Magazine: Crown Jewels of the Wire
P.O. Box 1003
Saint Charles, IL 60174
ph: 630-513-1544
fax: 630-513-8278
e-mail: mcd@crownjewelsofthewire.com
web: http://www.crownjewelsofthewire.com/
76-page monthly magazine of insulator and telephone and telegraph history; glass, porcelain; foreign columns; classified ads, show dates, etc.

Zyg Nilski
Nilski Partnership, The
Magazine: Morsum Magnificat
The Poplars
Wistanswick
Market Drayton, Shropshire TF9 2BA
U.K.
e-mail: zyg@morsum.demon.co.uk
web: http://www.morsum.demon.co.uk/
A bi-monthly English publication; journal dedicated to Samuel F.B.

Morse (1781-1872), "Father of the Morse Telegraph."

Telegraph Keys

Collectors

Thomas B. Perera
11 Squire Hill Rd.
Caldwell, NJ 07006-4718
ph: 973-226-9185
e-mail: pererat@alpha.montclair.edu
web: http://www.w1tp.com/
Wants to buy telegraph keys and apparatus; specializing in Civil War era, 19th century, land line, and wireless keys; has been collecting for over 40 years; has over 400 keys for trade.

Experts

Gil Schlehman
Gil Schleman Antiques
335 Indianapolis
Downers Grove, IL 60515-3119
ph: 630-968-2320
Noted collector and author of "Telegraph Key Review" column in the "Antique Radio Classified"; largest collection of "speed keys" in the world.

Suppliers

Tom French
Artifax Books
P.O. Box 88
Maynard, MA 01754-0088
ph: 978-562-5573
fax: 978-562-3043
e-mail: artifaxbooks@yahoo.com
web: http://home.fiam.net/tfrench/artifax.htm
Carries replacement knobs, paddles and rubber feet for old telegraph keys; the knobs can be used on hand keys or "bugs"; paddles and feet are good for Vibroplex, McElroy, Electric Specialty, Lionel and many other keys; send SASE for list.

TELEPHONE CARDS

(see also BANKING; CIVIL WAR ARTIFACTS, Currency; COINS & CURRENCY; CREDIT CARDS & CHARGE ITEMS; MONEYCARDS; WOODEN MONEY)

Clubs/Associations

Jim Wertheimer, Treas.
International Phonecard Collectors
P.O. Box 632
Millwood, NY 10546
e-mail: jhw20@cs.com
web: http://www.cardmall.com/ipc
A club for a special type of credit card collector focusing on phone cards.

International Telecard Association
904 Massachusetts Ave. NE
Washington, DC 20002-6228
ph: 202-544-4448 or 800-958-7824
fax: 202-547-7417
e-mail: inquiries@telecard.org
web: http://www.telecard.org
Trade association with collectors division; offers educational material.

Collectors

Dan Busby
P.O. Box 50188
Indianapolis, IN 46250
ph: 765-674-3301
fax: 765-674-3302
Wants to buy credit cards and telephone debit cards.

Dealers

Powell Associates
1270 Avenue of the Americas, Ste. 212
New York, NY 10020
ph: 800-528-8819
Large dealer in collectible telecards.

Ron Abler
5516 Maplefield Place
Alexandria, VA 22310-1891
ph: 703-971-9590 or 703-971-3524
Buys and sells U.S. and worldwide phonecards, specializing in first and early edition examples of telephone company issues.

James Moran
Telequest
1566 W. Algonquin, Ste. 115
Schaumburg, IL 60195-1575
ph: 847-991-1228
fax: 847-991-9938
e-mail: telequest@usa..net
Retails and wholesales U.S. telephone cards and international cards with U.S. themes; emphasis is on world, Disney, and scarce US cards.

Steve Eyer
P.O. Box 123 -MA
Mount Zion, IL 62549-0123
ph: 217-864-4321
fax: 217-864-3021
Buys and sells collectible telephone cards.

Experts

Bruce Harmon
ACME Telecards, Inc.
P.O. Box 450957
Fort Lauderdale, FL 33345
ph: 800-405-2263
fax: 954-742-9015
e-mail: acmetel@aol.com
web: http://www.acmetel.com
Appraiser, collector, dealer, expert specializes in collectible phonecards and Visa cash cards; also produces custom phonecards and gift cards.

Alan Cohen
Card Mall, The
1042 N. Mountain Ave., Ste. B339
Upland, CA 91786
ph: 909-981-6522
fax: 310-734-1529
e-mail: alan@cardmall.com
web: http://www.cardmall.com
Phone card dealer, collector and expert.

Internet Resources

Alan Cohen
Card Mall, The
1042 N. Mountain Ave., Ste. B339
Upland, CA 91786
ph: 909-981-6522
fax: 310-734-1529
e-mail: alan@cardmall.com
web: http://www.cardmall.com
Phone card site with dozens of dealers, collecting information, free classified ads, live chat, contests and more.

Terry Stewart
Collector Link
71 John St. East
Waterloo, Ontario N2J 1G2
Canada
ph: 519-745-1745
e-mail: stewart@collector-link.com
web: http://www.collector-link.com/
Catalogs over 2,000 trading card related web sites for: baseball, hockey, basketball, football, other sports, non-sports, phone cards, credit-debit cards, business cards, postcards.

Man./Prod./Dist.

Bruce Harmon
ACME Telecards, Inc.
P.O. Box 450957
Fort Lauderdale, FL 33345
ph: 800-405-2263
fax: 954-742-9015
e-mail: acmetel@aol.com
web: http://www.acmetel.com
Specializes in collectible phonecards and Visa cash cards; also produces custom phonecards and gift cards.

Star Telecom Network, Inc.
21243 Ventura Blvd., Ste. 241
Mission Hills, CA 91346
ph: 818-888-3880
fax: 818-888-3881
e-mail: info@startele.com
web: http://www.startele.com
Dealer, issuer, provider; leader in collectible phone cards.

Periodicals

Newspaper: Collectors' Advantage
1710 River Rd., Ste. 4D
Fair Lawn, NJ 07410
ph: 201-796-5552 or 800-VALUE-01
fax: 201-796-2250
e-mail: 102622.3501@compuserve.com
web: http://hmt.com/phonecards/tca/
A resource journal for the collectibles enthusiast.

Art Becker
Magazine: Art Becker's Telephone & Debit Card Journal
4542 E. Tropicana, #268
Las Vegas, NV 89121
e-mail: artbecker@artbecker.com
web: http://www.artbecker.com

Bill Jordan
Magazine: Premier
P.O. Box 2297
Paso Robles, CA 93447
ph: 805-227-1024
fax: 805-237-2530
e-mail: premier@premier-tele.com
web: http://premier-tele.com
A large format magazine on glossy stock with superb color photos of telephone cards; also sells collector telephone cards.

TELEPHONE COMPANY ITEMS

Bell-Shaped Paperweights

Experts

Jacqueline C. Linscott
3557 Nicklaus Dr.
Titusville, FL 32780-5356
ph: 407-267-9170
e-mail: bluebellwt@aol.com
Wants old, cobalt blue, bell-shaped paperweights used as giveaways by early telephone companies; author of "Blue Bell Paperweights, Telephone Pioneer Bells & Other Related Items", 1992 revised edition; $12 from the author.

TELEPHONES

(see also INSULATORS; TELEPHONE CARDS; TELEPHONE COMPANY ITEMS)

Clubs/Associations

Deborah Jan Thomas
Mini-Phone Exchange
Newsletter: Telephonically Yours
5412 Tilden Rd.
Bladensburg, MD 20710
Members interested in telephones as well as all types of items on which a telephone is depicted - postcards, ceramics, advertising, etc.; quarterly newsletter.

Paul McFadden
Telephone Collectors International, Inc.
Newsletter: Singing Wires
3207 E Bend Dr.
Algonquin, IL 60102-9664
ph: 847-658-7855
fax: 847-658-9360
e-mail: singwires@aol.com
web: http://www.voicenet.com/~tciplace/
For antique telephone collectors; sponsors two shows annually where old phones and related items are displayed, bought and sold; newsletter published monthly; journal "Switchers" published quarterly.

Ann Manning
Antique Telephone Collectors Association
Newsletter: Antique Telephone Collectors Newsletter
P.O. Box 94
Abilene, KS 67410-0094
ph: 785-263-1757 or 785-263-2681
e-mail: chuck@cybercomm.net
web: http://www.cybercomm.net/~chuck/atca.html
Dedicated to the preservation of historical telephony; membership includes monthly 8-12 page newsletter with free advertising for members, numerous ATCA-sponsored antique telephone shows each year; nearly 1200 members.

Collectors

William Boss
33 Hoffman Dr.
Kings Park, NY 11754
ph: 516-269-7839
e-mail: wbos@worldnet.att.net
All types of telephones and related ephemera including blue glass paperweights, signs, pay phones, and novelty phones.

Lydia M. Jackson-Fryer
608 Winans Way
Baltimore, MD 21229-1430
ph: 410-233-6231
fax: 410-233-6231
e-mail: lcfryer@erols.com
Wants to buy antique telephones from the 1920s through the 1950s.

Bob Hunter
15600 Andover Lane
Wake Forest, NC 27587-9778
ph: 919-528-3469
Collecting all types of phones: antique, novelty, toy, unusual; also wants related accessories and memorabilia.

Russ Pate
235 Sandpine Rd.
Indialantic, FL 32903-2117
ph: 407-777-1759 or 800-777-1759
fax: 407-777-9422
e-mail: rpate@harris.com
Wants to buy telephones and related items from 1876 to present; condition not important.

Paul G. Engelke
23399 Rio Del Mar Dr.
Boca Raton, FL 33486-8504
ph: 561-338-3332
e-mail: keytelco@bellsouth.net
Wants early wooden wall and candlestick phones, porcelain telephone signs, small coin phones, wooden coin phones, etc. but no paper.

Tom Vaughn
2016 Village Rd.
La Porte, IN 46350-7874
ph: 219-324-3494
fax: 219-325-4511
e-mail: phoneman@adsnet.com
Wants to buy pay-station and unusual old telephones; also wants porcelain telephone and telegraph company signs and badges.

John Huckeby
2440 W. CR 150 N
New Castle, IN 47362-9146
ph: 765-533-6369
fax: 765-533-6530
Old telephones, complete or parts.

Jon Kolger
6906 Meade Dr.
Colleyville, TX 76034-6416
ph: 817-329-5262
e-mail: jkolger@gte.net
Always buying COLORED PLASTIC Art Deco style telephones from the 1920s through the 1950s; also seeking pre-1900 mechanical telephones that work on the "two tin cans on a string" principle; also wants telephone related paper, books, etc.

Bill Hare
251 W. Capitol Ave.
Milpitas, CA 95035
ph: 408-942-5530
fax: 408-945-0887
e-mail: bill@dyz.com
web: http://www.dyz.com/phones/
Website has lots of information and pictures about old telephones.

Dealers

Bruce & Charlotte Mager
Waves
Chelsea Antiques Building
110 West 25th St., 10th Floor
New York, NY 10001-7401
ph: 212-989-9284
fax: 201-461-7121
e-mail: c1wave@aol.com
web: http://www.wavesradio.com/
Over 20 years experience specializing in vintage radios, phonographs, telegraphy, televisions, assorted electrical and mechanical apparatus, and related advertising memorabilia, books and pamphlets.

Becker's Bygones
ph: 914-635-2458
fax: 914-635-3253
web: http://www.antiquejunction.com/beckers/
In business for over 19 years buying, selling and restoring old telephones.

Jonathan Finder
Vintage Telephones
1203 East End Ave.
Pittsburgh, PA 15218
ph: 412-371-9608
e-mail: jon@oldphones.com
web: http://www.oldphones.com
Buys, sells, repairs 1928-1960 vintage telephones; each is restored to work on modern lines; guaranteed and original; no reproductions; selection varies as does availability.

Bruce Patterson
Phone Wizard
23 South Berlin Pike
Lovettsville, VA 20180-8502
ph: 540-822-4730
fax: 540-822-4733
e-mail: phonewizard@juno.com
Publishes a catalog ($3) providing genuine antique telephones, Art Deco telephones, and parts; offers restorations, conservation and repairs of all antique, old, and Western Electric telephones; visitors by appointment only.

Richard R. Marsh
Chicago Old Telephone Company
P.O. Box 189
Lemon Springs, NC 28355-0189
ph: 919-774-6625 or 919-775-5669
fax: 919-774-7666
e-mail: marsh@interpath.com
web: http://miraclemile.com/chicagophone/
Carries parts for old telephones; also repairs/restores and sells antique telephones; catalog available for free; also rents telephones to movies, TV and stage shows.

Rainbow Hirsh
20th Century Vintage Telephone Company
2780 Northbrook Place
Boulder, CO 80304-1432
ph: 303-442-3304
web: http://www.hollywoodphone.com/
One of the premier restorers of vintage (1910-1937) telephones; meticulous care and attention to authenticity is given to each instrument; also sells at major antique shows throughout the US.

Jim & Shirley's Antiques
146 N. Glassell St.
Orange, CA 92866
ph: 714-639-9662 or 562-598-1914
Buys and sells antique telephones and Victrolas.

Ron Christianson
Antique Telephones & Parts
P.O. Box 43
Cave Junction, OR 97523
ph: 541-592-4123
e-mail: bngholio@cdsnet.net
web: http://www.cavejunction.com/phones

Sheri Stritof
Roy's Phones
3705 E. College Way
Mount Vernon, WA 98273
ph: 360-424-4376
fax: 360-424-4378
e-mail: phones@nwlink.om
web: http://www.roysphones.com/
Buys, sells and repairs old telephones, including novelty phones.

Museums/Libraries

Georgia Rural Telephone Museum, The
P.O. Box 18878
Leslie, GA 31764
ph: 912-874-4786
web: http://www.sowega.net/%7Emuseum/
Has over 1,500 telephones from 1875 to present.

Illinois Bell's Oliver P. Parks Telephone Museum
529 South 7th St.
Springfield, IL 62721
ph: 217-789-5303
A private museum based on a personal collection and including over 100 antique telephones.

Janet Groninga
Museum of Independent Telephony
412 S. Campbell
Abilene, KS 67410
ph: 785-263-2681
fax: 785-263-0380
e-mail: dchs@ikansas.com
web: http://www.cc.ukans.edu/heritage/abilene/telephony.html
Established to illustrate pioneer spirit & ingenuity of the early independent companies who pioneered rural phone service; extensive collection of telephones and associated memorabilia, artifacts, photographs, documents.

Periodicals

John McDougald
Magazine: Crown Jewels of the Wire
P.O. Box 1003
Saint Charles, IL 60174
ph: 630-513-1544
fax: 630-513-8278
e-mail: mcd@crownjewelsofthewire.com
web: http://www.crownjewelsofthewire.com/
76-page monthly magazine of insulator and telephone and telegraph history; glass, porcelain; foreign columns; classified ads, show dates, etc.

Repair Services

Richard R. Marsh
Chicago Old Telephone Company
P.O. Box 189
Lemon Springs, NC 28355-0189
ph: 919-774-6625 or 919-775-5669
fax: 919-774-7666
e-mail: marsh@interpath.com
web: http://miraclemile.com/chicagophone/
Sells old restored telephones to public and collectors; restores old telephones; provides old telephones to movie companies, TV, stage shows, etc.; displays at top antique shows in major cities.

Paul McFadden
3207 E Bend Dr.
Algonquin, IL 60102-9664
ph: 847-658-7855
fax: 847-658-9360
e-mail: singwires@aol.com
web: http://www.voicenet.com/~tciplace/
Collects, repairs, specializes in old telephones.

Odis W. LeVrier
House of Telephones
2677 East Valley Dr.
San Angelo, TX 76903
ph: 915-482-0101
fax: 915-655-5681
e-mail: olevrier@aol.com
Repairs antique telephones and carries parts.

Suppliers

Ron & Mary Knappen
Phoneco, Inc.
19813 E. Mill Rd.
P.O. Box 70
Galesville, WI 54630-0070
ph: 608-582-4124
fax: 608-582-4593
e-mail: phonecoinc@aol.com
web: http://www.phonecoinc.com
Buys, sells, refurbishes any old telephone; also sells old and new parts, character phones, novelty phones; catalogs, history, price guide, diagrams and restoration help.

Art Deco

Collectors

Carl Ratner
550 Lamoka Ave.
Staten Island, NY 10312
ph: 718-317-1838
e-mail: artdeco@nyct.net
Buy, sell, trade telephones and parts; specializing in Art Deco phones of the 1920s through 1940s.

Candlestick

Experts

Howard Hazelcorn
6731 Ashley Ct.
Sarasota, FL 34241-9696
ph: 941-921-1815
Collects and specializes in candlestick phones.

Miniature

Collectors

Deborah Jan Thomas
5412 Tilden Rd.
Bladensburg, MD 20710
Interested in obtaining miniature telephones of all kinds as well as old postcards and trade cards depicting telephones.

Museums/Libraries

Deborah Jan Thomas
Miniature Telephone Museum
5412 Tilden Rd.
Bladensburg, MD 20710
A private museum based on a personal collection and including over 400 miniature telephones.

Novelty

Dealers

Bob Roberts
P.O. Box 152
Guilderland, NY 12084-0152
e-mail: hbv2020@compuserve.com
Wants to buy novelty transistor radios, e.g. Atlas Battery, Brut cologne, Budweiser, Pepsi, Coke, McDonald's, etc.; also wants telephones in unusual shapes, e.g. gas pumps, food items, cartoon characters, cars, etc.

Western Electric

Dealers

Cliff Sullivan
4902 W. Monte Cristo
Glendale, AZ 85306-2638
ph: 602-978-3551
fax: 602-843-3391
e-mail: suclif@worldnet.att.net
Wants items marked "Western Electric": telephones, telegraph, sound equipment, appliances, etc.; also wants old or unusual telephones, equipment, or telephone memorabilia.

TELEVISION SHOWS & MEMORABILIA

(see also AUTOGRAPHS; BROADCASTING; CHARACTER COLLECTIBLES; COWBOY HEROES; FAN CLUBS; GAMES, Board [TV Related]; MOVIE MEMORABILIA; PHOTOGRAPHS, Celebrity; PREMIUMS; SCIENCE FICTION; SPACE COLLECTIBLES; SUPER HEROES; TELEVISIONS; TOYS, Action Figures)

Collectors

Daniel Wachtenheim
P.O. Box 480444
Los Angeles, CA 90048
ph: 323-848-3053
e-mail: dwachte915@aol.com
Wants to buy 60s/70s TV related toys.

Scott Weiss
1158 26th St., #489
Santa Monica, CA 90403
ph: 310-442-0040
fax: 310-442-5530
e-mail: sweiss5905@aol.com
Wants to buy movie and TV promotional and advertising specialty gift items such as pin-back buttons, badges, cloisonne pins, cloth usher ribbons, paperweights, tokens, snow domes, ashtrays, statues, clocks, radios, flashlights, lighters.

Craig Dawson
115 Oakley Blvd.
Scarborough, Ontario M1P 3P8
Canada
ph: 416-751-3227
fax: 416-755-4977
e-mail: baddog@thebulletin.net
web: http://www.thebulletin.net
Wants to buy anything related to 1960 through early 1980s television shows: Charlies Angels, Bewitched, Beverly Hillbillies, Laverne & Shirley, MASH, Gilligan's Island, The Rookies, Munsters, Adam-12, Bonanza, The Patty Duke Show, etc.

Dealers

Stephen Albert
TVC Enterprises
P.O. Box 1088
Easton, MA 02334-1088
ph: 508-238-1179
e-mail: tvcollector@usa.net
web: http://www.angelfire.com/ma/tvcollector/home.html
28 pg. catalogs of TV, movie, rock 'n roll & other music, theater & other media-related collectibles & memorabilia for sale; send SASE.

Jon Allan
Elmer's Nostalgia, Inc.
3 Putnam St.
Sanford, ME 04073-2024
ph: 207-324-2166

Michael Torres
Howdy Do
72 E. 7th St.
New York, NY 10003
ph: 212-979-1618
e-mail: howdy72@aol.com
web: http://members.aol.com/howdy72/
A New York City shop that specializes in celebrity TV-related toys.

Jerry Ohlinger
Jerry Ohlinger's Movie Material Store, Inc.
242 W. 14th St.
New York, NY 10011-7206
ph: 212-989-0869
fax: 212-989-1660
Buys and sells motion picture photos and posters from 1920 to present; also TV photos; research services available; free lists available; complete lists of 100,000 black & white photos or of 100,000 color photos are $4 each.

Dennis & Mary Luby
Casey's Collectible Corner
HCR 31 Box 30
No. Blenheim, NY 12131
ph: 607-588-6464
e-mail: caseyscc@aol.com
web: http://www.csmonline.com/caseys/
Buys and sells collectible toys: comic characters, TV shows and personalities; also space and monster toys, sports collectibles, etc.

John Kachmar
Techno-Fantasy Traders
779 Carissa Dr.
West Palm Beach, FL 33411-3412
ph: 561-798-5978
fax: 561-798-5978

Bill & Joanne Bruegman
Toy Scouts, Inc.
137 Casterton Ave.
Akron, OH 44303-1543
ph: 330-836-0668
fax: 330-869-8668
e-mail: toyscout@akron.infi.net

Scott Curtis
52 Girls Collectibles
P.O. Box 6121
Chillicothe, OH 45601-6121

Jon & Carolyn Thurmond
Collectorholics
15006 Fuller
Grandview, MO 64030-4522
ph: 816-322-0906

Eddie Brandt's Saturday Matinee
5006 Vineland Ave.
North Hollywood, CA 91601
ph: 818-506-4242 or 818-506-7722
fax: 818-506-5649
A great source for stills, posters, and lobby cards.

J. Deson
P.O. Box 10013
Fullerton, CA 92838
Buys and sells movie and TV memorabilia by mail order; sends a list upon request; provide name of star or show you are interested in.

Harold Balde
Fungus Amungus
21 Wellington St.
Orangeville, Ontario L9W 2L2
Canada
ph: 519-942-3984
e-mail: kingpin@total.net
web: http://tilt.largo.fl.us/hbalde/
Collector and dealer of Classic TV shows; mostly from 16mm film with original commercials; specialty is 1950s and 1960s; hard-to-find and obscure TV shows; over 4,000 tapes.

Experts

Stephen Albert
TVC Enterprises
P.O. Box 1088
Easton, MA 02334-1088
ph: 508-238-1179
e-mail: tvcollector@usa.net
web: http://www.angelfire.com/ma/tvcollector/home.html
Consultant, freelance writer or researcher for production companies, books publishers etc. on the subject of TV nostalgia.

Ted Hake
Hake's Americana & Collectibles Auction
P.O. Box 1444
York, PA 17405-1444
ph: 717-848-1333
e-mail: Ted@hakes.com
web: http://www.hakes.com/
Author of "Hake's Guide to TV Collectibles"; always purchasing items for mail-bid auctions of Disneyana, historical Americana, toys, premiums, political items, character and other collectibles.

David Welch
P.O. Box 714
Murphysboro, IL 62966-0714
ph: 618-687-2282
fax: 618-684-2243
e-mail: PezDude1@aol.com
Wants 1950s-1960s TV show related items such as lunch boxes, games, toys, etc.; paying $3,000+ for rare items, especially super heroes.

Bill Morgan
World of TV Toys, The
P.O. Box 91-1491
Los Angeles, CA 90091
ph: 714-379-6791
e-mail: tvtoys@aol.com
web: http://www.tvtoys.com
Co-author of "Collector's Guide to TV Toys & Memorabilia 60s & 70s - 2nd Edition"; buys and sells; website has memorabilia for sale, collector's guide, online articles, links to TV show fan pages and celebrity web sites.

Internet Resources

Bill Morgan
World of TV Toys, The
P.O. Box 91-1491
Los Angeles, CA 90091
ph: 714-379-6791
e-mail: tvtoys@aol.com
web: http://www.tvtoys.com
Co-author of "Collector's Guide to TV Toys & Memorabilia 60s & 70s - 2nd Edition"; buys and sells; website has memorabilia for sale, collector's guide, online articles, links to TV show fan pages and celebrity web sites.

Museums/Libraries

American Museum of the Moving Image
35 Avenue at 36 Street
Astoria, NY 11106
ph: 718-784-4520 or 718-784-0077
fax: 718-784-4681
e-mail: info@ammi.org
web: http://www.ammi.org/
The only museum in the US devoted to the art, history, technology of film, television, video, interactive media; collection includes costumes, dolls, movie posters, magazines, TV sets, movie cameras, and other items of film & TV history.

Periodicals

George A. Carpinone, Ed.
Magazine: Celebrity Collector Magazine
P.O. Box 1115
Boston, MA 02117-1115
ph: 617-426-7724
fax: 617-426-7724
Interviews with classic movie stars, TV stars, and fan club presidents; exploration of Hollywood memorabilia collecting and collection care; contributions by readers; classified ads; beautifully designed as a collectible on glossy paper.

Stephen Albert
TVC Enterprises
Magazine: TV Collector, The
P.O. Box 1088
Easton, MA 02334-1088
ph: 508-238-1179
e-mail: tvcollector@usa.net
web: http://www.angelfire.com/ma/tvcollector/home.html
In-depth articles about old TV series, behind the scenes information, etc.; also collector ads for videotapes, memorabilia, etc.

Antique Trader Publications, Inc.
Newspaper: Big Reel
P.O. Box 1050
Dubuque, IA 52004-1050
ph: 800-334-7165 or 800-482-4155
fax: 800-531-0880
e-mail: atpzines@aol.com
web: http://www.collect.com/bigreel
A monthly tabloid for movie and television memorabilia collectors and fans: ads, news, current & nostalgic feature articles, obits, etc.

Charlie's Angels

Collectors

Bryan Thomas
171 N. Almont Dr., Apt. D
Beverly Hills, CA 90211
ph: 310-288-2109
Wants to buy "Charlie's Angels" memorabilia; also wants Farrah Fawcett items: pillows, beach towels, bean bag chairs, etc.

Jack Condon
P.O. Box 57468
Sherman Oaks, CA 91403
ph: 818-789-0862
fax: 818-501-1004
e-mail: ChrlAngels@aol.com
web: http://www.charliesangelsfan.com
Always looking to buy or trade "Charlie's Angels" memorabilia.

Dark Shadows

Clubs/Associations

Dark Shadows Festival
Newsletter: Shadow Gram
P.O. Box 92
Maplewood, NJ 07040-0092
ph: 973-762-7208
e-mail: webmaster@mpimedia.com
web: http://www.mpimedia.com/darkshadows/dark9.html
Interested in the "Dark Shadows" TV series; holds annual convention, Dark Shadows Festival.

Louis Wendruck
Dark Shadows Fan Club, The
Magazine: Dark Shadows Announcement, The
P.O. Box 69A04 - Dept. Mal
West Hollywood, CA 90069-0066
ph: 323-650-5112
e-mail: gayboylaca@writeme.com
web: http://members.tripod.com/~dsfc/
Fan Club for TV's Gothic soap opera originally from the 1960s; quarterly magazine; sells T-shirts, books, videos, photos, episode guides and memorabilia.

Periodicals

Sue Ellen Wilson
Newsletter: Dark Shadows Collectables Classifieds
6173 Iroquois Trail
Mentor, OH 44060-2903
ph: 440-946-6348
fax: 440-951-3056
A newsletter with ads for Dark Shadows memorabilia from old and new series; published 9 times per year.

Dennis The Menace

Collectors

Pete Nowicki
1531 39th Ave.
San Francisco, CA 94122-3015
ph: 415-566-7506
e-mail: portfire86@aol.com
Collector seeks all toys and collectibles relating to Dennis the Menace and his friends; no comics, please.

Doctor Who

Clubs/Associations

St. Louis Celestial Intervention Agency
Newsletter: Time Lord Times
P.O. Box 733
Saint Louis, MO 63188
e-mail: stlouiscia@hotmail.com
web: http://members.aol.com/tltimes/stlcia.html
One of the largest strictly Doctor Who clubs with local meetings in North America; excellent source for news and articles.

Collectors

Mark Phippen
Logopolis.com
U.K.
e-mail: mark.phippen@easynet.co.uk
web: http://easyweb.co.uk/~mark.phippen/quences.html
Avid "Doctor Who" collector; web site includes regularly updated release schedule of upcoming merchandise, a chronology of stories, articles, downloads, fan fiction and more.

Internet Resources

U.K.
web: http://www.bbc.co.uk.doctorwho/
"Who" News, alien fact file, forum, Who links.

Dukes Of Hazzard

Clubs/Associations

Aneesh A. Sehgal
Dukes of Hazzard Fan Club
Newsletter: Dukes of Hazzard Fan Club Newsletter
P.O. Box 29154
Chicago, IL 60629-9998
ph: 773-476-7211
fax: 708-489-2331
web: http://www.smartlink.net/~dstitz/Dukes_of_Hazzard/dukeclubs.html
Quarterly newsletter; also issues a fan club merchandise catalog.

Experts

Aneesh A. Sehgal
P.O. Box 29154
Chicago, IL 60629-9998
ph: 773-476-7211
fax: 708-489-2331
web: http://www.smartlink.net/~dstitz/Dukes_of_Hazzard/dukeclubs.html

Gilligan's Island

Clubs/Associations

Original Gilligan's Island Fan Club, The
e-mail: gilligan@san.rr.com
web: http://www.gilligansisle.com/
Gilligan's is still afloat - the Professor found a way to make a computer out of coconuts! A "castaway" membership includes a "Stuck on Gilligan's Island" T-shirt, a quarterly 16-page newsletter, color photo of the castaways.

Gilligan Fan Club
e-mail: Bob@BobDenver.com
web: http://bobdenver.com/
This site is jam-packed with Gilligan Island history, stories, memorabilia, live chats, etc.; created, designed and maintained by Bob Denver (Gilligan) and his wife, Dreama.

Gunsmoke

Collectors

Hank Clark
P.O. Box 812
Waterford, CA 95386-0812
ph: 209-874-2640
fax: 209-874-5750
Wants television and radio "Gunsmoke" items; autographs, photos, advertising, etc.

I Dream Of Jeannie

Collectors

Richard D. Barnes
1520 West 800 North
Salt Lake City, UT 84116-2019
ph: 801-521-4400
fax: 801-292-1947
Collector/historian wants "Jeannie" scripts, press photos, news articles, posters, books, toys, board games, etc.

Experts

Richard D. Barnes
1520 West 800 North
Salt Lake City, UT 84116-2019
ph: 801-521-4400
fax: 801-292-1947
Author of I.D. of J. works including "Going Hollywood", a collectors guide to I.D. of J., Barbara Eden and other Hollywood collectibles; also "Jeannie Guide", and "Diary of a Genie."

I Love Lucy

Clubs/Associations

Thomas J. Watson
We Love Lucy/The International Lucille Ball Fan Club
Magazine: Star Notes
P.O. Box 56234
Sherman Oaks, CA 91413-1234
ph: 818-981-0752
fax: 818-981-0757
e-mail: lucyfan@ix.netcom.com
web: http://www.lucyfan.com/
Quarterly magazine focusing on collectibles pertaining to the "I Love Lucy" TV show and to Lucille Ball and other characters.

Dealers

Cathy's Closet
101 Greenway
Mesquite, TX 75182-9597
ph: 972-226-1352 or 888-BUY-LUCY
e-mail: iselllucy@aol.com
web: http://www.lucystore.com/
Sells new "I Love Lucy" collectibles: Lucy Barbies, books, stamps, ceramics, clothing and more.

Experts

Ric Wyman
408 S. Highland Ave.
Elderon, WI 54429
ph: 715-341-6177
Expert within the world of Lucille Ball nostalgia; author of "For the Love of Lucy: The Complete Guide for Collectors and Fans" (ISBN #0-7892-0006-6); interested in purchasing any Lucile Ball or Desi Arnaz memorabilia.

Thomas J. Watson
P.O. Box 56234
Sherman Oaks, CA 91413-1234
ph: 818-981-0752
fax: 818-981-0757
e-mail: lucyfan@ix.netcom.com
web: http://www.lucyfan.com/
Collects and specializes in Lucille Ball memorabilia.

Museums/Libraries

Lucy-Desi Museum
212 Pine St.
Jamestown, NY 14701
ph: 716-484-7070
e-mail: laughs@lucy-desi.com
web: http://lucydesi.com/
Located in Lucille Ball's hometown, the museum tells the personal story of Lucille Ball and Desi Arnaz.

Laramie

Periodicals

Marcia A. Studley
Laramie Revisited
Newsletter: Laramie Revisited
2108 Lorenzo Ln.
Sacramento, CA 95864
e-mail: Marcia_Studley@prodigy.com
web: http://pages.prodigy.com/Orrymain/
The newsletter is about the Laramie television show and its stars; episode synopsis, interviews, related articles of the show and the Old West.

Lassie

(see also ANIMAL COLLECTIBLES, Dogs [Collies])

Collectors

Joan L. Neidhardt
331 Regal Drive
Abingdon, MD 21009
e-mail: JLNCollies@aol.com
Wants to buy anything relating to Collies or to Lassie; old, new, unique; toys, figurines, character collectibles.

Lost In Space

Clubs/Associations

Scott Beiner
Lost In Space Fan Club
Newsletter: Lost In Space Fan Club Newsletter
550 Trinity Place
Westfield, NJ 07090
ph: 908-789-7323

Flint Mitchell
Lost in Space Fannish Alliance
Newsletter: LISFAN
7331 Terri Robyn St.
Saint Louis, MO 63129
ph: 314-846-2846
e-mail: lisfan@i1.net
web: http://www.lisfan.com/
Membership is free.

Partridge Family

Collectors

Daniel Wachtenheim
P.O. Box 480444
Los Angeles, CA 90048
ph: 323-848-3053
e-mail: dwachte915@aol.com
Buys, sells, trades Partridge Family items: bus, record cabinet, guitar, dolls, etc.; also wants character drum sets (Monkees, Kaptain Kool, etc.) and 60s/70s TV related toys.

Private Eye

Collectors

Gary Pimenta
64 Lakeside Dr.
Tiverton, RI 02878-3111
Wants to buy memorabilia related to television private eye shows such as 77 Sunset Strip, Surfside 6, Hawaiian Eye; wants related toys, magazines, comic books, etc.

Private Eye (Man From UNCLE)

Clubs/Associations

Darlene Kepner
U.N.C.L.E. HQ
Newsletter: HQ Newsletter
234 Washo Dr.
Lake Zurich, IL 60047
Official fan club for the man/girl from U.N.C.L.E.; focuses on the "Man from U.N.C.L.E." reruns, the program and its memorabilia.

Periodicals

Lynda Mendoza
Journal: McCallum Observer, The
P.O. Box 313
Lansing, IL 60438-0313
ph: 708-895-0736
fax: 708-895-1184
e-mail: lsmtmo@juno.com
web: http://www.tezact.com/~divozenk/mccallum/
An authorized journal that contains information about actor David McCallum's present and past career; published four times each year.

Sky King

Collectors

Rod W. Carnahan
541 El Paso St.
Jacksonville, TX 75766
ph: 903-586-1355
e-mail: rodcarnahan_toys@tyler.net

Star Trek

Clubs/Associations

Starfleet
Newsletter: Starfleet Communique
200 Hiawatha Blvd.
Oakland, NJ 07436-3643
e-mail: Membership@sfi.org
web: http://ww.sfi.org/
International Star Trek and science fiction club with chapters in many major U.S. cities and overseas.

Russ Haslage
International Federation of Trekkers
Magazine: Voyages
P.O. Box 242
Lorain, OH 44052-0242
e-mail: ops@iftcommand.com
web: http://www.iftcommand.com/
International club interested in Star Trek; numerous regional chapters; known for its public and charity work.

Dan Madsen
Star Trek: The Official Fan Club
Magazine: Star Trek: The Official Fan Club Magazine
P.O. Box 111000
Aurora, CO 80042
ph: 303-341-1813 or 800-878-3326
web: http://www.starwars.com/
International Star Trek club.

Dealers

Cindy Oakes
34025 W. 6 Mile
Livonia, MI 48152
ph: 734-591-3252
Wants dolls, autographs and other Star Trek memorabilia; also dolls from Star Trek The Movie & New Generation series.

David Roberts
D & S Sci-fi Toy World
4701 NE 72nd Ave. #J222
Vancouver, WA 98661
ph: 360-891-7822
fax: 360-604-5746
e-mail: dnstoys@spiritone.com
web: http://members.aol.com/dnsroberts/index.htm
Specializes in Star Wars, Star Trek, Aliens and other sci-fi movie related toys and collectibles.

Experts

Larry Brooks
Playmates Star Trek Action Figure Page
e-mail: lbrooks2@email.unc.edu
web: http://www.unc.edu/~lbrooks2/playmate.html
Specializes in Star Trek Playmates action figures; website has a complete listing and price guide of all Star Trek Playmates figures; place and view buy/sell/trade ads.

Internet Resources

Star Trek: WWW
e-mail: comments@stwww.com
web: http://www.stwww.com/
Bills itself as "The Mother of All Star Trek sites."

Misc. Services

Star Trek Welcommittee
P.O. Box 12
Saranac, MI 48881-0012
e-mail: caryther@aol.com
International clearinghouse for Star Trek information (all generations); several departments offering help; please enclose SASE when requesting a reply.

The Addams Family

Clubs/Associations

Louis Wendruck
Munsters & the Addams Family Fan Club, The
Magazine: Munsters & the Addams Family Reunion, The
P.O. Box 69A04 - Dept. Mal
West Hollywood, CA 90069-0066
ph: 323-650-5112
e-mail: gayboylaca@writeme.com
web: http://members.tripod.com/~mafc/
Fan Club for the 1960s TV shows "The Munsters" & "The Addams Family"; quarterly magazine; sells T-shirts, photos, videos, records, postcards, memorabilia.

The Fugitive

Clubs/Associations

Texas Bob Reinhardt
F.U.G.I.T.I.V.E.S., The
Newsletter: Stafford Chronicle, The
HC 001 Box 222
Canyon Lake, TX 78133-9701
The Fugitives is a special interest group based upon the character of Dr. Richard Kimble as created by Roy Huggins, and brought to life by David Janssen; focus is on helping others as Dr. Kimble did; annual conventions.

Periodicals

Rusty Pollard
Newsletter: On The Run
P.O. Box 461402
Garland, TX 75046-1402
ph: 972-862-1304 or 214-922-1696
e-mail: rustypol@aol.com
Back issues of bi-monthly newsletter (available) devoted to the 1960s TV series "The Fugitive", its star, David Janssen, and his career; each newsletter covers three episodes; subscribers get free classified ad in each issue.

The Munsters

Clubs/Associations

Louis Wendruck
Munsters & the Addams Family Fan Club, The
Magazine: Munsters & the Addams Family Reunion, The
P.O. Box 69A04 - Dept. Mal
West Hollywood, CA 90069-0066
ph: 323-650-5112
e-mail: gayboylaca@writeme.com
web: http://members.tripod.com/~mafc/
Fan Club for the 1960s TV shows "The Munsters" & "The Addams Family"; quarterly magazine; sells T-shirts, photos, videos, records, postcards, memorabilia.

The Waltons

Museums/Libraries

Walton's Mountain Museum
P.O. Box 124
Schuyler, VA 22969
ph: 804-831-2000
e-mail: ralph@blueridgeweb.com
web: http://www.the-waltons.com/museum.html
School and hometown village of Earl Hammer, Jr., creator of "The Waltons" television series.

Twilight Zone

Museums/Libraries

Jim Loomis, Dir.
Ithaca College, Roy H. Park School of Communications
Ithaca College
328 Park Hall
Ithaca, NY 14850-8364
ph: 607-274-3632
fax: 607-274-1664
e-mail: loomis@ithaca.edu
web: http://www.ithaca.edu/tvr/
Rod Serling archives with videotapes and original scripts of most Twilight Zone episodes.

V

Clubs/Associations

Commander Diana
V Fan Club
Newsletter: Hyperlight Cable
8048 Norwich Ave.
Van Nuys, CA 91402-5616
ph: 818-901-1466
e-mail: katarra@aol.com
International club interested in the series "V"; several regional chapters located throughout the U.S.

Westerns

(see also COWBOY HEROES)

Collectors

Gary Pimenta
64 Lakeside Dr.
Tiverton, RI 02878-3111
Wants to buy pre-1970 Western television program collectibles and comic books including board games and toys based on Western TV shows.

X-Files

Clubs/Associations

Official X-Files Fan Club
Newsletter: X-Notes
100 W. Broadway, #1200
Glendale, CA 91210-1202

TELEVISIONS

(see also AUDIO-VISUAL; ELECTRICITY RELATED ITEMS; RADIOS; TELEVISION SHOWS & MEMORABILIA)

Clubs/Associations

Bruce Kelley
Antique Wireless Association
Newsletter: Old Timer's Bulletin
59 Main St.
Holcomb, NY 14469-9336
ph: 716-657-6260 or 716-657-7489
e-mail: n2rsm@frontiernet.net
web: http://www.ggw.org/freenet/a/awa/
One of the world's largest and oldest historical radio collector organizations; purpose is to document and preserve the history of radio, telegraph and television artifacts.

Barry Zimmerman, Treas./Mem.
Mid-Atlantic Antique Radio Club
Magazine: Radio Age
5825 Woodwinds Cr.
Frederick, MD 21702-7579
ph: 301-696-5561
e-mail: bcbelanger@aol.com
web: http://www.maarc.org/
Published monthly since 1975 for collectors interested in the history of radio and television; restoration, articles by early experts; free buy and sell ads; free sample.

Collectors

Tony & Lynn DeMara
40231 Day
Mt. Clemens, MI 48044

Doug Heimstead
1349 Hillcrest Dr.
Fridley, MN 55432

Carol Leeth
801 S. Webster #14
Anaheim, CA 92804

Dealers

Bruce & Charlotte Mager
Waves
Chelsea Antiques Building
110 West 25th St., 10th Floor
New York, NY 10001-7401
ph: 212-989-9284
fax: 201-461-7121
e-mail: c1wave@aol.com
web: http://www.wavesradio.com/
Over 20 years experience specializing in vintage radios, phonographs, telegraphy, televisions, assorted electrical and mechanical apparatus, and related advertising memorabilia, books and pamphlets.

P. Assenza
Retro Classic TV's
P.O. Box 2631
Lake Ronkonkoma, NY 11779
e-mail: info@antiquetvs.com
web: http://www.antiquetvs.com/

John Okolowicz
624 Cedar Hill Rd.
Ambler, PA 19002-1504
ph: 215-542-1597
e-mail: grillecloth@compuserve.com
web: http://www.grillecloth.com
Buys, sells, trades pre-1950 radios and TV's in unusual or ornate plastic or wooden cabinets; especially those made by Emerson or Stromberg Carlson.

John E. Kendall
Vintage Electronics
P.O. Box 436
Fallston, MD 21047-0436
e-mail: maloney@vintage-electronics.com
web: http://www.vintage-electronics.com
Wants radios from the 1920s through 1960s; buys, sells tube and transistor radios, tube audio, unusual TV's and other early odd electronics; also related items such as books, schematics, tubes, parts, advertising, odd test equipment.

Tommy Meers
GARMCo
fax: 404-297-8161
e-mail: garmco@mindspring.com
web: http://www.garm.com/garmradio.htm
Buys and sells vintage electronics

including antique tube, crystal and transistor radios, phonographs (record players), microphones, televisions and related collectibles; on Internet since 1996; worldwide insured shipping.

Ty Cutkomp
33 Oak Lane
Davenport, IA 52803
ph: 319-323-7263
Buys, sells, trades early televisions: Automatic, Atlas, Majestic, National Republic, Transvision, Silverton, Televue, Viewtone, and any 7" console TV.

Experts

Harry Poster
Vintage TV's
P.O. Box 1883
South Hackensack, NJ 07606-0483
ph: 201-794-9606
fax: 201-794-9553
e-mail: hposter@att.net
web: http://www.harryposter.com
Buying 1922 to 1960s TV's plus small & unusual 1960s/1980s sets including sphere and flying saucer shape; also wants pre-1940 TV dealer displays, empty boxes, manufacturers' literature, old color TVs and adapters; buys complete TV shops.

Glenn F. Bubenheimer
Glenn's Vintage T.V. Service
27851 Terrence
Livonia, MI 48154-3498
ph: 734-421-5574
fax: 602-661-8304
e-mail: gbuben@provide.net
Has collected pre-1953 and select 1950s TVs for over ten years and has repaired them for twenty years; considers himself an expert in values, history and theory; has over 165 pieces in his collection; also repairs.

Mike Brooks
7335 Skyline
Oakland, CA 94611-1121
ph: 510-339-1751
e-mail: deborahwb@aol.com
Buying tiny screen early models, especially wants pre-WWII mechanical spinning disc sets and mirror-in-lid TVs.

Museums/Libraries

Museum of Television & Radio
25 West 52nd St.
New York, NY 10019
ph: 212-621-6800 or 212-621-6600
web: http://www.mtr.org
Museum had two locations, one in New York city and one in Los Angeles.

Bruce Kelley
Antique Wireless Association's Electronic Communication Museum
59 Main St.
Holcomb, NY 14469-9336
ph: 716-657-6260 or 716-657-7489
e-mail: n2rsm@frontiernet.net
web: http://www.ggw.org/freenet/a/awa/
Open limited hours May through October; call or write before visiting; please enclose SASE if requesting a reply.

Larry Auman
Auman Museum of Radio & Television (R)
4316 Murray Rd. N.W.
Dover, OH 44622-7758
ph: 330-343-2297 or 330-364-1058
e-mail: latv@webtv.net
web: http://www.geocities.com/TelevisionCity/Set/1930/
Museum shows early days of electronic entertainment: 1940s movie theater, 1920s-1930s radios, over 300 different 1930-1950 TV's, and related items.

Museum of Television & Radio
465 N. Beverly Dr.
Beverly Hills, CA 90210
ph: 310-786-1000
web: http://www.mtr.org
Museum had two locations, one in New York city and one in Los Angeles.

Periodicals

John V. Terrey
Magazine: Antique Radio Classified
P.O. Box 2
Carlisle, MA 01741
ph: 978-371-0512
fax: 978-371-7129
e-mail: arc@antiqueradio.com
web: http://www.antiqueradio.com
Antique radio's largest monthly about old radios, Art Deco, TV's, ham equip. - '40s, '50s, books, telegraph, etc.; lots of ads.

Repair Services

David B. Johnson
2336 S. Kenilworth Ave.
Berwyn, IL 60402
ph: 708-484-2743
Vintage TV and radio repairs and restorations (electronics and cosmetics).

Suppliers

Antique Electronic Supply
6221 S. Maple Ave.
Tempe, AZ 85283-2856
ph: 602-820-5411
fax: 800-706-6789
e-mail: info@tubesandmore.com
web: http://www.tubesandmore.com/
Large catalog carrying tubes, supplies, capacitors, transformers, chemicals, test equipment, wire, parts, tools, books, etc.

TEXTILES

(see also CLOTHING & ACCESSORIES, Vintage; COVERLETS; FEED & GRAIN BAGS; LOOMS; MILITARIA, Uniforms; QUILTS; REP./REST./CONSER., Textiles; RUGS; SAMPLERS; SEWING ITEMS & GO-WITHS; SHAWLS; MILITARIA, Silk Embroideries; STEVENGRAPHS; TIE-BACKS)

Auction Services

Jo Kris
Skinner, Inc.
357 Main St.
Bolton, MA 01740-1104
ph: 978-779-6241
fax: 978-779-5144
e-mail: info@skinnerinc.com
web: http://www.skinnerinc.com
Established in 1964, Skinner Inc. is the fifth largest auction house in the US; has offices in Bolton and Boston, MA.

Book Sellers

Dennis Marquand
Dennis B. Marquand Books
P.O. Box 1187
Culver City, CA 90232-1187
ph: 310-313-0177
fax: 310-915-9922
e-mail: dmarquand@aol.com
web: http://www.rugbooks.com
Specialize in books on ethnographic textiles from around the world with a focus on Oriental rugs, embroideries, textiles from Central Asian, Navajo, Tibet, Guatemala, Africa.

Clubs/Associations

Costume Society of America, The
Newsletter: CSA News
55 Edgewater Dr.
P.O. Box 73
Earleville, MD 21919-0073
ph: 410-275-1619x or 800-CSA-9447
fax: 410-275-8936
e-mail: webmaster@costumesocietyamerica.com
web: http://www.costumesocietyamerica.com/
Dedicated to advancing the global understanding of all aspects of dress and appearance; also publishes the journal "Dress."

Kathy Buder
Knitting Guild of America, The
Magazine: Cast On
P.O. Box 1606
Knoxville, TN 37901-1606
ph: 423-524-2401 or 800-274-6034
fax: 423-524-8677
e-mail: tkga@tkga.com
web: http://www.tkga.com/
National association of hand and machine knitters; provides education for hand & machine knitters; "Cast On" contains articles, ads, seminars, correspondence courses, competition, etc.

Stephanie Kline Morehouse
Textile Group of Los Angeles, Inc.
894 South Bronson Ave.
Los Angeles, CA 90005-3605
ph: 323-939-2240 or 323-931-4987
fax: 323-931-4987
e-mail: TGLAinc@aol.com
Non-profit society formed in 1979 to provide a further the interest in all and any type of carpets, textiles or related arts; regular meetings, lectures, viewing private collections; textile design, conservation, history.

Dealers

Sonnie Cucinotti
Spirits in the Attic
201 Msgr. O'Brien Hwy.
Cambridge, MA 02141
ph: 617-738-6054
Wants to buy vintage and antique textiles.

Barbara F. Mitchell
Barbara's Antiques
P.O. Box 9
Micanopy, FL 32667-0009
ph: 352-466-3853 or 352-332-1175
Wants to buy "work of art" quilts in good condition; also wants handmade rugs, vintage fabrics and lace.

Diane McGee
Diane McGee Estate Clothing Company
5225 Jackson
Omaha, NE 68106-1331
ph: 402-551-0727
Mail order only; specializing in vintage linens and other textiles.

Billie & John McBride
South Texas Trading Company
P.O. Box 857
Port Aransas, TX 78373
ph: 512-749-6149
e-mail: STFNandTRADING@centuryinter.net
web: http://www.tam.ca/southtexas/
Specializes in vintage textiles, lace and accessories.

Meg Andrews
Meg Andrews, Costumes & Textiles
23, Cowper Rd.
Harpenden, Hertfordshire AL5 5NF
U.K.
ph: 44 1582 460107
fax: 44 1582 461112
e-mail: 106020.2035@compuserve.com
web: http://www.victoriana.com
Specializes in 18th/19th cent. English costumes & accessories, 19th cent. paisley shawls, Arts & Crafts textiles incl. William Morris, Chinese court costumes and textiles, worldwide hangings, 18th/19th cent. samplers.

Experts

Doris May
46 Crafts Rd.
Newton, MA 02161
ph: 617-734-7131
Can help in identifying and appraising textiles.

Evelyn Siefert Kennedy
Sewtique, Inc.
391 Long Hill Rd.
P.O. Box 1293
Groton, CT 06340-1293
ph: 860-445-7320 or 800-332-9122
fax: 860-445-1448
e-mail: sewtique@aol.com
web: http://members.aol.com/sewtique/home.htm
Specialist in restoration, preservation & conservation of apparel and textiles; full service by mail/phone or appt.; appraises textiles, laces, tapestries, etc.; removes spots & stains; teaches textile appraisal & restoration workshops.

Holly Van Sciver
130 Cascadilla Park
Ithaca, NY 14850
ph: 607-277-0498
Can help in identifying and appraising textiles.

Alda Horner
3700 Dean Dr., Unit #3301
Ventura, CA 93003
ph: 805-642-7953
Author of "The Official Price Guide to Linens, Lace, and Other Fabrics."

Ruth Van Arnam
2545 SW Terwilliger Blvd., Apt. 827
Portland, OR 97201-6309
ph: 503-244-3774
An expert with experience in appraising clothing, textiles, quilts and crochet.

Internet Resources

Textmart. Ltd.
Rushmere House
41 Ash Grove
Stapleford, Nottingham N59 6Gl
U.K.
web: http://www.textmart.com/
Online resource for antique textiles, ancient textiles, and vintage textiles; for dealers, interior designers, stylists, and collectors.

Museums/Libraries

Museum of American Textile History
491 Dutton St.
Lowell, MA 01854-4221
ph: 978-441-0400
fax: 978-441-1412
web: http://valley.uml.edu/lowell/historic/museums/textile.html
Outstanding collection of textiles and textile making machinery and equipment; tools, machines, prints, photographs, business records, industry periodicals, textiles, swatches, sample books, trade catalogs, etc.

Rhode Island School of Design Museum
224 Benefit St.
Providence, RI 02903-2723
ph: 401-454-6500
fax: 401-454-6556
e-mail: rbenefie@risd.edu
web: http://www.risd.edu/museum.html
Apparel, architecture, furniture, graphic design, industrial design, interior architecture, landscape architecture.

Currier Gallery of Art, The
201 Myrtle Way
Manchester, NH 03104
ph: 603-669-6144
web: http://www.currier.org/

Shelburne Museum, Inc.
P.O. Box 10
Shelburne, VT 05482-0010
ph: 802-985-3346 or 800-253-0191
fax: 802-985-2331
e-mail: museinfo@together.net
web: http://shelburnemuseum.org/
37 historic structures and exhibit buildings; diverse collection of American folk, fine, decorative and utilitarian art.

Anne R. Fabbri, Dir.
Philadelphia College of Textiles & Science, The Goldey Paley Design Center
4200 Henry Ave.
Philadelphia, PA 19144
ph: 215-951-2860 or 800-951-7287
e-mail: webmaster@philacol.edu
web: http://www.philacol.edu/paey/index.html
A repository for many historical textiles and textile-related artifacts.

Textile Museum, The
Newsletter: Textile Museum Bulletin, The
2320 S St. NW
Washington, DC 20008
ph: 202-667-0441
fax: 202-483-0994
e-mail: info@textilemuseum.org
web: http://www.textilemuseum.org/
Museum dedicated to furthering the understanding of mankind's creative achievements in the textile arts; rotating exhibits drawn largely from the museum's collections featuring works from the eastern and western hemispheres.

Colleen Callahan
Valentine Museum
1015 East Clay
Richmond, VA 23219
ph: 804-649-0711
fax: 804-643-3510
e-mail: valmus@mindspring.com
web: http://www.valentinemuseum.com
Largest costume and textile collection in the South.

Josie De Falla, Dir.
Maryhill Museum of Art
35 Maryhill Museum Drive
Goldendale, WA 98620-4601
ph: 509-773-3733
fax: 509-773-6138
e-mail: MaryHill@gorge.net
web: http://www.maryhillmuseum.org/
Romanian folk textiles, ecclesiastical embroideries, San Blas mola's and 1946 miniature haute couture mannequins.

Museum for Textiles, The
55 Centre Ave.
Toronto, Ontario M5G 2H5
Canada
ph: 416-599-5321 or 416-599-5515
fax: 416-599-2911
e-mail: info@museumfortextiles.on.ca
web: http://www.museumfortextiles.on.ca/
The only museum in Canada exclusively devoted to the collecting, exhibition and documentation of textiles from around the world.

Periodicals

HALI Publications, Ltd.
Magazine: HALI
Kingsgate House
Kingsgate Place, London NW6 4TA
U.K.
ph: 44 171 328 9341 or 44 171 328 1998
fax: 44 171 372 5924
e-mail: hali@centaur.co.uk
"HALI" is the leading bi-monthly international publication in the field of carpet and textile art; an invaluable encyclopedic source of information with original research articles, reviews of museum collections, etc.; high color.

Blankets

Experts

Barry Friedman
P.O. Box 55492
Valencia, CA 91385-0492
ph: 805-255-2365
Buys/sells pre-1945 Indian style wool or cotton blankets by Pendleton, Beacon, Capps, Esmond, Shuler & Benninghofen, American Indian Blanket Mills, Knight, Racine, Buell, Jacobs Oregon City, Provo; plus related catalogs and ads.

Embroidery

Experts

Ita Aber
4465 Douglas Ave, #8G
Bronx, NY 10471-3519
ph: 718-548-3355 or 212-877-7311
fax: 718-548-7888
e-mail: mjaberesq@aol.com
Specializes in old and new needlework; also repairs beadwork; author of "The Art of Judaic Needlework."

Museums/Libraries

Barbara Livenstein
Cooper-Hewitt Museum National Museum of Design, Smithsonian Institution
2 East 91st St.
New York, NY 10128
ph: 212-860-8400 or 212-849-8349
e-mail: liven@ch.si.edu
web: http://www.si.edu/organiza/museums/design/ndm.htm
Can identify old lace, but are not allowed to access value.

Repro. Sources

Elizabeth Creeden
Sampler, The
84 Court St.
Plymouth, MA 02360
ph: 508-746-7077
e-mail: sampler@ici.net
Has knowledge of 17th, 18th and 19th C. needlework in surface embroidery, needlepoint (tent stitch) evenweave stitching and crewel; reproduction and adaptations can be drawn, charted or designed and stitched; coat of arms, samplers, etc.

Embroidery (Stumpwork)

Clubs/Associations

Sylvia C. Fishman
Stumpwork Society
Newsletter: Stumpwork Society Chronicle
55 Ferncrest Ave.
Cranston, RI 02905-3510
ph: 201-224-3622
fax: 201-224-3075
Interested in antique stumpwork embroidery; restoration, preservation and collection.

Fabric

Dealers

Dan
Experienced Denim
P.O. Box 239
Fayetteville, AR 72702-0239
ph: 501-444-7541 or 800-336-4694
fax: 501-521-8331
e-mail: exd@edenim.com
web: http://www.edenim.com/
Wants '40s-'50s drapery (barkcloth) with tropical, mod geometrics, large flowered prints, many types of vintage fabrics; send SASE for free list of items wanted.

Eugenie Gelman
Genie's Fab Fabrics
U.K.
e-mail: genie@thebrighton.demon.co.uk
web: http://www.thebrighton.demon.co.uk
Buys, sells, collects original fabric from the 1950s to 1970s: curtains, cushions, remnants, rolls.

Lace & Linens

Clubs/Associations

International Old Lacers, Inc.
Magazine: International Old Lacers Bulletin
P.O. Box 554
Flanders, NJ 07836
e-mail: iolinc@aol.com
web: http://members.aol.com/iolinc/ioli.html

Dealers

Marsha Manchester
Milady's Mercantile
17 South Main St.
Middleboro, MA 02346
ph: 508-946-2121
Buys and sells linen and lace, and ladies accessories, i.e. bridal handkerchiefs, fans, shawls.

Shirley Frater
Arsenic & Old Lace
P.O. Box 367
Main Street
Damariscotta, ME 04543-0367
ph: 207-563-1414
Buys and sells all types of linens and lace: tablecloths, napkins, dresser scarves, hankies, hand towels, etc.; prefers in as-found condition.

Cynthia Cooper
Linen Room, The
81 Albany Turnpike, Rte 44
Canton, CT 06019
ph: 860-693-4478 or 860-677-5423
fax: 860-677-5423
e-mail: cyncooper@imagine.com
Extensive selection of antique and vintage linens, most in pristine condition: pillow cases, shams, linen sheets, coverlets, tablecloths, napkins, place mats, hand towels, handkerchiefs, curtains.

Lydia Reed
Wyndham Needleworks
Box 65, 233 Old Colony Rd.
Eastford, CT 06242
ph: 860-974-1214
Buys and sells linen and lace.

Pahaka September
Pahaka
19 Fox Hill
Upper Saddle River, NJ 07458-1314
ph: 201-327-1464
Buys and sells quality lace, curtains, bed and table linens, fabrics, embroidery, etc.; by appointment or mail order; sorry, no catalog.

Susan & Michelle Horowitz
Quilted Corner, The
124 Fourth Ave.
New York, NY 10003-4903
ph: 212-505-6568
e-mail: michelle@quiltedcorner.com
web: http://www.quiltedcorner.com/
Carries a wide assortment of vintage linens, tablecloths, napkins, tea towels, souvenir pillows, drapes and textiles.

Lois Lamb
Vintage Linens
203 Camelot Dr.
Simpsonville, SC 29681-5739
ph: 864-967-1088
e-mail: herblamb@sprintmail.com
web: http://www.vintagelinens.com
Wants to buy antique linens that are at least 50 years old; wants high quality linens only including pillowcases, sheets, bed covers, doilies, runners, cloths, napkins, lace curtains, etc.; linens with monograms always a plus.

Cornelia Powell
Cornelia Powell Antiques, Inc.
271 B East Paces Ferry Rd.
Atlanta, GA 30305
ph: 706-733-6073
Lace clothing, vintage and designer made from antique laces and bridal accessories.

Coria Fierbaugh
Sweethaven Lace
4681 Bloomfield Rd.
Taylorsville, KY 40071
ph: 502-477-8819
e-mail: sfierbaugh@acm.org
Collector, dealer and expert in antique lace and linen; also does repairs.

Sabine Casten
Lace Collection, The
558 Monroe
River Forest, IL 60305
ph: 708-366-0756
Buys and sells linen and lace; also interested in buttons.

Dewey Cornay
214 Lafitte Ave.
Lafayette, LA 70506
ph: 318-235-5352
Buys and sells linen and lace.

Karen Dawkins
Legacy Linens
1321 Dartmouth
Denton, TX 76201
ph: 940-382-5623 or 940-382-0181
fax: 940-591-0262
Wants to buy lace and fancy white linens in good condition; also baby clothes, textiles and pre-1960 print table cloths and kitchen towels gives lectures and seminars on vintage linens, lace, hats & jewelry.

Rebecca Nohe
Quartermoon Market
315 East Pikes Peak Ave.
Colorado Springs, CO 80903
ph: 719-630-8961
Buys and sells linen and lace.

Sue Morse
Emma's Trunk
1701 Orange Tree Lane
Redlands, CA 92374-2857
ph: 909-798-7865 or 909-864-8445
fax: 909-798-7386
Wants FANCY aprons, bedspreads, Christening gowns, collars, cuffs, doilies, handkerchiefs, napkins, etc.; write before sending items.

Jude Allen
Vintage Collection
356 Main St.
Half Moon Bay, CA 94019
ph: 650-712-0366
fax: 650-654-0842
Buys and sells linen and lace; also old yardage, buttons, quilts, sewing implements, sewing machines and miniature sewing machines.

Jules Kliot
Lacis
3163 Adeline St.
Berkeley, CA 94703-2401
ph: 510-843-7178
fax: 510-843-5018
Antique & historic textiles, lace from the 16th century, vintage garments and accessories; sells books and supplies for costume, lace and embroidery; also offers repairs and conservation services.

Experts

Marsha Manchester
Milady's Mercantile
17 South Main St.
Middleboro, MA 02346
ph: 508-946-2121
Author of "Vintage White Linens, A to Z" (Schiffer Pub.)

Evelyn Siefert Kennedy
Sewtique, Inc.
391 Long Hill Rd.
P.O. Box 1293
Groton, CT 06340-1293
ph: 860-445-7320 or 800-332-9122
fax: 860-445-1448
e-mail: sewtique@aol.com
web: http://members.aol.com/sewtique/home.htm
Specialist in restoration, preservation & conservation of apparel and textiles; full service by mail/phone or appt.; appraises textiles, laces, tapestries, etc.; removes spots & stains; teaches textile appraisal & restoration workshops.

Mary Lou Kueker
7005 Fitzpatrick Dr.
Laurel, MD 20707-3208
ph: 301-490-5432
Specializing in antique lace and linens; identification and appraisal for all textiles; also cleaning and repair of fine laces and linens.

Elizabeth M. Kurella
Old Lace & Linen Merchant, The
P.O. Box 222
Plainwell, MI 49080
ph: 616-685-9792
fax: 616-685-5043
e-mail: ekurella@accn.org
Buys, sells, and appraises lace and linens; offers many pieces of antique lace for sale; author of "The Secrets of Real Lace," and "Guide to Lace & Linens."

Misc. Services

Unique Art Lace Cleaners
5926 Delmar Blvd.
Saint Louis, MO 63112
ph: 314-725-2900
fax: 314-725-3142
Specializes in cleaning old textiles, linens and lace.

Museums/Libraries

Lace Museum, The
552 South Murphy Ave.
Sunnyvale, CA 94086
ph: 408-730-4695
e-mail: sherrigd@sherrisworkshop.com
web: http://www.thelacemuseum.org/
Textiles, lace, linen; guild classes, teaching, museum gift shop; purpose is to keep the art of lace making alive for future generations.

Needlework

Clubs/Associations

American Needlepoint Guild, Inc.
P.O. Box 1027
Cordova, TN 38088-1027
ph: 901-755-3728
fax: 901-755-3803
e-mail: anginfo@needlepoint.org
web: http://www.needlepoint.org/
An educational, non-profit organization whose purpose is educational and cultural development through participation in and encouragement of interest in the art of needlepoint; for all stitchers, whether amateur or professional.

Dealers

Carol Huber
40 Ferry Rd.
Old Saybrook, CT 06475
ph: 860-388-6809
fax: 860-388-6809
Buys and sells early needlework including samplers, pictures and related items.

Experts

Ita Aber
4465 Douglas Ave, #8G
Bronx, NY 10471-3519
ph: 718-548-3355 or 212-877-7311
fax: 718-548-7888
e-mail: mjaberesq@aol.com
Specializes in old and new needlework; also repairs beadwork; author of "The Art of Judaic Needlework."

Needlework (Judaic)

(see also JUDAICA)

Experts

Ita Aber
4465 Douglas Ave, #8G
Bronx, NY 10471-3519
ph: 718-548-3355 or 212-877-7311
fax: 718-548-7888
e-mail: mjaberesq@aol.com
Consultations, restorations and commissions; works with architects and decorators; lecturer, historian, author of book and many articles on same.

Tablecloths

Dealers

Susan & Michelle Horowitz
Quilted Corner, The
124 Fourth Ave.
New York, NY 10003-4903
ph: 212-505-6568
e-mail: michelle@quiltedcorner.com
web: http://www.quiltedcorner.com/
Carries a wide assortment of vintage linens, tablecloths, napkins, tea towels, souvenir pillows, drapes and textiles.

Paula Rubenstsein
65 Prince St.
New York, NY 10012
ph: 212-966-8954
Specializes in vintage tablecloths.

Tapestries

Dealers

Her Castle Tapestry
134 Nelson Street #E
Arroyo Grande, CA 93420
ph: 800-350-3850
e-mail: tapestry@fix.net
web: http://www.fix.net/~rwhaley/dida/
Sells large line of European tapestries: medieval, hunt scenes, nature scenes, florals, romantic scenes.

THANKSGIVING COLLECTIBLES

(see HOLIDAY COLLECTIBLES)

THEFT & FRAUD

(see ART THEFT & FRAUD)

THERMOMETERS

Clubs/Associations

Warren D. Harris
Thermometer Collectors Club of America
Newsletter: Thermometer Reference
6130 Rampart Dr.
Carmichael, CA 95608
ph: 916-966-3490 or 916-654-2097
fax: 916-966-3490
e-mail: jockobwca@aol.com
web: http://www.angelfire.com/ma/thermo6/

Collectors

Alan Cook
1307 Hogan Ln.
Round Rock, TX 78664
ph: 512-244-6874
Wants to buy wood, metal, and picture advertising thermometers.

Experts

Richard Porter
49 Zarahelma Road
P.O. Box 944
Onset, MA 02558-0944
ph: 508-295-5504
"The Thermometer Man"; his large collection featured in "Ripley's Believe It or Not" and the "Guiness Computer of World Records"; curator of the world's only thermometer museum; motto: "Always open, always free, with about 3000 to see."

Warren D. Harris
6130 Rampart Dr.
Carmichael, CA 95608
ph: 916-966-3490 or 916-654-2097
fax: 916-966-3490
e-mail: jockobwca@aol.com
web: http://www.angelfire.com/ma/thermo6/
Wants decorative pre-1930 non advertising, non commercial, non clinical thermometers of every kind; mercury-in-the-tube type preferred; also wants thermometer related ephemera.

Museums/Libraries

Richard Porter, Curator
Porter Thermometer Museum
49 Zarahelma Road
P.O. Box 944
Onset, MA 02558-0944
ph: 508-295-5504
World's largest private collection of thermometers from American and all over the world; representing over 100 manufacturers and featured in over 60 articles and 18 videos.

THERMOS BOTTLES

(see LUNCH BOXES)

THIRD REICH

(see NAZI ITEMS)

TICKETS

(see also MOVIE MEMORABILIA; MUSIC; PAPER COLLECTIBLES; SPORTS COLLECTIBLES; TRANSPORTATION COLLECTIBLES; WORLD'S FAIRS & EXPOSITIONS)

Dealers

Jim Crump
Ticket Place Collectibles
P.O. Box 767
East Freetown, MA 02717
ph: 508-763-3502
fax: 508-763-9291
e-mail: tickets@ticketplace.com
web: http://www.rarestuff.com
Specializes in unused tickets and stubs to sporting events, special events and concerts; wants to buy almost any kind of ticket or ticket stub out there; also has Elvis Presley ticket stubs for sale.

TIE BARS, CLIPS & TACKS

(see also CLOTHING & ACCESSORIES, Vintage; CUFF LINKS; GEMS & JEWELRY)

Collectors

Norman Landis
1315 Marbendale Ct.
Saint Louis, MO 63122

Dean Hodgdon
2920 E. 77th St.
Tulsa, OK 74136-8723
ph: 918-494-0225 or 918-665-6512
e-mail: d.hodgdon@worldnet.att.net
web: http://home.att.net/~d.hodgdon
Wants company pins or tie tacks with years of services and company names; buys and trades.

Harvey Whittam
29 Shelley Close
Langley
Slough, Berkshire SL3 8JW
U.K.
Collector of aviation and law enforcement tie tacks from around the world.

TIE-BACKS

Collectors

Sandie Bush
516 N. Brian St.
Santa Maria, CA 93454
ph: 805-925-9756
Wants to buy glass and metal curtain tie-back holders.

TIFFANY ITEMS

(see also GEMS & JEWELRY; GLASS, Art; LAMPS & LIGHTING, Tiffany/Handel/Pairpoint; SILVER)

Dealers

Bill Holland
William Holland Fine Arts
1554 Paoli Pike
West Chester, PA 19380
ph: 610-344-9848
fax: 610-344-06651
e-mail: bill@hollandarts.com
web: http://www.hollandarts.com/
Buys and sells Tiffany desk lamps and desk set pieces; no reproductions please.

Reyne Haines
Vintage Glass
405 Lafayette Ave.
Cincinnati, OH 45220
ph: 513-559-1405
fax: 513-651-0860
e-mail: reyne@tias.com
web: http://www.tias.com/stores/RHA/
Buys and sells Tiffany glass, lamps, bronze, jewelry and windows; also buys art of the same period.

Experts

Neustadt Museum of Tiffany Art, Inc., The
124 West 79th St.
New York, NY 10024
ph: 212-874-0872
fax: 212-874-0872
e-mail: nmtamuseum@aol.com
Permanent exhibition is at the Queens Museum of Art; also has traveling museum; offers research facilities.

Sylvia Kornblum
Team Antiques
P.O. Box 1052
Great Neck, NY 11023-0052
ph: 516-487-1826
Over 30 years experience in cataloging and selling Louis C. Tiffany, Tiffany Studios items by mail-order.

Internet Resources

Paul Doros
e-mail: pdoros@ix.netcom.com
web: http://www.geocities.com/Vienna/Choir/7564/
A detailed web site on the life and works of Louis Comfort Tiffany including a chronological history of Tiffany and Tiffany Studios.

Man./Prod./Dist.

Tiffany Co.
5th Ave. at 57th St.
New York, NY 10022
ph: 212-755-8000
web: http://www.tiffany.com/
Main Tiffany store; Tiffany items also retailed through regional stores.

Misc. Services

Tiffany & Co. Archives
15 Sylcan Way
Parsippany, NJ 07054
web: http://www.tiffany.com/intro/archive.htm
Collects, preserves, maintains and makes available documents that record the history of Tiffany & Co from the 1840s to present; provides research services to customers interested in historical information pertaining to Tiffany.

Museums/Libraries

Chrysler Museum, The
245 West Olney Road
Norfolk, VA 23510-1587
ph: 757-664-6200
fax: 757-664-6201
e-mail: museum@chrysler.org
web: http://www.chrysler.org

TILES

(see also BOOKS, Reference [Tiles]; CERAMICS)

Clubs/Associations

Prof. William Prescott, Mem. Sec.
Tiles & Architectural Ceramics Society
Magazine: Glazed Expressions
38 Church St.
Stony Stratford, Milton Keynes MK11 1BD
U.K.
e-mail: w.prescott@open.ac.uk
web: http://www.aimnet.com/~tcolson/webtiles.htm
Society serves the collector, historian, craftsman and conservator interested in decorated ceramics relating to buildings; also publishes biennial journal; magazine twice a year & a newsletter quarterly.

Collectors

Michael Padwee
P.O. Box 023138
Brooklyn, NY 11202-3138
ph: 718-499-4307
e-mail: mwpadwee@inch.com
Tile historian who collects American antique ceramic tiles; author of "A Guide to the Patterns and Markings on the Backs of United States Ceramic Tiles, 1870s to 1930s," and "Field Guide to Key Patterns on U.S. Ceramic Tiles" (1999).

Susan Frost
806 Rosedale Terrace
Austin, TX 78704-3159
ph: 512-447-2575 or 512-447-0407
e-mail: Reuter@io.com
web: http://www.io.com/~reuter/
Wants to buy San Jose Pottery and San Jose Mission Crafts tiles.

Dealers

Sandie Fowler
Antique Articles
P.O. Box 72
North Billerica, MA 01862
ph: 978-663-8083
fax: 978-663-8083
e-mail: artiles@earthlink.net
web: http://www.antiqnet.com/antiquearticles/
Carries a full range of tiles dating primarily from 1880 to 1930s; has both American and European tiles; also carries early Delft tiles c. 1700; has both single tiles and matching tiles including complete fireplace surrounds.

Karen Guido
Karen Michelle
P.O. Box 489
Bridgewater, CT 06752-0489
ph: 860-354-7197
e-mail: freesia@javanet.com
Over 3000 antique & collectible tiles in stock; specializing in American and English tiles from 1870 to 1940; stock encompasses fireplace surrounds and mantle accents, border tiles, works of art in ceramics, tile-topped tables, etc.

Pedro Leitao
Solar Antique Tiles
971 First Ave.
New York, NY 10022
ph: 212-755-2403
fax: 212-980-2649
e-mail: pleitao@aol.com
web: http://www.solarantiquetiles.com/
Large selection of original antique tiles that have been removed from buildings and palaces dating back to 16th century; also has a line of reproduction tiles in antique designs.

Ken Forster
5501 Seminary Rd., Ste. 1311 South
Falls Church, VA 22041
ph: 703-379-1142
Dealer in American art pottery and tiles, specializing in American tiles from 1860 to 1940; also Art Nouveau, Art Deco, Georg Jensen silver, and American Modernism.

Kathy Rae
3990 12 Mile Road, Ste. #1
Berkley, MI 48072
ph: 248-642-1274
Wants to buy 1880s-1940s tiles.

Richard Mohr
Richard Mohr Antiques
402 S. Coler Ave.
Urbana, IL 61801
ph: 217-367-7856
e-mail: r-mohr@uiuc.edu
Collects, buys, sells American art tiles, specializing in faience tiles, particularly those of the Arts & Crafts movement.

Ron Endlich
Tile Antiques
P.O. Box 4505
Seattle, WA 98104
ph: 206-632-9675
Tile search, appraisal, research services, and framing.

Michael Swann
Tile Image Gallery
85 Curzon St.
Derby, Derbyshire DE1 1LN
U.K.
ph: +44 1332 362770
e-mail: captain@derbycity.com
web: http://www.derbycity.com/michael/recept.html
Collector, dealer with web site having full color images of tiles, each with a brief description and each dated; an essential reference source for anyone interested in ceramic art, history or design, method of surface decoration, etc.

Experts

Chris Blanchett
Holly Tree House
18 Woodlands Rd.
Littlehampton, West Sussex BN17 5PP
U.K.
ph: +44 1903 717648
fax: +44 1903 717648
e-mail: clbanchett@lineone.net
Collector, historian and author on tiles and related subjects of all periods; research/identification undertaken; major library of tile-related materials; large reference collection of tiles, etc.

Man./Prod./Dist.

Dona Danziger
Clay Works, The
4058 S. Main St.
P.O. Box 352
Exmore, VA 23350
ph: 757-414-0567
fax: 757-414-0571
e-mail: clayworks@esva.net
web: http://www.esva.net/~clayworks
Hand painted pottery and art tiles in current studio productions; brochures and shipping available.

Periodicals

Joseph Taylor
Tile Heritage Foundation
Newsletter: Flash Point
P.O. Box 1850
Healdsburg, CA 95448
ph: 707-431-8453
fax: 707-431-8455
web: http://www.aimnet.com/~tcolson/pages/tileorgs/thfinfo.htm
Dedicated to promoting the appreciation for tiled surfaces; promotes preservation of rare & unusual ceramics; has library on old tiles; also publishes a magazine entitled "Tile Heritage."

Repro. Sources

Pedro Leitao
Solar Antique Tiles
971 First Ave.
New York, NY 10022
ph: 212-755-2403
fax: 212-980-2649
e-mail: pleitao@aol.com
web: http://www.solarantiquetiles.com/
Large selection of original antique tiles that have been removed from buildings and palaces dating back to 16th century; also has a line of reproduction tiles in antique designs.

California

Experts

Steve Soukup
California Crazed
P.O. Box 7662
Van Nuys, CA 91406-7662
ph: 818-787-5990 or 818-781-9262
Buys and sells California pottery and tiles: Catalina, Batchelder, Arequipa, Calco, Malibu, Claycraft, California Faience, S&S, D&M, CCPCO, GMB, Tropico, Taylor, Tudor, etc.

California (Malibu Potteries)

Museums/Libraries

Malibu Lagoon Museum
23200 Pacific Coast Highway
P.O. Box 291
Malibu, CA 90265-0291
ph: 310-456-8432
Features the boldly hued tileworks of Southern California's Malibu Potteries (1926-1932); also tile books.

Drain

Museums/Libraries

Mike Weaver Drain Tile Museum
P.O. Box 464
Geneva, NY 14456
ph: 315-789-3848 or 315-789-5151
Large collection of over 350 drain tiles - ceramic pipes used to drain excess moisture from farm land - dating from 100 B.C.

New Jersey

Experts

Helen Henderson
P.O. Box 577
Keyport, NJ 07735-0577
ph: 732-739-6799
Wants catalogs, literature, backstamps, maker's marks of New Jersey decorative and architectural tiles; collecting interests: Monmouth and Middlesex counties manufacturers.

Pardee

Collectors

Helen Henderson
P.O. Box 577
Keyport, NJ 07735-0577
ph: 732-739-6799
Specializes in tiles made by the C. Pardee Works, Matanan Tile Co., ATCO; conducting research on New Jersey tile firms and seeks information and photographs of the plant, tiles, backstamps, advertisements, etc.

Victorian

Experts

Pamela & Allan Luttig
Blue Boar Antiques
P.O. Box 423
Grand Ledge, MI 48837
ph: 517-626-6432

Zsolnay

Internet Resources

Federico Santi
Zsolnay Tile Museum, The Online
152 Spring St.
Newport, RI 02840-6806
ph: 401-841-5060
fax: 401-848-0953
e-mail: zsolnay@drawrm.com
web: http://www.drawrm.com
An on-line museum of Zsolnay ceramic tiles from the 1870s through WWI; pictures, articles and tile links; browse to www.drawrm.com/ztilemus.htm.

TIN COLLECTIBLES

(see ADVERTISING COLLECTIBLES; ADVERTISING COLLECTIBLES, Tins; BISCUIT BARRELS/JARS/TINS; COFFEE, Tins; FOLK ART, Tinware; MINING COLLECTIBLES, Cap Tins; PROPHYLACTICS, Tin; SMOKING COLLECTIBLES; TOYS, Tin; TYPEWRITERS, Ribbon Tins)

TITANIC MEMORABILIA

(see also NAUTICAL ANTIQUES; OCEAN LINER COLLECTIBLES)

Clubs/Associations

Edward Kamunda
Titanic Historical Society
Magazine: Titanic Commutator, The
P.O. Box 51053
Indian Orchard, MA 01151-5053
ph: 413-543-4770
Focuses on all aspects of the "Titanic", her sister ship the "Britannic", and the White Star Line.

Robert M. DiSogra, Pres.
Titanic International Society
Journal: Voyage
P.O. Box 7007
Freehold, NJ 07728-7007
ph: 732-462-1413 or 973-742-8747
fax: 732-462-1771
e-mail: rdisogra@hotmail.com
web: http://www.titanicinternational.org
Members interested in the history of RMS TITANIC, her passengers and crew; a reference source for all Titanic artifacts; world wide society; annual meetings; speakers available on history, artifact recovery, educational displays.

Collectors

Gary Robinson
82 Elm St.
Oneonta, NY 13820
ph: 607-431-4437 or 607-432-6893
fax: 607-431-4105
e-mail: robinson@digital-marketplace.net
Buys, sells and trades artifacts and ephemera relating to RMS Titanic and the White Star Line; also RMS Carpathia, Titanic's rescue ship.

Frederick Lingenfelser
814 Byram St.
Reading, PA 19606-1446
Buying anything related to the Titanic: newspapers, post cards, menus, books, photographs, letters from survivors, paintings, artifacts, etc.

Experts

Edward Kamunda
P.O. Box 51053
Indian Orchard, MA 01151-5053
ph: 413-543-4770
Wants newspapers, books, sheet music, artifacts.

Charles Ira Sachs
TransAtlantic Research
P.O. Box 8005
Universal City, CA 91618-8005
ph: 818-985-1345
fax: 818-985-1345
e-mail: onrs@earthlink.net
web: http://www.titanic.org/
Buys/sells/specializes/lectures on ocean liner and zeppelin history & memorabilia from the high seas (i.e. none from coastal or river steamers) dating from 1840 to 1960s; posters, postcards and related material for collectors/museums.

Internet Resources

Jon Ostrowski
RMS Titanic Web Ring
5 Dalby Close, Leegomery
Telford, Shropshire TF1 4FJ
U.K.
ph: 01952 256567
fax: c
e-mail: jonsosmgy@hotmail.com
web: http://titanicring.hypermart.net/
The Internet Titanic Ring was set up to serve as a Titanic site database; has pretty much everything one could want about Titanic.

TOASTERS

(see also ELECTRICITY RELATED ITEMS)

Clubs/Associations

Carl Roles
Upper Crust
Newsletter: A Toast to You
P.O. Box 529
Temecula, CA 92593
ph: 909-699-5139 or 909-699-8456
fax: 909-699-8119
e-mail: rocknroles@yahoo.com

Collectors

William Blakeslee
116 Bethlehem Pike
P.O. Box 56
Ambler, PA 19002-0056
ph: 215-646-6593
fax: 215-646-5459
e-mail: readferry@snip.net
Wants unusual electric toasters: Mecky, Trimble, Foldex, Coleman, Cozy, Monarch, Helion, Thoro, Birtman, Pelouze; send photo, markings.

Howard & Jane Hazelcorn
6731 Ashley Ct.
Sarasota, FL 34241-9696
ph: 941-921-1815
Authors of "Price Guide to Old Electric Toasters."

Uwe H. Breker
6731 Ashley Ct.
Sarasota, FL 34241-9696
ph: 941-925-0385
fax: 941-925-0487
e-mail: auction@breker.com
web: http://www.breker.com/
Wants to buy toasters: porcelain, ceramic, etc.

Richard Mathes
P.O. Box 1408
Springfield, OH 45501-1408
Wants old fireplace, stove top and pre-1940 electric toasters.

Oscar P. Barkhurst
3910 Brookside Dr.
Rapid City, SD 57702-2219
ph: 605-348-1354
Wants old, electric pre-1950 toasters; heart shaped, perch, roaster coffee pot combination, very old toaster ovens, unusual, odd. Send photo and information printed on the item.

Joe Lukach
7111 Deframe Ct.
Arvada, CO 80004-1168
ph: 303-422-8970
e-mail: jlukach@resortdesign.com
Collector wants vintage toasters in good condition; also wants items related to toasters such as advertising, catalogs, etc.

Dealers

Carl Roles
26245 Calle Cresta
Temecula, CA 92590
ph: 909-699-5139 or 909-699-8456
fax: 909-699-8119
Wants to buy vintage electric toasters and any item marked "Porcelier", especially Porcelier toaster, waffle irons, sandwich makers, coffee percolators, urns.

Experts

Helen Greguire
Helen's Antiques
103 Trimmer Rd.
Hilton, NY 14468-9305
ph: 716-392-2704

Jim A. Barker
ToasterMaster Antique Appliances
RR 5 Box 1375
Honesdale, PA 18431
ph: 570-253-1951
Wants interesting electric toasters 1908-1940; Porcelier, GE, Toastrite, Mecky, Pelouze; mechanical, push button, crank type, drop down; highest prices paid.

Museums/Libraries

Eric R. Norcross
Toaster Museum Foundation, The
Newsletter: Hotwire
1003 Carlton Ave., Ste. B
Charlottesville, VA 22902-5974
ph: 804-293-3569
e-mail: eric@toaster.org
web: http://www.toaster.org
A non-profit foundation dedicated to preserving toasters and toast-related paraphernalia.

Periodicals

Carl Roles
Newsletter: Toast To You, A
26245 Calle Cresta
Temecula, CA 92590
ph: 909-699-5139 or 909-699-8456
fax: 909-699-8119
A bi-monthly newsletter for vintage

electric toaster collectors and dealers; historic data, stories, old ads, photographs and collections; for both the advanced and beginning collector.

TOBACCO CARDS

(see ADVERTISING COLLECTIBLES, Trade Cards [Tobacco]; CIGAR BOXES, LABELS & BANDS; CIGARETTE COLLECTIBLES; CIGAR STORE COLLECTIBLES; LIGHTERS; MATCHBOXES & LABELS; MATCHCOVERS; MATCH SAFES; PIPES; SMOKING COLLECTIBLES)

TOBACCO COLLECTIBLES

(see also ADVERTISING COLLECTIBLES, Trade Cards [Tobacco]; MATCH SAFES; PAPER COLLECTIBLES; SMOKING COLLECTIBLES)

Clubs/Associations

Betty & Jim Ogburn
Piedmont Tobacco Memorabilia & Collector's Club
Route 1, Box 324
King, NC 27021
ph: 336-983-9729

Collectors

Dan Calandriello
53-C Beacon Village
Burlington, MA 01803-3843
ph: 781-229-9009
e-mail: dan@coe.neu.edu
Wants 1880s-1910 American tobacco posters showing card sets; tobacco cards; leathers from 1880s-1905.

David & Barbara Freiberg
Cerebro
P.O. Box 327
East Prospect, PA 17317-0327
ph: 717-252-2400 or 800-69L-ABEL
fax: 717-252-3685
e-mail: cerebro@cerebro.com
web: http://www.cerebro.com
Wants to buy tobacco paper items, cigarette cards, tobacco trade cards.

Betty & Jim Ogburn
Route 1, Box 324
King, NC 27021
ph: 336-983-9729

Cindy Porman
22044 Roosevelt Rd.
South Bend, IN 46614
ph: 219-291-6414
Wants Copenhagen Snuff, Weyman & Sons, Weyman Bros., Skoal Snuff, and Key Snuff tobacco items including crocks, pocket tins, store displays, metal and paper signs, and related advertising items.

Chris Cooper
Rt. 2 Box 55
Pittsburg, TX 75686-9516
ph: 903-856-7286
fax: 903-856-6879
web: http://www.collectoronline.com/club-TTCC.html
Wants tobacco tags, trade cards, tins, cigar cutters, ashtrays, billheads, caddies, labels, matchsafes, hammers, box openers, pennants, felts, key chains, bags, and most other tobacco advertising and ephemera.

Dealers

Mark Suozzi
P.O. Box 102
Ashfield, MA 01330
ph: 413-628-3241
fax: 413-628-3241
e-mail: marklyn@valinet.com
web: http://www.marklynantiques.com/
Buys and sell tobacciana: antique tin litho and paper signs from 1850-1920, tobacco canisters, political campaign subjects, figural iron and lead cigar ad cutters and gas lighters, tobacco wood trade signs and store figures.

Lenore Monleon
33 Fifth Ave.
New York, NY 10003-4338
ph: 212-475-7871 or 212-675-7771
Wants to buy tobacco collectibles: pocket match safes, tobacco humidors, enameled cigarette cases, etc.

Stephen C. Jones
P.O. Box 267
Homer, NY 13077-0267
ph: 607-753-8822
e-mail: stevejones@a-znet.com
Wants cigar box labels, lithographers sample books of cigar box labels, cigarette cards, tobacco trade cards, tobacco business cards, tobacco store signs.

J. Glen & Violet Moore
Main Street Antiques
47 W. Main St.
P.O. Box 627
New Market, MD 21774
ph: 301-865-3710
Buys and sells early American tobacco collectibles; large selections of signs, wood cigar boxes, pocket and other tins, plug cutters, counter displays, etc.; appointments preferred.

Willisia Holbrook
Armbrook Antiques
531 Doub Rd.
Lewisville, NC 27023
ph: 888-393-8025 or 336-945-9477
fax: 336-945-9914
e-mail: olestuff@armbrookantiques.com
web: http://www.armbrookantiques.com
Buys and sells early tobacco and smoking antiques; specializes in pre-1930s items; web site has full online catalog including descriptions and photos.

J. Jones
Hermit Tobacco Works Company
P.O. Box 669
Pioneer, OH 43554
ph: 517-567-2208
fax: 219-639-6035
e-mail: hermittob@aol.com
web: http://www.pipestand.com
Collector, dealer, expert buys and sells trade pipes and all tobacciana; anything Dunhill; cigar signs, fan hangers, full tins of tobacco.

Jeff Mogilner
Racine & Laramie, Ltd.
2737 San Diego Ave.
San Diego, CA 92110-2731
ph: 619-291-7833
fax: 619-297-6653
web: http://sandiego.sidewalk.com/link/10622
Buy, sell, collect antique tobacco pipes: meerschaum, clay, briar, porcelain, and related items.

Jars

Clubs/Associations

Charlotte Tarses
Society of Tobacco Jar Collectors
Newsletter: Tobacco Jar Newsletter
3011 Falstaff Rd. #307
Baltimore, MD 21209-2960
e-mail: jfigtobjar@aol.com
Purpose is to promote the collection and dissemination of information related to the manufacture, design, artistic merit, and historic, educational and cultural aspects of antique tobacco jars; annual convention.

Collectors

Melinda Bagley
6370 Kirby Ridge Cove
Memphis, TN 38119

Sandie Goodman
3021 Courtland Blvd.
Cleveland, OH 44122-2805
ph: 216-921-0400
Focuses on collecting tobacco jars, especially figural jars.

Mail Pouch

Collectors

Mike Boggs
2075 Beaver Valley Rd.
Beaver Creek, OH 45385-9521
ph: 937-426-2171
Wants to buy anything related to Mail Pouch Tobacco - any size, any condition; also interested in any chewing tobacco items, any packs of tobacco, anything before 1965, all brands.

Tags

Clubs/Associations

Chris Cooper
Tin Tag Collectors Club
Newsletter: Tin Tag Exchange, The
Rt. 2 Box 55
Pittsburg, TX 75686-9516
ph: 903-856-7286
fax: 903-856-6879
web: http://www.collectoronline.com/club-TTCC.html
Dedicated to learning more about chewing tobacco tin tags.

Collectors

John Mosely
408 Brook Dr.
Mount Airy, NC 27030-5163
Wants tin brand stamps from plug chewing tobacco; send description, condition, quantity and price.

Dealers

Lee Jacobs
P.O. Box 3098
Colorado Springs, CO 80934-3098
ph: 719-473-7101

Experts

Louis Storino
P.O. Box 189
Los Altos, CA 94023-0189
ph: 650-941-7663
fax: 650-941-8835
e-mail: storino@ix.netcom.com
Collector and author of "Chewing Tobacco Tin Tags;" wants to buy tobacco tags - tin and paper used to identify brands of plug chewing tobacco; also wants related plug tobacco advertising, cards, posters, etc.

Tins

Dealers

Richard & Ann Lehmann
Antique Station - Booth 8
194 Thomas Johnson Dr.
Frederick, MD 21702
ph: 301-253-3890
Specializes in cigar and tobacco tins.

Experts

Dick Crews
29 Cumberland St.
Boston, MA 02115-5313
ph: 617-247-1751
Buys, collects and deals in quality tobacco tins: pockets, canisters and cigar tins.

TOBY JUGS

(see CERAMICS [ENGLISH], Royal Doulton; COLLECTIBLES [MODERN], Toby Jugs)

TOKENS

(see also BANKING; CIVIL WAR ARTIFACTS, Tokens; COINS & CURRENCY; CREDIT CARDS & CHARGE ITEMS; GAMBLING COLLECTIBLES, Poker Chips & Gaming Tokens; MEDALS, ORDERS & DECORATIONS; SCRIP; WOODEN MONEY)

Auction Services

Bob Moffatt
P.O. Box 281
Auburn, MA 01501-0281
ph: 508-832-9707
fax: 508-832-2992
Conducts mail bid auctions of tokens, badges, and other historical Americana.

David M. Gale
C & D Gale
2404 Berwyn Rd.
Wilmington, DE 19810-3525
ph: 302-478-0872
fax: 302-478-6866
e-mail: cdgale@dol.net
web: http://www.cdgale.com/catalog/exonumia.htm
Conducts mail bid auctions of medals, tokens, religious items, trade checks, miscellaneous items, Civil War tokens and other exonumia. Issues fixed-price exonumia catalogs.

Bob Slawsky
P.O. Box 864
Windermere, FL 34786-0864
ph: 407-352-7807
fax: 407-352-BIDS
e-mail: WWGD54A@prodigy.com
Buys, sells, auctions tokens, medals, badges, small advertising items, political, World's Fair, Olympic items, encased coins, etc.

Harold Trainor
P.O. Box 13055
Fort Pierce, FL 34979
ph: 561-878-7376
fax: 561-878-3676
Conducts mail bid auctions of tokens, medals, pins, paper items, World's Fair and Exposition, beer & whiskey items, celluloid mirrors, political, fire department, Centennial items, automobilia, railroadiana, airline collectibles.

Kurt R. Krueger
Krueger Auctions
P.O. Box 275
Iola, WI 54945-0275
ph: 715-445-3845
fax: 715-445-4100
Specializing in the mail-bid auction of tokens, advertising, brewery items, Western Americana, postcards, World's Fair & Expo., autographs, sports, coins & currency, pinbacks, military memorabilia, automotive, Disneyana, toys, dolls, etc.

Dick Grinolds
P.O. Box 18002
Minneapolis, MN 55418
ph: 612-331-8246
Conducts periodic mail-in auctions of tokens, medals, GAR, ribbons.

Rich Hartzog
World Exonumia
P.O. Box 4143
Rockford, IL 61110-0643
ph: 815-226-0771
fax: 815-397-7662
e-mail: hartzog@exonumia.com
web: http://www.exonumia.com/
Wants any tokens, medals, exonumia: badges, buttons, World's Fair items, political items, banners, etc.; sample auction catalog $4.

Exocoin
P.O. Box 720900
Oklahoma City, OK 73120-0900
ph: 800-860-7558
fax: 405-721-1194
e-mail: webmaster@exocoin.com
web: http://www.exocoin.com/
Buys, sells merchant trade tokens, Civil War tokens; also political collectibles, World's Fair & Exposition items, rare coins, costume and estate jewelry, fine diamonds, and art glass.

Stephen P. Alpert
P.O. Box 66331
Los Angeles, CA 90066-0331
ph: 310-836-2482
fax: 310-836-5691
e-mail: spalpert@flash.net
web: http://www.flash.net/~spalpert
Conducts periodic auctions of tokens, medals, tags, credit cards, gambling chips, movie money, related coin-like items.

Clubs/Associations

Dennis P. Helmer
New Jersey Exonumia Society
Newsletter: Jerseyana
112 Carlton Ave.
Collingswood, NJ 08108-3501
Collectors of New Jersey tokens, medals, paper, etc.; annual meeting at convention; regional meetings at different coin shows.

David E. Schenkman, Ed.
Token & Medal Society
Journal: Token & Medal Society Journal
P.O. Box 366
Bryantown, MD 20617-0366
ph: 301-274-3441
e-mail: turtlehill@olg.com
Promotes and stimulates "exonumia", the study of non-government issue tokens and medals; an organization of collectors and researchers of tokens, medals and related items.

V. King
Indiana, Kentucky & Ohio Token & Medal Society
Newsletter: IKO-TAMS Newsletter
600 N. Colfax St., Apt. #233
Warsaw, IN 46580
ph: 219-372-3075
e-mail: frjones@kconline.com
A non-profit society for collectors of tokens, medals and other exonumia; meets four times per year; members have bourse tables at each meeting.

T.L. Batchelder
Michigan Token & Medal Society
Newsletter: Junk Box, The
P.O. Box 572
Comstock Park, MI 49321
Dedicated to stimulating and maintaining interest in the exonumia of the state of Michigan.

Edward C. Rochette, ExDir
American Numismatic Association
Magazine: Numismatist, The
818 N. Cascade Ave.
Colorado Springs, CO 80903-3279
ph: 719-632-2646 or 800-367-9723
fax: 719-634-4085
e-mail: nulty@money.org
web: http://www.money.org
Worldwide assoc. of collectors of coins, paper money, medals and tokens; over 30,000 members; offers collector services and benefits.

Stephen P. Alpert
California Association of Token Collectors
Newsletter: Token TOpics
P.O. Box 66331
Los Angeles, CA 90066-0331
ph: 310-836-2482
fax: 310-836-5691
e-mail: spalpert@flash.net
An informal club for collectors of tokens, medals, and other exonumia; meets bi-monthly in southern California.

National Token Collector's Association
Newsletter: Talkin' Tokens
P.O. Box 212
Shingletown, CA 96088
ph: 530-474-4168
e-mail: tokenguy@flash.net
web: http://www.flash.net/~tokenguy/
For collectors of merchant and trade tokens.

Scott E. Douglas, VP
Canadian Association of Token Collectors
273 Mill St. East
Acton, Ontario L7J 1J7
Canada
e-mail: scott.douglas@sympatico.ca
web: http://www.nunetcan.net/catc.htm

Collectors

Joe Copeland
P.O. Box 4221
Oak Ridge, TN 37831-4221
ph: 423-482-4215
e-mail: joenatca@juno.com
Wants to buy tokens from saloons, CCC camps, and all southeastern US.

Jerome Schaeper, Jr.
705 Philadelphia St.
Covington, KY 41011-1252
ph: 606-581-3729
Collects and appraises merchant "good for" trade tokens.

Rich Hartzog
World Exonumia
P.O. Box 4143
Rockford, IL 61110-0643
ph: 815-226-0771
fax: 815-397-7662
e-mail: hartzog@exonumia.com
web: http://www.exonumia.com/
Wants any tokens, medals, exonumia: badges, buttons, World's Fair items, political items, banners, etc.; collections and quantities wanted.

James E. Kattner
P.O. Box 11132
Spring, TX 77391
ph: 281-986-6916 or 281-376-4826
Wants to buy tokens issued by Texas saloons, bars, military forts, post traders, lumber companies, drug stores, barbers, general stores, and other merchants; also tokens picturing steers, elephants, eagles, The Alamo; read "Good For".

Forrest Stevens
2336 Douglas #1308
Salt Lake City, UT 84105
ph: 512-442-0669
e-mail: stevensf@ccsi.com
web: http://www.ccsi.com/~stevensf/fstokens.html
Wants information on tokens of all kinds, especially modern arcade tokens; trade lists available.

Dealers

Mark Gatcha
Token Trader, The
1225 Martha Custis Dr.
Alexandria, VA 22302
ph: 703-820-6025
e-mail: gatcha@cais.com
web: http://www.arrowweb.com/gatcha/tokens.htm
Token dealer and collector.

Cy Phillips, Jr.
S C Coin & Stamp Co. Inc.
P.O. Drawer 661180
Arcadia, CA 91066-1180
ph: 818-445-8277 or 800-367-0779
fax: 818-445-8278
Tokens, medals, coins, currency, badges, expo. and fair items, scrap gold and silver.

Dan M. Jacobson
P.O. Box 277101
Sacramento, CA 95827-7101
Issues periodic lists of tokens for sale.

Experts

David E. Schenkman
P.O. Box 366
Bryantown, MD 20617-0366
ph: 301-274-3441
e-mail: turtlehill@olg.com
Full time dealer recognized as one of the leading authorities in the field of tokens and medals; author of seven books, each of which is a standard reference; wants to buy tokens, medals, watch fobs, and advertising mirrors.

Bob Temarantz
2824 N. Bentley Ave.
Tucson, AZ 85716-5513
ph: 520-326-6704
fax: 520-741-9751
Buys and specializes in western state "saloon", military, "post trader", Indian trader, territorial (i.e. Tucson, A.T., Yakima, W.T.) tokens, "Good for" advertising pocket mirrors, etc.

Stephen P. Alpert
P.O. Box 66331
Los Angeles, CA 90066-0331
ph: 310-836-2482
fax: 310-836-5691
e-mail: spalpert@flash.net
web: http://www.flash.net/~spalpert
Co-author with Lawrence E. Elman of "Tokens and Medals, A Guide to the Identification and Values of United States Exonumia"; dealer in all types of tokens, medals, tags, credit cards, gambling chips, movie money, related coin-like items.

Internet Resources

Mark Gatcha
Token Trader, The
1225 Martha Custis Dr.
Alexandria, VA 22302
ph: 703-820-6025
e-mail: gatcha@cais.com
web: http://www.arrowweb.com/gatcha/tokens.htm
This site is dedicated to providing token collectors with a centralized source for buying, selling, collecting and learning about every different category of the token collecting marketplace.

Museums/Libraries

Edward C. Rochette, ExDir
Museum of the American Numismatic Association
Magazine: Numismatist, The
818 N. Cascade Ave.
Colorado Springs, CO 80903-3279
ph: 719-632-2646 or 800-367-9723
fax: 719-634-4085
e-mail: nulty@money.org
web: http://www.money.org
A museum collection including 400,000 items; largest numismatic circulating library with books and A/V material free to members.

Love

Clubs/Associations

Love Token Society
Newsletter: Love Letter
3200 Ella Lane
Manhattan, KS 66502
For love token collectors and enthusiasts; newsletter published bi-monthly.

Merchant

Collectors

Joe Hunt
2117 Bush Dr.
Huntsville, TX 77340
Wants all U.S. "Good For" tokens; no casino tokens or wood tokens.

Dealers

Jim & Rita Hinton
Collector's Choice
P.O. Box 104284
Jefferson City, MO 65110-4284
ph: 573-636-7567
Wants merchant tokens that say "Good For"; prefers those listing town names.

Sales Tax

Clubs/Associations

American Tax Token Society
Newsletter: ATTS Newsletter
6837 Murray Lane
Annandale, VA 22003
Interested in collecting tokens, scrip, punch cards, coupons, receipts, etc. relating to the history and collection of sales taxes.

Dealers

Tom Holifield
P.O. Box 713
Alderson, WV 24910-0713
ph: 304-445-7120
Buys and sells sales tax tokens and related materials; also wants any tokens from the state of Mississippi.

Transportation (Fare)

Clubs/Associations

Bob Schneider
American Vecturist Association
Newsletter: Fare Box, The
2548 Virginia Beach Blvd., #103
Virginia Beach, VA 23452
ph: 757-631-7990
fax: 757-631-7993
e-mail: mykidsplay@aol.com
web: http://www.fantasticprices.com/token/AVAinfo.html
A source to buy, sell and trade all sorts of tokens; specializing in transportation tokens from the Atwood-Coffee catalog.

Dealers

Bob Schneider
2548 Virginia Beach Blvd., #103
Virginia Beach, VA 23452
ph: 757-631-7990
fax: 757-631-7993
e-mail: mykidsplay@aol.com
web: http://www.fantasticprices.com/token/tokens.html
Buys and sells transportation tokens.

Experts

John M. Coffee
P.O. Box 1204
Boston, MA 02104-1204
ph: 617-277-8111
Co-author of the Atwood-Coffee "Catalogue of Transportation Tokens."

TOM'S PEANUTS

Dealers

Tina & Mark Richey
Spotted Horse Collectibles
12141 Couch Mill Rd.
Knoxville, TN 37932-1102
e-mail: shcollect@aol.com
web: http://members.aol.com/shcollect/homepage.html
Buys and sells memorabilia related to Tom Houston Peanut Co., maker's of Tom's Toasted Peanuts; interested in contacting other Tom's collectors.

TOOLS

(see also ARCHITECTURE & RELATED ITEMS; BLACKSMITHING ITEMS; DIAMOND EDGE; FARM COLLECTIBLES; FIREPLACE ITEMS; ICE INDUSTRY; HARDWARE; INDUSTRY RELATED ITEMS; KEEN KUTTER; LOGGING RELATED ITEMS; MACHINERY & EQUIPMENT)

Appraisers

Anthony Seo
Olde River Hard Goods
1345 Hazlewood Road
Wilkes Barre, PA 18701
ph: 610-377-5423
e-mail: tonyseo@postoffice.ptd.net
web: http://home.ptd.net/~tonyseo/
User, collector, and dealer in antique woodworking tools; specializes in wooden planes and good user tools; member of MWTCA, EAIA, and CRAFTS.

Steve Johnson
Union Hill Antique Tools
4521 243rd Ave. NE
Redmond, WA 98053
ph: 425-868-1532
fax: 425-868-1532
e-mail: Tooltimer@msn.com
web: http://www.tooltimer.com/
Appraiser, collector, dealer, expert specializing in the best hard-to-find antique woodworking, metalworking and turning tools and treadle equipment.

Auction Services

Barry Hurchalla
249 Creek Road
Boyertown, PA 19512
ph: 610-323-0333
e-mail: threebid4@aol.com
Conducts monthly tool auctions in Eastern Pennsylvania; auctions include early wood through Stanley; also sells to beginner and the advanced collector; sales usually have over 1000 tools; send $1 and SASE for list.

Tom Witte
Tom Witte's Antiques
P.O. Box 399
Mattawan, MI 49071-0399
ph: 616-668-4161
fax: 616-668-5363
Conducts on site and cataloged tool auctions in Indianapolis; also full line tool dealer.

Tony Murland
Tool Shop Auctions
78 High Street
Needham Market, Suffolk IP6 8AW
U.K.
ph: 011-44-1449-722992
fax: 011-44-1449-722683
e-mail: tony@toolshop.demon.co.uk
web: http://www.toolshop.demon.co.uk
Antique and usable tools sold mail order to users and collectors worldwide; three mixed quality tool auctions each year and one prestigious international tool auction every July; catalogues available.

David Stanley
David Stanley Auctions
Stordon Grange, Osgathorpe
Loughborough, Leicestershire LE12 9SR
U.K.
ph: +44-1530-222320
fax: +44-1530-222523
e-mail: Davidstanley@btinternet.com
Specializes in the buying, selling, collecting, appraising and auctioning antique and usable woodworking tools.

Book Sellers

Gary Roberts
Toolemera Press, The
1077 South Street
Roslindale, MA 02131
e-mail: groberts@shore.net
Buys and sells out-of-print books and ephemera on hand tools, machine tools, trades, industry and crafts; please send email request to be added to the private email list.

Jon Zimmers
Jon Zimmers Antique Tools
206 NE 24th
Portland, OR 97232
ph: 503-232-1565
e-mail: jonz@teleport.com
web: http://www.teleport.com/~jonz/
Collector and dealer specializing in antique tools for woodworkers and collectors; homepage has free classified ads, antique tools, tool-related books, and antique tool information.

Clubs/Associations

Elton W. Hall, Ex. Dir.
Early American Industries Association, The
Newsletter: Shavings, The
167 Bakersville Rd.
South Dartmouth, MA 02748-4198
ph: 508-993-4198
e-mail: 70610.2041@compuserve.com
web: http://www.eaiainfo.org/
Interested in old tools, implements, utensils, vehicles, "Whatsits"; and to discover, identify and preserve same; also publishes the magazine "Chronicle."

Judy Hughes, Sec.
New England Tool Collectors Association
Newsletter: NETCA Newsletter
11 1/2 Concord Ave.
Saint Johnsbury, VT 05819
Purpose is to promote and increase knowledge and understanding of early American trades and crafts, and of the tools with which they are associated; meeting held twice each year with swap and sale of tools.

John Whelan
Collectors of Rare & Familiar Tools Society (CRAFTS) of New Jersey
Newsletter: Tool Shed, The
38 Colony Ct.
New Providence, NJ 07974-2332
ph: 908-464-5424
e-mail: jmwhelwdpl@aol.com
web: http://members.aol.com/craftsofnj/
Members share information on tools and implements used in early trades and industries; newsletter published five times per year.

Sue Eckers
Early Trades & Craft Society, The
Newsletter: Good Tidings, Etc.
11 Blythe Place
East Northport, NY 11731-3219
ph: 516-368-0836

Bill Hermanek
Long Island Antique Tool Collector's Association
Newsletter: Workbench, The
31 Wildwood Dr.
Smithtown, NY 11787-3452
ph: 516-360-1216 or 516-265-1564
e-mail: BHermanek@aol.com
Promotes knowledge, appreciation, collection and exchange of antique tools and machinery.

Ted Kinsey, Sec./Treas.
Western New York Antique Tool Collector's Association
Newsletter: Talking Tools
3162 Avon Rd.
Geneseo, NY 14454
e-mail: kinsey@uno.cc.geneseo.edu
web: http://physics.sci.geneseo.edu/WNYATCA/info.htm

Bob Kendra, Pres.
Three Rivers Tool Collectors
Newsletter: TRTC Newsletter
310 Old Airport Rd.
Greensburg, PA 15601-5806
Newsletter, four meetings per year, old tool sales.

J. B. Cox
Potomac Antique Tools & Industries Association (PATINA)
Newsletter: Patinagram
6802 Nesbitt Pl.
Mc Lean, VA 22101-2132
ph: 703-821-2931
e-mail: jbjocox@erols.com
Organization for men and women having an interest in the tools, crafts, techniques or manufacturing processes of the past.

Jim Hollins
Richmond Antique Tool Society
2208 Lochwood Ct.
Richmond, VA 23233
ph: 804-550-1010
e-mail: jelliott@sycomtech.com
web: http://www.sycomtech.com/oldtool/

Fred Bair, Jr.
Society of Workers in Early Arts & Trades
Newsletter: Sweat Rag, The
606 Lake Lena Blvd.
Auburndale, FL 33823-2937
ph: 941-967-3262
fax: 941-967-3262
Members are largely those who do public demonstrations of early crafts, but membership is open to anyone; exchange knowledge of practices in crafts; promotes the finding, making and exchange of tools; annual directory.

George E. Woodard, Sec.
Ohio Tool Collectors Association
Newsletter: Ohio Tool Box
P.O. Box 261
London, OH 43140-0261
ph: 614-852-3180
Interested in tools used for any function including construction, writing, household, etc.

Carl Blair
Southwest Tool Collector's Association
712 South Lincoln Ln. Ct.
Mustang, OK 73064-4141
e-mail: swtca@swtca.org
web: http://www.swtca.org/
Purpose is to promote the collection and exchange of tools, implements and devices used by our forefathers.

Gregor Mszar, Sec.
Southwest Tool Collectors Association
1409 Circle Lane
Bedford, TX 76022

Cliff Fales, Sec.
Rocky Mountain Tool Collectors
Newsletter: Shavings, Sawdust, & Splinters
1435 S. Urban Way
Lakewood, CO 80228
e-mail: cfales@idcomm.com
web: http://www.unm.edu/~tr1005/index.htm
Approximately 200 members, generally, but not limited to, the Rocky Mountain area; promotes the collection, restoration, and study of tools of bygone crafts; about 6 meetings per year in Denver area, and 6 in Albuquerque area.

Larua Ptiney, Ed.
PAST (Preserving Arts & Skills of the Trades)
Newsletter: Tooltalk
2535 Grambling Way
Riverside, CA 92507
ph: 909-686-5825
fax: 909-781-4731
e-mail: editor@tooltalk.org
web: http://www.tooltalk.org

John Wells
Mid-West Tool Collectors Association
Magazine: Gristmill
P.O. Box 8016
Berkeley, CA 94707-8016
e-mail: tkissam@cstone.net
web: http://www.mwtca.org/
Largest club that is dedicated to antique tool collectors.

Jim Gillis
Pacific Northwest Tool Collectors
5022 Erskine Ave.
Seattle, WA 98136
ph: 206-937-4753
e-mail: ToolTimer@msn.com
web: http://www.tooltimer.com/PNTC.htm

Peter Wood, Mem. Ch.
Tool Group of Canada
Newsletter: Yesterday's Tools
7 Tottenham Rd.
Don Mills, Ontario MC3 2J3
Canada
ph: 416-444-4255
Members are interested in collecting antique tools: woodworking, metalworking, leatherworking, textiles, domestic tools, hunting/trapping, nautical, fishing, scientific, medical, railway, farm, etc.; meets five times a year.

Administrator
Tool & Trades History Society, Amberley Museum
Newsletter: Tools & Trades
60 Swanley Lane
Swanely, Kent BR8 7RG
U.K.

Collectors

Eric Brooker
611 First Crown Pt. Rd.
Rochester, NH 03867
ph: 603-335-2319
Wants to buy all-metal, flat handle screwdrivers with advertising; please send overall length and condition along with a description of both sides of the flat handle.

Bill Rigler
Rte. 2 Box 152
Wartrace, TN 37183-9406
ph: 931-455-1935
fax: 931-455-0029

Jay Bolante
3058 North Honore St.
Chicago, IL 60657-2050
ph: 773-327-5091
Collects and wants to buy foot or hand-operated tools and machines.

Larry Poffenberger
1604 E. 55th Place
Tulsa, OK 74105
ph: 918-745-9786
e-mail: lkp@rustytool.cnchost.com
web: http://www.rustytool.cnchost.com
Part time dealer, full time collector; specializes in Stanley (particularly Bed Rock planes) and other makes.

Carole Meeker
5702 Vacation Blvd.
Somerset, CA 95684-9324
ph: 530-620-7019
fax: 530-620-7020
e-mail: clm@inforum.net
Wants to buy rare and unusual small patented mechanical antiques, early American technology and occupational-related photography, advertising and catalogs.

Dealers

Peter & Annette Habicht
Falcon-Wood Woodworking Tools
1985 S. Undermountain Rd.
Sheffield, MA 01257-9643
ph: 413-229-7745 or 800-829-7741
fax: 413-229-0144
e-mail: peter@oldtools.com
web: http://www.oldtools.com/
Buys and sells old woodworking tools.

Patrick Leach
Superior Works, The
P.O. Box 43
Ashby, MA 01431
ph: 978-386-2436
e-mail: leach@supertool.com
web: http://www.supertool.com
Collector, dealer, expert, in antique tools from the mundane to the exotic; also manufacturer of high-quality reproduction tools; monthly email tool list of freshly picked goods sent upon request; shop where dealers, collectors, users shop.

Ted Smith
Quality Tool Store
P.O. Box 445
Dennis Port, MA 02639
ph: 508-398-3651 or 508-398-3443
Buys and sells tools.

Charles Bonanno
Vintage Tool House
P.O. Box 855
Suffern, NY 10901
ph: 914-352-1347
e-mail: vtoolhse@aol.com
web: http://www.tooltimer.com/vintage/
Buys and sells a large variety of woodworking hand tools: hand planes, spoke shaves, hand saws, chisels, boring tools, measuring devices, etc.; also a authorized Stanley tools and parts dealer, even for old tools.

William A. Gustafson
William A. Gustafson Antiques
P.O. Box 104
11643 Rte. 22
Austerlitz, NY 12017-0104
ph: 518-392-2845
fax: 518-392-4436
e-mail: oldtools@taconic.net
web: http://www.taconic.net/oldtools
Dealer, collector, specialist and appraiser of antique tools; also conducts tool auctions.

Martin J. Donnelly
Martin J. Donnelly Antique Tools
P.O. Box 281
Bath, NY 14810-0281
ph: 800-869-0695 or 607-776-9322
fax: 607-776-6064
e-mail: mjd@mjdtools.com
web: http://www.mjdtools.com
Buys and sells antique tools of all sorts; publishes a catalog of antique tools for sale, a fully-indexed, photo-illustrated reference guide and sales catalog; used as a price guide for collectors and dealers worldwide

Anthony Seo
Olde River Hard Goods
1345 Hazlewood Road
Wilkes Barre, PA 18701
ph: 610-377-5423
e-mail: tonyseo@postoffice.ptd.net
web: http://home.ptd.net/~tonyseo/
User, collector, and dealer in antique woodworking tools; specializes in wooden planes and good user tools; member of MWTCA, EAIA, and CRAFTS.

Frank J. Vasaturo
Hen House, The
2315 Marshall Road
Lansdowne, PA 19050
ph: 610-623-1075
fax: 610-623-1075
e-mail: sales@hen-house.com
web: http://www.hen-house.com
Buying and selling tools for 45 years: wood, metal working, precision tools, instruments and kitchen tools.

James Leavenworth
118 Laurel Road
Boyertown, PA 19512
ph: 610-689-5024
Deals in antique tools from various time periods; handforged tools and artifacts as well as planes, shaves, knives, catalogs, and layout tools; from 200 years old to 20th century.

Lee Richmond
Best Things LLC, The
12640 Magna Carta Road
Herndon, VA 20171
ph: 703-850-9900 or 703-391-0074
fax: 703-758-8889
e-mail: lee@thebestthings.com
web: http://www.thebestthings.com
Carries a large selection of antique tools for sale: Stanley tools, molding planes, British metal planes, wooden planes, and more.

Barb & Dan Fromer
Fromer's Antiques
P.O. Box 224
New Market, MD 21774-0224
ph: 301-831-6712
Buys and sells antique woodworking tools.

Don Boyer
141 Cottonwood Drive
Franklin, TN 37069
ph: 615-794-7860
e-mail: dnbyr@aol.com
web: http://www.cs.cmu.edu/~alf/en/tool-lists/boyer.txt
Collector, user of old tools with an emphasis on pre-WWII woodworking tools in excellent to new condition; always buying, selling, trading single tools or full shops; free on-line identification and appraisal from your descriptions.

Tom Witte
Tom Witte's Antiques
P.O. Box 399
Mattawan, MI 49071-0399
ph: 616-668-4161
fax: 616-668-5363
Conducts on site and cataloged tool auctions in Indianapolis; also full line tool dealer.

E.J. "Al" Renier
Renier's Antiques
P.O. Box 1323
Minnetonka, MN 55346-0323
ph: 612-937-0393
e-mail: nordicAl@aol.com
Buys and sells old woodworking tools; expert in Nordic Tools (author and lecturer.)

Bob & Maxine Finch
Two Chiselers
1864 Glen Moore Dr.
Lakewood, CO 80215-3038
ph: 303-232-1932
fax: 303-232-8826
e-mail: rffinch@aol.com
Buys, sells, collects tools; publishes periodic catalog, 36 to 40 pages, fully illustrated; authoring a book on the development of braces and boring tools.

David Zeidman
Tools 'n Rules
2828 Newlands Ave.
Belmont, CA 94002
ph: 650-591-4889
fax: 650-591-2587
e-mail: dz@toolsrules.com
web: http://www.toolsrules.com
Buys and sells antique wood and metal working tools for the collector and craftsman; specializes in ivory and boxwood folding rules; the web site has pictures of the actual tool available for sale.

E.D. "Dave" Paling
Tool Guy, The
227 Ney St.
San Francisco, CA 94112-1644
ph: 415-334-7295
Buys and sells quality used and antique woodworking and machinists tools

Allan Foster
Allan Foster Antique Tools
5200 Lawton Ave.
Oakland, CA 94618

John Marshall
For Love or Money
16693 NW Meadowgrass Ct.
Beaverton, OR 97006
e-mail: john@europa.com
web: http://www.europa.com/~john/
Buys and sells antique and collectible woodworking and other trade tools; member of PNTC and MWTCA.

Jon Zimmers
Jon Zimmers Antique Tools
206 NE 24th
Portland, OR 97232
ph: 503-232-1565
e-mail: jonz@teleport.com
web: http://www.teleport.com/~jonz/
Collector and dealer specializing in antique tools for woodworkers and collectors; homepage has free classified ads, antique tools, tool-related books, and antique tool information.

Steve Johnson
Union Hill Antique Tools
4521 243rd Ave. NE
Redmond, WA 98053
ph: 425-868-1532
fax: 425-868-1532
e-mail: Tooltimer@msn.com
web: http://www.tooltimer.com/
Appraiser, collector, dealer, expert specializing in the best hard-to-find tools and treadle equipment.

Bob Kaune
Antique & Used Tools
511 W. 11th
Port Angeles, WA 98362
ph: 360-452-2292
e-mail: bktools@olympus.net
web: http://www.olympus.net/bktools/
Has a large selection of quality vintage hand tools: planes, scrapers, spokeshaves, chisels, slicks, draw knives, saws, braces, drills, levels, squares, bevels, parts and other hard-to-find items; Stanley Bed Rock planes a specialty.

Charles Stirling
Bristol Design (Tools) Inc.
14 Perry Rd.
Bristol, BS1 5BG
U.K.
ph: +44 177929 1740
e-mail: stirling@ndirect.co.uk
Issues a catalog of tools for sale with

quality color illustrations of fine English and American tools; subscription is $20 (partly refundable) for 5 issues; stocks metal planes, molding planes, plow planes, chisels, spokeshaves, etc.

David Stanley
David Stanley Auctions
Stordon Grange, Osgathorpe
Loughborough, Leicestershire LE12 9SR
U.K.
ph: +44-1530-222320
fax: +44-1530-222523
e-mail: Davidstanley@btinternet.com
Specializes in the buying, selling, collecting, appraising and auctioning antique and usable woodworking tools.

Experts

William A. Gustafson
William A. Gustafson Antiques
P.O. Box 104
11643 Rte. 22
Austerlitz, NY 12017-0104
ph: 518-392-2845
fax: 518-392-4436
e-mail: oldtools@taconic.net
web: http://www.taconic.net/oldtools
Dealer, collector, specialist and appraiser of antique tools; also conducts tool auctions.

James H. Cooley
James H. Cooley Antiques
507 Joslin Hill Rd.
Frankfort, NY 13340
ph: 315-894-3483
e-mail: TizCooley@msn.com
Buys, sells, collects, identifies, appraises antique tools; member of Early American Industries Association for over 30 years; also Midwest Tool Collectors Association.

Ed Hobbs
4417 Inwood Rd.
Raleigh, NC 27603-3315
ph: 919-828-2754
fax: 919-828-6697
Appraises and specializes in tools; writes column for Antique Week; available for speaking and demonstrations on antique tools.

Don Boyer
141 Cottonwood Drive
Franklin, TN 37069
ph: 615-794-7860
e-mail: dnbyr@aol.com
web: http://www.cs.cmu.edu/~alf/en/tool-lists/boyer.txt
Collector, user of old tools with an emphasis on pre-WWII woodworking tools in excellent to new condition; always buying, selling, trading single tools or full shops; free on-line identification and appraisal from your descriptions.

John Walter
Tool Merchant, The
208 Front St.
P.O. Box 227
Marietta, OH 45750-0227
ph: 740-373-9973
fax: 740-373-9059
e-mail: toolmerchant@sprynet.com
web: http://www.thetoolmerchant.com/
Buys, sells and appraises antique and traditional woodworking tools; author of "Antique & Collectible Stanley Tools" (1990, The Tool Merchants.)

Internet Resources

Electronic Neanderthal, The
e-mail: Allan.Fisher@cs.cmu.edu
web: http://www.cs.cmu.edu/~alf/en/en.html
A repository of information on the use and preservation of old and antique woodworking tools: source of tools and materials, events, schools, organizations, books, and places to visit, links to related websites.

Museums/Libraries

American Precision Museum Association, Inc.
Newsletter: Tools & Technology
P.O. Box 679
196 Main St.
Windsor, VT 05089
ph: 802-674-5781
fax: 802-674-2524
e-mail: curator@americanprecision.org
web: http://americanprecision.org/
The museum focuses on machine tools, early American hand tools and their products, such as sewing machines, typewriters and guns.

Bucks County Historical Society
Newsletter: Penny Lots
84 S. Pine St.
Doylestown, PA 18901-4930
ph: 215-345-0210
fax: 215-230-0823
e-mail: bchs@philadelphia.libertynet.org
web: http://www.libertynet.org/bchs
Operates three Nat. Historical Landmarks; Mercer Museum has over 50,000 tools of Early American trades/crafts; Spruance Library has research material on trades & crafts; Fonthill Museum is a concrete castle laden with tiles & treasures.

Hunter M. Pilkinton
World O' Tools Museum
2431 Hwy. 13 So.
Waverly, TN 37185
ph: 931-296-3218
Always interested in old or odd mechanical tools; also related books and catalogs.

Periodicals

Magazine: Fine Tool Journal, The
27 Fickett Rd.
Pownal, ME 04069
ph: 800-248-8114 or 207-688-4962
fax: 207-688-4831
e-mail: CEB@FineToolJ.com
web: http://www.FineToolJ.com/
A quarterly magazine for tool collectors and craftsmen; features biennial absentee tool auctions.

Taunton Press
Magazine: Fine Woodworking
P.O. Box 5506
Newtown, CT 06470
ph: 800-283-7252 or 203-426-8171
fax: 203-426-3434
e-mail: smessenger@taunton.com
web: http://www.taunton.com/fw/index.htm
Publishes a bi-monthly "How-to" magazine written and illustrated by master craftsmen; also publishes a related line of books and videos; free catalog available.

Barry Abel, Ed.
Newsletter: Tool Ads
P.O. Box 33
Hamilton, MT 59840-0033
ph: 406-363-3805
fax: 406-363-4117
e-mail: airgunads@bitterroot.net
A monthly newsletter for buyers and sellers of all types of tools from hand tools to machinery, parts, accessories and related literature; contains only ads and auction notices.

Repro. Sources

Kevin Riddle
Mountainman Woodshop
Rte. 2
Eagle Rock, VA 24085
ph: 540-884-2197
Traditional Appalachian Mountain woodworking using original tools and techniques; products include farm tools, furniture, and toys; available for lectures and demonstrations.

Anvils

Collectors

Don Monnier
P.O. Box 772
Sidney, OH 45365
ph: 937-492-1420
Wants to buy small, paperweight size "anvils"; brass or iron; with advertising; will buy one or entire collections.

Bruce Cynar
10023 St. Clair's Retreat
Fort Wayne, IN 46825
ph: 219-489-5004
e-mail: oldtchnlgy@aol.com
Wants small brass anvils with advertising.

Experts

Dick Postman
10 Fisher Ct.
Berrien Springs, MI 49103
ph: 616-471-5426
Author of "Anvils in America."

Blow Torches

Clubs/Associations

Ron Carr
Blow Torch Collectors Club
Newsletter: Torch, The
3328 258th Ave. SE
Issaquah, WA 98029-9173
ph: 425-557-0634
e-mail: roncarr@prodigy.net
web: http://www.indy.net/~toper/BTCA
A group of blow torch collectors dedicated to preserving the history of blow torches and related material.

Collectors

Samuel G. Scroggs
1073 Stonybridge Dr.
Chambersburg, PA 17201-9093
ph: 717-263-5422
Wants pre-1900 and early 1900s brass blow torches.

Ron Carr
3328 258th Ave. SE
Issaquah, WA 98029-9173
ph: 425-557-0634
e-mail: roncarr@prodigy.net
web: http://www.indy.net/~toper/BTCA
Wants to buy brass blow torches; turn of the century brass torches, all models including gasoline, alcohol, and kerosene.

Clamps

Experts

Milt Boyd
Rose Wood Drive
Haverhill, MA 01832-1532
ph: 978-469-0973
fax: 978-469-0973
e-mail: ClampGuy@aol.com
Collects, specializes in wooden clamps (hand screws); author of articles on clamp makers; pamphlet on clamp collecting available on request; wants to buy catalogs of American clamp makers and examples of their work.

Machinist

Collectors

John Treggiari
ph: 978-744-2897
fax: 978-744-5572
e-mail: micrometer@juno.com
Serious collector wants to buy pre-1920 measuring and layout machinist tools: micrometers, surface gages, calipers, small patented vises; speed indicators, rules, catalogs, display items, etc.; tool boxes alone are not needed.

Dealers

John Walkowiak
3452 Humbolt Ave. S.
Minneapolis, MN 55408-3332
ph: 612-824-0785
Collecting woodworking tools, specializing in anything made by the Sandusky Tool Co., Ohio.

New Jersey

Experts

Alexander Farnham
78 Tumble Falls Rd.
Stockton, NJ 08559-1309
ph: 908-996-4179
Author of "Search for Early New Jersey Toolmakers", $27.50 ppd., hardbound, "Early Tools of New Jersey and the Men Who Made Them", $22.50 ppd., hardbound, and "Tool Collectors Handbook," $3.50 ppd. softbound.

Planes

Experts

Roger K. Smith
P.O. Box 177
Athol, MA 01331-0177
ph: 978-249-5990
e-mail: rksmith@tiac.net
web: http://www.tooltimer.com/roger/
Buys, sells and specializes in planes; send LSASE for free catalog; author of "Patented Transitional & Metallic Planes in America" - Vols. I and II;

John Whelan
38 Colony Ct.
New Providence, NJ 07974-2332
ph: 908-464-5424
e-mail: jmwhelwdpl@aol.com
Author of "The Wooden Plane - Its History, Form and Function" (Astragal Press) and "Making Traditional Wooden Planes" (Astragal Press).

Plumb Bobs

Collectors

Bruce Cynar
10023 St. Clair's Retreat
Fort Wayne, IN 46825
ph: 219-489-5004
e-mail: oldtchnlgy@aol.com
Focuses on plumb bobs, plumb lines and bobs with pulleys.

Stanley

Collectors

Bill Hermanek
31 Wildwood Dr.
Smithtown, NY 11787-3452
ph: 516-360-1216 or 516-265-1564
e-mail: BHermanck@aol.com
Wants to buy planes, levels, rulers, braces, marking gauges, etc.; also wants tool literature, catalogs, advertising; anything Stanley.

Experts

John Walter
Tool Merchant, The
208 Front St.
P.O. Box 227
Marietta, OH 45750-0227
ph: 740-373-9973
fax: 740-373-9059
e-mail: toolmerchant@sprynet.com
web: http://www.thetoolmerchant.com/
Author of the illustrated "Antique & Collectible Stanley Tools: A Guide to Identification and Value" - 1997 edition (8 1/2" x 5", 885 pages), current values on 2,500 tools, over 1,500 illustrations.

Internet Resources

Jay Sutherland
Stanley Bench Plane Dating Page
web: http://peta.ee.cornell.edu/~jay/ww/planes/
Web site to assist in learning roughly when a Stanley bench plane was made; plane images; history.

Periodicals

John Walter
Tool Merchant, The
Magazine: Stanley Tool Collector News
208 Front St.
P.O. Box 227
Marietta, OH 45750-0227
ph: 740-373-9973
fax: 740-373-9059
e-mail: toolmerchant@sprynet.com
web: http://www.thetoolmerchant.com/
40-page user/collector magazine; feature articles, research, 100s of select quality tools for sale, all with photos (lowest prices), user info., auction results, type studies, classified ads.

Tape Measures

Collectors

Janet Morphy
135 Wedgewood Dr.
Pittsburgh, PA 15229
ph: 412-366-6589
Wants to buy figural tape measures of metal, celluloid, porcelain.

Wes & Elaine Hart
963 Westhaven St.
Columbus, OH 43228
ph: 614-870-7141

Myron Huffman
12409 Wayne Trace
Hoagland, IN 46745
ph: 219-639-3290

Sherry L. Werdon
400 N. Washington
Lowell, MI 49331-1465
ph: 616-897-9580
Wants to buy figural tape measures; also wants unusual sewing items such as figural pin cushions, thimble holders, etc.

Wrenches

Clubs/Associations

E. Eloise Alton, Ed.
Missouri Valley Wrench Club
Newsletter: Missouri Valley Wrench Club Newsletter
613 N. Long St.
Shelbyville, IL 62565-1544
ph: 217-774-5002
Club collects and studies anything having to do with wrenches; a quarterly newsletter is published with information about wrenches, manufacturers, patents, etc.

Collectors

Robert Rauhauser
RR 2 Box 766
Thomasville, PA 17364-9622
Wants wrenches with names; especially cutout (see throughs) wrenches; any farm machinery wrenches; specialty wrenches.

Shockley
1529 E. 49th St.
Tulsa, OK 74105
Wants to buy small, odd, or unusual wrenches; send picture, length, and price.

Wrenches (Adjustable)

Collectors

Charles W. Wardell
P.O. Box 195
Trinity, NC 27370-0195
ph: 336-434-1145
Wants early "monkey" wrenches of unusual design. Many 1800-1900 inventors used clever schemes to make the repair of machinery a more pleasant task. Gripping a bolt or nut securely and having a quick release mechanism were important.

TOOTH FAIRY

Experts

Dr. Rosemary Wells, Ph.D.
1129 Cherry St.
Deerfield, IL 60015
ph: 847-945-1129
fax: 847-945-1125
e-mail: stardesk@aol.com
Expert and researcher on the history and lore surrounding the Tooth Fairy; has a large collection of TF related items.

Museums/Libraries

Dr. Rosemary Wells, Ph.D.
Tooth Fairy Museum
Newsletter: Tooth Fairy Tabloid
1129 Cherry St.
Deerfield, IL 60015
ph: 847-945-1129
fax: 847-945-1125
e-mail: stardesk@aol.com

TOOTHBRUSH HOLDERS

Dealers

Estelle Sharp
ESCO Enterprises, Inc.
441 E. River Oaks Dr.
Baton Rouge, LA 70815-4063
ph: 225-924-5089
fax: 225-924-5089
Buys and sells toothbrush holders.

Experts

Marilyn Cooper
P.O. Box 55174
Houston, TX 77255
Author of "The Pictorial Guide to Toothbrush Holders."

TOOTHPICK HOLDERS

Clubs/Associations

Toby Shugart, Mem.
National Toothpick Holder Collectors Society
Newsletter: Toothpick Bulletin
P.O. Box 417
Safety Harbor, FL 34695-0417
e-mail: LHSODER@aol.com
web: http://www.collectoronline.com/club-NTHCS.html
Society members interested in collecting toothpick holders of all shapes and materials; monthly newsletter, annual conventions.

Collectors

Judy A. Knauer
1224 Spring Valley Lane
West Chester, PA 19380-5112
ph: 610-431-3477
Collector, lecturer, and author on old glass toothpick holders; publishes "Toothpick Bulletin" monthly newsletter for and founder of National Toothpick Holder Collectors Society.

Lorraine Holt
2892 Sand Creek Highway
Adrian, MI 49221
ph: 517-265-4777

Fred Phelps
P.O. Box 217
Colesburg, IA 52035-0217
ph: 319-856-2025

Richard & Nancy Ryan
8801 Thorndale Ct.
Fort Worth, TX 76180-1620
ph: 817-498-9046
fax: 817-788-4532
e-mail: RARyan13@aol.com

Experts

Judy A. Knauer
1224 Spring Valley Lane
West Chester, PA 19380-5112
ph: 610-431-3477
Collector, lecturer, and author on old glass toothpick holders; wants to add to collection of old glass toothpick holders; buying one piece or entire collection; please describe, state condition and price.

TOURS/BUYING TRIPS

Misc. Services

Peter Manston
Travel Keys Tours
P.O. Box 160691
Sacramento, CA 95816-0691
ph: 916-452-5200
Buy antiques at the best fairs, flea markets, warehouses and antique centers in Europe; group tours or individual escorted travel.

TOWLETTES

Clubs/Associations

Michael Lewis
Modern Moist Towlette Collecting
3000 Highway 19A, Ste. 2
Mount Dora, FL 32757
e-mail: MoistTwl@aol.com
web: http://members.aol.com/MoistTwl/

TOY GUNS

BB Guns

(see also AIRGUNS)

Clubs/Associations

Jim Buskirk
Toy Gun Collectors of America
Newsletter: Toy Gun Collectors of America Newsletter
3009 Oleander Ave.
San Marcos, CA 92069-6128
ph: 760-599-1054
Focuses on pre-WWII American cap guns and spring/air BB guns (non-pellet guns or other high powered air guns); newsletter published quarterly: photos, information, articles; also free want ads for subscribers; quarterly newsletter.

Collectors

Bob Warner
P.O. Box 336
Lake George, MI 48633
ph: 517-588-4968
Wants old BB and pellet guns, any make: Daisy double barrel, Buffalo Bill, Buck Jones, Buzz Barton, 25 Pump, Texas Ranger, NRA, and Daisy toys.

Terry Burger
2323 Lincoln
Beatrice, NE 68310-3306
ph: 402-228-2797
Wants pre-1915, preferably cast iron-framed guns: Daisy, Atlas, Matchless, New Rapid, etc.

Mike Burleson
12048 CR 1168
Tyler, TX 75703
ph: 903-561-9343
e-mail: bbguns@tyler.net
Wants old or unusual American BB guns by Markham, King, Heilprin, Daisy or others.

Clay Tontz
4043 Nora Ave.
Covina, CA 91722
ph: 626-338-9976
Wants pre-1930 BB guns.

Experts

Jim Buskirk
3009 Oleander Ave.
San Marcos, CA 92069-6128
ph: 760-599-1054
Buys, sells, collects and specializes in BB guns and cap guns.

Museums/Libraries

Customer Service
Daisy Manufacturing Co., Air Gun Museum
211 South 8th St.
P.O. Box 220
Rogers, AR 72757
ph: 501-636-1200 or 800-643-3458
fax: 501-636-1601
e-mail: djohnson@daisy.com
web: http://www.daisy.com/
World's oldest and largest manufacturer of BB and pellet air guns; museum contains commemorative guns and collectibles.

Cap Guns

Clubs/Associations

Jim Buskirk
Toy Gun Collectors of America
Newsletter: Toy Gun Collectors of America Newsletter
3009 Oleander Ave.
San Marcos, CA 92069-6128
ph: 760-599-1054
Focuses on pre-WWII American cap guns and spring/air BB guns (non-pellet guns or other high powered air guns); newsletter published quarterly: photos, information, articles; also free want ads for subscribers; quarterly newsletter.

Collectors

George Fougere
67 East St.
North Grafton, MA 01536-1830
ph: 508-839-2701
Interested in cast iron and die cast cap pistols; no air rifles, please.

Ralph Perlberg
1 Strawberry hill
Andover, MA 01810

Bob Williamson
190 Washington St.
East Stroudsburg, PA 18301-2819
ph: 570-421-6957 or 570-421-8550
fax: 570-421-8605
Sells and buys rare and common cast iron cap guns, bombs, canes, cannons, BB guns (1860s to 1950s); also wants caps, boxes, catalogs, literature, etc.

Terry Burger
2323 Lincoln
Beatrice, NE 68310-3306
ph: 402-228-2797

Bill Hamburg
P.O. Box 1305
Woodland Hills, CA 91365-1305
ph: 818-346-1269
fax: 818-346-0215
e-mail: whamburg@aol.com
Wants to buy excellent to mint-in-box only; also buys cap gun boxes.

Experts

Jim Schleyer
P.O. Box 243
Burke, VA 22015-0243
ph: 703-569-4478
e-mail: schleyerjc@erols.com
Wants to buy older toy and cap pistols and holsters; will answer inquiries that are accompanied by SASE; has written extensively on the subject of toy guns; author of "Backyard Buckaroos - Collecting Western Toy Guns."

Charles W. Best
11523 Pine Valley Dr.
Franktown, CO 80116-8708
ph: 303-660-2318
e-mail: Budbest@aol.com
Collects 19th century cap guns; author of "Cast Iron Toy Guns & Capshooters"; advanced collector interested in early toy guns.

Jim Buskirk
3009 Oleander Ave.
San Marcos, CA 92069-6128
ph: 760-599-1054
Buys, sells, collects and specializes in BB guns and cap guns.

TOYS

(see also BANKS; CHARACTER COLLECTIBLES.; CHILDREN'S THINGS; DISNEY COLLECTIBLES; DOLLS; GAMES; KITS; MINIATURES; MOVIE MEMORABILIA; POPULAR CULTURE; PREMIUMS; RIDING TOYS; SOLDIERS, Toy; STEIFF; SUPER HEROES; TEDDY BEARS; TOY GUNS; TRAINS; TRUCKS)

Auction Services

Mildred Ewing
Skinner, Inc.
357 Main St.
Bolton, MA 01740-1104
ph: 978-779-6241
fax: 978-779-5144
e-mail: info@skinnerinc.com
web: http://www.skinnerinc.com
Established in 1964, Skinner Inc. is the fifth largest auction house in the US; has offices in Bolton and Boston, MA.

Martin Krim
New England Auction Gallery
P.O. Box 2273
Peabody, MA 01960-7273
ph: 978-535-3140
fax: 978-535-7522
e-mail: dlkrim@star.net
web: http://www.old-toys.com
Conduct mail-bid auctions with full color illustrated catalogs; specializes in sales of Disney, TV and cartoon items from 1920-1970: toys, wind-ups, robots, space toys.

Withington, Inc.
590 Centr Road
Hillsboro, NH 03244
ph: 603-464-3232
e-mail: withington@conknet.com

Herb & Barb Smith
Smith House Toy
P.O. Box 3903
Eliot, ME 03903
e-mail: toys@smithhousetoys.com
web: http://www.smithhousetoys.com
Conducts four specialty mail-bid toys and collectibles auctions each year.

Randy Inman
James D. Julia Auctioneers Inc.
Rt. 201, Skowhegan Rd.
P.O. Box 830
Fairfield, ME 04937
ph: 207-453-7125
fax: 207-453-2502
e-mail: jjulia@juliaauctions.com
web: http://www.juliaauctions.com
Conducts specialized auctions of toys and doll items and are one of the leaders in this field in North America.

Lloyd Ralston
Lloyd Ralston Toy Auction
400 Long Beach Blvd.
Norwalk, CT 06850
ph: 203-386-9399
fax: 203-386-9515
e-mail: lrgallery@aol.com
web: http://www.lloydralston.com/
Specializes in auctioning toys, dolls, games and trains.

Bill Bertoia
Bill Bertoia Auctions
1881 Spring Rd.
Vineland, NJ 08631
ph: 609-692-1881
fax: 609-692-8697
e-mail: webmaster@billbertoiaauctions.com
web: http://www.billbertoiaauctions.com/
Specializing in the auctioning of antique toys, banks, trains, and doorstops.

Christie's East
219 E. 67th St.
New York, NY 10021
ph: 212-606-0400
web: http://www.christies.com

Sotheby's
1334 York Ave.
New York, NY 10021
ph: 212-606-7000
fax: 212-606-7107
web: http://www.sothebys.com
Over 70 collecting areas are featured at Sotheby's auctions including toys, dolls, porcelain, furniture, silver, art, books; exhibitions are free and everyone is welcome; for a free copy of "Sotheby's Newsletter", call 212-606-7245.

Henry Kurtz
Henry Kurtz Ltd.
163 Amsterdam Ave., Ste. 136
New York, NY 10023
ph: 212-642-5904
fax: 212-874-6018
Specializes in the sale of jewelry, paintings, prints, silver, coins, stamps, toys (especially lead soldiers), and movie memorabilia.

Amory Spizzirri, Client Svc.
William Doyle Galleries
175 E. 87th St.
New York, NY 10128-2205
ph: 212-427-2730
fax: 212-369-0892
e-mail: info@doylegalleries.com
web: http://www.doylegalleries.com
Holds over 50 auctions annually of furniture and decorations, paintings and sculpture, jewelry, books and prints, couture and textiles, 20th century art & design, majolica, Lalique, Asian works of art and other specialty categories.

Ted Hake
Hake's Americana & Collectibles Auction
P.O. Box 1444
York, PA 17405-1444
ph: 717-848-1333
e-mail: Ted@hakes.com
web: http://www.hakes.com/
Always purchasing items for 8 mail-bid auctions per year covering hundreds of categories including toys, character collectibles, Disney, cowboy heroes, premiums, television, politicals, pin-back buttons, advertising and more.

Noel Barrett
Noel Barrett Antiques & Auctions, Ltd.
P.O. Box 1001
Carversville, PA 18913-0201
ph: 215-297-5109
fax: 215-297-0457
Specializes in the auction of toys, games, vintage advertising and country store items.

Ted Maurer
Successful Auction Management
1003 Brookwood Dr.
Pottstown, PA 19464-3022
ph: 610-323-1573 or 610-367-5024
e-mail: ted@maurerail.com
web: http://www.maurerail.com/auction.htm
Specializes in the auctioning of toys, trains and railroad related items.

Richard W. Opfer, Jr.
Richard Opfer Auctioneering, Inc.
1919 Greenspring Dr.
Lutherville Timonium, MD 21093-4113
ph: 410-252-5035
fax: 410-252-5863
e-mail: info@opferauction.com
web: http://www.opferauction.com/
Specializes in auctioning toys, dolls, games, black memorabilia, and advertising items; weekly estate auctions including antiques, fine art; monthly eclectic collector sales feature a wide variety of collectibles.

Perry R. Eichor
Eichor Associates
703 N. Almond Dr.
Simpsonville, SC 29681-3453
ph: 864-967-8770
fax: 864-228-2541
e-mail: kpmflyn@earthlink.net
Appraises and conducts auction sales of toys; member Antique Toy Collectors of America.

Ann Hays, ISA CAPP
Hays & Associates, Inc.
120 South Spring St.
Louisville, KY 40206-1953
ph: 502-584-4297
fax: 502-585-5896
e-mail: annhays@haysauction.com
web: http://www.haysautcion.com/
Conducts specialty toy and doll auctions; Ann Hays is a Certified Appraiser of Personal Property with the International Society of Appraisers; director of auction house antique and collectible toy and doll department for over 25 years.

American Eagle Auction Company
20060 US Highway 23N
Circleville, OH 43113-9732
ph: 740-477-3900 or 740-927-2368

Lewis & Lambright, Inc.
908 S. Centerville Rd.
Sturgis, MI 49091
ph: 616-651-1033
Specializes in the auctioning of trains, toys, farm toys and dolls.

James L. Jackson, ISA
Jackson's Auctioneers & Appraisers
2229 Lincoln St.
Cedar Falls, IA 50613
ph: 319-277-2256
fax: 319-277-1252
e-mail: jacksons@jacksonsauction.com
web: http://www.jacksonsauction.com
Conducts specialty auctions of antique toys (tin, cast iron, windup) and contemporary toys.

Kurt R. Krueger
Krueger Auctions
P.O. Box 275
Iola, WI 54945-0275
ph: 715-445-3845
fax: 715-445-4100
Specializing in the mail-bid auction of tokens, advertising, brewery items, Western Americana, postcards, World's Fair & Expo., autographs, sports, coins & currency, pinbacks, military memorabilia, automotive, Disneyana, toys, dolls, etc.

Butterfield & Dunning
755 Church Rd.
Elgin, IL 60123
ph: 847-741-3483
fax: 847-741-3589
e-mail: info@butterfields.com
web: http://www.butterfields.com

Joy Luke
Joy Luke Auction Gallery
300 E. Grove St.
Bloomington, IL 61701-5232
ph: 309-828-5533
fax: 309-829-2266
e-mail: robert@joyluke.com
web: http://www.joyluke.com/
Conducts periodic auctions specializing in the sale of toys, banks, trains and dolls.

International Toy Collectors Association
804 West Anthony Dr.
Champaign, IL 61822
ph: 217-351-9437
e-mail: Hugereturn@aol.com
Conducts periodic catalog auction sales of vintage toys.

Glenn Butler
Wallis & Wallis
West Street Auction Galleries
Lewes, East Sussex BN7 2NJ
U.K.
ph: 01273-480208
fax: 01273-476562
e-mail: wallisandwallis@mcmail.com
web: http://www.wallisandwallis.co.uk/
Britain's specialist auctioneers of diecast & tin plate toys & models including model soldiers.

Sotheby's
34-35 New Bond St.
London, W1A 2AA
U.K.
ph: 44 171 293 5000
fax: 44 171 293 5989
web: http://www.sothebys.com/
Conducts specialty auctions of tinplate toys, diecasts, trains, antique dolls, teddy bears, automata.

Clubs/Associations

Robert R. Grew
Antique Toy Collectors of America, Inc., The
Newsletter: Toy Chest
c/o Carter, Ledyard & Milburn
Two Wall St. - 13th Floor
New York, NY 10005
ph: 212-238-8803
fax: 212-732-3232
e-mail: grew@clm.com
An organization focusing on antique toys and games; since membership is by invitation only for established collectors, there is a waiting list; bi-monthly newsletter available only to members.

American Game Collectors Association
Newsletter: Game Times
P.O. Box 44
Dresher, PA 19025
e-mail: agca@agca.com
web: http://www.agca.com
Focuses on board and card games as well as puzzles, playing cards, tops, yo-yos, and action games; also publishes "Game Researchers' Notes" - reports on member's research.

Canadian Toy Collectors Society
Newsletter: Canadian Toy Collectors' Newsletter
91 Rylander Blvd., Unit 7, Ste. 245
Scarborough, Ontaria M1B 5M5
Canada
ph: 905-389-8047 or 905-388-4014
e-mail: ctcsweb@hotmail.com
web: http://www.ctcs.org/ctcshp.htm
Association for toy collectors worldwide; promoters of Canada's greatest toy collector's show & sale, promoter of C.T.C.S. "Limited Edition" Brooklin models; CTCS maintains large museum collection of early Canadian toys.

Collectors

Martin Krim
P.O. Box 2273
Peabody, MA 01960-7273
ph: 978-535-3140
fax: 978-535-7522
e-mail: dlkrim@star.net
web: http://www.old-toys.com
Wants wind-up and battery toys, toy cars, robots and space toys.

Mark Bergin
P.O. Box 3073
Peterborough, NH 03458-3073
ph: 603-924-2079
fax: 603-924-2022
Wants old toys: tin, metal, celluloid; wind-up toys of all kinds, battery operated toys, friction, robots, space toys, space guns, cars, buses, racers, motorcycles, boats, airplanes, character toys, etc.

Stephen Leonard
121 McKinley Ave.
Albertson, NY 11507
ph: 516-742-0979
e-mail: lentoydag@aol.com
Wants to buy antique mechanical toys, daguerreotypes, and music boxes.

Sanford Weltman
39 Branford Rd.
Rochester, NY 14618-1707
ph: 716-442-8810 or 716-473-2498
Buying old toys, one item or collection.

Larry Bruch
Larry Bruch Toys
P.O. Box 121
Mountain Top, PA 18707-0121
ph: 800-549-TOYS
e-mail: kinglar@aol.com
All kinds of pre-1960 toys wanted: German, American: metal cars, airplanes, boats; comic characters, cast iron toys and banks, etc.; also buying Tootsietoys, Dinky, and Smith-Miller; write for free 3-page illustrated want list.

Lee Woolf
321 Meeting House Lane
Narberth, PA 19072-2029
ph: 610-667-9378
Wants to buy electric trains, toy trucks and cars, lead figures and soldiers, Daisy BB guns, model race cars.

Ronald Wiener
1650 Arch St., 22 Floor
Philadelphia, PA 19103
ph: 215-977-2266
fax: 215-977-2740
e-mail: rwiener@wolfblock.com
Wants to buy toys, especially Marklin German toy trains and other Marklin toys, as well as other German toy trains and transportation toys and European and American tin toys (1890 to 1956).

Jim Conley
2758 Coventry Lane
Canton, OH 44708-1320
ph: 330-477-7725 or 330-499-9283
fax: 330-879-2950
Buys and sells cars, trucks, tin wind-ups, Buddy L, Metal Craft, Smith Miller, Tonka, Lehmann, Bing, Ives, Marx, etc.; also Fisher-Price, Gibbs toys, Japanese tin cars from the '50s and '60s; OK for sellers to call collect.

Jerry Peters
Chestnut Hollow, Ltd.
6060 Bordman Rd.
P.O. Box 6
Almont, MI 48003-0006
ph: 810-798-3158
Wants to buy robots, sci-fi related, aviation related, cars, trucks, wind-ups, battery operated, etc.; Rocketeer, Star Trek, Star Wars, Buck Rogers, King Kong, Universal movie monsters, actual movie props, autographs, movie posters.

Dr. Greg Zemenick
Dr. "Z"
1350 Kirts, Ste. 160
Troy, MI 48084-4852
ph: 248-642-8129 or 248-244-9430
fax: 248-244-9495
e-mail: drzzeezzi@aol.com
web: http://www.drzzeezzi.com/
Wants to buy early American (pre-1910) toys, banks, cigar store collectibles, tin toys, clocks; appraises, collects, sells, repairs.

Kenneth R. Chane
9755 Independence Ave.
Chatsworth, CA 91311-4318
ph: 818-407-0855
fax: 818-407-0850
e-mail: kschane@msn.com
Wants to buy ice cream vendors, baggage carts with figures, graffiti cars, tin lithograph toys.

Dealers

Leila Dunbar
Dunbar's Gallery
76 Haven St.
Milford, MA 01757-3821
ph: 508-634-8697 or 508-634-8097
fax: 508-634-8698
Mail order Americana - no reproductions; buys, sells and specializes in vintage character and comic toys, banks, advertising, automobilia, and Halloween related items.

Joan Berglund
Atomic Candy
2 Lynde St.
Salem, MA 01970
ph: 978-740-9544
fax: 978-740-9544
e-mail: atomicandy@aol.com
web: http://members.aol.com/atomichome/
Collector/dealer, specializes in 1950s-1970s collectible toys: Barbie, GI Joe, lunch boxes, diecast, Western, space, movie, TV, and comic character toys.

George Newcomb
Plymouth Rock Toy Co.
P.O. Box 1202
Plymouth, MA 02362
ph: 508-746-2842 or 508-830-1880
fax: 508-830-0364

Dan Dozier
ToyNet
23 Forest Ave.
Falmouth, MA 02540-4006
ph: 508-548-6342 or 508-548-0893
fax: 508-548-0893
e-mail: tintoys@dosierdesigns.com
web: http://www.toynet.com/
Vintage and new collectible toys from around the world; specializing in robots, space toys, and high quality handmade reproduction toy boxes; also sells art posters made from toy box graphics.

Robb Sequin
P.O. Box 1126
Dennis Port, MA 02639
ph: 508-760-2599
e-mail: rsequin@capecod.net
Wants to buy 1950s to 1970s toys and fun stuff, battery-operated, wind-up, character collectibles, etc.

David Epstein
S & D Classic Toys
54 Bennington Rd.
Cranston, RI 02920
ph: 401-351-3900 or 401-943-1931

Carl Lobel
P.O. Box 74A
Warren, VT 05674
ph: 802-496-4025
Wants to buy comic character wind-ups, Lehman, space toys, robots/astronauts, TPS wind-ups, 1930-1960 Japanese, plush bear wind-ups, unusual comic character items such as figurines, radios, clocks, and dolls.

Lloyd Ralston
Lloyd Ralston Gallery
400 Long Beach Blvd.
Norwalk, CT 06850
ph: 203-386-9399
fax: 203-386-9515
e-mail: lrgallery@aol.com
web: http://www.lloydralston.com/

Toyareum
1101 Asbury Ave.
Ocean City, NJ 08226
ph: 609-391-0480
A museum-like shop.

Bill Bertoia
1881 Spring Rd.
Vineland, NJ 08631
ph: 609-692-1881
fax: 609-692-8697
e-mail: bill@billbertoiaauctions.com

Raymond Schieber, Sr.
Toy Locators
5821 Diana Lane
Lake View, NY 14085
ph: 716-627-5840
e-mail: rschie7677@aol.com

Bob Smith
62 West Ave.
Fairport, NY 14450
ph: 716-377-8394
fax: 716-377-6019
e-mail: oldtoys@frontiernet.net
web: http://www.frontiernet.net/~oldtoys/
Avid collector and dealer of 1870-1970 toys: wind-up, automotive, European tin, pressed steel, early diecast, cast iron; specializes in Oh Boy, Tootsietoys, Dinky Toys, Hillclimbers, Wyandotte, and German tin toys.

Jacquie Henry
Antique Treasures, Toys & Dolls
2240 Academy St.
P.O. Box 17
Walworth, NY 14568-0017
ph: 315-986-1424
e-mail: jacqueline.henry@cwix.com
web: http://www.cyberattic.com/dealer/toysndolls
Buys and sells 1860-1960 toys; cast iron, lithographed tin, wind-ups, banks, candy containers, pressed steel toys, toy soldiers, dolls, games, etc.

Chris Savino
P.O. Box 419
Breesport, NY 14816-0419
ph: 607-739-3106
fax: 607-739-3106
e-mail: csavino@extrope.net
Wants to buy any childhood items: tin wind-ups, battery toys, cast iron toys, autos, trucks, marbles, robots; toys made in the US, Japan, Germany, France England; toys in original boxes bring more; call or write for an offer.

Phil McEntee
Where the Toys Are, Inc.
45 W. Pike St.
Canonsburg, PA 15317
ph: 724-745-4599
e-mail: wheretoysr@aol.com
web: http://www.wherethetoysare.com/
Expert and dealer in vintage and antique toys from Victorian era to baby boomer collectibles.

Bob Stevens
Keystone Toy Trader
529 N. Water St.
Masontown, PA 15461
ph: 724-583-8234
fax: 724-583-0604
Wants quality antique toys in all categories: early comic characters, cast iron, tin, diecast Tootsietoys, German penny toys, early German and European toys.

Jim Cox
Sussex Antique Toy Shop
107 Avenue L
Matamoras, PA 18336
ph: 570-491-2707
e-mail: toyfolks@erols.com

Philip Norman
Norman's Olde Store
126 W. Main
Washington, NC 27889
ph: 252-946-3448

Mark Clark
636 Dover Rd.
Clarksville, TN 37042-6006
ph: 931-645-9218
Wants to buy old toys, old marbles, comic character collectibles, lunch boxes, old Teddy Bears, fireworks, T.V. show related toys, robots and space toys, advertising collectibles, whiskey jugs, arrowheads and other artifacts.

Gordy Dutt
Gordy's
P.O. Box 201
Sharon Center, OH 44274-0201
ph: 330-239-1657
fax: 330-239-2991
e-mail: Gordys_kitbuilders@juno.com
web: http://www.gordyskitbuilders.com/
Wants to buy toys from the '50s to '60s: games, gum cards, model kits, gun sets, monsters, super heroes, cereal premiums, TV-related, cartoon toys, etc.

Bill & Joanne Bruegman
Toy Scouts, Inc.
137 Casterton Ave.
Akron, OH 44303-1543
ph: 330-836-0668
fax: 330-869-8668
e-mail: toyscout@akron.infi.net
Specializes baby-boom era toys from 1950s-60s: TV, cartoon, monsters, super heroes, games, cereal premiums, model kits, etc.; anything baby-boomer era.

Ed McDandal
Ed's Toy Shop
953 East Richmond
Kokomo, IN 46901
ph: 765-459-0325
fax: 765-459-0380
e-mail: edtoys@iquest.net
web: http://members.iquest.net/~edtoys/
Wants to buy old toys from the 1920s to 1930s; pressed steel cars and trucks, cast iron toys, wind-ups, live steam toys.

James May
Olde Tyme Toy Shop
120 S. Main St.
Fairmount, IN 46928
ph: 317-948-3150
Focuses on toys and related pop culture collectibles such as Star Wars.

Richard Trautwein
Toys N Such
437 Dawson St.
Sault Sainte Marie, MI 49783-2119
ph: 906-635-0356
e-mail: rtraut@portup.com
Collector, dealer, expert, appraiser wants tin and metal wind-up, battery operated, and electric toys: German, Japanese, or American; also gas operated toys and pedal cars and bikes.

Ed Janey
1756 65th St.
Garrison, IA 52229
ph: 319-477-8888
Always buying old toys, model kits, Western collectibles and toys, space toys, slot cars and car kits, lunch boxes, ad items, radios, Disney, soakies, etc.

Heinz Mueller
Continental Hobby House
P.O. Box 193
Sheboygan, WI 53082
ph: 920-693-3371
fax: 920-693-8211
e-mail: toys@classictintoy.com
web: http://www.classictintoy.com/
Extensive list of toy trains (catalog $5); parts list ($5); HO train catalog ($5); wants all types of toys and trains especially European; very large inventory of all types of toys; request web page information.

Jay Robinson
Chicago Kid
P.O. Box 529
Deerfield, IL 60015-0529
ph: 847-945-8691
Wants to buy old electric and wind-up trains; also old toy trucks and cars; wind-up and battery-operated toys.

Sue Tarrant
Pretty Good Toys
67 May Valley Lane
Fenton, MO 63026
ph: 314-349-9057
fax: 314-349-9162
e-mail: pgtoys@pgtoys.com
web: http://www.pgtoys.com
Buys and sells collectibles toys from 1960s to 1990s, specializing in Batman, Aliens, action figures, movie & TV collectibles, Star Trek, Star Wars, puzzles, records, advertising premiums.

Jon & Carolyn Thurmond
Collectorholics
15006 Fuller
Grandview, MO 64030-4522
ph: 816-322-0906
Buys, sells, trades TV Guides, Western items, Star Trek, military toys, banks, novelty radios, radio premiums, Disney, etc.

Jim Yeager
P.O. Box 413881
Kansas City, MO 64141
ph: 816-333-2839

Bill & Pam Shepardson
Vintage Toys
201 Schiller
Hermann, MO 65041
ph: 573-486-3903
Wants to buy toys: early tin, cast iron, paper litho, character toys.

Jim & Rita Hinton
Collector's Choice
P.O. Box 104284
Jefferson City, MO 65110-4284
ph: 573-636-7567

Tim Ullmen
TTotalin Toys
P.O. Box 1188
Ponchatoula, LA 70454
ph: 504-419-9172 or 800-441-2609
fax: 504-419-2361
e-mail: ttotalin@i-55.com
Buys and sells old pre-1970s toys, dolls, games, cars, etc.; tin, metal, friction, battery operated; collecting Flintstones, Hanna Barbera, Winnie the Pooh and any cartoon related items.

Marjorie Jeffreys
Going to Pieces
P.O. Box 390
Cibolo, TX 78108
ph: 210-659-2458
Buys and sells old games, toys, blocks and children's dishes and children's baking items.

John D. McKenna
McKenna Bros. Wholesale
801-803 W Cucharras St.
Colorado Springs, CO 80905
ph: 719-630-8732
Buys, sells & collects pre-1960 toys in all categories especially early American tin, cast iron automotive and horse-drawn toys.

Barrett Behnke
Barrett's Toys & Collectibles
7063 E. Blue Lake Dr.
Tucson, AZ 85715
ph: 520-290-2864
Wants to buy Wyandotte toys and other pressed steel and tin toys.

Richard Johnson
P.O. Box 27093
Prescott Valley, AZ 86312-7093
ph: 520-775-4714
fax: 520-771-9445
e-mail: toys@futureone.com
web: http://www.futureone.com/~toys/toy.htm
Tin toys, robots.

Louis Steinberg
Classic Hobbies & Toys
17632 Chatsworth St.
Granada Hills, CA 91344-5601

Brent Harelson
Santa Barbara Antique Toys
349 W. Felicita #241
Escondido, CA 92025
ph: 760-737-0004
e-mail: toys@antiquetoys.com
web: http://www.antiquetoys.com
Buys, sells and takes on consignment toys from 1890 to 1960: Hubley, Dent, Buddy L, Structo, Tonka, Bing, Marx, Schuco, Kingsbury, Dinky, Tootsietoy, Chein, Metalcraft, Smith-Miller.

Toys 'N' Stuff
P.O. Box 2037
San Bernardino, CA 92406
ph: 909-880-8558
fax: 909-880-8096
Wants to buy Star Wars, Gremlins, Planet of the Apes, GI Joe, Nightmare, Corgi & Dinky, character toys of all kinds, all other movie and TV related toys and memorabilia.

Kathleen Hehn
Gotta Have It! Collectible Toys
1215 S. Beach Blvd. #E
Anaheim, CA 92804
ph: 714-995-4151
e-mail: lenkathy@gte.net
web: http://home1.gte.net/lenkathy/
Everything you could want in collectible toys: dolls, GI Joe, monsters, cartoon characters.

Keith Cook
2920 22nd Ave.
Forest Grove, OR 97116
ph: 503-357-6009
e-mail: keithcook@earthlink.net
web: http://www.geocities.com/MotorCity/Downs/5659/
Buys and sells pressed steel toys; dedicated to the restoration/preservation of pressed steel toys: Tonka, Nyline, Structo, Buddy L; complete restoration service using finest materials and state-of-the-art processes; parts and decals.

Alicia & Jorge Valino
P.O. Box 1442
Montevideo, 11000
Uruguay
e-mail: vala@adinet.com.uy.

Experts

Richard Friz
Maddie's Muse
P.O. Box 472
Peterborough, NH 03458-0472
ph: 603-563-8155
e-mail: jmdfriz@top.monad.net
Author of "The Official Price Guide to Toys."

Darrow's Fun Antiques
1101 1st Ave.
New York, NY 10021-8737
ph: 212-838-0730
fax: 212-838-3617
e-mail: george@fun-antiques.com
web: http://www.fun-antiques.com/
Buys & sells antique games, toys, ad signs, animated art, jukeboxes, slot machines, comic watches, bicycles & memorabilia of all types.

Judith Katz-Schwartz
Twin Brooks Antiques & Collectibles
P.O. Box 6572
New York, NY 10128-0006
ph: 212-876-3512
fax: 212-876-3512
e-mail: twinb@msjudith.net
web: http://www.msjudith.net
Buys, sells, appraises wind-ups, character toys, board games, battery operated, Chein, Marx, Disney, obots, Japanese celluloid, space toys, etc.

Bob Smith
62 West Ave.
Fairport, NY 14450
ph: 716-377-8394
fax: 716-377-6019
e-mail: oldtoys@frontiernet.net
web: http://www.frontiernet.net/~oldtoys/
Avid collector and dealer of 1870-1970 toys: wind-up, automotive, European tin, pressed steel, early diecast, cast iron; specializes in Oh Boy, Tootsietoys, Dinky Toys, Hillclimbers, Wyandotte, and German tin toys.

Ted Hake
Hake's Americana & Collectibles Auction
P.O. Box 1444
York, PA 17405-1444
ph: 717-848-1333
e-mail: Ted@hakes.com
web: http://www.hakes.com/
Always purchasing items for 8 mail-bid auctions per year covering hundreds of categories including toys, character collectibles, Disney, cowboy heroes, premiums, television, politicals, pin-back buttons, advertising and more.

Harry L. Rinker
Rinker Enterprises, Inc.
5093 Vera Cruz Rd.
Emmaus, PA 18049-9554
ph: 610-965-1122
fax: 610-965-1124
e-mail: rinker@fast.net
web: http://www.rinker.com
Researches, writes about and appraises all forms of 19th and 20th century toys, games and puzzles.

Joseph E. Freed
6209 Sandy Forks Rd.
Raleigh, NC 27624-9534
ph: 919-847-7365
fax: 919-847-3822
Buys and specializes in toys; also published books about toys.

David Welch
P.O. Box 714
Murphysboro, IL 62966-0714
ph: 618-687-2282
fax: 618-684-2243
e-mail: PezDude1@aol.com
Wants 1950s-1960s tin robots; also 1930s-1960s Disney, Popeye, Betty Boop and monster toys; $10,000+ for rare items.

Earnest & Ida Long
Long's Americana
P.O. Box 90
Mokelumne Hill, CA 95245
ph: 209-286-1348
Specializes in toys, banks, games and other children's items; publishes "Dictionary of Toys, Vol I & II" and "Penny Lane."

R. Bailey
P.O. Box 251
Coventry, CV5 9YT
U.K.
ph: 0120 369 1212
Consultant to "Diecast Collector" magazine.

Internet Resources

John Kincade
Toy Market
P.O. Box 4096
Olathe, KS 66063
ph: 913-780-9298
e-mail: editor@toymarket.com
web: http://www.toymarket.com
A leading online resource dedicated to the toys and collectibles marketplace; buy, sell, trade toys and collectibles.

Eric G. Myers
Raving Toy Maniac
1115 Autrey St.
Houston, TX 77006
ph: 713-529-1726
e-mail: egm@toymania.com
web: http://www.toymania.com
Toy and action figure collector and expert with one of the Internet's most comprehensive toy collecting resources.

AntiqueTOY.com
204 Mize St.
Huntsville, TX 77340
e-mail: travis@antiquetoy.com
web: http://www.antiquetoy.com/
Internet magazine for toy collectors.

Man./Prod./Dist.

International Toy Center
200 5th Ave.
New York, NY 10010
ph: 212-675-3535
fax: 212-727-2065
Houses more than 1,500 manufacturers of toys, Christmas decorations, novelties, and products for every holiday.

Museums/Libraries

Fawcett's Antique Toy Museum
P.O. Box 1156
Waldoboro, ME 04572-1156
ph: 207-832-7398
Extensive collection of antique cartoon character toys; one of the finest Lone Ranger collections in the world on display.

Forbes Magazine Collection
62 Fifth Ave.
New York, NY 10011-8882
ph: 212-206-5549 or 212-620-2200
web: http://www.tfaoi.com/newsmu/nmus172.htm

Sheila Clark
Museum of the City of New York
1220 5th Ave.
New York, NY 10029-5221
ph: 212-534-1672
fax: 212-534-5974
e-mail: mcny@mcny.org
web: http://www.mcny.org/mcny/
Access by appointment; research fee charged.

Strong Museum, The
1 Manhattan Square
Rochester, NY 14607
ph: 716-263-2700
web: http://www.strongmuseum.org
Collection contains more than 500,000 objects: toys, doll houses, miniatures, household furnishings, and the world's most comprehensive collection of dolls.

Toy & Miniature Museum of Delaware
P.O. Box 4053
Route 141
Wilmington, DE 19807
ph: 302-427-8697
fax: 302-427-8654
e-mail: toys@thomes.net
web: http://www.thomes.net/toys/

Delaware Toy & Miniature Museum
P.O. Box 4053
Wilmington, DE 19807
ph: 302-427-8697
fax: 302-427-8654
e-mail: toys@thomes.net
web: http://www.thomes.net/toys/
A historical reference of antique and contemporary dollhouses, miniatures and sample furniture as well as dolls, toys, trains, boats and planes, both European and American from the 18th to 20th centuries.

Washington Dolls' House & Toy Museum
5236 44th St. NW
Washington, DC 20015
ph: 202-244-0024

Lake Erie Toy Museum
P.O. Box 860
Kellys Island, OH 43438
ph: 419-746-2451
fax: 419-281-7101
Features toys of many themes: comic strip characters, Disney, circus and amusement park, TV and cartoons, military, sports, construction, space, nursery rhyme, holiday seasons, superheroes, farm, dolls, dollhouses, boats, airplanes, etc.

Eugene Field House & Toy Museum
Newsletter: Field Notes
634 So. Broadway St.
Saint Louis, MO 63102
ph: 314-421-4689

Roger Berg
Toy & Miniature Museum of Kansas City
5235 Oak St.
Kansas City, MO 64112-2877
ph: 816-333-2055 or 816-333-9328
fax: 816-333-2055
e-mail: bergr@umkc.edu
web: http://www.umkc.edu/tmm/
Museum housed in an elegant mansion features collections of miniatures, antique dolls' houses and antique toys.

Denver Museum of Miniatures, Dolls & Toys
1880 Gaylord St.
Denver, CO 80206-1211
ph: 303-322-1053
fax: 303-322-3704
e-mail: ldsbc@aol.com
web: http://www.sni.net/start/dmmdt/
Displays miniatures, dolls and toys dating back to the 18th century.

Hobby City Doll & Toy Museum
1238 South Beach Blvd.
Anaheim, CA 92804
ph: 714-527-2323

Kate Bines
Bethnal Green Museum of Childhood
Cambridge Heath Rd.
London, E2 9PA
U.K.
ph: 0181-980-2415
fax: 0181-983-5225
e-mail: k.bines@vam.ac.uk
web: http://www.vam.ac.uk/index3.html
National collection of dolls, toys, games, puppets, and children's costumes.

Periodicals

Magazine: White's Guide to Collecting Figures
P.O. Box K46
Richmond, VA 23288
ph: 888-280-0389 or 804-285-0995
fax: 804-285-9420
e-mail: mwhite@whitesguide.com
web: http://www.whitesguide.com
Pricing authority covers modern figures including Disney Classics, Beanies, NASCAR, Star Wars, Bears, dolls, Kenner, Barbie.

Teri Steele, Pub.
Magazine: YesterDaze TOYS
P.O. Box 57
Otisville, MI 48463-0057
ph: 810-631-4593 or 800-336-9927
fax: 810-631-4567
web: http://www.thedaze.com
The monthly meeting place for toy collectors; if children played with it, this magazine covers it; old to not-so-old toys.

Antique Trader Publications, Inc.
Newspaper: Toy Trader
P.O. Box 1050
Dubuque, IA 52004-1050
ph: 800-334-7165 or 800-482-4155
fax: 800-531-0880
e-mail: jmkoenig@execpc.com
web: http://www.collect.com/toytrader
Monthly newspaper with information on how to buy, sell and trade all types of toys; market trends, the latest prices, "how-to" columns, listings of toy clubs and upcoming toy shows and auctions; also full of buy and sell ads.

Pat DuChene, PR
Krause Publications
Newspaper: Toy Shop
700 E. State St.
Iola, WI 54990-0001
ph: 715-445-2214
fax: 715-445-4087
e-mail: info@krause.com
web: http://www.krause.com/
A bi-weekly fully indexed newspaper containing classified ads for toys, tin soldiers, dolls, diecast toys, models, trains, etc.

Pat DuChene, PR
Krause Publications
Magazine: Toy Cars & Vehicles
700 E. State St.
Iola, WI 54990-0001
ph: 715-445-2214
fax: 715-445-4087
e-mail: info@krause.com
web: http://www.krause.com/
One-stop marketplace and information for collectors of scale vehicles: toy cars, trucks, farm toys, military vehicles, and construction vehicles; model kits, diecasts, motor sports, far toys, promotional models.

Dale Kelley, Ed.
Magazine: Antique Toy World
P.O. Box 34509
Chicago, IL 60641-0509
ph: 312-725-0633
fax: 312-725-3449
e-mail: atw@antiquetoyworld.com
web: http://www.antiquetoyworld.com/
A monthly magazine serving toy collectors and dealers; 200 or more pages of all types of toys including antique toys, banks, cast iron toys, tin wind-ups, comic toys, pedal cars; ads, articles, etc.

Hugh Murphy, PR
Beckett Publications, Inc.
Magazine: Hot Toys
15850 Dallas Parkway
Dallas, TX 75248
ph: 972-448-9018 or 800-840-3137
e-mail: hmurphy@beckett.com
web: http://www.beckett.com/

Brian Savage
Fun Publications
Newspaper: Master Collector
225 Cattle Barron Parc Dr.
Fort Worth, TX 76108
ph: 800-772-6673 or 817-448-9863
fax: 817-448-9843
e-mail: brian@mastercollector.com
web: http://www.mastercollector.com
Ads-only newspaper; dolls (antique and modern collectible), toys, banks, models, cars, Matchbox, monsters, puzzles, political, toy trains, etc.; subscribers receive free 30 word ad each month; published monthly; reaches 20,000.

Rick Polizzi
Magazine: Spin Again
4602 Morse Ave.
Sherman Oaks, CA 91423-3326
Quarterly publication on the world of toys, games, and collectibles.

Sandra Hood, Pub.
Newspaper: Antique & Collectables
P.O. Box 12589
500 Fesler St., Ste. 201
El Cajon, CA 92022
ph: 619-593-2925 or 619-593-2927
fax: 619-447-7187
e-mail: antiqunews@aol.com
web: http://www.collect.com/antiqueandcollectables
The largest monthly newspaper in Southern California covering the antiques & collectibles industry with focus sections on Nevada and Arizona; 72+ pages; events and show section, feature articles; columns, ads.

Verlag SpielzeugAntik
Magazine: Spielzeug Antik
Ubierring 4
Koln, D-50678
Germany
Focuses on antique & collectible toys; published six times per year.

Repair Services

Walter Allen
Specialty Castings
19 Mill Rd.
Boxford, MA 01921
ph: 978-887-9783
Reproduces items for collectors by casting in cast iron, bronze, brass or aluminum; all items created through the lost wax process; also mold making, parts modification, and shrinkage compensation.

Marc Olimpio
Marc Olimpio's Antique Toy Restoration Center
P.O. Box 1505
Wolfeboro, NH 03894
ph: 603-569-6739
e-mail: luckydog@worldpath.net
Specializes in early handpainted German and French-American tin toys, iron and pressed steel, and cast iron.

Frank Capozzi
6 Devon Rd
Bethpage, NY 11714-1107
ph: 516-938-9765
fax: 516-938-9197
e-mail: FRCapozzi@aol.com
Repairs toys; battery operated, friction, wind-ups; all work guaranteed; send toys for free estimate; return shipping and handling your only cost if no repairs made.

Gary J. Moran
3 Finch Court
Commack, NY 11725-4901
ph: 516-864-9444
Antique toy repairs, including battery operated, friction and wind-up toys; call or write for free estimate; broken toys purchased.

Ron Hanley
Mini-Motors
130 Main
Hobart, NY 13788
ph: 607-538-9926
Repairs pedal cars and automotive toys: repair work, nickel plating, pressed-steel vehicles such as Tonka and Buddy L.

Joe Freeman
Tin Toy Works
1313 N. 15th St.
Allentown, PA 18102-1068
ph: 610-439-8268
fax: 610-439-1288
Specializes in the repair of tin toys; tin toy autos, boats, merry-go-rounds, etc.; repairs mechanisms, makes missing parts.

Jerry Shook
6528 Cedar Brook Dr.
New Albany, OH 43054-9715
ph: 614-855-7796
fax: 614-855-7796
e-mail: gshook@ee.net
Makes rubber & plastic replacement parts for toys: wind-ups, robots, space toys, battery operated, etc.; also for dolls; send SASE and $2 for parts list.

Classic Tin Toy Company Restoration Shop
P.O. Box 193
Sheboygan, WI 53082
ph: 920-693-3371
fax: 920-693-8211
e-mail: toys@classictintoy.com
web: http://www.classictintoy.com/shop.htm
Repair and total restoration of all makes of old toys including tin, cast iron and tinplate trains; world's largest manufacturer of toy parts; catalog $10.

Keith Cook
Trucks by Keith
2920 22nd Ave.
Forest Grove, OR 97116
ph: 503-357-6009
e-mail: keithcook@earthlink.net
web: http://www.geocities.com/MotorCity/Downs/5659/
Dedicated to the restoration and preservation of pressed steel toys: Tonka, Nyline, Structo, Buddy L; complete restoration service using finest materials and state-of-the-art processes; parts and decals; toys for sale.

Suppliers

Julian Thomas
Thomas Toys
P.O. Box 405
Fenton, MI 48430
ph: 810-629-8707
e-mail: thomastoys@thomastoys.com
web: http://thomastoys.com
Carries antique toy car replacement parts; catalog $7.

Action Figures

(see also POPULAR CULTURE, Baby Boomer; TOYS, Playsets; TELEVISION SHOWS & MEMORABILIA, Star Trek)

Clubs/Associations

Action Toy Organization of Michigan
e-mail: michaelcrawford@provide.net
web: http://www.atomgroup.com/

Allied Collectors & Traders Indigenous to Virginia
e-mail: ajhays@pressroom.com
web: http://www.pressroom.com/~jah-net/activ.htm
Club of toy collectors and traders in and around the Washington DC area; goal is to avoid unethical practices of scalpers and hoarders; strength lies in establishing friendships with fellow collectors and trading toys 1 for 1 or at cost.

Texas Action Figure Ring
e-mail: docgordo@mail.utexas.edu
web: http://www.angelfire.com/tx/afring/

Society of Obsessive Female Toy Traders
e-mail: softt@geocities.com
web: http://www.geocities.com/Wellesley/5031/

South Eastern Action Figure Collectors Association
e-mail: mattw@groupz.net
web: http://expage.com/page/seafca

Collectors

Steve Almy
Galactic Highway
113 Colonial Parkway, Ste. B
Yorkville, IL 60560
ph: 630-553-2993 or 888-262-6304
e-mail: steve@galactic-hwy.com
web: http://www.galactic-hwy.com
Online web store for the serious action figure/toy collector and gaming players.

Dealers

John Marshall
P.O. Box 340
Rancocas, NJ 08073-0340
ph: 609-267-6903
Buys, sells, collects action figures.

411 Toys
16054 Sherman Way
Van Nuys, CA 91406
ph: 818-786-9760 or 888-411-TOYS
fax: 818-786-4655
web: http://www.411toys.com
Focuses on modern action figures, GI Joe, Star Wars; also Beanie Babies.

Doreend Rivera
Rene's Action Figures, Toys & Collectibles
993 Bradshawe Place
Monterey Park, CA 91754-4913
ph: 626-573-1614
e-mail: mistertoys@aol.com
web: http://members.aol.com/mistertoys/
An online source for 1,000s of action figures, toys and collectibles: Batman, cartoon, Simpsons, Spiderman, Marvel, superheroes, movie, comic, non-sport trading cards, monsters and more.

Brian Rachfal
Craddock's Non-Sports Cards & Collectibles
P.O. Box 7772
San Jose, CA 95150-3766
ph: 408-298-9070 or 408-629-3980
Buys, sells, trades Star Wars action figures, exclusive & regional playsets (Sears, J.C. Penny's, etc.), remote control items, diecast vehicles, gum cards and related memorabilia; also wants rare Star Trek & Indiana Jones toys & figures.

Experts

John Marshall
P.O. Box 340
Rancocas, NJ 08073-0340
ph: 609-267-6903
Author of "Backyard Heroes: Action Figures of the 1970s" (Schiffer); writes articles for "Collecting Toys" magazine.

Periodicals

James Tomlinson, Ed.
Lee Publications
Magazine: Action Figure News & Toy Review
556 Monroe Turnpike
Monroe, CT 06468-2309
ph: 203-452-7286
fax: 203-452-0410
AFN is a full size magazine dedicated to the collecting of action figures (plastic figures such as G.I. Joe, Captain Action, Star Wars, etc.) and toys from 1964 to present; articles, ads, shows, etc.

Tom Tumbusch
Tomart Publications
Magazine: Tomart's Action Figure Digest
3300 Encrete Lane
Dayton, OH 45439-1944
ph: 937-294-2250
fax: 937-294-1024
e-mail: office@tomart.com
web: http://www.tomart.com
Devoted to action figure collectibles; published bi-monthly.

Mike Shuffield
Phase II Publishing
Magazine: G.I. Joe Patrol
P.O. Box 2362
Hot Springs National Park, AR 71914
ph: 501-525-7149
e-mail: gijp@snider.net
A bi-monthly publication that brings you up-to-date information on action figure and related collectibles from Hasbro, Marx, Mego, Kenner, Mattel and many other action figure series; identify loose accessories; ads.

Suppliers

Steve Lundin
Action Figure Display Case Co.
P.O. Box 7954
Chicago, IL 60680
ph: 773-395-3395
fax: 773-395-3495
e-mail: actioncc@enteract.com
web: http://www.enteract.com/~actioncc
Manufactures high quality display cases for all 12" action figures; full color combat backgrounds or cityscapes for Barbie; perfect for gifts, home or office.

Action Figures (G.I. Joe)

Clubs/Associations

Brian Savage
G.I. Joe Collectors Club
Newsletter: G.I. Joe Collectors Club Newsletter
225 Cattle Barron Parc Dr.
Fort Worth, TX 76108
ph: 800-772-6673 or 817-448-9863
fax: 817-448-9843
e-mail: brian@mastercollector.com
web: http://www.mastercollector.com
100s of members worldwide; the source for G.I. Joe information and service; monthly newsletter; send SASE for more information; membership includes subscription to "Master Collector" newspaper and 30-word ad each month.

David S. Lane, II
G.I. Joe: Steel Brigade Club
Newsletter: Ammo Box
8362 Lomay Ave.
Westminster, CA 92683-3327
ph: 714-297-5042
e-mail: sbcommand@geocities.com
web: http://www.geocities.com/area51/corridor/9429
International club interested in the 1982-1994 3 3/4" G.I. Joe collection; newsletter published quarterly.

Collectors

Jeff Kowalski
P.O. Box 64
Pluckemin, NJ 07978
ph: 908-526-5033
Wants G.I. Joe: dolls, clothing, accessories, vehicles.

Dealers

John Kachmar
Techno-Fantasy Traders
779 Carissa Dr.
West Palm Beach, FL 33411-3412
ph: 561-798-5978
fax: 561-798-5978

Bob Cummings
5669 Chelsea Ave.
La Jolla, CA 92037
ph: 619-456-2556
e-mail: bobbystoin@aol.com
Wants to buy old boys' toys, especially GI Joe from the 1960s; pays most for collections in excellent to mint-in-box collection.

Tina Windeler
Cotswold Collectibles, Inc.
P.O. Box 249
Clinton, WA 98236
ph: 360-579-1223
fax: 360-579-1287
e-mail: cotswold@whidbey.net
web: http://www.whidbey.net/~cotswold/
Buys and sells 12" G.I. Joe and accessories, including replacement parts such as boots, helmets, soldier equipment, etc.; also a line of high quality custom military 12" figures, "The Elite Brigade"; free monthly illustrated catalog.

Experts

Joe Bodnarchuk
G.I. Joe Nostalgia Co.
62 McKinley Ave.
Kenmore, NY 14217-2414
ph: 716-873-0264 or 800-5GI-JOES
fax: 716-873-0264
e-mail: webmaster@bodnarchuk.com
web: http://bodnarchuk.com/headquarters_quarterly/magazine.html
G.I. Joe enthusiast and collector since 1964; pays big for mint collections of any size; quality a must.

James DeSimone
150 S. Glenoaks Blvd.
Burbank, CA 91510-1314
ph: 818-563-1179
Buys, collects, appraises, and specializes in G.I. Joe; author of "The New Official Identification Guide to G.I. Joe". Vols. 1, 2, 3.

Periodicals

Joe Bodnarchuk
Newsletter: Headquarters Quarterly
62 McKinley Ave.
Kenmore, NY 14217-2414
ph: 716-873-0264 or 800-5GI-JOES
fax: 716-873-0264
e-mail: webmaster@bodnarchuk.com
web: http://bodnarchuk.com/headquarters_quarterly/magazine.html
A quarterly publication focusing of G.I. Joe.

Agriculture Related

(see TOYS, Farm)

Airplane Related

(see also AIRLINE MEMORABILIA, Models [Desk])

Collectors

Perry R. Eichor
703 N. Almond Dr.
Simpsonville, SC 29681-3453
ph: 864-967-8770
fax: 864-228-2541
e-mail: kpmflyn@earthlink.net
Wants aircraft toys and literature; member of Antique Toy Collectors of America.

Dealers

Dan Wells
Dan Wells Antique Toys
P.O. Box 7
Goshen, KY 40026
ph: 502-292-1748
fax: 502-292-1749
e-mail: jagdan@aol.com
Wants to buy all miniature/toy aircraft, especially travel agency and factory models.

Mike Bowen
704 St. James Place
Noblesville, IN 46060
ph: 317-773-9069
e-mail: kbowen@iquest.net
Appraiser, dealer, collector, expert interested in any Aeromini/Aero Mini information or diecast planes.

Experts

G.R. Webster
P.O. Box 845
Greenwich, CT 06836-0845
ph: 203-629-5270
e-mail: grwebster@aol.com
Interested in airplane toys and models: diecast toys, ID models, travel agency and desk models, etc.

Arcade

Experts

Al Aune
Mannolla Publishing
4441 Shari Ann Lane
Minneapolis, MN 55443-3461
ph: 612-560-4290 or 612-421-5151
fax: 612-421-3618
Author of "Arcade Toys"; contains hard-to-find information about dating Arcade toys.

Automotive

(see AUTOMOBILIA; TOYS, Cars)

Battery Operated

Collectors

Beau S. Cassity
Kid in Me, The
9502 Avenel Rd.
Silver Spring, MD 20903-2308
ph: 301-434-8293
e-mail: nodkitty@aol.com
Specializes in pre and post WWII toys, especially battery operated; wants to buy all types of battery operated toys, including toys for parts; wants plastic toys and Japanese tin wind-ups.

Stuart Stein
P.O. Box 303
Frederick, MD 21705-0303
ph: 301-663-8369
fax: 301-663-8202
e-mail: steincpa@ix.netcom.com
Wants to buy Japanese battery toys from the 1960s.

Experts

Don Hultzman
5026 Sleepy Hollow Rd.
Medina, OH 44256-8309
ph: 330-225-2668
e-mail: don.hultzman@gte.net
Buys/sells pre-1970 battery operated and wind-up toys; wants toys in any condition; author of "Collector's Guide to Battery Toys"; also does expert repairs on battery operated toys; repairs are undetectable & guaranteed.

Repair Services

Dr. Day
Toy Doctor, The
RR 1 Box 202
Red Creek, NY 13143
ph: 315-754-8846
fax: 315-754-6238
e-mail: janeday@zlink.net
web: http://www.thetoydoctor.com
Repairs battery operated toys; robots and space toys a specialty; dealer discounts; caring for all battery operated toys; "The Toy Doctor" is a registered trademark.

Don Hultzman
5026 Sleepy Hollow Rd.
Medina, OH 44256-8309
ph: 330-225-2668
e-mail: don.hultzman@gte.net
Does expert repairs on battery operated toys; repairs are undetectable & guaranteed; also buys and sells pre-1970 battery operated and wind-up toys; wants toys in any condition.

Randy King
211 Park Ave.
New Castle, IN 47362
ph: 765-529-9297

Mike Czerwinski
825 Vistga Circle
Brea, CA 92621
ph: 714-990-4851
fax: 714-256-4525

Beanie Babies

Collectors

Bette Page
Front Parlor, The
300 Cemetery Rd.
Oakland, IL 61943
ph: 217-346-3533 or 800-346-5996
fax: 217-346-3533
e-mail: frntprlr@advant.com

Dealers

Jeana Massimino
701 Kennedy Dr.
Winchester, VA 22601
ph: 540-678-3978
Buy, sell, trade Beanie Babies.

Joe Elliot
World Beanie Babies News
336 Leaning Fenct Ct.
Pickerington, OH 43147
e-mail: 105541.2550@compuserve.com
web: http://www.geocities.com/EnchantedForest/3098/
Collectors, dealers, experts in Beanie Babies; the online service operating since December 1996 provides frequent news updates and a store directory for internet customers.

Bean Bag Store & More
Newsletter: Beanie Baby Times
6021 Lyndale Avenue South
Minneapolis, MN 55419
ph: 612-861-0102
e-mail: beanbags@bhome.com
web: http://www.bhome.com/times.htm
Has online bean bag newsletter.

411 Toys
16054 Sherman Way
Van Nuys, CA 91406
ph: 818-786-9760 or 888-411-TOYS
fax: 818-786-4655
web: http://www.411toys.com

Experts

Peggy Gallagher
80 Burr Ridge Parkway, Ste. 123
Hinsdale, IL 60521
ph: 847-298-2001
Author of "The Beanie Baby Phenomenon."

Internet Resources

Karen Sullivan
eBeanies On Line
6303 SW 116th Place, Unit D
Miami, FL 33173
ph: 305-598-6268
e-mail: eBeanies@aol.com
web: http://members.aol.com/ebeanies/index.htm
Lots of information and printable lists on this site; free classifieds, buy, sell, trade; latest information, rumors and links.

All BeJeanie
Software: BeJeanie
P.O. Box 2934
Danville, CA 94526
ph: 888-338-BEAN or 925-820-8000
fax: 925-820-1281
e-mail: mail@bejeanie.com
web: http://www.bejeanie.com/
Website and collector software for Beanie Baby collectors; also publishes Beanie Baby software that tracks original, monthly, and current values and details on unlimited collections of Beanie babies, Teenie Babies, Beanie Buddies & others.

Man./Prod./Dist.

Ty, Inc.
P.O. Box 5377
Hinsdale, IL 60522
ph: 708-495-1515 or 800-876-8000
e-mail: yourfriends@ty.com
web: http://www.ty.com/
Manufacturer of the Original Beanie Babies; great website with history, names, retirement dates, etc. of all Beanie Babies.

Periodicals

Andi Lucas, Ed.
Tuff Stuff Publications, Inc.
Magazine: Beans & Bears!
P.O. Box 3070
Richmond, VA 23228
ph: 804-266-0140 or 800-899-8833
fax: 804-264-4205
e-mail: beans@tuffstuffpubs.com
web: http://www.beansmagazine.com
Monthly magazine for collectors of bean bag collectibles including Ty, Warner Bros., Disney, Coca-Cola, etc.; also covers Teddy Bears collectibles; includes price guide for both bean bag and Teddy Bear collectibles.

<u>Magazine: White's Guide to Collecting Figures</u>
P.O. Box K46
Richmond, VA 23288
ph: 888-280-0389 or 804-285-0995
fax: 804-285-9420
e-mail: mwhite@whitesguide.com
web: http://www.whitesguide.com
Pricing authority covers modern figures including Disney Classics, Beanies, NASCAR, Star Wars, Bears, dolls, Kenner, Barbie.

Rosie Wells
Rosie Wells Enterprises, Inc.
<u>Magazine: Collectors' Bulletin</u>
22341 E. Wells Rd.
Canton, IL 61520
ph: 309-668-2211 or 800-445-8745
fax: 309-668-2795
e-mail: Rosie@RosieWells.com
web: http://www.RosieWells.com
Articles about today's collectibles: Lowell Davis, Anri, Dept. 56, Precious Moments, Cherished Teddies, Hallmark ornaments, Jan Hagara, Maud Humphrey, David Winter and more; organizes Beanie Fests for Beanie Baby collectors.

Suppliers

Union Products, Inc.
511 Lancaster St.
Leominster, MA 01453
ph: 978-537-1631 or 888-875-1071
e-mail: info@unionproducts.com
web: http://www.unionproducts.com
Sells Beanie Babies crystal clear plastic stackable boxes for storage and display.

Janice
RaynOrShyn Enterprises
P.O. Box 676
York, ME 03909
ph: 207-351-1876
e-mail: catalog@RaynOrShyn.com
web: http://www.RaynOrShyn.com/kids/
Get Beanie Baby accessories here: snacks, bed & breakfast, hammock, Beanie tag protectors, etc.

Bell

Collectors

Dr. Greg Zemenick
Dr. "Z"
1350 Kirts, Ste. 160
Troy, MI 48084-4852
ph: 248-642-8129 or 248-244-9430
fax: 248-244-9495
e-mail: drzzeezzi@aol.com
web: http://www.drzzeezzi.com/
Wants bell toys.

Boats & Outboards

Collectors

Robert McDonald
27-34 167 St.
Flushing, NY 11358-1126
ph: 718-762-2541 or 718-520-3914
fax: 718-520-2539
e-mail: jb6290@aol.com
Wants to buy 1950s-1960s outboard motor toys: battery operated, metal motors only; Evinrude, Johnson, Mercury, Scottatwater, Gale, Buccaneer, Oliver.

Brent Simmons
3212 Severn Wharf Rd.
Hayes, VA 23072
ph: 804-642-2076
Wants to buy toy outboard boat motors; any condition.

Jack Browning
214 16th St. N.W.
Roanoke, VA 24017-5516
ph: 703-890-5083 or 703-982-8680
fax: 703-342-1283
e-mail: jbrow9945@aol.com

Richard Gronowski
1100 Peninsula Dr.
Traverse City, MI 49686
ph: 616-941-2111
e-mail: rgrono3381@aol.com
Wants to buy toy metal outboard boat motors: Gale, Oliver, Johnson, Mercury, Scott, Evinrude, Wen-Mac, Sea-Fury.

Bubble Blowers

Collectors

Judith Schulz
533 Milwaukee Ave.
Burlington, WI 53105-1232
ph: 262-763-3946
Wants old bubble blowers and related packages, literature, drawings and pictures of bubble blowing; conducts the International Bubble Blowing Extravaganza Event.

Canadian

Clubs/Associations

Betty Holland
CTM Farm Toy & Collectors Club
<u>Magazine: Canadian Toy Mania</u>
P.O. Box 489
Rocanville, Saskatchewan S0A 3L0
Canada
ph: 306-645-4566
fax: 306-645-4566
Focuses on farm toys and dolls.

Cannons

(see also CANNONS; FIREWORKS MEMORABILIA; TOY GUNS)

Collectors

Ray Brandes
P.O. Box 1922
Norcross, GA 30096
e-mail: maloney@ray-vin.com
web: http://www.ray-vin.com

Experts

David Ross
Cannon-Mania
P.O. Box 552
Stratford, CT 06497
ph: 203-378-2582
e-mail: cannon@cannon-mania.com
web: http://www.cannon-mania.com/
Can identify and appraise older cast iron toy cannons.

Internet Resources

David Ross
Cannon-Mania
P.O. Box 552
Stratford, CT 06497
ph: 203-378-2582
e-mail: cannon@cannon-mania.com
web: http://www.cannon-mania.com/
A web site for those interested in small cannon, i.e. fine replicas that sit on a mantle, bookcase or desktop; also includes toys, salute cannon and cannon used on boats.

Museums/Libraries

Ray Brandes
Toy Cannon Museum
P.O. Box 1922
Norcross, GA 30096
e-mail: maloney@ray-vin.com
web: http://www.ray-vin.com
An online museum of toy carbide, firecracker, cap, blank and powder cannons.

Suppliers

Conestoga Company
P.O. Box 405
Bethlehem, PA 18016
Source for authentic Big-Bang cannons and parts.

Cars

(see also AUTOMOBILIA; MODELS, Cars; TOYS, Diecast)

Clubs/Associations

Peter H. Foss
Toy Car Collectors Club
<u>Newsletter: Toy Car Magazine</u>
33290 W. 14 Mile Rd. #454
West Bloomfield, MI 48322-3549
ph: 248-682-0272
fax: 248-682-5782
A club for collectors of toy cars such as Dinky, Corgi, Matchbox, Hot Wheels, Solido, Norev, Siku, Schuco, Gama, Rio, Auburn, Tootsietoy, Maisto, Ertl, banks, NASCAR, Tomica, Diapet, etc.

Tom Morgan
Post Car Registry
812 N. Third St.
Saint Peter, MN 56082
Dedicated to the preservation of plastic toy cars distributed through Post cereals from 1950-196; made by F&F Co. of Dayton, OH.

Antique Miniature Race Car Collectors
<u>Newsletter: Antique Miniature Race Car Collectors Newsletter</u>
10337 S. Cook
Oak Lawn, IL 60453-4630
ph: 708-425-4463
Quarterly newsletter.

Collectors

David K. Bausch
252 N. 7th St.
Allentown, PA 18102-4024
ph: 610-432-3355
fax: 610-820-9368
e-mail: oldtoy@aol.com
Major collector of automobile related material, especially automobile art.

Richard McCoy
2719 Lakeview Ave.
St. Joseph, MI 49085
Wants toy cars and boats 1900-1955; tin, pressed steel, wood.

Rick Ralston
99-969 Iwaena St.
Aiea, HI 96701-3249
ph: 800-486-9794 or 808-486-1243
fax: 808-486-1276
e-mail: ralston.hawaii@crazyshirts.com
web: http://www.ralstonantiques.com
Buys and sells pre-WWII toy vehicles.

Dealers

Dan Wells
Dan Wells Antique Toys
P.O. Box 7
Goshen, KY 40026
ph: 502-292-1748
fax: 502-292-1749
e-mail: jagdan@aol.com
Wants to buy all tin, cast iron, and early pressed steel automotive toys; also excellent condition or better early diecast, especially Hot Wheels, Dinky, Corgi, Matchbox, etc.

Trader Rick's Collectible Toy Cars
P.O. Box 161
Newark, IL 60541
ph: 815-695-9484
Wants to buy toy cars and model cars; also built or unbuilt car kits.

Experts

Steve Butler
2696 Brookmar Dr.
York, PA 17404-9489
ph: 717-792-4936
e-mail: evetstoys@aol.com
Buys, collects, appraises, specializes in automotive toys (cars and trucks)

1920-1960: iron, steel, cast metal, plastic; author & seller of "Promotionals 1934-1983"; promotional toy car and truck reference and price book; $22.65 ppd.

Clarence Young
Clarence Young Autohobby
302 Reems Creek
Weaverville, NC 28787-9792
ph: 828-645-5243
fax: 828-645-5243
e-mail: clarenceyoung@carhobby.com
web: http://www.carhobby.com/
Specializes in automotive promotional toys, mostly pot metal or plastic; sells "AUTOQUOTES"; also produces exclusive metal and/or resin toy cars.

Periodicals

Challenge Publications
Magazine: Car Toys
7950 Deering Ave.
Canoga Park, CA 91304-5063
ph: 818-887-0550
fax: 818-884-1343
e-mail: mail@challengeweb.com
web: http://www.challengeweb.com/
Bi-monthly magazine covers model cars of all types, sizes, materials, and vintage; also covers automobilia from automotive art and racing collectibles to pedal cars, porcelain signs, neon clocks, apparel, literature, gas pumps, etc.

Cars (Racing)

Book Sellers

Kevin Timothy
What It Is! Publishing
P.O. Box 1373
Marcus Hook, PA 19061-0373
ph: 610-485-1270
fax: 610-364-2331
web: http://www.ken-net.com/WII.htm
Book publisher with a main focus on slot cars; five titles.

Clubs/Associations

Jim Wallen, Sec./Treas.
United Federation of H.O. Racers Association
6800 W. Kilgore Ave.
Yorktown, IN 47396

Jason Boye
National Slot Car Racing Club
1903 Middlefield Rd. #3
Redwood City, CA 94063-2252
ph: 650-365-9345
e-mail: lemonzaco@aol.com
Regional chapters.

Collectors

Ira S. Kuperstein
22 Brush Hill Terrace
Butler, NJ 07405-2439
ph: 973-283-2420 or 800-526-5177
fax: 973-283-2426
e-mail: kuperstein@nac.net
Wants to buy miniature gas powered racing car models.

Gabriel Bogdonoff
46 Porter Rd.
Howell, NJ 07731-8614
ph: 732-363-4064
Wants toy race cars, gas powered, any condition; also wants big tin friction race cars and Smith Miller trucks in any condition.

Rick Burneson
435 1/2 South Orange Street
Mission Viejo, CA 92866-1611
ph: 714-997-1266
e-mail: phvg77a@prodigy.com
web: http://pages.prodigy.com/housa/index.htm
Collects and races H.O. scale electric slot cars.

Rod Thurgood
11 Perrins Lane
West Kempsey, New Sout Wales 2400
Australia
ph: (02) 6562 8209
fax: (02) 6562 6319
e-mail: simon@atomicnet.com.au
web: http://atomicnet.com.au/ascr/
Wants 1:64 scale (HO size) model diecast, plastic, slot cars that depict the 1:1 scale Dodge Daytona, Plymouth Superbird range of vehicles.

Dealers

William Sakas
P.O. Box 586
Wayne, NJ 07474
ph: 973-783-7174
e-mail: decobill@aol.com
web: http://www.machineage.com/decobill/
Buys and sells Aurora HO scale slot cars; buys one or entire collections.

Robert Budano
Bud's HO Cars Inc.
2 Westbrook Dr.
Cortlandt Manor, NY 10567
ph: 914-526-4950
fax: 914-526-4950

Robert Molta
SlotCarCentral
113 Herz St.
Syracuse, NY 13208-3026
ph: 315-428-1724 or 315-490-2386
fax: 315-428-1282
e-mail: rcmolta@msn.com
web: http://slotcarcentral.com
In the slot car hobby for over 15 years; 400 cars on display; sells or trades (preferred), appraises, collects, repairs.

John A. Clark
Slot Car Johnnie's
7634 Asden
Reynoldsburg, OH 43068
ph: 614-864-TJET
fax: 614-864-2800
e-mail: afx1afx@aol.com
Buys, sells, collects H.O. slot cars from the 1960s and 1970s; carries a large supply of slot cars in all scales as well as parts and accessories from used to Mint-In-Box; author of "HO Slot Car Identification and Price Guide."

Joel Vanderkork
Lots of Slots
503 Boal St.
Cincinnati, OH 45210
ph: 513-621-9353
Buys, sells, auctions, collects vintage slot cars.

Craig Reid
9116 E. Sprague #145
Spokane, WA 99206-3601
ph: 509-536-8489
e-mail: crtoys@cet.com
web: http://www.cet.com/~crtoys/
Collector and dealer of HO slot cars; also wants Star Trek, Transformers, action figures, etc.

Experts

Robert Molta
SlotCarCentral
113 Herz St.
Syracuse, NY 13208-3026
ph: 315-428-1724 or 315-490-2386
fax: 315-428-1282
e-mail: rcmolta@msn.com
web: http://slotcarcentral.com
In the slot car hobby for over 15 years; 400 cars on display; sells or trades (preferred), appraises, collects, repairs.

John A. Clark
Slot Car Johnnie's
7634 Asden
Reynoldsburg, OH 43068
ph: 614-864-TJET
fax: 614-864-2800
e-mail: afx1afx@aol.com
Buys, sells, collects H.O. slot cars from the 1960s and 1970s; carries a large supply of slot cars in all scales as well as parts and accessories from used to Mint-In-Box; author of "HO Slot Car Identification and Price Guide."

Internet Resources

Joe Bodnarchuk
HO Motoring & Racing Slotcar Magazine
62 McKinley Ave.
Kenmore, NY 14217-2414
ph: 716-873-0264
fax: 716-873-0264
e-mail: webmaster@bodnarchuk.com
web: http://www.bodnarchuck.com/ho_slotcar/motoring.html
The only on-line magazine devoted to the vintage slot car collecting hobby.

Chris Jennings
Slot Car Center, The
ph: 972-783-6792
e-mail: chrisj81@airmail.net
web: http://www2.clearlight.com/cgi-bin/cgiwrap/chrisj/Ultimate.cgi
An H.O. Car Bulletin Board.

Ben Bell
Slotside
7 Elizabeth St.
Thornhill, Ontario L4J 1X7
Canada
ph: 905-731-2218
fax: 905-731-5374
e-mail: slotside@shaw.wave.ca
web: http://www.tor.shaw.wave.ca/~slotside
Provides technical information for the dedicated slot racer together with a world wide directory of commercial tracks, interactive bulletin board, real time chat, and links to every meaningful slot car racing site on the web.

Periodicals

Art Zabrecky
Newsletter: Slot Car Trader
127 Island Dr.
Elyria, OH 44035-4777
ph: 440-322-7415
A newsletter dedicated to the 1/64 scale H.O. slot cars; collecting and racing news, new product reviews, subscriber-submitted articles; buy-sell-trade ad section.

Joel Vanderkork
Newsletter: Lots of Slots
503 Boal St.
Cincinnati, OH 45210
ph: 513-621-9353
A professionally produced monthly magazine for vintage HO slot car collectors.

John Ford
Am/Slot Racing
Magazine: Scale Auto Racing News
2608 Robert Road
Aransas Pass, TX 78336
ph: 512-758-7223 or 800-797-7223
fax: 512-758-1640
e-mail: fordpub@2fords.net
web: http://www.fordpub.com/sarn
Founded in 1979, world's oldest slot car magazine: new products, how-

to's, race reports, etc.; for H.O., 1/32 and 1/24 scale.

Rick Burneson
Newsletter: H.O. USA Newsletter
435 1/2 South Orange Street
Mission Viejo, CA 92866-1611
ph: 714-997-1266
e-mail: phvg77a@prodigy.com
web: http://pages.prodigy.com/housa/index.htm
For H.O. scale slot cars; free ads with membership.

Scale Auto
Magazine: HO Journal
P.O. Box 2051
Redmond, WA 98073
fax: 425-868-9865
e-mail: hoslots@scaleauto.com
web: http://www.scaleauto.com/HOJournal/

Rod Thurgood
Newsletter: Australian Slot Car Review
11 Perrins Lane
West Kempsey, New Sout Wales 2400
Australia
ph: (02) 6562 8209
fax: (02) 6562 6319
e-mail: simon@atomicnet.com.au
web: http://atomicnet.com.au/ascr/
Published four times per year and offering a comprehensive coverage of slot car racing and collecting in Australia; minimum of 36 pages; informative articles and lots of photos; free ads to subscribers; write for info.

Nick Sismey
Magazine: Derby H.O. Racing
80 Chaddesden Lane
Chaddesden, Derby DE21 6LN
U.K.
Monthly magazine.

Cast Iron

Repair Services

Arnie Prince
434 N. School St., #A
Lodi, CA 95240-1229
ph: 209-334-6101
fax: 209-3334-6111
e-mail: ironman45@softcom.net
Cast iron repair and restoration, cast iron welding, fabrication, and painting; buys cast iron toys and parts.

Character

(see also CHARACTER COLLECTIBLES; DISNEY COLLECTIBLES)

Auction Services

Martin Krim
New England Auction Gallery
P.O. Box 2273
Peabody, MA 01960-7273
ph: 978-535-3140
fax: 978-535-7522
e-mail: dlkrim@star.net
web: http://www.old-toys.com
Conduct mail-bid auctions with full color illustrated catalogs; specializes in sales of Disney, TV and cartoon items from 1920-1970: toys, wind-ups, robots, space toys.

Collectors

Martin Krim
P.O. Box 2273
Peabody, MA 01960-7273
ph: 978-535-3140
fax: 978-535-7522
e-mail: dlkrim@star.net
web: http://www.old-toys.com
Wants tin & celluloid toys from Japan, Germany, etc.; character items from TV shows, westerns, stars from the 50-60s; robot & space toys; plastic wind-up toys.

Dealers

Leila Dunbar
Dunbar's Gallery
76 Haven St.
Milford, MA 01757-3821
ph: 508-634-8697 or 508-634-8097
fax: 508-634-8698
Mail order Americana - no reproductions; buys, sells and specializes in vintage character and comic toys, banks, advertising, automobilia, and Halloween related items.

Dennis & Mary Luby
Casey's Collectible Corner
HCR 31 Box 30
No. Blenheim, NY 12131
ph: 607-588-6464
e-mail: caseyscc@aol.com
web: http://www.csmonline.com/caseys/
Buys and sells collectible toys: comic characters, TV shows and personalities; also space and monster toys, sports collectibles, etc.

Richard Trautwein
Toys N Such
437 Dawson St.
Sault Sainte Marie, MI 49783-2119
ph: 906-635-0356
e-mail: rtraut@portup.com
Collector, dealer, collector wants wind-up, battery, tin, pull, cast iron toys: Barney Google, Charlie Chaplin, Mickey Mouse, Donald Duck, Popeye, etc.

Character (Mickey Mouse)

Collectors

Debra Krim
P.O. Box 2273
Peabody, MA 01960-7273
ph: 978-535-3140
fax: 978-535-7522
e-mail: dlkrim@star.net
web: http://www.old-toys.com
Wants 1930s Mickey Mouse items: empty boxes, figurals, wind-ups, bisque figurines, games, jewelry, etc.

Comic

(see TOYS, Character)

Computer Programs For

Man./Prod./Dist.

Robert Sullenberger
Sully Enterprises
Software: Toy Collector, The
7451 Rozena Dr.
Longmont, CO 80503-9118
ph: 303-651-2074
A Windows program; generates reports based on brand name, scale size, etc.; maintains the cost and the appraisal value for each toy.

Construction Sets

Collectors

Wally Krocsko
P.O. Box 307
Atlasburg, PA 15004-0307
ph: 724-947-5671
Buys, sells, trades construction sets (Erector, Meccano, American Model Builder); must enclose a LSASE to get a reply to buy/sell/trade inquiries; please call evenings.

Arlan Coffman
1223 Wilshire Blvd., Ste. 275
Santa Monica, CA 90403
ph: 310-453-2507
e-mail: buildingtoys@earthlink.net
Wants architectural construction toys: Erector sets, building blocks, villages, Lincoln Logs & figures, etc.

Dealers

John Maleski
Space Toys
20289 canal
Grosse Ile, MI 48138
ph: 734-675-8322 or 313-2979-6089

Joel Perlin
1111 Acapulco Ct.
Oxnard, CA 93035-2601
ph: 805-985-5498
fax: 805-382-7665
e-mail: erector@vcol.net
web: http://www.vcol.net/erector/
Specializes in antique Erector, Mecanno and other construction toys; complete, sets, ephemera, and spare parts; buys, sells, reproduces.

Experts

Joel Perlin
1111 Acapulco Ct.
Oxnard, CA 93035-2601
ph: 805-985-5498
fax: 805-382-7665
e-mail: erector@vcol.net
web: http://www.vcol.net/erector/
Specializes in antique Erector, Mecanno and other construction toys; complete, sets, ephemera, and spare parts; buys, sells, reproduces.

Construction Sets (Blocks)

Clubs/Associations

George Hardy
Anchor Block Foundation
Magazine: Anchor House News
1670 Hawkwood Ct.
Charlottesville, VA 22901
ph: 804-295-4863
fax: 804-295-4898
e-mail: georgeh@ankerstein.org
web: http://www.ankerstein.org/
Anchor House Foundation is a club whose members have interests in and build with Anchor Blocks; quarterly newsletter.

Collectors

Paul Neuman
173 Chrystie St.
New York, NY 10021
ph: 212-228-2444 or 212-734-4274
fax: 212-780-9338
e-mail: sbogdonoff@aol.com
Wants to buy architectural toys, building block sets; wood, paper on wood, stone, metal, etc.

George Hardy
1670 Hawkwood Ct.
Charlottesville, VA 22901
ph: 804-295-4863
fax: 804-295-4898
e-mail: georgeh@ankerstein.org
web: http://www.ankerstein.org/
Collector of Richter's Anchor Stone Building Sets (Anker-Steinbaukasten).

Dealers

Arley Pett
Arley L. Pett Antiques
12 Beach Rd.
Gloucester, MA 09130-3214
ph: 978-283-2612
fax: 978-283-2612
e-mail: apett92117@aol.com
Buys, sells and collects Anchor stone blocks and puzzles.

Construction Sets (Erector)

Clubs/Associations

Jay Smith
A.C. Gilbert Heritage Society
Newsletter: A.C. Gilbert Heritage Society Newsletter
1440 Whalley, Ste. 252
New Haven, CT 06515
e-mail: ghseditor@aol.com
web: http://www.acghs.org/
For A.C. Gilbert toy enthusiasts, all items except American Flyer trains; Erector sets, chemistry sets, magic sets, Gilbert appliances and tools; send SASE for membership info; newsletter published quarterly; over 400 members.

Frank Hare, Ed.
American Flyer Collectors Club
Magazine: Collector, The
P.O. Box 13269
Pittsburgh, PA 15243-0269
ph: 412-221-2250
fax: 412-221-8402
For collectors of A.C. Gilbert Co. American Flyer and other toy trains (all pre-1966 manufacturers); also contains information about Gilbert Erector sets.

Southern California Meccano & Erector Club
Newsletter: Southern CA Meccano & Erector Club Newsletter
P.O. Box 7653
Porter Ranch Station
Northridge, CA 91327-7653
e-mail: pedwards@webnexus.com
web: http://www.erector.webnexus.com/
Publishes a very good quarterly newsletter; holds regional meetings.

Collectors

Jay Smith
5 Whittier Rd.
Lexington, MA 02173
ph: 781-861-7547
e-mail: LaserJay@aol.com
Editor of The A.C. Gilbert Heritage Society Newsletter.

Larry Yesner
285 Orchid Rd.
Levittown, NY 11756
ph: 516-579-7040
Wants Erector and Meccano sets; preferably the larger sets in mint or excellent condition.

James Mietlicki
146 Ridge Park Ave.
Cheektowaga, NY 14211
ph: 716-896-8047

Michael Wagner
Wagner & Sons Inc.
28 E. Willow St.
Carlisle, PA 17013
ph: 800-827-3948 or 800-821-7002
fax: 610-296-2258
e-mail: w5344@aol.com
web: http://www.wagnerandsonstoys.com/
Purchasing A.C. Gilbert Erector set parts, manuals, catalogs, dealer items, etc.; also purchasing construction sets by Meccano, Marklin, Ives, Bing and Metalcraft.

Dealers

Paul & Nancy Piontkowski
Pandy's Collectibles
16 Palmer St.
Medford, MA 02155
ph: 781-395-5569
e-mail: Pandyscol@aol.com
web: http://www.pandys.com
Buy, sell, restore Erector sets (1913-1963); also buys and sells parts, labels and manual.

Jay Robinson
Chicago Kid
P.O. Box 529
Deerfield, IL 60015-0529
ph: 847-945-8691
Buys construction sets; also wants electric trains of all types, toys, and robots.

Experts

Al Sternagle
RD 2 Box 400
Hollidaysburg, PA 16648-9230
ph: 814-695-7012
Sent $11.50 for "Erector Parts Illustrated," $7.50 for "Erector Advertising"; author of several articles about Erector sets; send LSASE for complete list of publications available.

Bill Bean
439 Claxton Glen Ct.
Kettering, OH 45429
ph: 937-435-6196 or 937-439-2600
e-mail: ErectrBean@aol.com
Author of "Greenberg Guide to Erector"; wants to buy Erector sets by A.C. Gilbert, Ives, and Bing; especially large sets in wood boxes and chests; also store displays and advertising pieces.

Museums/Libraries

Stephen Ebinger
Eli Whitney Museum
915 Whitney Ave.
Hamden, CT 06517-4036
ph: 203-777-1833
fax: 203-777-1229
web: http://www.eliwhitney.org/
Dedicated to helping children learn by doing; uses Gilbert's construction and chemistry ideas in their educational program.

Repro. Sources

Tiger Enterprises
379 Summer St.
Plantsville, CT 06479
Makes reproduction A.C. Gilbert Erector parts and sets.

Suppliers

Paul & Nancy Piontkowski
Pandy's Collectibles
16 Palmer St.
Medford, MA 02155
ph: 781-395-5569
e-mail: Pandyscol@aol.com
web: http://www.pandys.com
Buy, sell, restore Erector sets (1913-1963); also buys and sells parts, labels and manual.

Michael Wagner
Wagner & Sons Inc.
28 E. Willow St.
Carlisle, PA 17013
ph: 800-827-3948 or 800-821-7002
fax: 610-296-2258
e-mail: w5344@aol.com
web: http://www.wagnerandsonstoys.com/
The oldest and largest stock source of original Erector parts, manuals, catalogs and sets; send SASE for catalog.

Crayola Crayons

Museums/Libraries

Crayola Hall of Fame, Binney & Smith, Inc.
Two Rivers Landing
30 Centre Square
Easton, PA 18042-7744
ph: 423-515-8000 or 800-272-9652
e-mail: crayola@crayola.com
web: http://www.crayola.com/history/history.html

Diecast

(see also AUTO RACING MEMORABILIA; BANKS [MODERN]; MODELS; MODELS, Cars; MODELS, Trucks & Equipment [Winross]; TOYS, Cars; TOYS, Ertl Replicas)

Appraisers

Fred J. Hill, Jr., ISA CAPP
Koty Professional Auctioneers, LLC
P.O. Box 625
Freehold, NJ 07728-0625
ph: 732-751-0504
fax: 732-751-9190
e-mail: Bidtaker@compuserve.com
Specializes in diecast models and NASCAR collectibles.

Auction Services

Diecast Exchange, The
27 Oziers, Elsenham
Bishops Stortford, Hertfordshire CM22 6LD
U.K.
e-mail: webmaster@diecastexchange.com
web: http://www.diecastexchange.com/
An online auction service to sell your surplus models directly to other collectors.

Clubs/Associations

Diecast Exchange Club
Newsletter: Diecast Exchange Club Newsletter
P.O. Box 1066
Miami, FL 33780-1066

Peter H. Foss
Toy Car Collectors Club
Newsletter: Toy Car Magazine
33290 W. 14 Mile Rd. #454
West Bloomfield, MI 48322-3549
ph: 248-682-0272
fax: 248-682-5782
A club for collectors of toy cars such as Dinky, Corgi, Matchbox, Hot Wheels, Solido, Norev, Siku, Schuco, Gama, Rio, Auburn, Tootsietoy, Maisto, Ertl, banks, NASCAR, Tomica, Diapet, etc.

Mr. Dana Johnson
Diecast Toy Collectors Association
Newsletter: Diecast Toy Collector
P.O. Box 1824
Bend, OR 97701-1824
ph: 541-382-8410
e-mail: toynutz@teleport.com
web: http://www.toynutz.com/
Provides discounts on collector price guides, information on new products, model variations and values, resources for buying and selling, toy shows around the country; newsletter published monthly.

Martin Uden
Maidenhead Static Model Club
Newsletter: Wheel Bearings
The Old Marquis, London Road
Wollaston, Northants NN9 7QP
U.K.
ph: 01256-819141
Diecast collectors club; meets 3rd Monday of month; organizes Windsor International swap meet in January, June, September; visitors to UK welcome to attend club meetings.

British Model Collectors Association
P.O. Box 11
Norwich, NR7 0SP
U.K.
ph: 01693 505210 or 01693 701929
fax: 01603 507355
e-mail: bmca@swapmeet.freeserve.co.uk
web: http://www.swapmeet.freeserve.co.uk/
Focuses on transpiration models:

cars, planes, boats; Meccano Dinky Toys, Corgi.

Collectors

Paul M. Provencher
Spring Garden House
20115 Woodfield Road
Gaithersburg, MD 20882-1229
ph: 301-948-2858
e-mail: ppro@compuserve.com
web: http://ourworld.compuserve.com/homepages/ppro/index.html
Specializes in die cast vehicles of all types; can provide information about current and past die cast issues; writes Die Cast Insider column for Toy Trader magazine; moderates CompuServe's Die Cast & Toys section.

Frank Kocinski III
912 Linwood
Delta, OH 43515
ph: 419-822-9028
e-mail: windxi60@powersupply.net
web: http://www.powersupply.net/users/windxi60/hotwheel.html
Collector and trader of Hot Wheels, Matchbox, Johnny Lightning, and Racing Champions diecast cars.

Dealers

Toys for Collectors
P.O. Box 1406
North Attleboro, MA 02763
ph: 508-695-0588 or 508-695-6966
fax: 508-699-8649
e-mail: gklarwasse@aol.com
If you collect models of cars, trucks, fire trucks, construction equipment, cranes, buses, race cars, NASCARS, etc. this is the source for better quality 1/43 scale models as well as 1/50, 1/18 and 1/14 scale models.

Donald Amnott
Small Wheels of America
34 Huckleberry Lane
Southington, CT 06489
ph: 800-258-7776
fax: 860-621-8885
Diecast cars, trucks, planes and blimps by Ertl, First Gear, Spec-Cast, PEM; oil company tankers by Hess, Texaco, Servco and many others.

Arlene Scherff
Apple Patch Toys
7 Hyatt Rd.
Branchville, NJ 07826-4139
ph: 973-702-0008
fax: 973-702-1699
e-mail: molly@interpow.net
Specializes in diecast collectible airplanes by Arch, Inc., Scale Models, Ertl, Corgi, CDC (Armour Collection).

Kid Pontiac
P.O. Box 70
Blauvelt, NY 10913

Neil H. Waldmann
Neil's Wheels, Inc.
P.O. Box 354
Old Bethpage, NY 11804-0354
ph: 516-293-9659
fax: 516-420-0483
e-mail: neilswheels@i-2000.com
Authorized Matchbox collectibles center; send SA2SE for list of 2000 models and brochure on Magic Box Display System.

Francis "Lash" Lerew
325 Scenic Drive
Mechanicsburg, PA 17055

Diecast Toy Exchange
P.O. Box 268
York, PA 17405
ph: 717-846-8097

Steve Mullican
325 Elm Ave.
North Wales, PA 19454
ph: 215-699-2393
Matchbox, Dinky, Corgi, early Lesney products.

Kiddie Kar Kollectibles
1161 Perry St.
Reading, PA 19604
ph: 610-375-4780

Dan Wells
Dan Wells Antique Toys
P.O. Box 7
Goshen, KY 40026
ph: 502-292-1748
fax: 502-292-1749
e-mail: jagdan@aol.com
Wants to buy Hot Wheels, Dinky, Matchbox, Johnny Lightning, Corgi, and Lesney cars; excellent or better condition only.

Toy Collector Club of America
P.O. Box 368
Dyersville, IA 52040-0368
ph: 800-452-3303 or 319-875-9223
fax: 319-875-8056
For collectors of contemporary diecast banks and vehicles; gives collectors the opportunity to purchase diecast metal banks; newsletter lists what is available for purchase and discounts on products.

Tom Lavely
Neat Olde Stuff
16935 N. Main St.
P.O. Box 9
Galesville, WI 54630-0009
ph: 608-582-2082
fax: 608-582-2180
e-mail: tglavely@aol.com
Collector of diecast Tootsietoy ships, trains and airplanes (no cars or trucks.)

William Adorjan
P.O. Box 2494
Glenview, IL 60025
ph: 847-657-8502
e-mail: iaretoys@aol.com
web: http://members.aol.com/iaretoys
Buys, sells, collects and repairs antique die-cast and tin vehicles.

Dean Knight
Kathy's Kards
7700 E. 42nd Place
Tulsa, OK 74145
ph: 800-435-3570 or 918-664-3232
fax: 918-664-7018
e-mail: kathy@nascarshop.com
web: http://www.nascarshop.com
One of the largest racing collectibles companies in the U.S.; specializes in diecast of all makes; also carries cards and many racing related souvenirs.

Bob Lowry
Foss Company, The
1224 Washington Ave.
Golden, CO 80401
ph: 303-279-3373
fax: 303-278-9556
e-mail: BLowry@fossco.com
web: http://www.fossco.com/
Carries a large selection of diecast toys.

Ernie Wilson
10262 Foothill Blvd.
Lake View Terrace, CA 91342
ph: 818-899-2634 or 888-845-9744
fax: 818-899-6764
e-mail: info@burntrubber.com
web: http://www.burntrubber.com
NASCAR and NHRA diecast cars by Action and Revell.

Hu Arthur
Arthur's Collectible Toys
12422 107th Pl. NE
Kirkland, WA 98034
e-mail: arthurhu@halcyon.com
web: http://www.leconsulting.com/arthurhu/collect.htm
Collector, dealer and expert in diecast and other model and toy cars: Hot Wheels, Matchbox, Sizzlers, Takara, Tomica, Siku, MicroMachines.

Experts

Richard L. Heuser
Heuser Publishing Div. of Heuser Enterprises
508 Clapson Rd.
P.O. Box 300
West Winfield, NY 13491-0300
ph: 315-822-4804
fax: 315-822-4804
e-mail: toybanks@concentric.net
web: http://www.concentric.net/~Toybanks/
Buys, collects, appraises and specializes in modern collectible toy banks and diecast toys.

Douglas R. Kelly
17920 Ashton Club Way
Ashton, MD 20861
ph: 301-570-2206
Author of "The Die Cast Price Guide" (Antique Trader Books, 1997); Matchbox, Hot Wheels, Corgi, Tootsietoys, Winross, Schuco, Majorette, Burago, Danbury Mint, etc. from 1946 to present.

Paul M. Provencher
Spring Garden House
20115 Woodfield Road
Gaithersburg, MD 20882-1229
ph: 301-948-2858
e-mail: ppro@compuserve.com
web: http://ourworld.compuserve.com/homepages/ppro/index.html
Specializes in die cast vehicles of all types; can provide information about current and past die cast issues; writes Die Cast Insider column for Toy Trader magazine; moderates CompuServe's Die Cast & Toys section.

Mr. Dana Johnson
Dana Johnson Enterprises
P.O. Box 1824
Bend, OR 97701-1824
ph: 541-382-8410
e-mail: toynutz@teleport.com
web: http://www.toynutz.com/
Matchbox collector since 1961; author of "Matchbox Bluebook - A Collector's Guide to Current Prices"; "Hot Wheels Blue Book"; "Collecting Majorette Toys"; "Matchbox Toys, 1947 to 1998," available from author.

Internet Resources

John Miller
Mr. Bill's Diecast & Collectibles Newsletter
e-mail: John@collectible-info.com
web: http://www.collectible-info.com
Comprehensive web site of diecast related news, articles, prices, reader's questions, convention news, classified ads, editorials, upcoming shows and more: Ertl, Matchbox, Winross, Franklin and Danbury Mints, Hess, Racing Champions, etc.

Jay Olins
Diecast Car Collectors Homebase
Diecast Club, Dept. OWSM
P.O. Box 2480
Huntington Beach, CA 92647-2480
ph: 213-500-4355
e-mail: jay@via.net
web: http://www.diecast.org/
Dedicated to the collection of precision diecast cars, trucks, and motorcycles; website provides news, detailed illustrated reviews, comprehensive car lists, a Bulletin Board, Collector's poll, even its own online auction.

Man./Prod./Dist.

Lisa Greco, Cust. Ser.
Playing Mantis
3600 McGill St., Ste. 300
South Bend, IN 46619-3688
ph: 219-232-0300 or 800-MANTIS-8
fax: 219-232-0500
e-mail: lgreco@playingmantis.com
web: http://www.playingmantis.com
Johnny Lighting, Sizzlers, Polar Lights model kits.

Periodicals

Richard L. Heuser
Heuser Publishing Div. of Heuser Enterprises
Price Guide: Heuser's Price Guide to Official Collectible Banks
508 Clapson Rd.
P.O. Box 300
West Winfield, NY 13491-0300
ph: 315-822-4804
fax: 315-822-4804
e-mail: toybanks@concentric.net
web: http://www.concentric.net/~Toybanks/
Quarterly price guide features Ertl, First Gear, Liberty Classics, Spec Cast, Action Racing Collectibles, Gearbox, Crown Premium/Vees Collectibles, DG Productions and others; listed by name, no., quantity, color, year made and value.

Richard L. Heuser
Heuser Publishing Div. of Heuser Enterprises
Newsletter: Heuser's Quarterly Collectible Diecast Newsletter
508 Clapson Rd.
P.O. Box 300
West Winfield, NY 13491-0300
ph: 315-822-4804
fax: 315-822-4804
e-mail: toybanks@concentric.net
web: http://www.concentric.net/~Toybanks/
Focuses on modern diecast collectible banks and custom imprinted replicas; new issues; articles of interest to collectors; listing of dealers and manufacturers; listing of upcoming toy shows.

Deb Sipe
Spec Cast
Newsletter: Spec Tacular News
P.O. Box 368
Dyersville, IA 52040-0368
ph: 319-875-8706
fax: 319-875-8056
e-mail: info@speccast.com
web: http://www.speccast.com/
A quarterly focusing on farm toys and collectibles.

Jeff Atkinson
Newsletter: Traders Horn
1903 Schoettler Valley Rd.
Chesterfield, MO 63017-5203
ph: 314-532-3871
e-mail: thorn@gloryroad.net
The oldest, largest bi-monthly periodical dedicated to the sales, trading of diecast toy vehicles, promotional models, model kits; obsolete, rare, current automotive & other transportation miniatures and related memorabilia; all scales.

Cam Sinden
Newspaper: Collectors Gazette
Fleck Way
Thornaby
Stockton-on-Tees, Cleveland TS17 9JZ
U.K.
ph: +44 (0) 1642 762335
fax: +44 (0) 1642 762401
e-mail: info@icn.co.uk
web: http://www.icn.co.uk/cg.html
Published 10 times per year for toy and model collectors worldwide; covers tinplate toys, obsolete and modern diecast cars (Corgi, Dinky, Matchbox, EFE, Lledo, Days Gone, etc.) and models, trains, airplanes, ships, dolls, etc.

Mike Forbes, Ed.
Magazine: Diecast Collector
The Maltings, West Street
Bourne, Lincs. PE10 9PH
U.K.
ph: +44 (0) 1778 394748
e-mail: mike.f@warners.co.uk
web: http://www.diecast-collector.com/
Monthly English magazine brings a colorful and nostalgic approach to the world of diecast transportation models.

Repro. Sources

Deb Sipe
Spec Cast
P.O. Box 368
Dyersville, IA 52040-0368
ph: 319-875-8706
fax: 319-875-8056
e-mail: info@speccast.com
web: http://www.speccast.com/
Manufacturer or discast replica belt buckles, banks, tractors, trucks, vehicle and airplane banks and non-banks, limited editions, and specialty items.

Diecast (Brooklin)

Clubs/Associations

Roger Mateo
San Francisco Bay Brooklin Club
Newsletter: SFBBC Newsletter
P.O. Box 61018
Palo Alto, CA 94306-6018
ph: 650-591-9580
fax: 650-591-9580
e-mail: sfbbc@ix.netcom.com
Newsletter published every other month; current information on Brooklin models, upcoming specials; has international club membership.

Diecast (Corgi)

Clubs/Associations

Corgi Collector Club
14 Industrial Rd.
Pequannock, NJ 07440
ph: 973-694-5006
e-mail: breyerhrs@aol.com

Corgi Collectors Club of the Corgi Heritage Center
53 York St.
Heywood
Hochdale, Lancs OL10 4NR
U.K.
ph: 01706 365812

Man./Prod./Dist.

Corgi Classics
Harcourt Way
Meridian Business Park
Leicester, LE3 2RL
U.K.
ph: 0116 282 6622
fax: 0116 282 6633
web: http://www.corgi.co.uk/

Diecast (Hot Wheels)

Clubs/Associations

David Conley
Blues City Hot Wheels Club
4807 Walden Glen
Memphis, TN 38128
ph: 901-386-6077
fax: 901-386-6077
e-mail: CanyonRdr@aol.com
A club for adults who are interested in a fair exchange of Hot Wheels product and knowledge.

Collectors

Les Tin
Les' Hot Wheels Homepage
e-mail: detarr@mediaone.net
web: http://people.we.mediaone.net/detarr/
Website is geared for Hot Wheels collectors; contains information such as collector number lists, limited edition and promotional car list, condition calculator, and much more.

Jeff Hubbard
2900 91st St.
Sturtevant, WI 53177-2013
ph: 414-886-0477
Buys and sells older Hot Wheel cars and pre-1960 oil company highway maps.

Dealers

Rich Blaut
9533 W. 7 Mile Rd.
Northville, MI 48167-9106
ph: 248-347-3227
Buys, sells, trades Hotwheels by Mattel; cars, Sizzlers, Gran Toros.

Internet Resources

Randy
Hot Wheelin's Web Page
e-mail: detarr@mediaone.net
web: http://people.we.mediaone.net/detarr/
Website is geared for Hot Wheels collectors; lots of Hot Wheel links.

Periodicals

Mike Strauss
Newsletter: Hot Wheels Newsletter
26 Madera Ave.
San Carlos, CA 94070-2937
ph: 650-591-6482
fax: 650-591-7935
e-mail: hwnewsltr@aol.com
web: http://members.aol.com/HWNEWSLTR/index.html
Published bi-monthly; each issue contains articles covering history, new releases, club news, classified ads, promotions, Limited Editions, and anything else that has to do with Hot Wheels and the Hot Wheels collector community.

Diecast (Johnny Lightning)

Clubs/Associations

Lisa Greco
Johnny Lightning Club
Newsletter: NewsFlash
P.O. Box 3688
South Bend, IN 46619
ph: 800-626-8478 or 219-232-0300
fax: 219-233-3788
e-mail: algreco@playingmantis.com
web: http://www.johnnylightning.com/
For collectors of Johnny Lightning cars.

Periodicals

Tom Lowe
Playing Mantis
Newsletter: Johnny Lightning Newsflash
P.O. Box 3688
South Bend, IN 46619-3688
ph: 219-232-0300 or 800-626-8478
fax: 219-232-0500
e-mail: PlayingM@aol.com
web: http://www.johnnylightning.com/
For collectors of Johnny Lightning diecast collectible cars.

Diecast (Matchbox)

Clubs/Associations

Bob Fellows
American-International Matchbox Collectors & Exchange Club
Newsletter: A.I.M. Newsletter
532 Chestnut St.
Lynn, MA 01904-2717
ph: 617-595-4135
fax: 617-595-4007
Monthly newsletter.

Charles Mack
Matchbox U.S.A.
Newsletter: Matchbox U.S.A. Newsletter
62 Saw Mill Rd.
Durham, CT 06422-2602
ph: 860-349-1655
fax: 860-349-3256
e-mail: mtchboxusa@aol.com
Conducts annual conventions and shows; newsletter published monthly.

Everett Marshall
Matchbox Collectors Club
Newsletter: Matchbox Collectors Club Newsletter
Pearl Street
P.O. Box 977
Newfield, NJ 08344-0977
ph: 609-697-2800
fax: 609-697-0762
e-mail: mbroad@aol.com
Newsletter published quarterly.

Mike Appnel
Pennsylvania Matchbox Club
1161 Perry St.
Reading, PA 19604-2046

Bon Newmann, Sec.
Illinois Matchbox Collectors Club
P.O. Box 1582
Oak Lawn, IL 60455
ph: 815-469-4170
e-mail: jstmtchbx@aol.com
web: http://members.aol.com/jstmtchbx/imc.html

Bay Area Matchbox Collectors Association
P.O. Box 1534
San Jose, CA 95109
e-mail: staff@bamca.org
web: http://www.bamca.org/
Informal group of toy vehicle enthusiasts who hold meets to buy, sell, swap miniatures made by Matchbox, Hot Wheels, Dinky, Corgi, Ertl, Majorette, Tomica, and others as well as related items such as catalogs and boxes.

Rita Schneider, Mem.
Matchbox International Collectors Association, The
Newsletter: MICA Newsletter
P.O. Box 28072
Waterloo, Ontario N2L 6J8
Canada
ph: 519-885-0529
fax: 519-885-1902
Formed to stimulate interest among collectors of Matchbox Diecast Models and Matchbox related items as manufactured originally by Lesney Products Ltd. and later by Matchbox Toys.

Collectors

Charles Mack
62 Saw Mill Rd.
Durham, CT 06422-2602
ph: 860-349-1655
fax: 860-349-3256
e-mail: mtchboxusa@aol.com

Experts

Charles Mack
62 Saw Mill Rd.
Durham, CT 06422-2602
ph: 860-349-1655
fax: 860-349-3256
e-mail: mtchboxusa@aol.com
Author of "Lesney's Matchbox Toys Regular Wheels Yrs. 1947-1969" and "Lesney's Matchbox Toys - The Superfast Years 1969-1982."

Marshall Everett
Pearl Street
P.O. Box 977
Newfield, NJ 08344-0977
ph: 609-697-2800
fax: 609-697-0762
e-mail: mbroad@aol.com

Man./Prod./Dist.

Matchbox Inc.
8585 SW Hall Blvd.
Beaveton, WA 97008-6408
ph: 800-367-8926
web: http://www.matchboxtoys.com

Museums/Libraries

Charles Mack
Matchbox & Lesney Toy Museum
62 Saw Mill Rd.
Durham, CT 06422-2602
ph: 860-349-1655
fax: 860-349-3256
e-mail: mtchboxusa@aol.com

Marshall Everett
Matchbox Road Museum
Pearl Street
P.O. Box 977
Newfield, NJ 08344-0977
ph: 609-697-2800
fax: 609-697-0762
e-mail: mbroad@aol.com

Ertl Replicas

(see also TOYS, Farm)

Clubs/Associations

Ertl Collectors Club
Newsletter: Replica, The
P.O. Box 500
Dyersville, IA 52040-0500
ph: 319-875-2000 or 800-553-4886
e-mail: ertl@harwoodmarketing.com
web: http://www.ertltoys.com
Provides new product and historical information to collectors of Ertl replica toys.

Dealers

Clever Impressions
115 N Wernick St.
Covington, OH 45318-1741
ph: 800-762-5663
Buys and sells Ertl farm toys, die cast collectibles, NASCAR items, Ertl banks.

Man./Prod./Dist.

Ertl Co. Inc.
P.O. Box 500
Dyersville, IA 52040-0500
ph: 319-875-2000 or 800-553-4886
e-mail: ertl@harwoodmarketing.com
web: http://www.ertltoys.com
Manufacturer of Ertl diecast toys.

Periodicals

Richard L. Heuser
Heuser Publishing Div. of Heuser Enterprises
Newsletter: Heuser's Quarterly Collectible Diecast Newsletter
508 Clapson Rd.
P.O. Box 300
West Winfield, NY 13491-0300
ph: 315-822-4804
fax: 315-822-4804
e-mail: toybanks@concentric.net
web: http://www.concentric.net/~Toybanks/
Focuses on modern diecast collectible banks and custom imprinted replicas; new issues; articles of interest to collectors; listing of dealers and manufacturers; listing of upcoming toy shows.

Richard L. Heuser
Heuser Publishing Div. of Heuser Enterprises
Price Guide: Heuser's Price Guide to Official Collectible Banks
508 Clapson Rd.
P.O. Box 300
West Winfield, NY 13491-0300
ph: 315-822-4804
fax: 315-822-4804
e-mail: toybanks@concentric.net
web: http://www.concentric.net/~Toybanks/
Quarterly price guide features Ertl, First Gear, Liberty Classics, Spec Cast, Action Racing Collectibles, Gearbox, Crown Premium/Vees Collectibles, DG Productions and others; listed by name, no., quantity, color, year made and value.

Etch-A-Sketch

Clubs/Associations

Melissa Stahlman
Etch-A-Sketch Club, c/o Ohio Art Co.
1 Toy St.
P.O. Box 111
Bryan, OH 43506
ph: 800-641-6226
e-mail: segul@bright.net
web: http://www.world-of-toys.com

Farm

(see also BOOKS, Reference [Farm Toys]; FARM COLLECTIBLES; FARM MACHINERY; TOYS, Diecast; TOYS, Ertl Replicas; TOYS, Playsets; TRACTORS)

Auction Services

Larry Martin
P.O. Box 333
Clinton, IL 61727
ph: 217-935-8211 or 217-935-3873
Monthly toy auctions of farm toys, collector trucks, industrial equipment, sport cars, wind-up toys, pedal tractors and cars, farm advertising, literature and signs.

Clubs/Associations

David Semmel
Antique Engine, Tractor & Toy Club, Inc.
Newsletter: AETTC Newsletter
5731 Paradise Rd.
Slatington, PA 18080-4028
ph: 610-767-4768
Organized in 1986 with over 500 members; dedicated to preservation and enjoyment of old time farm engines, tractors and related toys; newsletter three times per year.

Michiana Farm Toy Collectors Club
1701 Berkey Ave.
Goshen, IN 46526

Collectors

Jim Proctor
1395 South Concord Rd.
West Chester, PA 19382
ph: 610-399-0802

Earl Terpstra
Terpbroson
RR 4, Box 151
Washington, IN 47501-9428
ph: 812-644-7140
Wants farm and construction toys and related memorabilia.

Dealers

George Mayer
Garden State Farm Toy Store
416 Route 40
Elmer, NJ 08318-2536
ph: 609-358-1144
fax: 609-358-1155
A complete hobby and collectors outlet: Ertl, Spec-Cast, Scale Models, 1st Gear, banks, farm tractors, trucks, planes, D.C. cars, race cars, etc.

Bossen Implement
300 Washburn Ave., Hwy 187 S
Lamont, IA 50650-9535
ph: 319-924-2880
Buys, sells, and appraises farm implements: John Deere, Case, New Holland, McCormick, Cat, AGCO, Ford, etc.

Warrren D. Jensen
Jensen Manuals
106 S. Broadway
P.O. Box 1203
Albert Lea, MN 56007
ph: 507-377-9363
fax: 507-377-9727
e-mail: jensales@wolf.co.net
web: http://www.deskmedia.com/jensales/

Museums/Libraries

National Farm Toy Museum
1110 16th Ave. SE
Dyersville, IA 52040
ph: 319-875-2727
Large collection of cast iron toys, farm toys manufactured worldwide, first Ertl toy ever made, complete Tru-Scale collection, etc.

Periodicals

Rick Larsen
Magazine: Toy Tractor Times, The
P.O. Box 156
Osage, IA 50461
ph: 515-732-3530
fax: 515-732-5135
Features farm toys with an emphasis on toy tractors; articles, ads, shows, new releases, etc.

Deb Sipe
Spec Cast
Newsletter: Spec Tacular News
P.O. Box 368
Dyersville, IA 52040-0368
ph: 319-875-8706
fax: 319-875-8056
e-mail: info@speccast.com
web: http://www.speccast.com/
A quarterly focusing on farm toys and collectibles.

Claire Scheibe
Magazine: Toy Farmer
7496 106th Ave. SE
Lamoure, ND 58458-9404
ph: 701-883-5206 or 800-533-8293
fax: 701-883-5208
e-mail: zekesez@aol.com
web: http://www.toyfarmer.com/
Toy Farmer sponsors the annual National Farm Toy Shoy in Dyersville, IA.

Ronald Mucher
Magazine: Small Farm Today
3903 W. Ridge Trail Rd.
Clark, MO 65243-9525
ph: 573-687-3333 or 800-633-2535
fax: 573-687-3148
web: http://www.datasys.net/edpak/small.html
A bi-monthly magazine for the small farmer; sometimes contains articles about collectible farm toys.

Betty Holland
Magazine: Tractor Classics CTM
P.O. Box 489
Rocanville, Saskatchewan S0A 3L0
Canada
ph: 306-645-4566
fax: 306-645-4566
Canada's bi-monthly farm toy magazine: toy show reviews, information on new and old farm toys, toy shows, collector of the month stories, price guides, cars, comics, dolls, display ads, classifieds.

Repair Services

Donald Walter
W2490 Country Highway A
Curtiss, WI 54422
ph: 715-654-5440
Repairs tin trucks, pedal cars and tractors; removes old paint, repaints, adds needed parts, etc.

Suppliers

Dakotah Toys
RR 1 Box 157
Madison, SD 57042-9614
ph: 605-256-6676
fax: 605-256-9093
web: http://www.dakotahtoys.com/
Catalog contains toy parts, decals, paints, kits, 1/64 items, books, scratch building materials, tools and diorama materials.

Fisher-Price

Clubs/Associations

Jeanne Kennedy
Fisher-Price Collectors Club
Newsletter: Gabby-Goose, The
1442 N. Ogden
Mesa, AZ 85205
ph: 602-396-2534
e-mail: fpclub@aol.com
Members study, research, discusses and write about Fisher-Price toys; preserve and promote the collection of Fisher-Price toys and related items; annual convention in conjunction with ToyFest in August in East Aurora, NY.

Collectors

John J. Murray
P.O. Box 29
Eden, NY 14057-0029
The foremost collector of older Fisher-Price toys; co-author with Bruce R. Fox of "Fisher-Price 1931-63"; send SASE for information on book.

Lee Kauffman
324 East Lynnwood St.
Allentown, PA 18103
ph: 610-797-0179
Wants to buy 1930-1970 Fisher-Price wooden pull toys; please state condition and price.

John Krupienski
5200 Hilltop Dr.
P.O. Box AA6
Brookhaven, PA 19015-1200
ph: 610-874-3003

Jeanne Kennedy
1442 N. Ogden
Mesa, AZ 85205
ph: 602-396-2534
e-mail: fpclub@aol.com

Dealers

Ted M.
Ted's Toys
ph: 716-675-5555
e-mail: tedstoys@buffalo.crosswinds.net
web: http://www2.crosswinds.net/buffalo/~tedstoys/
A professional dealer, expert and collector of Fisher-Price toys.

Terri Pointon
Two Kids And a Grownup
RR 6, Box 6523
Moscow, PA 18444
e-mail: tmp95@mindspring.com
web: http://tmp95.home.mindspring.com/
Buys and sells pre-1990 Fisher-Price Little People sets, pull toys, loose pieces, etc.; online web site includes price guide for toys bought and sold on an online auction site.

Internet Resources

Lanajean Vecchione, Ed.
Magical World of Fisher-Price
P.O. Box 138
San Mateo, CA 94401
ph: 650-344-9555
e-mail: elusive@best.com
web: http://www.best.com/~elusive/fisher_price/welcome.html

Man./Prod./Dist.

Fisher-Price, Inc.
636 Gerard Ave.
East Aurora, NY 14052
ph: 716-687-3000 or 800-432-5437
fax: 716-687-3667
e-mail: consumer@fisher-price.com
Manufacturer of Fisher-Price toys; may still have parts for older toys, call 800-432-5437 to find out.

German & Japanese

Collectors

Martin Krim
P.O. Box 2273
Peabody, MA 01960-7273
ph: 978-535-3140
fax: 978-535-7522
e-mail: dlkrim@star.net
web: http://www.old-toys.com
Wants German and Japanese toys c. 1900; also comic character toys, wind-ups, battery, etc.; celluloid, tin etc.

Guitars

Experts

Steve Evans
Jacksonville Guitar Center
1105 Burman Dr.
Jacksonville, AR 72076-4386
ph: 501-982-4933
e-mail: jvilguitar@aol.com
web: http://members.aol.com/jvilguitar
Buys and collects toy guitars with pictures printed on the guitar; also wants crank models with built-in music boxes such as: Beany & Cecil, Popeye, Casper, and others.

Museums/Libraries

Steve Evans
Jacksonville Guitar Center
1105 Burman Dr.
Jacksonville, AR 72076-4386
ph: 501-982-4933
e-mail: jvilguitar@aol.com
web: http://members.aol.com/jvilguitar
Large collection of vintage guitars on permanent display; includes over 100 cowboy guitars, c. 1930s-1950s, made with painted cowboy scenes showing Gene Autry, Roy Rogers, Buck Jones and others.

Horse-Drawn

Experts

Leon M. Weiss
Gemini Antiques Ltd.
P.O. Box 1752
2418 Montauk Highway
Water Mill, NY 11976
ph: 516-537-4565 or 212-316-6380
fax: 516-726-9366
e-mail: julgert@geminiantiques.com
web: http://www.geminiantiques.com/
Buys and sells mechanical still banks, cast iron toys, door stops, folk art and more.

Ideal Toy Co.

Clubs/Associations

Judith Izen
Ideal Toy Co. Collector's Club
Newsletter: Ideal Toy Co. Collectors Club Newsletter
P.O. Box 623
Lexington, MA 02173
e-mail: jizenres@aol.com
web: http://members.aol.com/jizenres/homepage/index.html
Send SASE for more information.

Jack-in-the-Box

Collectors

Douglas Zimmerman
4413 Longford Dr.
Sarasota, FL 34232
ph: 941-378-3266

Jacks

Collectors

Judith Schulz
533 Milwaukee Ave.
Burlington, WI 53105-1232
ph: 262-763-3946
Collects old and unusual jacks and pick-up sticks; coordinates the annual international jacks & pick-up sticks event and tournament each February.

Japanese

Internet Resources

Cool Japanese Toys
e-mail: cjtadmin@cooljapanesetoys.com
web: http://www.cooljapanesetoys.com/monthly/
News, editorial, articles, marketplace, buy and sell.

Kenner

Clubs/Associations

Ed Sterling
Girder & Panel Collectors Club
Newsletter: Girder & Panel Collectors Club Newsletter
P.O. Box 494
Bolton, MA 01740-0494
ph: 978-779-6058 or 978-779-6058
e-mail: ed@ma.ultranet.com
web: http://www.ultranet.com/~ed/
Club exists to document the history and production of Kenner Toys Girder and Panel toy sets; quarterly newsletter; buys and sell ads; ideal place to purchase and restore one of those 1960s toy construction sets.

Kinder Surprise

Collectors

Ann Brogley
P.O. Box 16033
Philadelphia, PA 19114-0033
ph: 215-824-4698 or 215-824-2350
fax: 215-824-4698
e-mail: mostprod@erols.com
web: http://www.geocities.com/Heartland/Hills/2081/
Collects Kinder Surprise figurines and toys, Kinder advertising and Kinder boxes; Kinder surprise toys are found in Ferrero chocolate eggs in many countries, but not in US.

Experts

Joachim Antona
Fuenfkirchener Str. 61
Tettnang, Baden-Wuerttemberg 88069
Germany
ph: +49-171-5294004
e-mail: antona@w-4.de
web: http://www.w-4.de/~antona/
Buys, sells, swaps Ferrero Kinder Surprise Egg toys; web site has Kinder surprise toy online auction.

Kobe

Collectors

Bob Vargas
P.O. Box 1284
Los Altos, CA 94023
ph: 650-949-3959
Wants to buy Japanese Kobe toys; send good photo and price.

Mattel

Collectors

Joedi Johnson
P.O. Box 565
Billings, MT 59101-0565
ph: 406-248-4875
fax: 407-248-4875
e-mail: starbase@mcn.net
Buying Mattel Thingmakers, Maker Paks, Play Paks, store displays, Plastigoop, carded molds; Fright Factory, Creep Crawlers, etc.; newsletter available; also wants Mattel Upsy Downsy dolls, accessories and books.

Monsters

Collectors

Neal Austinson
P.O. Box 1691
Windsor, CA 95492-1691
ph: 707-837-9685
Wants movie monster toys: Frankenstein, Wolfman, Creature From The Black Lagoon, etc.

Dealers

John Skerchock
P.O. Box 733
Bellefonte, PA 16823-0733
ph: 814-353-0565
Specializes in monster and science fiction collectibles from the 1960s to present; writes articles for "Scary Monsters" magazine and related publications.

Mr. Potato Head

Internet Resources

Ellen Holbrook
Mr. Potato Head Collectors' Page
c/o Fun First
P.O. Box 40447
Berkeley, CA 94704
ph: 510-841-1240
fax: 510-841-1210
e-mail: info@socko.com
web: http://www.fun1st.com/collectors.html
Mr. Potato Head history, photos, links; 1952 to present.

Ohio Art Co.

Clubs/Associations

Sharon Lazane
Ohio Art Collectors Club
Newsletter: Ohio Art Beat
18203 Kristi Rd., West
Liberty, MO 64068
ph: 816-781-5452
e-mail: slazane@aol.com
Club is for those interested in collecting toys made by the Ohio Art Co.; especially sand toys including pails, sieves or sifters, sprinkling cans, water pumps, sand molds, sand hoists or lifts, and sand mills.

Optical

(see also CAMERAS & CAMERA EQUIPMENT; KALEIDOSCOPES; MAGIC LANTERNS & SLIDES; OPTICAL ITEMS; STANHOPES; STEREO VIEWERS & STEREOVIEWS)

Auction Services

Michael Pritchard
Christie's South Kensington, Ltd.
85 Old Brompton Rd.
London, SW7 3LD
U.K.
ph: 0171 581 7611 or 0171 321 3279
fax: 0171 321 3321
e-mail: mpritchard@christies.com
web: http://www.cskart.com/
Specializes in the sale of optical toys such as persistence of vision devices, stereoscopes, magic lanterns/slides, etc.

Collectors

Uwe H. Breker
6731 Ashley Ct.
Sarasota, FL 34241-9696
ph: 941-925-0385
fax: 941-925-0487
e-mail: auction@breker.com
web: http://www.breker.com/
Wants to buy optical toys: magic lanterns, mechanical slides, stereoviewer, etc.

Dealers

Bryan W. Ginns
2109 Cty. Rte. 21
Valatie, NY 12184-6001
ph: 518-392-5805
fax: 518-392-7925
e-mail: the3dman@aol.com
Wants large collections of stereo views, old cameras, daguerreotypes, magic lanterns, optical toys; anything relating to photographics.

Marianne Schneider
Schneider's Toys & Fancy Goods
3217 Pinewyn Circle
Lancaster, PA 17601
ph: 717-285-3200
fax: 717-285-3853
e-mail: toy2biz@aol.com
Buys and sells optical toys: zeotropes, kaleidoscopes, praxinoscopes and theaters, magic mirrors, polyorama pantoptiques, artascopes, etc.

Paper

(see also PAPER COLLECTIBLES)

Dealers

Barb & Jonathan Newman
Paper Soldier, The
8 McIntosh Lane
Clifton Park, NY 12065
ph: 518-371-9202 or 518-371-5130
Paper toys bought and sold. Paper dolls, paper soldiers, toy theaters, planes, ships, paper and cardboard houses, etc.

Pedal Vehicles

(see BICYCLES & RELATED MEMORABILIA; RIDING TOYS)

Penny

Dealers

Bob Stevens
Keystone Toy Trader
529 N. Water St.
Masontown, PA 15461
ph: 724-583-8234
fax: 724-583-0604
Wants quality antique toys in all categories: early comic characters, cast iron, tin, diecast Tootsietoys, German penny toys, early German and European toys.

Pick-Up Sticks

Collectors

Judith Schulz
533 Milwaukee Ave.
Burlington, WI 53105-1232
ph: 262-763-3946
Collects old and unusual jacks and pick-up sticks; coordinates the annual international jacks & pick-up sticks event and tournament each February.

Playsets

(see also SOLDIERS, Toy; TOYS, Action Figures)

Collectors

Eric J. Reinkka
P.O. Box 170-198
Ozone Park, NY 11417-0198
ph: 718-835-9764
Wants to buy old toy soldiers, sets, playsets; Marx, Sears, Wards playsets, 1950s and 1960s model kits, battery/friction tinplate vehicles, G.I. Joe, guns, etc.; any nice military theme toy.

Dave Gall
7180 Broadview
Parma, OH 44134
ph: 216-524-9514
Wants Marx playsets: Gunsmoke, Johnny Ringo, Ben-Hur, Blue and

Gray; also many others such as westerns, military, space, etc.

David W. Francis
148 King St.
Wadsworth, OH 44281
ph: 330-335-3717
fax: 330-335-3617
e-mail: fphadv@bright.net
Wants to buy zoo and farm animal figures.

Thomas P. Terry
5894 Lakeview Ct. E.
Onalaska, WI 54650
ph: 608-781-1894
Collector wants to add to personal collection: complete or partial playsets by Marx, Ideal, Superior, etc.; Western Towns, Alaska, Jungle, Skyscrapers, Battle Action, etc.; also seeking boxed or bagged figure sets, blister cards, etc.

Dealers

Excalibur Hobbies, Ltd.
63 Exchange St.
Malden, MA 02148
ph: 781-322-2959
fax: 781-322-7910
Carries large selection of playset figures and accessories.

Paul Stadinger
STAD'S
815 North 12th St.
Allentown, PA 18102-1318
ph: 610-770-1140 or 610-433-7728
fax: 610-770-1740
e-mail: pestad@browser.net
STAD'S is a leading source for plastic figures from U.S. makers (Marx, MPC, Lido, Timmee, etc.) and foreign (Britains, Timpo, etc.); twice monthly catalog subscription is $4 for six months.

Stone Castle Imports
P.O. Box 141
Bardstown, KY 40004
ph: 502-897-0207
fax: 502-897-6415
e-mail: castle@toysoldiers.cc
web: http://www.toysoldiers.cc/
Carries a wide variety of toy soldiers and playsets.

Terry Geppert
4532 W. 102nd St.
Minneapolis, MN 55437-2611
ph: 612-831-7454

Experts

Tim Geppert
Colorado Quality Collectibles
2818 McKeag Dr.
Fort Collins, CO 80526
ph: 970-225-9782
Buys, sells, collects, appraises Marx playsets, plastic toy soldiers and figures; author of "Guide for Non-Metallic Toy Soldiers of the U.S."

Periodicals

Paul Stadinger
STAD'S
Magazine: Plastic Warrior
815 North 12th St.
Allentown, PA 18102-1318
ph: 610-770-1140 or 610-433-7728
fax: 610-770-1740
e-mail: pestad@browser.net
A British bi-monthly focusing on leading European plastic figures, firms (Britains, Timpo, etc.), reviews, Q&A, letters, news, ads, etc.

Thomas P. Terry, Ed.
Specialty Publishing Co.
Magazine: Plastic Figure & Playset Collector
P.O. Box 1355
La Crosse, WI 54602-1355
ph: 608-781-1894
e-mail: tompfpc@aol.com
The only magazines devoted to Marx Playsets (1950s-1970s) and related plastic toys and figures of the era; bi-monthly, 44+ pages, 8 1/2"x11" B&W format with articles, photos and factory reprints, articles, Q&A, ads, and more.

Plush

Collectors

Johanna & Sean Billings
P.O. Box 244
Danielsville, PA 18038-0244
ph: 610-760-8134 or 610-760-1814
fax: 610-760-8142
e-mail: bankie@concentric.net
web: http://www.facets.net/facets/freeserv-edu/rosebowl/
Wants to buy furry, plush stuffed soccer balls; any size, any color, any condition; will pay a couple dollars for each plus shipping; also wants unusual stuffed objects: stuffed crayons, toothbrushes, guitars, etc.

Periodicals

Scott Publications
Magazine: Soft Dolls & Animals
30595 Eight Mile
Livonia, MI 48152-1798
ph: 800-458-8237 or 248-477-6650
fax: 248-477-6795
e-mail: 104137.1254@compuserve.com
For the collector and creators of cloth dolls and animals; magazine stuffed with projects, loaded with good ideas; project patterns included.

Pullstring

(see TOYS, Talking [Pullstring])

PVC

(see also CHARACTER COLLECTIBLES; TOYS, Character)

Clubs/Associations

Colleen Lewis
PVC Collectors Club
Newsletter: PVC Collector
10120 Main St.
Clarence, NY 14031-2049
ph: 716-759-7541
fax: 716-759-7462
web: http://www.toyline.com/clubs/pcc
International club for PVC (rubber) collectors; quarterly newsletter with information, reviews, ads, etc. about PVCs including the "Archives", a detailed listing of PVCs by series with pictures; special offers for club members.

Dealers

Colleen Lewis
Buffalo Road Hobby
10120 Main St.
Clarence, NY 14031-2049
ph: 716-759-7541
fax: 716-759-7462
web: http://www.toyline.com/clubs/pcc
Carries a huge selection of PVC cartoon figures from Animaniacs, Hanna Barbera, Looney Tunes, and Pink Panther to Little Lulu, Zorro and more; imported from all over the world; catalog $2.

Renwal

Collectors

Mary Soelberg
29126 Laro Dr.
Agoura Hills, CA 91301-1635
ph: 818-889-9909
Advanced Renwal toy collector wants hard-to-find pieces, especially the Broom and Policeman; write with complete description and price; no broken items.

Russian

Dealers

George Francisco Paley
c/o Natural Way
Newsletter: Russian Toy Club
820-822 Massachusetts St.
P.O. Box 842
Lawrence, KS 66044-0842
ph: 785-841-0100
fax: 785-865-5466
Wholesale retailer and dealer; periodically published a newsletter for collectors of Russian toys - a rapidly changing environment and usually a situation of extremely limited availability.

Sand

Clubs/Associations

Sharon Lazane
Ohio Art Collectors Club
Newsletter: Ohio Art Beat
18203 Kristi Rd., West
Liberty, MO 64068
ph: 816-781-5452
e-mail: slazane@aol.com
Club is for those interested in collecting toys made by the Ohio Art Co.; especially sand toys including pails, sieves or sifters, sprinkling cans, water pumps, sand molds, sand hoists or lifts, and sand mills.

Collectors

Donald Gorlick
P.O. Box 24541
Seattle, WA 98124-0541
ph: 206-824-0508
Wants sand toys (not very old); small box-like toy containing a clown or trapeze artist which spins when the box is inverted.

Experts

Carole & Richard Smyth
Carole Smyth Antiques
P.O. Box 2068
Huntington, NY 11743-0861
ph: 516-673-8666
Authors of "Pails by Comparison," a study and price guide; available from the author for $28.50 ppd.

Schoenhut

Clubs/Associations

Pat Girbach, Sec.
Schoenhut Collectors Club
Newsletter: Schoenhut Newsletter
1003 W. Huron St.
Ann Arbor, MI 48103-4217
ph: 734-662-6676
fax: 734-662-6676
e-mail: aawestie@provide.net
Quarterly newsletter includes articles, prices and announcements of shows and events of interest to Schoenhut collectors.

Collectors

Gerken
414 W. Madison St.
Ann Arbor, MI 48103-4926

Dealers

Judith Lile
Judith Lile Antique Toys
346 Valleybrook Dr.
Lancaster, PA 17601
ph: 717-569-8175
Buys and sells toys, specializing in Schoenhut.

Harry R. McKeon, Jr.
18 Rose Lane
Flourtown, PA 19031-1910
ph: 215-233-4094
e-mail: toyspost@aol.com
Buys and sells Schoenhut items: dolls, games, circus animals, toys, accessories; anything Schoenhut except pianos.

Norman Bowers
1916 Cleveland St.
Evanston, IL 60202-1910
ph: 847-866-7165 or 708-333-7880
fax: 708-333-9561
Buys, sells, trades, and appraises Schoenhut items.

Science Fiction

Dealers

John Kachmar
Techno-Fantasy Toys & Cards
779 Carissa Dr.
West Palm Beach, FL 33411-3412
ph: 561-798-5978
fax: 561-798-5978

Scientific Laboratory

Collectors

Barry Lutsky
31 Longfield Dr.
Neshanic, NJ 08853
ph: 201-369-7367
e-mail: shmoomania@aol.com
Wants toys by A.C. Gilbert, Chemcraft; 1915-1950; also Erector Sets, chemistry, electricity/radio, engineering, magic & tricks, magnetism, meteorology, mineralogy, optics, physics, weather, etc.

Silly Putty

Dealers

Toysensations
P.O. Box 218
Woodbury, NY 11797
ph: 516-338-4929 or 516-338-2701
fax: 516-681-3612
Sells Silly Putty related items.

Man./Prod./Dist.

Binney & Smith, Inc.
P.O. Box 431
Easton, PA 18044
ph: 800-272-9652
This is the company that manufactures Silly Putty today.

Museums/Libraries

Crayola Hall of Fame, Binney & Smith
Two Rivers Landing
30 Centre Square
Easton, PA 18042-7744
ph: 423-515-8000 or 800-272-9652
e-mail: crayola@crayola.com
web: http://www.crayola.com/history/history.html
In addition to crayons, this museum also honors Silly Putty.

Space & Robot

(see also SPACE COLLECTIBLES)

Auction Services

Lloyd Ralston
Lloyd Ralston Toy Auction
400 Long Beach Blvd.
Norwalk, CT 06850
ph: 203-386-9399
fax: 203-386-9515
e-mail: lrgallery@aol.com
web: http://www.lloydralston.com/

Collectors

John Vahary, Jr.
41 Crosby Dr.
Battle Creek, MI 49014
ph: 616-965-0943
e-mail: johnjr1222@aol.com
Wants to buy space toys including Star WArs and Star Trek.

Christmas Catalog Collector, The
175 East Delaware, #7403
Chicago, IL 60611-1731
ph: 800-879-6948 or 312-337-3123
fax: 312-266-7982
Wants to buy 1925-1970 space toys and ray guns, Buck Rogers, Captain Video, Space Patrol, etc.; also wants toy/Christmas catalogs.

Dealers

Dan Dozier
Dozier Collectible Toys
23 Forest Ave.
Falmouth, MA 02540-4006
ph: 508-548-6342 or 508-548-0893
fax: 508-548-0893
e-mail: dandozier@dozierdesigns.com
web: http://www.dozierdesigns.com/museum.html
Collector, appraiser, dealer and resource for antique collectible toys, specializing in robots and space toys; also expert toy box reproduction and restorations.

John Maleski
Space Toys
20289 canal
Grosse Ile, MI 48138
ph: 734-675-8322 or 313-2979-6089
Wants to buy space toy buildings, ray guns, figures, premiums, 1950s TV space series' toys, Archer slot handed figures & accessories.

Bill O'Neil
Robots & Space Toys
P.O. Box 27637
Milwaukee, WI 53227
ph: 414-328-0592
fax: 414-546-6497
e-mail: info@spacetoys.com
web: http://www.spacetoys.com
Specializes in robots, ray guns, movie posters, and other sci-fi related collectibles.

Space & Robot (Ray Guns)

Dealers

Gary Kraut
Alphaville
226 W. Houston St.
New York, NY 10014-4846
ph: 212-675-6850
fax: 212-741-2609
e-mail: alphavil@mindspring.com
web: http://www.alphaville.com
Along with partner Steve Karchin buys and sells space toys.

John Maleski
Space Toys
20289 canal
Grosse Ile, MI 48138
ph: 734-675-8322 or 313-2979-6089
Wants to buy space toy buildings, ray guns, figures, premiums, 1950s TV space series' toys, Archer slot handed figures & accessories.

Experts

Gene Metcalf
211 S. Elm #F
Oxford, OH 45056
e-mail: metcalew@muohio.edu
web: http://jrscience.wcp.muohio.edu/gene/homepage.html
Ray gun collector and expert.

Leslie Singer
7 Shackleford Plaza, Ste. C
Little Rock, AR 72211
ph: 501-228-9982
e-mail: zenmotel@aol.com
Collects and specializes in pre-1960 space toys; author of "ZAP! Ray Gun Classics."

Internet Resources

Gene Metcalf
211 S. Elm #F
Oxford, OH 45056
e-mail: metcalew@muohio.edu
web: http://jrscience.wcp.muohio.edu/gene/homepage.html
Website has images of hundreds of toy ray guns from the US and abroad; traces the development of this toy and its social significance; lots of ray gun pages plus bulletin boards, buy/sell/trade pate, rotating gallery pages.

Steam/Hot Air

Collectors

Robin Corsiglia
Toy Steam Engines
5200 NE 9th Lane
Ocala, FL 34470
ph: 352-236-2635 or 352-680-3022
e-mail: marklinc@atlantic.net
web: http://members.atlantic.net/~marklinc/
Buys, sells and collects toy steam engines (stationary with real boilers and flywheels) and tin pop-pop boats, tin wind up boats, and tin battery boats; mainly collects buy also buys, sells, trades and gives out information.

Robin Corsiglia
Toy Steam Engines
5200 NE 9th Lane
Ocala, FL 34470
ph: 352-236-2635 or 352-680-3022
e-mail: marklinc@atlantic.net
web: http://members.atlantic.net/~marklinc/
Buys, sells and collects toy steam engines (stationary with real boilers and flywheels) and tin pop-pop boats, tin wind up boats, and tin battery boats; mainly collects buy also buys, sells, trades and gives out information.

Dealers

Diamond Enterprises & Book Publishers
P.O. Box 537
Alexandria Bay, NY 13607-0537
ph: 613-475-1771 or 800-481-1353
fax: 613-475-3748
e-mail: info@yesteryeartoys.com
web: http://www.yesteryeartoys.com
American and Canadian distributors of Mamod and Wilesco steam models; sales, parts and service.

Bruce J. Southmayd
Little Bill's Toys
9200 5th St. NE
Minneapolis, MN 55434-1107
ph: 612-786-0762
Steam toy collector and dealer.

Eureka, I Found It! Antiques & Collectibles
P.O. Box 2192
Petaluma, CA 94953-2192
e-mail: eureka@erueka-i-found-it.com
web: http://www.eureka-i-found-it.com
An online dealer specializing in vintage textiles and clothing, toy and model steam engines, buttons, fans, Art Deco, costume jewelry, toy sewing machines.

Experts

Richard Leach
26146 Redfield Road
Edwardsburg, MI 49112-9146
ph: 616-663-8844
Expert and collector of toy steam engines, hot air engines, toy electric

motors; author of "Weeden Steam Toy Pictorial Guide" and steam toy booklets and instruction sheets.

Submarine Related

Dealers

Tom Lavely
Neat Olde Stuff
16935 N. Main St.
P.O. Box 9
Galesville, WI 54630-0009
ph: 608-582-2082
fax: 608-582-2180
e-mail: tglavely@aol.com
Collector, dealer of toy submarines, sub memorabilia, photos, books, related items,

Super Hero

(see also CHARACTER COLLECTIBLES; COMIC BOOKS; PREMIUMS; SCIENCE FICTION; TELEVISION SHOWS & MEMORABILIA)

Collectors

Dale L. Ames
144 Russell Street
Worcester, MA 01610
ph: 508-755-3830
e-mail: gp@telegram.infi.net

Talking (Pullstring)

(see also DOLLS, Chatty Cathy)

Dealers

Bryin Dall
Pull This!
P.O. Box 2124
New York, NY 10009
ph: 212-777-1868
e-mail: PullThis1@aol.com
Buys and sells talking dolls and toys; anything that has a pull-string and talks (or used to); working or not; will also buy empty boxes, advertising, displays, and salesman samples.

Repair Services

Speak-Up
25 Statler Dr.
Shirley, NY 11967
ph: 516-924-6256
Source for repairing Chatty Cathy and Mattel talkers.

Kelly McIntyre
Chatty Cathy's Haven
19528 Ventura Blvd. #495
Tarzana, CA 91356-2917
ph: 818-881-3878
e-mail: cchaven@aol.com
web: http://www.chattycathyshaven.com
Repairs, buys and sells pullstring talkers.

Teenage Mutant Ninja Turtles

Collectors

John Vahary, Jr.
41 Crosby Dr.
Battle Creek, MI 49014
ph: 616-965-0943
e-mail: johnjr1222@aol.com
Wants toys that have Teenage Mutant Ninja Turtles on them.

Tin

Collectors

Jeff Dykes
6 Wildwood Terrace
Glen Ridge, NJ 07028
ph: 973-748-4990
e-mail: lja@viconet.com
Wants to buy German tin "penny" toys, German windups, trains, Steiff and teddy bears, and cast iron toys.

Dealers

Harry R. McKeon, Jr.
18 Rose Lane
Flourtown, PA 19031-1910
ph: 215-233-4094
e-mail: toyspost@aol.com
Buys and sells tin toys made by Martin, Bing, Lehmann, Gutherman, Ives, Strauss, etc.

David A. Hull
Small Town Coins & Collectibles
7498 E. Davison Rd.
Davison, MI 48423-2014
ph: 810-658-1992
fax: 810-658-2977
Dozens of original antique tin toys and Mint-In-Box for sale.

John D. McKenna
McKenna Bros. Wholesale
801-803 W Cucharras St.
Colorado Springs, CO 80905
ph: 719-630-8732
Buys, sells & collects pre-1960 toys in all categories especially early American tin, cast iron automotive and horse-drawn toys.

Internet Resources

Mark Kerr
Tinplate Temptations
30 Abercairn Rd.
Streatham
London, SW16 5AD
U.K.
e-mail: kerrmw@sbu.ac.uk
web: http://www.sable.co.uk/tinplate/
The essential site for collectors and lovers of tinplate toys, clockwork devices, and automata; new and antique.

Repair Services

Joe Freeman
Tin Toy Works
1313 N. 15th St.
Allentown, PA 18102-1068
ph: 610-439-8268
fax: 610-439-1288
Specializes in the repair of tin toys; tin toy autos, boats, merry-go-rounds, etc.; repairs mechanisms, makes missing parts.

Tinkertoys

Museums/Libraries

Kristan McKinsey
Evanston Historical Society
225 Greenwood St.
Evanston, IL 60201-4713
ph: 847-475-3410
web: http://www.adena.com/ehs/
Tinkertoys originated in Evanston, IL; Evanston Historical Society has the largest collection of Tinkertoys and related information in the country.

Tonka

Collectors

Two Guys
P.O. Box 9672
Mc Lean, VA 22102
ph: 800-244-0820
Buys, sells, trades Tonka cars, trucks, trains.

Dealers

Nancy Merrow
Champion Toys
RR1, Box 1858
Kennebunkport, ME 04046
ph: 207-985-2292
Mail order toys and automobilia.

Suppliers

Thomas Toys
P.O. Box 405
Fenton, MI 48430
ph: 810-629-8707
Sells replacement parts for Tonka trucks.

Toonerville Trolley

Clubs/Associations

Asa Sparks
Toonerville Trolley Collectors
Newsletter: Toonerville Times News
6045 Camelot Ct.
Montgomery, AL 36117-2555
ph: 334-270-0687
e-mail: asasparks@mindspring.com

Tops & Gyroscopes

(see also TOYS, Yo-Yo's)

Collectors

Bruce R. Middleton
Top Secret
5 Lloyd Rd.
Newburgh, NY 12550-5028
ph: 914-564-2556
Buys, sells, trades tops, yo-yo's, spinners, figurals, peg tops, supported tops, diablos, gyroscopes, etc.; seeks other collectors.

Don Olney
Toycrafter, The
1237 E. Main St.
Rochester, NY 14609-6941
ph: 716-288-9000 or 800-433-TOYS
fax: 716-654-7820
e-mail: topman@toycrafter.com
web: http://www.toycrafter.com/
Buys, sells, trades new and old tops; also wants top related ads, photos, books, photos and videos of people doing tricks with tops; author of "The Little Book of Tops," and "The Tops Discovery Kit."

Experts

Judith Schulz
533 Milwaukee Ave.
Burlington, WI 53105-1232
ph: 262-763-3946
Wants to buy unusual tops, gyroscopes and yo-yo's; also wants related ads, literature, and old packages; editor of "Spin-Offs", curator of a small museum about tops, gyros, and yo-yo's; top expert of MGM's video "My Summer Story."

Museums/Libraries

Judith Schulz
Spinning Top Exploratory Museum
Journal: Spin-Offs
533 Milwaukee Ave.
Burlington, WI 53105-1232
ph: 262-763-3946
2,000 tops, gyroscopes & yo-yo's on exhibit (antique and modern); top games & experiments to try; 35 types to spin; sales of unique tops; demos, live show at museum; "Spin-offs" is a playful research publication of history, facts, etc.

Transformers

Clubs/Associations

Tony Buchanan
TransMasters
Newsletter: Matrix
1215 S. Andrews Rd.
Yorktown, IN 47396-1002
e-mail: TransMasters@geocities.com
web: http://www.geocities.com/Area51/Dimension/8034/
International club interested in Transformers, comics, cartoons and toys.

Collectors

Maret Webb
4118 East Vernon Ave.
Phoenix, AZ 85008-2333
ph: 602-957-0653
fax: 602-957-1631
Wants to buy Hasbro and Bandai Transformers (transformation robot toys), and related cards, books, cookie jars, games, posters, etc. - ANYTHING featuring Transformers.

Transportation

Clubs/Associations

Tom Nefos
National Toy Connection
Newsletter: National Toy Connection
779 E. Merritt Island Cswy., Ste. 2346
Merritt Island, FL 32952
ph: 800-704-1232
fax: 800-704-1232
e-mail: natltoycon@aol.com
web: http://members.aol.com/NatlToyCon/ntc1.htm
For today's transportation/promotional toy collector & dealer; new product releases (inside information), toys of 50s through 70s, current prices, First Gear, Hess, Texaco, Ertl, Scale Models, industry news, hard-to-find products.

Dealers

U.S. Toy Collector
P.O. Box 172
Helena, MT 59624-0172
e-mail: ustoy@usa.com
web: http://www.geocities.com/MotorCity/Pit/4302/
Online resource focusing on toy trucks, cars, construction toys, transportation toys, etc.; the photo-marketplace of toy vehicles for sale; also has articles on toy history.

Jim & Nancy Schaut
Aquarius Antiques
7147 W. Angela Dr.
Glendale, AZ 85308-8507
ph: 623-878-4293
fax: 623-878-2458
e-mail: jnschaut@aol.com
web: http://members.aol.com/jr1955/web.html
Buys and sells transportation toys and memorabilia; toys, trains; buy and sell; publishes a quarterly catalog of one-of-a-kind items for sale; authors of "AMERICAN AUTOMOBILIA."

Experts

Tom Nefos
779 E. Merritt Island Cswy., Ste. 2346
Merritt Island, FL 32952
ph: 800-704-1232
fax: 800-704-1232
e-mail: natltoycon@aol.com
web: http://members.aol.com/NatlToyCon/ntc1.htm
Specialist, appraiser in transportation and promotional toys.

Transportation (Hess Trucks)

Dealers

Mark Scherzer
54 Gates Court
Matawan, NJ 07747-9716
ph: 732-290-1407
fax: 732-290-0636
Specializes in Hess Trucks from 1964 to present.

Trucks & Equipment

(see also GAS STATION COLLECTIBLES; TOYS, Tonka; TOYS, Transportation)

Collectors

Larry Bruch
Larry Bruch Toys
P.O. Box 121
Mountain Top, PA 18707-0121
ph: 800-549-TOYS
e-mail: kinglar@aol.com
All kinds of pre-1960 toys wanted: German, American: metal cars, airplanes, boats; comic characters, cast iron toys and banks, etc.; also buying Tootsietoys, Dinky, and Smith-Miller; write for free 3-page illustrated want list.

Bob Ford
4804 Bensalem Blvd.
Bensalem, PA 19020
ph: 215-638-0531
e-mail: modelts@icdc.com
web: http://www.icdc.com/~modelts/
Collects and sells Hess, Wilco, Servco, Texaco and other gasoline promotional toy trucks by Ertl and others; also collects Hess memorabilia.

Ferdinand Zegel
3449 N. Randolph St.
Arlington, VA 22207
ph: 703-524-2061
fax: 703-522-0414
e-mail: fzegel@starpower.net

N.W. Neill, Jr.
P.O. Box 38
Ennice, NC 28623-0038
fax: 336-657-8084
e-mail: saddlemtn@skybest.com
Wants to buy Tonka, Smith-Miller, Doepke model toys, any make of toy fire trucks.

Bill Whelan
P.O. Box 617
Daly City, CA 94017-2332
ph: 650-756-1189
Wants to buy scale model tractor/trailers & bobtails, 1/64th down to 1/100th and smaller, with company names, logos and advertising; especially Matchbox, Lledo, Herpa, Con-Cor, Viking, Winross, etc.

Dealers

Brandon Lewis
Buffalo Road Imports
10120 Main St.
Clarence, NY 14031
ph: 716-759-7151
fax: 716-759-7462
e-mail: bri@toyline.com
web: http://www.toyline.com/bri/
Specializing in construction scale models since 1978 with the largest selection available worldwide; stocks both current and discontinued models: NZG, Conrad, EMD, ATM, Old Cars, Zon, Diapet, Arpra, Minimac, CCM and more.

Periodicals

Claire Scheibe
Magazine: Toy Trucker & Contractor
7496 106th Ave. SE
Lamoure, ND 58458-9404
ph: 701-883-5206 or 800-533-8293
fax: 701-883-5208
e-mail: zekesez@aol.com
web: http://www.toytrucker.com/
Focuses on trucks and construction toys; sponsors an annual National Toy Truck and Construction Show in August.

Twist-Um

Collectors

Dale Abrams
960 Bryden Rd.
Columbus, OH 43205-1809
ph: 614-258-5258
fax: 614-258-6663
e-mail: TLAntiques@aol.com
web: http://ourworld.compuserve.com/homepages/da
Wants to buy Twist-Um toys - jointed figures, mostly animals, similar to Schoenhuts; made in Oakland, CA in the 1920s by the Twist-Um Toy Co.

Water Pistols

Collectors

Jean B. Hall
10 Alden Dr.
Norwood, MA 02062
ph: 781-762-3779
e-mail: jeanBhall@aol.com
Wants water pistols, especially Captain Video, Jaws, Pac-Man, St. Louis Exposition 1904, etc.; also TV Sci-Fi items.

White Knob Wind-Ups

Clubs/Associations

Kim Cole
White Knob Wind-Up Collectors Club
Newsletter: WKW Newsletter
61 Garrow St.
Auburn, NY 13021-4605
ph: 315-253-9131
Members trade information and white-knob wind-up toys; these toys get their names from the little white ridged knob at the end of a metal rod which extends from the body and winds the motor when rotated - no "on-off" switch.

Dealers

Robert Johnson
Comet Toys
2720 East 50th St.
Minneapolis, MN 55417
ph: 612-721-5256
fax: 612-721-5598
e-mail: comettoys@cometoys.com
web: http://www.comettoys.com/
Buys and sells tin toys, wind ups, and tin toy robots.

Richard Johnson
P.O. Box 27093
Prescott Valley, AZ 86312
ph: 520-775-4714

Lisa Gage
Great Wind-up, The
93 Pike #201
Seattle, WA 98101
ph: 206-621-9370
The Northwest's largest selection of wind-up toys - tin and other; full selection of collectibles from Paya and DBS lines of tin toys; interested in wind-up toys from all over the world.

Wooden

Collectors

Perry R. Eichor
703 N. Almond Dr.
Simpsonville, SC 29681-3453
ph: 864-967-8770
fax: 864-228-2541
e-mail: kpmflyn@earthlink.net
Wants to buy wooden toys made by Hustler, Rich, Ted Toy, Toy Tinkers and others.

Yo-Yo's

(see also TOYS, Tops & Gyroscopes)

Clubs/Associations

John Stangle, Pres.
American Yo-Yo Association
Newsletter: Yo-Yo Times
627 163rd St. South
Spanaway, WA 98387
ph: 707-542-YOYO
fax: 707-542-9696
e-mail: yotopia@sonic.net
web: http://ayya.pd.net
Association for yo-yo players and collectors; source for information and two publications: "AYYA News" (twice yearly) and "The Yo-Yo Times" (quarterly); Mr. Stangle is also a professional yo-yo entertainer!

Collectors

Les Gordon, II
6475 E 550 S
Whitestown, IN 46075-9696
ph: 317-769-3382
e-mail: lgordon@iei.net
Wants old yo-yo's and related pins, patches, advertisements, trophies, strings, books, paper, memorabilia, etc.

Jason Colwell
3508 N 2000 E Country Road
Ludlow, IL 60949
ph: 217-396-5014 or 217-359-6081
e-mail: jacolwel@uiuc.edu
web: http://www.ews.uiuc.edu/~jacolwel/
Want so buy old yo-yos (Duncan, Flores, Goody, Jewel, Alox, Hiker, Cheerio) and yo-yo relate items such as string, patches, pins, trophies, etc.

Bob Zeuschel
1638 Highland Valley Ctr.
Chesterfield, MO 63005-4919
ph: 314-537-3145
Wants yo-yo's by Duncan, Goody, Royal, Ja-Do, Flores, etc.

Bill Caswell
1512 Cherokee Place
Bartlesville, OK 74003
ph: 918-336-5130
e-mail: rosicas@juno.com
Wants old yo-yo's by Flores, Festival, Medalist, Cheerio, Hi-Ker, Duncan, Goody, Royal; especially wants jeweled and carved models.

Experts

Lucky Meisenheimer
7300 Sandlake Commons Blvd., Ste. 105
Orlando, FL 32819-8011
ph: 407-354-0478
e-mail: LuckyJ@msn.com
Buys old yo-yo's, singles, collections, and yo-yo memorabilia; also contest kits, store displays, patches, pins, awards, advertising, etc.

John Stangle
YO-topia
634 Echo Lake Way
Santa Rosa, CA 95401
ph: 707-542-9696
fax: 707-528-9696
e-mail: yotopia@yotopia.com
web: http://www.yotopia.com
YO-YO sales, service, collections, photos, events and much more: everything YO-YOs!

Museums/Libraries

Judith Schulz
Spinning Top Exploratory Museum
Journal: Spin-Offs
533 Milwaukee Ave.
Burlington, WI 53105-1232
ph: 262-763-3946
2,000 tops, gyroscopes & yo-yo's on exhibit (antique and modern); top games & experiments to try; 35 types to spin; sales of unique tops; demos, live show at museum; "Spin-offs" is a playful research publication of history, facts, etc.

International Museum of Yo Yo History
2947 E. Grant
Tucson, AZ 85716
ph: 520-322-0100
web: http://www.proyo.com/museum.htm
Featuring the Duncan collection, free admission.

National Yo-Yo Museum
320 Broadway
Chico, CA 95928-5322
ph: 530-893-0545
e-mail: info@nationalyoyo.org
web: http://www.nationalyoyo.org/
Over 1,000 yo-yos on display; free admission.

Periodicals

Stuart F. Crump, Ed.
Creative Communications, Inc.
Newsletter: Yo-Yo Times
P.O. Box 1519 - MAC
Herndon, VA 22070-1519
ph: 703-715-6190
e-mail: YoYoTime@aol.com
web: http://members.aol.com/yoyotime/
A quarterly publication loaded with information about current yo-yo events, leading yo-yo'ers, the latest publications and videos, and anything else related to yo-yos.

TOYS (MODERN)

Clubs/Associations

Toy Manufacturers of America, The
1115 Broadway, Ste. 400
New York, NY 10010
ph: 212-675-1141
fax: 212-633-1429
web: http://www.toy-tma.org/
The toy, puzzle and game manufacturers' trade organization; sponsors the annual American International New York Toy Fair which is only open to the trade and to the press.

Periodicals

Geyer-McAllister Publications, Inc.
Magazine: Playthings
51 Madison Ave.
New York, NY 10010-1603
ph: 212-689-4411
fax: 212-683-7929
web: http://www.d-net.com/playthings/
The unofficial trade journal for the toy industry; publishes a directory which lists manufacturers, their representatives, inventors and designers.

TRACTORS

(see also ENGINES; FARM MACHINERY; MACHINERY & EQUIPMENT, Road Making; TOYS, Farm)

Auction Services

Iron Horse Auction Co.
413 South Hancock St.
P.O. Box 1267
Rockingham, NC 28380
ph: 910-997-2248 or 800-997-2248
fax: 910-895-1530
e-mail: horse@infoave.net
web: http://www.auctionweb.com/ironhorse/
Conducts auctions specializing in the sale of antique steam engines, tractors and farm related items.

Clubs/Associations

Foothills Antique Tractor & Engine Club
105 N. Calderwood St.
Alcoa, TN 37701
ph: 423-982-6385
e-mail: tprather@utk.edu
web: http://web.utk.edu/~tprather/foothills.html
Meets monthly to share information on all brands of antique tractors, engines and farmstead and homestead equipment; several shows and community service projects as well; monthly newsletter; free classifieds on web site.

Sharon Gotcher
North Texas Antique Tractor & Engine Club
308 Gwendola
Mc Kinney, TX 75070
ph: 972-562-8697
e-mail: ntextrac@cyberramp.net
web: http://www.cyberramp.net/~ntextrac/index.htm
Meet regularly to share knowledge and interest in the tractors, engines and farm equipment that mechanized our early 20th century farms.

Jerry MacMartin, WebMaster
Early Day Gas Engine & Tractor Association, Inc.
Newsletter: National, The
570 Corliss Way
Campbell, CA 95008
ph: 408-378-4259
fax: 408-378-1390
e-mail: jemm@prodigy.net
web: http://www.ave.net/~edgeta/
A national organization with 90 regional "Branches" interested in early gas engines and tractors.

Collectors

Gary Dougherty
Gary's Antique Tractors
13502 92nd St.
Alto, MI 49302
ph: 616-765-3101
e-mail: gdougher@rbc.org
web: http://www.angelfire.com/mi/GarysOldTractors/
Collects and repairs tractors; web site is a down home, personal, friendly, antique tractor page with pictures and great links to other tractor sites.

Dealers

Larry Sikes
Rock Ridge Farm - The Florida Tractor Connection
1813 NW 97th Terr.
Pompano Beach, FL 33071
ph: 954-527-7360
e-mail: lsikes@gate.net
web: http://www.gate.net/~lsikes/
Collects, restores, buys and sells antique tractors, stationary engines and farm equipment.

Experts

Spencer Yost
Antique Tractor Internet Service
3160 MacBrandon Ln.
Pfafftown, NC 27040
ph: 910-924-6109
e-mail: yostsw@atis.net
web: http://www.atis.net
Appraiser, collector, expert specializing in tractors; also does repairs.

Dave Mowitz
1716 Locust St.
Des Moines, IA 50336
ph: 515-243-3327
Author of "Ageless Iron, Restoring Your Legacy" and the "Ageless Iron Restoration Guide" which lists sources for parts, paint, etc.

Internet Resources

Kate Smalley
Antique Tractor Resource Page
P.O. Box 896
Branford, CT 06405
e-mail: anttrac@antiquetractors.com
web: http://www.antiquetractors.com
A complete reference site for collectors and restorers of antique tractors, stationary engines and farm equipment; also provides web sites and advertising services for businesses and individuals.

Spencer Yost
Antique Tractor Internet Service
3160 MacBrandon Ln.
Pfafftown, NC 27040
ph: 910-924-6109
e-mail: yostsw@atis.net
web: http://www.atis.net
The oldest and most complete website on the Internet that specializes in antique tractors and farm equipment;

thousands of people access the site monthly to buy and sell and research farm equipment.

Yesterday's Tractors
P.O. Box 160
Chimacum, WA 98325
fax: 360-385-6721
e-mail: kim@yesterdaystractors.com
web: http://www.yesterdaystractors.com
Tractor registry, resources, parts & supplies, classifieds, hauling schedule, discussion groups, tractor show schedule, etc.

Periodicals

Stemgas Publishing Co.
Magazine: Gas Engine Magazine
P.O. Box 328
Lancaster, PA 17608-0328
ph: 717-392-0733
fax: 717-392-1341
e-mail: weidman@pptnet.com
web: http://www.stemgas.com/
G.E.M. is the leading magazine for antique tractor and gas engine collectors; articles, ads, auctions, models, Maytag gas engines, restoration tips, histories, auctions, suppliers, parts, etc.; published monthly.

Adept Resources
Directory: Who's Who in Antique Engines & Tractors
P.O. Box 2297
Elkhart, IN 46515
e-mail: dhaynes@adeptr.com
web: http://www.adeptr.com/
Source of people who are involved in some way with the antique engine and tractor hobby.

Dennis Polk
Dennis Polk Equipment
Magazine: Polk's "The Antique Tractor Magazine"
72435 SR 15
New Paris, IN 46553
ph: 219-831-3555 or 800-795-3501
fax: 219-831-5717
e-mail: sales@dennispolk.com
web: http://www.dennispolk.com/
Bi-monthly magazine covering the world of antique tractors; restoration, tractor pulls, auction results, collector stories, etc.

Barbara Schmidgall
Newsletter: Tractorcard Newsletter
1988 Willoughby Rd.
Mason, MI 48854-9491
ph: 517-676-1835 or 517-676-4030
Newsletter lists various sets of tractor cards which are available; tractor cards are trading cards with pictures of tractors on them.

Magazine: Engineers & Engines Magazine
2240 Oak Leaf St.
P.O. Box 2757
Joliet, IL 60434-2757
ph: 815-741-2240
fax: 815-741-2243
Bi-monthly magazine: tractors, gas, steam, farm machinery, railroad.

Newsletter: Hook, The
P.O. Box 16
Marshfield, MO 65706
ph: 417-468-7000
e-mail: thehook@pcis.net
web: http://www.pcis.net/thehook/
The magazine for antique and classic tractor pullers.

Magazine: Antique Power
P.O. Box 500
Missouri City, TX 77459
ph: 800-310-7047
fax: 281-261-5999
e-mail: antique@antiquepower.com
web: http://www.antiquepower.com
Has regular columns about farm toys, tractor restoration, farm literature collecting and tractor history; free ads for subscribers.

Newsletter: Western Antique Iron Trader
24696 SW Daniel Rd.
Beaverton, OR 97007
e-mail: Irontrader@inetarena.com
A monthly newsletter for people interested in antique tractors, stationary engines, and related equipment; contains many ads and show announcements for the Western states of WA, OR, and CA, as well as for British Columbia.

Suzanne Wright
Kelsey Publishing Ltd.
Magazine: Tractor & Machinery Magazine
Cudham Tithe Barn
Berrys Hill
Cudham, Kent TN16 3AG
U.K.
ph: 01959 541444
fax: 01959 541400
e-mail: info@kelsey.co.uk
web: http://www.kelsey.co.uk
A 64-page monthly British magazine dealing with all tractors and tractor-driven machinery; restorations, rallies, ploughing matches, auctions, runs and club event.

Repair Services

Gary Dougherty
Gary's Antique Tractors
13502 92nd St.
Alto, MI 49302
ph: 616-765-3101
e-mail: gdougher@rbc.org
web: http://www.angelfire.com/mi/GarysOldTractors/
Collects and repairs tractors; web site is a down home, personal, friendly, antique tractor page with pictures and great links to other tractor sites.

Suppliers

Bert Ruprecht
Paynesville Tractor Parts
P.O. Box 231
30203 State Hwy. 55
Paynesville, MN 56362
ph: 320-243-7443 or 800-445-0061
fax: 320-243-7664
e-mail: ptparts@lkdllink.net
web: http://www.lkdllink.net/~ptparts/ptparts.html
Sells used tractors and parts for old and collectible tractors.

Walt Unger
Walt's Tractor Parts, LLC
5654 Highway 15
Mexico, MO 65265
ph: 888-414-4043 or 573-581-4345
fax: 573-581-1078
e-mail: ungers@sockets.net
web: http://www.waltstractors.com
Online replacement tractor parts catalog.

Allis-Chalmers

Periodicals

Nan Jones
Magazine: Old Allis News
10925 Love Rd.
Bellevue, MI 49021-9250
ph: 616-763-9770
fax: 616-763-9770
A quarterly magazine for the Allis-Chalmers collector and/or enthusiast; Allis-Chalmers related articles, photographs, histories, restoration stories, suppliers ads, shows, auctions, etc.

Dennis Potter
Newsletter: Allis Connection, The
7011 E. Bethel Rd.
Elizabeth, IL 61028
ph: 815-598-3329 or 319-652-2949
e-mail: acbdeppe@caves.net

Case

Clubs/Associations

David Erb
J.I. Case Collectors Association
Newsletter: Old Abe's News
4004 Coal Valley Road
Vinton, OH 45686-9741
ph: 740-388-8895
Published quarterly.

Case Heritage Foundation
P.O. Box 5128
Bella Vista, AR 72714-0128
ph: 501-855-0312

Caterpillar

Clubs/Associations

Antique Caterpillar Machinery Owners Club
10816 Monitor-McKee Rd. NE
Woodburn, OR 97071
ph: 503-634-2496
fax: 503-634-2454

Cockshutt

Clubs/Associations

Donna Engel
International Cockshutt Club
Magazine: Cockshutt Quarterly
1506 Indian Lakes Rd.
Kent City, MI 49330-9430

Periodicals

John Kasmiski
Magazine: Golden Arrow Magazine
N7209 State Hwy. 67
Mayville, WI 53050
ph: 414-387-4578
Published quarterly; Cockshutt and Co-op.

Ferguson

Clubs/Associations

Ken Goodwin
Ferguson Club
Newsletter: Ferguson Club Journal
Denehurst, Rosehill Rd.
Stoke Heath, Drapton TF9 2JU
U.K.

Ford (N-Models)

Internet Resources

Neil Reitmeyer
Neil's Antique Tractor Page
P.O. Box 235
Stamford, CT 0538-0235
e-mail: neilreit@ptdprolog.net
web: http://home.ptd.net/~neilreit/

Periodicals

Neil Reitmeyer
Magazine: N-Newsletter, The
P.O. Box 235
Stamford, CT 0538-0235
e-mail: neilreit@ptdprolog.net
web: http://home.ptd.net/~neilreit/
A homespun newsletter in conversation format for enthusiasts of old Ford farm tractors and machinery; also for those with a general interest in antique farm tractors and machinery.

Fordson

Clubs/Associations

Ford/Fordson Registry & Collectors Association
645 Loveland Miamiville Rd.
Loveland, OH 45140
ph: 513-683-4935

Fordson Tractor Club
Newsletter: FTC Newsletter
250 Robinson Rd.
Cave Junction, OR 97523-9719
ph: 541-592-3203
Dedicated to the restoration, preservation, exhibition of the Fordson tractor; bi-annual newsletter, manuals, service bulletins, etc.

Tom Brent
Fordson Club
Newsletter: Fordson Club News
Box 150
Dewdney, British Columbia V0M 1H0
Canada

Gibson

Clubs/Associations

Gibson Tractor Club
4200 Winwood Court
Floyds Knobs, IN 47119-9225
ph: 812-923-5822

Gravely

Clubs/Associations

Steve Wilson
Gravely Tractor Club of America
110 North Main St.
Plymouth, MI 48170
ph: 313-316-1963
e-mail: sawilson@worldnet.att.net
web: http://www.iupui.edu/~harrold/Gravely/news.html

John Deere

Clubs/Associations

Dave Trumbauer
Two-Cylinder Club Worldwide
Magazine: Two-Cylinder
P.O. Box 10
Grundy Center, IA 50638-0010
ph: 319-345-6060 or 800-782-2582
fax: 319-345-2662
web: http://www.two-cylinder.com/
Over 20,000 members who collect John Deer literature and memorabilia, and who restore early John Deere tractors, engines, and implements; bi-monthly newsletter.

Collectors

Jim Proctor
1395 South Concord Rd.
West Chester, PA 19382
ph: 610-399-0802
Wants pre-1960 John Deere 2-cylinder tractors; also wants tractor sales literature.

Experts

Brenda Kruse
Bleeding Green
500 Cabezon Court
Gallup, NM 87301
ph: 505-722-2939
fax: 505-722-4788
e-mail: johndeere@BleedingGreen.com
web: http://www.BleedingGreen.com/
Connected to major collectors across the country; wants to hear from established collectors with unique items to be featured in the book and on the web site; serves as an online community for collectors of John Deere memorabilia.

Museums/Libraries

John Deere Historic Site
8393 S Main St.
Dixon, IL 61021
ph: 815-652-4551
Tour the restored John Deere home, as well as the archaeological display of his original shop complete with functioning blacksmith.

Periodicals

Deere & Company
Magazine: JD Journal
One John Deere Place
Moline, IL 61265-8098
ph: 309-765-8000
e-mail: jdj@deere.com
web: http://www.deere.com/aboutus/pub/jdj
John Deere corporate magazine; contains columns on John Deere related collectibles.

Magazine: Green Magazine
2652 Davey Rd.
Bee, NE 68314-9132
ph: 402-643-6269
fax: 402-643-3912
e-mail: grnswap@cnweb.com
web: http://www.cnweb.com/green/
For collectors of John Deere tractors, combines, implements, etc.; articles, ads, how-to's, restoration hints and tips, parts sources, farm toy auction notices, etc.

Massey-Harris

Periodicals

Keith Oltrogge
Newsletter: Wild Harvest
P.O. Box 529
Denver, IA 50622-0529
ph: 319-984-5292 or 319-352-5524
fax: 319-984-6408
e-mail: keitho@sbt.net
Published bi-monthly.

Minneapolis-Moline

Clubs/Associations

Loren Book, Treas.
Minneapolis-Moline Collectors Club, The
18581 600th Ave.
Nevada, IA 50201
e-mail: lgbook@nevia.net
web: http://www.netbci.com/users.tturner/mmcollectors/
For Minneapolis-Moline collectors and enthusiasts organized to exchange knowledge, memorabilia, parts, and history of the MM legacy.

Collectors

Wayne Fuder
RR2 Box 21
Foxhome, MN 56543
ph: 218-736-4769
Collects toys and memorabilia from Minneapolis Moline as well as items from Twin City, MTM, or Moline Plow Co.

Internet Resources

Tony Turner
Minneapolis-Moline Modern Machinery
111 CR 1752
Saltillo, MS 38866-9160
e-mail: tony@minneapolis-moline.com
web: http://www.netbci.com/users/tturner/
Web site dedicated to Minneapolis-Moline tractors and equipment; lists part sources, serial number cross references, images, message board.

Periodicals

Ken Delap II
Newsletter: Prairie Gold Rush
17390 S. SR 48
Seymour, IN 47274

Gaylen Mohr
Newsletter: Minneapolis-Moline Corresponder
3693 M Ave.
Vail, IA 51465
ph: 712-679-2491
fax: 712-677-2491
e-mail: gmohr@netins.net
web: http://www.netins.net/showcase/corresponer/mohr.htm
Published quarterly.

Oliver

Clubs/Associations

Hart-Parr/Oliver Collectors Association
Newsletter: Hart-Parr/Oliver Collector
P.O. Box 685
Charles City, IA 50616
web: http://www.hpoca.org/
Publishes quarterly magazine as well as quarterly newsletter relating to all types of equipment built by Oliver Farm Equipment including brand names Hart-Parr, Nichols & Shepard, Cletrac, Farquar, Ann-Arbor, American Seeding & Be-Ge.

Midwest Oliver Collectors
21576 US Hwy 52
Mount Carroll, IL 61053

Collectors

Larry D. Harsin
3426 170th St.
Estherville, IA 51334-9617
ph: 712-362-2966
Oliver collector and restorer.

Dennis Gerszewski
RR 1 Box 44
Manvel, ND 58256
ph: 701-699-3577
Wants Oliver literature and almost anything with the Oliver name.

Rick & Andrew Garnhart
6372 E Edwardsville Rd.
German Valley, IL 61039-9622
ph: 815-362-6531
Buy, sell, appraise Oliver tractors.

Dealers

McMillan's Oliver Collectibles
9176 U.S. Rt. 36
Bradford, OH 45308
ph: 937-448-2216

Rumely

Periodicals

Windstacker Productions
Magazine: Rumely Collector's News
12109 Mennonite Chruch Rd.
Tremont, IL 61568
ph: 309-925-3932
fax: 309-925-3312
e-mail: agboy@dpc.net
web: http://www.rumley.com/
Quarterly.

TRADING CARDS

Non-Sport

(see also ADVERTISING COLLECTIBLES, Trade Cards; BOTTLE CAPS, Milk; BUBBLE GUM CARDS; BUBBLE GUM & CANDY WRAPPERS; CARDS; COMIC BOOKS; PAPER COLLECTIBLES; POGS; SPORTS COLLECTIBLES)

Clubs/Associations

Christopher Benjamin
United States Cartophilic Society
Newsletter: Card Collectors Bulletin
P.O. Box 4020
Saint Augustine, FL 32085-4020
fax: 904-826-1600
Focuses on non-sport cards.

Collectors

Dan Calandriello
53-C Beacon Village
Burlington, MA 01803-3843
ph: 781-229-9009
e-mail: dan@coe.neu.edu
Wants 1930s era non-sports cards: gum, candy, silks, Mickey Mouse, Indian gum, Superman, Lone Ranger, all war cards; also wants Northeastern University, Boston, memorabilia 1898-1950s for upcoming 100th anniversary.

Becky Loechelt
3315 E. Lavey Lane #107
Phoenix, AZ 85032
Wants to buy TV non-sports trading cards, especially "Partridge Family", "Waltons", etc.; also wants 1960s and 1970s fan magazines, e.g. "Tigerbeat", "16", "Fave", etc.

Walter Koenig
P.O. Box 4395
North Hollywood, CA 91617-0395
e-mail: gineokw@aol.com
Wants to buy non-sports trading cards (gum, candy, character/comic) from the 1890s - 1950s.

Dealers

Mollie & John Witney
Non Sport Network
19 Lores Plaza #160M
New Milford, CT 06776
ph: 860-355-0259
fax: 860-355-0259
e-mail: nonsport@aol.com
Over 1700 card and set listings with high/low values as seen throughout the hobby; topical listings, artists' biographies, historical references; published quarterly.

Gary S. Frisch
Non-Sports Cards
24 Peachtree Ct.
Monmouth Junction, NJ 08852
ph: 732-329-9203
e-mail: gfrisch@new-directions.com
Buys, sells, and trades non-sports cards: sets, singles, wrappers, and boxes.

Jim Nicewander
Card Coach, The
P.O. Box 128
Plover, WI 54467-0128
ph: 715-341-5452
Wants Arm & Hammer/Church & Dwight trading cards, posters, and other related collectibles; publishes periodic catalog of cards and collectibles for sale; friendly, fast service since 1956.

Bob Conway
Card Attack, The
P.O. Box 260942
Lakewood, CO 80226-0942
ph: 303-988-7106
Buys, sells and trades bubble gum cards; non-sport specialist.

Doug Craddock
Craddock's Non-Sports Cards & Collectibles
P.O. Box 7772
San Jose, CA 95150-3766
ph: 408-298-9070 or 408-629-3980
Buys, sells and trades non-sports cards: 1930s - 1970s cards, singles, sets, wax packs, unopened boxes and wrappers. Main focus is 1950s-1960s. Finders fee paid for accumulations and collections purchased.

Ken Mitchell
710 Conacher Dr.
Willowdale, Ontario M2M 3N6
Canada
ph: 416-222-5808
Wants to buy gum, candy and non-sports trading cards.

Experts

Mollie & John Witney
Non Sport Network
19 Lores Plaza #160M
New Milford, CT 06776
ph: 860-355-0259
fax: 860-355-0259
e-mail: nonsport@aol.com
Operates search service through many on-line systems helping collectors locate cards; specializes in pre-1970 cards; buys and sells throughout the world; posts informative "press releases" of new releases; Internet NONSPORT@aol.com.

John Neuner
91-50 98th St.
Jamaica, NY 11421-2732
ph: 718-849-6114
fax: 718-849-5915
Author of "Non-Sport Wrapper Checklist and Price Guide."

Christopher Benjamin
P.O. Box 4020
Saint Augustine, FL 32085-4020
fax: 904-826-1600
Appraiser identifies and evaluates all US and foreign trading cards (fee charged), private and insurance inquiries welcome; author of "The Best Trading Card Guide Ever Issued", prices, descriptions, checklists, thousands of pictures.

Internet Resources

Robert Kohlbus
NonSport Card Collector
8706 Castlerock Ct.
Laurel, MD 20723
ph: 301-776-3769
e-mail: rkohlbus@home.com
web: http://24.3.47.19/nscc/
An on-line source for information on the hobby of non-sport card collecting: release dates, new set descriptions, free classifieds, set reviews and contests.

Terry Stewart
Collector Link
71 John St. East
Waterloo, Ontario N2J 1G2
Canada
ph: 519-745-1745
e-mail: stewart@collector-link.com
web: http://www.collector-link.com/
Catalogs over 2,000 trading card related web sites for: baseball, hockey, basketball, football, other sports, non-sports, phone cards, credit-debit cards, business cards, postcards.

Periodicals

Roxanne Toser
Roxanne Toser Non-Sport Enterprises, Inc.
Magazine: Non-Sport Update
4019 Green St.
P.O. Box 5858
Harrisburg, PA 17110-0858
ph: 717-238-1936
fax: 717-238-3220
e-mail: feedback@nonsportupdate.com
web: http://www.nonsportupdate.com/
Since 1990 the only magazine devoted entirely to non-sport trading cards; issued bi-monthly; covers everything on non-sports from older cards to what was printed yesterday; free promos in every issue; separate 32-page price guide.

Tuff Stuff Publications, Inc.
Magazine: Collect!
P.O. Box 3070
Richmond, VA 23228
ph: 804-266-0140 or 800-899-8833
fax: 804-264-4205
e-mail: tsonline@tuffstuffpubs.com
web: http://www.tuffstuffonline.com/subscribe.html
The complete monthly sports price guide publication for non-sports cards.

Barbara Schmidgall
Newsletter: Tractorcard Newsletter
1988 Willoughby Rd.
Mason, MI 48854-9491
ph: 517-676-1835 or 517-676-4030
Newsletter lists various sets of tractor cards which are available; tractor cards are trading cards with pictures of tractors on them.

Les Davis
Non-Sport Publication
Newsletter: Wrapper, The
1811 Moore Court
Saint Charles, IL 60174
ph: 630-443-9690
e-mail: monsterwax@aol.com
web: http://members.aol.com/TheWrapper/TheWrapper.html
Focuses on non-sports cards, wrappers and related items; 8 issues per year.

TRAILERS & RV'S

(see also GAS STATION COLLECTIBLES; HIGHWAY COLLECTIBLES; HOTEL COLLECTIBLES; MOBILE HOMES)

Clubs/Associations

Todd & Kristin Kimmell
Lost Highways Classic Trailer & Motorhome Club
Magazine: Lost Highways Quarterly
P.O. Box 43737
Philadelphia, PA 19106-7737
ph: 215-925-2568
fax: 215-925-5646
e-mail: info@losthighways.org
web: http://www.losthighways.org/
A classic trailer and motor home club; archives collects material relating to trailers, motor homes and auto camping from 1920s to 1960s.

Vintage & Classic Travel Trailers
3802 E. Fernwood Ave.
Orange, CA 92869
e-mail: creatived@vintage-vacations.com
web: http://www.vintage-vacations.com/
A club for owners and admirers of 1920 through 1960s travel trailers; rallies, vintage trailers for sale, stories, archives.

Collectors

Todd & Kristin Kimmell
P.O. Box 43737
Philadelphia, PA 19106-7737
ph: 215-925-2568
fax: 215-925-5646
e-mail: info@losthighways.org
web: http://www.losthighways.org/
Wants 1920s to 1960s trailer, mobile home and RV related material: trailer parks, trailer travel, motor homes, autocamping, tincan tourists, etc.; magazines, books, pamphlets, promos, film (16mm-8mm), photos, even old trailers.

Periodicals

Deals on Wheels Publications
Magazine: Truck, Race, Cycle & Recreation
P.O. Box 205
Sioux Falls, SD 57101
ph: 605-338-7666 or 800-334-1886
fax: 605-338-5337
e-mail: donnelson@dealsonwheels.com
web: http://www.dealsonwheels.com
Photo-ad magazine listing trucks, 4-wheel drives, cycles, race equipment, race cars, boats, recreation vehicles, trailers, jet-skis; classifieds.

Kelley Blue Book
Price Guide: Kelley Blue Book
5 Oldfield
Irvine, CA 92618
ph: 949-770-7704
fax: 949-837-1904
e-mail: kelley@kbb.com
web: http://www.kbb.com/indexv.html
Website offers current trade-in values for all makes and model cars for the past 21 years; also publishes printed value guides for cars, RV's, motorcycles, snowmobiles, motor homes, travel trailers, personal watercraft, etc.

Steve Ferguson, Ed.
National Automobile Dealers Association
Price Guide: N.A.D.A. Official Used Car Guide
P.O. Box 7800
Costa Mesa, CA 92628
ph: 800-544-6232
fax: 714-556-8715
e-mail: nada@nada.org
web: http://www.nada.org/
A series of value guides for domestic and foreign cars, trucks, vans, RV's, mobile homes, motorcycles, snowmobiles, and boats, small and large; also Heavy Duty Trucks and Aircraft Book, car clubs & organizations, museums.

TRAINS

(see also MODELS; RAILROADS; RAILROAD COLLECTIBLES)

Model

Clubs/Associations

National Model Railroad Association, Inc.
Magazine: NMRA Bulletin, The
4121 Cromwell Rd.
Chattanooga, TN 37421
ph: 423-892-2846
fax: 423-899-4869
e-mail: nmra@tttrains.com
web: http://www.mcs.net/~weyand/nmra/
International association with regional and divisional organizations; monthly newsletter; the NMRA's Kalmbach Memorial Library offers an extensive collection of resource material on both model and prototype railroading.

Shane Lambert
LaCrosse & Three Rivers Railroad Club, Inc.
624 Jackson Street
La Crosse, WI 54601-5374
ph: 608-784-5445 or 608-782-3496
e-mail: laxand3rivers@clubmember.org
web: http://www.rrdepot.com/l3rclub/
Club of model railroad enthusiasts; web site includes a wealth of information about the club and how they operate; also information on modeling seminary as well as modeling stories written by club members.

Dealers

Chuck
19910 Viking Ave.
Poulsbo, WA 98370
ph: 360-779-3200
fax: 360-779-2210
e-mail: trains@hurricane.net
Buys, sells, repairs, appraises and specializes in all kinds of model and toy trains.

Internet Resources

Shane Lambert
Coulee Web
P.O. Box 271
La Crosse, WI 54602-0271
ph: 608-784-5445 or 608-782-3496
e-mail: couleeweb@iname.com
web: http://www.rrdepot.com/Miscellaneous/webring.html
The Railroad Web Ring is designed to bring together web sites that contain information about prototype railroads, model railroading, rail fanning, railroad museums, and railroad historical societies/

Man./Prod./Dist.

Laura Sebastian-Coleman
Walthers Model Railroad Mall
5601 W. Florist Ave.
Milwaukee, WI 53281
ph: 414-527-0770 or 800-877-7171
fax: 414-527-0770
e-mail: custserv@walthers.com
web: http://www.walthers.com
Walthers has been a manufacturer and distributor of model railroad products since 1932; there are over 3,000 authorized Walthers dealers; distributes products from over 300 other manufacturers.

Periodicals

Andy Sperandeo
Kalmbach Publishing Co.
Magazine: Model Railroader
P.O. Box 1612
21027 Crossroads Circle
Waukesha, WI 53187
ph: 414-796-8776 or 800-533-6644
fax: 414-796-1615
e-mail: customerservice@kalmbach.com
web: http://www.modelrailroader.com
A monthly magazine for the toy train collector and model railroad enthusiast; articles, ads, hardware, models, track systems, structures, layout tips, techniques, plans and projects.

Kalmbach Publishing Co.
Magazine: Garden Railways
P.O. Box 1612
21027 Crossroads Circle
Waukesha, WI 53187
ph: 414-796-8776 or 800-533-6644
fax: 414-796-1615
e-mail: customerservice@kalmbach.com
web: http://www.gardenrailways.com
Covers all aspects of outdoor model railroading, including building and operating model trains, designing and landscaping railways, and selecting and maintaining plant material; published bimonthly; for advanced to beginner.

Suppliers

Con-Cor International, Ltd.
8101 E. Rersearch Court
Tucson, AZ 85710
ph: 520-721-8939
fax: 520-721-8940
e-mail: concor@azstarnet.com
web: http://www.all-railroads.com.concor/
Unique source for thousands of model railroad products; also books and videos related to railroads and railroading.

Model (N Gauge)

Periodicals

Newsletter: N Scale Collector, The
3535 Stine Road, #108
Bakersfield, CA 93309-6610
e-mail: Nscale@interpow.net
web: http://www.nscalecollector.com/
Website has lots of links to other N Scale resources.

Model (O Gauge)

Collectors

Joe Weber
604 Centre St.
Ashland, PA 17921-1332
ph: 570-875-4787 or 570-875-4401
Wants O-scale (Lionel size) toy trains, i.e. kits assembled by the enthusiast; made by Scalecraft, Lobaugh, Ferris, Hines, Max Gray.

Periodicals

Magazine: O Gauge Railroading
P.O. Box 239
Nazareth, PA 18064-0239
ph: 610-759-0406
fax: 610-759-0223
e-mail: OGaugeRwy@aol.com
web: http://members.aol.com/ogaugerwy/org.html
A bi-monthly magazine exclusively for the O Gauge collector and market.

Model (S Gauge)

Clubs/Associations

Bill Moore, Treas
National Association of S Gaugers
Newsletter: Dispatch, The
220 Swedesboro Rd.
Gibbstown, NJ 08027-1504
ph: 609-423-0198
e-mail: nasgdispatch@hotmail.com
web: http://trainweb.com/NASG/

Periodicals

Donald Heimburger
Heimburger Publishing Co.
Magazine: S Gaugian
7236 West Madison Ave.
Forest Park, IL 60130-1765
ph: 708-366-1973
The magazine focuses on S gauge (1:64 scale) model train operation, modeling, and collecting.

Toy

Appraisers

Brenda Wimperis
Greenberg Auctions
7566 Main St., Ste. 101
Sykesville, MD 21784-5826
ph: 410-795-4749
fax: 410-549-2553
e-mail: auctions@greenbergshows.com
web: http://www.kalmbach.com/greenberg/shows.html
Appraises and specializes in Lionel, American Flyer, Marx, LGB, Marklin, Williams, AMT, etc.

Auction Services

Bill Bertoia
Bill Bertoia Auctions
1881 Spring Rd.
Vineland, NJ 08631
ph: 609-692-1881
fax: 609-692-8697
e-mail: webmaster@billbertoiaauctions.com
web: http://www.billbertoiaauctions.com/
Specializing in the auctioning of antique toys, banks, trains, and doorstops.

Brenda Wimperis
Greenberg Auctions
7566 Main St., Ste. 101
Sykesville, MD 21784-5826
ph: 410-795-4749
fax: 410-549-2553
e-mail: auctions@greenbergshows.com
web: http://www.kalmbach.com/greenberg/shows.html
Specialist in toy trains: Lionel, American Flyer, Marex, Ives, LGB, HO, Marklin, etc.; publishes an auction catalog and accepts mail bids.

Heinz Mueller
Continental Auctions
P.O. Box 193
Sheboygan, WI 53082
ph: 920-693-3371
fax: 920-693-8211
e-mail: toys@classictintoy.com
web: http://www.classictintoy.com/
Specializes in auctions of toy trains and all toy-related items.

Clubs/Associations

Louis A. Bohn, Mem. Ch.
Toy Train Collectors Society
Newsletter: Century Limited
109 Howedale Dr.
Rochester, NY 14616-1534
ph: 716-667-1548
New York State's largest and most active organization devoted to the collection, preservation and operation of the treasured electric trains of days gone by; runs toy train meets across NY state.

Train Collectors Association
Magazine: Train Collectors Quarterly
P.O. Box 248
Strasburg, PA 17579
ph: 717-687-8976 or 717-687-8623
fax: 717-687-0742
e-mail: toytrain@traincollectors.org
web: http://www.traincollectors.org/
Purpose is to bring together persons interested in collecting and operating toy trains and related items; also publishes the "National Headquarters News" newsletter.

Electronic Model Railroaders Association
P.O. Box 7
Mount Clemens, MI 48046
ph: 810-544-0998

Toy Train Operating Society, Inc.
Magazine: TTOS Bulletin, The
25 West Walnut St., Ste. 308
Pasadena, CA 91103
ph: 626-578-0673
fax: 626-578-0750
e-mail: ttos@ttos.org
web: http://www.ttos.org/
Formed to further the toy train hobby and to promote fellowship; members receive "The Bulletin" magazine and "Order Board" admagazine.

Collectors

Walter Makolandra
70 Cass Ave.
Woonsocket, RI 02895-4739
ph: 401-765-4756
Collector seeks Lionel, American Flyer, Marklin, Bing and other trains and related items.

Neil K. Yerger
7 Farm Rd.
Wayne, PA 19087-3303
Wants to buy Lionel, American Flyer, Williams, K-Line, Weaver, etc. toy trains and accessories.

Bill Bean
439 Claxton Glen Ct.
Kettering, OH 45429
ph: 937-435-6196 or 937-439-2600
e-mail: ErectrBean@aol.com
Writes articles for the Train Collectors Association Quarterly.

Edwin Wilder
1409 1st St.
Port Townsend, WA 98368-3078
Model railroad car, locomotive, structure kits - used, old. Also old locomotives and toy trains.

Dealers

Evertt A. Chapman
Dad's Trains & Granddad's Too
7 Lee Rd.
Barrington, RI 02806
ph: 401-245-0523

Bookbinder's Trains Unlimited
P.O. Box 660086
Flushing, NY 11366-0086
ph: 800-955-8729
fax: 718-657-2264
web: http://www.netpage1.com/bookbinderstrains/
Sells Lionel and American Flyer toy trains via his internet website.

Charles Siegel
Train City
3133 Zuck Road
Erie, PA 16506
ph: 814-833-8313
fax: 814-838-3237
e-mail: trainmaiin@traincity.com
web: http://www.traincity.com/
Buys, sells and repairs pre-owned Lionel, American Flyer, Marex, and other tin type toy trains.

Don Morris
HTrains, Inc.
6901 US Hwy. 19N
Pinellas Park, FL 33781
ph: 813-526-4682
fax: 813-526-3439
e-mail: hrtrains@hrtrains.com
web: http://www.hrtrains.com
Full service model train shop; repair shop, research library, garden railroad, pre-owned antique trains, children's playroom, Brio, Thomas the Tank, classes, LGB, Lionel, Mikes Train House, Marklin.

Merri-Seven Trains
19155 Merriman
Livonia, MI 48152
ph: 810-474-5373
Buy, sell, trade, expert repairs, all gauges; thousands of original Lionel, American Flyer and other toy train parts in stock; large selection of post-war Lionel, Athearn and other new and used toy trains.

Trains & Things
106 East Front St.
Traverse City, MI 49684
ph: 616-947-1353
fax: 616-947-1411
e-mail: tctrains@traverse.net
web: http://www.tctrains.com/
Buys and sells Lionel, American Flyer, Marx, Matchbox; also operates train rooms in toy train museum.

Jay Robinson
Chicago Kid
P.O. Box 529
Deerfield, IL 60015-0529
ph: 847-945-8691
Wants to buy old electric and wind-up trains; also old toy trucks and cars; wind-up and battery-operated toys.

Pat Neil
Collectible Trains & Toys
109 Medallion Center
Dallas, TX 75214
ph: 214-373-9469 or 800-462-4902
fax: 214-373-1622
e-mail: ctt@airmail.net
web: http://www.trainsandtoys.com/
Buys and sells pre-WWII Lionel, Marklin, K-line, American Flyer, and other trains including trains made in Germany; also does repairs on all toy trains made from 1900 to present.

Bill White
Vintage Lionel Train Exchange
1600 Smith, Ste. 4230
Houston, TX 77002
ph: 713-951-0230 or 888-624-5549
fax: 713-951-0022
e-mail: comments@trainxchange.com
web: http://www.ghgcorp.com/lionel/lionel.html
Buy, sell, appraise, repairs, trade old electric trains; helps individuals sell their train for top dollar; specializes in top quality collector items and original boxes; supplier of investment grade trains to discriminating collectors.

Pat Wilson
Koya Designs
3445-A Divisadero
San Francisco, CA 94123
ph: 415-929-9173
e-mail: plwilson@sirius.com
Wants to buy toy trains; European antique or vintage; will do searches for collectors.

Experts

Richard Friz
Maddie's Muse
P.O. Box 472
Peterborough, NH 03458-0472
ph: 603-563-8155
e-mail: jmdfriz@top.monad.net
Author of "The Official Price Guide to Toy Trains."

Ron Hollander
129 Lincoln Street
Montclair, NJ 07042
Author of "All Aboard!" the story of the Lionel Train Company; will give free appraisal; send description, including manufacturer, type of car or engine, all numbers & lettering on any part of the car; include SASE for reply.

Bruce C. Greenberg
7566 Main St., Ste. 100
Sykesville, MD 21784-5826
ph: 410-442-1537
e-mail: brucegreenberg@erols.com
Appraises and specializes in Lionel, American Flyer, Marx, LGB, Marklin, Williams, AMT, etc.; author of 22 books concerned with American toy trains; appraiser with litigation experience.

Allan W. Miller
Antique Trader Books
207 Westover Ave., #307
Norfolk, VA 23507
ph: 757-625-5045
e-mail: alstrains@aol.com
Former managing editor of Greenberg Guides to Lionel, American Flyer, Marx, and LGB trains; former managing editor of Kalmbach Books; editor of "America's Standard Gauge Electric Trains"; author for "Vintage Rails" magazine.

Internet Resources

Trains, Trams & Railroading
P.O. Box 5297
Ormond Beach, FL 32175-5297
ph: 904-672-4534
fax: 904-672-9214
e-mail: trains@notry.com
web: http://www.notry.com/trains.htm
Lots of railroading and toy train links.

Large Scale On-Line
4595 E Highland Drive
Post Falls, ID 83854
e-mail: info@largescale.com
web: http://www.largescale.com
The largest site on the internet for large scale trains: live chat rooms, workshops, classified ads, voting center, and more.

Man./Prod./Dist.

MTH Electric Trains
7020 Columbia Gateway Dr.
Columbia, MD 21046
ph: 410-381-2580
fax: 410-381-6122
e-mail: sales@mth-railking.com
web: http://www.mth-railking.com
Manufacturer of the worlds finest O gauge trains; offers the best quality, variety, service, and value in the industry.

Museums/Libraries

National Toy Train Museum
P.O. Box 248
Strasburg, PA 17579
ph: 717-687-8976 or 717-687-8623
fax: 717-687-0742
e-mail: toytrain@traincollectors.org
web: http://www.traincollectors.org/
Has trains on display dating from the late 1800s to present; five operating layouts (one with hands-on buttons); gift shop and reference library also available.

Periodicals

Neil Besougloff, Ed.
Kalmbach Publishing Co.
Magazine: Classic Toy Trains
P.O. Box 1612
21027 Crossroads Circle
Waukesha, WI 53187
ph: 414-796-8776 or 800-533-6644
fax: 414-796-1142
e-mail: editor@classtrain.com
web: http://www2.classtrain.com/ctt/
A 9-times per year magazine with articles on collecting, repairing, & operating new & old Lionel, American Flyer, Marx, Ives, MTH, K-Line & other toy trains; ads, layouts, museums, collectors.

Newspaper: Collectors Gazette
Fleck Way
Thornaby
Stockton-on-Tees, Cleveland TS17 9JZ
U.K.
ph: +44 (0) 1642 762335
fax: +44 (0) 1642 762401
e-mail: info@icn.co.uk
web: http://www.icn.co.uk/cg.html
Published 10 times per year for toy and model collectors worldwide; covers tinplate toys, obsolete and modern diecast cars (Corgi, Dinky, Matchbox, EFE, Lledo, Days Gone, etc.) and models, trains, airplanes, ships, dolls, etc.

Repair Services

Joe Mania
Downtown Trains
17 Douglas Rd.
Freehold, NJ 07728
ph: 732-303-8299
fax: 732-303-8299
e-mail: joe@jlmtrains.com
web: http://www.jlmtrains.com
Repairs and restores all makes of toy trains.

Pat Neil
Collectible Trains & Toys
109 Medallion Center
Dallas, TX 75214
ph: 214-373-9469 or 800-462-4902
fax: 214-373-1622
e-mail: ctt@airmail.net
web: http://www.trainsandtoys.com/
Buys and sells pre-WWII Lionel, Marklin, K-line, American Flyer, and other trains including trains made in Germany; also does repairs on all toy trains made from 1900 to present.

Suppliers

Railroad Press Company, The
P.O. Box 2644
Novato, CA 94948
ph: 415-898-7030
fax: 415-897-2705
e-mail: info@railpress.com
web: http://www.railpress.com/
Toy train specialists carries books, stickers, signs, videos, whistles, stock certificates, coffee cups and much more for all Lionel, Flyer, Ives, Marx toy train fans.

Toy (American Flyer)

Clubs/Associations

Frank Hare, Ed.
American Flyer Collectors Club
Magazine: Collector, The
P.O. Box 13269
Pittsburgh, PA 15243-0269
ph: 412-221-2250
fax: 412-221-8402
For collectors of A.C. Gilbert Co. American Flyer and other toy trains (all pre-1966 manufacturers); also contains information about Gilbert Erector sets.

Internet Resources

Paul Yorke
7501 Springhaven Ave.
Indiantown, FL 34956
e-mail: yorke@gate.net
web: http://www.gate.net/~yorke/
Website has message board, mailing list, web links, Flyer related bookstore and chat sessions; information about American Flyer model trains collecting, restoring, selling and operating; also covered is "S" scale,

Toy (Floor)

Experts

Rick Ralston
99-969 Iwaena St.
Aiea, HI 96701-3249
ph: 800-486-9794 or 808-486-1243
fax: 808-486-1276
e-mail: ralston.hawaii@crazyshirts.com
web: http://www.ralstonantiques.com
Author of "Cast Iron Floor Trains;" available from the author by calling 800-TOY-TRAIN.

Toy (Hornby)

Clubs/Associations

Bob Field, Mem.
Hornby Railway Collectors' Association
Journal: Hornby Railway Collector, The
2 Ravensmore Road
Sherwood, Nottingham NG5 2AH
U.K.
ph: +44 (0) 115 962 5693
web: http://www.bigfoot.com/~HRCA
Members also receive "The Directory of Replacement and Repair Services."

Toy (Ives)

Clubs/Associations

Jo Ann Miller, Mem.
Ives Train Society, The
P.O. Box 59
6714 Madison Road
Thompson, OH 44086
ph: 440-357-1544
fax: 440-357-1544
e-mail: kjtra1ns@aol.com
web: http://members.aol.com/ivesboy/index.html

Toy (LGB)

Clubs/Associations

Ralph Wilcox, Mem. Ch.
LGB Model Railroad club
Newsletter: Big Train Operator
1854 Erin Dr.
Altoona, PA 16602-7612
web: http://www.lgb.com/lgb_mrrclub.html
A 2000+ member organization of LGB (Lehmann-Gross-Bahn) enthusiasts, mainly collectors.

Experts

Jack Barton
Buffington Publishing
1573 Landvater
Hummelstown, PA 17036
ph: 717-566-9400 or 717-566-9413
fax: 717-566-9428
e-mail: 73670.3673@compuserve.com
web: http://www.lgbtelegram.com
Writes "LGB Kollector" column for the "LGB Telegram" magazine; internationally known LGB collector.

Periodicals

Frances Buffington
Buffington Publishing
Magazine: LGB Telegram
1573 Landvater
Hummelstown, PA 17036
ph: 717-566-9400 or 717-566-9413
fax: 717-566-9428
e-mail: 73670.3673@compuserve.com
web: http://www.lgbtelegram.com
A quarterly magazine for LGB (Lehmann-Gross-Bahn) fans; features articles on collecting as well as a column called "LGB Kollector" in every issue.

Toy (Lionel)

Clubs/Associations

Lionel Operating Train Society
Magazine: Switcher
6366 West Fork Rd.
Cincinnati, OH 45247-5704
ph: 513-598-8240 or 216-747-5151
fax: 513-598-4778
e-mail: lotsbusinessoffice@juno.com
web: http://www.lots-trains.org/
The bi-monthly "Switcher" is loaded with layout designs, track plans, scenery construction, layout operating, maintenance, repair tips and techniques, building & rolling stock modification projects, club information & news.

Brenda Schlutow
Lionel Railroader Club
Newsletter: Inside Track, The
P.O. Box 748
New Baltimore, MI 48047
ph: 810-949-4100
e-mail: LionelMI@aol.com
web: http://www.Lionel.com
For model railroading enthusiasts; members receive newsletter published quarterly, club button, layout accessories and other exclusive items; a company sponsored club.

Lionel Collectors Club of America
Newsletter: Lion Roars
P.O. Box 479
La Salle, IL 61301-0479
ph: 815-654-1705
e-mail: mottlerm@conwaycorp.net
web: http://www.lionelcollectors.org/
Purpose is to promote and foster interest in Lionel electric trains.

Collectors

Robert L. Schultz
P.O. Box 62240
Cincinnati, OH 45242-0240
ph: 513-874-5583

Charles W. Casad
801 Tyler Ct.
Monticello, IL 61856-2246
ph: 217-762-2303
Wants American Lionel toy trains in O-gauge, O-27 gauge, and standard gauge trains; also wants any Lionel

accessories; all must be complete and operating, please.

Dealers

Gary D. Mosholder
Gary's Trains
186 Pine Springs Camp Road
Boswell, PA 15531-2421
ph: 814-629-9277
e-mail: jlytwins@floodcity.net
web: http://www.homepage.floodcity.net/users/gtrains
Buys and sells Lionel trains and accessories including Plasticville buildings; sends out periodical list of items for sale; also carries parts and does repairs.

Trainmaster
Newsletter: Trainmaster
5001-B NW 34th St.
Gainesville, FL 32605
ph: 800-613-4222 or 352-373-4222
fax: 352-373-4468
Major dealer in Lionel trains; buys and sells; national market maker in secondary Lionel trains; published bi-monthly.

Bill White
Vintage Lionel TrainXchange
1600 Smith, Ste. 4230
Houston, TX 77002
ph: 713-951-0230 or 888-624-5549
fax: 713-951-0022
e-mail: comments@trainxchange.com
web: http://www.ghgcorp.com/lionel/lionel.html
Buy, sell, appraise, repairs, trade old electric trains; helps individuals sell their train for top dollar; specializes in top quality collector items and original boxes; supplier of investment grade trains to discriminating collectors.

Sam Mattes
Sam the Toy Train Man
7253 Pondera Circle
Canoga Park, CA 91307
ph: 818-347-4753 or 818-347-4753
e-mail: sam@val.net
web: http://www.toytrains.com
Buys, sells, and appraises Lionel trains.

Experts

Ron Hollander
129 Lincoln Street
Montclair, NJ 07042
Author of "All Aboard!" the story of the Lionel Train Company; will give free appraisal; send description, including manufacturer, type of car or engine, all numbers & lettering on any part of the car; include SASE for reply.

Bill White
Vintage Lionel Train Exchange
1600 Smith, Ste. 4230
Houston, TX 77002
ph: 713-951-0230 or 888-624-5549
fax: 713-951-0022
e-mail: comments@trainxchange.com
web: http://www.ghgcorp.com/lionel/lionel.html
Buy, sell, appraise, repairs, trade old electric trains; helps individuals sell their train for top dollar; specializes in top quality collector items and original boxes; supplier of investment grade trains to discriminating collectors.

Man./Prod./Dist.

Lionel Co.
50625 Richard W. Blvd.
New Baltimore, MI 48051
ph: 810-949-4100
e-mail: LionelMI@aol.com
web: http://www.lionel.com

Museums/Libraries

Charles W. Casad
Rayville Model Train Museum
801 Tyler Ct.
Monticello, IL 61856-2246
ph: 217-762-2303
Above is mailing address; physical location is 217 W. Washington St., Monticello, IL.

Toy (Marklin)

(see also TOYS, Marklin)

Clubs/Associations

Marklin Club - North America
Magazine: Insider
P.O. Box 510559
New Berlin, WI 53151
ph: 414-784-8854
fax: 414-784-1095
e-mail: webmaster@marklin.com
web: http://www.marklin.com
Dedicated to serving the interests of the Marklin enthusiast; helps enthusiasts get the most from Marklin trains and model railroading.

Marklin Digital Special Interest Group
Newsletter: Digital SIG, The
P.O. Box 51319
New Berlin, WI 53151-0319
ph: 414-784-8854
fax: 414-784-1095
web: http://www.marklin.com/
Provides its members with in-depth knowledge and insight into the advanced Marklin Digital control technology.

Collectors

Ronald Wiener
1650 Arch St., 22 Floor
Philadelphia, PA 19103
ph: 215-977-2266
fax: 215-977-2740
e-mail: rwiener@wolfblock.com
Wants Marklin (German) metal toys and toy trains, 1895-1960 in original and excellent condition, especially pre-1942 O gauge; also other old metal toys in excellent condition.

Grant A. Kreinberg
108 Brae Court
Suisun City, CA 94585-1304
ph: 707-864-1823 or 916-552-8736
fax: 707-864-9240
e-mail: grantk@castles.com
Collector seeks "O" gauge Marklin and other European trains.

Man./Prod./Dist.

Fred Gates, Pres.
Marklin, Inc.
16988 W. Victor Rd.
P.O. Box 510559
New Berlin, WI 53151-0559
ph: 414-784-8854
fax: 414-784-1095
e-mail: webmaster@marklin.com
web: http://www.marklin.com/
Marklin, Inc. is the American subsidiary of Gebr. Marklin & Cie. GmbH and is the exclusive distributor in North America for Marklin products.

Toy (Marx)

Collectors

Bill Smith
56 Locust St.
East Douglas, MA 01516-2440
ph: 508-476-2015
Wants to buy all Marx trains and related items regardless of condition; especially interested in Marx train catalogs.

Mark Whipple
102 Clarette Rd.
Pittsburgh, PA 15237
ph: 412-366-9459
Collects Marx trains and Marx accessories; also other Marx toys.

Toy (Plasticville)

Dealers

Gary D. Mosholder
Gary's Trains
186 Pine Springs Camp Road
Boswell, PA 15531-2421
ph: 814-629-9277
e-mail: jlytwins@floodcity.net
web: http://www.homepage.floodcity.net/users/gtrains
Buys and sells Lionel trains and accessories including Plasticville buildings; sends out periodical list of items for sale; also carries parts and does repairs.

Bill Nole
319 Oak St.
Dunmore, PA 18512
ph: 570-343-2236

Dennis Teepe
6802 GLenkirk Rd.
Baltimore, MD 21239
ph: 443-832-5375
e-mail: dteepe@mail.bcpl.lib.md.us

TRAMP ART

(see also FOLK ART; HOBO COLLECTIBLES)

Dealers

Matt Lippa
Artisans
P.O. Box 256
Mentone, AL 35984-0256
ph: 256-634-4037
fax: 256-634-4037
e-mail: artisans@folkartisans.com
web: http://www.folkartisans.com
Buy and sell folk art, outsider art, fine art; Internet WWW site offers links to additional dealers; also offers non-profit clubs and museums with an outlet to post notices, press releases, calendar items, etc. at no charge.

Anne Foster
1913 Hyde St.
San Francisco, CA 94109
ph: 415-776-8865
Wants all kinds of tramp art including frames, boxes, miniature pieces of furniture, etc.

Experts

Michael Cornish
Cigar Box Antiques
92 Florence St.
Roslindale, MA 02131-2603
ph: 617-323-6029
Buys, sells and repairs tramp art (layered and notched objects made from recycled wood c. 1870-1940); seeks unusual or furniture pieces; co-writing a book on tramp art with Clifford Wallach; especially wants elaborate boxes.

Clifford Wallach
277 W. 10th St.
New York, NY 10014-2562
ph: 212-243-1007
fax: 212-929-1839
e-mail: tramprt@aol.com
Author of "Tramp Art, One Notch at a Time" published by Wallace-Irons; buys, sells exceptional forms of tramp art and other folk art and outsider art.

Helaine Fendelman
Helaine Fendelman & Assoc.
1248 Post Rd.
Scarsdale, NY 10583-2153
ph: 914-725-0292
fax: 914-472-2266
e-mail: HFendelman@aol.com
Writing a book on tramp art; co-author with Jonathan Taylor of "Tramp Art - A Art Phenomenon" (Stewart, Tabori & Chang, 1999).

TRANSPORTATION COLLECTIBLES

(see also AIRLINE MEMORABILIA; AIRSHIPS; AUTOMOBILES; AUTOMOBILIA; AVIATION; BUS LINE COLLECTIBLES; BUSES; GAS STATION COLLECTIBLES; LUGGAGE LABELS; OCEAN LINER COLLECTIBLES; RAILROAD COLLECTIBLES; STEAMBOAT COLLECTIBLES; STREETCAR LINE COLLECTIBLES; TRUCKS)

Clubs/Associations

Courtney Haydon
Transport Ticket Society
Journal: Transport Ticket Society Journal
4 Gladridge Close
Earley
Reading, Berks RG6 7DL
U.K.
ph: +44 118 9264109
e-mail: courtney@gladridgecl.demon.co.uk
web: http://www.btinternet.com/~transport.ticket
Interested in the collection and study of tickets, transfers, passes, tokens, and other items issued by companies in the fare collection process; also ticket issuing machines.

Collectors

Seth Bramson
330 N.E. 96th St.
Miami, FL 33138-2718
ph: 305-757-1016
fax: 305-895-8178
Buys all U.S. RR/trolley/steamship/ airline and bus memorabilia; all Floridiana and U.S. travel & destination material - things put out by boards of trade, chambers of commerce, cities, counties, towns, hotels, restaurants, businesses.

Dealers

Stephen Hansrote
Griffin Trading Company
159 Howell St.
Dallas, TX 75207
ph: 214-747-9234
fax: 214-747-0660
e-mail: griffintc@aol.com
web: http://members.aol.com/griffintc/website.htm
Buying and selling plane, train, automobile and ship collectibles; everything from advertising and signs to equipment and actual parts and supplies; also provides decor for national restaurant chains.

Scott Arden
Antiques & Artifacts
20457 Highway 126
Noti, OR 97461-9706
ph: 541-935-1619
Leading RR mail order dealer for 28 years; catalog $1; buys and sells fine old transportation items, mostly non-paper; consignment.

Museums/Libraries

Lowell G. Kjenstad
Cole Land Transportation Museum
405 Perry Rd.
Bangor, ME 04401-6725
ph: 207-990-3600
fax: 207-990-2653
e-mail: mail@colemuseum.com
web: http://www.colemuseum.org/
200 antique Maine vehicles, 2,000 photos of life in early Maine communities, covered bridges, Maine state WWII memorial, Ertl-Coles express trucks, military collection.

Charles Chiarchiaro
Owls Head Transportation Museum
Rte. 73 Box 277
Owls Head, ME 04854
ph: 207-594-4418
fax: 207-594-4410
e-mail: ohtm@midcoast.com
web: http://www.ohtm.org/
Founded in 1964 to collect, preserve and exhibit pioneer aircraft, ground vehicles, and engines significant to the evolution of transportation and/or the state of Maine.

Western Reserve Historical Society
10825 East Blvd.
Cleveland, OH 44106-1703
ph: 216-721-5722
fax: 216-721-0645
e-mail: pomerleau@wrhs.org
web: http://www.wrhs.org/
Oldest cultural institution in Cleveland, with a research/ genealogical library, costume wing, auto & aviation museum and restored mansion under one roof; special interest area in automobiles and aviation.

Henry Ford Museum
20900 Oakwood Blvd.
P.O. Box 1970
Dearborn, MI 48121-1970
ph: 313-982-6001 or 313-271-1620
fax: 313-271-9621
e-mail: webmaster@hfmgv.org
web: http://www.hfmgv.org/
Museum houses a collection of over one million three-dimensional artifacts, defined by the following general categories: agricultural and industrial production, transportation, communication, and domestic life.

Pate Museum of Transportation
P.O. Box 711
Hwy. 377
Pate, TX 76101
ph: 817-332-1161 or 817-396-4305
web: http://www.classicar.com/MUSEUMS/PATE/PATE.HTM

Rob Etherington
Forney Transportation Museum
4303 Brighton Blvd.
Denver, CO 80216
ph: 303-297-1113 or 970-482-7271
fax: 970-498-9505
e-mail: forney@info2000.net
web: http://www.forneymuseum.com/
Over 170 antique automobiles plus four steam locomotives (including "Big Boy" #4005) and many other transportation exhibits plus a gift shop containing transportation collectibles and souvenirs.

China

Experts

Richard Luckin
621 Cascade Ct.
Golden, CO 80403-1581
ph: 303-278-8669
fax: 303-215-0095
Collector of transportation china for over 30 years; author of "Dining On Rails," "Teapot Treasury", and "Mimbres to Mimbreno"; also designs and supplies china for private railroad cars and for business cars for various railroads.

Timetables

(see also AIRLINE MEMORABILIA, Timetables; RAILROAD COLLECTIBLES, Timetables)

Clubs/Associations

Norbert Shacklette, Mem.
National Association of Timetable Collectors
Newsletter: First Edition, The
125 American Inn Rd.
Villa Ridge, MO 63089-2153
e-mail: crts@worldnet.att.net
web: http://www.rrhistorical.com/naotc/
Interested in timetables from airlines, steamships, railroads, and bus lines.

Collectors

George Johnson
P.O. Box 1449
Lexington, VA 24450-1449
ph: 540-464-4326
fax: 540-464-4326
Wants to buy pre-1940 timetables; railroad, trolley, airline or bus; any quantity; also wants passes, catalogs, and depot postcards.

TRAPS

Clubs/Associations

Tom Parr
North American Trap Collectors Association, Inc.
Newsletter: TRAPS
P.O. Box 94
Galloway, OH 43119-0094
ph: 614-878-6011
Members interested in the preservation of all trapping devices (animal, fish, bird, insect), trap operations, trapping literature, fur trade industry memorabilia, sporting collectibles, trapping magazines and paper ephemera, etc.

National Trappers Association, Inc.
Magazine: American Trapper, The
P.O. Box 3667
Bloomington, IL 61701
ph: 309-829-2422
e-mail: trappers@aol.com
web: http://www.nationaltrappers.com/
Over 20,000 members promote conservation to preserve the natural resources of the US; magazine published bi-monthly occasionally contains articles about old trapping equipment and techniques.

Collectors

Ron Willoughby
1072 Rte. 171
Woodstock, CT 06281-2134
ph: 860-974-1226
fax: 860-974-3190
e-mail: swillo@neca.com
web: http://www.neca.com/swillo
Wants to buy oddly-shaped traps and bear traps; also buying all trapping paper and memorabilia as well as lure containers, smokers, advertising items, etc.; a very serious buyer.

Ron B. Frodelius
P.O. Box 125
Fayetteville, NY 13066-0125
Wants anything related to trapping; pre-1950 only: ads, books, catalogs, magazines, hunt-trader-trapper, fur-fish-game magazines, mouse traps, mole traps, rat traps.

Robert Kwalwasser
168 Camp Fatima Rd.
Renfrew, PA 16053-9104
ph: 724-789-7766
fax: 724-789-9771
e-mail: robert@tcis.net
Wants old gopher, mole, mouse, fly, minnow, and rat traps.

Terry Swartz
RD 1 Box 197 A
Blain, PA 17006
ph: 717-536-3733

Chuck Clift
103 Duck Cove
Elmore, AL 36025
ph: 334-285-6522
Collects animal traps - everything from mouse to bear traps; specializes in mouse, rat, gopher, mole, killer, glass minnows and glass fly traps; odd shaped traps; traps with teeth.

Archie H. Stevens, Sr.
2196 AuSable Pt. Rd.
East Tawas, MI 48730
ph: 517-739-7006
Wants antique traps: bear, wolf, handforged, Newhouse, any size.

Sam Delavan
RR 3
Glenwood, IA 51534
ph: 717-527-9513

Terry Burger
2323 Lincoln
Beatrice, NE 68310-3306
ph: 402-228-2797

Clay Tontz
4043 Nora Ave.
Covina, CA 91722
ph: 626-338-9976
Wants traps - from mice to moose; only the scarce and unusual.

Jim Gipe
21149 NE 212th Ave.
Battle Ground, WA 98604
ph: 360-687-2793

Jack Lay
101 Glenview Crescent, Box 243
Princeton, British Columbia VOX 1WO
Canada
ph: 250-295-6010

Dealers

William A. Russ
Russ Trading Post
23 William St.
Addison, NY 14801-1326
ph: 607-359-3896
Buys and sells antique traps including bear traps; also issues a catalog of hunting and trapping supplies.

Dennis Helman
6969 Wright Puthoff Rd.
Sidney, OH 45365
ph: 937-492-5769

Experts

Boyd Nedry
728 Buth Dr.
Comstock Park, MI 49321-8207
ph: 616-784-1513
Specializes in unusual animal traps or related items: fly, mouse, mole, minnow, bear, rat, gopher, cockroach, handcrafted; any material: wood, glass, metal, etc.; any age; also books and advertising on trapping.

Museums/Libraries

Charles E. Hanson, Jr., Dir.
Museum of the Fur Trade
Magazine: MFT Quarterly
6321 Highway 20
Chadron, NE 69337-9501
ph: 308-432-3843
fax: 308-432-5963
e-mail: museum@furtrade.org
web: http://www.furtrade.org/
Dedicated to the study of the American fur trade from colonial times to the present; furs, traps, trade guns, trade goods, Indians; not involved with present day trapping.

Periodicals

Pat DuChene, PR
Krause Publications
Magazine: Trapper & Predator Caller, The
700 E. State St.
Iola, WI 54990-0001
ph: 715-445-2214
fax: 715-445-4087
e-mail: info@krause.com
web: http://www.krause.com/
A monthly magazine about hunting, trapping and predator calling, and animal damage control.

Fly

Collectors

Ralph Finch
34007 Hillside Ct.
Farmington, MI 48335-2513
Wants to buy fly traps in odd colors, shapes and sizes.

Rat/Mouse/Fly

Collectors

Robert Kwalwasser
168 Camp Fatima Rd.
Renfrew, PA 16053-9104
ph: 724-789-7766
fax: 724-789-9771
e-mail: robert@tcis.net
Wants old mouse, fly, minnow, and rat traps.

Tom Edmonds
6306 East Pea Ridge Rd.
Huntington, WV 25705
ph: 304-697-5280
Wants antique mousetraps; prefers live catch or capture traps.

TRAPSHOOTING

(see also SPORTING COLLECTIBLES; TARGET SHOOTING MEMORABILIA)

Museums/Libraries

Trapshooting Hall of Fame & Museum
601 W National Rd.
Vandalia, OH 45377-1036
ph: 937-898-1945
fax: 937-898-5472

TRAVEL COLLECTIBLES

(see HIGHWAY COLLECTIBLES; HOTEL COLLECTIBLES; SOUVENIR & COMMEMORATIVE ITEMS)

TREASURE HUNTING

(see also ARCHAEOLOGY; BOTTLES; CIVIL WAR ARTIFACTS; COINS & CURRENCY; NAUTICAL ANTIQUES; PREHISTORIC ARTIFACTS)

Clubs/Associations

Bernard Grabowski, Treas.
Federation of Metal Detector & Archeological Clubs, Inc.
Newsletter: Quest, The
2206 Kimwood Lane
Rancho Cordova, CA 95670
e-mail: chasjone@erols.com
web: http://www.fmdac.com/
The FMDAC is composed of over 190 clubs; goals include the promoting and protecting of the metal detecting hobby.

Internet Resources

International Treasure Hunters Exchange
web: http://www.treasure.com/
A forum for treasure hunters to freely exchange information, research and treasure hunting information; site contains a list of treasure hunting and archaeology clubs.

Periodicals

Newsletter: Treasure Hunter's Gazette
14 Vernon Street
Keene, NH 03431
ph: 603-357-0607
fax: 603-352-1147
e-mail: gazette@monad.net
web: http://www.monad.net/~streeters/gazette.htm
An informative publication that discusses virtually any topic within the world of treasure hunting, including much metal detector information and prices.

Bob Weller
Magazine: Treasure Quest Magazine
1860 Forest Hill Blvd., Ste. 204
West Palm Beach, FL 33406
ph: 561-357-0930
fax: 561-357-0890
e-mail: galleon@treasurequestmag.com
web: http://www.treasurequestmag.com
Journal of the professional treasure hunter: archaeology, treasure hunting, shipwreck recovery.

Steve Anderson
People's Publishing Company
Magazine: Western & Eastern Treasures Magazine
P.O. Box 1598
Mercer Island, WA 98040-1598
ph: 800-999-9718 or 206-230-9224
e-mail: westeast@treasurenet.com
web: http://www.treasurenet.com/westeast/
The world's treasure hunting authority written by experts for metal detecting enthusiasts; improve your skills, upgrade equipment, research treasure sites, first hand accounts of coin, artifact, gold finds.

Greenlight Publishing
Magazine: Treasure Hunting Magazine
The Publishing House
Hatfield Peverel
Chelmsford, Essex CM3 2HF
U.K.
Published since 1977, this is the biggest selling metal detecting magazine in the U.K.; how-to's, site research, machines and equipment, historical and finds identifications, etc.

Suppliers

George Streeter
Streeter's Treasure Hunting Supply
14 Vernon Street
Keene, NH 03431
ph: 603-357-0607
fax: 603-352-1147
e-mail: gazette@monad.net
web: http://www.monad.net/~streeters/aboutstreeter.htm
Vendor of treasure hunting equipment and supplies.

TREES & SHRUBS

Appraisers

Russell E. Carlson, ASCA
Tree Tech Consulting
ph: 302-832-1911
fax: 302-836-1870
e-mail: treetech@tree-tech.com
web: http://tree-tech.com/
Registered arboricultural consultant and tree appraiser.

Lee L. Lesh
International Consulting Arborists, Inc.
1590 Oak Knoll Lane
Newcastle, CA 95658
ph: 800-379-9011
e-mail: LeeLesh@tree-expert.com
web: http://www.tree-expert.com/
Registered arboricultural consultant and tree appraiser.

Clubs/Associations

American Society of Consulting Arborists
1524 Shady Grove Rd.
Rockville, MD 20850
ph: 301-947-0483
fax: 301-990-9771
e-mail: asca@mgmtsol.com
web: http://www.asca-consultants.org/
Call for referral to local appraisers of trees and shrubs.

International Society of Arboriculture
P.O. Box 3129
Champaign, IL 61826-1329
ph: 217-355-9411
fax: 217-355-9516
e-mail: isa@isa-arbor.com
web: http://www.ag.uiuc.edu/~isa/
Publishes book "Guide for Establishing Values of Trees and Other Plants"; publishes catalog of arboriculture books, gifts, study guides, plant health manuals, brochures and videos; some members are trained tree appraisers.

TRENCH ART

(see also AMMUNITION & EXPLOSIVE ORDNANCE, Shell Casings)

Collectors

Ed Mickel
5011 Briargrove Ln.
Dallas, TX 75287-7408
ph: 972-407-6960
Collector of engraved shell casings and other items made from shell casings or parts of shell casings, bullets, rotating bands or shrapnel; especially interested in WWI items.

TRIBAL

(see AMERICAN INDIAN; ART, African & Tribal; ART, Indonesian; ART, Oceanic; PRECOLUMBIAN)

TRINKET BOXES

(see BOXES; FAIRINGS)

TRIVETS

(see also IRONS, Pressing)

Collectors

Carol Hansen
c/o Scientific American Magazine
415 Madison Ave., 1st Floor
New York, NY 10017
ph: 212-754-0598
e-mail: chansen@sciam.com
Doing research for an extensive trivet collector.

TROLLEY LINE COLLECTIBLES

(see RAILROAD COLLECTIBLES; STREETCAR LINE COLLECTIBLES)

TROLLS

(see also DOLLS; ELVES)

Collectors

Debbie Brown
541 South St. Clair St.
Painesville, OH 44077-3636
Wants old trolls & related items in any condition, any number: trolls, troll houses, handlebar covers, charms, outfits, animals, etc.; wants Greek God, PAN, statues, pictures, etc.

Sally Kimmel
1471 Lark Lane
Concord, CA 94521-2942
ph: 510-676-2857
e-mail: sallyraek@yahoo.com
Troll lover wants 1960s to 1990s trolls, any size, tailed trolls, animal trolls (especially monkey), charms, pencil tops, clothes, houses, etc. - anything with trolls; any condition; one piece or entire collections.

Ellen Schmidt
P.O. Box 601292
Sacramento, CA 95860-1292
ph: 916-455-7678
fax: 916-455-7678
e-mail: Trollaholic@Worldnet.att.net
Serious collector wants to buy 1960s trolls: animal trolls (cow, turtle, elephant, monkey, reindeer, etc.), tailed trolls, trolls in original outfits, store displays, and anything troll related.

Marci Van Ausdall
P.O. Box 946
Quincy, CA 95971
ph: 530-283-2770
e-mail: dreams@psln.com
Wants to buy pre-1960 Trolls, clothing, accessories; jewelry; unusual items.

Experts

Jeanne Niswonger
305 West Beacon Rd.
Lakeland, FL 33803
ph: 941-682-8484
Author of "Troll Dolls."

Man./Prod./Dist.

Minna & Johannes Kuuskoski
U.S. Trolls
2305 Market St.
Wilmington, NC 28403
ph: 910-251-2270
fax: 910-251-2270
e-mail: trollmagic@aol.com
web: http://www.trollforest.com
The Kuuskoski family started making Trolls in Finland in 1952 - these were known as the FAUNI-Trolls; still making these Trolls and the collection has grown; each Troll is handmade and has a "personality"; each comes with story-card.

Periodicals

Ellen Schmidt
Newsletter: Troll'n
P.O. Box 601292
Sacramento, CA 95860-1292
ph: 916-455-7678
fax: 916-455-7678
e-mail: Trollaholic@Worldnet.att.net
Newsletter for trollaholics; free 40-word ad for anyone with trolls for sale; also buys and sells trolls.

TROPHIES

(see ANIMAL TROPHIES; MORBID & ODD ITEMS; PINS, Award; SPORTING COLLECTIBLES)

TRUCK LINE COLLECTIBLES

(see TRANSPORTATION COLLECTIBLES; TRUCKS)

TRUCKS

(see also AUTOMOBILES; AUTOMOBILIA; FIRE FIGHTING MEMORABILIA, Apparatus; MILITARIA, Vehicles; TOYS, Hess; TOYS, Transportation; TRAILERS & RV'S; TRANSPORTATION COLLECTIBLES)

Clubs/Associations

Antique Truck Club of America, Inc.
Magazine: Double Clutch
P.O. Box 291
Hershey, PA 17033-0291
ph: 717-533-9032
Focuses on antique trucks and other commercial vehicles.

Larry L. Scheef, Man. Dir.
American Truck Historical Society
Magazine: Wheels of Time
P.O. Box 531168
Birmingham, AL 35253-1168
ph: 205-870-0566
fax: 205-870-3069
e-mail: aths@mindspring.com
web: http://www.aths.org/
Recognized by the American Trucking Association as the official archives for the trucking industry; collects & preserves the history of trucks, trucking, and its pioneers; many chapters throughout the U.S. and Canada.

Mike Anderson
Antique Aviation & Truck Society
4533 Highway 201
Ontario, OR 97914
ph: 541-889-2378

Collectors

N.W. Neill, Jr.
P.O. Box 38
Ennice, NC 28623-0038
fax: 336-657-8084
e-mail: saddlemtn@skybest.com
Wants to buy pre-1948 Dodge trucks, literature, ads, etc.; Dodge Power Wagons 1 ton 1946-1968; anything on Dodge cab-over trucks; also 1960-1970 big Dodge trucks.

Al Koenig
P.O. Box 6122
Rochester, MN 55903-6122
ph: 800-533-1702 or 507-367-4319
fax: 507-288-6859
Wants 1930s to 1950s truck drivers' cap badges; also wants any other trucking company badges, trucking company lapel pins, cloth emblems, and other trucking company memorabilia.

Museums/Libraries

Lloyd Van Horn
Van Horn Truck Museum
15272 North St.
Mason City, IA 50401-9292
ph: 515-423-9066 or 515-423-0550
fax: 515-423-2570
web: http://www.aerosite.net/vanhorn
Over 60 models of pre-1930 trucks; early gas engines, gas pumps, signs and mobilia, old country store items and early farm items; 1930 store front streets, circus room with large scale model circus one man spent 34 years making!

Hays Antique Truck Museum & Old Truck Town
2000 East Main St.
Woodland, CA 95776
ph: 530-666-1044
e-mail: hatm@wheel.dcn.davis.ca.us
web: http://www.dcn.davis.ca.us/go/hatm/
Dedicated to the preservation and display of antique trucks and the history of the trucking industry.

Periodicals

Trucking Publications Inc.
Magazine: Truck Buyers Guide
P.O. Box 1232
Morrisville, PA 19067
ph: 215-295-0770
fax: 215-295-4650
Regional photo-ad magazine listing wide assortment of trucks for sale.

Deals on Wheels Publications
Magazine: Truck, Race, Cycle & Recreation
P.O. Box 205
Sioux Falls, SD 57101
ph: 605-338-7666 or 800-334-1886
fax: 605-338-5337
e-mail: donnelson@dealsonwheels.com
web: http://www.dealsonwheels.com
Photo-ad magazine listing trucks, 4-wheel drives, cycles, race equipment, race cars, boats, recreation vehicles, trailers, jet-skis; classifieds.

Magazine: This Old Truck
P.O. Box 500
Missouri City, TX 77459
ph: 800-310-7047
fax: 281-261-5999
e-mail: antique@antiquepower.com
web: http://www.thisoldtruck.com/
Full color magazine covering all makes of light trucks and commercial vehicles 1980 and earlier.

Steve Ferguson, Ed.
National Automobile Dealers Association
Price Guide: N.A.D.A. Official Used Car Guide
P.O. Box 7800
Costa Mesa, CA 92628
ph: 800-544-6232
fax: 714-556-8715
e-mail: nada@nada.org
web: http://www.nada.org/
A series of value guides for domestic and foreign cars, trucks, vans, RV's, mobile homes, motorcycles, snowmobiles, and boats, small and large; also Heavy Duty Trucks and Aircraft Book, car clubs & organizations, museums.

Chevrolet

Clubs/Associations

National Chevy/GMC Truck Association
Newsletter: Pickups 'N Panels in Print
P.O. Box 607458
Orlando, FL 32860
ph: 407-889-5387
fax: 407-886-7571
e-mail: CHEVY55-72@ao.net
web: http://www.ao.net/CHEVY55-72/
An organization by and for 1911 through 1972 Chevrolet/GMC enthusiasts; national and local shows, local clubs.

Periodicals

Petersen Companies, Inc.
Magazine: Chevy Truck
3816 Industry Blvd.
Lakeland, FL 33811
ph: 941-644-0449 or 800-999-3269
e-mail: leeke@petersenpub.com
web: http://www.d-p-g.com/
Aimed at owners of Chevrolet full- and mid-size pickups and sport utility vehicles who seek to enhance performance and add individualized appearance to their truck; a bi-monthly, manufacturer-specific truck title.

Ford

Clubs/Associations

Cecil Harry, Pres.
Old Ford Truck Club
3425 Moria Dr.
Amelia, OH 45102
ph: 513-752-9717
e-mail: oftc@choice.net
web: http://users.choice.net/~oftc/

Ford Truck Club International
Route 3
Caledonia, Ontario N3W 2B9
Canada

White

Clubs/Associations

Leigh Knudson
Vintage White Trucks Association
719 Ohms Way
Costa Mesa, CA 92627
ph: 949-645-5938

TRUNKS

(see also LEATHER; LUGGAGE)

Dealers

Pat Morse
Trunk Shop, The
23 Ceres St.
Portsmouth, NH 03801
ph: 603-431-4399
fax: 603-664-9699
e-mail: pat@trunk.com
web: http://www.trunk.com
Refinishes and sells antique trunks.

Churchill Barton
Brettun's Village Trunk Shop
302 Lake Street
Auburn, ME 04210
ph: 207-782-0861 or 207-782-7863
e-mail: barton@ime.net
web: http://w3.ime.net/~barton/
Sells and refinishes trunks, suitcases, toolboxes, toy boxes, and wardrobes; web site has on-line help for do-it-yourselfer, info on trunk makers, and histories.

Stevens Antique Trunks
61 Harrington Ave.
Closter, NJ 07624
ph: 201-768-1463
e-mail: oldtrunx@aol.com
web: http://www.njmetronet.com/antiquetrunks/
Buys, sells and restores old trunks

Antique Trunk Co.
3706 W. 169th St.
Cleveland, OH 44111
ph: 216-941-8618
Buy, sell, trade, restore, and repairs old trunks; also carries repair supplies.

Duane S. Bietz
Les Meilleurs
6461 S.E. Thorburn
Portland, OR 97215-1378
ph: 503-238-6888
fax: 503-233-1602
e-mail: dbietz@aol.com
Collects and sells hard luggage and trunks; specialty pieces, cosmetic, cigar, liquor, shoe, hat, collar, and car trunks; any Louis Vuitton memorabilia and promotional items; email or write with photos for appraisals or to sell.

Internet Resources

Churchill Barton
Brettun's Village Trunk Shop
302 Lake Street
Auburn, ME 04210
ph: 207-782-0861 or 207-782-7863
e-mail: barton@ime.net
web: http://w3.ime.net/~barton/
Web site has on-line help for do-it-yourselfers, info on trunk makers, and histories.

Repair Services

Pat
Trunk Shop, The
23 Ceres St.
Portsmouth, NH 03801
ph: 603-431-4399
fax: 603-664-9699
e-mail: pat@trunk.com
web: http://www.trunk.com
Refinishes and sells antique trunks.

Doris Harroff
AAA Antique Shop
953 W. Market
U.S. 6 West
Nappanee, IN 46550-1801
ph: 219-773-4912
Buys, sells and restores trunks.

Laurie A. Root
Original Woodworks
360 North Main St.
Stillwater, MN 55082-5024
ph: 651-430-3622
e-mail: orgwood@iaxs.net
web: http://home.iaxs.net/orgwood/
Specializing in complete antique trunk repair and restoration; will transform your trunk inside and out into a treasured family heirloom.

Flora Keen
House of Antique Trunks
753 B Northport Dr.
P.O. Box 508
West Sacramento, CA 95691-0508
ph: 916-372-8228
Antique trunk restoration parts & accessories; doll trunk supplies; chromolithographs for lids; linings, adhesives, leather; repairs.

Suppliers

Charlotte Ford Trunks
P.O. Box 536
Spearman, TX 79081
ph: 806-659-3027 or 800-553-2649
fax: 806-659-5614
e-mail: trunks@charoletteford trunks.com
web: http://www.charoletteford trunks.com
Trunk parts supplier, refinisher; publishes a 60 page parts catalog.

Muff's Antiques
135 S. Glassell St.
Orange, CA 92866-1421
ph: 714-997-0243
fax: 714-997-1601
e-mail: muffs@earthlink.net
web: http://home.earthlink/~muffs/
Buys, sells, trades, repairs old trunks; also new and old repair parts, locks, keys, supplies; catalog $5.

TUMBLERS

(see GLASSES, Drinking)

TUPPERWARE

Experts

Kip White
752 Palm Dr.
Orlando, FL 32803
A leading collector and expert on Tupperware.

Man./Prod./Dist.

Tupperware World Headquarters
14901 South Orange Blossom Trail
Orlando, FL 32837
ph: 407-826-5050 or 800-858-7221
web: http://www.tupperware.com

TURNPIKE COLLECTIBLES

(see HIGHWAY COLLECTIBLES)

TV'S

(see TELEVISION SHOWS & MEMORABILIA; TELEVISIONS)

TWINS

(see BIRTH RELATED ITEMS)

TYPEWRITERS

(see also ADDING MACHINES; ADVERTISING COLLECTIBLES, Typewriter Related; CALCULATORS; OFFICE EQUIPMENT; PRINTING EQUIPMENT)

Appraisers

Richard Polt
3800 Victory Pky.
Cincinnati, OH 45207-4443
ph: 513-745-3274
e-mail: polt@xavier.xu.edu
web: http://xavier.xu.edu/~polt/typewriters.html
Will help anyone estimate the value of an antique typewriter; web site features classified ads for typewriters and related items, repair shops around the world, typewriter history, and much more.

Book Sellers

Barbara Lippman
1216 Garden St.
Hoboken, NJ 07030-4406
ph: 201-656-5278
Selling "American Typewriters: A Collector's Encyclopedia" by the late Paul Lippman.

Clubs/Associations

Darryl Rehr, Ed.
Early Typewriter Collectors Association
Magazine: ETCetera
P.O. Box 641824
Los Angeles, CA 90064
ph: 310-477-5229
fax: 310-268-8420
e-mail: dcrehr@earthlink.net
web: http://home.earthlink.net/~dcrehr/
An international club for collectors of old office equipment; provides contact with worldwide network of over 500 members; free ads.

Collectors

Peter Frei
P.O. Box 500
Brimfield, MA 01010-0500
ph: 800-942-8968 or 413-245-4660
web: http://www.peterfrei.com/
Wants to buy hand powered vacuum cleaners, pre-1875 sewing machines, typewriters, calculators, and adding machines.

Anthony Casillo
Antique Typewriter Collecting
325 Nassau Blvd.
Garden City, NY 11530-5313
ph: 516-489-8300 or 516-742-4919
fax: 516-489-6501
e-mail: typebar@aol.com
web: http://members.aol.com/typesite
Wants to buy old, unusual typewriters; is always glad to assist anyone who has questions about an old typewriter; can date and evaluate.

Anthony Casillo
Antique Typewriting Collecting
325 Nassau Blvd.
Garden City, NY 11530-5313
ph: 516-4898-8300 or 516-742-4919
fax: 516-489-6501
e-mail: typebar@aol.com
web: http://members.aol.com/typebar/collectible/typewriter.htm
Wants early typewriters and related items including adders, checkwriters, pencil sharpeners and other early office items including advertisements.

Frank Briola
P.O. Box 44022
Pittsburgh, PA 15205-0222
ph: 412-937-8787 or 800-372-6509
e-mail: americana@mail.com
Wants early or unusual typewriters.

Howard Hazelcorn
6731 Ashley Ct.
Sarasota, FL 34241-9696
ph: 941-921-1815
Collects and specializes in early typewriters; wants to buy typewriters made between 1873 and 1910.

Jerry Propst
P.O. Box 45
Janesville, WI 53547-0045
ph: 608-752-2816
fax: 608-752-7691
When writing, please include a LSASE if requesting a reply.

Mike Brooks
7335 Skyline
Oakland, CA 94611-1121
ph: 510-339-1751
e-mail: deborahwb@aol.com
20 year collector buying early oddball typewriters, braille writers, shorthand machines and other 19th century office machines; gladly provides free appraisals by telephone; call evenings.

Jim Rauen
6937 Glenview Dr.
San Jose, CA 95120-5437
ph: 408-268-2943
fax: 408-268-5475
Collects typewriters and some related office equipment, especially pre-1900; will buy, sell, trade, and answer inquiries on typewriter history and values.

Conrad & Terry Hamil
Typewriters
615 Grandridge
Grandview, WA 98930-1542
ph: 509-882-3617
e-mail: ninwoham@quicktel.com
Wants to buy typewriters, ribbon tins, typing collectibles.

Dealers

Sandy Sellers
P.O. Box 35
Glenburnie, Ontario K0H 1S0
Canada
ph: 613-542-5598
Wants to buy old typewriters and other lettering machines and related ephemera.

Experts

Hobart D. Van Deusen
28 The Green
Watertown, CT 06795-2118
ph: 860-945-3456
e-mail: rtn.hoby@worldnet.att.net
Collects and advises on antique typewriters and typewriter-related items: blotters, carbon paper boxes, erasing shields, letter heads, rulers, letter openers, etc.

Richard Polt
Classic Typewriter Page, The
3800 Victory Pky.
Cincinnati, OH 45207-4443
ph: 513-745-3274
e-mail: polt@xavier.xu.edu
web: http://xavier.xu.edu/~polt/typewriters.html
Will help anyone estimate the value of an antique typewriter; web site features classified ads for typewriters and related items, repair shops around the world, typewriter history, and much more.

Darryl Rehr
P.O. Box 641824
Los Angeles, CA 90064
ph: 310-477-5229
fax: 310-268-8420
e-mail: dcrehr@earthlink.net
web: http://home.earthlink.net/~dcrehr/
Wants pre-1915 typewriters & related advertising, especially typewriters w/o keyboards; send SASE for free information pamphlet.

Museums/Libraries

John Lundstrom, Assoc. Cur.
Milwaukee Public Museum
800 W. Wells St.
Milwaukee, WI 53233
ph: 414-278-2702
e-mail: jl@mpm.edu
web: http://www.mpm.edu/
Museum has a large collection of antique typewriters.

Periodicals

Mike Brown
Newsletter: Typewriter Exchange, The
P.O. Box 52607
Philadelphia, PA 19115
ph: 215-934-7998 or 215-677-5879
e-mail: typex1@aol.com
web: http://freenet.tlh.fl.us/~curtis7
For collectors of early office equipment; published quarterly.

Ribbon Tins

Collectors

Millie Vaccarella
1955 Hythe St.
Roseville, MN 55113
ph: 651-631-2201
Wants to buy or trade ribbon tins.

Darryl Rehr
P.O. Box 641824
Los Angeles, CA 90064
ph: 310-477-5229
fax: 310-268-8420
e-mail: dcrehr@earthlink.net
web: http://home.earthlink.net/~dcrehr/
Wants tins of all sizes and makes, especially those with unusual shapes & graphics; any amount; send description or photocopy.

Steve Hosier
44711 N. Cedar Ave.
Lancaster, CA 93534-3210
ph: 805-946-7118
Wants typewriter ribbon tins.

Experts

Hobart D. Van Deusen
28 The Green
Watertown, CT 06795-2118
ph: 860-945-3456
e-mail: rtn.hoby@worldnet.att.net
Wants typewriter ribbon tins - small tin boxes used from 1880s to 1950 with graphic designs on them; has duplicates to sell; will help identify; also collects and advises on typewriter-related items: blotters, carbon paper boxes, etc.

Periodicals

Hobart D. Van Deusen
Newsletter: Ribbon Tin News
28 The Green
Watertown, CT 06795-2118
ph: 860-945-3456
e-mail: rtn.hoby@worldnet.att.net
Quarterly; serves as a resource for collectors looking for information, current news, exchange of views, social intercourse with fellow collectors; enhances the buying, selling, pricing typewriter ribbon tins and related items.

Here are some tips when contacting someone listed in this book:

- When requesting information about a particular item, include a description (material, dimensions, maker's mark, model number, etc.) and a photo, sketch, or photocopy of the item in question.

- Always ask if there are charges for samples or for the services requested.

- When writing, please be sure to include a Large (#10 business size) Self-Addressed and Stamped Envelope (LSASE) if requesting a reply or the return of photographs.

- Never call collect unless otherwise directed. When calling, be considerate of time zone differences and always ask if the party you are calling has time to talk. When leaving an answering machine message, always instruct the party to call you back collect.

U-Z

U.S. POSTAL SERVICE ITEMS

(see POSTAL SERVICE ITEMS; POSTCARDS, Post Office Related; STAMP COLLECTING)

UFO'S & UNEXPLAINED PHENOMENA

(see also BOOKS, Metaphysics; MAGICIANS PARAPHERNALIA; MORBID & ODD ITEMS; SCIENCE FICTION)

Collectors

Lucius Farish
2 Caney Valley Dr.
Plumerville, AR 72127-8725
ph: 501-354-2558
e-mail: ufobooks@webtv.net
Wants books, booklets, periodicals, and tapes on UFO's, extraterrestrial life, Atlantis, Bigfoot, occultism, unexplained phenomena.

Museums/Libraries

International U.F.O. Museum & Research Center
114 N. Main
P.O. Box 2221
Roswell, NM 88202-2221
ph: 505-625-9495
fax: 505-625-1907
e-mail: iufomrc@iufomrc.org
web: http://iufomrc.org/

UFO Enigma Museum
6108 S. Main
P.O. Box 6047
Roswell, NM 88202-6047
ph: 505-347-2275

Periodicals

Lucius Farish
Newsletter: UFO Newsclipping Service
2 Caney Valley Dr.
Plumerville, AR 72127-8725
ph: 501-354-2558
e-mail: ufons@webtv.net
Current press reports of UFOs/ unexplained phenomena from around the world; newsclippings compiled in 20-page monthly issues; since 1969.

UMBRELLA COVERS

Museums/Libraries

Nancy 3. Hoffman
Umbrella Cover Museum
Tower View
105 Brackett Ave.
Peaks Island, ME 04108
ph: 207-766-4496
e-mail: ucm1@aol.com
web: http://www.portlandwebsmith.com/ucmuseum
Contains a collection of umbrella covers including sheaths, wrappers and pockets; donations welcome.

UNICORNS

Collectors

Diane Stephens
e-mail: diannestephens@webtv.net
web: http://www.univorncollector.com/
Great web site for the unicorn collector: legends, images of unicorn collectibles, bookstore, links, unicorns available for online purchase, and more.

VACUUM CLEANERS

Collectors

Peter Frei
P.O. Box 500
Brimfield, MA 01010-0500
ph: 800-942-8968 or 413-245-4660
web: http://www.peterfrei.com/
Wants to buy hand powered vacuum cleaners, pre-1875 sewing machines, typewriters, calculators, and adding machines.

Robert Kautzman
Kautzman Vacuum Cleaner Repair
3509 Fairchild St.
Alburtis, PA 18011-2631
ph: 610-682-4510 or 800-830-7996
e-mail: vachunter@aol.com
Collects hand crank and pump type vacuum cleaners: water, foot, steam and hand-powered; also 1900-1930 electric upright vacuum cleaners plus tanks and hand vacuums; also wants primitive carpet stretchers and tackers; does repairs.

Billy Lipman
7428 Park Heights Ave.
Baltimore, MD 21208
ph: 410-486-1969
e-mail: inkey@erols.com
Wants to buy antique vacuum cleaners: hand-pumped and hand-cranked vacuums; also VERY EARLY electric uprights and canister vacuums; also wants parts; call or send description; all calls returned.

Roger A. Proehl
205 East Joppa Rd. #1005
Baltimore, MD 21286-3221
ph: 410-296-4545
e-mail: brendafan@aol.com
Buys, sells and trades pre-1940 vacuums; Hamilton Beach, Bee Vac, Apex, Hoover Duster; old parts needed such as bags, brushes, etc.; wants anything unusual.

Dealers

Grant Aslett
Don Aslett's Antiques
P.O. Box 39
Pocatello, ID 83204
ph: 208-232-6212
fax: 208-232-6286
Wants unique cleaning collectibles: vacuums, household items, cleaners, sweepers.

Museums/Libraries

Ann Haines, Operations
Hoover Historical Center
Newspaper: Center News
1875 Easton St. NW
Canton, OH 44720-3331
ph: 330-499-0287 or 330-499-9200
fax: 330-494-4725
web: http://www.hoovercompany.com
Restored Victorian farmhouse was boyhood home of W.H. Hoover; displays trace history of Hoover family and cleaning devices with focus on Hoover vacuum cleaner technology; herb gardens; free tours and seasonal programs.

Veronica L. Krandl
Grand Rapids Public Museum
272 Pearl St. NW
Grand Rapids, MI 49504-5371
ph: 616-456-3977
fax: 616-456-3873
e-mail: staff@grmuseum.org
web: http://www.grmuseum.org/
World's largest collection of carpet sweepers representing over 150 manufacturers worldwide; archives and advertising collection of the Bissell Carpet Sweeper Company.

Don Aslett
Don Aslett's Cleaning Museum
311 South 5th Ave.
Pocatello, ID 83201
ph: 800-451-2402
fax: 208-232-6286
web: http://www.cleanreport.com/
Wants to buy vintage vacuums, commodes, cleaners in original packaging, ads, janitorial stuff, floor polishers, brooms, brushes, buckets, mops, posters suitable for museum.

Repair Services

Robert Kautzman
Kautzman Vacuum Cleaner Repair
3509 Fairchild St.
Alburtis, PA 18011-2631
ph: 610-682-4510 or 800-830-7996
e-mail: vachunter@aol.com
Collects hand crank and pump type vacuum cleaners: water, foot, steam and hand-powered; also 1900-1930 electric upright vacuum cleaners plus tanks and hand vacuums; also wants primitive carpet stretchers and tackers; does repairs.

VACUUM TUBES

(see RADIOS, Tubes for)

VALENTINES

(see also CARDS; ELVES; HOLIDAY COLLECTIBLES; PAPER COLLECTIBLES)

Auction Services

Evalene Pulati
Pulati Auctions
P.O. Box 1404
Santa Ana, CA 92702-1404
ph: 714-547-1355

Clubs/Associations

Evalene Pulati
National Valentine Collectors Association
Newsletter: National Valentine Collectors Bulletin
P.O. Box 1404
Santa Ana, CA 92702-1404
ph: 714-547-1355
The quarterly newsletter focuses on collecting valentines; identification, values, ads.

Dealers

David & Katherine Kreider
Kingsbury Antiques
P.O. Box 7957
Lancaster, PA 17604-7957
ph: 717-892-3001

Katherine Kreider
Kingsbury Antiques
P.O. Box 7957
Lancaster, PA 17604-7957
ph: 717-892-3001
One of the largest dealers of Valentines.

Experts

Evalene Pulati
P.O. Box 1404
Santa Ana, CA 92702-1404
ph: 714-547-1355
Author of "Illustrated Valentine Price Guides", updated in 1998, now available for $16.85 ppd.

VAMPIRES

(see HORROR, Dracula)

VAUDEVILLE MEMORABILIA

Collectors

Collector
6 Chancery Ln.
Chico, CA 95926
Wants original Vaudeville sheet music, posters, photos and movie memorabilia.

VENTRILOQUIST ITEMS

(see also PUPPETS; PERFORMING ARTS)

Collectors

Peter Kidd
P.O. Box 1188
Shirley, MA 01464-1188
ph: 781-894-4040
Wants ventriloquial figures; professional, full size; age and condition not critical; high level of articulation desired.

J. Thomas
1208 Main Street North
Southbury, CT 06488
ph: 203-263-2233
fax: 203-263-2233
Wants to buy ventriloquist's dummies; child-size figures in handcarved wood, prefers with old clothing and full bodied; also wants sculptured heads; send photo and include phone contact.

T. Keppler
145 Lake Ave.
Nesconset, NY 11767-1049
ph: 516-361-4957
Wants ventriloquist dolls: Jerry Mahoney, Knucklehead Smiff, Moe Howard, and other uncommon vents.

M.A. Denemark
12 Harbor Circle
Cocoa Beach, FL 32931
Wants magazine ads with Edgar Bergen and Charlie McCarthy (Coke, GE, etc.), arcade cards, any ventriloquist item.

Andy Gross
P.O. Box 6134
Beverly Hills, CA 90212-1134
ph: 310-362-4372 or 818-765-1305
fax: 310-820-3308
e-mail: apedoll69@aol.com
web: http://www.lamagictoy.com/
Wants ventriloquist dummies, any related items such as puppets, toys, games, photos, books, marionettes, and old pro & toy dummies, i.e. Jerry Mahoney, Knucklehead Smiff, Charlie McCarthy, Mortimer Snerd, Danny O'Day, Farfel, etc.

Museums/Libraries

Anne Roberts
Vent Haven Museum, The
33 West Maple Ave.
Ft. Mitchell, KY 41011-2616
ph: 606-341-0461
e-mail: info@venthaven.com
web: http://www.venthaven.com/
The museum is a collection of over 800 ventriloquist figures, pictures, playbills and memorabilia that is open to the public from May to September for guided tours by advanced appointment only.

VETERAN ITEMS

(see also BADGES; INDIAN WARS ITEMS; MEDALS, ORDERS & DECORATIONS; MILITARIA)

Civil War

Clubs/Associations

Andrew Johnson, CIC
Sons of Union Veterans of the Civil War
e-mail: amjohnson@juno.com
web: http://suvcw.org

Maitland Westbrook, Ex. Dir.
Sons of Confederate Veterans
P.O. Box 59
Columbia, TN 38402-0059
ph: 800-380-1896
fax: 931-381-6712
e-mail: exedir@scv.org
web: http://www.scv.org

Roger L. Heiple, Sec.
Civil War Veterans Historical Association
Newsletter: Veteran, The
P.O. Box 16
South Lyon, MI 48178
e-mail: mistergar@voyager.net
web: http://pages.prodigy.com/CGBD86A/garhp.htm
For those interested in preserving the memory of Union and Confederate veterans of the American Civil War; also memorabilia.

Collectors

Julie Brighenti
1036 Rostraver Rd.
Belle Vernon, PA 15012
ph: 724-929-7311
Wants Grand Army of the Republic items: badges, ribbons, canes, glass, gold testimonial badges, etc.; also W.R.C. and G.A.R. items.

Rance Hulshart
4000 Old Orchard Rd.
York, PA 17402
ph: 717-755-5334
Avid collector and scholar on Civil War veterans - their history, activities, organizations and related memorabilia.

David J. Maloney, Jr., ISA CAPP
P.O. Box 2049
Frederick, MD 21702-1049
ph: 301-695-8544
fax: 301-695-6491
e-mail: dave@maloney.com
web: http://www.maloney.com/
Wants Union and Confederate veteran-related items: Grand Army of the Republic, United Confederate Veterans, WRC, SUV; any related item.

Peggy Dillard
P.O. Box 210904
Nashville, TN 37221-0904
ph: 615-646-1605
Wants Confederate Veterans Reunion items.

Don Limpert
P.O. Box 524
Manchester, MI 48158
ph: 734-428-7400

Dealers

Charles Brecheisen
Trans-Mississippi Militaria
1004 Simon Drive
Plano, TX 75025-2501
ph: 972-517-8111
fax: 972-517-8111
e-mail: charlucv@flash.net
web: http://www.transmississippi.com
Buys, sells, trades anything to do with the Civil War, with a specialty in Civil War medical items: UCV, GAR, reunion items, paper, relics, photographs.

Experts

Roger L. Heiple
P.O. Box 16
South Lyon, MI 48178
e-mail: mistergar@voyager.net
web: http://pages.prodigy.com/CGBD86A/garhp.htm

Internet Resources

Roger L. Heiple, Sec.
Grand Army of the Republic Home Page
P.O. Box 16
South Lyon, MI 48178
e-mail: mistergar@voyager.net
web: http://pages.prodigy.com/CGBD86A/garhp.htm

Museums/Libraries

Grand Army of the Republic Civil War Museum & Library
4278 Griscom St.
Philadelphia, PA 19124-3954
ph: 215-289-6484
e-mail: garmuslib@aol.com
web: http://suvcw.org/garmus.htm
Civil War Museum & Library; artifacts, personal memorabilia, paintings, G.A.R. & S.U.V.C.W. records; open first Sunday or by appt.

Wisconsin Veterans Museum, The
30 W. Mifflin St.
Madison, WI 53707-7843
ph: 608-264-6086
e-mail: museum@mail.state.wi.us
web: http://badger.state.wi.us/agencies/dva/museum/wvmmain.html
Tells the story of men and women from the Badger State who served in America's conflicts from the Civil War to the Persian Gulf War; great collection of GAR memorabilia.

Paula Nelson
G.A.R. Hall & Museum/Meeker County Historical Society
Newsletter: G.A.R. Hall & Museum Newsletter
308 Marshall Ave. N
Litchfield, MN 55355
ph: 320-693-8911
Grand Army of the Republic (GAR) Hall built in 1885 by Union Veterans of the Civil War; maintained by Meeker Historical Society.

Grand Army of the Republic Memorial Museum
629 S. Seventh St.
Springfield, IL 62703
ph: 217-522-4373

Periodicals

Rance Hulshart
Newsletter: Campfire Chatter
4000 Old Orchard Rd.
York, PA 17402
ph: 717-755-5334
A 12-page newsletter published four times each year; focuses on all aspects of Civil War veteran activities with a focus on Union Civil War veteran memorabilia.

VETERINARY MEDICINE ITEMS

Auction Services

Mike Smith, D.V.M.
7431 Covington Highway
Lithonia, GA 30058-7611
ph: 770-482-5100 or 770-979-3239
fax: 770-484-1304
e-mail: petvetmike@aol.com
Conducts periodic auctions of animal and veterinary medicine collectibles.

Clubs/Associations

Mike Smith, D.V.M.
Veterinary Collectibles Roundtable
Newsletter: Veterinary Collectibles Roundtable Newsletter
7431 Covington Highway
Lithonia, GA 30058-7611
ph: 770-482-5100 or 770-979-3239
fax: 770-484-1304
e-mail: petvetmike@aol.com
Seeking collectors and consignors for newsletter and twice-yearly auctions of antique veterinary patent medicines and advertising; for collectors of

animal or veterinary medicine antiques.

Collectors

Dr. Fred Cesana
49 E. Main St.
Plainville, CT 06062
ph: 860-747-2759
Wants pre-1930 veterinary advertising items, cabinets, bottles with labels, etc.

Paul Ferraglio
3332 W. Lake Rd.
Canandaigua, NY 14424-2441
ph: 716-394-7663
fax: 716-394-5424
e-mail: p4alyo@aol.com
Wants to buy veterinary medicine items: old surgical instruments, animal medicine bottles and tins, pamphlets, display cabinets, signs.

Mike Smith, D.V.M.
7431 Covington Highway
Lithonia, GA 30058-7611
ph: 770-482-5100 or 770-979-3239
fax: 770-484-1304
e-mail: petvetmike@aol.com
Wants to buy animal and veterinary medicine collectibles.

Dealers

Willisia Holbrook
Armbrook Antiques
531 Doub Rd.
Lewisville, NC 27023
ph: 888-393-8025 or 336-945-9477
fax: 336-945-9914
e-mail: olestuff@armbrookantiques.com
web: http://www.armbrookantiques.com
Buys and sells early veterinarian antiques; specializes in pre-1930s items; web site has full online catalog including descriptions and photos.

Barbara Cole
October Farm
2609 Branch Rd.
Raleigh, NC 27610-9213
ph: 919-772-0482
fax: 919-779-6265
e-mail: octoberfarm@bellsouth.net
web: http://www.octoberfarm.com/
Buys and sells horse books and paper ephemera, especially relating to polo, carriages & driving, Morgan horses, American Saddlebred horses, and veterinary medicine; also old farm horse equipment and catalogs; mail order only.

Trenton Boyd
P.O. Box 517
Columbia, MO 65205-0517
ph: 573-882-2461 or 573-442-5235
fax: 573-882-2950
e-mail: vetlib@showme.missouri.edu
Interested in veterinary postcards including schools and military veterinary; also wants teratology cards that show animals with birth defects (e.g. five-legged calves); Red Cross dogs, Humane Association.

VIETNAM ITEMS

(see also MILITARIA; SOCIAL CAUSES, Hippie Items)

Collectors

Sylvia Marcotte-Cloutier
Sylvia Charles of Blythe
218 W. Hobson Way
Blythe, CA 92225-1619
ph: 619-922-3456
fax: 619-922-5651
Wants 1960 to 1970 material relating to Viet Nam, counterculture organizations, Civil Rights: diaries, letters, signed books, letters from military men sent home; documents, photos of sit-ins, marches, riots, demonstrations, etc.

Periodicals

Cowles Magazines, Inc.
Magazine: Vietnam
741 Miller Dr. SE, Ste. D2
Harrisburg, PA 20175
ph: 717-540-6617 or 800-829-3340
fax: 717-540-6706
e-mail: brentd@cowles.com
web: http://www.cowles.com/maglist.html
Covers the controversial Vietnam War from many perspectives for both veterans of the war and students of military and political history; published bi-monthly.

Clem Kelly
Newsletter: Vietnam Insignia Collectors Newsletter
501 West 5th Ave.
Covington, LA 70433
A bi-monthly publication of 9 pages concerned with the history and collectibles of the Vietnam War; include is one page of free ads from collectors and dealers.

VIEW BOOKS

(see ALBUMS; PAPER COLLECTIBLES)

VIEW-MASTERS

(see 3-D PHOTOGRAPHICA, View-Masters)

VINTAGE CLOTHING

(see CLOTHING & ACCESSORIES, Vintage)

VIOLINS

(see MUSICAL INSTRUMENTS, String [Violins])

VISUAL AIDS

(see OPTICAL ITEMS)

VOLKSWAGEN RELATED ITEMS

Collectors

Frank Konisky
RD 2 Third Ave. Extension
Rensselaer, NY 12144
ph: 518-465-0477
e-mail: pplkars@aol.com
Wants Volkswagon toys, models, etc.

Dan Morris
1225 Ramblewood Dr.
Annapolis, MD 21401
ph: 410-757-6430
e-mail: epstein73@aol.com
Collects European car club badges and vintage Volkswagon accessories.

Melissa Jess
3121 East Yucca St.
Phoenix, AZ 85028-2616
ph: 602-867-7672
fax: 602-867-7672
e-mail: vwstuff@juno.com
web: http://www.mindspring.com/~deasterw/jess/jess.html
Wants Volkswagen related items: models, literature, accessories, postcards, dealer items, Herbie Lovebug, VW memorabilia, etc.

Mike Wilson
23490 S.W. 82nd
Tualatin, OR 97062-9613
ph: 503-638-7074
fax: 503-638-6654
e-mail: rennopup@msn.com
Wants Volkswagen toys, memorabilia, literature, etc.

WAGONS

(see BICYCLES & RELATED MEMORABILIA; HORSE-DRAWN VEHICLES; RIDING TOYS)

WALKING STICKS

(see CANES & WALKING STICKS)

WALL POCKETS

Clubs/Associations

Janet Hausher
Wall Pocket Collectors Club
1356 Tahiti
Saint Louis, MO 63128
ph: 314-821-2745

Collectors

Bobbie & Alan Bryson
1 St. Eleanoras Ln.
Tuckahoe, NY 10707-1307
ph: 914-779-1405
e-mail: napkindoll@aol.com
Wants to buy glass wall pockets.

Experts

Pam Brin
8 Park Lane
Minneapolis, MN 55416-4340
ph: 612-920-3030
fax: 612-920-3031
e-mail: PGBallery@pbgallery.com
web: http://www.pbgallery.com

WALL STREET

(see STOCKS & BONDS, Financial History)

WALLACE NUTTING

(see also FURNITURE [ANTIQUE], Wallace Nutting; PRINTS, Wallace Nutting)

Auction Services

Michael Ivanovich
Ivankovich Antiques, Inc.
P.O. Box 2458
Doylestown, PA 18901-0760
ph: 215-345-6094
fax: 215-345-6692
e-mail: wnutting@comcat.com
web: http://www.wnutting.com
Largest auction service for Wallace Nutting prints, books and furniture; conducts 3-4 auctions/yr., each with 300-500 Wallace Nutting pictures.

Clubs/Associations

Bill Hamann
Wallace Nutting Collectors Club
Newsletter: Wallace Nutting Collectors Newsletter
P.O. Box 22475
Cleveland, OH 44122
e-mail: billhamann@aol.com
Helps members learn more about Wallace Nutting, the man and his works; please include a SASE when requesting a reply.

Dealers

Sharon Lacasse
Sharon Lacasse Antiques
1424 Osterville - W. Barnstable Rd.
West Barnstable, MA 02668
ph: 508-428-0562
e-mail: slacasse@capecod.net
web: http://www.capecod.net/wnutting/
Buying and selling pictures, books, furniture and all memorabilia relating to Wallace Nutting.

Experts

Michael Ivanovich
Michael Ivankovich Antiques, Inc.
P.O. Box 2458
Doylestown, PA 18901-0760
ph: 215-345-6094
fax: 215-345-6692
e-mail: wnutting@comcat.com
web: http://www.wnutting.com
Wants pictures, books, furniture; leading collector; conducts auctions of Wallace Nutting items; author of books on Nutting; also pictures that resemble Wallace Nutting works, e.g. those by Fred Thompson, David Davidson, Chas. Sawyer

Internet Resources

Jan K. Lineratore
Wallace Nutting Center, The
e-mail: nutting@www.wallacenutting.com
web: http://www.wallacenutting.com/
Great online Wallace Nutting resource: classifieds, furniture, letters, picture gallery, research material, chat.

WALLETS

(see BUSINESS CARD HOLDERS)

WARBIRDS

(see AVIATION, Military)

WASHING MACHINES

(see also ENGINES, Gasoline; MAYTAG)

Experts

Robert Seger
4351 Harriet Ave., S.
Minneapolis, MN 55409
ph: 612-822-3534 or 612-823-2388
e-mail: unimatic00@aol.com
Collector of and expert in early automatic clothes washing machines from the mid-1940s to the early 1960s; wants to buy vintage machines, parts and literature.

Lee Maxwell
35901 WCR 31
Eaton, CO 80615
ph: 907-454-3856
e-mail: oldewash@aol.com
web: http://www.oldewash.com/
Collector, appraiser of old washing machines, has collection of over 700 pre-1940 washing machines having wooden, copper or galvanized tubs; send pictures & description; condition not important so long as the machine is complete.

WATCH FOBS

Clubs/Associations

R.J. Rothlisberger
Midwest Watch Fob Collectors, Inc.
Newsletter: Watch Fob Collectors Newsletter
11895 Highway 99
Burlington, IA 52601-8521
ph: 319-752-6749
A group organized to preserve, collect and educate themselves about strap advertising watch fobs.

International Watch Fob Association, Inc.
Newsletter: International Watch Fob Association Newsletter
601 Patriot Place
Holmen, WI 54636
ph: 608-526-2328
e-mail: info@watchfob.com
web: http://www.watchfob.com/
Focus is on strap-type watch fobs; members receive 2 fobs and 2 newsletter per year; membership roster available; annual show in the Cleveland, OH area.

William "Bill" Mitchell
Canadian Association of Watch Fob Collectors
2 Elm Drive
Stoney Cree, Ontario L8G 3B4
Canada
ph: 905-664-4576
e-mail: mitchfobs@aol.com
Dedicated to the collection and preservation of advertising-type watch fobs.

Collectors

John Cline
609 N. East St.
Carlisle, PA 17013-2012
ph: 717-249-4253
Wants road or farm machinery-related fobs, or fobs advertising fur, traps, powder and gun companies.

Gary Call
259 South 3rd St.
Pocatello, ID 83201-6442
ph: 208-232-0228
e-mail: mrfob@webtv.net
Wants to buy any strap-type advertising watch fobs that are home product related including food and drink products; also wants livestock commission and livestock related fobs, and silo and grain elevator fobs.

Advertising

Dealers

Dave Beck
P.O. Box 435
Mediapolis, IA 52637-0435
ph: 319-394-3943
fax: 319-394-3943
Buys and sells advertising watch fobs, mirrors and pin-backs; send stamp for illustrated mail auction catalog.

Machinery & Equipment

Collectors

John Leite, Jr.
44 Glenwood Rd.
Brewster, MA 02631-2202
ph: 508-385-4905
Wants to buy watch fobs dealing with heavy equipment and trucking.

WATCH HOLDERS

Collectors

John Michels
1658 Hardwick Rd.
Baltimore, MD 21286-8128
ph: 410-825-3636
Wants to buy watch holders; send picture and price; photos will be returned.

WATCHES

(see also BOOKS, Reference [Watches]; CLOCKS; GEMS & JEWELRY; INSTRUMENTS & DEVICES, Scientific; WATCH FOBS; WATCH HOLDERS)

Auction Services

George Horan
Jones & Horan Auction Team
453 Mast Rd.
Goffstown, NH 03045
ph: 603-625-5314

Robert Schmidt
R.O. Schmidt Fine Arts
P.O. Box 1941
Salem, NH 03079
ph: 603-893-5915
fax: 603-893-9777
e-mail: roschmit@worldnet.att.net
web: http://www.pricelessads.com/roschmit/index.htm

Clubs/Associations

Jon Hanson, Pres.
Early American Watch Club
P.O. Box 81555
Wellesley Hills, MA 02481-1333
A specialty chapter within the National Association of Watch & Clock Collectors, Inc.; focuses on early American watches.

Paul Wadsworth, Pres.
American Watchmakers Institute
64 South Ave.
P.O. Box 933
Hilton, NY 14468
A specialty chapter within the National Association of Watch & Clock Collectors, Inc.

Thomas J. Bartels, ExDir
National Association of Watch & Clock Collectors, Inc.
Magazine: Bulletin of the NAWCC
514 Poplar St.
Columbia, PA 17512-2130
ph: 717-684-8261
fax: 717-684-0878
e-mail: patti@nawcc.org
web: http://www.nawcc.org
The NAWCC is a non-profit and scientific association founded in 1943 and now serving the horological interests of 38,000 members worldwide.

American Watchmakers-Clockmakers Institute
Magazine: Horological Times
701 Enterprise Dr.
Harrison, OH 45030-1696
ph: 513-367-9800
fax: 513-367-1414
e-mail: awi-info@awi-net.org
web: http://www.awi-net.org
For those interested in horology as a profession or avocation; monthly technical magazine, technical bulletins, training, public relations, networking.

British Watch & Clock Collectors Association
5 Cathedral Lane
Truro, Cornwall TR1 2SQ
U.K.
ph: +44 01872 41953
e-mail: FMMatEZI@aol.com
Geared mainly to the collector, but also solicits membership from restorers and repairers.

Collectors

Bob Arnell
P.O. Box 313
Grandview, MO 64030-0313
ph: 816-966-0544 or 816-213-4999
e-mail: bobstuff11@excite.com
Wants to buy wrist and pocket watches.

Dealers

Robert Beaver
Classic Touch Antiques
P.O. Box 27
Newport, RI 02840-0001
ph: 401-849-1717 or 401-846-9663
fax: 401-849-1717
Buys and sells early and complicated watches, wrist and pocket.

Irv Temes
Temes & Co.
338 N. Charles St.
Baltimore, MD 21201
ph: 800-722-5274 or 410-347-7600
fax: 410-685-3299
Buyers of high quality wrist watches and pocket watches, especially Rolex, Patek Philippe, Vacheron, Cartier, Tiffany, etc.; all conditions; please call or write for offer; member

Jewelers Board of Trade, our 19th year.

Peter Thurber
Ritzi & Thurber, Inc.
160 S. Beach St.
Daytona Beach, FL 32114
ph: 904-252-2552 or 904-226-8489
fax: 904-226-8490
e-mail: ritzi1881@earthlink.net
web: http://www.ritzi-thurber.com/
Founded in 1881, restorations and repairs are done to all watches on premises; fine mechanical wrist and pocket watches are purchased as well as watches for parts; carries a selection of pre-owned Rolex and other brands.

Ed London
Parke Lloyds International, Inc.
9408 NW 70 St.
Fort Lauderdale, FL 33321-3002
ph: 954-724-4274 or 954-726-4107
Buys watches.

Don Baker
Finer Times Vintage Timepieces
P.O. Box 273020
Tampa, FL 33688
ph: 813-963-5757
fax: 813-960-5676
e-mail: dontime@mindspring.com
web: http://www.finertimes.com
Buys and sells a large selection of vintage timepieces online: Rolex, Omega, LeCoultre, Hamilton, etc.; also sells a fine selection of horological related books and accessories.

Bill Marshall
Marshall Vintage Timepieces
255 Hiway Drive
Clinton, TN 37716-4431
ph: 888-267-4886
fax: 423-457-0051
e-mail: bill@timepast.com
web: http://www.timepast.com
Dealer, expert and repairer of vintage wrist and pocket watches.

Chris Hooper
www.chronometer.net
910 NLSD
Chicago, IL 60611
ph: 312-587-3219
e-mail: chris@chronometer.net
web: http://www.chronometer.net
Buys and sells vintage timepieces including pocket watches, wrist watches, marine chronometers, and ships' clocks.

Ron Geweniger
Old World Jewelers Ltd.
7438 W. North Ave.
Elmwood Park, IL 60707
ph: 708-456-7730 or 800-322-3871
e-mail: owltd@ix.netcom.com
web: http://www.antiqnet.com/oldworld/
Dealers in fine antique and estate jewelry and timepieces for over 20 years; featuring toy Swiss made watches; also new watches.

Maundy International
P.O. Box 13028 - RM
Shawnee Mission, KS 66212-3028
ph: 800-235-2866
Watches - buying Patek Philippe pocket & wrist watches and fine watches from USA & Europe; since 1976; specializes in railroad pocket watches.

Mike Stute
World Wide Watch Brokers
626 Meadowbrooke
Duncanville, TX 75137
ph: 972-709-7960
e-mail: lilthug@metronet.com
web: http://www.worldwidewatches.com
Selling all types of vintage and new wrist watches and pocket watches.

Robert M. Wingate
Wingate's Quality Watches
P.O. Box 59760
Dallas, TX 75229
ph: 800-842-8625 or 972-392-7676
fax: 972-392-2304
e-mail: wingates@tic-tock.com
web: http://www.tic-tock.com
Specializes in the purchase, sale and restoration of antique watches; in business since 1976.

Tim Sweet
M.O.S.T. Watch & Clock Co.
3010 Forest Trail
San Angelo, TX 76904
ph: 915-947-8196
e-mail: timekeep@gte.net
web: http://www.tritco.com/most/most1.html
Dealer, collector, expert, auction and repair services, appraiser offering all aspects of antique clock and watch services; website has an Internet Horology Club.

Paul K. Lonnquist
Texas Time
3076 Wauneta St.
Newbury Park, CA 91320
ph: 805-498-5644 or 805-480-2107
fax: 805-480-9514
e-mail: paul@dock.net
web: http://www.texastime.com/
Buys, sells, trades vintage watches, specializing in the more affordable brands; on the Internet for over 3 years.

Howard Markham
Howard Markham Professional Numismatist
5225 Canyon Crest Dr., Bldg 200, Ste. 254
Riverside, CA 92507-6301
ph: 909-686-2122 or 800-953-3027
Buys old pocket watches, either one piece or entire collections; wants railroad watches, wrist watches, older Rolex, Patek, Vacheron, etc.; will travel to buy larger collections.

Don Levison
Don Levison Antiques
P.O. Box 22262
San Francisco, CA 94122
ph: 415-753-0455
fax: 415-753-5206
e-mail: dlevison@juno.com
web: http://www.antiquehorology.com
Buys and sells antique and better quality pocket and wrist watches, clocks, music boxes, singing birds, and other small automata; also mercury barometers from the 17th century to present.

Steve Bogoff
Bogoff Antique Timepieces
P.O. Box 408
Mill Valley, CA 94942
ph: 415-383-8100
fax: 415-383-8112
e-mail: info@bogoff.com
web: http://www.bogoff.com
Buys, sells, appraises and has on-line catalog of complicated, rare, early, unusual, beautiful pocket watches, vintage wrist watches, small clocks, singing bird boxes and more.

Dave Morris
3388 Merlin Rd., Ste. 351
Grants Pass, OR 97526
ph: 541-955-8411
e-mail: dave@wattpottery.com
web: http://www.wattpottery.com
Wants to buy wrist and pocket watches, watch fobs, and any other related merchandise including parts, tools, paper ephemera.

Gloria Dekter
Ashton-Blakey Antiques & Collectibles
6021 Yonge St., Ste. 895
Toronto, Ontario M2M 3W2
Canada
ph: 905-886-5122
fax: 905-886-8566
e-mail: ashtonb@netcom.ca
web: http://www.ashton-blakey-antiques.com
A complete internet shop specializing in vintage wrist watches, antique pocket watches, watch fobs, chains; web site contains images of all items; also specializes in scientific instruments.

Johnny Wachsmann
Pieces of Time
1 - 7 Davies Mews
London, W1Y 1AR
U.K.
ph: (44) 171 629 2422 or (44) 171 629 3272
fax: (44) 171 409 1625
e-mail: info@antique-watch.com
web: http://www.antique-watch.com
One of London's leading dealers in antique, precision and pocket watches; has one of the largest specialist antique internet sites in the world; has produced a quarterly catalog since 1984.

Experts

Philip M. Poniz
European Watch & Casemakers, Ltd.
P.O. Box 1314
Highland Park, NJ 08904-1314
ph: 732-777-0111
fax: 732-777-0118
e-mail: horology@webspan.net
Does history and sales research on antique watches, clocks, musical boxes, and unusual mechanical objects of virtu.

Arthur Guy Kaplan
P.O. Box 1942
Baltimore, MD 21203
ph: 410-752-2090 or 410-664-8350
fax: 410-783-2723
Author of "The Official Price Guide to Antique Jewelry."

Joe Cohen
4250 Galt Ocean Dr., Apt. 9A
Oakland Park, FL 33308
ph: 954-561-2234
Specializing in 17th, 18th, and 19th century clocks and watches.

Cooksey Shugart
P.O. Box 3147
Cleveland, TN 37320-3147
ph: 423-479-4813
fax: 423-479-4813
Author of "The Complete Price Guide to Watches", an annual price guide and mini encyclopedia for watch terminology; includes history of past watch manufacturers.

Museums/Libraries

Nancy Connelly
American Clock & Watch Museum
Journal: Timepiece Journal
100 Maple St.
Bristol, CT 06010-5034
ph: 860-583-6070
fax: 860-583-1862
web: http://www.pricelessads.com/acwmuseum/
Preserves the history of American horology, especially Connecticut and Bristol's role; large displays of clocks & watches.

Patricia Tomes, Cur.
National Association of Watch & Clock Collectors Museum, Inc., The
514 Poplar St.
Columbia, PA 17512-2130
ph: 717-684-8261
fax: 717-684-0878
e-mail: patti@nawcc.org
web: http://www.nawcc.org
The Watch & Clock Museum of the NAWCC strives to illustrate the history of timekeeping from the 1600's to the present with a collection of more than 8000 horological items.

Periodicals

Magazine: Watch & Clock Review
2403 Champa St.
Denver, CO 80205-2621
ph: 303-296-1600
fax: 303-295-2159
Monthly magazine primarily for new and vintage watch and clock retailers; features articles on watches, clocks and shops; also ads for buyers, sellers, and restorers.

Magazine: Chronos
2403 Champa St.
Denver, CO 80205-2621
ph: 303-296-1600
fax: 303-295-2159
A quarterly publication primarily for the collector of fine timepieces, especially wrist watches.

Repair Services

Philip M. Poniz
European Watch & Casemakers, Ltd.
P.O. Box 1314
Highland Park, NJ 08904-1314
ph: 732-777-0111
fax: 732-777-0118
e-mail: horology@webspan.net
Restoration of watches, clocks, and music boxes; museum experience; can make any part and restore any watch; clients include Sotheby's, Cartier, collectors in USA, Asia and Europe; appraises, researches, lectures on watch making, fakes.

Kenzie Smith
Clock Shop, The
119 East St.
Frederick, MD 21701
ph: 301-698-8252
Repairs and restores all mechanical clocks and watches; references upon request.

Ferenc Bitt
European Watchworks, The
202 Loft Lane #185
Raleigh, NC 27609
ph: 919-845-4355 or 919-844-2878
e-mail: watchmaker@europeanwatchworks.com
web: http://www.europeanwatchworks.com/
Specializes in the repair and restoration of fine and antique watches; Bitt is a Hungarian watchmaker educated in the old world model of European craftsmanship; over 25 years experience

Sellers Watch Repair
163 Harper Rd.
Atlanta, GA 30315
ph: 404-627-1581
Expert watch repair.

Peter Thurber
Ritzi & Thurber, Inc.
160 S. Beach St.
Daytona Beach, FL 32114
ph: 904-252-2552 or 904-226-8489
fax: 904-226-8490
e-mail: ritzi1881@earthlink.net
web: http://www.ritzi-thurber.com/
Founded in 1881, restorations and repairs are done to all watches on premises; fine mechanical wrist and pocket watches are purchased as well as watches for parts; carries a selection of pre-owned Rolex and other brands.

Felix Zaltsberg
Right Time International Watch Center
1485 S. Colorado Blvd.
Denver, CO 80222
ph: 888-TIME-388 or 303-691-2521
fax: 303-782-9316
e-mail: felix@righttime.com
web: http://RightTime.com
A pre-owned and antique watch superstore; buys, trades, restores watches worldwide; four certified master watchmakers on premises to restore your favorite antique watch of clock; one year warranty on workmanship.

Swiss Watch Services, Inc.
1402 Third Ave., Ste. 714
Seattle, WA 98101
ph: 206-622-3643
fax: 206-622-7927
Complete overhauls, makes custom dials with diamonds, names, pictures; cuts crystals; specializing in all Swiss watches including Patek Philippe, Rolex, Audemars Piguet, Cartier, Movado, Piaget, Longines, etc.

Suppliers

Rick Dunnuck, VP
S. LaRose, Inc.
3223 Yanceyville St.
P.O. Box 21208
Greensboro, NC 27420-1208
ph: 336-621-1936
fax: 336-621-0706
e-mail: slarose@worldnet.att.net
web: http://www.slarose.com
Supplier of clock and watch parts.

Advertising

Dealers

Maggie Kenyon
M. Kenyon Co.
One Christopher St. 14-G
New York, NY 10014-3581
ph: 212-675-3213
e-mail: mke1629869@aol.com
Buying, selling, collecting comic/ character watches for over 30 years; included are sports, political and product promotion watches in addition to all comic watches; interested in all regardless of age; send SASE.

Periodicals

Sharon Iranpour
Newsletter: Premium Watch Watch, The
24 San Rafael Dr.
Rochester, NY 14618-3702
ph: 716-381-9467
fax: 716-383-9248
e-mail: siranpour@aol.com
Bi-monthly newsletter: a guide to the newest advertising and logo watches; promotional, advertising and character watch news; send LSASE for sample.

Character/Comic

Collectors

Arthur Moore
1004 Cheyenne Blvd.
Madison, TN 37115-4212
ph: 615-865-4806
e-mail: chance1@bellsouth.net
Wants to buy comic character and advertising watches in any condition.

David Welch
P.O. Box 714
Murphysboro, IL 62966-0714
ph: 618-687-2282
fax: 618-684-2243
e-mail: PezDude1@aol.com
Wants pre-1980 watches/clocks relating to sports, TV, cartoon, comic, movie characters with original boxes ONLY; also wants empty boxes; no political, please.

Dealers

Maggie Kenyon
M. Kenyon Co.
One Christopher St. 14-G
New York, NY 10014-3581
ph: 212-675-3213
e-mail: mke1629869@aol.com
Buying, selling, collecting comic/ character watches for over 30 years; included are sports, political and product promotion watches in addition to all comic watches; interested in all regardless of age; send SASE.

Experts

Norm Vigue
62 Bailey St.
Stoughton, MA 02072
ph: 781-344-5441
Want mint boxed character watches; also point-of-sale signs for same.

Man./Prod./Dist.

John J. Matteo, Jr.
Collectible Watch Co., Inc.
1100 Montrose Ave.
Charlottesville, VA 22902-6236
ph: 888-846-3101 or 804-984-5005
fax: 804-984-2777
e-mail: jdematteo@collectiblewatch.com
web: http://www.collectiblewatch.com
Producer of fine time pieces for the serious collector; limited edition writs and pocket watches; new collector tips every month; sports, historical, character.

Merk Harbour
Fossil
2115 Campbell Creek
Richardson, TX 75082
ph: 800-842-8621
e-mail: webguy@fossil.com
web: http://www.fossil.com/
Manufacturer of limited edition, collectible, and antique-looking classic watches and character watches including Roy Rogers and Superman.

Periodicals

Sharon Iranpour
Newsletter: Premium Watch Watch, The
24 San Rafael Dr.
Rochester, NY 14618-3702
ph: 716-381-9467
fax: 716-383-9248
e-mail: siranpour@aol.com
Bi-monthly newsletter: a guide to the newest advertising and logo watches; promotional, advertising and character watch news; send LSASE for sample.

Computer Programs For

Man./Prod./Dist.

John Christians
WatchWare
4130 Terrace Drive
Anchorage, AK 99502
ph: 907-243-8894
e-mail: watch@alaska.net
web: http://www.alaska.net/~watch/
Horological software for collectors or businesses; keep track of your collections with easy-to-use software; print reports for quick reference.

Dials

Repair Services

International Dial Co., Inc.
P.O. Box 970
Wilmington, OH 45177-2226
ph: 937-382-4535

Kirk Rich Dial Corporation
404 W. 7th St., Ste. 1215
Los Angeles, CA 90014
ph: 213-626-6840

Electric (Hamilton)

Dealers

Rene Rondeau
Rene Rondeau Hamilton Electric Watches
P.O. Box 391
Corte Madera, CA 94976-0391
ph: 415-924-6534
fax: 415-924-8423
e-mail: rene@rondeau.net
web: http://rondeau.net/
Buys, sells, and repairs Hamilton electric wrist watches from the 1950s and 1960s; author of "The Watch of

the Future", 2nd edition, hb, 168 pgs, 6"x9".

Pocket

Clubs/Associations

Clint Geller, Sec.
Pocket Horology
6347 Edby St.
Pittsburgh, PA 15217
ph: 412-521-8092
e-mail: CBGeller@aol.com
web: http://www.pricelessads.com/nawcc174/

Dealers

Alan Altman
It's About Time
96 Harmati Lane
P.O. Box 537
Bearsville, NY 12409-0537
ph: 914-679-2832
fax: 914-679-2832
e-mail: alanalt@ibm.net
web: http://bearsystems.com/time/
Buys and sells American and European pocket watches; call 800-399-0066 for orders only.

Stephen Miles
Miles Pocketwatches
P.O. Box 366
Philmont, VA 20131
ph: 540-338-5482
fax: 540-338-5483
e-mail: mileswatch@aol.com
web: http://www.miles-pocketwatches.com
Internet site for the selling of American and European pocket watches; specializing in complications such as repeaters and calendar watches.

Pat Gurley
Pat's Pocket Watches
744 N. Edward St.
Decatur, IL 62522
ph: 217-422-4427 or 217-875-9662
e-mail: pgurley@fgi.net
web: http://www.pocketwatch.com
Carries a great selection of railroad grade pocket watches; all original antiques; Ball, Elgin, Waltham, Illinois, Rockford, Hamilton, Howard, Hampden, and many others.

Manny & Liz Trauring
Modesto Horology
2900 Standiford Ave., #16B-318
Modesto, CA 95356
ph: 209-579-2824
fax: 209-579-0901
e-mail: watches@modesto-horology.com
web: http://www.modesto-horology.com
Among the world's leading horological dealers; offers a large selection of pocket watches and other horological items; see website for online catalog.

Robert Young
Pocket Watch.UK, The
U.K.
ph: 01795-843985
fax: 01795-843985
e-mail: info@PocketWatch.co.uk
web: http://freespace.virgin.net/robert.young10/
Specialist mail order dealers buying and selling the finest of antique and vintage pocket watches from England and Europe; also sells antique pocket watch stands.

Pocket Watch Stands

Dealers

Robert Young
Pocket Watch.UK, The
U.K.
ph: 01795-843985
fax: 01795-843985
e-mail: info@PocketWatch.co.uk
web: http://freespace.virgin.net/robert.young10/index4.html
Specialist mail order dealer in fine antique pocket watches stands.

Swatch

Clubs/Associations

Swatch Collectors Club, The
P.O. Box 7400
Melville, NY 11747-7400
ph: 800-U4S-WATC
web: http://www.swatch.com
Club for collectors of any Swatch-manufactured item such as watches, bicycles, sunglasses, wall hangings, telephones, and (in the future) automobiles; also sponsors a traveling Swatch museum.

Collectors

Carl F. Pflanzer
50 Gates Ave.
Gillette, NJ 07933
fax: 732-424-7814
e-mail: carl@njsystems.com
Wants Swatch watches and Swatch clothing; must be in excellent condition.

Timex

Appraisers

Carl Rosa
P.O. Box 310
Post Road Extension
Middlebury, CT 06762-0310
ph: 203-573-5714 or 800-225-7742
fax: 203-573-5139
e-mail: crosa@timexpo.com
web: http://www.timexpo.com/
Collector and appraiser of Timex watches, Ingersoll watches, Waterbury clocks and related memorabilia; also director and curator of the Timexpo Museum.

Museums/Libraries

Carl Rosa
Timexpo Museum
P.O. Box 310
Post Road Extension
Middlebury, CT 06762-0310
ph: 203-573-5714 or 800-225-7742
fax: 203-573-5139
e-mail: crosa@timexpo.com
web: http://www.timexpo.com/

Wrist

Collectors

Marc L. Ames
539 Lyme Rock Rd.
Bridgewater, NJ 08807-1670
ph: 908-526-7676
fax: 908-575-0880
e-mail: magames@ix.netcom.com
Wants to buy vintage wrist watches especially those in working condition; also wants current Rolex, Audemars, IWC, Breuget, Mueller, etc.

Dealers

Paul Duggan
Horological Artifacts
P.O. Box 63
Chelmsford, MA 01824-0063
ph: 978-256-5966
fax: 079-256-2497
e-mail: paul@pduggan.com
web: http://www.pduggan.com/
International watch buyers; wants fine watches such as Rolex, Patek Philippe, Vacheron, Cartier, Tiffany, Gubelin, Jules Jurgenson, Breuget, E. Howard, American Watch Co., LeCoultre, etc.

Roger J. Foti
Mark VII Technology, Inc.
1 Bery Lane
Wading River, NY 11792
ph: 516-929-3651
fax: 516-929-5499
e-mail: rjfoti2@pipeline.com
web: http://www.markvii.com
Buys and sells vintage and contemporary watches with an emphasis on Hamilton, Omega, Baume & Mercier, Ebel, Audemars Piguet, Oris, Fortis, Krieger.

Timothy Haines
Got the Time?
1077 Celestial St.
Rookwood Bldg. #3, Ste. 400
Cincinnati, OH 45202-1629
ph: 513-559-1405
fax: 513-651-0860
e-mail: relostrat1@aol.com
web: http://members.aol.com/ReyneH
Buying men's wrist watches; vintage and new; Rolex, Patek, Universal Geneva, Breitling Chronographs, Doctors watches, etc.; please call or fax list of items for sale.

Girard Sensoli
Girards Vintage Watches
217 W. Main
Brighton, MI 48116
ph: 810-220-0011
fax: 810-220-0012
e-mail: info@girards.com
web: http://girards.com
Watch collector, dealer repairer and watch show promoter for over 20 years; Rolex to Bulova; has an active web site selling watches; also organizes watch and collectibles shows, also listed on his web site.

Kris Meyer
Vintage Timepieces Worldwide
12900 Preston Rd., Ste. 500
N. Dallas Bank Bldg.
Dallas, TX 75230
ph: 800-833-3159 or 214-392-4281
fax: 214-392-4283
e-mail: watchworld@hotmail.com
web: http://www.watches-meyer.com
Wants wrist watches: Rolex, Patek Philippe, Vacheron & Constain, Audemars Piguet, Cartier, Tiffany, Piaget, all high grade pocket watches; chronograph, moonphase, repeating, triple calendars, military watches, world time zone, etc.

Armand Gandara
Armand's Timeless Treasures, L.L.C.
P.O. Box 12752
Scottsdale, AZ 85267-2752
ph: 602-443-1310
fax: 602-948-2614
e-mail: armand@armands-wathes.com
web: http://www.armands-watches.com/
Buys, sells, trades wrist watches, travel clocks, signs, wrist watch parts, movements and dials by Audemars Piguet, Boucheron, Breitling, Breuget, Cartier, Hamilton, Heuer, IWC, Jaeger LeCoultre, Longines, Patek Philippe, and others.

Periodicals

International Wristwatch USA
Magazine: International Wristwatch
P.O. Box 110204
Stamford, CT 06911-0204
ph: 203-352-1817
fax: 203-352-1820
A glossy magazine full of auction reports, ads, articles about old and new wrist watches.

Bruce Shawkey
Newsletter: Vintage Wrist Watch Report
P.O. Box 74
Evansville, WI 53536
Monthly newsletter.

WATER SPRINKLERS

(see also CAST IRON ITEMS; CLOTHES SPRINKLERS; GARDEN HOSE NOZZLES; IRONS, Pressing)

Collectors

Phyllis Burt
P.O. Box 681
New Canaan, CT 06840
ph: 203-798-2763
Wants to buy ceramic laundry sprinklers.

Experts

Richard Tucker
Argyle Antiques
P.O. Box 262
Argyle, TX 76226-0262
ph: 940-464-3752
fax: 940-464-7293
e-mail: lead1234@gte.net
Buys and sells figural cast iron items: windmill weights, shooting targets, water sprinklers; no repros. or repaired items wanted.

WATKINS COMPANY

Clubs/Associations

Watkins Collectors Club
Newsletter: WCC Newsletter
W24024 State Road 54/93
Galesville, WI 54630-8249
e-mail: beanpot@win.bright.net
For collectors of items, packaging and printed material made and distributed by the Watkins Company of Winona, MN.

WEANERS

Calf & Cow

(see also FARM COLLECTIBLES)

Collectors

Robert Rauhauser
RR 2 Box 766
Thomasville, PA 17364-9622
Wants calf and cow weaners; also hand milking machines.

Steve Deer
1503 Albin Pond
Greencastle, IN 46135
ph: 765-653-9437
Wants rare and especially homemade calf and cow weaners.

WEAPONS

(see AMERICAN INDIAN, Tomahawks; ARMS & ARMOR; CIVIL WAR ARTIFACTS; EDGED WEAPONS; FIREARMS; KNIVES; MILITARIA; POWDER HORNS; SWORDS; TARGET SHOOTING MEMORABILIA)

WEATHERVANES

(see FOLK ART; LIGHTNING PROTECTION COLLECTIBLES)

WEAVING EQUIPMENT

(see COVERLETS; SPINNING WHEELS; TEXTILES)

WEDDING COLLECTIBLES

(see BRIDAL COLLECTIBLES)

WESTERN AMERICANA

(see also AMERICAN INDIAN; ART, Western; BARBED WIRE; BOTTLES, Western Whiskey; COWBOY HEROES; ANIMAL COLLECTIBLES, Horses; LAW ENFORCEMENT MEMORABILIA, Police & Sheriff; LEATHER; OUTLAWS & LAWMEN; PAPER COLLECTIBLES, Western; SADDLES)

Appraisers

Pierre Bovis
AZ-Tex Cowboy Trading Co., The
P.O. Box 13345
Tucson, AZ 85732-3345
ph: 520-318-9512
fax: 520-318-0023
e-mail: boris@azstarnet.com
Buy, sells, appraises cowboy memorabilia, primitive arts, American Indian arts, Napoleonic artifacts.

Phil Moerschell
Western Collectables
P.O. Box 21
Bend, OR 97709
ph: 541-923-2140
fax: 541-923-9894
e-mail: phm3@coinet.com
web: http://www.westerncollectables.com
Collector, appraiser of Western Americana: cowboy spurs, bits and chaps, Indian baskets, beadwork, etc.

Auction Services

Engel Auction Co.
P.O. Box 1429
Ennis, MT 59729
ph: 406-682-4499
Conducts periodic auction of gunfighter and cowboy memorabilia.

High Noon
9929 Venice Blvd.
Los Angeles, CA 90034-5111
ph: 310-202-9010
Conducts periodic auctions of authentic cowboy and gunfighter memorabilia.

Clubs/Associations

Bobby Newton
Working Cowboy, c/o Chamber of Commerce
Newspaper: Rope Burns
P.O. Box 35
Gene Autry, OK 73436-0035
ph: 405-389-5350
Largest listing of western events: bit-spur-collectible shows & auctions, rodeos, roundups, western trade & trappings, etc.

Alvin G. Davis
American Cowboy Culture Association
4124 62nd Dr.
Lubbock, TX 79413-5116
ph: 806-795-2455
fax: 806-795-4749
e-mail: adavis@cowboy.org
web: http://www.cowboy.org/
Purpose is to promote all areas of cowboy culture; sponsors events relating to cowboys; sponsors National Cowboy Symposium & Celebration - held in September in Lubbock, TX.

National Bit, Spur & Saddle Collectors Association
Newsletter: NBSSCA Newsletter
P.O. Box 3098
Colorado Springs, CO 80934-3098
ph: 719-473-7101
Members interested in western Americana memorabilia; supports shows and auctions; Western artifacts and collectibles show and auction schedules.

Collectors

Dr. Anthony Sapienza
East 106 Ridgewood Ave.
Paramus, NJ 07652
ph: 201-262-6310
fax: 201-262-3990
e-mail: siringo45@aol.com
Wants Western Americana photos (CDVs, cabinet cards, real photo postcards) of famous Westerners such as outlaws, lawmen, Wild West performers; also wants photos of armed cowboys, Indians, lawmen, exhibition shooters posing with guns.

Jim Babchak
313 East 85 #4B
New York, NY 10028
ph: 212-861-1356
Wants to buy old cowboy stuff including cowboy boots, shirts, horsehair bridles, spurs, chaps, children's costumes from the 1940s and 1950s, anything Roy Rogers, Hopalong Cassidy or Gene Autry.

Lewis Leigh, Jr.
P.O. Box 4327
Leesburg, VA 20177
ph: 703-771-3081
fax: 703-771-1432
Wants papers, letters, journals, uniforms, weapons & flags of American soldiers, seamen, pioneers, adventurers: 1607-1919.

Ernest Hoodenpyle
P.O. Box 487
Walters, OK 73572
ph: 580-875-3080
Wants to buy old cowboy stuff: silver mounted spurs, horse hair bridles, rawhide items, gun belts, holsters, chaps, horn furniture, old catalogs, pre-1900 cowboy boots, etc.

Rusty Gilbert
P.O. Box 92
Adkins, TX 78101
ph: 210-649-3849
Wants highback saddles, chaps, fancy headstalls, old spurs and bits, rifle scabbards, iron stirrups, Western catalogs, cowboy items, Western style dinnerware.

George Foott
120 W. Park Ave.
Salida, CO 81201
Wants to buy early Western mining memorabilia (especially Colorado): photographs, maps, promotional pamphlets, books, mining directories, miners' candleholders; also wants Old West cattle brand books, saddle catalogs, cowboy items.

Bill Mackin
1137 Washington St.
Craig, CO 81625-1613
ph: 970-824-6717 or 970-824-6360
fax: 970-824-7175
Wants pre-1940s cowboy and tack items: guns, cartridge belts, chaps, law badges, neckerchiefs, brands and brand books, spurs, knives, quirts, cowboy boots, hats, neckerchiefs, vests, cuffs, gauntlets, gun and saddle catalogs, etc.

Elizabeth Clair Flood
P.O. Box 1006
Wilson, WY 83014
Specializes in the history, fashion and gear of old time cowgirls and rodeo women.

William Manns
Cowboy Antiques
P.O. Box 6459
Santa Fe, NM 87502-6459
ph: 505-995-0102
fax: 505-995-0103
e-mail: zon@nets.com
Wants to buy cowboy related antiques: pre-1930 spurs, holsters, hats, saddles, guns, catalogs, posters, photos, chaps, wild west show items, etc.; send photos and prices; offers free identification service if LSASE is provided.

Terry Ahlberg
1000 Irvine Blvd.
Tustin, CA 92680-3527
ph: 714-730-1000 or 949-654-1331
fax: 714-730-1752
e-mail: emailit@earthlink.net
Wants any art by Jo Mora (J.J. Mora), Ranger Buckle sets by Edward Bohlin, cowboy or Indian bookends.

Maria E. Raymond
Plow & Pen, Inc.
P.O. Box 251
Robbins, CA 95676-0251
ph: 530-735-6596
fax: 530-735-6112
e-mail: M_Raymond@compuserve.com
Wants items relating to the history of women in the U.S. West: 1st edition books, ephemera, photos, news articles, diaries, letters; especially interested in items relating to women of color.

Dealers

L.R. Kauffman
Treasure Hunt
P.O. Box 3862
Woodbridge, CT 06525-0862
ph: 203-387-8759
Wants pre-1900 western ephemera, view books, promotional booklets of towns and states; documents on mining, towns, Indians, Indian language material, emigrant guides, letters, etc.

Fred Neece, Jr.
1307 Hadtner St.
Williamsport, PA 17701-3707
ph: 570-323-4679
fax: 570-323-5293
Wants to buy old Western and cowboy items: boots, books, spurs, hats, leather cuffs, fancy shirts, chaps, holsters, art, Wells Fargo, Overland, Pony Express items, 1860s-1870s saddles, rodeo posters, etc.

Roger M. Crowley
Old West Shop
P.O. Box 5232
Vienna, WV 26105
ph: 304-295-3143
fax: 304-295-3143
e-mail: oldwestshop@citynet.net
web: http://www.oldwestshop.com/
Buys and sells Western movie memorabilia, Western books, Remington prints, badges; old and new.

Gilbert Lewis
Frontier Americana
6342 Foreset Hill Blvd.
West Palm Beach, FL 33415
ph: 561-697-2459 or 561-655-3619
fax: 561-697-9608
e-mail: shopro@bellsouth.net
web: http://www.frontieramericana.com
Buys and sells items from the Old West: gambling, saloon collectibles, weapons.

William Butts
Main Street Fine Books & Manuscripts
206 N. Main St.
Galena, IL 61035-2244
ph: 815-777-3749
fax: 815-777-8950
e-mail: msfb@galenalink.com
web: http://www.wcinet.com/msfbooks
Open shop dealing in autographs and out-of-print books in most fields; specializing in all aspects of American history; books and autograph catalogs issued regularly; member of A.B.A.A.

Sharon Myers
J & S Oldwestern Store, Saddle Shop & Museum
RR 1, Box 315-c-nt
Warsaw, MO 65355
ph: 660-438-2631
fax: 660-438-6517
e-mail: oldwest@iland.net
web: http://www.cowgirls.com/dream/oldwest
Over 200 antique saddles, hibacks, side-saddles, military, charro, etc.; Admission to museum if free; also 1300 Western collectibles for sale; 55 page catalog for $5.

Experienced Denim
P.O. Box 239
Fayetteville, AR 72702-0239
ph: 501-444-7541 or 800-336-4694
fax: 501-521-8331
e-mail: exd@edenim.com
web: http://www.edenim.com/
Wants Levis, denim jackets; also fabrics, textiles, bedspreads, '40s-'50s fancy cowboy boots and belts, tablecloths with Western or Mexican theme; will consider any condition; send SASE for free list of items wanted.

Ruppert Books
5909 Darnell
Houston, TX 77074-7719
ph: 713-774-2202
fax: 713-774-2202
Wants any pre-1980 books in dust jackets about Texas and country histories.

Early West, The
P.O. Box 9292
College Station, TX 77842
ph: 800-245-5841
fax: 409-764-7758
Buys, sells, trades Western American including documents, photos, in-print and out-of-print books, paper ephemera; catalog includes items relating to lawmen, cowboys, Indians, Texans, soldiers, explorers, and mountain men.

Kurt House
Cowboy Collectibles
218 Country Wood
San Antonio, TX 78216-1607
ph: 210-490-2433
fax: 210-490-3433
e-mail: cowboyhous@aol.com
Buys, sells, restores pre-1940 cowboy items: bits, spurs, guns, gunbelts, swords, badges, cattleman antiques, books, manufacturer's catalogs, photos, etc.; author of "Joe Bianchi and the Victoria Spur" (1997).

Paul E. Mix
P.O. Box 180182
Austin, TX 78718-0182
ph: 512-836-8005
fax: 512-835-1708
e-mail: paulmix@prodigy.net
Buys and sells Western Americana: books on antique barbed wire, Western Arcade cards, Tom Mix memorabilia, pin-back buttons, photos, branding irons, belt buckles; catalog for $3, refundable with first purchase.

Bill Overly
P.P. Box 1394
Loveland, CO 80539
ph: 970-622-9612
e-mail: troper@lanminds.net
Website provides links to Cowboy art, poetry and rodeo; also has available free advertising section for sale or wanted to buy western art and memorabilia.

Lee Jacobs
P.O. Box 3098
Colorado Springs, CO 80934-3098
ph: 719-473-7101

John Hartman
Globalarts
17897 Hwy. 160
Durango, CO 81301
ph: 970-247-5589
fax: 970-259-6020
e-mail: hartman@rmi.net
web: http://www.globalarts.com
Buys and sells antique Frontier memorabilia, Native American Indian items, Cowboy items; also Ethnic Rarities from around the world.

Brian Lebel
Old West Antiques & Cowboy Collectibles
1215 Sheridan Ave.
Cody, WY 82414-3629
ph: 307-587-9014
fax: 307-587-5393
e-mail: oldwest@cody.wtp.net
web: http://www.codyoldwest.com/
Issues three catalogs per year of western Americana collectibles: saddles, chaps, spurs, bridles, etc.; also auction news, ads.

William L. King
Bozeman Trail Gallery
214 N. Main
Sheridan, WY 82801
ph: 307-672-3928 or 307-672-8318
fax: 307-672-2616
e-mail: btg@bozemantrailgallery.com
web: http://www.bozemantrailgallery.com/
Buys, sells, appraises 19th-early 20th cent. Western art, especially by Joe DeYong, E.W. Gollings, Hans Kleiber; also wants No. Plains Indian beadwork and related items, cowboy equipment, Colt Bisley's, mod. 1885 Remington pistols.

Tyrone & Una Campbell
Una
7103 E. Main St.
Scottsdale, AZ 85251-4315
ph: 602-423-9160
Buys and sells antique American Indian weavings: Navajo, Pueblo and Hispanic weavings and folk art; specializes in appraising collections, consultations, and research of 19th & 20th C. Navajo weavings.

Old West Cowboy Store
427 E. Allen St.
Tombstone, AZ 85638
ph: 520-457-3166
Specializing in Western and cowboy memorabilia: cowboy gear, holsters, spurs, Old West star badges, old saddles, etc.

Pierre Bovis
AZ-Tex Cowboy Trading Co., The
P.O. Box 13345
Tucson, AZ 85732-3345
ph: 520-318-9512
fax: 520-318-0023
e-mail: boris@azstarnet.com
Buy, sells, appraises cowboy memorabilia, primitive arts, American Indian arts, Napoleonic artifacts.

High Noon
9929 Venice Blvd.
Los Angeles, CA 90034-5111
ph: 310-202-9010
Wants to buy cowboy collectibles: bits, spurs, chaps, braided horsehair, silver saddles, saddle bags, cuffs, tack catalogs, etc.

Roger V. Baker
P.O. Box 620417
Redwood City, CA 94062-0417
ph: 369-851-7188
Buys, collects and sells Western Americana: American Indian items, cowboy paraphernalia, firearms, knives, saloon antiques, gold rush, mining and other related items.

Hank Clark
Argent Express
P.O. Box 812
Waterford, CA 95386-0812
ph: 209-874-2640
fax: 209-874-5750
Buys/sells Western American paper, books, weapons, autographs, vintage coins, photographs, gold & silversmithing, conchos & buttons; anything Western.

Douglas Vincent
Far West Antiques
P.O. Box 371
Redmond, OR 97756-0070
ph: 541-923-1847 or 541-923-2140
fax: 541-923-3874
e-mail: farwest@empnet.com
web: http://www.farwestantiques.com
Buys, sells, trades in older Native American items and Western Americana inducing gambling collectibles; also collects native American beadwork, baskets, jewelry and Kachina dolls.

Dick Perier
Dick Perier - Books
P.O. Box 1
Vancouver, WA 98666-0001
ph: 360-696-2033
e-mail: dperier@aol.com
Wants to buy books relating to Alaska, Lewis & Clark, Western Americana.

Experts

Robert W.D. Ball
26 Byron Dr.
Avon, CT 06001-4507
Author of "Cowboy Collectibles and Western Memorabilia" (Schiffer Publishing Co.), "American Shelf and Wall Clocks, A Pictorial History For Collectors", and auction catalogs for firearms and militaria auctions.

Robert Phillips
1703 North Aster Place
Broken Arrow, OK 74012
ph: 918-254-8205
fax: 918-252-9362
Collector of cowboy memorabilia for over 30 years and has written a book as well as many magazine articles dealing with the subject.

Bill Mackin
1137 Washington St.
Craig, CO 81625-1613
ph: 970-824-6717 or 970-824-6360
fax: 970-824-7175
Author of "Cowboy and Gunfighter Collectibles" with 1993-94 updated price guide; sells books for Old West collectors by mail and at shows; over 45 years collecting; wants nice gun leather and cowboy gear; appraises, consults, lectures.

Warren Anderson
America West Archives
P.O. Box 100
Cedar City, UT 84721-0100
ph: 435-586-9497 or 435-586-7323
e-mail: awa@netutah.com
web: http://www.americawestarchives.com/
Buys and sells paper Americana associated with the Western US: old documents, letters, photos, stocks, maps, autographs, prints, etc.; author of "Owning Western History."

Robert H. Balderson
2830 Arden Way, #110
Sacramento, CA 95825
ph: 916-484-7906
fax: 916-484-7906
Specializes and appraises firearms, Western Americana, and Native American weapons; author of "Official Price Guide to Antique and Modern Firearms."

Museums/Libraries

Robyn G. Peterson
Rockwell Museum, The
111 Cedar St.
Corning, NY 14830
ph: 607-937-5386
fax: 607-974-4536
e-mail: Rmuseum@stny.lrun.com
web: http://www.stny.lrun.com/RockwellMuseum/
Largest display of American Western art in the Eastern U.S.; includes paintings, bronzes, firearms, Native American artifacts; also Frederick Carder's Steuben glass, antique toys; museum shop on premises.

Randy Donley
Donley's Wild West Town & Museum
8512 S. Union Rd.
Union, IL 60180-9661
ph: 815-923-9000
fax: 815-923-2253
web: http://www.wildwesttown.com/
Large display of all kinds of Americana, especially from the Wild West.

Pony Express Museum
914 Penn St.
Saint Joseph, MO 64503
ph: 816-279-5059
fax: 816-233-9370
web: http://www.ponyexpress.org/

National Cowgirl Hall of Fame & Western Heritage Center
111 West 4th, Ste. 300
Fort Worth, TX 76102
ph: 817-336-4475
fax: 817-336-2470
e-mail: webmaster@cowgirl.net
web: http://www.cowgirl.net

Ranching Heritage Center
Museum of Texas Tech
P.O. Box 43191
Lubbock, TX 79409-3191
ph: 806-742-0498 or 806-742-0500
web: http://interoz.com/lubbock/ranch.htm

Museum of Northwest Colorado
590 Yampa St.
Craig, CO 81625-2612
ph: 970-824-6360
fax: 970-824-7175
e-mail: musnwco@museumnwco.org
web: http://www.museumnwco.org/
One of the world's most extensive collections of fine antique cowboy gear, frontier guns and gun leather, spurs, badges, saddles, chaps, etc.; a public county museum in historic state armory site; free admission.

Deck Hunter, Dir.
Museum of the American Cowboy
P.O. Box 7006
Sheridan, WY 82801
ph: 307-674-8875
web: http://wave.sheridan.wy.us/~bucaroo/index.html
Devoted to the working cowboy; purpose is to preserve the history and lifestyle of the American working cowboy, with a special emphasis on the period between 1870 and 1910.

Gene Autry Western Heritage Museum
Magazine: Spur
4700 Western Heritage Way
Los Angeles, CA 90027-1462
ph: 323-667-2000
fax: 323-660-5721
e-mail: rroom@autry-museum.org
web: http://www.autry-museum.org/
Collects items relating to the American West, including Western film memorabilia.

Wells Fargo History Museum
333 S. Grand Ave.
Los Angeles, CA 90071-1504
ph: 213-253-7166
web: http://www.wellsfargohistory.com/

Round Up Hall of Fame & Museum
P.O. Box 609
Pendleton, OR 97801
ph: 541-278-0815

Periodicals

Cowles Magazines, Inc.
Magazine: Wild West
741 Miller Dr. SE, Ste. D2
Harrisburg, PA 20175
ph: 717-540-6617 or 800-829-3340
fax: 717-540-6706
e-mail: brentd@cowles.com
web: http://www.cowles.com/maglist.html
A bi-monthly magazine covering America's westward expansion - major events, interesting characters, and little-known incidents, as well as Western art, artifacts, and collectibles.

Cowles Magazines, Inc.
Magazine: Southwest Art
741 Miller Dr. SE, Ste. D2
Harrisburg, PA 20175
ph: 717-540-6617 or 800-829-3340
fax: 717-540-6706
e-mail: brentd@cowles.com
web: http://www.cowles.com/maglist.html
The best in contemporary Western, traditional, Native American and impressionist artists; published monthly.

Western Publications
Magazine: True West
P.O. Box 2107
Stillwater, OK 74076-2107
ph: 800-749-3369 or 405-743-3370
fax: 405-743-3374
e-mail: western@cowboy.net
Published monthly; explores the places and events that made the American frontier a vital part of our history; where to go and what to do to capture the spirit of the west.

Western Publications
Magazine: Old West
P.O. Box 2107
Stillwater, OK 74076-2107
ph: 800-749-3369 or 405-743-3370
fax: 405-743-3374
e-mail: western@cowboy.net
Published four times each year, takes you back to the good old days when the only friends you had were your six-gun and a bag full of gold dust; great stories of America's past.

Reid Slaughter
Magazine: Cowboys & Indians
8214 Westchester Dr., Ste. 410
Dallas, TX 75225
ph: 972-750-8222 or 800-982-5370
fax: 972-750-4522
e-mail: cowboysindians@msn.com
web: http://www.cowboysindians.com
The premier magazine of the West.

Magazine: Western Horseman
P.O. Box 7980
Colorado Springs, CO 80933
ph: 719-633-5524
fax: 719-633-1392
e-mail: edit@westernhorseman.com
web: http://www.westernhorseman.com/
Monthly magazine focusing on western horsemanship and lifestyle.

WEB Publications, Inc.
Magazine: American Cowboy
P.O. Box 6630
Sheridan, WY 82801-7102
ph: 800-369-0196 or 307-672-7171
fax: 307-672-7766
e-mail: cowboy@cowboy.com
web: http://www.americancowboy.com/
The magazine of Western living: profiles of famous country-western singers, rodeo stars, artists, cowboys;

coverage of today's western art & collectibles; auction results, history, travel, cowboy poetry, etc.; bi-monthly.

Magazine: American Cowboy Poet Magazine
P.O. Box 326
Eagle, ID 83616
ph: 208-888-9838
fax: 208-887-2986
e-mail: acpm@cyberhighway.net
web: http://www.cyberhighway.net/~rudy/acpm.htm
Focusing on true cowboy music and poetry; articles, poetry, events, music offered by those who live the life and not by Hollywood or Nashville entertainers; great modern day cowboy artists featured in each issue.

William Manns
Newsletter: Cowboy Guide
P.O. Box 6459
Santa Fe, NM 87502-6459
ph: 505-995-0102
fax: 505-995-0103
e-mail: zon@nets.com
Send SASE for Cowboy Guide which contains information about cowboy collectibles, upcoming cowboy auctions and shows, plus a list of dealers, museums and publications.

Ted Knorr, Ed.
Newspaper: Today's Old West Traveler
P.O. Box 2928
Costa Mesa, CA 92628
ph: 800-775-9378
fax: 714-540-2476
web: http://www.wyoming.com/~wyprod/cowboy/oldwest/
Find all things Western - upcoming events nationwide, adventures, dude ranches, cattle drives, cowboy collectibles, poetry, music, historic sites, museums, living history, movies, western wear, and more.

101 Ranch

Clubs/Associations

Ruth & Jerry Murphey
101 Ranch Collectors
10701 Timbergrove Lane
Corpus Christi, TX 78410
ph: 361-241-2213
fax: 361-241-6908
e-mail: jmurphey1@aol.com
101 Ranch memorabilia collectors; for many years the 101 Ranch had a traveling wild west show; stars who worked on the ranch or appeared in the show included Buffalo Bill, Tom Mix, Will Rogers, Hoot Gibson, Buck Jones and many more.

Collectors

Ogden's
P.O. Box 248
Sudbury, MA 01776
Wants memorabilia related to the 101 Ranch.

Annie Oakley

(see also WESTERN AMERICANA, Buffalo Bill; WESTERN AMERICANA, Wild West Show)

Dealers

Vivian & James Karsnitz
1428 Jerry Lane
Manheim, PA 17545-9353
ph: 717-665-4202
Buys and sells anything Annie Oakley.

Bits

Collectors

Jean Gayle
Three Horses
7403 Blaine Rd.
Aberdeen, WA 98520-7409
ph: 360-533-3490
e-mail: jgayle@techline.com
Buying fancy, ornamental, military, iron horse bits; also wants to buy bridle rosettes and old tack catalogs.

Boots

Collectors

Ed Soost
1331 Weverton Rd.
Knoxville, MD 21758
ph: 301-694-7325
Wants to buy vintage Western boots.

Internet Resources

Jennifer June
Cowboy Boot Web Page, The
190 El Cerrito Plaza, Ste. 273
El Cerrito, CA 94530
ph: 510-435-5863
fax: 510-601-5852
e-mail: newboots@dimlights.com
web: http://www.hooked.net/~jbalogh/BOOTS.HTM
Boot collector and expert maintains a website described as a "Tribute to Cowboy Boots" and the folks who make, wear, and admire them; updated monthly; custom makers, events, history, photos.

Buffalo Bill

(see also WESTERN AMERICANA, Annie Oakley; WESTERN AMERICANA, Wild West Show)

Collectors

Ogden's
P.O. Box 248
Sudbury, MA 01776
Wants memorabilia related to Buffalo Bill and Pawnee Bill.

Michael Del Castello
23842 Cabot Blvd.
Hayward, CA 94545-1661
ph: 510-265-3506 or 650-941-4643
fax: 510-781-3468
e-mail: mdc@mdc-vacuum.com
Wants to buy Buffalo Bill Cody items: posters, programs, photographs and artifacts relating to Buffalo Bill, Wild West Show memorabilia, Annie Oakley, Wells Fargo.

Museums/Libraries

Buffalo Bill Museum Inc.
P.O. Box 284
LeClaire, IA 52753
ph: 319-289-5580
LeClaire is the birthplace of Buffalo Bill.

Buffalo Bill Grave & Museum
987 1/2 Lookout Mountain Road
Golden, CO 80401
ph: 303-526-0747
e-mail: BuffaloBillsGiftShop@yahoo.com
web: http://www.buffalobill.org/

Buffalo Bill Historical Center
P.O. Box 1000
720 Sheridan Ave.
Cody, WY 82414-1000
ph: 307-587-4771
fax: 307-587-5714
e-mail: bbhc@wavecom.net
web: http://www.bbhc.org/
Dedicated to the history of William F. Cody; large collection of personal belongings, photos and documents.

Holsters

Repro. Sources

Old West Reproductions
446 Florence South Loop
Florence, MT 59833
ph: 406-273-2615
fax: 406-273-2615
e-mail: bachman@montananet.com
web: http://www.angelfire.com/mt/owr/
Faithful reproductions of 1849-1900 holsters, cartridge belts, saddles and more; send $3 for catalog; also seeking to buy original Western memorabilia, i.e. 1849-1900 holsters, cartridge belts, wrist cuffs, etc.

Photographs

Collectors

Tim Gordon, ISA
1750 W. Kent
Missoula, MT 59801-5508
ph: 406-728-1812
e-mail: stacey1165@aol.com
Wants early photos of the West: saloon interiors, cowboys, Indians, lawmen, hangings, etc.; also offers appraisal service.

Dealers

L.R. Kauffman
Treasure Hunt
P.O. Box 3862
Woodbridge, CT 06525-0862
ph: 203-387-8759
Wants pre-1900 western photos or stereo views of historical interest; special wants include Watkins, Jackson, Houseworth; stereos and views of towns, streets, mining, shops, etc. of 19th century Western America.

Southwest

Collectors

John W. Barry
Indian Rock Arts
P.O. Box 583
Davis, CA 95617-0583
ph: 530-758-2561
e-mail: jackbarr@pacbell.net
Wants traditional Pueblo pottery paintings, prints, photos; books on Southwest Tribes & Pueblos, Southwest archaeology, exploration and surveys of the West, Yellowstone, Grand Canyon, Yosemite tourism, photographs, old tourist items.

Dealers

Eller, ISA
Peter Eller Gallery & Appraisers
206 Dartmouth
Albuquerque, NM 87106
ph: 505-268-7437
fax: 505-268-6442
e-mail: pelgal@nmia.com
web: http://www.peterellergallery.com/
Specializes in works by Albuquerque artists and minor New Mexico artists, traditional and modernist, 1925-1965, for beginning and intermediate collectors; appraising art, antiques, Spanish Colonial, religious and SW Indian artifacts.

Texas Rangers

Museums/Libraries

Texas Ranger Hall of Fame & Museum
P.O. Box 2570
Waco, TX 76702-2570
ph: 254-750-8631
fax: 254-750-8629
e-mail: bjohnson@eramp.net
web: http://www.texasranger.org/
Nonprofit and educational museum and Hall of Fame dedicated to the history of the Texas Rangers; artifact collections, research library, and audio-visual presentations.

Wells Fargo

Collectors

Bartz
25101 Cineria Way
Eltoro, CA 92630
ph: 949-768-5503
Wants any authentic Wells Fargo items.

Wild West Show

(see also WESTERN AMERICANA, Annie Oakley; WESTERN AMERICANA, Buffalo Bill)

Auction Services

Kurt R. Krueger
Krueger Auctions
P.O. Box 275
Iola, WI 54945-0275
ph: 715-445-3845
fax: 715-445-4100
Conducts periodic specialized auctions of circus and Wild West Show memorabilia.

Collectors

Dr. Anthony Sapienza
East 106 Ridgewood Ave.
Paramus, NJ 07652
ph: 201-262-6310
fax: 201-262-3990
e-mail: siringo45@aol.com
Serious collector wants Wild West Show memorabilia: posters, programs, photographs, souvenir targets, pinbacks, etc.; especially dealing with trick shooters such as Annie Oakley, Capt. Bogardus, Doc Carver, Lillian Smith (Princess Wenona).

William Manns
Cowboy Antiques
P.O. Box 6459
Santa Fe, NM 87502-6459
ph: 505-995-0102
fax: 505-995-0103
e-mail: zon@nets.com
Wants to buy cowboy related antiques: pre-1930 spurs, holsters, hats, saddles, guns, catalogs, posters, photos, chaps, wild west show items, etc.; send photos and prices; offers free identification service if LSASE is provided.

Art Sowin
8436 Samra Dr.
Canoga Park, CA 91304
Wants Wild West Show memorabilia: Buffalo Bill, Annie Oakley, Wild West Show books, advertising, photos, programs, tickets, passes, souvenir items, etc.

Michael Del Castello
23842 Cabot Blvd.
Hayward, CA 94545-1661
ph: 510-265-3506 or 650-941-4643
fax: 510-781-3468
e-mail: mdc@mdc-vacuum.com
Wants to buy Buffalo Bill Cody items: posters, programs, photographs and artifacts relating to Buffalo Bill, Wild West Show memorabilia, Annie Oakley, Wells Fargo.

WHALES & DOLPHINS

Collectors

Steven G. King
Whales & Friends
P.O. Box 2660
Alameda, CA 94501-0660
ph: 510-796-8500 or 800-282-8686
fax: 510-865-0851
Wants to buy any items with images of whales or dolphins, alive or dead: books, photos, coins, stamps, posters, toys, videos, models, sculptures, etc.; when calling, ask for Steve King and mention you're calling about whale material.

Flipper

Collectors

John Fredriksen
461 Loring Ave.
Salem, MA 01970
Wants Flipper related toys, books, cards, games.

WHALING

(see also ENDANGERED SPECIES; NAUTICAL ANTIQUES; SCRIMSHAW; WHALES & DOLPHINS)

Experts

Sara Conklin
Nautical Appraisals
239 Sierra Pt. Rd.
Brisbane, CA 94005-1664
ph: 415-467-6249
fax: 415-467-6249
e-mail: sconklin2@earthlink.com
Managed the collections of the National Maritime Museum in San Francisco for ten years and is an expert in appraising whaling objects and scrimshaw.

Museums/Libraries

Librarian
Kendall Whaling Museum, The
Newsletter: KWM Newsletter
27 Everett St.
P.O. Box 297
Sharon, MA 02067-0297
ph: 781-784-5642
e-mail: staff@kwm.org
web: http://www.kwm.org
International collection of whaling artworks & artifacts specializing in paintings 1600-present, scrimshaw, tools, gear, prints, ship models, etc.

New Bedford Whaling Museum
18 Johnny Cake Hill
New Bedford, MA 02740-6317
ph: 508-997-0046
fax: 508-994-4350
e-mail: whaling@ma.ultranet.com
web: http://www.whalingmuseum.org/
A whaling and local historical museum.

Cold Spring Harbor Whaling Museum
P.O. Box 25
Cold Spring Harbor, NY 11724
ph: 516-367-3418
web: http://www.cshl.org/cshm/whale.htm

Sag Harbor Whaling & Historical Museum
Main Street
P.O. Box 1327
Sag Harbor, NY 11963
ph: 516-725-0770
Instruments, scrimshaw, ship models, tools, artifacts.

San Francisco Maritime National Historical Park, Museum & Library
Bldg. E, Fort Mason Center
San Francisco, CA 94123
ph: 415-556-9870 or 415-556-9871
fax: 415-556-3540
e-mail: safr_maritime_library@nps.gov
web: http://www.nps.gov/safr/local/lib/libtop.html

Pacific Whaling Museum
Sea Life Park
Waimanalo, HI 96795
ph: 808-259-7933

WHEEL TOYS

(see BICYCLES & RELATED MEMORABILIA; GO-KARTS; RIDING TOYS)

WHISKEY INDUSTRY ITEMS

(see also ADVERTISING COLLECTIBLES; DECANTERS, Figural Whiskey; CERAMICS [ENGLISH], Whisky Pitchers; GLASSES; PROHIBITION ITEMS; SALOON & BAR COLLECTIBLES)

Museums/Libraries

Seagram Museum Library, University of Waterloo
200 University Ave. West
Waterloo, Ontario N2L 3G1
Canada
ph: 519-888-4567
fax: 519-884-8009
e-mail: lhasting@library.uwaterloo.ca
web: http://library.uwaterloo.ca/seagrams/
Contains a large selection of documents donated by the Seagram Museum.

Jack Daniels

Collectors

Claude Bellar
1750 Keyes Road
Greenbrier, TN 37073
ph: 615-643-0290
fax: 615-643-0290
e-mail: cbellar@aol.com

Old Crow

Collectors

Judith & Bob Walthall
P.O. Box 4465
Huntsville, AL 35815
ph: 256-881-9198
Wants to buy Old Crow Whiskey items.

WHISTLERS

(see MUSIC BOXES, Birds & Bird Boxes [Singing])

WHISTLES

(see HORNS & WHISTLES)

WHITE HOUSE COLLECTIBLES

(see also PERSONALITIES [HISTORICAL]; POLITICAL COLLECTIBLES)

Clubs/Associations

White House Historical Association
c/o White House Visitor Center
1450 Pennsylvania Ave. NW
Washington, DC 20004-1005
ph: 800-717-1450 or 202-456-7041
web: http://www.whitehousehistory.org/
The association was founded in 1961 as a charitable nonprofit institution for the purpose of enhancing the understanding, appreciation and enjoyment of the White House.

Dealers

H. Joseph Levine
Presidential Coin & Antique Co. Inc.
6550-I Little River Turnpike
Alexandria, VA 22312
ph: 703-354-5454
fax: 703-914-0547
Wants include Presidential jewelry, Christmas cards, pens and White House glass, china, and paper items; also wants any item connected with Presidential inaugurations such as medals, ribbons, invitations, programs, buttons, etc.

China

Repro. Sources

United States Historical Society
25 E. Main St.
Richmond, VA 23219
ph: 804-648-4736 or 800-788-4478
fax: 804-648-0002
e-mail: dolls@ushsdolls.com
web: http://www.ushsdolls.com/

WICKER

(see also REPAIR/RESTORATION/CONSERVATION, Wicker)

Dealers

Cathryn Peters
Wicker Woman, The
531 Main Street
P.O. Box 61
Zumbro Falls, MN 55991
ph: 507-753-2006 or 888-WICK-R-WN
e-mail: Wickrwoman@aol.com
web: http://www.bright.net/~basketc/cp.html
Wicker dealer and expert; since 1975 specializing in the sale and restoration of wicker, cane and rush furniture; available to lecture, teach and write on antique wicker and seat weaving.

Repair Services

Cathryn Peters
Wicker Woman, The
531 Main Street
P.O. Box 61
Zumbro Falls, MN 55991
ph: 507-753-2006 or 888-WICK-R-WN
e-mail: Wickrwoman@aol.com
web: http://www.bright.net/~basketc/cp.html
Professional quality wicker restoration for over 23 years; specializing in Victorian period; also restores strand and sheet cane, natural and paper rush, and splint seats; dealer, teacher, speaker, writer on the subject of wicker.

Repro. Sources

Gale Poudrier
Yesteryear Wicker
7616 Investment Ct.
Owings, MD 20736
ph: 410-257-9387 or 800-597-7061
fax: 410-257-1306
World's only antique wicker reproduction specialist.

WIENER WERKSTATTE

(see MODERNISM)

WILDLIFE

(see ANIMAL TROPHIES; SPORTING COLLECTIBLES, Hunting & Fishing; TRAPS)

WINCHESTER COLLECTIBLES

(see also DIAMOND EDGE [SHAPLEIGH HARDWARE]; FIREARMS, Winchester; HARDWARE; KEEN KUTTER [SIMMONS HARDWARE])

Auction Services

Bob Simmons
Simmons & Company Auctioneers
40706 E. 144th St.
Richmond, MO 64085
ph: 816-776-2936 or 800-646-2936
fax: 816-470-5016
e-mail: simmons_auction@raycounty.com
web: http://www.raycounty.com/simmons/
Conducts annual specialty auctions of Winchester, Keen Kutter (E.C. Simmons Hardware) and Diamond Edge (Shapleigh Hardware) collectibles; has a well-established reputation for expertise and high quality merchandise.

Clubs/Associations

Barbara Huhn, Mem.
Hardware Companies Kollectors' Club
Newsletter: Winchester Keen Kutter Diamond Edge Chronicles
432 S. Gore St.
Saint Louis, MO 63119
ph: 314-968-0304
e-mail: gramma@mvp.net
web: http://www.raycounty.com/simmons/clubs/newsletter.htm
A non-profit organization to serve as an interactive information distribution center for collectors of E.C. Simmons/Keen Kutter, Winchester Store (non-gun), A.F. Shapleigh/Diamond Edge, Hibbard, and other hardware store brands.

Winchester Club of America, The
3070 S. Wyandot
Englewood, CO 80110

Museums/Libraries

Shozo Kagoshima, Dir. of Mkt.
Winchester Mystery House, Antique Products Museum
525 South Winchester Blvd.
San Jose, CA 95128
ph: 408-247-2000
fax: 408-247-2090
web: http://www.sfbayfun.com/winchest.html
Displays cutlery, flashlights, lawn mowers, fishing tackle, and farm tools manufactured by the Winchester Products company after WWI.

WINDMILL COLLECTIBLES

(see also FARM MACHINERY)

Collectors

Ohio Windmill & Pump Co.
8389 SR 534
Berlin Center, OH 44401
ph: 330-547-6300
fax: 330-547-8213
Interested in anything windmill: literature, salesman samples, wooden wheel windmills, etc.

James Gress
13174 U.S. 127
Paulding, OH 45879
ph: 419-399-5358
Wants to buy any kind of advertising or literature related to American windmills.

Dealers

Ohio Windmill & Pump Co.
8389 SR 534
Berlin Center, OH 44401
ph: 330-547-6300
fax: 330-547-8213
Aermotor windmills & towers; hand pumps, cylinders & accessories; windmill books & historic literature; antique wood wheel windmills; custom fabrication & historic recreations and restorations; authentic original windmill weights.

T. Lindsay Baker
Windmill Books & Sales
P.O. Box 507
Rio Vista, TX 76093-0507
Always buying windmill trade catalogs, brochures, price lists, parts lists, and advertising ephemera.

Museums/Libraries

Volendam Windmill Museum, Inc.
RD 1 Box 242
Milford, NJ 08848
ph: 201-995-4365

Clark County Historical Society
105 N. Thompson Ave.
P.O. Box 2157
Springfield, OH 45501
Focus is on the history of a local industry - windmills, hand pumps & accessories.

Dalley Windmill Collection, The
E. Star Route, Box 7
Portales, NM 88130
ph: 505-356-6263
Over 75 windmills from around the world.

Periodicals

T. Lindsay Baker
Newsletter: Windmillers' Gazette
P.O. Box 507
Rio Vista, TX 76093-0507
Only periodical in America devoted exclusively to windmills and wind power history; author of "A Field Guide to American Windmills."

Weights

(see also CAST IRON ITEMS)

Dealers

Doug Clemence
Treasure Chest
436 North Chicago
Salina, KS 67401-2020
ph: 785-827-9371 or 785-825-4111
e-mail: clemence@midusa.net
Sells, sells and trades old and reproduction windmill weights.

Experts

Don Lawrence
P.O. Box 1141
Boise City, OK 73933-1141
ph: 580-544-3103
Co-author with Rick Nidey of "Windmill Weights", available from author for $17 ppd.

Richard Tucker
Argyle Antiques
P.O. Box 262
Argyle, TX 76226-0262
ph: 940-464-3752
fax: 940-464-7293
e-mail: lead1234@gte.net
Buys and sells figural cast iron items: windmill weights, shooting targets, water sprinklers; no repros. or repaired items wanted.

WINES & WINE RELATED ITEMS

(see also CORKSCREWS)

Appraisers

William H. Edgerton
P.O. Box 88
Darien, CT 06820-0588
ph: 203-655-0566
fax: 203-655-8066
e-mail: wedgerton@aol.com

Auction Services

Amory Spizzirri, Client Svc.
William Doyle Galleries
175 E. 87th St.
New York, NY 10128-2205
ph: 212-427-2730
fax: 212-369-0892
e-mail: info@doylegalleries.com
web: http://www.doylegalleries.com
Holds over 50 auctions annually of furniture and decorations, paintings and sculpture, jewelry, books and prints, couture and textiles, 20th century art & design, majolica, Lalique, Asian works of art and other specialty categories.

Michael Davis
Davis & Co. Wine Auctioneers, Ltd.
1440 N Dayton St.
Chicago, IL 60622
ph: 312-587-9500
fax: 312-654-1800
Conducts six wine auctions per year.

Ben Ferdinand
Chicago Wine Company, The
5663 West Howard St.
Niles, IL 60714
ph: 847-647-8789
fax: 847-647-7265
e-mail: tcwc@aol.com
web: http://www.tcwc.com/
Specializes in the sale of rare and fine wines from around the world; wines offered in monthly live auctions and through various retail offerings; in business for over 25 years.

Butterfield & Butterfield
220 San Bruno Ave.
San Francisco, CA 94103-5018
ph: 415-861-7500
fax: 415-861-8951
e-mail: info@butterfields.com
web: http://www.butterfields.com/
Specialties include posters, toys, decorative arts, furniture, photography, etc.; the largest full service auction in the west.

Hobby Markets Online, Inc.
375 Alabama Street, Ste. 410
San Francisco, CA 94110
ph: 415-252-6040 or 415-252-6040
fax: 415-252-6044
e-mail: hobbyinfo@hobbymarkets.com
web: http://www.AuctionVine.com/
Online auction service selling the very best in fine and rare wines.

David Richardson
Richardson's Wine Auctions
15 Kingston Ave.
Richmond, Adelaide 5033
Australia
ph: 8351-7373
fax: 8351-7374
e-mail: david@erauctions.com.au
web: http://www.erauctions.com.au/
Australia's largest auctioneers and valuers of fine wines; conducts some auctions live on the internet.

Collectors

Colgin-Schrader Cellars
P.O. Box 372
Calistoga, CA 94515
Wants to buy wines and wine related items: coasters, tastevins, decanters, silver mounted clarets, corkscrews, cellarettes, related paintings and prints from all wine regions especially CA; also wants pre 1962 vintage wines.

Dealers

Derek White
769 Sumter Drive
Morrisville, PA 19067
ph: 215-493-4143 or 609-860-5380
e-mail: dswhite@marketsource.com
web: http://www.taponline.com/cork/cs.html
Active collector and dealer of antique corkscrews; specialty is rare, unusual mechanical and pocket figural corkscrews; will buy single items as well s entire collections; also wants wine-related items: funnels, bin labels, etc.

Experts

Mark Barlow
Winetiques
3107A Medlock Bridge Rd.
Norcross, GA 30071-1423
ph: 770-449-7610
fax: 770-449-1839
Buys, sells, specializes in wine related antiques: corkscrews, tasters, bottle holders, old bottles, coasters, advertising, books, art; anything related to wine or champagne.

Internet Resources

David Harmon
Wine.com
1475 Fourth St.
Napa, CA 94559
ph: 707-257-2093
fax: 707-252-6996
e-mail: dharmon@wine.com
web: http://www.wine.com/
A complete wine website for the collector of fine and rare wines; online auctions, sales and information.

Museums/Libraries

Greyton H. Taylor Wine Museum
8843 G.H. Taylor Memorial Dr.
Hammondsport, NY 14840
ph: 607-868-3610

WINGS

(see AIRLINE MEMORABILIA, Junior Crew Member Wings; AIRLINE MEMORABILIA, Pilots Wings; AVIATION MEMORABILIA, Military Insignia)

WIRELESS TELEGRAPHY

(see TELEGRAPH ITEMS)

WITCHES

(see also GHOSTS & HAUNTINGS; HALLOWEEN COLLECTIBLES; HORROR)

Salem

Museums/Libraries

Salem Witch Museum
19 1/2 Washington Square North
Salem, MA 01970
ph: 978-744-1692
e-mail: facts@salemwitchmuseum.com
web: http://www.salemwitchmuseum.com
Depicts life in 1692 and the aftermath of the Salem Witch Trials.

WIZARD OF OZ

(see also MOVIE MEMORABILIA)

Clubs/Associations

Jim Vander Noot
International Wizard of Oz Club, The
Journal: Baum Bugle, The
P.O. Box 266
Kalamazoo, MI 49004-0266
ph: 510-527-4222
e-mail: info@ozclub.org
web: http://www.ozclub.org
Promotes the study and collecting of items relating to L. Frank Baum (1856-1919), The Oz Books, toys, movies, etc.; educates its members about the writings of L. Frank Baum and other authors and illustrators who contributed to Oz books.

Collectors

Bill Stillman
981 Kings Way West
Hummelstown, PA 17036-8909
ph: 717-566-5538
fax: 717-566-7718
Long time collector wants anything related to Wizard of Oz from 1900-1960s.

Michael Gessel
P.O. Box 748
Arlington, VA 22216-0748
ph: 703-542-0462
Wants books, posters, games, and advertising related to "The Wizard of Oz"; also wants items by W. W. Denslow.

Tod R. Machin
P.O. Box 3416
Kansas City, KS 66103
ph: 913-362-0528
Wants OZ items: old toys, books, dolls, paper and movie items dating from 1900 to 1970.

Edwin Wilder
1409 1st St.
Port Townsend, WA 98368-3078
Wants to buy Wizard of Oz books by any author; also wants related books, ephemera, and Baum non-Oz books.

Dealers

Elaine Willingham
Beyond the Rainbow Wizard of Oz Collectibles
P.O. Box 31672
Saint Louis, MO 63131-0672
ph: 314-799-1724
fax: 314-271-2727
Specializing in current and older MGM Wizard of OZ and Judy Garland collectibles, videos, books, jewelry.

Experts

Jay Scarfone
981 Kings Way West
Hummelstown, PA 17036-8909
ph: 717-566-5538
fax: 717-566-7718
Wants all kinds of memorabilia from the 1939 movie "The Wizard of Oz"; ads, souvenirs, posters, lobby cards, coat hangers, dolls, etc.

Periodicals

Elaine Willingham, Ed.
Newsletter: Beyond the Rainbow Collector's Exchange
P.O. Box 31672
Saint Louis, MO 63131-0672
ph: 314-799-1724
fax: 314-271-2727
Articles, ads.

WOOD

(see also PYROGRAPHY; REPAIR/RESTORATION/CONSERVATION, Furniture; REPAIR/RESTORATION/CONSERVATION, Woodworking; WOODEN MONEY)

Clubs/Associations

Bill & Myrtle Cockrell, Sec./Treas.
International Wood Collectors Society
Magazine: World of Wood
2300 West Rangeline Rd.
Greencastle, IN 46135-7875
ph: 765-653-6483
e-mail: cockrell@indy.tds.net
web: http://www.woodcollectors.org/
Dedicated to the advancement of information regarding wood; members enjoy wood sample collecting, identification (dendrology) and woodworking; trade, buy, sell and auction wood samples.

Carvings

Collectors

Joe Iozzia
P.O. Box 1005
Pomona, NJ 08240-1005
ph: 609-652-8504
fax: 609-652-8888
e-mail: pinflyers@aol.com
web: http://members.aol.com/Pinflyers/anri.html
Wants to buy figural wood handcarved people, animals, elves, pirates, monks, etc.; nutcrackers, cigarette boxes, bookends, ashtrays, pipe holders, figurines, bottle stoppers, humidors and unusual figural handcarved items.

Philly Rains
1401 Brentwood Dr.
Harrison, AR 72601
ph: 870-743-2040
fax: 870-743-2120
e-mail: phillyr@yournet.com
web: http://members.aol.com/corkskrue/philly.htm
Expert in old ANRI Italian wood carvings, 1912 through 1970s; non-limited editions only, including nutcrackers, bar sets, figurines, napkin rings, smoking accessories, and bottle stoppers; appraisals $25 per item; no limited editions.

Steve Elliott
1600 Tennessee St.
Vallejo, CA 94590
ph: 707-552-8400 or 707-642-1949
fax: 707-552-0881
Wants to buy antique Black Forest wood carvings.

Man./Prod./Dist.

Les Ramsay
Linden Tree Woodcarving Gallery
41 Bradley Road
Jackson Center, PA 16133
ph: 724-662-3623
e-mail: lindentree@pathway.net
web: http://www.pathway.net/lindentree/
Hand carved wooden figures, doors, fireplace mantels and commissioned sculpture.

Repair Services

David Warther II
David Warther Carving Museum
2561 Crestview Dr. NW
Dover, OH 44622-7405
ph: 330-852-3455 or 330-343-1868
Restores wood and ivory carvings and turnings; specialty is in small objects in ivory: chess sets, finials, small turned items, insulators, handles, and finials of ivory on sterling hollow-ware.

Identification

Misc. Services

R. Bruce Hoadley, Ph.D.
Wood Identification Workshop, University of Massachusetts Div. of Continuing Ed.
Goodell Bldg, Box 33260
Amherst, MA 01003-3260
ph: 413-545-2484 or 413-545-1834
Offers four-day workshops in wood identification.

Society for the Preservation of New England Antiquities, The
Conservation Center
185 Lyman St.
North Waltham, MA 02154
ph: 781-891-4882
fax: 781-893-7832
web: http://www.spnea.org/
Performs wood and finish/coatings analysis; also offers conservation treatment of furniture and objects.

David P. Lindquist
Whitehall at the Villa
1213 E. Franklin St.
Chapel Hill, NC 27514-3307
ph: 919-942-3179 or 919-933-3305
fax: 919-942-6600
e-mail: whchnc@aol.com
Offers a wood identification course.

Dr. Michael Taras
215 S. Craggmore Dr.
Salem, SC 29676-4626
ph: 864-944-0655
Send a wood sample for identification.

Regis Miller
Forest Products Laboratory, U.S. Dept. of Agriculture, Forest Services
One Gifford Pinchot Dr.
Madison, WI 53705-2398
ph: 608-231-9236
e-mail: rmiller1@facstaff.wisc.edu
web: http://www.fpl.fs.fed.us/

Turnings

Man./Prod./Dist.

James Hoyt
Artistic Lathe Turnings
110 SE Riceway
Bend, OR 97702-1508
ph: 541-389-7395
fax: 541-317-1955
e-mail: woodtrix@usa.net
web: http://www.woodtrix.com
Lathe turnings of exotic, tropical and domestic woods: cups, boxes, bowls, goblets.

WOODBURNING CRAFT ITEMS

(see PYROGRAPHY)

WOODEN MONEY

Clubs/Associations

Robbin Quinn
International Organization of Wooden Money Collectors
Newsletter: Bunyan's Chips
5295 Beechwood Rd.
Ravenna, OH 44266-9119
ph: 330-296-6783
e-mail: rq83@aol.com
web: http://www.startext.net/homes/woodmoney/index.htm
Club of over 350 focuses on woods, wooden tokens, commemorative and official woods.

Matt Welch
American Wooden Money Guild
Newsletter: Old Woody Views
P.O. Box 30444
Tucson, AZ 85751-0444
ph: 520-886-0505
e-mail: matwelch@aol.com
"Lignadenarists" are interested in collecting wooden money.

Collectors

Norman Boughton
P.O. Box 93262
Rochester, NY 14692
ph: 716-292-5550 or 716-292-0128
e-mail: nordel@rochester.infi.net
Wants wooden money issued for celebrations, used as money or issued by restaurant chains such as McDonald's.

Herb Hornung
Old Time Wooden Nickels
P.O. Box 18362
San Antonio, TX 78218-0362
ph: 877-464-2535 or 210-930-1677
fax: 210-832-8965
e-mail: herb@wooden-nickel.com
web: http://www.wooden-nickel.com/
Buy, sells and manufactures wooden nickels.

Man./Prod./Dist.

Herb Hornung
Old Time Wooden Nickels
P.O. Box 18362
San Antonio, TX 78218-0362
ph: 877-464-2535 or 210-930-1677
fax: 210-832-8965
e-mail: herb@wooden-nickel.com
web: http://www.wooden-nickel.com/
Manufacturer of wooden nickels for business advertising, souvenirs, politics, tokens, clowns, banks, police, novelties, centennials, fairs and festivals, magicians, casinos, fraternal groups, Scouts, tourist attractions, etc.

Museums/Libraries

Wooden Nickel Historical Museum
345 Old Austin Rd.
San Antonio, TX 78209
ph: 210-829-1291
fax: 210-832-8965
e-mail: museum@wooden-nickel.net
web: http://www.wooden-nickel.net/museum/
Printing plates and dies, printing presses, engravings, and other memorabilia related to making wooden nickels; includes "round" and "flat" wooden nickels in various sizes from the beginning in 1930 to present; by appointment only.

WOODSTOCK

(see also SOCIAL CAUSES, Hippie Items)

Collectors

Cary Demont
P.O. Box 16013
Minneapolis, MN 55416
ph: 612-522-0957
e-mail: Caryd8@aol.com
Wants unusual Woodstock 69 concert related items: authentic T-shirt and windbreaker jackets worn by crew members, backstage passes, early fliers and mailers (especially for the Wallkill venue), 3-D items; no common tickets, posters.

WORLD WAR MEMORABILIA

(see MARINE CORPS ITEMS; MILITARIA, WWI Items; MILITARIA, WWII Items; NAZI ITEMS; RATIONING RELATED ITEMS)

WORLD'S FAIRS & EXPOSITIONS

Auction Services

Janice & Richard Vogel
Vogels, The
4720 SE Fort King St.
Ocala, FL 34470-1501
ph: 352-694-5776
fax: 352-694-7330
e-mail: vogels@atlantic.net
Bi-monthly mail order souvenir auctions: china, glass, spoons, mauchline, paper, World's Fair, fraternal.

Bob Slawsky
P.O. Box 864
Windermere, FL 34786-0864
ph: 407-352-7807
fax: 407-352-BIDS
e-mail: WWGD54A@prodigy.com
Buys, sells, auctions tokens, medals, badges, small advertising items, political, World's Fair, Olympic items, encased coins, etc.

Clubs/Associations

Michael R. Pender, Pres.
World's Fair Collectors Society, Inc.
Newsletter: Fair News
P.O. Box 20806
Sarasota, FL 34276-3806
ph: 941-923-2590
e-mail: wfcs@aol.com
web: http://members.aol.com/bbqprod/wfcs.html
Focuses on collecting and preserving materials pertinent to the history of World's Fairs and International expositions; bi-monthly newsletter contains articles, ads, etc.

Jim Thompson, Sec.
1904 World's Fair Society
Newsletter: World's Fair Bulletin
12934 Windy Hill Dr.
Saint Louis, MO 63128
e-mail: terryl@inlink.com
web: http://www.inlink.com/~terryl/
Purpose is to preserve the memories and memorabilia of the 1904 St. Louis World's Fair.

Collectors

Augyre T.
P.O. Box 1293
Bayonne, NJ 07002-6293
ph: 201-339-8375
e-mail: augyre.T@talk21.com
Buys 1939-40 and 1964-65 New York World's Fair, especially posters, signs and things unusual; also has some for trade/sale.

Ken Schultz
P.O. Box M753
Hoboken, NJ 07030
ph: 201-656-0966
fax: 201-418-8640
Wants all items relating to world's fairs and expositions.

Andy Rudoff
P.O. Box 111
Oceanport, NJ 07757-0111
ph: 732-542-3712
fax: 732-542-3712
Wants early (1851-1904) World's Fair items especially 1876 Centennial and 1893 Columbian Exposition; wants all items especially china, glass, and metal souvenirs; all other early U.S. and foreign fairs also considered.

Steve Sheppard
2500 Johnson Ave.
Bronx, NY 10463
ph: 718-549-1570
Wants to buy World's Columbian Exposition items: advertising, documents, letters, diaries, photographs, and other ephemera.

Henry Heiman, III
P.O. Box 316
South Salem, NY 10590-0316
Wants 1939-1940 New York World's Fair items.

Rusty Olimpo
P.O. Box 363
Mechanicsville, PA 18934-0363
ph: 215-345-5768
e-mail: oporx@aol.com
Wants to buy anything relating to the 1939-40 New York World's Fair.

Frederick Lingenfelser
814 Byram St.
Reading, PA 19606-1446
Wants to buy World's Fair items; specializes in 1893 Columbian Exposition: photographs, post cards, art work, maps, trinkets, tickets, etc.

Paul A. Jarrett
611 West Main
Waverly, TN 37185
ph: 615-296-3151
Wants to buy any type of memorabilia from the 1897 Tennessee Centennial Exposition including china, paper, glassware, badges, pins, medals, ribbons, tickets, etc.

Rick Rann
P.O. Box 877
Oak Park, IL 60303-0877
ph: 708-442-7907
e-mail: ukczech@aol.com
Wants to buy items from the 1933-1934 Chicago Century of Progress: uniforms, toys, ride tickets, pennants, etc.

Doug Woolard
11614 Old St. Charles Rd.
Bridgeton, MO 63044-3078
ph: 314-739-4662

Max Storm
529 Barcia Dr.
Saint Louis, MO 63119-1518
ph: 314-968-2810
e-mail: worldsfair@earthlink.net
web: http://home.earthlink.net/~worldsfair/
Wants any type of memorabilia from the 1904 St. Louis World's Fair: clocks, padlocks, postcards, watches, china, tickets, paper, stock certificates, etc.

Chuck Wasserman
11723 W. 101st
Shawnee Mission, KS 66214
ph: 913-492-5005
Expert and serious collector of 1904 St. Louis World's Fair memorabilia; specializes in spoons, ceramics, and glass; especially foreign exhibit material such as jasperware, Haviland Limoges, Nippon, and moriage.

Dealers

Thomas J. Diddle
Worlds Columbian Exonumist, The
802 North Rd.
Boynton Beach, FL 33435-3238
ph: 561-738-1992
fax: 561-733-4127
Buys, sells, trades all World Fair and Exposition collectibles and ephemera.

Bindy Bitterman
Eureka! Antiques
705 W. Washington
Evanston, IL 60202-2214
ph: 847-869-9090
Focuses on the Chicago World's Fairs and other Chicago memorabilia; a small shop - they send no lists but write detailed individual letters; SASEs get first attention.

William "Bill" Pieber
Best of Times Antiques
1010 Mallow Dr.
Ballwin, MO 63011-2365
ph: 314-227-8930
Buys and sells St. Louis World's Fair (1904) and Louisiana Purchase Exposition items; also all World's Fair items from 1915 Pan-Pacific, 1939 New York, and 1939 San Francisco.

Vivian Briggs
Briggs Antiques
4443 Linwood Place
Riverside, CA 92506
ph: 909-781-3121
fax: 909-781-3121
e-mail: drago120@aol.com
web: http://www.tias.com/stores/briggs/
Specializes in World's Fair items from 1856 to 1939 New York; has World's Fair items from 1856 to 1939 New York.

Experts

Richard Friz
Maddie's Muse
P.O. Box 472
Peterborough, NH 03458-0472
ph: 603-563-8155
e-mail: jmdfriz@top.monad.net
Author of "The Official Price Guide to World's Fair Memorabilia."

Harvey & Sandy Dolin
Harvey Dolin & Co.
5 Beekman St.
New York, NY 10038-2206
ph: 212-267-0216
Wants any item pertaining to the 1939 New York World's Fair and the Columbian Fair.

Judith Katz-Schwartz
Twin Brooks Antiques & Collectibles
P.O. Box 6572
New York, NY 10128-0006
ph: 212-876-3512
fax: 212-876-3512
e-mail: twinb@msjudith.net
web: http://www.msjudith.net
Buys, sells, appraises all categories of World's Fair memorabilia; looking for items from 1939 New York World's Fair.

Herbert Rolfes
2260 Chase Court
Mount Dora, FL 32757-6909
ph: 352-735-3947 or 352-735-3970
e-mail: ny1939@aol.com
Co-author of "The World of Tomorrow: The 1939 New York World's Fair."

Rich Hartzog
World Exonumia
P.O. Box 4143
Rockford, IL 61110-0643
ph: 815-226-0771
fax: 815-397-7662
e-mail: hartzog@exonumia.com
web: http://www.exonumia.com/
Pre-1940 items preferred; collections and quantities wanted.

D.D. Woollard, Jr.
11614 Old St. Charles Rd.
Bridgeton, MO 63044-3078
ph: 314-739-4662
Buy, sell, trade World Fair & Exposition memorabilia: major interest in older fairs - 1893 Chicago, 1904 St. Louis, etc.

Max Storm
529 Barcia Dr.
Saint Louis, MO 63119-1518
ph: 314-968-2810
e-mail: worldsfair@earthlink.net
web: http://home.earthlink.net/~worldsfair/
Collector, historian and appraiser; noted expert on the 1904 St. Louis World's Fair.

Chuck Wasserman
11723 W. 101st
Shawnee Mission, KS 66214
ph: 913-492-5005
Expert and serious collector of 1904 St. Louis World's Fair memorabilia; specializes in spoons, ceramics, and glass; especially foreign exhibit material such as jasperware, Haviland Limoges, Nippon, and moriage.

Museums/Libraries

Buffalo & Erie County Historical Society
25 Nottingham Ct.
Buffalo, NY 14216
ph: 716-873-9644

Atwater Kent Museum - the History Museum of Philadelphia
15 S. 7th St.
Philadelphia, PA 19143
ph: 610-922-3031
web: http://www.fieldtrip.com/pa/59223031.htm

Dan & Rose Amato
Christopher Columbus Museum
239 Whitney St.
P.O. Box 151
Columbus, WI 53925-0151
ph: 920-623-1992
fax: 920-623-1992
web: http://www.wistravel.com/columbus/
Features a collection of souvenirs from the 1893 World's Columbian Exposition of Chicago; wants to buy all quality Christopher Columbus items, old and new.

Dan & Rose Amato
1893 Chicago World's Columbian Exposition Museum
239 Whitney St.
P.O. Box 151
Columbus, WI 53925-0151
ph: 920-623-1992
fax: 920-623-1992
web: http://www.wistravel.com/columbus/
Focuses on the World's Columbian Exposition of 1893; over 2,000 pieces.

Keith R. Gill
Museum of Science & Industry
57th St. & Lake Shore Dr.
Chicago, IL 60637
ph: 773-684-1414
fax: 773-684-5580
Archives contains documents & photos of the 1893 Columbian Exposition and the 1933-1934 Century of Progress Exposition.

WRAPPERS

(see BUBBLE GUM & CANDY WRAPPERS)

WRITING INSTRUMENTS

(see BLOTTERS; GLASS, Whimsies [Pens]; INKWELLS & INKSTANDS; LETTER OPENERS; OFFICE EQUIPMENT; PENCILS; PENS; SEALS, Wax)

WWI

(see MILITARIA, WWI Items)

WWII

(see MILITARIA, WWII Items)

YACHTS

(see BOATS)

ZEPPELINS

(see AIRSHIPS)

Here are some tips when contacting someone listed in this book:

■ When requesting information about a particular item, include a description (material, dimensions, maker's mark, model number, etc.) and a photo, sketch, or photocopy of the item in question.

■ Always ask if there are charges for samples or for the services requested.

■ When writing, please be sure to include a Large (#10 business size) Self-Addressed and Stamped Envelope (LSASE) if requesting a reply or the return of photographs.

■ Never call collect unless otherwise directed. When calling, be considerate of time zone differences and always ask if the party you are calling has time to talk. When leaving an answering machine message, always instruct the party to call you back collect.

APPENDIX A

Appraisers

Listed in ZIP code order

The International Society of Appraisers is the largest nonprofit association of educated and trained personal property appraisers in North America. Its Accredited and Certified members are experienced and educated appraisers who evaluate all types of personal property (including antiques & collectibles , art, gems & jewelry, and machinery & equipment) to establish accurate values for such uses as buying and selling objects, insurance coverage, damage claims, estate and gift taxes, charitable donations, bankruptcies, casualty loss, equitable distribution, and expert witness testimony.

All appraisers listed below are Accredited Members of the ISA, and many have earned the coveted CAPP (Certified Appraiser of Personal Property) designation. The ISA is the only personal property appraisal association that has always prohibited the "grandfathering" of its members. All those listed have demonstrated appraisal competency through a mandatory education/testing program and are bound to abide by a rigid Code of Ethics and Appraisal Report Writing Standard. In addition, the ISA's affiliation with the University of Maryland University College insures that ISA appraiser education programs adhere to the highest standards of academia.

For additional information about the ISA or to locate a nearby appraiser, write the ISA at 16040 Christensen Rd., Suite 120, Seattle, WA 98188. You can also call 888-472-4732, fax 206-241-0436 or e-mail ISAHQ@cs.com. Check out the ISA web site on the Internet at **http://www.isa-appraisers.org** to search for an appraiser in your locale or to learn more about the ISA and its course offerings.

Please note that hundreds of appraisers who specialize in a particular field of expertise are also listed under those categories within the General Listings section of this Directory.

Karin Ann Esposito, ISA, GG (GIA)
KAE Gemological Services, Inc.
9003 Est. Hope, Lot 003
Christiansted, VI 00820
ph: 340-778-6634
fax: 340-778-6634
Gems, Jewelry

Walter P. Petreyko, ISA
Imagine
PO Box 819
Groton, MA 01450-0819
ph: 978-448-5044
fax: 978-448-5044
Antiques, Arts, Collectibles, Furniture, Jewelry

Kenneth P. Katz, ISA, GG (GIA)
Katz Group, The
PO Box 538, Apt 415
Worcester, MA 01602
ph: 508-753-5783
fax: 508-753-6696
katzgp@aol.com
Gold and Diamond Jewelry, Colored Gemstones, Pearls, Watches, Silver Tableware

Frank Lenz, ISA
c/o Sudbury Arts & Antiques
277 Bolton St
Marlborough, MA 01752-3949
ph: 508-481-4870
masstiques@aol.com
Antiques, Art, Personal Property, Estates, Auctioneer

Spencer Gordon, ISA
Spencer Marks
PO Box 303
East Walpole, MA 02032-0303
ph: 508-668-8969
73760.1470@compuserve.com
Non Appraising Member. Silver (American & English), Furniture (American & English), Fine Art, Ceramics, Glass, Decorative Arts & Accessories, Orientalia, Antiques

Robert D. Nordberg, ISA
Paul E. Saperstein Co., Inc.
148 State St
Boston, MA 02109
ph: 800-660-6553
fax: 617-227-4538
pesco@pesco.com
Machinery & Equipment, Auction

Michael E. Saperstein, ISA
Paul E. Saperstein Co, Inc.
148 State St
Boston, MA 02109
ph: 800-660-6553
fax: 617-227-4538
msaperstein@pesco.com
http://www.pesco.com
Machinery & Equipment, Auctioneer

Judith Dowling, ISA
Edo Gallery Of Asian Art
133 Charles St
Boston, MA 02114-3252
ph: 617-523-5211
fax: 617-523-5227
Asian Art (Japanese & Chinese), Korean

Peter J. Shemonsky, ISA, GG (GIA)
24 Horace St
Boston, MA 02128-1534
ph: 617-569-1502
fax: 617-846-4767
pshemonsky@aol.com
Gemology/Gemstones, Jewelry (Antique, Estate, Arts & Crafts, Modern), Silver (American & European)

Norman Hurst, ISA S-CAPP
Hurst Gallery
53 Mount Auburn St
Cambridge, MA 02138-5053
ph: 617-491-6888
fax: 617-661-0439
nhurst@compuserve.com
http://www.hurstgallery.com
Asian Art: Chinese, Indian, Japanese & Korean Ceramics, Sculpture, Painting, and Prints. Arts of Africa and Oceania, Melanesia, Micronesia, Polynesia, American Indian, Eskimo, Pre-Columbian Art, Greek, Roman, Egyptian, and Ancient Art

Martin D. Haske, ISA, GG (GIA)
Adamas Gemological Lab
PO Box 470828
Brookline Village, MA 02147-0828
ph: 617-232-5508
fax: 617-232-5508
adamas@gis.net
Diamond Grading & Evaluation with SAS2000 Spectrophotometer Analysis System, Scientific Expert Witness

Mary Westcott, ISA
239 Common St
Belmont, MA 02178-2944
ph: 617-484-3386
fax: 617-484-0628
Silver, Porcelain, Furniture, Paintings, Americana, Residential Contents, Victoriana, Fine Art, Antiques, Decorative Art & Accessories

Matthew Joel Fink, ISA
PO Box 728
Centerville, MA 02632-0728
ph: 617-552-7037
fax: 617-332-8042
Antiques, Residential Contents, Decorative Arts & Accessories, Ceramics, Glass, Furniture, Paper, Ephemera, Orientialia, Fabrics (Textiles), Jewelry (Estate), Art Deco, Art Noveau, Clothing, and Poster Stamps. Alt Phone: 617-965-5735

Patricia P. Coughlin, ISA
Antique And Estate Appraisals
22 Ash St
Hollis, NH 03049
ph: 603-465-3443
fax: 603-465-3732
Decorative Arts & Accessories, Antiques, Paintings, Furniture, Residential Contents: Estate, Insurance Apprasials, Resale, Estate Planning, Coordination of Contents Sales.

Judith Fineblit Anderson, ISA CAPP, GG, CG, CGA
Bijoux Extraordinaire, Ltd.
PO Box 1424
Manchester, NH 03105-1424
ph: 603-624-8672
fax: 603-624-8673
judi@jewelryexpert.com
http://www.jewelryexpert.com
Jewelry, Gemstones, Antique And Period Jewelry, Contemporary Jewelry, Designer Jewelry, Diamonds, Metals, Insurance and Estate Appraisals, Damage Claims, Expert Witness, Charitable Donation Reports, Consulting

Carlton C. Ham, ISA
Carlton C. Ham Personal Property Appraiser
PO Box 3502
Concord, NH 03302-3502
ph: 603-934-4913
fax: 613-934-5174
whtmtman@together.net
Antiques, Residential Contents, Postwar Automobiles

Lawrence E. Reynolds, Jr., ISA, GG (GIA)
G.M. Pollack & Sons
PO Box 910
Scarborough, ME 04070-0910
ph: 207-883-8455
fax: 207-883-8565
lerabr@msn.com
Diamonds

Ruth H. Isgro, ISA CAPP
Stone Hearth Antiques
PO Box 77
140 N Rd
Harmony, ME 04942-0077
ph: 207-683-3188
Antiques & Res. Contents. Specialty in Am. Furniture & Accessiories(18th-20th C.) Consultation work Preferred (how, when, where to disperse of your Estate). Summer Address: P.O. Box 77, Harmony, ME 04942, 207-683-3188 (Aprl to Nov15)

Evelyn S. Kennedy, ISA
Sewtique
391 Long Hill Rd
Box 1293
Groton, CT 06340-1293
ph: 800-332-9122
fax: 860-445-1448
sewtique@aol.com
http://www.tlqse/home.htm
Quilts, Tapestries, Textiles (Laces, Furs, & Leather), Needlework, Repairs, Restoration, Costumes

Trina McCandless, ISA CAPP, GG (GIA)
McCandless Custom Jewelry
100 Starr Hill Rd
Groton, CT 06340-3333
ph: 860-443-3039
fax: 860-443-3039
trina@unidial.com
Gemology/Gemstones, Designer Jewelry, Antique & Period Jewelry, Colored Gemstones, Diamonds, Pearls Custom Designs, Goldsmith Jewelry.

Harry B. French, ISA, CGA, GG, RJ
Henry C. Reid & Son
1591 Post Rd
Fairfield, CT 06430-5910
ph: 203-255-0447
fax: 203-255-0448
Gems, Jewelry, Insurance Replacement, Estate Appraisal

Raymond D'Alessio, ISA
Valuation Resources, Inc.
34 Fawn Brook Cir
Madison, CT 06443-2442
ph: 203-318-0435
raymond.dalessio@snet.net
Machinery & Equipment, Commercial Inventories

Kathleen Connolly, ISA
Village Antique Shop
61 W Main St
Plantsville, CT 06479-1522
ph: 860-628-2498
kconnolly@snet.net
Dolls, Toys, Victorian Furniture

Paul D. Indorf, ISA CAPP, GG, CGA
Peter Indorf Jewelers
1022 Chapel St
New Haven, CT 06510-2412
ph: 203-776-4833
fax: 203-777-8423
paulindorf@snet.net
http://www.peterindorf.com
Gemology/Gemstones, Jewelry, Diamonds, Pearls, Estate, Gold

Doreen A. Guerrera, ISA CAPP, CGA
Addessi Jewelry Stores
72 Elm St
New Canaan, CT 06840
ph: 203-966-8705
fax: 203-966-7615
Gemology & Gemstones, Pearls, Jewelry

Joan Gehl, ISA
19 Spring Hill Dr
West Orange, NJ 07052-2411
ph: 973-731-3264
Residential Contents, Furniture, Silver, Porcelain, China, Pottery

Elissa S. Cohen, ISA CAPP, GG (GIA)
Suburban Jewelers
126 E Front St
Plainfield, NJ 07060-1202
ph: 908-756-1774
fax: 908-756-6596
Gemology/Gemstones, Colored Stones, Diamonds (Loose & Mounted, Old Cut), Jewelry (Fine, Contemporary, Estate, & Karat Gold), Pearls (Cultured), Figurines (Lladro, All God's Children, & Precious Moments)

Patricia Sheeleigh, ISA
Patricia Sheeleigh Fine Arts
39 Old Eagle Rock Ave
Roseland, NJ 07068-1433
ph: 973-228-4362
fax: 973-228-6509
Sheeleigh-cleaver@compuserve.com
American Art (1810-1950), Paintings, Drawings, Watercolors, Prints, Etchings, Engravings, 19th C. European Paintings

JoAnne M. Whitteaker, ISA CAPP, GG (GIA)
American Appraisal Gem Lab
23 W Westfield Ave
Roselle Park, NJ 07204-2252
ph: 908-241-8800
fax: 908-298-0021
#3580@polygon.net
Consultant, Diamonds, Gemology/ Gemstones, Insurance/Damage Appraisals, Estates, Jewelry, Gold, Silver, Pearls, Watches, Jade, Art Deco, Art Nouveau, Native American Indian Jewelry

Zia Ghahary Ph.D., ISA CAPP
Zighom International Fine Arts
240 Heather Ln
AAA Appraisals
Franklin Lakes, NJ 07417-1111
ph: 888-299-5577
fax: 201-337-0404
Authenticate & Appraise: Paintings (Old Masters, 19th C.), Bronze & Clay Sculpture, Antiques - Pottery, Earthenware, Antique Glass, Islamic Works of Art, Miniature Paintings, Drawings, Illuminated Miniatures & Manuscripts, Oriental Rugs

William L. Scolnik, ISA
William L. Scolnik, Inc.
55 Long Hill Rd
Oakland, NJ 07436-2501
ph: 201-405-0719
wls@intac.com
Clocks, Watches (Antique), Horological Books & Tools

Diane R. Patalano, ISA
Country Girls Appraisal & Liquidation Service
PO Box 144
Saddle River, NJ 07458-0144
ph: 201-327-2499
fax: 201-327-2094
dp@microdsi.net
Country Girls Appraisal & Liquidation Service conducts appraisals for all legal purposes, estate, money, tag sale & auction specialist.

Richard Henion, ISA
Another Facet
150 W Pleasant Ave
Maywood, NJ 07607-1335
ph: 201-368-9433
Gems & Jewelry (Antique & Contemporary), Diamonds, Pearls, Insurance, Estate, Resale, Equitable Distribution, Purchase

Beth K. Meer, ISA CAPP, GG (GIA)
A Meer Design
PO Box 452
Cresskill, NJ 07626-0452
ph: 201-569-6589
fax: 201-569-3152
Gemology/Gemstones, Jewelry

Frederick J. Hill, Jr., ISA CAPP
Koty & Associates, LLC.
PO Box 625
Freehold, NJ 07728-0625
ph: 732-751-0504
fax: 732-751-9190
fhill09085@aol.com
Residential Contents; Estates, Specializing in Estate Tax Liability Reports; Model Cars, Diecast & Plastic, All Scales, Auto Racing, Collectibles, Auction Company

Bob Koty, ISA CAPP, CAI, GPPA
Koty & Associates, LLC
PO Box 625
Freehold, NJ 07728-0625
ph: 732-751-0504
fax: 732-751-9190
bidtaker@compuserve.com
Residential Contents, Specializing In Estate Liability Reports, Estates, Antiques, Personal Property Consultant, Auctioneer

Clara Koty, ISA CAPP
Koty & Associates, LLC.
PO Box 625
Freehold, NJ 07728-0625
ph: 732-751-0504
fax: 732-751-9190
75754.1156@compuserve.com
Residential Contents, Specializing In Estate Liability Reports, Estates, Antiques, Personal Property Consultant, Collectibles, Hummels, Buttons

Eldred A. Stenzel, ISA
10 Blue Hills Dr
Holmdel, NJ 07733-2218
ph: 908-946-8437
American Furniture, Ceramics, Residential Contents

Suzy McLennan Anderson, ISA
Heritage Antiques, Inc.
65 Main St
Holmdel, NJ 07733-2310
ph: 732-946-8801
fax: 732-946-1036
suzyfx@aol.com
Furniture (American), Textiles, Decorative Arts & Accessories, Estate Liquidations

Gregory E. Sherman, ISA CAPP, GG (GIA)
5 Island View Way, Apt 10
Sea Bright, NJ 07760-2253
ph: 732-345-9313
fax: 732-741-7250
105064.2243@compuserve.com
Diamonds, Colored Gemstones, Antique & Period Jewelry, Watches, Giftware, Silverware, Designer Jewelry, Estate Appraisals, Insurance Appraisals, Educational Lectures and Speaking Engagements

Victor Brown, Jr., ISA
Tri-State Auction Company
28 DeJager Dr
Augusta, NJ 07822-2111
ph: 201-702-0800
fax: 201-702-8666
TriStateAuction@compuserve.com
Antiques, Estates, Residential Contents, Collectibles, Toys, Decorative Arts & Accessories, Equipment, Real Estate, Auctioneer, Auction Company

Leon Castner, Ph.D., ISA CAPP
Castner Appraisal Service/NAL
PO Box 920
Branchville, NJ 07826-0920
ph: 973-948-3868
fax: 973-948-3919
castner@garden.net
Full Menu Inc. Normal Ins, Est., Div., or Forced Sale to Complex, Tech. Suites. Comm & Priv, work w/ Carriers, Adjusters, Homeowners. Multi-specialty w/strong background in Auction & Ed., Multi-val Reports, Blockage & Market Analysis

Victor Franco, Jr., ISA
Franco & Associates, Inc.
223B Stiger St, Ste 8
Hackettstown, NJ 07840
ph: 908-684-8599
fax: 908-684-8551
Household Contents, Furniture, China, Crystal

Brian Kathenes, ISA S-CAPP
National Appraisal Consultants
PO Box 482
Hope, NJ 07844-0482
ph: 800-323-5996
fax: 908-459-4899
Brian@nacvalue.com
http://www.nacvalue.com
Autographs, Collectibles (Baseball Cards, Sports & Space Memorabilia), Coins, Currency, Stamps, Postal History, Movie Memorabilia, Computer & Office Equipment, Documents & Manuscripts, Photography, Photographica

Loretta Carbonaro, ISA
Acquisition, Inc.
883 Cooper Landing Rd
Cherry Hill, NJ 08002-1722
ph: 609-663-1466
fax: 609-665-2247
Weapons, Jewelry, Beadwork (American Indian), American Glass (Paperweights, Lamps, etc.), American Paintings

Pamela T. Giles, ISA
Blue Skies Auction Co.
PO Box 567
Voorhees, NJ 08043-0567
ph: 609-354-0199
fax: 609-354-8150
bluskysnj@aol.com
Residential Contents, Estates

Benjamin A. Doerrmann, ISA
Benjamin Doerrman Auctioneers & Appraisers
131 Sherwin Rd
Sewell, NJ 08080-4431
ph: 609-478-2389
fax: 609-478-6606
Glass (Glassware), Furniture, Farm Machinery & Equipment, Auctioneer, Auction Company

Ronald E. Shaffer, ISA
Exemplars, Inc.
17 Pemberton Rd
Vincentown, NJ 08088-8811
ph: 609-859-0045
fax: 609-859-3477
Antiques, Americana, American Art, Barometers, Ceramics, Clocks, Decorative Arts & Accessories, American Furniture, Glass, Lamps & Lighting Fixtures, Needlework, Oriental Rugs, Paintings, Porcelain, Quilts, American Silver, Textiles

James Crawford, ISA
1017 Park Ave
Collingswood, NJ 08108-3236
ph: 609-854-3049
fax: 609-854-3049
crawford@cyberenet.net
Antiques, Furniture, Decorative Arts & Accessories, Residential Contents, Estate Property Consultant

C. Frederick Horbach, Ph.D., ISA
Shibui
280 Greenville Rd
Pittsgrove, NJ 08318-3722
ph: 609-358-3726
fax: 609-358-3726
Orientalia, Woodblock Prints, Porcelain, Cloisonne

Ralph S. Joseph, ISA CAPP, GG (GIA)
Jewelry Judge of Princeton, The
190 Nassau St
Rear Office
Princeton, NJ 08542
ph: 609-683-7730
fax: 609-683-7742
rjoseph@jewelryjudge.net
http://www.jewelryjudge.net
Gemology/Gemstones, Diamonds, Jewelry, Insurance Matters, Expert Witness Testimony; Appraisal Editor and Columnist - National Jeweler Magazine, Author of "The Jewelers Guide to Effective Insurance Appraising"

Jeffrey S. Litwin, ISA, MD
Litwin Antiques
PO Box 494
Princeton Junction, NJ 08550-0494
ph: 609-275-1427
fax: 609-275-1427
jsl58@home.com
Chess Sets, Chess Books, Chess Related Art, Chess Ephemera, Objet D'Art, De Vertu, Needlework, Decorative Arts & Accessories

Richard A. Newman, ISA
Newman Fur Appraisers & Consultants, Inc.
11 Penn Plaza, 5th Floor
New York, NY 10001
ph: 212-564-4733
fax: 212-564-4735
richn1@idt.net
Furs (Appraiser, Consultant, All Phases of the Fur Industry), Damage & Claim Consultants

Jerry R. Ehrenwald, ISA, GG (GIA)
Int'l Gemological Institute
579 5th Ave
New York, NY 10017-1917
ph: 212-753-7100
fax: 212-753-7759
IGI@interport.net
http://www.igi-usa.com
Gems & Jewelry, Independant Appraisals for Insurance, Estate Tax, Charitable Donation Purposes, and Court Qualified as an Expert Witness

Robert C. Aretz, ISA, GG (GIA)
Gem Appraiser's Laboratory, Inc.
608 5th Ave, Ste 403
New York, NY 10020-2303
ph: 212-333-3122
fax: 212-245-6915
galine@erols.com
Diamonds, Antique Jewelry, Colored Stones, Art Deco, Pearls, Natural Pearls, Watches

Theodore M. Baer, ISA
Theodore M. Baer, Inc.
608 5th Ave
New York, NY 10020-2303
ph: 212-245-6330
fax: 212-245-6331
Jewelry (Estate, Previously Owned, Contemporary), Diamonds, Precious Stones, Pearls, Gold

Judy Herman Appelbaum, ISA
301 E 63rd St, Apt 2J
New York, NY 10021-7736
ph: 212-319-3898
fax: 212-319-3961
Dolls, Doll Houses, Miniatures, Residential Contents, Collectibles

Thomas Dipasqua, ISA
401 Willow Rd E
Staten Island, NY 10314-1696
ph: 718-698-0099
Porcelain, Pottery, Ceramics, Glass, Toys, Collectibles, Residential Contents

Paul Marinucci, ISA
Paul D. Marinucci & Associates
5 Pheasant Rd W
Pound Ridge, NY 10576-2317
ph: 914-764-4609
fax: 914-764-4609
http://www.butterauction.com
Paintings, Watercolors, Drawings, Prints (Limited Edition), Residential Contents, Auctioneer and Owner Of Butterscotch Auction Gallery In Bedford, NY

Laura Shahinian, ISA, GG, NJA
E. Ross Jewelers
96 Kraft Ave
Bronxville, NY 10708
ph: 914-771-6485
fax: 914-771-6942
lljjerro@aol.com
Jewelry, Gemstones

William J. Jenack, ISA
W.J. Jenack Estate Appraisers/ Auctioneer
18 Hambletonian Ave
Chester, NY 10918-1023
ph: 914-469-9095
fax: 914-469-8445
wmjenack@frontiernet.net
http://www.jenack.com
Furniture (American & Continental), Fine Art (American & Continental), Jewelry, Books, Ephemera, Militaria, Toys, Decorative Arts & Accessories, Orientalia

Les Wolff, ISA
PO Box 650037
Flushing, NY 11365-0037
ph: 718-454-3956
fax: 718-454-3956
lwolff1823@aol.com
Sports Memorabilia (Autographs & Uniforms Used By Athletes), Paintings (Sports), Lithographs (Sports) & Cards

Gail Brett Levine, ISA CAPP, GG (GIA)
Auction Market Resource
PO Box 7683
Rego Park, NY 11374-7683
ph: 718-897-7305
fax: 718-997-9057
76766.614@compuserve.com
Gemology/Gemstones, Diamonds, Jewelry (Antique, Estate, & Contemporary), Consultant, Publisher of "Auction Market Resource For Gems & Jewelry", Polygon #2646

Nehme Frangie, ISA, GG (GIA)
17 Glenbrook Dr
Clifton Park, NY 12065-1908
ph: 518-383-3247
fax: 518-383-3247
105042.372@compuserve.com
Gemology/Gemstones, Diamonds, Jewelry, Estates

Ralph F. Passonno, Jr., ISA, CAI
Uncle Sam Auctions & Realty, Inc.
225 Pinewoods Ave
Troy, NY 12180-7246
ph: 518-274-6464
fax: 518-272-7189
Antiques, General Household, Trains, Knives, Real Estate, Business Inventories

Robert A. Doyle, ISA, CAI
Absolute Auction & Realty, Inc.
PO Box 1739
Pleasant Valley, NY 12569
ph: 914-635-3169
fax: 914-635-5140
hikerto@aol.com
Americana, Gambling Devices (Antique), Antiques, Collectibles, Auctioneer, Auction Co., Estate & Insurance Appraisals

Susan A. Doyle, ISA
Absolute Auction & Realty, Inc.
PO Box 1739
Pleasant Valley, NY 12569
ph: 914-635-3169
fax: 914-635-5140
hikerto@Aol.com
Antiques, Collectibles, Residential Contents, Auctioneer, Auction Co.

Bruce M. Lubman, ISA, GG (GIA)
Hummingbird Jewelers
20 W Market St
Rhinebeck, NY 12572-1403
ph: 914-876-4585
fax: 914-876-3177
Gemology/Gemstones, Jewelry, Silver (Holloware & Flatware)

Catherine M. Sankey, ISA CAPP
Catherine's Antiques
RR 4, Box 298
Auburn, NY 13021-8801
ph: 315-685-5306
katlyn@aiusa.com or
csankey@compuserve
Furniture, Shaker Artifacts, Personal Property

David E. Martin, ISA, GG (GIA)
Egon A. Ehrlinspiel, Inc.
210 E Fayette St
Syracuse, NY 13202-1936
ph: 315-471-8710
fax: 315-471-3226
Gemology/Gemstones, Diamonds, Jewelry (Gold)

Marlene J. Kirby, ISA
America's Attic, Inc.
308 Harry L Dr
Johnson City, NY 13790-1477
ph: 607-798-0084
fax: 607-798-0878
attic@spectra.net
Modern Furniture, Furniture 1900-1997, Residential Contents

Carol Higgins, ISA, GG (GIA)
Higgins Jewelers, Inc.
428 County Hwy 47
Oneonta, NY 13820-3213
ph: 607-433-2073
fax: 607-433-2073
Gemology/Gemstones, Diamonds, Jewelry (Estate, Late 19th & Early 20th C., Modern)

David W. Mapes, ISA CAPP
Mapes Auctioneers-Appraisers
1729 Vestal Pkwy W
Vestal, NY 13850-1196
ph: 607-754-9193
fax: 607-786-3549
76742.274@compuserve.com
Residential Contents, Furniture, 19th-20th C. Decorative Arts & Accessories, Toys, Auction House.

Sarah E. Blawat, ISA, GG (GIA)
Sarah Eve Blawat, GG (GIA)
PO Box 220
Buffalo, NY 14205-0220
ph: 716-854-6444
Jewelry (Antique, Period, & Estate), Antique Diamonds, Gemstones

Elizabeth Lisy Smith, ISA
Elizabeth Lisy Smith Antiques & Appraisals
PO Box 347
Bergen, NY 14416-0347
ph: 716-494-1867
lizsmith36@aol.com
Furniture (18th-19th C. American), Decorative Arts & Accessories (18th-19th C. American), Antiques, Residential Contents, Estates

Ann Marszalek, ISA
350 W Commercial St
East Rochester, NY 14445-2225
ph: 716-381-7170
anntiques@compuserve.com
Since 1984, Estate Sale Coordinator; Fund-raising expertise, Buys Antiques & Collectibles, Offers after-sale house cleaning

Michael Bruce, ISA
Bruce & Co.
52 N Main St
Fairport, NY 14450-1555
ph: 716-388-1080
fax: 716-388-9654
Residential Contents, Antiques, Estates, Auctioneer, Auction Co.

Duane E. Gansz, ISA, CAI-RES
Gansz Auction & Realty
14 William St
Lyons, NY 14489-1119
ph: 315-946-9492
Antiques, Household, Farm, Commercial, Guns, Toys, Machinery & Equipment, Estate Appraiser & Auctioneer For Real & Personal Property, Auction Co.

Paul R. Cassarino, ISA CAPP, FGA
Gem Lab, The
35 Charit Way
Rochester, NY 14626-1101
ph: 716-225-4527
fax: 815-377-8277
paulcass@rochester.rr.com
Diamonds, Gemstones, and Contemporary Jewelry. Alt Email: 102073.2774@compuserve.com, pcassarino@csi.com

Pamela E. Mayo, ISA
710 Washington St
Sewickley, PA 15143-1845
ph: 412-749-0760
fax: 412-201-1747
pandjr@usaor.net
Fine Art (American 18th-Early 20th C.), Art, Paintings, Watercolors, Drawings, Sporting Art, Southern Art

William M. Kline, III, ISA
Three Rivers Auction Co.
PO Box 6298
Pittsburgh, PA 15212-0298
ph: 800-976-4607
Furniture, Decorative Arts & Accessories, Ceramics, Victoriana, Antiques, Residential Contents, Estates, Consultant, Auctioneer, Auction Co., Americana, Arts & Crafts, Porcelain, Folk Art

Vivian A. Highberg, ISA
Hilding & Larson Emporium
1741 Partridge Run Rd
Pittsburgh, PA 15241-2823
ph: 412-854-1421
Lecturer, Antiques, Collectibles, Furniture, Glass, Pottery

Charles J. Behm, III, ISA
Behm's Auction Service
Rr 1, Box 142
Graysville, PA 15337-9304
ph: 412-428-3664
fax: 412-428-4946
Auctioneer, Auction Co/Gallery

Romayne Shay McMahon, ISA
Veronique's Antiques
124 S Market St
Mechanicsburg, PA 17055-6329
ph: 717-697-4924
fax: 717-697-9594
Residential Contents, Antiques, Silver, European Porcelain, Crystal, Steins, Clocks, Fine Metals (Refinishing & Repairs), Damage Claims, Estates, Divorce, Charitable Contributions

John W. Rockafellow, ISA
Essential Images
382 Schottie Rd
Littlestown, PA 17340-9748
ph: 800-660-8299
Furniture, Silver, Residential Contents, Antiques, Porcelain, Pottery, Ceramics, China, Textiles, Glass, Consultant, Damage Claims, Fine Art, Liquidator, Estates, Orientalia

Frank Michael Pereny, ISA
Saisho International
RR 5 Box 5002
Spring Grove, PA 17363-9101
ph: 717-763-4729
fax: 717-763-1875
saisho@worldnet.att.net
Asian Art, Pre 1940 Native American Art, Military Collectibles, Japanese Swords, Fittings

Jane E. Chaikowsky, ISA, GG (GIA)
Chaikowsky Gem & Jewelry Appraisals
1203 S 8th St
Allentown, PA 18103-4027
ph: 610-776-2770
Gemology/Gemstones, Diamonds, Jewelry (Gold)

Marguerite S. Glaser, ISA
Aston Auctioneers & Appraisers
1012 Westminster Rd
Wilkes Barre, PA 18702-9404
ph: 717-654-3090
fax: 717-654-3090
aston@epix.net
Residential Contents, Antiques, Furniture, Shaving Mugs, R.S. Prussia, Art Pottery, Porcelain (American & European), Majolica, Glass By C.F. Monroe & Co. (Wavecrest, Nakara, Kelva), Auctioneers

Susanne Porter, ISA, GG (GIA)
Diamond Creation
PO Box 1269
Doylestown, PA 18901
ph: 215-230-8979
bosu25597@aol.com
Gems, Jewelry, Estate Jewelry & Antiques, Collectibles

Robert C. Groves, ISA
Pig Pen Antiques
PO Box 618
4486 York Rd
Buckingham, PA 18912-0618
ph: 215-794-0957
fax: 215-794-7899
ppbbtbs@aol.com
Antique Furniture, Collectibles

Walter F. Vilsmeier, ISA
Vilsmeier Auction Co. Inc.
PO Box 339
Montgomeryville, PA 18936-0339
ph: 215-699-5833
fax: 215-628-8010
auction@vilsmier.com
Machinery & Equipment (Construction, Vehicles, Line & Industrial Supplies), Cars, Trucks (Construction)

Cindy Stephenson, ISA
Stephenson's Auction
1005 Industrial Hwy
Southampton, PA 18966-4066
ph: 215-322-6182
fax: 215-364-4395
Residential Contents, Furniture (American & European, 19th & 20th C.), Antiques, Collectibles, American Ceramics & Pottery

Leah Erickson, ISA
Appraisal Network, The
290 Montgomery Ave
Bala Cynwyd, PA 19004-2913
ph: 610-668-9000
fax: 610-667-2301
Antiques, Eskimo Art, Archeological Art, Residential Contents, Real Estate

Jeannette Wellons Smith, ISA
Jeanette Wellons Antiques
214 Airdale Rd
Rosemont, PA 19010
ph: 610-581-7016
GeeSmith@home.com
Antiques, Collectibles, Residential Contents

Jon D. Edelman, ISA
Edelman's Coins & Stamps
301 Old York Rd
Jenkintown, PA 19046-3210
ph: 215-572-6480
fax: 215-572-6482
Coins, Currency, Tokens, Stamps, Postal History, Jewelry, Picture Postcards, First Day Covers

David C. Rotenberg, ISA CAPP, CGA
David Craig Jewelers, Ltd.
Summer Square Shopping Center
Rt 413 332 Bypass
Langhorne, PA 19047
ph: 215-968-8900
fax: 215-579-2377
Diamonds, Gemology/Gemstones, Colored Stones, Jewelry, Pearls, All Areas of Gems, Jewelry and Related Arts

Steven E. Rosen, ISA, GG (GIA)
Sydney Rosen Company
714 Sansom St
Philadelphia, PA 19106-3261
ph: 215-922-3500
Gemology/Gemstones, Colored Stones, Jewelry, Diamonds

Helene M. Huffer, ISA
Elaine Cooper & Co., Ltd.
8609 Germantown Ave
Philadelphia, PA 19118-2828
ph: 215-248-3030
<<< ON SABATICAL DO NOT REFER>>> Gemology/Gemstones, Jewelry

Barry S. Slosberg, ISA
Barry S. Slosberg, Inc.: Auctioneers - Appraisers
2501 E Ontario St
Philadelphia, PA 19134-5327
ph: 215-425-7030
fax: 215-425-7039
bssauction@aol.com
http://www.users.aol.com/bssaution
Antiques, Silver, Jewelry, Fine Arts, Clocks, Collectibles, Furniture, Residential Contents, Machinery & Equipment, Business Liquidations, Bankruptcies, Real Estate, Business Valuation, Auctioneer, Auction Company

William H. Bunch, ISA
Auctioneer & Appraiser
11 N Brandywine St
West Chester, PA 19380-2805
ph: 610-696-1530
fax: 610-701-2486
Estate Appraisals of 19th-20th C. Furniture and Accessories, Clocks, Music Boxes, Oriental Rugs

Aurora A. Stuski, ISA, GG (GIA)
AAS Appraisal Lab, Inc.
110 S Schuylkill Ave
Eagleville, PA 19403-3144
ph: 610-630-3280
fax: 610-630-3498
arsappraisal@att.com
Jewelry (Contemporary & Estate)

Byron Grant Klein, ISA
A. Ludwig Klein & Son, Inc.
PO Box 145
Harleysville, PA 19438-0145
ph: 215-256-9004
fax: 215-256-9644
Porcelain, Glass, Jade & Fine Art Restoration

Timothy D. Schwer, ISA, CAI
Hunyady Appraisal Service
1440 Cowpath Rd
Hatfield, PA 19440-2645
ph: 215-361-9099
fax: 215-361-9212
Auctioneer, Construction Equipment & Machinery, Machinery & Equipment, Trucks

Dorothy L. Balzer, ISA
Accurate Auto Appraisals
PO Box 459
Bear, DE 19701-0459
ph: 302-836-5167
balzer_g@msn.com
Auto & Truck Appraisals

William Schuh, ISA, GG (GIA)
Independent Jewelry Appraisal Co.
124 Hunter Ct
Wilmington, DE 19808-1978
ph: 302-239-2255
fax: 302-429-5953
AppraiseDe@aol.com
Gemology/Gemstones, Diamonds, Jewelry, Pearls

Paul S. Cohen, ISA, GG, CGA
Continental Jewelers, Inc.
2209 Silverside Rd
Wilmington, DE 19810-4501
ph: 302-475-2000
fax: 302-529-7688
Contjewels@aol.com
Gemology/Gemstones, Diamonds, Jewelry (Gold, Platinum, Silver)

Rochelle F. McGrory, ISA
Continental Jewelers, Inc.
2209 Silverside Rd
Wilmington, DE 19810-4501
ph: 302-475-2000
Gemology/Gemstones, Diamonds, Jewelry

John Michael Overton, ISA
ESP Estate Services
3601 Connecticut Ave NW, Apt 421
Washington, DC 20008-2448
ph: 202-244-2609
fax: 202-244-2609
Estate Liquidations, Residential Contents, Estate Appraisals

Pennye K. Jones-Napier, ISA, FGA
Jewelry Appraisal Sciences
236 Walnut St NW
Washington, DC 20012
ph: 202-291-5575
fax: 202-291-5354
pennye@triratana.com
http://www.triratna.com
Gemstones, Diamonds, Jewelry, Antique & Contemporary Jewelry, Consultant, Alt Phone: 202-321-5575 Alt Email: pennye@ziplink.net

Barbara L. Spaid, ISA
Squirrel Cage
130 Chesapeake Ave
Prince Frederick, MD 20678-4473
ph: 410-535-1158
Furniture (Country), Residential Contents, Tapestries, Textiles (Linens), Needlework (Quilts)

Helen Margaret Huber, ISA
4512 Riverdale Rd
Riverdale, MD 20737-1940
ph: 301-229-2949
Collectibles, Glass, Residential Contents, and Antiques

Israel Heller, ISA
Heller Antiques Ltd.
5454 Wisconsin Ave
Chevy Chase, MD 20815-6901
ph: 301-654-0218
Jewelry, Silver, Judaica, Diamonds, Estates

Marilyn Rudden, ISA
A.M. Sales
9900 Harrogate Rd
Bethesda, MD 20817-1543
ph: 301-469-9437
fax: 301-469-7833
76232.2466@compuserve.com
Residential Contents, Estate Sales

Jane E. Heller, ISA
6204 Leeke Forest Ct
Bethesda, MD 20817-3346
ph: 301-493-6067
fax: 301-493-6076
janeheller@aol.com
Estate Sales

Ann D. Robertson, ISA
Ann Robertson Estate Sales
6815 Selkirk Dr
Bethesda, MD 20817-4921
ph: 301-229-7640
fax: 301-229-7565
baldwin@wizard.net
http://www.wizard.net/~baldwin
Furniture, Residential Contents, Estate Liquidation

Joan Braunstein, ISA, GG(GIA), FGA
J. Braunstein, Ltd.
PO Box 1474
Bethesda, MD 20827
ph: 301-299-7270
fax: 301-299-7270
Gemology/Gemstones, Jewelry (Antique, Modern), Diamonds, Pearls, Colored Stones

Carol K. Oshinsky, ISA
A Carol Oshinsky Sale
PO Box 34105
Bethesda, MD 20827-0105
ph: 301-299-3497
fax: 301-299-3497
ckoshinsky@erols.com
Estate Sales & Liquidations, Antiques, Residential Contents, Jewelry, Silver

Ellen W. Shea, ISA
Antiques Critiques, Inc.
PO Box 34586
Bethesda, MD 20827-0586
ph: 301-299-7314
fax: 301-299-2932
Fine Art, Decorative Arts & Accessories, Antiques, Residential Contents

Barry Rogers, ISA
Barry Rogers, Appraiser
16650 Georgia Ave
Olney, MD 20832-2418
ph: 301-570-0779
fax: 301-570-0779
Gemology/Gemstones, Glass (Antique), Porcelain, Ceramics, Appreciable Residential Contents, Personal Property, Auctioneer, Expert Witness, Furniture, Collectibles, Silver

Barbara M. Lessig, ISA CAPP
Lessig's Pleasant Valley Antiques
21000 Georgia Ave
Brookeville, MD 20833-1138
ph: 301-924-2293
fax: 301-570-1625
BMLessig@aol.com
Glass, Porcelain, Ceramics, Silver, Orientalia, Residential Contents, Furniture, Textiles, Advertising Items, Americana, Art Deco & Nouveau, Decorative Arts & Accessories, Ink Wells, Lamps & Lighting, Music Instruments, Etc.; Damage Claim

Erik Padison, ISA
15127 Frederick Rd
Rockville, MD 20850-1109
ph: 301-424-0053
Japanese Swords & Fittings, Arms & Armor, Oriental Art, Russian Art

Charles B. Goldstein, ISA CAPP
Charles Barry International
8 Hardwicke Pl
Rockville, MD 20850-3010
ph: 301-340-6775
fax: 301-340-1726
Fine Art,Paintings, Sculpture Original Prints; Lithographs Serigraphs Limited Editions; Reproductions Giclees Posters; Expert Witness, Litigation Support: Broad Evidence, Art Fraud, Definitions, Misrepresentation, Blockage, Appraisal Revi

Adrienne Moss, ISA
Moss Antiques
11510 Parkedge Dr
Rockville, MD 20852-3729
ph: 301-770-2383
Quilts, Antiques (American), Americana, Furniture & Accessories, Residential Contents

Dianne Gregg, ISA
Glassnob Antiques
10413 Gary Rd
Potomac, MD 20854-4101
ph: 301-299-6456
Glass (17th-20th C. European, & American Studio) Paperweights, Scent bottles, Arts & Crafts, Art Deco & Nouveau, Decorative Arts, Contemporary High Style Furniture, Russian Decorative Art, Art Glass, Porcelain, Silver, & Enamels

Janet Hanyak, ISA
About To Move Estate Sale
2510 Stratton Dr
Potomac, MD 20854-6231
ph: 301-251-9899
fax: 301-762-5252
Residential Contents, Furniture, Antiques, Estates (Liquidator)

Cynthia Monahan, ISA
Greenbrier Estate Sales
12740 Three Sisters Rd
Potomac, MD 20854-6331
ph: 301-948-1937
fax: 301-948-5558
Estates (Liquidation), Residential Contents, Antiques, Furniture

Susan D. Moran, ISA
Greenbrier Estate Sales
12811 Three Sisters Rd
Potomac, MD 20854-6351
ph: 301-948-1937
Residential Contents, Antiques, Furniture, Estate (Liquidation), Personal Property

Scott Dworsak, ISA
Seneca Creek Trading Co.
19351 Circle Gate Dr, Apt 302
Germantown, MD 20874-5239
ph: 301-540-6160
fax: 301-540-6160
scotdeni@erols.com
http://www.senecacreek.com
Furniture, Electronics, Appliances

Lindsey B. Johnson, ISA, DPS
1315 Carlsbad Dr
Gaithersburg, MD 20879-3203
ph: 301-216-0876
Prints, Paintings, Posters, Collectibles

Maria Denise Nelson, ISA, GG (GIA)
Inner Circle
PO Box 2465
Kensington, MD 20891-2465
ph: 301-530-9266
fax: 301-530-9266
innrcrcl@erols.com
Fine Jewelry, Gems, Diamonds, Pearls, Gold

Carol Waldman Silverman, ISA CAPP
Chelsea & Co.
2302 Musgrove Rd
Silver Spring, MD 20904-5219
ph: 301-384-1673
fax: 301-384-1673
chelsea@digizen.net
Furniture (Antique & Contemporary, American & European), Antiques, Decorative Arts, Americana, Silver, Residential Contents, Collectibles, Insurance, Damage Claims, Estates, Divorce, Office Furniture & Equipment

Gloria Schuetze, ISA
Estate Sales By Gloria/Happy Hunting Grounds
3904 Bel Pre Rd, Apt 4
Silver Spring, MD 20906-2825
ph: 301-460-8537
Residential Contents Liquidator, Jewelry (Antique), Dolls, American Pottery, U.S. Collectibles

Frank Ward Gaines, ISA
47 Philadelphia Ave
Takoma Park, MD 20912-4338
ph: 301-270-5810
Residential Contents, Antiques, Decorative Arts & Accessories

Janice H. Hull, ISA, CAI
Appraiser - Auctioneer
526 Baltimore Blvd
Westminster, MD 21157-6102
ph: 410-876-3694
fax: 410-876-5694
Estate Tax Liability, Insurance & Liquidation, Antiques, Residential Contents, Single Item or Estate

Fred J. Winer, ISA
Appraisal Alliance Service, Inc.
25 W Chesapeake Ave, Ste 200
Towson, MD 21204-4820
ph: 410-494-7000
fax: 410-494-8832
Furniture (Antique American), Glass (American Art Nouveau), Toys (Trains), Auctioneer, Auction Co.

Joan J. Hurt ISA
Arundel Appraisers & Estate Liquidators
9715 Philadelphia Rd
Baltimore, MD 21237-3427
ph: 410-686-9598
fax: 410-574-1585
Residential Contents, Furniture (18th-19th C.), Silver, Glassware, Quilts, Collectibles, Dinnerware

Peter J. Simonetti, ISA
Simonetti & Associates, Inc.
PO Box 72035
Baltimore, MD 21237-8035
ph: 410-682-3702
fax: 410-682-3738
Pete@Simonetti.com
Specializing in Transit/Household Goods, Fire, & Casualty Claims. Antiques, Collectibles, Art, Oriental Rugs, Decorative Arts, Fly Fishing Equipment, Residential Contents, Repairs, Restoration, and Conservation Services.

Joel Stuart Litzky, ISA
Walnut Leaf Enterprises, Inc.
62 Maryland Ave
Annapolis, MD 21401-1630
ph: 410-263-4885
litzky@toad.net
Antiques, Residential Contents, American Cut Glass, Porcelain (European & Oriental), Pottery, Ceramics, American Furniture

Mary Ellen Heibel, ISA
Personal Property Consultants
1009 Old Bay Ridge Rd
Annapolis, MD 21403-4228
ph: 410-267-7708
fax: 410-269-5909
104334.273@compuserve.com
Residential Contents, Furniture (English & American), Silver (Antique English & American), Metalware, Ceramics, Glass, Decorative Arts & Accessories, Antiques

Herman J. Grabenstein, ISA, GG (GIA)
604 Greene St
Cumberland, MD 21502-2700
ph: 301-759-9350
GEMSTONE@HEREINTOWN.NET
Gemologist & Appraiser Appraisals of Jewelry and Silverware, Replacement Values for Insurance, Fair Market Values for Probate of Wills and Trusts or for Division in Divorce Settlements

Robert H. Campbell, II, ISA
23095 Old Fairlee Rd
Chestertown, MD 21620-3842
ph: 410-263-5808
fax: 410-263-8427
Antiques, Boats & Yachts, Cars & Trucks, Construction Machinery & Equipment, Auctioneer

David J. Maloney, Jr., ISA CAPP
Frederick Appraisal, Claims & Estate Services
PO Box 2049
Frederick, MD 21702-1049
ph: 301-695-8544
fax: 301-695-6491
dave@maloney.com
http://www.maloney.com
Antiques, Residential Contents, Collectibles, Folk Art, Estates, Cars, Furniture, Silver, Americana, Insurance & Moving Damage Claims Service; Author Of "Maloney's Antiques & Collectibles Resource Directory"

Bruce M. Schuettinger, ISA
Antique Restorations, Ltd.
PO Box 244
New Market, MD 21774-0244
ph: 301-865-3009
fax: 301-865-3009
schuettinger@erols.com
Furniture, Conservator, Consultant, Antiques, Woodworking Tools (Antique)

Margaret H. Smith, ISA
M H Smith Appraisals & Estate Sales
12486 Skipper Cir
Woodbridge, VA 22192
ph: 703-551-4096
fax: 703-494-6582
mhsmith222@aol.com
http://www.mhs-appraisal-estsls.com
Estate Liquidations, Residential Contents, Antiques, Fine Art, Collectibles, Decorative Arts & Accessories, Estate & Insurance Appraisals

Mildred R. Shepherd, ISA
Shepherd Studio
5527 3rd St S
Arlington, VA 22204-1115
ph: 703-671-1789
102756.2015@compuserve.com
Repair, Restoration and Conservation of Ceramics, Glass, Ivory, Jade, and other Art and Decorative Objects

Priscilla A. Wells, ISA
Appraisal Associates
205 Yoakum Pkwy, Ste 314
Alexandria, VA 22304-3806
ph: 703-370-0832
fax: 703-370-0832
priswells@aol.com
Antiques, Residential Contents, Silver, Orientalia, and Glass.

Christopher Rasmus, ISA
Acuity Appraisers
6060 Farrington Ave
Alexandria, VA 22304-4826
ph: 703-370-2338
fax: 703-823-5587
crasmus@rasmus.com
Commercial Inventories, Machinery & Equipment, Office Furniture & Equipment, Computers, Electronic Equipment, Personal Property, Restaurant & Food Service Equipment

Angela Saunders, ISA, GG (GIA)
Silverman Galleries, Inc.
110 N Saint Asaph St
Alexandria, VA 22314-3100
ph: 703-836-5363
Estate Jewelry & Diamonds (Pre-18th C. to Modern), Estate Silver (18th C. to Later American, English & Continental), General Antiques & Period Art, Specializing in Items of and About Domestic Life, Culinary and Dining History Pre-1850

Maurice B. Silverman, ISA
Silverman Galleries, Inc.
110 N Saint Asaph St
Alexandria, VA 22314-3100
ph: 703-836-5363
Antiques, Jewelry (Antique & Modern), Silver, Paintings (18th-19th C.), Decorative Arts & Accessories,

Marybeth Rabung, ISA
501 Chapman St
Ashland, VA 23005-1113
ph: 804-798-7020
Antiques (18th to Early 20th C. American & European), Residential Contents, Fine Art (18th-20th C. Oil On Canvas, Watercolor, Sculpture, Prints), Decorative Arts & Accessories

Barbara Walter, ISA
Carousel Shoppe, The
8287 Reunion Dr
Mechanicsville, VA 23111-4539
ph: 804-770-0844
fax: 804-779-2452
China, Pottery, Porcelain, Glass (American), Costume Jewelry (19th-20th C.), Estate Sales, and Residential Contents

Patricia Loughridge, ISA
Patricia Loughridge Appraisal Services
13553 Canterbury Rd
Montpelier, VA 23192-2625
ph: 804-883-7708
fax: 804-883-7708
Antiques, Decorative Arts & Accessories, Residential Contents, Furniture, Consultant

David P. Staples, Jr., ISA, CAI
Appraisal, Auction, & Estate Services, Inc.
225 Gun Club Rd
Richmond, VA 23221
ph: 804-359-0688
fax: 804-359-2580
knightm@mindspring.com
Business/Commercial FF&E (Furniture, Fixtures, Equipment, & Inventories), Estate/Residential Contents (Antiques, Collectibles, Furniture, Jewelry, Art, etc.), Auctioneers, Brokers, Liquidators, Real Estate Auctions

Owen F. Valentine, ISA
Owen F. Valentine & Co.
6417 Rigsby Rd
Richmond, VA 23226-2916
ph: 804-282-2355
fax: 804-288-9209
Residential Contents, Auctioneer, 17th-18th C. Silver, Furniture, Porcelain

Elizabeth D. Bullock, ISA
Decorative Arts Associates, Inc.
6432 Roselawn Rd
Richmond, VA 23226-3115
ph: 804-285-0296
fax: 804-282-0818
Furniture (American & British), Silver, Decorative Arts & Accessories, Residential Contents

Christine N. Corbin, ISA CAPP
Motley's Auctions
4402 W Broad St
Richmond, VA 23230-3202
ph: 804-355-2100
fax: 804-359-6954
http://www.Motleysgroup.com
Residential Contents, Full Estate Services, Storage & Distribution Facilities

Christina M. Woolford, ISA, GG (GIA)
C.M. Woolford
PO Box 12342
Richmond, VA 23241-0342
ph: 804-644-1941
Gemology/Gemstones, Diamonds, Jewelry

Rebecca L. Holberg, ISA, GG, CGA
Southeast Gemological Lab
2621 Lake Ridge Xing
Chesapeake, VA 23323-3323
ph: 757-487-3092
fax: 757-487-3092
HZGS77A@prodigy.com
Jewelry, Antique & Period Jewelry, Estate Jewelry, Gold Jewelry, Pearls, Watches

Gail Wolpin, ISA
Phoebus Auction Gallery
4202 Manchester Rd
Portsmouth, VA 23703-4823
ph: 757-722-9210
gail@phoebusauction.com
http://www.phoebusauction.com
Residential Contents, Antiques, Auctioneer, Erotica, Black Memorabilia, Militaria, Art Glass, Primitives, Furniture, Textiles, Paintings

Suzanne M. Sellers, ISA CAPP
Suzanne M. Sellers Appraisal Service
2609 Wycliffe Ave SW
Roanoke, VA 24014-2335
ph: 540-342-3771
sussell@bellatlantic.net
Antiques, Residential Contents, Household Contents, Insurance, Liquidators, Estates

Richard Lynn Manley, ISA
Hall Associates, Inc.
PO Box 1294, Ste 1007
Bedford, VA 24523
ph: 540-982-0011
http://www.auctionservice.com/hall
Antiques, Residential Contents, Machinery & Equipment

Elizabeth N. Gladwell, ISA CAPP
Elizabeth N. Gladwell & Assoc L.L.C.
PO Box 28
Goode, VA 24556-0028
ph: 540-586-4567
fax: 540-586-4567
Engladwell@aol.com
18th-20th C. Decorative Arts (American, Continental & English), Residential Contents, Collectibles (including Fishing Tackle), Folk Art, Silver, Ceramics, Antiques, Furniture

R. Stephen Mullins, ISA
Spencer Road Antiques
2533 Kay Ln
Charleston, WV 25302-4315
ph: 304-342-2865
fax: 304-342-3367
mullinssr@aol.com
Glass (Depression Glassware), Furniture (Period), Residential Contents, Decorative Arts & Accessories

Mary Moore Maxwell, ISA, GG (GIA)
Antiquitus Jewelers
48 Washington Ave
Wheeling, WV 26003-6241
ph: 304-242-1661
fax: 304-242-1662
oldjewel@ovis.net
http://www.antiquitus.com
Gemology/Gemstones, Jewelry (Antique, Estate), Estate Liquidations, Repairs & Restoration

Ronald H. Young, ISA
Y.E.S., Llc., Inc.
PO Box 3353
Parkersburg, WV 26103-3353
ph: 304-428-3494
fax: 304-428-3291
Heavy Equipment, Trucks, Machinery, Personal Property, Oilfield Equipment, Construction Equipment, Forestry Equipment

Grace Kelly, ISA
Antique Appraisals
239 Oakwood Ct
Winston Salem, NC 27103-1905
ph: 910-725-7228
18th-20th C. Decorative Arts (American, English & Continental), Residential Contents, Collectibles, Folk Art, Silver, Ceramics, Antiques, Furniture

Cecil B. Price, ISA
Cecil B. Price Antiques & Appraisals
3640 Winding Creek Way
Winston Salem, NC 27106-4325
ph: 336-774-8026
fax: 336-774-8036
wprice@juno.com
Antiques, Residential Contents, Decorative Arts & Accessories, Collectibles, and Estate Liquidations.

Keith J. Pierce, ISA
Pierce Auction Service & Real Estate
274 Brookwood Dr
Winston Salem, NC 27127-9121
ph: 336-748-8400
fax: 336-764-1807
pierce@netunlimited.net
http://www.pierceauction.com
Residential Contents, Office Equipment, Coins, Antiques, Automobiles, Machinery

Joyce Berg, ISA
578 Ferarington Post
Pittsboro, NC 27312
ph: 919-542-0287
fax: 919-542-0287
joytag@mindspring.com
Porcelain, Furntiure, Funiture 20th C., Decorative Arts & Accessories

Carla S. Butler, ISA
Butler & Associates
PO Box 4510
Greensboro, NC 27404-4510
ph: 336-299-6509
fax: 336-299-6509
CSBUTLER@VNET.NET
Antiques, Residential Contents, Decorative Arts & Accessories, SIlver, Estate, Insurance, Equidable Distribution, Personal Property Sales, Downsizing and Relocation Services

Ridley Tyler Smith, ISA
Tyler-Smith Antiques
8 Leawood Ct
Greensboro, NC 27410-4217
ph: 336-294-2771
rtsmith@nr.infi.net
Ceramics (18th-19th C. American, English, & European), Furniture (18th & 19th C. English & American), Residential Contents, Antiques, Americana

Alan Folley Butler, ISA
Butler & Associates
PO Box 2818
Durham, NC 27715-2818
ph: 919-489-9342
fax: 919-489-9342
Antiques, Decorative Arts & Accessories, Residential Contents, Oriental Carpets, Personal Property Liquidation

J. Robert Boykin, III, ISA CAPP
Boykin Appraisals, Inc.
PO Box 7440
Wilson, NC 27895-7440
ph: 252-237-1700
fax: 252-237-2314
boykinappraisal@coastalnet.com
Residential Contents, Antiques, Decorative Arts & Accessories, Fine Art

RoseMary Starling, ISA
Berry Appraisals, Inc.
2207 Nash St NW, Ste C
Wilson, NC 27896-1783
ph: 252-291-6433
fax: 252-237-4115
Berryappraisals@cocentral.com
Residential Contents, Estates, Liquidators, Insurance, Damage Claims, Antiques, Carpets, Rugs, Furniture, Decorative Arts & Accessories, Silver

Melanie Smith, ISA
Seaside Art Gallery
PO Box 1
Nags Head, NC 27959-0001
ph: 252-441-5418
fax: 252-441-8563
seaside@interpath.com
http://www.seasideart.com
Animation Art, Fine Art, Paintings, Original Prints

Garland D. Stewart, III, ISA, GG (GIA)
Jewelry By Gail, Inc.
207 E Driftwood St
Nags Head, NC 27959-9172
ph: 919-441-5387
fax: 919-441-7082
jbgjewel@interpath.com
http://www.jewelrybygail.com
Gemology/Gemstones, Diamonds, Jewelry (Estate & Contemporary)

Dianne Groves Atkinson, ISA
AMC Auction Co., Inc.
PO Box 306
Concord, NC 28026-0306
ph: 704-782-3111
fax: 704-782-2399
Office Equipment & Furniture, Residential Contents, Medical Equipment, Auctioneering

C.D. Gallimore, ISA, CAI
AMC Appraisal Co. Inc.
PO Box 306
Concord, NC 28026-0306
ph: 704-782-7979
fax: 704-721-3527
cdatamc@aol.com
Textile Equipment, Machinery & Equipment, FF&E, Vehicles, Boats, Residential Furniture, Auctions. Toll Free: 800-938-2121

Charlie Klumpp, ISA
Ibis, Inc.
225 N Trade St
Matthews, NC 28105-1713
ph: 704-814-0117
fax: 704-366-8957
cpklump@aol.com
Furniture, Toys, General Antiques, Residential Contents, Stamps

Sue S. Whitaker, ISA, GG, CMG
Gemstones
316 S Washington St
Shelby, NC 28150-5402
ph: 704-484-0216
fax: 704-482-2255
Gemology/Gemstones, Jewelry, Gold, Watches, Pearls, Diamonds

Paul G. Hughes, ISA
Tudor House Galleries
1401 East Blvd
Charlotte, NC 28203-5817
ph: 704-377-4748
PAULH65304@aol.com
Paintings, Watercolors, Drawings, Porcelain, Ceramics, Residential Contents

Ronald L. Roberts, ISA
Dixie Sporting Collectibles
1206 Rama Rd
Charlotte, NC 28211-4345
ph: 704-364-2900
fax: 704-364-2322
gun1898@aol.com
Firearms (Modern & Antique), Hunting and Fishing Collectibles, Antique Furniture, Estate Liquidations, Advertising Items, American Indian, Civil War

Caroline T. Gray, ISA CAPP
Thistle, The
PO Box 220064
Charlotte, NC 28222-0064
ph: 704-365-4539
Furniture (18th-19th C. American and English), Silver, Porcelain, Ceramics, Residential Contents, Estates, Insurance

Vivian Riegelman, ISA CAPP
AAA Appraisal Co., Inc.
10612-D Providence Rd, PMB 225
Charlotte, NC 28277-0233
ph: 704-843-4033
fax: 704-843-7562
vivri@perigee.net
Residential Contents (Appreciable & Depreciable), Antiques & Collectibles (19th-20th C.), Furniture, Glass, Ceramics, Silver, Victoriana, Art Nouveau, Art Deco, Office Furniture & Equipment, Damage Claims, Divorce, Insurance, Estates

Louise W. Phillips, ISA CAPP
Alexander Appraisal Service
8206 1200 Providence Rd, Ste 387
Charlotte, NC 28277-9705
ph: 704-849-7352
fax: 704-841-7305
cymber@compuserve.com
Antiques, Ceramics, Decorative Arts & Accessories, Expert Witness, Furniture (19th & 20th C.), Residential Contents, Silver, Insurance and Divorce

John M. Lucas, ISA
13453 Woody Point Rd
Charlotte, NC 28278
ph: 704-588-0731
Oriental Rugs

Jane E. Wetmore, ISA
1600 Morganton Rd, Lot H3
Pinehurst, NC 28374-6846
ph: 910-692-8082
fax: 910-692-3688
Liquidations, Residential Contents, Antiques, Decorative Arts & Accessories, Estates

Joan Ray, ISA
Hastings Ray Gallery, Ltd.
166 NW Broad St
Southern Pines, NC 28387-4801
ph: 910-692-3050
fax: 810-692-5949
hastingsgray@pinehurst.net
http://www.hastingsray.com
Fine Art (Contemporary, Paintings, Sculptures, Glass, Art, Ceramics, Prints), Objects d'Art, Donation, Insurance, and Estates. Alt Emai: 112040.3064@compuserve.com

Bruce E. Price, ISA
Mike's Jewelers
222 Middle St
New Bern, NC 28560-2142
ph: 252-637-9775
fax: 252-637-2065
Jewelry, Diamonds

Louis Long, Jr., ISA
Royal Scot, Inc., The
PO Box 2107
Highlands, NC 28741-2107
ph: 828-526-5917
fax: 828-526-0650
Residential Contents, Furniture (American)

Joette M. Humphrey, ISA, GG (GIA)
Shelleys Jewelry/Shelly's Auction Gallery
429 N Main St
Hendersonville, NC 28792-4903
ph: 828-698-8485
fax: 828-693-4305
humphrey@a-o.com
Jewelry, Diamonds, Pearls, Colored Stones

Beverly J. Nash, ISA CAPP
Accessories & Antiques
PO Box 2537
Hendersonville, NC 28793-2537
ph: 828-698-0020
fax: 828-698-0020
bevnash@compuserve.com
Residential Contents (Appreciable & Depreciable), Collectibles, Toys (Promotional Cars), Furniture (Late 18th C. to Present American), Estate Liquidations

Zack C. Allen III, ISA
Heritage Unlimited
21 Miller Rd
Ashville, NC 28805
ph: 828-298-8203
allenzc@aol.com
Antiques, Fine Art, Collectibles

Marylen Sue Scott-McKenzie, ISA, GG (GIA)
MSSM Appraisals
PO Box 15978
Asheville, NC 28813
ph: 704-277-0722
Gemology/Gemstones, Diamonds, Jewelry (Colored Stones, Karat Gold), Watches (Rolex), Pearls, Estates

Mary Paula Newsome, ISA, GG (GIA)
Skatell's
1036 B Johnnie Dodds
Mt. Pleasant, SC 29464
ph: 863-849-8488
fax: 803-881-0022
PAULANEW@charelston.net
Gems, Jewelry, Diamonds

Libby Holloway, ISA
PO Box 4790
Beaufort, SC 29903
ph: 846-524-4297
Antique Furniture, Collectibles, Residential Contents

Nancy N. Richardson ISA, CGA, GG
Nancy N. Richardson, CGA
PO Box 6148
Hilton Head Island, SC 29938-6148
ph: 843-842-4560
fax: 843-842-4599
nrichar156@aol.com
Gemology/Gemstones, Diamonds, Jewelry, Watches, Antique & Estate Jewelry, Silver (Flatware & Tableware)

James Edwin Mason, ISA
Rosemont Antiques
115 Colton Crest Dr
Alpharetta, GA 30005
ph: 770-232-1721
JMSMJMTM@worldnet.att.net
American & English Furniture, Silver

Tonnie Marie Parrott, ISA
Appraisals & Estate Liquidations Unlimited
1155 Alcovy N Dr
Mansfield, GA 30055
ph: 770-788-7040
fax: 770-784-9641
parrottcol@aol.com
Furniture, Antique Jewelry, Glass, Toys (Antique & Collectible), Metal Items, Household Contents, Ephemera, Books, Porcelain, China, Estate Liquidation, FIrearms

Howard S. Avery, ISA
Avery Gallery, Inc.
390 Roswell St NE
Marietta, GA 30060-8208
ph: 770-427-2459
fax: 770-427-2446
Restoration of Paintings, Prints, Documents, Photos, Frames, Convex Glass Replacement, Contemporary American Paintings, Vance Miller & Harold Little Oils, Etchings by Harold Little & Luigi Kasimir

Lynn E. Wesch, ISA
Gingerbread Box, Inc., The
1050 E Piedmont Rd, Ste 148E
Marietta, GA 30062-4611
ph: 770-973-0104
fax: 770-977-0077
lewassets@worldnet.att.net
http://www.assest.bitshop.com
19th - 20th C. Decorative Arts & Accessories, European & American Paintings, Porcelain, Bronzes, Enamels, Silver, and Quilts. Antique Period & Costume Jewelry.

Melinda L. Wilson, ISA CAPP
Betty A. Wilson Appraisal Service
1682 Terrell Ridge Dr SE
Marietta, GA 30067-8443
ph: 770-434-0227
fax: 770-319-9191
76161.565@compuserve.com
American Indian, Art Deco, Antiques, Paperweights, Damage Claims, Insurance, Residential Contents, Primitives, Glass, Silver, Furniture, Porcelain, Ceramics, Russian Art, Disneyana, Estates & Sales

Andrea Boyles, ISA
Encore Antiques & Estate Sales
1014 Lake Charles Dr
Roswell, GA 30075
ph: 770-641-8967
fax: 770-594-9657
aboyles@mindspring.com
Antiques, Collectibles, Estate Sales, and Household Goods.

Sharon D. Boatwright, ISA
Board of Trade Fine Consignments, The
154 Victoria Way
Roswell, GA 30075-2951
ph: 770-640-7615
fax: 770-640-7675
Antiques, Furniture, Art, Decorative Items, and Collectibles

Larry G. Davenport, ISA
Roswell Clock & Antique Co.
955 Canton St
Roswell, GA 30075-3612
ph: 770-992-5232
Antiques, Clocks (Antique), Furniture (American & English)

Betty A. Wilson, ISA CAPP
Betty A. Wilson Appraisal Service
3912 Lake Dr SE
Smyrna, GA 30082-3471
ph: 770-434-0227
fax: 770-319-9191
Oreintal Rugs, Fine Art, Bankruptcy & Insurance Claims, and Animation

Nathan D. Williams, ISA
Williams Furniture Repair
4590 Lawrenceville Hwy
Tucker, GA 30084-3705
ph: 770-498-9580
Furniture, Repairs, Restoration, Preservation (Furniture)

W.C. Golden, Sr., ISA
Golden & Associates, Inc.
311 Independence Way
Woodstock, GA 30188-4154
ph: 770-924-8528
fax: 770-924-5991
wcgolden@mindspring.com
Silver, Art Glass, Art

Kimberly Moore, ISA
Board Of Trade, The
957 Rosedale Rd
Atlanta, GA 30306
ph: 770-640-7615
fax: 770-640-7675
Antique Furniture, Silver, Porcelain

Patricia Rittenmeyer, ISA
Reminiscent Rose Antiques
1032 Wildwood Rd NE
Atlanta, GA 30306-3017
ph: 404-892-9611
fax: 404-876-2585
patrittenmeyer@juno.com
http://www.atlantaappraiser.com
Antiques, Decorative Arts & Accessories, Residential Contents, 18th-19th C. Silver, Furniture, Ceramics, Costume Jewelry, Conference Coordinator, Damage Claims, Victoriana, Sewing Collectibles, Porcelain.

Carol F. Wallen, ISA
143 Battery Pl NE
Atlanta, GA 30307
ph: 404-222-9355
wallen0143@aol.com
Antiques and Residential Contetns

Sara William McDaniel, ISA
Atlanta Antique Appraisal Co
2076 Dellwood Dr NW
Atlanta, GA 30309
ph: 404-352-0193
fax: 404-352-0193
18th C. English Furniture, Chinese Export Porcelain, 19th C. French Furniture

Deborah B. Abernethy, ISA
Abernethy, Deborah B., Appraiser
1266 W Paces Ferry Rd, # 213
Atlanta, GA 30327
ph: 404-262-2131
fax: 404-262-0922
dbamm@aol.com
Furniture, Oriental Rugs, Porcelain

Carol C. Higdon, ISA
7005 Northgreen Dr NE
Atlanta, GA 30328-1453
ph: 770-396-6418
fax: 770-396-8534
higdon@ix.netcom.com
Fine Art, Paintings, Prints, Sculpture

Benita T. Green, ISA
1329 Nash Rd NW
Atlanta, GA 30331-1015
ph: 770-434-0227
fax: 770-319-9191
tanjanee@aol.com
Residential Contents, Memorabilia, Collectibles, Furniture

Mark Lee Maxwell, ISA
4186 Gladney Dr
Atlanta, GA 30340-4719
ph: 770-934-0573
Paintings, Watercolors, Drawings, Etchings, Frames, Furniture, Porcelain, Pottery

Eric T. Martin, Ph.D., ISA
American Appraisal Services
4470 Chamblee Dunwoody Rd, Ste 170
Atlanta, GA 30341-1422
ph: 404-256-5299
fax: 404-252-2768
Real Property

Louis V. Craig, ISA
Craig Restorations
4717 Roswell Rd, Apt O-2
Atlanta, GA 30342
ph: 404-257-1777
fax: 404-257-1777
Household Goods, China, Porcelain, Pottery, Glass, Prints, Paintings, Estate Sales, Repairs

Philip H. Hawkins, ISA
Depew Galleries, Inc.
4291 Briarcliff Rd
Atlanta, GA 30345-2060
ph: 404-874-2286
fax: 404-874-2285
General Household Contents, Antiques, Decorative Arts, Silver

Debra Freer, ISA
Freer & Associates, Inc.
PO Box 98327
Atlanta, GA 30359-2027
ph: 404-321-6369
fax: 404-636-8531
DFreer@netscape.net
Paintings, Prints, Sculpture, 19th-20th C. Fine & Decorative Art, Art Deco, Pottery, Art Glass, Art Nouveau, Arts & Crafts, Victoriana, Lalique, Icart, Muller Frere, Tiffany, Daum, Manuscripts - Margaret Mitchell 76641.212@compuserve.com

Bernard Doris, ISA, GG, RJ
Doris Diamonds, Inc.
487 Highland Ave
Augusta, GA 30909-3742
ph: 706-733-6747
fax: 706-731-9622
102573.2205@compuserve.com
Diamonds, Silver, Gemology/ Gemstones, Gold, China

Brian Goldman, ISA, GG (GIA)
Arvin's, Inc.
516 Poplar St
Macon, GA 31201-2717
ph: 912-745-3684
fax: 912-738-0062
Diamonds, Colored Stones

Beth A. Kinstler, ISA
Avalon Antiques
PO Box 9496
Savannah, GA 31412-9496
ph: 912-233-8488
fax: 912-233-9779
avalonant@aol.com
Generalist, Silver, China, and Crystal.

Norma Bajalia Cloud, ISA
Professional Auctioneers, Inc.
1114 Cloverhill Rd
Valdosta, GA 31602
ph: 912-242-5412
fax: 912-241-0952
Household Contents, Antique Furniture, Glassware, Porcelain

Michael J. Stevenson, ISA
PO Box 3032
Thomasville, GA 31799-3032
ph: 912-227-6020
fax: 912-227-6020
cframing@rose.net
Antiques, Furniture, and Residential Contents.

Shirley Northern, ISA CAPP
Northern Associates, Inc.
PO Box 1008
Ponte Vedra Beach, FL 32004-1008
ph: 904-285-2004
fax: 904-285-5905
s.northern@worldnet.att.net
Antiques, Residential Contents, Decorative Arts, Accessories, Collectibles, Americana, Porcelain, Pottery, Ceramics, Silver, Glass, Victoriana, Damage Claims, Estates. Alt Email:76162.2445@compuserve.com

Patricia K. Webb, ISA
Barclay/Scott Antiques
4 Rohde Ave
Saint Augustine, FL 32084-3221
ph: 904-824-2483
Antiques, Residential Contents

Virginia S. Stratford, ISA
Stratford Appraisal Service
300 Raintree Trl
Saint Augustine, FL 32086-5551
ph: 904-797-2224
Antiques, Collectibles, Residential Contents

Claudina G. Trump, ISA
Trump Personal Property Appraisals
1842 Juniper Dr
Edgewater, FL 32141-4015
ph: 904-405-2023
fax: 904-423-2175
deantrump@aol.com
Glass, Ceramics, Antiques & Collectibles, Residential Contents

Victoria Lee Golden, ISA
Renaissance Appraisal Ltd.
17220 NW 78th Ave
Alachua, FL 32165
ph: 904-418-0519
fax: 904-418-0519
goldes4@aol.com
Fine Art, European & American Paintings, Antiques, Antiquities, Bronzes, American Indian Artifacts. Insurance & Estate Appraisals. Consultant to Private or Corporate Collections.

Robert A. Dewar, ISA
Coronado Antiques & Collectibles
512 Canal St
New Smyrna Beach, FL 32168-7012
ph: 904-428-3331
fax: 904-423-9541
Insurance, Estates, Divorce, Antiques, Furniture, Glass, Pottery, Military Weapons, Modern Guns

Susan E. Fisher, ISA
Fisher & Powell
2111 River Blvd
Jacksonville, FL 32204-4413
ph: 904-387-4800
Decorative Arts & Accessories, Residential Contents, Household Goods, Damage Claims

Caroline Cay Powell, ISA
Fisher & Powell
2111 River Blvd
Jacksonville, FL 32204-4413
ph: 904-387-4800
fax: 904-387-0017
Residential Contents, Household Goods, Decorative Arts & Accessories, Damage Claims

Barbara Langston, ISA
B. Langstons Antiques, Inc.
2018 San Marco Blvd
Jacksonville, FL 32207
ph: 904-391-0022
fax: 904-642-9591
LinenLady@aol.com
Appraising Antiques, Residential Contents, Textiles, Collectibles, Silver, Victoriana, Costume Jewelry, Porcelain. Conducts Estate & Liquidation Sales. Retail Antique Shop. Estates Bought. Consignments Accepted.

Wayne D. Essick, ISA
4027 Dayrl Rd
Jacksonville, FL 32207-7140
ph: 352-372-9792
http://www.inetica.com/~irwayne/index.html
Antiques, Furniture, Pottery, Porcelain, Stamps, Coins

Annie L. Martin, ISA
Stellers Gallery
1409 Atlantic Blvd
Jacksonville, FL 32207-7216
ph: 904-396-9492
fax: 904-398-0329
annie.martin@worldment.att.net
http://www.stellersgallery.com
Fine Art, Antiques and Residential Contents, Italian Fine and Decorative Art

C. Sue Holley, ISA
Memories Revisited
2229 Mescalaro Wy
Jacksonville, FL 32246
ph: 904-221-0478
sholley4922@aol.com
Antiques, Fine Glass & China, Furniture, Art Work, General Residential Contents

Helen Brinson Covington, ISA
Flourishes
2224 S 1st St, Apt A
Jacksonville Beach, FL 32250
ph: 904-241-4357
hcoving755aol.com
Antiques, Jewelry

June C. Koontz, ISA
June C. Koontz Appraisals
3335 Lighthouse Point Ln
Jacksonville, FL 32250-2325
ph: 904-223-3232
Anitques, Estates, Collectibles, Fine Art, and Vintage Jewelry

Betty Lee, ISA
Treasure & Things
2147 Armistead Rd
Tallahassee, FL 32312-3101
ph: 904-385-1693
Residential Contents, Collectibles, and New & Used Furniture.

Jeff J. Hofmeister, ISA, GG (GIA)
Professional Jewelry Appraisals, Inc.
PO Box 38398
Tallahassee, FL 32315-8398
ph: 850-562-4253
fax: 850-562-1320
Gemology/Gemstones, Diamonds, Jewelry

Elnita W. Burke, ISA
6 Nine Gables Ln
Crawfordville, FL 32327-1116
ph: 904-926-3159
eburke1943@aol.com
Antiques, Collectibles, Residential Contents, Ceramics

Logan G. Adams, ISA CAPP
Specialists Of The South
PO Box 87
Panama City, FL 32402-0087
ph: 850-785-2577
fax: 850-872-8662
76652.31@compuserve.com
Antiques, Furniture, Residential Contents, Collectibles, Glass, Ceramics, Porcelain, Silver, Decorative Arts & Accessories, FF&E (Furniture, Fixtures, & Equipment), Consultant, Estate Sales, Liquidator, Damage Claims, and Speaker.

Richard J. Adams, ISA CAPP
Specialists Of The South
PO Box 87
Panama City, FL 32402-0087
ph: 850-785-2577
fax: 850-872-8662
Antiques, Furniture, Residential Contents, Glass, Ceramics, Porcelain, Clocks, FF&E (Furniture, Fixtures, & Equipment), Damage Claims, Restoration, Repairs, Estate Sales, and Liquidator.

Jean Mallory, ISA
Mallory Appraisals
6431 Gardenia St
Panama City, FL 32404
ph: 850-271-0933
fax: 850-265-3093
71561.1706@compuserve.com
Antiques, Residential Contents, Furniture, Ceramics, Primitives, Glass, Decorative Arts, Insurance, Collectibles

Carol W. Belcher, ISA
Belcher Appraisals
2410 Ashland Rd
Panama City, FL 32405-1013
ph: 850-785-7657
chwbelcher@aol.com
Antiques Dealer

Helen Brown Galloway, ISA
Helen Brown, Ltd.
107 Country Club Rd
Pensacola, FL 32507-3530
ph: 904-456-9049
Antiques, Fine Art, Estate Consultant, Expert Witness, Estate Liquidation

Joy E. Bell, ISA
Bell's Estate Liquidation Service
33 Bayshore Dr
Pensacola, FL 32507-3576
ph: 850-453-3189
fax: 850-438-3641
JBell88301@aol.com
http://www.worldofantiques.com/bells
Antiques, Estate Liquidation, Estate Consultant, Residential Contents, American Furniture

Irene Della Porta, ISA
Webs And Shadows Antiques
7218 SW 97th Ln
Gainesville, FL 32608-6301
ph: 352-379-1088
fax: 352-379-1088
Antiques, Collectibles, Silver, Estates, Residential Contents

Joan L. Henns, ISA
Joan L. Henns Estate Appraisal & Sales
6878 S Round Lake Rd
Mount Dora, FL 32757-9645
ph: 352-383-7373
jhenns@mailcde.com
http://www.estateappraisalandsale.com
Household Contents

Thomas A. Kemper, ISA
Kat, Inc.
2170 State Road 434 W, Ste 390
Longwood, FL 32779-4990
ph: 407-774-9900
fax: 407-788-0366
Corporate Equipment and Electronics, Office Furniture & Equipment, Scientific Equipment

Renis S. Paton, ISA
Heritage Sales & Appraisals, Inc.
1141 Via Capri
Winter Park, FL 32789-2659
ph: 407-644-6742
fax: 407-644-9133
Residential Contents, Estates, Insurance, Antiques, Decorative Arts & Accessories, Furniture

Beverly G. Graham, ISA
Graham's Appraisals & Estate Sales, Inc.
1401 Grove Ter
Winter Park, FL 32789-4030
ph: 407-599-0444
fax: 407-628-0370
Antiques, Collectibles, Residential Contents, Specializing in Estate Appraisals, Sales, and Insurance Appraisals.

Michael E. Leadlay, ISA
Park Place Antiques & Collectibles
50 N Grove St
Merritt Is, FL 32953-3440
ph: 407-454-6361
fax: 407-454-4187
ELLIOTT.LEADAY@GTE.NET
Antiques, Collectibles, Furniture

Harry Stampler, ISA
Stampler Auctions
2801 Evans St
Hollywood, FL 33020-1119
ph: 954-921-8888
fax: 954-927-2939
Art, Jewelry, Machinery & Equipment, Business Liquidations

Christine Girello, ISA
Antique Appraisers Of America
1641 NW 110th Ter
Pembroke Pines, FL 33026-2722
ph: 954-431-4150
fax: 954-431-7399
PJG1614@aol.com
Residential Contents (Appreciable & Depreciable), Furniture, Antiques, Collectibles, Glass, Porcelain, Silver, Orientalia, Insurance, Divorce, Estate Tax

Barbara B. Fisher, ISA
Fisher Auction Co.
431 NE 1st St
Pompano Beach, FL 33060-6264
ph: 954-942-0917
Antiques, Fine Art, Residential Contetns, Estates, Auction Co.

Diane P. Marvin, ISA
Diane Marvin Appraisal Svcs
4738 NW 5th Pl
Coconut Creek, FL 33063-6742
ph: 954-968-0003
fax: 954-968-0003
dmappraise@aol.com
Estate Specialist, Appreciable & Depreciable Residential Contents, Antiques, Collectibles Furniture, Crystal, Silver, China, Art, Complete Estate Liquidations, Insurance Appraisals, Damage Claims, Expert Witness, and Consultations.

Jack Abrahams, ISA
Jay Sugarman Auctioneers, Inc.
555 Oaks Ln, Apt 303
Pompano Beach, FL 33069-3724
ph: 305-651-0101
fax: 305-633-9669
Machinery & Equipment, Office Furniture & Equipment, Restaurant Equipment, Cement Equipment, Industrial Machinery Equipment

Craig M. Walters, ISA, GG (GIA)
Finis Gemological
36 NE 1st St, Ste 429
Miami, FL 33132-2492
Gemology/Gemstones, Jewelry, Diamonds, Color Grading

Jay Rumbaugh, ISA
4160 Poinciana Ave
Miami, FL 33133-6331
ph: 565-444-4931
fax: 305-663-3583
asaandisa@aol.com
Residential Contents, Antiques, Fine Art, Furniture, Silver, Decorative Arts & Accessories, Carpets & Rugs, Collectibles, Estates, Liquidators

Marina Whitman, Ph.D., ISA
3800 Toledo St
Coral Gables, FL 33134
ph: 315-445-5910
fax: 305-461-4820
marina2@aol.com
Fine Art, Islamic Art, Art History, Far Eastern Art, 20th C. Decorative Art

Frederic "Ric" H. Emmett, Jr., ISA
1622 Ponce De Leon Blvd
Coral Gables, FL 33134-4012
ph: 305-442-8743
fax: 305-443-3074
artdeco@modernism.com
Art Deco: Furniture, Glass, Lighting, Bronze, Porcelain. Prints & Paintings (20th C.)

Suzy Furman, ISA
Suzy Furman Fine Arts
1170 NE 97th St
Miami Shores, FL 33138-2558
ph: 305-759-3875
fax: 305-759-4521
Modern and Contemporary Paintings, Drawings, Prints, Sculpture

Lauraine Dunn-Glispin, ISA
Lauraine Dunn & Associates, P.A., Appraisers
68 NE 91st St
Miami Shores, FL 33138-2808
ph: 305-758-7174
fax: 305-756-5153
110015.2421@compuserve.com
Antiques, Fine & Decorative Arts, Estates, Expert Witness, Bronzes, Litigation Preparation, Industrial Inventory, Evaluation for Tax Exemption, Residential Contents, Machinery & Equipment, Dolls, Ceramics, Orientalia

Joan Baron, ISA
Baron's Antiques
1776 Bay Dr
Miami, FL 33141-4720
ph: 305-866-0502
fax: 305-868-9881
Residential Contents, Estates, Jewelry, Antiques, Silver, Porcelain

Sandra Steinberg ISA,
Owl's Roost Antiques
900 Bay Dr, Apt 116
Miami Beach, FL 33141-5630
ph: 305-864-5905
fax: 305-868-4604
Residential Contents, Antiques, Jewelry (Antique & Estate), Estates, Antique Wicker

Luis M. Garcia, ISA
1520 Trillo Ave
Coral Gables, FL 33146-2315
ph: 305-444-4931
fax: 305-448-2197
LGARCIAISA@AOL.COM
Antiques, Art, Estates, Oriental Rugs, Paintings, Decorative Arts & Accessories, Art Deco & Art Nouveau, Furniture, Jewelry, Objet d'Art & De Vertu, Residential Contents, Silver

Lorena Overstreet Allen, M.Ed., ISA
L. Allen Appraisal Studios, Inc.
9720 W Bay Harbor Dr, Apt 3
Bay Harbor Islands, FL 33154-1752
ph: 305-866-1023
Fine Art: American, Asian & European Art 15th-20th C. (Old Masters, Engravings, Minatures, Silhouettes), American/British Bird Prints; Chinese/Japanese Scrolls, Screens, Woodblocks, Jade, Porcelain; Art Nouveau/Deco - Educator/Consultant

Donald Kapner, ISA
United Appraisal Group, Inc.
17971 Biscayne Blvd, Ste 207
Point East Professional Bldg
Aventura, FL 33160-2532
ph: 305-931-5800
fax: 305-935-0020
uag@gate.net
Residential Contents, Fine Art, Office Furniture & Equipment, Insurance, Estates

Arlene Schwarz, ISA, GG (GIA)
United Appraisal Group, Inc.
17971 Biscayne Blvd, Ste 207
Point East Professional Bldg
Aventura, FL 33160-2532
ph: 305-931-5800
fax: 305-935-0020
uag@gate.net
Antiques, Jewelry (Antique, Period, & Costume), Residential Contents & Estates

Jerome Bengis, ISA
Jerry Bengis, Inc.
9860 SW 122nd St
Miami, FL 33176-4928
ph: 305-232-1143
fax: 305-251-1450
yascha7@netrox.net
Salvador Dali Graphics, Bronzes, Graphics by Picasso, Chagall, Miro, Warhol, and all Major Artists - Etchings, Lithographs - All Print Techniques, Surrealism, 45 rpm Records

Santo R. Blasi, ISA
Gold Coast Appraisers
18861 Biscayne Blvd
Miami, FL 33180-2839
ph: 305-935-1471
fax: 305-933-4146
Jewelry, Fine Art, Porcelain, Personal Property, Auctioneer

Jay T. Euster, ISA
Euster Appraisal Service
12555 Biscayne Blvd, Ste 905
N. Miami, FL 33181-2208
ph: 305-895-8985
fax: 305-899-9129
Personal Property, Residential and Commercial (20th C.)

J. Ellen Thompson, ISA
Heirloom Appraisals, Inc.
1800 NE 114th St, Apt 809
Miami, FL 33181-3417
ph: 305-893-1599
fax: 305-893-7686
JET1800@aol.com
Estates, Residential Contents, Silver, Porcelain, Crystal, China, Furniture

Sharon M. Kerwick, ISA
Kerwick Appraisals
1633 NE 24th St
Fort Lauderdale, FL 33305-1402
ph: 954-565-9031
fax: 954-564-0648
sharon@kerwick.com
http://www.kerwick.com
Oriental Rugs, Silver, Estates, Insurance, Damage Claims, Appraisal Reviews, Lectures

Sheila M. Bemis, ISA
14250 SW 23rd St
Fort Lauderdale, FL 33325-5431
ph: 954-424-8912
fax: 954-564-0648
smb333@aol.com
Residential Contents, Estates, Insurance, Antiques, Porcelain, Pottery, Silver

Gilbert Hall, ISA
Hall & Hall Appraisers, Inc.
5722 S Flamingo Rd, # 258
Cooper City, FL 33330-3206
ph: 954-443-8585
fax: 954-442-1790
gilbog@worldnet.att.net
American & European Art & Antiques, Cars, Commercial Inventories, FF&E, Latin American Art, Mobile Homes

Mary Lou Nicholas, ISA
Appraiser's International, Inc.
3805 S Dixie Hwy
West Palm Beach, FL 33405-2231
ph: 407-832-0099
fax: 407-832-4541
mlnicholas@aol.com
Estate Appraisals, Liquidation, Litigation Support, Antiques, Fine Art, General Household, Jewelry, Coins, Silver, Firearms, Furniture

Leonid A. Livshitz-Smith, ISA CAPP, GG, CG, MG
Mayor's Jewelers
9696 Vineyards Ct
Boca Raton, FL 33428
ph: 305-944-0458
fax: 954-454-6710
Gemology/Gemstones, Diamonds, Jewelry, Watches, Glass

Gabrielle Siman, ISA
2889 NW 24th Ter
Boca Raton, FL 33431-6202
ph: 561-852-4716
fax: 561-852-4716
gsiman@sprintmail.com
http://www.home.sprintmail.com/~gsiman/
Attorney & Art Historian; Sotheby trained Appraiser/Valuation Consultant. Handles Fine Art, Antiquities, Decorative Art. Specializes in 19/20th C. Painting; Private & Corporate Collections; Confidential Representation & Brokerage Services

Anthony Capodilupo, ISA
Anthony Capodilupo Fine Art
6706 Boca Pines Trl, #E
Boca Raton, FL 33433-7714
ph: 561-477-1210
fax: 561-477-1237
fineart@metroweb.net
Fine Art (American, European, & Latin American), Consultant, Litigation Management Alt Phone 800-393-1023

Amy L. Walter, ISA, GG (GIA)
PO Box 1513
Delray Beach, FL 33447-1513
ph: 561-274-4941
fax: 561-272-3722
Gemology/Gemstones, Diamonds, Pearls, Jewelry, Watches

Lucy L. Ullmann, ISA
Phoenix Appraisals
521 N Country Club Dr
Lake Worth, FL 33462-1005
ph: 561-969-1865
fax: 561-969-1309
hlullmann@aol.com
Residential Contents, Silver, American Furniture

Melanie M. Hill, ISA
Appraisal & Acquisition Assoc.
315 S County Rd
Palm Beach, FL 33480-4250
ph: 561-655-2494
fax: 561-655-5821
Antiques, Residential Contents, Decorative Arts & Accessories, Silver, Estates

Joel J. Cohen, ISA
Cohen Books & Collectibles
PO Box 810310
Boca Raton, FL 33481-0310
ph: 561-487-7888
fax: 561-487-3117
cohendisney@prodigy.net
http://www.cohendisney.com
Walt Disney Specialist, Expert, Buys, Sells, Appraises, Evaluates, Consults, Auction Advice or Representation, Broker, Exclusively Disney; Books, Animation Art, Ephemera, Figurines, Autographs, Toys, Convention, Collectibles, Disneyana

Harold G. Flutie, ISA
Professional Appraisal Services
7932 Shelby Cir
Boca Raton, FL 33496-1324
ph: 407-477-9989
fax: 407-997-0559
Antiques, Collectibles, Decorative Arts & Accessories, Residential Contents, Estates, Office Furniture and Equipment, Damage Claims Specialist

Ruth T. Garland, ISA
1721 Scotch Pine Dr
Brandon, FL 33511
ph: 813-685-4341
fax: 813-286-8820
Appraisals & Estate Liquidations, Antiques, Collectibles, Residential Contents

Nancy S. Hilbert, ISA
Nancy S. Hilbert, Inc.
1303 Brentwood Hills Blvd
Brandon, FL 33511-6157
ph: 813-689-2165
Residential Contents, Glass, China, Silver (Contemporary & Antique), Furniture (Contemporary & Antique), Estate Jewelry, Ceramics.

Daphne L. Rosenzweig, Ph.D., ISA
Rosenzweig Associates
PO Box 16187
Tampa, FL 33687-6187
ph: 813-988-0880
fax: 813-989-8091
rosetwig@aol.com
Asian Fine & Decorative Arts, Buddhist Art, Asian Ceramics, Chinese Painting, Islamic Arts, South & Southeast Asian Arts, Japanese Prints, Ivory, Jade, Minerals, and Orientalia.

Donald A. Bartlett, ISA
Omega Automobile Appraisals
115 18th Ave SE
St Petersburg, FL 33705-2805
ph: 727-894-5690
fax: 727-894-5690
Cars, Trucks (Antique, Classic, Special Interest, Specializing In Rolls-Royce & Bentley), Repairs, Restoration, Preservation (Auto Restoration), Consultant

Lornie Mueller, ISA, GG (GIA)
Lithos Jewelry
344 Corey Ave
Saint Pete Beach, FL 33706-1817
ph: 813-367-9010
fax: 813-367-9011
Lithos@tampabay.rr.com
http://www.lithosjewelry.com
Pearls, Appraisals, Repairs and Sales (Extensive Inventory of Natural Color, Cultured, Black South Sea Pearls), Contemporary Designer Jewelry, Montana Sapphires, Complete Gem Testing Lab, Diamonds

Rose Mueller, ISA, GG (GIA)
Lithos Jewelry
344 Corey Ave
Saint Pete Beach, FL 33706-1817
ph: 813-367-9010
fax: 813-367-9011
Lithos@tampabay.rr.com
http://www.lithosjewelry.com
Pearls, Appraisals, Repairs and Sales (Extensive Inventory of Natural Color, Cultured, Black South Sea Pearls), Contemporary Designer Jewelry, Montana Sapphires, Complete Gem Testing Lab, Diamonds

R. N. "Nancy" Huff, ISA
Treasure Hunters
1502 Buckeye Rd NE, Apt 1
Winter Haven, FL 33881-2768
ph: 941-294-1981
fax: 941-294-1981
zarraj@gate.net
All Types of Appraisals, Antiques, Jewelry, and Orientalia. Professional Estate Sales, Marketing and Finding Service

Jane de Lisser, ISA
Jane de Lisser Associates
1348 Alcazar Ave
Fort Myers, FL 33901-6617
ph: 941-334-8199
fax: 941-334-8799
Silver; American, English and Continental Furniture; Porcelain; Rugs & Textiles; Paintings; Residential Contents, Brokerage Services

Joy Kelley, ISA
Read & Kelley/ Amerivision
PO Box 3111
Fort Myers, FL 33918-3111
ph: 941-731-2201
fax: 941-731-3167
bubbadog@peganet.com
Residential Contetns, Czeck Forged Glass Figurines, Depression Era Furniture

Carol Pier, ISA
Pier & Co.
2000 Lambiance Cir, # 202
Naples, FL 34108-6737
ph: 941-566-2828
fax: 941-566-2866
Residential Contents, Decorative Arts, Collectibles, Antiques, Liquidator

Ina H. Baden, ISA
Palma Sola Appraisals & Sales, Inc.
1210 99th St NW
Bradenton, FL 34209-9730
ph: 941-792-8401
fax: 941-747-4457
Residential Contents, Probate & Insurance, Estate Sales, Collectibles

Kenneth R. McMillen, Jr., ISA
McMillen & Co.
PO Box 5111
Sarasota, FL 34277-5111
ph: 941-388-2392
Antiques, Fine Art, Residential Contents, Decorative Arts & Accessories, Estates, Insurance

Melissa Brookes, ISA, GG (GIA)
D & M Diamonds
PO Box 8924
Port Saint Lucie, FL 34985-8924
ph: 561-879-0814
dmdia@aol.com
Identification of Gemstones & Jewelry, Retail Replacement Value

Jayne Fertig, ISA
Antiques & Interiors
1158 NW Lombardy Dr
Port St. Lucie, FL 34986
JBF63@hotmail.com
Anitques, Fine Art, Jewelry

Debbie Pearl, ISA
PO Box 624
Stuart, FL 34995-0624
ph: 561-287-2434
DO NOT USE FOR REFERALS—ON SABATICAL
Residential Contents, Antiques, Collectibles, Figurines, Hummels, Decorative Arts & Accessories, Liquidation and Estate Sales

Nancy H. Ruzicka, ISA
R & R Associates
212 Hwy 191
Jemison, AL 35085
ph: 205-688-2055
fax: 205-688-2055
Household Contents, Porcelain, Furniture, Decorative Arts & Accessories, General Personal Property, Silver, Victoriana

Bill Carner, ISA CAPP
Birmingham Appraisal Services
400 Lance Way
Birmingham, AL 35206-3035
ph: 205-836-8009
fax: 205-836-8009
BillCarner@aol.com
Antique Furniture, Art & Cut Glass, Pottery, Porcelain, Silver, Insurance claims, Estate Evaluations & Sales, and Teaching Antiques. Alt Email: Bill Carner@aol.com

Lee C. Scott, ISA CAPP
Estate Services, Inc.
3716 Montrose Rd
Birmingham, AL 35213-3828
ph: 205-870-5522
lscapp@hotmail.com
Furniture (Antique American), Residential Contents, Estates, Antiques, Decorative Arts & Accessories

Frances S. Wheelock, ISA
3616 Brookwood Rd
Birmingham, AL 35223-5513
ph: 205-969-5888
Silver and Furniture

William C. Ornburn, ISA
Bill Ornburn Auctions
99 Gurley Rd
Decatur, AL 35603-6100
ph: 256-350-5305
Antiques, Residential Contents, Auctioneer

Steve R. Hewitt, ISA
Investment Appraisals
319 Morning View Dr
Harvest, AL 35749-9429
ph: 256-851-9293
stevnmik@aol.com
Empire, 19th C. Furniture, Coin Silver, Transfer Ware China Sheffield Plate, 19th C. Glass, Residential Contents, Furniture, Decorative Arts & Accessories

Spencer L. Glasgow, ISA
28867 Huntsville Brownsferry Rd
Madison, AL 35756-3629
ph: 205-232-4465
Auctioneer, Estates, Residential Contents, American Art Pottery, Cookie Jars

Jane W. Mabry, ISA CAPP
Antiques, Etc. Appraisals
PO Box 10045
Huntsville, AL 35801-3670
ph: 205-534-2282
74136.1045@compuserve.com
Residential Contents, Antiques, Collectibles, Furniture, Glass (Glassware), Pottery, Porcelain, Ceramics

Linda R. Pugh, ISA
Old South Antique Appraisals
121 Wildwood Dr
Cecil, AL 36013-3013
ph: 334-271-0727
107701.2605@compuserve.com
Antiques, Collectibles, Pottery, Residential Contents, Estate Sales

Kenneth R. Powell, ISA
Pro-Tech Appraisal Service
7670 Theodore Dawes Rd
Theodore, AL 36582
ph: 334-665-4991
fax: 334-665-4991
Auto, Personal Property, Home Damage Appraisals

Judy Stroud, ISA
Stroud & McHale Appraisals
391 Jones Mill Rd
La Vergne, TN 37086-2618
ph: 615-459-4727
Decorative Arts & Accessories, Antiques, Collectibles, Estate Sales

Carol Wamble, ISA
Wamble Appraising Service
337 Willow Bough Ln
Old Hickory, TN 37138
ph: 615-824-5985
Antiques, Collectibles, Residential Contents, Porcelain, Pottery, Glass, Silver: British and American, Decorative Arts, Furniture, Primitives, Art Deco, Art Nouveau, Americana, Books, Toys, Consulation, Estates, Insurance, Divorce

Carolyn LeRoy, ISA
Appraisals, Estate & Moving Sales
2720 Overhill Circle
Nashville, TN 37214
ph: 615-883-1240
LeRoyEstateSales@compuserve.com
Residential Contents, Antiques, Decorative Arts, Silver, and Estate Sales of Personal Property.

Taylor M. Watson, ISA CGA
Fischer Evans Jewelers
8 W 8th St
Chattanooga, TN 37402-2601
ph: 423-267-0901
fax: 423-267-3862
Gemology/Gemstones, Diamonds, Colored Stones, Jewelry (Diamond, Gold, Estate, & Colored Stones)

Margaret Gillespie, ISA
169 S Greer St
Memphis, TN 38111-3428
ph: 901-324-9839
fax: 901-327-8213
Art, Antiques, Appreciable Personal Property, Decorative Arts & Accessories, Furniture, Residential Contents, Dinnerware, Silver, Estates

Dan A. Sasser, ISA
Market Street Antiques Mall
414 N Market St
Paris, TN 38242-3405
ph: 901-642-6996
fax: 901-642-6996
Furniture, Antiques, Residential Contents, Collectibles, Estates

Patti A. Thompson, ISA
Way-Fil Jewelry
1123 W Main St
Tupelo, MS 38801-3453
ph: 601-844-2427
fax: 601-840-4791
thompson@cathymns.com
Gemology/Gemstones, Diamonds, Jewelry, Silver (Flatware), Liquidators, Antique & Period Jewelry

Celia Fleishhacker, ISA
Nostalgia Alley Antiques
214 W Main St
Tupelo, MS 38801-3918
ph: 662-842-2757
Antiques, Collectibles, Residential Contents, Victoriana, Toys, Antique Dolls, Ephemera, Medical

Samuel Kevin Hall, ISA
Samuel's
1505 Ingalls Ave
Pascagoula, MS 39567-5626
ph: 228-762-8593
fax: 228-762-8593
Furniture, Auction Sales, Retail Sales

Cynthia Morse Taylor, ISA
Cynthia Taylor Antiques
2376 MS Hwy #43
Silver Creek, MS 39663-9762
ph: 601-886-7128
Furniture, Glassware, Linens, Antiques

Ann G. Hays, ISA CAPP
Kenneth S. Hays & Associates, Inc.
120 S Spring St
Louisville, KY 40206-1953
ph: 502-584-4297
fax: 502-585-5896
annhays@haysauction.com
http://www.haysauction.com
Dolls, Doll Houses & Accessories, Victoriana, Auctioneer, Antiques

Kenneth S. Hays, ISA
Kenneth S. Hays & Associates, Inc.
120 S Spring St
Louisville, KY 40206-1953
ph: 502-584-4297
fax: 502-585-5896
kenhays@haysauction.com
http://www.haysauction.com
Estates, Antiques, Dolls, Doll Houses (Antique), Auctioneer

Elizabeth P. Coons, ISA CAPP
Elizabeth Coons Appraisals, Ltd.
6148 Ashgrove Rd
Nicholasville, KY 40356-9233
ph: 606-271-4790
fax: 606-271-4790
Antiques, Residential Contents

Grover Farr, ISA
Impressions of Berea, Ltd.
PO Box 123
Berea, KY 40403-0123
ph: 606-986-8177
impressions@20us.chaple1.com
http://www.eclectibles.net
Residential Contents, Costume Jewelry, Glass.

James S. Harris, ISA
James Harris Antiques & Appraisals
PO Box 672
Richmond, KY 40476-0672
ph: 606-623-9100
Jimant@ipro.net
Silver (American Coin & English), Glass (Cut), American Pottery, Art Glass, Heisey Glass, Porcelain, Ceramics, China, Residential Contents, Estates

Russell C. Pattie, ISA, GG, CGA
Miller & Woodward
2220 Nicholasville Rd, Ste 152
Lexington, KY 40503-2400
ph: 606-276-6100
fax: 606-276-6112
Jewelry, Gemology/Gemstones, Diamonds

Cecil W. Roeder, ISA
Plantation Antiques
678 State Rt 1245
Beaver Dam, KY 42320
ph: 502-683-3314
Rookwood2@aol.com
Specializing in Arts & Crafts Movement: American Art Pottery, Furniture, & Metalwork. Fine Art: Paintings, 19th-20th C. Prints & Posters. Ephmera: Books, Maps, Postcards, & Autographs. Historical American Indian Items.

Nathaniel Ludlum, ISA
What On Earth, Inc.
7323 Tucker Rd
Centerburg, OH 43011-9200
ph: 614-436-1458
fax: 614-436-0124
ludlum@ecr.net
Fossil & Mineral Collections, Natural History Items & Books, Gemstones, Jewelry, Jewelry Repair, Collection Curating & Consultation

David M. Baker, ISA, CGA
David Baker Creative Jewelers, Inc.
6672 Perimeter Loop Dr
Dublin, OH 43017-3204
ph: 614-764-0068
Jewelry

Joseph G. Balshone, ISA, GG (GIA)
Columbus Gemological Labs
463 E Town St
COLUMBUS, OH 43215-4757
ph: 800-209-4367
fax: 614-224-5630
76701.242@compuserve.com
Alt Bus 614-224-2404 Gemstones, Jewelry, Modern Firearms, Vintage Writing Instruments

Trent Bobbitt, ISA
Sandisfield House Liquidations
7295 Ober Ln
Chagrin Falls, OH 44023-1125
ph: 440-893-9195
Antiques, Furniture, Residential Contents, Liquidators, Estates, Decorative Arts & Accessories

Krystina M. Nielsen, ISA
Nielsen Jewelers, Inc.
753 Broadway
Lorain, OH 44052-1805
ph: 440-244-4255
fax: 440-244-5040
Jewelry (Gemstones), Diamonds, Pearls, Jewelry (Gold, Contemporary, Antique & Period), Gemology

Jeanette C. Bendula, ISA
30201 Royalview Dr
Willowick, OH 44095-4809
ph: 440-944-4355
fax: 440-951-7175
Antiques, Breweriana, Estates, Liquidators, Residential Contents, Silver

James I. W. Corcoran, ISA
Corcoran Fine Arts Limited, Inc.
2915 Fairfax Rd
Cleveland Heights, OH 44118-4015
ph: 216-431-0025
fax: 216-397-0222
corcoran@aol.com
Fine Art (16th-20th C. European, American, Canadian Paintings, Watercolors, Drawings, Prints, and Sculpture), Titanic Memorabilia, Insurance, Loss and Damage Claims, Expert Witness, Consultant on Sale and Deposition

Peggy L. Sebek, ISA
Century Antiques & Appraisals, Inc.
3255 Glencairn Rd
Shaker Heights, OH 44122-3407
ph: 216-991-2356
fax: 216-991-2935
peggylane@worldnet.att.net
Residential Contents, Antiques, Porcelain (American Beleek), Glass (Czechslovakian, Wavecrest), 19th-20th C. Furniture, American, British, & European Ceramics

Patricia H. Campbell, ISA
Western Reserve Appraisers & Liquidators
1851 King James Pkwy, Apt 226
Westlake, OH 44145-3429
ph: 440-899-0484
fax: 216-292-6780
dacque@aol.com
Residential Contents, American Pressed Glass, Art Glass, Royal Commemorative Memorabilia, Antiques, Collectibles, British Ceramics, Estate Liquidations

Jerry Michael Jarvis, ISA
Quaker & Associates
452 Dorset St
Akron, OH 44305-3151
ph: 330-784-9080
fax: 330-784-9133
Residential Contents, Furniture, Pottery, Glassware

Judy Pier, ISA
Pier & Co.
44 Castle Blvd, Ste 307
Alcron, OH 44313
ph: 330-864-8595
fax: 330-864-8044
Residential Contents, Furniture, Glass, Porcelain, Pottery, Ceramics, Decorative Arts & Accessories, Collectibles

Kathleen Wieschaus, ISA CAPP
Professional Appraisal Services
PO Box 9660
Canton, OH 44711
ph: 330-456-6600
fax: 330-875-2563
104575.1571@compuserve.com
Antiques, Decorative Art, Silver, Porcelain, Residential Contents. Alt Email: kwieschaus@aol.com

Judee Hill, ISA
Heirlooms Etcetera Antiques & Appraisals
631 Wayne St
Sandusky, OH 44870-2723
ph: 419-625-4442
fax: 419-626-4979
zappraiser@hotmail.com
Liquidations, Tag Sales, Estate Sales, Household Goods, Glass (Opression Era), Collectibles, Antique Consignments Accepted, Probate, Insurance, Divorce, Damage Claims, Pre-Damage. Alt Tel: 419-625-1821.

Maggie M. Beckmeyer, ISA, CAI
Auctions By Maggie, Inc.
2191 Cliff Rd
North Bend, OH 45052-9629
ph: 513-941-9519
fax: 513-941-9519
AVCMAG@webtv.net
http://www.auctionweb.com/maggie
Antiques, Residential Contents, Cars, Generalist, Estates, Real Estate

Jeanne E. Read, ISA
Squirrel's Nest, The
PO Box 342
Blanchester, OH 45107-0342
ph: 937-783-4411
fax: 937-783-4411
rread@erinet.com
Glass (Pattern & Depression), Ceramics (British & American), Antiques, and Residential Contents

Steven S. Early, ISA
Antique Appraisals
125 Winding Brook Ln
Terrace Park, OH 45174-1035
ph: 513-831-0072
Furniture, Glass (Victorian Art), Silver, Dolls, Doll Houses & Accessories (Antique Dolls)

Frederick W. Fehr, III, ISA, GG (GIA)
Richter & Phillips Co., The
202 E 6th St
Cincinnati, OH 45202-3228
ph: 513-241-3510
fax: 513-241-7054
http://www.richterphillips.com
Gemology/Gemstones, Diamonds (Loose & Mounted), Jewelry (Gold, Handmade Chains)

Angelia Dawn Miller, ISA, GG (GIA)
Raul Haas Jewelers
2709 Erie Ave
Cincinnati, OH 45208-2103
ph: 800-797-7285
fax: 513-321-3074
Estate, Antique & Modern Jewelry, Diamonds, Gemstones, Jewelry Design, Identification, Plotting, Reports, Estate & Insurance Appraisals, Insurance Replacement and Damage Reports. Toll-Free: 800-797-7285

Carrie Metz, ISA, GG (GIA)
2753 McKinley Ave, # 2
Cincinati, OH 45211
ph: 513-662-0718
fax: 513-662-0049
Gems & Jewelry, Jewelry Insurance Appraiser

Dorothy Koman, ISA
DK Estates Sales
10347 Lochcrest Dr
Cincinnati, OH 45231-2737
ph: 513-772-1247
Antiques, Collectibles, Residential Contents, Estates (Liquidations)

Mary E. Mecklenborg, ISA
Special Things Antiques
5701 Cheviot Rd
Cincinnati, OH 45247-7007
ph: 513-741-9127
Residential Contents, Antiques, Ceramics, Rookwood & Ohio Pottery, Post Cards, Glassware, China

Jean C. Renick, ISA
Jean C. Renick
PO Box 54619
Cincinnati, OH 45254-0619
ph: 513-474-7036
fax: 513-474-7037
jrenick@msn.com
Real Estate, Residential Contents, Antique & Period Jewelry, Estate Sales

Kenneth J. Rapp, ISA, GG (GIA)
Rapp Jewelers, Inc.
PO Box 222
Englewood, OH 45322-0222
ph: 513-836-6243
Gemology/Gemstones, Diamonds, Jewelry

Jane Fetters Warner, ISA
Warner's Blue Ribbon Book
7163 Frederick Garland Rd
Union, OH 45322-9621
ph: 937-698-4508
fax: 937-698-4508
jane@wbrb.com
http://www.wbrb.com
Swarovski Silver Crystal, Swarovski Selection, D. Swarovski, Swarovski Produced Pieces of Art and Chandeliers

Claudia Miller, ISA
Estate Sales Services
18 S Main St
Dayton, OH 45459-1331
ph: 805-940-1930
fax: 805-722-8767
Residential Contents, Generalist, Personal Property, Insurance Claims, Estate Liquidator

Robert Fessel, ISA, GG, FGA
Fessel's, Inc.
116 N Williams St
Paulding, OH 45879-1281
ph: 419-399-3398
fax: 419-399-3885
fessel@bright.net
Gemology/Gemstones, Diamonds, Jewelry (Diamond, Colored Stone, Gold And Other Precious Metal), Silver

Myron Noble, ISA
Myron Noble Appraisals
388 E 300 N
Anderson, IN 46012-1208
ph: 317-642-2681
Residential Contents, Estates, Antiques, Farm Equipment, Real Estate

Joyce Haverty, ISA
AA Professional Appraisals
43 Terrace Ct
Carmel, IN 46032-1544
ph: 317-843-1885
Art (19th-20th C.), Antiques, Americana, Indiana Art, Native American, Oriental Rugs, Silver, Residential Contents

Margaret L. Durrer, ISA
Durrer's Antiques
112 Brierley Way
Carmel, IN 46032-1852
ph: 317-844-8351
jldurrer@aol.com
Residential Contents, Silver, Glass (Glassware), Antiques, Linens, Needlework, Watches, Estates, Ceramics

David A. Budd, ISA
12210 Windsor Dr
Carmel, IN 46033-3142
ph: 317-872-4710
fax: 317-879-9732
Fishing Tackle (Antique), Flow Blue China, Furniture (Antique), Sporting Collectibles.

Michael J. Ellis, ISA CAPP, GG (GIA)
Ellis Jewelers
PO Box 208
Lebanon, IN 46052-0208
ph: 765-482-0520
fax: 765-482-0791
mellis@inmotion.net
Gemology/Gemstones, Diamonds, Jewelry, Pearls, Gold

Virginia Lucas, ISA
Trash To Treasures
5505 N Keystone Ave
Indianapolis, IN 46220-3457
ph: 317-253-2235
fax: 317-726-0932
102003.2755@compuserve.com
Appreciable & Depreciable Residential Contents, Antiques, Estate & Household Liquidations, Tag Sales, Insurance, Divorce, Moving, Consultant

Pamela L. Hickman, ISA, GG (GIA)
International Diamond & Gold
4026 E 82nd St, Ste A5
Indianapolis, IN 46250-4206
ph: 317-578-4653
fax: 317-578-9335
Gemology/Gemstones, Diamonds, Colored Stones, Rubies, Sapphires, Emeralds, Decorative Arts & Accessories, Insurance, Retail Jeweler

Mary J. Khamis-Rowe, ISA CAPP, GG (GIA)
Khamis Fine Jewelers
9763 Fall Creek Rd
Indianapolis, IN 46256-4713
ph: 317-841-8440
fax: 317-841-9210
KhamisRowe@aol.com
Diamonds, Gemstones, Pearls, Watches, Designer Jewelry, Gold, Antique Jewelry

Dalimira A. Cmiel, ISA
Camile, Inc.
2996 N Horseshoe Bnd
La Porte, IN 46350-7918
ph: 219-326-1121
fax: 219-326-1121
Residential Contents, Restaurant, Hospital & Nursing Home Equipment, Kitchen Primitives, Insurance Claims, Estate Sales

Ronald S. Cmiel, ISA
Camile, Inc.
2996 N Horseshoe Bnd
La Porte, IN 46350-7918
ph: 219-326-1121
fax: 219-326-1121
Furniture, Fixtures, & Equipment, Residential Contents, Collectibles, Cars, and Commercial Inventories.

Eileen R. Eichhorn, ISA, GG (GIA)
Eichhorn Jewelry, Inc.
130 N 2nd St
Decatur, IN 46733-1609
ph: 219-724-2621
fax: 219-724-9483
http://www.eichhornjewelry.com
Antique & Estate Jewelry

James C. Voors, ISA
Court Of King James
515 W Wayne St
Fort Wayne, IN 46802-2123
ph: 219-426-3234
Silver (Sterling, Sheffield, & Fused Plate), Furniture (Period), Ecclesiastical (Vestments, Sacred Vessels, Reliquaries, etc), Books, Jewelry

Sally A. Boose, ISA
Sally's Antiques
9417 Marydale Ln
Fort Wayne, IN 46804-4727
ph: 219-432-4025
fax: 219-432-4025
Residential Contents, Glass, Furniture, Porcelain, Pottery, Ceramics, China, Estates, Jewelry, Antiques

Tamara J. Strickler, ISA CAPP, GG (GIA)
Strickler Jewelers
140 N Dixon Rd
Kokomo, IN 46901-4100
ph: 317-452-4075
Gemology/Gemstones, Diamonds, Jewelry

John F. Burger, ISA
Burger & Associates
303 Ellen Ct
New Albany, IN 47150-4643
ph: 812-945-6650
fax: 812-945-6650
Bankruptcy Court Appraisals, Auctioneer, Residential Contents, Office Furniture & Equipment, Collectibles

Beverly S. Reed, ISA
Whale Antiques
230 Burks Ave
Bloomington, IN 47401-8458
ph: 812-332-2290
Antiques, Collectibles, Residential Contents

Chad Lage, ISA
1651 Olive St
Evansville, IN 47714
ph: 812-473-2988
visionHTE@yahoo.com
Decorative Arts, Collectibles, and Ceramics

Jeffery A. Vierk, ISA, GG (GIA)
Vierk's Fine Jewelry
1650 Main St
Lafayette, IN 47904-2919
ph: 765-447-0200
0430@polygon.net
Gemology/Gemstones, Diamonds, Jewelry, Gold, Coins

Richard L. Stout, ISA
Williams & Lipton Co.
101 Southfield Rd, Ste 302
Birmingham, MI 48009-1645
ph: 248-646-7090
fax: 248-646-7093
Machinery & Equipment (Metal Working, Restaurant, & Construction), Cars & Trucks, Auctioneer

Ruth F. Rattner, ISA
Art Advisory Services
1002 Ann St
Birmingham, MI 48009-1770
ph: 248-258-5335
fax: 248-540-9656
rrattner@aol.com
20th C. : Paintings, Prints, Sculpture, Drawings, and Ceramics

Charles M. Ellias, ISA, GG (GIA)
Astrein's Fine Jewelry
120 W Maple Rd
Birmingham, MI 48009-3322
ph: 248-644-1651
fax: 248-644-7477
cmeggisa@aol.com
Jewelry, Diamonds, Pearls, Colored Stones & Gemology, Watches, Insurance Replacements, Appraisals, Alt. Phone: (810)704-7055. Alt. Email: cmeggisa@compuserve.com

James R. Krol, ISA, GG (GIA)
Birmingham Gemological Services
251 E Merrill St, Ste 240
Birmingham, MI 48009-6153
ph: 248-644-8828
fax: 810-642-3358
We do not sell jewelry - Independant Appraisal of Jewelry from 1850 to present, Hours by appointment - specialty of 2nd Opinion Repairs on Diamond and Estate Jewelry and Insurance Reports

Jan Chandler Durecki, ISA
Appraisal Consultants
PO Box 380227
Clinton Twp, MI 48038-0062
ph: 810-566-0353
fax: 810-566-0353
75451.3253@compuserve.com
Furniture (Antiques-Contemporary) Appreciable & Depreciable Residential Contents, Golf Memorabilia, Estate Liquidations, Victoriana, Collectibles

James S. Britton, ISA, GG (GIA)
25800 Village Green Blvd, #203
Harrison Township, MI 48045-3012
ph: 810-791-8490
JBRIT9489@msn.com
Jewelry, Gemstones, Diamonds, Goldsmith

Joseph DelGiudice, ISA
DelGiudice Antiques
515 S Lafayette Ave
Royal Oak, MI 48067-2556
ph: 248-399-2608
fax: 248-399-7570
Art, Antiques, Etchings (Icart), Bronzes, Jewelry (Fine, Costume, & Estate), Art Deco & Art Nouveau, Furniture, Decorative Arts & Accessories, Silver, Crystal, Porcelain, Sculpture, Figurines, Estate Appraisals & Liquidators

Jerome S. Feig, ISA
Field Art Studio
24242 Woodward Ave
Pleasant Rdg, MI 48069-1144
ph: 248-399-1320
fax: 248-399-7018
JSFIELDART@AOL.COM
Restoration of Gilded Objects and Oil Paintings; Architectural Gilding, and Reproduction Gilded Frames

Matthew G. Virzi, ISA
Connoiseur Galleries, Inc.
1341 Wrenwood Dr
Troy, MI 48084-2656
ph: 810-274-0770
fax: 810-274-0740
Firearms, Paintings, Prints, Sculpture, Fine Art, Insurance Consultations, Collection Buyer, Liquidator, Licensed Firearms Dealer.

Darlene R. Hines, ISA
Nostalgia Days Gone By Antiques
116 W Main St
Brighton, MI 48116-1522
ph: 810-229-4710
fax: 248-476-0794
dh.nostalgia@usa.net
Antiques, Collectibles, Residential Contents, Estate Sales, China, Glassware, Furniture, Linen, Seminars/Classes. Alt Phone: 810-717-0220

Patricia "Trish" Davis, ISA
Red Lion Antiques
PO Box 2005
Dearborn, MI 48123-2005
ph: 313-274-3647
fax: 313-278-9805
Antiques, Estates, Households, Estate Liquidators, Collectibles

Mavis L. Mealy, ISA
Old Visions Antiques
15767 Minock St
Detroit, MI 48223-1228
ph: 313-538-5071
fax: 313-538-5071
ova@flash.net
Residential Contents, Antiques, Collectibles, Furniture, Glass, Jewelry, Pottery, Silver, Textiles, Toys, Estate Appraisals & Liquidations, Insurance.

Melinda Adducci, ISA, GG (GIA)
Joseph Dumouchelle Fine & Estate Jewellers
5 Kercheval Ave
Grosse Pointe Farms, MI 48236-3601
ph: 734-455-2856
fax: 734-455-2403
Joelindy@earthlink.net
Gemology/Gemstones, Jewelry, Diamonds, Gold, Silver, Antique & Period Jewelry. Alt Tel: 734-455-4555.

Barbara C. Seichter, ISA
B.C. Seichter, Inc., dba Le Chatelet
5 Shadow Ln
Bloomfield Hills, MI 48302
ph: 248-647-3660
Furniture (English & Continental), Porcelain, Pottery, Ceramics, (English, Continental, & Chinese Export)

Susan C. Gahan, ISA
Pour Mary's Antiques
5878 Dixie Hwy
Clarkston, MI 48346-3358
ph: 810-623-3250
fax: 810-623-3254
Costume Jewelry, American Pottery, Estate Sales

Marilyn M. Roberts, ISA
Marilyn Roberts' Antiques
8745 Central Pl
Freeland, MI 48623-9519
ph: 517-695-6508
Antiques, Collectibles, Crystal, Furniture, Porcelain, Pottery, Primitives, Quilts, Residential Contents, Insurance, and Estate Sales.

Jay Ann Mills-McDonald, ISA
Somewhere In Time Antiques
PO Box 638
Mayville, MI 48744-0638
ph: 517-673-5300
jaymc@mill.tds.net
Antiques, Residential Contents, Furniture, Home Furnishings, and 19th C. British Furniture.

Mark E. Hazlett, ISA
Antique Appraisals & Consignments
PO Box 578
Haslett, MI 48840-0578
ph: 517-339-1827
Antiques, Furniture, Books, Fine Art

Richard A. Bloomquist, ISA
375 Turner Rd
Williamston, MI 48895-9410
ph: 517-655-3380
wrbloomquist@juno.com
Estate Sales, Antiques, Furniture, Ceramics, and Residential Contents.

Martha McDonald, ISA
c/o Dunes Antiques Center, Inc.
12825 Red Arrow Hwy
Sawyer, MI 49125-9173
ph: 616-426-4043
fax: 616-426-8238
dunesantiques@qtm.net
http://www.dunesantiques.com
Antiques, Residential Contents, Art Glass, Pottery, Decorative Arts & Accessories

Frank T. Wieber, ISA
Consumers Engergy
115 W Trail St
Jackson, MI 49201-1314
ph: 517-788-7098
fax: 517-788-0769
Vehicles, Equipment, Trailers (Parts & Tools), Office Furniture

Timothy G. Bos, ISA
Timothy G. Bos Appraisal
4701 County Farm Rd
Jackson, MI 49201-9092
ph: 517-784-2177
Furniture, Collectibles, Residential Contents, Depression Era Glass (Glassware), Furniture Repairs, Restoration, Preservation (Antiques), 1850's-1900's

Duane A. Leet, ISA
E'leet Appraisals & Estate Sales
533 Colfax Ave
Grand Haven, MI 49417-1828
ph: 616-842-7677
Toy Dishes, Staffordshire China, R.S. Prussia China, Oil Lamps

Scott A. Miedema, ISA
Miedema Auctioneering Appraisals, Inc.
PO Box 453
Grandville, MI 49468-0453
ph: 800-527-8243
fax: 800-527-8243
Machinery & Equipment, Boats, Marine Equipment, Construction Equipment, Office Furniture & Equipment, Auctioneer

Chad A. Van Overloop, ISA
Miedema Appraisals, Inc.
PO Box 453
Grandville, MI 49468-0453
ph: 616-538-0367
fax: 616-538-5230
info@miedemaauctioneering.com
Machinery & Equipment, Heavy Construction, Industrial Equipment, Presses, Lathes, Farms, Trucks, Restaurant Equipment, Auction Services

Joan F. McLain, ISA
Antique Appraisers, Grand Traverse
PO Box 416
Eastport, MI 49627-0416
ph: 616-946-2534
fax: 616-946-2573
Residential Contents, Liquidators, Damage Claims, Insurance, Estates

Bonnie C. Beckman, ISA
Antique Emporium
565 W Blue Star Dr
Traverse City, MI 49684-8778
ph: 616-943-3658
antiques@gtii.com
http://www.antique-emporium.com
Glass (Art), Lamps, Lighting Fixtures, Antiques, Collectibles, Estates, Jewelry, Liquidators, Residential Contents, Auctioneer, Consultant, Damage Claims

Susan B. Feiger, ISA
Susan Feiger Appraisal Service
2513 Nelson Rd
Traverse City, MI 49686-8557
ph: 616-223-7386
fax: 616-223-7387
feiger@gtuii.com
Antiques (American & General), Residential Contents, Furniture, Silver, Glass, Porcelain, Pottery, Quilts, Estate Sales, Gas Station Collectibles

Judith A. Owen, ISA
Antique Appraisers, Grand Traverse
10332 Stoney Beach Pt
Traverse City, MI 49686-8584
ph: 616-946-2534
fax: 616-946-2573
Judy@AntiqueAppraisers.com
http://www.antiqueappraisers.com
Antiques, Decorative Arts, American Furniture, Silver, Breweriana

Marilynn A. Quick, ISA
Susan Feiger Appraisal Service
1036 Bayside Dr
Traverse City, MI 49686-9205
ph: 616-946-7811
American Antiques, Collectibles, Glass (American Art Glass), Estates (Estate Sales), Residential Contents

Debra Streeter, ISA
23806 W Le Duc Row
Brimley, MI 49715
ph: 906-437-5526
fax: 906-437-5262
dstreeter@up.net
Residential Contents, Antiques, Collectibles

Deborah Golden, ISA
Golden Era Sales, Inc.
3182 Twin Pine Rd
Grayling, MI 49738-6307
ph: 517-348-2610
Residential Contents (Appreciable & Depreciable), Estates, Insurance, Liquidators, Estate Sales

Robin Rose, ISA
Silver Lining Antiques
530 Ashmun St
Sault Ste. Marie, MI 49783
ph: 906-632-4929
fax: 906-632-6309
Antiques, Furniture (c. 1850-1950), Porcelain, China, Pottery (c. 1850-1990), Sterling & Silverplate Service (c. 1850-1950), linen, fabric, textiles (c. 1900-1950), jewelry (costume & fine)

Sara Jane Harwood, ISA
4403 63rd St
Des Moines, IA 50322-1927
ph: 515-276-2790
sallygwtw@earthlink.net
Art (American & European), Paintings, Drawings, Prints (19th C.), Sculpture (19th C.), All 20th C. Art Media

Sandra K. Bates, ISA
612 W Main St.
Sac City, IA 50583
ph: 712-662-7116
fax: 712-882-2542
sandra@pionet.net
Antiques, Collectibles, Residential Contents, Damage Claims Specialist

Jon E. Crisman, ISA
Jackson's Auctioneers
PO Box 585
Cedar Falls, IA 50613-0585
ph: 319-277-2256
fax: 319-277-1252
jacksons@corenet.net
Residential Contents, Antique Glassware, European & Continental Pottery & Porcelain, American Art Pottery

James L. Jackson, ISA
Jackson's Auctioneers
2229 Lincoln St
Cedar Falls, IA 50613-3277
ph: 319-277-2256
fax: 319-277-1252
jacksons@corenet.net
http://www.jacksonsauction.com
Russian Icons

Bruce C. Anderson, ISA, CGA
Thorpe & Co. Jewelers
501 4th St
Sioux City, IA 51101-1601
ph: 712-258-7501
fax: 712-258-8138
Jewelry Appraisals, Insurance, Estate, Division of Property, and MUVR(tm) Reports

Robert J. Biede, ISA
Antique Junction Mall
200 Timber Ln
Council Bluffs, IA 51503-1769
ph: 712-325-1055
fax: 712-622-9367
Antiques

Janelle V. McClain, ISA
CornerHouse Gallery & Frame
2753 1st Ave SE
Cedar Rapids, IA 52402-4804
ph: 319-365-4348
fax: 319-365-1707
mcclain.janelle@mcleod.usa.com
Fine Art; Specializing in the Regionalist Movement (Grant Wood, Marvin Cone, T.H. Benton and J.S. Curry)

Katherine Vandygriff, ISA CAPP, GG (GIA)
Katherine's
605 Sunset Dr
Muscatine, IA 52761-2778
ph: 319-263-6008
fax: 319-263-1050
jhk@muscanet.com OR
stephv@muscanet.com
Gemology/Gemstones, Diamonds, Jewelry, Pearls

Susan S. Pohle, ISA
Accurate Appraisals
621 N Main St
Mequon, WI 53092-1215
ph: 414-242-2054
Art, Ceramics, Furniture, Glass, Silver

Larry Gutbrod, ISA
Greater Northshore Appraisals & Auctions, Inc.
10030 N Sunnycrest Dr
Mequon, WI 53092-5419
ph: 414-512-9083
fax: 414-512-9084
lgutbrod@aol.com
Residential Contents, Fine Art, Insurance, Auctioneer, Auction Co.

Kent Anderson, Ph.D., ISA
Kent Anderson Fine Art
11298 Bridget Ln
Hales Corners, WI 53130-2426
ph: 414-425-2377
fax: 414-425-4154
Paintings, Drawings, Prints (Original), Sculpture, Artist's Books (Livre's D'Artist), Posters

Karen I. Halboth, ISA
Karen I. Halboth/Company Appraisals
20 Orchard St
Williams Bay, WI 53191
ph: 414-245-0217
fax: 414-245-0217
kih@pensys.com
General Lines of Antiques, Collectibles, American Glass, and Pre-1960's Van Briggle Pottery.

Brent Fraser, ISA
Fraser & Associates
5037 W Washington Blvd
Milwaukee, WI 53208-1702
ph: 414-476-1465
Residential Contents, Fine Art, Cars, Trucks, Antiques, Auctioneer

Teresa M. Schnell, ISA
434 Superior St
St. Paul, MN 55102-2900
ph: 651-222-6151
fax: 651-222-6267
Gems & Jewelry: Appraising, Repair and Sales

Mary F. Marsden, ISA
Mary Marsden & Associates
515 Lexington Pkwy S, Apt 503
Saint Paul, MN 55116-1742
ph: 612-699-4740
fax: 612-690-3191
Vintage, Modern, and 19th C. Residential Contents; Specialist in Fair Market Valuations for Legal Purposes. Offers Mediation Assistance and Referral Services for Specialized Needs

Mary Chumas Ernst, ISA
Mary's Appraisals
2016 Yorkshire Ave, Apt 106
Saint Paul, MN 55116-2585
ph: 612-698-6624
Antiques, Religious Items, Collectibles

Henry G. Swiggum, ISA
Henry Swiggum Fine Art Appraisals
14246 Glencove Trl
Saint Paul, MN 55124-5517
ph: 612-891-1514
fax: 612-891-1514
Fine Art, Sculpture, Prints & Paintings, Asian Art, Insurance Claims

Susan K. Rychlik, ISA, GG (GIA)
Gemological Resource
7097 Robinwood Bay
Woodbury, MN 55125-2724
ph: 612-339-5007
Jewelry, Estate Jewelry

Patrick Batzler, ISA
Patrick Batzler Appraisals
8118 Virginia Circle N
St. Louis Park, MN 55426
ph: 612-525-9590
fax: 612-417-9417
Antiques, Collectibles, Glassware, Furniture, Fine China, Primitives, Children's Items, Art Prints

Margaret G. Zirbel, ISA, GG (GIA)
Antiques On Grand
406 Ryan Dr
Bozeman, MT 59715-9278
ph: 406-586-6216
Jewelry, Estate Jewelry, Antiques

Mary M. Kuhrtz, ISA
101 Carriage Rd
Barrington, IL 60010-2205
ph: 847-304-8239
Furniture (18th C.), Decorative Arts, Residential Contents

Ellen M. Kornhauser, ISA, GG (GIA)
I.K. Design
141 S Northwest Hwy
Barrington, IL 60010-4684
ph: 847-381-8626
Gemology/Gemstones, Diamonds, Pearls, and Contemporary Jewelry.

Karen S. Rabe, ISA CAPP
Appraisal Specialists
PO Box 21
Lake Forest, IL 60045
ph: 847-356-2094
fax: 847-356-2139
ksrabe@ameritech.net
Antiques, Decorative Arts & Accessories, Residential Contents, Including 18th-20th C. Furniture, Ceramics, Glass, Collectibles, Metals, Sterling Silver, Damage Claims Specialist, Broker, and Consultant.

Sybil Tillman, ISA
Artco, Inc.
3148 RFD
Long Grove, IL 60047-9610
ph: 847-438-8420
fax: 847-438-6464
Fine Art, Contemporary American All Medium, 19th-20th C. American and European Paintings, Prints, Bronzes

Stuart M. Robertson, ISA, GG (GIA)
Gemworld International, Inc.
650 Dundee Rd, Ste 465
Northbrook, IL 60062-2758
ph: 847-564-0555
fax: 847-564-0557
stuartr@ix.netcom.com
http://www.gemguide.com
Gemology/Gemstones, Colored Stones, Contemporary Diamond Jewelry, Estate Jewelry, Pearls, Watches, Gold, Diamonds, Liquidators, Insurance, Gem Lab, Expert

Witness, Litigation Consultant. Alt Email: 102036.275@compuserve.com

Beatrice Weiskopf, ISA
Weiskopf Appraisal Services, Inc.
1343 Landwehr Rd
Northbrook, IL 60062-4353
ph: 847-509-9664
fax: 847-509-9606
104345.3271@compuserve.com
Antiques, Residential Contents, Decorative Arts & Accessories, Collectibles, Americana, Porcelain, Glass, Modern Glass, Pottery, Silver, Damage Claims, Autos, Ceramics

George S. Ison, ISA
2368 W Warren Ave
Palatine, IL 60067-4556
ph: 847-705-6455
Gemstones, Fine Jewelry

Judy F. Banasek-Bratton, ISA
Judy Bratton Appraisals
1013 Surrey Rd
Addison, IL 60101-1141
ph: 630-628-0650
fax: 630-628-0640
Antiques, Collectibles, Residential Contents, Post Cards, Liquidator, Estate Consultant

Elroy J. Sell, ISA, GG (GIA)
Appraisal Office Of Elroy J. Sell
679 W North Ave, Ste 101
Elmhurst, IL 60126-2147
ph: 630-833-7250
fax: 630-833-7255
Independant Appraiser of Gems, Jewelry, & Watches, Private Office or 'on-site' at Home, Office, or Bank, Insurance, Estate, Liquidation, & Consumer Confirmation of Price and Quality

Maryellyn Woodruff, ISA
Vanderbilt's Antiques
28 Richards St
Geneva, IL 60134
ph: 630-232-0810
Residential Contents, Antiques, Collectibles, Furniture Restoration, Estate Sales

Marcia P. Crosby, ISA
Marcia Crosby Antiques
477 Forest Ave
Glen Ellyn, IL 60137-4104
ph: 630-858-5665
Appreciable Residential Contents, Antiques, Americana, Furniture, 19th C. Art, Prints & Maps, Folk Art, American Country Furniture & Accessories, White Ironstone, Lighting, Books, Children's Items, Insurance, Damage Claims, Estates

Stephanie M. Dooley, ISA
SMD Arts, Inc
PO Box 598
Medinah, IL 60157-0598
ph: 630-529-3288
fax: 630-529-3440
Fine Art, Prints (19th & 20th C.), Engravings, Etchings, Sculpture, Paintings, Posters, Lithographs, Serigraphs

Carolyn Gianopoulos, ISA
Carole's Coach House Antiques
6N680 Palomino Dr
Saint Charles, IL 60175-8439
ph: 630-584-4374
fax: 630-584-0057
Residential Contents, Antiques, Furniture (19th & 20th C. American, European, Victorian, and Contemporary), Collectibles, Glass, Dinnerware, Damage Claims, Estate Sales

Maurice E. Fry, ISA
PO Box 95605
Hoffman Estates, IL 60195-0605
ph: 847-843-1533
fax: 847-882-8292
Founder ISA; Lifetime Member

Colin Sinclair Reed, ISA
Prairieland Estate Services
2674 Prairie Ave
Evanston, IL 60201-1435
ph: 847-869-3119
fax: 847-383-9256
Estates (including Liquidations)

Jane L. Baker, ISA
1431 SEWARD ST
Evanston, IL 60202-2077
ph: 847-864-2150
Appreciable & Depreciable Residential Contents, Antiques, Collectibles, Insurance, Estates & Household Liquidations

James F. Sunderland, Jr., ISA CAPP, GG (GIA)
James & Sons, Ltd.
239 Gold Coast Ln
Calumet City, IL 60409-6096
ph: 708-862-3800
Rare Coins, Diamonds, Jewelry (Antique)

Harry Carpenter, ISA
Days Of Yesteryear
2429 Dougall Rd
Joliet, IL 60433-1601
ph: 815-722-8014
yesteryear@prodigy.net
Antiques, Collectibles, Glass, Sports

David V. Trout, ISA
David V. Trout Appraisals
28 Monee Rd
Park Forest, IL 60466-2107
ph: 708-748-3518
Art (19th to Early 20th C.), American & European Paintings, Hudson River School, Indiana Artists, Midwest & Chicago Artists, Folk Art, Americana

Gloria Moroni, ISA CAPP
Gloria Moroni, Appraiser
21 Spinning Wheel Rd
Hinsdale, IL 60521-2930
ph: 630-986-1945
fax: 630-986-1954
76725.746@compuserve.com
Antiques, Residential Contents, Silver, Porcelain, Pottery, Ceramics, Antique Furniture, Glass, Estates, Restaurant Equipment

Jane F. Washburn, ISA CAPP
Washburn & Associates
5 Morgan Ct
Burr Ridge, IL 60521-8339
ph: 630-325-3115
fax: 630-325-2144
102444.364@compuserve.com
Residential Contents, Antiques, Decorative Arts & Accessories, Furniture, Consultant

Dinah J. Thompson, ISA
401 S Park Rd
La Grange, IL 60525-6110
ph: 708-354-8775
Arts & Crafts Era. Furniture, Pottery, Decorative Arts & Acccessories, Modern Movement

Judith M. Martin, ISA CAPP
M & M Sales
1405 Culpepper Dr
Naperville, IL 60540-8310
ph: 630-548-1436
fax: 630-548-1436
76571.2714@compuserve.com
Estate Sales, Collectibles, Depreciable & Appreciable Personal Property, Office Furniture & Equipment, Decorative Arts & Accessories, Collectibles

Farhad Radfar, ISA
Mir International Gallery & Appraiser Svcs.
332 N. Michigan Ave, 2nd Floor
Chicago, IL 60601
ph: 312-814-8510
fax: 312-814-8511
mirgallery@aol.com
http://www.mirgallery.com
Porcelain (Meissen, KPM, Vienna), Rugs, Furs, and Fine Arts.

Heidi A. Feithen, ISA CAPP, GG (GIA)
Chicago Gem Evaluation Services, Inc.
5 N Wabash Ave, Ste 1615
Chicago, IL 60602-4712
ph: 312-578-0440
fax: 312-578-0477
http://www.chicagogem.qpg.com
Gemology/Gemstones, Colored Stones, Diamonds, Jewelry, Pearls, and Minerals

Marilyn Dresser, ISA
Dresser International
680 N Lake Shore Dr, Apt 1401
Chicago, IL 60611-4483
ph: 312-642-4011
Fine Art, Antiques, Art & Crafts, Glass (European & American)

Maureen F. Perou, ISA
Estate Excellence
2673 N Orchard St
Chicago, IL 60614-1548
ph: 773-975-9400
fax: 773-975-9400
Antiques, Furniture, Residential Contents, Glassware, China

Donald Shannon, ISA
Graphic Appraisal Services, Inc.
9820 S Damen Ave
Chicago, IL 60643-1702
ph: 773-233-5235
fax: 773-233-2829
Printing Machinery & Equipment including Press Bindery and Electronic Repress Offset Gravure Flexographic Screen Print Web and Sheet Fed

Byla Simon Kunis, ISA
Oriental Treasures
2947 W Jarlath St
Chicago, IL 60645-1215
ph: 773-761-2907
fax: 773-761-0789
Chinese & Japanese Antiques, Porcelain, Jade, Ivory, Cloisonne

Mike MacIntosh, ISA
Heller Financial, Inc.
500 W Monroe St, Fl 29
Chicago, IL 60661-3630
ph: 312-928-8538
fax: 312-928-8742
mmacintosh@hellerfin.com
Machinery & Equipment, Graphics

Vernon C. Thomson, Jr., ISA
PO Box 80
Vermont, IL 61484-0080
ph: 309-784-8381
Residential Contents, Antiques, Collectibles, Decorative Arts & Accessories, Victoriana

Robin Yaw, ISA
Crystal Connection, The
8510 N Knoxville Ave, Ste 218
Peoria, IL 61615-2034
ph: 309-692-2221
fax: 309-692-2221
TCCLtd@aol.com
http://www.crystal.org
Swarovski Crystal Figurines

Stephen C. Johnson, Ph.D., ISA
Behavorial Images, Inc.
302 Leland St, Ste 101
Bloomington, IL 61701-5646
ph: 800-988-6427
fax: 888-735-8856
sjohnson@mediavalue.com
http://www.mediavalue.com
Audio-Visual Recorded Media, Literature, Equipment, Motion Picture Film & Video Moving Image Media, Disc & Tape Sound Recordings, Still Photography, Negatives, Transparencies, & Animation Cells.

Marcia Lenhart, ISA
9162 N 1450 East Rd
Georgetown, IL 61846-7505
ph: 217-662-8644
fax: 217-662-6899
dlenhart@danville.net
Antiques, Residential Contents, Jewelry, Auction Co.

Virginia Cannon, ISA CAPP
China House, The
801 W Eldorado St
Decatur, IL 62522-2122
ph: 217-428-7212
fax: 217-422-8906
76573.376@compuserve.com
Dinnerware, Silver (19th & 20th C.), Furniture, Glass, Fine & Decorative Art, Haviland China Matching; Alt Phone 800-342-9536

Edwin G. Walker, ISA
Walker Antiques & Collectibles
425 S Henderson
Mt. Zion, IL 62549
ph: 217-424-6228
fax: 217-424-3933
ewalker@mail.millikin.edu
Turn of the Century Decorative Arts & Antiques, 20th C. Paintings, Arts & Crafts

Sally Hatcher, ISA
Hatcher Appraisals
PO Box 616
Lincoln, IL 62656-0616
ph: 217-735-2649
Antiques, Tribal Art, Beadwork, Beads, Buttons

Lorraine R. O'Hern, ISA CAPP
700 E Miller St
Springfield, IL 62702-6329
ph: 217-523-0998
Antiques, American Furniture (18th-20th C.), Decorative Arts & Accessories, Residential Contents, Estate Sales

Deborah Lauer Toelle, ISA, CGA, GG
Stout & Lauer Jewelers
1929 W. Iles - Montvale Junct.
Montvale Junction
Springfield, IL 62704-4177
ph: 217-793-3040
fax: 217-793-8746
Gemology/Gemstones, Diamonds, Jewelry

Marian Erb, ISA
Locust Street Gallery
PO Box 508
Centralia, IL 62801-0508
ph: 618-533-1699
fax: 618-533-8616
Collectibles, Antiques, Residential Contents, Airplanes

Sharon Niles, ISA
Carousel Restorations, Inc.
14409 Manchester
Manchester, MO 63011
ph: 314-391-4900
fax: 314-391-3993
Carouselskn@msn.com
Procelain, Pottery, Dolls,

Susan Martin, ISA
Appraisal Affiliates, Inc.
1 Brisbane
Chesterfield, MO 63017
ph: 314-532-2223
fax: 314-647-2313
Serving the St. Louis Area. Toll-Free . Specializes in Residential Contents, Antiques, Collectibles, Jewelry, Artwork, Estate Sales.

R. L . Butler, ISA
Galerie Vollard, Ltd.
3438 Russell Blvd.,, Penthouse
St. Louis, MO 63104
ph: 314-773-3132
Antique, Contemporary & Fine Art Prints, Etchings, Lithographs, Silk Screens, Serigraphs, Engravings, Woodcuts, Limited Editions (French, English, American, European), Some Oils and Watercolors, Posters, Art, Impressionism, and Drawings.

Michele Campbell, ISA
Apex Appraisal Services
PO Box 21713
Saint Louis, MO 63109-0713
ph: 314-752-5039
fax: 314-752-0235
75562.1536@compuserve.com
http://www.apex.stlmo.com
Antiques, Residential Contents, Art, Collectibles, Appraisal Services, Auctioneer & Consultant

Carol M. Sumpter, ISA
Cardan's Doll Shop
3808 Loughborough Ave
Saint Louis, MO 63116-3015
ph: 314-351-7955
Dolls & Accessories (Antique & Collectible Dolls), Toys (Collectible)

Carl T. Roedel, Jr., ISA
Automobile Appraisal Service & Special Interest Autos
10097 Manchester Rd, Ste 203
St. Louis, MO 63122-1828
ph: 314-821-4015
fax: 314-821-4015
Machinery, Equipment, Investment Counselor, RV's, SUV's, Motorcycles, Mobile Homes, Trucks, Trailers, Cars (Antique, Classic, Vintage, Special Interest, Sports, Customs, Kits, Foreign, Muscle, Street Rods & Machines, Milestones & Replicas

James Roedel, ISA
Automobile Appraisal Services
1414 Frances Rd
Saint Louis, MO 63122-2305
ph: 314-821-4015
fax: 314-821-4015
Cars (Antique, Classic, Special Interest, Reproduction, Sports, Foreign, & Late Models), R.V's, Motor Homes, Trucks, Trailers, Recreational Boats, Machinery & Equipment

Ted R. Young, ISA, GG (GIA)
1501 SW 13th St
Blue Springs, MO 64015-5413
ph: 816-228-6197
Diamonds, Gemology, Gemstones, Jewelry, Pearls, Watches

Danny O'Brien, ISA
1816 E 135th St
Grandview, MO 64030
ph: 816-763-4741
Antique & Classic Cars, Custom Cars, and Firearms

Ronald I. Zoglin, ISA
Brookside Antiques
6219 Oak St
Kansas City, MO 64113-2292
ph: 816-444-4774
Woodblock Prints (Japanese), Orientailia, Ivory, Bronzes, Decorative Arts & Accessories

Susan B. Dixon, ISA
Better Than Bass
HCR3, Box 3344-5
Shell Knob, MO 65747
ph: 417-858-6538
Collectibles, Residential Contents

Richard S. McElvaine, ISA, GG, CGA
Maxon's Jewelry
2622 S Glenstone Ave
Springfield, MO 65804-3712
ph: 417-887-1800
fax: 417-887-3422
Gemology/Gemstones, Diamonds, Jewelry (Fine), Watches (Fine)

Ann J. Steinberg, ISA, GG (GIA)
PO Box 4665
Springfield, MO 65808-4665
ph: 417-887-9062
Gemology & Gemstones, Diamonds, Jewelry, Watches, Estates, Insurance

David M. Solomons, ISA
David M. Solomons, Antiques, Art, Appraiser
PO Box 266
Baldwin City, KS 66006-0266
ph: 913-594-4064
Art, Antiques, Vintage Items, Collectibles, Porcelain, Glass, Dinnerware, Residential Contents, Broker Agent

Susan H. Kearns, ISA, GG (GIA)
S.H. Kearns Co., Ltd.
6800 College Blvd, Ste 260
Overland Park, KS 66211-1532
ph: 913-491-1942
Fine Jewelry, Diamonds, Gemology & Gemstones, Colored Stones

Kathylee Cook-Roberts, ISA, GJG
Look By Cook, The
PO Box 25042
Shawnee Msn, KS 66225-5042
ph: 909-925-9548
fax: 909-925-9548
Jewelry, Diamonds, Colored Stones, Gemology, Gold

Robert L. Dunlap, II, ISA
Equity Standard
8237 E Kellogg Dr
Wichita, KS 67207-1811
ph: 316-689-8773
U.S. Coins & Currency (But Not Limited To), Gold, Bullion (Scrap & Other Forms)

Marvin Mann, ISA
219 SW 8th St
Plainville, KS 67663-3320
ph: 785-434-2492
mann@ruraltel.net
Antiques, Collectibles, Coins, Glass, Toys

Eric Bauer, ISA
Russell's Cleaning Services, Inc.
PO Box 644
Metairie, LA 70004-0644
ph: 504-832-1546
fax: 504-832-9958
Cleaning & Restoration, Rugs, Oriental Rugs, Draperies

J. William Rosenthal, MD, ISA,
New Orleans Eye Specialists
1320 Valence St
New Orleans, LA 70115-3934
ph: 504-891-1988
fax: 504-899-1895
Ophthalmic Instruments, Spectacles, Vision Aids, Edged Weapons, Steel Beaded Purses

Sherry L. Kohlert, ISA
605 N Alexander St
New Orleans, LA 70119-4511
ph: 504-486-0257
fax: 504-486-0257
kohlwin@sprynet.com
http://www.collectoronline.com
Antiques, Collectibles, Estate Sales

Ward J. Stewart, ISA
Stewart's Antiques
1000 Coolidge Blvd
Lafayette, LA 70503-2436
ph: 318-232-2957
Antiques, China, Porcelain (American & Continental), Crystal, Glass (Cut and Art), Furniture

Polly R. Enloe, ISA
Century Antiques & Appraisals
212 Miller St
Lafayette, LA 70503-2522
ph: 318-234-7146
Appreciable & Depreciable Residential Contents, Generalist in Personal Property

Thomas H. Shelton, II, ISA, GG (GIA)
1326 W Pinhook Rd
Lafayette, LA 70503-2906
ph: 318-234-4396
fax: 318-232-5320
tom@net-connect.net
Gemology/Gemstones, Jewelry (Estate), Diamonds, Metals (Precious)

Stephen H. Martin, ISA CAPP
1455 Charmaine Ave
Baton Rouge, LA 70806-7717
ph: 225-923-3437
fax: 225-924-0620
harding1@msn.com
Residential Contents, Antiques, Fine Art, Firearms, Cars, Trucks, Office Furniture & Equipment, Clocks, Auctioneer, Auction Co.

Phillip D. Peck, ISA
Revpro Appraisal Service
4021 Indian Run Dr
Baton Rouge, LA 70816-3571
ph: 225-755-7002
fax: 225-755-0302
revpro@compuserve.com
Heavy Trucks & Trailers, Farm Equipment & Machinery, Industrial, Manufacturing, Oil Field, FF&E, Restaurant Equipment, Machinery & Equipment, Industrial & Manufacturing, Drilling & Service Equipment

James W. Pharr, ISA
James Pharr Machinery Co.
PO Box 38385
Shreveport, LA 71133-8385
ph: 318-636-6050
fax: 318-636-6608
Construction & Related Equipment, Trucks, Oil Field Equipment, Cranes and Erection Equipment

Nancy R. Garot-Reynolds, ISA, GG (GIA)
Gallery G. Antiques
200 Court Sq
Dewitt, AR 72042
ph: 870-946-2593
<<< SECOND LISTING >>>
Gemology/Gemstones, Antique & Estate Jewelry, Pearls, Colored Stones, and Silver

Nancy R. Garot-Reynolds, ISA, GG (GIA)
Circa Collection, The
55 Stanfield Rd
Edgemont, AR 72044-9716
ph: 501-723-4605
fax: 501-723-4605
Gemology/Gemstones, Antique & Estate Jewelry, Pearls, Colored Stones, Silver

Shea Weidner, ISA
Heritage House Antiques
593 Crest Dr
Fayetteville, AR 72701-4256
ph: 501-582-5653
fax: 501-582-5653
sheacrain@compuserve.com
Residential Contents, Antiques, Decorative Arts & Accessories

Sally K. Atkinson, ISA
Legacy Estate Liquidators, LLC
1905 Whipporwill Ct, Ste 148
Edmond, OK 73013
ph: 405-748-3433
fax: 405-330-6285
gean@worldnet.att.net
Residential Contents, Estate Sales

Richard L. Watts, ISA
89er Antique Mall
810 E Warner Ave
Guthrie, OK 73044-3635
ph: 405-282-2661
richardwatts3@gte.net
Czech Collectibles, Depression Glass, 1904 World's Fair Collectibles

M. Lyn Livingston, ISA CAPP
Livingston & Associates, Inc. Appraisal & Estate Service
2809 NW Expressway, Ste 150
Oklahoma City, OK 73112-7079
ph: 405-722-1475
fax: 405-415-2114
lynl@keytech.com
Residential Contents, Antiques, Collectibles, Estates, Probate, Divorce, Damage Claims, Liquidation, Furniture, American Glass, Wave Crest, Vintage Radios Alt Phone 405-722-7034

Scott M. Gordon, ISA, GG GIA, FGA
Scott Gordon Jeweler
50 Penn Pl, Ste 334R
Oklahoma City, OK 73118-1841
ph: 405-843-7856
fax: 405-848-5921
alefbet@aol.com
Diamonds, Colored Stones, Contemporary & Period Jewelry From Victorian Onward

John C. West, ISA
West Of Boston
300 S Wyandotte Ave
Bartlesville, OK 74003-4038
ph: 918-336-3277
fax: 918-336-0178
woboston@ionet.net
Art, Antiques, Residential Contents

Tom E. Hill, ISA
The Woodshed
11367 E 61st St
Broken Arrow, OK 74012-1272
ph: 918-258-8553
fax: 918-250-5169
Hilte@aol.com
Furniture (1700's to Present), Repairs, Restoration, Preservation and Conservation of all Furniture, Wood Carvings, Specialty Veneer Inlays, Court Testimony, Damage Claims

Barbara S. Nance, ISA
Estate Collections by Barbara
2252 E 31st Pl
Tulsa, OK 74105-2210
ph: 918-742-7712
fax: 918-745-5843
barb@tulsa.oklahoma.net
Residential Contents, Estate Sales

Debora Riggs Grillot, ISA
Estate & Consignment Sales & Appraisals
1820 E 37th St
Tulsa, OK 74105-8109
ph: 918-743-4515
Oriental Textiles, Estate Liquidator

Pat Anderson, ISA
Anderson Appraisal Service
6529 E Pine Pl
Tulsa, OK 74115-4608
ph: 918-838-7779
Appreciable & Depreciable Residential Contents, Liquidation

Katherine R. Cibula, ISA
10537 S 69th East Ave
Tulsa, OK 74133-6721
ph: 918-299-3060
fax: 918-299-9577
Furniture & Accessories (Antique & Reproduction), Antiques (French & English), Art

William L. Lavendusky, ISA
WLL Fine Art
3345 S Harvard Ave, Ste 100
Tulsa, OK 74135-1800
ph: 918-747-5336
fax: 918-742-3425
Paintings, Bronze Sculpture, and Works on Paper.

Connie J. Fletcher, ISA
6711 S Quincy Ave
Tulsa, OK 74136-3803
ph: 918-492-1273
Residential Contents, Antiques, Collectibles, Trusts, Insurance, Liquidations

Janell Lyle, ISA
Lyle's Appraisals
11855 S 270th East Ave
Coweta, OK 74429-5828
ph: 918-832-7905
Antiques, Residential Contents

Peggy Morrow, ISA
Morrow Appraisals
1102 Roaring Springs Dr
Allen, TX 75002-1908
ph: 972-727-6110
Residential Contents, Estate Sales

Lorrie R. Semler, ISA CAPP
Semler Appraisals
2000 Via Corona
Carrollton, TX 75006-4615
ph: 972-416-3417
fax: 972-416-1122
semler@airmail.net
http://www.home1.gte.net/lenny/semler.htm
Residential Contents including Furniture, Antiques, Glass, China, Pottery, Insurance, Damage Claims, Estate Probate, Equitable Distribution

Brenda Simonson-Mohle, ISA
Signet Art
2211 High Point Dr
Carrollton, TX 75007-1705
ph: 972-306-1963
fax: 972-306-1963
sigart7@airmail.net
Fine Art, Decorative Art, 19th C. American & European Art, 20th C. American & European Art, Paintings, Drawings, Prints (Intaglio, Serigraph, Lithograph), Sculpture, Tapestries Alt e-mail sigart7@airmail.net

Bob Webb, ISA
Robert Webb & Associates, Inc.
2411 Glen Morris Rd
Carrollton, TX 75007-2016
ph: 972-306-8556
fax: 972-306-7970
Industrial Appraisals of all Personal and Real Property, as well as Business Evaluations.

Cynthia L. Webb, ISA
Robert Webb & Associates, Inc
2411 Glen Morris Rd
Carrollton, TX 75007-2016
ph: 972-306-8556
fax: 972-306-7970
Antiques

Beverly Morris, ISA
PO Box 112327
Carrollton, TX 75011-2327
ph: 972-221-4022
bjcollect@aol.com
Antique & Period Costume Jewelry, Antiques, Collectibles, and Residential Contents. Alt Tel: 405-722-1475.

Leonard Ciesla, ISA
Price Waterhouse
8101 Lynores Way
Plano, TX 75025-4333
ph: 972-867-6292
Machinery & Equipment

Marigold Lamb, ISA
Lamb Appraisals
106 Autumn Trl
Rockwall, TX 75032-8816
ph: 972-771-9664
fax: 972-771-9664
Furniture (European & British), Decorative Arts & Accessories (European & British), Residential Contents, Antiques

Timothy James Healy, ISA
Premier International Auctioneers
3001 Skyway Cir N, #140
Irving, TX 75038
ph: 972-870-9997
fax: 972-870-9994
2premier@flash.net
Oil Field Equipment, Construction Equipment, Trucks & Trailers, Auctioneeer, Machinery & Equipment

Frank Everts, Jr., ISA, GG, CG
Frank Everts & Associates
11846 Donore
Dallas, TX 75128
ph: 214-349-5577
fax: 214-553-0446
Gems & Jewlery, Fancy color diamonds, Faberge

James E. Hawkins, ISA
Cathy's Antiques & Estate Jewelry
500 Crescent Ct, Ste 150
Dallas, TX 75201
ph: 214-871-3737
fax: 214-922-3376
jamesh193@aol.com
Gems & Jewelry, Antiques & Residential Contents

Ellen Amirkhan, ISA CAPP
Oriental Rug Cleaning Co., Inc.
3907 Ross Ave
Dallas, TX 75204-5248
ph: 214-821-9135
fax: 214-821-9136
eaa1@airmail.net
Oriental Rugs

Janelle Stone, ISA
Janelle Stone Estate Services
4016 University Blvd
Dallas, TX 75205-1715
ph: 214-528-9797
fax: 214-696-0377
bstone@airmail.net
Anitques, Collectibles, Residential Contents, Furniture (Antique, British, American, European), Decorative Arts, Estate Liquidations, Estate Appraisals

Avie C. Kalker, ISA
5805 Birchbrook Dr, #202
Dallas, TX 75206-4507
ph: 214-373-7656
fax: 214-373-7656
Fine Art, Household Contents, Decorative Arts & Accessories, Furniture, Porcelain, Cut Glass, Art Glass, Silver, Watches, Books, Estate Settlement/Sales; Consultant & Broker; Damage Claims, Dealer. Alt Phone & Fax: 413-458-8422

Alan Winston Smith, ISA, GG (GIA)
Winston Studio & Imports
5914 Vanderbilt Ave
Dallas, TX 75206-6136
ph: 214-357-0081
fax: 214-821-8583
wsimports@aol.com
Expert Witness, Copyright, Jewelry, NAFTA, Arts & Crafts, Faberge, Consultant, Gemology/Gemstones, Jewelry, Religious Items, Silver, Fine Art 76657.11372compuserve.com

Kathy Finch, ISA
5815 La Vista Ct
Dallas, TX 75206-7211
ph: 214-824-4684
KLFELVIS@AOL.COM
Appreciable & Depreciable Residential Contents, Estate Liquidations, Perfume Bottles

Shelley S. Stevens, ISA
Orion Antiques Importers, Inc.
1435 Slocum St
Dallas, TX 75207-3810
ph: 214-748-1177
fax: 214-748-1491
ss@oriondallas.com
16th-19th C. French & Italian Antique Furniture, Chandeliers, Architectural Elements, Tapestries, Paintings and Garden Ornaments

Jerry W. Holley, ISA
Holley Appraisals
5600 W Lovers Ln, Ste 116
Dallas, TX 75209-4311
ph: 972-743-6071
fax: 214-350-4330
jwholley@aol.com
Antiques, English Furniture, European Furniture, Victorian Furniture, Antique Clocks and Watches, General Household Goods, Estate Sales, Licensed Auctioneer

James Arthur Rousseau, ISA
4930 Swiss Ave
Dallas, TX 75214
ph: 214-824-2359
Antiques and Residential Contents, Glassware, Furniture, Accessories

Vicki S. Harris, ISA
Gaither Harris Estate Sales
3521 Centenary Ave
Dallas, TX 75225-5014
ph: 214-373-0132
vickiharris@compuserve.com
Furniture, Residential Contents, Antiques, Collectibles, Estates

Barbara Gaither, ISA
Gaither Harris Estate Sale
2801 Lovers Ln
Dallas, TX 75225-7906
ph: 214-691-0670
fax: 214-691-6397
lyndon1@airmail.net
Estates, Liquidator, Antiques, Residential Contents, Furniture, Must Dial Ext: #11 On Fax Machine

Gail R. Barnett, ISA
Gail Barnett Interiors & Appraisals
5608 Palomar Ln
Dallas, TX 75229
ph: 214-750-7775
fax: 214-659-0003
gailnb@aol.com
Household Furnishings

Robert H. Banks, ISA
Banks Fine Art
3316 Royal Ln
Dallas, TX 75229-5061
ph: 214-352-1811
fax: 214-352-6360
artman2@ix.netcom.com
http://www.banksfineart.com
Paintings and Drawings (American & European), Prints (General), Fine Art, Sculpture, 19th-20th C. & Contemporary Artists.

James Erwin Jessup, ISA
JEJ Enterprises - The Appraisal Group
6015 Burgundy Rd
Dallas, TX 75230
ph: 214-265-7979
fax: 214-987-1984
theappraisalgroup@yahoo.com
Antiques, Collectibles, Decorative Arts & Accessories, Furniture, Glass, Office FF&E, Porcelain, Pottery, Ceramics, China, Residential Contents, Silver, Estates, Insurance, Litigation Support, Liquidators

Martilla "Tillie" Williams, ISA
Attic Galleries
9302 Canter Dr
Dallas, TX 75231-1406
ph: 214-348-5162
fax: 214-648-2848
Estate Sales, Moving Sales (General Household Goods)

Jerry Forrest, ISA CAPP, GG, CGA
Jewelry Forrest, Inc.
9100 N Central Expy, Ste 185
Dallas, TX 75231-5901
ph: 800-368-5376
fax: 214-750-1141
102152.2165@compuserve.com
AGS Certified Gem Laboratory, Replacement & Estate Appraisals, Loose Gemstone & Diamond Importer, Custom Handmade Jewelry, Platinum & Gold

Karan Carruth, ISA
Abbey and Carruth, Inc.
10135 Ferndale
Dallas, TX 75238
ph: 214-342-3746
fax: 214-348-5074
Residential Contents, Antiques, and Estate Sales.

John A. Buxton, ISA
BAACS Or Shango Galleries
6717 Spring Valley Rd
Dallas, TX 75240-8636
ph: 972-239-4620
fax: 972-239-9766
jbuxton@arttrak.com
http://www.arttrak.com
American Indian, African, Pre-Columbian, Oceanic, Expert Witness

Shirley B. Williams, ISA
10024 Chimney Hill Ln
Dallas, TX 75243-2906
ph: 214-369-5361
Estate Sales, Residential Contents, Antiques, Collectibles

Kenna Elkins Rosen, ISA
Rosen Appraisals & Estate Sales
9138 Loma Vista Dr
Dallas, TX 75243-7408
ph: 972-503-1436
Residential Contents, Bluebird China, and Dolls

Trudy Miller, ISA
Trudy Miller Antiques
4021 Morman Ln
Dallas, TX 75244-2602
ph: 972-490-5758
fax: 972-502-5134
Glass (All Types - Pattern to Art), American Silver (Sterling & Plate), Porcelain

Barbara Ann Samuel, ISA
Bas Antiques
4807 Troon Cir
Dallas, TX 75287
ph: 972-407-9171
Furniture (French & English), Antiques, Poreclain

Virginia Montfort, ISA
De Montfort's Fine Art
PO Box 820152
Dallas, TX 75382-0152
ph: 214-696-2615
Fine Art, Paintings, Watercolors, Drawings, Fine Prints, Objet D'Art, Porcelain, Estates, Insurance, Damage Claims Specialist

Belinda Hendley, ISA, GG (GIA)
Blue Diamond Appraisal & Design
1530 SSW Loop 323, Ste 104
Tyler, TX 75701
ph: 903-535-9161
fax: 903-510-2978
bdiamond@tyler.com
Gemology/Gemstones, Jewelry, Diamonds

Larry G. Lough, ISA
Appraisal Systems Inc.
PO Box 131270
Tyler, TX 75713-1270
ph: 903-839-7029
fax: 903-839-4909
Oil Field, Machinery & Equipment (Farm, Construction, Transportation, Industrial), Boats, Yachts, Livestock, Airplanes, Cars, Trucks, Auctioneer, Medical Equipment, High Tech, Computers, Restaurant & Food Equipment, Textiles, Forestry Equ

Guinn D. Henderson, ISA
Henderson Appraisal Associates
PO Box 131753
Tyler, TX 75713-1753
ph: 903-526-0500
fax: 903-526-0501
ghenderson@tyler.net
Cars, Trucks (Construction), Machinery & Equipment (Construction), Oil Field (Drilling Well Service, Pipeline Construction), Energy Equipment

John A. McClain, ISA
McClain & Associates
16138 Treasure Cv
Bullard, TX 75757-8008
ph: 903-825-3453
TwoJays@prodigy.net
Residential Contents, Silver, Porcelain, Furniture, Crystal, Art Pottery, Ceramics

Dana C. Staples, ISA
Dana C. Staples
909 Hunter Dr
Palestine, TX 75801-5014
ph: 903-723-5059
Residential Contents, Estates, Antiques, Furniture, Silver, Collectibles, Ceramics, Glass, Dinnerware, Decorative Arts and Accessories, Liquidators

Adelia Hale-Stanley, Ph.D., ISA
Hale-Stanley, Inc.
1800 Tennyson Dr
Arlington, TX 76013-6429
ph: 817-265-8990
fax: 817-265-8990
76331.1330@compuserve.com
Residential Contents, Collectibles, Glass, Porcelain, Ceramics, Office Furniture & Equipment, and Sports Collectibles

Richard I. Pongratz, ISA, GG (GIA)
Richard Pongratz Appraisal Services, Inc.
729 Grapevine Hwy, Ste 325
Hurst, TX 76054
ph: 817-545-6696
rpongratz@aol.com
Gemology/Gemstones, Jewelry, Diamonds, Colored Stones. Alt Email:71520.3327@compuserve. Pager #: 817-432-3753

Teresa Ellis, ISA
Mistletoe Quilts & Estate Sales
1205 Mistletoe Dr
Fort Worth, TX 76110-1018
ph: 817-926-9424
tquilts@cyberramp.net
Residential Contents, Quilts, Estate Liquidations

Nan B. Shelton, ISA CAPP
Assets Appraisal & Sales, Inc.
PO Box 121337
Fort Worth, TX 76121-1337
ph: 817-737-0680
fax: 817-737-8277
Residential Contents, Antiques, Silver, Furniture, Glass, Porcelain, Quilts, Collectibles, Victoriana, Decorative Arts, Estates, Insurance, Damage Claims, Liquidators

Gail Loveman Cohen, ISA, GG (GIA)
Charles Cohen Jewelers, Inc.
4747 S Hulen St, Ste 109
Fort Worth, TX 76132-1413
ph: 817-292-4367
fax: 817-370-8720
Gemology/Gemstones, Colored Stones, Diamonds, Pearls, Jewelry (Contemporary, Antique, Art, Period, Art Deco, Art Nouveau, Arts & Crafts, Victorian, Georgian), Gold, Insurance, Estates, Liquidation

Stanley P. Cohen, ISA, GG (GIA)
Charles Cohen Jewelers, Inc.
4747 S Hulen St, Ste 109
Fort Worth, TX 76132-1413
ph: 817-292-4367
fax: 817-370-8720
Gemology/Gemstones, Colored Stones, Pearls, Diamonds, Jewelry (Contemporary, Antique Art, Period, Art Deco, Art Nouveau, Arts & Crafts, Victorian, Georgian) Insurance, Estates, Liquidation

David T. Greener, ISA
Crown Estate Services
7313 Wind Chime Dr
Fort Worth, TX 76133-7039
ph: 817-292-0909
DGREENER@mindspring.com
Antiques, Decorative Arts & Accessories, Residential Contents, Glass, Porcelain, Silver, Estate Sales, Damage Claims, and Expert Witness.

Rick Russell, ISA
PREMIER International, Inc.
1309 Carrizo St
Bowie, TX 76230-3903
ph: 405-948-0777
fax: 405-948-1180
premier@theshop.net
Construction Equipment, Trucks, Trailers, Oil Field Equipment, Energy Related Equipment

Juliene T. Neese, ISA
Juliene Neese Antiques
1306 Kiowa Dr E
Lake Kiowa, TX 76240-9582
ph: 972-239-3451
fax: 972-934-8520
nescobrokerage@compuserve.com
Textiles, Needle Arts, Furniture (American), Residential Contents

Linda H. Richard, ISA
Cajun Collection
3308 White Oak Dr
Temple, TX 76502-3028
ph: 254-774-8608
cajun@vvm.com
Glass, Porcelain, Pottery, Ceramics, Collectibles, Antiques

Louis Edward Rork, ISA
Trappings
2503 W Ave K
San Angelo, TX 76901-3748
ph: 915-949-7078
Residential Contents

Dominique Kendall, ISA
4128 Albans Rd
Houston, TX 77005-1006
ph: 713-858-9716
Residential Contents, Estate Liquidation, Decorative Arts

Virginia L. McNeely, ISA
Estate Sale Management
2923 Wroxton Rd
Houston, TX 77005-4024
ph: 713-661-0449
fax: 409-234-5586
estate.sale@cwix.com
Professional Household Liquidation for those Moving, Retiring, or Settling an Estate. Appraisals, Probate Inventories, Attorney and Client References and Written Contracts Provided

Stephanie A. Reeves, ISA
Stephanie Reeves & Son Antiques
1436 W Gray, 605
Houston, TX 77019
ph: 713-526-7120
fax: 713-529-1310
steph97r@aol.com
Residential Contents, Personal Property

Marjorie M. Jennings, ISA
Appraisals & Estate Sales
2104 Brentwood Dr
Houston, TX 77019-3512
ph: 713-526-5829
Estate Sales & Appraisals, Residential Contents, Antiques, Silver, Insurance, Decorative Arts & Accessories

Sibley Kopmeier, ISA
Sibley Kopmeier Appraisal Assoc.
201 Vanderpool Ln, #99
Houston, TX 77024
ph: 713-465-2175
fax: 713-827-7424
Antiques, Decorative Arts & Accessories, Porcelain, 18th-20th C. Furniture, Collectibles

Sidney Taylor McKenzie, ISA CAPP
McKenzie Galleries & Commercial
7026 Old Katy Rd, Ste 161
Houston, TX 77024-2133
ph: 713-863-1213
fax: 713-863-1216
mcgaisidsr@aol.com
Residential Contents, Furniture, Commercial Equipment, Estates, Decorative Arts & Accessories

Winston A. McKenzie, ISA
McKenzie Galleries & Commercial
7026 Old Katy Rd, Ste 161
Houston, TX 77024-2133
ph: 713-863-1213
fax: 713-863-1216
mcgaisidsr@aol.com
Furniture, Decorative Arts & Accessories, Residential Contents, Furniture Repair, Restoration & Preservation, Damage Claims, Costumes & Textiles, Cars (Antique), Charitable Contributions, Office Furniture & Equipment

Lorian Welsh, ISA
Shamrock Estate Sales
3827 Linkwood Dr
Houston, TX 77025
ph: 713-661-4640
Estate Sales, Residential Contents, Antiques, Collectibles, Vintage Clothing, Real Estate

Shelley Sandler, ISA, GG (GIA)
Gemological Appraisers
21 Briar Hollow Ln, # 306
Houston, TX 77027
ph: 713-355-3552
fax: 713-355-8972
shelley@wt.net
Jewelry (Estate), Diamonds, Gemology/Gemstones

Rachel Pabst, ISA CAPP
Rachel Pabst Appraisal Associates
4032 Sul Ross St
Houston, TX 77027-5720
ph: 713-626-0179
fax: 713-877-1405
Antiques, Residential Contents, Americana, Estate, Furniture, Ceramics, Silver, Glass, Victoriana, Estate Sales

Jane C. Brennom, ISA
Zaisan Enterprises, Inc.
3240 Las Palmas St
Houston, TX 77027-5725
ph: 713-527-0124
fax: 713-527-0184
Antiques, Residential Contents, Furniture, Accessories, Collectibles, Porcelain, Pottery, Silver, Glass, Damage Claims, Estates

Beth Brownlee, ISA
2348 Southgate
Houston, TX 77030
ph: 713-667-8470
fax: 713-667-7919
bbrownlee@compuserve.com
Fine Art, Decorative Arts, Antiques, Residential Contents, and Estate Sales

Samuel Abraham, ISA
Abrahams Oriental Rugs
5120 Woodway Dr, Ste 6010
Houston, TX 77056-1791
ph: 713-622-4444
fax: 713-622-8928
abrahams.rugs@worldnet.att.net
Antiques, Carpets & Rugs (including Oriental), Needlework, Tapestries, Textiles, Silks, Porcelain, Pottery, Ceramics, China, Decorative Art, Accessories, Insurance, Investment Counselling, Auctioneer, Auction Co.

Rose Laurette Proler, ISA, GG (GIA)
Rose Proler, Inc.
5433 Westheimer, # 1105
Houston, TX 77056-5305
ph: 713-627-3098
fax: 713-627-0504
Diamonds, Pearls, Gemstones, Jewelry, Gemology

Diana P. Livingston, ISA
Diana P. Livingston Antiques
6255 San Felipe St
Houston, TX 77057-2809
ph: 713-974-2947
Antiques, Residential Contents, Liquidations, Estate Sales, Jewelry, and Fine Art.

R. Rebecca Moncrief, ISA
Becky Moncrief
2007 Sea Cove Ct
Houston, TX 77058-4228
ph: 281-333-3672
fax: 281-333-0201
becky@ufdc.org
Dolls, Doll Houses & Accessories (Antique & Modern), Toys, Miniatures, Antiques, Collectibles

Jane Cowan, ISA
Cowan & Company
2100 Tanglewilde, # 735
Houston, TX 77063
ph: 713-532-7203
fax: 713-532-7203
janecowan@cowanco.com
http://www.cowanco.com
Wildlife and sporting art, Gulf Coast wildlife artists, Cowan prints

Betty W. Boyd, ISA
Boyd Appraisal Service
2513 Gessner, #340
Houston, TX 77063-3206
ph: 713-827-0446
fax: 713-827-0446
Antiques, Furniture, Silver, Glass (Art), Household Goods, Residential Contents, Divorce Cases, Furniture, Oriental Rugs, Estates

O. Craig Fashoro, ISA
African Quintessence
6134 Havendale Dr
Houston, TX 77072-1524
ph: 281-495-9946
fax: 281-495-9946
104036.2665@compuserve.com
African Antiques and Artifacts, Contemporary African Art, African Fabric and Handmade Textiles

O. Craig Fashoro, ISA
African Quintessence
6134 Havendale Dr
Houston, TX 77072-1524
ph: 281-495-9946
fax: 281-495-9946
104036.2665@compuserve.com
African Antiques and Artifacts, Contemporary African Art, African Fabric and Handmade Textiles

June Adair, ISA
Adair Appraisals & Estate Sales
1311 Devon Glen Dr
Houston, TX 77077-3211
ph: 713-861-7711
fax: 281-496-6234
Americana, Antiques, Art Deco, Art Nouveau, Arts & Crafts, Bronzes, Carpets/Rugs, Ceramics, China, Clocks, Clothing, Collectibles, Consultant, Crystal, Damage Claims, Decorative Art, Dinnerware, Estates, Figurines, Lamps

Patricia Stone, ISA
Personal Property Appraisals
7622 Las Flores Dr
Houston, TX 77083-4462
ph: 281-561-8581
fax: 281-561-9794
stone@mayberryusa.net
http://www.mayberryusa.net/stoneappraiser
Residential Contents, Household Furniture, Antiques, Fine Art, Decorative Arts & Accessories, China, Crystal, Silver, Collectibles, Dolls, Corporate Contents, Office Furniture & Equipment, Divorce, Estate, Insurance

Roger Lewis Howard, ISA
River Oaks Antique Center
2030 Westheimer
Houston, TX 77098
ph: 713-520-8238
fax: 713-520-8247
Antique Furniture, Glass, China, Household Goods

Judy L. Robinson, ISA
Judy Robinson Gallery, Inc.
2828 Bammel Ln, Apt 208
Houston, TX 77098-1129
ph: 713-522-7509
fax: 713-522-7498
Estates, Family Distrubition, Residential Contents, Fine Art, Decorative Arts, Antiques, Collectibles, Coins, Textiles, Clothing, Modern Art, Jewelry, Antique Furniture, Complete Appraisal Service and Estate Sales.

Fred M. Nevill, ISA
Nevill Antiques
2828 Bammel LN, Apt 711
Houston, TX 77098-1131
ph: 713-529-8473
English & Continental Furniture, Glass, Porcelain), and Accessories, General Household Contents, Antiques, Probate, Divorce, Bankruptcy, Insurance, Estate Sales

Shirley Engelhardt, ISA
Shirley Englehardt, ASA, ISA
4132 N Boulevard Park
Houston, TX 77098-5002
ph: 713-522-8139
fax: 713-522-8139
Fine Art, Antiques, Collectibles

David E. Newman, ISA
Newman & Associates: Appraisers & Auctioneers
PO Box 42809
Houston, TX 77242-2805
ph: 713-521-7044
NEWMANASOC@AOL.COM
Antiques, 19th & 20th C. Furniture, Lamps, Lighting Fixtures, Object d'Art & de Vertu, Bronzes, Residential Contents, Damage Claims, Auctioneer.

Suzanne Staley, ISA
Fine Art & Antiques Appraiser & Broker
PO Box 1288
Houston, TX 77251-1288
ph: 713-222-6309
fax: 713-223-3116
104512.1256@compuserve.com
Fine Art, General Residential Contents, Silver, Folk Art

Beth Szescila, ISA CAPP
Szescila Appraisal Services
PO Box 692242
Houston, TX 77269
ph: 281-376-4338
fax: 281-251-0608
bethszescila@compuserve.com
Antiques, Residential Contents, Fine Art, Sewing Collectibles, Textiles, Quilts, Needlework, Furniture, Ceramics, Silver, Glass, Boxes, Victoriana

Kelly D. Toney, ISA
Vantage Business, Inc.
PO Box 79582
Houston, TX 77279-7279
ph: 713-984-7670
fax: 713-984-7671
Oil Field Equipment (Drilling & Production), Machinery & Equipment

Penny Millican, ISA
Town & Country Estates
5319 Holly St
Bellaire, TX 77401-4805
ph: 713-666-0970
fax: 713-666-2715
American Indian (Art, Artifacts, & Textiles), Western Art & Bronzes, Quilts, Toys, Costume & Estate Jewelry, Residential Contents, Estate Sales

J.R. Adair, III, ISA
Adair & Associates, Inc.
2330 Country Mile Ln
Richmond, TX 77469-1295
ph: 281-341-1780
fax: 281-341-5918
Antiques, Residential Contents, Estate (Liquidation)

Ferol L. Rogers, ISA
Ferol L. Rogers & Co.
PO Box 33279
Kerrville, TX 78029-3279
ph: 830-896-5959
fax: 830-896-2879
Residential Contents, Antiques, Furniture, Ceramics, Victoriana, Primitives

Linda Thompson, ISA
Lambert - Thompson Estate Sales
110 Rock Rose
New Braunfels, TX 78132
ph: 830-625-4997
fax: 830-625-4997
Gecko1@sat.net
Residential Contents, Antiques, Furniture, Jewelry, Auctioneer, and Estate Sales.

T. Kay Lambert, ISA
Lambert - Thompson Estate Sales
PO Box 312460
New Braunfels, TX 78137-2460
ph: 830-629-5655
Estate Sales, Antiques, Retail, Residential Contents, Furniture

Michael J. Stoffel, ISA
Hallmark Sales
520 N River
Sequin, TX 78155
ph: 830-303-5177
mstoffel@worldnet.att.net
Antiques, Residential Contents, Fine Art, Silver, Porcelains, Estates, Auctioneer

Anne C. Alexander, ISA
206 EMPORIA BLVD
San Antonio, TX 78209-4004
ph: 210-822-3463
fax: 210-822-3463
aalex@sbell.net
Residential Contents, Antiques, Estate Sales, Fine Art (19th - 20th C.), Furniture, Decorative Arts

Francois Duhau de Berenx, ISA
Francois de Berenx Art Advisor
115 E Wildwood Dr
San Antonio, TX 78212-1776
ph: 210-829-4567
fax: 210-829-4567
Antiques (French), Art (Oriental), Heraldic Works, Antique Books, Misc. Paper Items

Tara D. Kruse, ISA
Superior Auctioneers & Marketing, Inc.
11202 Disco
San Antonio, TX 78216-2860
ph: 210-499-0777
fax: 210-499-4217
Auctioneer, Cars (Antique & Vintage), Machinery & Equipment, Oil Field, Art & Collectibles

Tiffany Ann Kruse, ISA
Superior Auctioneers & Marketing, Inc.
11202 Disco
San Antonio, TX 78216-2860
ph: 210-697-0700
fax: 210-697-9744
tpierce@saami.com
http://www.saami.com
Cars (Antique & Vintage), Oil Field

James Puckett, ISA
Superior Auctioneers & Marketing, Inc.
11202 Disco
San Antonio, TX 78216-2860
ph: 210-499-0777
fax: 210-499-4217
http://www.saami.com
Machinery & Equipment (Oil Field & Related Equipment), Cars (Antique), Real Estate

Rudy M. Pena, ISA, GG (GIA)
Pena & Associates
7330 San Pedro Ave, Ste 544
San Antonio, TX 78216-6257
ph: 210-349-4367
fax: 210-366-1802
pena544@world-net.net
Gemology/Gemstones, Diamonds, Jewelry, Pearls, Estate Jewelry

Richard Casagrande, ISA CAPP
Casagrande Appraisals
8546 Broadway St, Ste 270b
San Antonio, TX 78217-6340
ph: 210-820-3535
fax: 210-820-3097
104411.545@compuserve.com
Residential Contents, Fine Art, Decorative Arts & Accessories, Antiques, Collectibles, Furniture, Consultant

Linda H. Roberts, ISA
Casagrande Appraisals
8546 Broadway St, Ste 270B
San Antonio, TX 78217-6340
ph: 210-820-3097
fax: 210-820-3535
104411.545@compuserve.com
Fine Art, Appreciable & Depreciable Residential Contents, Decorative Arts & Accessories, Antiques, Collectibles, Furniture, and Textiles.

Glen C. Skaggs, ISA CAPP
Classic Collections
74 Oakwell Farms Pkwy
San Antonio, TX 78218-1784
ph: 210-822-5305
Glass (American Cut), Porcelain, Pottery, Ceramics, Silver, Furniture

June W. Hayes, ISA
Heritage Estate Consultants
2703 Stone Edge St
San Antonio, TX 78232-4217
ph: 210-408-7068
fax: 210-496-8066
JuneHayes@aol.com
General Personal Property, Antiques, Antique Lace, Linens, Clothing, Dolls, Fans, Collectibles, Estate Liquidation, Speaker, Consultant

Larry Gumber, ISA
929 Misty Water Ln
San Antonio, TX 78258-6014
ph: 210-438-3597
Machinery & Equipment, Oil Field Equipment, Construction Equipment, Trucks & Trailers

Christopher B. Pierce, ISA
Superior Auctioneers & Marketing, Inc.
PO Box 792427
San Antonio, TX 78279-2427
ph: 210-499-0777
fax: 210-495-1319
cpierce@saami.com
http://www.saami.com
Oil Field Equipment (Drilling & Production), Machinery & Equipment, Classic & Antique Cars

Betty Gresham, ISA
Betty Gresham Antiques & Appraisals
10901 Leopard St
Crp Christi, TX 78410-2609
ph: 512-241-7062
Antiques, Porcelain, Pottery, Glass, Residential Contents, Estate (Liquidations)

Anita Eisenhauer, ISA
Anita's Antiques
11753 Up River Rd
Crp Christi, TX 78410-3320
ph: 512-241-7097
fax: 512-241-7098
105074.112@compuserve.com
Antiques, Residential Contents, Decorative Arts & Accessories, Estate Liquidations, Damage Claims

Joan D. Jones, ISA
Joan Jones Apprasials
PO Box 545
(Harlingen Area)
La Feria, TX 78559-0545
ph: 956-412-1336
Antiques, Mexican Colonial Art: Retablos & Santos, Oriental Rugs, Antique Furniture, Paperweights, Insurance, Estates, and Residential Contents.

Tom W. Carpenter, Jr., ISA
Lone Star Investments Corp.
PO Box 275
Marble Falls, TX 78654-0275
ph: 830-693-1618
fax: 830-693-1495
lonestar@tstar.net
Machinery & Equipment (Construction), Cars & Trucks, Airplanes

Haydee Allred, ISA
Austin Galleries
802 Pressler St
Austin, TX 78703-5130
ph: 512-495-9363
fax: 512-495-9119
ausgalleries@earthlink.net
Fine Art with Special Interest in - Regional Texas Artists - Escuela Libre del Mediterraneo, J. Torrents Llado (Spain)

Patricia Minter, ISA, GG (GIA)
Engaging Ideas L.L.C
811 Barton Springs Rd, # 220
Austin, TX 78704
ph: 512-469-9110
fax: 512-469-9120
Gemstones & Jewlery,

Corey L. Shaughnessy, ISA, GG (GIA)
Independent Jewelry Appraisers
5205 Wheeler Branch Cir
Austin, TX 78749-2265
ph: 512-451-3889
fax: 512-451-3850
Diamonds, Colored Stones, Contemporary Jewelry

Elisabeth W. Douglas, JD, ISA
China Coast, The
11266 Taylor Draper Ln, # 2024
Austin, TX 78759-3972
ph: 512-288-3043
fax: 512-345-8420
wien@texas.net
Oriental Fine & Decorative Art, South & Southeast Asian Art, Chinese & Japanese Furniture & Ceramics, Oriental Ivory & Jade, Asian Art, Chinese Export Art

Carol D. Littlefield, ISA
Remember When
PO Box 126
Flatonia, TX 78941
ph: 512-865-2563
carolitp@fais.net
19th C. Antiques, Estate Sales, Auction, Probate Court, Real Estate

Susan B. Eisen, ISA, GG (GIA)
Susan Eisen Fine Jewelry
7500 N Mesa St, Ste 208
El Paso, TX 79912-3515
ph: 915-584-0022
Antique & Contemporary Jewelry, American Craft Jewelry, Gemstones

Charles R. Rosvall, ISA
C.W. Rosvall Auction
1238 S Broadway
Denver, CO 80210-1504
ph: 303-722-4028
fax: 303-777-2032
rick80210@aol.com
Residential Contents, Cars, Trucks, Coins, Currency, Auctioneer

Mary Samora, ISA
Appriasals By Mary Samora & Associates
541 Williams St
Denver, CO 80218-3639
ph: 303-320-1019
Residential Contents, Antiques, Furniture, Estates, Collectibles, Memorabilia, Victoriana, Decorative Arts & Accessories

Nikki C. Jersin, ISA
Nikki Jersin & Associates
3265 S Pontiac St
Denver, CO 80224-2765
ph: 303-758-2121
fax: 303-758-4220
JollyJill@aol.com
Antiques, Silver, Furniture, Orientalia, Residential Contents

Deborah E. Arden, ISA CAPP
Arden Van Wijk Associates, Inc.
PO Box 2515
Evergreen, CO 80437-2515
ph: 800-554-6949
fax: 303-567-0698
debarden@ecentral.com
Prints & Paintings (Modern, Contemporary, Old Masters, 19th-20th C. American, European), Sculpture (American, Impressionist, Modern, 19th & 20th C.), Bronzes (19th-20th C.), Furniture (19th-20th C.) Residential Contents, Expert Witness

Harold G. Camp, ISA
Appraisal Specialties Of Colorado
PO Box 273062
Fort Collins, CO 80527-3062
ph: 970-282-9054
fax: 970-282-8969
70512.217@compuserve.com
Motor Vehicles: All Foreign & Domestic - Antique to Late Model - Cars & Light Duty Trucks, Motorcycles, Boats, Bus Conversions, Etc. Art: 19th-20th C. Paintings, Prints & Bronze Sculpture.

Elise C. Hersey, ISA, GG (GIA)
Elise C. Hersey, GG (GIA), Appraiser
PO Box 206
Niwot, CO 80544-0206
ph: 303-581-9988
fax: 303-444-5050
Diamonds, Gemology/Gemstones, Jewelry

Debra M. Jensen, ISA
Rominger Jewelry, Inc.
PO Box 231
208 Main
Sterling, CO 80751-0231
ph: 970-522-2587
rominger@sosinc.net
Gemology, Gemstones, Diamonds, Jewelry, Gold, Silver (Holloware & Flatware)

Christopher Jones, ISA
PO Box 50864
Colorado Spgs, CO 80949-0864
ph: 719-548-1876
Specialist in Southwestern Items Including: Jewelry, Pottery, Weavings, Carvings, and Fine Arts.

Tony F. Laughter, ISA, GG (GIA)
PO Box 6658
Viel, CO 81658
ph: 970-845-9198
fax: 704-364-8808
Gemology/Gemstones, Jewelry

Barbara E. Smith, ISA
Spring Creek Appraisals
1402 25th St
PO Box 1723
Cody, WY 82414-4010
ph: 307-587-2483
Antiques (Glass, Porcelain), Furniture, Residential Contents, Dinnerware, Glass, Silver (Flatware & Holloware)

Jay Proost, ISA
ASAA
PO Box 186
Twin Falls, ID 83303-0186
ph: 208-733-2323
fax: 208-733-2326
JPROOST@MICRON.NET
Farm Equipment, Livestock, Horses

Jan Wilson, ISA
Jan Wilson Gallery
PO Box 6649
Ketchum, ID 83340
ph: 208-622-7799
fax: 208-726-5975
jan@janwilsongallery.com
http://www.janwilsongallery.com
Fine Art

Anne L. Shneider, ISA
922 E Curling Ln
Boise, ID 83702
ph: 208-344-2618
Antiques, Collectibles, Appreciable & Depreciable Residential Contents, Appraisal & Estate Services

Jeanmarie Gorham, ISA
J.S. Gorham & Associates
5318 Redbridge Dr
Boise, ID 83703-3434
ph: 208-345-5114
jeangassoc@aol.com
Residential Contents, Antiques, Collectibles, Sterling Silver & Mexican Jewelry, American Art Pottery and Dinnerware (Wedgewood).

Sharon Wakefield, ISA CAPP, GG (GIA)
Northwest Gemological Lab
PO Box 8243
Boise, ID 83707-2243
ph: 208-362-3938
fax: 208-362-2889
sharon@gem-science.com
Jewelry, Gemology/Gemstones, Diamonds

Karolyn L. Weber, ISA
Appraisal Service, Inc.
2200 N Alvarado Rd
Phoenix, AZ 85004-1414
ph: 602-949-7798
Art, Fine Art, Etchings, Engravings, Prints, Residential & Office Contents, Insurance, Damage Claims, Estates, Testimony In Court (Expert Witness)

Gail Guidry, ISA
2216 E Cortez St
Phoenix, AZ 85028-1711
ph: 602-485-5028
perps@primenet.com
Photographs, Buttons, Czechoslovakian Pottery, Stamps/Postal History, Prints

Craig H. Jackson, ISA
Barrett-Jackson Auction Co, LLC
5530 E Washington St
Phoenix, AZ 85034-2105
ph: 602-273-0791
Residential Contents, Antiques, Ceramics, Dinnerware, Silver.

Wendy Rood, ISA
Wendy's Antiques
1724 N Spencer
Mesa, AZ 85203
ph: 602-464-8730
fax: 602-464-8730
jonwendy@aol.com
Antiques, Antique Dolls

Paul R. Barnes, ISA CAPP, GG, CG
Anderson Barnes Fine Jewelers
891 N Val Vista Dr, # 102
Gilbert, AZ 85234-3602
ph: 602-545-8585
fax: 602-545-8585
Gemology/Gemstones, Diamonds, Fine Jewelry, Expert Witness, Gold, Platinum, Colored Stones

Lorene A. Wilson, ISA
Appraisal Service, Inc.
6430 E Calle Redondo
Scottsdale, AZ 85251-4243
ph: 602-970-8765
fax: 602-949-0231
American Indian Artifacts, Collectibles, Residential Contents, Expert Witness, and Estate Sales.

Sindi J. Schloss, ISA, GG (GIA)
Int'l Gemological Appraisal Service
2933 N Hayden Rd
Scottsdale, AZ 85251-6614
ph: 602-947-5866
fax: 602-949-1676
Gems & Jewelry

Pat Sharpe, ISA
Pat Sharpe Enterprises, Inc.
5834 E Friess Dr
Scottsdale, AZ 85254-3116
ph: 602-953-3373
Antiques, Fine Art, Residential Contents, Estates, and Silver.

Randy Anderson, ISA
Anderson Fine Jewelers
13545 W Camino Del Sol
Sun City West, AZ 85375-4416
ph: 602-584-1546
fax: 602-584-8896
randersn@doitnow.com
Jewelry, Gemology/Gemstones, Gold, Watches, Diamonds

Diana M. Warren, ISA
5555 N Via Alcalde
Tucson, AZ 85718-5107
ph: 520-299-6645
dianawarren@msn.com
Residential Contents, Silver, Decorative Arts, Antiques.

Beatriz Bernal Castillo, ISA
Personal Property Appraisals
11765 N Cassiopeia Dr
Tucson, AZ 85737-3410
ph: 520-577-9779
Antiques, Fine Art, American Furniture, Estate Sales, Consultations

James L. Lamerson, ISA, GG, CGA
Lamerson's Jewelry & Lapidary Arts
105 N Cortez St
Prescott, AZ 86301-3015
ph: 520-771-0921
Gemology/Gemstones, Diamonds, Jewelry, Repairs & Restoration

Peter Eller, Ph.D., ISA
Peter Eller Gallery & Appraiser
206 Dartmouth Dr NE
Albuquerque, NM 87106-2114
ph: 505-268-7437
Pelgal@aol.com
Fine Art, Antiques, Fine Furniture, Silver, Fine China, Native American Rugs & Pottery, Spanish Colonial Artifacts, Pre-Columbian Southwest Pottery, Residential Contents

Kent W. McDonald, ISA
Appraisal & Connoisseur Assoc.
620 Sierra Dr SE
Albuquerque, NM 87108-3377
ph: 505-265-2842
fax: 505-266-0657
jshan@highfiber.com
Paintings (Southwestern & Contemporary), Fine Art, Sculpture (Southwestern & Contemporary), Drawings, Oil & Acrylic Paintings, Residential Contents, Furniture, Silver, Porcelain, Rugs, Office Furniture & Equipment, N M Estate Sale

Mary E. McDonald, ISA CAPP
Appraisal & Connoisseur Assoc. (ACA)
620 Sierra Dr SE
Albuquerque, NM 87108-3377
ph: 505-265-2842
fax: 505-265-2842
American Indian (Rugs, Jewelry, & Pottery), Residential Contents, Arts & Crafts, Antiques, Fine Art, Textiles

Claire N. Shuford, ISA CAPP, GG (GIA)
7400 Montgomery Blvd NE, Ste 36
Albuquerque, NM 87109-1519
ph: 505-884-3101
fax: 505-883-4889
jeweler@iex.net
http://www.estatejeweler.com
Gemology/Gemstones, Jewelry (Diamonds, Pearls, Antique & Period)

Larry Phillips, ISA, GG (GIA)
Phillips & Associates
2430 Juan Tabo Blvd NE
Albuquerque, NM 87112-1818
ph: 505-299-7999
fax: 505-299-7999
gemologist-appraiser.com/phillips/
American Indian Jewelry, Contemporary & Period Jewelry, Gemstones & Minerals, Diamonds, Watches,

Susan Tarman, ISA
Susan Tarman Antiques & Fine Art
923 Paseo de Peralta
Santa Fe, NM 87501
ph: 505-983-2336
fax: 505-983-2399
TARMANOKEEFE@NETS.COM
Furniture, Silver, Decorative Arts, Fine Art, Orientalia

Joan Caballero, ISA
Joan Caballero, Appraisals
PO Box 822
Santa Fe, NM 87504-0822
ph: 505-982-8148
fax: 505-982-7048
joan.caballero@gte.net
http://www.collectorsguide.com/jcaballero
Art (Antique & Contemporary Southwest American Indian: Jewelry, Pottery, Textiles, Paintings; Southwest Hispanic Furniture & Religious), Fine Art (Southwest Regional Paintings & Sculpture - Living & Deceased.)

Suzanne R. Clark, ISA
Rochelle Ltd.
PO Box 9107
Santa Fe, NM 87504-9107
ph: 313-737-0122
Native American Art, Oriental Art

Mike J. Grippo, ISA
M & M Automobile Appraisers
584 Groomspun St
Henderson, NV 89015
ph: 702-568-5120
fax: 702-568-5158
Cars (Collectible, Antique, & Custom), Machinery & Equipment, Trucks, Automotive Literature, Automotive Related Collectibles, Trains, Investment Counseling

Jeane Parris, ISA
Sugarplums, Etc.
2022 E Charleston Blvd
Las Vegas, NV 89104-2018
ph: 702-385-6059
fax: 702-388-1202
Antiques, Silver, Porcelain, Pottery, Ceramics, China, Collectibles, Decorative Arts & Accessories, Perfume Bottles, Residential Contents

Joanna S. Stearns, ISA CAPP, GG (GIA)
J. Stearns & Associates
7412 Silver Palm Ave
Las Vegas, NV 89117-1442
ph: 702-360-8991
fax: 702-360-8938
76333.2316@compuserve.com
Fine Art, Paintings, Drawings, Prints, Sculpture, Bronzes (Specializing In Western & Contemporary Southwestern), Fine Jewelry, Residential Contents

Ronald A. Urcioli, ISA CAPP, GG (GIA)
1541 Beech Grove Dr
Las Vegas, NV 89119-0368
ph: 702-260-0835
fax: 702-260-0835
rurci61386@aol.com
Diamonds, Gemstones, Gold and Silver Jewelry

Grace P. Lee, ISA, GG (GIA)
CG Prestige, Inc.
550 S Hill St, Ste 1302
Los Angeles, CA 90013-2414
ph: 213-629-4346
fax: 213-629-3199
Loose Colored Stones (Especially Ruby & Sapphire).

Homayoun Tony Molayem, ISA, GG (GIA)
Molayem & Associates, Inc.
10750 Wilshire Blvd, Apt 201
Los Angeles, CA 90024-4469
ph: 310-603-2600
fax: 310-603-9200
tonymolayem@msn.com
Antiques, Jewelry, 19th C. Porcelain, 19th C. Furniture

Michael L. Wertz, Jr., ISA
Wertz Bros., Inc.
11879 Santa Monica Blvd
Los Angeles, CA 90025-2211
ph: 310-477-4251
Estate Liquidator

Richard R. Silverman, ISA CAPP
838 N Doheny Dr, Apt 1102
Los Angeles, CA 90069-4851
ph: 310-273-3838
fax: 310-273-3843
Netsuke, Inro, Ojime. CAPP in Netsuke.

Benyamin Sassoon, ISA
Arte Galleries
9000 Wilshire Blvd
Beverly Hills, CA 90211-1809
ph: 310-858-7666
fax: 310-858-0525
Antiques, Paintings, Porcelain, Bronze, Marble, Furniture, Objet d'Art

Oscar Golbert, ISA, GG, AA
18 Karat Appraisers
139 S Beverly Dr, Ste 236
Beverly Hills, CA 90212-3028
ph: 310-278-1022
fax: 310-278-0803
Gemology/Gemstones, Diamonds, Pearls, Colored Stones, Fine Jewelry, Antique & Period Jewelry, Watches, Insurance and Estate Appraisals

Janet F. Cobert, ISA CAPP
Janet F. Cobert Appraisal Services
PO Box 2976
Beverly Hills, CA 90213-2976
ph: 310-470-2176
fax: 310-441-5939
asianart1@earthlink.net
Fine Art, Decorative Art & Accessories, Asian Fine & Decorative Art, Oriental Art, Orientalia, Japanese Prints, Oriental Lacquer, Ivory, Textiles, Procelain, Ceramics, Antiques & Residential Contetns, Damage Claims, Insurance, Exp. Witnes

Danusia Niklewicz, ISA CAPP, GG, FGA
Paradise & Associates
23852 Pacific Coast Hwy, Ste 549
Malibu, CA 90265-4879
ph: 310-829-5286
fax: 310-829-5286
danusia@pacificnet.net
Forensic Evaluation of Gems & Jewelry (Contemporary & Antique), Assignments - Basic to Complex. Consultant, Educator and Appraiser to the Public, Trade, IRS, Legal and Insurance, Expert Wit in Fed and Supr Courts, USPAP, 20 Years Experien

Elena Alcalay, ISA, GG (GIA)
Azel Gallery
916 Chautauqua Blvd
Pacific Palisades, CA 90272-3804
ph: 310-459-6022
fax: 310-459-0017
elenapac@aol.com
Jewelry, Silver, Insurance, Estates

Alexander Rose, ISA
Alexander Rose Appraiser And Consultant
PO Box 10536
Marina Del Rey, CA 90295
ph: 310-216-5735
fax: 310-216-0435
aruzicka@earthlink.net
European & American Fine Art & Antiques, including furniture, rugs, tapestries, ceramics, glass, silver, bronzes, sculpture, and paintings. Insurance and estate appraisals. Consultation services. Formerly with Sothbey's and Butterfield's

Linda Crum, ISA CAPP
Linda Crum Appraisal Service
4050 Katella Ave, Ste 111
Los Alamitos, CA 90720-3431
ph: 562-598-7688
fax: 562-594-9710
Estate Liquidations

Camille Mirielle Catalogne, ISA
1434 Brett Pl, Apt 67
San Pedro, CA 90732-5098
ph: 310-833-0183
fax: 310-541-8557
Antique & Vintage Jewelry

Barr L. Doty, ISA, GG (GIA)
1077 Pacific Coast Hwy
Seal Beach, CA 90740-6250
ph: 562-592-2007
fax: 562-592-2007
Gemstones, Jewelry

Robert G. Christie, ISA
Christie Antique Liquidators
1418 Baypoint Ave
Wilmington, CA 90744-1512
ph: 310-835-2290
fax: 562-439-5202
bookred@aol.com
Residential Contents, Antiques, Furniture, Jewelry (Costume), Collectibles

Warren Finley, ISA
Finley-Gracer Jewelers
5112 E 2nd St
Long Beach, CA 90803-5322
ph: 310-494-3949
fax: 310-434-5699
Diamonds, Colored Stones, Jewelry

Janet Lynn Greene, ISA
Estate Associates
545 Terraine Ave
Long Beach, CA 90814-1946
ph: 562-986-9692
fax: 562-490-3137
Estate Sales, Antiques, Residential Contents, Jewelry: Antique & Collectible.

William M. Novotny, ISA, CGA
Novoty's Antiques & Appraisals
2591 S 10th Ave
Arcadia, CA 91006-5063
ph: 818-446-9663
fax: 818-446-2503
Antiques, 19th-20th C. Furniture, Victoriana, Porcelain, Glass, General Residential Contents (appreciable & depreciable), General Art, Damage Claims

KerryAnn Plumer, ISA, GG (GIA)
Gem & Jewelry Appraiser
260 S Lake Ave, Ste 104
Pasadena, CA 91101-3002
ph: 626-796-7029
fax: 626-796-7029
kaplumer@earthlink.net
Graduate gemologist specializing in all types of jewelry. I have a portable labratory for on site examinations.

David B. Kushner, ISA
Tower Trading Company/Antiques on Holly
38 E Holly St
Pasadena, CA 91103-3905
ph: 626-449-1488
fax: 626-449-6955
76352.2075@compuserve.com
Clocks (19th-20th C.), Bronzes, Furniture (European & American), Silver, Porcelain, Residential Contents, Insurance Valuation & Loss Reconstruction, Estates, Insurance & Probate. Alt Email: ttchantiques@earthlink.net

Susan Burnett, ISA
411 Gordon Ter, Apt 3
Pasadena, CA 91105-1854
ph: 626-793-2023
fax: 626-793-2643
18th-19th C. Furniture (American, English, & French), Residential Contents

James Haddad, ISA
Poulsen Galleries, Inc.
910 San Pasqual St
Pasadena, CA 91106-3309
ph: 626-792-7410
fax: 626-792-7247
poulsengalleries@compuserve.com
Art (English, French & American), Paintings, California Plein Art Artists, Prints (All Periods & Rare), Graphics & Reproductions

Bonnie Dunlap, ISA
Estate Sales Unlimited
3400 Country Club Dr
Glendale, CA 91208-1154
ph: 818-957-1144
fax: 818-957-5202
Residential Contents, Antiques, Estates

Susan McCune, ISA, GG (GIA)
Gemfacets, Llc.
20649 Keswick St
Canoga Park, CA 91306-2028
ph: 818-348-6701
fax: 818-348-6701
Lapidary Art, Gemstones, Jewelry, Jewelry Design, Mineral Specimens, Leaded Glass Prisms, Glass & Acrylic Sculpture

Stuart Locascio, ISA, GG (GIA)
Appraisal Service, The
18345 Ventura Blvd, #206
Trazana, CA 91356-4241
ph: 818-343-9016
fax: 818-343-5320
essel@annex.com
http://www.polygon.net/~3537
Jewelry, Diamonds, Gemstones, Gold

Ron Stark, ISA
S/R Laboratories
31200 Via Colinas, Ste 210
Westlake Village, CA 91362-3939
ph: 818-991-9955
fax: 818-991-5418
srlabs@earthlink.net
Animation Art, Works of Art on Paper, Disney & Animated Collectibles

George E. Waldman, ISA
Waldman Appraisal Co.
22311 Ventura Blvd, Ste 117
Woodland Hls, CA 91364-1522
ph: 818-884-8073
fax: 818-884-8088
Antiques (Porcelain & Silver), Residential Contents, Real Estate, Objet D'Art & De Vertu, Clothing, Carpets & Rugs, Cloisonne, Dinnerware, Estates, Fine Arts

Jennifer Thornton-Davis, ISA, GG (GIA)
In Depth Appraisals
PO Box 56591
Sherman Oaks, CA 91413-1591
ph: 818-988-5583
fax: 818-988-4341
indepth260@earthlink.net
Gemology/Gemstones, Jewelry, Watches, Insurance, Estate

Richard K. Houston, ISA, GG, CGA
Houston Jewelers
14019 Ventura Blvd
Sherman Oaks, CA 91423-3511
ph: 818-783-1122
fax: 818-783-8740
Gemology/Gemstones, Diamonds, Jewelry

Robert Shaw, ISA
Diamond Jewelry, Inc.
16830 Ventura Blvd, Ste 248
Encino, CA 91436-1715
ph: 818-905-5602
fax: 818-784-7308
robtshaw@aol.com
Gemology/Gemstones, Diamonds, Jewelry, Insurance Mediation

Jessica La Mar, ISA
Cranberry House, The
12318 Ventura Blvd
Studio City, CA 91604-2406
ph: 818-506-8945
fax: 818-506-0776
lamaraprs@aol.com
Antiques, Residential Contents, Furniture, Pottery, Textiles

Pamela D. Scott, ISA
Robert S. Scott Co. Appraisers
PO Box 8725
Universal City, CA 91618-8725
ph: 818-763-6273
fax: 818-761-1056
Residential Contents, Fine Arts, Antiques

Shira J. Brem, ISA
Brem's Antiques
1131 Village Dr
Chino Hills, CA 91709-2250
ph: 909-629-4411
Estate Sales, 19th-20th C. Furniture, Collectibles, and Residential Contents.

Polly Anne Johanson, ISA
All About Antiques
511 Elizabeth Ave
Monterey Park, CA 91755-1403
ph: 626-288-5060
fax: 626-288-5060
paj@allaboutantiques.com
http://www.allaboutantiques.com
Residential Contents, General Insurance Claims & Coverage, Estate Taxes & Probate, Americana (Pottery, Porcelain, Glass), Estate Sales

Monica Y. Yeung, ISA, GG (GIA)
2640 Del Mar Heights Rd, # 128
Del Mar, CA 92014
ph: 619-635-2868
myeung@san.rr.com
Fine Jewelry, Diamonds, Gemstones, Pearls, Jade, Custom Design

Roberta L. Ely, ISA
Roberta L. Ely Appraisal Service
175 Beechtree Dr
Encinitas, CA 92024-4031
ph: 760-942-3480
Antiques, Decorative Art & Accessories, Residential Contents, Insurance, Estates, Hypothetical Appraisals For Loss.

Paul Joseph McConnell, ISA
Paul McConnell Appraisals
1910 Springdale Ln
Encinitas, CA 92024-4244
ph: 619-316-3433
fax: 714-492-6691
paulmcconn@earthlink.net
Antiques, Collectibles, Residential Contents, Hypothetical/Forensic Appraisals, Furniture

Kathleen DeBolt, ISA
Debolt Fine Art
18353 Sycamore Creek Rd
Escondido, CA 92025-2302
ph: 619-676-5913
fineart@adnc.com
19th & 20th C. American Art, California Impressionism, American Scene, New Mexico Modernists, Western Art. Alt Email: fineart@gateway.net

Annette L. Jones, ISA
DM Jones & Associates
2710 Summit Dr
Escondido, CA 92025-7522
ph: 760-745-0949
fax: 760-745-0629
Fine Art, Drawings, Etchings, Paintings, Prints, Sculpture

Valentina Arbab, ISA CAPP
Oriental Rugs Appraiser/Broker
9705 Blackgold Rd
La Jolla, CA 92037-1114
ph: 619-453-4686
fax: 619-457-3647
Carpets & Rugs; Oriental Rugs & Textiles (Old & New); Machine Loomed Rugs & Textiles (Old & New); European & American Tapestries (Old & New)

LaVerne M. Larson, ISA, GG(GIA), NJA
Gemological & Appraisal Services
4796 Marblehead Bay Dr
Oceanside, CA 92057-3409
ph: 760-967-8497
fax: 760-967-8497
M-L-Larson@worldnet.att.net
Gems & Jewelry, Antique & Period Jewelry, Gemology, Gemstones, Speaker, and Consultant

Taryn Wayne, ISA, GG (GIA)
Taryn's Treasures
PO Box 675453
Rancho Santa Fe, CA 92067-5453
ph: 619-481-1257
fax: 619-481-1257
Jewelry, Gemology/Gemstones

Paula J. Straub, ISA CAPP, GG (GIA)
GIA
1623 La Bonita Way, Apt F
San Marcos, CA 92069-4603
ph: 760-603-4000
pstraub@aol.com
<<<Non Appraising Member >>> Jewelry (Antique & Period, Estate, & Contemporary), Gemstones (Diamonds & Colored Stones), Pearls, Watches, Precious Metals, Estates (Wholesale & Retail), Consulting, Brokering, Expert Testimony

Carol Ursula McAndrew, ISA
Carol McAndrew
14415 Woods Valley Rd
Valley Center, CA 92082-7346
ph: 760-749-5406
fax: 760-749-7336
Antiques, Collectibles, Residential Contents, Forensic Appraisals (Wildfires)

Thom Underwood, ISA, GG (GIA)
San Diego Gemological Labs
3309 Juanita St
San Diego, CA 92105-3809
ph: 619-286-6614
fax: 619-286-7541
Jewelry (Contemporary & Estate), Gemstones, Diamonds, and Pearls.

Maureen E. Bush, ISA
12255 Caminito Mira Del Mar
San Diego, CA 92130
ph: 619-350-8157
mebush@san.rr.com
Glass, Porcelain, Pottery, Residential Contents

Diane G. Page, ISA, GCA
Page Appraisals, Antiques & Collectibles
PO Box 19789-285
San Diego, CA 92159
ph: 619-448-5696
fax: 619-448-6737
DianePage@compuserve.com
Antiques, Ceramics, Collectibles, Furniture, Porcelain, Residential Contents

Otto A. Mower, Ph.D., ISA
PO Box 22421
San Diego, CA 92192-2421
ph: 619-459-4021
fax: 619-452-2175
drmower@juno.com
Painting (Old Masters to 19th C.), Sculpture (Early Renaissance to 19th C.), Prints (Old Masters to 19th C.)

Marcia Osterkamp, ISA
Poulsen Galleries, Inc.
327 Terrace Dr
Brawley, CA 92227-3040
ph: 760-344-4810
fax: 760-344-4778
poulsengalleries@compuserve.com
19th & 20th C. Paintings, and California Plein Air Artists

Carl G. Nielsen, ISA, CGA
Nielsen's
PO Box 1028
Barstow, CA 92312-1028
ph: 760-253-3574
Gemology/Gemstones, Colored Stones, Diamonds, Jewelry (Gold, Antique, & Platinum), Pearls

Diane L. Bendis, ISA
Bendis Company Auctioneers
3410 La Sierra Ave, F 123
Riverside, CA 92503-5205
ph: 909-780-3418
fax: 909-780-7384
infor@bendisauctions.com
http://www.bendisauctions.com
Machinery and Equipment, Vehicles, Resturant Equipment, Furniture, Auctioneer Services

Richard G. Guest, ISA
Guest Fine Art
27289 Capilano Dr
Sun City, CA 92586
ph: 909-672-2217
Fine Art, Paintings & Prints (19th-20th C.), Appraisal & Consultation (Paintings & Prints), also Painting Restoration. Who's Who In Art.

Mary E. Colby, ISA
Mary Colby Appraiser of Fine Antiques
1710 Calle De Los Alamos
San Clemente, CA 92672-4305
ph: 714-492-2620
fax: 714-492-6695
mcolby@worldnet.att.net
Specialist in All Types of Antique Furniture, Porcelain, Silver, Glass, Decorative Arts and Accessories.

J. Dennis Mitosinka, ISA
Dennis Mitosinka's Classic Cars
619 E 4th St
Santa Ana, CA 92701-4705
ph: 714-953-5303
fax: 714-953-1810
Cars (Antique, Classic, Special Interest, & Late Model Exotic Cars), Automotive Memorabilia, All types of Vehicles & Transportation Automobiles, and Diminutive Values of Vehicles After Repairs Completed.

Jeffrey A. Donahue, ISA
Donahue & Associates
17251 E 17th St, Ste D
Tustin, CA 92780-1951
ph: 714-508-7780
fax: 714-508-7789
DonaAssoc@aol.com
Specializing in FF&E, Machinery & Equipment, Construction Equipment, Commerical Inventories, and Computers. Expert Witness and Appraisal Review.

Pearl Shiffman, ISA CAPP
Chatham Appraisal Service
PO Box 962
Tustin, CA 92781-0962
ph: 714-832-5101
fax: 714-544-6955
pchatham@ix.netcom.com
Sterling & Silverplate (19th-20th C.), Furniture (19th-20th C.), Antiques, Decorative Arts, Residential Contents, Office Furniture & Equipment

Noel L. Novak-Pilch, ISA
Novak, Pilch & Associates
17251 E 17th St, Ste D
Tustin, CA 92781-1951
ph: 714-508-7780
fax: 714-508-7789
Decorative Arts & Accessories, Fine Art, Residential Contents, Office Furniture & Equipment; For Insurance, Estates, Probate

Nancy Lee Pretty, ISA
Nancy Pretty And Associates
2629 Trieste Way
Fullerton, CA 92833-2047
ph: 714-526-6057
fax: 714-526-6595
jpretty@deltanet.com
Estate Sales Residential Contents, Antiques, Collectibles, Furniture, Glass, Porcelain.

Chris Hurst, ISA
Hurst Associates
PO Box 2064
Yorba Linda, CA 92885-3706
ph: 714-996-9212
fax: 714-572-0260
churst7300@aol.com
Antiques, Residential Contents, Victorian Furniture

Mike Aversa, ISA
Aversa Appraisal & Estate Services
18301 Piper Pl
Yorba Linda, CA 92886-2432
ph: 714-777-3848
mikjr@aol.com
http://www.antiqnet.com/aversa
Furniture, Stereo Photographica, Vintage Musical Instruments, Antiques, Collectibles, Residential & Business Contents, Professional Auctioneer

Carol L. Sherwood, ISA
1217 Beachmont St
Ventura, CA 93001-4227
ph: 805-648-7475
fax: 805-648-7218
anneteak@compuserve.com
Antiques, Nautical Items, Ship Models, Navigational Instruments, Pottery, Residential Contents. Alt Fax: 805-658-7758

Lynn Harding, ISA
Lynn Harding Antique Instruments Of The Profess. & Sciences
103 W Aliso St
Ojai, CA 93023-2603
ph: 805-646-0204
fax: 805-646-0204
Antique Scientific Instruments ie:Telescopes, Microscopes, Medical, Nautical, Pharmacy, Globes, Orreries, Planetariums, Scales, Weights, Calculating, Surveying, Engineering, Steam, Telegraphy, Models, Drafting, Electrical, Dials, Tools

Leslie V. AnnRenee', ISA
Peregrine Galleries
508 Brinkerhoff Ave
Santa Barbara, CA 93101-3441
ph: 805-963-3134
fax: 805-963-3134
leslie313@aol.com
http://www.peregrinegalleries.com
Estates, Residential Contents, Fine Art, Antiques, Silver Jewelry (Mexican & Danish), Costume Jewelry, Vintage Clothing, Dolls, Furniture, Paintings, Oriental Rugs

Marlene R. Vitanza, ISA
Peregrine Galleries
1133 Coast Village Rd
Santa Barbara, CA 93108-2724
ph: 805-647-6017
fax: 805-565-1919
mperegrine@aol.com
http://www.peregrinegalleries.com
Household Goods, Oriental Rugs, Fine Art (Oil Paintings, Watercolors), Silver, Jewelry, Dolls, American Indian Artifacts, Probate, Estates

Dan Turrentine, ISA
La Porte's Appraisal Service
PO Box 20
Pacific Grove, CA 93950-0020
ph: 831-375-9565
fax: 831-655-8259
Furniture, Silver (English & American), Art (California)

Sara Conklin, ISA CAPP
Maritime Appraisals
239 Sierra Point Rd
Brisbane, CA 94005-1664
ph: 415-467-6249
fax: 415-467-6249
sconklin2@earthlink.net
Ivory (19th C. American Scrimshaw), Nautical Items (Ship Models, Figureheads, Navigational Instruments, Tools), Alaskan Indian/Eskimo, Scientific Instruments

Lucia Mathieux, ISA
20 Acorn Dr
Hillsborough, CA 94010-6103
ph: 415-348-7971
French Furniture and Decorative Arts, Fine Art, Impressionist and Modern Paintings, Continental Furniture, Estates

Patricia Darrell Knight, ISA
Patrician Antiques
197 1st St
Los Altos, CA 94022-2707
ph: 415-948-5218
info@patriciananantiques.com
http://www.patriciananantiques.com
18th & 19th C. Porcelain, Pottery, Ceramics, (English, Continental & American), Silver (English, Continental & American), Furniture (English & Continental), Decorative Objects, Miniature Protrait Paintings, Old Sheffield Plate, Art Nouvea

David Greenaway, ISA
DGW Auctioneers
2250 Charleston Rd
Mountain View, CA 94043-1618
ph: 650-940-1664
fax: 650-940-1094
dgwauctioneersusa@compuserve.com
Residential Contents, Antiques, Fine Art, Decorative Art, Office Furniture & Equipment, Auction Service

Kathleen Greenaway, ISA
DGW Appraisal Service
2250 Charleston Rd
Mountain View, CA 94043-1618
ph: 650-940-1542
fax: 650-940-1094
dgwauctioneersusa@compuserve.com
Residential Contents, Antiques, Fine Art, Auction Services, Decorative Arts, Office Furniture & Equipment

Julia K. Nelson-Gal, ISA
826 Alvarado St
San Francisco, CA 94114-3116
ph: 415-641-8004
fax: 415-641-8053
JKNG@sprynet.com
Fine Art Photography, Photography Books, Collectible Photography (Historical & Decorative)

Rann Shinar, ISA
Shinar Fine Art
2538 Balboa St
San Francisco, CA 94121-2909
ph: 415-668-2303
fax: 415-668-1949
aartish@aol.com
Fine Art

Jackie F. Corsun, ISA
Romanitques
632 First St
Benicia, CA 94510
ph: 707-745-6533
Corsun5@aol.com
Antiques

Susan Raymond, ISA
Susan Raymond
510 A East H St
Benicia, CA 94510
ph: 707-747-0694
fax: 707-747-0694
susanraymond@earthlink.net
Antiques, Collectibles, Memorabilia

Maurice E. Woulf, ISA CAPP, GG (GIA)
Woulf & Ury Jewelers
10572 San Pablo Ave
El Cerrito, CA 94530-2893
ph: 510-524-3600
watchman55@hotmail.com
Gemstones, Jewelry, Silver, Watches & Clocks, Repairs, Consignments, Liquidation, Appraisal Review, Consultation, Federal Estate, Charitable Donation, Insurance, Customs, Confirmation of Pur. Value, Identification, Expert Witness

Shirley J. Filgate, ISA
S & H Antiques
130 J St
Fremont, CA 94536-2913
ph: 510-797-9690
Household Contents' Generalist, Antiques, Collectibles, Furniture, China, Pottery, Porcelain, Glass

Pamela M. Rechter, ISA
Heart & Home
5323 Nash Way
Castro Valley, CA 94546-1641
ph: 510-886-1163
fax: 510-583-1722
Residential Contents, Insurance, Estates, Identification and Evaluation

Darla J. Crockett, ISA
Darron's
32521 Seaside Dr
Union City, CA 94587-5149
ph: 510-487-3987
fax: 510-487-1944
roncorso@pacbell.net
Residential Contents

Gayle M. Bennett, ISA
G.M. Bennett, Appraiser
460 El Camino Real
Vallejo, CA 94590-3420
ph: 707-642-8404
Antiques, Collectibles, Ceramics, Furniture, Residential Contents, Estate and Insurance.

Lilly I. Bennett, ISA
Lilly Bennett, Estate & Moving Sales
460 El Camino Real
Vallejo, CA 94590-3420
ph: 707-642-8404
lillibe@aol.com
http://www.homes.com/via/estatesales
Glass (Art & Cut), Porcelain, Pottery, Ceramics, Dinnerware, Residential Contents, Estates

Barbara W. Spitzack, ISA
Appraisal Firm Of Barbara Spitzack, The
47 Quail Ct, Ste 101
Walnut Creek, CA 94596-5573
ph: 510-935-5251
fax: 510-934-0414
bspitzack@compuserve.com
Residential Contents, Antiques, Jewelry, Coins, Stamps, Clocks, Estates, Real Estate

Nancy Stacy-Trahan, ISA CAPP, GG (GIA)
Jewels By Stacy Appraisals
712 Bancroft Rd
Walnut Creek, CA 94598-1531
ph: 925-939-4367
fax: 925-939-4567
nancy@appraiser.net
http://www.jewelry-appraisal.com
Jewelry: Gemstones, Diamonds, Estate, Contemporary

Deborah Sanborn, ISA
D.A. Sanborn Decorative Arts
2512 9th St, # 12
Berkeley, CA 94710
ph: 510-549-9405
fax: 510-644-9734
Antiques and Personal Property.

Hideko Kirichi, ISA
PO Box 12122
Berkeley, CA 94712
ph: 510-527-7002
fax: 510-527-7980
Fine Art, Contemporary Art Prints, Modern Art

Patricia Saultman, ISA CAPP
309 Willow Ave
Corte Madera, CA 94925-1534
ph: 415-788-3344
fax: 415-945-0471
102202.1075@compuserve.com
American & European Paintings & Prints; English, European, French, and American Furniture; Fine Art, Residential Contents

Susan Bickford, ISA, GG (GIA)
Pacific Gemological Services
38 Miller Ave
Mill Valley, CA 94941-1927
ph: 415-381-5642
Gemology/Gemstones, Jewelry, Diamonds, Gold, Jade, Pearls

James M. Stephenson, ISA
Patos Enterprises
26 Eucalyptus Knoll St
Mill Valley, CA 94941-2257
ph: 415-388-5650
Residenitial Contents, Antiques, Furniture, Silver, Porcelain

Linda Sugar, ISA
Linda Sugar Furniture Service
403 Fair St
Petaluma, CA 94952-2519
ph: 415-388-2579
fax: 415-388-5082
Linsug@pacbell.net
Furniture, Antiques, Restoration, Transit Damage Adjustment, Claims

Nancy Burke Bosch, ISA
Bosch Appraisal Service
1610 Northstar Dr
Petaluma, CA 94954-6607
ph: 707-773-3970
fax: 707-773-3974
boschappraisal@compuserve.com
European & American Antique Furniture, Decorative Arts & Accessories, Appreciable Residential Contents, China, Crystal, Silver,

Wicker, Quilts, Lines, Estate Liquidation Mangement and Consultation. Alt Phone: 415-897-7185

Anita Venezia, ISA
Venezia Antiques & Appraisal Services
140 W Main St
The Opera House
Los Gatos, CA 95030
ph: 408-395-3153
fax: 408-842-6002
afvenezia@aol.com
Antiques, Residential Contents, Furniture, Silver, Porcelain, Glass, Textiles, Antique Jewelry

Julie K. Summerville,
Pacific Automobile Appraisers
PO Box 67421
Scotts Valley, CA 95067-7421
ph: 408-335-1322
fax: 408-335-2869
Trucks, Cars (Antique, Vintage, & Special Interest)

Doug Neale, ISA
Neale & Sons, Inc., Appraisers
PO Box 425
Saratoga, CA 95071-0425
ph: 408-867-3751
fax: 408-867-3782
nealesons@aol.com
Antiques, Residential Contents, Jewelry, Machinery & Equipment, Estates

William Hoefer, Jr., ISA, GG, FGA
Hoefers' Gemological Services
5016 Alan Ave, # B4
San Jose, CA 95124-5741
ph: 408-264-0670
fax: 408-264-0725
bhoefer@ix.netcom.com
http://www.appraiserunderoath.com
Gemology/Gemstones, Jewelry, Diamonds, Litigation Consultant, Valuation Methodology Researcher

Peter Getty, ISA
Peter Getty Antiques
305 Buena Vista Dr
Santa Rosa, CA 95404-2152
ph: 707-526-6737
American Art Pottery, Arts & Crafts, Furniture, Metal Work, Lighting, Residential Contents, General Antiques

Jeffrey Savage, ISA, GG (GIA)
John Brorsen & Associates
1711 Schaeffer Rd
Sebastopol, CA 95472-5546
ph: 707-824-1957
fax: 707-824-1956
jsavage@aol.com
http://www.savagesguide.com
Residential Contents (Appreciable), Silver, Jewelry, Decorative Arts (19th-20th C.), Antiques, Expert Testimony, Estate Sales, Online Database Research

Nelda R. Palmer, ISA
Nelda Palmer Appraisals
PO Box 295
Cutten, CA 95534-0295
ph: 707-443-0967
fax: 707-443-0967
102774.3072@compuserve.com
Silver, Porcelain, Pottery, Ceramics, Crystal, Glass, Residential Contents

Lavonne J. Fraga, ISA
Lavonne's Antiques
3703 Edythe Ct
Placerville, CA 95667
ph: 916-626-3425
Retail Antique, Collectibles. Alt Phone: 530-621-1952 & 530-626-3425

Brad S. Lomazzi, ISA
Western Railroad Collectibles
1300 Liberty Ct
Roseville, CA 95747-7440
ph: 916-782-6587
lomazzi@ibm.net
Railroad Collectibles, Other Transportation Collectibles (Airline, Bus, Steamship, Auto, ect.) Western Americana

Dennis West, ISA
D.B. West Auctioneers
PO Box 278
Woodland, CA 95776-0278
ph: 530-661-0490
fax: 530-661-2499
dbwest@mother.com
Bankruptcy Property, Auctioneer/Auction Co., Commercial Business Liquidators, Machinery & Equipment, Cars, Trucks, RV's, Boats, Airplanes, Restaurant, Office Fixtures/Furniture, Computers, Oil Field & Mining

Sylvia M. Fitzgerald, ISA
A.A.E.S
PO Box 2509, # E24
Sacto, CA 95812
ph: 916-448-2428
sylfitz@compuserve.com
Decorative Arts 1800-1940, Art Nouveau, Art Deco, Arts & Crafts, Art Glass, Art Pottery, Fine Porcelains, Antiques, Appraisals, and Estate Sales.

Merilee A. Thorman, ISA
Merilee Thorman Fine Arts & Antiques
1049 11th Ave
Sacramento, CA 95818-4014
ph: 916-448-0404
fax: 916-448-0303
106254.1601@compuserve.com
Fine Arts & Antiques, Probate, Charitable Donations, Estate Liquidation & Sales

J. Marlene White, ISA, GG, FGA, C
Grebitus & Sons
404 Spinnaker Way
Sacramento, CA 95831-3236
ph: 916-442-9081
fax: 916-427-7844
ideal@gowebway.com
Gemology/Gemstones, Jewelry, Diamonds, Pearls

Richard C. Frey, ISA
R T L H Enterprises
1275 East Ave
Chico, CA 95926-1020
ph: 530-343-4528
fax: 530-343-9380
rfreyrtlh@aol.com
Art (Paintings, Watercolors, Drawings, Prints, Sculpture), Japanese Swords, Photography (American Indian & 20th C.), Consultant (Art, Etc.), Residential Contents, Estate Liquidation, Expert Witness, Arbitrator

Frank J. Williams, ISA
United Auction Services
PO Box 89
Crescent Mills, CA 95934-0089
ph: 530-284-6176
Machinery & Equipment, Rolling Stock, Industrial and Commercial Assets, Investment Recovery Consulting, Auctions and Liquidations, Expert Witness

Robert F. Trapp, ISA CAPP, GG (GIA)
Robert F. Trapp Gemological Services
3219 Calistoga Dr
Chico, CA 95973-0193
ph: 530-892-1907
fax: 530-892-1907
BobTrapp@MSN.com
Independent Appraiser of Gems and Jewelry, Expert Witness, Consultant, AGA Certified Gemological Laboratory

Susanne L. Adams, ISA
Riverfront Art Gallery
16425 Trail Dr
Redding, CA 96001
ph: 530-246-4868
fax: 530-246-4910
charleib@snowcrest.net
Fine Art, Antiques, Restoration, Grapic Arts

Richard C. Frey, ISA
Riverfront Art Gallery and Custom Framing
2649 Park Marina Dr
Redding, CA 96001
ph: 530-246-4868
fax: 530-246-4910
rfreyrtlh@aol.com
<<< SECOND LISTING >>> Art (Paintings, Watercolors, Drawings, Prints, Sculpture), Japanese Swords, Photography (American Indian & 20th C.), Consultant (Art, Etc.), Residential Contents, Estate Liquidation, Expert Witness, Arbitrator

Ernest M. Schmidt, ISA
Paradise Auction
PO Box 10418
Hilo, HI 96721-5418
ph: 808-969-1831
fax: 808-935-8430
auctions@ilhawaii.net
http://web-factor:oom/paradise/
FF&E (Furniture, Fixtures & Equipment), Furniture (Antique & Contemporary), Restraunts, Liquidator Auctioneer, and Realtor.

Neola Caveny, ISA, GG (GIA)
Neola Caveny Gem & Jewelry Appraisals
42 Pua Ole St
Paia, HI 96779
ph: 808-579-8823
fax: 808-579-9769
neola@mauigateway.com
Gemology/Gemstones, Diamonds, Jewelry (Antique & Period)

David Chun Ying Leung ISA
Bishop Jewelry Inc
1164 Bishop St, Ste 119
Honolulu, HI 96813-2810
ph: 808-538-3356
fax: 808-536-6091
Loose Diamonds, Precious Gemstones, Semi-Precious Gemstones, Finished Jewelry, Jade Carving

Brenda Reichel, ISA, GG, NGJA,
Carats And Karats
1254 S King St
Honolulu, HI 96814-1921
ph: 808-593-8122
fax: 808-591-9124
flawless@lava.net
http://www.caratsandkarats.com
Gemology/Gemstones, Diamonds, Jewelry, Gold, Ivory, Jade, Minerals, Pearls, Silver, Estates, Insurance, Expert Witness

Karen Young, ISA
15005 SW Wheaton Ln
Beaverton, OR 97007
ph: 503-643-1701
estchq@aol.com
Estate Sales, Sewing Items, Thimbles, Textiles, Embroidery

Kathy Luck, ISA
Kathy Luck Estate & Moving Sales
221 NW 12th
Gresham, OR 97030
ph: 503-665-9505
luckk@gateway.net
Collectibles, Antiques, Ceramics, Furniture, Depression Glass

Elizabeth Estes, ISA
2722 SE Evans Ave
Troutdale, OR 97060-2428
ph: 503-666-1303
eestes54@aol.com
Estate & Moving Sales, Antiques, Collectibles, Residential Contents

Joan Johnson, ISA
Joan Johnson Antiques & Appraisals
PO Box 506
Cannon Beach, OR 97110
ph: 503-717-1824
fax: 503-436-9680
Antiques, Furniture, Linens, Decorative Arts & Accessories

Donald Schubert, ISA
Schubert's Art & Antiques
937 SW 10th St
Portland, OR 97205
ph: 503-294-3381
Fine Art, Antiques, 19th C. Photos. Alt Tel: 503-781-0305

Sandra J. Millius, ISA
1530 NE 48th Ave
Portland, OR 97213-2138
ph: 503-249-8585
Antiques Instructor - Antiques/ Collectibles Appreciation; Antiques Collectibles, Residential Contents, Glass, Postcards

Kimberly Jae Stimac ISA
Laurie's & Casey's Antiques
7840 SW Capitol Hwy
Portland, OR 97219-2466
ph: 888-244-6775
Retail Antiques, Collectibles

Richard J. Richter, ISA
Urban Kaos Antiques & Collectibles
750 NE 87th Ave
Portland, OR 97220
ph: 503-253-9195
fax: 503-253-9195
Military Regalia (16th C. to Present), Antique & Collectible Toys, Antiques

Nancy Draper, ISA
Draper & Draper Appraisals
5403 SW Hewett Blvd
Portland, OR 97221-2237
ph: 503-292-2485
Antiques, Fine Art, Residential Contents, Folk Art, Textiles, Estates, Decorative Arts & Accessories, Toys

Shari M. Keeler, ISA
Shari's Antiques
14914 SW 109th Ave
Portland, OR 97224-3602
ph: 503-684-3442
Residential Contents, Antiques, Estate Liquidation, Producer of an Antiques Show

Christine A. Zachary, ISA
Christine Zachary Appraisals & Sales
PO Box 82906
Portland, OR 97282-0906
ph: 503-234-8143
fax: 503-777-5813
chris24@teleport.com
Estate Sales, Antiques, Estate Jewelry, Tibetan Art & Artifacts

Al Gilbertson, ISA, GG, CGA
Gem Profiles
PO Box 191
Albany, OR 97321-0059
ph: 503-274-2895
fax: 503-274-2895
Gemology/Gemstones, Diamonds, Jewelry, Watches, Pearls

John Kimble, ISA
Kimble Auction & Appraisal
1192 Rio Glen Dr
Eugene, OR 97401-1871
ph: 541-334-5130
jkimble961@aol.com
Antiques & Residential Contents, Early American & Western; Machinery & Equipment, Farm & Ranch Equipment, Heavy Equipment, Automobiles

Candy Moffett, ISA
Alder Gallery
55 W Broadway
Eugene, OR 97401-3002
ph: 541-342-6411
fax: 541-683-9797
alderart@efn.org
Fine Art, Sculpture, Paintings, Antiques, Prints, Bronzes, Watercolors, Ceramics, Modern & Contemporary Prints

Ann Rogers Pfrender, ISA
PO Box 23036
Eugene, OR 97402-0424
Quilts and Quilted Textiles

Sherril A. Cavallo, ISA CAPP
Appraisal Specialists, The
1269 W 10th Ave
Eugene, OR 97402-4705
ph: 541-687-6882
fax: 541-687-4699
73021.3620@compuserve.com
Antiques, Art (Fine Art, Decorative Art, & Accessories), Ceramics, Collectibles, Furniture (American & European), Glass, Jewelry (Antique & Period), Residential Contents (Appreciable), Silver, Textiles

Randeen M. Cummings, ISA CAPP
Cummings & Associates
PO Box 5484
Eugene, OR 97405-0484
ph: 541-345-5856
fax: 541-345-8192
Residential Contents (Appreciable), Commercial Inventories (Office & Business Contents), Estates (IRS, Probate, or Disbursal), Insurance Arbitration & Equitable Distribution, Antiques, Fine Art, Jewelry (Estate)

Patricia J. Wright, ISA
PO Box 83
Phoenix, OR 97535-0083
ph: 541-535-2095
fax: 541-535-2363
jim&pat@ccountry.net
Antiques, Collectibles, and Estate Sales.

Vanita J. Hertager, ISA
PO Box 833
Phoenix, OR 97535-0833
ph: 541-535-7419
fax: 541-512-9739
hertager@ccountry.net
Antiques, Collector

Claudette R. Elliott, ISA
Cobwebs Removed, Inc.
29407 61st Ave S
Auburn, WA 98001-1213
ph: 253-863-1924
fax: 253-839-2913
cobwebs@wa.net
Oriental Ceramics (Satsuma), Salt & Pepper Shakers, Coins, Jewelry, Household Items

Paul G. Bailey, ISA
Antique Appraisal & Estate Sale Service - The Original
12819 SE 38th St, PMB 320
Bellevue, WA 98006-1395
ph: 425-746-2777
fax: 725-562-6673
Furniture (18th-20th C.), Ceramics, Silver

Kathleen M. Bailey, ISA CAPP
Antique Appraisal & Estate Sale Service - The Original
12819 SE 38th St, PMB 320
Bellevue, WA 98006-1395
ph: 425-746-2777
fax: 725-562-6673
<<< SECOND LISTING >>> Estates, Liquidators. Antiques, Americana, Furniture, Decorative Arts, Silver, Art Nouveau, Faberge, Glass, Ceramics, and Victoriana.

Scott Zema, ISA CAPP
Ark Limited Appraisals
1435 154th Ave NE, APT 3905
Bellevue, WA 98007-4458
ph: 425-486-6310
fax: 425-486-6310
KarenMills@worldnet.att.net
Fine Arts, Antiques, Appreciable Residential Contents, Orientalia, Damage Claims

Brill Lee, ISA
PO Box 244
Bellevue, WA 98009-0244
ph: 425-885-4518
fax: 425-885-2475
Native American, Western (Cowboy), Boy Scout Memorabilia, Photgraphy, Railroad & Toy Trains, Arts & Crafts, Furniture, Metalwork, Pottery, Art Glass, Lamp & Lighting Fixtures

Peggy Jewell, ISA
Another Man's Treasure
14509 33rd Dr SE
Mill Creek, WA 98012-5029
ph: 425-482-0358
amtantiques@msn.com
Antiques, Collectibles, Residential Contents, Decorative Arts & Accessories, ONLY LOCAL REFERRALS : Americana, Ceramics, Victoriana, Art Deco & Art Nouveau, Toys, Memorabilia, Ephemera, Estates, Consultant

David E. Hong, ISA
27327 NE Big Rock Rd
Duval, WA 98019-8206
ph: 425-788-7520
davehong@msn.com
Clocks, Pocket and Wrist Watches, Slot Machines, Firearms, Fountain Pens, Cash Registers, Watch Fobs

James M. Anders, ISA
Waterfront Auction Company
190 Sunset Ave S
Edmonds, WA 98020
ph: 425-670-0770
fax: 425-670-0820
Antiques, Collectibles, Residential Contents, Auctioneer

Duane L. Benoit, ISA
Milltown Antiques
18916 Olympic View Dr
Edmonds, WA 98020
ph: 425-771-9466
fax: 425-778-9642
DLB511@aol.com
Fine Art, Antiques, Residential Contents, Native American Baskets, Japanese Swords

Bette G. Bell, ISA CAPP
Guildmark Appraisal & Estate Sale Service, LLC
PO Box 952
Edmonds, WA 98020-0952
ph: 425-775-5650
fax: 425-670-6597
stashn33@gte.net
Antiques, Collectibles, Residential Contents, Quilts, Estates

Donald L. Jensen, ISA CAPP
Cotswold Appraisal Services
7216 Soundview Dr
Edmonds, WA 98026-5566
ph: 425-745-3941
fax: 425-787-0548
76533.1531@compuserve.com
Antiques, Art Glass (American & European), 19th C. Staffordshire Ironstone & Figurines, Residential Contents, Estates, Consultant

Margaret Minnick, ISA
4645 Forest Ave se
Mercer Island, WA 98040
ph: 206-236-1100
fax: 206-236-1100
MMINNICK@home.com
Antiques, Residential Contents

Kathleen D. Victor, ISA
Victor Appraisal Services
6356 138th Ave NE, Apt 209
Redmond, WA 98052-4558
ph: 425-882-9003
fax: 425-895-0789
Antiques, Consultant for Estate Liquidations, Antique & Period Jewelry, Collectibles, and Victoriana.

Barbara Norris Miller, ISA
Barbara Miller, Auntie M's Enterprises
21307 50th Dr SE
Woodinville, WA 98072
ph: 425-424-0337
dbmiller@compuserve.com
Estates, Antiques, Collectibles, Residential Contents

John F. Roberts, ISA
10418 SE 302nd St
Auburn, WA 98092-2537
ph: 253-735-8641
fax: 253-804-8655
105326.421@compuserve.com
Art History-First Edition Books, Depreciable & Appreciable Residential Contents, Antiques, Estates & Household Liquidations, Insurance

Nicole Roberts, ISA
10418 SE 302nd St
Auburn, WA 98092-2537
ph: 253-735-8641
fax: 253-804-8655
105326.421@compuserve.com
French Antiques, Depreciable & Appreciable Residential Contents, Antiques, Estate & Household Liquidations, Insurance

John C. Craughan ISA
Equipment Consulting Services
32009 162nd Ave SE
Auburn, WA 98092-5905
ph: 253-833-2462
fax: 253-887-8120
ecs@seatac.net
Machinery & Equipment (Consturction, Logging, Mining & Farm), Trucks, Cars (Special Interest), Consultant

Karen Lorene, ISA, NAJA
Facere Jewelry Art
1420 5th Ave, Ste 108
Seattle, WA 98101-2333
ph: 206-624-6768
fax: 206-624-2852
Jewelry (Antique)

Donald R. Bell, ISA
Aircraft Appraisal
2312 Minor Ave E
Seattle, WA 98102-3308
ph: 206-325-5929
fax: 206-325-6567
Aircraft, Airport Equipment, and Hanger Appraisals

Lynn T. McAllister, Ph.D., ISA
Lynn Mcallister Gallery
1202 Lakeview Blvd E, Apt 8
Seattle, WA 98102-4375
ph: 206-467-0277
Sculpture (15th-20th C.), Paintings, Watercolors, Drawings (European & American 16th-20th C.), Glass (19th-20th C. Art, & Studio), Prints (15th-20th C.), and Residential Contents

Kay Frances Hurd, ISA
Hurd Antiques Appraisals & Estate Services
8554 1/2 Greenwood Ave N
Seattle, WA 98103-3614
ph: 206-782-2405
fax: 206-364-0635
antiquek9@aol.com
Estate Sales Specialist & Tag Sale, Insurance, Antiques, Collectibles, Glass (Victorian to Depression Era), Jewelry, Furniture, Porcelain, Pottery, Hummels, Smalls, Decorative Arts & Accessories, Silver, Expanded Residential Contents Expe

Daniel W. H. Griffin, ISA
5542 33rd Ave NE
Seattle, WA 98105-2303
ph: 206-523-5928
Antiques, Appreciable Residential Contents, Church/Religious/ Ecclesiastical Goods, Decorative Arts & Accessories, Estate Jewelry, Funeral Art, Preservation (Consultation), Estate Management, Scandinavian Fine and Folk Arts, Textiles

Kathleen M. Bailey, ISA CAPP
Antique Appraisal & Estate Sale Service - The Original
9416 1st Ave NE, # 311
Seattle, WA 98115-0191
ph: 425-746-2777
fax: 425-746-3793
Estates, Liquidators. Antiques, Americana, Furniture, Decorative Arts, Silver, Art Nouveau, Faberge, Glass, Ceramics, and Victoriana.

Charles G. Barker, ISA
Chronos A.S.
1511 NE 97th St
Seattle, WA 98115-2320
ph: 206-526-1372
fax: 206-526-1391
2barks@msn.com
Medical Equipment, Office Furniture & Equipment

Scott D. Singer, ISA
Singer Galleries, Ltd
411 W Galer St
Seattle, WA 98119-3335
ph: 206-285-0394
fax: 206-283-5264
SingerAntq@aol.com
http://www.tias.com/stores/singer
Antiques, Estates, Insurance, Art (Asian), Furniture, Porcelain, Pottery, Ceramics, China, Glass, Silver

Norene Ott, ISA
Antique & Collectible Dolls Of Seattle
11921 26th Pl SW
Seattle, WA 98146-2408
ph: 206-246-2290
fax: 206-244-8007
SeniorOtt@aol.com
Antique Dolls & Bears, Collectible Dolls & Bears, Doll Minatures & Accessories, and Toys.

Christian A. Coleman, ISA CAPP
ISA Executive Director
16040 Christensen Rd, Ste 102
Seattle, WA 98188-2965
ph: 206-241-0359
fax: 206-241-0436
isa_hq@compuserve.com

Brenda J. Paquette, ISA
Final Appraisal Studios
914 Hoyt Ave
Everett, WA 98201-1324
ph: 425-259-3449
19th-20th C. Furniture, Paintings, Engravings/Etchings, and Decorative Arts.

Theresa K. Meurs, ISA
2515 Vining St
Bellingham, WA 98226-4231
ph: 360-734-8087
fax: 360-676-5330
104507.1474@compuserve.com
Estate Sales, Antiques, Collectibles, Residential Contents, and Silver (20th C.).

Jan W. Sabin, ISA
S&J Dog and Pony Show
1359 Crestview Dr
Camano Island, WA 98292
ph: 206-784-3950
dittany@gte.net
Firearms (Contemporary), Antiques, Residential Contents

James Prossick, ISA
Pierce County Public Works & Utilities
7911 122nd St Ct E
Puyallup, WA 98383
ph: 253-798-7250
fax: 253-798-2740
igprossick@aol.com
Machinery & Equipment, Business Valuation, Residential Contents, Toys, Vinyl Records, Roseville Pottery, Furniture, and Household Goods

Raymond N. Elliott, II, ISA
Cobwebs Removed, Inc.
1008 Mann St
Sumner, WA 98390
ph: 253-863-1924
fax: 253-839-2913
cobwebs@wa.net
Furniture, Pottery

Caren L. Carlson, ISA
CLC Enterprises, Inc.
31313 NW Paradise Park Rd
Ridgefield, WA 98642-8754
ph: 360-887-8686
fax: 360-887-8909
carlson@vancouver.wsu.edu
Dolls, Estate Jewelry, Auctions, Estate Sales

Sally Ambrose, ISA CAPP
PO BOX 536
11156 North Rd
Leavenworth, WA 98826-0536
ph: 509-548-7472
fax: 509-548-0240
sally@televar.com
Residential Contents, Americana, Victoriana, Quilts (Antique & Contemporary), Wearable Art, Needlework, Textiles, Sewing Collectibles

Doris A. Dickinsen, ISA
Dickinsen Appraisal Services
6009 Douglas Dr
Yakima, WA 98908-2739
ph: 509-966-1209
fax: 509-966-7525
DAD2770@aol.com
Residential Contents

Marilu Ferguson, ISA
4-Wheel Country Antiques, Inc.
5904 Cowiche Canyon Rd
Yakima, WA 98908-9466
ph: 509-966-0469
Furniture (Antique), Glass (Antique), Residential Contents, Estates, Damage Claims Specialist

Molly C. Griffith, ISA
Hidden House Sterling Shop
550 Zickler Rd
Zillah, WA 98953-9223
ph: 509-865-3353
Silver (American Flat & Holloware - Coin & Silverplate), Sterling (American 19th & 20th C. - Victorian)

Vincent C. Rundhaug, ISA, GG (GIA)
Columbia Gem & Jewelry
8390 W Gage Blvd, Ste 105
Kennewick, WA 99336-8105
ph: 509-783-6363
fax: 509-783-0211
vrundhaug@aol.com
Gemology/Gemstones, Contemporary Jewelry, Diamonds, Jewelry, Gold

Linda Lee Halterman, ISA
Halterman's Appraisal Services
PO Box 672330
Chugiak, AK 99567-0581
ph: 907-688-2175
fax: 907-688-2176
MPReichter@aol.com
Antiques, Residential Contents

Barbara B. Lines, ISA
Blades Appraisal Services, Ltd.
48 Par-La Ville Rd, Ste 810
Hamilton, HM 11
Bermuda
ph: 441-295-4822
fax: 441-295-4856
blades@ibl.bm
Paintings (19th-20th C.), Furniture (19th-20th C.), Silver (19th-20th C.)

Karen Becker, ISA, GG (GIA)
Forever Precious Fine Jewellers Inc.
730 Upper James St, Unit 1
Hamilton, ON L9C 2Z9
Canada
ph: 905-575-4415
fax: 905-575-9920
Estate Items, Antiques, Collectibles, Fine Art, Jewellery

Peter S. Blundell, ISA
Birdseye Estate & Appraisals
PO Box 6
Vernon, BC V1T 6M1
Canada
ph: 250-542-4540
fax: 250-542-4581
Furniture (N. American), Glass (Pressed & Cut), Straffrodshire, Earthenwares, Canadian Art, Kerosene Lamps.

Cameron Carter, ISA
Normac Appraisals
3642 W 26th Ave
Vancouver, BC V6S 1P1
Canada
ph: 604-221-8258
fax: 604-224-1445
normac@lightspeed.bc.ca
Machinery and Equipment apraisals. Insurance valuations for real estate, furniture, and equipment. Government porpery valuations.

Gary B. Coyle, ISA, MGGA
Coyle's Jewellery & Gifts, Ltd.
5876 Wyandotte St East
Windsor, ON N8S 1M8
Canada
ph: 519-945-1969
fax: 519-945-5980
gcoyle@mnsi.net
Gemology, Gemstones, Jewelry, Diamonds, Colored Stones

Charles T. Cripps, ISA CAPP
Townsend Antiques & Appraisals
15227 81 Ave
Edmonton, AB T5R 3P2
Canada
ph: 780-486-5012
fax: 708-484-2836
Furniture, Silver, Porcelain, Pottery, Residential Contents

Thomas L. G. Gibson, ISA
Gibson's Appraisers & Restoration
6319 Chebucto Rd
Halifax, NS B3L 1K9
Canada
ph: 902-429-3873
Antiques, Object d'Art & de Vertu, Residential Contents, Repairs & Restoration, Consultant in Decorative Arts & Accessories.

Kathy Gowans, B.Ed., ISA CAPP
Gowans Appraisal Service
RR #2
Red Deer, AB T4N 5E2
Canada
ph: 403-347-7199
fax: 403-346-5415
kgowans@telusplanet.net
Antiques, Collectibles, Pottery, Porcelain, Porcelain Restoration, Victoriana

Philip Grouchy, ISA
Fitzpatrick's Auctioneering
7 Mullaly St
St. John's, NF A1C 5H5
Canada
ph: 709-722-5865
fax: 709-722-9612
Auction@auint.net
http://www.silverweb.nf.ca/fitzpatricksauction
Residential Contents, Industrial, Vehicle, Auctioneer

Kathleen Laverty, ISA
Horizon Art Galleries
2020 Haro St, #106
Vancouver, BC V6G 1J3
Canada
ph: 604-689-5360
fax: 604-602-0844
klaverty@dowco.com
Paintings, Graphics, Sculpture, Drawings, Canadian Contemporary and Historical, American, British, European, Inuit, Native, Folk, Photography, Contemporary Ceramics, Animation

Doreen Millin, ISA
793 Montrose St
Winnipeg, MB R3M 3M5
Canada
ph: 204-945-3849
fax: 204-945-1684
dmillin@ach.gov.mb.ca
Canadian Visual Art & Craft

Kathryn Minard, ISA
Contemporary Fine Art Services, Inc
413 Dundas St E
Toronto, ON M5A 2A9
Canada
ph: 416-366-9770
fax: 416-366-8541
75263.2530@compuserve.com
Canadian Contemporary & Historical: Painting, Sculpture, Watercolour, Prints, Photography, Textiles, Ceramics & Craft; Canadian Indian & Inuit

Ian Muncaster, ISA
Zwicker's Gallery
5415 Doyle St
Halifax, NS B3J 1H9
Canada
ph: 902-423-7662
fax: 902-422-3870
Paintings, Watercolrs, Drawings (Especially Canadian), Graphics, Sculpture, Fine Art, Folk Art, Maps, and Historical Prints

Sheila Wills Osborne, ISA
Contemporary Fine Art Services
413 Dundas St E
Toronto, ON M5A 2A9
Canada
ph: 416-366-9770
fax: 416-366-8541
Canadian Contemporary & Historical: Painting, Sculpture, Watercolour, Prints, Photography, Textiles, Ceramics & Crafts, Canadian Indian & Inuit

Erik J. Peters, ISA
Maynards Industries Ltd.
415 W 2nd Ave
Vancouver, BC V5Y 1E3
Canada
ph: 604-876-6787
fax: 604-876-2678
erik@maynards.com
http://www.maynards.com
Canadian Historical & Modern Fine Art, Western European, British & American Fine Art

Lorraine Pierce-Hull, ISA
Pierce-Hull & Associates
PO Box 93
Ottawa, ON K7C 3P3
Canada
ph: 613-257-2987
fax: 613-253-0949
1phull@magi.com
Fine Art: Canadian Paintings, Prints, Sculpture. Paintings: British & European. Alt Email: 1phall@magi.com

James Poag, ISA CAPP, S-CAPP, GG, AA
James O. Poag Jewelers, Ltd.
PO Box 39
94 Frank St
Strathroy, ON N7G 3J1
Canada
ph: 519-245-1040
fax: 519-245-6073
james@poags.com
Gemology/Gemstones, Gold, Jewelry, Estates, Pearls, Insurance, Consultations, Clocks

Elinor A. Racine, ISA
Elin Racine
175 Bessborough Dr
Toronto, ON M4G 3J8
Canada
ph: 416-483-8675
fax: 416-483-2805
75317.2337@compuserve.com
Ceramics Experience, Appraisal of Donations to the Permanent Collection of Ceramics, Glass, 20th C. Studio Work

Elizabeth L. Reynolds, ISA
Reynolds Associates Limited
12 Kent Pl
St. John's, NF A1B 1V5
Canada
ph: 709-722-4546
fax: 709-722-2040
ereynold@pagemaker.com
Canadian (Especially Newfoundland) Paintings and Fine Art Prints; Etchings and Engravings; Old Newfoundland Photographs; Quilts

Judith Scolnik, ISA
Judith Scolnik Art Search
95 Thorncliffe Park Dr, Apt 2701
Toronto, ON M4H 1L7
Canada
ph: 416-421-4239
fax: 416-423-8057
Fine Art, Candian Art (Historical & Contemporary), American & European Master Graphics

Meyer K. Steiman, ISA CAPP
Carter's Auction Gallery
206 Princess St
Winnipeg, MB R3B 1L4
Canada
ph: 204-942-3397
fax: 204-943-8960
Residential Contents, Estates, Office Furniture & Equipment, Business Liquidators, Auctioneer

Dennis R. Storey, Jr., ISA, CAI
Forest City Auctions, Inc.
43 Chaucer Ct
London, ON N6K 1V1
Canada
ph: 519-641-2844
fax: 519-641-6143
Residential Contents, Estates, Machinery & Equipment (Restaurant), Business Evaluations, Auctioneer

Stephen P. Sweeting, ISA
Appraisal Associates
80 Richmond St W, Ste 1101
Toronto, ON M5H 2A4
Canada
ph: 416-368-4334
fax: 416-368-6679
aaci@pathcom.com
http://www.appraise.org
Fine Art, Antiques, Decorative Arts & Accessories, Residential Contents

Irene Szylinger, ISA
Art Research & Appraisals, Ltd.
62 Woodlawn Ave W
Toronto, ON M4V 1G7
Canada
ph: 416-964-6449
fax: 416-923-3366
Fine Arts: Paintings, Prints, Drawings, Sculpture, Decorative Arts, (19th-20th C. Canadian, American, & European Collections)

Dominic K. U. Tang, ISA, GG (GIA)
Polytech Enterprises, Inc.
1872 Walnut Crescent
Coquitlalm, BC V3J 7T1
Canada
ph: 604-931-7441
fax: 604-931-7441
Jewelry (Diamonds & Colored Stones)

William B. Whetstone, ISA
Thompson & Whetstone, Inc.
1117 Saint Catherine St W, Ste 900
Montreal, PQ H3B 1H9
Canada
ph: 514-289-9761
fax: 514-289-9332
76262.614@compuserve.com
Jewelry (Antique & Period), Silver (Antique), Coins (Ancient to 20th C.), Decorative & Fine Arts (19th-20th C.), Stocks, Bonds, & Certificates

Andrew Steven White, ISA
Andrew White Fine Art
#3 1396 W 71st Ave
Vancouver, BC V6P 3B5
Canada
ph: 604-261-4801
fax: 604-261-4801
anwhite@direct.ca
Canadian Fine Art (19th-20th C.), Modernist/Objet d'Art & De Vertu

Sheila D. Wilson, ISA
Wilson & Associates
VMPO 3022
Vancouver, BC V6B 3X5
Canada
ph: 604-685-2964
fax: 604-685-2974
dswilson@bc.sympatico.ca
Antiques, Decorative Arts & Accessories, Estates, Residential Contents

Edith Yeomans, ISA
Appraisal Associates
80 Richmond St W, Ste 1101
Toronto, ON M5H 2A4
Canada
ph: 416-368-4334
fax: 416-368-6679
aaci@pathcom.com
http://www.appraise.org
Fine Art, Antiques, Decorative Arts & Accessories, Residential Contents

Regine David, ISA
Garry Antiques
13 Rue D'aumale
Paris, 75009
France
ph: 140-100-987
Antiques, Faberge, Jewelry, Russian Art, Silver (Phone numbers should be proceded by 011-33)

Here are some tips when contacting someone listed in this book:

- **When requesting information about a particular item, include a description (material, dimensions, maker's mark, model number, etc.) and a photo, sketch, or photocopy of the item in question.**
- **Always ask if there are charges for samples or for the services requested.**
- **When writing, please be sure to include a Large (#10 business size) Self-Addressed and Stamped Envelope (LSASE) if requesting a reply or the return of photographs.**
- **Never call collect unless otherwise directed. When calling, be considerate of time zone differences and always ask if the party you are calling has time to talk. When leaving an answering machine message, always instruct the party to call you back collect.**

APPENDIX B

Auction Services

Listed in ZIP code order

The following firms offer on-site, gallery, Internet and/or mail-phone bid auction services for all types of personal property, antiques, collectibles, and art. Those who, in addition, conduct auctions specializing in a particular field are also listed under those categories within the General Listings section of this Directory.

Mac-Caro Antiques
P.O. Box 643
Lee, MA 01238-0643
ph: 413-243-4647
fax: 413-243-4687
Antique dealer, auction and appraisal service; estate liquidations.

Douglas Auctioneers
Rte. 5
South Deerfield, MA 01373
ph: 413-665-3530
fax: 413-665-2877
http://www.douglasauctioneers.com/
Auction sales year-round, specializing in antiques, fine art, estates, and appraising; also conducts Auctioneering School.

Skinner, Inc.
357 Main St.
Bolton, MA 01740-1104
ph: 978-779-6241
fax: 978-779-5144
info@skinnerinc.com
http://www.skinnerinc.com
Established in 1964, Skinner Inc. is the fifth largest auction house in the US; has offices in Bolton and Boston, MA.

Grogan & Company Auctioneers
22 Harris St.
Dedham, MA 02026
ph: 781-461-9500
fax: 781-461-9625
grogans@groganco.com
http://www.groganco.com/

Willis Henry Auctions, Inc.
22 Main St.
Marshfield, MA 02050
ph: 781-834-7774 or 800-244-8466
fax: 781-826-3520
wha@willishenry.com
http://www.willishenry.com/
Specializes in the sale of American antiques of all kinds, particularly Shaker, American Indian and early American.

F.B. Hubley
364 Broadway
Cambridge, MA 02139
ph: 617-876-2030

Shute Auction Gallery
850 W. Chestnut St.
Brockton, MA 02401
ph: 508-588-0022 or 508-588-7833
fax: 508-559-6687
Antique and custom furniture, art, silver, glass and china, collectibles, etc.

Eldred's
P.O. Box 796
East Dennis, MA 02641-0796
ph: 508-385-3116
fax: 508-385-7201
eldreds@capecod.net
http://www.eldreds.com/
Auctioneers and appraisers for over 45 years.

Gustave White Auctioneers
37 Bellevue
Newport, RI 02840-3207
ph: 401-841-5780

Collector's Sales & Services
P.O. Box 4073
Middletown, RI 02842
ph: 401-849-5012
collectors@antiquechina.com
http://www.antiquechina.com
Specialize in mail-bid auctions for historical Staffordshire, Quimper, American glass, French and American paperweights, bottles, etc.

Withington, Inc.
590 Centr Road
Hillsboro, NH 03244
ph: 603-464-3232
withington@conknet.com

Northeast Auctions
694 Lafayette Rd.
P.O. Box 363
Hampton, NH 03483
ph: 603-926-9800
fax: 603-926-3545

Paul McInnis, Inc.
356 Exeter Rd.
Hampton Falls, NH 03844
ph: 603-778-8989 or 800-242-8354
fax: 603-772-7452
Paul@PaulMcInnis.com
http://www.paulmcinnis.com/

Sanders & Mock Associates, Inc.
P.O. Box 37
Tamworth, NH 03886
ph: 603-323-8749 or 603-323-8784
fax: 603-323-8784
http://www.auctionweb.com/sanmock/
20+ years as leading auction house in Northern New England; antiques, fine arts, collections, paintings, rugs, vertu; on site auctions throughout New England and modern auction gallery in Chocorua, NH.

Thomaston Place Auction Galleries
P.O. Box 300
Business Rt. 1
Thomaston, ME 04861
ph: 207-354-8141
fax: 207-354-9523
johnh@kajav.com
http://www.kagav.com/

James D. Julia Auctioneers Inc.
Rt. 201, Skowhegan Rd.
P.O. Box 830
Fairfield, ME 04937
ph: 207-453-7125
fax: 207-453-2502
jjulia@juliaauctions.com
http://www.juliaauctions.com

Eaton Auction Service
RR 1, Box 333
Fairlee, VT 05045
ph: 802-333-9717

Winter Associates, Inc. Auctioneers & Appraisers
21 Cooke St.
P.O. Box 823
Plainville, CT 06062
ph: 860-793-0288
fax: 860-793-8288
Appraises and conducts estate liquidations of antiques, fine furniture, paintings, jewelry, porcelain, glass, etc.

Norman C. Heckler & Company
79 Bradford Corner Rd.
Woodstock Valley, CT 06282-2002
ph: 860-974-1634
fax: 860-974-2003
heckler@neca.com
http://www.heckleraction.com/
A full-service auction company for antique glass and bottles, period decorative arts, single art objects and estates.

Greg Manning Auctions, Inc.
775 Passaic Ave.
West Caldwell, NJ 07006
ph: 973-882-0004 or 800-221-0243
fax: 973-882-3499
gmauction@aol.com
http://www.gregmanning.com/
Since 1905, a leading auctioneer of Americana, glass, stoneware, and antiquities.

Lincoln Galleries
225 Scotland Rd.
Orange, NJ 07050
ph: 973-677-2000
fax: 973-677-1176
warehouses@aol.com
http://cybergsi.com/lincoln/

Berman's Auction Gallery
33 West Blackwell St.
Dover, NJ 07081
ph: 973-361-3110

Koty & Associates, LLC
P.O. Box 625
Freehold, NJ 07728-0625
ph: 732-751-0504
fax: 732-751-9190
Bidtaker@compuserve.com
Specializes in the auction sale of antiques, collectibles, household contents, estates, etc.; certified appraisers of appreciable and depreciable residential contents.

Castner's
P.O. Box 920
Branchville, NJ 07826-0920
ph: 973-948-3868 or 973-383-7044
fax: 973-948-3919
castner@garden.net
Specializing in the sale of local estate contents including antiques and residential contents; gallery auctions; on site auctions; estate liquidations in NJ, NY, and PA.

Dawson's
128 American Rd.
Morris Plains, NJ 07950
ph: 973-984-6900
fax: 973-984-6956
dawson1@idt.net
http://www.dawsonsauction.com/
Specializes in the auction sales of antiques, art, silver, jewelry, toys and collectibles.

Swann Galleries, Inc.
104 E. 25th St.
New York, NY 10010-2977
ph: 212-254-4710
fax: 212-979-1017
swann@swanngalleries.com
http://www.swanngalleries.com/
Oldest/largest U.S. auctioneer specializing in rare books, autographs & manuscripts, maps, atlases, photographs, and works of art on paper including vintage posters.

Christie's East
219 E. 67th St.
New York, NY 10021
ph: 212-606-0400
http://www.christies.com

Sotheby's
1334 York Ave.
New York, NY 10021
ph: 212-606-7000
fax: 212-606-7107
http://www.sothebys.com
Call 212-606-7000 on a touch tone phone to access a data base to obtain post-sale prices; have sale number and lot number handy.

Guernsey's Auction
108 East 73rd St.
New York, NY 10021
ph: 212-794-2280
fax: 212-744-3638
catalogues@guernseys.com
http://www.guernseys.com/
Auctions unique commodities and collections, e.g. vintage automobiles, marine art, animation cels, Soviet art, posters, etc.

Christie's
502 Park Ave.
New York, NY 10022
ph: 212-546-1000
fax: 212-980-8163
http://www.christies.com
Call 212-546-1199 on a touch tone phone to access a data base to obtain post-sale prices; have sale number and lot number handy.

Phillips Fine Art & Auctioneers
406 East 79th St.
New York, NY 10022
ph: 212-570-4830
fax: 212-570-2207
phillips@philmail.demon.co.uk
http://www.phillips-auctions.com
Acts as a liaison with the London home office; solicits objects for sale in England and Europe; conducts special appraisal days in New York.

Dorotheum
Dorotheergasse 17
Vienna, 1010
Austria
ph: 0431 515 60 x226
fax: 0431 515 60 x489
services@dorotheum.at
http://www.dorotheum.com
Specializes in the auction sales of antiques, art, jewelry and collectibles.

William Doyle Galleries
175 E. 87th St.
New York, NY 10128-2205
ph: 212-427-2730
fax: 212-369-0892
info@doylegalleries.com
http://www.doylegalleries.com
Holds over 50 auctions annually of furniture and decorations, paintings and sculpture, jewelry, books and prints, couture and textiles, 20th century art & design, majolica, Lalique, Asian works of art and other specialty categories.

Cohasco, Inc.
P.O. Box 821
Yonkers, NY 10702-0821
ph: 914-476-8500
fax: 914-476-8573
cohascodpc@earthlink.net
http://home.earthlink.net/~cohascodpc/index.html
In business over 50 years, specializing in paper collectibles, autographs, documents, Americana, ephemera, etc.; mail auction catalogs issued.

South Bay Auctions, Inc.
485 Montauk Highway
East Moriches, NY 11940
ph: 516-878-2909 or 516-878-2933
fax: 516-878-1863
info@southbayauctions.com
http://www.southbayauctions.com/

Patrick Thomas & Partners
858 Route 212
P.O. Box 119
Saugerties, NY 12477-0119
ph: 914-247-8888
fax: 914-246-0589
auctionptp@aol.com
http://www.ptpauctions.com/
Full service auction gallery specializing in American & European fine art, antique furniture, decorative arts, and collectibles; consignments from a single item to entire estates accepted.

Savoia's Auction Inc.
Rte. 23
South Cairo, NY 12482
ph: 518-622-8000
fax: 518-622-9453

Absolute Auction & Realty, Inc.
348 Main St.
Beacon, NY 12508
ph: 914-635-3169 or 800-551-5161
fax: 914-831-9671
hikertwo@aol.com
http://www.auctionweb.com/aar-ny/

Iroquois Auction Gallery
P.O. Box 736
Brewerton, NY 13029
ph: 315-668-2346
Semi-annual upscale art and antique auctions; also regular estate art & antique auctions; over 20 years of service; graduate of Sotheby's Style in Art course; always interested in buying quality art & antiques, paintings, art work, etc.

Mapes Auction Gallery
1729 Vestal Pkwy. West
Vestal, NY 13850-1156
ph: 607-754-9193
fax: 607-786-3549
davidmapes@compuserve.com
http://www.mapesauction.com
Auctions and appraisals since 1966: estates, collections, fine and decorative art, toys, jewelry, oriental rugs, American furniture, European furniture and decorations, Arts & Crafts; no modern collectibles.

Bronstein Appraisal Service
3666 Main Street
Buffalo, NY 14226
ph: 716-835-7666 or 800-642-2500
fax: 716-835-7419
value@Bronsteincorp.com
http://www.BronsteinCorp.com
Valuation and marketing of all types of chattels and realty since 1950.

Gansz Auction & Realty
14 William St.
Lyons, NY 14489-1119
ph: 315-946-6241
fax: 315-946-6747
Providing estate auction ervices for over 40 years: antiques, fine art, collectibles; also appraisals.

Samuel Cottone Auctions
15 Genesee St.
Mount Morris, NY 14510
ph: 716-658-3119
fax: 716-658-3152

Total Auction Services
RD #2 Box 173B
Cherry Tree, PA 15724
ph: 724-254-4514
fax: 724-254-5141
totalauction@yourinter.net
http://www.yourinter.net/totalauction
Complete auction service for estates, antiques, collectibles, firearms, businesses; on site or off.

Collectors Auction Services
RR2, Box 431
Oil City, PA 16301
ph: 814-677-6070
fax: 814-677-6166
manderton@mail.usachoice.net
http://www.caswel.com/
An absentee mail and phone bid auction handling quality antiques and collectibles.

York Town Auction Inc.
1625 Haviland Rd.
York, PA 17404
ph: 717-751-0211
fax: 717-767-7729
yorktownauction@cyberia.com
Antique & specialty auctions, lecture & appraisal services; antiques also purchased; American & English furniture, related specialties & accessories, Americana, folk art, jewelry, art, clocks & watches, militaria, steins, Oriental rugs.

Hake's Americana & Collectibles Auction
P.O. Box 1444
York, PA 17405-1444
ph: 717-848-1333
Ted@hakes.com
http://www.hakes.com/
Always purchasing items for 8 mail-bid auctions per year covering hundreds of categories including toys, character collectibles, Disney, cowboy heroes, premiums, television, politicals, pin-back buttons, advertising and more.

Conestoga Auction Company
768 Graystone Rd.
P.O. Box 1
Manheim, PA 17545
ph: 717-898-7284
fax: 717-898-6628
http;//www.rootsmarket.com/conestoga/

Roan Inc. Auction Gallery
RR 4 Box 118
Cogan Station, PA 17728
ph: 570-494-0170 or 800-955-ROAN
fax: 570-494-1911
info@roaninc.com
http://www.roaninc.com/

Skinner's Auction Company
3807 Margate Rd.
Bethlehem, PA 18020
ph: 610-868-985
fax: 610-868-9985
skinnauct@aol.com
http://www.skinnerauct.baweb.com
Auctioneers, estate liquidators, appraisers of antiques and collectibles; licensed and bonded; over 15 years experience.

Aston Trade Company, Inc.
1012 Westminster
Wilkes Barre, PA 18702
ph: 570-654-3090
fax: 570-655-2145
aston@epix.net

Nard Auctions
U.S. Rte. 220
Milan, PA 18831
ph: 570-888-9404
fax: 570-888-7723

Clinton-Ivankovich Auction Co., Inc.
P.O. Box 29
Ottsville, PA 18942
ph: 610-847-5432

Stephenson's Auction
1005 Industrial Blvd.
Southampton, PA 18966-4006
ph: 215-322-6182
fax: 215-364-0883
http://www.stephensonauction.com/
Weekly general auctions of residential contents; quarterly auctions of antiques and decorative arts; additional specialty auctions.

Freeman/Fine Arts of Philadelphia
1808 Chestnut St.
Philadelphia, PA 19103
ph: 610-563-9275 or 610-563-9453
fax: 610-563-8236
http://www.artlibrary.com/freeman/
America's oldest auction house: Continental, English and American furniture, paintings, silver and decorative arts; Oriental rugs, rare books, fine jewelry, Orientalia.

Pook & Pook, Inc.
P.O. Box 268
Downingtown, PA 19335-0268
ph: 610-269-0695 or 610-269-4040
fax: 610-269-9274
info@pookandpookinc.com
http://www.pookandpookinc.com/
Auction management and appraisal service; antiques appraised, purchased and sold on consignment.

Childers & Smith
1415 Horseshoe Pike
Glenmoore, PA 19343
ph: 610-942-2367
fax: 610-269-1036
annette@smithauctionco.com
http://www.smithauctionco.com
Full service auction company specializing in estates, antiques, collections, toys, vintage electronics, military, sports items, pottery, paintings, furniture, jewelry, music boxes, instruments.

Alderfer Auction Company
501 Fairground Rd.
P.O. Box 640
Hatfield, PA 19440-0640
ph: 215-393-3000
fax: 215-368-9055
auction@alderfercompany.com
http://alderfercompany.com
A full service auction and appraisal business, specializing in Pennsylvania antiques, fine art, fire arms, Americana, and collectibles.

Mid Atlantic Auctions & Appraisals, Inc.
P.O. Box 4365
Wilmington, DE 19807-0365
ph: 302-654-8776
fax: 302-654-5884
nedstinson@earthlink.net

Weschler's
909 E St. NW
Washington, DC 20004-2006
ph: 202-628-1281 or 800-331-1430
fax: 202-628-2366
http://www.weschlers.com/
A full service auction service for art, antiques, decorative accessories, household furnishings, and commercial liquidations; also specializes in the sale of European and American furniture and decorative art.

Asset Services International Co., Inc.
P.O. Box 40883
Washington, DC 20016
ph: 703-525-0396
fax: 703-243-5562
gd@asset-services.com
http://www.asset-services.com
Appraisal, auction, liquidation, sealed bid, receiver, trustee, conservator, expert witness, replevins, legal/ litigation support, management services, asset recoveries, due diligence, monitoring.

Sloan's Auction Galleries
4920 Wyaconda Rd.
Rockville, MD 20852
ph: 301-468-4911 or 800-649-5066
fax: 301-468-9182
sloans@sloansauction.com
http://www.sloansauction.com/
Oldest metropolitan Washington, DC auction house; sells fine art and antiques from quality estates and collections.

Hantman's Auctioneers & Appraisers
P.O. Box 59366
Potomac, MD 20859-9366
ph: 301-770-3720
fax: 301-770-4135
hantmans@digizen.net
http://www.hantmans.com/
Full service auction firm specializing in the sale of fine art and antiques with internationally advertised catalog auctions; certified appraiser for estate, insurance replacement, estate planning, family division.

Williams Auction & Appraisal Service
P.O. Box 381
Forest Hill, MD 21050
ph: 410-836-3031
fax: 410-836-1123
Wilri@erols.com

Richard Opfer Auctioneering, Inc.
1919 Greenspring Dr.
Lutherville Timonium, MD 21093-4113
ph: 410-252-5035
fax: 410-252-5863
info@opferauction.com
http://www.opferauction.com/
Specializes in auctioning toys, dolls, games, black memorabilia, and advertising items; weekly estate auctions including antiques, fine art; monthly eclectic collector sales feature a wide variety of collectibles.

Grant Harding Auctioneers
P.O. Box 215
Owings Mills, MD 21117-0215
ph: 410-833-8780
fax: 410-833-2794
jmcx84a@erols.com
Licensed and bonded appraiser in Maryland and Pennsylvania; on premises auctions a specialty.

Isennock Auctions & Appraisals, Inc.
4203 Norrisville Rd.
White Hall, MD 21161-9306
ph: 410-557-8052
fax: 410-692-6449
isennock@starix.net
http://www.isennockauction.com/

Alex Cooper Auctioneers, Inc.
908 York Rd.
Baltimore, MD 21204
ph: 410-828-4838 or 800-272-3145
fax: 202-364-0325
info@alexcooper.coom
http://www.alexcooper.com
Auctioneer of antiques, collectibles, fine arts, furniture, paintings, Oriental rugs and jewelry.

DeCaro Auction Sales, Inc.
8133 Elliott Rd.
Easton, MD 21601-7184
ph: 410-820-4000
fax: 410-820-4332
info@decaroauctions.com
http://www.decaroauctions.com

Trout Auctioneers Inc.
9801 Hansonville Rd.
Frederick, MD 21702
ph: 301-898-9899
fax: 301-898-3596

J.D. Compton Auctioneering
13833 Rockdale Rd.
Clear Spring, MD 21722
ph: 301-582-0727
fax: 301-582-6114
COMPTONAUC@aol.com

Auction Gallery, The
3140 W. Cary St.
Richmond, VA 23221
ph: 804-358-0500 or 804-359-0688
fax: 804-358-1280
knightm@mindspring.com
Auctions, appraisals, estate services; general interest and specialty collector events; targeted marketing; your site or ours; valuations for all purposes and functions.

Motley's Auctions, Inc.
4402 West Broad St.
Richmond, VA 23230
ph: 804-355-2100
fax: 804-359-6954
aon@motleys.com
http://www.thunderbid.com/motleys

Phoebus Auction Gallery
14-16 E. Mellen St.
Hampton, VA 23663
ph: 757-722-9210
fax: 757-723-2280
bwelch@phoebusauction.com
http://www.phoebusauction.com
Conducts auctions of antiques, collectibles, estates, furniture, decorative and fine arts, etc.

Ken Farmer Auctions & Estates
105A Harrison Street
Radford, VA 24141
ph: 540-639-0939
fax: 540-639-1759
kfarmera@aol.com
http://www.kenfarmer.com/

C & M Auctions, Inc.
1316 E. Washington Ave.
Vinton, VA 24179
ph: 540-343-4411 or 540-389-1969
fax: 540-343-5497
snoopy@roanoke.infi.net
Professional full auction service with weekly gallery auctions; specializing in on-site estate, furniture and merchandise auctions.

Riverbend Auction
P.O. Box 800
103 South Monroe St.
Alderson, WV 24910
ph: 304-445-2897 or 800-726-2897
fax: 304-445-2900
rivauction@newwave.net
http://www.riverbendauction.com

Historical Collectible Auctions
P.O. Box 975
Burlington, NC 27215
ph: 336-570-2803
fax: 336-570-2748
info@hcaauctions.com
http://www.hcaauctions.com/

Ausband Auction & Real Estate Co., Inc.
3744 Highway 213
Marshall, NC 28753
ph: 828-649-0400
sellatauction@yahoo.com
http://madison.main.nc.us/~hla/
Specializing in antiques, estates, collectibles, furniture and antique guns.

Robert S. Brunk Auction Services, Inc.
P.O. Box 2135
Asheville, NC 28802
ph: 828-254-6846
auction@rsbrunk.com
http://www.rsbrunk.com
Conducts sales of estates and fine antiques.

Skyland Antiques & Collectibles
30 Rosscraggon Rd.
Asheville, NC 28803
ph: 828-687-0407
fax: 828-687-0225
rapowell@brinet.com
Weekly auctions of antiques and household property.

Charlton Hall Galleries, Inc.
912 Gervais St.
Columbia, SC 29201
ph: 803-799-5678
fax: 803-733-1701
info@charltonhallauctions.com
http://www.charltonhallauctions.com
Full service auctioneers and appraisers, specializing in 17th, 18th, 19th century American, English, and

Continental furniture, paintings and decorative arts.

Gene Patrick Auction & Realty
1051 Cooley Bridge Rd.
Belton, SC 29627-9277
ph: 803-243-2394 or 803-338-5720
genepatric@aol.com
http://www.genepatrick.com/

Jim Depew Galleries
1860 Piedmont Rd.
Atlanta, GA 30324-4839
ph: 404-874-2286
fax: 404-874-2285
Weekly consignment and estate auctions of antiques and traditional furniture, accessories, porcelains, silver, crystal and jewelry.

Great American Auction, The
P.O. Box 4020
Saint Augustine, FL 32085-4020
fax: 904-826-1600
Lists sport and non-sport trading cards, cereal box prizes and premiums, bread end labels, etc. (fee charged.)

J & N Auctioneers
P.O. Box 656
Clarcona, FL 32710-0656
ph: 407-294-3980
fax: 407-294-7836
rosepast@bellsouth.net
http://members.tripod.com/~rosepast/

A Plus Auctions
3645 N US 1
Cocoa, FL 32926
ph: 407-639-4440
fax: 407-636-9809
info@aplusauctions.com
http://www.aplusauctions.com/
Florida-based auction center specializing in fine antique furniture, art glass, pottery, jewelry, estates, appraisals, liquidations, and bankruptcies.

Stampler Auctions
2801 Evans St.
Hollywood, FL 33020
ph: 800-330-BIDS or 954-921-8888
fax: 954-927-2939
Specializes in business liquidations.

Sloan's Auction Galleries
8861 NW 18th Terrace, Ste. 100
Miami, FL 33172
ph: 305-751-4770 or 800-660-4524
fax: 305-751-9171
sloans@sloansauction.com
http://www.sloansauction.com/

Albert Post Galleries
809 Lucerne Ave.
Lake Worth, FL 33460
ph: 561-582-4477
fax: 561-582-4476
A.PostGallery@juno.com
http://www.AlbertPostGallery.com
Associate Member, International Society of Appraisers; member National Auctioneers Association; auctioneer of fine arts, decorative arts, jewelry, collectibles; also offers restoration and conservation services.

Dawson's
44 Cocoanut Row
Palm Beach, FL 33480
ph: 561-835-6930
fax: 561-835-8464
dawson1@idt.net
http://www.dawsonsauction.com/
Specializes in the auction sales of antiques, art, silver, jewelry, toys and collectibles.

Burchard Galleries/Auctioneers
2528 30th Ave. N.
Saint Petersburg, FL 33713
ph: 727-821-11667 or 727-823-4156
fax: 727-821-1814
burchard@atlantic.net
http://www.burchardgalleries.com/

Kincaid Auction
3214 E. Hwy. 92
Lakeland, FL 33801
ph: 800-970-1977 or 941-555-1977
kincaid@kincaid.com
http://www.kincaid.com
On site auction liquidations of antique stores, restaurants, museums, estates, stores and manufacturers.

Brfeker - The Specialists
6731 Ashley Ct.
Sarasota, FL 34241-9696
ph: 941-925-0385
fax: 941-925-0487
auction@breker.com
http://www.breker.com/
German auction company specializes in the sale of old office equipment, scientific instruments and devices, photographica, and old technology including toasters, typewriters, sewing machines, tools telecommunications, etc.

Vintage Auctions
US Hwy 278
Blountsville, AL 35031
ph: 205-429-2457
fax: 205-429-2457
Holds regular bi-monthly auctions selling American & European antiques, glassware and collectibles; in-house facilities; computerized sales.

Kimball M. Sterling Inc.
125 W. Market St.
Johnson City, TN 37601
ph: 423-928-1471
fax: 423-928-8697
kimsold@tricon.net
http://sterlingsold.com

Taylor Auction & Realty, Inc.
P.O. Box 357
15229 Hwy. 51 N.
Grenada, MS 38901
ph: 601-226-2080
fax: 601-226-2080
tauction@network-one.com
http://www.taylorauction.com/

Hays & Associates, Inc.
120 South Spring St.
Louisville, KY 40206-1953
ph: 502-584-4297
fax: 502-585-5896
annhays@haysauction.com
http://www.haysautcion.com/
Conducts auction sales of toys, dolls, furniture, ceramics, antique clocks, music boxes, and silver

Garth's Auction, Inc.
2690 Stratford Rd.
P.O. Box 369
Delaware, OH 43015
ph: 614-362-4771 or 614-369-5085
fax: 614-363-0164
info@garths.com
http://www.garths.com
Specializing in Early American, English, Continental, Oriental antiques and accessories; paintings, fine art, folk art, American Indian, military, jewelry, toys, dolls, advertising, collectibles.

Apple Tree Auction Center
1616 West Church St.
Newark, OH 43055
ph: 740-344-4282 or 740-344-4603
fax: 740-366-3673
info@appletreeauction.com
http://www.appletreeauction.com/
Conducts large, quality antique auctions containing over 3,000 items every six weeks.

DeFina Auctions
1591 State Route 45
Austinburg, OH 44010
ph: 440-275-6674
fax: 440-275-2028
definaauction@ncweb.com
http://www.definaauctions.com

Wolf's Auctioneers
1239 West 6th St.
Cleveland, OH 44113
ph: 216-575-9653 or 800-526-1991
fax: 216-621-8011
auction@ewolfs.com
http://www.ewolfs.com/

Auctions by Maggie
2191 Cliff Rd.
North Bend, OH 45052
ph: 513-941-9519 or 800-745-3557
fax: 513-941-9519
aucmag@webtv.net
http://www.netis.com/auctions/maggie/

Lawson Auction Service
923 Fourth St.
Columbus, IN 47265
ph: 812-372-2571 or 800-283-4866
dlawson@lawson-acution.com
http://www.lawson-auction.com
Family-owned auction company serving southern Indiana with primary experience in real estate auctions, estate settlement, antiques, business liquidations, and farm equipment.

Curran Miller Auction & Realty, Inc.
4424 Vogel Road, Ste. 400
Evansville, IN 47715
ph: 800-264-0601 or 812-474-6100
fax: 812-474-6110
auctionx@evansville.net
http://www.cmillerauctions.com/
One of the Midwest's premier auction companies; specializes in the auction sale of antiques and collectibles.

DuMouchelle Art Galleries Co.
409 East Jefferson Ave.
Detroit, MI 48226
ph: 313-963-6255
fax: 313-963-8199
info@dumouchelles.com
http://www.dumouchelles.com/
A fine arts auction house; rugs, paintings, jewelry, porcelain, silver, art glass, toys, dolls, furniture, books, sculpture, etc.

Joseph DuMouchelle Fine & Estate Jewelry Auctions
5 Kercheval
Grosse Pointe Farms, MI 48236
ph: 313-884-4800 or 800-475-4367
fax: 313-884-7662
joelindy@earthlink.net
Specializes in the sale of fine and estate jewelry and small objects of art; large diamonds and colored stones, paintings, Oriental rugs, silver, antique furniture and sculpture, Russian objects of art.

Pro Auction Company
707 230th Street
Algona, IA 50511
ph: 515-295-7819
fax: 515-295-7742
proauct@ncn.net
http://www.proauctionusa.com
A complete auction and appraisal service serving north central Iowa.

Jackson's Auctioneers & Appraisers
2229 Lincoln St.
Cedar Falls, IA 50613
ph: 319-277-2256
fax: 319-277-1252
jacksons@jacksonsauction.com
http://www.jacksonsauction.com
Conducts auction sales of fine arts, furniture, art pottery, art glass, porcelain, toys, rugs, etc.

Tabaugh Auctions
1702 8th Ave.
Belle Plaine, IA 52208
ph: 319-444-2413 or 800-368-1292
Tubaugh_Auctions@belleplaineiowa.com
http://www.belleplaineiowa.com/tubaugh/

Milwaukee Auction Galleries
1919 N. Summit Ave
Milwaukee, WI 53202
ph: 414-271-1105

Schrager Auction Galleries, Ltd.
P.O. Box 10390
2915 North Sherman Blvd.
Milwaukee, WI 53210
ph: 414-873-3738
fax: 414-873-5229

Krueger Auctions
P.O. Box 275
Iola, WI 54945-0275
ph: 715-445-3845
fax: 715-445-4100
Specializing in the mail-bid auction of tokens, advertising, brewery items, Western Americana, postcards, World's Fair & Expo., autographs, sports, coins & currency, pinbacks, military memorabilia, automotive, Disneyana, etc.

Fischer Auction Company
238 Haywire Ave.
P.O. Box 667
Long Lake, SD 57457-0667
ph: 800-888-1766 or 605-577-6600
fax: 605-577-6500
kwag@nvc.net
http://www.fischerauction.com
Over 40 years in the auction and real estate businesses; auctions medical equipment, antiques, commercial and farm land; complete action service from setup to close.

Curt D. Johnson Auction Company
RR1 Box 135
Grand Forks, ND 58201
ph: 701-746-1378
fax: 701-746-1379
merfeld@grandforks.means.net
http://www.curtdjohnson.com
Over 29 years of auction experience.

Butterfield & Dunning
755 Church Rd.
Elgin, IL 60123
ph: 847-741-3483
fax: 847-741-3589
info@butterfields.com
http://www.butterfields.com
Premier mid-American auction firm selling antiques, fine art, jewelry, American Indian art, and real estate.

Hanzel Galleries
1120 South Michigan Ave.
Chicago, IL 60605-2301
ph: 312-922-6247
fax: 312-922-6792

Susanin's Auction
228 Merchandise Mart
Chicago, IL 60654
ph: 888-787-2646 or 312-832-9800
fax: 312-832-9311
info@susanins.com
http://www.susanins.com/

Joy Luke Auction Gallery
300 E. Grove St.
Bloomington, IL 61701-5232
ph: 309-828-5533
fax: 309-829-2266
robert@joyluke.com
http://www.joyluke.com/
Conducts regular auctions in fine and decorative arts.

Phillips-Selkirk
7447 Forsyth Blvd.
Saint Louis, MO 63105
ph: 314-726-5515 or 800-728-8002
fax: 314-726-9908
selkirk@primary.net
http://www.selkirks.com/

Robert Merry Auction Company
5501 Milburn Rd.
Saint Louis, MO 63129-3514
ph: 314-487-3992

Simmons & Company Auctioneers
40706 E. 144th St.
Richmond, MO 64085
ph: 816-776-2936 or 800-646-2936
fax: 816-470-5016
simmons_auction@raycounty.com
http://www.raycounty.com/simmons/
Conducts specialty and general line antiques and collectibles auctions.

Simmons & Company Auctioneers
40706 E. 144th St.
Richmond, MO 64085
ph: 816-776-2936 or 800-646-2936
fax: 816-470-5016
simmons_auction@raycounty.com
http://www.raycounty.com/simmons/

Manion's Auction House
P.O. Box 12214
Kansas City, KS 66112-0214
ph: 913-299-6692
fax: 913-299-6792
collecting@manions.com
http://www.manions.com
A mail-bid auction company specializing in militaria from all countries, Scouting memorabilia, toys, antique advertising, and all fine collectibles.

Woody Auction Company
P.O. Box 618
317 S. Forrest St.
Douglass, KS 67039
ph: 316-746-2694
fax: 316-746-2145

Neal Auction Co.
4038 Magazine St.
New Orleans, LA 70115
ph: 504-899-5329 or 800-467-5329
fax: 504-897-3808
nauction@nealauction.com
http://www.nealauction.com
Specializing in antiques and fine art, especially Southern Art, American 19th century furniture, French furniture, and decorative objects.

New Orleans Auction Galleries, Inc.
801 Magazine St.
New Orleans, LA 70130
ph: 504-566-1849 or 800-467-5329
fax: 504-566-1861
info@neworleansauction.com
http://www.neworleansauction.com/

Kelly Auction Service
3015 Alice Dr.
Batesville, AR 72501
ph: 870-698-0011
auction@cei.net
http://www.freeyellow.com/members3/pauldkelly/

2j Auction
3325 Eastman Dr.
Oklahoma City, OK 73112
ph: 405-840-2341
fax: 405-840-1057
jan@2jweb.com
http://www.2jweb.com
Online internet auction that is always open; current listings may include antiques, collectibles, vintage and antique jewelry, stamps, coins, toys, dolls, buttons, vintage clothing, pottery, art, advertising collectibles, etc.

C & C The Auction Company
4801 MacKelman Dr.
Oklahoma City, OK 73135-4135
ph: 405-670-1705
Specializing in the auction sale of antiques and collectibles.

Frederick Auction Service
Rt 1, Box 48
S Coffeyville, OK 74072
ph: 918-255-6738
lfrederick@terraworld.net
http://www.gunslinger.com/auction.html
Specializing in the auction sale of antiques and estates in SE Kansas and NE Oklahoma.

HCR 68 Box 745
Vian, OK 74962-9128
ph: 918-489-5164
waskow@midwestlink.net
http://www.antiqnet.com/diversified/
Conducts specialty auctions; watches, clocks, Russian items, bronzes.

Forres Meadows Auctioneers
P.O. Box 1287
Boerne, TX 78006-1287
ph: 830-816-3403
fax: 830-816-2311
forres@texas.net
http://forres.home.texas.net
Estate and antique auction; professional auctioneer serving Texas and the Hill COuntry since 1989.

America West Archives
P.O. Box 100
Cedar City, UT 84721-0100
ph: 435-586-9497 or 435-586-7323
awa@netutah.com
http://www.americawestarchives.com/
Auction catalogs offer rare & historical documents, letters, photographs, autographs, paper Americana, maps; specializes on Western U.S., however Eastern material also accepted.

Auktionshaus Michael Zeller
Bindergasse 7
Lindau (Bodensee), 8990
Germany
Fine art auctioneers.

Butterfield & Butterfield
7601 Sunset Blvd.
Los Angeles, CA 90046-2714
ph: 323-850-7500
fax: 323-850-5843
info@butterfields.com
http://www.butterfields.com/

Abamex Auction Co.
10050 Via de la Amistad #2452
San Ysidro, CA 92173
ph: 800-841-3364 or 619-279-2846
fax: 619-576-9577
auctions@abamex.com
http://www.abamex.com
Real estate auctions in Southern CA; also business asset auctions, art and collectibles auctions.

Mail Bid Auction
P.O. Box 414
Yucca Valley, CA 92286-0414
fax: 619-365-9668
Conducts mail-bid auctions of collectibles: books, coins, medals, Disney, theater, valentines, art, railroad, medical/dental, etc.; Continental U.S. only.

Bendis Companies, Inc.
3410 La Sierra Ave., Ste. F 123
Riverside, CA 92503
ph: 909-780-4436 or 909-780-3418
fax: 909-780-7384
info@bendisauctions.com
http://www.bendisauctions.com
Auctioneer and appraiser; general merchandise, vehicles, machinery, electronics, and more.

Kozma Appraisal & Auction Service, Inc.
25221 Wagner Way
Hemet, CA 92544-1724
ph: 888-650-6444 or 909-927-0405
fax: 909-927-6806
kaas@pe.net
http://www.jkozma.com
A full service auction and appraisal company for antiques, collectibles and fine arts, both American and European.

Butterfield & Butterfield
220 San Bruno Ave.
San Francisco, CA 94103-5018
ph: 415-861-7500
fax: 415-861-8951
info@butterfields.com
http://www.butterfields.com/
Specialties include posters, toys, decorative arts, furniture, photography, etc.; the largest full service auction in the west.

A & A Auction
925a 41St Ave.
Santa Cruz, CA 95062
ph: 831-476-1713
fax: 831-476-1835
webmaster@aaauctions.com
http://www.aaauctions.com
Preview and place bids and/or consign items in upcoming auctions at the Gallery in Santa Cruz.

Auction Center, The
2770B South Bascom Ave.
San Jose, CA 95150
ph: 408-292-6800 or 408-930-1502
fax: 408-292-1792
sales@vendetti.com
http://www.vendetti.com
Full service auction company liquidating numerous estates each year.

Markus & Markus Auctioneers & Appraisers
P.O. Box 788
Banks, OR 97106
ph: 503-681-0806 or 888-411-8999
fax: 503-693-9159
markus@jps.net
http://www.markusandmarkus.com
Specializes in the auction sale of antiques and collectibles; call for free consultation.

Waverly's
8196 SW Durham Road
Portland, OR 97224
ph: 503-603-0070
fax: 503-603-0071
info@waverlys.com
http://www.waverlys.com

Kunsthaus am Museum, Carola Van Ham
Carola Van Ham
Drusugasse 1-5
Cologne, D-50667
Germany
ph: 0221 925862-0
fax: 0221 925862-4
info@Carola-van-Ham.com
http://www.Carola-van-Ham.com
Specializes in the auctions sales of Old master and 19th century paintings, modern and contemporary art, objets d'Art, furniture, rugs, carpets, bronzes, sculptures, Art Nouveau, jewelry.

Waddington's
11 Bathurst Street
Toronto, Ontario M5V 2R1
Canada
ph: 416-504-9100
fax: 416-504-0033
info@waddingtonsauctions.com
http://www.waddingtonsauctions.com
Canada's oldest and largest auction house specializing in decorative arts, jewelry, antique furniture, Inuit and native Canadian arts, European and Canadian arts, books, militaria, Orientalia, toys, ceramics, etc.

Bonhams
Montepelier Street
London, SW7 1HH
U.K.
ph: 0171 393 3900
fax: 0171 393 3906
info@bonhams.com
http://www.bonhams.com

Christie's South Kensington, Ltd.
85 Old Brompton Rd.
London, SW7 3LD
U.K.
ph: 0171 581 7611 or 0171 321 3279
fax: 0171 321 3321
mpritchard@christies.com
http://www.cskart.com/
Regular sales of furniture, paintings, silver, jewelry, ceramics, textiles, books and collectibles; free verbal valuations weekdays.

Maynards Auctioneers
415 West 2nd Ave.
Vancouver, British Columbia V5Y 1E3
Canada
ph: 604-876-6787 or 604-531-0166
fax: 604-876-2678
Erik@Maynards.com
http://www.maynards.com
Quarterly auctions of Canadian, American & Western European fine art, antiques, silver, jewellery, china, glass, carpets and specialty collectables; Accredited Member of International Society of Appraisers.

Phillips Auction Gallery
101 New Bond St.
London, W1Y 0AS
U.K.
fax: 44 171 333 0510
http://www.phillips-auctions.com/uk/

INTERNET AUCTIONS

Amazon.com Auctions
info@amazon.com
http://auctions.amazon.com/

Antique Country
webmaster@antiquecountry.com
http://www.antiquecountry.com
An online auction site specializing in antiques & collectibles; offers users the ability to buy and sell their favorite antiques and collectibles online.

Auction Port Live Online Auctions
28 S. Pine St.
Dover, NH 03820
ph: 603-740-4938
fax: 603-740-4938
bid@auctionport.com
http://www.auctionport.com/
By your own auctioneer; view the live online auction; bid on antiques, collectibles, computers and more; 24 hour nonstop; free classifieds.

Auction Universe
ph: 203-741-5110
info@auctionuniverse.com
http://www.auctionuniverse.com

AuctionInc
2 Railroad Ave., Ste. 203
Glyndon, MD 21071
ph: 410-581-1110
fax: 410-363-8698
auctioneer@auctioninc.com
http://ai.wwcd.com/
An Internet on-line REAL-TIME customer to customer auction service; no member fees, no buyers fees; free seller startup allowance of $25 and a monthly gift into your personal account.

Beckett Interactive
15850 Dallas Parkway
Dallas, TX 75248
ph: 972-991-6657 or 800-840-3137
fax: 972-991-1574
auction@beckett.com
http://www.beckettxchange.com

Biddington's Inc.
240 Mountainside Rd.
Mendham, NJ 07945
ph: 212-838-3572 or 202-547-4520
webmaster@biddingtons.com
http://www.biddingtons.com
Upmarket, online auction and information site for buyers and sellers of art, antiques and fine collectibles.

BidFind
P.O. Box 8445
Saddle Brook, NJ 07663
ph: 973-881-9336
vision@2020.vsn.net
http://www.bidfind.com
Thousands of items indexed daily; use this site to search for online items from popular auction sites on the Internet.

Boxlot Online Auction
webmaster@boxlot.com
http://www.boxlot.com/
Comprehensive on-line collectibles auction service.

CityAuction, Inc.
153 Kearney, Ste. 207
San Francisco, CA 94118
ph: 415-951-0650
nikki@cityauction.com
http://www.cityauction.com
Internet online auction for all types of personal property including collectibles.

Classifieds2000, a Division of Excite
suggestions@classifieds2000.com
http://www.classifieds2000.com/
Internet classified ad categories include vehicles, general merchandise, antiques and collectibles; also Hot Auctions for art, antiques, Beanie Babies, books and magazines, coins and stamps, comic books, porcelain, glass, etc.

Collectit.net Auctions
info@collectit.net
http://www.collectit.net/osauction.shtml
Brought to you by Krause Publications, one of the world's largest hobby publishers.

coolcollectibles.net
P.O. Box 117094
Burlingame, CA 94011
ph: 650-635-1570
fax: 650-635-1580
rte66@ix.netcom.com
http://www.coolcollectibles.net
A leading edge on line auction service.

DealerNet, Inc.
P.O. Box 2952
Woburn, MA 01888-1752
ph: 781-942-4626 or 781-944-6514
fax: 781-942-2626
collectorweb@collectorweb.com
http://www.collectorweb.com
Internet web based services for collectors & dealers: page development & maintenance, management of monthly sales/auctions, database marketing, qualified buyers.

Eauctionexpress
17-21 West Front Street
Keyport, NJ 07735
ph: 732-203-1001
fax: 732-203-1004
info@keyportantiquemarket.com
http://www.keyportantiquemarket.com
Located in the largest indoor antique market in New Jersey; handles all aspects of auctioning items for you worldwide for $10 per item; also collects the money and ships.

eBay, Inc.
2005 Hamilton Ave., Ste. 350
San Jose, CA 95125
ph: 408-369-4839
staff@ebay.com
http://www.ebay.com
Online auction of antiques & collectibles and lots more.

eHammer
315 Peck Street
New Haven, CT 06513
ph: 203-426-4469 or 203-785-0441
info@ehammer.com
http://www.ehammer.com
Online antiques & collectibles auction.

Global Auction Online
auctioneer@global-auction.com
http://www.global-auction.com/

Internet Auction List
USAWeb@syspac.com
http://www.internetauctionlist.com
Largest list of online auction companies on the internet; lists hundreds of auctions, online and live, in this country and internationally; offers dozens of search categories and presents information in a very readable fashion.

L.A.O. Live Auction Online
Kelowna, British Columbia V1W 1R8
Canada
ph: 250-979-5101
markos01@home.com
http://www.liveauctiononline.com
Buy and sell collectible toys, timepieces, jewelry, comics, animation, kitchen collectibles, and much more through this online auction.

LiveBid.com
520 Pike Street., Ste. 1005
Seattle, WA 98101
ph: 206-440-5469
fax: 206-860-9195
info@livebid.com
http://www.LiveBid.com/
LiveBid.com is a direct connection to the auction floor; hear and follow the auctioneer with real-time internet interface.

NetCollect.com
1055 Ridgecrest Drive
Goodlettsville, TN 37072
ph: 615-859-5236
fax: 615-859-5238
Robwork@gono.com
http://www.netcollect.com
Internet member-based online auction and trade site.

Popula Company
500 North Orlando Ave.
Los Angeles, CA 90048
ph: 323-646-8289 or 213-445-7691
maria@popula.com
http://www.popula.com
On-line antique and collectible auctions.

Sothebys.com
1334 York Ave.
New York, NY 10021
ph: 212-606-7000
fax: 212-606-7107
http://www.sothebys.com
An on-line auction service.

Up4Sale Online Auctions
feedback@up4sale.com
http://www.up4sale.com/
Offers over 30,000 items for sale; you can also start you own auction for free.

Virtual Nostalgia Auction Company
1023 East 5th Ave.
Lancaster, OH 43130
ph: 740-654-6179 or 740-681-6151
webmaster@vnostalgia.com
http://www.vnostalgia.com
Internet auction service for memorabilia and nostalgia items such as gas station, soda, general store, barbershop, automobilia.

World-Wide Collectors Digest
2 Railroad Ave., Ste. 203
Glyndon, MD 21071
ph: 410-581-1110
fax: 410-363-8698
prod@wwcd.com
http://www.wwcd.com/

Here are some tips when contacting someone listed in this book:

■ When requesting information about a particular item, include a description (material, dimensions, maker's mark, model number, etc.) and a photo, sketch, or photocopy of the item in question.

■ Always ask if there are charges for samples or for the services requested.

■ When writing, please be sure to include a Large (#10 business size) Self-Addressed and Stamped Envelope (LSASE) if requesting a reply or the return of photographs.

■ Never call collect unless otherwise directed. When calling, be considerate of time zone differences and always ask if the party you are calling has time to talk. When leaving an answering machine message, always instruct the party to call you back collect.

APPENDIX C

General Interest Periodicals

Listed in alphabetical order

Each of the following general interest periodicals covers a wide range of subjects within the fields of antiques, collectibles, and art. Periodicals that focus on specific subjects are listed under those categories within the General Listings section of this Directory. Don't forget collector clubs when looking for periodicals. Most clubs publish excellent periodicals focusing on their areas of specialization.

19th Century Magazine
Victorian Society in America, The
Patricia Sproehnle
219 South 6th St.
Philadelphia, PA 19106-3719
ph: 215-627-4252 or 215-627-4253
fax: 215-627-7221
vicsoc@libertynet.org
http://www.libertynet.org/vicsoc/
Membership benefits include quarterly newsletter, semi-annual magazine, symposia on wide array of 19th century subjects, annual meeting; fostering appreciation in Victorian life through preservation and educational efforts; non-profit.

America's Most Wanted To Buy
Scott Meand
P.O. Box 17107
Little Rock, AR 72222
ph: 501-660-4030 or 800-994-9268
fax: 501-614-8017
amwc1@aol.com
http://www.mostwantedtobuy.com
Bi-monthly glossy cover magazine devoted entirely to specialty collector and dealer wanted-to-buy 1/8th page ads.

American Antique Collector
P.O. Box 454
Murrysville, PA 15668
ph: 724-733-3968
fax: 724-733-3968

American Antiquities Journal
Art Wilson
126 E. High St.
Springfield, OH 45502
ph: 937-322-6281 or 800-557-6281
fax: 937-322-0294
mail@americanantiquities.com
http://www.americanantiquities.com/journal.html
A monthly publication for the antiques enthusiast featuring articles, an events calendar or antiques shows and events.

American Country Collectibles
GCR Publishing Group, Inc.
Florian McCain, Ed.
1700 Broadway
New York, NY 10019-5905
ph: 212-541-7100 or 800-955-3870
fax: 212-245-1241
Published four times a year; focuses on collecting and decorating with collectibles.

American History Illustrated
Cowles Magazines, Inc.
741 Miller Dr. SE, Ste. D2
Harrisburg, PA 20175
ph: 717-540-6617 or 800-829-3340
fax: 717-540-6706
brentd@cowles.com
http://www.cowles.com/maglist.html
Feature articles on all aspects of American history; coverage of military, social, and political events and the forces that have shaped American history; published bi-monthly.

Antique & Collectables
Regional Antique Publications
Sandra Hood, Pub.
P.O. Box 12589
500 Fesler St., Ste. 201
El Cajon, CA 92022
ph: 619-593-2925 or 619-593-2927
fax: 619-447-7187
antiqunews@aol.com
http://www.collect.com/antiqueandcollectables
The largest monthly newspaper in Southern California covering the antiques & collectibles industry with focus sections on Nevada and Arizona; 72+ pages; events and show section, feature articles; columns, ads.

Antique & Collectible News
Lonnie J. Hinton
P.O. Box 529
Anna, IL 62906-0529
ph: 618-833-2158 or 800-833-2699
fax: 618-833-5813
reppert@midwest.net
A regional monthly with articles about antiques, collectors, quilts, history, crafts, craftsmen, special events, collector clubs and other topics of interest to collectors in IL, MO, KY IN MS and TN.

Antique Almanac, The
P.O. Box 1613
Bowie, TX 76230
ph: 940-872-6186 or 800-972-7730
fax: 940-872-3559
http://ww2.morgan.net/antique/
A local antiques newspaper serving the central Texas region: ads, calendar of events, columns.

Antique Collecting
Antique Collectors' Club, Ltd.
91 Market Street Industrial Park
Wappingers Falls, NY 12590
ph: 800-252-5231 or 914-297-1312
fax: 914-297-0068
webmaster@antiquecc.com
http://www.artbookservices.com/articles/antcol.html
A sophisticated English magazine of the Antique Collectors' Club, the parent organization for dozens of regional antiques clubs within the U.K.

Antique Collector & Auction Guide, The
Farm & Dairy Publishers
Susan Hogan, Ed.
185 E. State St.
Salem, OH 44460-2842
ph: 330-337-3419 or 330-337-3164
fax: 330-337-9550
A weekly insert to "Farm and Dairy" newspaper; serving the antiques and collectibles trade; ads, auctions, articles, etc.

Antique Dealer & Collectors Guide, The
Philip Bartlam, Pub.
P.O. Box 805
Greenwich
London, SE10 8TD
U.K.
ph: +44 (0)181 861 0690
fax: +44 (0)181 427 3454
http://www.antiques-on-line.com/publications/collectorsguide/index.html
An English glossy international monthly magazine for dealers and collectors: articles, ads, book reviews, auction reports, etc.

Antique Dealer & Collectors' Guide
Statuscourt Ltd.
P.O. Box 805
Greenwich, London SE10 8TD
U.K.
ph: (0) 181 691 4820
fax: (0) 181 691 2489
antiquesdealercollectorsguide@ukbusiness.com
http://www.ukbusiness.com/antiquedealercollectorsguide
Monthly English publication; the very latest on auctions, antiques fairs, exhibitions, and other events; informative articles on furniture, ceramics, silver, pictures, and collectibles; over 1200 fair and auction dates each issue.

Antique Finder Magazine, The
P.O. Box 16433
Panama City, FL 32406-6433
ph: 850-236-0543
fax: 850-914-9007

Antique Gazette
Regional Antique Publications
Catherine A. Turner, Editor
6949 Charlotte Pike, Ste. 106
Nashville, TN 37209-4200
ph: 615-352-0941
fax: 615-352-0941
Complete monthly antiques guide; shop/mall locator, show calendar, classifieds, articles; nationwide distribution; featuring the exclusive "Antiques Locator" - hundreds of quality antiques listed for sale with prices.

Antique Journal
Regional Antique Publications
Jeff Hill
1684 Decoto Rd., Ste. 166
Union City, CA 94587
ph: 800-791-8592
fax: 510-523-5262
AntiqueJrl@aol.com
http://www.antiqueinfo.com/journal/antique_journal.htm
The largest antique monthly serving California, Nevada, Southern Oregon and Nevada; complete listings of shows, shops and auctions; two editions - one for CA & NV, and one for the Northwest.

Antique Press, The
Robert Fiallo, Editor
12403 N. Florida Ave.
Tampa, FL 33612
ph: 813-935-7577
Florida's newspaper of antiques and collectibles; articles, maps, calendars, photos, book reviews, advertisements, etc. Published 18 times per year.

Antique Review
Regional Antique Publications
Nancy Bletner, Asst. Ed.
P.O. Box 538
Columbus, OH 43085-0538
ph: 614-885-9757 or 800-992-9757
fax: 614-885-9762
editor@antiquereviewohio.com
http://www.antiquereviewohio.com
A monthly newspaper serving the dealers and collectors of Mid-America: articles, shows, auctions, ads, etc.

Antique Shoppe, The
Bruce Causey
P.O. Box 2175
Keystone Heights, FL 32656-2175
ph: 352-475-5326 or 352-475-1679
fax: 352-475-5326
antshoppe@aol.com
Florida's monthly antiques newspaper; interesting and entertaining articles about antiques and collectibles, historical landmarks and places of interest, including maps to Florida's best antique shops; serves FL and parts of GA.

Antique Showcase
Trajan Publishing Corp.
Paul Fiocca
103 Lakeshore Rd., Ste. 202
St. Catharines, Ontario L2N 2T6
Canada
ph: 905-646-7744
fax: 905-646-0995
bret@trajan.com
http://www.vaxxine.com/trajan/
National magazine with diverse articles, show and auction reports, museum exhibits, book reviews, upcoming trends, etc.; also contains lots of display and classified ads for buyers of Canadian, US and European antiques; 9 times per year.

Antique Trader Weekly, The
Antique Trader Publications, Inc.
P.O. Box 1050
Dubuque, IA 52004-1050
ph: 800-334-7165 or 800-482-4155
fax: 800-531-0880
khusfloen@mwci.net
http://www.collect.com/antiquetrader
A weekly newspaper with ads, articles and news on the antiques and collectibles hobby; buy, sell, trade smarter; over 2,000 ads in every issue; comprehensive national show and auction calendars; special feature stories.

Antique Traveler, The
Zorah Publications, Inc.
Harold E. Johnson
P.O. Box 656
Mineola, TX 75773
ph: 800-446-3588 or 903-569-2487
fax: 903-569-9080
antique@lakecountry.net
http://www.antiquetraveler.com/
Serving the American Southwest antiques trade; ads, dealer directory, articles, show and auction schedules nation wide.

Antique Traveller
PCCS Publishing
Penelope Callender, Ed.
P.O. Box 5216
Herndon, VA 20172-1974
ph: 703-437-4971
fax: 703-707-0458
Bi-monthly newsprint magazine covering the MD, DC, VA area; articles of area interest including historic sites, antiques shows, dealer ads, etc.

Antiques & Art Independent
Tony Keniston
P.O. Box 1945
Comely Bank, Edinburgh EH4 1AB
U.K.
ph: 07000 765 263 or 800-976-5133 ex 173
antiquesnews@hotmail.com
http://www.antiques-uk.co.uk/magazine/aaiind.htm
Widest circulating publication covering the antiques trade in Britain.

Antiques & Auction News
Dennis M. Sater, Ed.
P.O. Box 500
Mount Joy, PA 17552-0500
ph: 717-492-2540 or 800-800-2833
fax: 717-653-6165
A weekly newspaper featuring antiques, collectibles, auctions, sales, shows and exhibits.

Antiques & Collectibles Shopper, The
Regina Guminik
7190 Brookridge
West Bloomfield, MI 48322
ph: 800-995-4864 or 248-865-0498
fax: 248-865-8798
grmtchees@aol.com
13 issues per year specializing in the Midwestern states of MI, PA, OH, IN, IL, IA, WI; 15,000 copies distributed by subscription and free bundles.

Antiques & Collecting Magazine
Lightner Publishing Corp.
Dale K. Graham, Pub.
1006 S. Michigan Ave.
Chicago, IL 60605-9840
ph: 312-939-4767
fax: 312-939-0053
lightnerpb@aol.com
Informative articles on antiques & collectors items; up-to-the-minute news in the field, auction results, ads, book reviews; published monthly; published since 1931; authoritative and informative articles on antiques and collectibles.

Antiques & The Arts Weekly (The Newtown Bee)
Bee Publishing Co.
R. Scudder Smith
5 Church Hill Rd.
P.O. Box 5503
Newtown, CT 06470-9987
ph: 203-426-3141 or 203-426-8036
fax: 203-426-1394
antiques@thebee.com
http://www.thebee.com/aweb/aa.htm
Leading weekly newspaper for auction advertising, show coverage, and other events in the world of antiques.

Antiques Info Magazine
Antiques Information Services Ltd.
P.O. Box 93
Broadstairs, Kent CT10 3YR
U.K.
ph: 01843 862069
fax: 01843 862014
john.ainsley@antiques-info.co.uk
http://www.antiques-info.co.uk/
Search for fairs and auctions, market surveys and forecasts, fair and auction news and prices, informational and advisory pages.

Antiques Magazine
H.P. Publishing
2 Hampton Court Rd.
Harborne, Birmingham B17 9AE
U.K.
ph: (01210) 681 8003 or (01210) 681 8000
fax: (01210) 681 8005
info@antiquesbulletin.com
A weekly English publication for dealers and collectors.

Antiques Trade Gazette
17 Whitcomb St.
London, WC2H 7PL
U.K.
ph: +44 (0) 171 930 9955
fax: +44 (0) 171 839 5297
info@atg-online.com
http://www.atg-online.com
A substantial weekly newspaper with articles, calendar of shows and sales, ads, etc. focusing on the English market; call advertising agent in New York at 212-764-8555.

Antiques West
Monka Publishing, Inc.
Editor
3450 Sacramento St., Ste. 618
San Francisco, CA 94118
ph: 415-221-4645
Upscale monthly newspaper serving the Western U.S. antiques & early fine arts markets; news and information on auctions, shows and events; substantive articles about antiques and art.

Antiques!
Antiques! Communications
Marni Andrews, Pub./Ed.
Box 1860
Ste 707, 27 Queen St. East
Toronto, Ontario M5C 2M6
Canada
ph: 416-944-3880
fax: 416-944-3872
marnia@msn.com
Glossy magazine from Canada.

AntiqueWeek - Central Edition
Mayhill Publications, Inc.
Tom Hoepf, Ed.
P.O. Box 90
Knightstown, IN 46148
ph: 765-345-5133 or 800-876-5133
fax: 800-695-8153
antiquewk@aol.com
http://www.antiqueweek.com
A leading antiques, auctions and collectors' newspaper published weekly every Monday in two regional editions, Eastern and Central.

AntiqueWeek - Eastern Edition
Mayhill Publications, Inc.
Connie Swaim, Ed.
P.O. Box 90
Knightstown, IN 46148
ph: 765-345-5133 or 800-876-5133
fax: 800-695-8153
antiquewk@aol.com
http://www.antiqueweek.com
A leading antiques, auctions and collectors' newspaper published weekly every Monday in two regional editions, Eastern and Central.

Antiquing Vermont & New England
P.O. Box 141
Essex Junction, VT 05453
ph: 802-872-5700 or 800-729-0767
fax: 802-872-5720
http://www.collectoronline.com/avtne/
A guide for buying and selling antiques in New England.

Apollo Magazine
1 Castle Lane
London, SW1E 6DR
U.K.
ph: 0171-233 6640
fax: 0171-233-6307
editorial@apollomag.com
http://www.apollomagazine.com/
The international magazine of art and antiques; an English monthly publication with detailed articles and glossy color photos; for U.S. postal subscriptions write P.O. Box 47, North Hollywood, CA 91603-0047.

Arizona Antique News
Ron Smisek, Ed.
P.O. Box 26536
Phoenix, AZ 85068
ph: 602-943-9137
A monthly publication designed for collectors and dealers; syndicated writers offer regional perspectives of the antiques hobby.

Arkansas Antiques
P.O. Box 575
Dardanelle, AR 72834
ph: 501-229-2493
fax: 501-229-2493
arktique@yell.com
Ads, calendar of events for the antique enthusiast in Arkansas.

Art & Antiques
2100 Powers Ferry Rd.
Atlanta, GA 30339
ph: 770-955-5656 or 800-274-7594
art&antiques@billian.com
http://www.billian.com/artantiques/
Glossy magazine focusing on the fine and decorative arts and in antiques: colorful ads, articles, auction reports, etc.

Auction Action News
Bob & Jeni Olsze
1404 1/2 East Greenbay St.
Shawano, WI 54166-2258
ph: 715-524-3076
fax: 800-580-4568
auction@auctionactionnews.com
http://www.auctionactionnews.com/
A weekly newspaper focusing on auction ads and informative articles with lots of photos and price results for antiques and collectibles (the rare as well as those commonly found items) at auctions in the WI, MI, IL, MN and IA area.

Auction Times
Regional Antique Publications
Jayne Skeff
1684 Decoto Rd., Ste. 166
Union City, CA 94587
ph: 800-791-8592
fax: 510-523-5262
AntiqueJrl@aol.com
http://www.antiqueinfo.com/journal/antique_journal.htm

Boulay 300, The
64 Sloane Street
London, SW1X 9SH
U.K.
ph: +44 171 245 6826
fax: +44 171 235 0577
boulay@boulay.co.uk
http://www.dir-dd.com/boulay300.html/
The definitive guide to the 300 most important lots at auction each month; latest trends, issues and late-breaking news in the world of art, antiques and collectibles.

Brimfield Antique Guide, The
Brimfield Antique Show Website
P.O. Box 442
Brimfield, MA 01010
ph: 413-245-9329
brimfieldp@aol.com
http://www.brimfieldshow.com/brimfield-publications.htm
Published 3 times per year; highlights any changes, news releases or other noteworthy information, etc. pertaining to the Brimfield Antique and Collectible shows.

Carolina Antique News
Phil Burrows, Pub.
P.O. Box 241114
Charlotte, NC 28224
publishr@concentric.net
http://www.antiquestoday.com/

Carter's Home, Antiques & Collectables
Carter's Promotions Pty. Ltd.
Locked Bag 3
Terrey Hills, New South Wales 2084
Australia
ph: (02) 9450 0011
fax: (02) 9450 2532

Collect It!
Collect it Ltd.
P.O. Box 3658
Bracknell, Berkshire RG12 1GE
U.K.
ph: +44 1344 868280
fax: +44 1344 86177
collectit@dial.pipex.com
http://www.worldcollectorsnet.com/collectit/
A monthly magazine for collectors of antique Royal Doulton to modern collectibles such as Lilliput, Wade, Disneyana and sports memorabilia; now available in the US and Canada; US call 800-221-3148; in Canada call 800-438-5005.

Collectibles Canada
Trajan Publishing Corporation
103 Lakeshore Rd., Ste. 202
St. Catharines, Ontario L2N 2T6
Canada
ph: 905-646-7744
fax: 905-646-0995
bret@trajan.com
http://www.vaxxine.com/trajan/

Collectibles/Flea Market Finds
GCR Publishing Group, Inc.
Cathy Cook, Ed.
1700 Broadway
New York, NY 10019-5905
ph: 212-541-7100 or 800-955-3870
fax: 212-245-1241
ccook710@aol.com
Published four times a year; focuses on fleamarket collectibles and 20th-century collectibles that are fun, affordable, and not the standard fare of other magazines: kitchenware, toys, vintage clothing; display ideas.

Collector Magazine
Frank Donadee
436 W. Fourth St. #222
Pomona, CA 91766-1620
ph: 909-620-9014
A monthly periodical; Southern California's most popular collecting newspaper; ads, calendar of events, auctions, service directory, etc.

Collector Magazine & Price Guide
Antique Trader Publications, Inc.
P.O. Box 1050
Dubuque, IA 52004-1050
ph: 800-334-7165 or 800-482-4155
fax: 800-531-0880
atpzines@aol.com
http://www.collect.com/collectormag
A monthly magazine featuring stories on hot collectibles, travel log of great antiquing towns, a 25-page price guide, an in-depth look at antique collecting with advice from experts, exclusive 25-page price guide in each issue.

Collector's Eye
Donna Kaonis, Ed.
6 Woodside Ave., Ste 300
Northport, NY 11768
ph: 516-261-4100 or 888-800-2588
fax: 516-261-9684
donnakaonis@worldnet.att.net
http://www.collectorseye.com/
Glossy, color magazine on today's most popular antiques and collectibles: advertising, sports memorabilia, folk art, comics, animation, pop culture; collector profiles, shows, auctions, trends, ads, etc.; published nine times a year.

Collector's Marketplace, The
Dorothy J. Graf, Ed.
P.O. Box 25
Stewartsville, NJ 08886-0025
ph: 908-479-4614
fax: 908-479-6158
cm@4-collectors.com
http://www.4-collectors.com
A bi-monthly publication for collectors and dealers; an international advertising publications; classifieds and display ads for buying and selling collectibles.

Collector, The
Lois Bowman, Ed.
P.O. Box 148
Heyworth, IL 61745-0158
ph: 309-473-2466 or 309-473-2940
fax: 309-473-3610
Monthly newspaper for those interested in antiques and collectibles; flea markets, shows, articles, event reviews, etc.; many ads for antiques businesses in the Illinois region; free "I Collect" and "For Sale" ads for collectors.

Collectors Journal
CarPac Publishing Co.
Kathy Root
1800 W. D St.
P.O. Box 601
Vinton, IA 52349-0601
ph: 319-472-4763 or 319-472-4764
fax: 319-472-3117
http://www.collectorsjournal.com/
Weekly auction paper for collectors and antique lovers; weekly auction and flea market calendar, auction results, and articles.

Collectors News
Collectors News Co.
Linda Kruger, Ed.
506 Second St.
P.O. Box 156
Grundy Center, IA 50638
ph: 319-824-6981 or 800-352-8039
fax: 319-824-3414
collectors@collectors-news.com
http://collectors-news.com
The monthly newsprint magazine for antiquers & collectors nationwide; complete show & sale calendar, articles, limited edition collectibles, expert advice, values, etc.; price guide in every issue.

Collectors' Advantage
1710 River Rd., Ste. 4D
Fair Lawn, NJ 07410
ph: 201-796-5552 or 800-VALUE-01
fax: 201-796-2250
102622.3501@compuserve.com
http://hmt.com/phonecards/tca/
A resource journal for the collectibles enthusiast.

Collectors' Classified
William Margolin
P.O. Box 347
Holbrook, MA 02343-0347
ph: 781-961-1463
ccmay1975@aol.com
Published monthly; all collectibles - especially cards, coins, stamps, books, memorabilia; published since 1975; free subscriber ads.

Collectors' Mart
Annie Morrel
Pargate House
27 High Street
Hampton Hill, Middlesex TW12 1BN
U.K.
ph: (0) 181 941 4512
fax: (0) 181 941 8630
cmart@easynet.co.uk
http://www.worldcollectorsnet.com/cmart/
A quarterly magazine of advertising collectibles and other collecting lines; THE leading international collectibles magazine in print; available by subscription.

Collezionare
Editoriale Tricolore srl
via Panfilo Castaldo No. 1
Reggio Emilia, 42100
Italy
ph: 0522557893
fax: 0522557825
collezio@tin.it
http://www.collezionare.com/
Monthly periodical written in Italian; covers antique fairs, markets, conventions, art exhibitions, auctions and auction results in Italy and abroad; also contacts in Italy and abroad to exchange, buy and sell antiques & collectibles.

Colonial Homes Magazine
Hearst Corporation, The
Editor
1790 Broadway
New York, NY 10019-1400
ph: 212-830-2919
fax: 212-586-2455
colonialhomes@hearst.com
A bi-monthly glossy magazine that focuses on architecture, decorating, crafts, collectibles, and antiques.

Cotton & Quail Antique Trail
Regional Antique Publications
Sharon Morris
205 East Washington St.
P.O. Box 326
Monticello, FL 32345-0326
ph: 800-757-7755 or 904-997-3880
fax: 904-997-3090
cottonq@worldnet.att.com
A monthly newspaper on antiques and collectibles; wide variety of general interest articles; covers the Southeast; 65,000 readers; distributed in over 2200 antique malls, shops and shows.

Country Accents
GCR Publishing Group, Inc.
Lorraine Shea, Ed.
1700 Broadway
New York, NY 10019-5905
ph: 212-541-7100 or 800-955-3870
fax: 212-245-1241
Published six times per year; focuses on decorating, crafts, collectibles, and antiques.

Country Collectibles
Harris Publications
Barbara Jacksier, Ed.
1115 Broadway
New York, NY 10010-2803
ph: 212-807-7100
fax: 212-627-4678
Jacksier@his.com
http://www.countrycollector.com/
Full-color glossy magazine; features collectibles, antiques, bread & breakfast getaways, people who collect, favorite recipes, and decorating with collectibles.

Country Home
Larry Erickson
1716 Locust St.
Des Moines, IA 50309-3023
ph: 515-284-2740
fax: 515-284-2552
lerickso@dsm.mdp.com
A monthly magazine with lots of ads and in-depth articles about antiques, collectibles, decorative accessories, reproductions, interior decorating and architecture.

Country Living
Hearst Corporation
224 West 57th St.
New York, NY 10019
ph: 800-876-8696 or 212-649-3500
hacl@hearst.com
http://www.hearstcorp.com/mag3.html
A monthly magazine that focuses on decorating, crafts, collectibles, and antiques.

Early American Homes Magazine
Cowles Magazines, Inc.
741 Miller Dr. SE, Ste. D2
Harrisburg, PA 20175
ph: 717-540-6617 or 800-829-3340
fax: 717-540-6706
brentd@cowles.com
http://www.cowles.com/maglist.html
All aspects of American life before 1850 and material culture, i.e. pottery, iron, textiles, furnishings, architecture, ornament, utilitarian objects in depth (formerly "Early American Life").

Finders & Pickers Newsletter
Bob Mel
P.O. Box 141
Fort Dodge, IA 50501-0141
Lists over 50,000 common items wanted by dealers, collectors, museums and others; non-mainstream tips, resources, profitable information; former Goldstar Estate Buyers Corp. associate, editor; sample copy $5.

Georgian Antique Digest
Soaring Eagle Publications
Connie Wills
P.O. Box 429
Thornbury, Ontario N0H 2PO
Canada
ph: 519-599-5017
fax: 519-599-5017
gad@lynx.org
A quarterly magazine with informational articles on antiques to whet the appetite of the collecting public; helps them become familiar with the shops and shows around South Central Ontario, close to the Eastern Great Lakes states.

Great Lakes Trader
Greg Wilcox, Pub.
P.O. Box 9
Williamston, MI 48895
ph: 517-655-5621 or 800-785-3637
fax: 517-655-5380
gltrader@aol.com
Michigan's prime antiques trade paper; monthly show listings, original articles on antiques and related items, monthly auction and show reviews, ads.

Hawaii Antiques, Art & Collectibles Quarterly
P.O. Box 853
Honolulu, HI 96808
ph: 808-591-0049
iw@ukulele.com
http://www.ukulele.com/haq.html

Historic Traveler
Cowles Magazines, Inc.
741 Miller Dr. SE, Ste. D2
Harrisburg, PA 20175
ph: 717-540-6617 or 800-829-3340
fax: 717-540-6706
brentd@cowles.com
http://www.cowles.com/maglist.html
A guide to great historic destinations that inspires people to experience history,not just read about it.

Hudson Valley Antiquer, The
Independent Publishing
Vicki Simons
P.O. Box 219
Hillsdale, NY 12529
ph: 518-325-4400
fax: 518-325-4497
A free newspaper published monthly; distributed at antiques businesses and other locations throughout the Hudson Valley; the only Hudson Valley antiquing paper extensively distributed in New York City; available by subscription.

JH All Hobbies
Jacques Herrijgers
1 Nachtegaallaan
Itterbeek, 1701
Belgium
A quarterly international publication for hobbyists, collectors and penpal seekers; a bilingual publication (English and French.)

Journal America
P.O. Box 459
Hewitt, NJ 07421
ph: 973-728-8355
fax: 973-728-7128
journal@warwick.net
http://www.ajournal.com
Articles on all types of antiques and collectibles; also questions and answers.

Journal of the History of Collections
Oxford University Press, Inc., c/o Journals Marketing Dept.
2001 Evans Rd.
Cary, NC 27513
ph: 919-677-0977 or 800-852-7323
fax: 919-677-1714
www-admin@oup.co.uk
http://www.oup.co.uk/jnls/list/hiscol/
An international journal devoted to the study of collections from palaces and household accumulations to systematic museum collections.

Kovels on Antiques & Collectibles
Ralph & Terry Kovel
P.O. Box 22200
Beachwood, OH 44122-0200
ph: 800-571-1555 or 800-829-9158
fax: 216-752-3115
kovels@usbrands.com
http://www.kovel.com
Focuses on antiques, decorative arts and collectibles; identification and buying tips, prices, reproduction alerts, etc.

Magazine Antiques, The
Brant Art Publications
575 Broadway
New York, NY 10012
ph: 212-941-2800 or 800-925-8059
fax: 212-941-2897
brantpubs@aol.com
A full-color monthly magazine featuring detailed articles about art and antiques.

Maine Antique Digest
Maine Antique Digest, Inc.
Sam & Sally Pennington
911 Main St.
P.O. Box 1429
Waldoboro, ME 04572-1429
ph: 207-832-7534
fax: 207-832-7341
mad@maine.com
http://maineantiquedigest.com/
The major monthly newspaper on antiques, art and Americana.

MassBay Antiques
Community Newspaper Company, Inc.
254 Second Ave.
Danvers, MA 02494
ph: 800-924-5141 or 781-433-8377
fax: 781-433-8202
mbantiques@cnc.com
Monthly newspaper: auctions, people, research articles, extensive calendar section.

Master Collector
Fun Publications
Brian Savage
225 Cattle Barron Parc Dr.
Fort Worth, TX 76108
ph: 800-772-6673 or 817-448-9863
fax: 817-448-9843
brian@mastercollector.com
http://www.mastercollector.com
Ads-only newspaper; dolls (antique and modern collectible), toys, banks, models, cars, Matchbox, monsters, puzzles, political, toy trains, etc.; subscribers receive free 30 word ad each month; published monthly; reaches 20,000.

Metropolitan Home
Hachette Filapacchi Magazines, inc.
1633 Broadway, 44th Floor
New York, NY 10019
ph: 212-767-5731

MidAtlantic Antiques Magazine
Lydia A. Stainback, Ed.
P.O. Box 908
Henderson, NC 27536-0908
ph: 252-492-4001 or 800-326-3894
fax: 252-430-0125
maantiques@hendersondispatch.com
http://www.maantiques.com/
A monthly newspaper for antiques, collectibles and the antiques trade; listing upcoming shows & auctions; display ads for shops and mail order items.

Mountain States Collector
P.O. Box 2525
Evergreen, CO 80439-2525
ph: 303-987-3994
fax: 303-674-1253
Primarily distributed through advertisers, but subscriptions are also available; focuses on the mountain states; show schedules, articles, columns, etc.

New England Antiques Journal, The
Jody Young, GM
4 Church St.
P.O. Box 120
Ware, MA 01082-0120
ph: 413-967-3505 or 800-432-3505
fax: 413-967-6009
visit@antiquesjournal.com
http://www.antiquesjournal.com
Monthly newspaper providing the best coverage of New England: shops listed geographically, shows, auctions and a wide range of feature material.

New Hampshire Antiques Monthly
Charles Wibel
P.O. 546
Farmington, NH 03835-0546
ph: 603-755-4568
fax: 603-755-3990
A monthly publication.

New York Antique Almanac
New York Eye Publishing Co.
Editor
200 E 72nd St.
New York, NY 10021-4537
ph: 516-371-3300
Antiques and collectibles trade newspaper with ads, articles, auction and show reports; nationwide coverage.

New York City's Antique News
P.O. Box 2054
New York, NY 10159-2054
ph: 212-725-0344
fax: 212-532-7294

New York-Pennsylvania Collector, The
Messenger-Wolfe Publications
George M. Ewing, Jr., Pub./Ed.
P.O. Box C
Fishers, NY 14453
ph: 716-924-8230 or 800-836-1868
fax: 716-924-7734
WolfePub@Frontiernet.Net
Informative articles on art, antiques & Americana; show and auction reviews; annual subject index in Jan.; monthly calendar of events.

Northeast Journal of Antiques & Art
Harold Hanson, Ed.
364 Warren St.
P.O. Box 635
Hudson, NY 12534
ph: 518-828-9327
fax: 518-828-9437
http://www.northeastjournal.com/
Focuses on the New York and New England area; articles, ads, show and auction calendar.

Official Museum Directory
Reed Reference Publishing
121 Chanlon Rd.
New Providence, NJ 07974-1541
ph: 800-521-8110
Profiles more than 7,600 American institutions in 85 categories; aquariums, historic homes, museums, zoos; handy for those looking for information about specific types of antiques, fine art & collectibles; annual.

Ohio Collectors' Magazine
Judy Hunolt, Ed. & Pub.
P.O. Box 1522
Piqua, OH 45356-1322
ph: 937-773-6063
j&jatocm@westnet.com
Focuses on the Ohio antique and collectibles market, including complete Ohio antique show schedules; published five times per year.

Old News is Good News Antiques Gazette, The
Bill Alexander, Ed.
P.O. Box 305
Hammond, LA 70403-1069
ph: 504-429-0575
fax: 504-429-0576
gazette@i-55.com
A monthly newspaper focusing on the heritage, antiques, collectibles and attractions of the South; antiques auctions and shows, stories on collections, shops and museums, historic attractions, etc.

Old Stuff
Donna L. Miller
P.O. Box 1084
Mcminnville, OR 97128-1084
ph: 503-434-5386
fax: 503-434-0990
oldstuffdr@aol.com
http://www.oldstuffnews.com/
Published 6 times/year; a newspaper about the antiques, collectibles, history, and nostalgia of the Northwest U.S.; lots of ads, articles, show and auction calendar.

Old Times, The
Tom Ratzloff
P.O. Box 340
Maple Lake, MN 55350-0340
ph: 800-539-1810 or 320-963-6010
fax: 320-963-6499
oldtimes@lkdllink.net
http://www.theoldtimes.com/
Monthly newspaper serving antiques collectors in MN, WI, and IA.

Pandora's Treasures
Pandora's Treasures
Pandora L. McKinnon, Ed.
4841 Martin Luther King Blvd.
Sacramento, CA 95820-4932
ph: 916-452-6728
pandora@cwia.com
http://homepages.go.com/~jewels4u2/paper.html
Monthly antique & collectible newsletter; contains articles in all areas of antiques: events, ads, color & black & white photos, new shop and mall ads, interviews, etc.; complimentary issue available by request.

Pop Culture Collecting
Oddesy Publications
Ev Phillips
510-A S. Corona Mall
Corona, CA 91720-1420
ph: 909-371-7137 or 800-99-ODYSSEY
fax: 909-371-7139
DBTOGI@aol.com
http://www.odysseygroup.com/collect.htm
A monthly magazine focusing on collecting autographs, movie memorabilia, movie posters, television, rock & roll, props, costumes, sports, space collectibles, animation art and more.

Renninger's Antique Guide
Editor
P.O. Box 495
Lafayette Hill, PA 19444-0495
ph: 610-828-4614 or 610-825-6392
fax: 610-834-1599
Newspaper covering antique shows, shops, flee markets and auctions catering primarily to the mid-Atlantic region.

Smithsonian Magazine
Smithsonian Institution
900 Jefferson Dr. SW
Washington, DC 20560
ph: 202-786-2900
webmaster@si.edu
http://www.si.edu/

Southeastern Antiquing & Collecting Magazine
P.O.Box 510
Acworth, GA 30101
ph: 770-974-6495 or 888-388-7827
antiquing@go-star.com
http://go-star.com/antiquing/index.htm
A monthly magazine.

Southern Antiques
Editor
P.O. Drawer 1107
Decatur, GA 30031-1107
ph: 404-289-0054 or 888-800-4997
fax: 404-286-9727
The South's leading monthly antiques and collectibles newspaper.

Today's Collector
Krause Publications
Pat DuChene, PR
700 E. State St.
Iola, WI 54990-0001
ph: 715-445-2214
fax: 715-445-4087
info@krause.com
http://www.krause.com/
Monthly magazine with the latest news and market reports for dozens of areas of collector interest; classified ads, nationwide auction results, updated auction & collectibles show calendar in every issue.

Traditional Home
Meredith Corporation
1716 Locust St.
Des Moines, IA 50309-3023
ph: 515-284-3762 or 800-374-8791
fax: 800-51302935
thgroup@mdp.com
http://www.designerfinder.com/
Focuses on a classic, refined and gracious way of living, interpreting tradition as a style choice and a way of life: interiors, architecture, renovation, gardening, collecting, cuisine, table settings, travel, new products featured.

Treasure Chest
Treasure Chest Publishing
David & Constance Donnelly
564 Eddy St.
Providence, RI 02903
ph: 212-496-2234 or 800-557-9662
fax: 401-647-0051
Daved@ids.net
http://www.cjeans.com/JAN1.HTM
A monthly information source & marketplace for collectors & dealers of antiques and collectibles; emphasis is on antique shop, show, auction and classified ads; distributed in the NY, NJ, PA, CT, MA, and RI area.

Trodler & Sammeln
GEMI Verlags GmbH
Pfaffenhofener Strasse 3
Reichertshafen, D-85293
Germany
ph: +49 (0)8441 40220
fax: +49 (0)8441 71846
Glossy monthly magazine focusing exclusively on the antiques market.

Unravel the Gavel
Kathy Greer, Ed.
14 Hurricane Rd. #1
Belmont, NH 03220-5603
ph: 603-524-4281
fax: 603-528-3565
Gavel96@aol.com
http://www.the-forum.com/gavel/
Focusing on the northern New England area: covers auctions, antiques and collectibles in NH, VT, ME, MA, plus upstate NY.

Upper Canadian, The
Bill Dobson
30 D Chambers St.
P.O. Box 653
Smiths Falls, Ontario K7A 5B8
Canada
ph: 613-283-1168
fax: 613-283-1345
uppercanadian@recorder.ca
http://www.uppercanadian.com/
A bi-monthly Canadian newspaper with auction and show coverage, educational content, photo-ads, show and auction calendar, restoration section, and price guides; presents current trends in the Canadian antiques and collectibles business.

Victoria
Hearst Corporation
224 West 57th St.
New York, NY 10019
ph: 800-876-8696 or 212-649-3720
http://www.hearstcorp.com/mag11.html
Glossy monthly magazine; home decorating, recipes, gardening, architecture, country living; some articles about antiques & collectibles.

Victorian Decorating & Lifestyle
GCR Publishing Group, Inc.
Florian McCain, Ed.
1700 Broadway
New York, NY 10019-5905
ph: 212-541-7100 or 800-955-3870
fax: 212-245-1241
A glossy bi-monthly magazine that focuses on decorating, crafts, collectibles, antiques, Victorian people and costumes.

Victorian Homes
Victorian Homes, Inc.
265 South Anita Dr., Ste. 120
Orange, CA 92868
ph: 800-999-9718
Glossy magazine with information sources for locating special items for restoring and decorating Victorian homes.

Vintage Collector, The
Elizabeth Lilien
P.O. Box 764
Hotchkiss, CO 81419-0764
ph: 970-872-2226
Western Colorado's information source for people who are passionate about collecting.

Vintage Times, The
Angelia Jordan
P.O. Box 7567
Macon, GA 31209
ph: 912-757-4755 or 888-757-4755
fax: 912-757-4755
antiques@mylink.net
http://www.mylink.net/~antiques/
A monthly newspaper focusing on the antiques & collectibles trade of the Southeast U.S.; articles, columns, ads, shop directories and maps, some modern collectibles; free calendar listings for auctions, shows and fairs.

Wayback Times, The
Jay Telfer
RR #1, 541 Rednersville Rd.
Belleville, Ontario K8N 4Z1
Canada
ph: 613-966-8749
fax: 613-966-8747
waybackt@intranet.ca
http://www.yourguide.net/buyandsell/waybacktimes_lead.html
Covering the Ontario area antique stores and B&Bs.

West Coast Peddler
West Coast Peddler, Inc.
P.O. Box 5134
Whittier, CA 90607
ph: 562-698-1718
fax: 562-698-1500
antiques@westcoastpeddler
http://www.westcoastpeddler.com/
Oldest monthly newspaper about antiques, the arts, and collectibles serving the Pacific States, California, Oregon, and Washington.

Western CT/Western MA Antiquer, The
Independent Publishing
Vicki Simons
P.O. Box 219
Hillsdale, NY 12529
ph: 518-325-4400
fax: 518-325-4497
A free newspaper published monthly; distributed at antiques businesses and other locations throughout Western CT and MA; available by subscription.

Yankee Magazine
Yankee Publishing Inc.
P.O. Box 520
Dublin, NH 03444
ph: 603-563-8111
dearyank@yankeepub.com
http://www.newengland.com/

Yesteryear
Michael Jacobi
P.O. Box 2
Princeton, WI 54968-0002
ph: 920-787-4808
fax: 920-787-7381
A monthly newspaper featuring articles and ads about antiques & collectibles; shop directory, extensive calendar of events covering flea markets, antique shows, etc.; covering the North Central states.

Here are some tips when contacting someone listed in this book:

- **When requesting information about a particular item, include a description (material, dimensions, maker's mark, model number, etc.) and a photo, sketch, or photocopy of the item in question.**
- **Always ask if there are charges for samples or for the services requested.**
- **When writing, please be sure to include a Large (#10 business size) Self-Addressed and Stamped Envelope (LSASE) if requesting a reply or the return of photographs.**
- **Never call collect unless otherwise directed. When calling, be considerate of time zone differences and always ask if the party you are calling has time to talk. When leaving an answering machine message, always instruct the party to call you back collect.**

APPENDIX D

Repair Services

Listed in ZIP code order

The firms listed below are professionals specializing in the repair and refinishing of damaged household goods. They are members of the *Claims Prevention & Procedure Council*, the only nonprofit association that is exclusively dedicated to claims prevention and claims handling in the moving and storage industry. The CPPC studies the reasons for loss and damage and researches methods to reduce these problems. The CPPC also addresses ways to properly handle claims once they do occur. Membership in the CPPC consists of the major van lines and carriers, local movers and warehousemen, shippers, insurance firms, adjustors, appraisers, repair services, transit attorneys, government facilities and others. For more information contact the CPPC at P.O. Box 1367, Englewood, FL 34295-1367. Call 941-473-CPPC, fax 941-473-2775, e-mail claimsnet@aol, or see their web site at **http://www.claimsnet.org**. Refer also to the REPAIR/RESTORATOIN/CONSERVATION section of this directory's General Listings as well as to the *Repair Services* listed under specific categories for additional repairers, restorers, and conservators.

Servicemaster/Quaboag Valley
Frank Lombard
23 Sturbridge Rd.
Brimfield, MA 01010
Phone: (413)245-310
Fax: (413)245-289

The Finishing Touch
Ray Blais
795 Westhampton Rd.
Northampton, MA 01060
Phone: (413)586-556

Furniture Medic
Carl Bryant
22 Porter Rd.
Littleton, MA 01460
Phone: (978)486-955
Fax: (978)486-955

Furniture Plus
Gerald Brodeur, Jr.
P.O. Box 356
N. Uxbridge, MA 01538
Phone: (508)278-791
Fax: (508)278-424

J.O.B. Finishing
Joseph Branzetti
3 Dundee Park Dr., #10
Andover, MA 01810
Phone: (978)470-180
Fax: (978)470-001

R. Bruce Hamilton Ant. Rest.
R. Bruce Hamilton
P.O. Box 815
West Newbury, MA 01985
Phone: (978)363-263
Fax: (978)363-263

Judd Refinishing
Robert Judd
25 Cliff Way
Dedham, MA 02026
Phone: (781)251-662
Fax: (781)251-071

Trefler & Sons Antique Rest.
Leon Trefler
99 Cabot St.
Needham, MA 02194
Phone: (781)444-268

Furniture Medic
Patrick Mahoney
743 Old Barnstable Rd.
E. Falmouth, MA 02536
Phone: (508)457-520

Bird's "Chem-Clean" Furn Rest.
Ed or Larry Mathews
402 Gifford Street
Falmouth, MA 02540
Phone: (508)548-537
Fax: (508)540-285

People In The Woods
Joseph Sabatino
1430 E. Main Rd.
Portsmouth, RI 02871
Phone: (401)683-930
Fax: (401)683-930

Furniture Medic
Jim Harrington
143 Watson Dr.
Portsmouth, RI 02871
Phone: (401)682-180
Fax: (401)683-068

Furniture Medic
Edward and Ida Trenn
1 Marla Court
Warwick, RI 02886
Phone: (401)827-068
Fax: (401)827-068

Jordan Furniture Repair
Jim Jordan
214 County Road
Bedford, NH 03110
Phone: (603)669-711
Fax: (603)645-622

Furniture Medic
Charles P. Matteson
P.O. Box 231
Strafford, NH 03884-0231
Phone: (603)664-530
Fax: (603)664-697

Furniture Medic
Larry Clements
8 Gloucester Hill Rd.
New Gloucester, ME 04260
Phone: (207)926-369
Fax: (207)926-379

Furniture Medic
Trevett Hooper
19 Freedom Parkway #3
Bangor, ME 04401
Phone: (207)848-500
Fax: (207)848-500

Furniture Medic
Richard G. Nangle
P.O. Box 365
Southwest Harbor, ME 04679
Phone: (207)244-001
Fax: (207)244-016

Interstate Furniture Repair
George Parker
Rr5 Box 2136
Farmington, ME 04938
Phone: (207)778-667
Fax: (207)778-294

Country Village Antique Rest.
Brad Witham
652 Williston Rd.
Williston, VT 05495
Phone: (802)878-826
Fax: (802)872-804

Furniture Medic
Greg Fowler
P.O. Box 5
Waterbury, VT 05676
Phone: (800)458-198
Fax: (802)244-194

Furniture Medic
Jim Jarvis
P.O. Box 248
Barton, VT 05822-0248
Phone: (802)525-110
Fax: (802)525-110

Furniture Medic
Stanley Mylek
23 Griswold Dr.
Windsor, CT 06095
Phone: (860)688-156
Fax: (860)688-156

Woodshed, The
Tom Selmecki
20 Parkview Dr.
Niantic, CT 06357
Phone: (860)739-680
Fax: (860)739-719

Furniture Medic
Terrence Flynn
561 Old Colchester Rd.
Uncasville, CT 06382
Phone: (203)848-297

Furniture Medic
Kenneth J. Shackford
19 Lasky Rd.
Beacon Falls, CT 06403
Phone: (203)723-067
Fax: (203)723-126

Furniture Rescue
Gregg Nodelman
15 Yale Court
Branford, CT 06405
Phone: (203)486-688
Fax: (203)481-140

Jim's Furniture Service
Jim Martin
2490 Black Rock Tpk. #321
Fairfield, CT 06430
Phone: (203)256-078
Fax: (203)256-078

Custom Furniture Refinishing
Michael Pellegrino
107 Richards Dr.
Monroe, CT 06468
Phone: (203)268-047
Fax: (203)261-744

Universal Conservation
Dimitri & Georgiana Nedelcu
267 Derby Ave.
Orange, CT 06477
Phone: (203)795-884
Fax: (203)795-884

Connecticut Claims Svc. Inc.
Marty Horowitz
78 Anthony Ct.
Bethany, CT 06524
Phone: (203)393-271
Fax: (203)393-048

C. Colagrossi Furn. R & R
Carl A. Colagrossi
P.O. Box 376
Waterbury, CT 06720
Phone: (203)757-079
Fax: (203)757-577

Alpha Interiors
Vincent Costabile
17 St. Mary's Lane
Norwalk, CT 06851
Phone: (203)846-916
Fax: (203)846-184

Guardsman Woodpro
John Galatro
185 Davenport Ridge Rd.
Stamford, CT 06903
Phone: (203)461-915

Guardsman Woodpro
Nancie Smith
478 Watchung Ave.
Bloomfield, NJ 07003
Phone: (973)338-553
Fax: (973)338-567

L & S Furniture Service
Stephen S. Minsk
P.O. Box 57
Cedar Grove, NJ 07009
Phone: (973)228-583
Fax: (973)228-356

Alfonso Furniture Repair
Matt Alfonso
P.O. Box 204
Garfield, NJ 07026
Phone: (973)478-889
Fax: (973)546-652

AE Nationwide Mechanical Rep
Tanja Heuring
184 Franklin Turnpike
Mahwah, NJ 07430
Phone: (800)631-717
Fax: (201)529-814

Guardsman Woodpro
Blanche & Paul Cordero
81 Deerfield Terrace
Mahwah, NJ 07430
Phone: (201)818-651
Fax: (201)818-651

Quality Repair/Inspection Svc
Tanja Heuring
184 Franklin Turnpike
Mahwah, NJ 07430
Phone: (201)995-600
Fax: (201)995-600

Furniture Medic
Donald Dopiriak
22 Maryann Rd.
Oak Ridge, NJ 07438
Phone: (973)208-808
Fax: (973)697-284

Preis Carpentry/Formica Work
Bob Preis
24 Davidson Ave.
Ramsey, NJ 07446
Phone: (201)825-695
Fax: (201)825-751

Furniture Medic
Duncan Peterson
879 West Park Ave., #226
Ocean, NJ 07712
Phone: (908)542-728
Fax: (908)542-225

Furniture Medic
Kendall Frantz
46 Prospect Circle
Atlantic Highlands, NJ 07716
Phone: (732)872-262
Fax: (732)872-262

Care Furniture Services, Inc.
Charles Martens
8 Adams Dr.
Denville, NJ 07834
Phone: (973)983-708
Fax: (973)983-708

Franco Furniture Repair Svc.
Victor Franco, Jr.
999 Willow Grove St., 8-A
Hackettstown, NJ 07840
Phone: (908)813-094
Fax: (908)852-131

Atlantic Restoration Co.
Dave Lindeblad
123 Statesville Quarry Rd.
Lafayette, NJ 07848
Phone: (800)729-143
Fax: (973)875-695

Furniture Medic
Drew Kelly
283-B Egg Harbor Rd. Ste. 178
Sewell, NJ 08080
Phone: (609)582-760
Fax: (609)589-982

Guardsman Woodpro
Horace Madrid
601 Aberdeen Layne
Toms River, NJ 08753
Phone: (732)349-684
Fax: (732)349-684

Furniture Medic
Bob Wieckowski
16 Fox Hill Rd.
Edison, NJ 08820
Phone: (908)549-173
Fax: (908)549-173

Servicemaster
Randy Lavoie
19 Kingwood Ave.
Frenchtown, NJ 08825
Phone: (908)359-227
Fax: (908)996-621

New York Piano Center, Inc.
Leopold Holder
121 W. 19th Street
New York, NY 10011
Phone: (212)229-260
Fax: (212)229-266

Artisan Furn. Rep. And Rest.
Cornell Antoine
128 Central Ave.
Staten Island, NY 10301
Phone: (718)273-028
Fax: (718)273-009

Carpenter And Pelton Inc.
Margaret Roddy
116 Radio Circle
Mt. Kisco, NY 10549
Phone: (914)666-800
Fax: (914)666-084

Amato's Furniture Repair
Steve Amato
847 Wilmot Rd.
Scarsdale, NY 10583
Phone: (914)723-647
Fax: (914)723-645

Furniture Medic
Donna Martinetti
239 Crooked Hill Rd.
Pearl River, NY 10965
Phone: (914)620-016
Fax: (914)735-402

Sebastian Restorations
Robert Cinquemani
118 New Hyde Park Rd.
Franklin Square, NY 11010
Phone: (516)354-605
Fax: (516)354-058

Guardsman Woodpro
Jason Kim
35-46 74th St., Suite 420
Jackson Heights, NY 11372
Phone: (917)838-838

New Masters Restoration, Inc.
Richard J. Hilzinger
243-28 132nd Rd.
Rosedale, NY 11422
Phone: (718)525-110
Fax: (718)525-110

Everett Burger
81-23 188th St.
Jamaica, NY 11423
Phone: (718)465-492

Rosini Furniture Service
John Rosini
232 Herricks Road
Mineola, NY 11501
Phone: (516)739-690
Fax: (516)739-699

Robert Kugelmass Tran Clm Svc
Robert Kugelmass
979 Van Buren St.
Baldwin, NY 11510
Phone: (516)379-298
Fax: (516)379-298

Furniture Medic
Joe Hoffman
200-18 East 2nd St.
Huntington Station, NY 11746
Phone: (516)385-790
Fax: (516)385-790

A & M Restoration
Carmine Auriemma
19 Broadoak Lane
Dix Hills, NY 11746-5901
Phone: (516)351-617
Fax: (516)351-497

J & J Woodworking & Furn. Svc.
Jeff Ritzmann
21 Dunn Ct.
Sayville, NY 11782
Phone: (516)563-445
Fax: (516)244-292

Furniture Medic
Fred Baldes
503 B Route 146
Altamont, NY 12009
Phone: (518)456-583
Fax: (518)861-016

Furniture Medic
Hiland Sanders
13 Garling Drive
Latham, NY 12110-2311
Phone: (518)783-536
Fax: (518)783-543

Atlantic Restoration Svc.
Michael Derocha
P.O. Box 102
Pleasant Valley, NY 12569
Phone: (914)471-229
Fax: (914)452-360

Finisher's Touch
Steve Fisch
10 W. Main St.
Wappingers Falls, NY 12590
Phone: (914)298-888
Fax: (914)298-894

J & S Invisible Repairs
Sylvia & James Sheehan
29 Elm Street
Glens Falls, NY 12801
Phone: (518)798-644
Fax: (518)745-593

Furniture Medic
Jim Doepp
4206 Fireside Dr.
Liverpool, NY 13090
Phone: (716)746-502
Fax: (315)622-749

Mario Citra Furniture Service
Carol A. Citra
328 N. Beech St.
Syracuse, NY 13203
Phone: (315)472-498
Fax: (315)424-005

Wood Finishers New York
Donald P. Levesque
108 Baum Ave.
N. Syracuse, NY 13212-2320
Phone: (315)452-337
Fax: (315)458-445

Furniture Medic
Richard Toombs
135 Edgehill Rd.
Syracuse, NY 13224
Phone: (315)445-110
Fax: (315)445-120

Furniture Refinishing
Marge Vanslyke
8963 Turin Rd.
Rome, NY 13440
Phone: (315)339-222
Fax: (315)334-956

Restorers Of America
Andrea Daley
P.O. Box 447
Salisbury Center, NY 13454
Phone: (315)429-309
Fax: (315)429-726

Furniture Medic
Stanley W. Robbins
P.O. Box 307
Adams Center, NY 13606
Phone: (315)583-633
Fax: (315)583-633

Furniture Repair Service
Jim Sullivan
Rd #1 Box 64B
Bainbridge, NY 13733
Phone: (607)639-132
Fax: (607)639-168

Paul Atkinson
15 Wellington
Kenmore, NY 14223
Phone: (716)832-626
Fax: (716)832-626

Guardsman Woodpro
Gus Hoogers
45 Southcross Trail
Fairport, NY 14450
Phone: (716)223-393
Fax: (716)425-712

Richard Dininny Cabinet Maker
Richard Dininny
912 Southport St.
Elmira, NY 14904
Phone: (607)734-351
Fax: (607)734-351

Furniture Medic
Ken Melegari
2015 Devonwood Dr., #E
Mckeesport, PA 15135
Phone: (412)751-408
Fax: (412)751-050

Furniture Medic
David Cappalonga
Rd #2, Box 291e
Connellsville, PA 15425
Phone: (724)626-179
Fax: (724)626-188

Furniture Medic
Gregory A. Budd
819 Chestnut St.
Waterford, PA 16441
Phone: (814)796-399
Fax: (814)796-399

Guardsman Woodpro
Clarence Wolfe
125 Juniper St.
Cornwall, PA 17016
Phone: (717)273-197
Fax: (717)279-077

Restoration Clinic
Gary Kopperman
5222 E. Trindle Rd.
Mechanicsburg, PA 17055
Phone: (717)691-888
Fax: (717)691-888

Furniture Medic
Todd Alleman
1331 Springview Drive
Chambersburg, PA 17201-9011
Phone: (717)263-871
Fax: (717)263-871

Furniture Medic
Jerry Barbour
1872 Atom Rd.
Delta, PA 17314
Phone: (717)456-980
Fax: (717)456-980

Mobile Furniture/Uphol Rep.
Tim Burns
11 Oak Lane
Stevens, PA 17578-9706
Phone: (717)336-339
Fax: (717)336-333

Furniture Medic
Pat Wucher
105 Winding Hill Rd.
Lancaster, PA 17601
Phone: (717)898-682
Fax: (717)898-682

Furniture Medic
Robert Shriver
28 Walton Court
Newtown, PA 18940
Phone: (215)968-772
Fax: (215)968-434

Guardsman Woodpro
Terry Kramlik
121 Park Ave.
Quakertown, PA 18951
Phone: (215)536-781
Fax: (215)536-783

Furniture Medic
Susan Brown
597 Creamery
Quakertown, PA 18951
Phone: (215)529-939
Fax: (215)529-964

Furniture Medic
John Szostak
501 Martin Ln
Dresher, PA 19025
Phone: (215)542-027
Fax: (215)653-083

Niki Francis Antique Rest.
John Swahn
515 W. Lancaster Ave.
Haverford, PA 19041
Phone: (610)525-500
Fax: (610)581-737

D & S Restoration Svcs. (Fm)
David Leininger
2128 Sanger St.
Philadelphia, PA 19124
Phone: (215)537-111
Fax: (215)537-155

Guardsman Woodpro
Lisa Zanchetti
5932 Pulaski Ave.
Philadelphia, PA 19144
Phone: (215)849-619
Fax: (215)849-509

Furniture Medic
Arthur Faber
249 Weat Lafayette St.
Norristown, PA 19401
Phone: (610)239-511
Fax: (610)239-512

Guardsman Woodpro
Bill Dauksys
27 Skyline Dr.
Audubon, PA 19403
Phone: (610)650-015
Fax: (215)751-908

A. L. Klein & Son, Inc.
Byron Klein
P.O. Box 145
Harleysville, PA 19438
Phone: (215)256-900
Fax: (215)256-964

Furniture Medic
Richard Garwood
344 Evergreen Dr.
North Wales, PA 19454
Phone: (215)661-153
Fax: (215)661-891

Able Furniture Re. Warr. Co.
Jospeh H. Kaiser
25 Shull Dr.
Newark, DE 19711
Phone: (302)737-772
Fax: (302)455-074

Guardsman Woodpro
Joe Day
P.O. Box 7901
Newark, DE 19714-7901
Phone: (302)234-774

A Refinishing Touch
Michael Shur
604 Hillcrest Avenue
Wilmington, DE 19809
Phone: (302)762-368
Fax: (302)762-419

Furniture Medic
Brad & Karen Osman
2787 Melchester Dr.
Herndon, VA 20171
Phone: (703)478-008
Fax: (703)478-293

Manoly Furniture Service, Inc.
Larry Manoly
8981 Hillary Ct.
La Plata, MD 20646
Phone: (301)843-595
Fax: (301)753-329

Manoly Furn Rep Svc
Bill or Carol Manoly
11605 Candor Dr.
Mitchellville, MD 20721
Phone: (301)805-422
Fax: (301)464-203

Furniture Medic
Richard Carapellatti
12222 Mccullagh Ct.
Upper Marlboro, MD 20772
Phone: (301)868-889
Fax: (301)868-889

Furniture Medic
Mike O'Dea
14672-J Southlawn Lane
Rockville, MD 20850
Phone: (301)315-200
Fax: (301)315-960

L.P. Oliver & Sons Inc.
L. Philip Oliver
P.O. Box 659
Clarksburg, MD 20871-0659
Phone: (800)752-216
Fax: (301)428-928

Furniture Medic
Stuart Pisarra
18775-U N. Frederick Ave.
Gaithersburg, MD 20879
Phone: (301)947-950
Fax: (301)947-950

Strip Joint Etc., Inc., The
Bob Maclellan
514-A Pulaski Hwy
Joppa, MD 21085
Phone: (410)679-079
Fax: (410)268-164

Artisian Restoration, Inc.
Pete Simonetti
P.O. Box 72035
Baltimore, MD 21237
Phone: (410)682-370
Fax: (410)682-373

Furniture Medic
Dave Kuykendall
4507 D. Metropolitan Ct.
Frederick, MD 21704
Phone: (301)662-733
Fax: (301)874-316

Guardsman Woodpro
Larry Johns
4149 Old National Pike
Mt. Airy, MD 21771
Phone: (410)549-345
Fax: (410)549-345

Glade Valley Furn. Repair
John C. Pyle
10464 Glade Road
Walkersville, MD 21793
Phone: (301)898-379

Paul's Furniture Repair
Paul Hirmer
16020 Fleetwood Dr.
Catlett, VA 22019
Phone: (703)594-326
Fax: (703)594-360

Albert Ibrahim Furn. Repair
Albert Ibrahim
6050 Rockton Ct.
Centerville, VA 22020
Phone: (703)968-338
Fax: (703)803-062

Servicemaster Of Arl'ton Etc.
Reece Conner, Jr.
14325-D Willard Rd.
Chantilly, VA 22021
Phone: (703)527-590
Fax: (703)968-056

Furniture Medic
Joseph Skinner
7911 Larrick Court
Springfield, VA 22153
Phone: (703)451-803
Fax: (703)913-322

Furniture Medic
Robert Demay
8355 Magic Leaf Rd.
Springfield, VA 22153
Phone: (703)912-654
Fax: (703)912-980

Furniture Medic
Mahamoud Osman
6000 Stevenson Ave., #4
Alexandria, VA 22304
Phone: (703)751-386
Fax: (703)212-723

Metal Magic
David Sisson
6647 S. Kings Hwy.
Alexandria, VA 22306
Phone: (703)660-918
Fax: (703)660-918

Furniture Medic
Stanley Wells
4113 Glouster Ln
Fredericksburg, VA 22408
Phone: (540)898-496

Furniture Medic
Jeff Tinsman
9 Lincoln Ave.
Berryville, VA 22611
Phone: (877)955-503
Fax: (540)955-503

Furniture Medic
Lester & Kim Robbins
5344 Duval Rd.
Kent's Store, VA 23084
Phone: (800)565-809
Fax: (804)457-280

Five Star Restorations
Orrin Tyler
3807 Timber Ridge Rd.
Midlothian, VA 23112
Phone: (804)744-710
Fax: (804)744-716

Harrison Furniture Service
James Jr. Harrison
3016 Lincoln Ave.
Richmond, VA 23228
Phone: (804)266-107
Fax: (804)262-170

Classic Touch Furn. Rep. Svc.
Whit Williams
P.O. Box 11163
Richmond, VA 23230
Phone: (804)358-001
Fax: (804)359-008

Guardsman Woodpro
Bill Putnam
P.O. Box 6285
Chesapeake, VA 23323
Phone: (757)382-720
Fax: (757)523-706

Smith Furniture Svc., Inc
Harold Smith
3618 Tidewater Drive
Norfolk, VA 23509
Phone: (804)623-002
Fax: (804)623-067

Craftsmanship By Weathersby
Mark Weathersby
9521 Shore Drive
Norfolk, VA 23518
Phone: (757)362-841
Fax: (757)362-901

Furniture By Lowell
Lowell A. Galumbeck
605-N Industrial Park Drive
Newport News, VA 23602
Phone: (757)874-797
Fax: (757)898-981

Guardsman Woodpro
Dick Slemmer
151 Princess Margaret Dr.
Newport News, VA 23602
Phone: (757)220-430

Pro-Finish
Tommy Nelson, Jr.
1006 East Third St.
Farmville, VA 23901
Phone: (888)385-576
Fax: (804)392-576

Furniture Medic
Troy Y. Miller
P.O. Box 11541
Roanoke, VA 24022
Phone: (540)982-867
Fax: (540)982-353

Rowe Furniture
Mark Spencer
239 Rowan St.
Salem, VA 24153
Phone: (540)375-490
Fax: (540)375-491

P & P Transit Claims
Stephan R. Phelps
P.O. Box 4196
Lynchburg, VA 24502
Phone: (804)385-636
Fax: (804)385-061

Woodco Furniture Restoration
Betty Somerville
Rt. 11, Box 539-E
Parkersburg, WV 26101
Phone: (304)485-157
Fax: (304)485-055

Upshur Restorations
Howard R. Pletcher, Jr.
40 Marion St.
Buckhannon, WV 26201
Phone: (304)473-050
Fax: (304)473-190

Carolina Furniture Specialist
Rick Davis
119 Howardtown Circle
Mocksville, NC 27028
Phone: (336)998-999
Fax: (336)998-999

J & M Furniture Repair
Jerry Mcentire
2527 White Fence Way
High Point, NC 27265
Phone: (336)454-610
Fax: (336)454-163

Furniture Medic
Tom Delvecchio
3005 Sussex Dr.
Jamestown, NC 27282-9069
Phone: (336)454-552
Fax: (336)454-031

Wood-Pro
Bill Brown
2005 Kildare Woods Drive
Greensboro, NC 27407
Phone: (336)889-828
Fax: (336)889-828

Day-Mar Furniture Repair
Mike Pennington
600 Stage Coach Trail
Greensboro, NC 27409
Phone: (336)632-900
Fax: (336)632-990

Furniture Medic
Jeff Johnson
2216 Leadenhall Way
Raleigh, NC 27603
Phone: (919)836-984
Fax: (919)836-995

Bishop Furniture & Upholst.
Bill Johnson
1128 N. Blount St.
Raleigh, NC 27604
Phone: (919)829-120
Fax: (919)829-130

Furniture Medic
Jeff & Beverly Bartholomew
5910-129 Duraleigh Rd., #178
Raleigh, NC 27612
Phone: (919)510-878
Fax: (919)510-023

Guardsmen Woodpro
Kathy Garahan
10608 Tredwood Dr.
Raleigh, NC 27614
Phone: (919)845-454
Fax: (919)676-866

Furniture Medic
Mark Stocking
P.O. Box 51817
Durham, NC 27717
Phone: (919)493-496
Fax: (919)493-496

The Finishing Touch
Dennis W. Bell
1033 West Gaston Avenue
Gastonia, NC 28052
Phone: (704)868-853
Fax: (704)868-854

American Woodworking Spl'ists
Michael Walter
2217 Chesterfield Ave.
Charlotte, NC 28205-6015
Phone: (704)372-100
Fax: (704)372-573

Guardsman Woodpro
Juan Dominguez
7031 Whitemarsh
Charlotte, NC 28210
Phone: (704)643-000
Fax: (704)643-945

Fixit Services
Sydney Charnley
P.O. Box 25813
Charlotte, NC 28229-5813
Phone: (888)729-436
Fax: (888)729-436

Furniture Medic
Greg Clark
9210 Hemingford Ct.
Charlotte, NC 28277
Phone: (704)332-289
Fax: (704)332-289

Piece By Piece Inc.
Beth O'Leary
244 Robeson St.
Fayetteville, NC 28301
Phone: (910)484-022
Fax: (910)484-599

Furniture Medic
Bud Steere
P.O. Box 197
Fayetteville, NC 28302-0197
Phone: (910)484-405
Fax: (910)484-599

Furniture Medic
Gary & Mary Herbold
201 King Richard Court
Jacksonvulle, NC 28546
Phone: (910)455-720
Fax: (910)938-208

Furniture Medic
Liston Beck
300 Rockledge Rd.
New Bern, NC 28562
Phone: (919)637-406
Fax: (919)637-406

Furniture Repair Works
Joe W. Mccarson,Jr.
142 Church St.
Asheville, NC 28801
Phone: (704)252-855
Fax: (704)252-868

Furniture Medic
John Humphreys
825-C Merrimon Ave., #146
Asheville, NC 28804
Phone: (828)255-802
Fax: (828)255-802

Colonial Woodworks Inc.
Steven T. Brantley
1709 Laurel St.
Columbia, SC 29201
Phone: (803)254-751
Fax: (803)765-264

Furniture Medic
Carl Cease
5816-A Shakespeare Rd.
Columbia, SC 29223
Phone: (803)786-066
Fax: (803)786-061

The Crafter's Corner
Richard Bennington
1701 Meeting Place Rd.
Charleston, SC 29405
Phone: (843)723-395
Fax: (803)723-395

Furniture Medic
Rob Beard
1375 Emerald Forest Pkway
Charleston, SC 29414
Phone: (803)763-996
Fax: (803)769-025

Furniture Medic
Robert Wilkins
5765 Rosewood Dr.
Myrtle Beach, SC 29575
Phone: (803)293-646
Fax: (803)293-646

Furniture Medic
E. Porter Huskey
P.O. Box 2161
Greenville, SC 29602
Phone: (864)292-626
Fax: (864)292-727

Mid-State Furniture Service
Bill Courtney
Rt. #4, Box 390
Pageland, SC 29728
Phone: (843)672-231
Fax: (843)672-355

Furniture Medic
Al Lopez
3550 Clarkston Indus. Blvd.
Clarkston, GA 30021
Phone: (404)370-111
Fax: (404)370-120

Jack Williams Mover's Clm Svc.
Jack Williams
2447 Kingsley Dr.
Marietta, GA 30062
Phone: (770)977-167
Fax: (770)973-608

Atlanta's Total Leather Care
Dan Rafuse
5990-B Unity Dr.
Norcross, GA 30071
Phone: (770)441-990
Fax: (770)447-006

Service Solutions Associates
William A. Smith
876 Lakeshore Dr.
Berkeley Lake, GA 30096
Phone: (770)849-077
Fax: (770)849-003

3r Artisans
Pat Weichold
4790 Coppedge Trail
Duluth, GA 30096
Phone: (770)476-515
Fax: (770)446-029

Aip Leath & Vinyl Rpr. Prods.
John Artemis
Po Box 2550
Acworth, GA 30102
Phone: (770)516-384

Guardsman Woodpro
Bob Jansen
3407 Chatsworth Way
Powder Springs, GA 30127
Phone: (770)427-424
Fax: (770)426-110

Yarbrough Furn. Rest., Inc.
Malcolm T. Yarbrough
1345 Cedarcrest Rd.
Dallas, GA 30132-2953
Phone: (770)975-366
Fax: (770)975-047

Furniture Medic
Rick Mckelvey
418 Rocky Ridge Dr.
Douglasville, GA 30134
Phone: (770)920-101
Fax: (770)920-879

Linton's Furniture Shops
Danny Linton
P.O. Box 1259
Holly Springs, GA 30142
Phone: (770)345-002
Fax: (770)345-652

Guardsman Woodpro
Don Balhoff
195 Lakemont Dr.
Fayetteville, GA 30215
Phone: (770)719-261

See Restorations Unlimited
Bill See
5879 New Peachtree Rd., #D
Doraville, GA 30340
Phone: (770)455-416
Fax: (770)455-030

Bentz & Weathersby Furn. Rep.
Steve Bentz
3691 Toxaway Court
Atlanta, GA 30341
Phone: (770)491-038
Fax: (770)414-937

Furniture Medic
Mickey Stephenson
P.O. Box 82152
Athens, GA 30608-2152
Phone: (706)546-114
Fax: (706)546-143

Leather Finesse, Inc.
Stephen Cohen
703 Westbury Ln
Bethlehem, GA 30620-2007
Phone: (770)868-833
Fax: (770)868-833

Furniture Doctor, Inc.
Bruce Smith
3345 Peach Orchard Rd.
Augusta, GA 30906
Phone: (706)793-071

Furniture Medic
Robert Peacock
P.O. Box 127
Butler, GA 31006
Phone: (912)745-617
Fax: (912)745-617

Furniture Medic
Richard & Cecilia Deborde
208 Catalina Dr.
Tybee Island, GA 31328
Phone: (912)786-462

Property Inspection Svc
Jim Blease
400 E. Hill Ave.
Valdosta, GA 31601
Phone: (912)247-847
Fax: (912)249-886

Central Florida Furniture Svc.
Glenn Camp
P.O. Box 283
Sparr, FL 32192
Phone: (352)351-494
Fax: (352)351-884

F. Michael Johnston Co.
F. Michael Johnston
7072 Eagle Perch Dr.
Jacksonville, FL 32244
Phone: (904)908-030
Fax: (904)908-030

Premiere Service Group
Michael Brown
11214 Sunny Hill Rd.
Tallahassee, FL 32312
Phone: (850)893-615

Specialists Of The South, Inc.
Logan Adams
544 E. 6th St.
Panama City, FL 32401
Phone: (850)785-257
Fax: (850)872-866

Furniture Medic
W. Edward Williamson
3411 Edinborough Ct.
Pensacola, FL 32514
Phone: (904)494-662
Fax: (904)484-352

Furniture Medic
David & Pauline Richard
719 Caribbean Way
Niceville, FL 32578-4046
Phone: (850)897-333
Fax: (850)897-660

Master Furniture Service
Marion Sack
P.O. Box 1421
Apopka, FL 32704
Phone: (407)884-909
Fax: (407)884-927

Schoenbauer's Restorations
David Schoenbauer
P.O. Box 161876
Altamonte Springs, FL 32716
Phone: (407)886-920
Fax: (407)886-129

Complete Furniture/Interiors
Mitch Treider
P.O. Box 1167
Titusville, FL 32781-1167
Phone: (800)569-114
Fax: (407)383-043

Total Leather Care F. Rep/Cln
John Demola
7425 Tufts Ct.
Orlando, FL 32807-6426
Phone: (407)678-877
Fax: (407)679-127

Furniture Medic
Genevieve Blurton
249 Ivey Lane, "B"
Orlando, FL 32811
Phone: (407)299-508
Fax: (407)293-218

Mobiletech Solutions
J. D. Koesar
2697 Environs Blvd.
Orlando, FL 32818
Phone: (407)292-729
Fax: (407)522-813

Furniture Medic
Darrell Bullock
1111 Park Manor Dr.
Orlando, FL 32825
Phone: (407)382-347
Fax: (407)277-544

Furniture Medic
Darrell Phillips
3956 Town Center Blvd., #138
Orlando, FL 32837
Phone: (407)857-380
Fax: (407)826-471

Merchants Services Co.
Eric A. Verzi
P.O. Box 780511
Orlando, FL 32878-0511
Phone: (407)380-283
Fax: (407)380-391

Furniture Medic
Kim Allen Nielsen
1498 Riviera Dr., N.E.
Palm Bay, FL 32905
Phone: (407)728-163
Fax: (407)727-023

Dowling's Claim Service
Lawrence M. Dowling
1040 Lassen Ave. N.W.
Palm Bay, FL 32907
Phone: (407)768-866
Fax: (407)728-904

Furniture Medic
Richard Bernstein
4055 Turtlemound Rd.
Melbourne, FL 32934
Phone: (407)253-941
Fax: (407)253-941

Transit Claim Repair
Larry Parks
1622 91st Ct.
Vero Beach, FL 32966
Phone: (561)569-330
Fax: (561)569-048

Furniture Medic
Richard Raines
2410 N. 56 Terrace
Hollywood, FL 33021
Phone: (954)981-966
Fax: (954)428-204

Elite Cleaning/Restorations
Charles Keller
5815 SW 21 St.
Hollywood, FL 33023
Phone: (954)964-290
Fax: (954)986-433

Personal Touch Claim Svc.
Barry Toder
6975 Nw 11th St.
Margate, FL 33063
Phone: (954)973-431
Fax: (954)973-433

American Refinishing
James West
5431 Nw 15th St, Bay 4
Margate, FL 33063
Phone: (954)970-002
Fax: (954)970-144

Furniture Medic
Tom Fleckenstein
6641 Nw 41st St.
Coral Springs, FL 33067
Phone: (954)340-327
Fax: (954)340-841

Professional Furniture Care
Dominic Pregi
1751 Blount Rd.
Pompano Beach, FL 33069
Phone: (954)970-735
Fax: (954)977-597

Woodcraft Custom Design
Allyn Schmidt
4100 N. Powerline Rd., I-5
Pompano Beach, FL 33073
Phone: (954)971-232
Fax: (954)971-665

Guardsman Woodpro
Marcello Russo
1550 Madruga, #330
Coral Gables, FL 33146
Phone: (305)667-104
Fax: (605)668-462

Petersen Restorations, Inc.
John R. Petersen
7345 S.W. 45 Street
Miami, FL 33155
Phone: (305)261-698
Fax: (305)261-923

Perfect Touch
Michael & Lenore Indell
711 Shiloh Terrace
Davie, FL 33325
Phone: (954)475-999
Fax: (954)475-952

Palm Beach Claim Service
Carl Germana
P.O. Box 17663
West Palm Beach, FL 33416
Phone: (561)471-500
Fax: (561)471-426

Craig's Limited, Inc.
Jack Craig
10642 St. Thomas Dr.
Boca Raton, FL 33498
Phone: (561)367-009
Fax: (561)368-100

Schalck Services, Inc.
William F. Schalck
P.O. Box 915
Lutz, FL 33548
Phone: (813)920-808
Fax: (813)920-937

Unique Finishing Services
James Jarrell
P.O. Box 2098
Valrico, FL 33595-2098
Phone: (813)685-162
Fax: (813)654-321

Resource Protection Consltnts.
Bobby L. Cates
P.O. Box 3417
Tampa, FL 33601-3417
Phone: (813)654-006
Fax: (813)655-082

Furniture Medic
John J. Ogden
913 East Skagway Ave.
Tampa, FL 33604
Phone: (813)930-670
Fax: (813)915-876

Artisan Furniture Services
Stephen Seaton
4001 Lynwood Ave.
Tampa, FL 33611
Phone: (813)839-899
Fax: (813)839-899

Southern Transit Repair. Inc.
Leon & Shirley Davis
5008 Linebaugh Ave., Suite 51
Tampa, FL 33624
Phone: (813)968-744
Fax: (813)968-514

Caribe Interiors, Inc.
Chris Scirica
1444 - 19 St. North
St. Petersburg, FL 33713
Phone: (813)896-594

Leather Medic
Kyle Life
11532 Mahogany Run
Fort Myers, FL 33913
Phone: (941)561-042
Fax: (941)561-213

Gino Germana & Son
Gino Germana
2200 Kings Hwy., Bldg 3-L, #67
Pt. Charlotte, FL 33980
Phone: (941)629-812
Fax: (941)624-288

Guardsman Woodpro
Dave Beutler
3326 Mystic River Dr.
Naples, FL 34120
Phone: (941)352-881
Fax: (941)352-595

Carrier Consultants
Kevin Blizman
1939 Racimo Dr.
Sarasota, FL 34240
Phone: (941)377-224
Fax: (941)377-216

Dependable Furniture Service
Jack Florian
1550 66th Ave. Dr. E.
Sarasota, FL 34243
Phone: (941)751-239
Fax: (941)751-998

Furniture Medic By Dearth
Andy Dearth
33514 E. Picciola Dr.
Fruitland Park, FL 34731
Phone: (352)728-626
Fax: (352)728-626

Furniture Medic
David Frank
1761 King George Dr.
Kissimmee, FL 34744
Phone: (407)870-552
Fax: (407)870-811

Furniture Clinic
Lori Donnelly
2497 S.W. Warwick
Port St. Lucie, FL 34984
Phone: (561)879-115
Fax: (561)878-947

Muns Furniture Repair
Sammie Muns
5986 Miles Spring Rd.
Pinson, AL 35126
Phone: (205)681-211
Fax: (205)681-211

Harrell Repair And Inspection
David S. Harrell
1074 Deaver-Walker Rd.
Trafford, AL 35172
Phone: (205)681-242
Fax: (800)681-334

Alabama Inspection/Repair Svc
Don Douglas
P.O. Box 320092
Birmingham, AL 35232
Phone: (205)595-670
Fax: (800)552-247

Furniture Medic
Steve & Corinne Healy
13302 Hyde Park
Huntsville, AL 35803-4015
Phone: (256)882-929
Fax: (256)882-929

Old Style Furniture
Steve Balkenbush
2381 Us Hwy 231
Wetumpka, AL 36092-4581
Phone: (334)567-430
Fax: (334)567-430

Guardsman Woodpro
Jay Wilkinson
8618 Sturbridge
Montgomery, AL 36116
Phone: (334)272-577
Fax: (334)272-577

Furniture Medic
Pete Grantham
438 E. Saunders Rd.
Dothan, AL 36301
Phone: (334)702-191
Fax: (334)702-053

Furniture Medic
Rusty Longhurst
1845 Harpeth River Dr.
Brentwood, TN 37027
Phone: (615)370-166
Fax: (615)309-983

The Leather Specialist
Miro Carminati
201 Gillespie Dr, #14305
Franklin, TN 37067
Phone: (615)771-564
Fax: (615)771-564

Guardsman Woodpro
Dan Looney
1003 Riverwood Place
Franklin, TN 37069
Phone: (615)595-198
Fax: (615)595-946

Project America S.E. Svc Co.
Judd Sulcer
1784 W Northfield Blvd #277
Murfreesboro, TN 37129
Phone: (615)895-600
Fax: (615)895-018

Furniture Restoration
Ronald K. Schneider, Sr.
4951 Sherman Oak Rd.
Nashville, TN 37211
Phone: (615)833-497
Fax: (615)833-501

Reynolds Restoration
Robert Moon
5543 Edmondson Pike #142
Nashville, TN 37211
Phone: (615)895-704
Fax: (615)867-639

Transit Claims Service
Keith Smith
P.O. Box 292181
Nashville, TN 37229
Phone: (615)952-990
Fax: (615)952-990

The Furniture Finisher
Hank Wolfe
2720 St. Lawrence Rd.
Chattanooga, TN 37421
Phone: (423)892-778
Fax: (423)499-558

Walkers Furniture Refinishing
Marion Walker
7160 Lee Hyw
Chattanooga, TN 37421
Phone: (423)899-391
Fax: (423)894-666

Guardsman Woodpro
Bill Fisher
P.O. Box 21134
Chattanooga, TN 37424-0134
Phone: (423)893-776
Fax: (423)894-571

Guardsman Woodpro
Steve Basler
1914 Belvedere Ct.
Maryville, TN 37803-2818
Phone: (423)681-514

Buck's Finishing Touch
Buck Delaney
8013 Shady Ln.
Powell, TN 37849
Phone: (423)947-285
Fax: (423)938-282

Chuck's Repair Service
Chuck Veach
P.O. Box 483
Stanton, TN 38069
Phone: (901)548-262
Fax: (901)548-262

Furniture Medic
Donnie Floyd
1852 Harbert
Memphis, TN 38104
Phone: (901)568-593
Fax: (901)729-265

Clay Uphol. & Refinish. Co.
Donald & Carlene Clay
2608 Poplar Ave.
Memphis, TN 38112
Phone: (901)454-714
Fax: (901)454-715

Furniture Medic
John A. Washburn
7278 New Briton Dr.
Memphis, TN 38125
Phone: (888)763-342
Fax: (901)624-582

Blake Soule Furn. Rest., Inc.
Blake Soule
2077 Thomas Rd., #12
Memphis, TN 38134
Phone: (901)377-364
Fax: (901)377-361

Frazier Claim Service
Dennis & Cindy Frazier
P.O. Box 7326
Jackson, MS 39282-7326
Phone: (601)371-982
Fax: (601)372-033

Excel Shop, Inc.
Steven Weber
112 Bauer Ave.
Louisville, KY 40207
Phone: (502)895-737
Fax: (502)895-737

Hoskins Furniture Service
Dave Hoskins
3809 Broadland Trail
Louisville, KY 40241
Phone: (502)361-714
Fax: (502)361-714

Old Kentucky Restorations
Bob Cairns
122 W. Lexington St.
Harrodsburg, KY 40330
Phone: (606)734-623
Fax: (606)734-623

Furniture Medic
Johnathon West
271 Gold Rush Rd., Unit H
Lexington, KY 40503
Phone: (606)278-668
Fax: (606)278-668

Furniture Medic Of Lex., Inc.
Bob Dickson
4633 Hickory Creek
Lexington, KY 40515
Phone: (606)221-076
Fax: (606)369-736

Furniture Medic
Steve Elias
158 Rue Thierry
Paducah, KY 42001
Phone: (502)554-009
Fax: (502)554-009

Dave's Restoration
David Howard
5215 S. Wilson Rd.
Elizabethtown, KY 42701
Phone: (502)737-820
Fax: (502)737-221

Guardsman Woodpro
Terry Mccreary
361 Slate Run Dr.
Powell, OH 43065
Phone: (740)548-204
Fax: (740)548-204

Furniture Medic
Robert F. Cadegan
1081 Briarcliff Rd.
Reynoldsburg, OH 43068-1753
Phone: (614)755-391
Fax: (614)755-231

Guardsman Woodpro
John Holt
12827 Stonecreek Dr.
Pickerington, OH 43147
Phone: (614)751-122

Wilson Furn. Svc.
Wm. A. Wilson
669 Powhatan
Columbus, OH 43204
Phone: (614)279-157

Furniture Fix, The
Earl Muenze
4930 Brittany Ct. E.
Columbus, OH 43229
Phone: (614)848-877

Furniture Medic
David Urton
5581 Satinwood Dr.
Columbus, OH 43229
Phone: (614)436-313
Fax: (614)844-578

Columbus In-Home Furn. Svc.
John A. Johnson
4555 Groves Rd., #25
Columbus, OH 43232
Phone: (614)863-524
Fax: (614)863-636

Furniture Medic
Hope Ann Ingalls
P.O. Box 101
Sparta, OH 43350
Phone: (800)984-856
Fax: (614)397-238

Furniture Medic
Chris Dziubek
1833 S. Holland Sylvania Rd.
Maumee, OH 43537
Phone: (419)861-167
Fax: (419)861-175

Ohio Furniture Conservation
John Meeker
311 1/2 W. Broadway
Maumee, OH 43537
Phone: (419)893-630
Fax: (419)385-776

Huenefeld Claim Services
Jeffrey D. Huenefeld
8908 Linden Lake Rd.
Sylvania, OH 43560
Phone: (419)829-627
Fax: (419)829-627

Fred Rickard Furniture Svcs.
Fred Rickard
P.O. Box 118055
Toledo, OH 43611
Phone: (419)729-255
Fax: (419)726-595

American Furniture Technology
Jim Nesmith
1172 Hidden Ridge
Toledo, OH 43615
Phone: (419)868-303
Fax: (419)868-641

Furniture Medic
Scott Vansparrentak
45289 Old Middle Ridge Rd.
Amherst, OH 44001
Phone: (440)984-230
Fax: (440)984-230

Guardsman Woodpro
Mark Mathes
1730 Gulf Rd.
Elyria, OH 44035
Phone: (216)365-496
Fax: (216)365-294

W.A. Born Furn Rest/Trnst Clms
Wilfred Born
3467 Tree Lane
Cleveland, OH 44070-1682
Phone: (440)779-556
Fax: (440)779-556

Pro Touch Up
James Grimes
33974 Beachpark
Eastlake, OH 44095
Phone: (216)951-587
Fax: (216)953-124

Furniture Medic
Robert Divincenzo
1996 W. 3rd St.
Cleveland, OH 44113
Phone: (216)621-602
Fax: (216)621-616

D & K Enterprises
Karen Garmon
Po Box 30651
Middleburg Heights, OH 44130
Phone: (440)243-635
Fax: (440)243-635

J.B. Jewitt Co., Inc.
Jeff Jewitt
11929 Abbey Rd., Unit G
North Royalton, OH 44133
Phone: (440)582-892
Fax: (440)582-850

Furniture Medic
James D'Amico
4487 Diplomat Dr.
Stow, OH 44224
Phone: (330)945-784
Fax: (330)945-800

Furniture Medic
David Byer
P.O. Box 871
Salem, OH 44460
Phone: (330)332-605
Fax: (330)332-605

Jim Anderson Furn. Touch Up
Jim Anderson
5163 Oakcrest Dr.
Youngstown, OH 44515
Phone: (330)792-478
Fax: (330)792-841

Justice's Finishing Line
Jim Justice
1432 Tumbleweed St., N.E.
Uniontown, OH 44685
Phone: (330)877-151
Fax: (330)877-177

Dunn's Furniture Service
C. David Dunn
4421 New Haven Rd.
Tiro, OH 44887
Phone: (419)562-545
Fax: (419)562-930

Artistic Furn. Restoration
Bill Ruble
5179 Layhigh Rd.
Hamilton, OH 45013
Phone: (513)889-000
Fax: (513)889-001

Old World Restorations, Inc.
Doug Eisele
5729 Dragon Way
Cincinnati, OH 45227
Phone: (513)271-545
Fax: (513)271-541

Furniture Medic
Bill Spahr, III
990 Cardinal Dr.
Enon, OH 45323
Phone: (937)864-565
Fax: (937)864-521

Pete's Furniture Repair
Brian Aycock
9155 N. Dixie Dr.
Dayton, OH 45414
Phone: (937)454-180
Fax: (937)454-180

Stone's Fine Wd/Leath Rpr Svc.
James T. Stone
6657 Brigham Sq.
Centerville, OH 45459-6924
Phone: (937)434-420
Fax: (937)434-009

Moving Services
Roy Bivens
6832 Baker Rd.
Athens, OH 45701
Phone: (614)593-669
Fax: (614)592-390

Guardsman Woodpro
Kent Hilty
7299 Cr 86
Findlay, OH 45840
Phone: (419)420-184

Guardsman Woodpro
Bill Dodd
14408 Crystal Creek
Noblesville, IN 46060
Phone: (317)773-779

Able Woodcrafters
Garry Bole
10643 E. 1000 North
Brownsburg, IN 46112
Phone: (317)291-209
Fax: (317)291-174

Action Furniture Repair
Jon Helm
1118 S. Sherman Dr.
Indianapolis, IN 46203-2205
Phone: (317)357-209
Fax: (317)357-295

Shambles Furn. Restor., The
Ron Sanders
7183 W. US 40
Cumberland, IN 46229
Phone: (317)894-707
Fax: (317)894-864

Guardsman Woodpro
Kerry Ingram
4720 W. Mary St.
North Judson, IN 46366
Phone: (219)896-359

Furniture Medic
Thomas J. Keevin
1402 Lincolnway
Valparaiso, IN 46383
Phone: (219)477-586
Fax: (219)548-882

Heeter Furniture Repair
Jerry W. Heeter
1545 W. Lusher
Elkhart, IN 46517
Phone: (219)293-870
Fax: (219)522-633

Kelly's Furn. Service, Inc
Lisa Kohne
P.O. Box 48
Wolcottville, IN 46795-0048
Phone: (800)868-487
Fax: (219)854-373

Guardsman Woodpro
John Hunter
5299 Sleepy Hollow Rd.
Newburgh, IN 47630
Phone: (812)858-490

Furniture Medic
Karen Cook
500 Wayne Ave.
Crawfordsville, IN 47933
Phone: (317)272-794
Fax: (317)272-794

Furniture Medic By Rgw
Gayle Roudabush
42285 E. Edward
Clinton Township, MI 48038
Phone: (810)412-333
Fax: (810)412-333

Guardsman Woodpro
Jim Mcpherson
227 Amelia
Royal Oak, MI 48073
Phone: (810)588-310
Fax: (810)583-697

Guardsman Woodpro
Jerry Champine
7640 Zeeb Rd.
Dexter, MI 48130
Phone: (313)426-948
Fax: (313)426-948

Dart's Finishing
Art Dart
8131 Emerald Lane West
Westland, MI 48185
Phone: (734)981-940
Fax: (734)981-940

Michigan Antique Preservation
Bill Witkowski
2034 Eureka Rd.
Wyandotte, MI 48192
Phone: (313)283-570
Fax: (313)283-431

Raschella's Custom Service
Domenica Raschella
1450 Grayton Rd.
Grosse Pointe Park, MI 48230
Phone: (313)882-543
Fax: (313)882-087

Furniture Medic
Leonard Reinhardt
867 University Place
Grosse Pointe, MI 48230
Phone: (313)884-100
Fax: (313)884-893

Furniture Medic
Robert J. Thomas
2177 Avon Industrial Dr.
Rochester Hils, MI 48309
Phone: (248)853-988
Fax: (248)853-295

Furniture Care Specialists
Al Sunshine
42495 Park Ridge
Novi, MI 48375-2660
Phone: (248)348-909

Furniture Medic
Mel & Darren Dzeidzic
216 Audubon Ave.
White Lake, MI 48383
Phone: (248)887-239
Fax: (248)887-014

Martin Furniture Refinishers
Daniel J. Martin
239 E. Walled Lake Dr.
Walled Lake, MI 48390
Phone: (248)624-308
Fax: (248)471-706

Hensler Furn. Refinishing Inc.
Gerald A. Hensler
3100 Christy Way
Saginaw, MI 48603-2225
Phone: (517)792-131
Fax: (517)249-529

Benno's Woodworking
Benno Trenkle
1813 S. Burdick
Kalamazoo, MI 49001-2715
Phone: (616)342-907
Fax: (616)342-622

Able Repairs
Duane Smith
9366 Bever Rd.
Delton, MI 49046
Phone: (616)623-870
Fax: (616)623-870

Guardsman Woodpro
Bob Gibson
P.O. Box 297
Stockbridge, MI 49285
Phone: (517)851-885

Guardsman Woodpro
Cindy Lear
101 Washington St., #140
Grand Haven, MI 49417
Phone: (616)842-430
Fax: (616)842-430

Expert Furn. Rest. & Repr, Inc
Stephen M. Smith
1123 Butterworth Sw
Grand Rapids, MI 49504
Phone: (616)458-171
Fax: (616)454-968

Guardsman Woodpro
Tony Ziegler
4999 36th Street Se
Grand Rapids, MI 49512
Phone: (800)496-637
Fax: (616)285-788

The Furniture Masters
Michael John Anderson
801 Woodmere
Traverse City, MI 49684
Phone: (616)941-436
Fax: (616)941-064

Fisher's Furniture Rep/Refin.
Michael R. Fisher
9791 E. Crain Hill Rd.
Traverse City, MI 49684
Phone: (616)946-861
Fax: (616)932-867

Guardsman Woodpro
Eric Schatz
7668 N. Lake Bluff
Gladstone, MI 49837
Phone: (906)428-981
Fax: (906)786-909

Furniture Medic
Gary & Stacy Kaiser
606 Topaz Dr.
Sergeant Bluff, IA 51054
Phone: (888)427-046
Fax: (712)943-452

Craig's Claims Service
John Craig
210 29th St., N.E.
Cedar Rapids, IA 52402
Phone: (319)363-880
Fax: (319)393-208

Woodworks
Anne Lesnet
309 W 2nd St.
Muscatine, IA 52761
Phone: (319)264-214
Fax: (319)264-214

Holzbauer & Sons Repair
Carl W. Holzbauer
W160n9636 Colonial Dr.
Germantown, WI 53022
Phone: (414)253-978
Fax: (414)253-464

Furniture Medic
Mark Young
West 2243 County Y
Lomira, WI 53048
Phone: (920)583-372
Fax: (920)583-420

Furniture Medic
Robert Harrold
5090 Brown St.
Oconomowoc, WI 53066
Phone: (414)567-072
Fax: (414)567-072

Mullaly Furn Finish./Rep Svc
Virginia Mullaly
5226 W. Donges Bay Road
Mequon, WI 53092
Phone: (414)242-255
Fax: (414)242-171

Nielsen's Furniture Service
Randy Nielsen
7186 Madaus Dr.
Lake Geneva, WI 53147
Phone: (414)248-108
Fax: (414)248-129

Guardsman Woodpro
Gerry Miller
6714 244th Ave.
Salem, WI 53168
Phone: (414)842-141
Fax: (414)843-285

Heartland Furniture
Bruce Gee
1923 Hawkinson Road
Oregon, WI 53575
Phone: (608)873-181
Fax: (608)873-181

Guardsman Woodpro
Doug Zadra
1143 E. Johnson St.
Madison, WI 53703
Phone: (608)294-988
Fax: (608)294-988

Furniture Medic
Wayne Stuckey
526 North St.
Madison, WI 53704
Phone: (608)249-497
Fax: (608)249-497

Guardsman Woodpro
Jim D'Amour
1114 Lacount Rd.
Green Bay, WI 54313-1337
Phone: (920)405-670

Woodcraft Furniture Service
Daniel Klein
P.O. Box 294
Appleton, WI 54912-0294
Phone: (414)757-530
Fax: (414)757-530

Furniture Caretakers
Brad Jelle
2045 63rd St. E.
Inver Grove Heights, MN 55077
Phone: (651)552-830
Fax: (651)552-830

Furniture Medic
Paula & Doug Erickson
2324 Lakearies Blvd.
White Bear Lake, MN 55110
Phone: (651)407-169
Fax: (651)653-620

Guardsman Woodpro
John O'Connell
1833 Lake Ln.
Arden Hills, MN 55112
Phone: (651)636-841
Fax: (651)636-841

Older's Furniture Svc.
Glen Older
P.O. Box 1052
Burnsville, MN 55337
Phone: (612)890-234
Fax: (612)894-434

Guardsmen Woodpro
Bruce Mathison
4015 W. 54th St.
Edina, MN 55424
Phone: (612)915-194

Furniture Doctor, The
Susan Johnson Hoffman
4465 Harbor Lane
Minneapolis, MN 55446
Phone: (612)557-651
Fax: (612)557-657

Guardsman Woodpro
Al & Mary Jo Toering
225 Fanelle Ave.
Sioux Falls, SD 57103
Phone: (605)332-348

Furniture Medic
Jack Vaupel
47310 Austin Ct.
Sioux Falls, SD 57108-8127
Phone: (605)743-510
Fax: (605)743-517

Furniture Medic
Robert & Kristi Mitchell
2202 2nd Ave. East, Unit A
West Fargo, ND 58078
Phone: (701)277-100

Serendipity Masters
C. Dale Apeland
2535 Glen Lake Rd.
Eureka, MT 59917
Phone: (406)889-365
Fax: (406)889-390

Ers Replacement Services
Norm Rosenthal
214 E. Scranton Ave.
Lake Bluff, IL 60044
Phone: (847)295-223
Fax: (847)295-211

Craft Antique Repair
Scott & Jan Kuba
204 North Old Rand Road
Lake Zurich, IL 60047
Phone: (847)438-339
Fax: (847)438-232

Furniture Medic
Pete Barbacovi
520 N. Seymour Ave.
Mundelein, IL 60060
Phone: (847)367-966
Fax: (847)566-051

Hanson Furniture Service
Bruce Hanson
P.O. Box 245
Woodstock, IL 60098
Phone: (815)728-880
Fax: (815)728-161

D & L Furniture Service Co.
Deloris & Larry Gilmer
P.O. Box 232
Elmhurst, IL 60126
Phone: (630)279-724
Fax: (630)279-892

Midwest Adjusting & Insp Svc
Dan Basich, Jr.
P.O. Box 7251
Westchester, IL 60154-7251
Phone: (708)345-484
Fax: (708)345-484

Furniture Medic
Brian K. Healy
685 Edenwood Dr.
Roselle, IL 60172
Phone: (630)539-244
Fax: (630)539-264

Furniture Medic
Roy Grimsley
125 W. Front, #134
Wheaton, IL 60187
Phone: (630)653-774
Fax: (630)653-751

Associates Claim Service Inc.
John Hozian
722 W. Lunt Ave.
Schaumburg, IL 60193
Phone: (847)985-172
Fax: (847)985-837

Furniture Medic
James Bandy
2528 W. 183rd St.
Homewood, IL 60430
Phone: (708)957-791
Fax: (708)957-853

Guardsman Woodpro
Richard and Pam Walters
912 South Center
Plano, IL 60545
Phone: (630)552-858
Fax: (630)552-858

Furniture Medic
Michael J. Morris
210 E. Kendall Dr.
Yorkville, IL 60560
Phone: (630)553-181
Fax: (630)553-183

Claimguard, Inc.
Mike Witkowski
215 W. Diehl Rd.
Naperville, IL 60563
Phone: (630)717-356
Fax: (630)717-374

Furniture Medic
John Ross
3823 Mallard
Naperville, IL 60564
Phone: (630)904-300
Fax: (630)904-300

Chicago Conservation Center
Heather Becker
730 N. Franklin, #701
Chicago, IL 60610
Phone: (312)944-540
Fax: (312)944-547

Bobcat Wood Refinishing
Bob Shannon
7745 S. Halsted
Chicago, IL 60620
Phone: (773)238-205
Fax: (773)238-920

Furn. Patching & Touch-Up Svc
Robert E. Dudle
7347 N. Damen Ave.
Chicago, IL 60645-2356
Phone: (773)262-962
Fax: (773)262-963

Superior Custom Rpr. Svc. Inc.
James Murphy
2514 W. Armitage
Chicago, IL 60647
Phone: (773)645-030

Furniture Medic
William Parsons, III
4428 N. Ottawa
Norridge, IL 60656
Phone: (708)452-702
Fax: (708)452-159

Weber Furniture Service, Inc.
David Mcnulty
5915 N. Ravenswood Ave.
Chicago, IL 60660
Phone: (773)275-906
Fax: (773)275-194

Furniture Medic
Dieter Off
8212 Oleander
Niles, IL 60714
Phone: (847)967-118
Fax: (847)967-119

Image Restoration Services
David Kummerow
127 W. Locust
Belvidere, IL 61008
Phone: (815)547-591
Fax: (815)547-641

Furniture Medic
Edward J. Schmit
713 S. Bench St.
Galena, IL 61036
Phone: (815)777-688
Fax: (815)777-472

Furniture Medic
Michael Thrasher
1994 First St. A, #108
Moline, IL 61265
Phone: (309)797-373
Fax: (309)797-374

Warner's Art Rest/Obj Of Art
Wayne Warner
RR 16, Box 557
Bloomington, IL 61704
Phone: (309)828-099
Fax: (309)829-878

R.L. Wills Claim Service
Robert L. Wills
R.R. 2, Box 157
Heyworth, IL 61745
Phone: (309)473-333
Fax: (309)473-330

Furniture Medic
Scott Knudsen
406 N. Edwin
Champaign, IL 61821
Phone: (217)352-417
Fax: (217)352-449

Furniture Medic
Bob & Tom Stanze
16048 Meadow Oak Dr.
Chesterfield, MO 63017
Phone: (314)532-023
Fax: (314)532-023

Hamlin's Porcelain Rest'n
Gloria Hamlin
377 Novara Dr.
Ballwin, MO 63021
Phone: (314)256-857
Fax: (314)256-860

Craig Dodge Restorations
Craig Dodge
1326 West Lark Industrial Pk.
Fenton, MO 63026
Phone: (314)349-800
Fax: (314)326-136

Maxfield's Furniture Repair
Larry Maxfield
35 St. Maurice
Florissant, MO 63031
Phone: (314)837-732
Fax: (314)837-637

Furniture Medic
Stuart A. Klearman
370 Fee Fee Rd.
Maryland Heights, MO 63043
Phone: (314)209-744
Fax: (314)209-744

Furniture Doctor, The
Robert Brannan, Jr.
5591 Ruth Dr.
House Springs, MO 63051
Phone: (314)942-290
Fax: (314)942-452

Workbench Refinishing
Norm Shoults
8631 Gravois Rd.
St. Louis, MO 63123
Phone: (314)843-422
Fax: (314)843-466

House Doctor, The
Bob Soell
9311 Sappington
St. Louis, MO 63126
Phone: (314)842-644
Fax: (314)843-610

Furniture Medic
James Keusenkothen
1011 Eagle Dr.
Jackson, MO 63755
Phone: (573)243-186
Fax: (573)243-244

Ms. Fix-It Furn. Repair/Rest.
Deborah L. Brunner
3193 W. 89th St.
Desoto, KS 66018
Phone: (913)583-195
Fax: (913)583-195

Furniture Medic
John L. Patton
13502 W. 115th St.
Olathe, KS 66062
Phone: (913)451-595
Fax: (913)451-036

Seigler Woodwrkng Specl'ties
Bobby W. Seigler
22734 SW Indianola Rd.
Douglas, KS 67039-8286
Phone: (316)746-314
Fax: (316)746-314

Furniture Medic
Jason Klassen
1354 S. Ridge Rd.
Wichita, KS 67209
Phone: (316)941-476
Fax: (316)942-573

Furniture Medic
Jerry Winkley
4821 N. Hydraulic
Wichita, KS 67219
Phone: (316)838-640
Fax: (316)838-640

Don's Refinishing & Furn. Rep.
Don Sindelar
3719 "Q" Street
Omaha, NE 68107
Phone: (402)731-322
Fax: (402)731-643

Furniture Medic
T. Davis Hill
14867 Shirley St.
Omaha, NE 68144
Phone: (402)697-707
Fax: (402)697-700

Hall Piano Co., Inc.
Dan Hall
901 David Dr.
Metairie, LA 70003
Phone: (504)733-886
Fax: (504)736-010

Weathersby Furn. Rep.
Shad Weathersby
P.O. Box 8486
New Orleans, LA 70182
Phone: (504)945-756
Fax: (504)947-897

Furniture Works
Al Reisz
216 Sunvalley Dr.
Slidell, LA 70458
Phone: (504)649-086
Fax: (504)649-086

Woodpecker Furn. Rest. Cntr.
Mike Dorsett
216 E. Texas Ave.
Rayne, LA 70578
Phone: (800)492-966
Fax: (318)334-800

Furniture Medic
Harry Marshall
183 Rye Dr.
Cabot, AR 72023
Phone: (501)374-360
Fax: (501)843-523

Mr. Honey Do, Inc.
Evia Breshears
P.O. Box 2200
Conway, AR 72033
Phone: (501)327-121
Fax: (501)513-121

Furniture Medic
Kim Blalock
185 Ridgefield Dr.
Ward, AR 72176
Phone: (501)371-074
Fax: (501)605-918

Davis Furniture Restorations
Stephen Davis
P.O. Box 1961
Fayetteville, AR 72702-1961
Phone: (501)521-597
Fax: (501)443-710

Furniture Medic
Glenn & Lynne Foster
1047 Glenn Lane
Fayetteville, AR 72703
Phone: (501)587-949
Fax: (501)587-949

Furniture Medic
John Hanlon
209 N. Blake Dr.
Oklahoma City, OK 73130
Phone: (405)848-558
Fax: (405)741-498

Heartland Full Claims Svc.
Larry & Donna Marks
5420 Nw 65th St.
Oklahoma City, OK 73132
Phone: (405)728-193
Fax: (405)728-293

Furniture Medic
Mike Stuber
315 E. Harvard
Enid, OK 73701
Phone: (580)242-456
Fax: (580)242-456

Woodshed, The
Tom Hill
11367 E. 61 St South
Broken Arrow, OK 74012
Phone: (918)258-855
Fax: (918)250-516

Furniture Repair Specialists
Richard Powell
P.O. Box 1231
Sand Springs, OK 74063
Phone: (918)241-305
Fax: (918)241-566

Reid's Furniture Repair
Dick Reid
2017 N. Broadway
Carrollton, TX 75006
Phone: (972)245-525
Fax: (972)245-440

Classic Refinishing, Inc.
Denny and Suzanne Harris
3700 Canon Gate Circle
Carrollton, TX 75007
Phone: (972)306-540
Fax: (972)307-779

Guardsman Woodpro
George Hislop
2040 W Sprg Crk Pkwy/141-291
Plano, TX 75023-4225
Phone: (972)527-739
Fax: (972)527-601

Furniture Medic
Bill Tekrony
4800 Glen Echo Dr.
Plano, TX 75024
Phone: (972)618-820

Dallas Central Services
Steve Hart
P.O. Box 250011
Plano, TX 75025-0011
Phone: (972)712-791
Fax: (972)712-791

M2 Construction
Mike Mcdaniel
P.O. Box 294641
Lewisville, TX 75029
Phone: (972)355-030
Fax: (972)355-030

Furniture Medic
John Stout
3516 Merritt Rd.
Sachse, TX 75048
Phone: (972)475-284
Fax: (972)475-308

D & D Restorations
David Rackley
412 Elwood St., #101-A
Irving, TX 75061
Phone: (972)579-982
Fax: (972)579-808

Malin & Malin, P.C.
Steven C. Malin
110 N. Tennessee St., #B
Mckinney, TX 75069
Phone: (972)529-533
Fax: (972)529-516

Piano Arts
Dan Reed
1909 Lilac Court
Richardson, TX 75080
Phone: (972)699-746
Fax: (972)644-130

Tovar Furniture Studio
Rick Martinez
6506 Walnut Hill Lane
Dallas, TX 75230
Phone: (972)243-346
Fax: (214)691-462

Claim Services International
Kathy Sherwin
7557 Rambler Rd. Ste. 800
Dallas, TX 75231-4165
Phone: (214)265-997
Fax: (214)265-987

Smith's Antiques/Refinishing
Cyndi Smith
3650 Garner Blvd.
Arlington, TX 76013
Phone: (817)265-704
Fax: (817)265-781

Furniture Medic
Roger Ballou
6009 Saddle Ridge Rd.
Arlington, TX 76016
Phone: (817)496-997
Fax: (817)492-959

Furniture Medic
Sam Mcclure
100 Mariah
Weatherford, TX 76086
Phone: (817)341-450
Fax: (817)613-989

Accent Furniture Repair
Andy Chapman
P.O. Box 543
Burleson, TX 76097
Phone: (817)572-027
Fax: (817)478-976

S.W.K. Speciality Wood Cons.
Stanley W. Kowalczyk
2208 Tierney Rd.
Fort Worth, TX 76112
Phone: (817)496-013
Fax: (817)496-423

Furniture Medic
Joe Gilley
5504 Dublin Ln.
N. Richland Hills, TX 76180
Phone: (817)581-035
Fax: (817)581-035

Guardsman Woodpro
Craig & Mary Watkins
103 Ranch Ct.
Argyle, TX 76226
Phone: (940)464-231
Fax: (940)464-101

Shumake & Associates/Int. Svc
Larry W. Shumake
P.O. Box 8703
Waco, TX 76714
Phone: (254)836-171
Fax: (254)776-721

Furniture Medic
Ken Hahn
1618 Conrad Sauer
Houston, TX 77043
Phone: (713)461-466
Fax: (713)468-274

Furniture Medic
Al Green
4003 Village Corner Dr.
Houston, TX 77059
Phone: (281)998-907
Fax: (281)998-907

Key Restoration Services
Karl E. Yehlik
20819 Essman #16
Houston, TX 77073
Phone: (281)443-668
Fax: (281)443-678

Furniture Medic
Paul Kaye
12466 Deep Spring Lane
Houston, TX 77077
Phone: (281)752-557
Fax: (281)752-556

West Houston Management
Bob Mueller
16360 Park Ten Place, #101
Houston, TX 77084
Phone: (281)492-857
Fax: (281)492-058

Guardsman Woodpro
Gary Wallace
18314 Cransley Dr.
Houston, TX 77084-3203
Phone: (281)345-681
Fax: (281)345-682

The Touch-Up Men
Bruce Eden
P.O. Box 711353
Houston, TX 77271-1353
Phone: (713)774-564
Fax: (713)774-121

Best Finishing Co. Inc.
Brian Blackstock
P.O. Box 90213
Houston, TX 77290
Phone: (281)580-862
Fax: (281)580-242

Guardsman Woodpro
James Woelbrueck
10203 Cantertro
Humble, TX 77338
Phone: (281)446-895
Fax: (281)446-895

Wakewood Furniture Shop
Zoe Higgins
2038 Little Cedar
Kingwood, TX 77339
Phone: (281)358-715
Fax: (281)358-171

Positive Micro Results
Paul M. Raybern
P.O. Box 429
New Waverly, TX 77358
Phone: (409)438-888
Fax: (409)438-888

Furniture Medic
Norman Fowlkes
2650 Old Louetta Loop, Ste 8
Spring, TX 77388
Phone: (281)651-948
Fax: (281)651-941

Tom Granger Restorations
Tom Granger
2218 Brae Ln.
League City, TX 77573
Phone: (281)338-827
Fax: (281)338-827

Furniture Medic
Jerry Kirks
30641 Royal Valance
Fair Oaks Ranch, TX 78015
Phone: (830)981-913
Fax: (830)755-863

Adonna's Repairs/Restoration
Adonna Wilkinson
1040 Lakefield Dr.
Canyon Lake, TX 78133
Phone: (830)935-204

Windmill Country Store/Wdwrks
Allison Sims
11027 Wetmore Rd.
San Antonio, TX 78216
Phone: (210)494-667
Fax: (210)402-069

Hampton Cabinets & Furn Rest.
Dan Price
6602 Topper Ridge #1
San Antonio, TX 78233
Phone: (210)590-226
Fax: (210)590-238

Furniture Medic
Al Clauss
6907 Timberhill
San Antonio, TX 78238
Phone: (210)509-372
Fax: (210)509-372

Absolute Furniture Renewal
Michael Gilley
3636 S. Alameda, Ste. B-178
Corpus Christi, TX 78411
Phone: (512)852-899
Fax: (512)854-810

Furniture Medic
Len Leslie
600 South Bell Blvd, Ste. 209
Cedar Park, TX 78613
Phone: (512)260-216
Fax: (512)336-956

R. H. Roloff & Co.
Robert H. Roloff
203 Woods Ln.
Cedar Park, TX 78613
Phone: (512)259-505
Fax: (512)259-505

Neuberger Furniture Service
Jim Neuberger
13704-1 Bullick Hollow Rd.
Austin, TX 78726
Phone: (512)258-991
Fax: (512)219-030

Bix Refinishing & Upholstery
Frank & Rosemary Bergen
816 W. Yager Lane
Austin, TX 78753
Phone: (512)837-167
Fax: (512)837-167

Furniture Medic
Garry Baccus
872 N. Us Hwy 385
Levelland, TX 79336
Phone: (806)799-855
Fax: (806)894-192

A Finishing Touch
Jeff Withrow
P.O. Box 98541
Lubbock, TX 79499
Phone: (806)744-242
Fax: (806)744-316

Master Craft
Brooks Smith
1300 S. County Rd. 1110
Midland, TX 79706
Phone: (915)682-825

Queen City Furniture Repair
Vern Sybesma
7447 S. Dowining Cir. W.
Littleton, CO 80122
Phone: (303)794-334
Fax: (303)794-174

Colorado D&S Enterprises, Inc.
Dale Slaughter
12483 Meade Way
Littleton, CO 80125
Phone: (303)791-161
Fax: (303)791-162

Craftsmen & Associates
Bill Munns
9612 Titan Park Circle, #5
Littleton, CO 80125
Phone: (303)683-000
Fax: (303)683-000

Rene Wahl Furn. Repair, Inc.
Rene Wahl
3085 Hamal Circle
Monument, CO 80132
Phone: (719)488-889
Fax: (719)488-885

Furniture Medic
Jeffrey S. Messer
4954 E. 41st Ave.
Denver, CO 80216
Phone: (303)321-655
Fax: (303)321-655

Lanier's Refinishing
L.R. (Randy) Lanier
9760b E. Alameda
Denver, CO 80231
Phone: (303)363-778
Fax: (303)343-693

Woodtech Services
David Weatherford
P.O. Box 4627
Breckenridge, CO 80424
Phone: (970)453-235
Fax: (970)453-308

Guardsman Woodpro
Matt Williams
P.O. Box 945
Erie, CO 80516
Phone: (303)828-921
Fax: (303)828-408

Guardsman Woodpro
Bill Matthews
4701 Crest Rd.
Ft. Collins, CO 80526
Phone: (970)217-710

Brooks Furniture Service
Bob Brooks
7 Via Sierra Grande
Manitou Springs, CO 80829
Phone: (719)685-509
Fax: (719)685-941

Furniture Medic
Rick Singer
7825 Burgess Rd.
Colorado Springs, CO 80908
Phone: (719)495-258
Fax: (719)495-282

Guardsman Woodpro
Mike Carroll
6575 Foxdale Circle
Colorado Springs, CO 80919
Phone: (719)488-870
Fax: (719)522-944

M T I Inspection Svcs.
W. H. Fullerton
P.O. Box 6999
Colorado Springs, CO 80934
Phone: (719)633-017
Fax: (719)685-593

Re-Nu House
James D. King
516 Fruitvale Ct., Unit D
Grand Junction, CO 81504
Phone: (970)434-137
Fax: (970)241-104

Furniture Doctor, The
Blake Brown
P.O. Box 51962
Idaho Falls, ID 83405-1962
Phone: (208)542-255

Artcraft Refinishing
Janet Wonacutt
4655 Macarthur
Boise, ID 83705
Phone: (208)342-414
Fax: (208)336-215

Furniture Doctors, The
Paul Malinauskas
2750 W. Prairie Ave.
Coeur D'alene, ID 83815
Phone: (208)772-643
Fax: (208)772-477

Call's Furniture Repair
Duane Thornton
P.O. Box 294
Pleasant Grove, UT 84062
Phone: (801)785-132
Fax: (801)785-171

Specialized Repair Co.
Ken Gallacher
12101 S. 1390 W.
Riverton, UT 84065
Phone: (801)254-277
Fax: (801)254-351

Guardsman Woodpro
Corey Hansen
906 W. 13120 South
Riverton, UT 84065
Phone: (801)446-822

Professional Furniture Svc Inc
Tim Martell
4010 Nw Grand Ave., #10
Phoenix, AZ 85019
Phone: (602)995-392
Fax: (602)995-393

Customer Claim Service
Jim Whitten
2105 E. Lone Cactus Drive
Phoenix, AZ 85024
Phone: (602)971-401
Fax: (602)569-179

Furniture Medic
Dave Wooden
4246 S. 37th St.
Phoenix, AZ 85040
Phone: (602)470-083
Fax: (602)470-084

Furniture Medic
Jason Jantzen
11221 S. 51st, #1038
Phoenix, AZ 85044
Phone: (602)961-533
Fax: (602)961-529

Quality Furniture Repair
Stephen Call
1039 E. 2nd Pl.
Mesa, AZ 85203
Phone: (602)962-427
Fax: (602)962-431

Artistic Finisher's East
Wade Denson
2350 E. Javelina
Mesa, AZ 85204
Phone: (602)892-634
Fax: (602)892-301

Lost Art Finishing
Richard L. & Peggy J. Bennet
3025 E. Dolphin Ave.
Mesa, AZ 85204
Phone: (602)830-491
Fax: (602)981-553

Guardsman Woodpro
Brian Nowakowski
9781 E. Desert Trail
Scottsdale, AZ 85260
Phone: (602)614-803
Fax: (602)614-803

Michael's Restorations
Matthew Martell
5230 W. Luke Ave., F-3
Glendale, AZ 85301
Phone: (602)934-925
Fax: (602)934-131

Complete Claim Service
David Mogensen
P.O. Box 6213
Glendale, AZ 85312
Phone: (602)362-891
Fax: (602)362-891

Furniture Medic
Don Soncrant
7739 E. Broadway, #67
Tucson, AZ 85710-3947
Phone: (520)290-331
Fax: (520)290-553

F.A.S.T. Services
Rick Freeman
116 N. Cortez
Prescott, AZ 86301
Phone: (800)610-587
Fax: (520)445-744

Furniture Medic
William Mcbride
314 Amherst Dr., S.E.
Albuquerque, NM 87106
Phone: (505)265-800
Fax: (505)232-806

Furniture Medic
James Wray
1423 Solano Dr., NE
Albuquerque, NM 87110
Phone: (505)262-000
Fax: (505)255-501

Bizzy Furn. Repair
Andy Vanetsky
12154 San Rafael, NE
Albuquerque, NM 87122
Phone: (505)856-107
Fax: (505)856-107

Furniture Medic
Ronald E. Hebert
1236 Chaco Ave
Farmington, NM 87401
Phone: (505)564-233
Fax: (505)564-480

Furniture Medic
Allan Cooper
1956 Mulberry
Las Cruces, NM 88001
Phone: (505)527-067
Fax: (505)527-063

Barbara Charlton Furn. Repair
Barbara Charlton
4205 Linniki St.
N. Las Vegas, NV 89030
Phone: (702)648-199
Fax: (702)646-184

Guardsman Woodpro
Stephen & Dianne Confer
3111 S. Valley View, A-201
Las Vegas, NV 89102
Phone: (702)251-444
Fax: (702)251-444

Furniture Medic
Brian Meaton
5430 S. Cameron St, Ste. 101
Las Vegas, NV 89118-2295
Phone: (702)579-011
Fax: (702)579-020

Tink's Decorative Art Studio
Andy Daniels
1536 "D" Street
Sparks, NV 89431
Phone: (702)359-085
Fax: (702)359-238

Rebel Forwarding
Pat Thibodeaux
2100 S. Alameda St.
Compton, CA 90221
Phone: (310)884-762
Fax: (310)635-426

Apex Furniture Restoration
Maxine Woody
15500 S. Main St.
Gardena, CA 90248
Phone: (310)217-877
Fax: (310)538-451

Mover Services
Linda Black
520 Washington Blvd., #377
Marina Del Rey, CA 90292
Phone: (310)822-183
Fax: (310)822-630

C.M.S. Enterprises
Robert Davies
2554 Lincoln Blvd., #819
Marina Del Rey, CA 90292
Phone: (310)306-741
Fax: (310)306-741

Claims Adjustment Technology
Linda Bluel
1805 W. 208th St., Suite 203
Torrance, CA 90501
Phone: (310)782-061
Fax: (310)782-375

West Coast Claim Service
Sandy Friend
P.O. Box 957
Artesia, CA 90702-0957
Phone: (562)924-733
Fax: (562)924-488

Drake Enterprises
Ty Drake
P.O. Box 21290
Long Beach, CA 90801-4290
Phone: (562)424-540
Fax: (562)424-640

Trolan & Trolan, Inc.
David Trolan
11711 Clark St, Unit 106
Arcadia, CA 91006
Phone: (626)357-530
Fax: (626)357-416

Trilco Claims & Antiques, Inc
Michael A. Trlica
617 S. Myrtle Ave.
Monrovia, CA 91016
Phone: (626)359-101
Fax: (626)357-431

Novotny's Contracting/Refin.
Gary Novotny
1106 1/2 W. Glenoaks Blvd.
Glendale, CA 91202
Phone: (818)500-857
Fax: (818)243-531

Al. D. Luongo Furn Rep/Refin
Albert D. Luongo
22819 Trigger St.
Chatsworth, CA 91311
Phone: (818)882-227
Fax: (818)882-014

Horton's Furniture Center
Richard Rosenberger
28210 Ave. Crocker, #306
Valencia, CA 91355
Phone: (800)948-934
Fax: (805)252-963

A Home Design
David Field
5220 Veloz Ave.
Tarzana, CA 91356
Phone: (818)757-776
Fax: (818)708-372

Southern Calif. Craftsmen
Walter Greenes
13910 Ventura Blvd.
Sherman Oaks, CA 91423
Phone: (818)907-754
Fax: (818)907-754

Matheis & Associates
Neil Matheis
7966 Surrey Lane
Alta Loma, CA 91701
Phone: (909)989-372
Fax: (909)941-158

Trlica And Associates
Jerry Trlica
2117 Foothill Blvd., #107
Laverne, CA 91750
Phone: (909)593-473
Fax: (909)593-473

Victor Leather Repair
Victor Calderon
1140 Centre Dr., "I"
Walnut, CA 91789
Phone: (800)836-405
Fax: (909)444-827

Furniture Medic
Gary & Betsy Carney
71 Corte Maria Ave.
Chula Vista, CA 91910
Phone: (619)426-195
Fax: (619)426-194

Furniture Medic
Ray Swann
2844 Dos Lomas
Fallbrook, CA 92028
Phone: (760)731-262
Fax: (760)731-100

Furniture Medic
Shawn Dolan
300 Enterprize St. Suite E
Escondido, CA 92029
Phone: (760)741-925
Fax: (760)735-640

Moving Damage Repair
Dwight Greene
P.O. Box 1027
Poway, CA 92074-1027
Phone: (619)486-423
Fax: (619)486-078

Jim Carrico Furniture Repair
Jim Carrico
2003 Bayview Hgts Dr, #107
San Diego, CA 92105
Phone: (619)262-703
Fax: (619)263-911

West Wood Work
William West
40321 Avenida Cerrovista
Cherry Valley, CA 92223
Phone: (909)845-865
Fax: (909)845-659

Pick Up The Pieces
Lawrence Vescera
711 W. 17th St., C-12
Costa Mesa, CA 92627
Phone: (949)645-995
Fax: (949)645-838

Furniture Artists, The
Mark Hedges
22600 Lambert #G 1403
Lake Forest, CA 92630
Phone: (949)770-836
Fax: (949)770-040

Guardsman Woodpro
Tom Beahm
24111 Pandora St
Lake Forest, CA 92630
Phone: (714)455-199
Fax: (714)455-199

Furniture Medic So. Cal.
Patrick O'Donnell
19182 Red Bluff Dr.
Trabuco Canyon, CA 92679
Phone: (949)766-032
Fax: (949)766-016

Stout's Finishing
Michael T. Stout
27758 Santa Margarita Pkw#114
Mission Viejo, CA 92691
Phone: (949)837-136
Fax: (949)830-392

Price's Finishing
Jim Price
23052-H Alicia Parkway #305
Mission Viejo, CA 92692
Phone: (949)858-196
Fax: (949)858-081

Claimtronics Network
Paul V. House
5308 W. Ballast Ave.
Santa Ana, CA 92704-1804
Phone: (714)839-144
Fax: (714)775-349

Furniture Medic
Gary Childs
1586 #E Morse Ave.
Ventura, CA 93003
Phone: (805)644-841
Fax: (805)643-830

Furniture Medic
Chuck Blackmon
3412 Stine Rd., #121
Bakersfield, CA 93309-6341
Phone: (805)397-519
Fax: (805)397-519

Ron Rogers Claims Service
Ron Rogers
10240 Atascadero Ave.
Atascadero, CA 93422
Phone: (805)461-529
Fax: (805)461-910

Bay Area Restoration
Al & Mary Ann Zajec
417 Casa Del Mar Drive
Half Moon Bay, CA 94019-1413
Phone: (650)728-166
Fax: (650)728-166

Furniture Medic
John Sappingfield
2731 Fair Oaks Ave.
Redwood City, CA 94063
Phone: (415)299-908
Fax: (415)299-908

Roderd Co.
Richard Roder
2161 Turk Blvd., #7
San Francisco, CA 94115
Phone: (415)922-954
Fax: (415)922-954

Villar Restorations
Luis Villar
3979 Regan Dr.
San Mateo, CA 94403
Phone: (650)349-168
Fax: (650)349-168

Clarke's Restoration
Steven Vorpahl
1493 Duncan Rd.
Concord, CA 94521
Phone: (925)672-998
Fax: (925)672-998

J & J Finishers/Shirley's Cs
Bill & Shirley James
771 Hampton Rd.
Hayward, CA 94541
Phone: (510)276-033
Fax: (510)317-023

Furniture Medic
William Lakman
34121 Langhorn Ct.
Fremont, CA 94555
Phone: (510)742-194
Fax: (510)742-194

Furniture Medic
Chris Gilbert
14439 Catalina St.
San Leandro, CA 94577
Phone: (510)352-505
Fax: (510)352-591

Bepler Furniture Service
Ron Bepler
606 43rd St.
Richmond, CA 94805
Phone: (510)231-018
Fax: (510)231-052

Linda Sugar Furniture Service
Linda Sugar
330 Miller Ave.
Mill Valley, CA 94941
Phone: (415)388-257
Fax: (415)388-508

Trans Bay Furniture Repair
Jim & Janice Jacobson
121 Santa Maria Drive
Novato, CA 94947
Phone: (415)892-452
Fax: (415)897-174

Dunne's Finishing Service
Dennis R. Dunne
2179 Stone Ave., Ste. #20
San Jose, CA 95125
Phone: (408)293-989
Fax: (408)293-107

Universal Furniture Services
Terry Jiminez
302 Toyon Ave., #F-270
San Jose, CA 95127
Phone: (408)937-162
Fax: (408)937-162

Furniture Medic
James T. Morrow
P.O. Box 8813
Stockton, CA 95208-8813
Phone: (209)931-844
Fax: (209)473-117

Zeiger Furniture Svc.
Rita Hilinski
P.O. Box 1210
Valley Springs, CA 95252
Phone: (209)772-702
Fax: (209)772-702

Furniture Medic
Pete Creamer
400 S. Jensen Rd.
Gustine, CA 95322
Phone: (209)854-694
Fax: (209)854-694

Furniture Medic
Robin Cowden
216 Fitch St.
Healdsburg, CA 95448
Phone: (707)431-242
Fax: (707)433-560

Freedom Services
Michael Matthew
Box 4581
Auburn, CA 95603
Phone: (530)367-412
Fax: (530)367-412

Martin's Classic Rest. Svcs.
Tony Martin
221 Sterling Oak Dr.
Galt, CA 95632
Phone: (209)745-698
Fax: (209)745-699

Raul Guzman Furniture Repair
Raul Guzman
1310 Large Oak Dr.
Placerville, CA 95667
Phone: (530)642-247
Fax: (530)642-274

A-Masters Touch
Walt Knighton
1866 Southwood Dr.
Vacaville, CA 95687
Phone: (707)449-366
Fax: (707)449-366

Furniture Medic
Meredith Churchwell
P.O. Box 588
Applegate, CA 95703
Phone: (530)878-211
Fax: (530)878-838

Carmel Restoration Svcs.
Carole & Mel Stanley
5037 C College Oak Dr.
Sacramento, CA 95841
Phone: (916)338-040
Fax: (916)338-012

Furniture Medic
Rick Brewster
20013 Red Bank Rd.
Red Bluff, CA 96080
Phone: (530)528-921
Fax: (530)528-290

Guardsman Woodpro
Randy & Kristi Gray
51-174 Kaaawa Park Lane
Kaaawa, HI 96730
Phone: (808)237-115
Fax: (808)237-117

Furniture Medic
Michael Morgan
94-1015 Anania Place
Mililani, HI 96789-2541
Phone: (808)623-580
Fax: (808)623-615

Classic Furniture Restoration
Steve Larimore
P.O. Box 395
Colton, OR 97017
Phone: (503)824-246
Fax: (503)824-246

Antique Refinishing Factory
Rich Adair
18797 Hwy 99E
Hubbard, OR 97032
Phone: (503)981-692
Fax: (503)981-692

Cady Co The/Robin Cady Assoc.
Robin Cady
1732 N.W. 25th Ave.
Portland, OR 97210
Phone: (503)227-285
Fax: (503)227-204

Furniture Medic
Dan Mackinnon
14750 Sw 81 Ave.
Tigard, OR 97224
Phone: (503)598-345
Fax: (503)624-205

Oregon Furniture & Claim Svc
Allen Darrow
P.O. Box 253
Independence, OR 97351-0253
Phone: (503)838-411
Fax: (503)838-380

Furniture Clinic, The
Don Frosland
2210 Hwy 99 North
Eugene, OR 97402
Phone: (541)689-026
Fax: (541)689-729

Oregon Restoration Co., The
David Wagar
P.O. Box 26314
Eugene, OR 97402
Phone: (541)935-383
Fax: (541)935-383

Furniture Doctor
John Yakel
1609 Sun Glo Drive
Grants Pass, OR 97527
Phone: (541)479-485
Fax: (541)479-485

The Finishing Touch
Jonathan Green
10258 Wagner Creek Rd.
Talent, OR 97540
Phone: (541)535-867
Fax: (541)535-867

Furniture Medic
Roy Delia
P.O. Box 1285
Kent, WA 98035
Phone: (253)859-013
Fax: (253)813-388

Spencer Corp.
Ray Spencer
23220 Maple Vly Hwy, SE, #3b
Maple Valley, WA 98038
Phone: (425)413-166
Fax: (425)413-165

International Claims Svc.
Mark Mcgriff
P.O. Box 75226
Seattle, WA 98125
Phone: (206)522-357
Fax: (206)729-084

Furniture Medic
George Lanphear
310 74th St. SW
Everett, WA 98203-4958
Phone: (425)347-727
Fax: (425)710-405

Artisan Furniture Service
Richard Conley
3214 114th St., N.W.
Gig Harbor, WA 98332
Phone: (253)857-758
Fax: (253)851-738

Town & Country Furniture Svc
Ron Lawrence
18421 Driftwod Drive East
Sumner, WA 98390
Phone: (253)826-032
Fax: (253)826-032

Furniture Medic
Bob Gustavson
1892 Brittany Ln., Sw #2336
Tumwater, WA 98512-0014
Phone: (360)786-882
Fax: (360)709-079

Guardsman Woodpro
Rennie Espinoza
10847 W. Sagewood Rd.
Nine Mile Falls, WA 99026
Phone: (509)465-380
Fax: (509)466-811

Shanahan & Sons Furniture
Terry Shanahan
S. 2206 Inland Empire Way
Spokane, WA 99224-4536
Phone: (509)624-785
Fax: (509)747-243

Furniture Medic
Brian Millar
225 Harrison Rd.
Pasco, WA 99301
Phone: (509)545-548
Fax: (509)545-399

Knapp Furniture Restoration
Lynn Knapp
1219 W. Pine
Walla Walla, WA 99362
Phone: (509)529-749
Fax: (509)529-749

Classic Furniture Restoration
Rusty Bridges
700 W. 58th Ave., "E"
Anchorage, AK 99518
Phone: (907)563-330
Fax: (907)563-468

Furniture Medic
Douglas Jones
RR#2
Stirling, Ontario K0K 3E0 Canada
Phone: (613)477-145
Fax: (613)477-194

Artistic Furn Touchup/Rep Svc
Lyle & Barb Stricker
Rr #1, Group Box 103
Havelock, Ontario K0L 1Z0 Canada
Phone: (705)778-320
Fax: (705)778-320

Guardsman Woodpro
Yvon Vincent
141 Dalhousie St.
Ottawa, Ontario K1N 7C2 Canada
Phone: (613)562-399
Fax: (613)562-076

Furniture Medic
Llewellyn & Sean Rowlands
1913 The Chase
Mississauga, Ontario L5M 3A2
Canada
Phone: (905)607-489
Fax: (905)607-069

Duvals' Furniture Repair
Robert Duval
5776 Greensboro Dr.
Mississauga, Ontario L5M-5V1
Canada
Phone: (905)812-002
Fax: (905)812-002

Furniture Medic Of Canada
David Messenger
6540 Tomken Rd.
Mississauga, Ontario L5T 2E9 Canada
Phone: (905)670-000
Fax: (905)670-007

Furniture Medic
Robert Field
7-3392 Wonderland Rd. S.
London, Ontario N6L 1A8 Canada
Phone: (519)878-317
Fax: (519)652-993

Guardsman Woodpro
Gerry Palmer
157 Pen. Est.
Sherwood Park, Alberta T8C 1H5
Canada
Phone: (403)464-488
Fax: (403)464-482

Furniture Medic
Gil Goodman
1748 Spruceview Ct.
Kelowna, British Col. V1V 1S8
Canada
Phone: (250)860-551
Fax: (250)860-696

Guardsman Woodpro
Ken Grist
53 Roundhill Ct.
London, Ontario W5Z 4N3 Canada
Phone: (519)668-079
Fax: (519)668-378

Here are some tips when contacting someone listed in this book:

■ When requesting information about a particular item, include a description (material, dimensions, maker's mark, model number, etc.) and a photo, sketch, or photocopy of the item in question.

■ Always ask if there are charges for samples or for the services requested.

■ When writing, please be sure to include a Large (#10 business size) Self-Addressed and Stamped Envelope (LSASE) if requesting a reply or the return of photographs.

■ Never call collect unless otherwise directed. When calling, be considerate of time zone differences and always ask if the party you are calling has time to talk. When leaving an answering machine message, always instruct the party to call you back collect.

INDEX

B

C

D

E

G

H

I

J

K

L

N

Q

R

T

U

V

W

X - Y - Z

Would you like to be included in the next edition of
Maloney's Antiques & Collectibles Resource Directory?

If you are a dealer, collector or expert, or if you offer specific services to the antiques and collectibles trade, please consider completing and submitting the form on the following page so that you too can be included in the next edition of this Directory. Specialty clubs, periodicals, and museums are especially encouraged to become listed. By the way, listings are **free** of charge.

Here is some information you should keep in mind when checking over your listings. Because of the overwhelming response, we must limit the number of listings for Collectors and Dealers to five per person. **If you are not the current official point-of-contact for your club/association or periodical, please forward these forms to the appropriate person or office.**

1. Specialty Area: This is the category under which your entry will be listed. Tell us your areas of interest and we'll see that you are placed under the proper heading(s). Remember, Dealers and Collectors are limited to five (5) listings per person.

2. Entry Type: Include the type of listing. Choices include appraiser, auction service, book seller, club/association, collector, dealer, expert, matching service, museum/library, periodical, supplier or parts, repair/restoration/conservation service, reproductions source, manufacturer/producer/distributor, Internet services or resource, or other (explain). While most entry types are self-explanatory, please note the following definitions as used in this Resource Directory:

"Collectors" buy or trade primarily for their own enjoyment, with any profit motive being secondary.

"Dealers" buy, sell, or trade. They may also be "collectors", but "dealers" anticipate making a profit.

"Experts" (while they may also be a "collector" and/or "dealer") are considered to be expert because they have lectured or written extensively on the subject, have authored books or articles, have been a curator at exhibits or have managed collections, have dealt extensively in the subject, appraise within a specialized field, have conducted lengthy studies on the subject, or otherwise have such a degree of experience that they are recognized within the trade as having an uncommonly high degree of knowledge about the subject.

"Internet Services" are services or products for the trade which are offered primarily through the Internet.

3. Point-of-Contact: Please provide your full name or the name of your company's or club's designated point-of-contact. Museums and auctions houses, please provide the names of your curators or specialty department heads, respectively, for each specialty area listed.

4. Business Name: List the exact name of your business, club/association, museum, publishing house, etc.

5. Address: Provide your mailing address. If you use a Post Office Box, you may also list a street address (for UPS) if you like. For publishers of periodicals, please provide the mailing address for your editorial or publisher's office, not the address to your subscription service.

6. Phone and Fax Numbers: People would often prefer to call you rather than write to you, so please list up to two phone numbers and one fax number. For periodicals, please provide phone/fax numbers to your editorial or publisher's office as well as your 800 subscription service number, if any.

7. E-mail and Internet: Please make sure to list this information if it is applicable, and to update it immediately should it change. Remember to PRINT CLEARLY so we don't make a mistake when entering your information.

8. Periodical: If the listing is for a periodical **or** for a club that publishes a periodical, please list your periodical's exact name, its format (newspaper, newsletter, magazine, journal, directory, price guide, etc.), and its frequency of publication.

9. Comment: *This is a most important field to fill out.* It gives the reader a flavor of your wants, what service you provide, what your club is all about, or what your periodical covers. Please provide a couple of concise sentences (up to 240 characters in length) to let the reader know more about yourself and/or the products or services you provide or seek. Include key words associated with your specialty area for more accurate computer searches.

Note about Books & Periodicals: ***Maloney's Antiques & Collectibles Resource Directory*** is published every other year, but **Maloney's** answers written and telephone inquiries between editions regarding information that is maintained in our database. We also provide answers to questions from callers made during radio talk shows, or received on-line. Plus, database information is also posted on our website at **www. maloneysonline.com**. In addition, we review any book or video received that is about antiques, collectibles, and related subjects such as auctions, antique repairs, etc. To ensure that our files are maintained between editions and that accurate information is being disseminated, it is important that we receive copies of your publications such as books, catalogs, videos, newsletters, newspapers, magazines, flyers, brochures, etc. **To be eligible for preferred referral status, please place *Maloney's* on your *permanent* mailing list for complimentary copies of your publications.** Please send them to Maloney's, P.O. Box 2049, Frederick, MD 21702-1049.

...oney's Antiques & Collectibles Resource Directory

Listing Registraion and Change Form

...is form is also available ONLINE at our web site http://www.maloneysonline.com

(Save and use this form for future additions or changes to your listings.)

1. List your SPECIALTY AREA (Please limit listings to five per Dealer or Collector). Make copies of this form if you have specialties in more than one area.

____

2. Check the ENTRY TYPE(S) that applies to this listing. More than one selection is OK:

_____	Appraiser	_____	Dealer	_____	Supplier of repair or replacement parts
_____	Auction Service	_____	Expert	_____	Repair/Restoration/Conservator Service
_____	Book Seller	_____	Matching Service	_____	Reproductions Source
_____	Club/Association	_____	Museum/Library	_____	Manufacturer, Producer or Distributor
_____	Collector	_____	Periodical	_____	On-line Service or Resource

Other (specify): ______________________

3. POINT-OF-CONTACT. Your name as you want it listed: ______________________

4. BUSINESS NAME of your company, club, association, publishing house, museum, etc.: ______________________

____

5. ADDRESS (Note: for periodicals, include your **Editorial** or **Publisher's** address (not your subscription service) and your toll-free subscription telephone number, if any):

Address: ______________________

____

City: ____________ State (or Province): ____________ Zip (or Postal Code): ____________

Country : ____________

6. TELEPHONE #1: (   )____________ TELEPHONE #2: (   )____________ FAX: (   )____________

7. a. E-mail address: ______________________

b. Internet website address: http:// ______________________

8. PERIODICALS (magazines, newsletters, newspapers, etc.) that you publish. **To ensure continued accuracy of your listing and to be eligible for preferred referral status, please make certain that complimentary subscriptions to your periodical are sent to Maloney's, Attn: File Editor, P.O. Box 2049, Frederick, MD 21702-1049 for review.**

Periodical Name: ______________________

Format (newsletter, magazine, journal, newspaper, etc.): ______________________

Frequency of publication: ____________

9. COMMENT LINE: (Describe your club, association, periodical, or service. For the collector or dealer, describe your wants. If you are an author, please list your most recent books dealing with this specialty area. Also, please attach catalogs, brochures, flyers, business cards, etc. that relate to this listing. 240 character limit.)

____

____

____

The above information gives an accurate and realistic description of my business or areas of interest. I understand that this information is for distribution in electronic and written form including publication in *Maloney's Antiques & Collectibles Resource Directory* published by Antique Trader Publications.

Date ____________ Signature ______________________ Title____________

Please complete and mail or fax to: Maloney's, P.O. Box 2049, Frederick, MD 21702-1049
phone: (301) 695-8544, fax: (301) 695-6491, e-mail: feedback@maloney.com